PERSONALITIES OF AMERICA

Personalities

of

America

First Edition

published by:

ABI

the **American Biographical Institute**

a division of
Historical Preservations of America, Inc.
205 West Martin Street, Post Office Box 226, Raleigh, North Carolina 27602 USA

Library of Congress Catalog Card Number 79-51997

International Standard Book Number 0-934544-06-9

Printed and bound in the United States of America by
Vail-Ballou Press, Inc., Binghamton, New York

Table of Contents

Preface

The American Biographical Institute is presenting with the First Edition, *Personalities of America*, the newest publication to round out its *"Personalities"* series. This edition is the first to cover the total national scope and solidify and augment all other regional American *"Personalities"* titles. Our editors have promoted and recognized individual endeavors of research and knowledge, and documented biographical facts for genealogists, biographers, reporters, historians, librarians, students, business consultants, and researchers in general. Providing several new features, the Governing Board of Editors has designed this First Edition as the first volume to be illustrated photographically. All biographees have been offered the option of portraits, thus making this work more personal and authoritative. The Board is also introducing a new concept of the State-Locator Index of all listed biographees, as well as a Roster of both our Honorary Editorial Advisory Board consultants and the ABI's members in Fellowship standing. In addition, a fourth appendix will present the Life Patrons, Life Fellows, Life Associates, and Annual Associates of the American Biographical Institute Research Association.

Recommendations for *Personalities of America* are received from our Media Research Department, Governing Board of Editors, Board of Directors, and nationwide advisors. Nominations are also filed by national universities and colleges; national, state, and local professional organizations, service, civic, and social organizations; individuals; businesses; and biographees. Nominees are contacted and personal submissions are reviewed by the Governing Board of Editors. All personal materials are handled with utmost professionality and all files of the Institute are kept in strict confidence and security in the ABI Library and Record Center.

Purchase of the First Edition is not a pre-requisite for inclusion. A listing fee or required reservation payment has never been allowed by the Board of Directors. Editorial evaluation by the Governing Board of Editors is the ultimate determinant of publication selection, without regard for race, sex, or creed. High policy standards have been strictly protected.

Qualified and consistent attention has been given to the preparation of individual documentation herein, as well as efficient proofing by a competent staff of copy editors. If an occasional error does occur, however, the Board offers its apologies in advance and its sole responsibility will be to correct such in the subsequent edition.

I express appreciation to all individuals throughout the nation who have contributed to the development and production of this book, and congratulate, on behalf of the Governing Board of Editors, the unique and committed individuals honored in this First Edition of *Personalities of America*.

J. S. Thomson
Editor-in-Chief
Governing Board of Editors

ABI Biographical Titles

Community Leaders of America
Notable Americans
Personalities of America
Personalities of the South
Personalities of the East
Personalities of the West and Midwest
The Book of Honor
The American Registry Series
International Youth in Achievement
The Directory of Distinguished Americans

Delineative Information

Individual biographical entries are arranged according to standard alphabetical practice and information for publication is consistently and uniformly presented in the categorical order as below. Coding symbols are clarified below as well.

Editors of the Institute make all attempts to edit accurately the information furnished by each biographee. In the rare event of an error by the publisher, the sole responsibility of the publisher will be to correct such in the subsequent edition of the publication.

Editorial evaluation is the ultimate determinant of publication selection. Admission in this series is based on the value of achievement or recognized outreach of endeavor.

All submissions and files at the Institute are maintained in confidence and adequate security.

Due to the quality of submitted photographs, some did not reproduce or print well and their appearance was not up to publication standards. These unsuitable photographs were, therefore, not included.

Biographical Codes

oc/	Occupation	ed/	Education
b/	Birth	mil/	Military Service
h/	Home Address	pa/	Professional Activities
ba/	Business Address	cp/	Civic & Political Activities
m/	Married-Wife or Husband	r/	Religious Activities
c/	Children	hon/	Other Honors & Activities, etc.
p/	Parents		

Table of Abbreviations

The Following Abbreviations and Symbols Are Frequently Used in This Compilation

AA	Associate of Arts	Am	American, America
AAAS	American Association for the Advancement of Science	AM	Master of Arts
		AMA	American Medical Association
AAC	Army Air Corps	AME	African Methodist Episcopal
AAF	Army Air Force		
AAHE	American Association of Higher Ed	Am Inst EE	American Institute of Electrical Engineers
AAHPER	American Association of Health, Physical Education and Recreation	Am Soc CE	American Society of Civil Engineers
AART	American Academy of Radiology Technicians	Am Soc ME	Am Soc of Mechanical Engineers
		Anal	Analysis, Analyst
AASA	American Academy of School Administrators	Anesth	Anesthesiologist
		ANG	Army National Guard
AAUA	American Association of University Administrators	Anniv	Anniversary
		AP	Associated Press
		APGA	American Personnel and Guidance Association
AAUP	American Association of University Professors	Apr	April
AAUW	American Association of University Women	Apprec	Appreciate, Appreciation
		Approp	Appropriations
AB	Bachelor of Arts	Appt	Appointment
ABA	American Bar Association	Appt'd	Appointed
Acad	Academy, Academic	Apt	Apartment
Acct	Accountant	ARC	American Red Cross
Acctg	Accounting	Arch	Architect, Architecture
Achmt	Achievement	Ariz	Arizona
ACLU	American Civil Liberties Union	ArM	Master of Architecture
		Ark	Arkansas
Activs	Activities	Art	Article, Artillery
Addit	Additional	ASAS	American Society for the Advancement of Science
Adj	Adjunct		
Adm	Administration, Administrative	ASCAP	American Society of Composers, Authors, and Publishers
Admr	Administrator		
Adv	Advisory	ASHA	American Speech and Hearing Association
Advmt	Advancement		
Advr	Advisor	Assessmt	Assessment
Advtg	Advertising	Assn	Association
Aeronaut	Aeronautical	Assoc	Associate
AESP	Association of Elementary School Principals	ASSP	Associaton of Secondary School Principals
AF	Air Force	Asst	Assistant, Assistance
AFB	Air Force Base	Astronom	Astronomy, Astronomical
AFCW	American Federation of Colored Women	Ath	Athlete, Athletic
		Atl	Atlantic
Affil	Affiliate, Affiliation	Att'd, Att'g	Attended, Attending
Agri	Agriculture	Atty	Attorney
Agst	Against	Aug	August
Agt	Agent	AUS	United States Army
Agy	Agency	Auth	Authority
AIA	American Institute of Architects	Aux	Auxiliary
		A-V	Audio-Visual
Ala	Alabama	Ave	Avenue
Alt	Alternate	AWC	American Women Composers

TABLE OF ABBREVIATIONS

The Following Abbreviations and Symbols Are Frequently Used in This Compilation

Awd	Award	Cand	Candidate
Awd'd	Awarded	Capt	Captain
		Cardiovas	Cardiovascular
BA	Bachelor of Arts	Cath	Catholic
Bach	Bachelor	Cav	Cavalry
Balto	Baltimore	CB	Bachelor of Surgery,
Bapt	Baptist		Citizen Band
B Agr	Bachelor of Agriculture	CC	Country Clb
B Arch	Bachelor of Architecture	CDA	Catholic Daughters of
Bat	Batallion		America
BBA	Bachelor of Business	CE	Chemical Engineer
	Administration	CEC	Council for Exceptional
BBB	Better Business Bureau		Children
BC	Bachelor of Chemistry	Cert	Certificate, Certification
BCE	Bachelor of Chemical	Ch	Church
	Engineering	Champ(s)	Champion(s)
Bch	Beach	Chapt	Chapter
BCL	Bachelor of Civil Law	Chatta	Chattanooga
Bd	Board	ChD	Doctor of Chemistry
BD	Bachelor of Divinity	Chd	Children
BDS	Bachelor of Dental Surgery	ChE	Chemical Engineer
BE	Bachelor of Education,	Chem	Chemical, Chemist
	Engineering	Chiro	Chiropractic
BEE	Bachelor of Electrical	Chm	Chairman
	Engineering	Chperson	Chairperson
BF	Bachelor of Finance	CIA	Central Intelligence
B'ham	Birmingham		Agency
Bibliog	Bibliography,	Cinc	Cincinnati
	Bibliographical	Cir	Circle
Bicent	Bicentennial	Cit	Citation
Biog	Biography	Clb	Club
Biol	Biology, Biological	Clin	Clinic, Clinical
Bk, Bkg, Bkr	Bank, Banking, Banker	Clk	Clerk
Bkkpg	Bookkeeping	Cmdr	Commander
Bkkpr	Bookkeeper	Cnslg	Counseling
Bklyn	Brooklyn	Cnslr	Counselor
Bldg	Building	Co	County
Bldr	Builder	CO	Commanding Officer
BLit	Bachelor of Literature	CoChm	Co-Chairman
BLS	Bachelor of Library	C of C	Chamber of Commerce
	Science	Col	College, Collegiate,
Blvd	Boulevard		Colonel
BM	Bachelor of Medicine	Com	Committee
BMus	Bachelor of Music	Comdg	Commanding
BPd, BPe	Bachelor of Physical	Comm	Commission
	Education	Com-man	Committeeman
BPW	Business and Professional	Commend	Commendation
	Women	Commr	Commissioner
Br	Branch	Commun	Community
Brit	Britain, British	Communs	Communications
BS	Bachelor of Science	Com-wom	Committeewoman
BSA	Boy Scouts of America	Conf	Conference
BSc	Bachelor of Science	Cong	Congress
BSED	Bachelor of Science in	Congl	Congressional
	Education	Cong of P's	Congress of Parents and
BT, BTh	Bachelor of Theology	& T's	Teachers
Bultn	Bulletin	Congreg	Congregational
Bur	Bureau	Conserv	Conservation
Bus	Business	Conslt	Consultant
		Consltg	Consulting
Cal	California	Consol	Consolidated

TABLE OF ABBREVIATIONS

The Following Abbreviations and Symbols Are Frequently Used in This Compilation

Constit	Constitution	Dist	District
Constrn	Construction	Dist'd	Distinguished
Cont'd, Cont'g	Continued, Continuing	Distn	Distinction
Contbr	Contributor	Div	Division, Divinity
Contbtg	Contributing	DLit, DLitt	Doctor of Literature, Letters
Conv	Convention		
Coop	Cooperation	DLS	Doctor of Library Science
Coor	Coordinator, Coordinating	DMD	Doctor of Dental Medicine
Corp	Corporation	DMus	Doctor of Music
Corr	Corresponding, Correspondence	DO	Doctor of Osteopathy
		Doct	Doctoral
Cosmetol	Cosmetology, Cosmetologist	Dr	Drive, Doctor
		DS, DSc	Doctor of Science
Coun	Council	DTh, DTheol	Doctor of Theology
Creat & Success Personalities	Creative and Successful Personalities of the World	DVM	Doctor of Veterinary Medicine
CPA	Certified Public Accountant	E	East
Cpl	Corporal	Ec	Economics
CPR	Cardio-Pulmonary Resuscitation	Ecol	Ecology
		Ed	Education
Crim	Criminal	EdB	Bachelor of Education
CSB	Bachelor of Christian Science	EdD	Doctor of Education
		Edit	Editorial
Ct	Court	EdM	Master of Education
Ctl	Central	Ednl	Educational
Ctr	Center	Edr	Educator
Cult	Cultural	EE	Electrical Engineer
Curric	Curriculum	Elect	Electrical, Electric Electronics
DAC	Daughters of the American Colonists	Elem	Elementary
		Emer	Emergency
DAR	Daughters of the American Revolution	Employmt	Employment
		EMR	Educable Mentally Retarded
Daugh	Daughter		
DAV	Disabled American Veterans	EMT	Emergency Medical Technician
DC	District of Columbia	Ency	Encyclopedia
DCL	Doctor of Canon Law	Eng	English
DD	Doctor of Divinity	EngD	Doctor of Engineering
DDS	Doctor of Dental Surgery	Engr	Engineer
Dec	December	Engrg	Engineering
dec	Deceased	Entomol	Entomology
Def	Defense	Envir	Environment, Environmental
Deg	Degree		
Del	Delegate	Epis	Episcopal
Dem	Democrat	Equipmt	Equipment
Denom	Denomination, Denominational	Est	Establish
		Establishmt	Establishment
Dept	Department	ETO	European Theater of Operations
Delinq	Delinquent, Delinquency		
Dermatol	Dermatology, Dermatologist	Eval	Evaluation
		Evang	Evangelical
Desc	Descendant	Exam	Examination
Devel	Development	Examr	Examiner
DIB	Dictionary of International Biography	Exc	Exchange
		Exec	Executive
Dic	Dictionary	Ext	Extension
Dipl	Diploma		
Dir	Director, Directory	FAA	Federal Aviation Agency
Dis	Disease	Fac	Faculty

TABLE OF ABBREVIATIONS

The Following Abbreviations and Symbols Are Frequently Used in This Compilation

Fam	Family	Ia	Ia
F&AM	Free and Accepted Mason	IBM	International Business Machines
FBI	Federal Bureau of Investigation	IEEE	Institute of Electrical and Electronic Engineers
FCC	Federal Communications Commission	Ill	Illinois
FDA	Federal Drug Administration	Inc	Incorporated
		incl	Include
Fdg	Founding	incl'g	Including
Fdn	Federation	Indep	Independent, Independence
Fdr	Founder	Indiv	Individual
Feb	February	Indpls	Indianapolis
Fed	Federal	Indust	Industry
Fest	Festival	Inf	Infantry
FFA	Future Farmers of America	Info	Information
		Ins	Insurance
FHA	Future Homemakers of America	Insp	Inspector
		Inst	Institute
Fin	Finance	Instn	Institution
Foun	Foundation	Instnl	Institutional
Frat	Fraternity	Instr	Instructor
Ft	Fort	Instrn	Instruction
Ftball	Football	Intell	Intelligence
FTC	Federal Trade Commission	Intells	Intellectuals
Furn	Furniture	Intl	International
FWB	Free Will Baptist	Intercont	Intercontinental
		Intergovtl	Intergovernmental
Ga	Georgia	Interpret	Interpretation
GA's	Girls' Auxiliary	Invest	Investigation
GE	General Electric	Investmt	Investment
Gen	General	IOOF	Independent Order of ODD FELLOWS
Geneal	Genealogy, Genealogical		
Geo	George	IPA	International Platform Association
Geog	Geography, Geographical		
Geol	Geological	IRA	International Reading Association
Gov	Governor		
Govt	Government	IRS	Internal Revenue Service
Govtl	Governmental	Isl	Island
Grad	Graduate, Graduated		
GSA	Girl Scouts of America	Jan	January
Gtr	Greater	JCD	Doctor of Canon Law
Guid	Guidance	JD	Doctor of Law
Gyn	Gynecology	jg	Junior Grade
		Jour	Journal, Journalism
Hd	Head	Jr	Junior
Hdqtrs	Headquarters	Jt	Joint
Hgts	Heights	Jud	Judicial, Judiciary
Hi	Hawaii	Judic	Judicature
Hist	History	Jul	July
Histn	Historian	Jun	June
Hlth	Health	Jurisd	Jurisdiction
Hon	Honor, Honorable	Jurisp	Jurisprudence
Hort	Horticulture	J of P	Justice of the Peace
Hosp	Hospital	Juv	Juvenile
HPER	Health, Physical Education and Recreation	Juv Delinq	Juvenile Delinquent
HS	High School	K	Knights
HUD	Housing and Urban Development	Kgn	Kindergarten
		K of C	Knights of Columbus
Hwy	Highway	K of G	Knights of the Garter
		K of P	Knights of Pythias

TABLE OF ABBREVIATIONS

The Following Abbreviations and Symbols Are Frequently Used in This Compilation

Ks	Kansas	Me	Maine
Ky	Kentucky	Mech	Mechanical
		Med	Medical, Medicine
La	Louisiana	MEd	Master of Education
LA	Los Angeles	Mem	Member
Lab	Laboratory	Meml	Memorial
Lang	Language	MENC	Music Educators National
Laryngol	Laryngological		Conference
LB	Bachelor of Letters	Merch	Merchant
LCA	Lutheran Church of	Metall	Metallurgical
	America	Meth	Methodist
LD	Learning Disabilities	Metro	Metropolitan
Ldg	Leading	Mfg	Manufacturing
Ldr	Leader	Mfr	Manufacturer
Ldrship	Leadership	Mgmt	Management
LDS	Latter Day Saints	Mgr	Manager
Leag	League	Mil	Military
Lectr	Lecturer	Min	Minister, Ministry
Legis	Legislative, Legislature,	Minn	Minnesota
	Legislator, Legislation	Misc	Miscellaneous
LHD	Doctor of Humanities	Miss	Mississippi
LI	Long Island	Mkt	Market
Lib	Library	Mktg	Marketing
Libn	Librarian	Mng	Managing
Lic	License	Mo	Missouri
Lic'd	Licensed	mo, mos	Month, Months
Lit	Literary, Literature	Mod	Modern
Lit(t)B	Bachelor of Literature,	Mont	Montana
	Letters	MPd	Master of Pedagogy
Lit(t)D	Doctor of Literature,	MPE	Master of Physical
	Letters		Education
LLB	Bachelor of Laws	MS, MSc	Master of Science
LLD	Doctor of Laws	MS	Multiple Sclerosis
Ln	Lane, Loan	Mt	Mount
Lng	Learning	Mtl	Mental
Lt	Lieutenant	Mtly	Mentally
Ltd	Limited	Mtn	Mountain
Lttrs	Letters	Mun	Municipal
Luth	Lutheran	Mus	Museum
LWC	League of Women Composers	MusB	Bachelor of Music
LWV	League of Women Voters	Mut	Mutual
Lwyr	Lawyer	Mvt	Movement
MA	Master of Arts	N	North
Mag	Magazine	NAACP	National Association for
MAgr	Master of Agriculture		the Advancement of
Maj	Major		Colored People
Mar	March	NAHPER	National Association of
MArch	Master of Architecture		Health, Physical Educa-
Mat(s)	Material(s)		tion and Recreation
Math	Mathematics	NAm	North America
MB	Bachelor of Medicine	NASA	National Aeronautical and
MBA	Master of Business		Space Administration
	Administrator	Nat	National
Mbrship	Membership	N Atl	North Atlantic
MC	Master of Ceremonies	Nat Reg Prom Ams	National Register of
MCL	Master of Civil Law		Prominent Americans
Md	Maryland	Nav	Naval
MDiv	Master of Divinity	NBC	National Broadcasting
MDS	Master of Dental Surgery		Company
Mdse	Merchandise	NC	North Carolina

TABLE OF ABBREVIATIONS

The Following Abbreviations and Symbols Are Frequently Used in This Compilation

NCNW	National Council of Negro Women	PdB	Bachelor of Pedagogy
NCPGA	North Carolina Personnel and Guidance Association	PDM	Master of Pedagogy
		PE	Physical Education
NCTE, NCTM	National Council of Teachers of English, Math	PeD	Doctor of Pedagogy
		Perf	Performance
ND	North Dakota	Period	Periodical
NE	Northeast	Perm	Permanent
NEA	National Education Association	Pers	Personnel
		Pgh	Pittsburgh
Neb	Nebraska	PharB	Bachelor of Pharmacy
Neurol	Neurology, Neurological	PharD	Doctor of Pharmacy
NG	National Guard	Pharm	Pharmacy, Pharmacist, Pharmacology
NH	New Hampshire		
NJ	New Jersey	PharmM	Master of Pharmacy
NIH	National Institute of Health	PhB	Bachelor of Philosophy
No	Northern	PhD	Doctor of Philosophy
NO	New Orleans	Phil	Philosophy
Nom	Nominee	Phila	Philadelphia
Nom'd, Nom'g	Nominated, Nominating	Philharm	Philharmonic
NM	New Mexico	Photo	Photography
NSA	National Security Agency	Photog	Photographer
NSAC	National Society for Autistic Children	Phy	Physical
		Phys	Physician
		Physiol	Physiologist
Nsg	Nursing	Pk	Park
NSF	National Science Foundation	Pkwy	Parkway
		Pl	Place
Num	Numerous	Placemt	Placement
NW	Northwest	PO	Post Office
NY	New York	PodD	Doctor of Podiatry
NYC	New York City	Polit	Political, Politics
		Pop	Population
OAS	Organization of American States	PR	Puerto Rico
		Pract	Practice
Ob	Obstetrics, Obstetrician	Precnt	Precinct
Occup	Occupation, Occupational	Predoct	Predoctoral
OCS	Officer Candidate School	Premed	Premedical
Oct	October	Pres	President, Presidential
OD	Doctor of Optometry	Presb	Presbyterian
OES	Order of Eastern Star	Presby	Presbytery
Ofc	Office	Preven	Prevention
Ofcl	Official	Prin	Principal
Ofcr	Officer	Prob	Problem
OLC	Oak Leaf Cluster	Prod	Product
Opports	Opportunities	Prodn	Production
Opthal	Opthalmology	Prodr	Producer
Optom	Optometry, Optometrist	Prof	Professor
Orch	Orchestra	Profl	Professional
Org	Organization	Prog	Program, Progress
Org'd	Organized	Proj	Project
Orgnl	Organizational	Prom	Prominent
Orgr	Organizer	Prot	Protestant
Orient	Orientation	Protem	Pro tempore
Orig	Original	Psycho	Psychology, Psychologist
Ornithol	Ornithology	Psychi	Psychiatry, Psychiatrist
Ortho	Orthopedic, Orthopedist	PTA	Parents and Teachers Association
Outstg	Outstanding		
		PTO	Pacific Theater of Operations, Parents and Teachers Organization
Pa	Pennsylvania		
Parliamentn	Parliamentarian		
Path	Pathology, Pathologist	Pt-time	Parttime

TABLE OF ABBREVIATIONS

The Following Abbreviations and Symbols Are Frequently Used in This Compilation

Pub	Publish, Publication	Ser	Service
Pub'd	Published	Sev	Several
Pubr	Publisher	Sgt	Sergeant
Pvt	Private	SI	Staten Island
		SJD	Doctor of Judicial Science
QMC	Quartermaster Corps	SM	Master of Science
Qtr(s)	Quarter(s)	So	Southern
Qtrly	Quarterly	Soc	Society
Que	Quebec	Sociol	Sociology
		Spch	Speech
Radiol	Radiology	Spec	Special, Specialist
RAF	Royal Air Force	Spkg	Speaking
RCAF	Royal Canadian Air Force	Spkr	Speaker
Rd	Road	Sprgs	Springs
Rdg	Reading	Sq	Square
Real Est	Real Estate	Sqdrn	Squadron
Rec	Recreation	Sr	Senior
Rec'd	Received	SS	Sunday School
Rccog	Recognition	S/Sgt	Staff Sergeant
Reg	Regional, Region	St	State, Street, Saint
Reg'd	Registered	Sta	Station
Rehab	Rehabilitation	Stab	Stabilization
Rel	Religion	Stat	Statistic, Statistician
Relats	Relations	STB	Bachelor of Sacred Theology
Rep	Representative		
Repub	Republican	STD	Doctor of Sacred Theology
Res	Research		
Reschr	Researcher	Subcom	Subcommittee
Resv	Reserve	Subst	Substitute
Retard	Retarded, Retardation	Sum	Summer
Ret'd	Retired	Supr Ct	Supreme Court
Rev	Reverend	Supt	Superintendent
RN	Registered Nurse	Supvn	Supervision
RR	Rural Route, Railroad	Supvr	Supervisor
Rt	Route	Surg	Surgeon, Surgery
Rts	Rights	Symp	Symposium
Rwy	Railway	Symph	Symphony
		Sys	System
S	South		
SF	San Francisco	TB	Tuberculosis
SAR	Sons of the American Revolution	Tchg	Teaching
		Tchr	Teacher
Sask	Saskatchewan	Tech	Technical, Technician
Savs	Savings	Technol	Technology, Technologist
Savs & Ln	Savings and Loan	Temp	Temporary
SB	Bachelor of Science	Terr	Terrace
SCA	Speech Communication Association	ThD	Doctor of Theology
		Theol	Theology
ScD, SD	Doctor of Science	TMR	Trainable Mentally Retarded
Sch	School		
Sci	DScience	Tnd	Trained
Scis	Sciences	Tng	Training
Scist(s)	Scientist(s)	Tnr	Trainer
ScM	Master of Science	Tour	Tournament
SDA	Seventh-Day Adventist	Trans	Transportation
Sec'dy	Secondary	Treas	Treasurer
Sect	Section	T&T	Telephone & Telegraph
Secy	Secretary	TV	Television
Sel	Selective	Twp	Township
Sem	Seminar, Seminary		
Sept	September	U	United

TABLE OF ABBREVIATIONS

The Following Abbreviations and Symbols Are Frequently Used in This Compilation

UDC	United Daughters of the Confederacy	VFW	Veterans of Foreign Wars
UF	United Fund	VI	Virgin Islands
UN	United Nations	VMD	Doctor of Veterinary Medicine
UNESCO	United Nations Educational, Science and Cultural Organization	Voc	Vocational
		Vol	Volunteer
		VP	Vice President
UNICEF	United Nations International Childrens Emergency Fund	Vt	Vermont
		W	West
UMW	United Methodist Women	w	With
Univ	University	WAC	Women's Army Corps
UPI	United Press International	Wash	Washington
US	United States	WAVES	Women's United States Naval Reserves
USA	United States Army		
USAAC	United States Army Air Corps	Wed	Wednesday
		Wel	Welfare
USAAF	United States Army Air Force	WHO	World Health Organization
		Wis	Wisconsin
USAF	United States Air Force	Wk	Week
USAFR	United States Air Force Reserve	Wkr	Worker
		Wkly	Weekly
USAR	United States Army Reserve	Wkshop	Workshop
		Wm	William
USASC	United States Army Signal Corps	WOW	Woodmen of the World
		WSCS	Women's Society of Christian Service
USCG	United States Coast Guard		
USMC	United States Marine Corps	WVa	West Virginia
USMM	United States Merchant Marine	W/W	Who's Who
		W/W Fin & Indust	Who's Who in Finance and Industry
USN	United States Navy		
USNR	United States Naval Reserve	W/W MW	Who's Who in the Midwest
		Wyo	Wyoming
USPHS	United States Public Health Service		
		Yg	Young
USS	United States Ship	Ygst	Youngest
USSR	Union of Soviet Socialist Republic	YMCA	Young Men's Christian Association
		YMHA	Young Men's Hebrew Association
VA	Veterans Administration		
Va	Virginia	Yr	Year
Val	Valley	Yth	Youth
Var	Various	YWCA	Young Women's Christian Association
VBS	Vacation Bible School		
VChm	Vice Chairman	Zool	Zoology, Zoologist, Zoological
Vet	Veteran, Veterinarian		

Personalities of America

First Edition

ABBASY, IFTIKHARUL HAQUE oc/-Surgeon; b/Oct 28, 1935; h/244 Eggleston Elmhurst, IL 60126; ba/Villa Park, IL; m/Karen G; c/Shameem A; p/Ikramul Haque (dec); Mumtaz Begum, Khairpurmirs, Pakistan; ed/MB; BS; pa/Surg Pract; FRCS(C); FACS; FICS; r/Islam; hon/Personalities of W&MW; DIB; W/W Midwest.

ABBOTT, BENJAMIN EDWARD JR oc/Business Executive; b/Dec 7, 1928; h/Rt #2, Box 116-B, Alpine, AL 35014; ba/Birmingham, AL; m/Ellianna; c/Celeni, Dawn, Mark, Scott; p/Benjamin E and Agnes C Abbott; ed/BAC Univ Fla 1953; mil/USNR 1953-55, Lt (jg); pa/Pres Profl Realty Sers Inc, DBA Realty World; VP, Dir Investors Corp Am, B'ham 1968-75, Intl Resorts Inc 1970-76; Pres Resort Properties Realty 1975-; Dir Pac Am Corp, San Fran, Life Ins Co Am, B'ham; Other Former Positions; Reg'd Profl Engr: Ala, Fla; Profl Assns; cp/Pi Kappa Phi; Ret'd Ofcrs Assn; hon/W/W S&SW; Personalities of S.

ABBOTT, JOHN DAVID oc/Clergyman; Church Official; General Superintendent; b/Sept 29, 1922; h/1413 Glendale Dr, Marion, IN 46952; ba/Marion; m/Gladys Irene Kirkendall; c/John David, Kenneth Wayne; p/John Wesley Abbott (dec); Mary Mabel Boggs (dec); ed/ThB; pa/Gen Supt, The Wesleyan Ch 1966-; Gen Secy-Treas 1962-66; Exec Dir, Pilgrim Pension Plan 1960-62;

Editor: *Pilgrim Yth News* 1960-62, *Sunday Sch Advance* 1960; Gen Secy of Sunday Schs & Yth 1960-62; Dist Supt, Delmarva Dist, Denton, Md 1953-60; Pastorates: Cambridge, Md 1950-53, Warren, Pa 1945

Richeyville/Bentonville, Pa 1944, Chestertown, Md 1943; r/Wesleyan; hon/Hon DD; Delta Epsilon Chi; Alumni Achmt Awd 1968.

ABDALLAH, SALAM MOHAMED oc/-Senior Research Engineer; b/Jul 6, 1944; h/115 W Saratoga Ct, Vernon Hills, IL 60061; ba/Granville; m/Mahasen Hussein; c/Waleed A, Tarek A; p/Mohamed Abdallah (dec); Farjdah Mohamed Ibrahim, Cairo, Egypt;

ed/BSME Univ Cairo 1966; MSME Univ Ill 1971; MS 1975, PhD 1976 Univ Ia; pa/Sr Res Engr, Owens-Corning Tech Ctr; Reg'd Profl Engr, Ohio; ASME; ASHRAE; ASEE; NSPE; OSPE; r/Moslem; hon/Sigma Xi; W/W Midwest; Notable Ams; NSF Postdoct Res Fellow; Commun Ldrs & Noteworthy Ams.

ABDULLAH, TARIQ HUSAM oc/Physician; b/Oct 23, 1941; h/PO Box 424, Panama City, FL 32401; ba/Panama City; c/Keith and Kyle; p/Huey C and Gladys D Milton; ed/BS; MD; mil/USAFR, Capt; USPHS Comm'd Corp, Surgeon; pa/Islamic Med Assn; Bay Co Med Soc; Bay Meml Med Ctr Staff; cp/Bd Trustees, Al-Akhbar Insts of Sci & Technol; Hon Consul for Guyana in SEn US; r/Islam; hon/Lane Col Alumni Awd; Acad Hons; W/W S&SW; Howard Univ Pres's Clb.

ABELS, MAC JON oc/Florist; b/Mar 17, 1930; h/1732 Sheffield Pl, Ft Worth, TX 76112; ba/Ft Worth; m/Patricia Anita; c/Lallene Rector, Melody Hubnik; p/Benjamin Joseph Abels (dec); Ida Laney Abels, Ft Worth, TX; ed/BS Tex Christian Univ; pa/Profl Commentators Intl; Am Inst Floral Design; TSFA; cp/Past Pres, Kiwanis; Jr

Col Adv Bd; r/Meth; hon/Hon Commentator, Teleflora Nat; Guest Spkr, AIFD 1973; Others.

ABERCROMBIE, BETTY WEBBER oc/-Professor; b/Jun 26, 1920; h/614 S McFarland, Stillwater, OK 74074; ba/Stillwater; c/Kay Titmas (Mrs Gary W), Mary Anneler; p/I I and Faye L Webber (dec); ed/MEd Phillips Univ; EdD Okla St Univ; pa/Prof & Asst Dir, Sch of HPELS, Okla St Univ; OAHPER; AAHPER; NAPEC; SAPEC; cp/Altrusa Clb; Repub; r/Presb; hon/OAHPER Awd; Grad Student of Excell, Okla St Univ; Altrusa Intl Awd; ARC Awd.

ABERNETHY, JOHN GREGORY oc/-Minister; Businessman; Gospel Singer-Evangelist; b/May 16, 1946; h/842 Eden Pl, Escondido, CA 92026; m/Claire Ellen Kennedy; c/Robin Lorraine, Rebekah Joy, John Jr; p/John Wayne Abernethy; E Lorraine Ethridge (Aldridge); ed/Pacific Christian Col; mil/USMC 1963-64; pa/Radio Announcer, KWSO, Wasco, Cal 1977-; Ordained Min 1969; Pastor: Wasco Christian Ch 1974-76, 1st Christian Ch, Elsinore, Cal 1968-70, Chs in Maricopa & Norwalk, Cal 1966-67; Life & Hlth Ins Agt 1971-74; Band Ldr (Vocalist & Trumpeters) 1959-61; Former Mem, Var Min Assns in So & Ctl Cal incl'g: Wasco Min F'ship, (Assoc) Orange Cal Christian Bus-man's Com, Shafter, Cal Christian Bus-man's Com; Canton Christian Conf 1975, 76; Prodr & Musical Dir, Wasco Bicent Choir Pageant 1976; Recorded *I Love America* w Wasco Bicent Choir 1976; Soloist & Group Mem Perf'g Gospel & Secular Music Throughout Cal & Ariz; Ch Choir Guest Dir;

hon/Outstg New Agt of Mo (Mar-May & Oct), Mutual Security Life 1971; Agt of Yr & New Agt of Yr, Collier Agy, Mutual Security Life 1971; Million Dollar Clb & Pres's Clb, Mutual Security Life 1971; Agy Rookie of Yr, Vreeland Agy, Banker's Life of Ia 1972; Million Dollar Clb & Premier Clb, Banker's Life of Ia 1972-73; Nat Hlth Ins Quality Awd, Nat Assn Life Underwriters 1973; Subject of Articles *Christian Standard* 1975, 76; Acad Hons; Commun Ldrs & Noteworthy Ams; DIB; Personalities of W&MW; Notable Ams; Men Achmt; Intl W/W Commun Ser; W/W Rel; Top Talent Dir (SD Co) 1961.

ABLES, JAMES WHIT oc/Highway Safety Patrol Administrator; b/Mar 5, 1928; ba/PO Box 958, Jackson, MS 39205; ed/Grad Miss St Univ; mil/AUS, Served in Korean Conflict as Infantry Ofcr; Ret'd 1969 w Rank of Major; pa/Miss Hwy Safety Patrol: Appt'd Dir Implied Consent Bur 1980, Dir Public Relats Bur 1978, Asst Dir Public Relats Bur, Other Positions; Formerly Assoc'd w Vicksburg (Miss) Police Dept, Capt of Detective Bur; Fed Hlth & Safety; Mem Railroad Grade Crossing Comm; Uniform Safety Ofcrs Assn; Tenn-Miss Peace Ofcrs Assn; Miss Law Enforcemt Ofcrs Assn; Spec Fac Instr Miss Law Enforcemt Tng Acad, Jackson; Nat Safety Coun; Instrumental in Directing Yg Men to Law Enforcemt Careers; Involved in Recruiting Tng Classes; Other Profl Activs; cp/Life Mem: NG Assn, VFW; Am Legion; Bd Advrs Farm Bur; Active Mem Army Resv; Past Noble Grand Indep Order Odd Fellows; hon/Var Awds for Work in Safety Ed, VFW (US); Others.

ABRAHAM, JOHN P oc/Professor; b/Apr 14, 1947; h/2820 Hibiscus, McAllen, TX 78501; ba/Edinburg, TX; m/Mercy Kutty; c/Thomas John, Mary Thankam; p/Philip P Abraham (dec); Thankamma Abraham, McAllen, TX; ed/BS; MT; MEd; pa/Prof, Pan Am Univ; Pres, Local Chapt ASMT; Book Reviewer for AJMT; cp/Sub Area Coun, Hlth Sys Agy; Bd Mem, Am Cancer Soc; r/Ch of Christ; hon/W/W Among Am Jr Cols; Noyes Foun F'ship.

ABRHAMSON, BERGLJOT oc/Retired Teacher; b/Mar 27, 1909; h/PO Box 1642, Clewiston, FL 33440; ed/BEd; pa/Former Tchr; Life Mem, NEA; Former Mem: St Ed Assn NY, Md Ed Assn, Fla Ed Assn; cp/Repub Party; Secy, Conservative Caucus; Security Coun; r/Prot; hon/10 Yr Cert & Plaque for AEA Mbrship; 5 Yr & 10 Yr Certs & Pins for 4-H Ldr at Fairs in Ariz & Fla; W/W: Elem & Sec'dy Ed, MW & Canada; Personalities of S; Intl Reg Profiles; Book of Hon; Personalities of S&SW; IPA; Commun Ldrs & Noteworthy Ams; World W/W Wom.

ABRAHAMSON, DIANE M oc/-Instructor; Coach; Athletic Trainer; b/Jan 5, 1952; h/Box 43, Hutsonville, IL 62433; ba/Robinson, IL; p/Roland A and Lois M Abrahamson, Wilmette, IL; ed/BS cum laude 1974, MA 1975 Wn Mich Univ; pa/Lincoln Trail Col: Instr, Ath Tnr, Volleyball, Softball, Swimming & Basketball Caoch; cp/GSA; hon/Acad Hons; Mortar Board; W/W: Among Students in Am Cols & Univs, Among Am Wom; Book of Hon; DIB; Reg Profiles; Intl W/W Commun Ser; Intl W/W Intells; World W/W Wom; Men & Wom Distn; Personalities of W&MW; Commun Ldrs & Noteworthy Ams; Notable Ams.

ABRAHAMSON, IRA A JR oc/Ophthalmologist; b/Jul 19, 1924; h/2766 Baker Pl, Cincinnati, OH 45206; ba/Cinc; m/Linda Aloe; c/Richard, Thomas, Susan; p/Ira and Fay Abrahamson, Cincinnati, OH; ed/BA; MD; mil/Ohio NG 1947-49; AUS Med Corps 1951-53; pa/Ophthalmologist; r/Jewish; hon/Author: 80+ Sci Articles, 2 Textbooks *Know Your Eyes,* Color Atlas of Anterior Segment; Sci Exhibit "Anterior Segment Eye Disorders" Rec'd Num 1st Pl and Gold Awds for Outstg Sci Exhibit at Num Med Soc Meetings; Barraquer Awd.

ABRAMOVITZ, JOSEPH HENRY oc/-

Sheriff; b/Jul 15, 1931; h/225 S Wood Neosho, MO 64810; ba/Neosho; m/Edwina; c/Toni Kim; p/Joseph Adam Abramovitz, Pierce City, MO; Mary Abramovitz, Neosho, MO; pa/Sheriff, Newton Co; r/Cath.

ABRAMOVITZ, MORTON I oc/Diplomat; b/Jan 20, 1933; h/Peabody, MA; m/Married; c/2; ed/BA Stanford Univ 1953; MA Harvard Univ 1955; mil/AUS 1957; pa/Nom'd by Pres Carter as US Ambassador to Thailand 1978; Dep Asst Secy of Def for Intl Affairs 1974-78; Polit Advr to CINCPAC 1973-74; Fgn Affairs Analyst, US St Dept 1971-73; Spec Asst, Ofc of Dep Secy of St 1969-71; Intl Economist, US St Dept 1966-68; Polit Ofcr, Hong Kong 1963-66; Consular-Economic Ofcr, Taipai 1960-62; w Intl Coop Adm 1958-60.

ABZUG, BELLA SAVITZKY oc/Lawyer; Lecturer; b/Jul 24, 1920; h/37 Bank St, NY, NY 10014; ba/NYC; m/Martin; c/Eve Gail, Isobel Jo; p/Emanuel and Esther Tanklefsky Savitsky (dec); ed/BA Hunter Col 1947; JD Columbia Univ 1945; pa/Atty 1945-70; cp/Mem US Ho of Reps 1970-76; Cand for US Senate 1976; Cand for Mayor, NYC 1977; Presiding Ofcr, Nat Com on Observance of Intl Woms Yr; Former Co-Chm, Nat Adv Com for Wom; r/Jewish; hon/Hon Degs from Hobart Col, William Smith Col, Hunter Col, Manhattan Col.

ACCURSO, ANTHONY SALVATORE oc/Artist; Illustrator; Painter; b/Apr 5, 1940; h/714-46th St, Brooklyn, NY 11220; ba/Same; p/Carl Joseph Accurso; Mary Innella Accurso (dec); ed/Bklyn Mus Art Sch; Sch of Art & Design, NYC; Pratt Inst; pa/Artist-Correspondent for ABC-TV News, WABC-TV News 1969-; Courtroom Artist; Illustrator for *Am Astrol, Horoscope Guide, Your Daily Horoscope;* Bibliog, Harry Reasoner (interviewer), "Trial Artists", Commentary, ABC-TV News 1974; Dick Cavett (interviewer), "On UFO's", *Dick Cavett Show, ABC-TV Wide World of Entertainment* 1973; Ilustrator for Feature Film, *Mysteries From Beyond Earth,* Constantin Films 1975 & ABC-TV Documentary 1977; Illustrator, "Courtroom Artists", *The Today Show,* NBC-TV 1976; Exhibits: Bronx Mus of Art in Coop w Metro Mus of Art, Notre Dame Law Sch, Harbor Gallery (Long Island, NY), Huntsville Mus of Art (Ala), Living Arts & Sci Ctr (Lexington, Ky); Traveling Exhbns: Watergate: Am Court-trials, Contemp Courtroom Artists; Graphic Artists Guild of NYC; IPA; Visual Artists & Galleries Assn of NYC; Accadamia Italia delle Artie del Laroro (Parma, Italy); Contbr to *Time, Newsweek, Nat Review, The Nation, Science Digest,* Others; hon/Best Portfolio, Sch of Art & Design; Intl Salon Awd, Biarritz, France; 10th Annual TV Illustration Awd, *Art Direction Mag;* Gold Medal, Accadamia Italia delle Artie del Laroro; Biogl Listings; Others.

ACKERMAN, CAROLYN S oc/Librarian; Business Executive; h/15 Bramshott Ct, Rockville Centre, NY 11570; ba/Hempstead, NY; m/Bruno; c/Susan, Barbara; p/Henry and Hannah (dec); ed/BA Hunter Col 1938; MA Columbia Univ 1940; MLS Long Island Univ 1966; pa/Libn, Hofstra Univ Lib; VP, Am-Finn Sauna of LI; Am Lib Assn; NY Lib Assn; Nassau City Lib Assn; AAUP; NY Tech Sers Libns; Other Profl Orgs; Served on US Sen Coms; Editor, Hofstra Lib Newslttr; Contbr to Profl Pubs; cp/Rockville Centre Heritage Com; hon/Phi Beta Kappa; Beta Phi Mu; Alpha Chi Alpha.

ACREA, JEANNETTE McQUOID oc/-Psychologist; b/Aug 8, 1909; h/1635 Rancho Ave, Glendale, CA 91201 ba/Glendale; m/Ivan; c/Douglas, (Foster Chd:) Robert Dean, Tom Dean, Steven Dean; p/Charles and Clara MacSweeney McQuoid (dec); ed/MA; PhD; pa/Am Psychol Assn; Cal St Psychol Assn; cp/Repub; r/Prot.

ADAIR, EDWIN ROSS oc/Diplomat; b/Dec 14, 1907; h/813 Three Rivers N, Ft Wayne, IN 46807; ba/Ft Wayne, IN;

m/Marian E Wood; c/Caroline Ann Dimmers (Mrs David A), Stephen Wood; p/Edwin L and Alice Prickett; ed/AB Hillsdale Col 1928; LLB George Washington Univ 1933; LLD Ind Inst Tech; mil/AUS 1941-45; pa/Law Pract, Ft Wayne 1933-; US Ambassador to Ethiopia 1971-74; Ind St Bar Assn; Ft Wayne Bar Assn; cp/Ind 4th Dist Mem, US Ho of Reps, 82nd to 91st Congs; Trustee, Hillsdale Col; Past Mem Bd Dirs: Parkview Meml Hosp, Eisenhower S'ship Fund; VFW; Am Legion; 33° Mason; Phi Alpha Delta; Past Nat Pres, Delta Sigma Phi; Past Del, Interparliamentary Union; US Del, 18th Gen Conf UNESCO 1974.

ADAIR, TOBY WARREN JR oc/Minister; b/Sept 8, 1922; h/6115 Rockhurst Dr, San Diego, CA 92120; ba/Spring Valley, CA; m/Ann Redden; c/Robin Lee Beynon; p/Toby Warren Adair (dec); Mildred Lee Adair, Shreveport, LA; ed/BS; MDiv; MRE; DMin;

mil/USAF, Pers Ofcr (Ret'd); pa/Pastor, Bancroft Bapt Ch; San Diego So Bapt Assn: Com on Moral Concerns, Cal Missions Com; San Diego Evang Assn; r/So Bapt; hon/Dist'd Flying Cross; Boss of Yr, Sierra Chapt ABWA 1975.

ADAMS, ANDREW STANFORD oc/-Government Official; b/Jul 8, 1922; h/1600 S Joyce St, Apt B-409, Arlington, VA 22202; ba/Wash DC; m/Anke; c/Arva, Anya; p/Edward L Adams (dec); Jane Eva Kurwolsky (dec); ed/Doct, Univ Cal Berkeley 1954; mil/USAAC 1942-45; pa/Staff Asst for Policy Budget & Adm, Ofc of Secy, US Dept Interior 1977-; US Commr of Rehabilitation Sers 1974-77; Dep Dir, Ed & Rehab Sers, Vets Adm 1973-74; Supt, Kans City Public Schs, Mo 1970-73; Dir, Ednl Affairs & Selection,

VISTA, OEO 1964-70; Asst Supt & Dir Ednl Sers, Clark Co Public Schs, Las Vegas, Nev 1962-64; Supt, Freedom Public Schs, Cal 1960-62; Supt & Prin, San Luis Obispo Co Public Schs 1956-60; Tchg Positions: Geo Wash Univ, Univ Va, Univ Mo, Univ Nev, Univ Cal, San Jose St Univ, Fresno St Univ, Cal St Polytechnic Univ; Conslt; Planning Commr, Santa Cruz Co, Cal 1960-62; Others; Mem & Ofcr Num Profl Orgs; cp/Var Civic Affils; hon/Var Achmt & Ser Awds.

ADAMS, BETSY oc/Biologist; Poet; b/May 1, 1942; h/6480 S State Rd, Saline, MI 48176; ba/Detroit, MI; p/Lorne Paul and Dora B Adams; ed/BS Univ Mich, Ann Arbor 1964; MS 1970, PhD Cand Wayne St Univ; MA Boston Univ; pa/Res Asst in Evolutionary

Ecol (current); Res Assoc in Biophysics, Wayne St Univ 12 Yrs; Creative Writing Tchr 3 Yrs; English Tchr, Nikkoli Gakkuin (Pvt Sch), Tokyo, Japan 1 Yr; Sci Editor, *Second Growth* Mag; Contbg Editor, *Snowy Egret*; Grad Level Sci Tchr; Seeking & Implementing Alternatives to Use of Animals for Biomed Resch & Related Areas; Pub'd Poetry in: *West Coast Poetry Review*, *NY Qtrly*, *Kansas Qtrly*, *Images*, *Dacotah Territory*, Others; hon/Author: *Histories* 1978, *Losing the Moon* 1978, Var Profl Articles.

ADAMS, BEVERLY DECKER oc/- Professor; Private Music Teacher; b/May 7, 1926; h/1418 Laird Ave, Salt Lake City, UT 84105; m/Theodore (Ted) N; c/Julia, Mark T, Sondra, Decker O; p/Harold A and Julia Hiatt Decker, Salt Lake City, UT; ed/BMus McCune Sch of Music & Art 1948; MMus 1966, PhD 1969 Univ Utah; pa/Prof: Brigham Young Univ 1973-, Westminster Col 1977-, Univ Utah Grad Sch 1969-70; McCune Sch of Music 1947-57; Organist: 1st Unitarian Ch, Salt Lake City 1966-, Guest Tabernacle Organist 1978; Fellow, Am Guild Organists; Cert'd Music Tchrs Nat Assn; Past Pres, Utah Music Tchrs Assn; Past Utah Chm, Am Guild Organists; Recitalist; Adjucator; Professional Accompanist; cp/Former Mem, Utah Symph Yth Adv Bd; r/Ch of Jesus Christ LDS: Gen Music Com-Organ Task Force, Bonneville Stake Organist, Bonneville Stake Relief Soc Bd, Bonneville Stake Primary Bd; hon/Phi Kappa Phi; Sigma Alpha Chi; Mu Phi Epsilon.

ADAMS, CAROLYN E oc/Dancer; b/Aug 16, 1943; h/144 W 121 St, NY, NY 10027; ba/NYC; p/Julius J and Olive A Adams, NY, NY; ed/BA Sarah Lawrence Col; pa/Prin Dancer w Paul Taylor Dance Co; Co-

Dir, Harlem Dance Studio w Julie Strandberg; cp/Co-Chm, Ctl Harlem Brownstone Presv Com; r/Epis; hon/Dancer of Mo, *Dance Mag* Nov 1970; Mademoiselle Merit Awd 1969; W/W Am.

ADAMS, CECILE NEOMIA oc/Educator; b/May 31, 1915; h/Rt 3, Box 123, Vacherie, LA 70090; m/Stanley; c/Milton James, Daryl Gerard, Tharis Bernard, Stanley Junior; p/Alfred and Clothilda Aubert Walker (dec); ed/BA So Univ; pa/Ret'd; Prin 22 Yrs; Tchr, St James Parish 36 Yrs; cp/Grandady, St Philip Chapt 45, K of PC; Pres, Les Dame of Amour Civ Clb; r/Cath: Secy St Philip's Altar Soc, Pres Ladies Aux, Tchr CCD Classes Sev Yrs; hon/Medal for Vol Hours, W St James Hosp; Apprec Plaque, La Tchrs Assn.

ADAMS, ERNESTINE oc/Editor; Writer; b/Apr 14, 1905; h/2818 Fondren, Dallas, TX 75205; ba/Dallas; p/Ernest James and Betty Cottengim Adams (dec); ed/BJ Univ Mo 1926; Postgrad Study: New Sch Social Res, Columbia Univ, NY Univ, So Meth Univ; pa/Editor, Energy Pubs Div, HBJ Inc, Dallas 1943-; Pubr, *Energy News* and *Energy Week* 1970-; Advtg Dept, Neiman Marcus, Dallas 1943; Owner, *Logan Co News*, Crescent, Okla 1930-37; Wom in Commun; Chi Omega; Pi Epsilon Tau; cp/Repub; Press Clb; Charter Mem, Desk & Derrick Clb; r/Presb: Deacon; hon/Named 1st Oil Wom of Yr, Intl Petrol Expn 1953; Edit Achmt Awd, Am Bus Press 1963; Matrix Awd, Theta Sigma Phi 1964; W/W Am.

ADAMS, HARLAND MORRISON oc/- Corporation Executive; b/Nov 26, 1932; h/7301 Belle Meade Island, Belle Meade Island, Miami, FL 33138; ba/Cocoa, FL; m/Scarlett Norris Huenergardt; c/Tiffany, Rhett Harland; p/James Trigg Sr Adams Sr;

Margaret Sanders Huenergardt; mil/AUS 1953-55, Cpl; pa/Chm Bd Dirs, Ky Fried Chicken of Fla Inc; Inst Food Technologists 1961-; cp/Mem & Patron, Am Acad Achmt; Wingate Lodge #161, F&AM; Knight Templar, 32° Scottish Rite; Mahai Temple AAONMS; r/Prot; hon/Ky Col; W/W S&SW.

ADAMS, HENRY HITCH oc/Writer; Educator; b/Mar 26, 1917; h/Ferry Farms, Annapolis, MD 21402; m/Catherine S; c/Catherine S Hartmann (Mrs James F Jr); Henry A S; p/Henry F and Susan H Adams (dec); mil/USNR Active WW II, Capt (Ret'd); pa/Ret'd Prof; Wrote 4 Vols of Hist of WW II & Biog of Harry Hopkins; r/Epis; hon/Pub'd Author.

ADAMS, HERBERT RICHARDS oc/Publisher; b/Apr 19, 1932; h/2679 Stewart Ave, Evanston, IL 60201; ba/Chicago, IL; m/Mary Ryan; c/Ashley Ward, Joshua, Lee Hampton, Rachel Ellis; p/Leander Hampton Adams (dec); Helen A Bates, Brookline, MA; ed/AB Colby Col; EdD Harvard Col; pa/Ordained Unitarian-Universalist Min 1968; Mgr for Devel, HS Div, Sci Res Assocs Inc 1975-; Min, Follen Commun Ch, Lexington, Mass 1967-75; English Teacher, Lexington HS 1968-69, Sr Editor, Ginn & Co 1962-68; Min, Ch of the Redeemer, Chelsea, Mass 1962-66; Other Former Pub'g & Min Positions; Past Dir, NCTE; Vis Tchr & Lectr at Var Cols & Sec'dy Schs; Author 2 Multi-Media Curric Kits; Unitarian-Universalist Mins Assn; cp/Former Mem, Lexington Town Meeting; ACLU; Bd Dirs, Clergy & Laity Concerned; Former Mem Bd Dirs, Theatre Workshop, Boston; Bd Dirs, Newton (Mass) Country Players; Active in Var Commun & Little Theatre Groups; r/Min-at-large, 1st Unitarian Ch of Chgo 1975-; hon/Coe Foun Award for Am Studies.

ADAMS, J T oc/Educator; Businessman; Musician; b/Jul 17, 1926; h/3522 Lakeside Dr, Rockwall, USA TX 75087; ba/Dallas, TX; m/Judy Gaye; c/Virginia Carol, John Christopher; p/Walter Eddie and Bessy Cordelia Adams (dec); ed/BA, MEd; mil/USN WW II; pa/Col Prof, E Tex St Univ 5 Yrs; Prog Dir & TV Sta Mgr, Dallas, Tex; Recording Artist, Word Records 20 Yrs; Composer: "Glory to God", "Prince of Peace", "Emmanuel" (All Christmas Cantatas), "Worthy is the Lamb" (Easter Cantata), *Something Else*, *Time Out* (Youth Musicals); Bus Exec, Bronston, Adams Movie Prodn Co; Pres, Eden Industries; Pres, Carol Pres Inc; Pres, Telecommuns of Am; cp/Nat Chm, Christian Citizens Ams; r/Bapt; hon/Valley Forge Feedoms Foun Awd.

ADAMS, JEAN oc/Journalist; b/Nov 19, 1936; h/Apt 102, 8806 Three Chopt Rd, Richmond, VA 23229; ba/Richmond; m/Martin R; c/Mason, LeSue; p/Willmer Mason (dec); Sue Forman Mason, Longview, TX; ed/BBA Univ Tex; MA, PhD Univ Colo; pa/Syndicated Columnist: U Feature Syndicate 1969-, *NY News*-*Chgo Tribune* Syndicate 1965-69; Chm of Bd & Exec Dir, Intl Fdn for Preventive Med 1977-; Pres, Am

Nutritional Guid Ctrs Inc 1978-; Co-Bus Mgr, Agt & Dir, The Georgetown Art Gallery, Wash DC 1977-78; Dir of Ed & Comuns, Inst of Preventive Med 1977-78; Chm of Bd, Contemporary Programs Inc 1969-; Feature Article Writer, *Family Weekly* Mag 1971-73; Other Past Positions; cp/Bd Mem: Nat All-Am Fam, Wash DC, Emerson Sch Bd, NYC, Nat Miss Am Teenager Pageant, Intl Foun for Preventive Med, Am Nutritional Guid Ctrs Inc; r/Bapt; hon/W/W Am Wom; Phi Delta Kappa; Sigma Iota Epsilon; Delta Pi Epsilon; Notable Ams of Bicent Era.

ADAMS, JOHN MELVIN JR oc/Association Executive; b/Sept 8, 1950; h/Rt 5, Box 505, Laurel, MS 39440; ba/Laurel; m/Darla Kay Fuller; c/John Melvin II, Trinity Kaye; p/John Melvin Sr and Gladys Bea Adams, Bentonia, MS; ed/AA SEn Jr Col; BA SEn Bapt Col; MDiv, DMin Cand Luther Rice

Sem; pa/Pastor, Lebanon Bapt Ch & 3 Other Chs 1970-; Dir, 6 Annual Yth-Ch Camps in Miss; Yth Author, *Miss Bapt Paper* 1975-1978; Yth Lectr; St Dir, Col Assn Bapt Students in Miss; Hi-Y Attendant, Benton HS; r/Bapt; hon/Author, *Christian Youth in a Modern World*; Selected Outstg Local Citizen, Wiggins, Miss.

ADAMS, JOHN QUINCY oc/Counselor; Assistant Professor; b/Jul 18, 1935; h/8140 Aberdeen Rd, New Orleans, LA 70126; ba/New Orleans; m/Lydia Sindos; c/Donna Lynn, John Sindos, Michael David; p/L A and Viola Coverson Adams (dec); ed/BS; MA; mil/AUS 1957-60; pa/Cnslr; Asst Prof & Chm Human Potential; Stockbroker; Salesman; Tchr; Prog Dir; Phi Delta Kappa; cp/Urban Leag; YMCA; Alpha Phi Alpha; r/Meth; hon/Worthing Foun Fellow; W/W Among Students in Am Univs & Cols; Magna Cum Laude Grad Dillard Col; W/W S&SW.

ADAMS, L WAYNE oc/Organizational Administrator; b/Mar 11, 1953; h/N-8 Quail Hollow Apts, W Columbia, SC 29169; ba/Columbia; p/Laylon C Adams (dec); Oris C Adams, Ware Shoals, SC; ed/Univ SC; pa/Exec Dir, SC Repub Party; cp/Jaycees; Former Chm, SC Col Repubs; Pi Kappa Alpha; r/So Bapt; hon/W/W: Am Polits, Am Univs & Cols; Outstg Yg Men Am.

ADAMS, LEROY oc/Minister; Educator; b/Nov 6, 1923; h/239 S Grant St, Wooster, OH 44691; ba/Smithville, OH; m/Helen; c/Theodore Lee, Rachel Ann; p/Frank Adams, Washington, PA; ed/BM Youngstown St Univ 1955; BD Oberlin Col 1964; MDiv Vanderbilt Univ 1973; Addit Study: Akron Univ, Kent St Univ; mil/AUS WW II, Cpl; pa/Pastor, 2nd Bapt Ch, Wooster; Tchr & Asst Prin, Boys Village Sch, Smithville; cp/Phi Mu Alpha; Trombonist, Youngstown Philharm Orch 7 Yrs; U Fund; Dir, YMCA; Wayne Co Cancer Soc; U Negro Col Fund; Commun Bandsman; Wayne Co Task Force; Chaplain, Wooster Rotary Clb; Dean, Christian Usher's Assn Am Inc; r/Bapt; Instr, No Ohio Bapt Dist Assn; hon/YWCA Plaque; BSA Pin.

ADAMS, MARIANNE KATHRYN oc/- Government Administrator; b/Jan 10, 1924; h/128 Grove Ave, Albany, NY 12208; ba/Albany; p/Harold J Adams (dec); Marion S Adams; ed/BA; MA; pa/NYS Acad Public

Adm; Am Soc Public Adm; NYS Acad Hlth Adm; Am Acad Hlth Adm; NYS Public Hlth Assn; Am Public Htlh Assn; Intl Pers Mgmt Assn; Albany BPW; Nat Assn Female Execs; cp/Co-Chm/Chm Dept U Way Campaigns; SPAC Vols; Albany Symphony Vanguard; r/Meth; hon/Lttr Commend, Secy Htlh, Ed & Welfare 1976; NYS Merit Awd 1962; Cert of Outstg Contbn, SUNY Albany Alumni Assn Bd Dirs 1978.

ADAMS, WILLIAM MANSFIELD oc/-Seismologist; Professor; b/Feb 19, 1932; h/355 Royal Hawaiian Ave, Waikiki, Honolulu, HI 96815; ba/Honolulu; m/Naoko Nakashizuka; c/Henele Iitaka, Alden Fernald; p/Shirah Devoy Adams, St Augustine, FL; Olive Colburn Adams; ed/AB Univ Chgo; BA Univ Cal-Berkeley; MS, PhD St Louis Univ; MBA Santa Clara Univ; pa/Seismologist & Prof of Geophysics, Univ Hawaii; Am Geophysical U; Acoustical Soc Am; Soc Exploration Geophysicist; European Assn of Exploration Geophysicists; Sigma Xi; Seismological Soc Am (Past Editor); r/Bapt; hon/Fulbright Grant; NATO Grant; UNESCO Expert in Seismology; Patents in Field.

ADDISON, HAROLD V oc/Title Analyst; b/Oct 12, 1922; h/4949 Skillman #152, Dallas, TX 75206; ba/Dallas; p/I T Addison (dec); Alline Lee Addison, Haughton, LA; ed/Grad La Tech Univ; Addit Study: Centenary Col, Richmond St Univ, Univ Denver; mil/AUS WW II; pa/Land Property Admr & Title Analyst, Sun Oil Co 1977-; Asst Land Mgr, Eason Oil Co, 1965-77; Gen Mgr,

Anabasco, Okla City, Okla 1958-65; w Land Dept, Marathon Oil Co, Shreveport, La 1953-58; Chm, Nat Assn Div Order Analysts; Okla City Assn Petrol Landmen; cp/Patron, Okla Mus Art; Shreveport Geneal Res Soc; Charter Mem Beta Zeta Chapt, Tau Kappa Epsilon; Others; r/Holy Cross Epis Ch; hon/Purple Heart; Bronze Star w OLC; Fleur de Lis; Hon Mem: Sigma Alpha Iota, NY Philharm Soc; Book of Hon; W/W S&SW.

ADE, WALTER FRANK CHARLES oc/-Professor; b/Oct 24, 1910; h/8021 Schreiber Dr, Munster, IN 46321; ba/Munster, IN; m/Eleanor Anne Shroeder; c/Virginia Anne Miller (Mrs Robert H Jr), George Leonard; p/Leonard Konrad and Bertha Pauline Rhode

Ade (dec); ed/BA Queen's Univ, Canada 1933; MA 1939, BPaed 1943, MEd 1945 Univ Toronto, Canada; PhD NWn Univ 1949; MScEd 1955, EdD 1960 Ind Univ; Postdoct Dipls; mil/RCAF 1942-45, Flying Ofcr;

pa/Purdue Univ: Prof Emeritus 1976-, Prof of Mod Langs & Ed 1959-76; Profl Translator 1963-; Prof of German, Ariz St Univ 1958-59; Studienprof English, Humanistic Gymnasium Noerdlingen, Bavaria, W Germany 1955-56; Assoc Prof of Mod Langs, Valparaiso Univ 1949-58; Other Past Tchg Positions; cp/Commun Lectr on Life in Fgn Lands; Past Mem Ednl Div, Munster C of C; Other Former Civic Activs; r/St Paul's Luth Ch; hon/Author: 12 Books, 75 Articles, Num Poems, Others; Num F'ships, S'ships & Grants incl'g: Fulbright F'ship, Purdue Univ Res Fdn Grant; DIB; W/W: Am, Ind, Am Ed, World, Midwest; Intl W/W Commun Ser; Intl W/W Intells; Intl Authors & Writers W/W; Intl Scholars Dir; Ldrs in Ed in Am; Ldrs in Humanities in Am; Commun Ldrs & Noteworthy Ams; Personalities of W&MW; Notable Ams of Bicent Era; Others.

ADLER, ERWIN ELLERY oc/Attorney; b/Jul 22, 1941; h/872 Norman Pl, Los Angeles, CA 90049; m/Stephanie Ruskin; c/Lauren Michelle, Michael Benton; p/Ben Adler (dec); Helen M Adler; ed/BA Univ Mich 1963; JD Harvard Law Sch 1966; LLM Univ Mich 1967; pa/Am Bar Assn; Cal Bar Assn; cp/Bd Dirs: Chd's S'ships Inc 1979-, Hollywood Civic Opera Assn 1975-76; r/Jewish; hon/Phi Beta Kappa; Phi Kappa Phi.

ADROUNIE, V HARRY oc/Environmental Administrator; b/Apr 29, 1915; h/126 S Broadway, Hastings, MI 49058; ba/APO San Fran, CA; c/Harry Michael, Vee Patrick; p/H A Adrounie (dec); Dorothy Adrounie; ed/BS 1940, BA 1959 St Ambrose Col; Command & Staff Col Air Univ USAF Maxwell AFB, Ala 1956-57; Addit Study; mil/USA and USAF 27 Yrs; Lt Col USAF; pa/Envir Spec, Sch of Public Hlth, Univ Hawaii; Dir Div Envir Protection, Chester Co, Pa Hlth Dept 1970; Dir Envir Hlth, Berrien Co, Mich 1975; Past Dep Cmdr, 1st Aeromed Evacuation Group TAC, Rec'd OLC to AF Commend Medal; Tech Dir, Large Org Selling Sers to Hosps & Other Med Care Facilities Throughout US 1968-70; Dep Cmdr, World Wide USAF Med Unit 1966-68; Acting Chm & Visiting Assoc Prof, Dept Envir Hlth, Am Univ, Beirut, Lebanon 1963-66 (Legion of Merit, Only Serman Appt'd as Univ Dept Chm); Cmdr Detachmts 10 & 11 1st Aeromed Trans Group

MATS 1961-63; Envir Hlth Spec USAF Surg Gen & USAF Envir Hlth Rep to Nat Acad Scis & US Interdept Com Nutrition for Nat Def, Conslt USPHS Mobilization Prof 1957-61; Rec'd USAF Commend Medal (last 2 Pos Resp for World Wide Opers of USAF); Envir Hlth Spec Med Div & Biol & Chem Warfare Spec in Spec Weapons Div Ofc Inspector Gen Hdqrs USAF 1953-56; Chief of Planning & Reporting Branch, Field Test and Meterology Div Ft Detrick, Md 1951-52; Preventive Med Ofcr, USA I Corps Japan 1947-50, Rec'd Commend for Responsibility for So ½ Japan 1947-50; Cmdr 20th Med Lab Ft Lewis, Wash 1946-47; Calhoun Co Hlth Dept Bacteriologist Spec TB Res Jan-Aug 1946; Base Med Inspector Lincoln AFB, Neb 1943-46; USA & USAF 1941- from Pvt to Lt Col; Only AF Med Ser Corps Ofcr Qualified as Med Adm Staff Ofcr, Staff Biomed Sci & Bio Envir Engr; Fellow: Am Public Hlth Assn, Royal Soc Hlth, AAAS; Nat Envir Hlth Assn: Life Mem, Bd Dirs, Pres;

Charter Mem Intl Hlth Soc, Bd Govs; Mem: NY Acad Scis, AAUP, Am Mgmt Assn, Assn Mil Surgs of US, NC Public Hlth Assn, Inst Sanitation Mgmt; Bd Dirs: (Chm) Chester Co Water Resources Auth, Pa Envir Hlth Assn, Legal & Public Relats Com Pa Hlth Coun & Envir Hlth Review & Study Com of Reg Comprehensive Hlth Planning Coun; Chm Sanitarians Reg Bd Pa; Pres Nat Assn Sanitarians 1961-62; Fdr-Diplomate, Am Acad Sanitarians; Mem Chester Co Bd Hlth; Fdr & 1st Pres, Mich Assn of Local Envir Hlth Admrs; Diplomate Am Bd Indust Hygiene; Chm, Pa Public Hlth Assn, Sect on Environment; Cert'd by Am Acad Sanitarian, Am Bd Indust Hygiene in Comprehensive Pract Indust Hygiene; Reg'd Sanitarian Sts: Cal, Pa, Mich, Nev, Others; Num Other Profl Activs & Ofcs; cp/Mem & Cert'd Rifle Marksmanship Instr, Nat Rifle Assn Am; Assoc Mem, Am Mus Nat Hist; Nat Geog Soc; Elks; Am Legion; USAF Assn; Num Other Civic Activs; hon/Am Men Sci; Walter S Mangold Awd 1963; W/W S&SW; Alumnus of Yr, Hastings HS, Mich 1961; Pub'd Author; Personalities of W&MW; Notable Ams; Commun Ldrs & Noteworthy Ams; Others.

AEREA, JEANNETTE MCQUOID oc/-Psychologist; b/Aug 8, 1909; h/1635 Rancho Ave, Glendale, CA 91201 ba/Glendale; m/Ivan; c/Douglas, (Foster Chd:) Robert

Dean, Tom Dean, Steven Dean; p/Charles and Clara MacSweeney McQuoid (dec); ed/MA; PhD; pa/Am Psychol Assn; Cal St Psychol Assn; cp/Repub; r/Prot.

AFUVAI, DIANNA SUE oc/May 21, 1947; h/1231 S Treece, Denison, TX 75020; ba/Denison; m/Al M; c/Shannon Corrie; p/A U and M Maxine Hagan, Mountain Grove, MO; ed/BS SW Mo St Univ; pa/Currently Working in Note Dept, St Nat Bk; Sec'dy Public Sch Tchr 6½ Yrs; r/1st Freewill Bapt Ch: Choir Dir.

AGER, ALMA CLYDE oc/Psychologist; h/PO Box 244, Ft Meade, SD 57741; ba/Ft Meade; m/Grant Neil; c/Wayne, Gary, Jerry, Norma, James; ed/AB Columbia Union Col 1944; AM Univ Redlands 1960; Univ So Cal 1967; pa/Clin Psychologist, VA Hosp 1975-; Psychologist, VA Hosp, Hot Springs, SD 1973-75; Clin Psychol Intern, VA Hosp, Brockton, Mass 1972-73; Chm, Dept Behav Sci, So Missionary Col 1965-72; Other Past Positions; Am Psychol Assn; SD Psychol Assn (Past Secy); SD Mtl Hlth Assn; Rep, Wom Psychologists for SD 1975-; hon/Profl Pubs; hon/Fed Res Grant; Am Men & Wom of Sci; W/W: Am Wom, Midwest, S&SW; Nat Social Dir; Men & Wom Distn; Commun Ldrs & Noteworthy Ams; DIB; Book of Hon; 2000 Wom Achmt; Intl W/W Commun Ser; World W/W Wom; Personalities of S; Lives of Tenn.

AGLI, ROSEMARY oc/Bookkeeper; b/Apr 11, 1947; h/350 Earle St, Central Islip, NY 11722; ba/Hauppauge, NY 11722; m/Roger S; c/Roger Paul, Sherry Marie; p/Armando Marra, Peabody, MA; Edna O'Leary, Cambridge, MA; cp/Suffolk Co Wom's Dem Caucus; Campaign Vol for Sch Bd Cand; Local PTA; WIBC Bowling Leag; r/Cath.

AGNEW, LOUISE CHRISTINA oc/Art

Educator; Painter; Photographer; Printmaker; Lecturer; Designer; b/Aug 17; h/880 N Lake Shore Dr, Chicago, IL 60611; ba/Chgo; m/Wallace G; c/Betty Lee Marquis; p/Frank Oscar Satterwaite (dec); Susan Wampler (dec); ed/BA; MA; PhD; pa/Art Critic; Nat Leag Am Pen Wom; Mem Var Photographic & Art Orgs; Ind Artists Clb; cp/Hoosier Saloon; Chgo Chapt, DAR; r/Presb; hon/Fellow, Royal Photog Soc, Great Britain; Assoc, Am Photo Soc.

AGRAWAL, CHANDRA P oc/Professor; Writer; Translator; Ethnomusicologist; h/2170-19 Cram Pl, Ann Arbor, MI 48105; ba/Ann Arbor; m/Rajendra K Aggarwala; c/Sandeep; p/Shri Ram and Savitri D Agarwal, Lucknow, India; ed/PhD Lucknow Univ, India 1961; BMus Prayag Music Acad, Allahabad 1964; Postdoct Fellow; Univ Toronto 1969-70, Ind Univ 1970; pa/Lectr, Dept of Humanities, Univ Mich 1973-; Asst Prof, Am Univ 1970-72; AAS; Mod Lang Assn; MAASL; SALA; WRC; cp/Active Ser in Sev Local Civic Orgs; hon/Author *Studies in Indian Literature and Culture* 1977, *Jaya Sankar Prasad* 1978, Profl Articles; Indian Writers; World W/W Wom; Dir Indian Wom Today; W/W Am Wom; Personalities of W&MW; Notable Ams; Commun Ldrs & Noteworthy Ams.

AGUILAR, RODOLFO JESUS oc/Architect; Civil Engineer; Real Estate Broker; Consulting Professor; b/Sept 28, 1936; h/4866 Whitehaven St, Baton Rouge, LA 70808; ba/Baton Rouge; m/Nellyn Carias; c/Rodolfo J, Richard A, Robert J, Noryn; p/Jesus Aguilar Cortes (dec); Nora Aguilar Martin, Metairie, LA; ed/BS 1958, MSCE 1960, BArch 1961 La St Univ; PhD NCSU 1964; pa/Pres, Aguilar & Assocs 1977-78; Conslt'g Prof, La St Univ 1974-78; Pres, Ter-Am Bank Holding Co 1975-77; Chm, La Arch Selection Bd 1975-76; cp/Chm of Bd, Commun Bank 1974-77; Chm Exec Com, Am Bank Houma 1974-77; La Bd of Commerce & Indust 1976-78; Baton Rouge Mtl Hlth 1976-78; r/Cath; hon/AIA 1st Pl Design Awd 1957; Halliburton Awd 1967; La Engrg Soc Outstg Engr 1972; Phi Kappa Phi; Sigma Xi; Tau Beta Pi; Chi Epsilon.

AHERN, HUGH STEPHEN oc/Research Specialist; b/Jul 22, 1894; h/Apt D-11, 220 Edgewood Terrace Dr, Jackson, MS 39206; ba/Jackson; m/Lillian; p/James and Hannah

Ahern (dec); pa/Res Spec for Var Pubs; Ret'd Fed Govt Employee; r/Cath; hon/Meritorious Ser Awd, US Dept Commerce; Other Cits from Fed Govt, Atlanta Chapt Am Mktg Assn & Atlanta Assn Fed Execs.

AHL, SALLY W oc/Associate Professor; b/Apr 6, 1938; h/PO Box 246, Tarkio, MO 64491; ba/Tarkio; ed/BS Cornell Univ; BA summa cum laude Barrington Col; MA, PhD Brandeis Univ; pa/Assoc Prof of Rel, Tarkio Univ; Soc Biblical Lit; Ancient Near En Epistology Study Group; Am Acad Rel; Am Oriental Soc; Speak at & Conduct Wkshops on Topics of Biblical Study; cp/4-H Ldr; Commun Chorale; r/Prot; SS Tchr, Ch Camp Ldr, Lay Ldr; hon/Awd for Excell, Am Bible Soc 1969; Mary E Hirshfield F'ship 1971-73; KCRCHE Grant 1978.

AHLGREN, ROY B oc/Printmaker; Art

Educator; b/Jul 6, 1927; h/1012 Boyer Rd, Erie, PA 16511; ba/Erie; m/Martha A; c/Deborah Sue, Alan Roy, David, Brian; p/Ann Ahlgren, Erie, PA; ed/BS Univ Pgh; mil/USN 1944-46; pa/Printmaker, Silk Screen Prints (Serigraphs); Created & Prod'd 100+ Exhbns; Num Nat & Intl Exhbns incl: Intergraphia "78", Katowice, Poland 1978, 7th Intl Print Biennale, Cracow, Poland 1978, Annual Print & Drawing Exhbn, Providence, RI Watercolor Clb 1976, Nat Print Exhbn, Michael C Rockerfeller Arts Ctr, St Univ Col, Fredonia, NY 1976, 20th Nat Print Exhbn, Hunterdon Art Ctr 1976, 11th Nat Print Exhbn, Silvermine Guild Artists, New Canaan, Conn 1976, Nat Juried Art Show, Shreveport, La 1975; Num Others; Exhbns; Prof, Edinboro St Col 1974; 1-Man Shows:

Chautauqla Art Ctr, NY 1978, Mutual Savings & Ln, Erie, Pa 1977, Antique Village Gallery, Lake Orion, Mich 1975, Okla Art Ctr, Okla City, Okla 1974, Newport Art Ctr, Newport Art Assn, Newport, RI 1974, Lighthouse Gallery, Tequesta, Fla 1973, Del Mar Col, Corpus Christi, Tex 1973, Others; Wks in Permanent Collection at Var Mus, Cols Art Ctrs & Other Instns incl'g: Erie Art Ctr, Erie, Pa, Seattle Mus Art, Seattle, Wash, Potsdam Univ, NY, Butler Art Inst, Youngstown, Ohio, Minn Mus Art, St Paul; Phila Watercolor Clb; Boston Printmakers; Phila Print Clb; Wkshops; cp/Bd Mem, Erie Art Ctr; r/Luth; hon/Num Art Awds; W/W Am Art; DIB; Dic Am Printmakers; Commun Ldrs & Noteworthy Ams; Am Art Dir; Artists USA; Dic Am Painters, Engravers & Sculptors; Others.

AHMED, ALICE PEARCE oc/Teacher; b/Sept 15, 1934; h/912 Highland Way, Bowling Green, KY 42101; ba/Bowling Green; m/Sheik Basheer; c/Ivy Amina; p/Clay Pearce (dec); Ivy Stagner Pearce, Alvaton, KY; ed/BS Wn Ky Univ 1957; MA Murray St Univ 1965; EdD Cand Univ Tenn, Knoxville; pa/Tchr: Warren E HS 1971-, Wn Ky Univ 1976, Warren Ctl HS, Bowling Green 1971, Tenn Technol Univ 1966-68, Others; 3rd Dist Bus Ed Assn, Ky: Pres, Past VP, Secy-Treas; Pi Omega Pi; Assn Tchr Edrs; Intl Soc for Bus Ed; NEA; KEA; Nat Bus Ed Assn; Delta Pi Epsilon; Former Advr: Beta Clb; Future Bus Ldrs Am; cp/Phi Gamma Mu; r/1st Bapt Ch: SS Tchr, GH Ldr, Music Dir; hon/Co-Editor *A Cookbook of Faculty Favorites* (Wn Ky Univ) 1977.

AIKEN, THOMAS WORTHEN oc/Consultant; b/Dec 21, 1920; h/424 Maryland Ct, Va Beach, VA 23451; ba/Va Beach; m/Sara Francis Simpich; c/Marcia Lynn A Hilkert, Charles Anthony, Joan Frances, James Worthen; p/James Buxton Aiken (dec); Nelle Brickhouse Jenkins (dec); ed/BA; mil/USAAF WW II; pa/Conslt in Mil Proj Mgmt & Fed Govt Grant Progs.

AILEY, ALVIN oc/Choreographer; Dancer; b/Jan 5, 1931; h/467 Central Park W, NY, NY 10025; ba/NYC; p/Alvin Ailey Sr (dec); Lula Elizabeth Cooper; pa/Bd Dirs: Black Theatre Alliance, Proj Return; hon/Mayor's Awd of Arts & Cult 1977; Hon Degs: Princeton Univ, Bard Col, Adelphi Univ, Cedar Crest Col, Colgate Univ; Spingarn Medal 1976; *Dance Mag* Awd 1975.

AINSWORTH, KATHERINE LAKE oc/-Writer; Lecturer; b/Nov 15, 1908; h/630 W Duarte Rd #57, Monrovia, CA 91016; m/Ed (dec); c/Shelia A Herron (Mrs Robert S), Cynthia Kate Lengyel; p/William A and Alice O'Neill Lake (dec); ed/BA UCLA 1931; Univ So Cal; pa/Book Reviewer; City Libn, Monrovia; cp/Past Mem, Monrovia Sch Bd; Dir, Hist Soc So Cal; Dir, Death Val 49ers; LA Corral of Westerners; r/Prot; hon/Hon Mem, Delta Kappa Gamma; Hon Citizen, Palm Springs, Cal; Author: *In the Shade of the Juniper Tree*, *McCollum Saga*, *The Man Who Captured Sunshine*.

AITKEN, MOLLY BENNETT-MARKS oc/-Fund Raiser; Homemaker; b/Jul 25, 1944; h/Green Gables Farm, Bigelow Rd, Athol, MA 01331; m/Gerard James II; c/Bridget Marks, Sean Marks, Frederick Marks, Jacqueline Marks, Gerard III; p/Mervin Dreux Bennett (dec); Valre Vasilas, Las Vegas, NV; pa/TV Personality; cp/Dist Commr, Riding for the Handicapped, LI, NY; r/Cath; hon/Cert of Merit, U Cerebral Palsy; Num Awds for Charity Work.

AKIN, RALPH HARDIE JR oc/Corporation Executive; b/Oct 18, 1938; h/10614 Deerwood, Houston, TX 77042; ba/Houston; m/Elaine Fleming; c/Laura Elizabeth, Michael Hardie, Jennifer Aimee; p/Ralph H and Darla S Akin, Shreveport, LA; ed/BS Centenary Col; MS Univ Tulsa; mil/AUS 1960-61, 1/Lt; pa/Pres, Akin Energy Corp; Am Assn Profl Landmers; Am Assn Petrol Geologists; r/Meth; hon/W/W; Personalities of S; W/W S&SW; Num Dist'd Ser Awds.

AKMAKJIAN, ALAN PAUL oc/Poet; Author; b/Jul 18, 1948; h/1919 Greenleaf Dr, Royal Oak, MI 48067; ba/Detroit, MI; ed/BS 1973, MA 1974, En Mich Univ; PhD Cand Wayne St Univ; pa/MLA; Detroit Classical Soc; Cranbrook Writers' Guild; Nat Soc Poets; Poetry Soc Mich; hon/Cert of Recog for Poetry 1977; Cranbrook Writers Guild Awd for Poetry 1978.

AL-ABDULLA, HAMID M oc/Physician; b/Apr 29, 1935; h/308 El Dorado Dr, Richmond, VA 23229; ba/Richmond; m/Linda; c/Safaa, Susan; p/Haj Mohammad Al-Abdulla, Diwaniya, Iraq; Fatima M Twaij, Diwaniya, Iraq; ed/MD Univ Baghdad, Iraq 1958; mil/Iraqi Army Med Corps 1958-59; pa/Cardiologist; Asst Chief of Cardiol & Dir Cardiovascular Lab, VA Hosp, Des Moines, Ia 1970-73; Instr: Case Wn Resv Univ 1968-71, Univ Baghdad 1959-61; Cardiologist, Highland View Hosp, Cleveland, Ohio 1968-71; Attending Physician: Richmond Meml Hosp, Retreat Hosp for the Sick, St Mary's Hosp, Henrico Doctors' Hosp; Fellow: Am Col Physicians, Am Col Cardiol, Am Col Angiol; Am Heart Assn; Richmond Acad Med; Med Soc Va; Richmond Soc Internal Med; Va Soc Internal Med; Am Soc Internal Med; cp/VP, Iraqi Grads Assn, Fairfax, VA; r/Moslem; hon/AMA Physician's Recog Awd 1969, 72, 75; Profl Pubs.

ALAND, KENT MERREL oc/Health Care and Real Estate Consultant; b/Jan 2, 1943; h/9093 Despain Way, Sandy, UT 84070; ba/Salt Lake City, UT; m/Sharon; c/Terri

Lyn, Trevor Montee, Troy Ernest; p/Montee Levi Aland (dec); Phyllis Zoppi, Sparks, NV; ed/BS Brigham Young Univ 1968; MPH Univ of Cal, LA 1970; mil/USPHS 1970-73,

Comm'd Ofcr; pa/Mgr Residential Sales, Lauritzen & Assocs Real Est 1977-; Dir, Ofc of Prog Devel 1974-77; Dir, Utah Cost Improvemt Proj 1973-74; Hosp Admr 1971-73; Am Hosp Assn; Utah Hlth Assn; Salt Lake Bd Realtors; cp/Secy, Repub Leg Dist; Granite Commun Coun Subcom on Zoning & Land Use; r/Ch of Jesus Christ LDS; hon/Superior Work Perf Awd, Asst Surg Gen, USPHS 1971; Outstg Yg Men Am; W/W: W, Hlth Care; Others.

ALBIN, RICHARD JOEL oc/Immunologist; b/May 15, 1940; h/5055 Culver St, Skokie, IL 60077; ba/Chicago, IL; m/Linda Lee Lutwack; c/Michael David; p/Robert Benjamin and Minnie Edith Gordon Albin, Chicago, IL; ed/AB Lake Forest Col 1962; PhD St Univ NY, Buffalo 1967; pa/Cook Co Hosp & Hektoen Inst for Med Res: Sr Sci Ofcr, Div Immunol 1976-, Dir Immunobiol Sect, Div of Urol, Dept of Surg 1973-75; Assoc Prof, Dept Microbiol, Univ Hlth Scis/Chgo Med Sch 1973-74; Sr Sci Staff & Clin Immunologist, Cook Co Hosp 1973-75; Conslt'g Med Staff: Meml Hosp of Springfield 1970-73, St Johns Hosp Dept of Pediatrics 1971-73; Asst Prof, Dept of Med, So Ill Univ Sch of Med 1971-73; Others; AAAS; Am Assn Cancer Res Inc; Fellow: Am Col Cryosurg, Inst Med Chgo; Am Assn for Clin Immunology & Allergy; Am Assn Immunologists; Transplantation Soc; Soc for Cryobiologists; Soc for Protozoologists; Chgo Assn Immunologists; NY Acad Scis; Reticuloendothelial Soc; Intl Soc of Cryosurg; Intl Soc of Chronobiol; Intl Assn Biol Standardization; Am Fdn for Clin Res; Assoc Editor *Low Temperature Medicine*; Asst Editor *Allergologia et Immunopathologia*; Guest Lectr; cp/BSA; Little Leag Baseball; Y-Indian Guides; r/Jewish.

ALBOUM, LAWRENCE oc/Artist; b/Dec 19, 1932; h/106 E 14th St, NY, NY 10003; ba/NY, NY; p/Abraham and Anna Alboum (dec); ed/BS NY Univ 1958; mil/AUS 1954-56; pa/1-Man Shows: Rabinovitch & Guerra Gallery, NYC 1975, Painters' Theatre Gallery, NYC 1971, Blanchard Gallery, NYC 1965; Group Exhbns: 47 Bond St Gallery 1976, Arte Fiera 78, Bologna, Italy 1978, Newark Mus, Newark Mus 1961, 64, Brooklyn Mus 1977, NOHO Gallery, NYC 1978, Others; Works in Collection: Smithsonian Instn, Num Pvt Collections; hon/Var Art Awds.

ALBRECHT, PAUL E oc/Professor Emeritus; Science Writer; b/Oct 27, 1910; h/1399 9th Ave, San Diego, CA 92101; m/(dec); ed/BS, MA, PhD Univ Chgo; pa/Univ Fla: Prof of Sociol 1960-75, Chm Dept of Family Life 1957-69; Res Prof, Auburn Univ 1951-57; cp/Coun on Aging, Sch of Social Wk, St Col San Diego; Vol Sers to Aged; r/Prot; hon/Var Hons.

ALBRECHT, RUTH E oc/University Professor; b/Oct 27, 1910; h/1399 9th Ave, San Diego, CA 92101; ba/Same; m/(dec); chd/(dec); p/(dec); ed/BS, MA, PhD, Univ of Chgo; pa/Prof of Sociology, Univ of Fla 1960-75; Head Dept Fam Life, Univ Fla 1957-69; Research Prof, Auburn Univ 1951-57; Now Prof Emeritus; Writer; r/Prot; hon/Var Awds & Hons.

ALBRIGHT, COOPER EUGENE oc/- Mechanical Engineer; ba/Aug 27, 1927; h/5723 Claridge Dr, Houston, TX 77096; ba/Houston; m/Gracie P; c/George Allen, Paul Randall, Carole Jean Barnard, (Stepchd:) Gary Lang Koger, Tanya Lee Bodo, Patricia Ann Sveda; p/George Cooper and Verlie Lurline Williams, Bastrop, LA; ed/ME; mil/USN 1945-46, 1950-51; pa/Houston Engrg & Sci Soc; Am Soc Mech Engrs; Nat Soc Profl Engrs; Tex Soc Profl Engrs; Reg'd Profl Engrs: Ala, La, Okla, Miss, SC, Tex, Wis; cp/32° Mason; Repub; r/So Bapt.

ALBRITTON, ROBERT BYNUM oc/- Lawyer; b/Feb 1, 1905; h/723 Albritton Rd, Andalusia, AL 36420; ba/Andalusia; m/Carrie Veal; c/William Harold III; p/William Harold and Anne Mashburn Albritton; ed/LLB Univ Ala

1930; pa/Mem Law Firm, Albrittons & Rankin 1930-; Dir & Gen Counsel: Plumbing Supply Co, Ala Textile Products Corp, Troy Textiles Inc, Enterprise Mfg Co, Evergreen Textiles 1938-68; Ala Law Inst Adv Com for Revision of Probate Code; Am Bar Assn; Ala Law Inst; Am Judic Soc; Ala Bar Assn; Covington Co Bar Assn; Ala Def Lwyrs Assn; World Assn Lwyrs; Farrah Law Soc; Am Acad Polit & Social Sci; Am Inst Mgmt; IPA; Kappa Sigma; Phi Detla Phi; cp/Past Pres, Andalusia Rotary Clb; Andalusia CC; Ft Walton Yacht Clb; Little Pine Hunting Clb; Bd Dirs, Univ Ala Law Sch; Pres's Cabinet, Univ Ala; r/Presb: Deacon; hon/W/W: Fin & Indust, World, S&SW, Am.

ALDERMAN, MINNIS AMELIA oc/Educator; Counselor; Psychologist; Business Woman; Executive; b/Oct 14, 1928; ba/Nevada Personnel, Ely Mtl Hlth Ctr, Ely, NV; p/Louis Cleveland Sr and Minnis Amelia Wooten Alderman; ed/AB Ga St Col for Wom 1949; MA Murray St Univ 1960; PhD Cand; pa/Psychologist: Nev Job Ser 1975-, Ely Mtl Hlth Ctr 1969-75; Owner: Knit Knook Shop 1970-, Mini-Mimeo 1969-, Minisizer 1969-71; Gift Gamut 1977-; Originator: Creative Crafters Assocs 1976, White Pine Sr Citizens Nutrition Prog 1974, White Pine Sr Citizens Ctr 1974, White Pine Rehab Ctr 1972; Dir Ret'd Sr Vol Prog 1973-74; Instr Guid, Cnslr-Ed, Psychol: Murray St Univ 1961-62, Univ Nev Ext 1963-67; Test Supvr, Ed Testing Ser ACT Prog, Univ Nev 1960-68; Cnslr, White Pine Sch Dist, White Pine HS, Ely 1960-68; Eng & Social Studies Instr, Sinking Fork Sch, Hopkinsville, Ky 1960; Other Former Tchg Positions; Cnslrs on Alcoholism, Addictions & Related Dependencies 1974-; Nat Fdn BPW Clbs 1961-, Sev St & Dist Ofcs Nev Fdn, Ely Clb Parliamentn & Past Pres; IPA; Precnt Reporter, ABC News 1966; APGA; NAWDC; Am Fdn Woms Clbs; Nat Fdn of Indep Bus, Dist Chm 1971-; Gt Basin Hlth Coun; White Pine Coun on Alcohol & Drug Abuse; NOW; Nat Assn for Female Execs; NEA Life Mem; AAUW; cp/Gov's Conf on Status of Wom; Gov's Comm on Mtl Hlth; White Pine Commun Concert Assn: Bd Dirs, Past Pres & VP; Common Cause; Commun Choir Dir; DAR; UDC; Nev St Employees Assn; Home Ec Adv Bd, Univ Nev Ext Ser; r/Ely Meth Ch: Choir Dir, Lay Ldr; hon/Delta Kappa Gamma; Alpha Chi, Sev Ofcs Beta Chapt; Mensa; Biogl Listings; Pub'd Author Articles & Pamphlets; S'ships; Grants Author for Sev Funded Projs.

ALDRICH, THOMAS ALBERT oc/- Corporation Executive; ba/Nov 30, 1923; h/302 Elmhurst Cir, Sacramento, CA 95825; ba/Sacramento; m/Virginia Elaine Peterson; c/Sharon Elaine Lingis, Pamela Kay Williams, Thomas Charles; p/John Albert and Georgia Opal Hilliard Aldrich, San Angelo, TX; ed/Grad Inst Meteorol Univ Chgo 1944; BA 1961, MS 1968 Geo Wash Univ; mil/USAF 35

Yrs, Maj Gen; pa/VP & Corp Rep, Anheuser-Busch, Inc; Cmdr, 22D AF 1975-78; Dep Chief of Staff Plans, Mil Alft Cmd 1974-75; Cmdr, Air Wea Sv 1973-74; Cmdr, US Forces, Azores 1971-73; VCmdr, Air Wea Sv 1970-71; Cmdr, 9th Wea Recon Wg 1968-70; Am Meteorol Soc; c/Am Security Coun; BSA; r/Bapt: Deacon, SS Tchr; hon/Dist'd Ser Medal; Legion of Merit; Order of Sword, USAF; Order of Merit, Portuguese Govt.

ALESIA, JAMES H oc/Judge; b/Jan 16, 1934; h/1025 S Lincoln Ave, Park Ridge, IL 60068; ba/Chgo, IL; m/Kathryn P; c/Brian J, Daniel J; p/Henry J Alesia (dec); Ethel M Alesia, Chgo, IL; ed/BS Loyola Univ 1956; JD IIT-Chgo Kent Coll of Law 1960; pa/US Adm Law Judge; Am Fed Bar Assn; Ill Bar Assn; Former Asst US Atty; r/Rom Cath; hon/Blue Key (Past VP Loyola Chapt); Others.

ALEXANDER, ANN M oc/Counselor; Therapist; b/Nov 6, 1923; h/52 Jupiter Way, Gladstone, OR 97027; ba/Portland, OR; m/Gerald N; c/Nancy Miller (Mrs Arthur), Timothy, Steven; p/Robert F and Lena Loynes Mott (dec); ed/MEd; pa/Cnslr & Marital & Sex Therapist; Coor, Human Sexuality Clin, Portland St Univ; Am Pers & Guid Assn; Am Col Pers Assn; Am Assn Marriage & Fam Cnslrs; Am Assn Sex Edrs, Cnslrs & Therapists; cp/Portland Area Bd Dirs, Zonta Intl; r/Meth; hon/W/W W.

ALEXANDER, ASHLEY HARRY oc/Farmer; Teacher; b/Nov 20, 1912; h/Rt 3, Box 28, Perry, OK 73077; ba/Perry; m/Beverly Sue; c/Ashley Jr, Alan, Artie; p/Harry and Rozetta Alexander (dec); ed/BA Ctl St Univ; mil/158th Field Arty Band 9 Yrs; pa/Band Dir & Tchr, Okla Schs 45 Yrs; Dir Student Entertainers, Stdt & Univ 22 Yrs; Musician & Evangelist for Overseas Revivals in 5 Countries; cp/Rotary; C of C; IOOF; Kappa Kappa Psi; Phi Delta Kappa; Civil Air Patrol; Mgr, 3 USO Overseas Shows from Okla St Univ; r/Bapt; hon/Dist'd Former Student, Ctl Univ.

ALEXANDER, FRED J oc/College Administrator; b/May 14, 1935; h/15 Indian Trail, Searcy, AR 72143; ba/Searcy; m/Claudette Harris; c/Joe Frederick, Beverly

Ellen, Denise Kay; p/Emory Clyde and Ellen Matilda Branum Alexander, Dodson, TX; ed/BS; MEd; EdD; mil/USNR; pa/Col Admr, Harding Col; AAHE; AACRAO; NACAC; r/Ch of Christ.

ALEXANDER, JAMES oc/Independent Bank Broker; Real Estate Developer; b/Jul 7, 1934; h/2488 Westridge Rd, Los Angeles, CA 90049; ba/LA; m/Marsha; c/Scott, Cara, Derek, Tim; p/Sandy and Moretta Alexander (dec); ed/AA Long Beach Col; mil/AUS; pa/Indep Bk Assns; cp/Dem; hon/Pub'd Articles on Bkg Indust.

ALEXANDER, LARRY J oc/Associate Professor; b/Jan 28, 1941; h/2784 Stage Coach, Fayetteville, AR 72701; ba/Fayetteville; m/M Anne; c/Jennifer, Brent, Suzie; p/Raymond Alexander (dec); M Catherine Alexander, Sherman, TX; ed/BA Austin Col 1964; MEd E Tex St Univ 1966; EdD Okla St Univ 1970; pa/Univ Ark: Assoc Prof Instrl Resources Ed 1976-, Assoc Prof of Ed 1972-74, Asst Prof 1970-71, Instr 1968-70; Asst Prof & Dir Audiovisual Ctr, Okla Christian Col 1967-78; Other Past Positions; AECT; ASCD; AAVA; TAET; AECT 7; AAHE; Active in Consltg & Wkshops; cp/Joslin Diabetic Assn; Diabetic Res; Polit Campaign Vol; r/Ch of Christ; hon/Outstg Yg Men of Am; Personalities of S; DIB; Intl W/W Intells; Book of Hon; W/W Am; Intl W/W Commun Ser; Num Profl Pubs.

ALEXANDER, WILMA JEAN oc/- Associate Professor; b/May 25, 1938; h/Rt 1, Towanda, IL 61776; ba/Normal, IL; m/Leslie W; c/Glenella Jean; p/Glen B Heavin (dec); Wilma M Heavin, Columbus, KS; ed/BS 1959,, MS 1967 Kans St Col of Pittsburg; EdD Okla St Univ 1973; pa/Assoc Prof, Dept of Bus Ed & Adm Sers, Ill St Univ; Ill Bus Ed Assn; N Ctl Bus

Ed Assn; Nat Bus Ed Assn; Assn of Records Mgrs & Admrs; Ctl Ill Word Processing Assn; Bloomington Normal Pers Coun; Conslt; Word Processing Time Mgmt, Secretarial, Records Mgmt; r/Assembly of God; hon/S'ship; Pi Omega Pi; Delta Pi Epsilon; Delta Gamma Sigma; Other Acad Hons; World W/W Wom Ed; Profl Pubs.

ALEXIS, MILDRED ELIZABETH oc/Educational Consultant; b/Aug 21, 1919; h/1811 S Pershing Rd, Lincoln, NE 68502; ba/Lincoln; m/Carl Odman; c/Caren; p/Arthur Leonard and Betsy Edith Leggett Craig (dec); ed/BS 1958; MA 1966; pa/Title I Basics Resource Reading & Math Specialist, Saratoga Elem Sch; Delta Kappa Gamma; Phi Delta Gamma; Phi Lambda Theta; ACE; CEC; NEA; Neb St Ed Assn; Lincoln Tchrs Assn; Pres, Neb En Coun Intl Reading Assn; cp/BPW Clb; Beta Sigma Phi; r/Luth; hon/Notable Ams; Outstg Ldrs in Elem & Sec'dy Ed.

ALEXOPOULOS, CONSTANTINE JOHN oc/Professor Emeritus; b/Mar 17, 1907; h/917 Calithea Rd, Austin, TX 78746; ba/Austin; m/Juliet Dowdy; p/John C and Chrysoula J Alexopoula (dec); ed/BS w hons 1927, MS 1928, PhD 1932 Univ Ill, Urbana; pa/Prof of Botany; Univ Tex, Austin 1962-76, Univ Ia 1956-62, Mich St Univ 1952-56; Assoc Prof: Mich St Univ 1947-52, Kent St Univ 1940-43; Asst Prof, Kent St Univ 1936-40; Other Past Positions; Mycological Soc Am: Life Mem, Past Pres; Past Pres, Botanical Soc Am; British Mycological Soc Am; Past Pres, Intl Mycological Assn; r/Greek Orthodox; hon/W/W Am; Intl Blue Book; Am Men & Wom of Sci; W/W World; Profl Pubs; Alpha Zeta; Fulbright F'ship; Sigma Xi; Others.

ALF, MARTHA JOANNE oc/Artist; Instructor; b/Aug 13, 1930; h/2866 Monarch St, San Diego, CA 92123; ba/Venice, CA; m/Edward F Jr; c/Richard F; p/Foster W and Julia V Powell; ed/BA 1953, MA 1963 San Diego St Univ; MFA UCLA 1970; pa/Art Instr, UCLA Extension 1971-; Num Group & 1-Wom Art Exhbns; Exhbns: 1-Wom Show, Newspace Gallery, LA 1976, 77, 78, 1-Wom Show, John Berggruen Gallery, San Fran 1977, 1-Wom Show, Jack Glenn Gallery, Newport Beach, Cal 1975, 1-Wom Show, Green Mountain Gallery, NYC 1973; Wks in Collection: Newport Harbor Art Mus, Cal, Fine Arts Gallery of San Fran, Greenville (NC) Mus of Art; r/Prot; hon/Included in Whitney Biennial, NYC 1975.

ALFORD, BETTY BOHON oc/Academic Administrator; b/Jun 9, 1932; h/2608 Glenwood, Denton, TX 76201; ba/Denton; m/Joe G; c/Mark Allen, Matthew Bohon; p/R J and Marie Bohon, Denton, TX; ed/PhD; pa/Nutrition Reschr; Pres, Tex Home Ec Assn; r/Bapt; hon/Profl Pubs.

ALGARD, OLE oc/Ambassador; b/Sept 9, 1921; h/10 Gracie Square, NY, NY 10028;

ba/NYC; m/Rigmor; c/Knut, Gro; p/Gabriel Algard (dec); Bertha Algard, Norway; ed/Law Deg Univ Oslo; Acad Intl Law, Hague; mil/Norwegian Resistance WW II; pa/Permanent Rep, Permanent Mission of Norway to UN 1972-; Norwegian Ambassador in Peking 1966-71; Counsellor of Embassy, Norwegian Embassy, Brussels, Permanent Rep to Coun of Europe 1964-66; Dep Permanent Rep, Permanent Mission of Norway to UN, NY 1961-64; Hd Div of E European Affairs, Polit Dept, Ministry of Fgn Affairs, Oslo 1956-61; Charge d'Affairs, Norwegian Embassy, Vienna 1951-56; Secy, Norwegian Embassy, Moscow 1947-50; Chm Spec Com on UN Finances 1972; Pres, Intl Conf Experts to Support Victims of Colonialism & Arpartheid, Oslo 1973; Chm Ad Hoc Com on Spec Programme 1974; Chm, Review & Appraisal Com 1975; Pres Bd Gov's, UN Spec Fund 1975-77; VP, 30th Session Gen Assembly 1975; VP, ECOSOC 1977; Pres, Security Coun, Apr 1979; hon/L'Ordre de la Couronne; L'Ordre de Leopold; Cmdr, Lion's Order & St Olav's Order.

ALGER, DON MCKAY oc/Administrator; Educator; b/Jul 26, 1939; h/1602 Stonybrook Pl, Columbia, MO 65201; ba/Columbia; m/Carolyn; c/Amy, Suzanne, Juliet; p/Almo Don and Wanda Alger, Provo, UT; ed/BS US Naval Acad; MS, PhD Univ Mo, Columbia; mil/USN; pa/Assoc Dir, Res Reactor Facility, Univ Mo; Asst Prof of Nuclear Engrg, Univ Mo; Am Nuclear Soc; Mo Soc Profl Engrs; Reg'd Profl Engr; Am Soc for Testing & Materials; r/Ch of Jesus Christ LDS; hon/Gen Elect Co Fellow 1974.

ALGER, FERRIS EUGENE oc/Physicist; b/Jan 15, 1913; h/Old York Rd, RD 1, New Hope, PA 18938; ba/Philadelphia, PA; m/Margaret Gaines; p/Samuel Ezra and Eppie Eugenia Alger (dec); pa/Experimental Physicist; Experience in Fundamental Res, Development, Engrg & Prodn, Specializing in Fields of High Vacuum, Ultra-High Vacuum, Vacuum Tubes, Vacuum & Hydrogen Furnaces, Glass & Metal Seals, Molecular Beams, Evaporated Thin Films, Nuclear Physics, Cryogenics, Physical Chem & Aerodynamics; Pioneering Developmts in Sev Fields; Exec Bd Action Com, Insts for Achmt of Human Potential; Other Positions w: IBM, Am Machine & Foundry Co, Polytechnic Res & Devel Co, Freed Radio Corp, Nat Union Radio Corp, Columbia Radiation Lab; Am Physical Soc; Am Ceramic Soc; Am Vacuum Soc; AAAS; cp/Fdg Mem, Classic Car Clb; Fdr, Isotta Fraschini Owner's Assn; Exec Bd, Vol Action Com for Insts for Achmt of Human Potential; Experimental Aircraft Assn; Pvt Pilot; Mensa; hon/Brazilian Gold Medal of Hon & Merit; Others.

ALGER, PHILIP LANGDON oc/- Electrical Engineer; b/Jan 27, 1894; h/1758 Wendell Ave, Schenectady, NY 12308; m/Catherine E Jackson (dec); 2nd Helen Jackson Hubbell (dec); c/John R M, Andrew Dugald Langdon, Augusta J, Anne V; p/Philip Rounseville and Louisa Taylor Alger (dec); ed/BS St John's Col 1912; BS Mass Inst Technol 1915; MS Union Col 1920; mil/AUS 1917-19; pa/Adj Prof to Consltg Prof of Elect Engrg, Rensselaer Polytechnic Inst 1959-70; Gen Elect Co, Schenectady: Conslt Engr, Medium A-C Motor & Generator Dept 1950-59, Staff Asst to VP of Engrg 1930-50, Asst Engr A-C Engrg Dept 1924-30, Devel Engr, Intro Motor Engrg Dept 1919-23; Other Past Positions; Math Soc; Am Soc Engrg Ed; Nat Soc Profl Engrs; Life Mem, Am Ordnance Assn; Fellow: ASME, ASQC, AAAS, IEE (British); Fellow & Life Mem, IEEE; cp/Newcomen Soc; Am Legion; Nat Mun Leag; Va Soc of the Cincinnati; r/Unitarian; hon/13 Patents; Hon DSc Univ Colo 1969; Alumni Awd of Merit, St John's Col 1970; Hon Mem, Tensor Soc of Gt Britain; Liberty Bell Awd, Schenectady Co Bar Assn 1974; Newspaper-Salute, *The Knickerbocker News - Union Star*, 1971; Engr of Yr, NY St Soc Profl Engrs 1966; Tau Beta Pi; Sigma Xi; Eta Kappa Nu; Lamme Medal, Am Inst Elect Engrs; Author: *More Tales of My Life and Family* 1977, The Human Side of Engineering 1972, Mathematics for Science & Engineering 1969, Others.

ALIBARUHO, GLORIA LINDSEY oc/- Professor; Consultant; b/Sept 9, 1942; h/634 62nd St, Oakland, CA 94609; ba/San Jose, CA; ed/Dudley William Thompson; c/Mukwatsibwoha; p/James Lamar Lindsey (dec); Rachaell Dunn Lindsey, Maywood, IL; ed/BA Univ Ill; MA Univ Edinburgh, Scotland; PhD Univ Cal, Berkeley; PhD Wright Inst; pa/Prof, San Jose St Univ; Owner, T A Assocs Conslitg Firm; Cal Wom in Higher Ed; cp/Pres, 62nd St Neighborhood Assn; Vol, Congman Ronald V Dellums; Wom's Equity Leag; r/Prot; hon/Fulbright F'ship; World W/W Wom; W/W W; Outstg Edr, St of Cal; SCUC Adm Fellow.

ALKANA, RONALD LEE oc/Professor; b/Oct 17, 1945; h/613 Bayside Dr, Seal Beach, CA 90740; ba/Los Angeles, CA; m/Linda Kelly; p/Sam Alkana, Thousand Oaks, CA; Madelyn Jane Davis, LA, CA; ed/PharmD Univ So Cal 1970; PhD Univ Cal, Irvine 1975; pa/Univ So Cal: Asst Prof Pharmacy (Pharmacol) 1976-; Univ Cal, Irvine: Res Asst Dir Div Neurochem 1976; Postdoct Fellow 1974-76; Reg'd Pharmacist: Cal, Nev; Soc for Neurosci; Am Col Clin Pharmacol; Res Soc on Alcoholism; Am Assn Adv Sci; Sigma Xi; cp/Expert Witness; hon/Merck Sharpe & Dohme Awd 1967, 1970; E A Steinhaus Meml Tchg Awd Biol Sci, Hon Mention 1974; Tchr of Yr, Univ So Cal Pharm III 1978; Others.

ALLEN, ALICE SHOECRAFT oc/- Supervisor; b/Aug 9, 1931; h/1635 S McCord Rd, Holland, OH 43528; ba/Toledo, OH; c/Wanda Shoecraft Washington; p/Homer Franklin and Etta Graham Fikes (dec); ed/Univ Toledo; Bowling Green Univ; pa/Supvr, Conciliation-Investigation; cp/Public Spkr; Resource Person; Notary Public 11 yrs; Legal Aid; Mayor's Adv Comm; Vol Coor, Hosp Outreach; Ohio Repub Coun; r/Prot; hon/Outstg Citizenship Awd, Toledo MNRA 1976; Pres's Pvt Resource Adv Comm, 1972.

ALLEN, ALMA COPPEDGE oc/- Professor; b/Mar 23, 1922; h/4402 Fielding Rd, Wilmington, DE 19802; ba/Media, PA; m/L B; c/Patricia, L B Jr; p/B C Coppedge, Winston-Salem, NC; Ivy L Coppedge (dec); ed/AB summa cum laude; AM; PhD; pa/Prof, Romance Langs, Delaware Co Commun Col; Pub'd Profl Articles; Lectr in Romance Langs; Mod Lang Assn; AATSP; AATF; Pres, Profl Wom's Org; cp/Bd Dirs: GSA, YWCA; r/Bapt; hon/Danforth Foun Doct F'ship; Col Valedictorian; Phi Sigma Iota; Alpha Kappa Mu.

ALLEN, ANNIE BELL oc/School Administrator; b/Nov 3, 1923; h/Rt 2, Box 292F, Okmulgee, OK 74447; ba/Okmulgee; p/Felix Taylor, Henryetta, OK; ed/Dipl E Kardos Fashion Inst 1951; pa/Dir, O K (Older Kids) Sch for Retarded & Handicapped; Missionary Work w Chd; Elder; cp/Past Pres, Okmulgee Co Assn for Retarded Chd; r/Ch of God; hon/Sev Awds from Okla Assn for Retarded Chd.

ALLEN, ARIS T oc/Physician; State Senator; b/Dec 27, 1910; h/111 Cathedral St, Annapolis, MD 21401; ba/Annapolis; m/Faye W; c/Aris T Jr, Lonnie W; p/James and Marietta Allen (dec); ed/MD; mil/USAF, Capt; pa/Pvt Med Pract, Annapolis 33 Yrs; Anne Arundel Gen Hosp Staff; Anne Arundel Co Med Staff; Am Acad Fam Phys; AMA; Monumental Med Soc; Past VP, Med-Chirurgical Fac of St of Md; Bd Dirs, Md Acad Fam Phys; cp/Past Mem, Anne Arundel Bd of Ed; Chm, Repub Md St Ctl Com; Com of Bicent Comm; Past Bd Dirs: BSA, NAACP (Life Mem), Anne Arundel Co Commun Col, Gtr Annapolis C of C, Others; Mem Md St Sen; Elected Md Leg 1966; Elected Md St Leg Minority Whip 1967, 68, 70, 71, 72, 73; Pres, Anne Arundel Gen Hosp Staff; hon/W/W: Am, World, Black Am, E, Am Polits; Paul Harris Fellow, Rotary Intl 1978; Frontier's Intl Humanitarian Awd 1977; 1976 NAACP Awd, Anne Arundel Co Brs; Monumental Med Soc Awd of Merit; Alpha Phi Alpha Frat Awd 1973; Salute to Aris Allen 1975.

ALLEN, DON L oc/Educational Administrator; b/Mar 13, 1934; h/3611 SW 63rd Ln, Gainesville, FL 32601; ba/Gainesville; m/M Winifred Rouse; c/Donny, Michael, Donny, Susan; p/William A Allen, Elon Col, NC; Gena D Allen, Burlington, NC; ed/DDS; MS; pa/Dean, Col of Dentistry, Univ Fla; Am Assn Dental Schs; Intl Assn for Dental Res; Am Dental Assn; Am Acad Periodontol; cp/Ldrship Gainesville; FLADPAC; r/Prot; hon/Intl Col Dentists; Omicron Kappa Upsilon; Am Col Dentists.

ALLEN, DONALD HAROLD oc/Student; b/Mar 5, 1958; h/49 Denwood Dr, Jackson, TN 38301; ba/University, MS;

p/David C Sr and Doris E Allen, Jackson, TN; ed/Univ Miss; r/Bapt; hon/Omicron Delta Kappa; Sigma Nu.

ALLEN, E ROSS oc/Naturalist; b/Jan 2, 1908; ba/St Augustine, FL; ed/Stetson Univ; pa/Dir Reptile Shows, St Augustine Alligator Farm; Fdr, Ross Allen Venom Lab; Est'd Reptile Inst 1929; Produced 90% of Snake Venom Used For Med Purposes During WW II; Discovered 8 Species of Reptiles & Amphibians; Taxidermist; Lectr; Made 105 News-reels, Featurettes, Shorts, Features, etc; TV Appearances on *Hobby Lobby*, *Bob Ripley's Believe It Or Not*, *I've Got a Secret*, *Wild Kingdom*, Others; Involved in Movies: *Tarzan Finds a Son*, *Crosswind*, *Killers of the Swamp*, *King of the Everglades*, *Distant Drums*, Others; Expeditions to Num Countries incl: Panama, Costa Rica, Peru, Brazil, Colombia, Cuba, Others; cp/Former BSA Scout Master; hon/BSA Silver Beaver; Pub'd 480+ Articles & Sci Papers.

ALLEN, EDGARD YAN oc/Pharmaceutical Environmental Control Chemist; b/Oct 18, 1914; h/8 Paulus Blvd, New Brunswick, NJ 08901; ba/New Brunswick; p/Andrew Jacob and Josephine Von Reimann Allen (dec); ed/BS in Pharm Fordham Univ 1939; MS in Pharm PCP & S 1942; pa/Pharm Envir Control Chem, E R Squibb & Sons Inc, New Brunswick; Am Pharm Assn; Am Chem Soc; Soc of Ec Botany; Am Soc of Pharmacognosy; Assoc Am Soc of Hosp Pharms; cp/Am Security Coun; Civil Def Phila World War II, K of C; r/Rom Cath; hon/Fellow: AAAS, Am Inst of Chems; Life Corporate Mem, Phila Col of Pharm & Sci; Life Fellow, Royal Soc of Hlth, Britain.

ALLEN, GARY IRVING oc/Educator; Administrator; b/Apr 7, 1942; h/965

Knollwood Rd, White Plains, NY 10603;

ba/Berkeley, CA; m/Elaine Irene Main; c/Michelle Irene, Elisa Joy, Scott Jeremy; p/Ralph W and Lois M Allen, Lockport, NY; ed/BS Cornell Univ; PhD SUNY Buffalo; pa/Dir, Intl Student Min Devel Base, Campus Crusade for Christ, Univ Cal, Berkeley; Lectr (Pt-time), Dept of Physiol, Univ Cal, Berkeley; Min to Intl Students; Neurophysical Study of Movemt Control; r/Christian.

ALLEN, GEORGE HOWARD oc/Publishing Executive; b/Jun 1, 1914; h/112 Pear Tree Point Rd, Darien, CT 06820; ba/NY, NY; m/Virginia Russell; c/Russell Lawton; ed/BS Univ Mass 1936; MBA Harvard Univ 1938; pa/Sr VP & Group Pubr, CBS Pubs 1977-; Pubr, Exec VP & Dir, Mag Div, Fawcett Pubs Inc, NY, NY 1966-76; Pubr 1964-66: *Better Homes & Gardens*, *Successful Farming*; Other Past Pub'g Positions; Past Pres, Am Mktg Assn, NY; Chm, Mag Pubrs Assn 1977-; Past Chm,

Pubrs Info Bur; Past Nat Bd Mem, Sales Promotion Execs Assn; Public Relats Soc Am; Advtg Res Foun: Past Chm, Dir, Secy-Treas; Past Mem Bd Dirs: Advtg Fed Am, Nat Assn Mfrs; cp/Chm Bd Trustees, Intl Student Exchange Prog, Yth for Understanding 1978-79; Past Mem Ed Com, US C of C; Past Dir, Harvard Alumni Assn; White Conf on Food, Nutrition & Hlth Panel Mem 1969; hon/Alpha Chi Alpha; Am Legion Ldrship Awd; Silver Anvil Awd, Am Public Relats Assn; Ia Mgmt Man of Yr 1965.

ALLEN, J GARROTT oc/Professor; b/Jun 5, 1912; h/583 Salvatierra, Stanford, CA 94305; ba/Stanford; m/Kathryn Shipley; p/James E and Susan H Garrott Allen (dec); ed/AB; MD; mil/Manhattan Proj 1944-46; pa/Prof of Surg, Stanford Univ; Major Mech & Surg Orgs; cp/Orgs Dealing w Social Policy; hon/Gold Medal for Sci Work on Control of Heparin Therapy w Protamine 1948; From Human Blood to Social Policy.

ALLEN, JOHN ELDRIDGE oc/Historian; Former Federal Government Official; b/Sept 11, 1911; h/S Miami, FL; m/Mary Edwards; c/Mark; p/Arthur and Annie Willis Allen (dec); mil/USN 1942-46, Lt Cmdr; pa/Transition Adv Panel for Carter-Mondale Nat Adm 1976-77; Mem Exec Br, US Govt 1939-59; Analyst & Writer, Depts of Army & Def 1948-57; Housing Asst, Univ Miami, Fla 1963-73; Editor & Histn, Allen Personal Papers & Hist Jours 1973-; cp/Fdg Mem: Patriotic Ed Inc, Renaissance Soc Am, US Capitol Hist Soc, US Supr Ct Hist Soc; Charter Mem: U Miami Alumni Fund Century Clb, US Olympic Soc; Dem; Assoc Am, Nat Archives of US; Cousteau Soc; U Clb Wash DC; Nat Trust for Hist Presv; r/Meth; hon/Book of Hon; Served on Var Dedication Coms; Personalities of S; Notable Ams; Intl W/W Commun Ser; Blue Book; Intl Scholars Dir; Intl Authors & Writers W/W; W/W Am; Pub'd Author.

ALLEN, KAREN SUE oc/Clinical Psychologist; Assistant Professor; b/Mar 12, 1943; h/3 Wood Fern Ln, Houghton, LA 71037; ba/Shreveport, LA; m/R Michael Allen; c/Brandwyd Michele; p/William A and Elizabeth Drowns, El Paso, TX; ed/BS; MS; PhD; mil/MSC 3 Yrs, Capt; pa/Asst Prof, La St Univ Med Sch; Fam Pract; Am Psychol Assn; Tex Psychol Assn; Film Series *Step

Behind Internationally Distributed; r/Bapt; hon/US Olympic Swimming Team, Mexico City 1959; S'ship.

ALLEN, L CALHOUN JR oc/Mayor; b/Feb 8, 1921; h/65 Tealwood, Shreveport, LA 71104; ba/Shreveport; m/Jacqueline S; c/Frances Olivia, L Calhoun III; p/L Calhoun Allen; Lel Goodwin Allen, Shreveport, LA; ed/BA Centenary Col; mil/WW II & Korean Conflict; USNR 32½ Yrs, Capt; La NG 1969-74; pa/Assoc'd w Allen Constrn Co before 1962; cp/Elected Mayor of Shreveport 1970, Re-elected 1974; Elected Shreveport Commr of Public Utilities 1962, Re-elected 1966; Past Pres: Shreveport Coun Navy Leag US, (Exec Bd Mem) Norwela Coun BSA, Southland Dixie Promenade of Forty & Eight, Holiday in Dixie; Shreveport Airport Auth; Downtown Devel Auth; Shreveport Kiwanis Clb; BPOE; Joppa Lodge F&AM; Shreveport Consistory Scottish Rite; El Karubah Shrine Temple; Past Dist VP, Naval Resv Assn; Exec Bd & Bd Dirs, La St Fair Assn; Chm, La St Fair Stadium Comm; Bd Dirs, Sports for Boys; Exec Bd: Shreveport Symph, Shreveport Beautification Foun; Others; r/1st Presb Ch: Mem, Elder; hon/W/W: Govt, Am, La, S&SW; Am Polits; Personalities of S; Outstg Ams; DIB; Cert of Apprec: Nat Safe Boating Com 1972, Shreveport-Bossier Voc-Tech Ctr 1976, Rotary 1975, Dept Vet Affairs 1975; Num Others.

ALLEN, LORETTA BELLE oc/Artist; b/Jun 22; h/1645 E 17th Pl, Tulsa, OK 74120; ba/Tulsa, OK; m/Clarence Canning; c/Jesse Davis Douglas II; p/Floyd LeRoy and Lillie Elizabeth Trumbly Broome (dec); ed/Num Courses: Art, Anatomy, Design, Writing, in Okla City, NY & Westport, Conn; pa/Columnist 1971-75; Designer for Dona Mfg Co 1935-37, 69-72; Book Illustrations for Mary McKinney Frye 1938-39; Tulsa Press Club 1977; cp/Mem Tulsa Civic Ballet; VP Assn Am Ed Cart Aux 1968-69; r/Unity Sch of Practical Christianity, Mo; hon/Exhibits: Okla City Art Ctr 1959, Perm Exhibit 1969-77, Others; Special Display of Family, Osage Co Hist Mus; Personalities of S.

ALLEN, LULLAVEE ROGERS oc/Educator; b/Sept 23, 1919; h/4004 Drakes Br Rd, Nashville, TN 37218; ba/Nashville; m/Howard Verdell; c/Howard Verdell; p/Will and Zeadie Earnestine Perry Rogers; ed/BS 1939, MA 1977 Tenn St Univ; Postgrad Study: Fisk Univ, Mehary Med Col, Vanderbilt Univ; pa/Tchr: Nashville Public Schs 1947-73, Stokes Sch 1972-, Decatur HS, Decaturville, Tenn 1939-44; Supvr, Chd's Detention, Nashville 1945-47; USO Hostess 1942-44; Metro Nashville Ed Assn; Tenn Ed Assn; Life Mem NEA; cp/Former Ldr, GSA; Former Sponsor, Jr ARC; Nat Coun Negro Wom; Couples Clb; Life Mem, Tenn St Alumni Assn; Nashville Sigma Shadows; Life Mem, Zeta Phi Beta Sorority; La-Comrade Bridge Clb; p/St Vincent DePaul; hon/W/W S&SW; Cert Apprec, Zeta Phi Beta; 10 Yr Ser Pin, Nat Jr ARC; 20 Yr Alumni Ser Awd, Tenn St Univ; Vol Ser Awd, Nat Cystic Fibrosis Foun..

ALLEN, ROBERT CHARLES oc/Corporation Executive; b/Aug 24, 1929; h/1061 Sunset Dr, Hollister, CA 95023; ba/Santa Clara, CA; m/Norma Jean Barko; p/Morris F Allen (dec); Florence E Allen, Canton, OH; ed/BS magna cum laude Kent St Univ 1956; mil/USAF 1947-53; pa/Pres: R&N Chem Co, Hollister, Cal 1962-, Bayside Refining & Chem Co, Santa Clara, Cal 1976-77, Chem Processors Inc, Santa Clara 1978-; Teledyne McCormick Selph, Hollister, Cal: Exec VP 1968-76, Mgr Explosives Div 1962-68, Sr Applications Engr 1959-62; Tech Rep, Explosives Dept, E I duPont deNemours & Co, Wilmington, Del 1956-59; Am Chem Soc; Am Inst Aeronautics & Astronautics; Am Def Preparedness Assn; hon/Sev Patents.

ALLEN, THOMAS G oc/Clergyman; b/Jul 28, 1945; h/1204 Indiana St, Pine Bluff, AR 71601; m/Aline; c/Nedra Roshan; p/Jessie L Brentley; Lottie M Brentley, Pine Bluff, AR; ed/AA Shorter Col 1971; BA Philander Smith Col

1973; BD Jackson Theol Sem 1976; pa/Pastor: St Paul AME Ch, Pine Grove AME Ch, Arkadelphia 1970-73, St Paul AME Ch, Hot Springs 1969; Past Field Secy, SNCC; VP, Jackson Co Assn Mins 1974; Dir Newport Dist ENE Ark Annual Conf, AME Ch; Min Del, Gen Conf AME 1976; cp/Newport Urban Coun; 32° Mason; Omega Psi Phi; Gen Adult Ed Adv Com, White River Voc Tech Sch 1977; r/AME; hon/Cert of Merit, U Supr Coun Masons 1971; W/W Among Black Ams; Intl W/W Intells; Book of Hon; DIB; Men Achmt; Commun Ldrs & Noteworthy Ams; Outstg Yg Men Am; Personalities of S.

ALLEN, VIRGINIA RUTH oc/Occupational Therapist; b/Feb 21, 1946; ba/Occupational Therapy Dept, Med Col of Ga, Augusta, GA 30904; p/Henry B and Ruth W Allen, Columbia, SC; ed/BS w distn Ind Univ 1967;

MHE Med Col of Ga 1977; pa/Med Col Ga: Asst Prof 1977-, Instr 1973-77; Highland View Hosp: Sr Therapist 1969-73, Staff Therapist 1967-69; Rehab Conslt; r/Presb; hon/Alpha Eta; Fellow, AOTA.

ALLEN, WILLIAM THOMAS oc/Regional Claims Superintendent; b/Jun 4, 1935; h/4029 Liberty Canyon Rd, Agouna, CA 91301; ba/Woodland Hills, CA; c/Tami Lynette, William Lawrence; p/Albert Jackson Allen (dec); Rohma Jackson Allen, Prescott Valley, AZ; ed/BSC Univ Ia; MS LaVerne Col; mil/USAR, Col; pa/LA Life & Accident Claim Assn (Past Pres); cp/Mem & Past Pres: 63rd Infantry Div Assn, Chapt 92 Resv Ofcrs Assn; VP, Bd Govs Hlth Agy of LA Co Inc; r/Meth; hon/Dist'd Mil Grad, Univ Ia; Hon Grad, Command & Gen Staff Col; Fellow, Life Mgmt Inst; Meritorious Ser Medal, USAR; Civic Awd, City of Redondo Beach.

ALLERS, FRANZ oc/Conductor; b/Aug 6, 1905; h/139 W 94th St, NY, NY 10025; ba/NYC; m/Janne Furch; c/Carol Chappell-Allers; p/Carl and Paula Allers (dec); ed/Grad Conservatory Praque; Grad Acad of Music, Berlin; mil/Czechoslovakian Army 1935-37; pa/Conducted Most Maj Am Symph Orchs, Metro Opera, Operattas, Musical Theatre, Others; cp/Lectr in Music & Theatres; hon/Antoinette Perry Awd for Best Conductor 1957, 61.

ALLISON, FRANK EDWARD SR oc/Architect; Planner; Investment Consultant;

b/Nov 7, 1929; ed/BArch Tex A&M Col 1951; pa/Pres, Allison Investmts Assoc'd Corp 1973-;

Allison Assocs AIA Archs/Planners/Conslts, Houston 1966-; Welton Becket FAIA: Proj Dir, NY Br 1963-66, Planning Dir & Proj Arch, Houston 1961-63; Prin, Allison Assocs AIA Archs/Planners/Conslts, Beaumont, Tex 1959-61; Proj Arch, Pitts, Mebane & Phelps, Beaumont, Tex 1954-59; Engrg Draftsman, H E Bovay Engrs, Houston, Tex 1953-54; Tex Soc Arch; Am Soc Planning Ofcls; Urban Land Inst; Nat Coun Archs Registration Bds; Am Insts Archs; Secy-Treas, Atrium Inc, Houston; Reg'd Arch: Tex, La, Ga; hon/Dist'd Student, Tex A&M; W/W: SW, Tex; Personalities of S; DIB; Men Achmt; Intl Reg Profiles; Commun Ldrs & Noteworthy Ams; Notable Ams Bicent Era; Intl W/W Intells; Am Inst Arch's Reg.

ALLISON, GRAHAM TILLETT JR oc/Educational Administrator; b/Mar 23, 1940; h/69 Pinehurst Rd, Belmont, MA 02178; ba/Cambridge, MA; m/Elizabeth; p/Graham Allison Sr, Charlotte, NC; Virginia Allison, Charlotte, NC; ed/AB magna cum laude 1962, PhD 1968 Harvard Univ; BA, MA Hertford Col Oxford Univ; pa/Harvard Univ: Dean John F Kennedy Sch of Govt 1977-, Prof of Polits 1972-77, Assoc Dean & Chm of Public Policy Prog John F Kennedy Sch of Govt 1975-77, Assoc Prof of Polits 1970-72, Asst Prof of Govt 1968-70, Instr in Govt 1967-68; Conslt: US Dept of Def, Ofc of Budget & Mgmt, Rand Corp; Vis Com on Fgn Policy Studies, Brookings Instn; Commr, Trilateral Comm; Coun on Fgn Relats; Edit Adv Com, *Washington Monthly*; Edit Bd: *World Politics* 1971-73, *Public Policy* 1970-72; hon/Author: *Essence of Decision: Explaining the Cuban Missle Crisis*, 1971, "Afterword" (w Richard E Neustadt) to Robert F Kennedy's *Thirteen Days* 1971, *Adequacy of Current Organization: Defense and Arms Control* 1975, *Remaking Foreign Policy: The Organizational Connection* 1976, Var Profl Articles; Harvard Scholar; Marshall Scholar; Harvard Govt Dept Prize Fellow.

ALLISON, WILLIAM LANDON oc/Minister; Eductor; b/Sept 15, 1921; h/1430 Watuaga St, Kingsport, TN 37664; ba/Bristol, TN; m/Virginia Murray; p/Walter R and Flora Carriger Allison (dec); ed/BSc ETSU; MEd Univ Miami; MREd Univ So Cal; EdD L Rice Sem; mil/AUS WW II S/Sgt; Chaplain USAFR; pa/Min, First Ch of God; Prof, Steed Col; Chm E Tenn Ministerial Assn of Ch of God, Anderson, Ind; NEA; TEA; KEA; Life Mem Mil Chaplains Assn; r/First Ch of God (Gen Ofc Anderson, Ind); hon/Warner So Col Awd; W/W Rel in Am; Commun Ldrs & Noteworthy Ams; Intl Register of Profiles.

ALLRED, WILLIAM DAVID oc/Attorney; Minister; Legislator; b/Nov 27, 1933; h/1608 Hayes St, Wichita Falls, TX 76309; ba/Wichita Falls; m/Patricia; c/Rebecca, Stephen, James; p/James V Allred (dec); Joe Betsy Allred, Wichita Falls, TX; ed/BA Tex Christian Univ; MS Columbia Univ; mil/USAR, Maj (Ret'd); Army Command & Gen Staff Col; pa/Atty; Writer; Lic'd Min, Christian Ch; cp/Mem Tex Ho of Reps 1967-; r/Disciples of Christ.

ALLSBROOK, JOHNNY FRANK oc/Highway Patrol Officer; b/Sept 3, 1929; h/144 Cajah Mountain Rd, Hudson, NC 28638; ba/Lenoir, NC; m/Janice M; c/Johnny F Jr, Ann Linder, Jo Ellen, Thomas Edward; p/John H Allsbrook, Edenton, NC; Annie Clyde Allsbrook (dec); ed/AA Beaufort Tech Inst; mil/USAF; pa/NC St Hwy Patrol: Sgt, Dist Supvr Troop F Dist III; r/Mormon.

ALLSHOUSE, GARY WAYNE oc/Design Engineer; b/Nov 3, 1944; h/RD 4, Box 254, Muncy, PA 17756; ba/Muncy; m/Judith Ann Newcome; c/Lynnanne Marie, Mark Wayne; p/Rufus Wayne Allshouse (dec); Theresa Yolanda Allshouse, Brookville, PA; ed/BS; MS; pa/Design Engr of Pulp Refining Equipmt; Reg'd Profl Engr, Pa; Past Mem: Am Soc Agri Engrs, Pa Soc Profl Engrs; cp/Secy, Muncy Creek Commun Fire Co; Past Secy & Parliamentn, Muncy Jaycees; r/Muncy U Meth Ch: Missions Coor; hon/S'ships; Co-Author of Am Soc of Engrs Blue Ribbon Ednl Aid Awd Pub 1970; W/W: E, Am; Notable Ams; DIB; Men Achmt.

ALLUKIAN, MYRON oc/Public Health Dentist; b/Jan 6, 1939; h/8 Oakview Terr, Boston, MA 02130; ba/Boston; m/Ruth F Losco; c/Myron III; p/Myron Sr and Mary Nahabedian Allukian, Newton Centre, MA; ed/BS; DDS; MPH; mil/USN 1964-66, Lt; pa/Diplomate, Am Bd Dental Public Hlth; Dental Hlth Chm, Am Public Hlth Assn; Am Assn Public Hlth Dentists; Pres, Mass Public Hlth Assn; Fellow, Intl Col Dentists; cp/Bd Dirs, Mass Citizens' Com for Dental Hlth; Bd Dirs, S Boston Commun Hlth Ctr; Boston Yg Men's Christian Union; hon/James M Dunning Awd, Mass Public Hlth Assn; Merit Awd, Mass Leag Neighborhood Hlth Ctr.

ALMENDAREZ, YOLANDA CARBAJAL oc/Educational Administrator; b/Mar 8, 1945; h/Apt 21, Camp Gary, San Marcox, TX 78666; ba/San Marcos; m/Valentin;

c/Valentin Jr, Denise; p/Lazaro and Abigail Carbajal, Goliad, TX; ed/BS; MS; pa/Dir, Bilingual Ed; TSTA; NEA; r/Cath; hon/Outstg Elem Tchr Am.

ALOSA, JANET ALLARD oc/Student; b/Feb 9, 1938; h/6 Auburn St, Concord, NH 03301; ba/Manchester, NH; c/Judith Ann, Matthew Robert; m/Robert E and Hildreth P Allard, Manchester, NH; ed/AA Colby Col 1957; BA Univ NH 1960; Masters Cand New England Grad Sch; pa/English Tchr, Concord HS 1960-64; Secy, AAUW; cp/Trustee, Concord Public Lib; Del, Repub Nat Conv

1976; Co-Chm, Wyman for Senate Com 1976; Past Pres, Concord Wom's Repub Clb; Chm, Nixon-Ford Com, Concord 1972; Secy, Repub City Com 1975; Chperson, Concord Mar of Dimes Walkathon 1978; Orgr, Concord Girls' Baseball Leag; Pres: Concord Wom's Clb, Colby Jr Col Alumnae Clb, NH Fed Wom's Repub Clb; r/Rom Cath; hon/W/W Am Polits.

ALSIN, JUNEAU JOAN oc/Photographer; b/September 12, 1933; h/PO Box 85, Agoura, CA 91301; ba/Agoura; p/Luther Suby (dec); Gladys Alsin, Mercer Island, WA; pa/Photojournalist: *Family Weekly*, *Elite*, *Woman's World*, *Writers Digest*, *Playgirl*, *CB Times*, *New West*; cp/Election Bd Judge; Tax Reform Com; r/Ch of Millenium: Min; hon/Nat Torch Soc Awd; Wn Photojournalist Awd; Personalities of W&MW; Commun Ldrs & Noteworthy Ams.

ALTIERI, PABLO I oc/Physician; b/May 16, 1943; h/El Retiro #19, Huamcao, PR; ba/Rio Piedras, PR; m/Emma; c/Pablo I II, Mariemma; p/Pablo Altieri and Monsita Nieto, Anasco, PR; ed/BS 1963; MD 1967;

mil/USAF; cpa/Dir Cardiovascular Lab, Univ PR; Pres Fac, Univ PR Med Sch; cp/Rotary Clb; r/Cath; hon/W/W; Most Dist'd Edr, PR C of C.

ALTMANN, ESTHER W NESBIN oc/- Retired; b/Aug 5, 1910; h/PO Box 102, San Marcos, CA 92069; m/John Charles Maxwell; p/Oscar A and Helen Schmandt Winter (dec); ed/BA Univ Buffalo 1931; pa/Ret'd; cp/Escondido Hist Soc (Hon Mem); hon/Outstg Ser to Ed Awd: Consuelo Lodge F&AM 1965, C of C 1972.

ALTVATER, HELEN M oc/Legal Secretary; Office Manager; b/Nov 24, 1920; h/7070 Pembroke, Reno, NV 89502; ba/Reno; m/Anthony C; c/Dale Anthony; p/Maurice and Lida Higgins, Reno, NV; ed/San Fran Secy Col; Inst of Chd's Lit; pa/Attend Legal Secy Sems; Pub'd Writer of Chd's Stories & Poetry; cp/Stella Woodall Poetry Soc; The Anthropol Soc; r/Cath; hon/Invited by Inst of Chd's Lit to participate in Writing Master's Prog & received diploma.

ALVARADO-TORRES, THILDA I oc/- Librarian; b/Aug 25, 1932; h/267 Isabel la Catolica, Hyde Park, Hato Rey, PR 00918; ba/Hato Rey; m/Juan Alvarado and Carmen Torres, Hato Rey, PR; ed/BA Univ PR 1951; MSLS Drexel Inst Technol 1955; pa/Libn, Dept of Ed, Hato Rey; Lectr & Conslt for Devel of Public Lib Sers in PR 1973-77; Public Lib Sers in PR: Dir 1957-73, Asst Dir 1956-57; Other Past Positions; cp/Popular Dem Party; r/Cath; hon/W/W Am.

ALVAREZ, MARCELO A oc/Certified Public Accountant; b/Aug 7, 1938; h/103 Naudain St, Philadelphia, PA; ba/Phila; m/Betty Lou Lovell; p/Marcelino Alvarez (dec); Isabel Garcia (dec); ed/BBA 1962, MBA 1965 Univ Miami; pa/Coopers & Lybrand 1965-: Ptnr 1971-, Mng Ptnr Brazilian Audit Pract 1971-75, Dir Latin Am 1973-78, Staff Dir for VP Domestic Opers 1978-; Am Inst CPAs; Fla Inst CPAs; Nat Assn Accts; Am Assn Spanish Spkg CPAs; InterAm Acctg Assn; Spchs to Confs & Govtl Groups; cp/Intl Ctr, Bd Trustees, Fla St Theater; Latin Am C of C, Miami; Am C of C for Brazil, Rio de Janeiro & Sao Paulo; hon/Beta Alpha Psi; Beta Gamma Sigma; W/W Brazilian Bus.

ALVAREZ, THELMA LUCIA oc/Social Worker; b/Jul 30; h/535 Lafayette Ct, Sarasota, FL 33577; ba/Sarasota; p/Benigno G and Antonia C Alvarez, Sarasota, FL; ed/AB Fla St Univ 1945; pa/Orientation Supvr, Reg 9, Fla St Social & Ec Sers; Libn, Reg 9 Lib 1970-73; Unit Supvr, Sarasota Co 1961-70; Unit Supvr, Sarasota Co 1961-70; cp/Migrant Sch Planning Bd; Sarasota U Need; Past Pres, Sarasota Altrusa Clb; Beta Sigma Phi; r/Cath; hon/W/W: Am Wom, S&SW; World W/W Wom; Intl W/W Commun Ser.

AMARA, LUCINE oc/Opera/Concert Artist; b/Mar 1, 1927; h/260 W End Ave, NY, NY 10023; ba/NYC; p/George and Adrine Kazanjian Armaganian (dec); ed/Studied w:

Bertha Roth (Violin), Stella Eisner-Eyn (Voice), Bobbi Tillander (Voice); pa/Dramatic Soprano w Metro Opera 1950-; Metro Opera

Credits incl: 6 New Prodns, 5 Opening Nights, 43 Texaco Broadcasts, 745 Total Onstage Perfs; Appearances with other Operas or Symphs incl: Stamford, Conn Symph 1978, Houston Opera Co 1974, Hartford, Conn Opera Co 1974, NC Opera 1973, Philadelphia Lyric Opera 1969, NY Philharm Concert 1969, Boston Opera Co 1967, Mexico City Opera 1966, Num Others; Travelled Internationally in Opera & Concerts Since 1947; Held Concerts in 40+ US Cities; Debut Recital as Dramatic Soprano, San Fran 1947; Recordings on Angel, Cambridge, Columbia, Metro Opera Record of the Mo Clb, RCA Victor, & Other Record Labels; Radio & TV Appearances; r/Armenian Apostolic; hon/1st Prize, Atwater-Kent Auditions 1948.

AMERASINGHE, HAMILTON SHIRLEY oc/Diplomat; b/Mar 18, 1913; h/10 Waterside Plaza, Apt 10D, NY, NY 10010; p/(dec); ed/BA w hons Univ London 1934; pa/Ambassador of Sri Lanka to Brazil 1973-; Permanent Rep of Ceylon (Sri Lanka) to UN 1967-78 (Pres, 31st Session of UN Gen

Assembly); Pres, Third UN Conf on Law of Sea 1973-; High Commr of Ceylon in India & Ambassador of Ceylon to Nepal & Afghanistan 1963- 67; Other Diplomatic & Govtl Positions; r/Buddhism.

AMES, JOHN DAWES oc/Investment Banker; b/May 7, 1904; h/600 Washington Rd, Lake Forest, IL 60045; ba/Chgo, IL; m/Constance Hasler; c/John D Jr, Knowlton, William; p/Knowlton Lyman and Adelaide Schroeder Ames (dec); ed/BA Princeton Univ 1928; mil/WW II, Lt Col; pa/Bkg; cp/Past Dir, Wallace, Murray, Clark Equipmt; Dir, Chd's Meml Hosp, Chgo; Nat Chm, Citizens for Eisenhower; r/Epis; hon/Meritorious Ser Awd, WW II; Am & Italian Bronze Stars.

AMES, RICHARD GALYON oc/Educational Administrator; b/Jun 2, 1935; ba/Hayward, CA; m/Sue Ann Roedell; c/Andrea Elizabeth; ed/Univ Richmond; BA Geo Wash Univ 1958; MA Am Univ 1962; PhD Univ NC-Chapel Hill 1970; pa/Cal St Univ, Hayward: Assoc Dean Acad Planning

1975-77, Assoc Prof of Sociol 1971-, Asst Prof 1969-71; Asst Prof, Syracuse Univ 1967-69; Instr, Univ So Cal 1965-67; Instr, Univ-NC Chapel Hill 1964-65; Other Past Positions; Am Sociol Assn; AAAS; Am Assn Univ Admrs; Pacific Sociol Assn; Conslt; cp/Hayward S Rotary; St Rose Foun; r/Presb; hon/Grants;

Num Cits; Co-Author: *Elementary Statistical Statistical Theory in Sociol*, 1976, *The Handicapped Children of Alamance Co* 1965; Pub'd Monographs, Book Chapts, Profl Articles, Book Reviews; Am Men & Wom Sci; W/W: Cal; W; Commun Ldrs & Noteworthy Ams; DIB; Men Achmt; Personalities of W&MW; Intl W/W Commun Ser; Intl W/W Intells; Men & Wom Distn.

AMIR-MOEZ, ALI REZA oc/Professor; b/Apr 7, 1919; ba/Dept of Math, Texas Tech Univ, Lubbock, TX 79404; p/Mohammad and Fatemeh Amir-Moez; ed/BA Univ Teheran 1942; MA 1951, PhD 1955 UCLA; mil/Iranian Army, Lt; pa/Prof of Math, Tex Tech Univ; Res in Math; Past Tchg Positions: Univ Cal LA, Univ Idaho, Queens Col of CUNY, Purdue Univ, Univ of Fla, Clarkson Col of Technol; Am Math Soc; Math Assn Am; Sigma Xi; Pi Mu Epsilon; Circolo Matermatico Di Palmero, Kappa Mu Epsilon; cp/Lubbock Gem & Mineral Soc; r/Moslem; hon/Medal of Hon, Persian Army 1937; Medal from Acad of Human Scis of Brazil; Pub'd Num Papers, Articles & Books; Author Plays: *Kaleelah and Demneh, Three Persian Tales*.

AMMAR, RAYMOND G oc/Professor; b/Jul 15, 1932; h/1651 Hillcrest Rd, Lawrence, KS 66044; ba/Lawrence; m/Carroll Ikerd; c/Elizabeth, Robert, David; p/Elias Ammar (dec); Nellie Ammar, Kingston, Jamaica;

ed/AB Harvard Univ 1953; PhD Univ Chgo 1959; pa/Prof of Physics, Univ Kans, Lawrence; NWn Univ: Assoc Prof 1964-69, Asst Prof 1960-64; Fellow, Am Physical Soc; AAUP; r/Epis.

AMMARELL, JOHN SAMUEL oc/- Corporation Executive; b/Mar 21, 1920; h/13001 SW 71 Ave, Miami, FL 33156; ba/Coral Gables, FL; ed/BA Muhlenberg Col; pa/Exec VP, Wackenhut Corp; Cert'd Protection Profl; Am Soc for Indust Security;

Chm, Pvt Security Sers Coun; Com Nat Security Cos; cp/Trustee, Newberry Col; Dir, Gtr Miami Crime Comm; Soc of Former Spec Agts of FBI; BPOE; Lambda Chi Alpha; Coral Gables CC; r/St Peter's Luth Ch; hon/W/W: Am, Fin & Indust; Commun Ldrs Am; Alumni Achmt Awd, Muhlenberg Col.

AMMER, WILLIAM oc/Judge; b/May 21, 1919; h/141 Pleasant St, Circleville, OH 43113; ba/Circleville; p/Moses S and Mary Schallas Ammer (dec); ed/BS 1941, LLB 1946, JD 1967 Ohio St Univ; mil/AUS 1942-46, Sgt; pa/Common Pleas Judge, Pickaway Co, Ohio; Assigned to Sit on Ct Assignmts in 30 Ohio Cos; Past Pres, Ohio Common Pleas

Judges Assn; Past Chm Crim Law Com, Ohio Bar Assn; Prosecuting Atty 1953-57; Past Pres, Pickaway Co Bar Assn; cp/Circleville Kiwanis Clb (Past Lt Gov); Repub; r/Meth; hon/Life Fellow, Kiwanis Intl; Beta Gamma Sigma; Superior Judicial Ser Awd, Supr Ct Ohio 1974, 75, 76.

AMMERMAN, GALE RICHARD oc/-Professor; b/Mar 6, 1923; h/RR 4, Box 76, Starkville, MS 39759; ba/Mississippi St, MS; m/Jane Loretta; c/Kathleen, John, Joe, Mark, Chris; p/Lyman Sylvania and Iva Mae Ammerman, Sullivan, IN; ed/BS; MS; PhD; mil/1941-46, 1/Lt; pa/Prof, Dept of Horticult, Miss St Univ; IFT; Exec Secy, Phi Tau Sigma; Alpha Zeta; Sigma Xi; cp/Dem; r/Cath; hon/Fac Res Awd, Miss St Univ 1978; IFT Indust Achmt Awd 1977; Awd of Merit for Res, Gamma Sigma Delta 1974.

AMORELLI, ANNA MARIE oc/-Principal; b/Sept 3, 1934; h/290 Green Ave, Lyndhurst, NJ; 07071; ba/Rutherford, NJ; p/Anthony and Rose Amorelli (dec); ed/BA; MA; pa/Prin, Pierrepont Sch; Former Positions incl Tchr & Guid Cnslr; Rutherford Ed Assn; Bergen Co Ed Assn; NJ Ed Assn; Past Pres, Rutherford Admrs Assn; Bergen Co Elem

Tchrs Assn; NJ Sch Admrs Assn; Nat Elem Sch Admrs Assn; Delta Kappa Gamma (Past Pres Theta Chapt); Profl Pubs; cp/Wom's Col Clb of Rutherford; ARC Course Instr; 1/VP, Ridgewood-Hackensack Chapt Zonta Intl; Astraea Jr Guild; Fdr & Past Pres, S Bergen Mtl Hlth Ctr; Others; r/Cath; hon/Cert of Ser NJEA; Wom of Yr, Zonta Intl; Commun Ser Awd, Lyndhurst Jrs; Edr of Yr Awd, VFW 1977.

AMOS, MARJORIE R oc/Association Staff Member; b/Jan 13, 1926; h/361 Ashley Ave, Charleston, SC 29403; ba/Charleston; c/Vertelle Kenion, Elease Goodwin, William Jerome, Wilford; p/William Rhodes, Charleston, SC; Mamie Boseman; pa/Staff Person, U Way; cp/Bd Trustees: Allen Univ, Reid House Ctr; Mem Co Coun & Judicial, Nat Dem Party; r/African Meth.

AMYX, KATHERINE McCLURE oc/-Author; Retired Postmistress; b/Oct 29, 1902; h/PO Box 89, Grassy Creek, KY 41435; m/Ora Boyd; c/Frank M Ferguson; p/Matthew B and Margaret Kilgore McClure (dec); cp/Author 7 Books of Poety & 1 Book Short Stories; cp/Past Regent, DAR; r/Bapt; hon/Num Awds for Poetry in US, England & Canada.

ANBINDER, PAUL oc/Publisher; b/Apr 19, 1940; h/144 Southlawn Ave, Dobbs Ferry, NY 10522; ba/NY, NY; m/Helen Myra Rabinowitz; c/Mark Harris, Jeffrey Todd; c/Tulea Herzel Anbinder (dec); Gussie Dandeshane Anbinder, Yonkers, NY; ed/BA Cornell Univ; pa/VP & Trade Editor, Ballentine Books & Dir Spec Projs, Random House & Alfred A Knopf 1975-; Harry N Abrams Inc: Pres 1974-75, Exec Editor 1969-73; Editor-in-Chief, Shorewood Pubrs 1964-69; Exec Coun Gen Pubg Div, Assn Am Pubrs; r/Temple Beth Shalom, Hastings-on-Hudson; hon/NYS Regents Tchg F'ship.

ANDERJACK, GEORGE MICHAEL oc/-Museum Administrator; b/Mar 7, 1945;

h/Box 3037, University Sta, Moscow, ID 83843; ba/Lewiston, ID; p/George F and Helen Anderjack, Metuchen, NJ; ed/BS 1966, Grad Study 1966-67 Seton Hall; Univ of Idaho 1974-; Addit Studies: Henry Francis du Pont Winterthur Mus-Univ of Del Sum Inst 1973, Williamsburg Seminar 1977; Studied in England; mil/AUS Lt 1967-69; USAR Capt 1969-; pa/Exec Dir Nez Perce Co Hist Soc; Luna House Hist Soc; Mus Conslt 1977-, Fed ACTION Vol 1976-77; Tchg Asst, Univ Idaho 1975-76; Dir Sandwich Glass Mus 1972-73; Instr Perth Amboy HS 1966-67, 1969-72; Asst, Ginsberg & Ginsberg, Inc 1958-66; Am Assn of Msu; Am Assn for St & Local Hist; Soc of Arch Histns; Nat Trust for Hist Preserv; Assoc Student AIA; cp/BPO Elks; C of C; hon/Pub'd Articles in *The Acorn* (Sandwich Hist Soc Jour): "Preserv of Antiques," Jul 1972, "Preserv of Antique Mats," Jun 1972, "Preserv of Mats," May 1972; W/W in E; Men Achmt; DIB; Mus Dir of Am Assn of Mus; Others.

ANDERSON, CARL WILLIAM oc/-Attorney-at-Law; b/Mar 15, 1901; h/30 Stonepine, Hillsborough, CA 94010; ba/Box 471 Burlingame, CA 94010; m/Audrey Marion; p/Charles Oscar and Ada Augusta Johnson Anderson (dec); ed/AB; JD; pa/San Mateo Co Bar Assn; Cal Bar Assn; Am Bar Assn; Trial Lwyrs Assn; City Atty, City of San Carlos 1942-51; Public Admr Atty 1935-37; cp/Past Mem, Repub Ctl Com; Fdg Mem, Peninsula Humane Soc; Dir, Crippled Chd & Adults of San Mateo Co 1939-78 (Past Pres); Past Pres, Burlingame Rotary Clb; Former Selective Ser Appeal Agt; hon/Congl Dist'd Ser Medal; 7 Cits for Public Ser; Others.

ANDERSON, DOUGLAS SCRANTON HESLEY oc/Business Executive; b/Aug 23, 1929; h/39 Vista Dr, Greenwich, CT 06830; ba/NY, NY; m/Elizabeth Bartram Radley; c/Katherine Scranton; p/Lloyd Douglas Hesley Anderson (dec); Alice Scranton Eastman Anderson (dec); ed/AB Harvard Univ 1951; NWn Univ; mil/USNR, Lt (Ret'd);

pa/Dir Corporate Devel, Sterling, Grace & Co 1973-; Gen Ptnr, The Anderson Co; Cert'd by Investmt Bkrs Assn Am; cp/Pres, Pecksland Rd Assn 1977-78; VChm, U Way, Greenwich 1977-79; Dir, Indian Harbor Assn 1979-; Elected Rep to Greenwich Town Meeting (RTM) 1979-; Assn Former Intell Ofcrs; r/Prot; hon/NROTC S'ship, Harvard Col.

ANDERSON, ELIZABETH WICKER oc/-Retired Home Economist; Educator; b/Dec 9, 1916; h/108 N Whitehead, Warrenton, GA 30828; m/William Alan; c/William Alan Jr, Laura Virginia A Whitelaw, John Wicker; p/George Madison and Ruth Clapp Wicker (dec); ed/BSHE; MEd Home Ecs; MEd Cnslg; EdS; pa/Former Home Economist & HS Cnslr; ASCA; GSCA (StSecy 1972-73); NEA; GAE (Unit Pres 1964-66); APGA; GPGA; cp/Title XX Citizens Planning Coun (Warren Co Chm 1977-79); Dist Coun St Planning Coun; Ga Lung Assn (Warren Co Chm 1972-79); Eastern Seal Soc 1974-79; r/Warrenton 1st U Meth Ch: Adm Bd 1973-79, Pres U Meth Wom 1979, 80; hon/Phi Upsilon Omicron; Kappa Delta Pi; GSCA 109th Dist Cnslr of Yr 1976.

ANDERSON, EVELYN ROCELLA oc/Teacher; b/Sept 30, 1953; h/Box 185, Palmer, TN 37365; m/Clayton Jr; p/Arthur and Mary Lou Creighton, Chattanooga, TN;

ed/BS; pa/HS Ecs Tchr; NEA; TEA; GCA; cp/Delta Zeta Sorority; OES; VP, Middle Tennessee Alumna Chapt, Grundy Co; Active in commun sports; Little Sister, Pi Kappa Phi; r/Bapt.

ANDERSON, GLORIA B oc/Programmer/Analyst; b/Jan 12, 1949; h/7986 Janna Lee Ave #303, Alexandria, VA 22306; ba/Arlington, VA; m/Reginald L; c/Eric C, Darcee M; p/Israel Sr and Martha Foster; ed/BS cum laude; cp/NAACP; Delta Sigma Theta; r/Bapt; hon/Scholastic S'ship; Acad Hons; Commun Ser Awd, Frontiers Intl 1974.

ANDERSON, GORDON LEE oc/-Sculptor; b/Jan 28, 1930; h/8642 Island Dr S, Seattle, WA 98118; p/Anton and Helen Anderson, Tacoma, WA; ed/BA, MA Univ Wash; mil/USAF, Ofcr; Inactive Resvs; pa/Sculpture for public & private sites; hon/Jury Prizes; Fellowships.

ANDERSON, HARRIET IDELL oc/-Retired Librarian; b/Mar 3, 1910; h/1322 Gamma St, Crosby, TX 77532; m/Leroy Lawrence; c/Terry William, Larry Alan, Gwendolyn Idell A Sharoff; p/William Jessie and Ella Wisenbaker Galbreath, Wharton, TX; ed/Baylor Univ; BS, MS Univ Houston; pa/English Tchr & Libn, Crosby HS 35 yrs; Taught English, Music & Art, Goose Creek Sch Sys 7 yrs; Taught US Fed Plan and Cont'g Ed 7 yrs; Prin, Wharton Co 1929; Tex Ret'd Libns: Pres 1978-79, Secy 1977-78; Chm, Friends of the Crosby Br, Harris Co Lib; Sponsor, Crosby HS & Jr HS Student Coun Wkshop 20 yrs; Instr, Student Coun Wkshop, Univ Houston 3 yrs; NEA; Tex Edrs Assn; Nat

Lib Assn; Harris Co Br Libn, Crosby; AAUW; Tex Lib Assn; cp/Pres, Crosby Sorosis Wom's Clb 1977-78; San Jacinto Dist Chm, Intl Clbs 1976-78; DAR Good Citizen Chm, Sammuel Sorrell Chapter, 1976-78; Past Ldr: CSA, GSA; Past Pres: Crosby Band Parents, Crosby PTA, Harris Co PTA, Crosby Garden Clb; Parliamentn, Harris Co Tchr Assn; Worthy Matron, Crosby OES; U Daughs Confed; Assn Ret'd Persons; Wom's Aux, Houston Bar Assn; Young Wom of Arts; r/1st Bapt Ch; hon/Life Mem: Nat PTA, St PTA; Selected 1 of Crosby's Outstanding Citizens; Delta Kappa Gamma; W/W: Tex Edrs, Sch Adm, Am Wom; Commun Ldrs & Noteworthy Ams; Personalities of S; DIB; Notable Ams; World W/W Wom; Acad Hons.

ANDERSON, HERBERT FREDERICK oc/Physician; Surgeon; b/Jul 15, 1902; h/4213 Poudre Canyon, Bellvue, CO 80512; m/Eugenia Clair Foote; c/Gene C Haynes, Shirley J Ammons, Jerry H, Anders Timm; p/Anders Christian and Ida Alvina Anderson (dec); ed/AB cum laude Hastings Col 1924; BSc Univ Neb 1928; MD Univ Neb 1930; Addit Study: Univ Ill, Tulane Univ, Ks Univ, Dallas Southern Clinic; pa/Ret'd Physician & Surg (Ophthalmol & Otorhinolaryngol); Adams Co Med Soc; Neb Med Assn; AMA; Neb Acad Ophthalmol; Otorhinolaryngology; NY Assn Scis; Conslt'g Staff & Surg, Hastings St Hosp; cp/Kiwanis: Bd Mem, VP; Bd Dirs: YMCA, Commun Concert Assn; Hastings Park Comm; r/Presby Ch: Elder, Bd Trustees, Choir Mem, Tenn Soloist; hon/Kappa Tau Phi; Alpha Kappa Kappa; 1977 Am Masters Athlete of Yr, AAU; 53 Age & Age Group World Records & 5 American Records in

Masters Track & Field; Commun Ldrs & Noteworthy Ams; Others.

ANDERSON, HOWARD PALMER oc/- State Senator; Attorney; b/May 25, 1915; h/1080 Mt Rd, Halifax, VA 24558; m/Mildred Graham Webb; ed/BA Col William & Mary; LLB Univ Richmond Law Sch; mil/WW II; USNR, Lt (sg); pa/Va Bar Assn; Halifax Co Bar Assn; Va St Bar; Va Farm Bur Fed; cp/Univ Richmond Laws Sch Assn; Sportsman's Clb, Halifax; Wilson Meml Ruritan Clb; Bd Trustees, Patrick Henry Meml Foun; Delta Theta Phi; Sigma Pi; VFW; Am Legion; Masons; Lions Clb; Halifax Co C of C; Past Mem, Halifax Co HS Booster Clb; Va Ho of Reps 1958-71; Va St Sen 1972-; r/Bapt; hon/Biogl Listings.

ANDERSON, JACK ROY oc/Business Executive; b/Feb 14, 1925; h/110 Lynwood Terrace, Nashville, TN 37205; ba/Nashville, TN; m/Rose-Marie J Garcia; c/Gail Ellen, Neil Robert, Barbara Ann; p/Roy L and Katherine Munson Anderson (dec); ed/BS Miami Univ 1947; MS Columbia Grad Sch Bus 1949; mil/USNR, Lt (jg); pa/Chm of Bd, Hosp Affiliates Intl Inc; Dir: Tulane Med Ctr Hosp & Clin, New Orleans, Hosp Underwriting Group Ltd, Bermuda; Trustee, River Oaks Foun; Chm Hlth Care Subcom, Employee Benefits Com, Fin Execs Inst; Nat Assn Corp Dirs; Trustee, Nat Com for Quality Hlth Care; cp/Vis Com, Vanderbilt Grad Sch Mgmt; Bus Adv Coun, Univ Miami; Columbia Bus Assocs; hon/Author, *The Road to Recovery* 1976.

ANDERSON, JAMES WILLIAM oc/- Pioneer Telvision Executive; Author; Real Estate Broker; Apartment Building Owner; b/July 29, 1926; h/701 NE 67th St, Miami, FL 33138; ba/Miami, FL; p/James W Anderson Sr (dec); Cecelia Anderson; ed/Grad St Louis Univ; mil/USNAC WW II, Ensign; pa/Owner/Mgr 18 Apts; w ABC-TV 20 yrs; Former Advtg Agy Employee; TV & Radio Appearances; Subject of Newspaper & Mag Articles; Curator, Lemon City; Lectr; hon/Author, *Jim Anderson's How to Live Rent Free Book*.

ANDERSON, JOHN BAYARD oc/Member United States House of Representatives; b/Feb 15, 1922; h/2711 Highcrest Rd, Rockford, IL 61107; ba/Wash DC; m/Keke Machakos; c/Eleanora, John Jr., Diane, Karen, Susan; p/E Albin Anderson, Rockford, IL; ed/BA Univ Ill 1942; JD Univ Ill 1946; LLM Harvard Univ 1949; mil/AUS Field Arty 1943-45; pa/Law Pract, Rockford, Ill 1946-48, 1950-52, 1955-56; St Dept Career Diplomatic Ser 1952-55; Winnebago Co (Ill) St's Atty 1956-60; cp/16th Dist Ill Rep, US Ho of Reps 1960-; r/Prot; hon/Phi Beta Kappa; Harvard F'ship; Hon Degs: Trinity Col, Wheaton Col, N Park Col & Theol Sem, Shimer Col & Geneva Col.

ANDERSON, KENNETH ALLEN oc/- Pastor; b/Jun 2, 1910; h/500 Sylview Dr, Pasadena, MD 21122; ba/Pasadena; m/Opal C; c/Gloria, Miriam, Corrine, Naomi, Bryant; p/Andrew Adolph and Karen T Anderson, Minneapolis, MN; ed/BA; CT; pa/Pastor, Galilee Luth Ch; Pres, W Dak Luth Dist; Pres, NE Ill Pastors' Conf; cp/Pres, Ortonville Mission; Kiwanis Clb; r/Am Luth; hon/Hon Award, Kiwanis Intl.

ANDERSON, MOSELLE WILCOX oc/- Extension Home Economist; b/Apr 17, 1917; h/Rt 2 N, Box 49E, Pocatello, ID 83201; m/Joseph S; c/Zee Ray, Jo Zelle Buffaloe (Mrs Vernon), Tyron W; p/William Harvey Wilcox, Pocatello, ID; Dora Mickelson Wilcox (dec); ed/BA Idaho St Univ; pa/Prof Emerita, Univ Idaho 1978; Am Home Ecs Assn; Gov's Housing Coalition; Steering Com, St Housing Coalition, Assn of Ext Home Economists; SE Idaho Housing Specialist; r/Ch of Jesus Christ LDS; hon/Superior Ser Awd, US Dept Agri 1973; Gamma Sigma Delta; Epsilon Sigma Phi.

ANDERSON, OWANAH PICKENS oc/- Consultant; b/Feb 18, 1926; h/2206 Berkeley, Wichita Falls, TX 76308; m/Henry J; c/4; ed/Univ Okla; pa/Conslt, US Dept Hlth, Ed & Wel; Ret'd Mgr of Fam-owned Bus & Property; cp/IWY: Chm Tex Coor'g Com, Co-chm Tex Del at Nat Wom's Conf, Cont'g Com, Steering Com; Nat Wom's Prog Devel Inc: Bd Mem, Fiscal Ofcr; HEW Secy's Adv Com on Rights & Responsibilities of Wom;

Wichita Falls Com on Status of Wom 1974-80; Chm, Nat Com on Indian Work, Epis Ch US; Am Indian-Alaskan Native Wom's Caucus; Orgr, N Tex Intertribal Coun; Del, Dem Nat Conv 1970; Charter Mem, Wichita Co Dem Wom; Tex Coastal Mgmt Adv Com; Nat Wom's Polit Caucus; LWV; Tex Wom's Polit Caucus; r/Epis: Diocesan & Parish Ofcr; hon/Outstg Tex Citizen Awd, Tex Lic'd Child Care Assn 1977; Outstg Citizen Awd (local), LWV 1976.

ANDERSON, SARAH ANDERSON oc/- Legislator (Retired); b/Jan 23, 1911; h/226 N 52nd, Philadelphia, PA 19139; m/Adolphus W Sr (dec); c/Helen A Thornton, Adolphus Jr, Mae A Parks, Sara A Mosley, Jean A Mallory, Brenda A Kendall; p/Henry A and Maud Smith Anderson (dec); pa/Tchr, Philadelphia Public Sch Sys; cp/Mem, Pa Ho of Reps 1954-72; Est'd Sickle Cell Anemia Proj at Chd's Hosp of Phila (Hon Chm), 1972; Co-sponsored Legislation for Fair Employment Practs, Rehab Ctrs for Job Tng, Commun Col Act & Helped Est St's Com on Status of Wom (1964); Sponsor, Pa ERA; Chm, Pa Hlth & Wel Com, 4 Yrs; Chief Sponsor, Legislation to Est Ctrs for Renal Dialysis Treatmt; Instrumentl in Expanding Mtl Hlth Facilities in Pa; Involved in Promoting Interests of Visually Impaired Persons; r/Presb; hon/Presented "Dist'd Citizen of Pa" Awd by Gov Milton Shapp; W/W: Among Wom, Among Black Ams; Num Other Hons.

ANDERSON, THOMAS HAROLD oc/- Instructor; b/Aug 31, 1941; h/Box 456 Owingsvilel, KY 40360; ba/Mt Sterling, KY; m/Jeanette Houermale; c/Paul Thomas; p/John and Ora Reed Anderson (dec); ed/AB; MA; pa/Montgomery Co Commun HS: Instr, Social Studies Dept Chm, Chm Profl Negotion Com, 2-term Fac Rep; Montgomergy Co Ed Assn: Past Pres, Past VP; Ky Ed Assn; Ctl Ed Assn; NEA; KEA Del 2 yrs; cp/Fdr & 1st Pres, Montgomery Hist Soc; Ky Hist Soc; Bath Co Hist Soc; Montgomery Co Yg Dems; Montgomery Co Bicent Comm; Sponsor, Montgomery Co Hi-Y; Campaign Wkr; r/Owingsville 1st Ch of God; hon/Outstg Sec'dy Edr Am; W/W S&SW; Ky Bicent Reg; Outstg Ser Plaque, Caveryn Comprehensive Care Bd Dirs; Hon Mem, Ky Ct Appeals.

ANDERSON, THOMAS J oc/Publisher; Rancher; b/Nov 7, 1910; h/Norton Creek Clb, Gatlinburg, TN 37738; ba/Pigeon Force, TN; m/Carolyn; c/Carol Porter (Mrs Sam Jr); p/Mrs William J Anderson, Nashville, TN; ed/BA Vanderbilt Univ; mil/USN WW II, Lt; pa/Profl Positions have incl'd: Securities Salesman, Advtg Mgr, Publisher, Editor, Public Spkr, Newspapers Syndicate Owner, Rancher; cp/Am Party: Pres Nominee 1976, Nat Party Chm 1972-78, VP Nominee 1972; hon/Hon LLB, Bob Jones Univ; Liberty Awd, Cong of Freedom; Author: *Straight Talk*; *Silence Is Not Golden - It's Yellow*.

ANDERSON, VERNON ELLSWORTH oc/Professor; b/Jun 15, 1908; h/25369 Carmel Knolls Dr, Carmel, CA 93923; m/Alice Parker; c/Mary A Bayhi (Mrs Larry); p/Frank E Anderson; Johanna Pearson; ed/BS w distn 1930, MA 1936 Univ Minn; PhD Univ Colo 1942; Hon DLitt Susquehanna Univ 1972; pa/Prof Ednl Ldrship, PT, Schs of Human Behavior & Ed, US Intl Univ, San Diego, Univ Md: Prof Emeritus, Dean Col of Ed 1955-70, Prof Ed 1955-73; Univ Conn: Assoc Prof to Prof Ed, Dir Curric Ctr 1946-55; Tchg Positions in Sums: Univs of Wash, Minn, Cal-Berkeley, So Cal, Colo, Puerto Rico, Okla, & Oreg St Sys of Higher Ed; HS Tchr & Prin, Askov & Elk River (Minn) Public Schs; Dean of Jr Col, Worthington; Curric Dir, St of Wash & Portland (Oreg) Schs; ASCD: Exec Com 2 Terms, Bd Dirs 2 Terms, VP, Chm 3 Coms, Mem 5 Others; Helped Org & 1st Exec Secy NW ASCD & New England ASCD; Md ASCD, WCCI, Profs of Curri; On Progs of Sev ASCD Nat Confs; Conslt Activs incl: USOE, AAAS, NCATE, Ednl Policies Comm, Job Corps; Advr to Doct Cands at Conn, Md & USIU; r/Luth Ch of Am: Bd Social Min's Comm on Ch-St Relats 1964-65, Conslt Long-Range Planning Task Force 1968, Conslt Proposed Ctl Objective for Parish Ed 1969, Bd Parish Ed 1963-73, Edit Com; U Luth Ch Am: Mem Long-Range Prog Parish Ed, Conslt'g 1956-59, Writer's Conf, Long-Range Progs of Parish Ed 1960; Luth Student Foun of Md & DC: Mem Exec Com 1957-60; Hope Evang Luth Ch, College Park, Md: Mem Ch Coun 1956-61, VP Ch Coun 1958-60, Hd Ch as VP 1959-60, Chm Pulpit Com 1959-60, Chm Com on Christian Ed & Lit 1956-57, Mem Bldg Com 1956-57, Evangelism Visitor 1956-57, Usher 1959-60, Christian Ed Com 1971-73; New England Conf, Augustana Synod: Comm on Parish Ed 1950-55, Conducted Triple T Wkshops & Ldrship Sems in Conn, Fac Sponsor, Luth Student, Univ Conn; Other Former Com Mbrships & Positions: Columbia Conf (Augustana Synod), Augustana Luth Ch, Portland, Oreg, Gloria Dei Luth Ch, Olympia, Wash; hon/Profl Pubs incl: 2 Texts & a Paperback: *Principles and Procedures of Curriculum Improvement*, *Principals & Practices of Secondary Ed* (Coauthor), & *Curriculum Guidelines in an Era of Change*; Other Profl Pubs; During his Deanship, Col of Ed Received AACTE Dist'd Achmt Awd for Excell in Tchr Ed; Upon Retiremt Received 18 Cits of Recog from St & Nat Profl Assns, Alumni Assns, & Md's Col of Ed, Summer Sch & Univ Col; Cert Dist'd Citizenship, Gov Md; Life Mem ASCD; Establishment of Vernon E Anderson Lecture Series, Col of Ed, Univ M Num Biogl Listings; Num Others.

ANDERSON, VIVIAN M oc/Teacher; b/Oct 4, 1926; h/Oakland Ave S, Box 303, Mt Juliet, TN 37122; ba/Mt Juliet; m/Corbett W; c/Lawrence O; Randy G, Regina; p/Ira Mitchell, Falkner, MS; Elora LaBarreare Mitchell (dec); BS, MEd, Addit Study Middle Tenn St Univ; pa/Bus Ed Tchr & Girls Coach, Ashland HS 1946-47; Bus Ed Tchr, Prentiss Co Sch Sys 1949-60; Elem Tchr, Wilson Co Sch Sys, Tenn 1960-; WCEA; TEA; NEA; cp/PTA; 11th Dist Co Commr, Wilson Co Ct 1978-82 (Minutes Com 1979-80, Planning & Zoning Com 1979-80); Mt Juliet City Beautiful Comm: Bd Mem 1979-87, Histn 1979-; r/1st Mt Juliet Bapt Ch: Woms Missionary Soc, Bible Sch Dept Hd, Tng U Yth Dir, GA Dir, Others; hon/Cand: Outstg Tchr Am 1956-76, Wilson Co 1976-77.

ANDERSON, W E "ANDY" oc/Retired; b/Dec 2, 1906; h/955 Sam Dealey Dr, Dallas, TX 75208; m/Mabel M; ed/BBA Tex A&M Univ 1927; pa/Film Prodr; Writer; Big Game Hunter; Wildlife Photog; Author Num Articles Pub'd in Wildlife Mags; Prodr Wildlife & Big Game Films: *Big Game Hunting in North America*, *Big Game Trails*; Dallas Woods & Waters Clb: Charter Mem, 1st Chm Big Game Hunting Com; Oak Cliff Lions Clb: Coms, Old Monarch Awd, Achmt Awd; SAR; Aggie & Century Clbs; Fdr Mem, Tex A&M Lttrmans Assn; Past Bd Mem YMCA; Others; r/Kessler Park Meth Ch: Mem, Adm Bd, Fin Com Chm, Stewardship Com, New Pledge Com; hon/Num Biogl Listings.

ANDERSON, WENDELL BERNHARD oc/Poet; Artist; b/Jan 10, 1920; h/RR 1, PO Box 1808, Las Cruces, NM 88001; ba/Las Cruces; m/Emily Ferry; p/Gustav B and Ebba Reed Anderson (dec); ed/BA Franklin Pierce Col 1969; Reed Col; Univ Oreg; pa/Dir & Operator, Harwood Foun Bookmobile, Univ N Mex, Taos 1949-51; Caseworker-Fam Sers, N Mex Dept Public Welfare 1965, 66, 69, 70-71; Social Wkr, Child Welfare Sers, N Mex Dept Social Sers 1971-75; Creative Writing

Tchr, Hampshire Co Sch, Rindge, NH 1966-68; w US Forest Ser in Oreg, N Mex & Mont 9 Seasons; w US Fish & Wildlife Ser 1 Yr; Fire Control Aide, US Nat Park Ser 1 Season; Poet & Writer 1939-; hon/"Ye Tabord Inne" Writers' Hon Soc; Peter B Allen Student Awd 1969; Acad Hons; DIB; Author: (Poetry Collects:) *The Heart Must Be Half Eagle* 1950, *Hawk's Hunger* 1952; Poetry Pub'd in Var Anthols incl'g *Turquoise Land, Poets West, Three on a Match,* & Others.

ANDRE, PAUL REVERE oc/Clergyman; b/Oct 25, 1935; h/1910 Lloyd St, Bellevue, NE 68005; ba/Bellevue; m/Anna Katherine Jones; c/Paul Revere Jr, Georgia Carol, Iva Elizabeth A Yarolimek, Katherine A; p/George Martin and Iva Elsie Andre (dec); ed/AA Ctl Col 1957; AB Greenville Col 1959; MDiv Asbury

Sem 1962; pa/Pastor, Bellevue Free Meth Ch; Served Previous Pastorates in Free Meth Chs in Ill, Ky, Wash & Neb; cp/Charter Mem, Nebraskans for a Constitutional Conv; Bellevue Rotary Clb: Pres, VP, Secy; hon/Acad Hons; Outstg Citizen of Omaha (Neb) 1976.

ANDREWS, BENNY oc/Artist; b/Nov 13, 1930; h/130 W 26th St, NY, NY 10010; m/Mary Ellen; c/Christopher, Thomas, Julia, p/George C Andrews, Madison, GA; Viola Andrews, Atlanta, GA; ed/BFA Chgo Art; mil/USAF 1950-54, S/Sgt; pa/1-Man Shows: Ulrich Mus, Wichita, Ks 1977, Wadsworth Antheneum, Hartford, Conn 1978, Handshake Gallery, Atlanta, Ga 1978, Pelham-Stoffler Gallery, Houston, Tex 1977, Lerner-Heller Gallery, NY, NY 1976-78, Gallery of Sarasota (Fla) 1975, 76, 77, 78, Num Others; Major Group Exhbns: Indianapolis Mus Art 1978, Wadsworth-Antheneum 1978, Whitney Mus 1976, Baltimore Mus Art 1974, Mus Modern Art 1968, 71, 77; Boston Mus Fine Arts 1970, 75, Others; Works in Collects: Mus Mod Art, NY, Detroit Inst Art, High Mus Art, Atlanta, NJ St Mus, Bklyn Mus, Mus of African Art, Wash DC, Ohara Mus, Japan; Guest Curator: NY Cult Ctr 1973, Studio Mus in Harlem, NY 1976; Illustrator: *I Am the Darker Brother* 1968, *The Poetry of Black America* 1794, *Ludell* 1975, *Appalachia Red* 1978; Asst Prof,

Queens College CUNY 1968-; Instr: New Sch for Social Res, NY 1965-69, Cal St Col, Hayward, 1969; Co-editor, *The Attica Book*; Art Critic, *Encore*; Pub'd Articles; Author *Between the Lines* 1978; W/W Am Art; Commun Ldrs & Noteworthy Ams; Art & Ethics; Black Artists on Art; 17 Black Artists; Afro-Am Artists: A Biographical Dir; Afro-Am Art; Others.

ANDREWS, CHARLES LAWRENCE oc/-Business Executive; b/Apr 23, 1914; h/520 Hickory St, Hollidaysburg, PA 16648; ba/Altoona, PA; m/Harriet G; c/Beatrice Janice Walker, Lucinda Gilmore Axtell; p/Lawrence and Sarah J Andrews (dec); ed/BS Univ Ill 1935; LLB LaSalle Ext Univ 1949; Masters NYU 1950; pa/Pres, Boyer Bros Inc, Div of Am Maize Prods; Bd Dirs, Taconic Farms; Inst Food Technologists; Am Mgmt Assn; Am Mktg Assn; Am Inst of Mgmt (Pres's Coun); IPA; Chgo Exec Clb; Sales Exec Clb; cp/Mason; Shriner; r/Presb; hon/All-Am Wrestling Team; Olympic Swimming Com.

ANDREWS, CLAUDE LEONARD oc/-Psychologist; Psychotherapist; Minister; b/Jan 3, 1943; h/309 St John St, Tarboro, NC 27886; ba/Tarboro; m/Carol Cooper; pa/Leland Waverly Andrews, Tarboro, NC; Annie Grey Hyde Andrews (dec); ed/BA St Andrews Presb Col 1965; MDiv Princeton Univ 1969; MEd Univ Ga 1972; PhD Cand; pa/Psychol & Psychotherapist, Creative Living Assocs; Presb Min; APGA; ACPA; APA; AMHCA; ASSECT; ACPE; NCPA; AENCP; Psychologist ENMHC; OGA; cp/Dem; Friends of Lib; Edgecombe Hist Soc; Edgecomb Mtl Hlth Assn; r/Presb; hon/Rucker Awd; Lucy Steele S'ship; W/W: Cols & Univs, S; Phi Kappa Phi; Kappa Delta Pi.

ANDREWS, FRAZIER LEE oc/Minister; Educator; Business Entrepreneur; b/May 3, 1933; h/221 Underhill Street, High Point, NC 27260; ba/High Point, NC; m/Lula T; p/Christopher C Andrews, Mobile, AL; Naomi K Andrews (dec); ed/BS Ala St Univ; MDiv Va Union Grad Sch Rel; pa/Pastor, 1st Bapt Ch, High Point; Nat Bapt Conv Inc; Rowan Bapt Assn of NC; Gen Bapt St Conv; Gen Bapt St Conv; Past Pres, Min's Conf High Point & Vicinity; Fdr & Pres, Antil Enterprises Inc; cp/Past Nat Bd Mem, So Christian Ldrship Conf; Mayan Order; Phi Beta Sigma; Am Astrological Assn; Exec Bd, Model Cities Comm; Chm, High Point Bus Devel Corp; Pres, Brentwood Shopping Ctr; Legal Aid Bd & Fam Sers Bur; Co-sponsor, London Wood Devel; Treas, High Point Ch Housing Inc; Hd Start Policy Coun Bd; ESSA Adv Com, High Point City Schs; Exec Bd, Model City Comm; hon/Ford Foun Grants; Hon Degs; W/W Among Black Ams; Outstg Personalities of S; Intl W/W Intells.

ANDREWS, IKE FRANKLIN oc/Member of United States House of Representatives; b/Sept 2, 1925; h/Cary, NC; ba/228 Cannon HOB, Wash DC 20515; m/Pat Goodwin; c/Alice, Nina Patricia; p/A A Andrews (dec); Ina Andrews, Boulee, NC; ed/BS Mars Hill Col; LLD Univ NC-Chapel Hill; mil/AUS ETO WW II; pa/Ptnr in Law Firm Andrews & Stone, Siler City, NC (Prior to Election to Congress); cp/Dem; NC 4th Dist Rep, US Ho

of Reps 1972-; Mem NC Ho of Reps 1961-71; Mem NC St Sen 1959; r/Bapt; hon/2 Combat Stars; Bronze Star; Purple Heart; Biogl Listings.

ANDREWS, THEODORA ANNE oc/-Librarian; Professor; b/Oct 14, 1921; h/2209 Indian Trails Dr, W Lafayette, IN 47906; ba/Lafayette; c/Martin H; p/Harry F and M Grace Ulrey, Lafayette, IN; ed/BS Purdue

Univ; MS Univ Ill; pa/Libn & Prof, Purdue Univ; Spec Libs Assn; Med Lib Assn; AAUP; cp/Purdue Wom's Caucus; Intl Wom's Yr Prog; r/Am Bapt; r/Johns H Moriatry Awd for Dist'd Libnship, Ind Chapt Spec Libs Assn.

ANDRIEKUS, LEONARDAS KAZIMIERAS oc/Poet; Catholic Priest; Editor; b/Jul 15, 1914; p/Kasimieras and Jonkute Barbora Andriekus (dec); ed/Doct Canon Law; Grad Pontifical Univ 1945; pa/Preacher; Lectr; Editor; Collaborator in Num Lithuanian Newspapers with Articles; Provincial Supvr, Lithuanian Franciscan Friars in Exile & Lithuania 1964-70; Author 5 Books of Poetry in Lithuanian & 1 Book of Selected Poems in English; Pres, Lithuanian Writers' Assn in Exile 1969-; Editor AIDAI (Monthly Mag in Lithuanian of Lit, Arts & Scis); r/Cath: Mem Order of Franciscan Friars; hon/$1,000 Literary Awd for Poetry, Lithuanian Writers' Assn in Exile 1960.

ANDRIKOPOULOS, BONNIE JEAN oc/-Oil and Gas Broker; b/Feb 22, 1935; h/635 Ash, Denver, CO 80220; c/Kari Kay, Toni Lynn; p/Delmar C Edson; Gladys Hoddix Edson, Kearney, NE; ed/RN 1957; BS Univ Wyo Col Nsg 1966; pa/Oil & Gas Lease Broker 1960-; Surgical Nurse, Memorial Hosp, Casper, Wyo 1957-59; cp/Lobbyist, Colo NOW 1973-75; Del-at-Large, Nat Wom's Polit Caucus; Bd Dirs, Blue Cross & Blue Shield, Colo; Past Chperson, Colo Comm on Wom; Ldrship Denver Assn; York St Ctr Bd; Nat Comm on Observance of Intl Wom's Yr; Others.

ANDRONIC, ALEXE oc/Physician; b/Nov 10, 1922; h/825 Pontiac Ave, Cranston, RI; p/Constantin and Lucia-Prudentza Andronic (dec); ed/MD Sch Med, Romania 1947; pa/RI Med Ctr-IMH: Jr Phys 1977-78, Sr Phys 1978; Westboro St Hosp, Mass: Sr Phys, Med Dir & Assoc Clin Dir (Med) 1973-74, Pres Med Staff 1973-74; Grafton St Hosp, Mass: Jr Phys 1966-67, Sr Phys 1967-73; Ho Phys & Resident, Fairlawn Hosp, Worcester, Mass 1965-66; Hosp Phys, Oltenitza 1951-64; Country Phys, Gen Pract, Romania 1949-51; AMA; Acad Psychosomatic Med; cp/VP Romanian Parochial; Smithsonian Assocs; Nat Hist Soc; Audubon Soc; Nat Trust for Hist Preserv; Am Mus Nat Hist; Nat Hist Soc; Early Am Soc; Am Law Enforcemt Assn; Others; r/St Nicholas Greek Orthodox Ch; hon/W/W E; Men Achmt; DIB; 4 AMA Awds; Profl Pubs.

ANDRONIC, JOHN CONSTANTIN oc/Senior Chemist; b/Aug 6, 1921; h/21 Commodore Rd, Worcester, MA 01602; ba/Worcester; m/Maria; c/Sandra, Michael; p/Constantin and Lucia Andronic (dec); ed/BS, MS Univ Bucharest, Roumania; mil/Former Capt, Roumanian Med Corp; pa/Sr Chem, Astra Pharmaceutical Inc; NY Acad Scis; Am Chem Soc; Pioneer in Antibiotic Field; ICAB Bucharest, Roumania;

Roumanian Orthodox Archdiocesy USA; r/Christian Orthodox; hon/Hons for Outstg Merit in Med Field; F'ship.

ANGUS, FAY DAPHNE oc/Author; Speaker; h/405 N Canon Dr, Sierra Madre, CA 91024; m/John S; c/Anne, Ian; p/Ernest William Westwood (dec); Amy Beatrice Westwood; pa/Author: *The Catalyst* 1979, *The White Pagoda* 1978, *Up to Heaven and*

Down to Earth 1977, *Between Your Status & Your Quo* 1975; Writer/Spkr for Confs & Clbs; cp/IPA; PEN; Nat Leag Am Pen Wom; Cal Fed Chaparral Poets; Evang Wom's Caucus; Ch Wom United; r/Bapt; hon/Intl W/W Wom.

ANTHONY, SANDRA HARRIS oc/- Businesswoman; b/Mar 17, 1947; h/425 Beasley Rd, Apt E-2, Jackson, MS 39206; ba/Jackson; c/Tony; p/Homer L Harris, Denver, CO; Angelean Washington, Brooklyn, NY; ed/BA Marycrest Col; MBA Cand Miss Col; pa/Mgr Force, Number Sers Dist, S Ctl Bell; Tougaloo Col Bus/Indust Cluster; S Ctl Bell's Spkrs Clb; Nat Writer's Clb, Jackson S Div; Of Future Telephone Co Pioneers of Am; Pt-time Col Recruiter, S Ctl Bell Telephone Co; cp/Pres, LesBelles Social Clb; Chm Polit Action Com, Intl Div Nat Coun Negro Wom; NAACP; Norwood Subdiv #3 Social & Civic Clb; Holy Farm Sch PTA; Bd Mem, Jackson, Miss Nat Coun of Negro Wom Former Bd Mem, Jackson Teen Pregnancy Ctr; r/Rom Cath; hon/DIB; Notable Ams.

ANTHONY, WILLIAM AUGUSTUS oc/- Physician; b/Oct 2, 1900; h/1203 Belvedere Ave, Gastonia, NC 28052; m/Katherine Williams; c/William Augustus Jr, Ann A Lathrop, Katherine A Whitaker; p/William Dixon and Margaret Whitesides Anthony (dec); ed/BA 1924, Doct Humanities 1977 Erskine Col; MD Med Col Va 1929; pa/Ret'd Phys; Ofcl Electrocardiographer, Gaston

Meml Hosp 20 Yrs; Chief of Staff, Gaston Meml Hosp 1951; Phys, Gaston Co Tubercular Clin 20 yrs; AMA; NC Med Soc; Gaston Co Med Soc; Fellow, Am Col Cardiol 1952; Tuberculologist & Thoracologist, Am Acad Tuberculosis Physicians; Fellow, Am Geriatrics Soc; cp/Past Pres, Gaston Co Heart Assn; r/Presb; hon/William L Balthis Awd, Gaston Co Heart Assn 1972.

ANTONY, YANCEY LAMAR oc/- Clergyman; b/Feb 13, 1922; h/PO Box 4241; ba/NY, NY; p/Clifford Elm Anthony, Ft Myers, FL; Tula Barton Anthony (dec); ed/AB

Samford Univ 1944; ThB So Bapt Theol Sem 1947; MA; ThM; ThD Pioneer Theol Sem 1956; PhD Accademia Universitaria Internazionale, Rome 1957; pa/Pres, So Univ 1957-71; Prof; Chair of Diplomatic Sci, Leonardo di Vinci Univ (Italy), Polit Sci, Danzig Univ; Pastor: Ctl Collegiate Bapt Ch, Ft Walton Bch, Fla 1956-67, Harsh Chapel Bapt Ch, Nashville, Tenn 1953-56, 1st Bapt Ch, Ft Walton Bch 1947-53, Walnut Grove Bapt Ch, Lodiburg, Ky 1945-47, Valley Grove Bapt Ch, Tuscumbia, Ala 1942-44; Dir: Ch Missions Fund Bapt Foun, Ch Devel Foun; Pres, Ft Walton Bch Min Assn; Pres, Better Govt Leag of Okaloosa Co, Fla; Moderator, Okaloosa Co Bapt Assn; Exec Bd, Fla Bapt Conv; Mem, Fla Bd of Social Wel 10 yrs (Chm 2 terms); r/Bapt; hon/Knights of Malta 1973;

Gold Medal of Labor, Netherlands; Acad of Sci, Rome; Intl Order of Legion of Hon of Immaculate; Royal Order of St Gereon; Royal Academy of Golden Letters; Great Chivalry Orders Association; Nobility Order of Kaspis; Order of Hereditary Nobility; Accademia Gentium Pro Pace; Accademia Gentium Populorum Progressei; Mozart Society; Der Orden Signum Fidei; Order du Merite Africain; Academia de Ciencias Humanisticas y Relaciones; Insittut des Relations Diplomatiques; Col & Aide de Camp, Gov of Miss; Lt Col & Aide de Camp, Gov of Ala; Spec Cit, W Los Angeles Col Sen; W/W: Am Cols & Univs, Am, Fla, World; Commun Ldrs & Noteworthy Ams; Outstg Floridians; Intl W/W Commun Ser; Men of Achmt; Intl Reg of Profiles.

ANTONOVICH, MICHAEL DENNIS oc/Businessman; b/Aug 12, 1939; h/3023 San Gabriel Ave, Glendale, CA 91208; ba/Glendale, CA; p/Mike and Frances Ann M Antonovich, Glendale, CA; ed/BA 1963, MA 1967; mil/AUS; pa/Proj Dir, Gregg-Gangi Devel 1979-; Instr: Cal St Univ-LA 1979, Pepperdine Univ 1979; Govt-Hist Instr, LA Unified Sch Dist 1966-72; Bd Dirs, George Miller Constrn Co 1975-; LA Commun Col Dist Bd Trustees 1969-73 (Served as Pres & VP); cp/Mem Cal St Assembly 1972-78; Repub Whip 1976-78; Del, Repub Nat Conv 1976; 1976 Repub Platform Com; Phi Delta Kappa; ARC; Kiwanis; Elks Lodge; Profl Edrs of LA; Sec'dy Tchrs of LA; Philadelphia Soc; Native Sons of the Golden West; Good Shephard Luth Home for Retarded Chd; Glendale C of C; Bd Govs, Glendale Symph Orch Assn; Others; r/Luth; hon/Outstg Legislator of Yr, Cal Repub Assembly 1973-74, 1974-75, 1976-77; Outstg Yg Men Am; W/W: Am Polits, Govt, Am, W; DIB; Personalities of W&MW; Notable Ams; Men Achmt; Man of Yr, So Cal Repub Heritage Groups Coun 1977; Legislator of Yr, LA Co Fed'd Repub Wom 1977.

ANZALONE, ALFRED MARK oc/- Administrative Librarian; Government Official; b/Apr 23, 1926; h/32 Hilltop Rd, Mendham, NJ 07945; ba/Dover, NJ; m/Helen Marie Pryzbylski; c/Susan, Nancy, Mark, Linda; p/Phillip and Anna Marie Anzalone; ed/Newark Col Engrg; Seton Hall Univ; BS Rutgers Univ 1960; MLS; mil/AUS 1944-46; Picatinny Arsenal; Adm Libn 1975-, Acting Chief 1974-75, Libn Plastics Tech Eval Ctr 1961-74, Lit Res Chemist Sci & Tech Info Br 1956-61, Asst Chief Planning 1956; Res Chem, 1951-56; Past Pres, Picatinny Arsenal Tech Assn; Am Chem Soc; Spec Libs Assn (Pres NJ Chapt); Am Soc for Info Sci; cp/Past Pres,

Kearny Area Jaycees; Alpha Phi Delta; NJ Alumni Clb (Past Pres); hon/Pub'd Profl Articles; Patents.

APEA, JOSEPH B K oc/Consulting Engineer; b/Aug 9, 1932; h/2650 Western Ave, Park Forest, IL 60466; ba/Chicago, IL; m/Agnes J; c/Kathleen K, Adwoa O, Abena O, Akuad N; p/Joseph Appia (dec); Nancy

Norman, Aburi, Ghana; ed/BSCE; SE; PE; pa/ASCE; NSPE; SEA; Exec Dir, Samuels, Apea & Assocs, Inc; cp/Intl Toastmasters Clb; r/Presb; hon/Commun Ldrs & Noteworthy Ams; DIB; Men Achmt; Personalities of W&MW; W/W Among Black Ams.

APELQUIST, RONALD WILLIAM oc/Educator; Safety Engineer; b/Apr 1, 1909; m/G Irene Randklev; ed/BE Wis St Univ 1932; ME Univ Wis; MA Univ Minn 1940; mil/Grad Command & Gen Staff Sch 1945; pa/Ret'd; Pt-time Instr, Minn Metro St Col, St Paul 1971-; Math Tchr, South HS, Mpls, Minn 1957-74; Public Sch Tchr, Minn & Wis 1932-42; Pt-time Instr, Ext Div, Inst of Technol, Univ of Minn 6 Yrs; Safety Engr & Mgr, Var Railroads 1946-57; Pers Cons & OCS Instr; Mbrships incl: VP, Gt Lakes Region, Vets of Safety Intl; Bd Dirs, Minn Safety Coun; Dir, Mpls Ret'd Tchrs Assn 1978-81; Past Pres, Douglas Co Tchrs Assn, Wis; Am MENSA; cp/Amateur Short Wave Radio; Morse Telegraph Clb Inc; hon/Profl Pubs; DIB; Men Achmt; Intl W/W Commun Ser; W/W Midwest.

APODACA, RUDY SAMUEL oc/- Attorney-at-Law; b/Aug 8, 1939; h/3300 West St, Las Cruces, NM 88001; m/Nancy; c/Cheryl Ann, Carla Renee, Cynthia Lynn, Rudy Jr; p/Raymond and Elisa Apodaca, Las Cruces, NM; ed/BS N Mex St Univ; JD Gerogetown Univ Law Ctr; mil/USAR, Capt; pa/Atty; Bd Dirs, Citizens Bk, Las Cruces; N Mex Bar; Assn Trial Lwyrs Am; Nat Legal Aid & Defender Assn; La Raza Nat Lwyrs Assn;

Am Inst Bkg; Rio Grande Writers Assn; Poets & Writers Inc; cp/Pres Bd Regents, N Mex St Univ; Gov's Coor'g Coun for Higher Ed; Advisor to Regents, Selective Ser, Dona Ana Co, N Mex; Mus of N Mex Foun; Las Cruces Symph Soc; Commun Arts Ctr; Intl Connoisseurs of Green & Red Chile; Las Cruces C of C; N Mex Aggie Sports Assn; r/Cath; hon/Phi Kappa Phi; Blue Key; Hons Grad; W/W Am Law; DIB; Author *The Waxen Image*.

APP, AUSTIN J oc/Educator; b/May 24, 1902; h/8207 Flower Ave, Takoma Park, MD 20012; ba/Takoma Park; p/August and Katherine Obermaier App (dec); ed/AB; MA,

PhD Cath Univ Am; mil/Corps of Engrs; pa/Ret'd Assoc Prof of English, LaSalle Col; Former Instr & Prof at Other Cols; Writer; Lectr; cp/Chm Pastorius Unit, Steuben Soc, Phila; Former Chm, Gtr Phila Captive Nations Com; Pres, Fed Am Citizens German Descent 6 Yrs; r/Rom Cath; hon/Univ Scranton Gold Medal "Outstg Edr of Men" 1939; European Freedom Prize, Volksunion, Munich, 1975; Author 8 Books & Num Articles, Reviews, & Pamphlets; Hon Pres, Fed Ams of German Descent; Hon Mem, German-American Nat Cong.

APPLEGATE, HARRY ALVIN oc/-Association Executive; b/Mar 1, 1925; h/3049 Sleepy Hollow Rd, Falls Church, VA 22042; ba/Reston, VA; m/Patricia F; c/Roger L, Ronald W, Russell K, H Randall; p/Cecil M Applegate (dec); Vinise J Applegate, Kelso,

WA; ed/BS, MS Kans St Tchrs Col; mil/USNR 1943-45; pa/Exec Dir, Distributive Ed Clbs of Am Inc; Lectr; Editor; Admr; Author; r/Meth; hon/Life Mbrship: Am Voc Assn, DECA Inc, NADET.

APPLEGATE, WALTER THOMAS oc/-Minister; b/May 17, 1931; h/54 S Arnold Ave, Prestonburg, KY 41653; ba/Prestonburg; m/Bonnie Jo Crawley; c/Angela Susan; p/Benjamin Lewis and Mildred Ellen Cooper Applegate, Maysville, KY; ed/AB Asbury Col; BD, MDiv, Asbury Theol Sem; DD Mo Bible Inst; pa/Pastor, 1st U Meth Ch 1975-; Former Pastorates: Lexington, Ky Dist 1972-75, Ashland, Ky Dist 1965-71, Maysville, Ky Dist 1959-64; Chaplain, Ky Vil Reform

Sch, Lexington 1956-68; Pres, Highlands Min Assn; Floyd Co Min Assn; Secy, Dist Bd Evangelism, U Meth Ch; Conf Bd, Discipleship Min Bd; Secy & Treas, Prestonburg Sr Citizens Housing & Prestonburg Ch Housing; r/U Meth; hon/Ky Col; W/W: U Meth Ch, Bluegrass, Am Rel, Intl Biogs, Intells, Commun Ser; Personalities of S; Commun Ldrs & Noteworthy Ams; Notable Ams; Men Achmt; Book of Hon; DIB; Intl Reg Profiles.

APPLETON, BOBBY J oc/Administrator; b/Apr 28, 1936; h/PO Box 347, Collinsville, AL 35961; ba/Birmingham, AL; p/Louie Appleton (dec); Alice Appleton, Collinsville; ed/BS Ala St Univ 1957; MSLS Kent St Univ 1971; EdD Univ Ala; pa/Dir of Lib Sers, So Jr Col of Bus & So Inst; Former Libn/Media Spec, C'ville HS & Elem; Former Media Spec & Reference Libn, Snead St Jr Col; Dir Lib & Media Ctr, Gilmour Acad (Gates Mills, Ohio) 1971-72; Dir Lib, St Joseph HS (Cleveland, Ohio) 1968-71; Other Former Positions; ALA;

AIMA; Ala Lib Assn; Past Treas, CLA; NEA; AEA; cp/Big Brothers Inc of Am; Mason; r/Collins Chapel UMC: Lay Spkr, Soloist, SS Tchr; hon/LHD, London Inst of Applied Res; W/W MW; Fellow & Scholar; Others.

APPLETON, CLYDE ROBERT oc/Music Educator; b/Nov 21, 1928; h/2010-3 Canterwood Dr, Charlotte, NC 28213; ba/Charlotte; p/Clyde and Cleo Hurst Appleton (dec); ed/BA cum laude Park Col 1954; MME Univ Ariz 1957; PhD NY Univ 1971; pa/Assoc Prof of Creative Arts, Univ NC-Charlotte 1978-; Asst Prof of Music, Purdue Univ 1973-78; Coor, Higher Ed Achmt Prog, Kittrell Col 1971-73; Asst Prof of Music, Wn Carolina Univ 1966-70; Vis Asst Prof of

Ed, NY Univ 1967; Asst Prof of Music, Shaw Univ 1962-66; Music Tchr, Public Schs in Mo, Ia & Ariz, 11 Yrs; Music Edrs Nat Conf; Nat Assn Jazz Edrs; Soc Ethnomusicology; hon/Pub'd Profl Articles; Best Prof of 1970, Wn Carolina Univ; Excell in Tchg Awd, Dept of Creative Arts, Purdue Univ 1973-74; Kappa Delta Pi Outstg Tchr Awd in Elem Ed, Purdue Univ 1975, 76, 77, 78; Hon Mem: Kappa Delta Pi, Kappa Kappa Psi; Outstg Edrs Am; W/W NC; Intl W/W Music; Men Achmt.

ARABIA, ANTHONY JOHN oc/-Educational Administrator; b/Feb 25, 1935; h/481 Farm Hill Ct, New Kensington, PA 15068; ba/Pittsburgh, PA; m/Rose Marie Cardiello; c/Vincent, Anthony Jr, Maria; p/Vincenzo Arabia, New Kensington, PA; m/Clorinda Arabia (dec); ed/AB; EdM; PhD; pa/Dir, Lng Resources Ctr, Sch Nsg, Univ Pgh; Immediate Past Pres, Pa Lng Resources Assn; Pres, Knowledge Devel Assocs; Editor *The Mentor*; Phi Delta Kappa; Parent Tchrs Guild; r/Mt St Peter Ch (Rom Cath); hon/Var Hons, Awds & Pubs.

ARAYA, PEDRO ALFONSO oc/Management Consultant; b/Jan 19, 1922; h/148 Maison Pl NW, Atlanta, GA 30327; m/Esther Emma Rousillion; c/Carla Francesca; ed/BS Chilean Naval Col 1943; BA Univ Chile 1943; MS Columbia Univ 1963; mil/Chilean Navy 1943-45, Lt; pa/Pres: Global Growth & Devel Corp, Wilmington, Del 1973-, Compania Argentina de Crecimiento y Desarrollo SAFI, Buenos Aires, Argentina 1975-; Coca-Cola Corp: Corp Conslt for Prodn & Opers, Atlanta 1970-, Mktg Mgr for SAm 1968-69, Asst Area Mgr for Mid-E, N Africa & SW Asia 1963-68, Indust Mgmt Conslt for Mexico & Ctl Am 1963, Gen Mgr Coca-Cola Export Corp, Venezuela 1961-63; Held Var Positions in Rubber & Plastics Indust incl'g: Dir, Chilean Rubber & Mfg Assn, Mng Dir, Fargosa SA, Chile, Pres, Allison Plastics Inc, Newark, NJ; Nat Soc Profl Engrs; Inst Food Technologists; Am Soc Agri Engrs; Engrg Inst Canada; Soc Mfg Engrs; Am Mgmt Assn; Nat Soc Corp Planning; Soc Gen Sys Res; Am Mktg Assn; Colo Sci Soc; Am Geophys Union; Forage Grass Coun Australia; Others; hon/Fellow, AAAS; Author: *How to Win Customers* 1963, Num Profl Papers, Articles; DIB; Notable Ams; Book of Hon; Outstg Atlantans; Intl W/W Commun Ser; Men Achmt; Nat Soc Dir; W/W S&SW; Intl Reg Profiles; Intl Bus-men's W/W; Commun Ldrs & Noteworthy Ams; Intl

W/W Intells; Personalities of S.

ARBOLEYA, CARLOS JOSE oc/Bank President; b/Feb 1, 1929; h/1941 SW 23 St, Miami, FL 33145; ba/Miami; m/Marta Quintana; c/Carlos Jr; p/Fermin Arboleya (dec); Ana Quiros, Las Villas, Cuba; ed/Havana Univ; Adv'd Study; pa/Pres, Barnett Leasing Co 1977-; Chm Bd & CEO, Barnett Bk BankAmericard Ctr, Miami 1977-; Pres & Chief Operating Ofcr & Dir, Consolidated Barnett Bks of Miami 1977-; Pres & Dir: Barnett Bk-Midway, Barnett Bk-Westchester 1975-76; Chm Bd, Barnett Bk BankAmericard Ctr 1975-76; Flagler Bk, Miami 1973-75; Pres & Dir, Pres & Chm Bd; Fidelity Nat Bk, S Miami 1966-73: Exec VP & Cashier, Pres & Dir, Pres & VChm Bd; Blvd Nat Bk, Miami 1962-66: Opers Ofcr, Pers Dir, Cashier, VP & Cashier, Secy to Bd Dirs; Other Past Positions; cp/Dir: Dade Co Assn for Retarded Chd, Miami Mar of Dimes, Nat Assn for Bank Audit Control, City Bk Clb (Past Pres), Am Arbitration Assn, 3rd Century USA Com, Miami Mus of Sci, Heart Assn Gtr Miami, Intl Affairs Action Com, Miami ARC, Others; Chm, Cath Com on Scouting-Miami Archidiocese; Bd Trustees: Barry Col, Mus of Sci & Space Transit Planetarium, 3rd Century USA, Leukemia Soc Am; Adv Bd: Univ Miami Sch of Bus Adm, Nat Alliance Bus Men; Num Others; r/Cath; hons/Bkr of Yr, Voters & Tax Payers Leag of Miami & Dade Co, 1978; Carlos J Arboleya Camping & Picnic Grounds named in His Hon by Miami Comm, 1978; Geo Wash Medal, Freedoms Foun 1973, 74, 75, 77; Keys to Fla Cities, 1970: Miami, Coral Gables, Miami Bch, Dade Co, S Miami; Num BSA Awds incl'g: Cuban Silver Fleur DeLis, Dist'd Ser Awd, Dist Awd of Merit, Silver Beaver Awd; Carlos J Arboleya Day, Jul 20, 1973, Hialeah, Fla; Outstg Achmt Awd, Haute Academie Internationale De Paris, France 1972; Bkr of Yr 1972, Nat Ec Devel Assn; *TV Guide* Mag's 1977 Personality of Yr Awd "Chin de Plata"; Fla Patriot Awd of Bicent Comm 1976; Gov's Medal, Fla 1976; Key to City, Jacksonville, Fla 1976; Horatio Alger Awd, Am Sch & Cols Assn 1976; Bus-man of Yr Awd, Channel 23 TV 1976; W/W: Fla, S&SW, Bkg, Fin & Indust, Commerce & Indust; Intl W/W Commun Ser; Fla Lives; Nat Social Dir; Personalities of S; Prominent Cuban Fams; 2000 Men Achmt; Featured in articles in: *Banking, Forbes, Life, Business Week, Newsweek, Time, Finance, Mudndo Latino*, Others.

ARBUCKLE, WENDELL SHERWOOD oc/Information Specialist; Professor Emeritus; h/4602 Harvard Rd, College Park, MD 20740; ba/College Park; m/Ruth W; c/J Gordon, Wendy Ellen Wood; p/Charles E and Julia Barton Arbuckle (dec); ed/BSA; AM; PhD; mil/ROTC; pa/Prof Emeritus 1972-; Prof, Univ Md 1949-72; Assoc Prof, NC St Univ 1946-48; Asst Prof, Tex A&M Univ 1941-46; Instr, Univ Mo 1936-41; Dairyman, Earlham Farms 1933-36; Inst Food Tech; Sealtest Adv Comm; Dairy Tech Soc Md & DC; ADSA; Gamma Alpha; Gamma Sigma Delta; Sigma Xi; cp/Kiwanis; BSA; Purdue Alumni Assn; r/Meth; hon/Md Dairy Shrine; Dairy Tech Soc; Dist'd Ser Awd; Life Mem ADSP; W/W: E, Mo, Am Ed; World W/W Authors; DIB; Contemporary Authors; Men & Wom of Sci; Book of Hon; Personalities of S; Author *Ice Cream*, Num Articles, Book Chapts.

ARCHIBALD, PATRICIA ANN oc/-College Professor; Botanist; b/Jul 18, 1934; h/Box 11, Spiceland, IN 47385; ba/Slippery Rock, PA; p/Stanley Ray and Babel Ellen Seed Archibald, Spiceland, IN; ed/BS 1953, MA 1963 Ball St Univ; PhD Univ Tex 1969; pa/Phycologist, Slippery Rock St Col; Edit Bd, Phycol Soc Am; Intl Phycol Soc; British Phycol Soc; cp/BPW; r/Meth; hon/Fulbright Tchg Exchangee 1962-63; IREX Res Exchangee Czech Acad Sci 1977; Nat Acad Sci Exchangee USSR 1978; Sigma Xi; Sci Fac F'ship, NSF 1967-68.

ARCHIBALD, REGINALD MacGREGOR oc/Professor; Physician; b/Mar 2, 1910; h/266 Ancon Ave, Pelham, NY 10803; ba/NY, NY; m/Evelyn Stroh; c/Ruth Minnie,

Lawrence Eben; p/Eben H and Minnie Archibald (dec); ed/BA w hons 1930; MA 1932; PhD Univ British Columbia 1934; MD 1939 Univ Toronto; pa/Prof & Sr Phys (Pediatric Endocrinol), Rockefeller Univ Hosp; Prof of Biochem, Johns Hopkins Univ 1946-48; Former Mem Edit Bd: *Jour Biol Chem, Child Devel, Jour Clin Endocrinol & Metabolism*; cp/Vol Med Advr, Madison Square Boys' Clb; r/Presb.

ARCHIMOVICH, ALEXANDER SINOVIOUS oc/Researcher; Educator; Editor; b/Apr 23, 1892; h/143 Mountain Rd, Rosendale, NY 12472; m/Kira B Zagurska; c/Tatiana, Kathrine, Eugen; p/Sinovious and Alexandra Archimovich (dec); ed/PhD St Univ Kiev, Ukraine 1938; pa/Hd Dept of Biol, Schevchenko Sci Soc in USA; Fellow & Hd Dept of Biol, Ukrainian Acad of Arts & Scis in USA; Mem Num Sci Socs in US, Germany & Spain; r/Orthodox; hon/Hon Mem: Inst for Study of USSR, Ukrininan Vet Med Assn.

ARD, HAROLD J oc/Library Administrator; b/Aug 26, 1940; h/804 Briarwood Dr, Jackson, MS 39211; ba/Jackson, MS; m/Terri Ann, Mark Alan; p/Jacob S Ard (dec); Hazel E Ard, Pana, Ill; ed/BS, Grad Study Ill St Univ; MSLS Rosary Col; pa/Lib Admr; MLA; SELA; ALA; Med Lib Assn; cp/Rotary Clb, Jackson; r/Riverside Meth Ch: Mem; hon/Pub'd Sev Articles.

ARDMORE, JANE KESNER oc/Author; Journalist; b/Sept 12, 1915; h/10469 Dunleer Dr, Los Angeles, CA 90064; ba/Los Angeles; m/Albert; c/Ellen; p/David L and Florence Behrend Kesner; ed/PhD Univ Chgo; pa/Contbr to Nat Mags: *McCall's, Ladies Home Journal*, Others; Wom in Communs; Hollywood Woms Press Clb; r/Jewish Christian; hon/Ind Univ Writers Conf Fiction Prize; Wom in Communs Headliner of Yr; Author: *Take My Life, The Dress Doctor, The Self Enchanted Portrait of Joan, To Love Is To Listen, Wom Inc, Julie*.

ARGUE, JOHN CLIFFORD oc/Attorney; b/Jan 25, 1932; h/1314 Descanso Dr, La Canada, CA 91011; h/Los Angeles, CA; m/Leah Elizabeth; c/John Michael, Elizabeth Anne; p/Mrs J Clifford Argue, Newport Beach, CA; ed/BA Occidental Col 1953; LLB USC Law Sch 1956; mil/AUS 1956-58; pa/Atty; LA Bar Assn; Cal Bar Assn; Am Bar Assn; Dir, Heritage Life Ins Co; cp/Chm, LA Olympic Com; Pres, So Cal Com for Olympic Games; VChm, Verdugo Hills Hosp Bd Dirs; Bd Dirs, Am Heart Assn, Gtr LA Affil; Phi Delta Phi; Alpha Tau Omega; Chancery Clb; Cal Club; Oakmont CC (Past Pres).

ARISS, ROBERT M oc/Museum Curator; b/Oct 23, 1908; h/2040 Mayview Dr, Los Angeles, CA 90027; ba/Los Angeles; m/Helen T K; p/Bruce W and Anna K Ariss (dec); ed/AB Univ Cal-Berkeley 1932; MA UCLA 1953; PhD Univ So Cal 1969; mil/USN 1942-45; pa/Ret'd 1974; Curator Anthrol, LA Co Mus Natural Hist; Asst Prof of Anthropol: USC 1953-58, San Fernando Val Col 1958-; cp/LA Co Conf Commun Relats; hon/Mu Alpha Nu; Sigma Xi; Alpha Kappa Delta; Cit of Outstg Ser for Exhibit Man in Our Changing World, LA 1952.

ARIYOSHI, GEORGE RYOICHI oc/- Governor of Hawaii; b/Mar 12, 1926; h/Washington Pl, Honolulu, HI 96813; ba/Honolulu; m/Jean Miya Hayashi; c/Lynn Miye, Todd Royozo, Donn Ryoji; p/Ryozo Ariyoshi (dec); Mitsue Yoshikawa Ariyoshi, Honolulu, HI; ed/BA Mich St Univ 1949; JD Univ Mich Law Sch 1952; mil/AUS; pa/Pres, Hawaii Bar Assn; Pres, Hawaii Bar Foun; cp/Gov of Hawaii; Former Lt Gov, Hawaii; Mem St/Territorial Sen; Mem, Territory of Hawaii House of Reps; Del to Constitutional Conv; Dir: Hawaii Ins & Guranty Co, Honolulu Gas Co, 1st Hawaiian Bk; hon/Dist'd Alumni Awd: Univ Hawaii 1975, Mich St Univ 1975; Hon LLD: Univ Philippines 1975, Univ Guam 1975; Hon DHL Univ Visayas, the Philippines 1977.

ARMSTRONG, ALICE CATT oc/- Publisher; Editor; Author; b/Feb 7; h/Cordell Views, 1331 Cordell Pl, Los Angeles, CA 90069; p/Charles Harmon and Florence Iles Parkenham Catt; ed/Art Inst Kans; pa/Pubr-Author-Editor, *Who's Who in Los Angeles County 1949-, Who's Who in California 1954-, Who's Who Enterprises 1961-, Who's Who Executives in California 1963*; Fdr-Pres-Dir, *Who's Who Hist Soc*; Guest Artist for Num Radio-TV Progs; Lectr; Author: *Who's Who - Dining and Lodging on the North American Continent 1958*, Chd's Books, Poems, Short Stories, Others; cp/OES; Cal St C of C; So Cal Wom's Press Clb; Nat Writer's Clb; Nat Soc Arts & Lttrs; Execs Dinner Clb, Beverly Hills; Nat Soc Magna Charta Dames; Bel Air Fed Repub Wom's Clbs; hon/Wisdom Awd of Hon, *Wisdom Mag* 1965; DIB; Countess of Kobrin; Dame of Grace, Hospitaller Order St John of Jerusalem; Wom of Achmt, LA Co Repub Wom's Clbs 1973; Dame of Grand Cross, Royal & Sovereign Order of St Laurent; Cal Wom of Achmt; W/W: Am Wom, World; Ency Dist'd Ams; World W/W Wom; Wom Achmt; Blue Book of Am (Charter); World W/W Commerce & Indust; The Writers Dir; Num Others.

ARMSTRONG, WILLIAM HARRISON JR oc/Realtor; b/Jul 14, 1945; h/113 Huntington Ln, Blacksburg, VA 24060; ba/Blacksburg; c/Amanda Anne, Andrea K, William Harrison III; p/William Harrison Sr and Mildred J Armstrong, Midland, VA; ed/BS Va Polytech Inst & St Univ; mil/USAF, Ofcr; pa/Nat Assn Realtors; Grad Realtors Inst; cp/Blacksburg

Jaycees; Blacksburg Housing Sub-com; C of C; Past Mem, Kiwanis; Past Pres, Jr Ofcr's Coun; Past Dir, Va Jaycees; Past Pres, Blacksburg Sports Clb; Orgr, Remember the 14 POW Campaign, San Antonio, Tex; r/Deist; hon/Dist'd Air Force Cadet, VPI 1968; Selected Blacksburg's Outstg Yg Man 1973; W/W S&SW.

ARNDT, HILDA C M oc/Social Work Educator; Consultant; b/Aug 7, 1912; h/2740 Morning Glory, Baton Rouge, LA 70808; p/William and Augusta Scherer Arndt (dec); ed/BA; MS; PhD; pa/Prof Emeritus, La St Univ; Social Wk Conslt, Manpower Br, NIHM; Social Work Conslt, Chd's Bur, HEW; Bd Dirs, La Chapt Nat Assn Social Wkrs; cp/Bd Mem: YWCA, Oper Hope; r/Meth; hon/Phi Beta Kappa; Dist'd Alumni Awd, Univ Chgo 1977; George Freeman Awd 1977; Alumni Awd, Wash Univ 1961; W/W Am Wom; Outstg Edrs.

ARNER, SAMUEL DEWALT oc/Artist; Poet; Archaeologist; Historian; b/Jun 17,

1900; h/PO Box 687, Cathedral City, CA 92234; ba/Cathedral City; m/Irene G; c/Paul, David, John; p/George W and Cora Elizabeth Arner (dec); ed/Legal Dipl LaSalle Ext Univ; Theol Dipl Bellevue Col & Zarefhath Bible Inst; Pre-Med Dipl, US Sch of Pharm; pa/Semi-ret'd; Archaeol Expeditions to Mex, SAm; Res in Egypt, Israel, Turkey, Greece & Italy; r/Prot; Former Mem Num Sci Socs; Fdr, Mus of Antiquities & Art, Palm Springs Heights, Cal; Owner, Extensive Pre-Columbian Art Collect; cp/Congressional Cand 1942; hon/W/W: Am, Cal, Hist Soc; Nat Reg Prominent Citizens; DIB; Intl W/W Art & Antiques; 2000 Men Achmt; Num Certs of Merit; Others.

ARNETT, HAROLD EDWARD oc/- Professor; b/Jan 20, 1931; h/2113 Delaware Dr, Ann Arbor, MI 48103; ba/Ann Arbor; m/Betty J; c/John B, Carl E, Melia L; p/Dumous C Arnett (dec); Amie Frobose (dec); ed/BS 1955, MS 1958, PhD 1962 Univ Ill; mil/USN 1948-52; pa/Sch of Bus Adm, Univ Mich, Ann Arbor: Prof of Acctg, Chm Dept of Acctg 1969-72; Conslt to Bus & CPA Firms 1955-; Cert'd Public Acct, Ill; CMA; Res Assoc, Am Inst CPAs 1960-62; Am Acctg Assn; Am Inst CPAs; Fin Exec's Inst; Mich Assn CPAs; Nat Assn Accts; cp/Walsh Col:

Com on Pers, Com on Academic Progress, Bd Trustees; Past Bd Dirs: Univ Fac Clb, Univ Employees Credit Union; Past Pres, Wines Sch PTO; Former CSA Cubmaster; Others; r/Presb; hon/Beta Alpha Psi; Beta Gamma Sigma; Chi Omega Iota; Phi Eta Sigma; Sigma Iota Epsilon; S'ship; Cert of Merit, Nat Assn Accts; Fac F'ship, Ernst & Ernst 1975; W/W: World, Midwest, Am; Notable Ams; Commun Ldrs & Noteworthy Ams; DIB; World W/W Authors; Personalities of W&MW; Intl W/W Commun Ser; Men Achmt; Writers Dir; Others.

ARNETT, JAMES EDWARD oc/Educator; Business Executive; Community Service Worker; b/Oct 3, 1912; h/691 Payne Ave, Akron, OH; m/Helen Mae Vallish; p/Haden Arnett (dec); Josephine Risner Arnett, Hendricks, KY; ed/AB 1947, MA 1955 San Jose St Col; EdS Stanford Univ 1959; PhD Colo St Christian Col 1973; mil/AUS 1942-45; Spec Acad Instr; pa/Self-employed 1973-; Tchr, Ellet HS & Innes Jr HS, Akron 1953-73; Supt, Moss Landing Sch Dist, Cal 1950-51; English Tchr of Fgn-Born Adults, Salinas, Cal 1950; Tchr & Cnslr, Salinas Public Schs 1947-50; Dir: E&E Insurers, Columbus, Ohio 1957-63, E&E Co 1962-76, E&E Life Ins Co 1962-76, E&E Casuality Ins Co 1962-76, Great Am of Dallas Fire & Casuality Co 1974, Great Am of Dallas Ins Co 1974, JC Penney Casuality Ins Co, Westerville, Ohio 1976; JC Penney Life Ins Co 1976; Conslt: JC Penney Casuality Ins Co 1976-77, JC Penney Life Ins Co 1976-77; Other Past Positions; cp/Campaign Wkr: Adlai Stevenson 1952, 56, John F Kennedy 1960, Jimmy Carter 1976; Dem Party Wkr; Smithsonian Inst Assoc; Ohio Soc NY; Capt, U Fund-ARC Campaigns, Akron Public Schs 1960-73; hon/Ky Col; Hon Citizen Boys' Town; Book of Hon; DIB; Commun Ldrs & Noteworthy Ams; Notable Ams of Bicent Era; W/W: Fin & Indust, Midwest; Intl W/W Commun Ser; 2000 Men Achmt; Nat Social Dir; World W/W Commerce & Indust; Personalities of S.

ARNOLD, DUANE JR oc/Utility Company Executive; b/Apr 24, 1950; h/3018 Terry Dr SE, Cedar Rapids, IA 52403; ba/Cedar Rapids; m/Mary Colleen Geraghty; c/Duane Joseph, Mary Brigid, Stephen Richard & Kevin Sutherland (twins); p/Duane and Henrietta Dows Arnold; ed/AA Wentworth Mil Acad 1970; Att'd Coe Col, Univ Iowa, LaSalle Ext Univ; pa/Iowa Electric Light & Power Co: Mgmt Trainee 1970-77, Supt of Transportation 1977-; Dir: Dows Real Estate Co 1974-, Dows Farms Inc 1974-; Dep Sheriff, Linn Co Sheriff's Ofc 1972-, Emer Bd 1976-; So Automotive Engrs; Edison Electric Inst (Transportation Com 1977-); Nat Assn Fleet Admrs; cp/ARC: Bd Dirs, Chm First Aid Com Grant Wood Chapt, Advr Disaster Com; Bd Dirs, U Cerebral Palsy Assn; CR C of C; r/Presb.

ARNOLD, LESTER E JR oc/Director; b/Mar 3, 1939; h/36 Troy View Lane, Williamsville, NY 14221; ba/Buffalo, NY; m/Ingrid S Andersen; c/Elizabeth, Andrew, Jennifer, Daniel; p/Lester E Sr and Evelyn W Arnold, Baltimore, MD; ed/BS Johns Hopkins Univ 1968; MBA SUNY 1971; LLB Washington Univ 1979; mil/Defense Dept (Critical Skills); pa/Dir Industl Engrg, Anaconda-Atlantic Richfield Co 1979-; Div Mgr, Carborundum/Kennecott Co 1976-79; Var Adm Positions, Hooker Chemical-Occidental Petro Corp 1968-76; Instr Positions, Hedwin Corp & Westinghouse Corp 1959-68; Instr/Lectr, SUNY; Dir/Trustee Sev Banks & 2 Corps; Reg'd Profl Engr in NY & Md; Pub'd Author; Am Inst Industl Engrs; Am Mgmt Assn; Nat Soc Profl Engrs; Others; cp/Buffalo C of C; Profl Athletic Clb; W'ville Sch Bd; Others; r/Prot; hon/Patentee; Phi Beta Kappa; Tau Beta Pi; Others.

ARNOLD, MARIETTA R oc/Service Representative; b/Feb 2, 1922; h/8133 Douglas, Corpus Christi, TX 78409; ba/E Stubbs, Edinburg, TX; c/James Logan, Gary Lee, Reagan Rowe; p/Mason and Frances Rowe (dec); ed/BS; pa/Am Bus Woms Assn; Intl Assn Pers in Employmt Security; Tex Public Employees Assn; cp/Edinburg C of C; Fiesta Hidalgo Com, Bazaar Com Chm; r/Ch of Christ; hon/Wom of Yr, Magic Citrus Val Am Bus Woms Assn 1979.

ARONOWITZ, ALFRED G oc/Writer; Journalist; b/May 20, 1928; h/Box 463, Englewood, NJ 07631; m/Ann Wolkensheim (dec); c/Myles Mason, Brett Hillary, Joel Roi; p/Morris Aronowitz (dec); Lena Goldman, Englewood, NJ; ed/BL cum laude Rutgers Univ Sch Journalism 1950; pa/Writer; Mag Editor 1978; Prodr, Country in NY Concerts, Lincoln Ctr, Madison Square Gdn 1973-76; Mgr, David Bromberg 1970-75; Columnist, *NY Post* 1969-72; Pop Music Critic: *Life* Mag 1968, *NY Times* 1967; Contbg Writer, *Saturday Evening Post* 1963-66; Chief Feature Writer, *NY Post* 1957-63; Reporter, *Newark (NJ) News* 1951-57; Editor, *Lakewood (NJ) Daily Times* 1950-51; hon/Phi Beta Kappa; Co-Author (w Pete Hamill), *Ernest Hemingway: The Life and Death of a Man* 1961.

ARORA, CHANDRA K oc/Environmental Administrator; b/Dec 17, 1935; h/437 Collinsford Rd, Tallahassee, FL 32301; ba/Tallahassee, FL; m/Santosh; c/Malay, Mala; p/Amar Nath and Kanti Devi Arora (dec); ed/BArch Univ of Roorkee 1963; MS Urban Planning 1971, MS Envir Engrg 1972 Univ Iowa; pa/Envir Adm, Fla Dept Envir Regulation, Tallahassee 1973-; Dir Planning, Model City Agy, Pikeville, KY 1972-73; Asst Prof of Arch: Birla Inst Technol, Pilani, India 1964-69, Benaras Hindu Univ 1963-64; cp/Dem; Naturalized US Citizen 1976; r/Hindu; hon/Rotary S'ship; Tchg Asst'ships; EPA Tng Grant.

ARRINGTON, ABNER ATMAN oc/- Utility Supervisor; b/May 25, 1922; h/21 St James Pl, Apt 23-A, Bklyn, NY 11205; ba/NY, NY; m/Christine O Lofton; c/Cheryl, Velda, Andrea, Arlene; p/Plumber and India Arrington, Bklyn; ed/LaSalle Sch for Bus Mgmt

1968; mil/USN 3rd Class Cook; pa/Gen'l Oper Super of Gas Oper, Con Edison Co; cp/Unity Dem Clb; Edison Anchor Clb; K of C; Paragon Commun Clb; PTA Recipient; hon/Outstanding Achmt Harlem YMCA; Commun Ldrs & Noteworthy Ams.

ARTHUR, GLADYS BEAN oc/Teacher; b/Sept 18, 1913; h/102 Collier St, Aiken, SC 29801; ba/Aiken, SC; m/Chester; c/Marlene JoAnne Brantley; p/Robert W and Ollie Heard Bean, Cullman, AL; ed/Grad Jacksonville St Col 1936; BS Ga St Col for Wom 1959; pa/Ret'd; Tchr: Aiken Co Sch Sys 1953-78, LA Co Schs, Long Beach, Cal 1947-52, Cullman Co, Ala Sch Sys 1936-41; Hd Paratroop Div in Def, Stoughton, Mass; NEA; SCEA; ACEA; Asst Libn, N Quincy, Mass; Libn, Milbrook Sch, Aiken; cp/Assoc Matron, OES 2 Yrs; Mother Advr, Rainbow Girls 4 Yrs; PTA; ARC; r/U Presb USA: Mem, SS Tchr, Adult SS Class Pres, Pres WOC; hon/Outstg Ldrs in Elem & Sec'dy Ed.

ASADZADEHFARD, MURLENE WALLACE oc/Educator; Administrator; b/Feb 2, 1948; h/2410 Iowa St, Davenport, IA 52803; ba/Bettendorf, IA; m/Asadollah; c/Soraya; p/James Murl and Norma Schillie Wallace,

Green Castle, MO; ed/BSE 1970, MA 1971 NMSU; pa/NEA; NBEA; IBEA; OEA; AVA; IVA; Pi Omega Pi; IPA; r/Ch of God; hon/World W/W Wom; W/W Ed; Personalities of W&MW; Grad F'ship; Other Acad Hons.

ASAM, JULIA McCAIN LAMPKIN oc/Scientist; Educator; b/Feb 27, 1931; h/PO Box 6212, Ft Myers, FL 33901; ba/Ft Myers; m/Joseph Jr; p/Charles Barnett and Julia McCain Lampkin, Tuscaloosa, AL; ed/BS 1952; MS 1954; PhD 1958; pa/Cancer Rschr; Author: *Lymphomas: Regression, Carcinogenesis, and Prevention* 1966, *Malignant Intrigue*, 1973, *Model Lymphomas* 1976 (All Books on Cancer Res), 20 Jour Articles; Am Assn for Cancer Res; cp/Spkr for Cancer Res in Commun; r/Bapt; hon/NSF Postdoct F'ship 1956-58; Nat Am Cancer Soc Grant 1963-66; US Patent.

ASBURY, CLAUD LOGAN oc/Minister; b/Jul 16, 1923; h/2507 Lamp Post Lane, Baltimore, MD 21234; ba/Parkville, Balto, MD; m/Frances Luella Bayne; c/Barry, Brenda A Keith, Jimmy (dec), William, Barbara; p/Claud Logan and Theodore Dolvin Asbury (dec); ed/AA Tenn Temple Col 1948; BA Miss Col 1951; BD SWn Bapt Theol Sem 1957; mil/USN WWII; pa/Min: P'ville Bapt Ch 1973-, Gibson Ave Bapt Ch (Wilmington, NC) 1968-73, Gibson (NC) Bapt Ch 1966-68, Others; Home Mission Bd (NC, Cal, Okla) 1947-50; 1st Treas, Iowa So Bapts 1957-59; So Bapt Conv; Bapt Conv of Md; Balto Bapt Assn (Chm Christian Life Com); VModerator & Secy, Pastors Conf, Pee Dee Bapt Assn of SC; Dir Public Relats, W'ton (NC) Bapt Assn & Assoc Dir Ch Tng 1968-69; Author Num Poems; Lyracist; cp/Fdr, Ctr for Intl Security Studies, Am Security Coun Ed Foun (Wash, DC); Pres, Restore Prayer & Bible to Schs & Law & Order to Am Inc (Wash, DC); Bd Dirs, Citizens for Public Prayer (Wash, DC); Nat Coalition for Prayer Amendment; Human Rights Com, Veterans Adm; Others; r/So Bapt; hon/Author, "Prayer & Bible Reading in Schs", Presented to US Senate & US Ho of

Reps, Pub'd in *Congressional Record*; Liberty Awd, Cong of Freedom Inc; Author of Asbury Resolution on Vol Prayer in Public Schs (Adopted by NC & SC Bapt St Convs); IPA; Biogl Listings.

ASCHER, MARY oc/Artist; m/David; p/Jacob and Naomi (dec); ed/BBA City Col, Leedes, England; MA NY Univ; Postgrad Study: NY Sch Applied Design for Wom, Hunter Col, Students Art Leag (Life Mem); pa/NY City Sec'dy Schs: Tchr, Dept Hd, Guid Dir, Adm Asst; Exhbns: Wizo Bldg, Tel Aviv, Israel (Permanent), Nat Arts Clb, NYC 1973, 12 Solo Exhbns (Oil, Watercolor, Prints, Drawings) in NY, Wash DC, Israel, 50 Solo Exhbns in USA; Juried NAWA Group Shows: Palazzo Vecchio, Florence; Salon Intl de la Femme, Cannes, France 1969, Mus Mod Art, London, Ontario, Canada, Mexican Exhbn Tour 1965, Royal Acad Galleries, Edinburgh, Scotland 1963-64, Royal Birmingham Soc Galleries, England 1963-64, Museo Nacional de Bellas Artes, Buenos Aires, Argentina, 1963, Exchange Exhbn w Japan 1960; Wks in Collects: Smithsonian Instn, Butler Inst of Am Art, Youngstown, Ohio, Norfolk (Va) Art

Mus, Nat Art Mus of Sport, NYC, B'nai B'rith Mus, Wash DC, NYC Public Lib, Fordham Univ, Bat Yam Mun Mus, Israel, Ein Harod Mun Mus, Israel, Interchurch Ctr, (Synagogues:) Rodeph Sholom, NYC, Bethel, New Rochelle, Var Pvt Collects; Past Pres, Am Soc Contemporary Artists; Chaplain & Active Artist Mem, Nat Soc Arts & Lttrs; Lectr on 12 Wom of Old Testament & Apocrypha; Adv Bd, NAWA 1972-76; r/Jewish; hon/W/W: Am, Am Art, Am Wom, Intl Jewry; World W/W Wom; 2000 Wom Achmt; Foremost Wom in Communs; Intl Dir Arts; Fellow, Royal Soc Arts; Huntington Hartford Foun F'ship 1960; Medal of Hon, Painters & Sculptors of NJ 1958; Burndy Corp Awd, Silvermine Guild, 1967; 1st Prize, Watercolor & Graphics, NLAPW Profl Artists Group; Num Others; Outstg Achmt Awd, Baruch Col Alumni Assn 1975; Career Achmt Awd, City Col Alumni Soc 1968; City Col 125th Anniv Medal 1973; Intl Wom's Yr Awd 1975-76; 1st Prize Oil, Womanrat Gallery, NYC.

ASHBAUGH, LAURA FRANCES oc/- Retired Professor; b/Nov 15, 1901; h/115 Wall St, Bethlehem, PA 18108; m/Frederick R (dec); p/Levi F and Alice Ida Wagner McDonough, Pine Grove, PA; ed/BA 1924, MA 1931 Univ Pa; Addtl Grad Study Lehigh Univ; pa/Ret'd; Instr of Math: Moravian Sem & Wom's Col 1924-29, Lower Merion Sr HS, Ardmore, Pa 1929-30; Prof of Math, Moravian Col for Wom, Bethlehem, Pa 1932-47; Lectr in Math, Lehigh Univ (Pt-time) 1943-44 & 3rd Sum Sessions 1945-46; cp/Vol for Var Fund Drs; r/Cathedral Ch of Nativity: Mem; hon/Pi Mu Epsilon.

ASHBY, JOHN EDMUND JR oc/Marketing Executive; b/Mar 5, 1936; h/3429 Cornell, Dallas, TX 75205; ba/Dallas; m/Martha; c/Vicki, Dana, Suzanne, Shellay, Elizabeth; p/John E Ashby (dec); Lillian Cox Weddington; ed/BBA Univ Tex; mil/USMC; pa/Sales & Mktg Execs; IPA; cp/Repub; Royal Oaks Clb; r/Presb; hon/Sales & Mktg Execs Awd; IBM Awd; W/W: World, Fin & Indust, S&SW; Men Achmt; DIB.

ASHCRAFT, JESSE MORRIS oc/Professor; b/Aug 14, 1922; h/4942 N College, Kansas

City, MO 64119; ba/Kansas City; m/Anna B Haley; c/Mark Henry, Anna Belle; p/(dec); ed/BA; BT; ThD; mil/USN WW II, Aircraft Pilot; USN Korean War, Chaplain; pa/Prof of Theol; Lectr; Writer; r/So Bapt; hon/Fellow, Am Schs Oriental Res; ATS S'ship Awd 1965-66.

ASHE, ARTHUR ROBERT oc/Professional Athlete; b/Jul 10, 1943; h/360 E 72, NY, NY 10021; ba/Wash DC; m/Jeanne-Marie Moutoussamy; p/Arthur Ashe Sr, Gum Spring, VA; ed/BS UCLA 1966; mil/AUS, 1/Lt; pa/Profl Tennis Player; Assn Tennis Profls (Pres 1976-77); cp/Nat Jr Tennis Leag; African Student Aid Fund; hon/US Jaycees TOYM.

ASHER, FRED M oc/Psychologist; Consultant; b/Jul 12, 1948; h/6817 John Dr, Ft Worth, TX 76118; ba/Irving, TX; p/J B and Maxine Asher, Ft Worth, TX; ed/BS, Univ Tex, Arlington; MS, PhD E Tex St Univ; pa/Psychologist & Conslt, Pvt Pract 1976-; Prof of Human Devel, Northlake Col 1976-; Dir of Cnslg, Univ Dallas Grad Sch 1976-; Univ Cnslr & Intern Supvr/Psychometrist, Tex A&I Univ, Kingsville, Tex 1974-76; Resident Cnslr, E Tex St Univ 1973-74; Cnslr Intern, Richland Col 1973-74; Instr, Univ Tex, Arlington 1972-73; Am Psychol Assn; Am Pers & Guid Assn; Am Assn Marriage & Fam Cnslrs; hon/Psi Chi; Phi Delta Kappa; Sigma Delta Pi (Pres 1973-74).

ASHER, VERNON oc/Justice of the Peace; b/Feb 10, 1915; h/1519 N Robinson, Cleburne, TX 76031; ba/Cleburne; m/Dovie King; p/James Washington Sr and Pattie Statton Asher (dec); mil/AUS WW II, PFC; r/Bapt; hon/W/W Tex; DIB; Personalities of S; Notable Ams of Bicent Era; Commun Ldrs & Noteworthy Ams; Men Achmt; Others.

ASHLAND, EMELYN IDA ANDREA oc/Educator; b/Sept 29, 1910; h/773 Marion Ave, Highland Park, IL 60035; p/Gustav A and Ida Frances Alex Ashland (dec); ed/BS 1931, SM 1933, Postgrad Study Univ Chgo; Postgrad Study: Univ Cal, Berkeley, Univ Colo; pa/Tchr: Chgo Public HSs 1937-76, Sterling Twp (Ill) HS 1936-37; Med Social Wkr, Unemploymt Relief Ser, Chgo 1934-35; Held Var Positions as Artist; Chgo Tchrs Union; Soc Circumnavigators (Charter); Pioneer in Traffic Safety Ed 1948-51; r/Bapt; hon/W/W Am Wom; Co-Author: *Development of Flower and Fruit of Myrica Rubra* 1950.

ASHMORE, PAMELA LYNNE oc/Administrator; b/May 31, 1951; h/415 Lexington Ave, Thomasville, NC 27360; ba/Thomasville; p/Harry L and Anne G Ashmore, Thomasville, NC; ed/BA NC St Univ; MEd Univ NC-Greensboro; pa/Coor, Davidson Co Coun on Status of Wom; cp/Thomasville Jr Wom's Clb: Yearbook Com, Report Com Chm, Public Affairs Com Co-Chm, Arts Fest Page for NCFWC, Conv Del; 1/VChm, Thomasville Precnt #3; Davidson Co Dem Exec Com; Davidson Com Dem Wom; Chm, City Players; Vol Mbrship Dr: YMCA, Zoo Telethon, Heart Fund; r/Grace Luth Ch: Mem, Former SS Tchr, Choir Mem, Vacation Ch Sch Tchr; hon/Young Career Wom of 1977, Thomasville BPW; Nom'd for 5 Outstg Yg Wom in NC, Thomasville Jaycettes; Featured in Profile Article in *Highpoint Enterprise*, 1977; Personalities of S.

ASHWORTH, BRENT FERRIN oc/Attorney; b/Jan 8, 1949; h/1001 S Main St, Payson, UT 84651; ba/Spanish Fork, UT; m/Charlene Mills; c/Amy Jo, John Dell, Matthew Ferrin, Samuel Mills, Adam Parrish; p/Dell S Ashworth, Provo, UT; Bette B Ashworth (dec); ed/BA cum laude Brigham Young Univ 1972; JD Univ of Utah 1975; mil/US Army Reserv 1969-75; pa/Amtec Indusrs Inc: VP (Legal) 1979-, Corp Secy 1977-, Gen Counsel & Chief Legal Ofcr 1977-; Assoc Atty w Frandsen & Keller Law Firm 1977; Asst Co Atty, Carbon Co (Price, Utah) 1975-77; Former Reals Estate Salesman; Other Former Positions; cp/Chm, Payson Public Safety Com; City Coun-man, Payson City; Commr, Payson City Planning Comm; Chm Ec & Industl Devel Com; SAR; Former Bd Mem & Gen Counsel to Bd Dirs, Carbon Co Nsg

Home; Others; r/Mormon: 1st Cnslr Bishopric, Bishop, Former SS Tchr, Former Asst Ward Organist, Others; hon/Phi Eta Sigma; Phi Kappa Phi; Pub'd Author; Art Dirs Excell Awd for Writing Annual Report, Amtec Indusrs Inc; Oratorical Awds, SAR; Others.

ASHWORTH, DELL SHEPHERD oc/Architect; b/Jul 20, 1923; h/1965 N 1400 E, Provo, UT 84601; ba/Provo; m/Bette Brailsford (dec); 2nd Faughn Montague Bennett; c/Brent F, Mark Shepherd, Anne Elizabeth, Christopher John; p/Paul P Ashworth; Jane Ferrin Ashworth, Salt Lake City, UT; ed/Brigham Young Univ: BA Univ Cal, Berkeley; mil/USAR 1940; USNR 1942-46; pa/Pres, TAG The Ashworth Group, Developers 1971-; Distributor, Panel Brick Co 1974-; Ptnr, TAG Real Est, 1971-; Owner, B Ashworth's (Fabric Store) 1973-; Owner: Dell S Ashworth & Assocs 1976, TAG Archs & Engrs 1971-75; Ptnr, Ashworth Archs 1953-71; Pract'g Arch 1949-; cp/Dir: Provo Indust Devel Corp, Utah Val Cult Ctr Com; Past Pres: Provo C of C, Provo Kiwanis Clb, Utah Val Chapt SAR; Others; hon/W/W: W, World; World W/W Commerce & Indust; DIB; Commun Ldrs Am; Intl W/W Commun Ser; Intl W/W Art & Antiques; 2000 Men Achmt; Personalities of W&MW; Intl Register of Profiles; Nat Register of Prominent Ams; Creative & Successful Personalities; Outstg Personalities W&MW; Men Achmt; Notable Ams of Bicent Era; Commun Ldrs & Noteworthy Ams; Commun Ldrs Am.

ASKEW, EDWARD L oc/Lawyer; b/Jul 15, 1950; h/928 Ridgecrest St, Montgomery, AL 36103; ba/Montgomery; p/William H Askew (dec); Dora L Askew, Montgomery, AL; ed/AA Selma Univ; BA Stillman Col; JD Howard Univ; pa/Asst Dean, Selma Univ; cp/Fdr, Ala Coalition of Concerned Citizens; r/Bapt; hon/W/W; Magna Cum Laude 1971; Phi Alpha Delta.

ASSATOURIAN, ALICE HUSISIAN oc/Editor; Research Consultant; Critic; Teacher; Lecturer; b/Sept 15, 1920; h/410 E 20th St, NY, NY 10009; m/Haig Gourji Khan; c/Seta A Buchter, Sona A Davidian, Lora; p/Leon Nishan Husisian (dec); Arax Zorian Husisian, Elmira, NY; ed/Gen Ed Dip w hons Boston Univ 1940; Premed Studies Clark Univ 1943-45; BS Columbia Univ 1964; MA NY Univ 1966; pa/Exec Asst to Pres Wallace W Atwood, Clark Univ, Worcester, Mass & Mr N Peter Rathvon, Pres RKO Film Corp, NYC (Res on Ednl Films) 1943-46; Edit Work on Manuscripts & Documents, Conf Sers Dept of UN, NYC 1955-57; CoFdr & CoOwner, Profl

Editing & Typing Sers, NYC 1960-; Guest Appearances on Radio & TV; Lectr, Cols & Univs; CoEdit w H G Assatourian *Children and Their Literature*; CoAuthor w H G Assatourian of "Experimental Trends in Soviet Armenia," presented at 89th Annual Conv of Mod Lang Assn Am, NYC 1974; Edit of Num Doct Dissertations & Books in Ed & Humanities; Author, *Procedure Manuals* for Grand Matron and Grand Officers of Daughters of Vartan; 1st Violinist & VP, Worcester Philharm Orch 1935-43; 1st Violinist, Phil Spitalny's All-Girl Orch, Springfield, Mass 1940-41; Nat Assn for Armenian Studies & Res; Mod Lang Assn Am; Secy, Armenian Profl Adv Coun NY 1976-; CoLdr w Husband of 91st Sem, Non-Slavic Peoples of the Soviet Union, 91st Annual

Conv of Mod Lang Assn Am, NYC 1976; Var Other Convs; Secy-Treas, Am Soc for Study of Peoples of Eastern Europe & Northern Asia; Nat Soc Lit & the Arts 1975-; cp/Past Mem, Armenian Folk Dance Soc, NY; Life Mem, Intl House, NYC; Past Dist Commr, GSA Coun Gtr NY-E Midtown Dist; Armenian Gen Benevolent Union, Advisor NY Chapt; Past Cotillion Chm, Constantinople Armenian Relief Soc, NYC; Patron & Com Mem, Intl Debutante Ball, NYC 1972-; Daughs of Vartan: Grand Recorder, Grand Coun 1971-73, Matron, Ani Chapt, Bayside, NY 1974-75, Gen Chm 34 Annual Conv NYC 1974, Grand Matron 1975-77; r/Armenian Apostolic Ch; hon/Spec Awd for Outstg Sers, GSA Coun of Gtr NY; Runner-up Woms Singles, US Paddle Tennis Assn Nat Tournament, Peter Cooper, NYC 1972; Gold Medal Ath Awd, Boston Univ 1940; Foremost Wom in Commun; 2000 Wom Achmt; World W/W Wom; Dir of Wom Scholars in Mod Langs; Dir of Am Scholars; W/W: Am, E, Fin & Indust; Intl W/W: Intells, Commun Ser; DIB; Commun Ldrs & Noteworthy Ams; Wom in Bus; Notable Ams of Bicent Era; Personalities of S; Book of Hon.

ASSATOURIAN, HAIG GOURJI KHAN oc/Research Consultant; Critic; Editor; Writer; b/Sept 19, 1911; h/410 E 20 St, 3A, NY, NY 10009; ba/NYC; m/Alice Husisian; c/Seta A Buchter, Sona A Davidian, Lora; p/Gourji Khan Assatourian (dec); Gayaneh Asdvatzadourian (dec); ed/AB Col of Emporia 1933; MA Columbia Univ 1936; MBA 1954, Postgrad Studies NY Univ; pa/Pres & Designer, Haig-Howard Corp, NYC, Mfgr Silverplated Holloware 1947-50; Pres, Haig Giftware Co, NYC, Mail Order Bus 1951-56; Plant Mgr, Laminated Fiberglass Corp of Am, NYC 1956-60; CoOwner, Profl Editing & Typing Sers, NYC 1960-; Author 2 Monographs: "Branch Banking in Relation to Business" 1936, "Problems in the Promotion of Mail-Order Business" 1954; CoEdit w Wife *Children and Their Literature*; Co-Author w Wife (Paper) "Expl Trends in Soviet Armenia" Presented at 89th Annual Conv, Mod Lang Assn Am, NYC 1974; Editor Num Doct Dissertations & Books in Ed & Humanities; Acad Polit Sci; Am Acad Polit & Social Sci; Am Judic; Soc; Bd Mem, Armenian Profl Adv

Coun 1976-; Nat Assn Armenian Studies & Res; Hon Bd Mem, Armenian Lit Soc, NY; Armenian Folk Dance Soc, NY 1948-56; VP, Armenian Gen Benevolent Union, NYC 1969, 1975-, Treas, Eastern Dist Com 1975, Advr NY Chapt 1978-; Public Relats Chm, "Thank-You Am" Bicent Com 1976; Primate's Com, Diocese of Armenian Ch, USA 1975-; Publicity Dir, Constantinople Armenian Relief Soc 1971; Patron & Com Mem, Intl Debutante Ball, NYC 1972-; Bd Dirs & Life Mem, NY Intl House Alumni; UN Assn of NY; Armenian Assembly 1973-; Cmdr, Etchniadzin Lodge, Knights of Vartan, Bayside, NY 1971-73; Gen Chm 56th Nat Convocation NYC 1974; Chm, Mid-Atlantic Interlodge Conf 1975-76; CoLdr w Wife, 91st Sem Non-Slavic Peoples of the Soviet Union, Mod Lang Assn Am Annual Conv, NYC 1976, Other Convs; Charter Mem & 1st Pres, Am Soc for Study of Peoples of En Europe & No & Ctl Asia; r/Armenian Apostolic Ch; hon/European Ser Medal w 3 Battle Stars; Good Conduct Medal; WW II Victory Medal; Men of Achmt; Notable Ams of Bicent Era; DIB; W/W E; Commun Ldrs & Noteworthy Ams; People Who Matter; Book of Hon; Intl W/W: Commun Ser, Intells; Dir Am Scholars.

ASTON, CHUCK oc/Consulting Petroleum Geologist; b/Mar 9, 1917; h/1505 Sandpiper, Palm Desert, CA 92260; ba/Palm Desert; m/Alyce; c/Wayne, Fred, Sharon, John, Mary Lou, Richard, Linda; p/Bert and Esther Hammond Aston (dec); ed/Petrol Geol; pa/Conslt'g Petrol Geologist 1939-; cp/City Coun-man, Palm Desert 1973-76; Rotary Intl; r/Epis; hon/FAAAS.

ASTON, KATHARINE OLINE oc/-Professor; b/Jun 25, 1917; h/University Inn, Apt 1807, 302 E John, Champaign, IL 61820; ba/Urbana, Ill; p/Walter Douglass and Carrie Oline Anderson Aston (dec); ed/AB Univ Kans 1937; PhD Bryn Mawr Col 1958; pa/Univ Ill, Urbana: Prof of English, English as 2nd Lang & Linguistics 1969-, Assoc Prof 1965-69, Asst Prof 1961-65, Instr 1958-61, Dir Progs English as Second Lang 1964-76, Acting U/I Acad Dir, Tchr Tng, Res & Materials Devel Prog (Co-sponsored by UIUC & Tehran Univ, Iran) 1974-76; Bur of Ed of Philippines: Vis Fulbright Lectr, ESOL, Tchr Tng in ESOL 1954-55; Other Past Positions; Consortium on Intensive English Progs; Tchrs of English to Spkrs of Other Langs; Nat Coun Tchrs of English; Linguistic Soc Am; AAUP; Nat Assn for Fgn Students Affairs-Assn of Tchrs of English as 2nd Lang; Reg Rep 1964-65, Prog Chm 1965-66, Secy 1966-67, VChm 1971-72, Chm 1972-73; Lectr; Conslt; Panelist; r/Cath; hon/Phi Beta Kappa (Past Pres & Past Secy, Ill Gamma Chapt); Profl Pubs; Kappa Kappa Gamma Omega Chapt S'ship Pins; Harry C Thurneau S'ship; Carl Schurz Meml Foun Prize; Germanistic Soc of Am F'ship; W/W: Am Wom, Oita Ken; Dir Am Scholars; 2000 Wom Achmt; World W/W Wom; Intl W/W Intells; World W/W Wom in Ed.

ATCHITY, KENNETH JOHN oc/Educator; Editor; Publisher; b/Jan 16, 1944; h/1733 Campus Rd, Los Angeles, CA 90014; ba/Los Angeles; m/Bonnie Fraser; c/Vincent, Rosemary; p/Fred and Myrza Achity, Kansas City, MO; ed/AB Georgetown Univ 1965; MPhil 1969, PhD 1970 Yale Univ; pa/Assoc Prof Comparative Lit, Occidental Col; Editor: *Contemporary Qtrly, The Dream Jour*; Contbg Editor, *San Fran Review of Books*; Guest Columnist, *LA Times*; Author Books of Criticism & Poetry; hon/Fulbright, Am Coun of Learned Societies, Nat Endowment for Humanities; Graves Awd.

ATCHLEY, EDWARD NOAH oc/Business Executive; b/Mar 27, 1935; h/502 Tivoli Ct, Altamonte Springs, FL 32701; ba/Sanford, FL; m/Sharon E; c/Teresa, Scott, Dean; p/Curtis B and Alma A Atchley, Knoxville, TN; ed/BA Univ Tenn; mil/USNR 1953-1961; pa/Pres, Cobia Boat Co; Bd Dirs, Boating Indust Assn; r/Prot.

ATKINS, CHARLES AGEE oc/Businessman; b/Apr 24, 1954; h/120 E 75th St, New York, NY 10021; ba/New York, NY; m/Frances Bellingrath; p/Orin Ellsworth and Kathryn Agee Atkins, Ashland, KY; ed/BA Univ NC 1975; MSc & PhD, London Sch of Ec; pa/Mng Partner, The Securities Group; Coun on Fgn Relats; Royal Inst Intl Affairs; Am Ec Assn; Am Fin Assn; cp/Nat Repub Senatorial Com; Trustee, Citizen's Budget Comm; Repub Senatorial Trust; Repub Nat Com; r/Presb; hon/John Motley Morehead Scholar; George C Marshall Scholar; Brookings Fellow; Phi Beta Kappa.

ATKINS, HANNAH DIGGS oc/State Legislator; h/PO Box 11628, Oklahoma City, OK 73111; ba/Okla City; m/Charles N; c/Edmund, Charles, Valerie; p/James T and Mabel Kennedy Diggs; ed/BS cum laude St Augustine's Col; BLS Univ Chgo Grad Lib Sch; Okla City Univ Sch Law; MPA Cand Univ Okla; pa/Law Libn, Chief of Gen Reference, Okla Dept Libs 1962-68; Instr of Law, Okla City Univ Law Sch 1962-68; Instr of Lib Sci, Univ Okla 1962-68; Br Libn, Okla City Public Libs 1953-56; Sch Libn, Kimberley Park Elem Sch, Winston-Salem, NC 1950-51; Reference Libn, Winston-Salem St Univ, Winston-Salem 1950; Other Past Positions; cp/Rep, Dist 97, Okla St Leg 1968-; Nat Com-

wom, Dem Nat Com 1976-; Exec Com, Nat Conf St Legs; Chwom, Nat Assn Black Wom Legs; VChwom, Nat Caucus Black Legs; Comm on Pres Nom & Party Structure of Nat Dem Com; Okla Chapt Nat Wom's Polit Caucus (Fdr); Comm on Del Selection & Party Reform, Dem Nat Com; Comm on Voting Rights, Dem Nat Com; Past Chwom, Okla Black Polit Caucus; Past Treas, Nat Black Polit Assembly; Nat Bd, ACLU; Sr Citizens Adv Coun; Exec Bd, Neighborhood Sers Org; r/Ch of Redeemer (Epis): Mem, Ch Wom United, Former Vestry Mem, Former SS Tchr; Lic'd Lay Reader, Diocese of Okla; hon/Phi Beta Kappa; Nat Citizen of Yr, Nat Assn Social Wkrs 1975; Nat Fdrs Ser Awd, Alpha Kappa Alpha Sorority 1970; Dist'd Ser Awd, Nat Link Inc 1972; Leg Conf Fellow, Rutgers Univ Eagleton Inst of Polits 1973; Hon Mem, Eta Phi Beta; Hannah Atkins Day, Univ of Okla 1975; Outstg Ser Awd, SWn Reg, Phi Delta Kappa 1976; Outstg Commun Ser Awd, So Reg, Nat Urban Leag 1971; Outstg Wom of Yr: Okla Soroptimist Intl 1965, Theta Sigma Phi 1968, Shawnee Chapt NOW 1976; Num Others.

ATKINS, WALTER J JR oc/Assistant Professor; b/Aug 5, 1943; h/Qtrs 4410 A, USAF Academy, CO 80840; ba/USAF Academy; m/Carolyn Ingram; c/Quentin A, Nicole J, Walter J III; p/Walter J and Annette R Atkins (dec); ed/BSEE Howard Univ 1965; MSEE 1971, PhD 1977 Univ Ill; mil/USAF 1966-, Maj; pa/Asst Prof of Elect Engrg, USAF Acad; IEEE; Optical Soc Am; cp/Alpha Phi Alpha; r/Presb; hon/Air Force Commends 1972, 75; W/W Black Am 1976; Intl Men Achmt 1976.

ATKINSON, ARTHUR SHERIDAN oc/Financial Consultant; Professional Director; b/Dec 5, 1918; h/2520 Broadway, San Fran, CA 94123; ba/San Fran & NYC; m/Didi Crutcher; c/Marsha Fay, Sheridan Earl; p/Arthur Garratt and Fay Mosher Atkinson; ed/BS w highest hons Univ Cal, Berkeley 1938; Postgrad Study Stanford Univ Sch Bus 1942-43; mil/AUS 1944; pa/Chm Bd, Atkinson & Assocs, NYC & San Fran 1955-; Chm & Pres, Botany Industs, NYC 1974-; Chm & Mng Dir, Crown Intl Group 1974-; Chm, Crown Fin Inc 1974-; Chm & CEO, Spl Earth Equipmt Corp, Emoryville, Cal 1976-;

Investmt Coun, Scudder, Stevens & Clark, San Fran 1953-55; Assoc, McKinsey & Co 1951-53; Investmt Advr to Regents, Univ of Cal; Chm (Acting), World Vision 1958-59; Chm: Devel & Tech Assistance Intl 1960-62, Univ Christian F'ship 1939-50, Fin Com of Bd - S S Pierce Co 1970-71; Dir, Intervarsity Christian F'ship 1953-56; Lectr on Profl Topics; Newcomen Soc; Nat Fed Fin Analysts Socs; Assn Corporate Growth; cp/Univ Cal Fac Clb; San Fran Stock Exc Clb; Brit Philos Soc; r/Presb: Bible Class Tchr, Christian Conf Spkr; hon/Selected by *Time* Mag & San Fran C of C as "1 of San Fran's 100 Ldrs of Tomorrow"; Alpha Beta Psi; Beta Gamma Sigma; W/W Am.

ATKINSON, BURNETT F oc/Musician; Educator; b/Jul 22, 1911; h/2402 Anaccepa, Santa Barbara, CA 93105; ba/Santa Barbara; m/Floryns; c/Howard, Clyde, George Marlowe; p/James F and Winifred Maude Birdie Burnett (dec); ed/BM Curtis Inst Music; BA Eastman Sch Music; mil/AUS; pa/Fac Mem: Univ Cal-Santa Barbara, Ventura Col, Music Acad of W; Play Solo Flute w Santa

Barbara Symph & Ventura Symph; Previously Played w: Phila Orch (10 Yrs), Mpls Orch, Chgo Orch, Los Angeles Philharm, Ballet de Monte Carlo, Phila Opera Co, Chgo Opera Co; cp/GASP; Repub; Mason; hon/Bronze & Gold Awds, SD.

ATKINSON, D FRANKLIN oc/Educator; b/Nov 15, 1930; h/806 Slone Dr, Marshall, TX 75670; ba/Marshall, TX; m/Barabara Ruth Harris; c/Ruth, Jean, David; p/Albert Dewey and Rosa Atkinson (dec); ed/BA 1952; BD 1955: ThM

1969; ThD 1958; pa/Assoc Prof of Rel, E Tex Bapt Col; Preacher; Writer; Assn Bapt Tchrs Rel; cp/Rotary Intl; r/S Bapt: La Bapt Conv Bd; hon/Tchr of Yr 1975, 77; W/W Am.

ATKINSON, INEZ W oc/Gift Shop Proprietor; b/Nov 8, 1927; h/PO Box 237, Pine Level, NC 27568; ba/Pine Level; m/Needham G; c/Joan I Dunbar; p/John T and Mary Williams (dec); ed/AAS Johnston Tech Inst 1978; pa/Work in Ceramic Shop, Inez Atkinson's Ceramic Gifts; Reg'd Barber, Beautician, Notary Public; Probation Vol; Future Secys Am; cp/4-H Clb Ldr; r/Bapt: Ch Treas, Editor & Pubr Ch Bulletin; hon/W/W Among Students in Am Voc & Tech Schs; Hons Grad; Other Acad Hons.

ATKINSON, NATALIE O oc/Instructor; b/Aug 27, 1920; h/3374 La Mesa Dr, San Carlos, CA 94070; p/Orlando and Anna Imel Atkinson (dec); ed/BA Univ Cal, Santa Barbara 1947; MA Stanford Univ 1952; pa/Instr; Cal Tchrs Assn; Cal Sci Tchrs Assn; Nat Marine Ed Assn; Nat Sci Tchrs Assn; cp/Oceanic Society; Acad of Sci; hon/Fulbright Exc Tchr to Austria 1962-63; Author *Marine Science Resource Handbook* 1978.

ATTALES, GERALD BRUCE oc/Farmer; b/Jul 28, 1938; h/Rt 6, Box 100, Ville Platte, LA 70586; ba/Ville Platte; m/Theresa Vidrine; c/Mitchell Jude, Lynette, Lisa Renee; p/Lawrence and Pearl Ardoin Attales, Ville Platte, LA; ed/Grad Shreveport Barber Sch 1959; pa/Rice & Bean Farmer, 5 Yrs; Profl Barber, Blue Point & Ville Platte, 16 Yrs; cp/Cand, Ward 1, Dist 1, Police Juror, Evangeline Parish, La; La Qtr Horse Assn; Jaycees; Ran Turnoi 10 Yrs; Turnoi Assn: VP 3 yrs, Bd Mem 4 Yrs; Evangeline Parish Cattlemen's Assn; Evangeline Parish Sheriff's Posse; C of C; Rotary Clb; K of C; Sacred Heart PTA; Sacred Heart Booster Clb; Evangeline Parish Farm Bur; r/Cath; Sacred Heart Ch: Usher; hon/Best Sportsmanship Trophey (Turnoi) 1970.

ATWATER, MILTON JR oc/Dental Technician; Rancher; b/Jan 3, 1927; h/Rt 2, Box 708, Rosharon, TX 77583; ba/Houston; c/Miltonetta, Ladye M; p/Milton and Rosie Lee Atwater (dec); mil/USN WW II; pa/Dental Lab Assn; Angus Assn; cp/U Negro Col Fund; r/Cath; hon/W/W Dental Lab; cp/U Negro Col Fund; r/Cath; hon/W/W Dental Lab; Cattle Breeders Hall of Fame.

AUBIN, BARBARA oc/Artist; Writer; Teacher; b/Jan 12, 1928; h/1322 W Cornelia, Chicago, IL 60657; ba/Chgo; p/Philip T and Dorothy Chapman Aubin (dec); ed/BA Carleton Col 1949; BAE 1954, MAE 1955 Sch of Art Inst of Chgo; pa/Tchr, Art Dept, Chgo

St Univ; Artist-in-Residence, St Louis Commun Col, Mar 1979; 20+ 1-Wom Exhbns incl'g Ill Arts Coun Gallery, Chgo 1975, Harper Col 1976; Group Exhbns incl: Fairweather Hardin Gallery, Chgo 1979, Springflield (Ill) Art Assn 1979, Hyde Park Art Ctr, Chgo 1978, Nancy Lurie Gallery, Chgo 1978, En Ill Univ 1977, Beverly Art Ctr, Chgo 1977, Ill St Mus 1976, Artists Guild of Chgo 1976, Num Others; Wks in Collects: Art Inst Chgo, Ball St Univ, Ernst & Ernst, Northwest Industs, Ill Tool Wks, Union Leag Clb-Chgo, Ill St Mus, Gould Inc, Continental Ill Nat Bank & Trust, Centre d'Art (Port-au-Prince, Haiti), Others; Co-editor, "Chgo Artists Coalition Newslttr"; Contbg Editor *Visual Dialog 1978;* Wom's Caucus for Art; hon/*George D Brown Fgn Travel F'ship 1955; Buenos Aires Conv Act Grant; Ill Arts Coun Proj Completion Grant.*

AUE, JULIA NEWTON oc/Housewife; Retired Educator; b/Oct 10, 1910; h/Rt 8, Box 276 A, San Antonio, TX 78229; m/Rudolph Jr; c/Betty Ann, Rudolph III; p/Joseph Samuel and Tillie Steinle Newton (dec); ed/BA; pa/Ret'd Schr Tchr; r/Presb; hon/1st Prize Patriotic Sem 1976.

AUERBACH, BARRY B oc/Dental Surgeon; b/Aug 16, 1916; ba/3322 Frederick Ave, Baltimore, MD 21229; m/Jean Alma Fretwell; c/Diane A Myers (Mrs Bob); p/Samuel L and Edith Handler Auerbach; ed/BS 1935, DDS 1939 Univ Md; mil/USNR 1942-46, Lt Cmdr; pa/Dental Pract Specializing in Prosthetics and Gen Dentistry; Staff Mem, St Agnes Hosp, Baltimore 1946-; Dental Surg Under Dr Albert Schweitzer, Lambarane, Gabon, Africa 1964; Res on Mouth Cancer; Am Dental Assn; Am Soc Clin & Exptl Hypnosis; Am Soc Psychosomatic Dentistry and Med; French Fed Dentaire Intl; Md Soc Med Res; Intl Soc Hypnosis; Am Acad Oral Roentgenology; Intl Soc Clin & Exptl Hypnosis; Assn Mil Surgs US; Am Acad Acupuncture Res; Nat Acupuncture Res Soc; Sigma Epsilon Delta; Lect'd in Japan, Hong Kong, Bangkok, India, Africa, Others; hon/Hon Mem: Pan Am Clipper Clb, TWA Ambassador Clb (Traveled Over 1 million Air Miles); Admiral, Am Airlines; Gorgus Odontological Soc (Hon Soc); W/W E.

AUGUST, RICHARD BRUCE oc/-Administrator; b/Jun 19, 1952; h/14007 Palawan Way #317, Marina Del Rey, CA 90291; ba/Los Angeles; m/Kathleen Leslie Perez; p/John Joseph and Patricia Adele Beaton August; ed/BSEE Univ So Cal 1973; MSEE Mass Inst Technol 1974; mil/USNR 1971-77; pa/Dir of Info Processing Techniques, Custom Application Sys Inc 1978-; Communs Analyst, Telecredit Inc 1977-78; Scist/Engr, Adv'd Products Div, Magnavox Govt & Indust Electronics Co 1977; Engr/Scist, Jet Propulsion Lab, NASA 1975-77; Res Assoc: Dept of Elect Engrg, Univ So Cal 1974-77, Dept of Elect Engrg, Mass Inst Technol 1974-75; Pres, Am Soc Engrs & Archs 1972; Conslt; cp/Repub; hon/Ser to Country, USNR 1973.

AULENBACH, W HAMILTON oc/Clergyman; b/Oct 4, 1898; h/660 W Bonita Ave, Apt 21A, Claremont, CA 91711;

ba/La Mirada, CA; m/Pearl F; c/Gretchen Frandsen, William H Jr, Dorothy Blunden; p/Louis Jeremiah and Ida Hamilton Aulenbach (dec); ed/BA; MT; DD; mil/USN WW I; pa/Epis Clergyman: Assoc Preacher, St

Christopher's, La Mirada 1976-; Asst Preacher, St James, So Pasadena, Cal 1975; Preacher-at-large; Vol Chaplain, Chino (Cal) Prison (Girls) 1974; Rector: Christ Ch & St Michael's, Germantown, Phila, Pa 1938, Locum Tenes 1970; Assoc Rector: Christ Ch, Cranbrook, Mich 1927, St Paul's, Flint, Mich 1926; Curate, St Asaph's, Bala, Pa 1925; Taught at Temple Univ, Phila; hon/Bronze Medal, Am Legion; Anthony Wayne Medal, Val Forge; *Philadelphia Tribune* Awd for Interracial Activities; Author: *Good Evening, My Friends!, Joy! Joy! Joy!, Love on the Highway, A Go Religion!*

AUSTEN, WILLIAM GERALD oc/Surgeon; b/Jan 2, 1930; h/163 Wellesley St, Weston, MA 02193; ba/Boston, MA; m/Patricia Ramsdell; c/Karl R, W Gerald Jr, Christopher M, Elizabeth P; p/Mrs Bertyl Arnstein, Akron, OH; ed/BS Mass Inst Technol 1951; MD Harvard Med Sch 1955; mil/USPHS Comm'd Corps 1961-62, Surg; pa/Harvard Med Sch: Edward D Churchill Prof of Surg 1974-, Prof of Surg 1966-74, Assoc Prof of Surg 1965-66, Assoc in Surg, 1963-65, Tchg Fellow in Surg 1960-61; Mass Gen Hosp: Chief Surg Sers 1969-, Vis Surg 1966-69, Chief Surg Cardiovascular Res Unit 1963-; Surg, Clinic of Surg, Nat Heart Inst, Bethesda, Md 1961-62; Pres: Am Heart Assn 1977-78, New England Cardiovascular Soc 1972-73, Mass Heart Assn 1972-74, Assn for Acad Surg 1970, Soc Univ Surgs 1972-73; Am Med Assn; New England Surg Soc; Am Surg Assn; Am Col Cardiol; Boston Surg Soc; Am Thoracic Surgs; Am Col Surgs; NY Acad Scis; Societe Internationale de Chirurgie; Mass Med Soc; Soc for Vascular Surg; Pan Med Assn; Am Acad Arts & Scis; Soc Clin Surg; Allen O Whipple Surg Soc; Am Trauma Soc; Italian Res Soc; New England Cardiovascular Society; Canadian Cardiovascular Soc; Inst of Med of Nat Acad Scis; Others; Edit Bd: *Circulation* 1972-, *The New England Jour of Med* 1972-, *Jour of Surg Res* 1967-74, *Am Jour of Surg* 1967-, *The Annals of Thoracic Surg* 1970-, *Review of Surgs* 1970-, *Annals of Surg* 1972-, *Current Problems in Surg* 1972-, *Minerva Medica* 1974-, *Excerpta Medica* 1976-; Num Vis Prof'ships incl'g: Duke Univ, Yale Univ, Tulane Univ, Baylor Univ, Univ NC-Chapel Hill, Univ Ala, Univ Md, Univ Chgo, Cornell Univ, Columbia Univ, NJ Col of Med, Univ Miami; hons/Hon Mem: Panhellenic Surg Soc, Canadian Cardiovascular Soc, Dutch Cardiol Soc; Fellow, Am Acad Arts & Scis; Markle Scholar in Acad Med; Outstg Yg Men Awd, Boston 1965; Nat Register Prominent Ams & Intl Notables.

AUSTIN, BARBARA ELIZABETH oc/Administrator; b/Aug 18, 1941; h/1069 Poplar, Jackson, MS 39202; ba/Jackson, MS; p/William Thomas Austin (dec); Mrs William Thomas Austin, Terry, MS; ed/BA magna cum laude Miss Univ for Wom 1963; Grad Study Jackson St Univ; pa/Univ Miss Med Ctr: Dir Public Relats & Info Sers 1978-, Assoc Dir Spec Sers & Campus Relats & Hd Info Sers 1973-76, Asst Dir Spec Sers & Campus Relats & Hd Info Sers 1973-76, Asst Dir Public Info 1969-73, Asst to Dir of Public Info 1967-73; Asst Dir of Public Relats, Belhaven Col 1964-67; Conslt: Camp Merri-Mac, Camp Rockbrook, Camp Ahoy (Black Mtn, NC) 1966-67, Peace Col (Raleigh, NC) 1973, SEn Public Ed Prog (Atlanta, Ga) 1977, Elon Col Instl (Elon Col, NC) 1978; Group on Public Relats, Assn Am Med Cols; Nat Fed Press Wom; Miss Press Wom; Col Public Relats Assn of Miss; Wom in Communs; Public Relats Assn Miss; cp/Bd Dirs, Hinds Co Kidney Foun; VP Bd Dirs, New Stage Theatre; Ed Com, Miss Task Force on Nurse-Midwifery; Public Relats Conslt, Aux to Miss Soc for Prevention of Blindness 1977; Media Campaign Conslt, Vol Jackson; Jackson Symph Orch: Conslt, Com Chm, Edit Staff, Former Mem Bd Govs; Jackson Symph Leag: Mem & Past Bd Mem; Miss Opera Assn: Mem, Past Editor; Miss Mar Dimes; Inter-Alumni Coun; Goodwill Aux; Jackson Co Opera Guild; Miss Arts Fest: Past Com Chm & Mem; Jackson Co Ballet Guild; U Givers Fund; r/Galloway Meml U Meth Ch: Public Relats

Com 1978; hon/W/W Am Wom; Outstg Yg Wom Am; Miss Press Wom: 1st Pl Layout Photog 1964, 1st Pl Dir Mail Comp w Lois Clover 1965, 66; Wom Achmt: 1st Pl w Maurine Twiss for Public Relats Innovation, Group on Public Relats, Assn Am Med Cols 1975; Sigma Tau Delta; Pi Tau Chi; Others.

AUSTIN, ELLA FRANCES NEAL oc/Teacher; b/Jun 2, 1920; h/129 So Hatton Ave, Lebanon, TN 37807; ba/Lebanon; m/James Harry; c/James, Mary Etta Skeen, Joseph, Rebecca Donnell, Andrew, Elizabeth Dickens; p/Thell Ross Neal (dec); Laura Etta Neal Johnson, Lebanon, TN; ed/BS Cumberland Col-George Peabody Col; David Lipscomb; pa/Tchr: Lebanon City Schs, Ho of Hope 1962-, Highland Hts Sch, 2 Summers

Kindegarten Tchr 1966-67, Pvt St Approved Kindergarten 1957-61, Wilson Co TMR Spec Ed Students for Assn for Retarded Chd 1961-62; Wilson Co Sys Prin: Grades 6-8 1941-42, Grades 1-3 1942-43, Grades 4-6 1943-44; Lebanon Ed Assn; Secy, Lebanon City Schs 1974-75; cp/Vol Tchr, YMCA Summer Camp 1963, 64, 65; Bd Dirs, Wilson Co Devel Ctr 1969-; r/Col St Ch of Christ: Mem, Presch Tchr, Vacation Bible Sch Tchr, Nursery Tchr, Former Bulletin Vol; hon/Spec Ed Grants.

AUSTIN, MICHAEL HERSCHEL oc/Lawyer; b/Nov 7, 1896; h/47 Richards Rd, Columbus, OH 43214; ba/Columbus; m/Inez; p/Michael Green and Willie Catherine Roberson Austin (dec); ed/LLB Univ Miss 1922; JD Ohio St Univ 1923; mil/USCG Aux WW I; pa/Gen Law Pract, Columbus 1924-; Ptnr, Pfeiffer & Austin 1927-30; Admitted to Bar: Miss 1922, Ohio 1924; Am Judic Soc; Assoc, Columbus Real Est Bd; Am Bar Assn; Ohio St Bar Assn; Columbus Bar Assn; Tax Sect, Am Bar Assn; Past Secy, Columbus Lwyrs Clb; IPA; cp/Am Legion: 12th Dist Judge Advocate 1967-70, 1975-76, Past Pres Big 4 Vets Coun, Past St Treas, Former Dist, Co & Post Cmdr; Pres, Past Cmdrs Clb 1961-62; Chm's Coun, Franklin Co Dem Party; Ohio St Alumni Assn; Univ Miss Alumni Assn; hon/Fellow, Truman Lib Assn; Outstg Legionnaire, 12 Dist Am Legion 1967; Hon'd at 50th Yr Banquet of Am Legion, Lancaster, Ohio 1968; Cross of Hon, U Daughs Confed 1944; W/W Midwest; W/W World; W/W Commerce & Indust.

AUSTIN, STANLEY STUART oc/Professor; Composer; Conductor; Corporation Executive; Cellist; Author; b/Aug 23, 1914; h/4 Hampton Rd, Trenton, NJ 08638; ba/Trenton; m/Dorothea J; c/David S, Peter S, Paul S, Ruth E; p/Arthur Thompson and Agnes E Austin (dec); ed/Artist Dipl; BS; MA; PhD Equiv; mil/USAF; pa/Musician-Prodegy (Violinist) at Age 6 (Cellist at 16); Composer; Conductor; Soloist; Trenton St Col: Dir Bands & Orch 1952-, Dept Chm & Grad Music Supvr 1957-; Spec Lectr, Columbia Univ Tchr Col 1944-52; Chm Music Dept: Wayne Sch 1938-41, Westwood HS 1943-52; Band & Orch Dir, Pompton Lakes HS 1934-38; Past Pres, Bergen Co Music Edrs Assn; Bd Dirs, Dela Music Edrs; Assn Col Profs; NY Symph Orch; MENC; Assn of Musicians of Gtr NY; ASCAP; Lionel Hampton/Counterpoint, Enterprises; Permanent Conductor, Jersey Pops Jazz Symph; Pres, Creative Arts Wkshop Inc; Pub'd Comps incl: Concerto Composed for Clarinet & Saxaphone & Symph Orch (Comm'd by NJ Atty Gen William F Hyland), Composition 1978 Heritage for New Hampshire, Bicent Comp "A Shot Heard Round the World" for Chorus and Symph Band, 3 Solos for All Band Instruments, 2 Solos w Band Accompaniment, 3 Marches for Band, Others; cp/Ed Task Forces; Conf Spkr; Spec Wkr Releaving Juv Delinquincy; Corp Pres for Helping Yth Get Started; r/Prot; Ch Choir Dir; hon/11 Ser Awds for Helping Combat Juv Deliquency; Ser Awds for Helping Fund Res (Cancer-Leukemia); Outstg Music Tchr Awds; 14 Merit Awds for Helping in Tchg of Tchrs; Intl W/W Tchrs; Tchr of Yr, NJ 1947; NJ Awd 1945.

AUTEN, MELVIN R oc/Pyschological Consultant; b/Sept 5, 1944; h/315 S 30th St, Muskegee, OK 74401; ba/Taft, OK; m/Carol Elaine; c/Krista Renae; p/Ray L Auten, Ada, OK; Mary Luciel Brown; ed/BSEd; MED; ABD; mil/Army NG; pa/Psychol Conslt, Okla Chd's Ctr; Am Col Pers Assn; Am Pers & Guid Assn; cp/Kiwanis; Dem; r/Bapt; hon/W/W S&SW; Personalities of S; Psi Chi; Phi Delta Kappa.

AVERBACH, BENJAMIN LEWIS oc/Professor; m/Gertrude M McCarthy; c/Paul Vincent, Anne Louise, Clare Frances; p/George Averbach (dec); Lillian Yves; ed/BS 1940, MS 1942, Rensselaer Polytech Inst; ScD Mass Inst Technol 1947; pa/Mass Inst Technol: Prof 1960, Assoc Prof 1953-60, Asst

Prof 1947-53; Editor, *Fracture* 1960; Conslt in Field; Pres, Intl Cong on Fracture; Del, Intl Inst of Welding; Am Phys Soc; Am Cryst Assoc; Fellow, Am Soc Metals; cp/Treas, Belmont Repub Town Com; r/Cath; hon/Howe Medal, ASM; Patentee in Field; 200 Tech Pubs.

AVERBUCH, PHILIP FRED oc/Physician; Orthopedic Surgeon; b/Nov 28, 1941; h/3180 NW 114 Terr, Coral Springs, FL 33065; ba/Tamarac, FL; m/Judith Hope; c/Amy Lynne, Robert Neil; p/Maurice and Dorothy Averbach, Lauderhill, FL; ed/BA Columbia Col; MD Tufts Univ; mil/AUS, Maj; pa/Univ Commun Hosp: Chief of Staff, Dir Physical Med; Treas, W Broward Phys Assn; cp/Bd Dirs, Fdn Jewish Philanthropies, U Fla, Ft Lauderdale; r/Jewish; hon/Fellow: Am Col Surgs, Am Acad Orth Surgs, Intl Col Surgs; Diplomate, Am Bd Orth Surgs; Developed New Type Plaster Cast.

AVERHART, LULA oc/Teacher; b/Apr 17, 1916; h/400 McClain St, Bessemer, AL 35020; ba/Fairfield, AL; p/Frank and Octavia Reese Averhart (dec); ed/AB Cum Laude Paine Col 1939; MEd Ala St Univ 1959; 6th Yr Deg Auburn Univ 1972; Double AA Cert Auburn Univ 1973; Addit Studies; pa/Tchr 38 Yrs F'field Bd Ed: Home Ec, Math, Social Studies, Spec Ed, Summer Sch Prin, Org Hist & Math Clbs, Advr Nat Hon Soc; Dir Tchr Tng Miles Col; Tchr Sewing & Basic Adult Ed; NEA; Ala Ed Assn; F'field Tchrs Assn; Ala St Sci Assn; Ala Assn Adult & Continuing Ed; cp/Civil Def Ed; Shelter Mgmt; Tchr Nutrition ARC; Fund Drives: Am Cancer Soc, Nat Mutiple Sclerosis, Ctrl Ala Chapt & Nat Leukemia Soc Inc; OES; YWCA; r/Mars Hill Bapt Ch: Mem, SS & Ch Secy, Yth Dir, Wom Bible Class Tchr, Ser Hon; Wom Day Spkr Num Chs; hon/HS Valedictorian; Chm Num

Hon Progs; Num S'ships & Stipends; 25 Yr Ser Award F'field Bd Ed; Class of 1942 Merit Awd; F'field Hall of Fame; Sel'd for Num Wkshops; Hon'd by Fairfield Bd of Ed for More Than 25 Yrs of Ser (38 Yrs); Pub'd Author: Num Profl Papers.

AVERSA, ALARICO oc/Artist; b/Mar 18, 1930; h730 Lorimer St, Brooklyn, NY 11211; ba/Bklyn; m/Anna Marchione; c/Serena, Frank; p/Francesco Aversa; Vincenza Tomassi; ed/Scenery Decorating Movie Picture Ctr, Rome; pa/Painter; Sculptor; Practicing Artist; Artists Equity Assn; Intl Soc Artists (UNESCO); cp/Nat Bd for Hist Preserv; Nat Adv Bd, Am Security Coun; r/Cath; hon/Livre D'or, Academie Intl de Lutece-Paris.

AVERY, DAVID ROGER oc/Pediatric Dentist; Dental Educator; b/Apr 20, 1940; h/1207 Donnybrook Dr, Carmel, IN 46032; ba/Indianapolis, IN; m/Myra Jean; c/Lisa Jean, Scott David; p/W Kenneth and Frieda R Farmer Avery (dec); ed/BS Purdue Univ 1963; DDS 1966, MSD 1971 Ind Univ Sch Dentistry; mil/USN 1966-68; USNR 1970-, Cmdr; pa/Pvt Pract: Gen Dentistry, Kokomo, Ind 1966, Pedodontics, Indpls 1974-; Ind Univ Sch Dentistry: Assoc Prof & Chm Dept of Pedodontics & Dir Post-doct Pedodontic Prog 1976-78, Assoc Prof & Chm Div of Undergrad Pedodontics 1973-76, Asst Prof & Chm Div of Undergrad Pedodontics 1971, Asst Prof & Acting Chm Div of Undergrad Pedodontics

1970, Others; Hosp Affils: Ind Univ Med Ctr Hosp 1976, McAfee Army Hosp, White Sands Missile Range, NM 1967-68; Am Acad Pedodontics; Am Dental Assn; Ind Dental Assn; Ind Soc Dentistry for Chd; Ind Soc Pedodontics; Am Assn Dental Schs: Secy, Chm-elect, Chm Coun of Facs; Indpls Dist Dental Soc; Intl Assn Dentistry for Chd; Others; cp/Purdue Univ Alumni Assn; Ind Univ Sch Dentistry Alumni Assn; r/King of Glory Luth Ch: Mem, Past Com Chm, Past Pres Ch Coun & Congreg; Participant, Indpls Schs Dental Inspections 1968-69; Past Mem: YMCA, Father & Son Y-Indian Guides; hon/Omicron Kappa Upsilon; Grants; F'ships; Assoc Editor & Co-Author of Textbook (w R E McDonald) *Dentistry for the Child and Adolescent* 1978.

AXAM, JOHN ARTHUR oc/Librarian; b/Feb 12, 1930; h/1803 Chew Ave, Philadelphia, PA 19141; ba/Philadelphia; m/Dolores; ed/BS Cheyney St Col; MSLS Drexel Univ; pa/Libn; Am Lib Assn; Pa Lib Assn; cp/U Way; Girl Scouts of Gtr Phila; r/U Meth; hon/Chapel of the Four Chaplains Awd.

AXEEN, MARINA ESTHER oc/Professor; b/Nov 29, 1921; h/4501 N Wheeling 2-114, Muncie, IN 47304; ba/Muncie; ed/BS St Cloud St Col 1945; BSLS 1949, MSLS 1953 Univ Minn; PhD Univ Ill 1967; pa/Ball St Univ: Chm & Prof Dept of Lib Sci 1969-, Assoc Prof 1967-69; Hd Reference Libn, St Cloud St Univ, St Cloud, Minn 1957-64; Hd Libn, Bethel Col & Sem, St Paul, Minn 1947-57; Public Sch Tchr, Duluth, Minn 1945-46; Am Lib Assn; Delta Kappa Gamma; AALS; ACRL; ILA; AIME; cp/Active in Civic Affairs; Polit Campaigner; r/Ch of Christ; hon/Sev pa/Active in Civic Affairs; Ill Lib Sch Alumni Assn; Bd Mem, Friends of the Muncie Lib; r/1st Bapt Ch: Christian Ed Bd; hon/Birdella Ross S'ship.

AXTON, FLORENCE GOTTHELF oc/Homemaker; Civic Worker; b/Mar 6, 1915; h/3131 E Alameda, Denver, CO 80209; c/Gordon T; p/Earl Gordon Gotthelf (dec); Agnes Rowena Noland Gotthelf, Denver, CO; ed/Ferry Hall Jr Col; Finch Col; PhD Colo St Christian Col 1972; pa/Past Merchandiser, Bonwitt Teller, NYC; Asst Dir, Drama Dept Finch Col 1936-37; cp/Travellers Aid Soc, NYC; Martha F Chison Res Lib on Dance; Colo & Co Repub Orgs; Ctl City Opera Ho Assn; L'Alliance Francaise; Bd Mem, Sewall Rehab Ctr; Denver Art Mus; Denver Press Coun; Histn, Denver Lyric Opera Guild; r/Ctl Christian Ch; hon/Pub'd Poetry & Recipes; hon/Hons & Awds from Cancer Soc, Mar Dimes, Denver Art Mus, Others; Commun Ldrs & Noteworthy Ams; W/W Am Wom; Personalities of W&MW; Intl W/W Commun Ser; Nat Register Prominent Ams & Intl Notables; DIB; Notable Ams of Bicent Era; Nat Social Register; Royal Blue Book; W/W W; Book of Hon; 2000 Wom Achmt.

AXTON, MAE BOREN oc/Public Relations Consultant; b/Sept 14; h/4215 Harding Rd, Nashville, TN 37205; ba/Nashville, TN; c/Hoyt, John Boren; p/Mark L and Mae Weatherall Boren (dec); ed/BS; BA; MS; MA; PhD Equiv; pa/Songwriter (Over 200 of her songs have been recorded incl'g the hit "Heartbreak Hotel" recorded by Elvis Presley); Author; Lectr; Sch Tchr 17 yrs; Public Relats Conslt (Current & Past Clients incl Jerry Reed, Dennis Weaver, Dolly Parton, Tony Orlando, Kenny Rogers, Crystal Gayle, Hoyt Axton); cp/Active in Civic Affairs; Polit Campaigner; r/Ch of Christ; hon/Sev Broadcast Music Inc Awds incl'g 4 for "Heartbreak Hotel"; Ky Col; Spec Tribute by NY Songwriters Hall of Fame; Tex Ritter Awd; Sev Hon Sheriff Awds incl'g Hon Ala Hwy Patrol Awd; Num Keys to Cities; Hon Lt Col Aide-de-Camp: Ala, Ga; Cert Apprec, Army Info Radio Ser; Dist'd Ser Awd, Austin, Tex; Hon Citizen, Austin, Tex; Spec Awd, Propeller Clb of US; Hon PhD, Peter Univ; Cert Awd, Walden Ho of Tenn; Outstg Oklahoman Awd; Snowmen's Leag of Am.

AYACHI, HELEN oc/Teacher; b/Dec 16, 1941; h/1004 W Stratford Dr, Peoria, IL 61614; m/Salah; c/Najet, Ramzy; p/Fred C and Dora M Castillo, Galveston, TX; ed/BA Tex Wom's Univ; MA Univ Houston; pa/Tchr; Coor Early Childhood Lng Prog 1971-77; Tchr, Ill Migrant Coun; Treas, Galveston Tchr Assn; Pres & Fdr, Galveston Assn Biling Ed; NEA; TSTA; NAYEC; TAEYC; TABE; NABE; AATSP; cp/Goals for Galveston Ed Task Force Com; Galveston Co Cult Arts Com; Vol Dep Voter Registrar; "Save Old Ctl" Restoration Com; Friends of Rosenberg Lib; r/Rom Cath; hon/Red Cross Vol Awd; Personalities of S; Spec Recog Awd, Galveston Assn Bilingual Ed; Galveston ISD Clearinghouse; Task Force Chm, Com for Needs of Mex-Am Students.

AYERS, ANNE LOUISE oc/Education Specialist; b/Oct 22, 1948; h/Beckley, WV; ba/Nat Mine Hlth & Safety Acad, Beckley, WV 25801; p/F Ernest and Gladys M Ayers, Shelton, WA; ed/BA Univ Ks 1970; MEd Seattle Pacific Univ 1971; EdD Studies William & Mary Univ; pa/Am Pers & Guid Assn; Federally Employed Wom; Nat Assn Wom Deans, Admrs & Cnlsrs; Nat Assn Student Pers Admrs; Nat Assn Col Admrs; Nat Def Trans Assn; cp/Indept Wom's Party; Cnslr Intern, Seattle Ctl Commun Col & Cnslr/Interviewer/Spch Therapist, Goodwill Indust 1971; Vol, Pacific Sch (for severely mtly retarded, spch handicapped & emotionally disturbed); r/Meth; hon/2 Ch S'ships; Humble Oil Ldrship S'ship; W/W: Am Wom, S&SW; Outstg Dist'd Personalities of S; Hon Mem, Va Sheriff's Assn; Pub'd Profl Articles.

AYERS, CURTIS PROPER III oc/- Proposal Manager; Chemical Engineer; b/Dec 10, 1942; h/14551 Bramblewood Dr, Houston, TX 77079; ba/Houston, TX; m/Kathryn Nix; c/Curtis Proper IV, Elizabeth Ferrell; p/Curtis Proper Ayers Jr (dec); Elizabeth O Ayers, Vicksburg, MS; ed/BS, MS Univ Miss; mil/USAR Chem Corps, Maj; pa/Proposal Mgr,

Davy Powergas Inc; Proposal Mgr, Kinetics Technol Intl Corp, Pasadena; Proposal Engr, J F Pritchard & Co 1975-76; Licensing, Res & Engrg Div, Miss Chem Corp 1970-75; Tech Ser & Devel, Dow Chem Co 1968-70; Ofcr Am Inst Chem Engrs; Reg'd Profl Engr, Tex; cp/Ofcr Lions Incl; Advtg & Sales Execs Clb; Am Legion; Univ Miss Alumni Assn; BSA Ldr; Alpha Tau Omega; r/Epis Ch: Ofcr; hon/Scabbard & Blade; Num Mil Hons; Profl Pubs.

AYERS, JAMES WILBUR oc/Self Employed; b/Apr 1, 1928; h/609 1st St, Atalla, AL 35954; ba/Atalla; p/Jay W Ayers, Atalla, AL; Thelma Harbin Ayers (dec); pa/Self-employed Yard Wkr & Coal Yrd Wkr; IPA; Writer; Songwriter; Poet; r/Presb; hon/Etowah Co Author at Gadsden Public Lib, Nat Lib Wk 1969; Hon Mem, Atalla Lion's Clb; St Record of Lttrs to Editors of Newspapers.

AYMAR, CATHERINE BEATRICE oc/Realtor; b/Nov 28, 1922; h/917 Kennard Way, Sunnyvale, CA 94087; ba/Santa Clara, CA; m/Clarence Phillip; c/Patrick Mercer; p/Morley Victor Pomeroy (dec); Jessie Edna Fredenburg Pomeroy, Midvale, ID; ed/GRI; pa/Santa Clara Val Chapt Wom's Coun Realtors; VP, Cal St Chapt Wom's Coun Realtors 1978; San Jose Real Est Bd; Sunnyvale Bd Realtors; Cal Assn Realtors; cp/Nat Jr Achmt Mktg Advr 1978; Quota Clb Intl; Vol, Mobile Blood Bank; Spch Judge for Commun HSs; r/Meth; hon/Var Profl Awds for Salesmanship; Wom of Yr 1977.

AYNES, EDITH ANNETTE oc/-Administrator; b/Apr 2, 1909; h/1125 Grand Concourse, Bronx, NY 10452; ba/Bronx; p/Andrew Festus (dec); Marian Pearl McIrvin (dec); ed/BS; MA; mil/AUS Nurse Corps 22 yrs;

pa/Admr, Non-profit Home for Aged; Nat Leag for Nursing; Gerontological Soc; Am Security Coun; Repub Nat Com; r/Christian; hon/Treas Awd; Legion of Merit 1952; Kiwanis & Lions Clb Awds; Army Commend Ribbons.

AZIZ, GEORGE KALIB JR oc/Roman Catholic Jesuit Priest; b/August 2, 1927;

h/1340 Tainter St, St Helena, CA 94574; ba/St Helena; p/George K Aziz Sr (dec); Lillian Essey Aziz, Brownsville, TX; ed/MA cum

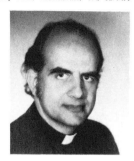

laude; STM cum laude; pa/Assoc Pastor, Diocese of Santa Rosa, St Helena Parish; Lead Ch Prayer; Preach in English & Spanish; Cnslg; Catechizing; Visit Sick; Moderator, Cath Action; Panelist; Authored & Produced Spec 13 Wk Series, *Challenge* 1975; Conslt; Cath Theol Soc Am; cp/Com on Inst in Morals in Public Schs, St Helena Sch Dist; Wkly Social Contact w Public Sch Students; r/Rom Cath: Mem Professed Soc of Jesus; Degree of Distn, Nat Forensic Leag 1953; HS Valedictorian & Winner Statewide S'ship.

B

BAATZ, CHARLES ALBERT oc/- Professor; Department Chairman; b/Apr 4, 1916; h/168 Village Rd, SouthOrange, NJ 07079; ba/South Orange; m/Olga Alexandra Kozoriz; c/Barry; Terry; p/Charles Frederick and Anna Lenheer Baatz; ed/AB; PhL; PhD Phil; pa/Seton Hall Univ: Chm Gen Profl Ed, Prof; Deacon; Author: *Philosophy of Education - Guide to Sources*; cp/Pres, Citizens for Responsive Govt; r/Rom Cath, Ordained Deacon 1975; hon/Assn of Tchr Edrs Spkr, Las Vegas 1978.

BABERO, BERT BELL oc/Parasitologist; b/Oct 9, 1918; h/2202 Golden Arrow Dr, Las Vegas, NV 89109; ba/Las Vegas; m/Harriett King; c/Bert Bell Jr, Andras Fanfiero; p/(dec); ed/BS 1949, MS 1950, PhD 1957 Univ of Ill; mil/AUS 1943-46; pa/Parasitologist, Univ of Nev; Mem: Am Soc Parasitols, Am Micros Soc, Helminthological Soc of Wash, Sigma Xi, Beta Beta Beta, Phi Sigma; cp/Man of Yr, NAACP 1969; Commr, Nev St Equal Rights Comm 1969; r/Prot; hon/Fellow, Tropical Med in Ctl Am 1969; Pres Rocky Mtn Conf of Parasitols 1975-76.

BABETTE, ANITA oc/Commercial Photographer; Company President; b/Aug 27, 1939; ba/3614 SW Third Ave, Miami, FL 33145; ed/Cert in Photography, Centro Superior de Artes Aplicadas 1961 Mexico City; BA 1962, MA Studies 1965 Wayne St Univ; Addit Studies Univ of Miami 1967-76; pa/Pres, Ad/Photographics Inc 1971-; Photog of Mag

Covers & Feature Articles; Contb'g Writer/Illustrator to Profl Jours; cp/Mem: Nat Assn of Wom Bus Owners, Wayne St Univ Alumni Assn, Fla Profl Photogs, SEn Profl Photogs Assn, Profl Photogs of Am, Intl Ctr of Photography, Others; hon/Cert of Merit, Salon of Photography, Fla Profl Photogs 1967, 69; Winner of *Industrial Photography* Mag "Why didn't I think of that?" Competition 1979.

BACCIGALUPPI, ROGER JOHN oc/- President, Chief Executive Officer; b/Mar 17, 1934; ba/PO Box 1768, Sacramento, CA 95808; c/John, Elisabeth, Andrea; p/Harry and Ethel Hutcheon Baccigaluppi, Burlingame, CA; ed/BS Univ of Cal-Berkeley 1956; MS Columbia Univ Grad Sch of Bus 1957; mil/AUS Active Duty 1957; pa/Pres & Chief Exec Ofcr; Dir: Nat Coun of Farmer Coop, Agri Coun of Cal; Mem Almond Bd of Cal; Arbitration Panel, Dried Fruit Assn; cp/Dir, Mercy Hosp Foun; Adv Bd, Nat Alliance of Bus-men; Dir, U Way of Sacramento; r/Prot.

BACHER, ROSALIE WRIDE oc/Vice Principal; b/May 25, 1925; h/265 Rocky Point Rd, Palos Verdes Estates, CA 90274; ba/Long Beach, CA; m/Archie O Jr; p/Homer Martin Wride, Palos Verdes Estates, CA; ed/AB, MA Occidental Col; pa/V-Prin, Jefferson Jr HS; Chapt Pres, Delta Kappa Gamma: Area Dir, St of Cal; Profl Affairs Chm; Pi Lambda Theta: Chapt Pres, So Cal Coun VP; Phi Delta Gamma: Pres Omicron Chapt, Univ of So Cal;

Phi Delta Kappa: Secy Long Beach Chapt; cp/AAUW; r/1st Ch of Christ, Scientist, Palos Verdes Estates; hon/Phi Beta Kappa.

BACHMAN, JERALD GRAYBILL oc/- Program Director; Research Scientist; b/Oct 20, 1936; h/2124 Stephen Terrace, Ann Arbor, MI 48103; ba/Ann Arbor; m/Virginia Arlene Ludy; c/Terri Lynne, Steven J, Jon Andrew; p/J Clarence and Harriett Mathias Bachman; ed/AB; MA; PhD; pa/Prog Dir, Res Scist: Survey Res Ctr, Inst for Social Res, Univ of Mich; Mem: Soc for the Psychological Study of Social Issues, Inter-Univ Sem on Armed Forces & Soc, Am Psychol Assn, AAAS, Soc of Sigma Xi; cp/Dir, VP, Property Owner's Assn; Dem Precnt Deleg; hon/Nat Sci Foun Fellow 1959, 60, 62; Num Res Grants from Founs & Govt Agies.

BACHMAN, LEONARD oc/Secretary, Pennsylvania Department of Health; b/May 20, 1925; h/2404 Bellevue Rd, Harrisburg, PA 17104; ba/Harrisburg; m/Sarah Jaffe; c/Emily, Joseph, Daniel, Jacob; ed/BS 1946 Franklin and Marshall Col; MD 1949 Univ of Md; mil/USNR AS/V-12 1943-46; USNR Lt/jg to Lt MC 1950-52; pa/Secy of Hlth, Commonwealth of Penna; Lectr of Anesthesia, Univ of Penna Sch of Med 1972-; Conslt in Anesthesia, VA Hosp, Philadelphia 1961-; Mem: AMA, Balto City Med Soc, Am Soc Anesthesiols, Penna Soc of Anesthesiols, Philadelphia Soc of Anesthesiols, Sigma Xi, NY Acad of Sci, Physiological Soc of Philadelphia, Others; cp/Ser'd on Proj Hope, Tunisia 1970; Dem Cand for US Cong, Del Co 1964; Bd Mem, Ctl Philadelphia Reform Dems 1967-; Mem Urban Coalition of Philadelphia; Chm, Gov's Hlth Care Task Force 1971-; Others; hon/Hon DHLs: Penna Col of Podiatric Med 1975, Hahnemann Med Col 1977; Hon DSci, Penna Col of Optometry 1977; Hon Visiting Prof of Anesthesia, Einstein Col of Med 1970; Others.

BACKSTROM, MARTHA CAROLYN MURPHREE oc/Retired Educational Administrator; b/Aug 20, 1916; h/2606 North Ridge Dr, Gautier, MS 39553; m/James Walton (dec); c/James Walton II; p/Stanley Thomas and June Elizabeth Byars Murphree; ed/BA cum laude Miss St Col for Wom (Renamed Miss Univ for Wom); pa/Ret'd; Former Sec'dy Sch Tchr, Green Co, Miss; Former Ednl Admr, Prog Coor, Green Co Sch Dist; cp/DAR; Colonial Dames XVII Century; Descs of the Mayflower Soc; r/Meth; hon/Editor: *The Ephemera*; Dist Rep, MSCW Alumnae; VP So Area, MUW Foun; 2000 Wom of Achmt; DIB; 500 1st Fams of Am; Hereditary Register of USA; Intl Scholars Dir; W/W: Am Wom, S&SW; Others.

BACKUS, CHARLES EDWARD oc/- Professor of Engineering; b/Sept 17, 1937; h/29 W Southern Ave, Mesa, AZ 85202; ba/Tempe, AZ; m/Judith Ann Clouston; c/Elizabeth, Amy, David Anthony; p/Clyde Harvey and Opal Daisy Backus, Mayer, AZ; ed/BSME 1959 Ohio Univ; MS 1961, PhD 1965 Univ of Ariz; pa/Ariz St Univ: Asst Prof of Engrg 1968-71, Assoc Prof of Engrg 1971-76, Prof of Engrg 1976-; Conslt Num Cos; Mem: AAAS, Am Nuclear Soc, Am Soc for Engrg Ed, Am Soc of Mech Engrs, IEEE, Intl Solar Energy Soc, Ariz Solar Energy Assn, Pi Mu Epsilon, Sigma Xi, Tau Beta Pi; Num Coms; Lectr; Res; Author Num Articles in

Profl Jours; cp/Frequent Spkr at Civic Functions; Commr, Ariz Solar Res Comm; r/1st U Meth Ch; hon/ASU Fac Achmt Awd 1976; W/W in West.

BADEER, HENRY SARKIS oc/University Professor; b/Jan 31, 1915; h/2808 South 99th Ave, Omaha, NE 68124; ba/Omaha, NE; m/Mariam Kassarjian; c/Gilbert Henry, Daniel Henry; p/Sarkis Badeer (dec); Persape Koundakjian (dec); ed/MD 1938 Am Univ of Beirut, Lebanon; pa/Prof of Physiology, Creighton Univ Sch of Med; Pubs in Profl Jours; cp/Ser'd on Coms of Ch, Choral Soc & Sanatorium in Beirut; Res Com, Nebr Heart Assn; r/Prot; hon/Rockefeller F'ship 1948-49; Student Am Med Assn Golden Apple Awd 1975.

BADGER, DANIEL DELANO oc/- University Professor; b/Apr 13, 1933; h/601 North Skyline Lane, Stillwater, OK 74074; ba/Stillwater; m/Betty Jo; c/Daniel D Jr, Samuel C, Jane E, David A; p/Daniel J and Grace D Badger, Birds Nest, VA; ed/BS w Hons 1954 Va Polytech Inst; MS w Hons 1958

Okla St Univ; PhD 1964 Mich St Univ; mil/USAR LtC, 2 Yrs Active Duty Germany; pa/Prof, Dept of Agri Ecs, Okla St Univ; Mem: Am Agri Ecs Assn, So Agri Ecs Assn; cp/Chm, Parks & Recreation Adv Bd, City of Stillwater 1972-77; r/Bapt; hon/Phi Kappa Phi; Alpha Zeta; Num Dist'd Ser Awds.

BADIK, ELEANOR ROSE oc/Artist; b/Oct 26; h/3685 E Sunset Blvd, Las Vegas, NV 89120; ba/Las Vegas; m/Michael (dec); c/Jamara, Michael; p/Henry (dec); Rose, New York, NY; pa/Pres, Las Vegas Art Leag 1967-68; Pres, Gallery Guild, Univ of Las Vegas 1969-70; cp/Pres, Nat Leag Am Pen Wom, Las Vegas Branch 1976-78; r/Cath; hon/Num Awds in Art incl'g: Nat Leag Am Pen Woms Art Show, Las Vegas 1975, Nat Leag Am Pen Wom Bicent Exhbn 1976: 1st Place Etching, Nat Leag Am Pen Woms Art Show, Las Vegas Art Mus 1976, 1st Place Oil, Las Vegas Art Mus Juried Am Mothers Show 1977, 78, 1st Place Oil, 1st Place Print.

BAEBLER, ARTHUR GEORGE oc/- Executive Vice President; b/1932; h/20 Fox Meadows, St Louis, MO 63127; ba/St Louis; m/Ivalea; c/Matthew, Andrew; p/Arthur P and Clara Henke Baebler, St Louis, MO; ed/BSME; MBA; pa/Exec VP, St Louis Regional Commerce & Growth Assn; Bd Dirs: Amtron Corp, 1st Mo Fin, RCGA Ser Corp; r/Rom Cath.

BAER, CHARLES GORDON oc/Public

Relations; b/Dec 21, 1955; h/3801 Forest Lane NE, Knoxville, TN; ba/Knoxville; p/Charles Arnold Baer, Decatur, TN; Bobbie H Baer, Knoxville, TN; ed/BA Polit Sci Univ of Tenn-Knoxville; pa/Dir, Lavidge & Assocs, Public Relats; Assoc, Am Enterprise Inst of Public Policy Res; cp/Secy, Knox Co Elect Comm; Chm, Fountain City Town Hall Inc; r/Meth; hon/2nd Place, Frank McClung Meml Spch Contest 1975.

BAER, MAX FRANK oc/Management Consultant; b/Nov 10, 1912; h/4201 Cathedral Ave NW, Washington, DC 20016; ba/Washington; m/Gertrude; c/(Stepchd:) Richard Rosenbaum, Randye Low; p/Bernard and Erna Baer (dec); ed/LLB; MA; EdD; JD; pa/Self-employed Mgmt Conslt; Past Pres, Nat Vocl Guid Assn; VChm Coun of Nat Orgs on Chd & Yth; r/Jewish, Life Mem Bd Mgrs, Adas Israel Cong, Wash; hon/Dist'd AZA Alumnus Awd 1974; Max F Baer Cult Ctr, Ossifiya, Israel; Gold Medal for Highest Hons in Hist 1930.

BAER, NORBERT SEBASTIAN oc/-Co-Chairman, Conservation Center; b/Jun 6, 1938; h/194 Ascan Ave, Forest Hills, NY 11375; ba/New York, NY; m/Janet De Pold; c/Diana M, Norbert S Jr; p/William F and Maria Baer, Brooklyn, NY; ed/BSc; MSc; PhD; pa/NY Univ Inst of Fine Arts Conservation Ctr: Instr 1969, Asst Prof 1970, Assoc Prof 1975, Co-Chm 1975; Editorial Advr & Assoc Editor: *Studies in Conservation*

1971-; Mem Conservation Com, Nat Endowmt for the Arts 1976, 77; Chm, Ad Hoc Visiting Com, Conservation Analytical Lab, Smithsonian Inst 1977-; Mem: Am Chem Soc, Instrumt Soc of Am, Sigma Xi; Fellow: Am Inst of Chems, Am Inst for Conserv, Intl Inst for Conserv; Lectr; Author Num Articles in Profl Jours; r/Prot; hon/Commun Ldrs & Noteworthy Ams; DIB; W/W in East.

BAERTSCHI, WALTER oc/Clergyman; b/Feb 1, 1926; h/714 Benedict St, Chillicothe, IL 61523; ba/Chillicothe; m/Frances E; c/Carol Eikum, Paul, Steven; p/Emil and Martha Baertschi (dec); ed/AB Theol Gordon Col; BD Luth Sem; STM Pastoral Cnslg Luth Sch of Theol; Cont'g Prog of Pastoral Ed; pa/Since Ordination, actively ser'd in Parish Ministry: Amery, Wis, Portland, Maine, Pittsburgh, Chicago; Currently at St Mark, Chillicothe; r/Luth Branch of Christian Ch.

BAERWALD, JOHN E oc/Director, Highway Traffic Safety Center; Professor; b/Nov 2, 1925; h/1421 Mayfair, Champaign, IL 61820; ba/Urbana, IL; ed/BSCE; MSCE; PhD; pa/Dir, Highway Traffic Safety Ctr; Prof of Transportation & Traffic Engrg; Conslt'g Traffic Engr; Bd Dirs Nat Safety Coun; Transportation Res Bd, Am Rd & Transportation Bldr's Assn; cp/Chm of C-U Mass Transit Dist; Ill Transportation Study Comm, Tech Adv Com; hon/Ill Secy of St's Public Ser Awd 1976.

BAFALIS, LOUIS ARTHUR "SKIP" oc/-Member, United States House of Representatives; b/Sept 28, 1929; h/7150 Estero Bldv, Fort Myers Beach, FL 33931; ba/Washington, DC; m/Mary Elizabeth Lund; c/Renee Louise, Gregory Louis; p/Louis

J and Vesta Bafalis; ed/BA St Anselms Col; mil/AUS Korean War to Rank of Capt; cp/Elected to 93rd Cong, 1972, Re-elected to each succeeding Cong; House Ways & Means Com & its Sub-Coms on Public Assistance & Unemploymt Compensation & Oversight; Active Conservationist; Fiscal Conservative; Red Cross; Lions Clb; JCs; Muscular Dystrophy Assn; r/1st Christian Ch; hon/Recog'd by: Nat Assoc'd Bus-men Inc, Am Fedn of Small Bus, Nat Fedn of Indep Bus, Others; 2-times Winner of "Watchdog of the Treasury" Awd, Nat Assoc'd Bus-men Inc; "Guardian of Small Bus" Statuette, Nat Fedn of Indep Bus; Cited by GOP colleages as "The Outstg Freshman in Fiscal Affairs"; Alumni Awd of Merit, St Anselms' Col.

BAGBY, MARVIN ORVILLE oc/-Chemist; b/Sept 27, 1932; h/209 S Louisiana, Morton, IL 61550; ba/Peoria, IL; m/Jean; c/Gary Lee, Gordon Eugene; p/Byron O Bagby (dec); Geneva F Bagby, Quincy, IL; ed/BS 1957; MS 1957; mil/AUS 1953-55; pa/Assoc Chem 1959; Chem 1960; Res Chem 1963; Sr Res Chem 1967;

Proj Ldr 1970; Res Ldr 1974; Tech Advr, Technologies for Fiber Use 1974-; cp/Former Mem Morton JCs; Former Mem AOCS; Mem: TAPPI, ACS, AAAS; Spec Assignmts, 1977 Joint Wkshop ACS/NRC, Cairo, Egypt; r/Morton U Meth Ch; hon/Perf Awd; AOCS Bond Awd; Hon Mention 1965.

BAGCHI, PRANAB oc/Research Chemist; b/Jan 14, 1946; h/3 Huntsman Way, Webster, NY 14580; ba/Rochester, NY; p/Phanin Dranath Bagchi (dec); Gita Bagchi, Calcutta, IN; ed/BSc Chem w Hons; PhD

Physical Chem; pa/Res Chem, Photographic Scist: Eastman Kodac Co; Mem Am Chem Soc; Fellow Chem Soc of London; hon/Am Chem Soc Petroleum Res Fund Fellow 1965-69; Nat Sci Foun Trainee 1969-70.

BAGGETT, AGNES oc/Secretary of State; h/3202 Montezuma Rd, Montgomery, AL 36106; ba/Montgomery; m/George Lamar (dec); p/John R and Leila Thomason Beahn (dec); cp/St of Ala: Elected Secy of St w/out run-off 1950, Elected St Auditor w/out opposition 1954, Elected St Treas 1958, Elected Secy of St 1962, Elected St Treas 1966, Re-elected 1970, Elected Secy of St carried every Co 1974; Sers on Bds: St Bd of Adjustmt, Healing Arts Bd, St Canvassing Bd, St Records Bd; 2-times Pres, Montgomery B&PW Clb; Mem: Ala Fedn of B&PW Clb, Am Legion Aux, 8 & 40 Salon, OES; r/Meth, Past SS Supt; hon/Named Career Wom & 1 of top 10 Wom in Montgomery 1963; DIB; W/W: Govt, Am Wom, S&SW, Am, US, Am Polits; World W/W of Wom.

BAGGETT, JIMMY D oc/Engineer; b/Jan 11, 1935; h/1114 Sproles Dr, Ft Worth, TX 76126; ba/Ft Worth; m/Glenda; c/Carolyn, Cathy; p/Frank B and Martha L Baggett, Ft Worth, TX; ed/MArch Equivalent; mil/Grad, Cmd & Gen Staff Col, Industl Col of Armed Forces; pa/Mem: Soc of Profl Engrs, US Comm, Intl Comm on Lge Dams, Soc of Am Mil Engrs; cp/Dallas-Ft Worth Fed Exec Bd; Fed Bus Assn; Metroplex Recreation Coun; NIRA; r/Bapt; hon/Certs of Achmt, SWn Divs Corps of Engrs; Fed Bus Assn; W/W: Tex, S&SW.

BAHILL, S LARRY oc/State Representative; Educator; b/Dec 10, 1943; h/3010 E 30th St, Tucson, AZ 85713; ba/Phoenix, AZ; m/Carol; c/Nathaniel; p/Stephen and Tracey W Bahill, Tucson, AZ; ed/BS 1969 No Ariz Univ; MEd 1970, 76 Univ of Ariz; mil/USNR 17 Yrs, Enlisted 11 Yrs, Ofcr (Lt) 6 Yrs; pa/Co Hlth Edr; Substitute Tchr; cp/St Rep, House Dem Ldr; Am Legion; K of C; Frat Order of Police Assocs; r/Cath; hon/Legislator of Yr 1977.

BAHM, ARCHIE J(OHN) oc/Professor Emeritus; b/Aug 21, 1907; h/1915 Las Lomas Rd NE, Albuquerque, NM 87106; ba/Albuquerque; m/Luna Parks Bachelor; c/Raymond John, Elaine Lucia; p/John Samuel and Lena Mary Augusta Kohn Bahm (dec); ed/AB Albion Col; MA, PhD Univ of Mich; pa/Prof of Phil Emeritus, Univ of New Mex; Mem Am Philosophical Assn Com on Intl Coop & its Secy for Asian Affairs; Author: *Interdependence, The Specialist, Comparative Philosophy, Ethics as as Behavioral Science, Metaphysics, An Introduction,* Num Others; r/Humanist; hon/Phi Beta Kappa; Phi Kappa Phi; Fulbright Res Scholar in Buddhist Philosophy, Burma; Fulbright Res Scholar in Indian Philosophy, India.

BAHR, GEORGE RICHARD oc/College Administrator; b/Mar 14, 1936; h/3725 48 Court, Meridian, MS 39301; ba/Meridian; p/George W Bahr, Cassopolis, MI; ed/BS; MS; EdD; mil/USMC 2nd VSAR Inactive, Capt; pa/Admr, Miss Col; Chperson, Profl Growth Com of Profl Devel Task Force, Miss

Pers Guid Assn; Mem Vol Task Force, Experimt in Intl Living; Mem: APGA, Am Col Pers Assn, Miss Pers & Guid Assn, Miss Public Jr Col Deans of Student Assn, Others; cp/Bd Dirs, Miss Mtl Hlth Assn; Mem: Lauderdale Mtl Hlth Assn, Adv Bd, Weems Mtl Hlth Ctr; r/1st Bapt Ch, Meridian; hon/Cnslr of Yr, Col Level 1978, Miss Pers Guid Assn.

BAHR, JEROME F oc/Writer; b/Oct 26, 1909; h/800 Hillcrest Dr, Santa Fe, NM 87501; p/(dec); ed/Univ of Minnesota; mil/USAF Major; pa/Speech Writer for 2 Presidents, USA & Others; Pub'd Author: *Holes in the Wall, The Lonely Scroundrel, The Linen Suit and Other Stories,* Num Others.

BAHR, LAUREN S oc/Senior Editor; b/Jul 3, 1944; h/444 E 82 St, Apt 8A, NY, NY 10028; ba/NY, NY; m/Jesse R Smith; p/Simon A Bahr (dec); Rosalind J Miller, Highland Park, NJ; ed/BA; MA; pa/Nat Bus Ed Assn; r/Jewish; hon/Mortarboard.

BAIKMAN, NELL T oc/Registered Nurse; b/Aug 27, 1914; h/3906 Lake View Rd, Little Rock, AR 72116; ba/Little Rock, AR; m/A F; c/Elizabeth B House, Robert A; p/Charles R and Cora Whiteside Teeter (dec); ed/BA; BSN; pa/ANA; ASNA; NLN; ALN; Ark Lung Assn; Psychiatric Nurse Educator; Every Child Immunization Prog; Others; hon/ASNA Hall of Fame; ASNA Nurse of Yr; ALN Merit Awd; Cit Medical Center & PN Assn.

BAILES, TRESSIE NONA oc/Retired Teacher; b/Aug 10, 1899; h/Rt 3, Box 121, Clay, WV 25043; p/Albert R and Martha J Bailes (dec); pa/Writer, Poetry; Tchr, 41 Terms, Elementary & HS; Writer for 2 Local Papers; Mem, IPA, DKG, Intl Soc WV Poetry Soc, KDP, Clover Poetry Soc Intl; r/Bapt; hon/World's W/W of Wom; Personalities of S; Pub'd Poetry in *New Voices in America Poetry*, *Clover Collections of Verse*, Others.

BAILEY, ARTHUR oc/Social Security Administration; h/Los Angeles, CA; ba/3375 S Hoover, Suite A, Los Angeles, CA 90007; p/William Henry Bailey and Winifred Towers (dec); ed/Att'd Carnegie Inst of Technology, Pittsburgh, Pa; Pittsburgh Acad, Pittsburgh, Pa; mil/USAF 1945-46; pa/Downtown Chorale, Pgh, Pa 1948-56; Profl Chorus; Pittsburgh Playhouse, Pgh, Pa 1958-59, Actor; cp/Black Porsche, Inc, Los Angeles, Ca, Dir of Public Relations 1976-; Prepare Weekly New

Releases Printed in Num Papers; Social Security Rep: Coordinated Social Services Interagency (Los Angeles, Cal), S Central Com on Aging (LA, Cal); Avalon-Central Area Planning Coun (LA, Cal), Others; Bd Mem, Junipero Sierra Lib Coun (LA, Cal), S Central Com on Aging (LA, Cal); hon/Outstg Performance Awd, Social Security Adm, Huntington Park, Cal 1976; Superior Performance Awd, US Corps of Engrg, LA, Cal 1960-61.

BAILEY, CHARLES WILLIAMS III oc/-Real Estate Executive; b/Jul 26, 1925; h/701 S Mashta Dr, Key Biscayne, FL 33149; ba/-Miami, FL; m/Dorothea L; c/Elizabeth M, Susan M, Charles Williams IV; p/Charles

Williams II and Katherine Ford Bailey, Spartanburg, SC; ed/BSEE; MS Electrical Tng; mil/AUS 1944-46; pa/Real Estate Investment, Devel, Mgmt, Brokerage; r/Prot; hon/W/W in S&SW.

BAILEY, ELIZABETH ELLERY oc/Mem,

Civil Aeronautics Board; b/Nov 26, 1938; h/4601 N Park Ave, Apt 1811, Chevy Chase, MD 20015; ba/Wash DC; m/James L; c/James L Jr, William E; p/Irving W Raymond (dec); Henrietta D Raymond, York Harbor, ME; ed/BA magna cum laude, Ecs; MS Maths; PhD Ecs; pa/Bd Editors, Am Ec Review, En Ec Assn; cp/Active in Schs for Child w Lng Disabilities; hon/Program Design Trainee Awd, Bell Labs; Doctoral Support Awd, Bell Labs.

BAILEY, EXINE MARGARET ANDERSON oc/Professor; Singer; b/Jan 4, 1922; h/17 Westbrook Way, Eugene, OR 97405; ba/Eugene; m/Arthur Albert; p/Joseph and Exine Anderson, Marshall, MN; ed/BS Univ Minn 1944; MA 1945, Profl Dipl 1951

Columbia Univ; pa/Prof Univ Oreg; Adm Positions; Profl Sing'g Perfs; Conductor Master Classes; Profl Orgs; cp/Lobbyist St Bd Higher Ed; Spkr to Legs & Communs; r/Prot; hon/Metro Opera S'ship; NY Sing'g Tchrs Awd; NYC Awd, Music Fdn.

BAILEY, HARRY HUDSON oc/Professor of Soil Science; b/Jan 22, 1921; h/501 Ridge Road, Lexington, KY 40506; ba/Lexington, KY; m/Ethyl C; c/Linda, Lee, Ruth; p/Bertie E Bailey (dec); Annie Lou Bailey, VA; ed/BS Va Tech 1942; MS 1949; PhD Michigan St 1956; mil/USAR, Retired Col; pa/Clay Minerals Soc; Soil Cons Soc Am; Am Soc Agronomy; Intl Soc Soil Sci; Soil Sci Soc Am; cp/Big Brothers/Big Sisters of Am; r/Bapt; hon/Certified Profl Soil Scientist 1978; Meritorious Ser Medal, AUS 1973; Great Tchr Awd 1969; Master Tchr Awd 1976.

BAILEY, HENRY JOHN III oc/Law Professor, Writer on Legal Subjects, Attorney; b/Apr 4, 1916; h/4156 Riverdale Rd, S, Salem, OR 97302; ba/Salem, OR; m/Marjorie Ebner; c/George W, Christopher G, Barbara W, Timothy P; p/Henry John and Lenore F Cahoon (dec); ed/BA Penn St, JD Yale; mil/AAF, WW II; USAFR, Retired Lt/Col; pa/Admitted to NY, Mass, Oregon, Am Bar Assn; Mem Unif Co Code Com of Corp Bank & Bus Law Section; Am Law Inst, Mem Editorial Bd, *The Practical Lawyer*; r/Cath; hon/Lecturer at Num Bar & Bus Group Meetings; Num Writings incl'g: *The Law of Bank Checks*, *Secured Transactions in a Nutshell*, *Bank Deposits and Collections*, Others.

BAILEY, JAMES L oc/Reading Department Head and Teacher (Remedial Reading); b/Jul 14, 1930; h/8517 Rolling Green Way, Fair Oaks, CA 95628; ba/North Highlands, CA; m/Ellen Jo; c/William, Patrick, Hope; p/Benjamen R Bailey (dec); Alpha Hill Bailey, Costa Mesa, CA; ed/MA, BA, Life Credentials (Elem, Sec'dy, Commun Col); pa/Dist Curriculum Com, Parents Adv Com; cp/Former Greentree Townhouse Bd Dir 1974-75; Grant Dist Bld Pres 1975; Robla PTA Pres 1970; Tierra del Oro Girl Scout Coun Site Chm 1964-77; r/Prot; hon/Outstg Ldrs in Elem & Sec'dy Schs 1976; Awd of Merit in Ed Am Assn for Excellence in Ed 1972; Title 1 Pilot Proj Intermediate Reading & Math Specialist Robla Sch Dist 1970-71.

BAILEY, LEO LYNN SR oc/Professor; b/Jan 17, 1922; h/431 W Kingsville, TX 78363; ba/Tex A&I Univ, TX; m/Lou Tudor; c/Lynn, Judy, Nora, Billy; p/L M Bailey and

Nora Stevens (dec); ed/BS, MA, PhD; mil/European Theater, WW II, Infantry Unit CO; pa/Phi Delta Kappa; Alpha Tau Alpha; cp/Past Gov, Dist 593, Rotary Intl; r/Meth; hon/Author, *Guide to Landscaping and Gardening*.

BAILEY, ROBERT EDSON oc/College Professor & Clergyman, United Presbyterian Church; b/Dec 7, 1927; h/904 Main St, Parkville, MO 64152; m/Annell Deanne; c/Robert Jr, Steven D, Scott T, Brian M, Sharon Elizabeth, Karen Lynn, Cherlyn Deanne; p/Edson Albert and Josephine Turner Bailey (dec); ed/BA Grove City Col 1950; BD

1953, MDiv 1972 Theol Sem of Univ of Dubuque; PhD Univ of Edinburg 1962; pa/Prof, Park Col 1965-; Univ of Dubuque 1956-65; Lecturer, St Paul Sch of Theology 1966-67, 1968-69; cp/Num Activities; Project Equality, Bd of Directors; r/U Presb (Ordained Clergyman); hon/Nom Various Prof Assn (AAR, SBL); W/W; DIB; Dir of Am Scholars; Num Others.

BAILY, NATHAN A oc/Senior Staff Vice-President Education, Mortgage Bankers Association of America; b/Jul 19, 1920; h/5516 Greystone St, Chevy Chase, MD 20015; ba/Wash DC; m/Judith; c/Alan Eric, Lawrence Joel; p/Sayl and Eleanor Baily (dec); ed/BS; MA; PhD; pa/Corporate Dir; Seminar Leader; Author; Lecturer; r/Jewish; hon/Phi Beta Kappa; Fellow, Am Inst of Banking Society for Religious Org Mgmt; Pell Gold Medal Dist'd Salesman's Awd; Num Others.

BAIN, EMILY JOHNSTON oc/Artist; Educator; b/Jul 28, 1911; h/834 Valley View Dr, Grand Prairie, TX 75050; ba/Prairie, TX; m/Robert E Zeigler (dec); 2nd Alonzo W Bain (dec); c/Nora Ann Zeigler, Emily Carolyn Bain; p/Daniel Roger and Necy Ann Hicks Johnston (dec); ed/MA Tulane Univ 1961; MA La St Univ 1940; BA NWn St Univ 1931; Addit

Studies; pa/Exhibit Art Works, Paintings, Art Tchr; cp/Adv Bd of Am Security Coun; Mem Wom's Clb of Grand Prairie, Tec; Delta Kappa Gamma; r/Prot: Christian; hon/Fellow La St Univ, Baton Rouge, La in Art Paintings Exhibited Lynn Kottler Galleries, NYC 1977; Invited by Other Galleries; Served as State Supervisor of Art for St Dept of Ed in La 1948-49.

BAINUM, PETER M oc/University Professor, Administrator; b/Feb 4, 1938; h/2400 Queens Chapel Rd, Hyattsville, MD

20782; ba/Washington, DC; m/Carmen Cecilia Perez; c/David Peter; p/Charles Bainum, Scottsdale, AZ; Mildred Salyer, St Petersburg, FL; ed/BS Texas A&M 1959; SM MIT 1960; PhD Cath Univ of Am 1967; pa/Howard Univ: Prof Aerospace Engrg 1973, Dir Grad Studies 1974; Conslt: John Hopkins Univ (Applied Physics Lab) 1969-72; WHF & Assoc Inc 1977; VP Pubs Am Astronautical Soc; AIAA: Assoc Fellow, Commun Action Com 1976-77, Astrodynamics Tech Com; Fellow Brit Interplanetary Soc; hon/Tau Beta Pi; Sigma Gamma Tau; Phi Kappa Phi; Phi Eta Sigma; Howard Univ Grad Sch Awd Exemplary Res 1976; Soc Auto Engr Teetor Awd (for Engr Edr) 1971; NASA/ASEE Sum Fac F'ship 1970-71.

BAIR, BARBARA oc/University Professor; b/Dec 28, 1924; h/1602 Pebble Dr, Greensboro, NC 27410; ba/Same; m/Donald; c/Stephen, Philip; p/Erwin and Lillian Cox Breithaupt (dec); ed/BMus; MMus; pa/Univ NC-Greensboro Current Assoc Prof Music Ed; Conslt: Early Childhood Assn, Forsyth Co, NC 1975; Asheville City Sch Staff Devel Wkshop, Asheville, NC 1975; NC Sch Sys for In-Ser Wkshop, Winston-Salem, NC 1977; NC Assn for The Ed of Young Chd 1978; Wake Co Sch for Devel Curric Guide in Music Middle Schs, Raleigh, NC 1977-78; Choral & Vocal & Ensemble Contests, Peace & Lenoir-Rhyne Col, NC 1976; Other Profl Assns; r/Prot; hon/W/W S&SW.

BAIRD, JAMES CATCHINGS JR oc/Legal Advisor; b/Sept 12, 1904; h/Running Knob Hollow Rd, Sewanee, TN 37375; ba/Same; m/Mary Louise; c/Anne B Chatoney (Mrs B J Jr), James III, Henry; p/James and Mary Long Baird (dec); ed/BS, LLD; mil/AUS Mil Intell WW-II, Capt; pa/Current Legal Advisor, Karatana Inc; Ch Cnslt; Admr; Fund-Raising Activs; cp/Civic Clb; EQB; r/Epis; hon/Phi Delta Phi; Dist'd Ser Awd (Fgn Awd), Dept of St 1954-63; W/W Am.

BAIRD, MAURA L oc/Writer; Editor; b/Jul 23, 1921; h/PO Box 415, Santa Cruz, CA 95061; ba/Santa Cruz; m/Thomas (dec); c/Lisa B Evans; p/Francis and Louisa Fensch

(dec); ed/BA Univ Cal-B; pa/Pub'd Author: Articles, Poems, Travel Column, Novel, Short Stories; cp/DAR; Fdg Pres Humane Soc Napa Co Inc; Other Humane Socs; r/Cath; hon/Phi Beta Kappa.

BAIS, DALJIT S oc/Consulting Engineer; h/987 New Dover Rd, Edison, NJ 08817; ba/New York, NY; m/Pammi; c/Monica, Rajeev Kumar; p/Thakur Kanwar Singh (dec); Daropadi Devi Bais, Edison, NJ; ed/BSc; MSc; MBA; pa/Profl Engr: NY, NJ; Am Soc Civil Engrs; Nat Soc Profl Engrs; NJ St Soc Profl Engrs; AIA: Chm Employmt & Relocation Com Engrg Coun 1975-76, CoChm Travel Coun 1976-77; cp/Former Treas Nat Exec Com; Pres Soc for Ednl, Cult & Tech Asst; Chm: Indian Ams for Public Affairs, Planning & Design Com of U Hindu Temple of NJ; r/Hindu; hon/Biogl Listings.

BAKER, BARTON oc/Lawyer; Lecturer; b/Jan 9, 1901; h/100 Brookwood Rd, Rochester, NY 14610; ba/Rochester; m/Bernice Dennis; c/Betty B Trost (Mrs Theodore); p/(dec); ed/LLB Cornell Univ;

PhD, DCL cum laude Chicago Law Sch; pa/Admitted to Bar: US Supr Ct & NY Cts; Former Assoc Editor *Cornell Law Review*; Editor: *Universal Scout & Universal Tribune*; Former Asst Law Libn Cornell Univ; cp/Foun Barton Baker Youth Ed Ctr; Var

Activs BSA; Dir Intl Bell Orch; Former Actor w Rochester Commun Players; Pres Cornell Clb; Adv Bd Salvation Army; Past Pres Rochester Intl Friendship Coun; r/U Meth Ch; hon/Awd of Achmt, Intl Assn of Fairs & Expositions; Pub'd Author.

BAKER, BERNICE MAUDE oc/Legal Secretary; Author; Book Reviewer; b/Apr 5, 1901; h/100 Brookwood Rd, Rochester, NY 14610; ba/Rochester; m/Barton; c/Betty B Trost (Mrs Theodore); ed/LLB: Hamilton Law Sch, Univ of Wyo, Cornell Univ; pa/Legal Sect

Barton Baker; Author *With Bells On*; Editor AAUW Mag; Contbr to Var Pubs; cp/DAR; Rochester Fdn Woms Clbs; Salvation Army Aux; Susan B Anthony Repub Clb; En Star; Bd of Vistors NY St Indust & Agri Sch; Other Civic Assns; r/Prot; hon/Civic Ctr Awd; Citizen of Day, Monroe Co Citizens Civic Com; Awd, Susan B Anthony Repub Clb.

BAKER, BETTY LOUISE oc/Educator; b/Oct 17, 1937; h/3214 W 85th St, Chicago, IL 60652; ba/Chgo; p/Russell and Lucille Baker, Chgo, IL; ed/BEd 1961, MA 1964, PhD 1971; pa/Tchr & Chm of Math Dept Hubbard HS; MAA; NCTM; ICTM; SSMA; ASCD; Kappa Delta Pi; Pi Lambda Theta; Chgo Tchrs Union; cp/1/VP & Prog Chperson Hubbard PTSA; r/Hope Luth Ch, Chgo: Organist, SS

Tchr; hon/Univ F'ship NWn Univ 1969-70; PTA S'ship 1960-61; Outstg Sr 1961; Dist'd Ser Awd & Life Mbrship ICPT; Contbr to Var Profl Jours; Biogl Listings.

BAKER, BETTY RUTH oc/Assistant Professor; b/Jul 20, 1937; h/4801 Sanger Apt #39, Waco, TX 76710; ba/Waco; p/Obie Baker (dec); Ruth Andrews Baker, Gilmer, TX; ed/BA 1959, MS 1968 Baylor Univ; Grad Study Tex Woms Univ; pa/Asst Prof Early Childhood Ed Baylor Univ 1971-; Kgn Tchr Gladewater Indep Sch Dist 1959-71; ACEI; NAEYC; Pres WAEYC 1975; EKNE; AAUW; AAUP; So Assn for Chd Under 6; Life Mbrships: TSTA, NEA; Tex Soc Col Tchrs Ed; Delta Delta Delta; cp/Mem Baylor Univ Fac Aths Coun; Mem Baylor Round Table; r/Bapt; hon/Delta Kappa Gamma; Phi Delta Kappa; Contbr *Baylor Edr*; Girl of Yr, Lambda Chi Chapt Beta Sigma Phi 1964.

BAKER, CARL GWIN b/Nov 27, 1920; h/Bauiaatrasse 1, 8702 Zollikon, Switzerland; oc/Physician; Cancer Researcher; m/Catherine Valerie; c/Cathryn, Jeannette; p/Edward Forest (dec); Naomi Taylor, Louisville, KY; ed/AB Univ L'ville 1942; MD Univ L'ville Sch Med 1944; MA, J C Childs Fellow, Univ Cal 1948; mil/USNR; US Public Hlth Ser, Asst Surgeon Gen (RAdm), Ret'd; pa/Med Dir, Intl Cancer Res Org, Ludwig Institut fur Krebsforschung, Zurich, Switzerland 1977-; Alcohol, Drug Abuse, & Mtl Hlth Adm, Interagy Com on Alcoholism & Alcohol Abuse 1976-77; HEW Task Force on Nat Guidelines in Hlth 1976-77; Nat Cancer Inst, Interagy Task Force on Cancer Control 1976-77; Dir Prog Policy Staff, Hlth Resources Adm, DHEW 1975-77; Sr Sci Advr for Prog Coor, Ofc Sci Affairs, Hlth Resources Adm, DHEW 1975; Editor, Cancer Res & Jour of Nat Cancer Inst; Secy, Div Biol Chem, Am Chem Soc; Sci Pubs: Cancer Res, Resolution of Amino Acids, Res Adm; Sev Corp Bd Dirs; Mem US Delegation to Soviet Union on USA-USSR Hlth Agreements 1972; Pvt Conslt, Med Res Adm 1973-75; Dir-at-Large, ACS 1970-73; Dir Nat Cancer Inst 1969-72; Num Com'ships, Num Other Profl Activs; Profl Assns; cp/Schs Com, Montgomery Co, Md; hon/Public Hlth Ser Meritorious Ser Medal; VP 10th Intl Cancer Cong; Res & Med Hon Socs; W/W: Govt, E; Am Men & Women of Sci; Ky Col; Bd Dirs, Am Assn for Cancer Res; Others.

BAKER, CARLETON HAROLD oc/Professor; b/Aug 2, 1930; h/4305 Golf Crest Ct, Tampa, FL 33624; ba/Tampa; m/Sara; c/Elizabeth, Janet; p/Harold Baker (dec); Loretta Baker, Oriskany, NY; ed/BA Syracuse Univ 1952; MA 1954, PhD 1955 Princeton Univ; pa/Prof & Chm Physiol Univ S Fla; Edit Bds: *Jour of Applied Physiol, Am Jour Physiol, Bloodvessels, Circulatory Shock*; Grad Com; Curric Com; Exec Com; Microcirculatory Soc; Other Profl Assns; cp/Bd Dirs Am Heart Assn; hon/Fla Affil Ser Awd 1974 & 1977; Pub'd Author.

BAKER, DANIEL R oc/Executive; b/Mar 19, 1932; h/Craftown, Hwy ba/7310 Craftown Rd, Fairfax Sta, VA 22030; m/June; c/David, Jill; p/Arthur and Kathy Baker, New York City, NY; ed/BA Brooklyn Col 1957; MS Am Univ 1969; mil/AUS Med Corps 1953-55; pa/Pres Baker & Baker Data Assocs; Computer Conslt; Real Est Broker; cp/VP Wash DC Tufts Clb; hon/BSA Eagle Scout.

BAKER, DOROTHY GILLAM oc/Writer; Educator; Speaker; Investigator Research; b/Jun 9, 1906; h/140 W End Ave (29F), New York, NY 10023; m/Melville (dec); p/Albert and Mae Fowler Gillam (dec); ed/BA Hunter Col; MA UCLA; PhD NYU Sch of Ed; mil/USCG Lt (jg) & Lt 1943-45; pa/Author *Transformation Or Catastrophe?* 1978; Lectr Grad Div Hunter Col 1953-60; Asst Prof: CCNY 1957-58, Long Isl Univ 1963-64; Theater Actress & Promotion 1930-40; cp/Promotion Dir & Lectr U China Relief & Other Var Agys; Former Cal St Secy of Am Vets Com; Keynote Spkr: World Citizens Assembly 1977, Fests Intl Coop Coun, SOLAR, People's Assembly & Plow Shares 1978; r/Universal.

BAKER, ELSWORTH FREDRICK oc/Psychiatrist; Medical Orgonomist; b/Feb 5, 1903; h/51 Hance Rd, Fair Haven, NJ 07701; ba/New York, NY; m/Marguerite Mayberry; c/Courtney, Allan, Michael; p/Niles and Ettie Cartwright Baker (dec); ed/MD cum laude Univ Manitoba; pa/Fdr Orgonomic Res Foun 1967; Fdr & Pres Am Col of Orgonomy; Fellow: Am Psychi Assn, Am Col of Orgonomy, Royal Soc of Hlth, AAAS; AMA; Med Coun of Canada; NJ Acad of Sci; Diplomate Am Bd of Psychi & Neurol; Pvt Pract Psychi & Med Orgonomy 1948-; Chief of Woms Ser St Hosp, Marlboro, NJ 1931-48; hon/NJ Tchrs English Awd for *Man In The Trap*; Wilhelm Reich Awd; K Cmdr of Justice of Sovereign Order; K of Malta; Num Biogl Listings.

BAKER, IRA L oc/Professor; h/1913 E 5th St, Greenville, NC 27834; ba/G'ville; p/Joseph Baker, China Grove, NC; Celia Baker (dec); ed/BA Wake Forest; MA Columbia Univ; MSJ Univ Ill; mil/Air Corps Spec Sers WW-II; pa/Prof ECU; Assn for Ed Jour; Soc for Profl Journalists; Sigma Tau Alpha; Former Nat Pres Alpha Phi Gamma; Soc for Col Journalists; Former Editor *The Collegiate Journalist*; Edit Bd *Scholastic Editor & C-JET*; cp/Del St Repub Conv 1958; r/Bapt; hon/Dist'd Newspaper Advrs Awd 1973; Pioneer Awd 1970; Nat Sch Press Assn; Golden Key Awd Columbia Univ Scholastic Press Assn.

BAKER, JAMES HALLEAD oc/Executive; b/Mar 17, 1933; h/645 Startouch Dr, Eugene, OR 97405; ba/Eugene; m/Barbara Jean; c/Gregory, Jeffrey, Angela; p/James and Gladys Baker (dec); ed/BS Univ Oreg 1959; mil/USN 1951-55; pa/Am Soc of Assn Execs; Radio Clb of Am; Oreg Soc of Assn Execs;

Oreg Logging Conf; Toastmasters Intl; Land Mobile Communs Coun; cp/Dist Chm Lane Co Repub Ctl Com; r/Christian: Past Pres Congreg, Bd Mem, SS Tchr; Pres Eugene Chapt of Full Gospel Bus News Assn; CoChm Charismatic Christian Couples; hon/JC of Mo; Univ Oreg Honor Roll.

BAKER, JAMES L JR oc/Aesthetic Plastic Surgeon; b/May 4, 1936; h/1216 Buckwood Dr, Orlando, FL 32806; ba/Winter Park, FL; m/Wiesje; c/Cynthia, Dana; p/James Sr and Dorothy Baker, Orlando, FL; ed/BS; MD; pa/Pvt Pract Aesthetic Surg 1971-; Hosp Staff Appts: Fla Hosp, Winter Park Meml Hosp, Chief Holiday Hosp, Other Profl Positions; Intl Soc Aesthetic Plastic Surg; Intl Acad Cosmetic Surg; Am Soc of Plastic & Reconstructive Surgs; Am Med Assn; Netherlands Am Med Assn; Cand Auditor Exec Com of Am Com of Am Soc of Aesthetic Plastic Surg 1977; Other Profl Assns; cp/Rotary Intl; Other Var Clbs; r/Prot; hon/Recipient F'ships; Beta Beta Beta; Clin Res Investigator Awd.

BAKER, JOHN STEVENSON oc/Author; b/Jun 18, 1931; ba/PO Box 16007, Minneapolis, MN 55416; p/Everette B and Ione M Baker; ed/BA cum laude Pomona Col, Claremont Cols 1953; Univ Cal Med Sch 1957; pa/Nu Sigma Nu; Pub'd Poems; Fiction: The Diary of Sesso-Vesucci, *Trace*; Mister Carcoleotes, *The Human Voice Qtrly*; Articles: Comml Sources for Hart Crane's *The River*, *Wis Studies In Contemp Lit*; Brief on Hart Crane & The Artists of Tech, *Trace*;

LeRoi Jones, Secessionist, and Ambiguous Collecting, Criteria for 1st Printings of LeRoi Jones, *The Yale Univ Lib Gazette*; Miscellaneous: Review of The Shape Of Content, Design Qtrly, Cliches, *Trace*, Psych, *The Jour Of Aesthetics & Art Crit*; Dir Exhbn & Author Catalog for Exhbn, Mpls Inst of Arts; Coauthor: "Electro'grams During Hypoxia In Healthy Men," "Electro'grams During Hypercapnia" Pub'd in *Archives Of Neurology*; "A Stat Analysis of 1 Yr of EEG in an Active 226 Bed Gen Hosp" and "AN EEG Analysis of 99 Hd Injuries in a 226 Bed Gen Hosp" Abstracts of Papers *Electroencephalography And Clin Neurophysiology*; hon/1st Prize, Jennings Eng Prize 1950, Pomona Col, Claremont Cols; Dist'd Ser Awd 1976, Minn St Hort Soc; Donations: Brahms Recordings to Bennington Col, Wild Plants to Minn Landscape Arboretum, Num Others.

BAKER, JUSTINE CLARA oc/Teacher; Student; b/Oct 1, 1939; h/816 Eaton Rd, Drexel Hill, PA 19026; ba/Phila, PA; m/Harold; p/Michael and Edna (Stepmother) Boni, Aldan, PA; Justine DeFlavia Boni (dec); ed/BA Immaculata Col 1963; MATM Villanova Univ 1970; MS Univ Pa 1973; pa/Math Tchr Penn Ctr of Phila YMCA; Doct Student Univ Pa; NCTM; Math Assn Am; Am Ednl Res Assn; Assn for Computing Machinery & Spec Interest Group on Computer Uses in Ed; World Future Soc; Pres Phi Delta Kappa 1977-78; r/Rom Cath; hon/Cert Recog, Phi Delta Kappa; Pres Awd, Phi Delta Kappa; World W/W Wom; Pub'd Author.

BAKER, KATHRYN TAYLOR oc/-Associate Professor; Director; b/Jan 5, 1925; h/1818 Mignon, Memphis, TN 38107; ba/Memphis; m/John; p/John Taylor (dec); Alma Wharey Taylor, Trenton, TN; ed/BS; MSSW; pa/Assoc Prof Univ Tenn Col Med; Dir Univ Tenn Child Devel Ctr; Intl Conf Social Wel; Nat Assn Social Wkrs; Nat Conf Social Wel; Univ Tenn Fac Clb; AAUP; Am Assn Mtl Deficiency; Other Profl Assns; Admissions Bd Arlington Devel Ctr; Nom'g Com Tenn Conf Social Wel; Adv Com Univ Tenn Sch of Social Work Alumni; Nom'g & Ldrship Com Nat Assn Soc Wkrs; cp/Bd Mem: Am Cancer Soc, Memphis Heart Assn, Nom'g Com Goodwill Industs, U Way Greater Memphis, Policy & Public Relats W Tenn; r/Ch of Christ; hon/Life Mbrship Sigma Kappa; Fellow Am Assn Mtl Definiency; Assoc Prof'ship Univ of Tenn Col Med; Editor.

BAKER, KERRY ALLEN oc/Engineer; b/Sept 21, 1949; h/824 Larry Ln, Decatur, GA; ba/Ellijay, GA; p/Austin and Betty Brooks Baker, Decatur, GA; ed/BIE Ga Tech 1971; MBA Ga St Univ 1973; mil/AUS 1973-77; USAR Presently CPT; pa/Div Engr Gold Kist Poultry; Am Inst Indust Engrs; Am

Mgt Assoc; Soc for Advmt Mgmt; Am Inst Plant Engrs; Soc Am Mil Engrs; cp/Masons; Sigma Phi Epsilon; Alpha Phi Omega; Gamma Beta Phi Soc; r/Bapt; hon/Pi Delta Epsilon; Arcom; Scabbard & Blade; Order of St Barbara; W/W S&SW.

BAKER, LURLINE JUANITA oc/Job Development Specialist; b/Oct 29, 1938; h/1008 E 9th St, Duluth, MN 55805; ba/Duluth; c/Michael, Kenneth, Keith, Darnell; p/Kelly and Gladys Berry Chambers, Los Angeles, CA; ed/BA Col St Scholastica 1971-74, cum laude, Spec Ed U MN 1974;

pa/Equal Opport Ofcr 1976; Duluth Sch Bd, Duluth Bus & Prof Wom; Altrusa Civic & Social; Adv Coun NAACP; Bd Ctr Drug & Alcohol; Duluth Shelter Wkshp; cp/Career Ed Task Force MN; Adv Coun Ec Status Wom; Del Dem Nat Conv; r/Bapt; hon/Mil Wife of Mo.

BAKER, MARILYN VIRGINIA oc/-Reporter; b/Sept 13, 1929; ba/2655 Van Ness Ave, San Francisco, CA 94109; c/Jeffrey, Chris; p/Charles Mansfield; pa/Reporter Los Angeles Examr 1945-49; Editor "The Spectator" LA & Beverly Hills 1949-59; News Dir Cameron Broadcasting LA & Palm Springs 1968-70; TV Newswom: KQED-TV SF 1970-74, KPIX-TV SF 1974-; Nat Acad of TV Arts & Scis; cp/Civic Com Restructure Voters Handbook; Bd Dirs Chinese Youth Affirmative Action; hon/Recipient Outstg Investigative Reporting Awd Univ Cal; Cert of Hon SF Bd Supvrs; Awd Outstg Achmt SF Chapt U Jewish Woms Coun; Dist'd Ser Medallion SF Chapt Nat Acad TV Arts & Scis; Emmy Investigative Reporting; Emmy Feature Reporting 1974 & 1977; George Foster Peabody Awd; Wom of Yr Awd SF Chapt Am Wom Radio & TV; Columbia-du Pont Cert.

BAKER, MARY JANE oc/Counselor; Advisor; b/Oct 6, 1944; h/Troy, AL; ba/Box 20, Suite 125, Adams Ctr, Troy St Univ, Troy, AL 36081; p/King and Allie Rinehart Baker, Centre, AL; ed/BS Jacksonville St Univ 1966; MA Univ Ala 1968; Further Grad Study Troy St Univ; pa/Troy St Univ: Counselor, Fgn Student Advr; Am Pers & Guid Assn; Troy Mtl Hlth Bd; So Col Pers Assn; Delta Kappa Gamma; Am Assn Univ Wom; Intl Students Cult Org; r/Meth.

BAKER, NORMAN OTTIS oc/Minister; b/Jan 31, 1918; h/PO Box 365, Waynesboro, TN 38485; ba/W'boro; m/Helen; c/Lavonne B McCollum, Donna B Willis; p/Carless and Ida Franks Baker (dec); ed/BA Union Univ; Grad Work SWn Theol Sem; pa/Ordained Min First Bapt Ch; Hosp Chaplain; Radio Min; Exec Bd; Tenn Bapt Conv; Chm Evangelism; Indian Creek Bapt Assn; cp/Rotary Clb; r/Bapt; hon/Awd, Exec Bd Tenn Bapt Conv; Contbr Var Mags & Papers.

BAKER, ORPHA MAE oc/Shop Owner; b/Apr 13, 1922; h/625 N Glendora Ave, Glendora, CA 91740; ba/Glendora; c/Philip Morris, Carol Obeoi, Laura Williams, Margaret Morris; p/Philip Phillips (dec); Beulah Bartolomew (dec); pa/Antique Shop Owner "The Time Door"; Artist; Sculptress; Mus Curator-Dir 1967-74; hon/Outstg Citizen Achmt Awd, Desert Caballeros Org; Citizen of Yr Wickenburg C of C; Prizes-Art.

BAKER, RAYMOND E oc/Executive; b/Sept 24, 1947; h/125 Maple St, Brookfield, MO 64628; ba/B'field; m/Carol Warnock; p/(dec); ed/BA Westminster Col; pa/Pres Pepsi-Cola Bottling Co; Treas Mo Pepsi-Cola Assn; Mo Soft Drink Assn; Exec Bd, Dir; cp/Pres B'field C of C; Chm Boy Scout Dr; Del Dem Nat Conv; r/Presb: Ruling Elder; hon/Outstg Young Man of Am; W/W: Mo, Am Polits, Fin & Indust, MW.

BAKER, TOMMYE PITTS oc/Professional Interior Designer; b/Sept 26, 1938; h/6920 Lakewood Blvd, Dallas TX 75214; ba/Same; m/Samuel; c/Paula B Stephens, Jerry; p/Thomas Chase (dec); Adelaide Pitts, Mexia, TX; ed/BS Tex Woms Univ 1961; pa/Tex Woms Univ: Assoc Prof, Dept Head, Adv Coun 1977; Other Acad Positions; Intl Platform Assn; Var Offices: Am Inst Interior Designers, ASID, Nat Home Fashions Leag, Am Assn Univ Wom; r/Ch of Christ; hon/Pub'd Author; Outstg Young Wom of Am Awd, Num Biogl Listings.

BAKER, WILLIAM DUNCAN oc/-Aerospace Engineer; b/Sept 27, 1950; h/PO Box 30711, Amarillo, TX 79120; ba/Amarillo; m/Martha; c/Gray, Ryan; p/Altred and Koma Baker, Amarillo, TX; ed/BS; pa/Nat Soc Profl Engrs; Tex Soc Profl Engrs; r/Bapt; hon/Sigma Gamma Tau, Tau Beta Pi; W/W S&SW.

BAKER, WILLIAM OLIVER oc/Executive; b/Jul 15, 1915; h/Spring Valley Rd, Morristown, NJ 07960; ba/Murray Hill, NJ; m/Frances Burrill; c/Joseph; p/Harold and Helen Stokes Baker (dec); ed/BS Wash Col 1935; PhD Princeton Univ 1938; pa/Bell Tele Labs: Pres 1973-, VP Res & Patents 1955-73, Phys Scis 1954-55; Other Positions; Conslt Nat Security Agy 1959-1976; Mgmt Adv Coun Oak Ridge Nat Lab 1970-; Nat Cancer Adv Bd 1974-; Conslt to Ofc Sci & Technol Policy 1977-; Gas Res Inst Adv Coun 1978-; Trustee Var Orgs; Num Univ Vis Coms; cp/Bd Higher Ed NJ 1967-; VChm 1970-72; r/Christian; hon/18 Hon Degs; ASTM Awd to Execs; Frederik Philips Awd (IEEE); Indust Res Man-of-Yr Awd; Gold Medal, AIC; Num Other Awds.

BAKHRU, HASSA oc/Professor; Director; b/Jun 2, 1938; h/12 California Ave, Albany, NY 12205; ba/Albany; m/Usha; p/Choithram and Heer Bakhru, San Diego,

CA; ed/PhD; pa/Assoc Prof Physics; Dir Nuclear Accelerator Lab; Reschr Nuclear & Atomic Physics; r/Hindu; hon/Frederick Gardner Cottrell Res Awd.

BAKKEN, HENRY H oc/Economist; Publisher; b/Mar 24, 1896; h/2218 Chadbourne Ave, Madison, WI 53705; ba/Madison; m/Clara Grimstad; c/James, David, Haakon; p/Halvor and Malla Nelson Bakken; ed/BA 1922, MA 1924 Univ Wis; Addit Studies; mil/AUS 1916-17; pa/Mimir Publs Inc: Ownr, Mgr; Univ Wis: Appt'd Emeritus Prof, Other Positions; Am Farm Ec Assn; Price Control Ofcr Allied Control Command; Ec Conslt Min Natural Resources, Honduras 1964-65; Conslt Weitz-Hettlesater Engrs; Other Profl Assns; cp/Mason (Shriner); r/Luth; hon/Contbr Articles Profl Jours; Author Pub'd Books; Fulbright Lectr, Finland, Norway 1962-63.

BALADA, LEONARDO oc/Composer; b/Sept 22, 1933; ba/Music Dept, Carnegie-Mellon Univ, Pittsburgh, PA 15213; c/Dylan; p/Jose and Lucia Balada, Spain; ed/Dipl (Composition) Juilliard Sch; pa/Composition Prof Carnegie-Mellon Univ; Composer Several Solo & Chamber Works & Ballets;

Symphonic Compositions: *Guernica, Steel Symphony, Ponce de Leon, Homage to Casals and Homage to Sarasate*; Works Performed By Maj Orchs Throughout USA & Europe; Guest of Several Instns Incl'd Aspen Inst, Univ Tel-Aviv, Min of Cult of Poland; Comms from Var Insts; hon/ASCAP Awds; Intl Prize: "City of Zaragoza," "City of Barcelona."

BALADAD, JUANITO T oc/Doctor; b/Sept 28, 1940; h/337 Hackberry Ct, Wood

Dale, IL 60191; ba/Northlake, IL; m/Purificacion; c/Mary Jane, Michelle Lynn, Juanito Jr; p/Roman and Filomena Baladad; ed/AA; MD; pa/Doctor Radiologist; RSNA; AMA; ISMS; CMS; r/Cath; hon/Notable Ams 1976.

BALAM, BAXISH SINGH oc/Professor; b/Aug 16, 1930; h/PO Box 256, Itta Bena, MS 38941; ba/Itta Bena; m/Marilyn Cogswell; c/Elisabeth, Gabrielle; p/Ram Singh Boparai and Rajinder Kaur, Shelby, MS; ed/BS 1951, MS 1953 Punjab Univ; PhD Ohio St Univ 1965; pa/Prof of Chem Miss Valley St Univ 1969-; Prof Punjab Univ 1953-66; Advr Intl Atomic Energy Agy of UN 1966-68; Conslt to Govt of Iran 1977-78; Conslt Several Intl Orgs; r/Sikhism; hon/Pub'd Author.

BALANIS, CONSTANTINE A oc/-Professor; b/Oct 29, 1938; h/120 Scenery Dr, Morgantown, WV 26505; ba/M'town; m/Helen; c/Erini; p/Apostolos Balanis (dec); Erini Balanis, Trikala, Greece; ed/BSEE; MSE; PhD; pa/Prof of

Elect Engrg WVU; IEEE; ASEE; RTCA; Eta Kappa Nu; Tau Beta Pi, Phi Kappa Phi; Sigma Xi; Assoc Editor of IEEE Transactions of AP/S; hon/W/W E; Men of Achmt; Am Men of Sci; Other Biogl Listings.

BALAS, EGON oc/Professor; b/Jun 7, 1922; h/104 Maple Heights Rd, Pittsburgh, PA 15232; m/Edith Lovi; c/Ann, Vera; p/Ignat and Boriska Balas; ed/DL Bolyai Univ; DSc Ed summa cum laude Univ Brussels; DU Univ Paris; pa/Prof of Indust Adm & Applied Math Carnegie-Mellon Univ 1968-; Assoc Editor *Operations Res* (1967-); Edit Bd *Revue d'Automatique, Informatique et Recherche Operationnelle* (1976-); Nat Res Couns Com on Recommendations for AUS Res 1977-; TIMS: Coun Mem, Chm Pubs Com; Lectr Inst Ec Sci & Planning; Visiting Opers Res Com to Univ Tel-Aviv 1975; ORSA; AMS; SIAM; SIGMAP; Conslt Fed Energy Adm; Other Profl Assns; hon/W/W: World, Am; Am Men & Wom of Distn; Recipient Grants; Ford Dist'd Res Prof, Carnegie-Mellon Univ; Res Fellow, Intl Computation Centre.

BALDERSTON, JEAN MERRILL oc/-Psychoanalyst; Poet; b/Aug 29, 1936; h/1225 Park Avenue, New York City, NY 10028; ba/Same; m/David; p/Frederick and Helen Merrill, Saco, ME; ed/BA Univ Conn; MA, EdD Columbia Univ; pa/Psychoanalyst Pvt Pract 1971-; Univ Tchg Psychol 1965-71: Douglass Col for Wom, Rutgers Univ, Montclair St Col, Hunter Col, Queens Col, Columbia Univ; Edit Staff *New*

York Qtrly 1971-76; Am Psychol Assn; Nat Coun Fam Relats; Am Assn Marriage & Fam Cnslrs; Emily Dickinson Soc; r/Prot; hon/W/W Am Wom, NE; Intl Dic of Biog; Pub'd Poet Num Lit Mags.

BALDINGER, CHARLENE LOIS oc/Counselor; b/Sept 24, 1948; h/830 Alexandria Pk, Apt 11, Ft Thomas, KY 41075; ba/Alexandria, KY; p/Bruce and Shirley Baldinger, Cold Spring, KY; ed/AB; MA En Ky Univ; pa/HS Guid Cnslr; NEA; KEA; CCEA; APGA; KPGA; NKPGA; r/Prot: Ch Coms, Choir, Tchr, Youth Advr; hon/W/W S&SW; Personalities of S.

BALDWIN, CHARLOTTE EADS oc/-Mayor; b/Jan 21, 1932; h/149 Forest Ln, Madisonville, KY 42431; ba/M'ville; m/-Stanley; c/Stuart, Ben; p/Edward and Maxine Cook Eads, Campbellsville, KY; ed/Assoc Deg C'ville Jr Col; BS cum laude Univ Evansville; pa/Mayor M'ville; Bd Dirs: Ky Mun Leag, M'ville C of C; cp/Past Pres Garden Clb of Ky Inc; Dem Exec Com of Hopkins Co; r/Meth; hon/Wom of Yr, M'ville; Outstg Layman's Awd, Ky Rec & Pk Soc.

BALDWIN, ESTHER LILLIAN oc/-Musician; Teacher; b/Mar 7, 1906; h/PO Box 114, Columbia, SC 29202; ba/Same; m/(dec); p/(dec); ed/PhD; pa/Nat Guild Piano Tchrs: Master Tchr, Adjudicator, Chm Columbia Chapt; Musicians Clb Am; Fellow Mem Intl Inst Arts & Lttrs; r/Epis, Mem Trinity Cathedral, Columbia; hon/Hall of Piano Guild USA; Life Mem & Bd of Govs Profl & Exec Hall of Fame; W/W: Am Wom, S&SW; Intl Dir; Royal Blue Book; Commun Ldr Am; Nat Register: Ednl Specs, Prominent Ams; Personalities of S.

BALDWIN, STANLEY C oc/Writer; Editor; Speaker; b/Dec 17, 1929; h/17901 S Lanter Ln, Oregon City, OR 97045; ba/Same; m/Marjorie Antoinette Iverson; c/Kathleen Bagley, Krystal Brown, Steven, Karen Kraus, Gregory; p/Leonard Brown (dec); Irma Toney, Portland, OR; pa/Editor *Stanley Baldwin Presents* (Novel Series); Former Editor Victor Books; Pres Oreg Assn Christian Writers; Originator 'Take Charge of Your Life" Sems; Fdg Pastor Calvary Com Ch Albany Oreg., Others; Author: *What Did Jesus Say About That, What Makes You So Special?, Bad Henry, Your Money Matters,* Others; r/New Hope Commun Ch; hon/W/W Rel; Dic of Biog; Others.

BALE, JAMES F oc/Superintendent; b/Jan 1, 1923; h/225 S Monroe, Rockford, MI 49341; ba/R'ford; m/Marilyn c/James Jr, Michael; p/Blanche Bale, Mattawan, MI; ed/BS Wn Mich Univ; MS Univ Mich; pa/Schs Supt; AASA; MASA; cp/Rotary, C of C; R'ford: City Planning Comm, Commun Foun; r/First Congreg Ch; hon/Boss of Yr Awd; IDEA F'ship, Col S'ship.

BALENT, RALPH oc/Engineer; Executive; b/Jan 23, 1923; h/4508 Park Allegra, Calabasas Park, CA 91302; ba/Canoga Park, CA; m/Elaine Barcroft; c/John, Diane; p/Albert and Edna Matson Balent, Garden Grove, CA; ed/BSME Univ Denver; MSME UCLA; mil/Sargeant Reconnaissance Platoon 714 1943-46; pa/VP & Gen Mgr Atomic Intl Div,

Energy Sys Group; Reg'd Profl Engr (Nuclear & Mech) St of Cal; cp/YMCA; Toastmasters; Little Leag; r/Presb; Elder; hon/San Fernando Valley Engr of Yr Awd; Outstg Engr Alumnus Awd, Univ Denver.

BALENTINE, JOHN LEROY III oc/Program Evaluator; b/Apr 14, 1948; h/400 Forrest Park Rd, B6-3, Madison, TN 37115; ba/Nashville, TN; m/Eva April; p/John Jr and Roberta Balentine, Los Angeles, CA; ed/BA; MA; PhD; pa/Am Mgmt Assn; cp/Aircraft Owners & Pilots Assn; US Ski Assn; Jr C of C; r/Jehovah's Witnesses; hon/Human Ser Awd; Cert Meritorious Commun Ser.

BALICK, BERNARD oc/Judge; b/May 14, 1940; h/2319 W 17th St, Wilmington, DE 19806; ba/W'ton; m/Helen; p/Simon Balick (dec); Jennie Balick, Miami Bch, FL; ed/BA Columbia Col 1958-62; JD Dickinson Sch of Law 1966; pa/Judge Superior Ct of St Del 1973-; Am Bar Assn; Del St Bar Assn; Pvt Pract 1966-69, 1971-72; Staff Atty Legal Aid Soc 1968-69; Asst Public Defender St Del 1969-71; City Solicitor City of W'ton 1973; cp/Congreg Beth Shalom Bd Dirs; Fac Advr Nat Jud Col; hon/Phi Beta Kappa.

BALISTRIERI, THOMAS JOSEPH oc/Counselor; Public Speaker; b/Dec 8, 1950; h/4311 Dunbarton Apt 16, Tampa, FL 33611; ba/Tampa; m/Sandra; p/Edward and Patricia Balistrieri, West Allis, WI; ed/BS Univ Wis-Oshkosh; MA Pacific Luth Univ; pa/Cnslr & Public Spkr Univ Tampa; ACPA; APGA; CPC; Presenter at Convs; cp/Mem Var Sports Clbs; Spkr to Civic Orgs; r/Cath; hon/Personalities of S; Var Awds.

BALL, CATHERINE BRODIE oc/Artist; Teacher; h/10,511 Birnham Rd, Great Falls, VA 22066; ba/Same; m/Lawrence Deeble; p/Fred and Lenore Ricketts Pierce (dec); ed/BA Univ Mich; MA Univ Wis; pa/Art Tchr; McLean & Vienna Va; Enamelist; McLean Art Clb; Pres, Corr'g Secy; NLAPW; AAUW; cp/Ed Chm Am Cancer Soc; r/Presb; hon/Wom of Yr, Arlington Va; Awd: Fairfax Fest of Arts, Palette Clb.

BALL, HAROLD G oc/Minister; b/Jun 29, 1944; h/Rt 1, Nelson, VA 24580; ba/Same; m/Geraldine Vess; c/Terry, Ronny; p/William and Nancy Holbert Ball, Newport, TN; ed/BA Carson-Newman Col; pa/SEn Sem Wake Forest NC; r/So Bapt; hon/Pi Tau Chi Soc; W/W Rel 1977.

BALL, IRIS GEORGIA oc/Executive; b/Oct 19, 1921; h/8723 Ramsgate Ave, Los Angeles, CA 90045; ba/LA; p/Cam and Oma Martin Ball (dec); ed/BA Cal St Univ 1973; MBA Pepperdine Univ 1975; pa/Mgr Equal Opport for Wom, Dart Industs Inc; Pers & Indust Relats Assn Inc; Am Soc Pers Admrs; Am Assn Univ Wom; Spec Agt Prudential Ins Co; Other Former Positions; cp/LA: Town Hall, World Affairs Coun; YMCA; r/Prot; hon/W/W: W, Fin & Indust, Am Wom, Am; Notable Am Awd; Dic Intl Biog; Other Num Biogl Listings.

BALL, ROBERT JEROME oc/Associate Professor; b/Nov 4, 1941; ba/Dept European Langs & Lit, Univ Hi, Honolulu, HI 96822; p/William and Pauline Ball, Floral Park, NY; ed/BA Queens Col 1962; MA Tufts Univ 1963; PhD Columbia Univ 1971; pa/Assoc Prof of Classics Univ Hi; Col of Arts & Scis Fac Senate; Fdr & Chm: Hi Classical Soc, Soc Augustan Poetry (Am Philological Assn); Chm Classics Div Univ Hi; hon/Assoc & Full Prof Awd, Univ Hi 1979; Pub'd Author.

BALLANTYNE, REGINALD MALCOLM III oc/Executive; b/Oct 2, 1943; h/1252 E Gardenia Dr, Phoenix, AZ 85020; ba/Phoenix; p/Reginald and Constance Martin Ballantyne, Westbury, Long Isl, NY; ed/BA Col of Holy Cross 1965; MBA Cornell Univ 1967; mil/USPHS Comm'd Hlth Sers Ofcr & Public Hlth Advr Comm Corps 1967-69; pa/Pres Mem Hosp 1976-; Bd Trustees; Mem Hosp; Exec VP 1974-76, Admr 1973-74; Coor Commun Hlth Tng & Demo Programs 1967-70; Bd Dirs: Ariz Hosp Assn,

CODAC, Maricopa Co Assn for Med Ed; Ariz Emer Med Sys Inc; Other Bd Positions; Pres Phoenix Reg Hosp Coun; Comm'd Ofcrs Assn of USPHS; Other Profl Positions; cp/Pres Phoenix Sunrise Rotary Clb; Hosp Chm Phoenix-Scottsdale U Way Campaign; Phoenix C of C: Bus & Govt Div Coun, Local Govt Fin Com; Ariz Clb; Num Civic Assns; r/Rom Cath; hon/W/W: W, Hlth Care; Outstg Young Men Am; Eagle Scout; Cert Merit & Achmt; Surg Gen Ofc of USPHS; Pub'd Author.

BALLARD, IRMA L PARRETT oc/Realtor; Developer; b/May 8, 1908; h/1815 Wm H-Taft Rd, Cincinnati, OH 45206; ba/Same; m/Francis James (dec); c/James, Francis Jr; p/Sherman and Sylvia Jones Parrett (dec); ed/Student: Ohio St Univ 1927, Leland Powers Sch 1928, Univ Cinc 1945; pa/Real Est: Ethel Daly 1946-47, R A Schrimer 1947, Owner City Wide Realty 1948; Home Bldr 1950-62; Pres: Balwin Hres Inc 1955-62, Jil Inc 1960-64; Cinc Real Est Bd; Intl Platform Assn.

BALLENGER, KENNETH LEIGH oc/Professor; b/Jul 28, 1921; h/506 Hawthorne, Fayetteville, AR 72701; ba/F'ville; m/Inez Ward; c/David, Joan; p/H L and Mary Ballenger (dec); ed/BA, BM

Hardin-Simmons Univ; MM Eastman Sch Music; mil/ETO 104th Inf Div WW-II; pa/Prof of Music Univ Ark; Dir Uarkettes; Tour: Europe 1964, 71, 74, Mexico 1968, 78, 79; cp/Past Pres F'ville Rotary Clb; r/Presb.

BALLENTINE, KRIM MENELIK oc/US Marshal; Chief Deputy; b/Oct 22, 1936; h/1 E Lafayette Plaisance, Apt 1403, Detroit, MI 48207; ba/Detroit; c/Taraka; p/Habib and Rose Ballentine, St Louis, MO; mil/AF 1954-58; pa/Nat Org Black Law Enforcemt Execs; Intl Assn Chiefs of Police; US Marshals Hist Soc; Am Acad Polit & Social Scis; cp/Dist Chm Detroit Boy Scouts Coun; Mark Twain Soc; Nat Urban Leag; r/Islam; hon/Boy Scouts Outstg Ser Awd; Dedicated Ser Awd Mathew-Dickey Boys Clb; W/W: Black Ams, Govt.

BALLER, ADOLPH oc/Pianist; Teacher; b/Jul 30, 1909; h/275 Lowell Ave, Palo Alto, CA 94301; ba/Same; m/Edith; c/Nina Lobban; pa/Prof of Music: Stanford Univ, San Francisco Conservatory; Composer; Fdr Alma Trio; Concert Pianist; Perfs: Europe, Russia, Czechoslovakia; Num Other Solos.

BALLEW, SUSIE LEE oc/Graduate Student; b/Oct 31, 1954; h/4620 Summit, #14 Kansas City, MO 64111; p/George Ballew, Fayette, MO; ed/BA Univ Mo-Columbia

1976; Grad Student Univ Mo; cp/Vol: Com for Equal Rts Coalition Grt KC, Staff Wkr for Kaye Waldo for City Coun Campaign; Del: Nat Yg Dems Conv, Mo Student Voter Registration Conf, TARGET Sems; Woms Polit Caucus of KC; Inst of Soc, Ethics & Life Scis; r/Christian; hon/W/W Am Polits; Personalities of W&MW; Outstg Yg Wom of Mo; Dist'd Ser Awd, Mo Yg Dems; Outstg Yg Wom of Am; Recipient Mo St Senate Resolution.

BALNICKY, ROBERT G oc/Minister; b/Apr 18, 1922; h/PO Box 4182, Chattanooga, TN 37405; m/Annette; p/(dec); ed/Am Legion Staff Col; Columbia Presb Theol Sem; Pensacola Jr Col; Fla St; Other Insts; mil/USN 1942-49; USNR 1950-54; pa/Robert G Balnicky Eval Assn Inc 1969-; Will Turner Electronics 1978-; Cnslg Ctr Dir; Indust Chaplain; Fdr & Pastor: Grace Ch, Trinity Bible Ch; Others; Mil Chaplains Assn; Youth for Christ; CoFdr, Past Chm Bd Dirs, Past Chm Pastors Adv Bd; Past Pres World Min F'ship Intl; Other Profl Assns; cp/Fraternal Order Police; CAP: Dep Chaplain, Master Air Observer, Escort Ofcr for Intl Air Cadet Exc to Japan; Other Positions; YMCA; "Sycamore Tree" Youth Ctr; Fla U Christian Action Inc; Am Legion; Forty & Eight Vets Org; Bd Dirs "Agape" House; r/Presb; hon/Grover Loening Aerospace Awd; Meritorious Ser Awd; W/W: Rel, S&SW; Other Biogl Listings; Pub'd Author; Four Chaplains Cit.

BALSIGER, DAVID W oc/Executive; Author; b/Dec 14, 1945; h/257 Brentwood St, Costa Mesa, CA 92627; ba/Santa Ana & Anaheim CA; m/Janie Francis; c/Lisa, Lori; p/Leon and Dorothy Balsiger, Buena Park, CA; ed/BA Nat Univ; LHD Lincoln Mem Univ; Num Other Insts; pa/Investmt Cnslr Balsiger Enterprises; Writeway Profl Lit Assocs: Gen Partner, Sr VP; Visiting Prof Nat Univ, San Diego, Cal; Former Exec Reschr Schick Sunn Classic Prodns Inc; Chief Photog/Feature Writer *Anaheim Bultn* 2 Yrs; Fgn Feature Correspondent for Mags & 13 So Cal Weekly Newspaper 1 Yr; News Editor *Logos Jour* 1 Yr; Bd Govs Lit Hall of Fame; Nat Soc of Lit & the Arts; Nat Writers Clb; Sev Motion Picture Credits; Author: *The Lincoln Conspiracy, In Search Of Noah's Ark, Beyond Defeat, The Satan Seller,* Others; cp/UCI Friends of Lib; Melodyland Christian Ctr; Nat Univ Alumni Assn; Diamond Mem Nat Univ Pres' Assocs; Past VP Pepperdine Yg Repubs; Christians for Polit Action; Repub Assocs of Orange Co; Cal Repub Assembly; Other Activs; r/Neo-Pentecostal; hon/Key to City of Costa Mesa, Cal; Outstg Commun Ser; Lit Hall of Famer: Nom'd & Elected 1977; Ldrship Cit, Pepperdine Univ Alumni Bd; Vietnam Apprec Cit, Am Soldiers in Vietnam; Writer of Mo, *Cal Writer* 1967; Num Biogl Listings; Pub'd Author.

BALTHROP, LLOYD KENNETH oc/- Missionary; Evangelist; b/Sept 7, 1925; h/601 Oakwood Pl NE, Albuquerque, NM 87123; ba/Owensville, MO; m/Winnie Jo Palmer; c/Lloyd Jr, Kirby, Pamela Bassett; p/Horace and Zula Belle Stafford Balthrop (dec); ed/BA cum laude Baylor Univ; BD SW Bapt Theol Sem; ThD, PhD So Bapt Theol Sem; pa/Dir & Preacher World Wide Evangelistic Crusades; Pastor 23 Yrs; Tchr 4 Yrs; Singer; Intl Platform Assn; cp/Col Aide-De-Camp NM Gov; r/So Bapt; hon/Top 10 Citizens NM; Outstg: Intl Evangelist, Missionary Aide, Rhodesia; Order of Ky Cols; Num Socs.

BALTHORPE, JACQUELINE MOREHEAD oc/Principal; b/Dec 2, 1928; h/16220 Delrey Ave, Cleveland, OH 44128; ba/Same; m/Robert Granville Sr; c/Robert Jr, Yvonne, Robin; p/Jack Morehead Sr, Springfield, OH; Minnie J Morehead (dec); ed/BSEd magna cum laude Ctl St Univ (Ohio) 1949; MAEd magna cum laude Case Wn Resg Univ 1959; PhD Cand; pa/VPrin Corlett Elem Sch, Cleveland; Alpha Kappa Alpha; Delta Kappa Gamma; Phi Delta Kappa; AAUW; Cleveland Coun Admrs & Supvrs; Local, St & Nat Assn Elem Sch Prins; Omega Psi Phi Wives; Jr Leag; cp/Supporting Mem: Friends of Lib, Coun of Human Relats, Proj Friendship of Juv Ct, Phyllis Wheatley, NAACP, YWCA, Urban Leag, Ctl St Col Alumni Assn; Case Wn Resv Univ Alumni Assn; Vol Num Commun Drives & Campaigns; Vol Tutor Glenville HS Scholars Clb; Lee-Harvard Commun Assn; Others; r/Meth; St John AME Clb; hon/HS Salutatorian; S'ship: Delta Sigma Theta; Valedictorian Elem Ed Dept, Ctl St Univ; Donor Jacqueline Morehead Balthrop S'ship for Highest Ranking Grad in Col of Elem Ed, Ctl St Univ; Alpha Kappa Mu; Zeta Sigma Pi; Sen Mer Rekh Frat; Outstg Tchr of Yr; Martha Holden Jennigs Foun Scholar; Citizenship Awd; Commun Ldr Awd; Dist'd Awd for Meritorious Sers; Biogl Listings.

BALZER, LARRY DALE oc/Physician; b/Apr 3, 1945; h/4103 Scottsdale Cir, Wichita Falls, TX 76302; ba/WF; m/Diana Kiser; c/Keli; p/Lawrence and Martha Wiens Balzer, Hooker, OK; ed/BS Panhandle St Col; MD Okla Univ; mil/USAF Flight Surg 1972-78; pa/Am Acad Fam Pract; Am Soc Clin Hypnosis; Tex Med Assn; Wichita Co Med Soc; r/So Bapt; hon/USAF Commend Medal; Okla St Med Assn S'ship; Marvin E McKee Awd; Top Student Sci Div.

BANCROFT, BARBARA AYLEEN oc/Counselor; b/May 27, 1944; h/678 Hawthorne NE, Salem, OR 97301; ba/Salem; m/Terrance Lee; p/Donald and Mildred Gillum, Astoria, OR; ed/BS Oreg Col of Ed 1969; Grad Work Cnslg 1973; pa/Voc Rehab Cnslr; Salem Rehab Facility: Supvr Grad Practicum Students, Dir Human Awareness/Sex Ed Prog, Conslt for Deaf & Hearing Impaired; Secy for Coun for Exceptl Chd; Exec Bd Dirs Living Opports; OSEA; cp/Adv Coun Goodwill Industs; Mtl Hlth Task Force; Smithsonian Assn; Natural Hist Mus; r/Bapt; hon/W/W Am Wom; Notable Ams; Personalities of W&NW; Num Other Biogl Listings.

BANCROFT, PETER oc/Author; Photographer; b/May 5, 1916; h/3538 Oak Cliff Dr, Fallbrook, CA 92028; ba/Same; m/Virginia Pomeroy; c/Martha, Edward, Robert, Barbara; p/Roy and Lillian Walker Bancroft (dec); ed/BA Univ Cal-SB; MS Univ So Cal; EdD Univ No Col; pa/Public Sch Tchr; VPrin; Prin Beverly Hills; Supt Num Schs; Author 'Worlds Finest Minerals

& Crystals"; Contbr Var Mags; White House Ednl Conf; Photog-Writer Hanna Barbera; Curator Mineralogy; cp/Pres: Girls Clb, Rotary; Bd Dirs Boys Clb; Lions Clb; Orch Assn; VP C of C; Symphony; UCSB Kern Co Alumni Assn; hon/Blue Key; UCSB Student Body VP; Prof of Yr, Bolivia; PTA Annual Awd; Edr of Yr, El Cajon; Am Fdn Mineral Soc Annual Awd.

BANDY, BETTE LINDE oc/Secretary; Pianist; Composer; b/Apr 16, 1926; h/4501

Walton Ct, Louisville, KY 40213; ba/L'ville; c/Betty Bowman, Parker III; p/Knud Linde, Pelham, TN; Alice Lasserre Stiles, Knoxville, TN; ed/Grad St Cecilia Sch Music 1943; Att'd John R Neal Col Law 1945-47; pa/Secy to VP & Tech Dir Standard Gravure Corp 1977-; Pianist & Composer Sacred and Secular Music Incl'g "Crucifixion in A minor;" Legal Secy & Bkkpr 1968-77; Former Ct & Conf Reporter AEC; Music Tchr; Jefferson Reporter: Humorous Columnist, Edit, Feature & Music; r/St Peters Epis Ch: Soloist, Asst Choir Dir, SS Pianist; Organist & Choir Dir: Okolona Presb Ch, Beechmont Presby Ch; Dir Music Kenwood Bapt Ch; hon/W/W Am Rel.

BANDY, JACK DONALD oc/Trial Lawyer; b/Jun 19, 1932; h/16411 Calahan St, Sepulveda, CA 91343; ba/Los Angeles, CA; m/Betty; c/Jean, Michael, Jeffrey; p/Homer Bandy (dec); Gladys Bandy, Van Nuys, CA; ed/BA Knox Col; LLB Univ San Fernando Valley Col Law; mil/AUS 1st Lt 82nd Airborne Div 1954-56; Active Resvs Capt 1958-62; pa/Cal St Bar; San Fernando Valley Bar; Am Soc Safety Engrs; cp/Former Pres PTA; YMCA; Little Leag; Precnt Wkr; hon/Certified Safety Profl; Life Ser Awd PTA.

BANGHAM, P JERALD oc/Associate Professor; Director; b/Jan 12, 1936; ba/Box 59, Alcorn St Univ; Lorman, MS 39096; p/Paul and Phyllis Bangham, London, OH; ed/BA 1957, MA 1959, PhD 1965 Ohio St Univ; pa/Alcorn St Univ: Assoc Prof Spch &

Theatre, Dir Theatre, Chm Spch-Theatre Area; Intl Fdn Theatre Res; Am Soc Theatre Res; Am Theatre Assn; US Inst Theatre Tech; cp/ACLU; AAUP; Sierra Clb; Audubon Soc; Nature Conservancy Rivers Unlimited; Envir Action; Friends of Earth; Common Cause; r/Presb.

BANIK, PROMILA oc/Solar Cell Operator; Registered Nurse; b/May 5, 1939; h/8606 Bradmoor Dr, Bethesda, MD 20034; p/Sambhu N; c/Sharmila, Kakali; p/E Roy (dec); Florence Roy, Bethesda, MD; ed/RN Delhi Univ (India); pa/Reg'd Nurse, Gangaram Hosp (India) 1965-67; Staff Nurse, Newfoundland Hosp (Canada) 1967-68; Solar Cell Operator, Solarex Company 1978-; CoAuthor w Husband of Cookbook; Lectr on Role of Wom in India; cp/Social Secy, Prabashi; Intl Friendship Wives; Nat Homemakers Assn; r/Hindu; hon/Clt for Commun Activs, Canada; SARI Demo at Smithsonian Inst & Bloomingdale's (Wash, DC); Dir'd India's Participation at Bicent Celebration Parade; Awds for Singing.

BANK, THEODORE PAUL II oc/Explorer; Anthropologist; Professor; b/Aug 31, 1923; h/1809 Nichols Rd, Kalamazoo, MI 49007; ba/K'zoo; m/Trina Lindenstein; c/Kristin; p/Ted Sr and Madlyn Huber Bank, Indian Wells, CA; ed/BSF 1946, MS 1950 Univ Mich; Postgrad Doctoral Studies Archaeology 1950-54; mil/USN Air Corps Fleet Weather Ctl 1944-46; pa/Exec Dir Am Inst Exploration 1954-; Prof Social Sci Wn Mich Univ; Dir: WMU's World Exploration Prog, Aleutian-Bering Sea Expeditions 1969-; Other Profl Positions; Intl Platform Assn; Am Heritage Res; Soc of Sigma Xi; Intl Com Urgent Anthropological & Ethnological Res; Edit Bd: *Mariah* 1976-, *The Explorers Jour* 1961-; Other

Profl Assns; r/Meth; hon/Recipient Grants; W/W: Am World, Marine & Freshwater Res,

Authors; Other Biogl Listings; Pub'd Author; Advr: Expedition Train'g Inst, Our World-Underwater, Exploration Clb of Hokkaido Univ; Lectr.

BANKS, IOLA K oc/Teacher; b/Aug 10, 1935; h/PO Box 41, Kenai, AK 99611; ba/Kenai; m/Lovell; c/Valencia, Jacqueline, Dorenda, Lovell Jr; p/Edd Kelly, Hodge, LA; Marie Kelly (dec); ed/BA, MA Univ Alaska; pa/Tchr: 3rd, 4th & 5th Grades Springfield, Mass 1967-70, 4th & 6th Grades Kenai Peninsula Borough Schs 1970-78; cp/Chm: Kenai Precncts 1, 2 & 3, House Dist 13 Kenai Peninsula; Del Nat Dem Conv; r/Bapt; hon/Cert 1953.

BANKS, GLENNA MAE oc/Educator; b/Oct 12, 1922; h/802 N Washington St, Stillwater, OK 74074; ba/S'water; m/Clarence; c/Jed; p/P C and Ida Smith (dec); ed/Okla St Univ; pa/Mgr Contracts & Grants Engrg Res, Okla St Univ; Soc Res Admrs; Am

Bus Woms Assn; Beta Sigma Phi; cp/YMCA; Heart Fund; UF Aide; Higher Ed Alumni Coun Okla; Vol Instr; Girl Scouts; r/Meth: Mem, Fin Com, Secy Adm Bd; hon/YMCA Ser Awd 3 Yrs; AUS Intell Sch; Orange and Black Quill; Mortar Bd; W/W Am Wom.

BANKS, ROSA MARIA TAYLOR oc/-Executive Assistant; b/Mar 19, 1942; h/1811 Forney Dr, Huntsville, AL 35806; ba/H'ville; m/Halsey; c/Kevin Bernard, Karmala La Taria; p/Eddie L Taylor (dec); Albertha Taylor, Ocala, FL; ed/AA; BS; MEd; EdD; pa/Assoc Prof of Bus Ed & Dept Hd, Oakwood Col; Exec Asst to Pres, Oakwood Col; Prof of Bus, Ala A&M Univ; Dir Long-Range Planning; Internal Auditor; Coor, Mgmt Prog; NBEA; Pres, SDA Bus Ed Assn; Ala Bus Ed Assn; Delta Pi Epsilon; Doctl Assn Edrs; College Bd; cp/Yth Spkr, NW Ala Commun Assn NAACP; r/SDA; hon/Pub'd Author; World W/W Wom; W/W Am Wom; Outstg Yg Wom Am; Others.

BANSEMER, RICHARD FREDERICK oc/Clergyman; Author; b/May 26, 1940; h/Box 10, Dillon, CO 80435; ba/Same; m/Mary Ann Troutman; c/John, Arron, Andrew; p/Reinhold and Oralee Ann Bansemer; ed/BA; BD; pa/Clergyman of Luth Ch in Am; Author: *People Prayers, The Chosen and the Changed*; cp/Chm Emer Med Sers Bd, Summit Co; r/Luth.

BARBA, HARRY oc/Educator; Writer; Publisher; b/Jun 17, 1922; h/47 Hyde Blvd, Ballston SPA, NY 12020; ba/Clifton Park, NY; m/Marian; c/Gregory; p/Michael and

Sultone Sarah Barba (dec); ed/BA Bates Col 1944; MA Harvard Univ 1951; MFA 1960, PhD 1963 Univ Iowa; pa/Edr: Marshall Univ 1968-70, Skidmore Col 1964-68; Other Profl Positions; Author: Novels, Short Stories, Reviews, Articles & Criticisms; Authors Guild Inc; Col Eng Assn; Conf Col Composition & Communs; Authors Leag Am Inc; Mod Lang Assn; Editor-in-Chief: *Maroon & White, Bates Garnet*; Bd Dirs Harvard Clb; Other Profl Assns; r/Christian Univeralist Humanist; hon/Recipient Grants; F'ship: Yaddo Residence, Univ Iowa, Fulbright Post-Doct, MacDowell Colony Residence; W/W E; Contemp Authors; Dir Am Scholars; Num Other Biogl Listings; Dist'd Vis Lectr, St Univ NY.

BARBEITO, MANUEL SERAFINO oc/Microbiologist; b/Jan 23, 1930; h/2105 Runny Meade Ct, Frederick, MD 21701; ba/Bethesda, MD; m/Eva Rebecca Rhoderick; c/David, Diane, Ronald; p/Jobino Barbeito, Freeland, PA; Almirinda DiPrino Barbeito (dec); ed/X-Ray Tech Franklin Sch Sci & Arts 1948; BS Penn St Univ 1956; Postgrad Studies; mil/USN 1948-52; pa/Microbiologist Asst Safety Mgr Nat Cancer Inst; Am Soc Microbiology; Sci Res Soc N Am; Am Acad Microbiology; cp/Scoutmaster; Former: Exec Com Frederick PTA, Com Chm CSA, Asst Scoutmaster BSA; r/Rom Cath; hon/W/W: Am, E; Adult Scoutmaster Awd, BSA; US Govt Outstg Perf; Quality Increase; USN Meritorious Ser.

BARBER, SANDRA POWELL oc/Lecturer; b/Dec 15, 1941; h/PO Box 131, Newburgh, IN 47630; ba/Evansville, IN; m/Charles Turner; c/Robin, James, Melissa, Gretchen, Derek, Katrina; p/Sanford Powell, Baltimore, MD; Mary Powell, Balto, MD; ed/BA; MA: History, Polit Sci; PhD Cand; pa/Lectr Polit Sci; Dir Ind Polit Sci Assn; Intl Studies Assn; cp/Lectr Am Polits; r/Meth; hon/Md St Tchrs S'ship; Pi Gamma Mu; Sloan Foun Grant; Worlds W/W Wom.

BARBOUR, WALWORTH oc/Diplomat; b/Jun 4, 1908; h/14 Grapevine Rd, Gloucester, MA 01930; ba/Same; p/S Lewis and Clara Hammond Barbour (dec); ed/BA Harvard 1930; pa/Former Diplomat; Ambassador to Israel 1961-73; r/Unitarian; hon/Fellow Weizmand Inst; LLD Dropsie Univ; Dr Humane Letters, Hebrew Union Col; PhD: Hebrew Univ, Tel Aviv Univ.

BARDIS, PANOS D oc/Professor; Editor; Author; b/Sept 24, 1924; h/2533 Orkney, Ottawa Hills, Toledo, OH 43606; ba/Toledo; m/Donna Jean; c/Byron, Jason; p/Demetrios Bardis (dec); Kali Bardis, Athens, Greece; ed/BA magna cum laude Bethany Col; MA Notre Dame Univ; PhD Purdue Univ; pa/Univ Toledo: Prof Sociology, Editor *Social Sci*; Var Edit Positions; Intl: Assn Fam Sociology, Inst

Arts & Lttrs, Pers Res; Nat: Coun Fam Relats, Soc Lit & Arts, Soc Pub'd Poets, Assn Standard Med Vocabulary; Num Other Profl Assns; cp/Former Chm Crime Reduction Com; r/Epis; hon/Awd Outstg Achmt Ed, Bethany Col; Outstg Tchg Awd, Toledo Univ; Pub'd Author: Couphos Prize; Awd *Seminario De Investigacion Historica Y Arqueologica*; W/W: Am Men Sci, World, Am Ed, Commun Ser; Num Other Biogl Listings.

BARETSKI, CHARLES ALLAN oc/-

Librarian; Historian; Educator; b/Nov 21, 1918; h/229 Montclair Ave, Newark, NJ 07104; ba/Newark; m/Gladys Edith von Nyitrai Yartin; p/Charles and Mary Ann Gorzelnik Baretski (dec); ed/BA Rutgers St Univ 1945; BS 1946, MS 1951 Columbia Univ Sch of Library Ser; Archival Admn Diploma 1951, Adv Archival Admn Diploma 1955 Am Univ; MA 1957, PhD 1958 (Polit Sci) Notre Dame; MA 1965 (Govt & Intl Relats), PhD 1969 (Polits) NYU; pa/Staff Newark Public Library 1938-; Archivist-Histn Am Coun of Polish Cult Clbs; Rutgers Univ: Fac Mem, Public

Admr, Polit Scist; Res Intern Nat Archives; Fdr & Dir Inst Polish Cult; Exec Dir Baretski Vol Tutorial Ser; Conslt US Pop Ethno-Hist Res Ctr; Res Panelist Nat Coun Commun Ser; Am Assn Jr Cols; cp/Pres Assoc'd Commun Couns Newark; Treas NJ Coalition Safe Communs; Coor Slavic-Am Hist & Cult Studies; r/Rom Cath; hon/Dist'd Citizenship Awd, Newark City Govt; Fdrs Day Awd, NYU; Nat Heritage Awd, J F Kennedy Lib for Minorities; Outstg NJ St Labor Ldr Awd; Dist'd Edr of Am Awd; Newark 2nd Annual Brotherhood Awd; Outstg Civic Ldrship of Newark; Contbr Var Jours & Books.

BARFIELD, MARGUERITE IRL oc/-Psychologist; b/Jun 20, 1938; h/12752 Huntingwick, Houston, TX 77024; ba/Houston; p/John Durham; Arline Durham, Houston, TX; ed/BA; MA; PhD; pa/Clin Psychologist; Cnslg: Marriage, Psychol; Indiv & Group Psychotherapy; hon/Phi Kappa Phi.

BARINGER, CLARA ELLEN oc/Educator; b/Jan 14, 1905; h/R2 Box 18, Crothersville, IN 47229; p/David and Anna Baringer (dec); ed/Dipl Ctl Norman Col 1928; Att'd Ind Univ; pa/Tchr Vernon Twp Jackson Co 1926-76; Phi Delta Sigma; Nat Ret'd Tchrs Assn; Farm Bur Ind St Tchrs; Other Profl Assns; cp/Jackson Co Ext Homemaker Clb; Reading Coun; 4H Clb Ldr; r/First Presb Ch: Mem, Elder, Former Treas, Organist, Ch Sch Tchr, UPW; Chm New-Albany Presb Chd; hon/Outstg Ldrs Elem & Sec'dy Ed; Gold Pin for Ser 4H Ldr; Plaque 50 Yrs Ser, Sch Bd & Commun; Silver Tray, Presb Ch; FFA Chapt Farmer.

BARKAN, ELLIOTT ROBERT oc/-Professor; b/Dec 15, 1940; h/1612 E Bonita Vista, San Bernardino, CA 92404; ba/SB; m/Esther; c/Ari, Liana, Yoni; p/Carl

and Tessie Barkan, Delray FL; ed/BA; MA; PhD; pa/Prof Cal St Col; Am Hist Assn; Org Am Hist; Immig Hist Soc; Am Sociol Assn; r/Jewish; hon/Fellow Woodrow Wilson; Phi Beta Kappa; Phi Alpha Theta.

BARKER, ELLIOTT SPEER oc/Author;

Consultant; Game Warden; b/Dec 25, 1886; h/343 Palace Ave, Santa Fe, NM 97501;ba/Same; m/Ethel; c/Roy, Florence Giers, Dorothy Elmore; p/Squire and Pricila Barker (dec); pa/US Forest Ranger & Supvr 1909-19; Rancher 1919-30; NM St Game Warden Dir G & F Dept 1931-53; Exec Secy

NM Wildlife Fdn 1958-68; Former Pres Wn Assn Game & Fish Commrs; Intl Assn Game, Fish & Conserv Commrs; r/Prot; Meth; hon/St Conservationist of Yr for NM, Nat Wildlife Fdn; Pres Emeritus NM Wildlife Fdn; Am Motors Corp Conservationist Awd; Hon LLD NM St Univ.

BARKER, MADELINE oc/Educator; Lecturer; Writer; h/2452 Baja Cerro Cir, San Diego, CA 92109; m/Kenneth Samuel; p/Daniel Pomeroy Taylor; Fannie Elliott Miller; ed/BA SD St Univ 1939; MA Geo Peabody Col for Tchrs 1950; Gen Tchg Credential: Sec'dy 1967, Jr High; pa/Tchr Var Public Schs 1942-72; Perfs: *Four Seasons Ballet, Nutcracker Suite, Mother Goose Ballet*; Num Other Perfs; Author: "Poems of Madeline", "Aladdin in Queen Elizabeths Ct"; Num Others; Jewel Sq Dance Clb: Dancer 27 Yrs, Public Relats, Soc Chm, Treas; Univ Cal SD Folk Danc'g; Al Gilbert Dance Camp Univ SD; Dir Showcase Singers 1978; Am Assn Univ Wom SD; SCAMBI Intl; Nat Leag Am Pen Wom Lectr; cp/SD Opera Guild; Peabody Col Alumni Assn; SD Ballet Publicity; r/Choir Mt Soledad Presb Ch; hon/W/W: Am Wom, W, Am; Nat Soc Dir; Lttrs Awds, Nat Leag Am Pen Wom; Writing Awds, Am Assn Univ Wom; Prizes: 1st, Orchid Show 27th SD Co, 3rd, Cal Lttrs, 3rd, Contra Costa Co Fair.

BARKLEY, FRED ALEXANDER oc/-Biologist; b/Nov 4, 1908; h/104 E Highland, Tecumseh, OK 74873; m/Elizabeth Ducker; c/Robert, William, Anne Powers, Jorge Araque; p/Alexander and Maie Webster Barkley (dec); ed/BA, MS Univ Okla; PhD Washington Univ; pa/Nat Vice-Chancellor Phi Sigma; Sigma Xi; Begonia Soc; r/Epis; hon/Fellow Tex Acad Sci; Soc Bot de Mex.

BARKLEY, G RICHARD oc/Electrical Engineer; b/Jul 15, 1934; h/1406 Massengale, Round Rock, TX 78664; ba/Austin, TX; c/Yvonne, Travis, Robin; p/George and Velma Lowry Barkley, Aurora, MO; ed/BS Okla St Univ 1960; Addit Studies; mil/AUS Signal Corps 1954-57; pa/Res Engr Doppler Sonar Dev Prog Univ Tex 1976-; Former: Vinyl Repair Franchisee, Examr Soc Security Adm, Reconciliation & Analysis Unit, Owner/Mgr El Rancho Motel, Engr Dynamics Pomona Div; Gen Dynamics Covair Div: Conslitg Engr AWACS Proj, EMC Engr Atlas, SLV & Centaur Missiles, Sub-Sys Engr Atlas Weapon Sys Missile Sites; IEEE.

BARKLEY, OWEN HERBERT oc/-Photographer; b/Aug 9, 1922; h/126 N Main, Climax, MI 49034; ba/Battle Creek, MI; m/Karen Ann; c/Matthew, Russell, Jeffrey; p/Kirk and Mabel Barkley (dec); ed/USN: Sch Photo, Electronics Sch; Nat Camera Repair Sch; mil/USN Chief Photog 1943-64; pa/Profl Photog; CoOwner K & O Photo Inc; Profl Photogs Am; cp/Pres Village of Climax; OES; Masonic Lodge; r/Prot; hon/W/W MW; Dic Intl Biog; Commun Ldrs & Noteworthy Ams; Other Biogl Listings.

BARKSDALE, LUCY ANN oc/Educator; b/Jul 3, 1942; h/PO Box 4156, West Biloxi Station, MS 39531; ba/Biloxi; p/Robert Barksdale, Summit, MS; Lucy Barksdale (dec); ed/BA; Addit Studies; pa/Migrant Tutor; Former 6th Grade Tchr; Sci Fair Clb; Am Fdn Tchrs; CoAuthor 6th Grade Sci Curr; Dir Elem Sch Sci Fairs; cp/PTA Talent Show Com; Alcohol & Drug Abuse Studies Assn; r/Mem First Bapt Ch Ocean Springs, Miss; hon/Outstg Tchr 1975-76; W/W Am Schs & Univs.

BARLOW, HERMAN ZULCH JR oc/Administrator; Conductor; b/Oct 8, 1949; h/2918 Nottingham, Houston, TX 77005; ba/Houston; c/Meredith; ed/BA Houston Bapt Univ; MEd Univ Houston; EdD Pacific Sts Univ; pa/Houston Bapt Univ: Assoc to Pres, Dean Admissions 1973-76, Acting Dean Admissions 1972-73, Admissions Cnslr 1972; Former: Resident Conductor Smph N Houston, Min Music Westbury U Meth Ch; Conductor: Overtures, Symphs, Suites, Choral; Guest Conductor Var Orgs; Nat Assn Col Adms Cnslrs; Am Assn Col Registrars & Admissions Ofcrs; Am Acad Arts & Scis; Am Choral Dirs Assn; Choristers Soc; F'ship U Meth Musicians; Other Profl Assns; r/Asst Choir Dir: Ch of St John Divine, First Presb Ch; Organist Victory Bapt Ch; Dir Music Northwoods Presb Ch; hon/Kappa Alpha; Former Pres, Omicron Delta Kappa; Dist'd Alumnus Awd 1974; W/W Am Univs & Cols; Outstg Young Men Am; Num Other Biogl Listings.

BARNARD, CLARE A oc/Real Estate Broker; b/Dec 31, 1927; h/Rt 1 Box 750, Lutz, FL 33549; ba/Land O'Lakes, FL; m/Henry Clay; c/Henry III, Matthew, David; p/Leon Amundson (dec); Charlotte Amundson, Toledo, OH; ed/AA Stephens Col 1948; pa/Land O'Lakes Bd Realtors; Chm RPAC;

Assn Realtors: Nat, Fla; Fla Real Est Exchangors; cp/Pasco Co: Bicent Chr, Repub St Com Wom; VChr 5th Congl Dist Repub Party Fla; Jr Leag Tampa Inc; Del Repub Nat Conv; Alumnae Bd Stephens Col; Easter Seal Guild Tampa; r/Epis.

BARNARD, GEORGE HUGH oc/Lawyer; b/Jun 14, 1909; h/181 E Lake Shore Dr, Chicago, IL; ba/Chgo; p/Julius and Martha Barnard (dec); ed/PhB 1930, JD 1931 Univ Chgo; mil/USNR Cmdr WW-II; pa/St Bar Assns: Chgo, Am, Ill; cp/Exec Clb Nav Order USNR Assn; Govs Comm Equal Rts for Wom; Coor Yachting PanAm Games Chgo; hon/USNR: Bronze Star, 2 Commend Ribbons.

BARNARD, JANET KAY oc/Educator; b/May 12, 1948; h/404 S Emery St, Heyworth, IL 61745; ba/Normal, IL; m/John Dennis; p/Harold and Alice Bressner, Pontiac, IL; ed/BS 1970, MS 1977 Ill St Univ; pa/Tchr Math 1970-; Ed Assns: Unit 5, Ill, Nat; PTO; Delta Kappa Gamma; Coun Tchrs Math: Nat, Ill; Supvr Student Tchrs & Undergrad Students; Ill St Univ, Ill Wesleyan Univ; Other Profl Assns; cp/Ill St Alumni Assn; Heyworth: Lioness Clb, Fed'd Woms Clb; Guernsey Breeders Assns: Ill, Dist 4; Christian Bus Woms Assn; Cand Promotion Com Sch Bd Election; Other Civic Assns; r/U Ch H'worth: Substitute SS Tchr, Sr High Yth Group Sponsor, Bible Sch Tchr, Greeter,

Liturgist, Reach Out Choir, Volleyball Team; Coun Mins; Reach Out Fellowship: Secy, Treas; hon/Outstg Yg Edr Awd, Normal Jaycees; Nat Outstg Ldr Elem & Sec'dy Ed; McLean Co 4H Ldrship Recog; Detroit Area Coun Tchrs Math; Pub'd Author; Num Biogl Listings.

BARNES, BEULAH DANIELS oc/Environmentalist; b/Apr 24, 1919; h/Rt 5 Box 255, Goldsboro, NC 27530; m/Joseph; c/Clarence, Luebert; p/Burke and Aldonia C Daniels (dec); pa/Envir Asst O'Berry Ctr; cp/Past Matron Lady Love Chapt OES; St Chairlady Histn Com; Past Most Noble Gov Naomi

Chapt Household of Ruth; 30 Yrs Extension Work; Wayne Co Coun: Pres 1978-79, VP 1976-77; Other Civic Assns; r/Mem Holly Green Missionary Bapt Ch, Dudley; Pres Ushers Bear Creek Assn; hon/Personalities S; A & P Ldrship Awd; Miss Bride Dist En Star; Miss Missionary Wkr Bear Creek Assn; Num Other Honors.

BARNES, BRUCE ERNEST oc/Manager; b/Jun 16, 1949; h/2-11E Lincoln Sq, New York, NY 10023; ba/NY; p/Earle Jr and Marion Barnes, Lowville, NY; ed/BS Syracuse Univ 1972; MBA Fairleigh Dickinson Univ 1974; pa/Prod Mgr Colgate Palmolive Co; AMBA Execs; cp/Syracuse Alumni Clb; NY SCUBA Assn; r/Presb.

BARNES, CHARLES EDWARD oc/Executive; b/Feb 25, 1933; h/4300 Bellwood Ln, Matthews, NC 28105; ba/M'thews; m/Molly Primm; c/Kristin, Stephan; p/W M and Glenna Viola Barnes, Rock Hill, SC; ed/Brevard Col; pa/VP Advtg, Promotion & Public Relats; Charlotte Advtg Clb.

BARNES, FRANCES RAMONA oc/Educator; b/Dec 23, 1931; ba/Menard Correctional Ctr, Menard, IL 62259; m/Clarence Edward; c/Robert, Carlena,

Quentin, Vicki; p/Ralph Henry, Steelville, MO; Alice Mae (dec); ed/BS; MA; pa/Reading Spec Edr; Intl Reading Assn; Coun Exceptl Chd; cp/Auxs: Eagles, VFW, Chester Mem Hosp; Girl Scout Asst Ldr; Band Boosters; r/Luth; hon/Kappa Delta Pi; W/W; Child Devel Profls, Wom; Other Biogl Listings.

BARNES, JIM WEAVER oc/Associate Professor; Poet; b/Dec 22, 1933; h/918 Pine St, Macon MO 63552; ba/Kirksville, MO; m/Carolyn Louise Turpin; c/Bret, Blake; p/Austin and Bessie Vernon Barnes,

Summerfield, OK; ed/BA; MA, PhD Univ Ark; mil/Okla Nat Guard 1950-51; pa/Assoc Prof Comparative Lit NE Mo St Univ; Poet-in-the-Schs: Mo, Ill, Ia; MLA; NCTE; r/Prot; hon/Nat Endowment Arts Creative Writing F'ship in Poetry; Pub'd Author.

BARNES, MAGGIE LUE SHIFFLETT oc/Nursing; b/Mar 29, 1931; h/Rt 1 Box 9-B, Hermleigh, TX 79526; ba/Snyder, TX; m/Lawrence; c/LaWayne Fagan; p/Howard and Sadie Dunlap Shifflett, Snyder, TX; ed/LVN; RN; AA; BSN; pa/Nsg East Evening Supvr; Procedure Com Emer Room Nsg Assn; cp/BSA; PTA; Sr Citizens; Cnslr & Bd Mem AAA; r/Apostolic Faith Ch; hon/S'ship Meth Sch Nsg; Wn Tex Col: Deans List, Pres' List; Num Biogl Listings.

BARNES, MELVER RAYMOND oc/Chemistry; b/Nov 15, 1917; h/Rt 1 Box 424, Linwood, NC 27299; ba/Same; p/Oscar and Sarah Rowe Barnes (dec); ed/BA UNC-CH; mil/AUS 1942-45; pa/Sci Lit Res; hon/Num Biogl Listings.

BARNES, RACHEL CARTER oc/Educator; b/Mar 13, 1895; h/613 Kansas, Oswego, KS 67356; m/Charles L; c/(Stepchd:) LaVada Hollyfield, Inez Latham; p/Jesse and Mary Carter (dec); ed/BS; Postgrad Studies; pa/Ret'd Eng & Spch Tchr Sec'dy Level; Ofcr Var Tchr Orgs; Delta Kappa Gamma Soc; cp/Wkr Repub Party; Ofcr Var Fed'd Clbs & Fraternal Orgs; r/Prot; Presb; SS Tchr, Elder; Pres UPW; Other Positions; hon/HS Valedictorian.

BARNETT, ED WILLIS oc/Artist-Photographer; Author; b/May 8, 1899; h/4322 Glenwood Ave, Birmingham, AL 35222; ba/Same; m/Lula White; c/Edith B Delavan, Roberta Colebeck, Melanie Parker; p/Samuel and Claribel O'Leary Barnett (dec); ed/Att'd Univ Ala; mil/USN: Lt Commdr 1941-46, US Nav Acad 1917-20; pa/Partner Barnett & Barnett Advtg Agy 1929-73; Pub'd Author & Photog; Fdr & Dir Fotos Intl; Dir

Photographic Dept Ala St Fair; Pres Ala Mus Photo; Fellow Photographic Soc Am; 1 Man Shows; Photographs Perm Collections: Metro Mus Art, NY Mus Mod Art, Seattle Mus Art, Kodak Camera Clb; Num Others; cp/Rotary Clb; r/Epis; hon/US Olympic Fencing Team 1928; Gold Medal Federation Internationale d'Art Photographique; Litzel Gold Medal; Commandeur d'Honneur Commanderie de Bon Temps de Medoc et des Graves; Osterreiche Gesellschaft fur Photographie; Num Other Hons.

BARNETT, FRANKLIN DEWEES oc/Doctor; b/Aug 1, 1935; h/9104 Nawassa Dr, Midwest City, OK 73130; ba/MWC; m/Louise B; c/Julie, Brian, Shelley, Kelly, Robert, Colin; p/Harry Barnett, Florence, KY; Elizabeth Barnett (dec); ed/BA; MD; mil/USAF 1962-64; pa/Med Dr Ob & Gyn; Med Assns: Am, Okla St, Christian; Am Col OB-GYN; Am Assn GYN Laparoscopists; Am Fertility Soc; cp/MWC Rotary Clb; r/Meth; hon/W/W: SW, Med Specs; Personalities S.

BARNETT, SAMUEL CLARENCE oc/Engineer; Educator; b/May 10, 1922; h/1938 Gotham Way NE, Atlanta, GA 30324; ba/Atla; m/Dorothy W; c/Daniel; p/Jesse Barnett (dec); Marguerite H Barnett, Fort Meade, FL; ed/BIE 1948, MS 1956, PhD 1962 Ga Inst Technol; mil/AUS 1942-45; pa/Prof Mech Engrg Ga Inst Technol; Dir Undergrad Sch Mech Engrg Ga Tech 1962-68; Asst &

Assoc Dean Ga Tech Undergrad Div 1968-72; Head Indust Engrg Tech Dept Sn Tech Inst 1972-75; Conslt Ga Power Co 1977; Fac Advr & Treas Tau Beta Pi; Fac Secy Phi Kappa Phi; Am Soc Mech Engrs: Fac Advr, Gen Awds Com; Other Profl Positions; cp/Past Pres Piedmont Hgts Civic Clb; Ansley Golf Clb; r/Presb; hon/Pi Tau Sigma; Phi Eta Sigma; Soc Sigma Xi; Pub'd Author.

BARNETT, WELDON I oc/Director; b/Dec 23, 1916; h/1207 S 18th St, Artesia, NM 88210; ba/Artesia; m/Jean Barbara Nelson; c/Donald, Susan (Mrs Mark Long); p/William and Ila Rogers Barnett (dec); ed/BA Howard Payne Univ 1945; BD SWn Bapt Theol Sem 1948; pa/Dir Missions Pecos Val Bapt Assn; Past Dir Missions Ks; Former Pastor: Tex, Cal & Ark; r/Sn Bapt; hon/W/W: Rel, Am Univs & Cols.

BARNEWALL, GORDON GOUVERNEUR oc/Dean; Professor; Editorialist; b/Feb 1, 1924; h/1675 S Birch St, Denver, CO 80222; ba/Denver; m/Sieglinde Gruber; c/Ann; p/William and Nancy Barnewall (dec); ed/BS; MBA; PhD; mil/1st Inf Div WW-II; pa/Col Bus UCD: Dean, Prof; Radio Editorialist & Commentator; hon/Peabody Awd; Pub'd Author.

BARNHARDT, WILLIAM H oc/Textiles; b/Feb 3, 1903; ba/3600 NCNB Plaza, Charlotte, NC 28280; m/Margaret McLaughlin; c/William, Nancy B Thomas, Charles (dec), John; ed/BE NC St Col 1923; pa/Former Pres, Treas & Dir: Am Realty Corp, Am Textile Corp, Barnhardt Brothers Corp, Barnhardt Elastic Corp, Novelty Yarns Corp; Others; Sn Webbing Mills Inc; Sharon Corp; Univ Hgts Inc; Num Other Profl Assns; cp/BSA: Reg Com, Adv Bd Mecklenburg Coun; YMCA: Past Pres, Bldg Com, 25 Yrs Exec Com; Campaign Chr Charlotte Citizens; Former VP U Commun Sers; Chr Capital Funds Bd; NY Ath Clb; Travelers Century

Clb; Metro Clb; Other Civic Assns; r/Myers Park Presb; Former Deacon, Elder, V Moderator; hon/Man of S 1973; Nat Conf Christian & Jews Awd; Charlotte YMCA Ser Yth Awd; BSA: Silver Antelope, Silver Beaver; Pi Kappa Phi; Newcomen Soc N Am; W/W: Am, Commerce & Indust, S&SE; Dedicated Bldgs & Books; Num Other Hons.

BARNHART, JOE EDWARD oc/Professor; b/Nov 1, 1931; h/606 Headlee Ln, Denton, TX 76201; ba/Denton; m/Mary Ann Shropshire; c/Ritschl, Linda; p/Clifford and Irene Snyder Barnhart (dec); ed/BA Carson-Newman Col; MDiv Sn Bapt Theol Sem; PhD Boston Univ; pa/Prof Phil N Tex St Univ; Proj Dir & Scriptwriter for Tex Com Humanities TV Drama; r/Naturalistic Humanism.

BARNHART, PHILLIP H oc/Minister; b/Jul 7, 1937; h/990 Cooper Lake Rd, Smyrna, GA 30080; ba/Smyrna; m/Sharon; c/Denise, Mark, Lisa, Kara, Kenneth, Amy; p/Harold Barnhart (dec); Hazel Barnhart; ed/BA; MDiv; pa/U Meth Min; Accredited Visitor World Meth Conf; cp/Mayors Adv Bd Atlanta; r/Meth; hon/W/W Am Cols & Univs; Pres Lttr Commend; Pub'd Author.

BARNHILL, LAURA RUTH oc/Manager; b/May 24, 1936; h/1570 Foxridge Run, Winter Haven, FL 33880; ba/Bartow, FL; c/Teresa Lea Lillie, William III, Curtis; p/Curtis Whittle (dec); Irene Prevatte, Ft Meade, FL; ed/Att'g Inst Fin Ed; pa/Branch Mgr First Fed Winter Haven; Coor Suncoast Soc Branch Mgrs;

Golden Gate Merchs Assn; cp/Chrperson U Way Com; Can-Do Clb; Dir Greater Bartow C of C; Crickett Clb; Bartow Booster Clb; En Star; Girl Scout Ldr; Den Mother Boy Scouts; Other Civic Assns; r/Bapt; hon/Awd Ser: Bartow Can-Do Clb, C of C; Merit Awd, Bartow Art Guild.

BARON, HOWARD N oc/Executive; b/Jun 16, 1922; h/2611 Bayshore Blvd, Tampa, FL 33609; ba/Tampa; m/Rebecca; c/Allen, Martin, Michael; p/Leon and Friede Baron (dec); ed/MA Univ La; mil/Capt Defence Army of Israel; pa/VP Intl; Conslt

Finland; Cnslr Fgn Trade; Coun Fgn Relats; Intl Dir Seald Sweet Growers Inc; cp/Dir Ellis Nat Bank Tampa; Univ Clb; Tower Clb; Fla Citrus Comm; r/Jewish; Hebrew; hon/Fgn Trade Man of Yr; K of White Rose, Finnish Decoration; Officier du Merit Agricole, French Decoration.

BARONE, STEPHEN S oc/Executive; b/Jun 25, 1922; h/8 Wren Ct, Old Brookville, NY 11545; ba/New York, NY; m/Maria

Regina Abbadessa; c/Vivian Dewey (Mrs R J), Anne Marie Tronolone (Mrs W V), Vincent; p/Vincent and Vincenzina Reina Barone (dec); ed/BA cum laude Holy Cross 1943; JD Columbia 1945; pa/Electronics Co Exec; RCA Corp: Sr VP Lic'g 1979, VP Lic'g 1972; Staff VP Intl Lic'g 1967; Div VP Lic Ops RCA Intl Div 1963; Dir & Chr Bd RCA Engrg Labs; Dir & Pres Labs RCA; Dir & VP RCA Res Labs; r/Rom Cath.

BARR, CHARLOTTE ANNE oc/Educator; h/8130 W 84th Pl, Oak Lawn, IL 60458; ba/Posen, IL; c/Darryl; p/Stanley and Lillian Barr (dec); ed/PhB 1934, MA 1953 DePaul Univ; Addit Studies; pa/Prof Emeritus Early Childhood Ed Chicago St Univ; Dist 143½: Dir Title I, Dir Title VII; Former Conslt Var Proil Orgs; Bd Dirs Ill Assn Higher Ed; Ill Ed Assn: Chr Col Sec, Bd Dirs, Pres Chgo Div; Assn Childhood Ed Intl; Child Study Assn Am; Pi Lambda Theta, Nat Soc Study Ed; Nat Assn Ed Yg Chd; Other Profl Assns; cp/Policy Adv Bd Parent Involvement; Exec Dir EdnlCoor Suburban Opport Sers; Ednl Dir Tri-Area Commun Action Agy; Leag Wom Voters; Dir Parent Adv Coun; Other Civic Assns; r/Rom Cath; hon/W/W: Am Wom, MD; Intl Biog; Delta Kappa Gamma; Pi Lambda Theta; Pub'd Author.

BARR, ELSIE S oc/Educator; Librarian; b/Feb 23, 1892; h/312 E Millett Ave, Mesa, AZ 85202; ba/Same; m/William Wesley (dec); c/William Jr, Burton; p/Frederick and Caroline Sueltz (dec); pa/Former Edr Public & Ch Schs; Dept Co Supt Schs; Libn City Lib; cp/Girl Scouts; Am Legion Aux; Vets WW I; Del Repub Convs; Secy & Dir ARC; Clerk Elections; Promoter Repub Cands; r/Presb; Libn; hon/Meritorious Awd; 1st Prize St Pub Contest Am Legion Aux; W/W Am Wom; Wom World; Num Other Biogl Listings.

BARR, NONA LEE oc/Educator; Speech Pathologist; Artist; b/Jul 11, 1934; h/2509 Ingrid Ln, Metarie LA 70003; ba/New Orleans, LA; m/Luther Laken; c/Lori; p/Joseph and Beulah Futrell Behel, Iron City, TN; ed/BS 1965, MA 1968 Univ Houston; Postgrad Studies; pa/Pvt Pract Spch Pathol; Former Spch Pathol: St Charles Gen, La Porte Indep Sch; Past Conslts: Unihlth Corp, Homemakers Greater NO; Spch & Hearing Assns: Am, Tex, La; Bd Dirs Am Acad Pvt Pract Spch Pathol & Audiology; Nat Coun Aging: Nat, Jefferson Parish, Metro NO; Nat Ed Assn; Coun Exceptl Chd; cp/USCG Wives Clb; Propellar Clb; Coms: Ethics, Mbrship, Fees, Ad Hoc, Communs Problems of Aged; r/Hickory Knoll Ch Christ; hon/Acad Pvt Pract Spch Pathol & Audiology; Sigma Alpha Eta Awd; Pub'd Author.

BARRERA, EUSTOLIA R oc/Reading Specialist; b/Dec 19, 1927; h/PO Box 615, Rio Grande City, TX 78582; ba/RGC; m/Benicio; c/Diana, Belinda; p/(dec); ed/BS; MS; MA; pa/CTA; TSTA; AAUW; cp/Cath Daughs; Boosters: Band, Freshman; r/Cath; hon/Outstg Ldrs Elem & Sec'dy Ed; Outstg Sers Awd, Band Boosters.

BARRET, RICHARD CARTER oc/Director; Author; Lecturer; b/Mar 19, 1916; h/"Lemon Fair" 14 Bank St, Bennington, VT 05201; ba/Same; m/Betty Oder; c/Tracy; p/Richard and Edith Carter Barret (dec); ed/AA Univ Toledo 1938; BA cum laude Middlebury Col 1950; mil/AUS Pvt-Capt Trans Corps 1942-46; pa/Author Num Books

Art; Lectr Edl TV; Sheldon Mus: Asst Curator 1949, Curator 1950; B'ton Mus: Asst Curator 1951-54, Curator 1954-60, Dir 1960-74; Fdr & Dir B'ton Mus Sch; Fac Sems: Sandwich Glass Mus, Old Sturbridge Village, Henry Ford Mus; Pvt Inst Arts & Crafts; Num Profl Assns; cp/Past Trustee Vt Hist Soc; Mil Order LaFayette; Asst Boy Scout Exec; Secy & Dir B'ton Battle Monument Assn; r/2nd Congreg, B'ton; Past Trustee; hon/Fellow Intl Inst Arts & Scis; W/W E.

BARRETT, CLAIRE RONDEAU oc/- Administrator; Educator; h/76 Lowell Ave, West Orange, NJ 07052; ba/South Orange, NJ; m/Clifford James; p/Charles and Gelia Tessier Rondeau (dec); ed/BS Tchrs Col; MS, PhD Fordham Univ; pa/Seton Hall Univ: Asst Dean 1976-, Assoc Prof Ed 1973-, Dept Chperson 1972-74; Former Guid Dir 1965-69; Cnslr Stella Viae Intl Col 1964-65; Num Other Profl Positions; Exec Coun Kappa Delta Pi; Exec Coun Intl Platform Assn; Am Israel Leag; Am Acad Rel; Am Assn Univ Profs; Am Profs Peace Mid E; cp/Fordham Alumni Assn; Am Cath Hist Soc; NY Chapt Christian Life Commun; r/Rom Cath; St Josephs Ch, WO; hon/Gold Medalist Christian Life Commun; PhD S'ship, Fordham Univ; W/W Am Wom; Commun Ldrs; Outstg Am Caths; Num Other Biogl Listings.

BARRETT, JOHN FRANCIS oc/Priest; b/Apr 24, 1933; h/64 Norfolk, Clarendon Hills, IL 60514; ba/Same; p/Francis Barrett (dec); Hildegarde Parr Barrett, Glen Ellyn, IL; ed/BA, STB, MA St Mary of Lake Sem; pa/Pastor Notre Dame Ch; Priests' Senate: Diocesan Conslt Joliet Bishop; Former Chr Diocesan Liturgy Com; cp/Former Nat Chaplain Dominic Clb; r/Rom Cath.

BARRETT, LEN GARY oc/Farmer; b/Sept 24, 1953; h/Rt #4 Box 221, Alexander City, AL 35010; ba/Same; m/Sandra Foshee; p/L G and Laura Jordan Barrett, AC, AL; pa/Feeder Pig Farmer; Tallapoosa Co Feeder Pig Assn; r/Christian; hon/Outstg Yg Farmer, T'poosa Co.

BARRETT, ROBERT OWEN oc/Sales Manager; b/Jun 2, 1944; h/519 Greenhill Ln, Berwyn, PA 19312; ba/King of Prussia, PA; m/Elisabeth Hayes; c/Susan; p/Edward Barrett, Norristown, PA; Elizabeth P Barrett (dec); ed/BA; MBA; pa/Asst Nat Comml Sales Mgr Lees Carpets Valley Forge Corp; Am Mgmt Assn; cp/Repub Nat Com; r/Presb.

BARRETT, WILLIAM ARVEL oc/Health Administrator; b/Aug 16, 1919; h/PO Box 155, Ila, GA 30647; ba/Athens, GA; m/Frances S; c/William (dec), Johnny, Perry, Joy; p/Lawrence Barrett (dec); Beatrice Barrett Holt, Rochester, MI; ed/BBA Sa St Univ; mil/USAR Maj; pa/Fellow Am Col Nsg Home Adm; Am Col Hosp Admrs; cp/Long Term Hlth Care Coun St of Ga; r/Bapt.

BARRICK, LOUISE GRIDER oc/Librarian; b/Apr 19, 1912; h/340 S 22nd St, Terre Haute, IN 47803; m/Harry T; c/Judith Stull (Mrs Robert), Thomas; p/John and Dean Grider (dec); ed/BS; Cert Lib Sci; pa/Lib Assns: Am, Ind; Vigo Co Public Lib Staff Assn; Bd Adult & Child Guid Clinic; cp/Sigma Kappa Alumna; Woms Dept Clb: VP, Chr Art Dept; Fac Wives Ind St Univ; Lundi Clb; Davis Park PTA; r/Centenary U Meth Ch: U Meth Wom, Adm Bd, Bd Trustees, Yg Woms Guild; hon/W/W: Am Wom, MW, US; Num Other Biogl Listings.

BARRIENTES, GUADALUPE oc/Medical Specialist; b/Oct 9, 1952; h/1614 14th St, Hondo, TX 78861; ba/Ft Richardson, AK; p/Manuel Barrientes (dec); Maria L Barrientes, Hondo, TX; ed/Att'd: Med Spec Sch, Airborne Sch; Att'g Univ Alaska; mil/AUS; pa/Airborne Med Spec; Paratrooper; Chr Nat Yth Am Gl Form; cp/Del Tex Gov Conf; Del Pres Nixon's Conf "Yth Apprec Wk"; r/Rom Cath; hon/Nations Outstg Yth 1972; W/W S&SW; Am Soldiers Spirit Awd Medal.

BARRON, DAVID MILTON oc/Actor; Musician; b/May 11, 1938; h/96 Hicks St, Brooklyn, NY 11201; m/Susan; p/R C and Mrs R C Barron, Canyon, TX; ed/BMus Baylor Univ; MMus Yale Univ; PhD Univ Ill; pa/Former Edr Sch Music Univ Ill; Opera & Concert Perfs USA & Europe; Recital Tours 19th & 20th Century Am Songs; Fests:

Warsaw Autumn Intl Fest Contemp Music, Charles Ives Centennial Fest-Conf; Musical Roles: Nicks Shadow, Don Giovanni, Papageno, Leporello, Don Alfonso, Alberich; Musical Comedies: Oklahoma, Fantasticks, Man of La Mancha; hon/Phi Mu Alpha; Alpha Chi; Pi Kappa Lambda; Phi Kappa Phi; Pub'd Author; Num S'ships.

BARROWMAN, KINO MARY oc/- Director; b/Nov 28, 1943; h/7441 SW 176 St, Miami, FL 33157; ba/Miami; m/John; c/Kino Anne; p/Goro Sakuma, Miami, FL; ed/AA Miami Dade Commun Col; BS Fla Atl Univ; MEd Fla Intl Univ; Doct Cand; pa/Dir Curric & Res U Tchrs Dade; Am Assn Higher Ed; Mtl Hlth Assn Dade Co Inc; Smithsonian Assocs; U Tchrs Dade; Fla Ed Assn/U; Am Fdn Tchrs;

cp/Kappa Omega; Asian-Am Caucus/NEA; Reg'd Lobbyist House & Senate; Leag Wom Voters; Tiger Bay; Floridians Casinos; Hemispheric Cong Wom; En Star; Dade Co Public Schs: Preferential Employmt Criteria Com, Early Childhood Ed Coor'g Coun, Pupil Progression Plan Com, Chperson UTD Curric Coun; Other Civic Assns; r/Cath; hon/Outstg Cath of Yr 1962; Spch & Debate S'ship Awd, Exchange Clb; Outstg Wom Dade Co.

BARROWS, MARGARET BENTLEY HAMILTON oc/Writer; Composer; b/Sept 6, 1920; h/2117 Jackson St NW Apt C, Olympia, WA 98502; c/David; p/David and Margaret Bentley Hamilton (dec); ed/Grad Sarah Lawrence Col 1941; (Hon) PhD Col St Christian Col; pa/Composer & Lyricist Num Compositions incl'g "Living w Arts", "Easter Carol", "Promised Land", "Month of June", Others; Staff Asst ARC Fgn Inquiry Ser; Pres Woms Farm Home Adv Com Sn Sts Coop;

Chm Coun En Centre & World Poets Resource Ctr; Orgr & Chr Intl Poets Wkshp; Bd Dirs World Poets Resource Ctr Corp; Lay Jury Detroit Artists Mktg; U Repubs Am; Fellow Intl Biog Assn; Nat Soc Lit & Arts; Nat Soc Arts & Lttrs; Intl Platform Assn; Am Guild Authors & Composers; Am Conservative Union; Nat Adv Bd Christian Crusade; Nat Voter Adv Bd Am Security Coun; Delta Omicron; Dir Sigma Gamma; cp/Capital Hill; Quota; Colonial Dames; Jr Leag; Pres Sarah Lawrence Alumnae Assn; r/Presb; Mem U Chs, Olympia; hon/Annual Mentor Poetry Awd; Art Awd, St Timothys Sch; Stage Design Awd, Jr Leag; Recipient Essay Awd, World Poets Resource Ctr; Pub'd Author.

BARRY, ARTHUR LELAND oc/Microbiologist; b/Aug 2, 1932; h/921 Sierra Madre, Davis, CA 95616; ba/Sacramento, CA; m/Diane Hollingsworth; c/Karen, Kathleen, William, Brian; p/Roy and Jean Dyment Barry (dec); ed/BS Gonzaga Univ 1955; MS Wash St Univ 1957; PhD Ohio St Univ 1962; pa/S'mento Med Ctr: Clin Microbiologist, Dir Microbiology Labs; Former Prof Microbiology Univ Cal-D; Lectr Clin Microbiology; Chr NCCLS Subcom Antibiotic Sensitivity Tests; r/Presb; hon/Pub'd Author.

BARRY, B AUSTIN oc/Professor; b/Jul 23, 1917; h/4415 Post Rd, Bronx, NY 10471; ba/Bronx; p/Michael and Veronica Gertrude

Kopaskie (dec); ed/BA; BCE; MCE; pa/Prof Civil Engrg Manhattan Col; ACSM; ASCE; ASEE; r/Rom Cath; hon/Chi Epsilon; Sigma Xi; Survey'g & Mapp'g Awd, ASCE.

BARRY, THOMAS MARTIN JR oc/Civil Engineer; b/Oct 8, 1926; h/4455 Confederate Pt Rd Apt 15A, Jacksonville, FL 32210; ba/J'ville; m/Shirley Anne Ackerman; c/Thomas, Patricia Barnes (Mrs Larry G); p/Thomas and Alice Laux Barry (dec); ed/BS US Mil Acad 1950; MSCE Univ Ill 1956; mil/USAAF 1944-45; AUS Comm'd 2nd Lt 1950 Ret'd Ltc 1971; pa/Am Public Works Assn; Insts: Bldgs & Grounds, Mun Engrg, Traffic Engrs; Past Pres Soc Am Mil Engrs.

BARSI, LOUIS MICHAEL oc/Administrator; h/197 Hill Ct, Hartland, WI 53209; ba/Waukesha, WI; p/Louis Barsi, Woodbridge, NJ; Mary Remak Barsi (dec); ed/BA Univ Okla; MA Ctl Mich Univ; MAEd Univ No Iowa; EdS Cand Univ Wis-S; pa/Coor Fin Aids Univ Wis-W'sha 1977-; Former Dean Students Mt St Clare Col 1969-76; Instr Muskegon Commun Col 1966-68; Other Profl Positions; Am Pers & Guild Assn; Pers Assn: Wis Col, Am Col; Mbrship Com WCPA; Univ Wis-W'sha: Hons Prog Com, Student Sers Com, Fin Aids Comm; Other Profl Assns; cp/Rotary Clb; Bd Dirs HANDS; r/Rom Cath; hon/Phi Alpha Theta; Phi Delta Kappa; Intl W/W: Intellectuals, Comm Ser; Num Other Biogl Listings.

BARSTOW, PAUL ROGERS oc/Professor; Director; b/Oct 22, 1925; h/"W Lodge" 280 Ctl St, Wellesley, MA 02181; ba/W'ley; c/Victoria, Julia; p/Robbins and Dorothy Rogers Barstow (dec); ed/BA magna cum laude Williams Col 1948; MFA Yale Sch Drama 1955; mil/AUS ETO 1943-46; pa/Dir Theatre W'ley Col; Theatre Studies: Prof, Dir Prog, Chr Dept, Lectr & Chr Spch Dept, Actor & Dir: Harvard Sum Players, Williamstown Theatre, Provincetown Playhouse,

Roundabout Repertory; Num Other Works; Actors Equity Assn; Am Fdn TV & Radio Actors; Screen Actors Guild; Nom'g Bd Am Theatre Assn; Former Pres New England Theatre Conf; Other Profl Assns; cp/Nat Gay Task Force; Gay Rts Nat Lobby; r/Metro Commun Ch, Boston: Vestry Mem, Clerk; hon/Phi Beta Kappa; Schumway Prize Eng; Pub'd Author.

BARTA, MARIE LAURA oc/Educator; b/Oct 4, 1917; h/223 E N, Manly, IA 50456; ba/Mason City, IA; p/Edward Francis and Katherine Koci Barta (dec); pa/Music Edr; 2nd VP Iowa Music Tchrs Assn; Chr Nat Guild Piano Tchrs; Dis Chr Iowa Music Tchrs; Del Am Col Musicians People to People Prog En & Wn Europe & Soviet Russia; Nat Adjudicator Am Col Musicians; cp/Pres Pilot Clb; r/Luth; hon/W/W: Am Wom, Wom World; Intl Music Dic.

BARTACHEK, JUDITH DIANE oc/-Educator; b/Jul 8, 1940; h/Box 221, Denmark, IA 52624; ba/Denmark; p/Louis Bartachek (dec); Helen Bartachek Schwabe, Belle Plaine, IA; ed/BA, MA Univ No Ia; pa/Elem PE Tchr;

Civilian Tchg Overseas Dependent Schs; PE & Ed Assn: Ia, Nat; FMEA; ISEA; NEA; IAHPER; AAHPER; Del ISEA Assembly; r/Christian; hon/PE Dept Awd; Wild & White Awd; Tchr of Yr, Ft Madison Ed Assn.

BARTALOS, MIHALY oc/Physician; Educator; b/May 27, 1935; h/1 Eastwoods Ln, Scarsdale, NY 10583; ba/New York, NY; m/Eva P; c/Michael, Gabriel, Gregory; p/Mihaly and Roza Knazovicky Bartalos (dec); ed/MD cum laude Univ Heidelberg; mil/USPHS Sr Surg 1968-70; pa/Med Geneticist; Tchr Columbia Univ 1970-; Former Tchr Howard Univ 1965-68; cp/Former CoPres Hungarian Freedomfighters Fdn; Past Pres Semmelweis Sci Soc; r/Prot; hon/Govt S'ships: Hungary, W Germany; Pub'd Author.

BARTEL, BRUCE ALLAN oc/Minister; b/Nov 10, 1943; h/310 E Harris St, Appleton, WI 54911; ba/A'ton; m/Kathleen Jepsen; c/Tami, Brian, Trina; p/Bernard Bartel, Madison, WI; Edith Bartel, Janesville, WI; ed/BS Wis St Univ 1966; MDiv Evang Theol Sem 1970; DMin Iliff Sch Theol 1978;

pa/A'ton Min Assn; Alaska Missionary Conf Coun Mins; Alaska Missionary Conf: Bd Pensions, Bd Ordained Min, Chr Global Mins; Instr Chapman Col Residence Ctr; cp/Kenai Peninsula Borough Bd Ed; Chr Bd Kenai Peninsula Commun Care Ctr; Assn of Couples Marriage Enrichment Anchorage, Alaska; r/U Meth; hon/Outstg Yg Men Am 1973; Citizen of Month.

BARTER, ALICE KNAR oc/Professor; b/Nov 11, 1918; h/7231 Wolf Rd #212C, Indian Head Park, IL 60525; ba/Chicago, IL; c/Andrea B Kopp; p/Harry and Marguerite Seraderian Shamlian (dec); ed/BA En Mich

Univ 1939; MA 1944, PhD 1957 Univ Mich; pa/Prof Eng Chgo St Univ; NCTE; NSSE; MMLA; AFT; Pi Lambda Theta; Num Univ Coms; cp/Bd Trustees Leag Wom Voters; Precinctwom Lisle Twsp Dem Org; Cand Sch Bd; r/Epis; hon/Pub'd Author.

BARTHOLOMEW, MARYANN oc/Specialist; b/Jun 22, 1943; h/220 S Norma, LaHabra, CA 90631; ba/Whittier, CA; c/Tracy, Brian; p/John and Ann Pershern, Maple Hts, OH; ed/BFA Ohio Univ; MA Cand Cal St Long Bch; pa/Spch & Lang Spec; r/Cath; hon/Personalities W&MW; Commun Ldrs & Noteworthy Ams; W/W Child Devel Profls.

BARTLETT, HALL oc/Motion Picture Executive; b/Nov 27, 1925; h/861 Stone Canyon Rd, Los Angeles, CA 90024; ba/LA; m/Lupita Ferrer; c/Cathy, Laurie Bramhall (Mrs Scott); p/Paul Bartlett (dec); Alice Hiestand Bartlett, Kansas City, MO; ed/Grad Yale Univ; mil/US Nav Intell 1942-46; pa/Prodr, Dir & Writer Motion Picture Features: *Navajo, Crazylegs, Unchained, Jonathan Livingston Seagull*; Num Other

Movies; Motion Picture Acad Arts & Scis; Acad TV Arts & Scis; Phi Beta Kappa; cp/Patron Music Ctr; Bd Dirs Huntington Hartford Theatre; Friends Lib; Cinema Circulus; Bel Air Country Clb; r/Presb; hon/13 Acad Awd Nominations; Film Fest Awds: Cannes, Venice, Edinburg, San Sebastian, Grand Price Intl Mosco Film Fest; Motion Picture of Yr Awd, Nat Conf Christians & Jews; Fgn Press Awds.

BARTLETT, JOE oc/Minority Clerk; b/Aug 7, 1926; h/6128 Long Meadow Rd, McLean, VA; m/Virginia Bender; c/Laura Lee, Linda Hobgood (Mrs James L); p/F Dorsey Bartlett (dec); Blanche Hacker Bartlett; Att'd: George Wash Univ, WVa Wesleyan Col; (Hon) LLD: Atlanta Law Sch, Salem Col; mil/USMC Brig Gen; USMCR; pa/Page House Rep 1941-44; Rep Chief Pages 1945-53; Reading Clerk 1953-70; House Rep Minority Clerk 1970-; Bd Govs Nat Repub Clb Capital Hill; Participant Def Strategy Sem Nat War Col; cp/Bd Dirs Fed Exec Inst Alumni Assn; hon/Dist'd Ser Awd, US Jaycees; George Washington Medal, Freedoms Foun Valley Forge; Pub'd Author.

BARTLETT-GOODRICH, HELEN ELIZ-

ABETH oc/Executive; b/May 26, 1921; h/-1105 Gardner, Las Cruces, NM 88001; ba/-Same; m/James Lynn; c/(Stepchd:) Harvey Bartlett II, John, Lynn Lyon (Mrs Warren), Bert, Gisela G Webb (Mrs Michael); p/Charles and Beulah Dawson Nesbit (dec); ed/Att'd Univ Mo; pa/Engrg Mgmt Firm Exec; Profl Bus Partners Goodrich-Bartlett & Assocs Adv Plann'g-Feasibility-Coordination Conslts 1973-; Chief Fiscal Ofcr LC Urban Renewal Agy 1968-73; Former Real Est Broker; Other Profl Positions; Secy Inland Missile Range Sec Am Inst Aeronautics & Astronautics; Chr Spec Events Skylab-Erts Conf; Past Pres Dona Ana Chapt Nat Legal Secys Assn; Nat Assn Indep Ins Agts; Am Def Preparedness Assn; Nat Adv Bd Am Security Coun; r/Presb; hon/Am Inst Aeronautics & Astronautics: Apprec Cert Outstg Contbns, Nat Sect Spec Event Awd; W/W: W, Fin & Indust, Am; Dic Intl Biog; Intl W/W Commun Ser; Pub'd Author.

BARTON, LARRY H oc/Salesman; b/Apr 17, 1940; h/PO Box 588 Shady Ln Dr, Talladega, AL 35160; m/Mary C; c/Larry; p/B W and Willie Ruby Barton, T'dega, AL; ed/LSU Sch Bank'g; AS Gadsden St; mil/AUS

E5-SP5; pa/Salesman Jim Preuitt Pontiac-Cadillac-GMC; cp/Bd Cerebral Palsy; Am Assn Wkrs for Blind; Chr Westside Com Bd Cattlemen Assn; r/Prot; hon/Cerebral Palsy Sponsor Awd; Recipient Boys & Girls Ranch Awd.

BARTON, NELDA ANN LAMBERT oc/Politician; b/May 12, 1929; h/1311 7th St Rd, Corbin, KY; m/Harold Bryan (dec); c/William (dec), Barbara, Harold Jr, Stephen, Suzanne; p/Eulis G and Ruby West Lambert; ed/Grad Norton Mem Infirmary Sch Technol; pa/Repub Nat ComWom Ky 1968-76; Reg'd Technologist; Bd Dirs Nsg Homes Inc: Hazard, Hillcrest, Williamsburg; Adv Com Repub Fdn Repub Wom; Repub Nat Com: Exec Com, Adv Coun; SubCom CoChm RNC Rules Review; Precinct CoCapt Whitley Co Repub Party; Num Other Profl Assns; cp/Pres: WKU Beta Omega Chi, Whitley Co Med Aux, Corbin Ossoli Woms Clb, Corbin Ctl Elem PTA; Chr: Hlth Careers Ky Med Assn Aux, Adv Com Cumberland Col Assoc Degree Nsg Prog; Corbin Commun Devel Com; Ky Comm Wom; Ky Colonels; Ind Sagamore; Cub Scout Den Mother; Num Other Civic Assns; r/First Christian Ch: Mem, Chr, Yth F'ship, Circle #2, Stewardship; Other Positions; hon/HS Valedictorian Awd; Ky Repub Wom of Yr; Thank You Awd, Bluegrass Coun Boy Scouts; Dwight David Eisenhower Awd; Nelda Barton Day; PTA Life Mbrship Awd; S'ship Wn Ky Univ.

BARTOVA, FLORENCE oc/Ballet Teacher; b/Sept 28, 1911; h/133-01 Sanford Ave, Flushing, NY 11355; ed/Pvt Ballet Schs England, Russia & Italian; pa/Child & Adult Perfer; Classical Ballet Tchr 30 Yrs; Dir Ballet Wkshp 1967-; Demos, Recitals & Charitable Perfs; Contbr: *Dance & Dancers, Dancing Times, Dance Mag USA, Dance News USA*; Pavlova Soc; Nat Assn Dance & Affil'd Artists Inc; hon/Recipient Num Pins, Medals, Awds & Certs Achmt Throughout Career.

BARTSCH, RICHARD ALLEN oc/Professor; b/Jun 7, 1940; h/2604 77th St, Lubbock, TX 79423; ba/Lubbock; m/Nadine L; c/Robert, Lisa; p/Harold and Myrtle Bartsch, Pendleton, OR; ed/BA 1962, MS 1963 Oreg St

Univ; PhD Brown Univ 1967; pa/Tex Tech Univ: Prof Chemistry 1978-, Assoc Prof 1974-78; Asst Prog Admr Petroleum Res Fund 1973-74; Asst Prof Washington St Univ 1968-73; NATO Postdoct Fellow Univ Wurzburg, W Germany 1967-68; hon/Excellence Tchg Awd, Tex Tech Dads Assn.

BARYSHNIKOV, MIKHAIL oc/Dancer; b/Jan 28, 1948; ba/c/o Edgar Vincent Assocs, 145 E 52nd St Suite #804, New York, NY 10022; p/Nicolai and Alexandra Kisselov Baryshnikov; ed/Ballet Schs: Riga, Kirov; pa/Prin Dancer: NYC Ballet 1978-, Am Ballet Theatre 1974-78; Guest Artist: Nat Ballet Canada, Royal Ballet London, Hamburg allet, Ballet Victoria, Eliot Feld Ballet; Num Others;

Orig Works Performed: "Medea", "Push Comes to Shove", "Pas de Duke", "Awakening"; Num Others; Produced & Choregraphed: "Nutcracker", "Don Quixote"; Other Profl Perfs; hon/Gold Medalist Varna Competition; First Intl Ballet Competition: Recipient Nijinsky Prize, Gold Medalist; Dance Mag Awd; Acad Awd Nomination Best Support'g Actor "Turning Point".

BASHORE, IRENEDIANNA SARAS oc/Researcher; Educator; Producer; h/PO Box 4040, Fullerton, CA 92634; p/John Saras (dec); Evangeline Lionudakis Saras, Modesto, CA; pa/Exec Dir Inst Dramatic Res; Editor-in-Chief On Stage; Playwright.

BASS, CHARLES DANIEL oc/Minister; b/Jul 14, 1934; h/2828 Chaswood, El Paso, TX 79935; ba/Ft Bliss, TX; m/Martha Latham; c/Daniel, Elizabeth; p/C B Bass (dec); Doris Center Bass; ed/BA Baylor Univ; MDiv

Golden Gate Bapt Sem; MS LIU; mil/Current Maj Active Duty; pa/Pastor Biggs Chapel #1; Pi Gamma Mu Nat Social Sci Soc; Mil Chaplains Assn; r/So Bapt; hon/Alpha Chi Soc; Bronze Star; Air Medal; Meritorious Ser Medal; Army Commend Medal.

BASS, HYMAN oc/Executive Director Congress for Jewish Culture; b/Nov 27, 1904; h/164 E 78th St, NYC, NY; ba/NYC; m/Sulamitis Kreplak; c/Vivian; ed/Tchrs Sem in Vilna, Poland & NYC; pa/Writer, Editor, Org Exec; Past Pres Jewish Book Coun of Am; CoEditor Lit mthy "The Zukunft"; Past VP Arbeiter-ring; Jewish Daily Forward Press Assn; Editor Derziungs Ency 1957-59; Bd Dirs "Forward" Pub'g Co 1971-; Assoc Editor Jewish Book Annual 1971-; cp/PEN Clb; Former Mem Com on Cult Affairs Jewish Wel Bd; Trustee Meml Foun for Jewish Cult Inc; Bd

Dirs Jewish Tchrs Sem; Adm Com Jewish Labor Com; hon/Shaban Lit Awd, Cong for Jewish Cult; Author 11 Books, the latest *Shreiber Un Verk* 1971.

BASSETT, HENRIETTA ELIZABETH oc/Educator; b/Mar 25, 1932; h/Rt 2 Box 180, Mesquite, TX 75182; ba/Same; p/Sidney and Edna Bassett, M'quite, TX; ed/BA Baylor Univ 1952; pa/Music Edr; Admr & Dir: Music Camp, Music Camp Acad; Former Music Instr M'quite Indep Schs; Chm M'quite Ctr Nat Play'g Auditions: Piano, Organ; Nat Guild Piano Tchrs; Nat Assn Organ Tchrs; Certified Tchr Music Tchrs Nat Assn: Piano, Organ, Theory, Composition; ACM; PGHF; cp/Chm M'quite Area Music Tchrs Assn; Baylor Alumni Assn; r/Bapt; Mimosa Ln Bapt Ch: Ch Organist & Pianist, SS Tchr, Dir & Ldr GA's/Girls Action, Staff GA's/Girls Action Ch Camp; Dir Plays & Musicals Var Bapt Chs; hon/Recipient: 13 Certs Intl Annual Composition Contest, 4 Harmony Certs Nat Guild Piano Tchrs; Intl W/W: Intells, Music; Notable Ams; Num Other Biogl Listings; Piano Guild Hall Fame; Pub'd Author.

BASSETT, JOHN WALDEN JR oc/Lawyer; b/Mar 21, 1938; h/600 Rosemary Ln, Roswell, NM 88201; ba/Roswell; m/Patricia Lubben; c/John III, Loren; p/John Bassett (dec); Evelyn Thompson Bassett, Roswell; ed/BA Stanford Univ; LLB Univ Tex Sch Law; mil/USAR Inf First Lt; pa/White House Fellows Assn; Bar Assns: Am, Tex, NM; cp/Bd Dirs St Marys Hosp; U Way Chaves Co: Past Pres, Bd Dirs; Roswell: YMCA, Plann'g & Zon'g Comm, Girls Clb; r/Past Mem Vestry & Foun St Andrews Epis Ch; hon/White House Fellows; Order Coif.

BASSFORD, FORREST RAYMOND oc/Consultant; b/Feb 2, 1906; h/927 Elmview Dr, Encinitas, CA 92024; ba/Same; m/Marian Horton; c/Marilyn, Karen B Kaytes, Dale; p/Horace and Vilura McGinness Bassford (dec); ed/BS Col St Univ 1929; mil/Wyo NG; pa/Livestock Pub & Promotion Conslt 1978-; Secy & Treas Livestock Pubs Coun; Former

Pubr *Charolais Journ*; Num Other Profl Positions; cp/Repub Party; Past Dir Wn Stock Show Assn; r/Epis; hon/Communs Awd, Nat Assn Farm Mgrs & Rural Appraisers; Top Choice Awd, Col Cattle Feeders Assn; Agriculture Alumnus Awd, Col St Univ; Gamma Sigma Delta; Beef Improvement Fdn Pioneer Awd; Citation Am Gelbvieh Assn; Others.

BASTAWI, ALY ELOUI oc/Professor; b/Oct 13, 1928; h/3103 Danbury Ct, Louisville, KY 40222; ba/L'ville; m/Khadiga Hamza; c/Akrum, Bassel; p/Abdel and Amina Abdel Ghafour Bastawi, Cairo, Egypt; ed/BDS Cairo Univ 1957; MSD Ind Univ 1963; DMD Univ L'ville 1975; pa/Dept Pedodontics: Prof, Chm; Former Prof: Stockholm Royal Col 1964, Cairo Univ 1969; Fellow World Hlth Org; Intl Col Dentists; Intl Dental Res; r/Islam; hon/FICD; MRSH; MAAP; OKU.

BASU, SAMARENDRA oc/Scientist; b/Jul 21, 1942; h/7 MacDonald Cir Apt 3, Menands, NY 12204; ba/Albany, NY; m/Helen Jean Sabat; c/Scott; p/Sachindra Basu (dec); Nihar Bala Basu Ghosh, Calcutta, India; ed/PhD; pa/Sr Res Scist Hlth Res;

Biophysics Soc Am; Am Soc Cell Biol; Electron Microscopy Soc Am; Am Microscopy Soc; r/Hindu; hon/Sloan Kettering Fellow; W/W: E, Am; DPI Stipend Holder, Gov Bengal.

BATA, EVELYN JOAN oc/Executive; b/Mar 22, 1931; h/5403 Queens Chapel Rd, Hyattsville, MD 20782; ba/Greenbelt, MD; m/John Jr; c/Constance Badillo, Lawrence, Cynthia; p/(dec); ed/BA, MEd, PhD Univ Md; pa/Exec VP Prince Georges C of C 1976-; Corporate Rep & Intl Partner Quality Inns 1960-; Lectr Var Univs & Sch Sys 1968-; Bata Assocs: Pres, Conslt Bus & Indust 1973-76; Pres: Metro Washington Coun Cs of C, Bus & Profl Woms Clb; Am Assn Univ Wom: Pres, Exec Com, Chm; Am Assn Univ Profs; Joint Bd Sci & Engrg Ed Greater Metro Area; Md Assn Travel Execs; Other Profl Assns; cp/Dir Am Red Cross; Urban Renewal Prog; Chm Crim Justice Com Leag Wom Voters; Coun U Way Prince Georges Co; Bd Trades; Md Nat Capital Park & Plann'g Comm Task Force; Hyattsville Woms Clb; Capitol Hill Lobbying Corps; Woms Polit Caucus; Num Other Civic Assns; hon/Wom of Yr 1974; BusWom of Yr, Dist'd Ldrship Awd; Prince Georges C of C: Outstg Ser Awd, Awd Excellence; Am Assn Univ Wom: Intl Woms Yr Awd, Meritorious Awd; W/W: E, Am Wom, Md Wom; Personalities S; Pub'd Author; Num Other Hons.

BATASTINI ARMANDO EMILIO JR oc/Social Worker; b/Sept 3, 1930; h/192 Eaton St, Providence, RI 02908; ba/Prov; m/Mary; c/Armando, Maria, Laurie; p/Armando and Katherine Batastini (dec); ed/BA Prov Col; MEd Boston Univ; mil/USN 1955-57; pa/Sch Social Wkr Prov Sch Dept; Hlth, Ed & Wel Coms: Govt Opers, Govs

Task Force Child Wel, Nsg Indust; Com RI Bicent Sports; cp/Past Chm 8th Rep Dis Com; Prov Col Alumni Assn; St Pius: Atl Coun, Basketball & Baseball Coach, Holy Name Soc, Clb Dominicana; Elmhurst Little Leag: Bd Dirs, Past Commr, Past VP; Prov Tchrs Union; Prov Col Commun Relats Com; Num Other Civic Assns; r/Cath; hon/CYO Man of Yr; W/W Am Polits; Sons Italy.

BATEMAN, JOHN ROGER oc/Executive; b/Sept 21, 1927; h/1015 Luxor, Corpus Christi, TX 78412; ba/CC; m/Dorothy Jane; c/David, Sally Baulch, Susan; p/Joseph and Bessie Jackson Bateman, Berkeley, CA; ed/BS, MBA Univ Cal-B; mil/Navy Aviator Lt jg 1945-50; pa/Investment Co Exec; CPA Cal; Tex Soc CPAs; Beta Alpha Psi; Beta Gamma Sigma; cp/Bd Rotary CC; Midtown Kiwanis; Trust Com Nat Repub Senatorial; Little Theatre CC: Pres, Treas, Dir; Bd Gov U Way

Coastal Bend: Bd Gov, Campaign Chm; Exec Coun USO; St Del Repub Party Tex; Dir Camp Fire Girls; r/Meth; hon/Phi Beta Kappa; F'ship Standard Oil Co; S'ship Univ Redlands.

BATES, ENID MAY oc/Associate Professor; b/Dec 15, 1927; h/1115 Creekmere, Canyon, TX 79015; ba/Canyon; m/Raymond W; p/Albert Buswell (dec); Enid Scott Buswell, Kingfisher, OK; ed/BFA, MEd Univ Okla; EdD Tex Tech Univ; pa/Assoc Prof Ed W Tex St Univ; Am Assn Univ Wom; VP Delta Kappa Gamma; Tex Panhandle Coun Intl Reading Assn; Nat Assn Ed Yg Chd; Nat Ed Assn; Tex Assn Col Tchrs; Tex Soc Col

Tchr Ed; Other Profl Assns; cp/Commun Adv Com Cont'g Ed Wom; Tex Child Care Amarillo Commun Coun; Profl Adv Com Tex Public Employee Tng Exc; Amarillo Bus & Profl Wms Clb; r/Meth; hon/Wom of Yr 1979; Amarillo Bus & Profl Woms Clb: Wom of Day, Wom Achmt; Boss of Yr, Nat Secys Assn; Scribes Soc: "Favorite Prof", Awd Ldrship, Ser & Acad Excell; Fac Excell Awd, W Tex St Univ; Num Biogl Listings.

BATES, JAMIE LOUISE oc/Cashier; Clerk; b/Sept 5, 1918; h/115 McCormick Dr, Sumter, SC; ba/Sumter; m/George F; c/Charles, Keith; p/James and Hattie Lester Bevers (dec); ed/AA Cand Sumter Area Tech Col; cp/Leag Woms Voters; Residential Chm Cancer Crusade; Am Cancer Soc: Bd Mem, Meml Chm; r/Meth; hon/Certs: March of Dimes, Cancer Crusade, Arthritis Foun, Heart Dr; Personalities S.

BATES, LURA WHEELER oc/Director; b/Aug 28, 1932; h/2802 Teresa Dr, Jackson, MS; ba/Jackson; m/Allen C; c/Carla B Clack; p/Carl Wheeler (dec); Ray Pace Wheeler, Caraway, AR; ed/BS Univ Ark; pa/Dir Adm Sers Assoc Gen Contractors Miss; Nat Assn Parliamentns; Nat Assn Wom Constrn: VP 1977-78, Chm NAWIC Manual Revisions

1978-79, Constrn Assoc Prog 1973-78; Other Positions; Jackson Chapt NAWIC: Pres 1963-64, Dir 1977-78, Secy 1959-60; cp/Christian Bus & Profl Woms Coun: Exec Com 1975-79, Secy 1978-79, Pres 1979-80; Delta Delta Delta; r/Hillcrest Bapt Ch: Mem, SS Tchr; hon/Outstg Mem, Jackson Chapt NAWIC; Outstg Mem, Region V NAWIC; Intl Platform Assn; W/W Wom; Personalities S.

BATES, PATRICIA LEE ESTILL oc/Executive; Artist; b/Sept 8; ba/Pawidol Collection, PO Box 7095, Albuquerque, NM 87104; m/William Colcord; c/William Jr, Patricia B Spragins; p/Paul Estill (dec); Opal

Lee Estill, Tulsa, OK; ed/AA Gulf Park Col 1945; BFA Okla Univ 1947; MA Univ NM 1960; pa/VP Bates Lumber Co; Pres Pawidol Collection; r/Presb; hon/W/W NM; Intl W/W: Art & Antiques, Intells; World W/W Wom.

BATISTA DE RODRIGUEZ, ADELAIDA oc/Professor; b/Feb 19, 1928; h/279A Machado, El Senorial, Rio Piedras, Puerto Rico 00926; ba/RP; m/Nicolas; c/Leticia; p/Justo Batista de Rodriquez (dec); Estebania Ortiz (dec); ed/BA w hons; MA; EdD; pa/Prof Grad Dept Col Ed Univ PR; Lectr; Career Guid & Ed; cp/Commun Activs; r/Rom Cath; hon/Num S'ships.

BATTERSBY, HAROLD RONALD oc/Educator; b/Nov 16, 1922; h/Box 80, Groveland, NY 14462; ba/Geneseo, NY; m/Betty Yertchenig O'hannesian; p/Eric Battersby (dec); Lilian Darnell Battersby, England; ed/BA Univ Toronto 1960; PhD Indian Univ 1969; Addit Studies; mil/RAFVR 1939-46; pa/Prof Anthropology & Linguistics St Univ NY; Res Altaic Studies; Dept Anthropology & Fgn Langs: Chm Linguistics Prog, Curric Com, Fac Adv Com Indep Study Linguistics 1970-71, Professorial Standards &

Ethics Com 1972-73; Other Positions; Former Fgn Correspondent *Survey Times*; Past Adv Dir & Editor *Turkish Post*; Former Eng Instr Istanbul Univ Med Fac; Num Others; F'ships: Am Anthropological Assn, Linguistic Soc Am, Royal Anthropological Inst Great Britain & Ireland, Royal Asia Soc; Am Oriental Soc; Hakluyt Soc; Intl Soc Oriental Res, Inst Ency Human Ideas Ultimate Reality & Meaning; Num Other Profl Assns; r/Epis; hon/Nat Trust Awd, Mod Near En Studies Toronto; F'ships Var Domestic & Fgn Socs; Recipient Num Res Grants; Num Biogl Listings; Pub'd Author.

BATTISTA, O(RLANDO) A(LOYSIUS) oc/Executive; Professor; Artist; Inventor; b/Jun 20, 1917; h/3725 Fox Hollow, Fort Worth, TX 76109; ba/FW; m/Helen Keffer; c/William, Elizabeth; p/(dec); ed/First Class Honors Degree McGill Univ 1940; ScD honoris causa St Vincent Col 1955; pa/Pres & Chm Res Sers Corp 1976-; Univ Tex: Adjunct Prof Chem, Dir Ctr Microcrystal Polymer Sci 1976-; Fdr & Pres Olympiads Knowledge Foun 1976-; Editor & Pubr *Knowledge* Mag 1976-; VP Sci & Technol Avicon Inc 1971-74; Pres & Chief Exec Ofcr Am Inst Chems 1977-79; hon/James T Grady Awd 1973; Chem Pioneer Awd 1969; Capt Achmt Awd 1971; Boss of Yr Awd, Nat Secys Assn; Fellow: NY Acad Scis, Nat Assn Sci Writers; Pub'd Author; Over 500 Patents.

BAUCOM, JAMES E oc/Minister; b/Feb 19, 1939; h/1411 Madison St, Radford, VA 24141; ba/Radford; m/Mary Lee Adams; c/Jimmy, Lee, Tim; p/Herbert Jr and Ruth Harrison Baucom, Littleton, NC; ed/BA Wake Forest 1961; MDiv 1964, DMin 1978 SEn Bapt Theol Sem; pa/Pastor First Bapt Ch; First VP Bapt Gen Assn; Va Bapt Salary Scale Com; Chm Va Bapt Campus Mins Com; Yth Com Bapt World Alliance; St Pres NC Bapt Student Union; Va Bapt Gen Bd: VChm Com Mins 1975-76, Chm 1976-77, Exec Com; Va Bapt Christian Life Com; cp/Pres: Meridian Pride Lions Clb, Radford Min Assn, Belle Heth PTA; Bd New River Mtl Hlth & Retardation; Chm Radford Mayors Com Indust Devel; Highlands Assn: Student Com, Nom'g Com, Adms Com; Other Civic Assns; r/First Bapt Ch, Radford; hon/W/W: Va, Rel; Personalities S; Men Achmt; Other Biogl Listings.

BAUER, CHARLES RONALD oc/Physician; b/May 16, 1943; h/7400 SW 134th St, Miami, FL 33156; ba/Miami; m/Rita Ehnes; c/Charles Jr, Kristen; p/Charles and Ann Kalmar Bauer; ed/BS Iona Col 1965; MD Univ WVa 1969; pa/Neonatologist Univ Miami; Am Acad Pediatrics; Am Med Assn; Fla Soc Neonatal Perinatologists; Fla Med Assn; r/Rom Cath; hon/Outstg Tchg Awd, Am Acad Pediatrics.

BAUER, JOSEPH CARL oc/Producer; Educator; Lecturer; ba/139 W Colorado Blvd, Pasadena, CA 91105; p/Joseph and Paulina Bauer; ed/BA; MA Occidental Col; pa/Pres Compendum Prodns; Produced & Dir 150 Intl Syndicated TV Progs; Num News Events Specs; Fac Mem Broadcasting Area Ambassadors Ext Jour Dept; Reschr Media Impact; Lectr Mass Commun Var Ednl, Civic & Profl Orgs; Fdr Ambassador Swingphonic Stage Band; Intl Platform Assn; Am Fdn TV & Radio Artists; Broadcast Ed Assn; Intl Commun Assn; Nat Acad TV Arts & Scis; TV Acad: Gov, Ofcr; Arts Coun; Broadcasting Assns; Intl Performers; Hypnosis Socs; Public Relats/Public Affairs Specs; Psychic Reschrs; hon/Intl Awds: Heart Fund, Goodwill Industs, BSA, USAF, NATO; Hon Mayor San Antonio; Keys Sev Cities; Commun Ldrs & Noteworthy Ams.

BAUER, RAYMOND G oc/Manufacturing Executive; b/Jun 19, 1934; h/132 Maple Ave, Haddonfield, NJ 08033; ba/Same; m/Jayne Whitehead; c/Linda; p/Robert and Florence Guyer Bauer Irwin, Ocean Grove, NJ; ed/AA Monmouth Col 1955; BBA Univ Miami 1958; mil/USAF Comm'd Ofcr Aux;

pa/Owner Ray Bauer Assocs Mfrs Reps; Am Mgmt Assn; cp/US Senatorial Clb; Repub Clb; Am Security Coun; AF Assn; Smithsonian Assocs; Friends H'field Lib; Nat Philatelic Soc; Lambda Sigma Tau; Lambda Chi Alpha; Arrowhead Racquet Clb; Iron Rock; Swim & Country Clb; r/Meth; Wesley Foun.

BAUM, CARL EDWARD oc/Electromagnetic Theorist; b/Feb 6, 1940; h/5116 Eastern SE, Unit D, Albuquerque, NM 87108; ba/Kirtland AFB, NM; p/George Baum, Syracuse, NY; Evelyn Bliven Baum, Coventry, RI; ed/BS 1962, MS 1963, PhD 1969 Cal Inst Technol; mil/USAF Comm'd 2nd Lt 1962; pa/Sci Advr AF Weapons Lab; Advr Num

AUS, Navy, AF & Tri-Ser Agys EMP; IEEE; Intl Union Radio Sci: US Nat Com, US Del Gen Assembly; Chm Tech Steering Com New Acad Sci; Tech Com Nat Conf Electromagnetic Scattering; hon/HS Valedictorian; Fellow Intl Biogl Assn; Dist'd Lectr IEEE Antennas & Propagation Soc; Tau Beta Pi; Soc Mil Engrgs Awd; Sigma Xi; Best Undergrad Engr Honeywell Awd; AF: Commend Medal, Res & Devel Awd, 10 Outstg Yg Men Am; Pub'd Author; Num Biogl Listings.

BAUM, CHARLES J oc/Priest; b/Jan 2, 1908; h/7 S Memminger St, Greenville, SC; ba/Same; ed/BA 1930, MA 1931, STB 1933 St Marys Univ; DD SEn Univ 1977; pa/Pastor Emeritus St Marys Ch; Ordained 1934; Former Assoc Pastor: Cathedral St John Bapt, St Josephs Ch Charleston, St Josephs Ch Anderson, St Peters Ch; Former Pastor: Ch St Louis, St Paul Apostle, St Marys Ch; First Resident Chaplain St Eugene Hosp; Dean

G'ville Deanery; Domestic Prelate Title Right Rev Monsignor; Vicar Rel Charleston Diocese; cp/Newman Clb Chaplain; Aux Chaplain Mil Ordinariate; Former Bd G'ville Co Mtl Hlth Assn; VP G'ville Christian Mins Assn; K Columbus & Faithful Friar 4th°; Supvr Bldg Prog Jr, HS & Covent St Marys Ch; G'ville Sertoma Clb; Charleston Diocesan Pastoral Coun; Bd Conslts Diocese; Chm Charleston Diocesan Commun Ecumenical Affairs; Diocesan Sch Bd.

BAUMANN, DANIEL BRUCE oc/Engineer; b/Mar 30, 1952; h/1713 Cedar Ridge Cir, Durant, OK 74701; ba/Durant; m/Delania; p/Bruce and Nell Baumann,

Perryton, TX; ed/BS Agri Engrg Tex Tech Univ 1974; pa/Civil Engr AUS Corps Engrs; Profl Engrs Socs: Nat, Tex; Phi Kappa Phi; cp/Durant Evening Lions Clb; Nat Rifle Assn; r/Meth.

BAUMBACH, DONALD OTTO oc/Edu-

cator; b/Jun 25, 1926; h/112 S Virginia St, Prescott, AZ; m/Leona Anderson; c/Timothy; p/Otto Baumbach (dec); Erna Zielke Baumbach; ed/BS Syracuse Univ 1954; MS 1959, PhD 1962 Pa St Univ; mil/AUS: Corporal 1944-46, S/Sgt 1947-50; pa/Asst Prof Chem; NY Acad Scis; Sigma Xi; Am Chem Soc; r/Mormon; Ch Jesus Christ Later Day Sts; hon/Fellow: Nat Urban Leag Sum Res, Allied Chem Corp, NASA Langley Res Ctr Res; Phi Lambda Upsilon; Sigma Gamma Epsilon.

BAWDEN, JAMES WYATT oc/Professor; b/Apr 23, 1930; ba/Dental Res Ctr Univ NC, Chapel Hill, NC 27514; m/Shirley Stevens; c/Steven, Michael, Timothy, David, Becky; p/Leland Bawden (dec); Rose Bawden Branscome; ed/DDS 1954, MS 1960, PhD 1961 St Univ Ia; pa/Alumni Dist'd Prof Dept Pedodontics 1977-; Univ NC Sch Dentistry: Dean 1966-74, Asst Dean & Coor Res 1963-66, Prof 1965-77; Other Positions: Former Pvt Pract 1956-58; Conslt USPHS Dental Tchg Facilities Constrn; Coun Dental Ed Am Dental Assn; Intl Assn Dental Res; Am Soc Dentistry Chd; Prog Com Am Acad Pedodontics; Am Assn Advmt Sci; cp/NC St Dental Soc; hon/HS Valedictorian; Phi Eta Sigma; Omicron Kappa Upsilon; Fellow Col Dentists: Intl, Am; Pub'd Author.

BAWDEN, MONTE PAUL oc/Scientist; b/Jun 3, 1943; h/17401 Chiswell Rd, Poolesville, MD 20837; ba/Bethesda, MD; m/Lynn Ann Sackett; c/Julie, Amy, Mandy, Katie; p/Norman Bawden; Nina Brown Morava; ed/BA Univ Cal-R 1965; PhD Rutgers Univ 1960; mil/USNR Active Duty: Comm'd Lt Med Ser Corps 1973, Comm'd Status Navy 1975; pa/Res Scist Parasitology & Serology Nav Med Res Inst 1973-; Lectr: Nav

Sch Hlth Care Adm, Hlth Scis Ed & Tng Command; Am Soc Parasitologists; Tropical Med & Hygiene Socs: Am, Royal; Helminthological Soc Wash; Soc Protozoologists; r/Prot; hon/Eagle Scout, BSA; Am Field Ser Student Abroad; Fellow Nat Sci Foun Undergrad Sci Ed Prog; Undergrad Student Res Assoc, Cal Heart Assn; Predoct F'ship Nat Defense Ed Act V, Title IV; Postdoct F'ship Public Hlth Ser; Nat Defense Ser Medal; Am Men & Wom Sci; Pub'd Author.

BAXTER, GENE KENNETH oc/Executive; b/Sept 4, 1939; h/10 Pebble Bch Dr, Ormond Bch, FL 32074; ba/Daytona Bch, FL; m/Laraine Mitchell; c/Gretchen, Aaron; p/Glen Sr and Mable Velhelmina Baxter, Meridian, IN; ed/AA Boise Jr Col 1959; BS Univ Idaho 1961; MS 1966, PhD 1971 Syracuse Univ; mil/Army Nat Guard: Idaho, NY 1957-65; pa/Engrg Mgmt Exec Gen Elect Co; Sect Ofcr IEEE; ASME; NSPE; Sigma Xi Res Soc; Lectr Num Nat Engrg Confs; r/Prot; hon/Machinery Mag Design Awd; Idaho St Engrg Examrs Raymond J Briggs Awd; Phi Kappa Phi; Tau Beta Pi; Phi Theta Kappa; F'ship Syracuse Univ; S'ship Boise Jr Col; Pub'd Author.

BAXTER, ROBERT FRANCIS oc/Doctor; b/Nov 14, 1926; h/Box 66, Vansant, VA 24656; ba/Grundy, VA; m/Nancy McFall; c/Frances, Robert (dec), Mary, Elizabeth, Nancy; p/Frank and Frances Felton Baxter; ed/BS Roanoke Col 1951; Addit Studies; mil/USSN 1943-46; pa/Med Dr Grundy Hosp

Inc; Chm Fam Pract & Med Dept; Intern Univ Va Hosp 1957-58; Staff Phys Grundy Hosp 1958-62; AMA; Acad Fam Pract; Va Med Soc; Am Soc Contemp Med & Surg; So Med Assn; Diplomate Am Bd Fam Pract; cp/Past Pres Buchanan Co Assn Mtly Retarded; Bd Vistors King Col; Pres Buchanan-Dickinson Med Soc; Buchanan Min Assn; Hlth Adv Com SW Va Commun Col; CoChm Fuel-A-Thon; Chm Christian Crusade; Liberal Dem Clb; Moose Home; hon/FellowAm Acad Fam Pract.

BAXTER, RUTH HOWELL oc/Educational Administrator; h/13349 Delaney Rd, Dale City, Woodbridge, VA 22193; ba/Washington, DC; m/Dudley H G; c/Robert, Astrid, Mava, Mova; p/Robert R and Georgie Murray Lassiter; ed/BS DC Tchrs Col 1958; MA Geo Washington Univ 1961; Cert of Ed 1965; Cert, Oslo Univ (Norway) 1970; pa/Tchr, DC Public Schs 1958-; Dir & Propr, Jewels of Ann Pvt Day Sch (Wash, DC) 1970-; Tchr, Newlands Infant (Southampton, England) 1965-67; Instr Math, Howard Univ; Dir, Early Childhood Ed Wkshop, Brent Elem Sch (Wash, DC) 1974; Tchr Adult Ed, Bel Air Sch (Woodbridge, VA) 1977; Ednl Instrn Licensure Commun Task Forces 1978; Mayor's Pre-White House Conf on Libs & Info Sers 1978; Exec HS Internship Prog, DC Public Schs 1978; Author, *A Norwegian Birthday Party*; Contbr to Chd's Pubs; Others; cp/Jack & Jill Clb; BPW; Zeta Phi Beta; hon/Fullbright Scholar; N Am Com of Oslo Scholar; Outstg Tchr of Yr, FTA; Outstg Contbn Awd, Nat Assn Negro Wom; Biogl Listings.

BAY, MAGDALENA CHARLOTTE oc/Writer; b/Aug 7, 1922; h/3410 Galt Ocean Dr, Ft Lauderdale, FL 33308; m/George; c/Helen; p/Aojust and Johanne Schiesojehies, Germany; pa/Freelance Creative Writer; Poet; Social Wkr; Nat Adv Bd; Am Security Coun; cp/Campaign Wkr Repub Nat Com; r/Prot; Luth.

BAYAZEED, ABDO FARES oc/Engineer; b/Aug 20, 1924; h/432 SE Queenstown, Bartlesville, OK 74003; m/Dorothy Gant; c/Fares, David, Raina, Jason (dec), Nadia; p/Fares Bayazeed (dec); Wahebah Azizieh (dec); ed/BS Univ Okla 1955; pa/Petro Engr Bartlesville Energy Res Ctr 1962-; Petro Engr: Layton Oil Co 1960-62, Sinclair Oil & Gas Co 1955-60; Soc Petro Engrs AIME; cp/Arrangements & Registration Sci Fair: Chm 1972, Judge 1968; Tech Career Adv Com; Bd Dirs; Chm Ed Com; Bartlesville YMCA; Yth Com; Advr Jr Hi-Y Clb; r/Muslim; hon/Awd, Wentworth Mil Acad; Pub'd Author.

BAYH, MARVELLA HERN oc/Former Representative; b/Feb 14, 1933 (dec 1979); h/Formerly of 2919 Garfield St NW, Washington, DC 20008; ba/Formerly of Wash DC; m/Birch E Jr; c/Birch III; p/(dec); ed/BS Ind Univ; pa/Spec Rep Am Cancer Soc; CoChperson Ind Div Am Cancer Soc Crusade; Nat CoChperson Cancer Soc Crusade; Bicent Reporter "Sunday" Show; cp/Nat Woms Polit Caucus; Mrs Lyndon Johnson's Beautification Spkrs Com; CoChperson Ind Easter Seal Campaign; Dir Senate Ind Girls St; Pi Beta Phi; hon/Ind Wom of Yr, Theta Sigma Phi; Outstg Yg Wom Nation; Hoo's Hoo Hoosier Woms Awd, Ind Soc; Pub'd Author; Num Biogl Listings.

BAYLESS, DAN J oc/Manager; b/Nov 6, 1939; h/7480 Johnson, Hollywood, FL 33024; ba/Ft Lauderdale, FL; m/Joan Cutrer; p/Milburn and Pauline Flannery Bayless (dec); ed/ABA Ft L'dale Univ; pa/Mgr & Pubs Modular Computer Inc; Certified Graphics Communs Mgr IPMA; In Plant Print'g Mgrs Assn; Broward Co Adv Bd Reprographics; r/Meth; hon/15th Annual Creative Awd; W/W S.

BAYLOR, RICHARD P oc/Businessman; b/May 1, 1925; h/318 Ballngee St, Hinton, WV; m/Margaret Jacque Clinebell; c/Jennifer; p/Lewis and Birdie McCreery Baylor (dec); ed/BS Concord Col; MA WVa Univ; PhD Col Divine Metaphysics; PsD Neotarian Col Phil of Neotarian F'ship; mil/USMC WW-II, Pacific Theatre; USAF Lt Korean War; pa/St

Senate 10th Dist; Wholesale Bus: Coal, Gas & Timber; Land Owner; Former Sch Tchr; cp/YMCA; Elks Lodge; Moose Lodge; Am Legion; Vets Fgn Wars; Phi Delta Pi; Epsilon Delta Chi; Disabled Am Vets; Marine Corps Leag; r/Ascension Epis Ch.

BEACH, DOROTHY R oc/Psychologist; b/Sept 24, 1933; h/523 Nantucket Dr, Temple Terrace, FL 33617; ba/Tampa, FL; m/Eugene Hamilton; c/Daryl Mattson, Dana Mattson; p/Lynn Rigdon, Brooklyn, NY; Mary Marine (dec); ed/BA 1970, MA 1972 Univ S Fla; EdD Nova Univ 1975; pa/Univ Cnslg Psychologist Univ S Fla; Am Pers & Guidance Assn; Am Assn Higher Ed; cp/Pres: Athens Soc, Pres Woms Survival Ctr Tampa Inc; Dir Chd's Home; hon/Phi Kappa Phi.

BEACH, PAUL COLE SR oc/Correspondent; b/Aug 2, 1907; h/5602 Meridian Hill Pl, Burke, VA 22015; ba/Washington, DC; m/Geraldine Brill; c/Mrs Alicia Porter, Paul Jr; p/William and Eva Houghton Beach (dec); ed/AA Vincennes Univ; BA Ind Univ; pa/Newspaper Correspondent US Senate & House Reps; Staff: WA Times, Post, Star, Alexandria Gazette; Indpls Star; cp/Majority & Minority Staff Dir; Jr Congl Com Print'g; r/Christian Scist; hon/US Senate Cert Awd.

BEACH, PAUL THOMAS oc/Manager; Interior Designer; b/Jul 21, 1956; h/514 W Tom Stafford, Weatherford, OK 73096; ba/W'ford; p/E D and Pauline V Beach, Humble, TX; ed/BMusEd SWn Okla St Univ; pa/Asst Mgr & Interior Designer Jacks Flowers & Gifts; Instr Var Design Schs; Pvt Instrn Vocal & Instrumental Music; cp/Bicent Tour'g Co; Univ Operas; r/Emmanuel Bapt: Jubilation Singers, Wesley Foun Choir Dir; hon/W/W Students Am Univs & Cols; Best Dressed Man Campus.

BEACHAM, LOUISE H oc/Counselor; b/Sept 14, 1931; h/20 Gaillard Dr, Tuskegee, Al 36083; ba/T'gee; m/Roman; c/Marilyn, Andre; p/Willie Harrison Sr (dec); Lillie Penn Harrison, T'gee; ed/BS 1952, MS 1965, MEd 1976 T'gee Inst; Addit Studies; pa/T'gee Inst: Intl Student Advr 1977-, Instr Foods & Nutrition 1977, Upward Bound Coor/Spec Progs 1974-77; Other Profl Positions; Am Tissue Cult Assn; Am Dietetic Assn; APGA;

VP & Mbrship Chm Am Assn Univ Wom; Phi Delta Kappa; cp/CoChm March Dimes Campaign; Rep U Negro Col Fund; T'gee Civic Assn; Secy T'gee Inst Local Alumni Assn; Orchid Social & Civic Club: Pres, VP, Treas; r/Greater St Mark Bapt Ch: VChm Bd Trustees, Former Pres Matrons; CoChm Impact Ch Wom U; hon/HS Valedictorian; Kappa Delta Pi; Achmt Awd Ser Clb & Commun Activs; Cert Merit Outstg Ser Mbrship Campaign NAACP; W/W S&SW; Pub'd Author.

BEACHAM, WOODARD DAVIS oc/Gynecologist; b/Apr 10, 1911; h/1527 S Carrollton Ave, New Orleans, LA 70118; ba/NO; p/Woodard and Ida Felder Beacham (dec); ed/BA; MS; MD; mil/USPHS Resv; r/Meth; hon/Univ Miss Alumni Hall Fame; Alpha Omega Alpha; Sigma Xi; Dist'g Ser; Am Col Obs & Gyns; John H Musser Awd; Am Col Surgs Med Records Awd; Apprec Awd, So Bapt Hosp; W/W: Am, S&SW, Am Ed; Num Other Biogl Listings.

BEAHON, MARY ANN EGGERS

oc/Editor; b/Oct 27, 1946; h/2920 Yellowstone Dr, Lawrence, KS 66044; ba/L'rence; m/Michael L; p/Joseph and Camillus Eggers, Two Rivers, WI; ed/BJ Univ Mo 1968; MS Univ Ks 1976; pa/Univ Ks: Editor *The Oread* 1976-, Writer/Editor Div Info Ofc Univ Relats 1975-76; Univ Mo-C: Editor Internal Pubs 1973-75, Asst Editor 1972-73; Other Profl Positions; Sigma Delta Chi; Wom Communs Inc; Secy L'rence Chapt

Alpha Chi Omega; cp/St Awds Chm Ks JCs Jaynes; Pres & Chm Bd L'rence JCs Jaynes; Publicity Chm L'rence Doll Collectors Clb; Vol Cystic Fibrosis Bikeathon; CoChm & Vol Com Cerebral Palsy Telethon; Other Civic Assns; r/Rom Cath; hon/Alpha Nu Chapt Alpha Chi Omega: Outstg Alumna, Ideal Sr; Columbia JCs Wives: Spokette Awd, Sparkette Awd; Gannett Newspapers S'ship; Kappa Tau Alpha; Kappa Alpha Mu.

BEALE, EVERETT M oc/Musician; Educator; b/Jul 7, 1939; h/104 Red Gate Rd, Tyngsboro, MA 01879; ba/Lowell, MA; m/Carol; c/Dawn, Tania; p/Minot and June Beale, N Abington, MA; ed/BM New Eng Conservatory; pa/Percussion Tchr & Musician; hon/World Symph Orch 1971.

BEAM, BITTENA CARTER oc/Bookkeeper; b/Jan 13, 1936; h/Rt 1 Box 63, Alligator, MS 38720; ba/Clarksdale, MS; m/John L; c/Cassandra, Nelda, John; p/Oris and Voncile Hortman Carter, Moultrie, GA; pa/Bkkpr Miss Limestone Corp; Former Telephone Operator Gold Leaf Telephone Co;

Quality Control Tester Electronic Compontants; Clerical Work: Tri-St Co, Trans World Ins Co; Other Profl Positions; cp/VFW: Ladies Aux, Chm Poppy Sales; Wahabi Temples Ladies Aux; r/Rena Lara Bapt Ch: Secy & Treas SS; hon/First Pl Bowling Team; Most Improved Bowler.

BEAMISH, PATRICIA MARY oc/Psychologist; b/Feb 19, 1952; h/900 Kirkwood Hwy Apt K-1, Newark, DE 19711; ba/Newark; p/Richard III and Josephine Beamish, N Miami, FL; ed/BA 1973, MEd & EdS 1975 Univ Fla; pa/Cnslg Psychologist Univ Del; Cnslr: WVa Univ 1977-78, W Liberty St Col 1976-77, Drug Abuse Fla Correctional Instn 1975-76; APGA; Chperson Cont'g Ed Com Am Mtl Hlth Cnslrs Assn; ASGW; ACES; cp/Tnr: Crisis Hotline, Gainesville Corner Drug Store; Dir G'ville Open House; r/Cath; hon/W/W S&SW; Personalities S.

BEAN, ALAN L oc/Astronaut; b/Mar 15, 1932; h/Fort Worth, TX; ba/Houston, TX;

c/Clay, Amy; p/Mr & Mrs Arnold Bean, FW; ed/BS Univ Tex 1955; mil/USN Capt Ret'd 1975; pa/Head Astronaut-Cand Opers & Tng Group; Acting Chief Astronaut Ofc; Former Backup Spacecraft Cmdr US Flight Crew Am-Russian Apollo-Soyuz Test Proj; Spacecraft Cmdr Skylab Mission II SL-3 1973; Lunar Module Pilot Apollo 12 1969; Backup Astronaut Gemini 10 & Apollo 9 Missions 1963; Fellow Am Astronautical Soc; Soc Experimental S Tex Wesleyan Col; EngD Univ Akron.

BEASON, DONALD RAY oc/Educator; b/May 27, 1935; h/2855 St Charles Ave, New Orleans, LA 70115; ba/NO; p/Sylvan Beason (dec); Jennie Vise Beason, Birmingham, AL; ed/BS 1957, MBA 1960 Univ Ala; Addit Studies; pa/Xavier Univ: Assoc Prof Acctg 1967-, Chm Dept Bus & Ec 1970-; Asst Prof

Acctg Jacksonville St Univ 1965-67; Instr Acctg NEn Univ 1963-64; Am Acctg Assn; So Bus Adm Assn; Am Inst Decision Scis; Nat Assn Mgmt Ed; Beta Alpha Psi; Omicron Delta Gamma; Other Profl Assns; r/Bapt; hon/Chi Alpha Phi; Sum Fac F'ship, Intl Bus Machines.

BEAUCHAMP, JEFFERY OLIVER oc/Executive; b/Jan 19, 1943; h/2636 Albans Rd, Houston, TX 77005; ba/Houston; m/Toni Nobler; p/Charles Kirkland and Lila Calk Beauchamp; ed/BSME 1969, MSME 1973 Univ Houston; MBA Cand Sam Houston St Univ; pa/Fdr & Pres Spare Parts Group 1978-; Proj Mgr Flour Engrs & Constructors 1974-78; Mech Design Chief Engr Malley Corp 1970-74;

Res Asst Univ Houston 1968-70; Other Profl Positions; Exec Bd Engrs Coun Houston; Tex & Nat Socs Profls Engrs; Am Soc ME; cp/Inst Intl Ed; Amnesty Intl, Intl Rescue Com & Common Cause; Houston Mus Fine Arts, LA Co Mus & Smithsonian; hon/Sigma Xi; Phi Kappa Phi; Pi Tau Sigma; Outstg Yg Engr of Yr, Sam Houston Chapt TSPE; W/W: Am, S&SW; Pub'd Author.

BEAVERS, MARY DAWN THOMAS oc/Artist; Poet; b/Sept 30, 1917; h/827 N Fairfax Ave, Los Angeles, CA 90046; ba/Same; c/Michael Chiechi, Gay B McBrearty (Mrs Jerome Jr); p/Chester and Arra McPherson Thomas (dec); pa/Portrait Painter; Photo Retoucher; Dir Mary Beavers Gallery; cp/Dep Registrar Voters; r/Epis; hon/W/W Am Wom; Notable Ams; Living Am Artists; Photogs Mkt; Num Other Biogl Listings; Aggie F'ship Awd; Hist Thomas Clan.

BEAZLEY, CURTIS EDWARD oc/Command Pilot; Meteorologist; b/Sept 13, 1928; h/3832 Rouse Ridge Rd, Montgomery, AL 36111; m/Sara Richardson; c/Rebecca, Sara; p/Curtis Beazley (dec); Louise McWilliams Beazley, Scooba, MS; ed/AA E Miss Jr Col 1946; BS Miss St Col 1951; BS Fla St Univ 1952; Addit Studies; mil/AUS 1946-48; USAF

Lt Col 1951-75; pa/Ret'd AF Ofcr; AF Assn; cp/Masonic Lodge; r/Bapt: Deacon, SS Tchr; hon/Sigma Gamma Epsilon; Sigma Pi; UN Ser Med; Republic Vietnam Campaign Med; Nat Def Ser Med; Korean Ser Med; Combat Readiness Med; AF Outstg Unit Awd; Num Other Mil Hons.

BECHTEL, JEAN ROBINSON oc/Dietetics Administrator; b/Mar 24, 1922; h/1015 12th St NE, Auburn, WA 98002; ba/Auburn; m/Kenneth Edgar; c/Dawn, Jeffrey, Mary, Ruth, Kenneth; p/John and Kathryn Dailey Robinson; ed/BS Siena Hts Col 1944; pa/Dir Dietetics Auburn Gen Hosp 1971-; Head Dietitian: Concord Commun Hosp 1964-68, Pittsburg Commun Hosp 1968-70; Theurapeutic Dietitian: Sequoia Hosp 1961-62, Kaiser Hosp 1963-64; Other Profl Positions; Am Soc Hosp Food Ser; Dietetic Assns: Am, Pt-time VP & Spkrs Bur Seattle; Admrs Am Hosps Assn; r/Rom Cath; hon/Pub'd Author.

BECK, ARTHELLO JR oc/Artist; Mental Health Worker; b/Jul 17, 1941; h/2801 Ramsey, Dallas, TX 75216; ba/Dallas; m/Mae Beck; c/Mashariki, Hodari; p/Arthello Beck (dec); Millie Beck, Dallas; pa/Mtl Hlth Wkr Mtl Hlth & Retard Ctr; Art Tchr; Assn Adv'g

Artists & Writers; Nat Conf Artists; cp/Bd Dirs Commun Ctr Arts So Meth Univ; hon/1 of 8 Leading Artists SW; Spec Merit Awd, St Fair Tex; 2nd Pl Awd, SWn Ceramic Show; 1st Pl, Black Art Exhibit; Fine Arts Awd, Com of 100; Cert Recog Art, Elite News; Featured Var Mags, Newspapers & TVs.

BECK, CLIFFORD WALLACE oc/Property Manager; Senator; b/Aug 12, 1908; h/1263 Beach Dr E, Port Orchard, WA 98366; ba/Same; m/Hope Grace; ed/Att'd Stanford Univ; mil/USN Nav Ordnance Engr; pa/St Dem Senator 26th Dist 1974-; House Rep 7 Terms; cp/Sons Norway; Elks; Eagles; Grange; Kiwanis; DAVs; Fleet Resv Assn; So Kitsap C of C.

BECK, GASPER PAUL oc/Engineer; b/May 6, 1915; h/118 S 5th Ave, Highland Park, NJ 08904; ba/N Brunswick, NJ; m/Ethel Nagy; c/Paul, Patricia Ladota (Mrs James), Christine Puk (Mrs John), Rose Mary Murphy

(Mrs Frank), Ilene Lassogna (Mrs Joseph); p/Andrew and Rose Kovacs Beck, Edison, NJ; ed/Att'd: Rutgers Univ, Am Sch Chicago; pa/Lic'd Profl Engr NJ; Soc Profl Engrs: Nat, NJ, Raritan Valley; cp/Coun-man 1963-72; Mayor 1972-76; Chm Civil Rts Com 1962-65; Chm Middlesex Co Conf Mayors; Bd Dirs NJ Conf Mayors; NJ Adv Coun Voc Ed; Dem Com-man; Treas Am Hungarian Foun; Bd Dirs Raritan Valley GSA; Capt U Fund Annual Dr; Lions Clb Intl; K of C; Other Civic Assns; r/Rom Cath; Parish Coun: St Ladislavs Ch, VP St Pauls Ch; hon/Spec Achmt Awd, Johnson & Johnson; Brotherhood Awd; Patents In Field.

BECK, HUBERT FREDERICK oc/Pastor; b/Jul 21, 1931; h/1405 Francis, College Sta, TX 77840; ba/CS; m/Betty Beaver; c/Kathleen, Cynthia, Mary, John; p/Louis Beck (dec); Martina Dierks Beck, Willisville,

IL; ed/BA, MDiv Concordia Sem; pa/Pastor Luth Ch Tex A&M Univ; Campus Min Assn: Nat, Luth; ITEST; cp/Chm Brazos Co Child Wel Bd; Kiwanis Clb; Citizens Adv Coun Bluebonnet Psychi Ctr; r/Luth; hon/Pub'd Author.

BECK, MICHAEL WARREN oc/Police Officer; b/Aug 17, 1942; h/412 Vine, Leavenworth, KS 66048; ba/L'worth; m/Lynda Joyce; c/Steven; p/Harvel and Esther Beck, Grayville, IL; ed/AA KC Commun Col; mil/USAF; pa/Patrol Sgt; L'worth Law Enforcement Assn; cp/Masonic Lodge; Fdr Big Brothers/Sisters L'worth; r/Meth; hon/Commun Ldrs & Noteworthy Ams; JCs Outstg Yg Ams 1978; Liberty Bell Awd, L'worth Bar Assn.

BECK, ROBERT ALFRED oc/Dean; b/Nov 1, 1920; h/2498 Slaterville Rd, Slaterville Springs, NY 14881; ba/Ithaca, NY; m/Mary K; c/Susan, Janice, Robin; p/Alfred Beck Jr (dec); Laura Beck, Milton, MA; ed/BS 1942, MS 1952, PhD 1954 Cornell Univ; mil/Field Arty 1st Lt 90th Inf Div 1942-45; pa/Dean Sch Hotel Adm Cornell Univ; E M Statler Prof Hotel Adm; Chm Hotel Sch Coms: Admissions, S'ship, Petitions & Student Pract; Spkr Sems & Cont'g Ed; Mgmt Conslt Var Orgs; Trustee & VP Ednl Inst Am Hotel & Motel Assn; Trustee Nat Inst Food Ser Indust; Adv Bd Hosp Foodser Admr Assn; Dir: Culinary Inst Am, Intl Inst Glion; Bd Govs Shannon Col Hotel Mgmt; Num Other Assns; r/Cath; hon/Phi Kappa Phi; Phi Delta Kappa; Ye Hosts; W/W: Am, E, Ed.

BECKER, PAUL ERDMAN JR oc/Administrator; b/May 4, 1917; h/806 Baylor Dr, Newark, DE 19711; ba/Newark; m/Claire

Atkins; c/Kip, Kenneth, Raymond; p/Paul Sr and Gertrude Evers Becker (dec); ed/BS US Nav Acad 1938; MBA Univ Del 1966; mil/USMC Lt Col 1938-60; pa/Univ Del: Admr, Asst Treas 1972-, Treas 1966-72, Bus Mgr 1964-66, Controller 1960-64; Univ Risk Mgmt & Ins Assn; cp/Govs Coun Pres & Execs; Govs Economy Com; Pres Ret'd Ofcrs Assn; Boy Scouts; Masons; Shriners; r/Epis; hon/David I Walsh Prize Highest Merit Mil Law; 6 Mil Campaign Medals; Pub'd Author.

BECKER, ROBERT DEAN oc/Educator; b/Dec 15, 1936; h/4100 Weeks Park Ln #278, Wichita Falls, TX 76308; ba/WF; m/Nickie; p/Marvin and Leona Becker, Colo Springs, CO; ed/BA 1967, MA 1969, PhD 1972 Univ Colo; mil/AUS 1955-57; pa/Asst Prof Hist MWn St Univ; Rocky Mtn Assn Advmt Slavic Studies; Wn & SWn Social Sci Assns; cp/Wichita Mtl Hlth Assn: Bd Dirs, Spkrs Bur Chm; Commun Coun; MSU: Fac Senate, Treas, Secy & Chm; hon/NDEA Title IV F'ship; Univ Colo Res Grant.

BECKLES, FRANCES N oc/Educator; Writer; b/Oct 27, 1939; h/200 Hialeah Dr, Glen Burnie, MD 21061; ba/Baltimore, MD; m/Melvin G Sr; c/Melvin Jr, Marc; p/Richard and Evelyn; ed/BA Morgan Univ 1962; MSW Howard Univ 1965; DSW Univ Pa 1975; pa/Author: *Twenty Black Wom*, "Black Wom Drs Md Scene", "Influence Mass Media Black Commun"; Num Other Profl Pubs; Assoc Prof Morgan St Univ 1970-; Howard Univ Sch

Social Work: Tchr & Dir 1968-70; Res Conslt: Greenleigh Assocs Firm 1972-73, Ed Testing Ser Princeton 1972; Tchr Univ Md Vista Prog 1966-67; Num Other Profl Positions; Assn Univ Profs; Assn Black Social Wkrs; Nat Assn Social Wkrs; Coun Social Work Ed; Md Press Assn; cp/Howard Univ Alumni Assn; Commun Hlth Coun Md; Wom Power; Nat Geographic Soc; Alpha Kappa Alpha; r/Cath; hon/Morgan St Univ Fac Res Awd.

BECKMAN, GAIL McKNIGHT oc/- Lawyer; Educator; Writer; b/Apr 8, 1938; h/Lenox Forest C400, 3200 Lenox Rd, Atlanta, GA 30324; ba/Atla; p/Irland and Elizabeth Beckman, Atla; ed/BA; MA; JD; Addit Studies; pa/ABA; St Bar Ga; Ga Assn Wom Lwyrs; cp/DAR; Nat Soc Colonial Dames; NW Ga Girl Scouts; Toastmasters; Jr Leag Atla; r/Presb; hon/Fulbright; Beta Gamma Sigma; Gamma Iota Sigma.

BECKMANN, GEORGE CLAUS oc/Executive; b/Aug 16, 1922; h/13108 Spanish Moss Rd, Savannah, GA 31406; ba/S'nah; m/Mary Helen Scranton; c/Barbara, Nancy; p/George Sr and Lucile North Beckmann (dec); ed/BS Ga Inst Technol; mil/USAAF 1st Pilot & Troop Carrier Command 1942-45; pa/VP & Admr St Josephs Hosp; VP Candler Gen Hosp 1973-78; Admr Ga Warm Springs Foun 1953-73; Am Col Hosp Admrs; Am Hosp Assn; Trustee: Ga Hosp Assn, Nat Amputee Golf Assn; cp/Rotary Clb; German Heritage Soc; S'nah Quarterback Clb; Chathan Co Emer Med Ser Adv Coun; Num Other Civic Assns; r/Luth Ch Redeemer, S'nah; Governing Coun; hon/Joe Avans Awd; Mich Awd 1977; Nat Amputee Golf Assn Awds; W/W S&SW.

BECKSTROM, HARRIETT MAE oc/Physician; Surgeon; b/Mar 10, 1925;

h/8443 Banguo Dr, Dallas, TX 75228; ba/Dallas; c/Martin II, Perry; p/Benjamin and Trena Perry, Dallas; pa/Dr Ostropathic-Anesthesiologist; Am Ostropathic Col Anethesiologist; Nat Ostropathic Assn; Tex & Dist 5 Ostropathic Med Assn; cp/Am Bus Woms Assn; OES; r/Zion Luth Ch; hon/Notable Ams; Nat Register Prominent Ams & Intl Notables; Dic Intl Biog.

BEDDINGFIELD, VALERIA GREEN oc/Postmaster; b/Oct 9, 1919; h/PO Box 343, Spring Hope, NC 27882; ba/SH; m/N W Jr; c/Patricia B Gupton, Curtis; p/Wilson and Senora Bryant Green (dec); cp/U Daughs Confederacy; r/Missionary Bapt; hon/-Personalities S; W/W Small Commun.

BEDROS, ARTEMIS BELIAN oc/Pianist; Educator; b/Mar 1; h/Rt 8 Box 5, Lumberton, NC 28358; m/Ohan Arteen; c/Nina, Ani; p/Sarkis and Haigouhi Behesnilian; ed/BM; Addit Studies; pa/Perfs Orchs, Concerts &

Chamber Groups; Judge Nat Piano Guild; NC Music Tchrs Assn; Delta Omicron; cp/Pres Commun Concert Assn; Fountainbleau Alumni Assn; Advr Lib Concert Series Robeson Co; r/Armenian Orthodox.

BEEBE, GERTRUDE A oc/City Official; b/Aug 9, 1903; h/1751 E Hill St, Signal Hill, CA 90806; c/Joseph Travers Jr, Constance Urquhart (Mrs Dale), John Travers; Anita Hillebrandt (Mrs William Jr), James Beebe; p/Fredrick and Margaret Robertson Potter (dec); ed/Att'd Univ Wyo; pa/Former Elem Sch Tchr; cp/Mayor 1974-75; City Coun-man 1968-76; City Clk 1966-68; Clk-in-Charge PO 1956-68; City Treas 1942-68; Repub Woms Clb; SH Elem Sch PTA; White Shrine Jerusalem; OES; r/Ch Latter Day Sts; hon/City Mayor Cit; Var Cits Civic Orgs.

BEELER, MARIAN BOWERS oc/Actress; Model; b/Apr 27, 1905; h/6132 Glen Holly, Hollywood, CA 90068; ba/Same; m/B J; c/William Thomas; p/William Bowers (dec); Gertrude Rice (dec); ed/BA Mo Univ; pa/Films: Day of Locust, The Greatest Story Ever Told, Inherit The Wind; Num Others; TV: The Little House on Prairie, Tom Sawyer, Burt Bacharach Spec, Twilight Zone; Theatre: Mrs Lincoln, The Man Who Came To Dinner; Man Called Peter; Hamlet; Wuthering Hts; Fam Portrait; Num Others; hon/Var Media Awds.

BEEM, JACK D oc/Attorney; b/Nov 17, 1931; h/175 E Delaware Pl, Chicago, IL 60611; ba/Chgo; p/Darrell Beem (dec); Margie Beem, Chgo; ed/BA Univ Chgo; JD Univ Chgo Law Sch; pa/Partner Baker & McKenzie 15 Yrs; ABA; Past Chm Intl & Fgn Law Com Chgo Bar Assn; cp/Dir Japan Am Soc; Visiting Com Ctr Far En Studies; MW Adv Bd; Inst Intl Ed; hon/Phi Beta Kappa.

BEESON, CONI IRENE oc/Filmmaker; b/Apr 19, 1930; h/99 W Shore Rd, Belvedere, CA 94920; m/Duane B; c/Craig, Tod, Kim; p/Richard Donelson (dec); Irene Nora Donelson, Twaine Harte, CA; ed/BA; hon/Film Fests, Smithsonian Inst & Wells Fargo Bank Awds Film Documentation.

BEETON, DIANA LAFAY oc/Director; Producer; b/Oct 17, 1934; h/315 E 68th St, New York, NY 10021; ba/NYC; p/John and Fay Beeton, E Windsor, NJ; ed/BA William &

Mary 1956; pa/Indep Casting & Music Prodn The Casting Couch; Casting Dir: Ogilvy & Mather Inc 1974-74, Howard Zieff Inc 1970-72, Foote, Cone & Belding Inc 1967-70, Papert, Koening & Lois Inc 1965-67; Admr Talent Assocs Ltd 1962-65; Asst Casting Dir & Talent Paymt Dept Batten, Barton, Durstine & Osborne Inc 1957-62; r/Presb; hon/Blue Ribbon Panelist Nat Acad TV Arts & Scis; W/W: E, Am Wom; Dic Intl Biog; Num Other Biogl Listings.

BEETS, SARA SULLENBERGER oc/Civic Leader; b/Aug 4, 1918; h/1717 Crockett Ridge Rd, Morristown, TN 37814; m/Henry Paul Sr; c/Henry Jr, John, George; p/John Sr and Etta DaVault Sullenberger (dec); ed/Att'd Carson Newman Col; mil/Am Nat Red Cross Overseas 1944-46; cp/Div VChm Vols ARC; Pres Hamblen Co Assn Preserv Tenn Antiquities; Hamblen Co Am Rev Bicent Com; Trustee M'town Hamblen Hosp; Chm Mother March; r/First U Meth Ch, M'town; Pres & Treas Woms Soc; Bd Stewards; hon/Am Nat Red Cross Overseas Cert; Medal Freedom.

BEGLEY, ROBERT JENNINGS oc/Executive; b/Dec 11, 1938; h/"Larwood" Rt 7, Richmond, KY 40475; ba/R'mond; m/Susan Scrivner; c/Leigh, Ashley, Robert; p/Robert and Vera Jennings Begley, R'mond; ed/Att'd Univ Ky & Univ Cinc; pa/Pres Drug Chain; Chm Govt Affairs Com Nat Assn Chain Drug Stores; cp/Bd Trustees: Midway Col, Cardinal Hill Hosp; Ofcr Affil'd Drug Stores; Bd Ky Retail Fdn; Affil'd Industs Ky; Ky C of C; Yg Pres Org; r/Christian Ch; hon/Outstg Yg Men Am Awd.

BEHRENS, JUNE YORK oc/Educator; Author; b/Apr 25, 1925; h/230 S Catalina Ave #402, Redondo Bch, CA 90277; ba/Same; m/Henry W; c/Terry, Denise; p/Mark and Aline Stafford York; ed/BA Univ Cal-SB 1947; MA Univ So Cal 1961; Addit Studies; pa/Elem Tchr: Cal 1947-54 & 1956-63,

Overseas Schs 1954-56; VPrin Los Angeles 1966; Reading Spec LA City Schs 1966; Author: Who Am I?, Earth Is Home, True Book Metric Measurement, A Walk In The Neighborhood; Num Other Pubs; NEA; AAUW; Cal Tchrs Assn; Authors Guild; Delta Kappa Gamma; r/Prot.

BELK, JOHN MONTGOMERY oc/Merchant; b/Mar 29, 1920; h/435 Hempstead Pl, Charlotte, NC 28207; ba/C'lotte; m/Claudia Watkins; c/Mary; p/William Sr and Mary Irwin Belk (dec); ed/BA Davidson Col; mil/AUS Lt WW-II & Korean Conflict; pa/Pres Belk Stores Sers Inc; World Bus Coun; Am Mgmt Assn; Past Chm

NRMA; Conf Bd Sister Cities; cp/Mayor C'lotte 1969-77; Sr Bd & Past Pres C of C; BSA Coun; Mint Mus Art; r/Presb; hon/NRMA Gold Medal Awd; Dist'd: NC Citizen, Eagle Scout, Alumnus Medal-Davidson; Ctl News Man of Yr.

BELL, BILLIE JOE oc/Attorney; b/Jul 14, 1941; h/1938 Lakeshore PO Box 682, Rockwall, TX 75087; ba/R'wall; m/Lucille Cross; c/Liana; p/Charles Bell, Freeport, TX; Lillie Constance, New Orleans, LA; ed/BA La St Univ 1968; JD Loyola Univ S 1970; LLM So Meth Univ 1971; mil/USN YN 2, E-5, 1959-62; pa/Crim Dist Atty R'wall Co; ABA; Bar Assns: Tex St, N Tex, La; cp/Past Pres & Dir R'wall C of C; Secy Royse City Indust Devel Foun; R'wall Co: Bd Realtors, Friends Lib, Dir YMCA, Hist Foun; Cir 10 Coun BSA; Rotary Clb; Past Pres R'wall Lions Clb; Num Other Civic Assns; r/First Christian Ch, Royse City; hon/W/W Tex; Personalities S.

BELL, CHARMIE POORE oc/Businesswoman; h/2312 Camelot Cir, Johnson, TN 37601; ba/Johnson City, TN; m/Jess W(dec); p/John and Virgie Poore, Bristal, VA; pa/Restaurant Owner Bell's Henny Penny; Profl Bus Woms Clb; cp/Christian Woms Clb; r/Bapt.

BELL, GEORGE GUICE JR oc/Executive; Artist; b/Oct 30, 1943; h/3527 Edmar Pl, Jackson, MS 39216; m/Robbie LeNoir Lloyd; c/George III; p/George Sr and Sharlyne Belle Whittington Belle, Jackson; ed/BA; Postgrad Studies; Grad Profl Schs; cp/Pres UN-Common Carrier Corp (Trailer Mftr); VP Geo Bell Carpets; Mftrs Sales Agt in SE to Distribute Carpet Paneling Sys 1973-; Pres Comml Logos; Bd Dirs Visions Inc; Lectr; Dir Home Bldrs Assn; Past Pres Kappa Alpha Order; Painter, Designer & Sculptor of Carpet Logos for Major Instns & Bus; Other Profl Assns; r/1st Bapt Ch: Deacon, Dir Col Dept; hon/W/W S&SW; Dist'd Sales Awd; Sales & Mktg Execs Jackson; Kappa Alpha Ct of Honor; Mil Decorations; Socs.

BELL, INEZ DICKERSON oc/Educator; b/Jun 10, 1927; h/2409 Bel Air Ave, Wilson, NC 27893; m/Laddie P; c/William, Donnell, Laddie Jr; p/Fred Dickerson, Wilson; Almeter Dickerson (dec); ed/BS Winston-Salem St Univ; Addit Studies; pa/Wilson Co Tech Inst: Tchr, Head Lng Lab Coor, GED Admr; NCCCAEA; NC St Employees Assn Inc; cp/Wilson Co: Ed Devel Coun, Bd Dirs Mtl Hlth Assn, Past 2nd VP Dem Wom; NC Employment Tng Coun; Delta Sigma Theta; r/Deaconess St John AME Zion Ch; Yg Adult Missionary Soc; Ch Wom U; hon/W'Salem St Tchrs Col: Miss "TC", 2nd Pl Miss Alumni.

BELL, JAMES MILTON oc/Physician; b/Nov 5, 1921; h/Hudsonview Old Post Rd, N Croton-on-Hudson, NY 10520; ba/Canaan, NY; p/Charles Bell Sr (dec); Lucy Barnes Bell; ed/BS NC Ctl Univ 1943; MD Meharry Med Col 1947; Intern Harlem Hosp 1947-48; Resident Winter VA Hosp 1953-56; mil/AUS Capt Med Corp 1951-53; Div Psychiatrist 1st Inf Germany; USAR Assigned Var Hosps 1976-77; pa/Psychiatrist Child & Adolesent Berkshire Farm Ctr & Ser Yth; Parsons Child & Fam Ctr: Staff Psychiatrist 1976-, Chief Conslt Psychiatry 1959-77; Am Soc Adolescent Psychi; Coun Psychi Pan-Am Med Assn; Coun Leg & Public Policy Nat Assn Mtl Hlth; Am Orthopsychi Assn; Com Psychi Facilities Chd & Adolescents Am Acad Child Psychi; Others; Participant Var Profl Meetings; Num Profl Pubs; cp/Rotary Clb; hon/Alpha Omega Alpha; Hon'd by Albany Home Chd; Pres Awd, Meharry Med Col; Cert Commend, Am Psychi Assn; Medals: Good Conduct, Am Campaign, WW-II Victory, Nat Def Ser, Army Resv Achmt; Num Biogl Listings.

BELL, JERRY SHERIDAN oc/Engineer; b/Jul 11, 1892; h/314 SW 67 Ter, Hollywood, FL 33023; ba/Same; m/Verda Ellen; p/Joseph and Emily Bell (dec); ed/PhG Valparaiso Univ 1914; MD Loyola Univ Sch Med 1918; Var Postgrad Studies; mil/Internship 1918-19; pa/Dir Dept Nuclear Med Mary Immaculate

Hosp 1964-74; Pvt Pract Roentgenology 1944-59; Clin Asst & Instr Dept Cardiology 1942-50; Num Other Profl Activs; Lic'd Var Sts; NY Co & St Med Socs; Am, Fla St & Broward Co Med Assns; r/Prot; hon/Cit Med Soc St NY; Contbr Var Med Lit.

BELL, LESLIE oc/Rancher; b/Aug 14, 1914; h/4445 E Flower St, Phoenix, AZ 85018; ba/Skull Val, AZ; m/(dec); c/Lawrence Garland, Leslie Garland; p/Herbert and Lillian Hirsh Baer (dec); ed/BA Stanford Univ; pa/Rancher L Bell Ranch; Horse & Cattle Breeder; Rodeo Sports Writer; Owner Talent Agy; CoOwner Theatrical Sch & Movie Distribution Co; cp/Cattlemens Assn; Cowbelles; Phoenix: Musical Theater Guild, Zoo Aux, Symph; Scottsdale Players; Other Civic Assns; r/Prot; hon/PhD.

BELL, LORRAINE PETTIES oc/Guidance Counselor; h/208 Bonita Dr, Memphis, TN 38109; m/Raymond Crittenden; c/Tammy, Raymond; p/Henry Petties, Cleveland, OH; Lula Porter Petties, Memphis; ed/BS LeMoyne Owen Col; MEd M'phis St Univ; Postgrad Work; pa/APGA; Nat & Tenn Ed Assns; M'phis Cnslrs; Direct Selling Assn; cp/Vol Am Cancer Soc; Delta Sigma Theta; Alpha Pi Chi; Theatre M'phis; r/Christian; hon/Kappa Delta Pi; W/W S&SW.

BELL, LOUISE MATHESON oc/Photography; Homemaker; b/Jan 21, 1919; m/James Bruce; c/Harold, James; p/Thomas and Lillie Hudson Matheson, Fairplay, SC; ed/Att'd Winona Sch Photo; pa/CoOwner & Operator Bell Studio 1948-76; SC & SEn Profl Photogs Assn; cp/SC Hertiage Trust Adv Com; Chm: Seneca Centennial & Hist Comm, Lunney Mus Bd Trustees; Treas Oconee Co Hist Soc; Seneca: Pres & VP Coun Clbs, Planning & Zoning Comm, CoFdr Band Booster Clb; U Daughs Confederacy; r/S'ca Bapt Ch; hon/Outstg Ser City S'ca; Patriotic Ser St & Country; SC Am Revolution Bicent Comm & Govs Awd; SC Travel Awd; Num Biogl Listings; Pub'd Author.

BELL, MAUD MELINDA oc/Educator; b/Jun 24, 1911; h/Hudsonview, Croton-on-Hudson, NY 10520; ba/St Albans, LI, NY; p/Charles Bell Sr (dec); Lucy Barnes Bell, Croton-on-Hudson; ed/BA cum laude Shaw Univ; MA Columbia Univ; pa/Sec'dy Sch Tchr Eng & French 1932-77; Apptmts: Robeson Co Tng Sch, Booker T Washington HS, Alexander Hamilton, Andrew Jackson, John F Kennedy; Chm Eng Dept; Reading Spec; Lic'd Real Est Assoc; Am Guid Cnslrs; NAACP; Chr Nat Coun Negro Wom; cp/Hon'd Daugh Ruler Elks; Fdr: Wom Am Inc, A J Legum Foun S'ship; Uptown Campaign Mgr Gubernatorial Election; Mbrship Com & Cnslr YWCA; Girl Scout Ldr; March of Dimes; Alpha Kappa Alpha; B&P Woms Clb; NYC Assn Tchrs Eng; Shaw Univ Nat Alumni Assn; Wom Voters Leag; r/AME St Johns, Norfolk; Supt Asbury U Meth Ch Sch; Student Bible Sch Tchr; Sponsor Bible Clb; hon/Wom of Yr 1950; 100 Wom NY, Hotel Americana 1975; Hon Shaw Homecoming 1973; Num Biogl Listings; Pub'd Author.

BELL, MICHAEL GEOFFREY oc/Chemist; b/Aug 12, 1947; h/2922 Camino Del Gusto, Santa Fe, NM 87501; ba/SF; m/Dori C; p/Wakeman Bell; Frances Bell (dec); ed/BC; pa/Forensic Drug Chemist; MW Assn Forensic Scists; r/Meth; hon/W/W W.

BELL, RICHARD G oc/Professor; Attorney; b/Jan 31, 1928; h/104 Belle Vista Ct, Winston-Salem, NC 27106; ba/WS; m/Evalyn C; c/R Gordon, Lavonn, Kenneth; p/Ralph and Ruth Bell, Bedford, OH; ed/BA Univ Ky 1949; JD 1951, LLM 1961 Case W Resv Univ; mil/1945-46; pa/Prof Law; Ohio, NC & Forsyth Co Bar Assns; cp/Past Treas & Dir Stratford Rotary Clb; Num Other Civic Assns; r/Centenary U Meth Ch, WS; hon/Paul Harris Fellow, Rotary Intl.

BELL, ROBBIE LLOYD oc/Instructor; Businesswoman; b/Nov 23, 1947; h/3527 Edmar Pl, Jackson, MS 39216; ba/Jackson; m/George Guice Jr; c/George III; p/William and Anna Wolfe LLoyd, Jackson; ed/BA cum laude Millsaps Col 1969; MEd Miss Col 1971; Postgrad Studies; pa/Owner UN-Common Promotions Ad Agy; Pt-time Instr Spch & Theatre Millsaps Col; r/First Bapt Ch.

BELLAMY, BEVERLY HICKS oc/Counselor; b/Jan 3, 1947; h/3298 F Covington Dr, Decatur, GA 30032; ba/Lawrenceville, GA; m/Glenn L; p/John and Dorothy Hicks, Newport Bch, CA; ed/BA Univ Cal-I; MEd Clemson Univ; pa/Elem Guid Cnslr; Nat Coun Tchrs Maths; APGA; Am Sch Cnslr Assn; Ariz: PGA, ASCA; cp/Epsilon Sigma; Alpha Alpha Kappa; r/Meth; hon/Tchr of Yr, RH Fulmer Mid Sch 1976.

BELLISTON, ANGUS HENRY oc/Executive; b/Apr 17, 1932; h/2714 N 880 E, Provo, UT 84601; ba/Spanish Fork, UT; m/Marcelle; c/Camille, Anne, Janine, James, Carl, Kathryn, Nathan; p/Albert Belliston (dec); Elsie Maughan Belliston, Provo; ed/BS Univ Utah; pa/Sr VP Zions 1st Nat Bank; Exec Com Utah Bkrs Assn; cp/Chr Snow Col Governing Bd; VP Utah Nat Parks Coun; BSA; r/Ch Jesus Christ Latter-Day Sts; hon/Phi Kappa Phi.

BELLO, TERESA ANN oc/Educator; b/Mar 12, 1943; h/23 Northgate Ave #1, Daly City, CA 94015; p/Juan and Michaela Bello, Stockton, CA; ed/BS San Jose St Univ; MS Univ Cal-SF; pa/Asst Clin Prof Nsg Dept Mtl Hlth Comm Nsg UCSF; Nat Spanish Spkg/Spanish Surnamed Nurses Assn; r/Cath; hon/Hispanic W/W Am; San Francisco Jilipino Nurses Assn.

BELLVILLE, MIRIAM PRISCILLA oc/Educator; Organist; h/508 N State St, Alma, MI 48801; ba/Alma; ed/BA Eureka Col; SMM Union Theol Sem Sch Sacred Music; pa/Assoc Prof Music & Organist Alma Col; cp/Organist Gratiot Co Comm Chorus.

BELOW, FRED JR oc/Musician; b/Sept 6, 1926; h/3977 S Vernon Chicago, IL 60653; ba/Chicago; p/Fred Below, Chgo; Dorthy Below (dec); ed/Att'd Col; mil/AUS 1944-50;

pa/Drummer; Perf'd w Chess & Checker Records & Num Musicians; Art; Photo; r/Bapt; hon/Liverpool Awd Best Drummer of Yr; *Blues Unlimited* Mag Awd.

BENCKENDORFF, NANCY L oc/School Psychologist; h/9959 S Leavitt, Chicago, IL 60643; ba/Markham, IL; p/Ernest Beck, Phoenix, AZ; Sarah Harvey, Wichita, KS; ed/BA Chgo St Univ; MA Govs St Univ; pa/Commun Prof Govs St Univ 1978; Sch Psychologist Prairie Hills Sch Dist 1978; Cnslr & Facilitator Reentry Wom Thornton

Commun Col 1978; Tchr Dist #132 1977; Grad Asst & Instr Chgo St Univ 1974-76; Dir & Tchr St Nicholas Pre-sch 1968-70; cp/Coun Cath Wom; YWCA; r/Rom Cath; St Nicholas Tolentine Ch, Chgo: Pres Coun Cath Wom Liturgy Com, Catechist, Extraordinary Min, Vicariate Coun Cath Wom, Chr Human Relats; hon/Grad Asst, Chgo St Univ.

BENDELL, LEE ROY oc/Executive; Colonel; b/May 1, 1927; h/23233 E Antler Dr, Diamond Bar, CA 91765; ba/Rosemead, CA; m/Gloria Epperly; c/Roy; Gayle B Ellis; p/Leroy and Altha Bendell (dec); ed/BS US Nav Acad 1950; MAEd Stanford Univ 1964; MSs 1966 & 1975 George Washington Univ; PhD Cal Grad Sch Theol 1979; mil/USMC 1945-75; USNA 1946-50, Plt Lt (WIA) Korea 1951, Co Cmdr Japan & Hawaii 1954-55, Tactics Instr Basic Sch Va 1956-58, Aide & Cmdt MC Schs 1959, Div Opns Off Okinawa 1960-61, Aide CINCLANT/CINCLANTFLT

1961-63; Staff USNA 1964-67, CO 3rd Bn 4th Mar in combat Vietnam 1967-68; HQMC Opers Analyst 1968-71; Ofcr in Charge R&D Computer Installation 1972-75; pa/VP Narramore Christian Foun; cp/Cub Scouts; PTA; CBMC; PDK; USNA Alumni; OCF; MC Assn; Spkr Var Civic Orgs; r/1st Bapt Ch, Pomoma: Mem, Trustee, Adult SS Tchr; Former Chs: SS Supt, Deacon, Elder, Ch Coms; hon/Awd Am Legion; Nat Championship LaCrosse Team; USNA; Purple Heart; Vietnam: Silver Star, Legion Merit, 2 Meritorious Unit Cits, Vietnamese Cross Gallantry; 2nd Legion Merit; Pub'd Author.

BENDER, BEVERLY STERL oc/Sculptor; b/Jan 14, 1918; h/Westchester Ave, Pound Ridge, NY 10576; ba/Same; p/Helen Sterl Bender, PR; ed/BA Knox Col; pa/Marble, Wood & Alabaster Animal Sculptor; 1 Man Shows; Nat Assn Wom Artists; cp/Burr Artists; Knickerbocker Artists; Pen & Brush; So Vt Art Ctr; Treas Soc Animal Artists; Jury Admissions Catharine Lorillard Wolfe; r/Prot; hon/Anna Hyatt Huntington Awd; Gold Medal Catharine Lorillard Wolfe; Sydney Taylor Meml Awds: Knickerbocker Artists, Anonymous Awd; Bronze Medal Pen & Brush; Num Biogl Listings.

BENDIK, JOHN JOSEPH oc/Priest; b/Oct 15, 1941; h/906 Main St, Stroudsburg, PA 18360; ba/S'burg; p/John and Helen Sterbinsky Bendik, Shavertown, PA; ed/BA St Meinrad Col 1963; MDiv St Meinrad Sch Theol 1972; pa/Campus Min E S'burg St Col 1970-; Diocesan Dir Campus Min; Priest' Senate & Bd Ed Diocese Scranton; Cath Campus Min Assn; Colleague Consultation Ser CCMA; cp/Bd Dirs Alpha Chi; Adv Bd

Sigma Pi; Monroe Co Clergy Assn; Chaplain Monroe Co Jail; Bd Dirs Am Cancer Soc; Other Civic Assns; r/Rom Cath; hon/Dist'd Ser Awd, Pocono Mtns JCs; Liberty Bell Awd, Monroe Co Bar Assn; Outstg Yg Man of Yr Awd, US Jr C of C; W/W Rel.

BENDURE, LEONA JENSEN oc/Piano Teacher; b/Sept 27, 1912; h/711 Euclid, Lawton, OK 73501; ba/Same; m/Lloyd K (dec); c/Donald, Lorene B Teed (Mrs Dan); p/James and Nettie Folley Jensen (dec); ed/BM; BME Univ Ks; Addit Studies; pa/Pi Kappa Lambda; Mu Phi Epsilon; Music Tchrs Assn: Nat, Var Ofcs Okla; cp/Lawton Woms Forum: 2nd & 3rd VP, Fine Arts Chr, Bd Dirs; Bd Symph Soc; Citizens Ed Coun; Initiator Vocal Music Ed Public Schs; r/Centenary Meth; VChr Adm Bd; hon/Howard Taylor Piano S'ship; Mu Phi S'ship; Num Biogl Listings.

BENEDICT, JOHN L oc/Systems Planner; b/Oct 28, 1952; h/10901 SW 42 Pl, Davie, FL 33328; ba/Miami, FL; m/JoAnna E; c/Jason, Jarret; p/Ralph Benedict (dec); Gloria Benedict, Davie; ed/BSEE Univ Miami 1971; MSEE Rensselaer Polytechnic Inst 1972; pa/So Bell T&T Co: Network Mgr Minicomputer Planning 1977-, Mgr Minicomputer Planning 1976-77, Mgr Network Maintenance Engrg 1975-76; Instr Profl Engrg Exam Review Course 1972-76; Other Profl Positions; Treas & VChr Reg Conv Am Inst Aeronautics & Astronautics; cp/K of C: Fla St Ceremonial Dir 1974-77, Dep Grand K 1976-77, Recorder Coral Gables Coun 1977; Others; Past Pres Engrg Sch Alumni Assn; Chief & Med Man Iron Arrow Soc; Student Chapt Pres Fla Engrg Soc; r/Rom Cath; hon/Tau Beta Pi; Eta Kappa Nu; Phi Eta Sigma; Omicron Delta Kappa Alumnus of Yr; Univ Miami: Brownell Awd, Gen Motors Scholar; K of Mo 1975; Cnslr of Yr, Columbia Squires 1974 & 1975; Num Biogl Listings.

BENHAM, JACK EDWARD oc/Executive; Author; b/Jan 18, 1925; h/558 NW 9 Ct, Boca Raton, FL 33432; ba/Miami, FL; m/June Gridley; c/Cynthia; p/Edward Benham; Mary Stanton; ed/Univ Cinc Col Engrg 1948; Att'd Num Other Univs; mil/USNR Yeoman 3rd Class 1945; Ohio St Guard Med Corp; pa/Pres JB Intl Mktg Corp 1971-; VP & Stockholder: Billie Rose Dinner Theatre 1969-71, Palmers Supplies Co Fla 1964-71; Paint Chem Bruning Paint Co 1956-74; Other Profl Positions; Author: *Beings, Boundaries & Beauty, Macaronical, Metaphorical, Montace*; Num Other Profl Pubs & Paintings; Bd: Sunburst Paints Ltd, Hercules Polymers Inc, E Bond Epoxies; NY Acad Scis; Am Chem Soc; Intl Platform Assn; Nat Adv Bd Am Security Coun; Former Chr So Soc Paint Technol; Past Pres Fla Paint & Coatings Assn; Past Nat Pres Nat Assn Chem Distributors; Other Profl Assns; cp/VChr UN Day; Fdr Boca Raton Elks Lodge; Masonic Lodge; JCs Intl Senator; Boca Raton JCs; US Senatorial Clb; hon/Fellow Am Inst Chemist; Salesman of Yr, So Soc Paint Technol; Num Biogl Listings.

BENJAMIN, ADAM JR oc/United States Representative; Author; b/Aug 6, 1935; h/2106 W 3rd Pl, Hobart, IN 46342; ba/Washington, DC; m/Patricia Ann; c/Adam III, Alison, Arianne; p/Adam and Margaret Benjamin, Merrillville, IN; ed/BS US Mil Acad 1958; JD Valparaiso Univ Law Sch 1966; mil/USMC Corporal 1952-54; AUS 1st Lt 1958-61; pa/Ind St: Rep 1966-70, Senator 1970-76; r/En Cath.

BENN, BRADLEY W M oc/Harpsichord Maker; b/Dec 21, 1937; h/4424 Judson Ln, Edina, MN 55435; ba/Same; m/Jenny Lou Dixon; c/Scot, Wendy; p/Louis and Florence Grove Benn, Louisville, KY; ed/BSEE, BSIE Washington Univ; pa/IEEE; Early Music Forum; Orgr Harpsichord Symp; Participant Fest Flanders.

BENNER, LORA MERLE oc/Musician; Educator; Author; b/Sept 23, 1907; h/1739 Randolph Rd, Schenectady, NY 12308; ba/Same; m/Philip E; p/Robert and Ethel Merriam Miller (dec); ed/Att'd Num Univs; pa/Tchr: Piano & Theory, Piano Pedagogy;

Author: *Theory Piano Students, Tchrs Ref, Benner Handbook*; Num Others; Ednl Advr Piano Tchrs; Lectr Wkshps Var Orgs; Fdr Am Piano Tchrs Assn; Part-Fdr NYSMTA; ASCAP; cp/Num Civic Assns; r/Indep; hon/World W/W: Musicians, Wom; Intl & Nat Biog Dics.

BENNER, PHILIP EDWARD oc/Engineer; b/Sept 17, 1904; h/1739 Randolph Rd, Schenectady, NY 12308; ba/Same; m/Lora Merle; c/Philip Jr, Edith B Stables; p/Philip and Amy Barth Benner (dec); ed/BEE Ia St Univ; pa/Ret'd Elect Engr Gen Elect Co; Inventor Benner Desalinator; Theta Xi; cp/Past Commodore S'ady Yacht Clb; Shrine; Elfun; hon/Phi Kappa Phi; Tau Beta Pi; Eta Kappa Nu; Num Patents.

BENNETT, BEVERLEY LOREE oc/Educator; b/Nov 19, 1926; h/740 Penn Ave, Ashland, OR 97520; ba/Ashland; p/Albert and Myrtle C Bennett, Dallas, OR; ed/BS; MS; Addit Studies; pa/Assoc Prof PE So Oreg St Col 1950-; OAHPER: VP So Dist 1959, Pres Elect 1965, Pres 1966; AAHPER: Chr Nat

S'ship Com 1968-69, Secy NW Dist 1968-70; AAUW; PEO; DKG; cp/Secy Govs Comm Wom; So Campfire Girl Coun; Sponsor & Dir Spec Olympics Jackson Co; Chr Task Force Affirmative Action; Worked Var Sum Rec Progs; r/Meth; hon/Outstg Wom Grad, Univ Oreg.

BENNETT, BOBBY oc/Radio Announcer; b/Jul 20, 1944; h/10933 Bucknell Dr, Silver Springs, MO 20902; ba/Washington, DC; m/Connie; c/Eric; p/Flavia M Payne, Pittsburgh, PA; ed/Att'd Col; pa/Chief Announcer WOL Radio; VP DJ Prodns; AFTRA Shop Steward; cp/Urban Leag; NAACP; NATRA; Black Unites Front; r/Meth; hon/Black Radio DJ Yr: Nat Reg Billboard Mag 1973 & 1977, Nat Bill Gavin Report 1974; NATRA Nat DJ Yr 1976.

BENNETT, BONNIE C oc/Office Assistant; b/Feb 29, 1956; h/515 W Liberty St, Covington, VA 24426; ba/C'ton; m/Donald E; p/Carl Cole, Selma, VA; Edith H Cole (dec); ed/AS Cand Dabney S Lancaster Commun Col; r/Epworth U Meth Ch.

BENNETT, CHARLES EDWARD oc/United States Congressman; b/Dec 2, 1910; h/400 W Bay St, Jacksonville, FL 32202; ba/Same; m/Dorothy Jean; c/Bruce, James, Lucinda; p/Walter and Roberta B Bennett (dec); ed/JD; mil/Capt Inf WW-II 1942-47; pa/Lwyr 1934-48; cp/St Leg 1941-42; r/Disciples Christ; hon/French & Philippine Legions; Bronze & Silver Stars; HHD; LLD.

BENNETT, IVAN FRANK oc/Physician; b/Sept 6, 1919; h/8452 Green Braes N Dr, Indianapolis, IN 46234; ba/Indpls; m/Audrey Poley; c/Ivan, Judith B Ransburg; p/Frank and Iva Bacon Bennett (dec); ed/BS Trinity Col; MD Jefferson Med Col; Cert Psychi; mil/AUS Capt, Chief Neuropsychi Ser 98th Gen Hosp 1946-48; pa/Sr Clin Investigator Lilly Res Labs; Prof Psychi Indpls Sch Med; Dir Lilly Psychi Clin; Assoc Staff Phys Dept Neuropsychi Marion Co Gen Hosp; AAUP;

Sigma Xi; Profl Adv Com Ind Assn Mtl Hlth; Controlled Substances Adv Com & Standing Com Study Mtl Hlth Laws St Ind; cp/Marion Co Assn Mtl Hlth: Bd Dirs, Exec Com, Profl Adv Com & Suicide Preven Ser Com; Bd Dirs & Exec Com Commun Addiction Sers Agy Inc; r/Presb; U Presb Metro Ctr Bd; Conslt Downtown Pastoral Cnslg Ser Inc Riley-Lockerbie Min Assn; hon/Fellow: Am Col Phys, Am Psychi Assn, Am Col Neuropsychopharmacology; Pub'd Author.

BENNETT, IVAN STANLEY oc/Director; b/Jan 27, 1949; h/2502 Belleview Rd, Burlington, KY 41005; ba/Covington, KY; m/Susan Lee; c/Jonathan; p/Ivan and Audrey Poley Bennett, Indianpolis, IN; ed/BA Thomas More Col; ED/LD, Cert Dir Pupil Pers Xavier Univ; pa/Dir Admissions & Release No Ky St Voc Sch; PGA: Am, Ky, So Reg & No Ky; cp/Repub; C of C; r/Luth; hon/Certs Apprec: APGA, SRPGA, KPGA, NKPGA; Dic Intl Biog; W/W S&SW; Personalities S.

BENNETT, MARGARET ELAINE oc/Psychologist; Author; b/Mar 11; h/PO Box 6087, Carmel, CA 93921; ba/Same; p/Towsend and Clara Arms Bennett (dec); ed/BA, MA, EdD Stanford Univ; pa/Conslt

Adult Ed Monterey Peninsula 1973-; Prof & Vis Prof Num Univs 1928-64; Psychologist Pasadena City Col 1958; Guid Conslt St Dept Germany 1951-52; r/Presb; Elder; hon/Phi Beta Kappa; Pi Lambda Theta; Meritorious Ser Cit; Nat Voc Guid Assn.

BENNETT, ROBERT F oc/Governor; b/May 23, 1927; h/Cedar Crest, Topeka, KS 66606; ba/Topeka; m/Olivia Fisher; c/Robert Jr, Virginia, Cathleen, Patricia; p/Otto Bennett (dec); Dorothy Dodds (dec); ed/BA 1950; LLB 1952; mil/USMC 1945-46 & 1950-51; pa/Former Mayor Prairie Village; Sr Partner Law Firm Bennett, Lytle, Wetzler & Winn; Ks St Senator; Am & Ks Bar Assns; cp/Chr Nat Repub Govs Assn; Prairie Village Optimist Clb; Topeka Consistory Scottish Rite Free Masonry; Univ Ks Alumni Assn; Past Pres Ks Leag Municipalities; Rotary Clb; Am Legion; VFW; r/Prot; hon/Ks of Yr, Topeka Capitol Jour Pubs; Citizenship Awd, Ks Engrg Soc; Outstg Citizen, Emporia St Col.

BENOVITZ, MADGE KLEIN oc/Civic Volunteer; b/Nov 26, 1934; h/840 Nandy Dr, Kingston, PA 18704; m/Burton S; c/Jane B Feinstein; p/Nathan and Esther Miller Klein, Kingston; ed/BA Wyo Sem & Wilkes Col 1956; pa/Pa St Rdg Adv Coun 1977-; Pa St Bd Ed: Coun Basic Ed, Voc Com; Pa St Adv Coun Voc Ed: Exec Com, Chperson Com Goals,

BENZINGER, THEODOR HANNES oc/Physician; b/Aug 23, 1905; h/6607 Broxburn Rd, Bethesda, MD 20014; m/Maria Henke; c/Robert Henke, Fay Ann, Rolf, Angela Stuempel (Mrs Rolf), Monica Utermann (Mrs Eckhard); p/Theodor and Alma Heincke Benzinger; ed/DSc Univ Tubingen 1929; MD Univ Freiburg 1933; pa/Conslt Nat Bur Standards 1970-; Dir

Bioenergetics Labs & Head Colarimentry Div Nav Med Res Inst 1947-70; Dir Aeromed Dept German AF Testing Ctr 1934-44; Other Profl Positions; Am Physiol Soc; Aerospace Med Assn; NY Acad Scis; Colloque Claude Bernard; German Physiol Soc; Soc German Natural Scis & Med; hon/Recipient: Golden Scheele Medal, Chem Soc Stockholm 1963, Humboldt Awd.

Chperson Com Eval; Citizens Comm Basic Ed: Exec Com, Chperson Staff Com; US Circuit Judge Nom'g Panel 3rd Circuit Ct; Other Profl Positions; cp/VP Wilkes-Barre Chapt Hadassah; Nat Coun Jewish Wom; Temple Israel Sisterhood; Woms Aux WB Gen Hosp; Pres Leag Wom Voters WB Area; Exec Com, Chperson Pers Policies Com; U Way Wyo Valley; Chr Planning Allocations & Resources Devel Com, Chr Rec & Social Devel SubCom, Chr Needs Assessment Com; Bd Trustees Kings Col; Flood Recovery Task Force; Ec Devel Coun NEn Pa: Exec Com, Tax Task Force; r/Jewish; hon/Penns Woods Girl Scout Recog Awd 1977; Num Biogl Listings.

BENSKINA, MARGARITA ORELIA (PRINCESS ORELIA) oc/Dancer; Poet; Manager; h/192-22 100th Ave, Hollis, Queens, NY 11423; c/Pearl Quintyne; p/Jose and Amelia Divins Benskina; ed/Att'g Queens Col; pa/Owner & Mgr Retail Rel Mdse Store; Composer: One Day, Un Dia; Author: No Longer Defeated & Other Poems, Inflammable Desire To Rebel, I Have Loved You Already, I Thank You Father, To Whom It May Concern; Choreographer; Vocalist; Former Personal Mgr Les Jazz Modes Quintet; Nat Coun Negro Wom; r/Cath; hon/John F Kennedy Lib Minorities Awd; Num Biogl Listings.

BENSON, LESTER R oc/Evangelist; b/Oct 1, 1943; h/1505 Madison St #62, Klamath Falls, OR 97601; ba/KF; m/Verna F; p/Ray Benson, Lansing, MI; Mary Benson (dec); ed/BA Warner Pacific Col; MDiv Anderson Sch Theol; pa/Pres Dir Child Evangelism F'ship; Past St Chr Bd Christian Ed; r/Ch of God, Anderson.

BENSON, MAVIS oc/Management; h/17079 E 59th Cir, Denver, CO 80239; ed/Wesleyan Col; pa/Prog Assoc Profl Lng Ctrs Inc 1977-; Pres B W Investmt Co 1969-76; Pres Candlewick Inc 1967-71; Mktg & Sales Gardinier & Co 1964-69; Other Profl Positions; cp/Pres: Darlettes Clb, Dee-Cees Clb, Zonta Clb Englewood-Littleton; Intl Toastmistress Clbs Inc; Royal Matron ADA Ct Order of Amaranth; Bus & Profl Woms Fdn; Am Bus Woms Assn; White Shrine; En Star; Spkrs Bur; Other Civic Assns; hon/Citizen Country Mexico & Cuidad de Juarez; Wom of Yr, Bus & Profl Woms Clb; Nom'd Colo Wom Achmt; Intl Sales & Mktg Dist'd Salesman Awd; Marquis & Nat Social Dir; DLB.

BENSON, WARREN STEN oc/Administrator; Professor; b/Aug 23, 1929; ba/Trinity Evang Div Sch, Deerfield, IL 60015; m/Lenore Ellis; c/Scot, Bruce; p/Sten and Evelyn Arneson Benson (dec); ed/BA NWn Col 1952; ThM Dallas Theol Sem 1956; MRE SWn Bapt Sem 1957; PhD Loyola Univ Chicago 1975; pa/Trinity Evang Div Sch: Assoc Dean Acad Affairs 1978-, Prof Christian Ed 1978-, Asst Prof 1970-74; Assoc Prof Dallas Theol Sem 1974-78; Ctl Reg Dir Gospel Light Pubs 1969-72; Other Profl Positions; Evang Theol Soc; Rel Ed Assn; MW Assn Hist Ed; Nat Assn Profs Christian Ed; hon/W/W Rel; Personalities S; Commun Ldrs & Noteworthy Ams.

BENSTOCK, BERNARD oc/Professor; Author; Critic; b/Mar 23, 1930; h/615 W Univ Ave, Champaign, IL 61820; ba/Urbana, IL; m/Sharon G; c/Kevin, Erika; p/Sol and

Lily Garde Benstock; ed/BA Brooklyn Col; MA Columbia Univ; PhD Fla St Univ; mil/AUS 1951-53; pa/Literary Critic; Pres James Joyce Foun; CoChm Intl James Joyce Symposia; hon/Fulbright Lectr.

BENTLEY, JAMES HARLEY oc/Director; b/Nov 17, 1941; h/433 Rinconada Ct, Benicia, CA 94510; ba/Concord, CA; m/Bonnie Bea; c/William, Virginia; p/James Bentley (dec); Virginia Titus Vlahos, Tarzana, CA; ed/AS Imperial Valley Col 1966; BA San Diego St 1969; MBA Cand John F Kennedy Univ; mil/USAF Corpsman 1959-63; pa/Dir Data

Processing; Head Stat & Engrg Sys Support Br 1975-79; Head Stat Eval Calibration Data 1972-75; Mathematician Computer Support 1969-72; Honeywell U Ser Group; Fed ADP Coun No Cal & Nev; cp/Bd Dirs Chapt 90 Nat Supvrs Assn; hon/Outstg Organic Chem Student Awd, IVC 1966.

BENTLEY, KENTON EARL oc/Director; b/Jun 1, 1927; h/15811 Dunmoor Dr, Houston, TX 77059; ba/Houston; m/Elizabeth Jule; p/Kenneth Bentley (dec); Mrs Isabell Norris, Houston; ed/BS Univ Mich 1950; PhD Univ NM 1959; mil/USN 1945-46; pa/Dir Sci & Applications Br Lockheed Electronics Co Inc; Am Chem Soc; Am Assn Advmt Sci; AAUP; Nat Mgmt Assn; r/Prot; hon/Los Alamos Res Fellow, Univ NM; Sigma Xi Rockefeller Foun Grant, Am Univ Beirut.

BENTLEY, RUTH SHEARER oc/Librarian; b/Jul 29, 1911; h/Rt 10 Box 515, London, KY 40741; m/C Frank; c/Kenneth (dec), Philip (dec), James, John, Joe (dec), Douglas; p/Thomas and Nora Powell Shearer (dec); ed/BA, MS Univ Ky; pa/Pres, VP & Treas: KASL, KLA; r/Ch of Christ; hon/Outstg Sch Libn Ky 1968.

BENTLEY, VIRGIL TEMPLE oc/Minister; Gerontologist; b/Apr 19, 1919; h/10715 Wyatt St, Dallas, TX 75218; ba/Mesquite, TX; m/Ann Ruth; c/Ann B Tippens (Mrs Darryl), John; p/James and Johnnie Bentley (dec); ed/BA; MLA; MA; pa/Author: The Beauty of Age; Lectr; Editor; cp/Public Relats Dir C of C; Co Chr Nat Foun Infantile Paralysis; r/Ch of Christ; hon/W/W: S&SW, Okla City.

BENZINGER, MARIA oc/Physician; b/Feb 18, 1918; h/6607 Broxburn Dr, Bethesda, MD 20034; ba/Washington, DC; m/Theodor H; c/Robert Henke, Fay Ann; p/Heinrich Gerhartz; Elisabeth Gerhartz, Berlin, Germany; ed/MD; pa/Chief Med Ofcr Anesthesiology DC Gen Hosp; r/Cath; hon/Num Awds Sci Exhibits.

BERARD, DAILEY J oc/Executive; b/Aug 9, 1929; h/110 Mountainside Dr, Lafayette, LA 70501; ba/New Iberia, LA; m/Nathalie Mary; c/Deadra, Karen, Angela; p/Blanc and Maude Berard, NI; ed/BCE; mil/AUS; pa/VP & Gen Mgr Houston Sys Mfg Co; LA Engr Soc; Reg'd Surveyor: Tex, La, Miss, Ga, Minn & Ala; cp/NI & Lafayette Chambers; La Intracoastal Sea Way Assn; Kiwanis Clb; Other Civic Assns; hon/Num Patents; Pub'd Author.

BERCHTOLD, LILLIAN HELEN oc/- Principal; b/Jan 14, 1912; h/541 Humes Ave, Aptos (Rio Del Mar), CA 95003; m/Werner E; c/Paul Stevens, Kathleen Martin (Mrs Dennis Sr); p/Alexander and Lillian Sheehy Schloesser (dec); ed/BA UCLA; MA

USC; Addit Studies; pa/Ret'd Asst Prin Hillsdale HS; Phi Beta; cp/Bd Dirs Goodwill Industs; SC Symph; Am Nat Red Cross; r/Mem Epis Ch; hon/Wom Achmt, San Mateo Soroptimist 1972; Wom Achmt, Santa Cruz Woms Clb 1976.

BERG, ERIC WILHELM oc/Administrator; b/Jul 28, 1921; h/1830 Pawnee Tr, Lakeland, FL 33803; ba/L'land; m/Regena May; c/Constance Plunkett, Eric III, Thomas; p/Peter and Judith Berg (dec); ed/BME Univ Enid 1947; MMus NWn Univ 1951; mil/AAC WW-II; pa/Asst Prin; Intl Soc Mus Ed Conf; Mus Ed Nat Conf; Fla Mus Ed Assn; Past Pres FEMEA; Phi Mu Alpha; cp/L'land Symph Orch Del Dem Nat Conv; Polk Co Dem Com; Del Fla Dem Conv; AF & AM; Former Pres L'land Concert Assn; r/Disciples of Christ; Choir Dir Beymer U Meth Ch.

BERG, JEAN HORTON oc/Author;

b/May 30, 1913; h/207 Walnut Ave, Wayne, PA 19087; m/John Joseph; c/Jean, Julie B Blickle, John; p/Harry and Daisy Horton Lutz (dec); ed/BS, MA Univ Pa; pa/Writer & Tchr Creative Writing; Author 47 Books for Yg People; cp/Leag Wom Voters; r/Christian Scist; hon/Jr Lit Guild; Medalion, City Philadelphia; Follett Awd; Alumni Awd Merit, Univ Pa.

BERG, JERALD ALLAN oc/Engineer; b/Mar 28, 1944; h/6439 Oaknut Dr, Houston, TX 77088; ba/Houston; m/Elizabeth Jean; c/Kim, Karen; p/John Berg (dec); Helen Muse Berg, Molaki, HI; mil/USAF; pa/Engr & Dir Mfg; Conslt Meml Univ.

BERG, JULIA IRENE oc/Nurse; b/1918; h/5353 Fillmore NE, Minneapolis, MN 55421; ba/St Paul, MN; m/Edmund (dec); c/Theresa, Edlona, Valkyr; p/Michael Hutney (dec); Mary Hutney, Rojovo; ed/Baccalaureate Nsg; pa/Reg'd Nurse Orthos, Surg & Treatment Gillette Chds Hosp 1977-; Fairview Hosp: Supvr Maternal & Infant Care 1975-77, Head Nurse Newborn & Premature Nursery 1960-75; Num Other Profl Positions; Am Nurses Assn; cp/Intl Platform Assn; r/Presb; hon/Notable Ams; Personalities W&MW; W/W Am Wom; Intl W/W Commun Ser; Other Biogl Listings.

BERG, LOUIS LESLIE oc/Investment Executive; b/Dec 27, 1919; h/1085 Park Ave, New York City, NY 10028; ba/Lyndhurst, NJ; m/Minnette; c/Sharon, Randee, Michel; p/Gustav and Hedwig Kohn Berg; ed/Att'd Univ Vienna & Col City NY; pa/Pres Gt Empire Corp 1946-; Bendalor Real Est Corp 1950-60; Netherlands Securities Co Inc 1959-62; Imported Automotive Parts Ltd; Num Other Profl Positions; Am Mgmt Assn; cp/Wings.

BERGER, LEONARD oc/Educator; b/Jun 15, 1947; h/PO Box 1245, Clemson, SC 29632; ba/Clemson; m/Ellen Welser; p/Charles and Ethel Berger, Deerfield Bch, FL; ed/BA 1968, MS 1970, PhD 1972 Temple Univ; pa/Assoc Prof Indust Psychol Clemson Univ; Dir Spkrs Bur; Conslt Reg Govt & Indust; Soc Advmt Social Psychol; Secy SC Psychol Assn; cp/Bd Dirs Greenville Zoo; Sertoma Clb; r/Jewish; hon/Edr of Yr; Best Tchr, Clemson Univ.

BERGER, MIRIAM E oc/Counselor; b/Apr 4, 1924; h/140-70 Burden Crescent, Jamaica, NY 11435; ba/New York, NY; m/Paul D; c/Suzanne, Elizabeth; p/Max and Tillie Easton, Jamaica; ed/BA; MSW; pa/Psychotherapist; Supervisory Status Am Assn Marriage & Fam Cnslrs; cp/Feminist Therapy Collective; Ethical Cult; hon/W/W Am Wom.

BERGERON, JIMMIE LEON oc/Physician; b/Nov 1, 1932; h/1023 Maranon Ln, Houston, TX 77090; ba/Houston; m/Lynn Ann; c/James, Micheil; p/Albert Ralph Bergeron (dec); Louise Neebrommer, Reardan, WA; ed/BS (Mech Engrg & Indust Engrg) Univ Wash-S 1955; MD 1968, Intern 1968-69 Emory Univ; Resident Baylor Col Med 1969-71; mil/AUS Trans Corps 1955-57; pa/Pvt Pract Med 1972-; Staff: Houston NW & NE Hosps, Meml Hosps; Num Former Profl Positions; Diplomate Am Bd Internal Med; Am Col Phys; Tex Med Assn; Harris Co Med Soc; Pres NHDC Inc; r/Luth; hon/Poet Laureat Maranon.

BERGGREN, PAUL WALTER oc/Minister; b/Aug 22, 1922; h/585 Old Crystal Bay Rd, Long Lake, MN 55356; ba/Minneapolis, MN; m/Dorothea Faye; c/Nancy, Susan, Jane; p/Walter Berggren, Boone, IA; Fern Temple Berggren (dec); ed/BA Kletzing Col; pa/Min Gospel; Evang Free Ch Am: Pastor & Treas Min Assn, Dir Ch Ext N Ctl Dist; Secy Overseas Mission; r/Prot; hon/W/W Rel; Personalities W&MW; Noteworthy Ams.

BERGGREN, VIRGINIA HERMA oc/Administrator; b/Jan 19, 1918; h/1023 Maranon Rd, Ojai, CA 93023; ba/Same; m/Stuart Gustav; c/Sonja B Baesemann; p/Daniel and Sarah Fullmer (dec); ed/BA; MS; pa/Ednl

Admr; cp/Var Polit Activs; Mbrship Num St & Local Orgs; r/Prot; hon/Outstg Dedication Ed, Cal.

BERGLEITNER, GEORGE C JR oc/Executive; Consultant; b/Jul 16, 1935; h/Red Rock Rd, Hobart, NY 13788; ba/Stamford, NY; m/Betty L; c/George III, Michael, Stephen; p/George Sr and Marie Bergleitner, Ft Myers, FL; ed/BBA; MBA; PhD; mil/AUS 11th Airborn Div; pa/Pres Delhi Chems Inc; Investmt Banker; Fin Conslt; cp/Intl Rotary Clb; Stamford Country Clb; Honor Legion; Downtown & NY Ath Clb; K of C; Moose Clb; r/Rom Cath; hon/Cert Apprec: Stamford Little Leag & Commun Hosp, Spec Olympics; JFK Meml Awd; NYC Police Legion; Ambassadore Clb, St Francis Col.

BERGSTEN, C FRED oc/Secretary; b/Apr 23, 1941; h/4106 Sleepy Hollow Rd, Annandale, VA 22003; ba/Wash, DC; m/Virginia Lee Wood; c/Mark; p/Carl and Halhaline Kirk Bergsten, Plattsburg, MO; ed/BA; MA; MALD; PhD; pa/Asst Secy to Treas Intl Affairs; Sr Fellow Brookings Inst 1972-76; r/Prot; hon/W/W Am; Outstg Yg Men Am; *Times* 200 Yg Am Ldrs; Pub'd Author.

BERKOWITZ, DAVID oc/Musician; b/Jun 9, 1915; h/180-44 80 Dr, Jamaica, NY 11432; ba/New York, NY; c/Lynn Dubal, Phebe B Tanners, Robert; p/Jacob and Lillian Berkowitz (dec); ed/St John Univ; mil/Merch Marine 1942-45; pa/Perf'd Num Musical Groups & Recording Cos; r/Am; hon/Var Musical S'ships & Contests.

BERLAND, THEODORE oc/Author; b/Mar 26, 1929; h/2729 W Lunt Ave, Chicago, IL 60645; ba/Same; m/Cynthia Rich; ed/BS Univ Ill 1950; MA Univ Chgo 1972; pa/Author: 11 Books, 5 Public Affairs Pamphlets, Num Articles; Sev Editorships; Lectr Var Orgs & Sems; Instr Practical Nutrition Columbia Col 1977-; Instr Sci Writing Medill Sch Jour NWn Univ 1973 & 1975; Chief Chgo Bur Med World News

1960-66; Authors Guild; Past Pres & Treas Soc Midland Authors; Chr Freelance Com Nat Assn Sci Writers; Overseas & Chgo Press Clb; Num Other Profl Assns; cp/Dir Indep Voters Ill; Dir Commun Action Indep Precnt Org; Cook Co Citizens Search Com; Alt Del ADA; Num Polit Coms; Bd: Jewish Commun Cts Chgo, Camp Chi, Alts Inc, Citizens Sch Commun; Pres: Citizens Against Noise, Mather HS Coun, Dist 2 Ednl Coun, N Town Commun Coun; Art Inst Chgo; Num Other Civic Assns; hon/Am Med Writers Assn;

Fellow, Achmt Med Writing Awd, 2 Beth Fonda Meml Awds; Cert Apprec, Vision Conserv Inst; Public Ser Awd Jour, Am Optometric Assn; Am Dental Assn: Meritorious Achmt Sci Writers Awd, 1st Pl Sci Writers Awd; Oper PUSH Excell Ed Awd; Commun Ser Awd Medal; Num Biogl Listings; Num Other Honors.

BERMAN, HERBERT LAWRENCE oc/Engineer; b/Jan 8, 1931; h/23-20 Bell Blvd, Bayside, NY 11360; ba/New York, NY; m/Pearl Marilyn; c/Stacey, Marcy; p/Moses and Bertha Berman (dec); ed/BCE Polytechnic Inst Brooklyn 1952; Addit Studies; pa/Furnace Engrg Spec Caltex Petro Corp 1972-; Mgr Proposal Engrg Alcorn Combustion Co 1969-72; Sr Engr Foster Wheeler Corp 1960-62; Lectr Am Inst Chem Engrs; Am Soc Mech Engrs; Am Assn Cost Engrs; Am Petro Inst; *Chem Engrg* Mag: Adv & Prod Res Panels; hon/Nat Geog Soc; hon/Order of Arrow.

BERNARD, BETTY oc/Physician; b/Aug 7, 1933; h/1866 Via del Rey, S Pasadena, CA 91030; c/Peter B Anthony, John Anthony; p/Raymond and Mildred Dowell Bernard, Encino, CA; ed/BA; MD; pa/Acad Phys, Pediatrics & Neonatology LAC-USC Med Ctr Wom Hosp; Reschr; Patient-care; Opera Assocs of LA; Profl Assns & Coms; Conslt'ship; Profl Pubs; hon/Biogl Listings; Nat Cystic Fibrosis Res Foun Ser Awd.

BERNARD, LOWELL FRANCIS oc/Director; Educator; b/Dec 14, 1931; h/244 Monticello Dr, Chagrin Falls, OH 44022; ba/Cleveland, OH; m/Diana Gypson; c/Deborah, Steven, Jocelyn; p/Francis Bernard (dec); Irma Bernard, Portland, OR; ed/BA 1955, MSPH 1959 UCLA; Addit Studies; pa/Dir C'land Hlth Ed Mus 1969-; Tchr Dept Commun Med Case Wn Resv Univ Sch Med 1969-; Addit Former Tchg Experience; Conslt Intl & Nat Orgs; Past Pres

& VP Am Assn Hlth & Med Mus; Past Pres InterMus Coun NE Ohio; Assn Sci & Technol Ctrs: Bd Dirs 1976-, Secy-Treas 1978-, Prog Chr C'land 1979; Lectr Num Wkshps; Num Other Profl Assns; cp/Bd Dirs C'land Chapt Epilepsy Foun Am; Greater C'land Growth Assn; Public Ed Com C'land Acad Med; Adult Ed Coun C'land; InterAgy Coun Smoking & Hlth; Harris Co Dental Mus; Poison Info Com; Motorbike Safety Com; r/Presb; hon/Mayor & IMC Pres Cits; Recipient Num Grants; W/W: Am, World; Nat Reg Prominent Ams; Pub'd Author.

BERNARDO, JOSE RAUL oc/Architect; Composer; Playwright; Lighting Engineer; b/Oct 3, 1938; h/240 W 98 St, New York, NY 10025; p/Jose and Luisa R Bernardo, NYC; ed/BMus Havana Conservatory 1958; BArch 1964, MMus Univ Miami 1969; MArch 1965, PhD Columbia Univ 1972; pa/Partner in Joyner/Bernardo Archs & Designers; Partner in JBBJ Music/Theatrical Prodns; Illuminating Engrg Soc; Am Inst Archs; cp/Fdg Partner, Org of Homosexual Men; r/Cath; hon/Author, *The Child: An Operatic Poem for the Stage* (1974); Composer: Concerto for Piano, Voices & Antiphonal Chamber Orchs (1975), Score for *Fat Angels* (Feature Film, 1980); Cimitas Fellow, Inst Intl Ed, United Nations; Lumen Awds in Lighting; Nat Opera Inst Awd; Am Music Ctr Awd; NY St Fellow; Others.

BERNHARDT, JOHN PETER ASHLEY oc/Attorney; b/Jun 11, 1946; h/Finders 1290 Old Earth Rd, Charlottesville, VA 22901; ba/Ch'ville; p/C Murray and Iris Ashley Bernhardt, Wash, DC; ed/Cert Intl Law London Sch Ec & Polit Sci 1967; BA summa cum laude Dartmouth Col 1968; JD Univ Va Sch Law 1973; mil/USNR Lt; pa/Assoc Dir Ctr Oceans Law & Policy; Lectr Law Univ Va Sch Law; CoChr ABA SubCom Polar Policy; DC Bar Assn; r/Epis; hon/Reynolds Fellow Intl Law, Trinity Hall Cambridge; Rufus Choate Scholar, Darthmouth Col.

BERNS, HARMON GORDON oc/Producer; Writer; b/May 20, 1947; h/129 W 95th St, New York, NY 10025; ba/Same; p/Jerome Berns, Chicago, IL; ed/BA 1969, MA 1971 NWn Univ; Harvard Law Sch 1974; pa/Prod & Dir: *Merlin, Waterhole, Blessed Mcgill & Las Vegas Strip*; Dir Theatre & Opera Lincoln Ctr; cp/Dir Arts Projs Foun; hon/Num Film & Theatre Awds; Men Achmt; W/W Prominent Ams; Black Belt Karate; AAU Champion Swimmer.

BERNSTEIN, LEONARD oc/Conductor; Pianist; Composer; b/Aug 25, 1918; ba/1414 Ave Ams, New York City, NY 10019; c/Jamie, Alexander, Nina; p/Samuel and Jennie Resnick Bernstein; ed/AB Harvard 1939; Grad Curtis Inst Music 1941; Studied Conduct'g w Fritz Reiner & Serge Koussevitsky; Studied Piano w Helen Coates, Heinrich Gebhard & Isabella Vengerova; Num Hon Degs Var Cols & Univs; pa/Toured Europe w Vienna Philharm Orch 1970; Charles Eliot Norton Prof Poetry Harvard 1972-72; Gala Bicent Tour Am & Europe w NY Philharm 1976; Frequent Conductor Israel Philharm Orch; Life Laureate Conductor Philharm; Num Other Profl Positions; Works Include: *West Side Story* 1957, *Mass* 1971, *Dybbuk NYC Ballet Co* 1974, *Suites No 1 & 2* 1974, *Slava* 1977, *Three Mediations from Mass* 1977, *Songfest* 1977; Num Others; hon/Recipient TV Acad Awd Yg Peoples Concerts 1960; TV Acad Awd Outstg Classical Music Prog 1976; Pub'd Author.

BERRETT, LAMAR CECIL oc/Professor; b/Mar 28, 1926; h/1032 E 400 S, Orem, UT 84057; ba/Provo, UT; m/Darlene Hamilton; c/Marla, Kim, Michael, Susan, LeAnn, Nathan, Even, Ellen, Jared; p/John Berrett (dec); Stella Wright, Salt Lake City, UT; ed/BS Univ Utah 1952; MS 1960, EdD 1963 Brigham Yg Univ; mil/2nd Inf Div 1944-46; pa/BYU: Prof Ch Hist & Doctrine; Dept Chm 1969-75, Dir Ch Hist TV Series 1967, Dir Inst Mormon Studies 1975-76; Am Profs Peace Mid E; Chapt Pres & VP Utah St Hist Soc; r/Ch of Jesus Christ Latter-Day Sts: Bishop & High Councilor; Sem Tchr 1953-62.

BERRIE, PETER MICHAEL oc/Zoologist; Consultant; b/Jan 1, 1939; h/116 Charles St, Fairbanks, AK 99701; ba/F'banks; m/Elaine Frances; c/Dayna, Erik; p/Albert Berrie, Harrisburg, PA; Juanita Eve (dec); ed/BA 1965, MS 1967 Univ Conn; PhD Cand Univ Ga; mil/AUS 1957-60; pa/Conslt: Survival Ser Comm IUCN 1976-, DAV-TRON Animal Radio-Telemetry 1970-; Envir Conslt Inst Marine Sci 1975; Adv Tech Editor *Mzuri Drumbeat* 1972-74; Num Other Profl Positions; Trustee Mammalian Res Assn 1973-; Am Soc Mammalogists; Am Assn Adv Sci; Arctic Inst No Am; British Ecol Soc; Wildlife Soc; cp/Intl Platform Assn; Fellow Explorers Clb; r/Prot; hon/LCS Res Fellow, Univ Ga; Beta Beta Beta; Pub'd Author.

BERRY, CHARLES ALDEN oc/Administrator; b/Sept 17, 1923; h/10814 Riverview Dr, Houston, TX 77042; ba/Houston; m/Addella Nance; c/Michael, Charlene B Forrester (Mrs David), Janice B Dudley (Mrs Jay); p/George and Vera Berry, Riverside, CA; ed/BA Univ Cal-B 1945; MD Univ Cal Med Sch-SF 1947; MPH cum laude Harvard Sch Public Hlth-B 1956; Cert'd Preventive Med 1957; pa/Pres Univ Tex Hlth Sci Ctr Houston 1974-; Dir Life Scis, Nat Aeronautics & Space Adm 1971-74; Dir Med Res & Opers NASA Manned Spacecraft Ctr 1966-71; Num Other Past Positions; Lic'd Cal & Tex; Num

Acad Appts; Var Edit Bds incl'g "Aerospace Med", Jour of Aerospace Med Assn & "Space Life Scis" Intl Jour of Biol & Med; Num Profl Assns; cp/Bd Dirs: SmithKline Corp, Nassau Bay Nat Bk, SWn Savs & Ln Assn; Earth Awareness Foun; Harris Co Med Soc; Delta Omega; Nu Sigma Nu; r/Meth; hon/Aerospace Med Assn: Arnold D Tuttle Awd, Louis H Bauer Fdrs Awd; USAF Cert Achmt by Surg Gen; Spec Aerospace Med Hon Cit, AMA; Hoyt S Vanderberg Trophy, Arnold Air Soc; Melbourne W Boynton Awd, Am Astronautical Soc; Gold Medal; Am Col Chest Phys, Czechoslovakian Acad Med; NASA Dist'd Ser Medal; Num F'ships; Num Biogl Listings; Pub'd Author.

BERRY, LEMUEL JR oc/Professor; b/Oct 11, 1946; h/715 E Harrison, Guthrie, OK 73044; ba/Langston, OK; m/Christine; c/Lemuel III, Cyrus; p/Lemuel Sr and Ethel Berry, Burlington, NJ; ed/BA w hons Livingstone Col 1965-69; MA 1970, PhD 1973 Univ Ia; pa/Prof & Chr Dept Music Langston Univ 1976-; Fayetteville St Univ: Chr Dept Music 1973-76, Chr Div Humanities 1973-75; Music Conslt F'ville & Cumberland Co Schs 1973-76; Other Profl Positions; Nat Soc Lit & Arts; Music Edr Nat Conf; Intl Soc Music Edrs; Okla Col & Univ Music Assn; Coun Res Music Ed; NAACP; Lectr incl'g Afro-Am Music Wkshops & Inst Technol & Higher Ed, Monterrey; cp/Lions Intl; Tri-M; Kappa Kappa Psi; r/Meth; hon/Author Num Pubs incl'g *Biogl Dic Black Musicians and Music Edrs & Afro-Am Music Resource Guide and Dir: A Source Book*; Num Biogl Listings.

BERRY, RALPH A oc/Minister; b/Jun 7, 1919; h/PO Box 5427, Lenoir, NC 28645; ba/Lenoir; m/Grace; c/Kenneth, Rachel B Henkle; p/Perry and Artie Berry (dec); ed/Dipl Fruitland Bapt Bible Inst; pa/Pastor

Missionary Bapt Ch of 1st Bapt Whitnel; Pastored Chs Tenn, Ky & NC; r/Bapt; hon/Cert Awds New Orleans Bapt Theol Sem: With Christ After The Lost, Bldg Better Chs & Heart of Old Testament.

BERRYMAN, ESTHER B oc/Artist; h/3450 Lake Shore Dr, Chicago, IL 60657; m/Gerald Howard; p/Charles and Goldie Bierman (dec); ed/PhB Univ Chgo; cp/N Shore Art Leag; Chgo Artists Coalition; Alumni Assn Sch Art Inst Chgo; Chm Art Exhibit Comm Chgo Woms Aid; hon/Cert Apprec Commissary Designs Worldwide Aus Installations; Patentee Chd's Ed Clock.

BERRYMAN, JAMES C oc/Professor; b/Sept 28, 1935; h/127 Evonshire, Arkadelphia, AR 71923; ba/Arkad; m/Mary Anne Pierce; c/James, Cathryn; p/Cleo Berryman (dec); Mrs Cleo Berryman, Arkad; ed/BA cum laude Ouachita Bapt Univ 1957; BD 1960, ThD 1964 SWn Bapt Theol Sem; pa/Ouachita Bapt Univ: Coor AIDP Prog 1969-, Prof Rel & Phil 1964-, Acting VP Acad Affairs 1969-70; Vis Prof Henderson St Univ & St Johns Home Mission Sem; Other Past Positions; Secy-Treas SWn Assn Bapt Tchrs Rel 1972-; Past Charter Pres OBU Chapt Am Assn Univ Profs; Am Acad Rel; Ark Phil Assn; Soc Biblical Lit; cp/Former Ofcs S Ft Civitan Clb: Bd, Pres, Lt Gov, Dist Chaplain, Gov Ozark Dist, Ed & Ldrship Tng Com, Civitan Intl; Num Others; Bd Arkad Commun Theatre; Chr Bd; Ctl Ark Devel Coun, Ark Housing Asst Corp; VP Arkad Min Alliance;

r/So Bapt; Dir SS 1st Bapt Ch, Arkad 1972-; hon/Outstg Edrs Am 1973 & 1974; Outstg Yg Men Am 1970-71; Ser Awd Cub Scouts Arkad; Ouachita Bapt Univ: Outstg Min Student 1956-57, Outstg Fac Mem 1970-71; Num Biogl Listings.

BERSIN, RUTH HARGRAVE oc/Consultant; b/Sept 16, 1939; h/5787 Highwood Rd, Castro Valley, CA 94546; ba/Hayward, CA; m/Richard L; p/Harold and Rowena Hullett Hargrave, La Porte, IN; ed/BS Ind Univ 1962; MA Colgate Rochester Div Sch 1965; pa/Conslt Intl Plasma Corp 1978-; Conslt Teijin Ednl Sys 1977; US Coor Bunka Pub'g Bur 1975-77; Dir Ednl Devel Ctr Commodore Ednl Sys 1974-75; Num Other Past Positions; Nat Writers Clb; AAUW; Am Lib Assn; Intl Reading Assn; r/Bancroft Ave Bapt Ch; Dir Christian Ed 1st Bapt Ch, LaPorte 1967; Commun Wkr Christ Ch Cathedral, Rochester 1966; Bd Christian Ed Coun Chs 1964-67; Bd Urban Min 1964-67; Num Other Positions; hon/Pub'd Author.

BERTONE, C M oc/Psychologist; b/Jul 12, 1930; h/PO Box 1432, Guilford, CT 06437; ba/Stratford, CT; m/Stacey; c/Kathleen, Victoria, Jenifer, Dana, Christopher; p/Anthony Dominic (dec); Dellora Dominic, N Bergen, NJ; ed/BS; PhD; pa/Res Psychologist Chief Human Factors; r/Past Pres Canoga Park Civic Assn; r/Rom Cath; hon/Woodrow Wilson F'ship Nominee; Pub'd Author.

BERTONI, DANTE H oc/Artist; b/Nov 13, 1926; h/52-02 8th Ave, Bay Ridge, NY 11220; ba/Long Island City, NY; m/Mae Henriksen; c/Rachel, Irene II; p/Victorio and Rosa Bertoni (dec); ed/Cert Parsons Sch Design; Addit Studies; mil/9th USAAF 584th Bomb Sq 394th Bomb Gr WW-II; pa/Packaging Design Artist; NACAL Com Salmagundi Clb; Exhibited w: Nat Acad

Design, Nat Arts Clb, Am Vets Artist Assn, Wash Sq Outdoor Art Exhibit, Long Bch Art Clb & Mus Fine Arts; Am Watercolor Soc; r/Rom Cath; hon/Louis E Seley NACAL Gold Medal; Num Awds Wash Sq Outdoor Art Exhibit; Salmagundi Prize; Num Other Painting Awds.

BERTONI, MAE HENRIKSEN oc/Artist; b/Dec 17, 1929; h/52-02 8th Ave, Brooklyn, NY 11220; ba/Same; m/Dante H; c/Rachel, Irene; p/Elias and Fanny Hodt Henriksen, Tonsberg, Norway; ed/Cert Parsons Sch Design; pa/Watercolor Artist; cp/Am Watercolor Soc; Hudson Valley Art Assn; Knickerbocker Artists Assn; Painters & Sculptors Soc NJ; Long Bch Art Assn; WSOAE; hon/Gold Medal, Catherine Lorillard Wolfe Art Clb; Wm Esty Purchase

Prize, Am Watercolor Soc; Still-Life & Landscape Awds, Hudson Valley Art Assn; Medal Excell, Long Bch Art Assn; Num Other Awds.

BERTRAM, JEAN DeSALES oc/Professor; Author; Artist; b/Sept 28; h/512 Arballo Dr, San Francisco, CA 94132; ba/SF; c/Larkin Bertram-Cox; p/Val and Ruth Bertram (dec); ed/BA UNC-G; MA Univ Minn 1951; PhD Stanford Univ 1963; pa/Prof Theatre Arts SF St Univ 1952-; Perf'g Impersonation &

Reading Artist; Dir Radio Broadcasting Studio Minn Voc HS 1951-52; Fdr Public Relats Dept Burlington Industs 1943-49; cp/Pres Phi Beta Kappa N Cal Assn; Secy Exec Bd Omicron Chapt Phi Beta Kappa, SFSU; r/Christian Sci; hon/Stanford-Wilson Fellow; Delta Phi Lambda; Pub'd Author.

BERTRAM, RANDALL BYRON oc/Attorney; b/Dec 31, 1912; h/115 Evelyn Ave, Monticello, KY 42633; ba/M'cello; m/Doris Huffaker; c/Randall, Judith; p/E and Maggie Ballenger Bertram (dec); ed/BA Centre Col; mil/WW-II Far E; pa/M'cello City Atty 1950-60; Am, Ky & 40th Jud Dist Bar Assns; r/Bapt.

BERTSCH, NED ANTHONY oc/Minister; b/Sept 20, 1933; h/84661 Trona Rd, Trona, CA 93562; ba/Same; m/Virginia Carol; c/Bryan, Paul; p/LaVerne Bertsch (dec); Velma Root Bertsch, Long Bch, CA; ed/BA Cal Bapt Col 1967; MDiv Golden Gate Bapt Theol Sem 1971; DMin Maranatha Bible Sem 1978; mil/USAF 1952-61; pa/Current Pastor 1st Bapt Ch, Searles Valley; Pastor: West Santa Rosa Bapt Ch 1971-72, 1st Bapt Ch Rodeo 1968-71, 1st So Bapt Hesperia 1966-68, Asst 1st Bapt Ch Banning 1964-66, Asst So Euclid Bapt Ch Ontario 1963-64; Staff Campus Crusade Christ 1972-78: Personal Asst Dir Intl Mins Ofc, Nat Coor Host Fams Mins, Coor Intl Stay Home Progs, Adm Coor Intl Exec Tours; r/Bapt; hon/DD London Inst 1973.

BETHARDS, BETTY JEAN oc/Lecturer; Author; Meditation Teacher; b/Sept 23, 1933; h/PO Box 6874, Tahoe City, CA 95730; ba/Novato, CA; m/Gregory L Huntington; c/Pam Naugle, Chris, David; p/Charles and Mildred Adams, Tucson, AZ; pa/Author: *Sacred Sword, There is no Death, Atlantis, Way to Awareness, Sex & Psychic Energy;* Lectr: San Quintin Prison, AMA, Nurses; Num TV & Radio Series: Meditation, Alt Drugs, Inner Awareness; r/All Rels; hon/San Quintin Apprec; Mind Excel.

BETHEA, BARRON oc/Lawyer; b/May 20, 1929; h/4963 Spring Rock Rd, Birmingham, AL; ba/Bessemer, AL; m/Phyllis Parker; c/Barron, Elizabeth; p/Malcolm Sr and Wilma Edwards Bethea (dec); ed/BS Univ Ala 1952; LLB 1953; mil/USAF 1st Lt 1954-56; pa/Elec Hardware Mfr Lwyr; Fdr & Chr Bd Barron Bethea Co Inc; Assoc Industs; Ala World Trade; cp/House Reps Ala 1962; Dec Exec Com 1958-62; r/Meth.

BETHEL, JAMES SAMUEL oc/Professor; Administrator; b/Aug 13, 1915; h/3816 E Mercer Way, Mercer Isl, WA 98040; ba/Seattle, WA; m/Marinelle Reeves; c/Ruth Anderson, James, John; p/(dec); ed/BS Univ Wash 1937; MS 1939, PhD 1946 Duke Univ; mil/USAAF Capt 1942-46; pa/Univ Wash: Dean Col Forest Resources 1964-, Prof

Forestry & Assoc Dean Grad Sch 1962-64; Head Spec Projs Sci Ed Nat Sci Foun 1959-62; Other Past Profl Positions; Soc Am Foresters; Am Assn Advmt Sci; Am Soc Quality Control; Intl Acad Wood Sci; Phi Sigma; Sigma Xi; Xi Sigma Pi; Gamma Sigma Delta; Num Other Profl Assns; cp/Past Pres Duke Univ Forestry Alumni Assn; Trustee Keep Wash Green Assn; Exec Bd & Chief Seattle Coun Boy Scouts; Mayors Com Seattle Zoo; Other Civic Assn; hon/Fellow: Inst Wood Sci, Soc Am Foresters, Intl Acad Wood Sci; SAF Forester of Yr, Puget Sound Section 1972.

BETTENCOURT, MARGARET ROWAN oc/Homemaker; b/Dec 1890; h/3815 Ave S, Galveston, TX 77550; m/Henry Joseph (dec); c/Dorothy Elfstrom, Henry; p/William and Kathleen Rowan (dec); r/Rom Cath.

BETTIS, DOROTHY D oc/Teacher; b/Feb 13; h/1861 Nabers Dr, Mobile, AL 36617; ba/Mobile; c/Victor Lett; p/James and Inez Holt Dillard (dec); ed/BS Ala St Univ 1956; MS Purdue Univ 1969; AA Univ S Ala 1976; pa/Tchr: Woodcock 1973-, Eanes 1970-73, Leinkauf 1969-70, E A Palmer 1963-68, Whitley 1962-63, E T Belsaw 1956-62; Nat & Ala Ed Assns; Edrs Study Assn; Am Lib Assn; Past Secy Mobile Co Tchrs Assn; cp/NAACP; Nat Coun Negro Wom; Nabers Dr Civic Improvement Clb; Mobile City Fdn Wom; YWCA; Delta Sigma Theta; r/Bethel African Meth Epis Ch; hon/NDEA Tchrs F'ships Purdue Univ & Univ Ks; Tchr of Yr, E A Palmer Elem Sch; 4 Human Relationship Awds, Springhill Col & Univ S Ala; Intl Paper Co S'ship, Tuskegee Inst; Num Biogl Listings.

BETTS, CLIFFORD ALLEN oc/Engineer; Consultant; b/Sept 12, 1889; h/2510 S Ivanhoe Pl, Denver, CO 80222; ba/Same; m/Edna Cantril; c/Allen, Edith, Marjorie Seiser (Mrs Virgil); p/Albert and Lila Malkin Betts (dec); ed/PhB Yale 1911; CE Wis 1913; pa/Civil Engr Moffat Tunnel, Owyhee Dam & Num Others; Pres DC Sect ASCE; Dir & Pres Wash Soc Engrs; Dir Colo Soc Engrs; Wash Acad Scis; Yale Engrg Assn; Chm DC Coun Engrs & Arch Coun; p/BSA Commun; Cosmos Clb; Dir Kiwanis Clb; r/Meth Epis; hon/Dist'd Ser Cit, Univ Wis 1976; Thomas Fitch Rowland Prize, ASCE 1932; Civil Engrg Hist & Heritage Awd 1975; Soc Awd, Wash Soc Engrs 1954; Granted Patent Ilinged Automatic Flashbd Gate; Pub'd Author.

BETTS, JO ANN oc/Educator; Consultant; b/Oct 8, 1947; h/PO Box 63, Gary, IN 46402; ba/Gary; p/Hobart Betts (dec); Mattie Betts, Gary; ed/BS 1970, MS 1974, Doctoral Cand Ind St Univ; pa/Tchr Reading Gary Commun Schs 1970-; Owner & Dir Reading Ctr Inc 1976-; Am Fdn Tchrs;

AAUW; cp/Gary Reading Coun; Eval Com NW Ind Sickle Cell Anemia Foun Inc; Coun Exceptnl Chd; Minority Bus Steering Com Gary; Delta Sigma Theta; r/St Timothy Commun Ch; hon/Featured Ebony Mag 1967 & 77; Silver Awd Most Unique Bus NW Ind, MBSC.

BEVERLY, LAURA ELIZABETH oc/Educator; b/Nov 26, 1935; h/150 Wash St Apt 6B, Hempstead, NY 11550; p/Sidney and Alma Logan, H'stead; ed/BA WVa St Col; MS Brooklyn Col; Addit Studies; pa/Tchr Spec Ed; Phi Delta Kappa; r/Bapt; hon/Dist'd Achmt, Intl Biogl Centre.

BEVILL, TOM oc/Legislator; b/Mar 27, 1921; h/1600 Alabama Ave, Jasper, AL 35501; ba/Wash, DC; m/Lou Betts; c/Susan, Donald, Patricia; p/Herman and Fannie Fike Bevill (dec); ed/BS 1943, LLB 1948 Univ Ala; mil/AUS Capt WW-II ETO 1943-46; USAR Lt Col 1946-66; pa/Congress 1967-; Ala & Am Bar Assns; cp/Lions Clb; Bd Trustees Walker Col; Mason; Shriner; r/Bapt; hon/Rhineland Campaign Ribbon w Battle Star; AUS Commend Ribbon; ETO Ribbon w Bronze Star.

BEX, BRIAN WILLIAM LOUIS oc/Executive; b/Feb 5, 1943; h/Leemookwanwi Manor, Cambridge City, IN 47327; ba/Knightstown, IN; m/Gail Eshenbaugh; c/Douglas, Charles, Kristopher; p/John and Jeanne Rowena Sharbeau Bex, Mechanicsburg, PA; ed/LLB Blackstone Law Sch 1967; Postgrad Studies; pa/Fdr Am Communs Network Knightstown 1967-; Pres Brian Bex Report Inc 1975-; Amerland Co 1971-75; Producer Num TV Shows; US C of C; Am Sociol Assn; Polit Affairs Soc; AF Assn; Am Soc Ind Edrs; Nat Hist Soc; Nat Buffalo Assn; Isaac Walton Leag Am; UN Intl Law Assn; cp/Bd Dirs Eisenhower S'ship Foun; hon/Recipient Awds: Nat Hist Foun, Freedoms Foun.

BHAJAN, WILLIAM RUDOLPH oc/Scientist; b/Jan 16, 1937; h/610 Dos Marinas I, Fajardo, PR 00648; ba/Univ PR; c/William Roshan, Indira Lymari; p/William and Lilian Baijnauth Bhajan, Corentyne, Guyana, South America; ed/BA InterAm Univ 1962; MSc Mich St Univ 1966; PhD Univ Waterloo 1970; Addit Studies; pa/Limnologist

& Envir Scist Ctr Energy and Envir Res 1975-; Conslt Envir Res & Application Caribtec Labs 1973-78; Num Past Tchg & Adm Positions; Intl Water Resources Assn; PR Water Pollution Control Assn; r/Anglican; hon/Beta Beta Beta; Intl Scholar, InterAm Univ 1960; Pub'd Author; Num Biogl Listings.

BHATKAR, AWINASH P oc/Scientist; b/Oct 10, 1944; h/437 Collinsford Rd, Tallahassee, FL 32301; ba/Gainesville, FL; m/Helga Sittertz; p/P G and Nirmalatai Bhatkar, Muramba, Maharashtra St, India; ed/BSc Univ Nagpur 1964; MSc IARI 1966; PhD Univ Fla 1973; mil/NCC & ACC India; pa/Envir Scist Univ Fla; TV Series & Newspaper Releases Envir Impact Species; Num Sci Assns; Intl Symposia; r/Universal; hon/Fellow Nat Res Couns India & Canada; Num Awds Sci Presentations; Acad S'ships; Sci Invitee German Sci Foun; Pub'd Author.

BIDART, MARY FLORECITA oc/Nun; b/May 4, 1904; h/Contemplative Sisters Precious Blood, Our Lady Nativity Monastery, New Riegel, OH 44853; p/Francis and Joacina Gliese Bidart (dec); ed/BS Univ Dayton 1948; pa/Assn Contemplative Sisters; Nat Del 1969, Chr 1st ME Reg Sem 1973; Monastery Contemplative Sisters New Riegel: Foundress 1955, Admr 1956-; Directress 1st Cath Info Ctr Dayton 1946-54; Num Other Past Profl Positions; r/Rom Cath.

BIDDLE, JANE LAMMERT oc/Educator; b/Oct 10, 1926; h/407 Mason St, Newark, NY 14513; ba/Newark; m/Thomas; c/Susan; p/Henry and Elsie Lammert (dec); ed/AB; MA; pa/Eng Tchr; AAUW; cp/Bd Trustees Commun Ctr; Pres & Bd Trustees Newark

Public Lib; Div Chm U Way; Wayne Co Woms Repub Clb; Treas, VP, Pres, Co Mbrship Chm; Del Repub Nat Conv; Bd Dirs Wayne Co Red Cross Com; Asst Friends Lib Newark; Publicity & Leg Chr Newark-Wayne Hosp Aux; Vol Rochester Meml Art Gallery; Num Other Civic Assns; r/Prot; Ch Choir; Pres Ch Cir.

BIDDLE, W(ALTER) SCOTT oc/Executive; b/Apr 12, 1927; h/1907 Yacht Puritan, Newport Bch, CA 92660; ba/NB; m/LaVonne Shepherd Wickman; c/Gary, Gregory, Cynthia Thurber, Shelley Trojillo, Bobbette

Wickman; p/Walter Biddle (dec); Marjorie Biddle, Santa Monica, CA; ed/AB, BBA Univ NM; mil/USNR 1945-46; pa/Pres Biddle Devel Inc; Pres Bldg Indust Assn; cp/Past Pres Cal St Jr C of C; r/Presb; hon/Deans Coun UCLA; JCI Senator.

BIDEN, JOSEPH R oc/United States Senator; b/Nov 20, 1942; h/6 Montchan Dr, Wilmington, DE 19807; ba/Wash, DC; m/Jill Tracy; c/Joseph III, Robert; p/Joseph Sr and Jean Biden, W'ton; ed/BA Univ Del 1965; JD Syracuse Col Law 1968; r/Cath; hon/10 Outstg Yg Men, Jr C of C; Chancellors Medal, Syracuse Col Law.

BIESER, ALBERT HOWARD oc/Executive; b/Jan 31, 1932; h/609 Carroll Dr, Garland, TX 75041; ba/G'land; m/Barbara; c/Scott, Frank III; p/Frank Bieser, Concordia, KS; Besse Bieser (dec); ed/BS; BSEE; MSEE; pa/Pres B E Industs Inc; hon/KME; Delta Sigma Pi.

BIEVER, BRUCE FRANCIS oc/Priest; Administrator; b/Jul 24, 1933; h/1404 W Wisconsin Ave, Milwaukee, WI 53233; ba/M'kee; p/Franklyn Biever (dec); Helene Biever, M'kee; ed/AB, MA, PhL, STL St Louis; MA; PhD Univ Pa; pa/Rom Cath

Priest; Admr & Provincial Superior Wis Province Soc Jesus; Bd Dirs: Conf Major Superiors Men, Jesuit Conf, Creighton Univ; Adv Coun, Univ Pa; r/Rom Cath; hon/Fellows: Danforth, George Loeb Harrison; Alpha Sigma Nu.

BIGDA, RICHARD JAMES oc/Consultant; b/May 15, 1930; h/6732 S Columbia Ave, Tulsa, OK 74136; ba/Tulsa; p/John and Ernestine Tweddle Bigda, Warren, MI; ed/BS Wayne St Univ; MSE Univ Mich; mil/AUS Chem Corps PFC 1953-55; p/Chem Mkt & Corp Devel Conslt; ACS; AIChE; AAAS; OSE; PE Okla & Tex; cp/Advr Philbrook Art Mus Am Indian Art; Former Okla Repub St Com-man.

BIGGERS, JOHN ALVIN oc/Executive; b/Oct 27, 1926; h/5372 Monalee Ave, Sacramento, CA 95819; ba/S'mento; m/Esther Debler; c/Curtis, Merlene & Marlene, Cavin; p/Alvin and Bessie Biggers (dec); ed/Att'd Ford Motor Inst; pa/Pres & Gen Mgr Gerlinger Motor Parts Inc; Past Chm S'mento Chapt Cal Auto Wholesalers Assn; Automotive Ser Indust Assn; cp/Past Chm Bus & Career Ed Com S'mento Co Schs; Preston Sch Industs; U Crusade Auto; Fin Com BSA; C of C; YMCA; Fairhaven Home Unwed Mothers; Other Civic Assns; r/Ch Nazarene: Secy S'mento Dist Adv Bd, Chm Dist Laymens Retreat Bd, Del 4 Intl Gen Assemblies; hon/Num Biogl Listings.

BIGGS, ODIE E oc/Teacher, Coach; b/Sept 9, 1929; h/1045 Longreen Ct, Kernersville, NC 27284; ba/Clemmons, NC; m/Joan Coleman; c/Debra Nell, Cynthia, Martha, Kathryn; p/(dec); ed/BS Okla A&M

Univ 1951; MA Ball St Univ 1972; mil/AUS 24 Yrs Ret'd Lt Col 1975; pa/Kappa Sigma; NC Coaches Assn; NC Edrs Assn; Ret'd Ofcrs Assn; Others; cp/W Forsyth Booster Clb; r/Cath; F'ship Christian Aths.

BIGLEY, CHRISTINE RUTH oc/Educator, Pastor; b/Oct 19, 1940; h/PO Box 203, Salem, IA 52649; ba/Mt Pleasant, IA; m/George Vincent; c/Michael, Thomas, Amanda; p/Jefferson and Lottie Blazer, McFarland, CA; ed/AA Bakersfield JC 1960; BSN 1963, MS 1965 UCSF Med Ctr; MDiv

Naz Theol Sem 1971; pa/Ia Wesleyan Col: Asst Prof Nsg 1976-, Acad Standards Com; CoPastor Salem Friends Ch 1975-; Num Past Positions; Assn Clin Pastoral Ed; Henry Co Min Assn; cp/Com Wom AAUW; Vol Crisis Intervention Cnslg; r/Soc Friends, Ia Yrly Meeting; hon/Nom'd Outstg Yg Wom Am.

BILBO, THOMAS E oc/Educator; b/Feb 12, 1944; h/133 Courtaulds Ave N, Saraland, AL 36571; ba/Mobile, AL; p/Prentiss Bilbo (dec); Doris B Adams, Moss Pt, MS; ed/BS Miss Coll 1966; MCS Univ Miss 1970; MEd Auburn Univ 1971; PhD Univ So Miss 1976; pa/Asst Prof Mobile Col; Nat Sci Tchrs Assn; Phi Delta Kappa; Audubon; r/Bapt; hon/Students Choice Nat Sci Div 1978.

BILLINGSLEY, DAVID LEWIS oc/Consultant; b/Nov 8, 1935; h/Rt 3 Box 618A, Keithville, LA 71047; ba/Shreveport, LA; m/Madora; c/David Jr, Carl, John, Madora Mae; p/L S and Hazel Billingsley, Houston,

TX; ed/BS, MS Univ Tex; pa/Intl Petro Conslt; Owner Billingsley Engrg Co; Pres La & Ark Sect Soc Petro Engrs 1964; Pres NW La Chapt Univ Tex Students Assn 1969; Others; r/St Marks Epis Ch, Shreveport, LA; hon/Tau Beta Pi; Sigma Gamma Epsilon.

BINFORD, LINWOOD THOMAS oc/Supervisor, Educator; b/Jun 12, 1908; h/2107 Lamb Ave, Richmond, VA 23222; ba/Richmond; m/Janie Quattlebaum; c/Mrs Lynette B Guilford, Linwood Jr; p/George and Bessie Anderson Binford (dec); ed/BA; MA; LHD; FIBA; pa/Staff Sch Ed & Psychol Va

Union Univ; Former Dir Ed Dept Seneca Col; Past Profl Positions; VEA; NEA; Nat Prins Assn; Nat Soc Study Ed; cp/Smithsonian Inst; Omega Psi Phi; Num Other Civic Assns; r/5th St Bapt Ch, Richmond: VChm Bd Deacons, Tchr, Mens Bible Class; hon/Fellow Intl Biogl Assn; Num Biogl Listings.

BINGHAM, JOHNELLA WOODS oc/Educator; b/Jun 11, 1928; h/420 Cross St, Cairo, IL 62914; ba/Cairo; p/John and Susie Woods (dec); ed/AB Lane Col; Postgrad Studies; pa/Tchr Elem Spec Ed; IEA: Human Relats Com, Ethnic Minority Caucus; NEA; VP CAT; cp/VP Egyptian Housing Devel Corp; Bd Sons & Daughs Charity Corp; Bd Dirs Commun Mtl Hlth Ctr; Bd Lwyrs Com Civil Rts Under Law; Past Matron OES; Pres Lane Col Alumni Assn; NAACP; Pres Cairo Woms Civic Leag; Num Other Civic Assns; r/Yth Dir Everdale Bapt Ch; Ch Clerk; Zion Dist Yth Congress: Trustee Bd, Yth Instr; hon/EHDC: $1 Million Awd Cert, W G Best Homes Awd; Num Biogl Listings.

BIOLCHINI, ROBERT F oc/Attorney; b/Sept 22, 1939; h/1744 E 29th St, Tulsa, OK 74114; ba/Tulsa; m/Frances Lauinger; c/Robert Jr, Douglas, Frances, Tobin, Thomas; p/Alfred Biolchini, Detroit, MI; Erma Biolchini (dec); ed/BA Univ Notre Dame 1962; LLB Geo Washington Univ 1965; mil/AUS Capt 1965-67; pa/Atty Partner Doerner, Stuart, Saunders, Daniel & Anderson 1968-79; Okla & Mich Bar Assns; cp/Pres Thomas Gilcrease Mus Assn; Bd Tulsa Ballet; Pres Monte Cassino Sch; r/Rom Cath; hon/Army Commend Medal 1967.

BIRCH, LONAH KAY oc/Director; b/Sept 19, 1941; h/12905 W 77th, Lenexa, KS 66216; ba/Kansas City, MO; m/C E II; c/Jennifer, Julie; p/Orville Watt, Columbia, MO; Mildred Tate Watt (dec); ed/BJ Univ Mo Sch Jour 1963; Postgrad Studies; pa/Asst Reg Dir Public Affairs & Communs; Reg Wom Bus Advocate; Fed Woms Prog Coor; Reg VII Adv Coun Coor; Asst Reg Dir Adm; Num Other Positions; Federal Info Coun; VP Public Relats

Soc Am; Wom Communs Inc; KC Bus Communicators; Proceedings Chrperson FEB/FWPC 3rd Nat Conf; r/Meth; hon/SBA: Nat Profl Excell Public Info, Meritorious Ser Awd, Reg VII Public Contact Awd, Reg VII 1975 Nom & 1977 Winner William A Jump Awd; Num Biogl Listings; Num Others.

BIRCH, ROBERT LOUIS oc/Librarian; b/Aug 9, 1925; h/3108 Dashiell Rd, Falls Church, VA 22042; ba/Wash, DC; m/Grace Kay; c/John, David, Paul, Mary, Joseph, Rose, Eve, Daisy; p/William and Anita Bowles Birch (dec); ed/MSLS; BA; mil/AUS 1951-53; pa/Reschr Lit Applications Human Memory Sys; cp/Pres Lincoln Group DC 1968-69; r/Cath; hon/Medal of Vets Polish Resistance, France; Spokesman of Yr Agri 1974; Mense Mace.

BIRCHFIELD, ROBERT BOYD oc/Manager; Engineer; b/Feb 10, 1940; h/3734 Capilano Dr, W Lafayette, IN 47906; ba/WL; m/Karen Kimbrell; c/Matthew, Weston; p/Homer Birchfield (dec); Gertie Birchfield,

Hillsboro, WV; ed/BSEE Purdue Univ 1966; MSEE US Nav Postgrad Sch 1973; mil/USN 1958-78; pa/Prog Mgr & Sales Engr Cts Microelectronics; IEEE; r/Prot; hon/Eta Kappa Nu; Nav Achmt Medal; W/W S&SW.

BIRD, AGNES THORNTON oc/Attorney; b/Sept 15, 1921; h/Box 647, Maryville, TN 37801; ba/M'ville; m/Frank; c/Patricia; p/E G and Anne Renfro Thornton, Olney, TX; ed/BS; MA; PhD; JD; pa/Atty Partner Firm Bird, Navratil & Bird; Am, Tenn & Treas Blount Co Bar Assns; cp/Chm Tenn Comm Status Wom; Bd Nat Assn Comms Wom; VChr Tenn Dem Exec Com; Dem Nat Com; Parliamentn Nat Fdn Dem Wom.

BIRKELBACH, MARY RUTH oc/Writer; b/May 17, 1935; h/Rt 1 Box 14, Georgetown, TX 78626; p/William and Marie Braun Birkelbach (dec); ed/Att'd Num Univs; pa/Intl Platform Assn; Intl Poetry Soc; Am Poetry Leag; CSSI; Nat & World Poetry Day Coms; r/Am Luth Ch; hon/Fellow Intl Biogl Assn; Num Intl & Nat Awds Poetry.

BIRNELL, DORISA LEON oc/Paralegal; b/May 6, 1947; ba/2304 Hancock Dr Suite 9, Austin, TX 78756; m/Howard; p/(dec); ed/Adm Mgmt; pa/Owner & Operator Leon PTG Spec 1964-79; Nat Assn Female Execs; cp/Austin Police Monitor; Dem Precnt Wkr & Election Judge; r/Cath; hon/Outstg Yg Dem, Small Bus Assn.

BIRRELL, VERLA LEONE oc/Professor;

Writer; Artist; b/Nov 24, 1903; h/2004 Wasatch Dr, Salt Lake City, UT 84108; ba/Same; p/James and Elfie Naylor Birrell (dec); ed/BS Univ Utah 1928; MFA Claremont Grad Sch; EdD Columbia Univ; pa/Prof Emeritus Univ Utah; Lectr Art, Archaeology, Interior Design & Textiles; Participant Num 1 Man Shows; cp/Sr Citizen Rehab Projs; Com Work Foster'g Arts; r/Ch Jesus Christ Latter Day Sts; hon/Nu Delta Sigma; Pub'd Author.

BISHOP, BERNICE ANGELINE oc/-Homemaker; b/Aug 23, 1914; h/165 Mayluth Rd, Johnstown, PA 15904; ba/Latrobe, PA; m/Gerald; c/Gerald, Rebekah B White; p/William and Edna Mitchell Beach (dec); ed/Evang Theol Sem 1939; cp/Friendship Sch; Pres PTA; r/U Meth Ch: Num Ldrship Positions.

BISHOP, BESSIE EMILY oc/Educator; b/Nov 4, 1925; h/709 Main St, Goodland, KS 67735; ba/G'land; m/Roy Shughart; c/Bonnie Casseday, Thomas, Susan Christmas, Randy, Paula; p/William and Marie Mast Watkins (dec); ed/BS Phillips Univ 1951; MA Univ No Colo 1969; pa/4th Grade Tchr 1971-; Pvt Piano, Voice & Theory Tchr 1948-; 3rd Grade Tchr 1968-71; Asst Tutor Eng Phillips Univ 1945-50; Guest Conductor Voice Chds Choir

Fest; Art Pub Soc; Intl Choristers Guild; Assn Disciple Musicians; Nat & Denver Area Music Tchrs Asn; Num Ed Assns; AAUW; cp/Fed'd Music Clb; Euterpean Soc; Camp Fire Girls Am; Guardian & Dist Music Dir; Den Mother Cub Scouts; Pres Join Our Yth PTA; r/1st Christian Ch, G'land: Dir Sr & Yth Choirs, SS Tchr, Asst Supt, Tchr Tng Supvr; Mountain Christian Ch, Lakewood: Vocalist, Organist; Soloist Voice Choir Intl Conv Christian Chs; hon/Cardinal Key Nat Soc; Varsity Sweetheart; Pub'd Author.

BISHOP, ELIZA H oc/Consultant; Researcher; b/Jun 18, 1920; h/629 N 4th, Crockett, TX 75835; ba/Crockett; p/William Bishop (dec); Carey LeGory (dec); ed/BA; pa/Hist Reschr; Owner EB Promotions; WICI; NFPW Inc; Pres Tex Press Wom Inc; Nat Hist Preserv Soc; cp/Crockett Zoning Com; Chm Co Hist Comm; Pres Hist Projs Houston Co; r/Epis: Vestry, Clk; hon/Wom Achmt, Tex Press Wom; Wom of Yr Crockett Pilots, Beta Sigma Phi; Dist'd Ser Awd, Tex Hist Preserv.

BISHOP, ROBERT MILTON oc/Executive; b/Jun 15, 1921; h/4 Kimball Cir, Westfield, NJ 07090; ba/New York, NY; m/Anne Selene Rowan; c/Donald, Anne B Bennett, Robert Jr, Elizabeth B Speed, Regina, Rowan; p/Milton and Florence Crofutt Bishop, Avon Park, FL; ed/BA Union Col 1943; MA Trinity Col 1955; mil/USAF Cadet & Pilot 1943-45; pa/Sr VP New York Stock Exc Inc.

BISHOP, SID G oc/Union Official; b/Nov 11, 1923; h/4414 Mid Ridge Dr, Fairfax, VA 22030; ba/Rockville, MD; m/Margaret Linkous; p/Clarence and Lillian Onks Bishop (dec); ed/Grad USN Trade Sch 1942; Cert Coll Labor Relats Concord Col 1961; mil/USN Aviation Radioman 1st Class 1941-46; pa/BRAC: Asst Intl VP 1973-, VP Communs-Trans Div 1969-73; 2nd VP Trans-Communs Employees Union 1968-69; Gen Chr C&O Virginian RR 1962-68; Other Past Positions; SubCom Labor Res Adv Coun Dept Labor; Com Productivity, Tech & Growth Bur

Labor Stats; AFL-CIO; Canadian Labor Cong; cp/Greenbriar Civic Assn; Dem; VFW; Elks; Masons; Royal Arch Masons; KT; Shriners; Chantilly Nat Golf & Country; hon/7 Battle Stars; 7 Area Medals; 2 Pres Cits.

BISON, LARRY GENE oc/Finger Print Expert; b/Oct 3, 1929; h/3620 Moreno Ave #107, La Verne, CA 91750; ba/Los Angeles, CA; m/Bobbie Kell; c/Steven, Darrel; p/David Bison (dec); Genevieve Romanski, Baldwin Park, CA; ed/AA E LA Commun Col; BS Cal St Univ; BTh Life Bible Col; MA, PhD Cal Grad Sch Theol; mil/AUS 1947-56;

USCGR 1976-; pa/Print Expert LA Police Dept; Instr LA Police Acad 1975-77; Intl Assn Identification; So Cal Assn Fingerprint Ofcrs; Am Crim Justice Assn; Advr Am Assn Police Chaplains; Fdr & Pres Far E Missionary Soc Inc; cp/Missionary & Coor Better Boys Soc; Bd Dirs: Dae Han Sam Sung Orphanage, Pusan Christian Home Orphanage; r/Prot; hon/W/W Rel; Men Achmt; Pub'd Author; Num Inventions.

BISQUERRA, JOSE oc/Psychiatrist; b/May 12, 1927; h/2506 Linwood, Temple, TX 76501; ba/Temple; m/Amalia Riaza; c/Maria, Jose; p/Jose and Dolores Vila Bisquerra (dec); ed/BA, BS Univ Barcelona 1948; MS, MD Univ Seville Sch Med 1955; PhD Univ Seville 1956; pa/Child & Adolescent Psychi; Pvt Pract 1978-; Chief Cotton & White Clin & Hosp 1972-77; Mtl Hlth Conslt Var Sch Dists, Hlth Ctrs & Couns;

Participant Num Confs; Profl Assns; hon/Recog Awds: AMA 7 Yrs, St Mo Div Mtl Hlth, Wn Mo Mtl Hlth Ctr, Univ Mo Sch Med, Dept Psychi; Outstg Phys of Yr, St Joseph St Hosp; Medal Outstg Humanitarian Ser: Georgetown & Kwakwani; Gold Medal: Guyana Miners Union, "We The People"; Humanitarian Ser Cross, Indian Tribes; Miguel De Cervantes, Intl Awd; Others; Biogl Listings; Pub'd Author.

BISSON, WHEELOCK ALEXANDER oc/Physician; b/Jan 5, 1898; h/2312 Park Ave, Memphis, TN 38114; m/Maude Lee Voorhies; p/George and Sarah Bisson; ed/BS Fla A&M Univ 1922; MD Meharry Med Col 1929; Intern Royal Cir Hosp; pa/Gen Pract 1933-; Clinitian Memphis Hlth Dept 1933-70; Vol St Med Assn; Tenn St Pres, Chm Trustee Bd, Chm TB & Leg Coms, Treas; 2nd VP Nat Med Assn; Am Thoracic Soc; Tenn Acad Sci; Am Assn Advmt Sci; Nat Public Hlth Assn; Am & Tenn St Med Assn; Nat Rehab Assn; cp/Former St Pres Tenn Elks; Secy Bluff City Med Soc; Memphis & Shelby Co Med Socs; NAACP; YMCA; BSA; Mason; King Frederick Concistory; Mystic Shrine;

Omega Psi Phi; r/Emmanuel Epis Ch: Active Mem; hon/Tenn Dr of Yr, Vol St Med Assn 1962-63; Vol St Med Jour Dedication; Practicioner of Yr Awd; Nat Med Assn; Meritorious Achmt Awd, Fla A&M Univ; Outstg Citizen Awd Tenn; Hon'd by Memphis 35 Yrs Ser; Fellow Intl Biogl Assn; Num Biogl Listings.

BIUNDO, JOSEPH JAMES JR oc/Educator; b/Sept 24, 1937; h/4808 Elmwood Pkwy, Metairie, LA 70002; ba/New Orleans, LA; m/Mary Cools; c/Elizabeth, Brenda; p/Joseph Biundo Sr; Ann Biundo Hammond, LA; ed/BS Univ Houston; MD La St Univ Med Sch; mil/USAR Capt 1967-73; pa/La St Univ Med Sch: Chief Sect Rheumatology & Rehab 1974-,

Assoc Prof Med 1975-; Dir Rehab Med & Voc Rehab Inst Charity Hosp 1975-; Dir Arthritis Unit Hotel Dieu Hosp 1978-; Fdr & Pres La Rheumatism Soc; Am Rheumatism Assn; Am Cong Rehab Med; La St & Orleans Parish Med Socs; Am Col Phys; Num Adm & Com Appts; Others; r/Cath; hon/Rho Chi; Alpha Epsilon Delta; Omicron Delta Kappa; Alpha Omega Alpha; Num F'ships; Recipient Grants; Pub'd Author.

BLACK, DONALD RAYMOND oc/Minister; b/Feb 7, 1934; h/871 Cheryl Ln, Kankakee, IL 60901; ba/Forsyth, IL; m/Doris Rickert; c/Timothy, Tiffany, Tory; p/William

Black (dec); Laura Kassing Black, Belleville, IL; ed/BS; MDiv; mil/USAF; pa/U Meth Min; Conslt Ldrship Devel; Chm Bd Ch & Soc; Bd Dirs U Meth Min Credit Union; cp/Treas Forsyth Yth Leag; Vol Fire Dept; r/U Meth.

BLACK, MARGARET C oc/Director; b/Aug 13, 1940; h/361 Blvd; Orangeburg, SC 29115; ba/O'burg; m/Roger; c/Gregory Winds, Franklin Winds, Darrell; p/Frank Mizzell (dec); Grace Sanders, O'burg; ed/BS; pa/Dir Public Relats; Nat Sch Public Relats Assn; cp/NAACP; Oper Push Dem Party; r/Bapt; hon/Pi Gamma Mu.

BLACK, SHIRLEY JEAN oc/Educator; b/Apr 20, 1935; h/1003 Rose Cir, College Station, TX 77840; ba/CS; m/Charles (dec); c/Cheri, Jeani; p/E Ray and Elena Ferrell, Tulsa, OK; ed/BA 1967, MA 1969, PhD 1974 Univ Okla; pa/Asst Prof Hist Tex A&M Univ; Pub'd Author: "Olivenza: An Iberian Alsace-Lorraine" The Americas; "The Silver Problem of 2nd French Empire: Motivation for Intervention in Mexico" The Austrian Yrbook; Num Others; Edit Advr Mil Affairs; Dir & Secy Wn Soc French Hist; cp/Del Tex 6th Congl Dist Repub Nat Conv; Dir Yth Ldrship Prog LA; r/Bapt.

BLACK, WENDELL RAY oc/Steelworker; Executive; b/Nov 15, 1953; h/PO Box 94, Myra, TX 76253; ba/Myra; p/David and Dorothy Black, Myra; pa/Pres Tribute Record Co; Gospel Music Min; cp/Chief Myra Vol Fire Dept; r/Myra Bapt Ch.

BLACK, WILLA BROWN oc/Farmer; b/Jul 9, 1895; h/702 Remmel Ave, Newport, AR 72112; ba/Same; m/William (dec); c/Emma B Walker, Willa B Murdock, Loretha B Jones; p/Alexander Brown (dec); Mary Brown (dec); ed/Att'd Fisk Univ & Philander Smith Col; pa/Ret'd Farm Owner; Tchr Tenn 5 Yrs; Ark Farm Bur; cp/Pres PTA; Orgr & Chm Coun PreSch Groups PTA Coun; City Mgr Adv Comm; Urban Renewal Bd; Newport City Beautiful Comm; White River & Crawleys Ridge Devel Coun; Sr Citizens Adv Coun; r/African Meth Epis: Treas.

BLACKBURN, BERTHA MAIDEN oc/Home Economist; b/Jan 3, 1924; h/1744 Sycamore St, Clarksdale, MS 38614; ba/C'dale; m/Samuel Lee; c/Myra, Linda; p/Cleveland and Melvina Maiden, C'dale; ed/BS; pa/Dir, Coor & Conslt Food Sers Prog; cp/Dist Advr Future Homemakers Am; CoChr Indep Cand; Zeta Phi Beta: St Dir, Pres Local Chapt; r/Bapt; hon/Commun Ser Awd 1975; Wom of Yr 1978; Humanitarian Awd 1979.

BLACKBURN, ELLA MAE oc/Educator; b/Oct 4, 1916; h/Rt 3 Box 116, Walters, OK 73572; m/John William; c/Teena Anderson (Mrs Charles), Peggy Heisch (Mrs John); p/John and Ora Morgan Askins (dec); ed/BS Okla Univ; Postgrad Studies; pa/Ret'd Tchr

Eng & Spch; Author: Stars From Dust, Ponder...ings, My Favorite Poets; Num Other Pubs; Great Plains & Okla Writers; Poetry Soc Okla; NAPS; Intl Acad Poets; cp/Past Pres Cotton Co Ret'd Tchrs; ORTA; NRTA; r/1st Bapt Ch: SS Tchr; hon/Personalities S; Intl W/W Poetry; Worlds W/W Wom.

BLACKBURN, ROBERT EARL oc/Missionary; b/Dec 15, 1929; h/234 Maywood Dr, Martinex, GA 30907; ba/Augusta, GA; m/Mildred Roberts; c/Elizabeth, Robert Jr; p/Veran Blackburn (dec); Lennie Blackburn, Valdostan, GA; ed/BA Mercer Univ 1951; MDiv SWn Bapt Theol Sem 1955; mil/Ga NG Chaplain 1955-58; pa/Area Missionary Augusta, Hephzibah & Kilpatrick Assns 1973-; Preached Num Crusades Worldwide; Pastor Trinity Bapt Ch 1968-73; Supt Tng Ga Bapt SS Dept 1961-68; Other Past Positions; Moderator Centennial Assn; Pres SW Ga Bapt Pastors Conf; cp/Kiwanis Clb; Pres Ga Alumni Assn SWn Sem; r/Bapt; hon/W/W Rel; Pub'd Author.

BLACKBURN, WILLIAM KENTON oc/Attorney; b/Jan 11, 1947; h/210 N 18th, Junction, TX 76849; ba/Junction; m/Glenda Mae; p/M C Blackburn (dec); Geraldine Blackburn, Junction; BBA 1969, JD 1971 St Marys Univ; pa/St Bar Tex; Am & Hill Country Bar Assns; cp/Rotary; Masonic Lodge; Lions Clb; C of C; r/Meth.

BLACKHURST, J(AMES) HERBERT oc/Educator; h/1901 E 13th Ave Apt 6D, Denver, CO 80206; ba/Same; m/Edna; c/Bonnie, Beverly, Marilynn, Donna, James, William, Thomas; p/William and Mary Dwyer Blackhurst (dec); ed/PhD; MA; PhD;

mil/France 1918; pa/Writer Ed & Phil; Works include: Body-Mind & Creativity, Introducing Stats As Way of Thinking, Humanized Geometry; Num Others; Past Pres Ia Phil Assn; SWn Phil Soc; Metaphysical Soc Am; Pi Delta Kappa; Kappa Delta Pi; r/Humanist; hon/Phi Sigma Tau.

BLACKSTON, JOE RONALD oc/Accountant; b/Apr 1, 1941; h/Farmsteads, Jasper, AL 35501; ba/Jasper; m/Carolyn; c/Paula, Jonathan; p/Jim and Charlene Blackston, Oakman, AL; ed/BS Univ Ala; pa/Public Acct; NSPA; AAPA; ANHA; AHA; cp/Pres' Clb; Dem; r/Bapt; hon/Olympics 1972; Good Citizen Awd 1973; Personalities S; Notable Ams; W/W Fin.

BLAHOVICH, JOSEPH SAMUEL oc/Clergyman; b/Jan 31, 1931; h/307 Arizona Ct, Vancouver, WA 98661; ba/Vancouver; m/Frances Arnott; p/Arthur Blahovich, Willowdale, Ontario; ed/BA Atl Union Col 1956; MA Andrews Univ 1959; pa/Pastor

Vancouver 7th Day Adventist Ch; Past Pastor Chs: NY, Ia, Wash & Oreg; cp/Exec Com N Pacific Union Conf; Sec'dy Sch Bd Oreg; r/SDA; hon/Fellow Intl Platform Assn; W/W Rel; Intl W/W; Commun Ldrs & Noteworthy Ams.

BLAIR, F JOE oc/Director; b/Jan 1, 1931; h/Rt 1 Box 54, Maramec, OK 74045; ba/Stillwater, OK; m/Marie; c/Elizabeth Stone, Roger; p/Hiram Blair (dec); Fern Richardson, Enid, OK; ed/BS Okla A&M Col; pa/Dir Univ Food Ser; NACUFS; Past Prog Chr, Secy-Treas, Pres; Okla (Bd Dirs, Past Pres) & Nat Restaurant Assns; Silver & Gold

Plate Soc; cp/Past Pres Kiwanis Clb; Masonic Lodge; OES; Order White Shrine Jerusalem; Okla Grand Assembly Intl Order Rainbow Girls: St Exec Com, Past St Visitor; Stillwater DeMolay Chapt: Chr Bd, DeMolay Dad; r/Christian; hon/DeMolay: Legion Hon,

Cross of Hon; Grand Cross of Color, Order Rainbow; IFMA Silver Plate Awd; Num Biogl Listings.

BLAIR, JOHN DOHERTY JR oc/Air Force Officer; b/Jan 5, 1938; h/3005 Mesa Rd, Willow Park, TX 76086; m/Sally Marie; c/Diane; p/John Blair, Oakhurst, NJ; Gladys Harrington Blair (dec); ed/MEd; BA; mil/Chief Mil Pers Ofc 1977-; Armed Forces Staff Col 1976-77; HQUSAF Pentagon 1972-76; AF Mil Per Ctr 1968-72; pa/APGA; Nat Voc Guid Assn; cp/Optimist Clb; r/Meth; hon/Strategic Air Cmd Sr Pers Mgr of Yr 1977.

BLAIR, MARIE LENORE oc/Reading Specialist; b/Jan 9, 1931; h/Rt 1 Box 54, Maramec, OK 74045; ba/Stillwater, OK; m/F Joe; c/Elizabeth Stone, Roger; p/Virgil Strode (dec); Ella Strode, Stillwater, OK; ed/BS Okla A&M Col; MS Okla St Univ; Addit Studies;

pa/Okla, Intl & Pres Cimarron Rdg Coun; NEA; OEA; SEA; Kappa Kappa Iota; Delta Lambda; cp/Dem; OES; White Shrine Jerusalem; St Exec Com Dist 6; Intl Order Rainbow Girls; r/Christian; hon/Grand Cross Color, Rainbow; Num Biogl Listings.

BLAKE, JEAN ALESTINE LLOYD oc/Educator; b/Nov 6, 1934; h/2628 Brookline Dr NW, Huntsville, AL 35810; ba/Normal, AL; m/John; c/Robert, Johnia; p/Astley Lloyd, St Mary, Jamaica; Zetilda

Henry, St Ann, Jamaica; ed/BA; MS; PhD; Dipl Ed; pa/Tchr Dept Physics & Math Ala A&M Univ; Nat & Ala Coun Tchrs Math; Pi Mu Epsilon; r/Seventh Day Adventist; hon/Personalities S; W/W World Wom.

BLAKE, SALLY MIRLISS oc/Free Lance Writer; b/Jun 11, 1925; h/200 Julia Ave, Mill Valley, CA 94941; ba/Same; c/Andrew, Gail; p/Samuel and Eve Lansman Mirliss (dec); ed/BS Boston Univ 1945; MA San Francisco St Univ 1964; pa/Author Novels, Short Stories & Features; Works Include: *A House Divided, Silence Is Golden, An Isl Babel, Where Mist Clothes Dream & Song Runs Naked*; Num Others; Profl Articles & Features; Public Info Ofcr, Cal St Intl Progs 1970-71; Asst Editor & Staff Writer, SF Jewish Bultn 1966-69; Asst Dir Public Relats, Jewish Wel Fdn SF 1965-66; Other Past Positions; r/Jewish; hon/O Henry Awd 1964; Residency Awd, Millay Colony for Art Inc; Num Biogl Listings.

BLAKE, TERRI (THERESA BLALACK) oc/Actress; Writer; b/Sept 10, 1903; h/570 N Rossmore Ave, Hollywood, CA 90004; ba/Same; m/Orange Russell Blalack (dec);

c/Russell, Ronald, David; ed/LA City Col; pa/Actress: *House in the Sea, Night Ct Day Ct, Hwy Patrol;* "Raid on Entebbie" TV Spec Movie; TV Show WKEF Ohio 1966; Num TV Commls 1974; Signed TV & Motion Pic Glen Shaw Agy 1977; Pub *You Too Can Do It;* Contbr Var Mags; Pub Spkr; Former Contract Bldr; Nat Leag Am Pen Wom; Intl Poetry Inst; Screen Actors Guild; cp/Hollywood C of C; OES; r/Hollywood St Thomas Epis Ch: Lectr, Woms Guild; Ordained Min, Universal Life Ch; hon/Wom of Yr; Intl Authors Guild; Meritorious Commun Ser Awd, City LA; Ever-Ythful Sr Inspiration of Yr, Gtr NY Citizens Soc; Awd Excell Participation Santa Claus Ln Parade Stars, Hollywood C of C; New Neighbor of Mo Awd, New Neighbors Leag; Worlds Most Glamorous Grandmother; Grandparents Day Proclaimed Hon of Her Birthday, City LA.

BLAKENEY, ROGER NEAL oc/Professor; b/Sept 16, 1939; h/576 Warsaw, Hitchcock, TX 77563; ba/Houston, TX; c/Christopher, Benjamin; p/C B Blakeney (dec); Flora McAnally Blakeney, Ft Worth, TX; ed/BS Tex A&M 1964; MA 1967, PhD 1969 Univ H'ton; mil/AUS Airborne 1960-62;

pa/Univ H'ton: Assoc Prof Orgnl Behavior & Mgmt 1968, Dir Masters Prog 1971, Coor Indust Relats Res 1972; Former Conslt Num Industs & Govt; APA; ITAA; Acad Mgmt; Ed Bd Transactional Analysis Jour; Num Presentations & Lectures; hon/Pub'd Author; Num Biogl Listings.

BLANCHARD, B EVERARD oc/Consultant; b/Oct 19, 1909; h/303 Astor Ct, Villa Park, IL 60181; ba/VP; m/Ann Quaglia; c/Sharon Reyn, David; p/(dec); ed/BS; MS; MA; DD; PhD; mil/USAF Ret'd Lt Col; pa/Conslt Ednl Adm & Res; Pres Villa Ednl Res Assocs; Phi Delta Kappa; Sigma Theta Gamma; Kappa Delta Pi; NEA; NSBA; Adv Bd Sev Orgs; cp/Aviation; r/Meth: Ret'd Clergyman; Supply-Pulpit Min Var Chs USA; hon/George Washington Medal & Cit 1960; Cits: US Pres, Phi Delta Kappa, Princeton Univ 1973, Notre Dame Univ 1968, NEA & NSBA Res 1960; Ky Cols.

BLANCHARD, PATRICK G oc/Executive; b/May 15, 1943; h/8109 Sir Galahad Dr, Evans, GA 30809; ba/Martinex, GA; m/Gwen Banks; c/Mary; p/John and Mildred Pollard

Blanchard, Appling, GA; ed/BBA Ga So Col; Postgrad Studies; pa/Pres Ga St Bank; Ga Bankers Assn; Banks Adm Inst; cp/Pres E Ga Lung Assn; Rotarian; Exc Clb; Martinex Merchs Assn; r/Bapt; hon/W/W Fin & Indust.

BLANK, RALPH JOHN oc/Banker; Lawyer; b/Apr 2, 1922; h/122 Forest Hill Blvd, W Palm Bch, Fl 33401; ba/WPB; m/Merry Lake; c/Pamela Hellin, Liisa, Michelle; p/Ralph Sr and Stella Kleinbeck Blank (dec); ed/BS & BA 1942, LLB & JD cum laude 1948 Univ Fla; mil/AUS Arty 1942-45; ETO; CIC 1951-52; Ret'd Lt Col Res; pa/Atty Sr Partner Firm Blank, Williams & Benn

1972-; Bd Dir Fla Atl Univ Endowment Corp; Chr Bd Citizens Bank Palm Co 1963-; Indiv Pract Law 1952-72; Home Ofc Counsel Am Fire & Casualty Co 1950-51; Assoc Mem Firm Moorehead, Pallot, Smith, Green & Phillips 1948-49; Am, Fla & Palm Bch Co Bar Assns; Am Trial Lwyrs Assn; cp/Fla House Reps 1956-60; Senate 1960-64; Civ Ser Bd W Palm Bch 1965-74; r/Meml Presb; hon/Air Medal 5 Oak Leaf Clusters, AUS.

BLANKENBAKER, RONALD GAIL oc/Physician; Educator; b/Dec 1, 1941; h/3104 Wesson Way, Tampa, FL 33618; ba/Tampa; m/Sharon Williams; p/Lloyd Blankenbaker (dec); Lovina Blankenbaker, Morocco, IN; ed/BS Purdue Univ 1963; MD 1968, MS 1970 Ind Univ; ed/BS Purdue Univ 1963; MD 1968, MS 1970 Ind Univ; mil/AF Resv Flight Surg Med Corp Major 1971-; Commdr: 930th TAC Hosp 1971-72, 931th TAC Clin 1972-75, 434th TAC Hosp 1976-; pa/Chm & Prof Dept Fam Med Univ S Fla 1977-; Editor Fam Pract Sect Med Info Sers Ref & Index Sers Inc 1976-; Med Advr New Hope Foun Am Inc 1974-; Other Past Profl Positions; Am Bd Fam Pract; Am, Fla & Ind Acad Fam Phys; AMA; Assn

Hosp Med Ed; Soc Tchrs Fam Med; Am Soc Allied Professions; Assn Ind Dirs Med Ed; Soc Prospective Med; Adv Bd: Med Pers Pool, Peoples Hlth Ctr, Profl Careers Inst & Ind Voc Tech Col; cp/Marion Co Med Assn; AF Assn; Chr Meals on Wheels; Ind Chapt Arthritis Foun; Treas & Secy Comprehensive Med Corp; Pres Exec Med Care; r/Prot; hon/Meritorious Ser Medal, USAF; Ky Col Comm, St Ky; Ser Mankind Awd, Golden Cir Sertoma Clb; Outstg Alumnus Awd, Mt Ayr HS; Outstg Exhibit Awd, Am Acad Fam Phys; Kappa Kappa Psi; VP Purdue Reamer Clb; Alpha Epsilon Delta; Pres Delta Rho Kappa; Num Res Grants; Pub'd Author.

BLANKINSHIP, ANN ROBERTA oc/Editor; b/Nov 5, 1948; h/9622 Jaywood Dr, Houston, TX 77040; ba/Houston; m/John Robert; p/Lennart and Allie Belle Larson, Dallas, TX; ed/BA 1970, MA 1972 Univ Tex; pa/Tech Editor Exxon Prodn Res Co; Wom Communs Inc; Soc Tech Communs; Univ Tex Ex-Students Assn; r/Mem Highland Park U Meth Ch, Dallas, Tex; hon/Kappa Tau Alpha; Hon'd Journ Day & Univ Tex Day; 3 Commends, Lockheed Electronics Co Inc.

BLASIUS, JACK MICHAEL oc/Executive; b/Feb 29, 1932; h/1017 W O Ezell Blvd, Spartanburg, SC 29301; ba/S'burg; m/Sybil Claire Watkins; c/Michael, Kimberly; p/Arthur Blasius (dec); Jessie Pate Blasius, Northport, AL; ed/BS 1954, MBA 1957 Univ Ala; mil/AUS ETO 2 Yrs; pa/Pres & Gen Mgr Batchelder-Blasius Inc; Former Indust

Salesman Kaiser Aluminum Corp; Soc Die Casting Engrs; Am Foundryman Soc; Inst Scrap Iron Steel; Aluminum Recycling Assn; cp/S'burg City Coun; Dir C of C; S'burg Devel Assn; Pres Clb Wolford Col; Clemson Iptay S'ship Donor; Exec Dirs Clb; Rotary; Atlanta Ath Clb; YMCA; Repub; r/1st Presb Ch; hon/Num Biogl Listings.

BLAYLOCK, DONALD LYNN oc/Minister; b/Jul 31, 1938; h/2815 Breckinridge Ln, Louisville, KY 40220; ba/Middletown, KY; m/Phyllis Joyce; c/Mary Donice; p/O R and

Mary Blaylock; ed/BA Carson-Newman Col; MDiv So Bapt Theol Sem; pa/Dir Bapt Student Week Ky Bapt Conv; Am Mgmt Assn; Writer & Composer Rel Works; r/So Bapt; hon/W/W Rel.

BLAZER, DAN GERMAN II oc/Educator; b/Feb 23, 1944; h/5102 Longleaf Dr, Durham, NC 27712; ba/Durham; m/Sherrill; c/Natasha, Trey; p/Dan Sr and Mary Blazer, Nashville, TN; ed/BA Vanderbilt Univ 1965; MD Univ Tenn 1969; MPH Cand Univ NC-CH; pa/Asst Prof Psychi & Psychiatrist Duke Med Ctr; Assoc Dir Progs Ctr Study Aging & Human Devel; Gerontological Soc; Christian Med Soc; Am & So Psychi Assns; So Med Assn; Num Other Profl Assns; cp/Bd Dirs: Concern Inc, African Christian Hosps Assn; Dir Tng Com Contact Inc; r/Mem Brooks Ave Rd Ch of Christ; hon/Sr Fellow Ctr Study Aging & Human Devel; W/W S&SW; Recipient Num Grants.

BLAZER, SONDRA KAY GORDON oc/Writer; b/Jun 2, 1937; h/3730 Beatrice Dr, Franklin, OH 45005; ba/Same; c/Sherry Irving (Mrs Jeffrey), Cynthia Bays, Robert Bays; p/John Gordon (dec); O Lillie Stewart Gordon, Middletown, OH; ed/AA magna cum laude Univ Cincinnati 1975; pa/Free Lance Writer & Journalist; Pt-time Bd Elections Warren Co; Correspondent *Franklin Chronicle* 1975-77; Editor *Warren Co Reporter* 1966-72; Reporter & Ch Editor *Middletown Jour* 1955-56; Intl Platform Assn; Intl Assn Psycho-Social Rehab Sers; Nat Coun Crime & Delinq; Ohio Cts & Corrections Assn; cp/Search Com Rollmans Psychi Inst; Pubs Com Univ Cinc; Warren Co Chr Ohio Easter Seal Soc; Bd Co Vistors; Safety Coun; Dirs Citizens Comm Dept Rehab & Corrections;

Chr Dist 1 Planning Coun Ohio Dept Mtl Hlth & Mtl Retardation; Num Other Civic Assn; r/U Meth Hunter Commun Ch: SS Tchr 1963-72, Secy Worship Comm 1973-75; hon/Alpha Sigma Lambda; Beta Sigma Phi; 1st Pl Intl Short Story Contest, 2nd Pl Intl Poetry Contest; Sev Awds Ohio Dept Hwy Safety Media Contest; Awd Writers Digest Intl Short Story Contest; Num Biogl Listings.

BLEND, HENRIETTA BORONSTEIN oc/Specialist; b/Mar 10, 1924; h/10419 Greenwillow Dr, Houston, TX 77035; ba/Houston; m/Jake; c/Stanley, Stuart, Sharon B Schomburg, Susan; p/Max and Sarah Boronstein (dec); ed/BSEd 1961, MEd 1963 Univ Houston; pa/Instrnl Spec Houston Indep Sch Dist; Past Pres Tex Classroom & Houston Tchrs Assn; NCATE Eval Bd; Budget Chrperson Houston Prins Assn; NEA; TASA; ASCD; TSTA; cp/Tex Polit Action Com; Park Bd Town of Village, Okla; r/Congreg Beth Israel, Houston, Tex; hon/Linz Awds; Everts Awds; Franklin S'ship; Fac Wives Scholar; Human Relats Awd; Fondren Tchr of Yr.

BLESSING, VINNIE MALETA oc/Teacher; b/Nov 10, 1928; h/327 W Melba, Gladewater, TX 75647; ba/G'water; c/Julia; p/Normal Hollaway (dec); Mary Hollaway, Seagoville, TX; ed/BA; BS; MEd; pa/Voc Adjustment Coor; NEA; TSTA; TCTA; CEC; TAVAC; cp/C of C; Camp Fire Ldr; Gregg Co Assn Retarded Citizens; r/Bapt; Tng Union Ldr; hon/Outstg Mem, GCARC; TARS Advr; CTA Ser Awd; Personalities of S.

BLIESNER, GUSTAV HENRY oc/Professor; Engineer; b/Oct 8, 1910; h/1555 E 2nd St, Newberg, OR 97132; ba/Same; m/Jessie Mildred Crumbaker; c/Vernita B Christianson, Robert, Lawrence, Marion; p/Gustav Bliesner (dec); Emma Stocks Bliesner, Spokane, WA; ed/BSEE 1933, PhD 1976 Wash St Univ; MSEE Ia St Univ 1946; EngD UCLA 1966; mil/USAF; GS-14 Lt Col AUS Corps Engrs; Chief EE Engrg Br SE Asia 1965-67; Asst Elect Design Chief AUS Engrg Dist 1957-62; pa/Ret'd Pres, Engrg Conslt & Ed Coor Gus Bliesner Engrg Inc; Profl Engr Meyer Engrg Conslts Inc 1977-78; Num Past Engrg Conslt & Tchg Positions; IEEE; ASEE; AAUP; Soc Am Mil Engrs; cp/Rotary Clb; Toastmasters; WSU Alumni Assn; AKL Frat; BSA; Downey, Cal & Portland Mgmt Clbs; r/Zion Luth Ch: Pres, Treas, Deacon & Trustee 1967-79; hon/Sr 1st Citizen Runner-Up, Newberg C of C; Fellow: FIBA, Intl Platform Assn; Tau Beta Pi; Num Awds USCE; Pub'd Author; Num Biogl Listings.

BLISS, EDWARD L JR oc/Journalist; b/Jul 30, 1912; h/14 Marlboro St, Newburyport, MA 01950; ba/Same; m/Lois Arnette; c/Lois B Abshire, Anne B Mascolino; p/Edward Bliss (dec); Minnie May Bortz (dec); ed/BA Yale; pa/Prof Emeritus Am Univ; Writer, Editor & Prodr CBS News 1943-68; Conslt CBS & Nat Public Radio; hon/Dist'd Tchr Jour Awd, Soc Profl Journalists 1977.

BLOCK, RONALD R oc/Counselor; Teacher; b/Jun 25, 1932; h/28044 Leona Dr, Elsinore, CA 92330; ba/Seal Bch, CA; m/Joyce; c/Tami; p/Al and Shirley Block, El Cajon, CA; ed/MA; mil/USNR; pa/Tchr Self-Help Progs Var Cols & Adult Schs; Cnslr Alcoholism; Spec Spkr Fund-Raising Groups; Vol Conslt; hon/Equal Employment Opport Humanitarian Awd; Spec Contbn & Achmt Awd Cnslg.

BLOOM, MELVYN HAROLD oc/Executive; b/Oct 20, 1938; h/445 Wolfs Ln, Pelham Manor, NY 10803; ba/New York, NY; m/-Priscilla Newman; c/Jeffrey, Alan, Steven, Bradley; p/William and Lillian Bloom, Skokie, IL; ed/BS 1958, MS 1950 NWn Univ; MA 1971, PhD Cand New Sch Social Res; Cert Public Relats Univ Cal 1965; mil/Ill Air Nat

Guard 1956-67; pa/Asst Exec VChm U Jewish Appeal; Sigma Delta Chi; Soc Prof Journalists Headline Clb; Am Jewish Public Relats Soc; Am Polit Sci Assn; cp/Prog Com Anti-Defamation Leag; r/Jewish; hon/Cit Secy of St 1965; Goldkey Awd, *P R News* 1977; Pub'd Author.

BLUE, DAVID ROBERT oc/Businessman; b/Sept 13, 1911; h/Rt 6, Laurel, MS 39440; ba/Laurel; m/Lillie; c/Jerriel, Eloise Morgan, Wendell, Doval, Louise Russell; p/David and Mamie Ward Blue (dec); pa/Owner & Operator Furn & Real Est Bus; Appraiser; Min; Former Tchr Sandersville HS; Evangelist; cp/Mason; Exc Clb; Nom Dem St Rep 1975; Past VP Miss Annual Conf C Meth Ch; S'ship Com So Meth Col; r/So Meth Ch: Elder, Relats Com, Chm Ch Ext & Public Morals Com; hon/Certs: Dale Carnegie Sch Effective Spkg, Ldrship Tng & Human Relats, Stock Mktg & Investmts Univ So Miss, Bus Mgmt Jones Co Jr Col, Pi Sigma Epsilon Conf.

BLUE, EDNA GOSSAGE oc/Writer; Counselor; h/12 Grassy Cove Rd Rt 3 Box 202, Crossville, TN 38555; ba/Same; m/William Francis; c/Dorothy Jordan, Daniel Gossage (dec), (Stepchd:) Roy Gossage Jr, Margaret Solomon, (Foster Child) Helen Kendall; p/Arthur and Lennie Bailey Jenkins (dec); ed/Att'd Num Cols & Univs; pa/Ret'd Sr Cnslr Tenn Dept Human Sers; Writer; Num Essays, Poems, Articles & Books; Columnist "Homesteads Hannah" *Cumberland Homesteader* 1935-39; cp/Chm New Eyes for Needy Prog; Past Pres Cumberland Co Bus &

Profl Woms Clb; Pres Anderson Co Parents Coun Celebral Palsy; Fdr Daniel Arthur Rehab Ctr; Pres Bd Dirs & CoFdr CC Girls Clb; Steering Com Fdr Hilltoppers Inc; CCARC; Janet Clark Meml Group Home Inc; Bd Dirs U Fund; Bd Dirs 4 Cs; CC Commun Playhouse; r/Homesteads U Meth Ch: Mem, Tchr, Num Comms, VBS Dir, Treas & Histn; U Meth Wom: Pres Homesteads Ch, Exec Ofcr Dist Level; hon/Mother of Yr, Anderson Co 1951; Cumberland Co: Wom Achmt 1963, Bicent Wom Hist 1976; Num Biogl Listings.

BLUM, JUNE oc/Artist, Director, Curator; b/Dec 10, 1939; h/899 E 21st St, Brooklyn, NY 11210; ba/Same; m/Maurice C; p/Charles Druiett (dec); Elsie Druiett, Cocoa

Bch, FL; ed/MA Bklyn Col; pa/Dir Wom Art 1976-; Curator Num Profl Orgs; cp/Orgr Shows Wom Artists Living Bklyn; r/Luth; hon/Anne Eisner Putnam Meml Prize, Nat Assn Wom Artists 1968; Sculpture Hon Mention, White Mtn Fest Arts 1977.

BLUMBERG, PHILLIP IRVIN oc/Administrator; b/Sept 6, 1919; h/791 Prospect Ave C-4, West Hartford, CT 06105; ba/WH; m/Janet Helen Mitchell; c/William, Peter, Lisa, Bruce; p/Hyman and Bessie Simons Blumberg (dec); ed/AB Harvard Col; JD Harvard Law Sch; mil/USAF Major JAGD Res; pa/Law Sch Dean Univ Conn Sch Law; Am Law Inst; Am & Conn Bar Assns; cp/Gov Grassos Com Review Jud Nominations; Dept St Adv Com Transnational Enterprises; Trustee Conn Bar Foun; Treas Harvard Law Review; hon/Phi Beta Kappa; Bronze Star Medal.

BLUNT, JANE ANTOINETTE LOMAX oc/Educator; b/Aug 15, 1926; h/1435 Talley Ave, Petersburg, VA 23803; m/Norman; p/Joseph Lomax, P'burg; Marie Lomax (dec); ed/BS; MEd; pa/Tchr Reading Progs; Cnslr Students in Personal, Ednl & Fin Problems; Ofc Tchr Orgs YEA; Reading & Spec Ed Orgs; Supvr Num Progs; cp/Zeta Phi Beta; NAACP; 6th Ward Voters Leag; Chm Commun Outreach Progs; Participant Christian Ed Bds; Supvr Yth Activs; Other Civic Assns; r/Good Shepherd Bapt Ch; hon/Safety Cert; W/W Am Wom.

BLYTHE, WILLIAM JACKSON JR oc/Politician; Broker; b/Aug 15, 1935; ba/2815 Greenridge #43, Houston, TX 77057; m/Charlene Cotton; c/Alison; p/William Sr and Bess Blythe, Huntsville, TX; ed/BBA Univ Tex-A; mil/AUS 8 Yrs; pa/House Reps St Legislature 1970-; Num Coms & Positions Each Term; cp/Past Pres Repub Victory Clb; Reg Dir Repub Party Tex St Hdqtrs; Repub Primary Election Judge Travis Co; Tex Yg Repub Fdn; Num Polit Affils; Advr: Am Security Coun, N Harris Co Col & Yg Ams Freedom; Houston Jr C of C; Nat Hist Soc; Harris Co Heritage Soc; SAR; Alumni Assn Univ Va; Univ Tex Longhorn Clb; Num Other Civic Assns; r/S Main Bapt; hon/Charles A Perlitz Jr Meml Awd, Houston Jr C of C; Liberty Awd, Congress Freedom Inc.

BOAL, SARA METZNER oc/Painter; b/Jan 10, 1896; h/246 Corona Ave, Pelham, NY 10803; ba/Same; m/Arthur McClure; c/Elizabeth, Arthur Jr; p/William and Elizabeth Brackman Metzner (dec); ed/BA Wellesley Col 1916; pa/Painter Fine Arts; Nat Arts Clb; Salmagundi Clb; Pres Catharine Lorillard Wolfe Art Clb 1965-68; Pen Wom; Pres Composer, Author & Artists Am 1970-72; cp/Trustee Hammond Mus; Pres Citizens Com Army, Navy & AF; r/Presb; hon/Fellow Royal Soc Art, London; Num Painting Awds.

BOATMAN, BECKY L oc/Instructor; b/Sept 29, 1955; h/11 Paisley Ln, Columbia, SC 29210; ba/Columbia, Cleveland, MS; ed/BS Delta St Univ; MA Cand Univ SC; pa/Police Instr SC Crim Justice Acad; Assoc'd Public Communs Ofcrs Assn; Intl Assn Wom Police; SC Law Enforcement Ofcrs Assn; Intl Assn Chiefs Police; r/Bapt; hon/Gooch S'ship; Num Biogl Listings.

BOATRIGHT, BARBARA REBA-HALL oc/Doctor; b/Apr 18, 1914; h/1007 E Lakeview Cir, Clinton, MS 39056; ba/Bay Springs, MS; c/Jean B Parker, Barbara B Little; p/John and Nan Gilbert Hall, Wagoner, OK; ed/Dr Chiropractic; pa/Am & Miss Chiropractic Assns; Sigma Phi Chi; r/So Bapt; hon/Chiropractic of Yr 1967; Num Biogl Listings.

BOBROW, EDWIN E oc/Executive; Consultant; b/Apr 28, 1928; h/4465 Douglas Ave, Riverdale, NY 11471; ba/Tew York, NY; m/Gloria Lefkowitz; c/Mark; p/Abraham and Emma Bobrow, Miami Bch, FL; ed/Grad Long Isl Univ; Att'd NY Univ Grad Sch; pa/Pres Mktg in Depth Inc; Chm Bd Bobrow Sales

Assocs Inc; VP Bobrow Realty Co; Lectr Var Profl Orgs; Soc Profl Mgmt Conslts; Am Mktg Assn; Authors Leag & Authors Guild; U Jewish Appeal Gtr NY; Nat Coun Salesmen's Orgs; Intl Platform Assn; CoFdr Mass Mdse Distributors Assn; Adv Bd Assn Sales Reps & Agts Inc; Num Other Profl Assns; cp/Bd Dirs Solidaridad Humana Inc; Ldrship Coun UJA; Bonds Israel; Hardware Affil'd Reps; Bd Dirs

Bus Games Group LI Univ Grad Sch; Vol Urban Consulting Group; Other Civic Assns; hon/St Israel Ldrship Awd; U Jewish Appeal Scroll; UJA Ldrship Cit; 2 Certs Highest Achmt Tchg, Univ Wisc; Dist'd Alumnus Awd, LI Univ; Mfrs Agts Nat Assns Spec Awd; Num Cits Inst Mass Mktg; Dist'd Ser Mktg Awd, Sales Execs Clb; Pub'd Author; Num Biogl Listings.

BODEY, GERALD PAUL oc/Physician; b/May 22, 1934; h/5023 Glenmeadow, Houston, TX 77096; ba/Houston; m/Nancy Louise Wiegner; c/Robin, Gerald Jr, Sharon; p/Allen and Mary Smith Bodey (dec); ed/AB magna cum laude Lafayette Col 1956; MD John Hopkins Univ Sch Med 1960; mil/USPHS 1962-66; pa/Prof Univ Tex Hlth Sci Ctr: Grad Sch Biomed Scis 1975-, Dental Br 1977-, Med Sch 1976-; Adjunct Prof Microbiology & Med Baylor Col Med 1975-; Univ Tex Sys Cancer Ctr: Med Dir 1977-, Chief Chemotherapy Br 1975-, Internist & Prof Med 1975-, Chief Sec Infectious Diseases 1971-; Conslt: Brooke Army Med Ctr 1971-, Hematology-Oncology Wilford Hall USAF

Med Ctr 1975-, Preven Med Div Space Flight Manned Spacecraft Ctr 1970-71, Comm Devel Comprehensive Cancer Care Ctr 1978-; Num Other Profl Positions; Edit Bds: Leukemia Res 1977-, Antimicrobial Agts & Chemotherapy 1975-77; Num Inst Coms & Symp Chrships; Am Soc: Clin Oncology, Clin Pharmacology & Therapeutics, Hematology, Microbiology; Am Assn: Advmt Sci, Cancer Res; NY Acad Scis; Intl Soc Chemotherapy; Intl Assn Study Lung Cancer; Other Profl Assns; r/Presb; hon/Fellow: Am Col Phys, Royal Col Med, Royal Soc Promotion Hlth, Am Col Clin Pharmacology; Am Chem Soc Prize; Awd Am Inst Chems; Merck Chem Prize; Robert B Youngman Greek Prize; Phi Beta Kappa; Sigma Chi; Num Biogl Listings; Others.

BOECKLIN, PEG PITMAN oc/Administrator; Consultant; b/Dec 11, 1910; h/52 Westgate Dr, Delaware, OH 43015; m/Roland (dec); c/Arnold; p/Laurence and Elise Aztle Pitman (dec); ed/AB Smith Col; pa/Ret'd Col Admr Ohio Wesleyan Univ; Orgr & Dir Num Wkshops & Sems; Profl Orgs; cp/Exec Bd: Help Anonymous, U Way, Area Coun Aging; r/Prot Epis; hon/Pub'd Author.

BOEHM, EDWARD GORDON JR oc/Administrator; b/Jan 30, 1942; h/4829 Powder House Dr, Rockville, MD 20853; ba/Wash, DC; m/Regina Ellen Evans; c/Evan, Andrew; p/Edward Sr and Catherine Boehm, Long Boat Key, FL; ed/BS; MEd; EdD; pa/Higher Ed Adm Am Univ; Nat Assn Student Pers Admrs; Nat Assn Col Admissions Cnslrs; Coun Advmt & Support Ed; cp/Bd Dirs Friends Nat Zoo; Nat Chr Wash Col Fair; r/Cath; hon/Omicron Delta Kappa; Pi Gamma Mu; Phi Delta Kappa; W/W: E, Am Cols & Univs.

BOGAN, CARMEN PAGE oc/Petroleum Landman; b/Jun 4, 1918; h/4415 Tibbs Ave, Shreveport, LA 71105; ba/S'port; m/James Miller; c/Carmen B Murrey, James Jr; p/Stanley and Christina Terrell Page (dec); ed/Att'd Murray St Univ & Draughons Bus Col; pa/Indep Petro Landman S'port 1974-; Asst Landman & Fin Advr 1961-74; Secy & Fin Advr Ind Oil Operator 1957-61; Am Assn Petro Landman; Ark, La & Tex Petro Landmen; cp/Past Pres Chapt X PEO; Former GSA Ldr; Repub; r/Broadmoor U Meth Ch, S'port: SS Tchr, Div Supt; UMW; hon/W/W S&SW; Personalities S; Dict Intl Biog.

BOGDANOWICZ, WALTER ANDREW oc/Engineer; b/Jun 16, 1912; h/9104 Burchfield Dr, Oak Ridge, TN 37830; m/Beryl Tucker; c/Mary, Cheryl, Don; p/Andrew Bogdanowicz (dec); Johanna Oscik (dec); ed/BSEE; mil/Army Signal Corps Tech Sgt; pa/Union Carbide: Chief EE & Supt EE Dept 1958-, Design Engr & Elect Conslt Engrg Div

1947-58; Gen Foreman Electromagnetic Plant Oak Ridge; Other Past Positions; Lic'd Profl Engr Mass & Tenn; Am Mil Engrs; cp/K of C; Intl Platform Assn; r/Rom Cath: Fin Secy, Commentator, Lectr, Cantor, Maintenance Chr, Bd Dirs; hon/Intercontinental Biogl Assn; Bronze Plaque, Armed Sers; Num Biogl Listings.

BOGGESS, LOUISE BRADFORD oc/Writer, Teacher, Lecturer; b/Mar 28, 1912; h/4016 Martin Dr, San Mateo, CA 94403; ba/Same; m/William Fannin Jr; c/Patricia B Blair, William III; p/Giles Bradford (dec); Hattie Corbett Bradford, Sweetwater, TX; ed/BA, MA Univ Tex; pa/Profl Writing Sers Offered Num Univs & Sems; Authors Guild; Cal & Burlingame Writers; Past Pres Profl Writing Sec AAUW; Am Cut Glass Assn; Nat Antique Glass Assn; r/Epis; hon/Phi Beta Kappa; Phi Lambda Theta; Phi Sigma Alpha; Jack London Awd, Cal Writers; Pub'd Author; Num Biogl Listings.

BOGLE, ENNIS ODELLE oc/Executive Secretary; b/Sept 1, 1925; h/3904 Highridge Dr, Austin, TX 78759; ba/Austin; m/James Owen; c/Jimmie Rhodes, Jerry, Russell; ed/Bus Col Deg 1946; Cert'd Assn Exec 1976; pa/Exec Secy Tex Med Liability Trust 1978-; Exec Dir: Tex Soc Profl Engrs 1963-78, Tex Assn Petro Retailers 1958-63; Exec Secy W Republic Life Insur Co 1955-57; Other Past Positions; Contbr Ala & Tex Profl Engr Jours; Former Pres & VP Town Lake Chapt Am Buswoms Assn; Zonta Clb Austin Zonta Intl: Bd 1975-76, Secy-Treas 1974-75; St Soc Admrs Coun Nat Soc Profl Engrs; Am & Dir Tex Soc Assn Execs; Toastmasters Intl; hon/Wom of Yr, Am Bus-woms Assn; Cert Exceptl Ser, Socs Annual Meeting 1965; Devotion & Ldrship, TSPE; Num Biogl Listings.

BOHLER, CLORINDA SCARPA-SMITH oc/Physician; b/May 1, 1923; h/2279 Wrightsboro Rd, Augusta, GA 30904; ba/Same; m/T Gordon; p/Jose and Maria Smith Scarpa (dec); ed/MEd 1941, BS 1942 Nat Coun Ed Min Ed; MD Univ Buenos Aires Sch Med 1950; pa/Phys Pvt Pract Specializing Endocrinology & Metabolic Dis 1972-; Att'g Phys Univ Hosp 1972-; Asst Prof Dept OB-Gyn Talmadge Meml Hosp & Med Col Ga 1965-69; Res Assoc Dept Physiol Med Col Ga 1960-65; Num Other Past Positions; Am Acad Fam Phys; Am Acad Gen Pract; AAUP; Am Fertility Soc; Am Med Woms Assn; r/Bapt; hon/Phys Recog Awd, AMA; Fellow Royal Soc Hlth; F'ship Argentinian Assn Progress Ciences; Recipient Num Grants; Pub'd Author; Num Biogl Listings.

BOHMFALK, JOHNITA SCHUESSLER oc/Educator; b/Mar 4, 1916; h/PO Box 883, Yorktown, TX 78164; m/Milton; c/Ida B Ullrich (Mrs James), Robert; p/John and Ida Jordan Schuessler (dec); ed/BA So Meth Univ 1938; pa/Ofcr: PTA, AAUW, Mins Wives Assn; cp/U Fund; Leag Wom Voters; Cancer Crusade; DRT; OES; Intl Platform Assn; Music Clb; Woms Fed'd Clb; Boy Scouts; Voter Registration; Genealogical Soc; Num

Other Civic Assns; r/S Bluff U Meth Ch, Corpus Christi, Tex: SS Tchr, Communion Steward, Chds Choir Dir, Yth Cnslr, Dir Vacation Ch Schs; U Meth Wom: Bd Christian Vocs, Secy Campus Min, Bd Christian Ed, Secy Mbrships, Chrperson Nominations; hon/Dean's Distn List; Delta Phi Alpha; Tex Merit Mother 1978; Intl Biogl Assn; Am Biogl Inst; Num Biogl Listings.

BOHNSDAHL, NAOMI C oc/Realtor; Teacher; Librarian; b/Aug 15, 1908; h/PO Box 546, Canton, NC 28716; ba/Canton; m/Gunnar William (dec); c/Eleanor Terrill (Mrs JB); p/Harwell and Mary Thompson Crumley (dec); ed/AB George Washington Univ; BS Univ NC; Realtors Lic Haywood Tech; pa/Haywood Co Bd Realtors; Ret'd Tchrs; Delta Kappa Gamma; Nat, St & SE Lib Orgs; cp/Canton Homemakers; Common Cause; Dem Party; r/Epis; hon/Num Ath Awds & Hon Soc Col.

BOITER, KENNETH ALAN oc/Administrative Aid; b/Oct 5, 1952; h/4271-A1 S 35th St, Arlington, VA 22206; ba/Wash, DC; p/William Jr and Florence Boiter, Spartanburg, SC; ed/BS Univ SC 1975; Addit Studies; pa/Leg Com & Res Aid Cong-man Carroll Campbell; Former Design Engr Mech Dept MBTB Archs & Engrs; Pipe Design & Analysis J E Sirrine Co 1976-68; ASME; SAE; ASHRAE; cp/Orgr & Co Exec Chr Wn Precnt 1978; Sptbg Co Repub Party Conv 1978; Del SC Repub Party Conv 1978; Participant Carroll Campbell Campaign; Coor Election Day Activs Sptbg Co; Poinsett Sertoma Clb; Org'd & 1st Chm Sptbg Co Yg Repubs; r/Bethlehem Bapt Ch, Roebuck, SC.

BOLEY, BOLAFFIO RITA oc/Artist; h/310 W 106th St, New York, NY 10025; ba/Same; m/Orville; c/Lucius, Bruno; p/Angelo & Olga de Scandiano; ed/Dipl Violin Conservatory; pa/Exhibits Num Mus; Pvt Collections; Murals, Collages & Assemblages; hon/CAAA Awd Excell.

BOLGER, ANNIE LAURIE MARVIN oc/Home Companion; b/Jun 17, 1928; h/903 N Holly Box 154, Searcy, AR 72143;

m/Robert Paul (dec); c/Eva Lopez, Robert, Raymond, Don, William, Dan; p/Alfred Marvin (dec); Eva Barton Marvin, Jonesboro, AR; ed/Grad Wash Sem; Grad Harcum Col; cp/Cancer Dr 1974-78; VRegent Little Red River Chapt DAR; Pres Phoenix Clb; Secy Sp Ed White Co; Campaigned Elections Cands 1976-78; r/Epis.

BOLTE, CARL EUGENE JR oc/Realtor; b/Feb 4, 1929; h/3548 Wyoming St, Kansas City, MO 64111; ba/KC; p/Carl Bolte Sr (dec); Muriel Eastman Bolte, KC; ed/BS 1951, AB 1955 Univ Mo; mil/USNR Capt & Insp Gen Readiness Command Reg 18 1976-; pa/Exec VP Paul Hamilton Co Realtors; KC Real Est Bd; Appraisers: Am Soc, Am Col Real Est, Nat Assn Cert'd Real Est; cp/Pres KC Rotary Clb; Immediate Past Chr Goodwill Industs; Secy Starlight Theatre; Salvation Bd; Dir St Bank Slater; ASCAP; Bd Dirs KC Mus; r/Country Clb Christian Ch: Deacon; hon/Fellow Harry S Truman Lib Inst; Omicron Delta Kappa; Pub'd Author & Composer.

BOLTON, THOMAS PORTEOUS oc/-Architect; City Planner; b/Oct 25, 1912; h/Rt 2 Box 219-A, Blackfoot, ID 83221; ba/B'foot; m/Patricia Irene Corney; c/Margaret Almeida, Katherine Dickman, Patricia Riley; p/William Bolton (dec); Harriett Oddie Burscough (dec); ed/BArch, Dipl Civic Design

Univ Liverpool; mil/British Royal Engrs Lt Col WW-II; pa/Former Pres Newfoundland Assn Archs; AIA; cp/Rotary Clb: Former VGov Dist 109, Pres Aylesbury, Mem B'foot; r/Ch of Jesus Christ Latter Day Sts: Mem; 70 Freeman City London; hon/Fellow: Royal Inst British Archs, Royal Town Planning Inst.

BOND, FLOYD ALDEN oc/Administrator; Professor; b/Aug 20, 1913; h/2533 Londonderry Rd, Ann Arbor, MI 48104; ba/AA; m/Jean Marrow; c/Richard, Robert; p/Isaac Bond (dec); Ada Wolfe Bond; ed/AB 1938, AM 1940, PhD 1942 Univ Mich; pa/Univ Mich: Dean Emeritus & Donald C

Cook Dist'd Prof 1979-; Dean & Prof Bus Ec 1960-78; Chm Dept & Prof Ec Stedman-Sumner Foun Pomona Col 1948-59; Conslt Govt Acctg Ofc; Pres Am Assn Col Schs Bus; Pres Wn Ec Assn; cp/Prog Chm Detroit Ec Clb; hon/Phi Beta Kappa; Beta Gamma Sigma; Num Fac F'ships; 4 Dist'd Prof Awds.

BONDURANT, BYRON LEE oc/Professor; Engineer; b/Nov 11, 1925; h/265 Franklin St, Dublin, OH 43017; ba/Columbus, OH; m/Lovetta May Alexander; c/Mrs Connie Jaycox, Richard, Mrs Cindy Gardino; p/Earl Bondurant (dec); Joyce Koneta Gesler

Chugiak, AK; ed/BAE 1949; MS 1953; mil/USN 1943-46; pa/Dean, Chm Dept & Prof Agri Engrg; Consltg & Intl Devel Agri Engrg; Reg'd: Profl Engr Me & Ohio, Land Surveyor Me, Fallout Shelter Analyst US; cp/PTA Activs; r/Prot; hon/Tau Beta Pi; Sigma Pi Sigma; Sigma Xi; Gamma Sigma Delta; Epsilon Sigma Phi; Fellow: Am Assn Advmt Sci, Inst Engrs, Worldwide Acad Scholars; Num Biogl Listings.

BONHAM, TAL D oc/Minister; b/Jul 20, 1934; h/1913 N Glade, Bethany, OK 73008; ba/Oklahoma City, OK; m/Clara Faye; c/Marilyn, Randy, Daniel, Tal David; p/Woodrow Bonham (dec); J B Trowbridge, Neosho, MO; ed/B & BA Okla Bapt Univ 1957; BD SWn Theol Sem 1958; ThD 1963; pa/Dir Dept Evang Bapt Gen Conv Okla 1973-; S Side Bapt Ch Pine Bluff 1964-73;

Pastor 1st Bapt Ch Marlow 1960-63; Ordained Min 1954; cp/Pres Marlow Min Assn; Moderator: Mullins Bapt Assn 1962, Harmony Bapt Assn 1965; Past Pres & Exec Bd Ark Bapt Conv; Pine Bluff Min Assn; Chaplain Babe Ruth World Series Ark; VChm Chapel Com Cummins Prison; r/So Bapt; hon/Dist'd Citizen, Pine Bluff 1970; Outstg Yg Man, Ark JCs 1970.

BONINE, VIVIAN WAY oc/Film Technician; Educator; Poet; b/Sept 28, 1912; h/2556 La Presa Ave, Rosemead, CA 91770; ba/Same; m/Arvel Earl; c/Patricia Small Webster, Billie Small Jones; p/John and Jennie Ellison Way (dec); pa/Exec Bd U Poets Laureate Intl; Former Matrix Printer Technicolor Corp; Cal St Poetry Soc; Cal Fdn Chaparral Poets; Past Publicity Chm Nat Fdn

St Poetry Socs; Poetry Soc Tex; Other Profl Assns; cp/Nat Repub Com; Pasadena Writers Clb; Hist Writer Crosby Co Hist Comm; Ralls Hist Mus Inc; Alumni Assns: W Tex St Univ, Tex Woms Univ, Baylor Univ; r/Prot; hon/Dr Arts & Lttrs honoris causa World Univ 1970; UPLI: Poet Laureateship Gold Crown Awd, Intl Wom of Yr 1975; Num Poetry Contest Awds Intl, Nat, St & Local Levels.

BONNER, JACK WILBUR III oc/Psychiatrist; b/Jul 30, 1940; h/27 Windsor Rd, Asheville, NC 28804; ba/A'ville; m/Myra T; c/Jack IV, Shelley Bliss, Katherine; p/Jack Jr and Irldene Turner Bonner, Corpus Christi, TX; ed/AA Del Mar Col 1960; BA Univ Tex honors 1961; MD Univ Tex SWn Med Sch 1965; Internship Univ Ark Med Ctr 1965-66; Residency Duke Univ Med Ctr 1966-69; mil/USAF Flight Surg Wing Psychiatrist 1968-72; pa/Duke Univ Med Ctr Highland Hosp Div: Med Dir 1975-, Asst Prof Psychi 1972-, Dir Outpatient Sers 1972-75; Staff Psychiatrist 1971-72; Conslt Psychi: A'ville

Vets Adm Hosp 1974-, Austin St Hosp 1969; Am & So Psychi Assn; Am Group Psychotherapy Assn; Am & So Med Assn; Am Col Psychiatrists; hon/Phi Theta Kappa; Diplomate Am Bd Psychi & Neurol.

BONNER, LILLY ANNELLE oc/Educator; b/Jan 17, 1919; h/1115 Adeline St, Hattiesburg, MS 39401; ba/H'burg; p/Martin Sr and Lilly Moseley Bonner (dec); ed/BS 1946, MA 1954 Univ So Miss; EDD Ind Univ 1964; pa/Prof & Dept Chm Dept Bus Ed Univ So Miss 1968-; Num Past Tchg Positions; Miss Ed Assn; Nat Assn Tchr Edrs Bus & Ofc Ed; Miss Bus Ed Assn; VP 1966-67, Pres 1967-68, Sr Col Rep 1970-71 & 1975-78; Nat & So Bus Ed Assns; Am & Miss Voc Assns; Pi Omega Pi; Delta Pi Epsilon; Delta Kappa Gamma; Public Relats & Chm Nom'g Com Phi Kappa Phi; Pi Tau Chi; cp/Bus & Profl Woms Clb; S'ship Com, Nat Bus Woms Week, Foun Com, Leg Com; VChm H'burg Mayors Com Status Wom; Univ So Miss Alumni Assn; H'burg Commun Concert Assn; r/Main St Bapt Ch; hon/Nom Dist'd Prof of Yr Awd; H'burg Chapt Bus & Profl Woms Clb: Wom Achmt, Nom Susan B Anthony Awd; Nom'd Outstg Edr Awd, So Bus Ed Assn; Most Outstg Bus Edr of Yr, Miss Bus Tchrs; Pub'd Author; Num Biogl Listings.

BONNER, OPHELIA CALLOWAY oc/Civic Leader; b/Sept 25, 1897; h/806 E Lomita, Flint, MI 48505; ba/Same; m/Charles; p/Alexander and Dolly Sharp Watson (dec); ed/Intl Coun Rel Ed; cp/Urban Leag; NAACP; Jefferson Commun Coun; r/Christ F'ship Missionary Bapt: SS Tchr, Missionary Soc, Chm Pastors Anniv Booklet 20 Yrs; Intl Coun Rel Coun; hon/Dedication Ophelia Bonner Park, Flint City Coun Resolution; Dedication Ophelia Bonner S'ship Fund, Jefferson Commun Coun; Liberty Bell Awds; Golden Cup, Yg Peoples Connections; Nat Assn Negro & Bus Wom Awd; Apprec Awd, PTA Jefferson Commun Coun; Commun Ed Dept Awd, Flint Bd Ed; W E Boise Humanitarian Awd, Urban Leag; NAACP Yth Coun Awd; Num Resolutions & Certs; Others.

BONNETTE, JEANNE DELAMARTER oc/Writer; b/Dec 29, 1907; h/8901 W Frontage Rd NE #235, Albuquerque, NM 87113; m/Arthur; c/Judith Best Barrick, Haven Best Tobias; p/Eric DeLamarter (dec); Rubee Wilson DeLamarter, Santa Fe, NM;

ed/Tchrs Cert; pa/Prodr *The Creative Process* KNME-TV 1971-75; 6 Books Poetry; Poetry Soc Am; NY Poetry Forum; Acad Am Poets; Poetry Socs: World, Past Pres NM St, Past Secy Nat Fdn St; St Lttrs Chm Nat Leag Am Pen Wom; hon/Zia Awd, NM Press Wom; Num Nat & St Awds Poetry & Short Stories.

BONNEY, ARTHUR PERES oc/Minister; Journalist; b/Jul 14, 1925; ba/QUMRAN 305, Bloomingburg, NY 12721; c/Michele, Marc, Lisa; p/Peres and Eva Rundlett Bonney (dec); ed/Wagner Col; mil/USAFR Capt WW-II & Korea; pa/Exec VP NY Acad Nutrition; Tchr Parapsychology & Nutrition; Pvt Conslt; ARE; Nat Chaplains Assn; Occupl Therapy Assn; Fla Psychical Res Soc; ICC; cp/Editor *Taxpayers Oper Publicity* News Orange Co Taxpayers Assn; Cnslg Projects; Orange Co Press Assn; Hudson River Fishermans Assn; Rountable; r/Fdr QUMRAN Congreg; Bd Dirs: Universal Listening Post, Spiritual Sci; Emissaries Divine Light; hon/Purple Heart.

BONNO, JAN HUFFCUT oc/Executive; b/Apr 22, 1946; h/31 Liberty, San Francisco, CA 94110; ba/San Mateo, CA; m/Charles Henri; p/W Harwood and Vernice Wood Huffcutt, Walnut Creek, CA; ed/BA (Hist & Polit Sci) SF St Univ 1969; pa/Asst VP; Investmt Portfolio Mgr; Fin Woms Clb SF; Cal

Savings & Loan Leag Investmt Com; Nat Org Wom; AAUW; cp/Commonwealth Clb SF; Leag Wom Voters; Advr Jr Achmt; Exec Com Mayoral Campaigns SF; Bd Dirs Friends Outside; r/Presb; hon/Ldrship Tng Prog, SF St Univ; W/W: Fin & Indust, Am Wom.

BONTEMPO, PAUL N oc/Executive; b/Mar 8, 1951; h/Florham Park, NJ 07932; m/Cheryl Pate; p/Salvatore and Gloria Bontempo, FP; ed/BBA Univ Notre Dame 1973; Postgrad Studies; pa/VP Braidburn Corp; Nat Org Wom; cp/Friends Public Broadcasting; Common Cause; K of C; UNICO; BPOE; Exec Com Morris Co Dem Com; NJ Adv Com Juv Justice & Delinq Preven; NJ Dem St Com; Dem Cand Assembly 1975; At Large Del Dem Nat Conv 1976; Num Other Civic Assns; r/Rom Cath.

BOOK, RONALD LEE oc/Attorney; b/Dec 3, 1952; h/12905 Cherry Rd, N Miami, FL 33181; ba/Miami Bch, FL; p/Harold and Delores Book, NM; ed/BA; JD Tulane Univ; pa/Delta Theta Phi; Am, Fla & Dade City Bar Assns; Am Judicature Soc; cp/Dade Dem Clb; Yg Dems; Fla & NM Track Clbs; r/Jewish; hon/Nat Mem of Yr, Delta Theta Phi; Audubon Soc Awd; NM JCs Outstg Citizen Awd; W/W Cols & Univs.

BOOKER, HENRY MARSHALL oc/Professor; b/Jan 12, 1935; h/111 Browns Neck Rd, Poquoson, VA 23662; ba/Newport News, VA; m/Porter Phillips; c/Mary DeMott, Sharon Sinclair, Paige Meriwether, Marshall; p/William Booker (dec); Evelyn Booker, Hampton, VA; ed/BA cum laude Lynchburg Col 1959; PhD Univ Va 1965; pa/Col Prof Christopher Newport Col; Intl, Am, So, En & Va Ec Assns; AAUP; Alpha Kappa Psi; cp/Lions Clb; r/Epis: Ch Choir, Vestry, SS Tchr; hon/Tchr of Yr 1975; Most Dedicated Christopher Newport Col 1975; Outstg Edr Several Yrs.

BOOKER, JANICE A oc/Executive; b/Dec 24, 1946; h/1234 Massachusetts Ave NW #423, Washington, DC; ba/Wash, DC; p/Boyce Booker (dec); Jewel Booker, Tryon, NC; ed/BS St Augustines Col 1968; MBA Am Univ 1977; pa/Assn Exec; ABA: Monthly Newslttr *Urban & Commun Ec Devel* 1975-, Ad Hoc Task Force Equal Credit Opport Act 1974-, Ctrs Bkg Ed Eval Com; Assn MBA Execs; Am Mgmt Assn; Nat Bus Leag; Nat Coun Urban Ec Devel; Awds Sel Com Commun & Campus Conf Nat Assn Devel Orgs; Trustee Intl Ser Agys Employee Pension Fund; cp/Smithsonian Inst; Wash Urban Leag: Bd Dirs, Treas, Chrperson Fin Com, Exec Com; Fin Com & Bd Dirs Wash Nat Zool Park; DC Woms Polit Caucus; Congl Black Caucus Annual Banquet; r/Epis; hon/Nat Awd 1975; Outstg Yg Wom Am; Pub'd Author; W/W: Wom, Black Ams.

BOOKER, MERREL DANIEL oc/Counselor; b/Jul 9, 1908; h/829 20th St NE, Washington, DC 20002; m/Erma Barbour; c/Merrel Jr, Sue; p/John and Esther Williams Booker (dec); ed/AB, BD Howard Univ; STM Boston Univ; pa/Pastoral Care Cnslr; Min;

Cert'd Chaplain; Prof; Author; Lectr; cp/Kiwanis; Alpha Phi Alpha; r/Bapt; hon/Grant Evanston Ill Mtl Hlth Assn.

BOOKS, EARL JAMES EUGENE oc/Counselor; b/Jun 22, 1942; h/8202 Martha St, Alexandria, VA 22309; ba/Ft Belvoir, VA; m/Hiroko; c/Julie; p/Cleo and Ruth Little Books, Dillsburg, PA; ed/BA 1970, MEd 1974 Univ Md; mil/USN Communs Intell Nav Security Group 1964-68; pa/Writer & Cnslr AUS Corps Engrs Engr Topographic Labs; Nat Assn Govt Communs; APGA; Am Col Pers Assn; Assn Cnslr Ed & Supvn; Nat Voc Guid Assn; Assn Humanistic Ed & Devel; Am Sch Cnslr Assn; Am Rehab Cnslg Assn; Assn Measuremt & Eval Guid; Nat Employmt Cnslrs Assn; cp/VFW; Am Legion; r/Luth; hon/AUS Sustained Superior Perf Awd; 8 AUS Suggestion Awds.

BOOKWALTER, KARL WEBBER oc/Educator; b/Dec 21, 1899; h/9815 E St Rd 45, Unionville, IN; m/Carolyn Weems; p/John and Barbara Cummings Bookwalter (dec); ed/AB Denver Univ 1925; MEd Columbia Univ; EdD NYU; mil/AUS 2nd Lt Inf; pa/Ret'd Prof Emeritus Ind Univ; Num Other Past Positions Ind Univ; Vis Prof: So Ill Univ 1970-71, Taiwan Normal Univ 1974; Editor *Phy Edr*; Nat Col PE Assn Men; Am Alliance Hlth, PE & Rec; NEA; cp/Lions Clb; Past Local Pres BSA; Am Red Cross; Chm Monroe Co Commun Chest Campaign; Chm Com Ed Prog USAF Acad; hon/Fellow AAHPER; Am Acad PE: Fellow, Hetherington Awd; BSA Order of Arrow; Silver Beaver; Silver Antelope; Delta Epsilon; Phi Delta Kappa; Phi Beta Sigma; Phi Epsilon Kappa; Phi Sigma; Kappa Delta Pi; Phi Kappa Chi; Pub'd Author.

BOONE, REBECCA ANN oc/Psychologist; b/Oct 27, 1938; h/1357 N Highland Ave NE, Atlanta, GA 30306; ba/Atla; p/Isaac Boone (dec); Irma Boone, Northport, AL; ed/BS; MEd; PhD; pa/Psychologist Pvt Pract; Conslt; Tchg; Conducting Groups Treatmt Phobias; hon/W/W S&SE.

BOPP, EDWARD oc/Engineer; b/Jun 2, 1918; h/2507 Marchese Way, Santa Clara, CA 95051; ba/Same; m/Vivian Belle Eastland (dec); c/Gordon; p/Daniel and Natalie Christina Heintz Bopp (dec); ed/BS Healds Engrg Col 1956; Num Dipls; pa/Pvt Pract

Design Conslt & Engrg Sers Conslt; Sr Assoc Bopp & Assocs 1952-; Design Engr: Morgen Design Inc 1977-78, Proj Support Engrg Co 1974-75, Bay Tech Sers Co 1972-74, Comprehensive Designers 1969-70; Other Past Positions; cp/Indep Order Foresters; hon/Pub'd Author; Devel Num Devices & Sys.

BORDALLO, RICARDO JEROME oc/Governor; b/Dec 11, 1927; h/Ofc of Gov PO Box 2950, Agana, Guam 96910; ba/Same; m/Madeleine M; c/Deborah; p/Baltasar and Josefina Bordallo, Tamuning, Guam; ed/Att'd Univ San Francisco; pa/Gov Guam; Owner Nat Automotive Parts Assn 1974; Housing & Apt Bldg Investmts 1974; Real Est Devel 1974; Former Pubr Guam Pacific Jour Daily Newspaper 1966; Chm & Bd Dirs Fam Fin Co Inc Gen Insur Agy 1959-74; Num Other Past Positions; Nat Geog Soc; Soc Intl Devel; cp/Chm Dem Party Guam 1971-73; Dem Party Nom Isls 1970; Del: Nat Dem Conv Chicago 1968, Leg Ldrs Conf Puerto Rico

1965, Nat Leg Conf Atlantic City 1964; Others; Num Guam Legs 1956-70; Guam C of C; AF Assn Guam; Navy Leag; Lions Clb; SKOL; Bd Dirs & Chm Am Red Cross; Yg Mens Leag; Spanish Clb; Tourist Comm; Rehab Ctr; Marianas Assn Retarded Chd; Liberation Day Com; r/Cath; hon/Intl Platform Assn; W/W Am.

BORDEN, WILLIAM HENRY oc/Accountant; b/Sept 13, 1894; h/5855 La Jolla Mesa Drive, La Jolla, CA 92037; ba/LJ; m/Lucie Caroline Knox; c/Louise Erickson, James, Caroline Oeland; p/James and Mary Tomkins Borden (dec); ed/BA; MA 1921 Wisc; mil/Corps Engrs Qtr Master Engr Sr Grade WW-I; Wis NG Capt QMC; pa/Ret'd Public Acct Wis; r/Presb; hon/Pi Gamma Mu; Wis Acad Scis, Arts & Lttrs.

BOREN, EDWARD DANIEL oc/Educator; b/Sept 2, 1936; h/1214 Stonewall, San Antonio, TX 78211; ba/SA; p/Mary Boren, Indianapolis, IN; ed/BA; STB Quincy Col; MA Univ Tex-SA; pa/Math Dept Head St

Francis Acad; Registrar Hales Franciscan HS 1969-73; Nat Coun Tchrs Maths; cp/Common Cause; r/Cath; hon/NSF Grants: Ill Inst Technol & DePaul Univ; Outstg Sec'dy Edrs Am Awd; Outstg Ldrs Elem & Sec'dy Ed.

BORETSKY, METODIJ oc/Civil & Environmental Engineer; b/Mar 12, 1927; h/8302 MacArthur Rd, Wyndmoor, PA 19118; ed/BS & MS, Drexel Univ 1964, 70, 74; Post-grad Studies; pa/Civil Engr, Cons Engrg Co (Doylestown, Pa) 1958-60; Civil & Structural Engr, US Forest Serv, Dept of Agri 1960-65; Structural Engr, US Army Corps of Engrs, Phila Dist 1965-70; Civil & Environmental Engr, N Div, Naval Facilities

Engrg Command, USN 1970-; Author of Tech & Profl Articles on Environment, Radio-active Waste, Pollution, Others; Am Soc Civil Engrs; Am Soc Mil Engrs; Ukrainian Engrs Soc of Am: Exec Bd 1972-79, Exec Bd Pres 1979-, Phila Br Pres 1966-67 & 1976-77; cp/Ukrainian Cong Comm of Am: Exec Bd 1967-68 & 1977; Ukrainian Nats Sport Clb "Tryzub": Exec Bd 1969-70; hon/Acad Achmt in Basic Sci & Gold Medal, Drexel Univ; Outstg Performance Awd, N Div, Naval Facilities Engrg Command, USN.

BORKAN, WILLIAM NOAH oc/Manager; b/Apr 29, 1956; h/3031 Prairie Ave, Miami Bch, FL 33140; ba/Miami, FL; p/Martin and Annabelle Borkan, MB; ed/BSEE 1977; pa/Mgr Electronic Diagnostics Inc N Am Biols 1978-; Design Engr Borktronics 1974-; Chief Design Engr Lumonics 1974-; Mgmt Tech Electronics 1976;

Num Other Past Positions; Am Assn Advmt Scis; Am Soc Heating & Refrigeration Engrs; Assn Energy Engrs; Soc Automotive Engrs; Delta Tau Delta; hon/W/W: S&SW; Am Cols & Univs; Num Patents.

BORMAN, IRIS oc/Medical Systems Specialist; b/Dec 14, 1943; h/132 Jane St, Englewood, NJ 07631; ba/New Hyde Park, NY; p/Murray and Shirley Greenberg Borman, E'wood; ed/Att'd Adelphi Col & Queens Col; pa/Conslt Ultrasound & Echocardiographic Sys Picker Corp 1976-; Med Sys Conslt Cardiac Monitoring Equipmt & Pacemakers Med Sys Div Gen Elect Co 1971-76; NE Reg Mgr Bio-Dynamics Inc 1968-71; Mycoplasma Reschr Supr Lab Kidney Transplants NYU Sch Med 1966-68; Technologist N Shore Hosp & Med Ctr NYC 1964-66; Contbr Num Articles Med Pubs; AAAS; Am Soc Microbiology; Intl Platform Assn; cp/Ft Lee Vol Ambulance Corps; Dem; r/Jewish; hon/W/W Am Wom.

BORRA, RANJAN oc/Communication Specialist; b/Oct 25; h/2705 Easton St, Hillcrest Hgts, MD 20031; ba/Wash, DC; m/Labanya; p/I N and Hemangini Borra; ed/BA Am Univ; MA Univ Md; pa/Area Communs Spec Lib Cong; Org & Participation Confs & Sems; Contbr Num Profl Jours; cp/Orgr Socio-Polit Groups; r/Hindu; hon/Son of Sub-Continent Awd, S Asia Sem.

BORSI, PETER N oc/Tele-Communications Specialist & Consultant; Historian; Museum Curator; b/May 2, 1916; h/111 N Alder Ave, Sterling, VA 22170; m/Grace; c/Frank, John, David; p/Joseph Borsi (dec); Teresa Henninger Borsi; ed/Cert Broadcast Engr/Communs Univ Wis-M 1937; Cert TV, Facsimile, Micro-Waves Grad Sch, Technol Inst, NWn Univ 1953; mil/AUS Army Signal Corps & Army Air Corps; pa/Curator/Lectr Telecommuns Mus, Lord Fairfax & No Va Commun Cols, etc; Sr Mem IEEE; Assoc-Conslt: Nat, DC Soc of Profl Engrs, Nat Def & Emergency Communs Resources, Others; Nat Assn Govt Communicators; Am Security Coun Foun; Coalition for Peace Through Strength; Assn Former Intell Ofcrs; Spec Forces Clb; Fairfax Co Coor Engrg Bd;

Smithsonian Instn Assn; Nat Ret'd Tchrs Assn; Radio Intell Div Assn; Antique Wireless Ass; cp/Bd Dirs Sterling Area Citizens Assn, Area Rep, Exec Secy 1973-74; Secy Leag for Constitutional Justice; Secy, Sub-Com Chm: Emergency Asst Com; Adv Coun Sci Ctr No Va Commun Col; Employees Rep & Advr Nat Fdn Fed Employees; Conslt & Advr Am Legion Boys St Americanism Com; Publicity & Public Relats Coor: Randolph-Macon Acad, Linton Hall Mil Acad, Other Ednl & Cult Instns; Am Revolution Bicent Assn; Am Legion; Disabled Am Vets; 4-H Clbs; Am Platform Assn; Former Positions w: PTA, BSA, Nat Chds Rehab Ctr; Rec Coun Co of Loudoun, Others; r/St Josephs Ch Com Mem; Activs Vol Chm; hon/Notable Ams of Bicent Era; POS; Nat Social Dir; DIB; "Old Timers" & "Old Old Timers" Recog Cits; Goodwill Ind Awd of Merit Cert; BSA Plaque Awd 1971; St Josephs Ct Cert for Com Work, etc; Am Bicent Prog Chm Awd; Pub'd Author; Num Others.

BORTHICK, MAVIS ARY oc/Counselor; b/Nov 21, 1914; h/613 Crestview Dr, Springfield, TN 37172; ba/Greenbrier, TN; m/Joseph William (dec); c/Joary B Hampton, Alice; p/Elbert Ary (dec); Eugenia Harder

Ary, Linden, TN; ed/BS MTSU 1939; MA Peabody 1956; Addit Studies; pa/Guid Cnslr Greenbrier Elem Sch 1970-; Conslt Sp Ed Robertson Co Schs 1975-79; Contbr Jour; RCEA; NEA; TEA; MTEA; APGA; TPGA; TSCA; RCSCA; BPW; cp/Task Force Guid Elem Schs Tenn; r/Missionary Bapt; SS Tchr: Red River Bapt Ch 1947-52, Spring Bapt Ch 1965-67; hon/BPW Wom of Yr; Cert Outstg Work, Field Enterprise Ed Corp; 1 of 4 Oustg Edrs, Robertson Co Schs; Grant Career Ed Wkshop.

BORTZ, LIBBY JOFFE oc/Social Worker; Educator; b/May 30, 1934; h/10 Lindenwood Dr, Littleton, CO 80120; ba/L'ton; m/Alan; c/Richard, Patricia; p/Morris Joffe (dec); Sarah Joffe, Miami Bch, FL; ed/BS Univ Mich 1957; MSW Univ Denver 1967; pa/Psychi Social Wkr; Pvt Pract Cnslg; Instr Arapahoe Commun Col; Conslt; Acad Cert'd SW; cp/Chperson: L'ton Housing Auth, Woms Resource Ctr; Pres Arapahoe Commun Col Governing Coun; U Way Governing Bd; r/Jewish; hon/F'ship Nat Inst Mtl Hlth; Outstg Citizen L'ton; W/W Am Wom.

BORUM, ELIZABETH ANN oc/Psychologist; b/May 4, 1930; h/1830 Lakeshore #304, Oakland, CA 94606; ba/Concord, CA; p/John Borum (dec); Helen Sheedy Borum, Oakland; ed/BA honors 1951, MA 1953 Univ Cal-B; pa/Am Acad Polit & Social Scis; Am Assn Advmt Sci; Soc Psychol Study Social Issues; Psychol Assns: Wn, Am Correctional, Am, Treas Bay Area Coun, Past Pres Contra

Costa Co, Task Force Reorg Cal St; cp/Pres E Bay Chapt People to People; Treas UN Assn; Past Pres Bus & Profl Woms Clb Berkeley; B'ley Mayors Bicent Com; Oakland Mus Assn; Am Civil Liberties Union; World Federalists Assn; r/Past Chm W Coast Coun Ethical Cult; Past Pres Bay Area F'ship Ethical Cult; Secy Yg Mens Christian Assn; hon/Fremont & Anchor Poetry Awds; Meritorious Ser, Bus & Profl Woms Clb.

BOSWORTH, MARGARET WAMSLEY oc/Educator; b/Jul 12, 1918; h/5 Sonora Dr, Pasadena, MD 21122; ba/Glen Burnie, MD; m/Charles Ebbert; c/David, Deborah; p/David and Mary Wamsley (dec); ed/AB Davis Elkins Col; Postgrad Studies; pa/Hearing Impaired Resource Tchr Oakwood Elem Sch; Conv Am Instr Deaf; NEA; Md & Anne Arundel Co Tchrs Assns; cp/TRIPOD; OES; Dem; r/Presb: Elder, Chm Worship Com; Past Pres Presb Woms Org; hon/W/W: Am Wom, E; Personalities S; Dict Intl Biog.

BOTT, HARVEY JOHN oc/Artist; b/Dec 28, 1933; h/5400 Meml Dr, Drawer 72, Houston, TX 77007; ba/Atlanta, GA; m/Margaret Deats; c/Gretchen LaVonna; p/John and Linda Dill Bott, San Antonio, TX; ed/BS; BFA; MS; MFA; MBK; Addit Studies; mil/AUS Counter Intell Corps Ed Spec & Propaganda Writer 1953-56; pa/Art Conslt Joint Art Ventures Inc 1976-; Art Therapy & Rehab Conslt Gulf Coast Reg Mtl Retardation Ctr 1973-77; Artist-in-Residence Loft-on-Strand 1969-; Chief Modeller Southwell Co 1962-66; Asst Instr Tex Col Arts & Industs 1959-60; Asst Instr Kunstverein Akademie 1955; Num Selected Exhbns incl'g: Bienville Gallery, Amarillo Art Ctr, Dusseldorf Kunsthalle, Alessandra Gallery, Pa Acad Fine Arts, Cal Palace of Legion of Hon, Dallas Mus

Fine Arts, Museen der Stadt, Guild Hall; Num Monographs, Essays & Res Papers; cp/Bd Dirs Houston Artists Equity; Mus Modern Art; Galveston & Tex Hist Foun; Am Civil Liberties Union; Artists Rights Today Inc; Tex Soc Sculptors; So Assn Sculptors; Contemporary Arts Mus; Rotary Intl; Num Other Civic Assns; r/Deist Advocating Evolutionary Humanism; hon/Soc Indust Designers $5000 Awd; Premier les plus Sculpture, Prix de Paris; Mrs Henry C Beck Awd, Dallas Mus Fine Arts; NY Govs Cit 1959; US VP Cits 1962, 64, 66, 67 & 68; Wis Govs City 1967; Tex Govs Cit 1967 & 68; US Pres Cit 1969; National Humanist Tribute, Jewish Voc Ser; Num Others; Recipient Grants & S'ships; Biogl Listings.

BOTT, MARGARET DEATS oc/Director; b/May 27, 1942; h/5400 Meml Drawer 72, Houston, TX 77007; ba/Houston; m/H J; p/Wayne and Margaret Deats, H'ton; ed/Univ H'ton 1964; pa/Dir Info Fed Land Bk H'ton; cp/Hist Foun; Galveston: Arts Coun, Conv & Vistors Bur, Past Bd YWCA; hon/Tex Med Assn Awd Med Reporting; Am Psychol Foun Social Ser Reporting; W/W Am.

BOTTEL, HELEN A oc/Columnist; Author; Lecturer; h/2060-56th Ave, Sacramento, CA 95822; ba/New York, NY; m/Robert; c/Robert, Rodger, Kathryn Bernhardt, Sue Peppers; p/Alpheus and Ellen Alexander Brigden (dec); ed/AA Riverside

Col; Addit Studies; cp/Cosumnes River Col Patrons Clb; Var Commun Ser Orgs Cal & Oreg; r/Presb; hon/Outstg Student Awd, Riverside Col; Govs Cit, Ga; 1st Pl Book *To Teens With Love,* Cal Press Clb; Num Awds Newspaper Feature Stories.

BOTTICHER, WILHELMINA WOTKYNS oc/Retired Microbiologist; b/Jan 14, 1916; h/3151 Mt Veeder Rd, Napa, CA 94558; m/Wilhelm Karl; p/Grosvenor and Wilhelmina Wotkyns (dec); ed/AB 1944, MS 1945 Univ So Cal; pa/Sigma Xi; Am Public Hlth Assn; Soc Med Technologists; cp/Pres Napa Val Chapt CAMLT; r/Prot; hon/Pub'd Author.

BOULTON, GRACE W oc/Homemaker; b/Oct 4, 1926; h/1701 NE 63rd St, Oklahoma City, OK 73111; m/Don C; c/Ann, Scot; p/W T and Grace Johnson Ward (dec); ed/BA Univ Okla; cp/Repub Nat Com-wom Okla; r/Disciples Christ.

BOURKE, GERARD JOSEPH oc/Chaplain; b/Jan 17, 1926; h/2345 E Manoa Rd, Honolulu, HI 96822; ba/Same; p/George Bourke (dec); Kathleen Tierney Bourke, Dublin, Ireland; ed/BA Nat Univ Ireland

1948; Lic Phil Jesuit Philosophate 1951; STL Jesuit Theologate 1958; MSEd 1972, PhD 1976 Fordham Univ; pa/Cath Chaplain Univ Hi & E-W Ctr; Pt-time Lectr Mercy Col 1974-78; Pt-time Cnslr: Mt St Vincent Col 1974-78, Fam Consulation Sers Archdiocese NY 1972-74; Col Chaplain Mt St Vincent Col 1972-78; Num Other Past Positions; APA; Am & Fordham Pers & Guid Assns; r/Cath; Soc Jesus-Jesuit; hon/Kappa Delta Pi; W/W: Rel, E; Pub'd Author.

BOUSLEY, GLORIA DIANA PARRISH oc/Educator; b/Dec 3, 1932; h/PO Box 125, Allendale, IL 62410; ba/Olney, IL; m/Donald; p/Thomas Parrish (dec); Cecilia Armstrong, Evansville, IN; ed/BA Univ E'ville 1953; MS Ind Univ 1958; PhD So Ill Univ 1977; pa/Bus Tchr Olney Ctl Col; Chrperson Div Bus & Human Devel; Vol Cnslr: So Ill Mtl Hlth Ctr, Ill Div Voc Rehab; Intl Soc Bus Edrs; Nat

Secys Assn; Am & Ill Voc Assns; Nat, Ill, En Ill & So Ill Bus Ed Assns; Bus & Profl Woms Org; cp/Olney Arts Coun; Past VP & Secy NW Territory Art Guild; Phi Mu; r/St Pauls Meth Ch of Christ; Mem; hon/Nat Ofc Mgmt Awd; Town & Country Awds Paintings; Delta Pi Epsilon; Iota Lambda Sigma; Phi Kappa Phi; Delta Kappa Gamma; Pi Gamma Mu; Pub'd Author; Num Biogl Listings.

BOUTTE, MARGARET ANN oc/Psychologist; b/Dec 22, 1946; h/1317 Jackson St, Mamou, LA 70554; ba/Starkville, MS; p/Charley Boutte (dec); Euna Boutte, Mamou;

ed/BA; MS; pa/Psychologist Ed Psychol Dept Miss St; SE & SW Psychol Assns; Nat Assn Sch Psychologists; r/Cath; hon/W/W: Intl, SW, Am Wom, Worlds Wom; Other Biogl Listings.

BOWDEN, ELIZABETH CHANDLER oc/Civic Leader; b/Jan 10, 1920; h/224 N 17th St, Mayfield, KY 42066; ba/M'field; m/Marion Douglas (dec); c/Elizabeth, Junion; p/Richard and Metta Chandler (dec); ed/BA cum laude Mid Continent Bapt Bible Col; pa/Ser Mil Fams Am Red Cross; cp/Coun Urban Renewal; Pres: M'field Coun Clb Wom, Pres Gtr Paducah Chapt Parents Without Partners; Secy Am Leg Aux; Ky Col; Duchess Paducah; Past Brownie Ldr; Bear Creek Girl Scout Coun; Past Nobie Grand Loyal Rebakah Lodge; Vol Worker Dem Party; r/1st Bapt Ch, M'field; Mem, SS Tchr: hon/Ky Cong Parents & Tchrs; Single Parent of Yr, Parents Without Partners; Gtr Paducah Chapt 1978 & 1979, Mason-Dixon Reg 1978 & 1979; Certs Apprec: M'field-Graves Co U Way, 1st Dist Ky Parents & Tchrs, Graves Co Bicent Com; Nat Deans List.

BOWEN, DEBORAH H oc/Secretary; b/Aug 26, 1953; h/309 Fulwood Blvd, Tifton, GA 31794; ba/Tifton; m/Cal Jr; c/Austin; p/John and Joyce Haman, Sumner, GA; ed/Assoc ABAC; pa/Secy St Dept Ed; Alpha Beta Gamma; cp/Pres Rosewood Garden Clb; r/Bapt; hon/ABAC: Fellow, "Miss Bus Exec", Hon Student.

BOWEN, ERNEST THOMAS HARRISON III oc/Priest; b/Nov 10, 1945; h/PO Box 812, Abbeville, SC 29620; ba/Same; p/Ernest II and Alma Stefanilo Bowen, Santa Monica, CA; ed/BA St Marys Col 1967; pa/Rom Cath Priest Sacred Heart Cath Ch; Pres McCormick Co Min Assn; Greenville Deanery Diocese Charleston: Voc Rep, Rep Priests Senate;

cp/Bd Dirs & Chaplain Rotary Clb; Chm Bd A'ville JCs; Chaplain Foothills CB Clb; r/Rom Cath; hon/Pres Awd, A'ville Rotary Clb; Outstg Accomplishment, US JCs; A'ville JCs: Dist'd Ser Awd, JC of Yr; SC JCs: Outstg Prog Dir, Outstg Local Pres, Faith in God Awd; K of C Coun: K of Mo, K of Qtr, Catholicity Awd; Pub'd Author; Num Biogl Listings.

BOWEN, MILDRED HAZEL oc/Farmer; Rancher; b/Nov 26; h/Antelope, TX 76350; m/Earl; c/Mary Jo Earline, Henry; p/James Frank; Mary Elmery; r/Bapt; hon/-Commonwealth Pa; St of Tex.

BOWEN, OTIS RAY oc/Governor; b/Feb 26, 1918; h/Bremen, IN 46506; ba/Indianapolis, IN; m/Elizabeth Steinmann; c/Rick, Judy, Tim, Rob; p/Vernie and Pearl Wright Bowen, Leiters Ford, IN; ed/AB Ind Univ 1939; MD Ind Univ Med Sch 1942; mil/Army Med Corps Capt Pacific Theater & Okinawa Campaign 1943-46; pa/Pvt Pract Med Bremen 1946-72; Former Staff: Bremen Commun, Parkview, St Josephs S Bend, St Josephs Mishawaka & Meml Hosp; Am & Ind St Med Assns; Ind Mtl Hlth Assn; cp/Chm Rep Gov Assn 1978-79; Exec Com Nat Gov Assn 1978-79; Exec Com Coun St Govts 1977-78; Chm Ed Com of Sts 1977-78; Com Fed Paperwork; Pres Com Sci & Tech; Adv Com Intergov Rel; Num Other Polit Positions; C of C; Am Leg; VFW; Kiwanis; Farm Bur; Alpha Omega Alpha; Phi Beta Pi; Delta Chi; Bd Trustees: Valparaiso Univ, Ancilla Col; Bd Dir Ctr Public Ser Anderson Col; r/St Pauls Luth Ch, Bremen; Past VP Congreg, Chm Bd Fin, Luth Ch Sch Bd; Indpls Chapt F'ship Christian Aths; hon/Merit Awd, Ind Public Hlth Assn; Alumnus of Yr, Ind Univ Sch Med; Dr Benjamin Rush Awd, AMA; Dist'd Ser Awd, FFA; Outstg Public Admr, Ind Soc Public Admrs; Num Hon Degs; Pub'd Author.

BOWER, TRUE GEHMAN oc/Retired Media Specialist; Librarian; Educator; b/Oct 17, 1916; h/8205 Wales Ave NW, N Canton, OH 44720; ba/Same; m/Aaron; c/Howard, Miriam B Poorman; p/Edwin and Daisy Waltz Gehman (dec); ed/AB Otterbein Col 1938; MSLS Case Wn Resv Univ 1953; r/Unity Ch; hon/Grant, HEA Act 1968; W/W: Am Wom, Worlds Wom; Dic Intl Biog; Nat Register Prominent Ams & Intl Notables; Foremost Wom Commun.

BOWERS, FAUBION oc/Writer; TV Producer; b/Jan 29, 1917; h/205 E 94, New York City, NY 10028; c/Jai; ed/Columbia Univ; Universite de Poitiers; mil/Major; pa/Author 12 Books; Prodr 30 TV Cult Progs CBS-TV; hon/Bronze Star; Oak Leaf Cluster.

BOWERS, SHARON FAYE oc/Manager; b/Jun 9, 1954; h/523 N Washington Ave, Cookeville, TN 38501; ba/C'ville; p/Lois Bowers, Alcoa, TN; ed/BS; pa/Stores Sales Mgr Pic'N Pay Inc; NEA; TEA; BCEA; r/1st Bapt Ch, C'ville.

BOWLES, DAVID STANLEY oc/Educator; b/Jun 30, 1949; h/1342 E 60 S, Logan, UT 84321; ba/Logan; m/Valerie; c/Penny-Anne, Simon; p/Stanley and Elsie Bowles, Upminster, Essex, UK; ed/BSc honors; PhD; pa/Res Asst Prof Utah Water Res Lab Utah St Univ; Instn Civil Engrs London; ASCE; Reviewer Water Resources Res AGU; AWRA: Chm Tech Prog, Reviewer Water Resources Bultn; Conslt Govt & Indust; r/Christian; Bapt; hon/Outstg Yg Man Am 1978; Pub'd Author.

BOWLES, HAZEL ELIZABETH oc/Educator; b/Feb 22, 1930; h/224 W S St, Jackson, MI 49203; ba/Jackson; m/Harry; c/Kipp, Lezlie B Sisson; p/George and Henrietta Patton, Asheville, NC; ed/BS; pa/Tchr Elem Grade 1; Mich Ed Assn; cp/Cancer Dr; Martin Luther King Jr S'ship Fund; Jackson Voguette Clb; Num Coms; Vol Work; r/U Peoples Ch; hon/Outstg Ldrs Elem & Sec'dy Ed; Notable Ams Awd.

BOWLING, FRANKLIN LEE oc/Physician; Pharmacist; Educator; Musician; b/Nov 2, 1909; h/1001 E Oxford Ln, Englewood, CO 80110; ba/Same; m/Ruth; c/Franklin Jr, William, Allen; p/(dec); ed/PhC, BS, MD Univ Colo; MS Univ Denver; MPH Harvard Univ; mil/USAF Col & Chief Flight Surg Med

Corps Ret'd 1967; Insp Gen 1952-55; Surg Gen 1961-66; Epidemiological Bd 1961-66; pa/Med Dir Colo St Govt 1967-74; Am Fdn Musicians; Secy-Treas & Past Pres Intl Hlth Soc; US Pharmacopeial Conv; Past Pres Fed Med Dirs; Fdr & Org Dir Nat Intercollegiate Bands; hon/Dist'd Ser Music Awd; Kappa Kappa Psi; Tau Beta Sigma.

BOWMAN, GEORGIANA HOOD oc/University Administrator; b/Jan 19, 1937; h/2671 Cleveland Ave, Columbus, OH 43211; ba/C'bus; m/Harris Claude; p/George Hood Sr (dec); Corinne Hunter Hood, Middletown, OH; ed/BSEd Wilberforce Univ 1965; MA 1973, PhD 1976 Ohio St Univ; pa/OSU: Coor Black Student Progs 1974-, Advr Num Student Orgs, Comm Minorities & Wom, Adv Com

Affirmative Action; Tchr C'bus Public Schs 1967-74; cp/Pres Nat Coun Negro Wom; Bd Dirs: Urban Leag, YWCA, Southside Settlement House; NAACP; Metro Dem Woms Clb; Pi Lambda Theta; Phi Delta Kappa; Cand C'bus Bd Ed; r/Prot;

hon/WCOL Black Spectrum Awd; Ser Awds: Delta Sigma Theta, Alpha Kappa Alpha, NAACP, Afro-Am; OSU Black Student Ch Awd.

BOWMAN, JOSEPH E JR oc/Media Specialist; Lecturer; b/May 22, 1950; h/PO Box 203, Brooklyn, NY 11213; ba/Schenectady, NY; p/Joseph and Violetto Bowman, Bklyn; ed/BA; MA; MLS; pa/Free-Lance

Prodr-Dir; Photog; Burund African Dance/Drum Troupe; NAACP; r/Christian; hon/NAACP; Outstg Achmt W/W Black Ams; Commun Ldrs & Noteworthy Ams; Men Achmt Intl Biogl Centre.

BOYCE, EMILY STEWART oc/Professor; b/Aug 18, 1933; h/1609 Sulgrave Rd, Greenville, NC 27834; ba/G'ville; p/Harry Boyce (dec); May Fallon Boyce, Rich Sq, NC; ed/BS, MA East Carolina Univ; MLS Univ NC-CH; pa/Prof Dept Lib Sci ECU; NC St Dept Public Instr; Spkr; Conslt So Assn Cols & Schs; Nat Org Wom; Num Profl Assns; cp/Leag Wom Voters; Pitt Co Humane Soc; Bd Dirs Wicker & Wood; r/Meth; hon/Beta Phi Mu; Phi Kappa Phi.

BOYCE, MONICA PLAXCO oc/Author; Instructor; b/Feb 18, 1893; h/Box 146 Colonial Lodge, Warrenton, NC 27589; ba/Same; m/J H (dec); c/James Jr; p/W A and Mary Whiteside Plaxco (dec); ed/AB Erskine Col 1914; pa/Owner & Editor Poetry Mag 1975-; Instr Poetry Technique; Author 4 Books Poetry & Num Articles; Former Tchr Piano Music; hon/US Savs Bond, Clover Press; 1st Pl Am-Eng Competition Poetry; Best of 7 Yrs Pub'd, Lanterne Form; Awd, Sidney Lanier Sonnet; 2000 Wom Achmt; Intl W/W Poetry; Other Biogl Listings.

BOYD, JULIA MARGARET oc/Church Leader; b/Mar 7, 1921; h/PO Box 455, Mt Olive, NC 28365; m/Shelton; c/Mary Bevan Berdine, Deborah Pearson; p/Isaiah and Mary Blackman Tart (dec); ed/BS East Carolina Univ; r/U Meth; Pres UMW 1st U Meth Ch, Mt Olive; Goldsboro Dist: Pres UMW, Coor Yth Min; Dist Coun Mins; NC Conf Coun Min & Yth Min; NC Conf Bd Ed; hon/W/W: Rel, Worlds Wom; Dic Intl Biog; Notable Ams; Personalities S.

BOYD, RANDALL oc/Lawyer; Banker; b/Jul 7, 1900; h/326-A Avenida Carmel, Laguna Hills, CA 92653; m/Jane Ellen; c/John, Harry, Robert; p/Walter and Jennie Denton Boyd (dec); mil/CAP: Lt & Flight Ldr; pa/Dir So Realty Co; Past Dir & Ofcr Bkrs Equipmt Co; Equitable Trust Co; cp/Former Dir Saddleback Commun Hosp; LA Ext Co; Yosemite Mtn Ranch Ltd; Golden Rain Foun; Lung Assn Orange Co; r/Presb: Elder.

BOYD, RODNEY CARNEY oc/Professor; Musician; b/Sept 27, 1943; h/2715 SW 19th, Topeka, KS 66604; ba/Topeka; m/Sylvia Louise Kendrick; p/Victor Boyd, Baton Rouge, LA; Ora Nell Causey (dec); ed/BME; MS; DMA Cand Boston Univ; pa/Prof Music Washburn Univ; Solo Bassoonist Topeka Symph Orch; Washburn Arts Quintet; Recitals Throughout E, S & MW; r/Meth; hon/2 F'ships; Berkshire Music Ctr.

BOYD, SALLIE McFERREN oc/Educator; b/May 11, 1924; h/2191 S Pkwy E, Memphis, TN 38114; ba/M'phis; c/Brenda Durham, Marilyn; p/Eugene McFerren (dec);

Estella McFerren, M'phis; ed/BS Lane Col 1969; pa/M'phis Public Sch Tchr; Nat, Tenn, W Tenn & M'phis Ed Assns; cp/Past Secy-Treas Cooper Pkwy Home Owners Assn; NAACP; GSA Scout Ldr; r/Mt Pisgah CME Ch: Mem, Cnslr; BR Danner Clb; hon/M'phis City Beautiful Comm Cert; Sch of Mo Contest Judge; Fed Grant Early Childhood Study.

BOYD, WILLIAM SEABORN oc/Physician; b/Sept 19, 1907; h/2315 Laurel Ln, Augusta, GA 30904; ba/Augusta; m/Katherine Elizabeth Kreps; p/William Boyd (dec); Martha Jones Boyd (dec); ed/BS magna cum laude Univ Ga 1932; MA Emory Univ 1934; MD Med Col Ga 1942; mil/USPHS Major Comm'd Ofcrs Corp; pa/Pvt Pract Phys Ob-Gyn; Asst Clin Prof Ob-Gyn Med Col Ga; St Josephs Hosp: Past Chief Ob-Gyn Ser, Past Chief Med Staff, Past Med Dir, Past Bd Trustees; cp/Secy Augusta Symph Leag; Originator & Sponsor William S Boyd Augusta Symph Nat Piano Competition; Past Pres Friends Augusta Lib; Exec Bd Pres Clb Univ Ga; r/Luth; Ch of Resurrection; Former Trustee Lowman Home, Luth Ch Am; hon/Diplomate Am Bd Ob-Gyn; Phi Beta Kappa; Alpha Omega Alpha; Phi Sigma: Outstg Non-Alumnus Awd, Newberry Col.

BOYEA, RUTHE WRIGHT oc/Educator; Director; b/Sept 22, 1918; h/105 Black Rock Ave, New Britain, CT 06052; ba/NB; m/Douglas Paul; c/Ruthe B Boiczyk, Douglas Jr; p/George and Ethel Alward Wright; ed/MS; BS; mil/USNR Ofcr Corps; pa/Ctl Conn St Col: Prof Sch Ed 17 Yrs, Prof Eng Dept 2 Yrs, Dir Woms Ctr 2 Yrs; Former Elem

Sch Tchr; Del Intl Woms Yr Conf; Intl Woms Yr Com; Rep Nat Woms Conf; Conn Ed Assn; AAUP: Exec Bd, Past Secy CCSC; AAUW: Past Pres NB Br, Past VP Conn Div, Chrperson Com Wom St Div; cp/Pres & Bd Dirs Local Leag Wom Voters; Bd Dirs Burritt Savs Bk; Commr Human Sers St Conn; r/Christian Prot; hon/Outstg Elem Tchr; F'ship AAUW.

BOYER, THEODORE STANLEY oc/Director; b/Sept 7, 1945; h/11322 Leesburg Pl, Louisville, KY 40222; ba/L'ville; m/Doris Pauline; c/Scott; p/Theodore Sr and Frances Boyer, Philadelphia, PA; ed/BS; MBA; EdS Cand; pa/Dir Fin Univ L'ville Dental Sch; Behavioral Sci & Fin Ofcrs Sects AADS; cp/Bd L'ville Am Red Cross; r/Cath; hon/Achmt Awd, Am Red Cross; Order Ky Cols; Intl Biogl Dic; Men Achmt; W/W S&SW; Personalities S.

BOYETTE, ROBERT E oc/Minister; Clergyman; b/May 24, 1917; h/11991-68th Ave N, Seminole, FL 33542; ba/Bay Pines, FL; m/Gladys; p/William Boyette (dec); Hettie Boyette, Meridian, MS; ed/BA; MDiv; MA; mil/European Theater WW-II 4½ Yrs; pa/Chaplain Vets Adm; APHA; Mil Chaplains Assn; Bd Dirs Assoc'd Cos; cp/Kiwanis Clb; Dem; r/Ch of God, Anderson, Ind; hon/Fellow Col Chaplains.

BOYKIN, JOHN WYANT oc/Professional Golfer; b/Jun 27, 1952; h/PO Box 919, Greenwood, SC 29646; ba/Same; m/Sandra; c/Daniel, Benjamin; p/R R and Geraldine Boykin, Savannah, GA; pa/Profl Golfers Assn Am; cp/Key Clb Intl: Lt Gov Ga Dist, Nom'd Intl Trustee; Soloist Savannah Symph

Orch; r/Main St Meth Ch, Greenwood; hon/Awd St Talent Contest, Ga Key Clb Conv; All-Conf Golf Team, NAIA; Outstg Col Aths Am.

BOYKIN, LORRAINE STITH oc/Nutritionist; b/Feb 1, 1931; h/1126 Tiffany Rd, Silver Spring, MD 20904; ba/Bethesda, MD; p/Benjamin Stith Jr (dec); Mabel Archer Stith, Creive, VA; ed/BS Va St Col 1951; MS 1954; MA NYU 1954; MA LIU 1964; EdD 1970; PhD; pa/Expert Nutrition Nat Inst Hlth; Former Asst Prof Hunter Col 1967-70; Tchr Home Ec NYC Bd Ed 1964-65; Nutritionist Clin NYC Dept Hlth 1960-64; Pratt Inst; Instr 1963-68, Asst Prof 1968-70; Other Past Positions; NYC Assn

Public Hlth Nutritionists; Am Dietetic Assn; NY St & Gtr NY Dietetic Assns; Assn Tchr Preven Med; Food & Nutrition Coun; Am Home Ec Assn; NYC Sch Home Ec; AAUW; AAUP; Inst Participant Intercult Communs; Am Acad Polit & Social Sci; Inst Food Tech; Kappa Delta Pi; Phi Chi; Pi Lambda Theta; Pi Gamma Mu; Delta Sigma Theta; Alpha Kappa Mu; Lambda Kappa Mu; cp/Evang Deaconess Hosp; Anti-Poverty Prog; Pres E Harlem & Chm Bklyn Nutrition Coms; r/Prot; hon/Awd Excell Tchg 1962; Fellow: AAAS; NY Acad Med; Am Public Hlth Assn; Royal Soc Hlth Eng.

BOYLE, PAUL MICHAEL oc/Catholic Priest; b/May 28, 1926; h/5700 N Harlem Ave, Chicago, IL 60631; ba/Rome, Italy;

p/Bartley and Mary Roche Boyle, Detroit, MI; ed/STD; JCD; pa/Superior Gen Congreg of Passion; r/Rom Cath; hon/Man of Yr, Canon Law Soc Am 1976.

BOYNTON, IRENE RUTH oc/Community Leader; b/Aug 11, 1908; h/3915 Texas, Vernon, TX 76384; m/Charles; c/Louis, Bobby, Marquita B Wright; p/Allan and

Gussie Connell Williams (dec); cp/Bus & Profl Woms Clb; Former Pres Wilbarger Co Woms Forum; Tex Fdn Woms Clb: Pres, 2nd & 3rd VP, Safety Chm; Vernon Garden Clb: Past Pres, Chm Ch Gardens Dist II Tex Garden Clbs Inc; Chaplain & Secy Am Leg Aux; Wilbarger Gen Hosp Aux; Sorosis Clb: Conserv Chm, Hands Up Prog Chm; Former Pres & VP Farmers Val Home Demo Clb; Election Precnt Wkr; r/1st Bapt Ch: Sr Adult Choir, Secy & Treas SS Class; hon/Blue Ribbon, Dist Conv Tex Fdn Woms Clb; Vernon Garden Clb: Blue Ribbons Flower Shows, Tri-Color Awds, 1st Pl Pres Report Dist II & St Tex Garden Clbs Inc.

BRACEWELL, MERVELL WINZER oc/Educator; b/Oct 21, 1927; h/1337 Rapides Dr, New Orleans, LA 70122; ba/NO; m/P J Jr; c/Jennifer; p/Charlie and Elvia Major Winzer, Homer, LA; ed/BSN Adelphi Univ 1957; MSN Cath Univ 1963; DPH John Hopkins Univ 1975; mil/USAF Nurse Corps 1 Lt 1954-56; pa/Prof Nsg La St Med Ctr Sch Nsg 1979-; Chm Div Nsg Dillard Univ 1973-79; NIH Fellow John Hopkins Univ Sch Public Hlth

1970-73; Nsg Instr Los Angeles Co Med Ctr Sch Nsg 1969-70; Dir Sch Nsg Firestone Med Ctr 1962-68; Other Past Positions; Nat & S La Leag Nsg; Nat Assn Woms Deans, Admrs & Cnslrs; Am Nurses Assn; Chi Eta Phi; cp/Repub; Adv Bd Cont'g Ed NO Public Schs; Steering Com: 1st Govs Conf La Wom, Govs 2nd Annual Conf Aging; Trustee Miss Indsl Col; r/Meth; hon/Freedmens Hosp Sch Nsg Alumni; USAF-NC; W/W Hlt Care.

BRADBURY, LYNN ALLEN oc/Minister; b/Nov 8, 1945; h/412 Front St, Vanceburg, KY 41179; ba/V'burg; m/Patricia Sue Brill; c/Keith; p/Dohn Bradbury (dec); Mildred Alexander, Chrisman, IL; ed/SLB Cincinnati Bible Sem; pa/Radio Devotions; cp/Lewis Co Min Assn; Sportsman Assn; r/Chs of Christ; Christian Chs; hon/Commun Ldrs & Noteworthy Ams; Personalities S; W/W Rel; Dic Intl Biog; Nom'd Men Achmt.

BRADDOX, MIAMAH MIETTA oc/Systems Analyst; b/Aug 1, 1952; h/1800 Greenwich Woods Dr #11, Silver Springs, MD 20903; ba/Wash, DC; m/Roy Lee; p/Stephen Tolbert (dec); Betty Carter, Monrovia, Liberia; ed/BA Harvard Univ 1973; pa/Staff Asst Sys Analyst Cannon House Ofc Bldg; cp/Tex St Soc; r/Cath; hon/Nat Achmt Scholar; Num Music Awds.

BRADEN, HENRY ENGLISH IV oc/Attorney; Senator; b/Aug 24, 1944; h/2932 Bell St, New Orleans, LA 70119; ba/NO; m/Michele Bordenave; c/Heidi, Remi, Henry V; p/Henry III and Irma Haydel Braden, NO; ed/JD Loyola Univ; pa/ATLA; LTLA; La St Bar Assn; cp/Exec Com Dem Nat Com; r/Rom Cath.

BRADFORD, LOUISE MATHILDE oc/Social Worker; b/Aug 3, 1925; h/5807 Joyce St, Alexandria, LA 71301; ba/A'ria; p/Henry and Ruby Pearson Bradford, A'ria; ed/BS La Tech Univ 1945; MS Columbia Univ 1953; Addit Studies; pa/Dir Social Sers St Marys Tng Sch 1978-; Adjunct Asst Prof Sociol La Col 1970-; La Fam Sers Soc; Social Sers Conslt 1966-78, St Conslt Day Care 1963-66, Child Wel Conslt 1959-63, Chds Case Supvr 1957-59; Others; Intl Coun Social Wel; Nat Assn Social Wkrs; Ctr La Pre-Sch Assn;

La Conf Social Wel; SW Reg Planning Com Am Public Wel Assn; So & La Assn Chd Under Six; cp/Former Bd Dirs Cenal Commun Action Com; Lectr Kgn Wkshops; Profl Adv Com Parents Without Partners; Pilot Clb Intl; DAR; Rapides Golf & Country Clb; r/1st U Meth Ch, A'ria; Kgn Com, Adm Bd; hon/Nat Assn Social Wkrs: Social Wkr of Yr Awd Ctl La Br 1974, Nom'd Nat Social Wkr Yr Awd 1974; Num Biogl Listings.

BRADSHAW, DAVID LEE oc/Professor; Minister; Counselor; b/Jun 8, 1939; h/711 Richardson, Artesia, NM 88210; ba/A'sia; m/LeEtta Marie Crow; c/Lorena, Donna, Davinna, Dwight; p/J H and Cuma Reeves Bradshaw, Oakland, CA; ed/BTh Minn Bible Col; pa/Prof A'sia Christian Col; Pastor Col Ch A'sia; Former Pastor: Med Lodge, Shattuck, Eads, Albert Lea; Student Recruiter: Manhattan Christian Col, A'sia Christian Col; cp/Dir & Bd Yth Camps; Explorer Com Chm BSA; r/Indep Christian Chs.

BRADSHAW, WILBERT CLINTON oc/Engineer; Consultant; b/Dec 6, 1909; h/1465 Harrison, Fresno, CA 93728; ba/Fresno; m/Clarice Buttner; c/John, Wilbert III; ed/BME Univ Mich 1929; pa/Mgmt Conslt & Owner W C Bradshaw Co 1952-; Conslt: Plumbing Heating Cooling Contractors Ctl Cal 1972-, Plumbing Indust Trust Fund 1972-; Secy: Ctl Nev Corp 1977-, Nat Geothermal Corp 1977-; Num Other Past Positions; Am Public Works Assn; Intl Slurry Seal Assn; cp/U Celebral Palsy Assn: Pres Cal 1958-60, Pres Fresno Co 1965-66, VP Nat 1960-72, Bd Dirs; Employmt Handicapped; Chm Cal Govs Com, Pres Com; Adv Coun: Cal Devel Disabilities, Chm Cal Dept Rehab; PTA; Kiwanis Clb; Sunnyside Country Clb; r/1st Congreg Fresno; hon/UCPA: Roger S Firestone Awd, Nat Ser Awd, Cal Humanitarian Ser Awd; Citizen of Yr, Phi Delta Kappa; St Aerie Humanitarian Awd, Order Eagles; Cal St Amateur Handicap Tour Champion 1938; Num Biogl Listings.

BRADY, DALE E oc/Engineer; b/Jan 27, 1943; h/1248 Neelys Bend Rd, Madison, TN 37115; ba/Nashville, TN; m/Phyllis Fern Tracy; c/Tracy, Matthew, Sharon; p/Eugene and Lillie Matthews Brady, Nebo, MO; ed/BS Mo Sch Mines 1966; MS Univ Tenn-N 1972; Postgrad Studies; pa/Computer Sci & Data Processing; Lectr & Conslt EDP Security and Auditing; Participant Intergovtl Tchg; Reschr; Am Cong Surveying & Mapping; Am Inst Indust Engrs; Assn Sys Mgmt; IEEE; cp/Fdr & Pres El Bus Choritable; r/Temple Bapt Ch: CBE Dir, Deacon, Yth Ldr.

BRADY, EMILY F oc/Specialist; h/PO Box 11, Clinton, NY 13323; p/John and Mary Hefferon Brady (dec); ed/BS cum laude Syracuse Univ; MA; pa/Promoter Study Brazilian Portuguese Lang; Comm'd Brazilian Govt Translate Book Intl Ed for UN; r/Rom Cath; hon/Num Grants incl'g US Ofc Ed, Inst Intl Ed & Dept St.

BRADY, WINIFRED B oc/Director; b/Nov 28, 1933; h/19 Spruce Ave, Bordentown, NJ 08505; ba/Trenton, NJ; m/Richard; p/Percy, Syracuse, NY; Eula (dec); ed/BS; MBA; pa/Dir NJ Job Sers; VP Reg II ASPA; Past St Pres NJ Fdn Bus & Profl Wom Inc; cp/Soroptimists Intl Inc; People to People Intl; Former Chair Burlington Adv Bd Status Wom; hon/Fellow US Civil Ser Comm.

BRAFFORD, WILLIAM C oc/Secretary; b/Aug 7, 1932; h/10 Fairfield Ln, Doylestown, PA 18901; ba/Trevose, PA; m/Katherine; c/William III, David; p/William Brafford (dec); Minnie Brafford, Pikeville, KY; ed/JD Univ Ky 1957; LLM F'ship Univ Ill 1958; mil/USA Counter-Intell 1st Lt 1954-56; pa/Secy & Gen Cnslr Betz Labs Inc; Am Soc Corporate Secys; Am, Ky, Ga, Pa & Ohio Bar Assns; US Superior Ct; r/Presb.

BRAGG, DENNIS W oc/Computer Scientist; b/Oct 13, 1946; h/6316 Loud Dr, Oscoda, MI 48750; ba/Same; m/Katherine; p/George Bragg Sr (dec); Delza Bethel Bragg, Orcutt, CA; ed/MBA San Diego St Univ 1978; BS Pepperdine Univ 1968; mil/USNA Lt; pa/Assn Computing Machinery; Data Processing Mgmt Assn; IEEE; r/Prot; hon/Sigma Alpha; Sigma Iota Epsilon; Beta Gamma Sigma; W/W: W, Am.

BRAKE, ZENOBIA S oc/Educator; Artist; Poet; b/Sept 16, 1902; h/2104 N Cal St, Stockton, CA 95204; c/Mary Ann Poletti; p/P E Sr and Myrtle Butler Schow (dec); ed/BA, MA Univ Tex; pa/1 Wom Shows; Juror Art Shows; CTA; NRTA; BAC; Pres Nat Leag Am Pen Wom; cp/Stockton: Art Leag, Fine Arts Gallery; Repub; hon/2 Awds Poetry; Pub'd Poems.

BRAMBLETT, LARRY R oc/Director; Lecturer; b/Nov 1, 1945; h/165 Citation Ct, Athens, GA 30605; ba/Athens; c/Allison, Jessica; p/H R and Arthelene Bramblett, Cumming, GA; ed/BBA 1967, MBA 1969 Univ Ga; PhD Cand Ga St Univ; pa/Col Bus Adm Univ Ga: Dir Small Bus Devel Ctr 1977-, Head Ext Sers 1975-77, Field Rep Sers 1971-75, Instrnl Supvr Waycross Ctr 1970-71, Instr Waycross Ctr 1969-70; Conslt & Advr Num Orgs & Govt; Chm Nat Univ Ext Assn Bus Indust & Labor Div; Pres Nat Small Bus Devel Assn; hon/"Stay & See Ga Prog Contbn Awd", St of Ga; Nat Univ Ext Assn Awd; Cited Most Widely Known Ser Profl Univ Ga, Citizens Ga; Pub'd Author; Num Biogl Listings.

BRAMWELL, HENRY oc/Judge; b/Sept 3, 1919; h/101 Clark St, Brooklyn, NY 11201; ba/Bklyn; m/Ishbel Brown; p/Henry Bramwell (dec); Florence Elva Bramwell, Bklyn; ed/LLB Bklyn Law Sch 1948; mil/AUS 1941-45; pa/US Dist Judge En Dist NY Appt'd 1974; Judge Civil Ct City NY 1966 & 1969-75; Asst Adm Judge 1974-75; Spec Hearing Ofcr Conscientious Objectors Dept Justice 1965-66; Asst US Atty En Dist NY 1953-61; Fed, Nat, Am, Bklyn & NY St Bar Assns; Inst Judicial Adm; r/Prot.

BRANCH, HIRA E oc/Surgeon; b/Dec 9, 1907; h/1014 Woodside Dr, Flint, MI 48503; ba/Flint; m/Alice; c/Barry, Mark Turpen; p/Edmund and Mable Branch (dec); ed/MD Univ Mich 1932; mil/AUS Resv Lt Col; pa/Ortho Surg; Detroit & Pres Flint Acads Surg; Mich St & Am Med Assns; Mich Ortho Soc; Detroit Acad Ortho; Clin Ortho Surg; Am Acad Surg; Societe Internationale De Chirugee Ortho et De Tramatoligie; cp/Rotary Clb; Chm Bd Med Care Ctrs Inc; hon/Fellow Intl & Am Cols Surgs; Diplomate Am Bd Ortho Surg; Liberty Bell Awd, Law Day; Cert Humanitarian Ser Awd, AMA; Med Cert Apprec Sers; Cit House Rep, US Cong; Cit & AUS Commend Ribbon.

BRANCH, FRANCES CHRISTIAN oc/Artist; b/Feb 7, 1901; h/111 Washington Ave, Charlottesville, VA 22903; c/John Sibley, Eugene Dew; p/John B and Lucille Sibley Christian; ed/BFA; mil/Maj WAC; pa/Portrait Painter, Collection incls: 1st Black Mayor, 1st Wom Mayor, 1st Black Student to enter Univ of Va, 1st Black to graduate from Univ of Va Law Sch, 1st Wom Grad of Univ of Va Law Sch, Others; Hon Exhbn, Cultural Dept of Mexican Nat Govt 1959; AAUW; CWU; cp/NAACP; FOCUS; DAR; Soroptimist Intl C'ville Albemarle Arts Assn; Am Leg Post 74; Cross of Nails, Friends of Alderman Lib; Mus of Fine Arts (Richmond); r/Epis; hon/Mother of Yr, USCPFA; Valiant Wom; AAUW Grant; Others.

BRANDEL, MARY HERMENGILD oc/Educator; b/May 15, 1905; h/15 S Union St, Delaware, OH 43105; ba/D'ware; p/Joseph Brandel (dec); Mary Brandel; ed/BS 1945, MA 1966 En Mich Univ; Addit Studies; pa/Rdg Spec & Tchr St Mary Sch 1972-78; Supvr & Conslt Franciscan Sisters Christian Charity 1969-72; Tchr: Holy Fam Col 1967-71, Prin Wisc & Ohio Schs 1950-68, Wisc & Mich Schs 1924-50; NCEA; NRTA; Ohio Mtl Hlth & Retardation Assn; cp/Bread for World; Am Security Coun; Cath Conf Ohio; r/Cath; Mem Ecumenical Inst & At/One/Ment; Perm Cert Tchg Rel Diocese Columbus; hon/Spec Ed S'ship Awd, Order Alhambra; Joseph P Kennedy Jr NCEA S'ship Awd; Ldrs Am Elem Ed; Outstg Ldrs Elem & Sec'dy Ed; Fdrs Cert, Ctr Intl Security Studies.

BRANDON, INMAN oc/Attorney; b/May 14, 1906; h/3488 Knollwood Dr NW, Atlanta, GA 30305; ba/Atla; m/Louise; c/Louise B Shane, Christopher; p/Morris Brandon (dec); Harriet Frances Inman (dec); ed/AB magna cum laude Univ Ga 1927; LLB Yale Univ 1930; mil/US Nav Resv Lt Cmdr Pacific Theater 1944-45; pa/Pract Law 1930-; Sr Partner Hansell, Post, Brandon & Dorsey; cp/Atla Commun Chest: Pres, Chm Dr; Chm U Appeal; Past Pres Atla Fam Ser Soc; Univ Ga Foun: Trustee Emeritus, Secy & Chm; CoFin Chm St Ctl Repub Com; r/Presb; hon/Univ Ga: Dist'd Alumni Awd, Sphinx; Phi Beta Kappa; Phi Kappa Phi; Phi Delta Phi; Phi Delta Theta.

BRANDSNESS, MARGARET CARSON oc/Consultant; Writer; b/May 15; h/3333 NE 34th St, Fort Lauderdale, FL 33308; ba/FL; m/Peter; c/Maggie Bobb (Mrs Herbert);

p/Robert Carson (dec); Margaret Hale (dec); ed/BA Vassar Col; pa/Travel Conslt; Feature Writer; cp/Fla Symph Soc; Mus of Arts; Friends of Lib; r/Epis; hon/Chicago Advtg Wom of Yr.

BRANHAM, HENRY HAMILTON oc/Administrator; b/Jan 31, 1938; h/1721 Glenview, Alvin, TX 77511; ba/Houston, TX; m/Barbara Lynn; c/Brad, Wade, Mark; p/Henry Branham (dec); Zelma Branham, H'ton; ed/BS SW Tex St Univ 1962; BS Univ H'ton 1968; pa/H'ton Hlth Dept: Asst Chief Water Pollution Control 1978-, Enforcement Chief Air Pollution Control 1967-78; Toxicologist Tex Dept Public Safety 1963-67; Chem Dow Chem Co 1962-63; Am Chem Soc; Am Inst Chem; r/Meth.

BRANNAN, ETHEL FORD oc/Professor; b/May 27, 1911; h/34 Holly Ct W, Pitman, NJ 08071; ba/Glassboro, NJ; m/(dec); p/Thomas and Helen Gooding Ford (dec); ed/BS cum laude 1952, MEd cum laude 1956 Glassboro St Col 1967-78; Prof Univ Buffalo 1965-67; VChrperson World Ed Coun; Conslt Social Studies Public Schs; Other Positions; cp/John Hopkins Hosp Com Friends; NCSS Intl Activs Com & Inter-Nation Exc Clb; UN Assn NJ; Town & Country Woms Clb; r/Meth; hon/Num F'ships; Gold Doct Key Dist'd Ser, Phi Delta Gamma; Kappa Delta Pi; Pi Lambda Theta.

BRANNOCK, DURANT YORK JR oc/Educator; b/Jun 19, 1932; h/205 Holly Ave, Clemson, SC 29631; ba/C'son; p/Durant Sr and Ruth Brannock, C'son; ed/AB Elon Col

1954; AM Duke Univ 1956; mil/USNR Ensign Lt 1956-63; pa/Asst Prof French Dept Langs C'son Univ; Am Assn Tchrs French; S Atl Mod Lang Assn; SC Conf Fgn Lang Tchrs; cp/C'son: Little Theatre, Music Clb; r/C'son U Meth Ch; hon/Fellow Nat Endowment Humanities.

BRANNON, THOMAS J oc/Director; b/Dec 26, 1937; h/14-D Heritage, Columbia, SC 29201; ba/C'bia; m/Sandra Annette Raines; p/J A and Lettie Emory Brannon (dec); ed/AA N Greenville Col 1958; BA Furman Univ 1960; Addit Studies; pa/Dir Public Relats SC Bapt Conv 1965-; Interim Pastor Amelia St Bapt Ch, Orangesburg 1964-65; Dir Public Relats SC St Trade Schs 1961-65; Dir Publicity G'ville Rescue Mission 1959-60; So Bapt Home Mission Bds Pers 1958 & 1961;

cp/Secy SC Chapt SEn Bapt Theol Sem Alumni Assn; Rotarian: Public Relats Chm, Bultn Editor, Student Guests Chm; Newspaper Publicity Coor Good News SC; So Bapt Public Relats Assn: Past Pres, Prog VP, Awds Chm; SBC: Public Relats Adv Com, Hist Soc; Alston-Wilkes Soc; r/So Bapt; hon/So Bapt Public Relats Assn: Awd Exceptl Achmt Total Public Relats Proj 1970 & 1972, Pub Photo Awd, Motion Picture Film Merit Awd, Letterhead Design 2nd Pl; Cert Apprec Press Pers, Alston Wilkes Soc; Outstg Yg Men Am; Pub'd Author.

BRANT, MARGARET G oc/Administrator; b/Sept 22, 1924; h/1237 8th St, Manhattan Bch, CA 90266; ba/Via Torrance, CA; p/Charles and Bessie Brant (dec); ed/Dipl Cal Hosp Sch Nsg; BS Univ So Cal; MS UCLA; Sup Cred Cal St Univ-LA; pa/Assoc Dean Nsg El Camino Col; Am Nsg Assn; Nat Leag Nsg; Assn Cal Commun Col Adm; cp/Am Heart Assn; Hlth Sys Agy; Wn Coun Higher Ed Nsg; Assoc Deg Dir So Cal; Torr Hlth Dist Adv Coun; r/Olivet Luth Ch, Inglewood, Cal; hon/Merit Awd, Am Heart Assn.

BRASCH, WALTER MILTON oc/Journalist; b/Mar 2, 1945; h/1707 S Pleasant Ave, Ontario, CA 91761; ba/Ontario; p/Milton Brasch; Helen Haskin Brasch (dec); ed/AB; MA; PhD; pa/Editor-In-Chief Brasch & Brasch Pubrs Inc; cp/Var Activs; r/Jewish; hon/Press Clb So Cal: Outstg Columnist, 1st Freelance; Mooradian Medal Humanistic Jour; Num Other Writing Awds; Res Grants: Temple Univ, Ohio Univ.

BRASEY, HENRY L oc/Director; Educator; b/Nov 25, 1937; h/3776 Aikenside Ave, Cincinnati, OH 45213; ba/Cinc; m/Anna Burney; c/Darrell, Jennifer; p/(dec); ed/AS 1969; BS 1972; mil/USMCR; pa/Asst

Dir Computer Instrnl Sers; Adjunct Assoc Prof Engrg Sci Univ Cinc; Pres Mid Mgmt Assn; ACM; cp/Ken-Sil Ath Assn; Var Local Campaigns; r/Bapt; hon/Ser Awd, Gothic Lodge.

BRASHEARS, MELVIN RICHARD oc/Scientist; b/Nov 11, 1945; h/332 Lester Ct, Santa Clara, CA 95051; ba/Palo Alto, CA; m/Victoria Lynn Fuqua; c/Robert, Richard; p/Robert and Gail Curtis Dollins Brashears, Perry, MO; ed/PhD, MS, BS Univ Mo; pa/Aerospace Scist Lockheed Missiles & Space Co; Am Inst Aeronautics & Astronautics; Nat Mgmt Assn; Tau Beta Pi; Pi Mu Epsilon; cp/Vol Num YMCA Activs; r/Bapt; hon/NASA F'ship; Nat Sci Foun S'ship; Outstg Yg Men Am; W/W S&SW; Men Achmt.

BRASWELL, J(AMES) RANDALL oc/-Chemist; Director; b/Jul 7, 1926; h/5321 Emily Dr, Columbus, GA 31904; ba/Same; m/Dagmar Enid Santiago; p/James Braswell (dec); Irma Pierson Braswell, C'bus; ed/AB Emory Univ 1948; BS summa cum laude C'bus Col 1972; MS Univ Fla 1974; mil/USNR 1944-46; pa/Royal Crown Cola Co: Mgr Quality Control Sers 1968-70, Dir Quality Control 1965-68, Tech Sers Staff 1949-65; Lab Tech Nehi Corp 1946 & 1949; Lab Asst Chem Dept Emory Univ 1948; Am Chem Soc; AAAS; AIBS; AWWA; Ga Acad Sci; WPCF;

Ga Water Pollution Control Assn; Phi Kappa Phi; cp/Past Pres, VP, Secy, Bd Dirs & Num Chmships C'bus JCs; Alumni Coun C'bus Col; Kiwanis; Bd Dirs Goodwill Indust, U Cerebral Palsy, Gtr Little Leag Baseball, Commun Safety Coun, Youth Craft Shop Inc; Bd Trustees Empty Stocking Fund Inc; Secy & Dir Chattahoochee Investmt Clb; U Givers Campaign; U Way Campaign; r/Bapt; hon/JCs Key Man Awd; Dist'd Ser Awd, C'bus JCs; Spark Plug Awd; Pres Spec Awd; Cit, Bd Dirs C'bus Col Alumni Assn; Cit, Bd Dirs UCP Muscogee Co, Ga Inc; Columbus Man of the Yr 1959; Pub'd Author.

BRAUDE, HERMAN M oc/Lawyer; b/Oct 16, 1939; h/6006 Neilwood Dr, Rockville, MD 20850; ba/Wash, DC; m/Marcey; c/Sherrie, Brett, Sharon; p/Arthur Braude, Brooklyn, NY; Sara Braude (dec); ed/BS Cooper Union 1961; JD Georgetown Univ Law Ctr; pa/Sr Partner Braude, Margulies, Sacks & Rephan; Law Clk US Sr Judge Samuel Whitaker; Editor *Georgetown Law Jour*; Chm Spec Com St & Local Public Contract Law Md Bar Assn; VChm Constrn Law Co Public Contract Sec ABA; hon/Charles Goodman Awd Humanities, Cooper Union.

BRAUDO, MARTIN FREDERICK oc/Financial Analyst; International Treasury; b/Jan 30, 1950; h/361-E Glendare Dr, Winston-Salem, NC 27104; ba/WS; p/J Leonard and Vera Perlstein Braudo, Glencoe, IL; ed/BA cum laude Kalamazoo Col 1971; MBA Univ NC-CH; pa/Former Import-Export Exec; cp/K Clb Alumni Assn; Student Govt K'zoo Col: Pres 1970, VP 1971; Optimist Clb; Soccer Clb; hon/F'ships: Bus Foun, Nat Heart Inst; Winifred Peake Jones Awd; Phi Beta Kappa; Phi Eta Sigma; Rotary Clb Group Exc Participant Austria.

BRAULT, RAYMOND WILFRED oc/Attorney General; b/Jun 10, 1927; h/22 Jefferson St, Helena, MT 59601; ba/Helena;

m/Wanda; c/Alan, Mark, Kelly; p/Armand Brault (dec); Viola Brault, Escondito, CA; ed/LLB; mil/USMC Inf-man; AUS Spec Agt Counter Intell Corps; pa/Spec Asst Atty Gen Mont Dept Agri; Num Law Enforcement Positions; Supreme Ct Mont 1960; US Dist Ct 1961; Interstate Commerce Comm 1963; US Tax Ct 1965; US Supreme Ct 1971; Am Acad Forensic Scis; Acad Paraphychol & Med; Am MENSA Ltd; Intl Assn Identification; Intl Chiefs Police Assn; St Bar Mont; Am, Mont & Wn Mont Bar Assns; Am & Mont Trial Lwyrs Assn; cp/Cub Scout Ldr & Pack Com-man; Boy Scout Com-man; r/Ordained Min; Nat Fdn Spiritual Scis; Var Ch Mins; hon/Dean's List Univ Mont; W/W: West, Intl Intells; Intl Men Achmt.

BRAUNAGEL, HELEN MAY oc/Artist; Author; Speaker; b/Apr 20, 1920; h/9208 Bridlewood #1, San Antonio, TX 78240; ba/Same; m/Henry Alois Jr; c/Jan Bull, Guy Bull; p/Theodore Langewisch (dec); Ethel Boercker, St Louis, MO; ed/BA Otis Art Inst; pa/Asst Brazilian Primitive Painting Exhibit Dept Spanish & Portuguese and Latin Am Ctr UCLA Semana de Arte Moderna Symp; Author *A Way Out Of Maze*; Moderator & Panelist Inst Study Wom Transition; Conslt Hosp Patients; Newspaper Inst Am; Portrait Clb NY; cp/Pres Bay W Commun Asst Homeless Youngsters; r/Luth; hon/Cert Merit, Fac Art Exhibit; Outstg Ser, Audie Murphy Meml Vets Hosp; W/W: Am, S&SW; Personalities W&MW; Intl Dic Arts.

BRAUNSCHWEIGER, HELEN RAYMOND oc/Artist; b/Nov 15, 1895; h/720 S Orange Grove #4, Pasadena, CA 91105; ba/Same; m/Walter (dec); c/Sumner Lapp; p/Clark and Helen Smith Raymond (dec); pa/Num Art Socs Los Angeles Area; cp/Pasadena Arts Coun; LA Chapt Freedoms Foun; r/Epis; hon/Awds: Am Artists Profl Leag, Am Inst Fine Arts, Artists SW & San Gabriel Fine Arts Assn; Degs: FIFA, FAAPL.

BRAXTON, HOWARD McCOY JR oc/Principal; b/Dec 9, 1940; h/903 Montpelier Dr, Greensboro, NC 27410; ba/G'boro; m/Patsy; c/Robert; p/Howard Sr and Leola Brown Braxton, Scotland Neck, NC; ed/AB Guilford Col 1963; MA Appalachian St Univ 1966; EdD UNC-G 1975; mil/USCG Aux; pa/Asst Prin Jackson Jr HS; Staff Com Jr HS Curric Com G'boro Public Schs 1976-77; UNC-G: Curric Com Devel Behavioral Objectives NC Hlth, PE & Rec Col Conf 1973-75; Num Staff Coms; NCAE; NEA; NC Assn Prins-Asst Prins; NASSP; cp/Chm NC St Asst Prins Conf; Bd Dir Pasquotank-Elizabeth City Chapt Am Nat Red Cross; Chm Albemarle Dist First Aid & Water Safety Com; Jr C of C; Albemarle Choral Soc; Guilford Col Vol Fire Dept; r/Starmount Presb Ch, G'boro: Mem; hon/W/W: Am Cols & Univs, Yg Men Am.

BRAZAUSKAS, PIUS oc/Catholic Prist; b/Nov 28, 1905; h/3959 Sheridan, North Bend, OR 97459; ba/Same; p/Pius Brazauskas, Pilviskiai, Lithuania; Katarina

Dispinigaityte, PL; pa/Chaplain Schs & Hosps; Asst Parishes; r/Rom Cath; hon/I and II Prizes Premium Art Oreg.

BRAZIEL, DELANO R oc/Educator; b/Jan 11, 1934; h/Rt 1 Box 359, Pitts, GA 31072; ba/Tifton, GA; m/Barbara; c/Marti, Del, Jim, Leslie; p/James and Estelle Braziel

(dec); ed/BS; MEd; mil/AUS 1956-58; pa/Math Instr Math Dept ABAC; MAA; AAUP; cp/Pres Pitts Civic Assn; CoSponsor Mu Alpha Theta Chapt; r/Meth; hon/Abraham Baldwin Col: Citizenship Awd, Valedictorian, Drama Awd; Univ Ga: Pi Tau Chi, Alpha Zeta, Most Proficient Agri Subjects Awd, Fellow NSF AYI; Auburn Univ: Drama Awd, Fellow NSF SI; Best Display Awd, Flatlanders Arts & Crafts; Men Achmt; Commun Ldrs & Noteworthy Ams.

BREAK, VIRGINIA HUFFMAN oc/Educator; b/Oct 16, 1925; h/308 N Smith, El Dorado, AR 71730; ba/ED; p/Madison Huffman (dec); Jessie Huffman, ED; ed/BA Hendrix Col 1947; MS Univ Ark-F 1953; Postgrad Studies; pa/4th Grade Tchr Retta Brown Elem Sch ED Public Sch Sys 28 Yrs; Unit Contbr Tchr Kit Elem Schs Ark St Dept Ed; Contbr Evolutionary Curric Guide ED Sch Sys; Retta Brown Sch Rep Exec Bds: ED Classroom Tchrs Assn, Ed Assn; Assn Childhood Ed Intl; AAUW; Alpha Phi; Delta Kappa Gamma; Num Other Profl Assns; cp/Champagnolle Chapt DAR: Ch American-ism & DAR Manual Citizenship Com, USA Bicent Com; Henry G Bunn Chapt UDC: VP, Histn, Chm Ed Com, Ch S'ship Com & Correspond'g Secy; S Ark Ballet Assn: Patron, Pres, VP, Bd Dirs, Others; Patron-Sponsor S Ark Symph; Sponsor Little Theatre ED; Beta Sigma Phi: VP, Chm Ways & Means Com, Chm Ser Com, Chm Courtesy Com & Treas; Sev Geneal & Hist Assns; Other Civic Assns; r/1st U Meth Ch, EL: Mem, CoChm & Secy Circle #5 WSCS, SS & VBS Tchr, Open Door SS Class, Pres & Soprano Sect Ldr Adult Choir, CoAuthor Ch Pubs, Music Com.

BREAUX, JOHN B oc/Congressman; b/Mar 1, 1944; h/4912 Kingston, Annandale, VA 22003; ba/Wash, DC; m/Lois Gail Daigle; c/John Jr, William, Elizabeth, Julia; p/Ezra and Katie Breaux; ed/BA Univ SWn La 1964; JD La St Univ 1967; pa/US Cong-man 7th Dist La; House Public Works & Trans Com; House Merch Marine & Fisheries Com; cp/Dem Policy & Steering Com; Demo Res Org; r/Cath.

BRECKEL, SUSANNE oc/Psychologist; b/Nov 9, 1925; h/Blessing Rd Bethlehem Terrace 124, Slingerlands, NY 12159; ba/Albany, NY; ed/BC Salve Regina Col; EdB Cath Tchr Col; MA 1958, PhD 1965 Boston Col; Addit Studies; pa/CoDir & Cnslg Psychologist Consultation Ctr Diocese Albany; Former Dir Psychol Sers & Head Psychol Dept Salve Regina Col; Past Pers Dir 800 Sisters of Mercy; Therapist Col Cnslg Ctrs & Pvt Mtl Hlth Facilities 12 Yrs; Conslt Num Orgs; APA; APGA; Am Soc Adlerian Psychol; Assn Humanistic Psychol; Wom Edrs; Intl Transactional Analysis Assn Inc; Intl Platform Assn; World Future Soc; Nat Assembly Wom Rel; hon/Pub'd Author; W/W: Am, Rel; Am Cath W/W.

BREDLOW, THOMAS GAYLE oc/Designer; Metal Worker; b/Oct 18, 1938; h/3524 N Olive Rd, Tucson, AZ 85719; ba/Tucson; p/Warren and Elizabeth La Ponsa Bredlow, Dallas, TX; ed/BA Tex A&M 1960; mil/Ordnance Corps 1st Lt; pa/Bd Artist Blacksmith Assn N Am; IPA; Guest Instr Arch & Anthropology Univ Ariz; cp/Mtn Oyster Clb; r/Closet Cath; hon/Recipient: Richard Quinnrel "WALLY".

BREIGHNER, HARRY DANIEL SR oc/Writer; b/Feb 27, 1909; h/2627 E La Palma #138, Anaheim, CA 92806; ba/Same; m/Doris Earnestine Sprague; c/H D, Archie, Diana Simmons (Mrs Ralph), Carol Parker (Mrs John); p/Harry and Ada Barber Breighner (dec); ed/USN Med Sch; mil/USN 1926-27; pa/Mayor Clinton 1951-55; Standard Oil Co Dealer 1933-54; Mgr Theaters 1955-56; Mgr Motels 1957-63; cp/Chm All City Events; Chm War Salvage DeWitt Co: Bd WW-II; Bus Men; Clinton Commun HS Bd; Rotary Clb; 32nd Deg Mason; Kiwanian; Past Pres YMCA; r/Christian; hon/Nat Awd WW-II; Writers Awd; Pub'd Author.

BREKKE, ARNOLD oc/Scientist;

Professor; Consultant; b/Jul 31, 1910; h/550 Ashland Ave, St Paul, MN 55102; ba/SP; p/Andrew and Anne Nyhus Brekke, St James, MN; ed/BS w Distns 1942, PhD 1952 Univ Minn; mil/USAF Meteorologist & Climatologist 1942-43; AUS Mil Intell G2 1944-45; pa/Lectr; Prof Metro Commun Col; Prof & Scist: Univ Minn, Univ Cal, Univ Md, Mich St Univ, Normandale Col, Europe; IPA; Ctr Study Presidency; Intl Peace Res Assn; Pres Clb; New Directions; Success Ldrs Spkrs Ser; Intl Order Michael Archangel; Am Security Coun; cp/UN Assn USA; World

Future Soc; Fac Advr Num Student Orgs; Common Cause; Knowledge Resource Contbr Nat Com for Effective Cong NCEC; r/Num Lectures & Panel Discussions Rel Groups & Orgs; hon/Gamma Sigma Delta; Alpha Zeta; Valedictorian Univ Minn; Fellow H S Truman Inst; Am Men Sci; Pub'd Author: *Devel Of Agri Policy, Ideology & Capitalistic Stability & Growth:* Revised Ed, Num Profl Articles; Intl Reg Profiles World Ed; Notable Ams Bicent Era; Honoris Causa K Chevalier Intl Order Michael Archangel; Ct of Hon; Fdrs Cert Grad Ctr Intl Security Studies, Am Security Coun Ed Foun; Fellow ABI; DIB; Book of Hon; Men Achmt; Intl W/W Commun Ser; Other Biogl Listings.

BRELAND, JAMES ANDREW oc/Director; b/Feb 10, 1927; h/200 Sostes Dr, Cleveland, MS 38732; ba/C'land; m/Billie; c/Brenda; p/Luther Breland, Union, MS; Onie Rice Breland (dec); ed/AA; BS; MEd; mil/AUS; pa/Dir Bapt Campus Min Delta St Univ 1951-; Pastor Bapt Chs 1950-51; r/Bapt; hon/Omicron Delta Kappa; W/W Rel.

BRELSFORD, JEANNE KAYE oc/Educator; b/Oct 28, 1943; h/8103 Ivan Reid Dr, Houston, TX 77040; ba/Houston; m/Ronald; p/L B and Williemae Clancy, Mexia, TX; ed/BA; MA; PhD Cand; pa/Fac Div Crim Justice Univ Houston; Acad Crim Justice Scis, Nat Coun Crime & Delinq; Am Bus Woms Assn; Tex Corrections Assn; AAUP; r/Ch of Christ; hon/W/W S&SW; Personalities: Dic Intl Biog; Num Ser Awds.

BRENNAN, RICHARD OLIVER oc/Lecturer; Author; b/Feb 25, 1916; h/9334 Briar Forest, Houston, TX; ba/Houston; m/Gloria Jean; c/Phyllis, Patricia, Michael, Junie, Patrick; p/William Michael and Coraalzora Brennan, Maple Hill, KY; ed/PhG; DO; Md; DPH; pa/Dir, Bellevue Metabolic Clinic; Lectr; Appearances on *Today Show;* Instr: Ks City Col of Osteopathic Med, Ks City Univ of Phys & Surgs, Okla Col of Osteopathic Med; Fdr & Past Pres, Alumni of Ks City Col of Osteopathic Med; Fdr & Past Pres, Tex Soc Gen Practioners; Fdr & Past Pres, Tex Soc Gen Practioners; Fdr & Past Pres, Nat Child Hlth Conf (KC); Fdg Mem, Bd Dirs, Intl Metabolic Soc; Intl Acad Applied Nutrition; Edit Bd: *Jour of Intl Acad Prev Med, Jour of NW Acad Prev Med;* Am Med Writers Assn; Staff Mem, Doctors Hosp (Houston); World Med Assn; Author: *Become Nutrition-Wise, Help for the Loser, Nutrigenetics,* Others; cp/Houston Rotary Clb; Arabian Shrine; r/Meth; hon/Fellow, Am Col GPs in Osteopathic Med & Surg; Fellow, Intl Col Applied Nutrition; Fellow, Intl Acad Prev Med; Fdrs Awd, Intl Acad Prev Med; Miller Biomedical Awd, Prev Med

Pioneer; Commend, City of Los Angeles; Others.

BRENNEMAN, MARY L BLACK oc/-Psychiatrist; b/Oct 14, 1923; h/7505 Whitlock Ave, Playa Del Rey, CA 90291; ba/W Los Angeles, CA; c/Gayne, James, Donna, Heidi; p/George and Laura Dryden Black (dec); ed/MPH Univ Pittsburgh Grad Sch Public Hlth 1956; MD Univ Toronto 1947; pa/Psychi Dir Penny Ln Inst Emotionally Handicapped Teenagers 1974-; Co Psychiatrist Crisis Prog 1973-76; Sch Phys Kaiser Perm Med Group 1957-58; Dir BCG Vaccine Prog 1950-54; Pediatrician Pittsburgh Pub Hlth Dept 1950-57; Psychi Staff: St Johns Hosp, Van Nuys Psychi Hosp, Commun Hosp N Hollywood; Am & S Cal Psychi Assns; LA Soc Adolescent Psychi; cp/Westport Bch Clb; Sieria Clb; Common Cause; Ctr Healing Arts; hon/Moonwalker Res Grant, Chd's Bur HEW; Pub'd Author; W/W: Am Wom, Worlds Wom.

BRENTLEY, MARY DELOIS oc/Payroll Officer; b/Jan 17, 1949; h/1803 E Circle Dr, Pine Bluff, AR 71603; ba/PB; p/Jessie and Lottie Brentley, PB; ed/BS Univ Ark 1971;

MEd; pa/Payroll Dir Univ Ark; Former Math Tchr Merrill Jr HS; Lic'd Real Estate Broker; cp/VP Ja' Da' Lam Des Social & Civic Clb; r/St Peters Cath Ch: Mem.

BRERETON, THOMAS F oc/Professor; b/May 21, 1945; h/112 Lindell, San Antonio, TX 78212; ba/SA; p/John and Lucy Brereton, Bronx, NY; ed/BSFS Georgetown Univ 1967; MRP 1970, PhD 1973 Syracuse Univ; pa/Prof Dept Urban Studies Trinity Univ; Am Inst Planners; cp/Num Vol Positions City SA; hon/Phi Beta Kappa.

BRESLIN, DONALD JOSEPH oc/Physician; b/Mar 16, 1929; h/48 Glen St, Dover, MA 02030; ba/Boston, MA; m/Evalynne Wood; c/Mark Nathaniel, Lisa Karen, Paul Andrew Scott; p/R H Breslin, Toronto, Canada; S T Dobkins, Canton, OH; ed/BA Yale Univ 1946; BA McGill 1950; MD 1954; pa/Asst Prof Clin Med, Harvard Med Sch; Lahey Clin Foun 1966-; Hd Dept of Peripheral Vascular Sect, Mng Editor Bulletin 1975-, Secy of Staff 1970-72; Pvt Pract (Canton) 1961-66; Am Heart Assn; cp/NE United Fund; hon/1st Class Hons, Hons Sci, McGill; Fellow, Mayo Clin; Res Fellow, Royal Postgrad Sch of Med, Hammersmith Hosp (London); Fellow, Am Col Physicians; Diplomate, Bd Internal Med.

BREVETTI, ANNE ANNA oc/Committeewoman; b/Nov 1, 1917; h/221 Waterford Crescent, Delray Bch, FL 33446; ba/Same; m/Vincent; c/Adrianne Reilly (Mrs Richard), Valerie Fiesel (Mrs Richard), Vincent II; p/John D'Addario (dec); Rosaria Varca (dec); ed/Grad NY Police Acad; Num Certs Nat Law Enforcement Acad; pa/Exec Com-wom Palm Bch Co; Corporate Security Mgr Nat Retail Corps; Former Police Reporter: *The Ldr Observer, The Long Isl Post;* Past Aux Policewom Police Dept Aux Forces Sect; Spec Investigator Dept Law; Num Other Profl Positions; Adv Coun USA Small Bus Adm; Adv Bd Am Security Coun; cp/Fdr & Dir Dwight D Eisenhower Repub Clb; Nat Secy Nat Repubs Italian Descent; Nat Fdn Repub Wom; Chm Nat Rep Heritage Groups Coun; Del Num Repub St & Nat Convs; US Senatorial Clb; Repub Party Fla; Repub Nat

Com; Repub Congl Com; Num Other Polit Positions; r/Cath; hon/L B Humanitarian Awd, Pres Borough Queens; Acad Awd, City NY; Dwight D Eisenhower Wom of Yr, Nat Repub Heritage Groups Coun; Nat Public Ser Awd, Repub Nat Com; Fdrs Cert, Ctr Intl Security Studies Am Security Coun Ed Foun; Cert Apprec, Palm Bch Co Bar Assn; Meml Awd, Repub Nat Delegation; Pub'd Author; Num Biogl Listings.

BREWER, SILAS H oc/Optical Physicist; b/Jan 4, 1929; h/524 Bonhill Rd, Los Angeles, CA 90049; ba/LA; m/Jimmie Helen; p/Jesse Brewer, Dallas, TX; Lenora Brewer (dec); ed/BS NWn Univ; Postgrad Studies; pa/Pres PAGOS Corp; Optical Soc: Am & So Cal; Am Inst Physics; Soc Photo-Optical Instrumentation Engrs; r/Meth; hon/Outstg Small Contractor, US Small Bus; 2 Patents.

BREWER, WILMON oc/Author; b/Apr 1, 1895; h/Great Hill, Hingham, MS 02043; ba/Same; m/Katharine More; p/Francis and Augusta Edwards Brewer (dec); ed/AB magna cum laude 1917, AM 1920, PhD 1925 Harvard; DScO Curry Col 1959; mil/Am Expeditionary Force Inf Ser 2nd Lt 1917-19; pa/Pubs: *Dantes Eclogues, About Poetry & Other Matters, Adventures in Verse, New Adventures, Adventures Further, Still More Adventures, Ovids Metamorpphhoeses in European Cult;* Editor *20th Anniversary Volume Am Poetry Assn;* Contbr Num Anthologies; Instr Eng Harvard 1923-24; Lectr Poetry; Cape Cod Writers Conf, Cooper Hill Conf; Pres Am Poetry Assn; Boston Authors Clb; cp/Dir & Past Sec Hingham Public Lib; r/Unitarian; 1st Parish, Hingham: Chm Parish Com; hon/Rhyme 'n' Rhythm Awd, Woodbury Room Harvard; Purple Heart; Accolade.

BREWSTER, ETHEL H oc/Public Official; b/Jul 30, 1889; h/725 W Galena Ave, Freeport, IL 61032; m/Harry (dec); p/Benjamin and Anna Young Heisler; pa/Circuit Clerk; cp/Pres Steph Co Humane Soc; Coun Aging; Bd & Histn Repub Woms Clb; Past Pres & Histn Quota Clb; Am Leg Aux; r/Presb; hon/Wom of Yr, ABWA; Cert Apprec March of Dimes; Meritorious Ser, Am Humane Assn; Cont'g Ser, Steph Co Nsg Home; Num Biogl Listings.

BREZINSKI, PAUL FRANK oc/Podiatrist; b/Mar 17, 1952; h/5440 N Panama Ave, Chicago, IL 60656; ba/Chgo; p/Frank and Therese Brzezinski, Chgo; ed/BS Bradley Univ; DPM Ill Col Podiatric Med; pa/Am Podiatry Assn; Ill Podiatry Soc; Am Public Hlth Assn; Am Assn Advmt Sci; cp/Instr ARC Water Safety; r/Rom Cath; hon/Ser Awd, ARC; Pub'd Author.

BRIAN, ALEXIS MORGAN JR oc/Attorney; b/Oct 4, 1928; h/1738 S Carrollton Ave, New Orleans, LA 70118; ba/NO; m/Elizabeth Louise Graham; c/Robert, Ellen; p/Morgan Brian Sr (dec); Evelyn Thibaut Tuller, NO; ed/AB 1949, JD 1956 LSU; MS 1954 Trinity Univ; mil/USAF 1951-55; pa/Partner Gen Law Pract Firm Deutsch, Kerrigan & Stiles 1961-; Am, La St & NO Bar Assns; Intl Assn Ins Counsel; La Assn Def Coun; Def Res Inst; Am Arbitration Assn; Phi Delta Phi; cp/LSU: Foun, Alumni Fdn, Law Sch Alumni Assn; Trinity Univ Alumni Assn; Intl House; La Civil Ser Leag; Yg Mens Bus Clb NO; WYES-TV Sponsor Clb; Asst Scoutmaster BSA; Bd Dirs: Goodwill Industs, Inter-Varsity Christian F'ship, Trinity Christian Commun, NO Bapt Theol Sem Foun; Gideons Intl; Com Bd So Bapt Conv; NO Bapt Theol Sem: Pres, Bd Dirs, Exec Com; NO Bapt Assn: Exec Bd, Trustees, Secy; r/1st Bapt Ch, NO: Deacon, Trustee, Tchr, Lay Preacher; hon/Num Biogl Listings.

BRICK, KATHERINE ADAMS oc/Aviation Writer; b/Aug 8, 1910; h/622 Golden Rd, Fallbrook, CA 92028; ba/Same; m/Frank Reeve (dec); c/Ruth Brick Macario; p/Oliver Menges (dec); Ruth Swift Linnell, Richmond, VA; ed/BS Boston Univ 1931; MA NYU 1938; Addit Studies; mil/WASP 2 Yrs; pa/POWDER PUFF DERBY: Bd 1951-, Ex-Officio-

Advr 1975-, Chm Bd 1961-75; FAA Safety Cnslr 1972-; FAA Woms Adv Com Aviation 1968-71; Participant Num Air Races incl'g Powder Puff Derbies 1955-59 & 1977; Institutor & CoChm Colt for Kim & Wom Korea 1962-63; Ninety-Nines; Pilots Assns: Nat, P-47 Thunderbolt, Australian Wom; Bd Dirs Aviation Space Writers Assn; Bd Dirs AF Assn; Am Aviation Hist Assn; San Diego Aerospace Mus; Airplane Owners & Pilots Assn; cp/Silver Wings; Teaneck; NJ Col Clb; Altrusa Intl; Wings Clb NYC; hon/Num Amelia Earhart Medals; Outstg Contbn Humanity, Sargent Col Alumni; Cert Commend, FAA; Paul Tissandier Dipl, Fdn Aeronautique Intl; Teterboro Aviation Hall of Fame; Pub'd Author; Num Biogl Listings.

BRIDGES, DOROTHY LOUISE oc/Postmaster; b/Jun 1, 1930; h/Hwy 22A PO Box 15, Milledgeville, TN 38359; ba/Same; m/H D; c/Terry, Deborah, Richie, Nicholas; p/Walter and Sallie Burns Rickman (dec); pa/Pres Tenn Chapt & Area Coor So Reg Nat Leag Postmasters; Del Tenn 1972-77; Page Nat Conv: Buffalo 1972, Dallas 1973, Hostess Com

Hollywood 1974, Chm Grand Banquet and Pres Reception Grand Rapids 1975, Phoenix 1976, San Juan 1977, Washington 1978; cp/OES: March of Dimes; Cancer Crusade; Red Cross; r/Milledgeville Meth Ch: Mem, Ladies SS Tchr, Ch Choir, Official Bd, Secy-Treas Bldg Fund; hon/Wom of Week, Hardin Co; Personalities of S.

BRIDGES, JAMES EDWARD JR oc/Educator; Supervisor; b/Dec 17, 1946; h/14007 Siniard Cir SE, Huntsville, AL 35803; ba/H'ville; p/Edward Bridges Sr, Catherine,

AL; Ethel Dees Bridges (dec); ed/BS; MS; MAS; mil/Ala Army NG; pa/Employment Cnslg Supvr; Pt-time Instr Bus Adm; ASPA; APGA; AMA; r/Presb; hon/W/W S&SW; Personalities S.

BRIDGEWATER, WALTER CLEVELAND oc/Reading Specialist; b/Mar 11, 1938; h/RR 8, Crawfordsville, IN 47933; ba/Indianapolis, IN; p/Walter Bridgewater (dec); Clarice Bridgewater, Scottsburg, IN; ed/BA Wabash Col; MA Ind Univ; PhD Cand Purdue Univ; pa/Rdg Spec Indpls Public Schs; Num Other Past Positions; Indpls & C'ville Ed Assns; Ind St Tchrs Assn; NEA; Ind Coun Tchrs Eng; Gtr Indpls & C'ville Area Rdg Couns; Ind St Coun; IRA; cp/C'ville Wabash Col Clb; Ind Univ Alumni Assn; Ind Soc; SAR: Montgomery & Scott Cos Hist Soc; Soc Ind Pioneers; Mason; Foun Christian Living; Adult Scout Ldr; r/Prot; U Meth; Lay Spkr Var Dist & Conf Coms; hon/Phi Delta Kappa; Delta Phi Alpha; Citizen Boys Town; Outstg Scouter

Awd, Lew Wallace Dist.

BRIDGMAN, JOYCE MARIE oc/Educator; h/2516 S 123rd E Ave, Tulsa, OK 74129; ba/Tulsa; p/Ray and Viola Bridgman, Enid, OK; ed/BMus Phillips Univ; MMus Univ Ks; DMA Cand Univ Wash; pa/Asst Prof Music Oral Roberts Univ 12 Yrs; Pianist Solo & Ensemble Recitals; Fac Advr & S'ship Chm Tulsa Alumnae & ORU Chapts; NMTA; OMTA; TAMTA; Mu Phi Epsilon; r/Pentecostal; Ch Organist & Pianist; hon/Recipient Num Acad & Music S'ships.

BRIEDE, ROBERT PAUL oc/Business Executive; b/May 8, 1923; h/249 Honey Ln, Battle Creek, MI 49015; ba/BC; m/Betty Marie; p/Paul and Mathilda Briede, Decatur, IN; ed/BS Purdue Univ; Postgrad Studies; mil/USN Capt Edy Prog WW-II; pa/Pres Briede Enterprises; Owner Elect Contracting Co; Estimator Sev Constrn Cos; Owner & Pres Motor Shop Elect Constrn Co; Nat Assn Elect Contractors; cp/Purdue Alumni Assn; Rotary; BC Country Clb; r/Cath; hon/W/W Am.

BRIEGER, ALTON oc/Administrator; b/Sept 13, 1927; h/104 Laurel Ln, San Marcos, TX; m/Ann Anderson; c/Jon, Karen; p/Robert Brieger (dec); Wilhelmine Brieger; ed/BA 1951, MA Tex Col Arts & Industs; Addit Studies; pa/SW Tex St Univ: Dean Student & Acad Sers 1975-, Dean Admissions and Registrar 1966-75, Assoc Prof Hist 1966-75, Acting Dean Students 1974; Dir Student Union Tex Col Arts & Industs 1951-64; Reg Rep Intl Assn Col Unions; Am &

Tex Assn Col Registrats & Admissions Ofcrs; Tex St Coun Am Col Testing Prog; Tex Assn Col Tchrs; Nat Bd Dirs & St Coun Am Col Test; cp/Univ Affairs Task Force; Rotary Intl; Asst Dist Commr BSA; Bd Dir: U Fund, 1st Nat Bank; Secy Charter Com San Marcos; Lambda Chi Alpha Fac Sponsor; r/Epis Ch: Sr Warden, Clk Vestry; Lic'd Lay Reader & Chalice Bearer 1969-; hon/Rotary Foun Grad F'ship, Univ Heidelberg; Awd Fac Devel Leave; Phi Alpha Theta; W/W Am Cols & Univs.

BRIGGS, EVERETT FRANCIS oc/Clergyman; Administrator; b/Jan 27, 1908; h/PO Box 86, Monongah, WV 26554; ba/Same; p/Thomas and Mary Hughes Briggs (dec); ed/STB Cath Univ Am 1932; MA cum laude Fordham Univ 1950; LHD Holy Cross Col 1950; mil/USN V-12 Tng Prog 1943-44; pa/St Barbaras Meml Nsg Home 1961-; WV Nsg Home Admr Adv Coun 1972-76; Pastor Cath Chs Monogah 1956-73; Dean Studies Maryknoll Col 1946-50; Instr Classical & Romance Langs Maryknoll Sem 1944-46; Supvr Kyoto Mission 1942-43; Diplomate Nichigo Bunka Gakko 1934; Pastor Cath Ch & Missionary Japan 1933-43; cp/Advr Ngo Dinh-Diem; Past Pres S Vietnam 1948-50; Recorder Am Royal Descent; r/Cath; hon/Cit Nat Conf Christians & Jews; 3 Cits & 2 Awds Am Freedom Foun.

BRIGGS, HILTON MARSHALL oc/President Emeritus; b/Jan 9, 1913; h/327 S 21st Ave, Brookings, SD 57006; ba/Brookings; m/Lillian; c/Dinus, Janice; p/John and Ethel Marshall Briggs (dec); ed/BS Ia St Univ 1933; MS 1935, Hon ScD 1963 ND St Univ; PhD Cornelle Univ 1938; pa/Pres Emeritus SD St Univ 1958-75; Dean Agri &

Prof Okla St Univ Univ Wyo 1950-58; cp/C of C; r/Meth; hon/Fellow: Am Soc Animal Sci, Am Assn Adv'd Sci; Alumni Achmt Awd, Nat 4-H Clb; Decoration Civilian Ser, Dept Army; Exceptl Ser Awd, USAF; Outstg SD Citizen; Portrait Saddle & Sirloin Clb Gallery; Dr Higher Ed Adm Univ SD 1973.

BRIGHT, VONETTE ZACHARY oc/Director; Author; Speaker; b/Jul 2, 1926; h/Arrowhead Springs, San Bernardino, CA 92414; ba/Same; m/William; c/Zachary, Bradley; p/Roy and Mary Waggoner Zachary, Coweta, OK; ed/BS Tex Woms Univ; Postgrad Studies; pa/Dir Great Comm Prayer Crusade; Bd Dirs Campus Crusade Christ; Former Tchr Los Angeles City Sch Dist; cp/Bd PTA; Adv Com Freedom Foun Val Forge; r/Campus Crusade Christ; Lausanne Com World Evangelization; hon/Chwom of Yr 1973; W/W Rel.

BRIGHTMAN, TOM C oc/Oil Producer; b/Dec 31, 1923; h/1346 Cordvadura, Graham, TX 76046; ba/Graham; m/Mae; c/Elaine Day (Mrs James), Bill, Fleda Brogdon (Mrs Gary); p/Thomas Brightman Sr (dec); Ola Brightman, Crane, TX; r/Prot: Ch Deacon.

BRIGHTWELL, JUANITA S oc/Director; b/Jan 4, 1918; h/1307 Hancock Dr, Americus, GA 31709; ba/Americus; m/Louie; ba/Mrs Claire Shaeffer; p/Robert Sumner (dec); Lottie Davis Sumner, Americus; ed/BSEd Ga Col; Master Libnship Emory Univ; pa/Dir Lib Sers; Am, SEn & Ga Lib Assns; Bus & Profl Woms Clb; cp/Magna Charta Soc; DAR; UDC; Am Camellia Soc; Azelea Garden Clb; Delta Kappa Gamma; Alpha Chi Omega; r/1st Bapt Ch; hon/Recipient Tchr Merit S'ship; Outstg Public Servant Awd, Americus Civitan Clb; Num Biogl Listings

BRINKLEY, ANGELINE ROSE oc/Homemaker; b/Jan 30, 1924; h/13206 Alpine Dr, Poway, CA 92064; m/Mardy; c/Jean Crist (Mrs Mike), Stephen Wilkinson, Joan Wilkinson, John & Paul Wilkinson; p/Max and Ersilia DeCarli (dec); cp/Fdr Vista Coor'g Coun; Poway Coor'g Coun: Advr, Fdg Chm, Set Master Calandar 1973, Heart Chm 4 Yrs, Capt 2 Areas 4 Yrs; Epsilon Sigma Alpha, Local Level: Pres 4 Chapts (Delta Nu, Theta Alpha, Theta Chi, Gamma Beta), All Coms, VP 3 Yrs, Treas, Secy, Ednl Dir, Histn, Publicity 7 Yrs; ESA, Reg Coun Level: Pres, 1 & 2/VP, Corresp'g Secy, Chaplain 2 Terms, Ways & Means Chm 3 Terms, Parliamentarian, Jr Past Pres, All Coms, Publicity Chm 4 Terms, PR Chm Million Dollar Bike Ride for 2 Rides, Others; ESA, Cal St Coun: By-Laws Com, St Mbrship Dir, IC Coun Credential Chm, Cal World Ctr Foun Cnslr, 49er Vol 2 Yrs, Cal St Coun Long Range Planning Com, Current CoChm San Luis Rey Reg Coun St Conv, Com Intl Conv, Hi; ESA, Intl Coun: Intl Coun Asst, IC Credentials Com; Vol: Vista Ranc_hero Days, Boys Clb Carnival; Vista Boys Clb Mothers Clb: Fdg Treas, PR Chm, Ofcr Installer; Vol Receptionist Palomar Fam Cnslg Ser; Chm Christians Baskets Poway; Chm All Ser Clbs & 3 Commun Clean-ups; Orgr & Chm SOC Save Our Country Day Cleanup; Poway Heart Dr: Chm 4th Yr, Capt 2 Areas 4th Yr; Capt Cancer Dr; Fund Raising Adv Com Poway, N Co Br San Diego Co Heart Assn; Heart Sunday Adv Com; TV Promotional Appearances; Radiothon Wkr St Jude Chds Hosp; Vol FISH Prog; Wkr Commun Emer Cupboard; Sigma Kappa Pi: All Ofcs Chapt Level, Coun; Provides Trans, Food & Other Sers Needy; Other Philanthropic Activs; r/Cath; hon/Dist'g Ser Awd, Poway JCs; Poway Wom of Yr; Grand Marshall Pow Wow Days Parade; Vol of Yr Awd, San Diego Co; Ser Awd, Heart Assn; Num Biogl Listings.

BRISBON, BOBBY LEROY oc/Professor; Administrator; b/Sept 10, 1935; h/237 Broad St Apt 6A, Sumter, SC 29150; ba/Sumter; p/John Brisbon, Portsmouth, VA; Melvina Dawkins Brisbon (dec); ed/AA Norfolk St 1955; BS Va St 1957; MA Case-Wn Resv Univ 1962; MAT Univ Va 1963; EdD Auburn Univ 1978; mil/AUS Capt 1958-62; pa/Prof & Ednl Admr Morris Col; AAUP; AAAS; ACPA; APGA; ATE; SCCPA; NEA;

SCEA; Phi Delta Kappa; Phi Chi; Alpha Phi Omega; r/Jehovah Bapt Ch: Mem; hon/Fellow Intl Biogl Assn.

BRISCOE, FRANK EARL oc/Executive; b/Jul 13, 1946; h/2020 N Main St, Nevada, MO 64772; ba/Nevada; m/Vickie Lynn; c/Shawn; p/Francis Briscoe; Irene Bell (dec); mil/USMC; pa/Pres & Owner Richardson Motor Co 1978-; Purchased Nev Volkswagen Inc 1976 & Honda Motor 1977; Past Dir Am Imported Auto Dealers Assn; cp/Nev Police Dept Aux Police Resv; C of C: Ambassadors Com, Orgr & Chm 1st Annual Turkey Shoot, Var Projs; CoChm & Treas Downtown Retail Merchs Assn; Chm & Comptroller Child Safety Prog; Treas Nev NOW Com; Past Bd Vernon Co Sheltered Wkshop; Chm Vernon Co Temporary Ambulance Ser 1978; Planning Com 1977-80; Fdr & Comptroller Miss Vernon Co Pageant Assn; Rotary Clb: Bd Dirs Commun Sers, Spkr Procurement Chm; JCs: Past Pres, Reg VI Dir, St Tng Coor, Comptroller Exercise Trl Proj & Annual Rodeo, Chm Bushwhacker Marathon Proj, Chm Miss Vernon Co Beauty Pageant; Elks; Am Legion; Lions Clb; Bd Dirs & Fin Chm U Fund; r/U Meth; hon/Govs Ldrship Awd 1978; Pace-Setter Awd, C of C; Top Mbrship Recruiter, Mo JCs; W/W Outstg Yg Men Am.

BRISTER, DOUGLAS WOODROW oc/Administrator; b/May 4, 1942; h/101 Lawnfield St, Mauldin, SC 29662; ba/Greenville, SC; m/Nettie; c/Douglas Jr; p/James and Doris Brister, Quitman, GA;

ed/BS 1966, MEd 1971 Tuskegee Inst; PhD Univ Tex 1876; mil/AUS Capt QMC 1966-70; pa/Col Admr G'ville Tech Col; Bd Dirs Phyllis Wheatley Ctr; r/Aravat Bapt Ch: SS Tchr, Pres Brotherhood; hon/Outstg Yg Men Am; Personalities S; Dic Intl Biog.

BRITT, CHESTER OLEN oc/Scientist; b/Jul 2, 1920; h/2708 Rae Dell Ave, Austin, TX 78704; ba/Austin; m/Patricia; p/Bevely Britt (dec); Ida Britt, Nashville, TN; ed/BS 1949, MS 1951, PhD Univ Tex; mil/USAAF; USAFR; pa/Res Scist Dept Chem Univ Tex; IEEE; AIP; AAS; Reg'd Profl Engr; hon/DFC & Air Medal W2/OLC; Pub'd Author; Num Biogl Listings.

BRITT, GEORGE G JR oc/Executive; b/May 19, 1949; h/906 S 60th St, Philadelphia, PA 19143; ba/Phila; m/Wanda Riveria; c/Bunny; p/George Sr and Mary Britt, Phila; ed/BA Cheyney St Col; Georgetown Univ Law Sch; pa/Chm of Bd, Nat Assn of Puerto Rican Yth; Owner Polit Conslt Firm, Geo Britt Jr & Staff; Assn MBA Execs; United Minority Enterprises Assn; Chm, Intl Ec Devel Forum; Chm, Coun for Equal Opportunity Bd; cp/SW Human Relats Coun; Edison HS Commun Adv Com; F'ship Comm; Dem Nat Com; Past Candidate for Mayor; Others; r/Bapt; hon/Hon Ky Col; Del to White House; Hon Citizen of Minn, WV, Ala, Ark, Ky, Tex.

BROADNAX, EVELYN JOSEPHINE oc/Educator; Civic Leader; ba/13024 Salinas Ave, Los Angeles, CA 90059; c/Patricia Henderson Stine; p/Austin White (dec); Emma Dockins, New Orleans, LA; ed/Xavier Univ; So Univ; BA LA Cal St Col 1952; Grad Work: UCLA, Pepperdine Univ, LaVerne Col; MA 1976, Dr Cand Pepperdine Univ; Credentials: Adm in Elem Ed, Pupil Pers Sers, Early

Childhood Ed, Major Social Scis, Gen Elem, Life Dipl in Ed on Kgn-Primary Level; Field Work in Adm, US Intl Univ, San Diego, Cal; Ext Study on "Open Classroom"; pa/Dir Aliso Cooperative Sch, LA Housing Sch 1972; Bd Dirs Friendship Day Camp, LA 1956; Cal Elem Ed Assn; Cal Tchrs Assn; NEA; Wkr on Curric Guide for Enterprise Sch Dist 1962; r/2nd Bapt Ch; hon/1 of 10 Best Dressed Wom, LA 1968; Commun Ser Awd, Indep Sq Foun Inc; Commends: Cal St Col as a Master Tchr Writing Guidelines for Student Tchrs; Chapman Col as a Master Tchr in Tng Tchrs; W/W Among Black Ams; Participant in PEDR Urban Exec Ldrship Prog from Carnegie Corp NY Grant; World W/W Wom.

BROADWAY, MONROE J oc/Minister; b/Aug 24, 1937; h/1205 Lorraine Dr, Redding, CA 96001; ba/Redding; m/Jackie Jean; c/Michael, Sharon, Carol; p/G W Broadway (dec); Hazel Broadway, Belton, TX; ed/BA Cal Bapt Col; MDiv SWn Sem; PhD cum laude Cal Grad Sch; mil/USAF 1955-60; pa/Sr Min 1st So Bapt Ch; Pastors Conf; Pres & Moderator Calvary Arrowhead Assn; Tchr Sem Ext Cal Bapt Col 1977-78; Org'd Inland Empire Singles; cp/CAP Chaplain; Lions; Bd Payson Mtl Hlth; VP & Coach Little Leag; Org'd Mission Work Navajo Indians; r/So Bapt; hon/Cert Apprec, Payson Old Time Music Assn; Num Ser Awds; Pub'd Author.

BROCCOLI, LOUIS VISCARDO oc/Engineer; b/Aug 27, 1931; h/831 Camino Dos Rios, Thousand Oaks, CA 91360; ba/Van Nuys, CA; m/Jo Ann Osborn Bettencourt; c/Mitchell, Viscardo, Kim, Susan, Rea; p/Viscardo Broccoli (dec); Inez Renzetti Broccoli, New London, CT; ed/BS US Merch Marine Acad 1955; MS W Coast Univ 1975; mil/USNR 1951-65; pa/Engrg Mgr Devel Mil Tactical Data Sys Litton Data Sys; cp/Dem; U Way Campaigner; r/Prot; hon/W/W: W, Intl Commun Ser; Personalities W; Dic Intl Biog; Men Achmt.

BROCK, VANDALL KLINE oc/Professor; b/Oct 31, 1932; h/2302 Amelia Cir, Tallahassee, FL 32304; ba/T'hassee; m/Frances Ragsdale; c/Geoffrey, Brantley; p/William Brock (dec); Gladys Lewis Brock, Decatur, GA; ed/BA Emory Univ 1954; MA 1963, MFA 1964, PhD 1971 Univ Ia; mil/US Air NG; USAFR 1957-67; pa/Prof Dept Eng Fla St Univ; Gen Editor & Pubr Anhinga Press; Fdr & Dir Apalachee Poetry Ctr; Fdr & Coor: T'hassee/Leon Co Poets Schs Prog, Fla Poets Prisons Prog; Editorial Bd *Poets in S/Conversations Within Word*; Poetry Editor *Nat Forum Phi Kappa Phi Jour*; Num Wkshops; hon/Fellow Intl Inst Creative Communs; Rockefeller FSU F'ship; Creative Writing F'ship, Fine Arts Coun Fla; 1st Prize Non-Students, Fla Poetry Contests; Borestone Mtn Poetry Awds 1972 & 1965; Num Others; Pub'd Author.

BROCK, WILLIAM ALLEN oc/Economist; b/Oct 22, 1941; h/1126 E 59th St, Chicago, IL 60637; ba/Same; m/Joan Elaine; c/Caroline; p/William and Margaret Brock, Cole Camp, MO; ed/AB w Hons Univ Mo 1965; MA, PhD 1969, MAIB Univ Cal-B; pa/Lectr Australia, Japan, Poland, Others; Currently Univ Chgo: Placemt Ofcr, NSF Grant "Intertemporal Ec"; Univ Chgo: Assoc Prof Ec 1972 & 75, Vis Assoc Prof Dept Ec 1971-72, Search Com, Admissions Com; Assoc Prof Ec & 2 Thesis Coms Cornell Univ 1974-76; Univ Rochester: Prof Ec & Math

1969-71, Vis Assoc Prof Ec 1973; Vis Lectr Tex A&M Univ 1968-69; Field Work & Stat Consltn Traffic Res Corp 1966; Engrg Aide Univ Cal Richmond Field Sta 1965; Stat Consltn Univ Mo 1962-65; Participant Num Wkshops & Confs; Presentations Profl Orgs & Univs; Assoc Editorships: *Jour Ec Theory*, *Intl Ec Review*; Reviewer: *Math Reviews*, *Zentralblatt fur Mathematik*; Econometric Soc: Fellow, Session Orgr for Dynamic Ec Summer Meetings 1976, Chm Session Ec Growth & Prog Com 1971; hon/Univ Mo: Curators Cert Recog 1960, Deans List 1965-65, Nat Sci Foun Traineeship 1965; Bernard Friedman Meml Prize, Univ Cal-B; Sherman Fairchild Dist'd Scholar; Pi Mu Epsilon; Num Grants; Pub'd Author.

BROCKHAUS, WILLIAM LEE oc/Executive; Lecturer; b/Jan 22, 1943; h/13802 W NW Passage, Marina del Rey, CA 90291; ba/Culver City, CA; ed/BS cum laude 1966, MBA 1967 Univ Mo; DBA Ind Univ 1970; Addit Studies; mil/USAF Comm'd Ofcr; pa/Chm Bd & Chief Exec Ofcr BC&A Enterprises Inc 1978-; Gen Partner Landmark Investmts Ltd 1978-; Chm Bd & Chief Exec Ofcr Edward Hyman Co 1976-78; Conslt Mgmt: Brockhaus, Carlisle & Assocs, Profl Mgmt Counsel 1971-78; Fac Dept Mgmt Grad Sch Bus Adm Univ So Cal 1971-76; Other Past Positions; Lectr Num Profl Orgs; Designer & Dir Num Major Res Projs; Acad Mgmt; Am Fin Assn; Am Psychol Assn; AMA; Soc Advmt Mgmt; Am Soc Tng & Devel; AAAS; Soc Entrepreneurship Res; Nat Coun Small Bus Mgmt Devel; Newcomen Soc NA; Nat Social Dir; Assn Corp Growth; hon/Beta Gamma Sigma; Sigma Iota Epsilon; Delta Sigma Pi Awd; Am Legion Awd; Univ Mo Curators Awd; Scabbard & Blade; Kawneer Co S'ship; Ind Univ & Ford Foun F'ships; Multiple USC Res Grants; CoDevel "Semantic Differential Org Diagnostic"; CoDevelr "Bus Enterprise Devel & Entrepreneurship Prog"; Pub'd Author; Num Biogl Listings.

BRODER, JUDITH TUSHNET oc/Physician; b/Jul 31, 1940; h/1905 Loma Vista Dr, Beverly Hills, CA 90210; ba/BH; m/Donald; c/Benjamin, Michael, Leah; p/Leonard Tushnet (dec); Fannie Tushnet, BH; ed/BS Univ Chicago; MD Univ Chgo Sch Med; pa/Los Angeles Psychoanalytic Soc; Am Psychi Assn; cp/Nat Orig Wom.

BRODERICK, GRACE MARGARET NOLAN oc/Scientist; b/5214 8th Rd S, Arlington, VA 22204; ba/Wash, DC; m/Francis Byrne; c/Grace; p/Emmett and Edna Burnet Nolan (dec); ed/BA Univ Buffalo 1947; MA Brigham Yg Univ 1950; JD Georgetown Univ 1956; Addit Studies; pa/Vanadium Spec US Bur Mines 1967-;

Geologist US Geol Survey 1952-67; Asst Mineralogy Pa St Univ 1950-52; Asst Geol Brigham Yg 1948; Export Clk Translator Carborundum Co 1947-48; Fellow AAAS; Am Inst Profl Geologists; Am Assn Petro Geologists; Geol Soc Wash; Delta Phi Alpha; Sigma Delta Epsilon; Kappa Beta Pi; Phi Delta Gamma; r/Rom Cath; hon/Spec Awd, US Bur Mines; Outstg Perf Awd, US Geol Survey.

BRODY, STUART MARTIN oc/Researcher; b/Jun 25, 1936; h/8 Timberlane Dr, Colonia, NJ 07067; ba/Summit, NJ; m/Helene; c/Russell, Elyse; p/Michael Brody, Queens Village, NY; Celia Brody (dec); ed/BS Queens Col; pa/Ciba-Geigy 1958-: Dir of

Operations of Chromatographic Analysis Labs; Contbr to Profl Jours; Presenter at Profl Confs; Am Pharmaceutical Assn; Soc for Applied Spectroscopy; NJ Chromatography Discussion Group; cp/Queens Col Alumni Assn; Fund Raiser for Dem Party; B'nai B'rith; r/Jewish; hon/W/W E; DIB; Others.

BROEKER, ANNIE BARR oc/Economic Evaluator; b/Dec 20, 1951; h/113-N Cay Ct, Angleton, TX 77515; ba/Freeport, TX; m/Roger John Jr; p/Decania Jr and Norma Barr, Leesville, SC; ed/BS Univ SC 1973; MBA Cand Univ Houston; pa/Past Mbrship Chm Local Chapt Tex Soc Profl Engrs; Soc Wom Engrs; TSPE; NSPE; AIChE; cp/Bronze Co Repub Clb; r/Presb; hon/W/W: Students Am Cols & Univs, S&SW, Am Wom; Personalities S; Dic Intl Biog.

BROMBY, CAROL HOGAN oc/Educator; b/Dec 31, 1950; h/639 Muscogee St N, Ft Meyers, FL 33903; ba/FM; m/Philip; c/Christopher; p/Robert and June Hogan, FM; ed/AA Edison Commun Col 1970; BA 1973, MA 1975 Univ S Fla; Doct Cand Nova Univ; pa/Tchr J Colin Eng Elem Sch 1975–; Basic Skills Resource Person 1976–; Past Tchr: Tanglewood Elem Sch 1974-75, Paul Mort Elem Sch 1973-74; Pilot Prog Devel Lng: Resources Specific Task Analysis; Devel Com Rdg Skills Record Cards; Assn Childhood Ed 1974- & Intl 1972–; cp/Worthy Advr Order Rainbow Girls; Orgr & Tchr After-Sch Baton Twirling; r/Presb; hon/Outstg Ldr Elem Sch.

BRONSON, OSWALD PERRY oc/Educational Administrator; b/Jul 19, 1927; h/709 Second Ave, Daytona Bch, FL 32014; ba/Daytona Bch; m/Helen W; c/Josephine B Vickers, Flora Helen, Oswald Perry Jr; p/Uriah Perry and Flora Hollinshed Bronson (dec); ed/BS Bethune-Cookman Col 1950; BD summa cum laude Gammon Theol Sem 1959; PhD NWn Univ 1965; pa/Pres, Bethune-Cookman Col; Pastor in Fla, Ga (U Meth Ch) 16 Yrs; Lectr & Tchr: Interdenominational Theol Ctr (Atlanta, Ga); Dir Field Ed 1964-68, VP 1966-68, Pres 1968-75; Author: Bd Dirs: Fla Assn Cols & Univs, Fund for Theol Ed, Nat Assn Equal Opportunity in Higher Ed; Indep Cols & Univs of Fla; Appt'd by Gov to Sch Bd of Volusia Co; Exec Com, So Reg Ed Bd; Chrperson, Div of Min, Fla Annual Conf of U Meth Ch; AAUP; VP, Am Assn Theol Schs 1968-70; Past VChm Bd Govs, Ga Assn Pastoral Care; Others; cp/Adv Com, Fla St Sickle Cell Foun Inc; Bd Dirs: United Negro Col Fund, Work Oriented Rehab Ctr, Inst of the Black World, Martin Luther King Ctr for Social Change, ARC, Others; Bd Trustees, Hinton Rural Life Ctr (Hayesville, NC); NAACP; Others; r/Meth; hon/Certs of Apprec, Bethune-Cookman Col; Alpha Kappa Mu; Theta Phi; Key to City of Orlando (Fla) & Ormond Bch (Fla); United Negro Col Fund Awd; Apprec Awds: Interdenominational Theol Ctr, Nat Black Am Law Students Assn, Billy Graham Crusade, C H Mason Theol Sem; Others.

BROOK, CHARLES ALBERT oc/Geologist; b/Mar 20, 1947; h/39112-A Sundale Dr, Fremont, CA 94538; ba/Menlo Park, CA; p/Lester and Delphia Brook, Sanger, CA; ed/AA; BA; MA; pa/Geologist US Geol Survey; Pacific Sect Geol Soc Am; Soc Ec Paleontologists & Mineralogists; N Cal & Peninsula Geol Socs; r/Bapt; hon/Outstg Student Awd, Phi Kappa Phi.

BROOK, DAVID oc/Educator; b/Apr 1, 1932; h/135 Hawthorne St Apt 6-H, Brooklyn, NY 11225; ba/Jersey City, NJ; p/Nathan Brook, Bklyn; Pearl Efros Brook (dec); ed/BA John Hopkins Univ; MA, PhD Columbia Univ; pa/Prof Dept Polit Sci Jersey City St Col; Dir Inst War & Peace; Exec Com Intl Studies Assn MAR; Columbia Univ Sem Problem Peace; hon/Wilton Park Fellow; Pub'd Author.

BROOK, NATHAN HARRY oc/Teacher; b/Sept 28, 1903; h/135 Hawthorne St Apt 6-H, Brooklyn, NY 11225; m/Pearl; c/David; p/Morris Brook (dec); Kate Weinstein (dec);

ed/BME; mil/Wis NG; pa/Tchr: Jr HS, Acad HS, Voc HS, Engrg Col; Taught: AA Prog, WPA Prog, War Tng Prog, Vets Tng & Reconversion Prog; Designer Tools & Dies; Engr: Time Study, Designing, Prodn, Indust; Chm Indust Arts Dept; hon/Outstg Work Tchg; Pub'd Author.

BROOKER, CYNTHIA CROCKER WARNER oc/Educator; b/Apr 1, 1909; h/8114 Carroll Ave, Takoma Park, MD 20012; ba/Same; m/Robert Morris; c/Richard Warner, Nancy Maher; 5 Stepchd; p/Frederick Crocker (dec); Sarah Mabel Allen (dec); ed/BS Elmira Col 1930; MA Am Univ 1933; pa/Fdr & Dir: Cynthia Warner Sch Ltd 1934-, Kaup Kelnearock 1940-; ABWA; AIMS; AISGW; cp/Former Regent Ft McHenry Chapt NSDAR; r/Prot; Christ Congreg Ch: Mem; hon/Nat Achmt Awd, Phi Delta Gamma; Dist'd Achmt Awd, Elmira Col; Num Biogl Listings.

BROOKS, BETTY JEAN oc/Administrator; b/May 17, 1950; h/1914 3rd Ave, Selma, AL 36701; ba/Selma; p/Mrs Edna Davis, Birmingham, AL; ed/Hlth Care Facility

Conslts Nsg Home Adm; Cert Reality Orient; pa/Admr W J Anderson Meml Nsg Home Inc; Ala Nsg Home Assn; Cont'g Ednl Sems; cp/Voters Leag; NAACP; Black Caucus Dallas Co; r/Luth; hon/Am Podiatry Awd.

BROOKS, JOHN oc/Manager; b/Sept 7, 1940; h/3005 Wellington Dr, Rocky Mount, NC 27801; ba/RM; m/Virginia Cashion; p/Roscoe Brooks, Harrogate, TN; Mamie

Brooks (dec); ed/BS Univ Tenn 1967; mil/USAF 1960-64; pa/Prog Engrg Mgr Abbott Labs; IEEE; NSPE; Chapt Pres PENC; r/Bapt.

BROOKS, JUNE BROOKS oc/Businesswoman; b/Jun 24, 1924; h/915 Stanley Ave, Ardmore, OK 73401; c/Claudia B Chappell, Rebecca, William; p/Major and Lillian Berry Brooks, Ardmore; ed/Att'd Num Insts; pa/Fdr & Owner June Brooks Oil & Gas Co; Okla Indep Petro Assn; Okla Petro Coun; Okla Chm Public Lands Am Assn Petro Landmen; Soc Petro Engrs; Indep Petro Assn Am: Bd Dirs, Spkrs Bur, Public Lands Com; Am Petro Inst; Tex Indep Prodrs & Royalty Owners Assn; Spkrs Bur Energy Res Assocs Dallas; Del World Petro Cong 1975 & 1979; AAUW; Intl Platform Assn; r/Presb; hon/Dist'd Ser Awd, Am Assn Petro Landmen; Okla Petro Coun Spkrs Awd.

BROOKS, TYRONE L oc/National Human Rights Leader; b/Oct 10, 1945; h/1315

Beecher St SW, Atlanta, GA 30310; ba/Atla; c/Tyrone Jr, Naheede; p/Mose Brooks; Ruby Brooks, Warrenton, GA; ed/BS; pa/SCLS: Orgr Oper Mil Prog, 12 Yr Vet; Pres Tyrone Brooks & Assocs; r/Bapt; hon/Outstg Yg Man Am.

BROOKS, VIRGINIA WALTON oc/Homemaker; b/Aug 6, 1904; h/Epping Forest Manor 3661 James Rd, Memphis, TN 38128; m/Berry Boswell Jr (dec); c/Virginia B Martin; p/Allan and Virginia Feild Walton (dec); pa/Nat Leag Am Pen Wom; cp/Colonial Dames Descendant of Most Noble Order of Garter; Magna Carta Dame Order of Crown of Charlemogne; Order of 3 Crusades; Num Civic Orgs; r/Christian Scist; hon/PhD, Lindenwood Col.

BROPHY, CHARLES A JR oc/Librarian; b/Jul 9, 1913; h/303 S Ardmore Rd, Bexley, OH 43209; m/Mary Jane Ruth Belt; c/Nancy Muldoon (Mrs James), Patsy Conrades (Mrs George); p/Charles Sr and Elizabeth Brophy (dec); ed/BS Ohio St Univ; BS Univ Ill; mil/AUS 1942-46; pa/Ret'd Head Libn Battelle Meml Inst; Compiler Titanium Bibliog; Spec Libs Assn; Soc Metals; cp/Past Bd Trustees Goodwill Industs; r/Prot.

BROSNAN, CAROL RAPHAEL oc/Reports Specialist; b/Jul 19, 1931; h/4201 Massachusetts Ave Apt 3030C NW, Wash, DC 20016; ba/Wash, DC; p/Basil Brosnan, Paterson, NJ; ed/Att'd: Montclair St Tchrs Col, George Washington Univ (Prof Helen Yakobson Dept Slavic Langs & Lits), Univ Va, Univ Oxford; mil/AUS Woms Army Corps 1953-55; pa/Reports Spec Nat Endowment Arts; Am Hist Assn; Am Assn Advmt Slavic Studies; Am Classical Leag; Tolstoy Foun; Phi Alpha Theta; hon/Artistic Achmt as Pianist, Yg Peoples Concert Series; Fellow Intl Biogl Assn; Certs Dist'd Achmt: Intl Biogl Centre, Am Biogl Inst; hon/Num Biogl Listings.

BROTHERS, JACK ANTHONY oc/Business Manager; b/Jun 4, 1943; h/53 Pyrex St, Corning, NY 14830; ba/Corning; m/Barbara Ziel; c/Timothy, Andrew; p/Jack Brothers (dec); Mary Brothers Kimble, Lake Havasu

City, AZ; ed/BS 1965, MS 1967 Mich Technol Univ; pa/Bus Mgr Corning Glass Works; Am Ceramic Soc; Am Geol Inst; cp/BPO Elks; r/Meth; hon/2 US Patents; W/W S&SW; Pub'd Author.

BROTHERS, JOYCE DIANE oc/Psychologist; h/1530 Palisade Ave, Fort Lee, NJ 07024; ba/New York, NY; m/Milton; c/Lisa; p/Morris and Estelle Rapoport Bauer; ed/BS Cornell Univ 1947; MA Columbia 1950; PhD

1953; pa/Asst Psychol Columbia 1948-52; Instr Hunter Col 1948-52; Res Proj Ldrship UNESCO 1949; CoHost TV Prog *Sports Showcase* 1956; Appearances TV Progs: *Dr Joyce Brothers 1958-63*, Conslt *Dr Brothers 1960-66*, *Ask Dr Brothers 1965-*; Columnist: N Am Newspaper Alliance 1961-70, Bell-McClure Syndicate 1963-70, *Good Housekeeping Mag* 1962-, King Features Syndicate 1970-; Appearances: Radio Sta WNBC 1966-69, NBC Radio Prog Emphasis 1966-75, Sta WMCA 1969-72, Monitor 1967-75, NBC Radio Network News Line 1975-, ABC Reports 1966-67; News Corr TVN Inc 1975-76; Spec Feature Writer Hearst Papers UPI; cp/CoChm Sports Com Lighthouse for Blind; Door-to-Door Chm Jewish Fdn Philanthropies; Fund Raising Com Olympic Fund; People to People Prog; Sigma Xi; hon/$64,000 Winner TV Prog $64,000 Question; Winner $70,000 TV Prog $64,000 Challenge; Mennen Baby Foun Awd; Newhouse Newspaper Awd; Am Acad Achmt Awd; Deadline Awd, Sigma Delta Chi.

BROWDER, JOHNIE MAE GOMILLION oc/Principal; Educator; b/Oct 2, 1919; h/Rt 1, McKenzie, AL 36456; m/Ralph; c/Ralph, Tempie; p/Thad Gomillion (dec); Irene Lee Gomillion, McKenzie; ed/BS Troy St Univ; MEd, AA Cert Guid Auburn Univ; pa/Prin W O Parmer Elem Sch 8 Yrs; Former Tchr & Guid Cnslr 22 Yrs; Guid Supvr Butler Co 6 Yrs; BCEA; AEA; NEA; ADESP; NAESP; ASCAS; Soc Wom Tchrs; Intl Platform Assn; cp/New Home Bapt Ch, McKenzie: Mem, Adult SS Tchr, Ch Treas; hon/Kappa Delta Pi; Delta Kappa Gamma.

BROWER, KAREN LEE oc/Counselor; b/Nov 17, 1952; h/229 Linda Dr, High Point, NC 27263; ba/Fayetteville, NC; p/Herman Brower, HP; Josie Gilliam Brower, HP; ed/BSHE Univ NC-G; MS; Cnslg Granted George Peabody Col Tchr; pa/Elem Sch Guid Cnslr Cumberland Co Public Sch Sys; APGA; NCPGA; ASCA; NEA; APA; NCSCA; SACUS; r/Bapt; hon/Omicron Nu.

BROWN, ANNETTE NETTIE oc/Editor; Author; Reporter; b/Jul 1, 1915; h/1454 S Hwy 86, El Centro, CA 92243; ba/EC; c/James, Mrs Mary Walker, George II, John, Jerry, Mrs Eleanor Van Gieson, Philp, Antone, Carl Black (Adopted); p/Antone and Mary Perry Cardoza (dec); ed/Gen Bus Held Col Bus 1937; mil/Navy Flight Demo Team Blue Angels 1968; pa/Pubr & Editor: *Imperial Val Wkly*, *Imperial Hometown Review* 1952-; Palo Alto News Editor 1935-36; Atwater Signal Reporter 1950; Tulelake Reporter News Editor 1950-52; LA Times Correspondent 1964-69; NAF EC Sandpaper Editor 1971-75; Blue Angels Serials 1973-74; Author *Grandma Wore Combat Boots: A Hometown Editor Looks Viet-Nam* 1969; r/Imperial Val Ch Rel Sci: Mem, Former Dir; hon/1st News: LA Press Assn, Theta Sigma Phi; 1st Wom Journalist Unusual Fields, Theta Sigma Phi; Ser Awd, Chief Nav Air Tng; Ser Awd, Navy Leag US; Commend Nav Air Facility; Ser Commend USAF Recruiting Command; Imperial Co Supvrs Ser Awd; Nat Parachute Test Range Ser Awd; Optimist Clb Newspaper Commend; Mother of Yr Awd, Fraternal Order Eagles.

BROWN, BARBARA JUNE oc/Administrator; Consultant; Editor; h/17781 15th Ave NW, Seattle, WA 98177; ba/Same; m/Elmer; c/Deborah, Robert, Andrea, Michael, Steven, Jeffry; p/Carl Rydberg (dec); Nora Rydberg, Milwaukee, WI; ed/BS 1955, MS 1960, EdD 1970 Marquette Univ; pa/Editor *Nsg Adm Qtrly* Jour, Aspen Sys Corp; Asst Admr Patient Care Sers Fam Hosp & Nsg Home, M'kee 1973-78; Assoc Clin Prof Nsg Adm Marquette Univ Col Nsg 1974-78; Nsg Conslt & Reschr; Pres Hosp Adm Assesmt Profile, M'kee; Participant Num Progs; Other Past Positions; Am Nurses Assn; Pres & Bd Am Soc Nsg Ser Admrs; Gtr M'kee Area Nsg Ed & Nsg Ser Adm Coun; Nat & Pres Wis Leag Nsg; cp/Marquette Univ Alumni Assn; Res & Devel Adv Com Marian Col; Med, Dental & Hlth Tech Adv Com M'kee Sch Bd; Gov Luceys Task Force Hlth & Hlth Planning; r/Cath; hon/Fellow Am Acad Nsg; Marquette Univ

Outstg Alumni Awd 1977 & Nat Alumni Merit Awd 1972; Alpha Tau Delta; Pub'd Author.

BROWN, BRUCE ROBERT oc/Artist; Educator; b/Jul 25, 1938; h/17 Sedgewick Dr, Honeoye, NY 14771; ba/Rochester, NY; c/Adam; p/Mack and Mary Brown, Forksville, PA; ed/BFA 1961, MFA 1964 Tyler Sch Fine Arts Temple Univ; pa/Assoc Prof Sculpture Monroe Commun Col 1968-; Preparing Film Sculpting Human Figure Sponsored Grant & F'ship SUNY; Head Sculpture Dept W Liberty St Col 1966-68; Painting Tchr Phila Public Schs 1964-66; Col Art Assn; IPA; Nat Soc Lit & Arts; So Sculptors Assn; cp/Rochester Print Clb; Adv Bd Shumann Meml Foun; Adv Bd Tyler Alumni Assn; hon/Num Art Awds, Cits, Contbns & Exhibns 1955-; Num Biogl Listings.

BROWN, CLARENCE J JR oc/Editor; Publisher; Congressman; b/Jun 18, 1927; m/Joyce Eldridge; c/Elizabeth (dec), Clarence III, Catherine, Roy; p/Clarence and Ethel McKinney Brown; ed/BA, Comm Nav Resv Duke Univ 1947; MBA Harvard Univ 1949; mil/USN: Korean War Theater 1950-52, V-12 WW-II 1944-46; pa/Brown Pub'g Co: Pres 1965-77, Bd Chm 1977-; Urbana *Daily Citizen*: Editor 1957-62, Pubr 1959-70; Franklin *Chronicle*: Editor 1953-57, Pubr 1957-59; Editor Blanchester *Star-Repub* 1949-53; Nat Chm Nat Newspaper Assn; Chperson Nat Urban Coalition; cp/US Cong-man 7th Dist Ohio 1965-; Joint Ec Com 1969-; House Com Interstate & Fgn Commerce 1967-; House Com Govt Opers 1966-; House Repub Task Force Election Reform 1973; 1 of 3 House Nat Adv Com Intergovtl Relats 1973-; Del 7th Congl Dist Repub Nat Conv 1972 & 1976;

Champaign Co Repub Exec Com; Other Polit Activs; Georgetown Univ Ctr Strategic & Intl Studies; Bd Vis Harvard Grad Sch Bus; Former Dir C of C: Blanchester, Franklin, Urbana; Trustee: Wilberforce Univ, Ohio Newspaper Assn, Freedoms Foun; Past Pres: Ctl Ohio Profl Chapt Sigma Delta Chi, Champaign Co Commun Improvement Corp, ARC Chapts Franklin & Urbana; Bd Mgrs AF Mus; Friends WCSU St Univ; Nat Mus Afro-Am Hist & Cult Planning Coun; Masons; Shrine; Rotary; Jr Order; Am Legion; VFW; Bd Dirs Capitol Hill Clb; Former Bd Urbana Commun Park Devel Bd; Former Chm Champaign Co Easter Seal Fund Dr; r/Trustee: 1st Presb Ch Urbana 1965-67, Nat Presb Ch Wash 1967-73; hon/US Delegation US-Polish Trade Conf 1976; Rep US Cong US-Mexican Interparliamentary Conf 1973; "Watchdog of Tresury" Awds; "Guardian of Small Bus" Awd 1972 & 1976; Aerospace Power Awd, Ohio AF Assn; BSA: Silver Beaver Awd, Dist'd Eagle Scout.

BROWN, DAVID MILLARD oc/Superintendent Schools; b/Oct 11, 1918; h/Box 195, Goodridge, MN 56725; ba/G'ridge; m/Helen Elise Fisher; c/David, Helen Faes, Tamara Rude; p/David Brown (dec); Elsie Wright Brown, Fergus Falls, MN; ed/MA Univ Minn 1952; EdD Univ ND 1957; mil/AUS 1st Lt Air Corps WW-II; pa/Past Pres & Secy Dist 31 Minn Assn Co Supts; cp/Justice of Peace; Mayor G'ridge; Chm Pennington Co IR; VP NW Reg Fire Fighters Minn; Past Pres & Zone Chm Lions Clb; r/Faith Luth Ch ALC.

BROWN, EDITH PETRIE oc/Physician; b/Jun 7, 1900; h/835 E Copper St, Tucson, AZ 85719; ba/Same; m/Howard Ray Osler; c/Margaret Fleming, Stanley; p/William and

Hattie Shontg Petrie (dec); ed/BS; MD; DH; FAAFP; pa/Pvt Pract Num Yrs; Initiation Measles Immunization Kenya; r/U Presb; hon/W/W: Am, World.

BROWN, GARRY E oc/Congress Representative; b/Aug 12, 1923; h/321 W Eliza St, Schoolcraft, MI 49087; ba/Wash, DC; c/Frances, Mollie, Amelia, Abigail; p/Lakin and Blanche Jackson Brown (dec);

ed/BA Kalamazoo Col 1951; JD George Washington Univ 1949; mil/AUS 2nd Lt Inf 1946-67; pa/Rep Cong 3rd Dist Mich 1967-; Mich St Senator 1962-66; Atty Partner Ford, Kriekard, Brown & Staton 1954-67; r/Presb; hon/Doct Humanities, Lawrence Inst Technol.

BROWN, GWENDOLYN RUTH oc/Music Educator; b/May 17, 1942; h/2433 N 3rd, Abilene, TX 79603; p/Earle and Alice Washburn Brown, Graham, TX; ed/BMEd; MEd; pa/Music Spec Abilene Indep Sch Dist; Tex Music Edrs Assn; NEA; Mu Phi Epsilon; cp/Jr Mem Chatqua Lit Social Clb; Sweetheart Abilene Evening Lions Clb; r/Christian; hon/W/W: Music & Musicians, Wom; DIB.

BROWN, HAROLD OGDEN JOSEPH oc/Professor; Minister; b/Jul 6, 1933; h/1311 Stratford Rd, Deerfield, IL 60015; ba/D'field; m/Grace Winifred Hancox; c/Cynthia, Peter; p/Harold Brown (dec); Mary Brown,

Hernando, FL; ed/AB magna cum laude 1953, STB 1957, ThM 1959, PhD 1967 Harvard; pa/Prof Theol Trinity Evang Div Sch 1975-; Min 1958-; Assoc Editor *Christianity Today* 1972-74; cp/Chm Christian Action Coun 1975-; r/Evang Prot; hon/Phi Beta Kappa.

BROWN, JAMES THOMAS JR oc/Engineer; b/Feb 12, 1947; h/2517 Cortland St, Waynesboro, VA 22980; ba/W'boro; p/Thomas and Mildred Brown, W'boro; ed/BS VPI & SU; mil/USMC Sgt 1968-74; pa/Engr Sys Analyst; DPMA; AMA; Bd Dir AIIE; cp/W'boro JCs: Dir 1974-76, Internal VP 1976-77, External VP 1977-78, Pres 1978-79, Chm Bd 1979-80; Va JCs: Reg Dir Skyline Reg 1979-80, St Bd Dirs 1978-80, St Exec Com 1979-80; Adv Bd W'boro Sr Ctr; Steering Com & Bd Dirs W'boro Affil Big Brothers/Big Sisters Am; U Way; Chm Citizens Com W'boro Planning Comm; Va St Yth Ldrship; C of C; Past Asst Scoutmaster BSA; r/Main St U Meth Ch: Mem; hon/USMC: Marine of Qtr, Meritorious Mast Outstg Duty, Nav Achmt Medal; W'boro JCs: Pres Awds, Top 10 Most Active, Keyman Awd, Outstg Pres Dist Awd; Va JCs: Outstg Ser Awd, Nom'd St Keyman Awd, Outstg External Programming; BSA: Eagle Scout, God & Country Awd.

BROWN, KATHRYN ANN oc/Professor; b/Jan 6, 1926; h/1733 N Dudney, Magnolia, AR 71753; ba/Magnolia; m/Ivan (dec); c/Kathy, Michael; p/Ervin Smith (dec); Katie Crow Smith, Linville, LA; ed/BS; MS; EdD; pa/Prof SAU; AAHPER; Ark AHPER; SAPECW; NAPECW; r/Bapt; hon/Danforth Awd; Kappa Delta Pi; W/W: Am Wom, Wom World.

BROWN, LOIS LORANE oc/Professor; Director; b/Mar 31, 1933; h/Box 507, Searcy, AR 72143; ba/Searcy; m/Herman Leon; c/Leon, Eldon, Linda, Vivian; p/Riley Morse (dec); Maye Morse; ed/MA San Diego St Univ; pa/Asst Prof Spec Ed & Psychol Harding Col; Dir Home Emotionally Disturbed Chd; Dir Chds Div Ark St Mtl Hlth; Coor Coun Ark St Spec Ed; Ednl Conslt 9 Co Area Sch Dists; Num Wkshops; Contbr Num Proposals & Plans; r/Ch of Christ; hon/Dist'd Tchr Awd, Harding Col.

BROWN, MAGGIE COLE oc/Educator; Principal; h/4221 NWn Pkwy, Louisville, KY 40212; m/Alton; c/Norma B Homes; p/David and Georgia Jones Cole; ed/Life Cert Wn Ky

Univ; pa/Ret'd Tchr & Prin ABC Pvt Schs; Pres LaRue Co Tchrs Assn; KEA NEA; cp/En Star; r/Bapt; hon/Personalities S; 2000 Wom Achmt; Intl W/W Commun Ser.

BROWN, MILLARD RAY oc/Professor; b/Jul 30, 1913; h/PO Box 325, Buies Creek, NC 27506; ba/BC; m/Dorothy Crane; c/David, Roger; p/John and Lucy Rogers Brown (dec); ed/BA cum laude; BD; ThM; MA; PhD; mil/AUS Chaplain 1942-46; USAR

Col 1946-73; pa/Prof Sociol Campbell Col; Chm Campbell Symp; Sociol Conslt; cp/Chm Harnett Co Task Force Juv Delinq; Precnt Com-man Dem Party; Lions Clb; r/Bapt; Clergyman; Interim Pastor Chs; hon/Golden Bough (Phi Beta Kappa).

BROWN, NATHANIEL B JR oc/Research Associate; b/Dec 18, 1947; h/1300 Gladys St, Fort Valley, GA 31030; ba/FV; m/Fredrena; c/Kenneth, Kysha, Kimberly; p/Nathaniel Sr and Lydia Brown, New Bern, NC; ed/BS; MS; PhD; pa/Res Assoc Dept Agri & Rural Devel FV St Col; AFEE; AAUP; SPLC; NIS; OBS; NAACP; cp/Teens Talk Commun Org; Dem Nat Party; r/Christian Meth Epis Ch; hon/Nat Urban Leag Res F'ship.

BROWN, OTHA N oc/Counselor; b/Jul 19, 1931; h/Shorefront Park, S Norwalk, CT 06854; ba/Stamford, CT; m/Evelyn; c/Darrick; p/Otha Sr and Elizabeth Gossitt Brown (dec); ed/BS cum laude Ctl St Col 1952; MA Univ Conn 1956; mil/AUS 1st Lt Psychol Warfare Ofcr 1952-54; pa/Guid Cnslr

Bd Edn 1962-; Tchr Pub Schs 1957-60; APGA; Spec Interest Group Sys Res; Reg'd Real Est Broker; cp/Dem Nat Conv: Del, Nat Rules Com; Perm Moderator & Chm Carter Pres Primary Slate; Dist Dem Com; City Coun-man N'walk; Conn House Reps; Majority Ldr Common Coun; Chm Com Human Rts & Opports; Chm Com Public Wel Corrections & Human Instns; Pres St Fdn Black Dem Clbs; Del Dem Nat Mini Conv; Del Dem St Rules Com; Cand Mayor N'walk; Fdr & Pres N'walk Dem Coalition; Bd Dirs 4-Town Drug Network; Bd Dirs Commun Mtl Hlth Bd; Trustee Univ Conn; NAACP; JCs; Elks; Masons; Yg Dems; Alpha Phi Alpha; r/Meth; hon/Yg Man of Yr, N'walk JCs; Outstg Yg Man of Yr, Conn JCs; Alpha Man of Yr Awd; Ldrship Awd, NAACP; Senator Edward W Brooke Awd; Alpha Kappa Mu; Phi Alpha Theta; Kappa Delta Pi.

BROWN, ROBERT JOSEPH oc/Government Executive; b/Sept 10, 1929; h/9311 Holly Oak Ct, Bethesda, MD 20034; ba/Wash, DC; m/Iolene Cecilia Gau; c/Mary, Joseph, Timothy, Patrick, Barbara, Susan, Thomas, Brenda; p/George Brown, Pasadena, CA; Eileen Bagley (dec); ed/AA Univ Minn 1951; pa/Exec Under Secy Labor; cp/Dem Party; r/Rom Cath; hon/Outstg Career Achmt, Dept Labor.

BROWN, ROBERT PAUL oc/Engineer; b/Jun 23, 1918; h/1502 Clarksdale Ct, Lexington, KY 40505; ba/L'ton; m/Helen; p/Robert and Olive Davis Brown (dec); ed/BS; mil/Corps Engrs Ret'd Lt Col; pa/VP & Chief Engr Congleton Concrete; Past Pres KSPE; r/Cath; hon/Ky Dist'd Engr Awd; Outstg Chm Awd, Ky Ready Mixed Concrete Assn.

BROWN, ROBERT WADE oc/Executive; b/Jun 2, 1933; h/7605 Meadowhaven, Dallas, TX 75240; ba/Dallas; m/Mozelle Rawson; c/Robert, Cindy, Cathy, Candy; ed/BA 1955, MS 1956 N Tex St Univ; Cert Completion Sales Analysis Inst; pa/Instr Chem NTSU 1951-55; Temco Aircraft Process Analyst 'A' 1955-56; Wn Co: Mgr, Res Chem 1956-64; Instr Math Odessa Jr Col 1958-59; Self-Employed 1964-; BPR Constrn & Engrg Inc

1964-70: Pres, Chm Bd; Robert Wade & Assocs: Pres & Owner; Pres & Chm Bd: Brown Foun Repair & Consltg Inc, Brown Fence Installation Inc, Webb Properties Inc, Brown Oil Prodn; ASCE; Soc Petro Engrs; Alpha Chi Sigma; Chm Bd Nat Home Improvement; Contbr Var Jours & Other Prodns; cp/Trustee Tex Tech Dads Assn; hon/Holder US Patents; Cert Meritorious Ser, Sch Petro Technol; Cert Proficiency, Wn Co; Pub'd Author; Num Biogl Listings.

BROWN, (ROBERT) WENDELL oc/- Attorney; b/Feb 26, 1902; h/29921 Ardmore, Farmington Hills, MI 48018; ba/Detroit, MI; m/Barbara Ann; c/Barbara Travis, Mary Fletcher; p/Robert and Jane Anderson Brown (dec); ed/AB Univ Hi 1924; LLB Univ Mich 1926; pa/Admitted Mich Bar 1926; Supreme Ct Mich 1926; US Supreme Ct 1934; 6th US Circuit Ct Appeals 1954; US Dist Ct 1927; En & Wn Dists Ct 1931; US Dept Justice; Bd

Immigration Appeals 1944; US Tex Ct 1973; Asst Atty Gen Mich 1931-32; Legal Advr Wayne Co Graft Grand Jury 1939-40; Asst Prosecution Atty Wayne Co 1940; Spec Asst City Atty Police Dept Invest 1951-52; Detroit Bar Assn: Dir, Treas, Secy, Pres; St Bar Mich: Chm, Var Coms; cp/Repub Nom House Reps; Nom'd Circuit Judge; Pres Oakland Co Repub Clb; F'ton Hist Soc; St Anthonys Guild Franciscan Friars; r/Presb.

BROWNE, ALICE PAULINE oc/Accountant; b/Jun 26, 1918; h/PO Box 672, Douglasville, GA 30133; ba/Same; c/Gerald Smetzer, Raymond & Jonathan Smetzer, Patricia S Gibson; p/James Sweeney (dec); Alice Crabb Sweeney Young; ed/BBA Univ Miami; pa/Writer Num Bus & Profl Articles; Delta Theta Phi; r/Christian Pilots Assn; Addicts Christian For Christ; hon/Deans List & Nat Hon Soc, Univ Miami.

BROWNE, JOSEPH PETER oc/Catholic Priest; Director; b/Jun 12, 1929; h/5410 N Strong St Apt 8, Portland, OR 97203; ba/P'land; p/George Browne (dec); Mary Browne, Detroit, MI; ed/AB; STL; STD; MSLS; pa/Univ Lib Dir; Past Pres Oreg Lib Assn; Cath Lib Assn; cp/Coun & Former St Chaplain K of C; r/Cath; hon/Beta Phi Mu; Oreg K of Yr 1973.

BROWNE, SHARON KAY oc/Educator; b/Sept 17, 1939; h/331 Arguello, San Francisco, CA 94118; ba/SF; p/John and Marjorie Kent Browne, Oceanside, CA; ed/BS; MS; Tchg Credentials: Regular Ed, Severely Handicapped, Lng Handicapped; pa/Asst Prof Dept Lng Disabilities; Reg'd Occupl Therapist; Am Occupl Therapy Assn; cp/Orton Soc; r/Christian; hon/S'ships; Grad Asst, Voc Rehab; W/W Am Wom; Excepl Edrs.

BROWNE, WALTER BROACH oc/Library Director; b/Feb 26, 1938; h/1504 Cruise, Corinth, MS 38834; ba/Corinth; m/Virginia Lund; c/William, Michael, Joly Starr, Elizabeth Starr; p/Willie Myers Browne, Tulsa, OK; ed/AB; BA; MLS; mil/AUS 1958-60; pa/Dir NE Reg Lib; Asst Dir Pike-Amite Lib; Lib Asst Grand Canyon Col; VP Sales Ariz Aerosol Co; cp/Chm Tourism Com Alcorn Co C of C; St Coor Miss Very Spec Arts Fair; C of C St Hwy Com; r/Presb; hon/Outstg Yg Libn Miss; Phi Beta Delta; Phi Theta Kappa; Past Pres Awd.

BRUCE, JERRY WAYNE oc/Executive Director; b/May 30, 1945; h/Rt 7, Box 174-X, Athens, AL 35611; ba/Lester, AL; m/Paul Faye Richey; c/Mary Lynn, Jay, Martha Faye; p/Ralph and Mary Edna Bruce, Dyersburg, TN; ed/BBA Memphis St Univ 1967; MBA Miss Col 1973; CPA Sts of Tenn, Miss & Ala; pa/Exec Dir, D E Jackson Meml Hosp; AICPA; Hosp Fin Mgmt Assn; Miss Soc CPAs; Ala Soc CPAs; Pi Sigma Epsilon; Am Acctg Assn; Am Acad Med Admrs; cp/Athens-Limestone C of C; Spec Lectr in

Acctg, Athens St Col; Yg Repubs; Assoc Mem, Fla Col Alumni Assn; r/Ch of Christ: SS Tchrs; hon/Dean's List, Holmes Jr Col.

BRUFF, BEVERLY OLIVE oc/Director; b/Dec 15, 1926; h/508 Tomahawk Trl, San Antonio, TX 78232; ba/SA; p/Albert Bruff (dec); Hazel Smith Bruff, SA; ed/BA Tulane Univ; Addit Studies; pa/Public Relats Dir SA Area Girl Scout Coun; Am Wom Radio & TV: Chapt Dir, Secy, Pres; Tex Public Relats Assn; Alamo Bus Communicators; Tex Press Wom:

Exec Bd Dirs, Dist Treas, Dist VP; Nat Fdn Press Wom; Wom Communs Inc: Histn, VP, Treas; Assn Girl Scout Exec Staff: Exec Bd, Public Relats Chm, VP, Nat Bd Dirs, Communs Chm; Speech Arts Assn SA: VP, Pres, Bd Dirs; cp/SA Soc Fund Raising Execs; Coun Pres; Coun Intl Relats; Zoning Commr Hill Country Vil; hon/Silver Spur Awd, Tex Public Relats Assn; Tex Press Wom St Writing Contests Awds.

BRUHN, JOHN GLYNDON oc/Administrator; b/Apr 27, 1934; h/416 1st St, Galveston, TX 77550; ba/G'ston; p/Margaret Treiber Bruhn, Phoenix, AZ; ed/BA Univ Neb 1956; MA 1958; PhD Yale 1961; mil/USAR 1957-63; pa/Univ Tex Med Br: Assoc Dean Commun Affairs, Prof Preventive Med & Commun Hlth 1972-; Fac Univ Okla Med Ctr 1962-72; Res Sociologist: Grace-New Haven Hosp 1960-61, Univ Edinburgh 1961-62; Conslt in Field; Papers Read Num Confs; Am Public Hlth Assn; Am Heart Assn; Royal Soc Hlth; Am Psychosomatic Soc; Assn Am Med Cols; Assn Tchr Preventive Med; AAAS; AAUP; SWn Sociol Assn; NY Acad Sci; Sigma Xi; Alpha Kappa Delta; Kappa Sigma; cp/Bd Trustees & Exec Com U Way; Bd & VChm G'ston Co Coor'd Commun; Rotarian; Bd Cult Arts Coun; Bd Dirs G'ston Performing Arts Enterprises; Num Other Civic Assns; hon/F'ships: Commonwealth Fund Yale Univ, USPHS, US Fulbright; Career Devel Awd, Nat Heart Inst; Pub'd Author.

BRUNER, INEZ W oc/Economist; h/Rt 1 Box 167-A, Porter, OK 74454; ba/Wagoner, OK; m/George; p/Hezzie and Susie Williams (dec); ed/MEd; pa/Ext Home Economists Assn; Home Ec Assn; Epsilon Sigma Phi; r/Wesley Meth Ch; hon/W/W Dist'd Ser Awd.

BRUTUS, DENNIS V oc/Professor; b/Nov 28, 1924; h/624 Clark St, Evanston, IL 60201; ba/E'ston; m/May; c/Jacinta, Marc, Julian, Anthony, Justina, Cornelia, Gregory, Paula; p/Francis and Margaret Bloemetjie Brutus; ed/BA distn, CED Fort Hare Univ; LLB Witwatersrand Univ; pa/Prof Eng & African Lit NWn Univ; Vis Prof Univ Denver; Dir Campaign Release S African Pol Prisoners; Pres S African Non-Racial Olympic Com (SAN-ROC); Ed Bds: Africa Today, The Gar, S&W; Publs: Mod Poetry Africa, African Writing Today, Protest Conflict African Lit, 7 S African Poets, Black Orpheus, China Poems, Strains, S African Voices, Stubborn Hope, A Simple Lust Letters to Martha; Num Socs.

BRYAN, EDWARD RAYMOND (May 27, 1978); oc/Former Engineer; h/Formerly of PO Box 2227, Garland, TX 75041; m/Ella; c/Terri B Gordon, Edward Jr, Patrick; p/Eldon Bryan (dec); Helen Ewing (dec); ed/BS E Ctl Univ 1962; Addit Studies;

mil/USN Korean War 4 Yrs; pa/Former Pres, Chief Exec Ofcr, Stockholder & Chm Bd Electronic Flo-Meters Inc 1970-78; Teledyne/Geotech; Intl Mktg Mgr 1968-70, Proj Engr 1966-68, Proj Engr & Group Ldr Mobile Seismic Stas 1962-64; Engr Team Ldr & Operator Seismic Stas US Geotech Inc 1962-64; Owner & Mgr Bryan Electric Co 1959-62; Num Papers Read Intl & Nat Orgs; Am & Dallas Geophysical Soc; Intl Union Geodesy & Geophysics; So Gas Assn; ITAD; AMA; Standards Review Bd & Sr Mem Instrument Soc Am; cp/Fdr Nat Security Coun; DAV; Elks; VFW; FFA; Speech Clb; HS Band Clb; r/Mem 1st Bapt Ch; hon/Num Medals & Battle Certs USN; Cert Recog Devoted & Selfless Consecration Ser Coun, Pres Carter.

BRYAN, JANE CAMPBELL oc/Analyst; Painter; b/Sept 29, 1925; h/14460 Misty Meadow, Houston, TX 77079; ba/Houston; c/Elizabeth, Carolyn, James; p/Langdon and Rhoda Trego Campbell (dec); ed/AB (Art & Psych) Case Wn Resv; CLU; pa/Computer Sys Software Analyst; Fellow Life Mgmt Assn Inst; Soc Cert'd Data Processors; AAUW; cp/Past Bd Trustees Union Co Psychi Clin; Past Ofcr & Trustee Summit Art Ctr; DAR; Leag Wom Voters; r/Presb; hon/Chi Beta Phi; Recipient Var Awds Juried St & Local Art Shows.

BRYAN, JANET MAJOR oc/Educator; Nutritionist; Consultant; b/Nov 22, 1922; h/527 Elberon Ave, Cincinnati, OH 45205; ba/Cinc; p/Emmette and Virginia Tillman Bryan (dec); ed/BA Ala Col 1944; MS Columbia Univ 1964; Postgrad Studies; pa/Am Dietetic Assn; APHA; AAUP; AAAS; Soc Nutritional Ser; Kappa Delta Pi; r/Prot; Meth & Presb; hon/Recipient Awd Merit; Dipl Commun Ser; Intl Biog; Notable Ams Bicent Era; Personalities W&MW.

BRYAN, SHARON ANN oc/Medical Writer; Editor; b/Dec 18, 1941; h/533 Via Del Monte, Palos Verdes Estates, CA 90274; m/James; c/Lisa, Holly; p/George Goll Jr, Gladstone, MO; Dorothy Henn Goll, Shawnee-Mission, KS; ed/BJ Univ Mo 1963; Dipl Stanford Radio & TV Inst; Postgrad Studies; pa/Am Acad Ophthalmology & Otolaryngology: Hist Writer 1972-, Editor Perceiver 1969-72; Manuscript Editor Transactions; Managing Editor Staffoscope 1965-66; Manuscript Editor & Writer Nonsci Sects NY5 Jour Med Med Soc St NY; cp/Soc Meml Sloan-Kettering Cancer Ctr; NY Hosp Woms Leag; Drs Wives Guild; Little Co Mary Hosp; r/Prot; hon/W/W Am Wom; World W/W Wom.

BRYANT, ALLETIS AUGBURN oc/Principal; Coordinator; h/1820 5th St NE, Winston-Salem, NC 27101; ba/WS; m/William; p/P T and Virginia Augburn (dec); ed/BS Elizabeth City St Univ; MA Columbia Univ; Addit Studies; pa/Asst Prin & Rdg Coor Konnoak Elem Sch; NEA; NC Tchrs; IRA; NC Asst Prins; r/Bapt; hon/Alpha Kappa Mu; Outstg Ldr Elem & Sec'dy Ed; Notable Ams Awd.

BRYANT, ANTUSA SANTOS oc/Professor; b/Aug 22, 1934; h/230 N Ash, Belle Plaine, MN 56011; ba/Mankato, MN; m/Benjamin; c/Benjamin Jr, Lori, Bobby; p/Andres and Mercedes Santos (dec); ed/BS magna cum laude 1954; MA 1957; EdD 1960; pa/Prof Spec Ed Mankato St Univ 1965-; Ednl Conslt; Reschr & Writer; AAMD; CEC; ARRM; MCGT; NAACP; hon/PEO Intl Peace Scholar; Meritorious Prof 1977-78.

BRYANT, CLAUDINE MOSS GAY oc/Physician; b/Nov 30, 1915; h/5030 Loughboro Rd NW, Wash, DC 20016; ba/Wash; m/James Marion; c/Gordon Gay, Spencer Gay; p/Fred Moss (dec); Rosa Mercer Moss; ed/BS William & Mary Col; MD Univ Va; pa/FAAFP; DC Pres, Leg Comm, & Del AAFP; Bd DC Med Soc; Past Pres AMWA; DOCPAC; AMPAC; cp/Pres Com Malpract Comm; Rep Pres Drug Abuse; Rep St Dept & US; Fdn Orgs Profl Wom; Zonta Clb; r/Epis.

BRYANT, ELIZABETH ANN oc/Equal Opportunity Officer; b/Feb 28, 1950; h/1152 Lombard Dr, Montgomery, AL 36109; ba/M'gomery; p/Percy Bryant (dec); Claire Kimbrough Bryant, Bay Minette, AL; ed/BS 1972, MA 1974 Univ Ala; pa/Equal Opport Ofcr M'gomery Commun Action Agy; VP Ala Equal Opport Ofcrs Assn; Ala Pers & Guid Assn; VP Univ Ala Chapt APGA; Nat & Ala Voc Guid Assn; r/Meth; hon/Outstg Achmt Awd, Tri-Co Yth Prog; Outstg Yg Wom Am; W/W S&SW; Personalities S; Dict Intl Biog.

BRYANT, JOHN WILLIAM oc/Educator; b/Jun 16, 1938; h/22 Abedar Ln, Latham, NY 12110; ba/Albany, NY; m/Mary Roberta Davis; c/John, Kevin; p/John Bryant, Rensselaer, NY; Margret O'Neil Bryant (dec); ed/BS; MS; mil/USAR; pa/Tchr Mtly Retarded Spec Ed Thomas S O'Brien Sch; NYS U Tchrs Assn; Albany Public Tchrs Assn; cp/Spec Olympics; K of C; r/Rom Cath; hon/Notable Ams; Dic Intl Biog; W/W Child Devel.

BRYANT, SYLVIA LEIGH oc/Poet; b/May 8, 1947; h/Rt 5, Box 498A, Madison Heights, VA 24572; ba/Lynchburg, VA; p/Hudley Bryant, Madison Heights, VA; pa/Editor/Pubr & Pres, Anthology Soc; Pub'd in The Poet, Adventures in Poetry Mag, Am Poet, Modern Images, Others; Fellow: Intl Acad Poets, Intl Biogl Assn, Anglo-Am Acad (hon); Poet Laureate, Stella Woodall Poetry Soc Intl; Am Poets F'ship Soc; U Poets Laureate Intl, Philippines; Others; r/Bapt; hon/W/W Poetry; Anglo-Am W/W; DIB; Literary Hall of Fame; Assoc Mem, Am Biogl Inst; Others.

BUCHANAN, JERRY MAJOR oc/-Author; b/Dec 10, 1923; h/#1 Nob Hill Dr, Vancouver, WA 98664; ba/Vancouver; m/Beverly Ann; c/Danny Smothers (dec); p/Herbert and Doris De Nully Buchanan (dec); mil/USMC WW-II 4 Yrs; pa/Writer & Pubr 'Towers Clb USA Newsletter'; Fdr Sales Tng Inc; Author: Writers Utopia Formula Report, Looking Back Country, Universe With Potential; r/Rel Philosopher; hon/W/W West.

BUCHANAN-DAVIDSON, DOROTHY JEAN oc/Science Writer; b/Dec 22, 1925; h/6278 Sun Val Pkwy, Oregon, WI 53575; ba/Madison, WI; m/Max Arthur Davidson; c/Scott, Janet, Nancy; p/John and Helen Huey Buchanan (dec); ed/BS; MS; PhD; pa/Sci

Writer Wis Clin Cancer Ctr; Sigma Xi; Sigma Delta Epsilon; Iota Sigma Pi; Anciens Eleves de l'Institut Pasteur; Am Med Writers Assn; Am Soc Preventive Oncology; cp/VFW Band; Oreg PTO; Forest Prods Leag; Kappa Delta; r/Presb Ch: Elder, Deacon.

BUCKALEW, LOUIS WALTER oc/Behavioral Scientist; Researcher; b/Apr 21, 1944; h/2412 Lauderdale Ct, Orlando, FL 32805; ba/Normal, FL; p/L W Buckalew Jr (dec); Maryruth Buckalew, Orlando; ed/BA; MS; mil/AUS Vietnam 2 Yrs; pa/Asst Prof Psychol Ala A&M Univ; Dir Psycho Res Lab; Conslt: Ala Public TV, Gerontolgy Progs; r/Epis; hon/Phi Chi; Kappa Delta Pi; AUS: Bronze Star, Num Commend Medals.

BUCKEL, RONALD PAUL oc/Roman Catholic Priest; b/Aug 6, 1939; h/5600 W Genesee St, Camillus, NY 13031; p/Clarence

Buckel, Syracuse, NY; Jane Smith Buckel (dec); ed/BA St Bonaventure Univ 19654; MA Syracuse Univ 1971; pa/Coor Preventive Drug Abuse Prog Onondaga Co Parochial Sch 1971-; cp/Chaplain: Onondaga Co Ancient Order Hibernians 1976-, Fairmount Fire Dept 1971-; Priest Senate; Reachout Drug Rehab Ctr; Camillus Yth Bd & Narcotic Coun; Camillus Ethics Bd; Teen Challenge; Drug Abuse Task Force; Bd Dirs Onondaga Co Mtl Htlh Dept; Fam Life Dept; Former Chm City Co Drug Abuse Comm; hon/W/W Rel; Man of Yr, W Genesee JCs.

BUCKLEY, HAROLD DONALD oc/Professor; b/Nov 25, 1929; h/2263 Edgewood Dr, Vineland, NJ 08360; ba/V'land; m/Thelma Weiderhold; c/Donna Mosovich, Darlene, Dean; p/Clifford Buckley (dec); Anna Buckley, Warminister, PA; ed/AB Kings Col 1951; MA Univ Denver 1957; MDiv Temple Univ 1954; EdD Syracuse Univ 1969; Addit Studies; mil/USAF Chaplain; pa/Cumberland Co Col: Dean Student Pers Sers 1969-74, Prof Psychol & Phil 1974-; Coadjutant Fac Psychol Glassboro St Col 1970-73; Assoc Dean

Students & Prof Psychol St Univ Col-O 1966-69; Dir Student Activs & Cnslr Mohawk Val Commun Col 1963-65; Psychologist; Philosopher; Cert'd Lectr Psychol Mtl Hlth NJ Dept Hlth; APA; APGA; ACPA; NVGA; NASPA; Yth Sers Com NJEA; cp/Exec Bd CCC Fac; Bd Dir Neighborhood House; Bd Mgrs Otsego Co Mtl Hth Assn; Exec Bd C'land Co Drug Abuse Clin; Budget & Admissions Com U Fund; Exec Com C'land Co Dem Org; Bd Trustees Black Studies Prog; Polit Cand; r/Am Bapt; Clergyman; hon/NSF Grant Psychol; Prof of Yr 1976-77 & 1977-78; Pub'd Author; Num Biogl Listings.

BUCKLEY, PAUL V oc/Superintendent; b/Oct 8, 1927; h/1898 Wren Ave, Corona, CA 91720; ba/Corona; m/Mary Lou; c/John, Peter, Mary; p/Verne Buckley (dec); Jennie Buckley, Sullivan, IN; ed/BS; MS; EdD Cand; mil/AUS 1946-47; pa/Assoc Supt Schs; Public Sch & Univ Adm Tchg; cp/Rotary Intl; r/Epis; hon/Num Awds Adm Assn & Pepperdine Univ.

BUCKNER, JOHN KENDRICK oc/Engineer; b/Jun 13, 1936; h/5408 Benbridge Dr, Fort Worth, TX 76101; m/Nancy Ann Smith; c/James, Bari; p/Roland Kendrick (dec); Lucille Buckner, Indianapolis, IN; ed/BA DePauw; MSAE Stanford Univ; pa/Engrg Mgr Aerospace Indust; AIAA; Tech Com Atmospheric Flt Mechanics.

BUCKNER, ROBERT oc/Social Services; b/Jul 27, 1938; h/PO Box 417, Gatesville, TX 76528; ba/Same; m/Darnell; c/Sharon, Sheryl, Sherrie, Stephanie, Shanna; p/Robert Buckner Sr (dec); Mary Buckner, Oklahoma City, OK; ed/BA Langston Univ 1961; MS St Louis Univ; Addit Studies; mil/AUS 1961-63; pa/Chief Social Sers G'ville St Sch Boys 1973-; Yth Devel Specs Langston Univ 1971-73; Correctional Treatment Specs El Reno Fed Reformitory 1969-71; Supvr Social Sers Boley St Sch Boys 1964-66; Conslt Elem & Sec'dy Schs; Nat Assn Social Wkrs; Child Wel Leag Am; Tex Correctional Assn; Am Public Wel Assn; Nat Assn Blacks Crim Justice Sys; cp/Kappa Alpha Psi; r/Bapt; hon/S'ship Langston Univ; W/W Am Cols & Univs.

BUCZKO, THADDEUS oc/Auditor;

b/Feb 23, 1926; h/47 Butler St, Salem, MA 01970; ba/Boston, MA; p/Ignacy and Veronica Brzozowska Buczko (dec); ed/BA w hons Norwich Univ; JD Boston Univ 1951; Addit Studies; mil/USN Asiatic-Pacific Theatre Opers WW-II; AUS Unit Tank Cmdr & Asst Staff Judge Advocate 3rd Armored Div Korean War; 94th USAR Cmd Chief Staff Col; pa/St Auditor Commonwlth Mass 1964-; Former Postmaster Salem; Mass House Rep 10th Essex Dist 6 Yrs; Atty Law; Admitted Pract Law: Mass 1951, US Dist Ct Dist Mass,

US Ct Mil Appeals; Supreme Ct USA; US Ct Claims; Fed, Am, Mass, Boston, Essex Co & Salem Bar Assns; Mass Trial Lwyrs Assn; Resolutions Com Nat Assn St Auditors, Comptrollers & Treas; Nat Assn Internal Auditors; Am Acctg Assn; Am Soc Mil Comptrollers; Past VP New Eng Intergovt Audit Form; Electronic Data Processing Assn; cp/Bd Fellows Norwich Univ; Former VP Norwich Alumni Assn; Boston Univ Nat Alumni Coun; Heart Assn; Cancer Soc; Mtl Hlth Assn; Cerebral Palsy Assn; Num Other Civic Assns; r/Rom Cath.

BUDGE, MELBA CORNWELL oc/Educator; b/Mar 31, 1898; h/109 S Main St, St John, KS 67576; ba/Same; m/Raymond LeClair (dec); p/John and Anna Welsh Cornwell (dec); ed/Ward-Belmont Music Conservatory; Nat Acad Msic; pa/Piano & Organ Tchr; Judge Am Col Musicians; NMTA; KMTA; NGPT; IBC; cp/People-to-People Confs; Repub Party; r/Meth; hon/Hall of Fame, NGPT.

BUFORD, OLIVETTE H oc/Educator; Editor; b/Nov 26, 1914; h/817 Holbrook Cir, Fort Walton Bch, FL 32548; m/Charles Duffy (dec); p/Arthur and Mabel Larson Holmes (dec); ed/BA magna cum laude 1936, MA 1940 Univ Ia; pa/Tchr Eng & Spch Ia, Ga & Alaska 13 Yrs; Ed Spec & Chief Tech Pubs Editor/Writer US Govt 20 Yrs; Rec Conslt ARC WW-II; Pres Fla St Div AAUW; cp/Govs Comm Status Wom; r/Epis; Mem St Simons-on-the-Sound; hon/Phi Beta Kappa; Zeta Tau Alpha; Nat Col Players.

BUHL, LLOYD F oc/Newspaper Publisher; b/Jan 9, 1918; h/3665 N Main, Deckerville, MI 48427; ba/D'ville; m/Rosamond; c/William, Robert, Marcia, Karl; p/William and Bessie Buhl, New Haven, MI; cp/Vil Pres; 8th Dist Chm Repub Party; r/Presb.

BUJAC, JAMES NORMAN JR oc/Engineer; b/Feb 10, 1926; h/989 Pike Ct, St Louis, MO 63138; ba/SL; m/Vera Clayton; c/Jane; p/James and Marguarite Roberts Bujac, Carlsbad, NM; ed/BSME NMSU 1953; mil/AUS Inf Capt 1944-47 & 1950-52; pa/Chief Power Generation & Trans Sys Sect AUS Troop Support & Aviation Mat Readiness Cmd 1977-; AUS Aviation Sys Cmd: Gen Engr Mat Release Br 1976-77, Chief Sys Assessmt Br 1973-76, Pollution Abatement Control Coor 1972-73, Chief Planning & Progs Br Directorate Res Test & Eval 1972-73, Gen Engr ECM Test Infrared Countermeasures Proj Mgr 1970-72, Aerospace Engr Aircraft Propulsion 1968-70; Other Positions; Paper Presentations Num Socs; Reg'd Profl Engr NM & Mo; Lic'd Fallout Shelter Analyst; Nat, Mo & Chapt Pres NM Socs Profl Engrs; AIAA; Profl Soc Protective Design; Soc Logistics Engrs; Intl Biogl Assn; cp/Assn Old Crows;

BPO Elks; Circle D'Escrime; Assn AUS; r/Vestry St Francis Epis Ch; hon/Herschel S Nelson Awd, SOLE; Cert Merit, DIB; Num Biogl Listings.

BULCAO, DOUGLAS WILLIAM oc/Legislative Assistant; b/Mar 8, 1942; h/1937 Rhode Isl Ave, McLean, VA 22101; ba/Wash, DC; m/Carolyn Farr; c/Christian, Scott; p/William and Olive Woodham Bulcao, Slidell, LA; ed/BA; pa/Leg Asst US Rep Joe D Waggonner Jr Wash, DC; r/Epis.

BULL, STANLEY RAYMOND oc/Professor; b/May 15, 1941; h/208 Devine Ct, Columbia, MO 65201; ba/C'bia; m/Diana; c/Melanie, Jeffrey, Julia; p/Raymond and

Nesla Bull, La Plata, MO; ed/BS; MS; PhD; pa/Prof Engrg Univ Mo; Am Nuclear Soc; Am Assn Physicists Med; cp/Rotary Intl; hon/Sr Fulbright-Hays Prof.

BULLARD, FRED MASON oc/Professor; b/Jul 20, 1901; h/206 W 33rd St, Austin, TX 78705; ba/Austin; m/Bess Mills (dec); c/Thais, Peggy B Marshall; p/Ezra and Lillie Mason Bullard (dec); ed/BS 1921, MS 1922 Univ Okla; PhD Univ Mich 1928; pa/Field Geologist Okla Geol Survey 1921-23; Conslt Geologist 1923-24; Univ Tex-A: Fac 1924-, Chm Dept 1929-37; Vis Prof Vassar Col 1949;

Fulbright Res Scholar Italy 1953; Fulbright Lectr Peru 1959; Lectr Am Assn Petro Geologists 1943-45; Vis Prof & Chief Party US Tech Asst Prog Univ Baghdad 1962-64; Fellow Geol Soc Am; Mineralogical Soc Am; Am Assn Petro Geologists; Phi Beta Kappa; Sigma Xi; Sigma Gamma Epsilon; cp/Kiwanis Clb; hon/Dist'd Tchg Awd, Col Arts & Scis Univ Tex; Pub'd Author.

BULLOCK, DOROTHY DODSON oc/Consultant; Minister; b/Aug 19, 1928; h/6501 E Aster Dr, Scottsdale, AZ 85254; ba/Phoenix, AZ; c/Pamela B Schlieter; p/Walter and Emma Dosdon; ed/BS Univ Ariz 1951; MA ASU 1969; Tchg, Cnslg & Supvg Certs; Cert'd Ariz Sch Psychologist; pa/Conslt Ed Conslt Cartwright Sch Dist 1974-; Tchr Spec Ed Grad Classes ASU 1976-77; Other Tchg Positions: Madison Sch Dist 1967-74, Epis Sch 1966-67, Prince Georges Co 1960-65, Am Sch Japan 1957-59, Anne Arundel Co 1954-56, Thatcher Public Schs 1953-54, Salt Lake City 1952-53, Madison 1951-52; Helped Organize Spec Ed Prog Good Samaritan Hosp 1973; Author *The Simplied Phonetic Approach*; Num Wkshops; AACLD; ACLD; APGA; NASP; CEC; Delta Kappa Gamma; cp/Cartwright Sch Adm Assn; Am Appaloosa Assn; Ariz Horsemans Assn;

r/Unity Ch Metaphysical Approach; Min & Dir Goodly New Thought Foun; hon/Ariz St Dept Spec Ed; Ariz Assn Chd w Lng Disabilities; 4-H Ldrship Awd; PhD USAU 1977; W/W West; Notable Ams Awd; Intl W/W Eng.

BULLOCK, WILLIAM JOSEPH oc/Professor; b/Dec 25, 1943; h/3011 Magnolia Pl, Hattiesburg, MS; ba/H'burg; m/Jane Lee; c/Mark, Leigh; p/Harold and Waneta Bullock; ed/BME cum laude 1966, MA 1968, PhD 1971 Fla St Univ; pa/Assoc Prof & Dir Choral Activs Dept Music Univ So Miss 1977-; NE Campus Music Dept Tarrant Co Jr Col: Prof 1968-77, Coor Vocal & Choral Music 1972-77; Student Intern Choral Dept Fort Lauderdale HS 1965; Tchrs Aide Music Dept Nova HS 1965; Choral Fest Dir: Six Flags Over Tex 1973-, Six Flags Over Mid-Am 1979-, Astroworld Choral Fest 1979-; Num Wkshops;

Guest Conductor Var Profl Orgs; Phi Mu Alpha; Kappa Delta Pi; Phi Delta Kappa; Am Choral Dirs Assn; Col Music Soc; Miss Music Edrs Assn; Am Choral Foun; cp/Dir Miss Yth Chorale 1978 Tour Europe; Bd Dirs Van Cliburn Intl Quadrennial Piano Competition; r/Meth; Chancel Choir Dir: Richland Hills Christian Ch Fort Worth 1970-71, 1st U Meth Ch of Hurst 1971-77; hon/Resolution Recog, Tex Jr Col Tchrs Assn; Tarrant Co Jr Col: Dist'd Ser Awds 1973 & 1977, St Jr Col Prof of Yr Nominee 1974; Musicianship Awd, Fla St Univ; F'ships: Tuesday Morning Musicale 1962 & 1963, Prospective Tchr Higher Ed Act Fla St Univ 1966; Pi Kappa Lambda; Phi Kappa Phi; Phi Eta Sigma; Pub'd Author; Num Biogl Listings.

BUNDRENT, DURWOOD CREED oc/Supervisor; b/Jul 4, 1030; h/1228 E Jefferson, Kokomo, IN 46901; ba/Kokomo; m/Hattie; c/Carol B Preston, Marcia, Patricia

Brisker, Durwood Jr, Bonnie, Byron, Cynthia, Donna; p/Chester Bundrent (dec); Opal Napier; ed/BS 1956; mil/AUS Korean Conflict 1952-54; cp/City Coun-man Kokomo 1968-76; r/Bapt; hon/GM Awd Excell Commun Ser.

BUNN, CHARLES IVY JR oc/Accountant; Educator; h/Rt 1 Box 102B, Spring Hope, NC 27882; ba/Rocky Mount, NC; m/Catherine; p/Florence Bunn, SH; ed/AB Duke Univ 1973; pa/Cert'd Public Acct; Acctg Tchr NC Wesleyan Col 1978-; Price Waterhouse & Co: Sr Acct Audit Div 1974-78, Instr Cont'g Ed Sems 1976-78; Instr Other Sems 1976-77; Am Inst Cert'd Public Accts; Fellow & Com Govt Affairs & Leg NCACPA; Am Acct Assn; Chi Delta Phi; cp/Chm 2nd

Congl Dist Caucus Yg Dems NC; Past Pres Yg Dem Nash Co; Dir, Pres & Secy NC Student Leg Alumni Assn; Treas So Nash Sr HS Alumni Assn; Coun Area Devel & Leg RM Area C of C; RM Breakfast Optimists Clb; Treas Twin Co JCs; NC Zool Soc; Iron Dukes Clb; r/Gibson Meml U Meth Ch, SH; hon/Lambda Chi Alpha; W/W Students Am Cols & Univs; Outstg Yg Men Am; Personalities S.

BUNSON, MARGARET R oc/Free Lance Author; Artist; b/Jul 25, 1930; h/131 Kuulei Rd, Kailua, HI 96734; ba/Honolulu, HI; m/Michael; c/Stephen, Matthew; p/Florence Anderson, Kailua; ed/BA; Postgrad Work; pa/Poet; Illustrator; cp/Sec Coalition Clergy & Laity; Hi St Crime Commr; r/Cath; hon/Tamiment Inst Awd; Num Lit Awds.

BUNTEN, CAROLYN MELBA oc/Businesswoman; b/Oct 7, 1937; h/307½ S Roan St, Elizabethton, TN 37643; ba/E'ton; p/Paul H and Doris M Bunten, Mountain City, TN; ed/Speedwriting & Secl Col 1966; pa/USDA/FmHA 1971-: Bd Dirs Co Ofc Assts & Co Ofc Clerks; FBI 1956-66; Pres BPW 1979-80; r/Doe Valley Bapt Ch: Tchr, Choir Mem, Dir Bible Sch.

BUNTING, JOHN JAMES oc/Physician; b/Nov 7, 1913; h/6307 So Rice, Bellaire, TX 77401; ba/Houston, TX; m/Katharyne Denton; c/Beverly Moor (Mrs Robert), John Jr, William; p/James and Doroa Smith Bunting; ed/BS Lafayette Col 1934; MD Univ Md 1938; Postgrad Studies; mil/USAAF Major 1942-45; pa/Phys Internal Med 1946-; Resident Jersey City Med Ctr 1940-41; Intern Resident Univ Hosp 1938-40; Staff: Meml Hosp, Meth Hosp, St Lukes Epis Hosp, Hermann Hosp, Jefferson Davis Hosp, St Joseph Hosp, Diagnostic Hosp, Rosewood Hosp, Twelve Oaks Hosp, Ben Taub Hosp, Ctr Pavilion Hosp; Assoc Prof Clin Med Baylor Med Sch 1947-; Assoc Med Univ Tex 1957-; Num Other Past Tchg Positions; Diplomate Am Bd Internal Med; Fellow: Am Col Angiology, ACP, Am Col Chest Phys; AMA; Am Heart Assn; Am Diabetes Assn; AAAS; Am Geriatrics Soc; NY Acad Sci; Tex Acad Internal Med; So Med Assn Episcopalian; Am & Tex Soc Internal Med; Assoc Editor *Med Records & Annals*; Edit Bd & Contbr *Book Hlth*; Contbr Num Other Profl Jours; cp/Pres Postgrad & Chm Publicity and Mbrship Med Assembly S Tex.

BURCH, LOREN WILLIAM oc/Editor; h/7406 E 3rd St, Tulsa, OK 74112; ba/Tulsa; m/Olive May; c/Phyllis (dec), Bryon, Marilyn Harkey, Loren Jr, James, (Stepchd:) Jerry, Raymond Holder; p/Henry and Emma Burch

(dec); ed/BA; BD; MA; mil/USAF Major 1943-69; pa/News Editor SE News; cp/Tulsa Press Clb; Kiwanis; Green County Ret'd Ofcrs Assn; Keystone Toastmasters; r/Prot; hon/Freedoms Foun Medal; AF Commend; Num Acad Awds.

BURCHARD, FORREST J oc/Farmer; Trucking; Lime Service; b/May 14, 1944; h/Rt 1, Melber, KY 42069; ba/Same; m/Joyce Rogers; p/Arch and Anna Jackson Burchard, Melber; mil/USAR 100th Div E-7 SFC 7 Yrs; pa/Ky Del Am Agri Mvmt; cp/Ky Cols; Cand St Senator Dist 1; r/Bible Bapt Ch, Paducah.

BURDETTE, PATRICIA ANN oc/Public Official; Manager; b/Aug 27, 1931; h/2602 Jefferson Ave, Point Pleasant, WV 25550; ba/PP; m/Wayne; c/Charles, Sandra Aide; p/Charles and Nellie Young Jones, PP; pa/City Clerk; Treas; Ofc Mgr Water & Sewer Plant; WVa Planning Assn; Bd Dirs WVa Mun Leag; Intl Treas Assn; cp/Woms Clb; Repub Woms Clb; Cancer Soc; PP Bicent Celebration; r/Presb; hon/Outstg W Virginians; W/W Am Wom.

BURG, LAWRENCE EDWARD oc/Stockbroker; Security Analyst; b/Apr 2, 1913; h/820 Elder Rd, Homewood, IL 60430; ba/Chicago, IL; m/Mary Ewing Glickauf; c/Kenneth, Bruce, Louise, Mary; p/Clifford Burg, Long Bch, CA; Hazel Russell Burg (dec); ed/Att'd Num Cols; mil/AUS 1941-45; pa/Commonwlth Edison Co: Salesman 1931-32, Dist Rep 1937-51; Salesman: Burg Typewriter Ser 1933, Williams & Meyes Co 1934-35, Standard Oil Co 1935-36; Owner & Pres Minit-Fry Potato Co; Mgr Res Dept & Asst Secy William M Tegtmeyer Co 1961-65; Reg'd Rep, Res Conslt & Mutual Funds Spec Woolard & Co 1965-; Owner Minit Calculator; Former Partner St Lawrence Chem Prds Co; Reg'd Rep Nat Assn Security Dealers; Stockbrokers Assn Chgo; Adv Coun Am Security Coun; cp/Am Contract Bridge Leag; Intl Platform Assn; Am Legion; US Chess Fdn; Toastmasters Intl; Repub; Nat Invest Com Aerial Phenomena; Aerial Phenomena Res Org; Homewood-Flossmoor Chess; Beverly Social; r/Christian Scist; hon/Granted Patent #3, 045, 906 Edwards Calculator 1962.

BURGE, ETHEL oc/Writer; Lecturer; Counselor; b/Feb 5, 1916; h/1352 W Pampa Ave, Mesa, AZ 85202; m/Floyd; c/Jeffery Lon, Jon Graham; p/(dec); pa/Author: *This Bus of Dressing, Your Personal Colorscope;*

Columns: *Fashion Strip, Spotlight, Peacock Alley;* Consist: Metro Sch Bus, Dartnell Corp; Exec Dir & Key-Note Spkr Woms Whirl; Personality Seminars; Banquet Circuit; Num Other Past Positions; hon/Golden Hat, NWn Univ.

BURGER, HENRY G oc/Anthropologist; Codifier Physical & Social Engineering; b/Jun 27, 1923; h/7306 Brittany, Shawnee Mission, KS 66203; ba/Kansas City, MO; ed/BA Pulitzer Scholar Columbia Col 1947; MA 1965, PhD St Doct Fellow 1967 Columbia Univ; mil/AUS Engrs Capt 1943-46; pa/Univ Mo: Prof Anthropology & Ed 1973-, Fdg Mem Univ-Wide Doct Faci 1974-; Former Anthropological Conslt: Prentice-Hall Inc, US Vets Adm Hosp; Adv Editor *Anthropology & Ed Qtrly* 1975-; Other Past Positions; Life Fellow: Am Anthropology Assn, Royal Anthropology Inst Gt Britain; Soc Profl Anthropologists; Am Ethnological Soc; Soc

Med Anthropology; Coun Anthropology & Ed; AAAS; AAUP; World Acad Art & Sci; Phi Beta Kappa; Num Other Profl Assns; Social Sci Spkr 59 Confs Am & Europe; Pub'd Author: Articles, Monographs, Books; r/Prot; hon/Nat Sci Foun Grant 1970; Num Biogl Listings.

BURGESS, FRANCES MARIAN oc/- Printer; Publisher; b/Feb 20, 1939; h/PO Box 4770, St Thomas, US Virgin Islands 00801; ba/Same; c/Michael, Patricia, David, Marianne, Melody, Mellisa, Norman Jr, Marlaine; p/Robert Dickson (dec); Frances Silemas (dec); ed/BA; cp/Alt Del Repub Nat Conv 1972 & 1976; Repub Territory Party; Leag Wom Voters; NSA; Civil Def; r/Prot.

BURKE, BILLY W oc/Pastor; b/May 1, 1932; h/1013 Alamosa, Carlsbad, NM 88220; ba/C'bad; m/Mary Ann; c/Jerry, Jan, Joel, Jeff; p/William and Mrs William Burke, Gonzales, TX; ed/BA Baylor Univ; MRE SWn Bapt Sem; DMin Luther Rice Sem Intl; pa/So Bapt Pastor Hillcrest Bapt Ch; Author *Clouds Can Be Beautiful*; Contbr *Outreach Mag*; cp/Min Alliance; Kiwanis; r/So Bapt; hon/J P Price Awd, SWn Bapt Sem.

BURKE, DANIEL ANTHONY oc/Director; b/Feb 20, 1944; h/42 Kerry Dr, Springfield, MA 01118; ba/S'field; m/Ellen Mary Snyder; c/David, Kevin, Patrick, Carolyn; p/John and Agnes Burke, S'field;

ed/BA St Anselms Col; MA Univ Conn; EdD Univ Mass; pa/Reg Dir Sp Ed Mass Dept Ed; Sp Ed Adv Com Mass Tchrs Assn; Coun Exceptl Chd; Phi Delta Kappa; cp/Deputy Sheriff; Sports Ofcl hon/Dean's List.

BURKE, GERARD PATRICK oc/Lawyer; Government Official; b/Apr 3, 1930; h/1117 Spotswood Dr, Silver Spring, MD 20904; ba/Ft Meade, MD; m/Ann Marie; c/Gerard Jr, Maura, Christine; p/Patrick and Mary Burke (dec); ed/AB Holy Cross Col 1952; JD Georgetown Univ 1958; Inst Comparative Law Univ Paris 1960-61; mil/Nav Ofcr 1952-57; pa/Admitted Bars: US Dist DC, US Ct Appeals DC, US Supreme Ct; Fed & DC Bar Assns; Intl Assn Chiefs Police; Asst Dir Nat Security Agy 1976-77; Pres & Exec Secy Pres Fgn Intell Adv Bd 1970-73; Past Pres NSA Intl Affairs Inst; cp/Phi Delta Phi; Chm US Savs Bond Campaign 1974; r/Cath; hon/NSA Exceptl Civilian Ser Awd 1969; William A Jump Foun Meritorious Awd.

BURKE, THOMAS J M oc/Jesuit Priest; Administrator; b/Nov 19, 1920; h/Fairfield Univ, Fairfield, CT 06430; ba/Same; p/Thomas and Catherine Cahill Burke (dec); ed/AB 1944, MA 1945 Boston Col; Lic Theol Weston Col 1952; SJ; PhD NYU 1962; pa/F'field Univ: Dean Grad Sch Corporate & Polit Commun, Fdr Ctr Advmt Human Commun, Dir Public Relats 1963-66; Dir Public Relats & Assoc Editor *Jesuit Missions* 1954-63; Tchr F'field Preparatory Sch 1945-48; Joined Soc Jesus 1938; Ordained Rom Cath Priest 1951; Sev Editorships; Public Relats Soc Am; Am Soc Public Adm; Intl Commun Assn Inc; Am Acad Polit & Social Scis; PRA; Soc Ed Film & TV; JESCOM; r/Cath; hon/Num Biogl Listings.

BURKE, YVONNE BRATHWAITE oc/Congresswoman; b/Oct 5, 1932; h/5132

Garth Ave, Los Angeles, CA 90056; ba/Inglewood, CA; m/William; c/Autumn; p/James Watson; ed/BA UCLA; JD USC; pa/Admitted Cal Bar 1956; Atty 1956-66: Police Comm, Atty McCone Comm; Num Others; cp/Cal St Assembly 1966-72; US Congress Rep 28th Congl Dist 1973-; hon/JD: Va St Col, Atlanta Univ; Wom of Yr: LA Times, Nat Assn Black Mfrs.

BURKES, WAYNE oc/Pastor; Legislator; m/Ruthine Ferguson; c/Ted, Tim; p/(dec); ed/BA, MEd Miss Col; MDiv New Orleans Bapt Theol Sem; Grad USAF Supply Spec Sch, Pilot Tng Sch & Disaster Control Sch Ofcrs; Grad Indust Col Armed Forces; mil/Miss Air NG Lt Col Command Pilot; pa/Pastor Bolton Bapt Ch; Former Tchr, Cnslr & Admr Staff Hinds Jr Col; Phi Delta Kappa; Kappa Delta Pi; cp/Rep Dist 31-I St Leg; Past Pres Hinds Jr Col Ed Assn; Past Gen Ins Co; Dir Pearl River Basin Devel Dist; Hinds-Madison Pastors Assn; Pres Clinton C of C; Past VP Miss NG Assn; Past Pres Bolton Rotary Clb; Bd Hinds Co Mtl Hlth Assn; Com-man BSA; Farm Bur; Masonic Lodge; hon/W/W: Rel, Polits.

BURKHALTER, KENNETH VENOY JR oc/Director; b/Nov 24, 1943; h/3101 Bender Rd, Texarkana, TX 75501; ba/T'kana; m/Mable; p/Kenneth and Mary Burkhalter,

Waskom, TX; ed/AS T'kana Col; BS E Tex St Univ 1975; pa/Dir Computer Sers Wadley Hosp; Tex Hosp Info Sys Soc; cp/Justice of Peace 1970-75; 1976 US Congl Cand; r/Prot.

BURKMAN, ERNEST JR oc/Professor; b/Oct 4, 1929; h/705 N Ride, Tallahassee, FL 32303; ba/T'see; m/Nancy; c/Laurie, Linda, Jan, Patty; ed/BS En Mich 1952; Masters Zool 1955 & MEd 1959, EdD 1961 Univ Mich; pa/Fla St Univ: Prof Ed 1960-, Dir ISIS Proj 1972-, Head Dept Sci Ed 1965-66, Dir Ednl Res Inst 1969-71, Dir Div Instrnl Design & Pers Devel 1972-74; Dir ISCS 1966-71; CoAm Dir Turkish Nat Sci LISE Proj 1961-65; Conslt Instnl Design & Sci Curric Matters Num Profl, Govtl & Corp Orgs incl'g: Ford Foun, UNESCO, USAID, Nat Sci Foun, US Dept Def; Participant Num Intl Symps; Former Editorial Bd *Jour Res Sci Tchg*; AAAS; NSTA; Phi Delta Kappa; AERA; NARST; NABT: Bd Dirs, Editor *News & Views*; hon/Fulbright Awd Uruguay; Pub'd Author; Num Biogl Listings.

BURMAHLN, ELMER FRED oc/Director Business Education; b/Oct 6, 1897; h/3716 Manton Dr, Lynchburg, VA 24503; m/Elizabeth Butler; p/John and Emma Klopfer Burmahln (dec); ed/BS Boston Univ 1930; MA NYU 1934; Addit Studies; pa/E C Glass HS L'burg: Dir Bus Ed & Controller HS Fins 1923-67; Treas L'burg Tchrs Clb 1935-52; Supvr Comml Ed Public Schs Houston 1922-23; Hd Comml Dept: Lead HS 1918-22, Escanaba HS 1917-18; Conslt & Contbg Editor *Catering World Mgmt Mag Inc* 7 Yrs; Moderator Indust Coun Panel Conf RPI 1952-56; Conslt & Advr Todays Bus Law Goodman & Moore Pitman Pub'g Corp 1956-75; Va St Comml Contest Mgr 1926-29; Bus Ed Assns: Nat, En, So, Va (Pres, Chm Bd Dirs 1931-34); Chm Va St Prodn Bus Ed; Va Ed Assn; NRTA; Nat Assn Penmanship Tchrs & Supvrs; Nat Handwriting Coun US; Am Voc Assn; Intl Soc Bus Ed; Am Acctg Assn;

Spkr City, St, So Nat Bus Ed Convs; Lectr Columbia, So & Nat Scholastic Press Assns; Nat Assns Accts: VP L'burg Chapt #151 1960-61, Mbrship Dir L'burg Chapt 1969-73, Charter Mem Richmond, Roanoke & L'burg; NAA Intl Execs Ser Corps; Conductor Fgn Tours & World Traveler; Exec Secy Clarence Hatzeld Arch 1914; cp/Kazim Temple; Naja Temple; 32 Deg Mason; K Templar Dakota Commandery }1; Master Mason Golden Star Lodge #9 AF&AM; Dakota Chapt #3 RAM; Black Hills Coun #3 R&SM; 100 Million Dollar Clb Shriners Hosp Crippled Chd Kazim Temple & Naja Temple; Auditor L'burg Shrine Clb; Track Meet Ofcl Local & St; Chm L'burg Gasoline Rationing WW-II; Houston Univ Clb & C of C; Univ Clb Seattle; Schoolmasters Clb; Boston Univ Alumni Assn; NYU Alumni Fdn; hon/Sigma Chi; Pub'd Author; Hon Legion of Hon, Intl Supr Coun Order DeMolay; Certs Apprec: Va Bus Ed Assn, L'burg Sch Bd; Num Biogl Listings; Climbed Pikes Peak Colo Springs 1918; Crossed Equator near Panama Canal 1915.

BURNAU, SUANNA JEANETTE oc/Educator; Mezzo-Soprano; b/Jan 22, 1938; h/7007 Gingerbread Ln, Little Rock, AR 72204; ba/LR; c/Jennifer; p/Anthony and Dimple Evans Flake, LR; ed/BSE 1960, MEd 1970 Univ Ark; pa/21 Operatic Roles, Oratorio, Musical Comedy, Concert Artist & Soloist w Chs, Temples & Symph Orchs; Ks City: Lyric Opera, Starlight Theatre, Civic Orch; Ark St Opera; Symphs: Joplin, Ark, Univ-Fayetteville; Tchr: Univ Ctl Ark 1965-74, Pulaski Co Spec Sch Dist, Little Rock Public Schs, Pvt Studio; NEA; MENC; NATS; AEA; VP Ark Tau Chapt Alpha Delta Kappa; cp/Little Rock Classroom Tchrs Assn; r/Bapt; hon/Chatham Opera S'ship, Am Fdn Music Clbs; W/W Am Wom; Intl W/W Music; World W/W Wom; Personalities S.

BURNETT, ALTA HAZEL oc/Educator; b/Mar 14, 1894; h/1103 NE 55th St, Seattle, WA 98105; p/George and Cora McKey Burnett (dec); ed/BA 1926, MA 1933 Univ Wash; pa/Tchr Public Schs St Wash 43 Yrs; Nat, Wash St & Seattle Ret'd Tchrs Assns; AAUW; cp/Sustaining Mem: Repub Nat Com 1971-, Repub St Com Wash; Garfield Co & Wash St Pioneer Assns; Nat Soc DAR; Univ Wash Alumni Assn; r/Christian Ch; hon/2000 Wom Achmt; World W/W Wom; Intl W/W Commun Ser; Commun Ldrs & Noteworthy Ams; Notable Ams; Dic Intl Biog; IBA Yrbook & Biogl Dic.

BURNETT, BARBARA ANN oc/Artist; b/May 7, 1927; h/5430 Lamar Ave, Mission, KS 66202; ba/Same; m/John E; c/W David Heiser; p/Roy I and Wilma A Carson Snyder, Merriam, KS; pa/Est'd Burnett Art Studio 1973; Num 1-person Gallery Shows; Paintings in 12 Art Galleries in MW; Accepted in Num Juried Shows in W & MW; Art Work in Num Pvt & Corporate Collections in US & Europe; Designed Christmas Card for Kansas City Chapt Heart of Am Heart Assn 1975; Tchr Adult Watercolor Classes, Kansas City 3½ Yrs; Num Watercolor Wkshops & Demos to Art Groups, Schs & Others; Pub'd in: "The Illustrator", "Rush County Kansas. . .A Century in Story & Pictures", "Johnson County Kansas, Its History in Painting & Prose"; NLAPW; Gtr Ks City Art Assn; Ks Watercolor Soc; hon/1st Pl Awds: Ks City Creative Art Exhibit 1970, GKCAA Artist of Mo 1972-77, GKCAA Metcalf Show Competition 1977, Mission Art Show 1977, Ks City Flower & Garden Show (Watercolor 1977, Naturalistic 1977), Lindsborg Art Show 1976, Best of Show Awds: Ks City Flower & Garden Show 1977, Bonner Art Show 1977, Fulton Art Show 1976; Biogl Listings.

BURNETT, DONALD EWING oc/Library Director; b/Feb 2, 1938; h/Box 471, Anna, IL 62906; ba/Anna; m/Carol Jane; c/Andrea, Laura; p/William Burnett (dec); Ottie Cotter Burnett Young, Jonesboro, IL; ed/BA, MA Murray St Univ; MLS George Peabody Univ; mil/USAR Inf Sgt 6 Yrs; pa/Beta Phi Mu; Phi Delta Kappa; NEA; ALA; LISN; cp/Stinson Lib Bd; Park Bd; Yg Dems; r/Presb: Session, Clk Session, Deacon,

Class Pres; hon/Outstg Tchr Awd; W/W.

BURNETTE, JERRY EDWARD oc/Administrator; b/Mar 24, 1944; h/175 Fisher St, Christiansburg, VA 24073; ba/Dublin, VA; m/Lois; p/William and Clara Burnette, Dublin; ed/BS Radford Col 1975; AAS Blue Ridge Commun Col; Att'd Num Police Schs; pa/Dept Head Adm of Justice Prog New River Commun Col 1976-; Waynesboro Police Dept 1969-74; Radford Army Ammunition Plant 1967-69; Ranger & Sworn Corrections Guard Va Div Parks 1965-67; Lectr Concepts of Mod Criminology; Reg'd Intl Criminologist; Acad Police Sci; Nat Law Enforcement Acad; Intl Assn Univ Fingerprinting; cp/Chaplain 1st Session Ctl Police Tng Sch; So Police Inst Alumni Assn; hon/Legion of Hon Awd, Police Dept; Intl Cert Merit Crim Invest; Outstg Contbns Security Tng; Phi Theta Kappa; Pub'd Author.

BURNS, JOHN LUTHER oc/Professor; b/May 25, 1932; h/212 Univ Dr, Jonesboro, AR 72401; ba/St Univ, AR; m/Naomi Jean Staley; c/Martha, Alan; p/(dec); ed/BS, MS Univ Tenn; PhD Univ Tex-A; mil/USNR 1952-54; pa/Prof Cnslr Ed & Psychol St Univ; Num Profl Assns; Papers Presented Convs; r/Bapt; hon/Pub'd Author.

BURNS, RICHARD LELAND oc/Consultant; b/Sept 22, 1930; h/6 Pacific, Piedmont, CA 94611; ba/San Francisco, CA; m/Nancy; c/Lisa, Shelley, Richard; p/Leland and Rachel Burns, Piedmont; ed/AB Stanford 1952; mil/AUS 1952-54; pa/Mktg Conslt Broadcast/Retail Advtg; Pres Clement & Schiller; N Cal Broadcasters; EB-SF Adv-Mktg Assn; SAWA Coun Founds; Nat Adv Com Am Humane; cp/Stanford Univ Assn; Stanford Mens Clb; Commonwlth Clb Cal; r/Presb; hon/JC Man of Yr; W/W Advtg; Advtg/Mktg Film Prodn; Pearl S Buck Foun; Am Medal, AUS.

BURNS, SALLY J oc/General Manager; b/Jan 19, 1925; h/111 Donna Dr, Mabank, TX 75147; ba/Garland, TX; m/Leonard Odell; c/James, Alton; p/Frank Gipe (dec); Velma Gipe, Moody, TX; ed/Draughn Bus Sch; pa/Ofc Mgr Garland Daily News 1952-54; En Hills CC Garland: Ofc Mgr 1955-61, Gen Mgr 1961-76; Gen Mgr Lakewood CC Dallas 1976-; Clb Mgrs Assn Am: Nat Bd, Ednl Chm St Tex, Rg 10 Dir 1976, Secy St Tex Lone Star Chapt; Secy & VP N Tex Reg Clb Mgrs Assn; Nat Clb Mgrs Assn: Dir-at-Large, Mbrship Chm Lone Star Chapt; cp/Pres Altrusa Clb; Soroptimist Intl; Precnt Chm Dem Party; Num Others; r/Bapt; hon/Altrusa Wom of Yr 1971; Hon Dept Sherrif; Outstg Clb Mgr St Tex; Num Biogl Listings incl'g W/W Am.

BURR, PATRICIA LEMAY oc/Professor; b/Aug 6, 1943; h/119 Park Dr, San Antonio, TX 78212; ba/SA; m/Richard; c/Ashley; ed/BBA 1966, PhD 1973 N Tex St Univ; MA Tex Woms Univ 1968; Certificat de Langue Francaise Univ Paris a La Sorbonne; Certificat de Scolarite L'Academie Pigier Univ Paris; pa/Col Bus Adm Univ Tex: Current Prof, Assoc Prof 1976, Asst Prof 1973; Guest Prof Sch Bank Mktg Colo 1978; Col Bus Adm N Tex St Univ: Tchr Dept Pers, Indust Relats & Law 1968-72; Pt-time Tchr Fashion Mdse 1966; Asst Admr Small Bus Adm 1977-; Economist Policy Analysis Cluster Carter-Mondale Transition Ofc 1976-78; Reschr Distribution Ec Inst 1971; VP Mkt Res Assocs; Other Past Positions; Bd Dirs Hixon Venture Capital; Bd Advrs World Trade Inst; SW & So Mktg Assns; Nat Coun Small Bus Mgmt Devel; Small Bus Adv Coun S Ctl Tex Dist Small Bus Adm; Am Acad Advtg; AMA; SWn Social Sci Assn; Tex Consumer Assn; cp/Bd Dirs Bus Resource Ctr; Gtr SA C of C; Mayors Comm Status Wom; City Mgr Adv Coun Wom; Public Affairs Coun Roundtable; YWCA; r/Presb; hon/Outstg Yg Wom Am 1971; Outstg Yg Ldr, SA Express; Silver Rose, Delta Gamma; AACSB-Sears Fellow, US Small Bus Adm; Music S'ship, Florence St Univ; World W/W Wom; Pub'd Author.

BURRELL, RONALD EUGENE oc/Ad-

ministrator; b/Sept 13, 1955; h/319 Twin Lakes Rd, Rock Hill, SC 29730; ba/RH; m/Beth Cruse; p/Kenneth Burrell (dec); Patricia Godrey Burrell, RH; ed/Att'd Univ SC & Winthrop Col; pa/Nsg Home Admr Meadow Haven Nsg Ctr 1978-; Asst Admr Annes Convalescent Home 1977-78; Former Student Rep Am Col Nsg Home Admrs; SC Hlth Care Assn; 3 Rivers Hlth Sys Agy; cp/Lions Clb; Christian Couples Clb; r/Northside Bapt Ch, RH.

BURTON, ARTHUR oc/Professor; b/Mar 10, 1914; h/8330 La Riviera Dr, Sacramento, CA 95826; ba/S'mento; m/Edith Hamilton; c/Vicki; p/Hyman Burton (dec); Martha Burton, Los Angeles, CA; ed/MA UCLA 1938; PhD Univ Cal-B 1940; pa/Prof Psychol Cal St Univ; Author 14 Books Clin Psychol; cp/Red Cross; Juv Crime Preven; r/Judaic; hon/Fulbright Nomination; Book-of-Mo.

BURTON, EDWIN CLARENCE oc/Educator; Administrator; b/Oct 21, 1907; h/203 N Tenn Rd, Cartersville, GA 30120; ba/Same; p/Andrew and Effie Carver Burton (dec); ed/AB Piedmont Col 1939; MA Peabody 1953; pa/Public Sch Tchr & Admr; Pres Ret'd Tchrs Assn; VP AARP; cp/VP Child Coun; Coun Child Abuse; r/Bapt.

BURTON, WILLIAM JOSEPH oc/Engineer; Professor; b/Mar 22, 1931; h/Rt 1 Box 193, Iva, SC 29655; ba/Chattanooga, TN; p/Emory and Olivia Copeland Burton, Iva; ed/BS 1957, MS 1964, PhD 1970 Univ SC; mil/AUS Corporal Mil Police Corps Berlin Command; pa/Proj Mgr TVA 1974-; Prof Univ Tenn 1971-74; Prof Tex A&M Univ 1970; Sr Proj Engr Allison Div Gen Motors Corp 1964-67; Sr Engr Lockheed Ga Co 1957-62; ASME; Soc Nav Archs & Marine Engrs; Reg'd Profl Engr Tenn; cp/Past Bd Exc Clb; S Caroliniana Soc; r/Prot; hon/Order of Engr; Tau Beta Pi; Pi Tau Sigma; Sigma Xi; Fellow Intl Biogl Assn.

BURTSCHI, MARY PAULINE oc/Writer; Educator; Historian; b/Feb 22, 1911; h/307 N 6th, Vandalia, IL 62471; ba/Vandalia; p/Joseph and Olivia Yoos Burtschi (dec); ed/BA St Louis Univ; MA Univ Ill-U; pa/Tchr Eng: Carlyle HS 1936-39, Effingham HS 1939-70; Pub'd Books used in HSs & Cols in Study of Hist & Lit: *Biogl Sketch Joseph Charles Burtschi 1962*, *Wilderness Capital Lincolns Land 1963*, *A Port Folio James Hall 1968*, *A Guide Book Hist Vandalia 1974*, *Seven Stories By James Hall (Editor) 1975*, *James Hall Lincolns Frontier World 1977*; Univ Ill Col Ed Assn: Field Rep 1969-70, Dir 1970-72, Secy & Treas 1972-; Fayette Co Ret'd Tchrs Assn; cp/VP Ill St Hist Soc; Past Pres & Dir Vandalia Hist Soc, Current Res Histn & VP; Past Pres Sir Thomas More Soc; Past VP Vandalia Woms Clb; Dir & Poetry Conslt Fayette Co Cult & Arts Assn; Past Chm Fayette Co Bicent Comm; Chm Fayette Co Bicent Coun; r/Cath; hon/Delta Kappa Gamma; Awds Profl Writing: Ill St Hist Soc 1965, Ill Sesquicentennial Comm 1968, Ill Bicent Com 1975; Dist'd Tchg, En Ill Univ; Hon'd Hist (Gave Address Unveiling 5 Oil Portraits Early Ill Ldrs); Outstg Vol Commun Ser, Ill Secy St; Dist'd Ser, Am Revolution Bicent Comm.

BURZYNSKI, STANISLAW RAJMUND oc/Physician; Director; b/Jan 23, 1943; h/5 Concord Cir, Houston, TX 77024; ba/Houston; m/Barbara; c/Gregory Stanislaw; p/Grzegorz Burzynski (dec); Zofia Burzynski, Houston; ed/MD w Distn Med Acad (Lublin, Poland); PhD; pa/Dir, Burzynski Res Lab 1977-; Pvt Pract Physician Spec'g in Internal Med 1977-; Baylor Col of Med: Res Assoc 1970-72, Asst Prof 1972-77; Med Acad (Lublin): Tchg Asst 1962-67, Intern, Resident Internal Med 1967-70; Am Heart Assn; AAAS; Am Assn Cancer Res; AMA; Fdn Am Scists; Harris Co Med Soc; Soc Neurosci; Tex Med Soc; Sigma Xi; cp/Past Pres Houston Chapt, Polish Nat Alliance; r/Cath; hon/Pub'd Author; Grantee: Nat Cancer Inst, West Foun.

BUSBEE, ELIZABETH DIVERS oc/Administrator; b/May 15, 1912; h/114 Taliaferro Ave, Rocky Mount, VA 24151; m/Charles (dec); p/Alfred and Bessie Ramsey Divers (dec); ed/BS Radford Col; Addit Studies; pa/Ret'd Dir Dept Social Sers; NASW; Va Conf Social Work; cp/Past Pres Leag Local Wel Exec; St Hlth Coor'g Coun; Bd Va, Area III Hlth Ser Agy; Rep Mtl Hlth Adv Coun; Past Pres C of C; Woms Clb; r/RM Christian Ch; Past Pres Christian Woms F'ship; hon/W/W: Va, Am, Dist'd Citizens NA, World Wom; Nat Social Dir; Dic Intl Biog; 2000 Wom Achmt; Commun Ldrs Va.

BUSBY, FLORENCE ROBINSON oc/Mayor; Judge; b/Jan 18, 1916; h/PO Box 233, Shubuta, MS 39360; ba/Shubuta; m/George Stephen (dec); c/George Jr, Florence B Fennell, Carolyn B Hayes, William; p/Calvin and Leila Robinson (dec); ed/Corr Deg LaSalle Univ; pa/Mayor Town Shubuta; Mun Judge; Miss Mun Exec Com; cp/Crim Justice Planning Div; E Ctl Planning & Devel; Shubuta Improvement Assn; E Ctl Rural Hlth Inc; Hlth Sys Agy; r/Bapt; hon/Personalities S; Dic Intl Biog; Bicent Fam.

BUSE, SYLVIA TWEEDT oc/Educator; b/Oct 8, 1926; h/2318 Dorchester Dr, Bartlesville, OK 74003; ba/Springfield, MO; m/Donald; c/Charles, Deborah, Sarah, John; p/Lloyd Tweedt (dec); Pearl Tweedt, Belvedere, CA; ed/BA 1948, MS 1961 Univ Cal-B; PhD Cand Okla St Univ; pa/Instr Psychol Dept SW Mo St Univ 1975-; Vol Conslt Cerebral Palsy Ctr 1977-; CoSupvr Diagnostic Clin & Instr Psychol Processes Sch Med Sci Univ Pacific 1970-74; Res Psychologist Intl Neurological Scis Pacific Med Ctr 1962-70; Psychometrist Birth Defects Clin Chds Hosp 1961-62 & 1964-65; Res Psychologist Inst Human Devel Univ Cal 1959-61; Am & Mo Psychol Assn; Jean Piaget Soc; Mo Assn Chd Lng Disabilities; cp/SW Mo St Univ: U Way Com, Grant Com; r/Luth; hon/Sigma Xi; Num Grant Awds Res Projs; Deans Grant Adv Bd.

BUSH, MARCIA KAY oc/Special Education Liaison; b/Feb 24, 1949; h/8736 W 70th, Merriam, KS 66204; ba/Kansas City, KS; p/Charles Bush (dec); Virginia Bush, Wichita, KS; ed/BS Univ Ks; pa/Tchr 1971-77; Presentor USA-Ks Conv 1979; Coun Exceptl Chd; Coun Admrs Spec Ed; Adv Bd Career Opport Ctr; Ks Assn Gifted; NEA; cp/Shawnee Mission Red Cross Vol; GSA; Alpha Delta Pi Alumni; r/Cath.

BUSH, WENDALL oc/Attorney; b/Dec 10, 1944; h/3785 Winchester Pk, Circle #8, Memphis, TN 38118; ed/AB, Philonder Smith Col; JD, Emory Univ; pa/Atty: Emory Univ Law Clin (Atlanta, Ga) 1969-71, Indpls Legal Serv (Ind) 1971-73, Equal Opportunity Comm (Memphis) 1973-; Am, Fed Bar Assns; Phi Alpha Delta; hon/Outstg Yg Men of Am; Outstg Sr, Philonder Smith Col.

BUSHA, CHARLES HENRY oc/Educator; Writer; b/Dec 13, 1931; h/Summit Dr, Rt 2 Box 175, Liberty, SC 29657; ba/Pendleton, SC; p/James Busha; Rosa Anderson Busha, Liberty; ed/BA Furman Univ 1958; MLS Rutgers Univ 1961; PhD Ind Univ 1971; mil/AUS 2nd Lt 1951-54; SCNG Capt

1954-67; pa/Edr Ofc Devel Tri-Co Tech Col; Author *Freedom versus Suppression &*

Censorship; Editor *An Intellectual Freedom Primer;* Beta Phi Mu; SEn Lib Assn; cp/Past Pres Liberty Arts Coun; Friends of Sarlin Commun Lib; Clemson Little Theatre; Dem; r/Unitarian-Universalist.

BUSHMAN, CLARENCE EARL oc/Educator; Musical Director; b/Feb 11, 1937; h/125 W Hunt Ave, Drawer 1015, Snowflake, AZ 85937; ba/Fort Worth, TX; m/Leena Kyllikki Makipaja; c/Preston, Lea; p/Garland and Gleenie Smith Bushman, Mesa, AZ; ed/Dipl NM Mil Inst; BA; MME; mil/7th Army Symph Orch Mgr Stuttgart, Germany; pa/Prof Humanities & Fine Arts; Chm Music Dept Northland Col; Conductor

N'land Symph Orch; NM Symph; St Louis Philharm; Prin Fgn Study Leag Resident Inst Switzerland & France; Am Recorder Soc; Am Guild Organists; cp/Rotary Intl; r/Ch of Jesus Christ Latter-Day Sts; Choir Dir, Organist; hon/Carillonic Bellmasters Stipend S'ship, Brigham Yg Univ; Hon Soc Grad; Intl W/W Music.

BUSKELL (BALES), ZELMA JEAN oc/Biologist; b/May 15, 1945; h/Apt 1, 18806 Walkers Choice R, Gaithersburg, MD 20760; ba/Wash, DC; m/John Emery Bales; p/Kelly Buskell Sr (dec); Edith Russell Buskell, Bristol, TN; ed/BS 1970; pa/Res Biologist & Tech Conslt Hepatitis Coop Studies Prog Vets Adm Med Ctr; ASMT; AIBS; AAUW; BPW; cp/E Tenn St Univ Alumni Assn Century Clb; Yg Repubs; Vol Boys & Girls Homes Montgomery Co; VAMCs Student Summer Aid Prog; FLEX-ED PROG Walt Whitman HS; r/Meth; hon/Pub'd Author.

BUSWELL, ARTHUR WILCOX oc/Physician; Surgeon; b/Jan 6, 1926; h/1047-7 Nysteen, Fort Wainwright, AK 99703; ba/FW; m/Jane Fuksa; c/Arthur, Robert, Barbara, Brian, Gayla, Richard; p/Albert Buswell (dec); Enid Scott Buswell, Kingfisher, OK; ed/BS Univ Okla 1950; MD Univ Okla Sch Med 1952; mil/AUS: WW-II 1944-46, 1st Lt Fitzsimons Army Hosp & 1st Armored Div 1952-54, Commdr 372d Med Det 1961-62, Chief Profl Sers Bassett Army Hosp 1963-65, Div Surg 1st Armored Div 1966-67, Div Surg 1st Inf Div Republic Vietnam 1967-68, Chief Experimentation Div & Human Factors Combat Devel Command Experimentation Command 1968-72, Chief Profl Sers Reynolds Army Hosp 1972-73, Commdr USA Med Dept Activs Fort Stewart/Hunter Army Airfield & US Army Hosp 1973-77, Chief Profl Sers Kenner Army Hosp 1977-78, Commdr US Army Med Dept Activs Alaska & Bassett Army Hosp 1979-; pa/Pvt Pract Med & Surg 1955-63; Chief Staff Kingfisher Commun Hosp 1957; Supt Hlth Kingfisher Co 1960-61; Del Okla St Med Assn 1960; Adjunct Asst Prof Med Sci Baylor Univ 1960; Phys & Surg Bassett Army Hosp 1979-; Fellow Royal Soc Hlth; Fdg Mem AUS Soc Flight Surgs; Aerospace Med Assn; Assn Mil Surgs US; cp/Bd Dirs Fort Stewart Fed Credit Union; Pres Sch Bd FS; hon/Legion Merit w 1 Oak-Leaf Cluster; Soldiers Medal Bronze Star w V & 1 Oak-Leaf Cluster; Meritorious Ser Medal w 3 Oak-Leaf Clusters Army Commend Medal; Vietnamese Decorations: Gallantry Cross w Palm, Armed Forces Medal, 1st Class Civic Action Medal.

BUSWELL, HENRIETTA ARLENE oc/Educator; b/Sept 24, 1916; h/332 E Marion St, Marengo, IA 52301; ba/Iowa City, IA;

p/Henry Buswell (dec); Bessie Beckler Buswell, Marengo; ed/BS 1944, MA 1951, PhD 1975 Univ Ia; pa/Univ Ia: Curric Coor Bur Instrnl Sers 1973, Asst Prof Bus Ed & Tchg Asst 1968-72, Coor *la Bus Edr,* News Editor Omicron Chapt *Delta Pi Epsilon Jour;* Univ Wis-Platteville: Asst Prof Bus Adm 1965-68, Secy Curric Com, Chperson Public Relats Com, Improvement Instrn Bd, Fin Com, Cand Tchr of Yr; Asst Prof Bus Radford Col 1958-65; Other Former Positions; Beta Gamma Sigma; Omicron Delta Epsilon; Delta Pi Epsilon; Pi Omega Pi; Gamma Alpha Chi; Alpha Delta Kappa; cp/Secy Deo Juvante Soc; Repub Polit Party; r/1st Presb Ch, Marengo; hon/Pub'd Author; Num Biogl Listings.

BUTCHER, LARRY LEE oc/Professor; Researcher; b/Feb 21, 1940; h/3186 Coldwater Canyon Ave, Studio City, CA 91604; ba/Los Angeles, CA; m/Sherrel Gwen; p/Frederick and Ellen Butcher, Troy, MI; ed/BA w Distns 1962, MS 1964, PhD 1967 Univ Mich; pa/Prof Dept Psychol UCLA 1969-; Reschr: Brain Histochem & Neurologic Disorders, Parkinsons Disease, Huntingtons Chorea; USPHS Postdoct Fellow Nat Inst Arthritis & Metabolic Diseases Dept Pharm Sch Med Univ Goteborg 1967-69; Reviewer Num Profl Jours; Am Soc Pharm & Experimental Therapeutics; Soc Neuroscience; Wn Pharm Soc; hon/Best Paper Awd, *Jour Microwave Power;* Chancellors Fac F'ship, UCLA; Num Res Grants.

BUTLER, MANLEY CALDWELL oc/US Congressman; b/Jun 2, 1925; h/845 Orchard Rd, Roanoke, VA 24014; ba/Roanoke; m/June Nolde; c/Manley, Marshall, Jimmy, Henry; p/W W Butler Jr (dec); Mrs W W Butler Jr, Roanoke; ed/AB Univ Richmond; LLB Univ Va Sch Law; mil/USN; pa/Am & Va Bar Assns; r/Epis; hon/Order of Coif; Phi Beta Kappa; JD Washington & Lee.

BUTLER, YVONNE JANET oc/Executive; b/Sept 26, 1946; h/151A Comml St, Provincetown, MA 02657; ba/Baltimore, MD; p/Victor and Helen Butler, Providence, RI; ed/BS RI Col 1968; MPA Cand Univ Balto; pa/Sr Dir & VP Prog Planning & Devel YMCA; APO; Black Chd Assn; Nat BANWYS; US Del World Cong Food & Devel; cp/Subarea Adv Coun Ctl Md Hlth Sys Agy; Campaign Wkr; r/Prot; hon/Recipient Grant Grad Studies; Commemoration Black YMCAs.

BUTTERFIELD, HUBER EDWARD oc/Executive; b/Mar 8, 1935; h/305 1st Ave, Troy, AL 36081; ba/Troy; m/Dorothy Ann; c/David; p/Jerome and Anna Minor Butterfield (dec); ed/Univ RI 1960; mil/USCG Resv 1952-60; pa/VP Mktg & Sales Hudson Industs Inc; Lectr Num Profl Orgs; IFMA; NRA; FOOD; ACFSA; Adv Bd Instnl Distribution Mag; cp/Sales & Mktg Execs Minneapolis; Zuhrah Shrine; Scottish Rite; Temple Lodge #18 AFAM; Minnetonka Shrine Clb; USCG Aux; r/Bethel Meth Ch, Mound, Minn.

BUTTINGER, JOSEPH oc/Writer; b/Apr 30, 1906; h/RR 1 Box 264, Pennington, NJ 085344; m/Muriel; p/Anthony and Maria Buttinger (dec); cp/Refugee Relief Work; hon/Golden Order Merit Republic Austria.

BUXBAUM, MARTIN oc/Writer; Poet; b/Jun 27, 1912; h/7819 Custer Rd, Bethesda, MD 20014; ba/Same; m/Alice Lee; c/Mrs Joan Galope, Mrs Alice Dick, Mrs Rosemary Redding, Mrs Roberta Walker, Mrs Martha Newpher, Mrs Kathleen Stubbs, Martin Lawrence, William; p/Ernest Buxbaum (dec); Sadie Harrell (dec); ed/MJ Cranston Univ; mil/DCNG 121st Eng; pa/Wkly Columnist; Author 10 Books & Num Jour Papers; Contbr Var Mags; Advr *Sunshine* Mag; Assoc Editor *Praying Hands* Mag; cp/Ky Col; Kiwanis; Md Press Assn; r/Indep Christian; hon/5 George Washington Medals, Freedoms Foun; Prin Medal Awd; Poet of Yr, Md 1967.

BUXTON, CHARLES ROBERTS oc/Editor; b/Mar 20, 1913; h/5215 Sky Trl, Littleton, CO 80123; m/Janet; c/Cynda

Wilcox (Mrs Philip Jr), Charles Jr, Richard, Janet; p/Harry and Lucielle Buxton (dec); ed/BA Oreg St Univ 1935; mil/AUS Lt Col 1940-45; pa/Ret'd Editor & Pubr Denver Post Inc; Dir InterAm Press Assn; Theta Chi; Phi Kappa Phi; cp/Past Trustee Denver Post Employees Stock Trust; Reg Bd Inst Intl Ed; MW & Denver Univ Res Insts; Newspaper Advtg Bd ANPA; Past Dir: Denver C of C, Sunday Metro Newspapers, Inst Newspaper Opers, Gravure Res Inst, Gravure Tech Assn; Mile High U Way; Eng Spkg Union; Kiwanis; Conv & Vis Bur; Perf'g Arts; Nat & Denver Bds Salvation Army; Cherry Hills Country Clb; Garden of Gods Clb; r/1st Presb Ch, Littleton; hon/Dist'd Ser Awd, Oreg St Univ; Gold Good Citizenship Awd, Colo Soc SAR; AUS: Bronze Star Medal, Silver Star Medal w Oak Leaf Cluster.

BYAM, MILTON S oc/Library Director; b/Mar 15, 1922; h/162-04 75 Rd, Flushing, NY 11366; ba/Jamica, NY; m/Yolanda; c/Megan, Roger; p/Charles and Sybil Byam (dec); ed/BSS cum laude CCNY 1947; MS w Hons Columbia Univ 1949; mil/AUS 92nd Inf Div 1943-45; pa/Am & NY Lib Assns; cp/Bd Dirs Coun Social Wel; r/Epis; hon/Bronze Star Medal, AUS.

BYERLY, JOAN B oc/Consultant; b/Aug 19, 1926; h/1945 4th St, Apt 37, Sparks, NV 89431; ba/Reno, NV; m/Joseph; c/John, Bruce; p/Jesse and Marie Banta; ed/BA Bradford Univ; pa/Lic'd Fin Conslt; Nat Conf Christians & Jews 1966-71; Stringer O&A Mktg News; Num Phases Newspaper Work *Carson City Nev Appeal;* Sec Mgr Sparks C of C; *Sparks Tribune;* Radio K-1 Gal Friday; Nat Fdn Press Wom; Am C of C Execs; cp/Intl Platform Assn; Bus & Profl Wom; Adv Bd Better Bus Bur; Reno Exc Clb; Reno Press Clb; St Public Inf Ofcr CAP; ARC; Publicity Fund Chm: Heart, Cancer, Polio; r/Prot; hon/Red Ribbon Awd, CAP; Ser Awd, Reno Air Races; 1st Pl Newspaper Picture Competition; W/W Am Wom; Personalities W&MW; Royal Blue Book; Dic Intl Biog.

BYGNESS, HAZEL ISABELLA oc/Piano & Organ Instructor; b/Feb 28, 1899; h/Goldfield Comm #5, Goldfield, IA 50542; ba/Goldfield; m/(dec); c/Harrold L; p/John S and O Edythe McCallum (dec); ed/Normal Piano Dipl, Chgo Univ; Intl Piano Tchrs Cert; Masters Piano Tchrs Cert; pa/Piano & Theory Instr, Boone Val Sch Sys (Rennick, Iowa) 9 Yrs; r/Meth: Ch Pianist & Organist 70 Yrs; hon/1st in St of Iowa w Record of 70 Yrs Ser as Ch Organist; Gold Wristwatch, UP Ch (Goldfield); ESO Sorority; PSI; World W/W Wom; Others.

BYINGTON, FREDERICK D oc/Director Private School; b/May 2, 1930; h/Suite P305, 1500 Locust St, Phila, PA 19102; ba/Same; p/Lt Comdr and Mrs H D Byington, LaJolla, CA; ed/BA Pomona Col; MS, MEd Univ So Cal; PhD Cand Univ Pa; pa/Pioneer in Spec Ed Lng Probs & Gifted; Conf Spkr Sec'dy & Spec Ed; Conslt Gifted Prog Phila Sch Dist; cp/Lions; YMCA; BSA; Repub; r/Christian Sci; hon/Phi Delta Kappa; Alpha Phi Omega; Alpha Tau Omega.

BYLER, GARY C oc/Legislative Assistant; b/Feb 9, 1957; h/4615 Paul Revere Rd, Va Bch, VA 23455; ba/Wash, DC; p/Clarence and Virginia Byler, VB; ed/BA cum laude Georgetown; pa/Leg Asst Senator John Warner; Dir Res & Policy Devel; cp/Campaign Wkr; Chm So Area Col Repub; r/Bapt; hon/Outstg Yg Man 1977, 78 & 79.

BYRD, ALMA C WEAVER oc/Educator; b/Sept 18, 1924; h/2327 Willow St, Columbia, SC 29203; ba/C'bia; m/Wallace; p/Ernest and Annie Spann Weaver, Aiken, SC; ed/AB Benedict Col 1944; MA C'bia Univ 1960; PhD Univ SC 1978; Sorbonne Cert 1960; pa/Tchr Benedict Col; AAUP; AAUW; cp/Pres Nat Coun Negro Wom Inc; CoFdr C'bia Area Sickle Cell Anemia Foun; Am Legion; Altrusa Clb SC Assn Woms & Girls Clbs; Daughs of Elks; r/Bapt; hon/Edrs Awd SC, NCNW; Phi Iota; Alpha Kappa Alpha.

BYRD, JAMES CALVIN oc/Media Coordinator; b/May 19, 1941; h/Box 273, Burnsville, NC 28714; ba/B'ville; m/Judy Wildermuth; c/James, Jeffrey; p/Charlie and Bertha Byrd; ed/AS; BS; MA; pa/Treas & Pres Yancey Co Unit NCAE; cp/CoFdr Yancey Yth Jamboree; r/Prot; hon/Yancey Co Tchr of Yr.

BYRD, JOSEPH KEYS oc/Counselor; b/Oct 3, 1953; h/802 Magnolia Ave B, Hattiesburg, MS 39401; ba/H'burg; p/Willie Byrd, New Orleans, LA; Mozell Keys, Meadville, MS; (Fosterparents) Mr & Mrs Lorman Harris, Meadville, MS; ed/BS William Carey Col; pa/Spec Progs William Carey Col: Field Cnslr 1976-, Ofc Mgr Tutor Coor 1975-76; Pi Kappa Delta; Theta Kappa Sigma; Nat Assn Tutorial Sers; Nat & Miss Ed Assns; cp/Nat Bapt Conv Am; Heart Fund; Cancer Crusade; Red Cross; Yg Dems; H'burg Little Leag; H'burg Yth Ser Bur; r/Bapt; hon/Excell Debater 1972; Notable Ams; Book Honor.

BYRD, ROBERT C oc/Politician; m/Erma Ora James; c/Mrs Mona B Fatemi, Mrs Marjorie B Moore; ed/JD cum laude Am Univ; pa/WVa House Dels 1946 & 1948; WVa Senate 1950; US House Rep 1952, 1954 & 1956; US Senate 1958 & 1964; Del-at-Large WVa Dem Nat Conv 1960; Secy Senate Dem Conf 1967 & 1969; Senate Majority Whip 1971, 1973 & 1975; Senate Majority Ldr 96th Cong 1977 & 1979; hon/W Virginian of Yr 1974 & 1977, *Charleston Sunday Gazette Mail*; 1 of 5 Best Public Servants Achmt Nation, Gallagher Pres Report; Outstg W

Virginian 1975 & 1977, Participants WVa Teen-Ager Pageant; 4th & 8th Most Influential Man US, *US News & World Report*.

BYRON, LEONARD J oc/Psychologist; b/Jun 18, 1915; h/PO Box 327, Sharon, CT 06069; ba/Sharon; m/G Anne; c/Thomas; p/(dec); ed/BESL 1937, STB, STL, STD magna cum laude 1944, PhB, PhL summa cum laude, PhD magna cum laude 1948 Laval Univ; BA Sorbonne 1939; BA Assumption Col 1940; Addit Studies; pa/Indust & Conslt Psychologist Byron Assocs Inc w Ofcs USA, Canada, France & Switzerland; Mtl Hlth & Mtl Retardation Conslt Num Indusls, Bus & Pvt Agys; cp/Repub Activs; Num Public Hlth Orgs; r/Prot.

BYRUM, JAMES KNOX oc/District Judge; b/Mar 4, 1904; h/1702 N Broadway, Shawnee, OK 74801; ba/Same; m/Thelma Spurgeon; c/Leah B Shankle (Mrs John); p/James and Leah Knox Byrum (dec); ed/AB

Okla Bapt Univ 1923; LLB Univ Okla 1927; mil/USNR Cmdr WW-II; pa/Mun Judge City Shawnee 1930-34; Judge Pottawatomic Co 1935-37; Judge 23rd Jud Dist Okla 1937-42 & 1947-71; Judge Okla Ct Tax Review 1947-55; cp/Okla Leg House Rep 1929; Bd Trustees Okla Bapt Univ; Past Pres & Bd Dirs Pott Co Hist Soc; Shawnee Lions Clb; Bd Dirs Shawnee Little Theatre Inc; r/Bapt; hon/Silver Beaver Awd, BSA; Dist'd Alumni Awd, Okla Bapt Univ.

BYSIEWICZ, SHIRLEY RAISSI oc/Professor; Librarian; h/S Plumb Rd, Middletown, CT 06457; ba/W Hartford, CT; m/Stanley; c/Susan, Walter, Karen, Gail; p/Kyriakos Raissi; Anna Gavalas; ed/BA, JD Univ Conn; MSLS So Conn St Col; pa/Univ Conn Sch Law: Law Libn, Prof Law; Pract Law w Brother John Raissi; Former Asst Prosecutor Town Enfield; Hartford Co Bar Assn: CoChwom Com Status Wom, Exec Bd; Conn Bar Assn: Num Coms, Treas; ABA; Nat Assn Wom Lwyrs: Cowom Law Day, Conn St Del, Chwom Intl Law Com; Task Force Govs Comm Status Wom; Woms Equity Action Leag; Advr & Conslt: Middlesex Co Bar Lib, New Haven Co Bar Lib, Meridan Co Bar Lib; New Eng Law Libns Assn: Pres, VP; Bus Mgr *Law Lib Jour*; Am Assn Law Libs: Exec Com, Former Chwom Microfacsimiles Com, Dir Inst Legal Biblio, Others; cp/Adv Bd & Treas *Alert Leg Review*; Former Exec Bd Auerbach Ser Bur Conn Orgs; Adv Com Conn Comm Reorg & Unification Cts; Bd Dirs CWEALF; Presider Task Force Comm Status Wom; hon/Recog Significant Contbns Law Lib, AALL; Outstg Law Day Prog Country, ABA; Pub'd Author; Num Biogl Listings.

C

CABELL, BENJAMIN BRYAN oc/-Pediatrician; b/Jul 22, 1935; h/2900 Rogers Ave, Ft Smith, AR 72901; ba/Ft Smith; m/Evelyn Ann Woods; c/Laura Ashley, Bryan Chastian, Scott David; p/Gerald E Cabell; Merle Bryan Cabell Clutter, Ft Smith; ed/BS Univ of S 1955; MD Tulane Univ Sch of Med 1959; mil/USN 1960-64 Lt, 1964-65 Lt Cmdr; pa/Ped Conslt for Art St Crippled Chd's Div; Asst Prof Univ Ark Med Ctr; FAA Med Examr; ACC Investigator; Conslt Seb Co Hlth Dept; cp/Bd Dirs Spec Lng Ctr for Chd w LD, Ft Smith Symph Assn; Mem Ark Coun on Arts & Humanities (Former Chair); r/Epis; hon/Fellow, Am Acad Pediatrics; Diplomate, Am Bd Pediatrics.

CACCAMISE, GENEVRA LOUISE oc/-Media Specialist; b/Jul 22, 1934; h/PO Box 241, DeLand, FL 32720; m/Alfred Edward; p/Herbert Oscar and Genevra Green Ball (dec); ed/BA Stetson Univ; MSLA Syracuse

Univ; pa/Elem Sch Media Specialist; Treas Volusia Co Assn for Media in Ed; AAUW; cp/Bd Trustees DeLand Public Lib; Hosp Aux; Magna Charta Dames; DAR; r/Epis; hon/Delta Kappa Gamma; DIB; Outstg Yg Wom Am; W/W: Am Wom, S&SW.

CADRECHA, MANUEL oc/Supervising Mechanical Engineer; b/May 18, 1919; h/4915 Windhaven Ct, Dunwoody, GA 30338; ba/Norcross, GA; m/Beatriz; c/Beatriz, Manuel; p/Alberto Cadrecha (dec); Dolores Suarez (dec); pa/Elect & Mech Engr; Conslt'g Engr EBASCO Sers Inc; cp/Repub; r/Rom Cath; hon/W/W S&SW.

CAESAR, SHARLYN ALICIA CHATON oc/Fashion Designer; b/April 6, 1947; m/Norman H Jr; chd/Alicia LaVonghn, DeBrauk M, Norman Anthony, Christopher Garfield, Konstance B; p/Johnnie Sr and Lillian Mae Boyd, Los Angeles, CA; ed/BA; MA; pa/Fashion Designer; Producer; Screen Writer; hon/W/W; IPA.

CAHILL, MARY PAULA oc/Retired Free-lance Writer; b/Jul 1, 1891; h/2381 W Nebraska, Tucson, AZ 85706; m/Matthew (dec); c/Paul; p/Hugh and Margaret Kelly

(dec); pa/Author: Mag Articles, Books of Poetry incl'g *Heart Beats, The Desert Speaks, Vagabond Gold, The Voice of Paula;* Also Book *The Fatima Story;* Lectr; World Poetry Soc; r/Cath Charismatic; hon/1st Prize, Nat Fdn St Poetry Soc Annual Contest.

CAIN, ELISE GASQUE oc/Teacher; Office Nurse; Homemaker; b/Apr 5, 1920; h/1309 E Cleveland St, Dillon, SC 29536; m/Rufus Haynes Jr; c/Walter Ewings Belk Jr, Carol Kay Marbert, Rufus Haynes III, Edina Elise, Carol Kay; p/Baker Fore and Carrie Lee Frierson Gasque, Dillon; ed/AB; pa/Tchr Dillon Jr HS, Avalon Acad; Dillon BPW Clb; cp/Crippled Chds Soc, Chm Dillon Co; Bd Mem Dillon Co TB Assn; VP Avon Study Clb; Pres: Pee Dee Med Aux, Dillon Co Med Aux, SC Med Assn Aux; Dist Pres SC Fdn Wom's Clb; Bd Mem Friends Francis Marian Col; Bd Dirs, VP Avalon Acad; Bd Dirs SC Indep Schs; Pres Seaboard Coastline Railroad Surgs Aux; Var Other Activs; r/U Meth Ch; hon/DIB; Personalities of S.

CAIN, JOSEPH A oc/Professor; Painter; b/May 27, 1920; h/402 Troy Dr, Corpus Christi, TX 78412; ba/Corpus Christi; m/Mabe; c/Jonizo C Calloway; p/T W Cain Sr (dec); Rose A Triplett, Perry, GA; ed/BA, MA Univ Cal-Berkeley; mil/USMCR Col, 32 Yrs Active & Resv; pa/Del Mar Col 1950-64 (Pt-time), 1965- (Full time): Prof Art, Chm Art; Tchr W B Ray HS 1950-64; Tchr Corpus Christi HS 1948-50; Has Exhibited throughout: US, Mexico, Canada, Japan, France; Exhbns incl: Radio City Music Hall Gallery, Grand Ctl Mod Gallery, Petite Gallery, Ligoa Duncan Gallery (NY & Paris, France), La Jolla Art Ctr, Otis Art Inst, Oakland Art Mus (Cal), Art Mus S Tex (Corpus Christi), Butler Inst Am Art (Youngstown, Ohio), Isaac Del Gado Mus (New Orleans), & Num Others; 1-Man Shows incl: Univ Oreg, Univ Tex, Williamantic St Col (Conn), Ind Univ, Centennial Art Mus, Laguna Gloria Mus, Incarnate Word Col, Baylor Univ, Tex Christian Univ, Others; Past Pres S Tex Art Leag; Fellow Royal Soc Arts, London (England); Bd Dirs Corpus Christi Fine Arts Colony; Tex Fine Arts Assn; S Tex Art Leag; Corpus Christi Art Foun; Ala, Cal & Tex Watercolor Soc; Beaumont Art Mus; Tex Jr Col Assn; Others; cp/Exhbn Chm Jewish Commun Coun; Appt'd to Mun Arts Coun by Mayor of Corpus Christi; Former Chm Mun Arts Comm; r/Ch of Christ; hon/Nat Soc Painters, Casein (NY): Alfred Newan Gold Medal Awd, Grumbacher 1st Awd, Sarah Goode Awd; Dixie Annual, Birmingham; Gold Medal Seton Hall Univ; Others.

CALCAGNI, FRANK J oc/Administrator; b/Oct 1, 1919; h/77 Melrose St, Cranston, RI 02910; ba/Cranston; m/Eugenia Robison (dec); c/Elizabeth C Searle, John Angelo; p/Angelo Calcagni (dec); Susie Petrucci Giusti, Cranston; ed/Bus Mgmt; mil/USAF Air Combat Intell, 4 Yrs WWII, 6 Yrs Resv;

pa/Dept Dir Dept Job Devel & Tng; Chm Manpower Planning Bd; C of C; Manpower Profls; Nat Pilots Assn; Others; cp/Rotary Clb Cranston; Trustee Citizens S'ship Foun Am; Pres RI Citizens S'ship Foun; Others; r/Cath; hon/86 Local, St & Nat Awds; Mil Decorations & Civilian; Commun & Org Awds.

CALDERON-SERRANO, ALFREDO oc/University Teacher; b/Jan 11, 1952; h/Cond El Residencial, Apt 201, Luna 67, Mayaguez, PR 00708; ba/Mayaguez; m/Rosa Nydia Padilla; p/Nicolas Calderon and Milagros Serrano, Hato Rey, PR; ed/BS Univ PR 1975; pa/Tchr Chem Dept Univ PR; HS Sci Tchr Colegio de la Milagrosa; Judge Reg Sci Fair 1976-78; NSTA; Colegio de Quimicos de PR; Am Chem Soc; Res Assoc Ctr of Energy &

Envir Res, Mayaguez; r/Cath; hon/Dean's List; F'ship, Searle; W/W S&SW.

CALDWELL, DAVID ORVILLE oc/Professor; b/Jan 5, 1925; h/601 Por La Mar Circle, 219A, Santa Barbara, CA 93103; ba/Santa Barbara; m/Paulette M; c/Bruce D, Diana M; p/Orville R Caldwell (dec); Audrey A Caldwell, Laguna Hills, CA; ed/BS Cal Inst Tech 1947; MA 1949, PhD 1953 UCLA; mil/USAAF 1943-46, Pvt to 2/Lt; pa/Prof Physics Univ Cal-SB 1965-; Lectr Univ Cal-Berkeley 1964-65; Vis Assoc Prof Princeton Univ 1963-64; MIT; Assoc Prof 1958-63, Asst Prof 1956-58, Instr 1954-56; cp/Served on Adv Bds: Dept Def, Dept Energy, Others; hon/Guggenheim F'ship; Ford Foun Fellow; NSF Sr Postdoct Fellow; Fellow, Am Phy Soc; Res Grants: AEC, ERPA, POE.

CALDWELL, LOUIS O oc/Professor; Director; Social Psychotherapist; b/Feb 6, 1935; h/1111 Loire Ln, Houston, TX 77090; ba/Houston; m/Mamie Ruth Carrico; c/Terri Lynn, Louis Regan, David Andrew, Paul Bradley; p/Lewis J and Sidney McDonald Caldwell, Houston; ed/BS; MEd; EdD; pa/Prof; Dir Christian Cnslg Ctr; Tex Psychotherapy Assn; Am Assn Marriage & Fam Cnslrs; r/Prot; hon/Contemp Authors; W/W: Tex, Rel; Outstg Edrs Am; Personalities of S; DIB.

CALDWELL, ROBERT GRAHAM oc/Professor; b/Nov 9, 1904; h/2421 Ohio Blvd, Terre Haute, IN 47803; m/LaMerle Sutton; p/Robert G and Rebecca Jane Caldwell (dec); ed/BS; MA; PhD; LLB; pa/Field Rep Fed Security Agy, Wash DC;

Prof Criminology & Crim Law Ind St Univ; Conslt; Author; Lwyr; cp/Masonic Order; Shrine; Police & Correctional Commun Activs; r/Bapt; hon/Harrison F'ship; Social Sci Res Awd; Sr Res F'ship Awd, Univ Chgo Col of Law.

CALDWELL, STRATTON FRANKLIN oc/University Professor; b/Aug 25, 1926; h/80 N Kanan Rd, Agoura, CA 91301; ba/Northridge, CA; c/Scott Raymond, Karole Elizabeth; p/Kenneth Simms Caldwell (dec); Margaret Matilda Peterson (dec); ed/BS 1951; MS 1953; PhD 1966; mil/USN Pharmacists Mate 3/C 1944-46; pa/Prof Cal St Univ; Fellow: Am Assn HPER, Am Col Sports Med, Canadian Assn for HPER; Charter Mem: Am Assn HPER Nat Foun, Am Assn for Advmt Tension Control; Assn for Transpersonal Psychol; Cal Assn for HPER; Nat Col PE Assn for Men; Num Ofcs held; Mem Var Edit Bds; Sigma Delta Psi; Phi Delta Kappa; Phi Epsilon Kappa; hon/Dist'd Ser Awd, Assoc'd Students, UCLA; Dist Ser Awd, Cal Assn for HPER; Silver Cir Awd, Alpha Tau Omega; Pub'd Author; DIB; Ldrs in Ed; Commun Ldrs & Noteworthy Ams; Intl W/W Commun Ser; W/W in W.

CALE, DAVID LEE oc/Businessman; b/Jul 16, 1945; h/PO Box 1095, Uniontown, PA 15401; ba/Same; m/Lillian Mae Gangware; ed/BA; pa/Owner Laurel Caverns (Natural Cave & Tourist Attraction); Past Pres: Laurel Highlands Inc, Pa Travel Assn; Bd Dirs Fayette Fest Assn; Mem Nat Cave Assn; Secy Pa Cave Assn; Host Nat Speleological Soc Nat Conv 1976; Formulator Cale's Rule for Planetary Distances 1965; Other Profl Activs; cp/Former Reg Easter Seals Chm; Bd Dirs Uniontown C of C; VP

Fayette Heritage; Bd Dirs U'town Rotary Clb; Pres Intl Relats Clb; hon/DAR Awd for Excell in Am Hist; Outstg Yg Men Awd; Life Mem, WVa Acad Sci; Herman Buck Man of Yr Awd 1975; Gov's Rep, Rotary Intl to Taiwan & Hong Kong.

CALHOUN, WILLIAM CARL oc/Pastor; b/Oct 28, 1949; h/20 Coachman Ct, Randallstown, MD 21133; ba/Baltimore, MD; m/Philathia Reese; c/William Carl Jr; p/William T Calhoun, Rantoul, IL; Myrtle L Johnson, Annapolis, MD; ed/BA Judson Col; MDiv Va Union Univ; pa/Pastor Trinity Bapt Ch 1974-; 1/VP Progressive Bapt Conv Md; Former Chaplain Frontiers Clb Balto; Bapt Min's Conf Balto; Interdenom Min Alliance Balto; Serves w Bapt Jt Com on Public Affair, Progressive Nat Bapt Conv, Wash DC; cp/Bd Mem Balto NAACP; Bd Mem NW YMCA Balto; r/Bapt; hon/Student Senate Ser Awd, Judson Col.

CALLAHAN, WILMA JEAN oc/Accountant; b/Feb 17, 1926; h/155 E 67th St, Los Angeles, CA 90003; c/Janice LaNell; p/Robert Anglin (dec); Essie Mae Givens Anglin, LA; pa/Acct, LA; Nat Soc Public Accts; Nat Assn Tax Conslts; cp/Adv Com on Sickle Cell Cnslg, LA Co Dept Hlth Sers, Vol Awd; Charter Mem & Ofcr Woms Aux, Mem Bd Dirs Sickle Cell Dis Res Foun, Vol Awd; r/Rel Sci of Mind; hon/Vol Awd, LA Dept Rec & Pks; Notable Ams.

CALLAWAY, CAREY SKINNER oc/-Biologist; b/Nov 22, 1929; h/1015 Shepherds Ln, Atlanta, GA 30324; ba/Atlanta; p/C W Sr and Janice Young Skinner (dec); ed/BS Univ Ala 1952; pa/Biologist Ctr for Disease Control (Pathol Div, Electron Microscopy) 1965-; Electron Microscopist Emory Univ Sch of Med 1961-64; Dance Instr City of Atlanta Rec Dept 1959-60; SE Electron Microscopy Soc: Fdg Mem, Com Mem; Electron Microscopy Soc Am; r/Cath; hon/Sigma Xi; Profl Pubs; W/W S&SW; Personalities of S.

CALLAWAY, HOWARD HOLLIS oc/-Resort Executive; b/Apr 2, 1927; h/Box 528, Crested Butte, CO 81224; ba/Same; m/Elizabeth Walton; c/Betsy C Considine, Howard Hollis Jr, Edward Cason, Virginia Hand, Ralph Walton; p/Cason J Callaway Sr (dec); Virginia Hand Callaway, Hamilton, GA; ed/BS West Point; mil/AUS Inf Ofcr 1949-53; pa/Pres Crested Butte Mtn Resort; Callaway Gardens, Pine Mtn, Ga: Exec Dir, Pres 1963-64; Pres Callaway Gardens 1966-72; Secy of Army, Wash DC 1973-75; Pres Ford Com, Wash DC, Chm 1975-76; Interfin Inc, Atlanta, Ga: Chm & CEO 1976; p/Mem of Cong, 3rd Dist of Ga 1965-66; r/Epis; hon/Medal for Dist'd Public Ser, Dept of Def.

CALLAWAY, JOHN WILSON oc/Insurance Broker; Real Estate Salesman; Retired Army Officer; b/Nov 1, 1915; h/165 Rue Fontaine, Decatur, GA 30038; ba/Atlanta, GA; m/Madeleine S; c/Frank F II, John W Jr; p/John S Callaway (dec); Frances W

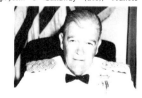

Callaway; ed/BS US Mil Acad; Army Command & Gen Staff Col; Armed Forces Staff Col; Nav War Col; mil/Inf Bat Cmdr; Chief of Staff, 1st Cavalry Div; US Mil Advr to NATO Ambassador; Post Cmdr, Fort McPherson (Ga); cp/Past Pres Rotary Clb W End, Atlanta; Chm Ft McPherson Mil Retiree

Coun; VP Atlanta Chapt Am Def Preparedness Assn; Atlanta Coun BSA; r/Presb; hon/4 Silver Stars; 2 Legions of Merit; 2 Bronze Stars; Army Commend Medal; Combat Inf Badge w Star; Greek Dist'd Ser Medal; Korean Dist'd Unit Awd; UN Awd.

CALLISON, THOMAS RAY oc/Sales Representative; b/Jun 28, 1946; h/6826 Burnley Dr, San Antonio, TX 78239; ba/Same; m/Charlotte Virginia Dooley; c/Martha Lucille; p/John Thomas Callison (dec); ed/BA Angelo St Univ; pa/Pres S San Antonio Tchr's Assn 1972-73; cp/Repub Party Nom, Bexar Co Comm Precnt 4 (1978); Del Repub Nat Conv 1976; Del Repub Tex St Conv 1974, 76, 78; Sustaining Mem Nat Repub Com; Charter Mem Repub Men's Clb Bexar Co; Other Polit Activs; r/Bapt; hon/W/W Am Polits; Personalities of S.

CALLNER, RICHARD oc/Artist; Professor; b/May 18, 1927; h/11 Davis Pl, Latham, NY 12110; ba/Albany, NY; m/Carolyn K; c/Joanna R, David K; p/Julius Callner (dec); Sarah Callner, San Jose, CA; ed/Cert FA Academie Julian, Paris; BS Univ Wis-Madison; MAFA Columbia Univ; mil/USNR 1945-46; pa/Univ NY-Albany: Prof A-t, Chm Art Dept; Pres Coun of Art; CAA; hon/Guggenheim Fellow; Art Work Rep'd in Collections incl'g: Phila Mus of Art, Cinc Mus, Detroit Art Inst, Mus Fine Art, Istanbul Turkey, Others.

CALUB, ALFONSO de GUZMAN oc/-Plant Breeder; b/Aug 1, 1938; h/5811 Skylark Dr, Alexandria, LA 71301; ba/Alexandria; m/Laura V Norcio; c/Janice Fides, Florence; p/Eduardo Club (dec); Juana de Guzman (dec); ed/BSA 1960, MS 1968 Univ Philippines; PhD Univ NH 1972; pa/Dir & Sr Plant Breeder, Alexandria Seed Co; Postdoct Fellow Univ Neb 1972-74; Grad Res Asst UNH 1969-74; Var Other Res Activs; Am Reg Cert'd Profls in Agronomy, Crops & Soils; Am Soc Agronomy; Crop Sci Am; Soil Sci Am; Coun for Agri Sci & Technol; Sigma Xi; Phi Sigma; r/Cath; hon/Contbr 14 Sci Articles to Profl Jours; Biogl Listings.

CALVERT, TOMMY oc/Urban Survey Specialist; Public Affairs Consultant; b/May 11, 1952; h/912 W French, San Antonio, TX 78212; ba/SA; m/William and Pearl Edwards, San Antonio; ed/Att'd San Antonio Col; pa/Public Affairs Conslt Barrio Betterment Devel Corp; Adv Conslt KEDA Radio & Urban Survey Spec; cp/Exec Com Tex Black Caucus; Treas SA Voters Action Leag; Yg Dems Bexar Co; Mem Black Unity Coor'g Coun; A Phillip Randolph Inst; SA Dem Leag; Mem Residents Org'd for Better & Beautiful Envir Devel; Del Dem Nat Conv 1976; Other Activs; r/Friendship Bapt Ch: Mem; hon/Cert of Recog for Outstg Commun Work, SA Housing Auth; Ambassador of Goodwill, Gov Dolph Briscoe 1976; Outstg Commun Ser Awd, Black Unity Coor'g Coun; Outstg Commun Ser Awd, Proj ABLE; Biogl Listings.

CAMERON, NINA RAO oc/Attorney; b/Apr 28, 1925; h/441 E 20th St, New York, NY 10010; ba/NYC; c/Scott; ed/BA Manhattanville Col of Sacred Heart 1945; Bach Law Brooklyn Law Sch 1950; pa/Dist Counsel US Immigration & Naturalization Ser, Dept Justice, NYC 1968-; Law Secy to Justice of Supreme Ct, St of NY 1967; Pvt Law Pract 1966, 1955-56; Dir UN Com of City of NY & Dir Consular Corps Com, City of NY, Asst Commr Dept of Public Events 1958-65; Appt'd Asst Dir of Commerce, City of NY 1956-58; Other Past Positions: Fed Bar Coun; ABA; Bar Assn City of NY; Wom's Bar Assn NY; NY Co Lwyrs Assn; Am Soc Italian Legions of Merit Inc (Chief of Protocol); cp/Exec Com Intl Debutante Ball; hon/Hon JD, Mexican Acad Intl Law, Univ Mexico; JFK Lib for Minorities Am Heritage Awd for Commun Ser; Guest of Govts of Spain, Greece & Portugal 1965; Other Hons.

CAMMARATA, JOAN FRANCES

oc/College Teacher; b/Dec 22, 1950; h/8303 Fourth Ave, Brooklyn, NY 11209; ba/NYC; m/Richard M Montemarano; p/Angelina Guarnera, Bklyn, ed/BA summa cum laude Fordham Univ 1972; MA 1974, MPhil 1977, PhD Cand 1977- Columbia Univ; pa/Tchg Asst Spanish Lit & Lang Columbia Univ; MLA; AATSP; Hispanic Inst; Contbr Article to *Bilingual Press;* hon/Columbia Univ: Univ F'ship, Pres' F'ship.

CAMP, KENNETH RAY oc/Consultant; Educational Lecturer; b/Apr 11, 1938; h/PO Box 1661, Jonesboro, AR 72401; ba/Same; m/Wanda Lee; c/Kendell, Kemuel, Janeene; p/John E Camp (dec); Gertrude L Camp, Rector, AR; ed/BSA, MSE Ark St Univ; pa/Fed Progs Conslt; Sch Tchr, Prin, Supt; cp/Mem Ark Ho of Reps; r/Ch of Christ: Deacon; hon/Outstg Yg Man of J'boro 1973.

CAMP, LOUISE PHIFER oc/Musician; Farmer; Homemaker; b/Mar 22, 1912; h/701 Oleander, Bakersfield, CA 93304; m/Wofford Benjamin; c/Wofford B Jr, Donald M, Addie Louise Segars, George William Wise, Sarah Cory; p/Charles McKnight and Louisa Williams Phifer (dec); ed/BA 1933, Hon HHD 1977 Limestone Col; pa/Secy W B Camp & Sons Inc 1956-; CoFdr Trenton (SC) Devel Corp 1950; Dir Bank of Trenton, Trenton, SC 1945-78; Farmer Edgefield Co, SC 1945-77; Soloist St John's Meth Ch, Augusta Ga 1953-55 & Presb Ch, Trenton 1934-55; Other Past Positions; Mem Nat Assn Bk Wom; Farm Bur: SC, Cal; AAUW; cp/Nat Exec Bd Gospel Music Assn; Rel Heritage of Am: Mem Exec Bd, Nat Treas; Dir John & Beverly Stauffer Foun; Trustee SC Foun Indep Cols Inc; Trustee Freedoms Foun at Val Forge; DAR; U Daughs of Confed; PEO; Bakersfield Wom's Clb; B'field Garden Clb; Philharm Assn, B'field; r/Presb Ch: Mem; hon/Outstg Cotton Grower of SC, SC Agri Ext Ser; Outstg Alumna Awd, Limestone Col; Awd, Freedoms Foun at Val Forge.

CAMPBELL, AGNES KNIGHT oc/Social Agency Executive; b/Jan 10, 1911; h/6515 Sherwood Dr, Knoxville, TN 37919; ba/K'ville; m/John Franklin (dec); p/George Allen and Nora Clark Knight (dec); ed/BS Tenn Tech Univ 1934; MSSW Univ Tenn-K 1953; pa/Exec Dir K'ville Travelers Aid Soc Inc; Nat Assn Social Wkrs; Profl Exec's Coun K'ville; Acad Cert'd Social Wkrs; Tenn St Conf Social Wkrs; cp/Gtr K'ville Nutrition Coun; Knox Co Assn on Alcoholism; r/1st Christian Ch; hon/Social Wkr of Yr, Knox Area Chapt Nat Assn Social Wkrs 1976; Dist'd Alumni Awd, Tenn Tech Univ.

CAMPBELL, BETTY JO oc/Bank Executive; b/Oct 21, 1933; h/#1 Fox Chase St, Rossville, GA 30741; ba/R'ville; m/James Ray; c/Denise Liebe, Jan; p/Melvin and Bessie Watkins, LaFayette, GA; pa/Rossville Bank: Asst VP, Auditor; Chm NW Ga Group Nat Assn Bk Wom; Am Inst Bkg; Cherokee Chapt Bk Adm Inst; Nat Assn Bk Wom; R'ville BPW Clb; cp/Better Housing Comm City of F'ville; Voc Ofc Tng Adv Bd, R'ville HS; r/Cedar Hill Bapt Ch: Mem; hon/Wom of Achmt, R'ville BPW Clb.

CAMPBELL, CALVIN ARTHUR JR oc/-Business Executive; Lawyer; Engineer; b/Sept 1, 1934; h/1320 N State Pkwy, Chicago, IL 60610; ba/Chgo; m/Rosemary P; c/Georgia Alta; p/Calvin Arthur Campbell, Midland, MI; ed/AB Williams Col 1956; SB MIT 1959; JD Univ Mich Law Sch 1961; pa/ABA; NY Bar Assn; Am Inst Chem Engrg; Ill Mfg Assn Bd Dirs; Am Mining Cong Bd Govs.

CAMPBELL, CAREY WALTON oc/-Neurological Surgeon; b/Oct 24, 1937; ba/Suite 5-A, 1532 Lone Oak Rd, Paducah, KY 42001; c/Phyllis Catherine; p/Brutus Randolph Campbell, Hattiesburg, MS; Maggie Smith Campbell (dec); ed/BS 1960; MD 1964; mil/AUS MC 1967-69, Mjr; pa/Am Assn Neurological Surgs; Cong Neurol Surgs; Intl Soc for Study of Lumbar Spine; cp/Bd Mem Paducah Art Guild; Masonic Lodge; hon/Cert'd, Am Bd Neurol Surgs; Essayist Med Sch Grad.

CAMPBELL, CHARLES GEORGE oc/Banker; b/Jul 16, 1895; ba/400 Main St, Mt Carmel, IL; m/Helen I Thompson; c/Claire Locke (Mrs David Jr), Joyce C Beals (Mrs Rodney); p/William T and Grace Calder Campbell; ed/Grad Ind Bus Col 1916; Att'd Univ Chgo 1920-22; mil/AUS 1917-19, AEF in France; pa/Am Savs & Ln Assn, Mt Carmel: Pres 1939-59, Dir 1937-; Dir Camray Inc, Mt Carmel, Mt Carmel Area Devel Corp; Dir Tri-Country Indsl Com 1965-67; Security Bk & Trust Co, Mt Carmel: VP 1937-59, Pres 1959-64, Dir; VP Vigo Motor Co, Terre Haute, Ind 1944-50; cp/Mayor Mt Carmel 1965-67; Mt Carmel C of C; Am Legion; Mason; Elk; Moose; Eagle; Kiwanis; r/Presb; hon/Biogl Listings.

CAMPBELL, CHARLES M oc/State Legislator; b/Oct 29, 1918; h/3215 Ala Ilima St, Hononlulu, HI 96818; m/Naomi S; c/Lori M; p/Lee and Lela Campbell; ed/BA; MA (Rel Ed); MA (Sociol); pa/Tchr; Past Pres Hi St Tchrs Assn; Past VP Assoc'd Classroom Tchrs Am; cp/Former City Coun-man Honolulu; Fdr & Chm Teen-Age Assembly of Am; Oper Aloha Inc; r/Meth.

CAMPBELL, GILLETTE (GILLY) SHELTON oc/School Teacher; Minister; b/Jul 20, 1927; h/PO Box 231, Swifton, AR 72471; ba/Same; m/Ruth Helen Warren; c/David, Charles, Carol; p/John DeKalb Campbell (dec); Beulah Evaline McFalls,

Paragould, AR; ed/BSE Univ Ark 1978; mil/USN 1945-47; pa/Sch Tchr; Libn; Assembly of God Pastor; Author Book of Poems, *Priceless Pearls in Poems*; Writer Gen Column for *Stone County Leader* (Newspaper), Mtn View, Ark; r/Assembly of God: Min; hon/W/W in Rel.

CAMPBELL, HELEN ALEXANDER oc/Retired Journalist; ba/PO Box 1064, Ojai, CA 93023; m/William Thomas (dec); p/Lucien Hugh and Mazie Just Alexander (dec); mil/USNR WWI; pa/Free-lance Journalist; cp/ARC (WWI, WWII); r/Epis; hon/Tennis Champion: Phila & Dist in Singles, Ladies Doubles & Mixed Doubles, 1912.

CAMPBELL, HUGH BROWN JR oc/Lawyer; b/Feb 19, 1937; h/1428 Scotland Ave, Charlotte, NC 28207; m/Mary Irving Carlyle; c/Hugh B III, Irving Carlyle; p/Hugh B and Thelma W Campbell, Charlotte; ed/AB Davidson Col; JD Harvard Law Sch; mil/AUS Maj, Resvs-Staff Judge Advocate, 108th Div; pa/Am, NC & 26th Judicial Dist Bar Assns; Chm 26th Judicial Dist Calendar Com; cp/Former Mem NC Gen Assembly; Past Pres Rotary; r/Epis: Vestryman; hon/Outstg Yg Men Am; W/W in Law.

CAMPBELL, MARIE MALLORY oc/Mathematics Teacher; b/Jan 5, 1939; h/3175 Guava St, Fort Myers, FL 33901; ba/N Fort Myers; c/Monique Patrice; p/Clarence and Lula Mallory, Daytona Bch, FL; ed/BS; pa/Math Tchr N Ft Myers HS; NEA; NCTM; Tchr Assn Lee Co; Fla Tchg Profession; cp/RSVP Adv Bd; Dunbar Day Care Adv Bd; Delta Sigma Theta Inc; Commun Relats Comm; r/Bapt; hon/Nom Lee Co Wom of Yr; Tchr of Month; Biogl Listings.

CAMPBELL, MARY LOU oc/Public Relations Consultant; b/Jan 17, 1928; h/6922

S Jeffery Blvd, Chicago, IL 60649; ba/Same; c/Cathleen Cynthia; p/Philip Bliss and Camille Ateman Moore, Waukegan, IL; ed/BA Univ Ill 1950; MA Univ Chgo 1957; pa/Public Relats Conslt 1977-; Dir Admissions & Pubs Sch of Art Inst of Chgo 1976-77; Pubs Editor NEn Ill Univ 1975-76; Pubs Editor Govs St Univ, Park Forest South, Ill 1973-75; Chgo Urban Prog Dir, NAACP 1971-72; Other Past Positions; Adult Ed Assn USA; Nat Assn Wom Admrs, Deans & Cnslrs; Publicity Clb Chgo; cp/Chgo Symph Soc; Chgo Urban Leag Wom's Bd; Bd Mem S Side Commun Art Ctr; Bd Dirs Planned Parenthood; r/Ch of St Paul & Redeemer (Epis); hon/W/W Am Wom; Pub'd Author.

CAMPBELL, RITA RICARDO oc/Economist; b/Mar 16, 1920; h/26915 Alejandro Dr, Los Altos Hills, CA 94022; ba/Stanford, CA; m/Glenn; c/Barbara, Diane, Nancy; p/David Ricardo (dec); Elizabeth Ricardo, Boston, MA; ed/PhD Harvard; pa/Sr Fellow Hoover Instn, Stanford Univ 1968-; Courtesy Appt, Hlth Sers Adm, Stanford Med Sch 1973-; Archivist & Res Assoc Herbert Hoover Archives,

Hoover Inst 1961-68; Other Past Positions; Bd Dirs Watkins-Johnson Co, Palo Alto, Cal; Mem Simmons Col Corp, Boston, Mass; Mem Adv Com Ctr for Hlth Policy Res, AEI, Wash DC; Others; cp/Mem Nat Citizens' Adv Coun on Status of Wom; Former Mem Task Force on Taxation, Coun on Envir Quality; Others; hon/Annual Alumnae Achmt Awd, Simmons Col; Nat Endowmt for Humanities Sr F'ship; Pub'd Author.

CAMPBELL, ROBERT CRAIG III oc/Attorney; b/Dec 11, 1942; h/128M Du Rhu Dr, Mobile, AL 36608; ba/Mobile; c/David, Brett; p/Joseph R and Gertrude Campbell, Drexel Hill, PA; ed/BA Georgetown Col 1964; JD Cumberland Sch of Law 1967; Certs of Attendance: NWn Univ Sch Law 1971, Ams for Effective Law Enforcemt Inc 1976; mil/AUS JAG 1967-69; pa/Atty for Bd of Sch Commrs, Mobile Co; Instr Univ S Ala 1974-; Asst Juv Judge Mobile Co Yth Ctr 1975-; Asst City Atty City of Mobile 1973-; Sr Partner Sintz, Pike, Campbell & Duke 1973-; Dist Atty Chief Asst St of Ala, Mobile Co 1971-73; Mobile Bar Assn; Ala St Bar Assn; ABA; Ala Trial Lwyrs Assn; Mobile Claims Assn; Ala Def Lwyrs Assn; Ala Crim Def Lwyrs Assn; Fed Bar Assn; Phi Alpha Delta; Alpha Beta Pi; Others; cp/Mirror Lake Racquet Clb; Var Campaign Activs; r/Cath; hon/Spec Asst Atty Gen, St of Ala; Hon Lt Col Aide de Camp, Gov St of Ala; Commend for Exceptionally Meritorious Ser, USS Ala Battleship Comm; AUS Commend Medal; Biogl Listings.

CANCRYN, ADDELITA oc/Retired; h/Box 189, c/o #1 Kokos Straede, St Thomas, USVI 00801; m/E Vernon; p/(dec); ed/BS; MA; pa/Musician: Organist, Choir Dir; cp/Mem Adv Coun U Way; VP Wom's Leag; r/Epis; hon/Outstg Edr, Wom's Leag (Spec Ser).

CANE, JULIA E oc/Retired Teacher; b/Feb 2, 1905; h/335 Freiling Dr, San Antonio, TX 78213; ba/Same; m/Joe L (dec); c/Bernard M, Andries C; p/Charles W and Josephine W Dickinson (dec); ed/BS, Battle Creek Col; Addit Studies; pa/Ret'd 1972; Tchr Phy Hlth, Biol & Physiol San Antonio (Tex)

Public Schs 1947-72; Tchr PE Lubbock Public Elem Sch 1941-47; Tchr PE Elem Div, Detroit, Mich 1929-33; Dir PE Dept YMCA, Kalamazoo, Mich 1927-28; NEA; Tex St Tchrs Assn; Local San Antonio Tchrs Assn; Ret'd Tchrs Assn; Am Poetry Leag; Dr Stella Woodall Poetry Soc; Social Chm, Chm Ways & Means Com, Chm Badge Com; World Poetry Leag; Pres, San Antonio Poets Assn 1979-80; Penn Wom (San Antonio) 1980; r/Travis Park Meth Ch, San Antonio: Mem, Choir; Chm UMW Downtown Group of Wom; hon/Pub'd Poet; 1st, 2nd & 3rd Places in Local Poetry Competitions; Bicentennial Medallion for Poem "The Eagles Nest", Dr Stella Woodall Poetry Soc; Poet Laureate Intl; Num Biogl Listings.

CANGEMI, JOSEPH P oc/Associate Professor; b/Jun 6, 1936; h/1305 Woodhurst Dr, Bowling Green, KY 42101; ba/Bowling Green; m/Married; c/2 Chd; ed/BS SUNY 1959; Master's Deg Syracuse Univ 1959-64; Adv'd Grad Study Wn Ky Univ 1970-71; Doct Ind Univ 1974; pa/Assoc Prof Col Ed Dept Psychol, Wn Ky Univ 1968-; Proj Dir Org Analysis: Lib Systems, Computer Sers Sys, Student Sers 1975-77; Universidad de Los Andes, Merida, Venezuela, Inter-Am Devel Bk, Wash DC & Wn Ky Univ; Asst Dir to Acting Dir (Tng & Devel) US Steel Corp, Orinoco Mining Div, Puerto Ordaz & Ciudad Piar, Venezuela 1966-68; Other Profl Positions; Conslt; Advr or Edit Bd Mem Var Pubs; Pub'd Author; hon/Dean's List, SUNY; 20 Awds for Sports; Decreto, St of Santander, Colombia, S Am; Cert, City of Bucaramanga (Colombia); Ky Col; Cert, US Army Armor Sch; Pi Kappa Delta; Others.

CANNADY, NIXON LOUIS oc/School Administrator; b/Mar 26, 1905; h/PO Box 36, Clayton, NC 27520; m/Flossie Davidson; c/Louis H; p/Milton and Annie Petiford Cannady; ed/BS Shaw Univ 1929, Cert Maj in Sci; Masters Sch Adm 1949, Spec Study in Adult Ed & Psychol 1954 Columbia Univ; pa/Prin: Ranson's Acad Sch 1929-30, Wilson's Mills Elem Sch 1930-31, Cooper HS, Clayton 1931-70; Exec Bd NC Tchrs Assn; Others; cp/Exec Bd Johnston Co Citizens Assn; Tri-City Housing Bd; Past Mem Neusick Dist Coul Scout Coun; CoOrgr 1st Black Boy Scout Troop Johnston Co; Former 1/7th Johnston Co 1st Boy Scout Coun; Orgr & Past Chm, Johnston Co Shaw Univ Alumni Clb; 1 of Orig

Trustees Johnston Tech Inst; Past Chm Mazie Byrd Shaw Univ Alumni Clb; Past Pres: Clayton Progressive Enterprises, Clayton Improvement Coun (Past VP); Former 2/VChm Johnston Co Dem Bd; Past CoChm Clayton Commun Day Care Ctr; Currently Mem Bd Dirs Res Triangle Housing Bd; Johnston Co Chm Howard Lee for Lt Gov; Num Other Activs; r/1st Bapt Ch, Clayton: Secy Trustee Bd, Chm Fin Com, Ch Auditor, Plaque for Sers to Ch 1974; Johnston Co Bapt Assn Trustee Bd & Exec Bd; hon/Cert Achmt Johnston Co Tng Sch; Plaque from Sch Fac for Sers to Chd; Silver Beaver Awd, 1 Black Recip Johnston Co; Cash Awds upon Retiremt; Parmi-Nous Clb, Local Girl Scouts; Plaque for Excellent Job in Ed, Johnston Co Citizens Assn 1977; Num Other Plaques; Cits *Smithfield Herald*; Cert Classroom Tchrs Dept of Ed for 25 Yrs Ser; Commun Action Medal for 500 Hrs Vol Work; Cert for Outstg Sers to Mankind, Shaw Univ; W/W NC; Num Others.

CANNON, HOWARD W oc/United States Senator; b/Jan 26, 1912; h/6300 Evermay Dr, McLean, VA 22101; ba/Washington DC; m/Dorothy P; c/Nancy Lee Bjornsen (Mrs Robert J), Alan H; p/Walter and Leah S Cannon; ed/BE Ariz St Tchrs Col; LLB Univ Ariz; mil/USAFR Maj Gen; pa/Admitted to Bar 1937; Reference Atty Utah St Senate 1939; Co Atty Washington Co (Utah) 1940; Law Pract Las Vegas, Nev 1946; Nev, Ariz & Utah Bar Assns; Nev Bd Bar Examrs 1950-55; Charter Mem So Nev Indust Foun; Elected Las Vegas City Atty 1949 (Re-elected 3 Consecutive Terms); cp/Mem US Senate; r/Ch of Jesus Christ LDS; hon/LLD: Ariz St Col, Univ Nev-LV; Univ Ariz: Dist'd Ser Awd, Alumni Ser Awd, 75th Anniv Medallion of Merit; H H Arnold Awd, AF Assn; B'nai B'rith Yth Sers Trans Man of Yr Awd 1977; Outstg Achmt Awd, Nat Security Indust Assn; Awd of Merit, Intl Aviation Clb; Others.

CANNON, LENA (LEE) F oc/Home Economics Specialist; b/Oct 12, 1918; h/525 Forestdale Dr, Auburn, AL 36830; ba/Auburn; m/R Y; c/Emilie, Bobby Jr, Leigh; ed/BS, MS WVa Univ; Further Study Univ Wis; pa/Home Ecs Specialist Ala Cooperative Ext Ser & Ala Public TV 1970-; Assoc Prodr & Hostess Ala Public TV (Auburn Univ) 21 Yrs; Asst Prof Foods & Nutrition, Sch of Home Ecs 22 Yrs; Nutrition Res Sch of Home Ecs, Univ Wis 5 Yrs; Home Ecs Tchr, Osage, WVa 4 Yrs; Am Home Ecs Assn; Am Wom in Radio & TV; Wom in Communs; Delta Kappa Gamma; Phi Upsilon Omicron; IPA; Ala Nutrition Coun; Ala Public Hlth Assn; VP Univ Clb; hon/Cit, Sch of Home Ecs, Auburn Univ; Pub'd Author.

CANOVA, SAYER JOSEPH oc/Pastor; b/Oct 6, 1921; h/119 Bigelow Dr, Edgewater, FL 32032; ba/Edgewater; m/Gene Frances; c/Courtney Gene, Jay Ross, Timothy, Charles, Grace Catherine; p/Stephen Frank

and Mary Canova; ed/BA John Brown Univ; MRE New Orleans Bapt Sem; mil/USN; pa/Pastor 1st Bapt Ch; Free-lance TV Sketch Artist; r/Bapt; hon/W/W in Rel; Personalities of S; Men of Achmt.

CANTERINO, SERAFINA oc/Registered Dental Hygienist; b/Aug 30, 1950; h/80 Rumsey Rd, Yonkers, NY 10705; ba/Scarsdale, NY; p/Emanuel and Matilde Canterino, Yonkers; ed/AAS SUNY; BS Manhattan Col; pa/Westchester Dental Hygienists' Assn: Bd Mem 1975, Pres Elect 1976, Pres 1977; r/Rom Cath.

CANTRELL, CLYDE HULL oc/Retired Director of Libraries, Professor; b/Sept 23, 1906; h/Box 290, 175 Woodfield Dr, Auburn, AL 36830; ba/Auburn; m/Ethel Marie Williams; c/Nancy Elizabeth C Lacy; p/James Volney and Sarah Nancy Florence Hull Cantrell (dec); ed/AB, ABLS, MA Univ NC; PhD Univ Ill; pa/Auburn Univ: Ret'd Dir Libs & Prof; Var Life Mbrships in Lib & Lit Socs; Pubr Articles, Books, Others; Former Archivist Ala Acad Sci; r/Anglican: Active Ch-man; Participant Var Convocations & Confs; hon/Phi Beta Kappa; Mu Beta Psi; Phi Sigma Iota; Sigma Delta Pi; Valedictorian HS Grad'g Class.

CANTRELL, LIZABETH STUPPI oc/Theatre Director; b/Apr 1, 1947; h/1615 Travis St, Amarillo, TX 79102; ba/Amarillo;

m/Donald Ray; p/F N and Virginia Fluhr Stuppi, Amarillo; ed/AB Wellesley Col; MFA Univ Tex-Austin; pa/Chd's Theatre Dir Amarillo Little Theatre; Co-Fdr Cantrell Freelance Advtg 1974-78; Radio Journalist; Actress 1972-74; w Brit Broadcasting Corp, London 1968-69; cp/PEO; DAR; r/St Andrew's Epis Ch, Amarillo; hon/Winner 11 Addy Awds for Advtg Excell.

CANTRELL, ROBERT WENDELL oc/Otolaryngologist; b/Apr 25, 1933; h/RFD 5, Box 385, Charlottesville, VA 22901; ba/C'ville; m/Lee Y; c/Mark L, Elizabeth L, Victoria L, Robert W Jr; p/Lloyd L and Ruby R Cantrell (dec); ed/AB 1956; MD 1960; mil/USN Med Corps 1961-76; USNR Med Corps 1976-, Capt; pa/Univ Va Sch Med, C'ville: Fitz-Hugh Prof & Chm Dept Otolaryngology & Maxillofacial Surg 1977-, Prof & Chm 1976-77; Lectr Audiol & Sph Pathol Cal St Univ, San Diego, Cal 1971-76; Assoc Clin Prof Surg/Otolaryngology Univ Cal, San Diego 1970-76; Other Past Positions; Fellow: Am Col Surgs, Intl Col Surgs, Am Acad Ophthal & Otolaryngology, Am Soc for Hd & Neck Surg, Am Soc Ophthal-Otolaryngological Allergy, Am Acad Facial Plastic & Reconstructive Surg, Am Laryngological, Rhinological & Otological Soc Inc; Acoustical Soc Am; Albemarle Co Med Soc; Am Audiol Soc; Am Broncho-Esophagological Assn; Am Coun Otolaryngology; Assn Mil Surgs; AMA; Am Neurotology Soc; ASHA; Assn Acad Depts Otolaryngology; Am Inst Physics; Other Mbrships; Bd Dirs: Am Acad Facial Plastic & Reconstructive Surg 1976-, Am Coun Otolaryngology 1977-, Am Soc for Hd & Neck Surg 1978-; Conslt; Edit Positions; Num Com Mbrships; cp/Mayor Oakmont, Md 1968-69; r/Epis: Vestry 1959; hon/F'ship, Am Heart Assn 1959; Hurron W Lawson Prize 1960; Plastic Surg Awd; Harris P Mosher Mem Awd, Am Laryngological, Rhino & Oto Soc Inc; W/W: W, S.

CAPELLAN, PRISCILLA FRANKLIN oc/Child Development Center Director; ba/2829 W Vernon Ave, Los Angeles, CA 90008; m/Married; c/2 Sons; ed/BEd Ariz St Univ; pa/Former Sch Tchr Ariz & Cal; Ret'd Fdr & Dir Do Re Me Child Devel Ctr; VChm Chinese Westside Ctr; AAUW; cp/Am Legion Aux Manila Unit #464; Filipino Am Commun; Layte-Samar Assn; Repub Woms Clb; Crenshaw C of C; Japanese Perfect Liberty; Sigma Gamma Rho; r/St Bernadette Cath Ch.

CAPONE, HELEN DIANA oc/Doctor of Medicine; b/Jun 1, 1927; h/5600 Cromwell Dr, Washington, DC 20016; ba/Wash DC; m/Maurice Anthony; c/Maurice, Marcus, Matthew, Martha, Michael, Martin; p/Zygmunt Preisler (dec); Monica Preisler, Oshawa, Ontario, Canada; ed/MD; pa/Doct Walter Reed Army Med Ctr; Fellow Am Col Physicians; Am Soc Internal Med; DC Med Soc; r/Rom Cath.

CAPOZZI, MARIAN R oc/Librarian; h/6802 Dunhill Rd, Baltimore, MD 21222; ba/Towson, MD; p/Daniel Capozzi (dec); Frances Jane Capozzi, Balto; ed/BS Univ Md 1949; MSLS Cath Univ Am 1967; pa/Supvr Lib Sers Balto Co Public Schs; Am Lib Assn; Assn for Lib Ser to Chd (2/VP 1976); Am Assn Sch Libns; Md Ednl Media Org; r/Cath; hon/Beta Phi Mu.

CAPPS, ANTHONY (CAPOZZOLO) oc/International Public Relations Executive; h/2715 Juniper Ave, Palm Springs, CA; m/Theresa Cecelia Harmon; p/Nicolo and Anna Solomone Capozzolo; ed/LA Bus Col; pa/Dance Dir, Choreographer, Prod Mot Pics, TV & Radio; Feat Profl Dance Team, Biltmore Bowl, Cocoanut Grove, LA, St Catharine Hotel, Catalina 1939-42; Dance Dir & Prodr NBC, ABC, KCOP-TV, Columbia Pics, 20th Century Fox & Cal Studios 1940-60; Govt Tours: PR, Cuba, Jamaica, Dominican Repub, Haiti 1954; Prod *Latin Holiday*, TV Series of Latin Am; Num TV Interviews on Rel & Polit Hist of Ballet & Opera of last 500 Yrs; Exec Dir Lockheed & Vega Aircraft Co Activs, Burbank, LA, Glendale, Pomona, Pasa, Bakersfield, Taft, Cal Plants; Intl Public Relats

Dir: Howard Manor, Palm Sprgs Key Clb, CC Hotel, Palm Sprgs Ranch Clb,; Fdr-Pres-Dir Tony Capps Enterprises; George Cameron Jr, Owner, Desert Sun Newspapers, KDES Radio, Palm Sprgs, Cameron Ctr & Cameron Enterprises & Oil Co, Burbank Radio Sta; Fdr-Pres Nat Artists & Art Patrons Soc of City of Hope; Est Anthony Capps Art Gallery Med Ctr; Bd Dirs: Opera Guild of the Desert, Palm Sprgs Pathfinders; Desert Art Ctr of Coachella Val; Palm Sprgs Desert Mus; AFTRA; Desert Press Clb; Other Profl Activs; cp/Fdr-Pres Tri-Co Chapt, Nat Ftball Foun & Hall of Fame; Charter Mem Eisenhower Meml Hosp Aux; Fdr-Pres Societe Culinaire Philanthropique Internationale; Nat Trust for Hist Preserv; Smithsonian Inst; Adv Bd Am Security Coun; Mem Num Clbs; Other Civic Activs; r/Cath; hon/Recipient 25 Awds & Plaques; W/W: Am, Cal, W; Intl W/W Commun Ser; Men of Achmt; Commun Ldrs & Noteworthy Ams.

CAPPS, NORMAN E oc/Executive; b/Jun 25, 1933; h/One Dunford Cir, Kansas City, MO 64111; ba/KC; m/Shirley Lee; c/Leane, Linda; ed/BS Univ Ks; Bach Fgn Trade Am Inst Fgn Trade; pa/Pres Elect Computer Prog'g Inst; Pres: Data Processing Mgmt Assn 1969-70, Assn for Systems Mgmt 1977-78; Past Pres Mo Assn Trade & Tech Schs; cp/Past Pres Ks City Breakfast Club; Pres Rotary Clb 13; Dir BBB of Gtr Ks City; Trustee Ks City Tumor Inst Foun; Former Dir Systic Fibrosis Foun Gtr KC; hon/Indiv Perf Awd, Data Processing Mgmt Assn; Merit Awd, Assn for Systems Mgmt; Recipient Awd for Meritorious Ser to Ks City Police Dept.

CAPPS, ROBERT VanBUREN oc/Minister; b/Aug 19, 1938; h/3 E Lake Dr, Haines City, FL 33844; ba/Lake Hamilton, FL; m/Nancy Patricia Radford; c/Joy Lynn; p/Homer Buren and Grace Ione Ward Capps, Lake Wales, FL; ed/BA cum laude Furman Univ 1960; BDiv SWn Bapt Theol Sem 1963; MDiv 1973; pa/Pastor Poynor, Tex Bapt Ch 1961-62; Assoc Pastor 1st Bapt Ch, Enterprise, Ala 1963-65; Pastor Pine Crest Bapt Ch, Tampa, Fla 1965-67; Evangelist & Fdr Van Capps Evangelistic Assn, Lake Hamilton, Fla 1967-; Mem Conf So Bapt Evangelists; Yth Week Pastor 1st Bapt Ch, Atlanta, Ga; St Music Dir Ga Bapt Student Union; r/So Bapt; hon/Scholastic Hon Soc, Emory Univ; Alpha Phi Gamma.

CAPPUCCI, DARIO TED JR oc/Veterinarian; Scientist; b/Aug 19, 1941; h/1077 Sanchez St, San Francisco, CA 94114; ba/Same; p/Dario and Julie Cappucci, San Francisco; ed/BS 1963, MS 1966, DVM 1965, Univ Cal-Davis; PhD Univ Cal-SF 1976; MPH Loma Linda Univ 1977; AS NY St Univ-Albany 1977; mil/USPHS Comm'd Corps 1966-68, Lt (sg); Duty at: NIH, Md, NCDC, Atlanta, Ga; pa/Currently involved in indep biomed res; Vet Conslt; Former Assoc'd w Cal St Depts Hlth & Food & Agric; Contbr Sci Articles to Profl Lit on Vet Med & Public Hlth; Num Affils w Nat, St & Local Profl Socs & Orgs relating to Vet Med & Biomed Res; r/Rom Cath; hon/Merit Awd, St of Cal; Alpha Zeta; Phi Zeta; Phi Kappa Phi; Sigma Xi; Delta Omega.

CARDOSO, ANTHONY A oc/Art Instructor; b/Sept 13, 1930; h/3208 Nassa St, Tampa, FL 33607; ba/Tampa; m/Martha; c/Toni Lynn, Michele Denise; p/Frank and Nancy Cardoso, Tampa; ed/BS; BFA; MFA;

pa/Art Instr Leto High, Tampa; Fine Arts Dept Hd Hillsborough Co Schs; CTA; FEA; Arts Cun; cp/Mem Dem Party; Platform Assn Wash DC; r/Cath; hon/Var Art Awds incl'g: Prix de Paris Intl, Smithsonian XXII Bienniel, Others; W/W Am Art.

CARDUS, DAVID oc/Professor; b/Aug 6, 1922; h/14314 Cindywood, Houston, TX 77029; ba/Houston; m/Francisca; c/Hellena, Silvia, Bettina, David; p/Jaume and Fernanda Pascual de Cardus, Barcelona, Spain; ed/MD; pa/Prof Med; Physician; Investigator; Contbr Articles to Profl Jours; r/Cath; hon/Grad Magna Cum Laude, Universidad de Barcelona

Med Sch; F'ships: French Govt, Brit Coun; Trainee in Math, Nat Insts of Hlth; 1st Prize for Exhibit on Clin Res, Am Urological Assn; Gold Awd for Sci Exhibit, Am Cong Rehab Med; August Pi i Sunyer Prize of Physiol, Inst d'Estudis Catalans; 1st Prize for Sci Exhibit, 5th Intl Cong of Phy Med.

CAREY, EILEEN FRANCES oc/Librarian; b/Dec 5, 1924; h/2320 Risen Dr, Cantonment, FL 32533; ba/Pensacola, FL; m/John Thomas; c/Thomas George, Michael John; p/George F and Veronica E Schenk Schumann (dec); ed/BSEd; MALS; pa/Libn Pensacola Jr Col; Past Pres W Fla Lib Assn; cp/Past Pres UWF Fac Wives; r/Cath; hon/Vis Libn, World Campus Afloat 1973.

CARGILL, O A (BUCK) JR oc/Lawyer; b/May 30, 1914; h/6305 NW 83rd St, Oklahoma City, OK 73132; ba/Okla City; c/Henson, Carol Lash, Christy C Best, John, Angela Beth, Jennifer, Kima; p/Otto A Sr and Delia Arnold Cargill (dec); ed/LLB Cumberland Univ 1934; mil/AUS 1943; pa/Admitted to Okla Bar 1935; US Dist Cts, Wn, Mo, En Dists, Okla, US Ct of Appeals, 10th Circuit, US Supreme Ct; Pract Okla City 1935-; Pres Buffalo Breeders Am Inc; Okla Charolais Breeders Inc; Fellow Intl Acad Trial Lwyrs; Am, Okla, Okla Co Bar Assns; Assn Trial Lwyrs Am; Okla Trial Lwyrs Assn; Nat Assn Crim Def Lwyrs; Am Judic Soc; Law-Sci Acad Am; cp/Okla City C of C; Dem; r/Bapt; hon/Gold Medal Awd, Law-Sci Acad Am; Biogl Listing.

CARGO, DAVID FRANCIS oc/Attorney at Law; b/Jan 18, 1929; h/750 Briarcliff Ln, Lake Oswego, OR 97034; ba/Portland, OR; m/Ida Jo; c/Veronica, David, Patrick, Elena, Eamon; p/Francis and Mary Cargo, Jackson, MI; ed/AB; MPA; JD Univ Mich; mil/AUS; pa/Mich, NM & Oreg Bars; cp/Former Gov NM (2 Terms); Former NM St Rep (2 Terms); r/Cath; hon/Conservationist of Yr 1970; NM Outstg Man of Yr, NM 1965.

CARLO, MICHAEL J oc/Professor; b/Dec 27, 1937; h/Box 10986 ASU Sta, San Angelo, TX 76901; ba/San Angelo; m/Mary Lynn; p/J F and Anne Carlo, San Antonio, TX; ed/BS 1961, BA 1961, MS 1962, PhD 1970 Tex A&M Univ; pa/Angelo State Univ: Prof Chem 1970-, Grad Fac 1971-; Res Assoc Thermodynamic Res Ctr, Tex A&M Univ Col Sta, Tex 1968-70; Asst Prof Chem: Angelo St Col 1967-68, Tarleton St Col, Stephenville, Tex 1965-67; Other Past Positions: Conslt'g Toxicologist; Tom Green Co Probation Dept, San Angelo 1976-, P&P Lab, San Angelo 1975-76, Wohler Livestock Prods Co, San Angelo 1975-76, St Prog on Drug Abuse, Austin, Tex 1974-, Others; AAUP, Bd Dirs

Angelo St Univ Chapt 1973-76; Tex Assn Col Tchrs: Pres Angelo St Univ Chapt 1974-75, VP Angelo St Univ Chapt 1973-74; Am Chem Soc; Instrument Soc Am; AAAS; Fed Am Scists; Fellow Tex Acad Sci; Other Profl Activs; cp/Lions Clb; Chm Mtl Hlth/Mtl Retard Drug Treatmt & Preven Adv Bd; Chm Concho Val Coun of Govts Reg Alcohol/Drug Adv Bd; Pres Halfway House Bd Dirs; Bd Dirs: San Angelo Coun on Alcoholism, Civic Theater, Coun for Human Growth & Devel; Holy Angels Cath Sch Bd of Ed; Var Past Activs; hon/Gamma Sigma Upsilon; Phi Delta Kappa; Sigma Xi; Num Biogl Listings; Pub'd Author.

CARLSON, ERMA WOOD oc/Author; Homemaker; h/PO Box 3777, Baytown, TX 77520; m/Carl Edward; p/William Walter and Ermina Young Wood (dec); ed/BS Minn Univ; BLS Drexel Univ; pa/HS Eng Tchr, Minn; Col Libn, Baytown, Tex; Author: "The Everlasting

Light, the King James Version of the Bible, Chronologically Condensed", "The Manifestation of God's Law of Abundance, from the Bible"; r/Christian Sci; hon/Carnegie Grant for Excell of Org of Baytown Col Lib.

CARLSON, HELEN HEDMAN oc/Life Insurance Counselor; b/Jan 21, 1910; h/1339 Hedmanway, White Bear Lake, MN 55110; ba/Minneapolis, MN; m/L Floyd; p/Daniel and Huldah Hedman (dec); ed/LUTC; pa/Nat

Assn Life Underwriters; Nat Assn Hlth Und; Pres Zonta Intl of St Paul 1978-80; cp/Bd Mem St Paul Chamber Orch; Dir Maplewood Commun Singers; r/Luth; hon/W/W Am Wom; London World Register.

CARLSON, MARY JEAN CALLERY oc/Author; Literary Consultant; Composer; Lyricist; Poet; Children's Choir Director; Business Consultant; h/Same; m/Thomas R, Jane Mary; p/Milton Charles Callery, El Cajon, CA; Myrtle Callery (dec); ed/Cert in Music McPhail Sch of Music, Mpls; Cert, Bus Mgmt, Control Data Corp Bus Inst 1970; Att'd: Wheaton Col, Writer's Inst, Decision Mag Writer's Sch; Grad Personal Dynamics Inst as Cert'd Coor Instr of Dynamics Inst Sems; pa/Case Reviewer, Placemt Advr, Hennepin Co Wel Dept; Adm Coor, Control Data Corp, Mpls 1968-72; Bus Conslt (Self-employed); Public Relats, Profl Promotor & Coor of Nat & Intl Convs & Tng Sems for large Corps 1970-74; Admr, Dir of Promotions, Mgr of Distributor Sers, Successful Living Inc, Intl Book Distributor Sers, Successful Living Inc, Intl Book Distributors 1972-74; Lit Conslt;

Free-lance Writer 1974-; Mem Hennepin Co Pers Bd, Appt'd by Co Bd for 4 Yr Term 1979; Chd's Choir Dir; Many Musical Compositions; Resource Person for Sev Pub'g Houses; Contbr of Articles, Prose & Poems to Var Jours; Instr in Rel Ed 1952-73; Pub'd Book: *Some People* (1976), Sequel *More About Some People* (forthcoming); Soloist, Lyric Soprano; Mem: NLAPW (Secy Minn Br), Minn Writers Guild, Minn Christian Writers Guild, Evang Press Assn, Metro Alert (Div of Fdn of Woms Clbs), Nat Assn Female Execs; cp/Former Hlth & Wel Chm, Mpls Sch; Active YMCA 20 Yrs, Other Yrs' Chapt Mpls 2 Yrs; Campaign Wkr; r/Edina Covenant Ch, Edina, Minn: Mem; hon/Voted Most Talented, HS Grad Class of 1948; Adv'd Cert of Merit for Dist'd Achmt, World W/W Wom; Biogl Listings; Lttrs of Apprec for Lit Contbns from: Pres Gerald Ford, Pres Jimmy Carter, VP Walter Mondale, late Sr Senator Hubert H Humphrey.

CARLSON, RICHARD WARNER oc/Mortgage Banker; Lecturer; Journalist; b/Feb 10, 1941; h/7956 Avenida Alamar, La Jolla, CA 92037; ba/San Diego, CA; m/Patricia Caroline Swanson; c/Roberta Hunt, Tucker McNear, Buckley Peck; p/Warner and Ruth Carlson (dec); pa/VP San Diego Federal; Former Awd-Winning Journalist & TV Anchorman; Former Staff Reporter: U Press Intl (San Francisco), Capitol Bur (Sacramento); Investigative Reporter KGO-TV, San Francisco 1966-70; News Anchorman "AM" Show 1967-69; Polit Editor, Hd Investigative Unit KABC-TV's Flagship Sta, Los Angeles 1971-75; Anchorman KFMB-TV, San Diego 1975; Other Profl Activs; Dir Cal Gen Mortgage Ser Co; Dir Del Mar News Press Inc; Cal C of C; San Diego C of C; VP, Dir, Mem Exec Com; Sigma Delta Chi; San Diego Press Clb; Co-Fdr A J Liebling Soc; VP Repub Bus & Profl Clb; Dir Motion Picture & TV Bur San Diego; cp/The City Clb; Senate Repub Adv Com; Citizens for Open Space, Former Chm; Fin Adv Com Jr Leag San Diego Inc; Mem Var Charitable Orgs & Social Clbs; Trustee La Jolla Country Day Sch; Dir La Jolla Chamber Music Soc; r/Epis; hon/San Diego Press Clb Awds: Best Documentary, Investigative Reporting; LA Press Clb Grand Awd, Investigative Reporting; George Foster Peabody Broadcasting Awd; Sev "Emmy" Awds; Sev "Golden Mike" Awds; Nat Hdliners Awd, Hunter's Point Riot Coverage; San Diego St Col Broadcasting Awd, Best Documentary Film; Num Assoc'd Press TV & Radio Awds.

CARLTON, RUBY STEWART oc/Secretary; b/Nov 17, 1918; h/302 Lynn St, Bluefield, VA 24605; ba/Bluefield; m/Charles S; p/Arthur Wade and Effie Linkous Stewart (dec); pa/Secy Bluefield St Col; Tchr Pvt Piano; cp/Bluefield Commun Concert Assn: 2/VP, Bd Dirs; Wom's Clb of Bluefield: Past Secy, Past Pres, Former Parliamentrn, Past 1/VP, Current Pres; Music Lovers' Clb Bluefield: Pres, Past Treas; Va Fdn Wom's Clbs: Ed Chm, Former Garden Chm SWn Dist; YWCA; Mercer Co Humane Soc; Former Mem: Beautification Comm Town of Bluefield, Bus & Profl Assn; Other Civic Activs; r/1st Bapt Ch, Bluefield: Mem; Organist/Choir Dir Graham Presb Ch, Bluefield 1972-; hon/Outstg Clbwom on Yr, Wom's Clb 1975; Biogl Listings.

CARMICHAEL, ARTHUR COMMONS JR oc/Insurance Executive; b/Sept 5, 1946; h/1585 Grant Rd, Los Altos, CA 94022; ba/Los Altos; m/Jean Caroline Heard; c/Arthur Commons III, Jennifer Marston; p/Arthur Commons Carmichael Sr (dec); Helen Cribari Carmichael Pettit; ed/BS Univ Oreg; mil/AF ROTC; pa/Pres Flamer & Co Ins Brokerage; Dir Neu Bros Grading & Paving Inc; Past Dir W H Burke & Co; Past Pres: Los Altos C of C, Foothill Ins Assn; Past Pres & Fdr Express Inc; Past Pres 778X ray, Inc; cp/Mayor & Coun-man City of Los Altos; Former Trustee: Foothill Col Augmented Bd, Los Altos Foun, Hope Thru Help; Past Pres Los Altos Kiwanis; Former Mem Repub St Ctl Com; r/Rom Cath; hon/Nicholas Van Utt Meml; Outstg Yg Men Am.

CARMICHAEL, TRUDIE ELAINE
oc/Housing Aide/Selector; b/Dec 10, 1953; h/48 Oliver St, Apt #9, Decatur, GA 30030; ba/Decatur; p/John Lewis Lyles, Winder, GA; Willie E Carmichael, Decatur; ed/BA; JD; pa/Nat Assn Hsg & Redevel Ofcls; SEn Reg Coun (Housing); cp/NAACP; Former Chperson Wom's Polit Caucus, Yg Dems Ga; Former Parliamentn Yg Dems of Ga; DeKalb Co Dem Com; Nat Fdn Dem Wom; Former Corr'g Secy Dem Wom of DeKalb; 3/VP Ga Fdn Dem Wom; Exec Com Yg Dems Am; Co-Chperson Minority Caucus-Reg 3; Del 1975 Yg Dems Am Conv (St Louis, Mo); Del 1975 1st St Charter Conv, Macon, Ga; Alt Whip 1976 Dem Nat Conv (NYC); Other Polit Activs; r/Bapt; hon/Hon Ky Col; Gov's Intern; Cert of Merit, Delta Theta Phi; Outstg Yg Wom Am; Ygest Alumni Awd, N Ga Col; W/W: Am Cols & Univs, Am Polits; Personalities of S.

CARNAHAN, JEAN ANN oc/Speech-Language Pathologist; b/Nov 12, 1954; h/1414 Dehart Ave, Coshocton, OH 43812; ba/Coshocton; p/William L and Gertrude Carnahan, Coshocton; ed/BA; MA; pa/Spch-Lang Pathologist Coshocton City Schs; E Ctl

Ohio Spch & Hearing Assn; Ohio Spch & Hearing Assn; AAUW; cp/Kent St Alumni Assn; r/St Paul's Anglican Ch, Coshocton; hon/Rho Lambda; W/W Among Am Cols Students.

CARNER, REBECCA L oc/Educational Consultant; Therapist; b/Oct 23, 1940; h/12955 SW 83 Ct, Miami, FL 33156; m/John D Goins; c/Anne Kathryn; p/Elbert S Brewer (dec); Annie Jewel Phillips Brewer, Ruston, LA; ed/BA 1961, MA 1962, EdD 1971 Univ Miami; pa/Dir Carner Conslts (Ednl Conslt, Cert'd Sex Therapist); cp/Pres Coral Gables ACLD; IRA; AMS; AASECT; r/Presb; hon/Epsilon Tau Lambda; W/W Am Wom; Notable Ams.

CARNEVALE, DARIO oc/Petroleum & Petrochemical Company Executive; b/Jan 11, 1935; h/1358 NE 138th St, N Miami, FL 33161; ba/Des Plaines, IL; m/Franca Nelken; c/Daniela, Flavia, Fulvia, Dario Jr; p/Emilio Carnevale (dec); Olinda Marcelli, Rome, Italy; ed/DEng Univ Rome (Italy); pa/Gen Mgr UOP Processes Intl Colombian Br at Bogota (Colombia); Mktg, Engrg Design & Proj Mgmt Oil Refineries & Petrochem Plants; r/Cath; hon/Advr to Colombian Govt for Petrol Refining-World Bank Meeting, Paris 1973; W/W Am.

CARNEY, FRANK NELSON oc/Professor; b/Jan 7, 1952; h/4387 Faronia, Memphis, TN 38116; m/Janice Stockdale; p/W H and Anna Louise Cobb Carney, Memphis; ed/BA magna cum laude 1974, MA 1977 Baylor Univ; pa/Pt-time Tchr Freshman Eng Baylor Univ 1974-77; Tchr Hong Kong Bapt Col 1977-78; Extramural Evening Lang Courses Taught to Chinese Bus-men & Bus-wom 1977-78; Proofreader for *MLA Handbook for Writers of Research Papers, Theses, and Dissertations*, 1977, Pub'd by Mod Lang Assn 1977; Charter Mem *Wilson Qtrly*; Mod Lang Assn; hon/Selected as Outstg Tchg Asst, Christine Fall Tchg Asst'ship Awd; Winner 1st Annual Robert A Markham Pipe Organ Competition, San Antonio, Tex; Dean Waco Chapt Am Guild Organists 1976-77.

CAROLINE, J C oc/Realtor; b/Jan 17, 1933; h/2501 Stanford Dr, Champaign, IL 61820; ba/Champaign; m/LaVerne; c/Janice, Jayna, Jolynn; p/Eugenia Gordon (dec); ed/BS; pa/Realtor Assoc; Pro-Ftball; cp/Urban Leag; Boys Clb; r/Bapt; hon/All Am, All Pro, SC Hall of Fame.

CARPENTER, ALLAN oc/Author, Editor, Publisher; b/May 11, 1917; h/Suite 4602, 175 E Delaware Pl, Chicago, IL 60611; ba/Chgo; p/John Alex and Theodosia Smith Carpenter (dec); ed/BA; pa/Author 126 Books which includes a book on each st, a book on each country of S & Ctl Am & Africa; Fdr

Teachers Digest Mag; Fdr Carpenter Pub'g House; Fdr Infordata Intl Inc; Fdr *Index to US Govt Periodicals*; Author Num Articles for Periodicals; Fdr Music Coun Metro Chgo; Pres Chgo Bus Men's Orch; Prin Bass Violist Symph Orchs; r/2nd Presb Ch, Evanston: Clerk of Session, Ruling Elder.

CARPENTER, CHARLES WHITNEY II oc/Educator; b/Jan 2, 1918; ba/Bloomsburg, PA 17815; ed/AB Cornell Univ 1943; MA Univ So Cal 1952; Dipl Indep Col Armed Forces 1961; PhD NY Univ 1968; pa/B'burg St Col: Prof Dept Fgn Langs 1969-, Assoc Prog 1966-69; Asst Prof Buena Vista Col (Ia) 1965-66; Instr: Univ Hi 1963-65, Univ Vt 1962-63; Asst Prof Bronx Commun Col 1959-62; Instr NY Univ 1956-59; Other Former Positions; Inst Germanic Studies (London); German Soc NY; Friends of Princeton Lib; Staten Isl Inst Arts & Scis; Bishop Mus Assn; Mod Lang Assn; AAUP; Am Assns Tchrs German & French; Hi Assn Lang Tchrs; Linguistic Soc Am; Delta Phi Alpha; cp/Mil Soc WWs; hon/Fellow, Pres' Coun of Am Inst Mgmt 1965; Life Mem, Am Ordnance Assn; Silver Order of Merit; Golden Medal of Spec Mbrship, Japanese Red Cross; Var Acad Awds; DIB; W/W MW; Nat Social Dir; Dic Am Scholars; Intl W/W Intells.

CARPENTER, DONALD BLODGETT oc/Property Appraiser; b/Aug 20, 1916; h/Box 87, Mendocino, CA 95460; ba/Mendocino; m/Barbara Adams; p/F Donald Carpenter, Burlington, UT; Gwendolen Blodgett Carpenter (dec); ed/PhB Univ Vt 1938; mil/USN 1942-46; Comm'd Ensign USNR 1942; Cmdg Ofcr USNR Unit 1967-68; Hon Ret as Lt-Cmdr 1968; pa/Appraiser, Property Tax (Cal) 1969-; ROA: Chapt Pres 1954, 56, St VP 1958-61; cp/Am Legion, Former Post Cmdr; Mendocino Cardinals Booster Clb; Rotary Intl; Selection Com Ftball Foun Hall of Fame; r/Cong; hon/DIB; W/W: Among Students in Am Univs & Cols, W, Commun Ser; Personalities W&MW; Cert of Merit, Kappa Sigma; Secy of Navy Commend w Ribbon; Commun Sports Man-of-Yr, Booster Clb; St Cit for Outstg Commun Ser Activs, Am Legion; Dist Gov Awds, Rotary Intl.

CARPENTER, JAMES ROBERT III oc/Store Manager, Administrator; b/Oct 19, 1948; h/2501 Meadow Ave, Atlanta, GA 30306; ba/Athens, GA; p/J R Jr and Dorthy Moore Carpenter, Elaine, AR; ed/BSBA; cp/Athen's Downtown Coun; C of C; r/Epis.

CARPENTER, MICHAEL KENNETH oc/Executive; b/Feb 2, 1941; h/1219 Oak Meadows Dr, Dallas, TX 75230; ba/Dallas; m/Ann Livingston; p/Eldridge K Carpenter, Jacksonville, FL; Mary Pendrey Carpenter,

Ralph, AL; ed/BSEE Univ Ala; pa/Pres Scientific Machines Corp; r/Bapt.

CARPENTER, WILLIAM LEVY oc/Engineer; b/May 26, 1926; h/227 Seven Oaks Dr, Greenville, SC 29605; ba/G'ville; m/Blanche Owen; c/Mrs R R Bouton, William O, Robert M; p/L L and Lucille O'Brien

Carpenter (dec); ed/BS US Nav Acad 1947; mil/USN 1947-53; USNR 1947; pa/Pres J E Sirrine Co, Architects-Engrs-Planners; NSPE; SCSPE; CESC; ACEC; TAPPI; PEPP; cp/Pres Gtr G'ville C of C; r/Prot.

CARPIO, LUZ M oc/Real Estate Sales Representative; b/Aug 3, 1924; h/3511 Russell, El Paso, TX 79930; ba/El Paso; m/Pedro; c/Cecilia, Peter; p/Feliciano Mendoza; Luz Bonilla; pa/Sales Agt Dewitt & Rearick, Realtors 1968-; Gen Ofc Clerk Triangle Elec Co 1946-66; Tex Assn Realtors; El Paso Bd Realtors; cp/Nat Dem Clb El Paso: Past Pres, VP, Secy & Chm; Bowie Alumni Assn: Secy, Treas, Capt; Former Dir Pan Am Pilot Clb; Mem Goals for El Paso Human Relats Task Force; Mexican-Am Dems;

Progressive Dems Clb; El Paso Wom's Polit Caucus; Law Enforcement Jamboree Day; Precnt Chm Dem Clb; Bd Mem El Paso Co Dem Exec Com; Dem Clb: Co Del, St Del, Gov's Conv Del; r/Cath; hon/Merit Awd for Outstg Work, Kathy White Chapt Nat Dem Wom's Clb; Bowie HS Alumni Plaque Awd for Secy Work; Cert of Apprec: El Paso City Coun Mayor's Adv Coun, El Paso Police Dept Yth Ser Div, Cathedral HS Mother's Clb; Biogl Co Plaque for Outstg Selected Citizens in SW; US Public Relats Ser Plaque for Selected W/W Citizen in Tex; Other Hons.

CARR, ELIZABETH STEPHENS oc/Shop Owner; Book Dealer; Artist; b/Oct 26, 1897; h/101 Royal Palm Dr, Leesburg, FL 32748; p/James W and Elizabeth Stephens Carr (dec); ed/AB Ind Univ, Butler Univ; Cincinnati Conservatory of Music; pa/Ret'd; Gift Shop Owner & Book Dealer; Gt Books Clb 13 Yrs; Apollo Musical Clb Chgo; cp/Repub Wom's Clb; Am Assn for Ret'd Persons; r/Disciples of Christ; hon/Hoosier Salon Exhibitor; Brown Co Art Gallery Exhibitor.

CARR, HOWARD ERNEST oc/Retired Insurance Agency Executive; b/Oct 4, 1908; h/3927 Madison Ave, Greensboro, NC 27410; ba/G'boro; m/Thelma Northcutt (dec); c/Howard Ernest; p/William Alexander and Gertrude Feathers Carr; ed/BS E Tenn St Univ 1929; MEd Duke 1935; Postgrad UNC 1938-39; mil/USNR 1942-46, Lt, Asst Hd Motion Picture Dept, Wash, to Capt 1951-54, as Hd Motion Picture Dept; Ret'd as Capt

1968; pa/Jefferson Standard Life Ins Co, G'boro 1947-77; Spec Rep 1947-54, Supr Agy G'boro 1964, Mgr 1964-67; Dir Activs 1st Presb Ch, G'boro 1946-47; Prin G'boro City Schs 1937-42; Other Past Positions; Nat, NC, G'boro Assns Life Underwriters; cp/NC Ldrs Clb; G'boro C of C; Mason; Kiwanis; Past Pres Everett's Lake Corp, Chm Guilford Co Bd Ed; Former VChm NC Gov's Com Ed; Former NC Rep White House Conf Ed; Mem Adv Com G'boro Div Guilford Col; Bd Dirs Cancer Soc; Past VP NC St Sch Bds Assn; Others; r/Presb: Elder; hon/Author *History of Higher Education in East Tennessee*, 1935; Nat Quality Awd, Nat Assn Life Underwriters; Boss of the Yr, Lou-Celin Chapt Am Bus Wom's Assn; Man of Yr Awd, NC Assn Life Underwriters.

CARR, JAMES ROGERS oc/Banker & Realtor; b/Jun 30, 1955; h/257 Maryland Dr, Richmond, KY 40475; ba/Richmond; p/Richard Igo and Elizabeth R Carr, Richmond; ed/En Ky Univ; pa/Asst Cashier Richmond Bank; Realtor & Salesman Don Foster & Assocs; Mem Ky Bd Realtors; r/Presb.

CARR, JESS oc/Novelist; b/Jul 27, 1930; h/1401 Madison St, Radford, VA 24141; m/Lois Ainslie Domazet; c/Marsha Ainslie, Susan Kay, Catherine Rae; p/Jesse C Carr Sr (dec); Flossie Elizabeth Carr; ed/Grad Coyne Radio Sch; mil/USMC Vet; pa/Lectr; Writer; Mem Var Lit Clbs; cp/City of Radford Com, Repub Party; r/Bapt; hon/Author 10 Books, 1 Made into Movie; Book Selected as 1 of 100 Outstg Books Pub'd in 1972.

CARR, OWEN C oc/College President; b/May 19, 1923; h/PO Box 810, Phoenixville, PA 19460; ba/P'ville; m/Priscilla Faye Seidner; c/Marilyn C Deaton, S David; p/Claud Carr (dec); Alvina Carr, Springfield, MO; pa/Pres Valley Forge Christian Col; Fdr & 1st Pres Christian Communs of Chgoland Inc, Channel 38, WCFC-TV; Nat Speed-the-Light Rep Intl Hdqtrs of Assemblies of God

(Springfield); St Dir Yth & Ed Ks Dist Assemblies of God 5 Yrs; Pastor: Ks, Tex & Ill; Pastor The Stone Ch of Chgo 6 Yrs; Asst Supt Ill Dist Assemblies of God throughout US; Missionary Evangelist in More than 30 Countries; Headed Nat Christ's Ambassador (Yth) Dept, S'field 3 Yrs; IPA; r/Assemblies of God; hon/W/W in Rel; Commun Ldrs & Noteworthy Ams; DIB.

CARR, PAT MOORE oc/Writer; Professor; b/Mar 13, 1932; h/1029 Kelly Way, El Paso, TX 79902; pa/El Paso; m/Duane; c/Stephanie, Shelley, Sean, Jennifer; p/Stanley and Bea Rawke Moore (dec); ed/BA cum laude, MA Rice; PhD Tulane; pa/Prof Univ Tex-EP; Author Books: *The Grass Creek Chronicle*, 1976, *Bernard Shaw*, 1976, *The Women in the Mirror*, 1977, *Mimbres Mythology*, 1978; Stories & Articles Have Appeared in: *Southern Review, Yale Review, Best Am Short Stories, Modern Fiction Studies, Modern Drama*; hon/Phi Beta Kappa; Lib of Cong Marc IV Awd; la Sch of Lttrs Short Fiction Awd; Tex Inst Lttrs Short Story Awd.

CARRAHER, CHARLES E JR oc/Teacher; Researcher; Administrator; b/May 8, 1941; h/2855 College Hill Ct, Fairborn, OH 45324; ba/Dayton, OH; m/Loyalea Velda Zimmerman; c/Charles, Shawn, Michelle, Erin, Heather, Colleen, Shannon; p/Charles E Carraher (dec); Addie Carraher, Ks City, KS; ed/BS Sterling Col 1963; PhD Univ Mo-Ks City 1967; pa/Prof & Chm Dept Chem Wright St Univ 1976-; Univ SD: Prof 1973-76, Chm Sci Div 1971-74, Assoc Prof 1970-73, Asst Prof 1968-70, Instr 1967-68; Am Chem Soc; AAAS; Fellow Am Inst Chemists; Indust Conslt;

HEFA; Spkr; Others; cp/Reviewer Ohio Bd of Ed; Adv Com Career Dayton Public Schs; r/Alliance Ch, Vermillion, SD: Ch Elder 1969-76, SS Supt 1970-74, Yth Dir 1968-70; Presb Ch: Urban Devel Com, Gtr Ks City Area; John Calvin U Presb Ch, Ks City, Ks: Ch Elder & Christian Ed Dir 1964-67; hon/Pub'd Author; Recipient Grants; Am Inst Chemists Student Awd; Kelsey Scholar; Num Biogl Listings.

CARRINGTON, FREDRICK MURRAY oc/Psychologist; b/Jul 19, 1948; h/13 Cerrato Ln, Texarkana, TX 75503; ba/Texarkana; m/Emma B; c/Cristi, Sunny; p/Murray and Eugenia Carrington, Cooper, TX; ed/BS; MS; PhD; pa/Chief Psychol Sers Fed Correctional Instn; Am Psychol Assn; Tex & SW Psychol Assns; Certn Bd Tex Corrections Assn; Lic'd Psychologist; Cert'd Correctional Cnslr; Kappa Delta Psi; Am & Tex Correctional Assns; hon/DIB; W/W in S&SW; Personalities of S; Notable Ams; Commun Ldrs & Noteworthy Ams.

CARRINGTON, LAURA ANN oc/School Teacher; b/Aug 25, 1946; h/RR3, Morris, MN 56267; ba/Morris; m/Thomas Louis; c/Anna, Matthew; p/Willie Henry and Marjorie Heldt Stock, Correll, MN; ed/BA Univ Minn 1967; pa/4th Grade Tchr Morris Public Schs; Morris Tchrs Assn: Mem, Past Secy, Mem Negotiating Com, Communs Coun, Govtl Relats Chair; cp/Stevens Co DFL Chm; Del to 7th Dist & St DFL Convs & Platforms Coms; r/Assumption Parish (Cath Ch): Mem, Rel Instr, Mem of Guild; hon/W/W in Am Polits.

CARRISON, MURIEL PASKIN oc/Professor; b/Apr 27, 1928; h/11371 Matinicus Ct, Cypress, CA 90630; ba/Dominguez Hills, CA; m/D A; c/Michael, Amy, Peter, David Lombrozo; p/Jacob Paskin (dec); Hattie Paskin, Seal Beach, CA; ed/BA; MA; PhD; pa/Prof Ed Cal St Univ-DH 1969-; Instr Long Bch City Col, Rio Hondo Jr Col 1968-69; Vis Asst Prof Ed 1967-69: Univ So Cal, Cal St Univ-LB, Cal St Univ-F; Other Past Positions; AAUP; Am Psychol Assn; Am Sociol Assn; Cal Assn Profs in Elem Ed; Nat Coun for Social Studies; NEA; Pacific Sociol Assn; Phi Delta Kappa; Sociol Ed Assn; Other Profl Activs; cp/Fair Housing Foun LB; Intl Host Progs; r/Cath; hon/Nat Def Ed Act Scholar; EDUCARE Scholar; Biogl Listings; Pub'd Author.

CARROLL, CHARLES EDWARD (BUTCH) oc/Insurance Agent; b/Jan 17, 1944; h/501 Graham St, Florence, SC 29501; ba/Florence; p/Robert Clinton Carroll (dec); Harriett Holland Carroll, Florence; ed/BS Clemson Univ; pa/Trainee Agt State Farm Ins; St Farm Tng Group 1977-78; Florence Sch Dist #1 Engr 1968-77; Tchr 1977 & 78; Energy Conservation Conslt 1968-; cp/Advr Jr Civitan Clb; Scoutmaster Scout Troop 475; r/1st Presb Ch: Mem; hon/BSA: Silver Beaver, Vigil Hon Member Order of Arrow.

CARROLL, DAVID WILLIAM oc/International Communications Consultant; b/May 16, 1949; h/18680 Harleigh Dr, Saratoga, CA 95070; ba/Saratoga; p/Cecil Thomas, Portland, OR; Florence Emily Grant Carroll (dec); pa/Conslt 1976-: Cal Microwave Inc, Siliconix Inc, SP Communs Inc, Bechtel Corp; VP Opers Transmedia Corp, Santa Clara, Cal 1977; Chm Bd & Conslt Vector Communs Inc, Sunnyvale, Cal 1977-; Var Past Positions; IEEE; AIIE; ACM; AES; Profl Photogs Am; Profl Photogs SF; Photo Soc Am; Nat Freelance Photog's Assn; Nikkor Clb; r/Prot; hon/NASA Awd, Space Communs & Elects; USAF Comz Europe Ground Safety Awd.

CARROLL, LILLIAN REBECCA oc/-Administrator; b/Oct 4, 1912; h/7 Surf Dr, St Augustine By-the-Sea, FL 32084; ba/St Augustine; m/Richard Parker (dec); p/-Richard Dunstan and Alice Cotton Fletcher; ed/RN Cert Mass Gen Hosp 1935; BS 1965, MA 1967 Boston Univ; Addit Studies Fla St Univ 1969-73; pa/Dir of Guid Dept for the Blind Fla Sch for Deaf & Blind 1968-; Co-Fdr & Co-Instr Cooperative Voc Guid Course for Visually Impaired FSDB & Div of Blind Sers 1969; Mount Ida Jr Col, Newton Centre, Mass: Hd Clin RN 1963-67, Hygiene Instr 1955-62, Dir & Instr Airline Tng Course 1952-64; Other Former Positions; Nat Rehab

Assn; Fla Voc Assn; Assn Classroom Tchrs; Life Mem Platform Assn; Nat Kiwi Clb: Chm Chapt Form 4 Yrs, Fdr Boston Chapt (held all ofcs, now Mem-at-Large), Nat 7th Biennial Conv Chm 1966; Fla Coun of Blind; cp/GSA: Troop Conslt on Ser Team, St Augustine Neighborhood 10 Yrs, Coor 4 Troops Girl Scouts in Dept for Blind 1968; Coor Pilot Prog for Visually Impaired, St Augustine HS 1977-78; Former Mem St John's Co Com on Drug Abuse; r/Epis; hon/S'ships incl: Boston Univ Trustee, Fla St Dept of Ed, Fla St Univ, Sum Tng Grant USOE, Gen Elect Sum Guid F'ship; Gateway Girl Scout Coun Silver Plate in Awd "In Apprec", 1978; Pub'd Author; Others.

CARSON, WILLIAM EDWARDS oc/-Engineer; b/Jul 31, 1930; h/2625 Morningside Dr, Clearwater, FL 33519; ba/Dunedin, FL; c/Kathryn E Reed, William E Jr, John Edwin; p/J E and Elinor E Carson, Danville, VA; ed/BSEE 1952, MS 1959 VPI; pa/NUS Corp,

Clearwater 1973-: Prin Engr, Proj Mgr Nuclear Power Plants; Staff Engr Nuclear Power Plants So Nuclear Engrg Inc, Dunedin, Fla 1971-73; Sr Elect Engr Nuclear Power Plants Burns & Roe Inc, Oradell, NJ 1971; Nuclear, Elect, Instrumentation, Propositions Engr (Nuclear Steam Supply Systems) Babcock & Wilcox Co, Lynchburg, Va 1957-71; Other Past Positions;

Sigma Xi; Am Nuclear Soc; Sr Mem IEEE; cp/Former Chm Yg Repub Fed of Va; Former Mem JCs; Former Mem Va repub St Ctl Com; Other Repub Party Activs; r/U Meth Ch; hon/Sev Tech Pubs; Men of Achmt; W/W S&SW.

CARSTEN, ARLENE D oc/Executive Director; b/Dec 5, 1937; h/1415 Via Alta, Del Mar, CA 92014; ba/San Diego, CA; m/Alfred J; c/Christopher Dale, Jonathan Glenn; p/Albert F and Ann Desmet, Rumson, NJ; ed/Alfred Univ; Univ Cal; pa/Exec Dir Inst for Burn Med 1972-; Dir Muskie for Pres Campaign (San Diego) 1972; Res Conslt CRM 1970; Piano Tchr 1964-71; Music & Arts Dir Evening Prog Deveraux Sch, Santa Barbara 1960; Info Coun on Fabric Flammability; Nat Fire Protection Assn; Am Burn Assn: Spec Mbrship, Mem Burn Preven Com; Guest Lectr; cp/Mtl Hlth Assn San Diego: Bd Dirs,

Chair of Public Ed Com, Chair Mbrship Com; Bd Med Quality Assurance, Psychol Exam'g Com; Fdg Mem Nat Burn Foun; Fdg Mem & Dir Citizens for Paramedics Inc; Bd Dirs Donated Organ Prog; Num Past Activs; hon/Hon Citizen (Key to City), Baton Rouge, La 1976; Spec Awd of Recog for Ser in Field of Mtl Hlth, San Diego Soc Clin Psychologists 1975; Cert of Apprec, San Diego Co Dept Substance Abuse; 1st Annual Commun Awd, Belles for Mtl Hlth, San Diego Mtl Hlth Assn; Spec Awd of Recog for Activs in Public Ed, San Diego Soc Safety Engrs; Pub'd Author; Num Biogl Listings; Others.

CARSWELL, DAVID CLEMENTS oc/Realtor; Insurance Agent; Developer; b/Apr 29, 1949; h/128 Gilbert Dr, Chipley, FL 32428; ba/Chipley; m/Mary Trawick; c/David Clements Jr; p/Elba Wilson Carswell, Chipley; Mabel Bagley Carswell (dec); ed/AA Chipola Jr Col; BS (Mktg), BS (Mgmt) Univ W Fla; Further Studies Univ Tampa; pa/Pres Carswell Realty Inc; Partner Foxmeadow Apts, Ltd; Nat Assn Realtors; Fla Assn Realtors; Chipola Area Bd Realtors; cp/Chipley City Coun: Mem, Pres; VP Carswell Fam Assn Worldwide; Past Pres Bd Dirs The Carswell Foun Inc; Edit Staff Carswell Chronicle; Nat Soc SAR; Sons of Confed Vets; r/Meth; hon/Eta Upsilon Chapt Delta Sigma Pi.

CARTER, EUNICE JANE oc/Assistant Trust Officer; b/October 19, 1932; h/303 Gober St, Houston, TX 77017; ba/Webster, TX; m/Calvin; chd/Greg, Kelle; p/Charlie C and Minnie Smith, Mt Pleasant, TX; ed/Am Inst of Banking Cert; Att'd Univ of Houston; pa/Secy-Treas & Owner, Downtown Body Shop Inc; Secy-Treas, Dreams Inc; cp/C of C (Clear Lake, Tex); Former PTA Exec Bd Mem; Toastmasters Intl; Am Bus Wom; Played Softball w Capital Nat Bank 8 Yrs; Active in Little Leag & Other Commun Activs; r/Bapt; Former Sunday Sch Tchr; hon/Beauty Queen; Mrs Trust Dept; Miss Shrine Circus; Football Sweetheart; Employee of the Month, Oct 1975; Wrote Article which won her Employer the Boss of the Yr Awd, Am Bus Wom; Travel.

CARTER, FRANCES TUNNELL oc/Professor; b/May 21; h/2561 Rocky Ridge Rd, Birmingham, AL 35243; ba/B'ham; m/John T; c/Wayne, Nell; p/D A and Mary Annie McCutcheon Tunnell (dec); ed/AA; BS; MS; EdD; pa/Prof Sch Ed Samford Univ; Exec Bd Ala Assn for Yg Chd 1972-; Reg Dir Kappa

Delta Epsilon 1976-78; Coun on Tchr Ed; Parliamentn Ala AAUW 1976-77; 2/VP (Mbrship) B'ham Br AAUW 1976-77; Editor Ala Tchr Edrs 1976-77; Ala Adv Com on Early Childhood Ed 1972-; Other Profl Activs; cp/Past Pres: B'ham Wom's C of C, B'ham Br Nat Leag Am Pen Wom, Jefferson Co Day Care Assn; Var Activs DAR; Former 1/VP Ala Writers Conclave; Histn & Charter Mem Wom's Chapt Freedom Foun; CAP: Info Ofcr & Editor Ala Wing, Lt Col, Others; Arlington Hist Assn; r/Bapt; hon/B'ham Wom of Yr 1977; Honoree in Hons Convocation, Univ Ala-B; 20-Yr Ser Awd, Samford Univ; Model w "Most Improvemt", Mannequins; Outstg Ser Awd, CAP; Vis Prof Awd, Hon Kong Bapt Col; Others.

CARTER, HELEN STRICKLER oc/Attorney at Law; Law Librarian; b/Jun 20, 1926; h/2913 Cutler Ave NE, Albuquerque, NM 87106; ba/Albu; m/Mitchel M; c/Shannon Louise, Joseph William, Ruth (dec); p/Charles William and Ruth Esther Long Strickler (dec); ed/BA Univ NM; JD Univ Utah; pa/Law Libn Univ NM Sch of Law Lib; DC Bar; St Bar NM; Am Assn Law Libs, Spec Interest Sect on Legal Assistance to Instnl Residents; NM Lib Assn; cp/Legal Conslt: Am Civil Liberties Union, NM St Penitentiary, Dept Corrections & Detention, NM St Lib; r/Presb; hon/Commun Ldrs & Noteworthy Ams; Intl W/W Commun Ser; Personalities W&MW; W/W: Am Wom, Am Law; World W/W Wom.

CARTER, JACQUELINE oc/Aviation Company Executive; b/Apr 8, 1945; h/411 Ridge Rd, San Carlos, CA 94070; m/Ronald Lee Walker III; c/Wayde Christian; p/James William and Margaret Sophia de Avila Carter; ed/BA Long Bch St Univ 1966; MA Stanford 1968; Postgrad Studies: Princeton 1969, Rutgers 1968-69; pa/Intern, Reporter San Francisco Examr 1966-67; Assoc Scope Documentary Film Prodns, Washington 1966-; Conslt Commun Relats Long Bch (Cal) Ofc Ed, San Jose 1970-72; Public Relats, VP Walker Aviation, San Carlos 1972-; Dir Public Relats Chd's Hosp, San Francisco 1972-74; Dir Film Fests Rutgers Univ (NJ) w Mus Mod Art 1969-70; Dir Ednl Fair Ofc Ed, San Jose 1971; Wom in Communs; Bay Area Soc Editors; Exptl Aircraft Assn; Aircraft Owner & Pilots Assn; Phi Beta; cp/Advr Explorer Prog BSA; Bd Dirs No Cal Hosp Assn; Former Ofcr Coun of Living Theatre, Long Bch; Fdr Nat Election Activity Team; Bd Mem Soroptimist Intl, Burlingame, San Mateo; hon/Pub' Author; Contbr Feature Articles to Num Newspapers & Mags; Named Miss Navy 1964; Biogl Listings.

CARTER, JOAN HASELMAN oc/Registered Nurse; Quality Assurance Coordinator; b/Apr 13, 1933; h/7 Williamsburg Rd, St Louis, MO 63141; ba/St Louis; m/Don E; c/Carol, Ann; p/Lewis and Kathryn Haselman (dec); ed/RN; BSN; MSN; pa/Quality Assurance Coor St Louis Univ Hosps; Fac Mem Am Nurses Assn, Wkshops on Implementation of Nsg Standards 1974-75; Coor Interdisciplinary Patient Audit Proj, St Louis Univ Hosps 1974-75; Nsg Conslt Hlth Indust Forums Inc, Clayton, Mo 1974-75; Clin Fac Jt Comm on Accreditation of Hosps 1974-75; Other Past Positions; Am Nurses' Assn; Mo Nurses' Assn; Am Heart Assn; St Louis Heart Assn: Bd Dirs, Res Com; Conslt; r/Rom Cath; hon/Pub'd Author; Mem Nsg Hon Soc.

CARTER, LEONARD CLYDE JR oc/Pastor; Businessman; b/Apr 4, 1935; h/PO Box 85, Daleville, VA 24083; ba/D'ville; m/Karen Schultze-Spohr; c/Claudia, Kermon, Leonard; p/Leonard C and Gladys Stone Carter, Bassett, VA; ed/BA Bridgewater Col; MTh Bethany Theol Sem; pa/Pastor Ch of Brethren, D'ville; Owner & Operator Lenglad Camping; Bd Dirs: Roy Stone Transfer Co, Smith Cattleguard Co; cp/Bd Dirs Commun Action Prog; Kiwanis; St Chm Weekday Rel Ed; r/Ch of Brethren; hon/Moderator En Dist Va Ch of Brethren; Pub'd Num Articles on Theol & Camping.

CARTER, LIZZIE E HILL oc/Minister; b/Feb 8, 1906; h/Calhoun, KY 42327; ba/Calhoun; m/Thomas E; c/Edna H Anderson (dec); p/Henry and Dora Bandy; ed/LPN; pa/Pentecostal Min, Founded Local Ch, Calhoun; Former Min Pentecostal Ch, Eldorado, Ill; r/Pentecostal; hon/Hon'd by Ch & Friends for 50th Yr Anniversary of Work in Ministry.

CARTER, MAXINE GOODMAN oc/Music Teacher; Organist; b/Feb 7, 1927; h/6455 Boeu F Trace, Alexandria, LA 71301; ba/Same; c/Jack T Jr, John M; p/John William Goodman (dec); Lula Simmons Goodman, Alexandria; pa/Church Organist; Funeral Organist; Tchr Sherwood Music Sch; r/Bapt; hon/Intl W/W Musicians.

CARTER, PRENTISS HENSON JR oc/Executive; b/May 29, 1931; h/Tall Timber Estates, Greensburg, LA 70441; ba/G'burg; m/Sadie W; c/Karlette, Kevin, Rhenette; p/Prentiss Henson and Rebecca Matthews Carter, G'burg; ed/BA SEn La Univ 1952; Md

Ed La St Univ 1954; pa/Tchr Public Sch, G'burg 1952-55; Asst Prin, G'burg 1955-57; Pres: Carter Ins 1953, Carter Real Est 1963, Carter Mobile Homes Inc 1973; VP St Helena Acceptance Corp 1963; La Mfg Housing Assn: Mem, Past Pres, Dir; r/Bapt; hon/Contbr Articles to Profl Jours; W/W S&SW.

CARTER, V L oc/Professor, Director; b/Oct 19, 1927; h/1621 E 38th St, Little Rock, AR 72206; c/Larry D, Michael R; p/Thomas Glasgow, Little Rock; ed/BS AM&N Col 1949; MS Univ Ark-F 1954; EdD N Tex St Univ; Further Studies; pa/Philander Smith Col: Assoc Prof Ed & Dir Student Tchrs 1964-, Acting Chm Div Ed 1966, 67, Prof Ed, Chm Div Ed 1970, 71-; Prof Ed Ark Bapt Col 1970-; Dean of Instrn Ark Bapt Col 1970-73; AAUP; Ark Merit Sys Coun; Phi Delta Kappa; Conslt: Mem Var Coms; cp/Urban Leag; OES; Spec Conslt Ec Opportunity Agy, Dallas Reg; U Way Pulaski Co, Former Chm Ed Sect; Ark Ec Opportunity Agy; Former Vol Probation & Parole Ofcr, Pulaski Co; Others; r/Mt Zion Bapt Ch: Bd Christian Ed, U Adult SS Class, Maids & Matrons Clb; Secy Bapt Tng Union 5 Yrs; hon/Miss Alumni, AM&N Col; So Ed F'ship; Ford Foun Grant; IBM F'ship; Female Fac-Mem of Yr, Philander Smith Col 1969-70; Honoree Morris Booker Meml Col for "Outstg Ser in Ed"; Author *How to Get a Career Job*, 1978; Philander Smith Col Student Govt Awd; U Way Pulaski Co Awd; Biogl Listings.

CARTER, WALTER HORACE oc/Writer; Journalist; b/Jan 29, 1921; h/101 Crescent St, Tabor City, NC 28463; ba/Tabor City; m/Lucile M; c/Linda, Russell, Velda;

p/Walter Raleigh and Waulena Lowder Carter (dec); ed/AB Univ NC-CH; mil/USN 1942-46; pa/Outdoor Mag Writer; Newspaperman; Bus-man; Fdr Atlantic Pub & Paper Co; cp/Rotary; Former JC; r/Bapt: SS Tchr; hon/Pulitzer Prize, 1952; 1 of 10 Most Outstg Yg Men in Am 1954.

CARTER, WARRICK L oc/Professor; b/May 6, 1942; h/43 Monee Rd, Park Forest, IL 60466; ba/Park Forest S, IL; m/Patricia; c/Keisha; ed/BS Tenn St Univ; MM 1966, PhD 1970 Mich St Univ; pa/Coor Music Prog, Univ Prof Music, Music Dept, Col of Cultural Studies; Mem Black Music Caucus; Nat Secy-Treas Nat Assn Jazz Edrs; Coor Ethnic Music for N Ctl Div MENC.

CARTER, WILLIAM BEVERLY oc/Diplomate; b/Feb 1, 1921; h/434 O St SW, Washington DC 20024; ba/Wash DC; m/Carlyn Brown Pogue; c/William Beverly III, (Stepchd:) Dion Pogue, Ann V Pogue; p/William Beverly and Maria Green Carter; ed/AB Lincoln Univ 1944; Att'd Temple Univ Sch Law 1946-47, New Sch Social Res 1950-51; pa/US Ambassador-at-Large for Liaison w St & Local Govts, Dept St 1979-; US Ambassador to: Repub of Liberia 1976-78, U Republic of Tanzania, Dar-es-Salaam 1972-75; Spec Asst to Asst Secy St for African Affairs 1975-76; Dep Asst Secy St African Affairs, Dept St, Wash 1969-72; Cnslr Embassy, Lagos, Nigeria 1966-69; Other Former Activs; Mem Subcom Preven Discrimination & Protection Minorities, UN 1972-; Mem, Acting Chm DC Bd Higher Ed 1972; Nat Newspaper Publrs Assn, Pres 1958; Am Fgn Ser Assn; Sigma Pi Phi; Kappa Alpha Psi; cp/Former Secy Pa Comm Civil Rts; Cand US Ho of Reps, 4th Congl Dist 1954; NAACP; Nat Urban Leag; Lincoln Univ Alumni Assn; Cosmos Clb Wash; hon/Order of African Redemption, Republic of Liberia.

CARUSO, PAUL JOHN oc/Managing Director; b/Jul 21, 1948; h/7 Sweet Hollow Rd, Huntington, NY 11743; ba/Port Jefferson Sta, NY 11776; m/Laurie; c/Kristy, Justin; p/Lucy Ross, New Port Richey, FL; ed/BS Monmouth Col; pa/Mng Dir, Univ Garden Apts; VP, U G Mgmt Corp; Apt House Coun; cp/Treas, West Hills Day Camp; cp/Phi Delta Sigma; Repub Com-man; r/Christian; hon/W/W E; Outstg Yg Men Am; Commun Ldrs & Noteworthy Ams.

CARVALHO, ALAN DEAN oc/Clergyman; b/Jan 9, 1936; h/603 Main St, Port Jefferson, NY 11777; ba/Port Jefferson; m/D Ann; p/John A and Marjorie Dean Carvalho; ed/AB Drew Univ 1958; MDiv Hartford Theol Sem 1961; Addit Study; pa/U Meth Ch Min; Pastorates incl: 1st U Meth Ch, Port Jefferson 1977-, Wesley U Meth Ch, E Norwich, NY 1966-77, (Assoc Pastor) 1st Meth Ch, Bridgeport, Conn 1962-66, (Assoc Pastor) 1st U Meth Ch, Stamford, Conn 1961-62, (Asst Pastor) 1st Meth Ch, Waterbury, Conn 1959-61; Asst Secy NY Annual Conf U Meth

Ch 1963-; Meth Sub-Dist Yth Advr 1964-66; Mem NY Annual Conf Comm on Min Support 1963-66; Rep to Conn Com on Campus Min 1963-66; B'port Pastor's Assn 1962-66; Other Profl Activs; cp/NY St Assn Fire Chaplains; 1st Dep Chief Chaplain, Other Positions; Oyster Bay-E Norwich Clergy Coun: Former Mem, Past Pres; Former & Chaplain E Norwich Vol Fire Co No 1 Inc; Former Mem

Commun Social Action Coun (Oyster Bay-E Norwich); Mem Port Jefferson Vol Fire Dept; Hon Mem Kiwanis Clb Port Jefferson Inc; Intl Conf Police Chaplains; Other Civic Activs; r/Meth; hon/Pi Gamma Mu; Pubs; Biogl Listings.

CARVALHO, JULIE ANN oc/Psychologist; Administrator; b/Apr 11, 1940; h/11668 Mediterranean Ct. Reston, VA 22090; ba/Wash DC; m/Joao; c/Alan R, Dennis M, Melanie D, Celeste A, 4 Stepchd; p/Daniel H and Elizabeth G Schmidt; ed/BA magna cum laude Univ Md 1962; MA George Wash Univ 1966; PhD Cand Univ Md 1968-73; pa/Leg Analyst HEW Ofc for Civil Rts 1977-78; Equal Opportunity Specialist Ofc of Secy, DHEW 1973-77; Prog Analyst/Specialist US Ofc of Ed 1970-73; Ed Prog Specialist Nat Ctr for Ednl Res & Devel, US Ofc of Ed 1969-70; Other Former Positions; Am Psychol Assn; Am Soc for Public Adm; Alliance for Child Care in Fed Agys; Federally Employed Wom, Nat Editor; Bd Dirs HEW Employees Assn; Bds for Ed of Gifted Chd; hon/Psi Chi; Phi Alpha Theta; Merit S'ship Commend, Wash Jr Acad Scis; Commends from Fed Ofcls; Num Pubs; Biogl Listings.

CARVER, JESSIE ALVIS oc/Businessman; b/Sept 6, 1920; h/206 delono Ave, Dunn, NC 28334; ba/Dunn; m/Mable Starling; c/Anthony Steven; p/Herbert Charles and Geneva Patterson Carver (dec);

ed/Acct'g & Bus Adm; mil/USCG 1942-45; pa/Owner-Operator Carver Equipment Co Inc; cp/St Cmdr, Nat Comm Fgn Relats; Am Legion; Adv Mem Dem Senate & House Com; r/Presb; hon/ETO Ribbon; 1 Battle Star; Good Conduct Medal; Others.

CARVER, RALPH DANIEL JR oc/Auto Parts Company Executive; b/Oct 7, 1932; h/1007 S 12th, Montrose, CO 81401; ba/Montrose; m/Myrlis Jean; c/Delphine, Robert, James, Steven; p/Ralph Daniel Carver (dec); Beulah M Hill Carver, Wheatridge, CO; pa/Pres, Chm of Bd C & C Auto Parts Co, Delta, Colo 1977-; Dir Rocky Mtn Automotive Wholesalers 1976-78; Land Developer 1972-; Chm of Bd, Pres C & C Author Parts, Naturita 1960-, Montrose 1969-72; cp/32nd Deg Mason; Elks; Dir 1st Nat Bank, Montrose; r/Meth.

CASALE, JOAN T oc/Writer; Lecturer; b/Oct 19, 1935; h/5468 Avenida Fiesta, La Jolla, CA 92037; ba/Same; m/Robert M Watkins; c/Victoria, Sandra; p/Jacob T Casale (dec); Sarah E Barr (dec); ed/BA Seton Hill Col 1957; cp/NOW, Past Pres San Diego Co; hon/Outstg Reference Book of Yr, Am Lib Assn 1975.

CASCARIO, ELIZABETH FRINZI oc/Psychologist; b/Nov 11, 1919; h/RD #3, Box 3323, Bangor, PA 18013; ba/Same; m/Matthew; c/Nicholas (dec), Carol C Wise; p/John Frinzi (dec); Liboria S Frinzi, Easton, PA; ed/BS cum laude E Stroudsburg St Col 1968; MEd 1969, EdD 1972 Lehigh Univ; pa/Pt-time Elem Guid Cnslr Pen Argyl (Pa) Area Sch Dist 1969-72; Pt-time Psychologist 1972-; Pvt Pract 1972-; Am Soc Clin Hypnosis; Am, Lehigh Val Psychol Assns; Mid-E Pa Sch Psychologists Assn; IPA; cp/Secy Northampton Co Mtl Hlth/Mtl Retard; r/Rom Cath.

CASE, PAUL CONWAY oc/Captain

Police Department; b/Jan 27, 1927; h/707 W Sunset Ave, Madison, NC 27025; ba/Madison; m/Mary; c/Larry W, Linda A; p/Fletcher C and Dottis L Case, Madison; mil/USN; pa/Capt Madison Police Dept; cp/Retard Chd; r/Bapt; hon/Personalities of S.

CASELLA, ROBERTA LEONARD oc/Librarian; b/Feb 5, 1932; h/3707 28th St, Lubbock, TX 79410; ba/Lubbock; c/Robert Joseph, John Paul, Geoffrey David, Melissa Noreen; p/Robert Elvin Leonard (dec); Nora Maxwell Leonard, Abilene, TX; ed/BS; MSLS Long Isl Univ; pa/Libn Tex Tech Univ Lib; Tex Lib Assn, Var Ofcs & Coms; cp/Pres 20th Century Clb, Lubbock; Chm Lubbock Wom's Clb Adv Bd.

CASH, GRACE oc/Free-lance Writer; b/Apr 13, 1915; h/Rt 2, Flowery Branch, GA 30452; p/Rufus Spencer and Lou Ella Deaton Cash (dec); ed/BA Brenau Col; pa/Ofc Secy, Am Leprosy Missions 1945-46, ARC 1947-48, Ga St Dept 1950-69; Author: *Highway's Edge* (1965), *Promise Unto Death* (1967); Pub'd 431 Stories in Var Mags & Jours; Author, "That Short Summer" (1981); 5 Short Stories Pub'd/Accepted at *Hoosier Challenger* 1980; Approx 200 Poems Pub'd since Jan 1981, incl'g 2 in *Mature Living*, So Bapt Pub; Haiku Pub'd in *Dragonfly, Brussels Sprout, Leanfrog, Echoes;* Poetry Pub'd in Num Anthols; r/Bapt; hon/Life Hon Mem, Mark Twain Intl Soc; Hon Citizen of Korea; Num Biogl Listings.

CASKEY, GUY DAVID oc/Minister; b/Jun 4, 1940; h/2303 Kipling, Baytown, TX 77520; ba/Baytown; m/Becky; c/Chiara, Jason; p/Guy V and Jessie Lee Caskey, Arlington, TX; ed/BA Abilene Christian Univ; Postgrad Work (in Swahili Lang) Tanzania Bible Col; Radio & TV Prodn NE La Univ; pa/Min 1960-; Currently Min Mo St Ch of Christ, Baytown; Rel Lectrs, Nat & Intl; Completed Constrn of Chimala Mission Hosp, Tanzania, E Africa 1963; Dir Univ Sch Biblical Studies, Monroe, La 1972-78; Worked in Game Conserv & Selection, E Africa 1962-63; cp/Guest Spkr to Civic Clbs & Sch Banquets; Former Secy Denton (Tex) C of C; Helped Foun Shady Acres Home for Homeless Chd, Denton 1967; r/Ch of Christ; hon/Author 4 Books: *Evangelistic Greek Word Studies, What Every Christian Should Know, The Church, Commentary on Hebrews.*

CASON, CLEO STARGEL oc/Chief Librarian; b/Jun 24, 1910; h/700 Watts Dr, SE, Huntsville, AL 35801; ba/H'ville; m/Charles Monroe Jr; c/Charles Monroe III; p/John J and Georgia Jones Stargel (dec); ed/LLB Am Sch of Law; pa/Chief Libn Madison Co Law Lib; Spec Libs Assn; SEn & Ala Lib Assn; cp/Mem Aladdin Clb, H'ville; r/Prot; hon/Miss Insurance of Am 1932; Army Meritorious Civilian Awd.

CASSIDY, MICHAEL EDWARD oc/-State Legislator; b/Sept 15, 1955; h/211 South St, Newry, PA 16665; ba/Harrisburg, PA; p/Francis V and Lois Juhl Cassidy, Atglen, PA; ed/Att'd Pa St Univ; cp/Mem Pa Ho of Reps; Former Dem Com-man; Former Mem Newry Borough Coun; SAR; Altoona Area C of C; Pa St Grange; r/Rom Cath; hon/Eagle Scout, BSA; Fac Awd, Pa St-Altoona Campus.

CASTANEDA, JAMES AGUSTIN oc/College Professor; Coach; b/Apr 2, 1933; h/5467 Loch Lomond, Houston, TX 77096; ba/Houston; c/Christopher James; p/Ciro Castañeda (dec); Edna M Sincock; ed/BA summa cum laude Drew Univ 1954; MA 1955, PhD 1957 Yale Univ; pa/Rice Univ: Asst, Assoc & Prof Spanish 1961-, Hd Freshman & Asst Varsity Baseball Coach 1962-, Chm Dept Classics (Italian, Portuguese, Russian & Spanish) 1964-72, Master Will Rice Col 1969-76; Asst & Assoc Prof Spanish & French Hanover Col 1958-61; Pres Ind Chapt AATSP 1960-61; Danforth Foun F'ship Prog 1969-; Mem Rdg Com, Interviewer, Mem Adv Coun; Pres Inst of Hispanic Cult of Houston 1972; Bd Dirs L'Alliance Francaise de Houston 1972-74; Pres Nat Fdn Mod Lang Tchrs Assn 1974; Am

Com Mod Humanities Res Assn; Exec Coun Am Assn Tchrs Spanish & Portuguese 1977-79; Var Vis Prof'ships; cp/Houston Small Bus Assn; r/Meth; hon/Danforth Grad F'ship; Fulbright F'ship; Named "Miembro Titular", instituto de Cultura Hispanica de Madrid; James Street Fulton Ser Awd, Will Rice Col; Alumni Achmt in Arts, Drew Univ; Pub'd Author.

CASTILLO, GUADALUPE MARIA oc/Teacher; b/Mar 12; h/157 Bertita St, San Francisco, CA 94112; ba/Oakland, CA; p/Doroteo Castillo (dec); Josefa Reyes Castillo, San Francisco; ed/AA SF Jr Col; BA SF St Univ; Grad Work: UC-B, SF St; Civil Rts Insts, U Cal-B; pa/Jr HS Tchr (Bilingual/-Bicult) Oakland Unified Sch Dist; Classroom Tchr & Cnslr Jefferson Elem Sch Dist (Cal); Classroom Tchr & Fgn Lang Dept Chwom, Patterson, Cal; OEA, Orgr & Fdr Chicano Caucus; Cal Tchrs Assn, Fdr Chicano Caucus; NEA: Fdg Mem Chicano Caucus, Mem Nat Task Force on Testing (Wash DC); Assn Mexican Am Edrs Inc: Pres Oakland Chapt 1969, Reg VP 1970, Mem St Exec Bd, Other Activs; Other Profl Activs; cp/SF Comm on Status of Wom: Coor'g Com, Pre-Screening Com on Talent Bank, Resource Talent Bank Task Force; Wom for Racial & Ec Equality; Concilio De Mujeres (Pres); r/Cath; hon/Awd for Contbn to Ed, Assn Mexican Am Edrs Inc, Santa Barbara, Cal; Pub'd Author; Biogl Listings.

CATES, ANNETTE BINGHAM oc/Librarian; b/Aug 4, 1939; h/4461 Blackwood Dr, Montgomery, AL 36109; ba/Montgomery; m/Curtis A; c/Curtis Anthony Jr, Daniel Frazier; p/Frazier Franklin Bingham (dec); Anna Riley Bingham, Montgomery; ed/AA; BS; MLS Univ Ala 1976; pa/Libn Ala Christian Sch Rel; Assn Ed, Commun Technol; Ala Instrnl Media Assn; Ala Lib Assn, Com on Ed 1978-79; Alpha Beta Alpha; r/Ch of Christ; hon/Var Biogl Listings.

CATES, CURTIS ANTHONY oc/Dean; b/Feb 8, 1941; h/4461 Blackwood Dr, Montgomery, AL 36109; ba/Montgomery; m/Annette Bingham; c/Curtis Anthony Jr, Daniel Franzier; p/Curtis C and Margaret J Cates, Montgomery; ed/AA, BS Ala Christian

Col; BS Livingston Univ; MS Samford Univ; MRE, GSRE Ala Christian Sch Rel; EdD Univ Ala; pa/Dean Acad Affairs, Prof Ala Christian Sch Rel; Evangelist; cp/Lectr; r/Ch of Christ; hon/Pi Tau Chi; Phi Delta Kappa; Kappa Delta Pi; IPA; Num Biogl Listings.

CATES, PAUL WILLIAM oc/Educator; Evangelist; b/Jul 25, 1930; h/Rt 2, Poplar Creek Rd, Oliver Springs, TN 37840;

ba/Same; m/Isobel; c/Bill, Peter, John, David, Kirk, Linda, Anne; p/Paul and Marjorie Cates, Providence, NJ; ed/BA N Ctl Col 1962; MA NEn Ill Univ 1965; PhD Loyola Univ 1972; pa/DePaul Univ: Psychol Ed Clin, Dir, Rdg, LD Prog Dir 1971-; Dir Proviso Area for Exceptl Chd 1968-71; Dir Psychol Ser Assn 1965-; CEC, Chapt Pres; IRA; Ill Admrs of Spec Ed; ASCD; Assn for Chd w LD; Am Assn Col Tchrs of Ed; AAUP; Freedom Univ: Exec VP, Prof; Pres Intl Assn for Christian Ed; r/Bapt; hon/Phi Delta Kappa; FICA, Cambridge Univ; Pub'd Author; Biogl Listings.

CATHCART, ALAN oc/Remedial Assistant; b/Mar 29, 1925; h/730 Fort Washington Ave, New York, NY 10040; ba/NYC; p/Ernest William Cathcart (dec); Alice Elizabeth Bergmann (dec); ed/BA 1944, MA 1945 Columbia; pa/Remedial Asst in Math Manhattan Commun Col; Am Math Soc; cp/Am Mensa, Ltd; r/Christian Sci.

CATHCART, MILDRED DOOLEY oc/Retired Teacher; Writer; h/Rt 3, Centerville, IA 52544; m/John C; c/Kerry Lee, Jean C Rosen; p/Ernest Lee Dooley (dec); Edith V Hughes (dec); ed/BS Drake Univ; pa/Pres Alpha Rho Chapt Delta Kappa Gamma; Pres Jerome YW Study Clb; Nat Leag Am Pen Wom; cp/St Joseph Hosp Aux; r/Prot; hon/Merit Mother of Ia; Luke Mallory Poetry Awd; Var Writing Awds; W/W Am Wom.

CATTELL, RAYMOND BERNARD oc/Research Professor; b/Mar 20, 1905; h/1350 Ala Moana Blvd, Honolulu, HI 96814; m/Karen; c/Hereward, Mary, Heather, Roderic, Elaine; p/Alfred Earnest and Mary Cattell, Devonshire, England; ed/PhD; DSc; pa/Res Prof in Psychol Univ Hi; Author 400 Res Articles, 36 Sci Books; r/Prot; hon/Darwin F'ship; Wenner-Gren Prize, NY Acad Sci; Hon Fgn Mem, Brit Psychol Soc.

CAUTHEN, DELORIS HELEN oc/Artist; b/Oct 4; h/2407 Wheat St, Columbia, SC 29205; m/John Kelley (dec); c/John Vaughan, Henry Jennings III; p/Robert Selden and Margaret Hurst Vaughan; ed/Rice's Col; Profl Art Studies; pa/Guild of SC Artists; Columbia Artists' Guild; Intl Soc Artists; Trenholm Art Coun; Wkshop Theatre, Columbia; Rep'd in Public Collections incl'g: Mint Mus of Art, Charlotte (NC), Columbia Mus of Art, Columbia, Univ SC, SC Nat Bank, Banker's Trust, SC Gov's Mansion, Columbia, Spring Mills, SC; cp/SC Gov's Coun of Advrs on Consumer Credit; Smithsonian Inst; r/Wash St Meth Ch, Columbia: Mem; hon/Winner 3 Person Show, Columbia Artists' Guild (4); SC Nat Bank Awd; Columbia Mus Purchase Awd, SC; Personalities of S; World W/W Wom.

CAVANAUGH, CAROLINE SEALE oc/Administrator; b/Jun 25, 1936; h/5311 Rexford Ct, Montgomery, AL 36116; ba/Montgomery; c/Reb Baber, Tab Baber, Cab Baber, Deb Baber, Mark, David, Doug, Chas; p/Mabel F Harman, Andalusia, AL; ed/Chem Engrg Ga Tech; Gen Sci Troy St Univ; pa/Dir Bur Publicity & Info St of Ala; cp/Pilot Intl; LWV; Am Legion Aux, Post 80; 1st Female Appt'd Mem Cabinet (by Gov F James); r/Prot; hon/Gamma Beta Phi; Lady of Month.

CAVE, MAC DONALD oc/Scientist;

b/May 14, 1939; h/40 Pine Manor, Little Rock, AR 72207; ba/Little Rock; c/Eric MacDonald, Heidi Lee; p/Edward H and Adeline M Cave, Radnor, PA; ed/BA Susquehanna Univ 1961; MS 1963, PhD 1965 Univ Ill; pa/Scist Dept Anatomy UAMS; Am Soc for Cell Biol; Am Assn Anatomy; hon/USPHS Predoct Fellow; Swedish-Am Exchange Fellow, Am Cancer Soc; USPHS Postdoct Fellow.

CAVITT, CORA JEAN oc/Teacher; b/Jun 17, 1930; h/401 E Hayes, Box 914, Morton, TX 79346; ba/Morton; m/Garland K; c/Kelly Leigh, Jennifer Kaye; p/Wilbur C Hill (dec); Ruth A Hill, Canyon, TX; ed/BS 1952, MEd 1970 W Tex St Univ; pa/6th Grade

Rdg & English Tchr; TSTA; TCTA; MCTA; Dumas Br AAUW: VP 1959, Pres 1960-62; IRA, Local Lubbock; cp/Tex Wom's Fed'd Study Clb; r/Meth; hon/Outstg Ldrs in Elem & Sec'dy Ed.

CAWEIN, KATHRIN oc/Artist; b/May 9, 1895; h/35 Mountain Rd, Pleasantville, NY 10570; ba/Same; m/Seabory Cone (dec); p/Henry and Barbara Franz Cawein; ed/MA hon Oberlin Col 1966; pa/Music Roll Editor, Music Interpreter w Var Musicians 1911-32; Tchr Co Ctr Work Shop 1935-36; Owner Studio for Chd 1950-55; 1-Man Shows incl: Berea Col (Ky) 1977, St Johns Ch, P'ville (NY) 1976, Oberlin Col, Oberlin (Ohio) 1975, Univ Tampa, Tampa (Fla) 1973, Others; Exhibited Group Shows: US, Eng, France, Italy, Ecuador; Rep'd in Perm Collections: Met Mus, Nat Mus, Wash, Pa St Univ, Tampa Univ, Oberlin Col; Illuminated Books; Nat Assn Wom Artists; Art Students Leag; Chgo Soc Etchers; Soc Graphic Artists; r/Epis; hon/Prizes for Etching; Nat Assn Wom Artists, Westchester Fdn Wom's Clbs; Prize for Dry Point, P'ville Wom's Clb; W/W Am Wom; Others.

CAWOOD, BILLIE JEAN oc/Instructional Supervisor; b/Feb 24, 1931; h/407 Ivy St, Harlan, KY 40831; ba/Harlan; m/Billy Joe; c/Stephanna Jane, James C; p/Clyde and Emma B Dixon (dec); ed/BS; MA; Addit Studies; pa/Past Pres; Ky Coun Tchrs Eng, Ky Assn Supvn & Curric Devel; cp/VP Harlan Wom's Clb; Dem; r/Meth: Ed Chm, SS Tchr; hon/Outstg Yg Edr, Harlan Co; Alpha Delta Kappa.

CAYCE, HUGH LYNN oc/Executive; b/Mar 16, 1907; h/413 53rd St, Virginia Beach, VA 23451; ba/Va Bch; m/Sally Gregory Taylor; c/Charles Thomas, Gregory Jackson; p/Leslie B and Carrie Elizabeth Cayce; ed/Wash & Lee Univ 1926-30; mil/AUS 1943-46; pa/Chm of Bd ARE Inc; Author; Lectr; r/Prot; hon/1st Citizen of 1964, Va Bch; Silver Beaver Scouting Awd, Tidewater Scout Coun.

CAZALAS, MARY WILLIAMS oc/Assistant United States Attorney; b/Nov 11, 1927; h/1116 City Park Ave, New Orleans, LA 70119; m/Albert Joseph; p/George Edgar Williams (dec); Mary Annie Staffey Williams, New Orleans; ed/RN; BS; MS; JD; pa/Asst US Atty, New Orleans 1971-; Gen Pract Law 1967-71; Legal Res 1965-71; Med Res 1961-65; Inst Maternity Nsg St Joseph's Infirmary Sch of Nsg, Atlanta, Ga 1954-59; Gen Duty Nsg 1948-68; ABA; Am Judic Soc; La St Bar Assn; New Orleans Bar Assn; Fed Bar Assn; Phi

Alpha Delta; Nat Assn Wom Lwyrs; Nat Hlth Lwyrs Assn; BPW Clb; Federally Employed Wom Inc; Num Ofcs Held; Participant Var Confs; cp/DAR; PEO; Am Heart Assn, La Inc; New Orleans Art Assn; Alumni Assns: Emory Univ, Oglethorpe Univ, Loyola Univ; r/Cath; hon/Commend from Guam Leg for Tchg in Forensic Psychi Conf, 1977; Rev E A Doyle Awd, Outstg Cardinal Key; Cert of Apprec, Fed Exec Bd; Superior Perf Awd, US Dept of Justice; Hon La St Senator; Law Review, Loyola Univ; Phi Sigma; Cardinal Key; Leconte Hon Sci Soc; Alpha Epsilon Delta; Biogl Listings; Pubs; Others.

CECCONI-BATES, AUGUSTA oc/Composer; b/Aug 9, 1933; h/Toad Harbor, Box 49-D, W Monroe, NY 13167; m/Robert N Bates Sr; c/(Stepchd:) Robert Jr, Daniel, Nancy; p/Peter T and Emily Romano Cecconi; ed/BA w hons 1956, MA 1960 Syracuse Univ; Addit Studies Cornell Univ; pa/Pvt Tchr Music 1976-; Music Specialist Syracuse Sch Dist 1968-; Prof Maria Regina Col 1964-65; Public Sch Music Tchr 1957-64; Music Dir Scuola Italiana, Middlebury Col 1956; Libn Syracuse Univ Sum 1956; Other Former Positions; Bd Dirs Soc for New Music, Syracuse; NY St Sch Music Assn, Adjudicator for Piano Auditions; MENC; LWC; Wom Composers Am; Sigma Alpha Iota; Phi Sigma Iota; Composed Cantata for Chorus, Soloists & Orch, Dedicated to Martin Luther King Jr, Premiered at Syracuse Sch Dist Music Fest 1974; Dir Programme of Own Compositions Under Auspices of Cherubini Soc of Rochester, Villa Perla for Gala Benefit of Centro Italiano 1977; Composed & Perf'd 4 Songs at Vt Music & Art Centre; Other Compositions & Perfs; cp/Old Tyme Fiddlers' Assn NY; Com Mem Centro Italiano, Rochester, NY; hon/Hon Mention, Stowe Inst Composition Competition; Intl Register Profiles.

CEDERBERG, ELFORD A oc/Congressman; b/Mar 6, 1918; h/Midland, MI 48640; ba/2306 Rayburn Bldg, Washington DC 20515; m/Married; c/2 Chd; mil/AUS 1941-45; 2/Lt-Capt; Var Positions Held; USAR Maj; pa/Mgr Nelson Mfg Co, Bay City; cp/Elected to 83rd Cong 1952-, Mem Var Coms; Appt'd Regent Smithsonian Insts & Mem Bd Visitors US Mil Acad West Point (by Spkr of Ho of Reps); Past Pres Lions Clb; Odd Fellows; Masons; Am Legion; VFW; r/Evang Ch.

CESSNA, JOHN CURTIS oc/Chemist; b/Apr 15, 1926; h/8066 Spieth Rd, Litchfield, OH 44253; ba/Parma, OH; m/Virginia Belle Anderson; c/Alan Eugene, Bonnie Lee; p/John Curtis Cessna (dec); Virginia Kintzler, Moline, IL; ed/BA cum laude Augustana Col; MS Ia St Col; mil/USNR 1943-46; pa/Am Chem Soc; Electrochem Soc; Nat Assn Corp Engrs; Profl Articles; r/Ch of Christ; hon/Patentee in Field; Phi Lambda Upsilon.

CHADWICK, JAMES DWIGHT oc/Police Detective Sergeant; b/Jun 12, 1952; h/1802 David Dr, Dalton, GA 30720; ba/Dalton; m/Deborah Marie; c/Christian Dwight; p/James Dennis and Ora Mae Chadwick, Dalton; ed/Assn Deg Cand; mil/USAF 6 Yrs; r/Pentecostal; hon/Exc Clb Ofcr of Yr 1978.

CHADWICK, MARGARET LEE oc/Educational Administrator; b/Apr 26, 1893; h/637 Via Horguilla, Palos Verdes Est, CA 90274; m/Joseph Howard (dec); c/Theodora, Joseph, David; p/Theodore Lee (dec); Anna Myrtilla Wray Lee; ed/AB Stamford; Grad Work; pa/Elem & HS Prin, Metropolis & Wells, Nev 1915-21; Fdr Chadwick Nursery Sch, San Francisco, Cal; Fdr & Dir Chadwick Sch, Palos Verdes Ests; Dir Margaret Lee Cnslg Ctr, Palos Verdes Ests; AAUW; CAIS; cp/ARC; LA Mus of Art; Num Conservation Groups; r/St Lukes Presb Ch: Elder; hon/Author; Wisdom Awd of Hon; Citizenship Awd for Outstg Ser to Commun, LA; Cert of Recog, Famous Writers Sch.

CHAGALL, DAVID oc/Writer; Researcher; TV/Radio Personality; b/Nov 22, 1930; h/PO Box 85, Agoura, CA 91301; ba/Los Angeles, CA; m/Juneu Joan Alsin; p/Harry

and Ida Coopersmith Chagall (dec); ed/BA Pa St; pa/Acad Polit & Social Sci; Judic Soc; Mark Twain Soc; Author's Guild; r/Millenium House Congreg, ULC: Mem; hon/Dist'd Hlth Jour Awd; Carnegie Awd; Noms for Nat Book Awd; Pulitzer Prize in Lttrs 1973; Poetry Prize, Univ Wis; Pubs incl: *Diary of a Deaf Mute*, 1960, 71, *The Century God Slept*, 1962, *The Spieler For The Holy Spirit*, 1973; Contbr Articles & Stories to Nat Mags & Newspaper Supplements; Poetry & Fiction in Jours & Reviews; Contb'g Editor: *Bestways* Mag & *Elite* Mag.

CHAHINE, ROBERT A oc/Physician; Educator; b/Feb 8, 1941; h/6111 Chimney Rock, Houston, TX 77081; ba/Houston; p/Antoine H and Jamileh Chahine, Beirut, Lebanon; ed/BS 1962, MD 1966 Am Univ of Beirut; pa/Former Postdoct Fellow: Univ Miami, Harvard, UCLA; Asst Prof UCLA 1972; Baylor Col of Med: Asst Prof of Med 1972-76, Assoc Prof of Med 1976-; Chief, Sect of Cardiol, VA Hosp; Lebanese Order of Physicians; Am Heart Assn; Houston Cardiol

Soc; AAUP; Am Fdn for Clin Res; AAAS; cp/Chm Com for Salvation of Lebanon; Bd Dirs Houston Chapt Am Heart Assn; r/Cath Ch: Mem; hon/Fellow: Am Col of Cardiol, Am Col of Phys, AHA Coun on Circulation, AHA Coun on Clin Cardiol; Num Pubs in Sci Jours w Ldg Res & contbns in: Coronary Artery Spasm, Unstable Angina, Hypertrophic Cardiomyopathy & Exercise Testing.

CHAIN, BOBBY LEE oc/Electrical Contractor; b/Sept 19, 1929; h/312 6th Ave, Hattiesburg, MS 39401; ba/H'burg; m/Betty Green; c/Robin Ann, Laura Grace, Bobby Lee Jr, John Webster; p/Zollie Lee and Grace Sellers Chain (dec); ed/BS Univ So Miss; mil/AUS 1950-51; pa/Dir Deposit Guaranty Nat Bank, Jackson, Miss; cp/VP Bd Trustees St Instns of Higher Lng; Former Dir H'burg C of C; Kiwanis; H'burg CC; Univ So Miss

Century Clb; Shriners; Elks; Univ Clb; Capitol City Clb (Jackson); Steering Com St Ldrship Prayer Breakfast; Bd Dirs H'burg Area Devel Corp; Interstate Oil Compact Comm; Newcomen Soc NAm; Former Mem Nat Adv Coun for Small Bus Adm; Alt Del to Dem Nat Conv 1964; r/1st Bapt Ch, H'burg; hon/Albert Gallatin Awd; Dist'd Ser Awd, Univ So Miss; Recog, City of H'burg; Outstg Ser Awd, Univ So Miss Alumni Assn; W/W S&SW.

CHAKRABARTY, RAMESWAR P oc/-Associate Professor; b/Jun 2, 1935; h/12127 David Dr, Silver Spring, MD 20904; ba/Jackson, MS; m/Sukla Goswami; c/Raj, Rishi; p/Ram Tarak and Krishna Mohini Chakrabarty (dec); ed/BS (hon) 1955; MS Univ Gauhati 1957; PhD Tex A&M Univ 1968; pa/Assoc Prof Dept Computer Sci Jackson St Univ 1976-; Asst Prof Statistics & Computer Sci, Univ Ga 1971-76; Other Past Positions; Dir Reg Res Conf on Numerical Analysis, Jackson (Funded by NSF) 1977; Reviewer Math Reviews; Am Statistical Assn; Assn Computing Machinery; Biometric Soc; Intl Assn Survey Staticians; Sigma Xi; Reschr; Conslt; r/Hindu; hon/Contbr 30 Papers in Nat & Intl Jours; Gold Medal Awd, Univ Gauhati; NSF Res Grant.

CHAMBERLAIN, CHARLES DEVERE JR oc/Professor; Physician; b/Apr 26, 1928; h/2601 Augusta, #16, Houston, TX 77057; ba/Houston; c/Anne Wesley, Mary Cravens, Laura Roberts, Charles Devere; ed/AB Univ Tex-A 1950; MD Univ Tex Med Br-G 1954; mil/USAMC Capt; pa/Current Clin Assoc Prof Univ Tex Hlth Sci Ctr, Houston; Active Staff Mem: Hermann Hosp, Diagnostic Ctr Hosp, Park Plaza Hosp, Meml Hosp, Twelve

Oaks Hosp, Rosewood Hosp; Courtesy Staff Var Hosps; Conslt'g Staff Houston Intl Hosp; AMA; Tex St Med Assn; Harris Co Med Soc; Houston Surg Soc; Diplomat Am Bd Surg; Am Col Surgs; Am Col Angiology; Am Geriatrics Soc; Am Soc Abdominal Surgs; Am Cancer Soc; Am Diabetes Assn; L Kraer Ferguson Surg Soc; Tex Traumatic Surg Soc; Pan Am Med Assn; Sigma Alpha Epsilon; Phi Chi; cp/Wash Co C of C; hon/Profl Pubs.

CHAMPLIN, H H oc/Oil Exploration Operator; Rancher; Investments; b/Jan 1, 1912; h/505 NW Gore Blvd, Lawton, OK 73501; p/Roy Frank and Frances Cobb Champlin (dec); ed/Att'd Univ Okla 1929-33; mil/USA 1933-67; 2/Lt to Col, Ret'd 1967; pa/Cattlemen Assn; Indep Oil Operators Assn; cp/Repub Party; r/Christian; hon/Legion of Merit, USA; Army Commend Medal.

CHAN, JULIE MAY TANG oc/Assistant Professor; b/Jul 23, 1941; h/6921 Dresden Cir, Huntington Beach, CA 92647; ba/Long Beach, CA; m/Lyman Gordon; p/Chester and Lee Tang, Los Angeles, CA; ed/BA UCLA 1963; MS Univ So Cal 1965; EdD Univ Colo 1970; pa/Asst Prof Sch Ed Cal St Univ-LB 1975-; Prodr AFN Public Ser Radio Broadcasts on Rdg for Parents 1971-74; Tchr NE Indep Sch Dist, San Antonio, Tex 1971; Other Past Positions; Pres Cal Profs of Rdg 1978-79; Pres Pi Lambda Theta, LA Field Chapt 1977-79; Am Ed Res Assn; Cal Rdg Assn; IRA; Mid-Cities Coun IRA; Nat Coun Reschrs in English; Orange Co Rdg Assn; So Cal Chinese Profs Assn; Toastmasters Intl; Conslt; Var

Edit Activs; Other Profl Activs; cp/AFN Radio Series for Parents on Rdg; EPIC Tutorial Prog, Sems for Parents; r/Presb; hon/Univ Colo Tuition S'ship; Elizabeth Wilson Awd for Outstg Wom Grad Students; Outstg Yg Wom Am; Profl Pubs; Phi Delta Gamma; Pi Lambda Theta; Kappa Delta Pi.

CHANDAN, RAMESH C oc/Scientist; Professor; b/Jul 5, 1934; h/5837 Smithfield Ave, E Lansing, MI 48823; ba/E Lansing; m/Premila; c/Mridula, Rohini, Anupama; p/Shiv Kumar and Padma Chandan, Delhi, India; ed/BSc; BSc w hons; MS w hons; PhD; pa/Assoc Prof Dept Food Sci & Human Nutrition Mich St Univ 1976-; VP Protein

Prodn & Tech Sers Purity Cheese Co, Mayville, Wis 1974-76; Mgr Res & Devel Dairylea, Syracuse, NY 1969-74; Other Past Positions; Fellow Am Inst Chemists; Am Chem Soc; Inst Food Technologists; Am Dairy Sci Assn; AAAS; r/Hindu; hon/US Del to Intl Dairy Cong, Paris, France 1978; Sigma Xi; Sigma Delta; Profl Pubs; Am Men & Wom of Sci; W/W: E, MW.

CHANDLER, CARL C JR oc/Chief of Police; b/Nov 5, 1950; h/1204 Proctor, Waco, TX 76708; ba/Waco; p/Carl C Sr and LaVerne Chandler, Waco; ed/AAS Sam Houston Univ; pa/Northcrest Chief of Police; McLennan Co Peace Ofcrs Assn; r/Meth; hon/Num Certs of Tng in Field of Law Enforcement.

CHANDLER, VIRGINIA GOODMAN oc/Occupational Therapist; b/Jan 10, 1930; h/11106 Shortmeadow, Dallas, TX 75230; m/Robert J; c/Ron Lee, Check Lee; ed/BA So Meth Univ 1951; Occupl Therapy's Registration Tex Wom's Univ 1953; pa/Dir Occupl Therapy Baylor Univ Med Ctr, Dallas 1968-; Pt-time Staff Therapist Parkland Meml Hosp, Dallas 1965-68; Dir Occupl Therapy Fla

Sanitarium & Hosp, Orlando, Fla 1962-65; Other Past Positions; Reschr; Conslt; Sem Participant; Instr Num Univs; Am Occupl Therapy Assn; Tex Occupl Therapy Assn; World Fdn Occupl Therapists; Am Heart Assn; Arthritis Foun; Chi Omega; Other Profl Activs; r/Meth; hon/DIB; W/W: Am Wom, S&SW; World W/W Wom; Pub'd Author.

CHANG, JAMES KUOHSIUNG oc/Manager; b/Nov 20, 1936; h/12203 Waldemar, Houston, TX 77077; ba/Houston; m/Jessie; c/Walan, Ellan, Sylan, Pelan; ed/BSCE, MSCE Univ Houston; Tng Univ Houston; Engrg & Constrn Mgmt Univ Denver; pa/Mgr of Projects; Tex Soc Profl Engrs; Tex St Awds Com, Chapt Dir Sam Houston; Nat Soc Profl Engrs;

cp/Houston-Taipei Sister City Com, Assn Concerned Am Chinese Profls; Chinese Profl Clb; Advr to Inst Chinese Cult; hon/Tex Soc Profl Engrs: Outstg Ser Awd, Outstg Yg Engr Awd; Commun Ldrs of Am.

CHANG, JEFFREY CHIT-FU oc/Educator; b/Jan 10, 1928; h/116 Woodhill Dr, Box 307, Boiling Springs, NC 28017; ba/Boiling Springs; m/Frances Lin; c/Paul W, Margaret J, John W; p/Chih-mao Chang (dec); Jui-ying Chih Chang, Taipei, Taiwan, China; ed/PhD Univ Ga; mil/Chinese Army; pa/Edr Gardner-

Webb Col; Am Statistical Assn; Inst Math Statistics; Soc Data Edrs; Chinese Statistical Assn; r/Presb; hon/Phi Kappa Phi; Men of Achmt; W/W: S&SW, NC; Commun Ldrs & Noteworthy Ams; Notable Ams; Personalities of S; Outstg Edrs of Am.

CHAO, JING oc/Physical Chemist; b/Nov 7, 1924; h/3415 Spring Lane, Bryan, TX 77801; ba/College Station, TX; m/Ping C M; c/William C H; p/Li Chi Chao; Pei Tsun Hsia; ed/PhD; pa/Physical Chemist Tex A&M Univ; Am Chem Soc; Sigma Xi; Fdn Am Scists; Am Soc for Testing & Mats; r/A&M U Meth Ch: Mem; hon/Grad w Hon, Carnegie-Mellon Univ; Am Men & Wom of Sci; W/W S&SW; Notable Ams of Bicent Era; Men of Achmt; Intl W/W Intells.

CHAPMAN, CAROLYN oc/Homemaker; b/Jan 26, 1924; h/5937 Memory Ln, Belleville, IL 62223; ba/B'ville; m/Robert Arthur; c/Diana Carolyn Miller, Victoria Christina Forness; p/Edward Samuel Nelson (dec); Mildred Mary McNeill (dec); cp/Chm St Clair Co Commun Mtl Hlth Bd 1970-; Designed & Operated Poll Watching Prog 1970-77; Appt'd to Ill Comm on Mtl Hlth & Devel Disabilities; r/Prot; hon/Outstg Citizen, St Clair Co; 1st Biennial Public Ser Awd, Ill LWV.

CHAPMAN, DOUGLAS K oc/Executive; b/Jan 10, 1928; h/175 Dickens Rd, Northfield, IL 60093; ba/Wheeling, IL; m/Doreen E; c/Laura E Kohler, Dawna L, Kevin D; p/Alfred D and Isabel Chapman, Toronto, Canada; pa/ACCO Intl Inc: Dir, Pres, Chief Exec Ofcr; ACCP Canadian Co Ltd: Chm, Pres, Dir; Dir & Chm: ACCO Co Ltd, ACCP Nederland BV; ACCO Mexicana, SA DE CV; VP, Dir; Dir & VP: ACCO Jamaica Ltd, C A ACCO Mfg: Nat Ofc Prods Assn: Dir, Past Chm Mfg Div; Past Pres: Canadian Ofc Prods Assn, Toronto Stationers; Dir & VP Bus Records Mfg Assn; Wholesale Stationers Assn; cp/Chgo Crime Comm; Execs Clb Chgo; Metro Clb; Mid Am Clb; N Shore CC; Mission Hills CC; Scorboro Golf & CC; Bent Tree CC.

CHAPMAN, JAMES ALFRED JR oc/Executive; b/Sept 30, 1921; h/825 Plume St, Spartanburg, SC 29302; ba/Inman, SC; m/Martha Cloud; c/Mary, Martha Marshall, Dorothy, James IV; p/James Alfred and Martha Marshall Chapman (dec); ed/BS Davidson Col 1943; LHD (hon) Presb Col 1975; LLD Wofford Col 1976; pa/Inman Mills: Plant Mgr 1946-54, VP 1954-64, Pres, Treas 1964-, Chm of Bd & Chief Exec Ofcr; Dir Textile Hall Corp, Greenville, SC; Trustee Inman-Riverdale Foun; Trustee J E Sirrine Textile Foun; So Textile Assn; SC Textile Mfrs Assn; Am Textile Mfrs Inst; cp/Mem Adv Bd Citizens & So Nat Bank SC; Trustee SC Foun Ind Cols; SC C of C; S'burg CC; Piedmont

Clb; Other Clb Mbrships; r/1st Presb Col, S'burg: Ruling Elder; Moderator Enoree Presby 1963; Trustee Presb Col, Clinton, SC 1964-73; hon/Biogl Listing.

CHAPMAN, JOHN SHERWOOD oc/Lawyer; b/Jul 6, 1936; h/2423 Hillway Dr, Boise, ID 83709; ba/Boise; m/Judith Day; c/Christina Jean, Heidi Suzanne, Elizabeth June; p/Marshall B Chapman (dec); Dorothy Jean Chapman, Twin Falls, ID; ed/BA Univ Idaho 1958; JD Stanford Univ Law Sch 1961;

mil/USAR JAG, Capt; pa/Idaho St Bar; 3rd Dist Bar Assn; cp/Chm: Boise U Way, Boise Planning & Zoning Comm; Dem Nat Comman, Idaho; Boise Rotary Clb; C of C; Bd Mem Boise Chapt ARC; YMCA; r/Epis; hon/Boise Yg Man of Yr 1965; Idaho St-man Citizen of Week 1977.

CHAPMAN, MICHAEL RAY oc/Minister; b/Aug 22, 1951; h/6708 Larkwood Ln, Chattanooga, TN 37421; ba/Chatta; m/Trudy Elaine; c/Shannon Michael; p/Ray C and Sara D Chapman, Laurens, SC; ed/BA summa cum laude Lee Col; ThM Luther Rice Sem; Doct Studies Faith Evang Luth Sem; pa/Pastor Chs in Cal & Hi 1973-76; Asst Pastor S Cleveland (Tenn) Ch of God 1972-73; St Yth & Christian Ed Dir for Chs of God, Hi 1974-76; Pastor Lee Hwy Ch of God, Chatta; cp/Former Vol Cnslr "Contact", Cleveland, Tenn; Former Chaplain Day of Hi St Senate; Exec Bd Mem Chatta Teen Challenge Ctr; r/Ch of God; hon/Biblical-Hist Awd, Lee Col; Ch of God: Yth World Evang Appeal Awd, Christian Ed Cit Awd; Alpha Chi; Pi Delta Omicron; Author & Contbr Articles to Rel, Yth & Profl Jours; W/W in Rel; DIB; Commun Ldrs & Noteworthy Ams; Men of Achmt.

CHAPMAN, MORRIS H oc/Minister; b/Nov 21, 1940; h/7613 American Heritage NE, Albuquerque, NM 87109; ba/Albu; m/Sarah Francis; c/Christopher, Stephanie; p/J Morris Chapman, Laurel, MS; Barbara C Chapman, Jackson, MS; ed/BMus cum laude Clinton Col 1963; MDiv 1968, DMin 1975 SWn Bapt Theol Sem; pa/Pastor 1st Bapt Ch, Albu; NM Bapt Conv: Pres, Mem Exec Bd; Mem Fgn Mission Bd, So Bapt Conv; cp/Chaplain Univ NM Basketball Team; Mem Albu Commun Coun; Rotary Clb; r/Bapt; hon/Colonel-Aide-de-Camp, Gov's Staff of NM; Stella P Ross Meml Awd for Evang, SWn Bapt Theol Sem; Outstg Yg Men Am; W/W Rel; DIB.

CHAPPELL, BETTE TYSON oc/College Professor; h/215 Church St, Willimantic, CT 06226; ba/Willimantic; m/Maro A (dec); c/(Stepchd:) Oliver Spaulding, Shirley C Mustard; p/Thomas Henry and Jean Alison Tyson (dec); ed/BS; MA; 6th Yr Cert; pa/En Conn St Col: Prof, Fac Senate Intern, Chperson Dept Early Childhood Ed (2 Terms); AAUP; En Sts Assn for Tchr Ed; AAUW, Chperson Com on Wom; r/Prot; hon/Pi Lambda Theta; Delta Kappa Gamma; Kappa Delta Pi; Num Biogl Listings.

CHAPPELL, JANIE oc/Realtor; b/Nov 22, 1929; h/1300 Live Oak, Lufkin, TX 75901; ba/Lufkin; m/Roy J; c/Nathan Wade, Jana Leigh; p/Percy D Bagwell (dec); Rosie M Bagwell Dykes, Lufkin; ed/Att'd Tex Realtors Inst; pa/Realtor 1965-; Lufkin Bd Realtors: Pres 1977, Bd Dirs 1972-78; Bd Dirs Tex Assn

Realtors 1972-78; cp/Angelina Co C of C: Bd Dirs, VP, Var Coms; Lectr; Mem Real Est Panels in HSs & Stephen F Austin Univ; r/Prot; hon/Life Mbrship Awd, Angelina Co C of C; Awd for Top Mbrship Salesman (in Under 100,000 Population Category), US C of C.

CHAR, WAI SINN oc/Dentist; b/Jun 14, 1902; h/"Woodrose" 780 Amana St, Honolulu, HI 96814; ba/Honolulu; m/Bertha Kam Yuk Lum; c/David Kingman, John Kingson, Cynthia Moonyeen Schwab (Mrs Gerald William), Claudia Moontoy Loo (Mrs Gary Y S), Douglas King Chee; p/Man Hoon and Yun Kun Wong Char (dec); ed/DDS; pa/In Charge Dental Dept Hunan-Yale Hosp, Changsha, Hunan, China 1926-27; Dentist in charge Shanghai Chinese Red Cross Hosp & Margaret-Williamsen Hosp) 1928-30; Assoc w Dr C Jackson Shanghai 1928-30; Dental Staff

Strong-Carter Dental Clin, Palama Settlemt 1930-34; Pvt Pract, Honolulu 1934-; Bd Dir Woodrose Condominium 1971-72; Pres Assn Honolulu Artists 1970; Life Mem St & Am Dental Assns; Honolulu Co Dental Soc; Acad Gen Dentistry; IPA; cp/Chinese Amateur Ath Assn; Am Chinese Clb; Creighton Alumni Clb; Hi Acad Sci; AARP; Sustaining Mem Nuuanu YMCA; Fdr Hi Chinese Jr C of C; Fdr Char Assn Hi; Downtown Improvement Assn; Nat Trust for Hist Preserv; Other Activs; r/U Ch of Christ; hon/Resolution of Merit, Hi C of C; Lttr of Commend, Pres Richard Nixon; Ltter of Commend for Org'g Hi Chinese Jr C of C, Senator Hiram Fong; Men of Achmt.

CHARLESTON, JO ANN NORMA oc/Community Services Instructor; b/Aug 20, 1930; h/7481 Buena Vista, Cucamonga, CA 91730; m/Kenneth R; c/Darrel, Jeffery, Leslie Egge, Stuart; p/Theodore and Erna Baer, Magalia, CA; ed/Cert Occupl Therapist; Art Cert; Att'd: Art Inst Chgo, Chaffey Col; pa/Mural Painter; Occupl Therapist Upland Convals Hosp 4 Yrs; Has Donated Murals to: Dept of Motor Vehicles, Upland Convals Hosp; r/Unitarian; hon/Sketches Chosen from St Contest for DMV Contest; Picture & Awd on Mural Plaque; Love Offering, Vineyard Bapt Ch (for Donated Mural).

CHARLTON, GEORGE N JR oc/Executive Director; b/Apr 12, 1923; h/1714 Lincoln Ave, Pittsburgh, PA 15206; ba/Pgh; m/Nadine; c/Lena L Coleman, George N III, Ronald L, Dianna L Jones, Susan E; p/George N Sr and Mildred F Charlton, Inglewood, CA; ed/BBA; mil/USAR WWII Vet, Lt Col (Ret'd); pa/Exec Dir Public Parking Auth of Pgh 1976-; Exec Dir Pgh Model Cities Prog 1973-76; Asst Exec Dir Pgh Model Cities Prog 1971-73; Other Past Positions; Inst of Trans Engrs (Mid-Atlantic Sect); Soc Am Mil Engrs; Mem Reg Pers Sers Adv Coun of SWn Pa; Instnl & Mun Pkg Cong 1977-; Allegheny Co Housing Auth: Asst Secy & Asst Treas 1977-; cp/Housing Auth City of Pgh: Mem, Treas, Bd Dirs; Mem Mayor's Ec Manpower Adv Com; Former Mem & Treas Commun Action Pgh Inc Bd; Mem St Cyprian-Alpha Lodge No 13, F&AM; AUSA; Pa Assn Notaries; Univ & City Mins; Pgh Br NAACP; Chadwick Civic Leag; VFW; Others; r/Presb; hon/Commun Ldr Awd, George Washington Carver Commemorative Day Com, Pgh; Cit in Recog of Ser in AUS, Gov Shapp; Meritorious Ser Medal for Ser in USAR, Pres of US; Selected as 1 of 25 Most Influential Blacks in Metropolitan Pgh, *Talk* Mag, 1975; Biogl Listings; Others.

CHARYNA, MYROSLAV oc/Priest; b/Mar 9, 1909; h/6934 Ditman St, Philadelphia, PA 19135; ba/Phila; m/Maria H Facjewycz; c/Chrystia T Senyk, Z Luba Kulczycky, Rostislav George; p/Jacob and Tecla Charyna (dec); pa/Pastor St Josapart's Ukr Cath Ch; Dean Phila Deanery; Hon Supreme Pres Ukr Cath Providence Assn; r/Cath; hon/Monsignor, Papal Chaplains, Chancery Conslt; Mem Archeparchial Adm Coun; Dir Archeparchial Press.

CHASE, HELEN CHRISTINA oc/Biostatistician; b/Mar 21, 1917; h/6417 15th St, Alexandria, VA 22307; ba/Rockville, MD; m/Donald Frederick Jr; p/Josef and Kristina Gerwich Matulic (dec); ed/AB; MS; DPH; pa/AAAS; Am Public Hlth Assn; Am Statistical Assn; Population Assn Am; r/Meth; hon/Fellow, Nat Heart Inst; F'ship, Univ Cal-B; Delta Omega.

CHASE, JOSEPH RUSSELL oc/Music Teacher; Music Therapist; Clinical Counselor; b/Mar 9, 1922; h/Salt Pond Rd, Eastham, MA 02642; ba/Same; p/Leslie E and Mabel Warren Cobb Chase (dec); ed/BS; MEd; RMT; pa/Music Tchr: Piano, Theory; Therapist; Co-Fdr Cape Cod Conservatory of Music & Art; r/Universalist-Unitarian; Former Pres Universalist Ch of E'ham; hon/George R Baker S'ship in Music; Tuition S'ship; Hon Fdrs Medal, Nat Guild Piano Tchrs; Fellow, Intl Biogl Assn; W/W in Music & Musicians Dir; Intl W/W Intells.

CHATFIELD, RUTH oc/Artist; Musician; b/Nov 2, 1918; h/6701 Woodcrest Dr, Austin, TX 78759; ba/SF; p/Henry and Sonia Chatfield (dec); ed/Grad NY Sch of Applied Design for Wom 1938; pa/Violinist; Artist McFadden Pubs, NYC 1939-41; Art Dir Fawcett Pubs, NYC 1941-44; Art Dir Doe-Anderson Advtg Agy, Louisville, Ky 1944-48; Free-lance Graphic Artist, SF 1948-65; Violinist w L'ville Symph Orch 1944-48; Violinist w Marin Symph Orch, Marin Co,

Cal 1962-; Exhibiting Fine Artist 1965-; 1-Wom Shows incl: 6 Galleries in SF, Pacific Grove Mus, Pacific Grove (Cal), St Mary's Col, Moraga (Cal), Villa Montalvao, Saratoga (Cal), Others; Num Juries & Invitational Shows & Group Shows; Artists' Equity Assn; Musicians' Union, Local #6; Former Mem: SF Wom Artists, Oakland Art Assn, Soc Wn Artists, Other Art Orgs; SF Gem & Mineral Soc Inc; hon/Medal for Most Outstg Student at Grad, NY Sch of Applied Design for Wom; Num Art Awds; Biogl Listings.

CHATTERJEE, JUNE CHACRAN oc/College Instructor; b/Jun 26, 1938; h/876 Santa Barbara Rd, Berkeley, CA 94707; m/Satyabrata; c/Mina Virginia; p/George Chacran, Newton, MA; ed/BA cum laude Colby Col 1960; MA UC-B 1963; pa/Spanish Instr Peralta Col for Non-Traditional Study, Berkeley 1976-; Instr in Spanish & ESL Contra Costa Col, San Pablo, Cal 1976-; Spanish Instr: Berkeley Adult Sch 1975-76, UC Ext-B (HS Corres Courses) 1974-; Other Past Positions; CATESOL; cp/Prabasi (Indian Cult Org); r/Armenian Orthodox; hon/Phi Beta Kappa; Recipient S'ships & F'ships; Profl Pubs.

CHAUDHURI, TAPAN KUMAR oc/Medical Researcher; Administrator; Teacher;

Clinician; b/Nov 25, 1944; h/315 Orange Plank Rd, Hampton, VA 23669; ba/Hampton; c/Lakshmi; p/Taposh K and Bulu Rani Chowdhury, San Antonio, TX; ed/MD; pa/VA Med Ctr, Assoc Prof & Chief Nuclear Med; cp/Chm & Mem Var Coms; r/Hindu; hon/Gold Medal, Silver Medal, Certs of Hon, Invited Spkr, Panel Discussant; Others.

CHAVERS, PASQUAL DEAN oc/College President; b/Feb 4, 1941; h/Hurley House, Bacone Col, Muskogee, OK 74401; ba/Muskogee; m/Antonia Navarro; c/Cynthia Christine, Monica Lynn, Celia; p/Luther C Chavers (dec); Dorothy M Byrd, Jacksonville, FL; ed/BA Univ Cal-B 1970; MA, PhD 1976 Stanford Univ; mil/USAF Navigator 1963-68; Capt; pa/Pres Bacone Col; Dir Native Am Studies Cal St Univ-Hayward; Tchr; Conslt; Pres Native Am S'ship Fund Inc; Partner Ind Ed Assocs; Chm Higher Ed Com, Cal Indian Ed Assn; Soc for Applied Anthropol; Am Indian Hist Soc; Am Indian Press Assn; Indian Ed Assocs; cp/Media, San Francisco Bay Area; Tng Staff/Bds in Indian Ed Progs; r/Bapt; hon/Num Pub'd Articles, Reports, Papers; Nat Hon Soc.

CHAVIS, EARL B oc/Executive; b/May 23, 1934; h/818 S Cashua Dr, Florence, SC 29501; ba/Florence; m/Potitsa Stefanakos; c/Sabrina, Dino, John, Patrice; p/Ulysses and Lena O Chavis, Pembroke, NC; ed/BSME; CM/GE; mil/USN; pa/Pres Chavis Tool & Mfg Co Inc; SME; Pres Clb; cp/VP AHCPA; Mason; En Star; CC; Past Pres JCs; r/En Orthodox; Pres Greek Ch, Florence; hon/W/W; Men of Achmt; IPA; Notable Ams.

CHEARY, BRIAN SIDNEY oc/Chemical Company Executive; Entomologist; b/May 25, 1936; h/2276 The Woods Dr, Jacksonville, FL 32216; ba/J'ville; m/Elisabeth Ann; c/Kelly, Craig Alan, Stacey Lynn; p/Sidney Eric Cheary, Bulawayo, Rhodesia; Esther Cheary (dec); ed/BS Cal-Poly; PhD Univ Cal-Riverside; pa/Exec Union Carbide Corp;

Entomol Soc Am; Entomol Soc Canada; Pacific Coast Entomol Soc; Soc Nematologists; Org of Tropical Am Nematologists; Assn Tropical Biol; Sigma Xi; Am Registry Profl Entomologists; cp/Repub; hon/US Fed Public Hlth Envir Scis F'ship; Nat Acad of Scis Res Grantee.

CHEESE, PAULINE STATEN oc/Card Counselor; b/Sept 12; h/PO Box 47823, Los Angeles, CA 90047; ba/LA; m/Lee (dec); c/Lee Jr; p/Paul E Staten Jr; Ellen Cathryn Staten (dec); ed/BS Fla A&M Univ; MA Pepperdine Univ; pa/Card Cnslr; r/Meth.

CHEESMAN, PAUL R oc/Professor; b/May 31, 1921; h/1146 Old Willow Ln, Provo, UT 84601; ba/Provo; m/Millie; c/Brian, Ross, Douglas, Larry, Lee Ann, Jay; p/Frederick and Ella Vera Cheesman (dec); ed/BA; MRE; DRE; mil/USNR; pa/Prof BYU; Profl Photogs Assn; Profl Tchrs Assn; cp/Lions Clb; r/Ch of Jesus Christ of LDS; hon/Hons Tchr of Yr.

CHEN, WAI-KAI oc/Professor; b/Dec 23, 1936; h/RR 1, Box 67, Athens, OH 45701; ba/Athens; m/Shirley S L; c/Jerome, Melissa; p/You-Chao Chen; Shu-Dan Chen, Athens; ed/BS, MS Ohio Univ; PhD Univ Ill; pa/Ohio Univ: Dist'd Prof Elect Engrg 1978-, Prof

1971-, Chm Elect Engrg Grad Com 1973-;
IEEE; Assoc Editor Transactions on Circuits &
Systems 1977-, Circuits & Systems Soc Com
on Prize Papers 1977-; SIAM; ACM; ASEE;
AAAS; Tensor Soc Gt Britain; MAA; Sigma
Xi; Phi Kappa Phi; Pi Mu Epsilon; Eta Kappa
Nu; Other Profl Activs; hon/Fellow Awds:
AAAS, IEEE; Ohio Univ: Excell in Tchg Awd,
Baker Fund Awd, Res Inst Fellow Awd; Lester
R Ford Awd, Math Assn Am; Outstg Edrs
Am; Others; Biogl Listings.

CHENAULT, W BLEWETT JR
oc/Consultant; b/Oct 27, 1917; h/3715
Dumbarton, Houston, TX 77025;
ba/Houston; m/Frances Burrell; c/William B
III, Charles Bruce, Harriot Elizabeth; p/W
Blewett and Clara Russell Chenault,
Beaumont, TX; ed/BA Univ Houston 1941;
mil/Alt Duty Manhattan Project, Oak Ridge,
Tenn 1944; pa/Plant Utilities Conslt, Houston
1977-; Petro-Tex Chem Co, Houston: Chem
Engr 1955-62, Utilities Supvr 1962-77; Sinclair
Rubber Inc, Houston: Chem Engr 1950-52,

Asst Purchasing Agt 1952-54, Chem Engr
1954-55; Other Past Positions; Lic'd
Stationary Engr, Tex; Mem Cooling Tower
Inst; Air Pollution Control Assn; Am Chem
Soc; Am Inst Chem Engrs; Water Pollution
Control Fdn; Nat Assn Corrosion Engrs; Sam
Houston Water Utilities Assn; cp/Houston C
of C; Delta Sigma Phi; Mem Var Clbs; Mason;
Shriners; OES; Tex Lodge of Res; r/Epis Ch,
Houston: Lay Rdr 1963-; hon/Contbr Articles
& Res Papers in Field; W/W S&SW.

CHENG, CHIA-CHUNG oc/Research
Scientist; b/May 5, 1925; h/10301 Overbrook,
Leawood, KS 66206; ba/Kansas City, KS;
m/Katherine; c/Amy Yu-wei, Anna Yumin,
Alice Yu-ray, Audrey Yu-hui; p/Kuo Liang
Cheng and Chui-Yuen Chien; ed/BS 1949; MA
1951; PhD 1954; pa/Dir Mid-Am Cancer Ctr
Prog, Univ Ks Med Ctr; Am Chem Soc;
cp/Chinese Assn of Gtr Ks City; hon/MRI-
CPS Sci Awd.

CHENG, JAMES CHESTER oc/Professor;
b/Apr 4, 1926; ba/San Francisco, CA 94132;
m/Marion; c/Alexander; p/Hsiao-quin Cheng
(dec); Hui-ying Tsao (dec); ed/BA St John's
(Shanghai); MA; PhD; pa/Prof Dept Hist San
Francisco St Univ; Am Hist Assn; Assn for
Asian Studies; Fdr Asian Studies on Pacific
Coast; cp/Prin Emeritus Palo Alto Chinese
Mandarin Sch; Pres Emeritus St John's Univ
Alumni Assn (Wn USA); Conslt Asia Bur,
KQED; Conslt US Ofc of Ed; Conslt Nat
Endowmt for Humanities; r/Confucianism;
hon/Brit Univs China Com Res Awd;
Cambridge Instn Res F'ship; Fulbright Sr Res
Professorship; Fulbright Intercountry
Lectureship; Am Coun Learned Socs Travel
Awd.

CHENNAULT, ANNA CHAN oc/Avi-
ation Consultant; b/Jun 23, 1925; h/2510
Virginia Ave NW, Washington DC 20037;
ba/Wash DC; m/Claire Lee (dec); c/Claire A,
Cynthia L; p/Y W Chan (dec); Bessie Jeong
Chan; ed/BA; pa/Pres TAC Intl 1976-; Bd
Dirs USA-ROC Ec Coun, CoChm Aviation &
Trans Com 1976-; Bd Dirs Wash Crossing
Foun 1977-; Bd Trustees People-to-People Intl
1976-; US C of C 1976-; Coun on Trends &
Perspectives 1976-; Intl Policy Com 1976-; Bd
Dirs Communs Corp of Am 1975-77; CoChm
US Coun for SE Asian Trade & Investmt
1973-; Bd Dirs DC Nat Bk 1972-; VP Intl
Affairs, The Flying Tiger Line Inc 1968-76;

Num Other Positions; Nat Coun of Fgn Policy
Assn; IPA; Flying Tiger Assn; Am Newspaper
Wom's Clb, Wash DC; Aero Clb of Wash DC;
Nat Leag Am Pen Wom; Writers' Assn, Free
China; Others; cp/USAF Wives Clb, Wash
DC; Friends of Chung-ang Univ; Nat Press
Clb; DC Repub Com; Repub Nat Fin Com;
Leag Repub Wom of DC; Fdg Mem Century
Clb, Nat Repub Heritage Groups; Others;
r/Cath; hon/Hon Fellow, Aerospace Med
Assn; Repub of Yr, DC; Repub Fdn 1st Annual
Awd; Awd of Honor, Chinese-Am Citizens
Alliance; Lady of Mercy Awd; Chosen 1 of
Am's 75 Most Important Wom, *Ladies Home
Journal*; Freedom Awd, Free China Assn; Num
Biogl Listings; Others.

CHERRY, GWENDOLYN SAWYER
oc/Attorney; State Legislator; b/Aug 27,
1923; h/2545 NW 46 St, Miami, FL 33142;
ba/Miami; m/James L; c/William, Mary;
p/W B Sawyer (dec); Alberta Sawyer, Miami;
ed/JD Fla A&M Univ 1965; MA NY Univ
1950; pa/Order of Wom Legislators; Am, Fla,
Dade Co Bar Assns; cp/Sigma Gamma Rho;
AAUW; r/Congreg; hon/Recog of
Accomplishmt in Govt Awd.

CHERTOW, DORIS S oc/County
Legislator; b/Apr 23, 1925; h/139 Sunnyside
Park Rd, Syracuse, NY 13214; ba/Syracuse;
m/Bernard; c/Andrew Henry, Richard Philip,
Marian Ruth, Douglas William, David Jacob;
p/Jacob and Ella Saltzman (dec); ed/BA
Hunter Col 1945; MA Radcliffe 1947; PhD
Syracuse Univ 1968; pa/Adult Ed Assn; NY St
Assn of Counties; cp/Literacy Vols; Legal Aid
Soc; Assn for Retarded; r/Jewish; hon/Phi
Beta Kappa; Post-Standard Wom of Achmt.

CHESSER, BARBARA JO oc/University
Professor; b/Feb 26, 1941; h/7700 Yankess
Hill Rd, R#8, Lincoln, NE 68516; ba/Lincoln;
m/Delton L; c/Christi; p/John Russell (dec);
Winnie Luttrell, Portales, NM; ed/BS summa

cum laude; MA; PhD; pa/Prof Univ Neb;
Reschr; Profl Orgs; Ofcr Nat Coun on Fam
Relats; r/Bapt; Tchr, Fin Com; hon/Author 2
Books, Num Articles in Profl Jours; Grad
Fellow, Univ Neb; Biogl Listings.

CHESSHER, FAYE BATEY oc/-
Administrator; b/Jul 28, 1921; h/1436
Mockingbird Ln, Seguin, TX 78155;
ba/Seguin; m/Daniel S; p/William Whit and
Harriet Callison Batey (dec); ed/BS 1962 Tex
Luth Col; MA 1967 SW Tex St Univ;
pa/Wom's Dir, Commun Affairs Dir KWED
AM-FM Radio; Past Pres Zonta Clb Seguin;
Dist 7 Tex Press Wom: CoChm Clb Publicity
Wkshop, Former Treas, Secy & Pres; Dir Tex
Press Wom St Bd; Decorations Chm 1978 Nat
Conv Nat Fdn Press Wom; cp/Adv Bd Voc Ed

Dept, Seguin HS; Bd Dirs Seguin-Guadalupe
Co Coliseum; Seguin Study Clb; Seguin
Conservation Soc; Mid-Tex Symph Soc;
Friends of Lib; Guadalupe Co Assn for
Retarded Citizens; Var Former Activs; r/1st
United Meth Ch, Seguin: Mem, Commun
Com, Former Mem F'ship Com; hon/3 1st Pl
Awds, Tex Press Wom's St Contest; 1st Pl,
Tex Nsg Home Assn's Media Competition for
Profl Jour; Abe Lincoln Awd Cert of Excell, So
Bapt Radio-TV Comm; Num Others.

CHI, WEN-SHUN oc/Research Linguist;
b/Mar 17, 1910; h/1545 Douglas Dr, El
Cerrito, CA 94530; ba/Berkeley, CA;
m/Ellen; c/Josephine, Francis, Franklin, Alice;
p/Chung Te Chi (dec); Shih Wang (dec);
ed/BA Tsing Hua Univ; MA Univ Wash;
pa/Res Linguist Univ Cal-B; Tchr of Chinese:

Univ Wash-Seattle, Stanford, Columbia, Univ
Cal-B; hon/Pub'd Author, Books incl:
Readings in Chinese Communist Documents,
1963 (3rd printing 1968), *Readings in Chinese
Communist Idealogy*, 1968, *Readings in the
Chinese Communist Cultural Revolution*,
1971, & *Chinese-English Dictionary of Con-
temporary Usuage*, 1977.

CHIENTAN, GOLD oc/Chinese Herb-
alist; Artist; b/May 13, 1916; h/1030 S
Alvarado St, Los Angeles, CA 90006; ba/LA;
m/Eleanor L; p/Yill C Chien, Shanghai,
China; M P Chu, Shanghai; ed/PhD S China
Univ; pa/Spkr Nat Hlth Fdn 1974 (San

Francisco, Cal); Organic Photo Exhibit at Cal
Mus of Sci & Indust, LA 1978; Profl Orgs;
cp/Lions Intl; Hwa Pei Benevolent Assn of So
Cal, LA; hon/1st Prize & Special Awd,
Pasadena Art Fairs, Cal 1975; Spec Awd,
Santa Monica Art Show 1976.

CHILDRESS, DENVER RAY oc/College
Professor; b/Feb 5, 1937; h/Rt One, Box 46,
New Market, TN 37820; ba/Jefferson City,
TN; m/Margaret Haynes; c/Kim D, Mark A;

p/Theodore Childress (dec); Edna Campbell Childress, Maryville, TN; ed/BS Maryville Col 1959; MM 1964, EdD 1975 Univ Tenn-Knoxville; mil/USAF; Tenn NG; pa/Col Math Prof; Tenn Math Tchrs Assn; Kappa Mu Epsilon; AAUP, St Conf Coms; NCTM; MAA; ETEA; cp/Jefferson Co Vol Contbrs; Dem; r/1st Bapt Ch, Jefferson City: Deacon, SS Tchr; hon/NDEA F'ship; Knapp Math Prize; Outstg Edrs Am; Am Men & Wom Sci; Personalities of S.

CHILDRESS, JAY WALTER oc/Psychotherapist; b/Jan 31, 1933; h/43 Windsor on the Marsh, Savannah, GA 31406; ba/Savannah; m/Beth Odess; c/Walter, John, Janelle, Merideth, Kimberly; p/Walter Jefferson and Nellie Stevenson Childress (dec); ed/BA Randolph-Macon; MS Va Comm Univ; Adv'd Dipl Smith Col; mil/USMC; pa/Psychotherapist, Marriage & Fam; ACSW; AAMFT; AGPA; AASECT; cp/Past Pres Savannah W Rotary Clb; Ga Marriage & Fam Cnslr Lic'g Bd; r/Meth; hon/NIMH S'ship & Grants; Superior Perf Awd, USVA.

CHILDS, FRANCINE C oc/Professor; b/Feb 8, 1940; h/4-204 Monticello, PO Box 821, Athens, OH 45701; ba/Athens; p/Nathan Rogers, Dallas, TX; Margaret Thomas, Amarillo, TX; ed/BS 1962; MEd 1970; EdD 1975; pa/Prof Afro-Am Studies; ASCD; Phi Delta Kappa; SESS; NCBS; AAUP; Alpha Kappa Delta; APGA; NCBF; Bd Dirs BHHVRD; Min's to Blacks in Higher Ed; U Campus Min; cp/LWV; Pres Athens Co Br NAACP; Chm Afro-Am Com Ohio Conf Brs of NAACP; Urban Leag; Coun on Human Rts; r/Bapt; hon/Ohio Univ: Dist'd Univ Prof, Resident Advr of Yr 1968; Cited as a Wom to Know in Dallas 1974; Most Outstg in Wom Affairs; Tchr of Yr; W/W S&SW; Others.

CHILDS, JOHN LAWRENCE oc/Retired Professor; b/Jan 11, 1889; h/4141 N Rockton Ave, Rockford, IL 61103; ba/NYC; m/Grace Mary; p/John Nelson and Janette Smith Childs (dec); ed/BA Univ Wis 1911; MA 1924; PhD Columbia Univ 1931; pa/Ret'd Prof Founs of Ed, Tchr Col Columbia Univ; Vis Prof: Univs Wis, Mich, Ohio, Ill 1954-66; cp/Fdr & 1st St Chm Liberal Party NY St; Am Fdn Labor Postwar Planning Com; Co-Editor The Social Frontier; hon/LHD, So Ill Univ; John Dewey Awd, Am Humanist Assn; Profl Pubs.

CHILES, JERRY EDWARD oc/Minister; b/Feb 20, 1946; h/614 Valley Dr, Dalton, GA 30720; ba/Dalton; m/Patsy Copeland; c/Elizabeth Ashley; p/James A and Ruth Bentle Chiles, Falmouth, KY; ed/BA Georgetown Col 1968; MRE 1970, Grad Specialist RE 1971 So Bapt Sem; pa/Min Music & Yth: Woodland Ave Bapt Ch, Lexington (Ky), 1st Bapt Ch, Lawrenceburg (Ky), Reidland Bapt Ch, Paducah (Ky); Min of Yth: 1st Bapt Ch, Decatur (Ga), 1st Bapt Ch, Dalton; 2nd VP Ga Bapt Rel Ed Assn 1978; Tchr Rel Ed at Sev Confs; cp/Drug Adv Coun, Whitfield Co (Ga); Supervise God & Country Prog; Chm Adv Comm Dalton Jr Col Bapt Student Union; r/So Bapt; hon/Outstg Col Aths of Am; W/W of Rel; Men of Achmt.

CHILTON, HOWARD GOODNER oc/Retired Business Executive; b/Nov 3, 1910; h/4226 Arcady Ave, Dallas, TX 75205; ba/Dallas; m/Margaret Harrison; c/Howard Jr, Evalyne Wynne C Baxter, Margaret Anne Wynne C Worsham; p/James Edward Robert and Evalyne Preuit Chilton (dec); ed/BBA

Univ Tex 1932; mil/USNR Lt; pa/Chilton Corp: Dir, Advr 1975-, Former Chm Exec Com; Dir Assoc'd Credit Burs 1947-; VP: Credit Bur Mgmt Co 1964-68, Credit Bur Sers 1968-69, Merchants Retail Credit Assn 1928-64; Pres Retail Merchs Assn Tex 1952; Pres & Dir: Assoc'd Credit Burs Am 1953-54, Assoc'd Credit Burs of Tex 1950; Mgmt Instr: Univ Ks 1953-54, Univ Ks, Univ Ill 1957; Instr Princeton Univ; Instr Univ NC; Secy Treas Fort Worth Retail Credit Exs 23 Yrs; cp/Life Mem Fort Worth C of C; Past VP Phi Kappa Psi; Rotary; Thalian; Past Commodore Dallas Sailing Clb; Others; r/St Michaels & All Angels Epis Ch: 1st Treas Men's Bible Class, Mem Money Counting Team; hon/Recipient (w brother) of Awd as Outstg Credit Bur Mgrs in Large Cities of US & Canada; Dallas Jr Chamber Diamond Awd; Intl Ser Awds, Credit Burs of Am; Biogl Listings.

CHING, ERNEST K S oc/Retired Sugar Plantation Surveyor; b/Jan 3, 1903; h/1414 Farrington St, Honolulu, HI 96822; m/Nancy Young; c/Patricia Milligan, Claire Mahuna, Richard K M; p/Ah Sen Ching and Ah Kyau Wong Shee; pa/Ewa Plantation Sugar Plantation: Clerk-Draftsman, Instrumentman 1921-28, Surveyor 1928-41, Chief Surveyor

1941-67; Warehouse Shipping Clerk Cal Packing Corp 1921; cp/Former Vol Dir Sports Ewa Plantation Co; Past Pres & Dir Tsung Tsin Assn; Past 1/VP Ket On Soc; Chinese C of C; U Chinese Soc; Past Pres Chun Wing Chin Tong Soc; Hlth Com Hi St Comm on Aging; Repub Party Activs; Var Activs Rotary Clb; r/1st Ch of Christ: Mem; hon/Paul Harris Fellow, Rotary Clb; Men & Wom of Hi; Men of Achmt.

CHIPAIN, GEORGE CHRIS oc/Orthodontist; b/Apr 24, 1935; h/421 Barclay Ct, Elmhurst, IL 60126; ba/Elmhurst; m/Joyce; c/Chris, Georgia; p/Chris Chipain (dec); Christine Chipain, Elmhurst; ed/DDS; MSD; pa/Orthodontist.

CHISOLM, CHARLES SMITH oc/Foundry Executive; b/Sept 10, 1916; h/1213 Peter Pan Rd, Lookout Mt, TN 37350; ba/Chattanooga, TN; m/Martha Gilbert; c/Betsy Silberman, John Grier, Catherine C; p/James S and Ernestine Chisolm (dec); ed/BS, MS Auburn; mil/Lt Col Arty; pa/Am Foundry Mens Soc; ASTM; cp/Planning Bd Lookout Mtn; r/Presb Ch in Am: Ruling Elder; hon/Omicron Delta Kappa.

CHOATE, HERBERT WADE oc/Executive: Mayor; b/Aug 19, 1932; h/2707 Crestline, Big Spring, TX 79720; ba/Big Spring; m/Toni LaRue Barron; c/Kyle Wade, Melody; p/John Harold Choate (dec); Vera Choate, Big Spring; ed/Draughon's Bus Col 1950-51; So Meth Univ 1951-53; Howard Co Col 1955-56; Univ Wis Sch for Credit Union Pers 1965-67; mil/AUS 1953-55; pa/Treas-Gen Mgr Citizens Fed Credit Union, Big Spring 1965-; Reg V Bd Mem Nat Credit Union Adm 1975-81; Credit Union Exec Soc; Credit Union Com 1973-77; Chm Bd Dirs Mems Ins Cos 1975-76; Bd Mem Tex Assn Fed Credit Unions 1970-76; Dir Credit Union Nat Assn Inc 1973-76; Pres Big Spring Chapt Credit Unions 1972-73; Others; cp/Mayor Big Spring 1972-; Other City Ofcs Held; Charter Mem Hilltop Clb; IOOF Lodge; Mustang Clb; AF Assn; Am Bus-men's Clb, Big Spring Chapt; Chm Big Spring Steering Com; Others; r/St Mary's Epis Ch, Big Spring: Vistry 1969-71;

hon/Outstg Man of Yr Awd, Rotary Clb 1974; Life Mem Delta Sigma Pi; W/W: Polits, Tex, Am.

CHOI, JEI YORK oc/Research Metallurgist; b/Jun 5, 1923; h/2727 Midtown Ct, Palo Alto, CA 94303; ba/Menlo Park, CA; m/Yun Han; c/Myong Suk, Soojin Paul; p/Byong Sang and Ko Bang Kim Choi; ed/BEngrg Kyushu Inst Technol 1944; BEngrg 1947, MEngrg 1953 Seoul Nat Univ; PhD Kyushu Univ 1962; pa/Res Staff Mem Raychem Corp, Menlo Park 1968-; Res Metallurgical Engr Carnegie-Mellon Univ 1967-68; Prof & Hd Metall Engrg Dept Han Yang Univ (Korea) 1964-67; Res Metall Engr

Carnegie Inst Technol 1962-63; Chief Metall Engrg Sect Sci Res Inst (Korea) 1957-60; Asst Prof Seoul Nat-Univ 1954-57; Mem Bd Nat Sci, Seoul City (Korea) 1967; Pres Korean Inst Metall Engrs 1965-69; Pres Korean Soc Heat Treatment Metals 1965-66; Am Inst Mining; Metall & Petrol Engrs; Am Soc for Metals; Sigma Xi; Pres Alumni Assn Metall, Seoul Nat Univ 1964-67; r/Korean Ctl Presb Ch, San Francisco; hon/Emperor Japan Awd 1944; Silver Star Wha Rang Decoration, Republic of Korea; Mu Song Chung Mu Decoration, Repub of Korea; Nat Invention Awd, Korea.

CHONG, ANSON oc/State Senator; b/Aug 8, 1938; h/Box 813, Honolulu, HI 96808; ba/Honolulu; p/Kim Fan Chong, Honolulu; Lily Winters, Honolulu; ed/BA Colgate Univ 1961; MA Columbia Univ 1963; mil/AUS 1956 pfc; pa/Conslt to Commun Orgs; cp/Bd Dirs: Atherton YMCA, UNA-USA (UN Assn of USA); r/Congreg; hon/Outstg St Legislator Awd, Eagleton Inst, Rutgers Univ.

CHONG, LUIS A oc/Corporate Director; b/May 14, 1930; h/59 Ethelbert Pl, Ridgewood, NJ 07450; ba/Hartford, CT; m/Vivian; c/Ana, Louis, Michael, Mary, Catherine, Paul; p/Issac and Maria Chong;

ed/BSME; pa/Corporate Dir Tech Planning U Technols Bldg; NA Soc for Corporate Planning; NEMA; AMA; NAS; cp/Bergen Co C of C; r/Cath; hon/W/W: Engrg, E.

CHOPRA, KULDIP PRAKASH oc/Professor; b/Mar 25, 1932; h/1372 W Little Neck Rd, Virginia Beach, VA 23452; ba/Norfolk, VA; m/Phyllis; p/Madan Gopal Chopra, Delhi, India; ed/BS w hons 1951; MS 1953; PhD 1960; pa/Prof Physics Old Dominion Univ 1969-; Vis Prof Va Inst Marine Scis 1972-; Prof Applied Physics Nova Univ (Fla) 1967-69; Other Acad Positions; Editor Va Jour of Sci 1977-; Sci Advr to Gov of Va; Reschr; Sci Conslt; Author; Spkr; cp/Guest

Spkr: Lions Clb, Jewish Ctr; hon/Var F'ships, S'ships; Fellow, Am Phy Soc; Melpar Author of Yr Awd 1964; Shelton J Horsley Res Awd, Va Acad Sci; Biogl Listings.

CHOW, CHEN-YING LEUNG oc/Artist; b/Mar 20, 1921; h/2740 Le Jeune Rd, Coral Gables, FL 33134; m/Chow Chian-Chiu; c/Chow Chee-Woo; p/(dec); ed/Dipl Art Tchr Tng Col (China); pa/Est'd Chow Studio, Miami, Fla; Former Prin Intl Studio Chinese Art, Hong Kong; Works Accepted & Displayed (w husband's work) at Nat Exhbn of Contemp Painters, China; Other Exhbns: Exhbns of Contemp Painters, London, 1937, Japan 1952, 58, Yugoslavia 1957-60, New Zealand, 1961, Canada 1963, Foster Art Gallery, Laguna Bch, Cal 1964, Hopkins Centre Art Gallery, 1966; Invited to Display Paintings at Galerie Des Deux Mondes, J F Kennedy Terminal, NY (by Tans World Airlines); Num Lectrs to Univs, Art Ctrs, Art Leags, Others; hon/Profl Pubs incl: *Easy Ways to do Chinese Painting, Chinese Painting No 2, Comprehensive Study in Chinese Painting* (pub pending at present); Color Movie Made of their Demonstration for Ednl Purposes; Biogl Listings; Others.

CHOW, MOOPING oc/Engineer; b/Dec 17, 1927; h/3091 Medina Dr, San Bruno, CA 94066; ba/SF; m/Lin-Lin Pan; c/George, Ellen, Betty; p/Shin Ting Chow (dec); Wee June Chi (dec); ed/BS Chiao Tung Univ 1947; MS Univ NC-CH 1961; Further Study; pa/Engr, City & Co SF 1969-; Participant in

Planning & Designing Var Plant Expansions & Improvemts around USA 1947-69; Am Soc Civil Engrs; Water Pollution Control Fdn; Diplomate, Am Acad Envir Engrs; Reg'd Profl Civil Engr, Cal; r/Christian Reformed; hon/Recipient F'ships; W/W in W; Intl W/W Commun Ser; Personalities of W&MW.

CHOY, YOUNG CHUL oc/Chief Engineer; b/Sept 14, 1941; h/3152 Cabo Blanco Dr, Hacienda Heights, CA 91745; ba/Pasadena, CA; m/Soon Ja; c/Nancy, Dennis; p/Kwang Ho Choy, Seoul, Korea; Keum Ja Park, Seoul; ed/BSEE Cal St Polytech Univ 1968; pa/Instrument Soc Am; cp/Esquire Golf Clb; r/Bapt; hon/W/W in W.

CHRISMAN, JAMES EDWARD oc/Dentist; b/Dec 5, 1916; h/906 Randall Dr, Normal, IL 61761; ba/Bloomington, IL; m/Ruth Catherine Henebry; c/James C, Daniel P, Robert A; p/Edward W and Clara A Chrisman (dec); ed/BS Davidson Col; DDS NWn Univ; mil/USCG 1942-46; pa/ADA; Ill Dent Soc; McLean Co Dent; Mennonite Hosp; cp/Am Cancer Soc; BSS; US Power Sqdrn; Mid Ill Sqdrn Cmdr; r/Luth: Coun Mem; hon/Silver Beaver, BSA; Exchange Clb Man of Yr.

CHRISMAN, PERRY OSWIN oc/Judge; b/Aug 5, 1935; h/1151 Plymouth Rd, Dallas, TX 75208; ba/Dallas; m/Marilyn Barron; c/Lori Paige, David Keith; p/L E Chrisman, Port Arthur, TX; Dorthea Chrisman (dec); ed/BA Baylor Univ; JD Baylor Law Sch; mil/USAFR; pa/Judge 44th Judic Dist Ct of Tex; Presiding Judge Dallas Co Dist Judges; cp/ARC; Mtl Hlth Assn; Dallas Heart Assn; Oak Cliff C of C; Juvenile Bd; Dallas Coun on Alcoholism; Dallas Assembly; U Way of Metro Dallas; r/Cliff Temple Bapt Ch: Deacon; Mem Bapt Jt Com; Mem SW Bapt Theol Sem; hon/Editor Tex Probate System,

Depend Adm; W/W: Am Cols & Univs, Selection Com; Outstg Yg Men Am.

CHRISTENSEN, JAMES MERLIN oc/-Radio Minister; b/May 1, 1937; h/3536 Burritt Way, La Crescenta, CA 91214; ba/Glendale, CA; m/Betty; c/Christine, Karlyne, Jeffrey,

Mark; p/Arthur and Dolores Christensen; ed/BA; MA; DD; pa/Nat Rel Broadcasters; r/Bapt; hon/Ia Farmer Deg 1955; DeKalb Awd; Hon DDiv.

CHRISTENSEN, JERRY MELVIN oc/Engineer; b/May 5, 1949; h/209 N Oregon St, Morton, IL 61550; ba/Morton; p/Melvin and Louise Christensen, Lake Preston, SD; ed/BS SD St Univ; pa/Livestock Housing Engr; Am Soc Agri Engrs; Nat Soc Profl Engrs;

Ill Soc Profl Engrs; Reg'd Engr in St of Ill; cp/Smithsonian Assocs; Dem; Nat Geographic Soc; Nat Rifle Assn; r/Luth; hon/DIB; Men of Achmt; Intl W/W Commun Ser; Intl Register Profiles; W/W MW; Commun Ldrs & Noteworthy Ams; Personalities of W&MW; Notable Ams; Book of Honor.

CHRISTIAN, GARY DALE oc/Professor; b/Nov 25, 1937; h/7827 NE 12th St, Medina, WA 98039; ba/Seattle, WA; m/Suanne C; c/Dale B, Carol J; p/Roy Christian (dec); Edna Christian Gonier, Eugene, OR; ed/BS; MS; PhD; pa/Prof Chem Univ Wash-S; Conslt; Res Interests in Analytical Chem, Clin Chem; Author 2 Textbooks, 1 Reference Book, Num Articles in Profl Jours; r/Prot; hon/Fulbright Scholar, Belgium.

CHRISTIAN, JAMES HOWARD oc/-Sales Manager; b/Jun 4, 1938; h/917 Kapapala Pl, Honolulu, HI 96825; ba/Honolulu; m/Patricia Ann; c/Kent, Jim, Kelly, Karen, John; p/Joseph Christian (dec); Thelma J Struchen, Ks City, MO; ed/BS Univ Mo-Rolla; pa/Mo Profl Engrg Soc; cp/PTA; r/Prot; hon/Var Awds; W/W in W; DIB.

CHRISTIAN, MAE ARMSTER oc/Faculty Member; b/Dec 22, 1932; h/2626 Lisa Dr SW, Atlanta, GA 30311; ba/Atlanta; m/Leopold; c/George C, Earle A; p/Josephine Spey, Thomasville, GA; ed/BS NY Univ; MS Bank St Col; EdD Univ Ga; pa/Fac Univ Ga; Dir Atlanta Tchr Corps; Lectr; Evaluator; Conslt in Early Childhood, US Mainland & Virgin Isls; AAUP; NAEYC; Phi Delta Kappa; Delta Sigma Theta; cp/NAACP; Dem Party; Wom's C of C; r/Meth; hon/Bronze Wom 1976; Bronze Wom Ed 1976; Ford Fellow; Num Dist'd Ser Awds.

CHRISTIAN, WALTER P oc/Adminis-

trator; b/Nov 19, 1946; ba/PO Box 703, Chatham, MA 02633; m/Barbara Pritchard; c/Katherine Rae, Walter Kenton; p/Walter P and Rae Gardner Christian, Mobile, AL; ed/BA; MS; PhD; pa/Dir May Inst for Autistic Chd 1978-; Pt-time Instr Depts Child Devel & Psychol Clark Co Commun Col, N Las Vegas, Nev 1977-78; Vis Prof & Mem Grad Fac Dept Spec Ed, Univ Nev, Las Vegas 1977-78; Adjunct Prof Dept Psychol Univ Nev 1977-78; Chief Psychologist Chd's Behavioral Sers, Las Vegas 1976-78; Other Past Positions; Am Psychol Assn, Div Experimental Analysis of Behavior 1975-; Assn for Advmt of Behavior Therapy; Nat Soc for Autistic Chd; MWn Assn Behavior Analysis; Rocky Mtn Psychol Assn; Num Other Profl Activs; r/Cath; hon/Recipient S'ships; Tchg Asst'ship, F'ship; Biogl Listings; Num Profl Pubs.

CHRISTIANSEN, MARJORIE MINER oc/Professor; b/Feb 28, 1922; h/94 Laurel St, Harrisonburg, VA 22801; ba/H'burg; m/Theodore L; c/Karen L; p/John E and Margaret W Miner, H'burg; ed/BS w distn 1949, MA Univ NM 1955; PhD Utah St Univ 1967; pa/Prof Home Ec James Madison Univ 1969-; Regina Sch of Nsg, Albuquerque, NM;

Sci & Nutrition Instr 1950-64; Project Dir 1966-69; Proj Dir & Adj Prof Nsg Univ Albuquerque 1969; Am Dietetic Assn; Reg'd Dietitian; Va Dietetic Assn: Pres 1974-75, Del 1976-; cp/Mem Adv Com on Spec Ed, H'burg Public Schs; r/Meth; hon/Utah St Univ Res Coun F'ship; Res Grant, Corn Prods Co; Other Grants.

CHRIST-JANER, ARLAND F oc/College President; b/Jan 27, 1922; h/President's Home, Stephens Col, Columbia, MO 65201; ba/Columbia; m/Sally Johnson; p/William Henry and Bertha Wilhelmina Beckman Christ-Janer (dec); ed/bA Carleton Col; BD Yale Divinity Sch; JD Univ Chgo Law Sch; mil/USAAC 1943-46, Pvt to Capt; pa/Pres Stephens Col; Trustee & Chm: Ednl Policy Com, Carleton Col, Acad Affairs Com, New Col; Trustee Stephens Col; Dir Am Republic

Ins Co of NY; Phi Beta Kappa; Century Assn NYC; Columbia C of C; Am Acad Arts & Scis; Cleveland Conf; Intl Assn Univ Presidents; Japan Intl Christian Univ-Men's Com; cp/Missourians for the Equal Rts Amendment; Bd Dirs Mus Assocs, Univ of Mo; US People's Fund for UN Inc; Nat Coun Wilberforce Univ's Pres Devel Coun; Newcomen Soc NAm; Rotary Clb Columbia; hon/LLD: Coe Col, Colo Col, Carleton Col; LHD: Monmouth Col, Curry Col.

CHRISTMAN, LUTHER oc/Professor;

h/19141 Loomis Avenue, Homewood, IL 60430; m/Dorothy Mary Black; c/Gary James, Judith Ann C Kinney (Mrs Thomas P), Lillian Jane; ed/BS 1948, EdM 1952 Temple Univ; PhD Mich St Univ 1965; pa/Rush Univ: Prof Nsg & Dean Col Nsg 1972-, Prof Sociol Col of Med 1972-76, Prof Sociol Col Hlth Scis 1976-; Sr Scist, Attending Staff Rush-Presb-St Luke's Med Ctr; VP Nsg Affairs Rush-Presb-St Luke's Med Ctr; Var Past Positions; Coun Adv'd Practitioners in Psychi & Mtl Hlth Nsg,

ANA; Am Sociol Assn; Am Nurses' Assn; New York Acad Scis; Soc for Applied Anthropol; AAAS; Biomed Engrg Soc; Nat Leag for Nsg; Conslt; Num Other Profl Org Activs; hon/Pub'd Author; Sigma Theta Tau; Alpha Kappa Delta; Fellow: Nat Leag for Nsg, Inst of Med of Chgo, Am Acad Nsg; Outstg Man Nurse in Nation, Nat Assn Male Nurses Establishmt; Portrait donated to Rush Univ Lib, Comm'd by Rush Nurses Alumni Assn; Vis Fellow, New Zealand Nurses Ednl & Res Foun; Biogl Listings; Others.

CHRISTMAS, BETH W oc/Administrator; b/Jul 4, 1944; h/PO Box 343, Metter, GA 30439; ba/Metter; m/Jack W; p/Pickens W Watson (dec); Mary Searson, Metter; ed/Ga So Col 1962-63; Addit Specialized Studies; pa/Exec Dir Genesis Housing & Commun Devel Cor 1974-; Prog Dir Altamaha Area CAA Inc, Reidsville, Ga 1972-74; Neighborhood Sers Ctr Dir Altamaha Area CAA Inc, R'ville 1971-72; Substitute Tchr Candler Co Bd of Ed, Metter 1971; Other Past Positions; Metter BPW Clb, Chperson Yg Careerist Prog; Nat CAA Exec Dirs Assn; Altamaha-Ga So Area Employmt & Tng Coun; cp/Candler Co Unit Am Cancer Soc, Chperson Media & Spec Events; Ga Human Rts Coun; Ga Residential Fin Auth Adv Coun; Ga Commun Action Assn; Ga Reg Hosp Bd, Savannah; Adult Ed Adv Bd; Gov's Coun on Human Relations Conf; Guest Spkr; Other Activs; hon/Outstg Yg Wom Am.

CHRISTNER, JANIECE oc/Executive; b/Sept 5, 1917; h/4215 Lakeside Dr, Dallas, TX 75219; ba/Dallas; m/(dec); c/W Russel; p/(dec); pa/Chm of Bd Christner Industs.

CHRISTOPH, MILDRED oc/Teacher, Librarian; b/Apr 18, 1915; h/1165 SW Blvd, Wichita, KS 67213; p/John Christoph (dec); Agnes Danler (dec); ed/AB; MA; pa/Tchr-Libn Christ the King Sch, Okla City; CLA; MW CLA; OLA; Pub'd Lib Sci HS Student

Handbook; cp/Okla Geneal Soc; Ks Geneal Soc; LOOPS; Right to Read Com, Right to Life Com; r/Cath; hon/Pubs incl: Christoph Fam Hist, 1977, The Danlers of Ks 1877-1977, 1978, Flusche Fam Hist, 1979; Math Grant, Ill

St; Outstg Ldrs in Elem & Sec'dy Ed; Notable Ams; Book of Honor; DIB.

CHRISTOPHER, THOMAS WELDON oc/University Dean; b/Oct 8, 1917; h/7 Pinehurst Dr, Tuscaloosa, AL 35401; ba/University, AL; m/Evelyn Montez Hawkins; c/Thomas Heflin; p/William Arthur and Ruby Thomas Christopher (dec); ed/AB Wash & Lee 1939; LLB Univ Ala 1948; LLM NYU 1950; SJD 1957; LLD Univ Ala 1978; pa/Dean Univ Ala Sch of Law; ABA; Assn Am Law Schs; Food & Drug Law Inst; hon/Author: Cases and Materials on Food and Drug Law, 2nd Edition 1973, Constitutional Questions in Food and Drug Laws, 1960, (w Leverett & Hall) Georgia Procedure and Practice, 1957, (w Dunn) Special Federal Food and Drug Laws, 1954; Contbr Num Articles to Legal Jours.

CHRISTOPHERSON, MARIE LUCILLE oc/Educator; b/Dec 8, 1922; h/318 Meek, Box 1032, Arkansas City, KS 67005; ba/Gore, OK; p/Oscar M Christopherson (dec); Sarah A Christopherson, Ark City; ed/BSEd 1953; MSEd 1959; PhD 1967; pa/Spec Ed; Pvt Tutoring; Past Mem Wichita (Ks) Hd Start Bd; NEA; Okla St Tchrs Assn; cp/Former Mem Wichita Commun Action Prog; Wichita Choral Soc; r/Rom Cath; hon/Grad Asst'ship, Cath Univ Am; NDEA Grant in Rdg, Tex So Univ.

CHRYSSAFOPOULOS, HANKA WANDA SOBCZAK oc/Geotechnical Engineer; b/Sept 24; h/5 Horizon Rd, #2002, Fort Lee, NJ 07024; ba/New York, NY; m/Nicholas; p/Stefan and Estacia Sobczak, Porte Alegre, Brazil; ed/Civil Engr 1951, Mech & Elect Engrg 1952 Univ Rio Grande do Sul; MS 1954, PhD 1964 Univ Ill; pa/Sr Engr Dames & Moore 1978-; Pvt Res 1967-77; Asst Prof Civil Engrg Cal St Univ-Long Bch 1965-67; Conslt'g Engr Woodward-Clyde-Sherard & Assoc, Ks City, Mo 1964-65; Other Past Positions; Am Soc CE; Geological Soc Am; Soc Wom Engrs; Conselho Reg de Engenharia, Agronomia e Arquitetura (Brazil); Intl Soc Soil Mechanics & Foun Engrg; Sigma Xi; r/Rom Cath; hon/Fulbright Scholar; Contbr Papers to Tech Pubs.

CHU, FLORENCE CHIEN HWA oc/Radiation Therapist; b/May 20, 1918; h/1500 Palisade Ave, Fort Lee, NJ 10021; ba/NY; m/Percy Tung; c/Shirley, Allan Tung; p/Shu Loh C Quang (dec); Kung Shu (dec); ed/MD; pa/Meml Hosp, NYC: Chm Dept Radiation Therapy 1976-, Attending Radiation Therapist 1969-, Assoc Att'g Radiation Therapist 1955-65, Clin Asst Radiation Therapist 1950-53; Att'g Radiologist NY Hosp, NYC 1974-; Other Profl Positions; Assoc Mem Sloan-Kettering Inst 1977-; Cornell Univ Med Col: Prof Radiol 1977-, Clin Prof Radiol 1973-77, Assoc Prof Radiol 1969-73, Others; Am Col Radiol; Radiol Soc NAm; NY Cancer Soc Inc; Am Assn for Cancer Res; Am Roentgen Ray Soc; NY Roentgen Soc; Am Soc Therapeutic Radiologists; Am Soc Clin Oncology Inc; Med Soc St NY; NY Co Med Soc; Am Radium Soc; Am Med Wom's Assn Inc; Radiation Res Soc; Other Mbrships; hon/S'ship; 1st Prize, Radiol Soc NAm for Sci Exhibit; Outstg Sci Achmt Awd, Am Chinese Med Soc; Num Profl Pubs.

CHU, TIEN-YUNG JULIAN oc/Environmental Engineer; b/Sept 1, 1979; h/7823 Celeste Ln, Hixson, TN 37343; ba/Chattanooga, TN; m/Ling Shirley; p/Chien-Chiu and Chien-I Chu, Taipei, Taiwan; ed/BS; MS; MS; pa/Envir Engr Tenn Val Auth; Am Inst Chem Engrs; Am Soc Civil Engrs; Am Water Pollution Control Fed; hon/DIB; Men of Achmt; W/W S&SW; Phi Tau Phi.

CHUANG, MARISA YUEN oc/Psychologist; Administrator; b/Mar 19, 1943; h/2820 Heathfield, Birmingham, MI 48010; ba/Detroit, MI; m/Vem L; c/Jessica Millie; p/Ah Hain Yuen, Toronto, Canada; Sin Chun Cheng; ed/MA Columbia Univ; PhD Cand Univ Mich 1980; pa/Admr Human Sers Agys; Asst Dir & Equal Employmt Opport Ofcr Wayne Co Dept of Substance Abuse Sers,

Detroit 1975-; Chief Planning & Analysis Bur Mich Dept Social Sers, Reg 9 1974-75; Res Dir Wayne Co Dept Social Sers, Detroit 1972-74; Other Former Positions; Psi Chi; cp/VP Org of Chinese Am Wom; r/Meth; hon/Dean's Hon List, Berea Col; 1st Prize Winner, Ky Intercollegiate Oratorical Contest; Outstg Yg Wom Am; Intl W/W in Music.

CHUN, DAI HO oc/Educator; b/Jan 8, 1905; h/1588 Laukahi St, Honolulu, HI 96821; p/Hin and Kwock Shee Chun (dec); ed/BA w hons 1930, MA 1937 Univ Hi; PhD Ohio St Univ 1947; mil/USAF 1942-45, Cmdg Ofcr, Lt Col (Ret'd); pa/Univ Hi: Emeritus Prof Ed 1970-, Asst, Assoc & Prof 1945-70; Conslt; Inst Dir E-W Ctr (Hi) 1961-70; Dir Intl Cooperation Ctr Hi (Gov's Ofc) 1956-61; Fellow Progressive Ed Assn; Var Edit Activs;

Res Fellow Jt Coun on Ec Ed 1952; Former Scholar & Vis Fellow Ohio St Univ; Other Profl Activs; cp/Mem Var Gov Orgs: Travel Indust Cong, Com on Post-War Reconstruction, Adv Com on Survey of Public Ed, Com on Ed Beyond HS, Coun on Intl Visitors, Adv Com on Peace Corps, Others; r/Prot; hon/Wisdom Hall of Fame; Wisdom Awd of Honor; Dist'd Ser Awd, Univ Hi Alumni Assn; Meritorious Unit Cit, USAF; Life Fellow, Intl Inst Arts & Lttrs; Nat Hon Socs; Biogl Listings; Others.

CHUNG, FRANK HUAN-CHEN oc/- Senior Scientist; b/Jul 20, 1930; h/18027 Tarpon Ct, Homewood, IL 60430; ba/Chicago, IL; m/Doris Chu-feng; c/Susan, Shirley, Sonia; p/Koe-yie and Chi-ming Chung, China; ed/BS; MS; PhD; pa/Sr Scist Sherwin-Williams Res Ctr, Chgo 1968-; Res Fellow Kent St Univ 1964-68; Instr 1954-57 & Lectr 1960-63 Chung Cheng Inst Technol, Taiwan; Other Past Positions; Am Chem Soc; Soc for Applied Spectroscopy; Am Crystallographic Assn; Treas MW Assn Chinese Engrs & Scists; hon/Lttr of Commend, AUS; Outstg Acad Record Awd & Kent Intl Achmt Awd, Kent St Univ; Res F'ships: NSF, NASA; Biogl Listings.

CHUNG, KYUNG CHO oc/Professor; Author; b/Nov 13, 1921; h/25845 S Carmel Hills Dr, Carmel, CA 93921; ba/Monterey, CA; m/Y S; c/In Ja, Jn Myung; p/Yang Sunhung (dec); Myung Ok Peng (dec); ed/BA

Seoul Nat Univ; MA NY Univ; MA Monterey Inst Fgn Studies; LLD; pa/Fac US Def Lang Inst; Dir Korean Res Coun; Advr Am-Korean Foun; r/Meth; hon/Superior Perf Awd; Cert of Achmt, US Govt.

CHUNG, MAY EVELYN KIRKPATRICK oc/Executive; b/Feb 15, 1925; h/1333 Lopaka

Pl, Kailua, HI 96734; m/(dec); c/Keven, Cherie, Mark, Laurie, Laui Kirk; p/Charles Kirkpatrick; Ivah C Pope Kirkpatrick, Medford, OR; ed/Bach; MPH; pa/Pres Hawaiian Hlth Foun; Chm Hono Co Med Aux Intl Hlth; CoFdr Castle Meml Hosp; cp/Honolulu Neighborhood Bd Comm; r/SDA; hon/Awd in Civil Def, Pres Kennedy; Biogl Listings.

CHURCH, AVERY GRENFELL oc/University Teacher; Author; b/Feb 21, 1937; h/351 Azalea Rd, Apt B-28, Mobile, AL 36609; ba/Mobile; p/Avery M and Eulah Lowe Church, Winston-Salem, NC; ed/BA cum laude Baylor Univ 1962; MA 1965, Addit Grad Work Univ Colo; mil/USN 1955-57; Hon Disch; pa/Univ S Ala, Mobile: Lectr Anthropol, Pres Fac Adv Com, Nom'g Com

Col Arts & Scis; Res Staff & Bd Dirs Sociol & Anthropol Sers Inst Inc, Mobile; Asst Prof Anthropol Memphis St Univ 1965-66, 1969-72; Sev Profl Orgs; Ala Acad Sci: VChm Anthropol 1975-76, VP 1976-77, Exec Com 1975-77; cp/Conslt; Panelist; Vol Work for Cands; r/Guest Lectr Sev Rel Orgs; hon/Alpha Chi; Alpha Kappa Delta; Sev F'ships; Sev Profl Papers & Pubs; Num Pubs & Sev Awds in Poetry; Biogl Listings.

CHURCH, AVERY MILTON oc/Minister; b/Jan 9, 1909; h/656 Sunset Dr SW, Winston-Salem, NC 27103; ba/Ferguson, NC; m/Ulah May Lowe; c/Milton Lowe, Avery Grenfell, John Whiteford, Martha Eulah; p/Noah Cleveland Church (dec); Frances Caroline Yates Church, Daytona Beach, FL; ed/BA Wake Forest Col 1930; ThM So Bapt Theol Sem 1939; ThD 1944; pa/Min Beaver

Creek Bapt Ch, Ferguson; Former Pastorates: 1st Bapt Ch, Wilkesboro, NC 1931-36, Waughtown Bapt Ch, W-S 1940-64, Parkway Bapt Ch, W-S 1965-74; Mem Gen Bd NC St Conv 1946-50; Pilot Mt Assn: VModerator 1945-46, Exec Com 1944-74; Pres W-S Bapt

Conf 1943-44; Others; cp/Former Mem Merits Com Old Hickory Coun BSA; Forsyth Clergy Assn; Allied Ch Leag; SW Commun Chs; r/Bapt; hon/Inter-Univ Study Tour of Israel, 1962; Contbr Articles to Rel Pubs & Local Newspapers.

CHURCH, LLOYD E oc/Oral Surgeon; b/Sept 25, 1919; h/7005 Glenbrook Rd, Bethesda, MD; m/Hildegard Cascio; c/Pamela Gail; p/Howard Church; ed/BA WVa Univ; Dental Degree Univ Md; Masters, PhD George Wash Univ; mil/AUS Dental Corps: Tex, Cal, Japan, China; pa/Fac Mem Dept Anatomy & Surg George Wash Univ; Fac Mem Univ Md Sch of Med, Asst Prof Anatomy; Almas Temple Rep to Phila Hosp; Fdr & Life Mem Intl Assn Oral Surgs; Chm 1st Res Com Am Soc Oral Surgs; Fellow: Am Col Dentists, Intl Col Dentists, Royal Microscopic Soc Gt Britain, Royal Soc Hlth Gt Britain, AAAS, Wash Acad Sci; Acad Med of Wash; Am Dental Assn; Other Profl Assnl Mbrships; cp/Cosmos Clb; Philosophical Soc Wash; Bethesda-Chevy Chase & Montgomery Co Cs of C; M C Crime & Drug Abuse Com; Bethesda-Chevy Chase Kiwanis Clb; YMCA; Am Cancer Soc; Reg IV Gov's Com on Law Enforcemt Planning Bd; Wash Hearing Soc Bd Dirs; Illustrious Potentate Almas Temple, Masonic Order; r/Bethesda U Meth Ch: Mem, Pres Men's Clb, Usher, Mem Bd Stewards, Adm Bd; hon/Phi Delta Theta; Psi Omega; Sigma Xi; Profl Pubs; Biogl Listings.

CIABATTARI, JANE DOTSON oc/Writer; Editor; b/Mar 27, 1946; h/1784 Filbert St, San Francisco, CA 94123; ba/SF; m/G Mark; c/Scott Antony; p/William Francis and Dorothy Bruner Dotson, Emporia, KS; ed/BA Stanford Univ 1968; pa/Mng Editor *California Living*; Media Wom (NY); Bay Area Profl Wom's Network; AAUW; cp/NOW; Former Press Ofcr Mont Gov's Status of Stanford Alumni Assn Wom Comm; hon/Nat Merit S'ship; Stanford Univ S'ship; Pub'd Articles in: *Seventeen*, *Redbook*, *McCall's*, Others.

CIANCONE, LUCY oc/Accountant; b/Jun 17, 1931; ba/1018 City Hall, Buffalo, NY 14201; ed/Bus Deg Stratford Bus Col 1950; Acct'g Deg Canisius Coll 1958; pa/Pvt Pract, Buffalo 1950-; Enrolled Public Acct, NY & Ont, Notary Public, St of NY; IPA; Nat Soc Public Accts; Past Pres Empire St Assn Public Accts; Bd Dirs CSEA; cp/Dem Cand Eric County Leg 1975; Smithsonian Inst; Nat Geog Soc; hon/World W/W Wom; Awd of Merit, Empire St Assn Public Accts.

CICCHINELLI, LOUIS FRANK oc/Social Research Psychologist; b/Jan 30, 1948; h/6989 S Valentia St, Englewood, CO 80110; ba/Denver, CO; m/Dorothea Graham; c/Lauren Christine; p/Anthony J and Mary A Cicchinelli, Latham, NY; ed/BA Canisius Col

1969; MA 1972, PhD 1974 Univ Denver; mil/Colo NG; pa/Social Sys Res & Eval Denver Res Inst, Univ Denver; APA; AAUP; Conslt to Ft Logan Mtl Hlth Ctr 1974-75; Res Assoc Computer Image Corp 1972-74; Instr Univ Denver 1972-76; r/Rom Cath; hon/NDEA F'ship.

CISARUK, ANDREW A oc/Urban Planner; b/Feb 20, 1908; h/8371 Fox Bay Dr, Union Lake, MI 48085; m/Marcia Rudnycka; c/Halyna, Jerome; p/John F and Sophia Cisaruk; ed/BA; Masters Deg in Correctional

Sci; PhD; pa/Engaged in Urban Planning & Devel; Current Chm Bd Dirs, Res Inst for Social Action, Fenton, Mich.

CISSIK, JOHN HENRY oc/Laboratory Chief; b/Aug 18, 1943; h/301 Dartmouth, O'Fallon, IL 62269; ba/Scott AFB, IL; m/Dorthothy Paulette Allen; c/John Mark; p/John Peter and Gladys Lucille Morre Cissik, McGregor, TX; ed/BA, MA Univ Tex-Austin; PhD Univ Ill; mil/USAF Biomed Scis Corps, Maj; pa/Chief Spec Procedures Lab; Course Dir USAF Cardiopulmonary Lab Tng Course; Mem or Chm Edit Bds for Sev Jours; Mem Sev Profl Assn Coms; AART; ATS; NSCPT; ASAHP; cp/Evans Presch Coms; Evans PTA; Am Heart Assn; hon/DIB; Book of Honor; W/W in MW.

CITRENBAUM, RONALD LEE oc/Computer Industry Executive; b/Jul 17, 1942; h/22835 Sparrow Dell Dr, Calabasas, CA 91302; ba/Los Angeles, CA; m/Sandra; c/David; p/Irvin and Pauline Citrenbaum, Baltimore, MD; ed/BES; MSEE; PhD; pa/VP & Dir Corp in Computer Indust; Tau Beta Pi; Eta Kappa Nu; Sigma Xi; cp/Tau Epsilon Phi; r/Jewish; hon/Md Senatorial F'ships & S'ships.

CIUCA, EUGEN oc/Sculptor; Painter; Critic of Art; b/Feb 27, 1913; h/21 Shore Lane, Bay Shore, NY 11706; ba/Same; m/Alice Caroline; p/Vasile and Victoria Comes Ciuca (dec); ed/Univ CLUJ-Romania 1934-38; Acad Fine Arts, Bucharest, Romania 1942-46; Dept Pedagogy Univ Bucharest 1944-46; pa/Fdr 4th Dimension in Arts 1970; 33 One-Man & 35 Intl Jt Exhbns in: Romania, Ungheria, Jugoslavia, Venezuela, Italy, Spain, USA; Pub'd Fourth Dimension in Arts Manifesto, 1977 (Rome, Italy); hon/Hon Citizen, Pontelongo-Padova-Italy; Hon Citizen, Mira Venezia, Italy; Golden Fram Awd, Cronaca, Rome for Fourth Dimension in Art Exhbn in Rome; Fellow Knight of Mark Twain Soc; European Reg of Arts (Rome); Intl W/W in Art; W/W in Am; DIB.

CIZEK, EUGENE DARWIN oc/Architect; Urban Designer; City Planner; Environmental Social Psychologist; Professor; Corporation President; p/Darwin and Malilda Fabianek Cizek (dec); ed/PhD; DSc; MCP; MUD; BArch; mil/USAF, ROTC; pa/Asst Prof Sch of Arch & Urban Studies Fac 1972-78; Num Arch Projects; Baton Rouge Chapt Am Inst Archs; New Orleans Chapt Am Inst Archs; Am Inst Archs; La Archs; Am Inst of Planners; AAUP; Var Exhbns; Num Com Mbrships & Ofcs Held; Reschr; hon/Vieux Carre Hon Awd for 830 Royal St Restoration Cizek, Freidrichs & Sigle, Archs & Landscape Archs; S'ship, Univ Cal-Berkeley; Outstg Alumni, Beta Rho Chapt, Phi Gamma Delta; White House Fellow Nom, LSU 1969; Fulbright Scholar, Holland; Henry Adams Awd, LSU; AIA Outstg Terminal Student in Arch, LSU; Profl Pubs; Biogl Listings; Others.

CLAAR, RICHARD LEE oc/Minister; b/Nov 19, 1926; h/Hillcrest Addition, Branson, MO 65616; ba/Branson; m/Kathleen C; c/Terry Lee, Richard Lee Jr; p/Lawrence McKinley and Millie Hayes Claar (dec); ed/Grad Dallas Bible Col 1954; Postgrad Moody Bible Inst 1973; mil/AUS WWII; pa/Min Branson Bible Ch 1959-; Former Pastorates: Dalton Bible Ch, Dalton, Wis 1958-59, Decatur Chapel Ch, Little Hocking,

Ohio 1956-58; Pres Dallas Bible Col Alumni Assn 1962-63; VP Wis Reg IFCA; Pres Ozark Reg IFCA; cp/Branson PTA; Mo Wel Comm; Branson Police Comm; Served on Mo Rehab Study; Former Treas Wilderness Ch Fund; r/Indep Fundamental Chs of Am; hon/Alumnus of Yr 1961, Dallas Bible Col; W/W in Rel.

CLAGUE, THOMAS EUGENE oc/Manpower Development Consultant; b/Jul 20, 1923; h/7808 W 103, Bloomington, MN 55438; ba/Same; m/Ann F; c/Karen, Brian, Candace C Garza (Mrs Pedro Jr), Kevin; p/Glenn Clague (dec); Hazel B Clague, Knoxville, IA; ed/BS Ia St Univ; mil/AUS 1943-46; pa/Am Soc Agri Engrs; Weed Sci Soc Am; SAE; cp/BSA; U Fund; Commun Concerts; Others; r/Presb & UCC: Choir Mem, Chm New Ch Bldg Com, Moderator.

CLAIBORNE, OLLIE ELLEN oc/Public Relations Director; b/Oct 12, 1941; h/105 Timberland Dr, Dalton, GA 30720; ba/Dalton; m/Lucien; c/Mike, Cindy, Lanore, Patsy; p/Kenneth and Leota Blankenhagen, Humbolt, KS; ed/Att'd Dalton Jr Col; pa/Public Relats Dir Whitfield Co Schs; Kgn Tchr 1972-77; Ga Schs Public Relats Assn; cp/Num PTA Activs incl'g: Sci Review Bd for Nat PTA 1976-77, Secy Comm on Org Ga PTA 1973-75, Comms Conf Chm 1976-77, VChm MOS Comm 1975-77, Goals Comm Chm 1977, Ldrship Tng Conf Chm 1977, St Del to Nat PTA Conv (from Ga PTA) 1976, Chm Campaign on Wheels 1976, Mem S'ship Com, Others; Former Mem: Whitfield Co Task Force, NW HS Rt to Read Task Force, Whitfield Co Sch Bd Hlth Com, Bank Boosters Exec Com, Dalton City Schs Adv Com, Others; Del to Gov's Conf on Ed 1977; NC St Human Relats Conf; Girl Scouts Com Mem; Num Other Civic Activs; r/Ctl Ch of Christ: Mem; hon/Daltons Wom of Yr 1977; WTTI Radio Citizen of Day (Feb 11, 1978); Ga PTA: Hon St Life Mbrship, Hon Fdrs; Dawnville PTA Apprec Awd; Sertoma Awd of Whitfield Co; NW Band Boosters Apprec Awd; Dalton-Whitfield Celebration Apprec Awd; Others.

CLANCY, JOHN P (JACK) oc/Professor; b/Jun 11, 1920; h/San Juan Capistrano, CA; ba/Mission Viejo, CA; p/E Earl Sr and Mary O'Brien Clancy (dec); ed/BA Univ Dayton 1948; BEd 1953, MEd 1956 Univ Toledo; MA Univ Detroit 1965; PhD US Intl Univ 1975; mil/AUS Parachute Troops 1942-45, S/Sgt Intell, Rhineland & Ctl Europe Campaigns; Combat Inf Badge; pa/Prof Hist Saddleback Commun Col 1969-; Tchr & Admr Public Schs 1954-69: Ohio, Mich, NY, Cal; Metallurgist Willys Motors, Toledo, Ohio 1950-54; Radio Announcer WABJ, Adrian, Mich 1948-50; AAUP; Alpha Gamma Sigma; Nat Hist Soc; Smithsonian Inst Assocs; cp/Elks; DAV; PAC; CIO; Vols for Adlai Stevenson 1952-60; hon/Eagle Awd, BSA; NDEA Grant, Mich St; Dean's List Var Cols; Debate Gavel, De Sales Col; Honoris Societatem Associationem Ad Promovendum Studium Latinum, 1939; Num Biogl Listings.

CLARE, STEWART oc/Research Biologist; Educator; b/Jan 31, 1913; h/405 NW Woodland Rd, Indian Hills in Riverside, Kansas City, MO 64150; ba/Same; m/Lena Glenn Kaster; p/William Gilmore and Wardie Stewart Clare (dec); ed/BA Univ Ks 1935; MS Ia St Univ 1937; PhD Univ Chicago 1949; Adv'd Study & Res: Univ Mo-Kansas City, Ks City Art Inst, MW Res Inst 1945-49; mil/USAAF Weather Sch 1942-43, Instr (Civil Ser), Meteorol & Weather Forecasting; Ensign USNR Malaria Res, Nav Med Ctr & S Pacific Isls 1943-45; pa/Res Biologist & Conslt 1974-; Prof Emeritus Biol 1974-; Prof Biol & Dir Biological Res The Col of Emporia (Ks) 1967-74; Lectr, Prof &/or Chmship Depts Biol or Sci Div: Ks City Col Osteopathic Med 1963-67, Rockford Col 1962-63, NY St Univ-Plattsburg-Twin Vals 1962-66, Mo Val Col 1961-62, Union Col 1958-61; Ed Res: Klipfontein Organic Prods Corp, Johannesburgh, S Africa 1957, Min Agri, Khartoum, Sudan, Africa 1955-56, Univ Adelaide, S Australia 1954-55, Univ Alberta, Canada 1949-53, Earlier Positions 1937-49;

Mem: Am Entomological Soc, British Assn for Admvt of Sci, NY Acad Scis; Life Fellow IBA; Fellow ABI; Fellow Explorer's Clb; Sigma Xi; The Sci Res Soc NAm; Phi Sigma; Psi Chi; Nat Assn Biol Tchrs; AAUP; Arctic Inst NAm; Am Polar Soc; Soc NAm Artists; Inter-Soc Color Coun; Nat Coun on Arts in Govt; Others; Res Projects: Physiol & Biochem of Arthropoda, Capillary Movemt & Particulate St of Matter, Res Collections, Chromatology-Theory & Sci of Color & Design; Res Artist Over 30 Exhibits of Color Designs, Paintings & Illustrations on Local, Nat & Intl Levels; Var Group Exhibits; Pvt Shows in Australia & Africa; hon/Dist'd Citizens Plaque, W/W Hon Soc Am; Cited for Contbns to Advmt of Higher Ed & Ser to Commun, Emporia Col; Outstg Edrs Am; Certs of Distn, Res Ctr, Nat Register of Prom Ams; Cert of Merit in Art & Dist'd Ser Awds for Ed & Res in Biol, Intl Biogl Centre; Creativity Recog Awd, Intl Pers Res; Num F'ships, Res Grants & Var Hon Positions; Num Biogl Listings incl Am Men & Wom Sci; W/W: Am, MW, Am Art; DIB; Commun Ldrs; Pub'd Author; Others.

CLARK, ALICE T oc/University Administrator; b/Mar 2, 1926; h/622 23rd Ave S, Grand Forks, ND 58201; ba/Grand Forks; c/-Fred, Sherrie, Gordon, Terrence, Laurie Anne, Riley; p/Melvin Billings Thompson (dec); Hazel Kirk Justesen Thompson, Salt Lake City, UT; ed/BS Univ Utah 1947; MEd 1960, PhD 1965 Brigham Yg Univ; pa/Asst VP for Acad Affairs Univ ND; APA; MPA; NDPA; AAUP; NARC; VARC; APGA; SPATE; ND St Hd Start Adv Com 1967-68; CAPPS Nat Org; AAMD; Appt'd to St Bd of Psychol Examrs, by ND Gov; Elected Commr to N Ctl Assn of Cols & Schs Comm on Instns of Higher Ed 1976; Auditing Com MWn Assn Grad Schs 1969-76; Coun of Grad Schs 1975-77; Wom Dean's Assn; AMCAP, Area Rep for Nat Org 1976-; Psychol Conslt; Other Profl Activs; cp/1/VP Dakota Dist Latter Day Saint Relief Soc, Grand Forks; Former PTA Mag Chm, Provo, Utah; Repub Party Activs; Other Former Activs; r/LDS; hon/Res Awd, Univ ND; Nat Def Ednl Act, 3-Yr F'ship; Alpha Phi Alumnae S'ship; Assoc'd Wom Student S'ship.

CLARK, BILL P oc/Manager Data Quality Assurance; b/May 15, 1939; h/6988 Hanover Pkwy, #300, Greenbelt, MD 20770; ba/Goddard Spaceflight Ctr; p/Lloyd A and Ruby L Clark, Dewey, OK; ed/BS 1961, MS 1964, PhD 1968 Okla St Univ; pa/Mgr Data Quality Assurance, NASA Landsat Proj, Computer Scis Technicolor Assocs; Am Phy Soc; AAAS; NY Acad Scis; hon/Post-doct Res Fellow, Univ Warwick, Coventry, England; Undergrad S'ships.

CLARK, CAROL LOIS oc/Educator; b/May 23, 1948; h/1861 Herbert Ave, Salt Lake City, UT 84108; ba/Sandy, UT; p/Norman W and Lois Colt Clark, Salt Lake City; ed/BA; MEd; PhD; pa/1st VP Delta Kappa Gamma; Curric Writer; Mem 1st Utah

Edrs Group in Egypt 1976; cp/Repub Voting Dist VChm; Country Rep; Tutoring Chm LDSSA; r/LDS: Ch Relief Soc Gen Bd; hon/Utah St Hist Soc Tchr of Yr 1975; Phi Kappa Phi; Alpha Xi Delta S'ship; LDS Ch Histn's F'ship; Biogl Listings; Others.

CLARK, DONALD EDWARD oc/Chairman County Commissioners; b/Apr 25, 1933; h/811 SW Broadway Dr, Portland, OR 97201;

ba/Portland; m/Shirley; c/Donald, Donna C Kincaid, Richard Paulus; p/Harold E and Vera Lang Clark, Portland; pa/Chm Bd Multnomah Co Commrs (Elected); pa/Chm Bd Multnomah Co Commrs (Elected); Author Num Articles in Profl Law Enforcemt Jours; cp/Mem City Clb; hon/Advr Pres' Comm on Law Enforcemt & Adm of Justice 1966.

CLARK, DOROTHY CORBIN oc/Registered Nurse; b/Oct 8, 1924; h/1075 E Elm Ave, Provo, UT 84601; m/Stanley Newell; c/S Corbin, David Crawford, Kevin Newell; p/John Whitbred and Ila Palmer Corbin, Moab, UT; ed/Cadet Nurse Corp 1943-46; pa/Leg Conslt Utah Nurse Assn 1971-; Mem Bd Trustees N-CAP for Am Nurses Assn 1975-; Pres Wom's Leg Coun Utah Co 1977-79; cp/Nat Gov Affairs Com, Arthritis Foun; Del to Co, St & Nat Rep Convs 1972, 76; r/LDS; hon/Ambassador of Goodwill to Philippines for Pres Ford 1975.

CLARK, EUGENE C oc/Ceramic Engineer; b/Oct 18, 1941; h/703 Orchard St, Hendersonville, NC 28739; ba/H'ville; m/Mary Elizabeth Adams; c/Mary Corry, Walter Emmett; p/Walter Nathaniel Clark, Washington, GA; Mary Helen Corry Clark (dec); ed/BS 1964, MS 1968 Ga Inst Tech; mil/AUS Inf Capt 1964-66; pa/Am Ceramic Soc; Keramos; Nat Inst Ceramic Engrs; cp/Cub Scouts; Lions Clb; Soc Mfg Engrs; r/Presb; hon/Keramos.

CLARK, FRED JR oc/Instrument Engineer; b/May 31, 1911; h/Aquetong Rd, Carversville, PA 18913; ba/Same; m/Clara E; c/Richard A (dec), Elizabeth Caddick; p/Fred and Julianna Clark (dec); pa/Instrument Engr, Ser Indust; cp/Fdr Fred Clark Mus & Art Gallery; r/Prot; hon/Buck's Cty Blue Book; W/W in Am.

CLARK, JAMES ARTHUR oc/Educator; b/Mar 12, 1895; h/2423 Va Bch Blvd, Norfolk, VA 23504; m/N Beverly; c/James A Jr (dec), Amelia C Mebane; p/John and Martha Clark (dec); ed/AB Livingston Col 1917; BS Howard Univ 1924; MA Columbia Univ 1936; Dr Inventing Patent Univ of Am Inc 1973; mil/Regimental Sgt Maj Pioneer Inf WWI, 1918; pa/Tchr St Univ Elizabeth City, NC 1929-40; Prin HS Ruthville, Va 1940-42; Booker T Washington HS 1942-62: Sci Tchr, Band Dir; Missionary to Liberia, Africa 1962-63; Tchr Jr Col, Greenville, Ala 1964-70; Cnslr & Tchr to Drug Addicts, Drug Abuse Ctr, Norfolk 1970-76; Phi Beta Sigma; cp/Am Legion Tchr Assn; Dem; r/AME; hon/Man of Yr Awd, Omega Phi Psi; W/W in Am; Inventor.

CLARK, JOHN RICHARD oc/Professor; b/Oct 2, 1930; h/11712 Davis Rd, Tampa, FL 33617; ba/Tampa; m/Anna Lydia Motto; c/Valerie Molly, Bradford Russell; p/Russell Leroy Clark (dec); Dorothy Myers Clark, Cape May, NJ; ed/BA Pa St Univ 1952; MA Columbia Univ 1956; PhD Univ Mich 1965; mil/USNR, Active Duty 1952-54 (Korea); pa/Prof Eng Univ S Fla; MLA; APA; SAMLA; ASECS; Other Profl Orgs; hon/3 Rackham F'ships, Univ Mich; Sum at Inst for Adv'd Study, Princeton; Author 2 Scholarly Books, 76 Articles, Num Book Reviews.

CLARK, JOSEPH DANIEL oc/Professor; Minister; b/Dec 20, 1931; h/1711 Hollyberry, Houston, TX 77073; ba/Houston; m/Sally Lou Caldwell; c/James Caldwell, Steven Daniel; p/James Earl and Nellie Carleton Clark, Greenville, TX; ed/BS 1957, MS 1961 Univ Houston; Postgrad 1964-68; DMin U Meth Theol Sem 1976; pa/So Bible Col, Houston: CoFdr, VP 1958, Hd Spch & Homeletics Depts 1958-, Bd Adm, Bd Dirs; Rep for Org & So Bible Col at Annual Meeting of Nat Assn Evangs; Tex Tchrs Assn; Am Assn Bible Cols; Contbr Articles to Rel Jours; cp/Former Chaplain Harris Co Commrs Ct; r/Prot; hon/Outstg Edrs Am; Personalities of S; W/W in Rel.

CLARK, JULIE ANN oc/Model; Student; b/Feb 24, 1962; h/16350 Hanna Rd, Lutz, FL 33549; p/Robert Julian Jr and Marie

Tramontana Clark, Lutz; ed/Berkeley Preparatory Sch; pa/Am Musical Theatre Co: Soloist, Featured Dancer; Teen Fashion Bd Model w Maas Brothers Dept Store; r/Presb; hon/1976 Bicent All Am Beauty, Fla St Pageant; Queen of Latin Am Fiesta, Led a Delegation of 36 Persons on Goodwill Trip to Spain, Morocco & Portugal Rep'g USA, Sum 1978; Others.

CLARK, LaVERNE HARRELL oc/Author; Photographer; Lecturer; b/Jun 6, 1929; h/4690 N Campbell Ave, Tucson, AZ 85718; ba/Same; m/L D; p/James Boyce Harrell (dec); Belle Bunte Harrell, Smithville, TX; ed/BA Tex Wom's Univ 1950; MA Univ Ariz 1962; Columbia Univ 1951-54; pa/Author & Photog 4 Books: *They Sang for Horses, The Face of Poetry, Re-Visiting Mari Sandoz Plains Indian Homeland,* & *Focus 101;* Also Var Articles, Short Stories & Reviews; Conslt to *Southwestern Literature Magazine* 1973-75; cp/Chm Lttrs Fiction Contest Pima Co HSs, Ariz 1976, 77; r/Epis; hon/8 Nat Writing & Photog Awds, Biennial Lttrs Contest, Nat Leag Am Pen Wom; 1st Pl Intl Folklore Awd, Univ Chgo; "Tucson Creative Writer of Yr", 1977.

CLARK, MARVIN RAY oc/Director; b/Dec 6, 1942; h/206 Ruggles, Temple, TX 76501; ba/Temple; m/Carol Little; c/Tonya Michelle, Tammy Rene; p/T R and Lola Wyly Clark, Sundown, TX; ed/BA Univ Houston; Systems Sci II, IBM SS Inst; pa/Dir MIS; Data Processing Mgmt Assn; DPMA: Pres 1977, Intl Dir 1979-80; r/So Bapt: Lic'd Min; hon/W/W: Tex, SW.

CLARK, ODIS MORRISON oc/Minister; b/Jan 23, 1944; h/409 Streamland, Danville, KY 40422; ba/Danville; m/Sharon Patrick; c/Brian, Jonathan, Amy; p/Leonard Clark (dec); Waldien Clark, Bagdad, KY; ed/AB Louisville Bible Col; pa/Min: Indian Hills Christian Ch 1976-, River Dr Christian Ch 1972-76, Mt Eden Christian Ch 1966-72; cp/Rotary Clb; r/Christian; hon/Cited for Ldrship, Salt River Christian Men's F'ship.

CLARK, ROBERT JULIAN JR oc/Civil Engineer; b/Jan 15, 1938; h/16350 Hanna Rd, Lutz, FL 33549; ba/Lutz; m/Marie Tramontana; c/Julie Ann, Robert Julian III; p/Robert Julian and Mary Challancin Clark, Tampa, FL; ed/CE Ga Inst Technol 1960; Masters Bus Prog Univ S Fla; pa/Secy/Treas

Tampa Steel Erecting Co; Nat Erectors Assn; Com of 100, Gtr Tampa C of C; cp/Latin Am Fiesta Assn; Carrollwood Clb; Ga Tech Alumni; Sigma Chi; Dem; r/Presb; hon/Krewe of Venus Debutante Presentation of Daughter; Krewe of Venus King's Guard; Latin Am Tour of Spain, Morocco, Portugal.

CLARK, RUTH MILLBURN oc/Professor; h/515 S 10th E, Salt Lake City, UT 84102; m/(dec); c/Marjorie C Alvey, Patricia C Olsen; p/Herbert W and Olive Branch Millburn (dec); ed/BA, MA Univ Utah; PhD Univ So Cal; pa/Univ Denver: Ret'd Prof Emeritus Speech Pathol, Dir Spch Clin; Past

Pres: Utah Spch & Hearing Assn, Colo Spch & Hearing Assn; cp/Bd Dirs Commun Meml Chapel Foun; r/Mormon; hon/Nat Zeta of Yr 1965; Var Univ Scholars; Hon Mem, S African Logopedics Soc; Fellow ASHA; Conslt Sev Univs.

CLARK, RUTH WALLACE oc/Teacher; Poet; b/May 13, 1939; h/Rt 1, Old Boston Rd, Lebanon Junction, KY 40150; ba/Shepherdsville, KY; m/Douglas Brian; c/Rebecca, Brian, Rex; p/Marvin J and Sarah Florence Wallace, Fisherville, KY; ed/AA Univ Ky; BS Univ L'ville; pa/Tchr Bullitt Co Bd of Ed; Ky St Poetry Soc; Nat Fdn Poetry Socs; World Poetry Soc; Intercontinental, Intl Poetry Soc; r/Unitarian; hon/Num Awds for Writing & Poetry incl'g 1975 & 1978 Awd for Outstg Poetry, NFSPS.

CLARK, VIRGINIA LYNN oc/School Improvement Program Facilitator; b/Apr 23, 1944; h/1041 Cornell Ave, Albany, CA 94706; ba/Oakland, CA; c/Lance Wesley, Jacob Josef, Catherine Nicole; p/Milton Meagher and Miron M Clark, Richmond, CA; ed/BA Univ Cal-Berkeley; MS Cal St Univ; Grad Work; Life Tchg Credential & Adm Credential, St of Cal; pa/Adj Prof Nova Univ, Ft Lauderdale, Fla; Oakland Ed Assn; Grievance Rep, Cal Math Coun; Mem Math Task Force Team; Math Textbook Eval for Cal; hon/Class Filmed for Nat TV Spec, *What's New at School.*

CLARK, WARREN SEELEY JR oc/Executive Director; b/Apr 13, 1935; h/253 N Friars Ct, Addison, IL 60101; ba/Chicago, IL; m/Virginia M; c/Drew Bradley, Gail Elizabeth, Neal Brian; p/Warren S and Martha W Clark, Goshen, CT; ed/BS w hons & distn Univ Conn 1956; MS 1959, PhD 1963 Ia St Univ; mil/USAR 1956-58, Maj MSC;

pa/Intersoc Coun of Am Public Hlth Assn; Dairy Indust Com; Chm 3-A Symbol Coun Bd Trustees; IAMFES; ADSA; cp/Chm Addison Bd of Review; Chm Addison Hosp Com; Mem Dist 88 Bd of Ed; r/Presb; hon/DFISA Fellow; Alpha Zeta Tall Corn Awd; Sigma Xi; Gamma Sigma Delta; Alpha Zeta.

CLARK, WAYNE DOUGLAS oc/City Engineer; b/Jan 5, 1936; h/632 Spruce St, Staunton, VA 24401; ba/Staunton; m/Shirley Anne; c/Sharon F, Karen A, Wayne D Jr;

p/Donald J and Mary F Clark, Staunton; ed/BA; mil/USAF 3 Yrs, 11 Months; pa/-Engrg, Surveying & Design; cp/Order of Eagles; Benevolent Proctective Order of Elks; r/Presb; hon/St Pres Frat Order of Eagles 1977-78.

CLARK, WILLIAM JAMES oc/Educational Administrator; b/Aug 7, 1931; h/12304 Melody Turn, Bowie, MD 20715; ba/Rockville, MD; m/Rachel Ann; c/Franklin Ray, Roxana, Steven Edward, Louis Matthew James; p/Louis Klarik and Margit Soltesz Clark, Grant Town, WV; ed/AB Fairmont St 1957; MEd Univ Ga 1961; mil/USAF 3½ Yrs; pa/Dir Div of Acad Skills; Phi Delta Kappa; ASCD; NCTM; NCSM; NEA; MSTA; MCEA; MCTM; hon/Outstg Edrs Am; Personalities of S; W/W Among Sch Dist Ofcls; DIB; Notable Ams; Commun Ldrs & Noteworthy Ams; W/W Among Students in Am Univs & Cols.

CLARK, WILLIAM MERLE oc/Baseball Scouting Supervisor; b/Aug 18, 1932; h/3906 Grace Ellen Dr, Columbia, MO 65201; ba/Same; m/Dolores Pearl; c/Patrick Sean, Michael Seumas, Kelly Kathleen, Kerry Maureen, Casey Connor; p/Merle William and Beulah Wilson Clark (dec); ed/BJ Univ Mo 1958; mil/AUS 1951-54, Korea (1 Yr); pa/Baseball Scouting Supvr, Cincinnati Reds; CoFdr Nat Corr Rec Assn; AAU Weightlifting Com 20 Yrs; Originated Nat Masters' Prog for Lifters 40-Over; Sports Ofcl 28 Yrs; Past Pres Mo Val AAU; Mo Sportwriters' Assn; Columbia Ofcls Assn; r/Unitarian-Universalist Ch; hon/John Pike Awd for Contbn to Prison Rec.

CLARKE, ANN NEISTADT oc/Consulting Engineer; b/Jul 27, 1946; h/Twin Springs Dr, Brentwood, TN 37027; ba/Nashville, TN; m/James Harold; p/Donald and Besse Neistadt, Holiday, FL; ed/BS Drexel Inst 1968; MA Johns Hopkins 1970, 71; PhD Vanderbilt Univ; pa/Conslt'g Engr AWARE Inc; ACS; Sigma Xi; WPCF; ASTM; Tenn Acad Sci; hon/Am Men & Wom in Sci; W/W S&SW.

CLARKE, WILLIAM R oc/Physician; b/Dec 10, 1921; h/180 Pearson, Water Tower Pl, Chicago, IL 60611; ba/Chgo; c/William R Jr, Gregory C, Clifton B; p/Henry A and Delia Clarke (dec); ed/MD; mil/AUS 1941-45, Cmdr; pa/Phys Internal Med; Roosevelt Meml Hosp: Pres Med Staff, Dir Med Studies; Tchr Chgo Med Sch; Instr through Assoc Prof 1957-; Am Soc Internal Med; Chgo, Ill, Nat, Prairie St, Am Med Assns; Bd Dirs Roosevelt Meml Hosp Hlth Plan; Mem Ill Dept Registration & Ed Nsg Opinions; cp/Dir & VP Better Boys Foun; Dir & Chm Exec Com Hyde Park Bank & Trust Co; Dir Step Sch Retard Chd; Dir Adlai Stevenson Inst of Intl Studies; Exec Coun BSA; Dir Urban Fund, Chgo Area Comml Bks; Dir 5050 S St Med & Shopping Complex; Former Commun Resource Advr DePaul Univ; r/Prot; hon/Friendship Awd; LuPalmer Foun; Silver Beaver Awd, BSA; Black Liberation Awd, Kuumba Wkshop; Pres' Awd for 25 Yrs Ser to Mankind, Meharry Med Col.

CLARKSON, HAZEL LILLIAN SANDERS oc/Educator; b/Nov 21, 1902; h/Rt 2, Box 302, Jamestown, KY 42629; m/James Arless; c/Curtis C, Viola C Thomas, Victor W (dec), Nelda C Walker, Lula C Peffey, Neleta C Jefferies; p/John Fletcher and Florence Elizabeth Sanders (dec); ed/AA; BS; ME; Addit Studies; pa/Elem Tchr 27 Yrs; Ceramicist 10 Yrs; Painter; Fam Hist Writer; Author, *Forgotten Acres or The Cochran Spawning Ground;* Nat Ret'd Tchrs Assn; KEA; Russell Co Chapt RTA; cp/Past 4-H Ldr; Wom's Vet Aux; Var Ednl Clbs; Nat Hist Soc; Ky Hist Soc; Nat Assn Ret'd Persons; Vol w Coun on Aging; r/Christian; hon/Hon Ky Col; Rec'd Awds from 4-H, Others; Fam Chosen for Book, *Ky Bicent Register* (1976); DIB; Others.

CLATANOFF, DORIS ANN oc/Associate Professor; b/Jan 29, 1932; h/1278 N 6 St, Seward, NE 68434; ba/Seward; m/Duane Bernhard; c/Clark, Craig; p/Fred R and Marie

F Goeller Risch, Howells, NE; ed/BA magna cum laude Midland Luth Col; MAE Wayne St Col; PhD Univ Neb-L; pa/Assoc Prof English Concordia Col; MLA; NCTE; Nat Assn for Humanities Ed; Soc for Study of MWn Lit; Willa Cather Foun; Neb Coun Tchrs of Eng; AAUW; cp/GFWC; LWML; St Dir for Miss Neb Nat Teen-Ager Pageant; Bd Trustees Midland Luth Col; Exec Com Midland Alumni Assn; IPA; r/Luth; hon/Admiral, Navy of Neb.

CLAUDEL, CALVIN ANDRE oc/Writer, Editor; b/Jul 7, 1909; h/PO Box 1083, Chalmette, LA 70044; ba/Chalmette; m/Alice McLeod Moser; p/Andre Emile and Leota Edwards Claudel (dec); ed/BA; MA; PhD; mil/USMCR; pa/Asst Editor *The New Laurel Review*; Assoc Editor *Claudel Studies*; Author *Fools and Rascals: Louisiana Folktales*; cp/VP St Bernard Hist Soc; r/Epis; Mem Epis Peace F'ship; hon/Phi Beta Kappa; French Acad Palms; Others.

CLAUSEN, HENRY CHRISTIAN oc/- Lawyer; b/Jun 30, 1905; h/36 San Jacinto Way, San Francisco, CA 94127; ba/Washington DC; m/Virginia Palmer; c/Henry Christian, Florian Elliot (Mrs William), Donald, Karen; p/Louis and Lena Clausen; ed/JD Univ SF 1927; Postgrad: Univ Cal-SF 1927-32, Univ Mich 1942-43; mil/AUS 1942-45, Served to Lt Col Judge Advocate Gen's Dept; Legion of Merit; pa/Admitted to Cal Bar 1927; Pract SF 1927-; Asst US Atty No Dist Cal, Chief Counsel for Chief Engr Joseph B Strauss (During Constn of Golden Gate Bridge) 1931-33; Law Assoc Judge George E Crothers, Thomas G Crothers, Francis V Keesling & Sons 1946-67; Nat Lwyrs Clb Wash; cp/Mason: Ks Templar, Shriner, Sovereign Grand Cmdr, Supreme Coun, Ancient & Accepte Scottish Rite of Masonry, So Juris, USA 1969-, Editor in Chief of Monthly Mag *The New Age*; Mem Var Clbs; Mem & Pres Cal Jr C of C; Pres SF YMCA; Trustee George Washington Univ; r/Congreg; hon/Contbr Articles to Pubs; Author: *Messages for a Mission, Masons Who Helped Shape Our Nation.*

CLAUSEN, ROBERT HOWARD oc/Ordained Clergyman; Author; Playwright; b/Dec 12, 1927; h/403 N Plum Grove Rd, Palatine, IL 60067; ba/Palatine; m/Elsbeth Margarete; c/Kristen Adele, Christopher Noel, Kara Michele; p/Walter P and Lydia

Clausen, El Paso, TX; ed/BA; MFA; mil/AUS Chaplain; pa/Pastor Immanuel Luth Ch, Palatine; Chperson Communs Com Luth No Ill Dist; Author & Dir Rel Plays; cp/Mem Palatine Rel Coun; r/Luth Ch-Mo Synod: Ordained Clergyman; hon/Phi Kappa Phi.

CLAUSON, ALBERTA AYER oc/Retired School Librarian; b/May 5, 1913; h/Rt One, Ashby, MN 56309; m/Bruce Kenmore; c/Bruce, Kay, Christopher; p/Charles E and Inez M Randall Ayer (dec); ed/BEd; Lib Sci Deg; pa/Life Mem Ret'd Tchr Minn; Delta Kappa Gamma; cp/Ottertail Co Mus Soc: Libn, Life Mem; Mem Local Ret'd Sr Vol Prog; Vol Wkshop, Gov's Ofc of Vol Sers; Other Civic Activs; r/Luth: Mem & Ofcr ALCW.

CLAVENNA, LeROY RUSSELL oc/- Chemical Engineer; b/May 12, 1943; ba/PO Box 4255, Baytown, TX 77520; m/Joyce Elaine Engelhardt; c/Michael, Andrew; p/Robert M

and Josephine M Clavenna; ed/BS Univ Ill 1966; PhD Univ Minn 1971; pa/Chem Engr Exxon Res & Engrg Co; Am Inst Chem Engrs; Soc for Profl Chemists & Engrs; cp/Am Heart Assn; CPR Intr; r/Rom Cath; hon/Rotary S'ship; Univ Ill Transfer Tuition S'ship; Univ Ill S'ship; NDEA F'ship; Minn Ind F'ship.

CLAWSON, DELWIN (DEL) MORGAN oc/United States Congressman; b/Jan 11, 1914; h/9117 Manzanar Ave, Downey, CA 90240; ba/Washington DC; m/Marjorie Anderson; c/Delwin L (dec), James B; p/Charles Moses Jr and Edna Allen Clawson (dec); pa/Mem US Ho of Reps, Cal 33rd Dist; cp/Past Pres & Past Lt Gov Kiwanis Intl; Mem Pk & Rec Comm; City Coun & Mayor, Compton, Cal; Mem LA Co Sanitation Dists; r/Mormon; hon/Citizen of Yr, Compton; Silver Beaver, BSA; Statesman of Yr, Nat Assn Ind Bus; Watchdog of Treasury.

CLAY, WILLIE B SR oc/Clergyman; Administrator; ba/77 W Washington St, Chicago, IL 60602; m/Ruth Davis; c/Gladys, Willie Jr, Jonathan, Margo, Lara; p/H C Sr and Clara Washington Clay (dec); ed/Grad Rust Col 1954; Att'd Gammon Theol Sem; Former Pastorates: Miss, Ind, Ill; Current Coun Dir No Ill Conf, U Meth Ch; Bd Trustees N Ctl Col; Bd Trustees Gammon Theol Sem; Mem Kendall Col Corp; Mem No Ill Conf Bd Missions; Mem Exec Com of Chgo Black Meths for Ch Renewal; Nat Black Meths for Ch Renewal; Del to Gen & Juris Confs 1972; Former Dist Supt Chgo So Dist; No Ill Conf Coun on Fin & Adm; Juris Coun Dirs' F'ship; Chperson No Ill Conf Dept Communs; Others; cp/Rotary Clb Chgo; Ck Fdn Gtr Chgo; Others; r/U Meth Ch; hon/Hon DDiv, Wiley Col; Recipient S'ship.

CLAYBAUGH, GLENN A oc/Sales Administration; b/Dec 10, 1927; h/1612 Russell Ave, Evansville, IN 47712; ba/E'ville; m/Mary Lou; c/Lloyd, Cynthia; p/Joseph H and Helen K Claybaugh (dec); ed/BS Univ Neb; MS Mich St Univ; PhD Ia St Univ; mil/248th Gen Hosp, APO 74, Clark Field, Philippines 1946-47; pa/Sales Adm Mead Johnson & Co; ADSA; AAAS; ASM; AMA; AAPA; NAPNAP; Fellow: APHA, RSM; cp/Boy Scout Com; U Way; Freedom Fest; r/Trinity U Meth Ch, E'ville; hon/Dist'd Gov Ind Dist, Kiwanis Intl 1976; Pres Awd, Mead Johnson & Co.

CLAYTON, SHERYL ANNE oc/Library Administrator; b/May 17, 1929; h/4831 Washington Park Blvd, Washington Park, IL 62204; ba/E St Louis, IL; c/Ruth C Robbins (Mrs Wendell Jr), Wynne T, Elbert G, Edgar M; p/Maurice L Howard, Washington Park; Mrs M L K Howard, Denison, TX; ed/BA; MSLS; MS (Cnslg & Guid); pa/Dir Public Lib; Am Lib Assn; cp/Bd Ed Mem Dist 184; Public Spkr; r/Christian Scist; hon/Ill Club Wom's Awd; Friend of Chd Awd; NACW Awd.

CLAYTON, WILLIAM HOWARD oc/College President; b/Aug 16, 1922; h/54 Adler Cir, Galveston, TX 77550; ba/Galveston; m/Dee; c/Jill, Greg; ed/BS Bucknell Univ 1949; PhD Tex A&M Univ 1956; mil/Royal Canadian AF 1940-43; USAF 1943-45; pa/Tex A&M Univ: Pres Moody Col 1977-, Provost Moody Col Marine Scis & Maritime Resources 1974-77, Dean Col Marine & Maritime Resources 1971-74, Assoc Dean Col Geoscis 1970-71, Prof Oceanography 1965-, Prof Meteorology 1965-, Other Positions, Prin Investigator Tex A&M Res Foun 1956-65; Other Profl Positions; Gulf Univs Res Consortium: Trustee Tex A&M Univ Sys 1971-, Chm 1977-79; Am Meteorol Soc; Am Geophysical Union; Simulation Couns; Sigma Phi Epsilon; Other Frat Orgs; cp/Galveston Marine Affairs Coun; Former Mem Bd Dirs Galveston C of C; Bd Dirs Bank of W; Commr Police & Fire Dept Civil Ser Bd, City of Galveston; Bd Dirs Galveston UF; Others; r/Prot; hon/Pub'd Author; Biogl Listings.

CLAYTOR, ANNE MARIE oc/Assistant Professor; b/Oct 29, 1925; h/16 Green Hill Rd, Morristown, NI 07960; p/Lester and

Constance Claytor (dec); ed/MA; EdD Rutgers Univ; pa/Asst Prof Ed Col of St Elizabeth Convent Sta; Exec Dir Inst for Ed of Wom; r/Cath; hon/Outstg Edr of Am; Grants: NSF, Ford Foun, NJ Dept of Ed.

CLEARY, JAMES WILLIAM oc/University President; b/Apr 16, 1927; h/19855 Septo St, Chatsworth, CA 91311; ba/Northridge, CA; m/Mary Augustyne; c/Colleen, Patricia, Janet; p/James W Cleary (dec); Mrs James W Cleary, Milwaukee, WI; ed/PhB; AM; PhD; mil/AUS Inf 1945-47; pa/Cal St Univ-N: Pres, Prof Speech Communication 1969-; Univ Wis: VChancellor for Acad Affairs, Prof Spch 1966-69, Asst Chancellor & Prof Spch 1965-66, Prof Spch Dept 1963-69, Other Positions; Parliamentn Am Assn St Cols &

Univs 1974-; Chm CSUC Chancellor's Coun of Presidents 1976-78; Fdg Chair & Mem Tri-Val Alliance for Higher Ed 1974-; Chm Wn Assn Schs & Cols Spec Com on Accreditation Standards 1977-78; Chm Am Assn St Cols & Univs Cult Affairs Com 1977-80; Other Profl Activs; cp/Mem Ad Hoc Com on City Fins, Los Angeles; Bd Dirs Val Fed Savs & Ln Assn; Former Mem Bd Dirs The Soc of Experimental Test Pilots S'ship Foun; Bd Dirs Am Inst Parliaments; Other Civic Activs; r/Rom Cath; hon/Var Tchg Awds; Mem Hon Socs; Pub'd Author; Biogl Listings.

CLEAVER, EDGAR M oc/Administrator; b/May 29, 1926; h/3442 E 84th Pl, Tulsa, OK 74136; ba/Tulsa; m/Jeanne; c/Lori C Broermaun, Janet C Vaughn, Victor, Mary Jo, Edgar T; p/Edgar M and Moitee Cleaver, Venango, NE; ed/AB 1952; MD 1954; Further Studies; mil/USNR; pa/Dir Wichita-Sedgwick Co Dept Commun Hlth, Wichita, Ks 1977-, Dir Public Hlth for Waco & McLennan Co (Tex) 1972-77; Dir Weld Co Hlth Dept, Greeley, Col 1968-72; Other Former Positions; AMA; Am Public Hlth Assn; Am Assn Public Hlth Physicians; Soc Tchrs of Fam Med; Christian Med Soc; Tex Med Assn; McLennan Co Med Soc; Ks Med Soc; Med Soc Sedgwick Co; Ks Public Hlth Assn; Other Profl Assnl Activs; cp/Past Pres Colo Assn Home Hlth Care Agys; Former Mem Profl Adv Com to Foun for Urban & Neighborhood Devel, Denver; Former Mem St Adv Coun to Tex Comm on Alcoholism; Former Mem Bd Dirs McLennan Co Comprehensive Hlth Planning Coun; Bd Trustees US Conf City Hlth Ofcrs; Bd Dirs Mid-Way Ks Chapt ARC; r/Bapt; hon/Cert of Cit, St of Tex Ho of Reps for Dist'd Ser; Personalities: S, W&MW; W/W in Tex.

CLELAND, JOHN GEORGE P oc/- Physician, Surgeon; b/Sept 18, 1898; h/14343 Clackamas Riv Dr S, Oregon City, OR 97045; ba/Oregon City; m/Beatrice C (dec); c/John Eastmore, Donald, Beverly Ann, Molly C Ellis; p/John Alexander and Mary S Gourlay Cleland (dec); ed/MD; CM; MSc; mil/RAF 2/Lt 1918; pa/Res; Phys; Writer; Orgl Activs; r/Epis; hon/Sci Exhibit, AMA, Hon Mention; Dist'd Ser Awd; 1st (Sr) Citizen, Oregon City 1969; Oreg Doct of Yr 1970; Prof Emeritus Ob-Gyn, Univ Oreg Med Sch.

CLEMA, JOE KOTOUC oc/Computer Scientist; b/Sept 23, 1938; h/6128 Martingale, Dayton, OH 45459; ba/Dayton; m/Mary Chipman; c/Jennifer Arta; p/Mr and Mrs Joe A Clema, Alvin, TX; ed/BS Univ Neb 1963; MS Univ Miami 1969; PhD Colo St Univ 1973;

mil/AUS Corps of Engrs 1963-67, Capt; pa/Computer Scist Simulation Tech Inc; Soc for Simulation; AAAS; Assn for Computer Machinery; Assn for Computer Programmers & Analysts Chapt Org, Denver-Fort Collins, Colo Area; IEEE; Nat Mgmt Assn; Sr Mem Am Inst Indust Engrs; AF Assn; hon/Rensselaer Medal for Sci & Math, Rensselaer Polytech Inst; Frankfurter Ldrship Awd, Univ Neb; Outstg Ofcr Chem Sch, US Army Ofcr's Tng Sch; W/W MW; DIB; Others.

CLEMENS, DAVID ALLEN oc/Clergyman; b/Aug 8, 1941; h/72 Knox Blvd, Marlton, NJ 08053; ba/Upper Darby, PA; m/Janice Bonino; c/Stephen, Daniel; p/Arleigh Allen and Mae Elizabeth Clemens, Woodbury, NJ; ed/BA magna cum laude Houghton Col; MA Nat Christian Univ; pa/Missionary 1963-66: Argentina, Paraguay, Brazil, SAm; Interim Pastor Richfield

Mennonite Ch (Pa) 1966-67; The Bible Club Movement Inc 1971-76: Missionary, Bible Tchr, Nat Rep; Dir Fam/Adult Mins Dept 1977-; Writer 4-Volume Book Series Titled *Steps to Maturity*; Bible Tchg/Preaching Tours: England, Belgium, Holland, Sweden, Spain, Mid East; r/Bapt; hon/W/W: Am Univs & Cols, Rel; DIB; Commun Ldrs & Noteworthy Ams.

CLEMENTS, LOUIE O oc/Student; b/-Dec 10, 1952; h/Lee Col, Box 908, Cleveland, TN 37311; ba/Cleveland; m/Susan; p/(Stepfather) Art and Alere Walters, Tifton, GA; ed/BA Cand Bible Ed & Missionary Ed Lee Col; mil/USN; r/Ch of God, Cleveland Penecostal; hon/Featured in Newspaper Articles after rescue feat.

CLEMENTS, RITA CROCKER oc/Civic Leader; h/Austin, TX; m/Gov William P Jr; c/Dan Bass, Bonnie Bass, Barbara Bass, Jim Bass; p/Mason and Florabel Crocker, Brady, TX; ed/Grad cum laude Univ Tex 1953; pa/Former Mem Bd Dirs Lange Co Investments; Real Est; cp/Nat Adv Coun for Ec Opport 1972-75; Nat Vol Ser Adv Coun, Chmships 1973-75; Past Pres Jr Leag Dallas Inc; Past Bd Mbrships incl'g: Ec Task Force of Goals for Dallas, KERA-TV, Wom's Adv Bd Univ Dallas, St Michael Sch, Adventure Trails for Girls, Ednl Opports, Dallas Soc for Crippled Chd, Hockaday Sch; Present Bd Mbrships: U Way Dallas, Winston Sch, Fine Arts Com Dept St, Wolf Trap Foun; Del Repub Nat Conv 1968; Repub Nat Com 1973-75; Org Chm Repub Party Tex 1966, 68, 72; Other Polit Activs; r/St Michael & All Angels Epis Ch, Dallas.

CLEMONS, MAE O oc/Educator; b/Oct 10, 1946; h/1215 Barcia St, Pensacola, FL 32503; ba/Pensacola; p/Ernest C Clemons (dec); Rosa L Clemons, St Petersburg, FL; ed/AA Gibbs Jr Col 1965; BA 1966, MEd 1969 Fla Agri & Mech Univ; PhD Fla St Univ 1974; pa/Pensacola Jr Col: Dir Writing Lab & Chperson Dept Rdg & Interim Studies 1978-, Asst Prof Eng 1976-77; Asst Prof Eng Berry Col 1974-76; Instr Eng Ed Fla St Univ 1972-74; Instr/Sch Coor for Proj Upward Bound 1967-68; Other Positions; Conslt; Lectr; NCTE; Conf on Eng Ed; NEA; Fla Ed Assn; Fla Coun Tchrs Eng; Fla Commun Col Rdg Coun; cp/Alpha Kappa Alpha; Links Inc; YWCA, Mem Nat YWCA So Reg Bd (2); r/Bapt; hon/Lambda Iota Tau; Num Cits, Awds &

Plaques from Var Social, Ednl & Civic Orgs; Profl Pubs; Biogl Listings.

CLENDENING, JOHN ALBERT oc/Geologist; Palynologist; b/Mar 6, 1932; h/1018 Tulip Tree Ln, Houston, TX 77090; ba/Houston; m/Cleo Dorothy; c/Kyra, Rebecca, Shawna; p/Charles Brady Clendening (dec); Florence M Clendening, Charles Town, WV; ed/BS; MS; PhD; mil/AUS 1951-54; pa/Fellow Geol Soc Am; Am Assn Stratigraphic Palynologists: Secy-Treas, VP 1976-77, Councilor 1975-76; r/Prot.

CLEVELAND, CROMWELL COOK JR oc/Chaplain Supervisor; b/Dec 6, 1948; h/1836 Fairmount Ave, Cincinnati, OH 45214; ba/Cincinnati; p/Cromwell C Sr and Gene Rickey Cleveland, Lee, KY; ed/BA Centre Col; MDiv Gen Theol Sem; pa/Specializing in Pastoral Care & Cnslg, Diocese of Mo; Assn Clin Pastoral Ed; r/Epis: Priest; hon/Westminster Catachism Scholar; Horace B Domegan Prize for Excell.

CLEVELAND, GAINES HIGHTOWER oc/Political Graphics Consultant; b/Jun 1, 1957; h/1916 Beach Dr, Gulfpont, MS 39501; ba/Washington DC; p/Dr and Mrs C Hal Cleveland, Gulfpont, MS; ed/BA Georgetown Univ; pa/Fdr & Partner Potomac Assocs; Graphics Conslt Graphic Communs Assocs; Communs Dir Col Repub Nat Com; Editor *The College Republican*; Dir Wash Campus News Ser; cp/Chm Nat Col Repub St Chm's Assn; Chm Miss Col Repubs; Chm Gulf Coast Jour Clb; r/Presb; hon/Miss St Debate Champ; Phi Eta Sigma; Univ Scholar; Phi Kappa Phi S'ship Awd.

CLEVELAND, GENE RICKEY oc/Type Setter; b/Oct 22, 1914; h/3564 Lansdowne Dr, Lexington, KY 40503; ba/Lexington; m/Cromwell Cook Sr; c/Cromwell Cook Jr; p/Homer Herron and Ruth Nystrom Rickey (dec); ed/Att'd Univ Chgo; pa/Type Setter Printing Sers, Univ Ky; cp/Pres Mins' Wives, Newport News, Va; Ctl Ky Wom's Clb; Pres Kiwanis Ladies, Newton, Ia; Profl Wkr ARC, WWII; r/Disciples of Christ.

CLEVELAND, HATTYE MAE oc/Occupational Therapist; b/Sept 22, 1911; h/22 Union Ave, Mount Vernon, NY 10550; m/John Marion Jr III; p/William Guy and Rosa lee Johnson (dec); ed/BS (Sci); BS (Home Ecs); Cert Occupl Therapy; pa/Supvr, Occupl Therapist; AOTA; WFOT; MNYD OTA;

NYS OTA; Pt Care Plann/Disch Comms; Shaw Univ Nat Assn, Local Chapt; cp/NCNW; LWV; WOM Task Force; Commun Coun Sers; Supt Coun Westchester; The Pres' Clb; r/Prot; hon/Alumni Achmt Awd, Shaw Univ; Nat Coun Negro Wom Inc; Montefiore Hosp & Med Ctr; IPA; Others.

CLEVELAND, OLLIE ANCIL JR oc/Economist; b/Feb 21, 1945; h/5 Colonial Cir, Starkville, MS 39759; ba/Miss St, MS; m/Martha; c/Mary Christina, Tres; p/Ollie A and A Bernice Cleveland, Lexington, MS; ed/BS 1967, MS 1970 Miss St; PhD Okla St 1976; mil/AUS Signal Corps, 1/Lt; pa/Agri Economist USDA 1970-71, 1972-77; Instr Univ Md 1972-77; Mktg Specialist Miss Cooperative Ext Ser 1977-; Agri Columnist; AAEA; SAEA; WAEA; MAEA; Gamma Sigma Delta; Alpha Zeta; Omicron Delta Kappa; cp/Commun Fund Chm; Rotary; Sch Bd; VFW; Am Legion; r/1st Bapt Ch; hon/Bronze Star; Miss

Sportsman of Yr.

CLEVENGER, ERNEST ALLEN oc/Manufacturing Executive; b/Oct 22, 1908; h/807 Hurricane Creek Rd, Chattanooga, TN 37421; ba/Chatta; m/(dec); c/Ernest Jr, Robert G, Michael Dale, Alice Cooper; p/(dec); ed/McKenzie Col; Cooke Sch Elect Engrg; Intl Corres Sch; Cadek Conserv Music, Univ Chatta; Dale Carnegie Ldrship Instrs' Sch; pa/Corley Mfg Co: Chm of Bd 1976-, Pres 1969, Bd Dirs 1947-, VP 1947, Sales Mgr 1939, Asst Sales Mgr 1934, Joined 1929; Nat Assn Mfrs; Forest Prods Res Soc; Am Wood

Preservers Assn; IPA; cp/Bd Trustees Boyd-Buchanan Sch; Rotary Clb Chatta; Gtr Chatta C of C; Dir TB & Respiratory Diseases Assn; Voc Ednl Adv Coun, Hamilton Co Voc Ed Gov'g Bd; Chatta Golf & CC; Former Activs; r/Brainerd Ch of Christ: Mem; hon/Tenn Outstg Man of Yr in Forestry 1957; Patriot's Medal, SAR; Ky Col; Tenn Col; Admiral of Fleet of Ky's Waterways; Exec of Yr, Chatta Chapt NSA 1978; Biogl Listings.

CLEVENGER, HORACE MARSHALL oc/Operations Research Analyst; b/Dec 21, 1913; h/21 Almeda Pl, Ferguson, MO 63135; ba/St Louis, MO; m/Roberta Walter; c/John Walter (dec), Robert Marshall, Donna Jean Phelps; p/Charles Henry and Edna Marcia Clevenger (dec); ed/BSA Purdue Univ; MS Ohio St Univ; pa/Opers Res Analyst (US

Govt); Dept of Army, St Louis, OPA & Statistician 1957-; Statistician Dept Agri, Columbus, Ohio 1941-53; Am Statistical Assn; Am Ec Assn; Opers Res Soc Am; Am Soc for Quality Control; cp/Mason; Past Pres Ferguson Toastmasters Clb; r/Immanual U Ch of Christ, Ferguson: Mem; hon/S'ship to Purdue Univ, 4-H.

CLEWETT, KENNETH V oc/Hospital Administrator; b/Jun 3, 1923; h/3102 E Highland Ave, Patton, CA 92369; ba/Patton; m/Margery Haas; c/Richard, Bruce, Curtis, Janet; p/Heber H Clewett Sr (dec); Thelma Clewett, Pomona, CA; ed/AA Pomona Jr Col 1943; Ensign Midshipmen's Sch, Columbia Univ 1944; BA Stanford Univ 1947; mil/USN 1943-46, Lt (jg); pa/Hosp Exec Dir Patton St Hosp 1976-; Hosp Admr Fairview St Hosp, Costa Mesa, Cal 1972-76; Sonoma St Hosp, Eldridge, Cal: Hosp Admr 1960-72, Pers Dir 1952-60; Asst Pers Ofcr Cal St Dept Mtl Hygiene, Sacramento, Cal 1950-52; Pers Examr Cal St Pers Bd 1947-50; Other Former Positions; Assn Mtl Hlth Admrs, USA, Canada & Mexico: Pres 1976, Wn Reg Gov 1967-72; Pres Redwood Empire Hosp Conf 1967; Fdg Pres Pers Assn Sonoma Co 1958; Bd Dirs: Assn Mtl Hlth Admrs 1967-72, 1974-76,

Comprehensive Hlth Planning Assn Sonoma Co 1968-72, Eldridge Foun for the Retarded 1969-72, Pers Assn Sonoma Co 1958-60, Sonoma Co Hlth Facilities Planning Com 1964-65; Adv Com on Hlth Care Curric George Wash Univ 1970-; Num Other Profl Activs; cp/Bd Dirs So Cal Col; San Bernardino Area C of C; Num Former Activs; r/San Bernardino Commun Ch, San Bernardino: Mem 1978-; Newport-Mesa Christian Ctr, Costa Mesa, Cal: Deacon 1975-76, Mem 1974-78; Others; hon/Outstg Ser Awd, Redwood Empire Hosp Conf; Citizens Awd of Yr, Val of Moon Tchrs Assn 1970; Hon Life Mem, Alpha Gamma Sigma; Biogl Listings.

CLIFTON, ROSE MARY oc/Extension Home Economist; b/Oct 11, 1940; h/PO Box 373, 608 Sunset Dr, Frederick, OK 73542; ba/Frederick; m/John P; c/Paulette, Connie; p/Mary Culver, Duncan, OK; ed/BS; pa/Ext Home Economist Okla St Univ; Nat & Okla Assns Ext Home Economists; Am Home Ecs Assn; cp/Ext Homemaker 4-H Clbs; Adult & Yth Ednl Progs; r/U Meth Ch: Mem; hon/BPW Wom of Month; Wom of Yr, Beta Sigma Phi.

CLINE, RAY STEINER oc/Educator; Writer; b/Jun 4, 1918; h/3027 N Pollard St, Arlington, VA 22207; ba/Washington DC; m/Marjorie Wilson; c/Judith M Fontaine, Sibyl W Halper; p/Charles and Ina May Steiner Cline (dec); ed/AB 1939, MA 1941, PhD 1949 Harvard Univ; pa/Govt Res: OSS 1942-45, Army 1946-49; Dep Dir for Intell CIA 1949-69; Dir Intell & Res St Dept 1969-73; Adj Prof & Exec Dir Strategic & Intl Studies Georgetown Univ; r/Prot; hon/Dist'd Intell Medal, Career Intell Medal, US Govt.

CLINEBELL, HOWARD oc/Professor; b/Jun 3, 1922; ba/Claremont Grad Sch; m/Charlotte Ellen; c/John, Don, Susan; ed/BA cum laude DePauw Univ 1944; BD summa cum laude Garrett Theol Sem 1947; PhD Columbia Univ 1954; Further Studies; pa/Sch of Theol Claremont: Prof Pastoral Cnslg 1959, Fac Mem Claremont Grad Sch, Dept Psychol & Dept Rel; Lectr Dept Rel Ed NY Univ 1955-57; Mem Sum Schs Facs: Garrett Theol Sem, Pacific Sch Rel, Iliff Sch Theol, Yale Sum Sch Alcohol Studies, Univ Utah Sch Alcohol Studies; Lectr; Co-Led (w wife) 7 Insts on Cnslg, India 1970; Wkshop Ldr for Cnslrs & Clergy in Other Countries; Guest Prof Univ Stellenbosch, S Africa 1978; Clin Dir Pomona Val Pastoral Cnslg & Growth Ctrs 1976-78; Dir: Claremont Area Pastoral Cnslg Ctr 1963-65, Pasadena Area Pastoral Cnslg Ctr 1959-63; Var Pastorates; Am Assn Pastoral Cnslrs: 1/Pres, Diplomate; Am Assn Marriage & Fam Therapists; Fellow Am Orthopsychi Assn; Am Soc Group Psychotherapy & Psychodrama; Intl Assn Group Psychotherapy; Assn for Humanistic Psychol; British Assn for Advmt of Pastoral Care & Cnslg, Coun Mem; Others Assnl Mbrships; Var Profl Activs; hon/4th Annual Awd, Assn Couples for Marriage Enrichmt; Spec Recog Awd, Cal Assn Marriage & Fam Therapists; Grants; Man of Month, Pastoral Psychol Mag, April 1962; Person of Yr, Dist'd Contbn Awd, Am Assn Pastoral Cnslrs 1974; Num Biogl Listings.

CLINGER, GRACE JUNE oc/Retired Teacher; Businesswoman; b/Jun 6, 1907; h/PO Box 433, 335 W Eisenhower Blvd, Loveland, OH 80537; p/Orrin Ace and Mary Ann Clinger, Loveland; ed/AB 1936; Master's 1938; Addit Studies; pa/Tchr 43 Yrs; Loveland Tchrs' Assn, Co & St; Nat Ret'd Tchrs Assn; AAUW; Philomatheon Clb; Motel Assn; Owned & Managed Trailer Ct 29 Yrs; Bldr of Homes; Owner Lakeview Apts 28 Yrs, Lake Side Motel 25 Yrs; Dealer: Amphicars 8 Yrs, Mobile Homes 10 Yrs; Distbr, Dealer Fascination Car; Other Profl Activs; r/Presb; hon/Skelly Agri Achmt Awd 1943; Num Recogs for Contbns; W/W Am Wom; Notable Ams; Commun Ldrs & Noteworthy Ams.

CLINTON, STEPHEN M oc/Teacher; Minister; b/Aug 21, 1944; h/5105 Louise, San Bernardino, CA 92407; ba/Arrowhead

Springs, CA; m/Virginia Ann; c/Matthew, Michael; p/Thomas Francis Clinton (dec); Bettie Lee Footy; ed/BA; MA; MDiv; PhD; pa/Dir Curric & Ext, Sch of Theol; Evang Theol Soc; IPA; cp/PTA; r/Evang Free Ch: Ordained.

CLINTON, WILLIAM CHRISTOPHER oc/Physicist; b/Aug 19, 1937; h/PO Box 1125, Rolla, MO 65401; ba/Rolla; m/Elizabeth P DeWandel; p/William Milford and Mary Avo Thorpe Clinton, Joplin, MO; ed/BA William Jewell Col 1966; mil/USAF Aeromed Res Lab, Med Lab Tech;

pa/Physicist US Bur of Mines, Rolla Metall Res Ctr; Microbeam Analysis Soc; Intl Metall Soc; Sigma Xi; Contbr Articles to Tech Jours; cp/Former Chm Rolla Combined Fed Campaign; Former Mem Bd Dirs: Rolla Civic Theatre, Alamogordo (NM) Players Wkshop; Rolla Lions Clb: Secy, Former Treas; Dist Gov Lions Dist 26-J.

CLIPPER, JOSEPH DANIEL oc/Photographer; Executive; b/Dec 3, 1937; h/6445 Luzon Ave NW, Washington DC 20012; ba/Wash DC; c/Juana Danita, Jannell Hope; p/Herman Stanley Clipper (dec); Viola Elizabeth Whitby, Wash DC; ed/Cath Univ; Doscher Country Sch Photo; Winona Sch Profl Photogs; Joseph Zeltsman Portrait Sch; mil/AUS 1961-63; pa/Portraiture Photog; Pres Clipper Assocs Inc; Former Secy Md Profl Photogs; Lectr; Profl Photogs Am Inc; Bd Dirs Md Profl Photogs; cp/Past Pres Armstrong Alumni Assn DC; Pigskin Clb Wash Inc; r/Rel Sci; hon/Pvt Collections of His Portraits: Philippine Isls, Caribbean Isls, Africa, US.

CLISE, DOROTHEA V oc/Registered Nurse; b/Feb 14, 1914; h/3025 N Meridian #506, Indianapolis, IN 46208; m/(dec); c/W Kent; p/Frederick A and Elva B McCallian (dec); ed/RN 1936; Att'd Taylor & Butler Univs; pa/Ret'd 1962, Supvn Med Res & Statistics; r/Presb; hon/W/W Am Wom.

CLOGAN, PAUL MAURICE oc/Professor; b/Jul 9, 1934; ba/PO Box 13348, N Tex Sta, Denton, TX 76203; m/Julie Sydney; c/Michael Rodger, Patrick Terence, Margaret Murphy; p/Michael and Agnes J Clogan (dec); ed/BA; MA; PhD; FAAR; pa/Prof Eng N Tex

St Univ; Editor *Medievalia et Humanistica*; Prog Com Mod Lang Assn Am; r/Rom Cath; hon/Sr Fulbright-Hays Res F'ships, Italy & France; Fellow: Nat Endowmt for Humanities, Am Coun Learned Socs, Am Philosophical Soc; Author 7 Books & Num Articles in Profl Jours.

CLOSSER, PATRICK D oc/Printer;

Businessman; b/Apr 27, 1945; h/3875 Dunhaven Rd, Dallas, TX 75220; ba/Dallas; p/E B and Helen M Thompson, Dunhaven; ed/Dipl Am Schs of Cinema; BFA; pa/TV, Radio, Film, Mission Fields; Printer; Intl Christian Broadcasters; SMPTE; cp/JCs; r/Epis; hon/Awd, Repub Party 1962.

CLOUDEN, LaVERNE CAROLE oc/Music Director; b/Dec 6, 1933; h/3851 E 151 St, Cleveland, OH 44128; ba/Cleve; m/Aubrey B; c/Norman, Nathan, Karen Duncan; p/Edward C Mosley, Los Angeles, CA; Virginia M Evans, Cleve; ed/BS, MA Case Wn Reserve Univ; pa/Dir Instrumental Music, John F Kennedy Sr; Wom Band Dirs Nat Assn; Ohio Music Edrs Assn; MENC; Dir: Mt Pleasant Musicians Guild, Cleve Band Masters Assn; Nat Bd Mem: Am Yth Symph & Chorus; Com Mem All-City HS Band; r/Prot; hon/Mu Phi Epsilon; Cert of Congrats, Mayor of Cleve; S'ship; Grad Cum Laude; Lecture Recital Clb Awd; Num Trophies; 1st Wom HS Band Dir, Cleve.

CLOUSE, JOHN D oc/Lawyer; b/Sep 4, 1925; h/819 S Hebron Ave, Evansville, IN 47715; ba/E'ville; m/Georgia Lynn; c/George Chauncey; p/Frank P Clouse (dec); Anna L Clouse, E'ville; ed/AB E'ville Col 1950; JD Indiana Univ 1952; mil/AUS 1943-46; pa/Assoc'd w Atty James D Lopp 1952-56; Pvt Pract of Law 1956-; Past VP, E'ville Bar Assn; Ser'd on Com on Implementation of Criminal Justice Act of 1964, Indiana St Bar Assn; Fellow, Ind Bar Foun 1979-; 2nd Asst City Atty, E'ville 1954-55; cp/Guest Editorialist: *E'ville Courier* 1978-, Radio Sta WGBF 1978-; Selden Soc; Past Pres, Civil Ser Comm of E'ville Police Dept; Judicial Nom'g Com, Vanderburgh Co; Appellate Rules Subcom, Ind Supreme Ct Com on Rules of Pract & Procedure; hon/Bronze Star; Pi Gamma Mu.

COALSON, JOYCE BASEY oc/Minister; b/Jul 4, 1943; h/6915 LaSalle, Austin, TX 78723; ba/Austin; m/Robert Lewis; p/Harold L and Norma Claar Basey, Greeley, CO; ed/BA Phillips Univ; MDiv Christian Theol Sem; pa/Min Christian Ch; Wom in Interim Min Proj: Served 4 Chs in Ks, Okla & Tex; r/Disciples of Christ: Bd Dirs Ch Fin Coun.

COATES, CHARLES R oc/Professor; b/Nov 2, 1915; h/RD 3, Box 55, Shippensburg, PA 17257; ba/S'burg; m/Lucille M; c/Charles R Jr, John Thomas, Christopher Scott; p/John Wesley and Hattie Price Coates (dec); ed/EdD Univ Va 1965; MEd William & Mary; mil/USN WWII, Korean Conflict, Meteorologist; pa/Prof Cnslg S'burg St Col; Ednl Advr Quartermaster Sch, Ft Lee, Va 1962-65; Supvr Guid Southampton Public Schs 1958-62; Other Former Positions; AAAS; NEA; APGA; Am Ednl Res Assn; IPA; Phi Delta Kappa; cp/Var Commun Activs; r/Meth; hon/Pub'd Author; Men of Sci; Ldrs in Ed; Dir Ednl Specialists; DIB; Contemp Authors; W/W in E.

COATIE, CHARLES E oc/Minister; b/Apr 14, 1929; h/1800 Carver Dr, Muncie, IN 47303; ba/Muncie; m/Ann Dennis; c/Shenita Gail, Sheila Ann, Charlotte Elain,

Beth Ann; p/Dixon C Coatie, Muncie; Hazel V Coatie (dec); mil/Staff Sgt AUS 1950-53; pa/Pres Charisma Cosmetic Plant; cp/Bd Dirs VNA; r/Ch of God in Christ; hon/W/W.

COBB, ANNETTA P oc/Retired Administrator; b/Sept 23, 1914; h/PO Box 3116, Durango, CO 81301; m/Elvin Thomas; c/John Frederick; p/Fred and Christella Fisher Carver (dec); ed/Att'd Col 3 Yrs; pa/Ret'd Dir III LaPlata Co Public Wel Dept; Hon Mem Colo Co Dirs Social Wel Assn; Former Com Mbrships, St of Colo Dept Social Sers; cp/Bd Mem: LaPlata Co Coun on Aging, Am Assn Ret'd Persons, Durango Chapt; Repub Party; Num Commun Ser Com Mbrships; r/Meth; hon/Citizen of Month, May 1966, Durango Herald Newspaper; Num Biogl Listings.

COBB, BERNICE COAR oc/Associate Professor; b/Jun 19, 1938; h/5327 Ave H, Fairfield, AL 35064; ba/Birmingham, AL; p/W H Coar (dec); Juanita Davis Rutledge,

Phenix City, AL; ed/BA; MA; PhD; pa/Assoc Prof Biol; AEA; NEA; cp/NAACP; r/CME; hon/Outstg Edr; Outstg Tchr Awd; Acad Excell, Delta Sigma Theta.

COBB, JAMES PETERSEN oc/Student; b/Aug 13, 1956; h/6409 Wildwood Dr, Brentwood, TN 37027; ba/Memphis, TN; p/James Richard and Marion P Cobb, Brentwood; ed/BA; Student SWn-Memphis; cp/Chm Tenn Col Repub; VP Kappa Alpha; Student Govt-at-Large Rep; Student Rep for Pres Energy Com; r/Presb; hon/Outstg Yg Man Am; Outstg Yg Am; Eagle Scout; W/W.

COBLENTZ, STANTON ARTHUR oc/Author; b/Aug 24, 1896; h/200 Glenwood Cir, D-3, Monterey, CA 93940; m/Flora B (dec); 2nd Emily C; p/Mayer and Mattie Arndt Coblentz (dec); ed/AB 1917, MA 1919 Univ Cal-Berkeley; pa/Author 60+ Books;

Contbr to Newspapers & Mags; Currently Book Reviewer Los Angeles Times; Editor Wings A Qtrly of Verse 1933-60; hon/Gold Medal for Poetry, Commonwealth Clb Cal; Winner $1000 Aware of Lyric Foun for Traditional Poetry.

COCHRAN, JOHN HENRY JR oc/Teacher; Author; Artist Photographer; b/Jul 23, 1929; h/4608 Herty Dr, Savannah, GA 31405; ba/Savannah; m/Hattie B; c/John H III, Donald Jerome, Christopher Oscar; p/John H Sr and Dora J Cochran, Atlanta, GA; ed/BA Paine Col; MA Atlanta Univ; EdD Univ Ga; 6th Yr Cert; mil/AUS 2 Yrs; pa/Tchr Div Ed Savannah St Col; CBTE; Tchr Adm, Res, Media, Supvn, Sci in Elem & Mid Sch, Curric; ASCD; GASCD; PDK; Coun Basic Ed; NSSE; Nat Alliance Black Sch Edrs; Nat Conf Artists; Ga Coalition Higher Ed; cp/Empty Stocking Fund; UF; NAACP; Commun Action; Y's Mens Clb Intl; r/Bapt; hon/Kappa Delta Pi Compatriot in Ed; So F'ships Fellow; Civic

Cits; Dist Grad, Paine Col; Danforth Assoc; Photogs in Perm Collection, DuSable Mus, Chgo, Ill; Biogl Listings.

COCHRAN, MARJORIE MITCHELL oc/Retired Elementary School Teacher; b/Jun 4, 1912; h/6201 Linwood Dr, Covington, GA 30209; m/Hulon L; c/Betty Jo C Ridley (Mrs W E Jr), Lynn C Thompson (Mrs Gerry); p/Stiles Edwin and Rosalee Thurman Mitchell (dec); ed/AB Univ Ga 1933; pa/Elem Public Sch Tchr Griffin-Spalding Co Schs 1933-36, 1952-72; Ga Assn Edrs 1952-72; NEA 1952-72; Secy Griffin Chapt Ga Assn Edrs; Helped Est Adult Night Elem Ed Classes, Griffin HS 1957;

AAUW 1955-65, Com Chm 1960; Del to NEA, Local Group 1955; Ret'd Tchrs Assn 1972-; cp/Ga St Mothers Assn; Am Mothers Com; Am Assn Ret'd Persons, Nat Mem, Local Mem; Covington Wom's Clb; Former Mem: U Daughs of Confed, PTA, Griffin Wom's Clb; Others; r/1st U Meth Ch, Griffin, Ga; UMW, Circle Ldr, Choir Mem, SS Tchr; 1st U Meth, Covington: UMW, Cir Mem; Wesley Meml Coun 1931-32; hon/Kappa Delta Pi; Merit Mother 1979; Ga St Mother 1979; WSB Radio Achmt Awd; Gov's Proclamation for Being Ga St Mother.

COCHRAN, SAMUEL LYNN oc/Electronics Engineer; b/Sept 30, 1949; h/PO Box 701, Dahlgren, VA 22448; ba/Dahlgren; m/Debra Lynne Garrett; p/Ray Samuel and Nellie May Harris Cochran, Midway, WV; ed/BSEE WVa Inst Technol; pa/Elects Test Engr Nav Surface Weapons Ctr 1974; Elects Design Engr Nav Weapons Lab 1973-74; Elects Engr Nav Air Rework Facility 1972-73; WVa Soc Prof Engrs; cp/Colonia Bch Moose Lodge No 1267; Rappatomac Shrine Clb AAONMS; ACCA Temple AAONMS; SW Fredericksburg Commandery No 1; COH Westmoreland Royal Arch Chapt No 41; Lodge Ed Ofcr Colonial Bch Masonic Lodge No 199, AF&AM; r/Bapt; hon/Awd for Directing: Plaza Suite, 1975 & The Banker's Dilemma, 1977; Bits & Pieces Commun Theater Ser Awd; W/W S&SW; DIB; Personalities of S; Men of Achmt.

COCHRAN, WALTER MARTIN oc/Physician; b/Aug 21, 1941; h/Rt 1, Box 215, Tahlequah, OK 74464; ba/Tahlequah; m/Lu Anne; c/Martin Wayne, Carl David, Don Edward; p/Claud Mayo Cochran (dec); Ardith McBrian, Miami, OK; ed/Okla Univ Grad Prog 1966-67; DOsteo Med Ks City Col Osteopathic Med & Surg 1967-71; BS NEn St Col 1962-66; mil/AUS Med Corps 3 Yrs, USAR 3 Yrs; pa/Diplomat Nat Bd Examrs; OOA Okla; AOA Am; Med Examr Cherokee Co; Pt-time Clin Instr; Am Col Gen Practioners; cp/JCs; Ducks Unlimited; Nat Scuba Diving Assn; r/Prot; hon/Kappa Mu Epsilon; Rho Theta Sigma.

COCKRELL, CLAUDE O'FLYNN JR oc/Executive; b/May 10, 1937; h/Box 90387, Nashville, TN 37209; ba/Same; c/Cana Lynn, Claude III; p/C O Sr and Audrey R Cockrell (dec); mil/USAF ANG 1958-64; cp/Pres Nashville Corrugated Box Inc; cp/Hd George Wallace Campaign; r/Presb.

COCKRELL, PEARL HAND oc/Freelance Writer; b/Jan 2, 1921; h/4408 Murray Hills Dr, Chattanooga, TN 37416; m/Harold R; c/Pamela C White, Jan C Mitchell, Donis C Schweizer; p/Arthur H and May J Hand (dec);

ed/Att'd: Massey Bus Col, Cleveland St Commun Col; pa/Nat Leag Am Pen Wom; Poetry Soc Tenn; Tenn Wom's Press & Author's Clb; Poems Have Appeared in Nat Periodicals incl'g: Home Life, Science of Mind, Progressive Farmer, Modern Maturity, The American, Music Ministry, National American Camellia Yearbook, Grit, The Braille Forum; r/Bapt; hon/2nd Book of

Poetry Pub'd 1978, Of Men and Seasons; Num Writing Awds & Hons incl'g those from: Utah St Poetry Soc, Nat Leag Am Pen Wom, Ala Writers' Conclave, Mid-S Poetry Fest, Freedoms Foun, Tenn Fdn Garden Clbs Inc, Nat Fdn St Poetry Socs, Ky St Poetry Soc, Cleve Creative Arts Guild, Author & Artists Clb, Others.

COE, WENDELL LYNN oc/Minister; b/Aug 25, 1915; h/1904 Seventh St, Tillamook, OR 97141; ba/Tillamook; m/Janet Barber; c/Harold Wallace, Samuel Barber, Martha Lynn C Parker; p/Earl B Coe (dec); Lela B Roberts, St Petersburg, FL; ed/AB Baker Univ 1941; STB 1944, STM 1944 Boston Univ Sch Theol; pa/U Meth Min, Pastor Chs: Dorchester & Lynn, Mass, Boise, Idaho, Portland, Oregon; Supt E Idaho Conf; cp/Rotary; Kiwanis; Trustee Wesley Foun Idaho St Univ; Dir Care Ctr, Tillamook; Trustee Oreg-Idaho UM Ch; Lt Col CAP; r/U Meth: Del to Juris Conf & Meth World Conf; Dist Coun Mins; hon/Dist'd Ser Awd, CAP.

COFER, LANELL oc/State Representative; Attorney; b/Mar 12, 1949; h/1514 Dalview, Dallas, TX 75203; ba/Dallas; p/Alvin and Jo Cofer, Dallas; ed/BA E Tex St Univ 1971; JD Thurgood Marshall Sch Law 1974; pa/Lic'd to Pract Law 1974; Dallas Crim Bar Assn; Tex Trial Lwyrs; Oak Cliff BPW Clb; Pvt Pract Law; cp/NAACP; Progressive Voters Leag; Black C of C Bd; Oak Cliff Chamber; Coun on Legal Ed Opports Awd; Dallas Mtl Hlth Task Force; Yg Dems; r/Bapt Ch.

COGGIN, JOAN C oc/Cardiologist; Associate Dean; Administrator; b/Aug 6, 1928; h/11495 Benton St, Loma Linda, CA 92354; ba/Loma Linda; p/Charles Benjamin Coggin (dec); Nanette Coggin, Loma Linda; ed/MD; pa/Loma Linda Univ: Assoc Dean Sch of Med Intl Progs 1975-, Assoc Prof Med 1973-, Fdr, Co-Dir & Cardiologist Heart Surg Team, VP Alumni Assn Sch of Med 1975-, Others; Org'd Heart Surg Affil w Evangelismos Hosp, Athens, Greece & Loma Linda Univ Sch of Med 1970-; Mem Pres' Adv Panel on Heart Dis (Appt'd by Pres Richard M Nixon) 1972-; Profl Resources Com, Am Med Wom's Assn 1972-; Bd Dirs TV Opers Bd of SDA Radio-TV Film Ctr 1972-; Pres Tel-Med Inc, San Bernardino Co Med Soc 1977-; Others; Am Col Cardiol; AMA; Am Heart Assn; Cal Med Assn; Assn for Advmt of Med Instrumentation; Med Res Assn Cal; AAUW; San Bernardino Co Med Assn; cp/World Affairs Coun; IPA; MUSES; Am Wom in Radio & TV; hon/Charles Elliot Weniger Awd for Excell; Outstg Wom in Gen Conf, SDA for Yr 1975; Alpha Omega Alpha; Gold Medal of Hlth, Min of Hlth, Repub of S Vietnam; Hon'd Alumnus, Sch of Med Loma Linda Univ; Outstg Wom of Yr in Sci, MUSES 1969; Num Others.

COHEN, AARON E oc/Typist; b/Jul 2, 1937; h/1 Bank St, NY, NY 10014; ba/NYC; p/Charles C Cohen, Provincetown, MA;

Tirea Karlis Cohen (dec); pa/Typist First Manhattan Co; Writer; Assoc Mbrship Poetry Soc NH.

COHEN, ANITA JAYNE oc/Supervising Employment Counselor; b/Sept 27, 1916; h/535 S Curson Ave W, Los Angeles, CA 90036; ba/LA; p/David Robert and Delphine Silberman Cohen (dec); ed/AB Univ Cal-Berkeley; MS Univ So Cal; pa/Supvr & Test Release Agreemt Specialist Reg Testing Prog, St of Cal Employmt Devel Dept; Mem LA Trade Tech Col Secretarial Sci Adv Com 1974-77; APGA; Nat Voc Guid; Nat Employmt Cnslrs Assn; Pres LA Pers & Guid Assn 1964-65; Exec Bd Nat Rehab Assn So Cal 1965-69; cp/UCLA Alumni S'ship Com, Hollywood Wilshire Area; r/Jewish; hon/St of Cal: Merit Awd, 25-Yr Ser Awd.

COHEN, ARMOND E oc/Rabbi; b/Jun 5, 1909; h/3273 Euclid Heights Blvd, Cleveland, OH 44118; ba/Cleve; m/Anne; c/Rebecca Long (Mrs Charles), Samuel J, Deborah (dec); p/Samuel and Rebecca Cohen (dec); ed/BA NY Univ 1931; Rabbi 1934, DDiv 1966 The Jewish Theol Sem Am; Master Hebrew Lit 1945; LLD Cleve St Univ Law Sch 1969; pa/Rabbi The Park Synagogue (Cleve Jewish Ctr) 1934-, Elected for life 1949; Vis Prof Pastoral Psychi The Jewish Theol Sem Am 1960-; Adj Prof Am Col in Jerusalem; Bd Govs

The Hebrew Univ of Jerusalem; Bd Dirs Inst Rel & Hlth; Edit Bd Jour of Rel & Hlth, NYC; cp/Bd Dirs Am Cancer Soc, Cuyahoga Unit; Bd Consumers Leag of Ohio; Bd Trustees Coun on World Affairs; Hon VP Zionist Org of Am; Appt'd by Gov Bricker as Public Mem of Adv Coun, Bur of Unemploymt Compensation (Reappt'd by 3 other Govs); r/Jewish; hon/Hon Fellow, Hebrew Univ Jerusalem; Author Books, Num Monographs & Articles on Rel & Psychi & Jewish Affairs; Others.

COHEN, DAVID oc/Executive; b/Oct 10, 1936; h/1322 Holly St NW, Washington DC 20012; ba/Wash DC; m/Carla; c/Aaron, Eve; p/Joseph and Gertrude Cohen, Silver Spring, MD; ed/BA Temple Univ; pa/Pres Common Cause; Assoc Fellow Calhoun Col, Yale Univ; Non-Lwyr Mem Ethics Com DC Bar; Former Mem Synthesis Panel of Nat Acad Scis' Com on Nuclear & Alternative Energy Systems; Mem Aspen Inst Com on Energy; Served on Secy of Treasury's Adv Com on Pvt Phil & Public Needs; Served on Wash DC Jewish Commun Relats Coun; r/Jewish.

COHEN, GAIL DEBBIE oc/Travel Agent; Personnel Director; h/Four Park Ave, New York, NY 10016; p/Sol and Dorothy Cohen, Lancaster, PA; ed/BA City Univ NY, Bklyn Col; pa/Pers Dir Movie Star Inc; Travel Agt; Owner Gail D Cohen Travel Agy, NY; IPA; cp/Coor Murray Hill Com Entertainmt Bur; Mem Murray Hill Com NYC; Entertainmt Bur U Jewish Appeal-Fdn of Jewish Philanthropies; Charter Mem Am-Israel Friendship Leag; Franklin Mint Collector's Soc; Patron Judaic Heritage Soc; Contb'g Mem Mus Mod Art; Assoc Mem Friends of NY Public Lib; Nat Travel Clb; Fulton Opera House; The Cousteau Soc; Vanderbilt Racquet Clb; Manhattan Plaza Racquet Clb; Yg Wom's Repub Clb, NY St; Social Chm, 1/VP, Acting Pres, Bd Govs, Rep to Var Sems, Convs, Meetings, Others; Del to Nat Repub Wom's Fdn Conv, Wash DC; Asst Secy NYC Yg Repubs; Co-Gov NY Co, Assn NY St Yg

Repubs; Bd Govs NY St Yg Repub Clbs Assn; Vol Repub Conslt, NYC; hon/Certs of Apprec: Yg Ldrship Div U Jewish Appeal, UJA-Fdn Jewish Philanthropies; Cert of Merit; Pres Sports Awd for Tennis; Fellow, IBA; Humane Awd, N Shore Animal Leag; Biogl Listings.

COHEN, IRWIN oc/Financial Economist; b/Feb 29, 1936; h/3555 Bruckner Blvd, Bronx, NY 10461; ba/NYC; p/Samuel and Gertrude Levy Cohen; ed/BS NY Univ 1956; MBA 1964, MA 1969, BS 1970 Col City NY; pa/Fin

Analyst; US SEC, NYC 1965-67, Fed Res Bk NY, NYC 1967-72, Prudential Ins Co Am 1973-74, SEC, NYC 1974-; Fellow World-Wide Acad Scholars (NZ); Math Assn Am; Am Fin Assn; Ec Hist Assn; Life Mem IPA; hon/Fellow: IBA, ABI; W/W in World.

COHN, PRISCILLA N oc/Associate Professor; b/Dec 14, 1933; h/1518 Willowbrook Ln, Villanova, PA 19005; ba/Abington, PA; c/Clifford Blair; p/S S Neuman (dec); Helen P Neuman, Philadelphia, PA; ed/BA; MA; PhD; pa/Assoc Phil; r/Jewish; hon/Author *Heidesgerisu Filosofia a traves de la Nada*, 1974; Contbr 2 Articles to *Texas Quarterly*.

COKE, C EUGENE oc/Scientist; Author; Educator; h/26 Aqua Vista Dr, Ormond Beach, FL 32074; ba/Ormond by the Sea, FL; m/Sally B Tolmie; p/Chauncey Eugene and Edith May Redman Coke; ed/BSc w hons Univ Manitoba; MS magna cum laude; Grad Student Yale Univ; MA Univ Toronto; PhD The Univ, Leeds, England; mil/Royal Canadian AF 1942-46, 2/Lt to Maj; pa/Coke & Assoc Conslts; Pres 1970-78, Chm 1979-; Vis Res Prof Stetson Univ 1979-; Dir Application Devel 1967-70; Dir New Prods Am Cyanamid Co Fibers Div 1963-67; Tech Dir Textiles Drew Chem Corp 1962-63; Guest Lectr Sir George Williams Univ 1949-59; Other Former Positions; Life Fellow: Royal Inst

Chem (Gt Brit), Chem Inst Canada, AAAS; Life Mem: NY Acad Sci, Am Assn for Textile Technol; Fellow: The Textile Inst (Gt Brit), Soc Dyers & Colourists (Gt Brit), NJ Acad Sci; Hon Life Mem Canadian Assn Textile Colorists & Chemists; The Fiber Soc; US Metric Assn; Fla Acad Scis; Chemists' Clb, NYC; Num Ofcs Held; cp/Past Pres Aqua Vista Corp Inc; Former Dir Gtr Daytona Bch Repub Clb; Former VChm N Peninsula Adv Bd to Co Coun; Former Dir N Peninsula Coun Assns; VChm The Group of Ten; Pres Repub Presidents Forum; Others; hon/Bronze Medals: Canadian Assn Textile Colorists & Chemists, Am Assn for Textile Technol; Hon Mem Edit Adv Bd, ABI; Profl Pubs; Num

Biogl Listings.

COKER, DAISY LINNIE oc/Dispatcher; Volunteer; b/Mar 14, 1923; h/222½ Tuscaloosa Rd, Columbus, MS 39701; ba/Columbus; m/Fred Charnell; c/George Clayton, Naomi Leva Campbell, Victoria Charlene Green; p/George and Naomi Garnet Williams (dec); cp/Full-time Vol; r/Prot.

COKINOS, GENEOS PETE oc/Engineering Consultant; Oil Producer; b/Jan 7, 1919; h/4675 Gladys St, Beaumont, TX 77706; ba/Beaumont; m/Lula; c/Peter, Elizabeth, Natalia, Nena, Katie; p/Panayotis Demetrios Cokinos, Parga, Greece; Elizabeth Vellianitis Cokinos, Paxos, Greece; ed/BS; mil/USAAF;

pa/Petrol & Geol Engrg Conslt; Pres Soc Petrol Engrs of AIME, Beaumont Spindletop Sect; cp/Pres Beaumont Tennis Assn; Downtown YMCA; r/Pres St George's Greek Orthodox Ch; hon/TAAF-55 Singles Champ in Tennis.

COLBERT, ANNIE JOSEPHINE SMITH oc/Teacher; b/Sept 19, 1906; h/3706 Las Cienega Blvd, Temple, TX 76501; m/Harry Leon; p/R T and Mary Dallas Henson Smith (dec); ed/BS Mary Hardin Baylor Col 1949; pa/Ret'd Tchr; Jr HS Math & Sci Tchr 4 Yrs; Primary & Elem Tchr 23 Yrs; Rep Field Enterprises Ednl Corp, World Book Div 17 Yrs; Tex Elem Prins & Supvrs Assn; Tex Classroom Tchrs Assn, VP Killeen, Tex Assn; Bell Co Br Assn for Childhood Ed Intl; All Ofcs, Br Rep at Intl Confs; Killeen Tchrs Fed Credit Union; Orgr, Pres 4 Yrs, Bd Dirs 6 Yrs; Secy Ctl Tex Chapt Credit Unions, Waco, Tex; Mem US Team of Tchrs in Normal Sch, San Luis Potosi, Slp Mexico (Tex ACEI); US

Team of Tchrs working w tchrs in public schs of Guatemala City, Cal; Pres Belton Br AAUW; Tex St Tchrs Assn; Tex Assn Math & Sci Tchrs; Nat Assn Ret'd Tchrs; Assn for Sci & Curric Devel; cp/Past Pres Commun Home Demonstration Assn; Chm Milam Co Home Demonstration Coun; Chm Milam Co Adv Bd Bryan Prodn Credit Assn; Temple Iris Soc; Tri-City Gem & Mineral Soc; Pres, Secy; Bell Co Sportsman's Clb; r/Bapt Ch: SS Tchr, Soloist, Ch Choir, Former Music Dir; hon/Superior Awd, Vocal Div, Tex Bapt Ch Music Fest; Poet; Author; Plaque Awd for Meritorious Ser, Tex Classroom Tchrs Assn; DIB; World W/W Wom; W/W Commun Ser; W/W Intells; Personalities of S.

COLBURN, GARY LEE oc/Political Public Relations Advisor; b/Oct 19, 1953; h/1626 S King, Denver, CO 80219; ba/Same; m/Irene Marie; p/Arthur M and Marian Colburn, Billings, MT; mil/AUS 1971-72,

Served in Stuttgart, Germany; pa/Polit Public Relats Advr on Reg Govt; St of Mont Pres, JC DECA; cp/Former Mem St Leg; r/Prot; hon/1st Pl, St of Mont Public Spkg.

COLBY, ROBERT LESTER oc/Psychologist; b/Jan 21, 1941; h/50 Blenheim Rd, Cambridge, Ontario, Canada N1S 1E8; ba/Brantford, Ontario; m/Bonnie; p/Allen M and Beatrice Kalkut-Colby, Bronx, NY; ed/BA; MS; pa/Dept Hd, Chief Behavioral Conslt Brant Co Bd of Ed 1969-; Pvt Pract, Reg'd Psychologist, Vancouver, British Columbia; cp/Advr Commun Free Sch; Participant in Establishing: Commun Wkr Tng Prog, Dir of Social Ser Wkrs & Skills; Formulation of Consumer Eval Sys of Social Ser Agys & Wkrs; Liaison between Commun Agys, Fed & Provincial Govtl Agys (to obtain funding); Assisted in Devel of Emer Crisis Telephone Ser; Participant Commun Oriented Rep Hlth Planning Coun; Adv Com on Ed of Exceptl Chd & Yth; Practicum Supvr Univ Guelph, Grad Dept Psychol; Others; hon/Psi Chi; Men of Achmt; Notable Ams; W/W.

COLE, EDDIE-LOU oc/Poet; Poetry Editor; b/Feb 2, 1909; h/1841 Garden Hwy, Sacramento, CA 95833; ba/Same; m/Ray Wehrner Howard; c/David Laurence Cole, Donna Ruth Stallings; p/James Raymond and Pearl White Neill (dec); pa/Poetry Editor; Illustrator; r/Luth; hon/139 Poetry Awds.

COLE, EUGENE ROGER oc/Free-lance Writer; Editor; Researcher; Clergyman; b/Nov 14, 1930; h/PO Box 272, Whiting, IN 46394; p/Bernard James and Mary Louise Rogers Cole, Euclid, OH; ed/BA 1954; MDiv 1958; AB 1960; MA 1970; pa/Ordained Rom Cath Priest 1958; Author: *Which End, the Empyrean?* (play), 1959, *April Is the Cruelest Month* (play), 1970, *Act & Potency* (poems), 1978; Editor *Grand Slam*, 1975; Guest Editor *Experiment*, 1961; Assoc Editor *The Harvester*, 1955; Contbr to 60 Jours; cp/Election Bd Lake Co, Ind; r/Rom Cath; Fdr/Proponent "Christian Ascriptualism"; hon/Annual Mentor Poetry Awd; Dragonfly Awd; Pro Mundi Beneficio Awd; PSA Monthly Awd; W/W.

COLE, JOHN DEAN oc/Educator; Clergyman; b/Apr 18, 1921; h/Weston Causeway, Zarephath, NJ 08890; ba/Zarephath; m/Marie Haffner; c/John Paul; p/Luke Chapen Cole (dec); Minerva Thatcher Cole, Lusk, WY; ed/BA Alma White Col 1945; MA 1973, PhD 1978 Univ Colo; pa/Dean Alma White Col 1977-; Pastor; Owner-Mgr C&C Pubs 1967-73; r/Pillar of Fire Ch: Clergyman; hon/Phi Delta Kappa; Men of Achmt; DIB; W/W: Bus & Fin, Rel.

COLE, MARGARET EVELYN oc/Emeritus Professor; b/Jun 10, 1910; h/1703 Ryan Ave, Murray, KY 42071; p/Stephen Wall Jr and Effie Jones Cole (dec); ed/BA Miss Univ for Wom 1932; MA Duke Univ 1943; PhD Vanderbilt Univ 1948; pa/Prof Biol Murray St Univ 1960-75; Tchg Fellow Vanderbilt Univ 1957-60; Asst Prof Biol & Chem Greensboro Col, G'boro, NC 1945-57; Sum Sch Tchr Physiol & Botany Univ Miss 1948; Sum Sch

Tchr Nature Study E Tex St Tchrs Col 1947; Tchr Biol, Chem & Physics DeKalb Co HS, Ft Payne, Ala 1942-45; Other Past Positions; Am Inst Biol Sci; Am Soc Zoologists; Am Ornithologists Union; Soc Systematic Zool;

Nat Ret'd Tchrs Assn; AARP; Contbr Articles to Jour of Tenn Acad of Sci & Transactions of Ky Acad Sci; r/1st Bapt Ch, Murray: Mem; hon/Medal for Essays; Charter Mem Upsilon Chapt Beta Beta Beta; Ldrs Am Sci; Am Men & Wom Sci; W/W: Am Wom, S&SW; DIB; 2000 Wom Achmt; Personalities of S.

COLE, PATRICIA DYESS oc/Artist; b/Oct 3, 1928; h/116 John St, Santa Cruz, CA 95060; ba/Same; c/Rebecca Tellin, Linda Caskey; p/Bert Rodrick Cole (dec); Sadie Van Praag (dec); ed/MS; pa/Artist, Own Studio, Tchr; Pres Los Gatos Art Assn; Rec Secy NLAPW; Past Pres BPW; Past Rec Secy Saratoga Contemp Artist; Santa Cruz Art Leag; Soc Wn Artist; cp/Vol Wkr: Hosp, w Retard Chd; r/Bapt; hon/32 1st Pl Awds; Silver Trophy Awd; Spec Awd, Soc Wn Artist; Other Art Awds; World W/W Wom.

COLE, WILLIAM JOSEPH oc/Clergyman; Professor; b/Jun 12, 1923; h/Marianists, PO Box 50504, Nairobi, Kenya; ba/Dayton, OH; p/James Vincent Cole, St Louis, MO; Clara Chrysostoma Dalton; ed/DTheol cum laude 1955; pa/Univ Dayton: Prof Theol

1956-, Chm Dept Theol 1961; Current Tchr Aquinas Sem, Nairobi, Kenya 3 Yrs; cp/Cath Interracial Coun; NAACP; SCIC; Pax Christi; Farmworkers; r/Rom Cath; hon/Asst to Provincial of Soc of Mary, Cincinnati Province.

COLEMAN, CLAUDETTE T oc/Nurse Educator; Assistant Professor; b/Jan 17, 1949; h/1053 Sea Cliff Dr N, Daphne, AL 36526; ba/Mobile, AL; p/Claude Arthur Coleman (dec); Mildred Mason Coleman, Mobile; ed/BSN Univ Ala 1971; MSN Univ Ala-Birmingham 1974; pa/Asst Prof Univ S Ala, Sch of Nsg; Am Nurses Assn; Nat Leag for Nsg; Sigma Theta Tau; Nurses' Assn of ACOG; Sustaining Mem Nat Student Nurses' Assn; Curric Com, Conslt Student Nurses Assn; cp/Sponsor Explorers Med Post, BSA; r/Woodmont Bapt Ch: Choir Mem, SS & Tng Union Ldr; hon/Outstg Yg Wom Am; W/W: Am Wom, Am, S&SW; Personalities of S; Commun Ldrs & Noteworthy Ams; World W/W Wom; Intl W/W Commun Ser.

COLEMAN, GEORGIA FORBES oc/Accountant; Tax Consultant; b/May 18, 1905; h/3559 Riverside Ave, Jacksonville, FL 32205; m/Lloyd O (dec); c/Georgia Leida

Yarbrough (Mrs F Rennie III), Mary Lloyd Toler (Mrs Roger H); p/John Walter Forbes (dec); Peity Rachel Lee (dec); ed/J'ville Col of Bus 1923-24; J'ville Jr Col Tax Sems 1971-75; pa/Acct R R Rosborough & Bro Inc, J'ville

1924-70; Milans Acct'g Ser 1965-70: Public Acct, Tax Conslt, Practioner; Self Employed Public Acct, Tax Practioner & Conslt 1970-; cp/Nat Trust Hist Preserv; Nat Hist Socs; Riverside-Avondale Preserv; Columbia Theol Sem Friendship Cir; Charter Mem Cummer Art Gallery; J'ville Friday Musicale; J'ville Symph; Spirit of "1976"; Wom's Clb J'ville; Sponsor & Contbr to Jefferson Davis Chapel, Nat Cathedral, Wash DC; Sponsor & Contbr to Chapel in Med Sch Univ Va; Am Security Coun; Voting Mem Nat Adv Bd; Fdr Inst Am Strategy; Ctr for Intl Security Studies; Others; r/Riverside Presb Ch, J'ville: Org'd Pre-Nursery Dept, SS Tchr, VBS Supt, Cir Chm, Others; hon/Num Certs of Apprec; Commun Ldr; Painters Add Writing Contest; 1st Pl, Dist Poetry Contest, Fla Fdn Wom's Clbs; UDC Cash Hist Awd; W/W: Am Wom, Indust; DIB; 2000 Wom Achmt; Others.

COLEMAN, HAROLD JOHN oc/Research Chemist; Project Leader; b/Dec 29, 1919; h/3118 E Oak Rd, Bartlesville, OK 74003; ba/B'ville; m/Elsie Nell Redden; c/Paul Eugene, Kenneth John, Cathy Sue; p/Virgil Allen Coleman (dec); Laura Ruth Shoemake Coleman, Emporia, KS; ed/BA Col Emporia; Grad Work Chem Okla Univ; mil/USN 1944-46; pa/US Dept Energy: Project Ldr, Res Chemist; Responsible for Res B'ville Energy Technol Ctr (DOE); Frequent Spkr at Sci

Meetings: Am Chem Soc, Am Soc for Testing & Mats, Am Petrol Inst; cp/BSA Ldr 23 Yrs: Cub Pack Ldr, Asst Scoutmaster, Currently Com Chm Active Boy Scout Troop 11, B'ville; Sch Bd Mem B'ville Indep Sch Dist 1-30; Pres-elect Okla St Sch Bds Assn; VP B'ville Limestone Lions Clb; Past Pres B'ville Garden Ctr; r/1st Bapt Ch, B'ville: Mem, Deacon, SS Tchr; hon/2 Ser Awds for Sci Contbns: US Dept Interior, US Dept Energy; Author or Coauthor 80+ Sci Papers.

COLEMAN, J WINSTON JR oc/Retired Engineer; Farmer; Building Contractor; Author; Historian; b/Nov 5, 1898; h/2048 Blairmore Rd, Lexington, KY 40502; ba/Same; m/Burnetta; p/John Winston and Mary Payne Coleman (dec); ed/BS Univ Ky 1920; ME 1920; LittD 1947; mil/ROTC WWI; pa/Ret'd: Engr, Farmer, Bldg Contractor; Author; cp/Sigma Nu; Omicron Delta Kappa; Phi Alpha Theta; r/Presb; hon/LittD, Lincoln Meml Univ; LHD En Ky Univ; LLD Transalvania Univ; Dist'd Alumni Awd, Univ Ky; W/W Am.

COLEMAN, LINDA E oc/Make-Up Artist; Fashion Coordinator; Radio & Television Announcer; b/May 17, 1947; h/119 Cedar, Morton, IL 61550; ba/Morton; m/Harold Kenneth; c/Teresha Dawn, Marcy Tanna; p/Claud Martin and Myrl Hankins Erwin, Rocksprings, TX; ed/Dipl Jour & Broadcasting; FCC First Class Radio-Telephone Lic; Elkins Inst 1971; pa/Owner Face First by Linda; Lectr on Fashions & Make-Up Techniques; Modeling Conslt; r/Christian.

COLEMAN, NANCY JEAN oc/Instructor; b/Aug 21, 1936; h/10285 Caskie Rd, Wayne, OH 43466; ba/Bowling Green, OH; m/Ronald L; c/Todd Alden, Robin Renee; p/S E and Mary B Hasselswerth Clark, Holland, OH; ed/BS 1958; MA 1959; pa/Pt-time Instr Art Bowling Green St Univ; VP Fabri-Kast Studios; r/Meth; hon/Delta Phi Delta.

COLEMAN, SARAH WILLIAMSON oc/Administrator; b/Dec 8, 1899; h/601 Edgewood St NE #625, Washington DC 20017; ba/Wash DC; m/R W (dec); p/William Eli and Kizzie Wearer Williamson (dec); ed/Grad Hampton Inst; Spec Study Univ Rochester; pa/Coor Sr Citizens Progs in Edgewood;

Missionary Liberia, W Africa 1924-64; cp/Nat Assn Colored Wom's Clbs; r/Beracah Bapt Ch, Wash DC: Mem; hon/Cit from Mayor of DC; Merit Awd; Cert of Apprec, Christian Rit Frat Inc, Wash DC; Achmt Awd of Dist'd Wom, Nat Assn Colored Woms Clb.

COLEMON, JOHNNIE M oc/Minister; Consultant; b/Feb 18; h/8601 S State St, Chicago, IL 60619; ba/Chgo; m/Don Nedd; p/John Haley (dec); Lula Parker, Chgo; ed/BA Wiley Col; Tchg Cert Unity Sch of Christianity; pa/Pastor Christ Universal Temple for Better Living; Former Tchr Chgo Public Sch Sys; Former Price Analyst Chgo Market Ctr; Guest Spkr Fest of Mind & Body, London, England; Mem Intl New Thought Alliance: Dist Pres, Bd Dirs, Chperson 60th Anniv INTA Cong; r/New Thought Metaphysician; hon/Hon DDiv; Resolution, House Bill, St of Mich 1978; Proclamation, "Johnnie Colemon Day", City of Chgo Feb 23, 1978; Key to City, Detroit, Mich; Excell in Rel, Push Foun "A Fam Affair"; Blackbook's Humanitarian, Blackbook Bus & Reference Guide; Biogl Listings; Others.

COLES, RICHARD W oc/Administrator; Biologist; b/Sept 16, 1939; h/11 Hickory Ln, Eureka, MO 63025; ba/Eureka; m/Mary Sargent; c/Christopher Sargent, Deborah Walton Coles; ed/Henry B and Katherine W Coles; ed/BA w highest hons Swarthmore Col; MA, PhD Harvard Univ; pa/Dir Tyson Res Ctr; Edr; AAAA; AIBS; Am Soc Zoologists; Ecol Soc Am; Am Soc Ornithologists; Am Soc Mammalogists; Secy-Treas Org Biol Field Stas; cp/House Spring PTA; Open Space Coun for St Louis; r/Quaker; hon/NSF & NIH Grad F'ships; Harvard Tchg Fellow; Outstg Yg Men Am.

COLEY, BETTY ANN oc/Librarian; b/Aug 4, 1933; h/331 Guittard, Waco, TX 76706; ba/Waco; m/Kenneth; c/Carol Ann; p/Bennie B and Louise L Gilbert, Dallas, TX;

ed/BS; MEd; pa/CoChm Dist TLA; ALA; SLA; SWLA; AAUW; Delta Kappa Gamma; r/Bapt; hon/Kappa Delta Pi; Pi Gamma Mu; Delta Kappa Gamma, Alpha & Zeta S'ships.

COLINS, CHRISTINE MILLAR oc/Social Worker; b/Apr 6, 1915; h/108 Park Ave, Kinston, NC 28501; ba/Kinston; m/Christopher; p/Thomas Spurgeon and Ione

Myrtle Lane Maynard (dec); ed/BA; MSSW; pa/Provide Social Sers for Mtly Retard/Developmentally Disabled & Fams; r/Meth Ch: Bd Mem, Comm for Race & Rel; hon/Recog Plaque for Ideas Submitted to St Dept of Human Resources.

COLINS, CHRISTOPHER oc/Social Worker; b/Sept 3, 1925; h/108 Park Ave, Kinston, NC 28501; ba/Kinston; m/Christine Millar; p/James Kollinites (dec); Mary Skipitaris Kollinites, Roslindale, MA; ed/BA; MSSW; mil/USAAF WWII, Corporal Lt Armored Cavalry; pa/Marriage Cnslg; Lectr on Alcoholism; Cnslg Mtly Ill; cp/Kiwanis Clb; r/Meth Ch.

COLLE, BARBARA W oc/Businesswoman; b/Sept 15, 1915; h/132 Patrician Dr, Spanish Fort Estates, AL 36527; ba/Mobile, AL; p/Henry C and Mena Ery Colle (dec); ed/Grad LaSalle Univ; pa/Owner: The Hutchings Brokerage Co & China Doll Inc (Pres); AL Wholesale Grocers Assn; Nat Food Brokers Assn; Quill & Scroll Hon Soc; Intl Trade Clb; cp/C of C; Mobile CC; World Traveler; hon/Mem Nat Hon Soc; Ldg Wom Ala; Ala's Dist'd Ldrs; Personalities of S; W/W: Ala Wom, Am Wom; Commun Ldrs & Noteworthy Ams; DIB; Nat Reg Prom Ams; Intl W/W Intells.

COLLIER, BETTY F oc/Homemaker; Political Leader; b/May 2, 1935; h/3656 Dill Dr, Drayton Plains, MI 48020; m/Nathan D; c/Linda, Tammy, Janice, Eric, Jennifer; p/Luther Wilson (dec); Desemer Wilson, Eva, AL; ed/BA; cp/Mem St Ctl Com Dem Party; Com Mem Mar of Dimes.

COLLIER, CHARLENE MITCHELL oc/Businesswoman; b/Mar 25, 1939; h/190 Glen Hills Rd, Meriden, CT 06450; c/John Wesley Jr, Pamela, Carol; p/Thomas T Mitchell (dec); Lillie Bell Bradford, Humboldt, TN; ed/BS Skidmore Col 1978; pa/EEO Specialist; Conslt, Formulation Exam St of Conn; Affirmative Action I & II Position; cp/Bd Dirs: U Way Meriden/Wallingford, Meriden Fam Sers Assn; Former Commr Meriden Housing Auth; Former Bd Mem Meriden Commun Action Agcy; Former Secy Meriden/Wallingford NAACP; Yth Advr Conn Fed Black Dem Clbs; LWV; r/Epis; hon/S'ships; BPW Wash DC, Capitol Higher Ed, Hartford, Conn.

COLLIER, GAYLAN JANE oc/Professor; b/Jul 23, 1924; h/2801 Princeton St, Apt 206, Ft Worth, TX 76109; ba/Ft Worth; p/Ben Vivian and Narcis Nura Smith Collier (dec); ed/BA Abilene Christian Univ; MA Univ Ia; PhD Univ Denver; pa/Prof Theatre Sch of Fine Arts, Tex Christian Univ; Am Theatre Assn; Directed a Play in Reg Fest, Am Col Theatre; cp/Dem; Var Civic Theatre Activs; r/Ch of Christ; hon/Best Actress, Col (3 Yrs); Alpha Psi Omega; Zeta Phi Eta; Directed Play to Rep US, Am Fest, Britain, Sum 1970; Dir Play, Reg ACTF Fest.

COLLIER, LOUIS M oc/University Teacher & Department Chairman; b/May 19, 1919; h/3031 Oak Forest, Shreveport, LA 71107; ba/S'port; m/Pearlie Beatrice May; c/James Bernard, Irving Orlando, Albert Jerome, Phillip Louis, Eric Wayne; p/Albert and Ludia Lewis Collier (dec); ed/BS Grambling St Univ 1954; MS Okla St Univ 1960; mil/Vet WWII, Sgt AUS; pa/St Comm by La Gov "La Sci Foun Bd"; Chm Sci & Math Dept Ctl HS, Calhoun, La 1955-62; So Univ, NO: Instr Physics & Math 1962-64, Asst Prof Physics & Math; Assoc Prof & Chm Physics Dept, So Univ, S'port 1967-72; La Ed Assn: Pres Sci & Math Dept, Sci Ed Ldrship Awd; AAAS; AAUP; AIP; NSTS; MAA; NCTM; cp/Secy Cooper Rd Civic Clb; S'port C of C; S'port Negro C of C; Am Legion: Exec Bd, Fin Ofcr, Chaplain Post 525; Geo Wash Carver Br YMCA: Exec Bd, Secy, Coop Mem Blue Ridge Assembly Bd; St Dir Ed, Phi Beta Sigma; Pres: S'port Bossier Chapt, Nat Pan Hellenic Coun, N S'port Kiwanis Clb; Vol Cnslr, Caddo-Bossier Juv Ct; Chm Adv Bd for Caddo Parish Sch Bd, Emer Sch Aid Act Prog (ESAA); VP Newton Smith PTA; Prog Dir Wkly Radio

Broadcast "Yth Want to Know"; Chm Bd Dirs, S'port Negro Joy Fund; Past Pres: Bd Dirs ("Yth Want to Know"), Cooper Rd Hlth Clb; VP 7th Dist Bicent Comm; Caddo-Bossier Commun Coun; S'port-Bossier Mayors Com on Yth Sers; Caddo Commun Action Agy: VP, Fin Com Chm; CCCA Bd Rep, Caddo Parish Police Jury; r/Dubach, La Liberty Hill Bapt Ch; hon/2000 Men Achmt; Sci Ed Ldrship Awd, Sci & Math Dept, La Ed Assn; Classroom Tchr Awd, Freedom Foun, Val Forge; Shell Merit S'ship, Stanford Univ; Personalities of S.

COLLINS, ALVIN OAKLEY oc/Professor; Minister; b/Aug 5, 1921; h/7902 Edgemoor, Houston, TX 77036; ba/Houston; m/Margaret; c/Gordon Wayne, Robert Graham; p/(dec); ed/BA Miss Col; ThM, PhD So Bapt Theol Sem; pa/Houston Bapt Univ; Chm Dept Christianity & Philosophy, Prof; ABTOR; AAUP; Soc Bible Lit; ASOR; AAR; r/So Bapt; hon/Omicron Delta Kappa; Biogl Listings.

COLLINS, CORLISS JEAN oc/Family & Child Counselor; b/Apr 7, 1938; h/8900 Sheringham Dr, Oklahoma City, OK 73132; ba/Same; m/William Edward Jr; c/Bryan Dwayne Barnes, Bryson Allen Barnes, Corliss Adora; p/Corliss Binning and Katherine Grace Evans Allen, El Reno, OK; ed/BS summa cum laude SWn St Col 1966; MSW Okla Univ 1968; pa/Pvt Pract 1972-; Fam Cnslr Sunbeam Home & Fam Ser, Okla City 1968-72; Wel Aide Concho Indian Agy 1964; Nat Assn Social Wkrs; Okla Hlth & Wel Assn; Okla Ed Assn; Child Devel Study Group, Univ Okla Hlth Scis Ctr, Okla City 1969-72; Acad Cert'd Social Wkrs; RSW; Okla Assn for Chd w LD 1970-77; Oklahomans for Gifted/Talented; cp/Okla Geneal Soc; Okla Hist Soc; Canadian Co (Okla) Geneal Soc; Okla City Chapt DAR; Num Other Activs; r/Putnam City Bapt Ch, Okla City: SS Tchr Adult Dept 1971-77; hon/Grad S'ship, Okla Univ; Pres' & Dean's Hon Rolls, SWn St Col; Alpha Phi Sigma; Personalities of W; 1st Pl Exhibit Awd for "Most Complete Geneal-Unpub'd", Okla St Fair; Commun Ldrs & Noteworthy Ams; NASW Profl Social Wkrs Dir.

COLLINS, COURTNEY W oc/Businessman; b/Mar 27, 1931; h/1238 Transaray Dr, Henderson, KY 42420; ba/Henderson; m/Dorothy L; c/Richard, Michael, Scott;

p/Lila Serler, Henderson; mil/USN; pa/Owner Collins Aluminum & Constrn Co 25 Yrs; Nat Fdn Small Bus; cp/Elks, Moose; r/Prot; hon/Ky Col.

COLLINS, DAVID RAYMOND oc/- Author; Teacher; Lecturer; b/Feb 29, 1940; h/3403 45th St, Moline, IL 61265; ba/Moline; p/Raymond A Collins (dec); Mary Elizabeth Collins, Moline; ed/BS, MS Wn Ill Univ; pa/Eng Tchr Woodrow Wilson Jr HS 1962-; Life Mem Ill Coun Ps & Ts; Past Pres Blackhawk Div Tchrs of Eng; Blackhawk Div Rep to Ill Ed Assn; Dir Moline Ed Assn; Life Mem NEA; Phi Delta Kappa; Ill Hist Soc; Fdr Miss Val Writers Conf; cp/Wn Ill Univ Alumni Bd; Secy Christ the King Parish Coun; r/Rom Cath; hon/Alumni Achmt Awd, Wn Ill Univ; Writer of Yr Awd, Quad City Writers Clb; Writing Awd, Ind Univ; Writing Awds, Judson Col; Writer of Yr Awd, Writers' Studio; Outstg Edr Awd, Ofc of Ill Ed; Pub'd Books incl: *George Washington Carver, If I*

Could, I Would, A Spirt of Giving, Charles Lindbergh, Flying Ace, Joshua Poole Hated School, Illinois Women-Born to Serve, Others.

COLLINS, DENNIS GLENN oc/Math Instructor; h/716 Dauphine St, Apt 3C, New Orleans, LA 70116; ba/NO; p/Glenn and Irene Collins, Hobart, IN; ed/BA Valparaiso Univ 1966; MS 1970, PhD 1975 Ill Inst Technol; pa/Math Instr Univ NO; Am Math Soc; Soc Photo-Optical Instrumentation Engrs; r/Luth; hon/NSF F'ship; Yale Grad Sch.

COLLINS, DOROTHY DOVE oc/Writer; Musician; b/Oct 1, 1917; h/Collinwood, Maxton, NC 28364; m/Neil Carmichael Jr; c/Neil Carmichael III, Judith C Millar; p/Rhett Pendleton Dove (dec); Blanche J Dove, Rowland, NC; ed/AA Campbell Col; BA Univ NC; pa/Public Relats Dir Carolina Mil Acad 1966-72; Assoc Journalist St Andrews Presb Col 1972-75; CoFdr & Tchr Maxton Music Acad 1975-77; Ch Organist 1955-65; St Cecelia Music Clb; cp/Org'g Dir Carolina Col Alumnae Assn (Meth Col, Fayetteville, NC); Former Dist Dir U Daughs of Confed, NC Div; Pres Campbell Col Friends of Lib; Former Mem Exec Bd Maxton Centennial Comm, Maxton Hist Soc; r/1st Presb Ch, Maxton: Mem, Dir Chd's Choir 1974-78, Publicity Dir Centennial Yr 1978.

COLLINS, DOROTHY SMITH oc/Administrator; b/Jul 25, 1934; h/6267 Rockhurst Dr, San Diego, CA 92120; ba/San Diego; m/Julius A (dec); p/A V Smith (dec); Betty V Yarborough Coatney, Oakland, CA; ed/BS; MEd; MLS; Cert in Media; pa/Tchr: Public Schs Houston 1955-57, Cleveland 1958-62, US Army Dependent Schs (Germany) 1963-66, Public Schs Lancaster, Cal 1967-69; Libn Public Schs: Cleve 1966-67, Palmdale, Cal 1969-74; Field Resource Libn Sec'dy Dept Ed SD Co 1974-; Coor Instrn Resource Sers (Sec'dy), Dept Ed, SD Co; Delta Kappa Gamma; Phi Delta Kappa; Mem Curric Com Reform Intermediate, Sec'dy Ed, Cal Dept Ed 1976-; ALA; Am, Cal Assns Sch Libns; AAUW; Pres 1972-74; Cal Soc Ednl Program Auditors, Evaluators; Am Soc Tng, Devel; Assn Cal Sch Amdrs; ASCD; NEA; Cal Tchrs Assn; Gtr SD Rdg Assn; cp/Delta Sigma Theta; Dem; r/Rom Cath; hon/W/W Am Wom.

COLLINS, EDWARD MILTON oc/Librarian; b/Feb 8, 1930; h/7969 N State Rt 48, Waynesville, OH 45068; ba/Kettering, OH; m/Virginia M; c/Donald, Judy, Janet, David; p/Irven and Beatrice Collins, Skyland, NC; ed/BA; MEd; MA LS; MA; pa/Libn Kettering Med Ctr; r/SDA.

COLLINS, J QUINCY JR oc/Executive; b/Jul 4, 1931; h/1500 Queens Rd, Charlotte, NC 28207; ba/Charlotte; c/Quincy III, Charles Lowell, William Robey; p/J Q Collins Sr (dec); Willie Marie Collins, Marietta, GA; ed/BS The Citadel 1953; mil/USAF Ret'd, Col; POW in Vietnam 1965-73; pa/VP Am Ins Mgmt Corp (Risk Mgmt) 1978-; Dir Bus Devel Soil Systems Inc, Marietta, Ga & Charlotte, NC 1975; Sr Account Exec US Underwriters Ins Agy, Atlanta 1977; AF Assn; Am Security Coun; Former Mem: Ga Bus & Indust Assn, Indep Ins Agts Assn; cp/Charlotte C of C; Congl Guard, 7th Dist Ga 1974, 76; St Myers Park Presb Ch; hon/2 Silver Stars;

Meritorious Ser Medal; Legion of Merit; Air Medal; 2 Bronze Stars; USAF Commend Medal; Purple Heart; Hon'd at "Quincy Collins Day", Concord, NC 1973; Introduced Pres Ford for Nat Freedom's Foun Awds, Atlanta; Grand Marshall for World 600 Auto Race, Charlotte; Guest on *To Tell the Truth*; Others.

COLLINS, JANET REED oc/Associate Professor; School Psychologist; b/Nov 20, 1919; h/683 Bent Oak Dr, Lake St Louis, MO 63367; ba/St Louis; c/Reed Stuart, David Penfield; p/Robert Findley and Martha Johnson Reed (dec); ed/BA 1941; MAEd 1962; PhD 1973; mil/USN 1943-46, Full Lt; pa/Assoc Prof Ednl & Devel Psychol Maryville Col; APA; AERA; Phi Delta Kappa; NAGC; NARC; cp/Am Legion; r/Unitarian; hon/Phi Beta Kappa; Sociol Prize; Regents Awd for Excell in Tchg, Wichita St Univ; W/W Am Wom; World W/W Wom.

COLLINS, MARTHA LAYNE oc/Court Clerk; h/Route 4, Versailles, KY 40383; ba/Frankfort, KY; m/Bill; c/Stephen, Marla Ann; p/Everett and Mary Taylor Hall, Shelbyville, KY; ed/BS Univ Ky; pa/Clerk Ky Supreme Ct; Nat Assn Appellate Ct Clerks; BPW Clb; cp/Secy Ky Dem Party; Former Dem Nat Com-wom; Ky Chwom 51.3 Com, Carter for Pres; r/Versailles Bapt Ch: Mem, SS Tchr; hon/Wom of Yr, Woodford Co BPW 1977; Hon'd for Ser, Licking Val Girl Scouts.

COLLINS, NANCY W oc/Corporate Development Officer; b/Dec 20, 1933; h/1850 Oak Ave, Menlo Park, CA 94025; ba/Stanford, CA; c/James Quincy III, Charles Lowell, William Robey; p/Ward W Whisnant, Charlotte, NC; M B Whisnant, Charlotte; ed/AB; MS; pa/Stanford Univ: Corporate Devel Ofcr of Grad Sch Bus, Asst Dir Sloan Prog, Grad Sch Bus 1968-; Oriental Tour Dir: Tokyo, Hong Kong, Bangkok, Singapore 1965; Prog Dir for Area Ldrs GSA, Hampton, Va 1959-61; Other Past Positions; Am Mgmt Assn; AAUW; Kappa Delta; Overseas Press Clb; cp/Drafting Com San Mateo Charter Review Com; r/Trinity Epis Ch; hon/Res Grant, The Richardson Foun; F'ship to Grad Sch, Cornell Univ; Profl Pubs; Num Biogl Listings.

COLLINS, ROBERT HILLIARD III oc/Executive; b/May 5, 1935; h/2387 Kimridge Rd, Beverly Hills, CA 90210; ba/Signal Hill, CA; m/Emily Banks; p/Robert H Jr and Nancy Morgan Collins, Oakland, CA; ed/BSME 1957, MBA 1959 Stanford; mil/USNR 1957-59; pa/Pres Sanitary Landfill Methane Recovery Org; Am Inst Mech Engrs; Am Soc Mining Engrs; cp/Stanford Alumni Assn; Jonathan Clb; r/Epis.

COLNY, JEAN POINDEXTER oc/-Author; Editor; b/Jul 26, 1907; h/27 Chesynut St, Brookline, MA 02146; ba/Same; m/Fletcher H (dec); c/Antonia C Shoham, Peter Fletcher, Jean P II; p/Charles Edward Poindexter (dec); Lena Von Steinhoff (dec); ed/AB Wellesley Col; pa/Author 14 Hardbound Books; cp/Duxbury Hist Comm; Boston Bicent Com; Garden Clbs; r/Epis; hon/Hon PhD, Colo St Univ.

COLOMBI, VIOLA MARIE oc/Homemaker; Volunteer; Civic Worker; b/Aug 13, 1913; h/2863 Richmond Rd, Beachwood, OH 44122; m/Christopher A (dec); c/Christopher

A Jr, Licia M and Lucia B; p/Joseph Famiano (dec); Bernadine Gentile (dec); ed/BS Case Wn Resv Univ; pa/Past Pres: Adv Bd Cleveland Wom's Orch, Adv Bd Cleve Assn Chd w LD; Bd Mem Nat Conf Christians & Jews; Bd Dirs: DePaul Home for Unwed Mothers, Great Lakes Shakespeare Fest; Bd Mem Metro YWCA; Pres Acacia CC Wom's Golf Assn; Mem Beachwood Bd Ed 10 Yrs; Past Pres Wom's City Clb of Cleve; Num Other Civic Activs; r/Cath; hon/"Halo of the Week", Milton Widder of Cleve Press; Wom of Achmt, Interclb Coun 1964; "Goodwilly" Statuette, Goodwill Industs; Cert of Apprec, Cleve Chapt Wom's Coun of Nat Assn Real Est Bds; 1st Citizenship Awd, Beachwood Civic Leag; 2000 Wom of Achmt; Nat Reg Prom Ams; DIB; Num Others.

COLSKY, JACOB oc/Physician; b/Dec 5, 1921; h/8220 SW 52nd Ave, Miami, FL 33143; ba/Miami; m/Irene Vivian Belen; c/Liane Caryl, Arthur Spencer, Andrew Evan; p/Abraham Samuel and Jennie Shefsky Colsky (dec); ed/Memphis St Col 1940; MD Univ Tenn Med Sch 1944; mil/AUS Med Corps 1945-47, Lt to Capt; pa/Univ Miami Sch Med: Clin Prof Oncology 1975-, Clin Prof Dept Med 1974-, Clin Assoc Prof Med 1966-74; Cedars of Lebanon Hosp, Miami: Chief of Med 1977-, Dir En Cooperative Oncology Group 1977-, Dir Med Oncology Sect 1972-, Att'g Phys 1961-; Exec Com Comprehensive Cancer Ctr St of Fla 1973-77; Mem Cont'g Med Ed Com Dade Co Med Assn 1977-; Att'g Phys Jackson Meml Hosp 1957-; Conslt: Bapt Hosp, Mt Sinai Hosp, VA Hosp, Miami; Pvt Pract Internal Med & Med Oncology, Miami 1957-; Other Profl Positons; AMA; Fellow: NY Acad Med, Am Col Physicians, Bklyn Soc Internal Med (Former); Diplomate: Am Bd Internal Med, Med Oncology Am Bd Internal med; NY Acad Sci; AAAS; Am Fdn for Clin Res; Am Assn for Cancer Res; Am Geriatrics Soc; Fla Med Assn; Affil Royal Soc Med, London, England; Others; hon/W/W in S&SW.

COMEAUX, ALLEN JOSEPH oc/Captain, Businessman; b/Jul 10, 1935; h/202 S Bourque St, Delcambre, LA 70528; ba/Delcambre; m/Barbara Lucille Naquin; c/Charles J Lovell Jr (Stepson); p/Rene J and Eleda Blanchard Comeaux, Delcambre; pa/Owner & Captain Shrimp Trawlers; Pres A J Comeaux Inc; Mem Delcambre Shrimp Assn; cp/Fgn Mission Soc; r/Cath.

COMEAUX, BARBARA LUCILLE NAQUIN oc/Secretary-Treasurer; h/202 S Bourque St, Delcambre, LA 70528; ba/Delcambre; m/Allen J; c/Charles J Lovell Jr; p/Willie J Naquin Sr (dec); Adelle LaBlanc Bergeron, New Orleans, LA; pa/Secy-Treas A J Comeaux Inc; cp/Fgn Mission Soc; r/Cath.

COMOLA, JACKIE PETERMANN oc/Training Consultant; b/Aug 8, 1937; h/1301 Cliffwood Rd, Euless, TX 76039; ba/Dallas, TX; c/James Paul II, Jon Ronald; p/John Winfred and Flo Petermann (dec); ed/BA; MA; PhD Cand; pa/Exec Bd Mem & Prof Devel Com, Am Soc for Public Admrs; Task Force Mem, Am Inst Planners; Am Soc for Tnrs & Developers; Others; cp/Planning & Zoning Com, City of Euless; Crusade Chperson, Am Cancer Soc; hon/Var Acad, Profl & Commun Awds.

COMPTON, ROGER E oc/Clergyman; b/Dec 10, 1932; h/400 Linden Ln, Mattoon, IL 61938; ba/Mattoon; m/Sara Jo; c/Beth, Lisa, Lori, Eric; p/Earl E and Marie Compton, Dayton, OH; ed/AB; MDiv; MA; DD; pa/Pastor 1st Bapt Ch, Mattoon 1971-; Gen Bd Am Bapt Chs/USA; Gtr Rivers Reg ABC; Bd Mgrs, Profl Standards Comm; cp/Rotarian; Dir Mtl Hlth Ctr; Wesley Towers Trustee; Salvation Army; Vis Nurses Assn; r/Am Bapt Chs; hon/Ch of Yr 1964; DDiv, Judson Col 1978.

COMSTOCK, RUTH B oc/Retired; b/Nov 17, 1903; h/124 Burns Terr, Penn Yan, NY 14527; m/Herbert G (dec); c/Ann C Crandall (Mrs Stuart F), Alan B; p/William

Wesley and Hanna Brewer Boies (dec); ed/BS; MA; pa/Prof Emeritus, Ext Specialist, Cornell Univ, Itahca, NY; cp/Meals-on-Wheels; Yates Co Planning Bd; Hist & Geneal Soc Bd; r/Meth; hon/World W/W Wom.

COMTY, CHRISTINA MARY oc/Physician; b/Aug 10, 1930; h/9180 Vincent Cir, Bloomington, MN 55431; ba/Minneapolis, MN; m/John Marvin Nygren; c/Pierre Rene, Beatrice Marie-Rachelle; p/William Robert Charnock (dec); Monica Johnsson, New South Wales, Australia; ed/BS, MBBS London; LRCP; MRCS; MRCP (Edinburgh); MD (London); pa/Specialist in Internal Med & Nephrology; Am Soc Artificial Internal Organs; Am Soc Nephrol; Brit Med Assn; Canadian Soc Nephrol; European Dialysis & Transplant Assn; Intl Soc Nephrol; Med Res Soc, London; Royal Col Physicians, Edinburgh; Royal Soc Med, London; cp/Minn Val CC; r/Cath; hon/Royal Free Hosp: Charlotte Brown Prize, Cunning Awd; Brit Heart Foun Res F'ship; Florence Stoney Prize; Others.

CONGER, BERNARD WALLACE oc/Management Consultant; b/Sept 4, 1907; h/475 Montevallo Dr NE, Atlanta, GA 30342; ba/Same; m/Louise James; c/Barry Louise C Gunby Sheffield; p/Clyde Wallace and Mabel Watts Conger (dec); ed/AB, LLB Geo Wash Univ; pa/Mgmt Conslt, Tng & Devel Ga Power Co 1973-; Pract Law Washington DC 4 Yrs; w US Govt 31 Yrs, Ret'd; Mgmt Tng Instr Atlanta Sch Sys 1967-73; Reg Tng Ofcr Fed Aviation Agy 1960-66; Asst Reg Tng Ofcr US Post Ofc Dept 1955-60; Reg Tng Ofcr IRS 1953-55; Reg Pers Ofcr Civil Aeronautic Adm 1946-53; Pers Diplomate, ASPA 1977-80; cp/Local Civic Clbs; r/Presb; hon/Spec Recog Awd for Contbns to Adult Ed in Ga, Ga Adult Ed Coun.

CONIBEAR, JO W oc/Secretary; b/May 15, 1937; h/1125 E Lk Parker Dr, Lakeland, FL 33801; m/Richard H; c/Jo Linda C Snell (Mrs J Leroy), Richard David, Amelia Ann; p/Frank Oliver and Dorothy Ford Wintermute, Lakeland; ed/Att'd Polk Commun Col; pa/Secy to Dist Mgr of Radio Shack; Former Positions: Travel Agt, Reporter Radio Sta, Hostess TV Show, Ofc Mgr, Receptionist & Bookkeeper for Law Firm; Lakeland BPW Clbs; cp/Fla Fdn Wom's Clbs (FFWC): (Sorosis Clb:) Publicity Chm, Sponsor to Jr Clb, 1st VP, Pres; C P Ser Guild: Local Bd Mem, Orgnl Chm, 1st Pres; Lakeland Day Nursery; BSA; Lakeland Physically

Handicapped Clb; Ctl Fla Comprehensive Hlth Planning Coun; Heart of Fla Girl Scout Coun; DAR; Exec Secy Polk Co Chapt Mar of Dimes; U Way Budget Com Mem; Polk Co Hlth Planning Coun; Former Sch Grey Lady ARC; Cancer Dr; Mem St of Fla's HRS Dist Human Rts Advocacy Coun; Beta Sigma Phi; Jaycee-ettes; PTA; Lakeland Gen Hosp Aux; Coor'g Coun of Wom's Orgs; Num Other Civic Activs; r/All Saints Epis Ch; Epis Chwom; hon/1963 Outstg Mem, Jr Sorosis; 1968 Lakeland's Wom of Yr; Keys to City of Lakeland 1967, 71; Dist'd Citizen Awd, Hacienda Girls' Ranch; Ser Awd, Lakeland Com on Employmt of Handicapped; Cert of Apprec, Lakeland Physically Handicapped Clb; George Washington Hon Medal, Freedoms Foun at Val Forge; Biogl Listings.

CONLEY, GEORGE EMERY oc/Attorney; Oilman; Rancher; b/Nov 28, 1933;

h/9712 E Hilltop Rd, Parker, CO 80134; ba/Parker; m/Julie Ann; c/John, Paul, Kevin; p/Helen Conley, Upland, CA; ed/BA; MBA Wharton; JD; mil/USMC, Intell; pa/Am & Colo Bars; Phi Delta Phi; cp/Parker C of C; Am Tax Reduction Movement; r/Hilltop Commun Ch, Parker; hon/Order of the Coif.

CONLEY, JOHN W oc/College President; b/Feb 15, 1932; h/5934 Birchmont Dr, Houston, TX 77092; m/Dolores; c/Konni, Kerri; p/Hollie Conley, Wheelersburg, OH; Dora Conley (dec); ed/BA; MTh; DD; mil/Intell 1951-53; pa/Pres Gulf Coast Bible Col; Mem & Ofcr Sev Ednl Socs; cp/City-Wide Crusade Spkr; r/Ch of God: Exec Coun, Gen Ser Div; hon/Awd of Merit, St of Ky; Gov's Commend, WVa.

CONNAWAY, INA LEE WALLACE oc/Artist; Writer; Teacher; b/Dec 27, 1929; m/Charles Earl; c/Richard Earl, Robert Wallace; p/Lee Oliver and Edith Cloe Slaughter Wallace (dec); ed/BA Geo Wash Univ; pa/Artist: Painter, Sculptor; Am Artist Profl Leag; Nat Soc Arts & Lttrs; IPA; *Lasting Americana*; cp/DAR; r/Epis Ch; hon/Honorarium, US Mil Acad; Gold Medal, Accademia Internazionale Leonardo da Vinci.

CONNELL, JAMES F L oc/Professor; Consulting Geologist; b/Jun 25, 1920; h/Box 144, 452 Crestview Dr, Montevallo, AL 35115; ba/Montevallo; m/Martha Matthews; c/James J C; p/(dec); ed/BS La St Univ; MS, PhD Univ Okla; mil/USN; Royal Canadian Army; British Army; AUS; pa/Prof Geol Univ Montevallo; Am Inst Profl Geologists; Paleontological Soc; Paleontol Res Instn; Soc

Vertebrate Paleontologists; Gulfcoast Sect Soc Ec Paleontologists & Mineralogists; Ga Geol Soc; Ga Acad Sci; Yorkshire Geol Soc; Sigma Xi; RESA; AAAS; Sigma Epsilon; Phi Sigma; Gamma Theta Upsilon; Ala Consortium for Higher Ed; Others; cp/US Nav Inst; Royal Regiment of Canada Assn; F&A Mason; r/Meth; hon/Author 23 Books & Scholarly Articles; Var Mil Hons.

CONNELL, LOUISE FOX oc/Retired Editor, Author; b/Nov 14, 1890; h/240 E 82 St, Apt 21D, NY, NY 10028; m/Richard (dec); p/Hugh F and Virginia Herrick Fox (dec); ed/AB Barnard Col, Columbia Univ; pa/Ret'd Mag Editor; Author Hlth, Wom's Probs Articles; Writer for Herbert Hoover, Wash DC, WWI; cp/Gave Blood for Wounded WWII; Working for Equal Rts, Peace; r/All Souls Unitarian Ch, NYC: Deacon; hon/Medal for War Work; Biogl Listings; Awd Plaques 4 Biogl Insts.

CONNELL, SUZANNE McLAURIN oc/Librarian; Author; b/Sept 12, 1917; h/502 Brunswick St, Southport, NC 28461; c/John Alexander (dec); m/John Bethea and Aleine McLeod McLaurin (dec); ed/AB Wom's Col Univ NC-G 1938; AB Univ NC-CH 1940; pa/Ret'd; Civil Ser Libs 22 Yrs; Hosp Libn 14 Yrs; Lib Asst Mt Pleasant Br Public Lib 1940-41; Hd Circulation & Hd of Ext Greensboro (NC) Public Lib 1962-63; Pt-time Asst Reference Wilmington (NC) Lib 1967-75; Am Lib Assn; NC Lib Assn; SEn Lib Assn; Pres Assn Hosp & Instn Libs, ALA 1955-56; cp/Var Vol Activs; r/Meth; hon/Phi Beta Kappa; Pub'd Author.

CONNELLAN, THOMAS KENNEDY JR oc/Behavioral Psychologist; b/Jun 15, 1942;

ba/3125 Geddes Ave, Ann Arbor, MI 48104; m/Sandra Sherlock; c/Avis Murphy; p/Thomas K and Florence Rhea Connellan, Grosse Ille, MI; ed/BBA; MBA; PhD; mil/Instr Army Adjudent Gen's Sch; pa/Acad Mgmt; Author; Lectr; Conslt; r/Presb.

CONNELLY, MICHAEL ROBERT oc/Attorney; b/Oct 28, 1947; h/15606 Treasurer St, Baton Rouge, LA 70816; ba/Baton Rouge; m/Marilyn Memory; c/Sean Michael, Patrick Devlin; p/Roy E Connelly, New Orleans, LA; Marjorie B Connelly (dec); ed/BA; JD LSU; mil/USAR 1/Lt; pa/Baton Rouge Bar Assn; Law Day Com; Spkrs Bur; Nat Justice Foun; cp/Nat Dir Citizens Com for the Right to Keep & Bear Arms; Nat Dir Counsel for Inter-Am Security; Former Exec Dir La Conservative Union; Former Nat Secy Yg Ams for Freedom; Atty Baton Rouge Right to Life; Alt Del Repub Nat Conv 1976; Nat Dir 2nd Amendment Foun; Others; r/U Meth; hon/Hon Cert Awd, Freedoms Foun; Geo Wash Hon Medal, Freedoms Foun; Ser Above Self Awd, Baton Rouge Rotary; Yg Ams for Freedom: Outstg Achmt Awd, Advocate of Freedom Awd; Outstg Yg Men Am.

CONRAD, LARRY ALLYN oc/Attorney; b/Feb 8, 1935; h/7153 N Meridian St, Indianapolis, IN 46260; ba/Indpls; m/Mary Lou Hoover; c/Jeb Allyn, Amy Lou, Andrew Birch, Jody McDade; p/Marshall Conrad and Ruby Rooksby Conrad, Muncie, IN; ed/AB Ball St Univ 1957; LLB Ind Univ Sch of Law 1961; mil/NG 1952-62; pa/Law Clerk 1957-61; Campaign Mgr Bayh for Senate Com 1962; Leg Asst US Senator Birch E Bayh Jr 1963-64; Chief Counsel US Senate Judiciary Subcom on Constitutional Amendments 1964-69; Secy of St, St of Ind 1970-; cp/Dem Nom for Gov of Ind 1976; Bd Dirs: PACE, Ind Am Revolution Bicent Com, Hemophilia of Ind Inc, Mus of Indian Heritage; Adv Bd NW Ind Sickle Cell Foun; Former Hon St Chm Mar of Dimes; Life Mem NAACP; Mem L W Freeman Chapt Nat Paraplegic Foun; Hon Mem U Auto Wkrs; r/Presb.

CONSTABLE, LORAINE LODER oc/Bookstore Owner-Manager; b/Feb 19, 1914; h/1151 N Atlantic Blvd, Apt 5B, Fort Lauderdale, FL 33304; ba/Ft Lauderdale; m/Bruce John; p/Elwood Hill and Mary Harnish Loder (dec); ed/AB maga cum laude NY St Col for Tchrs; MA Columbia Univ;

pa/Owner-Mgr The Christian Book Store 1959-; Pres Math & Physics Clb, Albany; cp/Alumni Assn, Albany; Fdr's Clb, Rosemead, Cal; Air Raid Warning Ser, WWII; Repub; Others; r/Presb; hon/Signum Laudis, NYS Col for Tchrs; W/W: Am Wom, S; World W/W Wom.

CONTRERAS-BORDALLO, FERMIN oc/Banker; h/Box 3074, Mayaguez, PR 00708; ba/San German, PR; m/Gisela Gomez; c/Fermin, Omar, Gisela, Mariana; p/Benigno Contreras and Argelia Bordallo, Mayaguez; ed/BBA MBA; pa/Sr VP Banco Central y Economias; Cert'd Comml Lender, Am Bkr Assn; cp/Mayaguez Hilton Tennis & Swimming Clb; Others; r/Cath.

CONWAY, DWIGHT COLBUR oc/- Chemistry Professor; b/Nov 14, 1930; h/1909 Bee Creek, College Station, TX 77840; ba/Col Sta; m/Diane Coulter; c/Kathleen, Karyn, Michael, Patrick; p/Dee Conway, Heber, CA; Ruth E Holmes, Fallbrook, CA; ed/BS Univ Cal-B; PhD Univ Chgo; pa/Chem Prof Tex A&M Univ; Alpha Chi Sigma; Am Chem Soc; Am Soc Mass Spectrometry; Chm Local Sect Am Chem Soc; Sigma Xi; Am Phy Soc; cp/Chm Cub Scout Pack; r/Meth; hon/Outstg Tchr, Standard Oil of Ind; Phi Beta Kappa.

CONYERS, J C oc/Drilling Engineer; b/Oct 31, 1937; h/14115 Kingsride, Houston, TX 77079; ba/Houston; m/Dinah Gunter; p/Joe Crump and Ellie Evelyn Conyers, Gainesville, TX; ed/BS Tex Technol Univ; pa/AAPG; SPE; ASME; HGS; r/Bapt; hon/Alfred P Sloan Scholar; Am Petrol Inst Scholar.

CONYERS, JOHN JR oc/Congressman; b/May 16, 1929; ba/Washington DC; p/John and Lucille Conyers; ed/BA 1957, JD 1958 Wayne St Univ; mil/AUS 1950-54, 2/Lt Corps of Engrs; Combat & Merit Cits, Korea; pa/Mem US Ho of Reps, Re-elected in 1976 to 7th Term; Sr Mem House Judiciary Com; Chm Subcom on Crime; Govt Opers Com Manpower & Housing & Legislation & Nat Security Subcoms; Sponsor Var Leg; cp/Kappa Alpha Psi; r/Tabernacle Bapt Ch: Mem; hon/Hon LLD, Wilberforce Univ; Rosa Parks Awd for Civil Rts Activs, Dr Martin Luther King Jr.

COOK, BLANCHE HELEN McLANE oc/Artist; b/Jul 1, 1901; h/915 Pleasant Ave, Yakima, WA 98902; m/Harry Christian; p/Alva Randolph and Eva Wynn McLane; ed/Art Deg; BA; MA; Moore Col of Art 1928; pa/Artist; Pvt Art Instr 1930-; Free-lance Comml Artist 1928-; Portrait Painter 1928-; Works Exhibited in Var Galleries & Mus; Rep'd in Sev Public & Pvt Collections; Wilson Jr HS, Sch Dist 7, Yakima: Art Instr 1961-66, Chm Art Dept 1962-66; Art Instr, Cnslr Moxee Elem Sch, Dist 90 1959-60; Tchr (Pt-time) Moore Col Art, Philadelphia, Pa; Tchr (Pt-time) Baldwin Sch, Bryn Mawer, Pa; Other Former Positions; Profl Assns; Intl Leag Am Pen Wom, Yakima Val Chapt: Fdr, Past Pres; CoFdr: Larson Gallery Guild, Yakima Val Art Assn; Donor Blanche McLane Cook Art Lib to Bleyhl Commun Lib, Grandview, Wash; Delta Kappa Gamma, Theta Chapt; Other Profl Affils; cp/OES; Other Civic Affils; hon/2nd Popular Vote NW Annual, Seattle 1947; 2nd Traditional Awd, Spokane 1954; Others.

COOK, BLANCHE WIESEN oc/Histor-ian; Journalist; b/Apr 20, 1941; h/240 W 98th St, New York, NY 10025; ba/NYC; p/David Theodore Wiesen (dec); Sadonia Ecker Wiesen, NYC; ed/BA Hunter Col; MA, PhD Johns Hopkins Univ; pa/Histn & Journalist John Jay Col; Syndicated Columnist *One Woman's Voice*, Anderson-Moberg Syndicate, *NY Times Features*, 1972-76; Am Hist Assn: Exec Coun, Res Com 1975-77; Conf on Peace Res in Hist: VP 1976-78, Exec Secy 1970-73, Secy to Coun 1973-75; Org of Am Histns, Mbrship Com 1972-75; Conslt Inst for World Order 1970-78; Rdr & Examr Doct Prog, Albert Schweitzer Col, Chur, Switzerland 1970-73; Mem Columbia Univ Sem on Am Civilization 1970-; Inter-Univ Sem on Armed Forces & Soc 1974-; Columbia Univ Sem on Wom & Soc 1976-; Intl Peace Res Assn; Am Studies Assn; AAAS; Consortium on Peace Res Ed & Devel; The Berkshire Wom's Hist Assn; Coor'g Com of Wom in Hist Profession; Others; cp/Exec Bd Wom's Intl Leag for Peace & Freedom; hon/Phi Alpha Theta; Pi Sigma Alpha; F'ships.

COOK, CHARLES EBERLE oc/Professor; b/Oct 8, 1926; h/3409 Chimney Rd, Manhattan, KS 66502; ba/Manhattan; m/Barbara; c/Charlesa Whitaker, Kevin Cook, Leah Ann; p/Charles D and Martha Cook, DuQuoin, IL; ed/BA; MDiv; DDiv; pa/Prof Christian Mins Manhattan Christian Col 1979-; Min: Sr Min Ctl Christian Ch, Mesa, Ariz 1968-79; Min: Town & Country Christian Ch, Wichita, Ks 1963-68, 1st Christian Ch, Junction City, Ks 1955-63, 1st Christian Ch, Greenwood, Ind 1954-55; Evangelist Barnes-Cook Evangel Team 1952-53; Other Former Activs; Bd Trustees Manhattan Christian Col 1965-68; 1st Pres Christian Evangelizing Assn of Ks; Christian Missionary F'ship; Bd Dirs 1954-, Pres 1965-68, Chm Fields Com, Long Range Com; Bd Dirs European Evang Soc; Ariz Home & Fam Com; Bd Assocs Emmanuel Sch Rel; Bd Trustees Pacific Christian Col; Coor Ariz MA in Mins Prog, Pacific Christian Col; Wn Assn Christians for Psychol Studies; Others; cp/Fdg Pres Junction City YMCA; Former Mem Bd Dirs Mesa YMCA; Chm World Ser Com; Others; r/Christian; hon/Yg Man of Yr Awd, JCs; Ser to Yth Awd, YMCA; Others.

COOK, DORIS MARIE oc/University Professor; b/Jun 11, 1924; h/1115 Leverett, Fayetteville, AR 72701; ed/BS 1946, MS 1949 Univ Ark; PhD Univ Tex 1968; CPA: Okla 1947, Ark 1954; pa/Jr Acct Haskins & Sells, Tulsa, Okla 1946-47; Univ Ark, F'ville: Instr Acctng 1947-52, Asst Prof 1952-62, Assoc Prof

1962-69, Prof 1969-; Am Acct'g Assn; Am Inst CPAs; VP Ark Soc CPAs; Beta Alpha Psi: Newslttr Editor, Nat Coun, 1st Wom to Ser as Nat Pres; Pres Delta Kappa Gamma; Contbr to Profl Jrnls; hon/Certs: 25 Yrs Meritorious Ser, Ark Dept Higher Ed, Alpha Kappa Psi; 30 Yr Cert, Univ Ark; World W/W Wom.

COOK, INA BOYD oc/Psychiatrist; b/Dec 12, 1911; h/12339 Longworth, Houston, TX 77024; ba/Same; m/(dec); c/Pauline, Rodda C Downie; p/William T and Ina Reeves Boyd (dec); ed/BA; MD; pa/Psychiatrist; r/Epis.

COOK, JEANNINE SALVO oc/Library Director; b/Apr 11, 1929; h/40 Seabrook Ln, Stony Brook, NY 11790; ba/Setauket, NY; m/Donald Carter; c/Carter Steven; p/Ernest August and Edith Agatha Lombardo Salvo; ed/AB Hunter Col 1951; MLS Columbia 1958; Adv'd Lib Deg 1973; pa/Brookhaven Dirs' Assn; Public Lib Dirs' Assn Suffolk Co, Exec Bd; cp/Three Vil Comm & Yth Coun, Bd Mem; r/Setauket U Meth Ch: Coun on Mins, Bd Mem; hon/Lib Public Relats Coun Awd for Best Budget Brochure.

COOK, KENNETH JOHN oc/Executive; b/Sept 4, 1941; h/3195 Deerfield Rd, Deerfield, IL 60015; ba/Milwaukee, WI; m/Sandra; p/Kenneth A and Ruth L Cook, Milwaukee, WI; ed/BSEE Purdue 1964; MBA Claremont Grad Sch 1967; pa/Exec Tech Commun Ken Cook Co; STC; ASTD; ITC; r/Meth; hon/Robert G Frank Awd for Outstg Contbns in Field of Tech Commun.

COOK, LEE WILLIAM oc/Major; b/Feb 11, 1943; h/7555 Sunbury Rd, Westerville, OH; ba/Langley AFB, VA; m/Gayle Ann; c/Christopher Lee, Brian Scott; p/Harry Lee and Bessie Alice Cook, Westerville; ed/BA Ohio St Univ 1965; Assoc Elec Engrg Nat Tech Sch 1970; BA Univ Md 1974; mil/USAF Elects

Instr, Keesler AFB, MS 1966-70; Opers Ofcr, Wiesbaden AB, FRG 1970-74; OIC DCA AUTODIN, Norton AFB, Cal 1974-77; Chief Contigency Plans HQ TAC, Langley AFB 1977-; Major Regular Line; pa/Past Pres German/Am Philatelic Assn, Wiesbaden Chapt; Past Pres German/Am Radio Clb, Wiesbaden Sect; Am Radio Relay Leag; USAF Mil Affil Radio Sys; HQ TAC Command MARS Dir; AFCEA; RACES/AREC; Others; cp/BSA: Eagle Scout, Tng Commr, Scoutmaster; Comm Conslt to Fontana HS Dist, Cal; Past Pres Radio Clbs: Biloxi, Miss, Selma, Ala, Wiesbaden FRG, San Bernardino, Cal; r/Presb/Mormon; hon/Outstg Boy Scout Tnr; Adult Tng Awd; Nom'd for 10 Outstg USAF Communicators for 1976; Ohio Hist Soc Foun Awd; USAF Communs Ser Outstg Achmt Awd for Radio Communs Ser in Vietnam; USAF Commend Medal w 2 OLC; Others.

COOK, RICHARD OMAR oc/Sculptor; b/Sept 16, 1951; h/337 E Main, Fredericksburg, TX 78624; ba/Same; p/Mr and Mrs Richard Cook Jr, San Antonio, Tx; ed/BA w hons Univ Tex; pa/Sculptor Bronze Art; cp/Mem 4th US Meml Cavalry Regiment (Tex); r/Cath.

COOKE, JAMES LOUIS oc/Professor; b/Sept 20, 1929; h/6235 Westgate Dr, Beaumont, TX 77706; ba/Beaumont; m/Ina Lee Crowell; c/Diane, Linda; p/E B Cooke (dec); Vita Heasley Cooke, McLean, TX; ed/BSEE; MSEE; PhD; mil/AUS Signal Corps 1953-55; pa/Prof Elect Engrg Lamar Univ; IEEE; r/U Meth Ch; hon/Regent's Prof, Lamar Univ.

COOKE, JERRY (GERALD) NICHOLS SR oc/Nov 25, 1935; h/837 W Marion St, Shelby, NC 28150; ba/Charlotte, NC; m/Shirley Virginia Holland; c/Jeri Catherine, Sara Eyvette, Gerald Jr, June Christine; p/Robert Hoyle Cooke (dec); Christine Nichols Cooke, Shelby; pa/Collector of Antiques: Books, Coin, Collectibles, Obsolete Automobiles, Owner/Mgr/Pres Cooke Enterprises &

Nostalgia Unlimited; Owner Obsolete Autos & Parts; Am Numismatic Assn; NHRA; Nat Hist Soc; Nat Trust for Hist Preserv; Fdr 3 Auto Clbs; cp/Nat Rifle Assn; Shelby Coin Clb; Earl Gun Clb: VP, Charter Mem; Repub; Com Wkr, Mar of Dimes; r/Meth; hon/Num Auto Awds; Point Champ UTA & ITA; Featured in: *Car Life & Rod & Custom*; Men of Achmt; W/W in S&SW.

COOKE, ROBERT WAYNE oc/Teacher; Educator; b/Nov 2, 1927; h/38 Westcott St, Inwood, NY 11696; ba/Cedarhurst, NY; m/Marion Edna Childs; c/Wayne Allen, Cheryl Ann, Ruth Yvonne, Robert Timothy; p/E Minor and Jessie E Cooke, Inwood; ed/BS; MS; Dipl in Bible & Missions; pa/Asst Dean Students; Supvr Testing; Nat Edr's F'ship; cp/Intl Students Inc; r/Christian: Lay Preacher; Bible Tchr.

COOLE, WALTER ALTON oc/Instruc-tor; b/Jul 6, 1929; h/1325 Shirley Pl, Mt Vernon, WA 98273; ba/Mt Vernon; m/Marjorie Josephine Wrinch; c/Barbara Ruth Richman, Walter Allen, Valya Lara; p/Walter A Coole (dec); Ruth M Coole, Mt Vernon; ed/BA Trinity Univ; MA Univ Tex; mil/AUS 1952-55, 1/Lt; pa/Instr Philosophy The Open Classroom, Skagit Val Col;

cp/Active in Early Civil Rts Movemt; r/Unitarian.

COOLEY, ADELAIDE NATION oc/Artist; Writer; b/Apr 18, 1914; h/3308 N Bigelow St, Peoria, IL 61604; m/William Jr; c/Marcia C Blevins, Susan C Fargo, William C; p/Carl DeLos Nation (dec); Ivo Nation Dutton, Peoria Heights, IL; ed/BS Univ Wis; Postgrad

Study Bradley Univ; pa/Painter; Potter; Lectr; Writer (Book & Mag Articles); Radio & TV Art News 1969; cp/Selection Com, Civic Ctr Sculpture; Fdr Public Art Com; Former Pres Peoria Art Guild; r/Meth; hon/Outstg Wom in Art, Peoria YWCA; Ldrship in Arts Awd, Peoria; Prizes for Painting & Pottery.

COOLEY, CAROLYN A oc/Secretary; Homemaker; b/Jun 28, 1956; h/1106 S Park, Little Rock, AR 72202; m/J F; c/Stephen Lamar; cp/Vol Wkr Cystic Fibrosis Foun 1976, 78; Inspirational Trio (Singing Group); Assoc Mem Ark Constable's Assn; NAACP; Spec Investigative Aid for Circuit Clerk's Ofc, Pulaski Co; hon/Hon Probation Ofcr & Investigator N Little Rock Mun Ct; Certs of Merit & Recog, Pulaski Co & Constable's Ofc Dist 3-A; Men & Wom of Distn.

COOLEY, J F oc/Minister; Educator; Civil Rights Activist; b/Jan 11, 1926; h/1106 S Park, Little Rock, AR 72202; ba/Same; m/Carolyn A Butler; c/Virginia M Lewis, James F, Gladys M Taylor, Franklin D, Stephen Lamar; p/James F Cooley (dec); Martha Buie (dec); ed/AB 1953, BD 1956, MDiv 1973 Johnson C Smith Univ; MA En Neb Christian Col; Addit Studies; mil/AUS 1944-46; Sev Decorations, 2 Battle Stars; pa/Shorter Col: Polit Sci Dir, Min of Ser, Dean Men, Acad Dean 1969-73; Chaplain Tucker Intermediate Reformatory 1971; Public Relats Ofcr Ark Bapt Col; Assoc'd w: Allen Temple AME Ch, W Helena, Ark 1976, W End Presb Ch, Arkedelphia 1975-76; Other Positions; Ark Tchrs Assn; IPA; Nat Com Black Churchmen; Nat Sheriff's Assn; Ark Law Enforcemt Assn; Nat Conf Christians & Jews; Juv Correctional Assn; Min Alliance Gtr Little Rock; Other Profl Activs; cp/Early Am Soc; Urban Leag; Vets Org; Nat Hist Soc; ACORN; SANE; Am Security Coun; Ark Coun on Human Relats; Com for Peaceful Co-Existence; Wel Rts Org; St Dem Party; NAACP; Masons; Others; r/Meth; hon/Hon Citizen N Little Rock; "Dr J F Cooley Week" in N Little Rock, Mayor Eddie Powell Mar 28, 1977-Apr 3, 1977; Num Certs of Merit & Apprec; "Dr J F Cooley's Day", Gov Pryor Jan 11, 1977; Biogl Listings; Num Others.

COOLEY, NANCY CAROL oc/Admissions Counselor; b/Jul 7, 1956; h/405 Gordon St, LaGrange, GA 30240; ba/LaGrange; p/Charles L and Addie S Cooley, Decatur, GA; ed/BA; pa/Admissions Cnslr LaGrange Col, Recruites HS Students; r/Meth; hon/Dean's List; Kappa Delta; Pi Kappa Phi Little Rock; Miss Greek; Alpha Tau Theta; Grad Cum Laude.

COOLIDGE, RICHARD ARD oc/Professor; b/Nov 1, 1929; h/2212 Dogwood St, Nacogdoches, TX 75961; ba/Nacogdoches; m/Penny; c/Alicia Shelley, Jonathan Scott; p/Harold L and Eatha Ingersoll Coolidge, New Port Richey, FL; ed/BMus; MMus; DMus; mil/AUS Signal Corps 2 Yrs; pa/Prof Music Stephen F Austin St Univ; Pub'd Composer, Author; Pianist; hon/Delius Composition

Awds, Jacksonville, Fla.

COOMBES, MARIEL oc/Business Owner; b/Aug 5, 1938; h/8707 Lillian Ln, PO Box 641, Tolleson, AZ 85353; ba/Tolleson; c/Scott Craig Goodwin, William Cullen, Anna Maria, Joel Howard; p/William N Turner, Palos Verdes Pen, CA; Mary Lincoln, Phoenix, AZ; pa/Pres Ariz Steel Fabricators Assn; cp/Repub Party, Former Dist Coor, Oreg; r/Restored Ch of Jesus Christ of LDS; hon/Mensa, Intertel.

COOMBS, C'CEAL P oc/Business Administrator; Notary Public; Civic Worker; b/Aug 8; h/Yakima, WA; m/Bruce Avery; c/Keith Avery, Glinda C Mason; p/Perry Edwin Phelps (dec); Flora L Coney (dec); ed/BS Univ Idaho; Att'd Wash St Col; cp/Past Pres: Wash St Friends for Libs, Mary Chilton Chapt Nat Soc Colonial Dames of XVII Century; Former Mem Intl Relats Am Lib Assn; Am Lib Trustee Assn: Former Mem White House Conf Com, Spkr's Bur; Former Mem: Intl Fdn Libs, Hist Socs-Res, Yakima Co Law & Justice Bd, Wash St 4-H Foun Bd; Former Rec'g Secy Wash St Soc Nat Soc Colonial Dames XVII Century; Former Adv Mem Gov's Conf on Libs; Yakima C of C, Agri Aviation & Leg Coms; Wash St Leg Coms; hon/Hon Life Mem: Nat Cong PTA, Yakima Val Reg Lib, Wash Lib Assn; Yakima Co Wom of Achmt; Spec Ser Cit, Yakima City Coun; Wash St Wom of Achmt, Zonta Intl; Intl Trustee Cit, Am Lib Assn; Cit of Merit, Wash St Lib Trustee Assn; Ldrship Awd, Wash St Coun Crime & Delinq; Outstg Ser Awd, Wn Correctional Assn; Wash St Gov's Ser Awd; Spec Awd, Wash St Coun Crime & Delinq; W/W Am Wom.

COOMBS, THELMA H oc/Educator; Pianist-Organist; b/Jun 9, 1907; h/308 N "C" St, Wellington, KS 67152; ba/Same; m/A J Jr (dec); c/Anne Elgar Kopta (Mrs Nikola); p/Wilbert and Anna Luella Hughes (dec); ed/BMus Friends Univ; Post Grad Studies: Am Conservatory, Chgo Univ, Longy Sch of Music; pa/Tchr Friends Univ 1930-37: Piano, Organ, Theory Classes; Tchr Organ Wichita St Univ 1944-54; Tchr Public Schs New York

City 1961-62; Organist & Choir Master: Ks, New England; TV & Radio Appearances; Organ Dedicatory Recitals, Solo Organ & Piano Recitals Throughout Mid-W; Nat Music Tchrs Assn; Nat Guild Piano Tchrs; Ks Music Tchrs Assn; Wichita Piano Tchrs Leag; Past Sub-Dean Am Guild Organists of Ks; Saturday Afternoon Music Clb Wichita; Mu Phi Epsilon; Charter Mem Beta Sigma Phi; cp/Composer Wellington Song for Centennial Celebration 1971; Chd's Piano Music; Former Ldr Camp Fire Girls; r/Meth.

COON, THOMAS FRANCIS oc/Retired, Former Administrator; b/Aug 2, 1918; h/13 Margaret Court, Dumont, NJ 07628; m/Helene M; c/Patricia Berardo, Maureen, Deborah Magnotta; p/James E and Mary A Coon (dec); ed/BS NY Univ; mil/USNR Lt (sg), Naval Intell; Former Supv'g Spec Agt, Ofc of Nav Intell; pa/Former Dir Bergen Co (NJ) Police & Fire Acad; Former Supv'g Spec Agt Waterfront Comm of NY Harbor; Past Pres Soc Profl Investigators; Past Nat VP Am Fdn Police; cp/Former Co Campaign Mgr Dem Cands in Bergen Co (Freeholder, Gov, Others); r/Cath; hon/Phi Alpha Kappa; Citizen of Month Awd, Detectives Crime Clin Metro NYC; Mem Conslt'g Edit Bd of

Abstracts on Police Sci, Pub'd in Netherlands; Editor *The Bulletin*, Pub'd by Soc Profl Investigators.

COONS, ELDO J JR oc/Manufacturer; b/Jul 5, 1924; h/1315 North St, Oswego, KS 67356; ba/Oswego; m/Betty June Muntz; c/Cheryl Ann, Roberta Annette, Valerie Lucille; p/Eldo J Coons (dec); Ruby Allison Coons; ed/Univ Cal-Berkeley; mil/AUS 1943-46; pa/Pres Coons Mfg Inc, Oswego

1971-; Chm of Bd Borg-Warner Corp 1968-71; Pres Coons Custom Mfg Inc, Oswego 1957-68; Nat Field Dir Nat Hot Rod Assn, Los Angeles, Cal 1954-57; Sgt Pomona Police Dept 1948-54; Owner C & C Constrn Co, Pomona, Cal 1946-48; Am Inst Mgmt, Fellow Pres' Coun; Yg Pres' Org; Appt'd by Gov to Adv Com for St Architects Assn; r/Epis; hon/PhD, Colo St Christian Col; Exec & Profl Hall of Fame; Rec Vehicle/Mobile Homes Hall of Fame; Ldg Men in USA; Nat Social Dir; 2000 Men Achmt; Life Mem, IBA; Nat Reg Prom Ams & Intl Notables; W/W: MW, Commerce & Indust; DIB; Personalities W&MW; World W/W Fin & Indust.

COOPER, ARTHUR EARNEST oc/Pastor, Moderator; b/Jan 24, 1905; h/Box 802, Muskogee, OK 74401; ba/Muskogee; m/Esther Mae; c/Juanita Jenkins, James, Annabelle Street, Lowell E, Larry, Rick, Kathleen Treanor; p/James T and Ollie Ann

Cooper, Viola, AR; ed/Grad Mt Home Bapt Col; Att'd Ctl Sem; mil/18th Field Arty; pa/Pastor Oldham Meml Bapt Ch; Dist Mgr; Staff Mgr, Wash Nat Ins Co 20 Yrs; cp/Dem Election Judge, St Louis, Mo; r/Bapt: Pastor, Tchr, Moderator; hon/Guest Spkr; Others.

COOPER, CHARLES DEWEY oc/Professor; b/Jan 11, 1924; h/4235 Barnett Shoals Rd, Athens, GA 30605; ba/Athens; m/Willie Johnson; c/Norma Louise, Virginia Claire, Edward Howell; p/Grady Talmadge and Lela Howell Cooper (dec); ed/BS Berry Col 1944; MA 1948, PhD 1950 Duke Univ; mil/USN 1944-46; pa/Prof Physics Univ Ga 1961-; ASOP 1956-61; ASTP 1950-55; Res Fellow Harvard 1954-56; Sigma Xi; APS; AAPT; AIP; AAAS; Conslt Oak Ridge Nat Lab 1966-; hon/Navy Commend Medal; Michel Res Awd, Univ Ga.

COOPER, CRAVEN LEROY oc/Counselor; b/Nov 10, 1937; h/1428 S Sawyer Ave, Chicago, IL 60623; ba/Chgo; c/Gregory Scott, Craven Leroy, Brenda Ellen; p/Craven L Cooper (dec); Leona N Prince, Chgo; ed/BA Chgo St Univ; pa/Cnslr City of Chgo DHS Manpower Unit; APGA; IPGA; NACD; cp/Bd Dirs LPPAC; Sally Smith S'ship Foun;

r/Christ Tabernacle MB Ch; hon/Vol Awds: Safer Foun, Pace Inst; Vol of Yr Awd, Pace Inst & City of Chgo; Great Guy of Day Awd, WGRT Radio Sta; Achmt Awd, DHS Lawndale Commun Ser Ctr.

COOPER, DANIELLE CHAVY oc/Educator; b/Dec 11, 1921; h/1146 Seaview Ave, Pacific Grove, CA 93950; ba/Monterey, CA; m/Wilmer A (dec); c/Laurel Martine; p/Henry Paul Chavy (dec); Jeanne Camille Vasselin, Perpignan, France; ed/PhD Univ So Cal 1963; mil/French AF, Liaison Ofcr & Interpreter, WWII; pa/Prof French Monterey Inst of Fgn Studies; Pres French Alliance of Monterey Peninsula; AATF; Alpha Mu Gamma; Phi Sigma Iota; Pi Delta Phi; SPFA; MLA; r/Cath; hon/Chevalier des Palmes Academiques, French Cult Awd.

COOPER, GEORGE WILLIAM NOEL SR oc/Retired; b/Jul 21, 1896; h/7307 St Charles Ave, New Orleans, LA 70118; m/Helen Edith de Lessaps Derbes; c/George William Jr, Helen Edith; p/Harvey Hottel Sr and Carrie Beeler Noel Cooper; ed/MD; oc/Ret'd Physician; Ret'd Chief Med Ofcr; Poet Laureate Emeritus of La; Pres Emeritus, La St Poetry Soc; r/Cath; hon/Biogl Listings.

COOPER, HERBERT PRESS oc/Professor; Administrator; b/Feb 18, 1887; h/114 Riggs Dr, Clemson, SC 29631; m/Sara Louise McCrary; c/Sara Louise Shigley, Herbert Press Jr, Mary Elizabeth Acock, Thomas Reid; p/Mars Lafayette and Isabel Vanbrackle Smith Cooper (dec); ed/S Clemson Col 1911; MS Univ Wis 1916; PhD Cornell Univ; pa/Clemson Univ: Prof Emeritus Agronomy,

Dean Sch Agri, Dir SC Experiment Sta, Emeritus; cp/Mem 1st Sta Nutrition Com (SC); Anderson (SC) Kiwanis Clb: Past Pres, Mem 44 Yrs; r/Clemson U Meth Ch: Mem; hon/Dist'd Agronomist; Pres Am Soc Agronomy 1950; Recog'd as 1 of 10 Ablest Chemists in Fert Res 1947; Pres Assn So Agri Wkrs 1939; Man of Yr in Ser to SC Agri Progressive Farmer.

COOPER, JAMES VERNON oc/Administrative Director; b/Feb 23, 1936; h/Rt 1, Box 310, Greenwood, MO 64034; ba/Kansas City, MO; m/Hazel Dean; c/Dan, Verna, Marie, Jason, Dawn; p/Gus Sewell Cooper, Ks City, MO; Ava Frances Norton, Harrison, AR; ed/BA Ark Polytech Col 1962; MSW Univ

Tenn 1966; mil/USMC; pa/Adm Dir Highlands Child Placement Ser, Ks City 1969-; Social Ser Supvr Ark St Wel Dep, Little Rock, Ark 1966-69; Cnslr Christian Cnslg Ctr, Ks City, Mo 1974-75; Instr Johnson Co Commun Col, Overland Park, Ks 1973-75; Instr Ctl Mo St Univ, Ks City Br 1972-75; Clin Mem Am

Assn Marriage & Fam Cnslrs, Clairmont, Cal; Pastor NW Assembly of God Ch, N Little Rock 1967-68; Assoc Pastor 1st Assembly of God Ch, Russelville, Ark 1968-69; cp/Former Mem Ark Govs Comm on Early Childhood Devel; Former Rep to White House Conf on Rural Am; r/Assemblies of God: Ordained Min; hon/Men of Achmt; Notable Ams; W/W in Rel.

COOPER, JANET SHARI oc/Graduate Assistant; b/May 17, 1956; h/Knob Creek Rt, Melbourne, AR 72556; p/Lonnie G and Margie D Cooper, Melbourne; ed/BSE 1978; MA 1979; pa/Grad Asst in Basketball So Ark Univ; PEMM Clb-SAU; Wom's Rec Assn; r/Bapt; hon/All-AWISA Basketball; Dean's List, SAU; All-AWISA Volleyball; Valedictorian; W/W Among Students in Am Cols & Univs.

COOPER, JOHN NELSON oc/Knife Maker; b/Jan 16, 1906; h/Rt 8, Box 653,

Lufkin, TX 75901; p/George W and Rosina Bernd Cooper (dec); mil/AUS 4 Yrs; cp/Mason; r/Prot.

COOPER, LEE P oc/Writer; Real Estate Broker; b/Nov 4, 1926; h/1711 Highland Rd, Fredericksburg, VA 22401; ba/F'burg; m/E Randolph; p/(dec); ed/BA Mary Washington Col; Further Studies: Univ Mexico (Mexico City) & Univ Heidelberg (Germany); pa/Chd's Writer; Maj Books incl: *The Chinese Language*, 1971, *The Pirate of Puerto Rico*, 1972, *Five Fables from France*, 1970, *More Fun with Spanish*, 1967, *Fun with German*, 1965, Others; Nat Soc Lit & the Arts; Sigma Kappa; Contbr to *The Instructor Mag*; hon/Va St Awd, AAUW; Personalities of S; The Writers Dir; World W/W Wom; Dir Brit & Am Writers; DIB; Commun Ldrs & Noteworthy Ams; W/W: Am Wom, S&SW; Others.

COOPER, LUTHER GRADY oc/Ordained Minister; Professor Emeritus; b/Jul 10, 1902; h/1800 College St, Newberry, SC 29108; ba/Newberry; m/Miriam Greever; c/Kathryn C Link, John Walton, Virginia C Schott; p/John Francis and Martha Page Cooper (dec); ed/AB Roanoke Col; AM Univ SC; STM Union Sem; BD Luth Sem; PhD Hartford Theol Sem; pa/Pastor Luth Chs; Missionary in China, Am Luth Mission 1928-48; Pastor SC 1948-57; Prof Rel & Philosophy Newberry Col 1957-73; Currently Asst Pastor Luth Ch; cp/Former Mem Rotary & Lions Clb; Mem Bd of Coun on Aging; Civic Leag; Hist Soc; r/Lutheran; hon/Jacobus F'ship, Hartford Sem; Acad S'ship, Union Sem; Hon DDiv, Newberry Col; Citizen of Yr, Newberry Co 1977.

COOPER, REGINALD R oc/Physician; b/Jan 6, 1932; h/201 Ridgeview Ave, Iowa City, IA 52240; ba/Ia City; m/Jacqueline; c/Pamela, Douglas, Christopher, Jeffrey; p/Eston and Kathryn Cooper, Dry Fork, VA; ed/BA; BS; MS; MD; mil/USN 1960-62, LCDR; pa/Phys Univ Hosps; cp/Rotary; r/Presb; hon/Kappa Delta Awd for Outstg Orthopaedic Res; Exc Fellow to England 1969.

COOPER, ROBERT ELBERT oc/Court Justice; b/Oct 14, 1920; h/196 Woodcliff Circle, Signal Mountain, TN 37377; ba/Chattanooga, TN; m/Catherine Kelly; c/Susan C Hodges, Bobbie C Martin, Kelly Ann, Robert E Jr; p/John Thurman and Susie Inez Hollingsworth Cooper, Chatta; ed/BA

UNC-CH 1946; JD Vanderbilt Sch of Law; mil/USNR 1941-46, Lt Cmdr; pa/Tenn Supreme Ct: Justice 1974-, Chief Justice 1976-77; Tenn Ct Appeals 1960-74, Presiding Judge 1970-74; Judge Tenn 6th Judic Circuit 1953-60; Chair Tenn Judicial Coun 1967-; Tenn Judicial Standards Comm; cp/Past Master Highland Park Masonic Lodge; Scottish Rite Mason; Knight Templar; York Rite Mason; Past Potentate Alhambra Shrine; Metro YMCC, Former Dir; r/Presb Ch USA: Ruling Elder; hon/Phi Beta Kappa; Order of the Coif; Red Cross of Constantine; Royal Order of Scotland, Royal Order of Jesters.

COOPER, ROBERT PERRY oc/Pastor; b/Oct 25, 1946; h/4639 Glenn St, Charleston Heights, SC 29405; ba/CH; m/Ava Mignon Guinn; c/Julie Kassette, Elizabeth Suzanne, Robert Troy; p/Homer George Sr and Margarette Rose Lundy Cooper, Phila, MS; ed/BA; MDiv; pa/Pastor 1st Original Free Will Bapt Ch, CH; Mem Local, St & Nat Assns Free Will Bapts; Asst Moderator SC Conf FWB; Mem Ordaining Coun Dist Conf; r/FWB; hon/Notable Ams; W/W: SC, Rel.

COPELAND, AMANDA oc/Teacher, Educator; b/Aug 13, 1928; h/2108 Shoshoni, Jonesboro, AR 72401; ba/State University, AR; m/Charles; c/Charles Walker (dec), Ravania Lynn, Nancy C Womack; p/Walker and Elsie Grady Baldridge (dec); ed/BSE; MSE; EdD; pa/Nat Bd Advrs Outstg Elem & Sec'dy Tchrs Am; Nat Assn St Supv of Bus & Ofc Ed: Adm & Supv Sect, Chm 1974, VChm 1973, Secy 1972; NBEA; SBEA; AVBOE; AVA; ABEA: St Chm 1972-75, St VP 1970-71, St Secy 1969-70, Dist Dir 1966-67, Asst Dist Dir 1965-66; St Chm FBLA-PBL 1972-75; Alpha Delta Kappa: Jonesboro Chapt, Rec'g Secy 1976-77, Pres 1972, VP 1970-71, Little Rock Chapt, Rec'g Secy 1972-73; St Chapt Chm, St Ways & Means Com 1976; Bd Advrs Craighead Co Adult Ed Ctr; cp/Altrusa Intl; Red Cross Swimming Tchr; r/Ch of Christ: SS Tchr; hon/Pub'd Author; Certs of Apprec: Utah St Univ, Tex Dept Ed; Best Talk, Dale Carnegie Class; Mistress of Ceremonies, St Staff Sem of Voc Ed 1972; Var Acad Hons; Personalities of S; Notable Ams Bicent Era; DIB.

COPELAND, CAROLYN DAVIS oc/Learning Disabilities Supervisor; Consultant; b/Feb 19, 1947; h/7882 Pheasant Hill, West Chester, OH 45069; ba/Hamilton, OH; m/William Mack; c/George Edward, Carolyn Elaine; p/George Joseph and Antonia Bowrys Davis, Enfield, CT; ed/BA Our Lady of the Elms 1968; MS S Conn St 1973; pa/LD Supvr Butler Co Bd of Ed; Assn for Chd w LD; CEC; Ohio Assn of LD/BD Supvrs; Butler Co Prins Assn; r/Cath.

COPELAND, DRUSILLA GAIL oc/Teacher; b/Nov 21, 1955; h/1861 W 600 N #44, Salt Lake City, UT 84116; ba/SLC; p/Maple L and Harriette M Copeland, Birmingham, AL; ed/BS Elem Ed; pa/Tchr SLC; cp/Former Hosp Vol, B'ham, Ala; r/Bapt; hon/Pi Gamma Mu; Hyptia.

COPELAND, WILLIAM MACK oc/Attorney; b/Jan 21, 1937; h/7882 Pheasant Hill Dr, West Chester, OH 45069; ba/W Chester; m/Carolyn; c/George, Carolyn; p/John H and Margaret E Copeland, Columbia, TN; ed/BA So Colo St Col 1965; MS Univ Colo 1969; JD Chase Col of Law No Ky Univ 1977; mil/USAF, Ret'd Ofcr; pa/Am

Col Hosp Admrs; Am Acad Hlth Admrs; Charter Mem & Charter Pres Dayton Admrs Group; ABA; Am Assn Hosp Attys; Nat Hlth Lwyrs Assn; Am Soc Law & Med; Hosp Systems Soc; Gtr Cinc Hosp Coun; Bd Trustees, Exec Com; Ohio St Bar Assn; Cinc Bar Assn; Butler Co Bar Assn; Sigma Iota Epsilon; r/Prot; hon/AF Commend Medal, Outstg Achmt; AF Commend Medal, 1st OLC, Outstg Achmt; Outstg Jr Ofcr of Qtr, Mil Airlift Command; Outstg Ser Awd, Dayton Admrs Group; Meritorious Ser Medal, Outstg Ser Awd; Am Jurisprudence Awd, Chase Col of Law.

COPPEDGE, JOSEPHINE M oc/Consultant; b/Jan 31, 1919; h/3750 Harrison St, #305, Oakland, CA 94611; p/James Eaton and Elizabeth Easton Morrison (dec); ed/RN Capital City Sch Nsg 1939; BA Cal St Univ-San Jose 1953; MS Univ Colo 1956; EdD Univ So Cal 1977; mil/AUS Nurse Corps; pa/Indep Conslt: Mgmt, Ednl Adm, Nsg Ed & Adm 1977-78; Kaiser Foun Sch of Nsg: VP & Dir Sch of Nsg 1973-76, Conslt & Dir Tng 1973-76, Dir Sch Nsg 1957-73, Assoc Dir Ed & Curric Devel 1956-57; Num Other Profl Positions; Nat & Cal Leags for Nsg; Am & Cal Nurses' Assns; Nat Leag for Nsg Coun of Baccalaureate & Higher Deg Progs; Adv Nsg Conslt Kaiser Foun Intl; Am Assn for Higher Ed, Wash DC; Mem & Fac Advr Trainex

Corp; Adv Bd Kaiser Foun Res Inst; Nsg Adv Coun Cal St Univ-Hayward; Var Com Mbrships; cp/Nat Fdn BPW Clb Inc, Leg & Public Relats Coms; Adv Mem Dept Mtl Hygiene Alameda Co; Am Security Coun, Nat Voter Adv Bd, Wash DC; Smithsonian Inst; Nat Hist Soc; Cal Acad Sci; Nat Assn Lit & Arts; r/Presb; hon/Wom of Achmt, BPW Clb Inc, Oakland, Cal; Hon PhD, Colo St Christian Col; Cert of Commend, USAF Recruiting Ser; Achmt Awd, Kaiser Foun Med Entities Mgmt Assn; Grad Summa Cum Laude; Grad w Distn; Pub'd Author; Num Biogl Listings; Others.

COPPERSMITH, MIMI UNGAR oc/Advertising Executive; b/Jun 11, 1933; h/325 Homan Ave, State College, PA 16801; ba/St Col; m/W Louis; c/Carol Barash, Nan Barash; p/Max Ungar (dec); Tillie Ungar, Wilkes-Barre, PA; ed/BA Pa St Univ; pa/Pres Barash Advt'g Inc; Theta Sigma Phi; Delta Sigma

Rho; Omicron Delta Kappa; Mortar Bd; cp/Trustee Pa St Univ; Bd Dirs Pa C of C; Blue Cross of Pa; Commun Sers of Pa; Pa for Effective Govt; r/Jewish; hon/Grand Nat Debating Champ while in Col; Outstg Ser Awd, UF; Awd for Commun Ser, Kiwanis Clb.

COPPES, LEONARD JOHN oc/Minister;

b/Jun 26, 1939; h/Box 55, Harrisville, PA 16038; ba/Same; m/Diana Lee; c/Keil David, Kristina Marie, Kellie Elizabeth; p/Lloyd J and Rose M Coppes, Las Vegas, NV; ed/BA Bethel Col 1961; BD Bethel Theol Sem 1964; ThM Princeton Theol Sem 1965; ThD Westminster Theol Sem 1968; PhD Cand Dropsie Univ; pa/Min Orthodox Presb Ch; Chm Cands & Credentials Com Ohio Presby-Orthodox Presb Ch; Pres Dianconal Mins Com Orthodox Presb Ch; Pres Diaconal Consltn Com Nat Assn Presb & Reformed Chs; r/Orthodox Presb; hon/Coauthor *The Amsterdam Philosophy: A Preliminary Critique,* 1971; Author: *Who Will Lead Us?,* 1977, *Whatever Happened to Biblical Tongues,* 1977, *Who is Jesus Christ,* 1977, *What is Faith,* 1976.

CORAN, AUBERT Y oc/Chemist; b/Mar 24, 1932; h/477 Greenhaven Cl, Akron, OH 44313; ba/Akron; m/Susan; c/Stephen, Jeffrey, Sigma; p/Jack J and Edith Coran, Brentwood, MO; ed/BS; MS; pa/Chemist; AAAS; ACS; Editor *Rubber Chemistry & Technology;* Past Chm Akron Polymer Lectr Group, Akron Polymer Confs; r/Jewish; hon/Dist'd Monsanto Fellow; Holds 50 US Patents.

CORBITT, GRETCHEN JOHNSON oc/Retired School Teacher; b/Dec 20, 1920; h/PO Box 303, Ridgecrest, NC 28770; m/John C; c/Nathan John, Alzada Mae, Gretchen Evangeline, Rebekah Angela; p/Leondias L Johnson, Magnolia, NC; Picolo Garner Johnson (dec); ed/AB Meredith Col; pa/Ret'd Sch Tchr; Columnist "Reflections", Weekly Newspaper; Pres Christian Wom's Bus Clb; cp/Dir Foothills Chd's Theatre; VP McDowell Co NC Symph Chapt; r/So Bapt; hon/Author *No Woman Had Gone;* World W/W; Musician, Wom; W/W: Am Wom, S&SW; Book of Honor.

CORCORAN, M JEROME oc/Sister of Religious Order; Administrator; b/Apr 21, 1916; h/Ursuline Motherhouse, 4250 Shields Rd, Canfield, OH 44406; ba/Youngstown, OH; p/Austin J and Rose A Corcoran, Youngstown; ed/BA, MA Cath Univ Am; PhD Case Wn Resv Univ; pa/Dir: Millcreek

Child Ctr, Vol Instrs in GED Ed Inc; Assn Child Care Dirs; NCTE; Nat Assn Ed of Yg Chd; Instr Y'town St Univ; cp/Ohio Citizens' Coun; Urban Leag; NAACP; Mayor's Human Relats Com; r/Rom Cath: Nun; hon/B'nai B'rith Wom of Yr; Mahoning Co Bar Assn Annual Awd; Urban Ser Awd; Vol Ser Awd.

CORDARO, JOHN (JB) BENEDICT oc/Food-Nutrition Economist; b/Oct 7, 1941; h/1336 Buttermilk Ln, Reston, VA 22090; ba/Washington DC; m/Elizabeth Ann; c/Susan Marie, Gregory Edward, Michael Patrick; p/Joseph B and Lucille Rita Cordaro, Shreveport, LA; ed/BSS Loyola of S; MS Cornell; pa/Food Group Mgr, Food Prog Mgr & Bd Staff for Senator Hubert H Humphrey, US Cong/OTA 1971-, 1974-78; Agy for Intl Devel: Chief Agri Prog, Tech Assistance Bur 1972-74, Food-Nutrition Economist, Agri Ecs-Sector Planning 1972, Spec Nutrition Prog Assessmt 1971-72; Other Profl Positions; Inst Food Technol; AAAS; cp/Dem Party, Former Staff Mem for Senator Humphrey; r/Rom Cath; hon/Ks of C F'ship for Grad Study, Georgetown Sch Fgn Ser; Outstg Perf Awds; Congl Staff Oberserver; Others.

CORDERO, ROQUE oc/Professor; Composer; b/Aug 16, 1917; h/308 Clay St, Normal, IL 61761; ba/Normal; m/Elizabeth Lee Johnson; c/Dimitri Jose, Rogelio Miguel, Ricardo Lee; p/Pablo and Maria de Jesus Cordero (dec); ed/BA magna cum laude Hamline Univ 1947; pa/Prof Music Ill St Univ 1972-; Musical Advr Peer-So, New York City

1969-72; Prof Ind Univ 1966-69; Conductor Nat Orch Panama 1964-66; Dir Nat Conservatory, Panama 1953-64; hon/Guggenheim; LLD, Hamline Univ; Koussevitzky Recording Awd; Interam Music Contest, Costa Rica; Latin Am Music Contest, Venezuela.

CORDOVA, RONALD MICHAEL oc/State Legislator; b/Aug 18, 1946; h/21845 Michigan Ln, El Toro, CA 92630; ba/El Toro; m/Mariann; c/Danielle; p/Reuben and Lya Cordova, Beverly Hills, CA; ed/AB Dartmouth Col; Cert, Univ Stockholm (Sweden); JD Univ So Cal Sch of Law; pa/St Bar Cal; Cal Dist Attys Assn; cp/Cal St Assemblyman; r/Jewish; hon/Diplomate, Nat Col Dist Attys.

COREA, CHICK oc/Musician; b/1941; ba/Los Angeles, CA; c/Liana; p/Armando and Anna Corea, Boston, MA; ed/Att'd Columbia Univ & Julliard; pa/Apprenticed, Orchs of Billy May & Warren Covington; Joined Stan Getz Band 1966; Recorded 1st Solo LP 1966 *Tones for Joan's Bones* (currently circulated as *Inner Space*); Joined Miles Davis' Band 1968; Formed Group "Circle" 3 Yrs Later; Former 1st "Return to Forever", Recorded Sev Albums; Formed New "Return to Forever" 1977; Var World Tours; Performed at White House; Albums Recorded incl: *Delphi, Secret Agent, The Mad Hatter, Musicmagic, My Spanish Heart, The Leprechaun, Ny Mystery, Romantic Warrior, Where Have I Known You Before, Hymn of the Seventh Galaxy,* Others; r/Scientologist; hon/Playboy Music Poll Awd for Best Jazz Keyboardist; Grammy Awd for Best Perf by a Group; Jazzman of Yr, *Swing Jour,* 1978; Top Electric Keyboard, Contemp Keyboards; Top Pianist, Record World; Num Others.

CORLEW, JOHN G oc/Attorney-at-Law; b/Jul 13, 1943; h/1115 Westwood, Pascagoula, MS 39567; ba/Pascagoula; m/Elizabeth Lee; c/John Scott, William Heath; p/E A and Margaret Swann Corlew, Pascagoula; ed/BA Univ Miss 1965; JD Vanderbilt Univ 1968; pa/Pres Jackson Co (Miss) Bar Assn 1974; VP Miss Chapt Fed Bar Assn 1972; cp/Miss St Senate; Chm Leg Audit Com 1978; r/Meth.

CORLISS, JACK ARTHUR oc/Library Administrator; b/May 6, 1933; h/PO Box 1165, Arlington, TX 76010; ba/Arlington; m/Barbara Ann Mann; p/Annie Corliss, San Antonio, TX; ed/MA Baylor Univ 1961; mil/USAF 1953-60, Capt; pa/Dir Libs Arlington Public Lib; Am, SW, Tex, Tarrant Reg Lib Assns; Tex Mun Leag; Public Lib Div; cp/Gt SW Rotary Clb; C of C; hon/Nom'd Tex Libn of Yr 1973.

CORMIER, ROMAE JOSEPH oc/Mathematics Professor; Realtor; b/May 17, 1928; h/125 Delcy Dr, DeKalb, IL 60115; ba/DeKalb; m/Sue; c/Ivan, Richard, Landall, Darrin; p/Arthur J and Marie Anna Cormier, Canada; ed/BS; MA; AM; mil/AUS 1952-54; pa/Math Prof NIU; Am Math Soc; Math Assn

Am; Tensor Soc; NCTM; Editor *Jour of Rec Math;* cp/Stagecoach Players; r/Free Apostolic; hon/Spoke Awd, JCs.

CORNELL, GEORGE WASHINGTON II oc/Columnist, Author; b/Jul 24, 1920; h/250 First Ave, New York, NY 10009; ba/NYC; m/Jo Ann; c/Marion E, Harrison R; p/Charles H Cornell (dec); Gladys M Cornell, Oklahoma City, OK; ed/AB Univ Okla 1943; LHD Defiance Col 1962; mil/AUS 1944-47, 2/Lt Inf; pa/Rel Columnist Assoc'd Press; Author: *They Knew Jesus,* 1957, *The Way and its Ways,* 1963, *Voyage of Faith,* 1964, *Punctured Preconceptions* (w Doublas Johnson), 1972, *Behold the Man,* 1974, *The Untamed God,* 1975; Rel Newswriters Assn; Am Newspaper Guild; r/Epis; hon/Rel Heritage in Am Faith & Freedom Awd; Rel Newswriters Supple Meml Awd; Nat Rel Public Relats Coun Awd; Jim Merrill Rel Liberty Awd.

CORNETT, FRANCES (FRAN) BERNICE oc/Poet; Restaurant Work; b/Apr 27, 1937; h/1754 Algonquin Pkwy, Louisville, KY 40210; c/Dawn, Tracy, Sandra; p/Morgan S and Edna Hampton Boggs, Louisville; pa/Pres Ky Poets 1975-78; Editor *Pegasus Mag* 1976-;

Pres Ky St Poetry 1975; cp/Jeff Co Repub Wom; Precnt Capt; Campaign Activs; Past Pres L'ville Fire Prevention Coun; r/Bapt; hon/Ky St Poetry Soc: 1st Pl, 2nd Pl, Gold Pin; Var Haiku Awds; Pub'd 200+ Poems in US & Canada.

CORNETT, LEOTA RAE oc/Retired Educator; b/Sept 14, 1911; h/2228 Denniston Ave, Roanoke, VA 24015; c/Carl MacRae, Joanna C Dunn; p/John Rae, Jarratt, VA; Addie Barlett; ed/BS Mary Washington Col; Grad Studies; pa/NEA; VEA; Exec Bd REA 3 Terms; Classroom Tchrs; PTA; Va Art Ed Assn; St & Nat Rdg Assns; Nat Assn for Advmt Humane Ed; IPA; cp/Red Cross Yth Sponsorship 24 Yrs; Art Renaissance Soc; Roanoke Fine Arts Assn; Sci Mus Assn; Roanoke Val Opera Soc; Nat Wildlife Fdn; Local, St & Nat Repub Party, Del to Nom'g Conv in Va; Mtl Hygiene Assn; r/Greene Meml U Meth Ch: Mem; hon/Alpha Phi Sigma; Delta Kappa Gamma; Pro Mundi Beneficio Medal; Mother of Yr, Roanoke Val; Author *A Survival Kit for Grade School Teachers.*

CORNFORTH, ROBERT MAYO oc/Marketing Executive; b/Sept 3, 1914; h/201 Vanderpool, Houston, TX 77024; ba/Houston; m/Viviah; c/Robert Jr, Carol, Cathy; p/Charles and Gertrude Cornforth (dec); ed/BS Univ Tenn; MS MIT; MBA

NWn; mil/AUS Corps of Engrs, Lt Col; pa/Dir of Mktg H K Ferguson, Houston 1976-; Former Profl Positions; Nat Petrol Refiners

Assn; Am Petrol Inst; Am Inst Chem Engrs; cp/Repub; Univ Clb NY; Houston Clb; Houston Racquet Clb; r/Presb; hon/Sigma Chi; Phi Kappa Phi; Tau Beta Phi; Omicron Delta Kappa; Beta Gamma Sigma; Chem W/W; W/W: Engrg, Fin & Indust, S&SW, W.

CORPUZ-AMBROSIO, ERLINDA BALANCIO oc/Physician, Pediatrician; h/502 Parkersburg Rd, Spencer, WV 25276; ba/Spencer; m/Pedro N Ambrosio; c/Cecilia, Ruth; p/Ricardo R and Petro B Corpuz, La Union, Philippines; ed/BS; MD 1965; Internship Ch Home & Hosp, Baltimore, Md 1965-66; pa/Pediatric Residency & Chief Resident AECOM, Lincoln Hosp, Bronx, NY; AMA; WVa St Med Assn; Parkersburg Acad; Chief of Staff: Roane Gen Hosp 1975-76, Secy Med Staff Roane Gen Hosp, Spencer 1971-74, 1978, 79; Yeshiva Univ, Lincoln Hosp, Bronx: Asst Instr 1968-69, Instr 1969-70 Pediatrics, AECOM; Lic'd to Pract NY & WVa; Diplomate Am Bd Pediatrics; r/Rom Cath; Pres Parish Coun Holy Redeemer Cath Ch 1978-79; hon/Pre-Med Hon Soc; Entrance Scholar & Col Scholar, Univ Philippines.

CORR, MICHAEL WILLIAM oc/Scientist; Poet; h/511 Lake Washington Blvd S, Seattle, WA 98144; ba/Seattle; c/Anders; p/William John and Cecilia Genevieve Corr, Seattle; ed/BS Antioch Col 1963; MA Univ Wash 1965; pa/Res for Univ Wash Med Sch

1966; Editor's Cir Kyoto Univ 1968; AAAS, Com on Envir Alterations 1969-73; Guest Lectr Dept Biol Wash Univ, St Louis, Dept Anthropol; CoEditor & Coauthor *Energy and Human Welfare;* Lectr Doshisha Univ Lit Dept 1974-76; Scist The Quinault; Num Other Pubs.

CORTEZ, MARTIN LYNN oc/Teacher; Salesman; b/Sept 11, 1945; h/Rt 1, Box 103 #2, Raceland, CA 70394; ba/Raceland; m/Anna B; p/Alcide and Edna R Cortez (dec); ed/BA 1969, MEd 1978 Nicholls St Univ; pa/Tchr; Salesman (Trophies); Phi Delta Kappa 1978; cp/Raceland JCs; Raceland KCs; r/Rom Cath; hon/Outstg Local Pres in La; Outstg Yg Edr; Outstg World Book Div; JC of Yr; Others.

CORTLANDT, LYNN oc/Artist; h/1070 Park Ave, New York, NY 10028; ed/Chouinard Art Inst; Jepson Art Inst; Art Students' Leag NY; Art Sch Pratt Inst; Columbia Univ Sch of Painting & Sculpture; Hans Hofmann Sch Fine Arts; China Inst in Am; Pvt Instrn; pa/Rep'd Var Mus, Libs incl'g: Metro Mus of Art (NY), Stedelijk Mus, Amsterdam, Netherland, Musee Nat d'Art Moderne, Paris, France, Bklyn Mus, Baltimore Mus Art, Fogg Mus of Art, Cambridge, NY Public Lib, Boston Public Lib, Others, Public & Pvt Collections; Fellow: Royal Soc Arts (London), Intl Inst Arts & Lttrs (Germany); Adv Mem Marquis Biogl Lib Soc; Comitato Internazionale, Centro Studi e Scambi Internazionali (Italy); Knight of Mark Twain (Intl); Acad Polit Sci; Am Acad Polit & Social Sci; Ctr for Study of Dem Instns; IPA; Am Judic Soc; Nat Trust for Hist Preserv; Painters & Sculptors Soc NJ; Phila Water Color Clb; Pen & Brush Clb; Allied Artists Am; Others; Intl Exhbns incl: Kunst Mus at Bern, Switzerland, Lisbon, Portugal, Mun Mus of Art, Tokyo, Japan, Naples, Italy, Paris, France, Rio de Janeiro, Brazil, Others; Nat Exhbns; Titles of Maj Paintings incl: *If Indeed There Was a Beginning, La Vie Dans La Vie,*

The Discovery, Echo Through the Ages, Fantasia, Te Deum, The Earliest Time, Doorway in the Distance, Silent Journey, Estrada A Belo Horizonte, Others; hon/Intl W/W; DIB; Blue Book; W/W: World, Europe, Am, Art, Am Art; Other Biogl Listings.

COSNOTTI, RICHARD LOUIS oc/- Minister; b/Jan 27, 1952; h/1140 Park Ave, New York, NY 10028; p/Frank Paul and Mary Louise Paich Cosnotti (dec); ed/BS Brigham Yg Univ 1973; MDiv Princeton Theol Sem 1976; pa/Asst Min Brick Presb Ch, NYC 1976-; Chaplain Hosp Chaplaincy, NYC 1976-; Dir Good News Communs, NYC 1978-; Vis Lectr Inst of Theol, Cathedral Ch of St John the Divine, NYC 1978-; Asst to the Min Hebron U Presb Ch, Pittsburgh, Pa 1975; Asst to Min Flatbush Reformed Ch, Brooklyn, NY 1973-75; Asst to Min Orem & Am Fork

Commun Chs, Orem & Am Fork, Utah 1971-73; NYC Presby: Ecumenical Relats Com 1977-, Social Concerns Com 1977-, Maj Mission Fund 1978-; Chm Princeton Univ Career Panel on Rel, Cnslg & Social Work 1978-79; Am Acad Rel; Soc Biblical Lit; Coun on Rel & Intl Affairs; Hymn Soc Am; Am Sociol Assn; Presb Assn Musicians; Presb Hist Soc; Eta Omicron Chapt Alpha Phi Omega; Var Musical Pubs; cp/Repub; Princeton Clb of NY; Knickerbocker Repub Clb, NYC; Univ Clb, Pgh, Pa; r/Presb; hon/Pub'd Sermons; Kiwanis Support of Ch Awd; En Star Rel Ldrship Awd; Alpha Kappa Delta.

COSPER, BARRY FLOYD oc/Minister; b/Jun 11, 1951; h/Box 62, New Liberty, KY 40355; m/Cathy Ann Gibbs; c/Melissa Ann; p/Cecil W and Bernice Rogers Cosper, Graham, AL; ed/BA Samford Univ 1974;

MDiv Cand So Bapt Theol Sem; pa/VP Owen Co (Ky) Min Assn; Mem Owen Co Min Exec Com; r/So Bapt; hon/W/W in Rel; Personalities of S; Men of Achmt.

COSTA, SYLVIA ALLEN oc/Marketing Executive; b/Jan 3, 1937; h/230 Fair Haven Rd, Fair Haven, NJ 07701; ba/Atlantic Highlands, NJ; m/John; c/Michele Dianne, Antony Allen; p/Charles and Dorothy Allen, Aitkin, MN; ed/BA Univ Minn; pa/Dir of Mktg; IABC; Sales & Exec Clb NY; r/1st Presb Ch; Deacon; hon/Author 2 Books; W/W Am Wom.

COSTELLO, EVELYN M oc/Hospital Executive; b/Mar 23, 1922; h/1060 Southern Pkwy, Ormond Beach, FL 32074; ba/Ormond Bch; m/Richard J; c/Sharon Anne, John Maurice; p/Otto A Schwenn (dec); Carrie M Schleret (dec); ed/RN; mil/AUS Nurse Corp 1945-46; pa/Dir of Purchasing; ASHPMM;

NAHPM; FHPMMA; SEHCPA; Secy/Treas FHPMMA; cp/Syracuse Univ Alumni Assn; IPA; r/Rom Cath; hon/W/W Am Wom; World W/W Wom.

COTHRAN, GLADYS WILLIAMS oc/College Professor; b/May 6, 1920; h/2417 Athens Rd, Olympia Fields, IL 60461; ba/Chicago, IL; m/Tilman C; c/Brenda Faye, T Christopher Jr; p/Joseph S Williams Sr (dec); Rose W Liggett, Chgo; ed/AB Univ Ark-Pine Bluff; MS Ind Univ; Cert of Adv'd Study Univ Ill; pa/Prof Bus Kennedy-King Col, Chgo 1970-; Clark Col, Atlanta, Ga: Chm Dept Bus Ed & Ofc Adm 1969-70, Acting Chm 1965-69, Assoc Prof Bus & Supvr Student Tchrs 1961-70, Asst Registrar & Freshman Composition Tchr 1959-61; Assoc Prof Bus & Supvr Student Tchrs Univ Ark-PB 1952-59; Mem Fac Coun City Cols Chgo; Kennedy-King Fac Coun, Rec'g Secy; Var Com Mbrships; cp/Former VChm Laymen's Coun Westside Commun Ch, Atlanta; Former Den Mother & Den Ldr Coach, Pack 372, CSA, Atlanta Coun; Vol Wkr E Chgo Child Day Care Ctr, E Chgo Hgts, Ill; r/Meth; hon/Most Popular Fac Mem, Clark Col; Campus Chapt Ldrship Awd, Sigma Gamma Rho; Achmt Awd, E Chgo Hgts Child Care Ctr.

COTTON, CYNTHIA LEE oc/Homemaker; b/Jun 9, 1952; h/Rt 2, Box 163, Linden, TN 37096; m/Bruce; c/Tracy Lee, Jeffrey Bruce; p/Paul E Jones, Fairburn, GA; Mary R Jones, Memphis, TN; ed/Att'd: DeKalb Col, Univ Hi; cp/Perry Co Jaycettes; Chm Heart Fund; En Star; Home Demonstration Clb; r/1st U Meth Ch, Linden.

COTTON, THOMAS ROBERT oc/Minister; b/Jan 1, 1945; h/Rt 5, Box 625-A, Waycross, GA 31501; ba/Waycross; m/Gloria Jean; c/Jonathan, Samuel, Jeremy; p/BA Asbury Col 1967; MDiv Asbury Theol Sem 1970; pa/Pastor Jamestown U Meth Ch; Evangelist; FGBMFI Spkr; CFO Coun Mem; r/U Meth.

COTTONE, RONALD ANTHONY oc/Counselor; b/Mar 5, 1949; h/214 W 15th St, #105, Minneapolis, MN 55403; p/John W and Dorothy K Cottone, Benton Harbor, MI; ed/BA magna cum laude 1971, MA 1973 Baylor Univ; MDiv Princeton Theol Sem; pa/Group Cnslr Univ Minn Med Sch; cp/Bd Dirs Minn Zool Soc; Vol Neighborhood Involvemt Prog, Mpls; Minn St Chperson Baylor Nation-wide Public Relats Prog; hon/Alpha Chi; Robinson Foun Awd Winner.

COUCH, JAMES VANCE oc/College Professor; b/Mar 16, 1946; h/Rt 1, Box 442, Dayton, VA 22821; ba/Harrisonburg, VA; m/Linda Sue; c/Christopher Clifton; p/Clifton Couch (dec); Betty Couch; ed/BA; MS; PhD; pa/Assoc Prof Psychol James Madison Univ; Pres-elect Va Psychol Assn; Num Other Assns; cp/Vol Activs; r/Epis; hon/Num Pubs.

COUCH, M DOUGLASS oc/Realtor; Developer; Consultant; b/Aug 27, 1916; h/67 Bay Tree Ln, Los Altos, CA 94022; m/Robert Ann Brunn; c/1 Son, 1 Daugh; ed/Att'd: Am Inst Bkg 1936-40, Univ Cal; Dipls, Cal Assn Realtors 1960-70; pa/Doug Couch Gen Contractors Inc 1946-; Doug Couch Inc Realtors 1951-; Doug Couch Dev & Investmt Co Inc 1960-; Cal Real Estate Mktg Inc 1972-; Pres (2) Palo Alto Real Est Bd; Pres Mtn View Bd Realtors; Nat Assn Home Bldrs 1960; Intl Real Est Fdn; Foothill Commun Col Real Est Adv Comm; hon/Hon Life Dir, Cal Assn Realtors; Realtor of Yr, Palo Alto Bd Realtors 1957; Men of Achmt.

COUGILL, MARY ANN oc/Teacher; b/May 29, 1935; h/RR #1, Kendallville, TN 46755; ba/K'ville; m/Jack Allen; c/Gwyn, Lisa, Angela, James; p/Angelo C Stefoff (dec); Hildreth M Stefoff, Mishawaka, IN; ed/BS Ball St Univ; MS St Francis Col; pa/Spec Ed Tchr No Side Sch; CEC; cp/Kappa Kappa Kappa Inc; r/Meth; hon/World W/W Wom; DIB; W/W: Child Devel, MW, Am Wom.

COULTER, WILLIAM GODDARD

oc/Editor; Publisher; b/Feb 12, 1928; h/George Hill Rd, Lancaster, MA 01523; ba/Clinton, MA; m/Joyce M; c/James, Carolyn, Constance, Candance, Christopher, Catherine; p/Craven H Coulter (dec); Barbara G Coulter, Duxbury, MA; ed/BS; mil/AUS 1951-53; pa/Sigma Delta Chi; cp/Past Pres Clinton Rotary Clb; Masons, Blue Lodge; r/Epis; hon/New England Press Assn: 2nd Prize Best Column Awd 1976, 1st Prize Best Column Awd 1977.

COUNTER, BENJAMIN FRINK oc/-Executive; b/May 16, 1912; h/PO Box 208, Ft Lupton, CO 80621; ba/Ft Lupton; m/Marjorie L; c/Ann Tate (Mrs Brad), Benjamin T, James Dana, Karna; p/Ben T and Marguerite F Counter (dec); ed/Colo St Univ; mil/AUS European Theatre, Served to Maj; Bronze Star for Bravery; pa/Pres Ft Lupton Canning Co;

Dir Nat Food Processors Assn 3 Terms; Pres Rocky Mtn Food Processors Assn 1963-; cp/Ft Lupton Sch Bd; Mem Weld Co (Colo) Exec Com; Past Pres Weld Co Bd Hlth; Former Secy Platte Val Soil Conservation Dist; Past Pres: Old Guard Soc, Ft Lupton Rotary Clb; Am Legion; r/Meth; hon/Alpha Tau Omega; Scabbard & Blade.

COUSINS, ALBERT NEWTON oc/Professor, Department Chairman; b/May 7, 1919; h/2595 Charney Rd, University Heights, OH 44118; ba/Cleveland, OH; m/Rose D; c/Julia, Daniel; p/Harry and Anna Cousins (dec); ed/AB Ohio St 1942; MA 1949, PhD 1951 Harvard; mil/AUS 1942-46; pa/Prof & Chm Dept Sociol Cleve St Univ; Author *Urban Life*, 1979; cp/Pres Bd Trustees U Area Citizens Agy; r/Universalist; hon/Phi Beta Kappa; Medal of Merit; NSF F'ship.

COUTS, WOODY CHARLES oc/Probation Officer; Child Care Worker; Student; b/Nov 20, 1956; h/412 E State, Newcomerstown, OH 43832; ba/Kent, OH; p/Woodrow W Couts (dec); June E Couts, N'town; ed/BA (Polit Sci); BA (Corrections); Assoc Deg; pa/Probation Ofcr; Child Care Wkr; cp/Kent Dems; Upward Bound Prog; hon/Polit Sci Hon; Crim Justice Hon; Sociol Hon.

COUTTS, FRANCES ISABEL oc/Retired Elementary Teacher; Tennis Teacher; b/Sept 30, 1905; h/3 Park Rd, Oglesby, IL 61348; m/Francis W; c/Barbara Hall, June Whalen, William; p/James and Mabelle Pine (dec); ed/BE NIU; pa/IEA; USTA; Tennis Tchr & Player 40 Yrs; cp/Wom's Clb; UF; CROP; r/Grace U Meth Ch; hon/Tennis Trophies; Ill Coaches' Hall of Fame.

COUTURE, DELORES MARY oc/Evangelist; Businesswoman; b/Oct 9, 1934; h/2055 E Lake Rd, Atlanta, GA 30307; ba/Same; m/David Arthur; c/Patrick John, Steven Keith, Cynthia Ruth, Victoria Rae; p/Phillip Grodins (dec); Ruth Fox, Chicago, IL; pa/Profl Model 1965-68; CoFdr (w husband) Intl Messianic Outreach; Fdrs 1st Messianic Jewish SS Class, Atlanta Region; Tchr Jewish Evangel; Spkr Christian Wom's Clbs; Former Bd Mem Atlanta's Northside Christian Wom's Clb; Informal Ambassadress of Goodwill to Israel; Holy Land Tour Ldr; TV & Radio Appearances; r/Hebrew Christian; 1st Bapt Ch, Atlanta: Mem.

COVAL, NAOMI MILLER oc/Orthodon-

tics Specialist; h/30 Westover Pl, Lawrence, NY 11559; c/Payson Rodney, Mark Lawrence, Ilya Sandra; p/Jacob Paul and Bertha Blumstein Miller; ed/BA Univ Chgo 1939; DDS Columbia Univ Dental Sch 1943; pa/Instr NYU Dental Sch; Lectr; Editor Intl Jour Ortho 1962-65; VP & Secy Intl Acad Ortho; VP NY Assn Wom Dentists; Editor *Dentistae*, 1948; Am Assn Dental Editors 1963-66; Fellow: Soc Oral Physiol & Occlusion, Royal Soc Hlth; Chperson Long Isl Com for Flouridation of Water; Fdn Dentaire Intl; Pan Am Med Assn; Am Dental Assn; 1st Dist Dental Soc 1943-59; 10 Dist Dental Soc 1960-; Nassau-Suffolk Acad Dentistry; Am Acad Oral Med; NY Assoc Assn for the Professions; Charter Mem Am Soc for Study of Ortho; Columbia Univ Dental Alumni Assn; Nat Assn Wom Dentists; Fdn Am Orthodontists; Brit Soc for Study of Ortho; Att'g Dentist: NY Infirmary 1964-50, Peninsula Hosp Ctr 1967-; Am Soc for Preventive Dentistry; Assn for Wom in Sci; cp/Past Pres: Five Town Am Jewish Cong, Lawrence HS PTA, Five Towns Aux Peninsula Gen Hosp; UN Assn USA; IPA; Charter Mem Am Cancer Soc Art Show; ARC; Am Field Ser; Wayfarer's Clb; Wildlife Soc Kenya; Nat Geographic Soc; Natural Hist Soc; Nat Coun Jewish Wom; AAAS; Num Others; hon/-William Jarvie Soc for Dental Res; 1st Wom Selected to Rep Ofcl Dentistry on TV; Del to Oral Hygiene Comm; 1st USA Wom Dentist Invited to Give Univ Sem in Socialist-Soviet Bloc; Num Biogl Listings; Pub'd Author.

COVELL, CRANSTON EDWARDS oc/Army Officer; Educational Administrator; b/Mar 21, 1913; h/1810 Sevilla Blvd, Atlantic Beach, FL 32233; m/Betty Jean Williams; c/Tanna Jean Pidgeon (Mrs John), Mary Alice Friese (Mrs William); p/Charles William Covell; Ruth Louise Parsons; ed/BA Hamilton Col 1935; MA NY Univ 1947; Addit Grad Studies: Univ Buffalo, Univ Wash, Univ Mexico, Harvard Univ; mil/AUS Lt Col; Dir Mil Instr Tng Prog, US Mil Acad; Asst to Acad Dean, US Mil Acad; pa/NY St Ednl Dept: St Supvr Sec'dy Schs, Dir Sch Adm Ldrship Tng Prog; cp/Dir Emer Sch Assistance Prog, Duval Co Sch Bd, Jacksonville, Fla; Pres Duval Co Repub Men's Clb, J'ville; Del to Repub Nat Conv, Ks City 1976; Secy-Treas J'ville Bchs-Mayport Coun of Navy Leag of US; VP Bchs Chapt Toastmasters Intl; VP Players by the Sea, J'ville; Bd Trustees J'ville Epis HS; Var Campaign Activs; r/Palms Presb Ch, J'ville: Ruling Elder, Mem of Session.

COVERT, RICHARD LEE oc/Teacher; b/Nov 14, 1947; h/3533 King's Point Terr, Lansing, MI 48917; ba/Lansing; p/C Edgar and Janet C Covert, Lansing; ed/BA, MA Mich St Univ; mil/USMC 1969-71; pa/Tchr Bassett Park Jr High Re-entry Ctr; Tchr Harry Hill HS, Lansing; Lansing Sch Ed Assn; Bldg Rep, Public Relats Dept Chm; Pres & Fdr Am Foun for Christian Mins; Pres Capital Area Rel Cable TV Assn Inc; Pres & Fdr R L Covert Enterprises Intl Inc; Broker 1st Fin Credit, Shawnee Mission, Ks; cp/Lansing JCs; Repub Party, Cand St House; r/Pres E Lansing, MSU Chapt of FGBMFI, SS Tchr; hon/Mich Scholastic Chess Leag; Pres Cent Mich Chess Leag.

COVINGTON, RICK oc/University Administrator; b/Mar 1, 1954; h/725 Cedar Lane Rd, Greenville, SC 29611; ba/G'ville; m/Betty Wilson; p/John R and Priscilla

Covington, Georgetown Univ; pa/AB 1976, MHE 1977 Morehead St Univ; pa/Dir Sports Info & Promotions Furman Univ; Former Asst SID Morehead St Univ; Former SID Ft Hays St Univ; Rep Morehead St Univ Com on Intercollegiate Aths; Col Sports Info Dirs Am; Ftball Writers Am; US Basketball Writers Assn; Baseball Writers Assn Am; Nat Ftball Foun & Hall of Fame; Asst Press Dir Ohio Val Conf Indoor Task Champs 1977; Asst Press Dir Ky St HS Baseball Tour 1975, 76, 77; Pres Dir Nat Gymnastics Champs 1978; Pi Kappa Phi; r/So Bapt; hon/Pi Kappa Phi Archon Gavel; Outstg Frat Sr & Brother; Outstg Yg Kentuckian; W/W Am Cols & Univs; Outstg Teenagers Am.

COWARD, RAYMOND oc/Attorney; Poet; Writer; Lecturer; b/Feb 10, 1909; h/1022 S Cooper, Suite 202, Arlington, TX 76013; ba/Same; m/Phyllis Lee Furr (dec); c/Raymond Lynn, Janet Anne; p/Emmett Timothy and Mary Alice Gentry Coward (dec); ed/BA Coe Col 1933; MBA Univ Ala 1966; JD Univ Ia 1935; Grad Work: Univ Mich & Univ Vienna (Austria); mil/AUS, Served all Ranks, 2/Lt Cavalry to Col, JAG Corps; Ret'd 1963; pa/Tchr: Tex Wesleyan Col, Fort Worth 1968-69, Univ Tex-Arlington 1966-67, Univ Ala 1965-66, La St Univ 1963-65; Spec Agt FBI 1941-43; Gen Pract Law, St of Ia 1935-41; Admitted: Ia Bar 1935, Bar of DC 1956, US Ct of Claims, US Ct of Mil Appeals, Supreme Ct of US 1948; ABA: Com Mbrships, Adv Com on Law Day 1974-; cp/32nd Deg Mason; r/Prot; hon/Merit Awd, ABA; Mem ABA Com that received George Washington Medal Awd, Freedoms Foun Val Forge; Awd'd Gold Three Gallon Donor's Pin for Vol Blood Donations, ARC; Mil Hons; Biogl Listings; Author Var Articles.

COWEN, EMORY L oc/Professor; b/Apr 20, 1926; h/32 Aberthaw Rd, Rochester, NY 14610; ba/Rochester; m/Renee Senna; c/Richard Jon, Peter Rolf, Lisa Allyson, Andrew Philip; p/Philip and Rose Cowen (dec); ed/MA; PhD; mil/USN 1944-46; pa/Univ Rochester: Prof Psychol 1960-, Dir Ctr for Commun Study 1969-, Prof Psychi (Med Sch) 1967-, Prof of Ed (Col of Ed) 1973-; Other Positions; Past Pres Genesee Val Psychol Assn; St Psychol Assn; En Psychol Assn; APA; Conslt VA 1955-; Mem NY St Bd Examrs in Psychol 1962-68; NSF Vis Scist Prog; APA Vis Conslt Prog; Mem Psychol Tng Subcom NIMH 1964-68; Adv Editor Jour of Conslt & Clin Psychol 1967-76; Assoc Editor Am Jour Commun Psychol; Other Profl Activs; hon/Phi Delta Kappa Res Awd; Dist'd Contbns Awd, Genesee Val Psychol Assn; Res Awd, APGA; Recipient F'ship; Profl Pubs.

COWEN, GERALD PRESTON oc/Teacher; b/Jan 12, 1942; h/621 N Claud St, Bolivar, MO 65613; ba/Bolivar; m/Mary Johnson; c/Kimberly Gayle, Lara Elizabeth; p/James

Preston and Louise Bryan Cowen, Mobile, AL; ed/BA Miss Col; ThM, ThD New Orleans Bapt Theol Sem; pa/Tchr SW Bapt Col; Assn Bapt Profs of Rel; Soc Biblical Lit; r/Bapt.

COWLEY, AU-DEANE SHEPHERD oc/Social Work Educator; Administrator; b/Feb 8; h/1931 S Moor Dr, Salt Lake City, UT 84117; ba/SLC; m/Carter; c/David Carter, Cardeane Veniece, Michael William, Phillip Earl; p/Earl Budge Shepherd (dec); Jhoun Chugg; ed/BA; MSW; PhD; pa/Current Dir Practicum & Asst Prof Grad

Sch Social Work Univ Utah; Clin Mem Am Assn for Marriage & Fam Therapy; Coun on Social Work Ed; Nat Assn Social Wkrs; Nat Conf on Social Wel 1976; Utah Assn Marriage & Fam Cnslrs; Utah Assn Mtl Hlth; Utah Sociol Soc; Utah St Conf on Human Sers; Wom in Social Work; Cert'd Social Wkr, St of Utah; Num Other Profl Activs; cp/Dist Coor Cancer Drive; Area Chm Heart Fund Drive; Alumni Assn Grad Sch Social Work; Former Chperson Interpersonal Relats Com, Commun Sers Coun; Appt'd by Gov as Mem Marriage & Fam Cnslr Bd for St of Utah; Mem 10-Person Fam Ct Study Task Force, St of Utah; Others; hon/Item Writer, Nat ACSW Exam; Social Wkr of Month in Area of Commun Org, Nov 1977; Chosen to be Listed on Pres Carter's *Talent Bank*, Dem Nat Com, 1977; Valedictorian, Social Work Class 1969; F'ship: George Corey Meml Awd, Outstg Sociol Student of Yr 1966; Phi Kappa Phi; Biogl Listings; Profl Pubs; Others.

COWPERTHWAITE, BLANCHE HALLACK oc/Real Estate, Mortgage Banking; b/Jul 6, 1919; h/1625 E 3rd Ave, Denver, CO 80218; ba/Denver; m/Arthur Taylor; c/-Arnold Stephen, Charles Hallack, James Moorhead, Jill Taussig, Arthur T Jr; p/Arnold Stephen and Gertrude Fletcher Hallack Taussig (dec); ed/AB; Grad Work; pa/-Realtor, VP Cowperthwaite & Co; Nat, Colo & Denver Bds Realtors; Dir: S Colo Nat Bank, Mtn Bell; Mem Comm on Judicial Qualifications of St of Colo; St Bd for Commun Cols & Occupl Ed; Pres & Acting Dir Va Neal Blue Ctrs for Colo Wom; AAUW; BPW; Former Mem: Manpower Adv Coun Denver, Mtn Bell Bd Advrs, Reg Coun Small Bus Adm, Bd Capital Improvemts Prog, City & Co Denver; cp/Colo Comm on Wom; Bd Trustees Colo Wom's Col; Bd Dirs Colo Acad; hon/Hon Mem, Delta Kappa Gamma; Intl W/W Commun Ser; W/W Am Wom; World W/W Wom; Commun Ldrs & Noteworthy Ams.

COX, ANNA (NICKY) oc/Homemaker; b/Oct 20, 1944; h/Route 1, Four Oaks, NC 27524; m/Jerry; c/Vince, Clark; p/Herman and Myrtle Vinson, Roseboro, NC; ed/BS E Carolina Univ; pa/Former Johnston Co Home Ec Ext Agt; cp/S Johnston Sch Adv Coun; Johnston Co Commun Sch Coun; Johnston Co Schs Planning Coun; Four Oaks PTA; Johnston Co Farm Bur Wom's Com; Four Oaks Scout Den Mother; r/Meth; hon/Outstg Yg Fam Awd, Cooperative Coun of NC.

COX, BERTHA MAE HILL oc/Teacher; Author; b/Mar 10, 1901; h/1130 N Winnetka, Dallas, TX 75208; m/Willis L; p/Marshall Victor and Ollie E Phifer Hill (dec); ed/BS 1935, MS 1950 N Tex St Univ; pa/Ret'd Tchr; Dallas Assn for Childhood Ed: Mem, Pres 1938, St Secy-Treas 1940; Past Pres Spch Arts Tchrs; Kappa Delta Pi; Delta Kappa Gamma; Life Mem: NEA, TSTA; Author 5 Books; Edited 9 Books; cp/PTA; Dem; r/Meth: Pres Wesleyan Ser Guild, Tchr Ch Sch; Author Ch Sch Mat; hon/Dallas Tchr of Yr 1950; Plaque in Ch for Founding Day Sch, Kessler Park U Meth; Hon Life Mem: Wesleyan Ser Guild, Tex PTA.

COX, BILLY RAY oc/College Administrator; b/Nov 12, 1935; h/9 Magnolia, Searcy, AR 72143; ba/Searcy; m/Patty Ann Overman; c/David, Dale, Kimberly Ann; ed/Bach's Deg summa cum laude Harding Col 1958; Master's Deg (Univ Scholar) So Meth Univ 1961; Doct Deg; 5 CPA Certs; pa/Harding Col: VP, Dir Am Studies Prog, Fac Mem; Tax Bus Conslt, No Ark; Vis Lectr Univ Ark Indust Res & Ext Ctr; Former Gen Opers Mgr Dallas Ceramic Co; Formerly Assoc'd w Ernst & Ernst, CPAs; Mem Am Inst CPAs; Bd Mem: White Co Guaranty Savs & Ln Assn, El Dorado Coffee Co, Harbin Ctr Inc, White Co Ser Corp, Ctl Ark Mortgage Co, The Mad Butcher Inc; cp/Bd Mem: Happy Hills Boys' Ranch, Zambia Christian Col, Yg Ams for Freedom, Nat Security Coun, Ark Foun Assoc'd Cols, Searcy Rehab Housing Inc, Christian Sr Housing Foun; hon/Spec Bicent Speech, "The Rebirth of a Nation - 1976" Received Prin Awd, Freedoms Foun at Val Forge (as Outstg Public Address in Am during

1975); 1976 Speech, "Beyond '76 - The Healing of the Land" Won George Washington Hon Medal, Freedoms Foun.

COX, CATHERINE NEFF oc/Social Worker; b/Sept 28, 1896; h/315 Fourteenth St NW, Canton, OH; m/Vance David McCormac (dec); 2nd Herbert J; c/Vance David McCormac (dec), Elizabeth Annette, Thomas Neff, Peter William, Herbert Earl, Susan Catherine; p/Peter and Susan Elizabeth Williams Neff; ed/Att'd Kindergarten Col of Wn Resv Univ; Postgrad Work Kent St Univ; pa/Tchr Canton & Stark Co (Ohio) Schs; Caseworker ARC; Dir City Wel; Sub-Div Mgr Aid for the Aged; Dir Sr Citizens Prog Stark Co; Ret'd 1964; cp/Vol Work: Sr Citizens, Massillon St Hosp; Public Spkr to Ch Groups & Sr Citizens; Former Mem City Commun Coun; ARC; Dir Jr Red Cross Work; Rep to Ohio Cong of P's & T's on Gov's Comm to Study Needs of Schs; Fdr & 1st Pres Stark Co Coun PTA; Repub Party; r/Epis Ch: Mem, Pres Epis Ch Wom, Diocese of Ohio, Pres Province of MW; hon/Ohio Lives.

COX, DEAN FREEMAN oc/Auto Body Repair; b/May 13, 1927; h/404 S Dekalb, Corydon, IA 50060; ba/Corydon; m/Willa Jeane Grimes; c/Cheryl Christine, Joyce Ann, Jeffrey Keene; p/John Anderson and Myrtle Annis Cox (dec); mil/USNR WWII, S Pacific, SGM USAR; pa/Owner Auto Body Shop; Coor St of Mo, Newland Prod; cp/Chm Ia Vets Coun; Adv Bd Ia Vets Home; Dist Com Am Legion, Dept of Ia; Wayne Co, Dist 93 Chm Dem Party (Ia); r/Bapt; hon/AUS Commend Medal; Outstg Achmt Awds in Scouting.

COX, DONALD EMERY oc/Chemical Engineer; b/Jun 12, 1921; h/369 W Saxet Dr, Corpus Christi, TX 78408; ba/Corpus Christi; m/M Chauncey; c/Albert Emery, Anita Emily C Ekstrand, Raymond Emery; p/William Emery and Vera Hall Cox (dec); ed/BSChE Okla St Univ 1943; pa/VP & Gen Mgr Refinery Terminal Fire Co, Corpus Christi 1978-; w Chem Div PPG Industs 1943-78; Conslt on Engrg, Ec & Envir Studies 1978-; Pres Lower Nueces River Water Supply Dist 1972-; Am Inst Chem Engrs: Mem 1943-, Chm Coastal Bend Sect 1978; Am Chem Soc; S Tex Engr's Clb; cp/Mem Coastal Bend Coun Govts; Envir Quality Com, COG; BSA, Gulf Coast Coun; Cactus & Succulent Clb; Air Pollution Control Assn; Tex Water Conserv Assn; Num Former Activs; hon/Ser to Soc, Nat Awd, AIChE; PPG Industs: Corporate Citizen of Yr 1976 (worldwide), Commun Ser Awd.

COX, EDWIN III oc/Professional Engineer; b/Oct 31, 1931; h/7111 Pinetree Rd, Richmond, VA 23229; ba/Richmond; m/Sally Dreyfus Carr; c/Virginia Meade, Edwin Carr, James Maxwell, William Hatcher; p/Edwin Cox (dec); Virginia DeMott Cox, Aylett, VA; ed/BS Va Mil Inst 1953; MChE Univ Va 1960; mil/USAR 1966-, Col; pa/Nat Soc Profl Engrs; Am Inst CE; Am Water Works Assn;

Water Pollution Control Fdn; Air Pollution Control Assn; Am Inst Chemists; Am Chem Soc; Am Soc for Metals; Am Soc for Testing Mats; Inst of Metals (London, England); Soc Chem Indust (London); Fertilizer Soc (London); Fertilizer Round Table; cp/Sons of Revolution in Va; Hist Richmond Foun; Va Hist Soc; Soc of Colonial Wars; r/St Stephens Epis Ch.

COX, ELINOR DRIVER oc/Director of Recreation; b/Dec 19, 1907; h/310 Parkwynn Apts, Ridley Park, PA 19078; ba/Chester, PA; p/Robert Miller and Edith Driver Cox (dec); ed/BS, MS; pa/Supvr Rec (full time) 1966-, Supvr Rec (pt-time) 1942-66; Smedley Jr HS: Dean of Girls 1953-66, Dir PE 1928-53; Fellow Am Pk & Rec Soc; Nat Assn Sec'dy Sch Prins; Pa Pk & Rec Soc; Rec Promotion & Ser Inc; Nat Writers Clb; IPA; Wilderness Soc; Nat

Wildlife; Intl Wildlife; Defenders of Wildlife; World Wildlife; Life Mem SPCA; Intl Rec Assn; Nat Soc Arts & Lttrs; r/Christ Epis Ch, Ridley Park: Mem; hon/Pub'd Author; Awds of Merit, Dept of Rec; Hon PhD, Colo St Col; Fellow, Intercontinental Biogl Soc; Cit, Nat Fdn Mar of Dimes; Wom of Yr, B'nai B'rith 1963; Cits: ARC, Am Cancer Soc, Am Heart Assn; Dist'd Ser Awds: Chester Ed Assn, Rotary Clb; Num Biogl Listings; Others.

COX, ELIZABETH L oc/Sales Assistant; Free-lance Research/Editoral Work; b/Sept 20, 1927; h/390 Morris Ave, Summit, NJ 07901; ba/New York, NY; p/William H D Cox, Ft Myers Beach, FL; Josenia Elizabeth Larter Cox (dec); ed/BA Univ Vermont; MA

NY Univ; pa/Sales Asst WMCA Radio; Am Polit Sci Assn; Spec Libs Assn; Newspaper Guild; cp/Summit Civil Rts Comm; Union Co (NJ) Adv Bd on Status of Wom; Wom's Polit Caucus; NJ Fdn Repub Wom; Summit Repub City Com; r/Epis; hon/W/W: Am Wom, E.

COX, HARDIN CHARLES oc/Senator; b/Mar 4, 1928; h/602 W Calhoun, Rock Port, MO 64482; m/Virginia Ann Heifner; c/Charles Bryan, Mark Hardin; p/BS Univ Mo-Columbia; mil/AUS 1946-48, Japan Occup Force Signal Corps, Corporal; US Arty 1952-53, US Forces in Korea, 1/Lt; pa/Operator: Cox & Sons Ins Agy, Hardin Cox Real Est, Farm Loan Agy; Secy-Treas Farmers Mutual Ins Co, Rock Port; Farmers Mutual Hail Ins Co; Columbia Mutual Ins Co; cp/Elected to Ho of Reps 1964-72, Elected to Senate 1974, Num Coms; Sigma Chi; QEBH; Ancient F&AMs; Shriner; Am Legion; Mo Univ Alumni Assn; r/Rock Port Luth Ch: Mem; hon/Omicron Delta Kappa; Mo Press 1st Pl Best Personal Column for Weeklies 1969; 4-H Meritorious Awd; Mo Conserv Fdn Leg Awd.

COX, IRENE DICKSON oc/Teacher; b/Oct 12, 1917; h/Rt 1, Box 6, Grassy Creek, NC 28631; m/George Dewey; c/Bill Dickey, Nathalia Sue; p/John Alexander Dickson (dec); Ruby Thompson Dickson, Jefferson, NC; ed/BS Appalachian St Univ 1938; Certn Spec Ed Radford Tchrs Col 1973; Postgrad Work: ASU 1972, Radford St Tchrs Col;

pa/Tchr Eng & French: Lansing (NC) HS 1938-39, Mtn Park Sch, Mtn Park, NC 1939-40; Eng Tchr: Va-Carolina Sch, Grassy Creek 1940-60, Ashe Ctl Sch, Jefferson 1961-67; Tchr Spec Ed Mount Rogers Sch, Whitetop, Va 1971-76; cp/Charter Mem U Daughs of Confed; DAR: Past Pres Va-Carolina Commun Inc; Former Registrar Grassy Creek Precnt; Former Mem NC Ext Homemakers Assn; Others; r/Grassy Creek Bapt Ch: Mem, Yg People's Tchr 1954-60; pa/Cert of Apprec, Nat Beta Clb, Spartanburg, SC; Recipient S'ships; W/W: Biogl Record-Child Devel Profls, S&SW; World W/W Wom; Personalities of S.

COX, JACK C oc/Oceanographer; b/Nov 16, 1951; h/6281 Bright Plume, Columbia, MD 21044; ba/Columbia; m/Margaret Ann;

p/Arthur C and Noma Fay Cox, Quincy, IL; ed/BS; MS; PhD Cand; pa/Oceanographer ARCTEC; AGU; ASCE; SNAME; NACE; r/Presb; hon/Davis Fellow.

COX, JEAN ELIZABETH oc/Secretary; Homemaker; b/Jul 11, 1937; h/Rt 6, 411 Marcia Dr, Goldsboro, NC 27530; ba/G'boro; m/Willard Thomas; c/Michael Thomas, Melinda Jeanne, Rhonda Lynne; p/Arthur Harrelson and Mary Pinson McQueen, Loris, SC; ed/Att'd: Limestone Col, Wayne Commun Col; cp/Wom's Dem Party; So Wayne Wom's Clb; r/Bapt: SS Tchr; hon/Rep'd Wom in Paper on Mother's Day; Awds for Art; Cand for Mrs Am.

COX, JOSEPH MASON ANDREW oc/Publisher; Professor; Poet; Writer; b/Jul 12, 1929; h/801 Tilden St, Bronx, NY 10467; ba/Bronx; c/Terrance McRae, Kelly Ann; p/Hiram Cox (dec); Edith C Henderson (dec); ed/BA; LLB; PhD; pa/Authors Leag Am; Exec Bd Poetry Soc Am; cp/N Bronx Dem Clb; r/Unitarian-Universalist; hon/Intl Poet Laureate; Gold Medal for Poetry; Fellow, Intl Acad of Poets; Has Read Poetry at White House; Rep'd US at World Poetry Conf at Expo "67"; Intl Poets Shrine; Daniel S Mead Intl Essay Awd; Pres Johnson's Great Soc Writer's Awd; The Master Poets Awd; The World Poets Awd; Others.

COX, MARYGRACE oc/Educator; b/Oct 29, 1910; h/413 E 5 Ave, Jerome, ID 83338; c/Janet C Peterson, William Brackett, Camille Grace C Irwin, Carolyn Zorah C Matsuoka; p/James Ira and Mary Grace Brackett, Reubens, ID; ed/BS Univ Idaho; pa/Jerome Ed Assn; Pres Idaho Ed Assn; NEA; Cong P's & T's; Life Mem IRA; BPW Clb; cp/Civic Clb; Toastmistress Clb; Jerome Art Guild; Pres Gem St Writers Guild; Dem Wom Assn; r/Jerome U Meth; hon/Commun Ldrs of Am; BPW Achmt Awd; World W/W Wom; A Brackett Fam Dir.

COX, NANCY INGLE oc/Administrative Secretary; b/Jan 11, 1941; h/708 45th Ave N, Nashville, TN 37209; ba/N'ville; m/Andrew W; c/Nancy D Lamb, Charlotte W, Joyce Rena, Andrew David; p/Sanford Thurlo Ingle (dec); Willie Nelson Ingle, Sheffield, AL; ed/N Ala Bus Sch; Addit Studies: Univ N Ala, Belmont Col, Univ Tenn-N'ville; pa/Adm Secy The Urban Observatory of Metro N'ville; Former Mem Nat Secys & Legal Secys of N'ville; cp/PTA; r/Park Ave Bapt Ch, N'ville: Mem; hon/Honor Soc.

COXE, NELSON Y oc/Arbitrator;

Industrial Relations Consultant; b/Oct 6, 1912; h/Clearwater Park, Covington, VA 24426; ba/Same; m/Mary Lee; c/Keren, Rowena Anderson; p/Edward H and Keren-Happuch Coxe (dec); ed/BS Lehigh Univ 1934; pa/Pvt Indust Relats Conslt; Formerly Assoc'd w: G E, Schenectady, NY, Westvaco Corp, Mechanicville, NY & Covington, Va; Former Instr R P I, Troy, NY; Nat Labor Panel of Am Arbitration Assn; cp/Treas UF; Chm Leag of Older Ams; r/Presb; hon/Hudnall Citizenship Awd; Boss of Yr Awd.

CRABTREE, ARTHUR BAMFORD oc/Professor; b/May 5, 1910; h/H10 Radwyn Apts, Bryn Mawr, PA 19010; ba/Villanava,

PA; m/Hanna; c/Martin; p/George and Harriet Crabtree (dec); ed/BA; BD; DTheol; pa/Prof Rel Studies Dept Villanova Univ; r/Bapt.

CRAHAN, JACK B oc/Executive; b/Aug 24, 1923; h/1195 Arrowhead, Dubuque, IA 52001; ba/Dubuque; m/Peggy F; c/Patricia M, Colleen Mary, Kevin Furey; p/J F and Ann B Crahan, Long Lake, MN; ed/BA; mil/USMC Maj; pa/Exec VP; cp/Bd Dirs: Dubuque Bank & Trust, Loras Col, Xavier Hosp; r/Cath.

CRAIG, JOHN DAVID oc/Administrator; b/Nov 10, 1935; h/4821 Gaviota, Encino, CA 91436; ba/Los Angeles, CA; m/Nancy; c/Carrie, Matthew, Jennifer; p/George N and Kathryn L Craig, Brazil, IN; ed/AB 1957, JD 1970 Ind Univ; mil/USAR 1957-65; pa/Dir Corporate Affairs AM Intl Inc; Spec Agt FBI; NBC Coor Talent & Prog Adm 1961-66; Asst Gen Counsel Assocs Corp 1970-72; Pvt Pract 1972-78; Instr Constitutional & Media Law Ind Univ 1972-75; Fdr Ind Forum; Phi Beta Kappa; Am, Ind, Los Angeles Trial Lwyrs; Am Judic Soc; ABA; Cal & Ind Bar Assns; cp/Cal Rep Ctl Com; Cal & Ind Rep Platform Comm; LA Coun World Affairs; LA Public Affairs Ofcrs; LA Rotary #5; hon/Sherman Minton Court Awd; Others.

CRAIG, VERNON EUGENE oc/Lecturer; Entertainer; Author; b/Jan 7, 1932; h/323 Ihrig Ave, Wooster, OH 44691; ba/Same; m/Ruth Lavonne; c/Vicki Lynn, Scott Gregory, Brenda Lee; p/Orville and Leona Thomas Craig, Middletown, OH; pa/Lectr on Mind Control; Coauthor (w Brad Steiger): *Life Without Pain & Komars Secrets of Pain Control;* cp/Dover Exchange Clb; r/Mormon: Elder; hon/Outstg Yg Man 1966; Ky Col; Rec'd Tiemyer-Augustine Awd; Outstg St Chm, US JCs; Num Biogl Listings.

CRAIG-HOLMES, ANN PRESTON oc/Cytogeneticist; b/Nov 13, 1939; h/7707 Bankside, Houston, TX 77071; ba/Same; m/John G Holmes; c/Stacey Elizabeth; p/R T and Elizabeth Craig, Glade Spring, VA; ed/BS; MS; pa/Res Asst Med Genetics Ctr Grad Sch of Biomed Scis, Univ Tex, Tex Med Ctr, Houston 1967-; Res Asst Dept Pediatrics Stanford Med Ctr, Palo Alto, Cal 1964-67; Lab Technician Dept Human Genetics Univ Mich, Ann Arbor, Mich 1961-63; Other Former Positions; Am Soc Human Genetics; Am Soc for Cell Biol; r/Prot; hon/Mortar Bd; W/W Am Cols & Univs; Merit S'ship, Univ Tex Grad Sch Biomed Scis.

CRAIN, ADA ELIZABETH oc/Retired Teacher, Librarian; b/Sept 18, 1904; h/400 Cedar River Dr, Lot 21, Fowlerville, MI 48836;

p/(dec); ed/BS SW Mo St Tchrs Col; MEd Univ Mo; cp/Sr Citizens Coun; Vol Hillcrest St Hosp; Garden Clb; r/Meth; hon/F'ville's Most Outstg Citizen, VFW Post; Notable Ams Bicent Era; W/W Am Wom; World W/W Wom; 2000 Wom Achmt.

CRAIN, HAZEL MAE oc/Educator; b/Mar 22, 1926; h/1641 Devoe Dr, Lincoln, NE 68506; ba/Lincoln; p/Arthur P Crain (dec); G Pearl Tunis Crain, Lincoln; ed/BSE; ME; PhD Colo St Univ; pa/Edr Univ Neb; Am

Home Ecs Assn; Neb Home Ecs Assn; Am Voc Assn; Neb Voc Assn; Delta Kappa Gamma; r/U Ch of Christ; hon/Outstg Edrs; Neb Voc Ed Awd; Hon'd by Am Voc Assn; Delta Kappa Gamma S'ship.

CRANDALL, IRA CARLTON oc/Consulting Engineer; b/Oct 30, 1931; h/5754 Pepperridge Pl, Concord, CA 94521; ba/Walnut Creek, CA; m/Jane Leigh Ford; c/Elizabeth Anne, Amy Leigh, Matthew Garrett; p/Carlton F and Claire H Crandall, De Land, FL; ed/BSRE 1954, BSEE 1958 Ind Inst Tech; BSEE US Nav Postgrad Sch 1962; LLB Blackstone Sch Law 1970; MA Piedmont Univ 1967; PhD Univ Sussex; mil/USNR 1949-72; Comm'd Ensign 1955, Active Duty 1955-72, Ret'd as Lt Cmdr 1972; Presently Inactive Duty Nav Air Resv Unit; Navy Univ Cit; Navy Expeditionary Medal; Armed Forces Expeditionary Medal; Nat Def Ser Medal; Vietnam Ser Medal; Vietnam Cross of Valor; Other Mil Hons; pa/Conslt'g Engr; Fellow Am Col Engrs; Sr Mem Am Inst Tech Mgmt; Charter Mem Assn Energy Engrs; IEEE; US Nav Inst; Soc Am Mil Engrs; Assn Naval Aviation; cp/YMCA; PTA; SAR; Optimists; Resv Ofcrs Assn; Repub; r/Meth Ch: Mem; hon/Hon DSSc, Piedmont Univ; Hon DLitt, St Matthew Univ; Hon EdD Mt Sinai Univ; Pi Upsilon Eta; Gamma Chi Epsilon; SAR: War Ser Medal, Silver Good Citizenship Medal; Pres Cit, Optimist Intl; Num Biogl Listings.

CRANDALL, VERN J oc/Professor; b/Mar 18, 1939; h/1224 E 700 South, Provo, UT 84601; ba/Provo; m/Linda Rae; c/Lance Vernon; p/Bliss H and Mildred Johnson Crandall, Provo; ed/BA w hons Brigham Yg Univ 1963; MSc Ks St Univ 1966; PhC 1968, PhD 1972 Univ Wash; pa/Brigham Yg Univ: Assoc Prof Computer Sci & Statistics 1974-; Asst Prof 1968-74; Innovation Enterprises Inc: VP, Treas & Dir 1969-; Mortgage Sers Inc: Secy, Dir 1975-; Statistical Conslt Inst Logopedics, Wichita, Ks 1964-65; Other Former Positions; AAAS 1968-70; Am Statistical Assn: Mem 1963-, Treas Utah Chapt 1976-77; Wn NAm Reg Biometric Soc; Inst Math Statistics; Pattern Recog Soc; Soc for Computer Simulation; cp/Former Mem Lions Intl; Repub; r/Ch of Jesus Christ of LDS: Lifetime Mem, Mission Pres, Bishopric, St Exec Secy, Others; hon/Recipient S'ships & Traineeships; Outstg Yg Men Am.

CRANE, CHARLES ARTHUR oc/Minister; b/Jul 4, 1938; h/2216 Wyoming Ave, Caldwell, ID 38605; ba/Caldwell; m/Margaret Lucile; c/Carol E, Douglas G, Steven A; p/Claude C Crane (dec); Jessie L Edwards, Sweet Home, OR; ed/BA; MA; MDiv; CPE; DDiv; pa/Prof Boise Bible Col; Author 2 Pub'd Books; cp/Kiwanis Intl; r/Christian Ch; hon/W/W: Rel, World, W.

CRANE, FRANCES HAWKINS oc/Paint-

er; b/Jul 8, 1928; h/5058 Wingfoot, Corpus, Christi, TX 78413; ba/Same; m/Gene Calvin; c/Cynthia Susan C Rogers, Cheryl Elizabeth; p/Henry Cleo Hawkins (dec); Laura Elizabeth Hawkins, Corpus Christi; ed/pa/Free-lance Artist; r/Bapt; hon/World W/W Wom; DIB; Top Art Awds in Local, St, Nat & Intl Shows.

CRANK, WINFRED DONALD oc/Sales Representative; b/Apr 11, 1932; h/104 Redwood Dr, Hot Springs, AR 71901; ba/Hot Springs; m/Kathleen; c/Robin, Christopher, Martin Dockery, Shelly Dockery; p/John Crank (dec); Luda Crank, Puxico, MO; ed/BS; Chartered Life Underwriter; pa/Sales Rep Metro Life Ins; Pres Hot Springs Life Underwriters Assn; Ctl Ark Chapt Soc Chartered Life Underwriters; Former VP Ark Assn Life Underwriters; Former Chm Ark St Sales Cong; Instr Bus Ins Course Life Underwriters Tng Coun 1975-77; cp/Housing Chm Nat Gospel Singing Conv; r/Oaklawn U Meth Ch: Dir Music, Yth Cnslr; hon/Ch Fam of Yr 1976.

CRANNY, TITUS FRANCIS oc/Clergyman; b/Apr 15, 1921; h/Graymoor, Garrison, NY 10524; ba/Same; p/Daniel and Teresa Clarke Cranny; ed/BA; MA; STL; STD; pa/Tchr, Writer; Am Cath Theol Soc; Ecumenical Soc of Mary; Intl Marian Acad; Franciscan Ednl Conf; r/Cath; hon/Author Sev Books incl'g: *Book of Meditations*, *Father Paul and Christian Unity*, *Fr. Paul: Apostle of Unity*, Others.

CRAVEN, DOUGLAS CHARLES oc/-Electrical Engineer; b/Sept 8, 1952; h/1013 Ambrose Ln, Hixson, TN 37343; ba/Daisy, TN; m/Pamela June Vick; c/Stephen Douglas; p/Charles C and Cora Beatrice York Craven, Cookeville, TN; ed/BS Tenn Technol Univ 1974; pa/Elect Engr Tenn Val Auth; IEEE; Am Nuclear Soc; Tau Beta Pi; Phi Kappa Phi; Order of the Engr; Eta Kappa Nu; r/Burks U Meth Ch: Mem Adm Bd, Sports Comm, Stewardship Com, Sonshire SS Tchr; hon/Putnam Co True Gentleman 1970; Engrg Devel Scholar; Upper Cumberland Sci Fair Scholar.

CRAWFORD, CLAN JR oc/Lawyer; b/Jan 25, 1927; ba/Ann Arbor, MI; m/Alice Biship Berle; c/Peter, Lloyd, David; ed/Grad cum laude Univ Sch, Shaker Heights (Ohio) 1944; AB Oberlin Col 1948; JD Univ Mich 1952; pa/Credit Reporter Dun & Bradstreet Inc, Cleveland, Ohio 1948-50; Admitted to: Mich Bar 1953, US Dist Ct 1953, US 6th Circuit Ct of Appeals 1954; Pract Law Ann Arbor 1953-, (w Roscoe O Bonisteel 1953-57, sole practitioner 1957-); 1st Asst Washtenaw

Co Prosecuting Atty 1955-57; Washtenaw Co Bar Assn; St Bar Mich; ABA, Var Coms; Lectr; cp/Former Ann Arbor City Coun-man; Former Chm Ann Arbor Civic Art Com; Former Mem Ann Arbor Zoning Bd Appeals; Former Chm Ann Arbor Sesquicentennial Beautification Com; Ann Arbor Civic Theatre; Sierra Clb; Mich Soc Planning Ofcls; Tri-Co Sportsmen's Leag; Trout Unlimited; Steering Com for ENACT Envir Teach-In, Univ of Mich 1970; Other Civic Activs; hon/Author 3 Books.

CRAWFORD, DAVID WRIGHT oc/-Teacher; Playwright; b/Aug 15, 1951; h/508 S Spring, Tyler, TX 75702; ba/Tyler; m/Toni K Cassaday; p/Ira Melvin and Bonnie Wright Crawford, Tyler; ed/AA Tyler Jr Col; BS N

Tex St Univ; MA Stephen F Austin St Univ; pa/Tchr Tyler Jr Col; Tex Ednl Theatre Assn; Theatre Dir, Lighting Design; Produced Off-Broadway at Provincetown Playhouse "Plumage", 1978; r/Green Acres Bapt Ch, Tyler; hon/2nd, Tex 1-Act Play Contest; Premiered 2 plays at NY & Tex.

CRAWFORD, JAMES FRANKLIN oc/Economist; b/May 16, 1920; h/1096 Clifton Rd, Atlanta, GA 30307; ba/Atlanta; m/Miriam Weirick; c/Cathy Ann, David; p/Frank M Crawford, Tabor, IA; Loie Marie Yerger Crawford; ed/AB Peru Col 1941; MA Univ Colo 1952; PhD Univ Wis 1957; mil/USN 1942-46, Lt (jg); pa/Prof & Chm Dept Ecs Ga St Univ; Pres Atlanta Chapt Indust Relats Res Assn 1978-79; Mem Exec Com Atlanta Ecs Clb; cp/Commun Disputes Settlemt Panel, Am Arbitration Assn; Reg 3 Ec Stabilization Com, Ofc of Emer Planning; Bd Trustees Ga Coun on Ec Ed.

CRAWFORD, MAXINE GRACE oc/Administrator; b/Jul 24, 1918; h/1502 Cedar Hill Dr, Dallas, TX 75208; ba/Dallas; m/Raymond Lee Sr; c/Raymond Lee Jr, Jerry John; p/Adolphus Earl Grace (dec); Mary Catherine Hays (dec); ed/BFA, MLA So Meth Univ; pa/Dep Admr US Dist Ct for No Dist Tex; AAUW; Bd Dirs Dallas Fed Bus Assn; Nat Fed Ct Clerk's Assn; cp/Dallas Co Hist Soc; Daughs of Repub of Tex; Life Mem: SMU Alumni Assn, SMU Mother's Clb; Poetry Soc Tex, Dallas Chapt; r/Highland Pk Presb Ch, Dallas; hon/Contbr art & photo to *Tex Hist Award Winning Essays*, 1971-76; Intl W/W Among Intells.

CRAWFORD, SHIRLEY EAGLEY oc/-Associate Professor; b/Aug 2, 1933; h/RD#3, 253 Nelson Rd, Canastota, NY 13032; ba/Morrisville, NY; m/Jack; c/Kathleen, Jonathan, Mary; p/Karl C and Nellie Fairburn Eagley (dec); ed/BS Pa St Univ; MAT Rollins Col; PhD Col Envir Sci & Forestry; pa/Assoc Prof Biol SUNY; Mem NSF Review Com; Exec Com NYS Reg II Biologists; Participant 2 NSF Grants; Resource Com Nat Assn for Envir Ed; cp/Chperson Madison Co Water Quality Mgmt Comm; Madison Co Hlth Systems Coun: Chperson Hlth & Envir Status Com, Bd Dirs; r/Epis; hon/Phi Kappa Phi; Pa St Wom's Chem Hon; Recipient 1976 SUNY Fac Res F'ship; Outstg Edrs Am Awd; W/W Am Wom; Outstg Female Fac; EPA Cert of Apprec.

CRAWFORD, WILLIAM EDWIN oc/Seminary Administrator; b/Dec 19, 1918; h/3800 Ashford, Fort Worth, TX 76133; ba/Fort Worth; m/Inez Gilliam; c/Dan Reavis, Bob Floyd; p/W E and Mattie Heard Crawford (dec); ed/BA Baylor Univ; BD SWn Bapt Theol Sem; mil/AUS Chaplain, Capt; pa/Dir Devel SWn Bapt Theol Sem; Nat Soc Fund Raisers; r/Bapt; hon/DIB; W/W: Rel, S&SW.

CRAWLEY, WESLEY V oc/Professor; b/Mar 1, 1922; h/104 Dogwood Dr, Greenville, NC 27834; ba/G'ville; m/Fanchon Milne; c/John M, James W; p/(dec); ed/AB; MS; mil/USAAF 1941-46, Capt; pa/Prof Art E Carolina Univ; Sculptor, Known for Portraits & Figures; cp/Bd Dirs G'ville Art Soc; r/Presb; hon/Num Public & Pvt Comms.

CRAY, CLOUD LANOR JR oc/Grain Processor, Distiller; b/Nov 7, 1922; h/RR #1, Atchison, KS 66002; ba/Atchison; m/Sara

Jane Hunter; c/Karen Lee C Seaberg, Susan Hunter C Robbins, Cathy Lynn C Freund; p/Cloud Lanor Cray, Atchison; Edna Reinoehl Cray (dec); ed/BS cum laude Case Inst Technol 1943; mil/AUS Signal Corps 1944-46; pa/Pres Atchison Leather Prods Co 1976-; Pres Wheat Gluten Indust Coun 1975-; Dir Security Benefit Life Ins Co 1974-; World Bus Coun 1973-; Alt Dir Distilled Spirits Coun 1973-; Dir Ks Power 0 Light Co 1972-; Pres MW Grain Processing Equipmt Co 1972-; Other Profl Positions; Distillers Feed Res Coun: Dir 1949-72, Pres 3 terms; Yg Pres Org; Other Pres Org; cp/Former Dir & VP Unified Dist #409 Sch Bd; Former Trustee Col Emporia (Ks); YMCA Atchison: Former Dir, Former VP & Pres; Trustee Atchison Hosp Assn; Former Mem Human Relats Comm Atchison; Var Repub Party Activs; r/Presb; hon/Atchison's Outstg Yg Man of Yr 1948; Dist'd Ser Awd, Distillers Feed Res Coun; Atchison Liberty Bell Awd; W/W: MW, World of Commerce & Indust; Commun Ldrs Am; Notable Ams.

CREE, ALLAN oc/Petroleum Consultant; b/Jul 10, 1910; h/Box 3945, West Sedona, AZ 86340; ba/Same; m/Margaret S; c/Robert Boone II, Mary Catherine C McCormick (Mrs Lloyd E); ed/AB No Ariz Univ 1933; MA Ohio Univ 1935; PhD Univ Colo 1948; Att'd: Univ Ariz, Stanford Univ, Colo St; pa/Petrol Conslt W Sedona 1972-; Assoc Petroconslts, Geneva, Switzerland 1974-; Bd Dirs: OSEC Inc, Oklahoma City, Okla 1976-, Ulster Petrols Ltd, Calgary, Alberta 1974-, OSEC Petrol AG, Munich 1972-73; Coor Intl Exploration Cities Ser Intl Inc, Tulsa, Okla

1970-72; Mgr Exploration Intl Div, Cities Ser Oil Co, Bartlesville & Tulsa, Okla 1966-70; Other Former Positions; Am Men Sci; Am Assn Petrol Geologists: Past Pres & Past Secy En Sect, Past Rep En Sect & Mont Dist; Assn Profl Geol Scists, Pres Okla Sect 1971; Geol Soc Am; AAAS; Mont, Wyo, Tulsa Geol Socs; Life Mem NEA; Adv Com for Dept Geol, NY Univ; Am Mus Natural Hist, NY: Bd Dirs, Dept Micro-Paleontol; Mont Oil & Gas Conserv Comm; Am Assn Petrol Geologists' Strategic Com for Public Affairs; Other Profl Orgs; cp/Ariz Hist Soc; Mem Var CCs; B'ville (Okla) C of C; hon/Sigma Xi; Kappa Delta Pi; Sigma Gamma Epsilon; Alpha Psi Omega; Phi Tau Theta; Alpha Phi; Presentations & Pubs.

CREEK, JERRY WAYNE oc/Pastor; b/Apr 4, 1948; h/Rt 4, Sherman, TX 75090; ba/Sherman; m/Judy Tate; c/Jasen Tate; p/Gurstel and Ruth Creek, Glen Carbon, IL;

ed/BS So Ill Univ; MDiv SWn Bapt Theol Sem; pa/Pastor Luella 1st Bapt Ch; BSU Evangelist; Instr New Testament Grayson Co

Col; cp/Staff Mem Boy's Clb; r/So Bapt; hon/W/W in Rel.

CREEKMORE, FREDERICK HILLARY oc/Attorney; b/Nov 12, 1937; h/261 Bridgeview Cir, Chesapeake, VA 23320; ba/Chesapeake; m/Margery Keith Buchanan; c/Marystuart, Hillary, Carla; p/Allie and Ruth Creekmore, Chesapeake; ed/BA Richmond Col, Univ Richmond 1960; JD TC Williams Sch Law, Univ Richmond 1963; pa/Atty; Past Pres Chesapeake Bar Assn; cp/Past VP Chesapeake Gideon Camp; Past Pres: Chesapeake Civitan Clb, Great Bridge JCs; Mem Va Ho of Dels 1974-; Bd Dirs Chesapeake Hlth Systems Inc; Great Bridge Royal Arch Chapt 82; Great Bridge Masonic Lodge No 257; Former Mem Bd Dirs: Tidewater Heart Assn, Cystic Fibrosis Foun Tidewater Chapt; r/Great Bridge Presb Ch: Mem, Elder; hon/Outstg Pres, Region I, Va JCs.

CREER, THOMAS LASELLE oc/Clinical Psychologist; b/Nov 2, 1934; h/8043 E Oberlin, Denver, CO 80237; ba/Denver; m/Patricia J Plummer; c/Jennifer, Matthew; p/Laselle L Creer, Provo, UT; ed/BS; MS; PhD; mil/AUS 1956-58; pa/Num Psychol & Sci Activs; r/LDS.

CREGGER, MILDRED RODGERS oc/Associational Administrator; b/Jan 7, 1922; h/Creggwood Pl, Rt 2, New Castle, VA 24127; ba/Roanoke, VA; m/Morris McClure; c/Morris McClure Jr; p/Martel O and Bessie Lee Owen Rodgers, Roanoke; ed/Att'd: Roanoke Col 1942, NYU 1945, Va Poly Inst 1949; pa/YWCA Roanoke Val Camp-on-Craig: Dir Hlth, PE & Rec Dept 1957-, Adult Dir 1956-57, Activs Coor 1953-56; Advt'g & Public Relats Sports Ser Co, Buffalo 1941-46; cp/Roanoke Val Safety Coun; Chm Water Safety Comm ARC; Roanoke Val C of C; BPW; Former Activs; r/Meth: Former SS Tchr; hon/Hon/Chief Seabee Resv Nav Mobile Constrn Battalion 23 Detachmt 0223; W/W Am Wom; Personalities of S.

CREMORA, GOUDA oc/Physician; Sex Therapist; b/May 11, 1943; h/1800 Taylor Ave #412, Seattle, WA 98109; ba/Same; p/Alfred Cremora, Seattle; Elizabeth Cremora-Dinsmore; ed/BS Universidad De Santa Larca (Pedillo, Spain) 1967; MD L'Institut De Suisse-Roman (Basil, Switzerland) 1973; pa/Dir NW Sex Clin; cp/Secy-Treas Queen Anne Restoration Soc.

CRENSHAW, TENA LULA oc/Medical Librarian; b/Dec 15, 1930; h/1408 SE Bayshore Dr, #1012, Miami, FL 33131; ba/Miami; p/Herbert Joseph Crenshaw; Nellie Wicker; ed/BS Fla So Col; MLS Univ Okla; pa/Med Libn Louis Calder Meml Lib Sch of Med, Univ Miami; Former Hd Sers to Public A W Calhoun Med Lib, Emory Univ, Atlanta, Ga; Res Info Analyst, Res Info Specialist, Lockheed Missiles 0 Space Co, Palo Alto, Cal 1966-68; Other Former Positions; Med Lib Assn; Spec Libs Assn; Spec Libs Assn, Biol Scis Div; Am Soc for Info Sci; Ga Lib Assn; SEn Lib Assn; Ga Hlth Scis Lib Assn; r/Epis; hon/Univ Okla S'ship.

CRESSON, RUTH ELIZABETH HAYNER oc/Homemaker; Former Astronomer; b/Apr 16, 1918; h/32 Amherst Ave, Swarthmore, PA 19081; m/William J Jr; c/Charles O, Richard H; p/DeEldon E Hayner, Philadelphia, PA; Elizabeth Heerd Hayner (dec); ed/BA Mt Holyoke Col; MA Mills Col; pa/Astronomer US Nav Observatory, Wash DC; Astronomy Instr Mt Holyoke Col; r/Meth; hon/F'ship Awd for Grad Study 0 Astronomical Assistance at Mills Col, Cal.

CREWS, ESSIE J oc/Librarian; h/Rt 1, Box 322, Hilliard, FL 32046; ba/Same; m/J A; c/Robert Johnson, Cheryle C Pearson; p/Stephen Owen and Ola Ellen Weaver Raulerson (dec); ed/AB, MS Univ Fla; MS Fla St Univ; pa/NEA; PTA; Alpha Delta Kappa; cp/Dem; r/Ch of God: Mem, Tchr; hon/Fla Personalities; W/W: Am, Ed.

CRIADO, VALENTIM B oc/Artist; Writer; b/Mar 31, 1931; h/119 Globe Ave,

San Antonio, TX 78228; ba/Paris, France; p/Valentim Criado and Herminia Hernandez, San Antonio, TX; ed/Masters: Nuclear Energy, Cosmic Energy; p/USMC; pa/Painter, Sculptor; hon/Cosmonaute Satellite Awd.

CRIHAN, IOAN G oc/Electronics Engineer; b/Mar 8, 1931; h/417 E 64th St 4G, New York, NY 10012; m/Marietta Enescu; ed/Grad Radar Dept Tech Mil Acad (Romania) 1955; Grad Utilization of Radioisotopes Romanian Acad 1968; pa/Elects Engr Bucharest Univ, Romania; Radiation & Solid State Lab, NY Univ; Owner Art Restoration & Irradiating Preservation Inc, NYC; Creator of 1st Pvt Co in World to Apply Nuclear Radiation Statue Preserv of Work of Art; Assisted in Restoration of Statue of Liberty, NYC; Fdn Am Scis; IEEE; Assn for Preserv Technology (Canada); Preserv League of NY St; Others; cp/US Senatorial Clb; Nat Repub Senate Com; Am Security Coun Nat Adv Bd; Legis Adv Com, NY St Senate; IPA; r/Orthodox; hon/Patentee; Mem, Intl Biogl Assn; Life Patron, Am Biogl Inst; Intl W/W Intells; Men of Achmt; Others.

CRIM, CLAIRE GAMBLE oc/Home-maker; Civic Worker; b/Jun 3, 1914; h/7920 Hayden Dr, Knoxville, TN 37919; ba/Same; m/Henry Frank; c/Barbara C St John; p/Frank Carlton and Robbie Lucile Hughes Gamble (dec); ed/Att'd Ks City Col; Spec Adm in Govt Tng, Rock Isl Arsenal 1942; pa/Ofc Mgr Oil Co, Birmingham, Ala 1942; Redstone Arsenal, Huntsville, Ala 1942-45; Civilian Chief of Property Div; cp/Hist Presv

& Restoration; Presentation Com for Teen Bd, K'ville; Art Coun K'ville; Dulin Art Gallery; Preserv of Tenn Antiquities; James White Fort, Blount Mansion Assn; Chm Knox Co Coun of Regents, DAR; Sr Pres Isaac Anderson Soc, Chd of Revolution; Knox Co Lineage Res Asst, DAR; Others; r/Church St U Meth: Class Ofcr; hon/Hon'd at Mayor's Dinner for 10 Yrs Ser on Teen Bd Presentation Dance Com; Cmdg Ofcr Redstone Arsenal for Dist'd Ser.

CRIM, JOHN WINTHROP oc/Professor; b/Nov 9, 1924; h/3421 Seminole Dr, Columbus, GA 31907; ba/Columbus; m/Jean Beresford; c/Lucinda C Hill, Martha Winthrop; p/William D Crim (dec); Susan Copland Crim, Ann Arbor, MI; ed/BME; MBA; PhD; mil/USNR Ret'd; pa/Prof Bus Mgmt Columbus Col; Acad Mgmt; Am Compensation Assn; r/Epis; hon/Cert'd Mgr.

CRIPPEN, EDWARD FILMORE oc/Med-ical Consultant; b/Nov 9, 1921; h/1265 N Michigan Ave, Howell, MI 48843; ba/Howell;

m/Kathryn S; c/Janie C, Edward F, Frederick A, Joel S, Ember L, John N; p/Glen L and Margaret A Crippen (dec); ed/BS Mich St Univ 1943; MD 1950, MPH 1961 Univ Mich; mil/USAR, Lt Col 1975; pa/Med Conslt, Fam Pract Intl Hlth & Occupl Med; MAFP, Hlth Sers Coun; AMA; MSMS; APHA; AQMA; Livingston Co Med Soc; Vis Com, Univ Mich Med Alumni; cp/Del Nat Repub Conv 1960; Rotary Clb, Howell; Explorers Clb; Intl Dwarf Tree Assn; Mich Adac Fam; r/Luth; hon/Bd Cert'd, Fam Pract & Preventive Med; W/W: W, Med Specialties.

CRISMAN, MARY FRANCES B oc/Librarian; Director Emeritus; b/Nov 23, 1919; h/6501 Burning Tree Ln, Tacoma, WA 98406; m/Fredric Lee (dec); p/Lindon Arthur and Mary Cecelia Donnelly Borden (dec); ed/BA (Hist) 1943, BA (Libnship) 1944 Univ Wash; pa/Dir Emeritus Tacoma Public Lib; Am Lib Assn, Var Ofcs & Coms; Pacific NW Lib Assn, Var Coms; Wash Lib Assn: Past Treas, Exec Bd; Past Mem Exec Bd Urban Libs Coun; cp/Past Pres Tacoma Clb; Quota Intl; Pres Friends of Tacoma Public Lib; Past Pres Tacoma Lodge Ladies Aux Intl; Trainworkers Union; Tacoma Symph Guild; AAUW; Others; r/Rom Cath; hon/DIB; Notable Ams Bicent Era; W/W: Am, W, Am Wom.

CRISPIN, CHARLES HONNOLD oc/Retired Architect, Minister, Writer; b/Jul 26, 1914; h/4954 Kahala Ave, Honolulu, HI 96816; ba/Same; m/Zilda Guimaraes; c/Helen, Alessandra, Cristina, Eric, Angela Adriana; p/Egerton Lafayette Crispin (dec); Angela Shipman (dec); ed/Att'd: Stanford Univ, Univ So Cal Col of Arch; pa/Am Inst Aeronautics & Astronautics, NY; Am Soc Landscape Archs, Wash DC (Hi Chapt); Engrng Assn Hi; Scarab Arch Frat; Arch Guild, Univ So Cal; cp/Gen Soc Colonial Wars, Gov Hi Soc; Gen Soc Sons of Revolution, Cal Soc; Baronial Order of Magna Charta; Mil Order of Crusades; Order of Augustan Eagle; Welsh Soc Philadelphia; Geneal Soc Pa; Hist Soc Pa; Nat Trust for Hist Preserv; AF Assn; Navy Leag US; Intl Oceanographic Foun; Honolulu Acad Arts; Stanford Clb Hi; Waikiki Yacht Clb, Honolulu; Other Civic Mbrships; r/Min, Nonsectarian; hon/Knight, KCR.

CRISTIANO, ESTHER R oc/Artist; Writer; Poet; Columnist; b/Oct 1, 1915; h/7271 Katella #89, Stanton, CA 90680; m/Joseph; c/John, Robert, Barbara; p/Joseph and Lottie Charlotte, Detroit, MI; pa/Pres Writers Clb; Writer of Lyrics for Music; r/Universal; hon/1st Awd, Poetry, Sculpture; Wom of Achmt; W/W Wom; Plaque for Poetry; Total 19 Awds.

CRISTOBAL, ADRIAN LORETO oc/Retired Guam Senator; US Postal Service Station Contractor; b/Dec 10, 1921; h/10 Ungaguan St, Barrigada, Guam 96913; ba/Barrigada; m/Concepcion Torres Finona; c/Carmen, Adrian Jr, John; p/Adriano Maria and Carmen De Leon Untalan Cristobal (dec);

mil/USN 1941, Enlisted Seaman; Prisoner-of-War & Vet WWII; Hon Released as Musician 1st Class 1946; pa/Exec Asst Ricky's Auto Co, Agana, Guam 1969-72; Public Relats Conslt, Comml Port Guam 1967-69; Chm Guam Ec Devel Comm 1961-62; Proprietor/Mgr Nito's Store & Market, Barrigada, Guam 1950-67; Other Former Positions; cp/Senator Guam Leg 1970-76: Minority Ldr 1975-76, Mem

Inter-Govtl Relats Com Nat Conf St Legs 1975-76, Other Com Mbrships; Former Mem Ctl Exec Com Dem Party of Guam; Former Dem Nat Com-man Guam; Elks Lodge 1281, Agana; Yg Men's Leag Guam; Others; r/Rom Cath; hon/Outstg Ser Awd, Future Farmers Am; US Navy Good Conduct Medal; Am Pacific-Asiatic Campaign Victory Medal; WWII Medal.

CRITCHLOW, SUSAN MELISSA oc/-Advertising Executive; b/Dec 24, 1950; h/-5318 Ortega Forest Dr, Jacksonville, FL 32210; ba/Orange Park, FL; m/Warren H Jr; p/James C and Mildred E Pringle Barley, Tampa, FL; ed/BA 1972, MA w hons 1973 Univ S Fla; pa/Pres SC&A, Orange Park 1977-; Dir Info Sers Gtr Orange Park Commun Hosp, Orange, Fla 1974-; Coor Public Relats St Luke's Hosp, J'ville 1974; Asst Public Relats Dir Goodwill Industs N Fla Inc, J'ville 1973-74; Other Former Positions; Fla Public Relats Assn; Pres IABC, NE Fla Bus Communicators; Bd Mem Fla Hosp Assn's Public Relats Coun; Past Pres Gtr J'ville Hosp Public Relats Coun; Public Relats Soc Am; cp/Pilot Clb Orange Park, Treas; Am Cancer Soc Bd Dirs, Clay Co Unit; Alumni Assn Univ S Fla; r/Epis; hon/Fla Hosp Assn: Gold Awd, Silver Awd; Fla Public Relats Assn: Cert of Merit, 1st Place Maj Promotions, 2nd Place Minor Promotions; Crusade Cit, Am Cancer Soc; W/W S&SW.

CRITELLI, IDA JOANN oc/College Teacher; b/Feb 1, 1940; h/153 Junefield Ave, Cincinnati, OH 45218; ba/Cinc; m/Thomas Andrew Schick; c/Michele Maria Schick, Michael Montague Schick; p/Giuseppe and Maria Martino Critelli, Highland Park, MI; ed/BA summa cum laude Nazareth Col 1961; MA 1963, PhD 1965 Marquette Univ; pa/Edgecliff Col, Cinc: Lectr in Phil 1977-, Assoc Prof Phil 1969-70; Lectr in Phil George Mason Univ, Fairfax, Va 1975; Asst Prof Phil

Xavier Univ 1968-69; Free lance Writer/Lectr 1968-; Other Former Positions; Kappa Gamma Pi; Am Cath Phil Assn; Am Phil Assn; Inst of Soc, Ethics 0 Life Scis; cp/Former CoChm Xavier Univ Forum Lecture Series; Former Mem Edit Adv Com *St Anthony Messenger* Mag; Former Mem Bd Trustees: Birthright of Cinc, Nazareth Col (Kalamazoo, Mich); Former Mem Adv Coun Nazareth Col; r/Rom Cath; hon/Coauthor 1 Book *Unmarried and Pregnant--What Now?*, 1977; Contbr Articles & Book Reviews to Mags.

CROCKER, DOROTHY BRIN oc/Registered Music Therapist; Piano Teacher; Composer; b/Jul 29, 1913; h/2-20-6 Lakeside Dr, Fairfield Bay, AR 72088; m/Harold Ford; c/Hal Kenneth, Thomas Edward; p/Maurice

Rene and Elma England Brin (dec); pa/Dir Music & Music Therapy Shady Brook Schs 1948-66; Mem Music Fac So Meth Univ 1950-70; Pres Nat Assn Music Therapy 1957-59; Pres Dallas Music Tchrs Assn 1967; Pres SWn Music Therapy; Am Soc for Group Psychotherapy & Psychodrama; cp/Spkr for Civic Clbs; Vol Wkr: Mtl Instns, Hosps for Crippled Chd; Conslt Sch for Blind Chd; r/Epis; hon/Hon Life Mem: Nat Assn for Music Therapy, Jr Pianists Guild; Awd of Merit, Mu Phi Epsilon.

CROCKETT, ANNE ALLEN oc/Educator; b/Aug 26, 1933; h/2552 Cherosen Rd, Louisville, KY 40205; ba/L'ville; p/Waller Allen Crockett (dec); Lide Chenault Crockett; ed/BA; MA; Adv Cert; EdD Cand; pa/Edr Brown Ed Ctr; Phi Delta Kappa; Delta Kappa Gamma; AASA; NASSP; KASA; ASCD; cp/Wom's Clb; Trustee Brooklawn Chds Clb; Filson Hist Clb; r/Prot; hon/John Hay Fellow; GE Fellow; Lily Fellow; Mem-at-Large, CEEB, So Reg.

CROCKETT, H DALE oc/Clergyman; b/Feb 17, 1933; h/306 Prospect, Berea, KY 40403; ba/Berea; m/Ruth Alice Bays; c/Bruce Michael, Mark Stephen, Laura Ellen, Philip Colin; p/Charles Randolph Crockett (dec); Gladys Robinett Crockett, Marion, IL; ed/BA Union Univ; MDiv SEn Bapt Theol Sem; DMin San Francisco Theol Sem; Addit Studies: Iliff Sch of Theol, Oxford Univ; pa/Pastorates: Fountain Meml Bapt Ch, Washington DC, 1st Bapt Ch, Sioux City, Ia, NWn Am Bapt Ch, Detroit, Mich, Union Ch, Berea Col, Berea; Parish Devel Conslt; Contbr to Rel Pubs; Dir Personal Growth & Christian Ed Wkshop; cp/World Hunger Coor & Spkr; r/Am Bapt (No); hon/High Commend for Doct Dissertation.

CROMEENES, JAMES RICHARD oc/Counselor, Farmer, Politician; b/Mar 12, 1934; h/29 Marberry Dr, Metropolis, IL 62960; ba/Metropolis; m/Mary Ann Korte; c/J Chris, Cindy Ann; p/Reed F and Elle A Baker Cromeenes, Metro; ed/AS; BBA; MRE; mil/AUS Security; pa/Mem Var Profl Orgs; cp/City Alderman 3 Terms; Del to Nat Repub Conv 1976; r/Am Luth.

CROMER, CHARLES MARION oc/Poetry, Philosophy, Singing, Music; b/Sept 15, 1943; h/117 Bostick Dr, Longview, TX 75602; p/Hiram Elisha and Mary Jackson Cromer, Longview; pa/Writer Poems; Pianist; r/Bapt; Former Yth Ldr & Bible Sch Wkr; hon/S'ship, Le Tourneau Col.

CROOKE, STANLEY THOMAS oc/Associate Director; b/Mar 28, 1945; h/110 Scottholm Blvd, Syracuse, NY 13224; ba/Syracuse; m/Nancy Alder; c/Evan Christopher; p/Robert E and Catherine E Crooke, Indianapolis, IN; ed/BS; MS; PhD; MD; pa/Assoc Dir Res & Devel Bristol Labs 1977-; Clin Asst Prof Dept Med Upstate Med Ctr 1977-; Var Former Positions; AAAS; Am Assn for Cancer Res; Am Soc for Microbiol; Cancer & Acute Leukemia Group B; Am Soc for Clin Pharm & Therapeutics; Am Soc for Pharm & Experimental Therapeutics; Am Soc for Clin Oncol; Other Profl Activs; hon/NCI Grant; Outstg Lectr in Basic Sci, Baylor Col of Med; Instnl Res Awd, Nat Cancer Inst; So Med Assn Res Awd; Public Hlth Ser Postdoct & Predoct F'ships; Pub'd Author.

CROSBY, FRED McCLELLAN oc/Furniture Company Executive; b/May 17, 1928; h/2530 Richmond Rd, Beachwood, OH 44122; ba/Cleveland, OH; m/Phendalyne Tazewell; c/Fred Jr, James, Llionicia; p/Fred D and Marion C Crosby, LaPuenta, CA; mil/AUS 1950-52, S/Sgt, Hon Disch; pa/Pres CEO, Crosby Furniture Co Inc; Bd Trustees: Minority Ec Devel Corp (Chm), Cleveland Bus Leag (Secy), Ohio Furnishings Assn (Pres), Coun of Smaller Enterprises (Secy), 1st Bank Nat, Loan & Discount Comm (Chm), Ohio Coun Retail Merchs, Gtr Cleve Growth Assn, Cleve Bus Leag; Mem-at-Large Nat Home Furnishings Assn; cp/Nat Bus Leag; Buckeye Exec Clb, St of Ohio; Bd Trustees: Hiram House, Coun for Ec Opports in Gtr Cleve,

Woodruff Hosp, Cleve Automobile Clb, Goodwill Industs, Var Former Orgs; Cleve Coun on World Affairs; Cleve Coun on Human Relats; Harvard Bus Sch Clb Cleve; Mid-Day Clb Cleve Inc; Wn Resv Hist Soc; Cleve Concert Assn; CoChm NAACP Freedom Fund Dinner Dr; Bd Trustees Fdn for Commun Planning; Others; hon/Man of Yr, 13th Dist Civic Leag 1977; Cert of Apprec for Civic Involvement, Mayor of Cleve 1976; Outstg Am Awd; YMCA Pres' Awd (2); Whitney M Young Awd, Urban Leag Cleve; Deus Optimus Awd, Pentecostal Ch of Christ; Prog in Bus Awd, Nat Coun of Negro Wom; Biogl Listings; Others.

CROSE, JAMES GREGORY oc/Engineer; b/Mar 27, 1938; h/3117 S Pacific Ave, Santa Ana, CA 92704; ba/Santa Ana; m/Judith Kaye Phelps; c/Steven Scott, Douglas Todd, Gregory Neil; p/Paul T and Eithel Z Smith Crose, Washington MO; ed/BS Wash Univ 1960; MS 1962, PhD 1967 Univ Ill; mil/AUS, to Capt; pa/Dir Adv Technol Prototype Devel Assoc Inc; ASCE; AIAA; Applied Mechanics Reviews; Am Acad Mechanics; r/Bapt; hon/NDEA Fellow; Assoc Fellow, AIAA; Sigma Xi; Phi Kappa Phi; Tau Beta Pi; Phi Eta Sigma.

CROSS, IRVIE KEIL oc/Minister, Editor, School Administrator; b/Mar 21, 1917; h/9649 Foster Rd, Downey, CA 90242; ba/Bellflower, CA; m/Johnnie Maxine Sharp; c/Johnnie Keilene C Barnes, Irvie Irviene C McCombs; p/William Earl and Bertha Frances Harris Cross, Texarkana, AR; ed/ThM; ThD; DD; mil/Tex Guard 194?-48, Chaplain, Capt; pa/Pastor; Adm VP Cal Missionary Bapt Inst; Editor Bapt Sentinel; Pres Am Bapt Assn; cp/Pres C of C (Ky); Pres Guild Artists & Craftsmen (Ky); r/Missionary Bapt; Pres En Bapt Assn; Moderator Cumberland River Assn; hon/Pioneer Awd, Ky Col; Ark Traveler; USAF Cit; W/W: Rel, S&SW, Ky.

CROSS, ROBERT MICHAEL oc/Banking Executive; b/Nov 26, 1938; h/25276 Arcadian, Mission Viejo, CA 92691; ba/Irvine, CA; m/Judy; c/Michael, David; p/Dolly Cross, Seal Beach, CA; ed/BS Univ Wis 1963; mil/USN, Hon Disch; pa/Pres Bkrs Investors Group Inc (Investmts); Gov Cal Chapt Am Inst Bkg Reg 4 1978; Pres Bayside Merchs Assn; Am Soc Pers Adm 1968-71; cp/Past Pres Saddleback Val Aquatics Swim Team; Former Dir Newport Harbor C of C; r/Intl W/W Commun Ser; W/W: W, Fin & Indust, Am Cols & Univs.

CROSSER, CAROLYN HAYS oc/General Manager; b/Feb 27, 1943; h/740 Paris Pike, McKenzie, TN 38201; ba/McKenzie; m/Joe E; c/Tony, Deon, Casey; p/Bob Hays (dec); Belle A Hays, Darden, TN; ed/Att'g Bethel

Col; pa/Gen Mgr WKTA Radio; Salesperson; Former Hairdresser; BPW Clb; Nat Assn Am Wom in Radio & TV; cp/Col Gov's Staff; r/1st Bapt Ch: Mem, Former SS Tchr; hon/Supersales Person 1978.

CROTTS, MARCUS BOWMAN oc/- Engineer; b/Aug 6, 1931; h/10 Gomar Ln, Winston-Salem, NC 27106; ba/W-S; m/- Margo Jackson; c/Van, Laura; ed/BME NC St Univ; MSME Univ Ill; mil/USAF, Lt in Aircraft Maintenance Engrg; Korean Vet; pa/Partner Crotts & Saunders Engrng Inc; Owner Crotts Enterprises Inc; Formerly Assoc'd w: Duke Power Co, Babcock & Wilcox Co, Wn Elect Co; Dir Am Machine

Tool Distributors Assn; Am Soc Mech Engrs: Life Mem, VP, Mem of Coun; Soc Mfg Engrs: Life Mem, Nat Dir; Profl Engrs NC; NC Soc Engrs; Numerical Control Soc; Instn Prodn Engrs (London, England); Past Pres W-S Engrs Clb; Lic'd Reg'd Profl Engr: NC, SC, Va; cp/W-S C of C; Past Clb Pres Rotary; Forsyth CC; Pvt Pilot; r/1st U Ch of Christ, W-S: Mem, Brotherwood Activs, Chm Bldg Com; Bd Govs Nazareth Chds Home; hon/Awd of Merit, SME; Pub'd Author; W/W in Engrg.

CROTTS, STEPHEN MICHAEL oc/- Ordained Minister; Writer; b/Apr 14, 1950; h/PO Box 187, Charlotte Ct House, VA 23923; ba/Same; m/Kathryn; c/Claire, Bryan; p/George and Betty Crotts, Graham, NC; ed/BA Furman Univ; MDiv Emory Univ; pa/Min Presb Ch USA; Frequent Guest Preacher; Author 5 Books; cp/Repub; r/Presb.

CROUCH, ANNA BELLE oc/Professor; b/Nov 11, 1918; h/411 Union St, Murfreesboro, NC 27855; ba/M'boro; p/Joseph Earl Sr and Iva Mae Crouch (dec); ed/BS SE Mo St Univ 1942; MRE So Bapt Theol Sem 1947; MA Columbia Univ 1967; pa/Chowan Col: Prof Spch 1961-, Prof Profl Devel 1960-69, 1975-77, Prof Rel 1959-63, Prof Music 1958-62, Prof Hygiene 1960-63, Asst Dean of Wom 1958-66; Dir Music & Ed

Rosemary Bapt Ch, Roanoke Rapids, NC 1955-58; Dir Music: M'boro Bapt Ch 1966-71, Branchville Bapt Ch, Va 1973-74; Spch Correctionist Southampton Public Schs, Va Spring 1970; NC Spch & Drama Assn; So Spch Commun Assn; Spch Commun Assn Am; Other Former Activs; cp/M'boro Hist Assn; M'boro Wom's Hist Leag; NC Hist Preserv Soc; Chowan Col Commun Concert Assn; Chowan Col Spkrs Bur; Chowan Col Wom & Wives Clb; Wom's Div M'boro C of C; M'boro Fed'd Wom's Clb; Coastal Plains Devel Assn Travel & Rec Com; Other Civic Activs; r/M'boro Bapt Ch: WMU, Adult SS Tchr & Supt, Ch Choir; hon/Dir Chowan Col

Hist Pageant "Through the Yrs", 1961 & 73; World W/W Wom in Ed; Personalities of S; W/W S&SW; Contbr to Var Denom Pubs; Others.

CROUCH, PHILIP ANDREW oc/Minister, Educator; b/Dec 6, 1916; h/R22, Box 244D, Springfield, MO 65803; ba/S'field; m/Hazel Conway; c/Mark, Wedge; p/(dec); ed/BA; MA; DD; pa/Assemblies of God: Min, Missionary 1937-57, Edr 1957-; r/Assemblies of God; hon/DDiv 1977.

CROW, MARY LYNN oc/Professor, Director; b/Aug 30, 1934; h/5000 Fall River Dr, Fort Worth, TX 76103; ba/Arlington, TX; p/Herman G and Harriet Copeland Cox, Fort Worth; ed/BA summa cum laude 1956, MEd 1967 Tex Christian Univ; PhD N Tex St Univ 1970; pa/Univ Tex-A: Dir Fac Devel Resource Ctr & Prof of Ed 1978, Dir Fac Devel Resource Ctr & Assoc Prof Ed 1973-77; Pvt Pract Psychol 1973-77; Other Former Positions; POD Network: Exec Dir 1977-78, Core Com 1977-80; Am Psychol Assn: Ednl Psychol Div, Psychol of Wom Div; Tex Psychol Assn; APGA; Tex Pers & Guid Assn, Var Activs; Am & Tex Sch Cnslrs Assn; Am Assn for

Cnslr Ed & Supvn; Tex Assn Cnslr Edrs & Supvrs; Tex Assn Tchr Edrs; Tex Soc Col Tchrs Ed; Tex St Tchrs Assn; Tex Assn Col Tchrs; Am Assn Higher Ed; Delta Kappa Gamma; Phi Delta Kappa; cp/Forum Ft Worth; Tarrant Co Humane Soc; Action for Foster Chd, Former Mem Exec Com; hon/Piper Prof of Tex 1975; S'ship, Ldrship Ft Worth; Nat Awd, APGA; Outstg Tchr at UTA 1972; Doct S'ship, N Tex St Univ; Phi Theta Kappa; Valedictorian, Tex Christian Univ 1956; Arlington Female Newsmaker of Yr 1975; A'ton *Citizen-Journal*; Face of Arlington 1976, *Arlington Daily News*; Others.

CROWDER, CAMELLIA HUFFMAN oc/Staff Assistant; b/Oct 1, 1940; h/Rt 2, Box 56, Fincastle, VA 24090; ba/Roanoke, VA; m/Steve E; c/Steven Edward; p/Walter W and Irene Craft Huffman, Roanoke; ed/Grad Nat Bus Col; pa/Staff Asst Hon M Caldwell Butler, Mem of Cong; Past Pres Roanoke Val Legal Secys Assn; r/Bapt; hon/Roanoke Val Legal Secy of Yr 1965; Va St Legal Secy of Yr 1967.

CROWE, HILDA FAYE oc/Registered Nurse; Instructor; b/Oct 11, 1935; h/200 Oakland Dr, KosciusKo, MS 39090; ba/Kosciusko; m/James N; c/Rene, Loiuse; p/Thomas Jefferson Peoples (dec); Eva Malone McDaniel, Philadelphia, PA; ed/Grad Studies: Univ So Miss, Miss Col Univ; pa/Instr Hlth Occups Jr Col; Miss Nurses Assn; Am Nurses Assn; Nat Assn Reg Emer Med Tech; Miss Emer Med Sers; Co-Owner Ctl Ofc Supply Co, Kosciusko & Phila; Kosciusko BPW Clb: Pres, Mbrship Chm, Club Hostess, Exec Bd, Bd Dirs, Others; Miss Emer Cardiac Care Com; Attala Co Heart Assn; Miss CPR Quality Control Com; Attala Co Heart Assn; Miss Heart Assn; Bd Dirs Miss Lung Assn; Miss Div Am Cancer Soc; Bd Dirs Cathy Collins Blood Bank; Spkrs Bur Kosciusko-Attala C of C; Kosciusko Little Theatre; Hostess Natchez Trace Fest Hospitality Booth; Miss St Univ Alumni Assn; Kosciusko Band Boosters Clb; Others; r/1st U Meth Ch: Mem, Choir Mem, Robe Chm; Good Shepherd Neighborhood Chm; Participant Commun Easter Sers; Instr Disaster Response Team, N Miss Meth Conf;

hon/Wom of Achmt, Kosciusko BPW Clb; 1978 Outstg Citizen, Attala Co; 3rd Place "Wom of Achmt", Miss Fdn BPW Clbs.

CROWLEY, FRANCES FELICIA oc/Educator; b/Mar 22, 1921; h/515 N Sprigg, Cape Girardeau, MO 63701; ba/Cape Girardeau; m/Cornelius Joseph; c/Robert, Veronica; p/Oscar Geyer (dec); Mathilda Crastan (dec); ed/BA; MA; PhD; pa/Prof Mod Langs Semo St Univ; Past Pres Cape Girardeau Writers' Guild; cp/Mem SE Mo Coun on the Arts; r/Presb; hon/Phi Sigma Iota.

CROWLEY, RALPH MANNING oc/Psychiatrist, Psychotherapist, Psychoanalyst; b/Nov 13, 1905; h/7 W 96th St, Apt #2E NY, NY 10025; c/Stephen F, Michael Anderson, Daniel Yost, Jonathan R, Patrick M; p/Frances Manning and Ada Fuller Crowley (dec); ed/BA 1926; MA 1928; MB 1933, MD 1934 NUMS; mil/USNR 1942-46, Lt Cmdr; pa/Pvt Pract 1936-; Psychi Conslt Var Agys; Vis Psychi Roosevelt Hosp; Vis Lectr Albert Einstein Sch Med; Fellow Emeritus W A White Inst Psychi; cp/Var Conservation Activs; Nat Peace Acad; Common Cause; Nature Conservancy; hon/Hon Staff Mem, Sheppard & Enoch Pratt Hosp, Towson, Md; Phi Beta Kappa; Alpha Omega Alpha.

CROWTHER, ROBERT HAMBLETT oc/Consultant; b/Mar 17, 1925; h/4205 W 91st St, Prairie Village, KS 66207; ba/Same; m/Mary Nan McKeever; c/Philip Everett, Deborah Marie, Hugh Gordon; p/Louis Everett Crowther, Mayfield Hgts, OH; Julia

Emeline Hamblett Crowther (dec); ed/BChemEngrg; MS; mil/USAAF 1943-46; pa/Conslt in Energy, Ecs & Hydrocarbon Processing; Am Inst Chem Engrs; Am Petrol Inst; hon/Sigma Xi; Phi Lambda Upsilon; W/W MW; DIB.

CROZIER, VIVIAN oc/Photographer; b/Sept 3, 1920; h/Box 68, Roosevelt, NJ 08555; ba/Hightstown, NJ; m/Robert; p/Maurice and Elizabeth DeLisser Samburg; pa/Contbr Fashion Photos to: Mademoiselle, American Girl, Bazaar, Others; hon/World W/W; W/W Am Wom.

CRUM, PATSY YOUNG oc/Reading Coordinator; b/Mar 29, 1934; h/Rt 9, Surtout Rd, Greeneville, TN 37743; ba/G'ville; m/Paul Edward; c/E Grant, Patrick W; p/Leon G Young (dec); Evelyn Brinkley Young, Roan Mountain, TN; ed/BS; MA; pa/Rdg Coor G'ville City Schs; Alpha Delta Kappa; NEA; TEA; IRA; TIRA; Right-to-Read; cp/En Star; Commun Concerts Assn; Greene Co Hist Trust; UF Rep; r/Christian Ch; hon/Personalities of S; W/W: Child Devel Profs, Am Cols & Univs; World W/W Wom.

CRUM, PAUL EDWARD oc/Public Health, Environmentalist; b/Aug 19, 1933; h/Rt 9, Surtout Rd, Greeneville, TN 37743; ba/G'ville; m/Patsy Young; c/E Grant, Patrick W; p/Paul Crum (dec); Kate R Crum, G'ville; ed/BA E Tenn St Univ; pa/Tenn Environmentalist Assn; NEA; Tenn Public Hlth Assn, Chm Envir Sect; cp/Masonic Order; Kerbela Shrine; Scottish Rite; Elks; Moose; Chm Park Comm; TSSAA Ftball Ofcr; Kinser Klown Korp, Lt; r/Christian Ch: SS Ofcr.

CRUMB, ANNE MARIE THERESA

oc/Medical Technologist; b/Dec 20, 1946; h/1110-0 St, Troy, NY 12182; ba/Albany, NY; m/John Kenneth; c/Richard Kenneth, Michele Lynn; p/Frank M Tarsa (dec); Mary J Tarsa, Mechanicville, NY; ed/BS; MT (ASCP); pa/Med Technol St Peter's Hosp (Microbiol Lab); Am Soc for Med Tech; Empire St Assn for Med Tech: Treas, Bd, Noms Chair; Capital Dist Chapt ESAMT: Pres, VP, Secy, Newslttr Ed, Const & By laws Chair, Mbrship Chair; Infection Control Com SPH; cp/Citizens Choice; WCCS Mother's Clb; Nat CB Law Enforcemt Org; r/Rom Cath; hon/Outstg Med Tech; W/W: World, Am Wom; Notable Ams; World W/W Wom.

CRUMBLY, JOHN QUANTOCK oc/-Priest; b/Nov 2, 1916; h/12 George St, A3, Charleston, SC 29401; m/Meda C; p/Frank W and Anna Walden Crumbly (dec); ed/BDiv; MDiv; pa/Epis Priest; Rector & Chaplain Diocese of SC; Diocese Upper SC; Diocese S Fla & Diocese Wash; r/Epis; hon/W/W in Rel; Men of Achmt; DIB.

CRUMBO, MINISA oc/Artist; b/Sept 2, 1942; h/6630 E 60th Pl, Tulsa, OK 74145; ba/Tulsa; p/Woodrow and Lillian Hogue Crumbo; ed/Att'd Tex Wn Univ, Univ Colo-Boulder, New Mex Acad Fine Arts, Sch Visual Arts (NYC); pa/1-Wom Shows: Gilcrease Inst of Am Hist & Art (Tulsa) 1976, Tulsey Town Gallery (Tulsa) 1975, USSR 1978-79, Roy Clark Ranch Party-TV Spec 1976, Pottawatomie Agri & Cultural Ctr (Shawnee, Okla) 1977, Okla Gov's Spec Showing 1976, Adobe Gallery (Las Vegas, Nevada) 1977; Pvt Collections in US & Europe; Guest Instr, Taos Pueblo Day Sch Ctr; Native Am Ch, 1st Indian Art Show to Tour Soviet Union; Others; hon/Work Rep'd in Perm Collections: Heard Museum (Phoenix, Ariz), Gilcrease Inst Am Hist & Art, Philbrook Art Ctr (Tulsa); Graphics Awd for Pencil Drawing, "Creek Woman", 29th Am Indian Exhbn at Philbrook Art Ctr.

CRUMP, KENNY SHERMAN oc/Professor; Consultant; Researcher; b/Oct 13, 1939; h/1729 Hodges Rd, Ruston, LA 71270; ba/Ruston; m/Shirley Edmondson; c/Faith, Tanya, Casey; p/Sherman and Travis H Crump, Haynesville, LA; ed/BS; MA; PhD; pa/Statistical & Math Conslt & Res; r/Bapt.

CRUMP, RICHARD LOY oc/Principal; b/Sept 2, 1935; h/2313 Dogwood Ln, Orange Park, FL 32073; ba/Jacksonville, FL; m/Betty Abernethy; c/Jon Richard; p/Richard Lexington Crump (dec); Effatta D Crump, Mt Holly, NC; ed/BS Wn Carolina Univ; MAT Jacksonville Univ; EdD Nova Univ; mil/USN 4 Yrs, Ofcr; pa/Prin Jr HS; NASSP; FASA; FASSP; Phi Delta Kappa, Past Pres J'ville Chapt; r/Presb: Elder; hon/DIB; Personalities of S; W/W S&SW.

CRUNK, BIRDA FLORENCE oc/Homemaker; h/317 St Charles St, San Antonio, TX 78202; m/Robert L; c/Robert Fredrick, John Fitzgerald, Lynn Denise; p/William A and

Novella Reed (dec); pa/Poetess; r/Bapt; hon/Recipient Certs for Vol Sch Work, from Ch for Writing a Book, from Poetry Soc & Amateur Songwriters & Poets.

CRUSE, HELOISE II P oc/Columnist; b/Apr 15, 1951; h/San Antonio, TX; ba/New York, NY; p/Marshal H Cruse, San Antonio; Heloise Bowles (dec); ed/BA; pa/Columnist

King Features; Tex Press Woms Assn; hon/Hon Chair, SWT Parents Clb.

CRUSIUS, MILTON WOOD oc/Geologist; Geophysicist; Writer; b/May 9, 1922; h/7139 Galleon, Houston, TX 77036; ba/Houston; m/Lois L; c/Timothy, Bryan; p/Milton W Crusius Sr (dec); Georgie G Dahlberg, Fort Pierce, FL; ed/BS Univ Tex-Austin 1949; mil/USN 1940-46, Gunner's Mate; Vet Pearl Harbor Dec 7, 1941; pa/Humble Oil & Refining Co (now Exxon Co USA), Houston: Geophysicist 1949-64, Data Analyst 1966-70, Tech Writer Earth Scis 1970-; Geologist & Geophysicist Argus Oil Explorations Africa Ltd, Cape Town, S Africa 1964-66; Soc for Tech Commun, Chm Houston Chapt 1974-75; Am Assn Petrol Geologists; cp/Advsr Explorer Post, BSA; r/Prot; hon/Author (w Dearl T Russell) Geology of El Rancho Crime, 1963; Contbr. Articles on Geol of S Africa to Profl Jours; W/W S&SW.

CRUZ, CARLOS oc/Entomologist; b/Dec 24, 1940; h/Rt 1, BZN-L-18, Aguadilla, PR 00603; ba/Isabela, PR; m/Elsa Iris; c/Claribel, Brenda; p/Carlos and Aurora Cruz, Aguadilla; ed/BSA; MS; PhD; pa/Res; Tchg; cp/Sev Civic Coms; r/Cath; hon/Var.

CUELHO, ANTIE JOSEPH oc/Artist; Novelist; Short Story Writer; Poet; b/May 20, 1943; h/Box 214, Big Timber, MT 59011; m/Mae; c/Ira, Eli, Rhonda, Rusty; p/Arthur J Cuelho, Riverdale, CA; Ida Cuelho (dec); ed/AA; pa/Editor: Black Jack Mag, Valley Grapevine Mag; Pubr Seven Buffaloes Press; hon/Pushcart Awd.

CUERVO, ROBERT FELIX oc/Political Scientist; b/Aug 1, 1948; h/85-44 111 St, Richmond Hill, NY 11418; p/Felix J and Phyllis Cuervo, Richmond Hill; ed/BA 1970, MA 1973 St John's Univ; mil/USN 1970-72, Navy Dept, Wash DC; pa/Am Polit Sci Assn; Ctr for the Study of the Presidency; cp/Public Relats Dir Native New Yorkers' Hist Assn; r/Rom Cath; hon/Grad Asst'ship, St John's Univ; Earhart Foun F'ship.

CUFF, WILLIAM AUBREY oc/Retired Teacher; b/Aug 8, 1897; h/Danielsville, GA 30633; m/Ruby Rogers; p/Virgil and Levinia Cuff (dec); ed/BSEd, MA 1933 Univ Ga; mil/USAAF 1942-46; Instr Aviation Cadets Cochran Field, Ga 1942-43; Transferred to Enlisted Resv Corps, Employed by Secy of War in Classification & Wage Adm until 1946; pa/Univ Ga: Asst Prof Bus Adm & Chm Secretarial Studies Dept 1957, Ret'd 1963; Pres Athens Bus Col (after retiremt); Tchr Emanuel

Col 1964; Tchr Bus Ed, Knoxville, Tenn 1934-42; Other Former Tchg Positions; Contbr to Tchr's Manual 1954; Pub'd Letter Writing Handbook 1957, Revised & Reprinted 1960; Lecture Staff of Inst of Life Ins for Course in Fam Fin 1958; Secy Tenn Bus Ed Assn 3 Yrs; 10th Dist Dir Ga Bus Ed Assn 2 Yrs; NEA; GEA; GBEA; DHE; AAUP; Phi Kappa Phi; Phi Beta Kappa; Other Profl Activs; r/Meth; hon/Hon'd by Gregg Pub'g Div of McGraw Hill in Connection w Diamond Jubilee Celebration of Gregg Shorthand; Hon DLit, Brantridge Forest Sch.

CUKJATI, JOSEPH FRANK oc/Veterinarian; b/Oct 29, 1936; h/1609 Canyon Oaks St, Irving, TX 75061; ba/Irving; m/Helen Charlene Lillig; c/Joseph John, Julie

Ann, Christopher Lee, Curtis Allen; p/Joseph John and Julia Virginia LeRoy Cukjati; ed/BS Ks St Univ 1958; DVM 1960; mil/USAF 1960-62, Capt; pa/Assoc: Vine Vet Hosp, Chapel Hill, NC 1962-63, Bogue Animal Hosp, Wichita, Ks 1963-64, Ridglea Animal Hosp, Ft Worth 1964; Owner: Story Rd Animal Hosp, Irving 1964-, N Irving Animal Clin, Irving 1971-; Conslt J & L Ranches, Girard, Ks 1960-75; Am & Tex Vet Med Assns; Dallas Co Vet Med Assns: Dir 1970-75, Secy 1973-74, Pres 1976-77; Am Animal Hosp Assn; Am Vet Radiol Assn; cp/Former Mem Bd Dirs Prevention Cruelty to Animals, Dallas; Irving C of C; Ks St Univ Alumni Clb; Alpha Gamma Rho; hon/W/W S&SW.

CULBERSON, RANDALL EDWARD oc/Engineer; b/Apr 25, 1952; h/966-2 Marcus Dr, Newport News, VA 23602; ba/Surry, VA; m/Rebecca Ann Williams; p/Reid Taylor and Betty Lou Hands Culberson, Miami, FL; ed/BSEE summa cum laude Univ Fla 1974; AA Miami Dade Jr Col 1972; Further Studies: Univ Fla, Univ Miami, US Navy Nuclear Power Sch; mil/USN 1974-76, Ofcr, Nav Reactors Div; pa/Nuclear or Elect Engr Va Elect &

Power Co, Surry Nuclear Power Sta 1976-; Conslt'g Engr-Designer Donald Weeks & Assocs 1971-72; IEEE; Am Nuclear Soc; Nat Soc Profl Engrng; Fla & Va Engrng Soc; cp/VEPCO: Fire & First Aid Team, Golf Team; Dir Hampton Rd JCs; NCAA Soccer Ofcl; Va HS Ftball & Soccer Ofcl; US Soccer Fdn Ofcl; Repub Party; r/Bapt; hon/Patent Pending for Invention of Mobile Nuclear Generation Plant; Var Acad Hons; Personalities of S; W/W of Am.

CULLUM, RIXIE T oc/Medical Volunteer Liaison; b/Sept 10, 1922; h/2932 Oak Knob St, Tyler, TX 75701; m/Felder W; c/Maureen Leverenz; p/William B Tisdel (dec); Cora B Tisdel, Beckworth, CA; ed/Att'd: Univ Hi, Univ Md; cp/Mem St Gov'g Bd Tex Assn Hosp Auxs Inc, Austin; Pres-elect Med Ctr Hosp Aux, Tyler; Bd Dirs: Smith Co Chapt

Am Cancer Soc, Mtl Hlth Assn Tyler; Tyler Woms Forum; Mem & Past Ofcr: Ctl E Tex Orchid Soc, Rose City Organ Clb; r/1st Christian Ch, Tyler; Mem, Chancel Choir; hon/Hon'd for Outstg Ser to Cause of Cancer Control, Am Cancer Soc; Dist'd Citizens Day Honoree, Tyler.

CULPEPPER, JETTA C oc/Librarian; h/Rt 8, Murray, KY 42071; ba/Murray; p/Palmer and Reva Culpepper, Murray; ed/BS; MA; MLS; EdS; pa/Libn Murray St Univ; Ky Lib Assn; SEn Lib Assn; Others; r/U Meth; hon/Biogl Listings.

CULPEPPER, RICHARD ALAN

oc/Assistant Professor; b/Mar 2, 1946; h/8507 Para Ct, Louisville, KY 40222; ba/L'ville; m/Jacquelyn; c/Erin Lynn, Rodney Alan; p/Hugo H and Ruth C Culpepper, L'ville; ed/BA cum laude Baylor Univ 1967; MDiv So Bapt Theol Sem 1970; PhD Duke Univ 1974; pa/Asst Prof New Testament Interpretation So Bapt Theol Sem 1974-; Res Asst for W D Davies 1971-73; Pt-time Instr Dept Rel Duke Univ 1971; Pastor Macedonia Bapt Ch, Madison, Ind 1968-70; Soc Biblical Lit; Assn Bapt Profs of Rel; SS Lesson Illustrator; r/Crescent Hill Bapt Ch, L'ville; Mem, Deacon; hon/Author *The Johannine Sch*, 1975; Also Articles & Book Reviews; Outstg Yg Man Am.

CULYER, RICHARD C III oc/Associate Professor; Author; b/Feb 12, 1939; h/Rt 3, Box 80, Mt Gilead, NC 27306; ba/Hartsville, SC; m/Gail B; c/Ginger; p/Brice R (Stepfather) and Virginia F Smith, Oakboro, NC; ed/BS 1959, MA 1963 Appalachian St Univ; PhD Fla St Univ 1974; pa/Assoc Prof Ed Coker Col 1976-; Free-lance Curric Conslt 1974-76; Asst Dir Rt to Read Dept of Ed, St of Fla 1973-74; Tchg Fellow Fla St Univ 1972-73; Other Former Positions; NC Coor IRA 1975-81; Pres: NC Coun for IRA 1971-72, Gtr Appalachian Coun IRA 1970-71, Montgomery

Co Coun of IRA 1977-78; Editor Conf Proceedings NCCIRA 1971-; IRA: Leg Com 1976-78, Parents & Rdg Com 1974-76; Mem Implementation Bd RISE, NC Cong of P's & T's 1972-73; Chperson Var Coms; cp/BSA: Former Asst Scoutmaster, CoLdr & CoOrgr Explorer Scouts; Past VP Ctl Sch PTA, Kings Mtn, NC; r/Wesleyan: SS Tchr; hon/King's Mtn: Dist'd Ser Awd, Yg Man of Yr 1965; Pres Cit of Merit, NCCIRA; W/W in Commun Ser; Commun Ldrs & Noteworthy Ams; Personalities of S; Num Profl Pubs.

CUMMING, ROGER A oc/Teacher; h/75 Chestnut Hill Rd, Rochester, NH 03867; ba/Takoma Park, MD; p/Alexander Gray and Hannah Cumming, Rochester, NH; ed/BA Columbia Union Col 1968; Cert'd in Reading, Spec Ed, English; MA Equiv, Montgomery Co Public Schs; pa/Artist at Parker Marine Co (Alton Bay, NH) 1978-80 (summers); Tchr of Spec Ed, Reading, Math, English, Social Studies & Sci, Montgomery Co Public Sch Sys 1972-: Takoma Park Jr HS 1972-77, Northwood HS 1978-80; Former Tchr: Washington (DC) Public Sch Sys, DC Village, Mtl Hlth Ward of DC Gen Hosp; Other Former Positions; Soloist at Var SDA Chs in New England 1956-; Featured Soloist, Afro-Am Bicent Chorus, Kennedy Ctr (Wash, DC) 1975-76; Member, "Promusica", Perf'd in England, Holland, Germany, Austria, Switzerland, France; Other Perfs w SDA Choirs throughout USA; Am Guild Musical

Artists; cp/All-Star Softball Player, Takoma Park Amateur Ath League; Outfielder, Montgomery Co Fastpitch Softball A League; r/Sligo SDA Ch: Student Pastor & Min, SS Tchr, Deacon, Others; hon/1st Prize Music Fair, Atlantic Union Col; 1st Prize Autumn Fair (Art), Columbia Union Col.

CUMMINGS, CHARLES BARTON JR oc/Tuba Player; University Professor; b/Jul 10, 1946; h/4550 60th St, San Diego, CA 92115; ba/Same; m/Pamela Jean; p/Charles B Cummings Sr (dec); Ruth R Cummings, Newport, NH; ed/BS Univ NH 1968; MM Ball St Univ 1973; mil/AUS Band Prog 1968-71; pa/Tubist San Diego Brass Quintet; ECC

Philharm; Fac Mem San Diego St Univ, Pt Loma Col Ednl Cult Complex; Recordings: CRYSTAL & CAPRA; Author Num Articles & Reviews; Recitals at Carnegie Hall & throughout US; r/S Congreg Ch, Newport; hon/Arion Foun; US Army Commend Medal; Wm J Bell Meml S'ship; Others.

CUMMINGS, CONRAD M oc/Executive; b/Jul 1, 1933; h/10626 Glenway, Houston, TX 77070; ba/Houston; m/Beverly H; c/Ross, Constance, Leigh C Ford; p/Horal Carson and Gladys Martin Cummings, Shreveport, LA; ed/BS Tex A&M Univ; mil/AUS 2 Yrs, 1/Lt; pa/Sr VP Indep Oil & Gas Co, McRae

Consolidated Oil & Gas Co; Am Petrol Inst; Soc Petrol Eng; Indep Petrol Assn Am; Mid-Cont O&G Assn; La Assn Indep Prodrs & Royalty Owners; Tex Indep Prodrs & Royalty Owners; r/Presb; hon/Notable Ams; Personalities of S; W/W S&SW.

CUMMINGS, DONALD EUGENE oc/Officer in Dental Corp; b/Jun 28, 1949; h/Rt 4, Box 230, Portland, TN 37148; ba/Anchorage, AL; m/Deborah Williams; c/Anthony Michael, Kelly Michele; p/Charles

B and Kathleen P Cummings, Portland; ed/BS Tenn Tech Univ 1971; DDS Univ Tenn 1975;

mil/USAF Dental Corp Capt; pa/ADA; Former Mem Dental Ecs Adv Bd; r/Meth; hon/W/W in SE.

CUMMINGS, PATRICIA C oc/Executive; h/3224 Lake Anderson Ave, Orlando, FL 32806; c/Laura Marie; p/John Daniel and Lottie Marie Calhoun, Colquith, GA; ed/BA Fla St Univ 1963; pa/Ramada Inn SW/Hospitality Mgmt Corp 1972-78: Dir Sales & Mktng/Reg Dir Mktng HMC; Dir Sales US Holiday Inns: Tex, Mexico, Dallas, Tex 1971-72; Royal Coach Motor Hotel, Dallas 1968-71: Mktng Coor, Dir Public Relats; HS Tchr Dougherty Co Sch Systems, Albany, Ga 1964-68: Ctl Fla Hotel Sales Mgmt Assn: Pres, Secy, Bd Dirs; Intl Hotel Sales

Mgmt Assn; Bon Vivant; Am Soc Travel Agts: Rep, Allied Mem; Fla Hotel & Motel Assn; IPA; Allied Mem: Ontario Motor Coach Assn, Nat Tour Brokers Assn; Discover Am Assn; Nat Assn Motor Bus Owners; Am Mgmt Assn; Orlando Tourist Assn; Wom in Travel; Am Hotel & Motel Assn; cp/Orlando C of C, Action Team; hon/Outstg Salesman of Yr 1975, Hospitality Mgmt Corp; Order of the Flying Orchid, Delta Air Lines Inc; Admirality Awd, Sea World Fla Inc; Intl Bus-men W/W; Num Biogl Listings.

CUMMINS, KENNETH BURDETTE oc/Professor; b/Jul 27, 1911; h/421 S Center, New Washington, OH 44854; ba/Kent, OH; p/Royal Clinton and Pearl Rilda Rittenour Cummins (dec); ed/AB Ohio Wesleyan Univ; MA Bowling Green St Univ; PhD Ohio St Univ; pa/Prof Math Kent St Univ; NCTM; Math Assn Am; Program Spkr; Wkshop Ldr; Author Book on Tchg Math; Contbr Articles to Jours; cp/Dir New Wash Commun Chorus, NW Commun Band; r/Meth; hon/Phi Beta Kappa; Sigma Xi; Dist'd Tchg Awd, Kent St Univ Foun & Alumni Assn.

CUNNINGHAM, BEATRICE oc/Seamstress, Musician, Beautician; b/Dec 17, 1939; h/333 Center St, Itta Bena, MS 38941; ba/Itta Bena; c/Larry, Jeannetta, David, Nathanial, Yvonnie; ed/Bus Deg Miss Val St Univ 1970, Secy Deg; pa/Self-employed, Seamstress, Musician; Beautician; r/4 Chs; hon/Personalities of S.

CUNNINGHAM, PAUL JOHNSTON oc/Surgeon; b/Oct 10, 1928; h/5101 Denver Dr, Galveston, TX 77550; ba/Galveston; m/Billie Jane; c/Suzanne, Cynthia, Paul Raymond; p/Paul C and Marie J Cunningham, Princeton, KY; ed/BS; MD; mil/USAFR Capt; pa/Med Asst Prof Surg UTMB; cp/Tex St Repub Exec Com; r/Bapt.

CUNNINGHAM, R WALTER oc/Executive; b/Mar 16, 1932; ba/2000 S Post Oak, Suite 1300 Houston, TX 77056; m/Lo Ella; c/Brian Keith, Kimberly Anne; p/Walter W and Gladys Cunningham, Venice, CA; ed/BS 1960, MS 1961 UCLA; mil/USNR 1951-52; Fighter Pilot USMCR 1952-56; NASA Astronaut 1963-71; Mem Crew 1st Manned Apollo Spacecraft; pa/Sr VP/Dir Engrng; Dir Univ Savings Assn; Soc Experimental Test Pilots; cp/Aviation Com Houston C of C; Houston Am Revolution Bicent Comm; hon/NASA Exceptl Ser Medal; Haley Astronautics Awd; Navy Astronaut Wings; Am Legion Medal of Valor; UCLA Alumni Profl Achmt Awd; Author *The All American Boys*, 1977.

CUNNINGHAM, WILLIAM oc/Executive; h/2131 Valley Wood Pl, Charlotte, NC 28216; ba/Charlotte; c/William Ronald, Kenneth, Gary; mil/USN, Ret'd Vet; pa/Pres Hatchett & Cunningham Assocs Inc; Pres Charlotte Bus Leag; Exec Com Durham Col; cp/Johnson C Smith Univ Alumni Assn; NAACP; U Negro Col Fund; Johnson C Smith 100 Clb; Am Legion; Fleet Resv Assn; r/Parkwood Instnl CME Ch: Chm Bd Trustees.

CURATOLO, ALPHONSE FRANK oc/Architect; b/Sept 20, 1936; h/5525 N Virginia Ave, Chicago, IL 60625; ba/Chgo; p/Joseph and Pearl Loizzo Curatolo; ed/BA Univ Ill 1961; mil/AUS 1961; pa/Architect Masonite Corp, Chgo 1963-66; Chief Designer-Architect Playboy Clbs Inst, Chgo 1966-; Exec VP, Hd Architect Intl Design Studios Inc; AIA; Assn Reg'd Archs; Nat Coun Arch Registration Bds; Mensa; cp/Repub; r/Rom Cath; hon/Mar of Dimes Awd; Awd for Lake Geneva Playboy Resort AIA; Earl Prize for Outstg Arch Design; Instns Awd for Outstg Design, Lake Geneva; Trophy for Outstg Entertainer of Yr 1968-69, Universal Artists, Chgo; Arch Awd, Lighting Inst; Winner Var Karate Championships; Named Golden Gloves Fighter of Yr 1968; Biogl Listings.

CURL, SAMUEL E oc/University President; b/Dec 26, 1937; h/2602 E Maine, Enid, OK 73701; ba/Enid; m/Betty; c/Jane, Julie, Karen; p/Clay Curl (dec); Elva Curl, Tolar, TX; ed/BS 1959; MS 1961; PhD 1963; mil/AUS 1959, Active Duty 2/Lt; Currently Capt AUS Ret'd Resv; pa/Pres Phillips Univ; Coauthor 2 Books; Author or Coauthor 75 Res Articles & Abstracts; cp/Rotary; Enid C of C; Dir NW Okla Blood Inst; r/Christian Ch: Elder; hon/Univ Mo Fac-Alumni Gold Medal Awd; Am Coun on Ed Fellow.

CURLER, MARY BERNICE oc/Writer; b/Dec 4, 1915; h/8156 Waikiki Dr, Fair Oaks, CA 95628; m/Albert Elmer; c/Daniel Jay, Dawna Dee; p/Charles Ether and Josephine Babette Meier Davis (dec); pa/Free-lance Writer Fiction & Non-fiction for Var Nat Pubs Over 20 Yrs; Writing Instr Cosumnes River Col, Sacramento 1971-77; Asst Dir & Instr Sierra Writing Camp 1975, 76, 77; Am Soc Journalists & Authors; Cal Writer's Clb: Pres, VP, Prog Chm, Secy, Bd Mem 12 Yrs; Author *Story of a Medal--A Family Heritage*, 1976; Contbr Mags incl'g: *House Beautiful, Writer's Digest, Lady's Circle, McCalls, American Girl, Christian Science Monitor, Grit*, Others; Playwrite *Mazie's Red Garter*; hon/Lit Achmt Awd, Sacramento Reg Arts Coun; W/W Am Wom; World W/W Wom.

CURRAN, CONNIE LEA oc/College Administrator; Nurse Educator; b/Sept 16, 1947; h/5178 Parkridge Dr, Oakland, CA 94619; ba/San Francisco, CA; m/Arnold E Mattis; c/Melissa C Mattis; p/Patrick J Curran, Berlin, WI; Kathleen Crimmings, Berlin; ed/BS; MSN; EdD; pa/Univ San

Francisco 1977-: Assoc Dean Nsg Cont'g Ed & Res, Assoc Prof; Loyola Univ Sch Nsg 1974-77: Chm Dept Med-Surg Nsg, Asst Prof; Loyola Univ Med Ctr 1975-77: Acting Dir Nsg Staff Devel, Coor Nsg Res; Other Former Positions; Am Nsg Assn; Cal Nurses' Assn; Am Ed Res Assn; Soc for Res in Child Devel; Am Cancer Soc, Ill Com for Profl Ed; Am Heart Assn, Com for Profl Ed; Nat Assn for

Wom Deans; Am Assn for Higher Ed; Conslt; Wkshops; r/Cath; hon/Grad w Highes Hons from Master & Doct Studies; Profl Pubs.

CURREY, VIRGINIA MAY oc/Professor; b/May 6, 1927; h/931 E Mitchell, Arlington, VA 76010; ba/Dallas, TX; m/Donald P (dec); c/Amy, Ellen, James; p/Paul Anderson (dec); Mable Anderson; ed/BA; Masters Intl Affairs;

PhD; pa/Prof Dept Polit Sci So Meth Univ; SW Social Sci Assn; Wom Studies Assn; cp/Dem; St Bd Ed, 24th Dist Tex; r/Unitarian; hon/Friend of Freedom, Dallas Chapt Ams U for Separating Ch & St.

CURRY, MARY EARLE LOWRY oc/Homemaker; Poet; Free-lance Writer; b/May 13, 1917; h/1244 Naples Ave, Cayce, SC 29033; m/Peden Gene; c/Eugene Lowry, Mary Earle (dec); p/Ullin Sidney and Mary Sloan Earle Lowry (dec); pa/Author 2 Books Rel Poetry: *Looking Up*, 1949, *Looking Within*, 1961; Contbr to Var Pubs incl'g: *Yearbook of Modern Poetry, Poets of Am*,

Poetic Voice of Am, Poetry Digest, Poetry Anthology of Verse, Greenville News, Fort Mill Times, Intl Anthology on World Brotherhood and Peace, Others; Centro Studi Scambi International Roma; cp/Former Mem Aux Rotary, Charleston, SC; r/U Meth: UMW Org, Meth Min's Wives Clb; hon/Intl W/W Poetry; DIB; World W/W Wom; W/W: Am Wom, S&SW; Personalities of S; Commun Ldrs & Noteworthy Ams.

CURRY, PEDEN GENE oc/Church Administrator; b/Jan 7, 1919; h/1244 Naples Ave, Cayce, SC 29033; ba/W'boro; m/Mary Earle Lowry; c/Eugene Lowry, Mary Earle (dec); p/Justus States Curry (dec); Jennie Richardson McDowell, Fountain Inn, SC; ed/AB Furman Univ; BD Candler Sch Theol; pa/Supt Walter Dist U Meth Ch, SC 1974-; Pastor Num Chs incl'g: N Charleston (SC)

1971-74, Main St, Columbia (SC) 1966-71, Duncan Meml, Georgetown (SC) 1962-66, St John, Ft Mill (SC) 1959-62, Others; SC Meth Activs: Conf Bd Missions 1978, Comm Res & Planning 1971-73, Conf Bd Min 1960-76, Others; cp/Former Chm Mtl Hlth Assn, Georgetown; Past Pres: G'town Min Assn, N C'ton Min Assn; Former Chaplain N C'ton Rotary; r/U Meth.

CURTIS, BETTIE JEAN oc/Teacher; b/Jul 8, 1935; h/412 W John St, Orange, TX 77630; ba/Orange; m/James I; p/Shelton Broussard, Orange; Ophelia Broussard (dec); ed/BA Wiley Col; MA Tex So Univ; pa/Tchr 21 Yrs; Former Med Secy Orange Meml Hosp; Former Tchr Tex So Univ (Sum Session); Former Ct Reporter; Other Former Positions; Tex St Tchrs Assn: Life Mem, Exec Com, Chm St Profl Rts & Responsibilities Com 2 Terms, Dist V Dir, 2/VP Orange Co Unit I, Secy Orange

Co Unit I; W Orange-Cove Classroom Tchrs Assn: 1/VP, Pres, Secy; Secy Orange Co Coun Classroom Tchrs Assn 2 Yrs; NEA; Tex & Nat Bus Ed Assns; cp/Delta Sigma Theta; Bd Dirs: UF, Orange C of C, Lamar Tchr Ctr; Mem Top Ladies of Distn; r/Mt Olive Bapt Ch: Fin Secy; hon/Awd for Yrs of Successful 0 Dedicated Ser; Tchr of Yr, W Orange-Cove CISD 1972 & 1978; Bus Ed Tchr of Yr, Dist V 1973.

CURTIS, DOROTHY STEVENSON oc/Nurse; b/Mar 12, 1941; h/868 Troxel Rd, Lansdale, PA 19446; ba/Same; m/A Kenneth; c/William Kenneth, Karen Althea; p/Victor James and Mary Violet Goddard Stevenson, Providence, RI; ed/RN Beverly Hosp 1961; BS En Col 1977; pa/Hd Nurse Beverly Hosp, Beverly, Mass 1961-63; Pvt Duty Nsg, Boston, Mass 1964-67; Evening Supvr Deering Nsg Home, Hingham, Mass; Pvt Duty Nsg Morris Manor, Plymouth Meeting, Pa; Am Nurses Assn; Nurses Christian F'ship; Assn Chd w LD, Secy 1978; cp/Conslt Gateway Films,

Valley Forge; Former Mem Exec Coun PTA; Worcester Racquet Clb; r/Lower Providence Bapt Ch, Eagleville, Pa: Bd Christian Ed.

CURTIS, JOHN HAROLD oc/Associate Professor; Marriage & Family Therapist; b/Jun 28, 1937; h/1100 Williams, Valdosta, GA 31601; ba/Valdosta; p/Orville R Curtis, Peoria, IL; Dorothy M Curtis, Peoria; ed/BA MacMurray 1959; MDiv Boston Univ 1962; MA Ind St Univ 1969; PhD Fla St Univ 1972; pa/Assoc Prof Sociol Valdosta St Col; NCFR; SCFR; GCFR; AAMFT; GAMFT; AASECT; AAUP; SSS; r/U Meth: Min; hon/Alpha Kappa Delta.

CURTIS, JOYCE MAE oc/Professor; Coach; b/Aug 27, 1937; h/2501 Garfield, Abilene, TX 79601; ba/Abilene; p/Robert J and Maudie Lowman Curtis, Fort Worth, TX; ed/BS 1959, MS 1960 NTSU; PED Ind Univ 1970; pa/Abilene Christian Univ: Prof PE, Volleyball Coach; Life Mem: Delta Psi Kappa, AAHPER; SAPECW; NAPECW; TAHPER; Treas TAIAW 1970-; r/Highland Ch of Christ; hon/Outstg Edr Am; Personalities of S; W/W S&SW.

CURTISS, GEORGE C oc/Painter; Museum Curator; Art Gallery Director; b/Feb 15, 1921; h/832 NE 124 St, N Miami, FL 33161; ba/Same; m/Jerry Gerda Tolksdorf-Anderson; c/Birgit Martha, Jorn John, Gregory Arthur; p/Hans John and Martha Ludwig Curtiss (dec); ed/Baccalaureat Dipl; BFA; MA; pa/Portrait Painter; Curator Sci Mus; Art Galleries Dir-Owner; Author Cartoon Book; Tchr Arts; r/Luth; hon/Medals & Prizes; Lttrs of Commend; DIB; Others.

CURZON, DANIEL oc/Writer; Teacher; h/511 Capp St, San Francisco, CA 94110; ed/PhD Wayne St Univ; pa/Pub'd Books: *Among the Carnivores, The Revolt of the*

Perverts, Something You Do in the Dark, The Misadventures of Tim McPick; hon/Cable Car Awd (for Drama), SF.

CUTHRELL, CARL EDWARD oc/Minister; Teacher; Administrator; b/Aug 13, 1934; h/307 Agusta Dr, Newport News, VA 23671; ba/Hampton, VA; m/Naomi Lorene Marshall; c/Byron Eugene; p/Cecil Edward Cuthrell (dec); Edna Catherine Post, Maple, NC; ed/BDiv; LLB; MA; BA Pub Adm; mil/AUS: Korean War, Germany; pa/Min Rescue Evang Friends Ch; cp/SAR; Sons of Confed; Mil Order of Stars & Bars; Repub; hon/Scouter's Awd; Silver Beaver, BSA.

CUTLER, ALLAN HARRIS oc/Professor; b/Oct 16, 1939; h/c/o Jacob Cutler, 1014 S Alfred St, Los Angeles, CA 90035; ba/LA; m/Helen Marie; p/Jacob and Ruth Cutler, LA; ed/BA; BRE; BHL; PhD; JD Cand; pa/Prof Medieval & Renaissance Ctr UCLA; Am Hist Assn; Am Judic Soc; cp/So Cal Dem Chperson's Cir; S Cal Am Jewish Cong, Gov'g Coun; r/Jewish; hon/F'ships & Grants: Nat Endowmt for the Humanities, Am Phil Soc, Am Coun Learned Socs, Danforth Foun, Others.

CUTTER, CHARLES RICHARD III oc/Professor; b/Feb 8, 1924; h/2425 Charboneau, Waco, TX 76710; ba/Waco; m/Phyllis Marie; c/Cynthia C Wheeler, Marcia C Walker; p/Charles R and Mary E Cutter (dec); ed/BA Baylor Univ; BD, PhD SWn Bapt Theol Sem; mil/USAAF 3 Yrs, Navigator, 35 Combat Missions in Europe; pa/Prof Classics Baylor Univ 1958-; Proprietor Cutter Feed Mkt 1946-51; Am Philological Assn; Soc Biblical Lit; Classical Assn; cp/Var Positions YMCA; r/Bapt: Ordained Preacher 1950, Pastored Chs 1955-72; hon/The Reverend Jacob Beverly Stiteler Prof of Greek; Air Medal w 5 OLC.

D

DAARUD, BERTHA MAE oc/Retired Public School and Music Teacher; b/Dec 6, 1897; h/624 Wedgewood Dr, Columbus, OH 43228; m/(dec); p/Albert J Williams (dec);

Elizabeth Hire (dec); ed/Public Sch Cert; pa/Public Sch Tchr 16 yrs; Music Tchr 54 yrs; r/Prot; Wom Aglow; hon/Sev Hon Certs: Nat Piano Guild, Am Col Musicians.

DABBS, MIRIAM ADAIR oc/Artist; Journalist; Housewife; b/May 6, 1908; h/321 Maple, Clarksdale, MS 38614; m/Chester Norwood; c/Willis Norwood; p/Watie McIntosh and Betty Pearson Adair; ed/MA; pa/Art Shows in Paris, NYC, Philadelphia & Mid-South; Features for Local Mag *Here's Clarksville*; Newspaper Writer; 4 1-man Art Shows in Paris; cp/Clarksdale Beautification Comm; Clbs; r/So Bapt: Active in Local Ch; hon/Nat & Intl Art Awds; Critics Choice, Mus of Modern Art, Paris; Others.

DAGGETT, BRADFORD I oc/Executive; Educator; b/Feb 20, 1933; h/128 Sharbot Dr, Pittsburgh, PA 15237; ba/Pittsburgh; m/Janette A; c/Michael P, Cheryl A;

p/Donald and Mildred Daggett, Prescott, IA; ed/BS Long Island Univ 1965; mil/AUS; pa/Dir, Art Inst of Pgh; Post Sec'dy Educ Planning Comm; r/Presb; hon/Bronze Star.

D'AGNESE, HELEN JEAN oc/Artist; b/Jul 6, 1922; h/1683 Knob Hill Ct, NE, Atlanta, GA 30329; ba/Atlanta; m/John J; c/John, Linda, Diane, Michele, Helen, Gina, Paul; p/Leonardo and Rose Redavid De Santis; ed/CUNY; Oakland Art Inst; pa/1-man Shows: Maude Sullivan Gallery, El Paso 1964, John Wanamaker Gallery, Phila, Pa 1966, Univ NM 1967, Karo Manducci Gallery, San Francisco 1968, Tuskagee Inst Carver Mus 1968, Lord & Taylor Gallery, NYC 1969, Harmon Gallery, Naples, Fla 1970, Fountainbleau, Miami 1970, Reflections Gallery, Atlanta 1972, Williams Gallery, Atlanta, Ga 1973, Americana Gallery, Tex 1977, Howard Gallery, Ameila Island, Fla 1978, Others; Exhibited in Group Shows: Musseo des Artes, Juarez, Mex 1968, Benedictine Art Show, NYC 1967, SE Contemp Art Show, Atlanta 1968, Atlanta Univ 1969; Nat Judaic Theme Exhbn 1976; Annual Bible Heritage Art Exhibit, Marietta, Ga 1975 & 1976, Garden Gallery, Atlanta, Art World, Amelia Isl, Fla; Exhibiting: Red Piano Gallery, Hilton Head, SC, Terrace Gallery, 1975, Kraskin Gallery, Atlanta; Represented in Perm Colections: Gov's Mansion, Atlanta, DeKalb Lib, Atlanta, Mario Spada Gallery, Juarez; Series of Liturgical Paintings Exhibited

at Var Chs, & Mus Contemp Art, Vatican, Rome, Italy; Judge Art Show Mt Loretto Acad, El Paso 1967; Art Demonstration & Lectr Margaret Harris Sch, Atlanta 1970; El Paso Art Assn Conslt Atlanta Arts Coun 1968-; Loaned Painting Gtr Atlanta Arts Coun 1974-; cp/Atlanta Lawn Tennis Assn; Tennis, Fencing Clbs; hon/Rep'd in Permanent Collection of US Pres Jimmy Carter; W/W: Am Wom, S; World W/W of Wom; Notable Ams of Bicent Era; Commun Ldrs & Noteworthy Ams.

DAILY, JAMES LEE oc/Business Systems and Forms Representative; b/Apr 16, 1944; h/3835 Camelot Cir, Decatur, IL 62526; ba/Decatur, IL; m/Diane L; p/Robert E and Dee Daily, Dayton, OH; ed/AS; BS; mil/AUS 6 yrs, Sgt; cp/Recreational Advr, Poker Players of Ohio; r/U Meth.

DALDIN, HERMAN J oc/Executive; b/Jan 22, 1912; h/514 Sunset Dr, Clinton, MI 49236; m/Ruth E; p/John and Mary Daldin (dec); ed/Kent St Univ; Mich St Univ; Univ Mich; mil/US Army, Ser'd S Pacific; pa/Owner, Pres & Gen Mgr, Star Hotel Co Inc; Dist Supvr, Dept Hd, Pres & Mgr of Chain of Hotels comprising 203 Units (Largest Chain of Hotels in the World); cp/Chm Col & Univ Com, Ec Clb of Detroit; Pres Mich Chapt, IPA; Bd Dirs, Circumnavigators Clb 6 Yrs; Adcraft Clb of Detroit; Elks Clb of Ann Arbor; Others; r/Cath; hon/Sev Dist'd Ser Awds.

DALE, RICHARD oc/Political Scientist; b/Oct 22, 1932; h/Union Hill, Rt 4, Carbondale, IL 62901; ba/Carbondale; m/Doris C; p/Edgar and Elizabeth K Dale, Columbus, OH; ed/AB Bowdoin Col 1954; MA Ohio St Univ 1957; MA 1961, PhD 1962 Princeton Univ; mil/Enlisted Man in US & W Germany w 3rd Inf Div of AUS 1957-59; pa/So Ill Univ, C'dale: Assoc Prof, Dept Polit Sci 1971-, Asst Prof 1967-71, Adj Prof 1966-67; Asst Prof, Dept Polit Sci, No Ill Univ, DeKalb 1963-66; Instr, Dept of Govt, Univ NH, Durham 1962-63; Mem Num Profl Orgs; Adv Bd Univ Press of Am 1976-; Many Paper Presentations; Ext Res & Travel; Pub'd Author: Books, Articles & Chapts in Jours, Books & Annuals, Review Articles & Essays, Book Reviews; cp/Treas Shawnee Group, Gt Lakes Chapt of Sierra Club; r/Prot; hon/Biogl Listings.

DALLIANIS, JEAN DEMAS oc/Real Estate Company Executive; b/Dec 30, 1940; h/Lincolnwood, IL; ba/5695 N Lincoln Ave, Chicago, IL 60659; m/Harry T; c/Irene Lorraine, Thomas Harry; p/Charles William and Helen Alice Kyriakopulos Demas, Chgo; ed/BA NWn Univ 1962; pa/Tchr Von Steuben HS, Chgo 1962-65; Ideal Real Est & Inst Brokerage Inc, Chgo: Secy-Treas 1965-72, VP & Exec Dir 1972-, Dir Corp Relocation 1975-; Dir Ideal Realty Co, Realtors; Nat Assn Realtors; Realtors Nat Mktg Assn; Ill Assn of Realtors; Chgo Real Est Bd, Mem Sales Coun 1977-; N Side Real Est Bd; N Suburban Chgoland Real Est Bd; VP 1975-76, Pres 1977-78, Dir 1978-; RELO/InterCity Relocation Ser, Chgo Metro-area Chm 1975-76; Nat Indep Fee Appraisers; Sr Mem Cert'd Review Appraiser; cp/Lincolnwood (Ill) Commun Coun; Past Treas L'wood Homeowners Assn; L'wood Bicent Com;

Precnt Capt L'wood Commun Action Party; Friends of Lib L'wood Com; L'wood PTA; LWV; r/Greek Orthodox, Sts Peter & Paul, Glenview, Ill: SS Tchr 8 Grade 1976-77, Dir Bd Ed; hon/Biogl Listings.

DALTON, GLENN LAQUE oc/Attorney; b/Jun 20, 1953; h/12753 Willow Trail, Black Jack, MO 63033; ba/St Louis, MO; m/Diane Kilgore; c/Roderick Kirkland, Laque Kennard; p/U G III and Helen Louise Dalton,

Pine Bluff, AR; ed/BA Hendrix Col 1974; JD Wash Univ Sch Law 1977; pa/Am Bar Assn; Mo Bar Assn; Metro Bar Assn, St Louis; cp/Trustee, Hendrix Col; Asst Scoutmaster, BSA; r/AME.

D'AMATO, AL oc/Pastor; b/Mar 12, 1930; h/3383 Watkins Rd, Columbus, OH 43207; ba/Columbus; m/Constance Holmes; c/Dawn, Albert Jr, Bette, John Paul, Jill, Gina, Harold, Heidi; p/Alexander and Edith Rose D'Amato (dec); mil/AUS 1951-53; pa/Pastor,

Hope Bapt Ch; Pres, Hope Tapes & Publications; cp/Bd Selectmen, Abington, Mass 1958-63; r/Bapt; hon/W/W Rel; Men Achmt; DIB; Commun Ldrs & Noteworthy Ams; Personalities of W&MW; Notable Ams; IPA.

DAMON, CAROLYN ELEANORE oc/Research Chemist; b/Aug 16, 1937; h/3100 S Manchester St, Apt 540, Falls Church, VA 22044; ba/Wash DC; p/Glenn H and Eleanore G Damon, Arlington, VA; ed/BA Western Col 1959; MS Purdue Univ 1964; pa/Res Chem, US Customs Serv; Accredited Profl Chem; Expert Govt Witness in Crim Litigation; cp/Ofcr & Past Ofcr of 3 Tech or Civic Orgs; hon/S'ships; F'ships; 1st Annual Awd, Am Chem Soc (Local Sect).

DANCEY, HARRY LEO oc/Theatre

Administrator; b/Nov 20, 1953; h/2205-A S Tyler, Amarillo, TX 79109; ba/Amarillo; p/Harry Jr and Jewel Reed Dancey, Port Isabel, TX; ed/BA w hons E Tex St Univ; pa/Mng Dir, Amarillo Little Theatre; Am

Theatre Assn; SW Theatre Conf; Tex Non-Profit Theatres; Tex Ed Theatre Assn; cp/Explorer Post Ldr, Amarillo Fine Arts Coun; hon/Alpha Chi; Alpha Psi Omega; Personalties of S; Pub'd Articles.

DANIEL, EDITH SHORT oc/Postal Clerk; b/Nov 30, 1978; h/PO Box 22, Black Creek, NC 27813; m/Marvin Elliott; c/Marvin Anthony, Dennis Timothy, Ted Stuart; p/Emmitt W Short (dec); c/Cora Hayes Short, Wilson, NC; pa/Postal Clk; cp/Pres & Dist Dir, PTA; Charter Mem, Coastal Plain Devel

Com; Chm, Local Commun Devel Com; Pres, NC Ext Homemakers 1978; Co Adv Com, Concerned Citizens for Better Schs; Com to Improve Cts; Worthy Matron & Dist Dep Grand Matron, OES; 5 Time Del, Ext Homemakers Nat Conv; r/Bapt: Pres Wom's Aux, Adult SS Tchr 20 yrs; hon/A&P Ldrship Awd; HS Valedictorian; Co Wom of Yr.

DANIEL, EUNICE BACON oc/Retired; b/Jan 31, 1922; h/23 Culverton Ct, Savannah, GA 31406; m/Curtis Warren (dec); p/John Henry and Marietta Bacon (dec); ed/Computer Ed Inst; Drake Univ; la St Univ; Kirkwood Commun Col; pa/Ret'd Chief, Interview Unit, VARO, Houston, Tex; r/Asbury U Meth Ch: U Meth Wom, Coor Fam Mins; hon/W/W Wom; Commun Ldrs & Noteworthy Ams; Notable Ams of Bicent Era; Personalities of W&MW; Career Ser Awd for 25 Yrs Ser to US Govt; Supr Perf Awds; Others.

DANIEL, JOYCE ANN oc/Teacher; b/Oct 1; h/5105 Avenue M, Galveston, TX 77550; m/H Michael; c/Monique; p/William C Sr and Hilda Hunter, Galveston, TX; ed/BS; MA; pa/Tex St Tchrs Assn; NEA; AAUW; Tex Assn Improvemt Reading; cp/NAACP; Dem Party: Precnt Secy; r/Rom Cath: Nat Soc

Knights of St Peter; hon/Mother of Yr, Hon Mrs Prairie View Univ; Black Cath Commun Concerns Awd.

DANIEL, ROBERT WILLIAMS JR oc/United States Congressman; b/Mar 17, 1936; h/Brandon Plantation, Spring Grove, VA 23881; ba/Wash DC; m/Sally Lewis Chase; c/Robert, Charlotte, Nell; p/Robert Williams Daniel (dec); Charlotte Bemiss (dec); ed/BA Univ of Va; MBA Columbia Univ; mil/AUS; r/Epis; hon/Phi Beta Kappa.

DANIEL, SAMUEL M oc/Psychotherapist; b/Mar 9, 1929; h/600 W End Ave, NY, NY 10024; m/Erna; p/Michael Daniel (dec); Errusha Daniel, Bombay, India; ed/MSW; pa/Nat Assn Social Wkrs; Cert'd Social Wkr; Fellow, NY St Soc Clin Social Work Psychotherapists Inc; r/Jewish.

DANIELS, DAVID H JR oc/Physician; b/Sep 1, 1941; ba/1770 N Orange Grove Ave, Pomona, CA 91767; m/Doris Jean Brown; c/David Henry, Dorothy Jean, Doreen Jeanette, Danny Herbert, Dora Jane; ed/BS Philander Smith Col 1963; MD Univ of Ark Med Sch 1967; pa/Dir of Cardiopulmonary Ser, Cardiac Catheterization Lab & Coronary Care Unit, Doctors Hosp (Montclair, Cal) 1974-; Dir of Cardiopulmonary Ser, Coronary Care Unit, Chino Gen Hosp (Chino, Cal) 1974-; Hosp Appts: Pomona Valley Commun Hosp, San Antonio Commun Hosp, Ontario Commun Hosp, Martin Luther King Gen Hosp, Others; Bd Status: Bd of Med Examrs St of Cal, Bd Med Examrs Wash (DC), Bd Med Examrs Ark; Contbr to Profl Jours; AMA; Nat Med Assn; San Bernardino Co Med Soc; Am Heart Assn; Others; hon/Alpha Kappa Mu; Beta Kappa Chi; Others.

DANIELS, ROGER DALE oc/Technical Director; b/May 20, 1938; h/131 Poinciana Lake, Jackson, TX 77566; ba/Freeport, TX; m/Judith Smith; c/Craig, Phillip; p/Henry D and Murvel Lynch Daniels, S. Point, OH; BSChe VPI&SU; pa/AIChe; ACS; ASME; cp/C of C; Little Leag Baseball; r/Prot. hon/Pres Awd 1974.

DANIELS, ROSE LYNN oc/Professor; b/Oct 17, 1939; h/2 Hackensack St, B-3, Wood Ridge, NJ 07075; ba/Wayne, NJ; p/George L Daniels, Hollywood, FL; Janet A Daniels, Harrisburg, PA; ed/BA cum laude William Patterson Col 1970; MA 1971, PhD 1975 Ohio State Univ; pa/William Patterson Col: Prof of Hlth Sci, All Col Sen, Ath Assn, Master Planning Coun, Fac Forum, Ath Policy Coun, Computer Adv Com, Res & Adam Devel Com; Contbg Editor, *Hlth Ed*; Com for Completed Res, AAHE; cp/Bd Trustee, Venereal Disease Ser Org; Ed Com, Passaic Co Chapt Am Cancer Soc; hon/NDEA Fellow, Ohio St Univ.

D'ANJOU, HENRY GENET oc/Pastor; b/Nov 18, 1922; h/229 Willett Ave, Port Chester, NY 10573; ba/Port Chester; p/Ignace

d'Anjou (dec); Anne de Folque, Port Chester, NY; ed/DST; SSL; PhD; pa/Pastor, Sacred Heart of Jesus Church; r/Rom Cath.

DANKO, BOHDAN oc/Librarian; b/Jul 6, 1929; h/5 Gilbert Ave, New Haven, CT 06511; m/Wasylka Shramenko; p/Wasyl

Shmata (dec); Sophie Danko, New Haven, CT; ed/BA Univ Conn 1956; MSLS Conn St Col 1970; pa/Contbr to Profl Jours; AAUP; Conn Lib Assn; cp/Ukrainian Cong Comm; Ukrainian Nat Sch; Symon Petlura Institut; r/Ukrainian Cath; hon/Ukrainians of NAm; W/W E; DIB; Commun Ldrs & Noteworthy Ams; Men Achmt.

DANNELLEY, PAUL EDWARD JR oc/- Journalist; Educator; b/Dec 25, 1919; h/#107 300 Hal Mudrow Dr, Norman, OK 73069; ba/Norman; m/Delaine C; p/Paul E III, Shannon Gay; p/Paul E Sr and Arran Neal Dannelley, McPherson, KS; ed/BA McPherson Col 1941; MA Wichita St Univ 1970; mil/USN 1941-43; USNR; pa/Assoc Prof of Jour, Univ Okla; Past Pres, SPJ/Sigma Delta Chi Chapt, Wichita; Past Pres, Kans Profl Chapt, PRSA; Past Mem, PRSA Assembly; cp/Trustee, Kans Med Foun; Advr, Small Bus Adm Exec Com, Okla; PR Conslt, Okla Nursing Assn; r/Epis; hon/Outstg Edr Awd, Okla Educl Assn 1974; Okla Univ Outstg Fac Awd, Wom in Communs 1975; Okla Univ Outstg Fac Awd, Student Press Assn 1975.

DANNENBERG, ARTHUR M JR oc/- Professor; b/Oct 17, 1923; h/12 Lake Manor Ct, Baltimore, MD 21210; ba/Baltimore; m/Aileen Hart; c/Arlene, Andrew, Audrey; p/Arthur M Dannenberg, Philadelphia, PA; Marion L Dannenberg (dec); ed/BA; MD; MA; PhD; mil/USN 1954-56, LCDR; pa/Prof of Expmtl Pathol, Johns Hopkins Univ Sch of Hygiene 1973-; Assoc Prof, Dept Pathol, John Hopkins Univ Sch Med 1964-; Assoc Prof, Dept Radiol Scis, John Hopkins Univ Sch of Hygiene & Public Hlth 1964-73; hon/Profl Pubs; F'ships.

DANNOV, FRED oc/Attorney; Municipal Judge; b/Apr 30, 1930; h/1123 Falcon Dr, Columbia, MO 65201; ba/Columbia, MO; m/Nita; c/David, Dana; p/Edward and Rae Dannov, Lakewood, CA; ed/BA, MA, JD Univ of Mo; mil/AUS; pa/Boone Co Bar Assn; Mo Bar Assn; Mun Judge, City of Columbia, Mo.

DANOFF, DUDLEY SETH oc/Urologic Surgeon; b/Jun 10, 1937; h/1821 Loma Vista Dr, Beverly Hills, CA 90210; ba/Los Angeles; m/Hevda; p/Alfred and Ruth Danoff, Rancho Mirage, CA; ed/Grad summa cum laude Princeton Univ 1959; MD Yale Univ Sch Med 1963; pa/Adult & Pediatric Urology Pract w Danoff, Holden & Silver Urology Group, LA; Hosp Staffs: UCLA Med Ctr, Cedars-Sinai Med Ctr, Midway Hosp, Brotman Meml Hosp, Temple Hosp, Century City Hosp, LA New Hosp; Fellow, Am Col Surgs; Diplomate, Am Bd Urology; Am Fertility Soc; Sigma Xi; Soc Air Force Clin Surgeons; Am Urologic Assn; Societe Internationale D'Urologie; Am Assn Clin Urologists; LA Urologic Soc; Transplant Soc So Cal; LA Co Med Assn: Pres-elect Dist 1, Bd Govs; AMA; Am Urologic Assn Wn Sect; cp/Phi Delta Epsilon; Nat Ldrship Cabinet, U Jewish Appeal; Am Friends of Hebrew Univ; Am Technicon Soc; Bd Dirs, Guardians of Courage: Am-Israeli Public Affairs Com; r/Jewish; hon/Phi Beta Kappa; Alpha Omega Alpha; Others.

DANSBY, HUDDIE oc/Land Surveyor; b/Jun 11, 1941; h/2808 Dowell Ct SW,

Birmingham, AL 35211; ba/Bessemer, AL; m/Dorothy J; c/Joseph A, Huddie A, Belinda A, Wililam A, Jessie E, John T; p/Joseph Afenious and Sarah Ann Dansby, Uniontown, AL; pa/Land Surveyor; r/Bapt.

DARBY, HARRY oc/Industrialist; Farmer; Stockman; b/Jan 23, 1895; h/1220 Hoel Parkway, Kansas City, KS 66102; ba/Kansas City; m/Edith Marie Cubbison; c/Harriet Gibson (Mrs Thomas H), Joan Edwards (Mrs Roy A), Edith Marie Evans (Mrs Ray), Marjorie Alford (Mrs Eugene D); p/Harry and Florence Isabelle Smith Darby (dec); ed/BS 1917, ME 1929 Univ Ill; mil/AUS 1917-19, 2/Lt to Capt; pa/Chm Bd Dirs, Darby Corp & Leavenworth Steel Inc; Dir, Piping Contractors Inc; Pres, Dir & Bd Chm, Darby Railroad Cars Inc; ASCE; Am Soc Agri Engrs; Soc Am Mil Engrs; Nat Soc Profl Engrs; Kans Soc Profl Engrs; Engrs Clb, Kans City; Kans Engrg Soc; Past Mbr, St Bd Engrng Exmrs; cp/US Sen from Kans 1949-50; Repub Nat Com 25 yrs; Chm, Kans St Hwy Comm 1933-37; Del Chm to Num Repub Nat Convs; Spec Ambassador for US Pres to attend inaugural ceremonies for Venezuelan Pres Betancourt 1959; Chm Bd Trustees, Eisenhower Foun; hon/DHL: St Benedict's Col 1963, Westminster Col 1964, Kans St Univ 1966, Washburn Univ 1968; Dr Commercial Scis Baker Univ 1975; Dist'd Ser Cit, Univ Kans Alumni Assn 1971; Kansan of Yr 1962; Kansas City (Kans) Man of Yr 1965; Alumni Hon Awd, Univ Ill Col of Engrng; Fellow Awd, ASME; Chm Emeritus, Am Royal Assn; Named Mr American Royal for 50 Yrs Serv; Hall of Fame of Great Westerners, Nat Cowboy Hall of Fame 1978.

DARBY, WESLEY ANDREW oc/Pastor; Teacher; b/Sept 19, 1928; h/5628 N 11th Ave, Phoenix, AZ 85013; ba/Phoenix; m/Donna Maye; c/Carolyne D Eymann, Lorena Elizabeth M Bass, Andrea M Perdue; p/A L

Darby; ed/BA ASU; mil/CAP, 1/Lt; pa/Pres, Conserv Bapt Foun; VP, Ariz Bapt Conv; cp/Chm Ariz Breakfast Clb; Precnt Capt, Repub Party; r/Conserv Bapt.

DARITY, EVANGELINE ROYALL oc/Educational Administrator; b/Jun 16, 1927; h/105 Heatherstone Rd, Amherst, MA 01002; ba/Concord, NC; m/William Alexander; c/William Jr, Janiki Evangelia; p/Ossie Jenkins Royall; ed/BS Barbaer Scotia Col 1949; MEd Smith Col 1969; EdD Univ Mass, Amherst 1977; pa/VP Student Affairs, Barber Scotia Col 1978-; Asst to Class Deans, Smith Col, Northampton, Mass 1968-67; Am

Pers & Guid Assn; Nat Assn Wom Deans, Cnslrs & Admrs; cp/LWV; hon/Hon Mem, Order of Valkyries, Univ NC-Chapel Hill; W/W: E, Am Wom; DIB; Commun Ldrs Am; World W/W Wom.

DARNELL, EDNA ERLE oc/Librarian; b/Mar 4, 1925; h/2114 Orr St, Poplar Bluff, MO 63901; ba/Poplar Bluff, MO; m/Willie; c/Willie Jr, Daralina Ann; p/W L and Ora Burnley, Poplar Bluff, MO; ed/BS 1960, MA 1967 Murray St Univ; EdS George Peabody Col 1971; pa/Libn, Three Rivers Commun

Col; Lib Sci Tchr: Murray St Univ, SE Mo St Univ; Sch Libn; Public Libn; Acad Libn; cp/Wom's Clbs; PTA; GSA Ldr; Gov's Conf on Libs, Mo; Dem Wom; r/Temple Bapt Ch: SS Tchr, Nom'g Com, Ch Libn; hon/Num Ser Awds for Ch Activs; Ldrship Awds.

DARGUSCH, CARLTON SPENCER oc/Attorney; b/Aug 19, 1900; h/271 N Columbia Ave, Columbus, OH 43209; ba/Columbus, OH; m/Genevieve Johnston; c/Carlton Jr (dec), Evelyn Byrd Lanphere (Mrs Charles A); p/Julius Herman and Etta Burnham Dargusch (dec); ed/LLB Ind Univ 1925; mil/AUS 1940-47, Lt Col-Brigadier Gen; pa/Atty, Dargusch & Hutchins (Tax Specialists); Dir, Clark Grave Vault Co; Cons, Engrng Manpower Comm; Atty to Commr, Ohio Dept of Taxation 1925-37; Asst Dir, US Ofc Def Mobilization 1955-57; cp/Trustee, Ohio St Univ 1938-59, 1963-65; r/Epis; hon/Dist'd Ser Medal 1946; Army Exceptl Civilian Ser Awd 1950.

DARRACOTT, HALVOR THOMAS oc/Government Official; b/Aug 21, 1910; h/3325 Mansfield Rd, Falls Church, VA 22041; m/Margaret Jane Mitchell; c/Hattiejane, William Michael, James Patrick; p/Charles William and Allie Mae Moore Darracott; ed/BS Drury Col 1933; MS Univ Ark 1939; mil/AUS 1941-62, 2/Lt to Col; pa/Ret'd; Chief Communs & Control Sys, Ofc Sys Devel, HQs AUS Devel & Readiness Command, Alexandria, Va 1975-79; AUS Adv'd Materials Concepts Agy, Alexandria: Chief Communs-Electronics Div 1974-75,

Supvr Phys Sci, Chief Technol Forecasting Div 1971-74, Chief Ops Analysis Div 1968-71; AUS Material Command HQs, Wash DC: Sr Supervisory Phsy Scist in Tech Forecasting 1964-68, Supervising Gen Engr 1964; Other Govt Positions; Am Math Soc; AAAS; Am Inst Physics; Am Acad Polit & Social Sci; Assn US Army; Fellow, Wash Acad Sci; IEEE; Kappa Delta Pi; Sigma Pi Sigma; Armed Forces Communs & Electronics Assn; Wash Ops Res Coun; cp/Mason; Kiwanis; hon/Cert Apprec, Ft Dix 1962; W/W S&SW; Pub'd Profl Articles.

DASH, JAMES ELLIS oc/Educational Consultant; b/Sept 20, 1948; h/212 S Alfred St, Alexandria, VA 22314; p/Ellis E Dash; Maxine E Dash, Delmont, PA; ed/BME 1970,

MM 1973 Morehead St Univ; Postgrad Study Univ Va; pa/Ednl Music Conslt, Perf'g Arts Abroad Inc, Kalamazoo, Mich 1978-; Band Dir, Fairfax Co Public Schs 1973-78; Nat Thespian Soc; Nat Band Assn; Past Exec Bd Mem: Va Music Edrs Assn, Fairfax Co Band Dirs Assn; Va Band & Orch Dirs Assn; Music Edrs Nat Conf; Phi Mu Alpha; cp/Order of DeMolay; Sigma Pi; hon/Personalities of S; Notable Ams; Intl W/W Music; Asst Dir, All-Am Wind Band 1977; Asst Dir & Staff, US Col Wind Band 1977 & 78; Others.

DAUBE, DAVID oc/Professor; b/Feb 8, 1909; ba/Boalt Hall, Univ Cal, Berkeley, CA 94702; c/Jonathan, Benjamin, Michael; p/Jakob and Selma Ascher Daube; ed/Dr Jur w distn Univ of Gottingen 1932; PhD Univ Cambridge 1936; MA 1955, DCL 1955 Univ Oxford; pa/Prof of Law, Univ Cal, Berkeley;

r/Jewish; hon/Hon Degs: Univ Edinburgh, Univ Paris, Univ Leicester, Hebrew Union Col, Univ Munich; Fellow: British Acad, Am Acad Arts & Scis, World Acad Art & Sci; Hon Fellow: Oxford Univ Ctr for Postgrad Studies, Royal Irish Acad; Corres Fellow, Acad of Scis, Gottingen; Others.

DAUBE, JONATHAN M oc/College President; b/Nov 23, 1937; h/200 Pomeroy Ave, Pittsfield, MA 01201; ba/Pittsfield; m/Linda; c/Andrew, Katherine, Matthew; ed/MA w hons Univ Aberdeen, Scotland 1957; MAT Equiv Univ London 1958; EdD Harvard Univ 1968; pa/Pres, Berkshire Commun Col 1978-; Dir Grad Progs in Ed, Union Grad Sch, Union for Experimenting Cols & Univs, Yellow Springs, Ohio 1975-78; Temporary Dir, Union Grad Sch-1 1976; Supt Schs, Martha's Vineyard Sch Superintendency Union & Martha's Vineyard Reg HS Dist, Mass 1970-75; Other Past Positions; hon/Profl Publs.

DAVID, KEITH RAYMOND oc/Professor; b/Aug 20, 1929; h/1029 Broadmore Ln, Liberty, MO 64068; ba/Liberty; m/Donnaretha Aduddel; c/Kevin Lee, Gerald

Lynn, Kim Alan, Philip Brian; p/Floyd M and Edna G David (dec); pa/Prof, William Jewell Col.

DAVIDGE, BILLY LLOYD oc/Administrator; b/Jul 14, 1927; h/PO Box 448, Natalbany, LA 70451; ba/Baton Rouge, LA; m/Nell Lafleur; c/Billy L Jr, Deborah Nancy D Piediscalzo, Kurt LaRay; p/Thomas H and Lela Nancy McAlpin Davidge (dec); mil/-USNR; pa/Chief, Intl Sers Ofc & Public Works Dept of Transportation & Devel, St of La 1960-; Surveyor, E V McCollam & Co

1947-51; Chief Surveyor: E V McCollam & Co 1951-60, Sun Oil Co 1960; r/Prot; hon/W/W S&SW.

DAVIDSON, MABEL ELIZABETH oc/Author; Professional Speaker; b/May 20, 1901; h/Villa Maria, Apt 102, 1739 SE 46th Ln, Cape Coral, FL 33904; ba/Colfax, IN; m/Dwight L; c/Evelyn Potvoricky; p/Richard M and Lida Jane Steele Farlow; ed/Famous Writers' Sch; pa/Author 3 Books; Profl Spkr; Intl Cong on Arts & Communication; IPA;

cp/Past Pres & 35-Yr Mem Intl Travel Study Clb; Intl Toastmistress Clb; Isaac Walton Aux; Co & St Hist Socs; DAR; Homemaker's Clb; Book Lovers Clb; Repub Clb; Rotary Ann; r/U Meth; hon/World W/W Wom; DIB; Book of Hon; Alt Spkr, Nat Contest in Cal, Intl Toastmistress Clbs; Others.

DAVIS, AGNES MARION oc/Librarian; b/Apr 14, 1923; h/Draper's Meadow Apts B-3 NW, Balcksburg, VA 24060; ba/Blacksburg; p/Charles William Davis (dec); Elma A Sarber Davis, Blacksburg, VA; ed/BS; MA (LS); pa/Libn, Va Polytech Inst & St Univ; ALA; SELA; VLA; AAUP; AAUW; Delta Kappa Gamma; Kappa Delta Pi; r/Blacksburg Presb Ch; Deacon 1977-79.

DAVIS, ALICE V oc/Music Teacher; Lecturer; b/Jul 24, 1918; h/Rt 1, Box 57, Omaha, TX 75571; m/Joseph Marion Davis; c/Joe Lane, Jerrol Porter; p/Walter H and

Lena Porter Gunn (dec); ed/Sr Col Dipl (Piano); pa/Tchr; Performer; cp/Sr Citizens Coun; r/Meth Ch: Organist, Lectr; hon/W/W; Piano Guild Hall of Fame; Commun Ldrs & Noteworthy Ams.

DAVIS, ALEXANDER SCHENCK oc/Architect; b/Jan 3, 1930; h/928 Contra Costa Dr, El Cerrito, CA 94530; ba/1057 Solano Ave, Albany, CA 94706; m/Nancy Barry Davis; c/Arthur Barry, Laurel Margaret, Pamela Alexander; p/William Schenck and Amelia Francisco Davis; ed/AA; BA; MA Univ Cal, Berkeley; mil/USCG 1953-55; pa/Am Inst Archs; cp/Rotary Clb; C of C; r/Prot; hon/D Zelinsky & Sons Grad Scholar in Arch 1955-56; Other Acad Hons.

DAVIS, BERTHA G oc/Artist; h/715 Gaylewood Dr, Richardson, TX 75080; ba/Richardson; m/Irving (dec); c/Sylvia D Caplan, Doryn Z Davis; p/Abraham and Dvora Germaize; ed/Pan Am Col; Art Inst of San Miguel Allende, Mex; pa/Oper, Art Gallery, Houston, Tex 1969-72; Asst Mgr, Art Intl, Houston, 1972-75; Asst Mgr, Kirt Niven Gallery, Dallas; 1-Wom Shows; Group Shows; Tex Fine Art Assn; Richardson Civic

Art Assn; SW Watercolor Soc; Artist Sculptors Contemporary Soc; Art League of Houston, Houston Art Assn; hon/W/W.

DAVIS, CAROLE ELIZABETH Mc-REYNOLDS oc/Artist; b/Mar 4, 1942; h/518 Poplar Tree Rd, Longmeadow, Starkville, MS 39759; ba/Starkville; m/Frank Marvin Sr; c/Frank Marvin Jr, Lewis McReynolds; p/John Andrew Sr McReynolds, Starkville, MS; Elizabeth Lewis McReynolds (dec); pa/Miss Arts Assn; AAUW; cp/Chi Omega Alumni Assn; Civic League, Starkville; Miss St Univ Wom's Clb; r/Trinity Presb Ch; hon/W/W Am Cols & Univs; Outstanding Yg Wom Am; Phi Kappa Phi; Cardinal Key; Acad Hons.

DAVIS, CHARLES RONALD oc/Pastoral Counselor; Administrator; b/Jun 11, 1940; h/18227 NE 176th, Woodinville, Wa 98072; ba/Seattle, WA; m/Nancy Jean Johnson; c/Barbara Jean, Paul Erik; p/Charles Wilbert Davis (dec); Robert Wielage, San Diego, CA; ed/BA; MDiv; Cert Clin Cnslg; pa/Dir, Yokefellow Cnslg Ctr; Instr; Sharing Group Ldr; r/Luth; hon/W/W Rel; W/W Commun Ser.

DAVIS, CURTIS CARROLL oc/Writer; h/16-R, The Carlyle, 500 W Univ Pkwy, Baltimore, MD 21210; ed/BA Yale Univ 1938; MA Columba Univ 1939; PhD Duke Univ 1947; mil/USAAC 1942-46, Capt; USAR 1946-76, Lt Col; pa/Writer (Biographer, Historian & Essayist) 1950-; Editor: *The End of an Era*, John Sergeant Wise 1965, *Belle Boyd in Camp and Prison* 1968, *The Knights of the Golden Horse-Shoe*, William Alexander Caruthers 1970; Pub'd Articles: *Am Heritage, Jour of So Hist, Civil War Hist, Intell Digest, William & Mary Qtrly, Va Cavalcade*, Others; Pub'd Reviews: *Am Lit, Am Hist Review, NY Times Book Review, Cath Hist Review*, Others; Contbr to Var Ref Wks; Manuscript Soc; Am Hist Assn; Am Assn St & Local Hist; Nat Book Critics Cir; Va Hist Soc; Authors Leag Am Inc; NC Hist & Lit Assn; Exec Com, Edgar Allan Poe Soc; Chm Lib Com, Md Hist Soc; hon/Phi Bet Am Scholars: Hist; Intl Authors & Writers W/W; Writers Dir; Others; Opers Ofcr, CIA 1947-49; hon/Bronze Star; Pres Unit Cit; Phi Beta Kappa; Author: *Chronicler of the Cavaliers: A Life of the Virginia Novelist, Dr William A Carruthers*, 1953, *The King's Chevalier: A Biography of Lewis Littlepage*, 1961, *That Ambitious Mr Legare: The Life of James M Legare of South Carolina, including a Collected Edition of His Verse*, 1971, *Revolution's Godchild: The Birth, Death, and Regeneration of the Society of the Cincinnati in North Carolina* 1976.

DAVIS, DANELLA BETH oc/Editor; b/Aug 1, 1939; h/2809 W 28 #131, Amarillo, TX 79109; ba/Amarillo, TX; m/Bob D'Wayne; c/Malia Parnell; p/Oscar B Porter, Tenaha, TX; Ella Freeman, Ft Stockton, TX; pa/Editor, Employee Mag, Pioneer Corp; Intl;

Assn Bus Communicators; Tex Press Wom; Nat Fed Press Wom; Wom in Communs; Nat Assn Exec Females; cp/Amarillo C of C; Repub Party; Desk & Derrick Clb, Amarillo; r/Presb; hon/Num Awds, Tex Press Wom; Biogl Listings; Addy Awd 1977; Others.

DAVIS, DONALD FRED oc/Art Instructor; b/Nov 14, 1935; h/3116 Madison, Baton

Rouge, LA 70802; ba/Baton Rouge; m/Anna Mae; c/Anthony, Angela, Derek, Michael, Miriam; p/Annabelle Davis, Baton Rouge, LA; ed/BA; MEd; PhD Cand; mil/USN 1952-56; pa/Art Instr; NAEA; LAEA; Phi Delta Kappa; r/Meth; hon/Cum Laude Grad; Cited for Outstg Contbns to Arts, Links Inc 1971.

DAVIS, EGBERT LAWRENCE III oc/Attorney; b/Dec 30, 1937; h/321 Banbury Rd, Winston-Salem, NC 27104; ba/Winston-Salem; m/Alexandra Holderness; c/Alexandra, Bert, Lucinda, Pam; p/Egbert Lawrence and Eleanor Layfield Davis, Winston-Salem, NC; ed/AB Princeton Univ; LLB Duke Univ Law Sch; MBA George Wash Univ; mil/AUS 1963-65, Capt; pa/Atty, Womble, Carlyle, Sandridge & Rice 1963-; Am Bar Assn; Forsyth Co Bar Assn; NC Bar Assn; Am Judicature Soc; cp/Elected: NC Ho of Reps 1970, 1972, NC Sen 1974, 1976; Cand, US Sen 1978; Winston-Salem Rotary Clb; Winston-Salem C of C; Trustee, NC Bapt Hosp; Bd Visitors, Duke Med Ctr; Cystic Fibrosis Adv Comm; Bd Dirs, NC Mtl Hlth Assn; r/Bapt; hon/Winston-Salem Jaycees Dist'd Ser Awd; NC & US Jaycee Freedom Awd; Comm on Employmt of Handicapped's Citizen of Yr Awd.

DAVIS, ERNEST JR oc/Pastor; b/Sept 16, 1937; h/62 Cottage St, Poughkeepsie, NY 12601; ba/m/Dorothy; c/Gay M, Ernest S, Joy M, Jason B, Christopher B; p/Ernest Sr and Freedie C Davis, Morristown, TN; ed/No Bapt Sch Rel; Rutgers Univ; Newark St Col; MDiv 1974, DMin Study 1978- Andover Newton Theol Sch; pa/Pastor: Smith St AME Zion Ch 1976-, 2nd Ch John Wesley AME Zion Ch, Attleboro, Mass 1975-76, Hood Meml AME Zion Ch, Providence, RI 1974-76, Lincoln Congreg Ch, Brockton, Mass 1970-74; Asst Pastor, Calvary Bapt Ch, Morristown, NJ 1968-70; Black Min Alliance, Poughkeepsie 1976-; cp/Pres, Poughkeepsie Housing Redevel Corp; Dutchess Co Hd Start Policy Coun on Ednl Progs 1976-; Pres & Fdr, RUSH (Rescue Underfed Starving Humans), 1968-; Bd Dirs: Dutchess Co Com for Economic Opportunity, Dutchess Co Soc for Mtl Hlth Inc; Dutchess Co NAACP; Mayor's Commun Relats Comm 1977-; Num Others; r/AME Zion Ch; hon/W/W Rel; Soc Dist'd Am HS Students; Others.

DAVIS, EVELYN MARGUERITE BAILEY oc/Church Organist; Pianist; Vocal Soloist; Harpist; Music Instructor; Bible Teacher; Composer; h/4 Rancheo Dr, St Charles, MO 63301; ba/St Charles; m/James Harvey; p/Philip Edward Bailey (dec); Della Jane Morris Bailey (dec); pa/Organist, Vocal Soloist & Floral Arranger, Faith Missionary Bapt Ch; Instr in Piano, Voice, Organ & Chromaharp; Directed Yth Orch; Conducted Yth Choir; Played for Weddings, Funerals, Revivals, Conferences; Music Instr, Bible Bapt Christian Sch; Bible Tchr; Composer: "I Will Sing Hallalujah", "I Am Alpha and Omega", "Prelude to Prayer", "O Sing Unto the Lord a New Song", "O Come Let Us Sing Unto the Lord", "O Lord, Our Lord, How Excellent Is Thy Name!", "My Shepherd", "The Lord Is My Light and My Salvation"; r/Bible Bapt Ch; hon/Life Fellow Intl Biogl Assn; Num Biogl Listings.

DAVIS, FRANCE A oc/Pastor; Teacher;

b/Dec 5, 1946; h/1912 Meadow Dr, Salt Lake City, UT 84121; ba/Salt Lake City; m/Willene Witt; c/Carolyn Marie, Grace Elaine, France Albert II; p/John H Davis; Julia A Davis, Waynesboro, GA; ed/AA Laney Col 1971; AA Merritt Col 1972; BA Univ Cal, Berkeley 1972; BS Westminster Col 1977; MA Univ of Utah 1978; mil/USAF 1966-70; pa/Tchg Fellow & Instr of Communs, Univ Utah; Ordained Bapt Min 1971; Pastor, Calvary Bapt Ch 1974-; Moderator, Utah-Idaho Nat Bapt 1976-; cp/Chm OIC; Utah Bd Corrections; r/Bapt; hon/Tchg Cit 1974; Pres Awd, NAACP 1975; Commun Ser Awd 1975; Eccles Fellow 1978; W/W W.

DAVIS, FRANCIS RAYMOND oc/Pastor; b/Feb 10, 1920; h/40 Elizabeth St, Dansville, NY 14437; ba/Dansville; p/Frank Raymond Davis Sr (dec); Ruth Donovan Davis, Rochester, NY; ed/BA St Bernard's Sem & Col 1941; MSLS Cath Univ Am 1953; pa/Pastor, St Mary's Rom Cath Ch 1978-; Pastor, Our Lady of Lourdes, Elmira, NY 1969-78; St Bernard's Sem, Rochester, NY

1950-69: Libn, Prof of Lit, Prof of Spch; Asst Pastor, St Ambrose, Rochester, NY 1945-50; Elmira & Vicinity Ministerial Assn 1960-74 (Sec-Treas 1970-72); Dansville Ministerium 1978-; cp/Chemung Co Gen Ed Bd, Diocese of Rochester 1971-78; Exec Com, Chemung Co Coun for Aging 1972-76; Adv Bd, Chemung Co Ofc for Aging 1973-78; hon/Beta Phi Mu; Fellow, Intl Biogl Assn; Fellow, Am Biogl Inst.

DAVIS, JOHN CLARENCE JR oc/Minister; b/June 14; h/1728 Fair Dr, NE, Knoxville, TN 37918; m/Alma Coleen Beets; c/John Clarence III; p/John Clarence Sr and Cora Jane Martin Davis; ed/Att'd: Univ Tenn-K'ville, NWn Univ; BS Univ Cal 1958; MA magna cum laude Kingdom Bible Inst 1959; PhD Univ Cal 1960; mil/AUS 1951-53, Chaplain; Founded *The Chaplain Hour* Radio & TV Armed Forces Network Prog; pa/Ordained 1959; Pastorates: Stamps Meml Bapt Ch Atlanta 1959, Glenbrook Bapt Ch Atlanta 1959-61, Forest Park Bapt Ch, Druid Hills Bapt Ch; Interim Supply Pastor, Knox Co, Tenn 1970-; Midland So Bible Conf; Knox Co So Mins Conf; Life Mem Atlanta So Bapt Mins Conf; Several Appts to US Civil Ser; Spkr for *Look at Your Bible* Radio Prog 1966-; Writer Column "Reach Out, Am" for *Knoxville News-Sentinel* 1973-75; cp/Former Chaplain: CAP, Am Legion Post K'ville, USCG Aux; Chm Div of Rel Affairs USCG Aux; K'ville Bd Chaplaincy; Nat Alumni Assn of Univ Tenn; NWn Univ Alumni Assn; Assn for Adv'd of Higher Lng in Theol Ed; Nat Rel Broadcasters Assn; r/So Bapt; hon/Hon DLitt, Meth Univ Glendale (Cal); Dist'd Cit for Excellent Broadcasting in Public Affairs, AUS; Bicent Writers Awd, Bicent Comm of Ky; Nat Thespian Dramatic Hon Soc Awd; Cert of Merit, Heart Fund; Cert of Apprec: Tenn Bar Assn, Pilot Clb, JCs; Dist'd Public Ser Awd; Deafness Res Foun, ARC; Civitan Intl Public Benefactor Awd; Ky Col; Hon Citizen Boys Town; W/W Rel; Nat Rel Broadcasters Blue Book of Ofcl Info.

DAVIS, JOHN ISAAC oc/Clergyman; b/Aug 22, 1927; h/1415 Orange Ave, National City, CA 92050; m/Rosie Lee; c/Helen Harris, Glenn Isaac; p/Willie and Maud Davis (dec); ed/Peter's Bus Col; Ill Univ; Bapt Inst; pa/Fed Inspector for US Navy; Nat Evangelist for Ch of God in Christ; Pres of Men's Coun of Gtr Israelite COGIC

1975-80; Ecumenical Coun 1970-76; Orgr of Heavenly Vision COGIC in Chgo 1956 & San Diego 1960; cp/Pres Sch Adv Com, Hoover HS; Chm of Bd, Yth Dept of So Cal 1973-80; Orgr, Yg People Willing Workers in the United Dist 1961; Pres, COPA 1958; r/Pentecostal; hon/Cert of Awd, Yth Dept of So Cal; Trophy, Israelite Ch of God in Christ; DIB; Others.

DAVIS, JULIA ELIZABETH oc/English Teacher; b/Oct 8, 1914; h/403 Wilson, Richland, WA 99352; ba/Richland; m/Edward S; c/Gloria D Tinder, Shirley Anne D Lawrence-Berrey; p/Edward H and Alma Bizzell Brown (dec); ed/BS, Addit Studies; pa/Eng Tchr Columbia HS; Dept Chm for 10 Yrs; Delta Kappa Gamma; REA: Exec Bd, Profl Affairs Com, S'ship Com, Rep Coun; Richland Sch Dist: Lang Arts Com, Curric Coor'g Com; Chperson Columbia HS Lib Com (5 Yrs); Prin's Adv Com (6 Yrs); cp/AAUW; r/Meth; Ctl U Prot Ch: Mem; hon/Outstg Ldrs Elem & Sec'dy Ed; Commun Ldrs & Noteworthy Ams.

DAVIS, LENWOOD G oc/Educator; ba/Newark, DE; ed/BA 1961, MA 1968 NC Ctl Univ; Univ Ghana, Africa 1969; NWn Univ 1970; Carnegie-Mellon Univ 1978; pa/Asst Prof, Black Am Studies, Univ Del 1977-; Asst Prof, Black Studies Dept, Ohio St Univ 1974-77; Instr, Hist & Black Studies, Portland St Univ 1970-72, 1973-74; Acting Dir Black Studies Ctr & Instr Hist, Portland St Univ 1971-72; Instr, Hist, Livingston Col 1968-70; Conslt; Acad Polit Sci; African Assn for Black Studies; Ohio Black Polit Assembly; Nat Coun Black Studies; Edrs in Africa Assn;

AAUP; Others; cp/Fdr & Past Pres, Rowan Co Chapt NCCU Alumni Assn; Fdr & Pres, Ore Afro-Am Hist Soc 1972; hon/Piedmont Univ Ctr Scholars F'ship 1969; HEW F'ship 1970; DIB; Living Black Authors: A Biographical Dir; The Writers Dir; Outstanding Edrs Am; Dist'd Achmt for Inclusion in Men Achmt; Phi Alpha Theta; Author: *I Have A Dream: The Life and Times of Martin Luther King, Jr* 1973, *The Black Woman in American Society: A Selected Annotated Bibliography*, 1975, *The Black Family in the United States: A Selected Annotated Bibliography*, 1978, Book Reviews, Articles.

DAVIS, LOWELL LIVINGSTON oc/-Thoracic & Cardiovascular Surgeon; b/Dec 14, 1922; h/800 W 1st St, Los Angeles, CA; m/Barbara Helen Allen; b/Dec 14, 1922; h/800 W 1st St, Los Angeles, CA; ba/Los Angeles; p/Jordan and Mary Emma Wright Davis (dec); ed/BS; MS; MD; mil/USNR, Capt; pa/Pvt Pract Thoracic Surg; r/Prot; hon/FACS; FACC; FCCP; FICS; W/W W.

DAVIS, MATTIE oc/Counselor; Professor; b/Apr 8, 1942; h/PO Box 3731, Columbia, SC 29230; p/Prophet Davis (dec); Eugenia Davis, Columbia, SC; ed/AB; MA; PhD; pa/Dir of Cnslng; Prof; r/Meth: SS Tchr; hon/Outstg Yg Wom Am 1978; W/W S&SW.

DAVIS, MOLLIE CAMP oc/Associate Professor; b/Mar 2, 1932; h/4700 Aspen Ct, Charlotte, NC 28210; ba/Charlotte; c/William E Jr, Sidney C, Stephan Powell; p/A Sidney Camp (dec); Sarah F Camp,

Newnan, GA; ed/AB Hollins Col 1953; MAT Emory Univ 1965; PhD Univ Ga 1972; pa/Queens Col: Chm & Assoc Prof, Dept of Hist 1975-, Asst Prof of Hist 1972-75; Vis Prof, Wom's Hist, Winthrop Col 1975; Asst Prof of Hist, W Ga Col 1969-72; Am Hist Assn; Am Studies Assn; Org Am Histns; Oral Hist Assn; So Hist Assn; Ga Hist Soc; Hist of Ed Soc; So Assn Wom Histns; Num Others; Scholarly Papers Presented; Panelist; cp/Nat Wom's Polit Caucus; Past Chm, Dem Wom of Coweta Co; Civil Liberties Union; LWV; NOW; Wom's Equity Action Leag; r/Bapt; hon/Grants; F'ships; Phi Alpha Theta; Ford Foun Fellow 1963-65; Vis Lilly Scholar, Duke Univ 1976-77; Others.

DAVIS, NATHANIEL oc/State Department Advisor; b/Apr 12, 1925; h/613 Hudson St, Hoboken, NJ 07030; ba/Newport, RI; m/Elizabeth Kirkbride Creese; c/Margaret Morton, Helen Miller, James Creese, Thomas Rohde; p/Harvey Nathaniel and Alice Marion Rohde Davis (dec); ed/AB Brown Univ 1944; MA 1947, PhD 1960 Fletcher Sch of Law & Diplomacy; Addit Studies: Columbia Univ, Cornell Univ, Middlebury Col, Universidad

Ctl de Venezuela; mil/USNR 1944-46, Lt (jg); Tchr: Naval War Col 1977-, Howard Univ 1962-68, Univ Br Centro Venezolano-Americano 1961, Tufts Col 1947; St Dept Advr to Naval War Col 1977-; US Ambassador to Switz 1975-77; Asst Secy of St for African Affairs 1975; Dir Gen, US Fgn Ser 1973-75; US Ambassador to: Chile 1971-73, Guatemala 1968-71; Sr Staff, Nat Security Coun 1966-68; US Min to Bulgaria 1965-66; Other Fgn Ser Positions; Am Fgn Ser Assn (VChm Bd Dirs 1964); Coun on Fgn Rels; Am Hist Assn; r/U Ch of Christ; hon/Phi Beta Kappa; Hon LLD Brown Univ; Profl Pubs.

DAVIS, PHILLIP REUBEN oc/Office Manager; b/Apr 18, 1941; h/3107 Auburn Cir, Jeffersontown, KY 40299; ba/Savannah, GA; m/Kay; c/Frank, Monica & Michelle; p/Frank M Davis (dec); Kathleen Davis, Waynesville, NC; ed/HS; mil/AUS 1963-66; USAR 1966-73; USCGR 1973-, Petty Ofcr; pa/Ofc Mgr, Ford Motor Credit Co 1969-;

Protl Musician w Own Band (The Champions) 1959; Formed Reuben Madison Band in Savannah; cp/Worshipful Master, Zerubbabel Lodge #15, Savannah 1978; 1/Sgt, Alee Shrine Patrol 1978; r/Davis Chapel Meth Ch, Waynesville, NC: Mem.

DAVIS, POLLY ANN oc/Professor; b/Nov 11, 1931; h/4301 John Reagan, Marshall, TX 75670; ba/Marshall; p/Robert Sidney Davis (dec); Olive Marie Flanagan (Mrs R S Davis), Marshall; ed/BA Blue Mountain Col 1953; MA Univ of Miss 1954;

Univ Ky 1963; pa/Prof & Chm Dept Hist & Polit Sci, E Tex Bapt Col; Am Assn St & Local Hist; Org of Am Histns; Soc Hist Ed; So Bapt Hist Soc; Am Hist Assn; Author, *Alben W Barkley: Senate Majority Ldr & VP* (1979); Contbr Aritcles Profl Jours; hon/Dissertation Year Fellow, So F'ships Fund; Haggin Scholar; Univ Scholar; DIB; Intl Authors & Writers W/W; World W/W Wom; Outstg Edrs Am; Num Others.

DAVIS, ROBERT CARTER JR oc/Physician; b/Sept 21, 1939; h/3219 Nancy Creek Rd, Atlanta, GA 30327; ba/Atlanta; m/Hulda Maruillie; c/Edward Campbell IV, Kathleen Morgan Robert C III; p/Robert Carter and Hilda Brown Davis (dec); ed/MD; mil/AUS, Maj; pa/Am Col Gastroenterology; Am Col Phys; Am Soc for Gastrointestinal Endoscopy; cp/Bd Trustees, Med Assn Atlanta; Past Pres, Emory Univ Med Alumni Assn; r/Rom Cath; hon/Alpha Omega Alpha; W/W Ga; Outstg Yg Men Am 1974.

DAVIS, ROBERT JAMES oc/Astrophysicist; b/Oct 26, 1929; h/307 Pleasant St, Belmont, MA 02178; ba/Cambridge, MA; m/Ruth; c/Carolyn, Deborah, Paul, Elizabeth; c/Harry C Davis, Sarasota, FL; Margaret Davis (dec); ed/AB; AM; PhD; mil/USNR, Lt; pa/Space Astronomy; Astronomical Photometry; Astronomical Spectroscopy Historian; Intl Soc for Philos Enquiry; r/Park Ave Congreg Ch: Vice-Moderator; hon/Gen Elect Coffin F'ship; Harvard Detur Awd; Fed Outstg Ser Awd.

DAVIS, ROBERT L oc/Administrator; b/Jan 29, 1938; h/2301 Hill N' Dale, Irving, Tex 75062; ba/Dallas; m/Patricia A; c/Lee Ann (dec), Melinda Kay, Anthony Howard; p/Sidney Lee Davis; Gladys Clara Vaught; ed/BA So Meth Univ 1961; BD Perkins Sch Theol 1963; ThM Brite Div Sch 1978; pa/Lic'd Meth Min 1955; Dir, Dept of Pastoral Care, Dallas Co Hosp Dist 1979-; Dir, Div of Ordained Min, Bd of Higher Ed & Min, U Meth Ch 1975-79; Dir of Chaplain's Ser, Barnes Hosp, St Louis, Mo 1971-75; Dir, Dallas Co Hosp Dist, Dallas, Tex 1968-71; Assoc Chaplain, Harris Hosp, Ft Worth, Tex 1965-68; Other Past Positions; Past Pres, Tex Assn Hosp Chaplains; Past Secy, SW Reg Assn for Clin Pastoral Ed; Conslt; cp/Past Dir, Dallas Co Suicide Prevention Ctr; Past Chperson, Dallas Chapt Acad Rel & Mtl Hlth; Past Dir, Dallas Co Unit Am Cancer Soc; Bd Pres, Flynn Park PTO; Past Dir, St Louis Unit Am Cancer Soc; Others; hon/W/W: Tex, Rel, Intells; DIB; Personalities of S; Men Achmt; Commun Ldrs & Noteworthy Ams; Profl Pubs.

DAVIS, ROBERT PICKENS oc/Retired Minister; Project Editor; b/Dec 23, 1911; h/9413 Treetop Ln, Richmond, VA 23229; ba/Richmond; m/Lila Ross Norfleet; c/Lila Ross, Rebecca Cooper D Davidson (Mrs James E); p/Walter Pickens and Sadie Lenorah McCardell (dec); ed/AB Davidson Col 1932; BD 1935, ThM 1941, ThD 1958 Union Theol Sem; pa/Proj Editor, Hist Records for Synod of Virginias; cp/Bd Dirs, Va Mtl Hlth Soc; Charter Mem & Chaplain, Civitan Clb of Va Bch; Chaplain, GSA Round-up 1965; Princess Anne Co GS Coun 5 yrs; r/Presb; hon/Ser Awd Cert, Highland Commun Mins, Louisville, KY 1977.

DAVIS, RONALD BYRON oc/Minister; Evangelistic Speaker; Merchant; b/Nov 27,

1943; h/PO Box 39308, Cincinnati, OH 45239; ba/Cincinnati; m/Ruby Marie Bove; c/Angela Marie; p/Byron C Davis (dec); Hannah M Davis, Fremont, NE; ed/BSEd Midland Luth Col; BD, MDiv NWn Luth Theol Sem; pa/Owner-Mgr, Christ Centered Book, Gift & Supply Store; Fdr-Dir, Christ Centered Mins; Spkr, *The Power of Faith* Radio Prog; Author, *A Doing Faith* Newspaper Column; Nat Fed Indep Bus; Chm, Fremont Dist Child Evangelism F'ship; Nat Assn Evangels; Christian Booksellers Assn; cp/Incorporator & Bd Mem, Dodge Co Assistance Line; Fremont Child Abuse & Neglect Com; r/Evangel Ch Alliance & Conservative Congreg Christian Conf: Min; hon/W/W Rel; Men Achmt; Notable Ams; DIB; Personalities of W&MW; Commun Ldrs & Noteworthy Ams.

DAVIS, SARA JACQUELINE oc/Teacher; Librarian; b/Sept 9, 1926; h/4536 Carriage Hill Ln, Columbus, OH 43220; ba/Columbus, OH; ed/BS Ohio St Univ; MEd Xavier Univ; pa/OEA; NEA; COTA; Past Pres; FCHEA, CHETA; CWTBL; Past Pres, Past Treas; cp/Ohio St Univ Alumni Assn; LPGA Vol; r/Meth.

DAVIS, WILLIAM CLAUDE oc/Linguist; b/Mar 5, 1929; h/640 Esmeralda, Fallon, NV 89406; ba/Fallon; m/Dorothy; c/Wes, Jane; p/Claude Elza Davis (dec); Serena Nichols Hancock (dec); ed/PhD Ohio Christian Col 1972; mil/USAF; pa/Fdr-Dir, "Explorers Intl Clb"; Writer; Lectr; r/Prot; hon/Fellow IBA.

DAVIS, WILLIE L oc/Administrator; b/Feb 20, 1947; h/292 N Ashley, Bourbonnais, IL 60914; ba/Kankakee, IL; m/Amelia; c/Willie; p/James Davis, Stephens, AR; Tessie Rae Davis (dec); ed/BA; MA; EdD Cand; pa/Admr, Sch-Commun Communications; NABSE; Kankakee Co Admin Assn; cp/Kankakee Jaycees; NAACP; Men of Progress Clb; r/Prot.

DAVIS, ZADIE AURELIA oc/Retired Educator; b/Oct 2, 1902; h/PO Box 1235, Thomasville, GA 31792; p/John Joseph and Emma Jane Roddenberry Davis (dec); ed/BS Ga St Col for Wom; MS Fla St Univ; pa/Former Tchr & Prin; cp/Yth Ctr Bd 5 yrs; Nocturne Garden Clb; Am Camellia Soc; Ga

Hist Soc; Thomasville Entertainmt Foun; Thomasville Exec Clb; DAR; Thomas Co Hist Soc; Ga Geneal Soc; Smithsonian Instn; r/1st Bapt Ch: Mem, SS Tchr 25 yrs; hon/Kappa Detla Pi; Delta Kappa Gamma; 5-Time Tchr of Yr; Var Hons for Ser to Ed; Others.

DAVISSON, MONA JUNE GARNER

oc/Linguist; Professor; b/Jan 29, 1937; h/315 W Rutgers Ave, Melbourne, FL 32901; ba/Melbourne; m/Myron Fay; c/Sanford Fay; p/Joshua Sanford and Geneva Margaruetta Grimes Garner, Melbourne, FL; ed/AA WVa Bus Col; BA Eng; BA Commerce; pa/Linguist & Prof of Eng, Fla Inst Technol; Mod Lang Assn; AAUP; Fla Forensic Assn; Am Bus Wom's Assn; AAUW; Assn Fla Toastmasters; cp/Melbourne Area C of C; Pres, Flowerbox Inc; Indian River Jubilee Assn; r/Ch of Christ; hon/Personalities of S; W/W S&SW; DIB; W/W Intl Ed.

DAVY, GLORIA JEANNE oc/Registered Nurse; b/Dec 19, 1943; h/PO Box 124, Brunswick, ME 04011; ba/Brunswick; p/Arthur and Yvonne Jeanne Elizabeth Davy, White Salmon, WA; ed/BS; pa/Nurse, Parkview Meml Hosp; r/Seventh-day Adventist.

DAWLEY, ROBERT MICHAEL oc/College Instructor; Orchestra Director; Music Educator; Violinist; m/Ofelia Vasquez; p/Morris Dawley (dec); Grace F Carrow, Springville, NY; ed/BM Eastman Sch of Music, Univ Rochester; MA NE Mo St Univ; Doct Study: Univ Ariz, Univ Ill; pa/Dir,

Hillsdale Col Commun Orch; 1st Violinist w Tucson Symph 1975-76; Supvr of Music Student Tchr, Univ Ill 1976-78; cp/Reg XIV Orch Chm, Tex Music Edr's Assn 1973; r/Prot; hon/Phi Delta Kappa; Pi Kappa Lambda; Meritorious Ser Awd, Tex Ed Agy 1973.

DAY, BETH F oc/Writer; b/May 25, 1924; h/35 E 38th St, NY, NY 10016; ba/NYC; p/Ralph L Feagles (dec); Mary A West (dec); ed/BA Univ Okla; pa/Author 24 Pub'd Books, Articles in All Major Mags - US & Abroad; Bd Mem, Soc of Mag Writers (Now Assn of Jrnlsts & Authors); cp/Bd Mem, CCP Dance Co, Manila, Philippines; hon/Doct Lttrs Philippine Woms Univ; Dame Officier, Chaine des Rotisseurs.

DAY, DELBERT EDWIN oc/Professor; b/Aug 16, 1936; h/Box 357, Rolla, MO 65401; ba/Rolla; m/Shirley Ann Foraker; c/Lynne Denise, Thomas Edwin; p/Edwin Raymond and Doris J Day; ed/BS Univ Mo, Rolla 1958; MS 1960, PhD 1961 Penn St Univ ; mil/AUS Corps Engrs, 1/Lt; pa/Prof, Ceramic Engrg, Univ Mo, Rolla; Conslt; Am Ceramic Soc; Am Soc for Engrg Ed; Nat Inst of Ceramic Engrs; Sigma Xi; Tau Beta Pi; Phi Kappa Phi Sigma Gamma Epsilon; Others; cp/Past Pres, Rolla Kiwanis Clb; Rolla Comma U Fund; Rolla City Bd Adjustmt; Advr, Explorer Scout Post 82; hon/Am Men Sci; W/W: MW, Engrg Ed;

DIB; Creative & Successful Personalites of the World; Commun Ldrs Am; Engrs of Distinction.

DAY, JOHN H oc/Artist; Educator; b/May 27, 1932; h/22 E 89th St, NY, NY 10028; ba/Wayne, NJ; p/Kenneth Knowlton and Josephine Hamblin Day; ed/BFA 1954, MFA 1956 Yale Univ; pa/Prof of Painting, William Patterson Col; Public & Pvt Collects: Mus Mod Art (NYC), Whitney Mus Am Art, Chase Manhattan Bk (NYC & Paris), Mr Anthony Perkins, Mrs Robert Benjamin, Mr & Mrs Richard Rodgers, ABC (NYC), Mrs Raymond Cartier, Sheldon Meml Art Gallery, Musee Pompidou, Am Coun Learned Socs, Num Others; Num Exhbns; Num Group Shows incl: Musee Pompidou, Whitney Mus Am Art, Mus Mod Art (NY), Hudson River Mus, Bklyn Mus, Alonzo Gallery Nordness Gallery, Yale Univ, Flint Inst Arts, Hunterdon Art Ctr, Annual New England Exhbns, Finch Col; Wks Reviewed in: *Art & Artists, Newsday, Long Island Free Press, The Artery, East Hampton Star, Art International, Invitational*; hon/Num Art Awds; MacDowell Fellow, Fribourg S'ship; French Govt S'ship.

DAY, RANDALL L oc/Administrator; b/Apr 6, 1955; h/2570 Murfreesboro Rd #C9, Nashville, TN 37217; ba/Nashville; ed/Mr & Mrs A D Day Jr, Union City, TN; ed/BS Univ Tenn; pa/Dist Exec Dir, Tenn Div Am Cancer Soc; cp/Jaycees; Univ Tenn Alumni Assn; r/Meth; hon/W/W Am Cols & Univs.

DAYE, CHARLES EDWARD oc/Associate Professor; b/May 14, 1944; h/Rt 6, Box 89, Chapel Hill, NC 27514; ba/Chapel Hill; p/Eccleasiastes and Addie Roberts Daye; ed/BA w high hons NC Ctl Univ 1966; JD w hons Columbia Univ 1969; pa/Assoc Prof of Law, Univ NC Sch Law; NY St Bar; US Ct Appeals 6th Circuit; US Ct Appeals DC Circuit; US Dist Ct for DC; NC St Bar; Nat Acad Trial Lwyrs; Pres, NC Assn Black Lwyrs 1976-; cp/NAACP; Bd Dirs: NC Ctr for Public Policy Res, In-Chu-Co Housing Devel Corp; Durham Com on Affairs of Black People; Chm, Dem Precnt Org; Durham Co Dem Exec Com; Others; r/Bapt; hon/Profl Pubs; Harlan Fiske Stone Scholar; Order of Coif.

DAYRINGER, RICHARD LEE oc/Associate Professor; b/Feb 3, 1934; h/3221 Dorchester, Springfield, IL 62704; ba/Springfield; m/Evelyn Janet; c/Stephen, David, Deborah, Daniel, James; p/Joe and Sara Davringer, Cassville, MO; ed/AA; AB;

MDiv; ThD; pa/Assoc Prof of Med Humanities & Fam Pract, So Ill Univ Sch of Med 1974-; Dir, Dept of Pastoral Care & Cnslg Bapt Meml Hosp, Kansas City, Mo 1965-74; Instr, Rel & Pastoral Cnslg, Univ Mo, Kans City Sch Med 1971-74; Other Past Positions; Clin Mbr, Am Assn Marriage & Fam Cnslrs; Am Assn Pastoral Cnslrs; Assn for Clin Pastoral Ed; Past Pres, Assn Mo Chaplains; Kans City Bapt Assn; Soc for Hlth & Human Values; Inst Soc, Ethics & Life Scis; Others; hon/Commun Ldrs & Noteworthy Ams; DIB; Dir Am Scholars; Intl W/W Commun Ser; Men Achmt; Notable Ams; W/W: Rel, Kans; Grants; F'ship; S'ship; Profl Pubs.

DEADMON, GERTRUDE VALIVIA oc/Educator; b/Aug 28, 1927; h/1906 N Cheyenne Ave, Tulsa, OK 74106; ba/Tulsa;

m/Robert Dee Sr (dec); c/Robert Dee Jr; p/Theodore R Owens Sr; Sue Ella Owens (dec); ed/BA Bishop Col; MTA Univ Tulsa; Addit Studies; pa/Mgmt Recruiter/Interviewer, Okla City Pers Dept 1976-; Ednl Adm Sers Conslt, Lloyd E Rader Diagnostic/Evaluation Ctr; Assessment Intake Cnslr, Human Resources Devel Dept (Okla City) 1975-76; Adm Asst, Div of Ec Opportunity, Comprehensive Drug Treatment Prog for St of Okla 1972-75; Prin, Holmes Elem Sch (Tulsa) 1970-72; Adv Spec for Human Relats Dept, Tulsa Public Schs 1967-68; Other Past Positions; Author, "TULSAPAC Improving Human Race Relats in the Classroom", Adopted by Tulsa Public Schs; TV Panelist on Human Relats; Currently Writing Novel; Early Childhood Ed Assn; Nat Inst Mtl Hlth; Past Mem: NEA, Okla Edn Assn, Nat Prins Assn; Others; cp/NAACP; YWCA; Fine Arts Apprec; Book of the Month Clb; BPW; Others; hon/Elem Tchr of Yr 1967.

DEAL, WILLIAM SANFORD oc/Minister; Author; Counselor; Freelance Writer; h/11326 Ranchito St, El Monte, CA 91732; ba/El Monte; m/Myrna Allen; c/Evangeline Sue Shelton (Mrs Larry); p/Marcus Virgil and Lacy Eva Miller Deal (dec); ed/AB Taylor Univ; ThB Roosevelt Grad Sch; ThM Defenders' Sem; MA Pasadena Col Grad Sch; ThD Pacific Wn Univ; pa/Dist Supt, Wesleyan Chs 16 yrs; Pres, Wn Pilgrim Col, El Monte 2 yrs; r/Wesleyan; hon/W/W: Oreg, Cal, Far W; 2000 Men Distn; DIB; Others.

DEAN, DONALD EDWIN oc/Consulting Engineer; b/Feb 13, 1926; ba/565 W 5th Suite 1, San Pedro, CA 90731; c/Steven, Michelle, Jeanette, Craig; p/Theodore Edwin Dean (dec); Gladys Ernst Dean, Pacific Grove, CA; ed/AA; BS; mil/AUS; pa/Fluid Power Soc (Past Mem Bd Dirs); Soc Plastics Engrs (Past Mem Bd Dirs); Reg'd Profl Engr; r/Prot; hon/Technol Awd, Soc of Plastics Engrs 1978.

DEAN, FRANCIS HILL oc/Landscape Architect; b/Oct 1, 1922; h/31591 Mar Vista Ave, S Laguna, CA 92677; ba/Newport Beach, CA; m/Carolyn Bower; c/Gary Edward, Tamara Ellen, 4 Stepchd; p/John S P and Ethel Hill Dean (dec); ed/BS Univ Cal, Berkeley 1948; MLA Univ So Cal 1981; mil/USAF 1942-45, Capt; pa/Landscape Arch Pvt Pract 30 yrs; Num Public & Pvt Projs; Am Soc Landscape Arch; Lic'd Landscape Arch, Cal; Vis Lectr & Critic; Fac Mem, Cal Polytech Univ 1976-; Advr; Spkr; Panelist; Profl Juries; cp/S Laguna Civic Assn; Town Hall; Others; hon/Awds for Profl Work; Sigma Lambda Alpha; Coun of Fellows, Am Soc Landscape.

DEAN, HALSEY ALBERT oc/Chief Field Operations; b/Apr 23, 1916; h/7816 Birnam Wood Dr, McLean, VA 22102; m/Lydia Margaret Carter; c/Halsey A Jr, John Carter, Lydia Margerae Carter; p/James Frank and Pinkie Estelle Creasy Dean; ed/BS; EdM; EdD; mil/USN WW II Lt (jg); pa/Dir Va Credit Union Leag; CUNA; CSG; CUNA; Supply; CUNADATA; Chief Field Opers, VA Ctl Ofc;

cp/Life Mem, Univ Va Alumni Assn; VPI Alumni Assn; Lynchburg Col Alumni Assn; 8 Gallon Blood Donors Clb, ARC; Am Legion 40 & 8; Clb s Clb Credit Union Nat Assn; Bd Dirs, Intl Credit Union Ser Inc; r/Bapt: Bd of Deacons, Past Supt of SS; hon/WW II Asiatic Pacific, Def & Philippine Liberation Medals; Personalities of S.

DEAN, LLOYD oc/Counselor; Minister; b/Aug 17, 1930; h/Rt 6, Box 498, Morehead, KY 40351; ba/Morehead; m/Arvetta Plank; p/Bert T and Minty Creech Dean, Morehead, KY; ed/BS 1958; MA 1959; mil/USAF 1953-57; pa/Cnslr, Rowan Co HS 1970-79; Pastor, U Pentecostal Ch Hays Crossing "Cobblestone Ch in the Woods" 1963-; Past

Pres: RCPGA, CCEA, EKPGA; cp/Rowan Co HS: 4-H Ldr, Histn Clb Ldr; APEBP Ldr; cp/Pres, Rowan Co Hist Soc 1977-79; Repub; Notary Public; Pastor, Morehead U Pentecostal Ch 1957-69; Editor, Ky Dist New 1957-69; UPC SS Dir, Ky 1957-69; UPC Secy & Treas, Ky Dist 1969-73; hon/Hon Mem FFA; 4-H Awds; Others.

DEAN, LYDIA MARGARET CARTER oc/Author; Food & Nutrition Consultant; b/Jul 11, 1919; h/7816 Birnam Wood Dr, McLean, VA 22101; ba/Wash DC; m/Halsey Albert; c/Halsey Albert Jr, John Carter, Lydia Margerae; p/Christopher C and Hettie Gross Carter; ed/BS Madison Col 1941; MS Va Poly Inst & St Univ 1951; Postgrad Study: Univ Va, Mich St Univ; pa/Food & Nutrition Consultant, Nat Hdqrs ARC, Wash DC 1967-; Dir, Dept Nutrition & Dietetics, SWn Va Med Ctr, Roanoke 1960-67; Commun Nutritionist, Roanoke, Va 1953-60; Assoc Prof, VPI 1946-53; Pres, Carter & Dean Assocs; Cons & Assoc Dir, Am Dietetic Assn 1975-; Coor New Deg Prog, Univ Hawaii 1974-75; BPW; Am Home Econs Asns; AAUW; IPA; Food Sers Execs Assn; Others; hon/Author, *The Complete Gourmet Nutrition Cookbook* 1978, *Community Emergency Feeding* (w Virginia McMasters) 1972, *How to Help My Child Eat Right* 1978, Profl Articles; W/W Am.

DEAN, ROBERT GAYLE JR oc/Musician; Composer; Arranger; Producer; Author; b/Nov 22, 1939; h/PO Box 110546, Nashville, TN 37211; ba/Nashville; p/R Gayle and Helen Y Dean, Nashville, TN; mil/AUS 1957-59; pa/Bus interests incl: Dean's List Pub'g Co, Owlofus Music Inc, Myownah Music Inc, Camera Five Pub'g Co, Soul, Country & Blues Record Co, Cross Co Records & Co Soul Records; Nat Electoral Bd, Nat Acad Recording Arts & Scis; Nashville Songwriters Assn; Intl Nat Acad Recording Arts & Scis; Country Music Assn; Am Fed Musicians; cp/Am Rifle Assn; Jewish Relief Fund; Repub; Pete Fountain's Half Fast Walking Clb; r/Bapt.

DEAN, WANDA ELIZABETH oc/Assistant Professsor; b/Jan 29, 1953; h/2415 E Jolly Rd #7 Lansing, MI 38910; ba/E Lansing, MI; p/Abel Jr and Dorothy P Dean, Richmond, VA; ed/BA; MA; PhD; pa/Asst Prof of Commun Hlth Sci, Mich St Univ; Mich Assn Non-White Concerns; Nat Alliance of Black Edrs; Am Pers & Guid Assn; Mich Pers & Guid Assn; Assn Black Psychologists; Mich Assn Black Psych; Assn Non-White Concerns; cp/NAACP; Oper PUSH; Elizabeth Harris Chap #86; OES; PHA; Delta Sigma Theta; r/Bapt; hon/William H Madella Awd; W/W Midwest; Lincoln Univ Ser Awd; Alpha Chi Hon Soc.

DeANDREA, LOIS LUCILE oc/Registered Nurse; b/Nov 29, 1916; h/1501 Meyers Rd, Irving, TX 75060; ba/Irving; m/(dec); c/Yvonne, Linda; p/John H and Effie Lucile Parkerson (dec); ed/BS; MA; pa/Reg'd Nurse; Tex St Tchrs Assn; Dallas Area Sch Hlth Assn; Am Sch Hlth Assn; cp/Jetset Toastmistress;

Wom's Div C of C; ARC Instr in Mother Baby Care & −st Aid; CPR; Dir, Irving Aid's Bd; ARC Disaster Nurse Cadre; r/Presb.

DEANIN, RUDOLPH DRESKIN oc/Professor; b/Jun 7, 1921; h/Box 466, Westford, MA 01886; ba/Lowell, MA; m/Joan Marie Berkoff; c/Nancy Elwell, Alice; p/Zalman Samuel and Sonya Sophie Dreskin

Deanin (dec); ed/AB Cornell Univ 1941; MS 1942, PhD 1944 Univ Ill; pa/Prof of Plastics, Univ Lowell; Am Chem Soc; Adhesion Soc; Soc Plastics Eng; Plastics Ed Foun; New England Soc Coatings Technol.

DEASON, DONNA DAVIS oc/Teacher; b/Jul 15, 1951; h/2602 Longhorn Rd, Waycross, GA 31501; ba/Waycross; m/William Edward; c/Christi Mechelle; p/Dewey D and Martha Z Davis, Milledgeville, GA; ed/BS; MEd; pa/Tchr, 1st Meth Kindergarten; Okegenokee Assn for Yg Chd; GAE; NAE; cp/Choir; Childbirth Parent Ed Assn; Intl Childbirth Ed Assn; r/Bapt; hon/Personalities of S.

DEATON, FAE ADAMS oc/Mental Health Team Member; Artist; Writer; Teacher; b/Feb 19, 1932; h/819 Colonial Ave #6, Norfolk, VA 23507; ba/Norfolk; c/Dorothea Fae Stein Krause, Caroline Louise Stein Werth, Erich Charles Stein; p/Charles Sizemore and Dorothea Lucia Adams Deaton, Norfolk, VA; ed/BS Salem Col 1953; MSEd Old Dominion Univ 1975; MSW Cand Norfolk St Col; pa/Admissions Release Bd, Norfolk Lakehouse Girls Detention Ctr; Bd Mem, Tidewater Chapt Va Coun on Social Welfare 1978-81; Tidewater Profl Child Abuse Comm; Tidewater Rape Info Sers (TRIS); Tidewater Mtl Hlth Assn; Nat Assn Social Wkrs; Am Am Pers & Guid Assn; Va Pers & Guid Assn; Hampton Roads Pers & Guid Assn; Am Sch Cnslrs Assn; Va Elem Sch Cnslrs Assn; Nat Leag Am Pen Wom; Alaska Press Clb; Others; cp/Va Opera Guild Assn; Chrysler Mus; hon/Acad Hons; W/W S&SW; Others.

DeBAKEY, LOIS oc/Professor; Writer; Edicotr; ba/Baylor College of Medicine, 1200 Moursund, Houston, TX 77030; p/S M and Raheeja Z DeBakey (dec); ed/BA Newcomb Col Tulane Univ; MA, PhD Tulane Univ; pa/Prof of Scientific Communs, Tulane Univ Sch of Med, New Orleans, La; Lectr in Scientific Communs, Tulane Univ Sch of MEd, New Orleans, La; Edic Bd *Cardiovascular Res Ctr Bultn* and *Biosciences Communication;* Biomed Lib Review Com, Nat Lib of Med; Exec Coun of Comm on Cols, So Assn Cols & Schs; Former Mem Panel of Judges for Writing of NCTE; Num Profl Orgs Incl'g: AAAS, Am Soc for Info Sci, Nat Assn Sci Writers, Soc for

DeBAKEY, SELMA oc/Professor; ba/- 1200 Moursund Ave, Houston, TX 77030; p/S M and Raheeja Z DeBakey (dec); ed/BA Newcomb Col; Grad Studies Tulane Univ; pa/Prof of Sci Commun, Baylor Col of Med, Houston; Editor, *Cardiovascular Res Ctr*

Tech Commun; Edited Num Med & Sci Articles, Chapts & Books; Sr Author *The Scientific Jour: Editorial Policies & Practices;* Conductor of Progs in Sci Commun at Annual Profl Meetings, Var Med Schs & Hosps throughout US, Canada & Abroad; r/Epis; hon/Phi Beta Kappa; Dist'd Ser Awd, Am Med Writers Assn 1970; Biogl Listings.

DeBAKEY, MICHAEL E oc/Cardiovascular Surgeon; b/Sept 7, 1908; h/5323 Cherokee St, Houston, TX 77005; ba/Houston; m/Katrin Fehlhaber; c/Michael M, Ernest O, Barry E, Denis A, Olga Katerina; p/Shaker M and Raheeja Zorba DeBakey (dec); ed/BS 1930, MD 1932, MS 1935 Tulane Univ; pa/Certs: Am Bd Surg, Am Bd Thoracic Surg, Nat Bd Med Examrs; Acad Affils: Instr, Assoc 0 Asst Prof Surg Tulane Univ; Pres, Dist'd Ser Prog, Prof & Chm Cora Webb Mading Dept Surg Baylor Col Med; Clin Profl Surg Univ Tex Dental Br 1971-72; Hosp Affils: Dir Nat Heart & Blood Vessel Res & Demo Ctr, Houston; Sr Att'g Surg Meth Hosp Houston, Surg in Chief, Ben Taub Gen Hosp; Editorial Bd, Nat & Intl Med Jours Incl'g: Iranian Cardiovascular Jour (Hon Chm), New Technique for Audiovisual Ed for Surgs; Bd Govs Am Acad of Achmt; Pres 1959 Am Assn Thoracic Surg; Fdg Mem Am Heart Assn; Dir 1966 Assn for Advmt of Med Instrumentation, Bd Dirs 1968 Bio-Med Engrng Soc, Adv Coun 1968-69 Houston Heart Assn, Pres 1964 Nat Assn on Standard Med Vocab, Bd Govs 1965 Soc for Cryobiology, Pres 1954 Soc for Vascular Surg, Pres 1952 SWn Surg Cong; Com for Prevention of Heart Disease, Cancer, Stroke, Am Heart Foun; Hon Sponsor Draper World Population Fund; Bd Advrs Intl Med

Complex of Iran; Adv Bd Nat Coun Drug Abuse; Ofc of Technol Assessmt Hlth Adv Com; Hon Chm Art Rooney Benefit Dinner; Asociacion Mexicana de Cirugia Cardiovascular A C (Hon Mem); Albert Lasker Clin Med Res Jury Awds Chm 1973; Citizens for Treatmt of High Blood Pressure Chm 1974; Intl Heart & Lung Inst Sci Adv Com; Nat Insts Hlth Nat Heart & Lung Adv Coun 1974; Hon Fellow Royal Col Surgs England; Hon Mem Acad of Med Scis USSR; cp/Press Clb Houston; Rotary Clb; hon/Hon DSc Hahnemann Med Col & Hosp Phila 1973; Baylor Alumni Dist'd Fac Awd Soc Contemp Med & Surg 1973; Baylor Alumni Dist'd Fac Awd; Lions Intl Spec Awd; Intl Prize "La Madonnina" NYU Med Col of Dent, Alumni Awd; USSR Acad Sci 50th Anniv Jubilee Medal; Lib Human Resources; Alpha Omega Alpha; Alpha Pi Alpha; Omicron Delta Kappa; Phi Beta Pi; Phi Lambda Kappa; Sigma Xi; Hon LLD; AMA Dist'd Ser & Hektoen Gold Awds, Eleanor Roosevelt Humanities Awd, St Jude Man of Yr & Medal of Freedom Press Awds; Tex Med Ctr Medallion 1972; Rotary Clb Dist'd Citizen Awd 1972; Am Col Chest Phys Pres Cit; Michael DeBakey Day, Baylor Col of Med; St Francis Hosp F'ship Awd, Roslyn, NY; Dir Ednl Specs; Intl Scholars Dir; Intl W/W Commun Ser; Intl W/W; Ldrs Ed; Nat Reg Prom Ams & Intl Notables; Outstg Edrs Am; W/W: Am, Am Col & Univ Adm, Sci, World; Personalities of S.

Bulletin; Co-Dir, Courses in Sci Commun at Med Schs & Med Soc Meetings in US & Abroad; hon/Author, *Current Concepts of Breast Cancer,* 1967.

DEBUSMAN, PAUL MARSHALL oc/Librarian; c/Dec 6, 1932; h/2934 Grinstead Dr, Louisville, KY 40206; ba/Louisville; m/Amelia; c/Amelia Anne, Melanie; p/Paul Louis Debusman (dec); Lillian G Debusman, Wichita, KS; ed/BA; MDiv; MSLS; PhD; pa/Am Theol Lib Assn; Metroversity Ref Libns Com; cp/Crescent Hill Commun Coun; r/S Bapt.

DECHAMPLAIN, GLADYCE CATHY WILSON oc/Educator; Research Scholar; Writer; Investment Consultant; Real Estate & Land Development Consultant; h/622 Highlands Terr, Piedmont, CA 94611; ba/Piedmont; m/Frederic Edwin de Champlain; c/Patricia Ann de Champlain; p/John Elkane and Hattie Lee Wood Wilson (dec); ed/BS Univ Cal, Berkeley; MA Columbia Univ; pa/Artist; Writer; Instr; Conslt; Nat Assn Real Est Bds, Cal Assn Realtors; Oakland Bd Realtors; Cal Tchrs Assn; Fdr: de Champlain Med Pers, Phys Therapy Reg'd; Admr, Howland Convalescent Hosp; Est'd Phys & Surgs Telephone Exch; Notary Public; cp/DAR; Fdr, Baby Nurses' Clb of Cal; Dir, Slumber Home for Pre-Sch Child Rearing; Oakland C of C; Rel/Prot; hon/Most Outstg Wom in Bus & Profl Area, Oakland C of C; Grant; Notable Ams of Bicent Era; Notable Ams; Commun Ldrs & Noteworthy Ams; DIB; World W/W Wom.

de CHAMPLAIN, PATRICIA ANN oc/Educator; Real Estate Broker; Financier; h/622 Highlands Terr, Piedmont, CA 94611; ba/Piedmont; p/Frederic Edwin de Champlain (dec); Gladyce Cathy Wilson de Champlain, Piedmont, CA; ed/BA w hons Univ Cal, Berkeley; MA Middlebury Col; pa/Pres & Broker-Owner, Crocker Highlands Real Est & Investmt Co; Nat Assn Real Est Bds; Cal Assn Realtors; Oakland Bd Realtors; Pres, de Champlain Translators & Interpreters; Fgn Lang Spec; Notary Public; cp/DAR; Fgn Lang Instr, ARC; r/Prot; hon/Phi Beta Kappa; Fulbright S'ship; W/W: Am Wom, W; World W/W Wom; DIB; Notable Ams; Personalites of W&MW; 500 1st Fams Am; Book of Hon; Commun Ldrs & Noteworthy Ams.

DE CONCINI, DENNIS oc/United States Senator; b/May 8, 1937; h/Arizona; ba/4104 Dirksen Senate Ofc Bldg, Wash DC 20510; m/Susan Margaret Hurley; c/Denise, Christina, Patrick Evo; p/Evo and Ora Webster DeConcini, Tucson, AZ; ed/BA Univ Ariz 1959; LLB Univ Ariz Col of Law 1963; mil/Adj Gen Corps 1959-60, 2/Lt; Judge Advocate Gen Corps, Army Resv 1964-67; pa/Mem US Sen 1976-; Pima Co Atty 1972-76; Mem Law Firm DeConcini & McDonald 1968-73; cp/Pima Co Dem Ctl Com 12 Yrs; Dem St Exec Com 10 yrs; Del, Dem Nat Conv 1974; r/Rom Cath; hon/Co Atty of Yr 1975.

DECKER, ROBERT D SR oc/University President; b/Nov 10, 1922; h/RR 5, Box 267, Bemidji, MN 56601; ba/Bemidji; m/Jacqueline; c/R David Jr, D Lynn D Rud, Jack M; p/C M Decker (dec); Mrs C M Decker Kyle, TX; ed/BS; MEd; PhD; mil/AUS

1942-46, 1/Lt; USAR, Lt Col (Ret'd); pa/Pres, Bemidji St Univ; Contbr to Profl Pubs incl'g *Tex Outlook*; cp/Bemidji Area C of C Agri Com; Rotary Intl; cp/BSA; Masonic Lodge; r/U Meth Ch: Chm Pastor-Parish Com; hon/Sev Mil Medals; Biogl Listings.

DE CROW, KAREN oc/Attorney; Author; Editor; Lecturer; ed/BS NWn Univ 1959; JD Syracuse Univ 1972; pa/Atty; NY St Bar; Onondaga Co Bar Assn; Writer, En Reg Inst for Ed 1967-69; Textbook Editor, L W Singer Co 1965-66; Social Studies & Adult Ed Editor, Holt, Reinhart & Winston Inc 1965; Newsletter Writer & Book Editor, Ctr for Study of Liberal Ed for Adults 1961-64; Editor, American Soc Planning Officials' *Zoning Digest* 1960-61; Fashion & Resorts Editor, *Golf Digest* 1959-60; TV Appearances; Conslt; cp/NOW: Nat Pres 1974-77, Nat Bd Mem 1968-77; Mayoral Cand, Syracuse, NY 1969; Ad Hoc Com for Human Rights; Nat Bd Mem, Gay Rights Nat Lobby; Bd Advrs, Working Wom V; Endorser, Coalition Against Racism; hon/W/W: Am, Am Wom; DIB; Commun Ldrs & Noteworthy Ams; 1 of 200 Future Ldrs of Am, *Time* Mag 1974; 1 of 50 Most Influential Wom in Am, Newspaper Enterprise Assn; Author: *Sexist Justice* 1974, *The Young Woman's Guide to Liberation* 1971, Num Articles.

DECUIR, LARRY BRENT oc/Student; b/Feb 19, 1959; h/2240 13th St, Port Neches, TX 77651; p/Albert J and Pollie Reynolds Decuir, Port Neches, TX; ed/BBA Cand Lamar Univ; pa/Am Soc Pers Adm; cp/Student Govt; r/Exec Coun, Bapt Student Union, Lamar Univ; hon/Phi Eta Sigma; Acad Hons.

DEDMON, RICHARD KENDRICK oc/Actor; Writer; Gentleman Farmer; Arabian Horse Breeder; b/Oct 16, 1947; h/Rt 6, Fairview Farms, Shelby, NC 28150; m/Sandra Schenck; p/A V Dedmon (dec); Lizzie Lee Dedmon, Shelby, NC; ed/BA Univ NC-Charlotte 1969; pa/Pres, Barnyard Press; cp/Pres, Shelby Commun Theatre; r/Bapt; hon/Author: *Frances the Pig, Cramp the Donkey*.

DEDOWICZ, CHRISTINE DOROTHY oc/Registered Nurse; b/Mar 30, 1949; h/3721 S Wenonah, Berwyn, IL 60402; ba/Berwyn; p/Edward Thaddeus and Dorothy Stephanie, Berwyn, IL; ed/AAD Morton Col; BSN Cand Lewis Univ; pa/Reg'd Nurse, MacNeal Meml Hosp; Nurse's Assn Am Col Obstetricians & Gynecologists; Ill Assn for Maternal & Child Hlth; cp/Wom's Aux, MacNeal Meml Hosp; Adv Bd, Triton Col LPN Prog; r/Cath; hon/W/W Am Wom; World W/W Wom.

DeFELICE, DAVE JOHN JR oc/Principal; b/Jul 10, 1943; h/PO Box 95, Raceland, LA 70394; ba/Houma, LA; m/Mona M; p/Dave J Sr and Lolita H DeFelice, Raceland, LA; ed/BS La St Univ; MEd Nicholls St Univ; pa/Prin; Lafourche Tchrs Inc; La Assn Edrs; Nat Elem Prins Assn; La Elem Prins Assn; Phi Delta

Kappa; PTC; cp/Raceland Jaycees; NSU Alumni Coun; LSU Alumni; r/St Hilary Cath Ch; hon/Oustsg Elem Tchrs of Am; DIB; Outstg Men Am; Men Achmt; W/W Among Elem Sch Prins; Personalities of S.

DeFOREST, JULIE MORROW oc/Artist; Poet; Writer; h/Vernon Manor Hotel #302, 400 Oak St, Cincinnati, OH 45219;

m/Cornelius W (dec); p/Cornelius W and Rosalie Carolyn Morrow; ed/BA Wellesley Col; AM Columbia Univ; pa/Painting; Writing; 6 1-man Exhbns in NYC; 1-man Shows: Jersey City Mus, Loring Andrews Gallery, Cinc, Farnsworth Mus-Wellesley Col, Others; Allied Artists Am; Nat Arts Clb; Wom's Univ Clb, NYC; Cincinnati MacDowell Soc; Profl Artists of Cinc; Other Exhbns: Nat Acad Design, Pa Acad, Corcoran Gallery, NY World's Fair, Bklyn Mus, Cinc Art Mus; Wks in Permanent Collects: Columbia Univ Lib, Xavier Univ, Howard Univ, Fisk Univ, Univ Cinc, Cinc Art Mus, Cinc ARC HQs, Am Christian Col, Others; cp/Cinc Town Clb; Cinc CC; DAR; hon/FRSA; Awds for Art & Poetry; W/W: Arts, Art & Antiques, NY, Am Art, Am Wom; DIB; 500 1st Fams Am; Nat Soc Dir; Intl W/W Commun Ser; Others; Author *Belfry Chimes and Other Rimes* 1974.

De GAETANO, CAROLYN HALL oc/Singer; Actress; Teacher; b/Aug 22, 1924; h/2119 Beaufait, Grosse Pointe, MI 48236; ba/Grosse Pointe; m/Armand L (dec); c/Mark, Douglas; p/Joseph M and Rose Elizabeth Hall (dec); ed/BA Univ Pgh; Julliard Sch Music; pa/Contralto Soloist, 1st Congregational Ch, Detroit; cp/Detroit Fine Arts Soc; Detroit Theatre Arts Soc; Tuesday Musicale; Grosse Pointe Symph Wom's Com; r/Prot; hon/Univ Pgh Hall of Fame; Pi Lambda Theta; Kappa Kappa Gamma; Theta Alpha Phi; Mortar Bd.

De GAISH, MELADE S oc/Vocational Administrator; b/Dec 24, 1933; h/Box 664, Portland, TX 78374; ba/Gregory; m/Mary Darlene Ganem; c/Mark Steven, Miriam Ann, Darlene Ann, Brett John, Debra Ann; p/Shaeen Shaff DeGaish (dec); Lurece Samara DeGaish, Corpus Christi, TX; ed/BS Tex Tech

Univ; MS Tex A&I Univ; mil/AUS 1957-59; pa/TSTA; NEA; AVA; TVTA; TADSOET; NCLA; Tex St Bd Voc Adm; cp/Dem; Past Pres, Lions Clb; Bd Dirs, Lions Clb; VP, Invesco 74 Inc; r/Cath; hon/Outstg Ser Awd, Robstown Ind Sch Dist; Lion of Yr 1975; W/W S&SW; Personalities of S.

De GENARO, GUY JOSEPH oc/Associate Professor; b/Nov 20, 1921; h/3 Berkshire Rd, Richmond, VA 23221; m/Jennie Jennings; c/Marsha Jean Blakemore; p/Ralph DeGenaro (dec); Madeline DeGenaro, Hamden, CT; ed/BS; MBA; PhD; mil/USAF, Lt Col; pa/Assoc Prof of Mgmt, Va Commonwealth Univ; Acad Mgmt; VP & Bd Mem, Soc for Advmt Mgmt; cp/Bd Dirs, Va Affil Am Heart Assn; Soc for Prevention of Blindness; hon/Outstg Edrs Am.

De GENARO, JENNIE JENNINGS oc/Educator; b/Jan 27; h/3 Berkshire Rd, Richmond, VA 23221; ba/Highland Sprgs, VA; m/Guy J; c/Marsha Jean Blakemore; p/Thomas Pankey and Frances Birtha Jennings (dec); ed/BS E Tex St Univ; MS Ind Univ; pa/Elem Supvr for Spec Progs, Henrico Co Schs; Pub'd Profl Articles; AAUW; cp/LWV; r/Meth; hon/Alpha Delta Kappa; Pi Lambda Theta; hon/W/W Va; Personalities of S; Hon Grad.

DEGENER, VENETA M oc/Publisher; Advertiser; b/May 10, 1922; h/7101 Roseland Dr, Des Moines, IA 50322; ba/Des Moines; m/LeRoy H; c/Judy Fontana, Kent

Oestenstad, Larry Oestenstad; p/Engle O and Rosalie Bollman (dec); pa/Ins Advtg Conf; Bus Communicators Ia; Mutual Ins Communicators; Ins Wom Des Moines; NAMIC Public Rels Com; cp/C of C; Des Moines Toastmasters; r/Prot; hon/Dist'd Edit Experience; Merit Awd, Nat Assn Ins Wom.

De GRAFFENREID, MARION F oc/- Financial Manager; Tax Consultant; b/Jul 31, 1951; h/853 N Ridgewood Pl, Los Angeles, CA 90038; p/Marion Sr and Ruby W DeGraffenreid, Los Angeles, CA; ed/AA 1974, BA 1977 Thomas Edison Col; pa/Controller, Consumer TV & Audio Inc 1976-78; Owner/Bookkeeper, Hope Ceramics, Kans City, Mo 1971-74; Instr, Univ Mo, Kans City 1972-74; Nat Acct'g Assn; Am Inst Managerial Acct'g; cp/Art Critic; r/Disciples of Christ; hon/W/W Bus & Fin.

DeGREGORIO, ROBERT EUGENE oc/Attorney; b/Feb 22, 1951; h/14 Bob-o- Link Lane, Northport, NY 11768; ba/Northport; p/Peter J and Fulvia A DelVecchio DeGregorio, Northport, NY; ed/BA magna cum laude CW Post Col; JD Hofstra Univ Sch of Law; pa/Suffolk Co Bar Assn; Suffolk Co Coun on Juv & Criminal Justice; cp/Downstate VP, NY St Yg Dems; CoChm, Suffolk Co Yg Dems; Chm Legis Action Com, N'port/E N'port Sch Bd; Past Mem, Huntington Yth Bd; hon/W/W: Am Politics, Students in Am Cols & Univs.

de HAAN, JOHN oc/Editor; Publisher; b/Nov 20, 1920; h/Huntington Beach, CA 92648; ba/Huntington Beach; m/John, David; p/Gilbert A and Mary Scott de Haan (dec); mil/AUS WW II & Korean Conflict; pa/Editor; Publr; Dir, World-wide Assn for Anomalous Sci Phenomena; r/Lamaistic, Lotas Lama, White Lodge of Tibet; hon/ Purple Heart; Army Commend Medal.

DEINHARDT, CAROL LUCY oc/Psy- chologist; Administrator; b/Nov 8, 1946; h/2901 Esplanade Ave, New Orleans, LA 70118; ba/New Orleans; m/Anthony Richard Mawson; p/John and Hazal Hoag Deinhart, Ridge, NY; ed/BA Stanford Univ; MA Harvard Univ; pa/Dir, Wom's Ctr for Gtr New Orleans 1975-; Asst Prof, City Col, Loyola Univ 1975-; Dir/Psychologist, Child Devel Ctr, SE La Hosp, Mandeville, La 1973-75; Psychologist, Salem Hosp, Salem, Mass 1972-73; Tutor, Harvard Univ 1971-75; cp/Exec Bd: La Cystic Fibrosis Res Foun 1977-, Opportunity 1977-; hon/Nat Social Sci Res Coun/NIMH F'ship; Ford Foun Res Grant; YWCA Bicent Achmt Awd 1976; Outstg Yg Wom Am; World W/W Wom; Nat Sci Foun Grad F'ship.

de la HUERGA, JESUS oc/Clinical Pathologist; b/Nov 25, 1915; h/1414 Lincoln, Evanston, IL 60201; ba/Chicago, IL; m/Jayne; c/Carmen, Carlos, Luis, Mario, Victoria; m/Jesus and Luz de la Huerga (dec); ed/MD; PhD; pa/Clin Pathologist, Univ Ill Med Sch; Dir of Lab; Pres, Dominican Med Assn; r/Cath; hon/Hon Consul, Dominican Repub; Others.

DeLANGE, KENNETH ALLEN oc/- Corporation Executive; b/Jan 20, 1935; h/306½ E 32nd St, Joplin, MO 64801; ba/Joplin; m/Margaret Ann; c/Lisa Michelle; p/Leo and Ruby DeLange, Girard, KS; ed/BS

Pittsburg St Univ 1956; mil/USMC, Sgt; pa/Pres, DeLange Industs; Exec VP, Pittcraft Printing Inc; Pres: Rental Ranches Inc, Meml Pub'g Co; Advertising Fed Am; Profl Photographers Assn Am; cp/C of C; Shrine; r/Meth; hon/*Printers Ink* Mag Silver Medal Awd as Outstg Man of Yr; Num Jaycee Awds; Others.

De La PENA, CORDELL AMADO oc/-Physician; Pathologist; b/Apr 30, 1934; h/209 Candlelight Dr, Clarksburg, WV 26301; ba/-Clarksburg; m/Erlinda Lapuz; c/Leslie B, Nina J, Cordell Jr; ed/MD; mil/PHS 1959-60, 1961-63; pa/FCAP; ASCP; IAP; AMA; WVMA; WVPA; cp/Aid; C of C; r/Cath; hon/Diplomate, Am Bd Anatomic & Clin Pathol.

de la SIERRA, ANGELL O oc/University Professor; Biophysicist; b/Feb 28, 1932; h/Box 2060, Cayey, PR 00633; m/Judith Ann; c/5; ed/BS Univ PR, MS CUNY; PhD St John's Univ; Vis Prof, Fac of Med, Univ PR; Chm Fac Natural Scis, Univ PR Cayey; Former Prof of Biophysics, Georgetown Univ Med Sch; Other

Past Positions; NY Acad Sci; Radiation Res Soc; Sigma Xi; Biophys Soc; Pres, Consulti8ng Bd of Technol & Voc Tng, Cayey; Num Profl Pubs; hon/W/W Am; Intl W/W Commun Ser; Personalities of S; Author: *Notes on a Biopsychosociology of Man, Theory & Practice in Anatomical Physiology.*

de la TORRE de SAN BRAULIO, (COUNT) ENRIQUE CARLOS IV (de la CASA y GARCIA-CALAMARTE), oc/Diplomat; Lawyer; Professor; Writer; b/Sept 17, 1906; h/"Holladay" 2602 Walker Ln, Salt Lake City, UT 84117; m/Maria-Luisa; ed/LLD; PhD; LittM; AB; BSc; pa/Mbr Fgn Ser; Former Envoy Extraordinary & Min Plenipotentiary; Acting Ambassador; Former Off, Cavalary Off, Royal Horse Guard of the King; Royal Acad Jursiprudence & Legislation. hon/Knight of the Mil Order of St John; Knight of Justice of the Sovereign Mil Order of Malta; Pub'd Author; Biogl Listings.

de la TORRE de SAN BRAULIO (The Countess), MARIA-LUISA (GARZON de la CASA) oc/Author; Educator; Publisher; m/Enrique Carlos IV; h/"Holladay" 2602 Walker Ln, Salt Lake City, UT 84117, USA; ed/BA Tex St Coll for Wom; BA BS, Inst San Isidro, Madrid, Spain; PhD Univ Ind; pa/Served Var Appts at: Marylhurst Col, Univ Utah; Ed & Publr, *Revista Iberica*; Hons/Pub'd Author; *Lady Mil Order of Kts of St John; Lady of Hon & Devotion, Sovereign Order of Malta; Dame Grand Cross of Justice, Sovereign Mil-Teutonic, Order of Levant, London;* Biogl Listings.

DeLAY, WAYNE TILDEN oc/Corporation Executive; b/Apr 1, 1919; h/1154 Brookwood Ln, Nashville, TN 37220; ba/Nashville; m/Iva Pettus; c/Cheri Ann & William Tilden; p/William Tilden and Emma McPeak DeLay, Lascassas, TN; ed/BA, BS Union Univ 1941; pa/Owner: Conway Metal 1946-, Sherman Concrete Pipe Co 1949-; Plant Mgr, Universal Concrete Pipe Co 1944-49; Supvr Constrn, H K Ferguson Co, Cleveland 1941-43; Nat Corrugated Pipe Assn; Am Concrete Pipe Assn; cp/Exec Bd, Middle Tenn BSA; Chm, Assn Bapts for Scouting; Nashville C of C; Masons; Shriners; Presidents Clb; Richland C of C; Sertoma; r/Bapt; hon/W/W S&SW.

DELCO, EXALTON ALFONSO JR oc/Academic Dean; b/Sept 4, 1929; h/1805 Astor Pl, Austin, TX 78721; ba/Austin; m/Wilhelmina Ruth; c/Deborah Diane, Exalton Alfonso III, Loretta Elmirle, Cheryl Pauline; ed/AB; MS; PhD; mil/46th Surg Mobile Army, Landstuhl, Germany; pa/Acad Dean, Huston-Tillotson Col; Soc Sigma Xi; cp/Bd Mem, Holy Cross Hosp; r/Cath; hon/Stoye Prize, Am Soc Ichthyologists & Herpetologists 1960.

DELGADO, RAMON LOUIS oc/College Professor; b/Dec 16, 1937; h/16 Forest #107, Montclair, NJ 07042; ba/Montclair; p/Eloy V and Hildegard Delgado, Winter Haven, FL; ed/BA cum laude Stetson Univ 1959; MA Dallas Theatre Ctr 1960; MFA Yale Sch Drama 1967; PhD So Ill Univ 1976; pa/Assoc Prof of Spch & Theatre, Montclair St Univ;

Dramatists' Guild; Am Theatre Assn; Speech Commun Assn; cp/Playreader, Whole Theatre Co; hon/Fellow, Wasserman Midwest Profl Playwrights Workshop 1978; David Lib Awds, Am Col Theatre Fest 1976-78; Nat Play Awds from Samuel French; Theta Alpha Phi; Others; Pub'd 7 Plays incl'g *Once Below A Lighthouse* and *Waiting for the Bus;* Nat Playwrights Dir; Outstg Edrs Am.

DELGADO de TORRES, ALMA oc/Lawyer; b/May 16, 1913; h/4th St D 28, Hnas Davila Dev, Bayamon, PR; ba/Bayamon; m/Manuel Torres Reyes (dec); c/Manuel; p/Luis Mario Delgado Lugo and Maria Pasapera Tio (dec); ed/Commercial Dipl 1933; BA 1937; LLB & JD 1940; Addit Studies; pa/Lwyr in Pvt Legal Ofc 1940-44; Judge, Min Ct 1944-45; Assoc Lwyr, Div of Opinions, Dept of Justice 1946-47; Mun Judge 1948-50; Dist Atty 1950-56; Pvt Pract 1956-65; Dist Judge 1965-75; Pvt Pract 1975-; Asst Prof, InterAm Univ 1970-75; PR Bar Assn; Secy, Bayamon Lwyrs Assn 3 times; InterAm Lwyrs Assn; Others; cp/Pres, BPW Clb of Bayamon 1970-71; Altrusa Clb; Parents Assn Lasalle Cath Sch 1970-74; Others; r/Cath; hon/Pub'd Author; Plaque, PR Bar Assn; Lwyr of the Yr 1970; BSA Awd; Awds from Masonic Lodge, Altrusa, BPWC, Others.

DELLI, HELGA BERTRUN oc/Editor; b/Jul 17, 1928; h/408 W 34st NY, NY 10001; ba/Bronx, NY; p/Johannes Delli (dec), Elfriede Tamme Delli, Germany; ed/PhD Free Univ Berlin 1957; MS 1978; pa/Editor; Music & Art Historian; Var Editorial Positions in Music & Art Pubs in Germany 1957-, US 1960-; Asst Prof, Concordia Tchrs Col, 1972-73; Var Other Tchg Positions; Asst Editor, Art Index, H W Wilson Co, NY 1973-76; Editor, Biographical Index, H W

Wilson Co, NY 1977-; Am Musicol Soc; ALA; hon/Clawson Mills Res F'ship, Metro Mus Art 1969-70; Profl Pubs.

DE LONG, HAROLD WILLIAM oc/Writer; Lecturer; Actor; Producer; Diplomat; Executive; b/Dec 7, 1920; ba/Delbay Prodns, 143-15 Hillside Ave, Jamaica, Long Island, NY 11435; ed/St Mary's Univ; Univ Pa; Nat Foun Funeral Ser; Govt Schs; mil/USAAF 1942-46, PTO; 3 Bronze Stars w OLC; Pres Unit Cit; In Field of Intell, Cmdr in Chief G-2 1946-48; Counter Intell Corps 1942-48; pa/Pres & Owner Delbay Prodns, Pa; Secy-Treas & Owner "Casket Ser Inc", NY 1959-; Diplomat Fgn Ser, Ofc Mil

Attache, Am Embassies in Syria, Jordan, Lebanon, Poland 1948-54; Nat Known Writer/Lectr; Presenter One-Man Shows at Venues throughout US; Perfs incl: "Hats Off to Laughter", "The Pa Dutch", "Fashion & Fabrics", "Whistle Stop Willie", "We Make a Little Visit to the Pa Dutch", Others; Phi Theta Pi; Nat Soc Arts & Lttrs; Chm Ways & Means Com, NY Chapt; CAAA; IPA; Bus Mens Clb; cp/Intl Lions Clb; Intl Rotary; Wyomissing Clb; Rdg CC; hon/Man of Yr, Lions Intl, Rdg, Pa 1958; DIB; Royal Blue Book; IPA W/W in Spkrs World; 2000 Men Achmt; Others.

DEL PERCIO, GLORIA M oc/Officer; Banker; Data Processing Manager; b/Oct 22, 1926; h/122 First Ave, Kings Park, NY 11754; ba/Huntington Sta, NY; p/Antonio and Filomena Del Percio (dec); ed/Certs Achmt in Data Processing: NY Univ, Nassau Commun Col, NY Inst Technol, Wabash Col; pa/Data Processing Mgr, Citibank, NA; Nat Assn Bank Wom; cp/NOW; r/Cath; hon/W/W Am Wom; Awardee of 3 Yr Exec Devel Prog, Wabash Col.

DEL VALLE, HELEN C oc/Professional Artist; Designer; Colorist; Poet; Writer; b/Sept 22, 1933; h/PO Box 958, Chicago, IL 60690; p/(dec); ed/BJ; MFA; pa/Taught Art, Hist & Math, 2 yrs; VP & Membrship Chm, Am Soc Artists; hon/Awds in Portraiture, Landscape, Seascape, Florals, & Still Life in Oils & Watercolor in US & Europe.

de MALDONADO, QUINONES AIDA oc/Extension Home Economist; b/Nov 11, 1934; h/PO Box 286, Los Piedras, PR 00671; ba/Las Piedras; m/Teodoro; c/Teodoro Jr, Orlando, Aidita; p/Marcos Quinones and Delores Alejandre, Junco, PR; ed/BS; MS; PhD; pa/Ext Home Economist; Acad Sen, Univ PR; Phi Lambda Theta; Omicron Nu; Phi Delta Kappa; Epsilon Phi; cp/Am Legion Aux; r/Cath; hon/Nat J C Penney F'ship 1970.

DEMAREST, BRUCE ALVIN oc/Professor; b/May 29, 1935; h/8423 E Jamison Cir N, Englewood, CO 80110; m/Elsie; c/Starr, Scott, Sharon; p/Clifford Demarest (dec); Dorothy Demarest; ed/BS Wheaton Col; MS Adelphi Univ; MA Trinity Evang Div Sch; PhD Univ of Manchester; mil/USNR, Lt; pa/Prof; Tyndall Soc for Biblical Res; Evang Theol Soc; Inst for Biblical Res.

de MARZIA, VIOLETTE oc/Educator; Foundation Executive; Author; h/Box 93, Marion Sta, Pa 19066; ba/Merion Sta; ed/Ecole Superieure Gatty, Brussels; Priory Ho Sch, St Johns Wood, London; Hampstead

Conserv, Hampstead, London; Polytechnic Sch, London; pa/The Barnes Foun: Dir of Ed, Lectr, Mem & VP Bd Trustees; Editor, The Barnes Foun Art Dept Jour; hon/W/W: Am Wom w World Notables, Am Wom, E; World W/W Wom; Intl Reg Profiles; Notable Ams of Bicent Era; Intl W/W Intells; Commun Ldrs & Noteworthy Ams; DHL Lincoln Univ 1969; DFA St Joseph's Col 1970; Chevalier de l'Ordre des Arts ed des Lettres, French Min of Cultural Affairs 1973; Cert of Legion of Hon, Chapel of Four Chaplains 1967; "Super Achiever", Phila 1978; Co-author: (w Albert C Barnes & John Dewey) *Art and Education*, (w Albert C Barnes) *The French Primitives and Their Forms, The Art of Henri-Matisse, The Art of Renoir, The Art of Cezanne;* Contbr to Profl Jours.

de MESNE, EUGENE oc/Writer; Editor; Publisher; Book Designer; Critic; Artist; ba/Box 8776 Boston, MA 02114; ed/Grad w hons Newspaper Inst; London Sch Jrnlsm; pa/Writes Under Pseudonym Julian Ocean; Editor: *N/Press* 1973-75, Writer's Profit 1972-73; Editor & Columnist, *In-Crowd* 1972; Editor, *Person to People* 1968-72; Freelance Writer 1966-68; Nat Writers Clb; Clover Intl Soc; Writers Amalgamated; Artists/Authors Intl; Intl Poetry Forum; Contemporary Novelists; Intl Fiction Soc; Others; hon/DIB; Contemporary Authors; Intl Platform Soc Dir; Intl Authors & Writers W/W; Men Achmt; Intl W/W Poetry; NAm Prize for Poetry; NY Hall of Fame Prize; Clover Intl Soc Awds 1973, 75; Writers Amalgamated Awd; Garretson Prize Poet 1976; Others; Author: *Lost Moments, Sad Dunfrey, Thoughts from 1536, Orbis Romanus, Mood Haiku, Three Hearts, Expressions of a Night Person,* Others.

DEMETRIOUS, MARY oc/Administrator; b/Feb 27, 1950; h/112 Wells St, Darlington, SC 29532; ba/Columbia, SC; ed/BA Randolph-Macon Wom's Col; pa/Projs Coor, St Reorg Comm; Am Soc for Public Adm; cp/VChm, SC Dem Party 1976-78; Dem Nat Com; Assn of St Dem Chm; Exec Com, SC Coun for Human Rights; ERA/SC Adv Coun; r/Greek Orthodox; hon/DAR Citizenship Awd, W/W Am Wom; W/W Am Polits; Outstg Yg Wom Am 1978.

DEMETRIUS, JAMES KLEON oc/College Professor; Critic; Book Review Editor; b/Aug 23, 1924; h/Suite 507, 516 Fifth Ave, NY, NY 10036; ba/NYC; p/James Demetrius (dec); Liz Dee Stephens (dec); ed/BA Bklyn Col 1948; MA 1949, PhD Cand Columbia Univ; mil/USAF; pa/Dean, Latin Am Col 1972-; Past Positions: Interboro Col 1972-74, St Francis Col 1971-72, Bloomfield Col 1963-68, Washington Col 1962-63, Widener Col

1959-62, Iona Col 1952-59, Polytechnic Prep Country Day Sch 1949-51; Spkr; Classical Assn Spain; AAUP; Am Classical Leag; Soc for Ancient Greek Philos; Royal Inst Philos; Am Assn Tchrs of Spanish & Portuguese; Hellenic Soc London; Medieval Soc Am; Others; cp/Assoc Mbr, Nat Wildlife Fed; r/Presb; hon/Gold Plaque for Excell in Tchg, St Francis 1971; Plaque for Excell in Tchg, Bloomfield Col 1968; W/W: World, Am, World Authors; Dir Am Galleries; DIB; Nat Social Dir; Commun Ldrs & Noteworthy Ams; Notable Ams; Intl W/W Commun Ser; Men Achmt; F'ships; Author: *Greek Scholarship in Spain and Latin America* 1966.

De MICHELE, MARGARET M oc/Retired; b/Mar 3, 1921; h/9409 Old Marlboro Pike, Upper Marlboro, MD 20870; m/Joseph A; p/Lawrence and Elizabeth O'Connell Connelly (dec); pa/Ret'd 1976; Former Adm Asst to Sen Mike Mansfield; Secy to Congman James F O'Connor 1940-45; r/Cath.

DE MOURA CASTRO, LUIZ CARLOS oc/Associate Professor; b/Mar 16, 1941; h/3745 W Biddison, Ft Worth, TX 76109; ba/Ft Worth; W Hartford, CT; m/Bridget Mary; c/Marilia, Beatriz, Iracema; p/Luis Gonzaga Pereira DeMoura Castro, Rio De Janeiro; Maria Passos De Moura Castro; ed/Fed Univ of Rio de Janiero; Brazil Conserv of Music; Liszt Acad of Music; mil/Marines, Lt; pa/Assoc Prof of Piano: Tex Christian Univ, Hartt Col of Music; Music Union Brazil; Concert Mgmt: Brazil, Portugal, Italy; Concertizes Annually in Switz, US, Canada; Lectr on Music in 4 Langs; Radio & TV Progs; Bartok Ensemble; Fdr, Annual Intl Piano Summer Course "Corsi Di Interpretazione Pianistica", N Italy; Contbr to *Calvier;* Asst to Chm, Van Cliburn Competition; r/Rom Cath; hon/Pi Kappa Lambda; Music Tchr of Yr 1972, 1975 Ft Worth; Hon Prof, Brazilian Conserv Music; W/W Music.

DENISE, MARGARET ETHEL oc/-Musician; Civic Worker; b/Sept 30, 1887; m/Malcolm F; c/Malcolm Lawrence, Theodore Cullom, Warren Pritchard (dec); ed/-Ferris St Col; cp/Past Pres: Lansing Symph Orch, Greater Lansing Commun Concerts Assn, Lansing Matinee Musicale; Mich Fed Music Clbs: Mem, Pres SE Mich Dist 1944-45, Hon Life Mem Adv Coun; Nat Fed Music

Clbs: Life Mem, Past Pres Chapt #34, Past Presidents Assembly 1948-49; Edward W Sparrow Hosp Wom's Assn (Life Mem); Kresge Art Gallery, Mich St Univ; Metropolitan Opera Guild; Sponsor, Denise Alumni Bus & Profl Wom; Patroness, Sigma Alpha Iota; r/Presb Ch; hon/Hon Life Mem: Golden Eagle Alumni Soc Ferris Col, Lansing Town Hall Assn; Others.

DENIUS, FRANKLIN WOFFORD oc/Attorney at Law; b/Jan 4, 1925; h/3703 Meadowbank, Austin, TX 78703; ba/Austin; m/Charmaine Hooper; c/Frank Wofford, Charmaine D McGill; p/Samuel F Denius (dec); Frances C Denius, Athens, TX; ed/BBA; LLB; pa/Ptnr, Law Firm of Clark, Thomas, Harris, Denius & Winters 1949-75; Dir: Capital Nat Bank Austin, Delhi Intl Oil Corp, So Union Co, Supron Energy Corp; Dir-Secy & Fdr: TeleCom Corp, Tex Capital Corp; Past Chm Bd Dirs, Aztec Oil & Gas Co; Former Gen Counsel: Delhi-Taylor Oil Corp, Delhi Pipeline Corp, Tex Capital Corp; Past Dir &

Men Exec Com, Delhi Taylor Oil Corp 1964; St Bar Tex; Travis Co Bar Assn; Am Bar Assn Tex Utilities Lwyrs Assn; Atty, Tex HS Coaches Assn; Legal Coun, Better Bus Bureau; Dir, Tex Res Leag; cp/Past Pres: Yg Men's Bus Leag of Austin, Longhorn Clb Austin, Headliners Clb, U Way; Chm Bd, U Way Austin, 1973; Austin C of C; Athens C of C; Bd Trustees, Schreiner Col; Burnt Orange Clb; Univ Tex Chancellor's Coun; r/Westminster Presb Ch: Mem, Past Chm Bd Deacons, Past Chm bd Elders, Fin Com Chm, Trustee; hon/Outstg Yg Man Austin, Jaycees 1959; W/W: Tex, Commerce & Indust, Am, S&SW; Am Politics; Purple Heart; Silver Star w 2 OLC; Pres Unit Cit; European Theatre Ribbons w 5 Battle Stars; French & Belgium Crox de Guerre; 1 of 10 Most Decorated Vets of WW II.

DENNER, HELEN VIRGINIA KESSEL oc/Professor; b/Nov 10, 1929; h/Box 840, Extreda St, Rio Grande Bible Inst, Edinburg, TX 78539; m/Frederick John; c/Mary Ann, Deborah Lee; p/Ervin G Kessel (dec); Anna G Kessel; ed/BA Bible Ed 1954; BA Spanish 1976; Spanish Cert 1961; Literacy Tchr Cert; pa/Prof, Rio Grande Bible Inst; Cert'd Dental Asst; r/Bapt.

DENNIS, CHERRY NIXON oc/Artist; Painter; Etcher; b/Sept 2; h/Rt 1, Box 304-B, Lakeview Add, Wagoner, OK 74467; m/Thomas L "Jack" (dec); p/Howard T Nixon (dec); Ida May Pierson (dec); ed/Univ Tulda; Okla St Univ; Univ N Mex; pa/Exhbns incl: Midwestern Exhib, Kans City, Mo, Nat Watercolor & Print Ann Oakland Art Gallery, Cal, Philbrook Art Ctr, Tulsa, Okla, Nat Representational Art Ann, Thomas Gilcrease Inst, Tulsa, SWn Biennial, Mus NM, Sante Fe, Long Beach Art Ann, Cal, Others; St, Reg & Nat Juried Shows; Art Instr in Etching & Drawing, Philbrook Art Ctr 1940-41; cp/Pres, Alpha Rho Tau Art Frat; Pres & Bd Chm, Adah M Robinson Mem Fund 1967-69; Pub Info Ofcr, Civil Air Patrol, Okla Wing 1950-56; r/Christian; hon/Cert of Apprec, Univ Tulsa 1968; Watercolor Awd, Philbrook Art Ctr; Graphic Awds, New Art Leag 1972.

DENNIS, DOROTHY oc/Home Economist; Consumer Educator; h/62 Grove St, Somerville, NJ 08876; ba/Bridgewater, NJ; c/Robert, Roger, Russell (dec); p/Robert H Denton, Council Bluffs, IA; ed/BS cum laude 1968; MEd 1975, MBA Cand Rutgers Univ; Univ Laval; pa/Home Economist & Consumer Edr, Rutgers Univ 1969-; Adm Secy & Res Asst, Rutgers Ctr on Alcohol Studies 1963-69; Conslt, US Metric Assn 1976-; Guest Prof, Univ of Pretoria, Repub of S Africa; Daily Consumer Ed Radio Prog, WBRW, Sommerville, NJ 5 yrs; OES; Intl Fed Home Ecs; NJAEHE; Zonta Intl; AHEA; NAEHE; NJHEA; cp/Former Pres, Middlesex, NJ Bd of Ed; Past Pres, Middlesex PTA; LWV; hon/Epsilon Sigma Phi; Kappa Delta Pi; Dist'd Ser in Home Ec Awd, Somerset Co, NJ; S African Bur of Standards Metric Edr US Recog.

DENNIS, FRANCIS ALFONSO oc/Diplomat; b/Aug 24, 1926; h/3507 Fulton St NW, Wash, DC 20007; ba/Wash DC; m/-Evangeline B; c/Francis Alfonso Jr, Florence Charlotte, Beryl Evangeline, Baromi Albert; p/N Theodore Dennis and Catherine Louise, Careysburg, Liberia; ed/BA; mil/Liberian Armed Forces, 1/Lt; pa/Ambassador of

Republic of Liberia to USA; r/Bapt; hon/Decorated by Govts of France, Britain, Ivory Coast & Liberia; Hon LLD.

DENSFORD, CHARLES F oc/Rancher; Land Broker; Columnist; b/Jan 26, 1907; h/PO Box 174, Pipe Creek, TX 78063; ba/Pipe Creek; m/Cora G; c/Dolores D Fender, Charles F Jr, James T, Elena D Watkins, Daniel D; p/James W and Pearl L Densford (dec); ed/BS; mil/USAF 35½ Yrs, Col (Ret'd); pa/W Point Soc S Tex; Order of Daedalians; Assn Grads USMA; Ret'd Ofcrs Assn; cp/Life Mem, Nat Rifle Asns; Tex Rifle Assn; Past Chm, Bandera Co Repub Com; Past Cdr, Bandera Am Legion Post 157; r/Prot; hon/Freedoms Foun Awd; Cong of Freedom.

DENT, MYRA LENA oc/Business Proprietor; b/Dec 18, 1923; h/Rt 3, Box 369, Stafford, VA 22554; ba/Stafford; m/Estrel R (dec); c/Dorothy Darlene Baetz, Donald Dale (dec), Dennis Duane, Debra Diane Fitzgerald,

Dena Dolinda Burnell, Gary Estrel; p/Edwin W and Lillian T Killinger (dec); ed/HS; Grad Nsg Sch; pa/Owner-Operator, Dent's Grill; Other profl activs incl: Tax Computation, Bookkeeping, Bus Mgmt & Import-Export; cp/Active in Commun Ser; r/Epis.

DENT, V EDWARD oc/Business Executive; b/Oct 17, 1918; h/Honey Hill Rd, Old Lyme, CT 06371; ba/NY, NY; p/Florian E and Loretta M Castone Dent; ed/BS Univ Wis 1940; mil/AUS 1941-46, 1/Lt; pa/Sci & Med Pub'g Co Inc 1977-, Cinemed Sys Inc 1977-, Subsidiaries Benton & Bowles Inc, NYC; Chm

Bd Medicus Communs Inc 1972-; Exec Dir, Nat Sci Network, NYC 1964-72; Exec VP, L W Frohlich & Co Intercon Inter Inc, NYC 1949-72; Mng Editor, Pharm Pubs, McGraw-Hill Co, NYC 1946-49; cp/Bd Dirs, Aston Magna Foun; PTO; Met Mus; Mus Primitive Art; Pharm Advt Clb NYC Clb; hon/Biogl Listings.

de PLANQUE, E GAIL oc/Physicist; b/Jan 15, 1945; h/13 Bowdoin St, Maplewood, NJ 07040; ba/New York, NY; p/Martin W de Planque (dec); Edna Gilroy de Planque (dec); ed/AB cum laude Immaculata Col 1967; MS Newark Col of Engrg (now NJ Inst Technol) 1973; PhD Cand, NYU; pa/Physicist, Environmental Measurements Lab, US Dept of Energy 1967-; Am Nuclear Soc: Bd Dirs, 1977-, Nat Exec Com 1978-, Nat Prog Com 1974-77, Radiation Protection & Shielding Div Exec Com 1976-79, NY Metro Sect Exec Com 1976-78; Hlth Physics Soc; Am Physical Soc; AAAS; Assn Wom in Sci; NY Acad Scis; cp/AAUW; Dep

Foreman, Essex Co 15th Grand Jury; hon/Am Men & Wom Sci.

DERR, MARY LOUISE oc/Associate Editor; b/May 19, 1917; h/3410 Everett Dr, Boulder, CO 80303; ba/Boulder; m/Vernon E; c/Michael E, Katherine M, Louise E, Carol J; p/Ralph O and Jessie B Sherwood Van Atta

(dec); ed/BA Mary Baldwin Col 1940; pa/Assoc Editor, *The Weaver's Jounal*; Freelance Writer; cp/Publicity Chm, Boulder Reg ARC; r/Epis; hon/Writing Awds.

DERRINGTON, KENNETH EDWARD oc/Minister; b/Nov 16, 1922; h/360 Fourth Ave W, Madison, WV 25130; ba/Madison; m/Etta Lanora; c/Kenneth Royal; p/Edward Royal Derrington, La Canada, CA; Rosali Freeman Derrington (dec); ed/Bible Bapt Sem; ThG Pioneer Theol Sem; MDiv Luther Rice Col; mil/USN 20 yrs; pa/Pastor: W Madison

Bapt Ch 1977-, 2nd Bapt Ch, Ravenswood, W Va 1963-77, (Asst) Calvary Bapt Ch, Jacksonville, Fla 1963, Bible Bapt Ch, Pace, Fla 1960-63, 1st Bapt Ch, Del City, Okla 1955; Chaplain, Jackson Gen Hosp 1968-77; Pres, Fundamental Pastors of W Va 1965-68; Chm Bapt Bible F'ship of W Va 1969-71; BBFI Missions Com 1976-78; Chm BBF of W Va 1977-; hon/W/W Rel.

DERUCHER, KENNETH NOEL oc/Assistant Professor; b/Jan 24, 1949; h/Apt 1211, 13006 Old Stagecoach Rd, College Park, MD 20811; ba/College Park; m/Barbara; p/Kenneth John Derucher, Gowanda, NY; ed/BS Tri St Univ; MS Univ ND; PhD Va Tech Univ; pa/Asst Prof of Civil Engrg, Dept of Civil Engrg, Univ Md; ASCE; ASTM; TRB; CEPA; AAAS; ASEE; SESA; r/Rom Cath; hon/Intl W/W Commun Ser; Book of Hon; DIB; Notable Ams.

DESAI, VEENA BALVANTRAI oc/Obstetrician & Gynecologist; b/Oct 5, 1931; h/12 Harbor View Dr, RFD #1, Portsmouth, NH 03801; ba/Portsmouth; m/Vinay D Gandevia; c/Vijay V Gandevia; p/Balvantrai P Desai

(dec); Maniben B Desai, India; ed/MBBS; DGO; MD; MRCOG; FACOG; FACS; Diplomate Am Bd Obstetrics & Gynecol; Fellow Am Soc Colposcopy & Cervical Pathol USA; pa/Pvt Pract, Ob-Gyn; NH Med Soc; Portsmouth Med Soc; Am Med Wom's Assn; Nat Soc Lit & Art; Brit Med Assn; Birmingham & Midlands Obstetrical & Gyn Soc, UK; IPA; Pres Desai Prof Assn; r/Hindu; hon/W/W Am Wom; World W/W Wom; Physician's Recog Awd, AMA 1977; Cert of Cont'g Profl Devel, Am Col Ob-Gyns 1977, 79; Other Prizes & Awds; Contbr to Profl Jours.

DeSALVO, LOUISE A oc/Educator; b/Sept 27, 1942; h/1045 Oakland Ct, Teaneck, NJ 07666; ba/Teaneck; m/Ernest J; c/Jason, Justin; p/Louise B and Mildred N Sciacchetano, Ridgefield, NJ; ed/BA; MA; PhD; pa/English Coor, MA Tchg Prog, Fairleigh Dickinson Univ; hon/Walter B Anderson F'ship; Nancy Higginson Dorr Awd for Tchg Excell.

DESMOND, TERRENCE T oc/Teacher; b/May 18, 1944; h/2718 Pioneer, DeKalb, IL 60115; ba/Sycamore, IL; m/JoAnn; c/Tracy, Courtney; p/Walter C Desmond (dec); Eileen A Desmond, Waukegan, IL; ed/BA 1968, MS 1970 No Ill Univ; pa/Tchr; DeKalb Co Bd: VChm Rules Com, VChm Safety & Law Enforcemt Com, Past Mem Fin Com; Life Mem, NEA; cp/DeKalb Co Jaycees: Pres 1973-74, Sustaining Mem; DeKalb Co Farm Bur; LWV; Pres Gov'g Bd, Kishwaukee YMCA; Past Bd Mem, DeKalb Lng Exch; Dist Chm, Kishwaukee Commun Hlth Ctr Fund Dr; Ill Coalition for Polit Honesty; Leg Asst to St Rep Richard Mautino; hon/Phi Delta Kappa; W/W Am Polits; Commun Ldrs & Noteworthy Ams; Sears Foun F'ship; Outstg Yg Men Am Awd; Ldrs Am Elem Ed Awd 1972; Recog'd for Ser to Commun Mtl Hlth, Ben Gordon Ctr 1975.

DESSAUER, HERBERT C oc/Professor; b/Dec 30, 1921; h/7100 Dorian St, New Orleans, LA 70127; ba/New Orleans; m/Frances Jane Moffatt; c/Dan Winston, Rebecca Lynn, Bryan Clay; p/Herbert Andrew Dessauer (dec); ed/BS 1949, PhD 1952 La St Univ; mil/USAAF 1942-46, 1/Lt; pa/La St Univ:

Prof of Biochem 1963-, Act'g Hd Dept Biochem 1977-78, Instr-Prof 1953-63; Conslt, VA Hosp, New Orleans 1962-; Res Assoc, Dept Herpetol, Am Mus Nat Hist, NYC; Am Physiol Soc; Soc Systematic Zool; AMA; Am Soc Ichthyol & Herpetol; Soc for Expmtl Biol & Med (Past Secy & Chm So Sect); hon/Phi Kappa Phi; Sigma Xi; Fellow: Herpetologist's Leag, AAAS.

DETZEL, WILMA MARIE oc/Administrator; b/Sept 3, 1911; h/3417 Ellsworth Ave, Erie, PA 16508; ba/Erie; m/Arthur Frank; c/Donald Arthur; p/Henry and Mary Carnelly, Beaver Falls, PA; ed/BS Geneva Col; Grad Study Univ Pgh; pa/Wom's Physical Dir, Glenwood Park YMCA; Conslt Wom's Fitness, YMCA; cp/Bd Mem, Meth Towers; r/Meth; hon/World W/W; W/W Am Wom; Dist'd Ser Awd, Geneva Col.

DEUPREE, JEAN DURLEY oc/Educator; b/Nov 9, 1942; h/1118 Surrey Rd, Papillion, NE 68046; ba/Omaha, NE; p/Joseph E and

Virginia L Deupree, Big Rapids, MI; ed/BS Ferris St Col; PhD Mich St Univ; pa/Fac Mem in Pharmacol, Univ Neb Med Ctr; Am Soc for Advmt Sci; Am Chem Soc; Am Soc for Neruochem; Am Soc for Pharmacol & Expmtl Therapeutics; Altrusa Clb of Omaha; cp/Participate in Altrusa Clb Ser Projs; r/Cath.

DEUTSCH, PAUL MICHAEL oc/Rehabilitation Psychologist; b/May 23, 1949; h/3900 Rose of Sharon Dr, Orlando, FL 32808; ba/Orlando; m/Nancy Wayman; p/Samuel Paul and Elaine Simpson Deutsch; ed/MRC; pa/Am Cong Rehab Med; Nat Rehab Cnslrs Assn; Fla Rehab Cnslrs Assn; Am Rehab Cnslrs Assn; Am Pers & Guid Assn; r/Jewish; hon/Eta Rho Pi; Pi Lambda Theta; Rehab Sers Adm Fellow 1971-72.

DEUTSCH, STUART THOMAS oc/- Teacher; b/Aug 9, 1949; h/60th E Linden Ave, Apt 3B, Englewood, NJ 07631; ba/NY, NY; p/Karl A and Roselle H Deutsch, Rochester, NY; ed/BA 1971, MA magna cum laude 1974 SUNY Fredonia; pa/Eng & Hist Tchr; Bd Dirs, Camp Loyaltown Inc 1978; cp/Brighton Yth Agy 1969-73; r/Temple Beth El, Rochester; hon/Steuben Soc of Am Awd for German 1967; Alumni Awd, SUNY Fredonia 1974; Commun Ldrs & Noteworthy Ams.

DeVANE, EVELYN GAYNELLE oc/Professor; Administrator; b/Sept 21, 1941; h/902 Valley Dr, W Chester, PA 19380; ba/Cheyney, PA; c/Freddia Gaynelle; Herbert Morrell and Gladys Lowe DeVane, Philadelphia, PA; ed/BME cum laude Howard

Univ; MA Columbia Univ; PhD 1978 Univ Ghana, W Africa; pa/Prof, Cheyney St Col; Dir, World Cults Ctr; Bd Govs, Consort for Intl Ed; Intl Studies Assn; Intl Soc for Music Ed; Pi Kappa Lambda; cp/Alpha Kappa Alpha; Intl Leag for Human Rights; r/Prot; hon/Del to Festac '77 (2nd World Fest Black & African Arts & Cults).

DEVERA, ADELE KING oc/Teacher; b/Dec 1, 1917; h/8227 S Prairie Ave, Chgo, IL 60619; ba/Chgo; oc/Tchr; m/Mitchell W Pryor; c/Miriam Devera Lyttle; p/John Howard King, Chgo, IL; Mary Chatman King (dec); ed/BA; MA; pa/Public Sch Tchr; Lectr in Fields of Ed, Human Relats & Rel-Sci; cp/Ed Com, 1st Congl Dist; r/Congl Ch, Park Manor: Mem; hon/Recog'd by US War Dept 1950; Execll in Tchg, Ill St Bd Ed; Outstg Tchr; Phi Delta Kappa; Blue Ribbon Home Beautiful Awd.

DeVERE, JULIA ANNE oc/Specialist Teacher; b/Nov 2, 1925; h/950 Chehalis Dr, Sunnyvale, CA 94087; ba/San Jose, CA; m/Robert E; c/David E; p/Goodlet C DeVere (dec); Anna Fairbanks Bonjour, Onaga, KS; ed/BA 1957, MA 1961 Univ Denver; pa/Spec Tchr in Lng Ctr-Public Elem Sch; Delta Kappa

Gamma; PTA; Coun for Exceptl Chd; Foun for Except Chd; NEA; CTA; Cupertino Ed Assn; cp/Repub; Fund Dr Vol: Cancer Soc, Muscular Dystrophy, Retarded Ch, Others; Unity Rebekah Lodge #232; r/U Brethern; hon/St & Co 4-H Awds; Delta Kappa Gamma S'ship; Biogl Listings.

DEVEREAUX, ELIZABETH BAKER oc/Assistant Professor; b/Oct 1, 1926; h/18 Pembroke Ln, Huntington, WV 25705; ba/Huntington; c/Gregory Charles, Jan Renee D Lantz, Steven Mitchell; p/Harry Claybourne Baker (dec); Mrs O G Bishop, Ft Pierce, FL; ed/BS Ohio St Univ 1949; MSW W Va Univ 1976; pa/Asst Prof, Dept Psychi,

Marshall Univ Sch Med; Occupl Therapy Conslt, Huntington VA Med Ctr; Am Occupl Therapy Assn: Exec Bd, Chm Fiscal Adv Com, Ednl Liaison to External Agys, Fees Com, Nat HQs Housing Com; cp/Past Mem Var Civic Bds, Parkersburg, WVa; hon/AOTA Roster of Fellows; Dist'd Ser Awd, Nat Assn Activity Therapy & Rehab Prog Dirs 1978; W/W: Am Wom, E.

DeVINE, MACK B oc/Corporation Executive; m/Shirley Fitzpatrick; c/Charles, Cynthia; p/Charles D and Nell B DeVine, Pensacola, FL; ed/BS Jacksonville St Univ; Univ S Fla; Harvard Univ; mil/AUS; pa/Pres & Dir, Am Agronomics Corp: Pres & Dir 1977-, VP & Chief Operating Ofcr 1976-77; Chief Fin Ofcr, Great So Equipmt Co Inc, Tampa, Fla 1975-76; Secy-Treas, Automatic Merchandising Inc, Tampa, Fla 1971-74; Am Acctg Assn; Nat Acctg Assn; Am Mgmt Assn;

Presidents Assn; Aircraft Owners & Pilots Assn; Bd Dirs: Am Agronomics Corp, Am Orange Corp, Am Intl Food Corp, Coastland Corp, Funshine Corp; hon/Army Commend Medal; W/W S&SW.

DeVITO, ALBERT KENNETH oc/- Educator; Composer; Author; Arranger; Editor; Publisher; b/Jan 17, 1919; h/361 Pin Oak Ln, Westbury, NY 11590; ba/Westbury; p/- Ralph and Rose Abronze DeVito; ed/BS, MA NY Univ; PhD Midwestern Univ; mil/AUS 1941-45; pa/Am Choral Dirs Assn; Am Soc

Composers, Authors & Pubrs; Assoc'd Musicians Gtr NY; Assm Music Tchrs Leag Inc; Phi Mu Alpha Sinfonia; Piano Tchrs Cong NY Inc; NY St Sch Music Assn; cp/Nat Geographic Soc; hon/MusD En Neb Christian Col; Book of Hon; Men & Wom Distn; Contemporary Am Composers; Personalities of Am; Notable Ams; W/W E; Intl W/W Intells; Intl W/W Commun Ser; Commun Ldrs & Noteworthy Ams; Fellow, Intl Biog Assn.

DEVLIN, JANE oc/Poet; b/Jul 1, 1908; h/939 Coast Blvd, Suite 6D, La Jolla, CA 92037; ba/Same; m/Gerald G Griffith; p/Joseph Lowell and Katherine Warren Sherwood Cox (dec); pa/Assoc Editor & Book Reviewer, *Chgo Daily News* 1924-36; Resident Poet Laureate, Bridgewater Hotel & Radio Sta WEBH (Chgo) 1933-39; Author Poetry Books: *Gypsy Lyrics* (1935), *Read Me a Poem* (1960); Contbr Poetry to Var Jours; Incl'd in Sev Anthols incl'g: *Am Sonnets & Lyrics* (1941), *Poems for Radio* (1945); Composer/Lyracist: "Summer's Promise", "You Are Spring", "Near to Me"; Collaborations w Frank Loren Graves (music): "Together", "Lovely Lady", Others; Collaboration w Isaac Van Grove (music): "Africa", "Life is a Song", "Singing Sea", Others; Pres & Charter Mem, Nat Leag Am Pen Wom 1958-60; Assoc Editor & Reporter, *Sandpiper News* (La Jolla) 1966-68; Nat Songwriters Guild 1950-52; Others; cp/San Diego Opera Guild; Social Sers Leag of La Jolla; Nat Wildlife Fdn; Belles for Mtl Hlth Assn Aux (San Diego); Others; hon/SW Region Nat Leag Am Pen Wom: 2nd Prize in "Song", 2nd Prize in "Choral Groups", 1st Prize in "Poetry"; Biogl Listings; Others.

de VRIES, MARGARET GARRITSEN oc/Economist; Historian; b/Feb 11, 1922; h/10018 Woodhill Rd, Bethesda, MD 20034; ba/Wash DC; m/Barend Arie; c/Christine, Barton; p/John Garritsen (dec); Margaret Garritsen, White Bear Lake, MN; ed/BA Univ

Mich 1943; PhD Mass Inst Technol 1946; pa/Economist & Histn, Intl Monetary Fund (30 yr assn w this org); Author Sev Vols of Hist of Intl Monetary Fund; Prof, George Wash Univ; hon/Phi Beta Kappa; Phi Kappa

Phi; Num Scholarly Socs; Alumni Assn Univ Wom Schlr.

DEWBERRY, INEZ STEPHENS oc/-Special Education Teacher; b/Aug 28, 1915; h/Rt 1, Box 100, Lineville, AL 36266; m/James Lawrence; p/Oscar Lee Stephens (dec); Bessie Gibson Stephens, Lineville, AL; ed/BS;

Postgrad Study Univ Ala; pa/Tchr; AEA; NEA; REA; CTA; r/Bapt; hon/Child Devel Profls; Personalities of S&SW; Notable Ams; Commun Ldrs & Noteworthy Ams.

DEWEESE, CHARLES WILLIAM oc/-Administrator; b/Oct 7, 1944; h/309 Ash Grove Ct, Nashville, TN 37211; ba/Nashville; m/Mary Jane; c/Dana; p/James Philip Deweese, Asheville, NC; Faye Warren Deweese (dec); ed/BA Mars Hill Col; MDiv, PhD So Bapt Theol Sem; pa/Dir Edit Sers, Hist Comm So Bapt Conv; Vis Prof, Acadia Divinity Col 1978; cp/Gallon Donor Clb, ARC; r/So Bapt; hon/Men Achmt; Notable Ams; Personalities of S; DIB; Commun Ldrs &

Noteworthy Ams; W/W: Rel, Ky, Among Students in Am Univs & Cols; Outstg Yg Men Am; Outstg Ams S; Davis C Woolley Meml Awd, S Bapt Conv 1972; Others; Author, *A Community of Believers: Making Church Membership More Meaningful* 1978; Co-Author, *Faith, Stars and Stripes* 1976.

DEWIRE, NORMAN (NED) EDWARD oc/Administrator; b/Mar 5, 1936; h/34 W Dixon Ave, Dayton, OH 45419; ba/Dayton; m/Shirley Woodman; c/Cathy Lynn, Deborah Kay; p/Ormsby Dewire, Cincinnati, OH; Lucille Binder Dewire (dec); ed/BSEd w hons Ohio Univ 1958; MDiv w hons Boston Univ 1962; DMin McCormick Theol Sem 1979; pa/Gen Secy, Gen Coun on Ministries, U Meth Ch 1975-; Exec Dir, Jt Strategy & Action Coms 1969-75; Exec Secy, Detroit Conf Bd Missions & Ch Ext 1967-69; Pastorates: Ctl

U Meth Ch, Detroit, Mich 1962-75, Charlton City U Meth Ch, Worcester Co, Mass 1958-62, Jacksonville U Meth Circuit, Athens Co, Ohio, 1957-58; cp/Newcomen Soc NAm; Bd Trustees, U Theol Sem; Edit Adv Group, *Interpreter* Mag; Gov'g Bd, Nat Coun Chs; Nat Rural Housing Coalition; U Way of Dayton; r/U Meth Ch: Ordained Clergyman; hon/Kappa Delta Pi; Nat Meth S'ship Sem Awd; Public Ser Awd, US Dept of Justice; DD Adrian Col 1976.

DEWTON, JOHANNES LEOPOLD oc/-Librarian; b/Sept 27, 1905; h/4201 Seventh Rd S, Arlington, VA 22204; ba/Wash DC; m/-Hedwig Marianne Strauss (dec); c/Elizabeth Ann Cordaro (Mrs John B), Doris Jean; p/Eduard Deutsch (dec); Elsbeth Brauchbar (dec); ed/JurD Vienna Univ, Austria 1927; BSLS 1941, MS 1944 Univ Ill; mil/US Strategic AF in Europe 1945, Col; pa/Libn, Lib of Cong; Author of Var Articles in Lib & Legal Jours; r/Jewish; hon/Superior Accomplishmt Awd, Lib of Cong 1947; Dist'd Ser Awd, Lib of Cong 1974.

DeYOUNG, MURIEL HERRICK-MAURER oc/Professional Artist; Teacher; b/Mar 12, 1916; h/2605 Frederick Blvd, Delray, FL 33444; ba/Delray Bch; m/John "Charles"; p/Louis Charles Maurer (dec); Anna Barbara Beck Maurer, Pompano Bch, FL; ed/Ringling Sch Art; Farnsworth Sch Art; pa/Fine Artist in Oil & Acrylic: Landscape, Still Life, Portrait; Life Sketching; Tchr, De Young Fine Arts Sch; Former Tchr, Crystal Lake Beach Clb, Pompano, Fla; Num Group Exhbns & 1-man Shows; Wk Featured in Local Shows incl'g: Art Inst (Ft Lauderdale), Parker Playhouse,

Deerfield Bch Shrine Clb, Shaams Galerie, Delray Art Leag, Art Guild of Boca Raton, Boynton Civic Ctr, Ctr for the Artists - Boca Raton, Jordan Marsh - Ft Lauderdale, Others; Wks in Public & Pvt Collects; Fdr & Past Pres Delray Bch Br, Nat Leag Am Pen Wom; Past Pres: Ft Lauderdale Br Nat Leag Am Pen Wom, Delray Art Leag; r/Presb; hon/World W/W Wom; Book of Hon; Wom Achmt; Personalities of S; Commun Ldrs & Noteworthy Ams; DIB; Intl Register Profiles; W/W Am Wom.

DEYNES, WANDA N oc/Administrator; b/Feb 1, 1940; h/A #54 Vista Alegre, Ponce, PR 00731; ba/Ponce; m/Jose R; c/Wanda Marie, Frances Dianne, Mae Lynn, Jose R III, Joanne Marie; p/Cesar F Navajas (dec); Emma Souffront de Fleurian, Ponce, PR; ed/Cath Univ; pa/Public Relats Dir, Hosp Dr Pila; In Charge of Fund Raising Campaign; cp/Exchangettes Clb; New Dem Party: Mem, Fin Com; Alternate Del, Dem Nat Conv 1976; Carnival Com, Ponce & San Juan; 4th of July Festivities; Destellos de la Moda; r/Cath.

DEYRUP, ASTRITH JOHNSON oc/Artist; b/Apr 22, 1923; h/395 Riverside Dr, NY, NY 10025; ba/NYC; p/Alvin and Edith Henry Johnson (dec); ed/AB Barnard Col 1944; MA Columbia Univ 1947; pa/Art Fac, The New Sch; Adj Prof, Col of New Rochelle; r/Prot; hon/Author: *Getting Started in Batik* 1971, *Complete Book of Tie-Dyeing* 1972, *Tie Dye and Batik* 1974; World W/W Wom; W/W Ed.

DIAMANT, HERBERT ARTHUR oc/Municipal Bond Portfolio Trader;

Marketer; b/Jan 26, 1957; h/c/o Top Notch Estate, 15 White Birch Rd, Weston, CT 06883; ba/Greenwich, CT; p/David S and Martha M Diamant, Weston, CT; ed/BS Georgetown Univ 1978; pa/VP of Mktg, Diamant Investmt Corp; SW Conn Chapt, Am Mktg Assn; Conslt for Dir Print & Motion Picture Media, Ofc Asst Secy Def for Public Affairs, US Dept Def 1978; Gen, Fin & Opers Prin, Nat Assn of Securities Dealers & Boston Stock Exch; cp/Georgetown Univ Alumni Assn of Conn; ARC; Saugatuck Harbor Yacht Clb; Res Asst, US Sen Select Com on Small Bus 1975-79; hon/W/W Among Students in Am Univs & Cols; Outstg Yg Men Am; Presidential Sports Awd for Sailing 1976.

DIAMANT, MARILYN CHARLOTTE oc/-Businesswoman; Singer; b/Aug 16, 1933; h/63 Aspen Rd, Swampscott, MA 01907; ba/Marblehead, MA; m/Bruce; c/Mark Gary, Glenn Steven, Daniel Ethan, Andrea Dale; p/Abraham and Frances Sherman, Lynn, Mass; ed/BA New England Conservatory Music; cp/Alternate Del, Dem Nat Conv 1976; Permanent Mem, Dem Nat Credentials Com; Cand, Mass Ho of Reps 1976; Cand, Dem Nat Com-Wom 1976; Reg IV Area Ment Hlth & Retard Bd; Pres Gtr Boston Chapt, Nat Soc Autistic Chd; Cong Chevra Tehillim: Pres, Life Mem; VP, B'nai B'rith; Cong Ahabat Sholom, Lynn, Mass; Life Mem, Hadassah; r/Jewish; hon/Wom of Yr, Lynn Item 1972; W/W Am Polits.

DIAMOND, HARVEY J oc/Executive; b/Dec 7, 1928; h/6929 Folger Dr, Charlotte, NC 28211; ba/Charlotte; m/Betty L; c/Michael, Beth, David, Abby; p/Harry B Diamond (dec); Jeannette D Diamond, St Petersburg, FL; ed/BS Univ NC-Chapel Hill; mil/AUS 1952-54; pa/Pres, Plasti-Vac Inc; Chm of Bd & Gen Mgr, Diamond Supply Inc; Soc Plastic Engrs Inc; Nat Electric Sign Assn; cp/Chm, Mecklenburg Dem Party 1974-75; Del, Dem Nat Conv 1972; US Trade Mission 1967; Past Dir, Nat Conf Christians & Jews; r/Jewish; hon/Dist'd Ser Awd, Mar Dimes 1966; Dist'd Serv awd, Nat Electric Sign Assn 1979; W/W in US Fin & Indust.

DIAS, DONALDO DE SOUZA oc/-Student; b/Sept 19, 1936; h/2311 Stone Dr, Ann Arbor, MI 48105; ba/Ann Arbor; m/-Norma Leitao; c/Monica De Souza, Luciana De Souza; p/Indalecio De Souza Dias, Rio de Janerio, Brazil; Erika Scheid Dias (dec);

ed/PhD Student; Eng Fed Univ Rio de Janeiro 1960; MS Univ Mich 1978; pa/IBM Brazil: Sci Mgr 1971-77, Sys Analyst 1961-70; Asst Prof, Cath Univ Rio de Janeiro 1968-76; Intl Fed Info Processing; r/Cath; hon/Author 2 Tech Books; Intl Authors & Writers W/W.

DICKERSON, LOREN LESTER oc/Electronics Engineer; b/May 11, 1918; h/PO Box 95, Denville, NJ 07834; ba/Dover, NJ; m/Charlotte Adelaide Perry; c/Charlotte Angela, Caitilin Mary, Loren Lester III; p/Loren L Sr and Alice M Dickerson (dec); ed/BS Emory Univ 1939; PhD Mass Inst Technol 1942; Univ Ala, Huntsville; pa/Electronics Engr, Armament R&D Command, Dover, NJ 1978-; Physicist, Metrology & Calibration Ctr, Redstone Arsenal, Ala 1976-78; Aerospace Engr, Gen Engr & Physicist, Ballistic Missile Def Sys Command, Huntsville 1970-76; Chem & Res Aerospace Engr, AUS Missile Command, Redstone Arsenal 1960-70; Res Dir, Reynolds

Metals Co, Sheffield, Ala 1953-60; Conslt, Textiles Mfg Mountrie, Ga 1947-53; Res Engr, Reynolds Metals Co, Longview, Wash 1945-47; Others; Am Nuclear Soc; Fellow, AAAS; cp/L'Alliance Francaise: Past VP, Past Dir; Twickenham Hist Presv Dist Assn; Hist Huntsville Foun; Small Voices Com for Park Presv in Zoning; Commun Ballet Assn: Dir, Past VP; Past Dir, Huntsville Film Forum; Trustee, The Arts Coun Inc, Huntsville 1964-74; hon/Phi Beta Kappa; Sigma Xi; Am Men Sci; S'ships; Mensa; W/W S&SW; Personalities of S; Others.

DICKIE, LOIS GALBRAITH oc/Professor; b/Jun 18, 1906; h/216 W Monument Ave, Hatboro, PA 19040; ba/Elkins Park, PA; m/John Thayer (dec); p/Thomas R and Eleanor Patton Galbraith (dec); ed/BA; MA; PhD; pa/Prof of English, Faith Theol Sem; r/Bible Presb; hon/World W/W Wom in Ed.

DICKINSON, JUNE McWADE oc/Organizational Executive; b/Jun 26, 1924; h/2904 E Lake Rd, Livonia, NY 14487; ba/Livonia; m/Howard L McWade (dec); Esther B McWade, Rochester, NY; ed/Masters; pa/Pres & Chm of Bd, Schumann Meml Foun Inc; Reg'd Profl Music Therapist; Composer; Writer; cp/Advocates for the Arts Lobbyist; Nat Assn Music Therapy; ASCAP; Proj Dir, Casterbridge Village Fine Arts; r/Epis; hon/Order of Merit, Fed German Repub; Commun Ldrs of Am; Notable Ams; W/W Am Wom; World W/W Wom.

DICKSON, NAIDA RICHARDSON oc/Writer; Puzzlesmith; Illustrator; Newspaper Syndicate Co-Director; b/Apr 18, 1916; h/17700 Western #69, Pasadena, CA 90248; ba/Pasadena; m/C Eugene; c/Charles E, Clarence E; p/Charles E and Daisie Stout Richardson (dec); ed/BS 1940, MS 1944 Utah

St Univ; pa/Operate Newspaper Feature Syndicate; Construct Puzzles for Mags; Author 11 Chd's Books, 1 Adult Book; cp/Vol, Right to Life Lines; r/Ch of Jesus Christ LDS; hon/S'ship.

DICKSTEIN, JACK oc/Chemist; b/Dec 14, 1925; h/318 Keats Rd, Huntingdon Valley, PA 19006; ba/Naugatuck, CT; m/Pauline G; c/Jeffrey L, John F, Andrea E, Cindy L; p/Aaron Dickstein (dec); Anna Cohen, Philadelphia, PA; ed/BS; MA; PhD; pa/Am Chem Soc; AAAS; Am Inst Chem; NY Acad Scis; Franklin Inst; Fed Am Scists; cp/Smithsonian Inst; r/Jewish; hon/Sigma Xi; Phi Lambda Upsilon; Phi Eta Sigma.

DI CORLETO, HELEN THERESA oc/Educational Consultant; b/Apr 6, 1918; h/90 Kane St, W Hartford, CT 06119; ba/Hartford;

p/Francesco and Rosina Scavullo DiCorleto (dec); ed/BS Ctl Conn St Col 1941; MA NYU 1951; pa/Freelance Ednl Conslt; Hartford Asst Dir, Elem Ed 1965-67; Dir, Elem Ed 1967-70; Clin Suprvr, Univ of Hartford 1970-71; Educ Agt Tchr, Peace Corps 19781-72; Dir, Title III, Tch Interactive Lng Ctr 1972-75; Am Assn Sch Administrators; NEA; Zonta Intl; Delta Kappa Gamma; r/Rom Cath.

DIEDOLF, JOHN T oc/Music Director; Real Estate Salesperson; b/Nov 11, 1932; h/197 Middle Rd, Blue Point, LI, NY 11715; ba/Bayport, NY; m/Robert Howell; p/A L J and Lillian Scanzillo; ed/Julliard Sch Music; Yale Sum Sch Music; BM Yale Univ; MA, Profl Dipl Columbia Univ; Paris-Am Acad Music, France; Adelphi Col; pa/Band, Orch, & Choral Dir, Bayport-Blue Point Sch Dist 12 yrs; Other Past Tchg Positions; Recitals; Ch Soloist 3 yrs; Conductor, Annual Arts Fest, Blue Point Sch 8 yrs; Vocal Dir, Dormike Prodns; Salesperson: Zangren Realty, Hewlett, NY, Island Green Realty, Middle Island, LI, NY; NEA; NY St U Tchrs; Suffolk Co Music Ed Assn; Bayport-Blue Point Ednl Assn; Bd Dirs: BDB Realty Corp, Barmajo Realty Corp; cp/LWV; La Union Hispanica; Steuben Soc Am; Yale Clb, NYC; Soc for Preserv of Long Isl Antiquities; Bay Area Friends of Fine Arts; Suffolk Co Hist Soc; Vols for Animal Welfare; Blue Point Repub Clb; Cand, NY St Leg 1976; Others; hon/Fulbright S'ship Audition Finalist.

DIEFENDERFER, OMIE TILTON oc/Retired Teacher; b/Jun 1, 1910; h/828 Third, Fullerton, PA 18052; p/Eugene E and Omie A Tilton Diefenderfer (dec); ed/BS (Ed) 1931, BS (Art) 1952, Katztown Tchrs Col; MEd Temple Univ 1955; pa/Ret'd Tchr, Whitehall-Coplay Sch Dist; Conslt, Title I Prog 1966-77; Tchr & Rdg Spec 1931-77; PTA; NEA; Whitehall Ed Assn; Lehigh Val Assn for Chd w Lng Disabilities; Intl Reading Assn; 1st Aid Instr & Air Raid Instr, WW II; Introduced Gillingham-Stillman Approach for Chd w LD in Auditory-Visual Perceptual Prog 1966-77; cp/Majority Inspector, Election Bd Dist 4; 2/VP, Repub Clb; Secy, Whitehall Twp Bicent Com; Cnslr, YWCA Camp; r/St John's UCC, Fullerton, Pa: Tchr Ladies Bible Class, Deaconess, VP Chancel Choir, Ch Histn; hon/Golden Deeds Awd, Whitehall Exch Clb 1968; Life Mbr, Fullerton PTA; Wom of Yr Awd, St Johns UCC 1967; Recog'd by Lee Valle Sch for Brain Injured Chd 1970; Cert of Recog, Pa St Assn for Chd w LD 1971; Cit, Katztown St Col Gen Alumni Assn 1972; Others.

DIENER, URBAN LOWELL oc/Professor; b/May 26, 1921; h/750 Sherwood Dr, Auburn, AL 36830; ba/Auburn; m/Mary Jacqulyn Maund; p/Urban Edward Diener (dec); Ethel H Diener, Fremont, OH; ed/BA Miami Univ 1943; MA Harvard Univ 1945; PhD NC St Univ 1953; pa/Prof of Mycotoxicol & Plant Pathol, Dept of Botany & Microbiol, Auburn Univ; Am Phytopathol Soc; Am Soc for Microbiol; AAAS; Ala Acad of Sci; Am Peanut Res & Ed Assn; Edit Bd, Am Phytopathol Soc; Life Mbr, AAAS; Pres: Ala Acad Sci 1976-77; Auburn Chapt Sigma Xi 1978-79; cp/BSA: Dist Commr, Dist Fin Chm, Exec Bd Chattahoochee Coun; Auburn Lions Clb; Past Pres, Auburn Men's Camellia Clb; Auburn U Fund: Dr Chm 1977-78, VP 1978-79; Auburn Lodge #76, F&AM; Pres, E Ala Shrine Clb 1976; Others; r/Auburn U Meth Ch: Choir, Meth Men, Ch Bd; hon/Silver Beaver Awd, Chattahoochee Coun BSA; Dist Awd Merit; Phi Sigma; Anna Ames Meml Scholar, Harvard Univ; Sigma Xi; Gamma Sigma Delta; Fellow, AAAS; Golden Peanut Res Awd, Nat Peanut Coun; Phi Kappa Phi.

DIETHRICH, EDWARD BRONSON oc/Cardiovascular Surgeon; b/Aug 6, 1935; h/4819 E Hummingbird Ln, Paradise Valley, AZ 85253; ba/Phoenix, AZ; m/Gloria; c/Tad, Lynne; p/Thurmon C and Nina K Diethrich; ed/AB 1956, MD 1960 Univ of Mich, Ann

Arbor; pa/Dir & Chief of Cardiovascular Surg, Ariz Heart Inst; Baylor Col of Med: Asst Prof of Surg 1967-71, Instr 1966-67, Asst Instr 1965-66; Hosp Staff: St Joseph's Hosp & Med Ctr, Phoenix, St Luke's Hosp Med Ctr, Phoenix, Phoenix Meml Hosp, Phoenix Bapt Hosp; Am Col Angiol; Assn for Acad Surg; Am Heart Assn; Soc for Vascular Surg; Michael E DeBakey Intl Cardiovascular Soc; Soc Thoracic Surgs; Nu Sigma Nu; Fellow: Am Col Cardiol, Am Col Chest Physicians; hon/Frederick A Coller Awd 1963; Hektoen Gold Medal Awd, AMA 1970; Notable Ams; Nat Reg Prominent Ams; Sev Film Awds; Pub'd Profl Articles.

DI GIROLAMO, RUDOLPH GERARD oc/Professor; Administrator; b/Jan 26, 1934; h/1050 Ralston Ave, Belmont, CA 94002; ba/Belmont; c/Christopher; p/Mrs C DiGirolamo, Dumonth, NJ; ed/BS Mount St Mary's Col; MS St John's Univ; PhD Univ Wash; pa/Prof & Chm, Dept Biol Scis, Col of Notre Dame 1970-; Dir, Marine Resources Ctr, Col of Notre Dame 1970-; Univ Wash, Seattle: Res Assoc Prof, Dept of Sanitary Engrg 1969, Lectr, Marine Microbiol 1967-69, Trainee, Shellfish Sanitation 1964-69; Tchg Asst, St John's Univ 1956-57; NY Acad Sci; AAAS; Am Soc Microbiol; Am Soc Malacologists; Intl Oceanographic Foun; Am Fisheries Soc; r/Rom Cath; hon/Profl Pubs; Intl Dir Envir Sci; Am Malacologists; Am Men & Wom Sci; W/W: Ecol, W; Others.

D'IGNAZIO, SILVIO FREDERICK III oc/Writer; Consultant; Executive; b/Jan 6, 1949; h/202 Barclay Rd, Chapel Hill, NC 27514; ba/Chapel Hill; m/Janet Letts; c/Catherine Shum; p/Silvio Frederick Jr and Elizabeth McComas D'Ignazio, Moylan, PA; ed/BA w hons Brown Univ; MA Fletcher Sch Law & Diplomacy; pa/Pres, Household Info Sys; Lectr on Coming Personal Computer Revolution; cp/Bikeways Conslt, Town of Chapel Hill; r/Cath; hon/Var F'ships & Grants for Res, Civic Renewal of Small Towns; 2 Pub'd Books on Computers: *Catie and the Computer* 1979, *Home Computer Fun* 1979.

DI GRAPPA, GERALD PETER oc/Clinical Social Worker; b/Jan 29, 1921; h/1601 Kiowa Dr, Big Spring, TX 79720; ba/Big Spring; m/Mary Maxine Clark; ed/BA; MA; mil/USMCR; USPHSR; pa/Clin Social Wkr; ACSW; NASW; cp/Bd Dirs, Cath Charities.

DI JANNI, JOHN ALBINO oc/Musician; h/14 Verano Loop, El Dorado, Santa Fe, NM 87501; ba/Santa Fe; m/Helen K Rupp; c/John Charles, Robert A; p/Albino Di Janni (dec); Regino Porpora Di Janni; pa/Prin Violist, Santa Fe Orch; Fdr, Santa Fe String Quartette; Soloist, Chamber Orch, Albuquerque; Viola Instr: St John's Col, Col of Santa Fe; Metro Opera: Ret'd 1975, Orch Pers Mgr 1969-75, Prin Viola 1936-75, Mem Viola Sect 1935-36, Extra 1931-35; Fac Prof: Mich St Univ Cong of Strings, Skidmore Col 1965-69; Violist, La String Quartette 1929-31; r/Prot.

DILL, DAVID BRUCE oc/Physiologist; b/Apr 22, 1891; h/303 Wyoming St, Boulder City, NV 89005; ba/Boulder City; m/Olive Lillian Gassel; 2nd Chloris Luella Fuller Gillis; c/David Bruce Jr, Elizabeth D Horvath (Mrs Steven M); p/David White and Lydia Dunn Dill (dec); ed/BS Occidental Col 1913; MA Stanford Univ 1914; PhD Univ Nev, Las Vegas 1925; mil/AUS 1941-45, Maj to Col; pa/Res Prof, Univ Nev, Las Vegas 1977-; Dir, Lab of Applied Physiol, Boulder City 1966-77; Res Scholar, Ind Univ 1961-66; Dep Dir Med Res, AUS Chem Res & Devel Labs 1947-61; Harvard Univ: Dir Res Fatique Lab 1927-47, Prof Indust Physiol 1938-47, Assoc Prof Indust Physiol 1936-38, Asst Prof Biochem 1927-36; Other Past Positions; Fellow: Am Acad Arts & Scis, AAAS; Am Soc Biol Chems; Fed Am Soc Expmtl Biol; Am Physiol Soc; Am Inst Biol Scis; Assoc Fellow, Am Acad Phys Ed; hon/DSc Occidental Col 1959; LHD Univ

Nev, Las Vegas 1972; Hon Fellow: Am Col Sports Med, Am Col Cardiol; Phi Beta Kappa; Phi Lambda Upsilon; Aerospace Med Hon Cit, AMA; Author: *Life, Heat, and Altitude* 1938, *Physiology of Muscular Excerise* (w A V Bock) 1931.

DILLARD, EMIL LEE oc/Educator; b/-Mar 14, 1921; h/74 Rutland Rd, Hempstead, NY 11550; ba/Garden City, NY; m/Leona M Sneed; p/Oscar Winfiled Dillard (dec); Mabel Dollie Brooks Dillard, Arlington, KS; ed/BA; MA; PHD; mil/USAAF; pa/Edr, Adelphi Univ; AAUP; MLA; Am Studies Assn; Nat Coun Tchrs English; cp/ACLU; Common Cause; r/Unitarian; hon/Outstg Edr Am.

DILLER, PRISCILLA BERDYNE TJADEN (PEG) oc/Technical Illustrator; Theatrical Designer; Consultant; b/Jan 23, 1926; h/2370 San Marco Dr, Hollywood, CA 90068; m/David Henry; c/Marselline Anne, Paul John; p/George Bernhardt and Elda Maxwell Wade Tjaden, Colton, SD; pa/Costume Designer, Cleveland; Tech Illustrator, Azusa, Cal; Tech Illustrator & Art Supvr, Frank Mayer Engrg & Luric Industs, LA, Cal; Co-Fdr, RotoWing, LA; Co-Owner, Designer

Dream Factory, LA; cp/Sch Commun Adv Coun; Cal Cong Parents & Tchrs; Sch Res Histn; Parliamentary Rules Advr; Bicent Coor; Integration Coun; Tech Art Conslt; Jobs Daughs; r/Meth; hon/Le Cerc le Concours d'Elegance, Blind Chd's Ctr; Bicent Salute to Wom; Hon Ser Awd & Life Mbrships, Cal Parents & Tchrs; Le Conte Acad Awd; Others.

DILLEY, GREGORY D oc/Electronic Engineer; b/Feb 28, 1949; h/Ogden, UT; ba/3750 Airport Rd, Ogden, UT 84403; m/K Geniel; p/William G and Jean Dilley, Ogden, UT; ed/BS Cand; pa/Electronic Design & Mfg Co Exec; Audio Engrg Soc Inc; Soc Motion Picture & TV Engrs; VChm, Utah Audio Engrg Soc Inc; cp/Utah Corvette Clb; r/Presb; hon/W/W W; S'ship, Weber St Col; Future Scist of Am Awd.

DILLEY, WILLIAM G oc/Manufacturer; b/Jun 6, 1922; ba/770 Wall Ave, Ogden, UT 84404; m/Jean; c/Gregory D, Karen K; p/William G and Ethel M Dilley; ed/BS Univ Colo; mil/USAAF & USAF, Ofcr; pa/Fdr & Prin, Spectra Sonics (Electronic Design & Mfg Firm); Former Chief Electronics Engrg for Thor, Atlas D, Atlas E, Atlas F, Titan I, & Titan II Intercontinental Ballistic Missle Sys & Minuteman Engrg Test Facilities; Conslt & Lectr in Electronics Field; 14 US & Fgn Patents; Pub'd 250+ Profl Papers & Articles; Holder of US & World Aircraft Speed Records; Sr Broadcast Engr; Audio Engrg Soc Inc; Nat

Assn Broadcasters; Soc Motion Picture & TV Engrs; Soc Reg'd Inventors; Aircraft Owners & Pilots Assn; Nat Aeronautic Assn; IPA; cp/Ogden Golf & CC; Mt Eyrie Racquet Clb; Pi Kappa Alpha; Caterpillar Clb; hon/Dist'd Flying Cross; Air Medal w 9 OLC; Army Commend Medal; Belgian Fourraguerre; Dist'd Alumnus Awd, Univ Colo 1977; W/W: World, Fin & Indust, US, W; Notable Ams: Notable Ams of Bicent Era; Intl Reg Profiles; Intl W/W Intells; DIB; Intl W/W Commun Ser; Nat Social Dir; Commun Ldrs & Noteworthy Ams; Personalities of W&MW; Book of Hon; Engrs of Distn; Men Achmt; Fellow: Audio Engrng Soc, IBA, ABI.

DILLIN, JAKE THOMAS JR oc/Administrator; b/Aug 19, 1945; h/7529 Compass Dr, Orlando, FL 32807; ba/Orlando; m/Married; c/Traci; p/Jake Thomas and Beatrice B Ervin Dillin; ed/BS; Grad Study; pa/Holiday Div, Orlando Reg Med Ctr Inc: Adm Dir Pharmacies 1979-, Lab Adm Dir 1976-79; Pres, Ctl Fla Biologicals Inc, Orlando & Tampa 1974-76; Doctors Lab Sers Inc, Tampa 1972-74: Toxicologist, Lab Mgr, VP, Bd Dirs; Others; Diplomat & Bioanalyst Lab Dir, Am Bd Bioanalysis; Charter Mbr: Med Electronics & Data Society, Society Biomed Equipmt Technicians; Am Assn Clin Chemists; Am Soc Law & Med; Am Soc Quality Control, Intl Soc Blood Transfusion, Paris; Clin Lab Mgmt Assn; Assn Drug Detection Labs; cp/Fdr & Pres, Fla Jacguar Clb; Jacguar Clbs NAm; Tampa Jaycees; Jaquar Drivers Clb, England; E-Jag NAm; Past Pres Bd Dirs, YMCA Lakemont Gymnastic Team; Orlando Choral Soc Messiah Chorus; US Gymnastics Fed; 1-Man Photographic Art Shows; hon/Dist'd Ldrs in Hlth Care; Clin Chems Recog Awd 1978; DIB; Personalities of S; Others.

DILLINGHAM, MARJORIE CARTER b/Aug 20, 1915; m/William Pyrle; c/William Pyrle Jr (dec); Robert Carter, Sharon D Martin; ed/PhD Fla St Univ; pa/Tchg Positions: Duke Univ, Univ Ga, Fla St Univ, Panama Canal Zone Col, St George's Sch (Havana, Cuba), Fla Sec'dy Schs; Formerly Dir'd Traveling Spanish Conservation Classes Throughout Spanish-Speaking World; Nat Pres, La Sociedad Honoraria Hispanica 2 yrs; Pres: Fgn Lang Div Fla Ed Assn 2 yrs, Fla Chapt Am Assn Tchrs Spanish & Portuguese, Alpha Lambda Chapt Delta Kappa Gamma 2 yrs, Big Bend Area Coor'g Coun Delta Kappa Gamma, Fgn Lang Tchrs of Leon Co (Fla); Presented Profl Papers; hon/Phi Kappa Phi; Sigma Delta Pi; Beta Pi Theta; Kappa Delta Pi; Alpha Omicron Pi; Delta Kappa Gamma.

DILLMAN, GEORGE F oc/Financial Consultant; Investor; b/Sept 5, 1934; h/13361 Peyton Dr, Dallas, TX 75240; ba/Richardson,

TX; m/Virginia; c/Leesa, Mitchell, Louise, Laura; p/Wilbur M and Meadie A Dillman; pa/Gen Mgr; Fin Conslt; Investor.

DILLON, RAE EVELYN oc/Broadcast Journalist; b/Jun 21, 1949; h/850 Lindbergh Dr, #P-2, Jackson, MS 39209; ba/Jackson; p/Anglon and Rose Dillon, Jackson, MS; ed/BA; pa/Documentary Prodr; Soc Profl Journalists; Sigma Delta Chi; Am Wom in Radio & TV; r/Holiness; hon/Nat Mtl Hlth Assn Media Excell Awd 1977; Ms Broadcasters Assn Best Documentary Awd; St Mtl Hlth Awd.

DILLON, VIOLA MAY oc/Educational Administrative; b/Oct 19, 1900; h/8350 Greensboro Dr, Apt 1-520, McLean, VA 22102; m/Dale C (dec); c/Joanne D Lichty, Robert Sherwood; p/William Burke and Nora Shaw Sherwood (dec); ed/AB George Wash

Univ; pa/Ret'd; Supvry & Adm Prin, Elem Schs, Fairfax Co, Va 1943-66; Past Mem: Fairfax Co Ed Assn, Va Ed Assn, NEA, PTA; Life Mem, Fairfax Co & Va Elem Prin Assn; cp/BSA; GSA; Past Staff Mem, Va Girls' St; Overlee Knowles Citizen Assn; r/Columbia Bapt Ch: Supt Jr Dept, SS Tchr, Choir Mem.

DI LUZIO, JEAN BAPTISTE oc/Educational Administrator; b/Jun 7, 1925; h/2551 W Lake Rd, Erie, PA 16505; ba/Erie; p/Anthony and Ermelinda DeDionisio DiLuzio (dec); ed/BA Villa Maria Col; MA Wn Resv Univ; pa/Col Admr; VP for Fin & Planning; Nat Assn for Col & Univ Bus Ofcrs; Soc for Col & Univ Planning; EACUBO; cp/Bd Trustees: Cath Social Sers, Erie Diocesan Cemetary Bd, St Mary Home of Erie; r/Rom Cath: Sister; hon/Fulbright Grant; Outstg Sec'dy Edrs Am.

DI MUCCIO, MARY-JO oc/Librarian; b/Jun 16, 1930; h/720-C Blair Ct, Sunnyvale, CA 94087; ba/Sunnyvale; p/Vincent and Theresa Yovino Di Muccio, Mountain View, CA; ed/BA; MALS; PhD US Intl Univ 1970; pa/City Libn, Sunnyvale; Past Pres, Cath Lib Assn; Secy-Treas, Peninsula Lib Assn; ALA; Spec Lib Assn; Cal Lib Assn; Public Lib Execs of Ctl Cal; Continuing Lib Ed Network & Exch; cp/VP Exec Bd, Sunnyvale Commun Sers; VP, Sunnyvale BPW Clb; Pres, Soropimist Clb; U Way Allocation Bd; Secy Bd Dirs, Brookline Homeowners Assn; r/Cath; hon/Lib of Human Resources of Am Bicent Res Inst.

DIXON, EVA CRAWFORD JOHNSON oc/Library Administrator; b/Aug 28, 1909; h/506 Kelson Ave, Marianna, FL 32446; ba/Marianna; p/William Alpheus and Willie Crawford Johnson (dec); ed/ABE w hons; MA; mil/WAC 2 yrs; pa/Lib Admr, Chipola Jr Col Lib; Past Chm, Fla Ed Assn Hon Socs; Past Pres, Jefferson Co Ed Assn; Nat Lib Assn; Fla Lib Assn; Fla Assn Sch Libns; Life Mbr, NEA; Fla Ed Assn; Fla Assn Public Jr Cols; Chipola Dames; Nat Assn Parliamentns; cp/Chipola Dames; Marianna Wom's Clb; Fla Wom's Clb Dist II; IPA; r/Marianna Presb Ch; hon/Kappa Delta Pi; Hon Life Mbr, WOC, PCUS; PhD Colo St Christian Col; Intl Pers Res Creativity Awd; Var Cits.

DIXON, FREDDIE BROWN SR oc/Minister; b/Jun 6, 1944; h/1201 Hackberry St, Austin, TX 78702; ba/Austin; m/Barbara Watson; c/Freddie B Jr, Douglas L; p/Ernest T Jr and Lois F Dixon, Topeka, KS; ed/BA Philander Smith Col; MDiv, Interdenominational Theol Ctr; pa/Pastor; Wesley U Meth Ch, Austin 1973-; Assoc Pastor, 1st U Meth Ch 1970-73; Pastor, Jones Chapel U Meth Ch 1970-73; Field Instr, Perkins Sch Theol Intern Prog, So Meth Univ 1975-76; Tchr, Sch of Christian Missions U Meth Wom, 1974, 75 & 77; Conslt & Participant in Wkshops, Forums, Sems & Panels; cp/Alpha Phi Alpha; 32° Prince Hall Mason; Commr, City Planning Com, Austin, Tex; Adv Bd: Travis Co MH-HR Drug Abuse Prog 1976-78, Maplewood Commun Sch 1976-78, Adult Basic Ed, Austin

Commun Col 1975-; Past Pres Bd Dirs, Austin Area Urban Leag Inc 1977-; Past Mem, Bee Co Kiwanis; hon/W/W Rel; Intl W/W Commun Ser; Cert Appres, Austin Assn Tchrs Inc 1978; Human Relats Awd for Outstg Contbns in Area of Human Relats 1977-78; Outstg Yg Men Am.

DIXON, PAUL RAND oc/Commissioner; b/Sept 29, 1913; h/5911 Carlton Ln, Wash, DC 20016; ba/Wash DC; m/Doris Busby; c/David Leslie, Paul Randall; p/James David and Sarah Munn Dixon (dec); ed/AB Vanderbilt Univ 1936; LLB Univ Fla Law Sch 1938; mil/USNR 1942-45; pa/US Fed Trade Comm: Commr 1961-, Chm 1961-69, Trial Atty 1938-42, 1946-57; Coun & Staff Dir, US Sen Antitrust & Monopoly Subcom 1957-61; Asst Football Coach, Univ Fla 1937-38; Fla St Bar; Tenn St Bar; Fed Bar Assn; Nat Lwyrs Clb; cp/George C Whiting Masonic Lodge #22; Alpha Tau Omega; Past Pres, Wash DC Chapt, Vanderbilt Univ Alumni Assn; Kenwood Golf & CC; Naval Ofcrs Clb; Nashvile Quarterback Clb; Tenn St Soc; r/Metro Meml U Meth Ch; hon/Phi Delta Phi; Pub'd Profl Articles; W/W: Am, S&SW, Govt, Am Polits; Nat Reg Prominent Ams; Personalities of S; DIB; Intl W/W; Men Achmt; Intl W/W Commun Ser; Blue Book; Martindale-Hubble Law Dir; Current Biog Yearbook; Commun Ldrs & Noteworthy Ams; Others.

DIZER, JOHN THOMAS JR oc/Professor; b/Nov 7, 1921; h/10332 Ridgecrest Rd, Utica, NY 13502; ba/Utica; m/Marie Leerkaup; c/John Thomas III, Jane E, William D, Ann E, Mary L; p/John T Dizer (dec); Eunice Haven Dizer, Montclair, NJ; ed/S Northeastern; MS, PhD Purdue Univ; mil/WW II & Korean Conflict, Lt (sg); pa/Prof & Hd, Mech Dept, Mohawk Val Commun Col; Pres, NYS Engrg Tech Assn; Gen Chm, Mohawk Val Engr Exec Coun 1977; cp/Dir, Oneida Hist Soc; Trustee, Plymouth-Bethesda UCC; BSA; ed/U Ch Christ; hon/Outstg Engr Awd, NSF India Prog; Others.

DMOCHOWSKI, LEON L oc/Physician; Scientist; b/Jul 1, 1909; h/3311 Grennoch Ln, Houston, TX 77025; ba/Houston; m/Sheila; c/Roger; p/Roman and Ludmila Dmochowski (dec); ed/MD Univ Warsaw 1937; PhD Univ Leeds, England 1949; pa/Phys-Scist, Dept Virol, Univ Tex Sys Cancer Ctr, MD Ander-

son Hosp; Tumor Virol Res; Edit Bd, *CANCER*; cp/Nat Bd Trustees, Leukemia Soc Am; r/Cath; hon/Americanism Awd, DAR 1969; Alfred Jurzykowski Awd in Med 1971; Dist'd Ser Awd, Univ Tex Sys Cancer Ctr, MD Anderson Hosp 1974; Dist'd Ser Awd, Am Assn for Cancer Res SW Sect 1977.

DOAN, ELEANOR LLOYD oc/Publicist; Writer; b/Jun 4, 1914; h/1240 Moncado Dr, Glendale, CA 91207; ba/Glendale; p/Fred and Gladys Doan (dec); ed/BA; Grad Study; pa/So Cal Book Publicists; Wom's Nat Book Assn; cp/Repub Wkr; r/Presb; hon/Wom of Yr, Glendale News Press; Commun Ldrs & Noteworthy Ams; Chi Delta Phi; Kappa Tau Alpha; Runner-up for Gold Medallion Book Awd, Juvenile Div.

DOBBS, VIRGINIA ELIZABETH

oc/Bookkeeper; Secretary; Office Assistant; p/Charles Alvin and Rosa Bishop Dobbs (dec); ed/Crump Commerce Col; Ky Bus Col; Asbury Col; pa/Lena Madisen Phillips BPW Clb; cp/Charter Mbr, Jessamine Hist Soc; r/Disciples of Christ: Deaconess, Tchr, 3-Time Pres & Charter Mbr, Ch Woms F'ship; hon/Ky Col; Awd for 37 Yrs as Bkkpr at 1 Bus.

DOCK, WILLIAM oc/Consultant in Medicine; Educator; Physician; b/Nov 1, 1898; ed/BS Washington Univ 1920; MD Univ Chicago 1923; pa/Full-time Conslt in Med VA Hosp, NYC 1969-73; Chief Med Div VA Hosp, Brooklyn 1963-69; St Univ NY: Prof Emeritus Med 1963-73, Prof Med (Long Isl Col Med) 1944-63; Prof Pathol Cornell Univ (NY) 1941-44; Stanford Univ: Prof Pathol 1936-41, Assoc Prof Med 1928-36, Asst Prof 1927-28,

Instr 1926-27; Resident Stanford Hosp, San Francisco 1925-26; House Ofcr Peter Bent Brigham Hosp, Boston 1922-24; Am Col Physicians; Am Acad Arts & Scis; Am Soc Clin Investigation: Mem Emeritus, Pres 1941-42; Mem Emeritus Am Col Cardiol; Harvey Soc; NY Acad Med; Soc for Experimtl Biol & Med; hon/Num Profl Pubs.

DOCKERY, CHRISTINE oc/University Administrator; Educational Consultant; b/May 1, 1942; h/2834 Dufton Loop, Tallahassee, FL 32303; ba/Fayetteville, NC; m/Charles Billings; p/William and Evelyn Dockery, Laurinburg, NC; ed/BS cum laude NC Ctl Univ 1963; MA Columbia Univ; PhD Fla St Univ 1976; pa/Assoc Prof & Chperson, Bus Ed Dept, Fayetteville St Univ 1977-; Asst Prof & Chperson, Bus Ed Dept, Fla A&M Univ 1971-76; Bus Ed Tchr, Jr HS, High Point, NC 1965-69, W B Wicker HS, Sanford, NC 1963-65; Nat Bus Ed Assn; So Bus Ed Assn; NC Bus Ed Assn; Intl Soc Bus Edrs; Adult Ed Assn USA; Am Voc Assn; Assn Tchrs Ed; Bd Dirs, Nat Assn Black Adult Edrs; cp/NAACP; Urban Leag; Alpha Kappa Alpha; SCLC; Black Caucus Nat Subcom on Housing, Minority Enterprise & Economic Devel; r/Bapt; hon/World W/W Wom in Ed; Delta Pi Epsilon; Pi Gamma Mu; Pi Omega Pi; Outstg Yg Wom Am.

DOCTER, CHARLES ALFRED oc/Lawyer; b/Aug 5, 1931; h/9810 Hillridge Dr, Kensington, MD 20795; ba/Wash DC; m/Marcia Kaplan; c/Will Henry, Michael Warren, Adina Jo; p/Alfred Docter (dec); Annie Rothchild Docter; ed/BA magna cum laude Kenyon Col 1953; JD Univ Chgo Law Sch 1956; mil/USN 1956-59, Lt (sg); pa/Bar Assn DC; Md St Bar Assn; Admitted to Bar: DC 1959, Md 1962, Ohio 1959; cp/Md Ho Dels 1967-78; r/Jewish; hon/Haym Salomon Awd.

DODDS, EDNA CORDER oc/Educator; b/Sept 2, 1907; h/515 Honor Ave, Clarksburg, WV 26301; m/John Mann (dec); c/Sue D Michaels, John P, JoAnn D Richardson; p/Grover Cleveland and Mamie Harris Corder (dec); ed/AB Univ Ky; MA WVa Univ; pa/Ret'd Tchr; NEA; SEA; ARSE; W Va Ed Assn; AAUW: Pres 2 yrs, VP 2 yrs; cp/Charter Mem, Leag for Ser; Bd Mem, WVa Arthritis Foun; Orgr & Pres, N Ctl Arthritis Foun 1974-; Del, W Va St Meeting 1976; Clarksburg CC; YWCA; Clarksburg Wom's

Clb; r/1st U Meth Ch: SS Tchr 4 yrs, Nursery Supvr 2 yrs, Ofcl Bd Mem; hon/Personalities of S; Commun Ldrs & Noteworthy Ams; Citizen of Yr, Arthritis Foun of W Va 1975.

DODSON, DON C oc/Professor; Administrator; b/Feb 22, 1942; h/105 Hemlock Dr, Boone, NC 28607; ba/Boone; m/Carol Daniel; c/Robert Daniel; p/R J and L L Dodson, Bonham, TX; ed/BA; MA; PhD Univ Tenn, Knoxville; pa/Prof & Assoc Dir Bur of Ec & Bus Res, Walker of Bus, Appalachian St Univ; Mem & Ofcr, Var Profl Socs; Editor *Appalachian Bus Review*; Conslt; Pub'd Profl Articles; Bd Editors: *Jour Hlth & Human Resources Adm, Soc & Edr*; hon/Nat Hon Awd, Am Acad Hlth Adm 1978; Pi Sigma Alpha; Phi Alpha Theta.

DODSON, RONALD FRANKLIN oc/-Administrator; b/Feb 14, 1942; h/2918 Bain Pl, Tyler, TX 75701; ba/Tyler; m/Sandra Jim Roberson; c/Diana Lynn, Debra Kay; p/Benjamin F and Vera Eubank Dodson, Paris, TX; ed/AA; BA; MA; PhD; pa/Chief, Dept of Cell Biol & Envir Scis, Univ Tex Hlth Ctr 1977-; Chief, Depts of Expmtl Pathol & Envir Scis, E Tex Chest Hosp, Tyler 1976-77; Baylor Col of Med: Adj Asst Prof 1977-, Asst Prof 1971-77, Instr 1970; Am Heart Assn (Fellow, Stroke Coun); British Brain Res Assn; NY Acad Sci; AAAS; Am Men & Wom Sci; SW Sci Forum; Soc Neurosci; SW Sci Forum; Am Chem Soc; Tex Acad Sci; cp/Bd Dirs, Tex Gulf Coast Chapt, Cystic Fibrosis Fdn 1976-77; Bd Trustees, NE Tex Chapt, Nat MS Soc; Chm Med Adv Com, NE Tex Chapt Nat MS Soc 1977-; hon/Profl Pubs; Am Men & Wom Sci; Men Achmt; DIB; Personalities of S; Notable Ams; W/W: Am, S&SW; Commun Ldrs & Noteworthy Ams.

DOERMANN, RALPH WALTER oc/-Professor; b/Jun 25, 1930; h/2474 Seneca Park Pl, Columbus, OH 43209; ba/Columbus; m/-Laurel Ackermann; c/Roger James, Gail Marie, Richard Carl, William Frederick; p/Carl Martin and Cora Knupke Doermann (dec); ed/AB Capital Univ; BD Luth Theol Sem; PhD Duke Univ; mil/USNR 1952-54, Communs Ofcr; pa/Prof of Old Testament & Archaeol, Luth Theol Sem; Am Schs Oriental Res; Soc Biblical Lit; Archaeol Inst Am; Nat Assn Prof Hebrew; cp/Ohio Civil Rights Comm; r/Am Luth Ch: Ordained Min; hon/Phi Beta Kappa; James B Duke Fellow; Frederick A Schiotz Fellow; Annual Prof'ship, Albright Inst Archaeol Res, Jerusalem.

DOGGER, ADA RUTH CAROLYN oc/-Educator; Scientist; b/Nov 4, 1925; h/710 Winhall Way, Silver Spring, MD 20904; oc/Educator; Scientist; m/James Russell; c/Allen James, Stuart Jon, Gary Robert (dec); p/John H Emde, Sussex, WI; Ada K White, Milwaukee, WI; ed/BS 1963, MS 1965 ND St Univ; pa/Am Soc for Microbiol; Coun for Exceptl Chd; Ga Ed for Hearing Impaired; cp/Am Security Coun; Vol, Alexander G Bell Assn for Deaf; Dir Vols & Info Coor, HEAR Foun; r/Presb; Anthroposophist; hon/NIH Fellow; Phi Kappa Phi; W/W Am Wom; Intl W/W Wom; W/W S; Notable Ams; Commun Ldrs & Noteworthy Ams; Lions Awd.

DOHRING, GRACE HELEN oc/Executive; h/24028 Union, Dearborn, MI 48124; m/Albert A; c/Charles, Deborah, Joan; p/Frederick Henry and Martha Helen

Johnson; ed/Doct Chiropractic; Doct Naturopathic (Cert'd); Practioner, Doct & Master Neuropathy; pa/Pres, Doctor's Supply Intl (Acupuncture Supplies); 3 Patents; 30+ Copyrights; Nat Small Bus Assn; Nat Assn for Female Execs; Kyoto Pain Inst, Japan; German Acad for Auricular Med; Intl Acupuncture Soc; Acupuncture & Res Soc; Charter Mem: Acupuncture Ryodoraku Assn, Am Chiropractic Assn; Tchr & Lectr; cp/Past Matron, Ashlar Chapt OES #378; Den Mother; Asst Ldr, GSA; hon/W/W: Among Am Wom, Fin & Indust, Chiropractors Intl; Intl W/W Intells; Personalities of W&MW; DIB; World W/W Wom; Men & Wom Distn; Dist'd Ldrs in Hlth Care; Wom in Bus.

DOI, NELSON KIYOSHI oc/Lieutenant Governor; b/Jan 1, 1922; h/2030 Mauna Pl, Honolulu, HI 96822; ba/Honolulu; m/Eiko Oshima; c/David Tadashi, Katherine Aiko; p/Tadaishi and Chieno Kurata Doi (dec); ed/BS 1946, JD 1948 Univ Minn; pa/Sr Judge, 3rd Circuit Ct, Hawaii 1969-73 (Chm Circuit Cts Rules Com); Atty, Pvt Pract, Hilo, Hawaii 1954-68; Hawaii Co: Co Atty 1953-54, Dep Co

Atty 1949-53; Nat Conf Lt Govs; Nat Assn Secys St; Am Bar Assn; Hawaii St Bar Assn; Hawaii Co Bar Assn; cp/Lt Gov, Hawaii 1974-; Chm, Hawaii Crime Com 1977-; Territorial & St Sen, Hawaii 1954-69 (Sen Pres 1963-64, Floor Ldr); Del, Hawaii Constnl Conv 1950, 1968; Del to Wash DC for Hawaii Statehood; Dir: Hawaii ARC, Hawaii Tuberculosis Assn; Others; hon/Gamma Eta Gamma.

DOLL, DIXON R oc/Executive; ed/BSEE cum laude Kans St Univ; MSE, PhD Univ Mich; pa/Pres, DMW Telecommunications; Adj Staff, IBM Sys Res Inst, NYC; Grad Fac: Univ Mich, En Mich Univ; Fdr & Tech Dir, Intl Communs Corp's ICC Inst, Miami; Lect'd throughout Europe, SAm, US & Canada; Assn for Computing Machinery; IEEE Communs Profl Socs; hon/Author: *Data Communi-*

cations-Facilities, Networks and System Design, Num Papers & Jour Articles; NSF Scholar.

DOLL, MARGUERITE E oc/Retired Professional Librarian; Professional Artist; b/Jun 30, 1911; h/105 Lowery, #30, Hot Springs Nat Park, AR 71901; p/Charles F and Grace Chapman Doll (dec); ed/BA Univ Ill; MA No Ill Univ; pa/Intl Soc Artists; Ark Arts Ctr; So Artists Assn; cp/SAA: Former Prog Chm, Former CoChm Printmaking; Chm Ark Arts & Humanities Art Wkshop 1974; Exhibiting Artist Fine Arts Ctr Gallery, Hot Springs Nat Pk 7 Yrs; Friends of Lib, Tri-Lakes Lib; r/Prot; hon/Former Mem Hon Socs; Var Prizes Art Shows; Biogl Listings.

DOLLAHITE, DAVID RIDLEY oc/Administrator; Educator; b/Apr 22, 1941; h/3031 Zola, San Diego, CA 92106; c/David Andrew; p/Kenneth J Dollahite (dec); Pat Gabbert, Denison, TX; ed/BS Tex Christian Univ 1963; MS So Ill Univ 1973; MBA Nat Univ 1979;

mil/USAF 13 yrs, Maj; pa/Admissions Cnslr, Nat Univ 1976-; Equal Opportunity & Treatmt Ofcr, Charleston AFB, SC 1974-76; Chief of Analysis Br, Internal Info, Mil Airlift Command, Scott AFB, Ill 1972-74; Chief of AF DC-9 Pilot Tng Sch 1969-72; hon/Outstg Yg Men Am, US Jaycees 1977; Dist'd Flying Cross; 7 Air Medals.

DOLLAR, DENNIS EARL oc/State Representative; b/Aug 22, 1953; h/PO Box 1411, Gulfport, MS 39501; ba/Gulfport; m/Janie S; p/Bennie E and Dorothy S Dollar, Gulfport, MS; ed/AA Miss Gulf Coast Jr Col; BA Univ Miss; cp/St Rep, Dist 45-A; Jaycees; Lions; Homebuilders Assn; Friends of Lib;

Hosp Adv Bd; Dixie Yth Baseball Coach; St Manpower Sers Coun; Harrison Co Employmt & Tng Coun; Miss Gulf Coast Jr Col Alumni Assn; Univ Miss Alumni Assn; r/Bapt: Deacon, SS Tchr; Phi Kappa Phi; ODK; Dist'd Ser Awds; Personalities of S; W/W Am Polits.

DOMBROWSKI, MADGE COHEA oc/Photographer; Writer; b/Sept 6, 1918; h/421 N 12th St, Frederick, OK 73542; ba/Frederick; m/Casey William; c/Carol Kitchen, Linda Edgell, Peggy Porter, John Casey, Alan Wayne; p/William E and Clyde Greer Cohea (dec); ed/BS Okla Col for Wom; pa/Co-owner, Cohea Photography Studio 41 yrs; Writer: Lawton Pub'g Co, Wichita Falls Pub'g Co, Okla Pub'g Co, WTAT Radio Sta; cp/Publicity Chm: Arts Fest, Bicent, Heart Fund, Others; Hd of Publicity & Beautification, C of C; r/1st Christian Ch: SS

Tchr 28 yrs, SS Supt, Revival Coor, Com Mem, Ch Sweetheart; hon/Frederick's Most Useful Citizen; BPW Clb Wom of Mo; Hon'd by DeMolay, Scouts, FFA Yth; Wom of Yr, Black Kat Klub; W/W SW, Am.

DOMEC, ETHEL McDONALD oc/Registered Nurse; b/Mar 10, 1920; h/3898 Dryden Rd, Port Arthur, TX 77640; ba/Port Arthur; m/Samuel Domec; c/Colleen Clare Conover, Michael Douglas, Robert Neil; p/John Walton and Roberta Epps McDonald (dec); ed/RN St Mary's Hosp; Our Lady of the Lake Col;

Lamar Univ; pa/Reg'd Nurse; Quality Assurance-Risk Mgmt Coor; Am Nurses Assn; Tex Nurses Assn; cp/Tex Poetry Soc; Nat Poetry Soc; r/Cath; hon/Intl W/W Poetry; Nat W/W Poetry; World W/W Wom; Commun Ldrs & Noteworthy Ams.

DOMENICI, PETE VICHI oc/United States Senator; b/May 7, 1932; h/Rockville, MD; ba/405 Russell Sen Ofc Bldg, Wash DC 20510; m/Nancy; c/Lisa Ann, Peter, Nella, Clare, David, Nanette, Paula & Helen; p/Cherubino Domenici (dec); Alda Vichi Domenici, Albuquerque, NM; ed/BA Univ NM; JD Univ Denver Law Sch; pa/Indep Busmen; Nat Assn Bus; cp/US Sen: Budget Com, Com on Energy & Natural Resources, Ranking Minority Mem-Select Com on Aging; Mayor, City of Albuquerque 1967; US Del, 1st World Food Conf, Rome 1975; 1st Interparliamentary Del from US to Soviet Union; r/Cath; hon/Named Albuquerque's Outstg Yg Man 1967-68; Hon'd by: Leag United Latin Am Citizens Nat Ed Sers Ctr, Nat Fed Indep Bus, Nat Assn Bus, Others.

DOMSTEAD, MARY M oc/Freelance Writer; b/Jul 29, 1928; h/425 N 19th St, Duncan, OK 73533; m/Billy R E; c/Billy Eugene, Brenda June Wagner; p/Jefferson Wesley and Lucille Elleen Wadley (dec); pa/Christian Writers Guild; pa/Rep: Keepsake Clippings, Gatesville, Tex, Sangamon, Taylorsville, Ill; cp/Cnslr, Campfire Girls, Ardmore, Okla 1962; r/New Testament Christian Ch; Jr Dept Supt, Ch Secy 1977.

DONAHEY, JEAN ELIZABETH oc/Educator; b/Mar 22, 1906; h/619 River St, W Brownsville, PA 15417; p/Tracy T and Elizabeth Percy Donahey (dec); ed/BS; MEd; pa/Ret'd Cnslr & Social Studies Tchr; Past Pres: Brownsville Ed Assn, Fayette Co PSEA, Fayette Co Cnslrs Assn, SW Reg Pupil Sers; Secy, SW Reg PSEA 1964-71; cp/Nat Dir, Intl Thespian Soc; Brownsville Hist Soc; Brownsville Reading Cir; r/Presb; hon/Pi Gamma Mu; Alpha Psi Omega; Delta Kappa

Gamma; 2000 Wom Achmt; DIB; W/W Am Ed.

DONAHUE, GRACE HELEN SERVERINO oc/Educational Administrator; b/Apr 26, 1927; h/Barmore Rd, LaGrangeville, NY 12540; ba/Poughkeepsie, NY; c/Robert Brandon, Scott Vincent, Sean Elliot; p/Maurice Joseph and Mary Catherine Condon Serverino (dec); ed/BS Syracuse Univ 1949; pa/Prin, Noxon Rd Sch 1970-; Asst Prin, Arlington Ctl Sch Dist, Poughkeepsie 1955-70; Classroom Tchr 1952-66: Arlington Ctl Sch Dist, Ballston Spa Ctl Schs (NY),

Junction City Sch Dist (Kans), Colo Sprgs Sch Dist (Colo), Muscogee Co Sch Dist (Ga); Nat Assn Elem Sch Prins; Sch Admrs Assn NY; Pres, Dutchess Co Sch Admrs Assn; Mid-Hudson Sch Study Coun; Arlington Admrs Assn; Phi Delta Kappa; Conslt; Panelist; Task Force Mem; cp/Vol, Dutchess Co Chapt Am Heart Assn; Adv Bd, Astor Child Guid Clinics; Commun Rep, Dutchess Co Hd Start Policy Coun; PTA; Zonta Intl; hon/World W/W Wom; Notable Ams; W/W Am Wom; DIB; Commun Ldrs & Noteworthy Ams; W/W E; Book of Hon.

DONAHUE, HAYDEN H oc/Psychiatrist; b/Dec 4, 1912; h/1101 Westbrooke Terr, Norman, OK 73069; m/Patricia; c/Erin Kathleen, Kerry Shannon, Patricia Marie; p/(dec); ed/BS 1939; MD 1941; pa/Chief Conslt in Psychiatry, Okla St Penitentiary 1963-; Conslt: Okla St Crime Bur 1964-, Base Hosp (Tinker Field) 1964-; Dir, Okla Inst for Mtl Hlth Ed & Tng; Dir Dept of Mtl Hlth, St of Okla 1970-78; Med Doctor; Former Engr; Staff Mem & Adv Com Mem, Univ Okla Chd's Hosp 1975-; AMA; Fellow & Com-mem, Am Psychi Assn; Am Bar Assn; Comm on Mtly Disabled, Exec Com, Prog Com, SubCom on Legis, Edit Bd for *Mtl Hlth Reporter*; Nat Assn Mtl Hlth Prog Dirs; Fellow, AAAS; Fdg Fellow & Past Holder Num Ofcs, Am Col Psychiatrists; Soc of Med Conslts to Armed Forces; Others; pp/Pres' Com on Employment of Handicapped (Advr to Okla Com); Med Adv Bd, United Cerebral Palsy Assn of Okla; Gov's Com on Chd & Yth; Bd Dirs, Wesley Foun; Capitol Improvements Com, City f Norman; Bd Dirs, C of C; Others; r/Methodist; hon/Fellow: Am Assn Mtl Deficiency, Am Psychi Assn, Am Geriatrics Soc; "Donahue Apprec Day" Ordered by Gov, St of Okla; Outstg Ser Awd, Okla Assn Mtl Hlth; Okla Hall of Fame; Hon Chief to Choctaw Nation for Outstg Ser to Indian Tribes of Okla; Bowis Awd, Am Col Psychis; Commends by Okla St House & Senate; A H Robins Commun Ser Awd, Okla St Med Assn; Num Biogl Listings; Others.

DONALDSON, FLETCHER WILLIAM oc/Professor; b/Oct 30, 1912; h/521 Sharondale Dr, Tullahoma, TN 37388; ba/Tullahoma; m/Myrtle N; c/Patricia A Goltz, Rebecca J Rubke; p/Alpheus F and Elizabeth Donaldson (dec); ed/AB; MA; PhD; mil/CAC WW II, Capt; pa/Prof of Computer Sci, Univ Tenn Space Inst; Adj Prof, Dept of Surg, Meharry Med Col; Pres, Med Sys Corp; Fellow, Soc for Advanced Med Sys; Assn for Computing Machinery; IEEE; Acting Dir, Tenn Opers, Apollo Applications Res Inst; cp/Commun Concert Assn; r/Luth, Mo Synod: Elder; hon/Kappa Delta Pi; Pi Mu Epsilon; Phi Delta Kappa; Sigma Xi; Alpha

Gamma Epsilon.

DONALDSON, LORAINE oc/Professor; h/1170 Pine Ridge Rd NE, Atlanta, GA 30324; ba/Atlanta; p/Lonnie M and Lois Lorene Donaldson (dec); ed/MA; DBA; pa/Prof of Ecs, Ga St Univ; Author; Rschr; Conslt in Ecs; cp/Govt Conslt; Neighborhood Civic Assn; r/Cath: Ch Wk; hon/Acad S'ships; F'ships.

DONALDSON, MARY HOWE oc/Educator; Homemaker; b/Dec 17, 1923; h/PO Box 55, Oakland, MS 38948; m/James S; c/Rebecca D Herlep, Joel; p/E B Howe Sr, Oakland, MS; ed/Memphis St Univ; pa/Subst Tchr; Former Clerical Typist, Sears-Roebuck, Memphis; cp/Rep, Nat Fed'd Clb Com; Nat Ldrship Fdn; Nat Great Awakening Bd; Nat Kidney Fdn Bd; Am Legion Aux; r/Bapt; hon/Cit from Pres Nixon 1970; Hon'd for Wk w Mtl Retard, Heart Dr, Cancer Dr.

DONALDSON, MYRTLE NORMA oc/Music Teacher; Church Organist; m/Fletcher W; c/Patricia A Goltz, Rebecca J Rubke; p/E Otto and Eleonore Schneider, Austin, TX; ed/AB Univ Ariz; pa/Cert'd Music Tchr; Tenn Music Tchrs Assn; Cert'd Keyboard Arts Tchr; Pres, Highland Rim Commun Concert Assn; cp/Nat Soc Lit & Arts; Tullahoma Wom's Clb; Tullahoma Music Clb; Tullahoma Fine Arts Ctr; Luth Soc for Music Worship & Arts; r/Luth Ch, Mo Synod; hon/Delta Phi Alpha.

DONEGAN, CHARLES EDWARD oc/Attorney; Arbitrator; b/Apr 10, 1933; h/212 Laura Ln, Chgo Heights, IL 60411; ba/Chgo; m/Patty Lou Harris; c/Carter Edward; p/Arthur C Jr and Odessa Arnold Donegan (dec); ed/BSC Roosevelt 1954; MSIR; JD Howard Univ 1967; LLM Columbia Univ 1970; pa/Vis Prof of Bus Law, Ohio St Univ; Am Bar Assn; Fed Bar Assn; Wash Bar Assn; Chgo Bar Assn; Cook Co Bar Assn; cp/NAACP; Urban Leag; Alpha Phi Alpha; r/Unitarian; hon/Ford Fellow, Columbia Univ 1972; Nat Endowmt for Humanites, Yale Univ 1972.

D'ONOFRIO, JOHN FRANCIS oc/Music Educator; b/Nov 27, 1917; h/20 Brandon Ridge Dr NW, Atlanta, GA 30328; ba/Atlanta; m/Mary Ruth Whitmire; c/Joe, Glenda, Linda; p/(dec); ed/Grad w hons New England Conserv Music; mil/AUS 1944-46;

pa/Tchr: Piano, Theory, Harmony, Group Theory, Group Piano, Pre-sch Music Instrn; Atlanta Music Tchrs; Ga Music Tchrs Nat Assn; Adjudicator NGPT; Guild Tchr, Progressive Series Piano Lessons; Pro-Mozart Soc Atlanta; hon/Intl W/W Music; Personalities of S.

DONOVAN, MARGARET HENDERLITE oc/Piano Instructor; Pianist; b/May 6, 1925; h/1872 Reichert Ave, Sauk Village, IL 60411; ba/Park Forest, IL; m/Russell John; c/Russell Jr, Peter, Rachel, Margaret, Tammy; p/Peter Baxter Henderlite (dec); Jessie Newton Henderlite, Walnut Creek, CA; ed/AA; BM w highest hons; MM; Doct Study; pa/Adjudicator, Nat Guild Piano Tchrs; Soc

Am Mus; Ill St Music Tchrs; Lakeview Musical Soc; Sigma Alpha Iota; r/Presb; hon/W/W Am Wom; W/W Musicians; Intl W/W Commun Ser; Intl W/W Music & Music Dictionary; DIB; S'ship 'T' Awd, Tarleton St Univ; Sigma Alpha Iota Dist'd Grad; Hahstaedt Gold Medal Piano Awd.

DONOVAN, ROBERTA MARIE oc/-Freelance Writer; Photographer; b/Sept 4, 1921; h/Box 519, Lewistown, Montona 59457; ba/Lewistown; c/James E, Robert I, Patricia Ann Wilbur, Mary Ruth Murchie, Joyce, Jeanne; p/Ike Messier (dec); Ruth Messier, Lewistown, MT; pa/Correspondent: *Billings Gazette*, *Great Falls Tribune*; Editor, *Lewistown News-Argus* 12 yrs; Stringer, Assoc'd Press; Writer: *Denver Post*, *Grit*, Other Nat & Reg Pubs; r/Meth; hon/Author: *Ike--Boy of the Breaks*, *Mystery Stalks the Prairie*; Mont Press Wom of Yr 1968; 100+ St & Nat Writing Awds.

DONZE LENA M oc/Teacher; Author; b/Aug 4, 1904; h/3521 Race, Ft Worth, TX 76111; ba/Ft Worth; m/Anthony J; p/Anthony and Susan Parker Maserang (dec); ed/BS; MS; pa/Ret'd Tchr; AAUW; Tex St

Tchrs Assn; Rejebian Book Review Clb; Birdville Ret'd Tchrs; cp/Pres's Clb; r/Rom Cath; St George Ch: Mem; hon/Hon Life Mem, Tex Cong PTA for Ser to Chd & Yth; Author: *Elizabeth's Children*.

DOORNBOS, ROY JR oc/Corporation Executive; b/Sept 14, 1926; h/5136 Truemper Way #6, Ft Wayne, IN 46815; ba/Huntington, IN; m/Gayle J Scott; p/Roy Sr and Johanna Doornbos, Comstock Park, MI; ed/BS Ctl Mich Univ; MA, EdD Univ No Colo; pa/Pres,

Recreation Mgmt Corp; Life Mem, AAHPER; Leg Com, IAHPER; Nat Parks & Rec Assn; Pres, Mich Jr Col Ath Assns; Reg 21 Dist Chm, NAIA; cp/Bd Dirs: Limberlost GSA Coun, Rotary Intl; r/Christ's Ch at Georgetown; hon/Carlson Awd; S'ships; Toastmaster of Yr, Flint, Mich 1963; Kappa Delta Pi; Phi Delta Kappa; Phi Epsilon Kappa.

DOPICO, ELVIRA MARTA oc/Educational Administrator; b/Oct 20, 1923; h/1400 SW 90 Ave, Miami, FL 33174; ba/Miami; p/J Claudio Dopico (dec); Marcelina Dopico, Miami, FL; ed/MS Barry Col 1969; pa/Area Supt, S Area Dade Co Public Schs; Delta Kappa Gamma; Kappa Delta Pi; Nat Adv Bd, Sonrisas Biling TV Prog; KLAN, Austin, Tex; cp/Treas, U Fam & Chd's Sers; Exec Bd: BSA of S Fla, Cuban Mus Arts & Cult; Fam Sers Assn Am; r/Rom Cath; hon/Lincoln Marti Awd, Dept HEW 1971; Premio Juan J Remos 1973; Premio Jose de la Luz Caballero 1978; Others.

DORE, MARY D oc/Administrator; b/-Jan 16, 1933; h/2472-J Chartres Dr, Gastonia, NC 28052; ba/Charlotte; p/William Daniel Dore, FL; ed/BA 196, MEd 1972, PhD 1974 Univ NC-Chapel Hill; pa/Dir & Incorporator, Mary Dore Ctr for Human Potential Inc 1978–; Sacred Heart Col: Asst Prof of Psychol 1975-78, Dir & Fdr Inst for Study of Exceptl Chd & Adults 1975-78, Dir Cnslg & Human Relats & Asst Prof in Charge of Prog Planning 1974-75; Former Elem & HS Tchr; Conslt: Gaston Co Juv Ct 1975-78, Gaston Co Public Sch Sys 1975-76, Charlotte Diocese Parochial Schs 1975–, NC St Dept Voc Rehab 1975–; Assn for Humanistic Ed & Devel; Am Rehab Cnslrs Assn; Charter Mem, Assn for Specialists in Group Wk; NC Pers & Guid Assn; Nat Assn Sch Psychologists; NC Psychol Assn; Others; hon/W/W S&SW; Profl Pubs.

DORFF, MARCELLA ADABELLE oc/-Missionary; b/Mar 14, 1923; h/1445 Boonville Ave, Springfield, MO 65802; ba/Salatiga, JaTeng, Indonesia; p/Walter Dorff, Detroit Lakes, MN; ed/BA N Ctl Bible Col; MA Grad Sch Assemblies of God; pa/Fdr & Dir, Bible Sch, Java, Indonesia; Tchr 1953–; r/Assemblies of God: Missionary.

DORGAN, BYRON LESLIE oc/State Tax Commissioner; b/May 14, 1942; h/224 Apollo Ave, Bismarck, ND 58501; ba/Bismarck; m/Judy; c/Scott, Shelly, Nathan; p/Emmett and Dorothy Dorgan, Bismarck, ND; ed/MBA; BS; pa/Chm, Gov's Comm on

Commercial Air Transport; St Bd Equalization; Chm, Multistate Tax Comm 1972-74; Pres, MW Assn Tax Admrs 1970; Exec Com, Nat Assn Tax Admrs 1972-75; pa/Elected St Tax Commr 1972, Re-elected 1976; Dem Cand, US Ho of Reps 1974; hon/ND Nat Ldrship Awd Excell.

DORIAN, HARRY A oc/Banker; Attorney; b/Jan 3, 1928; h/18 Meredith Rd, Green Hill Farms, PA 19151; ba/Philadelphia; m/Alice; c/Harry Jr, Stephen, Paul, James, Alexia; p/Bernard and Violet Dorian, Philadelphia, PA; ed/BA Penn St Univ; MBA NY Univ; JD Syracuse Univ Law Col; mil/AUS; pa/Am Bar Assn; Am Bankers Assn; Pa Bankers Assn; Phila Lwyrs Clb;

cp/Knights of Vartan; Order of Ahepa; Bd Trustees, Pierce; r/Prot; hon/Man of Yr, Ararat Square Clb; CTF Merit, Order of Ahepa.

DORNETTE, RALPH MEREDITH oc/Professor; b/Aug 31, 1927; h/5642 Jessup Rd, Cincinnati, OH 45239; ba/Cincinnati; m/Betty Jean Pierce; c/Cynthia Anne; p/Paul A and Lillian B Dornette (dec); ed/AB Cinc Bible Col; MA, MDiv Cand Cinc Christian

Sem; pa/Prof of Christian Mins, Cinc Bible Col; Devel Ofcr, Cinc Bible Sem; VP, NAm Christian Conv 1972; r/Christian; hon/Churchman of Yr Awd, Pacific Christian Col 1975; Author 3 Books.

DOROUGH, VERA LEONA "LE" oc/Registered Nurse; b/Nov 24, 1932; h/719 18th Ave E, Cordele, GA 31015; ba/Cordele; m/Kermit Sanders; c/Karen Leigh, Kathryn Lynn, Kermit Sanders Jr, Joseph Lawton;

p/Joseph Preston and Martha Holloway Coleman, Rochelle, GA; ed/RN; pa/Reg'd Nurse, Crisp Co HS; Instr: EMT, CPR, 1st Aid; cp/Bd Dirs: Crisp Co Chapt Am Cancer Soc, Ga Lung Assn; cp/Past Mem Jaycees; Vol: Ga Chapt Am Heart Assn, ARC; BPW Clb; r/Penia Bapt Ch; r/Wom of Achmt, BPW Clb 1978.

DOROUGH, VIRGINIA ANN oc/Programmer; Analyst; b/Dec 26, 1930; h/2140 Shadybrook Ln, Birmingham, AL 35226; ba/Birmingham; p/Joe S and Gladyce W Dorough, Shadybrook Ln, Birmingham, AL; ed/BS Univ Ala 1952; Sch of Bkg of S, La St Univ; Am Inst Bkg; Ga St Univ; pa/Programmer-Analyst, Ctl Computer Sers Inc 1978–; Sys Mgr, 1st Ala Bancshares 1977-78; 1st Ala Bk, B'ham: Sys Mgr 1975-76, Asst Cashier 1969-70, Sys Analyst 1967-75, Programmer 1965-67; Other Past Positions; Nat Assn Bank Wom; Am Inst Bkg; Assn Computing Machinery; Data Processing Mgmt Assn; Past Pres, Am Soc Wom Accts;

Past Pres, Mtn Brook BPW Clb; Spkr; cp/Bluff Park OES; AAUW; Soroptimist Intl, B'ham; Past Pres Xi Upsilon Chapt, Beta Sigma Phi; Smithsonian Assoc; Arlington Hist Assn; Freedoms Foun; B'ham Mus Art; hon/Bausch & Lomb Hon Sci Awd; Dist V Ofcl Fam Awd, Am Inst Bkg 1967; So Reg S'ship, Nat Assn Bk Wom 1970; W/W: Computers & Data Processing, Am Wom, S&SW; Personalities of S; Ala's Dist'd; World W/W Wom; DIB; Nat Reg Prominent Ams; Nat Social Dir; Commun Ldrs & Noteworthy Ams; Others.

DORSEY, HAROLD WINSTON oc/Minister; b/Dec 31, 1916; h/2400 Forest Ave, Ashland, KY; m/Irene Cochran; c/Edwin Cochran (dec); p/Earl V Dorsey, Shelbyville, KY; Angie Hancock (dec); ed/AB Ky Wesleyan 1938; h/MTh Candler Sch Theol Emory Univ; pa/Pastor & Dist Supt, Ky Annual Conf; cp/Kiwanis 27 yrs; ARC; r/U Meth; hon/Hon DD Ky Wesleyan; Ky Col.

DORSEY, LOIS LEE oc/Florist; Funeral Directress; b/Sept 24, 1918; h/1602 Brighton Rd, Pittsburgh, PA 15212; ba/Pittsburgh; m/Frank; c/Leon Lee; p/Leon R and Roxlanie Martin Lee (dec); ed/Pgh Inst Mortuary Sci; Duff Bus Col; Duquesne Univ; pa/Florist, Lee's Floral Shop; Nat Secy, Nat Funeral Dirs & Morticians Assn; Iota Phi Lambda (Secy Pi Chapt); IPA; cp/Adv Coun: WQED TV; Pgh Better Bus Bur; NS C of C; Exec Wom's Coun Gtr Pgh; U Mtl Hlth Soc; Fund Dr Vol: Mar Dimes, Muscular Distrophy, Am Heart Assn, Jewish Nat Hosp, Am Cancer Soc, r/Bethel AME Ch: Trustee; hon/World W/W Wom; W/W Am Wom; Commun Ldrs & Noteworthy Ams; Cert of Merit, Shriners 1976; Cert Apprec, Imperial Ct Daugh of Isis 1978; Hon'd as Past Matron, Allies Chapt OESPHA 1976; Outstg Negro Wom from Imperial Daughs of Isis 1974; Others.

DORSEY, MICHAEL A oc/Assistant Professor; b/Jul 31, 1949; h/108 Cedar Ln, Starkville, MS 39759; ba/St University, MS; m/Susan L; c/Shea, Nicholas; p/D L and Betty Jane Dorsey, Rotunda W, FL; ed/BS En Ill Univ 1971; MA, MFA Bowling Green St Univ 1972, 1973; pa/Asst Prof of Art, Dept of Art, Miss St Univ; 80+ Intl, Nat & Reg Art Exhbns; r/Rom Cath; hon/10 Awds in Nat & Reg Juried Art Competitions.

DORWEILER, PAUL LAWRENCE oc/Writer; Photographer; b/Jan 11, 1934; h/4106 Woodbine Ln, Brooklyn Center, MN 55429; ba/Bklyn Ctr; m/Jean Carole; c/Kevin, Pamela, Lisa, Kimberly; p/Peter Dorweiler (dec); Dora Dorweiler; ed/BA Univ Minn; Mankato St Univ; NWn Inst; mil/USN 1951-56; pa/Writer's Wkshop; cp/Commun Emer Assistance Prog; r/Cath; hon/W/W; DIB; Nat Social Dir; St & Nat Awds for Pubs by Soc for Tech Communs.

DOSICK, WAYNE DAVID oc/Rabbi; b/Aug 6, 1947; h/6110 Travers Way, San Diego, CA 92122; ba/La Jolla, CA; m/Rona; p/Hyman and Roberta Dosick, San Diego, CA; ed/BA; BHL; MAHL; pa/Rabbi, Cong Beth El; Bd Dirs, U Jewish Fed SD; Bd Dirs, SD Bur Jewish Ed; Bd Dirs, Jewish Fam Ser; VP, San Diego Rabbinical Assn; r/Jewish; hon/Ldrship Awd, Univ Judaism 1976.

DOSTER, HAROLD CHARLES oc/College President; b/Mar 6, 1931; h/303 Wilshire Blvd, Wilson, NC 27893; ba/Wilson; m/June Carolyn Marken; c/Deborah Renee, Diana Christine, Donald Marken, Denise Elizabeth; p/Donald Doster (dec); Mary Smith Doster, Ashland, OH; ed/AB Bethany Col; BD Yale Univ; MA, PhD Univ Mich; pa/Pres, Atlantic Christian Col; Higher Ed Bds in Mo; N Ctl Accrediting Assn; Ch Gen Bd & Reg; cp/Kiwanis; Rotary; BSA Coun; r/Disciples of Christ: Ordained Min; hon/Alumni Achmt Awd in Ed, Bethany Col 1973; Biogl Listings.

DOTTERER, RICHARD ALLEN oc/Playwright; Director; Educator; b/Dec 27, 1945; h/1508 Marie Terr, Arlington, TX 76010; ba/Arlington; p/T Kenneth and Roberta

Smith Dotterer; ed/BA Tex Christian Univ 1966; MFA Univ Okla 1968; Sec'dy Cert Univ Tex-Arlington 1973; pa/Freelance Writer & Playwright 1966-; Play Dir & Opera Stager 1968-; Sec'dy Sch Tchr 1974-; Dramatics Instr, Arlington YWCA 1968-69; Columnist, *Arlington Daily News* 1969; Dir, Producers Theatre Co 1974-77; Dramaticists Guild Am; Authors Leag Am; Alpha Psi Omega; ANTA; Dir, SW Theatre Conf Playwrights Proj 1972-74; r/Meth; hon/Commun Ldrs & Noteworthy Ams; Personalites of S; Book of Hon; Intl Men Achmt; Var Writing Awds.

DOUGHERTY, WILLIAM HOWARD JR oc/Banker; b/Dec 23, 1930; h/3801 River Ridge Rd, Charlotte, NC 28211; ba/Charlotte; m/Audrey Snider; c/Deborah Jean, David William, Kathy Louise; p/William Howard and Mary Stencil Dougherty, McKeesport, PA; ed/BBA cum laude Univ Pgh 1952; mil/USAF, 1952-54, Lt; pa/NC Nat Bk Corp: Pres 1974-, VChm 1973-, Exec VP 1968-74, Sr VP 1967-68; Dir: NCNB Corp, NC Nat Bk,

NCNB Mortgage Corp, NCNC Mortgage S Inc, TranSouth Fin Corp, Coca-Cola Bottling Com Consol; Pres & Dir: NCNB Properties Inc, NCNB Plaza Charlotte Inc; Bd Trustees, Tri-S Mortgage Investors; Assn Resv City Bkrs; Fin Execs Inst; Am Inst Cert'd Public Accts; Dir, Assn Bk Holding Cos; Trustee, Fin Acct'g Foun; cp/Trustee: Pfeiffer Col, Johnson C Smith Univ; Chm Bd Trustees, Carmel Acad; NC Natural & Economic Resources Bd; Dir: Mercy Hosp, Univ Res Park, Carmel CC, Charlotte Ath Clb; Chm, U Way Campaign 1979; r/Myers Park Presb Ch.

DOUGLAS, BARTON THRASHER oc/Attorney-at-Law; b/Mar 23, 1908; h/PO Drawer 1228, Gainesville, FL 32602; ba/Gainesville; m/Monica K; c/Barton A J; Zach H II, Alexander S II, Monica K; p/James B and Rebecca Isabelle Douglas (dec); ed/LLB, JD Univ Fla; mil/USNR, Lt Cmdr (Ret'd); pa/Ret'd Atty; Am Bar; FlaBar; 8th Judicial Bar (Past Pres); Tex Bar; Am Judic Soc; Acad Law & Sci; Fed Bar; Matrimonial Lwyrs.

DOUGLAS, DEANNA MAE oc/Assistant Professor; b/Jul 20, 1949; h/326 Critz, Starkville, MS 39759; ba/Miss St Univ, MS; p/Allison A and Elouise Douglas, Gulfport, MS; ed/BFA Univ So Miss; MFA Univ Miss; pa/Asst Prof of Art, Miss St Univ; 18 Nat/Intl Juried Art Exhbns; cp/Phi Kappa Phi; hon/W/W S&SW; World W/W Wom Edrs; Outstg Yg Wom Am.

DOUGLAS, WILLIAM RICHARD oc/Biomedical Consultant; b/Dec 16, 1914; h/PO Box 7, Bronx, NY 10451; ba/NY, NY;

c/Cheri, Yvonne, Marilyn, Mia, Katherine; p/(dec); ed/PhD; MSc; CP(UK); mil/AUS 1941-45, Warrant Ofcr; pa/Clin Chemist; Sr Res Scist; Fellow, Aerospace Med Assn; Intl Mem, Com on Space Res; cp/Sustaining Mem, Am-Scandinavian Foun; r/Unitarian-Universalist; hon/Fellow, Am Inst Chems.

DOUGLASS, KATHERINE MOONEY oc/Librarian; b/Aug 26, 1910; h/2011 Bryant Ave, Colorado Springs, CO; m/Harold Eugene; c/Gregory Charles France and Marie Kidd Mooney (dec); ed/BS Ind Univ 1934; BLS Univ Ky 1948; NDEA Inst Libns Univ Denver 1966; pa/Libn: Holmes Jr HS, Ill St Water Survey, Urbana, Ill, Post Libn, Ft Knox, Ky, Indpls Public Lib, LA Public Lib, US Naval Air Sta, Corpus Christi, Tex, Evansville Ordnance Plant, Evansville, Ind; Libn-Tchr, Madison Twp Sch, Mishawaka, Ind; Tchr, Shawswick Consol Sch, Bedford, Ind; Am Lib Assn; Colo Sprgs Lib Assn; NEA; AARP Chd's Reading Round Table; Beta Phi Mu; AAUW; Colo Ret'd Tchrs Assn; Colo Sprgs Ret'd Tchrs Assn; cp/Storytelling Day Participant, Patrick Henry Elem Sch 1978.

DOUGLASS, RICHARD BARY oc/Minister; b/Jan 19, 1936; h/Rt 2, Box 138, Okarche, OK 73762; ba/Oklahoma City, OK; m/Marilyn Sue Lacy; c/Brooks, Leslie; p/Charles and Myrtle Mae Douglass, Anadarko, OK; ed/BA magna cum laude Okla Bapt Univ 1958; BD SWn Bapt Theol Sem 1962; Univ Okla, Norman; SWn Bapt Theol Sem; pa/Min, Putnam City Bapt Ch; Bd Dirs, Bapt Gen Conv Okla; Pres, Ctl Okla Multi Media Assn Bd Mem, Okla City Christian Cnslg Ctr; cp/F'ship Christians in Arts; Bd Trustees, Okal Bapt Univ; Past Mem: Rotary, Kiwanis, Okla City Jaycees; Gov's Com on Employmt of Handicapped; IPA; Nat Ho Reps Com on Appts to W Point Acad; Chaplain, Mayor's Com on Employmt of Handicapped, Okla City; r/So Bapt; hon/8 Awds, Freedoms Foun; Outstg Yg Men Am; Men Achmt; DIB; W/W Rel; Profl Pubs.

DOW, MARGUERITE RUTH oc/Professor; b/Jun 13, 1926; h/1231 Richmond St, Apt 909, London, Ontario N6A 3L9, Canada; ba/London; p/Gordon Russell and Beatrice Bott Dow (dec); ed/BA 1949, BEd 1971, MA 1970 Univ Toronto; pa/Fac of Ed, Univ Wn Ontario: Prof of English & Drama 1972-, Assoc Prof 1965-72; Tchr, Ontario HSs

1950-65 (Hd English Dept, Laurentian HS, Ottawa 1959-65); cp/Bd Govs, Theater Foun, Ottawa 1961; r/Bapt; hon/Profl Pubs; IBA; Life Fellow, Life Patron; Life Fellow, Intl Inst Commun Ser; Fellow, World Acad, New Zealand; Life Mem, U Empire Loyalists' Assn, Canada; DIB; Intl W/W Commun Ser; Fdr-Fellow Silver Medal, Intl Inst Commun Ser 1975; Fellow, ABI.

DOWELL, MARY RUTH oc/Educational Administrator; b/Jan 2, 1932; h/219 Bailey, Dumas, TX 79029; ba/Dumas; m/Chester; c/Tracie Ann, Chester Barry, Amy Jan, Jamie Lu; p/Wilbur C Hill (dec); Ruth Hill, Canyon, TX; ed/BS; MEd; pa/Cnslr, Dumas Jr HS; CTA (Prog Chm & Secy, Local Chapt); TSTA (Secy, Local Chapt); NEA; ACLD; CEC; TPGA; cp/C of C; r/Meth.

DOWLER, JAMES ROSS oc/Company Executive; b/Apr 19, 1925; h/3303 Riverlawn

Dr, Kingwood, TX 77339; ba/Houston, TX; m/Helen Jean Ernst; c/Ross Matthew; p/Emery Ross Dowler (dec); Ethel Burroughs Dowler, Champaign, IL; ed/BS, MS Univ Ill; mil/USAAC 1934-45; USAF 1951-53, Maj; pa/Advtg & Promotion Mgr, Shell Chem Co; hon/Author: *Partner's Choice, Fiddlefoot Fugitive, Laredo Lawman, Copperhead Colonel*; r/Meth.

DOWNING, THOMAS NELMS oc/Attorney; Former Congressman; b/Feb 1, 1919; h/Newport News, VA; m/Virginia Dickerson Martin; c/Susan Nelms, Samuel Dickerson Martin; p/Samuel Downing (dec); Mrs Joseph Phillips, Hampton, VA; ed/BS, MS Univ Ill; LLB Univ Va; mil/AUS WW II; pa/Mem Law Firm, Bateman, Downing, Redding & Conway, Newport News; Former Pract'g Atty w Firm of Downing, Andrews & Durden;

Former Subst Judge, Munic Ct, Warwick; Am Bar Assn; Newport News Bar Assn; Va St Bar Assn; cp/US Ho of Reps: Elected 1958, Mem 87th-95th Congs, Var Com Assignments; Bd Dirs: C & P Telephone Co, Atlantic Permanent Savings & Loan Assn, 1st & Merchants Nat Bk of the Peninsula; Nat Dem Clb; Resv Ofcrs Assn; Warwick Moose Assn; VFW; Univ Va Alumni Assn; Va Mil Inst Alumni Assn; Assn AUS; Others; hon/LLD Col William & Mary; Silver Star; 5 Battle Stars; Hon Mem: AHEPA, Ft Eustis Ofcr's Open Mess, Propeller Clb US.

DOYLE, BRIAN BOWLES oc/Physician; b/May 20, 1941; h/4419 N Vacation Ln, Arlington, VA 22207; ba/Rockville, MD; m/Margaret Ready; c/Mairin McCready; p/Joseph Bernard and Margaret Kelley Doyle, Boston, MA; ed/BA; MD; mil/AUS, Maj; pa/Clinician; Administrator; Tchr; Writer; Editor; r/Cath.

DRAGONETTE, JESSICA oc/Soprano; Radio & Television Star; Recording Artist; Author; h/350 E 57th St, NY, NY 10022; m/Nicholas Meredith Turner; pa/Pioneered in Radio, 1st 1-Act Plays, Shakespeare, Others; Star, Radio's 1st Singing-Acting Thriller Series *Vivian, the Coca Cola Girl*; Wkly 1-hour Nat Concert Tours, Cities Service Hour, 7 yrs; 1st Intl Broadcast, *Hello Germany*; *Farewell to Amelia Earhart* Broadcast; 1st Artist Ever

Televised in US; Star, 1st TV Commercials; Films Appearances: *Gulliver's Travels, Big Broadcast of 1936*; hon/Ribbon of Order Isabella the Cath, Spain; Lady, Grand Cross; Equestrian Order, Holy Sepulchre of Jerusalem; Princess Signing Bird of Crow Tribe Indians; Pro Ecclesia et Pontifico Medal, Pope Pius XII; Hon Col, USAF; Voted Star of Stars in Nat Radio Polls for 8 Consecutive Yrs; Author; *Your Voice and You, Faith is a Song*;

Recorded Album: *With Love, Jessica Dragonette* 1977; W/W Am; World W/W Wom.

DRAGSTEDT, CARL ALBERT JR oc/Teacher; Coach; Sportswriter; b/Apr 21, 1921; h/1422 Gibson Dr, Orlando, FL 32809; ba/Orlando; m/Louise Graham; c/Marsha L Ferguson, Carl A III, Laurel M Kimrey, Graham L, Leslie C Hansen, Dana S, Carla J; p/Carl A Dragstedt, Park Ridge, IL; Ethel J Dragstedt (dec); ed/BA Univ Chgo; BS w high hons Univ Md; MA Rollins Col; mil/AUS, Maj (ret'd); pa/HS Tchr; Coach; Sportswriter; Instr, Fla So Col; NEA; Assn Former Intelligence Ofcrs; Nat CIC Assn; cp/Repub; r/Pinecastle U Meth Ch: Mem, Past Bd Mem; hon/Outstg Sportswriter, Fla Ath Coaches Assn; Outstg Sportswriter, Col Swim Coaches Assn.

DRAKE, JOSEPHINE ELEANOR oc/- Accounting Technician; Author; b/Jul 20, 1931; h/PO Box 115, Andover, NJ 07821; m/Paul E; c/Paul Edmund, Judith Ann, Patricia Ann, Robert Edmund; p/John Hall Stickle (dec); Bertha Ellen Messler Stickle, Andover; ed/Certs: Dover Bus Col 1967, Pa St Univ, Rutgers Univ, Eng-Lang Inst Am; Addit Studies; pa/Originator & Owner Jo's Book Ser 1973- (Pubs Own Manuscripts); Cert'd Pesticide Applicators, NJ Dept Envir

Protection; Author Manuscripts & Poetry incl'g: *Autobiography of Josephine E Drake, The Trail of No Return, My Love of the Woods, Genealogy of John B Drake, Love Speaks* (Volume of Poetry), *Evolution, What's Your Choice?* (Record), "Sleep My Baby" (Poem), Others; ASCAP; IPA; World Assoc Mem Nat Wildlife Fdn; Nat Writers Clb; cp/Am Legion Aux Unit #86; NJ Turfgrass Assn; Sussex Co Soil Conservation Dist; No Hills Organic Gardening Clb; Garden St Hort Soc; Sussex Co Assn Retard Citizens; hon/S'ship, Home Ecs Ext Adv Coun Rutgers Univ; ORTHO, Chevron Chem Co; Biogl Listings.

DRAPEAU, JEAN oc/Mayor; Lawyer; b/Feb 18, 1916; ba/Ville De Montreal, Montreal H2Y 1C6 Canada; m/Married; c/3 Sons; ed/Arts Deg Univ Montreal 1938; Att'd Fac of Law Univ Montreal 1938-41; pa/Admitted to Pract Montreal Bar 1943; Pract Law Crim & Civil Cts; Appt'd to Queen's Counsel 1961; Public Prosecutor 1950; Hon Mem ABA, Other Intl & Nat Orgs; cp/Mayor Montreal 1957-60, 1962-; Fdr Montreal Civic Party 1960; hon/Hon Degs: Univ Moncton, Univ Montreal, McGill Univ, Sir George Williams Univ, Laval Univ, Boswell Inst Loyola Univ-New Orleans; Gold Medal, Royal Arch Inst Canada; Created Companion of Order of Canada; Sr Canadian Rep at Intl Bur of Exhbns (Paris); Others.

DRAPER, CECIL NORMAN oc/Administrative Officer; b/Oct 30, 1922; h/502 Ivy Cir, Alexandria, VA 22302; ba/Washington, DC; m/Ellaree Cox; c/Ronald J, Dennis C, Robert W, Norma Jean; p/Cecil N Draper (dec); Helen Pulman Zeller, Alexandria; ed/BS Am Univ 1951; Att'd Indust Col Armed Forces 1957; mil/USN Med Corpsman WWII; pa/Adm Ofcr NASA Hdqtrs, Ofc Space Tracking & Data Systems; Former Exec Bd Mem Wash Chapt Soc for Advmt of Mgmt; DC Fdn Musicians; cp/Va Cong P's & T's: St Treas, Budget Com Chm, St Bd Mgrs; VP:

Alexandria Fdn Civic Assns, Taylor Run Citizens Assn; Alexandria Hosp Corp; T C Williams High PTSA; Var Former Activs; r/1st Christian Ch, Alexandria: Deacon, Former Chm Min of Ed; hon/Alexandria Civitan Clb Citizenship Achmt Awd; NASA Hq Space-Ship Earth Awd for Civic Activs; Life Mbrship, St PTA.

DRAPER, HOWARD DENNIS SR oc/Retired Elementary School Principal; b/Oct 2, 1917; h/591-E Winding Creek, Fayetteville, NC 28305; m/Ethel T; c/Howard Dennis Jr; p/(dec); ed/BS, MA E Carolina Univ; pa/Ret'd Prin Oakdale Elem Sch, Spring Lake, NC; Pt-time Belk's (Cross Creek Mall), F'ville; NC Assn Edrs; NEA; AARP; NC Prin's Assn; r/Haymount U Meth Ch, F'ville: Mem, Adm Bd; hon/Plaque, Spring Lake C of C.

DRAPER, LINE BLOOM oc/Artist; Educator; b/Nov 15; h/3134 Lakeview Dr, Delray Bch, FL 33444; ba/Same; m/Glen C; c/Andre L Bloom; c/Leopold and Mathilde T Voisin (dec); ed/Ecole des Arts Decoratifs (Verviers, Belgium); Academie Royale des Beaux Arts (Tournai, Belgium); Bowling Green St Univ; Skowhegan Sch Art; Addit Studies; pa/Artist: Painter, Printmaker, Enamelist, Engrosser; One-Man Shows incl: McInnis Galleries 1970, Studio 100, Boca Raton, Fla 1978, Defiance Col (Wom's Art Comm) 1975, Toledo Edison Co Art Gallery 1975, Elliott Mus, Stuart, Fla 1977, Others;

Touring Exhbns incl: Spectrum Traveling Shows 1975, 77, Nat Painters in Casein Touring Exhbn 1969-73, Am Artist Assn Traveling Exhbn, Printmakers Nat Traveling Exhbn, Others; Am Watercolor Soc; Art Interests Inc; Charter Mem Intl Soc Artists; NWn Ohio Watercolor Soc; Intl Inst Toledo; Fdn Art Socs: Past VP, Rec'g Secy; Nat Leag Am Pen Wom Inc, Boca Raton; Toledo Artists' Clb: Past Pres, Life Mem; Toledo Mus Art; Toledo Wom's Art Leag; Zonta Delray Bch; Charter Mem Port Clinton Artists' Clb; Others; IPA; cp/Planned Parenthood; Audubon Soc; Samagama Clb Presidents; Toledo Orch Assn; St Vincent's Hosp Guild; Others; r/Unitarian; Pub'd Work; Rep'd in Pvt Collections incl'g: Univ Toledo, Intl Inst, Miami Chds Ctr, Toledo Hosp (Claxton Hall), Others; Var Awds, Toledo Mus Art; Hon Awd for Outstg Contbn to Art & Ser, Toledo Fdn Art Socs; Var Awds, Toledo Artists' Clb; Hon Mention, Schuss Mtn Nat Art Fest; Biogl Listings; Num Others.

DRAPER, MARIAN E oc/Teacher; h/RFD, Rowley, IA 52329; ba/Walker, IA; m/Gordon (dec); p/William H and Katie L K Gardner (dec); ed/BA; pa/Tchr Kgn, 1st & 2nd Grades Cono Christian Sch; Helped Start Tipton Christian Sch, Became 1st Tchr; Supv'd Pract Tchg Upper la Univ Student 1975; Others; r/Reformed Presb; hon/Outstg Ldrs in Elem Ed; Notable Ams; Personalities W&MW; DIB; Intl W/W Commun Ser.

DRAPER, MARJORIE F oc/Businesswoman; h/816 Keel St, Martinsville, VA 24112; ba/M'ville; m/Ralph D; p/F G and Nannie B Frost; ed/Att'd Patrick Henry Commun Col; pa/Employed at E I duPont; Am Bus Wom's Assn, M'ville Charter Chapt; cp/Rebecca Lodge; Pythians; r/Wesley U Meth Ch; hon/Wom of Yr, M'ville Charter Chapt ABWA.

DRAPER, THOMAS JOHN oc/Writer; b/Jul 30, 1928; h/2 E 82 St, New York, NY 10028; p/Thomas John and Maria Demmink Draper (dec); ed/BA Amherst Col; Certificat Sorbonne; MA Johns Hopkins Univ; mil/AUS Intell; pa/Playwright; Intl Ecs Editor Fed Resv Bk (NY) 1968-76; Assoc Editor *Columbia Jour World Bus* 1967-68; Other Edit Positions; Former Intl Economist; Contbr to: *The Yale Review, The NY Times, Editions de L'Herne*; 2 Plays Produced; cp/Fdr-Secy Neighborhood Assn to Preserve 5th Ave Houses; Dir Registry for Hlth Res; r/Christian; hon/Commun Ldrs & Noteworthy Ams; DIB.

DRENOSKY, LILLIAN F oc/Educator; b/Jul 14, 1918; h/32 Harbor Rd, Westport, CT 06880; ba/Norwalk, CT; m/William; c/William F; p/Harry and Anna C Friedgen (dec); ed/BS Col of New Rochelle 1940; MA Columbia Univ 1942; 6th Yr Dipl Univ Bridgeport 1972; pa/Dept Chm Norwalk HS;

Life Mem: NEA, CEA, CBEA; NTA: VP 1962-64, Rec'g Secy 1959-62; cp/Former Mem: Cen Cur & Instr Com, U Credit Union Supvy Com; Mem: Pract Arts Adv Coun, Adm Mgmt Soc; Others; r/Cath; hon/Cooperating Tchr Awd, Univ B'port; Outstg Ldr in Am Ed; Notable Ams; Commun Ldrs & Noteworthy Ams.

DRES, DEMETRIOS WILLIAM oc/- Psychotherapist; Psychology/Social Work Researcher; b/Sept 20, 1947; h/349 S Peck, LaGrange, IL 60525; ba/Chicago, IL; m/Maria Irene; p/William and Mary Dres; ed/BA Univ Ill 1970; MS George Williams Col 1976; MSW Univ Chgo 1977; pa/Therapy for Indiv; CPLES; Conslt to Social Ser Agys; Reschr Transcult Probs of Adaptation; Nat Assn Social Wkrs; Acad Cert'd Social Wkrs; hon/Awd of Recog for Acad Achmt, Ill Hellenic Profl Soc; Cert'd Social Work, St of Ill.

DREWRY, JOHN ELDRIDGE oc/Dean Emeritus; b/Jun 4, 1902; h/447 Highland Ave, Athens, GA 30606; ba/Athens; m/Miriam Thurmond; p/William and Verdi Harrell Drewry (dec); ed/AB; BJ; AM; pa/Henry W Grady Sch Jour, Univ Ga: Dean Emeritus 1969-, Dir & Dean 1940-69, Prof 1930-, Assoc Prof 1926-30, Adj Prof 1924-26, Instr 1922-24; Book Reviewer *Atlanta Constn* 1939-, Others; Var Other Newspaper Activs w: Athens *Banner-Herald*, Atlanta *Journal*, Assoc'd Press; Am Assn Tchrs Jour; Am Coun Ed Jour; Ga Ed Assn; Newcomen Soc; Coun on Res in Jour, AASDJ; Other Profl Activs; cp/Dem; Past Pres Rotary; Mem Clbs; r/1st Bapt Ch, Athens: Mem, Former Deacon; hon/Phi Beta

Kappa; Phi Kappa Phi; Sigma Delta Chi; Kappa Tau Alpha; Names to Dixie Bus Hall of Fame for Living; Dist'd Ser Awds: Univ Ga Alumni Soc, Ga Press Assn, Ga Assn Broadcasters; Pub'd Author; Biogl Listings.

DRIEVER, STEVEN LEIBY oc/Educator; b/Apr 27, 1947; h/4831 W 78th St, Prairie Village, KS 66208; ba/Kansas City, MO; m/Pat; c/Steven; p/Lawrence S and Frances L Driever, Upper Montclair, NJ; ed/BA w distn Univ Va 1969; MS NWn 1970; PhD Univ Ga 1977; mil/USMCR 1970-76, Capt; pa/Univ

Mo-KC: Asst Prof Geography, Dir Urban Affairs Prog; Assn Am Geographers; Mo Acad Scis; Conf Latin Am Geographers; Sigma Xi; r/Presb; hon/Phi Kappa Phi; Intl W/W Intells; Men of Achmt; Men & Wom Achmt; DIB; W/W Among Students in Am Univs & Cols.

DRINKWATER, ROBERT EDWARD oc/Executive; b/Dec 30, 1935; h/10 Brush Hill Rd, Smoke Rise, Kinnelon, NJ 07405; ba/New York City, NY; m/Clare Burns; c/Robert Edward Jr; p/George Adolph Drinkwater (dec); Clare C Drinkwater, Medford, MA; ed/BS NEn Univ; pa/VP Bide A Wee Homes, NYC 5 Yrs; r/Repub; Chm En Reg Bd Am Humane Assn; r/Epis.

DRISCOLL, MARY H MIGOTTI oc/-Operatic Singer; Homemaker; b/Dec 12, 1934; h/3271 Brittan Ave, San Carlos, CA 94070; c/Vivian, Valerie, Veronica; p/Walter Migotti

(dec); Piery Migotti, Watsonville, CA; ed/BMus w Spec Sec'dy Credential; pa/-Concerts SF Bay Area, Switzerland; r/Christian; hon/Num Music Awds; Pi Kappa Lambda; Mu Phi Epsilon.

DRISKELL, CLAUDE EVANS oc/Dentist; b/Jan 13, 1926; h/6727 S Bennett Ave, Chicago, IL 60649; ba/Chgo; m/Naomi; c/Isaiah, Ruth, Reginald, Elaine, Yvette

Michele; p/James E Driskell, Chgo; Helen Elizabeth Driskell; ed/BS; BSD; DDS; mil/AUS 1944-46; pa/Dental Nat Editor & Journalist; Dental Conslt Hlth Sers Chgo Bd of Ed; St Editor Lincoln Dental Soc Pub Jour; Adj Prof Chgo St Univ (Univ Without Walls); cp/VP Jackson Pk Highlands; r/Presb; hon/Nat Hon Soc; F'ship, Acad Gen Dentistry; 5 Nat & Local Dental Awds.

DRISKELL, HERMIONE MARIE oc/-Assistant Professor; b/Feb 16, 1922; h/804 McGuire, Monroe, LA 71203; ba/Ruston, LA; p/Herman Lamar and Emma McCoy Driskell, Monroe; ed/BA; MA; MS; pa/Asst Prof Tchr

Ed & Lib Sci, La Tech Univ; Profl & Civic Orgs; r/Bapt; hon/Nat S'ship, Kappa Kappa Iota; Hon Socs; Hon Mem, Angel Flight, O'Donnell Sqdrn, La Tech; Delta Kappa Gamma Intl.

DROWN, EUGENE ARDENT oc/Forest Management Specialist; b/Apr 25, 1915; h/5624 Bonniemae Way, Sacramento, CA 95824; ba/Sacramento; m/Florence Marian Munroe; c/Linda Harriet Oneto, Margaret Ruth; p/Frank A and Jessie K Drown, Randolph, VT; ed/BS Utah St Univ 1938; Postgrad Indust Col Armed Forces 1956-58; MS Command & Gen Staff Col 1961; mil/AUS 1941-45, Res Comm Ofcr, Lt Col Air Def Arty, SW Pacific; pa/Park Ranger Yosemite Nat Pk 1940-47; Forest Ranger US Forest Ser 1948-56; Forest Mgmt & Devel Specialist US Bur of Land Mgmt 1956-; Soc Am Foresters; Am Inst Biol Scists; Nat Soc Profl Engrs; cp/Former Commr, Troop Ldr BSA; Former First Aid Instr ARC; Mason; Shriner; r/Meth Ch: Mem 1930-, Cert'd Lay Spkr; hon/Lic'd Land Surveyor & Profl Engr, Res & Devel Coor US Army w Univ Cal-D 1961-66; Xi Sigma Pi; Phi Kappa Phi; Mil Decorations; Biogl Listings.

DRUMMOND, MALCOLM McALLISTER oc/Project Engineer; b/Sep 22, 1937; h/60 Marberth Dr, Henrietta, NY 14467; ba/Rochester, NY; m/Linda Jerome Banning; c/Heather Lynn; p/George James and Winifred Ethel Drummond, Middlesex, England; ed/BS w Hons City Univ (London, England) 1961; pa/Proj Engr, Sybron Corp, Taylor Instrument Co 1972-; Tech Rep, Tymshare Inc (Rochester) 1970-72; Sr Engr, Gen Dynamics (Rochester) 1966-70; British Fgn Ofc 1964-66; Royal Radar Establishment (England) 1961-64; Sr Mem, IEEE (Chm Rochester Sect 1979-80); Fdr & Past Chm Computer Soc, IEEE; Dir, Rochester Engrg Soc 1979-; Sr Mem, Instrument Soc of Am; AMA; IPA; Others; cp/Christian Sci Min, Veterans Adm Hosp (Canadaigua, NY); Repub Nat Com; Am Security Coun; Others; r/Christian Sci; hon/Pub'd Author; W/W Fin & Indust; 1st Prize for Best Speech, Dale Carnegie Course; Others.

DUBEY, SATYA DEVA oc/Statistical Scientist; Executive; b/Feb 10, 1930; h/7712 Groton Rd, Bethesda, MD 20034; ba/Rockville, MD; m/Joyce Lura Tubbs; c/Jay Dev, Dean Dev, Neal Narayan; p/Jagdish N and Sahodara D Dubey, Bihar, India; ed/BS w hons; PhD; pa/Chief Statistics Eval Br Bur of Drugs, US Dept HEW 1973-; Acting Dir Div Biometrics 1975-76; Assoc Prof Dept Indust Engrg & Opers Res NY Univ 1968-73; Other Former Positions; Dep VChm

NY Univ Chapt AAUP; Adv Bd Mem Biometric Soc ENAR 1974-76; Fdg Mem Indian Soc Theoretical & Applied Mechanics; Charter Mem Intl Assn Survey Statisticians; Sr Mem Am Inst Indust Engrs Inc; Am Soc Quality Control; Sigma Xi; Fellow: AAAS, Royal Statistics Soc; cp/Chm: Indian Dels to Mich St Univ UN, Ed Com Univ Howland Cooperative House; Mem 700 Intl Clb; r/Jesusian: Full Gospel Bus Men's F'ship Intl; Am Sci Affil; hon/Food & Drug Adm Commendable Ser Awd; Apprec Cert: Am Soc Quality Control, IEEE; Creativity Recog Awd, Intl Personality Res; Biogl Listings; Profl Pubs.

DU BOIS, WILLIAM L oc/Writer; Producer; Director; b/Aug 30, 1934; h/8738 Holloway Dr, West Hollywood, CA 90069; ba/Same; m/Lucia Luciani; p/Nellie Du Bois, White Plains, NY; ed/Masters Cand; mil/AUS, USMCR 1954-62; pa/Dir Photo US Labor Dept & Meta/4 Prodns 1977; Dir Play *The Stoop*, Writers Guild Theatre W, Beverly Hills, Cal; Actor Film *Boss's Son*, 1978; Robert Lawrence Prodns: Prodn Asst, Film Editor; Prodn Asst Talent Assocs; Prodn Asst Nat Screen Ser; Roger Wade Prodns: Assoc Prodr, Prodn Coor; Film Camerman Wardell Gaynor & Assocs; Camerman WPIX-TV Channel 11; Other Former Positions; Mem Nat Small Bus Assn 1977; cp/Former Mem Town Hall Cal; Watts Tng Ctr: Original Fdr, Former Chm of Bd; r/Presb; hon/CINE Eagle Cert for Film; Intl W/W Commun Ser; W/W: W, Am; DIB.

DU BOSE, JERRY DAVIS oc/Assistant to US Representative; b/Mar 30, 1954; h/100 Folger St, Clemson, SC 29631; ba/Spartanburg, SC; p/Kelly J and Faye G DuBose, Clemson, SC; ed/BA Clemson Univ;

pa/Asst to US Rep Carroll A Campbell Jr; Mgr S'burg Co "Campbell for Cong" 1978; cp/Former Org Dir SC Repub Party; Other Former Repub Party Activs; r/Clemson 1st Bapt: Mem; hon/Outstg Yg Men Am; Personalities of S.

DU BROFF, DIANA D oc/Attorney; Columnist; Television Producer; b/Mar 4, 1909; h/12 W 72 St, New York, NY 10023; ba/Same; c/William, Elinor; ed/BS; LLB; pa/Law Pract (Fam & Supreme Cts St of NY); Assoc'd w Legal Aid Soc 4 Yrs; Admitted to Pract: Supreme Ct US, US Ct of Claims, US Dist Cts So & En Dists NY; Past Chperson Fam Law Com Bronx Wom's Bar Assn; NY St Trial Lwyrs Assn: Past Chperson Fam Law Com, Past CoChperson Matrimonial Ethics Com; Fam Law Com ABA; Matrimonial Panel Am Arbitration Assn; Diplomate Am Acad Matrimonial Lwyrs; Leg Sect Fam Law Com NY St Bar Assn; Am Judges Assn; Fed Bar Coun; Nat Assn Wom Lwyrs; Small Claims

Arbitrator; Alumni Dir Bklyn Law Sch; Writer Weekly Column "Let's Look at the Law"; Former Adj Prof Fam Law City Col; Pres & Fdr Nat Org to Insure Support Enforcemt; Inst for Pract Justice; Other Profl Activs; hon/Mem Am Soc Dist'd Persons; Profl Pubs; Biogl Listings.

DUBSKY, VACLAV PAUL oc/Travel Trade Executive; b/Jan 3, 1943; h/2618 NW 47 Terr, Fort Lauderdale, FL 33313; ba/Miami, FL; m/Zdenka; c/Michael V, Andrea Z; p/Vaclav and Francisca Dubsky, Carlsbad,

Czechoslovakia; ed/MBA Prague Sch Ecs 1965; pa/Travel Res; AIEST; cp/Fdr & Orgr Annual S Fla Travel Show, Miami; r/Prot; hon/Tourist Ofc Dir of Yr, Student Am Travel Awd Com 1973; Man of Yr, World Travel Awd Com NY 1974.

DUDLEY, GEORGE WILLIAM oc/Psychologist; b/Jul 18, 1943; h/1323 Iris Ln, Lewisville, TX 75067; ba/Dallas, TX; m/Carol Ann Lorenzen; c/Suzann Christine; p/(Foster) Lester A and Dorothy Boyd, Wrightstown, NJ; ed/BA Baylor Univ; MS N Tex St Univ;

mil/USMC; pa/Dir Field Testing & Res; SWn Psychol Assn; APGA; NVGA; AMEG; AMHCA; Inst for Adv'd Study in Rational Psychotherapy; Am Soc Tng & Devel; Assn Humanistic Psychologists; hon/DIB; Men of Achmt; Notable Ams; Personalities of S; W/W S&SW.

DUDLEY, GLENNA TOLBERT oc/Deputy Commissioner; b/Dec 3, 1944; h/115 McClellon Rd, Greenfield, IN 46140; ba/Indianapolis, IN; m/Mark M; p/Thomas G and Cassie L Tolbert, Tazewell, TN; ed/AB 1967; MA 1973; JD; pa/Dep Commr Ind Dept Revenue; Nat Assn Tax Admrs; Wom in Communs; cp/Hancock Unit Am Cancer Soc; G'field Co Clb Wom's Assn; IU Wom's Clb; Pres-elect Kappa Kappa Kappa; Fdg Mem Hoosier Heartland Theatre; r/Bradley U Meth Ch: Adm Bd; hon/Gov's Fellow; 1968 CASPER Awd; Spot News Awd, Ind News' Photogs Assn.

DUDLEY, WILLIAM M oc/Insurance Representative; b/Dec 24, 1921; h/3801 Sheringham Pl, Lynchburg, VA 24503; ba/L'burg; m/Elizabeth Leininger; c/E Jarrett D Henderson, Rebecca L D Godsey, James Forest, William L (dec); ed/BS Univ Va 1950; mil/USAAC 1942-45, 1/Lt; pa/Asst Reg Mgr Equitable Life Assurance Soc US, Sr Sales Conslt; Former Profl Ftball Player; Former Bd Mem Life Underwriters Assn; cp/L'burg Est Planning Coun; L'burg C of C; Past Chm Red Cross Campaign; Former Bd Mem: YMCA, Seven Hills Sch, Heart Assn, Cancer Soc, L'burg Scholastic Ftball Leag; Former Mem Ho

of Dels; Dir Automobile Clb Va; Chm St Va's Ath Comm; Bd Visitors Univ Va; Pres Nat Ftball Leag Alumni Assn; Others; r/1st Presb Ch: Mem, Deacon; hon/Recipient Awd, F'ship Christian Aths (Los Angeles, Cal); Life & Qualifying Mem, Million Dollar Round Table; Hon'd w Testimonial Dinner, L'burg C of C; "Sammy" Awd, Nat Sales Exec Clb; Elected to Var Halls of Fame; Others.

DUDLEY, WILLIE MARGURIE oc/- Teacher; b/Jul 7, 1925; h/361 Tompkins Ave, Brooklyn, NY 11216; ba/Bklyn; p/L J and Rozeina E McRae (dec); ed/BA Bklyn Col 1975; pa/Alpha Kappa Alpha; Bd Dirs Shirley Chilholm Day Care Ctr, Bklyn; cp/Vol Wkr Chd's Hosp, Belrose (Long Isl), NY; r/Siloam Presb Ch: Mem, Chancel Choir, Deaconess; hon/Tchr of Yr, Sardis Elem Sch, Sardis, Ga 1956.

DUERKSEN, MABLE VOGT oc/Teacher; Writer; Farmer; b/Jan 4, 1928; h/Box 147, Corn, OK 73024; ba/Corn; m/Vernon (dec); c/Sharon Ann, Timothy, John, Debbie; p/John C and Lena Esther Penner Vogt, Cordell, OK; ed/BA SWn Okla St Univ 1972; cp/Safety Chm Okla Ext Homemakers Coun; WCEHC: Former Public Info Chm, Former

Mem Hlth & Safety Com; Former Chm of Corn, Red Cross; Former Mem Town Bd (Corn); r/Mennonite Brethren Ch; hon/1st Place, Nat Safety Awd, Nat Ext Homemakers Coun; Cit of Meritorious Ser Awd in Safety, Nat Safety Coun.

DUFF, W JACK oc/Rancher; Legislator; b/Oct 22, 1913; h/Rt 1, Box 62, Adams, OR 97810; ba/Same; m/Ruth Thompson; c/F Duane, J Bart, James H; p/Frank and Nina Jean Jack Duff (dec); ed/Att'd Adcox Trade Sch; pa/Rancher; cp/St Rep, Dist 57; Law Enforcemt Coun; Var Agri Coms; Sch Bds (Local & St); r/Presb: Trustees, Session; hon/Outstg Citizen Awd, Pendleton, Oreg 1967.

DUFFEY, PAUL A oc/Minister; b/Dec 13, 1920; h/2252 Allendale Rd, Montgomery, AL 36111; ba/Montgomery; m/Louise C; c/Melanie Hutto (Mrs David J), Paul Jr; p/Geo Henderson and Julie M Duffey (dec); ed/AB; MDiv; DD; pa/U Meth Min; Pastor; Dist Supt; Mem Judic Coun, Var Bds; cp/U Way; YMCA; Commun Coun; r/U Meth; hon/DD, B'ham So Col.

DUGAN, CHARLES C oc/Physician; b/Jan 24, 1921; h/8696 Thousand Pines Cir, W Palm Beach, FL; ba/WPB; m/Ruth L; c/Charles II, Douglas, Dain, Timothy, Jay; p/Charles E Dugan; Wilhelmina Clark; ed/AA Wentworth Jr Col 1940; AB Cornell Univ 1942; MD Jefferson Med Col 1946; Var Other Studies; mil/USAF, Qualified Pilot, 1/Lt to Lt Col, Var Assignmts; pa/Pvt Pract Dermatology & Allergy, WPB 1959-; Conslt: Banyan Psychi Inst, Lake Worth, Fla, Bethesda Meml Hosp, Boynton Bch, Fla; Hosp Appoinmts: Palm Bch Gardens Commun Hosp, Palm Bch Gardens, Fla, Good Samaritan Hosp, WPB; Fellow: Am Acad Dermatol, Am Col Preven Med, Am Acad Allergy, Am Col Allergy, Assn Clin Immunology & Allergy; Assoc Fellow Aerospace Med Assn; AMA; Am Assn Cert'd Allergists; Fla Allergy Soc; Am Assn Dermatol Allergy & Immunol; S Ctl Dermatol Assn;

Num Other Profl Assns; cp/Var Alumni Assns; F&AM; Resv Ofcrs Assn; WPB C of C; Sigma Alpha Epsilon; Phi Theta Kappa; Sailfish Clb; Buyers & Sellers Assn; NW Bus Assn; Repub Clb Palm Bch; Nat Travel Clb; Am Angus Assn; WPB Sanction Bur; Others; hon/Profl Pubs; Num Biogl Listings.

DUGAN, CONSTANCE MARIE oc/Elementary Teacher; b/May 1, 1948; h/265 S Fellowship Rd, Maple Shade, NJ 08052; ba/Maple Shade; p/Arthur J and Iviline Davis Dugan, Maple Shade; ed/BA; Alliance Francaise Paris (Sum) 1974; Intl Sum Sch Trinity Col (Dublin, Ireland) 1975; Grad Study Glassboro St Col 1974-76; Addit Studies; pa/4th Grade Tchr OLPH Sch; Trenton Diocesan Report Card Com 1973-76; Vol Work Proj Commun Ctr, Cork, Ireland Sum 1974; cp/Former Mem Maple Shade Bicent Planning Com; r/Vol Rel Ed Tchr 1970-76; hon/Alpha Mu Gamma; Outstg Ldrs in Elem & Sec'dy Ed; Mem Leeds Univ Music Soc Chorus 1976-77; Intermediate Div Finalist Eng Country Dance Competition (Darlington, England); Semifinalist No Univs' Div Ballroom Dancing Competition, Leeds Univ; Del to Brit Nat Union of Students Easter Conf; Others.

DUGAN, MILDRED CLAIRE oc/Educator; Businesswoman; b/Sept 21, 1929; h/7158 Tamarack Rd, Fort Worth, TX 76116; ed/Hugh Dugan Jr (dec); Truman C (Stepfather) and Florine S Dugan Stubbs, Ft Worth; ed/BA Tex Christian Univ 1951; MD SWn Med Sch Univ Tex 1955; Postgrad Deg (Adolescent Med) Harvard Med Sch 1962; pa/N Tex Chapt Nat Cystic Fibrosis Res Foun: Med Advr 1972-75, Bd Mem 1973-75; Conslt Pediatrician Ft Worth Public Sch Bd Spec Ed 1968-70; CHAP Ofcr & Med Advr 1967-69; Com for Coor Chds' Activs Tarrant Co Med Soc 1972-73; USAF, Civil Ser, Carswell Hosp, Ft Worth 1956-59, 1962-73; Other Profl Activs; Diplomate Am Bd Pediatrics; Fellow: Am Acad Pediatrics, Tex Acad Pediatrics, Royal Soc Hlth (England), Pediatric Sect Pan Am Med Assn; Charter Mem Soc Adolescent Physicians; Am Med Wom's Assn; Med Wom's Intl Assn; Tex Assn Chd w LD; Am Public Hlth Assn; Am Sch Hlth Assn; Am, Tex, So Med Assns; Tex Public Hlth Assn; Tex Chapt Am Assn Physicians & Surgs; Others; cp/Nat Geographic Soc; Am Heritage Soc; IPA; Fed Bus Assn; Ft Worth Zool Soc; Am Mus Natural Hist; Var Alumni Assns; Others; r/Westbridge Bapt Ch: Charter Mem 1965, Orgr & Tchr Col & Career Class 1965-66; Others; hon/Spec Ser Awd, SAC, Carswell CHAP Work; SAC Lttr of Apprec; Num Biogl Listings; Profl Pubs.

DUIGNAN, PETER J oc/Curator; Director; Stanford, CA 94305; ba/Stanford; m/Frances; c/Kathleen, Patricia, Peter, Frances, Sheila, Rose; p/peter J and Delia C Duignan, San Francisco, CA; ed/BS cum laude; MA; PhD; mil/AUS S Pacific Theater 1944-46; pa/Hoover Instn, Stanford Univ: Dir Med E Res Prog 1977-, Curator Mid E Collection 1977-, Sr Fellow Hoover Instn 1968-, Stella W & Ira S Lillick Endowed Curatorship 1968-, Curator Africana 1966-, Others; African Studies Assn: Bd Dirs 1965-68, Lib & Archives Com 1960-64, Policy & Plans Com 1963-66; Am Hist Assn; Assn Res Libs 1965-; r/Cath; hon/Recipient F'ships & Grants; Num Profl Pubs.

DUKES, DOROTHY oc/Beautician; b/Jan 24, 1926; h/4181 Burns, Detroit, MI 48214; ba/Detroit; m/Leonard; c/Charlie Mae Johnson. Lauretta; p/Charlie Dixon (dec);

Elizabeth Jackson (dec); ed/Tchr Cert Detroit Bible Col; cp/Wom's Conf of Concern; r/SW Mich Ch of God in Christ Evang; hon/Wom of Yr, Mich Chronicle Ch 1973.

DUKES, LAURETTA oc/Student; b/Jul 10, 1960; h/4181 Burns, Detroit, MI 48214; c/Ann Michelle; p/Leonard and Dorothy Dukes, Detroit; ed/Att'd Wayne St Univ;

cp/Mich St Commun Choir; Yth Div Wom Conf of Concerns; r/Ch of God in Christ; hon/Miss Vnac 5 Queen, COGIC (Rep'g Intl SS Dept).

DULANEY, ALLENA FAYE oc/Income Tax Consultant; b/Feb 14, 1934; h/RD #3, Box 334, Moundsville, WV 26041; ba/M'ville; m/Glenn Duane (dec); c/Marirobin Arvell D

Riggle, Kevin Duane; p/Sanford Roy Yoho, Clewiston, FL; Audra Arvell F Yoho, Proctor, WV; cp/Marshall Co Dem Wom's Clb; M'ville C of C; r/Ch of Christ; Mem; hon/W/W S&SW.

DULANEY, ANNIE HARVEY oc/Retired Teacher; b/Apr 23, 1903; h/209 Birch, Gassaway, WV 26624; c/John Thorpton, Brian Hale; p/L T and Georgia H Harvey (dec); ed/AB WVa Wesleyan Col; pa/Ret'd Tchr Elem Schs, Tchr & Prin 31 Yrs; Ret'd Tchrs Assn, St & Nat; Ret'd Sch Employees Assn; cp/Elk Val Ext Homemakers; WVa Poetry Soc; Elk River Chapt DAR, Former Chaplain; Braxton Co Sr Citizens Assn; r/Gassaway Bapt Ch: Mem; hon/Author *Dandelions and Roses* (Book of Poetry), Hist Articles, Others; Var Prizes in Poetry Exhibits.

DULEEP, KODENDERA SUBBIAH

oc/General Surgeon; b/Mar 22, 1934; h/Brierwood Rd, Silvermine, Norwalk, CT 06850; ba/Westport, CT; m/Ganga; c/Anuradha, Arundathi, Annapurna; p/K B Subbiah (dec); Kitty Subbiah, Bangalore, India; ed/MB BS; pa/Fellow: Royal Col Surgs Edinburgh & Glasgow; DABS; Fairfield Co, Conn & Norwalk Med Socs; AMA; Conn Soc Am Bd Surgs; r/Hindu; hon/MacDonald Awd, Norwalk Hosp.

DULEY, ALVIN J oc/School Psychologist; b/Jan 12, 1916; h/75-5724 Alahou St, Kailua-Kona, HI 96740; ba/Kailua-Kona; p/Earl J Sr and Mary C Duley, Fond du Lac, WI; ed/BS Utah; MA Ariz; Grad Studies Univ Hi; pa/Hi Dist Trv Sch Psychol (K-12); Societe Canadienne De Psychologies, Exper & Applied

Divs; Hi Psychol Assns; APA; IRA; Nat Assn Gifted Child; Life Mem, GCRA; CRSC; cp/Univ Wis Alumni; Am Acad Polit & Social Scis; Hi-Y Ldrs F'ship; hon/Scouting Awds, Catalina Coun; Men of Achmt; DIB; IPR Awd; Personalities W&MW; W/W in W; Others.

DULISCH, MARY L oc/Veterinarian; b/-Jun 28, 1952; h/Lansing, MI; ba/E Lansing, MI 48824; p/A and L Dulisch; ed/AA; BS; DVM Univ Ill; pa/Veterinarian Veterinary Clin Ctr; Resident-Instr Veterinary Surg; Freelance Med Illustrator; r/Rom Cath, St John's Student Parish.

DUNAWAY, MARIO ALBERTO oc/-Teacher; b/May 28, 1951; h/10116 Kirwood, El Paso, TX 79924; ba/El Paso; c/Leah C, Katherine; p/Gordon L and Mary R

Dunaway, El Paso; ed/BS; pa/UTEP: Coach Boys Baseball, Asst Intramural Sports; Karate Instr; r/Cath; hon/Hon Mem, Govs Coun on EMS (NM); PBBS Awd in Curric, MIT & Biol Dept, UTEP.

DUNBAR, JAMES C oc/Doctor of Medicine; b/Nov 11, 1921; h/806 E 9th St, Mountain Home, AR 72653; ba/Mtn Home; p/Felton F and Eilleen L Dunbar, Mtn Home;

ed/MD; mil/USNR MC, Lt Cmdr, Ret'd; pa/Pvt Pract; Baxter Co, Ark & Am Med Assns; cp/Dem; r/1st Christian Ch; hon/W/W in Am; Men of Achmt.

DUNCAN, BERT LOGAN oc/Retired Minister; Student Contemporary Society; Essayist; b/Sept 12, 1913; h/2531 E 7th St, Bloomington, IN 47401; m/Edith Halsey; c/Beverly; p/Jonathan Marshall and Mary Elizabeth Logan Duncan (dec); ed/AB Wm Jewell Col 1936; ThM So Bapt Theol Sem 1939; Postgrad Study: Div Sch Univ Chgo, Ind Univ, Univ Va; mil/USNR 1943-46 Chaplain, PTO; pa/Min: 1st Congreg Ch Constantine, Mich 1958-62, Oak Park Congreg Ch Traverse City, Mich 1962-67, Brownhelm Congreg Ch Amherst, Ohio 1967-70, Orient Congreg Ch

Orient, LI, NY 1970-71; Local Min Assns: Radio Secy, Exec Coun; Cnslr or Dean Sum Yth Ch Camps 7 Yrs; Ednl Com Area Coun Chs, Traverse City; Lorain, Ohio Com Clergy & Laymen Concerned about Vietnam; Lorain Co Conf Rel & Soc; Wn Reserve Assn Ohio Task Force for Peace; Cleveland Area Peace Action Coun; cp/Num Civic Activs; Former Mem Steering Com Repubs & Dems United for Peace; r/1st Unitarian Ch, Louisville, Ky: Cont'g Ed Com, Active Sunday Morning Forums & Evening RAP Sessions, Currently Active in Prog in Ed Group & Wkshops; Unitarian-Universalist Ch of Bloomington, Ind; hon/IPA; Intercont Biog Assn; Sev Biog Listings.

DUNCAN, GERTRUDE I oc/Educator; b/Dec 4, 1896; h/4661 Plumosa Dr #69, Yorba Linda, CA 92686; m/Clarence B (dec); c/Jean Hollingsead (Mrs Robert A), Robert B; p/Burke Hamilton and Ariadne Hartley Samuels (dec); ed/BA Univ No Ia; MA

Columbia Univ; EdD Temple Univ; pa/Ret'd Edr; Tchr Ed Conslt 1970; Tchr Ed Advr Pa Dept Ed, Harrisburg, Pa 1960-70; Asst Prof & Supvr Wom's Activs Temple Univ, Philadelphia, Pa 1923-48; Other Former Positions; AAHPER; En Assn PE for Col Wom; AAUW, H'burg Br; Former Coms incl Ed, Col S'ship, Pa St Mass Media, Higher Ed, St Mass Med; Pa St Ed Assn, Exec Com; Am Acad Polit & Social Sci; IPA; Exec Bd AAUW, Placentia-Yorba Linda Br; Others; cp/Yorba Linda Sr Citizens Assn; Smithsonian Inst; Participant Orange Co Studies for Rapid Transit; Am Security Coun; Repub Party; Former Conslt Gov's Com on Ed (Pa); Other Former Activs; r/Garden Grove Commun Ch, Garden Grove, Cal; hon/Cert of Recog for 17½ Yrs Pa Ser; Cert of Apprec, Com for Survival of Free Cong; Fdr's Cert, Ctr for Intl Security Studies (Am Security Coun Ed Foun); Biogl Listings; Others.

DUNCAN, INEZ BOYD oc/Teacher; b/Aug 22, 1924; h/Rt 1, Box 1069, Orangeburg, SC 29115; ba/O'burg; m/Charles R; p/John H and Luvicer B Boyd (dec); ed/AB; MS; 40 Postgrad Hours; pa/Rdg Spec; ABE Tchr; SCEA Unified; Publicity Chm Edisto Rdg Coun; cp/Vol Var Campaigns & Drs: Beautification, Cancer, Heart; GSA; Voter-Registration Proj; r/Bapt: Ch Sch Tchr; hon/Num Certs for Scout'g Projs & VBS.

DUNCAN, VIRGINIA B oc/Administrative Manager; b/Jun 9, 1924; h/174 Harrison Ave, Sausalito, CA; m/Bruce G; c/John C, Michael G, Timothy B; p/Theodore and Maurine Bauer, Lansing, MI; ed/BA Univ Mich; pa/Adm Mgr Legal & Ins Dept Bechtel Group of Cos, San Francisco, CA 1976-; Prodr/Dir KQED 1961-74; Pres Candide Prodns Inc 1967-; Mem Media Panel Nat Endowmt for Art, Washington, DC 1973-; Bd

Dirs Corp for Public Broadcasting 1975-; Carnegie Comm on Future of Public Broadcasting 1977; cp/Bd Dirs/Trustees: Katharine Branson/Mt Tamalpais Sch, Yosemite Inst (Yosemite Nat Pk); Former Mem Bd Dirs/Trustees: Marin Co Day Sch, Town Sch for Boys (SF), Conard House, SF Conserv of Music, Others; hon/Screening at Am Film Fest *Ski Touring* 1972; Emmy Awd, Nat Acad TV Arts & Sci, SF Chapt 1971; CINE Golden Eagle Awd; Rdr's Digest Foun Awd; NET Awd for Excell Indiv Contbn to Outstg TV Programming; Biogl Listings; Others.

DUNCAN, WILLIAM A oc/Consultant; b/Apr 20, 1916; h/3366 E Date St, Brea, CA 92621; m/June; c/Geine Ensley, Jan Moores, Charles, Kathy Shelton, Cindi Heinecke;

p/William and Geine Fossett Duncan (dec); ed/Att'd Alex Hamilton; mil/US 6th Army WW-II; pa/Procurement Conslt; McDonnel Douglas Mgtmt Assn; cp/Repub Clb; Pres 39ers F'ship Clb; r/Yorba Linda U Meth Ch; hon/Dist'd Ser Awd, Los Angeles Sheriffs Dept; City Coun Commend, City of Brea; Man of Yr Awd 1948; Douglas Aircraft: Profl Perf Awd, Personal Achmt Awd; Pres Cit AUS; Num Biogl Listings.

DUNCAN, WILLIAM ADAM JR oc/Consultant; b/Apr 27, 1918; h/2239 Headland Dr, East Point, GA 30344; ba/Same; m/Edna Shaw; c/Robert, Malcom, Adam; p/W A Duncan, East Point, GA; Milner Sammons Duncan, Conyers, GA; ed/BA; BD; mil/AUS WW-II ETO; USAFR; pa/Conslt So Bapt Chs; Dir Assns Progs & Devel 24 Yrs; Pastor; Var Denom Positions; Assn Work Conf: VP, NC Dir; Pres & Fdr Triad Missions Conf NC Bapt Conv; cp/CAP; Greensboro Commun Coun; Conservative Caucus; 2nd Amend Foun; r/So Bapt; Ordained Min 1946; Missionary; hon/Lttrs Commend Cmdg Ofcrs; Interscholastic: SE Boxing Team, Lightweight Champion Jr Col Assn; 5 Mil Medals WW-II.

DUNCAN, WILLIAM NEIL oc/Associate Professor; b/Oct 14, 1932; h/1748 Westridge Dr, Hurst, TX 76053; ba/Fort Worth, TX; m/Anna Garrett; c/Susan Jewella, Andrew Neil; p/B E Duncan (dec); Mrs B E Duncan, Ft Worth; ed/BA David Lipscomb Col 1953; MA Geo Peabody Col for Tchrs 1954; EdD N Tex St Univ 1976; Addit Study; pa/Assoc Prof Eng Tex Wesleyan Col, Ft Worth; Pres Ft Worth Coun Tchrs Eng 1964-66; Tex Jt Com Dists X & XI: Pres 1970-71, Secy 1967-69, CoChm 1969-70; Former St Chm Tex Jt Eng Com for Sch & Col; AAUP, TWC Chapt: Pres 1971-72, Profl Ethics Chm 1969-70, VP 1970-71; Bd Dirs NCTE 1963-66; Sponsor Sigma Tau Delta, Tex Wesleyan Col 1968-; NEA; Tex Coun Tchrs Eng; Tex Eng Assn; Life Mem Tex Jt Eng Com for Sch & Col; S Ctl Col Eng Assn; CCCC; Col Conf Tchrs Eng; Phi Delta Kappa; Kappa Phi Kappa; Other Profl Activs; cp/Phi Chi Alpha; Former Chm UF, Tex Wesleyan Col; Former Judge Clb Projs, St Optimist Clbs; hon/Hon Admiral Tex Navy; Hon Life Mbrship, Tex Jt Com; So Recipient NDEA Inst in Eng, Boston Univ; Profl Pubs; Biogl Listings.

DUNHAM, DANIEL BENTLEY oc/Deputy US Commissioner; b/Apr 18, 1936; h/9457 Garnett Ln, Ellicott City, MD 21043; ba/Washington DC; m/Susan; c/Janice, Rebecca, David; p/Marshal G and Josephine Anne Dunham, Nampa, ID; ed/BS 1962, MS 1963, EdD 1970 Oreg St Univ; mil/Sr Chaplain's Asst 1959-60; pa/Dep US Commr Bur Occupl & Adult Ed, US Ofc of Ed, Dept HEW 1978-; Asst St Supt, St Dir Voc-Tech Ed, Md St Dept Ed; Oreg Dept Ed: Asst St Dir Career & Voc Ed, Coor Spec Occupl Progs, Career & Voc Ed; Other Profl Positions; Oreg Coun Voc Admrs, Org'g Pres 1966; Oreg Voc Assn, Pres 1970-71; Oreg Manpower Assn; NCLA; Am Voc Assn; Nat Conf RCU Dirs, Nat Secy-Treas 1972-73; Nat Assn Black Ams in Voc Ed; Nat Assn St Dirs Voc Ed, Leg Com; Others; Conslt; Nat Adv Com on Corrections Ed Curric Devel; Num Other Profl Activs; cp/Vol Instr Salem Commun Schs Prog; Girls City & Area Softball Leags; Coach Little Leag Baseball; "Tom Thumbs" Square Dance Clb, Ellicott City, Md; Ofcl St of Oreg Livestock & Horse Show Judge; Others; r/U Presb Ch: Ruling Elder, Mem & Chm Sev Ch Coms, Mem Nat Coun U Presb Men; hon/Profl Pubs.

DUNKEL, FRANK DONALD oc/Executive; b/Oct 20, 1927; h/25 Ethel Ct, Redwood City, CA 94061; ba/Foster City, CA; m/June C; c/Lisa K, Bradley D, Jill A; p/John Dunkel (dec); Theresa Dunkel, Chicago, IL; ed/PhB Univ Chgo 1948; Postgrad Studies: Univ Wis 1949, UCLA 1954-55; mil/AUS 1951-52, S/Sgt 24th Inf Div, Korea; pa/VP Purchasing Lyons Restaurant Inc (Consolidated Foods Corp); Dir Am Purchasing Soc 1977-78; Nat Assn Purch Mgmt 1977-78; cp/Former Chm LA JCs Yth Awds Com; r/Presb; hon/CPE Certn;

Exec Ldrshp Lab, UCLA.

DUNLAP, ESTELLE CECILIA DIGGS oc/Educator; Mathematician; b/Sept 26, 1912; h/719 Shepherd St NW, Washington, DC 20011; m/Lee A; c/Gladys D Kimbrough, Dolly D Sparkman; p/John F and Mary F Diggs (dec); ed/BS DC Tchrs Col 1937; MS Howard Univ 1940; pa/Instr & Hd Math Dept Garnet-Patterson Jr HS 1941-56; Math-Sci Instr MacFarland Jr HS 1956-72; Vis Lectr Math DC Tchrs Col; NCTM; Am Math Soc; VP Benjamin Banneker Maths Clb; AAAS;

Nat Def & Preparedness Assn; NEA; AAUW; Nat Ret'd Tchrs Assn; Other Assns; cp/Smithsonian Resident Assn; IPA; Nat Urban Leag; Fdg Mem Nat Hist Soc; Am Mus Natural Hist; Am Soc Dist'd Citizens; Adv Bd Am Security Coun; Charter Mem Repub Congl Clb; Nat Trust for Hist Preserv; Acad Polit Sci; Inst for Am Strategy; Nat Audubon Soc; Jacques Cousteau Soc; Salvation Army Assn; Am Film Inst; Nat Police & Firefighters Assn; Fdg Mem US Senatorial Clb; Num Others; r/Cath; hon/NSF F'ship; Cert of Awd: US Sch of Music, Lib Human Resources of Am Bicent Res Inst; Certs of Apprec: Superior Ct DC, US Dist Ct, Inst for Am Strategy; Cert of Merit, DIB; Contbr to *Talent* Mag; Others.

DUNLAP, JANE B oc/Communications Consultant; b/Jun 24, 1921; h/PO Box 834, Wilmington, OH 45187; ba/Kent, OH; m/James F; c/Laurel D-Miller; p/Carl M Boring (dec); Damaris Boring, Wilmington, OH; ed/BA NY Univ; MA, EdD Univ Akron; pa/Conslt: Cuyahoga Commun Col, Kent RE&D; AAUW; Am Assn Supvn & Curric Devel; Phi Delta Kappa; cp/Repub Party; LWV; r/Quaker; hon/Sev Profl Pubs; Reader of Paper, Canadian Ed Cong; Acad Hons.

DUNLAP, LYNN HAWKINS oc/Writer; b/May 20, 1940; h/1415 Emerald, Longview, TX; ba/Longview; b/Mary Ruth; c/Karen, Hawkins; p/W L and Margalrite Hawkins Dunlap, Lufkin, TX; ed/BA Univ Miss; pa/Writer Longview *News Jour*; Sigma Delta Chip; hon/Freedom of Info Awd, AP; Nom'd for Pulitzer.

DUNN, DOROTHY FAY oc/Educator, Administrator; h/504 E Chalmers, Champaign, IL 61820; ba/Chicago, IL; p/Lafayette and Jeannettie T Dunn (dec); ed/BS Univ Ill 1939; MSPH Univ NC-CH 1946; PhD Purdue Univ 1962; Further Studies; pa/Current Reg Prof Mgr for Consumer Affairs, Food & Drug Adm, Rev V; Home Mgmt Supvr US Dept Agri; Civilian Instr USAF; Pers Utilization US Fed Civil Ser Comm. Chgo Reg: Home Ecs Field Rep Univ

Wis Ext; Other Former Positions; Am Coun on Consumer Interest; Am & St Home Ecs Assns; Assn for Consumer Res; Fdn Unified Sci Edrs; Nat Coun Home Ecs Admrs; Nat Comm on Commun Hlth; Nat Assn Ed Broadcasters; Nat Coun on Smoking Behavior; Others; hon/Fellow: Am Public Hlth Assn, AAAS, Am Sch Hlth Assn, Am Col Hlth Assn, Soc Public Hlth Edrs; Omicron Nu; Kappa Delta Pi; Sigma Delta Epsilon; Merit Awd, US Civil Ser Comm; Commendable Ser Awd, FDA; USPHS Comm'd Resv; Profl Pubs; Biogl Listings.

DUNN, ROBERT GARVIN oc/Aerospace/Chemical Engineer; b/Jul 30, 1917; h/121 Redder Ave, Dayton, OH 45405; ba/Wright-Patterson AFB, OH; m/Dora Frances Gambill; c/Robert Garvin Jr (dec), Linda Lee, Karen France; p/George Thomas Dunn Jr (dec); Gladys A Dunn, Lake Village, AR; ed/BS La St Univ 1942; MS 1949, PhD 1964 Ohio St Univ; mil/USAF 1943-46, 1951-53; pa/W-P AFB: Branch Chief AF Flight Dynamics Lab 1975-, Lab Dir Aerospace Res

Labs 1974-75, Dep Lab Dir Aerospace Res Labs 1965-74, Others; Am Inst Aeronautics & Astronautics; The Combustion Inst; Am Chem Soc; cp/Mem & Ofcr Local Kiwanis Clb; Former Mem Bd Dirs Dayton Christian Ctr; PTA; HS Commun Coun; Past Cub Scout Com-man; r/Trinity Bapt Ch: Trustee, Chm Bldg Com, Mem Adv Bd; Am Bapt Chs USA, Nom'g Com for Ohio 3rd Election Dist; Others; hon/AF Meritorious Civilian Ser Medal; Sci Achmt Awd, USAF; Engrg Achmt Awd, Nat Engrs' Week, Miami Val Area 1971; USAF Nom for Nat Civil Ser Leag Career Ser Awd; Others.

DUNN, ROSS oc/Textile Business Executive; b/Sept 19, 1931; h/Rte 2, Box 923, Lanett, AL 36863; ba/West Point, GA; m/Rosa; c/Martin De Rosseau, Rosephanye Tolandra, Kennedy Fitzgerald, Wilfred Julian; p/Arthur Dunn Sr, LaGrange, GA; Petronis

Dunn, Shawmut, AL; ed/BS, MAdm Supvn Ala St Univ; mil/AUS 1952-54; pa/Employee Relations Specialist 1978-, Pers Asst Pers Relats Dept WP Pepperell 1974-78; Admr Asst Muscogee Co Sch Dist (Ga) 2 Yrs; Asst Supt Macon Co Sch Sys 1 Yr; Sch Prin Johnson Elem Sch, WP 3 Yrs; Other Former Positions; NEA; Muscogee Co Assn; Ga & Ala Ed Assns; Textile Ind Pres; cp/Chambers Co Val Br NAACP; Dir & Pres Huguley Water Sys; Dir: Drew Rec Ctr, Goodwill Ind, Ala Hlth Sys Agy (Gadsden, Ala); Chattahoochee Val Area Assn for Retard Chd; Bd Mem Chambers Co Pensions & Security, LaFayette, Ala; Jr Achmt, Lanett, Ala; ARC, WP; Exec Bd Geo H Lanier Coun BSA, WP; CoChm Chambers Co Child Abuse; Val C of C; Val Chapt Ala St Univ Alumni; Silver Beaver, BSA; Other Civic Activs; hon/BSA Dist Awd of Merit; NAACP: 100 Mbrship Awd, Pres Awd, Cit Awd; Man of Yr Awds; Dem Clb Ala Awd; W/W Among Black Ams; Others.

DUPIN, CLYDE C oc/Evangelist; Newspaper Columnist; b/Feb 22, 1933; h/1241 Woodbrook Dr, Kernersville, NC 27284; ba/K'ville; m/Grace E; c/C Wesley, Kenneth, Joy Beth; p/Kendrick and Polly Dupin (dec); ed/Att'd: U Wesleyan Col, Evansville Univ; pa/Pres Clyde Dupin Reachout Mins Inc; Writer Wkly Newspaper Column "Rel Viewpoint"; Bill Glass Evangel

Assn: VP, Crusade Dir; Pastor Trinity Wesleyan Ch E'ville, Ind 1959-69; Formerly Conducted Sunday Morning Radio Prog; Past Pres Gtr E'ville Assn Clergymen; Former Mem Bd Dirs Tri-St Yth for Christ Inc; Del Intl Conf (2); cp/Mem Sch Bd; Pres Clergymen's Assn; r/Wesleyan Ch: Ordained Min; hon/Outstg Min Alumni Awd, U Wesleyan Col 1965.

DUPREE, LEONARD LARKIN oc/Associate Pastor; b/Sept 29, 1941; h/3857 Greenway, Shreveport, LA 71105; ba/S'port; m/Jacquelyn Jennings; c/Leonard Larkin Jr, Elizabeth L; p/Joseph Howard and Evelyn Mae Suggs Dupree, Americus, GA; ed/BA; MDiv; DMin; pa/Assoc Pastor 1st Bapt Ch,

S'port; Exec Comm Fannin Co Bapt Assn (Tex); Exec Comm NW La Assn; S'port Min Assn; S'port Area Nat Conf Christians & Jews; Assn Clin Pastoral; cp/Lions Clb; Red Cross; BSA; Am Rose Soc; S'port Citizen's Comm on Blood Supply; Rotary Clb; r/Bapt; hon/HS Valedictorian; Valedictorian Jr Col Class; Phi Theta Kappa; Outstg Yg Men Am Awd.

DURAND, HUGO G oc/Sales Eng; b/Jan 24, 1930; h/5717 Tanglewood Dr, Corpus Christi, TX 78412; ba/Corpus Christi; m/Alma Anne; c/Danielle Yvette, Nicole

Annette; p/Armand and Emma Durand, Lubbock, TX; ed/BBA Univ Tex; mil/AUS 1/Lt Arty; pa/Sales Eng Future Metals Inc; Former Public Relats & Sales Rep Phoenix Supply Co; cp/Cal-Anna Lions Clb: Past Pres, Secy-Treas; Pres Longhorn Clb CC Chapt (UT); Longhorn Clb Century Mem (UT); Bd Dirs Boys Clb; Co Rep UF; Nat Rifle Assn: Instr, Pistol, Rifle & Hunter Safety; PTA St Pius Sch; Nat Moderate Dem: Nat Chm 4 Yrs; St Chm Moderate Dems Tex 4 Yrs; Nueces Co Dem Exec Com; Nat Del to Dem Conv; Charter Mem Jefferson-Jackson Study Group; r/Rom Cath; hon/Personalities of S; Dist'd Awd, Univ Tex (Ath Dept); Apprec Awd, Longhorn Clb; W/W in Tex; DIB; 2000 Men Achmt; Intl Reg W/W; Intl Men Achmt.

DURBNEY, CLYDROW JOHN oc/Gospel Minister; Pastor; b/Sept 27, 1916; h/8244 Addington Dr, Berkeley, MO 63134; ba/St Louis, MO; m/Mattie Lee; p/Earl Elmer and Conetta McKenzie Durbney (dec); ed/AB; BD; STM; DMin Cand; mil/AUS 3 Yrs; pa/Ghetto Evangelist Ch on Wheels 1952-; Asst Pastor Ctl Bapt Ch 1954-; Instr Wn Bapt Bible Col Ext Ctr 1954-67; r/Bapt; hon/Eagle Scout Awd; Cert of Achmt in Min, Antioch Dist Woms Conv; Diamond Jubilee Awd, Ferrier Harris Home; Dist'd World Ser Awd, CBC; Yth Awd, CBC; Num Biogl Listings.

DURDEN, THOMAS LAMAR oc/Music Instructor; b/Mar 16, 1939; h/PO Box 253, Cleveland, GA 30528; ba/Cleve; p/Mrs Ivey Durden Sr, Sandersville, GA; ed/BMus 1960, MMusEd 1961 Univ Ga; 6th Yr Adv'd Study Music Ga So Col 1970; pa/Instr Choral & Instrumental Music Truett-McConnell Col, Cleve 1977-; Pt-time Instr Music Emanuel Co Jr Col, Swainsboro, Ga 1975-77; Full-time Dir

Music & Yth 1st Bapt Ch, S'boro 1972-77; Other Former Positions; Ga Music Edrs Assn: Bd Dirs 1969-72, Chm Dist I 1969-72, Instrumental Chm Dist I 1968-69; Eval Com So Assn Cols & Schs 1972; Lectr; Adjudicator Ga Bapt Conv Music Dept; r/Bethlehem Bapt Ch, Clarkesville, Ga: Mem; hon/Judge Preliminaries Miss Am Pageant (Ga); Outstg Yg Men Am; Recipient US Govt Appointmt for Overseas Tchg 1970; Others.

DURNIL, GORDON K oc/Attorney at Law; Political Consultant; b/Feb 20, 1936; h/9301 N Delaware St, Indianapolis, IN 46240; ba/Indpl; m/Lynda L; c/Guy S, Cynthia L; p/J Ray Durnil (dec); E Merle Durnil, Indpls; ed/BS 1960, JD 1965 Ind Univ; mil/AUS Korea; pa/Sales Rep: Moore Bus Forms Inc 1960, Franklin Life Ins Co 1956; Atty; Legal Aid Com Ind St Bar Assn; Dep Marion Co Prosecutor 1965-66; VP Ind Ornamental Iron Works Inc 1960-65; Justice of Peace Washington Twp 1967-70; Spec Asst

Ofc Bus Sers, US Dept Commerce 1971; Am Assn Polit Conslts; cp/Num Campaign Activs; Del 1976 Repub Nat Conv; Legal Com on Election Laws, Marion Co Repub Com; Former Mem Bd Dirs Nora Sertoma Clb; Spkr Var Repub Ldrship Confs; Fund Raiser Var Repub Cands & Coms; Past VChm Marion Co Election Bd; Num Others; r/Northminster Presb Ch: Mem; hon/W/W Am Polits.

DUROSKA, EMILIA O oc/Public Relations Work/Cultural; Author; Composer; Instructor; b/Dec 20; h/70 Haven Ave, New York City, NY 10032; p/John and Emily Duroska, Saugerties, NY; pa/Tutor E & W Coasts (USA); Edit & Translation Work in Spanish & Slovak; Tchr; Anthropol Soc; Composers, Artists, Authors Am; cp/NY Hort Soc; Metro Mus Art; Pubs incl: "Lotus Pool", "At the Feet of Isis", "Carousel", Others; r/Christian; hon/Blue Ribbon for Poetry; Med for Excell in Spanish Lang; DIB; Other Biogl Listings.

DURRETT, MADISON WINFREY oc/Clergyman; b/Apr 8, 1915; h/Rt 1, Box 30, Lebanon, VA 24266; ba/Same; m/Carmen Elsie Gibbs; c/Dale Dwight, Glen Winfrey; p/James Madison Durrett, Otisco, IN; Myrtie W Durrett (dec); ed/BA E Tex Bapt Col 1949; MDiv So Bapt Theol Sem 1973; pa/Former Pastor: Tex, Ind, Ohio, Va; Dir Assnl

Missions New Lebanon Bapt Assn; Ordained So Bapt Min; Dir New Lebanon Sem Ext Ctr 1963-74; Appalachian Reg Working Com 1968-; Russell Co Mins' F'ship; cp/Bd Dirs Russell Co Hd Start; Adv Bd Va Alcohol Safety Action Prog; r/So Bapt: Ordained Min

1948; hon/DIB; Notable Ams; Personalities of S; W/W: Rel, Am Univs & Cols.

DYAR, WILLIAM HELLER oc/Minister; h/1015 Wendover Cir, Winston-Salem, NC 27104; ba/W-S; m/Virginia C; c/Barbara S; p/J G Dyar, Seneca, SC; Marfinjane Siebern Dyar (dec); ed/AB High Point Col 1951; BD Duke Univ 1957; MTh Wake Forest Sem 1958; DMin 1975; Grad Works; mil/USAF, Lt Col; Nat Chaplain's Com; pa/Dir Dept Pastoral Care Centenary U Meth Ch, W-S 1971-; Former Pastorates: SC, Va, NC; Other Former Positions; Var Ch Ofcs Held; Min Assnl Ofcs Held; IPA; Soc Biblical Lit; SEn Fam Life Assn; Others; cp/Ruritan; Civitan; Wel & Charity Bds; VChm Town Bd Commrs (Rescue, Va); Lib Bds; CAP-USAF; Nat Dir Chaplain Radio Nets; r/U Meth; hon/Red, White & Blue Ribbons; Exceptl Ser Awd; 20-Yr Awd; Profl Pubs; Biogl Listings.

DYER, GEORGE CARROLL oc/Retired Vice Admiral, US Navy; b/Apr 27, 1898; h/4 Chase Rd, Annapolis, MD 21401; m/Adaline Shick; c/Mary D Corrin, Georgia D Burnett, Virginia D Smith; p/Harry Blair and Georgia Mortimer Dyer (dec); ed/BS US Naval Acad 1918; Naval War Col; Nat War Col; Addit Studies; mil/USN 1915-55; Line Ofcr Submarines, Deep Sea Diver, Submarine Rescue Ship, Destroyer; Mine Layer, Cruiser, Battleship; Staff Cmdr, Destroyers; Staff Cmdr, Battleforce; Staff Cmdr-in-Chief & Chief of Naval Operations; cp/Pres, US Naval Acad Class of 1919; Pres, US Naval Acad Alumni Assn; Cmdr-in-Chief, Mil Order of World Wars; Bd Dirs, Ret'd Ofcrs Assn; Pres, Abenaki Tower & Trail Assn; Soc of the *Cincinnati*, St of Va; r/Epis; hon/Dist'd Ser Medal; US Legion of Merit; Purple Heart; Cmdr of British Empire; Most Exalted Order of White Elephants (Thailand); Cross of Naval Merit, Great Ofcr (Peru); Mil Order of Merit (Italy); Others.

DYESS, STEWART WOOD oc/Assistant Director; b/Dec 25, 1933; h/2110 56th St, Lubbock, TX 79413; ba/Lubbock; m/Dessie Mae Votaw; c/George Stewart; p/Bonnie Burk Dyess (dec); Dottie Wood Dyess, Lubbock; ed/BS 1965, MSLS 1966 E Tex St Univ; EdD Tex Tech Univ 1977; mil/AUS 1957-63 (Resv); pa/Asst Dir Lib Sers Tex Tech Univ Lib; Am Lib Assn; Tex Lib Assn: Life

Mem, VP, Pres Elect, Adm Round Table 1978-79, Chmships Var Coms; SWn Lib Assn; SW Acad Lib Consortium, Editor SWALC Newslttr 1977-; Tex Coun St Univ Libns; Tex Assn Col Tchrs, Var Coms; cp/Lubbock Rotary Clb; 32° Masons; r/1st Bapt Ch, Lubbock; hon/Phi Delta Kappa.

DYKSHOORN, MARINUS BERNARDUS oc/Parapsychologist; Consultant; Lecturer; b/July 10 1920; h/2400 Johnson Ave, 14-E, Riverdale, Bronx, NY 10463; m/Cora; c/Helga; p/Jacobus and Lena van der Houwen-Dykshoorn, Holland; ed/Agri Dipl 1937; Autodidact, Parapsychology, Clairvoyant & Crim Justice; pa/Conslt & Investigator in Criminology as a Parapsychologist; Lectr for Univs & Civic Orgs; Author, *My Passport Says Clairvoyant* (1974); cp/Free Masons Scottish Rite; 32° Mason; Dep Sheriff of Kansas 1975; Dep Sheriff of WV 1978; Past Mem, Sheriff's Assn of NC; Spec Dep Sheriff, St of Oregon 1976; r/Rom Cath; hon/Dist'd Citizen Awd, Boulder Co Sheriff's Dept (Colo); Psi Chi; Hon Capt, Sheriff's Dept of Colo; Hon Mem, Colo Police Dept; Hon Chief of Police, St of Tenn; Hon Sheriff of Tenn; Hon Capt of Police, New Orleans (La); Biogl Listings; Others.

DYKSTRA, GAIL LYNN oc/Student; b/Dec 7, 1955; h/16101 School St, South Holland, IL 60473; ba/Evanston, IL; p/Harry Jr and Marlys Jean Dykstra, S Holland; ed/BS NWn Univ; pa/Asst Prodr Radio Sta WMBI, Chicago; WNUR, E'ton: Announcer, Engr, Prodr; cp/Past Pres Gamma Phi Beta; r/Prot; hon/Outstg Yg Wom Am; Phi Eta Sigma; Nat Hon Soc Bible Cols.

DYMALLY, MERVYN M oc/Teacher; Lieutenant Governor; b/May 12, 1926; h/1425 Commons Dr, Sacramento, CA 95825; ba/Sacramento; m/Alice Gueno; c/Mark, Lynn; p/Andrew Hamid Dymally; Andreid Richardson; ed/BA; MA; PhD; pa/Lt Gov St of Cal 1975-; Tchr 1955-61; Adj Prof Golden Gate Univ, San Francisco; cp/Former St Senator & Assemblyman; CoFdr Jt Ctr for Polit Studies; Urban Affairs Inst; Nat Conf Black Elected Ofcls; Bd Regents Univ Cal; Bd Trustees Cal St Univ & Cols; r/Epis; hon/LLD, Univ W LA; JD, Lincoln Univ; LLD, Cal Col Law; Phi Kappa Phi.

E

EADIE, DONALD oc/Electronic Engineer, Computer Consultant; Author; Professor; b/Jan 12, 1919; h/2111 Lanai Ave, Belleair Bluffs, FL 33540; ba/Same; m/Ruth Hill; c/Susan Ruth E Willis, Carol Ann; p/Erskine R Eadie (dec); Louise B Shank, S Plainfield, NJ; ed/BSEE Lehigh 1941; MSE Univ Fla 1954; mil/US Armored Force; USAAF 1941-46, 2/Lt to Capt; pa/Sr Mem IEEE; Profl Engr Fla; cp/Former Commr, Belleair Bluffs; Civitans; Dir Belleair Bluffs, Property Owners' Assn; r/Presb; hon/Newtonian Soc (Col); Author Sev Articles & 3 Books: *Introduction to the Basic Computer*, 1968, *Modern Data Processors and Systems*, 1972, & Theory and Operation of Minicomputers, 1979.

EAKIN, THOMAS CAPPER oc/Sports Promotion Executive; b/Dec 16, 1933; h/3706 Traynham Rd, Shaker Hgts, OH 44122; m/Brenda Lee Andrews; c/Thomas Andrews, Scott Frederick; p/Frederick William and Beatrice Capper Eakin (dec); ed/BA Denison Univ 1956; mil/AUS 1956-58, Specialist 4th Class; pa/Pres TCE Enterprises, Shaker Hgts 1973-; Dist Mgr Hitchcock Pub'g Co, Cleveland, Ohio 1970-72; Reg Bus Mgr Chilton Pub'g Co, Cleve 1969-70; Other Former Positions; Fdr & Pres Golf Intl 100 Clb 1970-; Fdr & Dir: Cy Young Mus 1970-, "TRY" Target/Reach Yth 1971-; Fdr & Pres Ohio Baseball Hall of Fame 1976-; Trustee

Newcomerstown Sports Corp; Hon Dir Tuscarawas Co Old Timers Baseball Assn; Other Profl Activs; cp/Trustee Tuscarawas Co Hist Soc; Bd Dirs Wahoo Clb; Fellow IBA; Former Mem Cleve Indians Old Timers Com; Adv Bd: Camp Hope, Cuyahoga Hills Boys Sch; Cleve Coun on Corrections; Others; r/1st Bapt Ch of Gtr Cleve: Bd Mem 1966-69; hon/Commend, City of New Orleans (La); Certs of Merit: St of La, Tuscarawas Co Am Revolution Bicent Comm; Apprec Awd, Am Revolution Bicent Adm; Awd of Achmt, Ohio Assn Hist Socs; Gov's Awd for Commun Action, Ohio Gov 1974; Proclamation Awd, "Thomas C Eakin Day", City of Cleve 1974; Num Others; Biogl Listings.

EARLES, PAT S oc/Instructor; b/Nov 5, 1938; h/525 Joe Clifton, Paducah, KY 42001; m/Melvin; c/Cheryl; p/Knox Brinn (dec); Ruby Brinn, Paducah; ed/Early Childhood Ed Paducah Commun Col, Murray Univ; pa/PE Instr; NEA; KEA; PEA; Am Bus Assn; Beta Sigma Phi; Ky Cong of P's & T's; cp/Girl Scout Ldr 14 Yrs; PTA: Pres Paducah City, 1st Dist, Local Unit & St, 3rd VP Ky; Mem Beau Creek Girl Scout Coun; Adult Mem Yg Histns; Paducah Sum Fest; r/Clement St Ch of Christ; hon/Life Mem: Ky PTA, Nat PTA; Thanks Badge, GSA; Ky Col; Dutchess of Paducah.

EARMAN, JOHN GARY oc/Principal; b/Aug 13, 1934; h/2905 N Alliance Ln, Woodridge, VA 22193; ba/Alexandria, VA; m/Geraldine Walker; c/Steven, Margaret Lynn, Matthew; p/Carpenter B Earman (dec); Margaret M Earman, Harrisonburg, VA; ed/BS; MA; mil/USAR 1956-62; pa/Elem Sch Prin; Fairfax, Va & Nat Ed Assns; PTA: Mem 1960-78, Treas 1963-64; Mem Dept Sch Prins;

Forum Spkr Longwood Col 1971; cp/Cub Scouts; Dale City Little Leag: Former Commr, Umpire, Coach; Former Mem Dale City Elem Sch Adv Com; BPO Elks, Former Treas; r/Meth; hon/Human Relats Awd, Fairfax Ed Assn; Personalities of S; Commun Ldrs of Va.

EAST, ANNA MARY oc/Retired Teacher, Writer; b/Sept 23, 1904; h/111 E Clinton St, Clinton. MO 64735; m/(dec); c/Ira

Jr, Kathleen Smith; p/Roy Condra Simmons (dec); Laura Francis Simmons, Clinton; ed/BA; pa/Ret'd, Tchr & Writer; IPA; r/Bapt; hon/IBC F'ship.

EAST, DANIEL SIDNEY oc/Postmaster; b/Dec 14, 1922; h/103 West St, Rutherford, TN 38369; ba/R'ford; m/Dora (Nadean); c/Caprice, Daniel II, Bradley, Felicia; p/Arther Roy and Ruth Rebecca East (dec); ed/Erie, PA; ed/Oberlin Col; Erie Conservatory of Music; mil/37 Months Cannon Co, 98th Div; pa/Postmaster, Post Ofc R'ford; Music Tchr; Entertainer: Radio, TV; Super Mkt Mgr; cp/Lions Clb; Past Pres Rotary Clb; Scoutmaster 13 Yrs; r/Meth; hon/Dist'd Ser Awd, JCs; Order of Arrow, BSA.

EATON, BLAINE HASKIN oc/Executive; Farmer; b/Mar 12, 1913; h/Taylorsville, MS; ba/So Pine Electric Power Assn, Taylorsville, MS 39168; m/Elaine Ford; c/Emmett Howard, Suzanne Jordan, Mark Haskin (dec), Sarah Faye Buys, Elvie Ford McMorris; p/Lavell K and Annie Stringer Eaton (dec); ed/AB Jones Jr Col; Addit Studies; mil/USN 2 Yrs; pa/Mgr, So Pine Elect Power Assn 1958-; Mgr, Mize Branch Smith Co Bank; Mgr, Miss Rural Elect Coops 4 Yrs; Bd Dirs, S Miss Elect Power Assn 1978-79; Chm Legis Com, Nat Rural Elect Coop Assns 1960-; cp/Adm Asst to Senator James O Eastland, US Senate; Mem Miss Ho of Reps; Mason; Shriner; Lions Clb; 4-H Adv Coun; r/So Bapt: Deacon, SS Tchr; hon/Alumnus of the Yr, Jones Jr Col 1979.

EAVES, ELSIE oc/Civil Engineer; b/May 5, 1898; h/18 Third Ave, Port Washington, NY 11050; ba/Same; p/Edgar Alfred and Katherine Elliott Eaves (dec); ed/BS(CE) Univ Colo 1920; pa/Mem Intl Adv Edit Bd "Engrng & Process Ecs", Elsevier Sci Pub'g Co, Amsterdam, Netherlands 1977, 78; Conslt to Plan & Budget Org, Tehran, Iran, Exec Vol Intl Exec Ser Corps, NY 1974; Civilian Advr on Housing Costs Nat Comm on Urban Probs, Wash DC 1968-69; Conslt on Est'g Nat Bldg News Ser, Harrisville, NH 1964-65; Other Former Positions; Am Soc CE: Fellow, Mem Nat Applications Review Com 1968-, Secy Nat

Com on Estimating & Cost Control (Constrn Div) 1960-69; Am Assn Cost Engrs: Life Mem, Chm Intl Cost Index Com 1965-69; Colo Soc Engrs, Denver; Queens Chapt NY St & Nat Socs Profl Engrs; Soc Wom Engrs: Secy-Treas, Bd Trustees 1959-74, Mem 1975-; Wom's Engrng Soc Gt Britain, London; cp/Bd Trustees N Shore Sci Mus, Plandome Manor, NY; Wom's Coun NY Public Lib; r/Christian; hon/Cert of Recog for Pioneering, Soc Wom Engrs; Ser to Country Awd, Intl Exec Ser Corps; Univ Colo: George Norlin Silver Medal, Dist'd Engrng Alumnus Awd, 2nd Annual Arthur J Boase Meml Lectr for Dept of Civil & Envir Engrs, Chapt Hon Mem Chi Epsilon; Ser to Country Awd, Intl Exec Ser Corps; Hon Life Mem, Am Assn Cost Engrs; Tau Beta Pi; Awd of Merit, Am Assn Cost Engrs.

EBINGER, JOHN B oc/Attorney, Counselor at Law; b/Jul 10, 1894; h/341 Spruce Dr, Brookings, OR 97415; ba/Brookings; m/Teddy Lee Magruder; p/Paul and Marie Maag Ebinger; ed/Univ Oreg; LLB Willamette Univ 1930; pa/Admitted to Oreg Bar 1930; Pract'd Law, Tillamook, Oreg 1930-35; Spec Trust Rep 1st Nat Bk, Portland, Oreg 1936-38; Pract'd Law Klamath Falls, Oreg 1938-57, Brookings 1957-; Oreg Leg Interim Com Wildlife Resources 1946-48; Orgr, Exec Dir Com for Preserv St & Local Govt, Chgo 1953-56; Author of

Amendment to Article V, US Constitution, Sponsored by Com for Preserv of St & Local Govt, to Provide Alternate Method for Proposing Amendments by Sts; Oreg St Bar, Bd Govs; ABA; Am Judic Soc; Izaak Walton Leag; Past Pres Oreg Div, Pacific Coast Coun, Nat Dir; Am Trial Lwyrs Assn; cp/Nat Geog Soc; Am Forestry Assn; Smithsonian Instn Nat Assocs; Nat, Oreg Hist Socs; Brookings C of C; Nat Audubon Soc; Delta Theta Phi; Elk; Rotarian, Past Pres Brookings; City of Portland Clb; Commonwealth of Cal Clb; hon/Commun Ldrs & Noteworthy Ams.

ECKERT, ERNST R G oc/Regents' Professor Emeritus, Director; b/Sept 13, 1904; h/60 W Wentworth Ave, W St Paul, MN 55118; ba/Minneapolis, MN; m/Josefine Binder; c/Rosemarie Christa E Koehler, Elke, Karen E Winter, Dieter; p/Georg and Margarete Pfrogner Eckert; ed/Dipl-Ing 1927, Dr-Ing 1931 German Inst Technol; Dr habil Inst Tech (Danzig) 1938; Docent Inst Technol (Braunschweig) 1940; pa/Univ Minn: Regents' Prof 1966-, Dir Thermodynamics & Heat Transfer Div, Mech Engrng Dept 1955-, Prof Mech Engrng Dept 1951-; Conslt Nat Adv Com for Aeronautics Lewis Flight Propulsion Lab, Cleveland. Ohio 1949-51; Conslt Power

Plant Lab, USAF, Wright-Patterson AFB, Ohio 1945-49; Other Former Positions; Am Soc for Engrg Ed; Am Inst Aeronautics & Astronautics; Wissenschaftliche Gesellschaft fur Luft-und Raumfahrt; Am Soc Mech Engrs; NY Acad Scis; Adv Conslt; US Rep Aerodynamics Panel Intl Com of Flame Radiation; Hon Edit Bd Am Div Commonwealth & Intl Lib of Sci, Engrg & Liberal Studies; Var Editorial Positions; Sigma Xi; Pi Tau Sigma; Tau Beta Pi; Nat Acad Engrng; Nat Comm on Fire Prevention & Control; Num Other Profl Activs; hon/Fellow, NY Acad Scis; Adams Meml Mbrship Awd, *Welding Jour,* Am Welding Soc (Miami, Fla); Vincent Bendix Awd, Am Soc for Engrng Ed; DSc: Polytech Inst (Iasi, Romania), Univ Notre Dame; Num Cits; Num Profl Pubs: Articles & Books.

ECKMAN, BERTHA ELIZABETH oc/Educator; h/RD 4, Berlin, PA 15530; ba/Berlin; p/Frank and Augusta Olson Eckman, Berlin; ed/BS; Elem & Sec'dy Cert; pa/Tchr Garrett & Somerset, Pa; Supv'g Tchr of Student Tchrs Cal St Col; NEA; Pa St Ed Assn; Pres Somerset Area Ed Assn; Pres Alpha

Delta Chapt Delta Kappa Gamma; cp/Somerset Co Repub Wom; r/St Michael's Luth Ch: Lay Pres; Pubr Christian Ed Yr Books 1956-; Former Secy Somerset Co Coun of Christian Ed; hon/Nat Register Prom Ams; W/W: Am Wom, E; World W/W Wom; Intl W/W Commun Ser.

ECKMAN, CAROL ANN oc/Assistant Professor; b/Jan 11, 1938; h/Lot 56, 129 Woodward Ave, Lock Haven, PA 17745; ba/Lock Haven; p/Frank and Grace Eckman, Rockwood, PA; ed/BS Lock Haven St Col 1959; MS WVa Univ 1965; Addit Studies; pa/Lock Haven St Col 1974-: Asst Prof PE, Wom's Basketball Coach; Ind Univ Pa, Indiana, Pa 1972-74: Prof PE, Field Hockey &

Wom's Basketball Coach; Other Former Positions; AHPER; Nat, En, NY St, Pa St Assns PE for Col Wom; En Assn Intercollegiate Aths for Wom; US Field Hockey Assn; NEA APSCUF; Pres Hudson Val Field Hockey Assn; Basketball Chm Pa, Div of Girls' & Wom's Sport; Basketball Chm En Assn Intercollegiate Aths for Wom; Exec Bd USFHA; Other Profl Activs; r/Luth; hon/Kappa Delta Pi; Coached W Chester St Col to DGWS, Nat Invitational Wom's Basketball Championship 1969.

EDDINGTON, ALAN MICHAEL oc/Priest; b/Feb 6, 1944; h/140 Walnut St, Weirton, WV 26062; ba/Weirton; p/Carl Clayton and Margaret Hoehn Eddington,

Witt, IL; ed/BA Quincy Col 1968; MDiv St Louis Univ 1971; pa/Rom Cath Priest; Diocesan Dir of Scouting; Senator, Senate of Priests; cp/Asst Reg Supvr N WVa EMS Agy; EMT Instr; r/Rom Cath; hon/Nat Reg Emerg Med Technicians.

EDELEN, MARY BEATY oc/State Legislator; b/Dec 9, 1944; h/311 Canby St, Vermillion, SD 57069; ba/Dierre, SD; m/Joseph R; c/Audra Angelica, Anthony Callaghan; p/Donald W Beaty, Vermillion,

SD; Marjorie H Beaty, Vermillion; ed/BA Univ SD; MA Trinity Univ; pa/Former Hist Lectr Univ SD & Yankton Col; AAUW; cp/Mem SD Ho of Reps; Order of Wom Legs; SD Wom's Polit Caucus; PEO; OES; r/U-Ch of Christ.

EDELSON, DAVID oc/Mental Health Superintendent; b/Jan 28, 1919; h/Plum Hollow Rd, RFD #1, Dixon, IL 61021; ba/Dixon; m/Miriam; c/Richard, Jeffrey; p/Max and Freida Epsten Edelson (dec); ed/BA Wash Sq Col Arts & Sci, NY Univ 1948; MA NY Sch Social Wk, Columbia Univ 1950; MHA NWn Univ 1958; mil/AUS 1942-45; pa/Mtl Hlth Supt Dixon Devel Ctr; Fellow Am Assn on Mtl Deficiency; CEC; Nat Assn Supts of Public Residential Facilities, Bd Dirs 1976-77, 1977-78; Lee Co Mlt Hlth Assn; Lic'd as Nsg Home Adm, St of Ill; hon/Jewish; hon/Liaison Mem, Nat Assn Supts of Accreditation Coun for Facilities for MR; Ldrship Awd, Ill Assn for Retard Citizens; Gov'd Adv Coun on Retard 1963.

EDIGER, MICHAEL LEE oc/Assistant Residence Hall Director; b/Jan 10, 1956; h/220 W 11th, Hutchinson, KS 67501; ba/Hays, KS; p/Roland M and Theresa Ediger, Hutchinson; ed/AA Hutchinson Commun Jr Col; BA summa cum laude Fort Hays St Univ; pa/Asst Residence Hall Dir & Prog Coor, McMindes Hall; Advr Residence Halls Assn; CoChm Residence Hall S'ship Com; Advr Nat Residence hall Hon, Ft Hays Chapt; Ks Assn Student Pers Admrs; r/Ft Hays Cath Campus Ctr: Parish Coun Secy 1977-78; hon/Phi Theta Kappa; Mortar Bd; Phi Alpha Theta; Phi Kappa Phi; Nom'd Most Outstg Ft Hays Hist Undergrad, 1978; Recipient Sev S'ships; Biogl Listings.

EDINGER, STANLEY EVAN oc/Commissioned Officer; Clinical Chemist; b/Aug 9, 1943; h/404N, 12000 Old Georgetown Rd, Rockville, MD 20852; p/Louis and Lenore Edinger, R'ville; ed/BS cum laude Bklyn Col 1964; MA 1969, PhD 1970 NY Univ; mil/USPHS 1976-, Sr Sci Ofcr (Cmdr); pa/NY Univ: Tchg Fellow 1964-66, Res Asst 1966-70; Tech Translator & Editor; Asst Chemist Mt

Sinai Hosp 1971-76; Conslt (Lab Scis) Profl Exam Ser 1975-76; Sr Scist USPHS 1976-; Sr Scist Hlth Care Fin Adm 1977-; DHEW Rep to NCCLS; HCFA Rep to Public Hlth Ser; Clin Lab Task Force; Project Ofcr DHEW Profl Exam Prog for Clin Lab Technologists & Cytotechs; Am Inst Chem: Chm Mbrship Com, Councilor, Auditor NY Sect; Am Chem Soc; Am Assn Clin Chem; AAAS; Assn Mil Surgs US; APHA; NCHLS; ACS, Com on Envir Analytical Methodologies; cp/Dir Bklyn Col Chem Alumni Assn, NYU; Bklyn Col Alumni Assn; Annapolis Nav Sailing Assn; hon/Fellow, Am Inst Chemists; Honors Scholar, NYU; Profl Pubs; Biogl Listings.

EDMONSON, HAROLD W oc/Priest; b/Aug 16, 1925; h/4218 N Stanton, El Paso, TX 79902; ba/El Paso; m/Ava V; c/H Alan, Jeffrey S, Sarah J; p/Willard F and Ruth B Edmonson, Plainfield, IN; ed/BS 1948, Postgrad Work Canterbury Col; MS Ind Univ 1953; Att'd Epis Theol Sem 1959-61; Addit Studies; mil/Navy Air Cadet 1943-44; Navy Ofcr Tng 1944-45, Navy Communs Sch, USS Grainger, USS Antietam, 58th Task Force Pacific 1945-46; pa/Assoc Rector & Canon Pro-Cathedral Ch of St Clement, El Paso 1975-; Rector St Paul's, Las Vegas, NM 1969-75; Rector: Ch of St Peter, Rockport

(Tex) 1964-68, Ch of Messiah, Gonzales (Tex) 1962-64; Dean & Instr Cuttington Col, Suacoco, Liberia 1956-58; Other Former Positions; Diocesan Bd Christian Ed 1962-67; Diocesan Bd Camps & Confs 1966-68; Diocesan Bd Social Concerns 1968; Spiritual Dir Diocesan Cursillo 1970-72; Bd Dirs Highland Univ, Campus Min 1970-73; Fdg Mem: ESP Res Assocs, Little Rock (Ark) 1969-79, Order of Unknown Saints 1971-79; IPA; Soc Former Special Agts of FBI Inc 1978-79; Bd Dirs Campus Min UTEP 1978-79; Diocesan Task Force for Evangel & Renewal; Others; hon/Book of Honor; DIB; Intl W/W Commun Ser; Commun Ldrs & Noteworthy Ams; People Who Matter; Men of Achmt; W/W Rel.

EDMUNDS, NIEL ARTHUR oc/University Professor; b/Sept 19, 1931; h/1625 Brent Blvd, Lincoln, NE 68506; ba/Lincoln; m/Carol Jean; c/Jane Elizabeth, Ann Louise; p/Niel R Edmunds, Arvada, CO; Helen Edmunds, Lisbon, IA; ed/BAE 1958, MSE 1960 Neb St Tchrs; EdS Univ SD 1967; EdD Utah St Univ 1969; mil/AUS; pa/Univ Neb: Assoc Prof Gen Voc Tchr Ed, Dir Intl Voc Ed Sem; Neb St Col System: Div Chair, Dean, Asst VP; AVA; AIAA; ACIATE; St Orgs; cp/Mason, PM; Comml Clbs; Kiwanis; r/St Marks Meth Ch, Lincoln: Mem; hon/IA Tchr of Yr 1965; Laureate Awd, Epsilon Pi Tau; Adj Fac, Nat Acad for Voc Ed, Ohio St Univ.

EDMUNDS, PALMER DANIEL oc/Lawyer; Teacher; b/Oct 29, 1890; h/PO Box 317, Gilman, IL 60938; m/Sarah Shepard; p/Amos and Mary Campbell Edmunds (dec); ed/AB, LLD Knox Col; LLB Harvard; LLD Piedmont Col; mil/WWI, 1/Lt 109th Inf; Capt ORC; pa/Commr Supreme Ct of Ill 1929-32; Hearing Commr Def Prodn Adm 1951-53; Fac John Marshall Law Sch, Chgo 1926-76; r/Congreg; Mem Com for Continuation of Congreg Christian Chs in US; hon/Mem 1978 Class City of Chgo Sr Citizens Hall of Fame.

EDSE, ILSEDORE MARIA oc/Associate Professor; b/Oct 16, 1918; h/5693 Olentangy Blvd, Worthington, OH 43085; ba/Columbus, OH; m/Rudolph; c/Klaus-Peter, Franziska; p/Rudolf Edse (dec); Erna Edse, Bonn, Germany; ed/BS cum laude 1952, MA 1954, PhD 1960 OSU; pa/Assoc Prof German Lang & Lit; TV Writer & Prodr, Performer; Radio Prodr; Advr Student Coun; r/Prot; hon/Tchr of Yr, OSU; Emmy Awd Nom 1964, 68; TV "Visit to German", "Ja! German Spoken"; Others.

EDSON, CARROLL ANDREW oc/Former Manager; h/Dec 29, 1891; h/20 N Spruce St, Apt A-1, Batavia, NY 14020; m/Hazel Howard Partridge (dec); c/Stuart Patridge (dec), Lucile Elizabeth Smith, Virginia Crane, David Hatch; p/Andrews W Edson (dec); Cynthia Francelia Paine (dec); ed/BS; MA; mil/AUS Col, Ret'd; pa/Ret'd, Former Mgr Social Security Ofc; cp/Former Boy Scout Exec; Kiwanis Clb; Past Pres Am Assn Ret'd Persons Chapt; Past Pres Local Chapt Ret'd Ofcrs Assn; r/Congreg: Ch Clerk, Former Moderator, Others; hon/Order of Arrow; Outstg Sr Man in Commun Ser, Tucson, Ariz; Others.

EDWARDS, BRIAN ALFRED oc/Naval Officer; Mechanical Engineer; b/Jul 18, 1943; h/3712 Seamist Dr, Gautier, MS 39553; ba/Pascagoula, MS; m/Mary Marcella Hill; p/Alfred William and Evelyn May Edwards, Stuart, FL; ed/BA; BS, MSME; mil/USN Lt Cmdr; Var Shipboard & Shore-based

Assignments; Currently Serving in New Constrn; cp/Miss St Hunter Safety Instr; Former Boy Scout Com-man; r/Luth-Mo Synod; hon/Hon LLD; Nat Def Ser Medal; Vietnam Ser Medal; Cross of Gallantry w palm, Repub of Vietnam.

EDWARDS, CECILE HOOVER oc/Human Ecology Administrator & Teacher; h/3910 44th St NW, Washington DC 20016; ba/Wash DC; m/Gerald A; c/Gerald Jr, Adrienne, Hazel; p/Ernest Jack and Annie Jordan Hoover (dec); ed/BS; MS; PhD; pa/Admr & Tchr Sch Human Ecology Howard Univ; Am Inst Nutrition; Am Home Ecs Assn; Am Dietetic Assn; Soc for Nutrition Ed; Nat Inst Sci; Sigma Xi; Intl Fdn Home Ecs; r/Epis; hon/Cited for Contbns to Sci, Nat Coun Negro Wom; Awd for Dist'd Sci Res, NC A&T St Univ; Ia St: Home Ecs Alumni Centennial Awd, Alumni Achmt Awd; Alumni Merit Awd, Tuskegee Inst.

EDWARDS, CYNTHIA ADELE oc/Publishing Company Executive; b/Dec 15, 1946; h/336 E 50th St, New York, NY 10022; ba/NYC; p/John A and Elynore Walters Edwards, La Jolla, CA; ed/BA Ohio Wesleyan Univ 1969; pa/Macmillan Pub'g Co Inc, Sch

Div: Dir Advt'g Sers 1977-, Sr Copywriter 1970-72; Dir Advt'g & Promotion Noble & Noble, NYC 1972-77; Holt, Rinehart & Winston, NYC: Asst to Dir Lib Sers Div 1969-70, Publicity Asst Sum 1968; Other Former Positions; cp/Am Contract Bridge Leag; Dem; r/Presb; hon/Biogl Listings.

EDWARDS, E DEAN oc/Banking Executive; h/806 W Michigan Ave, Apt 308, W, Jackson, MI 49201; ba/Jackson; m/JoAnn; c/Paula Stormont, Vincent; p/E J and Susie B Huff Edwards, MI; ed/Assoc Bus Deg Jackson Commun Col; Grad Bkg & Fin Univ Wis; mil/USN WWII; pa/The Midwest Bk, Jackson: Chm of Bd, Pres, Incorporator; Litchfield St Savings Bk, Litchfield, Mich: Chm Bd, Dir; BancShares Corp, Mich: Chm Bd, Pres, Incorporator; Chm Sev Bk Adv Bds;

Indep, Am & Mich Bankers Assns; Wolverine Banking Clb; cp/Jackson C of C; Mem & Past Pres L'field Rotary Clb; Dir Hillsdale Co Agri Fair Assn; Adv Com Jackson Bus Univ; Am Legion; Mich Space Ctr, Jackson: Chm, Dir, Incorporator; Jackson CC; Arbor Hills CC; Town Clb Jackson; Adv Coun Mich 4-H Foun; Bd Trustees Jackson Commun Col; F&AM, 32° Mem Scottish Rite; r/L'field Meth Ch: Mem, Past Chm Bd Trustees; Fellow, Spring Arbor Col; Dist'd Ser Awd, Jackson Commun Col; Cert of Apprec, Inter-Lakes Lions Clb; J Howard Acton Clb, Am Cancer Soc.

EDWARDS, EDITH BUCKNER oc/-Homemaker; b/Mar 3, 1894; h/PO Box 141, Pipe Creek, TX 78063; m/Jesse William (dec); c/William E, Jesse B; p/Robert E and Florence Hinds Buckner (dec); ed/CAF-3; pa/Tchr; Pianist; Artist; Poet; Genealogist; cp/Heritage Geneal Soc; Bandera HD Clb; Am Legion Aux; VFW Aux; DAR; Daughs of Colonial Dames XVII Century; Magna Charta Dames; Daughs of So Ancestors; r/Bapt, Pipe Creek.

EDWARDS, EDWIN W oc/Governor; b/Aug 7, 1927; ba/Baton Rouge, LA; m/Elaine Schwartzenberg; p/Clarence and Agnes Brouillette Edwards; ed/Grad La St Univ Law Sch; mil/USN Air Corps WWII; pa/Pract Law, Crowley, La 1949-64; Gov of La 1972-; Nat Govs' Conf: Com on Natural Resources & Envir Mgmt, Task Force on Fgn Trade & Tourism, Rural & Urban Devel Com, Host 1975 Conf (Held in New Orleans); Energy Com So Govs' Conf; Former Chm Interstate Oil Compact Comm; St CoChm Ozarks Reg Comm; Former Mem US Ho of Reps; Former Mem Crowley City Coun & La St Senate; cp/Crowley Lions Clb; Intl Rice Fest; Gtr Crowley C of C; Am Legion.

EDWARDS, JACK oc/Legislator; b/Sept 20, 1928; ba/2439 House Ofc Bldg, Washington, DC 20515; m/Jolane Vander Sys; c/Susan Lane, Richard Arnold; ed/BS 1952, LLB 1954 Univ Ala; USN Sch 1947-48; mil/USMC 1946-48, Corp; USMC 1950-51, Sgt; pa/Pract Law, Mobile, Ala 1954-64; Former Secy Mobile Bar Assn; Pres Mobile Jr Bar Assn; US Ho of Reps 1964-; Appropriations Com, Sr Repub Def Subcom, Secy Ho Repub Conf; Other House Activs; cp/Bd Regents Spring Hill Col, Mobile; Bd Dirs Ala Coun on Ec Ed; Past Pres Mobile C of C; Former Judge, Ten Outstg Yg Men Am 1974; Gen Chm Am's Jr Miss Pageant 1970; Former Div Chm UF; Bd Trustees Choral Arts

Soc, Wash DC; Others; r/Presb Ch: Elder; hon/Hon Mem: W Mobile Kiwanis, Mobile Lions Clb; Outstg Yg Men Am, US JCs 1964; Man of Yr (Ala), Nat Fdn Indep Bus-men 1972-73; Watchdog of Treasury Awd; Guardian of Small Bus Awd, 94th & 95th Cong.

EDWARDS, MARY JANICE oc/Administrator; b/May 30, 1939; h/308 Killington Dr, Raleigh, NC 27609; ba/Raleigh; p/Jack W and Melba H Edwards, Smithfield, NC; ed/BS; MA; MEd; pa/NCAWDAC; SCPA; NASP; NAWDC; NCCPA; cp/Zonta Intl; r/Bapt; hon/W/W.

EDWARDS, MATTIE S oc/Associate Professor; b/Apr 16, 1931; h/11 Highland Cir, Westfield, MA 01085; ba/Springfield, MA; m/E Zeno; c/Zenia, Tanise; p/Chester Smith (dec); Essie Lawson Smith, Roxboro, NC; ed/BS; MA; EdD; pa/Assoc Prof S'field Col; Adv Comm on Ednl Pers for St of Mass; IRA; Assn Supvrs & Curric Devel; cp/Bd Trustees Baypath Jr Col; Bd Dirs Dunbar Commun Ctr; Urban Leag S'field; NARCP; r/Bapt.

EDWARDS, RAY CONWAY oc/Physicist; Chemist; Engineer; b/Sep 1, 1913; h/396 Ski Trail, Kinnelon, NJ 07405; ba/Pompton Plains, NJ; m/Marjorie Baisch; c/David, Douglas, Diane, Ruth, Robert (dec), Helen; p/Ernest Alfred and Augusta Ann Fee Edwards; ed/BA Univ of Cal-LA 1935; pa/Fdr, Chm of Bd & Pres, Edwards Engrg Corp 1947-; Life Mem, Am Soc Heating, Refrigeration & Air Conditioning Engrs Inc; Contbr 2 Chapts to ASHRAE Guide, Air Distribution & Noise Control; Contbr to Other Profl Pubs; hon/Lic'd Profl Engr in NY, NJ, Va & Pa; Holder 25 Patents.

EDWARDS, ROBERTA ELAINE oc/Office Manager; b/Feb 16, 1931; h/Rt 2, Box 147, Astoria, OR 97103; ba/Astoria; m/Clarence; c/Linda Corbin Wilkinson, John E Corbin, Steven D, Jeffrey A, Karen M; p/Forrest and Vera E Babbidge, Cumberland Center, ME; ed/Att'd Westbrook Jr Col; pa/Former Realtor, Secy; Current Ofc Mgr Cox Cablevision Corp; cp/Var PTA Activs; YMCA: Bd Mem 3 Yrs, Rec'g Secy 1 Yr; Am

Field Ser, Astoria 2 Yrs; Rainbow Mother's Clb 4 Yrs; Toastmasters Intl, Var Activs; Rotary Anns, Astoria; Advr to Miss Clatsop Co Pageant Ct, Astoria 4 Yrs; BSA: Troop 510 Com 2 Yrs, Vol Secy Ft Clatsop Field Ofc 2 Yrs; Former Blue Bird Ldr; Others; r/Immanuel Luth Ch, Knappa, Oreg: Mem; 1st Luth Ch, Astoria: Choir Mem, Soloist, Kgn Music Tchr; hon/Scouter's Wife Awd; HODAG Awd in Scouting; Toastmasters Intl: Outstg Area Gov Awd, Communs & Ldrship Awd, Able Toastmasters Awd.

EDWARDS, VIRGINIA LEE oc/Writer, Editor, Translator, Interpreter; b/Nov 15, 1942; h/2915 Connecticut Ave NW, Washington, DC 20008; ba/Wash DC; c/Maria, Ruy, Consuelo, Neila; p/Joseph Castro and Virginia Anne Moser Edwards, St Louis, MO; ed/BA Vassar Col; pa/Editor, Translator/Interpreter (Spanish), Dept of Commerce, Wash DC; Contbr to Sev Books & Mags incl'g The Home Birth Book, 1977; cp/DC Notary Public; hon/Grad w Hons,

John Burroughs Sch; Finalist, Nat Merit S'ship Exams.

EGAN, MARY JOAN oc/Assistant Professor; b/Jun 23, 1932; h/417 Summit St, Grove City, PA 16127; ba/Slippery Rock, PA; m/Joseph J; p/Ernest T Girlinghouse (dec); Vida Louise McGee Girlinghouse, Jena, LA; ed/BA Univ Ala; MA, PhD Cath Univ Am; pa/Asst Prof Eng Slippery Rock St Col; Asst Prof Centenary Col La 1969-72; Instr Univ Md 1966-69; Book Reviewer: *Choice*, 1972-, Mod Fiction Studies 1978-; Mod Lang Assn; Wallace Stevens Soc; Irish Am Cult Inst; Assn Pa St Col & Univ Facs; cp/Dem Party; hon/Cath.

EGAN, ROBERT LEE oc/Physician, Radiologist; b/May 9, 1920; ba/1365 Clifton Rd NE, Atlanta, GA 30322; m/Mary Alice; c/Kathleen Louise, Deborah Ann, Cheryl Lynn, Melissa Jean, Patricia Lea; p/Philip Kearny and Camilla Roach Egan; ed/MD Univ Pitts 1950; mil/USNR 1937-38, 1944-46, 1950-51, Lt (jg); pa/Emory Univ, Atlanta: Prof Radiol 1967-, Assoc Prof 1965-67, Chief Mammography Sect, Dept Radiol 1965-; Meth Hosp Ind, Indianapolis: Radiologist 1962, Fac Mem; Other Former Positions; Toronto Radiol Soc; Minn Radiol; Bay Dist Surg Soc, Los Angeles, Cal; hon/3rd Annual Wendall G Scott Meml Lecture, 14th Annual Conf on Detection & Treatmt of Early Breast Cancer, Am Col Radiol, San Juan, PR 1975; Dist'd Ser Awd, Am Cancer Soc; Am Men of Sci; Am Men of Med; Who's Important in Med; Hon Mem Asociacion de Radiologos de Centro America.

EGGLESTON, LOUISE MAVIS WAY oc/Teacher; b/Apr 26, 1888; h/537 Westover Ave, Norfolk, VA 23507; m/Aubrey Laurens; p/Alfred Hudnell Way; Laura Graham Cootes; ed/Doct's Deg Athens Col; pa/Tchr

of Prayer; Pres Emeritus Koininia Foun 1956-70; Author 40 Books; Ldr Interdenom Prayer Group, Ghent Meth Ch; Spkr Num Groups & Tours; Past Pres World Literacy Foun Inc; r/U Meth; hon/Hon's Throughout Lifetime for Num Achmts.

EGGLETON, JOHN EDWARD oc/Professor; College Campus House Director; b/Apr 29, 1932; h/2105 S Ave I Pl, Portales, NM 88130; ba/Portales; m/Phyllis; c/Phillip, Paul, Steven; p/Claude Eggleton (dec); Alyce Emily Eggleton Huff (dec); ed/BA magna cum laude Ky Christian Col; BD cum laude Butler Univ; MA Case Wn Resv Univ; PhD Univ Ia; pa/En NM Univ (ENMU): Prof Rel, Dir Christian Campus House; Min; Writer; r/Christian Ch: Mem; hon/Outstg Edrs Am; Intl Theta Phi.

EGLITIS, IRMA oc/Professor; Doctor; b/Oct 13, 1907; h/123 E Lane Ave, Columbus, OH 43201; ba/Columbus; m/John Arnold; p/Juris Georgs and Elizabete Liepinsk; ed/MD; Dipl Latvian Bd Dermatology & Veneral Diseases; pa/Ohio St Univ: Full Prof Col Med 1967-, Assoc Prof 1962-67, Asst Prof 1956-62, Instr 1952-56; Instr Human Gross Anatomy Ernst Moritz Arndt Univ, Fac of Med, Greifswald, Germany 1944-45; Other Former Positions; Am Med Wom's Assn; Nat

Chm Resolutions Com 1972, Nat Constitution & Bylaws Com 1970, Nat Chm Med Oppors & Pract Com 1968, Others; Columbus Med Wom's Assn, Var Ofcs; Am Assn Anatomists; Coun of Inst for Res in Vision; r/Ev-Luth; hon/Fellow, Ohio Acad Sci; Sigma Xi; Ohio St Univ: Pre-Clin Dist'd Tchg Awd, (Med Students), Nom'd Pre-Clin Prof of Yr, (Col of Med Students), 1975, Nom'd Outstg Tchg Awd, Sr Med Class, Nom'd Pre-Clin Dist'd Tchg Awd, Med Class of 1974, Dist'd Ser Awd (Col of Dentistry), Awd from Col of Med; DIB; Commun Ldrs & Noteworthy Ams.

EHLERT, ARNOLD DOUGLAS oc/Librarian; b/Apr 22, 1909; h/1262 Camillo Way, El Cajon, CA 92021; ba/El Cajon; m/Thelma A; c/A Benjamin, Susan E Bissonnette, Eunice Y Castle; p/Richard J and Cora E Hakes Ehlert (dec); ed/AB; MSLS; ThD; pa/Dir Libs Christian Heritage Col & The Inst for Creation Res, El Cajon; r/Prot; hon/Beta Phi Mu.

EHRENKRANZ, ELAINE oc/Professional Painter, Art Dealer; b/Jul 29, 1930; h/Coral Gables, FL; ba/PO Box 430852, S Miami, FL 33143; m/N Joel; c/Wendy, Corinne, Andrea, Fred; p/Sam and Lillian C Simonhoff, Miami, FL; ed/BA Cornell Univ; Grad Work; pa/Owner Ehrenkranz & Hammond Inc, Dealer in Oriental Japanese Art Objects

(Netsuke); 10 One-man Shows incl'g: Miami Mus of Mod Art, Lowe Mus & Norton Gallery, Palm Bch; Num Pvt Collections; Exc Shows w Yokahama, Japan; r/Jewish; hon/1st Prize, Lowe Art Gallery Mems Show; 2nd Prize, Soc of 4 Arts, Palm Bch; Gen Capital Awd, Lowe; Others.

EHRHARD, HUGH-BERT oc/Public Health Laboratory Director; b/Jun 3, 1920; h/4925 Chase Ave, Downers Grove, IL 60515; ba/Chicago, IL; m/Marjorie N; c/Theodore W; p/Theodore H and Mary E Ehrhard (dec); ed/BA; MA; MPH; DrPH; mil/USN Hosp Corps; pa/Chief Div Labs Ill Dept Public Hlth; Am Soc for Microbiol; Nat Reg Com for Nat Reg Microbiologists; Am Public Hlth Assn; Ill Soc Microbiol; Assn St & Territorial Public

Hlth Lab Dirs; Conf Public Hlth Lab Dirs; Sigma Xi; r/Meth.

EHRLICH, HELÈNE HEDY oc/Educator; Author; Literary Critic; b/Feb 1, 1924; h/265 Riverside Dr, New York, NY 10025; ba/New Brunswick, NJ; m/Irvin; c/Henri Rene, Sylvie Beatrice; p/Chaim Hercko and Freida Nirenberg Scheibe; ed/BA Hunter Col 1958; Degre avance langue francaise Sorbonne (Paris) 1961; MA 1962, PhD 1971 Columbia Univ; pa/Edr Rutgers Univ; Tchg in Am Univs 1960-; Writing & Pub'g in Field of French Lit & Lit Criticism; Former Asst Libn NY Bd Ed; Former Chm French Clb; Lectr; Org'd Inderdisciplinary Symposium 1967; AIMAU; AILA; ACLA; hon/Nom'd for W W S'ship; S'ship, Cult Div Conf of Jewish Mat Claims Against Germany; Res Grant, Rutgers Univ Res Coun.

EICH, WILBUR FOSTER III oc/Pediatrician; b/Jun 26, 1938; h/201 Flurnoy Ave, Florence, AL 36530; ba/Florence; m/Eugenia G; c/Paul F, Mark S, Donna E; p/Wilbur Foster Jr and Lula D Eich, Florence, AL; ed/BA Huntingdon Col 1960; MD Tulane Univ 1964; mil/USN 1965-71, LCDR, MC; pa/Pediatrics & Devel & Behavioral Med; cp/Trustee H'don Col; r/Epis.

EINACH, CHARLES DONALD oc/Advertising Agency Executive; b/Jul 1, 1929; h/301 E 66th St, New York, NY 10021; ba/NYC; m/Elen Simon; p/Joseph and Esther Riva Einach (dec); ed/BA Univ Buffalo 1951; MA Syracuse Univ 1953; pa/Nadler & Larimer

Inc, Advt'g, NYC: Sr VP Account Sers 1977-, VP-Account Supvr 1971-77; Grey Advt'g Inc, NYC: VP-Account Supvr 1969-71, Acct Supvr 1967-69, Account Exec 1963-67; Dir Advt'g, Sales Promotion & Public Relats J Nelson Prewitt Inc, Rochester, NY 1960-63; Other Former Positions; Nat Acad TV Arts & Scis; r/Jewish.

EISEL, JOYCE MARY oc/Associate Administrator; b/May 21, 1941; h/1156 Robinhood Ln, Norman, OK 73069; ba/Norman; c/Patrick Glenn, Randall Scott, Gregory Alan, Timothy David, Wendy Lauraine; p/Joseph Coleman (dec); Loraine Kradenski, Cliffside Park, NJ; ed/BS Miss St Univ 1972; MA Univ Okla 1975; Postgrad Study La Verne Col (Cal) 1976; Addit Studies; pa/Assoc Admr Okla Reg Red Cross Blood Ser 1977-; Dir Donor Resources Devel ARC 1975-77; Genetic Sers Coor Wichita Falls Mtl Hlth Mtl Retard Ctr; Other Former Positions; Bd Dirs Nat Human Relats Assn; Am & Tex Home Ecs Assns; Planning Com ARC, Nat Donor Resource Conf; Nat Tng Course Pers

Adm in Blood Ctrs; Edit Bd *Intl Human Relats Jour;* BPW Assn; cp/Miss St Univ Alumni Assn; Civitan; Univ Okla Alumni Assn; Norman C of C, Mbrship Com; Mtl Hlth Assn; Nat Assoc Smithsonian Instn; Former Mem Wichita Falls Mus Bd; Former Tchr Filipino Negrito Tribesman (1967); Cancer Crusade Vol; CFC Keyman; Former Chm Christmas Tows for the Underprivileged; Former Little Leag Team Mother; Others; r/St Joseph's Rom Cath Ch, Norman: Parish Lector & Eucharistic Min, Parish Coun; hon/Wom of Yr 1977, BPW Org; Commun Ldrs & Noteworthy Ams.

EISENHART, CHARLES ROBERT oc/College President; Town Councilman; b/Mar 12, 1912; h/238 Bay St, Glens Falls, NY 12801; m/Judith A Russell; c/Charles Robert Jr, Judith A Smullen, John B; p/John A and Nellie V Eisenhart (dec); ed/PhD Muhlenberg 1933; MA Albany St 1940; EdD Columbia Univ 1954; DHH Defiance Col 1961; mil/USAFR Col (Ret'd;); pa/Ret'd, Fdg Pres Adirondack Commun Col; cp/Coun-man, Town of Queensbury; r/Presb; hon/Silver Anniv Awd, Hartwick Col; AFR Cit; Resolution of Apprec, St Univ NY.

EISENMANN, LOIS ELEANOR oc/Language Arts Teacher; b/Aug 1, 1936; h/19188 Morocco Rd, Petersburg, MI 49270; ba/P'burg; m/Dale; c/Deborah, Cheryl; p/Oscar McPherson (dec); Grace McPherson, Toledo, OH; ed/AS Spring Arbor Jr Col; BS Greenville Col; MS Univ Toledo; pa/NEA;

Mich, Monro Co, Summerfield Ed Assns; IRA; Mich & Monroe Co Rdg Assn; Assn for Supvn & Devel; r/Free Meth; hon/DIB; World W/W Wom; W/W Child Devel Profs; Intl W/W Intells; Notable Ams; Personalities W&MW; Commun Ldrs & Noteworthy Ams; Book of Honor.

EISENSTEIN, ALFRED oc/Retired, Composer; Licensed Professional Civil Engineer; b/Nov 14, 1899; h/18900 NE 14th Ave, N Miami Beach, FL 33179; m/Mercedes; p/Marcus and Louise Eisenstein (dec);

ed/Dipl; pa/Composer Light Classical Music; Appearing in Concerts, Radio & TV; cp/Benefit Concerts; r/Hebrew; hon/Spec Awd, ASCAP; Cert of Merit, Cambridge, England.

EISS, ALBERT FRANK oc/Educational Consultant; b/Feb 2, 1910; h/118 Alice Ln, Carrollton, GA 30117; ba/C'ton; m/Lorene M; c/Roger L, Michael A, Kathryn G Byrd; p/Albert G Eiss (dec); Frances D Bort (dec); ed/BA Houghton Col 1933; MA St Lawrence Univ 1942; PhD NY Univ 1954; pa/Pres Innovations Inc (Devel'g Ednl Mats, Conslt to

Schs); cp/Vol Work for Var Orgs; r/Meth; hon/Cit, Nat Sci Supvrs Assn; 2000 Men Achmt; DIB.

EJIMOFOR, CORNELIUS OGU oc/College Professor; b/Oct 10, 1940; h/Cottage 48, Tuskegee Inst, AL 36088; ba/Tuskegee Inst; m/Priscilla Loveth; c/Cornelia, Carolina, Cornelius Jr, Priscilla Jr; pa/Osuji and Helen Ejimofor, Imo State, Nigeria; ed/BA w highest hon Wilberforce Univ; MPA Univ Dayton; MA, PhD Univ Okla; pa/Tuskegee Inst: Prof Dept Polit Sci 1977-, Assoc Prof & Hd Polit Sci

1972-76; Asst Prof Polit Sci William Paterson Col 1970-72; Univ Okla: Grad Asst 1969-70, Grad Res Asst 1968-69, Instr Polit Sci Edward Waters Col 1967-68; Other Former Positions; AAUP; ASPA; APSA; Exec Com Mem ASPA, Montgomery Chapt; cp/Dem; r/Rom Cath; hon/William Paterson Col Fac Res Awd; Univ Okla: Polit Sci Res Grant, Grad F'ship; Inst Intl Ed Devel F'ship; Sev S'ships; W/W in World; Men of Achmt.

EKREN, MARGUERITE MARTHA oc/College Professor; b/Jan 14, 1922; h/249 Elm Park Ave, Elmhurst, IL 60126; p/Einar B and Martha L Ekren (dec); ed/MA; pa/Prof Elmhurst Col; Sigma Tau Delta; cp/Am Civil Liberties Union; Dem; r/Unitarian; hon/2 Grad F'ships, Univ Minn; Valedictorian, HS Class; S'ship.

ELAM, J PHILLIP oc/Numismatic Investment Consultant; b/Feb 2, 1947; h/16 Central Ave, Winchester, KY 40391; ba/Same; p/James M Elam, Winchester; Pauline Fredric Warner Elam Woosley, Winchester; ed/Numismatics Res Wellsley 1968; pa/Establishmt of Numismatic Sems & Socs throughout Ky, Tenn & Ind; cp/Yg Repubs Clb; Cand for Local Ofcs; r/Epis; hon/Yg Numistmatist of Yr 1962; Best of Show, Bluegrass Numismatic Soc; W/W Ky Numismatics Awd for Promoting Hobby.

ELDER, JEAN KATHERINE oc/Associate Professor; b/May 30, 1941; h/1400 Gray St, Marquette, MI 49855; ba/Marquette; p/Clarence A and Katherine M Samuelson, Iron Mt, MI; ed/BS 1963, AM 1966 Univ Mich; pa/No Mich Univ, Marquette: Assoc Prof Dept Ed (Present), Coor Title IX to Ofc of Pres 1975-76, Asst Prof Dept Ed 1972-76; Project Dir Specialized Ofc 3, Assoc Scist Wis Res & Devel Ctr for Cognitive Lng, Univ Wis, Madison, Wis 1976-77; Other Former Positions; CEC; Fellow Am Assn on Mtl Deficiency; Am Assn for Ed of Severly/Profoundly Handicapped; Assn for Spec Ed Technol; Am Psychol Assn; Mich Assn Edrs of Lng Disabled; Var St Coms; AAUW; cp/Upper Peninsula Mich Areawide

Comprehensive Hlth Planning Assn; Bd Mem Child & Fam Ser of Upper Peninsula Mich; hon/US Ofc Ed Doct F'ship, Univ Mich; Pi Lambda Theta; Phi Delta Kappa; Delta Kappa Gamma; Appt'd to Pres' Com on Mtl Retard 1976; Biogl Listings.

ELDER, MARK LEE oc/University Research Administrator; Free-lance Author; b/May 3, 1935; h/1157 Robinhood Ln, Norman, OK 73069; ba/Norman; m/Wanda; c/Staci; p/Mark Gray Elder (dec); Ethel R Kiker, Oklahoma City, OK; ed/BA 1965, MA 1973 Univ Okla; mil/AUS 1954-56; pa/Univ Okla: Sponsored Progs Admr, Ofc of Res Adm 1978-, Security Supvr 1977-, Assoc Dir Ofc Res Adm 1976-78, Others; Conslt; Spkr; Judge; Nat Coun Univ Res Admrs; Soc Res Admrs; Authors Guild; Authors Leag; Wn Writers Am; Okla Writers Fdn; Other Profl Activs; hon/Profl Writing Awd, Univ Okla; Pub'd Author; W/W S&SW; Contemp Authors; DIB; Personalities; S, W&MW; Intl Authors & Writers W/W; W/W in Am.

ELDRIDGE, JESSIE CANNON oc/Poet; b/Mar 8, 1914; h/35 Maple St, Kingston, MA 02364; ba/Same; m/Warren Sanford (dec); c/Richard Sanford, William George, James Warren, Charles Prescott; p/Arthur G and Ella Mailman Cannon (dec); pa/Kingston Telephone Answering Ser; Mass St Poetry Soc; Am Poetry Leag; Rhode Isl Writer's Guild; NY Writers Guild; Author 26 Books of Poetry, 2 Pub'd: *To A Dream Aspiring* & *Wheel Chairs and Roses*; r/Christian Scist; hon/Poem Buried in Time Capsule (to be dug up in 100 Yrs); Gold Medal; Contbr Poems to Mags, Newspapers; Others.

ELEBASH, HUNLEY AGEE oc/Clergyman; b/Jul 27, 1924; h/1905 Live Oak Pkwy, Wilmington, NC 28401; ba/W'ton; m/Maurine Ashton; c/David Hunley, Brett Randolph E Gibbons (Mrs James); p/Eugene Perrin and Ann Hunley Elebash (dec); ed/BS Univ of S 1944; BD 1950; DD 1969; mil/USMC 1/Lt; pa/Diocese of E Carolina: Rector, Exec Secy, Bishop Coadjutor, Diocesan Bishop; r/Epis Ch: Ordained Priest 1951, Consecrated Bishop 1968.

ELFSTROM, DOROTHY BETTENCOURT oc/Executive Secretary; b/Sept 8; h/3815 Ave S, Galveston, TX 77550; ba/G'ton; m/Walter W (dec); c/Dorothy E Bailey, Bill, Henry; p/Henry Joseph and Margaret Catherine Bettencourt (dec); ed/Grad Draughon's Bus Col; pa/Columnist for *Daily Sun*, Galveston Co Newspaper 7 Yrs; Alt Poet Laureate St of Tex & Poet Laureate Galveston Co; Song Composer; Author Book *Seeker*; r/Cath; hon/Hon PhD; Book *Challenge of the Seasons* Took 1st Pl, Tex Fdn Press Wom Contest & 1st Pl, Nat Fdn Press Wom Contest.

ELG, ROBERT GEORGE oc/Administrator; b/Mar 15, 1947; h/317 Masonic St, Dyersburg, TN 38024; ba/Same; c/Pamela Jean, Dawn Michele; p/George Elg (dec); Ruth E L Johnson Elg, Mira Loma, CA; ed/AA; AS; BA; mil/USN, Hon Disch, Interior Communication Sys; pa/Dir D'burg Teen Challenge; Min to Yth; Jail Min; cp/Min Assn, Cnslr Police Dept; r/Christian.

EL GHAMRY, MOHAMED T oc/Analytical Chemist; b/Dec 3, 1937; ba/USREP/JECOR, APO, NY 09038; m/Sandra Ann Turner; p/Abdel Aziz Ghamry & Fatima M Khalil; ed/BS Univ Cairo (Egypt) 1959; PhD Imperial Col Sci & Technol (London Univ) 1967; pa/Sr Res Chemist & Hd Chem & Analysis Sect AWRC, US Dept Agri, IPD Sci & Ed Adm, Hyattsville, Md 1976-; Advr for Res Students & Postdoct Fellows; Former Asst Supt Chem Div for Min Agri, Dakki, Cairo, UAR; Former Tchr Sci & Math, Mecca, Saudi Arabia; Former Instr Imperial Col Sci & Technol; Former Harvard Chief of Party & Dir Res Labs, Harvard Univ Sch Public Hlth, Dept Nutrition; Other Former Positions; Dir Var Projs; Am Chem Soc; Intl Assn Dental Res; Brit Soc Analytical Chem, Bioanalytical Chem, Dental Chem, Nutrition Chem, Spectroscopy & Electrochem; Sr Mem Chem Inst Canada; Participant Intl Conf Lysine Fortification in Tunisia 1973; hon/Pub'd Author; Biogl Listings.

EL HAGE, SAMI G oc/Doctor; Professor; b/Oct 16, 1943; h/701 Bering Dr, #1102, Houston, TX 77057; ba/Houston; p/George and Marie El Hage (dec); ed/OD; PhD; DSc; pa/Eye Doct, Prof; r/Cath; hon/Biogl Listings.

ELIANDER, KEVIN SPURLIN oc/Data Processing, Education; b/Oct 10, 1947; h/18245 SW Pacific Hwy, Sherwood, OR 97140; ba/Tigard, OR; p/Harry F and Valda Eliander, Beaverton, OR; ed/AA Multnomah Jr Col 1968; BA Pacific Luth Univ 1970; MST Portland St Univ 1978; pa/Cert'd Key Punch Operator Wn Bus Univ 1977; p/Secy Beaverton Grange 324; Tigard Lions Clb; Noble Grand Charity Oddfellows Lodge 75; Pres Blvd Toastmasters Clb; Area Gov Area 16 Toastmasters ATM; Precnt Com-man GOP; r/Christ the King Luth Ch, Tigard; Mem; hon/Winner Oreg St Grange Serious Spkg Contest; Winner Wn Reg Serious Spkg Contest; Able Toastmaster Awd; Mem Winning Deg Team, Yth Oreg St Grange Deg Team 1978.

ELIAS, HAROLD JOHN oc/Artist; b/Mar 12, 1920; h/1800 McCann Rd, Longview, TX 75601; m/Marian L; c/Dennis H, David B; p/John Harold and Rose Francis Elias (dec); ed/BFA, MFA, Hon PhD; mil/USAF 1941-45; pa/Asst Prof Art; Artist; Lectr; Former Chm "Fine Arts Fest" SWn Mich; Cult Com "Mich Week"; Reg Dir "Am Art Week" 5 Yrs; Appt'd to Mich's St Coun for the Arts; Appt'd to Tex Comm on Arts &

Humanities; Past Pres E Tex Fine Arts Assn; 200+ One-Man Shows in Museums & Galleries, incl'g: Art Inst Chgo, Baltimore Mus Art, Creative Gallery (NY), Denver Art Mus, Detroit Inst Art, Pa Acad Fine Art, Others; Rep'd in Pvt Collections & Permanent Collections of: Univ Idaho, Ill St Mus, Univ Ill, Massillon Mus (Massillon, Ohio); hon/Work Selected for Metro's "Am Art Today" & 1953 Intl Sculpture Competition, Brussels, Belgium; DIB; W/W Am Art; Men of Achmt.

ELIASON, PHYLLIS MARIE oc/Missionary; b/Dec 21, 1925; h/Box 20217, Main Facility, Guam 96921; ba/Same; m/Albert Augustus (dec); c/Phyllis Worthen (Mrs John), James Eliason, Nancy Wilkins (Mrs W D), Albert Augustus Jr; p/John Sylvester Underhill (dec); Catherine Males, Broderick, CA; ed/BA; MEd; pa/Instr Simpson Col Ext Sch; Tchr Micronesia Bible Sch; AAUW; CEC; APGA; Bd Dirs Simpson Col, Guam; cp/VP Guam Girl Scout Coun; Christian Wom's Clb; Guam Shell Clb; r/Prot; Dir Child Evangel F'ship Micronesia; hon/Hon Mem, Huntsville, Ala; Chi Omichron Gamma Col Hon Soc.

ELKINS, DOV PERETZ oc/Family Therapist; Lecturer; Educator; Consultant; Rabbi; b/1937; ba/PO Box 8429, Rochester, NY 14618; c/Hillel, Jonathan, Shira; p/Ed and Bertha Elkins (dec); ed/BA; MHL; DMin; mil/AUS Chaplain 1964-66; pa/Fdr & Dir Growth Assocs (Human Relats Conslt'g Firm); Rabbi Temple Beth El, Rochester 1972-76; Spiritual Ldr Jacksonville (Fla) Jewish Ctr 1970-72; Rabbinical Assembly; Nat Coun on Jewish Ed; Nat Conf Jewish Communal Wkrs; Assn for Humanistic Psychol; Assn for Transpersonal Psychol; Assn for "Creative Change in Rel & Other Social Systems; Am Soc for Tng & Devel; r/Jewish; hon/Jewish

Book Coun Awd; Author & Editor 15 Books incl'g: *Humanizing Jewish Life: Judaism and the Human Potential Movement, Series in Experiential Education;* Contbr to Profl Jours.

ELKINS, LARRY OWEN oc/Chemical Engineer, Civic Service; b/Sept 28, 1937; h/1 Wimbledon Way, Shalimar, FL 32579; ba/Eglin AFB, FL; m/Patricia Jones; c/Larry DeWayne, Patrick Owen; p/Ezra Byford Elkins (dec); Mazell Brown Elkins, Old Hickory, TN; ed/BS 1959, MS 1962, PhD 1966 Vanderbilt; pa/USAF Systems Command, AF Armament Lab, Eglin AFB: Chem Engr 1967-72, Chief High Explosives Processing Lab/Chem Engr 1972-77, Dir Progs & Support, Res & Devel Labs 1977-; Dacron Plant: Chem Engr in charge of res & devel, Res & Devel Lab 1965-67, Chem Engr in charge of prodn 1962; Chem Engr Charge of Prodn: E I DuPont Cellophane Plant, Old Hickory, Tenn 1960-61, Ashland Oil Refining Co, Canton, Ohio 1959; Other Former Positions; Am Inst Chem Engrs; Am Chem Soc; Am Def Preparedness Assn; Sigma Xi; Kappa Mu Epsilon; cp/Beta Clb; Dem; r/Ch of Christ; hon/W/W S&SW; Notable Ams; Men of Achmt; Outstg Perf Awd, Eglin AFB.

ELLER, ARMENA MORSE oc/Retired; b/May 9, 1895; h/3073 Orange Ave, Oroville, CA 95965; m/Willard Henry (dec); c/Willard Morse; p/Thomas Oliver Morse; Leila Althea Allen Dawes; ed/BA Univ Cal-B; Grad Study Univ Hi; pa/Sci Illustrator Univ Cal-B 1925-28; Sci Illustrator Pineapple Res Inst, Honolulu 1928; Arch Designer Lake Bldg Corp 1929-35; Art Staff Roosevelt High, Honolulu, Designer Gumps, Honolulu 1941-56; cp/Univ Hi Fac Wom's Clb: Former Treas, Past Pres; Former Mem Bd Dirs Uluniu Wom's Swimming Clb, Waikiki, Honolulu; Sustaining Mem Repub Nat Com 1960-78; Mem Repub Senatorial Com Clb 1975-78; Repub Congl Com Clb 1975-78; DAR; Nat Adv Bd Am Security Coun; Nat Conservative Union; Former Mem: Nat Rt to Work Union, Maui (Hi) Repub Leag, Repub St Ctl Com Cal, Cal Repub Assembly; Num Other Polit Activs; r/Epis; hon/Cert of Merit, Cal Leg (Presented by Gov Ronald Reagan 1973).

ELLIG, BRUCE ROBERT oc/Executive; b/Oct 15, 1936; h/One Dawn Rd, Norwalk, CT 06851; ba/New York; m/Marie Phillip Claditis; c/Brett Robert; p/Robert Louis Ellig, Manitowoc, WI; Lucille Marie Westphal, Manitowoc; ed/BBA; MBA; pa/VP Compensation & Benefits, Pfizer Inc; Conf Bd's Coun on Compensation; NAM's Employee Benefits & Compensation Policy Com; Charter Pres: NY Assn Compensation Adms, En Reg Am Compensation Assn; Past Pres, NY Pers Mgmt Assn; Participant 1976 Pres Quadrennial Pay Comm Study of Employee Benefit Progs for Top Fed Employees; Spkr: Pers Wkshops, Sems & Confs throughout US; Tchg Positions: NYU, New Sch for Cont'd Ed; Pub'd Author; Conslt'g Editor, AMACOM's *Compensation Review;* r/Rom Cath; hon/Recog'd as 1 of Leading Compensation Experts in Country, Am Compensation Assn; Accred't Pers Diplomate Cert, ASPA; Hon Socs; W/W E.

ELLINGTON, CHARLES PORTER oc/-Agronomist; b/Dec 24, 1924; h/5014 Forest Glade Ct, Stone Mountain, GA 30087; ba/-Atlanta, GA; m/Margaret Bean; c/Martha Feldman, Charles P Jr; p/Henry Hill and

Annie Porter Ellington (dec); ed/BS Univ Ga 1950; MS Univ Md 1952; PhD Pa St Univ 1964; mil/USN 1942-46; pa/Am Soc Agronomy; Crop Sci Soc Am; Mem Meat & Poultry Inspection Adv Com, US Dept Agri; Pres NE Assn St Depts Agri; Chm Plant Indust Com Nat Assn St Depts Agri; Mem Ext Com on Org & Policy of Nat Assn St Univs & Land Grant Cols; Chm Envir Quality Subcom of Ext Com on Org & Policy; cp/Vol Yth Work; Rotary Clb; r/Prot; hon/Alpha Zeta; Phi Kappa Phi; Epsilon Sigma Phi; Gamma Sigma Delta; Man of Yr in Ga Agri, Fed Land Bank 1976.

ELLIOT, LARION J oc/Catholic Priest; School President; b/Sept 7, 1919; h/4701 N Himes Ave, Tampa, FL 33614; ba/Same; p/Francis B Elliot, Maplewood, LA; Enola Marie Hanemann Elliot (dec); ed/BS Spring Hill Col; STL St Louis Univ; pa/Pres & Alumni Dir Jesuit HS; Bd Mem Intl Ednl Devel Inc, NY, NY; Secy Priests' Senate-Diocese of St Petersburg; cp/Mem Fam Sers, Gtr Tampa C of C; r/Rom Cath; hon/W/W S&SW.

ELLIOTT, EMANUEL JOHN oc/Executive; b/Jun 28, 1929; h/143 Variety Tree Cir, Altamonte Springs, FL 32701; ba/Orlando, FL; m/Callie A; c/John E, Michael A, Marc G, Artemis Julia; p/John E Elliott (dec); Julia K Elliott, N Kingstown, RI; ed/Bach Arts & Law; mil/AUS; pa/Pres & Chm of Bd; Nat Asphalt Pavement Assn; Constrn Indust Mfrs Assn; CIMA Rep & VChm Energy Adv Coun, ARTBA; cp/Orlando C of C; Com of 200; Chm Political Action Com, Past VP Kiwanis; r/Greek Orthodox.

ELLIOTT, GEORGE ALGIMON oc/Veterinary Pathologist; b/Jun 6, 1925; h/4430 Romence Rd, Portage, MI 49081; ba/Kalamazoo, MI; m/Marguerite Hammond; /Kathleen Van Zandt, Elizabeth Sullivan, Jennifer Lee; p/George A Elliott (dec); Mattie S Elliott, Ashton, MD; ed/DVM Univ Ga 1953; MS Univ Pa 1957; pa/USN 1945-46; pa/Res Scist The Upjohn Co 1962-; Asst Prof: Vanderbilt Univ 1960-62, Univ Pa 1959-60; cp/Past Pres & VP PTA Local Chapt; r/Southridge Reformed Ch, Portage: Mem, SS Tchr.

ELLIOTT, MARJORIE REEVE oc/Teacher, Composer, Poet, Artist; b/Aug 7, 1890; m/4085 Highbridge Rd, Oneida, NY 13421; ba/Same; m/Charles H; c/Mrs W J Alford, Charles H, William; p/Charles H and Maude G Fox Reeve (dec); ed/MusB; DMus; pa/Nat Leag Am Pen Wom: Mem Nat Bd 12 Yrs, Contest Chm; Nat Bd Fdn Music Clbs, Nat Bd

Mem 1966-78; Author & Composer 400 Texts & Songs; Composer Full-length Opera; cp/Ill Fdn Woms Clbs; r/Rel Sci; hon/Centennial Awd, City of Syracuse, NY; "The George Arents Awd", Syracuse Univ; Hon Mem, Mu Phi Epsilon, NYC; Ursa Maj Awd, Alpha Phi; 2000 Wom of Achmt; World W/W Wom.

ELLIOTT, RENA McQUARY oc/Piano Teacher; b/Jul 27, 1904; h/443 Poplar, Sonora, TX 76950; ba/Sonora; m/Albert Cecil (dec); c/(Stepsons:) William Marion, James Webster; p/William T McQuary (dec); Minnie Lou Lacy (dec); ed/BA; BMus; MA; pa/Classroom Tchr; Music Ed; Music Supvr; Tex St Chm Music Ed Assn; Mem Other Profl Clbs; r/Bapt; Ch Pianist, SS Tchr; hon/Hall of Fame, Nat Piano Guild; W/W Am Wom; Intl

W/W World of Music.

ELLIOTT, SHIRLEY ANN WHITE oc/Office Education Instructor; b/Nov 4, 1939; h/7538 N 16th Dr, Phoenix, AZ 85021; ba/Glendale, AZ; c/Gregory Jr, Deborah, Carlton; p/Thomas W and Laura M White, Phoenix; ed/BEd; MBA; pa/Ofc Ed Instr Glendale Commun Col; pa/ABEA; NBEA; Delta Pi Epsilon; cp/Typewriting Judge, FBLA (Ariz); Judge Miss Ariz Pageant/-Glendale/Peoria Pageant; r/Unitarian; hon/Dean's List; Best-dressed Col Student (Female), Chgo Tchrs Col 1958.

ELLIOTT, STEPHEN MARION oc/Real Estate Development & Investment; b/Oct 15, 1945; h/9204 Flickering Shadow Dr, Dallas, TX 75243; ba/Dallas; m/Carol Anne; p/John Franklin and Winifred Key Elliott, Fort Worth, TX; ed/BBA Univ Tex-Arlington 1968; Real Est Cert So Meth Univ 1974; Further Studies: CBM; CPM; pa/Self-employed in Real Est 1976-; VP Baldwin-Harris Inc, Dallas, Tex 1971-76; Asst Property Mgr Mayflower Investmt Co, Dallas 1969-71; Proj Mgr San-Suz Apts, Arlington, Tex 1968-69; Asst Proj Mgr Coronado Apts, A'ton 1966-68; Life Mem Delta Sigma Pi; Chm IREM Income/Expense Analysis: Suburban Ofc Bldgs 1977-78; Agy Mgmt Com BOMA Intl 1976-77; Chm Transp Com 1977 BOMA Conv, Dallas; Dallas Chapt BOMA: Prog Chm 1976-78; Bd Dirs 1975-78; Inst Real Est Mgmt 1976-78; Bd Dirs NWDCCC 1974-77; r/Presb; hon/NWDCCC: Most Mbrships Sold (2), Largest Amount in Chamber Mbrships, Pavemt Pounder Awd, Teamwork Awd; Outstg Yg Men Am; W/W: S&SW, Am.

ELLIS, AILEEN VIRGINIA oc/Librarian; h/35E 10th St, Shalimar, FL 32579; ba/Eglin AFB, FL; p/Cale D and Josephine Hyder Ellis (dec); ed/AB Milligan Col; BS, MA Peabody Col; pa/Spec Libs Assn: Pres & Secy-Treas Ala Chapt, Secy Mil Libns Div, Secy Fla Chapt; Fla Lib Assn, Secy Col & Spec Libs Div; SEn Lib Assn, Chm Spec Libs Sect; VP W Fla Lib Assn; Am Lib Assn; Intl Fdn Lib Assns & Instns; AAUW, VP Fla Div; cp/DAR; r/Presb; hon/Outstg Awd, Dept AF.

ELLIS, ELLA THORP oc/Novelist; Teacher; b/Jul 14, 1928; h/1438 Grizzly Peak, Berkeley, CA 94708; ba/Same; m/Leo; c/Steven, David, Patrick; p/William D Thorp (dec); Marion Yates Thorp, San Luis Obispo, CA; ed/BA UCLA; MA San Francisco St Univ; pa/Tchr Creative Writing SF St Univ 1977-78; Other Acad Appts incl: Univ Cal Ext 1976-77, Holy Names Col Ext Fall 1976, Acalanes Adult Sch 1975-77, 1972-75; Panelist Participation incls: UC Symposium "Chd's Books in Transition" 1976, Am Lib Assn

Annual Meeting (SF) 1975, Wn Booksellers' Annual Meeting (SF) 1975, Univ Cal Symposium "Turn on to Rdg", 1974, Others; Spkr Var Occasions incl'g: Santa Barbara Annual Schs & Lib Conf 1976, Redwood City Lib Conf 1976, Annual Meeting Soc Chd's Book Writers 1975, Authors' Fest, Burlingame Schs & Libs 1975, 76, Others; Author 5 Pub'd Novels; r/Prot; hon/Jr Lit Guild Selection for *Celebrate the Morning* (Pub'd 1972); Am Lib Assn Hon Book for *Roam the Wild Country* (Pub'd 1967).

ELLIS, HOWARD EDWARD oc/Real Estate Broker; Commercial Photography; b/Jun 23, 1914; h/52 26th St NW, Atlanta, GA 30309; ba/Atlanta; m/Priscilla Martin; c/Susan Roger E Proctor; p/Edward B and Maude Sweet Ellis (dec); ed/BS; mil/USN Cmdr, Ret'd; pa/Sr VP First Equities Corp; The Summit Group Inc: Sr VP, Gen Partner; Gen Partner First Equities Assocs; Owner Ellmar Assocs; cp/Dir Atlanta Better Bus Bur; Soc for Preven of Blindness; Bd Sponsors Alliance Theater; Buckhead Bus Assn; r/Covenant Presb Ch; hon/WSB Beaver Awd; Kenmore Hall of Fame; Achiever, Atlanta U Way.

ELLIS, MARY L oc/Executive; b/Nov 25, 1933; h/7210 Windsor Ln, Col Hgts Ests, W Hyattsville, MD 20782; ba/College Park, MD; p/E N and Beatrice K Ellis, Glencoe, OK; ed/BS 1955, MS 1961 EdD 1970 Okla St Univ; pa/Ellis Assocs Inc 1975-: Fdr, Chperson Bd, Pres; Dir Wash Ofc Tech Ed Res Ctrs 1968-75; Dir Field Sers Am Voc Assn 1965-68; Reg Field Coor Manpower Devel & Ng Prog, Dept HEW US Ofc of Ed 1962-65; Other Former Positions; Am Gov'g Bds Assn; APGA; Am Soc for Tng & Devel; Am Tech Ed Assn; Am Voc Assn; Assn Commun Col Trustees; Md Voc Assn; Nat Coun Adm Wom in Ed; Prince George's Adv Com on Voc Ed; Conslt; r/Bapt; hon/Dist'd Lectr, So Ill Univ; Voc Edr of Yr, Md Voc Assn 1974; Hon Am Farmer Deg, Future Farmers Am 1975; Outstg Ser Awd to Field of Career Ed, Prince George's Co IWY; Adv Bd Bd of Md; Dist'd Ser Awd, Ctr of Voc Ed, Ohio St Univ; Hon Deg; Outstg Edrs Am.

ELLIS, MICHAEL oc/Theatrical Producer; b/Oct 25, 1917; h/963 Eve St, Delray Beach, FL 33444; m/Mary Elizabeth Walker; c/Sandra, Gordon, Thomas; p/Alexander and Mollie Fein Abrahamson; ed/BA Dartmouth 1939; MA Drew Univ 1973; pa/Actor & Stage Mgr Broadway Shows; Prodr 5 Broadway Shows w James Russo 1948-53, *Come Blow Your Horn* (w William Hammerstein) 1961, *The Advocate* (w William Hammerstein) 1963, *The Beauty Part* 1962, *Absence of a Cello* (w Jeff Britton) 1964, *The Paisley Convertible* 1967, *The Girl in the Freudian Slip* 1967; Var Off Broadway Prodns; Owner & Operator Bucks Co (Pa) Playhouse (now St Theatre Pa 1959) 1954-64; Prodr *Angela* (w Elliot Martin) 1969; Mng Dir Parker Playhouse, Ft Lauderdale, Fla 1973-76; Fdr (w wife) Package Ctr & One of a King, Delray Bch 1975-; cp/Mem Adv Bd Hopkins Ctr, Dartmouth; Former; Trustee Solebury Sch; Past Pres Delray Bch Tennis Ctr; hon/Biogl Listings.

ELLIS, PAUL DARNELL JR oc/Insurance-Real Estate Broker; b/Aug 5, 1911; h/4912 Carol Lane NW, Atlanta, GA 30327; ba/Atlanta; m/Miriam Florence; c/Paul Darnell III, Vicky E Allen, Judith E Mitchell; p/Paul Darnell and Martha Villepique Ellis (dec); ed/BS US Nav Acad; LLB, LLM Atlanta Law Sch; mil/USN, Ret'd LCMDR; Prof Aviation; pa/Re-Org'd Buckhead Bus Assn (Past Pres); Est'd 1st Mini-Park in Buckhead; Instigator in Upgrading Bus Dist; cp/CoOrgr Buckhead-Uptown Atlanta Assn; Past Pres Buckhead Civitan Clb; Former Gov N Ga Dist Civitan Intl; CoFdr Northside Hosp; Org'd Atlanta Chapt US Nav Acad Alumni; r/Bapt; hon/Citizen of Yr 1977, Buckhead Rotary Clb; Sigma Delta Kappa; Admiral Piedmont Navy; Lt Col on Govs' Staffs.

ELMORE, MARY LOUISE oc/Farmer; b/Mar 28, 1942; h/Rt 1, Box 181, Bee Branch, AR 72013; ba/Same; m/Jackie M; c/Michael

M; p/William W Bolinger (dec); Dorinda M Bolinger, N Little Rock, AR; pa/Acropolis Chapt Am Bus Wom's Assn: Scrapbook Chm 1972, Bultn Chm 1973, Mbrship Chm 1974, Prog Chm 1975, VP 1976, Pres 1977, Del to Conv 1977-78; Bid Chm 1977-78; cp/Ark Dem Wom: Former Secy, Past St Pres; Former Mem: St Dem Party Exec Com, Nat Fed Dem Wom; Former Cand Pul Co Sch Bd Dirs; r/Bapt; hon/Wom of Yr, ABWA Acropolis Chapt 1977; Apprec Awd, Dem Wom; Outstg Wom Am; Personalities of S; W/W Am Politics.

ELSON, EDWARD LEE ROY oc/Clergyman; b/Dec 23, 1906; h/4000 Cathedral Ave NW, Washington, DC 20016; ba/Wash DC; m/Helen Chittick; c/Eleanor Heginbotham (Mrs Erland), Beverly Gray (Mrs Frank M Jr), Mary Faith MacRae (Mrs Duncan), David Edward; p/Leroy and Pearl Edie Elson (dec); ed/AB Asbury Col; MTh Univ So Cal 1931; mil/AUS Ret'd Chaplain 1961, Col; pa/Nat Presb Ch, Wash: Min 1946-73, Pastor Emeritus 1973-; Chaplain US Senate 1969-; Pastor, Former Pres & Mrs Eisenhower, Mems of Cabinet & Other Govt Ofcls; Other Positions; Pub'd Author; Presb Rep World Alliance of Presby & Reformed Chs; Past Pres: Mil Chaplains Assn, Wash Fdn Chs; Former Nat Chaplain DAV; Phi Chi Phi; Theta Sigma; Chi Alpha; Am Soc Ch Hist; Ch Ser Soc; Acad Rel & Mtl Hlth; Others; cp/Eng-Spkg Union; Mil Chaplains Assn; Assn US Army; Newcomen Soc NAm; IPA; Scottish Am Heritage; US Capitol Hist Soc; Pa St Soc; Life Mem Kiwanis Intl; YMCA; Saint Andres's Soc Wash DC; Other Civic Activs; r/Presb; hon/Dist'd Citizen of Yr, City of Los Angeles, Cal 1975; Hon Citizen Var Cities of US; Edward L R Elson Monumental Wall at Nat Presb Ch, Wash; Freedoms Foun: Hon Medal Awd (for Book), Prin Sermon Awd; Clergy Ch-man of Yr, Rel Heritage Am 1954; Others.

EMANUEL, JAMES ANDREW oc/University Professor; Poet; b/Jun 15, 1921; c/James Jr; p/Alfred A Emanuel (dec); Cora A Emanuel, Denver, CO; ed/BA summa cum laude Howard Univ 1950; MA NWn Univ 1953; PhD Columbia Univ 1962; mil/93rd Inf Div WWII; pa/Assoc'd w City Col NY 1957-, Current Prof English Dept; Fulbright Prof, Grenoble, France 1968-69; Warsaw, Poland 1975-76; Vis Prof Univ Toulouse, France 1971-73; Poet; Literary Critic; Anthologist; Editor; hon/John Hay Whitney Opport Fellow; Eugene F Saxton Meml Trust Fellow.

EMBRY, CARLOS BROGDON JR oc/Businessman; Writer; Judge; b/Jul 29, 1941; h/Old Hartford Rd, Box 202, Beaver Dam, KY 42320; ba/Beaver Dam; m/Wanda Lou; c/Laura Ann, Barbara Ann, Carlos B III;

p/Carlos B Embry Sr (dec); Zora R Embry, Beaver Dam; ed/BA Wn Ky Univ; BD Alder Univ; MA Edison Col; pa/Past Pres Ky Weekly Newspaper Assn; Ky Co Judges Assn; Nat Soc Poets; cp/Mayor Beaver Dam 1970-73; Treas Repub Party Ky; VChm Green River Transp Coun; r/Bapt; hon/Outstg Yg Repub in Nation 1973-75; George Washington Hon Medal, Nat Freedoms Foun; Nat Winner, PE Fitness Ldrship Awd, US JCs.

EMERSON, GERALDINE MARIELLEN oc/Gerontologist; Medical Scientist; Medical Educator; b/Dec 30, 1925; h/2800 Vestavia Forest Pl, Birmingham, AL 35216; ba/B'ham; m/Jack Drew (dec); c/William Kenneth; p/William S Blakely; Buna L Thornton Blakely, Jacksonville, FL; ed/PhD Univ Ala 1960; pa/Assoc Prof Biochem UAB Med Ctr; Ofcr Profl Orgs; Author Num Papers & Book *Aging*; Citrus Grower; Dir Am Investors Ins Co, B'ham; cp/Adv Coun Ret'd Sr Vol Prog; hon/Var Cits.

EMERSON, ROBERT BISCAL oc/Research Scientist; b/Mar 17, 1909; h/1560 Stephens Ave, Baton Rouge, LA 70808; ba/Same; m/Opal D; c/Robert B Jr, Jin; p/Winiford F Sr and Robert P Emerson (dec); ed/MS La St Univ 1950; Grad Army Command Gen Staff Col 1948; DD; mil/AUS 1935-1962; Instr or Dir for Command & Gen Staff Subjects, Ft Sill, Okla 1953-57, Ft Sam Houston, Tex 1957, Cmdr Ofcr 4225 Logistical Command (C) 1957-62; Ret'd 1962; pa/Owner Emerson Testing Labs, Baton Rouge 1948-, Rschr Parapsychol & Biophysics; Assoc Chemist: Hurst Labs, St Petersburg 1936-38, Gable Clin Labs, St P'burg 1930-38; Sr Res Chemist, Staff Res Assoc, Chem Aluminas, Kaiser Chems, Baton Rouge 1953-74; Other Former Positions; Am Phys Soc; Am Chem Soc; Nat Geog Soc; Fla Soc Med Technicians; TAPPI; AAAS; Inst Fundamental Studies Assn; IPA; Ctr Integrative Ed; So Rubber Group; Mil Order World Wars; Am Theosophical Soc; Nat Ret'd Tchrs Assn; Am Parapsychol Res Foun; Acad Parapsychol & Med; Num Other Profl Assns; hon/Phi Eta Sigma; Phi Lambda Upsilon; Phi Kappa Phi; Sigma Pi Sigma; Patentee in Field; W/W S&SW.

EMMER, JOHN WILTZ oc/Periodontist, Preventive Dentistry; b/Apr 27, 1903; h/343 Hilltop Cir, New Iberia, LA 70560; ba/New Iberia; m/Allene G; c/Karen S; p/Albert G and Marie Wiltz Emmer (dec); ed/AB; DDS; FRCH; mil/NG; pa/Past Pres 3rd Dist Dental

Assn; Rschr Preventive of Smooth Surface Decay of Teeth; cp/Rotary: Former Mem, Past Pres Local Unit; r/Cath; hon/Fellow, Royal Col of Hlth; DIB; W/W: La, Am, S&SW.

EMRICK, RAYMOND TERRY oc/Professor; b/Aug 9, 1915; h/108 Dogwood Dr, Olney, IL 62450; ba/Olney; p/Terry C Emrick (dec); M Pearl Emrick, Paris, IL; ed/BS, MS Ind St Univ; PhD Walden Univ; pa/USAF 1942-45, 1951-52, Ret'd Ofcr; pa/Prof Psychol, Ed & Human Relats; IPA; Phi Delta; IBA; AAUP; WUMAA; cp/Ret'd Ofcrs' Assn; Resv Ofcrs Assn; Mil Order World Wars; VFW; Am Legion; Soc Comm'd Ofcrs; r/Christian; hon/Acad Hons, ISU; Tchg Fellow, ISU; Men of Achmt; Commun Ldrs & Noteworthy Ams; Book of Honor.

ENGEL, ELIOT L oc/State Legislator; b/Feb 18, 1947; h/4100-11 Hutchinson River Pkwy E, Bronx, NY 10475; ba/Bronx; p/Philip and Sylvia Bleend Engel; ed/BA Hunter Col CUNY 1969; MS Lehman Col 1973; pa/NYC Public Schs 1969-76: Guid Cnslr, Tchr, Dept Chm; cp/Mem NY St Assembly 1977-, Chm Assembly Com on Sr Citizens Transp Needs; Dem Dist Ldr; VChm Bronx Co Dem Exec Com; r/Jewish; hon/Man of Yr, FDR Ind Dem Clb 1976; Man of Yr, New Dem Clb Co-op City 1977; Awd, Hubert Humphrey Ind Dem Clb; Zionist Org Am.

ENGEL, RANDY V oc/Researcher; Writer; b/Dec 31, 1939; h/RD #3, Export, PA 15632; ba/Export; m/Thomas K; c/Dawn, Teresa, David, Regina, Tricia; p/Sebastion and Mary Fernandez Vignone, Bronxville, NY; ed/BS; pa/Exec Dir US Coalition for Life; Editor Profile Reporter; Pres Intl Foun for Genetic Res; r/Rom Cath: Chm Loaves & Fishes; hon/Dist'd Ser Medal, Vietman Coun on Fgn Relats.

ENGELMANN, CHARLES FRANK oc/Senior Pastor; b/Nov 23, 1946; h/13191 Silver Birch Dr, Tustin, CA 92680; ba/Tustin; m/JoAnn Marie; c/Christina Marie, Julia Lynne, Charles Frank Jr, Suzanne Michelle; p/Alfred F and Barbara Ann Engelmann, Madera, CA; ed/AA; BS; BA; MDiv; MRE; MA; DMin Cand; pa/Num Denom Positions; cp/Rotary; C of C; r/So Bapt; hon/Outstg Yg Men Am; W/W Am Cols & Univs; Cert of Merit-Dist Com Awd, Napa, Cal.

ENGLE, PATRICIA A oc/Construction Company Executive; b/Jul 30, 1931; h/1701 E RD Mize, Blue Springs, MO 64015; m/George I; c/6 Chd; p/Frederick Alexander and Hildred Viola Brown Pendleton; mil/USNR 1948-52; pa/w Eaton Metal Prods Co, Billings, Mont 1949, AEC, Los Alamos, NM 1949-51 & Safety Drivers Ins Co, Ks City, Mo 1951-52; w M-Wn Constrn Co of Mo, Raytown 1960-; CoOwner, Secy-Treas 1970-; CoOwner G P & M Constrn Co; Pres Constrn Wom's Assn 1980-81; Nat Exec Secys Assn; Am Bus Wom's Assn; hon/W/W: MW, Fin & Indust.

ENGLISH, ROBERT JAMES oc/Television Newsman; b/Apr 28, 1948; h/1419 Mimosa, Abilene, TX 79603; ba/Abilene; m/Patricia Ann; p/Robert March and Ressie Davis English, Ft Worth, TX; ed/BA Abilene Christian Univ 1971; pa/Newsman KRBC-TV, Abilene; Pub'd Poet; Mag Free Lance Writer; cp/Abilene Black C of C: Former VP & Exec Dir; Mem Taylor Co Grand Jury 1977-78; Original Mem Abilene Cult Arts Coun; Del Tex Dem Conv 1976; Former Bd Mem & VP Abilene Elderly Day Care Ctr; Campaign Activs; Other Civic Activs; r/Ch of Christ; hon/Pres Invitation to Inauguration of Jimmy Carter; Dist'd Cit, U Negro Col Fund; Cit for Commun Ser, Abilene VFW; DIB; Outstg Yg Men Am; Notable Ams; W/W Am Univs & Cols.

EPLEY, WILLIAM ARNOLD oc/Associate Professor, Department Chairman; b/May 18, 1939; h/108 Woodridge Cir, Pineville, LA 71360; ba/P'ville; m/Linda Morrison; c/David Eric, Allen Morrison; p/Ernest L and Ruth S Epley, Gadsden, AL; ed/BM Samford Univ 1962; BCM 1964, MCM 1965, DMA 1976 So Bapt Theol Sem; pa/La Col: Assoc Prof Music, Chm Dept Music; Dir L'ville Yth

Choir; Fdr-Dir L'ville Boys' Choir; Dir Choral Act Univ L'ville; Ky Opera Assn; Hanover Col; r/Cres Hill Bapt Ch, L'ville: Ch Musician 1965-76; pa/Dist'd Citizen, L'ville; Artist Awd, NATS.

EPPES, THOMAS ALLAN oc/Engineering Manager; b/Aug 14, 1948; h/2816 Cheshire Ln, Carrollton, TX 75006; ba/Irving, TX; m/Tera Elaine; c/Tommy Allan Jr, Tera Lynn, Elissa Anne; p/Fred T and Betty R Eppes, El Paso, TX; ed/BSEE 1970; MSEE 1971; PhDEE 1976; pa/Eta Kappa Nu; Tau Beta Phi; Phi Kappa Phi; r/Meth; hon/Opport Awd S'ship; Alcoa Alum S'ship.

EPPS, ANNA CHERRIE oc/Professor; Director; b/Jul 8, 1930; h/3333 Annette St, New Orleans, LA 70122; ba/NO; m/Joseph Sr; p/Ernest Sr and Anna L Johnson Cherrie, Prentiss, NO; ed/BA; MS; PhD; Tulane Univ: Dir Med Ed Reinforcemt Univ Med Ctr 1969-, Prof Dept Med Sch of Med 1975, Assoc Prof 1971, Asst Prof & USPHS Fac Fellow 1969-71; Other Former Positions; Am Soc Clin Pathologists; Am Soc Med Pathologists; Am Assn Blood Bks; AAUP; Albertus Magnus Guild; Washington Helminthological Soc; Am Soc Bacteriologists; Sigma Xi; Am Soc Tropical Med & Hygiene; Musser-Burch Soc; Num Hos & Res Appts; Num Com & Bd Appts; Reschr; hon/Awd for Meritorious Res, Interstate Postgrad Med Assn of NAm; Ldrs in Am Sci.

EPREMIAN, EDWARD oc/Executive Director; ba/2101 Constitution Ave, Washington, DC 20418; m/Mary; c/Barbara, Jeffrey; ed/BS MIT 1943; MS Rensselaer Polytech Inst 1947; Carnegie Inst Technol 1951; pa/Exec Dir Comm on Sociotech Systems, Nat Acad of Scis, Nat Res Coun 1976-; Union Carbide Metals Div: Dir New Ventures 1973-76, Mgr Speciality Prods 1971-72, Mgr Tantalum Prods 1970-71; Other Former Positions; AAAS; Am Soc for Metals; Am Inst Mining, Metall & Petrol Engrs; Sigma Xi; Phi Kappa Phi; Orgr & Co-Editor *Columbium and Tantalum*, 1963; Mem Adv Coun Col Engrng Univ Md 1978-; Bd Trustees Webb Inst Nav Arch & Marine Engrng 1976; Bd Dirs Acta Metallurgica 1971-73; Other Profl Activs; hon/Fellow: Am Soc for Metals, AAAS; Author 14 Tech Papers.

EPSTEIN, ALVIN oc/Artistic Director; Actor & Director; b/May 14, 1925; ba/Guthrie Theater, Vineland Pl, Minneapolis, MN 55403; p/Harry and Sonia Epstein; mil/AUS WWII; pa/Artistic Dir Guthrie Theater; Actor & Dir Broadway, Off-Broadway, US Tours & Reg Theatres, TV, Theatres in Paris & Tel-Aviv; hon/Obie Awd; Brandeis Univ Creative Arts Awd.

EPSTEIN, DAVID MAYER oc/Musician; b/Oct 3, 1930; h/54 Turning Mill Rd, Lexington, MA 02173; ba/Cambridge, MA; m/Anne; c/Eve, Beth; p/Joshua Epstein, E Meadow, NY; Elizabeth Epstein (dec); ed/Prof Music Mass Inst Technol; Conductor; Composer; Music Dir Worcester Orch; Worcester Fest; Music Dir Harrisburg Symph Orch 1974-78; Guest Conductor w Maj European & Am Orchs incl'g: Royal Philharm (London), Czech Radio Orch, Bamberg Symph, Bavarian Radio Orch, Vienna Tonkuenstlerorchester, Cleveland Orch, New York City Centre; hon/Fromm, Ford & Rockefeller Foun Awds & Grants; NY St Coun for Arts Comm; Boston Symph Orch Comm;

Mass Arts & Humanities Fdn Grant; ASCAP Awds 1963-.

ERB, RICHARD L L oc/General Manager; b/Dec 23, 1929; h/10 Fairfax Ct, Charleston, SC 29407; ba/C'ton; m/Jean E; c/John R, Elizabeth A, James E, Richard LL Jr; p/Louis H Erb, Walnut Creek, CA; Miriam L Erb (dec); ed/BA Univ Cal 1952; mil/USAR 1952-54, Lt Arty, Instr The Arty Command; pa/Gen Mgr Resort Devel Commun; Adv Bd Univ SC Hotel Sch; SC Innkeepers Assn: Dir Ed, Bd Dirs; Dir C'ton Travel Coun; Human Relats

Coun, C'ton; Am Hotel & Motel Assn; Caribbean & VI Hotel Assns; Caribbean Travel Assn; Intl, Va & Williamsburg Hotel Assns; Other Profl Activs; cp/Beta Theta Pi; Golden Horseshoe Clb; German Clb; r/Congreg; hon/Contbr Articles to Trade Jours; Extraordinary Ser Merit Awd, Am Hotel & Motel Assn; Merit Awd, VI Hotel Assn; W/W S&SW.

ERICKSEN, SYLVIA M oc/Special Education Teacher; b/Oct 10, 1914; h/6806 Meadowbrook St SE, Rochester, MN 55901; ba/Rochester; m/Chris; c/Barbara Eads, Patricia Jones, Kathy Schuetz, W A, Cindy; p/Albert Christensen (dec); Martha Simonsen;

ed/BS; Cert in Spec Ed; pa/Spec Ed Tchr, AAP Resource; MEA; NEA; REA; Assn for Retard; Coun English Tchrs; CEC; cp/Alpha Delta Kappa; r/Luth; hon/Personalities W&MW; World W/W Wom; W/W Am Wom; W/W Child Devel Profls.

ERICKSON, ELLSWORTH BURCH oc/Professor; b/Feb 14, 1924; h/2338 E 15th Ave, N St Paul, MN 55109; ba/St Paul, MN; m/H Dian; c/Sheryl, Kent, Valerie, Cynthia (dec), Kurt, Laura, Beret, Erik; p/Julius T and Isabelle Erickson, N St Paul; ed/BS 1949, MEd 1951 Univ Minn; mil/US Air Corps 1943-45 (Italy); pa/Current Tchr Art/Photo Mounds

View HS, N Suburban, St Paul; Bd Dirs Minn Alliance for the Arts in Ed: St Task Force for Elem Tchr Cert in Art; Judge Chd's Art for Nat Art Calendar; Chperson Position Paper Com & Curric Devel K-Grade 6, Art Edr's Minn; Fdr & Dir Studio 621, Art Resource, Res, Ctr & Gallery, St Paul; cp/VFW; DAV, St Paul; r/St Mark's Luth Ch, N St Paul: Mem, Bd Deacons, Choir Mem; hon/Pubs; Notable Ams; DIB; Intl W/W Commun Ser; Book of Honor; Intl W/W Intells; Others.

ERICKSON, FRED HARVEY oc/Minister; b/Oct 9, 1942; h/213 Buckingham Dr, Indianapolis, IN 46208; ba/Indpls; m/Cheryl Kay Hall; c/Shelley Renee; ed/BTh NW Christian Col 1965; MDiv 1969, STM 1971 Christian Theol Sem; pa/Dir Communs The Ch Fdn of Gtr Indpls 1973-; Lectr Communs Christian Theol Sem 1974-76; WISH TV, Indpls 1970-73: Studio Cameraman, Film Editor, Prodr-Dir; Min 1st Christian Ch,

Veedersburg, Ind 1968-70; Other Former Positions; World Assn for Christian Commun; Assn Reg Rel Communicators, VP 1975-76, Pres 1976-; Rel Public Relats Coun; UNDA-USA; Broadcast Ed Assn; Publi-Cable; Bd Mgrs Commun Comm, Nat Coun Chs; Ind Broadcasters Assn; Commun Com Ind Coun Chs; Inter-Rel Task Force on Cable TV; Ctl Ind Chapt Rel Public Relats Coun, VP for Prog; Disciples Peace F'ship; Bd Dirs Coun on Christian Unity; Disciples Amateur Radio F'ship; Num Others; cp/Bd Dirs PuppetVision Inc; BdDirs New World Communs; Commun Adv Bd Indpls Mus Art; Others; r/Disciples of Christ.

ERICKSON, J IRVING oc/Chaplain, Librarian, Hymnologist; b/Jul 19, 1914; h/3456 W Berwyn, Chicago, IL 60625; m/Myrtle Ann; c/Karin Ann Deitrick, Jenanne Inez Anderson; p/Fritz Erickson (dec); Jennie Olivia Midtlyng (dec); ed/BA Wheaton Col; MA Univ Chgo; MLS Rosary Col; Grad N Park Sem; pa/North Park Col & Theol Sem: Chaplain & Prof Rel 1947-61, Chaplain-Libn 1961-72; Pastor: Glen Ellyn (Ill) Covenant Ch 1946-48, Wiley Hgts (Wash) Covenant Ch 1941-44; r/Evang Covenant Ch: Chm Hymnal Comm 1967-73, Chm Covenant Comm on Ch Music & Worship 1975-; hon/Dist'd Ser Awd, N Park Col & Theol Sem; Author, *Twice-Born Hymns*, 1976.

ERICKSON, PATRICIA LOEBERL oc/Pediatric Nurse Practitioner; Public Health Nurse Director; b/Nov 13, 1935; h/2415 5th St NE, Salem, OR 97303; ba/Dallas, OR; c/Michael Anthony; p/Darius Silvester Orton (dec); Grace Marie Orton, Salem; ed/BS Univ Portland; PNP Univ Wash; pa/Am Nurses Assn; Act'g Secy Oreg Conf of Commun Hlth Nurse Supvrs; cp/Mar of Dimes Com; Local Mtl Hlth Assn; r/Rom Cath; hon/St Vincent's Hosp Awd.

ERICSON, CAROLYN REEVES oc/Museum Curator; b/May 12, 1931; h/1614 Redbud St, Nacogdoches, TX 75961; ba/Nacogdoches; m/Joe Ellis; c/Linda Diane, Joseph Reeves, John Ellis; p/Jonathan Floyd and Emma Cornelia Barrett Reeves, Nacogdoches; ed/BS; pa/Curator Stone Fort Mus Stephen F Austin St Univ 1972-; Ldr Geneal Wkshop, Corpus Christi, Tex; Editor Geneal Query Column which appears in 5 E Tex newspapers weekly; Nacogdoches Co Hist Survey Com; Tex Assn Museums; Tex Cath Hist Soc; Tex St, Heart of Am, Nacogdoches, E Tex, Dallas, Ft Worth

Geneal Socs; E Tex Hist Soc; Tex Folklore Soc; Other Profl Activs; Secy Nacogdoches Landmark Preserv Com; cp/Sovereign Colonial Soc Ams Royal Descent; Colonial Order of Crown; Magna Charta Dames: Past Colony Regent, Past St Rec'g Secy; Num Ofcs Held Colonial Dames XVII Century, Daughs of Republic of Tex; Order of Wash; Assoc Nat Archives; Univ Wom's Clb; r/1st Meth Ch; hon/Property Asst'ship, Ill Wesleyan Univ; Pres Delta Psi Omega, Monticello Col; W/W Am Wom.

ERLENBACH, JOHANNA MARIA oc/Actress; b/Jun 29, 1947; h/3000 Park Pl, Evanston, IL 60201; ba/Marion, NC; p/Julius and Johanna Erlenbach, Evanston; ed/Mem Equity Co, Flat Rock Playhouse 1969-77; Dir Vagabond Chd's Theatre 1969-77 (Sums); Vis Artist: Randolph Tech Inst, Asheboro, NC 1975-77, McDowell Tech Inst, Marion 1977-78; r/Luth; hon/Property Asst'ship, Ill Wesleyan Univ; Pres Delta Psi Omega, Monticello Col; W/W Am Wom.

ERLENBORN, JOHN N oc/Member of Congress; b/Feb 8, 1927; h/Glen Ellyn, IL; ba/Washington, DC 20515; 421 N Co Farm Rd, Wheaton, IL 60187; m/Dorothy C Fisher; c/Debra Lynn, Paul Nelson, David John; p/John H and Veronica Moran Erlenborn; ed/Ind St Tchrs Col 1944-45; Univ Ill 1945-46; JD Loyola Univ Col Law 1949; mil/USN, Active Duty 2 Yrs, Inactive Duty 4 Yrs; pa/Admitted to Ill Bar 1949; Began Pract w Ofc of Joseph Sam Perry, Wheaton 1949-50; Asst St's Atty, DuPage Co (Ill) 1950-52; Partner Law Firm Erlenborn & Bauer, Elmhurst 1952-63 & Erlenborn, Bauer & Hotte 1963-71; cp/Mem Ho of Reps, 14th Dist Ill 1965-; Var Com Assignmts; Former Rep Ill Gen Assembly; Mem DuPage Area Coun BSA; Mem & Former Ofcr THB Post, Am Legion, Elmhurst; hon/Hon Law Degs: Elmhurst Col, St Procopius Col.

ERLICH, ELIZABETH ANN oc/Freelance Artist; b/May 23, 1945; h/89-20 183rd St, Hollis, NY 11423; p/Ovidii Erlicht (dec); Margaret Erlich, NYC; ed/BA Wheeling Col;

MA Cand St John's Univ; pa/Outdoor Exhibits, Washington Square, NY; cp/Vol Commun Sers; r/Meth; hon/Red Cross, Mar of Dimes, Art Prizes in Col.

ERNEST, DAVID JOHN oc/Department Chairman, Professor; b/May 16, 1929; h/Crest Rd, Rt 5, St Clous, MN 56301; ba/St Cloud; m/Prudence Ellene Michael; c/David Michael, Stephen John, Bryan James, Christopher Scott; p/Rudolph J and Sylvia Rose Ernest, Berwyn, IL; ed/BMEd Chgo Musical Col 1951; MS Univ Ill 1956; EdD Univ

Colo-B 1961; pa/St Cloud St Univ 1963-; Chm Dept Music, Prof Music & Music Ed; Chm Div Fine & Applied Arts Glenville St Col, WVa 1961-63; Instr Univ Colo-B 1956-58, 1959-61; Other Former Positions; Phi Mu Alpha; Phi Delta Kappa; NACWPI; World Future Soc; Am Ednl Res Assn; Nat Coun on Measuremt in Ed; Intl Soc Harpsichord Bldrs; AAUP; St Cloud Art Coun; MENC; Minn Alliance for Arts in Ed; Num Other Profl Activs; r/Presb; hon/Danforth Assoc; Fulbright Scholar to France; Full S'ship, Chgo Music Col; Biogl Listings; Pubs.

ERNOUF, ANITA B oc/Teacher; b/Feb 22, 1920; h/312 Randolph St, Farmville, VA; ba/F'ville; m/Edward; c/Edward III, Roderic; ed/BA Hunter Col 1944; MA 1946, PhD 1970 Columbia Univ; Addit Study Mex, Spain, France; pa/Longwood Col, F'ville: Prof, Chm Dept Fgn Langs; French, Spanish & Portuguese Examr US Postal Sers; Res Asst Hispanic Inst, Columbia Univ 1945-47; Assoc Prof Hollins Col 1947-60; Universidad Iberoamericana; Tchr Grad Sems (Sums) & Dir of Thesis Intl Dept; Past Pres F'ville Dist Chapt AAUW; Alpha Delta Kappa: VP Alpha Delta Chapt 1972-74, Pres 1974-76; Mod Fgn Lang Assn of Va: Pres-elect 1972, Pres 1973; Pres-elect Mod Fgn Lang Assn Va 1977; Pres Va St Coun on Study Abroad 1977; Sgt-at-Arms St Alpha Delta Kappa 1977; ACTFL; VEA; NEA; LEA; V-PAK; AAUW; AATSP; cp/F'ville Woms Clb; Sponsor YWCA 10 Yrs; hon/Personalities of S.

ERWIN, A JEAN HOCKING oc/Professor; b/Dec 15, 1920; h/Glenwood Ests, Rt 4, Martin, TN 38237; ba/Martin; m/Kenneth (dec); p/William James Hocking, Toronto, Ontario, Canada; Margaret Pearl Logan Hocking (dec); ed/BA; MS; PhD; pa/Prof Child Devel Fam Relats Sch Home Ecs, Univ Tenn-M; AAUP; Life Mem AHEA; CHEA;

IFHE; NAEYC; NCFR; SACUS; SRCD; TAEYC; THEA; Omicron Nu; Phi Kappa Phi; cp/Adv Com Easter Seal Soc for NW Tenn; r/U Ch of Canada; Meth Ch, Martin: Adm Bd, Past Pres UMW; hon/Gen Foods' Awd; DIB; Notable Ams; Intl W/W Commun Ser; W/W S&SW; World W/W Wom in Ed.

ERWIN, WILLIAM WALTER oc/Executive; Farmer; b/Sept 28, 1925; h/RR2, Box 173, Bourbon, IN 46504; ba/Etna Green, IN; m/June Bramlet; c/Hope, Lewis, James; p/Lewis Erwin (dec); Eleanor Fribley Erwin, Bourbon; ed/BS Univ Ill; mil/USAF 1943-45; pa/Pres & Mgr Triple "E" Farm Inc; Asst Secy of Agri (Appt'd by Pres) 1972-75; Headed US Delegation to Intl Conf on Planning & Devel of Rural Areas, Plovdiv, Bulgaria 1974; Agri

Conslt to William Ruckelshaus (Admr of Envir Protection Agy) 1971-72; Dir Foun for Am Agri; Purdue Farm Policy Study Group; St & Nat Farm Bur Field Crop Com 1960; cp/Mem Ind St Senate 1964-68; Former St Chm Ind Yg Repubs; Lions Clb; Masonic Lodge; Shrine; Scottish Rite; Am Legion; Former Bd Mem Bashor Home for Boys; r/U Meth Ch; hon/Nat Winner JCs Outstg Yg Farmer Awd; FFA Hon St Farmer.

ESBERGER, KAREN ANN KAY oc/Registered Nurse; Educator; b/Jan 17, 1948; h/Box 116, Midlothian, TX 76065; ba/Dallas, TX; m/Michael; p/James Tolivar Kay Jr (dec); Phama Duke Kay, Midlothian; ed/BSN

Baylor Univ; MSN Univ Tex-Austin; PhD N Tex St Univ; pa/Fac Mem Baylor Univ Sch Nsg; Am & Tex Nurses Assns; Gerontological Soc; Tex & Nat Leags for Nsg; cp/Baylor Alumni Assn; Baylor Nurses Alumni Assn; Dallas Unit Am Cancer Soc; r/1st Bapt Ch: Mem, Ch Pianist; hon/J Harry Phillips S'ship.

ESCHNER, EDWARD G oc/Radiologist; b/Jun 3, 1913; h/755 Orchard Park Rd, W Seneca, NY 14224; ba/Buffalo, NY; m/Ailene; c/Edward G Jr, Lorene E Hengel, Reinold M, Nancy Ann Cy, Betsey M Ball; ed/Herman P

and Clara C Eschner (dec); ed/MD; mil/AUS Lt; NY St Guard Reservs Col; pa/Ret'd Dir Radiol Dept E J Meyer Meml Hosp; Ret'd Hd Dept Radiol SUNYAB; cp/Mason; OES; Buffalo Consistory; Shrine; Jesters; r/Prot.

ESKENS, ESTHER PAULINE oc/Registered Nurse; State Legislator; b/Nov 30, 1924; h/15 E 10th, Lovell, WY 82431; ba/Cheyenne, WY; m/Henry R; c/Joan, Henry II; p/Paul G Brown, Manhattan, KS; Viola Brown (dec);

ed/Nsg Dipl; pa/ANA; Wyo Nurses Assn; Dist 9 Nurses Assn; BPW; cp/Mem Wyo Ho of Reps; Order of Wom Leg; Fdn Woms Clbs; AMA Aux; Wyo Med Soc Aux; r/Cath; hon/Wom of Yr, BPW 1973-74.

ESKUT, BILLIE LEE oc/Minister; Educator; b/Dec 3, 1931; h/5709 Fair Oaks Ave, Baltimore, MD 21214; ba/Balto; m/Frances J; c/Ginger Kay, Vicky Lee, Ruth-Ann, Sandra Lynn, Frances Janice, William Lee; p/Kathleen B Eskut, Balto; ed/BA; MA; mil/USAF 1950-54; pa/Dept Hd Math Balto

Polytech Inst; Assoc Prof Univ Balto; NEA; PSTA; MSTA; BTU; Past VP Chesapeake Chapt Inst Envir Scis; cp/Explorer Scouts; Balto Tchrs Union; PTA; r/Christian: Min; hon/Nat, Intl Judge Sci Fair; Featured Spkr, Nat IES Conv; Fellow: IBA, ABA.

ESPARZA, THOMAS oc/Sports Director; h/8115 16th Ave, Edinburg, TX 78539; ba/E'burg; m/Esther LaMadrid; c/Tommy Jr, Steven, Teylene; ed/BS, MS Tex A&I Col; PhD Am Intl Open Univ; mil/USN WWII; pa/Dir Intramural Sports Pan Am Univ, E'burg 1968-; Former Asst to Sch Supt, E'burg; Former Hlth, PE & Rec Conslt E'burg Schs; Past Pres: E'burg Tchrs Fed Credit Union, Pan Am Univ Fed Credit Union; Former Mem Rep

Assembly HPER Assn Tex; Life Mem: NEA, Tex St Tchrs Assn, Tex Assn Col Tchrs; Nat Intramural Assn; Auditing Com Tex Assn for HPER; Hd Nat PE & Sports Week Com; cp/VP Am Cancer Soc Unit E'burg; Bd Dirs: Hidalgo Co Hist Soc, Hidalgo Co Housing Auth; Am Legion: 15th Dist Baseball Chm, Baseball Div Chm, Resolution Assignmts Com (Tex), Americanism Com (Tex); Steering Com Metro Bank, McAllen, Tex; Other Former Activs; hon/Hon'd by Gov's Com on Physical Fitness; Num Biogl Listings.

ESPINA, ANGEL BEAUNONI (Stage name Noni Espina) oc/Concert Singer, Professor, Composer, Scholar-Author; h/1866 Cedar Ave, New York, NY 10453; p/Angel C and Wencesline S Espine, Philippines; ed/BSE; MA; SMM; PhD; pa/Adj Prof NYC Univ 1974-; Vis Prof Univ Redlands 1971-72; Prof Music Jacksonville St Univ 1967-71; Vis Prof

Univ Colo 1966-67; Exec VP Col of Maasin 1965-66; Asst Prof Music Drury Col 1963-65; Other Acad Positions; Num Solo Recitals 1951-; USA, Ctl Am, Far E; Choral Conductor Num Choirs in USA & Philippines; Judge Yg Artists Auditions (NY), Music Fests; Composer: Songs, Operas, Operettas, Choral Arrangemts; Painter, Num Art Exhibits; Mem Wash Square Art Show 4 Seasons; Poet; Soloist: Fests, Radio, TV, Records; hon/Author; Dist'd Awd; Press Clb Awd of Hon; Cult Pioneer Awd; Biogl Listings.

ESPOSITO, KATHY ANN oc/Administrator; b/Nov 24, 1950; h/Yonkers, NY; ba/201 Palisade Ave, Yonkers; p/Louis J and Jean C Esposito; ed/BA; MA; MA; pa/Admr Spanish Foun Bilingual Prog; Phi Sigma Iota; Phi Delta Kappa; r/Rom Cath; hon/Dean's List Cand.

ESPOSITO, LUIGI oc/Catholic Priest; Associate Pastor; Educator; b/Aug 23, 1940; h/3600 Claremont Ave, Baltimore, MD 21224; ba/Balto; p/Pasquale and Colomba Esposito, Balto; ed/BA Collegio Bianchi (Naples, Italy); MDiv Mary Immaculate Col; MLA Johns

Hopkins; pa/Chaplain: KOC, CWV, Retreat Group BPD; Marriage Cnslr; Yth Cnslr; HS Prof; Assoc Pastor; Sons of Italy, Others; cp/BSA Instnl Rep; Com-man, GSA; r/Cath; hon/Ethnic Awds, Local Awds; W/W; Men of Achmt.

ESSENWANGER, OSKAR M oc/Physicist; Adjunct Professor; h/610 Mountain Gap Dr, Huntsville, AL 35803; ba/Redstone Arsenal, AL; m/Katharina D; c/Marianne, Angelika; p/Oskar and Anna Essenwanger (dec); ed/BS; MS; PhD Equiv; mil/German

AF 1939-45; pa/Supvy Res Physicist MIRADCOM; Adj Prof Envir Sci; Res in Statistical Analysis of Atmospheric Data, Climatology; r/Rom Cath; hon/Missile Command Sci Achmt Awd; Sigma Xi; Outstg Reschr Awd, UAH; Cert'd Quality Engr; Cert'd Conslt'g Meteorologist; Fellow, IBA.

ESSLINGER, W GLENN oc/Professor; b/Oct 21, 1937; ba/Carrollton, GA 30118; ed/BS 1962, MS 1964, PhD 1966 Univ Ala; pa/Chm-Elect Bd Regents, Adv Com on Chem Univ System of Ga 1978-79; W Ga Col, C'ton: Prof Dept Chem 1977-, Chm Dept Chem 1973-78, Assoc Prof 1971-77, Act'g Chm Dept Chem 1972-73, Asst Prof 1968-71; Instr Chem Experimental Prog (NSF Grant Sponsored), Oak Mtn Acad, C'ton 1970-71; Mem Num Coms; Am Chem Soc; Ga & Ala Acads Sci;

ACS Organic Exam Com; Ga Sect ACS: Nom'g Com, Herty Awd Com; Profl Wkshops; cp/Kiwanis Clb C'ton: Oper Drug Alert Com, Former Mem Bd Dirs; Conslt Southwire Co, C'ton; Fac Advr Delta Tau Delta; Conslt on Drug Probs, C'ton Sch Sys; Spkr to Civic Clbs, Schs, PTA, Ch Groups; Fdr SPEED Prog C'ton; Conslt Willard-Grant Press; Judge; Others; r/Tabernacle Bapt Ch: Deacon, Ch Choir, SS Tchr; hon/Sigma Xi; F'ship; Gamma Sigma Epsilon; Pi Mu Epsilon; Outstg Yg Edr, JCs; Outstg Ldr in Drug Ed, St of Ga Kiwanis; Dir NSF Grant; Boy Scout Awd for Drug Ed; Outstg Kiwanian; W/W in Am; Num Pubs; Biogl Listings.

ESTERGREEN, MARION MORGAN oc/Writer; Historian; Editor; h/PO Box 343, Taos, NM 87571; ba/Same; m/Paul H (dec); c/Sheryl M; p/Frances Marion and Glennie Holland Morgan (dec); ed/BA; MA; pa/Author *Kit Carson: A Portrait in Courage*, Other Books, Num Free-lance Articles to Mags & Newspapers; cp/Chm Kit Carson Meml Park Adv Bd; r/Presb; hon/Poet Laureat NM; 3rd Prize, NLAPW; Num Prizes.

ESTES, ERNEST LATHEN III oc/- Department Head; b/Mar 21, 1942; h/219 Carey Ln, Friendswood, TX 77546; ba/- Galveston, TX; m/Mary K; c/Arron Judson, Erika Nichol; p/Ernest L Jr and Lillian Lansen Estes, Racine, WI; ed/BA Lawrence Univ; MA; PhD Univ NC; pa/Hd Dept Marine Scis Moody Col; Marine Geochemist.

ESTILL, ANN H M oc/Assistant Professor; ba/2039 Kennedy Blvd, Jersey City St Col, Jersey City, NJ 07305; p/Don V and T Christine Estill, Kalamazoo, MI; ed/BMus Wn

Mich Univ; MA Columbia Univ; pa/Asst Prof Music Jersey City St Col; Coloratura Soprano; Sev Opera Roles; Radio & TV Appearances; Other Perfs; r/Meth; hon/Dean's Hon Awd, Sigma Alpha Iota; Phi Delta Kappa; DArts S'ship.

ESTIS, WILLIS CLEVE oc/Mental Health Counselor; b/Apr 3, 1946; h/404 Lakemont Dr, Rt 2, Ohatchee, AL 36271; m/Bess Roberts; p/Willis Pace and Essie Vines Estis, Pleasant Grove, AL; ed/BS 1969, MA 1973, EdD 1977 Univ Ala; mil/AUS 1969-71; pa/Am Psychol Assn; APGA; Nat Rehab Assn.

ESTRADA, DORIS EVELYN oc/Former Librarian; b/Dec 13, 1923; h/5349 E Hobart St, Stockton, CA 95205; m/Frank M; c/Denise Kelly (Mrs Charles III), William, Alan; p/William and Nettie Goss Perkins, Fanshawe, OK; ed/AA; BA; MLS; pa/Former

Libn II Stockton Public Lib; Secy Yg Peoples Cooperative Lib Assn; Author *Periwinkle Jones*, Short Plays & Stories; cp/Former Mem PTA; r/Reorg'd Ch Jesus Christ LDS; hon/3rd Pl, Princeton Theol Sem, Nat Competition for a Drama of Rel Significance.

ETHELL, JEFFREY LANCE oc/Aviation Writer; Commercial Pilot; Baptist Minister; b/Sept 29, 1947; h/2403 Sunnybrook Rd, Richmond, VA 23229; ba/Same; m/Bettie T; c/Jennifer Brooke, David William, Julie Christine; p/Ervin C and Thelma Jean Ethell, Myrtle Beach, SC; ed/BA King Col; pa/Aviation Writer, Sev Books & Mag Articles Pub'd Yrly; Cnslr Troubled Yth, Marriage; Charter Pilot; cp/Evangel Caucus for Polit Reform; r/Bapt; hon/Cert'd Scuba Diver; Biogl Listings.

EUDALY, NATE JR oc/Foreign Missionary; b/Sept 10, 1955; h/PO Box A-138, Managua, Nicaragua; ba/Ft Worth, TX; p/N H and Marie Saddler Eudaly, El Salvador, Ctl Am; ed/BA cum laude Baylor Univ; Grad Study SWn Sem 1977-78; pa/Rel Ed, Fgn Missionary Ser; SWn Rel Ed Assn; Sociedad Honoraria Hispanica; cp/Ft Worth Civic Orch; Am Field Ser; r/James Ave Bapt Ch: Worship Ldr, Choir; hon/1st Pl, AATSP Nat; Dean's List, Baylor; Mu Alpha Theta.

EURICH, ALVIN CHRISTIAN oc/Educator; Psychologist; b/Jun 14, 1902; h/Hubbell Mountain Rd, Sherman, CT 06784; ba/New York, NY; m/Nell P; c/Juliet Ann, Donald Alan; p/Christian H and Hulda Steinke Eurich; ed/BA; MA; PhD; mil/USNR Cmdr; pa/Pres Acad Ednl Devel 1963-; VChm Bd Ednl Facilities Labs Inc; Pres Aspen Inst Humanistic Studies 1963-67; Exec Dir Ed Div Ford Foun 1958-64; Ford Fund Advmt Ed: VP 1951-64, Bd Dirs 1952-67; Other Former Positions; Trustee Penn Mutual Life Ins Co; Conslt US Govt Agys during & following war yrs; Supr Var Ednl Surveys; Mem or Conslt Var Comms incl'g: Hoover Comm, Pres Truman's Comm Higher Ed, Pres Kennedy's Task Force Ed; Chm Surg Gen's Comm Nurses; Conslt: NASA, AID, Peace Corps; Chm US Nat Comm UNESCO; Vis Prof Var Univs; Vis Fellow Clare Col, Univ Cambridge (England); Bd Dirs Am Lovelace Foun, Belgian Am Foun; Fellow: AAAS, Am Psychol Assn, Aspen Inst; Sigma Xi; Phi Delta Kappa; cp/Univ Clb; Century Clb, NYC; Cosmos Clb (Wash); Athenaeum Clb (London); hon/Contbr to Ednl Jours, Gen Periodicals; Author or Coauthor Books & Studies in Ed; Outstg Achmt Awd, Univ Minn; Times Square Clb 4th Annual Awd; Annual Awd, NY Acad Pub Ed.

EVANS, BEATRICE SINGLETON oc/Guidance Counselor; h/1736 Walker Ave, Orangeburg, SC 29115; ba/O'burg; m/Robert Shaw; c/Robert Shaw II, Frederick Marshall Gary, James Malcolm; p/Nathaniel and Bertha S Singleton, Florence, SC; ed/BS; MS; pa/APGA; Assn Non-White Concerns; SC Pers & Guid Assn; cp/Dem; NAACP; OES; VFW Ladies Aux; Bd Mem U Way; Nat Assn Univ Wom; Links Inc; Delta Sigma Theta; Nat Coun Negro Wom; Jack & Jill; Mtl Hlth Adv Coun; Daughs of Isis; r/Mt Pisgah Bapt Ch; hon/U Way Vol Awd; Noteworthy Ams Plaque.

EVANS, BRUCE A oc/Library Administrator; b/Aug 6, 1947; h/Townhouse #11, Corinth, MS 38834; ba/Corinth; m/Carol K; p/Albert and Claire, Oklahoma City, OK; ed/BA SUNY-Stony Brook 1969; MSLS Fla St Univ 1974; pa/USAF 1969-73; pa/Asst Dir NE Reg Lib; Miss Lib Assn: Mem 1974-, Intellectual Freedom Com 1975, VChm Public Lib Sect 1977-78, Chm 1978-79; Miss Museums Assn; 1st Pres-elect Alcorn Co Libn's Cooperative 1976-77; Chm NE Reg for 1st Very Spec Arts Fair 1977-78 (Handicapped); Var Ldrsh Positions; Local Newswriter, Contbr Articles on Rel, Theatre & Hlth, Nat Polits 1974-; cp/Civitan; Local Little Theatre: Actor, Stage Hand; EEO Ofcr NE Reg Lib; Vol: Mar of Dimes, Cancer Drive; Ofcr Local Cancer Soc Unit; r/Cath: Parish

Coun Mem & Pres; Rel Ed Instr; 1 of 2 Dels to Miss Cath Conv 1975; hon/Personalities of S.

EVANS, EDWIN CURTIS oc/Physician; Practicing Internist; b/Jun 30, 1917; h/500 Westover Dr NW, Atlanta, GA 30305; ba/Atlanta; m/Marjorie; c/Nancy, Edwin, Marjorie, Jane and Jill, Carol; p/Watt Collier and Bertha Chambers Evans (dec); ed/BS Univ Ga 1936; MD Johns Hopkins Univ Sch Med 1940; mil/AUS 1942-46, Disch as Maj, Med Corps; pa/Cert'd Am Bd Internal Med 1951,

77; Clin Assoc Prof Med Emory 1972-; Chief of Staff Ga Bapt Hosp 1973-79; Diabetes Assn Atlanta, Pres 1958-59; Ga Diabetes Assn, Pres 1965-66; Am Inst Internal Med, Pres 1972-73; Am Col Physicians, Fellow; Med Assn Atlanta, Pres 1973-74; So Med Assn, Chm Exec Coun 1978-79; Inst of Med, Nat Acad Scis 1977.

EVANS, H C JR oc/College President; b/Aug 18, 1927; ba/Banner Elk, NC 28604; c/Mark Richard; ed/BA cum laude Carson-Newman Col 1950; MA Columbia Univ 1951; EdD Univ Tenn 1958; Addit Grad Work; mil/USAAC, USAFR 23 Yrs Ser; Lt Col USAFR; Liaison Ofcr Resv Ofcr Tng Corps; pa/Pres Lees-McRae Col 1967-; Dir Buck Hill Falls Sum Camp, Buck Hill Falls (Pa) 1961-67; Carson-Newman Col, Jefferson City, Tenn: Dir Tchr Ed, Prof Ed & Chm Dept Psychol-Ed 1963-67; Placemt Dir & Assoc Prof 1962-63, Assoc Prof 1961-62; Prin: Robert Elem Sch, Morristown City Schs 1958-61, Rose Elem Sch, M'town 1955-56; Other Former Positions; Past Pres: Tenn Guid Cnslrs, M'town Ed Assn; Ofcl Del to Tenn's White House Conf on Ed; Prin's Study Coun; Chm Nom'g Com Tenn Elem Prin's Assn; VP E Tenn Elem Prin's Assn; Adv Com NC Com on Intl Cooperation; Higher Ed Panel Am Coun on Ed; Exec Com: NC Assn Jr Cols, NC Foun Ch-Related Cols, Appalachian Consortium, NW Reg Ed Ctr; Life Mem: NEA, Tenn PTA; Bd Govs Highland Univ; Commun Adv Bd Upward Bound/Spec Sers; Other Profl Activs; cp/Kiwanis: Former Gov Carolinas Dist, Intl Coun, Chm Spec Sers Com & Gov's Flying Squad (Carolinas Dist), Carolinas Dist Key Clb Com, Others; Num Activs Scouts; Bd Dirs NC Nat Bk, Banner Elk; Bd Advrs Newland Br, Watauga Savs & Ln; CAP: Former Mem, Capt; Exec Panther Sprgs Rec Devel Com; Chm Co Wide Muscular Dystrophy Assn; Bd Dirs Civic Music Assn; Past Pres Century Clb M'town; Former Mem Bd Dirs M'town JCs; Others; hon/Tenn Tchr of Yr 1957; Airman of Yr, Outstg Resv Airman in USAF 1958; Yg Man of yr, M'town, Tenn 1955; Ambassador at Large, M'town C of C; Col Aide de Camp, Gov Buford Ellington's & Gov Frank

Clement's Staffs, Tenn; Man of Yr, Avery Co, NC 1974.

EVANS, JOHN DERBY oc/Telecommunications Executive; b/Jun 3, 1944; h/1023 Delf Dr, McLean, VA 22101; ba/Arlington, VA; m/Susan Allan; p/Edward S and Florence A Evans, Charlottesville, VA; ed/AB Univ Mich 1966; mil/USN 1967-70, Lt; Hd, TV Sect, Off of Chief of Nav Ops, Wash DC 1969-70; pa/Pres Evans Communs Systems Inc, Wash DC 1970-72; VP & Gen Mgr Am TV &

Communs Corp, Capitol Cablevision Corp, Charleston, WVa 1972-76; Reg Mgr Mid-States Reg, ATC 1973-76; Spec Telecommuns Conslt to Asst Secy, HEW, Planning & Evaluation, Wash DC 1976; VP & Ops Off, Arlington Telecommuns Corp, A'ton 1976-; Chm Adv Coun WVa Ednl Broadcasting Auth's, Soc Motion Picture TV Engrs; hon/Biogl Listings.

EVANS, JOHN J oc/Management Consultant; Executive; b/Mar 1, 1940; ba/1936 Elmsbury Rd, Westlake Village, CA 91361; m/Jennie Trees Nutt; c/Todd, Karlyn, Jane, Mark; ed/BA Centenary Col; MBA Pepperdine Univ Sch Bus & Mgmt; Grad Syracuse Univ Grad Sch Sales Mgmt & Mktg; Further Studies; pa/Pres Evans & Co, Mgmt Conslts, Westlake Village; Yg Pres' Org; Pres Assn; Aspen Inst; Conf Bd; Los Angeles Sales & Mktg Execs Assn; Past Pres Shreveport

SMEA; Past Pres SW Coun SME; Syracuse Univ Grad Sch Sales Mgmt & Mktg: Fac Mem, Trustee; cp/Former Chm Yth Opport Ctr Coun; Past Pres Mtl Hlth Ctr Bd; Fdr & Chm Bd of Shreveport-Bossier Conv & Tourist Bur; Dir C of C; Bd Mem: Red Cross, Vol Ser Bur, Assn for Mtl Hlth; Former Div Chm UF; Syracuse Univ Grad Sch Sales Mgmt & Mktg Alumni Assn; S'port Clb; S'port CC; Arizona Clb; Century Clb Ft Worth; hon/Dist'd Salesman Awd; Top Prodr Awd for Chamber Work.

EVANS, JOSEPH ROBERT oc/Minister; b/Jul 25, 1924; ba/PO Box 265, Brush, CO 80723; m/Dorothy Luke; c/Lorilee Anne, James Ratcliff, Elizabeth Anne; p/Joseph Ratcliff and Mary Frances Wilson Evans (dec); ed/Min Rankin Presb Ch; Pastoral Cnslr; cp/Rotary Intl; C of C; r/Presb; Developer of Ednl/Cnslg Ctr; hon/W/W in Rel.

EVANS, LOUISE oc/Clinical Psychologist; Lecturer; Real Estate Developer-Investor; ba/127 W Commonwealth, Fullerton, CA 92632; m/Tom R Gambrell; p/Henry Daniel Evans (dec); Adela Pariser Evans; ed/BS NWn Univ 1949; MS 1952, PhD

1955 Purdue Univ; Diplomate, Am Bd Examrs Profl Psychol 1966; pa/Staff Conslt in Clin Psychol Martin Luther Hosp, Anaheim, Cal 1963-; Psychol Conslt to Fullerton Commun Hosp 1961-; Pvt Pract, Fullerton 1960-; Clin Res Conslt to Epis City Mission, St Louis, Mo 1959; Other Former Positions; Intl Coun Psychologists Inc: Fellow, Secy 1973-76, Past Secy 1962-64, Mem-at-Large Bd Dirs 1977-, Com Spec Interests of Wom 1977-; Del to US Pres' Traffic Safety Conf 1964; Del to Cal Gov's Traffic Safety Conf 1964; Fellow: Royal Soc Hlth, AAAS, Am Orthopsychi Assn, Am Psychol Assn; IPA; AAUP; Sigma Xi; Cal St Psychol Assn; Orange Co Psychol Assn; Orange Co Soc Clin Psychologists, Num Ofcs; Los Angeles Co Psychol Assn; LA Soc Clin Psychologists; Am Acad Polit & Social Sci; Am Judic Soc; Alumni Assn Menninger Sch Psychi Rehab Intl USA; Life Mem Purdue Univ Alumni Asn; Ctr for the Study of the Presidency; Fellow, World Wide Acad Scholars; cp/Var Civic, Ser, Ednl, Cult, Rel & Col Orgs 1950-; Donor to Var Org'd Charities; hon/Fellow: IBA, ABI; 1 of 5 Purdue Alumni Selected to Receive 1st Purdue Alumni Assn Citizenship Awds; Ser Awd, Yuma Co, Ariz Hd Start Prog; Dist'd Ser as Ldr in Advancing Psychol Internationally 1968; Adv Mem, Marquis Lib Soc; "Miss Heritage", Heritage Pubs 1965; Recipient S'ships; Intl W/W Commun Ser; DIB; Num Other Biogl Listings.

EVANS, LYLE KENNETH oc/Pedodontist; Pecan Grower; b/Jun 1, 1935; h/7254 Blanco Rd, San Antonio, TX 78216; ba/SA; c/Jonathan Carter; p/L K and Margaret Kelly Evans, Gainesville, TX; ed/Univ Tex; Doct Baylor Univ Col Dentistry 1962; Post-doct Cert Univ Rochester 1966; mil/AUS Dental Corps Capt 1962-64; pa/Am, Tex Dental Assns; SA Dist Dental Soc; Tex Pedodontic Assn; SWn Soc Pedodontists; Am Acad Pedodontics; Am Soc Preventive Dentistry; Am Soc Dentistry for Chd; Tex Pecan Growers Assn; cp/YMCA Ftball Coach; Delta Sigma Delta; Kappa Alpha; hon/Cert Achmt US 5th Army 1964; Clin Awd Tex Dental Assn; Cert Apprec San Antonio Dist Dental Soc; W/W: Tex, S&SW; DIB; Men Achmt; Intl W/W Commun Ser; Book of Honor; Outstg Ams in S; Notable Ams Bicent Era.

EVANS, MARILYN BAILEY oc/State Legislator; h/321 Lynn Ave, Melbourne, FL 32935; ba/Melbourne; m/Hugh; c/Hugh Jr, Cecile, Daniel, Mary Louise; p/Cecil C and Augusta Bailey, Jacksonville, FL; ed/BA Duke Univ; Fla Tchg Cert; Fla Real Est Lic; pa/Brevard Substitute Tchg, Ctl Jr HS & Melbourne HS; Real Est Salesperson Evans-Butler Realty Inc; Fla Rep for AAUW; Nat Pilot Prog to Determine Needs of Sr Ams; Melbourne Br AAUW, Leg Chm; cp/Mem Fla Ho of Reps 1976-78; Var Coms; LWV; Melbourne Area of C, 1st Wom Booster Mem 1971; Dist XII Mtl Hlth Bd Mem; Cousteau Soc; Concern Inc; Philanthropic Ed Org; Fla Forestry Assn; Nat Repub Legs Assn; Repub St Com-wom; Former Mem: Am Leg Exc Coun, Nat Leg Task Force for Wom; Fla Fdn Repub Wom, Leg Com; Nat Fdn Repub Wom: Bd Dirs, Sr Am Proj Chm; Brevard Co Repub Exec Com; Srs Nutritional Aid Prog Adv Coun; Life Mem Friends of Eau Gallie Lib; Other Civic & Polit Activs; r/U Meth: UMW Melbourne Dist Leg Del, Tallahassee & Wash DC; hon/Juv Guid Awd, Brevard Co PTA Coun; Hdstart Cert of Apprec for Vol Work; Hon Life Mem, Wom's Soc Christian Ser; Wom of Yr, Melbourne Area C of C 1976;

Good Govt Awd, Melbourne JCs; Personalities of S; Notable Ams; W/W in Am Polits.

EVANS, MARTHA ALICE oc/Retired Teacher; b/Jan 2, 1912; h/2613 Smallhouse Rd, Bowling Green, KY 42101; ba/Bowling Green; m/Evan C (dec); c/Evan C Jr, Martha C E Glenn, Mereil M E Mayhew (dec); p/George Caleb and Rosa Robert Head (dec); ed/AA, MA, Rank I (30 Hrs above MA) Wn Ky Univ, Duke Univ; pa/Former Tchr Warren Ctl HS; Ret'd 1977; Past Pres Dist Classroom

Tchrs; Former Sponsor Future Tchrs & Jr Classical Leag; Past Pres Bowling Green Br AAUW; cp/Former Activs: Garden Clb, Mothers Clb (Lit), Dem Precnt Ofcr; Current: Treas Woodman of World Grove, Sponsor Rangerettes Yth Woodman Group; r/St Street U Meth Ch, Bowling Green: Mem, Choir Mem, Ch Sch Tchr, Circle Ldr, Conf & Dist Ofcr, U Meth Wom, U Ch Wom; hon/Phi Theta Kappa; Pres Delta Chapt, Delta Kappa Gamma.

EVANS, PATRICIA (PAT) TERRELL oc/Administrator; b/Jun 5, 1931; h/546 Magnolia Wood, Baton Rouge, LA 70808; m/Harry L; c/3 Chd; ed/BA w hons SEn La Univ 1953; Addit Studies; pa/Dir La Bur for Wom (Appt'd by Gov Edwards) 1974-; Ed & Info Dir St Div Mtl Hlth 1973-74; TV News Reporter 1972-73; Wrote, Filmed, Edited & Produced 64 TV Documentaries 1963-72; Other Profl Positions; La Wom's Conf for Intl Wom's Decade: Temporary Convenor & Mem St Coor'g Com, Chair St Delegation, Com of Conf; Wom in Communs Inc, Var Ofcs; cp/Bd Mem La Wom's Polit Caucus; Former Chair St Adv Bd on Mtl Hlth; Fdr & Mem Baton Rouge Mayor-Pres' Comm on Needs of Wom; Bd Dirs Baton Rouge YWCA; Baton Rouge Mtl Hlth Assn; Former Mem Baton Rouge Stop Rape Task Force Adv Bd; Former Mem & Secy La Comm on Status of Wom; Fdr & Bd Mem Wom in Polits; Sponsor Narcotics Anonymous La Correctional Inst for Wom; Former Chperson Baton Rouge Symph Yth Concerts; Others; hon/Narcotics Anonymous Awd; Mtl Hlth Awd for Outstg Contbn to La Mtl Hlth Assn; Ser Awd, Cystic Fibrosis Res Foun; Contbn to Wom's Awd, NOW; Dist'd Ser Awd, Wel Rts Org; Hon'd by Assn of Wom Students, So Univ; Biogl Listings.

EVANS, RAYMOND oc/Professional Engineer; b/Dec 29, 1925; h/Rt 1, Box 39, Raeford, NC 28376; m/Marie Elizabeth Grzymkowski; c/6 Daughs; ed/BS 1953, PhD 1973 Univ Ala; mil/USNR 1943-46, 1951-52; pa/Design & Proj Engr Gen Elect Co, Syracuse, NY 1956-63, Huntsville, Ala

1965-66; Sr Prod Engr Raytheon Co, Portsmouth, RI 1966-70; Proj Engr Savanna Army Depot, Ill 1971-73; Var Engrg Posts, Airborne Div US Army, Ft Bragg, NC 1973-76, Dir Facilities Engrg 1975-, Chief Envir Ofc 1976-; hon/Recipient Accent on Value Awd, Gen Elect Co 1964; Men of Achmt.

EVANS, RODNEY EARL oc/University Administrator; b/May 15, 1939; h/3826 Warwick Ct, Norman, OK 73069; ba/Norman; c/Mark, Scott, Cynthia; p/Hubert E Evans (dec); L Beatrice Evans; ed/BA; MBA; PhD Mich St Univ; mil/USAF Capt.

EVANS, THEDA oc/Artist; Musician; b/Mar 6, 1928; h/325 Glen Ridge Rd, Havertown, PA 19083; ba/H'town; m/Martin J; c/Bonnie, Wendy; pa/Lectr on "The Traditions in Painting"; Art Tchr; Contralto in Choir; Violinist in String Orchs; Tchr of Modeling; Exec Secy; Div Ldr, Chd's Camp; One-man Shows incl: Fleisher Art Meml, Pa Mil Col, Provident Nat Bk, Wallingford Art Ctr, Greenhill in Lower Merion Gallery, Simon Gratz High, Liberty Fed Gallery, W Phila Fed Gallery, Park Art, Wanamaker's Wilmington, Sacred Heart Convent, Others; Group Shows incl: Philadelphia Art Alliance, Phila Sketch Clb, Juried Annuals, Woodmere Juried Show, Allens Lane Juried Show, Newman Clb, Univ Pa, Lasalle Col, Drexel Inst, WCAU Art Fest, Others; Works included in Num Pvt Collections; Nat Forum Profl Artists; Nat Leag Am Pen Wom Inc; Friends of Barnes Foun; Phila Art Alliance; Da Vinci Art Alliance; hon/Best Painting of Yr, Phila Art Alliance; Gold Medal, Plastic Clb; Gimbel Brill Purchase Prize; Da Vinci Art Alliance Awd; Num Others; Biogl Listings.

EVERETT, ELDA JEAN oc/Free-lance Writer; Homemaker; b/Oct 11, 1928; h/Rt 3, Box 18, Snyder, TX 79549; m/Jess; p/James Obert and Marie Turner Littlepage (dec); ed/Att'd: Tex Wom's Univ & McMurray Col; pa/Ednl Dir 1st U Meth Ch 1960-64; Dep Clerk Scurry Co Tax Ofc 1955-60; Snyder Writer's Guild: Orgr, Charter Mem, 1st Pres; Charter Mem Scurry Co Poetry Soc; Writer Weekly Column "A Little About One or Two Hundred Things", Snyder Daily News 1975-76; Column "Pioneer Profiles" 1973 & "Know Your Country" 1978, Snyder Daily News; Other Profl Activs; cp/Scurry Co Hist Comm: Mem 10 Yrs, Editor "Scurryly Speaking" 6 Yrs, Current Chm; r/1st U Meth Ch, Snyder: Mem, SS Tchr, Vol Wkr; hon/Poetry Pub'd in The Atlar, Anthology of Am Poetry, Book VIII, Magic of the Muse, A Treasury of Modern Poetry & Lyrical Voices, Intl Poetry Anthology; Winner Ribbons for Cooking & Handwork, Scurry Co Fair; W H O O (We Honor Our Own) Awd, Snyder; 1st Lady of Yr, Lambda Kappa Chapt Beta Sigma Phi Intl 1976.

EVERETT, WARREN S oc/US Government Official; b/Oct 19, 1910; h/340 Watkins Ln, Battle Creek, MI 49015; ba/Battle Creek; m/Ruthmary Francis; c/Mary E Graham, Judith E McKee, Warren D; p/Carl S and Effie Barton Everett (dec); ed/BA; BS; MS; mil/AUS Corps of Engrs, Col Ret'd; pa/Govt Ofcl DPDS-MM, Fed Ctr; Am Soc Civil Engrs; Soc Am Mil Engrs; Nat Soc Profl Engrs; r/Prot; hon/US Fgn Mil Decorations; Fellow: ASCE, SAME.

EVERIDGE, MARY JIM oc/Community Activities Coordinator; b/Dec 16, 1930; h/502 E DeVane St, Plant City, FL 33566; ba/Tampa, FL; m/James Ralph Sr; c/James R Jr, Mary Elizabeth Stine; p/James Franklin Smith (dec); Mary Ellen Hancock Miles, Plant City; ed/Att'd: Fla So Col, Univ Fla, Fla St Univ; pa/Commun Activs Coor Hillsborough Co Chd's Sers 1972-; Mgr & Tax Info Clerk Hillsborough Co Tax Assesor's Ofc 1968-72; Ext Wkr Plant City Neighborhood Ser Ctr 1967-68; Other Former Positions; Fla Fdn BPW Clbs, Num Ofcs; cp/Fla Coor ERA Fla Steering Com; Past Pres Dem Woms Clbs Fla Inc; Former Rec'g Secy Hillsborough Co Dem Wom's Clb; Former Mem Fla Host Com

Dem Nat Conv; Past Treas Hillsborough Co Yg Dems; Other Polit Activs; Hillsborough Commun Mtl Hlth Ctr Bd; Hillsborough Co Bd Consumer Affairs & Appeals; Leukemia Soc Am, Var Ofcs; Dir Travelers Aid Soc Inc; Hillsborough Co Sch Desegration Com; SERVE Bd Dirs; Exec Secy Hillsborough Co Chd's Sers Vol Leag Inc; Bd Dirs Steppin' Stone Farm Inc; Profl Ldrs Assn for Yth Prog Com; Others; r/1st U Meth Ch, Plant City: Mem, Past Pres Wom Soc Christian Ser, Yth Cnslr; hon/Diana Awd Hillsborough Co, NOW, Tampa Chapt; Good Govt Awd, Plant City JCs; Wom of Yr, H'borough Co Dem Wom's Clb 1974; Life Mem, PTA; Commun Ser Awd, Plant City Jr Wom's Clb; Cert of Commend for Outstg Vol Ser, Wom in Commun Ser Inc; Wom of Yr, E H'borough Co Civic Clbs; Num Biogl Listings.

EVES, JAMES H JR oc/Personnel Director; b/Jul 6, 1936; h/116 Briarcliff Rd, Mt Lakes, NJ 07046; ba/Morris Plains, NJ; m/Courtney; c/Kimberley, James, Heather; p/James H and Lillian S Eves, S Harpswell, ME; ed/BS Cornell Univ 1958; mil/USMC 1/Lt, Hon Disch 1961; pa/Pers Dir Personal Prods Div Warner-Lambert Co; Mem Var Pers Assns; r/Epis; hon/Poetry Pub'd 40+ Mags & 5 Anthologies; Intl W/W in Poetry.

EVRIDGE, CAROLYN HALDANE oc/Watercolorist; b/May 3, 1943; h/9202 W Kentucky Pl, Lakewood, CO 80226; ba/Same; m/Kenneth L; c/Dawn Bernice, David Kenneth; p/David M and Dorothy K Haldane, Berwyn, IL; pa/SWn Watercolor Soc (Dallas, Tex); Foothills Art Ctr, Golden, Colo; Mountainside Art Guild, Lakewood, Colo; Denver Allied Arts Guild, Denver, Colo; Rocky Mtn Liturigal Arts Assn, Denver; N Platte Val Artists Assn, Scottsbluff, Neb; Wind River Val Art Guild, Dubois, Wyo; Intl Soc Artists; cp/Bd Dirs Lakewood Hist Soc; Vol Artists, Belmar Mus, Lakewood; r/Meth; hon/Winner Sev 1st & 3rd Places at Art Shows; Also Hon Mentions & Merit Awds.

EXTON, WILLIAM JR oc/Management Consultant; Author; Lecturer; b/Mar 15, 1907; h/RFD, Dover Plains, NY 12522; ba/NYC, NY; m/Katherine; c/William III; p/William Gustav and Florence Nightingale Augusta Phillips Exton (dec); ed/BA; MA; mil/USNR Capt, Ret'd; pa/Fdr & Past Pres Soc Profl Mgmt Conslts; Fdr & Past Secy Inst of Mgmt Conslts; Fdr & Past Chm Coun of Mgmt Conslt'g Orgs; Co-Fdr & Chm Univ Sem on Org & Mgmt, Columbia Univ; hon/Elected Fellow, Soc Profl Mgmt Conslts.

EYRAMYA, CARMEN STANLEY oc/Concert Pianist; Opera Singer; Educator; b/Jan 17; h/200 Winston Dr, Apt 1210, Cliffside Park, NJ 07010; ba/Cliffside Park; m/Ben; c/Dawn Elizabeth, Stanley Richard; p/George Hamilton and Frances Kniffin Stanley, Flossmoor, IL; ed/BMus Am Conservatory Music; NWn Univ Sch Music; Juilliard Sch Music; Boston Conservatory Music; Columbia Univ; Hunter Col; Pvt Study; pa/Chd's Parts w NY Metro Opera Co; NYC Ctr Opera; Chgo Opera; San Carlo Opera & Others; Ldg Roles w "All Chd's Grand Opera Chgo"; Ldg Parts Chd's Civic Theatre Prodns by Chgo Drama Leag; TV Appearances; Radio Broadcasts; Concert Appearances w NY Choral Soc at Carnegie Hall; Wrote Music Reviews for Star Pubs, William Press, Others; Adjudicator Contests

& Competitions; Tchr Music at Own Music Studio; Pres: Bach Beethoven Brahms Jr Music Clb, Jr Lyrics Music Clb Chgo, Chgo Music Study Jr Clb; Secy Chgo Chapt Mu Phi Epsilon; Fac Mem Nat Guild Piano Tchrs; Am Col Musicians; Soc Am Musicians; Chgo Artists' Assn; NY Choral Soc; IPA; Intl Soc for Contemp Music; Nat Fdn Music Clbs, Bd Dirs Ill Fdn; Piano Tchrs Cong NY Inc; Lyric Opera Chgo Suburban Chapt; Chautauqua (NY) Sum Choir; cp/Secy Yg Repub Clb; Alpha Delta Pi; Troop Ldr GSA; Chm Commun Ser Unit; PTA; r/Prot; hon/Gold Medal Winner, Chgo-land Music Fest Piano Contest; All St Winner, Nat Fdn Music Clbs Competitions for Ill; Am Legion Medal & Awd; Life Fellow, IBA; Biogl Listings.

EYRING, HENRY oc/Distinguished Professor; b/Feb 20, 1901; h/2035 Herbert, Salt Lake City, UT; ba/SLC; m/Winifred Brennan; c/Edward Marcus, Henry Bennion, Harden Romney, Eleanor Gwendoline, Patricia Margaret, Joan Morag, Bernice Heather; p/Edward Christian and Caroline Romney Eyring; ed/BS; MS; PhD; pa/Univ Utah: Dist'd Prof Chem & Metall 1966-, Dean Grad Sch & Prof Chem 1946-66; Asst & Assoc Prof Chem Princeton Univ 1931-38; Lectr Chem Univ Cal 1930-31; Other Acad Positions; Deutsche Akademie der Naturforscher 1975; Intl Acad Quantum Molecular Sci; Nat Sci Bd 1962-68; Am Chem Soc; Am Acad Arts & Scis; AAAS; Nat Acad Sci; Am Phil Soc, Rheology; Editor Annual Review Phy Chem 1956-75; Other Mbrships; r/Ch of Jesus Christ LDS: Gen SS Bd Mem 1946-71; hon/Phi Lambda Upsilon; Sigma Xi; Hon Mem: Chemist Clb (NY), Chem Soc (London), Korean Chem Soc; Dist'd Alumni Awd, St Bd of Commun Cols Ariz; Joseph Priestley Medal, Am Chem Soc 1975; Theodore William Richards Medal, NE Sect ACS; Joseph Priestley Celebration Awd, Dickinson Col; William Gardner Awd, Utah

Acad Scis, Arts & Lttrs; Num Other Hons; Profl Pubs; Biogl Listings.

EYSTER, HENRY CLYDE oc/College Professor; b/Jul 10, 1910; h/417 S Sage Ave, Mobile, AL 36606; ba/Mobile; m/Dora May Trexler; c/Richard Alan; p/Roy I and Mary Susan Reed Eyster (dec); ed/AB cum laude; MA; PhD; pa/Mobile Col: Prof Biol, Dist'd

Lectr; Former Tchg Positions: NC St Univ, Univ SD, Antioch Col; Col Tchg 22 Yrs; Rschr 20 Yrs; Reschr, Plant Physiologist Kellering Foun; Sr Res Biologist Monsanto Res Corp; cp/Lions Clb Intl, Mem Yellow Springs (Ohio) Chapt; Dem; r/Meth; hon/Outstg Edr Am; Men of Achmt.

EZELL, EARL GEER oc/Realtor; Appraiser; b/Apr 8, 1919; h/150 Bellwood Ln, Spartanburg, SC 29302; ba/S'burg; m/Sarah Elizabeth Bridges; c/Lynn Elizabeth, Kim Annette; p/Walter Orlando and Nora Pettit Ezell, S'burg; ed/BS Wofford Col 1942; Postgrad Weaver Sch RE 1960; Grad Sch Savs & Ln 1964-66; pa/Am Inst Real Est Appraisers, Gov'g Coun 1974; Soc Real Est Appraisers, VGov 1973-74; S'burg RE Bd;

Cert'd Review Appraisers; cp/S'burg Rotary Clb; r/1st Bapt Ch: S'burg: Deacon 1947-79; hon/Omega Tau Rho Medallion, Nat Assn Realtors; Merit Awd, S'burg Chapter Adm Mgmt Soc.

EZZO, CAROLYN oc/Educator; h/2900 Lake Ave, #1816, Lakewood, OH 44107; ba/Lakewood; p/Michael James Ezzo (dec); Marjorie Loftis Ezzo, Columbus, OH; ed/BS in Ed 1951, MA 1967 Ohio St Univ; Addit Studies; pa/Elem Prin & Conslt to Kgn Tchrs, Lakewood Bd of Ed 1967-78; Instr Baldwin-Wallace Col, Berea, Ohio 1966; Kgn Tchr Lakewood Bd of Ed 1956-67; Other Former Positions; Project Dir Interdist Ednl Aide Tng Prog, Lakewood 1970-71; Project Dir Vol Ednl Aide Tng Prog, Lakewood 1971-72; Curric Writing; Var Chperson Activs; Nat Assn Elem Sch Prins; Ohio Dept Elem Sch Prins; Am Assn Elem Kgn Nursery Edrs; Lakewood Org Sch Admrs; Lakewood Elem Sch Prins Assn; Elem Sch Prins Assn Gtr Cleveland; cp/Community Communs Chperson, Lakewood; r/Meth; hon/Phi Delta Kappa; Delta Kappa Gamma; Recipient S'ships; Adm Ldrship Awd, Martha Holden Jennings; Dist'd Edr Awd, Inst for Devel of Ednl Activs Acad of Fellows; W/W Am Wom; Others.

F

FABER, JOHN JR oc/Scientist; b/Sept 5, 1941; h/122 S Cass Ave, Westmont, IL 60559; ba/Argonne, IL; c/Jamie Alane; p/John Faber (dec); Emily Garner, Dallas, TX; ed/AAS; BEE; PhD; mil/USAF 1959-63; pa/Scist Argonne Nat Lab; Am Crystallographic Assn; Am Soc for Metals; Former Student Pres Am Ceramic Soc; r/Prot; hon/Tau Beta Pi; Eta Kappa Nu; Lab Assoc, Argonne Nat Labs 1972-73; Contbr to Profl Pubs.

FABIAN, JOSEPHINE CUNNINGHAM oc/Author; Historian; Playwright; Collaborator (History) National Park Service; b/Dec 6, 1903; h/29 S State St Apt 415, Salt Lake City, UT 84111; ba/Same; m/Harold P (dec); p/Joseph Henry Cunningham (dec); Mary Elizabeth Landrigran (dec); ed/Grad Lincoln (Neb) Sch of Bus & Newspaper Inst Am; pa/Nat Leag Am Pen Wom, Past VP SLC Chapt; Col Andrews S Roman Rdg Room for Blind, SLC; Dir, Past Pres; Utah Heritage Foun; Utah Hist Foun; Fort Douglas Mus Foun; r/Cath; hon/Utah Fine Arts Inst: 1st Prize for Novel, *Jackson Hole Story*, , 1st Prize for Play, *Old Salt Lake Theatre*; Bicent Awd for story about Salt Lake Br, Nat Leag Am Pen Wom.

FACCI, DOMENICO A oc/Sculptor; b/Feb 2, 1916; h/240 W 4 St, NY, NY 10014; ba/NYC; m/Penelope; c/Robert; p/Anthony and Grace Polimeni Facci (dec); mil/USAAF WWII, Camouflage Engr; pa/Tchr; Designer, Model-Maker; Portrait Sculptor; Fellow Nat Sculpture Soc; Other Profl Orgs; r/Cath; hon/Over 35 Mil Awds, Cits, Hons.

FAGAN, HENRY EARL oc/Bank Executive; b/Feb 24, 1937; h/PO Box 201, Redwater, TX 75573; ba/Redwater; m/Dorothy; c/Gregory, Robyn, Tammy, Cynthia, Nancy, Keeley; p/Sidney Earl Fagan (dec); Delia E Fagan, Redwater; ed/BA Stephen F Austin; pa/Pres & Chm Bd Guaranty Bond St Bk; Pres Texarkana Security Inc; Pres Fagan Enterprises; Chm Bd Bowie Co St Bk, Hooks, Tex; Partner Fagan-McEntire Ins & F&M Properties; cp/Pres Four Sts Fair Assn; r/Redwater Meth Ch: SS Tchr & Supt; hon/Charter Mem, Soc of the Confed; Life Mem, Nat Rifle Assn; Hon Mem, Tex Assn Tex Future Farmers Am.

FAIR, VIVIAN ROSE oc/Educator; b/Jan 10, 1942; h/116 View Bend Rd, Johnson City, TN 37601; ba/Elizabethton, TN; p/Clarence E and Kathryn L Fair, Elizabethton, TN; ed/BA Univ Tenn; MA E Tenn St Univ; Addit Studies Univ Intl (Saltillo, Mexico); pa/Alpha Delta Kappa; 1st Tenn Dist Tchr Spelling Task Force; Tenn Ser Option Task Force for Ed of Handicapped; So Assn Cols & Schs (Tenn Comm); r/Prot.

FAIRBANK, JANE DAVENPORT oc/Editor; b/Aug 21, 1918; h/141 E Floresta Way, Menlo Park, CA 94025; ba/Stanford, CA; m/William Martin; c/William Martin Jr, Robert Harold, Richard Dana; p/Harold Edwin and Mildred Foster Davenport (dec); ed/AB magna cum laude Whitman Col 1939; pa/Editor: *Radar Maintenance Manual* (2 Vols), 1945, *Second Careers for Women, A View from the San Francisco Peninsula*, 1971, *Second Careers for Women, Vol II: A View of Seven Fields from the San Francisco Bay Area*, 1975; cp/Fdg Mem Bay Area Consortium on Ednl Needs of Wom; Past Pres: Stanford Fac Wom's Clb, Woodside HS PTA; hon/Phi Beta Kappa; Mortar Bd; Hon Life Mem, Cal Cong of P's & T's.

FAIRBANKS, HAROLD VINCENT oc/Professor; b/Dec 7, 1915; h/909 Riverview Dr, Morgantown, WV 26505; ba/M'town; m/Marilyn Elizabeth Markussen; c/Elizabeth Muriel, William Martin; p/Oscar William Fairbanks (dec); Muriel Adelaide H Fairbanks (dec); ed/BSChE; MS; pa/WVa Univ: Prof Metall Engrg 1955-, Assoc Prof 1949-55, Asst Prof

1947-49; Asst Prof Chem Engrg Dept Rose Polytech Inst 1942-47; Other Former Positions; Res in Applying Ultrasonic Energy to Drying, Filtering & Heat Transfer Processes; Assoc Chm Dept Chem Engrng 1973-; CoDir Mats Sci & Engrg Grad Prog 1962-69; Advr for Mining & Metall Engrg Dept, Taiwan Provincial Cheng Kung Univ, Tainan, Taiwan, China 1957-59; Conslt; Acoustical Soc Am; Am Chem Soc 1941-61; Fellow AAAS; Am Inst Chem Engrs; Am Inst Metall Engrs; Am Ordinance Assn; Charter Mem: Am Powder Metallurgy Inst, Intl Metall Soc; Instrument Soc Am; Hon Mem Chinese Inst for Engrs; Am Soc for Testing & Mats; Am Soc for Metals; Am Soc for Engrg Ed; IEEE; Nat Assn Corrosion Engrs; Other Profl Assns, Ofcs Held; r/Presb; hon/Sigma Xi; Tau Beta Pi; Phi Kappa Phi; Phi Mu Alpha; Applied Metall Lab Named in His Hon for Adv Help given to Nat Cheng Kung Univ; Biogl Listings; Num Profl Pubs.

FAIRBANKS, JUSTIN FOX oc/Artist; College Teacher; b/Jul 12, 1926; h/803 Church St, Thatcher, AZ 85552; ba/Thatcher; m/Beth T; c/Daniel Justin, Janet Ann, Julie Bea, Robert Kenneth; p/Avard T and Maude F Fairbanks, Salt Lake City, UT; ed/BA 1953, MFA 1957 Univ Utah; mil/USN 1944-46; USAFR 1953-60, 1/Lt; pa/En Ariz Col: Art

Dept Hd 1973-78, Art Tchr 1969-78; Art Tchr Col En Utah, Price, Utah 1967-68; Owner-Mgr Artistic Bronze Casting Studio 1965-69; Asst to Art Dept Hd Univ Utah-SLC 1955-65; Other Former Positions; Nat Coun Art Admrs; Art Progs for Ednl TV, SLD; Days of '47 Parade Judge, SLC; Beauty Contest Judge; cp/Trustee Wire Mus & Hist Assn, SLC; Dir Pioneer Craft House, SLC; Com-man BSA; r/LDS: SS Pres, SS Tchr, Men's Group Pres, Missionary; hon/Ser Awds: DECA, Pioneer Craft House, Days of '47 Parade.

FAIRLEIGH, JAMES PARKINSON oc/Associate Professor; b/Aug 24, 1938; h/5 Rosewood Ln, Cumberland, RI 02864; ba/Providence, RI; m/Marlane Paxson; c/William Paxson, Karen Evelyn; p/W M and M P Fairleigh, St Joseph, MO; ed/BM, PhD Univ Mich; MM Univ So Cal; mil/AUS 1960-62, 2/Lt-1/Lt; USAR 1963-66, 1/Lt-Capt; pa/Rhode Island Col: Assoc Prof Music, Music Dept Com, Curric Com; Am Musicological Soc; MENC; Soc for Music Theory; CMS; r/Meshanticut Park Ch, Cranston, RI: Min of Music; hon/Phi Beta Kappa; Phi Kappa Phi; Pi Kappa Lambda; Phi Eta Sigma.

FAIRLEY, ROBERT LEONARD oc/Minister; b/Dec 31, 1940; h/1648 Tierra Buena, San Jose, CA 95121; ba/Redwood City, CA; m/Mary Ann McFadden; c/Fredrick, Ralph, Michael, Lori; p/Leonard Earl Fairley (dec); Luesther Barnes Fairley, San Jose; ed/BA; MDiv; DMin; mil/USN; pa/So Bapt Conv; Nat Bapt Conv USA Inc; cp/Nat Com of HS Awds; r/Bapt; hon/Men of Achmt; Intl W/W Commun Ser; Personalities W&MW; Commun Ldrs & Noteworthy Ams; W/W Am Rel.

FAKO, NANCY JORDAN oc/Musician; Free-lance Artist, Teacher; b/May 19, 1942; h/337 Ridge, Elmhurst, IL 60126; m/Martin John; c/Lisa, Laura, Nancy, Margaret; p/Robert Jordan (dec); Olga Visca Jordan, Elmhurst; ed/BMus Ind Univ 1963; pa/Musician, French Horn; Former Mem: Fla Symph, Houston Symph, Chgo Symph, Lyric

Opera Orch Chgo; Former Fac Mem Nat Music Camp, Interlochen, Mich; Mem Adv Coun Intl Horn Soc; r/Prot; hon/Mem Hon Music Sorority.

FALCONE, ALFONSO BENJAMIN oc/Physician; b/Jul 24; ba/2240 E Illinois, Fresno, CA 93701; m/Patricia Jeanne Lalim; c/Christopher Laurence Lalim Falcone, Steven Benjamin Lalim Falcone; p/Baldassare and Elvira Galluzzo Falcone (dec); ed/AB w distn, MD w hons Temple Univ; PhD Univ Minn; mil/AUS; USN; pa/Physician, Endocrinology & Metabolism; Biochemist; AMA; Fellow ACP; Am Soc Biol Chemists; Am Soc Internal Med; Sigma Xi; Phi Lambda Upsilon; cp/Fresno Arts Ctr; hon/Post-doct Fellow, Nat Inst of Hlth, Univ Minn; Diplomate, Am Bd Internal Med.

FALCONER, MARY W oc/Author; b/Mar 14, 1898; h/494 Richmond Ave, San Jose, CA 95128; ba/Same; p/Gerard C Falconer (dec); Mary W Rode (dec); ed/Dipl, Tchg Cert 1918 Univ So Miss; RN Mountainside Hosp Sch Nsg 1921; BA 1941, MA 1951 San Jose St Univ; pa/Former Tchr HS Home Ec, Clara, Miss 1918-20; Gen Nsg & Tchg of Nsg, NYC 1921-25; Gen Nsg Pract, Cal 1925-27; Tchr & Asst Dir, O'Conner Hosp Sch Nsg 1927-32, 44-63; Supvr & Asst Dir Nurses, Santa Clara Valley Med Ctr 1932-40; Cal Nurses Assn: Pres Local Chapt 1942, Bd Dirs 1936-42; Dir Nurses, Reid Meml Hosp, Richmond, Ind 1943-44; Ret'd 1963; Am Nurses Assn; Am Pharm Assn; Nat Leag Nsg; AARP; Fellow Intl Inst for Commun Ser; r/Cath; hon/Dist'd Citizens Awd 1958; Pub'd Author: *The Drug, The Nurse, The Patient, The Current Drug Handbook, Aging Patients: A Guide to Their Care, Patient Studies in Pharmacology: A Guidebook*; Num Nat & Intl Awds.

FALK, CAROLYN ROSENSTEIN oc/Microbiologist; b/Apr 28, 1902; h/169 E 69th St, Apt 8D, New York, NY 10021; m/K George (dec); p/Louis and Pearl Asher Rosenstein (dec); ed/BA Smith Col; pa/Ret'd Microbiologist; Bur of Labs, Dept Hlth, Dept of NY 1923-57; Fellow: AAAS, APHA; SAM; NY Acad Sci; AMWA; Royal Soc Promotion of Hlth; Contbr to Sci Jours; cp/Former Chm Metro Br ACU; Former Secy Bd Gov Finger Lakes Conf; St Mary En Province; Pres Friends of St Mary's-in-the-Field; Class Fund Agt Smith Col; Former 1st Aid Instr ARC; r/Epis; Manhattan Div Coun of Chs, NYC: Past VP, Mem-at-large; Bd Mgrs Coun of Chs NYC; Others; hon/Dist'd Ser Awd, Coun of Chs NYC; Mem APHA Ldrship Recog.

FAMARIN, SALLY BASIGA oc/Real Estate Executive; b/Nov 11, 1923; h/2207 28th Ave, San Francisco, CA 94116; m/Carsiolo Tagle; c/Sally Ann Davis (Mrs Andrew Glenn), Catherine Rizotto (Mrs Bruce David), Rodolfo Carlito, Rose Marie; p/Severo Ranili and Serapia Seno Dabon Basiga, Cebu, PI; ed/Grad So Col (PI) 1941; Postgrad Chamberlain Real Est Sch 1960, Harlowe Real Est Sch 1962, Anthony Sch Gen Ins 1961; H & R Block Income Tax Course 1975-; pa/Naturalized US Citizen 1952; Acctg, Bkkpr, Mgr Ladies Home, Cebu 1946-50; Vol Wkr, Vets & Marine Hosps w Regular Vets Assn Post 15, SF 1953-60; Real Est Salesman House of Homes Realty, SF 1960-61, U Homes Ins Sers 1962-, Notary Public; Owner, Operator Famarin Realty (U Home Realty) 1962-, SF 1965-, Becoming 1st Filipino Wom Realtor; Pres-Owner, Far E Am Travel Inc 1972-; Owner, Operator Sallys Sunset Villa, SF 1972-74; Cebu Assn Cal: Fdr, Pres Emeritus,*Gold Pin, Other Hon Awds; Other Profl Assns; cp/Landmarks Preserv Adv Bd; Commr, Plaque Recog & Testimonial Banquet & Ball from Marina Dizon Lodge 81; Exec Gen Chm, Fiesta of Santo Nino de Cebu, SF; Hermana Mayor, Fiesta of Santo Nino de Cebu, Basilica Minore, Cebu City; Mayor Moscones Screening Com on Bds & Comms, SF City & Co; Child Hlth & Disability Prevention Adv Bd; Orgr 1st Filipino Indep Polit HQs, SF; Initiated Philippine Gardens, Golden Gate Pk, SF, Cal 1976; Chm or Active Wkr in Num Polit Campaigns & Causes; Num

Others; hon/Num Biogl Listings; Only US Awardee, 4th Centennary Celebration of Cebu; 1st Filipino to Hold 3 Important Positions in SF City & Co; Resolutions: Cal St Leg & Senate, Spkr Cal Assembly, Mandaue City Coun (Cebu); Cert Hon, Bd Supvr SF City & Co; "The Famarin Story in Am" Pub'd in Hon; Famarin Bicent Commemorative Flag in Hon; Num Certs Apprec; Featured in Num Pubs; Contbr of Articles & Poems to Filipino & Am Pubs; Dist'd Citizen Awd; Outstg Plaque Merit, Filipino & Am Soc of Cal; 1st Wom Awd'd Ofcl Seal of Mandaue City for Generosity & Liberality to Mandaue City & People 1977; Authored & Endorsed, Intl Hotel Landmark Preserv, SF (1st Filipino Landmark in US) 1977; 1st Filipino Awd'd Meml Plate Awd by R C Howe as Patriot of the USA; Coor Cebu Assn of Cal Inc Chapts in Diff Countries, Cities, US; Author Hist of Santo Nino de Cebu in US & Hist of Cebu Assn of Cal Inc; Authored & Endorsed, Santo Nino de Cebu as Nat Shrine for Filipinos in USA (Nat Reg of Cult & Hist Places); Fdr, Pres Emeritus & World Emissary, Filipino Fiesta, Santo Nino de Cebu, SF, Cal (USA); Donor Traditional Carroza (Carriage) for Traditional Procession, Santo Nino de Cebu, SF, w Mayor Eulogio E Borres, Cebu City, Rep of Philippines; Commend, Fdr & Pres Emeritus, World Emissary, Cebu Assn of Cal Inc, Aug 13, 1977; Fdr Mandaue Assn de Santo Nino, Rep of Philippines, May 13, 1978; Responsible for Replica Donation, Image of Santo Nino de Cebu, So Cal Chapt, Cebu Assn of Cal, Inc May 26, 1978, Donated by Gov Eddie Gullas, Cebu, Rep of Philippines; Fdr, Filipino & Am Friends Forum, SF 1972; Testimonial Banquet & Dist'd Ser Awd, Cebu Assn Cal Inc (for multifarious achmts), SF 1976; Num Others.

FANT, SADIE PATTON oc/Language & Speech Pathologist; b/Jan 26, 1933; h/1122 Waterworks Rd, Columbus, MS; m/Arnold Lee; c/Richard Lee, Frances Yvonne Yarbrough (Mrs Charles Ronald); p/Samuel Hoyle and Mary Francis Parker Patton; ed/BS 1956, MS 1968 Miss St Col for Wom; Cert Clin Competence in Spch Pathol (ASHA) 1971; Ednl Specialist Deg Miss Univ for Wom 1975; pa/Lang & Spch Pathologist Columbus (Miss) Public Schs 1968-; Owner & Dir Fant Nursery Sch 1965-66; Tchr: Knee High Kgn 1963-65, 5th Grade W Lowndes Elem Sch, Columbus 1960-62, Others; ASHA; Miss Spch & Hearin Assn; Lowndes Co, Miss, Nat Assns for Retard Citizens; Am Law Enforcemt Ofcrs Assn, Citizen Band Posse; Miss Chapt Am Law Enforcemt Ofcrs Assn; Pvt Detective 1976-; Examr for Miss Dept Ed on Miss Univ for Wom Reg Screening Team; Lang/Spch Conslt & Hearing Impaired Conslt, Miss Univ for Wom Spec Ed Reg Screening Team; VP

Lowndes Co Assn for Retard Citizens; cp/Charter Mem Lowndes Co Emer Radio Net; Trojan Citizens Band Radio Clb; Altrusa Intl; r/Southside Bapt Ch, Columbus: Dir Ch Tng, Yth SS Tchr, Adult Tng Ldr, Flower & Entertainmt Coms; hon/W/W Child Devel Profls; Personalities of S; Commun Ldrs & Noteworthy Ams; World W/W Wom.

FANTOZZI, LYNN COLLINS oc/Instructor; b/Dec 6, 1946; h/9111 Indian Sch Rd NE, Albuquerque, NM 87112; ba/Albu; m/Victor P; p/N G and Mary Lee Collins, Santa Fe, NM; ed/BA; MA; pa/Classroom Instr Psychol & TV Prodn Albu Public Schs; Rocky Mt Psychol Assn; Spch Commun Assn; Intl Commun Assn; Nat Forensic Leag; NM Spch Commun Assn; hon/Phi Kappa Phi; Notable Ams; W/W Am Wom; Personalities W&MW; Commun Ldrs & Noteworthy Ams; Intl W/W Commun Ser; World W/W Wom.

FARAH, CAESAR ELIE oc/Professor; b/Mar 13, 1929; h/3847 York Ave S, Minneapolis, MN 55410; ba/Mpls; m/Marsha Bernadette McDonald; c/Ronald, Christopher, Ramsey, Laurence, Raymond, Alexandra; p/Sam Farah (dec); Laurice N Farah, Portland, OR; ed/BA; MA; PhD; mil/Resv Ofcr Tng; pa/Prof Univ Minn; Conslt on Mid E; cp/Former Repub Com-man, Oreg; r/Greek Orthodox: Ch Pres; hon/Fulbright Hayes to Turkey; Fellow: Am Phil Soc, Royal Asiatic Soc.

FARIAN, BABETTE SOMMERICH oc/Artist; b/Jun 6, 1916; h/34-48 81 St, Jackson Hts, NY 11372; ba/Same; m/Robert A; c/Robert A Jr; p/Hugo and Clara Hart Sommerich (dec); ed/NY Sch Fine & Applied Art; Cooper Union Sch Art; Mod Mus Art Sch; Pvt Studies; pa/Instr Colo & Design Cooper Union Sch of Art; Asst Addison Lamar, Color Conslt; Asst Hd of Studio Manhattan Shirt Co; Designer Hanscom Fabrics, Krasom Co; Contbr to Var Profl Jours; Group Exhibs incl: S Bay Art Gall, Atelier Gall of Contemp Art, Martha's Vineyard Fair, Artists Equity Assn NY, US Fine Arts Registry; Am Artists Profl Leag, Woms Interart Ctr, Pinch Penny Gall (Rochester); 6 One-Wom Shows; US Fine Arts Registry; Gotham Painters; Artists of Am; Jackson Hgts Art Clb; Perm in Collection of Tamassee DAR Sch, Wom's Fine Art Mus; Gotham Painters; Borr Artists; Composers, Author & Artists Am; Nat Leag Am Pen Wom; Intl Beaux Art; r/Unitarian; hon/Medal for Best Oil, Gotham Painters; 5 1st Prizes, 3 2nd Prizes, Martha's Vineyard Fair; Grumbacher Prize, Jackson Hgts Art Clb; CAAA Awd Oil; Intl Wom's Yr Awd; 1st Prize, Wall St Artists; 2nd Prize, Golden Age Art Exhibit; 1st Prize, Nat Art Leag (Oil); Awd of Merit, Nat Leag Am Pen Wom; Monetary Prize, Intl Soc Artists; Wom Artists in Am; Intl W/W Art & Antiques; W/W Am Wom; W/W Am Art; World W/W Wom.

FARISS, MARY E ADKINS oc/Artist; Businesswoman; b/Jun 27, 1933; h/7304 Middlebury Cove, Austin, TX 78723; ba/Austin; m/James Lee Jr; c/Joe Leslie, Jill Leigh; p/Earl Leslie and Mae Ella Warren Adkins, Gatesville, TX; ed/Tex Sch Fine Arts; pa/Owner Sign Shop; hon/Biogl Listings.

FARKAS, JACK JOHN S oc/Artist; Herbalist; Teacher; b/Nov 11, 1948; h/22 Knollwood St, Monroe, CT 06468; ba/Fairfield, CT; m/Claudia M Smith; p/John J and Helen T Karafa Farkas, F'field; ed/BFA; MFA; pa/Bd Dirs: F'field Arts Comm, F'field C of C, VAAF; 8 One-Man Exhbns; Work Rep'd in Num Public & Pvt Collections in US & Europe; cp/Coor F'field Fest of Arts; r/Cath; hon/Num Awds.

FARLEY, DOROTHY A oc/Educator; Nurse; b/May 6, 1929; h/305 Olcott St, Orange, NJ 07050; Dipl Lincoln Hosp Sch Nsg 1949; MS NY Univ 1957; MA Tchrs Col Columbia Univ 1963; DNSc Boston Univ 1971; Cert'd Clin Specialist in Psychi Nsg, Soc for Clin Specialists in Psychi-Mtl Hlth Nsg of NJ St Nurses Assn 1973; pa/Staff Nurse & Asst

Hd Nurse Obstetrics & Med-Surg Units, Var NJ Hosps 1949-57; Asst Hd Nurse Med Surg Unit St James Hosp, Newark, NJ 1961; Former Instr Psychi Mtl Hlth Nsg Monmouth Med Ctr Sch Nsg, Long Branch, NJ & St Michael's Hosp Sch Nsg, Newark; Asst Prof Allied Hlth Div Dept Nsg, Essex Co Col, Newark 1970-73; Chief Psychi Nsg & Clin Assoc Prof NJ Med Sch Commun Mtl Hlth Ctr 1973-; Am Nurses Assn, NJ Constituency; Nat Leag Nsg; NJ Leag for Nsg; Black Nurses Assn Inc NY; Nat Black Nurses Assn; ANA Coun Adv'd Practitioners in Psychi Nsg; NJ St Nurses Assn: Bd Dirs, Chperson Psychi Mtl Hlth Div of Pract 1974-76, Chperson Minority Caucus 1973-76; Past Mem & Past Pres NJ Bd Nsg; cp/Bd Dirs: Essex Co Heart Assn, Lewis H Loeser Meml; hon/Intl Reg Profiles; World W/W Wom; Book of Honor.

FARMAKIS, GEORGE LEONARD oc/Resource Specialist; b/Jun 30, 1925; h/752 Trombley Rd, Grosse Pointe Park, MI 48230; ba/Highland Pk, MI; p/Michael and Pipitsa Farmakis (dec); ed/MA 1966, PhD 1971 Wayne St Univ; MA Univ Mich 1978; mil/Mich NG, Cpl Grade V 1948-51; pa/Resource Specialist (Ed); Am Hist Assn;

NCTM; Nat Coun Social Studies; Acad Polit Sci; Am Phil Assn; Phi Delta Kappa; IRA; IPA; Nat Assn Admrs of St & Fed Ed Progs; Mod Green Studies Assn; cp/Univ Mich & Wayne St Univ Alumni Assns; PTA; r/Greek Orthodox; hon/Spec Commend, US Ofc of Ed; DIB; W/W MW; Men of Achmt; Outstg Ldrs in Elem Ed & Sec'dy Ed; Personalities of W&MW; Notable Ams; Intl W/W Commun Ser.

FARQUHAR, CLYDE RANDOLPH oc/Stock Broker; Executive; b/Aug 19, 1921; h/823 Alhambra Ct, Sugar Land, TX 77478; ba/Houston, TX; m/Mary Elisabeth Gage; p/George Randolph Farquhar (dec); Edith Rowena Harris (dec); ed/BS Duke Univ 1950; MS NC St Col 1952; mil/USAF 1940-47;

USAFR, Ret'd Maj; pa/VP Underwood, Neuhaus & Co; Var Geol Socs 1952-62; Var Fin Orgs 1962-78; cp/Var Commun, Civic & Polit Activs 25+ Yrs; Repub Co Chm Ft Bend Co (Tex); Others; hon/Explorers Clb; Fellow, Royal Geographical Soc (England).

FARRAR, MARGARET MARIAN oc/Educator; Reading Consultant; b/Feb 3, 1911; h/5162-34th St NW, Washington, DC 20008; ed/BA Dillard Univ; MEd Boston Univ; PhD Laurence Univ; pa/DC Public Sch Sys: Rdg Conslt 1969-80, Rdg Specialist 1967-69, Kgn Tchr 1960-67; New Orleans Public Sch Sys: Supt Student Tchrs 1950-53,

Vets Prog Tchr 1950-59, Sum Sch Prin 1950, Kgn Tchr 1937-60, 1931-37; NO Tchrs Assn, Pres 1949-52; Wash Br Nat Assn Univ Wom: Pres 1967-71, VP 1966-67; Geo Wash Univ Chapt Pi Lambda Theta, Alpha Theta: Pres 1973-74, VP 1972-73, Chm Nat Nom'g Com 1978-79; NEA; NCTE; NCTM; ASALH; AAUW; ACEI; IRA; NSPI; AERA; NCME; ASCD; cp/Past Pres DC Friends of Liberia; Aux Howard Univ Hosp; Fellow IBA; hon/Pub'd Author; Biogl Listings.

FARRELL, ODESSA WRIGHT oc/Retired Educator; h/4620 Kossuth Ave, St Louis, MO 63115; ba/St Louis; p/Reuben Q and Anna L Smith Wright (dec); ed/BA; MA; MA + 30; pa/Retired from A-V Div-Curric Sers St Louis Public Schs; Former Fac Mem Dunbar Elem Sch, Negro Hist Sch for Grades 4-8, Vashon High, Wash & Hadley Tech HSs; Former Hd Social Studies Dept Sumner HS; Former Lectr in Ed Cal St Univ-Hayward; CoFdr Stowe Societas Alumnarum; Appt'd to Com to Make Comprehensive Study of Public Sch Fin, Prog'g & Redistrict'g (Mo St Bd Ed); Nat, St & Gtr St Louis Couns for Social Studies; Bd Dirs & Pres Coun of Presidents of Nat & Intl Orgs; Mo St Tchrs Assn: Mem, Ofcr, Com Mem Local & St Divs; Nat Assn Univ Wom: Local Pres, Sect Dir, Nat Rec'g Secy, Nat 1/VP, Nat Pres, Currently Employmt Resource Coor; IPA; VP Ret'd Sch Employees St Louis; AAUW; cp/Bd Dirs Heritage House Redevel Corp Inc; Bd of Control of Aid to Victims of Crime; NAACP; US China People's Friendship Assn; Planning Com 1968, 70 White House Confs Gtr St Louis; Participant 1970 White House Conf Washington DC; Former Mem Gov's Com on Chd & Yth; Others; r/St James AME Ch: SS Tchr, Dept SS Supt, Secy Trustee Bd, Chaired 5 Wom's Day Sers; Mo Annual Conf AME Ch: Pres Christian Endeavor Leag, Supt SS, Pres Lay Org St Louis Booneville Dist, Ldr Lay Delegation to 1960 Gen Conf; Others; hon/World W/W Wom; Commun Ldrs Am; AME Ch Wom in Action; W/W Among Black Ams; Intl Reg Profiles, NAm Edition.

FARWELL, HAROLD FREDERICK JR oc/Teacher; b/Apr 9, 1934; h/PO Box 152, Cullowhee, NC 28723; ba/Cullowhee; m/Joyce; c/Douglas George, Beth Elene, Amy Kathleen, Ellen Claudia; p/Harold F and Dorothy Delma Cobb Farwell, Pompano Beach, FL; ed/BA; MA; PhD; mil/USN 1956-58; pa/Tchr Eng Dept Wn Carolina Univ; Prose Editor *The Arts Jour*; cp/Local 2437 Am Fdn Tchrs: Pres, Treas; r/Christian; hon/Acad F'ship, Wis; Res Awds.

FASCELL, DANTE B oc/Member of Congress; b/Mar 9, 1917; h/Miami, FL; ba/2354 Rayburn Bldg, Washington, DC 20515; m/Jeanne-Marie Pelot; c/Sandra Jeanne Diamond (Mrs Frank), Toni Francesca, Dante Jon; p/Charles Fascell (dec); Mary Fascell, Coral Gables, FL; ed/JD Univ Miami 1938; mil/Fla NG 1941, Comm'd 2/Lt 1942, African, Sicilian & Italian Campaigns; Disch'd Capt 1946; pa/Atty; ABA; Fed, Fla, Coral Gables, Dade Co Bar Assns; Omicron Delta Kappa; cp/Mem US Cong 1954-; Former Fla St Rep; Mem US Delegation to 24 Gen Assembly of UN 1969; CoChm US Delegation Belgrade Conf 1977-78; US Chm US-Canadian Inter-Parliamentary Group; Chm Comm on Security & Cooperation in Europe 1976-; Other Com Mbrships; Am Legion; Lions Clb Intl; Loyal Order Moose; Miami Chapt Mil Order World Wars; Miami, Gtr Miami, S Dade, Fla Cs of C; Bd Dirs "Close-Up"; Adv Coun on Latin Am Affairs, Ctr for Strategic & Intl Affairs; Coun on Fgn Relats; Project Hope; Hist Assn S Fla; Iron Arrow Soc; Others; r/Prot; hon/Dist'd Ser Awd, Coun Jewish Fdns; "Connie Awd", Soc Am Travel Writers; Golden Shofar Awd, Am Jewish Cong, SE Reg; Italian-Am of Yr 1977, The Italians Inc; Cit for Support to Hungarians, Am Hungarian Fdn; Man of Yr 1977, Gtr Miami Bch C of C; Freedom Awd, Nat Conf on Soviet Jewry; Num Other Hons.

FATEMI, NASROLLAH S oc/University Administrator; Educator; b/Jun 15, 1910;

h/47 Chestnut Ridge Rd, Saddle River, NJ 07458; ba/Teaneck, NJ; m/Shayesteh; c/Faramarz, Fariborz, Farivar; ed/BA Stuart Meml Col 1932; MA Columbia Univ 1949; PhD New Sch for Social Res 1954; pa/Fairleigh Dickinson Univ 1955-: Chm Social Sci Dept 1960-64, Dean Grad Sch 1965-70, Dir Grad Inst Intl Studies 1971-; Other Acad Positions: Princeton Univ 1950-55, The Asia Inst 1947-49, Stuart Meml Col 1933-36; Ec & Polit Advr to Permanent Delegation of Iran to US; Iran's Del to UN; Other Positions w Iran; Intl Assn Univ Pres: Mem Steering Com NAm Coun 1975-, Bd Dirs 1975-; Chm Exec Com Inter-Univ Centre for Post-Grad Studies, Dubrovnik, Yugoslavia 1972-; Fellow Royal Acad Arts & Scis (London); cp/Bd Dirs NJ UF Bergen Co; Former Mem Bd Trustees N Jersey Cult Coun; Envir Com Saddle River, NJ; r/Moslem; hon/Cit for Outstg Ldrship, Intl Assn Univ Pres; Outstg Edrs Am; Hon LLD, Kyung Hee Univ (Seoul, Korea); Cit for Best Iranian Work "Sufi Studies", UNESCO & Intl Book Yr 1972; Pub'd Author.

FATHIE, KAZEM oc/Physician; b/Nov 11, 1929; h/4324 Fox Meadow Dr SE, Cedar Rapids, IA 52403; ba/Cedar Rapids; m/Birgitta R M; c/Arman, Arezo, Ramin; p/Hossein and Eshrat Nasrolahzadeh Fathie, Tehran, Iran; ed/MD Univ Tehran 1955; Resident Surg Luth Deaconess Hosp, Chgo 1957, Harper Hosp, Detroit 1957-58; Other Resident Positions; Pract Med (Specializing Neurosurg) St Luke's Hosp, Cedar Rapids 1963-; Chief Dept Neurosurg Mercy, St Luke's Hosps; Pres Neurol Neurosurg Inst, Cedar Rapids; Fellow ACS, Cong Neurol Surgs; Intl Cong Neurol Surgs; World Med Assn; AMA; Linn Co, Ia Med Socs; MS Soc; Am Assn Neuro-Radiol; Am Assn Heart Dis & Stroke; Swedish Royal Med Soc; Iranian Med Soc; World Col Surgs; Num Other Profl Activs; cp/32° Mason; Rotary; Lions; Dank of USA; Viking of USA; Cedar Rapids Study; hon/Contbr Articles to Med Jours; Author *Shocks and Treatment* (in Persian), 1955, *Book of Koran*, 1959.

FAULK, LILLIAN T oc/Teacher; b/Aug 3, 1912; h/508 Gibson, W Memphis, AR 72301; m/Raymond B (dec); p/Charles D and Aurelia Tibbels (dec); ed/BSE; MA; EdS; pa/Local, St & Nat Ed Assns; Assn for Supvn

& Curric Devel; IRA; Nat Elem Sch Prin's Assn; cp/W Memphis Quota Clb; Mem, Secy W Memphis Civic Auditorium Comm; r/Bapt; hon/Favorite Tchr in Ark; W Memphis Wom of Yr 1965; Elem Sch Named After Her, "Lillian T Faulk Elem Sch", 1978.

FAULKNER, BERNICE TAYLOR oc/Pub-

lic Health Nursing Director; b/Jan 28, 1935; h/9230 Merrill, Chicago, IL 60617; c/Alvin, Ricardo; p/Peter Taylor (dec); Viola Casamor, Chgo; ed/BSN, MSN SIU; mil/AUS Resv Nurse Corp, Maj; pa/Alpha Kappa Alpha; APHA; IPHA; Ill Assn Nurse Admrs; SIU Sch Nsg Curric Com; St Commun Col Nsg Adv Com; Hlth Systems Agy Mem; cp/SIU Alumnae Assn; Hd St Adv Bd; r/Luth; hon/Resv Ofcr Yr 1975; Outstg Commun Achmt; Wom of Achmt; Outstg Ser for Better Hlth Care.

FAUST, NINA HOPE oc/Teacher; b/Mar 12, 1951; h/PO Box 2391, Anchorage, AK 99510; ba/Anchorage; p/George Sr and Rosemarie Faust, Anchorage; ed/BA Alaska Meth Univ 1973; pa/Math Tchr West HS, Anchorage; Alaska Conservation Soc; Sierra Clb, Exec Bd Mem Local Chapt; Anchorage Coun Math Tchrs; NEA; Sophomore Class Advr; Human Relats Fac Facilitator; cp/Alaska Public Interest Res Group; Alaska Ctr for the Envir; Common Cause; Tennis Coach; hon/1973 Mixed Doubles & Wom's Singles, St Champion (Alaska).

FAVRET, J RAYMOND oc/Executive; b/Sept 18, 1923; h/5440 Moeller Ave, Cincinnati, OH 45212; ba/Cinc; p/James Raymond and Helen Gilligan Favret, Cinc; ed/BA, BS Athenaeum of Ohio; STL, STD St

Thomas (Rome); pa/Pres The Athenaeum of Ohio; Chm Consortium for Higher Ed in Rel Studies; Treas Accredited Theol Schs Ohio & Ind; cp/Trustee Metro Area Rel Coalition of Cinc; Past Pres Priests' Senate Archdiocese of Cinc.

FAWBUSH, JOHN RAY oc/Labor Employee; b/Oct 3; h/105 Main St, La Grange, KY 40031; ba/Same; pa/Key Markett Sq Labor Employ; r/Bapt.

FAWCETT, GEORGE D oc/Newspaper General Manager; Businessman; b/Jul 21, 1929; h/602 Battleground Rd, Lincolnton, NC 28092; ba/Maiden, NC; m/Shirley P; c/Laurie, Chris, (Stepchd:) Kelly Freeman, Mark Freeman; p/T G Sr and Katie Lee Fawcett (dec); ed/AA Lees McRae Col; BA Lynchburg Col; mil/AUS Inf 1954-56, Panama Canal Zone; pa/Gen Mgr Maiden Times (NC) Newspaper 4 Yrs; Owner-Mgr Super Sub Sandwich Shoppe, L'ton; Profl YMCA Dir 20 Yrs: NC, RI, Mass, Pa, Fla, Tenn; cp/Maiden Lions Clb; Former Kiwanis Mem; JCs; NICAP; APRO; CUFOS; r/St Luth Epis Ch; hon/Most Ath Sr Nom, L'burg Col; JC Man of Yr Nom, Woburn, Mass; NC St Dir MUFON,

Mutual UFO Network Inc, Seguin, Tex; Pub'd Author; Personalities of S; W/W S&SW.

FAWCETT, LESLIE CLARENCE JR oc/Certified Public Accountant; b/May 12, 1920; h/428 Hammond Ave, San Antonio, TX 78210; ba/SA; p/Leslie C Fawcett Sr (dec); Estelle V Fawcett, San Antonio; ed/BBA, MBA Univ Tex-Austin; mil/AUS Signal Corp 1942-45, ETO; pa/Partner CPA Firm; Am Inst CPAs; Tex Soc CPAs; r/U Presb Ch USA: Ruling Elder, Clerk of Session.

FAWCETT, MRS ROSCOE KENT (MARIE ANN FORMANEK) oc/Homemaker; Civic Leader; Philanthropist; b/Mar 6, 1914; h/North St & Hawkwood Ln, Greenwich, CT 06830; m/Roscoe Kent; c/Roscoe Kent Jr, Peter Formanek, Roger Knowlton II, Stephen Hart; p/Peter Paul and Mary Ann Stepanek Formanek (dec); ed/Hon PhD: Hamilton St Univ 1974, Colo St Christian Col 1973; cp/Bd Dirs: Merry Go Round for Aged, Merry Go Round Mews for Elderly, Greenwich Philharmonia, MS Soc, Cerebral Palsy, Nathaniel Witherell Aux; Greenwich Hosp: Weekend Vol Chm, 2 Yrs, Ser Cit, Var Coms, Woms Clb of Greenwich; Chm Every Dr: ARC, Commun Chest, Mtl Hlth, Leukemia, Muscular Dystrophy; Wkr w Mtly Retarded Chd at Milbank Sch; Supr Ct Jury Duty 24 Wks; Danced in Every Benefit in Mpls Since Age 15; Participating Mem Huxley Inst for Biosocial Res; York Clb, NY; r/Cath; hon/Wom of Yr 1967 Soroptimist Clb; Commun Ser Awd U Cerebral Palsy Assn, Fairfield Co Inc 1972; Marquis Biog Lib Soc Adv Mem; Intl Biog Assn; Reference Source Lib Human Resources, Am Bicent Res Inst; Conn St Dept Hlth Cits 1974, 75; Hon Soc Am; Polit Sci Cert Awd Harvard Univ 1976; IPA; Great Britain's Coronation Edition Royal Blue Book; 2000 Wom Achmt; W/W: E, Am Wom, Conn, Am, US; Intl W/W Commun Ser Awd for Dist'd Ser to Commun; World W/W Wom; Nat Social Dir; DIB; Nat Reg Prom Ams & Intl Notables; Marquis W/W; Intl Reg Profiles.

FAWCETT, NOVICE G oc/University President Emeritus; Educational Consultant; b/Mar 29, 1909; h/3518 Rue de Fleur, Columbus, OH 43221; ba/Columbus; m/Marjorie Keener; c/Mary Joan (dec), Jane Elizabeth; p/John Henry and Mary Allie Lampson Fawcett; ed/BS magna cum laude Kenyon Col 1931; MA Ohio St Univ 1937; Addit Studies; pa/Ohio St Univ: Pres Emeritus

1972-, Pres 1956-72; Ednl Conslt 1972-; Acting Commr for Higher Ed St of Ind 1973-74; Supt Schs, Columbus 1949-56; Other Former Positions; Past Mem S'ship Bd Timken Roller Bearing Co Ednl Fund Inc; S'ship Bd Ford Motor Co S'ship Fund Prog; Past Mem Ed Policies Comm NEA; cp/Past Trustee AF Mus Foun; Dir Columbus Area C of C; Devel Com for Gtr Columbus; Former Dir Ohio C of C; Bd Govs Intl Ins Sems Inc; 33° Mason; Newcomen Soc; Ath Clb Columbus; Ohio St Univ Fac Clb; Kit Kat Clb; Rotary Clb Columbus; Others; hon/Novice G Fawcett Chair in Ednl Adm, Est'd by Ohio St Trustees 1972; Hon Lifetime Mbrship, Varsity "O" Assn; Outstg Citizen Awd, Bldg Indust Assn Ctl Ohio; Columbus Awd in Recog of Dist'd Commun Ser, Columbus C of C; Num Hon Degs; Hon Socs; Others.

FAWELL, MICHAEL K oc/Attorney at

Law; b/Jan 13, 1940; h/28 W 180 Indian Knoll Trail, W Chicago, IL 60185; ba/Lombard, IL; m/Judith Ann; c/Amy Louise, Michael John; p/Walter R Fawell (dec); Mildred G Fawell, W Chgo; ed/BS; JD; pa/Ill & Du Page Co Bar Assns; r/Prot.

FAY, THOMAS J oc/Rehabilitation Counselor; b/Sept 8, 1944; h/175 Southaven Ave, Medford, NY 11763; m/Jewel E; c/2 Chd; p/Patrick F and Rita M Fay; ed/BA Cath Univ Am; MA Universite Laval (Quebec); PhD Fordham Univ; pa/Prof St Bernard Col, Culman, Ala 1963-64; Vis Prof Drew Univ, Madison, NJ 1969; St Johns Univ, NYC: Joined Staff 1967, Current Chm Phil Dept; Current Rehab Cnslr Pilgrim Psychi Ctr, W Brentwood, NY; Am Cath Phil Assn: Pres Metro Reg Chapt 1975-; Com of Present Status & Future of Profession, Am Phil Assn 1974-76; ARCA; APGA; AMEG; AMBAE; Pres Pilgrim Fed Credit Union; Exec Bd Public Employees Fdn; r/Rom Cath; hon/Pub'd Author; Delta Mu Delta; Biogl Listings.

FEAGLES, GERALD FRANKLIN oc/Account Manager; b/Dec 8, 1934; h/1702 N 155th St, Basehor, KS 66007; ba/Overland Pk, Ks; m/Eleanor Jean; c/Gerald F Jr; p/George Joseph and Florence Ada Johnson Feagles, Fairplay; ed/Att'd Ks City Jr Col 1953-55; pa/Account Mgt E F Hauserman Co; Prodrs Coun 1970-73; Assoc'd Gen Contractors Inst 1970-75; Constrn Specifications Inst 1970-75; cp/Ks Univ Alumni Assn; BSA; r/Bapt; hon/W/W MW; DIB; Commun Ldrs & Noteworthy Ams.

FEATHERSTONE, JESSIE ANNA ROAN oc/Retired Classroom Teacher; b/Jun 14, 1904; h/1213 Arp St, Commerce, TX 75428; m/Patrick Earl (dec); p/Jesse J and Ida Louella Smith Roan (dec); ed/BA 1931, MA 1947 E Tex St Univ; pa/HS Tchr: Sr Eng, Jour, Spch, Drama; Freshman Eng E Tex St Univ; cp/OES; Vol Var Civic Drs; Chm UF Dr; DAR; Other Civic Activs; r/1st Christian Ch: Elder, Ch Sch Tchr, Pres Christian Wom F'ships; hon/Delta Kappa Gamma (Pres); AAUW; Worthy Matron OES; Pi Pi; Personalities of S; Others.

FECHEK, THERESA A oc/Administrator; h/#476, 7201 Wood Hollow Dr, Austin, TX 78731; ba/Austin; p/Frank J Fechek; Mary B Fechek (dec); ed/BS Clarion St Col; MA Case-Wn Resv Univ; PhD Ohio St Univ; pa/Coor

Prog Sers Delta Kappa Gamma Soc Intl; Spec Libs Assn; World Future Soc; Kappa Delta Pi; cp/Work w Orgs Involved w Improvemt of Ed; r/Cath; hon/Martha Holden Jennings Scholar Awd, Cleveland, Ohio.

FEDERICO, PETER GEORGE oc/Educator; b/Nov 26, 1939; h/118 Crump Rd, Exton, PA 19341; ba/Aston, PA; m/Margaret Louise; c/Peggie, Christine, Peter, Taryn, Celeste; p/Marcello Federico (dec); Aurelia Federico, Villanova, PA; ed/AB 1962, MA 1969 Villanova; pa/Advmt of Higher Ed, Our Lady of Angels Col; Nat Conslt to Cols & Hosps; Nat Bd Dirs Worldwide Marriage Encounter; cp/Bd Dirs Philadelphia Archdiocesan Fam Life Bur; r/Rom Cath; hon/Nat Prom Ams; W/W Among Admrs in Am Cols & Univs.

FEENEY, ROBERT EARL oc/Professor; b/Aug 30, 1913; h/780 Elmwood Dr, Davis, CA 95616; ba/Davis; m/Mary Alice; c/Jane, Elizabeth; p/Bernard Cyril and Loreda McKee Feeney (dec); ed/BS NWn Univ 1938; MS 1939, PhD 1942 Univ Wis; mil/AUS 1943-46, Capt & Cmdg Ofcr, Wound Res Team; pa/Univ Cal-Davis 1960-: Prof Dept Food Sci & Tech, Biochemist Agri Experiment Sta; Vis

Prof Dept Biochem Univ Bergen, Bergen, Norway 1976; Dist'd Vis Prof Depb Biochem Meml Univ Newfoundland, St John's, Newfoundland, Canada 1978-79; Univ Neb-Lincoln: Prof Chem & Chm Dept Biochem & Nutrition 1953-60; Other Former Positions; r/Prot; hon/3 Res Grants, Nat Insts Hlth; Awd for Dist'd Achmt & Ser in Agri & Food Chem, Am Chem Soc Div Agri & Food Chem; Feeney Peak, Queen Maude Mtn Range, Antarctica 1968; Superior Ser Awd, US Dept Agri; Pub'd Author.

FEINDT, MARY CLARISSA oc/Registered Land Surveyor; Land Title Abstractor; b/Mar 9, 1916; h/PO Box 18, Charlevoix, MI 49720; ba/Same; m/John L; c/Lawrence R; p/Ernest R and Lila M Bastian (dec); ed/AB Albion Col; BS, MS Univ Mich; pa/Past Pres Mich Land Title Assn; Past Mem Bd Govs Am Land Title Assn; Bd Dirs Mich Soc Reg'd Land Surveyors; Life Mem: Mich Engrg Soc, Am Cong on Surveying & Mapping; Soc Wom Engrs; Am Soc CE; cp/Charlevoix Co Surveyor 1942-; r/Prot.

FEINSTEIN, ABRAHAM J oc/Rabbi Emeritus; b/Sept 27, 1893; h/925 McCallie Ave, Chattanooga, TN 37403; ba/Chatta; m/Lillian B; c/Dee F Shacter (Mrs Herman); p/Samuel and Sima Bayle Feinstein (dec); ed/BA; MA; DD; DHUM; mil/Civilian Chaplain Fort Oglethorpe; Civilian Chaplain Red Stone Arsenal; Mem Mil Adv Com; pa/Lectr Tenn Wesleyan Col; Prof Univ Chatta; Lectr Girl's Preparatory Sch; Lectr Jewish Chautauqua Soc; Ctl Conf Am Rabbis; Spkr Num Rel & Civic Groups; Sponsor Hillel Foun; cp/Former SEn Chm War Labor Bd; Rotary Clb; Fam Ser Agy; B'nai B'rith; Traveler's Aid; Nat Conf Christians & Jews; r/Jewish; hon/Cits: Tenn Colleagues, Bnai Brith; Hon'd by Chatta Jewish Commun.

FEINSTEIN, EDWARD oc/Mortgage Banker; b/Jun 21, 1923; h/120 S Prospect Dr, Coral Gables, FL 33133; ba/Miami, FL; m/Shirley; c/Brian, Mark, Deborah, Eric; p/Robert Feinstein, Miami; Bertha Feinstein (dec); ed/BBA Univ Miami 1947; mil/USNR Supply Corps 1943-46, Lt (jg); pa/Pres: Heritage Corp S Fla, InterAm Title Corp; Pres Mortgage Brokers Assn S Fla 1964-66; Pres Mortgage Bkrs Assn Gtr Miami 1971-72; Lectr Univ Miami; cp/Consumer Credit Cnslg; Pacesetter, Nat Conf Christians & Jews;

Cerebral Palsy Telethon; U Way Cit; Golden Gloves; Bd Trustees Univ Miami Alumni Assn; Soc Univ Fdrs; Others; r/Jewish; hon/Mortgage Broker of Yr 1966; USN Middleweight Boxing Champ 1944; Other Boxing Achmts; Profl Pubs; W/W S&SW; Personalities of S.

FELDMAN, HARVEY W oc/Writer; Social Researcher; Ethnographer; b/Jul 1, 1929; h/4382 Howe St, Oakland, CA 94611; ba/Oakland; p/Charles S and Fannie Enoch Feldman, Pittsburgh, PA; ed/BA Univ Pgh; MSW Columbia Univ; PhD Brauders Univ; mil/AUS 1953-55; pa/Social Reschr, Brown & Feldman Assocs; Soc for Study of Social Probs; Nat Assn Social Wkrs; hon/Fellow, Drug Abuse Coun; NIMH F'ship; DIB; W/W in E.

FELDMAN, LEON oc/Public Affairs Official, US Government; b/Oct 5, 1929; h/3950 Lake Shore Dr, Chicago, IL 60613; ed/BS Univ Wis 1955; MA Univ Chgo 1961; pa/Dir Commun Relats Michael Reese Hosp & Med Ctr; Acct Exec Cooper & Golin Inc; Asst Reg Dir Public Affairs, Chgo MW Ofc, US HEW 1967-; Public Relats Soc Am; Soc Profl Jrnlsts; Chgo Headline Clb; Publicity Clb Chgo; hon/Contbr to Sev Profl Jours; Awds: Publicity Clb Chgo, Wel Public Relats Forum for Film on Nsg; 1st Awd, Wel Public Relats Forum for HEW brochure on day care; Cit, HEW Reg Dirs; DIB.

FELDSHER, HOWARD M oc/Educator; Composer; Director; b/Jul 11, 1936; h/8 Peace Dr, Middletown, NY 10940; ba/Montgomery, NY; m/Eileen Sinkowitz; p/Sylvia Feldsher, M'town; ed/BS Ithaca Col; MA Columbia

Univ; mil/AUS Band's Men 1959-61; pa/Dir Pub Aulds Music Pubrs; 13 Pub'd Articles on Music & Music Ed; 19 Pub'd Music Compositions; r/Jewish; hon/F'ship, Univ Utah; Outstg Yg Men Am; Intl W/W in Music.

FENN, CARL E oc/Professor; b/Nov 29, 1931; h/208 Jana Rd, Macomb, IL 61455; ba/Macomb; m/Linda; c/Scott, Lori, Kristi; p/Weaver C Fenn, Carson, IA; Bertha Fenn (dec); ed/EdD; mil/USN 1953-55; pa/Prof Spec Ed Wn Ill Univ; CEC; Am Assn on Mtl Deficiency; cp/Lions Clb; r/Reorg'd Ch of Jesus Christ of LDS.

FENN, RICHARD LEE oc/Minister; b/Dec 23, 1934; ba/786 Channing Ave, Palo Alto, CA 94301; m/Joan; c/Richard Lee, Robert Bruce, Carolyn Joan Grace; p/Vincent A and Esther B Fenn, Hendersonville, NC; ed/BA Columbia Union Col 1956; MA Am Univ 1960; pa/Min Palo Alto SDA Ch; SDA

Chaplain to Stanford Univ; cp/Mem 3 Sch Bds; Hines Cooperative Studies Human Rts Com; VA Hosp, Palo Alto; r/SDA; hon/Hon Citizen, City of Bethlehem.

FENSKE, VIRGINIA E oc/Retired Administrator; b/Dec 14, 1909; h/920 Fenske Dr, Olympia, WA 98506; m/Hugo; ed/AB Univ Ill 1931; MA Univ Chgo 1941; Postgrad Studies; pa/Ret'd 1973; St Coor Adult Progs Sect Wash St Dept Social & Hlth Sers 1967-73; St-wide Supvr Lic'g Vol Child Care Agys, Olympia 1945-67; Other Former Positions; Nat Assn Social Wkrs, Past Chapt Prog Chm

(Olympia); Am Acad Cert'd Social Wkrs; Wash Assn Social Wel; Am Public Wel Assn; Child Wel Leag Am; cp/Charter Bd Mem Wash St Employees Credit Union; Charter Mem Lady Lions Clb; Daughs of Nile; OES, Chapt 36; Altrusa; r/Gloria Dei Luth Ch; hon/Profl Pubs; DIB; 2000 Wom Achmt; World W/W Wom; Personalities W&MW; Commun Ldrs & Noteworthy Ams; Intl W/W Commun Ser; W/W Am Wom.

FERBER, ROBERT R oc/Solar Research Project Manager; b/Jun 11, 1935; h/5314 Alta Canyada Rd, La Canada, CA 91011; ba/Pasadena, CA; m/Eileen M; c/Robert Jr, Lynne; p/Rudolf F Ferber (dec); Elizabeth J

Ferber, Cape Coral, FL; ed/BS Univ Pgh; MS, PhD Carnegie-Mellon Univ; pa/Sr Mem IEEE; ISES; cp/Former Sch Bd Mem; r/Luth; hon/Buhl Foun F'ship; NDEA F'ship.

FERGUS, PATRICIA MARGUERITA oc/Retired Educator; Writer; b/Oct 26, 1918; h/510 Groveland Ave, Minneapolis, MN 55403; p/Golden M and Mary A Fergus (dec); ed/BS 1939, MA 1941, PhD 1960 Univ Minn; pa/Mount St Mary's Col, E'burg: Former Assoc Dean of Col & Prof of English & Writing; Univ Minn: Asst Prof Eng 1972-79, Dir Writing Ctr 1975-77, Coor Writing Conf 1975; NCTE: Reg Judge 1974, 76, 77, St Coor

1977-79; Minn Coun Tchrs Eng: Secy Leg Com 1973-, Chperson Careers & Job Opports Prog 1977-79; Spec Task Force on Tchr Licensure; St Dept Ed Liaison Com 1978-79; Pi Lambda Theta; AAUW; AAUP; Nat Writers Clb; Assn Wom Writers; Reviewer for Pub'g Cos; Free-lance Editor; r/St Olaf Cath Ch, Mpls; hon/Univ Minn: Twin Cities Student Assembly Awd for Outstg Contbn, Ednl Devel Grant, Horace T Morse-Amoco Foun Awd for Outstg Contbns to Undergrad Ed; Profl Pubs; Biogl Listings.

FERGUSON, ELIZABETH RYBURN oc/Instructor; b/Nov 7, 1934; h/Rt 7, Box 715, Pine Bluff, AR 71603; ba/Pine Bluff; m/Silas A; c/Gregory Monroe, Kimberly Karen; p/James Monroe and Hazel Evelyn

West Ryburn (dec); ed/BS; MEd; PhD Cand; pa/Instr Clothing, Textiles & Fashion Merchandising Univ Ark; AHEA; AATCC; ACPTC; ASTM; ABWA; cp/Ldr Willow Pride 4-H Clb; Com to Revitalize Inner City; r/Bapt; hon/Tex Doct F'ship; World W/W Wom.

FERGUSON, EVA DREIKURS oc/Professor; ba/Edwardsville, IL 62025; c/Rodney A, Beth E, Bruce E, Linda J; p/Dr Rudolf Dreikurs (dec); pa/Prof Dept Psychol So Ill Univ; Author 1 Book & Num Articles in Psychol; Conslt'g Editor JIP; Res in Experimental Psychol of Lng & Motivation; Lectr on Adlerian Psychol; hon/Notable Ams.

FERGUSON, EVELYN COOK oc/Writer; Editor; h/432 N Avenida Felicidad, Tucson, AZ 85705; ed/Att'd: Wash St Univ, NY Univ; pa/Assoc Editor *Jack and Jill* Mag, The Curtis Pub'g Co, Philadelphia, Pa 1946; Editor *Stories, Trailblazer,* The Westminster Press, Phila 1951-61; Author Books for Yg People incl: *The Lost Chd of the Shoshones, The Sign of the Anchor, Undergroung Escape, Captive of the Delawares, The River Spirit and the Mtn Demons, The Extraordinary Adventures of Chee Chee McNerney;* Short Stories Contb'd to: *Jack and Jill, Boy's Life, Stories to Remember;* Short Story "Grandma Tilbury" Used by Ofc of Audio Ed, Empire St FM Ednl Network; Books Pub'd Abroad; r/U Presb Ch, Phila: Ret'd Mem Staff, Bd of Christian Ed; hon/Mem Col Hon; *Underground Escape* Chosen for James Weldon Johnson Meml Collection, Countee Cullen Br NYC Lib; Num Biogl Listings.

FERGUSON, HARRY oc/Professor; b/May 1, 1914; h/3224 Fairway Dr, Dayton, OH 45409; ba/Cincinnati, OH; m/Helen B Baker; p/Robert and Isabella Gamble Ferguson (dec); ed/BS Boston Univ 1939; AM Harvard Univ 1949; PhD Univ Pgh 1958; pa/Prof Math & Engrg Sci Univ Cinc 1959-; Applied Mathematician & Aeronautical Res Engr Wright Patterson AFB 1950-59; Author Res Papers; Am Math Soc; Math Assn Am; Soc Indust & Applied Math; Soc Natural Philosophy; Am Soc Engrg Ed; Alpha Tau Omega; VP & Part-Owner Ferguson Sales Inc, Alpha, Ohio; Harvard (Dayton) Clb; Mason; Shriners; r/Christ U Meth Ch, Kettering, Ohio; hon/Am Men of Sci; Men of Achmt; W/W MW; Am Men & Wom Sci.

FERGUSON, KAREN ANNE oc/Bio-chemist; b/Oct 25, 1942; h/289 Kaymar Dr,

Tonawanda, NY 14150; ba/Buffalo, NY; p/Earl W and Roxana C Hodge Bunn, Nebo, IL; ed/BS w high hons Wn Ill Univ 1963; PhD Bryn Mawr 1971; pa/Biochemist SUNY; Support by Res Grant, Nat Insts Hlth 1976-78; Engaged in Tchg & Res; Am Chem Soc; AAAS; cp/NOW; hon/Valedictorian, Pittsfield HS 1959; Outstg Fac Awd, En Ill Univ; W/W Am Wom; Outstg Yg Wom Am.

FERLINZ, JACK oc/Physician; b/Feb 18, 1942; h/16792 Talisman Ln, Huntington Beach, CA 92649; ba/Long Beach, CA; p/Anthony and Maria Ferlinz; ed/AB Harvard; MBA NEn; MD Boston Univ; pa/Fellow: AHA,ACC, ACP, ACCP; Am Soc for Clin Pharm & Therapeutics; Am Fdn Clin Res.

FERRELL, EXCELL OSBORNE III oc/Executive; b/Feb 17, 1944; h/112 Fairforest Dr, Rutherfordton, NC 28139; ba/R'ton; m/Paula Barnes; c/Christopher Scott; p/E O Jr and Bertha L Ferrell, Durham, NC; ed/BSEE NC St Univ; MBA UNC-G; mil/AUS; pa/Mgr Duke Power Co; cp/Pres R'ton-Spindale C of C; VP Rutherford Co U Appeal; VP R'ton Kiwanis Clb; R'ton Appearance Comm.

FERRIER, RICHARD B oc/Associate Professor; Artist; b/Mar 29, 1944; h/1628 Connally Terr, Arlington, TX 76010; ba/A'ton; c/Sean Brooks; ed/BArch Tex Tech Univ 1968; MA Univ Dallas 1972; pa/Assoc Prof Arch Univ Tex-A 1968-; Arch/Assoc William S Austin 1976-; R B Ferrier Commun Conslts 1974-; Designer Ralph Kelman Archs 1969-70; Designer Engrg Assoc, Lubbock, Tex 1966-68; Other Former Positions; AAUP; The Cousteau Soc; Judge Dallas Chapt AIA, Ken Roberts Delineation Competition 1975; Var Exhbns; cp/Am Civil Liberties Union; hon/W/W S&SW.

FERRIS, CHARLES BIRDSALL oc/Civil Engineer; b/Mar 5, 1904; h/42 Silverbrook Rd, Shrewsbury, NY 07701; ba/NYC; m/Larua Soper; p/Charles and Florence Birdsall Ferris; ed/BS NYU 1926; CE 1927; Further Studies; mil/NYNG 1925-41; USAR; Mil Hons; pa/Pres: Ferris Constrn Co, NYC 1948-, Ferris Constrn Co, White Plains, NY, Charles B Ferris Inc, NYC 1951-; Secy-Treas Flagsim Co Inc, White Plains 1951-58; Other Former Positions; Propr: Charles B Ferris Assoc Archs & Engrs, NYC, C B Ferris Assn, Geneva, Switzerland, Paris, NYC 1951-, Pres 1960-; Conslt & Dir Operats Housing & Redevel Bd Charge Urban Renewal & Slum Clearance, NYC 1960-62; Reg'd Profl Engr: NY, NJ, Mass, Pa, Conn, Wis, Fla; Ret'd Arch-Engr, Geneva, Switzerland; ASCE; Soc Lic'd Profl Engrs; Res Ofcrs Assn; cp/SAR; Am Legion; Mil Order World Wars; NY Soc Mil Order Fgn Wars; Sojourners; Am C of C, Paris; Assn US Army; Mason; Mem Sev Clbs; r/Epis: Warden; hon/Works incl: Barnert Meml Hosp, Paterson, NJ, Hosps in Europe, Var Col Campus Bldgs, Mil Bases, Libs, Schs; Others; W/W in Am.

FERSHT, RENA SCHER oc/Scientist; b/Dec 16, 1938; h/3749 Buena Park Dr, Studio City, CA 91604; ba/Woodland Hills, CA; m/Samuel N; c/Karen Hadas, Sherri Nicole; p/Abraham Scher (dec); Chaya Stock, Safad, Israel; ed/BSc 1962, MSc 1964 Technion, Israel Inst of Tech; PhD Cal Inst Tech 1968; pa/Prin Investigator Devel & Design Fluid Bearings. Guid & Control

Systems Div, Litton Systems 1972-; Sr Engr Underwater Acoustics, Tetra-Tech Inc 1971; Other Former Positions; Am Inst Aero & Astronautics; Sigma Xi; hon/Amelia Earhart Awd; Achmt Awd in Sci, YWCA Ldr Luncheon III.

FIELD, ELIZABETH ASHLOCK oc/Former Government Official; b/Nov 27, 1915; h/150 SE 25th Rd, Apt 10A, Miami, FL 33129; m/Henry Lamar (dec); c/Elizabeth F Wassell (Mrs John Randolph Jr); p/Jesse Vernon and Felecia Bruner Ashlock (dec); ed/Little Rock Jr Col; Wash Univ; pa/Dir Hist House, Angelo Marre House; Dir Commemorative Comm-Ark; Ark First St Capitol, Confed Capitol, Wash, Ark; cp/Coun of Intl Visitors, Hist Assn So Fla; Dade Co Commun Devel Bd; Dade Heritage Trust; r/St Thomas Epis Ch, Miami; hon/Awd of Merit, ARC; Quadaw Qtr Awd; Book of Honor.

FIELD, MARY oc/Librarian; Sister of Religious Order; h/7900 W Division St, River Forest, IL 60305; ba/Same; p/Henry Augustus Field; Georgia Coakley Field, Wisconsin Dells, WI; ed/BA, MALS Rosary Col; MA Univ Wis; pa/Chief Libn Rosary Col; Am Lib Assn; Ill Lib Assn; r/Rom Cath.

FIELDER, MILDRED oc/Free-lance Author; b/Jan 13, 1913; h/2525 Bay Vista Ln, Los Osos, CA 93402; ba/Same; m/Ronald G; p/Robert A, John A; p/William and Edna Verna Edzards Craig (dec); pa/Author of Hist Books & Articles; Books incl: *Poker Alice*, 1978, *Plant Medicine and Folklore*, 1975, *Sioux Indian Leaders*, 1975, *Deadwood Dick and the Dime Novels*, 1974, Others; Poems

Pub'd in Anthologies; Life Mem Soc Am Histns; SD Poetry Soc, Former Reg VP; Life Mem SD Hist Soc; Nat Leag Am Pen Wom, Sev Nat Ofcs Held; Former Mem: Lawrence Co Hist Soc, Wn Writers Am; Assoc Mem NY Poetry Forum; Cal Fdn Chaparral Poets; cp/Repub; r/Presb; hon/Num Awds, incl'g 45 Nat.

FIELDS, JOAN ROSS oc/Chemical Company Executive; b/Jan 18, 1930; h/303 E 57th St, New York, NY 10022; ba/LIC, NY; c/Larry M, Paul B; p/Albert and Etta Lery Ross, Palm Beach, FL; ed/BS Adelphi Univ; Cert'd Early Childhood Ed; pa/NY Assn Wom Bus Owners; cp/Yg Profl Com USA; r/Jewish; hon/Valedictorian, Colby Acad; W/W Am Wom; World W/W Wom.

FIGERT, PETER A oc/Director Instrumental Music; b/Jun 11, 1930; h/Odessa, TX; ba/Odessa; m/Elaine Hunt; c/Mark, Michael, Anne, Amy, Alex; p/R L

Figert Sr (dec); Marie Figert, Tucson, AZ; ed/BS 1952, MA 1957 Ball St Univ; Doct Cand Univ Colo; mil/38th Div Band; pa/Assoc Prof Music Odessa Col; Tchr: Manchester Col, Howe Mil Sch, Sev Public Schs Ind; Pres Phi Delta Kappa; Other Profl Assns; cp/Pres Civic Concert Assn; Bd Pres Mus, Friends of Lib; Dir Bicent Band; r/St Johns Epis Ch; Dir Music; hon/World W/W Musicians; W/W: Tex, S.

FIGG, ROBERT McCORMICK JR oc/Lawyer; Retired Dean & Professor of Law; b/Oct 22, 1901; h/1522 Deans Ln, Columbia, SC; m/Sallie Alexander Tobias, Robert M III, Emily F Dalla Mura, Jefferson Tobias; ed/AB Col Charleston 1920; Columbia Univ Law 1920-22; pa/Dean & Prof Law Univ SC Sch of Law 1959-70; Sr Counsel Robinson, McFadden, Moore & Pope, Columbia 1971-; Gen Counsel SC St Ports Auth 194-72; Spec Circuit Judge 1957, 75, 76; Others; SC Bar, Ho of Dels; ABA: Ho of Dels 1971-73, Com on Fair Trial-Free Press, Others; Am Law Inst; Am Judic Soc; World Assn Lwyrs; cp/Former Mem SC Ho of Reps; Pres Col Charleston Foun 1970-72, Hon Life Chm 1972-; Elector Hall of Fame for Gt Ams 1976-; Grand Master of Masons SC 1972-74; Trustee: Saul Alexander Foun, Columbia Mus Art & Scis; hon/Fellow, Am Col Trial Lwyrs; Phi Beta Kappa; Phi Delta Phi; Blue Key; Hon LLD, Univ SC; Hon LittD, Col C'ton; Pub'd Author.

FILICKY, JOSEPH GEORGE oc/Production Superintendent; b/Mar 18, 1915; h/Forest Hills, Clifton Forge, VA 24422; ba/Covington, VA; m/Margaret Elizabeth Walsh; c/Sandra Lee F Hebenstreit, Necia Jo-Ann F Kaufman; p/Stephen and Julia Cintel Filicky (dec); ed/BCE NC St Univ 1940; Addit Studies; pa/Westvaco Corp (formerly WVa Pulp & Paper Co): Prodn Supt, Asst Prodn Supt, Quality Control Mgr 1964-, Chem Engr 1946-63; Hercules Power Co, Radford Ordnance Works, Radford, Va 1944-45: Devel Chemist, Shift Supvr (Prodn); Other Former Positions; Lectr; Instr; AAAS; AARP; NACCCA; Nat Roster Sci & Specialized Pers; Am Water Works Assn; Am Inst Chem Engrs; cp/LOA; Former Mem Tyrone Sportsmen's Assn; Purple Order of Pump Primers; Allegheny CC; r/St Joseph Cath Ch; hon/S'ship; Hon Socs; Pub'd Author.

FINCH, BERNIE O oc/Physician, Craniologist; b/Dec 27, 1939; h/Rt 1, Box 96, Rapid City, SD 57701; ba/Rapid City; m/Judy Mae; c/Lynn, Noel, Bernie Scott, Arne, Jennifer; p/Gerald F and Myra Jean Finch, Indianapolis, IN; ed/BA Bob Jones Univ; ThB Berea Sch Theol; MA St Andrew's Col; DC NWn Col Chiropractic; pa/Applied Kenesiologist, Craniologist; London & Cos Soc Physiologists; cp/Profl Bowhunters Soc; Pvt Pilot; CAP Capt; Black Belt; Chinese Kung Fu Soc; Am Mtn Men; r/Open Bible Ch.

FINCH, CLIFF oc/Governor; b/Apr 4, 1927; m/Zelma Lois Smith; c/Janet Herrington, Virginia Anne, Charles Clifton, Stephen Nicholas; ed/Law Deg Univ Miss Sch Law 1958; mil/AUS WWII; pa/Gov Miss 1976-; Dist Atty 17th Circuit Ct Dist 1964-72; Miss & Am Bar Assns; Past Pres Miss Dist & Dist Atty's Assn; Former Mem Bd Dirs Nat Dist Atty's Assn; Assoc Editor *Am Trial Lwyrs Jour*; cp/Former Mem Miss Ho of Reps;

Masons; Lions Intl; Civitans; Moose; Odd-Fellows; Am Legion; VFW; r/Bapt.

FINCH, DONALD GEORGE oc/Poet; Songwriter; b/Jun 30, 1937; h/506 NE Monroe, Peoria, IL 61603; ba/Peoria; p/Lloyd Lindo Finch (dec); Jean Finch, Peoria; mil/USAF; pa/Peoria Poetry Clb; Pub'd 5 Books of Poetry; r/Meth; hon/W/W: MW, Intl Poetry.

FINCHER, FORREST TRUMAN oc/Free-lance Artist; Barber/Stylist; Art Teacher; b/Sept 22, 1940; h/222 S Buffalo, Canton, TX 75103; ba/Canton; c/Forrest Bryan; p/Raymond Fincher; Rachel Fincher, Canton; ed/Tyler Jr Col; Tex En Univ; cp/Canton Lions; Tex Hist Soc; r/1st U Meth Ch; hon/Artist of Yr; Personalities of S.

FINCHER, GLEN EUGENE oc/Education-al Administrator; b/Oct 29, 1935; h/4003 Bellwood Dr NW, Canton, OH 44708; ba/Canton; m/Sue Ann; c/Debra Sue, Glen Eugene; p/Kadez Fincher (dec); Bernice Fincher, New Philadelphia, OH; ed/BS; MAdm & Supv; PhD; pa/Phi Delta Kappa; NCTM; NEA; Ohio Ed Assn; E Ctl Ohio Profl Edrs; cp/Former Mem: Chd's Com Stark Co Mtl Hlth Coun, NE Five Co Reg Coun on Alcoholism; r/Prot; hon/St of Ohio S'ship; PTA (St) S'ship; Nat Def F'ship.

FINE, RICHARD I oc/Attorney; b/Jan 22, 1940; h/14013 Captain's Row, Marina Del Rey, CA 90291; ba/Los Angeles, CA; p/Jack and Frieda Fine; ed/BS Univ Wis 1961; JD Univ Chgo 1964; PhD Univ London, London Sch Ecs & Polit Sci 1967; Certs; Further Studies; pa/Admitted to Bar: Ill 1964, DC & US Supreme Ct 1972, Cal 1973; Current Pvt Pract of Law, LA; Spec Counsel Govtl Efficiency Com (LA) 1973-74; Chief Antitrust Div City Atty's Ofc 1973-74; Prof Intl, Comparative & EEC Antitrust Law, Univ Syracuse Law Sch Overseas Prog (Sum) 1970-72; Trial Atty US Dept Justice, Antitrust Div, Fgn Commerce Sect, Spec Litigation Sect, Cleveland Field Ofc 1968-72; LA Co Bar Assn; CoChm Antitrust Com 1975-77; Ill St Bar Assn; ABA: Mem Sect Antitrust Law, Chm Subcom on Intl Antitrust & Trade Regulations, Intl Law Sect 1972-77, VChm Com on Intl Ec Orgs 1975-77; St Bar Cal; DC Bar; Am Soc Intl Law; Am Fgn Law Assn; Intl Law Assn; Brit Inst Intl & Comparative Law; World Peace Through Law Ctr; hon/Phi Delta Phi; Num Profl Pubs.

FINK, AARON oc/Business Executive; b/Apr 1, 1916; h/20 Crestwood Dr, Maplewood, NJ 07040; m/Roslyn Lamb; c/2 Chd; ed/AB Johns Hopkins Univ 1938; Hon PhD Hamilton St Univ 1973; pa/Current Mem Adv Bd Nat Paper Box Assn & Serves as Chm of Plant Opers & Manpower Com; Pres NJ Box Paper Box Bur 1954, 55; VP & Gen Mgr Essex Paper Box Mfg Co Inc, Newark, NJ 1945; Other Former Positions; US Del to Conf of Mfrs, Paris, France 1954; Spec Ec Mission to Italy 1954; Appt'd as Charter Mem to Pres's Coun of Am Inst Mgmt 1953; Fellow IBA; Nat Assn Mfrs; Am Geophy Union; Soc for Advmt of Mgmt; Tech Assn Paper & Pulp Indust; Am Soc for Quality Control; Am Inst Aeronautics & Astronautics; Math Soc Am; Am Statistical Assn; Nat Assn Cost Accts; Am Inst Corporate Controllers; Chaine des Rotisseurs; Paper Indust Mgmt Assn; Planning Execs Inst; Am Water Resources Assn; cp/Crestmont CC; W Orange Clb; Boca Raton Clb; Gt Oak Yacht Clb; Princeton Clb NY; hon/Biogl Listings.

FINLEY, EVELYN ANNE oc/Assistant Professor; b/Jan 23, 1937; h/Rt 1, Box 144, Sherrill, AR 72152; ba/Pine Bluff, AR; p/E M and Lucille Finley, Calhoun, LA; ed/BS; MS; EdS; pa/Asst Prof HPER, UAPB; Am Alliance for HPER; So Dist AAHPER; AWISA; SAPECW; Ark AHPER; cp/LWV; SE Spec Olympics; r/Meth.

FINN, WILLIAM F oc/Physician; b/Jul 23, 1915; h/3 Aspen Gate, Manhasset, NY 11030; ba/Manhasset; m/Doris Henderson;

c/Neil, Shanon, David; p/Neil A Finn (dec); Catherine M Finn, Westunken, NJ; ed/BA; MD; mil/AUS 1944-46, Capt; pa/Gynecolo-gist; Att'g Obstetrician-Gynecologist St Francis Hosp 1979; Courtesy Staff Manhasset Med Ctr 1959-; Conslt Obstetrics/Gynecol Mercy Hosp 1951-; Att'g Obstetrician-Gynecologist N Shore Univ Hosp 1959-; Former Hosp Appts; Assoc Prof Clin Obstetrics & Gynecol Cornell Univ Med Col 1971-; AMA; NY St, NY Co, Nassau Co Med Socs; Diplomate Am Bd Obstetrics & Gynecol; Am Col Obstetricians; NY Acad Med; NY Acad Sci; Am Assn Gynecol Laparoscopists; Am Geriatrics Soc; Others; Soc for Life & Human Values; Foun Thanatology; Am Phil Assn; cp/Manhasset Interfaith Coun; Bd Mgr Ch Charity Foun; Trustee Village Plandome Manor; NY St Maternal & Child Wel Com; Plandome CC; Other Civic Activs; r/Epis; hon/25 Yr Ser: N Shore Univ Hosp, NY Hosp, Dept Obstetrics & Gynecol N Shore Univ Hosp; Recipient F'ship; Pub'd Author; Biogl Listings.

FINNEY, CLARA oc/Businesswoman; b/Apr 14, 1930; h/454 Catalina, Youngstown, OH 44504; ba/Y'town; m/Frank (dec); c/Francine Joy; p/Arthur Huff (dec); Clara Huff, Y'town; pa/Owner & Operator Finney's Transfer & Storage Co; Independent Movers Assn; Nat Assn Negro BPW; cp/Jr Civic Leag Woms Org; Ohio Police Chiefs Assn; Ohio Frat Police Assn; Bd Mem Gilead House Neighborhood Settlemt; Y'town Arts & Cult Assn; Y'town Urban Leag; NAACP; Ohio Black Polit Assembly; r/Bapt; hon/Awd for Neighbor Achmt, Y'town Police Relats Assn; "Outstg Wom in Profile" Series, Y'town *Vindicator* Newspaper; Certs: YMCA, Hagstrom House, Goodwill Rehab Ctr Vol Sers.

FIORAVANTI, NANCY ELEANOR oc/Assistant Trust Officer; b/Apr 10, 1935; h/19 Harvard St, Gloucester, MA 01930; ba/Gloucester; p/Richard J and Evelyn G Fioravanti, Gloucester; pa/Asst Trust Ofcr Cape Ann Bk & Trust Co; Nat Assn Bank Wom; cp/Treas Art Adv Com Sawyer Free Lib; r/Cath, Our Lady of Good Voyage Ch, Gloucester: Mem.

FIORE, GENEVIEVE NATALINA oc/Executive Director Emeritus; b/Jan 20, 1912; h/3171 W 36th Ave, Denver, CO 80211; m/John R; c/David, Roxanna, Philip; p/Lorenzo and Anna Carleo D'Amato (dec); pa/Ret'd 1974; Exec Dir (Emeritus) Colo Div UNA, USA-UNESCO, Int Hospitality Ctr, Spkr Sers on UN 1961-74; Reg II Rep Commun Sect Nat Assn Fgn Student Affairs 1966-68; Est'd Fgn Lang File 1960; Activated Colo Coun UNESCO 1952, Started Intl Hospitality Ctr & Spkr Sers on UN 1952; Other Former Positions; Bd Mem People-to People 1975; Moderator Panel of Ams, Nat Conf Christians & Jews, YWCA & Denver Comm on Commun Relats 1975-; Att'd Gen Meeting of Experiment in Intl Living, Siena, Italy 1962; Assoc Mem Colo Coun on Arts & Humanities; Pres Colo Coor'g Coun of Wom's Orgs 1970-72; Other Profl Activs; cp/CoOrgr Denver U Yth Hostel; Var PTA Activs; Del Denver Dem Co Convs & St Dem Convs; Del to St Sems of Colo Fdn Jane Jefferson Dem Clbs; Others; Colo Polit Caucus; Nat Wom's Conf (Houston) 1977; Chair Colo Plan of Action Coun for Colo Wom's Conf IWD 1976-77; Other Civic Activs; r/Cath; hon/Plaques: Steele Commun Ctr, U Vets Coun; Cert of Awd. Colo Fdn Jefferson Dem Clbs; 1 of

60 Colo Wom Featured in *Hidden Heroines*; Public Ser Awd, Intl Wom's Yr, US-Denver Reg PO; Hon Mem Mortar Bd; Others.

FIRESTONE, O JOHN (JACK) oc/University Professor; b/Jan 17, 1913; h/375 Minto Pl, Ottawa, Ontario, Canada; ba/Ottawa; c/Brenda Ruth, Catherine Paula, Bruce Murray, John Mitchell Peter; p/Bruce and Regina Seaman Firestone; ed/MA McGill Univ 1942; Postgrad Studies; pa/Univ Ottawa: Prof Ecs 1960-, VDean Fac Social Scis 1964-70; Economist Candn Govt 1942-60; Other

Former Positions; Candn Pol Sci Assn; Ec Hist Assn; Candn Hist Assn; Am Ec Assn; Am Acad Polit & Social Wlth; Assn for Evolutionary Ecs; Inst Public Adm; Candn Tax Foun; cp/Cercle Universitaire d'Ottawa Clb; Rockcliffe Park Tennis Clb; hon/Author Num Profl Articles & Govt Reports, Studies & Books; Canadian W/W.

FIRL, DONALD HAROLD oc/Curriculum Specialist; b/Jun 28, 1926; h/2104 Fifth Ave NE, Rochester, MN 55901; ba/Rochester; m/Veryl Bowen; c/Cara Leeper (Mrs James), Heidi Hilton (Mrs Steven L), Jared, Christopher, Thomas, Jennifer; p/Max Richard Firl (dec); Henrietta Diercks Firl, Red Wing, MN; ed/BA Gustavus Adolphus; MS

Ks St Univ; Ed Spec No Univ Ia; mil/10th Armored Corps & War Crimes Div 3rd Army WWII; pa/NCSM; NCTM; Editor *The Mathematics Student*, NCTM; Author Random House Math, AJ Nystrom Elem Math Charts; Contbr Articles to Profl Jours; Genealogist; Free-lance Writer; Photog; r/LDS: Elder; hon/Metric Spkr, Nat Bur Standards; Pi Mu Epsilon; Tchg F'ship, Ks St Univ; NSF F'ships.

FISCHER, ROGER RAYMOND oc/State Legislator; b/Jun 1, 1941; ba/Box 195, Main Capitol Bldg, Harrisburg, PA 17120; m/Catherine Louise Trettel; c/Roger Raymond II, Steve Groegory; p/Raymond and Louise Fischer, Washington, PA; ed/BA Wash & Jefferson Col 1963; Grad Work Carnegie Inst Technol; mil/USAFR Capt; pa/Res Engr Jones & Laughlin Steel Res; cp/Mem Pa Ho of Reps 1966-, Mem Var Coms; Former Adv Mem Wash Sch Bd; Bd Dirs City Mission; Boy Scout Merit Badge Cnslr; Wash, Canonsburg & Palanka Sportsmen's Clbs; Am Legion; Wash Lodge #164 F&AM; Other Civic Activs; r/Luth Ch Am: Lay Asst.

FISER, JAMES RONALD oc/Biology Teacher; b/Oct 4, 1938; h/56 Pennsylvania Ave, Port Jervis, NY 12771; ba/Port Jervis; m/Roberta Dolores Westfall; c/Frances

Kathleen, Loretta Dolores; p/James Henton Fiser (dec); Kathleen Peerey Fiser, Tupelo, MI; ed/BS cum laude Lambuth Col 1960; MS St Univ NY; mil/USAF 1961-66, Biomed Sci Corps, Lt; pa/Biol Tchr Port Jervis HS; Port Jervis Tchrs Assn; NY St U Tchrs; Am Fdn Tchrs; Sci Tchrs Assn NY St; Nat Sci Tchrs Assn; AAAS; Am Assn Blood Bks; cp/Port Jervis Lodge 328, Masons: Chaplain, Past Master; Neversink Chapt 186 Royal Arch Masons; D&H Square Dance Clb; r/Drew U Meth Ch: Mem, Past Lay Ldr, Current Ed Chperson, Coun on Mins, Adm Bd; Mem Orange Co Camp-Gideons; hon/W/W in Rel.

FISHBEIN, HAROLD J oc/Executive Director; b/Nov 23, 1898; h/660 Mariposa-#210, Mt View, CA 94040; ba/Los Altos, CA; m/Elise P; c/Stephan M, Elise P (dec); p/Benjamin and Fannie Gluck Fishbein; ed/PhB; LLB; mil/AUS 1918-19, Sgt 1st Class Task Corps; pa/Lectr; Trade Assn Dir; Indust Advr Needle & Shoe Industs; Field Dir ARC, S Pacific 1942-45; Dir UNRRA & Intl Refugee Org, Germany 1945-48; r/Jewish; hon/Phi Beta Kappa; Cong Awd, Cal Assn Maternal & Child Hlth; Am Arbitration Assn; Awd of Hon, Am Red Mogen David for Israel.

FISHBURN, CHARLES GEORGE oc/Naval Officer; Adjunct Faculty; b/Oct 3, 1941; h/9446 Cloverdale Ct, Burke, VA 22015; ba/Washington DC; m/Patricia Alice Miller; c/Charles Richards, Barbara Jean; p/Charles G and Ruth Alma Holmes Fishburn, Spokane, WA; ed/BS 1963; BS 1968; MSA 1973; mil/USN Lt Cmdr; pa/Adj Fac George Mason Univ; MBA Execs Assn; cp/Smithsonian Assoc; Audit Com Amhurst Homeowners; PTA; r/Cath.

FISHER, ADA SIPUEL oc/Professor & Chairperson; h/4009 Spring Lake Dr, Oklahoma City, OK 73111; ba/Langston, OK; m/Warren W; c/Charlene L Factory, Bruce T; p/Travis B and Martha B Sipuel (dec); ed/BA Langston Univ; MA, JD Univ Okla; pa/Currently Prof & Chm Social Sci Dept Langston Univ; Sum Coor Ednl Advmt Prog for Commun Action Prog, Okla City 1974; Instr Assoc Deg Prog (Law Enforcemt

Pers) Okla St Univ 1973; Conslt; Edit Advr in Res & Writing of Documentary Hist *Black Hist in Okla*; Adv Com to Okla Regents of Higher Ed on Civil Rts; Okla Bar Assn; Assn Am Histns; Okla Ed Assn; NEA; Assn Okla Histns; Alpha Kappa Alpha; cp/NAACP; hon/Certs of Merit: Am Civil Liberties Union, UN Org, The Chgo Defender; Awd, Intl Wom's Conv of Chs of God in Christ; The Ada Lois Sipuel Fed'd Clb, McAlister, Okla (1950); W/W in Black Am.

FISHER, CARL A oc/Catholic Priest; b/Nov 24, 1945; h/1130 N Calvert St, Baltimore, MD 21202; ba/Same; p/Peter W Sr and Evelyn C Fisher, Pascagoula, MS; ed/AA Epiphany Col 1966; AB St Joseph's Sem Col 1969; MA Oblate Col 1972; MS Am Univ 1974; mil/USNR; pa/Lectr; Writer; Editor; cp/Soc of St Joseph; NAACP; Nat Urban League; Public Relats Soc of Am; Media Guild of Balto; Vocation Dirs Assn (En); Coor'g Coun of Balto; Improvement Assn of Balto; Adv Com, Balto Social Sers Dept; Mtl Hlth Clin Bd; Civic Action Com Mem; PUSH; hon/Nat Commun Ser Awd, Phi Beta Sigma; Dist'd Ser Awd, United Negro Col Fund; Cath

Communications Scholar of the Yr 1973; Rec'd Top 10 Black Newsmakers Awd.

FISHER, CHARLES HAROLD oc/Technical Consultant; Research Professor; b/Nov 20, 1906; ba/Salem, VA 24153; m/Lois C; p/(dec); ed/BS Roanoke Col 1928; MS 1929, PhD 1932 Univ Ill; Cert Am Mgmt Assn 1961; pa/Adj Res Prof Roanoke Col, Salem 1972-; Dir USDA So Utilization Res Div, New Orleans, La 1950-72; Res Group Ldr USDA Reg Lab, Philadelphia, Pa 1940-50; Other Former Positions; Am Chem Soc; Am Inst Chemists: Pres 1962-63, Chm of Bd 1963, 1973-75; Am Inst Chem Engrs; The Chem Soc (London); AAAS; Chemists Clb (NY); Conslt; cp/C of C, Intl House, Round Table Clb (NO); Roanoke Col Alumni Assn; Cosmos Clb (Wash DC); hon/Hon Mem, Am Inst Chemists; Chem Pioneer Awd; Herty Medal; So Chemists Awd; Hon DSc Degs: Roanoke Col, Tulane Univ; Pub'd Author; Biogl Listings.

FISHER, HOWARD L oc/Creative Services Director, Royal Division; b/Jun 20, 1936; h/Rt 7, Paschal Ests, Murfreesboro, TN 37130; ba/Nashville, TN; m/Joan Delores; c/Pamela, Penny, Christina, Howard Jr, Joni, Angela; p/Clyde Cecil and Mary J Fisher, (dec); ed/Grad: Gen Mtrs Indust Design Prog, Elects Inst Technol; r/Bapt; Gospel Singer; hon/2 Addy Awds, Ctl UA Advt'g Clb; 5 GM Awds; 2 1st Pl Awds, WVa Am Legion Poster Contest; Stereo Album in Top 40, S Cal 1976.

FISHER, JEWEL T oc/Marine Service Officer; b/Oct 31, 1918; h/PO Box 183, Port Lavaca, TX 77979; ba/Port Lavaca; m/King; c/Ann F Boyd, Linda F LaQuay; p/Thomas M

Tanner (dec); Minnie F Dunks, Port Lavaca; ed/Tex Luth Col; pa/Ofcr King Fisher Marine Ser; cp/Trustee Champ Traylor Meml Hosp; Pvt Pilot; Artist; r/Bapt.

FISHER, MARJORIE HELEN oc/Librarian; b/Nov 27, 1924; h/917 N Walnut St, Plymouth, IN 46563; ba/Plymouth; m/Delmara (dec); c/Madge Denise Gaines, Deljon Ray; p/James Cleo and Isie May Sutton Hardwick (dec); ed/AB; pa/Libn Plymouth HS; Rep Gov's Conf on Libs; Dir Lib Sers Plymouth Commun Sch Corp; hon/Var S'ships.

FISHER, MARK LAURENCE oc/Administrator; b/Apr 29, 1940; h/1229 Arbor Vista Dr, Atlanta, GA 30329; ba/Atlanta; m/Barbara Ladin; c/Joanne, Jonathan; p/Bennie B and Florence S Fisher, New Haven, CT; ed/BA Franklin & Marshall Col 1962; MA Tchrs' Col; EdD Cal Wn Univ 1977; Profl Dipl 1964, 69; pa/Dir Jewish Voc Ser Atlanta, Jewish Wel Foun; APGA; Nat Voc Guid Assn; Am Sch Cnslrs Assn; cp/Alumni Admissions Adv Bd, Franklin & Marshall Col; r/Jewish; Mem Congreg Beth Jacob, Atlanta; hon/Nat Meritorious Ser Cit, Nat Conf Synagogue Yth.

FISHER, MARY HANNAH oc/Artist; Illustrator; Teacher; b/Jan 29, 1910; h/831 N Venice Ave, Tucson, AZ 85711; m/John E; c/Jane, John; p/Wallace Fahringer (dec); Ella M Horton (dec); pa/Tchr Arts & Crafts; Writer; Poet; Art Mem Nat Leag Am Pen Wom; Ariz & Fla St Poetry Socs; cp/Bd Mem

GSA, Ed Com Mem; Repub; r/Quaker; hon/Art Medallion Awd, Intl Conf on Sc.

FISHER, THOMAS G oc/Attorney at Law; b/May 15, 1940; h/227 Brown, Remington, IN 47977; ba/R'ton; m/Barbara; c/Anne Corwin, Thomas Molnar; p/John C and Bonnie G Fisher, Holly, MI; ed/AB Earlham Col 1962; JD Ind Univ 1965; pa/Pres: Jasper Co Bar Assn 1973, Ind Prof Attys Assn 1977; cp/Rotary Clb, Rensselaer, Ind; r/Presb; hon/OYMA.

FISHMAN, JOSEPH oc/Physician; b/Apr 12, 1930; h/7351 SW 27th Ct, Davie, FL 33314; ba/N Miami Bch, FL; c/Renata; p/Moe and Florence Fishman, Montreal, Canada; ed/BS; MS; MD; CM; pa/Clin Asst Prof Med Univ Miami Sch Med 1973-; Pvt Pract in Internal Med, Endocrinol & Metabolism, Nuclear Med, N Miami Bch 1973-; Sr Att'g Phys Parkway Gen Hosp, N Miami Bch; Att'g Phys N Miami Gen Hosp, N Miami; Var Former Positions & Hosp Appts; Endocrine Soc; Am Col Physicians; Fellow Royal Col Phys (Canada); Dade Co, Fla Med Assns; Nassau Co & NY St Med Socs; r/Hebrew; hon/Profl Pubs.

FISHMAN, SUSAN oc/Writer; Public Relations; b/Apr 12, 1939; h/1245 Humboldt St, Denver, CO 80218; p/Jack Fishman (dec); Jeanne Lichstein, Flushing, NY; ed/BA; cp/Polit Campaign Mgr 1979, Denver Mun Election; Fund-Raising for Non-Profit Agys; hon/World W/W Wom; W/W Am Wom; Personalities W&MW; Nat Fdn Press Wom: 2nd Pl, 1st Pl; 1st Pl Colo Press Wom; Alfie Awd, Denver Ad Fdn; 1st & 2nd Pls, Colo Broadcasters Assn.

FITCHUE, LEAH GASKIN oc/Program Administrator; b/Jun 27, 1940; ba/Princeton, NJ 08540; c/Ebony; p/Joseph Matchett, Fort Meyers, FL; Rose Lee Jones, Newark, NJ; ed/BA Douglass Col; MS Univ Mich; EdD Harvard Univ; pa/Prog Admr Ednl Testing Ser; Col for Human Sers: Asst to Pres 1977-, Coor'g Tchr 1976-77; Trenton St Col: Assoc Prof 1977-, Adm Liaison 1977-; Mem Admissions Com Grad Sch of Ed Harvard Univ 1971-72; Mem Comm on Adm Decentralization & Commun Participation, Philadelphia Bd Ed 1969; Phi Delta Kappa; cp/Delta Sigma Theta; LS Odom Inspirational Choir; Intl Wom's Poetry Fest Com; r/Meth; hon/Grad Fellow, Univ Mich; Urban Leag Fellow; Ed & Social Policy Fellow, Grad Sch Ed, Harvard Univ; Pub'd Author.

FITE, BONETA LEBEAU oc/Social Worker (Retired); b/Aug 20, 1915; h/2705 NW 115th, Oklahoma City, OK 73120; m/James Bateman Jr (dec); c/James Bateman III, Carolyn F Johnson; p/Joseph A and Maud Eva Reddin LeBeau (dec); ed/BA Brigham Yg Univ 1938; MA Univ Ks 1966; LB LaSalle Ext

Univ 1973; pa/Social Wkr Bur Indian Affairs, Pawnee Agy 1962-; Conslt Bi-St Mtl Hlth, Kay Juv Sers, Kay Co Juv Ct Indian Tribes, USPHS 1962-75; Tchr Eugene, Oreg 1961-62; Other Profl Positions; Exec Bd Kay Co Juv Sers 1972-; Exec Bd Kay Coun Social Agys 1963-; Accredited Coun Social Wkrs; Nat Assn Social Wkrs; Reg'd Social Wkrs; Okla Hlth Wel Assn; cp/Former Del Wom's Prog; r/Mormon.

FITE, ELWIN oc/University Administrator; b/Nov 25, 1913; h/Rt 3, Box 311, Tahlequah, OK 74464; ba/Tahlequah; m/Mildred; c/Barbara Anne Scearce, James E; p/Austin R and Minnie B Fite (dec); ed/EdD; MM; BS; mil/USNR; pa/NEn St Univ: Tchr, Dean, VP, Pres; Pres Edr's Groups; cp/Kiwanian; C of C; Devel Couns; r/Christian; hon/Dist'd Citizen; St Awd of Merit.

FITTING, MARJORIE A PREMO PICKERING oc/Professor; b/Nov 29, 1933; h/8305 Chianti Ct, San Jose, CA 95135; ba/San Jose; m/Frederick N; c/William Pickering, David Pickering, John Pickering; p/Ellis J and Dorothy J Prock Premo; ed/BS; MEd; AM; PhD; pa/Prof Math San Jose St Univ; NCTM; Math Assn Am; Am Math Soc; Dir & VP Metra Instruments Inc; Phi Kappa Phi; cp/Spkr Local Schs & Bus Meetings; r/Unitarian; hon/NSF Sci Fac Awd; Wom of Yr, Santa Clara Co 1975.

FITTON, H NELSON JR oc/US Government Official, Educator; h/5624 Glenwood Dr, Alexandria, VA 22310; ba/Washington DC; m/Bernice Jeanette Sutton; p/Harvey Nelson Fitton Sr; Ada Hortense Marshall, Alexandria; ed/BA; MA; mil/USN; pa/USDA, Pubs Div; Am Assn Agri Col Editors; Cooperative Editors Assn;

World Future Soc; Soc for Tech Commun; Nat Press Clb; Assn Tchrs Tech Writing; World-Wide Acad Scholars; Nat Assn Lit & Arts; Nat Assn Govt Communicators; Fellow, IBA; cp/Fairfax Hosp Assn; No Va Fam Ser; Clermont Woods Commun Assn; Va Square Dancers; r/Presb; Old Presb Meeting House, Alexandria; Elder; hon/Alice Douglas Goddard Awd for S'ship in Lit, Geo Wash Univ; Superior Ser Awd, USDA.

FITTS, LEONARD DONALD oc/Administrator; b/Aug 19, 1946; h/1105 Hudson Ave, Voorhees, NJ 08043; ba/Camden, NJ; m/Sherrell Adrienne, Thomas; p/William Leonard and Mary Alice Brown Fitts, Faunsdale, AL; ed/BS 1961, MEd 1964, Postgrad Studies 1964-65 Tuskegee Inst; EdD Univ Pa 1972; mil/USAF Communs Ofcr 1961-63; pa/Dir Spec Sers Camden City Bd Ed 1975-; Psychol, Fla Parent Ed Model Follow Through, Phila Bd Ed 1971-75; Tchg Fellow Univ Pa 1969-71; Admr Equal Employmt Opports Prog, RCA, Camden/NYC 1968-69; Other Former Positions; Nat Assn Sch Psychologists, Mem Var Coms; APA; APGA; Camden Co Guid & Pers Assn; CEC; Assn Spec Ed Admrs; NJ Assn Pupil Pers Admrs; Phi Delta Kappa; cp/Lions Clb; Adv Coun Lng Resources Ctr; Adv Chm Al-Assist Recovery & Cnslg Prog, SE Neighborhood Hlth Ctr; Bd Mem Lincoln Day Nursery; Bd Dirs Nat Foun Mar of Dimes, SW NJ Chapt; r/Bapt; hon/Recipient S'ships & Grant; Cert of Appres; VP (Hubert Humphrey) Task Force on Yth Motivation; Cert of Recog, Nat Assn Sch Psychologists; Delta Air Line Ser Awd; Cert of Apprec, Project Follow Through; W/W in E; Others.

FITZGERALD, ERNEST A oc/Minister; b/Jul 24, 1925; h/1921 Virginia Rd, Winston-Salem, NC 27104; ba/W-S; m/Sarah Frances Perry; c/James Boyd, Patricia Ann; p/Rev & Mrs James B Fitzgerald; ed/AB cum laude Wn Carolina Col 1947; BD Duke Div Sch 1951;

Hon DDiv High Point Col 1968; pa/Sr Min Centenary Ch, W-S 1966-; Former Pastorates: Sylva, NC, Liberty, NC, Calvary Ch, Asheboro, Abernethy Ch, Asheville, Purcell Ch, Charlotte, Grace Ch, Greensboro; Joined W NC Conf 1946; Chm WNC Conf TV, Radio & Film Comm 4 Yrs; WNC Conf Comm on Christian Social Concerns; Evangel Mission, Dominican Repub; Search Com for New Pres, Pfeiffer Col; WNC Conf Bd Pensions; WNC Conf Com on Meth Info; VChm WNC Com on Conf Structures; Bd Visitors Duke Div Sch; Bd Trustees Inst for Homiletical Studies; Ofcl Visitor World Meth Conf, London, England 1966; Other Profl Activs; cp/Mason; Former Mem: Asheville & Greensboro Kiwanis Clbs, W Charlotte Rotary Clb, Sylva Lions Clb; Current Mem W-S Rotary Clb; Past Pres W-S Torch Clb; Bd Trustees U Way Forsyth Co; hon/Boss of Yr Awd, Olde Salem Chapt Am Bus Wom's Assn; Dist'd Alumni Awd, Pfeiffer Col; Forsyth Co Dist'd Alumni Awd, Duke Univ; Student Awd for Outstg Ser to Sch as Mem of Bd of Trustees, Pfeiffer Col; Pub'd Author; Biogl Listings.

FITZGERALD, GERALD JOSEPH oc/Writer, Reporting Broker; b/May 8, 1910; h/1400 N Lake Shore Dr, Chicago, IL; p/George Francis FitzGerald, Catherine Veronica Walsh (dec); ed/Univ Chgo 1936; LLB John Marshall Law Sch 1946; JD Blackstone Col of Law 1946; Hon LLD Univ E Fla 1971; Grad w Dipl US Treas Dept's Gen & Adv'd Tng Schs 1959 & So Police Acad 1969; mil/Admiral on Staff Gov Dwight P Griswold; pa/Former Reporting Broker US Dept of Justice, US Atty & US Anti-Trust Div & St's Atty of Cook Co; hon/Commodore US Submarine Fleet, Commodore G & M Fleets; Author *The FitzGerald Earls of Desmond, Nebraska Admirals, Candyland* & Other Works; Cited by US War Vets, Secy of St & Chgo Hist Soc; Hon Man-Silver Awd, Camp Hastings as Group Ldr & Wrestling Champ; Liederman Medal Awd for Strength & Endurance; Intl Biog Cert for Dist'd Ser in Mil Hist; Commun Ldrs of Am.

FITZGERALD, HAROLD ALVIN oc/Columnist; Former Publisher; b/Aug 3, 1896; h/148 Ottawa Dr, Pontiac, MI 48053; ba/Pontiac; m/Elizabeth M; c/Howard, Richard, Nancy Connolly; p/(dec); ed/AB; mil/USAF WWI, 2/Lt; pa/Newspaper Columnist; Mag Articles, Contbr to *Saturday Evening Post*; r/Epis; hon/Hon Deg, Univ Mich; Top Pontiac Citizenship Awd.

FITZGERALD, JOSEPH MICHAEL JR oc/Attorney; b/Oct 9, 1943; h/618 NE 58 St, Miami, FL 33137; ba/Miami; m/Lynne; p/Joseph M and Grace Fitzgerald, Coral Gables, FL; ed/BS Mt St Mary's; JD Cath Univ Am; LLM Univ M; mil/Civilian Intell Analyst, Def Intell Agy; pa/Am, Fla & Dade Co Bar Assns; cp/Dir Fla JCs; Miami Kiwanis; r/Cath; hon/W/W Am Law; Outstg Yg Men Am.

FITZGERALD, TERENCE SEAN oc/Physician; b/May 18, 1941; h/26 Pasture Ln, Darien, CT 06820; ba/Stamford, CT; m/Jacqueline Diane Hussey; c/Timothy Sean, Carrie Lee, Shannon Dee; p/Robert G Fitzgerald (dec); Jane Boudreau Fitzgerald, St Albans, VT; ed/BA 1963, MD 1968 Univ Vt; mil/AUS 1972-74; Chief Allergy Sect, US Army Gen Hosp, Ft Gordon, Ga; Conslt Allergist to Surg Gen, US Army Hlth Ser Reg III; Maj; pa/Phys Specializing in Allergy &

Clin Immunol; Clin Instr Med NY Med Col, Flower & Fifth Ave Hosps, NYC; Assoc Att'g Staff Greenwich Hosp, Greenwich, Conn; Spec Courtesy Staff Norwalk Hosp, Norwalk, Conn; Assoc Att'g Staff St Joseph's Hosp, Stamford; Assoc Att'g Staff Stamford Hosp, Stamford; Am Acad Pediatrics; Am Col Allergists; Am Acad Allergy; N Eng Soc Allergy; NY Allergy Soc; SEn Allergy Assn, Affil Mem; Conn St Med Soc; Fairfield Co Med Assn; Greenwich & Stamford Med Socs; r/Rom Cath; hon/Recipient Sev F'ships; Profl Pubs.

FITZPATRICK, ALAN JOSEPH oc/-Psychologist; b/May 16, 1937; h/5900 Evers, San Antonio, TX; ba/San Antonio; m/G Nadine; c/Michael, Shaun; p/Joseph A and Julia E FitzPatrick, San Antonio; ed/BS NEn Univ 1962; MEd Shippensburg S Coll 1967; PhD Univ Mo; mil/USAR Med Ser Corps, Maj; pa/Bexar Co Psychol Assn, Secy 1977-78; cp/Past Pres Tex St REACT Coun; r/Cath; Deacon Cand; hon/NDEA F'ship, Univ Mo.

FLACK, CHARLES ZORAH JR oc/Insurance & Real Estate; b/Jul 11, 1936; h/122 Forest Hills Dr, Forest City, NC 28043; ba/Forest City; m/Jane Sawyer; c/Charles Zorah III, Blair Thornton, Thomas Cooper; p/Charles Zorah and Blanche Thornton Flack, Forest City; ed/BS Univ NC-CH 1958; pa/Charles Z Flack Agy Inc, Real Est-Ins; Dir: NWn Bk, Forest City 1965, Isothermal Devel Inc; Former Dir Forest City Co Inc; St & Nat Assns: Real Est Bds (Realtor), Mutual Ins Agts; Nat Inst Real Est Brokers; Rutherford Co Bd Realtors: VP 1978, Pres elect 1979; cp/Univ

Bd Govs Univ NC; Dir U Appeal R'ford Co; Former Dir Isothermal Hlth Coun; Mem R'ford CC; Co Chm John F Kennedy Meml Dr; Former Mem R'ford Co Planning Com; Chm Town Forest City's Planning & Zoning Comm; Charter Mem N St Caucus; Past Pres R'ford Co Yg Dem Clb; Dem Precnt Com-man & Ofcr; Del Dem Nat Conv 1976; Order Eagles; Kappa Alpha; Others; r/1st U Meth Ch, Forest City: Mem, Pastoral Relats Com, Adm Bd, Chm Fin Com, Past Pres Meth Men, Past Chm "Every Mem" Canvas, Former SS Tchr; hon/Hon Admiral, Tex Navy; Ky Col; Hon Life Mbrship, Forest City JCs; Senator, Jr Chamber Intl; Order of Long Leaf Pine; Dist'd Ser Awd, Forest City; Biogl Listings.

FLAHERTY, SUSANNE ALICE oc/Social Worker; b/May 30, 1921; h/401 Douglas, Park Forest, IL 60466; ba/Tinley Park, IL; m/John J; c/Michelle, Catheen, Christine, Laureen; p/Raymond R and Myrle Rahel Taxlinger (dec); ed/BA; Grad Work; pa/Nat Assn Social Wkrs; Am Acad Cert'd Social Wkrs; Reg'd Clin Social Wkr; Ill Cert'd Social Wkr; AAUW; Ill Wel Assn; BPW; Adv Bd Moraine Val Col; cp/YWCA; Interracial Groups; PTA; Bowling Groups; GSA; Blue Birds; Farm Bur; LWV; Mother's Clb, Alpha Chi Omega; Pi Beta Phi; r/Prot; hon/Awd for Outstg S'ship, Citizenship & Ser, DAR; Yrbook Dedication; E Ill Tennis Champ; Pub'd Author; Num Biogl Listings.

FLAKER, JAMES HENRY oc/Management Consultant; b/Nov 21, 1915; h/107 Greer Cir, Milford, CT 06460; ba/Milford; m/Elois Kathryn Pearson; c/Philip George,

Kathy May Gage (Mrs Harlan); p/George William and May Amos Flaker (dec); ed/Att'd Columbia Col 1934-38; pa/Pres G&F Assocs, Milford 1978-; Chief Quality Engrg Avco Lycoming Div, Stratford, Conn 1963-78; Supvr Quality Engrg Kaman Aircraft, Bloomfield, Conn 1961-63; Other Former Positions; Conslt; Lectr in Field; Am Soc for Quality Control; Mem 1952-, Reg Dir 1976-77, VP 1977-79; cp/YMCA Indust Mgmt Div, Prog & Ednl Coms; Spkr; Milford Yacht Clb; Masons; OES, Past Patron; Elks; r/St Peters Epis Ch, Milford; Mem, Former Vestryman; hon/Fellow, ASQC; R Shaw Goldthwait Awd, NE Quality Control Coun; Dist'd Recog Awd, Nat Mgmt Assn; W/W: Engrg, E.

FLANDERS, ELEANOR CARLSON oc/Investment Counselor; Homemaker; b/Mar 27, 1916; h/917 Third Ave, Longmont, CO 80501; m/Laurence Burdette Jr; c/Laurel F Umile, John Carlson, Lynette F Moyer, Paul Laurence; p/Carl E and Laura Pine Carlson, Santa Barbara, CA; ed/BA Univ Colo; pa/Examr of Credits, Univ Colo Admissions; Investmt Cnslr 1st Nat Bk Trust Dept; AAUW; cp/Bd Ed; Hosp Aux; Mlt Hlth Clin; Bd Dirs St 4-H Foun; Colo Mothers Comm;

Pres Sunset Golf Assn; Pres St Vrain Hist Soc; Sunshine Clb; PEO; Fdr & VP Repub Roundtable, Longmont; C of C, Task Force Proj '80; Den Mother; Secy Univ Colo Alumni Assn; Others; cp/Congreg Ch: Deaconess; SS Tchr, Pres Wom's Soc; hon/Colo Mother of Yr 1973; Juv Ct Awd; Dist'd Citizen, Colo Hist Soc; Alumni Recog Awd, Univ Colo; HS Valedictorian; Theta Sigma Phi; S'ship, Vassar Col Fam Inst.

FLATT, JANE DEE oc/Executive; Publisher; b/Aug 8, 1945; h/1172 Park Ave, New York, NY 10028; m/S Thomas; c/Jessica Toonkel; p/Oscar and Marion Dietler Dystel, Rye, NY; ed/BA cum laude Wash Square Col; pa/VP & Pubr The World Almanac; hon/Phi Beta Kappa.

FLEISCHMAN, ALAN ISADORE oc/Clinical Biochemist; b/Aug 10, 1928; h/36 Hawthorne Pl, Montclair, NJ 07042; ba/Trenton, NJ; m/Margot Ilsa Becker; c/Stephen Howard, Jack Gerald; p/Louis and Sarah Schloss Fleischman, Encinitas, CA; ed/BS; MA; PhD; mil/USAR, Lt Col, Ret'd 1978; pa/Clin Biochemist Div Commun Hlth Sers, NJ St Dept Hlth; Am Soc for Clin Chem: Pres NJ Sect 1976, Nat Councilor 1975-; NJ Inst Chemists: Secy 1976-77, St Councilor 1974-76, Pres-elect 1978-79; Chm Com on Hosp Lab Accreditation Nat Acad Clin Biochem 1978-; Diplomat Am Bd Clin Chem; Am Chem Soc; Am Oil Chemist's Soc; Am Heart Assn; Intl Soc Cardiol; AAAS; Am Inst

Biol Scis; Am Inst Nutrition; NY Acad Scis; r/Hebrew; hon/Clin Biochemist of Yr 1978, NJ Sect Am Soc for Clin Chem; Meritorious Ser Medal, Dept of Army; Sigma Xi; Recipient F'ships; Biogl Listings; Num Profl Pubs.

FLEMING, DERYL RAY oc/Clergyman; b/Sept 1, 1937; h/7921 Ellet Rd, Springfield, VA 22151; ba/Annandale, VA; m/Beverly; c/Michelle, Christopher; p/L R and Estelle Fleming; ed/BA Baylor Univ 1959; BD So Bapt Theol Sem 1963; pa/Sermons Pub'd: *Master Sermon Series*, *Models for Ministers*, *Abingdon Marriage Manual*, *Abingdon Funeral Manual*; r/Bapt.

FLEMING, KATHLEEN ANN oc/Dental Hygienist; Landscape Consultant; Plant Broker; Antique Dealer; b/Aug 20, 1948; h/17622 Wild Oak Dr, Houston, TX 77090; ba/Spring, TX; m/John Preston; p/Eugene R and Irene H Literski, Milwaukee, WI; ed/BS; Tex Cert'd Nurseryman 1978; pa/Am & Tex Dental Hygienists Assns; Tex Assn Nurseryman; Intl & Am Carnival Glass Assns; Heart of Am Carnival Glass Assn; r/Christian; hon/Sigma Phi Alpha, Past Pres AAK Chapt.

FLEMING, LOIS DeLAVAN oc/Public Library Consultant; b/Jan 25, 1928; h/Rt 3, Box 162, Quincy, FL 32351; ba/Tallahassee, FL; m/Philip J; c/Mark William, Philip J Jr, Richard DeLavan; p/Millard Terry and Willa Metta Lucille Symons DeLavan; ed/BA 1950; MS 1965; Adv'd Master's LS 1968; Doct Study 1976; pa/Conslt St Lib Fla; Am Lib Assn; SEn Lib Assn; Fla Lib Assn; Adult Ed Assn US; Nat Assn Parliamentarians; r/Christian Sci; hon/Beta Phi Mu.

FLEMING, RONALD HOWARD I oc/Publisher; Producer; Professor; b/Oct 16, 1944; h/1490 Jefferson Ave, Buffalo, NY 14208; ba/Buffalo; m/Carolyn Cook; c/Ronald H II, Solomon Nixon James, Jasmin Alikhan; p/Cleveland Fleming (dec); Ophelia Fleming Lewis, Buffalo; ed/BA; pa/Pubr "Fine Print News"; Prodr & Host "Bldg a Decent Future", ½ Hour TV Public Ser Prog, WKBW

TV; cp/Vol Dir Coor Sr Citizens Activs; Tchr Wkly 1 Hour Bible Class Sr Citizens Ctr; Buffalo C of C; Operation PUSH; Lester Lodge 4 AF&AM; r/St Mark AME Zion Ch; hon/Cert Apprec, USN Recruiting Command, Nat Alliance Bus-men; Outstg Commun Ser, Afro Am Police Assn; Cert Gratitude, More Black Harmony; Cert Apprec, USMC, Nat Rifle Assn Am.

FLETCHER, ANDRIA JANE oc/Professor; b/Oct 20, 1944; h/4064 Olive Knoll Pl, Claremont, CA 91711; ba/La Verne, CA; c/Melissa; p/Nancy N Miller, San Carlos, CA; ed/AB 1966, MA 1968, PhD 1978 UCLA; pa/La Verne Col: Assoc Prof Dept Hist & Govt 1971-, Dir Polit Studies Ctr 1976-, Dir Pre-Law Prog 1973-76, Task Force on Col Governance, Pres' Adv Coun, Adm Cabinet & Exec Coun, Others; Lecture Tour on African Hist 1977-78; Dir City Govt Internship Prog 1973-; Mem Arms Control & Fgn Policy Sem, RAND Corp, Santa Monica 1971-; Conslt to Cal Dept Commerce 1971; Lectr Cal St Univ-Fullerton 1970-71; Other Former Positions; Am, Wn, & So Cal Polit Sci Assns; AAUP; Mun Mgrs & Public Admrs Assn; NOW; cp/Mem US Jr Wightman Cup Team (Tennis) 3 Yrs; Currently Active Player Claremont

Tennis Clb; Vol Work; hon/NDEA Nat F'ship; Soroptimist Intl F'ship; Alpha Phi Intl F'ship; Outstg Student at UCLA Awd; Outstg Yg Wom of Achmt in So Cal Awd; Intl W/W: Intells, Wom in Ed; Personalities W&MW; Profl Pubs.

FLETCHER, DIXIE CHAFIN oc/Registered Nurse; b/May 11, 1950; h/2525 Brookwater Cir, Birmingham, AL 35243; ba/B'ham; m/Oliver Mayo III; p/Richard and Ann Chafin, Lu Goff, SC; ed/BS NWn St Univ 1972; pa/Ala Nurses Assn; Am Nurses Assn; cp/Vol: Cancer Soc, Mar of Dimes, Arthritis Foun; r/Meth; hon/Personalities of S; W/W Am Wom; World W/W Wom.

FLEYSHER, ELLEN oc/Deputy Police Commissioner; b/Jun 5, 1944; h/91 Central Park W, New York, NY 10023; ba/NYC; p/Maurice H and Mollie Helper Fleysher, Buffalo, NY; ed/BA cum laude St Univ-B 1966; MA Annenberg Sch Communs, Univ Pa 1968; pa/Dept Police Commr, Public Info NYPD 1978-; Correspondent & Anchor WCBS-TV 1974-77; Reporter NY Daily News 1969-74; NY Press Clb; Newswom's Clb NY; Gtr NY Ath Assn; Road Runners Clb; hon/Hon DHL, Marymount Col of Tarrytown; Jr C of C Awd, NYC; NYC Ret'd Detectives Assn Recog.

FLICK, PAUL JOHN oc/Artist; Art Instructor; b/Feb 5, 1943; h/4032 Lyndale Ave S, Minneapolis, MN 55409; p/P J and C A Flick, Mpls; ed/BA 1970, MFA 1972 Univ

Minn; mil/USMC; pa/Have Shown in 30+ Art Shows; Num Comms; Rep'd in Num Collections; Pres Artists' Equity Assn Minn 1976-77; Bd Dirs AEA 1977-78; hon/W/W Am Art.

FLICKER, PAUL LEO oc/Physician; b/Aug 7, 1935; h/Hunterdon Co, NJ; m/Eda Z Gilgore; c/Blair Marc, Scott Randall, Jonathan Seth, James Kevin; p/Jacob I Flicker; Sarah Applebaum; ed/MD Jefferson Med Col 1955; Att'd Univ Pa Undergrad Col Fine Arts; Internship Univ Colo Med Ctr 1959-60; mil/USPHS 1964-66; Asst Chief & Dep Chief Dept Orthopedics, USPHS Hosp, Staten Isl, NY; pa/Pract Orthopedic Surg, Somerset Med Ctr, Somerville, NJ 1968-; Former Orthopedic Surg, Manhasset, NY; Current Instr Prosthetics & Orthotics NY Univ Med Ctr Sch Prosthetics & Orthotics; Former Positions; Asst Med Dir Matheny Sch for Crippled Chd, Peapack, NJ; Diplomat Am Bd Ortho Surg; Fellow: Am Acad Ortho Surgs, Am Col Surgs; Am Acad Cerebral Palsy; Am Acad Neurol Ortho Surgs; Intl Assn for Study of Pain; En Ortho Soc; NJ Ortho Soc; AMA; NJ St Med Soc; Somerset Co Med Soc; hon/DIB; Dir Med Specialists; W/W in E; Men of Achmt.

FLICKINGER, BONNIE GORDON oc/Writer; Lecturer; Teacher; Translator; Interpreter; b/Jul 27, 1932; h/31 Nottingham Terr, Buffalo, NY 14216; c/Burt III, Catherine F Schweitzer, Marjorie F Ford; p/C George and Violet S Gordon, Buffalo; ed/BA; MEd; pa/Contbr Articles to: *Mod Lang Jour, Buffalo News, Courier-Express*; Tchr Univ St NY-B; cp/Dist Del US Tennis Assn (Dist 14); r/Presb: SS Tchr, Adult Bible Lectr; hon/Cum Laude Soc; Delta Phi Alpha; Pi Lambda Theta; World W/W Wom.

FLOOD, DOROTHEA REHFUSS oc/Artist; b/Feb 5, 1913; h/9 Ensis Rd, Port Royal Plantation, Hildeon Hd Isl, SC 29928; ba/Same; m/Carl F; c/Carol Joan; p/Emil and Emma Louise Gullman (dec); p/Painter & Writer; Former Art Coor Pa Mil Col (Now Widener Col); Free-lance Art Feature Writer for Var Local Papers; Paintings in Collections in US, S Africa, SAm, France & Puerto Rico; Other Profl Activs; r/Prot; hon/Cits, Ldrship Tng Com En Pa Camping Assn; Good Neighbor Awd, New Garden Sch (Pa); Gallo Awd, Rehobeth Art Leag.

FLORA, JAN LEIGHTON oc/Rural Sociologist; b/Feb 6, 1941; h/710 Lee St, Manhattan, KS 66502; ba/New York, NY; m/Cornelia Butler; c/Gabriela Catalina, Natasha Pilar; p/Leonard and Billie Hazel Flora, Quinter, KS; ed/BA Univ Ks 1963; MS 1967, PhD 1971 Cornell Univ; pa/Rural Sociologist Ford Foun; Rural Sociol Soc; Latin Am Studies Assn; cp/ACLU; Amnesty Intl; hon/Fgn Area Fellow.

FLORENCE, FRANKLIN DELANO WINSTON oc/Minister; b/Jan 15, 1942; h/218 N Hale St, Mt Victory, OH 43340; ba/Mt Victory; m/Janet Gaye Freeman; c/David, James, Stephen, Daniel, John Mark; p/Robert Neuton Florence (dec); Ethel Mae Florence, Cynthiana, KY; ed/BA Cincinnati Bible Col; pa/Min Ch of Christ; Chaplain Hardin Co Home for the Aged; Evangelist; Pres Hardin Co Min Assn 1978; cp/Exec Ofcr Cub Scouts; CROP Hunger Walk Chair; Chm Cistic Fibrosis Bike-a-thon; r/Ch of Christ; hon/Ky Cols; DIB; Personalities W&MW; W/W in Rel; Men of Achmt; Commun Ldrs & Noteworthy Ams.

FLOTO, WILLIAM MATHEW oc/Executive; h/1535 Fisher Dr, Liberty, OH 44425; ba/Warren, OH; m/Peggy Virginia Pepall; c/Cheri Virginia, William Howard, Steven Mathew; p/Fredrick Francis Floto, San Gabriel, CA; Addeene Lake Kung, Penn Val, CA; ed/AA Fullerton Col; Prod Mgmt Cert UCLA; mil/USAF 1951-55; pa/Pres Rec Industs; Past Pres Am Prod Inv Control Soc; cp/Dir YMCA; Indian Guide Prog, Northbrook, Ill; r/Prot; hon/Patentee in field.

FLOWER, JOSEPH R oc/Clergyman; Denominational Executive; b/Mar 1, 1913; h/2306 S Lone Pine Ave, Springfield, MO 65804; ba/S'field; m/Mary Jane; c/Joseph Reynolds Jr, Mary Alice, Paul William; p/J Roswell Flower (dec); Alice Reynolds Flower, S'field; ed/Ctl Bible Col; pa/Gen Secy Gen Coun Assemblies of God; Dist Supt NY Dist Assemblies of God 1954-75; r/Assemblies of God.

FLOWERS, DONNA LEE oc/Realtor; b/Jan 18, 1931; h/6170 14th NE, Salem, OR 97303; ba/Salem; m/Wayne E; c/Ronda Lee, Karon Anne, Terri Lynn; p/Albert George and Carolyn Mefford Cheney (dec); ed/Grad Realtors Inst, Nat Assn Realtors; cp/Nat Assn Realtors: Dir, Mem Equal Opport Policy Com; Oreg Assn Realtors: Dir, Affirmative

Action Com, Consumer Ed Com; Wom's Coun Realtors: St Chm Mbrship Com, Former Oreg St & Salem Pres, Oreg VP & St Secy, Oreg Gov Nat WCR; Am Bus Wom's Assn; cp/Mem Personal Fin Adv Bd, St Dept of Ed; Toastmasters Intl; hon/Omega Tau Rho, NAR; Mother-in-Law of Yr; W/W Am Wom;

Notable Ams; Dist Ser Awd, World W/W Wom.

FLOYD, BERNICE D oc/Retired School Teacher; b/Apr 25, 1900; h/1211 Mary St, Waycross, GA 31501; m/Thomas Lovic (dec); c/Lucie F Hinson (Mrs L C), Claire F Girolame (Mrs N A) (dec); p/Sherman Lee and Lucy Moore Drawdy (dec); ed/AB Ga Tchrs Col; MA Columbia Univ; pa/Past Pres Delta Kappa Gamma; AAUW; NRTA; Pres's Adv Coun Waycross Jr Col; Waycross BPW; cp/past Pres Waycross Wom's Clb; DAR; UDC; OES; r/Meth; hon/Rosenwald S'ship; Mother of Yr; Star Tchr; W/W Am Wom; Nat Social Dir; Personalities of S; Royal Blue Book; DIB; Notable Ams Bicent Era; Commun Ldrs & Noteworthy Ams.

FLOYD, DOROTHY FAYE oc/Proof Operator; b/Apr 6, 1940; h/206 N Glenwood, Midland, TX 79703; ba/Midland; m/Joy Max; c/Joy Mac Jr, Paul Timothy; p/Haskel Howard and Mary Louise Miller, Melissa, TX;

ed/Comml Bus Col; pa/Proof Operator 1st Nat Bk 1977; cp/5th VP Tex Bapt Conv for Deaf; Adv Bd W Tex Panhandle Reg Sch for Deaf; Secy Permian Basin Coun for Hearing Impaired; r/1st Bapt Ch, Midland; hon/Employee-of-Month, 1st Nat Bk.

FLOYD, ELDRA MOORE JR oc/Attorney; b/Jul 19, 1920; h/411 Kenwood St, Hartsville, SC 29550; ba/H'ville; m/Eugenia C; c/Michael H, Cindy M, E M III, Eugenia, Ruth H; p/Eldra Moore and Augusta Blake

Floyd (dec); ed/BA; LLB; JD; mil/USNR (Ret), LCDR; pa/Exec Com SC Bar; ABA; Intl Bar; Assn Ins Attys; cp/Lions Clb; Mason; Shriner; Bd Ed Darlington Co; Exec Com D'ton Co Dem Party; Former Mem D'ton Co Comm; r/Epis.

FLOYD, JOHN ALEX oc/Senior Horticulturist; b/Feb 21, 1948; h/8604 4th Ave S, Birmingham, AL 35206; ba/B'ham; p/John Alex Sr and Louise Johnson Floyd, Selma, AL; ed/BS; MS; PhD; pa/Ala Nurserymen Assn; Am Soc Hort Sci; Am Hort Soc; Gtr B'ham Nurserymen Assn; Garden Writers Am; B'ham Botanical Soc; r/Presb; hon/J B Edmond Awd; Gamma Sigma Delta; Garden Clb Ala S'ship; Florist Assn S'ship; Pi Alpha Xi; Outstg Yg Men Am.

FLOYD, WINFORD RAY oc/Minister; b/Apr 1, 1932; h/1242 Thomas Blvd, Elizabethton, TN 37643; ba/E'ton; m/Frances Juanita; c/Myra Hogan, Rebecca Ange, Elisa, Sherri; p/Albert Ray Floyd, Norfolk, VA; Elsie Gantt Floyd (dec); ed/BA Milligan Col;

pa/Pastor: Highland Pines Free Will Bapt (FWB) Ch, Hamlet (NC) 1952-56, 1st FWB Ch, E'ton 1959-69, 1973-, Bethany FWB Ch & Bethany Christian Sch, Norfolk 1969-73; Ordained 1950; Chm Appalachian Preaching Mission 1967; Mem Nat Fgn Missions Bd Nat Assn FWB 1963-68; Evangelist; Conf Spkr; Trustee FWB Chd's Home, Greenville, TN; cp/Former Chm Citizen's Adv Com, E'ton; r/FWB; hon/Genn Gov's Cit Awd; Notable Ams; Intl W/W Commun Ser; Men of Achmt; IPA.

FLY, ANDERSON B oc/Mining Company Executive; b/Nov 27, 1923; h/PO Box 30400, Amarillo, TX 79120; ba/Amarillo; m/Celia Patterson; c/Charles B, Gerald W; p/Fritz Z and Gladys McCandless Fly, Phillips, TX; ed/BS; Addit Studies; mil/USN 1943-45, Combat Aircrewman; Dist'd Flying Cross (2); Air Medals (2); pa/Pres & Gen Mgr Marine

Metals Inc, Amarillo 1977-; Pres & Gen Mgr Hydro-Jet Sers Inc, Amarillo 1959-; Chief Civilian Instr (Guid Sys Elects Repairman Course) USAF 1955-59; Other Former Positions: Soc Mining Engrs, AIME; hon/Pubs in Sci & Tech Jours; Patentee in field; W/W: S&SW, Fin & Indust; DIB.

FLY, CLAUDE LEE oc/Consultant; b/Jun 23, 1905; h/415 S Howes St, Fort Collins, CO 80521; ba/Same; m/Miriam R; c/Maurita Ellen Kane, John M; p/Anderson Beauregard and Emmeline Josephine Lowery Fly (dec); ed.BS; MS; PhD; mil/Okla NG 1923-25; ROTC 1923-26; pa/Conslt in Soil & Water Resource Devel & Mgmt; Chapt Pres & Ofcs Soil Conservation Soc; Nat Pres Am Soc Agri Conslts; ASAE; ASA; SSSA; cp/Lions Clb; Salvation Army; Precnt Chm Repub Party; r/Christian; Meth Ch; hon/Sigma Xi; Gamma Sigma Delta, Dist Ser Awd; Fellow, Am Inst Chemists; Fellow, SCSA; Hon Life Mem, ASA; Num Cits; Nat 4-H Alumni Awd; Notable Ams; DIB; Others.

FLYNN, MARTHA CONNELLY oc/Nursing Administrator; b/Aug 30, 1921; h/225 St Paul's Ave, Jersey City, NJ 07306; ba/Jersey City; m/Thomas A; p/Howard J Connelly (dec); Cora D Connelly, Jersey City; ed/BSN; MS; pa/Dir Dept Nsg Jersey City St Col; Am Nurses Assn; Nat Leag for Nsg; AAUP; Am Public Hlth Assn; Assoc Deans Baccal Sch of Nsg, NJ; NJ Coun for Sch Nurse Ed; NJ Bd Nsg Subcom, Revision of Standards for Schs of Nsg; Bd Dirs NJ St Nurses Assn, Constituency 7; Adv Com St Francis Sch Nsg; Task Force for 80s, Jersey City St Col; Subcom on Acad Prog & Structures, Mid Sts Assn Preparation; Other Profl Activs; cp/Am Heart Assn, Nsg Coun; Hudson Co Inser Ed Coun; Action for Indep Maturity; r/Rom Cath; hon/Phi Delta Kappa; Commun Ldrs & Noteworthy Ams.

FLYNN, MICHAEL FRANCIS oc/Priest; Clinical Psychologist; Teacher; b/Dec 2, 1935; h/653 W 37th St, Chicago, IL 60609; ba/Chgo; p/Michael J Flynn (dec); Mary Ellen Lydon Flynn, Chgo; ed/BA 1955, BS 1958 St Bonaventure Univ; MA De Paul Univ 1966; PhD Loyola Univ Chgo 1974; pa/Diagnostic Conslt Chgo Police Dept 1978-; Asst Prof Ill Sch Profl Psychol 1977-; Diagnostic Conslt Marriage Tribunal, Chancery Ofc Cath Archdiocese of Chgo 1974-; Asst Prof Dept Psychi Univ Ill Med Sch, Chgo 1974-; Staff Psychologist & Dir Tng for Psychol Dept, W Side VA Hosp, Chgo 1974-; Former Positions;

Am & Ill Psychol Assns; Ill Group Psychotherapy Soc; Bd Dirs Assn Chgo Area Tng Ctrs in Clin Psychol; Reg'd Psychologist, St of Ill 1969-; Pres Assn Chgo Area Tng Ctrs in Clin Psychol 1978-79; cp/11th Ward Dem Com; r/Cath; hon/Personalities W&MW; Notable Ams; Men of Achmt; DIB; W/W: MW, Rel.

FOCH, NINA oc/Actress; Educator; b/Apr 20, 1924; ba/PO Box 1884, Beverly Hills, CA 90213; m/Michael Dewell; c/Schuyler Dirk; pa/Motion Picture Appearances incl: *Mahogany*, 1976, *Such Good Friends*, 1971, *Spartacus*, 1960, *Cash McCall*, 1959, *The Ten Commandments*, 1956, *You're Never Too Young*, 1955, *Executive Suite*, 1954, *An American in Paris*, 1951, Others; Broadway Plays incl: *Second String*, 1960, *King Lear*, 1950, *Twelfth Night*, 1949, Others; Appeared Am Shakespeare Fest in *Taming of the Shrew* & *Measure for Measure*, 1956; Appeared w San Francisco Ballet & Opera in *The Seven Deadly Sins*, 1966; Actress TV 1947-, Perfs incl: *The Wonderful World of Disney*, *The Name of the Game*, *Hawaii Five-O*, *Barnaby Jones*, *Columbo*, *I Spy*, *Mod Squad*, *Gunsmoke*, *The Steve Allen Show*, *The Outer Limits*, *Dr Kildaire*, *The Trailmaster*, Others; TV Panelist & Guest: *The Tonight Show*, *Dick Cavett*, *Merv Griffin*, *The Mike Douglas Show*, *The Dinah Shore Show*; Assoc Dir *The Diary of Anne Frank*, 1959; Adj Prof Univ S Cal 1966-68; Artist-in-Residence: Univ NC 1966, Ohio St Univ 1967, Cal Tech Inst 1969-70; Sr Fac Am Film Inst 1973-77; Adj Prof Univ S Cal 1978-; Fdr & Tchr The Nina Foch Studio, Hollywood 1973-; Fdr & Actress Los Angeles Theatre Group 1960-65; Bd Dirs Nat Repertery Theatre 1967-75; Exec Com for Fgn Film Awd, Acad Motion Picture Arts & Scis 1973-; Hon Chm LA Chapt Am Cancer Soc; Bd Govs H'wood Acad TV Arts & Scis; hon/Nom'd for Academy Awd for Supporting Perf in *Executive Suite*, 1954.

FOGELMAN, ANNA FLORENCE oc/Nutritionist; h/PO Box 58001, Houston, TX 77058; ba/Galveston, TX; m/Charles Edward Pulliam; p/George Franklin and Ruth Amelia Swartley Fogelman, Claymont, DE; ed/BS Univ Del 1950; Dietetic Internship Frances Stern Food Clin, Boston, Mass 1952; MPH Univ Cal-Berkeley 1957; mil/WAVES 1944-46, Yeoman; pa/Nutritionist Dept Obs/Gyn Univ Tex Med Br, Galveston 1963-; Dietary Dir Tex Nutrition Survey 1968-69; Nutrition Conslt Md St Dept Hlth, Baltimore, Md 1960-63; Nutritionist Charlotte-Mecklenburg Hlth Dept, Charlotte, NC 1957-60; Other Former Positions; Am Dietetic Assn; Tex Dietetic Assn, Exec Bd 1968-69; S

Tex Dietetic Assn: Pres-elect 1968-69, Chm Prog Com 1968-69, Pres 1969-70, Commun Nutrition Sect Com 1974-, Chm Constitution Com 1974-, Histn 1976-77; Am Home Ecs Assn; Tex Home Ecs Assn, Var Ofcs; Houston Area Home Ecs Assn; Am Public Hlth Assn; So Br APHA; Tex Public Hlth Assn, Food & Nutrition Sect; Inst Food Technol-Tex Sect; Nutrition Today Soc; Soc for Nutrition Ed; Ofcs Held Tex St Nutrition Coun; cp/Beta Sigma Phi; Intl Clbs; r/Presb; hon/Girl of Yr, Pasadena Preceptor Alpha Rho Chapt, Beta Sigma Phi 1974-75; Girl of Yr Dickinson Xi Theta Zeta Chapt, Beta Sigma Phi 1966-67; 1 of 10 Most Outstg Grads Sch of Home Ecs, Univ Del.

FOGLIO, FRANK oc/Real Estate Developer; Lecturer; Author; b/May 21, 1921; h/3553 Syracuse Ave, San Diego, CA 92122; ba/Same; m/Julia C; c/Frank Jr, Marilyn J F Crudo; ed/Dipls: Skadron Col Bus 1958 & 60, Anthony Schs Real Est 1962, Sharpe Inst Fin Devel 1970 & 71; Others; pa/Lectr & Fund Raiser 1970-; Real Est Devel 1957-60; Pt-Owner Meat Processing Plant, Fontana, Cal 1955-; Engrg Dept Swift & Co 1952-55; Train Electrician Pa RR 1945-52; IPA; cp/Oral Roberts Univ: Bd Regents, Fdg Exec Bd, Chm

Fac & Sem Coms; Pres' Coun, So Cal Bible Col; Coun Mem Evangel Col, Springfield, Mo; Numismatic Assn Cal; Am Numismatic Assn; Nat Rifle Assn; ARC, Magen David for Israel Red Cross; Millionaire's Press Clb; Diamond Key Life Mem, Pres' Assocs of Nat Univ; Cal St Dem Ctl Com; r/Mem, Dir Full Gospel Bus Men's F'ship Intl; hon/Hon Life Mem Nat Univ Alumni Assn; Key to City of San Bernardino; Chosen as Spkr for EXPO 76, Pgh, Other Spkg Engagemts; Author *Hey God*; Biogl Listings.

FOLEY, GERALD KEVIN oc/Catholic Priest; b/Jan 15, 1932; h/3801 Grand Ave, Des Moines, IA 50312; ba/Des Moines; p/William and Alma Perras Foley, Kelliher, MN; ed/BA; BS; MA; MSW; pa/Dir Nat Cath Rural Life Conf; Chperson Edwin V O'Hara Inst on Rural Min; r/Nat Exec Bd Cath Engaged Encounter.

FOLEY, KEVIN MICHAEL oc/Research Scientist; b/Nov 22, 1942; h/540 Dussel Dr, Maumee, OH 43537; ba/Maumee; m/Jeanne Ann; c/Tony, Keith, Brian; p/Matthew J and Mary Alice Foley (dec); ed/BS Xavier Univ; PhD Purdue Univ; JS Capital Univ; pa/Am Assn Cereal Chemists; Inst Food Technologists; Am Oil Chemists Soc; Am Chem Soc; Inst for Briquetting & Agglomeration; Toledo Patent Law Assn; Chm Lucas Co Med Malpractice Arbitration

Panel 1976, 78; r/Cath; hon/Order of Curia; Xavier Freshman Chem Awd; Phi Lambda Upsilon; Patentee; Pubs.

FOLLINGSTAD, HENRY GEORGE oc/College Professor; Scientific Research Consultant; b/Jan 6, 1922; h/3506 Garfield Ave S, Minneapolis, MN 55408; ba/Mpls; m/Helen Jane Chrislock; c/Carl Martin, Sharon Ruth, Karen Joy, Daniel Mark, Nancy Ellen; p/Henry Adolf and Lottie Regina Johnson Follingstad (dec); ed/BEE w high distn 1947, MS 1971 Univ Minn; mil/USAAF 1943-46, Radar Maintenance; pa/Assoc Prof Math Augsburg Col, Mpls 1962-; Sci Res Conslt Honeywell Systems & Res Ctr, Mpls 1964-; Elects Res Conslt N Star Res & Devel Inst, Mpls 1965-66; Other Former Positions; IEEE: Sr Mem 1960-, Mem 1948-60; Math Assn Am; Tau Beta Pi; Sigma Pi Sigma; Former Mem IPA; cp/Former Trustee Luther Col Bible & Liberal Arts, Teaneck, NJ; r/Luth; hon/Patentee in field; HS Valedictorian; Num Profl Pubs; DIB; Men & Wom of Distn; Men of Achmt; Personalities W&MW; Commun Ldrs & Noteworthy Ams; W/W MW.

FONTAIN, GREGORY (Rt Rev Archimandrite) oc/Priest; Language Instructor; h/PO Box 139, Wayne, PA 19087; ed/PhB, AB, STM, Colegio Serafico, Colegio de los RR HH Mariastas, Columbia, En Theol Sem; pa/Instr French Serafico Col, Christobal Colon Col, Colombia, SAm 1950; Epis Acad, Philadelphia, Pa 1958-61; Haddonfield Mem HS 1961-62; Asst Prof Spanish, French, Latin & German, VFMA, Wayne, Pa 1962-; Spiritual Advr Orthodox Cath F'ship, Bryn Mawr Col; Rector Sts Peter & Paul Albanian Orthodox Cath Ch, Phila 1967-70; Rep

Chaplancies Comm, Canonical Orthodox Cath Bishops Am; Fdr Acad Am Poets; Bd Dirs Acad Leonardo da Vinci, Rome; Classic Soc, Phila; Centro Studi e Scambi Internazionali; Am Poetry Leag; Pa Poetry Soc; Am Poet F'ship Soc; Christian Writers Leag; hon/Contbr of Poems to Anthols & Rel Jours & Radio; Gold Plaque, Broadway Spanish Ch (for ser to Spanish Commun of Camden, NJ); Gold Medal, Order of Anthony Wayne, VFMA; Conferred Title "DANAE", Intl Clover Poetry Assn, Wash DC; Biogl Listings.

FONTENOT, MARTIN MAYANCE JR oc/Environmental Chemist, Engineer; b/May 30, 1944; h/9024 Staring Ct, Baton Rouge, LA 70810; ba/St Gabriel, LA; m/Christel Yvonne; c/Martin III, Brodi Lin, Arloe Phillip; p/Mayance Fontenot, Los Angeles, CA; Hazel G Chvetien, Mamou, LA; ed/BS; MS; ME; pa/ACS; ISA; AIHA; APCA; BRAIDG; IMC; cp/Home Assn Jr Achmt; r/Rom Cath; hon/Fellow, Am Inst Chemists; Var Col S'ships.

FOOSE, DON HOLT oc/Executive; b/Nov 1, 1942; h/104 Beechwood Pl, Parkersburg, WV 26101; ba/P'burg; m/Peggy Wamock; c/Don Edward II; p/Don Edward Foose (dec); Helen Blanch Foose, Beckley, WV; ed/BA Marshall Univ; Grad Geo Wash Univ & Georgetown Univ; pa/Quaker St Oil Refining Corp: Dist Land Mgr 1975-, Asst Land Agt 1974-75; C & O Ry, Huntington, WVa: Asst Cost Engr 1969-70, Asst Track Supr 1970, Track Supr 1970-71, Asst Div Engr 1971-73, Asst Dir Labor Relats 1973-74; Ohio,

WVa, WVa Ind Oil & Gas Assns; Am Assn Petrol Landmen, Pres Benedum Chapt 1977-; Nom Dir Indep Oil & Gas Assn WVa; cp/P'burg JCs; Kiwanis; Elks; Masons, 32°; Repub; Mem Nemesis Temple AAONMS, P'burg; hon/Ky Col; W/W S&SW.

FORBES, FRED WILLIAM oc/Architect, Engineer; b/Aug 21, 1936; h/PO Box 443/465 Lamplighter Pl, Xenia, OH 45385; ba/Xenia; m/Carolyn L; c/Talerie Bliss, Kendall Robert; p/Kenneth S and Phyllis C Forbes, N Port, FL; ed/BS Univ Cinc 1960; MS Cand Univ Dayton; pa/Greene Co Profl Engrs Soc: Past Pres, Past VP; Past Nat Dir Am Astronautical Soc; Fellow Brit Interplanetary Soc; Chapt Com Mem Am Inst Archs: Past Com Chm

Ohio Soc Profl Engrs; Past Com Mem Nat Soc Profl Engrs; Former Pt-time Instr Univ Dayton; cp/Kiwanis Clb; "Spirit of 74" Com; Former VP Xenia Area C of C; r/Presb: Former Session Mem, Elder; hon/Patentee; Exceptl Civilian Ser Awd, USAF; Victor A Prather Awd, Am Astronautical Soc; Ohio Yg Engr of Yr 1970, Ohio Soc Profl Engrs; Pub'd Author; Others.

FORD, CLARA AGNES oc/Homemaker; b/Oct 8, 1924; h/PO Box 203, Foxworth, MS 39483; m/James M; c/James E, Candace L, Stephen P; p/Paul E and Nancy Moree Sylvest (dec); r/Rom Cath.

FORD, CLYDE GILPIN oc/Chemist, Materials Scientist; b/Aug 27, 1933; h/3716 S 98th E Ave, Tulsa, OK 74145; ba/Tulsa; m/Virginia Lee McClung; p/William Clyde Ford (dec); Mildred Ann Ford, Jonesboro, AR; ed/BA Ark St; MS Okla Univ; PhD Univ Tex; mil/AUS 1955-57, Lt, Pers Psychologist; pa/Sr Res Chem Int Paper; Engr Spec LTV; Mem Tech Staff Rockwell Intl; Mgmt Devel Chm Nat Mgmt Assn; Chm Elec Am Chem Soc, Tulsa Chapt; r/Bapt; hon/Woodruff Gold Medal, Art St; Others.

FORD, ELMER LEE oc/Retired Professor; b/Jan 2, 1894; h/3202 Alexander Ave, Shreveport, LA 71104; m/Eva E; p/Robert Lee and Mamie J Ford (dec); ed/BA, MA Samford Univ; Doctorate Lyon Univ (France); mil/French Army; pa/Prof Emeritus Fgn Langs Centenary Col La 1929-61; Other Acad Positions incl: King Col 1967-68, Miss Col 1922-29, Howard Payne Col (Hd Mod Langs) 1916-17; Mod Lang Assn; Am Tchrs French; AAUP; Am Fgn Policy Assn; Sigma Nu; Alpha Chi; Phi Sigma Iota; Other Profl Activs; r/Bapt; hon/Pub'd Author; IBA; W/W Am; Dir Am Scholars; W/W Am Ed.

FORD, GORDON BUELL JR oc/Educa-

tor; Author; Financial Management Specialist; b/Sept 22, 1937; h/PO Box 7847, Saint Matthews Sta, Louisville, KY 40204; ba/L'ville; p/Gordon B and Rubye Ann Allen Ford, L'ville; ed/AB Princeton Univ 1959; AM 1962, PhD 1965 Harvard Univ; pa/Prof Linguistics SEn Res & Devel Corp, L'ville, Chgo (Ill) & Palm Bch (Fla) 1973-; Reimbursemt Fin Mgmt Specialist Humana Inc, The Hosp Co, L'ville 1978-; hon/Phi Beta Kappa.

FORD, HAROLD EUGENE oc/United States Congressman; b/May 20, 1945; h/3631 Shady Hollow Ln, Memphis, TN 38116; ba/Memphis; m/Dorothy Bowles; c/Harold Eugene Jr, Newton Jake, Sir Isaac; p/Newton J and Vera Ford, Memphis; ed/BS; AA; pa/US Rep, 8th Dist St of Tenn; House Ways & Means Com, Select Com on Aging, Select Com on Assassinations, King Subcom; cp/Mtl Hlth Bd; Shelby Co Commun Action Agy; Trustee Rust Col; r/Bapt; hon/Majority Whip, TN St Leg, 87th Gen Assembly; Fellow, Harvard Inst Polits, Harvard Univ; Outstg Yg Man of Yr Awd, Memphis JCs 1976.

FORD, JUDITH ANNE oc/Physical Educator; Former Miss America; b/Dec 26, 1949; h/1540 Whitney Blvd, Belvidere, IL 61008; m/Edwin C Johnson; c/Bradley Edwin, Brian Ford; p/Virgil and Marjorie Visser Ford, Belvidere; ed/SWn La Univ 1967-68; BS cum laude Univ Ill 1973; pa/Began Competition in Swimming & Diving at 8 Yrs Old; Adv'd to Jr Olympics; US Gymnastics Team 1965; Rep'd US in Intl Gymnaestrada, Vienna; Competed Natly & Intly on Trampoline, Won Num Medals & Trophies; Instr, Hd Life Guard Belvidere Swim'g Pool Sums 1963-68; Fair Queen: Boone Co 1966, Ill St 1967; Miss Ill 1968; Miss Am 1969, Ext Travel; Ambassadress Nat Bowling Coun 3 Yrs; Pres' Coun on Phy Fitness & Sports; Nat AAU Com on Trampolining; Nat Jr Olympics Trampoline Com; Coaching Staff Spec Olympics Inc; Num Appearances as Spkr, Model, Hostess, Judge, TV Talk Show Guest, Comml Actress, Dir & Asst in Gymnastic & Sports Clins, Others; hon/Featured on Mag Covers & in Num Feature Stories; Alpha Lambda Delta; Phi Kappa Phi; Nom for BSA Outstg Nat Yg Am Awd 1971; Ofcl Chaperone for US Trampoline Team 1972; Trophy for Outstg Contbn to Nat PE Progs, Am Ftball & Basketball Conf 1972; Cit Prot Foun of Gtr Chgo Bus Ldrs; Biogl Listings.

FORD, LEE ELLEN oc/Attorney at Law; b/Jun 16, 1917; h/824 E Seventh St, Auburn, IN 46721; p/Arthur W Ford (dec); Geneva M Ford, Butler, IN; ed/BS w hons Wittenburg Univ 1947; MA Univ Minn 1949; PhD Ia St Col 1952; JD Univ Notre Dame 1972; Postgrad Studies Ohio St Univ; pa/Atty at Law, St of Ind 1972-; Hd Cytogenetics Lab Inst for Res in Mtl Retard, NY 1968-69; Editor Civil Rts & Animal Rts Pubs by Ford Assocs Inc; Adm Personal Aide to Gov of Ind 1973-75; Manpower Economist, Nev 1966-68; Prof, Res & Writing in Cytogenetics 1961-69; Assoc Prof 1952-61; Bar Assns: Am, Ind, DeKalb Co; Assn Wom Trial Lwyrs; Am Trial Lwyrs; Others; cp/Vol Atty: Butler (Ind) City Park & Rec Bd (former), DeKalb Co Humane Soc, Butler City Plan Comm (former); Ind Fdn of Humane Socs; DeKalb Humane Soc; Humane Soc of US; Wom's Equity Action Leag; Nat Wom's Polit Caucus; Dog Breeder & Tnr, Pioneer in Tng Companion Collies for Blind Chd; Vol Bd Mem: Ind Civil Rts Com Adv Coun on Status of Wom, Bd Dirs Assn Migrant Opport Sers; Pres's Coun on Drug Abuse & Num Other Drug Abuse Adv Couns; Chperson Proj Equality in Ind; r/Mem Luth Ch of Am, Ind-Ky Synod; Exec Bd Ind Coun of Chs & Chperson Div of Missions & Sers; hon/Author 600+ articles & volumes in Num Spec Fields of Expertise; Editor Volumes on Wom's & Persons Equal Legal Rts & Var Pubs in Popular Mags on these subjects.

FORD, LENA BRADLEY oc/Educator; Associate Professor; b/Dec 5, 1901; h/3901 Wilshire Dr, Abilene, TX 79603; m/Hoyt (dec); p/Walter E and Angie Bird Canon Bradley (dec); ed/BA magna cum laude 1934,

MA 1950 HSU; mil/Civilian Tchr Nurses Cadet Corps 1942-45, Hendrick Meml Hosp, Abilene; pa/Ret'd; Tchr Hardin Simmons Univ 1945-71; cp/Abilene Assn Mtl Hlth: Past Pres, Former Mem Adv Bd, St Bd; r/Bapt; hon/Meritorious Ser to Cadet Nurses Corps; Devoted Ser, Abilene Assn Mtl Hlth.

FORD, MARY VIRGINIA oc/Teacher; b/May 2, 1929; h/2944 Hood St, Columbus, GA 31906; ba/Columbus; p/Frand and Vera Ford (dec); ed/BS; DH; MA; STS; Addit Studies; pa/Kendrick High: Biol Tchr, Supv'g Student Tchrs in Sci; Tchr Biol, Anatomy, Physiol Spencer High 1960-70; Sci & Civics Tchr Marshall Jr HS 6 Months; Other Former Positions: Am & Ga Dental Hygienist Assns; Sigma Phi Alpha; Meharry Med Col Alumni Assn; Phi Delta Kappa; NEA; Ga & Muscogee Assns Edrs; Ga Classroom Tchrs Assn (Sci); GAE; PACE; Other Profl Activs; cp/NAACP; Alpha Kappa Alpha, Num Ofcs & Activs; Continental Socs Inc; Urban Leag; U Negro Col Fund Dr; Var Activs YMCA; Other Civic Activs; r/4th St Bapt Ch: Mem, Ofcs on S'ship Com; hon/S Atlantic Reg Ldrship & Ser Awd, Tampa, Fla; "Mary V Ford Cluster Four Coor Awd", Est'd by Gamma Tau Omega Chapt; Cert of Recog, Gen Missionary Soc 1st African Bapt Ch; Cert of Apprec & Book for Role in Ch; DIB; Book of Honors; Others.

FORD, RUTH VAN SICKLE oc/Artist & Teacher; b/Aug 8, 1898; h/69 Central Ave, Aurora, IL 60506; ba/Same; m/Albert G; c/Barbara Jane F Turner; p/Charles P and Anna Van Sickle (dec); ed/AWS; DFA Aurora Col; pa/Pres-Dir Chicago Acad Fine Arts 1937-60; Am Watercolour Soc; Am Artists Profl Leag; Conn Acad; Grand Ctl Galleries; Chgo Painters & Sculptors; Salon of Wom Painters; Nat Assn Wom Artists NY;

Philadelphia Water Colour Clb; Chgo Soc Artists; Rockport Art Assn; Hon Mem Artists Guild of Chgo; 1st Wom Mem Palette & Chisel Acad; Num One-Man Shows inclg: Art Inst Chgo, Grand Ctl Galleries (NYC), Mexico City CC, Centre d'Art (Port-au-Prince, Haiti); Rep'd in Many Collections; r/Prot; hon/Fine Arts Bldg Prize; Art Inst, Chgo & Vicinity Shows Awd; Conn Acad Show; Awds of Merit; 2nd Prize, Fla Intl; Purchase Awd, Artists Guild Medal, 1st Prize, Palette & Chisel Clb; Silver Medal for Water Colour; Hon Mentions; Others.

FORD, WILLIAM GERALD FRANCIS oc/Chemist; b/Dec 27, 1946; h/2 S 28th, Duncan, OK 73533; ba/Duncan; m/Laura; c/William Patrick; p/Harold and Evelyn Ford, Trenton, NJ; ed/BA Okla City Univ 1969; PhD Tex A&M Univ 1975; pa/Am Petrol Inst; Am Chem Soc; Soc Petrol Engrs; cp/Duncan JCs; Ks of C; r/Rom Cath; hon/Pres Awd of Hon; W/W.

FORDHAM, DONALD KEITH oc/Evangelist; b/Oct 15, 1950; h/245 Blalock, PO Box 355, Mountain View, GA 30070; ba/Forest Park, GA; m/Shirley Alice Waldrop; c/Angela Joy; p/Aubry Donald and Sarah E Reece Fordham, Forest Pk; ed/BA; MDiv; r/So Bapt.

FORDHAM, WILLMON ALBERT oc/Minister; b/Nov 13, 1926; h/101 Oak St, Petal, MS 39465; ba/Petal; m/Ethel Hover; c/Albert Jr, Gary W; p/W E and Lura Hatten

Fordham, W Monroe, LA; ed/BA William Carey Col; MDiv New Orleans Bapt Theol Sem; mil/USN 1944-46; pa/Pastor 1st Bapt Ch, Petal; cp/Drug Ed Counsel; Petal C of C; Instnl Rep, BSA, Troop 68; r/So Bapt; hon/Cert of Apprec, Miss Bapt Conv Bd; DIB; Men of Achmt; W/W in Rel; Commun Ldrs & Noteworthy Ams.

FORDNEY, MARILYN TAKAHASHI oc/Educator; Author; b/Dec 22, 1936; h/3821 Ocean Dr, Oxnard, CA 93030; ba/Ventura, CA; m/Alan; p/Toshio James and Margaret O'Brien Takahashi, Los Angeles, CA; ed/CMA-AC; pa/Edr Ventura Col; Author 3

Textbooks: *Insurance Handbook for the Medical Office, Medical Transcription: Techniques & Procedures, The Administrative Medical Assistant*; Parliamentn Am Assn Med Assts, Cabrillo-Ojai Val Chap; r/Rom Cath; hon/Outstg Wom of Yr Awd, BPW Oxnard.

FORDYCE, PHILLIP RANDALL oc/Executive; b/May 28, 1928; h/2805 St Leonard Dr, Tallahassee, FL 32312; ba/Tallahassee; m/Lois Marilyn Lamb; c/Deborah, Marilyn, Natalie, Kerry, Timothy; p/Russell S Fordyce (dec); Agnes Fordyce, Sebring, FL; ed/BS 1951, MS 1954 Butler Univ; mil/USMC 1946-48; pa/Asst Chief Exec Ofcr & Dir Intl Progs, FSU; AAAS Ed Sect; Assn for Ed Tchrs in Sci; Nat Assn Biol Tchrs, Pres 1963; Phi Delta Kappa; Kappa Delta Pi; cp/Kiwanis; r/Prot; hon/Outstg Edr Awd.

FOREHAN, L MARIE FARROW oc/Teacher; b/Feb 2, 1926; h/503 Welty St, Greensburg, PA 15601; ba/Irwin, PA; m/Clayton Levenworth; c/David Farrow, James Richard, Michael William, Henry Ira; p/Ira D and Clara A Dopp Farrow, Groton, VT; ed/BS Univ Vt; pa/Home Ecs Tchr W Hempfield Jr HS, Irwin; Sewing Instr Adult Evening Sch, G'burg; Bishop Method Sewing Instr Joseph Horne Co, Pittsburgh, Pa; Botany

Lab Asst Univ Vt, Burlington; Assisted w Bishop & Arch Sewing Textbooks; Writer Courses Var Bishop Method Classes; Co-Developer "Practical Arts Prog for 7th Grade", Adopted by Hempfield Schs; Local, St & Nat Ed Assns; Am Home Ecs Assn; cp/PTA; Concerned Citizens for Better Schs; BSA: Den Mother, Com-wom; 4-H Ldr; Mother's March Chm, Mt Pleasant Twp, Pa; FISH; Westmoreland Co Philatelic Soc; Wn Pa Geneal Soc; Others; r/Meth Ch: Lay Spkr, Mem Ed Comm; Vacation Ch Sch Dir, Vt Congreg Conf; hon/Omicron Nu; E L Ingalls 4-H Prize, Univ Vt; Phi Beta Kappa; Wom of Yr Contestant, G'burg; Delta Kappa Gamma; Outstg Ldrs Elem & Sec'dy Ed; World W/W Wom.

FOREMAN, GERTRUDE EVELYN oc/Librarian; Associate Professor; b/Aug 8, 1932; h/1905 Sargent, St Paul, MN 55105; ba/Minneapolis, MN; p/Curtis L and Elsie Snyder Foreman; ed/BA, MA Univ Minn; pa/Univ Minn: Assoc Prof, Libn Bio-Med Lib; ASIS; ALA; MLA; AAUP; r/Luth.

FORESTER, JEAN MARTHA BROUILLETTE oc/Librarian; b/Sept 7, 1934; h/PO Box 304, Eunice, LA 70535; ba/Eunice; m/James Lawrence; c/Jean Martha, James Lawrence; p/Joseph Walter Brouillette (dec); Thelma Brown Brouillette, Baton Rouge, LA; ed/BS La St Univ; MA Geo Peabody Col for Tchrs; pa/Asst Libn LeDoux Lib, La St Univ-E; La Lib Assn; Delta Kappa Gamma; Alpha Beta Alpha; Phi Gamma Nu; cp/Eunice Assn for Retard Chd; OES; U Daughts of Confed; Phi Mu; r/Bapt; hon/Carnegie Fellow, Peabody Col.

FORESTI, ROY JR oc/College Professor; b/Mar 25, 1925; h/301 Willington Dr, Silver Spring, MD 20904; ba/Washington, DC; m/Barbara; c/Lois, Carl; p/Roy Foresti (dec); Katherine Foresti, Baltimore, MD; ed/BE

Johns Hopkins 1947; MS Carnegie-Mellon 1948; PhD Penn St 1951; mil/AUS Signal Corps 1944-46; pa/Prof, Chm Chem Engrg Dept Cath Univ; Am Inst Chem Engrs; Am Chem Soc; Am Soc Engrg Ed; r/Rom Cath; hon/Tau Beta Pi; Sigma Xi.

FORET, GEORGE JOSEPH oc/Businessman; b/Sept 28, 1947; h/PO Box 503, Raceland, LA 70394; ba/R'land; m/Eloise B; c/Jed Anthony; p/George J Sr and Gladys U Foret, R'land; mil/AUS 1967-69; 1 Yr Ser in Vietnam; pa/Co-Owner Winner's Cir Trophy Shop; Participant Bus Profl Convs; cp/JCs; Ks of C; VFW; r/Cath; hon/US Army Commend Medal; Ath Awds for Var Sports.

FORKNER, CLAUDE ELLIS oc/Physician; Educator; Foundation Executive; b/Aug 14, 1900; h/PO Box 820, Deland, FL 32720; ba/Same; m/Marion DuBois; c/Claude Ellis Jr, Helen Sturges Farley, Lucy Greene; p/Allen and Lucy Forkner (dec); ed/BA, MA Univ Cal-B; MD Harvard Univ; mil/Pvt 1918, 1/Lt (Resvs) 1922-27; NY NG 1927-29; AUS Col 1943-45, Conslt to Surg Gen, AUS; pa/Clin Prof Med Emeritus Cornell Univ Med Col; Pres The Med Passport Foun Inc; Conslt; Life Mem: AMA, NY Co Med Assn, NY St Med Assn, NY Acad Med, Am Col Physicians; Assn for Advmt of Med Instrumentation; Intl Soc for Hematology; AAAS; NY Med & Surg Soc; NY Cancer Soc; Pan Am Med Assn;

Royal Soc Hlth (London); Assn for Hlth Records; Soc for Computer Med; Other Profl Activs; cp/Mem Bd Trustees Emeritus Tchrs' Col, Columbia Univ; Bd Dirs Damavand Col Foun; Mem Pres Cnslrs Stetson Univ; Mem Harvard Univ Overseer's Com to Visit the Center for Mid En Studies; Others; r/Presb; hon/Medal of Honored Merit, Repub of China; Royal Order of Homayun (Ks) of Iran; Gold Medal, Harvard Med Alumni Assn; Sigma Xi; Fellow, NY Acad Scis; Hon Mem, Rotary Intl (DeLand, Fla); Pub'd Author.

FORMAN, JOSEPH CHARLES oc/Executive Director & Secretary; b/Dec 22, 1931; h/77 Stanton Rd, Darien, CT 06820; ba/NYC; m/Ursula Weston; c/Diane, Steven, Mary; p/Joseph O and Marie Smith Forman (dec); ed/SB MIT 1953; MS 1957, PhD 1960 NWn Univ; mil/USAF 1954-56 (Active Duty), Resigned as Capt 1965; pa/Exec Dir & Secy Am Inst Chem Engrs; AIChE; ACS; NSPE; SCI (London); ASAE; EJC Bd; cp/Lake Bluff, Ill: Sch Bd Planning Com, Num Others; r/Prot; hon/Fellow of AIChE; Tau Beta Pi; Sigma Xi.

FORMAN, MAX L oc/Clergyman; b/Mar 6, 1909; h/2860 S Ocean Blvd, Palm Beach, FL 33480; ba/Palm Bch; m/Diana Slavin (dec); 2nd Sade Fischbein; c/Gayl (dec), Cyrelle, Barr H, Donna; p/Isaac and Celia Bernstein Forman (dec); ed/BA cum laude Univ Pa 1930; Rabbi; MHL 1934; DD Jewish Theol Sem Am 1966; pa/Rabbi Conservative Jewish Congreg, Phila, Los Isl & Palm Bch; Vis Prof: Comparative Rel En Bapt Sem 1942-43, Crozier Theol Sem 1943-44; Lectr: Col Jewish Studies, Phila 1939-41, Fla Atl Bapt Col 1977; Bd Dirs Rabb'l Assembly 1956-58; Chm Queens Div RA 1960-62; Pres Rabb'l Coun Palm Bch Co 1976-78; Hadassah Assocs; Am Friends of Hebrew Univ; Zionist Org Am; Org for Rehab & Train; Am Acad Polic & Social Sci; r/Jewish; hon/Zelosophic Hon Soc 1929-30; Soc Alumni Prize, Univ Pa; Prizes in Bible, Hist & Talmud; Man of Yr, Jewish Fdn NY 1955; Israel Solidarity Awd, PB; Ben Gurion Awd.

FORMANEK, ELIZABETH MARY oc/Homemaker; h/4452 Portland Ave, S Minneapolis, MN 55407; p/Peter Paul and

Mary Ann Stepanek Formanek (dec); pa/Homemaker; r/Austrian Cath: Var Ch Activs; hon/Commun Ldrs & Noteworthy Ams; Notable Ams.

FORMANEK, LUELLA HELEN oc/Homemaker; b/Aug 11, 1924; h/4452 Portland Ave, Minneapolis, MN 55407; p/Peter Paul and Mary Ann Stepanek Formanek (dec); ed/Univ Minn; pa/Model, NYC 1946-55; Traffic Expert, Ill Ctl RR, Mpls 1957-64; Former Fed Employee; cp/USO Vol; Semper Fidelis Vol; Greenwich, Conn: Merry-Go-Round Clb, Gold Ring Clb, Chm, G'wich Hosp; ARC; Mpls Commun Chest; Vol St Marys Hosp Aux; Vol Mar Dimes; Wom in Ser to Ed; Soroptimist Clb; r/Nat Coun Cath Wom; Cath Jr Leag; hon/Nat Social Dir; Notable Ams Bicent Era; Commun Ldrs & Noteworthy Ams; DIB; World W/W Wom; Intl W/W Intells.

FORMELLER, SHIRLEY ANNE oc/Mathematics Supervisor; b/May 24, 1927; h/2111 Oak St, Northbrook, IL 60062;

ba/N'brook; m/Klemens Roman; c/John George Reba Jr; p/Stanley Oscar Samuelson (dec); Clara Pauline Lundgoot Samuelson, N'brook; ed/BS No Ill Univ 1948; MS Univ Ariz 1950; pa/NCTM; Former Dir Ill Coun Tchrs Math; Sch Sci & Math Assn; Math Assn Am; r/Luth; hon/Kappa Delta Pi; Pi Mu Epsilon; Sigma Zeta; Grad Cum Laude; 4 NSF Grants; Jandell S'ship; Ill Tchr S'ship.

FORNIA, DOROTHY LOUISE oc/Administrator; Professor; b/Feb 14, 1918; h/6941 Driscoll St, Long Beach, CA 90815; ba/LB; p/Joseph V Fornia (dec); Margaret A Fornia, Los Angeles, CA; ed/BS 1941, MA 1944 Ohio St Univ; EdD Univ So Cal; pa/Prof Cal St Univ; Dir Grad Studies & Res Sch of Applied Arts & Scis 1966-; Sch Applied Arts & Scis: Adv Coun 1966, Chm Grad Coun 1966, Chm Res Com 1973-77, Res Assoc 1973-, Chm Symposium on "Critical Gaps in Human Nutrition" 1978, Fac Devel Com 1977-; Mem Univ Archives Com 1977-; Sub-Com Intl Progs, Sub-Com Admissions & Eval 1976-; Adv Coun BA in Human Devel 1976-; Chm Gerontology Res & Study Project 1976- Chm Univ Grad Coun 1974-; Other Univ Activs; Mem Bd Dirs Geriatric Hlth Care Sys Inc, St Mary's Hosp, LB 1978-; Mem Dirs Agy Progs on Aging, LB 1977-; Ed Consortium on Gerontology, Cal St Univ-Northridge 1977-; Others; r/Presb; hon/Phi Kappa Phi.

FORTT, INEZ JULIA LONG oc/Writer; Librarian; h/3870 Watkins Ln, Eugene, OR 97405; m/James Gill; c/Elizabeth Margaret F Beairsto, Thomas Alden; p/Frederick A Long (dec); Elizabeth Maria Schmaltz (dec); ed/Grad Milwaukee St Tchrs Col (now Univ Wis-M); Deg in Social Work Univ Oreg; pa/Author *Early Days at University of Oregon, History Tour thru Oregon*; Libn in Charge of Oreg Collections, Univ Oreg 13 Yrs; St Pres Nat Leag Am Pen Wom; cp/Rubison (Repub Party); Hist Soc; AARP; Sr Vol; r/Epis; hon/Sr Wom of Yr 1977; Awds: Lane Co Pioneer Mus, Lane Co Hist Soc; "Inez Long Fortt S'ship", AAUW; W/W Am Wom; Hon Life Mem, Lane Co Hist Soc.

FOSS, LUKAS oc/Composer; Conductor; Pianist; Lecturer; b/Aug 15, 1922; h/1140 Fifth Ave, New York, NY 10028; ba/NYC; m/Cornelia B; c/Christopher, Eliza; p/Martin and Hilde Schindler Foss (dec); ed/Yale Univ Music Sch; Curtis Inst Music; Lycee Pasteur (Paris); pa/Music Dir-Conductor Brooklyn Philharm 1971-; Vis Prof Music Manhattan Sch Music 1972-73; Music Advr-Conductor Jerusalem Symph 1972-75; Vis Prof Music Harvard 1969-70; Dir-Conductor: Stravinsky Fest, NY Philharm 1965, Franco-Am Fest 1964; Other Former Positions; Guest Conductor Maj Symph Orchs in US, Canada, Europe, Russia, Japan, Israel, Mexico & SAm; Guest Composer, Conductor & Lectr 100+ Am & Canadian Cols & Univs; Acad-Inst of Arts & Lttrs; hon/3 Hon Docts; 2 NY Music Critics' Cir Awds; 9 Composition Awds incl'g: Guggenheim F'ship, Prix de Rome Ditson Awd for Conductor who has done most for Am Music; NY St Coun on Arts Grant; NYC Awd for Spec Contbn to Arts; Num Printed Compositions; Pub'd Articles.

FOSTER, ATWOOD oc/Minister; b/Apr 9, 1908; h/1220 NE 17th Ave, Portland, OR 97232; ba/Portland; m/Dorothy Carolyn Gutekunst; c/David Atwood, Judith Marilyn; p/James E Foster (dec); Nannie Ann Suttle

(dec); ed/Bible Col; pa/Pastor Mins in Wash & Oreg 1931-42; Oreg Dist Assemblies of God: Dist Secy 1937-42, Supt 1942-56; Nat Treas Assemblies of God USA 1956-58; Fdr & Pres Ch Ext Plan 1950-74; r/Assemblies of God; hon/Hon Mem, Delta Epsilon Chi, Bethany Bible Col; W/W in Rel.

FOSTER, CARNO AUGUSTUS oc/Road Car Inspector; h/235 Sterling St, Brooklyn, NY 11225; ba/Bklyn; m/Phyllis; c/Maria, Philip, Stephen; p/Fitz Herbert and Elizabeth Foster; ed/Dipl Utilities Engrg Inst (Chgo); pa/Road Car Inspector NYC Transit Auth; Former Real Est Operator (Bklyn); Former Mgr Grocery Establishmt (Bklyn); cp/Orgr Block Assns, Bklyn; Ofcr U-Care Coor'g Coun, Bklyn; Ofcr Lafayette Gardens Coor'g Coun, Bklyn; Ofcr Bedford Stuyvesant Polit Leag, Bklyn; Pres Adelphi Civic Assn, Bklyn; Former Trustee & Mem Exec Coun Barbados Wkrs' Union; Former Pres Grand U Order of Odd Fellow, Barbados; Others; hon/Author "Justice in Man"; Intl Register of Profiles.

FOSTER, CAROLINE ROBINSON oc/Executive; b/Oct 2, 1937; h/5778 Honor St, Mobile, AL 36608; ba/Mobile; c/Robin Caroline, Edward Eugene Jr; p/Lucius Waite Robinson (dec); Vassar Bowling Robinson, Chickasaw, AL; ed/Att'g Univ S Ala; pa/Exec Asst to Mobile Co Commr; Goodwill Indust Mobile Area Inc 1968-79: Pers Dir, Asst to Pres; Mobile Gen Hosp 1966-68: Secy to Dir,

Asst Dir Social Ser; Other Former Positions; Mobile Pers Assn: Bd Dirs 1972-74, Secy-Treas 1975-76, VP 1976-77, Pres 1977-78; Am Soc Pers Adm; Secy Indust Mgmt Coun 1977-78; Pers & Indust Relats Sem, Cont'g Ed, Univ Ala 1974-76; Other Profl Activs; cp/Notary Public; Del to Russia, YMCA Sponsored US/USSR Exc of Mgrs 1978; Nat Rehab Assn; Mem Mobile Co Repub Exec Com, Dist 100; Former Judge Future Bus Ldrs of Am Contest 1978; Mobile Repub Clb Mobile Co; Others; r/Spring Hill Bapt Ch: Mem, Com on Coms, Sanctuary Choir; hon/W/W: S&SW; Am Wom; Others.

FOSTER, DUDLEY EDWARDS JR oc/College Professor; Department Chairman; b/Oct 5, 1935; h/2235 San Marco Dr, Los Angeles, CA 90068; ba/San Fernando, CA; p/Dudley E Foster, Port Hueneme, CA; Margaret DePoy Foster (dec); ed/AB 1957, MA 1958 UCLA; Fellow, Trinity Col of Music, Univ London; pa/Los Angeles Mission Col: Prof, Chm Dept Music; NEA; AFT; Am Musicological Soc; Mediaeval Acad Am; IPA; cp/Town Hall of Cal; r/Anglican.

FOSTER, EDWIN POWELL oc/Civil Engineering Professor; b/May 7, 1942; h/3101 Knobview Dr, Nashville, TN 37214; ba/N'ville; m/Joyce Lane; c/Cathleen Margaret, Patricia Ann, Michael Patrick; p/Edwin Powell Foster (dec); Mary Alice Foster, N'ville; ed/BE, MS, PhD Vanderbilt Univ; pa/Univ Tenn-N: Assoc Prof, Coor Civil Engrg 1968; Engrg Res Assoc NASA/Langley Res Ctr, Hampton, Va 1977-78; Engr-Analysis Sect AVCO Corp Aerostructures Div, N'ville 1968; Other Former Positions; Engrg Conslt; Pres Am Soc CE, Sect N'ville; Am Acad Mechanics; r/Rom Cath; hon/Alumni Outstg Tchg Awd, Univ Tenn Alumni Assn; NASA/ASEE Sum Fac F'ship; Tchr Excell Awd, Univ Tenn-N Chapt, Tenn Soc Profl Engrs; NSF Traineeship; Vanderbilt Univ S'ship; Men of Achmt; W/W S&SW.

FOSTER, FLORENCE PEREY oc/Early Childhood Educator; Child Development Specialist; Consultant; h/810 Harding St, Westfield, NJ 07090; m/Gerald R; c/Brian G; p/John Hubert Perey (dec); Florence L Perey, Westfield; ed/BS; MA; pa/Conslt for USOE/Dept of HEW; NAEYC; OMEP; AERA; NSSE; CEC; IPA; NJAEYC; NJAKE; NJ Nutrition Coun; Assn for Chd of NJ; NJACLD; NJ Reading Tchrs; Others; cp/Mem Var St Task Forces Relating to Chd & Fams; r/Prot; hon/Outstg Edr Am; W/W Commun Ser; World W/W Wom; Intl W/W Intells.

FOSTER, HELEN LAURA oc/Geologist; b/Dec 15, 1919; h/270 O'Keefe St, Palo Alto, CA 94303; ba/Menlo Park, CA; p/Stanley Allen and Alice Mary Osborn Foster (dec); ed/BS 1941, MS 1943, PhD 1946 Univ Mich; pa/Geologist US Geol Survey; r/Prot; hon/Outstg Alumni Awd, Univ Mich.

FOSTER, HOLLAND oc/Artist; b/Feb 15, 1906; h/75 Country Clb Ln, Woodstock, NY 12498; Palm Springs, CA; ba/Same; m/Dora Lucinda Ransom; c/Norman, Homer, Robert, "Cappy", Susan Neff (Mrs Wilfred); p/Homer A and Beatrice C Holland Foster (dec); ed/BA, MA St Univ Ia; mil/USN 1926-30; pa/Painter; r/Unitarian; hon/Cert of Merit in Painting; DIB.

FOSTER, JULIA F oc/Free-lance Home Economist; b/Apr 8, 1908; h/1108 Rathbun Dr, Minden, LA 71055; ba/Same; c/Raymond F; p/George Harlan and Emma Kemp Fincher (dec); ed/BS La St Univ 1927; Grad Work: Univ Fla-Gainesville 1943, Fla St Univ 1946; pa/Ret'd, Free-lance Home Economist 1973-78; Pa Power & Light Co (Ctl En Pa): Coor-Consumer Ed 1972-73, Dir Home Ser 1961-72; Sr Home Economist Fla Power Corp, Orlando, Fla 1960-61; Other Former Positions; Am Home Ecs Assn, Chm Wel & Public Hlth; Fla Home Ecs Assn, Exec Bd, Com Mem; Ill Home Ec Assn, Conslt; Pa Home Ecs Assn; Food Coun, Jacksonville, Fla; AAUW; Chgo Nutrition Assn; Mem Chgo Caterers Clb; Nat Restaurant Assn (Chgo); Nat Home Demonstration Agts Assn; Others; cp/Altrusa Clb, J'ville; Toastmistress Clb, Sarasota, Fla; Wom's Aux Civic Def, Sarasota; Pilot Clb Intl; Beta Sigma Phi; Others; r/Bapt; hon/1st Pl Awd for Yth Ed Prog, Edison Elect Inst; Awd for Consumer Ed Prog on Laundering, AHLMA; Lifetime Hon Mbrship, Philadelphia Chapt EWRT; Awd, Allentown C of C; Others.

FOSTER, LOWELL WALTER oc/Executive; b/Oct 22, 1919; h/3120 E 45th St, Minneapolis, MN 55406; ba/Mpls; m/Marion J; c/Michael, Janette, John; p/Walter J Foster (dec); Ferne C Tallman, Mpls; ed/Att'd Univ Minn; mil/USCG Acad 3½ Yrs, WWII

(Overseas); pa/Pres & Dir Technol Concepts & Engrg Intl; Engrg Conslt; Teacher; Author 13 Books, Num Tech Papers; Standardization Exec; Rep (USA) to Intl Stds Meetings; USA & Intl Standardization Devel & Mgmt; cp/PTA; Boy Scouts; r/Luth; hon/Leo B Moore Awd; Fellow; Dist'd Ser; Num Ser Awds, Profl Engrg Socs.

FOSTER, MARIETTA ALLEN oc/Researcher; b/Feb 10, 1934; h/1642 Wesleyan Hills Dr, Macon, GA 31210; m/Charles Edward; c/Thomas, Michelle; p/Joseph

Thomas Allen (dec); Marietta Sowell Allen, Macon; ed/BS; MS; Postgrad Work toward PhD; pa/Social Wkr, Reschr Yoga Healing Techniques, Foster Chiropractic Clin, Macon 1971-77; Conslt Mid Ga Cnslg Ctr, Macon 1976-77; Guid Cnslr Wilkes Co, NC Sch Sys 1970; Child Devel Specialist NC St Univ, Raleigh (NC) 1965-69; Est'd Meml S'ship, NC St Univ 1970; Social Wkr NC St Woms Prison, Raleigh 1962-65; Other Former Positions; cp/CSA Raja Yoga; Sidda Yoga Dham; Public Lectr Spiritual Symbols; Cong of Astrological Orgs; Am Fdn Astrologers; Fla, Atlanta Assn Astrologers; UNCG Alumni Assn; Am Home Ec Assn; Former Precnt Chm; Other Former Mbrships & Ofcs; r/Meth; hon/Omicron Nu; Roxie King Scholastic S'ship; Bordens Scholastic Awd; Deans List; Cert of Merit, CCRS Astrol Ctr, Cal; Biogl Listings.

FOUNTAIN, NELLIE LEE oc/Science Bookstore Manager; b/Nov 17, 1921; h/9209 Heatherdale Dr, Dallas, TX 75243; ba/Dallas; m/Jesse R; c/Barbara F Miller; p/James Etheridge and Vera Mae Whitaker Stark; pa/Mgr Major's Sci Books Inc, Dallas 1957-; Conslt in Field; r/Christian Ch: Mem; hon/W/W Am Wom.

FOURCARD, INEZ GAREY oc/Executive Director; Artist; h/1414 St John St, Lake Charles, LA 70601; ba/LC; m/Walden Arthur Sr; c/Chrystal Frances, Sharon Lynne, Walden Arthur Jr, Andrea Renee, David Marguard, Anita Lynne; p/G W and Lucille C (Stepmother) Garey, LC; ed/BFA 1963, Masters in Spec Ed Studies McNeese St Univ; pa/Exec Dir SWn Sickle Cell Anemia Foun Inc 1974-; Spec Adv Com of Spec Ed, Calcasieu Sch Bd; VP La Assn Sickle Cell Anemia; Artist, "Madonna Series" 7 Paintings, Last Series Finished 1974; cp/Calcasieu Parish Bicent Com; hon/Num 1-Man Shows; 1st Prize La Art Comm 1964; 15 Paintings w Eminent Black Artists of La Exhibited 1976; HS Valedictorian; Hon Citizen, Ft Worth, Tex; Awd of Merit, LC Deanery Human Relats Coun; Awds for Work w Sickle Cell Anemia: Sigma Gamma Rho Soc, La Assn Sickle Cell Anemia; Outstg Commer Ser Awds: Phi Beta Sigma Frat, Delta Sigma Theta Sorority; Num Certs of Merit; Biogl Listings.

FOWLER, BETTY JANMAE oc/Writer; b/May 23, 1925; h/N 7105 G St, Spokane, WA 99208; ba/Spokane; m/Leonard Joseph; c/Sherry Mareth Connors; p/Harry and Mary Jacques Markin (dec); ed/Att'd Stratton Bus Col 1942-43, Columbia Univ 1945-47; pa/Mem Public Relats Dept GSA (NYC) 1961-63; Adm Asst to Editor-in-Chief Scholastic Mags, NYC 1963-68; Adm Dir Leonard Fowler Dancers, Fowler Sch Classical Ballet Inc, NYC 1959-78; Tchr Ballet 1959-61; Editor Bultn, Kiwanis Weekly Pub, Spokane 1978-; cp/Adm Secy Kiwanis Clb; Instr Spokane Falls Commun Col; hon/W/W Am Wom.

FOWLER, DAVID PAUL oc/Mechanical Engineer; b/Nov 28, 1924; h/1726 E Union Bower Rd, Irving, TX 75061; ba/Irving; m/Mary Emma Welsh; c/Sharon Ruth, Judy Renee, John Welsh, Nancy Jean, Mary Ann; p/Clyde John and Irene Flotia Locklear Fowler (dec); ed/BS/ME Tex A&M Univ 1948; mil/USN 1945-46, S 1/c; pa/Assoc Mem Instrument Soc Am, Pres N Tex Sect 1969; cp/Am Mensa Ltd; Election Clerk Repub Party; r/Luth: Past Pres Local Congreg;

hon/Co-Inventor US Patents.

FOWLER, MEL oc/Sculptor; b/Nov 25, 1921; h/PO Box 255, Liberty Hill, TX 78642; ba/Same; c/James Everett, Robert Michael, William Wade; p/Walter Fowler, Marble Falls, TX; Thelma Gregory, Austin, TX; ed/Att'd: Univ Tex, Univ Md, SWn Univ, Norfolk Sch of Art; mil/USAF Fighter Pilot; pa/Num One-Man Exhbns incl'g: Hanging Marble Sculptures, Galerie Monika Beck, Homburg, Germany 1978, Abilene Fine Arts Mus, Abilene (Tex) 1977, Galerie Monika Beck, Homburg-Schwarzenacker (Saar) Germany 1977, St of Tex Ho of Reps 1977, Savoy, Kaiserslautern, Germany 1977, US Cong, Wash DC 1976, Others; Group Exhbns; Intl Sculpture Soc; So Assn Sculptors; Tex Soc Sculptors; Tex Fine Arts Assn; Artists Equity Assn-Nat; Artists Equity Assn NYC; hon/W/W: German Art, Tex; Num Prizes & Awds; Public Sculpture Comms.

FOWLER, SANDRA oc/Writer; Poet; b/Feb 4, 1937; h/West Columbia, WV 25287; p/Okey Donley and Jean Roach Fowler; pa/Pub'd Book *In The Shape of Sun*; Contbr to: *Bitterroot, Am Bard, Cyclo Flame, Poesie Europe, World Poet, Ocarina, Premier Poets, Parthenon Poetry Anthol,* Others; Current Cont'b Editor Spec Edition of *Ocarina* which will feature photos, biogl data & poems of 100 Am Poets of Distn; World Poetry Soc Intercont; Avalon World Arts Acad; Hon Rep Centro Studi E Scambi Internazionali; r/Fundamentalist: SS Tchr; hon/Medal of Honor, Centro Studi E Scambi; Hon Fellow, Academia Pax Mundi, Israel; Biogl Listings.

FOWLER, W LeRAY oc/Senior Minister; b/Oct 30, 1923; h/3610 Durness, Houston, TX 77023; ba/Houston; m/Rosemary Turner; c/David Mark, Stephen Douglas; p/W T Fowler (dec); Lorena Fowler. Mt Calm, TX;

ed/BA; MA; BD; DD; pa/Sr Minister W Univ Bapt Ch; Exec Bd Tex Bapts; Annuity Bd So Bapt Conv; Human Wel Comm; Ednl Coor Bd; Dir Bapt Standard; r/So Bapt; hon/George Washington Awd for Sermon; 3 Freedom Foun Awds for TV.

FOWLER, WATSON RODNEY oc/Educator; Psychologist; b/Jan 30, 1938; h/3428 Betty Ln, Chattanooga, TN 37412; ba/Chatta; m/Ann Carter Bass; c/Travis Lindley-Park, Margaret Alyse, Shannon Marie; p/Watson Francis and Margaret Elizabeth D Fowler; ed/BS Lock Haven St Univ 1965; MA Cal St Univ-San Diego 1968; EdD Ball St Univ 1974; mil/AUS 1957-59; pa/Asst Prof Cnslr Ed Univ Tenn-C 1976-; Asst Prof Psychol Ball St Univ, Germany, Eng, Greece, Spain 1974-76; Police Psychologist Del Co Police, Muncie, Ind 1973-76; Other Former Positions; Conslt: Ind St Police, Muncie Police, Cambridge Home, Ind Wom's Prison, Weathers Med Corp, Parkridge Hops, Hamilton Co Police, Chatta; Exec Dir Green River Crime Coun, Ky 1969-71; Am Assn Sex Edrs, Cnslrs, Therapists; APGA; Assn Cnslr Edrs & Supvrs; Am Assn Correctional Psychologists; Assn for Specialists in Group Work; Ind Assn Profl Police Ofcrs; Tenn Psychol Assn; Tenn Assn Pers & Guid Wkrs; Lookout Mtn Pers & Guid Assn; cp/Mem Var Clbs; hon/Named to Outstg Journalist Chair, Lock Haven St Col 1963, 64; Ky Col; Fellow, Am Acad Crisis Interveners; Biogl Listings.

FOWLES, BETH H oc/Consultant; b/Oct

23, 1913; h/7520 Curtiss Ave, Sarasota, FL 33581; ba/Same; m/George A; c/Carol Ann Savires, Barbara Lee Brown; p/Edward J Henniker (dec); Emily Stuart; ed/BS; MS; PhD; pa/Conslt in Med Arch; Bd Dirs Am Phy Therapy Assn; cp/Com Nat Easter Seal Soc; r/Prot; hon/Charter Centennial Cit for Outstg Ser, Boston Univ.

FOX, ABRAHAM H oc/Motel & Real Estate Executive; b/Oct 6, 1918; h/1714 E 19th St, Cheyenne, WY 82001; ba/Cheyenne; m/Donna; c/Stuart Lee, Ivan Dennis, Ellen Randy, Danielle Marie; p/Samuel and Bertha Fox (dec); mil/US Army; pa/Acct, United Airlines 1945-46; Owner Fox Realty Co 1958-; Exec: Fox Properties of Wausau, Fox Enterprises Inc, FFICO Inc; Owner, Firebird Motor Hotel & Restaurant (Minnehaha Court until 1973); Pres, Motel Assn (2 times); Dir, Wyom Motel Assn 6 Yrs; Reg Coor, Friendship Inns Intl 1971-; cp/Mason; Var Ofcs: Wyom Consistory, OES, Elks Clb, Moose Clb, B'nai B'rith, Am Legion, Cheyenne C of C, Others; hon/W/W: Am, W, Fin & Indust, Commun Ser; Intl W/W Intells; Other Biogl Listings.

FOX, DANIELLE DALEY oc/Floral Designer; b/Nov 17, 1949; h/18 Cromwell Pkwy, Summit, NJ 07901; ba/Summit; p/Daniel Daley Fred (dec); Clara Reheis Fox, Summit; ed/BA Finch Col; pa/Floral Designer

Flavia's Creations; Author: *Extension-An Anthology of Modern Poetry*; cp/Finch Alumni Assn; Jaguar Clb Am; r/St Theresa's Rom Cath Ch, Summit: Mem; hon/DIB; World W/W Wom; W/W Am Wom.

FOX, DICKIE LEE oc/College Professor; b/Nov 22, 1944; h/123 Waverly Way, Athens, TX 75751; ba/Athens; m/Susan Jean; c/Julie, Richard; p/Alfred and Mary Alice Fox, Odessa, TX; ed/BS, MS, MEd, PhD E Tex St Univ; mil/USMC Capt, Naval Aviator; pa/Eng & Rdg Prof Henderson Co Jr Col; Compliance Ofcr for Non-Discrimination of Handicapped; Conslt; cp/Kiwanis; hon/Profl Pubs; Intl W/W in Poetry; W/W Among Students in Am Univs & Cols; DIB.

FOX, GERALD G oc/City Manager; b/Nov 11, 1932; h/2703 Amherst, Wichita Falls, TX 76308; ba/Wichita Falls; m/Dolores Condon; c/Stephen, Gerald Jr, Carol; p/John E Fox (dec); Dolores Chess Fox, Kenosha, WI; ed/BA Beloit Col; MPA Ks Univ; mil/AUS Corps of Engrs 1954-56, Duty in France; pa/City Mgr Wichita Falls 1969-; City Mgr, Fayetteville, Ark 1966-69; City Mgr, Camden, Ark 1963-66; Other Former Positions; Tex Mun Leag: Com for Future, Human Resources

Adv Com, Leg Com; Intl City Mgmt Assn: Mun Mgmt Policy Com 1973, VP & Bd Dirs 1973-75, Com on Profl Conduct 1974-75; Mun Fin Ofcrs Assn; Am Soc Public Adm; Tex City Mgmt Assn: Bd Dirs 1971-73, S'ship Com Chm 1970-73, St Adv Bd for Acad for Profl Devel 1975-77, Chm Com on Profl Conduct 1977-78; Urban & Reg Info Systems Assn: Pres 1973-74, Bd Dirs 1972-75; Nat Mun Leag; Tex Innovation Group, Chm Exec Com 1978-79; cp/Rotary Intl; Bd Dirs (all Wichita Falls Affils): Bd of Commerce & Indust, Boys Clb, Mus & Art Ctr; Div Campaign Chm & Bd Dirs UF; CoChm Nat Conf Christians & Jews; r/Cath; hon/Omicron Delta Kappa; Annual Awd for Outstg Fin Adm, Tex Mun Adv Coun, Ennis, Tex; Cert of Conformance (for Annual Fin Report), Mun Fin Ofcrs Assn of US & Canada; Runner-up Mgmt Innovation Awd, Intl City Mgmt Assn; Selected as 1 of 10 Members to 2nd ICMA European Task Force to Visit & Study European Cities in England, Holland, & W Germany 1977; Biogl Listings; Pub'd Author.

FOX, H RONALD oc/Librarian; b/Apr 12, 1938; h/112 W 16th St, Grand Island, NE 68801; ba/Grand Isl; p/Wesley anf Margaret Fox, Kilgore, NE; ed/BA Neb Wesleyan Univ 1962; Grad Study Kearney St Col 1965-67; MLS Univ Okla 1968; Further Studies; pa/Libn VA Hosp, Grand Isl; Am, Neb & Med Lib Assns; Midcontinental Reg Med Lib Group; cp/Mason; York Rite Masonic Bodies; OES; Shriner; YMCA; Kiwanis Intl; VA Employees Assn; Repub Party; r/U Meth; hon/Lttr of Commend, FY, VA Lib Serv, Wash DC; Poetry Pub'd in Col Literary Mags; W/W: MW, Neb; Men of Achmt; Commun Ldrs & Noteworthy Ams; Nat Social Dir; Notable Ams Bicent Era.

FOX, HEWITT BATES oc/Oil & Gas Producer; b/Oct 24, 1922; h/233 Cape May Dr, Corpus Christi, TX 78412; ba/Corpus Christi; m/Margaret Standifer; c/Frederick H II, Douglas Standifer; p/Frederick H and Lorena Bates Fox, New Orleans, LA; ed/BA, BS, MA Univ Tex-Austin; mil/AUS 1942-46; pa/AAPG; CC Geol Soc; cp/Order of Arrow; BSA; r/Grace Presb Ch, Corpus Christi: Ruling Elder; hon/Sigma Gamma Epsilon.

FOX, LAURETHA EWING oc/Retired Associate Professor; b/Apr 25, 1910; h/1410 SW 35 Pl, Gainesville, FL 32608; p/Leslie Evans and Mary Ellen McMaster Fox (dec); ed/BS Westminster Col 1931; MS 1932, PhD

1934 Univ Ill; Postdoct Vanderbilt Univ Sch Med; pa/Ret'd Assoc Prof Pharmacol Univ Fla Col of Med; Reschr; Fla Foun Future Scists; r/Presb; hon/Pa St S'ship; Scholar, Univ Ill; Arthur D Little Fellow, Vanderbilt Univ Sch Med.

FOX, LUCILLE MONTROSE oc/Public Relations Specialist; b/May 30, 1929; h/6 Berkshire Rd, Rocky Hill, CT 06067; ba/Wethersfield, CT; m/Frank R; p/Louis Montrose (dec), Rose V Montrose, W'field; ed/Bus Mgmt; pa/Past St Chm Public Relats Conn Fdn BPW; Past VP Pyguag BPW Clb; Zonta Intl; Public Pers Assn Gtr Hartford; Past VP Chapt 22, Conn St Employee's Assn; Natural Resources Coun Conn; Gt Meadows Conservation Trust; Conn Public Hlth Assn; Nat & Local Mem Wom in Communs Inc; Liaison to: Conn Hist Comm, Am Revolution Bicent Comm; Antiquarian & Landmarks Soc Inc of Conn; VP Ctl Conn Chapt Wom in Communs; cp/Former Chm: Rocky Hill Pk

Comm, Swimming Pool & Teen Ctr Study Com of Rocky Hill; Charter Mem Wom's Com Nat Conf Christians & Jews Gtr Hartford; Mem Gov's Envir Policy Com; VChm Pk & Rec Adv Bd, Town of Rocky Hill; Trustee Bicent Coun of 13 Original Sts; Nat Mem Metro Opera Guild; Hon Mem Conn Fly Fisherman's Assn; Pres Conn Italian-Am Cult Assn; Others; r/Cath; hon/Certs of Achmt: Fed'd Garden Clbs Conn Inc, Conn St Pers Dept, Speechcraft, Conn Dept Pers & Adm; Humane Awd, N Shore Animal Leag; Cert of Ofcl Recog for Outstg Ser, Am Revolution Bicent Comm of Conn; DIB; Others.

FOX, MARGARET GERTRUDE oc/University Professor; b/Mar 31, 1912; h/Rt 2, Box 74, Prairie du Chien Rd, Iowa City, IA 52240; ba/Ia City; p/George E and E Gertrude Jacobs Fox (dec); ed/BS Univ Minn 1933; AM Columbia Univ 1940; PhD Univ Ia 1949; pa/Univ Ia: Assoc Prof 1949-57, Prof 1957-, Dept Chperson 1974-78, Univ Senate,

Fac Wel Com, Mem Other Coms; Am Acad PE: Pres, Secy-Treas, Bus Mgr; Am Alliance for HPER: Bd Dirs, Res Coun; Ctl Dist Assn for HPER: Pres, VP for Hlth, VP for PE, Dist Rep; Ia Assn for HPER; Nat Assn for PE of Col Wom, Leg Bd; Ctl Dist Assn PE of Col Wom; Assoc Editor *Research Quarterly*; Contbr to 5 Books, Articles in Profl Pubs; Fed'd BPW Clb; Radio & TV Appearances; cp/ARC; r/Meth; hon/Hon Fellow, AHPER; Hon Awds: Ctl Dist Assn HPER, Ia Assn HPER; Delta Kappa Gamma; Pi Lambda Theta; Kappa Delta Pi; W/W Am Wom; World W/W Wom; DIB.

FOX, MARY ELIZABETH oc/Journalist; Professor; Lecturer; h/Plantation Sq #C-3, 2411 S 61st St, Temple, TX 76501; p/J S and Frances West Fox (dec); ed/BA; BS; MA; Addit Studies; pa/Free-lance Writer; Book Reviewer; cp/Del to Co, St & Nat Convs Dem Party; r/Meth; hon/Biogl Listings.

FOX, PORTLAND PORTER oc/Consulting Engineering Geologist; b/Aug 10, 1908; h/500 Hiwassee Ave NE, Cleveland, TN 37311; ba/Same; m/Sarah Pearl Monk; p/William Ross and Dora Mayes Fox (dec); ed/BS Univ NC; pa/Bd Conslts: Des Dam (Iran), Swift Dam, Blenheim-Gilboa, Northfield, Bear Swamp, Rock Isl & Gathright Projects; VP Tenn Acad Sci 1945; r/1st Christian Ch; hon/Wisdom Hall of Fame; Sigma Xi; Am Men of Sci; W/W.

FOX, ROXANNE ELAINE oc/Research Assistant; b/Jun 22, 1946; h/110 E "H" St, Brunswick, MD 21716; ba/Frederick, MD; m/Raymond Dale; c/Rodney Redford; p/William Ralph and Ruth G Elliott, Alexandria, VA; ed/AA; BS; pa/Res Asst, Mgr Cancer Biol Prog Animal, Facility, Frederick Cancer Res Ctr; Am Assn for Lab Animal Sci; Frick Co Soc for Advmt of Tech; r/Epis; hon/Personalities of S; W/W Am Wom.

FOX, SAMUEL oc/Professor; Attorney; Certified Public Accountant; b/Mar 18, 1908; h/115 E Delaware Pl, Chicago, IL 60611; ba/Chgo; m/Genevieve Kubreener; c/3 Sons; ed/PhB Univ Chgo 1924; JD 1927, LLM 1928 Loyola Univ Law Sch; MBA Univ Chgo Grad Sch Bus 1947; PhD Univ Notre Dame 1950; pa/Prof Acctg Roosevelt Univ, Chgo 1973-; Prof Acctg & Mgl Law Univ Ill 1946-73; Vis

Prof Am Univ Beirut, Lebanon 1963; Lectr Beirut Mgmt Col 1963; Vis Prof Al-Hikma Univ, Baghdad 1963; Cost Acctg Conslt AID, Lima, Peru 1967; Acting Chair Acctg Dept Univ Wis-Eau Claire 1968; Am Assn Attys & CPAs; Assoc Editor Lexet Scientia; Others; Ill St Bar Assn; hon/Most Outstg Tchr Univ Ill-Chgo; Num Profl Pubs; Biogl Listings.

FOX, SANDRA ELAINE oc/Nursing Administrator; b/Apr 23, 1947; h/PO Box 296, Senoia, GA 30276; ba/Newman, GA; m/Harry Malcolm Schaffer Jr; p/Thomas A and Emily R Fox, Senoia; ed/RN; AA; BSN; MS; pa/Nsg Inser Ed Coor; Am Assn Critical Care Nsg; r/Bapt; hon/Top Student Awd, LPN Class 1968; Top Tchr Awd, RN Prog, Gordon Jr Col; World W/W Wom; Personalities of S; W/W Am Wom.

FOX, THEODORE A oc/Orthopaedic Surgeon; b/Feb 16, 1913; h/1170 Oak St, Winnetka, IL 60093; ba/Chicago, IL; m/Marcella Schaeffer (dec); c/Susan Rose, Nancy Beth; p/Albert Fox (dec); Jennie Fox, Chgo; ed/BS Univ Chgo 1933; MD Rush Med Col, Univ Chgo 1937; mil/USNR Ret'd, Cmdr (MC); pa/Assoc Prof Ortho Surg Abraham Lincoln Sch Med Univ Ill-C; Ill Masonic Med Ctr: Att'd Orth Surg, Dir Ctr for Sports Med, Chm Ortho Sect; Former Ortho Surg & Conslt Chgo Bears Ftball Clb; Chm Former Subcom on Ath Injuries, Chgo Com on Trauma; Am Col Surgs; Fellow: Am Acad Ortho Surgs, Am Col Surgs; AMA; AAAS; Clin Ortho Soc; Am Med Writers Assn; Latin Am Soc Ortho & Traumatology; Am Geriatric Soc; Others; hon/Sigma Xi; Profl Pubs.

FOXE, ARTHUR NORMAN oc/Psychiatrist; Editor; Author; b/Jun 28, 1902; h/9 E 67th St, NYC, NY 10021; ba/Same; m/Jane Millicent Langeloh; c/Jon L; p/David and Jennie Nash Foxe; ed/MD Jefferson Med Col 1927, Gold Medal in Physiol 1925; mil/SATC WWI, USAMRC 1927-33 1/Lt, Sel Ser Rehab Prog Exam'g Phys 1943-44; pa/Intern & Resident 1928-30, Asst Vis Phys 1930-32 Bellevue Hosp, NYC; Instr Neurol Bellevue Med Col 1930-32; Phys St Lawrence St Hosp 1933; Psychi & Dir Classification Great Meadow Prison, Comstock, NY 1933-39; Conslt Psychi: Mt Carmel Home 1947-57, Trinity Chapel Home 1957-62, Mary Manning Walsh Home 1956-62; Att'g Psychi Gracie Sq Hosp 1961-; Pvt Pract Glens Falls & NYC 1933-; Mem: Am, Pan-Am Med Assns, Com on Prisons Am Psych Assn, Authors Leag Am, Author Guild, Adv Coun Assn for Help of Retard Chd 1948-; Bd Dirs Assn from Commun Guid Sers 1956-, AAAS, Am Orthopsychi Assn, Am Group Therapy Assn, Am Acad Forensic Sci, Nat Coun Fam Relats, Res Coun Probs of Alcohol, Am Col Sports Med, NY Acad Med, Royal Soc Hlth; Num Others; Life Mem, VP 1948 am Psychopath Assn; Lectr Am Inst 1941, Awd of Lectureship 1951; Councillor 1952-56, VP 1970 Med Correctional Assn; Acad Psychosomatic Med: Fdr, Exec Com, VP 1962, Chm Credentials Com; Fellow IBA; Diplomate Am Bd Psychi & Neurol, Am Bd Legal Med; Num Editorships incl'g Assoc Editor *Archives of Crim Psychodynamics* 1950-57 & *Corrective Psychi & Jour of Soc Therapy* 1968-; cp/Fellow Intl Poetry Soc; r/Epis; hon/Royal Blue Book; DIB; 2000 Men Achmt; Dir Brit & Am Writers; Yrbk & Biog Dir, Nat Cyclo Am Biol; W/W: NY, E; Contemp Authors; World Biog Am Men Med; Intl World W/W; Nat Social Dir; Biog Dir Am Psychi Assn; Dir Med Spec; Alpha Omega Alpha; Blue Ribbon Panel Nat Acad TV Arts & Scis 1970; Pub'd Author Num Books; Intl W/W Commun Sers; Am Authors Today; Intl Reg W/W, Lausanne, Switzerland.

FOXWORTH, CHARLES LEONARD oc/Associate Professor; b/Aug 4, 1932; h/2203 Greenbriar, Ruston, LA 71270; ba/Ruston; m/Lois Mae Hudson; c/Judy Clare F Ray, Charles David (dec); p/Mamie Foxworth, Nederland, TX; ed/BA E Tex Bapt Col; MA Univ Houston; PhD La St Univ; pa/La Tech Univ: Chm Sec'dy Ed 1970, Assoc Prof Tchr Ed;; Chm Humanities Dept ENMU-

Roswell 1969; Pres La Coun Social Studies 1973; VP Tech Chapt AAUP; Pres Linc Parrish Coun for Social Studies 1977; Est'd Social Studies Resource Ctr, LTU; r/Emmanuel Bapt Ch, Ruston; hon/Tchr of Yr, ENMU-R 1965, & 1969; Outstg Edr in Col of Ed, LTU 1973; Biogl Listings.

FOYLE, DOLORES HARTLEY oc/- Homemaker; Civic Leader; b/Jun 17, 1928; h/5030 E Mockingbird Ln, Scottsdale, AZ 85253; m/Charles Martin Jr; c/Edward, Charles III, Michael, Donna Marie; p/David Hartley Dewitt (dec); Lillian D Galpine, Augusta, GA; ed/BS ASU; cp/VChwom St Repub Party; Nat Repub Conv: Del 1972, Mem Credentials Com; Chm St Get-Out-the-Vote; Campaign Coor All Levels Polit Campaigns; 1st Wom Appointed to Maricopa Co Planning & Zoning Comm; St Planning Assn; Bicent Com, Scottsdale & Paradise Val; St & Nat Assns Parliamentns; Pres Woms Clbs; Chm Citizens Com, S'dale; VP St Fdn Repub Wom in Ariz; Civic Fund Drs; Camp Fire Girls: Asst Ldr, Sponsor; Ariz Town Hall Acad; r/Cath; hon/W/W Polits S&SW, Am Polits; Personalites W&MW.

FRANCIS, ELIZABETH LINCOLN oc/Faculty Member; b/Aug 4, 1927; h/Box 266, Boykins, VA 23827; ba/Murfreesboro, NC; m/Gilbert W; c/Gilbert W Jr, Richard L, Jeffrey King; William E Jr (Stepfather) and Elizabeth G O'Neil, Richmond, VA; ed/Baccalaurate in Arts Hollens Col; pa/Chowan Col: Tchr Profl Devel 1969–, Curric Coor Merchandising Mgmt Prog 1976–; cp/CoChm Dem Party, 4th Dist (Va); Composor Polit Campaign Songs; Pres Boykins Union Wom's Clb; Cub Scout Den Mother 8 Yrs; r/Boykins Bapt Ch, Boykins: Choir Dir.

FRANCIS, MARILYN A oc/Writer; b/Jan 26, 1920; h/PO Box 263, Cottonwood, AZ 86326; ba/Same; p/Roy Brooke and Ruth Needles Francis (dec); ed/BS Ohio Univ 1941; pa/Free-lance Writer 1955–; Contbr 300+ Poems in Nat Periodicals; Pub'd 6 Books; Nat Leag Am Pen Wom; Poetry Soc Am; cp/Bd Trustees Verde Val Guid Clin; Ariz St Behavioral Hlth Adv Coun; r/Prot; hon/Cit'd for Dist'd Attainmts in Lit, Ohio Univ; Num Nat Poetry Prizes; Intl W/W in Poetry.

FRANCIS, MARION DAVID oc/Senior Research Scientist; b/May 9, 1923; h/10018 Winlake Dr, Cincinnati, OH 45231; ba/Cinc; m/Emily Liane; c/William Randall, Patricia Ann; p/George Henry Francis (dec); Marian Flanagan Francis, BC, Can; ed/BA; MA; PhD; pa/Sr Res Scist Miami Val Labs; Ohio Acad Sci; Fellow Am Inst Chemists; AAAS; Am Chem Soc; Soc Nuclear Med; NY Acad Sci;

cp/Past Local Chm, Capt U Appeal; r/Rom Cath; hon/Phi Lambda Upsilon; Gamma Alpha; Chemist of Yr 1977, Cinc Chapt ACS.

FRANCIS, NEVILLE ANDREW oc/Civil Engineer; Public Administrator; b/Oct 10, 1925; h/1133 Cramer Ct, Baldwin, NY 11510; ba/NYC; m/Christobelle Elain; c/Neville Andrew Jr, Houghton David; p/James Theophilus and Theckla Adina Francis, Antigua, W Indies; ed/BS; MPA; cp/Royal AF (England) 1943-47; pa/Resident Engr St of NY; Former Instr Field of Bldg Constrn & Engrg (Pres' Manpower Tng Prog), Port Auth NY; Gull-Slattery & Horn Constrn Cos: Former Surveyor, Estimator, Asst Project Engr; Formerly Assoc'd w Lizza & Sons Inc, Oyster Bay, NY; Am Inst Planners; Am Soc Planning Ofcls; Am Soc for Public Adm; Am Acad Polit & Social Sci; Profl Engrs Soc Barbados, W Indies; Am Concrete Inst; Inst for Certn of Engrg Technicians (Nat Soc Profl Engrs); Others; cp/Dem Party; Notary Public; r/Unity Ch of Christianity, Valley Stream, NY: Chm Bd Dirs, Bldg Com; hon/Pub'd Author.

FRANCIS, SHIRLEY A oc/Livestock Company Secretary-Treasurer; b/Nov 8, 1934; h/PO Box 365, Cheyenne, WY 82001; ba/Same; m/Edward; c/Linda F Uzzell, John Arthur II; p/John M and Cleo L Hunter, Cheyenne; pa/Secy-Treas Francis Livestock Co; Past Pres Zonta Clb; cp/Former Chm Laramie Co Repub Ctl Com; Former St Com-wom, Rep'g Laramie Co on Wyo Repub Ctl Com; Guest Lectr Univ Wyo Taft Inst of Lng 1976, 77; Fed'd Wom's Clbs: Past Pres Town & Country Leag (Cheyenne), Past Dist Pres Wyo Fdn Wom's Clbs, Var Coms; Past Pres Laramie Co Cowbelles; Past Pres Chapt S PEO; Orgr & 1st Chm Laramie Co Safety Coun; Past Chm Wyo Assn Wom Hwy Safety Ldrs; r/Prot; hon/Outstg Yg Wom Am; W/W Am Polits; Personalities W&MW.

FRANCISSE, ANNE EUDOXIE oc/Political Scientist; Actress; Teacher; b/Jul 27, 1930; h/PO Box 3383, Hollywood,CA 90028; p/Camille Francisse (dec); Marie Piron (dec); ed/MA; pa/Actress (Anne Francissi); Has Appeared in Var TV & Film Prodns; Edr Los Angeles Co Public Schs 1964-69; Am Polit Sci Assn; Am Fdn TV & Radio Artists; r/Prot; hon/World W/W Wom; W/W Am Wom; Intl W/W Commun Ser; Personalities W&MW; Commun Ldrs & Noteworthy Ams; Notable Ams; DIB; Omicron Chapt Phi Delta Gamma; Acad Players Dir; APSA Biog Dir; Others.

FRANCKE, HARRY CARL oc/Retired Chemical Engineer; City Councilman; b/Dec 7, 1909; h/201 Manhattan Ave, Oak Ridge, OK 37830; ba/Oak Ridge; m/Margaret Lipp; c/Claude R C, Carole R B F Goss; p/Charles L and Grace Huffstetter Francke (dec); ed/BS Hanover Col; Postgrad Work: Univ Louisville, Purdue Univ, Princeton Univ; mil/USNR, Ret'd Lcdr, Cmdg Ofcr, WWII;

pa/Engr 48 Yrs, Gold Mining Opers in Philippine Isls to Nuclear Energy Facilities in Oak Ridge; cp/City Coun-man 20 Yrs, Oak Ridge; Past Mem Tenn Mun Leag Bd Dirs; Bd Dirs Anderson Co Commun Action Comm; Past Pres & Dir Anderson Co Comm on Aging; Chm Anderson Co Civil Ser Bd; Nat Leag Cities; Oak Ridge Del to Gov's Conf on Aging 1978; Elks Clb; VP AARP; r/1st U Meth Ch; hon/Civic Ser Awd, Eagles Lodge; Columbus Awd for Civic Work; Pub'd Author; Mag Indust Res Awd.

FRANCOEUR, ROMAINE D oc/Hospital Administrator; b/Aug 5, 1938; h/8 Kasper Dr, Loudonville, NY 12211; ba/Albany, NY; c/Paul David; p/Wheeler Davis (dec); Rose A Nadeau (dec); ed/BA Col of St Rose 1979; pa/Dept Hd Ctl Supply Albany Med Ctr Hosp; Mem New Prod Eval Com, Cheseborough Ponds Inc; Am Hosp Assn, Grantee 1977; NEn NY Chapt Ctl Ser Pers Grantee 1976; Ctl Ser Pers, Ednl Chm NEn NY Chapt; Am Hosp Assocs Res; Hosp Infection Control Com; Parenteral Nutrition Com; Prod Eval Com; r/Cath; hon/W/W in E.

FRANCOIS, EWART IAN oc/Corporate Manager; b/Jul 24, 1935; h/Schillhammer Rd, Jericho, VT 05465; ba/Williston, VT; m/Anna Ginette; c/Graham, Mathew, Maxine;

p/Theodore Agustus Francois (dec); Ellen Honeychurch Francois, Newport Richie, FL; ed/Cert Indust Mgmt & Adm McGill Univ 1972; pa/Corporate Mgr Quality Assurance; r/Anglican.

FRANK, RUTH MARIE FINLEY oc/Civic Worker; Interior Designer; b/May 14, 1925; h/924 Ridgewood Rd, Bloomfield Hills, MI 48013; m/Harold L; c/Gale F Adise (Mrs Stephen Zachary), Kate F Cohen (Mrs Steven Michael); p/Abe H Finley (dec); Dorothy Seidenberg; ed/Syracuse Univ 1943-46; pa/VP Ruth & Harold Frank Interiors Inc 1948–; Commentator *Design for Women*, WWJ-TV 1950-51; Am Fdn Radio & TV Artists; Assoc Mem Americana Fine Arts Com, Dept of St; cp/BSA: Nat Bd Dirs, Nat Coun, Gen Chm 2nd Loan Exhbn Am Furn & Decorative Arts, Nat Nom'g Com, Num Other Local, Area & Nat Ofcs, Cert of Thanks 1956, 63, Thanks Badge 1974; Hon Chperson Grosse Pointe Univ Liggett Antiques Show; Bd Dirs Mich Area Syracuse Univ Alumni Assn; Adv Bd Wom for U Foun; Trustee Detroit Hist Soc; Gov's Spec Adv Com on Narcotics & Dangerous Drug Abuse, Mich Comm on Law Enforcemt & Crim Justice; Nat Trust for Hist Preserv; Nat Archery Assn; Num Other Civic & Spec Interest Activs; r/Detroit Bd Dirs, Nat Coun Jewish Wom 1968-70; hon/Outstg Public Ser Awd City of Detroit 1953; Commr's Civilian Cit #8 Detroit Police Dept 1961, 1st Recip Commr's Cert Apprec 1971; Outstg Alumna Awd Syracuse Univ 1975; Num Other Ser Awds; Biogl Listings.

FRANK, SAM HAGER oc/Educator; b/Jul 23, 1932; h/Chancellor's Home, Louisiana State University, Alexandria, LA; ba/Alexandria; m/Ellen Wilson Snow; c/Marian Elizabeth; p/Edward Lloyd and E Louise Frank, Bradenton, FL; ed/BA 1953, MA 1957 FSU; PhD Univ Fla 1961; mil/AUS 1954-56; pa/Chancellor La St Univ-A; cp/Rotary, Torch Intl; Dem; r/Epis; hon/Fulbright Prof in India 1965-66; Phi Kappa Phi.

FRANKEL, GEORGE JOSEPH oc/- Aerospace Engineer; b/Jan 3, 1923; h/26 Fountain Ln, Jericho, NY 11753; ba/Bethpage, NY; m/Miriam Dorothy Josephson; c/Paul Jay, Alice F Pratt, Lee Jeffrey; p/Joseph and Celia Simon Frankel (dec); ed/BME CCNY 1944; Grad Studies PIB 1968; pa/Aerospace Engr Grumman Aerospace Corp; Am Inst Aeronautics & Astronautics: Assoc Fellow, Chm Long Isl Sect 1976-77; Sr Mem Inst Envir Scis; Nat Fire Protection Assn, Chm Tech

Com on Fire Hazards in Oxygen-enriched Atmospheres 1966-; Am Nat Metric Coun, Chm Engrg Subsector Aerospace Sector Com 1976-; Gen Chm Am Inst Aeronautics & Astronautics/Am Soc for Testing & Mats/Inst Envir Scis/Nat Aeronautics & Space Adm Space Simulation Conf 1973, Tech Prog Chm 1975; Am Vaccum Soc; Pi Tau Sigma; Others; cp/Brichwood Civic Assn Jericho Inc: Past Pres, Former Mem Bd Dirs; BSA; hon/AIAA Long Isl Sect Basil Staros Awd.

FRANKLIN, CALVIN G oc/Colonel; b/Mar 31, 1929; h/San Diego, CA; ba/Washington, DC; m/Betty Marie; c/Gail, Steve, Kevin; p/Scott and L B Gail Franklin (dec); ed/AA; BA; MBA; PhD Cand USIU; mil/US Army War Col; Indust Col Armed Forces; Command & Gen Staff Col; Others; pa/Dir MOBEX Task Force & Chief Mobilization Improvemt Mgmt Ofc, Mobilization Planning Div, DCSOPS, US Army Forces Command; Var Other Mil Assignmts; Fdr & Pres Biomed Technologies Inc; Mgmt Conslt Aero Space Reliability Field 2 Yrs; Others; Past Secy Nat Mgmt Assn; Inst Envir Scis: Bd Dirs, Past Ednl Chm San Diego Chapt; Am Soc for Quality Control; cp/Intl Rotary Clb: Treas, Former Mbrship Chm; r/Prot; hon/Gen Dynamics Elects: Certs of Commend, Pres Awd; Nat Mgmt Assn: Excell Awd, Pres Awd; Profl Pubs; Var Mil Decorations.

FRANKLIN, CECIL LOYD oc/Professor; Priest; b/Aug 2, 1927; h/1704 S Humboldt St, Denver, CO 80210; ba/Denver; m/Gae Robinson; c/Catherine, Paul; p/Marion C Franklin (dec); Ellen Batts Franklin; ed/AB Phillips Univ; STB, STM, PhD Harvard Univ; pa/Ordained Priest 1957; Prof Dept Rel Studies Univ Denver 1966-; cp/Rocky Mtn Meml Soc; Dem; r/Epis.

FRANKLIN, HAROLD ALONZA oc/Educator; b/Nov 2, 1932; h/640 Old Montgomery Rd, Apt 21, Tuskegee, AL 36083; ba/Tuskegee Inst, AL; m/Lilla Sherman; c/Harold Alonza II; p/George and Eugenia Willaims Franklin, Talladega, AL; ed/AB; MA; PhD; mil/USAF 1951-58; pa/Edr Col of Arts & Scis Tuskegee Inst; Assn Social & Behavioral Scists; Ala Hist Comm; Ala Leag for Advmt of Ed; Ala Ctr for Higher Ed; Inst for Ser to Ed; cp/Talladega Co Improvemt Assn; E Ala Planning Comm; Talladega Co Overall Ec Comm; Commun Life Inst; Talladega Co Br NAACP; Ala Coun on Human Relats; Black Coalition Talladega Co; Ala Dem Conf; Talladega Co Dem Exec Com; Talladega Co Ala St Univ Alumni Assn; r/AME of Zion Ch; hon/Recipient S'ships; Sigma Rho Sigma; Tchr of Yr, Talladega Col 1975-76; Christian Yths F'ship Awd; Biogl Listings.

FRANKLIN, WILLIAM H III oc/-Accountant; b/Oct 2, 1946; h/2120 Pinehurst Dr, Newberry, SC 29108; ba/N'berry; m/-Carolyn S; c/Brian D, Kevin A; p/William H Jr and Sara B Franklin, N'berry; ed/BS; CPA Cert; mil/SC NG 1968-74; pa/Cert'd Public Acct; AICPA; SC Assn CPAs; NC Assn CPAs; cp/Masonic; York Rite Masons; Shriner; r/Luth; hon/W/W S&SW.

FRANKLYN, GASTON JOSEPH oc/Educator; Administrator; b/Dec 16, 1936; h/2000 Talbot Rd W, Windsor, Ontario, Canada N9A 6S4; c/2 Chd; p/George and Doris Franklyn; ed/BA Sir George William Univ 1961; MEd Univ Toronto 1963; PhD Univ Ottawa 1971; Addit Studies; pa/Sev Positions w St Clair Col Ed 1973-; Sec'dy Sch Tchr Eng & Social Studies Sir John Franklin Sch, Yellowknife, NW Territories 1964-68; Sec'dy Sch Tchr Eng & Geometry D'Arcy McGee Boys Sch, Montreal 1962-64; Primary Sch Tchr St Dominic's RC Sch, Morvant, Trinidad 1954-57; Other Former Positions; Mem Num Col Coms; VP Windsor/Essex Br Canadian Mtl Hlth Assn 1974-76, Pres 1976-78; Ontario Assn for Curric Devel; Canadian Mtl Hlth Assn; Ontario Ed Assn; Am Assn Higher Ed; Tri-Co Psychol Assn; AASA; Phi Delta Kappa; cp/Former Mem Prog & Budget Review Com U Commun Sers,

Windsor; Windsor Rep on Ed Com, Nat Black Coalition of Canada; hon/Contbr to Profl Jours; Tchr of Yr; Notable Ams.

FRANKS, DOROTHY SEYBOLD HARWARD oc/Retired Social Worker; b/Dec 12, 1911; h/706 Cherry, Mt Carmel, IL 62863; m/Richard H Harward (dec); 2nd Ben H (dec); c/Patrick G Harward; p/Charles C and Thresa Knoerr Seybold (dec); pa/Ret'd Civil Ser, Social Worker; Wabash Co & Cook Co; Former Mem BPW Clb; cp/Former

Activs: BSA, PTA; r/Luth Ch; hon/Hon'd for Essay Written on Fam for Bicent by US Commemorative Gallery; Plaque & Cert of Apprec, Franks Flag, Meml Plate; Essay Entered into Book *Impressions* by The Am Hist Soc to be Entered into the Lib of Cong; World W/W Wom; Personalities W&MW; Intl Registry of Profiles, World Edition.

FRANTZ, ANN BROWNING oc/Training Instructor; b/Oct 23, 1950; h/Box 41, Frontier Ct, Summersville, WV 26651; ba/Craigsville, WV; p/Richard A and

Louraine Martin Frantz, Montgomery, WV; ed/AB; MS; pa/Tng Instr Island Creek Coal Co; r/Presb; hon/W/W Am Wom; Personalities of S; World W/W Wom.

FRANTZ, OLIVE S oc/Bank Executive; b/Jul 9, 1914; h/108 W Douglas Ave, Naperville, IL 60540; ba/Chicago, IL; p/Milton A and Pearl Wessling Frantz (dec); ed/BA w hon N Ctl Col 1938; pa/Harris Bank: Adm Asst, Investmt Mgr; N Ctl Col: Asst Registrar 1938-42, Registrar 1942-43; Am Bus

Wom's Assn; cp/N Ctl Col Alumni Bd; Dir N'ville-NCC Commun Concert Assn; Secy Barrington Pk Camp Meeting Assn; r/Grace U Meth Ch: Com on Missions; No Ill Conf U Meth Ch: Bd Trustees, Bd Evangelism; hon/W/W Rel; Wom of Yr, Am Bus Wom's Assn.

FRANZ, JERRY LOUIS oc/Physician; b/Aug 5, 1943; ba/7711 Louis Pasteur, 801, San Antonio, TX 78229; m/Jennie Heim; c/Tracy, Eric; ed/BS Ohio No Univ 1965; MS Univ Fla 1967; MD Univ Ky Col Med 1971; pa/Thoracic & Cardiovas Surg; Am Med Soc, Student Affil 1967-71; Affil: Fayette Co Med Soc 1971-72, Bexar Co Med Soc 1972, AMA 1974; Tex Med Assn; Cand Group Am Col Surgs 1972; Am Assn for Acad Surg; Aust Soc; Am Col Chest Physicians; Cooley Cardiovas Soc; Bexar Co Hosp: Tissue Com, Operating Room Standards Com; Cardiovas Diseases Com Tex Med Assn; hon/Profl Pubs & Presentations.

FRAUENS, MARIE oc/Semi-Retired Editor; Researcher; Technical Writer; b/Jul 10, 1902; h/923 E Capitol, Washington, DC 20003; ba/Same; p/Frank Henry and Amanda Stansch Frauens (dec); ed/AA; BJ; MA; Postgrad Studies; mil/USNR Ofcrs Sch; Hon Grad Indust Col Armed Forces; USNR: Comm'd Lt (jg) 1943, Perm Rank Lt Cmdr 1949, Lt Cmdr (Ret'd) 1965; pa/Liaison Ofcr USN & US Armed Forces Inst; Tng Ofcr Res & Devel in Fire Control Radar, USN Bur of Ordnance; Histn Fire Control Radar USN Bur Ordnance; Tng Ofcr Nav Resv Tng Pubs Project; Tchr Prin & Dir All Extra-Curric Activs Wardell (Mo) HS; Math Editor Row, Peterson & Co, Evanston, Ill; Chief Editor HS Prog McGraw Hill Book Co, NYC; Tng Dir John I Thompson & Co, Wash DC; Tchr Writer Tactical Doctrine Dept of Navy, Wash DC; Adm Ofcr Ofc of Dir Res & Engrg, Ofc Secy of Def; Other Edit Activs; Res; cp/YWCA, Ks City, Mo; Cnslr Italian Commun Settlemt House, Chicago, Ill; Bd Dirs Nav Gun Factory Wel & Rec Assn; Swimming Instr Pk Bd Ks City (Mo); Reschr Mo St Hist Soc, Columbia; Others; r/Christian; hon/Pi Gamma Mu; Sev Mil Medals.

FRAZIER, LOYD D oc/Administrative Director; b/Aug 12, 1912; h/24600 Clay Rd, Katy, TX 77450; ba/Houston, TX; m/Marjorie; c/Larry, Robert, Carla, Connie, Melinda; p/Delie Frazier, Houston; ed/BS; pa/Adm Dir Harris Co DA Ofc 1972-; Chief Dep Harris Co Sheriff's Ofc 1949; Inst in Criminol Univ Houston 1947; Asst Supt Bur Ident Houston Police Dept 1940; Other Former Positions; Tex Dist & Co Attys Assn; Tex Crime Preven Assn; Nat Dist Attys Assn; SE Tex Assn for Identification & Investigation; Tex Div Intl Assn for Identification; Tex Narcotic Assn; Pharm Soc; Tex St Bar Comm on Revision of Penal Code; Tex Police Assn; cp/Masons; Shrine; PTA Houston; Harris Co Mtl Bd Dirs; Harris Co Fed Credit Bd Dirs; Houston Livestock Assn; Past Pres IAI; r/Meth; hon/Police Awds: B'nai B'rith, Nat Optimist Intl, Tex Govs Ofc, NBC Radio; Biogl Listings.

FRAZIER, WINFRED BRUCE oc/Sales Representative, Business Executive; b/1180 E St #507, Hayward, CA 94541; ba/San Mateo, CA; p/Winfield Guy and Mary Jane Frazier, Salem, OR; ed/AA Cal Concordia Col 1969; pa/Sales Rep Philip Morris, USA, San Mateo; Pres: Am Entertainmt Co (Recording Co), Hayward 1976, Frazier's of Cal (Mail Order Firm), Hayward 1975-; Gen Mgr The Green Lantern Corp, Hayward 1975-76; Featured Skater w Ice Capades, Los Angeles, Cal 1975; Customer Ser Supvr *The Oakland Tribune*, Oakland, Cal 1969-74; Conslt in Fields of Musical Recording & Mail Order Merchandising; Nat Assn Retailers; Nat Assn Perf'g Arts; cp/Exec Com Mem Downtown Hayward Flan'g Team; Am Philatelic Soc; Loyal Order of Moose, Castro Val, Cal; Assoc, Smithsonian Inst, Washington, DC; Consumer's Union Am; Repub Party; r/Luth; hon/Recip PRO DEO ET PATRIA (For God & Country) Awd, BSA; W/W in W.

FREAS, ANNIE BELLE HAMILTON oc/Businesswoman; b/Aug 9, 1904; h/3003 Natchez Trace, Nashville, TN; m/Maurice Henry; p/James N and Emma B McLaughlin Hamilton; ed/Grad Martin Col 1923 (Underwood Typewriter Co Medal); pa/Co-Owner & Bookkeeper Husband's N'ville Gen

Contracting Firm 1958-; Secy & Gen Bkkeeper Freas & Houghland Gen Contractors Inc 1963-; Secy-Treas Freas Constrn Co Inc 1967-; Former Bkkeeper, Hd Acct'g Dept & Asst Comptroller 1925-58: T L Herbert & Sons, W G Bush & Co, Sangravl Co N'ville; Other Former Positions; Wom in Constrn: Charter Mem N'ville Chapt, Dir 1961-63, VP 1963, 64, Pres 1965, Reg #2 Dir 1966, Chm Chapt Activs, Bd Dirs Nat Assn 1966-, Chaired Coms; cp/Zonta Intl, Var Ofcs & Activs; Nat Trust for Hist Preservn; Ladies Hermitage Assn; Assn for Preservn Tenn Antiquities; Tenn Botanical Gardens & Fine Arts Ctr; IPA; Cheekwood YWCA; r/Downtown Presb Ch, N'ville: Charter Mem, Pres Wom of Ch 1961-63, Life Mbrship Pin & Cert for Outstg Work; hon/1st Lady of the Day, WLAC Radio Sta; Wom in Constrn: Wom in Constrn of Yr 1965, Cert of Apprec (for work as Chm of Career Day Vanderbilt Univ); Other Certs of Apprec & Merit; Biogl Listings.

FREDERICK, CAROLYN ESSIG oc/Public Relations Consultant; Lecturer; h/326 Chick Springs Rd, Greenville, SC 29609; ba/Same; m/Holmes Walter; c/Carolyn Williamson (Mrs John Grant), Rosa Margaret Smith (Mrs Glen Clayton); p/Philip Martin and Lillian Hall Essig (dec); ed/BA Agnes Scott Col; pa/Former Newspaper Writer, Advt'g & Public Relats Exec; Conslt 1954-; Asst Dir G'ville Commun Chest & Coun 1950-53; Asst Dir G'ville Symph Orch & Assn 1954-70; AAUW: SC St Pres 1959-61, Br Pres

1944, 57, Nat Coms; cp/Mem SC Ho of Reps 1967-76, Mem Sev Coms; Initiator Arts Fest G'ville 1969; Pres Appointee to Adv Comm John F Kennedy Ctr for Perf'g Arts 1970-76; SC Rep to So Reg Ed Bd 1977-81; Nat Leag Am Pen Wom; Num Civic & Human Sers Bds; r/Presb; hon/Career Wom of Yr 1967, Zonta; SC Wom of Yr 1970, SC Status of Wom Conf; Robert W Beatty Outstg Ser to Yth Awd; Outstg Alumnae Awd, Agnes Scott Col; SC Press Assn Awd.

FREDERICK, JONATHAN ELBERT oc/US Army Officer; b/Feb 12, 1941; h/155E Gardiner Rd, West Point, NY 10996; ba/WP; m/Louise Pendleton; c/Cynthia Lynn, Jonathan Christopher; p/Elva L and Madeline B King Frederick, Central Point, OR; ed/BS NM St Univ 1963; MS Oreg St Univ 1969; mil/AUS Lt Col; US Mil Acad: Asst Prof for Opers 1979-80, Instr Physics 1977-80; cp/BSA, Cubmaster Pack 23; r/WP Epis Congreg: Vestryman, Lay Rdr; hon/AUS Bronze Star; Air Medal; Jt Ser Commend Medal; Commonwealth of Va Profl Engr.

FREDERICK, MARGIE GARRETT

oc/Accountant; b/Oct 3, 1926; h/675 E 33 St, Hialeah, FL 33013; ba/Hialeah; m/A Collins; c/Ronald S, Karen E Sampson (Mrs Gary), Beverly C; p/Walter Terry Garrett, Murfreesboro, TN; Lillian Johnston Garrett, Leesburg, FL; pa/Pres Margie Frederick Income Tax & Acctg Ing; Am Bus Woms Assn; Dir & Ofcr Sev Corps; Mem Var Geneal Socs; cp/Pilot Clb Intl; Hialeah C of C; Better Bus Div (Dade Co); r/Hialeah Ch of Christ: Mem; hon/W/W S&SW.

FREDERICKS, DONALD GREY oc/-Minister; b/Nov 1, 1930; h/3224 Patterson, Flagstaff, AZ 86001; ba/Flagstaff; m/Donna; c/Denice, Debra, Daniel, David; p/Raymond

J and Hilda Fredericks, New Castle, PA; pa/Gen Dir U Indian Missions Inc; Pastor; Conf Spkr; cp/Bd Trustees 2 Public Schs, Navajo Reservations.

FREE, HELEN M oc/Laboratory Director; b/Feb 20, 1923; h/3764 E Jackson Blvd, Elkhart, IN 46514; ba/Elkhart; m/Alfred H; c/6 Chd; p/James Murray, Clearwater, FL; Daisey Piper; ed/AB; MA; pa/Dir Specialty Test Systems Ames Co 1976-; Miles Labs: Ames Growth & Devel Sr New Prods Mgr Microbiol Test Sys 1974-76, New Prods Mgr 1969-74, Clin Test Systems or Chem Test Sys, Am Tech Sers 1966-69, Ames Prod Devel Lab 1964-66, Others; Am Chem Soc: St Joseph Val Secy Secy, Chm, Councilor 1971-, Div Biol Chem, Div Chm, Mktg & Ecs, Others; Am

Assn for Clin Chem; Assn Clin Scists; Am Soc for Med Technol; Fellow: Am Inst Chemists, AAAS; The Chemists Clb (NYC); Iota Sigma Pi; cp/UF; Kappa Kappa Kappa; Elkhart Concert Clb; Bd Dirs Altrusa Clb Elkhart Co; AAUW; Ind St Hlth Coor'g Coun; No Ind Hlth Sys Coun; NOW, Elkhart Co Chapt; Bd Dirs YMCA; Other Civic Assns; r/1st Presb Ch: Elder 1974-, Chperson Stewardship Campaign 1974; hon/Profl Achmt Awd in Nuclear Med, Am Soc for Med Technol; Honoree at Hons Ldrship Luncheon #1, YWCA Elkhart Co; "Bellringer's Awd", Elkhart UF; Profl Pubs; Biogl Listings; Others.

FREED, CURTIS B oc/Assistant Professor; b/May 15, 1933; h/8059 Esterbrook Dr, Nashville, TN 37221; ba/Martin, TN; m/Shirley E; c/Philip Thomas, Frederick Ray; p/William F Freed (dec); Ida P Freed, Souderton, PA; ed/Dipl Nsg Pa Hosp Sch Nsg for Men: BS Rutgers St Univ 1967; MS Vanderbilt Univ 1973; Addit Studies; pa/Asst Prof Nsg Univ Tenn-Martin; ANA; Tenn St Nurses Assn, Dist 3: Bd Dirs, Del to Conv 1975, 76, 77, Secy Psychi-Mtl Hlth Special Interest Group 1975-77; Tenn St Nurses Assn Coun on Pract 1975-76; Nsg & Hlth Progs

Com N'ville Chapt ARC 1974-77; Sigma Theta Tau; Var Spkg Engagemts; Wkshops, Sems, Presentations; cp/Vanderbilt Univ Alumni Assn; Rutgers Univ Col Nsg Alumni Assn; r/Bapt: Former Deacon, Former SS Supt, SS Tchr, Former Yth Ldr; Others; hon/Nat Inst Mtl Hlth Grants (2); Outstg Proficiency in Psychi Nsg, Pa Hosp Sch Nsg; Profl Pubs.

FREEDMAN, DAVID NOEL oc/Professor; b/May 12, 1922; h/PO Box 7434, Liberty Sta, Ann Arbor, MI 48107; ba/Ann Arbor; m/Cornelia; c/Meredith Anne, Nadezhda, David Micaiah, Jonathan Pryor; p/David and Beatrice Goodman Freedman; ed/BA, ThB, PhD; pa/Univ Mich, Ann Arbor 1971-: Prof Biblical Studies, Dir Prog on Studies in Rel; Vis Prof Hebrew Univ, Jerusalem 1976-; Prof Old Testament Grad Theol Union 1964-71; San Francisco Theol Sem: Prof Old Testament 1964-70, Dean of Fac 1966-70, Acting Dean of Sem 1970-71, Gray Prof of Old Testament Exegesis 1970-71; Other Former Tchg Positions; Pres Soc for Biblical Lit 1975-76; Johns Hopkins Univ Centennial Scholar 1976; Editor: Anchor Bible Series 1971-, Bultn of the Am Schs of Oriental Res 1974-, Dir of Pubs, Am Schs of Oriental Res 1974-; Edit Conslt, Genesis Proj 1973-; Chm Coun on Study of Rel in Mich Schs 1972-; VP Am Schs of Oriental Res 1970-; Tech Conslt Milberg Prodns 1961-; Secy-Treas Biblical Colloquium 1958-; Mem Num Learned Socs; Lectr Num Univs; Pubs: (CoAuthor:) An Explorer's Life of Jesus 1975, The Mountain of the Lord 1975, William Foxwell Albright: Twentieth Century Genius 1975, Num Others; Many Editorships; hon/Hon Degs; F'ship; Carey-Thomas Awd 1965.

FREEDMAN, GERALD STANLEY oc/Physician; Consultant; b/May 28, 1936; h/104 Riverview Ave, Branford, CT 06405; ba/Newhaven, CT; m/Karen Kristen; c/David Jordan, Julia Alexandra; p/Martin and Adele Freedman, Mt Vernon, NY; ed/BME; MD; pa/Indsl Conslt Mem Conn Computerized Tomography Task Force 1978-; Dir Radiol Temple Med Ctr, New Haven 1978-; Yale Univ Sch Med, New Haven: Assoc Clin Radiol 1978-, Fac 1968-77; Other Former Positions; Trustee Soc Nuclear Med; Radiol Soc NAm; Am Col Radiol; Am Col Nuclear Physicians; Editor Tomographic Imaging in Nuclear Med, 1973, Mgmt Concepts in Nuclear Med. 1977; Contbr Articles to Profl Jours; hon/Patentee; Biogl Listings.

FREELAND, PHILLIP LOY oc/Executive Director; b/Oct 2, 1951; h/300 S 17th, Frederick, OK 73542; ba/Frederick; p/Albert and Retha Freeland, Frederick; ed/BS; pa/Exec Dir Turning Point Inc; Criminal Justice Coor'g Coun, Okla Assn Yth Sers Inc; cp/JCs, Dir Nat Project Mainstream; Child Wel Leag; NCCD; Dir UF; r/Bapt.

FREELAND, ROBERT LENWARD JR oc/Executive; b/May 5, 1939; h/565 Roosevelt, Gary, IN 46404; ba/Gary; m/Carolyn J; c/Robin, Brandon; p/Robert Freeland Sr, Gary; Mamie O Freeland, Gary; ed/Cert Real Est Ind Univ; pa/Pres Gary

Common Coun; Nat Leag Cities; St Chm Nat Black Caucus; cp/Frontiers Intl; NAACP; Urban Leag; Minority Bus-men Assistance Corp; Nat Bus Leag; BSA; r/Cath; hon/Fab Awd; NAACP Awd; Firefighters Awd; Outstg Yg Man Awd, Ind JCs; W/W in Govt.

FREEMAN, ARTHUR MERRIMON III
oc/Physician; Psychiatrist; Professor; b/Oct
10, 1942; h/3233 E Briarcliff Rd, Birmingham,
AL 35294; ba/B'ham; m/Linda Poynter;
c/Arthur Merrimon IV, Katherin Leigh,
Edward Todd; p/Arthur Merrimon Jr and
Katherine Lide Freeman, B'ham; ed/AB
Harvard Univ 1963; MD Vanderbilt Univ
1967; Psychi Fellow Johns Hopkins Univ
1968-72; mil/USN 1972-74, Lt Cmdr; pa/Univ
Ala: Prof Psychi Dept 1977-, Exec Com Dept
Psychi; Chief Psychi VA Hosp, B'ham; Asst
Prof Psychi Stanford Univ 1974-77; Chief
Resident Psychi Johns Hopkins Hosp 1971-72;
cp/Bd Mem: E Side Mlt Hlth Ctr, Creative
Schs; Spkr; r/Canterbury Meth Ch; hon/Nat
Merit S'ship, Harvard; Fellow, Karolinska
Inst; Fellow, Univ London; Cert'd Am Bd
Psychi; Examr Am Bd Psychi; Conslt'g Editor
Jour Operat Psychi.

FREEMAN, DONALD McKINLEY
oc/Professor, Department Chairman; b/Apr
22, 1931; h/2317 E Michigan St, Evansville, IN
47711; ba/E'ville; m/Ina Benner; p/Major
McKinley and Bertha Wright Freeman,
Asheville, NC; ed/BA cum laude Wake Forest
1954; MA Univ RI 1955; PhD Univ NC-CH
1964; pa/Univ E'ville: Igleheart Prof, Chem
Dept Polit Sci/Public Policy; Am, So, MWn &
SWn Polit Sci Assns; Former Mem Bd Editors
Wn Polit Sci Qtrly; cp/Bd Dirs Commun
Action Prog E'ville; Mayor's Citizens Adv
Com, E'ville; Dir'd Field Work, Var Studies;
r/Presb; hon/Nat Conv F'ship, Dem Nat Conv
1964; Grants; Pub'd Author.

FREEMAN, DORIS BLANTON oc/-
Teacher; b/Apr 5, 1912; h/329 Charlotte Rd,
Rutherfordton, NC 28139; m/George L; c/-
Charles L; p/Burrell Blanton, Ellenboro, NC;
Maggie McKee Blanton, Shelby, NC; ed/BS;
pa/Tchr 45 Yrs; Ret'd 1977, Rutherfordton

Elem Sch (Rutherford Co Sch Sys); NEA;
NCAE; CTA; Classroom Tchrs; Kappa Iota;
NC Ed Assn; cp/PACE; PTA; Wom's Clb;
r/Bapt; hon/Personalities of S; W/W
Commun Ser.

FREEMAN, FRED RANDALL oc/Pastor;
b/Jan 23, 1947; h/PO Box 125, Guyton, GA
31312; ba/Guyton; m/Shirley Jean Ansley;
p/Fred and Elise Montford Freeman,
Glenwood, GA; ed/Theol Bapt Bible inst;
pa/Pastor Pine St Bapt Ch, Guyton;
Effingham Co Min Assn; Pres Mid Bapt
Pastors' Conf 1974-; Mid Bapt Assn;
cp/Guyton 5th Sunday Morning Civic
Breakfast clb; r/So Bapt; hon/W/W in Rel;
Personalities; Notable Ams; Cits, Billy
Graham Sch Evangel, Birmingham, Ala &
Atlanta, Ga; Adv'd Dipls.

FREEMAN, HAROLD F oc/Editor-in-
Chief; b/Mar 1, 1918; h/912 Newcastle Ave,
Westchester, IL 60153; ba/W'chester;
m/Esther Lucille; c/Harold Philip; p/Harold F
Freeman (dec); Leona Frances Powell (dec);
ed/ThB; mil/85th Inf Div, 339 Inf Regiment,
Co F (Italy), WWII; pa/Editor-in-Chief *Voice*
Mag, Ofcl Jour Indep Fundamental Chs of
Am; Pastor: Vallejo Bible Ch, Vallejo, Cal
1964-77, Salina Bible Ch, Salina, Ks 1956-64,
Grace Bapt Ch, St Louis, Mo 1948-56; IFCA:
Pres Ks Reg, Secy, VP, Pres No Cal Reg, Nat
Exec Com 1968-71, 1972-75, Rec'g Secy (Nat)
1968-71, 1972-75; Bd Mem Bible Ch Crusade,
Santa Rosa, Cal 1965-77; Adv Bd Chinese
Bible Evangel, SF: Missionaries for Christ Intl,

Bd Mem; Bd Mem Ill Bible Ch Mission; Adv
Bd Servicemen for Christ, Vallejo, Cal;
Others; r/Indep; hon/Contenders Awd, Am
Coun Christian Chs; Combat Infantryman's
Badge; 3 Battle Stars.

FREEMAN, HUGH WARD oc/Vending
Manager; b/Aug 28, 1948; h/9001 Patterson
Ave #118, Richmond, VA 23229; ba/Same;
m/Teresa Ann Clayton; c/Ann Martin;
p/Henry Ward Freeman, Anniston, AL;
Jacqueline Laughridge Harrelson (dec);
ed/Assoc Bus Adm; mil/USN 4 Yrs;
cp/Former Mem Pulaski JCs; r/Epis;
hon/Outstg Yg Men Am Awd; Cert of Merit,
Pulaski JCs; Spoke Awd, Cand's Clb, Va JCs.

FREEMAN, JAMES GOODRICH
oc/Beverage Company Executive; h/1 Buxley
Ct, Fredericksburg, VA 22401; ba/F'burg;
m/Nancy Hill; c/James Goodrich Jr, Virginia
Ann; p/Rodney and Virginia Ann Freeman,

F'burg; ed/BS Huron Col; pa/Pres Chatham
Beverage Co; VP Freeman Beverage Co; Va
MAIT Beverage Assn; cp/Huron Col Alumni;
Va JC Ofcr; Chm Bd F'burg JCs; r/Bapt;
hon/Outstg 1st Yr JC, Va JCs; Top 10 Outstg
1st Yr JCs, US JCs; Outstg Yg Men Am.

FREEMAN, JEROME WARREN
oc/Professor; h/PO Box 148, Danville, KY
40422; ba/Chackasha, OK; m/Helen Beatrice;
c/Jerome Warren Jr, Michael L; p/George L
and Ida Helen Freeman (dec); ed/BA; MEd;
MA; EdD; pa/Prof & Dir Deaf Ed Univ Sci &
Arts of Okla 1975-78; Asst Supt 1972-74; Prin

1969-71; Supv'g Tchr 1966-68; Tchr of Deaf
1952-65; Lectr; CAID; CEASD; NFSD;
r/Bapt; hon/Phi Delta Kappa; Hanson
Ldrship Awd; W/W Am Cols & Univs.

FREEMAN, LEONARD MURRAY
oc/Physician; Educator; b/Apr 20, 1937; h/65
Oak Dr, E Hills, NY 11576; ba/Bronx, NY;
m/Marlene; c/Eric Lawrence, David Robert;
p/Joseph and Tillie Freeman, Miami Beach,
FL; ed/BA NYU 1957; MD Chicago Med Sch
1961; pa/AECOM: Prof Radiol 1977, Assoc
Prof 1974-77, Asst Prof 1967-72, Instr Radiol
1965-67, Co-Dir Div Nuclear Med 1965-,
Other Positions; Montefiore Hosp & Med Ctr:
Chief Dept Nuclear Med 1976-, Adj Att'g
Radiologist 1967-76, Att'g Radiologist 1977-;
Bronx Mun Hosp Ctr & HAECOM: Asst Att'g
Radiologist 1965-67, Assoc Att'g Radiologist
1967-77, Att'g Radiologist 1977-; Soc Nuclear
Med: VP 1977-78, Editor "Newslines" 1977-78,
Chm Task Force on Future Directions in
Nuclear Med 1977-78, Pres 1979-80;
Diplomate: Am Bd Radiol, Am Bd Nuclear

Med, Am Bd Radiol; Edit Conslt Physicians
Desk Ref for Radiol & Nuclear Med 1970-;
Lectr: USPHS Hosp 1967-77, St Barnabas
Hosp for Chronic Diseases 1967-, Beth Israel
Med Ctr 1974-, Maimonides Hosp 1975-,
Others; Fellow Am Col Radiol; Am Col
Nuclear Phys; Assn Univ Radiol; Radiol Soc
NAm; Other Profl Assns; Var Edit Positions;
r/Hebrew; hon/Dist'd Alumnus Awd, Chgo
Med Sch; Hon Mem, Tex Radiol Soc; Hon Life
Mem, Pan Am Med Assn; Hon Chapt Mem, S
African Nuclear Med Soc; Hon Life Mem,
Long Isl Soc Nuclear Med Technologists; Num
Pubs.

FREEMAN, RALPH CARTER JR
oc/Investment Counselor; Certified Public
Accountant; Certified Management
Consultant; b/Mar 6, 1937; h/235 Kulamanu
Pl, Honolulu, HI 96816; ba/Honolulu;
m/Nancy Lynn; c/Ralph Carter III, Allyson

Louise, Stephens Cordell, LeAnna Torbert;
p/Ralph C and Alice C Freeman, LaGrange,
GA; ed/BBA; pa/Am Inst CPAs; Hi & Ga
Socs CPAs; Inst Mgmt Conslts; Intl Assn Fin
Planners; Nat Assn Securities Dealers;
cp/Trustee Honolulu Theatre for Yth; C of C;
r/Prot.

FREESE, HOWARD LEE oc/Executive;
b/Dec 9, 1941; h/2729 Hampton Ave,
Charlotte, NC 28207; ba/Charlotte; c/Laura
Katharine, Daniel Friedrich, Matthew
Stephen; p/Floyd H and Alice O Freese,
Adrian, MI; ed/BS Columbia 1965; MBA
Syracuse 1972; pa/VP Luwa Corp; Am Inst
Chem Engrs, Chm Ctl Carolinas Sect 1974-75;
Am Chem Soc; Chem Mktg Res Assn; Am
Mgmt Assn; cp/Mkt Task Force Charlotte C
of C; Mason; Shriner; r/Presb; hon/Order of
the Owls; Theta Tau; Beta Gamma Sigma;
W/W: Engrg, S&SW; Author & Coauthor 6
Tech Papers.

FREEZE, ELIZABETH BOULDIN
oc/Resource Teacher; b/Oct 1, 1942; h/4506
Belvoir Dr, Greensboro, NC 27406;
m/Wayne; c/1 Son; p/Edgar and Jewel
Bouldin; ed/BA Elon Col 1964; Grad Work;
pa/Tchr Mtly Retard & LD, Alamance &
Guildford Cos 1964-70; Resource Tchr Mtly
Retard & LD 1970-77; Resource Tchr LD
1977-; Guilford Co Assn Edrs: VP 1972-73,
Pres 1973-74, Parliamentn 1975-76; Guilford
Co Assn Classroom Tchrs, Pres-elect 1978-79;
Mem St ACT Govt Relats Com 1978-79; Chm
G'boro NCAE Elections Com 1975-76; ACT
PRR Com 1976-77; Orgr 1st Co NCAE-ACT
Newslttr & Served on Coms; Sch Fac Rep
NCAE & Del to 7 St NCAE Convs; Nat Assn
Edrs & Classroom Tchrs; Nat, St & Local
Assns for Chd w LD; cp/PTA; Guilford Co
EMR-LD Curric Com; Sch Assessmt Com
Chm; Sch Chm U Way Campaign; Cub Scout
Den Mother; Campaign Wkr for Polit Cands;
Repub Party Precnt Chm; Others; r/Immanuel
Bapt Ch, G'boro: GA Dir, WMU Dir, Exec
Coun Mem, Nom'g Com, SS Class Pres, Host
Fam for Intl Students, Sum Bible Day Camp
for Chd Dir, Tchr Home & Fgn Mission Study
Courses; hon/Pub'd Author; Biogl Listings;
Co Terry Sanford Awd for Creativity &
Innovation in Tchg; Selected by NC as 1 of 12
Master Tchrs.

FREEZE, MATTIE ELIZABETH
oc/Teacher; b/Oct 1, 1942; h/4506 Belvoir
Dr, Greensboro, NC 27406; ba/McLeansville,
NC; m/Roger Wayne; c/John Franklin;

p/James Edgar and Emma Jewel Bouldin, Pittsboro, NC; ed/BA; pa/Tchr LD M'ville Sch; NEA; Started 1st NCAE-ACT Co Newslttr; PACE Interviewing Team; NCAE-ACT Com Mem; ACLD; NCAE Elections Com Chm; ACT PRR Com Chm; St ACT Gov Relats Com; Guilford Co NCAE: Pres, VP, Parlimentn; Pres-elect Guilford Co ACT; cp/Gov's Inaugural Ball; Cub Scouts; Little Leag Baseball; Precnt Chm Repub Party; Polit Party Campaign Wkr; Host Fam to Intl Students; r/Bapt: GA Dir, Sum Bible Day Camp Dir, SS-Tng Union Tchr, Assnl Cnslr Resident & Day Camp, Others; hon/Terry Sanford Awd for Creativity; Intl W/W Commun Ser; DIB; Personalities S; Notable Ams; Commun Ldrs & Noteworthy Ams; W/W Child Devel Profls; Book of Honor.

FREIBERT, LUCY M oc/Associate Professor; b/Oct 19, 1922; h/2121 Cherokee Pkwy, Louisville, KY 40204; ba/L'ville; p/Joseph A Freibert (dec); Amelia J Freibert, Jackson, MS; ed/AB Spalding Col 1957; MA

St Louis Univ 1962; PhD Univ Wis 1970; pa/Assoc Prof Eng Univ L'ville; Mod Lang Assn; Nat Wom's Studies Assn; Nat Org Wom; Melville Soc; cp/Ky Civil Liberties Union; Wom's Agenda; r/Cath.

FREILINGER, JAMES EDWARD oc/Executive; b/Mar 11, 1939; h/1107 Shore Rd, Cape Elizabeth, ME 04107; ba/Portland, ME; m/Mary Catherine Danoski; c/Sarah Anne, Peter Joseph; p/Otto P and Martha Jane Hancock Freilinger, Aurora, IL; ed/BA (Phil); BA (Theol); CLU; pa/Pres-Gen Agt Cameron, Freilinger, Chartered 1973-; Co-Gen Agt Mass Mutual Life Ins Co, Me Agy 1976-; Agt NWn Mutual Life Ins Co, Chicago, Ill & Portland, Me 1969-74; Asst Mgr Continental Ill Bk & Trust Co, Chgo 1967-69; Tchr & Asst Hdmaster Marmion Mil Acad, Aurora, Ill 1963-67; Life & Qualifying Mem Million Dollar Round Table: So Me Life Underwriters; Past Pres, Current Nat Com-man & Bd Mem, Former Chm LUPAC; Former Mem Bd Dirs Me Assn Life Underwriters; Me Chapt Chartered Life Underwriters; Me Estate Planning Coun; cp/Am Heart Assn, Me Affil: Exec Com, St Fund Raising Chm; Former Mem Review Com Cath Convocation Diocese of Me; Chm Bd Rel Ed, Diocese of Me; r/Rom Cath; hon/W/W in E; Nat Quality Awd; Nat Sales Achmt Awd.

FREIMAN, MARSHALL oc/Doctor of Dental Surgery; b/Apr 14, 1941; h/9439 N Broadmoor Rd, Bayside, WI 53217; ba/Milwaukee, WI; m/Donna M; c/Karen Ann, Debbie Kim; p/Edward A and Mildred Freiman, Lauderhill, FL; ed/DDS; mil/Capt; pa/Blue Cross Dental Conslt; Pres & Chm Bd: Westport Dental Group, Westport DentaCare Group; r/Bayside Firefighters Assn, Fire & Rescue; hon/W/W in MW.

FRENCH, JEANA TURNER oc/Educator; b/Feb 22, 1947; h/3509 Turkey Run Ln, Tallahassee, FL 32312; ba/Tallahassee; m/John H Jr; p/C A and Myra H Turner, Tallahassee; ed/BS 1967, MS 1970, PhD 1972 Fla St Univ; pa/IRA; Nat Coun Social Studies; Nat Assn for Ed of Yg Chd; Assn for Supvn & Curric Devel; Assn for Childhood Ed; cp/FSU: Former Mem Col of Ed Bd Dirs, 25th Commemorative Anniv Comm; Fla Dem Credentialing Com; r/Meth; hon/Phi Delta Kappa; Kappa Delta Pi; Phi Kappa Phi; Alpha

Delta Gamma; W/W Am Wom.

FRENCH, RUTH EVELYN oc/Retired Educator; b/May 27, 1905; h/2 Grove St, Proctor, VT 05765; p/Charles Elliot and Grace Worden French; ed/PhB 1927, MA 1941 Univ Vt; pa/Atlantic City (NJ) HS: Eng Tchr 1946-58, Hd Eng Dept 1958-70, Dir Drama 1946-70; Spch & Drama Tchr Northampton HS, Mass 1942-46; Other Former Positions; CoDir 5 Pageants Held in Atl City Conv Hall; Tchr Atl Commun Col 1963-65; Past Pres NJ Assn Tchrs Eng; NJ St Div Delta Kappa Gamma; Atl City Br AAUW; Pres Rutland Co Ret'd Tchrs Assn 1974-76; cp/Pres Proctor Hist Soc; Served as Stage Dir Commun Concerts Series, Atl City; r/Union Ch of Proctor: Trustee 1974-; hon/Pub'd Author; Intl Reg Profiles; World W/W Wom.

FRENCH, SUSAN FLETCHER oc/-Professor; b/Sept 26, 1943; ba/Davis, CA 95616; c/Sarah H; p/Robert L and Betty B Fletcher, Seattle, WA; ed/AB Stanford Univ 1964; JD Univ Wash 1967; pa/Prof Law Univ Cal-D; Bd Editors *Barrister* Mag (ABA); hon/Order of Coif; Articles Editor, *Washington Law Review*, 1966-67.

FREUNDT, ALBERT HENRY JR oc/Clergyman; Educator; b/Jun 14, 1932; h/415 Trailwood Dr, Clinton, MS 39056; ba/Jackson, MS; m/Alene Doss; c/Albert Henry III, James Calvin; p/Albert Henry Freundt (dec); Jewel Saturday Freundt

Pennington, Savannah, GA; ed/BA King Col; MDiv Columbia Theol Sem; pa/Reformed Theol Sem, Jackson: Prof Ch Hist & Policy, Chm Dept Hist Theol, VP Denom Affairs; r/Presb Ch US; Stated Clerk: Presby of Ctl Miss, Synod of Mid-S.

FREY, BARBARA R oc/University Administrator; b/Jun 14, 1921; h/1982 Delaware Ave, Buffalo, NY 14216; ba/Buffalo; p/Ernest B and Ruth B Frey, Hamburg, NY; ed/BEd; MEd; EdD; pa/VP for Acad Affairs St Univ Col-B; Mis Sts Assn; NCATE; ASCD; cp/Zonta Clb Intl; r/Prot; hon/Delta Kappa Gamma; Phi Delta Kappa; Pi Lambda Theta; Kappa Delta Pi; Outstg Edr 1971.

FREY, EDITH TURNER oc/Educator; b/Feb 27, 1912; h/Rt 14, Box 469 D, Cullman, AL 35055; m/William Martin; c/Frank Turner, William M; ed/Miss St Col for Wom 1929-30; Univ Miami 1930-37; BA w hons 1946, MA 1952 St Univ Ia; Univ Glasgow (Scotland) 1964-65; MA Ohio St Univ 1967; Assoc Prof Eng Campbell Col, Buies Creek, NC 1967-; Tchg Asst Ohio St Univ 1965-67; Dean of Wom Col of Wooster 1961-64; Other Former Positions; NCTE; Delta Kappa

Gamma: S'ship Chm, Mbrship Chm; Delta Pi Epsilon; Pi Omega Pi; AAUW; Nat Assn Wom Deans & Cnslrs 1956-66; NC Lit & Hist Assn; S Atl Mod Lang Assn; NC, Va Eng Assns; cp/Mem at Large Campbell Col Liaison Mem; Former Mem Altrusa; Friends of Col Inc, NC St Univ; r/Presb Ch: Ruling Elder; hon/Outstg Edrs Am.

FREY, THOMAS L oc/Associate Professor; b/Oct 31, 1936; h/612 W Ohio, Urbana, IL 61801; ba/Urbana; m/Beverly A; c/-Stephen T, David T; p/Thomas R and Dorothy B Frey, Carthage, IL; ed/BS 1958; MS 1959; PhD 1970; Accredited Rural Appraiser & CPA; pa/Assoc Prof Agri Fin Univ Ill; cp/Past Chm Boy Scout Troop Com; Rotary Intl; r/Meth; hon/Dist'd Undergrad Tchg Awd, Am Agri Ec Assn; Ensminger-Interst Outstg Tchr Awd, Nat Assn Cols & Tchrs of Agri; Outstg Tchr Awd, Ctl US Reg, NACTA; Tchr Fellow, NACTA.

FRICK, (ALMA) ELIZABETH oc/Retired Librarian; b/Jan 18, 1913; h/212 Redan, Houston, TX 77009; p/Herman and Maud Price Frick (dec); pa/Ret'd Houston Public Lib 1971 (Poet Clerk, Catalog Dept); City Clerk, Lehigh, Okla 1942-43; cp/Sugar Ration Bd, Lehigh; Former Mem City Election Bd, Lehigh; r/Zion Luth: Active Mem; hon/HS Valedictorian; Poet-Laureate, Houston Public Lib; Intl W/W Poetry; Others.

FRICK, KENNETH EUGENE oc/Businessman; Executive; b/Apr 30, 1920; h/Rt One, Box 318, Arvin, CA 93203; ba/Arvin; m/Margaret Ann Janes; c/Linda Ann, Gail Elizabeth, David Janes; p/Forrest and Ruth McKay Finlayson Frick, Bakersfield, CA; ed/BS Univ Cal 1941; mil/USAF Capt 1941-45; pa/Owner Kenmar Farm; Partner Killdeer Farms; Exec VP Wn Cotton Growers Assn 1978-; USDA: Admr Agri Stabilization & Conservation Ser 1969-77, Exec VP & Bd Dirs

Commodity Credit Corp; Chm Standing Com Intl Cotton Adv Com; Del Intl Inst Cotton 1969-77; Food & Agri Com C of US 1978-; Nat Cotton & Cottonseed Res Adv Bd 1961-63; Pres Cal Planting Cottonseed Distributors 1963-68; Chm Res Com Nat Cotton Coun 1967-68; Bd Mem Cotton Inc 1965-68; cp/Mem Natural Resources Coun Repub Nat Com; Rotary; Former Mem Sch Bd, Arvin; hon/Pers Mgmt Improvemt Cert; Dist'd Ser Awd, USDA.

FRICK, MARGARET ANN JANES oc/Businesswoman; b/Apr 14, 1923; h/Rt One, Box 318, Arvin, CA 93203; m/Kenneth E; c/Linda Ann, Gail, David; p/Max Janes; Mary Stannard, Bakersfield, CA; ed/AA 1943, Elem Credential 1944 Univ Cal; Co-Owner Kenmar Farms 1947-; Elem Tchr Elk Hills, Cal 1944-46; X-ray Lab Cowell Hosp, Univ Cal-B 1943; AAUW; Cal Wom for Agri; cp/Bd Mem Kern View Foun Mtl Hosp; Former Mem Vol Staff White House Communs; Pres & Fdr Saturday Adventurers (for elem chd); Delta Delta Delta; Jr Leag; LWV; Japanese Intl Clb; Fdg Bd Mem "Repub Woms Fed Forum", Wash DC; Former Mem "Welcome to Wash" Intl Govt Clb; Other Civic Activs; hon/Pub'd "Welcome", Booklet for Adm Families, 1974.

FRIDDLE, DALE J oc/Minister; b/Dec 5,

1931; h/1490 29th Ave NW, New Brighton, MN 55112; ba/New Brighton; m/Ellen Jane; c/Diane Kay, Steven Dale; p/Ralph Friddle (dec); Thelma Friddle, Wilkinson, IN; ed/BA, BTh Minn Bible Col; MDiv Lincoln Christian Sem; pa/Com Mem NAm Christian Conv; Secy Bd Trustees Minn Bible Col; Minneapolis Min Assn; Advr Univ Christian Foun; r/Christian Ch; hon/Chiefs Awd of Merit, Mpls Police Dept.

FRIED, HERB G oc/Advertising Executive; Entertainment Promoter; b/Jun 21, 1938; ba/588 Fifth Ave, New York, NY 10036; m/Priscilla; c/David, Jennifer; p/Julius and Clara Fried; ed/BA; MBA; mil/USAR; pa/MBCA; EST.

FRIEDDLANDER, WALTER ANDREW oc/Professor Emeritus; b/Sept 20, 1890; h/6437 Regent St, Oakland, CA 94618; ba/Berkeley, CA; m/(dec); c/Dorothee Mindlin; pa/Prof Emeritus Social Wel Univ Cal-B; hon/Social Wkr of Yr, Oakland City Coun; Gold Medal, NASW.

FRIEDLIEB, LESLIE AARON oc/Advertising & Marketing Executive; b/Sept 16, 1936; h/292 Clermont Terr, Union, NJ 07083; ba/Union; m/Rosie Colombo; c/Katharine, Jennifer; p/Theodore and Gertrude Friedlieb, Kew Gardens, NY; ed/BS Queens Col CUNY 1959; MBA Baruch Col CUNY 1971; Addit; pa/Pres Advt'g & Mktg Communs Co; Editor NJ Bus & Profl Advt'g Assn Newslttr 1965-66; Am Mktg Assn, Communs Com; Am Mgmt Assn, Packaging Adv Com 1965-; NJ Mfr's Assn; cp/Dem Clb; Cosmo Clb; hon/Author Articles; Sigma Alpha Mu; Awds in Printing, Graphics & Design; W/W: Packaging, E.

FRIEDMAN, ALAN WARREN oc/-Professor; b/Jun 8, 1939; h/7202 Running Hope Cir, Austin, TX 78731; ba/Austin; m/-Maxine T; c/Eric Lawrence, Scot Bradley, Lorraine Eve; p/Leon and Anne Friedman, Lauderdale Lakes, FL; ed/BA Queens Col 1961; AM NY Univ 1962; PhD Univ Rochester

1966; pa/Prof Eng Univ Tex-A; Sr Fulbright Prof Univ Lancaster 1977-78; Dir Plan II (UT's Hons Prog); cp/Fdr & Chair Neighborhood Assn; Chair Dem Precnt Conv & St Del; Bd Mem Hillel Foun; r/Jewish; hon/Nat Endowmt for Humanities F'ship; UT Res Grants; Omicron Delta Kappa.

FRIEDMAN, JACOB SANDER oc/Rabbi; b/Jan 14, 1933; h/1207 Lawrence Ave, Ocean, NJ 07712; ba/Ocean; m/Carminda; c/Raymond, Anita F Lupow, Carol; p/Joseph and Ruth Friedman, Jersey City, NJ; ed/BA Trinity Univ; MA Univ Ind; Rabbi Rabbi Jacob Joseph Sem; mil/AUS 1951-54; pa/Currently Spiritual Ldr Temple Beth Torah, Ocean 1965-; Asst Rabbi & Yth Dir Congreg Sons of Israel, Jersey City; Spiritual Ldr: Congreg Kneset Israel, Kittanning, Pa, Tree of Life Congreg, Uniontown, Pa; Steering Com No NJ U Synagogue Am Yth Comm; Intl Ctl Yth Comm U Synagogue of Am; Indep Rabbinate Am, Nat Treas 1975; Past Pres Shore Area Bd Rabbis; Fdg Mem & Former Dean Solomon Schechter Sch Ctl NJ; cp/Nat Dep Chaplain Jewish War Vets; Post Chaplain Jewish War Vets Post 125; Past Pres Exc Clb Long Br; Chm Commun Relats Coun Fdn Monmouth Co; Chaplain Wanamasse Fire & First Aid Squads; r/Jewish; hon/Israel's Man

of Yr Awd, St of Israel Bonds 1975; Articles Pub'd; Coauthor Weekly Bible Study Series, 1974; W/W in Am; Intl W/W.

FRIEDMAN, JULIAN RICHARD oc/Attorney-at-Law; b/Oct 9, 1936; h/Star Rt #1, Box 25W, Bluffton, SC 29910; ba/Savannah, GA; m/Em Olivia Bevis; c/Sheldon Arthur, Esther Bess; p/W Leon and Evelyn Sarah Friedman, Savannah, GA; ed/BA Emory Univ 1956; JD cum laude Univ Ga Sch Law 1959; LLM NY Univ Law Sch 1964; mil/Ga Air NG Capt; pa/Admitted to Ga Bar 1958; Assn W Leon Friedman, Savannah 1959, 1961-63; Cheatham, Bergen & Sparkman, Savannah 1960; Adams, Adams, Brennan & Gardner, Savannah: Assoc 1965-, Partner 1968; r/Jewish; hon/Nat Hon S'ship, Univ Chgo Law Sch; Tchg Fellow, NY Univ Law Sch; Phi Delta Phi; Outstg Grad Awd; Henry Shinn Meml Awd; Phi Beta Kappa; Phi Kappa Phi.

FRIEDMAN, LINDA E oc/University Administrator; b/Jun 30, 1944; h/2364 Holly, Fayetteville, AR 72701; ba/F'ville; p/Sam and Harriet Friedman, Boynton Beach, FL; ed/BA Univ Colo 1966; MA Univ NM 1968; pa/Univ Ark: Asst Dir Housing 1976-, Asst Dean Students 1968-76; Nat Assn Student Pers Admrs Reg IV-W, Dir Profl Devel; Nat Assn Wom Deans, Cnslrs & Admrs; Mortar Bd Dirs of Communs; cp/LWV; Wom's Polit Caucus; r/Jewish; hon/Mortar Bd; W/W: Am Wom, Among Students.

FRIEDMAN, LORA R oc/Educator; b/Nov 29, 1930; h/38 Bonita Dr, Newport News, VA 23602; ba/Newport News; p/Milton Moskowitz (dec); Esta Borofsky Moskowitz, Orlando, FL; ed/BS CCNY; MA;

EdD Univ Fla 1967; pa/Edr Christopher Newport Col; AAUP; AAUW; IRA; VCRE; AERA; AAHE; cp/Bd Mem YWCA; Tidewater Epilepsy Assn Bd; Campaign Coor; hon/Delta Kappa Gamma; Phi Delta Kappa; Kappa Delta Pi; Pi Lambda Theta; Ser Plaque, Newport News Rdg Coun.

FRIEDMAN, PHILIP HARVEY oc/Clinical Psychologist; b/Oct 4, 1941; h/46 Red Rowen Ln, Plymouth Meeting, PA 19462; ba/Phila; m/Teresa Jean Molinaro-Friedman; c/Mathew Alan; p/Leonard and Miriam Rosalyn Friedman; ed/BA Columbia Col 1963; MA 1965, PhD 1968 Univ Wis; pa/Pvt Pract Psychotherapy, Phila & Plymouth Meeting 1974-79; Dir Tng Fam & Chd's Ser of CATCH CMHC, Phila 1979; Jefferson Univ, Dept Psychi & CMHC, Phila: Prog Admr 1978, Asst Prof 1977, Instr 1975, Sr Fam Therapist 1973; Child Psychologist NW Mtl Hlth Ctr, Phila 1971-74; Clin En Pa Psychi

Inst, Phila 1969-73; Fellow Am Orthopsychi Assn; Am Psychol Assn; Assn Marriage & Fam Therapists; Am Acad Psychotherapists; Assn Humanistic Psychol; Am Fam Therapy Assn; Pa Psychol Assn; Phila Soc Clin Psychologists; cp/Cert'd Tchr Siddha; Yoga; Common Cause, ACLU; r/Jewish; hon/NIMH Post-doct; Res F'ship; W/W in E; Pub'd Papers.

FRIEDMAN, RICHARD NATHAN oc/Lawyer; b/Jun 13, 1941; h/Miami, FL; ba/100 N Biscayne Blvd, Miami, FL 33132; m/Catherine H; c/Melissa D; p/Martin Harry Friedman (dec); Caroline Friedman Shaines, Miami; ed/BA 1962, JD 1965 Univ Miami; LLM Georgetown Law Ctr; pa/ABA; Fed, Fla, Dade Co, Intl, Inter-Am Bars; Unified Bar DC; Am Soc Intl Law; World Peace Through Law; Adj Prof Univ Miami Sch Law; Columnist "Securities Today", Miami Review, Business Ldr; Arbitrator NYSE Inc; cp/Fdr & Pres: Am Stockholders Assn Inc, Stop Transit Over People Inc; Charter Mem Pres' Clb, Univ Miami; Univ Miami Endowmt Com; Others; hon/Certs of Apprec: Lions Clbs, Kiwanis Clbs, Rotary Intl Clbs, Dade Co Bar Assn, Others; Cert of Merit, Dade Co Bar Assn; "Ride-a-long" Prog, Richard N Friedman Week (1978), City of Homestead, Fla; Hon Citizen, St of Tenn.

FRIEND, EDITH OVERTON oc/Extension Home Economist; b/Jun 5, 1928; h/Lovingston, VA 22949; ba/L'ton; m/Warren Glenn; c/Kathryn Louise, Mary Elizabeth (dec), Samuel Warren (dec); p/George Hiram Overton (dec); Carrie Elizabeth Overton, L'ton; ed/BA Asbury Col; MA WVa Univ; pa/Ext Home Economist VPI&SU 1968-; Instr Home Ecs Concord Col 1966-68; Home Ec Tchr Mercer Co Bd Ed 1966; Other Former Positions; Nat Home Demonstration Agts Assn, Nat Chm St Pres' Group 1958; WVa Wom Ext Wkrs Assn: St VP 1957-58, St Pres 1959-60; WVa Home Ecs Assn: Chm Ext Sect 1956-58, St Mbrship Chm 1958-60; Nat & Va Assns Ext Home Ecs; Am Sch Food Ser Assn; Am & Va Home Ecs Assns; E Ctl Dist Ext Home Economists, Secy 1970; Epsilon Sigma Phi, Alpha Gamma Chapt; Sigma Phi; Va Del to NAEHE Meeting, Miami, Fla 1971; Pres-elect Va Ext Ser Assn Inc 1978; Others; cp/Beta Sigma Phi; Former Scrapbook Chm Nelson Co Garden Clb; Former Mem WVa Univ Home Economists Alumnae Assn; Asbury Col Alumni Assn; OES, Chapt #95, Former Worthy Matron; Past Pres Cranesville Homemaker's Group; Other Civic Activs; r/Wesleyan U Meth Ch; Pres Wom's Soc Christian Ser 1969-71; hon/DIB; 2000 Wom Achmt; World W/W Wom; Intl W/W Commun Ser; Notable Ams Bicent Era; Personalities of S; Royal Blue Book; Nat Reg Prom Ams; W/W Am Wom; Commun Ldrs of Va.

FRIIS, ERIK J oc/Editor, Publisher; b/Apr 5, 1913; h/19 Shadow Ln, Montvale, NJ 07645; m/Sylvia K; c/Erik S, Elin S; p/(dec); ed/BS; MA; pa/Editor Emeritus Scandinavian Review; Editor & Pubr Scandinavian-Am Bulletin; Gen Editor "The Lib of Scandinavian Lit"; Translator Books from Scandinavian Langs; r/Luth; hon/K's Cross 1st Class Finnish Order of the Lion; K's Cross 1st Class Norwegian Order of St Olav; K's Cross Icelandic Order of Falcon; K's Cross 1st Class

Swedish Order of N Star; Hall of Honor, Norwegian-Am Mus, Decorah. Ia; US Medal of Antarctica Ser; Arts & Lttrs Awd, Finlandia Foun; Others.

FRIMER, NORMAN E oc/Educator; Administrator; b/Aug 3, 1916; h/1220 E W Highway, Silver Spring, MD 20910; ba/Washington, DC; m/Esther; c/Aryeh, Dov, Shael; p/Ber and Rose Frimer (dec); ed/BS cum laude Ill Inst Technol 1941; Ordination Hebrew Theol Col 1941; DHL Yeshiva Univ 1953; pa/Intl Dir B'nai B'rith Hillel Founs 1975-78; Nat Coor B'nai B'rith Hillel Founs, NY Metro Area 1968-75; Vis Prof Dept Judaic Studies Brooklyn Col, CUNY 1972-74; Other Profl Positions; Edit Bd *Tradition Mag,* 1970-; Staff Lectr B'nai B'rith Adult Ed Insts; Co-Fdr: Jewish Yth Coalition on Judaism (Key 73 Era), Jewish Fac CUNY; Del Brussels II Conf on Soviet Jewry; Others; Formr Nat VP Rabbinical Coun Am; cp/Former Mem Adv Coun NY St Senate Com on Higher Ed; Former Del World Zionist Cong; r/Jewish; hon/S'ship, Univ Chgo; Valedictorian, ITT 1941; Phi Delta Kappa; Pub'd Author.

FRINK, CHARLES RICHARD oc/Administrator; b/Sept 26, 1931; h/26 Pawson Landing Dr, Branford, CT 06405; ba/New Haven, CT; m/Roberta Manchester; c/Calvin R, Richard O, Aletta L; p/Richard J and Marjory L Frink, Dryden, NY; ed/BS 1953, PhD 1960 Cornell; MS Univ Cal-B 1957; mil/USN 1953-56, Served to Lt (jg); pa/Soil Chemist; VDir Conn Agri Exp Sta; r/Prot; hon/Res & Conservation Awds; Phi Kappa Phi; Conn Acad Sci & Engrg.

FROHNAPFEL, WILHELMINA oc/Sister of Religious Order; Administrator; b/Sept 11, 1919; h/St Mary of the Springs Convent, N Nelson & Johnstown Rd, Columbus, OH 43219; ba/Columbus; p/Henry and Agatha Haid Frohnapfel (dec); ed/BS Ohio Dominican Col 1953; MS Ohio St Univ 1957; Postgrad Studies; pa/Dir Diocesan Sch Food Ser for Diocese of Columbus 1965-; Tchr: Elem Schs 1939-49, Sec'dy Schs 1949-65; Actd Bd & Chm Mbrship Ohio Nutrition Coun 1971-75; Am, Ohio, Columbus & Franklin Co Home Ecs Assns; Nat Cath Home Ecs, Treas 1967-71; Adv Com on Ed J C Penny Co, Columbus; cp/Former Mem Columbus Epilepsy Assn; r/Rom Cath; hon/10 Yr Ser Pin, Diocese of Columbus; Notable Ams; W/W Sch Dist Ofcls.

FROMBERG, LaVERNE CHARLOTTE RAY oc/Artist; Teacher; b/May 6, 1930; h/1205 N Glenwood Ave, Peoria, IL 61606; ba/Same; m/Gerald (dec); c/Paul Ray, Robert Mathew, Steven Bruce; p/Verne F Ray, Port Townsend, WA; Julia W Orvis, Seattle, WA; ed/BFA, MFA Univ Wash-Seattle; pa/Instr Art Bradley Univ, Peoria 1954-57; Lectr Ill St Univ, Normal 1969-71; Dir Ed & Ext Lakeview Mus, Peoria 1973-77; Instr Art Lakeview M 1977-; One-Wom Shows Fulton Gallery, NYC 1964, 65, 66, 67; Collection Lib of Cong; cp/Bd Mem Peoria Assn for Autistic Chd; Nat Del for Peoria Assn Autistic Chd; hon/Best of Show Awd, New Orleans Art Mus Annual 1954.

FROMMHOLD, LOTHAR WERNER oc/Physicist; b/Apr 20, 1930; h/4706 Ridge Oak Dr, Austin, TX 78731; ba/Austin; m/Margareta Mercedes; c/Sebastian, Caroline; p/Karl Otto Walter Frommhold, Hamburg, Germany; Karoline Frommhold (dec); ed/PhD; pa/Physicist Physics Dept Univ Tex-A.

FROST, WILLIAM P oc/University Professor; b/Jun 26, 1932; ba/Dayton, OH 45469; p/Nicolas Vrasdonk; Catharina Vrasdonk-Leering, Holland; ed/MA; DrsThl; pa/Prof Rel Studies Univ Dayton; Chm CTS, Louisville Reg; Author: *Roots of Am Rel, Transcendental Ethics, Visions of the Divine, The Future Significance of Civilization, Nature & Rel;* Contbr Articles to Prof Jours; r/Cath.

FRUMKIN, GENE oc/Associate Professor; b/Jan 29, 1928; h/3721 Mesa Verda Ave NE, Albuqueque, NM 87110; ba/A'que; c/Celena, Paul Samuel; p/Samuel and Sarah Blackman Frumkin (dec); ed/BA UCLA; pa/Assoc Prof Eng Univ NM; AAUP; r/Jewish.

FRUMKIN, ROBERT MARTIN oc/Behavioral Science Professor; b/Mar 20, 1928; h/19171 Lesure St, Detroit, MI 48235; ba/Detroit; c/Judith; p/S A Frumkin, Irvington, NJ; Anna Gruber Frumkin (dec); ed/BA Upsala Col 1948; MA 1951, PhD 1961 Ohio St Univ; mil/USN Hosp Corps 1946-47; WWII Victory Medal; pa/Behavioral Sci Prof Shaw Col; Exec Dir Pearson Res Inst; cp/Fdr & Current Chperson Mid E Friendship Leag; r/Humanistic Judaism; hon/Men of Achmt; Contemp Authors; Am Men & Wom Sci; W/W: MW, World Jewry.

FRY, JOHAN TRILBY oc/Occupational Therapist; Educator; b/Apr 27, 1937; h/333 Sharon Dr, Cheshire, CT 06410; ba/Hamden, CT; c/Eluned, Erik, Kari Pihl; p/Paul A and Mary G Gifford, N Quincy, MA; ed/AA Westbrook Col; BS Tufts Univ; MA Wn Mich Univ; pa/Edr Quinnipiac Col; New England Occpal Therapy Ed Coun: Chm Steering Com 1977, Secy 1978; Conn Occpal Therapy Assn, Chm Comm on Ed; Am Occpal Therapy Assn; Assn Rehab Tchrs; Am Assn Wkrs for Blind; Am Fdn Tchrs; cp/Vol: UF, Heart Assn, Am Cancer Soc; r/Prot; hon/HEW Grantee.

FRY, MALCOLM CRAIG SR oc/Religious Administrator; b/Jun 6, 1928; h/534 Brewer Dr, Nashville, TN 37211; ba/N'ville; m/Myrtle Mae Downing; c/Pamela Mae, M Craig, Rebecca Dawn, Matthew Dwight; p/Dwight Malcolm Fry, Brenham, TX; Josephine Adrienne Fry (dec); ed/ThB Bible Bapt Sem 1959; BS Austin Peay St Univ 1962; MEd Univ Ariz 1969; DMin Luther Rice Sem 1978; mil/AUS 1946-48; USAF 1951-57; pa/Nat Assn Free Will Bapts (FWB): Gen Dir Ch Tng Ser, Gen Dir, Treas Bd 1972-, Dir Curric & Res Bd Ch Tng Ser 1971-72; Pastorates: 1st FWB Ch, Tucson, Ariz 1964-71, Ashland City, Tenn 1961-62, Bryan, Tex 1958-59, Lake Charles, La 1955-58; Others; Prog Writer Adult & Teen Tng Mag Nat Assn FWB 1963-; Secy-Treas Tucson Chapt Nat Assn Evangelicals 1965-78; Moderator Ariz Assn FWB 1965-67, 69-71; Evangel Phil Soc; cp/Kiwanian; r/FWB; hon/Phi Delta Kappa; Hon Doct Laws & Lttrs, Clarksville Sch Theol; Pub'd Author; W/W in Am.

FRYE, WALTER CARSON oc/Production Manager; b/Feb 13, 1913; h/413 Canyon St, Plainview, TX 79072; ba/P'view; m/Eleanor Lynette; c/Joe Billy, Jeanne

Carolyn Gaither; p/Roy Jesse and Mamie Bolin Frye (dec); pa/Prodn Mgr P'view *Daily Herald;* r/Grace Presb Ch: Elder; hon/Sweepstake APME Contest; Others.

FRYREAR, DONALD WILLIAM oc/-Research Engineer; b/Dec 8, 1936; h/Rt 1, Box 319, Big Spring, TX 79720; m/Sherry; c/Debbie, Kenneth; p/William Alfred and Marjori Fryrear, Hoxtun, CO; ed/BS Colo St Univ; MS Ks St Univ; pa/ASAE; ASA; SCSA; AAAS; cp/Lions; Gideons; r/Bapt; hon/Outstg Student; Lion of Yr 1973.

FU, LORRAINE S oc/Assistant Professor; b/Jan 7, 1939; h/175 Adams St, Brooklyn, NY 11201; ba/NY; m/Lee-Shien Lu; c/Michael Lu; p/Kang Lo (dec); Yen Fu, NYC; ed/BS Hunter Col; MS NY Univ; PhD Polytechnic Univ Bklyn; pa/Asst Prof Math Pace Univ 1977-; Hunter Col: Asst Prof Math 1971-76,

Lectr Math 1964-67; Corr'g Secy NY Kappa, KME 1978-; Am Math Soc; Math Assn Am; Soc Indsl & Applied Math; Sigma Xi; cp/Commun Sch Bd 13, NYC Bd of Ed; Former Mem, Former CoChperson Fin Com.

FUCHS, HELMUTH HANS oc/Associate Professor; b/Aug 25, 1931; h/804 Front St, Dunellen, NJ 08812; ba/Farmingdale, NY; p/Hans and Alycia Fuchs, Dunellen, NJ; ed/BS Loyola Univ Chgo; MS NM St Univ; PhD Fordham Univ; mil/USN 1952-54; pa/Assoc Prof Chem Dept SUNY; Am Chem Soc; Sigma Xi; Phi Lambda Upsilon; Soc for Applied Spectroscopy; r/Prot.

FUDALA, JANET BARKER oc/School Administrator; b/Nov 20, 1935; ba/1610 Blaine St, Port Townsend, WA 98368; m/John; c/Teresa F Simon, Stephen, Theresa Barker Freeman, Marie Barker; p/Lawrence K and Bernice I O'Neill, Page, AZ; ed/BA, MA Univ Ariz; PhD Univ Wash; pa/Dir Spec Ed/Spec Progs Port Townsend Sch Dist; Pres Wash St CEC; VP Wash Assn for Chd w LD; Leg Councilor ASHA; Wash Assn Sch Admrs; Zeta Phi Eta; Wash Assn Wom in Adm; Assoc Editor *Language, Speech & Hearing Services in Schools, Teaching Exceptional Children;* Diagnostic Supvr WACLD Diagnostic Ctr; Adj Fac: Seattle Univ, Seattle Pacific Univ, Wn Wash Univ; r/Rom Cath; hon/Author Num Tests & Profl Articles; Dist'd Ser Awd, Zeta Phi Eta; Am Spch & Hearing Foun Grant; Zeta Phi Eta Foun Grant; Delta Kappa Gamma S'ship; Ariz Wom's S'ship; W/W Am Wom.

FUDENBERG, H HUGH oc/Educator; b/Oct 24, 1928; h/675 Fort Sumter Dr, Charleston, SC 29412; ba/C'ton; m/Betty Sams Roof; c/Drew Douglas, Brooks Roberts, David Melton, Hugh Haskell; p/Nathan and Frances Chachowitz Fudenberg; ed/AB UCLA 1949; MD Univ Chgo 1953; pa/Prof & Chm Dept Immunology & Microbiol Med USC, C'ton 1975-; Prof Bacteriol & Immunol Univ Cal-Berkeley 1966-75; Univ Cal Sch Med, San Francisco: Dir Immunol Unit 1962-, Prof Med 1966-, Assoc Prof 1962-66, Asst Prof Med 1962-66; Other Former Positions; Fellow AAAS; Am, Brit Assns Immunologists; Am Soc for Human Genetics; Am Soc for Clin Investigation; Am Assn Physicians; Intl Soc Blood Transfusion; Intl, Am Socs Hematology; SE Cancer Res Assn; Edit Bd Biochem Genetics, Clin & Exptl Immunol, Am Jour Human Genetics; Mem Expert Adv Panel on Immunol WHO 1962-; hon/Pasteur Medal Inst Pasteur (Paris); Robert A Cooke Meml Medal, Am Acad Allergy; Dist'd Ser Awd, Univ Chgo Med Alumni; Biogl Listings; Pub'd Author.

FUDGE, EDWARD WILLIAM oc/Publisher; Author; b/Jul 13, 1944; h/#4 Sandra Ln, Athens, AL 35611; m/Sara Locke; c/Melanie Anne, Jeremy Locke; p/Benjamin Lee Fudge (dec); Sybil Short Fudge, Bulawayo, Rhodesia; ed/AA; BA; MA; pa/Soc Biblical Lit; Evangel Theol Soc; r/Christian; hon/Outstg Yg Men Am; W/W in Rel.

FUDIN, CAROLE ELLEN oc/Clinical Social Worker; Educator; Thanatologist; b/Apr 6, 1947; h/145 E 15th St, New York, NY 10003; ba/NYC; p/Charles and Mildred Roseman, Bayside, NY; ed/BA; MSW; PhD Cand; pa/Rutgers Univ Grad Sch Social Work; Instr Univ Ext Div, Profl Credits Prog 1978-, Coadjutant Master's Deg Prog 1978-79; Instr Am Acad McAllister Inst Funeral Ser Inc, NYC 1976-; Pvt Pract Psychi Social Wkr,

NYC 1973-; Psychi Social Wkr: Bklyn Ctr for Psychotherapy 1976-77, Cath Charities Guid Inst, Bronx, NY 1971-72; Other Former Positions; Reschr; Assoc Mem: Soc Clin Social Work Psychotherapists, Foun of Thanatology; NASW; ACSW; Columbia Univ Sem on Death; hon/Dean's List, LIU; Doct Qualifying Exams, Rec'd Hons; Pub'd Author; W/W Am Wom.

FULGHAM, SCOTT DOUGLAS oc/Research Associate; b/Dec 2, 1953; h/9825 Starlight, Dallas, TX 75220; ba/Dallas; m/Deborah Wood; p/Fred Gerald and Janice Bell Fulgham, Media, PA; ed/AAS Lon Morris Col 1974; BS Univ Houston 1976; PhD Cand SWn Med Sch; pa/Res Assoc (Cardiovas Physiol), SWn Med Sch; Fellow: AAAS, Am Physiol Soc; cp/Yg Dems; r/U Meth Ch: Lay Rep to Annual Conf 1978; hon/Hairgrove S'ship, LMC; Mitchell F'ship, SWn Med Sch; W/W Am Jr Cols.

FULLER, ALBERT CLINTON (CLINT) oc/Executive Assistant; b/Jun 14, 1920; h/944 Henderson Rd, Louisburg, NC 27549; ba/Washington, DC; m/Louise; c/Albert Lawrence; p/Butler Vancer and Chloe W Fuller (dec); ed/Att'd NC St Univ; mil/USAAC WWII, S/Sgt; pa/Exec Asst to US Senator Jesse Helms (NC); Newspaper Editor; Mem Senate AA Assn; cp/Chm Franklin Co Dem Party; Rotary; Pres Bus Assn; Chm Bd Ed; r/Bapt; hon/Man of Yr; Tarheel of Week; 1st Pl, NC Press Assn; Others.

FULLER, BRENT DAVIS oc/Research Geophysicist; b/Jan 16, 1936; h/Hawthorne Hill Rd, Newtown, CT 06470; ba/Ridgefield, CT; m/Doris A; c/Kristin A; p/Burnett O Fuller, Yonkers, NY; Elizabeth J Fuller, Kingston, NY; ed/BS Mich Tech Univ 1964; MS 1966, PhD 1970 Univ Cal; mil/USCG 1953-57; pa/Profl Staff Schlumberger-Doll Res 1975-; Sr Geophysicist Newmont Exploration Ltd 1969-75; Soc Exploration Geophysicists; European Assn Exploration Geophysicists; Assoc Editor Jour *Geophysics*; cp/Bd Dirs Newtown Fish & Game Clb; r/Newtown Congreg Ch; hon/NSF Fellow; Mobil S'ship; Intl Minerals & Chem Corp S'ship; Num Profl Pubs.

FULLER, GERALD RALPH oc/Federal Veterinarian; b/Sept 8, 1919; h/6612 N Grove Ave, Oklahoma City, OK 73132; ba/Okla City; m/Glenda Richardson; c/Gerald R Jr, Gilbert Ronald, Barbara Ann Shurtz, Glen Robert, Gordon Ross, Gene Raymond, Grant Richardson; p/Horace Ralph Fuller (dec); Hortense McClellan Fuller, Mesa, AZ; ed/BS Univ Ariz 1941; MS 1943, DVM 1954 Tex A&M; mil/Ariz NG 1939-40; AUS 1943-46, 2/Lt; USAR 1946-71, Lt Col Vet Corp; pa/Meat & Poultry Inspector: Tex, Okla, Ark; USDA 1953-79; Instr Agri Ariz St 1946-50; AVMA; NAFV, Pres Okla Chapt 1974-78; Alpha Zeta; cp/BSA, Scoutmaster 10 Yrs; Dem; r/LDS: High Priest, Mesa, Ariz, Stake Missionary, Bishopric, Ft Worth, Tex (2 Yrs),

High Coun, Little Rock, Ark (11 Yrs); hon/Eagle Scout; Pub'd Author.

FULLER, JAMES HOWE oc/Surgeon; b/Oct 14, 1939; h/2858 McGregor Blvd, Ft Myers, FL 33901; ba/Ft Myers; m/Rena Morris; c/James Howe, Steven Bradley, Kimberley Lynn (dec), Jennifer Michelle, Jeffrey Michael, David Patrick; p/J Virgil and Francis Virginia Fuller, Bardwell, KY; ed/AB; MD; mil/Maj Med Corps 1970-72; pa/Fellow: Am Cols Surgs, Am Acad Ophthal & Otolaryngol; AMA; Fla Med Assn; Fla Soc Otolaryngol; r/1st Christian Ch, Ft Myers: Chm Bd Elders & Deacons.

FULLER, JOSEPH DORCAS III oc/College Administrator; b/Aug 30, 1947; h/1709 Archer, Sherman, TX 75090; ba/Sherman; m/Charlotte Ann Smith; c/Joseph Edward; p/J D Jr and Elizabeth King Fuller, McOreeney, TX; ed/BA cum laude TCU 1969; MA Univ Tex 1971; PhD Cand; pa/Dir Public Relats Austin Col; CASE; NCCPA; SPS-SDX; ACP; ICUT; cp/Sherman C of C; Boys Clb; r/1st Bapt Ch, Sherman: Mem; hon/Num Jour Awds; DIB; Personalities of S; Notable Ams Bicent Era.

FULLER, MELVILLE W oc/College Professor; b/May 3, 1933; h/13711 Rivercrest Dr, Little Rock, AR 72212; ba/LR; m/Judith Scott; c/Greg, Alison; p/Mrs M W Fuller, Alexander City, AL; ed/BS; MEd; PhD; mil/AUS; pa/Prof Univ Ark; NSTA; AETS; CESI; ASTA; AAAS; Phi Delta Kappa; r/Bapt; hon/Donagley Foun Travel Grants; Inovative Tchg Awds; NSF Grants; NSTA Nom.

FULLER, MELVIN L oc/Executive; b/Mar 30, 1921; h/121 N Fir St, Ventura, CA 93001; ba/Same; m/Louise; c/Tanya, Deborah, Lee; p/Leroy Fuller (dec); Lettie Lee Campbell, Ventura; ed/BA; mil/AUS Capt; pa/Pres Inventors Wkshop Intl; Pres Inventors Lic'g & Mktg Agy; Control Date-Univac & Litton Industs; r/Scientologist.

FULLER, RAY W oc/Biochemical Pharmacologist; b/Dec 16, 1935; h/7844 Singleton Dr, Indianapolis, IN 46227; ba/Indpls; m/Sue Brown; c/Ray W II, Angela Lea; p/Lloyd M and Wanda Fuller, Anna, IL; ed/BA; MA; PhD; pa/Biochem Pharmacologist Eli Lilly & Co; Am Soc Biol Chemists; Am

Soc for Neurochem; Am Chem Soc; Am Soc for Pharm & Experimental Therapeutics; Endocrine Soc; Soc for Neurosci; Intl Soc for Neurochem; NY Acad Scis; AAAS; Edit Bd: *Circulation Res*, *Jour of Neural Transmission*, *Life Scis*; Mem Basic Pharm Adv Com, Pharm Mfrs Assn Foun; r/U Meth; hon/NSF Fellow; Sigma Xi; Phi Lambda Upsilon.

FULLWOOD, JOSEPH MICHAEL oc/Attorney; b/Jun 3, 1946; h/Rogers' Ct, Hendrix St, Lexington, SC 29072; ba/L'ton; m/Mary Diane; p/Edwin Charles and Katherine Tully Fullwood, Wellsboro, PA; ed/BA Mansfield St; JD Univ SC; pa/Atty, Firm of H Hugh Rogers; ABA; SC Bar Assn; L'ton Bar Assn; SC Trial Lwyrs Assn; Mem Cont'g Legal Ed Com SC Bar Assn; Phi Delta Phi; cp/L'ton JCs; L'ton Sertoma Clb; L'ton Arts Assn; SC Yg Dems; r/Rom Cath; hon/Outstg Yg Men Am; W/W Students Am Univs & Cols.

FULTON, ALVENIA MOODY

oc/Nutritionist; Naturopath; b/May 17, 1918; h/1953 W 63rd, Chicago, IL 60636; ba/Chgo; m/O M (dec); cp/Robert Edward Gray (dec); p/Richard M and Mihala W Moody (dec); ed/BS; BTh; ND; pa/Minister; Lectr; Innovator of Fultonia Weight Loss Diet; cp/LWV; NAACP; Urban Leag; r/AME; hon/Preventive Pioneers, Amra Mae Cory Awd; Prince Hall Grand Lodge AFAM Hlth Awd; Notable Ams.

FULTON, FRED FRANKLIN oc/Artist; Engineer; b/Sept 27, 1920; h/5121 Harlan Dr, El Paso, TX 79915; m/Mary E; c/Sharon Ann Rosenthal, Susanne Jean Paulson, Kathy Joyce Sutton, Fred Timothy; p/Fred Fulton; ed/Bach Indust Engrg, Bach Civil Engrg; mil/USN; USAF; pa/Cedam-El Paso Art Assn; Carlsbad Art Assn; cp/NE El Paso Civic Assn; Citizens for Preven of Crime; r/Mormon; hon/Purple Heart; Personalities W&MW; Commun Ldrs & Noteworthy Ams; W/W Am Art.

FULTS, ANNA CAROL oc/Professor; b/Dec 24, 1912; h/Rt 1, Box 183, Murphysboro, IL 62966; ba/Carbondale, IL; m/Ibrahim M Khattab; p/Jefferson D and Annie Mary Fults, Tracy City, TN; ed/BS Univ Tenn; MS Cornell Univ; PhD Ohio St; pa/Prof So Ill Univ; AHEA; AVA; IVHETA; AERA; cp/Wom's Ctr; r/Unitarian-Universalist; hon/SIU Alumni Gt Tchr 1972.

FUNDERBURK, DAVID B oc/College Professor; b/Apr 28, 1944; h/Box 514, Buies Creek, NC 27506; ba/Buies Creek; m/Betty Jo Swaim; c/Britt, Deana; p/Guy B Funderburk, Pageland, SC; Vesta Young Funderburk,

Aberdeen, NC; ed/BA; MA; PhD; pa/Prof Campbell Col; USIA Fgn Ser Staff Ofcr, Romania; cp/Precnt Chm Repub Party; r/Bapt; hon/Fulbright, Am Coun Learned Socs & Intl Res & Excs Bd Fellow.

FUNG, ADRIAN K oc/Professor; b/Dec 25, 1936; h/2913 Sage Brush Dr, Lawrence, KS 66044; ba/Lawrence; m/Jean; c/Lindy, Sally; p/Yum-Tien Fung; Man-Fan Chan; ed/PhD EE; pa/Prof EE Dept Univ Ks; Sr Mem IEEE; US Comm URSI; hon/Am Men of Sci; Ldr in Am Ed.

FUNK, JAMES E oc/University Administrator; b/Nov 8, 1932; h/1845 Blairmore Ct, Lexington, KY 40502; ba/L'ton; m/Jill; c/Lynn, Lori, Jimmy, Lisa, John; p/Nicholas J and Agnes S Funk, Cincinnati, OH; ed/CME Engr 1955; MSChE 1958; PhD 1960; pa/Univ Ky: Assoc VP for Acad Affairs, Coor Energy Res; Fdg Mem Intl Assn for Hydrogen Energy; *Intl Jour Hydrogen Energy*: Chm Pubs Com, Mem Edit Bd; Chm Ky St Bd Registration for Profl Engrs & Land Surveyors 1975-78; Reviewer: *Sci Mag* (Articles & Discussion), NSF Proposals; Mem US Team Participating in Intl Energy Agy Implementing Agreemt on Hydrogen Prodn Res & Devel; Conslt; Chm Var Meetings; Gov's Policy Adv Com on Energy; r/Christian; hon/Westinghouse Fellow in Reactor Enrgr; 4 Patent Disclosure Awds; Pittsburgh Sect Am Nuclear Soc; Univ Ky Res Fellow; Sr Fulbright-Hays Scholar; Dist'd Alumnus Awd, Univ Cinc Col of Engrg.

FUNK, LISA ANN oc/Automatic Transmission Specialist; b/Sept 21, 1957;

h/PO Box 189, Greenville, VA 24440; p/Francis and Audrey Funk, G'ville; ed/AAS Blue Ridge Commun Col 1977; r/G'ville Bapt Ch.

FUNKE, FRANCIS JOSEPH oc/Professor; b/Jun 11, 1915; h/7146 Ballantrae Ct, Miami Lakes, FL 33014; ba/Miami; m/Bertha Sainz; c/John A (dec); p/Anthony Funke (dec); Caroline A Reimer (dec); ed/AB magna cum laude Butler Univ 1973; MA Univ Wis 1938, Univ Pa 1940, Geo Wash Univ 1953-54; PhD Fla St Univ 1964; pa/Prog Fgn Langs; Am Assn Tchrs Spanish & Portuguese; Mod Lang Assn; S Atl Mod Lang Assn; Fla Fgn Lang Assn; Nat Hist Soc; Fla St Alumni Asn; Cnslr & Pres Kappa Delta Pi, Gtr Miami Chapt 1970-74; cp/Bd Mem Ecumenical Fests Gtr Miami; Hispanic Cult Com, Mayor of Miami; Past VP & Pres Instituto de Cultura Hispanica of Miami; r/Our Lady of Lakes Ch: Choir; Ecumenical Fest Gtr Miami Choir; hon/Recipient S'ships & Asst'ship; Phi Kappa Phi; Kappa Delta Pi; Sigma Delta Pi; Pi Delta Phi; Alpha Mu Gamma; Biogl Listings.

FUNN, COURTNEY H oc/Library Administrator; b/Nov 30, 1941; h/6523 Rolling Ridge Dr, Seat Pleasant, MD 20027; ba/Bowie, MD; c/LaMarr Troinette; p/Jerry L and Evelyn B Harris, Seat Pleasant; ed/BA; MA; MLS; pa/Bowie St Col: Dir Lib 1969-, Asst Prof Music & Acting Dir Lib 1967-70; AAUW; Am, Md, DC Lib Assns; AAUP; Am Soc for Info Sci; St Bd Mem Md AAUW 1977-; Cnslt; Other Profl Activs; cp/LWV; hon/Cert of Apprec, Student Govt Assn Bowie St Col; Alpha Kappa Alpha; Kappa Delta Pi; Beta Phi Mu; Wom of Yr, Fisk Univ 1962-63; Biogl Listings.

FUQUA, HUGH G oc/Educator; Administrator; b/Dec 3, 1926; h/452 E North St, Geneseo, IL 61254; ba/Geneseo; m/Lillie L Eldridge; c/Allen L, Martin L, Gina D; p/Marshall L Fuqua (dec); Artis Hill Fuqua, Murray, KY; ed/BS 1950, MS Murray St Univ 1955; EdSpec Wn Ill Univ 1972; pa/Elem Coor & Prin 1966-79; Jr HS Prin, Riverdale Schs (Millsdale, Ill) 1959-66; Tchr & Coach, Cairo Schs (Cairo, Ill) 1954-59; Tchr & Coach, Blodgett HS (Blodgett, Mo) 1951-54; Tchr, Parma HS (Parma, Mo) 1950-51; Phi Delta Kappa; Prins Assn; Nat Assn Sec'dy Sch Prins; Life Mem, PTA; cp/Alumni Assns of Murray St Univ & Wn Ill Univ; Kiwanis; r/Ch of Christ: Former Elder; hon/Hon Mention, Outstg Admr of Ill.

FUQUA, J B oc/Executive; b/Jun 26, 1918; h/3574 Tuxedo Rd NW, Atlanta, GA 30305; ba/Atlanta; m/Dorothy Chapman; pa/Fuqua Indusls Inc: Chm of Bd, Chief Exec Ofcr; Chm Bd Fuqua TV Inc; Dir Ctl Ga Railroad; Chief Execs Forum; World Bus Coun; The Conf Bd; cp/Former Mem Ga Leg; Former Chm Dem Exec Com Ga & Dem Party Ga; Bd Trustees Ga St Univ Foun; Bd Trustees: Hampden-Sydney Col, Duke Univ; Past VP Yg Pres' Org; Former Mem Bd Dirs

Atlanta C of C; Past Pres Augusta C of C; Former Mem: Augusta Aviation Comm, Ga Sci & Technol Comm, Bd Visitors Emory Univ; Others; hon/Ga Pioneer in Broadcasting Awd; Boss of Yr Awd, Augusta Jr C of C 1960; Broadcaster Citizen of Yr, Ga 1963; Golden Plate Awd, Am Acad Achvmt; Hon LLD, Duke Univ, Hampden-Sydney Col.

FURNESS, EDNA LUE oc/Professor Emeritus; Free-lance Writer; b/Jan 26, 1906; h/725 S Alton Way, Denver, CO 80231; p/Frank A and Nellie Swanson Furness (dec); ed/BA, MA, PhD Univ Colo; Grad Studies Nat Univ Mexico; pa/Prof Lang & Lit: Univ Wyo, Neb (Kearney) St Col; Vis Prof Sum Sessions: Adams St Col, Univ Denver, Univ Tenn-Chattanooga, Ctl Mich Univ; Life Mem

NEA; NCTE; Phi Sigma Iota; Kappa Delta Pi; Author *Spelling for the Millions*, & Num Articles in Jours & Anthologies; r/Prot; hon/Trustee F'ship, Smith Col; Rockefeller F'ship Inter-Am Studies; Coe Fellow in Am Studies; Delta Kappa Gamma Postdoct F'ship; US Ofc Ed Humanities Grants; *Poet Lore* Translation Prize.

FURR, QUINT E oc/Executive; b/Sept 21, 1921; h/9232 3 Oaks Dr, Silver Spring, MD 20901; ba/Beltsville, MD; m/Helen W; c/Tiffany Lee Grantham, Quentin C, Robert Luther, (Stepchd:) Pamela Lacy, Erik Erickson; ed/Grad Belmont Abbey Col; BA Univ NC; Att'd Univ NC Law Sch; mil/USNR WWII, Korea, Lt (jg); pa/VP Corporate Mktg Textilease Corp; Reg Mgr: Top Value Enterprises, J F Pritchard Co; Nat Adv & Sales Prom Mgr Wn Auto Supply Co; Prom Rep Sears Roebuck & Co; SMEI, Washington, DC; IIL, Chm Mktg Com 1974-76; Phi Kappa Alpha; cp/Moose Clb; Elks Clb; Am Legion; VFW; hon/Winner Mktg Awds; 1st Pl, Textile Leasing Indust; Biogl Listings.

FUSELER, ELIZABETH ANNE oc/Librarian; b/Jun 15, 1947; h/PO Box 1613, Galveston, TX 77553; ba/Galveston; p/Demitry J and Adah M Pollock, Philadelphia, PA; ed/AB; MS; pa/Tex Lib Assn, Marine Sci Libns Assn; SWLA; AAUW; cp/Galveston Hist Foun; r/Epis; hon/Outstg Yg Wom Am.

FUSON, BENJAMIN WILLIS oc/Retired Professor; b/Feb 17, 1911; h/Box 354, Rt 1, Louisa, KY 41230; m/Daisylee McClure; c/Linda Lee, David Willis; p/Chester G and Phebe Meeker Fuson (dec); ed/BA; MA; PhD St Univ Ia 1942; pa/Prof Eng Ks Wesleyan Univ, Salina, Ks 1960-76, Ret'd Emeritus; Pt-

time Lectr Asian Lit Univ Ky Commun Cols 1976-79; Vis Prof Eng Kobe Col, Nishinomiya, Japan 1966-67, 1973-74; Others; Mod Lang Assn; Nat Coun Tchrs Eng; Mo Assn Tchrs Eng; Ks Assn Tchrs Eng; r/Soc of Friends; hon/Dist'd Awd, Nat Univ Ext Assn; Pub'd Author.

FUTRELL, JOHN CARROLL oc/Clergyman; Educator; b/Oct 14, 1927; h/Mt 5, 3001 S Federal Blvd, Denver, CO 80236; ba/Same; p/George R Futrell (dec); Martha Rose Futrell, Oklahoma City, OK; ed/AB; PhL; AM; STL; STD; pa/Staff Mem Min Tng Sers; Vis Prof Theol Iliff Sch Theol, Denver 1977; Adj Prof Theol Regis Col, Denver 1976; Prof Spirituality St Louis Univ 1974-76; Vis Prof (Sum) Spiritual Theol St Paul Maj Sem.

Jogjakarta, Indonesia 1972; Others; Dir Rel Renewal Progs in: US, Europe, Far E, Australia, Africa, & Latin Am 1968-78; Mem Am Assistancy Sem on Jesuit Spirituality 1970-72; Chief Resource Person St Louis Archdiocesan Prog for Priestly Spirituality 1970-72; r/Rom Cath; hon/Cert as Outstg Edr of Am; W/W in Rel; Personalities W&MW; Am Cath W/W; DIB; Men of Achmt.

G

GADDIS, ROGER GARY oc/Professor; b/Nov 9, 1946; h/600 Lee St, Kings Mtn, NC 28086; ba/Boiling Springs, NC; m/Susan Avery Woodall; c/David Benjamin; p/A A and Minalee Gaddis (dec); ed/BA; MA; PhD; pa/Prof Gardner-Webb Col; Conslt; Lectr; cp/Former Mem Bd Dirs Kiwanis Clb, Kings Mtn; Bd Dirs Sun Co (Touring Musical Group); r/1st Bapt Ch, Kings Mtn: Mem; hon/Grad Ednl Res Tng Prog F'ship.

GADE, CLIFFORD W oc/Clergyman; b/Nov 10, 1934; h/1909 Hogeboom Ave, Eau Claire, WI 54701; ba/Eau Claire; m/Heidi Sievers; c/Dorothy, Werner, Stephen, Rebecca; p/Louis H and Dorothy Hellis Gade (dec); ed/BTheol Concordia Theol Sem; mil/USMC 1952-56; pa/Clergyman Luth Ch-

Mo Synod; Chm Dist Bd Missions N Wis Dist-LCMS; Campus Coor N Wis Dist-LCMS; Var Former Activs; cp/Chaplain CAP (Capt); Former Mem Bd Dirs Burnett Co Chapt ARC; Chm Regulatory Com Wis Wn Tri-Co Network; BSA; Antigo Area C of C; Am Legion; r/Luth Ch-Mo Synod; hon/Commun Ldrs & Noteworthy Ams; Other Biogl Listings.

GAFFNEY, BILL GRANT oc/Attorney-at-Law; b/Jun 16, 1922; h/10118 Lynbrook Hollow, Houston, TX 77042; ba/Houston; m/Marnel Wright; c/Grant Wright, Beverly Gay Fedigan, Brenda Kay Kocurek; p/Frank Bernard Gaffney (dec); ed/LLB So Meth Univ; mil/USN 1942-46; pa/Am, Tex & Houston Bar Assn; Comml Law Leag Am; Life Fellow, Tex Bar Foun; PAD Law Frat; cp/JCs: Pres, Former Nat Dir; Pres Intl Ks of Round Table; Am Legion Counsel; r/Presb; hon/W/W: Am Law, Tex; DIB; Men of Achmt.

GAGE, LOIS WAITE oc/Associate Director; Professor; b/Mar 8, 1922; h/3697 Maple Dr, Ypsilanti, MI 48197; ba/Ann Arbor, MI; c/Nancy Marie, John Barry; p/Roy Waite (dec); c/Agnes McGregor (dec); ed/BS; MA; PhD; mil/USNR Staff Nurse; pa/Assoc Dir Primary Care/Commun Med & Prof Nsg; St & Univ Adv Coms; Chm Mtl Hlth Sect Am Public Hlth Assn 1978; Mem Jt Pract Comm (Mich) 1978; Appraiser Div of Ednl Resources & Progs 1977-; Nat & Intl Consultations 1972-; Book Reviews; r/Cath; hon/Kappa Delta Pi; Pi Lambda Theta; Sigma Theta Tau; Fellow: APHA, Am Acad Nsg; W/W: Am Wom, Hlth Care; Pub'd Papers.

GAILLARD, WILLIAM LUCAS oc/Land Surveyor; b/Jul 22, 1912; h/1 Limehouse St, Charleston, SC 29401; ba/C'ton; m/Daisy Williams; c/Eleanor G Rogers, Marianne G Clare, W Lucas Jr; p/John Palmer and Eleanor Lucas Gaillard (dec); ed/BS Fla St Christian Col; pa/Author Chapt on Surveying, Standard Handbook for Engrs; cp/St Andrews Soc SC Soc; Gov Col Wars SC; hon/Hon DEngrg.

GAINER, RUBY JACKSON oc/Counselor, Dean; Reading Consultant; h/1516 W Gadsden St, Pensacola, FL 32501; ba/Pensacola; m/Herbert P; c/Ruby Paulette, James Herbert, Cecil Primus; p/William and Lovie Jones Jackson (dec); ed/BS Ala St Univ;

MA Atlanta Univ; hon/Woodham High: Cnslr-Dean; Life Mem NEA; Fla Ed Assn; FTP-NEA; Polit Caucus NEA-PAC; cp/LWV; Dem Wom; St Dem Party; Wom Caucus; Black Caucus; r/Mt Zion Bapt Ch; hon/Hon Doct Degs; Tchr of Yr; Mother of Yr; Wom of Yr; Citizen of Yr; Edr of Yr; Most Progressive Black Wom.

GALAMAGA, DONALD PETER oc/-Executive Director; b/Mar 14, 1938; h/30 White Rock Rd, Warwick, RI 02889; m/-Margot C; c/4 Chd; p/Peter and Mary Galamaga, St Clair Shores, MI; ed/AB Holy Cross Col 1959; MPA Univ RI 1971; mil/USNR Current Cmdr; Chm SEn New England Recruiting Dist Assistance Coun (Composed of Bus & Govt Ldrs in Area); pa/Exec Dir Mgmt & Support Sers RI Dept Mtl Hlth, Retard & Hosps, Dep Asst Commr of Ed for Budget 1973-78; Instr Grad Sch Public Adm Univ RI 1972-; Prog Budget Specialist RI Dept Ed 1971-73; Mem 3 Man Implementation Team to Implement Wide Ranging Improvemts at Adult Correctl Instns in RI Aug-Dec 1977; RI & Nat Chapts Am Soc for Public Adm 1972-74, 1978-80; cp/Former Budget Panel Mem U Way; Former Bd Dirs Res Bur RI Coun of Commun Sers; Armed Forces Writers Leag: Mem, Free-lance Writer; Chm & Mem St Kevin Parish Coun, Warwick; hon/Creative Public Adm Awd, RI Chapt ASPA; Cert of Commend, Navy Recruiting Command; Certs of Apprec: Assn for Systems Mgmt, Inst Mgmt & Labor Relats; Pi Sigma Alpha; Cit, Cmdr Cruiser Destroyer Forces US Atl Fleet; Benedict Joseph Fenwick Awd, Holy Cross Col; Navy Full S'ship to Holy Cross Col; Num Commend Lttrs for Perf of Duty & Public Spkg; Pub'd Author; Commun Ldrs Am.

GALANFFY, ADEL MARTHA oc/Department Head; b/Feb 20, 1925; h/104 W Briarwood Ln, Harker Heights, TX 76541; ba/Killeen, TX; m/Louis A (dec); c/Daniel Peter, Adam Louis; p/Laszlo Toth (dec); Maria Racz, Debrecen, Hungary; ed/Perf'g Artist's & Music Tchr's Dipl, Franz Liszt Conservatory Music, Budapest, Hungary; pa/Hd Music Dept Ctl Tex Col; Tchr: Piano, Theory, Harmony; Conslt Music Tchrs; Adjudicator Nat Piano Guild; 150 Duo-Piano Concerts under Commun Concerts Inc; Lectr; r/Christian; hon/DIB; Hungarians in Am; Dir Ednl Specialists; Intl W/W Music; Piano Guild Hall of Fame; W/W Am Wom.

GALBRAITH, LILYAN KING oc/Professor; h/47 Water St, Smithfield, PA 15478; p/Jasper T and Iona Ewing King (dec); ed/BS, MS WVa Univ; EdD Pa St Univ; pa/Hd Home Ec Ed: Mansfield St Col (Pa), Wn Mich Univ, Mich & SD St Univs; Prof

Home Ec Ed: Wn Ky Univ, WVa Univ; AAUW, Uniontown, Pa: Ednl Foun Chm 1973-74, Pres 1974-76, Histn 1976-; BPW Clb: Leg & Bylaws Chm 1973-74, Histn 1974-76, Public Relats Comm 1977-78; Delta Kappa Gamma: Hospitality Com 1971-72, Profl Affairs Com 1972-74; Fayette Co Home Ecs Assn: VP 1975-77, Pres 1977-79; r/U Meth Ch, Smithfield: Trustee 1972-75, Bd Ed Chm 1977-, Adm Bd 1977-, SS Tchr 1977-, Choir 1976-, VP UMW 1971-79, Nom'g Com, Connelsville Dist UMW 1976-79; hon/Kappa Delta Pi; Kappa Omicron Phi; Pi Lambda Theta; Delta Kappa Gamma; Cit of Merit, Devoted Ser to Voc Home Ec SD; SD Home Economist of Yr 1968.

GALE, JAMES ELWIN oc/Management Consultant; b/Dec 8, 1948; h/1608 32nd St NW, Washington, DC 20007; p/James S and Helen A Gale; ed/BS Clarkson Col Technol 1970; MS Geo Wash Univ 1974; pa/Sr Assoc Planning Res Corp & Energy Analysis Co 1979-; Conslt Logistics Mgmt Inst 1978-79; Proj Mgr Hitman Assocs 1976-78; Proj Ldr Wilbur Smith & Assocs 1974-76; Staff Mem Metro Wash Coun Govts 1973; Engr Gen Elect Co, Knolls Atomic Power Lab 1970-72; Am Soc Mech Engrs, Clarkson Pres 1969-70; Am Planning Assn; Opers Res Soc Am; VP Pi Mu Sigma 1969-70; cp/Smithsonian Assocs; hon/Pi Tau Sigma; Urban Mass Trans Fellow, US Dept Trans; Author Num Tech Documents & Reports; W/W in E; Commun Ldrs Am.

GALE, STEVEN H oc/Educator; b/Aug 18, 1940; h/Rt 4, Box 190-G, Gainesville, FL 32601; ba/G'ville; m/Kathy Johnson; c/Shannon Erin, Ashley Alyssa; p/Norman A Gale; Mary L Haase; p/BA Duke Univ 1963; MA UCLA 1965; PhD Univ So Cal 1970; pa/Assoc Prof Eng Univ Fla-G; Author: 2 Books, 1 Text, Num Articles, Reviews, Fiction, Poetry & Drama; Scholarly Papers Delivered; cp/Little Theatre: Actor, Dir; Track Ofcl; HS Ftball Ofcl; hon/Fulbright (Liberia 1973-74); Spec Advr Liberian Min of Ed; Danforth Assoc; Chi Delta Pi; Tchr & Res Awds & Grants.

GALL, LORRAINE S oc/Microbiologist; Visiting Associate Professor; Microbiological Consultant; b/Jun 16, 1915; h/B149 7321 Brompton, Houston, TX 77025; ba/Houston; p/Otto W Gall (dec); Vida S Gall, Houston, TX; ed/BS; PhD; pa/Baylor Col Med: Vis Assoc Prof, Sr Microbiologist; Sigma Xi; Phi Kappa Phi; Sigma Delta Epsilon; Soc Indust Microbiologists; Am Soc Microbiologists;

IPA; r/Epis; hon/Am Men of Sci; DIB; World W/W Commerce & Indust; W/W: NC, Am Wom, Am Ed, E; Creative & Successful Personalities; Personalities of: S, MW; Men of Achmt; World W/W Wom; NAm Intl Reg Profiles; Notable Ams; Book of Honor; Author 100+ Sci & Popular Articles; Coauthor 'Instrumented Approach to Microbiological Analysis of Body Fluids (in press).

GALLAGHER, BLANCHE MARIE oc/Sister of Religious Order; Professor; h/6363 Sheridan Rd, Chicago, IL 60660; ba/Chgo; p/John Joseph and Blanche Jacobson Gallagher (dec); ed/MFA Cath Univ Am; BA Mundelein Col; pa/Prof Art Mundelein Col; Lectr on Paintings: Tokyo (Japan), Kathmandu (Nepal), Kyoto (Japan), Old Delhi (India), Honolulu (Hi), Taipei

PERSONALITIES OF AMERICA

(Taiwan); One-Person Exhibits of Paintings: Univ Colo, Univ Chgo, Clarke Col; cp/Bd Title III ESEA, St of Ill 1968-74; r/Rom Cath; hon/Lilly Foun Awd Travel Grant to Res Mandala Forms in India, Nepal, Burma & Sri Lanka; Awd for Painting in Venice, Giorgio Cini Foun, Venice, Italy; Ford Foun Study Awd for Oriental Studies.

GALLAGHER, HELEN KIZIK oc/Teacher; b/Feb 5, 1916; h/124 Hecla St, Uxbridge, MA 01569; ba/Uxbridge; m/James; c/Elaine Doyle (Mrs John J Jr), Paul; p/Juluis and Vera Bobick Kizik (dec); ed/BS Ed; pa/Tchr Whitin Sch; NEA; MTA; Past Secy UTA; cp/VFW Aux: Treas, Sr Vice); Den Mother Cub Scouts; Asst to Brownie Troop Ldr; r/Rom Cath; hon/Outstg Ldr in Am Ed.

GALLAGHER, PATRICK FRANCIS oc/Anthropologist; Professor; b/Apr 18, 1930; h/3025 Dana St, Berkeley, CA 94705; ba/Caracas, Venezuela; c/Patrick Francis III, John Vincent, Lisa Bridge, Molly Alison, Kingman Cruxent; p/Hugh Vincent Gallagher (dec); Mary Caroline Denne Gallagher, Turtle Creek, PA; ed/BA summa cum laude Univ Pittsburgh 1957; PhD Yale Univ 1964; mil/USNR 1950-54, Seaman; pa/Prof Depto

de Antropologia IVIC; Prof & Chm Dept Anthropology George Washington Univ; Lectr Am Anthro Assn; Vis Lectr Prog; Coun Am Anthro Assn; hon/Fellow: Org Am Sts, Anthro Assn Am, Royal Anthro Inst Gt Britain & Ireland, AAAS; Pres: Phi Beta Kappa, Sigma Xi; Univ Fellow; Brady Fellow; Sterling Fellow; Fellow Yale Univ; Grants, NSF; Specialist *Intl Review of Bibliography;* Editor *Am Antiquity.*

GALLAGHER, PATRICK J oc/Building Inspector; b/Jun 28, 1915; h/125 S 72nd St, Tacoma, WA 98408; ba/Tacoma; m/Mable Beth Stauffacher; c/Patrick Charles, Theresa Reisenauer, Michael Jon, Robert Bruce, Gregory Dennis, Celine Brown; p/Charles and Annie Ferry Gallagher (dec); ed/BS Wash St Univ; pa/UGN Jt Com for Progress; cp/Bd Dirs Tacoma Sportsman's Clb; Dem Precnt Com-man; St Legislator; Ks of Columbus; r/Cath.

GALLEZ, DOUGLAS WARREN oc/Professor; Associate Dean; b/Apr 28, 1923; h/202 Princeton Ave, Mill Valley, CA 94941; ba/San Francisco, CA; m/Marcele R; c/Leslie, Paul, John; p/Isaac Cornelius Gallez, Long Beach, CA; Vivien Marie Gallez (dec); ed/BA 1944; MA 1956; MA 1957; PhD 1975; mil/Grad US Mil Acad (West Point) 1944, 20 Yrs Comm'd Ser, Ret'd 1964; pa/SF St Univ: Prof Film, Assoc Dean/Opers, Sch Creative Arts; AAUP; Soc for Cinema Studies; Univ

Film Assn; Am Film Inst; Soc Motion Picture & TV Engrs; r/Epis; hon/Commend Medal, AUS; Screen Prodrs Guild/*Look* Mag Inter-Collegiate Film Awd; Screen Prodrs Guild/Jesse Lasky Meml Awd.

GALLIANO, VERNON FREDERICK oc/University President; b/Apr 26, 1923; h/Box 2001, Nicholls St Univ Sta, Thibodaux, LA 70301; ba/Same; m/Josephine B; c/Vernon Jr, Timothy, Gregory, Jonathon; p/Emile and Josephine Vega Galliano (dec); ed/BS; MS; PhD; mil/USN; pa/Univ Pres Nicholls St Univ 1963-; Dean of Ed Nicholls St Col 1960-63; SWn La Inst: Prof Agri Ed & Dir Tchr Tng 1954-60, Supv'g Tchr 1948-54; Other Former Positions; Mem Comm on Cols So Assn Cols & Schs; Mem Adv Bd for Nat Ocean Industs Assn; Mem Prog Planning Com Comm on Cols, SACS 1975; La Tchrs' Assn &

Dept Higher Ed; Phi Delta Kappa; Com on Envir Am Assn St Cols & Univs; Var Former Profl Activs; cp/Bd Govs So Edr's Corp; La St Coun for Devel of French in La; Bd Commrs Hosp Ser Dist No 3, Lafourche Parish; Bd Dirs Citizens Bank & Trust Co, Thibodaux; Thibodaux C of C; Am Legion; VFW; Coun Trustees Gulf S Res Inst; Others; r/Cath; hon/Best Edr Awd, River Parishes Chem Indust Coun 1972; 1 of 20 Admrs in US to Participate in Am Assn Sch Admrs Intl Field Study (Europe), 1971; King of Krewe of Christopher, Mardi Gras, 1969; Blue Key; Delta Mu Delta; Phi Kappa Phi; Pub'd Author; Biogl Listings; Others.

GALLOWAY, LOUIE ALTHEIMER III oc/Engineer; b/Feb 3, 1936; h/410 Elmwood Dr, Lafayette, LA 70503; ba/Lafayette; m/Harriett Laws; c/Louie Altheimer IV, Nina Victoria, Mack Laws; p/Louie A Jr and Jessie Laws Galloway, Pine Bluff, AR; ed/AB Hendrix Col; MS, PhD Case Inst Tech; pa/Chief Engr Petrol Assocs Lafayette Inc; Rheological Studies; cp/Rotary Clb Lafayette; Repub; r/Meth; hon/Hon Grad, Hendrix Col; NSF Fellow; Centenary Col: Keen Prof Physics, Tchr of Yr 1967.

GALLOWAY, RAY MAYES oc/Insurance Executive; b/Nov 27, 1926; h/113 Hilldale Ln, Goldsboro, NC 27530; ba/G'boro; m/Lillian; c/Margaret, Melissa; p/Raymond and Helen Galloway (dec);

ed/BA Duke Univ; mil/USN WWII, Korean; pa/Chartered Property Casualty Underwriter; cp/Past Pres: Kiwanis Clb, Wayne U Way, G'boro Arts Coun; r/Presb Ch: Elder; hon/4 St Soaring Records.

GALLOWAY, REX FARMER oc/University Department Chairman; b/May 11, 1936;

h/308 Oak Dale Dr, Murray, KY 42071; ba/Murray; m/Frances Inez Taylor; c/Andrea Kaye, John Harding; p/Harding and Hattie Lee Galloway, Murray; ed/BS Murray St Univ 1963; MBA Memphis St Univ 1966; DBA Miss St Univ 1970; mil/USAR 6 Yrs, Hon Disch'd 1964; pa/Chm Dept Mgmt Murray St Univ; Acad Mgmt; So Mgmt Assn; MW Acad Mgmt; Am Inst Decision Scis; Data Processing Mgmt Assn; MW Bus Adm Assn; Ky Acad Computer Users Assn; cp/BSA; r/Bapt; hon/Beta Gamma Sigma; Phi Kappa Phi; Sigma Lambda Iota; Pi Sigma Alpha; Outstg Alumnus Zeta Lambda Chapt, Alpha Tau Omega; Mil Commend for High Proficiency Score 1959.

GALLUP, GRANT MORRIS oc/Priest; b/Jan 28, 1932; h/1619 W Warren Blvd, Chicago, IL 60612; ba/Same; p/Allan M and Eleanor Else Wilhelmina Daumitz Gallup (dec); ed/BA magna cum laude Alma Col 1954; MDiv Seabury-Wn Theol Sem 1959; mil/AUS 1954-56; pa/Epis Priest; Curate Ch of Atonemt 1959-61; Vicar St Andrew's Ch 1961-; r/Epis.

GALVIN, HOYT R oc/Executive; Library Consultant; b/Feb 26, 1911; ba/2259 Vernon Dr, Charlotte, NC 28211; m/Mary Elizabeth; c/Douglas G, Jane Ann; ed/AB Simpson Col 1932; BS Univ Ill 1933; Cert Brookings Inst Ctr for Adv'd Studies 1967; pa/Lib Conslt (Pt-time) 1957-70, (Full-time) 1971-; Lib Sch Tchg: Columbia, Emory, Pittsburgh, Syracuse; Hd Libn (Half-time) Univ NC-C 1967-68; Dir Public Lib Charlotte & Mecklenburg Co 1940-71; Other Former Positions; Am Lib Assn: 2nd VP 1969-70, Pres Lib Adm Div 1965-66; Pres: SEn Lib Assn 1962-64, NC Adult Ed Assn 1957-58, NC Lib Assn 1942-43; Chm Ala St Lib Bd 1939-40; Others; cp/Charlotte C of C; Former Chm Hist Com & Ed Com; Past Pres Rotary Clb Charlotte; hon/Yg Man of Yr, Charlotte JCs 1942; Outstg Public Libn Awd, SEn Lib Assn; Alumni Achmt Awd, Simpson Col; AIA/ALA/NBC Lib Bldgs Awd Jury 1964, 66; Cert of Merit, Charlotte Jr Wom's Clb; Cert of Recog, Nat Conf Christians & Jews; W/W in Am; Pub'd Author.

GAMMAGE, ROBERT (BOB) ALTON oc/Attorney-at-Law; b/Mar 13, 1938; h/1606 Antigua Ln, Houston, TX 77058; ba/Houston; m/Judy; c/Terry Lynne, Sara Noel, Robert Alton Jr; p/Paul Gammage (dec); Sara Ella Gammage, Houston; ed/AA Del Mar Col; BS Univ Corpus Christi 1963; MA Sam Houston St Univ 1965; JD Univ Tex Sch of Law 1968-; mil/AUS 1959-60; USNR 1965-, Lt Cmdr; pa/Atty at Law 1968-; Instr Govt San Jacinto Col 1969-70; Adj Prof Law S Tex Col Law 1971-73; Univ Corpus Christi 1965-66; Dean

of Men, Dir Student Activs; Sam Houston St Univ 1963-65: Tchg Fellow, Dir Frats; cp/Mem US Ho of Reps 1977-79; Former Mem Tex Ho of Reps & Tex Senate; r/Bapt; hon/Outstg Senator, 63rd Tex Leg 1973; Dist'd Alumnus, Univ Corpus Christi; Num Dist'd Ser Awds.

GAMSON, LELAND PABLO oc/Economics Assistant, Editor; b/Dec 30, 1950; h/4970 Battyer Ln #507, Bethesda, MD 20014; ba/Washington, DC; p/Arthur L and Anita G Gamson, Bethesda; ed/BA Hiram 1973; MEd American Univ 1974; mil/USNR; pa/Ecs Asst, Editor AS IS; Phi Delta Kappa; cp/Fed Poets; Boy Scout Cnslr; r/Quaker; hon/Pi Gamma Mu; Omicron Delta Kappa; Dir Am Poets; Freedom Foun Spch Awd; Gold Quill.

GANDRUD, EBENHARD STEWART oc/Executive; b/Oct 19, 1902; h/517 E School St, Owatonna, MN 55060; ba/Owatonna; m/Edith M Christensen; c/Linda G Stoddard, Dale E; p/Albert E and Kari Dahlen Gandrud, Detroit Lakes, MN; ed/BS Univ Minn;

mil/War Manpower Comm WWII; pa/Co Pres; Am Soc Agri Engrs; NAM; Minn C of C; cp/Sons of Norway; Elks; Rotary; Mem Exec Bd Gamehaven Coun BSA; r/Luth; hon/Awd for Outstg Contbn to Am Agri Cong of US; Silver Beaver Awd, BSA; 70 Patents in field.

GANDY, EDYTHE EVELYN oc/Attorney; State Lieutenant Governor; b/Sept 4, 1922; h/727 Arlington St, Jackson, MS 39202; ba/Jackson; p/Kearney C Gandy (dec); Abbie Whigham Gandy, Jackson; ed/LLB; pa/Lt Gov Miss 1976-; Commr Ins 1972-76; St Treas 1968-72, 1960-64; Commr Public Wel 1964-67; Asst Atty Gen; Atty St Dept Public Wel; Pvt Pract Law; Forrest Co, Hinds Co, Miss St, Am Bar Assns; Hattiesburg BPW Clbs; Former St Pres Miss Fdn BPW Clbs; Miss Wom's Cabinet of Public Affairs; Miss Ofcl Wom's Clb; Former Mem: AAUW, Am Assn Wom Accts, Miss Farm Bur, Am Public Wel Assn, Miss Conf Social Wel; Mem Var Comms; cp/Former Mem Altrusa Clb; Univ Miss & Univ So Miss Alumni Assns; r/1st Bapt Ch, Jackson: Active Mem; hon/Named 1 of Top 10 Wom of Mid-South for Decade of Sixties; Wom of Yr, Jackson 1964; Life Mbrship, Miss Cong of PTA; Biogl Listings.

GANDY, GERALD LARMON oc/Educator; Counseling Psychologist; b/Feb 9, 1941; h/300 Southern Ct, Richmond, VA 23075; ba/Richmond; m/Patricia Kay Haltiwanger; p/Larmon Brinkley and Ruby Wylene Vickers Gandy, Jacksonville, FL; ed/BA Fla St Univ; MA, PhD Univ SC; mil/AUS Med Ser 1963-66, Served to Capt; pa/Univ Prof; Author; Conslt; Admr; Profl Orgs; cp/Mem St & Fed Adv Coms; r/Prot; hon/Num Hon Socs; Spec Awds.

GANGSTAD, EDWARD OTIS oc/Research Administrator; b/Dec 18, 1917; h/7909 Greeley Blvd, Springfield, VA 22152; ba/Washington, DC; m/Ruth Margaret Fletcher; c/James Otis, John Erik, Karl Edward, Lillis, Mamie; p/John Otis and Della B Gangstad (dec); ed/BS 1942, MS 1947 Univ Wis; PhD Rutgers Univ 1950; mil/Capt AUS Air Force; pa/Botanist in charge of Aquatic Plant Control Prog, Ofc of Chief of Engrs; Former Prin Agronomist Hoblitzelle Agri Lab Tex Res Foun, Dallas, Tex; Editor/Author

CRC Press; Res done w: Univs Wis & NJ, US Dept Agri (Fla), Ofc Nav Res, Dept of Def, Others; cp/Toastmasters Intl; Repub Nat Com; r/Unitarian: Secy Bd of Control, Gtr Wash Area; hon/Cert of Achmt, AUS; Fellow: AAAS, AIC; Ldrs in Sci; Am Men of Sci; W/W; Men of Achmt; DIB; Contbr to Num Profl Pubs.

GANN, LOUISE WEEKS oc/Counselor; Clinical Psychologist; b/Nov 9, 1927; h/103 1st Ct SE, PO Box 414, Hamilton, AL 35570; ba/Montgomery, AL; m/John William (dec); c/Virginia G Scott (Mrs Charles W), Carolyn G Shotts (Mrs E Larry); p/William Shirley and Martha J Shellnut Weeks, Hamilton, AL; ed/BS Florence St Univ 1949; MA Elem Ed 1964, MA Cnslg, Guid & Psychol 1966, PhD 1971 Univ Ala; pa/Cnslg Psychologist IV, Div of Social Sers St of Ala, Med & Diagnostic Ctr, Montgomery; Cnslg Psychologist IV & Coor Consultation, Ed & Staff Inservice, NW

Ala Mtl Hlth Ctr, Hamilton 1971-75; Conslt Cnslg, Guid & Testing Ala St Dept of Ed, Montgomery 1967-71; Instr Cnslg & Guid Univ Ala Grad Sch, Tuscaloosa Sum 1970; Asst'd in Setting up 1st Freshman Orientation Prog for Univ Montevallo Sum 1967; Dir Voc Guid Marion Co Sch Sys, Hamilton 1966-67; Other Former Positions incl'g: Elem Tchr, Elem Prin; Kappa Delta Pi; Sigma Tau Delta; Alpha Delta Kappa; APGA; Ala APGA; AEA; NVGA; Ala VGA; ACES; So ACES; Ala CES; APA; SEPA; Ala Psychol Assn; cp/Toll Gate Chapt OES, Hamilton; r/1st Meth Ch, Hamilton; hon/S'ships; Biogl Listings.

GANSBERG, JUDITH M oc/Writer; b/Oct 20, 1947; h/421 Glenbrook Rd, Stamford, CT 06906; ba/Same; m/Robert J Burger; p/Martin and Agatha Gansberg, Rutherford, NJ; ed/BA Univ Mich; MA Univ Md; pa/Asst Editor Tennis Mag; Asst Prof Col New Rochelle; r/Jewish; hon/Am Film Fest Awd; Phi Kappa Phi.

GANTNER, ROSE KARLO oc/Assistant Professor; Licensed Marriage & Family Therapist; b/Dec 16, 1943; h/6801 Trapper Way, Midland, GA 31820; ba/Columbus, GA; m/Charles John Jr; p/Milan M and Laura Mamula Karlo; ed/BS Slippery Rock St Col 1965; MEd Univ Pgh 1968; Postgrad 1970-71; EdD Auburn Univ 1976; Cert in Cnslg Ga St Univ 1973; pa/Pvt Pract Marriage & Fam Therapist; Asst Prof Psychol; Pres Ga Assn Specialists & Group Work; APA; APGA; AAMFT; cp/Columbus Mayor's Comm on Status of Wom; Coor Crisis Hot Line, Columbus; r/En Orthodox; hon/Ser Awd; Civilian Ser Awd, Dept of Def; Career Wom of Yr, Chattahoochee Val BPW Clb; Personalities of S; W/W S&SW.

GANUS, CLIFTON L JR oc/College President; b/Apr 7, 1922; h/208 S Cross, Searcy, AR 72143; ba/Searcy; m/Louise Nicholas; c/Clifton L III, Deborah Duke, Charles Austin; p/Clifton and Martha Jewel Ganus (dec); ed/BA Harding Col; MA, PhD Tulane Univ; pa/Pres Harding Col; Bd Mem: 1st Security Bk, Finest Foods; cp/Lions Clb; Bd Mem C of C; r/Ch of Christ: Min, Elder; hon/7 Washington Medals for Address, Freedom Foun Val Forge; Outstg Alumnus, Harding Col.

GANUS, LOUISE NICHOLAS oc/-Homemaker; b/Feb 10, 1922; h/208 S Cross, Searcy, AR 72143; m/Clifton Loyd Jr; c/Clifton Loyd III, Deborah Lynn G Duke (Mrs J Richard), Charles Austin; p/Austin C Nicholas (dec); Pearl Matthews Nicholas, Searcy; ed/BA Harding Col; pa/Sec'dy Sch Tchr; cp/"City Beautiful" Com, C of C; Charter Mem Co Meml Hosp Aux; Have Worked w: PTA, GSA, Cub Scouts; AAUW; Greenkeepers Garden Clb; Searcy Garden Clb Coun; Assoc'd Wom for Harding; r/Ch of Christ; hon/Dist'd Alumnus Awd, Harding Col Alumni Assn; Remarkable Wom of Ark; W/W Am Cols & Univs; Harding Col Hon Soc.

GAPOSCHKIN, PETER JOHN ARTHUR oc/Computer Programmer; b/Apr 5, 1940; h/1660 Bay Rd, Palo Alto, CA 94303; ba/Monterey, CA; p/Sergei I and Cecilia H P Gaposchkin, Lexington, MA; ed/BS MIT 1961; MA (Astronomy) 1965, MA (Physics) 1966, PhD 1971 Univ Cal-B; pa/Computer Programmer Fleet Numerical Weather Ctl; Assn for Computing Machinery; Data Processing Mgmt Assn; Am Math Soc; Sigma Xi; Am Astronomical Soc; r/Unitarian, Friends; hon/Upper Deans List, MIT; Hon Mention, NSF F'ship Competition; Competent Toastmaster Awd.

GARABEDIAN, MARTHA ANN oc/Graduate Teaching Assistant; Student; b/Dec 8, 1953; h/1 West St, East Douglas, MA 01516; p/Charles and Sadie Garabedian; ed/BA summa cum laude Worcester St Col 1975; MA 1978, PhD Cand Univ Conn; pa/Grad Tchg Asst Dept Romance & Classical Langs Univ Conn; Am Assn Tchrs Spanish & Portuguese Inc; Mod Lang Assn; Bd Dirs Spanish Cult Soc Worcester (Mass); hon/Nat Hon Soc; Dean's List, Worcester St Col; Fdg Pres Kappa Kappa Chapt Sigma Delta Pi; French Consulate Book Awd; German Consulate Book Awd; Mem & Histn Gamma Chi Chapt Kappa Delta Pi; Danforth F'ship Nom; Sum Doct F'ships; Phi Kappa Phi; Predoct F'ship; Contbr Critical Essay to The Am Hispanist; W/W Among Students in Am Univs & Cols; Commun Ldrs Am; World W/W Wom.

GARCIAGODOY, MANUEL oc/Industrialist; Surgeon; b/Sept 2, 1908; h/1100 Los Angeles Dr, El Paso, TX 79902; ba/El Paso;

m/Irene Arroyo De; c/Irene Rosario, Manuel Emilio, Beatriz Eva; p/Justo G Garcia and Rosario Godoy (dec); ed/Ret'd Surg; Industrialist.

GARDNER, BARRY LYNN oc/Telephone Technician; b/Mar 28, 1946; h/Rt #1, Box 282-C, Rocky Mount, NC 27801; m/Shirley Batts; c/Lisa Lynn, Barry Scott, Ashley Todd; p/Ralph and Nona Mae Lamm Gardner,

Lucama, NC; ed/Grad Carolina Bible Inst; mil/USAF Acad 1964-65; USAFR 1965-70; pa/Pastor Floods Chapel Free Will Bapt 1974-78; cp/Nash Co Chm Mt Olive Col Fund; Repub Party: Poll Judge, Precnt Chm, Nash Co Secy, Dist Exec Com Mem, St Exec Com Mem, Cand for US Ho of Reps; r/Floods Chapel FWB Ch: Mem; Ordained Min Original FWB NC; hon/Nat Beta Clb: Sr Class Histn, Salutatorian.

GARDNER, BILLY DEAN oc/Chief Fiscal Officer; b/Sept 29, 1936; h/405 Frio, Portland, TX 78374; ba/Corpus Christi, TX; m/Carline Uselton; c/Kathy Lynn, Jeffrey Douglas; p/Troy W and Grace Johnson Gardner, Nashville, TN; ed/BBA; MBA;

CPA; pa/Chief Fiscal Ofcr Corpus Christi St Univ; TASSCUBO; NACUBO; cp/Past Dir Kiwanis; Little Leag; Kids Inc; Canyon Boys Clb; r/Bapt; hon/Notable Ams; Personalities of S; W/W S&SW.

GARDNER, E CLAUDE oc/College President; Minister; h/372 Mill St, Henderson, TN 38340; ba/Henderson; m/Delorese Tatum; c/Phyllis Ann Hester (Mrs Sam), Rebecca Sue Cyr (Mrs Larry), Claudia Elaine Goodson (Mrs Mark), James David; p/Edna Rowe, Paragould, AR; ed/AA; BS; MA; Addit Grad Study; pa/Pres Freed-Hardeman Col; Bd Dirs Chester Co Bk, Henderson; cp/Bd Dirs Chester Co C of C; r/Ch of Christ; hon/Blue Key; Alpha Chi; Ky Col; Hon Degs; Alumnus of Yr, F-HC 1972; Civitan Citizen of Yr 1976.

GARDNER, WILLIAM LEONARD oc/Retired; b/Nov 22, 1902; h/109 Rosehill Cir, Staunton, VA 24401; m/Mabel S; c/Mrs Manley P Caldwell Jr, Mrs Coleman D Carter; p/Benjamin F and Rosa Alice Gardner (dec); ed/AB; ME; mil/Lt Col, Ret'd; pa/Ret'd as Supt Emeritus Augusta Mil Acad; Author, Pub'd 1 Book; cp/Kiwanis; Masons; Other Activs; r/Bapt; SS Tchr, Chm Fin Com, Deacon; hon/Cited as Outstg Tchr of French, Fr Govt.

GARELLICK, ARWIN F B oc/Poet-Lyricist; Retired Head Librarian & Editor; b/Aug 18, 1921; h/100 Dewey St, Richford, VT 05476; ba/Same; m/Charles D Bashaw (dec); 2nd Jack L Garellick (dec); c/Dawn-Linnie Bashaw Mennucci; Alson Charles Bashaw; p/Alson B and Linnie A Fletcher (dec); ed/Hon Dipl (Arts & Lttrs), Athens, Greece; pa/Co-Fdr Music Mission for World Peace Inc 1963; 1st Wom Editor *Vermont Odd Fellow* Mag 11 Yrs; Life Mem Hellenic Writer's Clb, Athens, Greece; Am Soc Composers, Author & Pubrs; World Poetry Soc Intercontinental; Vt Lib Assn; Intl Press Assn; IOOF; Poetry Soc Vt; Cal Fdn Chaparral Poets; Ina Coolbrith Cir; Author *Remembered Winds*, 1963 (Book of Poetry); Contbr to Poetry Jours; Exhibited twice by invitation, Intl Outdoor Poetry Show, New Orleans; Other Profl Activs; cp/4-H Yth Ldr 21 Yrs, Diamond Pin & Cert; hon/George Washington Hon Medals (3); Annual ASCAP Popular Panel Awds for Lyrics (12); Grand Ole Opry Trust Fund Awd; Richard Rodgers Music Foul Awd; Prime Min Israel & India Music Awds; King of Thailand Music Awd; Viola Hayes Parsons Awd; Robert Frost Awd/Cert; Prairie Poet 1st Prize Awd; Intl Cloverleaf Anniv Awd; Dr Arthur Hewitt Meml 1st Prize Awd; Certs of Merit; Intl & Am W/W; Num Others.

GARIBAY, ELISA SALAZAR oc/-Homemaker; b/Nov 17, 1946; h/200 W Estes, Midland, TX 79701; m/Edward F; c/Edward Jr, Cipriano; p/Mike B and Lila L Hernandez,

Midland; cp/PTA: Room Mother, Carnival Wkr, Vol Tchr's Aide, City Coun Rep, Del to Dist & St Convs, Current Crockett Elem Sch's Vol Chm; r/Cath; hon/Tex Life Mem PTA.

GARMEL, MARION BESS SIMON oc/Journalist; b/Oct 15, 1936; h/226 E 45th, Indianapolis, IN 46205; ba/Indpls; m/Raymond; p/Marcus and Frieda Alfman Simon (dec); ed/BJour Univ Tex 1958; pa/Journalist *Indpls News*; Wom in Communs Inc; Soc Profl Journalistis; Nat Fdn Press Wom; cp/Hadassah; r/Jewish; hon/1st Pl Criticism: Nat Fdn Press Wom 1974, 78, Indpls Press Clb 1978; 2nd Pl Columnist, Indpls Press Clb 1972.

GARNER, GERALD J oc/Attorney; b/Dec 17, 1936; ba/260 Harrison Ave, Harrison, NY 10528; c/Robyn, Scott, Graig; p/Louis and Anne Garner; ed/BS; LLB; JD; pa/ABA; NY St Trial Lwyrs; DC Bar Assn; cp/Dep Treas Repub Party, Coun; Nat Adv Coun; Coun Dept Labor; r/Harrison Jewish Commun Ctr: Bd Dirs; hon/Arthritis Awd; W/W: Am Jewery, E.

GARNER, LA FORREST DEAN oc/Dentist; Teacher; b/Aug 20, 1933; h/6245 Riverview Dr, Indianapolis, IN 46260; ba/Ipls; m/Alfreida; c/Deana Yvette, Thomas La Forrest, Sanford Ernest; p/Sanford G Garner (dec); Fannie M Garner, Muskogee, OK; ed/DDS Ind Univ 1957; MS 1959;

pa/Orthodontist; Intl Lectr; Author; Clinician; Chm Dept Orthodontics IUSD; cp/Bd Dirs Ind Boys Clb; Vis Nurse Assn; Bd Dirs: YMCA, Ind Hlth Careers; r/Witherspoon U Presb Ch; hon/Nat Pres Omicron Kappa Upsilon; Fellow, Am Col Dentist; Sigma Xi.

GARNER, MARIE GRILLO oc/Volunteer; Investigator; Chief Appraiser; b/Mar 6, 1924; h/1214 Old Boalsburg Rd, State College, PA 16801; ba/Same; m/John A; c/John A Jr, M Judy, Evelyn A and Peggy Jeanne; p/Joseph J and Mary J Grillo (dec); ed/PSU Voc Ed Pa St Sch Aeronautics; mil/Sp Duty Civilian, AAF, AAF Air Power Show, Others; pa/Investigator for Treas of Pa; Chief Appraiser for Co; cp/Dem St Com Mem Centre Co; Area Chm Dem Com St Col; HHH Chm Ctl Pa 1972; Del to Nat Dem Conv; r/Cath; hon/1 of 10 Outstg Wom in Pa (Pres J F Kennedy) 1962; Cert & Pin for Outstg Contbn to Yth in Pa;

W/W: Am Polits, Am Wom; World W/W Wom.

GARNER, (MILDRED) MAXINE oc/Professor; Resident Counselor; b/Mar 15, 1919; h/123 N Asheboro St, Liberty, NC 27298; ba/Briar, VA; p/Robert M Sr and Maize V Kimrey Garner; ed/BA Wom's Col Univ Nc 1939; MA Columbia Univ, Union Theol Sem 1946; PhD Univ Aberdeen (Scotland) 1952; pa/Prof Rel, Resident Cnslr; Fac Devel Sem Banaras Hindu Univ, Varanasi, India Sum 1977; Fellow Am Inst Indian Studies, Poona, India 1962-63; Fellow Prog Adv'd Rel Studies, Union Theol Sem 1955-56; cp/Repub; r/Bapt; hon/Phi Beta Kappa; Fulbright Scholar.

GARNETT, ADRIENNE WILMA oc/Artist; b/Jan 7, 1936; h/126 Beaufort Pl, New Rochelle, NY 10801; ba/Same; m/W Gordon; c/Lianne Ritter, Louis Ritter, Stephen, Joan, Jeffrey; p/M H and Florence W Schlang, Palm Beach, FL; pa/Sculptor, Painter, Craftsman, Art Instr; Exhbns; Works Rep'd in Pvt & Comml Collections across Country; hon/1st & 2nd Prizes for Paintings, Drawings & Sculptures in Num Juried Art Shows.

GARRARD, THOMAS EDWARD oc/Executive; b/Aug 28, 1904; h/1418 Country Clb Rd, McAlester, OK 74501; ba/McAlester; m/Allece; p/Frank Field Garrard (dec); Kate Oliver (dec); ed/SB MIT 1928; pa/Tom Garrard Investmts 1977-; Mng Trustee 1977-; J G Puterbaugh Testamentary Trust, Puterbaugh Foun; McAlester Fuel Co: Ret'd 1977, Chm Bd 1974, Pres 1963, VP & Dir 1950, Asst to Pres 1948; Other Former Positions; Dir: McAlester Fuel Co, Alene Oil Co, McAlester, Brazos Yg Corp, McAlester, 1st Nat Bk & Trust Co, McAlester; Tex Bd Profl Engrs; VP Mid-Continent Oil & Gas Assn; Indep Petrol Assn Am; Am Petrol Inst; cp/ARC, Dir Pittsburg Co, Okla Chapt; Dir Boys' Clb McAlester; Frontiers of Sci Foun Okla Inc: Dir En Okla Chapt, Co Trustee St Org; Dir McAlester Hosp Foun Inc; Trustee Okla Hlth Scis Foun Inc, Okla City; Okla Public Expenditures Coun, Okla City: Trustee, Exec Com; Okla Med Res Foun, Okla City: Trustee, Exec Com, Sci Com, Chm Devel Com; Dir McAlester U Way; Kiamichi Area Voc-Tech Sch Dist No 7, St of Okla, Bd Mem Zone 1; Vols in Corrections; Okla St Sch Bds Assn Inc; MIT Clb Okla; Navy Leag US; Am Security Coun; BSA; Alumni Assn MIT; AARP; Am Radio Relay Leag Inc; C of C: McAlester, US; En Okla Hist Soc; Others.

GARRETTO, LEONARD A JR oc/Insurance Sales Executive; b/Apr 13, 1925; h/39 Rose Hill Ave, New Rochelle, NY 10804;

ba/Englewood Cliffs, NJ; m/Theres R; c/Deborah, Mark, Michael, Paula, David; p/Leonard Garretto Sr (dec); Evenia Garretto, Dix Hills, NY; ed/BEE Manhattan Col 1951; mil/AUS 1943-45, Tech 5th Grade; pa/Reg Sales VP Wis Nat Life Ins Co 1975-; VP Reg Sales Somerset Capital Corp, NYC 1972-75; Gen Mgr David Gracer Co, NYC 1970-72; Other Former Positions; Nat Assn Life Underwriters; Am Soc Notaries; Reg'd Prin Nat Assn Securities Dealers; r/Rom Cath.

GARRISON, ETTA JOSEPHINE oc/Civic Leader; Volunteer; b/Feb 22, 1905; h/5116 N Winnifred St, Tacoma, WA 98407; m/Lee C (dec); c/Lee C Jr, William Douglas; p/William and Josephine Veronica Kuzman Ganz (dec); cp/Precnt Com-man; Mem Ruston Planning Com; Bd Mem Larchmont Sr Ctr; Pierce Co Commun Action Com; Pierce Co Social Sers Adm Bd; Coun-wom Town Ruston 1969-76; Pierce Co Drug Alliance; 6th Congl Dist Dir Repub Woms Clbs; Pres: Pierce Co Repub Wom's Clb, City-wide Garden Clb, Delphinium Clb; Dist Orgr Capitol Dist Garden Clbs; Others; r/Holy Cross Cath Ch, Tacoma: Mem; hon/Plaque for Working w Blind 12 Yrs; Park Named after Mrs Garrison & Husband; Spec Cup Awd for Org'g 150 Garden Clbs (in 18 Months).

GARRISON, WILLIAM DOUGLAS oc/Computer Analyst; Educational Consultant; b/Aug 6, 1937; h/4208 S 252nd Pl, Kent, WA 98031; ba/Kent; m/Kayellen Sinclair; c/Gwendolyn Judith, Thomas William Sinclair; p/Lee C Garrison (dec); Etta Ganz Garrison, Tacoma, WA; ed/AB Harvard; MEd CWSC; PhD Univ Wash; pa/Analyst Boeing Computer Sers; Fac Mem Univ Wash; Conslt to Sch Dists; Grad Cost III Study, Coun Grad Schs of US; cp/Exec Dir Wash St Literacy Inc; King Co Fire Commr; r/Hillcrest Presb Ch: Mem; hon/Harvard Nat Scholar; Harvard Varsity Clb; NSF Fellow.

GARRISON-McDOWELL, MARGARET FRANCES oc/Author; Educator; b/Feb 20, 1905; h/3311 E Ustick Rd, Caldwell, ID 83605; m/Willard A McDowell; c/2 Chd; p/Lemuel Addison and Mary Firth Garrison; ed/BA 1928, PhD Equiv 1963 Univ Cal; MA Col Idaho 1954; pa/Public Sch Tchr: Council, Idaho 1928, Hot Springs, NM 1945-50, Nampa, Idaho 1951-55, Oakland, Cal 1955-65; Public Relats Dir St NEA, Idaho 1955; Prodr Radio Progs on Conservation (CBS) & Am Constitution 1934, 57; St Chm Idaho & Canyon Co Nat Ret'd Tchrs Assn 1974-75; HEW Treasure Val Grants Review Com 1974-76; Delta Kappa Gamma; NRTA; AARP; cp/Former Sr Girl Scout Ldr; Former Mbrship Chm Mayor's Bldg Com for Sr Citizens' Hall, Caldwell, Idaho; Nat Trust for Hist Preserv; Audubon Soc; The Nature Conservancy; Ctr for Envir Ed; Sierra Clb; Solar Lobby; Nat Pks & Conservation; r/Prot; hon/Col S'hip; 50 Yr Mbrship Cit, DAR, En Star & Rebekah; Profl Pubs; Personalities of W&MW.

GARSIDE, JO-ANN DOREEN oc/Educator; b/Mar 21, 1941; h/1108 40th St W, Birmingham, AL 35218; ba/B'ham; p/James P Garside (dec); Alice Richard Garside Sullivan; ed/BS Ala Col; MA 1972, EdD 1976 Univ Ala; pa/Assoc Prof PE B'ham-So Col; Review & Writing Team *Ala Hlth Ed Curric Guide* 1971-72; Ala St Assn AHPER: VP Hlth 1973-74, Treas 1974-75, VP PE 1975-76; Mem Prog Implementation Task Force St Sch Hlth Ed; Adv Com ASAHPER; Nat Outdoor Ed Conf 1977, Var Coms; cp/Planning Com Jefferson Co & N Ala Spec Olympics; r/Epis; hon/Kappa Delta Pi.

GARSZCZYNSKI, SUZANNE M oc/-Clinical Chemist; Laboratory Director; b/Jan 20, 1947; h/Apt C2 S 6th St, Lehighton, PA 18235; ba/Palmerton, PA; p/John and Florence Garszczynski, Wyomissing, PA; ed/BS; PhD; pa/Lab Dir Palmerton Hosp 1974-; St Joseph Hosp, Rdg, Pa: Clin Chemist 1971-73, Instr Microbiol, Biochem, Anatomy & Physiol (Sch Nsg) 1972-73, Instr Clin Chem (Med Tech Sch) 1972-73; Clin Chemist Pathol Sers Inc, Mt Penn, Pa 1971-73; Other Former Positions;

Am Chem Soc; Am Assn for Clin Chem; Phila Sect AACC; Am Soc for Med Technol; ASMT: Pa, Lehigh Val; Assn Clin Scists; Assn for Practitioners in Infection Control; Med Lab Observer's Profl Adv Panel 1978-79; Other Orgs; hon/World W/W Wom.

GARTHOFF, RAYMOND LEONARD oc/Foreign Service Officer; b/Mar 26, 1929; ba/Dept of St, Washington, DC 20520; m/Vera Alexandrovna Vasilieva; c/Alexander Raymond; p/Arnold Alexander Garthoff

(dec); Margaret L Frank Garthoff, Alexandria, VA; ed/AB Princeton Univ; MA, PhD Yale Univ; pa/US Ambassador to Bulgaria; hon/Dist'd Hon Awd, US St Dept; Superior Hon Awd.

GARTLAND, BEVERLY PATTERSON oc/Assistant Professor; b/Mar 7, 1941; h/8508 Carriage Hill Dr, Warren, OH 44484; ba/Youngstown, OH; m/Dennis Joseph; c/Dennis Joseph II; p/Russell Wallace and Leona Keyser Patterson, Niles, OH; ed/BA Youngstown St Univ 1964; MA Ohio St Univ 1967; Doct Studies Univ Ky; pa/Asst Prof Sociol Y'town St Univ; Am, N Ctl, Allegheny Val, Ctl Ky Sociol Assns; Ohio Ed Assn; NEA; Lectr to PTA on Violence in Our Cult & Chd; cp/Mem Child Abuse Preven Bd Trumbell Co; Pres LWV Trumbull Co; Advr to Howland Sch Levy Opinion Survey Com; r/Cath; hon/Dustheimer Awd in Astronomy, Y'town St Univ.

GARTNER, LAWRENCE MITCHEL oc/Professor; Director; h/One Normandy Rd, Larchmont, NY 10538; ba/Bronx, NY; m/Carol Blicker; c/Alex David, Madeline Hallie; p/Samuel Gartner, Madison, CT; Bertha Gartner (dec); ed/AB Columbia Univ; MD Johns Hopkins Univ; pa/Albert Einstein Col Med: Prof Pediatrics, Dir Div Neonatology; Med Res, Tchg--Newborn Med & Liver Diseases in Chd; cp/Trustee Am Liver Foun; hon/Alpha Omega Alpha; Phi Beta Kappa; Mosby & Appleton Century Crofts Book Awds; Career Devel Awd, Nat Inst Hlth Awd; Chd's Liver Foun.

GARY, GAYLE H M oc/Communication Executive; b/Dec 23, 1920; h/1212 Fifth Ave, New York City, NY 10079; m/Arthur John; c/Sandra Gayle M; p/Michael H Summers (dec); Lilian E Summers, NYC; ed/Att'd: Univ Miami 1939, NYU 1940-43, Columbia 1944-46; pa/Pres & Owner Gayle Gary Assocs (Radio & TV Conslts) 1954-; Interviewer & Prodr Syndicated Radio Prog "Views & People in the News"; Public Relats Soc Am; Intl Radio & TV Execs Soc; Nat Inst Social Scis; Rel Public Relats Soc Am; Wom in Radio & TV; Nat Soc Lit & Arts; Am Inst Mgmt; IPA; Bd Mem Ldrship Foun; Other Profl Assns; cp/Bd Mem Vols in Action; 1976 Nat UN Day Com; Fdn Repub Wom; Repub Com 100; Chm Public Relats Nat Coun Wom's Nat Repub Clb; Exec Com Hope Cotillion; Nat Dir Nat Radio-TV Com for Am Observance of Human Rts Week; GSA; Mem Spec Events Eleanor Roosevelt Mem Foun Com; Exec Com Hope Cotillion; Fund Raising Com Wom U Hosp Fund; Nat Adv Com Medico; Patron Activs Com Wom's Aux, NY Infirmary; Hort Soc NY; Sea Org; Chwom Patriotic Leag; Navy Leag; Eng Spkg Union; Repub; Exec VP Wom's Chess Clb NY; Other Civic Activs; r/Ch of Scn: Min, Ordained 1977; St Bartholomew PE Ch: Pres Guild 1954-56,

Convocation & Diocesan Ofcr 1954-; hon/Num Biogl Listings.

GATES, BETTY RUSSELL oc/Professional Artist; b/Aug 10, 1927; h/4900 Wondol Ct, Hurst, TX 76053; ba/Same; m/David W; c/Jerry R (dec), David E, Patricia A, Julie Lynn, Russell, Lisa, Alexander; p/Robert Russell, Hunt, TX; Lela Creekmore, Tulsa, OK; pa/Tchr; 35 Yrs Comml & Fine Art Experience; cp/Var Civic Activs; r/Unity; hon/St & Nat Awds; World W/W Wom; Intl W/W Intells; Personalities of S.

GATHINGS, EZEKIEL C oc/Attorney at Law; b/Nov 10, 1903; h/1705 Fairway Dr, West Memphis, AR 72301; ba/W Memphis; m/Tolise Kirkpatrick; c/Tolise Kirkpatrick Norwood, Joseph Royston; p/Melville W and Virgie Eva Garner Gathings (dec); ed/JD Univ Ark; pa/Indiv Pract Law: W Memphis 1969-, Earle, Ark 1930-31; Partner Firms: Shafer & Gathings, W Memphis 1933-39, Cooper & Gathings, Earl & W Memphis 1931-33, Others;

Ark, Am Bar Assns; Ark Trial Lwrys Assn; Am Judic Soc; Ark Bar Foun; cp/Mem W Memphis Port Auth; Former Mem US Ho of Reps; Former Mem W Memphis Flood Control Com; r/Bapt; hon/50th Anniv Medal, Fed Land Bank 1967; Cit for Being Watch Dog of Treasury, Nat Assn Bus-man; Cit for Meritorious Ser, Ark Farm Bur Fdn; Dist'd Ser Awd, W Memphis Rotary Clb.

GATHINGS, PAUL ERVIN oc/Store Manager; College Instructor; b/Jan 21, 1923; h/1008 W 21st, Odessa, TX 79763; ba/Midland, TX; m/Margaret Faye; c/Susan, John, Kay Smith, Wanda Canon, Brenda Swerison; p/Tom Ervin and Ruby Booth

Gathings (dec); ed/AS; mil/USN WWII; AUS Korea; pa/Lectr; Poetry Instr; Writer; Tex Poetry Soc; cp/Lion's Clb; VFW; Am Legion; IPA; hon/1st Pl Nortex Prize for Poetry; 3rd Pl, World Poetry Contest; 21 Battle Ribbons (2 Wars); Intl W/W: Living Poets, Intells; Men of Distn; Acad Am Poets.

GATTI, CORINNE S oc/Home Tutor; b/Apr 25, 1949; h/92 Lindberg Ave, Staten Island, NY 10306; ba/Same; m/Richard J; p/Thomas F and Marylyn J Gatti, SI, NY; ed/BA Notre Dame Col St John's Univ; MS Richmond Col SI 1978; pa/Home Tutor Eng; Reg Co-Chperson "Readathon Prog"; cp/Secy Thompkinsville-St George Bd of Trade; r/Rom Cath; hon/Reg Sci Awd, Ford Foun; Masland Duran Cover Girl; Editor & Contbr *Poetry Art Jour of Notre Dame Col*; Contbr Pubs to: *Clover Intl Poetry Anthology, Nat Poetry Review, "Glasswork" of Staten Isl, Staten Isl Poetry Anthology*; DIB.

GATTONE, VINCENT H oc/Technical Director; b/Apr 27, 1908; h/Edgemere Rd, Rt 4, Box 354, Easton, MD 21601; ba/Cambridge, MD; m/Ardita Pizzi; c/Antonette Saul, Vincent H II, Elvira Josephine Burlingham; p/Anthony and Josephine Gattone (dec); ed/PhG 1929; BS (Chem) 1932; BS (Pharm); MS; Grad Work: Univ Pa, Temple Univ, Univ Wash; mil/Nat Roster Specialized Sci Pers, Wash DC; pa/Tech Dir Specialty Gases & Lab Lif-O-Gen; Md Pharm Soc: Trustee, Com Mem; Rec'g Secy En Shore Pharm Soc; Conslt; cp/Franklin Inst Philadelphia; Lions Intl, Easton; Elks; r/Presby Ch Easton: Deacon; hon/Fellow, AAAS; Var Res Accomplishmts; W/W in E; Pub'd Author.

GAUL, THOMAS JOSEPH oc/Executive; b/Apr 11, 1942; h/162 Ten Eyck St, S Plainfield, NJ 07080; ba/Clifton, NJ; m/Faith Frances; c/Renee Andrea, Dana Lynn; p/Joseph G Gaul (dec); Mary Gaul, Woodbridge, NJ; ed/BA La Salle Col; MBA Seton Hall Univ; mil/AUS Spec Forces 1966-68; pa/Mktg/Planning Mgmt; Bd Dirs

Am Mktg Assn; Spkr: Am Mktg Assn, Am Mgmt Assn; Guest Lectr: Rider Col, Mgmt Devel Inst; cp/Toastmasters Intl; Bd Dirs Pilgrim Covenant Nursery Sch, S P'field; r/Pilgrim Covenant; hon/Mktg Man of Yr 1971, 78; Toastmaster of Yr 1970; W/W: E, Intly.

GAUMER, VERONICA G oc/Author; h/930 Downing #311, Denver, CO 80218; ed/BA Univ Colo; pa/Asst Exhbn Chperson Colo Lib Assn; cp/DAR; ERA Colo; hon/Pubs: *Thoughts Carried by the Wind*, 1977, (Poem) "Living as Defined as Dying", 1978; Fellow, IBC.

GAUNT, DONA OPHELIA JENNINGS oc/Teacher; Librarian; b/Feb 2, 1931; h/508 N Broadway, Canton, OK 73724; ba/Canton; m/Leslie H; c/Janet R Black; p/William Fred Jennings (dec); Ruth L Jennings, Lexington, OH; ed/BA 1971, MA 1975 SWOSU; pa/OEA; NEA; OCTE; NCTE; Kappa Kappa Iota; NW Okla Dist OEA Del; Designed & Set up Elem Lib Canton Elem Sch; cp/Gov's Adv Panel for Handicapped Chd; CoOrgr & VP Custer Co Assn for Retarded Chd; Mem City Lib Bd; r/Canton 1st Christian Ch: Mem, Jr High Yth Sponsor; hon/Full S'ship, Kappa Kappa Iota.

GAUNY, RONNIE DEAN oc/Physicist; b/Jun 12, 1947; h/10007 Kirkwren Ct, Houston, TX 77089; ba/Houston; m/Peggy Ann; c/Tamatha Anne, Ronnie Dean Jr; p/Van C and Nina A Gauny, San Antonio, TX; ed/BS; MS; pa/Supv'g Hlth Physicist Houston Lighting & Power Co; Hlth Physics Soc; Am Nuclear Soc; EEI-HPTF; FRHP; r/Civic Clb; Soccer Assn; r/Ch of LDS; hon/Nat Physics Hon Soc.

GAUTREAUX, MARCELIAN FRANCIS oc/Chemical Industry Executive; b/Jan 17, 1930; h/1662 Pollard Pkwy, Baton Rouge, LA 70808; ba/BR; m/Mignon Alice; c/Marc, Marian, Kevin, Andree; p/Marcelian Francis Gautreaux (dec); Mary Eunice Terrebonne Gautreaux, BR; ed/BS ChE magna cum laude 1950, MS 1951, PhD 1958 La St Univ; pa/Ethyl Corp, BR: Sr VP 1974-, Bd Mem 1972-, VP Res & Devel 1969-74, Gen Mgr Res & Devel 1966-68, Others; Nat Acad Engrg; Am Inst Chem Engrs: Nat Com, Mem Local

Sect, Ofcr & Exec Com; Soc Engrg Sci, Bd Dirs 1972-75; Soc Chem Indust; cp/Former Mem Bd Trustees La Arts & Sci Ctr; Bd Dirs Commun Concerts; Baton Rouge CC; City Clb; Camelot Clb; LSU Centurion; r/Cath; hon/Annual Meml Awd, CMRA; Charles E Coates Meml Awd, Local Chapts Am Inst Chem Engrs & Am Chem Soc; PACE Awd; Cit for Outstg Res, SEn Sect Am Soc Engrg Ed; Awd for Best Presented Paper, Nat Annual AIChE Meeting 1952.

GAVIN, ROSEMARIE JULIE oc/Sister of Religious Order; Educator; b/Jan 26, 1917; p/Michael Joseph Gavin; Rose Estelle Gardner; ed/AA Col Notre Dame 1937; BEd cum laude UCLA 1939; MA Cath Univ Am 1952; PhD Stanford Univ 1955; pa/Col Notre Dame: Tchr Ed, Eng & Psychol 1953-, Dir Evening Div 1966, Chm Tchg Ed Com 1960-69, Dir Grad Studies 1968-, Acad Dean 1968, Bd Trustees 1968-, Dir Sum Session 1961-66, Chm Grad Studies Com 1970-, Tchg Ed Com 1960-; Var Former Profl Positions; AAUP; NSSE; AAHE; Pi Lambda Theta; Delta Epsilon Sigma; Com to Restructure Cal Coun for Ed of Tchr 1962-64; Dir Annual Interdiscip Symposia 1963-66; Ed TV w KPIX 1963-66; Secy-Treas Nat Cath Ed Assn SW Reg Unit 1962-68; Tchg Profl Standards Com St of Cal 1963-69; San Mateo Co Com on Tchg Ed for Fam Life Ed 1966; Served on Cal St Dept of Ed Re-accreditation team to UCB 1969; NCATE Team to Univ Puget Soung 1974; cp/Former Mem: San Mateo Co Pace Forum, Planning Bd Conf on Rel & Peace; r/Cath; hon/Named Commun Ldr in Aging, San Mateo Co; Guest Spkr; Profl Pubs; Biogl Listings.

GAWIENOWSKI, ANTHONY MICHAEL oc/Associate Professor; b/Oct 24, 1924; h/902 E Pleasant St, Amherst, MA 01002; ba/Amherst; m/Clotilda Brewington; c/John, Anthony Jr, Margaret, Mary, Peter; p/(dec); ed/BS Villanova Col 1948; MS 1953, PhD

1956 Univ Mo-Columbia; mil/USNR 1944-46, Lt (jg); pa/Assoc Prof Biochem Univ Mass; Endocrine Soc; Am Chem Soc; AAUP; Phi Lambda Upsilon; Gamma Alpha; cp/BSA; Mtl Hlth Assn; r/Cath; hon/Fellow, AAAS; Sigma Xi; Gamma Sigma Delta.

GAY, ANNA BELLE GRAHAM oc/Homemaker; b/Jun 4, 1922; h/844 Aldino-Stepney Rd, Aberdeen, MD 21001; m/Herman Paul; c/Paul, Martha, Nancy, John; p/Waymon C and Maggie Bailey Graham (dec); ed/BA magna cum laude Winthrop Col 1942; pa/Computer-Mathematician Aberdeen Proving Gd 1942-45; Substitute Tchr; cp/Bd Dirs Harford Co TB Assn; Past Pres Md PTA;

Former Mem Bd Dirs Ctl Md Heart Assn; Appt'd (by Gov) to 5-Yr Term on Bd of Ed Public Schs Harford Co & Bd Trustees Harford Commun Col; r/U Meth: SS Tchr, Christian Social Concerns Chm, WSCS; Pres Baltimore E Dist U Meth Wom (Balto Conf); hon/Wom of Yr, UMW 1977; Listed in "Outstg Ladies We Hold Dear" (Booklet of Harford Co Homemakers' Coun); Resolutions of Apprec, Bd Ed & Bd Trustees; Ctl Md Heart Assn: Meritorious Ser Awd, Public Relats Awd, "Outstg Heart Vol"; Hon Life Mem, Nat PTA & Md PTA; Plaques of Apprec (2), BSA; W/W Cols & Univs.

GAY, CLARA FLOURNOY oc/Retired Writer, Poetess; b/Dec 19, 1907; h/507 Rosebud Dr, Natchitoches, LA 71457; c/Louise Wilcox Clay, Robert Wilcox Jr; p/James Pattson and Clara Johnson Flournoy (dec); ed/Hon Doct'd Deg in Lit; pa/Edit Writing; Poems, Books; cp/Adv Bd Nutrition N Triple Govt Proj; r/Epis; hon/Boswell-Order of Gracian (Rome, Italy); Poem in Congl Record; Others.

GAY, NANCY ANN oc/Assistant Professor; b/May 23, 1942; h/4533 Chaha Rd, #141, Garland, TX 75041; ba/Dallas, TX; p/Donald G and Virginia C Gay, Dallas; ed/BA; MS; EdD; pa/Asst Prof Spec Ed E Tex St Metroplex Ctr; CEC; Phi Delta Kappa; Tex

Assn for Chd w LD; cp/Vol Am Diabetic Assn; WEAL; hon/US Overseas Dependent Schs Europe: Outstg Tchr, Sustained Superior Tchg; Kappa Delta Pi; Sigma Tau Delta; Work in Jean Piaget Ctr, Univ Geneva (Switzerland) 1976-77.

GAY, WILLIAM TEAGUE oc/College Professor; Author; b/Sept 29, 1899; h/1513 College Ct, Montgomery, AL 36106; ba/Same; m/Lena Claire Butler (dec); c/Frances G Lyon, William T Jr, Robert Stirling, George Marion; p/John Floyd and Julia Teague Gay (dec); ed/BS 1921, LLB 1923, MA 1928, JD 1969 Univ Ala; Further Studies;

mil/USN; Midshipman US Nav Acad 1917-19; USAAC Capt WWII; pa/Writer; Assoc Prof Pembroke (NC) St Col (to 1966); Camp Ednl Advr Civilian Conservation Corps 1935-37; Engr Ala Hwy Dept 1934-35; Hd Eng Dept Ga St Col-Tifton 1930-33; Other Former Positions; Acad Am Poets; AAUP; World Future Soc; Edward Bellamy Meml Assn; cp/Polit Campaign Activs; r/Bapt: Unitarian Universalist; hon/Wall Plaque Engraved w Running Records: Age 75 at Masters Track Meet, Montgomery, Ala 1975 (1 Mile in 8 Min 18.6 Seconds, 3 Miles in 26 Min 58.2 Seconds); 6 Trophies Track Meets; Life Mbrship, Nat Jogging Assn; Medal for Age 76 Record 100 Yd

Dash in 20.1 Seconds, 1976; Pub'd Author; Biogl Listings..

GAZIN, CHARLES LEWIS oc/Paleobiologist Emeritus; b/Jun 18, 1904; h/6420 Broad St, Brookmont, MD 20016; ba/- Washington, DC; m/Elisabeth H (dec); c/Margaret A G Schellhous, Chester L, Barbara J G Neubauer; p/Charles Edward and

Janie Frances Gazin (dec); ed/BS 1927, MS 1928, PhD 1930 Caltech; mil/USAAF WWII, Maj; pa/(Vertebrate) Paleobiologist Emeritus Nat Mus Natural Hist; hon/Prize, Cordilleran Sect Geol Soc Am; Legion of Merit.

GAZZOLA, RICHARD PETER oc/- Teacher; b/Mar 26, 1945; h/16 Fernwood Ave, Rye, NY 10580; ba/Yonkers, NY; p/- Peter V and Edna D Soldwedel Gazzola, Rye; ed/BA, MS Fordham Univ; pa/Sci Tchr Longfellow Mid Sch; Nat Sci Tchrs Assn, Conv Evaluating Com 1978; Sci Tchr Assn NY St; Yonkers Fdn Tchrs, Asst Bldg Rep 1977-; NY St U Tchrs; Coun Long Isl Edrs; Edrs to Africa Assn; cp/Smithsonian Inst; Nat Audubon Soc; Nat Wildlife Fdn; Am Mus Natural Hist; NY Zool Soc; Fordham Univ Alumni Assn; US-China Peoples Alumni Assn; Var Ofcs Longfellow PTA, Yonkers Coun PTA & Westchester Dist PTA; hon/NY St PTA; Tchr F'ship, Hon Life Mbrship; Outstg Tchr, L'fellow Mid Sch; Outstg Commun Ser Awd, Nat Afro-Am Labor Coun, Westchester Chapt; S'ship; Biogl Listings.

GEDDES, LaNELLE EVELYN oc/Professor, Assistant Department Head; b/Sept 15, 1935; h/400 N River Rd, #1724, W Lafayette, IN 47906; ba/W Lafayette; m/Leslie A; p/Carl O Nerger (dec); Evelyn B Nerger, W Lafayette; ed/BS; PhD; pa/Purdue Univ: Prof Nsg, Asst

Hd Dept Nsg; Lectr; Writer; AAAS; Am Assn Critical Care Nurses; Am Nurses Assn; cp/Am Heart Assn, Ind Affil: Chm Nsg Ed Com, Bd Dirs; r/Univ Luth Ch, W Lafayette; hon/Recipient F'ships; Sigma Pi; Sigma Theta Tau; Phi Kappa Phi; Dept Tchg Awd; James Dwyer Undergrad Tchg Awd, Purdue Univ.

GEE, ZILPHIA TONI oc/Instructor, Clinical Director; b/Dec 11, 1941; h/9900 Georgia Ave #516, Silver Spring, MD 20902; ba/Washington, DC; m/Lloyd Powell, Port Arthur, TX; Georgiana Powell Manson, Port Arthur, TX; ed/BA Huston-Tillotson Col 1963; MA Cath Univ Am 1973; PhD Cand Univ Pittsburgh; pa/Howard Univ: Instr, Clin Dir Spch & Hearing Clin; ASHA; AAUW; Alpha Kappa Alpha; cp/Nat Coun Negro Wom; Communs Confs; Var Vol Activs;

r/Cath: Ch Lector; hon/Cert Competence in Spch Pathol; World W/W Wom; DIB; Intl W/W Commun Ser; Notable Ams.

GEER, PATRICIA BOYLE oc/Operations Analyst; b/Jul 29, 1924; h/2064 Sky Farm Ave, Vicksburg, MS 39180; ba/V'burg; m/Paul Raymond; c/J Michael, Karen G Recker, Paul G Childers; p/Alfred Louis and Marguerite Comer Boyle (dec); pa/Social Security Adm: Opers Analyst 1976-, Field Rep 1973-75, Claims Rep 1971-72, Adm Aide 1962-70; Atlanta Reg Mgmt Assn 1978; BPW Clb, Var Ofcs; cp/Girl Scout Ldr 7 Yrs; PTA Pres 6 Yrs; Former Mem Bd Dirs ARC; Agy Keyman U Givers; Former Treas Phi Alpha Kappa; Super Dog Div, Miss St Univ Bulldog Clb; Assn Miss St Alumni; r/1st Christ Ch, V'burg: Pres CWF 1968-70, Deaconess, Ch Clerk, SS Supt 2 Yrs, SS Tchr 15 Yrs; Bus Wom's Commr Miss Christians Chs 1971; Registrar Miss St Conv Christian Chs 1971; hon/High Quality Awd, SSA.

GEHRES, HELEN ROOP oc/Homemaker; Geneaologist; Former Secretary; b/Feb 20, 1921; h/1026 Elm St, Van Wert, OH 45891; ba/Van Wert; m/Walter Arnold; p/Samuel Rufus and Bessie Ogg Roop (dec); pa/Author 1 Pub'd Book on Fam Geneal; Other Pubs; cp/Isaac Van Wart DAR: Ofcr, Libn, Chm; Van Wert Co (Ohio) Hist Soc; Wells Co (Ind) Hist Soc; Former Dem Dep Clerk Bd Elections, Van Wert; Dem Wom's Clb; Former Dem Precnt Election Ofcl; Pres Van Wert Co Woms Dem 2 Yrs; r/1st U Meth Ch, Van Wert: Mem, SS Tchr, Former Chm Ch Histns; hon/W/W: Am Wom, Am Polits; Commun Ldrs & Noteworthy Ams; DIB.

GEHRING, JOHN WILLIAM JR oc/Physicist; Manager; b/Sept 22, 1928; h/365 Harvard Ln, Santa Barbara, CA 93111; ba/Goleta, CA; m/Suzanne Jean; c/John William III, Thomas G, Ronald B, Jeffrey J; p/John William Sr and Dorothea Gehring, Santa Barbara; ed/BS; pa/Mgr EG&G Inc; ADPA; AIAA; ASM; cp/Elks; C of C; Repub; r/Cath; hon/Patentee in field; Author 2 Books; W/W: Am, S&SW.

GEIGER, LOREN DENNIS oc/School Band Director; Professional Tuba Player; b/Jan 23, 1946; h/15 Park Blvd, Lancaster, NY 14086; ba/Orchard Pk, NY; m/Elaine Louise Sivers; p/Carroll Chester and Edith Lucille Swedenborg Geiger, Orchard Pk; ed/BMus 1968; MMus 1970; pa/Sch Band Dir Orchard Pk Ctl Sch; Prin Tuba: Orch Pk Symph, Amherst Symph, Clarence Symph, 20th Century Band; Music Edrs Nat Conf; Am Fdn Musicians; NY St Sch Music Assn; Tubists Universal Brotherhood Assn; Intl Mil Music Soc; Nat Band Assn; Contbr to Profl Jours;

Editor/Pubr, "Boombah Herald" Newslttr; Composer/Arranger over 200 Works for Band; r/Calvinist; hon/Pi Kappa Lambda.

GEIGLE, RALPH C oc/Retired City School Superintendent; b/Oct 25, 1911; h/1444 O, Reading, PA 19604; m/Ferne E; c/Frances L Geigle-Bentz, Suzann L Sager; p/(dec); ed/BA 1935, PedD 1959 Susquehanna Univ; MA Columbia Univ 1940; EdD Geo Wash Univ 1950; mil/USN Comm'd Ofcr WWII, Post-War Yrs; Nav Intell 1943-50, Anti-Sub Patrol 1943; pa/Supt: Rdg City Schs 1956-74, Oakmont Boro Schs (Allegheny Co) 1953-56; Supv'g Prin Susquenita Jt Schs, Duncannon & Marysville, Pa 1952-53; Grad Inst Res Pa St Univ 1951; Instr Fgn Langs

(Slavic) US Nav Resv Classes, Nav Communs Sta, Wash DC 1948-50; Other Former Positions; Participant Nat Fgn Policy Conf on Edrs, Dept of St 1966, 67; cp/Chm Ed Comm Nat Coun on Alcoholism; Chm Daniel Boone Dist BSA; Chm World Ser Rdg; Chm Pers Comm/Lung Assn; YMCA; 33rd Deg Mason; r/Luth; hon/Num Cits incl'g: Lehigh Univ Sch Study Coun, Rdg City Group & Phila Phillies, Armed Forces & Vets' Orgs, Lycoming Col Alumni Assn, Susquehanna Univ Alumni Asn, US Treasury Dept, YMCA, Others; Profl Pubs; Biogl Listings.

GEISINGER, WILLIAM ROBERT oc/Economist Analyst; b/Oct 21, 1908; h/108½ S Monroe St, Troy, OH 45373; ba/Troy; c/Harry Clifford, William Robert G Jr; p/William Morris and Glada Belinda Hawthorne Geisinger (dec); ed/AB Dartmouth Col 1930; Geo Wash Univ 1952; PhD

Hamilton St Univ 1973; pa/Ec Analyst-Forecasting; Am Ec Assn; Am Statistical Assn; AAAS; Foun for Study of Cycles; cp/Lions Clb; Masonic-York, Scottish Rite; Shriner; Moose; Waco Hist Soc; Troy Hist Soc; Former Dir, Mem Coun Boy Scouts; r/Presb; hon/Biogl Listings.

GEIST, HAROLD oc/Clinical Psychologist; b/Jul 22, 1916; h/2255 Hearst Ave, Berkeley, CA 94709; ba/Berkeley; p/Alexander and Edna Liebhaber Geist, Miami Beach, FL; ed/AB; AM; PhD; mil/AUS 1942-46; pa/Staff Psychologist Gladman Meml Hosp & Foun, Oakland, Cal 1970-; Psychologist Epis Homes Foun 1969-; Sr Clin Psychologist Napa St Hosp, Imola, Cal 1966-; Conslt; Panelist; Profl Pubs; Pres Div II Ed & Tng Div, Cal St Psychol Assn 1976-; Editor Div II Newslttr, CSPA 1975-; Dir Am Psychol Assn Tennis Clb 1975-; AAAS; APGA; Profl Mem Nat Voc Guid Assn; Nat Rehab Assn; Inter-Am Psychol Assn; Chief Edit Conslt Wn Psychol Ser, LA, Cal 1967-; Prin Investigator

Num Res Projs; Lectr San Francisco St Col, SF, Cal 1966-; Pvt Pract, Berkeley; Other Profl Positions & Activs; r/Hebrew; hon/Biogl Listings.

GELTZ, CHARLES GOTTLIEB oc/- Forester; Educator; b/Feb 21, 1896; h/1521 NW 7th Ave, Gainesville, FL 32603; m/- Mildred Harry; c/Charles, Betty Anne Swanson (Mrs Joel D), Helen Reilly (Mrs Ralph L), Jane Keenan (Mrs William T); p/William and Mary Ditter Geltz; ed/BS Pa St Forest Sch 1924; MSF Univ Cal 1927; Att'd Duke Univ; mil/WW I, Mexican Border, US Cavalry; WW II, Adj Gen Corps; Ret'd Maj USAR; pa/Forester, Ala Comm of Forestry 1924-25; Instr Forestry, Registrar, NY St Forest Ranger Sch, Col of Forestry, SUNY, Wanakena, NY 1925-27; Res Asst, Div of Forestry, Univ Cal 1926-27; Jr Forester, US Forest Ser 1927-29; Instr Forestry, St Forest Sch, Pa Univ 1929-30; Asst Prof, Purdue Univ 1930-34, Assoc Prof 1934-36; Dir Purdue Forestry Sum Camp 1930-42; Prof Silviculture, Sch Forestry, Univ Fla-Gainesville 1946-66; Prof Silviculture Emeritus, Univ Fla 1966-; Vis Prof-Conslt,

Univ Ky 1967-68; So Reg Coun for Nat Sch Forestry & Conserv, Wolf Springs Forest, Minong, WI; Operator, Owner, Charles G Geltz Assocs, Forestry-Wildlife-Outdoor Rec Conslts; Conslt Forest Rec & Fam Camping, Fla Fam Camping Assns; Outdoor Rec Conslt to Dir Resources Progs Dept Interior 1961-63; Fla Gov's Resource Use Ed Com; Reg'd Forester, Ga & Fla; Fellow Am Geog Soc; Soc Am Foresters (Forester of Yr Awd, Fla Sect 1966); Am Forestry Assn; Fla Forestry Assn (Hon Life, Dir Exec Bd); Forest Farmers Assn; Fla Forestry Coun (Secy) (Nat for 1936-38); Xi Sigma Pi; Phi Sigma; Phi Delta Kappa; Kappa Delta Pi; Alpha Phi Omega; Scabbard & Blade; cp/Mason (32 Deg, Shriner); Ret'd Ofcrs Assn; Neighborhood Commr BSA; Boy Scout Commr for Sunland Tng Ctr 1949-66; r/Epis; Lay Reader; hon/BSA: Unit Cit Awd & Plaque, Commend Ribbon, Silver Beaver Awd; Wisdom Awd of Hon, The Wisdom Soc 1970.

GENOA, JOHN JR oc/Teacher; b/Sept 15, 1944; h/1606 Bolton St, Baltimore, MD 21217; p/John Jr and Ethel M Genoa, Danville, PA; ed/AA York Jr Col 1965; BS 1968, Masters Bus Ed 1972 Bloomsburg St Col; pa/Bus Ed Tchr Balto Co Public Schs; Former Mktg Rep Bk of Hanover & Trust Co; Former Tchr Bald Eagle & Hanover Public Sch Dists; cp/Del Dem Nat Conv 1976; Life Mem Demolay; Hanover Area JCs; Hanover Area C of C; Patmos Lodge F&AM; Caldwell Consistory 32°; Irem Temple Shrine; Treas Hanover Area Dem Clb; Staff Mem Miss Md S'ship Pageant; Judge Miss WVa Pageant; Other Pageant Activs; r/Meth; hon/W/W Am Polits; Danville News Awd; Faith in G&O Awd, Pa JCs.

GENOVA, DAVID JOSEPH oc/Professor; Concert Pianist; b/Jun 17, 1943; h/1587 Locust St, Denver, CO 80220; ba/Denver; m/Laura Katherine; c/Eric David; p/Joseph Charles and Marian Genova, Pueblo, CO; ed/AA So Colo St Univ 1963; BMus 1965, MMus 1967 Univ Colo; pa/Assoc Prof Music Univ Denver 1978-; Accompanist Intl Artists; Lectr; Specialist 20th Century Music; r/Rom Cath; hon/Univ S'ships; Spec Music Awds; Grad F'ships; Pi Kappa Lambda.

GENSKOW, JACK K oc/Rehabilitation

Counselor; Educator; b/Mar 19, 1936; h/1916 Claremont, Springfield, IL 62703; ba/S'field; m/Lillian Margret; c/Karen Marie, Kenneth Dean; p/Harvey M and Marie V Genskow (dec); ed/BS; AM; PhD; pa/Assoc Prof Sangamon St Univ; Rehab Psychologist; UW-Stout R&T Ctr Adv Coun; Past Pres Ill Rehab Assn; Ill Psychol Assn, Ethics Com Chm; r/Prot; hon/Marlene Nelson Rehab Awd, Ill Rehab Assn; Others.

GENTRY, ALWYN HOWARD oc/University Professor; Research Botanist; b/Jan 6, 1945; h/4252 Botanical, St Louis, MO 63110; ba/St Louis; m/Julie Alice; c/Darrell, Diane; p/S Merle Gentry (dec); Goldie S Gentry,

Manhattan, KS; ed/BA; BS; MS; PhD; mil/Served 1969-70; pa/Secy Flora Neotropica; Authority on Tropical Am Plants; r/Meth; hon/Res Grants: NSF, Nat Geographic Soc.

GENTRY, DORIS GARNER oc/Businesswoman; Hospital Administrator; b/Feb 29, 1928; h/1243 Morgan Dr, Lakeland, FL 33801; ba/Lakeland; m/G B Jr; c/Bonnie G Dube, G Bryan III, Russell Garner, Kevin David; p/Russell Robert Garner (dec); Irma Padgett Garner, Lakeland; pa/CoOwner Season's Greetings Shoppe; Utilization Review Coor Lakeland Gen Hosp; BPW; cp/OES; ZEF Clb; Former Girl Scout Ldr, Brownie Ldr & Cub Scout Mother; r/1st Bapt Ch: Former SS Tchr, BTU Ldr; hon/Num Awds in Arts & Crafts.

GEORGE, PRESTON W oc/Retired, Civil Engineer; b/Oct 4, 1906; h/1812 S Rankin, Edmond, OK 73034; m/Margaret Prestridge; c/Burnis Argo, Margaret Jackson; p/Absalom E and Maude Farrar George (dec); ed/BS Okla St Univ 1931; pa/Civil Engr: Bur Reclamation Okla City (Plans & Reports) 1941-73, Okla

Hwy Dept 1932-41, Corps of Engrs 1929; Freelance Photog & Writer of Railroads & Hists; cp/Radio Amateur; Former Square Dance Caller & Instr; Amateur Archaeologist;

r/Bapt; hon/Gold Trowel Awd, Outstg Amateur Archaeologist, Okla.

GERBERICK, DAHL ANTHONY oc/- Data Processing Manager; b/Jun 14, 1945; h/1174 Flintlock Rd, Diamond Bar, CA 91765; ba/Los Angeles, CA; m/Stella Marie; c/Christina Marie, Anthony Dahl, Theresa Marie; p/Dahl Irwin Gerberick (dec); Dolores Elaine Gussette, S Pasadena, CA; ed/BS Loyola Univ 1969; MBA Cal Polytech Univ 1979; pa/Assn for Computing Machinery: Chm Los Angeles Ombudsman Com 1971-75, Chm Ombudsman Com on Privacy & Security

1974-76, LA Chapt Exec Coun 1971-76, Chm Nat Ombudsman Com 1975-78, Conceived & Devel'd ACM Film on Real Capabilities & Limitations of Computers 1978-79, VChm LA Chapt 1978, Chm LA Chapt 1979; EDP Auditors Assn; Data Processing Mgrs Assn; cp/Dem; r/Rom Cath; hon/Spec Cert of Apprec, Inst Internal Auditors; Outstg Mem Awd, Assn for Computing Machinery; Spec Achmt Awd, Supt LA City Schs; Guest Spkr; Author *Privacy, Security, and the Information Processing Industry*, 1976; W/W in W.

GERHARDT, LOUISE BURGER oc/Retired Secretary; h/5 S Belle Grove Rd, Catonsville, MD 21228; m/Clinton Francis (dec); p/John Frederick Sr and Elizabeth Anna Henkel Burger (dec); ed/Certs in Writing & Art; pa/Ret'd, Former Adm Secy & Personal

Secy to Dir Public Works, Baltimore, Md; Art Classes in Studio; Artist Mem Nat Leag Am Pen Wom; r/Mt Vernon U Meth Ch, Balto: Mem, Adm Bd, Coor Art Dept; hon/1st, 2nd & 3rd Pls & Hon Mentions in Watercolor Exhbns; 1976 Biennial Awd as Author of Carroll Br Hist.

GERLA, MORTON oc/Business & Engineering Executive; Consultant; b/Jul 11, 1916; h/764 Pipes Ct, Northfield, OH 44067; ba/Cleveland, OH; m/Miriam Kleeger;

c/Harry Seymour, Lisa Joy; p/Harry and Jennie Levy Gerla (dec); ed/BME; pa/Exec Gould Inc, Ocean Sys Div; ASME; ASM; Reg'd Profl Engr: Ohio, NY; Mem Exec Standards Coun Am Nat Standards Inst 1974-75; cp/Lectr; 1st Pres & Orgr NY Sect Am Rocket Soc; Former Mem Bd Dirs New Sch Assocs NY; r/Hebrew; hon/Civilian Commend, Navy Dept; Tau Beta Pi.

GERSHOWITZ, SONYA oc/Nursing Home Administrator; b/Jul 30, 1940; h/140 W Lafayette Ave, Baltimore, MD 21217; m/Irvin; c/2 Chd; p/David and Rose Ziporkin; ed/RN Sinai Sch Nsg 1960; AA Catonsville Commun Col; BS, Master's 1978 Univ Md; Holder Nsg Home Admr Lic; pa/Current Adm Dir Chai Mgmt Co Inc (Provides Mgmt Sers to Nsg Homes); Owner & Admr: Lafayette Square Nsg Ctr Inc, Gtr Pa Ave Nsg Ctr Inc, Fed Hill Nsg Ctr Inc; Dir Nurses Multi-Med Convalescent & Nsg Ctr, Towson, Md 1974-75; Dir Nurses Mt Sinai Nsg Home 1968-71; Dir Nsg Ashburton Home, Baltimore 1963-64; Other Former Positions; Num Spkg Engagemts; Conslt; Mem St Task Force on Nosocomial Infections; Am Col Nsg Home Admrs; Fellow, Pres-elect 1978; Mem White House Conf on Aging 1971; Am & Md Nurses Assns; Univ Md & Sinai Hosp Nurses Alumni Assns; Am & Md Hlth Care Assns; S Baltimore Bus'men's Assn; cp/Labor Market Adv Com Mayor's Ofc Manpower Resources; Walters Art Gallery; Mt Royal Improvemt Assn; Md Law Enforcemt Ofcrs Inc; Am Fdn Police; Leag Md Horsemen; hon/W/W: Hlth Care, Am Wom, Fin & Indust; Book of Honor.

GERSHOY, EUGENIE oc/Artist; b/Jan 1, 1901; h/Hotel Chelsea, 222 W 23 St, New York, NY 10011; ba/Same; p/Morris and Miriam Gershoy (dec); pa/Artist: Sculptor, Painter, Graphics-Lithographs, Silk Screen; Art Tchr: New Orleans Art Sch, San Francisco Sch Sys, SF Inst Fine Art; Indiv Exhbns incl: Pantechnicon Gallery, San Francisco, Cal, Gumps Galleries, SF, Raymond & Raymond Galleries, SF, Robinson Gallery, NYC; Group Exhbns incl: Intl Wom's Exhbn, Wom's Art Ctr, NYC 1975, Galerie Intermieure, Zurich, Switzerland, SF Wom Artists, Annual Exhbns, Bayonne Commun Ctr, Bayonne, NJ, Others; Mus Invitational Exhbns incl: Metro Mus of Art, Phila Mus of Art, Baltimore Mus Art (Balto, Md), Newark Mus, Newark, NJ, Meml Art Gallery, Rochester, NY, Dallas Mus, Dallas, Tex, SF Mus Art, Others; Instnl Collections incl: Whitney Mus Am Art, NYC, Metro Mus Art, NYC, Nat Collection Fine Arts, Smithsonian Instn, Washington, DC, Chicago Art Ctr, Delgado Mus Art, New Orleans, Others; Var Pvt Collections; hon/Recipient S'ships; Purchase Prize, Delgado Mus, NO; Mention, SF Mus Art; Recipient F'ships; Biogl Listings; Others.

GERSONI, DIANE CLAIRE oc/Writer; b/Apr 16, 1947; h/c/o Edelman, 301 E 78th St, New York, NY 10021; m/James Neil Edelman; c/Michael Lawrence; p/James Arthur and Edna Krinski Gersoni, Forest Mills, NY;

ed/BA cum laude Vassar Col 1967; pa/Author; Lectr; Book Reviewer; Conslt in field; cp/Vassar Clb NY; r/Jewish; hon/Author *Sexism and Youth* (Chosen as 1 of 9 Best Ed Books of 1974 by *Am Sch Bd Jour*).

GERSTMAN, JUDITH R oc/Psychoanalyst; Educator; b/May 22, 1949; h/770 Ocean Pkwy, Brooklyn, NY 11230; p/Harold

and Helen Gerstman; ed/BA Bklyn Col 1972; MA Long Isl Univ 1973; Postgrad Work Manhattan Ctr for Adv'd Psychoanalytic Studies; pa/Pvt Pract Psychoanalysis, Bklyn 1974-; Therapist Manhattan Ctr for Adv'd Psychoanalytic Studies, Bklyn 1974-77; Chd's Cnslr Long Isl Univ LD Ctr 1972-73; Social Work Asst Coney Isl (NY) Hosp 1968-69; APGA; Jt Coun on Mtl Hlth; Nat Accreditation Assn Psychoanalysis; hon/Notable Ams; W/W: Am Wom, E; Commun Ldrs & Noteworthy Ams.

GESELL, THOMAS FREDERICK oc/Associate Professor; b/Apr 28, 1940; h/3115 Broadmead, Houston, TX 77025; ba/Houston; m/Diane W; c/Thomas Richard, Barbara Corinne, Eric Andrew; p/Carl F and

Clara Elizabeth Gesell, Mission, TX; ed/BS; MS; PhD; mil/ANG; pa/Assoc Prof Hlth Physics; Tchg & Res on Public Hlth Aspects of Envir Radioactivity; r/Prot; hon/AEC, USPHS & NSF F'ships.

GESSEL, STANLEY P oc/Professor, Associate Dean; b/Oct 14, 1916; h/8521 Latona NE, Seattle, WA 98115; ba/Seattle; m/Beverly Ann; c/Susan, Paula, (Stepchd:) Patti, Pamela, Michael; p/Gottlieb and Esther Heyrend Gessel; ed/BS Utah St Agri Col; PhD Berkeley; mil/USAF 1942-46 Capt; pa/Univ Wash: Prof, Assoc Dean 1948-; Reschr Col of Forest Resources 1966-; Var Former Positions; Del to Union of Forest Res Orgs, Chm Quantitative Site Factors Wkg Group 1967-;

Dir Tropical Forestry Course, Org for Tropical Studies 1968; Univ Del to Univ Coun on Water Resources 1968-; Forestry Advr Taiwan 1974; Fellow AAAS; Editor Soils & Forestry, NW Sci; VChm & Chm Puget Sound Sect Soc Am Foresters 1967-73; Forestry Rep for Univ Wash on McIntire-Stennis Forest Reg Prog; Former Chm Div Forest Soils, Am Soc Agronomy; Others; hon/Hon Life Mem, NW Sci Assn; Hon Alumnus, Univ Wash; Profl Pubs.

GESSNER-ASTEN, ERIKA V oc/Freelance Educator; Homemaker; b/May 17, 1928; h/1678 N Forge Mt Dr, Valley Forge, PA 19481; m/Dietrich V Asten; c/Peter E Asten, Sylvia M Asten; p/Oswald Gessner (dec); Else Gessner, Berlin, Germany; ed/Tchr's Certs 1951, 72; PhD Free Univ (Berlin) 1961; pa/Courses in Hist of Music & Theory in Col Level & Sec'dy Level Schs Based on Rudolf Steiner's Phil; r/The Christian Commun, Devon, Pa; hon/Berlin Airlift Meml S'ship for Postgrad Studies, NYU.

GETMAN, CLYDE J oc/Chaplain; Pastoral Counselor; Educator; b/Aug 3, 1940;

h/850 Warder Ave, St Louis, MO 63139; ba/St Louis; m/Suzanne Marie Randall; c/Karen Elizabeth, Kristen Ruth, Kimberly Sue, Kevin Randall; p/Clyde J and Ruth I Wagner Getman, Binghamton, NY; ed/AAS Broome Tech Commun Col 1961; BA Barrington Col 1965; MDiv Gordon-Conwell Theol Sem 1970; DMin Andover Newton Theol Sch 1972; pa/St Louis St Hosp: Chaplain 1974-, Dir Clin Pastoral Ed 1976-; Am Assn Marriage & Fam Cnslrs: Clin Mem, Reg Prog Com; Am Assn Pastoral Cnslrs: Fellow, Mem Reg Com on Parish Concerns; Am Prot Hosp Assn: Fellow Col Chaplains, Certn Review Coms; Assn for Clin Pastoral Ed; Assn for Humanistic Psychol; Others; r/Delmar Bapt Ch St Louis: Mem, SS Tchr, Choir, Bd Christian Ed, Bd Trustees; hon/Byington Fellow New Testament Studies; Del to US Cong on Evangel; Del to Intl Cong on Pastoral Care & Cnslg; Biogl Listings.

GEWALD, ROBERT M oc/Concert Manager; b/Mar 8, 1934; h/441 E 20th St, New York, NY 10010; ba/NYC; c/Antony; p/Samuel Gewald (dec); Gertrude Gewald, NYC; ed/BA Wash Sq Col; MA NY Univ; pa/Gen Mgr Sum of Music on the Hudson Fest; ASOL; ACUCCA; NEC; cp/Leag NY Music; Intl Cult Foun; hon/Berg Prize for Hist; Am Legion Good Govt Awd; Cerebral Palsy Awd; Hon Doct, U Christian Col.

GHATTAS, SONIA R oc/Educator; Lecturer; b/Aug 20, 1942; h/3855 Boyce Ave, Los Angeles, CA 90039; p/Rezk Ghattas and Solange Khouzam; ed/BA Univ Alexandria (Egypt) 1965; MA Cal St Univ-LA 1973; PhD Univ Cal-I 1979; pa/Tchr, Translator & Interpreter; Cal Inst Technol, Pasadena, Cal 1979-: Lectr in French, Instr French Lang & Lit; Univ Cal-I: Assoc to Humanities Core Course 1977-79, Tchg Asst Dept French & Italian 1974-77; Tchr French Chd's Village, Monterey Park, Cal 1973-74; Other Former Positions; Am Assn Tchrs French; Mod Lang Tchrs Assn; ASCD; AAUW; Mgmt Clb Cal Inst Technol; Pi Delta Phi; cp/Cal St Univ-LA & Univ Cal-I Alumni Assns; Student Rep UCI; Alliance Francaise; Vol Interpreter UCI Med Ctr; Vol Interpreter Julia Ann Singer Presch Psychi Ctr, LA; r/Holy Trinity Cath Parrish, LA; hon/Hon Student, Univ Alexandria; Silver Medal for Spelling Bee; Cert of Apprec, Julia Ann Singer Presch Psychi Ctr for Vol Interpretation Eng/Arabic/Eng; Biogl Listings; Pub'd Author; Others.

GHERING, MARY VIRGIL oc/Sister of Religious Order; Librarian; b/Jul 18, 1910; h/2335 Grandview Ave, Cincinnati, OH 45206; ba/Cinc; p/Henry Christian and Frances Emily Sharp Ghering (dec); ed/AB Ctl Mich Univ 1935; MS Marquette Univ 1948; PhD Cand Fordham Univ 1959; PhD St Thomas Inst 1968; pa/Libn St Thomas Inst 1968-; Aquinas Col, Grand Rapids, Mich: Prof

Chem 1949-68, Chm Dept Phy Scis 1959-63; Tchr Sci & Math HSs Mich 1931-49; Fellow Am Inst Chemists; Am Chem Soc; Sophie de Marsac Campau Chapt (Grand Rapids); Telephone Coor Common Cause Cong Dist #2 (Ohio); r/Mem Sisters St Dominic, Grand Rapids 1929-; hon/Sci Fac F'ship, NSF to Fordham Univ.

GIAIMO, ROBERT NICHOLAS oc/Attorney; US Representative; b/Oct 15,

1919; h/North Haven, CT; ba/2207 Rayburn House Ofc Bldg, US Ho of Reps, Washington, DC 20515; m/Marion F Schuenemann; c/Barbara Lee; p/Rosario and Rose Scarpulla Giaimo (dec); ed/AB Fordham Col 1941; LLB Univ Conn 1943; mil/AUS WWII, 1/Lt; Capt Judge Adv Gen Corps, USAR; pa/Admitted to Conn Bar 1947; Pract New Haven; cp/Mem US Ho of Reps 1958-, Var Com Mbrships; Dem.

GIAMMERSE, JACK JR oc/Mathematician; b/Feb 11, 1954; h/4601 Sweetbriar St, Baton Rouge, LA 70808; p/Jack Giammerse Sr (dec); ed/BA La St Univ-BR; pa/Math Assn Am; Am Math Soc; r/Epis; hon/Pi Mu Epsilon; Sigma Pi Sigma; Mu Sigma Rho; La St Univ Freshman Hons Awd.

GIBBES, WILLIAM HOLMAN oc/Attorney; b/Feb 25, 1930; h/6143 Martha's-Glen Rd, Columbia, SC 29206; ba/Columbia; m/Frances Virginia Hagood; c/Richard H, William Holman, Lynn; p/Ernest Lawrence and Nancy Watson Gibbes, Hartsville, SC; ed/BS 1952, LLB 1953 USC; Postgrad Studies Univ Va 1954; mil/AUS Col, 12th JAG Det, Fort Jackson, SC; pa/Admitted to: SC Bar 1953, US Supreme Ct Bar 1959, US Ct Appeals 1965; Asst Atty Gen SC, Columbia 1957-62; Mem Firm Berry, Lightsey & Gibbes, Columbia 1962-71; Pvt Pract Law, Columbia 1971-; Secy & Gen Counsel SC Credit Ins Assn, Columbia 1963-; ABA; SC Bar Assn: Exec Com 1961-62, Chm Com on Referral 1975-78; Richland Co Bar Assn, Chm Memls Com 1976; Euphradian Soc; Omicron Delta Kappa; Kappa Sigma Kappa; Pi Kappa Alpha; Yg Lwyrs Clb; cp/YMCA; USC Alumni Assn; Columbia C of C; Kiwanis; Mem Var Clbs; r/Epis; hon/James Patterson Awd.

GIBBONS, JEAN DICKINSON oc/Educator; b/Mar 14, 1938; h/7 Woodridge, Tuscaloosa, AL 35401; ba/University, AL; m/John S Fielden; p/John Dickinson; c/Alice Dickinson, St Petersburg, FL; ed/BA Duke; MS; PhD Va Poly Inst; pa/Edr Statistics Univ Ala; Am Statistical Assn; Inst Math Statistics; hon/Fellow, ASA; Phi Beta Kappa; Fulbright Scholar; Pi Mu Epsilon; Phi Kappa Phi; Chi Alpha Phi.

GIBBS, CARROLL ROBERT oc/Writer; Lecturer; b/Jun 13, 1949; h/417 12th St SE, Washington, DC 20003; p/Carroll R and Dora G Gibbs (dec); ed/Att'd Univ DC; mil/E-5 Radar Operator Hawk Air Def Sys; pa/Freelance Writer; Lectr, Presented Exhibits Var Ednl Instns incl'g: Martin Luther King Jr Meml Lib, Howard Univ (Wash DC), No Va Commun Col (Alexandria Campus), Watha T Daniel Lib (Wash DC), The Ctr for Black Ed (Wash DC), Frederick Douglass Nat Meml Home, Others; Var Bus, Social or Civic Orgs incl'g: Fort Washington Pk (Md), Monument

Grounds (Wash DC), Dept HEW, Dept Trans (UMTA), Others; Conslt; Author Books, Film Scripts, TV Scripts, Others; Asst Tech Advr to Francis Thompson Co (for film); Monthly Column *Metro* Mag "Washington News Briefs"; Pub'd Writings incl: "Conspiracy, Harassment and Murder" *Metro* Mag, "The First Black Army Officer", *Armed Forces Jour Intl*, "Blacks In the Union Navy", *All Hands*, Mag of USN; Others; r/Rom Cath; hon/Cert of Achmt, AUS Med Ctr; Cert of Apprec, Nat

Coalition of Involved People; Others.

GIBBS, JEANNE OSBORNE oc/Poet; Writer; b/Jun 1, 1920; h/809 Pinetree Dr, Decatur, GA 30030; ba/Same; c/Robert Allan, Marilyn Osborne; p/Virgil Waite and Daisy Hampton Scruggs Osborne (dec); ed/BA Agnes Scott Col; pa/Past Pres Atlanta Writers Clb; *Atlanta Constitution*: Edit Staff 1942, Book Reviewer 1945-48; Book Reviewer *The Atlanta Journal* 1946-49; Feature Writer & Proofreader *The New London* (Conn) *Day* 1943; Poetry Editor Banner Press 1956-58; Book Editor *Georgia* Mag 1957-73; r/Druid Hills Bapt Ch, Atlanta; hon/Literary Achmt Awd, Ga Writers Assn; Author of Yr in Poetry, Dixie Coun of Authors & Journalists 1971; Author of Yr, Atlanta Writers Clb 1971; Robert Martin Awd, NY Poetry Forum; Westbrook Awd, Ky St Poetry Soc; Poetry Soc Ga: John Clare Awd, Katherine H Strong Prize, Eunice Thomson Awd, Jimmie Williamson Awd; 300 Poems Pub'd in Newspapers, Mags, Anthologies; Others.

GIBSON, CHARLES WALTER oc/Pastor; b/Feb 16, 1930; h/6407 Moon Ln, Richmond, VA 23234; ba/Richmond; m/Reva Jean Taylor; c/Charles Michael, Stephen Taylor, Dwayne Watkins; p/Virginia Gibson Boynton, Richmond; ed/Att'd Univ Richmond 1948-52; mil/Corps of Cadets, Regimental Capt Qtrmaster; pa/Pastor: Oak Grove Bapt Ch, Richmond 1971-, Emmanuel Bapt Ch, Manassas, Va 1967-71, Bethlehem Bapt Chapel, Richmond 1966-67, Cosby Meml Bapt Ch, Richmond 1953-61, Graceland Bapt Ch, Clayville, Va 1951-53; Va Bapt Gen Assn: Ch in Urban Ctrs Com, Chm Hillside Ctr Subcom 1977-78; Richmond Bapt Assn: Exec Com 1973-, Bapt Ctrs Com 1971-; Pres Southside Mins, Richmond 1972-; Var Former Denom Activs; cp/Pres Woodstock Civic Assn; Ofcr PTA; Ed Com Richmond Chapt Nat Foun for Illietus & Colitus; r/Bapt; hon/Personalities of S; Notable Ams; W/W: S&SW, Rel.

GIBSON, CURTIS A oc/Life Support Systems Engineer; b/Nov 5, 1929; h/2806 Oxford Dr, Springfield, OH 45506; ba/Wright-Patterson AFB, OH; p/Frank Z

and Helen W Cox Gibson (dec); ed/CHE Univ Cinc 1952; pa/Life Support Sys Engr USAF; Am Def Preparedness Assn; Intl Acad Profl Bus Execs; cp/BSA; r/Luth; hon/Silver Beaver Awd, BSA.

GIBSON, EVERETT KAY JR oc/Planetary Scientist; b/May 13, 1940; h/1015 Trowbridge Dr, Houston, TX 77062; ba/Houston; m/Morgan Shott; c/Bradford Pierce; p/Everett K and Lillie Ivey Gibson, Stephenville, TX; ed/BS 1963, MS 1965 Tex

Tech Univ; PhD Ariz St Univ 1969; pa/NASA Johnson Space Ctr: Analytical Geochemist 1975-, Lunar Sample Prin Investigator 1971-, Space Scist 1970-75; Univ Houston: Instr Ctr for Cont'g Ed 1977-, Adj Prof Dept Geol 1976-; Vis Prog Mgr Earth Scis Div Nat Sci Foun, Wash DC 1979; Am Chem Soc; Am Geophysical Union; Meteoritical Soc, Secy 1974-80; AAAS; Mineralogical Soc Am; Div Planetary Sci Am Astronomical Union; Intl Assn Geochem & Cosmochem; Phi Lambda Upsilon; Sigma Xi; Conslt; cp/Former Dir Clear Creek Basin Auth; hon/Fellow: Meteoritical Soc, Sigma Xi; Outstg Lectr, SE Sect Am Astronomical Soc; NASA Cert of Recog for Lunar Sample Prin Investigator Work; Tex Pacific Oil Co S'ship.

GIBSON, JAMES EUGENE oc/Physicist; b/Nov 25, 1940; h/150 Stoney Ridge Dr, Longwood, FL 32750; ba/Orlando, FL; m/Marilyn Kay; c/Jeffrey, David, Sheri; p/William A and Ruth L Gibson, Treasure Isl, FL; ed/AB; MS; pa/Dir Army Mil Sys Div Intl Lasar Systems Inc; Am Def Preparedness Assn; cp/Orange Co Sportsmans Assn; US Power Sqdrn; Cub Scout Ofcr; hon/W/W S&SW.

GIBSON, JOHN ALBERT JR oc/Agricultural Extension Agent; b/Jun 1, 1944; h/Rt 3, 25 Mayo Sub-Div, Nashville, NC 27856; ba/N'ville; m/Dureatta F; c/Sireatta J; p/John A Sr and Lillie H Gibson, Rowland, NC; ed/BA; pa/Agri Ext Agt Nash Co Agri Ctr 1974-; Ins Salesman Mutual of Omaha Ins Co, New Brunswick, NJ 1973-74; Other Former Positions; Nat Assn Co Agri Agts; cp/Twin Co JCs: Pres, Past Internal VP; Former CoChm Nash Co Heart Fund Dr; Commun Devel Soc Am; Rocky Mt-Nash Co Red Cross Blood Dr; NEED Inc Commun Ser Ctr Adv Bd; CoLdr & Sponsor Brownie Troop (N'ville); N'ville Citizens Adv Com; Nash Co Parents Adv Com Title I; r/Metro Bapt Ch, Rocky Mt; hon/Twin Co JCs Rookie of Yr 1976-77.

GIBSON, JOHN THOMAS oc/Assistant Professor, Department Chairman; b/Sept 19, 1948; h/43 N Anton Dr, Montgomery, AL 36105; ba/Montgomery; m/Mayme Voncile; c/John T Jr; p/Herman F Gibson (dec); Lillian P Gibson, Montgomery; ed/BS 1970, EdM 1971 Tuskegee Inst; EdS 1972, PhD 1973 Univ Colo-Denver; mil/AUS Field Arty, Hon Disch Capt 1978; pa/Ala St Univ: Asst Prof, Chm Dept Ednl Adm 1973-, Dir Lab Experiences 1973-75, Coor Fed Relats 1975-76, Chm Senate Com on Planning & Devel Fac Senate 1975-77; Others; Am Assn Univ Admrs; Phi Delta Kappa; cp/Bellingrath Exec Commun Coun; Ala Dem Conf; Elks: Secy, Mem; 32° Mason; Shriner; Kappa Alpha Psi; r/1st Congreg Ch: Treas, Bd Trustees; hon/Kappa Delta Pi; JC Outstg Yg Men Am; Montgomery Pan-Hellenic Coun Achmt Cit; Achm Awd So Reg, Kappa Alpha Psi; Outstg Edr Am; F'ships; S'ship; Profl Pubs; Commun Ldrs & Noteworthy Ams; W/W US; Men of Achmt; Others.

GIBSON, JOHN VIRGIL JR oc/Teacher; Realtor; b/Jul 27, 1920; h/703 Elaine Dr, Wake Village, TX 75501; ba/Wake Village; m/Lynda; c/John C, James C, (Stepchd:) Bill St Claire, Rene St Claire; p/John Virgil and Ruth Gibson, Charleston, AR; ed/Bachs Deg; mil/USAF WWII; pa/Liaison Ofcr Am Fdn Tchrs; cp/PTA: Life Mem, Pres; Charter Mem JC Com; Pres Wildlife Assn; Ofcr Elks; r/Prot, Pres SS; hon/Tex Ed Outstg Tchr; W/W in S.

GIBSON, MILTON EUGENE oc/Physician; Cardiologist; b/Jul 11, 1939; h/5640 Danbury Dr, South Bend, IN 46614; ba/S Bend; m/Gloria Jean; c/Kevin Scott, Bradley Mark; p/Maurice Gibson (dec); Mary Gibson, Valparaiso, IN; ed/BA Valparaiso Univ; MD Ind Univ; mil/AUS 1966-68; Bronze Star; pa/Dir Cardiac Catheterization Lab, Dir Cardiol Sers Meml Hosp; Co-Dir Cardiac Care Unit St Joseph's Hosp; Assoc Fellow Am Col Cardiol; Am Col Physicians; Chm Dept Med Meml Hosp; cp/Adv Coun MW Chamber Orch; r/Prot; hon/Meritorious Ser Awd, Am Heart Assn.

GIBSON, ROBERT (BOB) oc/Security Manager; b/Mar 6, 1945; h/8621 Oakwood Dr, Lakeland, FL 33801; m/Gail; c/Sharon (Stepsons:) Bill, Randy, Charles; p/Robert E and Ruby C Gibson, Statesville, NC; pa/ASIS; Am Soc Indust Security; cp/Lakeland C of C; r/Assembly of God; hon/DECA Mem of Yr 1963; Personalities of S.

GIBSON, VERDA KAY oc/Businesswoman; b/May 17, 1927; h/2418 7th Ave, Pueblo, CO 81003; ba/Same; m/Howard Glen; c/Frances, Patricia, Howard (Brian), Sheli, Erik; p/Francis H Fingado, Denver, CO; Donna Galbraith Apple, Ordway, CO; pa/Owner-Mgr Pride City Welcoming Ser; Free-lance Writer; Piano Tchr; cp/Originator Colo St Fair Silver Queen Activs; C of C Nsg Home Reserved Areas; C of C & Colo St Fair Parade Task Force Com; Colo St Fair Centennial-Bicent Task Force; Sharmar Nsg Home Resident Advocate; Pueblo Metro Mus Assn; Postal Commemorative Soc; Cub Scout Den Mother; Past PTA Pres; Others; r/LDS; hon/Pueblo Sunshine Awd Aug 1977; Vol of Yr Awd, Sharmar Nsg Home; Notable Ams; Plaque, Colo St Fair & Centennial Exposition.

GIBSON, WELDON B oc/Business Executive; b/Apr 23, 1917; h/593 Gerona Rd, Stanford, CA 94305; m/Helen Mears; c/2 Chd; p/Oscar and Susie Bailey Gibson; ed/Grad Wash St Univ 1938; MBA 1940, PhD 1950 Stanford Univ Grad Sch Bus; mil/USAF WWII, Dir Mat Requiremts 4 Yrs; Col; pa/SRI Intl: Exec VP & Bd Dirs 1960-, VP 1959-60, Assoc Dir 1955-59; SRI: Dir Ecs Res 1947; Assoc'd w Burroughs Corp, San Francisco 1946; Other Former Positions; Creator SRI Intl Assocs Plan; Originator & CoDir SRI's Worldwide Opers Intl Indust Conf; Dir Sev Bus Firms; Am Ec Assn; Soc for Intl Devel; cp/Japan-Cal Assn; Pacific Basin Ec Coun; SF Bay Area Coun; hon/Medal of Legion of Merit; Order of Cmdr of Brit Empire; Intl Reg Profiles; Book of Honor; Pub'd Author.

GIDDENS, BEULAH M oc/Newspaper Editor; b/Dec 26, 1921; h/PO Box 333, Burgaw, NC 28425; ba/Burgaw; m/John O; c/Judy G Schutt; p/Garris Lee Pridgen (dec); Beulah Jones Pridgen, Wilmington, NC; r/So Missionary Bapt Ch: Mem; hon/Hons from: JCs, Lions, USAF, AUS, 4-H; W/W: NC, SE, USA; Others.

GIDUZ, ROLAND oc/Editor, Writer; b/Jul 24, 1925; h/Box 31, Chapel Hill, NC 27514; ba/Chapel Hill; m/Helen Frances Jeter; c/William Roland, Robert Baker, Thomas Tracy; p/Hugo Giduz (dec); Edith May Baker (dec); ed/AB Univ NC-CH 1948; MS Columbia Univ 1949; mil/AUS 1943-45, Pvt 100th Inf Div (ETO); pa/Newspaper Reporter & Editor; Pubr; Alumnor; cp/Rotary; Toastmasters; BSA; Dem; Former Mem Chapel Hill Bd Aldermen; Mayor Pro-tem 1964-69; hon/Outstg Yg Men; Mass Media F'ship; Fund for Adult Ed, Harvard Univ; Ser to Mankind Awd, Chapel Hill; 25 Yr Apprec Awd, Sta WCHL; Silver Beaver, BSA.

GIES, FREDERICK JOHN oc/Professor, Dean; b/Sept 4, 1938; h/4565 137th Ave SE, Bellevue, WA 98006; ba/Seattle; m/Margaret Meads; c/Frederick Meads, Edward Michael, Nicholas John, Maria Louise; p/Leo M Gies (dec); Gertrude E Gies, Osage Bch, MO; ed/BA DePaul Univ 1960; MEd 1964, EdD

1970 Univ Mo-Columbia; pa/Seattle Univ: Prof, Dean Sch of Ed; Conslt; Public Spkr; Author 50+ Jour Articles, Monographs, Eval Studies & Funded Projs; cp/Fac Adv Com Wash Coun for Post Sec'dy Ed; r/St Madeline Sophie Ch (Cath), Bellevue; hon/Num Prof & Public.

GIL, DAVID GEORG oc/Professor; b/Mar 16, 1924; h/29 Blossomcrest Rd, Lexington, MA 02173; ba/Waltham, MA; m/Eva A Breslauer; c/Daniel Walter, Gideon Ralph; p/Oskar and Helene Weisz Engel (dec); ed/BA Hebrew Univ; MSW, DSW Univ Pa; pa/Prof Social Policy Brandeis Univ; VP Assn

for Humanist Sociol 1978-79; cp/Socialist Party; New Am Movemt; Movemt for New Soc; War Resisters Leag; F'ship of Reconciliation; hon/UN F'ship; Res Awds, US Dept HEW; Author: *Violence Against Chd, 1970, Unravelling Social Policy/The Challenge of Social Equality, 1976, Beyond the Jungle, 1979*.

GIL, EMIGDIO ANTONIO oc/Executive; b/Jul 27, 1944; h/1511 18th St, Key West, FL 33040; ba/Key West; m/Katy Lou; c/Denise, Emigdio II; p/Antonio and Catherine Gil, Key West; ed/RRC; pa/Tony's Sheet Metal & Roofing Co: 1st VP in Charge of Opers 1977-, Supvr-Estimator 1962-76, Roofer 1961-62, Others; Fla Roofing, Sheet Metal & Air Conditioning Assn 1976-; Notary Public; cp/Bd Dirs Teenage Clb No 551; Intl Order DeMolay; F&AM; Key West JCs; Assoc Mem Lower Keys Devel Corp; Sons of Italy; Key West JCs Sustaining Mem; r/Key West Bapt Temple; hon/JCs: Speak Up Awd, Spark Plug Awd, JC of Qtr 1975, JC of Yr 1975-76, Chm of Yr 1975-76, JC of Qtr, JC of Month, Ofcr of Yr 1977, Key Man of Yr (Local Clb) 1976-77, Outstg Yg Men Am, Others.

GILBERT, JUDY MAVIN oc/School Principal; b/Sept 9, 1943; h/Rt 1, Box 372, Lincolnton, NC 28092; ba/L'ton; p/Mike J and Bessie H Gilbert, L'ton; ed/AB Lenoir Rhyne Col; MA; EdS Appalachian St Univ; pa/Elem Sch Prin; NCAE (Local Unit): Fac Rep 1965, 66, 67, Treas 1971-72, PACE Coor 1972-73, Leg Chm 1973-74, 1975-76, Local Lobbying Team 1975, 77; NCAE Dist II Lobbying Team 1975, 77; Dist II ACT, Govtl Impact Com Chm 1976-77; ACT (Local Unit) Citizenship Com Chm 1970; Secy-Treas Lincoln Co Prins 1977-78; SACS, NC Com on Late Childhood/Early Adolescent Ed 1969-70; cp/Secy NC Human Relats Coun; Var Ofcs Alpha Delta Kappa; Lincoln Co Mus Art; Former Mem Lincoln Co Commun Chorus; Former Ldr Howard's Creek 4-H Clb; Former 1st VChm Vale Precnt; Yg Dems; Pres Lincoln Co Dem Wom; Others; r/Hulls Grove Bapt Ch: Tng Union Ldr, Pianist, Supt Yth Dept SS, Bible Sch Tchr, Study Course Tchr, Yth Dir 1973-75, Asst Dir Sr Choir, Budget Com, Lib Com, Co-Histn; hon/Tchr of Yr: L'ton City Schs 1973, NCAE-ACT Dist II 1973; Outstg Yg Wom Am; Personalities of S.

GILBERT, ROBERT LEE oc/Engineering, Construction Project Controls; b/Oct 9, 1944; h/3 Skyview Dr, Mt Airy, MD 21771; ba/Gaithersburg, MD; m/Juliet Tressler; c/Robert Lee; p/Irwin Hellings and Anna Marie W Gilbert; ed/BS The Citadel 1966; MS Ga Inst Tech 1968; MBA Univ Pitts 1974; mil/AUS 1968-69, Served to 1st Lt CE; pa/Reg'd Prof Engr Pa; Cost & Schedule Supr

Bechtel Power Corp, G'burg 1974-; Proj Engr Michael Baker Jr Inc Conslt Engrs, Beaver, Pa 1971-74; Sr Engr AT&T, White Plains, NY 1970-71; ASCE; hon/Biogl Listings.

GILBREATH, ALICE MARIE oc/Free-lance Writer; b/Apr 8, 1921; h/1100 Grandview, Bartlesville, OK 74003; m/Rex E;

c/Rex Jr, Tommie Sue; p/Alfred and Nanna Nielson Thompson (dec); mil/AUS; r/Presb.

GILDRED, VICTORIA oc/Executive; b/Feb 8, 1934; h/11 Island Ave, Miami Beach, FL 33139; m/Albert; c/John, William, Victoria; p/Guillermo Petersson and Susana Rivadeneira (dec); pa/Pres, Victoria Gildred Foun for Latin Am Hlth & Ed; Chm, Public Hlth Co, Partners of Am (Fla-Colombia Partners); Intl Coor, Univ of Miami Sch of Med (Ob-Gyn Dept); cp/Gov's Coun for Intl Devel; r/Cath; hon/Hon Consul of Columbia to Miami Beach; Order "Los Lanceros", Govt of Colombia (SAm).

GILES, BARBARA ANN oc/Professional Writer; b/Jan 25, 1944; h/PO Box 155, Black Mt, NC 28711; ba/Same; m/Carl H; p/Dalton H and Helen Williams, Murray, KY; ed/BS 1965, MS 1966, MA 1967 Murray St Univ; PhD USM Sussex (England) 1972; pa/Gen Mgr Channel 2, Union City (CATV Sta) 1973-74; Author 2 Books: *Purposeful Persuasion* & (Coauthor) *Bewitching Jewelry: Jewelry of the Black Arts*; Contbr Var Pubs incl'g: *National Star, Modern People, Dude,* & Cato's *Advtg, Mktg, Motion Picture, Photo, Public Relats & Writing Encyclopedia*; Communs Conslt to Broadcasting Stas & Public Relats Agy; Tchr Gen & Specialized Spch Courses, TV Advtg, Mass Communs Univ Tenn-Martin 1968-75; Spch Tchr Murray HS, Murray, Ky 1966-68; Former Model & Profl Ballet Dancer; hon/DIB; Personalities of S; World W/W Wom; Ky Col.

GILES, CARL HOWARD oc/Free-lance Writer; b/Mar 13, 1938; h/PO Box 155, Black Mt, NC 28711; ba/Same; m/Barbara Ann; c/Sheldon; p/William C and Thelma Fields Giles, Big Stone Gap, VA; ed/BSJ Fla So Col 1962; MSJ WVa Univ 1965; Addit Studies; pa/Author 12 Books incl'g: *Writing Right--To Sell, Advising Advisers, The Student Journalist and Feature Writing, Journalism: Dateline, The World,* Others; Contbr to Var Pubs incl'g: *Holiday, So Living, Coronet, Nat Parks Mag, Resources, Nat Enquirer, Modern People,* Others; Tchg Positions: Terry Parker HS, Jacksonville, Fla 1962-64, WVa Univ, Morgantown, WVa 1964-65, Univ Tenn-Martin 1965-; Kappa Tau Alpha; Sigma Delta Chi; Assn for Ed in Jour; Other Profl Orgs; hon/AEJ-ABP Mag F'ship; Wall St Jour Newspaper Fund F'ship; 3 Writing Awds; Tenn Squire; Ky Col; W/W Fin S&SW; Contemp Authors; DIB; Personalities of S; Notable Ams Bicent Era; Others.

GILES, WILLIAM MITCHELL oc/General Manager; b/Apr 8, 1943; h/210 Pine St, Essexville, MI 48732; ba/Bay City, MI; m/Elaine Alexander; c/Ashley Lynn, Mary Elaine, Amanda Nicole; p/Olin S Giles (dec); Evelyn Love Giles, Charlotte, NC; ed/AA Univ NC-Charlotte 1963; BSIM Clemson Univ 1965; pa/Gen Mgr Wolverine Knitting Inc; Sr Mem Am Inst Indust Engrs; Sr Mem Soc Mfg Engrs; cp/Rotary Intl; US JCs; BPOE Lodge #88; Intl Assn Lions Clbs; r/Meth; hon/Cert of Mert; Am Cancer Soc; US Patentee; Author "Yield Book for Mathematical Progressions for the Textile Industry"; W/W; Notable Ams.

GILFILLEN, GEORGE C JR oc/Executive; b/Oct 31, 1919; h/2230 S Patterson Blvd, Dayton, OH 45409; m/(dec); c/George C III, Mary Kimbrough G Coughnour; ed/Cornell Univ; pa/Chm of Bd E F MacDonald Co (Multi-Mktg Org), Dayton; cp/Bd Mem: Mercersburg Acad (Bd Regents), M'burg, Pa, 3rd Nat Bk & Trust Co, Dayton, Boys' Clb Am (Nat), Dayton Philharm Assn, Dayton Area C of C; Trustee (Dayton Orgs): U Appeal, One Hundred Clb, Aviation Hall of Fame; Dayton CC; Dayton Bicycle Clb; 32° Mason; NY Ath Clb; Newcomen Soc; Miami Val Skeet Clb (Dayton); Area Progress Coun (Dayton); Montgomery Co Hist Soc; Sustaining Mem Ohio Bankpac; Adv Bd Miami Val Coun BSA; YMCA Steering Com; Corporate Mem U Hlth Foun, Dayton; Ohio Foun Indep Cols, Dayton; Other Civic Activs; hon/W/W: Am, Intl.

GILL, ELIJAH (MRS) oc/Foster Home Care; b/Jan 23, 1908; h/Rt 1, 125, Shaton, SC 29742; ba/York, SC; m/(dec); c/Pauline G McKnight, Josephine G Kennedy, Charles (dec); p/Samuel and Nancy Ashley, York; r/Presb: SS Tchr, Var Ch Activs.

GILL, ROBERT MONROE oc/Assistant Professor; b/Mar 11, 1949; h/Col View Apts #4, Radford, VA 24141; ba/Radford; m/Salle Ann; p/C Edward and Harriet Monroe Gill, Richmond, VA; ed/BA cum laude Wash & Lee Univ 1971; MA 1973, PhD 1975 Duke Univ; Addit Studies; pa/Asst Prof Polit Sci Radford

Col; Sum Instr Colo Col; Fac Affairs Coun; Pre-Law Advr Liberal Studies Com; cp/Fac Advr Tau Kappa Epsilon; r/Anglican Cath, St Peter's Ch, Christiansburg, Va; hon/Grants; Nat Merit Lttr of Commend; Finalist, "Dissertation of Yr" 1976; Pub'd Author.

GILL, TRUDI H oc/Artist; b/Apr 7; h/IV Johann Strauss G, Vienna, Austria; ba/Same; m/Irvin; p/(dec); ed/Att'd Art Students Leag (NY); Former Short Story Illustrator *Harper's Mag*; Life Mem Am Fine Arts Soc; US Exhbns incl: Albuquerque, Cleveland, Dallas, NY,

Provincetown; Works on Display in Public Art Collections: Coral Gables, Evansville, NY; Exhibited Mus of 20th Century, Vienna; cp/Charter Mem Am Wom's Assn Vienna; Var Charity Orgs; r/Christian.

GILLESPIE, KATHRYN A oc/Teacher; b/Jun 23, 1949; h/320 N Illinois Apt 10, Peoria Heights, IL 61614; ba/Chillicothe, IL;

p/Wilbur G and Anna O Gillespie, Rockbridge, IL; ed/BS Ill St Univ 1971; pa/Tchr LD & Educable Mtly Handicapped S Grade Sch; Peoria Assn for Chd w LD; No Peoria Co Assn for Chd w LD; r/Rom Cath; hon/Tchr of Yr, Peoria Co 1974-75; Num Biogl Listings.

GILLET, PAMELA ALICE oc/Executive Director; b/Mar 29, 1943; h/6958 Hamilton Dr, Niles, IL 60648; ba/Palatine, IL; m/Lloyd; p/William Boyd Kipping; Alice Clara Kipping, Chicago; ed/BEd; MA; PhD;

pa/Exec Dir Spec Ed Cooperative; Col Lectr; Pres Ill CEC; Wkrshop Ldr; Adv Bd ACLD; Author; cp/Conslt to Commun Groups about Handicapping Conditions; r/Luth; hon/Outstg Spec Edr 1975; Am Legion Citizenship Awd.

GILLIATT, CECIL LEE oc/Retired Florist, Educator; b/Jan 6, 1905; h/202 Gilliatt St, Shelby, NC 28150; ba/Same; m/Rosalynd Nix; c/Lee, Ben; p/Theorore Robert and Della May Gilliatt (dec); ed/BS Ks St Univ; Hon DHL; pa/Tchr Durham HS; Owner & Mgr Gilliatt's Greenhouses & Gift's; Nat Sch Bds Assn: Dir So Reg 6 Yrs, Exec Com 3 Yrs, Secy-Treas 1971-72, Pres 1976-77; Past Pres NC Sch Bds Assn; Shelby City Sch Bd; Past Pres: NC St Florist Assn, So Retail Florist Assn, Shelby Merchs Assn; Past Dist Rep Florist Transworld Delivery; cp/Past Pres: Shelby C of C, Cleveland Co UF, Cleve Co ARC, Cleve Co Assn Govtl Ofcls; r/1st Bapt Ch: Former Deacon; hon/Man of Yr, Shelby 1952; Dist'd Ser Awd, NC Florist Assn; Gold Medal Awd, Outstg Achmt Floral Indust.

GILLIOM, BONNIE LEE CHERP oc/Consultant; Writer; Professor; b/Mar 1, 1933; h/2495 Haverford Rd, Columbus, OH 43220; m/M Eugene; c/Gregor William, Julia Lee; p/Gregor Leonard Cherp (dec); Rella Hildegard Jacobs Cherp; ed/AB Heidelberg

Col; MA, PhD Ohio St Univ; pa/Conslt & Writer in Movemt Ed; Adv Coun to Ohio Dept Ed; Nat Dance Assn; Heidelberg Fellows; NW Coun on Human Relats; Author Sev Books; hon/Kappa Delta Pi; Pi Delta Epsilon; Pi Lambda Theta; IERT 1st Pl Awd; Best Instrnl TV Series; World W/W Wom.

GILMAN, BENJAMIN ARTHUR oc/Member US House of Representatives; b/Dec 6, 1922; h/PO Box 358, Middletown, NY 10940; ba/Washington, DC 20515; c/Jonathan, Harrison, Susan, David; p/Harry and Esther Gold Gilman (dec); ed/BS Wharton Sch Bus & Fin, Univ Pa 1946; LLB NY Law Sch 1950; pa/Asst Atty Gen NY St Dept Law 1953-55; Atty NY St Temporary Comm on Cts 1955-57; Atty Adv Com NY St Div's St Ctr,

M'town 1962-67; M'town, Orange Co, NY St & Am Bar Assns; Assn Bar City NY; Am Trial Lwyrs Assn; cp/Mem US Ho of Reps 1973-, Mem Var Coms; Former Mem NY St Assembly; Former Mem Bd Dirs: Goldenarea Hosp Funds, Orange Co Heart Assn, Temple Sinai; Former Bd Chm M'town Little Leag; Past VP Orange Co Mtl Hlth Assn; VFW; Am Legion Post #151; BPOE; Orange Co Repub Com; Intl Narcotic Enforcemt Ofcrs Assn; Pres Capitol Hill Shrine Clb; Zeta Beta Tau; Hon VP Hudson-Del Boy Scout Coun; Pres NY Soc Wash; Others; hon/Cert of Hon Apprenticeship, Carpenters Jt Apprenticeship Com, Rockland & Orange Cos; Humanitarian Awd, Lt Walter Lipman Post #756 Jewish War Vets & Ladies Aux; Dean's Medal, NY Law Sch Alumni Assn; King of Hearts Awd, Orange & Rockland Div Am Heart Assn; Cert of Apprec, Pres' Com on Mtl Retard; Dist'd Ser Awd, Marine Corp Leag; Others.

GILMAN, DAVID ALAN oc/Professor; b/Sept 26, 1933; h/500 Gardendale Rd, Terre Haute, IN 47803; ba/Terre Haute; m/Elizabeth Ann Barlow; c/Ruth Ann, Thomas Alan, William Michael; p/Albert Maynard and Ruth Edna Gilman (dec); ed/BS Ind St Tchrs Col; MAT Mich St Univ; PhD Pa St Univ; mil/AUS Counter Intell Corps; pa/Prof Ind St Univ; Author 130 Pubs & 3 Books; cp/Ldrship Terre Haute; r/Meth; hon/Caleb Mills Dist'd Tchg Awd; Ind Ednl Res Assn Ser Awd.

GILMORE, JAMES W oc/Detective; b/Jul 28, 1932; h/PO Box 913, Harrison, TN 37748; ba/Same; m/Evelyn B; c/Ronnie, Tammy, Mike, Chris; p/Leonard W and Sally M Gilmore, Harrison; ed/Bus Adm; mil/USAF 4 Yrs, 9th AF; Disabled Vet; cp/St & Local Polit Activs; r/Bapt.

GILMORE, LAURENE S oc/College Dean; h/1853 43rd St, Birmingham, AL 35208; ba/University, AL; c/Harry, Patricia Clayton, Benjamin; ed/BSN Vanderbilt Univ 1945; MSN 1955, EdD Cand Univ Ala; pa/Prof & Dean Capstone Col Nsg Univ Ala 1976-, Samford Univ Sch of Nsg 1972-76; Assoc Dir Hlth Manpower & Ednl Dir, Ala Reg Med Progs 1968-74; Chm Dept Nsg & Div Hlth Related Technol, Jefferson St Jr Col 1963-68; Ed Dir: B'ham Bapt Hosp Sch Nsg 1948-63, Univ Hosp Sch Nsg 1960-63, S Highland Infirmary 1945-60; Coun of Preven of Dis & Hlth Care, St Com Public Hlth; Adv Com on Hlth Manpower, St Dept Ed; Task Force on Hlth Manpower, Ala Hlth Study Comm; Proj Dir: Samford Univ Open Curric, Rural Hlth Nsg; Hlth Plan'g B'ham Manpower Com; Chm Nsg Com, Lawson St Jr Col; Hlth Plan'g B'ham Manpower Com; Chm Nsg Com, Lawson St Jr Col; W Ala Hlth Coun Exec Com; Past Pres: Ala Bd Nsg, Ala Leag Nsg; Ofcr, Mem Num Other Nat & St Profl Assns; cp/Task Force on Ed, B'ham C of C; Feasibility Study: Proj Dir Samford Univ, Univ Ala; Tuscaloosa Commun Ctr; Guatemala Alliance; Tuscaloosa Pilot Clb; hon/Hon Ed Assn; Sigma Theta Tau; Cand B'ham Wom of Yr; W/W: S, Ala w Notable People; Pub'd Author.

GILPIN, DOROTHEA HAYMAN oc/Educator; b/Aug 26, 1921; h/915 E Pratt Dr, Palatine, IL 60067; ba/Gurnee, IL; m/William Russell; c/Judith Anne G Frederick, Jane Leslie G Leith; p/Frank Hayman (dec); Margaret Patton Hayman, Palatine; ed/BA Eureka Col 1959; Univ Ill-

Urbana 1967; pa/Chm Media Ctr Warren Twp HS 1967-; Lit for Yg Adults Univ Ill 1967; Libn K-12 Commun Consolidated Sch Dist 15 1965-67; Tchr Grades 3-8 Ill Val Unit Sch Dist, Chillicothe, Ill 1955-65; Dept Navy US Govt, Gt Lakes, Ill 1943-45; Am & Ill Lib Assns; Ill Assn Sch Libns; Ill Public Lib Dirs Assn, Exec Bd 1969-, Secy 1973-75; Am Fdn Tchrs; Am Lib Trustees Assn; Public Lib Trustee Awd of Yr Comm, Ill Public Lib Dirs Assn; cp/Trustee Palatine Public Lib Dist, Var Ofcs; r/Bahaii; hon/Best Trustee Awd, Univ Ill; Author Policy Manual, Palatine Public Lib Dist.

GIMENEZ, MIGUEL ANGEL oc/Lawyer; b/Oct 7, 1929; h/Serrania A-4, Garden Hills, Bayamon, PR 00619; ba/Old San Juan, PR; m/Bessie Cruz; c/Lizzette, Benilith, Miguel A, Alberto J, Bessie F; p/Miguel A Gimenez; Ana Munoz; ed/BA Niagara Univ; LLB Mercer Univ; mil/AUS 1952-54; pa/Atty Gen PR; Superior Ct Judge 1969-76; Pvt Pract 1962-69; Atty Crim Div & Prosecuting Atty Justice Dept 1957-62; Law Clerk to Asst Justice Supreme Ct PR 1957; r/Cath.

GINGERY, BURNEIL E oc/Educational Administrator; b/Oct 24, 1916; h/1232 Starview Ln, Lincoln, NE 68512; ba/Lincoln; m/Gwendolyn; c/Linda Sue G Swanson; p/Charles R and Johanna Gingery (dec); ed/BS; MS; pa/AUS 1942-45; pa/Voc Ednl

Supvn & Adm; Neb Voc-ag Assn; Neb Voc Assn, VChancellor's Citizens Com; cp/Past Pres Capital City Kiwanis; r/Meth Ch: Mem; hon/Hon Am Farmer Awd; Life Mem: Kiwanis Neb (Ia Foun), FFA Alumni; Dist'd Pres, Ia Kiwanis.

GIOLITO, CAROLYN HUGHES oc/Staff Assistant; h/13912 Northgate Dr, Silver Spring, MD 20906; ba/Washington, DC; m/Caesar A; c/Glenn, Antoinette; p/C T Hughes (dec); Eunice Brown Hughes, AL; ed/BS Ala Col; Geo Wash Sch Law 1956-58; pa/Staff Asst (Projs Ofcr) to Senate Maj Ldr, Senator Robert C Byrd (WVa); Adm Asst to Other Polit Ldrs; IPA; Adm Assts Assn US Cong; r/Presb; hon/Personalities of S; W/W: Govt, E, S, Am.

GIPS, WALTER F (TERRY) oc/Legislative Assistant; b/Feb 11, 1951; h/92 Brookstone Dr, Princeton, NJ 08540; ba/Washington, DC; p/Walter F and Ann Gips, P'ton; ed/BA Claremont Men's Col; MS Univ Cal-Davis; pa/Leg Asst to US Rep John Krebs; Am Agri Ecs Assn; cp/Dir & Fdr Sacramento Commun Garden Prog; Secy Yolo Co SPCA; hon/Claremont Men's Col Alumni Awd for Student Citizenship.

GIRARD, JUDITH oc/Reading Specialist; b/Oct 24, 1938; h/2905 Parfet Dr, Lakewood,

CO 80215; ba/L'wood; m/John; p/John Anderson, Wauwahosa, WI; ed/BA; MA; EdD; pa/Pres: Jefferson Co Coun IRA, Colo Coun IRA; Assoc Dir Rocky Mtn Rdg Specialist Assn; r/Meth; hon/Finalist, Colo Tchr of Yr 1970; Alpha Phi; Outstg Sec'dy Edr Am; Keep Colo Beautiful Awd.

GIRAUDIER, ANTONIO oc/Writer; Painter; Musician; b/Sept 28, 1926; h/215 E 68th St, NYC, NY 10021; p/Antonio Giraudier Ginebra (dec); Mrs D Giraudier, Palm Beach, FL; ed/BLitt Belen Jesuits, Havana 1944, Vedado Inst, Havana 1944; Grad Univ Havana Law Sch 1949; Pvt Art Studies; pa/Singer & Piano; 1-Man Exhibits: Smolin Gallery, NYC 1965, New Masters Gallery, NYC 1967, Avanti Galleries, NYC 1968, 69, 71, 73, 74, Palm Bch (Fla) Towers 1969, Univ Palm Bch 1970; 2-Man Exhbns: Welfleet Gallery, Cape Cod, Mass 1967, Welfleet Gallery, Palm Bch 1968, Avanti Galleries 1972; Num Group Exhbns US & Europe 1964-; Rep'd Perm Collections: Fordham Univ, Lincoln Ctr, NY & Bronx, NY, Univ Palm Bch, Greenville (SC) Mus Art, Am Poets F'ship Soc, Ill; Num Pvt Collections US & Europe; Art Wk Reproduced in 41+ Pubs in USA, Switzerland, Spain, Germany, Italy, & France; Smithsonian Inst; Nat Trust Hist Preserv; Ill St Poetry Soc; Pres Am Poets F'ship Soc; Portsmouth Arts Coun; Author

Num Books Poetry, US, Cuba, Europe 1957-; Written 2000+ Poems-prose; Contbr Poetry to Compilations & 50+ Anthologies; 26 Readings USA & Abroad; Composer & Lyracist 12 Songs; Words & Music; Over 500 Musical Gatherings; Own Musical Compositions; Books in 50+ Libs; Owner 2500+ Art Works; hon/NAm & World Edit Intl Reg of Profiles; W/W: E, Am, Chgo, Am Art; Men Achmt; Notable Ams of Bicent Era; Other Biogl Listings; Premier Prix de Printemps, Paris 1959; Hon Mention Prairie Poet Collection 1972; Hon Mention Maj Poets Contest 1972; Laureat Margerite d'Or, Paris 1960; Danae Lit Designate 1973; Cert of Merit: DIB, Men Achmt, Am Poets F'ship Soc 1973; Hon Men L'Orientation Litteraire, Paris; Dipl & Medal, Intl Commun Ser; Dipl Intl Biogl Assn; Life F'ship: Intl Biogl Assn, Intl W/W Commun Ser; 2 Certs of Awd in Envir Contest & Maj Poets Contest, USA; Num Others; Writings in Approx 80 Books Group of Individual, Pub'd or Booked for Pub.

GIROD, ALBERIC O oc/Company President; b/Sept 5, 1950; h/F-J-1 Villa Verde, Guaynabo, PR 00657; ba/Old San Juan, PR; m/Gretchen; c/Desha M; p/Oscar M and Olga Rossello, Miramar, PR; ed/MBA Harvard Sch Music; pa/Pres Girod Trust Co; Chm Bd Catano Fed; Dir Ahrens Aircraft Inc; Dir Caribbean Pacific Co; cp/Mortgager Bkrs Assn; Bkrs Clb; r/Cath.

GIROIR, MARCELLINE EVANS oc/Banking Executive; b/Aug 24, 1937; h/3 Longfellow Ln, Little Rock, AR 72207; ba/LR; p/C J Giroir Sr, Pine Bluff, AR; Marcelline E Giroir (dec); ed/BA magna cum laude; pa/Sr VP Pulaski Bk & Trust Co; Nat Assn Bk Wom; Bk Mktg Assn; Sales & Mktg Exec Assn; cp/LR C of C; Bd Dirs: Ark Orch Soc, Ark Opera Theatre, Yth Homes Inc; r/Rom Cath.

GISH, SANDRA LOUISE oc/Researcher; b/Oct 29, 1950; h/1726 Grand Ave, St Paul, MN 55105; p/Roger E and Louise L Gish,

Champaign, IL; ed/BS w high hons Univ Ill 1974; pa/Res Staff Minn Spec Sch Dist #287; Minn Theatre Inst of Deaf: Actress, Instr, Interpreter, Writer, Sign Lang Translator, Sign Lang Dir 1976-79, Dir Ednl Progs 1977, Bd Dirs 1976-79, Incorporator 1976; Tchr Mpls Spec Sch Dist #1 Hearing Impaired Prog 1974-76; Tchr Camp Tamarac Prog for Hearing Impaired & Mtly Retard Students 1975; Instr Manual Communs Parkland Jr Col, Champaign, Ill 1972-74; Lectr: Minn CEC 1976, Minn Assn Edrs of Hearing Impaired 1976, Univ Ill 1974; Judge Miss Deaf Minn Pageant 1976; Demonstrator: Minn Exceptl Chd's Art Fair 1976-77; Suburban Hennepin Co Voc Tech Schs 1975-76; Num Other Former Positions; hon/Wom of Yr, Minn Jr Nat Assn of Deaf 1977; Certn, Reg'd Interpreter & Translator for Deaf.

GITTLER, JOSEPH BERTRAM oc/Retired Professor; Dean; Author; b/Sept 21, 1912; h/29 Briarfield Dr, Great Neck, NY 11020; ba/NYC; m/Susan; c/Josephine, Peter, Sophia; p/Morris and Toby Gittler (dec); ed/BS; MA; PhD; pa/Vis Prof & Spec Lectr Univ Hiroshima (Japan) 1979-80; Dist'd Vis Prof Dept Sociol George Mason Univ St Univ Va (Fall Semester) 1979; Yeshiva Univ: Ret'd 1978, Prof Sociol Ferkauf Grad Sch Humanities & Social Scis 1966-78, Dean Ferkauf Grad Sch Humanities & Social Scis 1966-77; Queensborough Col CUNY: Dean Fac & Prof Social Scis 1961-66, Dir Col Discovery Prog; Other Former Positions; Fellow: Soc for Values in Higher Ed, NY Acad Scis, Am Sociol Assn; Coun of Fellows Crozier Sem, Chester, Pa 1961-70; Bd Trustees Ctr for Urban Ed 1968-72; Edit Bd Activs; Bd Dirs New Future Foun; En Sociol Soc; Soc for Study of Social Probs; En Assn Col Deans & Advrs of Students; Nat Coun for Social Scis; Assn for Higher Ed; Exec Coun Intl Org for Study of Group Tension; Coun Grad Schs US; cp/Adv Bd Rose F Kennedy Ctr for Mtl Retard; Chm Exec Com Max Weinreich Ctr for Adv'd Jewish Studies; Former Mem Com on Univ Relats Ofc of Mayor, NYC; r/Judaism; hon/Phi Beta Kappa; Phi Kappa Phi; Walter B Hill Prize in Phil; Awd for Poetry Writing; Pi Mu Epsilon.

GLASBERG, H MARK oc/Physician; Psychiatrist; b/Oct 11, 1937; h/480 Park Ave, New York, NY 10022; ba/Same; m/Paula Drillman; c/Scot Bradley, Hilary Jennifer; p/Joseph and Elsa Glasberg, NY; ed/BA; MS; MD; mil/AUS 1961-63, Lt Col Med Corps; pa/Asst Prof Psychi Mt Sinai Sch Med; Att'g Psychiatrist St Vincents Hosp; Mem Panel Indep Psychiatrists NY Co; r/Hebrew; hon/Spec Fellow in Psychi, Nat Inst Mtl Hlth; Spec Res Awd, Postgrad Div St Univ NY Col Med.

GLASER, KURT oc/Professor; b/Aug 19, 1914; h/7354 Tulane Ave, University City, MO 63130; ba/Edwardsville, IL; c/Jeffrey, Kristin, Robin, Angela; p/Otto Charles and Dorothy Merrylees Glaser (dec); ed/AB 1935, AM 1938, PhD 1941 Harvard Univ; pa/Prof Govt So Ill Univ; Assoc Editor *Modern Age* (Phila) & *Plural Socs* (The Hague); cp/Repub Cand for Cong, Ill 24th Dist 1962; r/Unitarian; hon/Fulbright Lectr, Univ Kiel (Germany) 1966-67; Author: *Czecho-Slovakia: A Critical History*, 1961, *Victims of Politics: The State of Human Rights*, 1979.

GLASS, IRIS J oc/Dietitian; b/May 11, 1941; h/1401 W Oak, El Dorado, AR 71730; ba/El Dorado; m/Bud; c/Kristi Michelle, James Stephen; p/James H and Henrietta Clark, Waldo, AR; ed/BS; MS; pa/Am Dietetic Assn; St Advr HEIFSS; Adv Bd S Ark Univ-Tech Br; r/Bapt.

GLASSMAN, ARMAND B oc/Physician; Educator; b/Sept 9, 1938; h/167 Broad St, Charleston, SC 29401; ba/C'ton; m/Alberta C Macri; c/Armand P, Steven B, Brian A; p/Rosa Ackerman, Paterson, NJ; ed/BA; MD magna cum laude; pa/Med Univ SC, C'ton: Prof & Chm Dept Lab Med, Dir Clin Labs, Med Dir Mt & MLT Progs; Var Former Acad Positions; Fellow: Am Col Physicians, Am Soc Clin Pathol, Col Am Pathologists, Am Col

Nuclear Med; Am Assn Blood Bks; AMA; So Med Assn; Am Assn Pathologists & Bacteriologists; Intl Acad Pathol; Assn Schs Allied Hlth Profs; Am Soc Med Technologists; Am Geriatrics Soc; Am Acad Oral Med; C'ton Med Soc; SC Med Assn; Bd Dirs Acad Clin Lab Physicians & Scists; Others; cp/Bd Dirs Franklin C Fetter Fam Hlth Ctr; C'ton Hist Soc; hon/Num Profl Pubs; Hon Mention, Yg Investigator of Yr 1971, SNM; W/W S&SW.

GLASSMAN, JAMES HENDRIX oc/Minister; b/Dec 5, 1925; ba/1102 Ash, Mission, TX 78572; m/Beth June Upham; c/James Francis, Anne Cathleen; p/Willard Glassman (dec); Myra Glassman, Portland, OR; ed/BA Univ Wash 1949; ThM Dallas Theol Sem 1953; PhD Univ Edinburgh (Scotland) 1958; mil/AUS WWII, Investigator Counter Intell Corps; pa/Min 1st Presb Ch, Mission 1978-; Sr Min Val Commun Presb Ch, Minneapolis, Minn 1969-78; Fac Mem Univ Wyo, Laramie 1965-69; Min: Univ Presb Ch, Laramie 1964-69, Trinity U Presb Ch, Seattle, Wash 1958-64; Asst Min Larbert-Dunipace Ch of Scotland 1956-57; Other Former Min Positions; Mem Presby of Del Salvador; Mem & Reviewer Am Soc Ch Hist; Scottish Ch Hist Soc; cp/Rotary; Am Legion; r/Presb Ch US (South); hon/Man of Yr, Northgate Rotary Clb Seattle 1964; Recog & Achmts in Aths; Pub'd Author; Num Biogl Listings.

GLATZ, MYRON LEE oc/Pastor; Educator; b/Oct 4, 1939; h/10th & Birch St, Douglas, WY 82633; ba/Douglas; m/Mary Jeneane; c/Lorell, Sharlyn, Robbin; p/Martin L Glatz; Ruth L West, Bakersfield, CA; ed/BA; pa/Pastor 15 Yrs; Pres Calvary Bapt Acad; cp/Com Man Repub Party; C of C; r/Bapt.

GLAUS, MARLENE ANNE oc/Teacher; Lecturer; Author; b/Nov 24, 1933; h/4575 W 80th St Cir, Minneapolis, MN 55437; ba/Mpls; p/Vernon LeRoy Glaus, Mantorville, MN; Ardis Menora Mott, M'ville; ed/BS; pa/Tchr Centennial Sch; Life Mem: NEA, MEA, REA; Judge Minn Tchr of Yr 1979; cp/Lectr; Tchr Evening Classes on Art Objects for Control Data Creative Lng Ctr; r/Congreg; hon/Runner Up 1974 Minn Tchr of Yr; W/W: Am Wom, Yg Am Wom.

GLAZE, DIANA GLADYS LISOWSKI oc/Intermediate School Principal; b/Jun 29, 1939; h/1409 Stafford Rd, Sherwood, AR 72116; m/Johnny E; p/Roman and Appolonia Lisowski; ed/BS, MA, Ed Specialist; pa/Intermed Sch Prin, Little Rock Sch Dist, Little Rock, Ark 1976-; Tchr Little Rock Sch Dist 1970-76; Substitute Tchr Milwaukee Public Schs (Wis) 1969-70; Other Former Positions; AEA, Human Relats Comm; AAUW: Br VP, Leg Chm, Wom's Com Chm; ACE; IRA; AAESP; Prin's Roundtable: Secy 1977, Negotiations Chm 1979; cp/Alumni Assns: Univ Wis, St Mary's Acad; PTA: Life Mem, Textbook Selection Com, Curric Guid Com; Am Wom's Polit Caucus; ERA Coalition; Bd Mem Panel of Am Wom; N Little Rock Dem Wom's Clb; Urban Leag; Altar Soc; r/Cath 1st Communicant Class Tchr; hon/Kappa Kappa Iota; Kappa Kappa Iota Conclave; Bowling & Golf Awds; Outstg Yg Wom Am; Personalities of S.

GLAZER, FREDERIC JAY oc/Library Administrator; b/Feb 20, 1937; h/114 Sheridan Cir, Charleston, WV 25314; ba/C'ton; m/Sylvia L; c/Hoyt, Hilary; p/M H

and Charlotte Esther Glazer, Miami, FL; ed/BA 1954, MLS 1964 Columbia Univ; mil/AUS 1960-62; pa/Dir WVa Lib Comm; Am Lib Assn; SEn Lib Assn; WVa Lib Assn; cp/Past VP Tidewater Literary Coun (Va); Former Chm Residential Cancer Dr, Kanawha Co (WVa); hon/Reg III Outstg Citizen Awd, HEW; Pres Cert of Apprec for Vol Ser to Proj Hd Start.

GLEIM, PAUL S oc/Manager of Engineering; b/Dec 20, 1923; h/8 Cumberland Pl, Richardson, TX 75080; ba/Dallas, TX; m/Gene; c/Gregory Paul, Gere; p/Alva A Gleim (dec); Phoebe D Gleim, Wheelersburg, OH; ed/BS w hons; mil/AUS; pa/Electrochem Soc; cp/Meth Ch: Adm Bd; hon/Num Patents in Semiconductors.

GLEITZ, GEORGE PHILLIP oc/Attorney at Law; b/Jul 11, 1943; h/918 Elm St, Bowling Green, KY 42101; ba/Bowling Green; m/Nancy Marie; c/Geoffrey; p/Elmer and Pauline Gleitz (dec); ed/BA Wn Ky Univ; JD Univ Louisville; mil/AUS 1967-69; pa/Am, Ky & BG Bar Assns; Ky Acad Trial Attys; cp/Bd Chm Cumberland Trace Legal Sers; JCs; r/Luth; hon/W/W S&SW.

GLENN, CAROLYN LOVE oc/Teacher; b/June 30, 1933; h/2310 Don Andres Ave, Tallahassee, FL 32306; ba/Tallahassee; p/Lawson Hilman and Geneva Foster Glenn, Raleigh, NC; ed/BME & Cert in Voice, Fla State Univ; pa/Pvt Tchr of Choral Music; Former Music Tchr in Public Schs (Elem, Jr & Sr HS); Recital at Carnegie Hall (NYC) 1965; Perf'd Concerts in NC, NJ, Ga & Fla; Former Instr of Pvt Voice Lessons on HS & Col Level; Church Soprano Soloist; r/St Paul's United Meth Ch; hon/Delta Kappa Gamma; Rockefeller Foun Grant to Oberlin Univ.

GLENN, JUDY N oc/Real Estate Broker; Teacher; b/Aug 26, 1955; h/2111 Hickory Rd, Corinth, MS 38834; ba/Corinth; m/William G Sr; c/Kelly C, William Gary Jr; p/Charlie and Velma Newborn, Corinth; ed/Grad Realtor's Inst; pa/Tchr Alcorn Co Vo-Tech Ctr; Nat

Assn Realtors; BPW Clb; cp/Mbrship Com C of C; Dorcas Cir; r/Harper Rd Christian Ch; hon/Outstg Sales Ldr, Nelda Parrish & Assocs; Corinth Yg Career Wom; Yth Ldrship Harper Rd Ch.

GLESER, GOLDINE C oc/Professor & Director; b/Jun 15, 1915; h/3604 Lansdowne Ave, Cincinnati, OH 45236; ba/Cinc; m/Sol M; c/Leon J, Malcolm A, Judith A G Klein; p/Julius and Lena Goldberg Cohnberg (dec); ed/AB; MS; PhD; pa/Univ Cinc Col Med: Prof Psychol, Dir Psychol Div, Dept Psychi; Reschr; Conslt; r/Jewish; hon/Phi Beta Kappa; Pi Mu Epsilon; Sigma Xi; Fellows Grad Sch UC; Grants: Founs Fund for Res in Psychi & US Dept HEW.

GLICK, PERRY AARON oc/Retired Entomologist; b/Dec 21, 1895; h/Ft Brown Resaca Apts 4005, Brownsville, TX 78520; m/Jessie Odom (dec); c/Dorothy Provine (Stepdaugh); p/M M and Eva Alice Morgan Glick (dec); ed/Park Col 1915-16; Univ Ks 1919-20; AB 1921, MS 1922 Univ Ill; mil/Tex St Guard 1944-45; pa/Asst Entomologist Ariz Comm of Agri & Hort 1922-23; Insp Fed Hort Bd: NY, Phila, Wash DC 1923-25; Asst Entomologist Bur of Entomol: Tallulah, La 1925-36 & Tifton, Ga 1936; Asst & Assoc Entomologist, Bur Entomol Plant Quarantine,

Waco, Tex 1939-50; Entomologist, Col Sta, Tex 1950-58; Entomol Res Div, Pink Bollworm Invests, Brownsville, Tex 1953-56; Ret'd 1965; Conslt; Entomological Soc Am: Fellow, Chm Mbrship Com 1958; Fellow: Tex Acad Sci, Royal Entomol Soc London, AAAS; Ecological Soc Am; Intl Lepidopterists' Soc; Sigma Xi; Author Num Papers; Contbr Var Profl Jours; cp/Intl Good Neighbour Coun; Nat Adv Bd Am Security Coun; Others; r/Presb; hon/US Dept Agri: Cert of Apprec Awd, Length of Ser Awd; Nom'd for Superior Sers Awd; Dist'd Alumnus Awd, Park Col; DIB; Ldrs in Am Sci; Who Knows-& What; Royal Blue Book; Personalities of S; Nat Reg Prom Ams; Others.

GLICKMAN, DAN oc/US Representative; b/Nov 24, 1944; h/442 Hawthorne St NW, Washington, DC 20016; ba/Wash DC; m/Rhoda; c/Jonathan, Amy; p/Milton and Gladys Glickman, Wichita, KS; ed/BA Univ

Mich; JD George Wash Univ; pa/Mem US Ho of Reps: House Agri & Sci & Technol Coms; cp/1979 St Campaign Chm Ks Easter Seals Soc; Wichita Area C of C; Past Pres Wichita Bd of Ed; r/Jewish.

GLINES, DON EUGENE oc/Educational Administrator; b/Nov 25, 1930; h/1501 3rd St, Sacramento, CA 95814; ba/Sacramento; m/Ruth; c/Laurie, Harlan; p/C E Glines (dec); Helen J Porter, Westminster, CA; ed/BS; MS; PhD; mil/AUS; pa/Dir Ednl Future Projs;

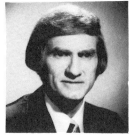

Conslt Prog Planning & Devel Cal St Dept Ed; Writer of 6 Pub'd Books & Num Pub'd Articles; Spkr; Pres Nat Coun on Yr-Round Ed; cp/World Future Soc; Cousteau Soc; Envir Action; hon/Recog'd for Achmts, *Nat Observer.*

GLOVER, ARTHUR LEWIS JR oc/College Counselor; b/Sept 29, 1912; h/4701 Don Miguel Dr, Los Angeles, CA 90008; ba/Culver

City, CA; m/Beatrice Louise Jones; c/Beatrice Louise; p/Arthur and Lucile Lewis Glover (dec); ed/AB, MA, ME, EdD Cand Nova Univ; mil/AUS 1942-46; pa/Phi Delta Kappa; Bd Dirs Didi Hirsch Clin; cp/Past Pres Culver City Lions Breakfast Clb; r/Westminster Presb Ch; hon/Man of Yr: Lions Clb 1973, Omega Psi Phi 1970.

GLOVER, BETTY S oc/Professional Musician; Teacher; b/Jan 24, 1923; h/8791 Cottonwood Dr, Cincinnati, OH 45231; p/Thomas J Semple (dec); Lillie L Semple, Cinc; ed/BM; MM; pa/Bass Trombonist Cinc Symph Orch; Adj Assoc Prof Conservatory of Music, Univ Cinc, Conductor Brass Choir; hon/Pi Kappa Lambda; Sigma Alpha Iota.

GLYNN, NEIL HELD oc/Corporate Vice President; b/Mar 22, 1928; h/24 Quail Rd, Osterville, MA 02655; ba/Centerville, MA; m/Arlene Terese; c/Steven Arlen, Diane Louise; p/Berkley Perham and Regina Louise Glynn, Hyannis, MA; ed/BS Univ of NH; mil/USAF, Ret'd 1/Lt; pa/VP in charge of Mktg Green Co Inc; Hanslin-Glynn Assn: Past Pres & Chief Exec Ofcr, Past Sales Mgr & Salesman; Mass Div Gen Motors, Lowell Br Mgr; Nat Assn Home Bldrs: Past Chm Spec Com for Mktg, Past Mem Indust Promotion

Com, Past Chm Mktg Coun; Inst of Residential Mktg; Nat Assn Real Est Bds; Nat Assn Real Est Editors; Leg Com Home Bldrs Assn Mass; Lic'd Real Est Broker; Dir Cape Cod Bldrs & Contractors Assn; cp/Past Dir Cape Cod C of C; Am Forestry Assn; Sierra Clb; Nat Pks & Conserv Assn; Mass Audobon Soc; r/Prot; hon/Nat Assn Home Bldrs: Sales Mgr of Yr Awd 1966, Best Idea of Yr Awd; Mem Million Dollar Cir; Bill Molster Awd; Owens-Corning Fiberglass Spec Awd; Biogl Listings.

GOBAR, ASH oc/Professor; Author; b/Apr 7, 1930; h/989 Holly Springs Rd, Lexington, KY 40504; ba/L'ton; m/Anne; c/Penelope, Peter, Karina; p/Imir and Salia Gobar (dec); ed/AB Col Wooster; MA Univ Chgo; PhD Univ Wis 1959; pa/Prof Phil Transylvania Univ; Am Phil Assn; World Cong Phil; Author Books, Treatises, Essays; r/Christian Ch; hon/Fellow, Univ Geneva (Switzerland); Grant, Am Phil Soc; Outstg Edrs Am.

GOBETZ, GILES EDWARD oc/Professor; Research Executive; Author; Editor; b/Jul 25, 1926; h/29227 Eddy Rd, Willoughby Hills, OH 44092; ba/Kent, OH; m/Milena Osenar; c/Emily, Maria, Margaret; p/Albert and Terezija Gobetz (dec); ed/MA Washington Univ 1955; PhD Ohio St Univ 1962; pa/Prof

Sociol & Anthropology Kent St Univ; Dir Slovenian Res Ctr Am Inc; Assoc Editor *Intl Jour of Contemp Sociol;* VP DTK; cp/Var Civic Activs: Yth Devel, Delinq Preven, Commun Improvemt Projs; r/Rom Cath; hon/Outstg Edr Am; Achmt Awd; Men of Achmt; Nat Reg Prom Ams.

GOCEK, MATILDA ARKENBOUT oc/Library Director; Publisher; Newspaper Columnist; Historian; Author; b/Feb 18, 1923; h/RD#5, Box 41, Dunderberg Rd, Monroe, NY 10950; ba/Suffern, NY; m/John A; c/Ruth Ann Robinson (Mrs Sam), Dianne McKinstrie (Mrs Ralph), John Jacob; p/Jacob R Arkenbout; Mathilda E Meyer; ed/AA; BA; MLS; PhD; pa/Lib Dir Suffern Free Lib; Lib Assn Rockland Co; Rockland Co Public Libns; RCLS Dirs Assn; cp/Trustee: Tuxedo Park Day (Sch), Mus Village in Orange Co; r/Presb; hon/Exell in S'ship; Poetry Awd, *Idiom Mag.*

GODBEY, WILLIAM GIVENS oc/- Professor; h/Alaska Meth Univ, Anchorage, AK 99504; m/Helen Persis Isberg; c/Will Emeth; pa/Prof Chem & Physics; hon/FAIC; FIBA; Sigma Xi; Gamma Sigma Delta; Armsey Excellence in Tchg 1968; F'ship, Am Inst Chemists; Gold Medal Awd Comm 1972-73; NW Pacific Dir of Yr Photographic Soc Am 1976; Notable Ams.

GODDARD, DEAN ALLEN oc/Minister; Christian Educator; b/Feb 19, 1942; h/1804 S Melrose St, Casper, WY 82601; ba/Casper; m/Mary L; c/Rebekah Marie, Matthew Dean; p/Fay F and Dorothy A Goddard, Medford, OR; ed/BA Bob Jones Univ; pa/Pres Calvary Bapt Christian Sch, Casper 1977-; Pastor: Calvary Bapt Ch, Casper 1977-, Mid-Cities

Bapt Temple, Downey, Cal 1971-77, Galilee Bapt Ch, Portland, Oreg 1965-68, 1st Bapt Ch, Woodland, Wash 1964-65; r/Indep Bapt; hon/Fratres In Christo Awd, Phi Kappa Pi; Commencemt Awd, Pacific Coast Bapt Bible Col; W/W Am Cols & Univs; Notable Ams; DIB.

GODFREY, DOROTHY DOUD oc/Home Economist; h/3035 125th Ave NE, Bellevue, WA 98005; ba/Bellevue; c/Jane G Rhinehart; ed/BS; pa/Intl Home Ecs Dir Rena-Ware Distributors; hon/Phi Kappa Phi; Omicron Nu; W/W Am Wom.

GODFREY, JOHN CARL oc/Medicinal Chemist; Executive; b/Mar 11, 1929; h/215 Manor Dr, Syracuse, NY 13214; ba/Same; m/Nancy Jane Williams; c/Laura Alexis, Helen Rebecca, Sabrina Lee; p/Carl H and Ruth Emma James Godfrey (dec); ed/BA Pomona Col 1951; PhD Univ Rochester 1954; pa/Pres Godfrey Sci & Design Inc; Chm Syracuse Sect Am Chem Soc; Editor *Syracuse Chemist;* cp/Pres Technol Clb Syracuse; hon/Phi Beta Kappa; 1st NSF Fellow on Chem.

GODWIN, PAUL MILTON oc/College Educator; b/Jun 18, 1942; h/15459 Old Hickory Blvd, Nashville, TN 37211; ba/N'ville; m/Mary Mae Wolfe; c/Katherine Elizabeth, Kimberly Ann; p/Walter F and Mamie Viola Godwin, Hot Springs, AR; ed/BA Ark Tech 1964; MA 1969, PhD 1972 Ohio St Univ; mil/AUS 1964-66 2/Lt, 1/Lt; USAR 1966-70; pa/Belmont Col: Assoc Prof Music, Band Dir 1975-; Band Dir: Lee Sr HS,

Marianna, Ark 1972-73, Lewisville, Ark 1966-67; Var Col Coms; Fac Advr Phi Mu Alpha Sinfonia; Composer; Judge Solo & Ensemble Contests; Former Mem Exec Com, Mid Tenn Sch Band & Orch Assn; Tenn Music Edrs Assn; MENC; Soc for Music Theory; Col Band Dirs Nat Assn; Col Music Soc; cp/Citizens Adv Com, Local Elem Sch; Elks; r/Crievewood U Meth Ch: Mem, SS Tchr & Ofcr, Choir, Former Mem Adm Bd; hon/Outstg Edrs Am; W/W S&SW.

GOETCHEUS, JOHN STEWART oc/Orthopaedic Surgeon; Educator; b/May 14, 1938; h/Partridge Hill, Essex, CT 06426; ba/Essex; m/Janice Berg; c/Amy Lisabeth, Gregory John; p/L Frederick and Elizabeth Gibson Goetcheus, Essex; ed/AB w distn

DePauw Univ; MD Case Wn Resv Univ; mil/USAF MC Capt; pa/Instr Ortho Surg Yale Sch Med; Diplomat Am Bd Orth Surg; Fellow Am Acad Orth Surg; En Orth Assn; cp/Essex Rotary; r/1st Congreg Ch, Essex.

GOETHERT, BERNHARD HERMAN oc/Educator; Scientist; Engineer; b/Oct 20, 1907; h/1702 Sycamore Cir, Manchester, TN 37355; ba/Tullahoma, TN; m/Hertha Tod; c/Hella G Lacy, Winfried Herman, Wolfhart Bernhard, Reinhard Karl; p/Bernhard August and Elise Rickmeyer Goethert (dec); ed/BSME Tech Univ Hannover 1930; MSAE Tech Univ Danzig 1934; PhD Tech Univ Berlin 1938; pa/Univ Tenn Space Inst, Tullahoma: Dean Emeritus, Dir Aeroacoustics & Prof AE 1975-, Dean & Prof Aerospace Engrg 1971-75, Dir & Prof Aerospace Engrg 1964-71; Chief Scist AF Systems Command, Andrews AFB, Md 1964-66; Other Former Positions; cp/Rotary Intl Clb; r/Luth; hon/Humboldt Awd for US, Sr Scists, Humboldt Foun on Behalf of W German Govt; 1st Recipient "Simulation & Ground Testing Awd", Am Inst Aeronautics & Astronautics; Hon Mem, German Assn for Aeronautics & Astronautics; Plaque of Hon, Tech Univ Aachen (Germany); Others.

GOFF, LOUELLA HOLLAND oc/Secretary; Retired Teacher; b/Dec 16; h/321 E Cherry St, Covington, VA 24426; m/William E; c/4 Chd; p/John H and Mary Lou Howell Holland; ed/Christian Col; Wilberforce Univ; pa/Pres Local Br AARP; cp/Pres Alleghany Players; r/1st Bapt Ch, Covington; hon/Hon'd by: NAACP, NOW, OES; Personalities of S.

GOGGINS, HORACE oc/Dental Surgeon; b/May 14, 1929; h/1635 W Main St, Rock Hill, SC 29730; ba/Rock Hill; m/Juanita W; c/Horace W II; p/Ulysses Goggins (dec); Mattie L Goggins, Greenwood, SC; ed/BS; DDS; mil/AUS 1954-56, Capt DC; USAR Maj

(Ret'd); pa/Nat Dental Assn; Palmetto Dental Soc; SE Analgesic Soc; cp/Life Mem: NAACP, Alpha Phi Alpha; Sigma Pi Phi; Dem; r/Mt Prospect Bapt Ch: Deacon; hon/Personalities of S; W/W: S&SW, Among Black Ams.

GOINS, MARY G oc/Principal; b/Sept 8, 1929; h/19102 Northwood Ave, Carson, CA 90746; ba/Compton, CA; m/Lee A Randle; c/Angela Marie Goins; p/Clofar and Olivia Guillory (dec); ed/BA; MA; pa/Assn Compton Unified Sch Admrs; Assn Cal Sch Admrs; cp/Var Civic Activs; r/Cath; hon/Finer Womanhood Awd, Xavier Univ; Life Hon Awd, PTA.

GOLAN, LAWRENCE PETER oc/Engineer; h/12 Andrews Rd, Randolph, NJ 07801; ba/Florham Park, NJ; m/Helen I; c/Lisa, Wanda, Lawrence; p/Joseph and Frances Golan, Hillside, NJ; ed/BSME, MSME WVa Univ; PhD Lehigh Univ; pa/Engr Exxon Res &

Engrg Co; Instr: WVa Univ 1962-64, Lehigh Univ 1964-68; Adj Assoc Prof Co Col Morris 1970-73; Mech Engr Picatinny Arsenal 1961-62; ASME; AIChE; Sigma Xi; ASEE; cp/Randolph Rec Hd Track Coach; Past Prin CCD; r/Cath; hon/Pub'd Author; W/W in E.

GOLANY, GIDEON S oc/Professor; b/Jan 23, 1928; h/292 Douglas Dr, St Col, PA 16801; m/Esther; c/Ofer, Amir; p/Jacob and Rajena Golany; ed/BA 1956, MA 1962, PhD 1966 Hebrew Univ, Jerusalem, Israel; Univ N Colo 1971-73; MS Technion-Israel Inst Technol, Haifa, Israel 1966, Thesis w Distn; DipCP Inst Social Studies, The Hague, Netherlands 1965; mil/"Hagana" Underground Movemt 1946-48; Israeli Army 1948-50; War of Indep 1948; Sinai War 1956; 6 Days War 1967; pa/Pa St Univ: Prof Urban & Reg Plan'g 1970-, Chm Grad Prog 1970-76, Sr Mem Grad Sch Fac; Vis Prof of Urban & Reg

Plan'g, Inst for Desert Res, Ben-Gurion Univ of the Negev, Israel 1975-76; Res Planner Ofc Reg Resources & Devel, Cornell Univ 1968; Other Acad Appts; Conslt Gideon Golany Assocs 1970-; Partner Plan'g Team Ofc, Haifa, Israel 1964-69; Mem, Fdr Kibbutz Bea'ri, Negev, Israel 1946-52; Num Other Conslt & Plan'g Positions, US & Israel; Papers Presented Var Intl Confs; Author Num Books, Articles, Papers, Other Profl Works; Am Inst Planners; Am Soc Plan'g Ofcls; Canadian Inst Planners; Overseas Mem Assn Engrs & Archs in Israel; r/Jewish; hon/DIB; Men Achmt; Intl W/W; Commun Ser, Intells; W/W Am.

GOLD, KENNETH R oc/General Manager; b/Aug 9, 1934; h/17230 SW 90 Ave, Miami, FL 33157; ba/Miami; m/Olga Ann;

c/Victoria, Rebecca, Jennifer; p/Vernon Gold (dec); Irene Gold, Southgate, MI; ed/AB; MSBA; mil/USN 1952-56, Anti-Sub Aviation Sqdrns; pa/Gen Mgr Cincom Latin Am; r/Presb.

GOLD, MILTON oc/Marketing Executive; b/Aug 5, 1922; h/135 Grandview Ave, Edison, NJ 08817; ba/Lancaster, PA; m/Shirley A Spivack; c/Sandra L Loveless; p/Max and Sarah Lippmanowitch Gold (dec); ed/EE; mil/USAF 1942-45; pa/Mktg Dir Intl Signal & Control Corp; IEEE; Armed Forces Elects & Communs Assn; AF Assn; Am Def Preparedness Assn; Nat Contract Mgmt Assn; cp/BPOE; IOOF; r/Jewish; hon/Cert of Merit, Nat Small Bus Assn; W/W in E.

GOLD, SHARLYA oc/Librarian; Specialist; Writer; h/805 Sir Francis Ave, Capitola, CA 95010; ba/Santa Cruz, CA; m/Leonard; c/Alison, Sheridan, Hilary, Darien; p/Albert H Isenberg (dec); Selma Isenberg Shott (dec); ed/BA Univ Cal-

Berkeley; MA San Jose St Univ; pa/Lib/Media Specialist Gault Sch; Nat Leag Am Pen Wom; Authors Guild Am; cp/Bd Mem YWCA Santa Cruz; r/Jewish; hon/Beta Phi Mu; Author 3 Books; *Time to Take Sides*, Jr Lit Guild Selection.

GOLDBERG, ARTHUR ABBA oc/- Investment Banker; b/Nov 25, 1940; h/83 Montgomery St, Jersey City, NJ 07302; ba/New York, NY; m/Jane E; c/Ari Matthew, Shoshona Eve, Benjamin Saul, Talia Akiva; p/Jack Geddy and Ida Goldberg; ed/BA w hons Am Univ 1962; LLB Cornell Law Sch 1965; pa/Matthews & Wright Inc: Exec VP & Mgr Mun Fin 1970-, Dep Atty Gen St of NJ 1967-70; Pract'g Atty, Jersey City 1967-; Adm

Asst to Cong-man Michael A Feighan (D-Ohio) 1966-67; Other Former Positions; Chm Nat Leased Housing Assn; Adv Bd Mem Housing & Devel Reporter; Gen Counsel NJ Chapts NAHRO & MFOA; ABA, NJ & Conn Bar Assns; Fed Leg Com Public Securities Assn; Dir Titan Industs; cp/Chm CASE (Com for Absorption of Soviet Emigrees); Treas Hebrew Free Loan NJ; CoPres New Synagogue; hon/Profl Pubs.

GOLDBERG, LILLIAN oc/Writer; Playwright; Poet; Lyricist; Social Worker; b/Oct 19, 1917; h/PO Box 391005, Miami Beach, FL 33139; p/Isaac and Yetta Goldberg (dec); ed/Att'd New Sch for Social Res; Att'd Brooklyn Col (Evening Sessions); pa/Ret'd Adm Asst Bklyn Col; Social Wkr; Ct Stenographer Domestic Relats Ct, Bklyn; Author: *Love the Land* & *So What's Wrong in Dreaming*; Former Editor Interfaith Pub *The*

Religious World; Former Columnist: *Bklyn Eagle*, *Blvd News*, *Jewish Ctr News*, *Jewish Examr*, Others; Lyricist: "Miami Bch is Paradise" & "Israel, the Wonderland"; Translator "Simone me Dimona" (from Hebrew to Eng); Public Relats Dir Chd's Aid Soc; cp/Vol Publicity Interns for Peace; Campaign Activs; Others; r/Jewish; hon/B'nai B'rith Awd; Awd for Play "Tillie Goes to Israel", Miami Bch Sr HS; Awd for Poem "Florida, Florida, Come to Its Shores", Gov Askew.

GOLDBLATT, BARRY LANCE oc/- Marketing Executive; b/Jul 29, 1945; h/42 Phelps Ave, New Brunswick, NJ 08901; ba/New Brunswick; p/Samuel and Joan Charlotte Morton Goldblatt, Menlo Park, CA; ed/BS 1967, MBA Univ So Cal; pa/Mktg Exec Johnson & Johnson; USC: Commerce Assocs, MBA's; Am Mktg Assn; Assn MBA Execs; Vol Urban Conslt'g Group; Zeta Zeta Tau; cp/New Brunswick Hotline; Pres USC NJ Alumni Clb; r/Jewish; hon/Outstg Sr, USC; W/W E.

GOLDER, ESTHER BARNES oc/Rancher; b/May 29, 1899; h/5075 N Calle La Vela, Tucson, AZ 85718; ba/Oracle, AZ; m/Lloyd W Jr; c/Lloyd W III, Nancy Winnell G Hillman; p/George Dallas and Winnifred Phillips Barnes (dec); ed/BS Univ Ill; Further Studies; pa/Owner & Mgr 4 Cattle Ranches, Ariz; Ariz Cattle Growers Assn; Designed & Built 1st & 2nd Sects Chateau Apt Hotel, Oak Park, Ill 1927, 29; Nat Leag Am Pen Wom; cp/Nat Soc New England Wom; Nat Soc Magna Charta Dames; Former Regent George Rogers Clark Chapt DAR, Oak Park, Ill; Former Art Editor Univ Ill Yrbook; r/Universalist; hon/Var Prizes for China Painting; Ranch Selected as Outstg Example of Desert Home by *Ariz Highways*.

GOLDIN, AUGUSTA oc/Educator; Author; Journalist; b/Oct 28, 1906; h/590 Bard Ave, Staten Island, NY; ba/Staten Isl; m/Oscar; c/Valerie, Kenneth; p/Jack Reider (dec); Fanny Harris (dec); ed/BA Hunter Col; MS CUNY; EdD Columbia Univ 1947; pa/Prin NYC Public Schs 1971-; Asst Prof Ed St John's Univ SI Campus 1974; Columnist SI Advance 1968-; Reviewer of Lit & Audio Mats *Scholastic Tchr*; Contbr: *Instr Mag* & *Grade Tchr*; Author 11 Books, Short Stories; Freelance Lectr; Nat Audubon Soc; Am Mus Natural Hist; Authors Guild; Nat Coun Adm Wom in Ed; hon/Outstg Sci Book for Chd Awd for *Grass the Everything Everywhere Plant*, Nat Sci Tchrs Assn & Chd's Book Coun.

GOLDMAN, BERT A oc/Dean, Professor; b/Apr 4, 1929; ba/Greensboro, NC 27412; m/Phyllis; c/Lisa, Linda; p/Clara Goldman; ed/AB; MEd; EdD; mil/AUS 1951-53; pa/Univ NC-G: Dean, Prof; Lic'd Psychologist; hon/Author 2 Pub'd Books & Num Articles.

GOLDMAN, MARTIN JEROME oc/- Consulting Engineer; b/Aug 9, 1936; h/Wixon Pono Rd, Mahopac, NY 10541; ba/New York, NY; m/Rhea; c/Hali, Geri, Beth, Michelle; p/Hyman and Shirley Goldman; ed/BME; mil/AUS 2 Yrs; pa/ASHRAE; NSPE; SAME; r/Hebrew.

GOLDMAN, SIMON oc/Broadcasting Executive; Station Owner; b/Jan 18, 1913; h/2153 Winch Rd, Lakewood, NY 14750; ba/Jamestown, NY; m/Marilyn Fink; c/R Michael, Gail M, Paul; p/Isaac and Ida Goldman (dec); ed/BS magna cum laude Syracuse Univ 1935; mil/AUS 1943-45, Communs Div 37th Army; pa/Pres: WJTN & WWSE, Jamestown, NY, WSYB & WRUT, Rutland, Vt, WVMT, Burlington, Vt, WLKK & WLVU, Erie, Pa, J'town Cablevision Inc 1965-70; Treas Am Info Network Affil Assn; Dir Commun Broadcasters Assn 1970-; Pres Troika Devel 1972-; Charter Mem Bd Dirs Am Info Network Affils Assn (Treas) 1968-; Var Former Activs; cp/Bd Dirs: Fredonia Col Foun, J'town Commun Col, Wn NY Anti-Defamation Leag, J'town Area Devel Corp, Operation Jobs, Erie Co Savs Bk; Pres J'town

Chapt Syracuse Univ Alumni & Action Planning Com, City of J'town; Chautauqua Co C of C; Chautauqua Agri Assn; Nat Coun USO; Am Legion; Mt Moriah Lodge; J'town Shrine Clb; Moon Brook CC; YMCA; Chautauqua Lake Yacht Clb; J'town Boys Clb; Chautauqua Coun BSA; Adv Coun St Div Human Rts; Sigma Delta Chi; UF; U Negro Col Fund; Others; r/Jewish; hon/Nat Conf Christians & Jews Brotherhood Awd; Biogl Listings.

GOLSTEIN, JANE oc/Assistant Dean; b/Oct 19, 1944; h/205 La Fontenay Ct, Louisville, KY 40223; ba/L'ville; m/Archie W Faircloth; p/Irvin and Beatrice Moseson Goldstein, L'ville; ed/BSC; MAT; CPS; pa/Univ L'ville: Asst Dean Sch Bus 1978-, Lectr Ofc Mgmt 1970-, Mgmt Univ Col 1973-, Asst to Dean Sch of Bus 1976-78, Adm Asst Sch Bus 1972-76, Others; Conslt; Nat Bus Ed Assn; Am Bus Commun Assn; Num Spchs & Sems; hon/Article Pub'd in *The Secretary*, Oct 1976; World W/W Wom.

GOLDSTEIN, MAXINE SHAPIRO oc/Homemaker; Civic Leader; b/Aug 25, 1926; h/PO Box G, Milledgeville, GA 31061; m/Jacob Louis; c/Marcia G Stein (Mrs Charles), Harriet G Greenhut (Mrs Gordon); p/Harry Shapiro (dec); Sadie Shapiro Millner, Jacksonville, FL; ed/Grad J Col Augusta; Univ Ga; Hedgerow Theatre Sch of Dramatic Art; pa/Former Woms Dir Augusta Radio Sta, Hosted Daily Radio Show; cp/CoFdr & Pres: M'ville Jr Wom's Clb, M'ville Civic Woms Clb, Designers Critique (Macon), M'ville Little Theatre, M'ville Hadassah; Mem Mayors Comm Downtown Revitilization; Rec Dept Allied Arts Coun; Former Bd Mem: Red Cross, Cancer Soc, Mtl Hlth Assn, Heart Fund; OES; Temple Beth Isreal Sisterhood; Town & Country Garden Clb; Mid Ga Judges Coun; B'nai Brith; Old Capitol Hist Soc; Am Guild Flower Arrangers; Am Land Trust; Ga Fdn Dem Wom; Nature Conservancy; Mem St Comm Bur Indian Affairs; St Dem Com; St Affirmative Action Com; Mem Charter Comm Dem Party; 8th Congl Dist Dir Ga Fdn Dem Wom; Former Mem Govs Comm on Status of Wom; Fdr Baldwin Co Dem Wom; Treas; Ga Fdn Dem Wom, Jewish Patients Benefit Fund, Ctl St Hosp; Other Civic Activs; r/Jewish; hon/W/W Am Polits; Personalities of S; DIB; Intl W/W Commun Ser.

GOLDWIN, ROBERT A oc/Resident Scholar; Administrator; b/Apr 16, 1922; h/1565 44th St NW, Washington DC 20007; ba/Wash DC; m/Daisy Lateiner; c/Nancy Harvey, Jane Bandler, Elizabeth, Seth; p/Alexander and Sed Goldwin (dec); ed/BA St John's Col 1950; MA 1954, PhD 1963 Univ Chgo; mil/US Cavalry 1942-46, Pvt to 1/Lt; pa/Am Enterprise Inst: Resident Scholar, Dir Sem Progs 1976; Spec Conslt to Pres of US 1974-76; Advr to Secy of Def 1976; Spec Advr to Ambassador US Mission to N Atl Treaty Org, Brussels, Belgium 1973-74; Dean & Charles Hammond Elliott Tutor St John's Col, Annapolis, Md 1969-73; Other Former Positions; Mem Bd Fgn S'ships 1977-; Bd Overseers' Com to Vis Dept of Govt, Harvard Univ 1975-; Bd Trustees Woodrow Wilson Intl Ctr for Scholars, Smithsonian Inst 1975-76; r/Jewish; hon/Medal for Dist'd Public Ser, Dept Def 1977; Profl Achmt Awd, Univ Chgo Alumni Assn 1977; Awd of Merit, St John's Col Alumni Assn 1977; Fellow: Guggenheim Foun, Fund for Adult Ed; Others.

GOLIKE, GLEN DALE oc/Minister; b/Oct 30, 1926; h/767 Loma Way, Santa Maria, CA 93454; ba/Santa Maria; m/Judith Ann; c/Gary, Scott, Dale; p/Robert R and Dela R Golike (dec); ed/Bible Inst Dipl; BA

Westmont Col; pa/Pastor Pine Grove Bapt Ch; Chm Coun of Nine Cal Assn Regular Bapt Chs; Coun Bapt Mid-Missions; Bd Trustees Los Angeles Bapt Col, Newhall, Cal; Wn Bapt Col, Salem, Oreg; Pastor 4 Bapt Chs 1954-.

GOLLUB, MONICA oc/Administrator; b/Jul 5, 1943; h/125 E 72 St, New York, NY 10021; ba/NY; p/Gerald Edwin; c/Michael Scott; p/Hans M F Schulman, Alicante, Spain; Gerda Lang Schulman, Riverdale, NY; ed/BA cum laude; pa/Dir Opers Statewide Wkrs' Compensation Bd; cp/Former Mem Gov'g Coun Am Jewish Cong; Former Chperson Wom's Com Metro Coun (AJC); Campaign Coor & Fund Raiser Var Polit Campaigns; Citizens Com; r/Jewish; hon/Phi Beta Kappa; Cert of Merit; Pi Delta Phi; World W/W Wom.

GOLSH, GENEVIEVE oc/Artist, Lecturer, Writer; b/Apr 5, 1900; h/PO Box 288, Valley Center, CA 92082; m/Marcus; p/Edward and Emma Vaughn; ed/St Joseph's Acad; Univ of Cal-Berkeley; ca/Ceramics Artist; Lectr on Indian Lore & Culture; Author Chd's Indian Stories, Versesfor Christmas & Gift Cards; Works in Leather Tooling, Creates Copper & Aluminum Art Works; Writes Column of Indian Lore "Smoke Signals" for *The Valley Roadrunner*; cp/Friends of Pala Mission; IPA; Nat Leag of Am Pen Wom; Ft Stutter Chapt, OES; Escondido Wom's Clb; Dos Valles Garden Clb; Pauma Valley Wom's Clb; Gen Fedn of Wom's Clbs, Wash DC; Casa de Cuna Chd's Home Soc; r/Cath; hon/Works Exhibited at: Cal St Fair 1954, SWn Museum, Los Angeles, Museum of Man, San Diego, Lazy-H-Sky Ranch Gallery 1956, 58, 60, 62, Desert Art Gallery, Palm Desert, Saddleback Art Gallery, Santa Ana 1964, Others; 4 Awds of Merit, Palomar Dist Wom's Clbs; Wom of Yr, Nat Leag Am Pen Wom; Freddie Awd, *Popular Ceramics* Mag; 2000 Wom of Achmt; World W/W of Wom; W/W in Cal; Intl Register of Profiles.

GOMES, ALBERT oc/Guidance Counselor; Private Therapist; b/Dec 26, 1944; h/Ridge Rd, Newtown, CT 06470; ba/Trumbull, CT; m/Kathleen; c/Natalie Kate; p/Albert and Benlinda Gomes, Danbury, CT; ed/BS Wn Conn St Col 1962; MS Univ Bridgeport 1972; CAS 1974; Gustalt Dipl So Conn St Col 1977; NEA; CEA; TEA; APGA; ASCA; Guest Lectr Univ B'port; Cnslr Beacon House; cp/JCs Am; Big Brothers; r/Rom Cath; hon/Tchg F'ship; W/W in E.

GOMEZ, BERRIOS, NELIDA oc/Business Executive; b/Nov 6, 1935; h/32 #312 Villa Nevarez, Rio Piedras, PR 00927; ba/San Juan, PR; c/Edmund Santiago G, Conrado Santiago G, Norman L Santiago G, Yamira Del Carmen Santiago G; p/Salomon Gomez (dec); Josefa Berrios (dec); ed/BBA; MAS; pa/Exec in Acctg & Fin; Ateneo de PR; Assn Cooperative Edrs; Nat Assn Public Accts; hon/Hon Matricula, Univ PR; Biogl Listings.

GONANO, JOHN ROLAND oc/Physicist; b/Jan 21, 1939; ba/Ft Belvoir, VA; m/Joyce Dove; c/Gina M, Dawn M, John R Jr; p/Lezelle and Mary Fuss Gonano (dec); ed/BS w hons WVa Univ; PhD Duke Univ;

pa/Physicist AUS Mobility Equiptmt R&D Command; Am Phy Soc; r/Boyds (Md) Presb Ch: Elder, Trustee; hon/Sigma Pi Sigma; Sigma Xi; MENSA.

GONZALES, CHARLES JOHN oc/Architect, Planner; b/Oct 20, 1941; h/60 Washington St, Santurce, PR 00907; ba/San Juan, PR; m/Leticia Rodriguez DeSevilla; c/Carlos Jose Juan, Mari-Angel Catalina, Carlos Manuel Lucien Ricardo; p/Carlos Gonzales (dec); Ricarda Martinez, New York, NY; ed/BS CCNY 1965; Masters (Urban & Reg Planning) magna cum laude Univ PR 1976; mil/AUS 1965-68, Hawk Guided Missiles; pa/Conslt'g Architect: Ofc Eduardo Figueroa Archs, Ponce, PR 1977-, La Casa Del Libro Mus, San Juan 1972-; Designer Bell Book & Candle Bookstores, San Juan 1977-; Ofc Pablo Quinones (Archs), San Juan 1976-: Sr Arch & Planner, Pers Dir; Other Former Positions; PR Del to XIth Cong Interam Planning Soc, Guayaquil, Ecuador 1976; Spec Asst to PR Secy of Commerce, San Juan 1977; PR Planning Soc: Pres 1978-, VP 1977-78; Interam Planning Soc; Am Planning Assn; Profl Mem Nat Rec & Park Assn; Nat Soc Pk Resources; Assoc Mem Mus Natural Hist; Metro Assn Urban Designers & Envir Planners; cp/Nat Hist Soc; Alumni Assn City Col; Bd Dirs Condominium Washington Co; Ecuardor Sporting Clb (NYC); Nat Col Soccer Referees PR; r/Rom Cath; hon/Merit Awd, PR Govt's Dept Instrn.

GONZALEZ-ALCOVER, JOSE CARMELO oc/Executive; Professional Engineer; b/Jun 1, 1937; h/Sauco 1959 San Ramon, Rio Piedras, PR; ba/Dorado, PR; m/Maggie M; c/Marga Mari, Lissette, Marisol; p/Antonio Gonzalez; Ruperta Alcover Pol; ed/BSME; mil/AUS 1962-64, 1/Lt; pa/Pres & Gen Mgr Mfg Indust; Bd Dirs: E L Mfg Corp, E L Caribbean Inc, Elso Inc; Am Mgmt Assn; Col Engrg PR; C of C PR; Soc Mfg Engrs; cp/Former Mem Bd Dirs "Movimiento por un Mundo Mejor"; r/Cath.

GONZALEZ, AURORA oc/School Counselor; b/Apr 6, 1932; h/1415 Matagorda, Dallas, TX 75232; p/Raul M and Aurora S Gonzalez, Edcouch, TX; ed/BS, MEd; pa/Classroom Tchrs Dallas Fac Rep; Bd Dirs Dallas Assn Cnslrs; BPW; cp/Dallas Edrs Polit Action Com Bd; U Way; Altrusa Intl; r/Rom Cath; hon/Personalities of S; W/W S&SW.

GONZALEZ, RAFAEL A oc/College Professor; Author; b/Nov 17, 1922; h/Calle Josefa Mendia 500, Urb Los Maestros, Rio Piedras, PR 00923; ba/Rio Piedras; m/Josefina; c/Marta J and Milagros; p/Enrique Gonzalez Ramos; Emilia Torres Valentin; ed/BA; MA magna cum laude; PhD magna cum laude; pa/Prof Univ PR; Editor Revista Cayey; Secretario Sociedad de Autores; cp/Tchr & Lectr Yoga; r/Cath; hon/Premio Bolivar Pagan for Novel *El retrato del otro*, 1976.

GOOD, MARY LOWE oc/Educator; b/Jun 20, 1931; h/Rt 1, PO Box 139, Sorrento, LA 70778; ba/Baton Rouge, LA; m/Bill J; c/Billy John, James Patrick; p/John W Lowe; ed/BS St Col Ark; MS, PhD Univ Ark; pa/Boyd Prof Div Engrg LSU 1978-; Univ New Orleans: Boyd Prof Dept Chem 1974-78, Prof Chem 1963-74; Other Former Positions; Am Chem Soc: Past Chm & Councilor La Sect, Past Secy Nat Meetings & Div Activs Com,

Mem Edit Bd *Chem & Engrg News*, Others; Fellow: Am Inst Chem, Chem Soc London; Alpha Chi Sigma, Nat Initiate at Large; Invited Spkr Var Intl Meetings; Mem Review Panels & Adv Coms; Other Profl Activs; cp/Zonta Intl: Past Pres Clb New Orleans, Mem Amelia Earhart F'ship Com; Former Mem: Bd Dirs Oak Ridge Assoc'd Univs, Jt Sch Bd St Paul 1st Eng Luth Sch; r/1st Eng Luth; hon/Mem Hon Socs; Recipient Grants & F'ships; Herty Awd, Ga Sect ACS; Tchr of Yr Awd, Delta Kappa Gamma 1974; Encyclopedia of Am Wom; AIC Hon Scroll La Chapt 1974; Dist'd Alumni Cit, Univ Ark; Garvan Medal, Am Chem Soc; Biogl Listings; Profl Pubs; Others.

GOODEN, WILLIAM J oc/Bowling Proprietor; b/Feb 28, 1934; h/1306 S 8th St, Kingfisher, OK 73750; ba/Kingfisher; b/LaDonna Jane Kramer; p/Mark William, Lori Karen, John Kramer, David Josiah; p/Francis W and Lillian Ruth Gooden, Kingfisher; ed/BS Okla St Univ 1957; mil/USAF 3 Yrs; Maj USAFR; pa/Pres Okla St Bowling Proprietors Assn, Nat Dir 6 Yrs; cp/Chm Kingfisher Co Repub Party; St VChm Okla Repub Party; Past Pres: K'fisher Lions Clb, K'fisher C of C, K'fisher JCs, Red Carpet Country, K'fisher Co Great Artists Series,

SAR; BSA: Advr Explorer Troop, Chm Roman Nose Dist, Mem Gt Salt Plains Exec Bd; Bd Govs Okla Coalition for Clean Air; Chm City Bd Adjustmt; Water Safety Instr Red Cross; Masonic Lodge; OES; Elks Lodge; All-Sports Assn; Okla Heritage Assn; Sportsman's Clb; r/Christian Ch: Deacon, Elder, Chm Ch Bd, St Bd; Past Intl & St Pres Christian Men's F'ship; hon/Outstg Yg Oklahoman, St JCs; Nat Pres Awd, Lions; Dist Awd of Merit, BSA; Dist'd Ser Awd, K'fisher JCs; Layman of Yr, Okla Christian Ch Men; Outstg Lion, Dist 3-A & K'fisher Clb; Others.

GOODWIN, CARLTON BYRON oc/Minister; b/Jan 14, 1919; h/505 Wimer Cir, Pittsburgh, PA 15237; ba/Pgh; m/Pauline F; c/Everett C, Carline A, Catheen D; p/Charles M and Grace L Goodwin (dec); ed/BA; BDiv; DDiv; pa/Pres Am Bapt Exec

Mins; Exec Com Am Bapt Nat Staff Coun; cp/Chm Sr Aides Adv Coun Allegheny Co, Pa; World Affairs Coun; UN Assoc; r/Am Bapt Chs USA; hon/Hon DD, Alderson Broaddus Col.

GOODWIN, DAVE oc/Insurance; Journalist; Consultant; b/May 14, 1926; h/721 86th St, Miami Beach, FL 33141; ba/Surfside, FL; m/Selma R; c/Ari E; p/Paul Goodwin (dec), Anna Goodwin, Miami Bch; ed/BBA

Univ Miami 1949; mil/USNR 1944-46; pa/Sr Mem Intl Assn Fin Planners; Former Mem Bd Regents Col Fin Planning; Am Risk & Ins Assn; Spkr Num Ins & Consumer Convs; Num Articles; cp/Bd Ed Hebrew Acad; Chm Ins Com Miami Bch Taxpayers Assn; CoChm Univ Miami Consumer Affairs Inst; r/Jewish.

GORAKHPURWALLA, HOMI DHUNJISHAW oc/Educator; b/Aug 5, 1937; h/-2112 Colorado Ave, Kingsville, TX 78363; ba/K'ville; m/Anita M Fuegener; c/Catherine Anita, Ashley Homi; p/Dhunjishaw H and Katy D Gorakhpurwalla (dec); ed/BS; BSEE; MSEE Purdue Univ; pa/Tex A&I Univ: Chm & Assoc Prof Elect Engrg 1977-, Assoc Prof Elect Engrg 1970-77; Devel Engr DorRan Elects Inc 1969-70; Asst Prof Dept Elect Engrg SD St Univ, Brookings, SD 1966-69; Other Former Positions; Reschr; hon/Eta Kappa Nu; Tau Beta Pi; Num Profl Pubs.

GORDLEY, MARILYN CLASSE oc/Artist; Teacher; b/Aug 4, 1929; h/105 Dalebrook, Greenville, NC 27834; ba/G'ville; m/M Tran; c/Scott Tran, Lillian Claire; p/Henry B Classe (dec); Ailma Classe, St Louis, MO; ed/BFA; MFA; pa/Tchr Sch Art E Carolina Univ; Exhibiting Artist; Wom's Caucus on Art; Col Art Assn; r/Epis; hon/1st Prize, Springs Art Contest, Lancaster, SC; Smithsonian Travel Awd; Irene Leache Meml Awd.

GORDLEY, METZ TRANBARGER oc/Artist; Teacher; b/May 24; h/105 Dalebrook, Greenville, NC 27834; ba/G'ville; m/Marilyn Classe; c/Scott Tran, Lillian Claire; p/C Metz Gordley, Jacksonville, IL; ed/BFA; MFA; mil/AUS 1953-55; pa/Tchr Sch of Art E Carolina Univ; Exhibiting Artist; hon/NC Print & Drawing Soc Awd; Watercolor USA Traveling Awd.

GORDON, ETHEL M oc/Administrator; Teacher; b/Nov 16, 1911; h/2221 Marguerette St, Columbia, SC 29204; ba/Columbia; m/Maxie S Sr; c/Maxie S Jr, Thomas A; p/Robert O and Olivia B McAdams (dec); ed/BA Benedict Col 1939; MEd Temple Univ 1955; Addit Studies: Harvard Univ, Mich St Univ; pa/Benedict Col: Tchr, Study Area Dir Elem Ed; IRA; Assn Tchr Edrs; Instl Rep AACTE; Phi Delta Kappa; cp/LWV: Christian Action Coun; Nat Assn Univ Wom; Life Mem NAACP; r/Nat Bapt USA Inc: Histn Wom's Conv Aux; VP Wom's Ednl & Missionary Conv SC; Corr'g Secy Gethsemane Wom's Conv; hon/Cit for Outstg Christian Ser, SC Mins' Wives Assn & Benedict Col Wom's Nat Conv; DHL, Morris Col; Pub'd Author.

GORDON, GARY HOWARD oc/University Professor; b/Aug 31, 1941; h/3300 Hillcrest Dr #118, San Antonio, TX 78201; ba/San Antonio; p/Howard and Lorna

Gordon, Waukon, IA; ed/BA 1963; MA 1965; PhD 1972; pa/Prof St Mary's Univ; Phi Alpha Theta, Intl Relats Advr; r/Congreg Ch; hon/Local Awds.

GORDON, GEORGE N oc/Administrator; b/Nov 11, 1926; h/Helfrich Springs Apts, 900 Mickley Rd, Whitehall, PA 18052; ba/Allentown, PA; m/Nancy L Davis; c/Diane, Harry, Jennifer; p/Harry Allan Gordon (dec); Rebecca Cohen (dec); ed/BS 1952, MA 1953, PhD 1957 NY Univ; mil/AUS

1944-45; pa/Dir Inst Communs, Muhlenberg, Cedar Crest Cols; Prof Commun Arts; Author; Lectr; Conslt; hon/Ednl Specialist, US Info Agy in Warsaw 1972; Winner Ednl Press Assn Awd, Best Feature Article.

GORDON, GILBERT oc/Professor, Department Chairman; b/Nov 11, 1933; h/190 Shadowy Hills Dr, Oxford, OH 45056; ba/Oxford; m/Joyce Elaine; c/Thomas M, Susan L; p/Walter and Catherine Gordon, Clearwater, FL; ed/BS Bradley Univ; PhD Mich St Univ 1957; pa/Prof & Chm Dept Chem Miami Univ 1973-; Prof: Univ Ia 1967-73, Univ Md 1960-67; Am Chem Soc; Chem Soc London; Conslt: Nat Bur Standards, Edgewood Arsenal, Olin Corp, Intl Dioxcide; Ia Acad Sci; Ohio Acad Sci; Phi Kappa Phi; Omicron Delta Kappa; Sigma Xi; Others; r/Luth; hon/Vis Prof to Japan, Japanese Soc for Promotion of Sci; Var Edit Positions; Pub'd Author; Biogl Listings.

GORDON, GUANETTA STEWART oc/Writer; b/Oct 4; h/11847 Hacienda Dr, Sun City, AZ 85351; m/Lynell F; c/Stewart, Krista Sharon Morris (Mrs Reginald); p/Samuel Lewis Stewart (dec); Minnie Anna Brown (dec); ed/Baker Univ, Univ Ks; pa/Author 6 Volumes of Poetry: *Songs of the Wind, Under the Rainbow Arch, Shadow Within the Flame, The Aurora Tree, Petals From the Moon, Above Rubies*; ; Dramatist; Lectr; Poet; Nat Leag Am Pen Wom: Past Pres Alexandria Br, Nat Insignia Chm 1978-80, Nat 1/VP 1970-72, Nat Res Chm 1966-68, Other Positions; Poetry Soc Am; Poetry Soc Va; World Poetry Soc; MW Fdn Chaparral Poets; Am Poetry Leag; The Ks Authors; Ariz St Poetry Soc; r/Luth; hon/Ks Poet of Yr 1966; Num Poetry & Prose Awds; Biogl Listings.

GORDON, HARRY WILLIAM oc/-Pharmacologist; Biochemist; Executive; b/Mar 31, 1924; h/210 E 181 St, New York, NY 10457; ba/Farmingdale, NY; m/Rosalind; c/Bebe Gail; p/Abraham and Elsie Gordon, New York; m/BS; MS; PhD; mil/AUS WWII; pa/VP, Sci Dir DEL Labs Inc; Sigma Xi; ACS; AAAS; NY Acad Scis; hon/Fellow AAAS; PA Sci Comm.

GORDON, ROBERT THOMAS oc/Surgeon; b/Feb 13, 1950; h/4936 W Estes, Skokie, IL 60077; p/David and Eunice Gordon, Skokie; ed/BS w highest distn 1971, MD w highest distn 1972 NWn Univ; pa/Chief Resident Cardio-Thoracic Surg NWn Univ Med Sch, NWn Univ Hosps 1977-; NWn Univ Med Sch: Instr Gen Surg 1976-77, Instr Cardio-Thoracic Surg 1977-; Conslt & Reschr in field; Bd Cert'd, Am Bd Thoracic Surg 1980; Chief Dept Cardiac Surg, Lutheran Gen Hosp

(Park Ridge, Ill); Staff (Cardio-Vascular-Thoracic Surg); Edgewater Hosp (Chgo), Mount Sinai Hosp (Chgo), Holy Fam Hosp (Des Plaines, Ill), Highland Park Hosp, N Suburban Med Ctr (Schaumburg, Ill), Others; Surg's Opinion Panel, *Contemp Surg* 1980; Staff Assoc Nat Inst Hlth HEW 1974; Other Former Positions; Fellow: Med Scist Life Ins, NWn Univ Med Res; AMA; Chgo Med Assn; Ill St Med Soc; Flying Physicians Assn; IPA; Luth Gen Hosp Men's Assn; Luth Gen Hosp Adv Bd; Alpha Omega Alpha; Phi Eta Sigma; Diplomate Nat Bd Med Examrs; Bd Cert'd Am Bd Surgs; Contbr Articles Profl Jours; Other Profl Activs; cp/NWn Univ & NWn Univ Med Sch Alumni Assns; US, Chgo Dist Tennis Assns; hon/Contbr Num Articles to Profl Jours; Physician's Recog Awd, AMA; Phi Beta Pi Scholar; Frederick K Rawson Jr Scholar; Hoffman LaRoche Awd; Macy Foun Res Fellow; Biogl Listings; Patentee.

GORDON, WILLIE JORDAN oc/Homemaker; b/Jun 15, 1891; h/193 Hale St NE, Atlanta, GA 30307; m/McCallister (dec); c/Mary G Thompson, McCallister Jr, Asa, Sarah G Butler, Fincher, Billie; p/James D and Mary Overton Jordan (dec); cp/Pres Inman Park Wom's Clb 13 Yrs; Treas Bass Commun Coun; Grandmother's Clb; Vol: Red Cross, TB Assn, Mar Dimes, Cancer Soc, Commun Sers, YWCA, Ga Assn for Retard Chd, Salvation Army Aux; Life Mem PTA; Adv Coun Nat Yth Courtesy Foun Inc; r/Inman Park Bapt Ch; hon/Lib Dedicated to Her; Personalities of S; World W/W Wom.

GORE, HENRY ANTHONY oc/Professor; b/Feb 11, 1948; h/3194 Topaz Ln SW, Atlanta, GA 30331; ba/Atlanta; p/Billy L and Bernice Burney, Atlanta; ed/BA Morehouse Col; MA, PhD Univ Mich; pa/Prof Math Morehouse Col; Am Math Soc; Math Assn Am; Assn for Symbolic Logic; r/Bapt; hon/Phi Beta Kappa; Outstg Edr Am; Outstg Yg Man Am; Prof of Yr 1977, 78.

GORE, LOUISE CANTRELL oc/Homemaker; Author; Retired; b/May 21, 1917; h/6530 N 3rd Ave, Apt 3, Phoenix, AZ 85013; m/John L; c/Donald, Barbara Young, Ethelyn Holland, Stephen, Gregory; p/Charlie and Ethel Hood Cantrell (dec); pa/Author *Soul of the Bearded Seal*, 1967; Judge Poetry Contests; Contbr to Var Poetry Mags; r/Prot; hon/-Hon'd in Alaska Centennial Salute of Alaska & N Country Authors; Spec Awd (Nonfiction Div), Alaska Press Clb; 1st Prize Poetry Book Div, Ariz Press Wom; Spec Medallion Awd, Exposition Staff 1967 Alaska Centennial Exhibit, US Dept of Commerce; 1st Prize Poetry Div, Leag Alaskan Writers; Others.

GORIN, ROBERT MURRAY JR oc/-Educator; b/Oct 29, 1948; h/51 Somerset Ave, Garden City, NY 11530; p/Robert Murray and Vivian Margaret Schleider Gorin, Garden City; ed/AB, MA Xavier Univ; MS Ed Hofstra Univ 1974; MA Fordham Univ 1978; ABD St Louis Univ 1978; mil/AUS 1968-69; pa/Social Studies Tchr: Bellmore-Merrick 1974-77, 1978-, Ctl HS Dist 1977-78, Rockville Centre Sch Dist; AHA; SHA; OAH; APS; AASLH;

Ctr for Study of Presidency; Am Heritage Soc; LI, NY & Nat Coun for Social Studies; Soc for Hist Ed; Inst Soc, Ethics of Life Scis; cp/Metro Opera Guild; Civil War Round Table NY; Nat Trust for Hist Preserv; Xavier, Hofstra & Fordham Alumni Assns; Repub; r/Rom Cath; hon/Phi Alpha Theta; Taft Scholar, Robert A

Taft Inst of Gov; W/W in E.

GORMAN, JOYCE MARIE oc/Social Worker; b/Feb 22, 1932; h/730 8th St, New Orleans, LA 70115; ba/NO; p/Lebbeaus and Ophelia Miller (dec); ed/BA; CSW-SW; MSW; pa/NASW; AAUW; cp/Urban Leag; LLOGG; r/Cath; hon/Offeramus Medal, Mt St Scholastica Col.

GORMAN, M ADELE FRANCIS oc/College Administrator; Sister of Religious Order; b/Jan 28; h/Our Lady of Angels Convent, Aston, PA 19014; ba/Aston; p/John Divin and Marguerite Meyer Gorman (dec); ed/AB cum laude Col Notre Dame Md; MA Villanova Univ; PhD Univ Notre Dame; Cert (Archival Mgmt) Univ Denver; pa/Admr Our Lady of Angels Col; CoChm Com on Hist in Classroom, Am Hist Assn; Nom'd for Pres AHA; Tchg Com, AHA & Am Cath Hist Assn; Ofcr Other Local, St & Nat Orgs; cp/Ch Hist Sub-com, Bicent Com, Nat Conf Cath Bishops; Former Co Chm Reg Comprehensive Hlth Planning Coun; Sub Area Coun Hlth Systems Agy; Others; r/Rom Cath; hon/George Washington Hon Medal (2); Univ S'ship; 2nd Prize Essay Awd, Thomas Edison Contest; Profl Pubs; Biogl Listings.

GORMLEY, MICHAEL BRODT oc/Surgeon; b/Dec 3, 1943; h/3615 Saul Rd, Kensington, MD 20195; ba/Washington, DC; p/Raymond Joseph and Helena Brodt Gormley; ed/AA; BS; DDS; pa/Oral & Maxillo Facial Surg; Lectr; Former Dir Oral Surg Kings Co Hosp, Brooklyn, NY; cp/Notary Public, St of Md; Comm on Aging; r/Cath; hon/Num Pubs & F'ships; Diplomate, Am Bd Oral & Maxillo Facial Surg; Biogl Listings.

GOSLEE, REBA ELENA oc/Nurse; b/Nov 23, 1926; h/736 S Park Dr, Salisbury, MD 21801; ba/Salisbury; m/Howard I; c/Jane McMillan, Salisbury; ed/RN Md Gen Hosp 1947; BSN 1969, MSN 1975 Univ Md; pa/Deer's Hd Hosp: Dir Nsg Ser 1969-, Supvr 1956-69, Staff Nurse 1950-56; Other Former Positions; Am Nurses Assn; Md Soc Hosp Nsg Admrs; cp/Univ Md Alumni Assn; Sigma Theta Tau; r/Bapt; hon/Phi Kappa Phi.

GOSPODARIC, MIMI (MARY J) oc/Educator; b/Aug 13, 1899; h/901 Sherwood Pl, Joliet, IL 60435; p/Frank and Mary Teran Gospodaric, Austria; ed/Att'd: Univ Chgo 1917-18, Art Inst Chgo, Chgo Musical Col 1919-23; BA Univ Cal 1926; Addit Studies; Former Asst to Hd Designer, Sebastian Bichele of J Milhening, Chgo (Mfr of Diamond & Platinum Jewelry); Former Hd Designer H C Akers; Formerly Assoc'd w B Altman Co, NYC; Former Hd Dept Arts & Crafts or Dramatic Art &/or PE Chgo Pks, Metro Chgo YWCA, GSA, Col Mt Scholastica, Others; Former Wel Ofcr Jugoslav Refugee Hosp, Sinai Desert Egypt; Former Vol 123rd Gen Hosp USA (Naples, Italy), 13th Scotische Gen Hosp (Cairo, Egypt) & New Zealand Mil Camp (Maadi, Egypt); Wel Ofcr Jugoslav Refugee Gen Hosp 1944-45, Created & Est'd Occupl Therapeutic Activity Dept & Interdep Diversionary Activs Ctr; Mem Adult Ed Tchrs Staff Joliet Twp HS 1951-76; Free-lance Designer 1923; Intl Assn for Tchrs Eng for Spkrs of Other Langs, Charter Mem; hon/Book of Honor; Personalities W&MW; World W/W Wom; Men & Wom of Distn.

GOTHIA, BLANCHE oc/Librarian; b/Oct 27, 1930; h/9000 Bellaire Blvd, Houston, TX 77036; ba/Same; p/Elton Joseph Gothia, Port Arthur, TX; Blanche Landry Gothia (dec); ed/BA Dominican Col 1960; MLS Tex Wom's Univ 1973; pa/Sister of Rel Order; St Agnes Acad: Media Coor 1969-, A-V Dir 1967-69; Prin, St Anthony's Cathedral Sch (Beaumont, Tex) 1965-67, Tchr 1964-67; Tchr in Elem & Sec'dy Schs of Tex 1950-69; CoChm Legis Com in Tex, Assn Ednl Communs & Technol; Pubs Com, *Tex Lib Jour*; Nat Conslt on Sch Lng Resource Ctrs;

Tex Com for White House Conf on Lib & Into Sers 1978-79; Adv Bd, HS Sect, Nat Cath Lib Assn 1979-; ALA; Am Film Inst; Houston Area Film Tchrs Assn; Others; cp/CoDir, HAFTA; Past Chm, Bishop Byrne Unit CLA; r/Cath; hon/W/W: Am Wom, S&SW, Am, US, Tex; World W/W Wom; Lib of Human Resources of Am Heritage Res Assn; Other Biogl Listings.

GOULD, JAMES JOHN oc/Technical Consultant; b/Nov 8, 1933; h/1332 Broad St, Grinnell, IA 50112; ba/Des Moines, IA; m/Jean Letch; c/John P; p/R T and Florence H Gould, Harlan, IA; ed/BA Simpson Col 1957;

MA Univ No Ia 1971; mil/AUS 1957-59; pa/Tech Conslt Dept Public Instrn; NEA; ISEA; APGA; NVGA; ATSU; AEDS; ASCU; cp/Masonic Lodge; Dem; r/Meth Ch, Grinnell: Adm Bd 1976-78; hon/Key Man Awd, JCs.

GOULDTHORPE, KENNETH ALFRED oc/Editor; Writer; Editorial and Publishing Consultant; b/Jan 7, 1928; h/30 Fifth Ave, New York, NY 10011; ba/NY; m/Judith Cutts; p/Alfred Edward and Frances Elizabeth Gouldthorpe, Welling, Kent, England; ed/City & Guilds of London Cert, Univ London; mil/Royal Navy, Minesweepers, Mediterranean Theater; pa/Editor & Assoc Pubr *Ambiance* Mag 1977; Mng Editor *Penthouse* Mag 1973-76; Mng Editor *Signature* 1970-73; Other Former Positions; Guest Instr The New Sch (Parsons Sch of Design, NY), Tchg Course in Edit & Graphic Design Approaches; r/Epis; hon/Pulitzer Prize Nom 1956; Sev Hons & Awds from Profl Socs & Instns.

GOULIAN, DICRAN oc/Professor; Surgeon; b/Mar 31, 1927; h/50 Crows Nest Rd, Bronxville, NY 10708; ba/NYC; m/Jean Marie; c/Linda Susan, Dicran III, Beverly Ann, Elizabeth Jean; p/Dicran Goulian Sr (dec); Shamiram Goulian, B'ville; ed/AB; DDS; MD; mil/USN 1944-45, Seaman 1st Class; pa/Prof Surg Cornell Univ Med Col; Att'g Surg-in-Charge Plastic Surg NY Hosp-Cornell Univ Med Ctr; Dir Tng Prog in Plastic Surg, NY Hosp; r/Prot; hon/William Jarvie Soc, Columbia Univ.

GOWDY, ANNI C oc/Realtor; Writer; b/May 8, 1931; h/2900 El Camino Ave, Las Vegas, NV 89102; ba/LV; c/Addison Walton, John Frances Burraughs, Thomas Kerr, Frederick Gerard Burroughs; p/Angelo Pomone (dec); Ella Mae Kerr (dec); pa/Owner & Broker Gowdy & Assocs Realtors; Camarillo Bd Realtors; Past Chm Public Relats & Publicity Chm Pvt Property Week; LV Bd Realtors; cp/C of C; r/Cath; hon/Num Civic & Profl Awds; Others.

GOWINGS, DAN DOUGLAS oc/College Professor; b/Jun 6, 1923; h/2810 W Twickingham Dr, Muncie, IN 47304; ba/Muncie; m/Chrystal Marie Bragg; c/Dana Irene, Mark Gerard, Bruce Allen; p/Henry Lee Gowings (dec); Margaret Irene Gowings, Muncie; ed/BS; MPH; PhD; mil/USN 1941-46; Current Lt Col USAFR; pa/Prof Dept Physiol & Hlth Sci Ball St Univ; Reschr; cp/Commun Sers; 33° Scottish Rite; r/Meth; hon/Outstg Edr; Merit Awd for Public Adm.

GRABER, HARRIS DAVID oc/Regional Sales Manager; b/Mar 31, 1939; h/80-51 249th St, Bellerose, NY 11426; ba/West Caldwell,

NJ; m/Esther Feldman; c/Donald Irwin, Gregory Stuart, Monique Cheryl, Roy Scott; p/Charles Graber; Ella Shapiro Graber; ed/MBA St Johns Univ 1979; BS cum laude CUNY 1975; AS Queensborough CC 1973; pa/Reg Sales Mgr Aerospace Prods Conrac Corp, Systems-E Div; Assn MBAs; Tech Mktg Soc; hon/Var Hons & Awds for Contbn to Proj Apollo.

GRACY, ROBERT WAYNE oc/Professor & Chairman; b/Dec 30, 1941; h/1414 Windsor Dr, Denton, TX 76201; ba/Denton; m/Lynn; c/Delaney, Kimberly; p/William Carl and Rubylee Gracy, Upland, CA; ed/BS; PhD; pa/N Tex St Univ: Current Prof & Chm Biochem, Prof Chem & Basic Hlth Scis 1975-76, Assoc Prof Chem & Basic Hlth Scis 1973-75, Others; Vis Prof Dept Physiol Chem Univ Wurzburg (W Germany) 1975-76; Prof Biochem & Acting Chm Div Biochem Tex Col

Osteopathic Med 1976-; Other Former Positions; Am Soc Biol Chemists; AAAS; NY Acad & Tex Acads of Sci; AAUP; Sigma Xi; Alpha Chi Sigma; Tri Beta; Reschr; Mem Var Dept & Univ Coms; cp/Chm N Tex Diabetics Res Inst; hon/Nat Insts Hlth Res Career Devel Awd; Fellow Alexander von Humboldt Foun; NTSU Chem Awd for Outstg Res & Tchg; Postdoct Fellow, Damon Runyon Cancer Foun; NDEA Predoct Fellow; Pub'd Author; Res Grants.

GRADISAR, HELEN MARGARET oc/College Administrator; b/Jul 1, 1922; h/657 Chestnut St, Bridgeville, PA 15017; ba/Pittsburgh, PA; p/Frank L Gradisar (dec); Elizabeth H Gradisar, B'ville; ed/BS Duquesne Univ 1944; pa/Carlow Col: Dir Instnl Res 1978-, Registrar & Dir Instnl Res 1977-78, Asst Dean Col & Registrar 1974-77, Registrar 1968-74; Other Former Positions; Assn Instnl Res; NE Assn Instnl Res; Former Mem Am Assn Collegiate Registrars & Admissions Ofcrs; Am Alumni Coun; r/Rom Cath.

GRADY, JOHN DONOVAN oc/Manager; b/Dec 28, 1940; h/1141 Magnolia Ln, Libertyville, IL 60048; ba/Zion, IL; m/Eileen Marie; c/John Donovan, Robert James; p/John Donovan Grady; Estelle Sylvia Grady, Freehold Twp, NJ; ed/BS US Merchant Marine Acad; mil/USNR Lt (jg); pa/Mgr Westinghouse Nuclear Training Ctr; Exec Com, Reactor Opers Div Am Nuclear Soc; cp/Past Pres Plum Borough (Pa) Kiwanis Clb; Mgr L'ville Little Leag; r/St Joseph's Rom Cath Ch; hon/Personalities of W&MW; W/W in MW.

GRAF, LEONARD GRANT oc/Medical Scientist; b/Sept 25, 1918; h/40 Prospect St, Lancaster, NH 03584; ba/Lyme, NH; m/Irene Lolita Gersch; c/Cheryl Ann, Kevin Leonard; p/Leonard H and Edith R Graf, Villa Park, IL; ed/BA; MS; mil/Mil Instr, Med Dept Enlisted Tech Sch; Chief Lab Ser, Camp Campbell, Ky; Resv Col; Conslt to Army Surg Gen in Lab & Pathol Scis; pa/Fac Norwich Univ; Lab Mgr: NEn Vt Reg Hosp, St Johnsbury, Vt, N Country Hosp, Newport, Vt; Secy Chgo Sect, Biol Photographic Assn; Exec Bd Chgo Sect; Am Assn Clin Chems; Am Assn Blood Bks; AAAS; Am Chem Soc; Am Inst Chems; Intl Soc Clin Lab Techs; Clin Lab Mgmt Assn; cp/Conservative Caucus; Am Def Preparedness Assn; Past Pres Aurora Chapt, Resv Ofcrs Assn; r/7th Day Adventist Ch; Mem; hon/Fellow Am Inst Chems; Profl Chem Accredited Nat Registry Clin Chem;

Meritorious Ser Medal for Duty w Surg Gen; W/W E.

GRAFTON, CONNIE ERNESTINE oc/Special Librarian; b/1913; h/235 E 22nd St, New York, NY 10010; ba/NYC; p/Louis D and Connie Imogene Newton Grafton (dec); ed/BA; BALS; MALS; MA; pa/NAPCAE; r/Judaism; hon/St (Va, Ia) Adult Ed Awds; Reg (SE, MW) Adult Ed; Va Wom of Yr.

GRAGG, HENRY WILLIFORD oc/- Executive; b/Jun 11, 1914; h/109 Church-wardens Rd, Baltimore, MD 21212; ba/Balto; m/Grace Bailey; c/France Ann Uhlenhopp; p/Ovvie Harvey Gragg (dec); Ruth Graves Williford (dec); ed/LLB; mil/USMC WWII Capt; pa/Chm of Bd USF&G Cos; HO: Chm of Bd 1978, Chm of Bd & Pres 1972, Pres 1970, Sr Exec VP, Bd Dirs 1963, Exec VP 1959, VP-Dir (Res & Review) 1956; HO & AD: Asst VP-

Assoc Agy Dir 1955, Asst Agy Dir 1953; Other Former Positions; cp/Bd Govs Presb Eye, Ear & Throat Hosp; Bd Trustees: Gtr Balto Med Ctr, Goucher Col; Bd Dirs: 1st Nat Bk Md, Provident Savings Bk of Balto, Am Stores Co, Noxell Corp; Chm Gen Assembly Compensation Comm, St of Md; Mem Univ Tenn Devel Coun; r/Presb.

GRAHAM, BRUCE M JR oc/City Manager; b/Dec 11, 1936; h/211 Bouvart Cr, Winchester, KY 40391; ba/Winchester;

m/Jean; c/Missy, James, Bruce III; p/Bruce M Graham, Copperhill, TN; ed/BS, MA Ctl Mich Univ; pa/ICMA; Ky & Mich Chapts ICMA; r/Meth.

GRAHAM, LOLA BEALL oc/Free-lance Photographer, Poet; b/Dec 11, 1896; h/225-93 Mt Hermon Rd, Scotts Valley, CA 95066; ba/Same; m/John Jackson (dec); c/Billy Duane, John Thomas, Helen Marie, Donald Jackson, Beverly Ann; p/John Gainer and Della Reid Beall (dec); ed/Tchr's Credentials; pa/Primary Tchr; r/Commun Covenant; hon/Nat Awds in Poetry; Hon Mbrship, Eugene Fields Soc & Intl Mark Twain Soc.

GRAHAM, NANCY GUILFOIL oc/- Businesswoman; b/Mar 13, 1931; h/110 Poplar St, Berea, KY 40403; ba/Berea; m/J Donald; c/Suzanne Shannon; p/John Andrew Guilfoil (dec); Lula Baesler Guilfoil, Lexington, KY; ed/BS Univ Ky; pa/Home Demonstration Ext Agt 1953-55; Dir: Appalachian Bookstore & Resource Ctr, Coun of So Mts 1962-76; cp/Group Ldr Recovery Inc, Lexington, Ky; r/Prot: Ch Organist; hon/Intl Yth Exc Student to France 1953.

GRAHAM, VIRGINIA BRYANT

oc/College Professor; h/PO Box 232, Buies Creek, NC 27506; ba/Buies Creek; m/George Sylvester (dec); c/Virginia Lydia; p/Grover Richard and Minnie S Bryant (dec); ed/AB w hons; MA; PhD Univ Cinc 1942; pa/Prof Dept English Campbell Col; Nat Col Eng Assn; NC-Va Col Eng Assn; AAUW; cp/Harnett Co Arts Coun; hon/Phi Beta Kappa; Phi Kappa Phi; Delta Phi Alpha; Hon Mention, Col Arts Poetry Contest 1967.

GRANAHAN, JOHN JOSEPH oc/Invest-ment Executive; b/Jan 11, 1936; h/1385 Old Marlboro Rd, Concord, MA 01742; ba/-Boston, MA; m/Kathryn; c/John, Kevin, Robert, Brian; p/Joseph A and Mary C Granahan, Glenside, PA; ed/AB St Joseph's Col; pa/Sr VP-Investmts; Chartered Fin Analyst; Boston Fin Analysts; r/Cath.

GRANT, ALICE BOYLE oc/Patron of Fine Arts; Philanthropist; b/Aug 18, 1911; h/Cumberland Ridge, Bullard, TX 75757; m/Lloyd W; c/Stephen LLoyd, Andrew Merritt; p/James Lee Robinson (dec); Rebecca Hopkins Robinson Boyle (dec); ed/BA Univ Cincinnati 1932; Cert Jour 1947; pa/NEA; Ohio Ed Assn; NCTE; Nat Coun for Ec Ed; Assn for Supvn & Curric Devel; APGA; Nat Voc Guid Assn; Tex Pers & Guid Assn; Piney Woods Cnslrs; cp/Alumna Prep Dept Cinc Col-Conservatory of Univ Cinc; Patron: Dallas Grand Opera Assn, Tyler (Tex) Civic Theater, Tyler Commun Concert Assn; Friend: NY Public Lib, Metro Opera Guild (Nat Mem); Sustaining Mem Tyler Wom's Forum; Wom Com Dallas Theatre Ctr; Mem: Mus Fine Arts (Boston), Tyler Mus Art; DAR; Var Former Activs; r/Epis; hon/AAUW Drama Ldrship Awd; Chi Delta Phi; Kappa Delta Pi.

GRANT, ANN BAUM DUDLEY oc/Registered Nurse; b/Sept 6, 1941; h/Rt 2, Box 505, Kinston, NC 28501; ba/Kinston; m/Charles Roberts; c/Margaret Ann, Rhonda Rene; p/William Swindell Dudley Jr (dec); Rachel Baum Dudley McGrath, Engelhard, NC; ed/Nsg Dipl; pa/Caswell Ctr: Lead Nurse 1978-, Hd Nurse 1976-78; Sampson Co Meml Hosp, Clinton, NC: Hd Nurse 1970-76, Supvr 1965-70, Staff Nurse 1962-65; Cert'd Emer Med Techn 1974-78; Adv Com Assoc Deg Nsg Dept Sampson Tech Inst 1972-76; Procedure Book Com (1973) & Coauthor Pediatric Procedure Book for Sampson Co Meml Hosp; Att'd Num Wkshops; cp/Mem Parents for Advmt of Gifted Ed (PAGE); r/Trinity U Meth Ch: Mem, VChm UMW, Com for Ecumenical Affairs 1978, 79; hon/Recog for Outstg Achmt in EKG & Coronary Care Course 1976; Outstg Grad Awd, Lenoir Meml Hosp Sch of Nsg 1962; Forty & Eight Clb S'ship 1959; HS Hons; Biogl Listings.

GRANT, LOWELL DEAN oc/Minister; b/Oct 12, 1935; h/112 N Almer, Caro, MI 48723; ba/Caro; m/Shirley Ann Hughes; c/Luann, Sheila, Gary, Rachael, David; p/William Hershall and Mell Juanita Grant, Cambridge City, IN; ed/BRE Grand Rapids Bapt Col 1966; MDiv magna cum laude Grand Rapids Sem 1969; pa/Bd Mem Lake Ann (Mich) Assn Regular Bapt Chs Yth Camp 1978-; Coun of Twelve En Mich Regular Bapt Chs: Moderator 1978, VModerator 1977-78, Secy 1974-76; Mem Coun of Thirteen Mich Regular Bapts 1975-76, 1978-; Saginaw Val Truth for Yth: Pres 1977-, VP 1975-76, Exec Bd 1974-75; Bd Dirs Bapt Acad Grand Rapids 1971-73; Other Former Activs; r/Bapt:

Ordained by Moline Bapt Ch 1970; hon/Christian Ser Awd, Grand Rapids Bapt Col; Bapt Sem Grand Rapids: Pres' Awd, Lehman Strauss Expository Preaching Awd, Leon J Wood 21-Day Holy Land Tour; Biogl Listings.

GRANT, PETER HENDRICKS oc/- Psychologist; Lecturer; Author; b/May 5, 1935; h/2037 Caminito Capa, La Jolla,CA 92037; ba/La Jolla; c/Peter A, Kari A; p/Leo B and Lucille Grant, Midland, MI; ed/BA; MA; PhD; pa/Am Psychol Assn; Psychologist Pvt Pract; Lectr Univ Cal; cp/Bd Mem YMCA; Pres Optimist Clb; hon/Pub'd Author.

GRANT, VERNE oc/Professor; b/Oct 17, 1917; h/2811 Fresco Dr, Austin, TX 78731; m/Karen Alt; c/Joyce, Brian, Brenda; ed/AB 1940, PhD 1949 Univ Cal-Berkeley; pa/Prof Botany Univ Tex-Austin 1970-; Univ Ariz, Superior, Ariz 1968-70: Dir Boyce Thompson SWn Arboretum, Prof Biol Scis; Prof Biol Inst Life Sci Tex A&M Univ, College Station 1967-68; Other Former Positions; Am Soc Naturalists; Genetics Soc Am; Soc for Study of Evolution: VP 1966, Pres 1968; Botanical Soc Am; Lund Botanical Soc; Intl Soc Plant Taxonomists; Am Soc Plant Taxonomists; SWn Assn Naturalists; Mem Var Edit Bds; Reschr; hon/Fellow, Am Acad Arts & Scis; Commun Ser Awd & Medal, London; Cert of Merit, Botanical Soc Am; Mem Nat Acad Scis; Phi Beta Kappa Awd in Sci; Nat Res Coun F'ship; Profl Pubs.

GRANT-EASTER, EVONNE (BUNNY) ELLA oc/Student; b/Dec 4, 1946; h/105 S 36th St, Boulder, CO 80303; m/Larry A; p/John D Easter, Viburnum, MO; Ollie Mae Easter (dec); ed/Grad Crim Investigation Div Sch AUS; Grad Bur Narcotics & Dangerous Drugs 1970; Current Study Colo Univ- Boulder; mil/AUS 5 Yrs, Ret'd Disabled Vet; pa/Personalizied Ed Prog (PEP): Staff Mem, Tchr PEP Methods; cp/Lectr Colo Univ; Var Vol Activs; r/Budhist; AUS Oak Leaf & Cluster; Armed Forces Day Queen, Ft Huachuca, Ariz; Nat Amputee Golf Queen 1971.

GRASER, EARL JOHN oc/Director; h/1601 Hanging Moss Ln, Monroe, LA 71201; ba/W Monroe; m/Marianne; c/Cathy Ann; p/Ottomar and Irene Graser (dec); ed/BS Univ Cincinnati; mil/USN Aviation; pa/Olinkraft Inc: Dir Indust Design, Multiple Packaging 1977-, Mgr Packaging Systems 1975-77, Mgr Prod Devel 1966-75; Mgr Structural Design Olin Corp 1961-66; Other Former Positions; Bd Dirs Am Soc Innovators in Technol; Packaging Inst USA; World Packaging Org; Am Mgmt Assn; Nat Soft Drink Assn; Master Brewers Assn; Soc Soft

Drink Technologists; cp/Aircraft Owners & Pilots Assn; Nat Assn Awareness in Music; USCG Aux, Flotilla Cmdr; CAP; Secy-Treas Aero Nutz Sailplane Assn; Monroe Little Theatre Assn, Bd Dirs 3 Yrs; Set Design Dir Miss La Pageant; Monroe Fine Arts Foun; Amateur Organist Assn Intl; Others; hon/Top Package of Yr, *Packaging Design* Mag 1971; Package of Yr Awd, *Food & Drug Packaging* Mag 1972; Olinkraft Awd, Inventor of Yr 1971; Patentee; Biogl Listings; Pub'd Author.

GRAUBARD, MARK AARON oc/Pro- fessor; Historian of Science; b/Jan 5, 1904; h/2928 Dean Pkwy, Minneapolis, MN 55416; ba/Mpls; m/Ann Wolfe; c/Jane Strovas, Maya Eldredge; p/Mendell and Fanny Graubard (dec); ed/PhD Columbia Univ; pa/Ret'd Prof Hist of Sci Univ Minn; Lectr: Univ Kyoto (Japan), Univ W Indies, Nat Foun for Humanities; cp/Cand for Sch Bd; r/Philosophical Christian; hon/Logic Medal, CCNY; George Washington Hon Medal, Freedoms Foun.

GRAUMANN, MARY KATHLEEN oc/Administrator; b/May 16, 1945; h/22604 Lutheran Ch Rd, Tomball, TX 77375; ba/Cypress, TX; m/Wayne E; p/E C and Luetta G Graumann, Dunnellon, FL; ed/BS Concordia 1970; MEd Tex A&I Univ 1976; pa/Dir Ed Good Samaritan Luth Home; Assn for Chd w LD; cp/Repub Party; r/Luth Ch- Mo Synod.

GRAUMANN, WAYNE E oc/Pastor; b/Oct 22, 1948; h/22604 Lutheran Ch Rd, Tomball, TX 77375; ba/Same; m/Mary Kathleen Werner; p/Emil Graumann (dec); Leonora Graumann, Granite, OK; ed/AA St John's Col 1968; BS Concordia 1970; MDiv Concordia Theol Sem 1974; pa/Pastor Luth Parish; Concordia Hist Inst; cp/Rotary Clb; r/Luth Ch-Mo Synod.

GRAVENS, DANIEL LEE oc/Microbi- ologist; Manager; b/Feb 6, 1937; h/28 Parkland Ave, St Louis, MO 63122; ba/St Louis; m/Carol; c/Christopher, Laura, David; p/Charles L and Georgia C Gravens, Ludlow, KY; ed/BA; MA; pa/Vestal Labs: Sr Microbiologist, Prod Mgr Profl Prods; Lab Supvr Surg Bacteriol Lab Barnes Hosp, Wash Univ Sch Med; Pres Mo Br Am Soc for Microbiol; APIC; Am Acad for Microbiol; Fac Mem Forest Pk Commun Col 1975; Other Profl Activs; hon/Awd, Nat Assn Med Environmentalists; W/W MW; DIB; Commun Ldrs & Noteworthy Ams.

GRAVES, HAROLD BOYD oc/Minister; District Superintendent; b/Oct 12, 1927; h/200 Gardenview Dr, San Antonio, TX 78213; ba/San Antonio; m/Bettie Eby; c/Harold B Jr, David Wayne, Brenda Joyce Johnson, Cheryl Ann Alderman, James T; p/James E and Johnnie Boyd Graves (dec);

ed/BA; mil/USN 1945-46; pa/Dist Supt, Bd Trustees Bethany Nazarene Col, Bethany, Okla; Bd Dirs TANE; SE Reg Rep Intl Yth Ch of Nazarene 1964-68; Pres Dist Yth Tenn Dist Ch of Nazarene 1960-68; Trustee Olivet Nazarene Col 1970-73; VP Billy Graham Crusade, Gary, Ind 1972; r/Ch of Nazarene.

GRAVES, MARY JO oc/Landscape Contractor; b/Aug 26, 1928; ba/311 W May St, Vivian, LA 710832; m/Cleve Verlon; c/Cleve Verlon Jr, Sandra Lynn Lindsay (Mrs Buchannan Harrison III); p/Wells Albert and

Stella Mae Wright; ed/Henderson St Tchr's Col; pa/Horticulturist Beautification Implementation, Town of Vivian 1973-; Partner (w husband) N Caddo Drug 1954-; Former Tchr; Bd Mem Caddo-Bossier Conv & Tourists Bur; Landscape Design Critics Coun; Nat Coun St Garden Clbs Inc; Accredited Flower Show Judge; Trails Adv Coun; cp/N Highlands Garden Clb; LGCF Judges Coun; Redbud Fest; NW La Hist Soc; Var Former Activs; r/Presb; hon/Awd of Apprec, Gov 1975; Bronze Honorium Tree, Redbud Pk; Savings Bond Winner, Dist 7 Beautification Slogan Contest; Commun Achmt; Grants; Sev Flower Show Awds; Biogl Listings.

GRAVLEE, LELAND CLARK JR oc/Physician; b/Apr 1929; h/1717 11th Ave S, Birmingham, AL 35205; ba/B'ham; c/Jan, Luann, Leland Clark III; p/Leland Clark Gravlee, Fayette, AL; Mary Annie Gravlee (dec); ed/BS Auburn Univ 1951; MD Univ Ala 1955; mil/USN 1946-48, All Navy Playoff 1947; pa/AMA; FACOG; Jefferson Co Med Soc; Ala Ob-Gyn Soc; SCOG; Chief of Staff S Highlands Hosp; Clin Prof Ob-Gyn Univ Ala; Asst Prof Univ Ala Med Sch; Guest of Russian Govt, Moscow (Hlth Fair) 1974; cp/B'ham Rotary Clb; B'ham CC; r/Mountainbrook Bapt Ch: Deacon; hon/Patentee; Pub'd Author; AOA, Outstg Resident Aw, Univ Ala Med Ctr 1958; W/W SE.

GRAY, BRYAN JAMES oc/University Professor; b/Aug 9, 1942; h/2803 Nottingham, Denton, TX 76201; m/Sally E; c/Dianne E, James R; p/Ada C Gray, Victoria, BC, Canada; ed/BPE; MS; DEd; pa/Bd Dirs Assn for Advmt in Hlth Ed; AAHPER; r/Unitarian.

GRAY, LAWRENCE ALSTON oc/- Executive; b/Jul 6, 1948; h/2093 NE Tompkins St, West Linn, OR 97068; ba/Washington, DC; p/Paul Michael Gray, Seattle, WA; Olive O Alston Gray (dec); ed/Att'd Portland St Univ 1966-68; mil/USN 1968-72, Discharged E-5 Journalist; pa/Pres GAP Communs Inc (Wash News Bur); Commentator WHO-Des Moines, KEX-Portland (Oreg), WWTC-Twin Cities (Minn); Correspondent Assoc'd Press Radio; Wash Radio & TV Correspondents Assn; Nat Assn Progressive Radio Announcers; Two Newspaper Town Com; Nat Citizen's Com for Broadcasting; Alt Newspapers; cp/Alt Del to 1976 Dem Nat Conv; Var Campaign Activs; GI Cnslg; Drug Cnslg; Vietnam Moratorium Com; Others; hon/W/W in Am Polits.

GRAY, LAWRENCE EDMUND oc/- Administrator; b/Jul 4, 1948; h/1311 W 187 Pl, Gardena, CA 90248; ba/Carson, CA; p/- Woodrow and Margaret Gray; ed/BA Cal St Univ-Dominguez Hills 1970; pa/Dir Student Devel Cal St Univ-DH; Student Pers Assn Cal; Nat Assn Student Pers Admrs; Am Assn Higher Ed; Cal Pers & Guid Assn; Org Cnslg Ctr Dir in Higher Ed; hon/Men of Achmt; Intl W/W Commun Ser; W/W Am.

GRAY, MILTON H oc/Lawyer; b/1910; h/420 Lakeside Pl, Highland Park, Chicago, IL; m/Florence A Subin; c/James S, Roberta Katz; ed/BA, JD NWn Univ; pa/Partner Law Firm Altheimer & Gray; VP & Dir Blackstone Mfg Co; Secy & Dir Noma-World Wide Inc, Alloy Mfg Co; ABA Coms: Corporate Law & Acctg 1971-, Fed Regulation Securities 1961-, St Regulation Securities 1961-; Chgo Bar: Bd Mgrs 1966-68, Pres 1971-72; Special Master

US Dist Ct 1973-; Chgo, Ill, Am, Intl Bar Assns; World Assn Lwyrs; Am Judic Soc; Order of Coif; cp/Var Activs BSA; Nat Adv Coun; Mem Var Clbs; hon/Dist'd Eagle Scout Citizen; NWn Univ Alumni Awd of Merit; Pub'd Author; Biogl Listings.

GRAY, NOLAN KENNETH oc/General Engineer; Physicist; Naval Flight Officer; Director Land Development Corporation; b/Jul 31, 1935; h/108 W Baldwin Rd, Panama City, FL 32405; ba/Panama City; m/Ann Patterson; c/Brian L, Eric A; p/John S Gray, Okawville, IL; Ouida Cope Gray (dec); ed/BA So Ill Univ 1963; MS Univ So Cal 1974; Addit Studies; mil/USN 1954-57, Discharged Radioman 1st Class; USNR 1958-, LCDR;

pa/Monitor 1978 Three Rivers Sci & Engrg Fair & Talent Search; Proj Engr Var New Minesweeping Systems/Techniques; Guest Lectr Mine Warfare Staff Ofcrs Sch; Spkr; Conslt; Dir & Partner Panama City (Fla) Land Devel Corp; Owner & Operator Home Rental Property; cp/Mem Nav Coastal Systems Ctr Clbs: Elects, Rod & Gun, Automobile Tune-Up; r/Bapt; hon/Author 62 Tech Reports; Meritorious Unit Commend, Secy of Navy; Var Mil Awds; Men of Achmt; W/W S&SW.

GRAY, RICHARD ALAN oc/Film Director; Still Photographer; b/Jan 17, 1938; h/7340 Harrison, Kansas City, MO 64131; ba/KC; m/Kathleen Coel; p/William Clinton Gray (dec); Geneva Nordica Gray, KC; ed/BA Univ KC 1959; MA UCLA 1962; ba/Stringer Photog *Newsweek* Mag 1973-; Capricorn Prodns, KC 1971-; Film Prodr, Dir, Cinematographer, Still Photog; Instr Film Aesthetics & Film Prodn KC Art Inst 1971-72; Other Former Positions; Soc Motion Picture & TV Engrs 1961-67; Univ Film Assn 1962-71; KC Film Critics' Cir; Adv Com Print Soc Friends of Art, Nelson-Atkins Art Gallery 1978-; Films Dir'd incl: *Where Do I Go From Here?, Patients Need You, Land of the Chinook, For All the People, The Harry S Truman Lib*, Others; One Man Shows incl: Sheldon Meml Art Gallery, Lincoln (Neb), Hallmark's, KC, Mt St Scholastica Col, Atchison (Ks), Others; Var Group Shows; cp/Former Mem KC Ski Clb; r/Presb; hon/Cert of Participation, Am Film Fest; Cert of Excell, Anaheim Film Fest; Awd of Merit, Nat Com on Films for Safety; Chris Awd, Columbus Film Fest; Pub'd Photos; Eagle Scout; Biogl Listings; Others.

GRAYSON, EDWIN M oc/Real Estate Broker; Insurance Counselor; b/Dec 20, 1931; h/3170 E Iona Rd, Idaho Falls, ID 83401; ba/Idaho Falls; m/Elaine Diana; c/Christine, Michelle, Brenda, Cindy, Marjorie, Jolene; p/William Thomas and Marjorie Jane Grayson (dec); ed/Grims Sch of Bus; Idaho St Univ; mil/USN BM-PO; pa/Grayson Bldrs Inc; Landco Inc Ariz; Bd Dirs, Pres 1977-78; St, Local, Nat Real Est Bd; cp/Former Mem Repub Precnt Com; Elk; Mason; Shriner; r/Presb; hon/Kiwanian Ser Awds.

GREAVES, RICHARD LEE oc/Professor; b/Sept 11, 1938; h/910 Shadowlawn Dr, Tallahassee, FL 32312; ba/Tallahassee; m/Judith Rae Dieker; c/Sherry Elizabeth, Stephany Lynn; p/David M and Frieda E Greaves, Glendale, CA; ed/BA summa cum laude; MA magna cum laude; PhD Univ London; pa/Prof Eng Hist Fla St Univ; Am Hist Assn; Am Soc Ch Hist; Am Soc for Reformation Res; Hisns of Early Mod Europe;

cp/Dem Party; hon/Love Meml Prize, Conf Brit Studies; F'ships: NEH, ACLS, Clark Lib, Mellon Foun.

GRECO, ALBERT NICHOLAS oc/- Executive Director; b/Jun 15, 1945; h/183 S Queen St, Bergenfield, NJ 07621; ba/New York, NY; m/Elaine Anne; c/Albert, Timothy; p/Albert C and Nellie M Greco, Morrisville, PA; ed/BA, MA Duquesne Univ; PhD Studies NY Univ; mil/USAF ROTC; pa/Exec Dir Metro Lithographers Assn; Dwight-Englewood Sch: Dir Devel 1978-79, Prin HS 1975-78, Prin Sum Sch 1971-78, Others; Am Film Inst; Am Hist Assn; cp/B'field Little Leag Umpire; r/St John's Rom Cath Ch: Fund Raising; hon/Phi Alpha Theta; Dean's List, Duquesne; W/W in E; Others.

GREEAR, YVONNE ETNYRE oc/Librarian; b/Jun 19, 1921; h/3449 Greenock, El Paso, TX 79925; ba/El Paso; c/Yvonne Patricia Ramage (Mrs C H), Kathryn Lynn Loewenstein (Mrs W A), Julie G Carrillo; p/Mentor and Carrie Geoth Etnyre (dec); ed/BFA; MLS; pa/Libn Univ Tex-El Paso; Tex Lib Assn; Spec Lib Assn; Am Name Soc; SCMLA; hon/Libn of Yr, Border Reg Lib Assn 1968.

GREEN, BILLY JACK oc/Minister; b/Aug 8, 1940; h/2181 Meadow Wood Ct, Marietta, GA 30062; ba/Marietta; m/Lee Grant; c/LeAnne, Angela Kay; p/B H Green, Birmingham, AL; Audrey Ruth Bradley Green, Orlando, FL; ed/AA Clark Col; BA Miss Col; BD Golden Gate Sem; Further Studies; pa/Min Music Eastside Bapt Ch,

Marietta; Ga Bapt Music Conf; Hymn Soc Am; Choristers Guild; GMA; SBCMC; Son of Jubal; r/So Bapt; hon/Outstg Yg Man Am; Favorite Son, 1st Bapt Ch, B'ham; Miss Bapt Musician of Yr 1970; Outstg Yg Men Am; Pub'd Author; Recorded 3 Albums; W/W in Rel.

GREEN, CHESTER R oc/Executive; b/Jul 9, 1915; h/427 Sheridan Rd, Kenilworth, IL 60043; ba/Glenview, IL; m/Doris Moore; c/Chester William, Susan G Findley; p/William Walter Green (dec); Ruby Culpepper Green, Albany, GA; ed/Harvard AMP 1955; mil/USNR; pa/Sr VP Kraft Inc; Chm Assn Nat Advertisers; Bd Am Advt'g Fdn; Fac Adv Bd Intl Acad Merchandising & Design; r/Winnetka Bible Ch, Winnetka, Ill.

GREEN, DEE M oc/Counseling Psychologist; b/Feb 6, 1913; h/1204 E Market, Searcy, AR 72743; ba/North Little Rock, AR; m/Zelma B; c/Carol Ann; p/(dec); ed/BA Harding Col 1948; MA Peabody Tchrs Col 1949; EdD Denver Univ 1961; mil/34th Inf Div 1942-45; pa/Cnslg Psychologist VA Hosp; r/Prot; hon/Bronze Star.

GREEN, EDITH oc/Member of US Congress; b/Jan 17, 1910; h/8031 Sacajawea Way, Wilsonville, OR 97070; c/James S, Richard A; p/James Vaughn and Julia Hunt Starrett (dec); ed/Willamette Univ; BS Univ Oreg; pa/US Rep (3rd Congl Dist Oreg) 1955-75, Mem Var Coms & Subcoms; Bd Dirs: Pacific NW Bell Telephone, Seattle, Wash, Benjamin Franklin Savs & Ln, Portland, Oreg, Oreg Physicians Ser, Foun for Study of Pres & Congl Terms; Bd Trustees Linfield Col, Oreg; Adv Bd Univ Oreg Hlth Scis Ctr, Portland; Review Com Oreg Commun Foun; Congl Del to Var Confs; cp/Var Campaign Activs;

hon/Num Hon Degs; Hon Mem Var Hon Socs; 1st Citizen Awd, Portland; Awd, Oreg Broadcasters Assn; AAUW Annual Achmt Awd; Simon LeMoyne Medal, LeMoyne Col, Syracuse, NY; Abram L Sachar Awd, Nat Wom's Com Brandeis Univ; Others.

GREEN, EMMA ALICE oc/Librarian; b/Sept 20, 1916; h/3704 Clearwell, Amarillo, TX 79109; ba/Amarillo; p/Roy J and Eliza K Green (dec); ed/BLS; pa/Past Pres Tex Mun Libns' Assn; Dir Tex Mun Leag; Tex, SW, Am Lib Assns; cp/Altrusa Clb Amarillo; C of C; r/LDS; hon/Tex Libn of Yr 1977.

GREEN, ERNESTINE R oc/Reading Teacher; b/Mar 27, 1938; h/245 Woodbridge, Buffalo, NY 14214; ba/Buffalo; m/Judge Samuel L; c/Beth; p/Eugene and Bertha Riddick, Hempstead, NY; ed/BS; MEd; pa/Rdg Tchr W Herteh Mid Sch; NEA; Push for Excell; AKA; Buffalo Tchrs Fdn; cp/Bd Dirs Buffalo Div for Yth; Del Dem Nat Conv 1975; Bd Dirs St Philips Boys Choir; Chm Sister City, Cape Coast Ghana; r/Bapt.

GREEN, GALEN LEE oc/Writer; Poet; Educator; Songwriter; b/Apr 30, 1949; h/3050 St Johns Ct, Columbus, OH 43202; ba/Same; p/Harry and Margaret Green, Wichita, KS; ed/BA Wichita St Univ; MA Univ Utah; pa/Editor & Pubr *Fireweed* 1975-; Poetry Wkshop Dir Creative Arts Prog Ohio St Univ 1975-; Resident Writer Poets-in-the-Schs Prog Ohio Arts Coun 1975-; Composition Instr Columbus Tech Inst 1976; Creative Writing Instr Ohio Dominican Col 1975; S Side Settlemt, Columbus 1974-75; Tchr, Writer, Commun Wkr; Res Correspondent, Keystone Mutual Funds, Boston, Mass 1972-73; Author 3 Books: *World-Weary Polka*, 1977, *You're Never the Same Person Twice*, 1975, *Apple Grunt*, 1971; Contbr Stories & Poems to Over 40 Mags; cp/Big Brothers Assn; hon/Recipient William Allen White Sch of Jour Awd for Interviewing; Contemp Author; Men Achmt; Dir Am Fiction Writers; Dir Am Poets; Intl W/W Poetry.

GREEN, GERALDINE D oc/Attorney; Secretary; b/Jul 14, 1938; ba/515 S Flower St, #3000, Los Angeles, CA 90071; p/Edward Chisholm (dec); Lula Chisholm, Bronx, NY; ed/BBA City Col NY 1964; JD St John's Univ 1968; pa/Atlantic Richfield Co 1972-: Sr Atty (Fin), Asst Corporate Secy; IBM Corp 1968-72: Staff Atty (Data Processing Div, LA) 1972, Atty (Fed Systems Div, Gaithersburg, Md) 1969-71, Others; LA Bd Traffic Commrs; ABA; Black Wom Lwyrs Cal; Cal, Nat Bar Assns; Fin Lwyrs Conf; Langston Law Clb; LA Wom Lwyrs Assn; Nat Legal Aid & Defender Assn; Phi Alpha Delta; Other Former Activs; cp/NAACP; So Poverty Law Ctr; US Olympic Soc; LA Urban Leag; Treas Beverly Hills/Hollywood Br NAACP; Legal Com Wn Reg NAACP; Others; YWCA Cert of Achmt; NAACP Freedom Awd Cit; Commun Ser Awd, LA Urban Leag; Biogl Listings.

GREEN, LACY AUGUST oc/Priest; b/Jun 11, 1925; h/302 Railroad St, Rosedale, MS 38769; ba/Same; p/Lacy August and Elizabeth Gutierrez Green (dec); ed/BA; pa/Rom Cath Priest; Cnslg & Guid; cp/Rosedale Chm Miss Mtl Hlth Assn 1979; r/Rom Cath.

GREEN, RICE ANDREW oc/Executive; b/Jul 15, 1928; h/238 Park Rd, Webster

Groves, MO 63119; ba/Clayton, MO; m/Irene Abbay; c/Linda Abbay, Robert Andrew, Russell Alan; p/Horace Jewel and Winona Suddeth Green (dec); ed/BS Univ Ark 1950; mil/USAF 1954-56, 1/Lt; pa/Exec SWn Bell Telephone 1977-; Partner Green & McGuire Investmt Co 1976-; Pres G&M Constrn Co 1976-; Var Former Positions; cp/Rotarian; Webster Groves Police Commr; Webster Groves Hist Soc; Var Polit Activs; r/Presb.

GREEN, ROLAND JAMES oc/Free-lance Writer; b/Sept 2, 1944; h/629 W Oakdale, Chicago, Il 60657; ba/Same; m/Frieda A Murray; p/James E Green, Ypsilanti, MI; Bertha M Green, Ypsilanti; ed/BA w high hon Oberlin Col 1966; MA Univ Chgo 1968; pa/Writer, Specializing in Sci Fiction & Fantasy; Sci Fiction Writers Am.

GREEN, S WILLIAM oc/Member of Congress; b/Oct 16, 1929; h/755 Park Ave, New York, NY 10028; ba/Washington, DC; m/Patricia Freiberg; c/Catherine Ann, Louis Matthew; p/Louis A Green; Evelyn Schoenberg; ed/BA magna cum laude Harvard Col 1950; JD magna cum laude Harvard Law 1953; mil/AUS 1953-55, 1/Lt; pa/Admr Housing & Urban Devel II 1970-77; Admitted to: DC Bar 1953, NY Bar 1954; Law Secy to Judge George T Washington 1955-56; Mem US Ho of Reps (18th Congl Dist NY) 1978-, Var Com Mbrships; Treas Assn of Bar City of NY 1976-78; Bd Dirs NY Leg Ser Inc; cp/Fdg Mem Jewish Assn for Sers for Aged; Former Chm Com on Devel Fdn of Jewish Philanthropies; Trustee Montefiore Hosp & Med Ctr; Overseer: Ctr for NYC Affairs New Sch, Albert Einstein Col Med; Adv Com Harvard Univ John F Kennedy Sch Govt; Adv Com NYU Grad Sch Public Adm; Mem Temple Emanu-El; Jewish War Vets; Others; r/Jewish; hon/Phi Beta Kappa.

GREEN, STANLEY BRUCE oc/Administrator; Teacher; b/Aug 24, 1937; h/1000 N Hayes, Searcy, AR 72143; ba/Searcy; m/Betty Joyce; c/Gregory, Todd, Stacy; p/Elliott H Green, Pasadena, TX; ed/BS cum laude Univ Houston 1959; pa/Harding Col, Searcy: Dir Public Relats 1971-, Dir Spec Events & Sports Info 1968-71, Instr Art 1965-, Dir Comml Art 1966-68; Other Former Positions; NAIA-SIDA: Nat Pres 1974-76, Nat VP 1972-73, Nat Secy-Treas 1970-72; AIC-SID; Am Col Public Relats Assn; Kappa Delta Phi; Kappa Pi; Ftball Writers Am; US Basketball Writers Assn; Col Sports Info Dirs Assn; US Collegiate Baseball Writers Assn; Other Profl Activs; cp/Kiwanis Intl; r/Col Ch of Christ, Searcy: Mem; hon/Cert of Achmt, Denver (Colo) Art Dirs Show; Certs of Merit, Houston Artist Guild Show; 1st Pl, CASE Nat 1975; Var Other Design Awds; Biogl Listings.

GREENAN, GARY COLLINS oc/Educator; City Planner; b/Jun 13, 1941; h/3617 Bayview Rd, Coconut Grove, FL 33133; ba/Coral Gables, FL; m/Linda Lou; c/Trevor, Tyler, Trent; p/Charles Greenan (dec); Heliece Greenan, Tampa, FL; ed/Bach Landscap Arch; Masters City & Reg Planning; pa/Edr Univ Miami; Planning Conslt; cp/Bd Coconut Grove Civic Assn; r/Meth; hon/Selected to Prepare Nat Site Planning Standards for Arch Graph Standards.

GREENAWAY, MILLICENT DICKENSON oc/Educator; b/Feb 26, 1921; h/219 Wainwright St, Newark, NJ 07112; m/Simon; c/3 Chd; p/Charles and Theresa Dickenson; ed/BA, MA; pa/Dir & Hd Tchr New Hope Devel Day Care Ctr; Tng Early Childhood Parents & Wkrs; Former Elem Tchr & Handicraft Tchr, Antigua, W Indies; Public Spkr; Bridal Conslt; Notary Public; Dressmaker; cp/No Chapt Univ Black Wom; Emer Com to Save Childcare in Newark; Notaries Assn; r/Franlin-St Johns U Meth Ch: Bd Mem, SS Tchr, Pres Theatre Guild; hon/Recog Awd, Emer Com to Save Childcare Newark; Outstg Dir Awd, Day Care Coor'g Coun Essex Co; Outstg Female Supvr Awd, Mt Carmel Guild; Awd, Bd Dirs & PTA New Hope Devel Day Care Ctr; W/W Child Devel Profls; Notable Ams.

GREENBERG, FRANK JOSEPH oc/Psychotherapist; Educator; b/Jun 15, 1933; h/Dorchester, MA; ba/Same; m/Elizabeth Irene Bowser; c/Robin Elizabeth, Diana Rose, Anita Louise, Linda Ann (dec), Frank Joseph Jr, Daniel Jacob Harold; p/Benjamin J Greenberg, Windham, NH; Mary E Greenberg (dec); ed/BA Sociol Brentwood Col 1958; PhD Phil 1963, DD (hon) 1963 Brantridge Forest Sch; BD Felix Adler Mem Univ 1964; LLB Blackstone Sch Law 1967; EdM Col & Adult Cnslg 1970, PhD Indust Psychol 1971, EdD Col & Adult Cnslg 1971, MCrim Natural Sci Emphasis 1972, DCrim Natural Sci Emphasis 1972; LLD (hon) Thomas A Edison Col 1972; LHD (hon) 1972, DCS (hon) 1973 London Inst Applied Res; Num Addit Courses; mil/USCG: Seaman 1950-54, Nat Defense Ser Medal; pa/Palm Bch Psychotherapy Tng Ctr, W Palm Bch, Fla 1974-; Thomas A Edison Col 1972-: Prof, Dir, VP, Dean of Cont'g Ed, Fac & Adm; Subst Sch Tchr Beverly Public Sch Sys, Beverly, Mass 1970-71; Cnslg Psychol & Clin Psychotherapist, Beverly 1963-; Tax & Security Acct, Beverly & Dorchester 1956-; Life Fellow: Alpha Psi Sigma Soc, Am Acad Behavioral Sci, Assn Social Psychol, Delta Epsilon Omega Hon Soc, Fla Psychoanalytic Inst, Gracie Inst Hypnosis; Life Mem: Am Assn Advmt Criminology, Criminological Execs Clb, Nat Psychol Assn, Thomas A Edison Col Alumni Assn; Am Assn Higher Ed; Am Bd Examrs Psychotherapy: Life Mem, Dipl, Pres; Voting Mem Am Ednl Res Assn; Charter Mem: Am Parapsychol Res Foun; Am Soc Notaries; Am Studies Assn; Life Mem & Fellow Soc Frat Order Lambda Epsilon Chi; Col Mem Nat Sic Tchrs Assn; Comprehensive Mem Nat Soc Study Ed; Assoc Mem Nat Soc Public Accts; Life Mem & K Cmdr Justice Order St John Jerusalem; Sustaining Mem Soc Profs Ed; Num Creative Pubs & Compositions; Active in Nontraditional Exptl Ednl Res, Devel, Adm & Curr Planning & Implementations-Area of Spec in Higher Ed; Diplomate: Behavioral Sci & Psychoanalysis Fla Psychoanalytic Inst, Clin Psychotherapy Palm Bch Psychotherapy Tng Ctr; AAAS; Am Assn Univ Admrs; Assn Ednl Communs & Technol; ASCD; Biblical Archaeol Soc; Intl Assn Hydrogen Energy; Am Sec/Intl Solar Energy Soc; Measuremts & Control Soc; Med Electronics & Data Soc Am; NE Solar Energy Assn; Soc Advmt Ed; Soc Intercult Ed Tng & Res; cp/Navy Leag US; Bd Dirs, Other Ofcs Universal Human Rights Foun Inc; US Naval Sea Cadet Corps; Fdg Past Pres Beverly Chapt Indoor Sports Clb; US Nav Inst; World Future Soc; Life Mem Am Studies Res Ctr, Hyderabad, India; 32°, SPRS, Mass Consistory, Scottish Rite Masonic Bodies in Val of Boston, Mass; hon/W/W: US (Plaque), Intl Commun Ser (Plaque, Dipl Hon), E (Cert Hon); Men Achmt; DIB (Cert Merit); Fdr-Fellow Medal & Commun Ser Dipl, Hon Intl Inst Commun Ser; Cmdr Intl Order Sursum Corda; Order St John Jerusalem: Purple Rosette, Maltese Cross, Acad Accolade & Laureate Magna Cum Laude; Min Plenipotentiary, Imperial Order Constantine; Cert Merit Bureau Bus Practice; IPA; Ref Source in Am Heritage Res Assns Lib of Human Resources.

GREENBERG, STAN SHIMEN oc/Scientist; Teacher; b/Sept 14, 1945; h/6427 Airport Blvd, Mobile, AL 36609; ba/Mobile; m/Patricia Ann Diehm; c/Jonathan Michael, Kristen Ann; p/Louis Myer and Anna Pinckosowitz Greenberg, Brooklyn, NY; ed/BS magna cum laude; MS; PhD; pa/Med Sch Prof; Res in High Blood Pressure; cp/VP Mobile Co High Blood Pressure Coun; r/Epis, Cath; hon/Career Devel Awd, Hypertension Br, NHLBI, USPHS.

GREENE, JOHN THOMAS oc/Marriage & Family Counselor, Psychotherapist; b/2918 Woodside Dr, Tallahassee, FL 32312; m/Nellie Pell; c/John Elbert, Harold Pell; p/John Jefferson Greene (dec); Sallie Jane Roberts Griffin (dec); ed/AB, BD, MA Duke Univ; PhD Univ NC; pa/Marriage Cnslg; Emeritus Prof Fla St Univ; Meth Min; Pres SEn Coun on Fam Relats 1975-77; r/Meth; hon/Pi Gamma Mu; Theta Phi.

GREENE, ROBERT FORD oc/Director of Athletics; Author; Sports Consultant; Educator; b/May 20, 1931; h/2500 Johnson Ave, 12F, Riverdale, NY 10463; ba/Greenvale, NJ; m/Joan Hope Ewers; p/John Joseph Greene (dec); Helen Williamson Ford (dec); ed/BS St Univ NY 1954; MA Columbia Univ 1955; DEd w hons UCLA 1970; mil/USMC 1950-51, Korean Conflict; pa/Dir Aths C W Post Col 1978-; Conslt US Sports Acad & Dir Nat Sports Prog in Mid E 1977-78; Dir Aths CCNY 1975-76; Other Former Positions; Author: Tennis Drills, 1976, Tennis Tactics, 1978; Editor Mid E Sports Sci Symposium Jour 1978; Contbr Num Articles to Jours & Mags; cp/Intl House Assn; Bd Dirs Spuyten Duyvil Assn; Interrel Foun; Commun Org; US & En Tennis Assns; Colonial Hgts Tennis Clb; r/Epis; hon/Fac Assoc Awd, CCNY; Coach of Yr, Metro Tennis Conf & CCNY; Patent Awd for Dissertation Res; Biogl Listings; Others.

GREENE, WILLIAM W oc/Clergy; Professor; Missionary; b/Aug 5, 1929; h/PO Box 18144, Ft Worth, TX 76118; ba/Same; m/Joy Lovell; c/Billie Doris Van Duyn; p/William W and Mildred Pharr Greene (dec); ed/BS 1961, MA 1962, DEd 1965 Univ Ga; Addit Studies; pa/Pastorates incl: Atmore, Ala, Thomas, Okla, Wharton, Tex, Athens, Ga, Santa Ana, Cal; Bethany Bible Col, Santa Cruz, Cal 1969-76: Prof Ed & Psychol, Chm Dept Psychol, Dir Tchr Ed; So Cal Col, Costa Mesa, Cal 1967-68: Dean of Admissions, Prof Sci; SEn Bible Col, Lakeland, Fla 1962-67: CoChm Music Dept, Prof Sci & Ed, Dir Cnslg; Dir Devel Far East Adv'd Sch of Theol, Manila, Philippines 1978-; Prin S Pacific Bible Col, Suva, Fiji 1975-77; Spec Lectr Oxford Univ, London, England 1975 (Sum); Other Missionary Positions; NEA; APA; Phi Delta Kappa; cp/First Aid Instr ARC; Rotary Intl; r/Assemblies of God; hon/Phi Theta Kappa; Kappa Delta Pi; Phi Kappa Phi; Res Grant; Biogl Listings; Others.

GREENFELD, YESHAYAHU oc/Principal; b/Jun 1, 1947; h/6358 Ebdy St, Pittsburgh, PA 15217; ba/Pgh; m/Devora; c/Ayelet, Taly; p/Moshe and Zipora Yehuda; ed/MEd; mil/Israeli Army; pa/Hillel Acad Pgh: Prin 1976-, Acting Prin 1976, Asst Prin Hebrew Studies Dept 1975-76, 1976-77, Tchr Hebrew Dept 1974-75; Tchr Hebrew Dept Yeshiva Achei Tmimin, Pgh 1974-75; Other Former Positions; Participating Author & Editor Action Prog for Nat Emer Conditions: A Manual, Nat Ednl Com Min of Ed & Cult, St of Israel 1971; r/Jewish; hon/Pub'd Author; Nat Ed Awd, Min of Ed & Cult, St of Israel.

GREENLEE, BETTY oc/Retired Savings & Loan Executive; b/Apr 8, 1920; h/108 Woodridge Dr, Hot Springs, AR 71901; m/Elmer H; p/Harold Hyde and Mabel Warren Bailey; ed/Hot Springs Bus Col 1943; Inst Fin Ed; Grad Sch Savs & Ln Ind Univ 1972; pa/1st Fed Savings, Hot Springs: Bd Dirs 1960-, Chief Fin Ofcr 1978, Exec VP 1977, 78, Sr VP 1976, VP 1959, Corporate Secy 1946, Asst Secy 1945, Teller & Clerk 1943; Ark Savs & Ln Leag: Treas 1959-65, Dir 1955-57; Nat Secys Assn: Former Mem, Pres, VP, Secy, Treas; Former Mem Garland Co Legal Secys Assn; Am Bus Wom's Assn; BPW Assn; Nat Assn Fin Mgrs Soc for Savings Instns Inc; SWn Reg Conf Fin Mgrs Soc for Savings Instns; Ark Chapt Fin Mgrs Soc for Savings Instns; cp/YWCA; Former Mem Epsilon Sigma Phi; Former Mem Hot Springs Woms' C of C; Former Dir & Treas Garland Co UF Campaign; Pilot Clb; r/Southside Ch of Christ; hon/Personalities of S.

GREENLEE, JACOB HAROLD oc/Missionary; Professor; h/715 Kennedy Ave, Duncanville, TX 75116; ba/Greenwood, IN; m/Ruth Bernice Olney; c/Dorothy Morrison (Mrs William), Lois Stuck (Mrs James), David; p/Jacob Greenlee, Melbourne, FL; Ethel Jarrett Greenlee (dec); ed/AB; BD; MA; PhD; pa/Missionary OMS Intl; Prof New Testament Greek; Intl Translation Conslt Sum Inst Linguistics; Author 5 Books & Num Pub'd Articles; r/U Meth; hon/Sr Fulbright F'ship, Oxford Univ; Dist'd Alumnus Awd, Asbury Theol Sem.

GREENSPAN, ADAM oc/Physician; b/May 28, 1935; h/61-35 98 St, Rego Park, NY 11374; m/Renata Gelber; c/Ludwig-Bernard; p/Bernard Greenspan (dec); Eugenia Greenspan; ed/MD 1958; MEd, ScD 1965;

pa/Radiologist Hosp for Jt Dis Orth Inst; Assoc Prof Radiol Mt Sinai Sch of Med; Fellow NY Acad Med; hon/Pub'd Author; Physician's Recog Awds, AMA.

GREENSTEIN, MICHAEL oc/Manager, Engineer; b/Nov 6, 1947; h/1117 Holcomb St, Watertown, NY 13601; ba/W'town; m/Linda Renee; c/Evan Seth; p/Leo and Sylvia Greenstein, Brooklyn, NY; ed/BEngrg; MBA; pa/Mgr Mfg & Indust Engrg; Soc Automotive Engrs; Am Soc Mech Engrs; Nat Soc Profl Engrs; cp/BSA; r/Jewish; hon/Awd for Effective Presentation, Gen Elect Co; W/W S&SW.

GREENSTEIN, TEDDY oc/Associate Professor; b/Mar 16, 1937; h/3000 Ocean Pkwy, Brooklyn, NY 11235; ba/Newark, NJ; p/Sam and Serena Greenstein, Bklyn; ed/BChE; MChE; PhD; pa/Assoc Prof Chem Engrg; r/Jewish; hon/NYU Fdrs Day Awd; Sigma Xi; Omega Chi Epsilon.

GREENWALD, BARRY S oc/Clinical Psychologist; b/Jul 24, 1937; h/312 N Elmwood, Oak Park, IL 60302; ba/Chicago, IL; m/Marjorie; c/Jessica, Jeffrey; p/Edward Greenwald (dec); Claire Greenwald Molinas, Margate, FL; ed/AB cum laude Ohio Univ 1959; MA 1961, PhD 1965 Univ Mich; pa/Clin Psychologist Student Cnslg Ser Univ Ill; APA; hon/Silver Cir Awd for Excell in Tchg.

GREENWALD, DOUGLAS oc/Consulting Economist; b/Jun 5, 1913; h/315 W 70 St, New York, NY 10023; ba/Same; m/Bette Ann; p/Max Greenwald (dec); Florence Semansky, NYC; ed/BA Temple Univ 1934; MA, PhD Geo Wash Univ; mil/AUS 1942-46, Combat Engrs European Theatre; pa/Former VP Ecs McGraw Hill Pub'g Co; Author;

Editor; Fellow: Nat Assn Bus Economists, Am Statistical Assn; Pres NY Chapt Am Stat Assn; Pres Metro Ec Assn; Chm Fed Statistics Users Conf; Conslt: Pres' Coun on Ec Advrs, Jt Ec Com on Cong, US Dept Commerce, US Bur Labor Statistics, US Treasury Dept; r/Jewish; hon/Forecasting Awds.

GREENWALD, HERBERT A oc/Owner Advertising Agency; b/May 4, 1919; h/2133 Campus Rd, Beachwood, OH 44122; ba/B'wood; m/Gloria; c/Marc, Gary; p/Samuel and Selma Greenwald (dec); ed/BBA Wn Resv Univ; mil/AUS 1942-44;

cp/Exec Dir Hgts Area C of C; r/Jewish; hon/Bd Govs IPA.

GREENWOOD, CHARLES HUDDIE oc/Educator; b/Jul 30, 1933; h/2504 W Lincolnshire, Muncie, IN 47304; ba/Muncie; m/Theresa M; c/Lisa Renee, Marc Charles; p/Huddie and Lida Greenwood (dec); ed/EdD; mil/AUS; pa/Asst Dean Undergrad Progs, Assoc Prof Adult & Commun Ed; Am Assn Higher Ed; Phi Delta Kappa; Assn Acad Affairs Admrs; ASCD; cp/Bd Mem: Kiwanis Intl (Muncie-2/VP), YMCA (Muncie), Jr Achmt E Ctl Ind, Fam Cnslg Sers; r/Meth; hon/Outstg Fac Mem; Ind's All Am Fam; Commun Ldrs & Noteworthy Ams; W/W in Ind.

GREER, MARTIN LUTHER oc/Minister; b/Jul 24, 1918; h/Box 27, Cross Plains, IN 47017; m/Martha May Morrison; c/Patricia G Tharp (Mrs Van K Jr), David Ray, Susanna G Fein (Mrs Joshua), Jane G Fultz (Mrs Joseph), James Martin, Martha Joellyn, William Luther; p/David Hunter Greer (dec); Charity Louise Wardroup Greer, Newport, TN; ed/AA Tenn Wes Col 1938; BA Univ Chgo 1940; BD 1944, MDiv 1972 Garrett Bible Inst; MA St Univ Ia 1956; pa/Pastor: S Ind U Meth Conf (Cross Plains) 1978—, WVa U Meth Annual Conf 1966-78; Others; Asst Prof Eng

WVa Wes Col 1965-70; Instr Eng, Lit & Spch Freeport (Ill) Commun Col 1963-64 & Canton (Ill) Commun Col 1964-65; Other Former Positions; Mem Ia-Des Moines Meth Conf; WVa Col Coun; NCTE; AAUP; Freeport Ed Assn; Ill Assn Classroom Tchrs; Am Studies Assn; WVa Assn Col Eng Tchrs; Other Assns; cp/Former Mem: Bd Dirs Upshur Co (WVa) Homes Corp, Commun Action Coun, Buckhannon Commun Theatre, Buckhannon Commun Choir; Var Activs BSA; Lions; Masons; Dem; r/U Meth Ch: Min, Former SS Tchr; hon/Sigma Tau Delta; Pub'd Author.

GREER, RACHEL DEAN oc/Professor; b/Apr 7, 1938; h/Rt 1, Box 144, Sherrill, AR 72152; ba/Pine Bluff, AR; p/Edward and Dorris Greer, Benton, AR; ed/BSE; MSE;

EdD; pa/Prof Hlth, PE & Rec Univ Ark-PB; AAHPER; So Dist AAHPER; Ark AHPER; SAPECW; Delta Psi Kappa; AWISA; cp/VIPS; LWV; r/Bapt; hon/Ark HPER Hon Awd.

GREGERSON, DORIS ELAINE oc/Interpretive Naturalist; Poet; b/Nov 23, 1923; h/1417 Circle Dr, Albert Lea, MN 56007; ba/Albert Lea; m/Jim; c/Amy Froiland (Mrs Tom), Pam Erickson (Mrs Ron), Jay, Cathy, Julie Orth (Mrs Kenneth), Kristin; p/Andrew J and Lillie A Larson, Albert Lea; pa/Interpretive Naturalist Helmer Myre St

Park; Leag Minn Poets; MW Fdn Chaparral Poets; Acad Am Poets; Intl Poetry Soc; cp/Albert Lea Audubon Soc; Minn Ornithologists' Union; r/Luth; hon/World W/W Wom; Intl W/W in Poetry; Men & Wom of Distn.

GREGERSON, EDNA J oc/Associate Professor; b/Aug 1, 1917; h/94 E Mount Hope, St George, UT 84770; ba/St George; m/Owen Louis; c/Ned Owen; p/Edward LeRoy Jensen (dec); Laura M Gore, St George; ed/AA; Bach; Masters; pa/Assoc Prof Humanities, Eng & Lit Dixie Col 1962-78; Guest Lectr Writers' Wkshop SUSC 1972 (Sum) & 1973 (Spring); Conducted 1st 3 Annual Writers' Wkshops Dixie Col 1973-75 (Sum); Conducted Wkshop on Chd's Lit Utah Acad Scis, Arts & Lttrs, Weber St Col 1976; Other Former Tchg Positions; UASAL: Life Mem, Chm Annual Spring Meeting 1977, Fellow World Acad 1977, Chm Com to Initiate Jr Acad Arts & Lttr 1977-78, Others; Utah Hist Soc; Utah Folklore Soc; So Utah Poetry Soc; Utah St Poetry Soc; Leag Utah Writers; Mem & Advr So Utah Heritage Writers Guild; Delta Kappa Gamma; Future Bus Ldrs Am, Snow Col Chapt: Charter Mem, Charter Pres; So Utah Tchrs Assn; UEA; NEA; AAUP; NCTE; Utah Coun Higher Ed; IPA; Num Others; cp/Gunnison Val Lady Lions; Am Civic & Beautification Com; Life Mem Nat Coun St Garden Clbs; Utah Assoc'd Garden Clbs; Guest Spkr; Contest Judge; Gunnison Val JayCettes: Charter Mem, Secy; Others; r/LDS Ch: Mem; St George Ward: Former Music Dir, Vol Wkr Geneal Lib, Others; hon/Outstg Tchr of Yr, Dixie Col Alumni Assn; Tchr of Qtr, Dixie Col Paper Staff Spring 1975; Marcell Augsburger Awd for Outstg Contbn to St Beautification; Pub'd Author; Guest Spots on Radio & TV; Biogl Listings; Others.

GREGOR, HAROLD LAURENCE oc/-Artist; Professor; b/Sept 10, 1929; h/1116 E Jefferson, Bloomington, IL 61701; ba/Normal, IL; c/Kathy Lynn, Matissa Suzanne; p/Robert McKay and Annie Malcolm Gregor (dec); ed/BS Wayne St Univ 1951; MS Mich St Univ 1953; PhD Ohio St Univ 1960; mil/AUS 1951-53; pa/Prof Art Ill St Univ; Exhibits: Tibor De Nagy Gallery (NYC), Nancy Lurie Gallery (Chicago), Sawyer Gallery (San Francisco); r/Unitarian; hon/Num Exhbns US & Abroad; Work included in Num Pvt & Public Collections; Recipient NEA Grant.

GREGORIAN, VARTAN oc/Educator; Professor; b/Apr 8, 1935; h/408 Drew Ave, Swarthmore, PA; ba/Philadelphia, PA; m/Clare Russell; c/Vahe, Raffi, Dareh; p/Samuel B Gregorian, Teheran, Iran; ed/AA; BA, PhD Stanford; pa/Univ Pa: Dean Fac Arts & Scis, Tarzian Prof Hist, Asst to Pres 1972; Vis Assoc Prof Hist UCLA 1968; Assoc Prof Hist Univ Tex 1968-72; Others; Am Assn Higher Ed; Nat Humanities Fac; Assn for Advmt Slavic Studies; Am Hist Assn; cp/World Affairs Coun Phila; Public Com for Humanities in Pa; hon/Golden Medal of Hon, City & Province of Vienna, Austria; Am Coun of Ed Fellow; Univ Tex Students Cactus Tchg Excell Awd; Danforth Fdn E H Harbison Outstg Tchg Awd; F'ships; Others.

GREGORIO, PETER ANTHONY oc/Grocery Executive; Artist; b/Jul 29, 1916; h/149 Bosphorus Ave, Tampa, FL 33606; ba/Tampa; m/Marie Blanton; c/Frank Allen, Carole Teresa; p/Frank Gregorio, Chicago, IL; Teresa Marotta (dec); mil/USAF Capt; Air Medal, 6 Clusters; pa/Bk Dir Ellis Nat Bk (Tampa); Painter & Graphic Artist; r/Cath; hon/Exhibits include: Col Vatican Lib (Rome) 1977, Am Bicent Exhbn (Paris) 1976, Rochester Fest Rel Arts (NY) 1972, Hillsborough Art Fest 1976-77-78; Awd Merit, H'borough Art Fest; Personalities of S; W/W S&SW; Fla From Indian Trail to Space Age; Pioneer Fla.

GREGORIUS, BEVERLY J oc/Physician; Educator; b/Jun 21, 1915; h/10635 Landale St, N Hollywood, CA 91602; ba/Glendale, CA; m/(dec); c/Joan G Jones; p/Henry and Arline Pruette (dec); ed/BS Madison Col 1935; MD 1947, MS 1952 Loma Linda Univ; Addit

Studies; pa/Assoc Clin Prof Ob-Gyn: Loma Linda Univ 1953-, USC Med Ctr 1960-; Dir Ob/Gyn Grad Ed Glendale Adventist Med Ctr 1976-; Fellow: Intl Col Surgs, Am Col Surgs, Am Col Ob-Gyn; Diplomate Am Bd Ob-Gyn; Assn Prof Gyn & Obs 1978; Royal Soc Med (London) 1973; Intl Fertility Assn 1951; LA Assembly Ob-Gyn 1955; LA Ob-Gyn Soc 1965; Staff Mbrships: St Joseph's Med Ctr (Burbank), Glendale Adventist Med Ctr (Glendale), Los Angeles Co-USC Med Ctr; r/SDA; hon/DIB; World W/W Wom; 2000 Wom in Distn; W/W: Am Wom, W; Notable Ams.

GREGORY, DENNIS A oc/Life Insurance; b/Oct 16, 1941; h/1213 Wooten, Colorado Springs, CO 80915; ba/Colo Sprgs; m/Kathy London; c/Eric Allen, Mark Alan; p/Ronald D and Elizabeth M Gregory, Decatur, IL; ed/BME Ind Univ; MA Adams St Col; Further Studies; mil/USAF-ROTC; pa/Pres Colo Springs Tchrs Assn; Colo Sprgs Bd Realtors; cp/El Paso Co Repub, Ctl Com; 5th Congl Dist Ctl Com; r/Meth; hon/Personalities W&MW; W/W World of Music.

GREGORY, LYDIA MAY JENCKS oc/-Retired College Librarian; b/Nov 6, 1903; h/39 Angeline St, S Attleboro, MA 02703; m/William; p/G Dallas and Florence Perkins Jencks (dec); ed/BS Univ RI; MA Brown Univ; Addit Studies; pa/Libn Tchr Franklin (NY) Ctl Sch; Asst Libn & Registrar NY St Univ, Genesco; Hd Libn Maine St Univ, Gorham; cp/St Libn Mass DAR; Pres Mass Chd of Am Revolution; Nat Chaplain Daughs of Am Colonists; Secy Trustees Attleboro Public Lib; Mem A'boro City Com; Repub; r/Congreg.

GREGORY, SHEILA ESTHER oc/Executive; b/Jun 21, 1943; h/13532 Wynant Dr, Westminster, CA 92683; ba/Westminster; m/Steve; c/David, Travis; p/Weston W and Esther A Holman, Troy, NH; ed/Whitley Col Ct Reporting; Golden West Col; pa/Co-Owner & VP Stenotype Operators Inc; Former Exec Secy McDonnell Douglas Astronautics Co; Cal Ct Reporters Assn; Assoc Mem Nat Shorthand Reporters Assn; Hotel Sales Mgmt Assn; Orange Co Trials Lwyrs Secys Assn; cp/Soroptimist Intl Westminster; Orange Co, Westminster Cs of C; Anaheim Conv Bur; Fdr Am Behcet's Foun; r/Garden Grove Commun Ch; hon/Cert of Accomplishmt, Stenotype Tchr's Course; Certs, Bd Dirs & Amassadors Clb Westminster C of C; Cert of Apprec, Career Fair 1976.

GREIG, WALTER oc/Attorney; President Emeritus of College; b/Nov 16, 1906; h/1223 Washtenaw Ave, Ypsilanti, MI 48197; m/Married; c/2 Chd; ed/BBA 1960, MBA 1961, Hon BS 1949, Hon DS 1962 Cleary Col; Hon DCS Drake Col Fla 1964; mil/AUS Active Duty 1941-46, WWII; Tex NG 1921-24, 1927-28; Ret'd AUS as Lt Col 1966; pa/Passed Tex Bar 1931; Pract'd Law 1931-41; Mich Bar 1946-; Admitted to US Supreme Ct Pract 1942; Lwyr in Detroit 1946-47; Ins-Adjuster, Citizens Mutual Ins Co 1947; Exec Secy Mich Liquor Comm, Lansing 1947-49; Cleary Col: Asst to Pres 1949, Exec VP 1951, Trustee & Ofcr Bd Trustees (Secy) 1950-70, Pres & Treas Bd Trustees 1970, Ret'd as Pres 1974, Pres Emeritus; Bus Conslt; Atty; cp/Former Chm Boy Scouts Fund Raising Dr; Past Pres Ypsilanti Area Indust Devel Corp; Nat Adv Bd Am Security Coun; Life Mem Ret'd Ofcrs Assn; Ann Arbor Chapt #6 Royal Arch Masons: High Priest, Other Positions; Cmdr Geo Wash Post #88 Am Legion; Masonic Lodge; Caravan Shrine Clb; Ypsilanti Area C of C; Mil Order Fgn Wars; Ypsilanti Kiwanis Clb; Detroit Ec Clb; Christian Bus Mens Clb; Royal Order Scotland; Former Mich Indust Ambassador; Pres, Detroit, Toledo, Ann Arbor Chapt Tex Univ Ex-Students Assn; Num Other Activs & Ofcs; hon/Recipient 33rd Deg Hon Mem Supreme Coun, N Masonic Jurisd; Scottish Rite; Legion of Hon Cert, Ypsilanti Kiwanis Clb; Hon Ky Col; Num Biogl Listings; Others.

GREIVE, WILLIAM HENRY oc/Chemist;

b/Dec 30, 1933; h/1441 Bradshaw Ct, Maumee, OH 43537; ba/Toledo, OH; m/Teresa; c/Roger, Susan; p/Henry F and Bernadine Greive (dec); ed/BA Univ Toledo 1976; mil/USMC 1954-57, Sgt; Good Conduct Medal; pa/Am Chem Soc; Sigma Xi; Soc Plastics Engrs; ASTM; Chm Plastics Analysis Group SPE 1969; cp/Former Mem Pk Com, Maumee; Former Scoutmaster; Repub Precnt Com; r/St Paul's Epis; hon/Num Scouting Awds.

GRENNEY, WILLIAM JAMES oc/Engineer; b/Aug 10, 1937; h/1716E 1600N, Logan, UT 84321; ba/Logan; m/Sally Ruth; c/-Michael, Judith, Pamela; p/Hamilton Grenney (dec); Bernice L Grenney, Corvallis, OR; ed/BS Mich Tech Univ 1960; MS 1969, PhD 1972 Oreg St Univ; mil/USN 1962-68, Civil Engrg Corps, Lt; pa/Hd Civil Engrg Utah St Univ 1977-; Dir Water Qual Systems IFG, US Fish & Wildlife 1978-; Chm Bd & Pres Intermountant Conslts 1973-78; r/Presb; hon/Outstg Reschr Col Engrg, Utah St Univ; Sigma Xi; Chi Epsilon; Blue Key.

GREULICH, KATHRYN SULLIVAN oc/Inventory Control Specialist; Buyer; b/Jun 2, 1954; h/1217 W 10th St, Erie, PA 16502; ba/Erie; m/Joseph Frank Jr; p/Raymond J and Celestine T Sullivan, Erie; ed/BA Villa Maria Col; cp/Kappa Gamma Pi; r/Rom Cath; hon/St Catherine Medal; W/W Am Cols & Univs; Outstg Ed Maj Awd; Outstg Yg Wom Am.

GRIDLEY, BERYL SMITH oc/Educator; Association Executive; h/Judson Pk, Seattle, WA 98188; m/Henry Norman (dec); p/George W and Alzona M Smith; ed/AB cum laude 1923, MA 1931 Univ Wash; Postgrad Sch Social Work Univ Wash 1935-37 & San Francisco St Col 1955; pa/Girls Advr Cleveland HS, Seattle 1924-28; Prin Woodside Sch for Handicapped Chd, Highline Sch Dist 1951-65; Caseworker Fam Cnslg: Seattle 1937-39, King Co Juv Ct, Seattle 1939-40, 1943-46; Caseworker, Dir Fed Transient Bur,

Seattle & Portland 1932-35; Consumer Rep OPA, West Coast 1941-43; Asst St Dir Mtl Hlth, St of Wash 1946-49; Adm Wom in Ed; AAUW; Nat Assn Social Work; Wash Soc Mtl Hygiene; Am Assn Mtl Deficiency; Royal Soc Hlth London; Wash Assn Retard Chd; Exec Dir King Co Chapt 1965-70; cp/Former Mem King Co Adm Bd for Mtl Hlth-Mtl Retard; hon/Mortar Bd; Pi Lambda Theta; Delta Kappa Gamma; Awd, Alpha Chi Omega; Matrix Awd, Theta Sigma Phi; Wom of Yr, Burien C of C; Biogl Listings.

GRIFFEN, JOYCE JONES oc/Professor; b/Apr 8, 1926; h/Rt 4, Box 902, Flagstaff, AZ 86001; ba/Flagstaff; m/William Bedford; c/Ellen, Jennifer; p/Lloyd E and Mabel W Jones, Denver, CO; ed/BA; MA; PhD; pa/Prof No Ariz Univ; Fellow: Am Anthropol Assn, Soc for Applied Anthropol; Wn Hist Assn; AAUP; Ariz Hist Adv Comm, Hist Sites Review Com; Bd Dirs Ariz Humanities Coun; cp/Former Mortar Bd Advr, NAU; Coconino Citizens Assn; hon/Danforth Fellow; Pub'd Author.

GRIFFIN, GEORGE ANN oc/Doctoral Student; Computer Systems' Analyst; b/Nov 12, 1950; h/2700 Wayside Dr, Evansville, IN 47711; ba/E'ville; p/George T Griffin (dec); Evelyn B Griffin, E'ville; ed/BA cum laude

Univ E'ville 1971; MEd Univ Louisville 1976; PhD Cand Univ Ky; pa/Computer Systems Analyst Gaither, Koewler, Rohlfer, Luckett & Co; APGA; Assn for Specialists in Group Work; cp/Mtl Hlth Assn in Vanderburgh Co: Bd Dirs, Chm Ed Com, Christmas Gift Lift Com, Public Policy Com; Wesselman Pk Nature Ctr Soc: Bd Dirs, Mbrship Chm; Jr Leag E'ville; E'ville CC; Petrol Clb; Vol SWn Ind Mtl Hlth Ctr; Daughs of Nile; OES; Others; r/Cath; hon/Grad Dean's Cit, Univ L'ville; Phi Kappa Phi; Kappa Mu Epislon; Alpha Lambda Delta; W/W in MW; Others.

GRIFFIN, KATHLEEN MARY oc/Speech-Language Pathologist; Audiologist; b/Oct 1, 1943; h/3343 Dent Pl NW, Washington, DC 20007; ba/Rockville, MD; p/Edward and Jean E Fleming, Milwaukee, WI; ed/BS Univ Wis; MA Stanford Univ; PhD Univ Oreg; pa/Dir Res & Profl Devel Dept; ASHA; cp/Altrusa Intl; r/Rom Cath; hon/Fellow, ASHA; Am Men & Wom Sci; W/W: Am Wom, E.

GRIFFIN, LUCILLE SLAUGHTER oc/Retired Teacher, Stock Broker, Insurance Representative, Farm Manager, Civic Leader, Businesswoman, Lecturer; b/Jun 3, 1911; h/633 Chestnut St, Henderson, KY 42420; m/Charlie Clay; c/Lawanna Ginger; p/John William and Eva Pearl H Slaughter; ed/Grad Bethel Col; Addit Studies: Wn Ky Univ, Univ Ky-Henderson, Univ Evansville; pa/Com Chm BPW Clb; cp/Life Mem Assoc'd Country Wom of World; Bd Dirs ARC; DAR: Local Ofcr 13 Yrs, Chapt Regent, Dir Ky's 1st Dist, Mem Ky Chapt Regent's Clb; OES; White Shrine; Past 1/VP Henderson Wom's Clb; Com Chm Garden Clb; Pres John William Slaughter Chapt Ky Soc US Daughs of 1812; Pres Henderson Music Clb; Ohio-Wabash Val Hist Soc: VP, Life Mem; VP Evening Belles Homemaker's Clb; Nat Hist Soc; Assocs of Smithsonian Inst; Nat Audubon Soc; U Daughs of Confed; Lectr; Others; r/Bapt: SS Tchr, Ch Libn, Pianist, Yg People's Supt, Dir VBS, Ch Coun; Others; hon/Ky Col; Named Nat Master Farm Homemaker 1963; Biogl Listings.

GRIFFIN, ROBERT P oc/United States Senator; b/Nov 6, 1923; ba/353 Russell Senate Ofc Bldg, Washington, DC 20510; m/Marjorie Anderson; c/Paul, Richard, James, Martha; p/J A and Beulah M Griffin; ed/AB, BS 1947, LLD 1963 Ctl Mich Univ; JD 1950, LLD 1973 Univ Mich; LLD: En Mich Univ 1969, Albion Col 1970, Wn Mich Univ 1971, Grand Val St Col 1971, Detroit Col Bus 1972, Detroit Col Law 1973; LHD Hillsdale Col 1970; JCD Rollins Col 1970; EdD No Mich Univ 1970; DPub Ser Detroit Inst Technol 1971; mil/AUS WWII, 71st Inf Div; pa/Pvt Pract Law Traverse City, Mich 1950-56; AMich St Bar; cp/Elected to Ho of Reps 1956, Re-elected 1958, 60, 62, 64; Appt'd to Senate 1966 (to fill open position), Elected 1966, 72; Mem Var Coms; Am Legion; Kiwanis Clb; Repub; r/Prot; 1 of 10 Outstg Yg Men Am, US JCs; Num Others.

GRIFFING, WILLIAM E oc/Motion Picture Producer; b/Jul 20, 1928; h/32 MacLeod Ln, Bloomfield, NJ 07003; ba/Orange, NJ; m/Janet; c/William, Cynthia, Russell, Tina; p/Chester Griffing (dec); Charlotte Griffing, Red Hook, NY; pa/Pres Creative Prodns Inc 26 Yrs; Scriptwriter; Cinematographer; Dir; r/Prot; hon/W/W in E.

GRIFFITH, CHARLES ALLEN oc/Physician; Clinical Professor; b/May 13, 1921; h/12806 NE 34th Pl, Bellevue, WA 98005; m/Dolores; c/Sharon, Judy, Debra, Patsy; p/C A and R P Griffith (dec); ed/BA; MS; MD; mil/AUS Maj; pa/Clin Prof Surg Univ Wash; Pioneer in Parietal & Selective Vagotomy; r/Epis; hon/Hon Recog for Contbns to Gastric Surg, World Cong Gastroenterology (Madrid) 1978.

GRIFFITH, ERNEST S oc/Editor; Writer; b/Nov 28, 1896; h/1941 Parkside Dr NW, Washington, DC 20012; ba/Same; m/Margaret D (dec); c/Margaret Earley (Mrs George), Alison Tennyson, Lawrence SC, Julia

Abernethy (Mrs David) (dec), Stephen L; p/George and Elizabeth Griffith (dec); ed/AB Hamilton; DPhil Oxford; LittD (Hon) WVa Wesleyan; LHD (Hon); pa/USN Aviation WWI; pa/Am Polit Sci Assn: Chm Res Com, VP; Nat Acad Public Adm; Dir Leg Ref Ser, US Cong; Pres Wash Coun Social Agys; US Nat Comm, UNESCO; r/Meth; Del to World Coun Chs; hon/Rhodes Scholar; Pi Kappa Alpha; Others.

GRIFFITH, MARGARET ARNOLD oc/Retired Piano Teacher; Homemaker; Free-lance Writer; Watercolorist; b/Feb 1, 1912; h/4324 Evergreen Ln, Annandale, VA 22003; ba/Same; m/Kelley E; c/Kelby E Jr, Ross A, Lynne G Marks; p/Herman Ross Arnold (dec); Sallie Curb Arnold, Annandale; ed/BA, MA; pa/Piano Tchr 1965-75; Free-lance Writer; Nat Leag Am Pen Wom; cp/Annandale PTA; cp/Annadae Bapt & Ravensworth Bapt Chs: Charter Mem; hon/Pub'd Author; Algernon Sydney Sullivan Awd, Judson Col; Art Awds; World W/W Wom.

GRIFFITH, MARY C oc/Attorney; h/1820 E Colfax Ave, Denver, CO 80218; ba/Denver; ed/BA 1938, JD 1941 Univ Col; mil/USNR Ret CDR, Gen Chm WAVE Reunion 1953; pa/Atty Law Ofcs John L Griffith-Mary C Griffith; Trustee Denver Bar Assn 1955-57; Mem Judic Coun St of Col 1957-58; BPW; cp/Bd Ethics for City Employees (Appt'd by Mayor); Former Mem: Colo Comm on Status of Wom, Wom's Adv Com on Def Manpower (Dept of Labor), Legal Aid Exec Bd, PEO Foun Fund for Colo, Bd YMCA; Altrusa Intl: Past 2/VP, Former Gov Dist 10, Former Chm Com; Others; r/1st Bapt Ch, Denver: Trustee 1947-50; hon/Delta Sigma Rho.

GRIFFITHS, DONALD MORGAN oc/-Artist; Gallery Owner; b/Jan 16, 1935; h/7225 Quail Rd, Fair Oaks, CA 95628; ba/Citrus Heights, CA; m/Alynne; c/Robin, Jeffrey, Donald; p/Harry D Griffiths (dec); Viola L Griffiths, Casa Grande, AZ; ed/BA 1967; MA 1970; mil/USMC 1952-55; pa/Art Dirs Clb, Sacramento, Cal; Phi Delta Kappa; Resident Artist Rio Linda Union Sch Dist; r/Epis; hon/Gold Medal Awd, Nat Competition (Watercolor); "Best of Show"; Artists USA; W/W: W, Am; Intl W/W Commun Ser; Men of Achmt.

GRIGGS, PATSY ANN oc/Nurse, Midwife; b/Apr 9, 1947; h/PO Box 3522 CRS, Johnson City, TN 37601; ba/Johnson City; p/Virgil Griggs (dec); Annie Griggs Brownfield; ed/Nsg Birmingham Bapt Hosp; Univ Ala-B; Nurse-Midwifery Ponce Dist Hosp, Ponce, PR; Internship Commun Hosp,

Springfield, Ohio; pa/Nurse TIOP Proj, Meml Hosp Inc; Instr ETSU Col Med, Dept Psychi; Am Col Nurse-Midwives; Am Nurses Assn; S Perinatal Assn; Am Public Hlth Assn; Tenn Nurses' Assn; NCNP Special Interest; Chperson Tenn Chapt ACNM; Interorg Affairs Com ACNM; Nurse-Midwifery Liaison to Tenn Nurses Assn; r/Bapt.

GRIGLAK, MARTIN SAMUEL oc/Labor Union Executive; b/Jan 13, 1927; h/206 S Ninth St, Connellsville, PA 15425; ba/C'ville; m/Rita J Pernatozzi; c/Nancy Ann, Martin J, James R, Janet Lee; p/Martin A Griglak (dec); Fannie R Nieberg (dec); ed/Att'd: Waynesburg & Pa St Cols; r/USN 1944-46; pa/Active Arbitrator 13 Yrs; Collegiate Lectr; Public

Spkr; Former Exec Secy Fdn Telephone Wkrs Pa; cp/Bd Mem C'ville Hosp; Former Chm Dem Party; Former Planning & Zoning Commr; Redevel & Urban Renewal; Others; r/Rom Cath; hon/Num Plaques & Awds for Outstg Ser to Commun; DIB; Men of Achmt; Commun Ldrs & Noteworthy Ams; W/W.

GRIGSBY, RONALD DAVIS oc/Associate Professor; b/Feb 28, 1936; h/3707 Warren Cir, Bryan, TX 77801; ba/College Station, TX; m/Nancy Jane; c/Lynn E, Brian P, Debra C, David R, Steven A, Jonathan C, Sara J; p/Logan Charles and Helen Dorothy Davis Grigsby (dec); ed/BS (Zool), BS (Chem), PhD Univ Okla; pa/Assoc Prof Biochem Tex A&M Univ; Charter Mem Am Soc for Mass Spectrometry; Alpha Chi Sigma; Am Chem Soc; NY Acad Scis; SW Sci Forum; IPA; hon/Phi Lambda Upsilon; Sigma Xi; Vis Scist, Atlantic Reg Lab, Nat Res Coun of Canada, Halifax, Nova Scotia 1973-74.

GRILLOT, FRANCIS A JR oc/Marketing Manager; b/Feb 3, 1935; h/1841 Center Dr, Carpentersville, IL 60110; ba/Arlington Heights, IL; m/Mary Ellen; c/Timothy, Tammy, Jacqueline, Janetta; p/Francis Grillot (dec); Eleanor Grillet, Parsons, KS; ed/AA Parsons Jr Col; BSChE Ks St Univ; MS Wichita St Univ; mil/USAR 1954-62; pa/NSPE; AIChE; WPCF; AWWA; cp/Lions; Repub Com; r/Rom Cath.

GRIMES, DOREEN oc/University Professor; b/Feb 1, 1932; h/3202 Lindenwood, San Angelo, TX 76901; ba/San Angelo; p/Clarence and Berta Keaton Grimes, San Angelo; ed/BMus 1949, MMus 1950 So Meth Univ; PhD N Tex St Univ 1966; pa/Angelo St Univ: Prof, Chm Fac Senate; Bd Dirs Tex Assn Music Schs; Composer 250+ Musical Works incl'g "Mass of the Good Shepherd"; Tex Music Edrs Assn; Tex Music Tchrs Assn; Tex Theory Assn; Soc for Music Theory; Col Music Tchrs; MENC; Sigma Alpha Iota; Phi Kappa Phi; cp/Past Pres Dist 11 Tex Fdn Music Clbs; Precnt Secy Dem Party; r/Meth; Organist-Choirmaster Epis Ch of Good Shepherd, San Angelo 6 Yrs; hon/S'ship Est'd in Her Hon, Weatherford Col, W'ford (Tex) 1978; Wom of Yr, ENMU.

GRINSTEAD, AUDREY HUDSON oc/Director of Guidance; b/Nov 9, 1926; h/666 Timberlake Dr, Danville, VA 24541; ba/Danville; p/Arthur F Hudson (dec); Minnie B Hudson, Virgilina, VA; ed/BS; MEd; pa/Golden Leaf Chapt VPGA; VSCA; VACES; VPGA; APGA; BPW Clb; cp/Colonial Garden Clb; Timberlake Wom's Clb; r/N Fork Bapt Ch; hon/Delta Kappa Gamma; Phi Delta Kappa.

GRINSTEAD, LEONARD S oc/Electrical Engineer; b/Dec 27, 1939; h/245 Sleepy Hollow Dr, Canfield, OH 44406; ba/Warren, OH; m/Patricia A; c/Leonard Mark, Mary Patricia; p/Sylvester L Grinstead (dec); Dorothy Grinstead, Youngstown, OH; ed/AAS; mil/USN 1957-60; pa/AISE; TCIMA; ASM; r/Cath.

GRISSETT, J RAY oc/Consultant; Minister; b/Aug 29, 1931; h/616 Cherry St, Jackson, MS 39205; ba/Jackson; m/Thelma Saucier; c/Jerry Ray Jr, Jayne, Michal Thresa; p/A F and Mary E Grissett, Hattiesburg, MS; ed/BA; BD; MDiv; pa/Min Miss Bapt Conv Bd; Owner J & G Cattle Corp; Bd Dirs Wax USA; cp/Rotary Clb, Ofcr, Former Com

Mem; Masonic Order; Exec Com BSA; r/So Bapt: Pastor; hon/Cit for Spec Ser, Red Cross; Gideons Intl Cert; Order of Arrow Awd, BSA.

GRKOVIC, GEORGE M (SKIP) oc/Public Administrator; b/Jun 1, 1946; h/PO Box 96, Grand Junction, CO 81501; ba/Grand Junction; p/George and Eugenia V Grkovic, Leesburg, VA; ed/BS Colo St Univ 1971; MPA Univ Colo 1978; pa/Assoc Dir Wn Colo, Colo Dept of Local Affairs; Am Soc for Public Adm; r/Epis; hon/Colo Grad Merit Scholar.

GROAH, LINDA KAY oc/Nursing Director; b/Oct 5, 1942; h/5 Mateo Dr, Tiburon, CA 94920; ba/San Francisco, CA; m/Patrick Andrew; c/Nadine, Maureen, Patrick, Marcus, Kimberly; p/Joseph D and Irma J Rozek, Cedar Rapids, IA; ed/BA; pa/Univ Cal-SF: Nsg Dir Operating & Recovery Rooms 1974-, Clin Instr Dept Biodysfunction 1975-; Dir Postgrad Course Operating Room Nsg (6-Month Course, Annual) 1978-; Dir Operating Rooms Med Ctr Ctl Ga, Macon, Ga 1973-74; Asst Dir Nsg Ser Michael Reese Hosp, Chicago, Ill 1969-73; Other Former Positions; Am Nurses Assn; Assn of Operating Room Nurses; Nat Leag for Nsg; Num Ofcs Held; Conslt; Am Cynamid Co Nurse Panel 1969-; Ednl Mat Proj Appraisal Panel, Nat Lib Med (Avline) 1977-; Operating Room Res Inst, Fairnwood, NJ 1978-; Other Profl Activs; cp/Redwood HS PTA; hon/World W/W Wom; W/W Am Wom; Pub'd Author.

GRODBERG, MARCUS GORDON oc/Technical Director; h/111 Hyde St, Newton, MA 02161; ba/Needham, MA; m/Shirley M; c/Joel, Kim, Jeremy; p/Isaac and Rosalie Grodberg (dec); ed/AB Clark Univ 1944; MS Univ Ill 1948; pa/Tech Dir Hoyt Lab, Div Colgate-Palmolive Co; Sponsor Num Sci Studies; Mem Num Dental, Med & Profl Socs; cp/Vol UF; r/Jewish; hon/Patentee; Cert of Merit for Dist'd Ser to Ldrship in Pharm Res; Ellis S'ship.

GRODMAN, PYRRHA GLADYS oc/Certified Pathologist; ba/PO Box 853, Monroe, LA 71201; ed/MD Wom Med 1948; pa/Pathologist & Dir Labs Monroe Med Diagnostic Labs 1965-, St Joseph's Inf, Atlanta & Med Diag Res Labs, Atlanta 1962; Other Former Positions: Conslt Pathologist: Conway Hosp, Monroe, Madison Parish Hosp, Tallulah, La; Clin Assoc Dept Pathologist (Ore) 19557-57 Instr Dept Pathol Emory 1958-; AMWA; Am Assn Med Instrumentation; AGerS; AABB; RCP (Eng); Am Assn Abdom Surgs; Intl Med Wom's Assn; Am Soc Cytology; Air Medics Med Aviation Assn; AMA; SMA; CAP; ASCP; PAMA; Royal Soc Hlth (F); Others; hon/Dir Med Specialists.

GRODY, WILLIAM CHARLES oc/Educator; b/Jan 16, 1948; h/1505 Concord Pl 3A, Kalamazoo, MI 49009; ba/Hopkins, MI; p/William P and Elsie Betty Grody, Union Pier, MI; ed/BA 1970, MA 1978 Wn Mich Univ; pa/MEA; NEA; Chief Negotiator HEA; cp/Del to St Polit Conv; Sum Rec Prog Coor; Advr Close-Up Prog; hon/Former Mem Kappa Delta Pi.

GROGAN, JAMES TILLMAN JR oc/Dentist; b/Sept 30, 1938; h/1800 Tennyson, Arlington, TX 76013; ba/Arlington; m/Lynn; c/James III, Dawn; p/J T and Allene Grogan, Bloomburg, TX; ed/BA NTSU 1961; DDS Baylor Univ 1965; Dipl Criswell Bible Inst Theol 1974; mil/Capt 1965-68; Nat Def Ser Medal; pa/ADA; TDA; AGD; AES; AOS; cp/Kiwanis Clb; Masonic Lodge; Scottish Rite; York Rite; Shrine; NTSU Alumni Assn; r/1st Bapt Ch: Deacon, SS Tchr; hon/Fellow, Acad Gen Dentistry; Biogl Listings.

GROGAN, STANLEY JOSEPH JR oc/Educator; Executive; b/Jan 14, 1925; h/2585 Moraga Dr, Pinole, CA 94564; ba/Same; m/Mary Skroch; c/Mary Maureen; p/Col and Mrs Stanley J Grogan, Washington, DC; ed/AA 1949, BS 1950, MA 1955 Am Univ; MS Cal St-H 1973; EdD Nat Christian

Univ 1973; mil/USAFR, Ret'd Col, WWII, Korea; Air Medal (2 OLC); UN Ser Medal; Korean Ser Medal; pa/Pres SJG Assocs Intl, Commun Specialists; Profl Lectr; Commun Prof Nat Univ Grad Studies, Belize; Acad Inst Course, Ala; Aerospace Writers Assn; Others; cp/Sr Mem CAP; Oakland-Fukuoka Sister City Soc; San Francisco Ad Clb; Commonwealth Clb Cal; hon/Cit, Repub of Korea; Cert, Comm Rel Germany; Outstg Sec'dy Edr; Biogl Listings.

GROSECLOSE, ELGIN oc/International Financial Consultant; Author; b/Nov 25, 1899; h/4813 Woodway Ln NW, Washington, DC 20016; ba/Wash DC; m/Louise Williams; c/Sarah Theodoropoulos (Mrs Peter), Nancy Witherspoon (Mrs Herold), Hildegarde Bender (Mrs Earl), Suzy Labaugh (Mrs Kenneth); p/Manasseh Clarence and Della Groseclose (dec); ed/AB 1920; MA 1924; PhD 1928; pa/Fin Conslt 1944-; Author Books & Articles; Nat Economists Clb; r/Epis; hon/Nat Book Awd; Near E Medal; W/W in World.

GROSS, EMILY GERTRUDE oc/Piano Instructor; Church Organist; b/Apr 12, 1925; h/104 Turtle Creek, Waco, TX 76710; ba/Same; m/Francis Burdett; c/Ronald (dec), Timothy; p/William Lowrey (dec); Alma G Lowrey Lyon; ed/AA; BMus; MMus; pa/Nat Piano Guild; Nat Music Tchrs Assn; Pres Waco Music Tchrs Assn 1974-76; Theory Com Tex Music Tchrs Assn 1977-78; Organist-Choir Dir: 1st Meth, Morristown (Tenn) 1946, Westminster Presb, Waco 1963-66; Organist: Lake Shore Hills Presb 1967-77, 1st Luth, Waco 1978; cp/DAR; UDC; r/Presb; hon/Finalist Tchrs Div, Intl Piano Recording Competition; Pub'd Author; Biogl Listings.

GROSS, JAMES DEHNERT oc/Pathologist; b/Nov 15, 1929; h/54 Sunset Dr, Streator, IL 61364; ba/Streator; p/Max A Gross (dec); Marion Riehm, Hudson Lake, IN; ed/BS w hons Univ Chattanooga 1951; MD Vanderbilt Univ 1955; Addit Studies; mil/USN 1955-68, Adv'd to LCDR, MC; pa/St Mary's Hosp, Streator: Instr Cont'g Med Ed Prog 1974-, Dir Labs 1962-; Chief of Lab US Nav Hosp, Memphis, Tenn 1959-62; Instr Dept Pathol & Microbiol Univ Tenn Med Sch, Memphis 1960-62; Other Former Positions; Fellow: Col Am Pathologists, Assn Clin Scists (Fdg Fellow), Am Soc Clin Pathologists; AMA; Ill Med Soc; LaSalle Co Med Soc; Pathologist Advr Ill Med Technologists Assn, Joliet Br 1967-68; Others; cp/Advr ARC; Former Mem Rotary Clb; Ks of C; Others; r/Cath; Parish Coun St Anthony's Ch, Streator 1969-72; hon/Col & Univ Valedictorian; Univ Chatta: Blue Key, Voted "Most Likely to Succeed" (by Student Body), Best Pledge (Sigma Chi), Others; Profl Pubs; Biogl Listings.

GROSS, JOHN HAMMES oc/Research Director; b/Jan 27, 1923; h/1766 Mountainview Dr, Monroeville, PA 15146; ba/M'ville; m/Phyllis J; c/Jeffrey J; p/Charles F Gross (dec); Anna E Gross, Bethlehem, PA; ed/BS; MS; PhD; mil/USNR WWII, Ofcr; pa/Dir Res US Steel Corp (Res Lab); ASM; ASTM; IRI; Sigma Xi; cp/M'ville Hosp Auth; r/U Ch of Christ: Lay Min; hon/Comfort A Adams Lecture, ASM Fellow.

GROSSNICKLE, WILLIAM FOSTER oc/Professor; b/Mar 19, 1930; h/1105 Oakview Dr, Greenville, NC 27834; ba/G'ville; m/Betty Depp; c/Carol Anne, Mark Earl; p/Foster E Grossnickle, Melbourne, FL; Blanche D Grossnickle (dec); ed/BA; MA; PhD; mil/AUS; pa/E Carolina Univ: Prof Psychol 1970-, Assoc Prof 1965-70; Instr (Pt-time) Geo Washington Univ 1963-65; Corporate Employmt Mgr Blue Bell Inc, Greensboro, NC 1958-62; Other Former Positions; APA, Divs 8, 14; Var Ofcs & Coms, SEn & NC Psychol Assns; Am Soc Tng & Devel 1974-77, Current Mem En NC Chapt; Conslt; r/Meth; hon/Sigma Xi; Psi Chi; Delta Phi Alpha; Profl Pubs; Biogl Listings.

GROSVENOR, GERALDINE oc/Scholar; Poet; Researcher in Early American History;

b/Aug 21, 1918; h/10799 Sherman Grove Ave, #39, Sunland, CA 91040; c/Larry Dennis, Richard Lynn; p/William Bennett and Lavinia Ruth Lay Grosvenor; pa/Pt-Owner Hunn Engrg Mfg; Am Fgn Ser 1967-76; Fgn Affairs 1966-67; Am Acad Arts & Scis 1964-65; World Affairs Coun, LA Chapt 1963-75; MIT 1975-76; Atlantic Coun US 1974-75, Previous Mbrship 1967-75; Am Public Hlth Assn; NATO; Inst World Affairs: USC, March AFB; UN, LA; Ensalen Inst; Viewpoints Inst; Carnegie Endowmt for Intl Conciliatory Peace; Cal Pan Am Assn; Pan Am Union; Cal Fdn Chaparall Poets; Santa Monica Writers Clb; Hollywood Pen Wom; Poets Haven; Franklin Mint: 3 Yr Mem, Gold Pin; LA Area ABMAC; Intl Soc for Gen Semantics (DATA); Univ Denver Sch Intl Studies (Africa); UCLA-Univ Ext Painters, Poets, Artists; Am Col of Arms; Am Forestry Assn; Propylean Soc; Nat Soc Arts & Lttrs; LA Chapt, Santa Monica Chapt; Fellow Royal Soc St George, England; Psychedelic Review; WAIF; Huntington Lib Rare Books Readers Clb; Augustan Soc; U Inventors & Scists; Pres Circle, LA; Am Judic Soc; Patroness: Libs, LA Ctl Lib, Morningside Park Lib; Acad Polit Sci, Columbia Univ; H S Truman Lib: Hon Fellow, Bronze Pres Medal; Hon, Inst for Intl Policy; Others; cp/Music Ctr Fdrs Circle; Hollywood Wilshire Symph; Cult Clb Cal; Save the Redwoods Leag; Chds Bapt Home So Cal; Num Geneal Socs; Variety Clb; Mayors Coun for Intl Visitors & Sister Cities; Nat Travel Clb; Sev Woms Clbs; Intl Soc Toastmistressess of Inglewood; Smithsonian Inst Fdrs Circle; US Olympic Soc; Hon Mem, Bronze Pin, Silver Medalist; Others; r/Prot; Evang Crusades Inc; hon/Hon Certs Recog & Apprec, U Inventors & Scists for Res in Fields of Nuclear Physics & Astro-Physical Deductions; Hon Cert: ASIL, APHA; Gold Seal Cert, Hon, Acad Polit Sci, Columbia Univ; Am Biogl Inst; Notable Ams Bicent Era; Am Scholars; Town & Gown, USC; W/W: Am Wom, Cal; DIB; World W/W Wom; IPA; Others.

GROTJAHN, MARTIN oc/Psychoanalyst; Psychotherapist; b/Jul 8, 1904; ba/416 N Bedford Dr, Beverly Hills, #209, CA 90210; m/Etelka; c/Michael; p/Alfred and Charlotte Grotjahn; ed/MD; Tng Analyst; mil/AUS Maj; pa/Prof Emeritus Univ So Cal; hon/Sigmund Freud Awd; Diplomate, Bd Psychi.

GROUT, GERALDINE ISABEL oc/College Professor; Editor; b/Jun 16, 1923; h/Main St, South Lancaster, MA 01561; m/John Marshall; p/Ashley G and Lula E R Hale (dec); ed/BS, MEd Boston Univ; EdD Ind Univ; pa/Lic'd Nsg Home Admr; Editor Atlantic Union Gleaner; Prof; Nat Bus Ed Assn; AAUP; Nat Registry Med Secys; r/SDA; hon/Pi Omega Pi; Delta Pi Epsilon; Fellow: Am Col Nsg Home Admrs, Am Acad Med Admrs, Intercont Biogl Assn; Biogl Listings.

GROVES, MORTON DAN PATRICK oc/Product Manager; Educator; Investor; b/Mar 20, 1940; h/14091 Saratoga Ave, Saratoga, CA 95070; ba/Santa Clara, CA; m/Kathryn Susan Stern; p/Truman Algie and Rita Arline Nichols Groves, Matador, TX;

ed/BA 1961, BSEE 1962, MSEE 1964, PhD 1967 Rice Univ; mil/USNR LCDR; pa/IEEE; ACM; AOC; USNI; AOPA; cp/Foothill Col DP Adv Bd; Mason; r/Prot; hon/Sigma Xi, Nat Merit Scholar; Fellow NSF.

GRUBER, JEROME MARTIN oc/Mechanical Engineer; b/Jul 21, 1919; h/711 Cheyenne Dr, Franklin Lakes, NJ 07417; ba/Wayne, NJ; m/Dale Ann Perrett; c/Jerome M Jr, William J, Jeanne M, James B, Suzanne J, Judith A; p/John Francis and Anna Marie H Gruber (dec); ed/BS Univ Wis 1941; mil/AUS Corps of Engrs 1941-46; pa/Reg'd Profl Engr: Mass, Wis, NJ; Life Mem Soc Nav Arch & Marine Engrs; Fellow Am Soc ME; Am Soc Nav Engrs; Am Soc Lubrication Engrs; hon/ASME Dist'd Ser Awd; Life Mem, SNAME; Bronze Star, AUS.

GRUBERG, MARTIN oc/Professor; b/Jan 28, 1935; h/247 Sullivan St, Oshkosh, WI 54901; ba/Oshkosh; m/Rosaline; p/Benjamin Gruberg (dec); Mollie Gruberg, New York, NY; ed/BA; PhD; pa/Univ Wis: Prof Polit Sci, Former Chm Polit Sci Dept; Other Acad Positions; Agt Adjudicator US St Dept (NY Passport Agy) 1960-61; AAUP: St Secy 1975-79, Pres Chapt 1972-73, Secy UW-O Chapt 1973-74, 1974-77; Wis Polit Sci Assn:

Pres 1974-75, VP & Prog Chm 1973-74; Panelist Am Polit Sci Assn ("Wom & Public Policy") 1975; Conslt; Other Profl Activs; cp/Past Pres Oshkosh Human Rts Coun; hon/Author Wom in Am Polits, 1968; Other Profl Pubs; Grantee; Grad Cum Laude; NYS S'ship; Student Govt Maj Awd; CCNY Hist Dept Del to 6th Student Conf on US Affairs; Buckvar Awd; Steigman Awd; Book Cited by US Supreme Ct; Biogl Listings.

GRUE, LEE MEITZEN oc/Poet; Forum Director; b/Feb 8, 1934; h/828 Lesseps St, New Orleans, LA 70117; m/Ronald David; c/Celeste, Ian, Teal; p/LeRoy and Bernice McCullar Meitzen (dec); ed/BA Univ New Orleans 1963; pa/Dir NO Poetry Forum; Dir NEA Poet's Rdg Series 1977; cp/Lit Coor Wom's Arts Fest 1978; hon/Mayor's Key to NO; 1st Prize (Short Story), Deep South Writer's Conf; W/W in Wom; Poets & Writers Dir.

GRUNDY, J(OHN) OWEN oc/Archivist; Journalist; b/Mar 8, 1911; ba/Jersey City Public Lib, 472 Jersey Ave, Jersey City, NJ 07302; p/J Owen and Julia E Salter Grundy; ed/Student Cooper Union; pa/Archivist JC Public Lib 1968-; City Histn, JC 1973-; Spec Asst to Mayor; Lectr in Field; Adj Polit Sci JC St Col 1976; Pres & Editor Greenwich Village News 1959-61; Other Former Positions; Chm Mun Hist Dists Comm, JC; cp/Fdr & Secy Greenwich Village Fresh Air Fund; Trustee Spec Social Sers (NYC); Pres JC Mus; Others; hon/Recipient Var Commun Ser Awds; Hon Mem, Phi Alpha Theta; Author History of Jersey City, 1976, Articles & Monographs; W/W in E.

GRUNKEMEYER, FLORENCE BERNADETTE oc/Professor; b/Jan 19, 1928; h/-1520 W Main St, Muncie, IN 47303; ba/-Muncie; p/Frank J and Rose C Grunkemeyer, Batesville, IN; ed/BS 1963, MS 1965 Ind Univ; PhD Ohio St Univ 1971; pa/Prof Bus Ed & Ofc Adm Ball St Univ; ABCA; DPE; N-CBEA; NBEA; IBEA; IVA; Chm Dept Communs ad hoc Com; r/St Mary's of the Rock Cath Ch, Batesville: Mem; St Mary's Cath Ch, Muncie: Mem; hon/FBLA-PBL: St Chm Emeritus, St Advr 1972-76, St Chm 1976-78.

GUENTHER, CHARLES JOHN oc/Poet; Translator; Educator; b/Apr 29, 1920; h/2935

Russell Blvd, St Louis, MO 63104; m/Esther G Klund; c/Charles J Jr, Cecile, Christine; p/Charles R and Hulda C S Guenther (dec); ed/AA Harris Tchrs Col; BA, MA Webster Col; pa/MW Reg VP Poetry Soc Am; Past Pres: Mo Writers' Guild 1973-74, St Louis Writers' Guild 1959, 1976-77, St Louis Poetry Ctr 1974-76, Gtr St Louis Chapt Spec Libs Assn 1969-70; Dir McKendree Writers' Conf 1969-73; hon/Cmdr, Order of Merit, Italian Republic 1973; James Joyce Awd, Poetry Soc Am; Mo Lib Assn Literary Awd.

GUERRANT, DORIS JEANNE oc/-Psychologist; b/Sept 23, 1931; h/2415 S Jefferson St, Roanoke, VA 24014; ba/-Roanoke; c/Priscilla Jeanne, Diana Nadine, Douglas Gordon, Margaret Anne; p/William Speer (dec); Matilda Eichhorn; ed/BA cum laude Roanoke Col 1968; MS Radford Col 1972; pa/Psychologist OMNI House; APA; Va Psychol Assn, Chm Public Relats Comm; r/Presb.

GUGLIELMINO, PAUL JOSEPH oc/Professor; b/May 19, 1942; h/734 Marble Way, Boca Raton, FL 33432; ba/Boca Raton; m/Lucy Margaret; c/Joseph Allen, Margaret Rose; p/Carl and Rose Guglielmino; ed/BA; MA; DEd; mil/USAR Capt; pa/Dir & Asst Prof Ctr for Mgmt & Profl Devel Col Bus & Public Adm, Fla Atl Univ 1977-; Pres Guglielmino & Assocs (Mgmt Conslt'g Firm) 1978-; Proj Coor Nat Endowmt for Humanities Grant 1977; Grad Tchg Asst Col

Bus Adm Univ Ga 1974-76; Owner Natly Franchised Ser Bus, Savannah Area & St of Ga 1971-74; Other Former Positions; Am Soc for Tng & Devel: Nat Mem, Bd Dirs, Broward/Palm Bch Chapt; Nat Univ Ext Assn; Am Mktg Assn; Adult Ed Assn US; Former Assoc Mem Public Relats Soc Am; Former Mem Am Col Relats Assn; Lectr; Var Profl Presentations; hon/Univ Ga: Doct Tchg Asst'ship, Master's Level Res Asst'ship; Pub'd Author; Biogl Listings.

GUHL, DALE THANE oc/Salesman; Poet; Public Relations; b/Oct 2, 1911; h/407 Fifth St, New Cumberland, PA 17070; p/George and Carrie E Guhl (dec); ed/Vet WWII; pa/Bus Rep Retail Clerks Union, Local 1436, Harrisburg, Pa; Past Pres Pa Poetry Soc; Current Pres Keysner Poets; Del to H'burg Area Arts Coun; H'burg Area Adult Ed Coun; H'burg Ctl Labor Coun; York Co Ctl Labor Coun; r/Luth; hon/Author Volume of Poetry *Turn Your Dogs Loose*, Winner of Va-Burley Miller Meml Awd; Other Prizes.

GUILLAUME, ALFRED JOSEPH JR oc/University Professor, Dean; b/Apr 10, 1947; h/7361 Cranbrook Dr, New Orleans, LA 70128; ba/NO; m/Bernice Forrest; c/Alfred Joseph III; p/Alfred Joseph Sr and Anna Trena Saizon Guillaume, NO; ed/BA; AM; PhD; mil/AUS; pa/Xavier Univ La: Dean Freshman Studies & Admissions, Asst Prof French; Am Assn Tchrs of French; S Ctl Mod Lang Assn; Col Lang Assn; Am Assn Collegiate Registrars & Admissions Ofcrs; Nat Assn Col Deans & Registrars; r/Rom Cath; hon/Fulbright-Hays Lang Tchg Asst'ship (Marseilles, France) 1974-75; Recipient F'ships; French Govt Awd, Xavier Univ La; Pub'd Author.

GUINIER, EWART oc/Professor; b/May 17, 1910; h/29 Robinson St, Cambridge, MA 02138; ba/Cambridge; m/Eugenia Paprin;

c/Clothilde Yvonne, Lani, Sary, Marie; p/Howard Manoah Guinier (dec); Marie French, Brooklyn, NY; ed/BS cum laude; MA; JD; mil/AUS 1942-46; pa/Prof Afro-Am Studies Harvard Univ; Life Mem Nat Bd Assn for Study of Afro-Am Life & Hist; Org Am Hist; cp/Life Mem NAACP; Alpha Phi Alpha; hon/Hon AM, Harvard Univ; Carter G Woodson Awd.

GULATI, JAGJIT oc/Data Processing Administrator; b/Oct 8, 1939; h/4017 Ridgedale Dr, Greensboro, NC 27405; ba/G'boro; m/Margaret Prevtt; c/Annita Belle; p/Mithe Shah Gulati (dec); Sita Devi Gulati; ed/BEd; MA (Lit); MA (Eng); pa/DPMA; Former Mem ACM; Chm DBA Team; cp/Mem Woodridge Assn, G'boro; r/Hindu; hon/1st & 2nd Prizes, Poster Painting.

GULLAN, ANN MARY oc/Associate Professor; b/Jul 4, 1913; h/Quincy, IL 62301; ba/18th Col, Quincy; p/Anthony and Theodosia Gullan (dec); ed/BS Viterbo Col 1952; MEd Marquette Univ 1960; Postgrad Work; pa/Quincy Col: Assoc Prof Ed & Dir Rdg Ctr 1968-, Originator Rdg Ctr; Mt Senario Col, Ladysmith, Wis 1960-68: Acad Dean, Pres; Other Former Positions; Miss Val Rdg Coun; Ill Rdg Coun; IRA; Col Instrs Rdg Profls; Nat Assn for Study of Ed; Conducted Profl Wkshops; Rdg Conslt to Sev Public Sch Systems; Fed'd BPW Clb; r/Rom Cath; hon/Huck Awd for Sers to Quincy Commun; Leg Cit, St of Wis; Biogl Listings.

GULNAC, JON CRAWFORD oc/Minister; h/Box 196, RD4, Johnstown, PA 15905; ba/Same; m/Kathryn Suzanne Greer; c/-Rebekah Ellen; p/Harry E Gulnac, Ridgway, PA; Dorothy E Gulnac (dec); ed/BA; MDiv; pa/Former Min-at-Large Frankin Dist Coun on Mins; Substitute Tchr; cp/Vol Fireman; r/U Meth; hon/W/W in Rel; Commun Ldrs & Noteworthy Ams.

GUMER, INDERPAL SINGH oc/Estimating Engineer; b/Oct 17, 1942; h/5507 Edgebrook Forest, Houston, TX 77088; ba/Houston; m/Manjit Kaur; c/Saminderpaul Singh, Anjleen Kaur; p/Prem Singh and Harbans Kaur, Ludhiana, India; ed/BS 1971; MS 1973; pa/Estimating Engr Bechtel Power Corp, Houston; cp/Treas Sikh Ctr of Gulf Coast Area 1978; r/Sikhism; hon/Senator, Univ Student Govt 1970-71.

GUNDERSON, GERALDINE MAXINE oc/Registered Nurse; b/Jan 11, 1921; h/2019 Philo Rd, Urbana, IL 61801; ba/Urbana; ed/Dipl & Cert Eagle Grove Jr Col 1940; Dipl Luth Deaconess Sch Nsg 1945; BS Univ Minn 1950; MS Drake Univ 1971; pa/Reg'd Nurse Carle Foun Hosp, Urbana; Dept Hd Nsg Indian Hills Commun Col, Ottumwa, Ia 1976-77; Floor Nurse Luth Gen Hosp, Park Ridge, Ill 1973-76; Instr Gyn & Endocrinol Ia Meth Hosp, Des Moines, Ia 1964-66; Other Former Positions; Am Nsg Assn; Secy of St Gen Duty Nurses Ia 1958-59; Nat Leag Nurses; Ia Nurses Assn; IPA; cp/Pres Luth Daughs of Reformation; Pres Luth Leag; r/Am Luth Ch; hon/Contbr to Var Pubs; Biogl Listings.

GUNN, MARY LAURA oc/Sister of Religious Order; Hospital Administrator; b/Jan 20, 1927; h/1006 Ford Ave, Owensboro, KY 42301; ba/O'boro; p/John F and Selmena D Gunn (dec); ed/BS Our Lady of Cincinnati Col 1951; MHosp Adm St Louis Univ 1960; Addit Studies; pa/Admr Our Lady of Mercy Hosp, O'boro; St Mary's Meml Hosp, Knoxville, Tenn: Admr 1963-66, Asst Admr & Pers Dir 1960-63, Instr Sch Nsg 1952-56; Other Former Positions; Bd Dirs Tri-St Hlth Planning Coun 1970-76; Green River Mtl Hlth-Mtl Retard Adv Coun 1970-; Am & Cath Hosp Assns; Am Col Hosp Admrs; Hlth Adv Bd Sisters of Mercy, Province Cinc; Trustee Ky Hosp Assn; cp/Bd Dirs: Wn Ky Reg Blood Bk, O'boro C of C; Bd Mem O'boro-Daviess Co Mtl Hlth Assn; Exec Com Coun of Commun Sers Execs; Mem Green River Dist Sub-Area Adv Coun-Ky-HSA-W; O'boro Tourist Comm; Other Civic Activs; r/Rom Cath; Mem Sisters of Mercy, Louisville, Ky Inc 1976-; hon/Ky Col; Biogl Listings.

GUNN, WILLIE COSDENA THOMAS oc/Counselor; b/Dec 24, 1926; h/1511 Church St, Flint, MI 48503; m/Willie James; c/John Henderson III; p/Fletcher Sr and Mattie Gideon, Seneca, SC; ed/BS Benedict Col; MEd Univ Mich; Master's Guid & Cnslg Univ Mich; Further Studies; pa/Guid Cnslr Flint Open Sch; Pt-time Instr Social Sci Dept Mott Commun Col; Former Fin Asst VA Hosp, Ann Arbor, Mich; Emerson Jr HS: Former Tchr Sci, Eng, Social Studies & Civics, Guid Cnslr; Nat Coun Social Studies; Mich Coun Tchrs Eng; Negro Hist Assn; Nat Bd Nat Assn Media Wom, VP Flint Chapt; Life Mem Nat Assn Negro BPW Clbs Inc; U Tchrs Flint; Mich Ed Assn; NEA; Genesee Area Pers & Guid Assn; Mich Sch Cnslrs Assn; Mich Pers & Guid Assn;s Mich Assn Wom Deans & Cnslrs; AAUW; cp/Life Mem Zeta Phi Beta; Past Pres Gamma Delta Chapt Phi Delta Kappa; Former Mem Bd Dirs Urban Leag; Past Pres Urban Leag Guild; Former Bd Mem NAACP; Past Pres Interracial Discussion Group Flint; Mich Alcohol Studies Alumni Assn; Past VP Dort-Oak Park Neighborhood House Coun; Secy Just Us Bridge Clb; Others; r/Christ F'ship Bapt Ch: Past Pres Bd Ed, Mem & Asst Dir Mass Choir, Others; hon/Recipient Var S'ships; Cert of Achmt in Res on Alcoholism, Univ Wis; Outstg Contbn in Flint Voter Registration Dr; Commun Ser Awd, Mar of Dimes; Key to City, Flint; Citizen of Month; Tchr of Month; Biogl Listings; Num Others.

GUNNIN, BILL LEE oc/Structural Engineer; b/Jan 19, 1943; h/432 Lowell Ln, Richardson, TX 75080; ba/Dallas, TX; m/Virginia Murphy; c/Michael, Christopher;

p/Royce Gerald Gunnin (dec); Mary Morrow Gunnin, Dallas; ed/BS 1965; MS 1967; PhD 1970; pa/Reg'd Profl Engr Tex Am Soc CE; Am Concrete Inst.

GUNNINGS, THOMAS SYLVESTER oc/Professor; b/Assistant Dean; b/Feb 8, 1935; h/1000 Blanchette Dr, East Lansing, MI 48823; ba/E Lansing; m/Barbara Bryd; c/Sonya Renita; p/Garfield and Marie Gunnings, Gastonia, NC; ed/BA Winston Salem Tchrs Col; MEd Oreg St Univ; PhD Univ Oreg; pa/Mich St Univ: Prof Psychi, Asst Dean Col Human Med, Exec Dir Urban Cnslg Mtl Hlth Prog; APA; APGA; Chm Awds Com; Bd Dirs Assn Non-White Concerns in Pers & Guid; Assn Black Psychologists; Nat & Mich Alliances Black Sch Edrs; Mich Assn Black Psychols; Nat Coun Med Edrs; cp/Operation PUSH; NAACP; r/Bapt; hon/Gov's City; Prof Ser Awd; Commun Ldrs & Noteworthy Ams; W/W: MW, Hlth Care.

GUNTER, EVELYN COLEMAN oc/-Minister; Marriage Counselor; Teacher; b/-Dec 18, 1919; h/1321 Sun Swept Dr, Union City, TN 38261; m/J H Sr (dec); c/John Herbert Jr (dec); p/Charlie and Frances Coleman (dec); ed/BS cum laude Bethel Col 1965; Spec Ed Cert Memphis St Univ; pa/Ret'd Tchr Spec Ed; NEA; TEA; Min's Assemblies of God; Home Missionary; Conslt Spec Ed; cp/4-H Clb Ldr; PTA; r/Assemblies of God; hon/Jaycette S'ship; Top Tchr Spec Ed, Tenn; HS Valedictorian; Personalities of S; Commun Ldrs & Noteworthy Ams; Others.

GUNTER, LESTER WILLIAM oc/Artist; h/1764 Bartow Ave, Bronx, NY 10469; ed/Jamaica Sch of Art; Art Students League of

NY; Nat Acad Fine Art; Studied under Mayo Cousins, Robert Sawyers, Robert Brackman, Robert Phillipp, Hugh Gumpel, Julian Levi, Jacob Lawrence; pa/1-Man Shows incl: Acts of Art Gallery (Greenwich Village, NY), Albert Einstein Col of Med (NY), Gallery in the Valley (Jamaica, West Indies), Jamaica Acts of Art Gallery; Jamaica Contemp Assn (Kingston); St Andrew Parrish Lib; The Inst of Jamaica, Park Plaza Galleries; hon/Artwork Chosen for Exhbn & Auction for Annual Fund-raising, Jackie Robinson Foun; Tribute Exhbn sponsored by Ala St Univ; Exhibited in Observation of Black History Month, World Trade Ctr; James Augustus Suydam Bronze Medal for Best Figure Painting, Nat Acad Fine Art.

GUNTER, WILLIAM DAWSON JR oc/State Treasurer; Insurance Commissioner; b/Jul 16, 1934; h/3802 Leane Dr, Tallahassee, FL 32308; ba/Tallahassee; m/Teresa Arbaugh; c/Joel, Bart, Rachel; p/William Dawson Sr and Tillie Gunter, Orlando, FL; ed/BSA Univ Fla 1956; mil/AUS, Outstg Hon Grad of Basic Army Adm; pa/Sr VP Southland Equity Corp, Orlando; Pres Southland Capital Investors Inc, Orlando; cp/St Treasurer & Ins Commr, St of Fla 1976-; Mem US Cong 1972-74; Former St Senator; JCs; Ctl Fla Fair Assn; Orlando Area C of C; Orange Co Farm Bur; Sportsman's Assn; Kiwanis Clb; Masons; U Appeal; r/Bapt; hon/1 of Fla's 5 Outstg Yg Men, St JCs; Univ Fla Hall of Fame; Fla Blue Key; St JC Good Govt Awd for Outstg Public Ser.

GUPTA, VENU GOPAL oc/Professor; b/Apr 3, 1934; h/744 Highland Ave, Kutztown, PA 19530; ba/K'town; m/Sunita Aggarwal; c/Sunil, Sanjiv; p/L Ram Dass and Ram Piari, Punjab, India; ed/BA w hons, MA, MEd Punjab Univ; BEd Delhi Univ; PhD Ga St Univ; pa/Prof Psychol & Cnslg K'town St Col 1974-; Tchg & Res Fellow Ga St Univ, Atlanta, Ga 1972-74; Asst Prof Psychol, Ednl Psychol & Cnslg En Ky Univ, Richmond, Ky 1968-72; Other Former Positions; APA; Am Ednl Res Assn; APGA; Assn for Cnslr Ed & Supvn; AAAS; Intl Coun on Ed for Tchg; AAUP; Intl Assn for Cross-Cult Psychol; Intl Assn Applied Psychol; Phi Delta Kappa; Am Mtl Hlth Cnslrs Assn; cp/Lectr; r/Hindu; hon/Commend Awd, Am Soc Dist'd Citizens (Beverly Hills); Dipl of Hon for Commun Ser, London; Creativity Recog Awd, Intl Pers Res (Los Angeles); Outstg Edr of Am; Biogl Listings; Others.

GURBAXANI, SHYAM H oc/Professor; b/Dec 28, 1928; h/12413 View Ct NE, Albuquerque, NM 87112; ba/Los Alamos, NM; m/Shannon Katherine Rawlings Howard; c/Andrew Raj, Brian Mohan, Catherine Shannon; p/Hassomal Gurbaxani and Kishni Kundanmal, Bombay, India; ed/BS; MS (Physics); MS (EE); PhD; pa/Prof Elect Engrg & Compt Sci; Dir Ctr for Grad Studies; Cnslt Govt & Indust; cp/Webalos; Baseball Little Leag; hon/Cert of Merit, AF; Vis Scist; Others.

GURICH, CONNIE G oc/Director; b/May 7, 1940; h/1616 Wimbleton Dr, Bedford, TX 76021; ba/Dallas/Ft Worth Airport, TX; m/Roger J; p/Jesus Gacta (dec); Lupe T Segovia, La Habra, CA; ed/BA Cal St Univ-LA; JD S Bay Univ; Dipl AF Sch Acct'g & Fin; mil/USAF; pa/Am Airlines Inc: Dir of Properties 1977-, Mgr Properties 1976-77, Premium Flight Attendant 1968-76, Others; Real Est Investor 1966-; ABA, Cal; Los Angeles Bar Assn; S Bay Bar Assn (Cal); Foun for Ec Res (NY); Editor *The Advocate*, S Bay Univ 1973-74; cp/Contb'g Editor Yg Friends of the Arts (NY); hon/Am Airlines: Awd for Excell, Hearing Ofcr for New Mgmt Pers; W/W Am Wom.

GURNSEY, RONALD ALLEN oc/Engineer; Scientist; b/Oct 31, 1931; h/1746 Westwind Way, McLean, VA 22102; ba/-Rockville, MD; m/Suzanne Linn; c/-Stephanie, Eric, Lois, Cynthia, Grant, Stephen; p/Grant O Gurnsey, Big Lake, AK; Ina M Gurnsey (dec); ed/BS; MS; mil/USN 1953-65, Comm'd Ofcr; pa/Tech Dir; Prin;

Staff Engr; Corp Ofcr; cp/Citizens Assn; Ofcr & Bd Dirs Charitable Org; r/Bapt; hon/Adaptive Control Patent Co-holder.

GUSTAFSON, ANITA VIRGINIA oc/-Teacher; b/Jan 31, 1917; h/554 Irwin St, Galesburg, IL 61401; ba/G'burg; p/Carl J and Anna Gustafson (dec); ed/BS; pa/Lng Ctr Tchr; Am Lib Assn; Ill Lib Assn; Nat, Ill & G'burg Ed Assns; AAUW; BPW; cp/Ill Hist Assn; r/Luth; hon/Alpha Delta Kappa; Hon Life Mbrships, Ill Cong PTA; Outstg Elem Tchrs Am.

GUSTAFSON, LEIF VALENTINE oc/-Engineer; Scientist; Inventor; b/Dec 31, 1911; h/39-133 One Horse Way, Palm Desert, CA 92260; m/Joan Miller; c/Glenn Nordhal, Linda Margaret Strauss; p/Oscar G and Olga A Gustafson (dec); ed/BS; mil/AUS Engrs, Designer of 59 Semi-Permanent Hwy & Railroad Bridges in Europe; pa/Cnslt'g Engr 1976-; Dep Dir, Public Works, American Samoa 1974-76; Gen Mgr, ESCO Intl (Guam & Saipan) 1970-74; Cnslt'g Structural Engr, USAF Ballistic & Space Sys Divs 1962-65; Pres & Owner, Leif Engrg & Constrn Corp 1961-69; Chief Structural Engr, EBASCO (Electric Bond & Share Co), NYC 1947-52; p/Past Pres, Swedish Clb of Los Angeles; r/Prot; hon/Nat Recog for Pre-stressed Concrete Design; Major Designer of Minute Man ICBM Launching Concept; Major Design Contbr & Chief Engr for Atlas ICBM Launching Sys; Inventor, "Hydro-Launched" Missile Facility Sys; CoAuthor of ASTM Specification using Pozzolon in Concrete Mixes; Inventor of "Ultra-Sonic" Electrostatic Precipitator; Inventor of Wet Sys Gustafson Electrostatic Precipitator; Inventor of K-G Knob Conveyor.

GUSTAFSON, MARJORIE LILLIAN oc/Associate Professor; b/Apr 17, 1920; h/1419 Lakelawn Dr, So Jacksonville, IL 62650; ba/J'ville; ed/AB Knox Col; MA Univ Ill; Addit Studies; pa/Assoc Prof Fgn Langs MacMurray Col; Am Assn Tchrs French;

Delta Kappa Gamma; AAUW; cp/Col Hill Clb; Fulbright Alumni Assn; hon/Phi Beta Kappa; Fulbright Exc Tchr; Pi Delta Phi; Alpha Lambda Delta; Dir Am Scholars; W/W: Am Wom, MW; Ill Lives; Intl Scholar's Dir.

GUSTASON, GERILEE oc/Associate Professor; b/Jul 5, 1939; h/704 Underwood St NW, Washington, DC 20012; ba/Wash DC; p/Arthur D Gustason (dec); Martha G Hewett, San Bernardino, CA; ed/BA Univ Cal-Riverside 1960; MA Gallaudet 1963; MS Cal St Univ-Northridge 1968; MA Univ Md 1970; PhD Univ So Cal 1972; pa/Assoc Prof Ed Gallaudet Col, Dir New Students Sum Prog 1977, 78; Cnslt in Field; Coauthor "Signing Exact English"; hon/Outstg Yg Wom; W/W Am Wom.

GUTHRIE, ANNIE MAXEEN DANSBY oc/Educator; College Administrator; h/5811 Portal, Houston, TX 77096; m/Rufus Kent; c/Annie, Kent; p/D W Dansby, Frankston, TX; Angeline Douglas (dec); ed/BA, MEd; pa/Dir Career Placemt & Cooperative Ed N Harris Co Col, Houston; APGA; Nat Voc Guid Assn; SWn Placemt Assn; Tex Jr Col Tchrs Assn; Cooperative Ed Assn; Tex Cooperative Ed Assn; r/Epis.

GUTHRIE, MARION B oc/Artist;

Bookkeeper; h/127 W Hillendale Rd, Kennett Square, PA 19348; ba/Same; m/W F Jr; c/Robert, Thomas W, James A; p/Chas P and Marion L Boyd (dec); ed/Dipls Art Schs; cp/Vol Guide Brandywine River Mus; r/Epis; hon/Num Awds for Paintings.

GUTHRIE, RICHARD A oc/Physician; b/Nov 13, 1935; h/4961 N Hillcrest, Wichita, KS 67220; ba/Wichita; m/Diana W; c/Laura, Joyce, Tammy; p/Merle and Cleona Marie Guthrie, Phoenix, AZ; ed/AA Graceland Col; MD Univ Mo; mil/USN 1960-63; pa/Phys, Specialty Pediatrics, Subspecialty Endocrinol & Diabetes in Chd; Acad Med in Pediatrics 1963-; Prof & Chm Dept Pediatrics UKSM-W 1973-; St Dir Hd Start, Ks 1974-76; Am Acad Pediatrics; MW Soc Pediatric Res; Soc Pediatric Res; Lawson-Wilkins Pediatric Endocrine Soc; cp/Optimist Clb, Columbia, Bd Dirs; Am Diabetes Assn: Former Mem Bd Dirs, Past Pres Ks Affil; Former Treas Mo Diabetes Assn; M & I Proj w Co Hlth Dept, Wichita; Dir Pediatric Prog Mid Am All Indian Ctr; r/Reorg'd Ch Jesus Christ LDS: Ordained Lay Priesthood; hon/Nat Hon Soc; Lambda Delta Sigma; Mosby Awd; Soc Pediatric Res; Outstg Ser Awd, ADA Ks Affil; Outstg Edr Am Awd; Best Diabetic Tchr Awd, Wichita St Univ PA Prog.

GUTHRIE, RUFUS KENT oc/Professor; b/Jul 4, 1923; h/5811 Portal, Houston, TX 77096; ba/Houston; m/Maxeen; c/Annie Lynn, Rufus Kent Jr; p/John Thomas and Annie Guthrie (dec); ed/BA, MA Univ Tex-Austin; PhD Baylor Univ Col Med; mil/USNR 1943-46, Lt (jg); pa/Prof Microbiol & Ecology Univ Tex Sch Public Hlth, Houston 1975-; Tchg, Res & Adm: N Tex St Univ 1954-69, Clemson Univ 1969-74; Vis Scist Tex Public Schs 1956-62; r/Epis; Bd Dirs Canterbury Ctr, Denton, Tex 1958-62, Vestryman 1958-68; hon/NSF Sci Fac Fellow; Fellow, Am Acad Microbiol.

GUTIERREZ-MAZORRA, JUAN FRANCISCO oc/Anesthesiologist; b/May 12, 1944; h/2208 Baxter Cir, Birmingham, AL 35216; ba/B'ham; m/Candice E Snyder; c/Lara Alicia, Jana Francesca; p/Francisco Alberto Gutierrez-Pelaez and Maria Eugenia Rissett Mazorra-Vega, B'ham; ed/BS NEn Univ 1965; MD WVa Univ Sch Med 1969; Univ Ala Hosps & Clins, B'ham: Anesthesia Resident 1970-72, Chief Resident 1972-73; mil/Nav Submarine Med Ctr, Groton, Conn 1973-75; pa/Anesthesiologist-in-Chief The Chd's Hosp, B'ham; Am Chem Soc; Am Inst Chem Engrs; Am Med Soc; Intl Anesthesia Soc; Am Col Chest Physicians; Am Acad Pediatrics, Anesthesia Sect; Am Soc Anesthesiologists; Med Assn St of Ala; Jefferson Co Med Assn; Jefferson Co Soc Anesthesiologists; r/Rom Cath; hon/US Nav Cit for Outstg Perf in Devel of Anesthesia-Respiratory Care Facilities at Nav Submarine Med Ctr 1975; Phi Kappa Phi; Tau Beta Phi; Sears B Condit Awd, Outstg Engrg Student; Others.

GUTKOWSKI, SIBYL NICHOLS oc/Administrative Assistant; b/Mar 9, 1924; h/3625 Aurora, Fort Worth, TX 76117; ba/Fort Worth; m/Frank H; c/Elizabeth Larimae Elting, Nicky Dane Cooper, Patricia Ann Hickman; p/William Ernest and Rosa Nelson Nichols, Ft Worth; pa/Adm Asst 1st Nat Bk Ft Worth; Am Bus Woms' Assn; Past Pres Ft Worth Poetry Soc; Poetry Soc Tex; Nat Fdn St Poetry Socs Inc; Acad Am Poets; Charter Mem Poets Tarrant Co; Corres Editor "The Clock" (Later Changed to "Landmark") 12 Yrs; Former Reporter *Ashcrescent News*; r/Bapt; SS Tchr 22 Yrs; hon/Poems, Biog & Photo Pub'd in "First Edition" Pub'd by 1st Nat Bk Ft Worth; Var Recogs for Lit Works; Personalities of S; Notable Ams; World W/W Wom.

GUY, C WILLIAM II oc/Executive; b/Mar 23, 1945; h/14551 Morrison St, Sherman Oaks, CA 91403; ba/Same; m/Katherine Hambright; c/Robert William, Cynthia Eva; p/C W Guy (dec); Helen Ogle Guy, Northridge, CA; ed/BA; AA; pa/Pres Intl Exec Search Firm; VP Paul R Ray & Co

Inc, Los Angeles; Past Pres Am Envir Assn; World Affairs Coun; Am Mktg Assn; Am Soc Pers Admrs; Past Chm Adv Bd Local Chain Indep Bks; cp/Pres Outreach Love; r/Nat Adv Bd Rel Yth Org; hon/Life Mem, Cal S'ship Fdn; Guest Lectr & Editorials; Biogl Listings.

GUYER, CHARLES GRAYSON II oc/Counseling Psychologist; h/1400A Chunn's Cove Rd, Asheville, NC 28805; ba/A'ville; m/Nancy P; c/Nikki Johnna; p/Charles Grayson and Mildred Workman Guyer, High Point, NC; ed/BA 1972, MA 1974 Appalachian St Univ; EdD Col William & Mary 1978; pa/Blue Ridge Commun Mtl Hlth: Crisis Team Ldr, Dir Psychodiagnostics; Pvt Pract Cnslg, Psychotherapy, Norfolk, Va 1976-78; Act'g Dir Psychol Sers Human Resource Inst, Norfolk 1975-76; Staff Psychologist HRI, Norfolk 1974-76; Adj Fac: En Va Med Sch 1976-, Wn Carolina Univ 1978-, Old Dominion Univ 1975-76, Norfolk St Univ 1977-78; r/Meth; hon/1st Bd for Nat Certn of Profl Cnslrs; W/W S&SW; Personalities of S.

GUYEWSKI, NORMAN M oc/Firefighter; Sculptor; b/Oct 7, 1924; h/5801 Maco, Galveston Island, TX 87550; ba/Galveston Isl; m/Celina B; c/Stewart, Gary; p/Luke and Emma Guyewski (dec); ed/Certn Univ Houston; mil/AUS WWII 3 Yrs; USAF 3 Yrs Active Resv; pa/Small Arms Instr; Fire Fighter; Sculptor; cp/Halfway House for Teenagers; Galveston Hist Foun; Former Mem Co Cult Arts Galveston; r/Orthodox; hon/4 Bronze Stars; Pres Unit Cit (WWII); Ser Ribbons; Var Awds for Sculpture Exhbns; Personalities of S.

GUYTON, GENEVA oc/Beautician; b/Mar 31, 1920; h/4116 W 21st Pl, Chicago, IL 60623; m/Brazie; c/Mary Van Smith, Margaret Jean, Annie Francis Austin, Micheal M, Ricky T; p/Ivory and Adeline Burt, Koscuisko, MS; cp/Yth Advr Metro MBC; r/Bapt; hon/Cert of Apprec for Outstg & Dedicated Sers to Yth.

GUYTON, RICKY TYRONE oc/Student; Hospital Laboratory Assistant; b/Jul 14, 1957; h/4116 W 21st Pl, Chicago, IL 60623; p/Brazie and Geneva Guyton, Chgo; ed/Student Biogl Sci NWn Univ; cp/Pres Older Boys' & Girls' Conf; Pres MW Bapt Yth Conf; VP Chgo Northwood River Dist; r/Bapt; hon/Nat Hon Soc.

GUZMAN, ALBERTO PORRATA oc/Executive; b/Oct 30, 1942; h/St 17 T25, Urb Las Delicias, PO Box 7606, Ponce, PR 00731; ba/Ponce; m/Carmen G Roda Rodriguez; p/Virgilio Porrata and Raquel Guzman, Ponce; ed/BBA Cath Univ PR; pa/Pres Ponce Rental Equipmt Corp; VP Isl Med & Hosp Supply Inc; cp/Ponce CC; William Shooting Clb; Dept of Commerce; Dir Shelters S Area, Civil Def PA, Vol Corps; New Progressive Party; r/Cath; hon/Cert; Trans in Indust, Indust Relats, Mind Control Inst.

GWALTNEY, MILDRED oc/Assistant Professor; b/Jun 1, 1946; h/621 Cabell Dr, Apt 4, Bowling Green, KY 42101; ba/Bowling Green; ed/BA Longwood Col 1967; MLS Geo Peabody Col 1970; EdD Cand Univ Ky; pa/Asst Prof Dept Lib Sci & Instrnl Media Wn Ky Univ 1971-; Tchr/Libn Henrico HS, Richmond, Va 1967-71; SEn & Ky Lib Assns; Ky Sch Media Assn; 3rd Dist Libns; Var Univ Coms; cp/Wom's Clb Bowling Green; r/Presb Ch, Bowling Green: Mem, Wom's Assn, Cir Secy; hon/Mortar Bd; Alpha Psi Omega; Beta Phi Mu; Biogl Listings.

H

HABBERTON, JOHN oc/Executive; b/Apr 20, 1912; h/80 Park Ave, New York, NY 10016; ba/NYC; m/Eugenia F Sweeney; p/Frank Hastings and Jean Clementine MacAllen Habberton; ed/BA Univ Va; Univ Colo; mil/USN WWII, Lt (sg); Flag Lt to Cmdr N China Forces 1946; pa/Pres Bus Coun for Intl Understanding 1958-; Assoc Exec Dir CARE Inc NYC 1956-59; Dean Col de l'Europe Libre (US Free Europe Com), Strasbourg, France 1955-56; Spec Asst Fgn Aid US Int Coop Adm, Ankara, Turkey 1951-55; Other Former Positions; VP & Sponsor Arms of Friendship (US-USSR Relats); Mid-Atl Clb (NY); US Nat Planning Assn; Del UNESCO Task Force on Int Ed; Chm Mbrship Comm Turkish-Am Assn, Ankara; hon/US Info Ser Dist'd Ser Awd; Commend Lttrs: Pres Eisenhower, Kennedy, Johnson, Nixon; Biogl Listings.

HABBOUSHE, CHRISTA PARHAD oc/Physician, Pediatrician; h/1229 Waverly Rd, Gladwyne, PA 19035; ba/Philadelphia, PA; m/Fawzi P; c/Reem-Ann, Fatin-Mary, Dina, Joseph; p/Malcolm Parhad (dec); Szabba Parhad, Gladwyne; ed/MD; MBChB; pa/Phys Hahnemann Hosp; Asst Prof Pediatrics Hahnemann Med Col & Hosp; r/Luth Prot; hon/Phys Recog Awd, AMA.

HABERECHT, ROLF oc/Executive; b/Jun 4, 1929; h/10984 Crooked Creek Dr, Dallas, TX 75229; ba/Dallas; m/Ute; c/Michael, Caroline; p/Olga Haberecht; ed/PhD; MBA; MS; pa/VP Tex Instruments Inc; Electrochem Soc, Var Ofcs; cp/Bd Trustees St Mark's Sch of Tex; r/Luth; hon/Beta Gamma Sigma.

HABIG, MARION ALPHONSE oc/Historian; Priest; Franciscan Friar; Writer; Editor; b/Jun 28, 1901; h/5045 S Laflin St, Chicago, IL 60609; ba/Chgo; p/Philip and Adelheid Dittmaier Habig (dec); ed/BA; MA Loyola Univ; LG Athenaeum Antonianum (Rome, Italy); pa/Assoc Editor Franciscan Herald Press, Chgo; Editor *Lesser Brothers* (Qtrly); Histn St Louis-Chgo Province Franciscans; Author 25 Pub'd Books; cp/CoFdr Old Spanish Missions Hist Res Lib, San Jose Mission, San Antonio Tex 1971; r/Rom Cath; hon/Marian Medal, Univ Dayton; La Bahia Awd, Sons of Repub of Tex; Hon Mem, Inst Historique et Heraldique de France; Gallery Living Cath Authors; Hon Mem, Eugene Field & Mark Twain Socs.

HACKAMACK, BEATRICE IRENE oc/Consultant; b/Oct 28, 1921; h/205 Joanne Ln, DeKalb, IL 60115; ba/Same; c/Lawrence C; c/Susan Ann Dugan, David Lee; p/Louis H and Edna Brown Littlefield (dec); ed/AA; Undergrad Degree; mil/WAC, Recruiter; pa/CMRS Conslt; Writer; Univ Wom; cp/Fam Ser Guild; Kishwaukee Hosp Aux; r/1st U Meth Ch; hon/Alpha Gamma Sigma, Valedictorian Awd.

HACKAMACK, DAVID LEE oc/Student; b/May 8, 1958; h/205 JoAnne Ln, DeKalb, IL 60115; p/Lawrence and Beatrice Hackamack,

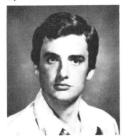

DeKalb, IL; ed/BS En Ill Univ; pa/Soc for Advmt of Mgmt; APICS; cp/Col Repubs; r/Meth; hon/Simmons Meml Awd, EIU.

HACKENBERG, LARRY MICHAEL oc/Architect; Author; Teacher; b/Feb 27, 1942; h/Rt 6, Box 210-A, Charlottesville, VA 22901; ba/Same; c/Tyson Noll; p/Roy L and Geraldine E Hackenberg, Three Rivers, MI; ed/BArch; Masters Landscape Arch; pa/Pvt Arch; r/Christian; hon/Biogl Listings.

HACKETT, WILLIAM DAVID oc/Company President; b/Oct 12, 1918; h/3130 NW Forest Ln, Portland, OR 97229; ba/Portland; c/Toni N Sheneman, Pati L Smith, Peter A, Mari D; p/Fred A and Lena S Hackett (dec); ed/Geo Wash Univ; mil/AUS 22 Yrs, Inf Ofcr in Combat Command & Staff Positions to Gen Staff Level; pa/Pres Bill Hackett Co Inc; Nat Sporting Goods Assn; Wn Winter Sports Reps Assn; Am Alpine Clb; Fellow Am Geographical Soc; Arctic Inst of NA; Mazamas; Clb de Exploraciones de Mexico; Other Worldwide Mtn, Polar & Exploration Clbs; hon/Silver Star Medal; Bronze Star w OLC; Army Commend Medal; 10th Mtn Div during WW II; Condor de Oro for being 1st Am to Reach Summit of Highest Mtn in Wn Hemisphere by Argentina; Led, Participated Mtn Expeditions to 6 Continents & 84 Countries; 1st Man to Stand on 5 Continental Summits; Contbr Num Papers & Articles to Jours & Pubs; Pub'd Author.

HACKNEY, HOWARD SMITH oc/Farmer; County Executive Director; b/May 20, 1910; h/2003 Inwood Rd, Wilmington, OH 45127; ba/W'ton; m/Lucille; c/Albert M, Roderick Allen, Katherine Ann Becker; p/Volcah M and Gusta Anna Smith Hackney (dec); ed/BS cum laude Wilmington Col;

pa/Co Ext Dir ASCS; NASCOE; St & Nat Dir Duroc Swine & Southdown Sheep Assns; cp/W'ton Col Agri Adv Com; r/Quaker; hon/Chi Beta Phi Sci Awd; Ohio St & MW Area NASCOE Awd for Ser to Agri; Num Awds for Livestock.

HACKNEY, JAMES ACRA III oc/Truck Body & Trailer Manufacturing Executive; b/Sept 27, 1939; h/220 Alderson Rd, Washington, NC 27889; ba/Wash; m/Constance Garrenton; c/Kenneth, Jane; p/James Acra Jr and Margaret Hodges Hackney; ed/BS (Mech Engrg) magna cum laude 1961, BS (Indust Engrg) magna cum laude 1962 NC St Univ; mil/AUS Ordnance Corps 1963-65, Served to 1/Lt; pa/Hackney & Sons Inc: Pres & Chief Exec Ofcr 1970-, Exec VP & Gen Mgr 1965-70, Asst Gen Mgr 1963-65, Chief Engr 1961-63; Dir: NC Nat Bk, Wash 1975, En Area Hlth Ed Ctr Inc, Greenville (NC) 1977-, NC Engrg Foun Inc, Raleigh (NC) 1977-, Others; Reg'd Profl Engr: NC & Ks; Nat Soc Profl Engrs; Profl Engrs

NC; NC Soc Engrs; Am Inst Indust Engrs, En NC Chapt; Am Mgmt Assn; Truck Body & Equipmt Assn; Profl Photogs Am; cp/BSA, Var Activs; Past Pres US Hwy 264 Assn; Former Mem: Coastal Plain Devel Assn Inc, City of Wash Zoning & Planning Comm; Trustee Beaufort Co Hosp; Mem: Beaufort Co Indust Mgmt Coun; Wash C of C; Wash Yacht & CC; Brook Val CC (G'ville); r/1st U Meth Ch, Wash: Mem, Adm Bd; hon/Silver Beaver Awd, E Carolina Coun BSA; Outstg Yg Alumnus, NC St Univ; Nat Yg Engr of Yr, Nat Soc Profl Engrs 1971; Outstg Yg Engr in NC, Profl Engrs NC; NC Small Bus-man of Yr, US Small Bus Adm 1971; Dist'd Ser Awd, Wash JCs.

HADA, JERRIANNE oc/School Librarian; b/Dec 19, 1944; h/1209 W Caddo, Cleveland, OK 74020; ba/Cleve; p/David Leroy and Thelma Rader Hada, Hardtner, KS; ed/BS NWn Okla St Univ; MS Emporia St

Univ; pa/NEA; OEA; Secy Cleve Classroom Tchrs; OLA; OASLMS; cp/Delta Kappa Gamma; Tulsa Geneal Soc; r/U Meth Ch; hon/World W/W Wom; NDEA Grant.

HADDOCK, JAY LAMAR oc/Research Soil Scientist; b/Dec 19, 1903; h/188 N 3rd E, Logan, UT 84321; ba/Logan; m/Pearl Richards; c/Glen Richards, Jay Larry, David Lee, John Martin; p/Edward John and Mary Ward Haddock, Bloomington, ID; ed/BS 1930; MS 1932; PhD 1942; pa/Conslt US Steel (Geneva) 1971; Conslt Stauffer Chem Co

1970-71; Res Soil Scist ARS, USDA 1945-68; Assoc Prof Wash St Col 1944-45; Other Former Positions; cp/Former Chm Plant Physiol Sect Am Soc Sugar Beet Tech; Past VP Soc Sigma Xi, Utah St Univ Chapt; Former Del to Repub St Conv; Former Scout Master; Others; r/Ch of Jesus Christ LDS; hon/Cert of Spec Commend, Sigma Xi for Excell in Res.

HADGOPOULOS, SARALYN POOLE oc/University Professor; Author; b/Aug 31, 1931; h/2309 Treasure Island Dr, Virginia Beach, VA 23455; ba/Hampton, VA; c/John George deHaven; p/G Grady Poole (dec); Sarah W Shaw, Va Bch; ed/BS Columbia Univ 1955; MA NY Univ 1961; PhD Emory Univ 1965; pa/Prof Geo Wash Univ; Author "Poems of N Africa" 1973, "Poems of Greece" 1975, "The Crystal Mandala" 1976, "Imagination's Wine" 1977; r/Meth; hon/W/W Am Wom.

HADLEY, ROSA LOUISE oc/Associate Professor; b/Sept 14, 1930; h/4903 Alburta Rd NW, Huntsville, AL 35806; ba/H'ville; p/Dennis and Rosetta Hadley, Thomasville, GA; ed/BS Fort Val St Col 1951; MA Columbia Univ 1959; EdD Wayne St Univ

1972; pa/Assoc Prof Ed & Music Oakwood Col; Ala Coun on Tchg of Composition; SEn Reg Assn Tchr Edrs; Ala Assn Tchr Edrs; Assn for Supvn & Curric Devel; r/SDA; hon/Awd for Outstg Work, Harris Home for Chd (H'ville); Tchr of Month, Detroit Ed Assn 1968; S'ship, Delta Sigma Theta; Student of Month, Fort Val St Col; Biogl Listings.

HADLEY, WAYNE NELSON oc/Clergyman; b/May 6, 1919; h/130 W High St, Somerville, NJ 08876; ba/Same; m/Virginia M Jominy; c/Lawrence H, Christine M Laquintano, Karen V, Ronald A; p/Bert Nelson and Ruth O Hadley (dec); ed/BS Univ Mich; BD, MDiv, DD En Bapt Theol Sem; pa/Sr Pastor 1st Bapt Ch, S'ville; cp/Chm Co Am Cancer Soc; Chaplain Fire Co; VP S'ville Sr Citizens Housing; r/Am Bapt; hon/Dist'd Alumni Awd; En Sem.

HAFEN, BRUCE CLARK oc/College President; b/Oct 30, 1940; h/459 E 350 South, Rexburg, ID 83440; ba/R'burg; m/Marie Kartchner; c/Jonathan, David, Tom, Emily, Sarah, Mark, Rachel; p/Orval Hafen (dec); Ruth C Hafen, St George, UT; ed/AA Dixie Col; BA Brigham Yg Univ; JD Univ Utah; pa/Pres Ricks Col; Brigham Yg Univ: Prof Law 1975-, Assoc Dir (Hons Prog) 1971-73, Asst to Pres 1971-76, Asst Dean J Reuben Clark Law Sch 1973-74, Others; Former Mem Law Firm; ABA 1967-71; Utah St Bar Assn; r/LDS: Dir Planning & Eval 1976-78; hon/Order of the Coif, Univ Utah Col of Law; F'ship; Profl Pubs; Others.

HAGEN, ORVILLE WEST oc/Labor Commissioner; b/Sept 26, 1915; h/1528-N 19th, Bismarck, ND 58501; ba/Bismarck; m/Astrid Berg; c/Orvis Wayne, Mylo Leroy, Ellyn Marie, Lana Jo; p/Oscar W Hagen (dec); Carrie Scollard (dec); pa/ND St Labor Commr; cp/Former St Senator & Lt Gov; r/Luth.

HAGGARD, WILLIAM HENRY oc/Meteorological Consultant; b/Nov 20, 1920; h/Box 9306, Asheville, NC 28805; ba/Same; m/Martina W; c/William H Jr, Robert H; p/Howard Wilcox and Josephine Foley Haggard (dec); ed/BS Yale; Cert Prof Met;

MIT; MS Univ Chicago; Grad Work Fla St Univ; mil/USN 1942-45, 1951-54, Ret'd as Capt; pa/Meteorologist US Govt 1947-75; Conslt 1976-; cp/Rotarian, Former Dist Gov; Red Cross; U Way; r/Presb; hon/U Way Awds; ESSA Top Mgmt Awd.

HAGOOD, LACY EDMUNDS oc/Military Officer; b/Jun 25, 1921; h/12208 Cliffwood Ct, Clifton, VA 22024; m/Margaret E Vaughn; c/Lacy E Jr, Peggy E, Elizabeth A; p/John Thomas and Emma Clay Haygood (dec); ed/BS Elon Col 1945; MA Command & Gen Staff Col 1971; mil/AUS, Progressed from Pvt to 1/Sgt; Att'd Inf OCS, Comm'd 2/Lt to Col; Currently Ranked Colonel; cp/Meet Dir Am-Canadian All Star Swimming Champs 1964; Swimming Com Congl CC, Washington, DC; r/Meth; hon/Mid-Weight Golden Gloves Champion (Piedmont, Raleigh & Burlington, NC); Army Light Mid-Weight Boxing Champ; Mem US Army Inf Sch Hall of Fame, Ft Benning, Ga.

HAHN, LORENA GRACE oc/Registered Professional Nurse; Certified Critical Care

Nurse; b/Apr 16, 1914; h/2431 Sichel St #207, Los Angeles, CA 90031; p/Albert Hicks and Myrtle Mae Bingham Barnes (dec); ed/RN; CCRN; pa/Critical Care Nurse White Meml Med Ctr; Am & Cal Nurse Assns; Reg 6 Am Assn Critical Care Nurses; Nat Critical Care Inst of Ed; Supv'g Nurse Maternity & Dept of Neonatology; cp/PTA; Sr Citizens Groups; Salvation Army; Repub; Lectr; Nurses Alumni Assn; OMS Intl Inc; r/Wesleyan; Oriental Missionary Soc Inc; hon/Outstg Employee Awd; Dedicated Ser Awd, White Meml Med Ctr; 35 Yr Ser Awd, LACUSC Med Ctr; Nat Hon Soc; Notable Ams; Hon Life Mem, Nurses Alumni Assn; World W/W Wom; W/W Am Wom.

HAHN, RALPH CRANE oc/Executive Consulting Engineers; b/Nov 9, 1927; h/1111 Williams, Springfield, IL 62704; ba/S'field; m/Jane Stroud; c/Lindsay, Charles, Alice; p/Lindsay Ralph Hahn (dec); Amanda Louisa

Hahn, S'field; ed/BS, MS Univ Ill; mil/AUS 1946-47, 1952-54; pa/Pres Ralph Hahn & Assoc (Consltg Engrs); Am Soc CE; Nat Soc Profl Engrs; Am Conslt'g Engrs Coun; cp/Trustee Univ Ill; r/Bapt; hon/Eminent Conceptor Awd, Ill Conslt'g Engrs Coun (to RHA).

HAHN, RICHARD DAVID oc/Architect, Land Planner; b/Mar 23, 1937; h/9617 Oak Pass Rd, Beverly Hills, CA 90210; ba/Same; m/Daisy Gerber; c/Lesley Jeannette; p/William D and Jane E Hahn, Los Angeles, CA; ed/UCLA; USC; mil/AUS, French Interpreter; pa/AIA, Local, St & Nat; Reg'd NCARB; Lic'd: Cal, Colo; Contbr to AIA Res Inst Solar Study; hon/Dean's List, USC; Winner HUD/Oper Breakthrough; Nat Homes Awd; Delta Sigma Phi.

HAHN, RUTH FREEMAN oc/College Professor, Department Chairperson; b/Jul 23, 1920; h/1119 W 40 St, Erie, PA 16509; ba/Erie; m/Raymond W; c/Raymond, Richard, Joseph, Marilyn; p/James A and Jennette Freeman (dec); ed/BS; MA; Further Studies; pa/Am Acad Polit & Social Sci; AAUW; Kappa Gamma Pi; cp/Bd Dirs: U Way, Erie Co Coun for Alcohol & Drug Abuse; r/Rom Cath; hon/Outstg Edrs Am; Alumnae Career Awd, Villa Maria Col.

HAHON, NICHOLAS oc/Research Microbiologist; b/Mar 24, 1924; h/1373 Headlee Ave, Morgantown, WV 26505; ba/M'town; m/Katheryn E; c/Nicolette Kay; p/Samuel A and Catherine Hahon (dec); ed/BS Johns Hopkins Univ; mil/AUS 1943-46; USN Med Ser Corps 1952-58 (Resv); pa/Res Microbiologist USPHS Appalach Lab, Occupl Safety Hlth; AAAS; Am Soc Microbiol; Sigma Xi; NY Acad Scis; Tissue Cult Assn; r/Cath; hon/RESA Awd; Fellow, Am Acad Microbiol; Kellogg Scholar; Achmt Awd, Commun Soc Am; Registry, Am Bd Microbiol.

HAIGH, BERTE ROLPH oc/Geologist; b/Jan 15, 1890; h/1605 N Midkiff Rd, Apt 264, Midland, TX 79701; ba/Midland; m/Caroline S; p/John Rolph Haigh (dec); Adelaide Addie Eudora (dec); ed/BS; mil/Cal NG: Inf 1910-17, Coast Arty 1917, Fed Mexican Border 1914, 16, WWI, 52nd Am Trn 1917-19, Overseas (France), 1918; pa/Semi-Ret'd; Geologist Dixie Oil Co (now Amoco) 1926-28; Asst Prof Geol & Engr 1928-34, Univ Tex Lands 1934-62, Chief 1954-62, Conslt 1962-76; cp/Kiwanis Clb; Mason; r/Prot;

hon/Life Mem, Am Geoph Un; Perm Base Petrol Hall of Fame; Others.

HAIGHT, HILDRED DRAY oc/Engineer; b/Sept 17, 1912; h/329 Second Ave, Hill n Dale, Brooksville, FL 33512; ba/B'ville; m/Robert B; p/James Henry and Icel Hutchison Dray (dec); ed/BS Purdue Univ 1940; pa/Engr Regulatory Div SW Fla Water Mgmt Dist 1965-; Adm Dir Geophysical Inst, Univ Alaska 1952-62; Asst to Comptroller Ladd AFB, Alaska 1947-52; Other Former Positions; AAUW; cp/Sr Mem SWE; Girl Scout Coun; r/Prot; hon/World W/W Wom; Hon Life Mem, DSK.

HAIRSTON, PETER WILSON oc/Judge; b/Aug 2, 1913; h/Rt 2, Box 391, Advance, NC 27006; ba/Lexington, NC; m/Lucy Dortch; c/George R, Peter W Jr; p/Peter W and Elmer G Hairston (dec); ed/AB; LLB; mil/1942-46, Pvt to Capt; ETO; 5 Battle Stars, Purple Heart, Bronze Star; pa/Superior Ct Judge; ABA; NC Bar Assn; cp/Former Mem NC House; Former Mem Real Est Lic Bd, NC Ins Adv Bd; r/Epis; hon/Phi Beta Kappa; Law Review; Others.

HALABY, RAOUF JAMIL oc/Assistant Professor; b/Nov 22, 1945; h/1205 Caddo #27, Arkadelphia, AR 71923; ba/A'phia; m/Rachel D; c/Ramzy T; p/Jamil Halaby (dec); Katrina Halaby, Redwood Shores, CA;

ed/BA; MSE; EdD; pa/Asst Prof Eng Ouachita B Univ; Dir Exc Prog; Intl Student Advr; cp/Lions Clb; r/Bapt; Var Ch Work; hon/Outstg Yg Men Am; W/W S&SW; Personalities of S; W/W Am Cols & Univs.

HALBE, DONALD JAMES oc/Treasurer; b/Jan 18, 1944; h/59 N Spring, Glen Ellyn, IL 60137; ba/Franklin Park, IL; m/Doris Joan; c/David James, Douglas Jay; p/William George Halbe (dec); Margaret Barbara Halbe, Chicago, IL; ed/Roosevelt Univ 1965-68; Intl Corres Schs 1968-69; pa/Am Inst Corporate Comptrollers; hon/W/W MW.

HALE, ARNOLD WAYNE oc/Educator; Counselor; Educational Specialist; b/Sept 2, 1934; h/10412 Firethorn Ln, Austin, TX 78750; ba/Same; m/Mary Alice Mauricio; c/Colleen Ann, Zola Lucille, Alexander Winfred; p/Archiebald William and Alvena Lucille Williams Hale; ed/BA Univ SD 1959; MEd Our Lady of the Lake Univ San Antonio 1971; MEd 1973; BS Univ St of NY 1976; AA Austin Commun Col 1979; mil/AUS: Infantryman Resv Component 1952-53, Active Inf-man 1953-55, Inf-man Resv Component 1955-59; Direct Comm to 2/Lt 1959, Adv'd to Major 1973; Var Staff & Mgmt Positions Med Ser Corps 1959-67, Med Advr Mil Assistance Command, Vietnam 1967-68; Ed Specialist Med Tng Ctr, Ft Sam Houston (Tex) 1968-73; Hosp Cmdr 86th Combat Support Hosp, Ft Campbell, Ky 1973-75; Med Advr Tex Army NG 1975-77; Ret'd 1977; cp/Lng Resources Specialist Milam Co Common Sch Dist, Milam Co (Tex) 1977-78; Psychol Instr Austin Commun Col, Austin 1977-; Christian Biblio-Cnslr Edr 1978-; Bibliotherapy Discussion Group; Bibliotherapy Com Am Lib Assn; APGA; NEA; Tex St & Tex Jr Col Tchrs Assns; Ret'd Ofcrs Assn (Life); Nat Guard Assn Tex (Life); cp/Maj & Med Advr CAP; Masons; Sigma Theta Epsilon; Indep Dem; r/Christian; hon/Num Mil Decorations; Hons Sem, Univ SD; Phi Alpha Theta; Duke of Paducah Awd, Paducah (Ky); Biogl Listings.

HALE, SELDON HOUSTON oc/Business Manager; b/Jun 11, 1948; h/111 Hidalgo Ln, Arlington, TX 76014; ba/Ft Worth, TX; m/Kay Ellen Moler; c/Emily Michelle, Denise Kathline; p/Woster Seldon Jr and Geraldine L Sacra Hale (dec); pa/Bus Mgr Bruce Lowrie Chevrolet Inc; Am Mgmt Assn; Gen Motors Soc Sales Execs; cp/Tex St Yth & Govt Prog; US Golf Assn; A'ton F'ship Christian Aths; Former VChm Greenville 4th of July Celebration; r/Meth; hon/A'ton F'ship Christian Aths: Dedicated Ser Awd, Mbrship Prodr Awd; Dedicated Ser Awd, A'ton YMCA; Outstg Ser Awd, Tex St Yth & Govt Prog.

HALES, CELIA ELAINE oc/Librarian; b/Sept 6, 1946; h/PO Box 96, Zebulon, NC 27597; p/Thomas Edwin and Joyce Hill Hales, Zebulon; ed/BA, MA Duke Univ; MLS E Carolina Univ; PhD Cand Fla St Univ; pa/Am Lib Assn; cp/LWV; r/U Meth Ch; hon/Tchg F'ship, E Carolina Univ; Grad Asst'ship, Fla St Univ.

HALES, LOYDE WESLEY oc/Professor; b/Mar 9, 1933; h/1410 SW Broadway, Portland, OR 97201; ba/Portland; m/Annie King Loudon; c/Loyde W II, Lavinia Anne, Lydia Elizabeth; p/Thomas Wesley Hales (dec); Lola Alice Bretches Hales, Cogan Sta, PA; ed/BS 1956, MS 1960, EdD 1964 Univ Ks; mil/USN 1956-59, Ret'd Lt, USNR; pa/Prof Ed, Ed Res & Eval Portland St Univ; Author (w J C Marshall) *Classroom Test Construction*, 1971, *Essentials of Testing*, (w B J Fenner) *Ohio Work Values Inventory*, 1973; Num Articles & Papers; AEKA; NCME; PDK; APGA; NVGA; OERA; AAUP; r/Prot; hon/Exc Scholar, Univ Aberdeen (Scotland); Ohio Univ Res Inst Fellow; Fulbright Sr Res Scholar.

HALEY, FRANK P oc/Engineer; b/Jun 23, 1925; h/409 W 9 St, Upland, CA 91786; ba/Brea, CA; m/Andrea H Von Juhasz; c/Lisbeth, Ella; p/Leslie Szerdahelyi, San Pedro, CA; Magdalena Reothy; ed/MS; PhD; BSBA; pa/Sr Engr FMC Corp; Mgr Upland Engrg; SME; NSPS; cp/Dem; CTC; r/Rom Cath; hon/GS May Co Grantee; SBA Awd; Others.

HALEY, JOHNETTA RANDOLPH oc/Associate Professor; b/Mar 19, 1923; h/7326 Stanford, St Louis, MO 63130; ba/Edwardsville, IL; m/David; c/Karen, Michael; p/John A Randolph (dec); Willye E Smith (dec); ed/BSME Lincoln Univ 1945; MMus So Ill Univ 1972; pa/Assoc Prof Music So Ill Univ; Col Music Soc; MENC; Mu Phi Epsilon; AAUP; Mo Music Edrs Assn; Nat Choral Dirs Assn; Assn Tchr Edrs; Mid-W

Kodaly Music Edrs; Org Am Kodaly Edrs; Alpha Kappa Alpha; Pi Kappa Lambda; cp/NAACP; Urban Leag; U Negro Col Fund; Nat Chm Cleveland Job Corps Support Com; Top Ladies of Distn Inc; Bd Mem Metro YWCA; Adv Coun Danforth Foun Ldrship Prog; r/Coun Luth Chs; hon/Dist'd Citizen Awd, St Louis *Argus* Newspaper; Ser Awd, Mo Music Edrs; Gold "N" Awd, Nipher Jr HS; Duchess of Paducah Awd, Paducah, Ky; Signel Hon Awd for Commun Ser, St Louis *Sentinel Newspaper; Biogl Listings*.

HALEY, KAREN LOUISE oc/Deputy Juvenile Officer; b/Oct 29, 1948; h/5453 Delmar, Apt #217, St Louis, MO 63112; ba/St Louis; c/David and Johnetta Haley, St Louis;

ed/BA; MA; pa/Dep Juv Ofcr Probation Dept, 22nd Judicial Circuit Ct; Assn Black Psychologists; cp/Vol Mtl Hlth Assn; Alpha Kappa Alpha; U Negro Col Fund; YMCA; YWCA; Fisk Univ Nat Alumni Assn; r/Luth; hon/Certs of Apprec: Ctl Reg Alpha Kappa Alpha, Gamma Omega Chapt Alpha Kappa Alpha; Spec Recog, Yth Min Luth Ch, Mo Synod; Awds: Mariner GSA, YMCA Ldrship Prog.

HALFON, ANN H oc/Retired Librarian; b/Sept 16, 1916; h/1400 St Charles Pl, Pembroke Pines, FL 33026; m/Raymond; c/Jerald, Robin H Licht; ed/Abraham and Rachel Halfon (dec); ed/MLS Columbia Univ; BA Hunter; Addit Studies; pa/Ret'd Asst Dir Libs, NYC; Author/Prodr Media Film Prog on Libs; Am Lib Assn; cp/Book Leag of NY; Local Civic Assn; City of Hope; hon/DIB; Foremost Wom in Am; Bronze Ser Awd, Coun of Dirs, NYC Bd of Ed; W/W: Am Wom, E.

HALFORD, MARGERY ARBAUGH oc/Music Editor; Writer; Lecturer; Teacher; b/Jun 9, 1927; h/1641 Marshall, Houston, TX 77006; m/Richard James; c/Cassandra; p/Harry F Jr and Grace F Arbaugh; ed/Peabody Conservatory of Music; Certn (Piano & Harpsichord Tchg) Music Tchrs Nat Assn; pa/Var Music Editions Pub'd by Alfred Pub'g Co NY; Houston Harpsichord Soc; CoFdr, Past Pres, Fest Dir, Prog Coor; Tex & Houston Music Tchrs Assns; Am Musicological Soc; r/Epis; hon/Contbr Articles to Profl Jours; DIB; Intl W/W in Music & Musicians' Dir.

HALL, ALICE CLAY oc/Poet; Artist; Author; Dramatic Reader; Lecturer; b/Dec 25; h/109 Saddletree Rd, San Antonio, TX 78231; m/Vernon Addison; c/Mrs G Urbach Sr;

p/John William and Gertrude Lee Butler Clay (dec); cp/PTA; Fine Arts; r/Christian; hon/Hon'd for Dist'd Achmt in Poetry & Art; Fellow 3 Orgs.

HALL, ANN LOUISE oc/Journalist; Author; b/Jun 17, 1946; h/40 Croydon Ct, Wallingford, CT 06492; m/Daniel Waldron; c/Christopher Wagner, Jonathan Lyman; p/Frank Eichinger (dec); Katharine E Heldmann, Port Richey, FL; ed/BA Syracuse Univ 1968; pa/Book Reviewer 1974-; Free-lance Writer 1978-; Mem The Courant St Capitol Bur 1971-73; Ed Reporter *The Courant* 1969-71; Other Former Positions; Wom in Communs Inc; Pres Syracuse Univ Chapt 1967-68, Pres Conn Profl Chapt 1972-73, Exec Bd Mem & Job Bank Dir Conn Profl Chapt 1973-; Contbr to *Encyclopedia Yrbook* 1969; r/Rom Cath; hon/Fac Awd for Ser to Sch of Jour, Syracuse Univ.

HALL, ANTHONY WILLIAM JR oc/- State Representative; b/Sept 16, 1944; h/3709 Rio Vista, Houston, TX 77021; ba/Houston; m/Carolyn Joyce Middleton; c/Ursula Antoinette, Anthony William III; p/Anthony W Hall Sr (dec); Quintanna Alliniece, Houston; ed/BA Howard Univ; mil/AUS 1967-71, Capt; Purple Heart; 3 Bronze Stars; pa/Dir Hlth Testing Prog So Tex Laborers' Dist Coun Hlth & Wel Trust Fund; Adv Bd Dirs Standard Savs & Ln Assn; Partner CHL Enterprises; cp/St Rep, Dist 85 1973-, Mem Var Coms; Martin Luth King Jr Commun Ctr Adv Coun; Bd Dirs: Houston Urban Coalition, Houston Coun on Human Relats, Riverside Lions Clb, Houston BPM Clb,

Operation Breadbasket (Houston); Houston Area Urban Leag; Harris Co Dems; Nat Hon Adv Com Voices in Vital Am; Nat Mun Leag; Kappa Alpha Psi; Houston Citizens C of C: Bd Dirs, Exec Com Mem; Houston Exec Bd Mem U Negro Col Fund; Mason; YMCA, S Ctl Br; Others; r/Bapt; hon/Dist'd Ser Awd, Beta Psi Omega Chapt Alpha Kappa Alpha; Dist'd Commun Ser Awd 1975, Tex So Univ Ex-Students' Assn; Susan B Anthony Awd, Harris Co Wom's Polit Caucus; Recog Awd in St Govt, ILA Local 872; Cit for Outstg Ser, NAACP Houston; Black Achiever Awd, S Ctl YMCA (Houston); Num Biogl Listings.

HALL, DAVID ALVIN oc/Psychiatrist; b/Nov 16, 1937; h/1673 Via Del Rey, So Pasadena, CA 91030; ba/SP; m/Kay Frances; c/Bryan Kent, Gregory Scott; p/Robert D and Helen M Hall; ed/BA; MD; pa/Chm Jt Conf Com, Ingleside Mtl Hlth Ctr; r/Meth; hon/Cert'd, Am Bd Psychi & Neurol.

HALL, EDWIN ARTHUR JR oc/Certified Tree Farmer; b/Feb 11, 1909; h/Indian Mountain Estate, Brackney, PA 18812; ba/Same; m/Freida Stein; c/Marlyce Dodd, Edwin A III, Charles Milton, David R, Marriet Bowser, Grichard, Eric Ashley; p/Edwin Arthur Sr and Harriet Babcock Hall (dec); cp/Former Mem: NY City Coun, 76th-82nd Congs, Sch Bd; r/Epis; hon/Winner NY-New England Area Oratorical Contest, A P Gianinni Foun & Am Inst Bkg.

HALL, FREDERICK COLUMBUS oc/- Plant Ecologist; b/Apr 19, 1927; h/*Golden Girl*, Hayden Isl Moorage, RM Unit, PO Box 3623, Portland, OR 97208; ba/Portland; c/Wayne F, Conlee H Steenberg; p/Nelson C and Carol C Hall, Phoenix, AZ; ed/MS

Purdue Univ 1951; MS 1956, PhD 1966 Oreg St Univ; mil/USMC 1944-45, 1951-54 (Ofcr); Ret'd from Resvs; pa/Plant Ecologist US Forest Ser, Portland; Forest & Non-Forest Ecological Investigation; Led USFS Reg Ecol Prog; hon/USDA: Superior Ser, Cert of Merit.

HALL, INEZ JEAN oc/Author; Lecturer; Businesswoman; b/May 7, 1930; h/1733 W 38th St, Anderson, IN 46013; ba/Richmond, IN; m/Phillip R II; c/Phillip R III, David T II, Katrina, Philomena, Dondeena; p/Granville P Kidd, Franklin, Ohio; Livia Clair Smallwood Kidd (dec); ed/BA; MA; EdD; pa/Edr-Lectr-Writer: Ind Univ, Ball St Univ, Anderson Col; r/1st Ch of God; hon/Lambda Iota Tau; Kappa Delta Pi; Hons in Langs; Biogl Listings.

HALL, JUDY A oc/Administrator; b/Oct 1, 1938; h/12231 Mentz Hill Rd, St Louis, MO 63128; ba/Alton, IL; m/Robert E; c/Keith J Bennett, Kristin D Bennett; p/Roy M Ragan, Kirkwood, MO; Margaret E Ragan (dec); ed/BA; MSW; PhD Cand; pa/Reg Dir Chd's Home & Aid Soc Ill; NASW; APGA; MASW; St Louis PGA; cp/MENSA; r/Bapt; hon/Phi Beta Kappa; 1st Lady of Day, WRTH; World W/W Wom; W/W: MW, Intells, Sch Dist Ofcls.

HALL, MILDRED VERZOLA oc/Social Worker; b/Jul 2, 1915; h/2460 LaSalle Gardens N, Detroit, MI 48206; ba/Detroit; m/Thomas N; p/Compton W and Gussie M Rowland (dec); ed/BA; MSW; pa/Acad Cert'd Social Wkrs; NASW, Detroit Chapt Social Work Coun; cp/NAACP; OES; r/Meth; hon/Arne Erickson Awd, Fam Ser Detroit &

Wayne Co; 25 Yr Ser Awd, St of Mich.

HALL, MONA MARIE oc/Retired Educator & Librarian; b/Jul 15, 1917; h/150 Roosevelt Rd, Jacksonville, AR 72076; p/John C and Tilda Criswell Hall (dec); ed/BA Ark Col 1947; MALS Peabody Col 1957; Addit Studies: Univ NC, Univ Okla, Univ Ark; pa/Ret'd 1976; Tchr Ark Schs 14 Yrs; Libn 18 Yrs; HS 10 Yrs, So Bapt 4 Yrs, Asst Libn UCA 4 Yrs, Ret'd from J'ville Jr HS N; ARTA; NRTA; JRTA; NEA; AEA; PACT; ALA; Ark Lib Assn; AAUW; WNBA; cp/Dem; r/Bapt: Secy, Treas, Tchr, Secy & Asst Secy Classes, Choir; hon/25 Yr Ser Awd, Ark Col; Lifetime Cert, Ark St Bd Ed; Cert of Merit, Pulaski Co Spec Sch Dist; Personalities of S; Commun Ldrs & Noteworthy Ams; World W/W Wom; W/W Lib Ser in US; Others.

HALL, ROBERT ARTHUR oc/State Legislator; b/Apr 15, 1946; h/9 Adams St, Fitchburg, MA 01420; ba/Boston, MA; p/Robert R and Dorothy Hall, Lunenburg, MA; ed/BA; mil/USMC 1964-68, Vietnam 1966-67; Present USMCR Corporal; cp/St

Senator, Mem Coms: Post-Audit, Public Safety, Commerce & Labor, Govt Regulations, Election Laws, Local Affairs; Mem F'burg Repub Com; hon/Sportsman of Yr, Worcester Co; Outstg Yg Men Am; Deans Key, MI-Wachusett Commun Col.

HALL, ROBERT MALCOLM oc/Judge; b/Jan 14, 1944; h/520 N Monroe, Williamsport, IN 47993; ba/W'port; m/Jeanette Kemp; c/Richard M, Kevin M; p/Richard M and Evelyn L Hall, Veedersburg, IN; ed/AB Ind Univ 1966; JD Ind Univ Sch of Law 1969; pa/Bar Assns: Ftn Co (Pres 1972-73), Warren Co, Ind & Am; Ind Judges Assn; Nat & Ind Coun Juv Ct Judges; Am Judic Soc; cp/Repub; r/Prot.

HALL, SAMUEL JONATHAN III oc/Real Estate; Merchant; Tree Farmer; b/Jul 10, 1916; h/602 Broadway, Ashford, AL 36312; ba/Ashford; m/Mary Kimball Egbert (dec); c/Samuel J IV, Joan H Godfrey; p/Samuel J Hall (dec); Dixie E Vaughn (dec); ed/BS Univ Ala; mil/AUS 1941-46, 1253rd Combat Engr Battalion; pa/Nat Assn Realtors; Farm & Land Inst; cp/Am Legion; BPO; Elks; VFW; r/Presb Ch US; hon/5 Mil Medals incl'g ETO Medal w 2 Bronze Stars.

HALL, WILFRED McGREGOR oc/Engineering Executive; b/Jun 12, 1894; h/4600 Prudential Tower, Boston, MA 02199; m/Anne Gertrude Jones; c/2 Chd; ed/BS Univ Colo 1916; DEng Tufts Univ 1955; pa/Chas T Main Inc, Boston: Dir 1943-, VP 1953-57, Pres & Chief Exec Ofcr 1957-72, Chm & Chief Exec Ofcr 1972-; Fellow Am Soc Civil Engrs; Mass Soc Profl Engrs; US Comm on Irrigation & Drainage; US Comm on Large Dams, Former Dir; Past Dir Engrg Sch Univ Colo; cp/Past Dir Mass Heart Assn; hon/George Westinghouse Gold Medal, Am Soc Mech Engrs; George Nolin Awd, Univ Colo; Author: *The Niagara - Adm and Construction Mgmt, Hydroelectric Devel in Turkey*; Notable Ams; Men Achmt; DIB.

HALLET, JEAN-PIERRE oc/Explorer; Sociologist; Naturalist; Author; Producer; Lecturer; b/Aug 4, 1927; h/PO Box 1067, Malibu, CA 90265; m/Marc, Bernard; p/Andre Hallet (dec); Berthe Hallet, Brussels, Belgium; ed/Agronomy, Sociol; mil/Belgian Resistance

1942-43, Army 1944-45; pa/Fdr-Pres The Pygmy Fund 1974; Owner Jean-Pierre Hallet's Pvt Gallery (African Arts), Malibu 1975-; Prodr 2 Ednl Films for *Encyclopaedia Britannica* 1975; Prodr, Dir Feature Documentary *Pygmies* 1973; Org'd Jean-Pierre Hallet's Spec Safaris (leads each sum) 1969-; Lectr Var Orgs in US & Fgn Countries 1961-; Num Other Profl Activs; hon/Humanitarian of Decade, ACF 1977; Hon Citizenship, Sev Sts & Cities; Fellow Mem, World-Wide Acad Scholars; Mayor's Commend (for saving Pygmies from extinction), Los Angeles; K of Mark Twain; Hon Mem, Honolulu Adventurers' Clb; Recipient Best Book Awd, ALA; Most Outstg Spkr of Yr, LA Adventurers' Clb 1965; 2000 Men Achmt; Num Other Awds & Certs of Merit & Apprec.

HALLIBURTON, JOHN ROBERT oc/Attorney at Law; Electronics Business Executive; b/Jul 31, 1934; h/PO Box 278, Rockwall, TX 75087; ba/Dallas, TX; m/Julia Ella Bateman; c/Cherie Ann, John Robert II, Rhonda Marie; p/Ralph E and Mary Smith

Halliburton, Shreveport, LA; ed/BS Centenary Col La; JD So Meth Univ; LLM Geo Wash Univ; mil/AUS (Regular Army) 1955-59, 1/Lt; pa/St Bar Tex; DC Bar Assn; r/Rom Cath; hon/Dist'd Mil Grad; ODK; Phi Delta Phi; W/W: S&SW, Am Cols & Univs.

HALLUM, ROSEMARY oc/Teacher; Educational Writer; Consultant; b/Oct 2; h/1021 Otis Dr, Alameda, CA 94501; ba/Oakland, CA; p/Fred F Hallum, Alameda, Edna B Hallum (dec); ed/BA; MA; PhD; pa/Tchg, Writing, Conslt'g; Tchr Disco Classes; cp/Spkr; Demonstrations; Wkshops; Others; r/Cath; hon/Phi Beta Kappa; Delta Kappa Gamma; ASCAP, S'ships.

HALO, HUGO H oc/Physician; b/Apr 9, 1930; h/162 E Hill Dr, Cranston, RI 02920; ba/Cranston; m/Marie; c/Deborah, Teresita, Marisa; p/Macario Halo (dec); Justa Hona Halo, Manila, Philippines; ed/MD; pa/RI Med Ctr, Inst Mtl Hlth: Clin Dir Geriatric Unit 1978, Clin Dir Female Ser 1975, Acting Dir Med Ed 1975, Clin Dir Adolescent Unit 1972, Dir Dept Group Therapy 1968-71; Psychi Conslt Providence Diocese (Elem & HS) 1972; Dir Child Study & Guid Clin St Mary's Sch, Cranston 1971; Other Former Positions; Am, Canadian, World Psychi Assns; AMA; RI & Providence Med Soc; Assn Philippine Pract'g Physicians in Am; Philippine Med Soc; MCU Alumni Assn; Fellow Royal Soc Hlth (London, England); r/Rom Cath; Cert of Merit for Mtl Hlth Res, DIB; Cert of Invaluable Ser, St Mary's Sch of Cranston; Notable Ams; W/W E; Intl Reg Profiles; Intl W/W Commun Ser; Commun Ldrs Am; Profl Pubs.

HALPERN, TEODORO oc/Dean, Professor; b/Sept 5, 1931; h/760 Cottage Pl, Teaneck, NJ 07666; ba/Mahwah, NJ; m/Marta; c/Patricia, Pablo G, Marcelo; p/David Halpern (dec); Fanny Wahrsager (dec); ed/MSc 1958; Dipl Physiker 1961; Dr rer nat, PhD 1961; pa/Ramapo Col NJ: Dean Schs, Prof Physics, Dir Sch Theoretical & Applied Scis; VP Fund Raising AFS, Teaneck Chapt; Bd Dirs HIP Gtr NY, Washington Hgts Ctr; Bd Trustees The Early Lng Ctr; Secy Argentine Phy Soc; Others; Clin Analyst; Hematologist; Lectr Socio Polits Nuclear Power; hon/Author *Fisicoquimica de Metales*, 1962, Other Pubs; Patentee in field; F'ships; Others.

HALSTEAD-McFARLAND, DIANE CLAIRE oc/Director; b/Mar 21, 1940; h/-57A Valley Hill Rd, RD #1, Malvern, PA 19355; ba/Allentown, PA; m/C Ross McFarland; p/Ernest Ray and Lucile A Halstead, Winchester, WI; ed/MS; PhD; pa/Microbiol/Immunology; Am Soc Microbiol; ASM En Br; Am Soc Clin Pathologists; Specialist Am Acad Microbiologists; Wom in Med, Theta Mu Chapt; r/Luth: Mem Altar Guild; hon/Dean's List; W/W Am.

HAM, BEVERLY J TOTMAN oc/Executive; Consultant; b/Jun 18, 1934; h/2207 Newport Bch, CA 92660; ba/Newport Bch; m/George A; c/Timothy, Gregory, Phillip, Jerry Jr; p/John O and Mabel H Jordan (dec); ed/BA Ohio St Univ; pa/Resort & Restaurant Mgmt 1968-71; The Bradford Group, Exec Search: Sr Assoc 1971-72, Sr VP 1973-78, Fdr, Chm of Bd 1979; Pres & Dir, Career Images Pers Ser 1979; Wom in Bus; Am Mgmt Assn; Nat Restaurant Assn; Cal Restaurant Assn; cp/Nat Dir, AASK, NTL; Orange City C of C; Speakers Bur; r/St Lukes Epis Ch: Past Secy.

HAMACHEK, ALICE LAVONNE oc/-Associate Professor; b/Oct 22, 1942; h/2157 Tamarack, Okemos, MI 48864; ba/Mt Pleasant, MI; m/Don E; ed/BS 1964, Master's 1970 Ctl Mich Univ; PhD Mich St Univ 1972; pa/Assoc Prof Elem Ed Ctl Mich Univ; IRA; Mich Rdg Assn; NCTM; Phi Delta Kappa; Rdg Conslt; cp/Big Sisters of Am; r/Prot; hon/Outstg Yg Edr Am; Outstg Edrs Am.

HAMACHEK, DON E oc/Professor; Psychologist; b/May 6, 1933; h/2157 Tamarack, Okemos, MI 48864; ba/East Lansing, MI; m/Alice L; c/Debbie, Dan; p/Evans O Hamachek, Sault Ste Marie, MI;

Marvis Hamachek, Sault Ste Marie, MI; ed/AB; MSW; PhD; pa/Prof Mich St Univ; Author; Pvt Therapy Pract; r/Prot; hon/Phi Kappa Phi; Outstg Alumnus, Lake Superior Col.

HAMBERGER, LOREN DAHLHAMER oc/Journalist; b/Mar 2, 1958; h/4429 Rena Rd, Apt 104, Forestville, MD 20023; m/Donald M Jr; p/Charles H and Gloria L Dahlhamer, Hagerstown, MD; ed/BS Towson St Univ 1980; pa/Editorial Asst; Freelance Writer & Poet; Sigma Delta Chi; Anthology Soc; Intern Writer, *Daily Mail* Newspaper 1978; Pub'd 5 Poems in Anthol Soc Annual Yrbook; r/Prot; hon/Bicent Yth Debate Awd; Dist'd Dean's List Awd.

HAMBOURGER, LINDA S MINTZ oc/College Administrator; b/Jan 2, 1946; h/443 Richmond Park West, Cleveland, OH 44143; ba/Cleve; m/Paul D; p/Richell P and Rose Z Mintz; ed/BA Univ Cinc 1970; pa/Inter-Univ Purchasing Coun; Nat Assn Ednl Buyers; Purchasing Mgmt Assn.

HAMILTON, CHARLES GRANVILLE oc/Minister; Historian; Poet; Newscaster; Statesman; b/Jul 18, 1905; h/Aberdeen, MS 39730; ba/Same; m/Mary Elizabeth Casey; p/Augustus W and Mary C Frey Hamilton (dec); ed/AB Berea; BD, MDiv Columbis; MA Univ Miss; PhD Vanderbilt; DD; mil/Chaplain 155th Inf WWII; pa/Author 32 Books: Rel, Poetry, Hist, Govt; Editor 20 Books; Contbr Var Books; Author 114 Pamphlets & Num Articles; Editor *Churchman, Jour Monroe History*;

cp/Chaplain Gen Sons Confed Vets; Former Floor Ldr Miss House; Former Del Sev Dem Nat Convs; Others; hon/Min of Yr; Ky & Miss Col.

HAMILTON, CHRISTINA DEE oc/Music Specialist; Music Studio Owner; b/Nov 30, 1935; h/516 N Fess, Bloomington, IN 47401; ba/B'ton; p/Stanley and Mildred M Hamilton, B'ton; ed/BS Miami Univ; MS Ind Univ; pa/Former Pvt Piano & Organ Studio; MENC; IMEA; MCEA; ISTA; NEA; Orff Shulwerk Assn; cp/Former Mem Yg Repubs; r/Meth; hon/IPA; Intl W/W Music; Wom of Achmt; W/W World Intells.

HAMILTON, ETHEL MACY oc/Retired Teacher; b/Jun 16, 1908; h/925 Cedar St, McMinnville, OR; m/Milton D; c/Janet Hartling (Mrs Norman), Scott Macy; p/Walter and Olive Macy (dec); ed/BS; pa/Life Mem: OEA, NEA; Former Ofcr assn Oreg Geographers; cp/Local C of C; Local VRegent DAR; Treas Newmac Toastmistress; Others; r/1st Presb Ch, M'ville: Mem, Pres Guild; hon/25 Yr Ser Awd, Pythian Sisters; Ofcrs Awd, Assn Oreg Geographers; Former Girl Scout Ldrs Awd; Yamhill Co Tchrs Retiremt Awd.

HAMILTON, EUGENE LEVERETT oc/Newspaperman; b/Aug 13, 1917; h/25 Lakeshore Dr, Tuscaloosa, AL 35401; m/Mary Frances Hammons (dec); 2nd Beverly Sanders Purser; c/Mary Alice, Betty Jean; p/Leverett John and Floy Mae Stout Hamilton; mil/AUS 1941-45, PTO;

pa/Tuscaloosa *News*: Conslt, Advr 1970-, Gen Mgr 1966-70, VP 1954-, Bus Mgr 1953, Advtg Mgr 1951-53; Advtg Exec Clearwater (Fla) *Sun* 1947-51; Advtg Exec Myers Dept Store, Clearwater 1945-47; Others; cp/Am Legion; Tuscaloosa CC; Var Former Activs; r/Presb; hon/W/W S&SW.

HAMILTON, MADRID TURNER oc/Social Worker; Educator; h/136 Geneva Ave, San Francisco, CA 94112; m/Norman Woodrow; c/1 Son; p/Paul and Mary Hubert Turner; ed/AB Spelman Col; MSW Atlanta Univ; Doct Tng Var Univs; pa/Assoc Prof Sociol & Ethnic Studies Univ Redlands (Cal); Former Prof'ships: Morehouse Col, Atlanta (Ga) & SF St Univ; Pres Hamilton Enterprises (Conslt'g Firm), SF; Reg Rep Fam Ser Assn Am; Reg Dir Planned Parenthood Fdn Am; Developed Mobile Unit Fam Planning Ser, Public Hlth Soc; Former Prog & Activs Dir'ships Phila & NY YWCAs; Former Conslt NYC Dept Public Hlth; Lic'd in Real Est; Am Acad Polit & Social Sci; Nat Assn Social Wkrs; Am Public Hlth Assn; cp/Var Adv Coms NYC Urban Leag; U Negro Col Fund; Spelman Col Alumnae; Bd Dirs SF YWCA; Relands YWCA; Nat Bd YWCA; U Way Redlands; Cal Gov's Population Study Comm; Zeta Phi Beta; hon/Human Resource Awd, Am Heritage Foun; Hon'd as Million Mile Traveler; Pub'd Author; Biogl Listings.

HAMILTON, MARGARET MARIE oc/Bookkeeper; b/Oct 7, 1938; h/1701 19 Ave No, Tex City, TX 77590; m/Leonard; c/Steven, Elizabeth, Mark Shawn; p/Will R and Marie Bearden, Tex City; cp/Girl Scouts: Troop Ldr, Orgr & Conslt, Assn Chm; Galveston Co Hist Com: Secy, Marker Chm; Tex City Hist Comm; Tex Hist Comm; Tex City Heritage Assn: CoFdr, Pres 2 Terms,

Secy, Bd Mem, Restoration Chm; Galveston Co Bicent Comm; CoChm Tex City 1976 Birthday Celebration; Heritage Com Tex City Jubilee Celebration; Others; r/Meth Ch: Choir, Comm of Ed, Comm on Missions, Attendance Secy; hon/Jr Wom of Yr, BPW; Best Com Mem, Tex St Hist Comm; Notable Ams.

HAMILTON, MARY ELIZABETH oc/-Educator; b/Mar 23, 1924; h/7 DeSoto Cir, Texarkana, TX 75503; ba/Texarkana; m/Carl C; c/Carla Elizabeth, Nakata, Leslie Lane H Webster, Mary Janine, Michael William; p/George W Daniels (dec); Virginia Billingslea Daniels, Augusta, AR; ed/BS; MS; EdS; EdD; pa/Instr, SW Ark Tchr Ctr; Phi Delta Kappa; Alpha Delta Kappa; Texarkana Reading Coun; IRA; Nat Bus Ed Assn; Mtn-Plains Bus Ed Assn; Classroom Tchrs Assn; Ark Ed Assn; NEA; Assn Supvn & Curric Devel; Assn Tchr Edrs; cp/Friends of Lib; ERA; AAUW; r/Trinity Presb Ch; hon/BS cum laude; F'ship, Ks St Univ; Others.

HAMILTON, MARY ELIZABETH CASEY oc/Editor; Retired Math Teacher; b/Sept 14, 1910; h/Meridian, Monroe & Maple, Aberdeen, MS 39730; ba/Same; m/Charles Granville; p/John Lucas and Anna Cordelia Frank Casey (dec); ed/BA Miss St Col for Wom; Grad Work; pa/Editor *Jour of Monroe Co History*; Pres Monroe Co Hist Soc; cp/Pres Aberdeen Wom's Clb; Chm City Beautiful Com; Registrar & Am Heritage Chm DAR; Horizons Chm Bicent; Dir Artists Guild; Miss Humanities Com Wkshop; Gov's Conf on Ed; Del Dem Convs; r/Epis; hon/Aberdeen Wom of Yr 1976; Clbwom of Yr 1979.

HAMILTON, THEOPHILUS ELLIOTT oc/University Administrator; b/Feb 6, 1923; h/221 Wilson Ave, Ypsilanti, MI 48197; ba/Ypsilanti; m/Fannie Lee; c/Millicent Allyse; p/George Elliott and Sarah Louise Hamilton (dec); ed/BMus; MA; SpecA Sch Adm; mil/5th Army 92nd Div, 366th Inf WWII; pa/En Mich Univ: Asst Dir Career Planning & Placemt Ctr 1969-, Asst Dir Pers Dept 1967-69; Asst Prin Highland Park Public Schs (Mich) 1964-67; Other Former Positions; Mich Col & Univ Placemt Assn: Mem 1969-, Secy & Treas 1972-73; Assoc Mem Mich Assn for Sch Admrs; Assoc Mem Gt Lakes Assn for Col & Univ Placemt; Former Mem: Col & Univ Pers Assn, Sch Admrs & Prin Assn; Past Pres Pickford Sch Tchrs' Assn; Kappa Alpha Psi; Fac Advr Delta Nu Chapt Kappa Alpha Psi, En Mich Univ; Mem En Mich Univ Appeal Judic Bd; cp/Ypsilanti Twp Planning Comm; Former Mem Washtenaw Co Commun Agy Assn; r/Luth; Mem Social Min Com, Mich Synod Luth Ch Am; hon/Alumni Achmt Awd, Kappa Alpha Psi; Dedication Commun Ser Awd, Kappa Alpha Psi; Best Tchr Awd, En Mich Univ Pers; W/W Among Black Ams.

HAMLAR, PORTIA Y T oc/Attorney; Professor; Publisher; b/Apr 30, 1932; h/748 Great Oaks Blvd, Rochester, MI 48063; ba/Detroit, MI; c/Eric L; p/Harper Council Trenholm (dec); Portia T Jenifer, Los Angeles, CA; ed/BA Ala St Univ 1951; MA Mich St Univ 1953; JD Univ Detroit 1972; pa/Atty Chrysler Corp Legal Dept; Prof of Law; ABA; Detroit Bar Assn; Motor Vehicle Mfrs Assn; Org Resources Cnslrs OSHA Lwyrs Group; r/Epis; hon/Univ Detroit Law Review; Alpha Kappa Mu.

HAMMER, LILLIAN oc/Poet; Writer; h/15 Elmwood St, Albany, NY 12203; m/Jack; c/Ruth, Helen; p/(dec); ed/Gen Col Ed; pa/U Poets Laureate Intl; Am Soc Writers; World Poetry Soc Intercontinental; Nat Soc Lit & the Arts; Centro Studi e Scambi Internazional; Pierson Meltier Assocs; Belles-Lettres Soc; Nat Mem Smithsonian Assocs; hon/World Belletrist Awd for Poetry; Belletrist Scroll, Life Mbrship; Gold Medal of Honor; Trophy World Poetry Awd for Poetry, Intl Poetry Centre IB-SL; Poetry Hall of Fame, World Poetry Lib Acad Contemp Poets; Num Others.

HAMMER, NORMAN LYLE oc/Pastor;

b/Nov 2, 1912; h/333 Lewers St, Honolulu, HI 96815; ba/Honolulu; m/Virgie T Olson; c/Sheryl Ann Sack, Stephen Lyle, Sonja Joanna Latawiec; p/Peder Hammer (dec); Anna Cecelia Tosseland (dec); ed/BA Bethany Col 1937; pa/Luth Pastor; cp/Former Mem Honolulu Mayor's Adv Comm; r/Luth; hon/Dist'd Ser Alumni Awd, Bethany Col.

HAMMERSCHMIDT, JOHN PAUL oc/Business Executive; Member of Congress; b/May 4, 1922; h/PO Box 999, Harrison, AR 72601; ba/Washington, DC; m/Virginia Sharp; c/John Arthur; p/Arthur P Hammerschmidt, Harrison; ed/The Citadel; Okla St Univ; Univ Ark; mil/USAAC Entered 1942; Pilot 3rd Combat Cargo Group, China-India-Burma Theatre; Air Medal w 4 OLC; Dist'd Flying Cross w 3 OLC; 3 Battle Stars; pa/Bldr & Bldg Supplies Dealer; Chm of Bd Hammerschmidt Lumber Co, Harrison; Past Pres: Ark Lumber Dealers, SWn Lumberman's Assn (Ks City, Mo); Former Nat Dir Nat Lumber & Bldg Mat Dealers; cp/US Rep 3rd Dist Ark 90th-96th Congs, Mem Var Coms; Former Chm Harrison City Planning Comm; Past Pres Boone Co Indust Devel Corp; BPO Elks; Am Legion; VFW; Boone Masonic Blue Lodge No 314; 32° Mason; Pi Kappa Alpha; Scimitar Shrine; Am Fdn Small Bus, Adv Com; Adv Bd Pres Classroom for Yg Ams; Others; r/Presb: Ordained Elder & Deacon; hon/Hon Mem, Future Farmers Am Alumni Assn.

HAMMETT, ARTHUR B J oc/Banker; Author; Industrialist; b/Oct 23, 1902; h/701 N Washington St, Victoria, TX; 2500 E Las Olas Blvd, Ft Lauderdale, FL; ba/Victoria, TX; m/(dec); c/Jacqueline Gaylord, Jo Anne Huff; p/Benjamin J and Rena Mae Hammett (dec); ed/Var; mil/Admiral Tex Navy; Cmdr USNR WWII; pa/Author Var Books; r/Prot; hon/Var Mil & Civilian.

HAMMETT, EUGENE KIRBY oc/Ballet Master; Choreographer; Artistic Director; b/Apr 24, 1937; h/3222 Tidewater Dr, Norfolk, VA 23509; ba/Same; p/Eugene K Hammett (dec); Irene Hammett Norman, Winston-Salem, NC; ed/Black Mtn Col; NYU; Wake Forest Ballet Sch; Am Ballet Theatre; Sch Am Ballet; pa/Pres Va Dance Week; Chm: Va Dance Fest, Intl Azaela Fest Ballet Gala; Pres Tidewater Ballet Assn; r/Christian Sci; hon/White House Ctr for Intl Azaela Fest Perfs; US Jewish Commun Ctr Ser Awd; Choreographic Mention, Varna, Bulgaria.

HAMMOND, JAY S oc/Governor; b/Jul 21, 1922; ba/Juneau, AL; m/Bella Gardiner; c/Heidi, Dana; ed/Pa St 1940-42; Grad (Biol Scis) Univ Alaska 1948; mil/USN 1942-46; Marine Fighter Pilot WWII; Hon Disch as Capt; pa/Homesteader Lake Clark, Comml Fisherman, Master Guide, Air Taxi Operator 1956-74; Pilot Agt US Fish & Wildlife Ser 1948-56; Others; cp/Elected Gov of Alaska 1974; Mayor Bristol Bay Borough 1972-74; Former Mem Alaska St Senate & Alaska Ho of Reps.

HAMMOND, RUSSELL IRVING oc/Retired University Professor; Former Dean; b/Aug 29, 1908; h/816 S 17th St, Laramie, WY 82070; m/Ola Arline; c/DiAnn Arline; p/Walter and Dora Claussen Hammond (dec); ed/BA; MA; EdD Columbia Univ 1942; mil/USN 1944-46, Lt (sg); pa/Ret'd Univ Prof (30 Yrs), Former Dean of Grad Studies in Ed; Supt of Schs 10 Yrs; St Dir Nat Ret'd Tchrs Assn; cp/Past Pres Laramie Lions Clb; Lobbyist Wyo Leg 4 Yrs; r/Meth; hon/Dist'd Mem, Coun of Ednl Facility Planners.

HAMMONS, DONALD R oc/Industrial Engineer; Research Consultant; b/Mar 16, 1922; h/2604 Arbor, Bryan, TX 77801; ba/College Station, TX; m/Genevieve; p/Cecile Lee Hammons, Gallatin, TX; ed/BS Tex Tech Univ 1951; mil/USAAC 1942-46; pa/ASAE; Food Dist Res Soc; Reg'd Profl Engr: Okla, Tex; hon/DIB; Men of Achmt; Personalities of S; W/W: Am, S&SW.

HAMNER, SHARON BOONE oc/Genealogical Record Searcher; b/Jul 31, 1939; h/111 Reynard Dr (Colthurst Farm), Charlottesville, VA 22901; ba/Same; m/Charles Edward Jr; c/Diana, Clifton; p/Joseph Wilson Boone, Toomsboro, GA; Edna Reed Pierce, Milledgeville, GA; ed/BSHE cum laude 1961, MEd 1963 Univ Ga; Addit Studies; pa/Pres Hamner Res Sers; Cert'd Geneal Record Searcher; Nat Geneal Soc; Albemarle Co Hist Soc; Former Home Ec Tchr; cp/DAR; Albemarle Co (Va) Tax Equalization Bd; Sr Ctr Bd; Citizens for Albemarle; 4-H Vol; r/Epis, Ch of Our Saviour: Mem, Former Vestry Person, Christian Ed Dir.

HAMPTON, CAROL DEAN oc/College Professor; b/Apr 19, 1929; h/103 Lamont Rd, Greenville, NC 27834; ba/G'ville; m/Carolyn H; c/Frederick B; p/Fred D Hampton (dec); Nettie Hampton, Carterville, IL; ed/AB; MSEd; EdD; mil/USAF 4 Yrs; pa/Prof Sci Ed Dept E Carolina Univ; Supvr Student Tchrs in Sci; Sci Conslt; cp/Chm Pitt Co Chapt NC Zool Soc; r/Luth; hon/St Chm NABT, Outstg Biol Tchr Awd Prog; Phi Delta Kappa.

HAMPTON, CAROLYN HUTCHINS oc/Professor; b/Dec 11, 1936; h/103 Lamont Rd, Greenville, NC 27834; ba/G'ville; m/Carol D; c/Frederick Bennett; p/Hugh Caldwell Hutchins (dec); Mary Elarnor Patton Hutchins, G'ville; ed/BS Appalachian St Univ 1959; MS 1961, PhD 1963 Univ Tenn; pa/E Carolina Univ: Prof Sci Ed 1976–, Assoc Prof 1970-76, Asst Prof 1966-70; Asst Prof Natural Sci Longwood Col, Farmville, Va 1965-66; Dir

OBIS Resource Ctr 1975–; Other Former Positions; Sigma Xi; Delta Kappa Gamma; Nat Sci Tchrs Assn; Am Inst Biol Sci; NC Acad Sci; NC Sci Tchrs Assn; AAUP; r/Our Redeemer Luth Ch, NC Synod: Luth Ch Wom, NC Synod Com on Envir Concerns, Ch Coun; hon/Dir Var Sci Projs & Progs; Recipient Sev F'ships; Gustaf-Ohaus Awd for Innovations in Col Sci Tchg Awd, NSTA Conv (Los Angeles, Cal) 1975; Profl Pubs.

HAMPTON, OPHINA (PEGGY) L oc/Registered Nurse; b/Nov 19, 1924; h/500 Oak Ave, S Pittsburg, TN 37380; ba/S P'burg; m/Newton Scott Sr; c/N Scott Jr, George L, J Tom; p/Oscar R Lawson (dec); Mary L Vann (dec); ed/Dipl Baroness Erlanger Hosp (Chattanooga, Tenn); Postgrad (CCU) St Mary's Hosp (Knoxville); pa/RN S P'burg Mun Hosp; AACCN; ANA; Supvr CCU & EKG-EEG Dept; Editor Hosp Newslttr *Happenings*; cp/BEH Alumni; Chm "Wom for Brock"; Den Mother, Cub Scouts; r/Presb: SS Tchr; hon/"Operation Pincushion", JC Awd; W/W Am Wom.

HAMRA, SAM F JR oc/Attorney at Law; b/Jan 21, 1932; h/2704 S Marlan, Springfield, MO 65804; ba/S'field; m/June; c/Sam F III, Karen Escine, Michael Kenneth, Jacqueline Kay; p/Sam Farris and Victoria Hamra; ed/BS Univ Mo Bus Sch 1954; LLB Univ Mo Law Sch 1959; mil/AUS Field Arty 1954-56, 1/Lt; pa/Greene Co Bar Assn: Treas 1966-67, Bd Dirs 1974-77; Mo & Am Bar Assns; Pres Legal Aid Assn, Greene Co 1976-77; cp/S'field C of C; Former Mem Bd Dirs, Chm Var Coms; Masons; Scottish Rite, Shrine; Charter Mem Pres' Clb Drury Col, S'field; Mem Mo Savs & Ln Comm; Former Mem Fin Com Dem Nat Com; Mo Fin Coor Carter-Mondale Campaign 1976; Del Dem Nat Conv 1972; Var Campaign Activs; Other Civic Activs; r/St James Epis Ch: Bd Dirs (Vestry) 1962-64, 1969-71;

hon/Outstg Yg Man of Yr: S'field 1966, Mo 1967; Nom'd for Am's 10 Outstg Yg Men of Yr 1967; Biogl Listings.

HAMRICK, CHARLES ROBERT oc/Advertising Coordinator; b/Oct 8, 1946; h/9405 Mariner's Ridge Dr, Fort Wayne, IN 46819; ba/Fort Wayne; m/Linda Ann Weaver; c/Michelle, Marie, Heather; p/William J and Mary Hamrick, Terre Haute, IN; ed/BA w hons; MSEd; pa/Advt'g Coor J C Penney Co; Distributive Ed Progs in Advt'g & Market; Charter Mem Intl Soc Artists; Lectr Ind Univ; Featured Work: Paintings Ayres Spring Art Fair 1972, Woodcut 16th Annual Wassenburg Art Mus Show, Van Wert, Ohio 1972, Weaving & Constr Satirical & Sensual Art Exhibit, Ind Univ 1975, Weavings The Love Tennis Tour Invitational Art Exhibit 1978; cp/Former Chm Parent Adv Com Pleasant Ctr Sch; Former Hd Judge Annual Art Fair; hon/Delta Epsilon Sigma; Intl W/W Commun Ser; W/W Students in Am Cols & Univs; Notable Ams; DIB; Fellow, ABI.

HAMRICK, JOYCE McCLESKEY oc/Assistant Professor; b/Feb 11, 1945; h/1 N Palafox Suite 420, Pensacola, FL 32501; ba/Dothan, AL; m/Robert Augustus; p/Benjamin C and Mary Jane McCleskey, Gulf Breeze, FL; ed/BA Univ W Fla 1969; MS 1970, PhD 1972 Univ So Miss; pa/Troy St Univ: Asst Prof Rdg (Dothan) 1975-78, Dir Rdg Ctr (Ft Rucker) 1972-75; Univ So Miss: Grad Tchg Fellow 1971-72, Coor Adult Basic Ed Media Ctr 1969-70; Other Former Positions; IRA; Ala Rdg Assn; Kappa Delta Pi; Phi Delta Kappa; Prog Chm Nat Rdg Conf Session 1978; cp/Essay Judge Assn of US Army S'ship Contest 1977; Coor Dothan READ-A-THON, Ctl Ala Chapt Nat MS Soc 1978-79; r/Prot; hon/Ctl Ala Chapt MS Patient Achmt Awd; Commun Ldrs & Noteworthy Ams; Notable Ams Bicent Era; Personalities of S; Outstg Edr Am; W/W Intells.

HANCE, KENT R oc/US Congressman; ba/1039 Longworth Bldg, Washington, DC 20515; m/Carol; c/Ron, Susan; ed/BBA Tex Tech Univ; LLB Univ Tex-Austin; pa/Lubbock & Am Bar Assns; Atty; Prof Tex Tech Univ, Regent W Tex St Univ; pa/Mem US Cong, 19th Dist Tex; Tex Boys' Ranch; SW Rotary Clb; Lubbock Lions; Water Inc; C of C; Tex Tech Century Clb; r/Bapt; hon/Counsel Awd, Univ Tex-A Sch of Law; Outstg Prof, Tex Tech Univ.

HANCOCK, GEORGE H SR oc/Retired; b/Nov 15, 1912; h/1003 N Alleghany Ave, Covington, VA 24426; m/Dorothy V; c/George Jr, Ralph, Nancy, Dottie, Ronald, Michael; p/Asa B Hancock (dec); Lucy E Hancock, Chattanooga, TN; pa/Ret'd, Installer-Repairman C'ton Exc of Clifton Forge-Waynesboro Telephone Co (36 Yrs Ser); r/Calvary Bapt Ch.

HANCOCK, GERRE EDWARD oc/Educator; Musician; b/Feb 21, 1934; h/1170 Fifth Ave, New York, NY 10029; ba/NYC; m/Judith Eckerman; c/Deborah Steger, Lisa Judith; p/Edward Ervin Hancock (dec); Flake Steger Hancock, Lubbock, TX; ed/BMus Univ Tex 1955; Masters Sacred Music Union Theol Sem 1961; pa/Fac Mem: Yale Univ, New Haven (Conn) & The Juilliard Sch, NYC; Fellow Am Guild Organists; Past Pres Assn Anglican Musicians; r/Epis: St Thomas Ch: Organist, Master of Choristers; hon/Pi Kappa Lambda; Rotary F'ship for Intl Study (Paris, France).

HANCOCK, IAN FRANCIS oc/University Professor; b/Aug 29, 1942; ba/Austin, TX 78712; m/Lee Swee-Lian; c/Julian, Adrian, Meilinne; p/Redjo and Kathleen Hancock; ed/PhD; pa/Prof Dept Eng Univ Tex-A; Editor *Jour of Creole Studies*; Linguistic Soc Caribbean Exec; cp/Intl Gypsy Com Exec.

HANDLER, SHIRLEY W oc/College Professor; b/Jan 2, 1925; h/203 E Crockett, Marshall, TX 75670; p/George A Handler, Marshall; Shirley W Handler (dec); ed/AA; BA; MA; PhD; pa/E Tex Bapt Col 1947–: Prof

Biol, Chm Div of Sci & Math; AAAS; Am Soc Human Genetics; Tex Acad Sci; cp/Pres Marshall Symph Soc; Reg VP Shreveport Symph; Pres Harrison Co Am Cancer Soc; Beta Sigma Phi; Secy Marshall Commun Concert Assn; r/Meth; hon/Girl of Yr, Marshall Beta Sigma Phi 1967; Wom of Achmt, BPW; Outstg Edr Am; Commended for Ser, Marshall Commun Concert Assn; 1 of 4 1977 Hdliners, Longview Profl Chapt Wom in Communs Inc; Am Men of Sci; DIB; W/W: Am Wom, Am Ed.

HANEBRINK, EARL LEE oc/Professor; b/Mar 24, 1924; h/4112 Oakhill Ln, Jonesboro, AR 72401; ba/St Univ, AR; m/Sue; c/John, Lisa, Lori, Kay; p/Harry H and Augusta Hanebrink (dec); ed/BS SE Mo St Univ 1948; MS Univ Miss 1955; EdD Okla St Univ 1965; mil/AUS 1943-46, Asiatic Pacific Theater of Opers; pa/Prof Biol St Univ Ark; Am Ornithologists' Union; Sigma Xi; Phi Delta Kappa; Phi Sigma; Tri-Beta; cp/Conslt in Envir Studies; r/Meth; hon/Outstg Edrs Am; Notable Ams Bicent Era; Intl W/W Commun Ser; Men of Achmt.

HANFORD, WILLIAM EDWARD oc/Chemist; b/Dec 9, 1908; h/4956 Sentinel Dr, Bethesda, MD 20016; ba/Same; m/Lorraine Harwood Easom; c/William E Jr, Ruth Harwood (dec); p/Thomac C and Irene L Hanford (dec); ed/BS Phila Col Pharm & Sci; MS, PhD Univ Ill; pa/Past Pres Indust Res Inst; Am Inst Chemists; Dir Am Chem Soc; Dir Sigma Xi; r/Presb; hon/Chem Indust Awd, SCI; Gold Medal, AIC; DS, Alfred Univ & Phila Col Pharm & Sci.

HANKINS, ANNA LOU oc/Nurse; b/Nov 23, 1907; h/Rt 1, Box 298, Vernon, AL 35592; m/Grover W (dec); c/Grover W Jr, Michael A; p/Archie E and Ida Dobbins Sartor (dec); ed/Nsg Dipl; pa/Ret'd Nurse; Worked in Public Hlth 35 Yrs; ASNA; ANA; cp/Dem; UDC; Homemaker Clb; r/So Bapt; hon/Nom'd Nurse of Yr 1967; Orchid Awd, Lung Assn; Wom of Yr 1977.

HANKINS, BETTIE JANET MERCER oc/Writer; b/Sept 7, 1942; h/Rt 1, Box 8-D, Ola, AR 72853; ba/Ola; m/Leon Emory; c/Angie Beth; p/Perry Monroe Mercer, Ola; Annie Elizabeth Tanner Mercer (dec); ed/BA Cand Ark Tech Univ; pa/Author 2 Pub'd Chd's Books: *The Selfish Elf & Tabby*; Photog & Feature Writer for Local Pubs; cp/Chm Fin Com Ola PTA; Cand Sch Bd; C of C: Former Secy, Bd Mem; Former Chm Mothers March, March of Dimes; Former Chm Yell Co Arthritis Foun; Charter Mem NAm Indian Foun; r/Ola U Meth Ch: Mem.

HANKINS, JOHN ERSKINE oc/Retired Teacher; b/Jan 2, 1905; h/RR 1, Oxford, ME 04270; m/Nellie E Pottle; c/Margaret, Thomas, John David; p/James Thomas Hankins (dec); Roma McKenzie (dec); ed/BA Univ SC 1924; MA 1925; PhD Yale 1929; pa/Eng Tchr: Univ Ks-L 1930-56, Univ Me-O 1956-70; Fulbright Lectr Univ Leyden 1953-54; Author: *The Character of Hamlet* 1941, *Shakespeare's Derived Imagery* 1953, *Sorree and Meaning in Spenser's Allegory* 1971, *Backgrounds of Shakespeare's Thought* 1978; r/Epis; hon/Phi Beta Kappa; Guggenheim F'ship.

HANKINSON, MEL DARWIN oc/Head Basketball Coach; b/Jan 28, 1943; h/403 S Bolivar, Cleveland, MS 38733; ba/Cleve; m/Joan Carol Cherry; c/Chad Brian, Joshua Dean; p/Melvin William Hankinson, Ambridge, PA; Arlene Bessie Hankinson; ed/BS; MS; pa/Hd Basketball Coach Delta St Univ; Former Positions; F'ship Christian Aths; Nat Assn Basketball Coaches; Spkr Danish Fdn Basketball Coaches 1977; cp/Nat Multiple Sclerosis Com; Run Roanoke Col Sum Basketball Camp (Approx 300 Boys); Main Spkr YMCA Annual Fund Raising Dr, Roanoke; Num Spkg Engagemts; r/Presb: Elder; hon/Phi Delta Kappa; Sportsman of Yr, Wn Pa Ofcl's Assn; Profl Pubs; Others.

HANKLA, VELMA CASH oc/Church Organist; Choir Director; Teacher Piano & Organ; b/Jul 7, 1910; h/PO Box 426,

Tazewell, VA 24651; m/(dec); c/1 Daugh; p/Walter Thomas and Rebecca Harriett Henninger Cash; ed/BMus; pa/Ch Organist, Choir Dir, Contralto Soloist & Pianist 60+ Yrs; Nu Chapt Phi Theta Kappa; Bd Mem Va Fdn Music Clbs; Pres Tazewell Music Clb; Former Pres Helen Trinkle Music Clb, Wytheville, Va; All Am Univ Wom; hon/Commun Ldrs & Noteworthy Ams; Hist Lives of Va.

HANKS, JESSE MACK oc/School Superintendent; b/Oct 8, 1901; h/9824 Eastridge, El Paso, TX 79925; ba/El Paso; m/Robbie Holloway; c/Jesse Parmer and Maggie Ruth Hanks (dec); ed/BS SW St Univ; MA Sul Ross St Univ; mil/AUS Maj WWII; pa/Ysleta HS: Former Tchr, Coach, Prin; Current Supt Schs Ysleta Indep Sch Dist; Life Mem: NEA, St & Nat Cong P's & T's; Tex St Tchrs Assn, Mem St Exec Com 6 Yrs (El Paso Area); Trans-Pecos Tchrs Assn, Past Pres; E El Paso Edrs Assn; Tex Assn Sch Admrs; Am

Assn Sch Admrs; 1 of Original Mems Coun & Exec Com SWn Cooperative Ednl Lab (Serving Ariz, NM, Okla, W Tex); cp/Ysleta Lions Clb: Charter Mem, Past Pres; Past Pres Knife & Fork Clb El Paso; Yucca Coun BSA; E EP YMCA; Nat Conf Christians & Jews; Former Bd Mem: EP Mus of Art, EP Fam Wel Ser, EP Safety Coun; Masonic Lodge; EP C of C; r/Ysleta U Meth Ch: Mem & Past Pres Ofcl Bd, Past Pres Bd Trustees; hon/Conquistador Awd for Outstg Ser, City of El Paso; St Awds as Outstg Admr: Future Farmers, Future Homemakers, DE Clbs Tex, Voc Agri Tchrs Assn Tex; Others.

HANSEN, EDWARD A oc/Clergyman; College Administrator; b/Apr 17, 1917; h/3211 Flag Ave N, New Hope, MN 55427; ba/Minneapolis, MN; m/Shirley M Bondo; c/Lee Anne, Linda; p/Albert and Anna C Nelsen Hansen (dec); ed/BA; BD; MDiv; DD;

pa/Bishop Emeritus; Current Dir Devel Golden Val Luth Col; Chm Home Coun World Mission Prayer Leag; Mem Inter-Luth Comm on Worship 1967-97; r/Am Luth Ch; hon/DDiv, St Olaf Col; Dist'd Alumnus, Dana Col.

HANSEN, HERBERT EDWIN oc/Director; b/Oct 29, 1920; h/11839 Durrette, Houston, TX 77024; ba/Houston; m/Marietta Hewitt; c/Marean Romaine, Donna Hewitt, David Christman; p/Maruis and Romaine Hansen (dec); ed/BA; MBA; JD; mil/Lt Cmdr, USNR; pa/Dir, Middle East Inst; Dir, ANERA (Wash, DC); Dir & Adv Bd Mem, Intl Bus Diplomacy, Georgetown Univ; Comm on Fgn Relats; r/Prot; hon/Phi Beta Kappa; Sigma Delta Psi; AB Summa Cum Laude.

HANSEN, JO ANN BROWN oc/Scientific Administrator; b/Jul 7, 1929; h/4926 E Bermuda, Tucson, AZ 85712; ba/Tuscon; m/Gordon Eddy; c/Erling Wilhelm II; p/William Brown (dec); Stefi Marie Shillingburg, Albuquerque, NM; ed/BS 1950, MS 1954, PhD 1966 Univ Ariz; pa/Univ Ariz: Res Assoc Cancer Ctr Div & Dept Internal Med 1977-, Proj Dir Sci Career Wkshop 1976-77, Res Assoc Dept Pharm (Col Med) 1975-76, Instr Dept Microbiol 1954-55; Conslt; VP Hansen's Auto & Tool Supply 1958-;

Other Former Positions; Am Soc Microbiol (Nat & Ariz Br); Ariz Acad Sci; AAAS; Am, Ariz & US-Mexico Border Public Hlth Assns; Assn for Wom in Sci; Sigma Delta Epsilon; Other Profl Activs; cp/Com of 100 St Joseph's Hosp; Mem Conslt Cadre Ariz Dept Ed; Mensa; AAUW; Repub Wom's Caucus: Fdr, Past Pres, Mem Exec Bd; NOW; Good Govt Leag; Chi Omega; Ninety-Nines; Others; r/Epis; hon/Recipient Grants; Iota Sigma Pi; 1 of Delegation (20 Profl Ariz Wom) to Visit People's Republic of China 1976; F'ship; Fdr's Fellow, AAUW; Biog! Listings; Profl Pubs.

HANSEN, JUNE ALLSHOUSE oc/Public School Teacher; b/Jun 30, 1920; h/3027 Hwy 508, Onalaska, WA 98570; ba/Onalaska; m/Steve; c/Holly June, Heather Harriett; p/John I and Pearl T Allshouse (dec); ed/BS; BEd; pa/Onalaska Ed Assn; AHEA; AAUW; cp/Toastmistress; OES; Literary Clb; 4-H Ldr; Repub Clb; r/Prot; hon/Outstg Elem Tchr Am; Ambassador to Oslo; Min-Grant in Career Ed.

HANSEN, KATHRYN G oc/Retired Social Adjustment & Art Coordinator; Businesswoman; b/Nov 5, 1909; h/2240-0-Via Puerta, Laguna Hills, CA 92653; ba/Same; m/Ralph E; p/Edmund and Margaret Gibbon (dec); ed/BSEd; MEd; Equiv Doct Deg; pa/Owner Bus in Art, Writing, Selling; Former Social Adjustmt Tchr & Art Coor 5 HSs (under Juris of Ct); Dir Proj Fam Life 1956-69; Former Sch Tchr; Chm Programme Brochures Ill Ed Assn (Chgo) 1965; Fdr Chgo Ed News; Life Mem NEA; Life Charter Mem NEA for Larger Cities; Delta Kappa Gamma: Life Mem, Pres Alpha Omega Chapt 1960-62; Fdr & Orgr Alpha Kappa Gamma Co Coor'g Coun 1963; Del all Ill & Nat Ed Assn Convs; Life Mem Chgo Art Ed Assn; Exceptl Chd's Assn; Adult Ed Assn (Univ Chgo); Secy AAUW (Cal) 1970-71; Others; cp/Former Chm Wom's Clb (Cal); Eliso Clb; Former Chm Laguna Hills Art Assn; Mem Smithsonian Inst; Golden Rain Hist Records Com, Laguna Hills Leisure World 1977-78; Currently Writing Book; r/Secy Laguna Hills Rel Coun 1975-78; hon/Press Prize, for Fdg Chgo Ed News; Profl Pubs; Var Dinners given in her honor for activs; Commun Ldrs & Noteworthy Ams; Intl W/W Intells; Intl Reg Profiles World Edition; Notable Ams; Intl Social Reg.

HANSEN, SUSAN MARIE oc/Sales Recruiter; b/Feb 2, 1948; h/133 Bordeaux Ct, Lake Elmo, MN 55042; ba/St Paul, MN; p/Robert M and Marjorie L Hansen, Pleasanton, CA; ed/Bachs Univ Cal-B 1970; Masters Cal St Univ-H 1977; pa/Sales Recruiter 3M Ctr (Staffing); cp/Alpha Chi Omega Alumnus; Ofcr E Bay Craftsmen's Clb 2 Yrs; Others; r/Rom Cath; hon/Sales Rep of Month, 3M Printing Prods Div.

HANSEN, WILLIAM FREEMAN

oc/Scholar; b/Jun 22, 1941; h/804 S Lincoln, Bloomington, IN 47401; ba/B'ton; m/Marcia Jean Cebulska; c/Inge Margrethe; p/William Freeman and Helen Marian Hansen, Santa Cruz, CA; ed/AB 1965, PhD 1970 Univ Cal-B; pa/Ind Univ: Assoc Prof Classical Studies & Fellow Folklore Dept 1977-, Asst Prof & Fellow 1970-77; hon/Hon Fellow, Am Scandinavian Foun; Younger Humanist Fellow, Nat Endowmt for Humanities; Fellow, Am Coun of Learned Socs.

HANSON, BERNOLD M (BRUNO) oc/Executive; b/May 7, 1928; h/1613 West Pecan, Midland, TX 79701; ba/Midland, TX; m/Marilyn Miller; c/Karen, Gretchen, Eric; ed/BS Univ ND 1951; MA Univ Wyom 1954; pa/Pres, Hanson Corp 1974-; Pres, Hanson Exploration Co Inc 1971-75; Pres, Hanson & Allen Inc 1966-74; Consltg Geologist & Independent Oil Operator1960-; Humble Oil & Refining Co: Dist Geologist (New Orleans, La), In charge of Proj (Alaska), Dist Geologist (Midland) 1955-60; Other Former Positions; Conslt in Tex, NM, ND, Ecuador, Nigeria, Norway, UK, Indonesia, Others; Profl Pubs; Am Assn Petro Geologists: Chm Profl Standards Com, Chm Contg Ed Com, Secy Profl Sect, Environ Com, Others; Am Inst Mining Engrs (Petro Sect): Am Inst Profl Geols, Advr of Fin; Sigma Xi; SW Fdn Geological Socs; Soc of Independent Profl Earth Scists; Others; cp/Life Mem: Univ of Wyom Alumni Assn & Wyom Sci Camp Alumni Assn; Midland C of C; Lions Clb; Nat Rifle Assn (Life Mem); BSA: Eagle Rank w 3 Palms, Order of Arrow, Former Asst Scoutmaster, Scoutmaster, World Jamboree in Japan, Silver Beaver Awd, Others; r/Holy Trinity Epis Ch (Midland); hon/Sigma Gamma Epsilon; Hon Life Mem, W Tex Geol Soc; W/W: SW, Fin; Others.

HANSON, FREDDIE PHELPS oc/Retired School Teacher; Poet; b/Jan 8, 1908; h/775 W Roger Rd, Tucson, AZ 85705; m/Philip Hanson (dec); c/Philip J, Ormand (dec); p/Thomas and Maude C Phelps (dec); ed/BA; MA; pa/Tchr Washington Sch Dist, Phoenix 1952-73 (Ret'd); Writer Short Stories, Articles & Poetry Contbg to Maj Pubs; Supt Ariz's St Lib & Archives; Poetry Pub'd in India, Italy, Britain & Other Countries; Contbr to Ariz Hwys; Reads Poetry over Radio Sta KHUAT, Tucson; Ext World Travel; Num Profl Mbrships incl: NLAPW, Phoenix Writers Clb (Past Pres), World Poetry Soc; cp/Ariz Pioneer Hist Soc; r/Metaphysician, Tucson Ch of Rel Sci; hon/NLAPW Contest Winner (Poem "Cattails") 1943; Book of Poetry ded'd to her by Centro Studi E Scambi Internazionale, Rome, Italy 1976; Pi Gamma Mu; Kappa Delta Pi; Book of Poetry Westard Whoa in progress; Intl W/W Intells; Book of Honor; W/W: Poetry, W; World W/W Wom; Cert Apprec, St of Ariz; Personalities W&MW.

HANSON, JOHN ROBERT oc/College Teacher; b/Feb 14, 1936; ba/Binghamton, NY 13901; m/Patricia Selover; c/Jeffrey, Marcianne; p/Robert A and Alyce M Hanson, Jamestown, NY; ed/BM, MA, PhD Eastman Sch of Music (Univ Rochester); pa/Asst Prof Music Theory SUNY-B 1977-; Asst Prof Eastman Sch Music 1970-77; Asst Prof Carroll Col 1966-70; Instr Music Ks 1960-64; Fdr & Pres Music Theory Soc NY St; Coun of Col Music Soc; Am Guild Organists; r/Ch Choir Dir & Organist; hon/Res Grant, Dept Ed HEW; Author Music Fundamentals Workbook.

HANSON, NORMA LEE oc/Free-lance Writer; Farmer; b/Feb 3, 1930; h/RR1, Goodridge, MN 56725; ba/Same; m/Lynn; c/Michael; p/Fred and Lena Sawyer Kruckow, Backus, MN; ed/Grad Bus Col; mil/WAVES; pa/Fac Northland Commun Col; Pres Minn Wom for Agri; Past Pres Minn Fdn BPW Clbs; Horse Trainer; cp/Secy Minn Zool Bd; Chm Reg Envir Ed Coun; Secy Deer Park Garden Clb; Chm Tri-Co Humane Soc; Mem Northland Commun Col Bd; Bd Mem Goodridge Area Hist Soc; Pres: Dist & Local PTA, Pennington 4-H Coun, Deer Park Garden Clb; Others; r/Luth; hon/Awd of

Merit, Minn Hort Soc; Alumni Awd for Ldrship, 4-H; Life Mem, Minn Parent Tchr Student Assn.

HANSON, ROBERT LEONARD oc/Office Products Industry Executive; b/May 19, 1937; h/3010 Margo, Northbrook, IL 60062; ba/Wheeling, IL; m/Mary Frances; c/Linda, Michael, Jeffrey, Karyn, Tracy; p/James L Hanson, Chicago, IL; Thyra H Hanson, Traverse City, MI; ed/AA NWn Mich; BS Ferris Col; mil/AUS 1961; pa/ACCO Intl Inc, Chgo 1972-: VP Mats Mgmt & Asst to Pres; VP & Gen Mgr ACCO Canadian Co Ltd, Toronto 1969-72; VP Fin ACCO Div Gary Industs, Chgo 1966-69; Other Former Positions; cp/Pres Wheeling Area C of C & Indust; Dir: Wheeling Indust Devel Group, NW Commun Hosp Foun (Arlington Hgts, Ill), Rotary Clb Wheeling, Windham Home Owners Assn; Gen Mgr N Suburban Jr Varsity Hockey Leag; Coach Northbrook (Ill) Bantom AA Hockey Clb; N'brook Vol Pool; Mem Scarboro Golf & CC (Toronto); hon/Paul Harris Fellow, Rotary Intl Foun Men of Achmt; Biogl Listings.

HAPP, LAWRENCE RAYMOND oc/-Welding & Materials Engineer; b/Mar 11, 1945; h/3428 S Westwood, Springfield, MO 65807; ba/S'field; m/Susan Jean Beste; c/Brian Lawrence, Donald William, Debra Suzanne, Gregory John; p/Albert William and Mary M Becker Happ, Wyanet, IL; ed/BS Univ Ill 1968; pa/Welding & Mats Engr Paul Mueller Co, S'field 1974-; Trane Co, LaCrosse, Wis: Welding Engr 1969-73, Promotion to Sr Welding & Quality Control Engr 1973-74; Other Former Positions; Am Welding Soc: Chm Ozark AWS Sect 1974-78, Prog Chm Ozark AWS Sect 1974-79, Ednl Com Mem Ozark AWS Sect 1977-79, Other Activs; Am Soc Mech Engrs; Am Soc for Metals; Am Soc for Testing of Mats; Mo Solar Energy Assn; Nat & Mo Socs Profl Engrs; Others; cp/Active in: Birthright, Right to Life 1973-; Former Mem: JCs, Peoria Co Ct Cons Prog; Mem Citizens for Decent Lit; r/Rom Cath; Cursillo Movemt; Scripture Study Groups; Var Activs on Local, Reg & Nat Level; hon/W/W in MW; Personalities W&MW; Men of Achmt; DIB; Intl W/W Commun Ser.

HAQUE, AZEEZ C oc/Physicist; b/May 8, 1933; h/5995 Forestview Dr, Columbus, OH 43213; ba/Columbus; m/Malika H; c/Kifi Z, Masarath N; p/C Abdul Nabi (dec); Shahzadi Nabi, Bangalore, IN; ed/PhD; MSc; BSc w hons; pa/Brown Univ: Fellow, Prof Physics; Scist Min of Def, India; Am Phy Soc; Am Vacuum Soc; cp/Pres Islamic Foun Ctl Ohio; r/Islam; hon/Tait Meml Prize; Others.

HAQUE, MALIKA HAKIM oc/Physician; Pediatrician; b/Mar 24, 1940; h/5995 Forestview Dr, Columbus, OH 43213; ba/Columbus; m/C Azeez; c/Kifizeba, Masarath N; p/S A and R Hakim, Madras, India; ed/MD; MBBS; pa/Pediatrician Columbus Chd's Hosp; Ctl Ohio Pediatric Soc; Ambulatory Pediatric Assn; Am Acad Pediatrics; cp/Pres Ladies' Aux IFCO; r/Islam; hon/Physicians' Recog Awds; Sev Gold Medals for 1st Pl Standing in Surg, Pediatrics, Ob/Gyn.

HARALICK, ROBERT M oc/Professor; b/Sept 30, 1943; h/3117 Longhorn Dr, Lawrence, KS 66044; ba/Lawrence; m/Linda Shapiro; c/Tammy-Beth; p/David and Yetta Haralick, Sun City, AZ; ed/BA 1964; BSEE 1966; MSEE 1967; PhD 1969; pa/Prof Elect Engrg & Computer Sci Univ Ks-L (Space Technol Bldg); IEEE; Computer Soc; cp/Kiwanis; hon/Eta Kappa Mu: Outstg Yg Engr, Hon Mention; DOW Chem Outstg Fac.

HARBOUR, PATRICIA MOORE oc/Executive Director; b/Dec 31, 1941; h/11035 Ring Rd, Reston, VA 22090; ba/Washington, DC; m/Wendell; c/Lisa, Wenda; p/Payton H Moore, Roanoke, VA; Jenny H Moore (dec); ed/BFA, MEd, Doct Cand; pa/Exec Dir DHEW Secretariat for Intl Yr of Child; Delta Kappa Gamma Intl; Phi Delta Kappa, Reston Chapt; cp/Bd Dirs Big

Sisters Am; Nat Links Inc; cp/Bapt; hon/1 of 10 Most Outstg Wom in USA 1975; HEW Secy's Cit for Meritorious Ser.

HARDESTY, PATRICIA E oc/Speech Pathologist; University Professor; b/Aug 25, 1931; h/204 Vennard Ave, Lafayette, LA 70501; ba/Lafayette; m/Patrick G; c/Idell Lacambe, Shann Patrick Jr; p/R C Edwins (dec); Mary C Edwin, St Louis, MS; ed/PhD 1971; pa/Tchr Univ SW La; r/Presb; hon/Outstg Ed; Thibodaux Wom of Yr 1971; Personalities of S.

HARDIN, CLIFFORD MORRIS oc/Executive; b/Oct 9, 1915; h/10 Roan Ln, St Louis, MO 63124; ba/St Louis; m/Martha Love Wood; c/Susan Wood (Mrs L W), Clifford W, Cynthia Milligan (Mrs R), Nancy Rogers (Mrs D L), James A; p/James Alvin Hardin, Knightstown, IN; Mabel Macy Hardin (dec); ed/BS 1937, MS 1939, PhD 1941 Purdue Univ; pa/VChm of Bd & Dir Corporate Res Ralston Purina Co; Bd Dirs: Ralston Purina Canada Inc, Intl Assn Agri Economists, Alpha Gamma

Rho; Bd Trustees: Rockefeller Foun, Intl Agri Devel Ser, Farm Foun, Am Assembly, Univ Neb Foun; Nat Adv Coun Monell Chem Senses Ctr; Indust Res Inst; Food & Agri Com, US C of C; Ec Policy Coun, UN Assn of US; Former Secy of Agri, US; Others; cp/Bd Dirs: St Louis Symph Soc, Arts & Ed Coun Gtr St Louis, U Way Gtr St Louis; hon/DSc: Purdue Univ, ND St Univ, Mich St Univ; LLD: Creighton Univ, Ill St Univ; DHL, Univ Neb; Doct Honoris Causa, Nat Univ Columbia (Bogota).

HARDIN, JAMES NEAL oc/Professor; b/Feb 17, 1939; h/132 Norse Way, Columbia, SC 29206; ba/Columbia; p/Mr and Mrs James N Hardin, Greeneville, TN; ed/MA; PhD; mil/Arty 1967-69, to rank of Capt; pa/Prof Univ SC; Author Sev Monographs & Articles; hon/von Humboldt Stipend; Var Res Grants.

HARDING, RALPH oc/Consultant; b/Sept 9, 1929; ba/1475 W Hays, Boise, ID 83702; m/Willa Conrad; c/Ralph D, Cherie, Charlene, John Kennedy, Cozette; p/Ralph W and Katherine O Harding; ed/Grad Brigham Yg Univ; Grad Work: Brigham Yg Univ, Idaho St Univ; mil/AUS Korean Conflict, Earned

Comm at Ofcr Cand Sch; Served in Korea as Mem 7th Inf Div; pa/Presently Assoc'd w Killebrew & Harding Inc; Conslt Var Bus & Indust Assns; Former Fdr, Pres & Chm Bd Harding Livestock & Land Co, Blackfoot, Idaho (sold to Harris Farms Inc 1975); Former

Staff Auditor; Nat Com on Mil Food Ser Systems; Coms for Grocery Mfrs Am; Nat Canners Assn; Am Nat Cattlemen's Assn; Pres Dehydrated Food Indust Coun; Dir Idaho Cattle Feeders Assn; cp/Former Mem Idaho St Leg; Former Dem Nat Com-man, St of Idaho; Former St Cand for US Senate; Elks Lodge; Am Legion; AF Assn; C of C; r/LDS; hon/Presented w Highest Awd Bestowed Upon Civilian, USAF.

HARDLEY, GARY KAYE oc/Clinical Social Work Administrator; b/Dec 30, 1931; h/1035 Locust Ave, Charlottesville, VA 22901; ba/Staunton, VA; m/Wilma Culpepper; c/Kay Gibson, Bill, Brenda,

David, Gary Paul; p/Mr and Mrs Arnold Hardley, Tarpon Sprgs, FL; ed/BS; MSW; EdD; pa/Clin Social Work Admr Wn St Hosp; Pres Va Assn Marriage & Fam Therapy; cp/Rotary; VChm C'ville Sch Bd; r/Prot; hon/Coun of Pres, AAMFT.

HARDON, JOHN ANTHONY oc/Priest; Professor; b/Jun 18, 1914; h/St Ignatius Residence, 53 E 83 St, New York, NY 10028; ba/Jamaica, NY; p/John and Anna J Hardon (dec); ed/BA; MA; STD; pa/Rom Cath Priest; Prof Theol St John's Univ; VP Inst on Rel Life; Dir Retreat; r/Rom Cath; hon/Papal Medal; Cath Press Assn; Medallion Slovak World Cong.

HARGRAVE, LEVI MARLIN oc/Retired Teacher; b/Nov 23, 1911; h/3609 47th St, Lubbock, TX 79413; m/Ruth A; c/Patricia R Brown, Eunice Jean Carlton; p/Levi Frank and Lena Hargrave (dec); ed/BS, MS Tex Tech Univ; pa/Tchr 42 Yrs; Tex Tech Univ 31 Yrs; cp/Supt Livestock Shows, Tex; r/Meth; hon/Outstg Agriculturalist W Tex, Tex Tech Univ.

HARITUN, ROSALIE ANN oc/University Professor; b/May 30, 1938; h/206 N Oak St, Apt 8, Greenville, NC 27834; ba/G'ville; p/George and Helen Ternosky Haritun, Great Bend, PA; ed/BME Baldwin-Wallace Conservatory Music 1960; MS Univ Ill 1961; EdD Tchr's Col (Columbia Univ) 1968; Addit Studies; pa/Asst Prof Music E Carolina Univ 1972-; Music Instr Title I Instrumental

Music Proj, NYC Bd of Ed 1971-72; Instr Music Ed Temple Univ, Philadelphia, Pa 1968-71; Other Former Positions; Clarinetist/Saxophonist G'ville City Sum Orch 1975-76; Clarinetist Sigma Alpha Iota Alumni Woodwind Quartet, SAI Alumni Chapt, Phila 1970-71; Other Perfs; Conslt; Adjudicator: En NC Jr High Choral Fest 1978, HS Choral Fests 1976-78, Orch Fest 1976-78, Others; Evaluator; Lectr/Spkr; cp/Mem Steering Com for City Commr Cand, G'ville 1978; Former Dir Patchogue City Music/Recorder Clb, Patchogue, Long Isl, NY; Others; r/Indep Missionary Bapt; Landmark Bapt Ch, G'ville: Dir Adult Choir 1975-78; hon/Annual Mbrship, Intl Biogl Soc; World W/W Wom in Ed; DIB; Outstg Yg Wom Am; Personalities of S; W/W S&SW.

HARKINS, BOBBYE ROBERTS oc/Florist; b/Nov 1; h/4065 Boxwood Cir, Jackson, MS 39211; ba/Jackson; m/John Patrick (dec); c/John Jr, Johnnita H Cook, Walter Michael; p/William Walter and Drusilla Walker Roberts, Mt Olive, MS; ed/RN; pa/Pres Ctl Allied Florists Miss; Owner, Mgr 2 Florist Shops; Miss Florist & Nurseymens Assn; So Florist Assn; FTD Assn; Teleflora Florist Assn; cp/Colonial Dames XVII Century: Past St Pres Miss Soc, Past Pres Rev Samuel Swayze Chapt, Parliamentn Gen; Nat Soc Magna Charta Dames; Past Ofcr Magnolia St Chapt DAR; Chd of Am Rev: Ofcr Miss Soc 4 Yrs, Sr Pres Gen Hummingbird Soc 4 Yrs; Past Pres W D Holder Chapt UDC; Am Clan Gregor Soc; DAC; UCD War of 1812; Bd Mem: Hinds Co Kidney Foun, Miss St Horseshow Assn; Knife & Fork Clb, BSA Ldr 13 Yrs; Past Pres: Etruscan Clb, Jackson Opti-Mrs Luncheon Clb, La Merienda Luncheon Clb; Jackson Symph Leag; Keep Am Beautiful; Goodwill Industs Aux; Miss Bapt Hosp Alumnae Assn; Hinds Co Fdn Woms Clbs; Le Jeunesse Luncheon Clb; Past Bd Mem: ARC, GSA, Mtl Hlth; r/Cath; hon/Hereditary Register of USA; Personalities of S.

HARKNESS, REBEKAH WEST oc/-Composer; Philanthropist; Executive; b/Apr 17, 1915; ba/4 E 75 St, New York, NY 10021; c/Allen West Pierce, Anne Terry Pierce, Edith Hale; p/Allen T West; Rebekah Semple; pa/Pres & Dir William Hale Harkness Foun (Supporting Med Res); Fdr Rebekah Harkness Foun (Sponsors Ballet & Dance Progs throughout US); Harkness Ballet: Fdr 1964, Pres, Artistic Dir 1965; Opened Harkness House for Ballet with Academy for a More Beautiful Nat Capitol; Dir Pres' Coun Yth Opport, Wash DC; Trustee John F Kennedy Ctr for Perf'g Arts; Composer: (Tone Poem) "Safari" 1955, "Mediterranean Suite" 1957, "Musical Chairs" 1958, (Ballet) "Jour to Love" 1958, "Gift of the Magi" 1958, Others; hon/Ofcr Merite Culturel et Artistique, France 1966; NYC Handel Awd; NYC Bronze Medal of Apprec; Marquis de Cuevas Prize, Universite de la Dance, Paris; Congl Record Cits; Am Indian & Eskimo Cult Foun Shield Awd; Cits, White House; DC Dept Correction; 2000 Wom Achmt; Others.

HARLLEE, JOHN oc/Management Consultant; b/Jan 2, 1914; h/Oakley, Front Royal, VA 22630; ba/Washington, DC; m/Jo-Beth Carden; c/John Jr; p/William C and Ella Fulmore Harllee (dec); ed/BS; mil/Grad US Nav Acad 1934; USN 1934-59, Rear Admiral (Ret'd); pa/Chm Fed Maritime Comm 1961-69; Mgmt Conslt (Maritime) 1969-79;

cp/Exec Dir San Francisco Bicent 1974-75; Former Dir Org Ams for Energy Indep; Former Chm Citizens for Kennedy, No Cal; r/Presb; hon/Silver Star; Legion of Merit; Navy Commend Ribbon; Pres Unit Cit (Cmdg Ofcr); Man of Yr, NY Fgn Freight Forwarders; Spec Commend, Fed Bar Assn.

HARLOWE, WILLIAM WALTON JR oc/Chemist; b/Apr 1, 1935; h/11106 Burr

Oak Dr, San Antonio, TX 78230; ba/SA; m/Joyce; c/Kristin; p/William W Sr and Irma Harlowe, Brownwood, TX; ed/BS; MS; mil/USNR; pa/The Sci Res Soc Am; r/Meth.

HARMAN, ESTELLE KARCHMER oc/Executive; b/Sept 11; ba/522 No La Brea Ave, Los Angeles, CA 90036; m/Samuel; c/Deborah Ann, Alexis Melinda, Eden Kay; p/Alexander and Ethel Ray Karchner; ed/AA LACC; BA UCLA; MA USC; pa/Pres Estelle Harman Actors Wkshop Inc (Owner/Dir); Former Instr UCLA; Former Hd of Talent Universal Studios; ANTA; AETA; NATTS; IPA; Am Film Inst; hon/Zeta Phi Eta; Mortar Bd.

HARO, MICHAEL S oc/College Professor; Health Counselor; b/Feb 27, 1943; h/-16414 Havenhurst, Houston, TX 77059; ba/-Houston; m/Lynne Y; c/Michaael S II, Scott William; p/Alphonso S Haro (dec); Angeline T Haro, Hamlet, IN; ed/BS; MS; EdS; PhD; pa/Am Sch Hlth Assn: Pres 1973-74, Gov'g Coun 1976-79; cp/Bd Dirs: Bay Area Com on Drugs & Alcohol, Am Heart Assn Clear Lake City Unit; r/Rom Cath; hon/Dist'd Ser Awd; ASHA.

HARPER, ED (TREE TOP) oc/Dispatcher; b/Dec 7, 1933; h/Rt 3, Box 110, Ellisville, MS 39440; ba/Laurel, MS; c/Robert F, David; p/Bob and Mildred E Harper (dec); ed/BS; pa/Dispatcher G&G Oil Field Ser; Employed at Phy Therapy Dept Jones Co Commun Hosp; Pvt Tchr; Writer; Former Sch Tchr & Ath Coach: Jones Co, Laurel City Schs, Smith & Wayne Cos; cp/Laurel Order of Moose; Cand for Justice of Peace; r/Bapt; hon/Handicapped Citizen of Yr, St of Miss.

HARPER, JAMES CUNNINGHAM oc/Teacher, Bandmaster; b/Feb 17, 1893; h/203 Norwood St SW, Lenoir, NC 28645; m/Charlotte Critz (dec); c/Lucy H Grier, James C, George F, Mrs George E Stone;

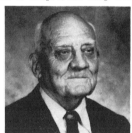

p/George F and Frances C Harper (dec); ed/BS, LHD Davidson Col; MA Univ NC; mil/AUS WWI, Capt Inf; pa/Ret'd; Band Dir Lenoir HS; Pres Am Bandmasters Assn; cp/Chm Lenoir Br, 1st Union Bk; r/Presb; hon/Hon Life Pres Assn.

HARPER, MITCH VAN oc/Politician; b/Apr 24, 1956; h/939 Main St, New Haven, IN 46774; ba/New Haven; p/Homer H and Erna V Harper, New Haven; ed/AB Ind Univ-B; pa/Bd Dirs E Harper & Son Funeral Home Inc; Reg'd Emer Med Technician; cp/Repub Nom Ind Ho of Reps 14th Dist 1978; Staff Mem Ind House Majority Staff 1978; Intern Rep Dan Quayle 1977; Var Former Polit Activs; Allen Co Yg Repubs; Allen Co Repub Clb; Allen Co-Fort Wayne Hist Soc; Nat Trust for Hist Preserv; r/U Meth.

HARPER, PAUL GORDON oc/Senior Systems Analyst; b/Aug 7, 1947; h/RR #1, Box 122, Brandenburg, KY 40108; ba/Tampa, FL; m/Shelia Mays; c/George, Dana, David, Jack; p/Paul R Jr and Alta May Harper, B'burg; pa/Sr Systems Analyst Jim Walters Corp; Data Processing Mgmt Assn; cp/Mason; r/Bapt.

HARPSTER, V AILEEN oc/Executive; b/Aug 12, 1930; ba/Intl Res Inst, 5623 N 16th St, Omaha, NE 68110; m/George Richard; c/7 Chd (5 Foster Chd); p/John Richard and

Goldie Marguerite Walling Norman; ed/BA; MS; MTh (2); DTh (2); PhD; DHL; MD; Hon Doct Humanities; DDiv (2); DPsychol; Hon DDiv (2); PhD Cand Ed; pa/Pres Intl Res Inst 1971-; Mem Reorg'd Ch Jesus Christ LDS & Pastor/Fdr Restored Ch Jesus Christ; Fellow: Brantridge Forest Sch, IBA, Intl Acad Poets,; Intl Chaplains Assn; Intl Assn Pastoral Psychologists; Am Inst Clin Psychologists; Ch Gospel Min; World Ch Leag; Calvary Grace Chs Faith & Bible Inst; Alpha Pi Omega; Nat Assn Female Execs; Neb Psychi Inst; cp/Omaha Area Coun on Alcoholism; Douglas Co (Omaha) Hlth Dept Forum; Univ Neb Med Ctr Commun Hlth Ed Prog; Clarkson Hosp Aux; Salvation Army Aux; Spiritual Frontiers F'ship; Univ Neb Alumni Century Clb; Joslyn Art Mus; Smithsonian Instn; Omaha Opera Angels; Omaha Symph Guild; hon/Author: *Treatise on Theol* (Book of Poetry), Num Articles & Papers; Biogl Listings.

HARRELL, BARBARA ELLEN TUCKER oc/Registered Brangus Cattle Breeder; Ranch Office Manager; b/Apr 2, 1944; h/Sabinal Canyon Ranch, Western Bandera Co, Utopia, TX 78884; ba/Same; m/John Kenneth Sr; p/Cecil Martin and Ethel S Tucker; ed/Att'd San Antonio Col, Univ Tex; pa/Intl Brangus Breeders Assn; Charter Mem IBBA Aux; cp/Bandera C of C; Fine Arts Clb; Bandera Chapt DAR; Michael Upchurch Chapt CDXVIIC; San Antonio Colony Magna Charta Dames; Capt Francis Eppes I Chapt DAC; Albert Sidney Johnston Chapt #2060 UDC; San Antonio Geneal & Hist Soc; Nat VP Tex Soc So Dames of Am; r/Epis; hon/Outstg Jr Mem, Tex Soc DAR 1978; Outstg Jr Mem, Tex & Nat Socs Colonial Dames XVII Century.

HARRELL, CHARLES H oc/Executive Director; b/May 1, 1932; h/116 N Breazeale Ave, Mount Olive, NC 28365; ba/Mt Olive; m/Faye; c/Rene, Charles Jr, Kelly; ed/BS East Carolina Univ; Further Study Univ Ky; pa/Exec Dir Med Park Nsg; Mt Olive Col: Treas, Bus Mgr 1963-78, Other Activs; Internal Auditor Burlington Indust 1960-63; Field Auditor NC Dept Revenue 1957-60; NC Fin Aid Admrs; NAFAA; SASFAA; So & Nat Assns Col & Univ Bus Ofcrs; cp/Optimist Clb; C of C; Kiwanis Clb; Exc Clb; JCs; Master Mason; Wayne Co Scottish Clb; 32° Scottish Rite; Shriner Sudan Temple; Wayne Co Shrine Clb; Goldsboro CC Bd Dirs; r/U Meth Ch Mt Olive; hon/NC Fdr's Awd, Bd of Heart Fund; Today's Outstg NC Citizen, WNCT-TV; Personality of Week, G'boro News Argus; Biogl Listings.

HARRELL, DAVID LYNN oc/Mechanical Engineer; b/May 7, 1953; h/6245 Renwick #149, Houston, TX 77081; ba/Houston; m/Carmen Valentin-Miranda; p/I D and Shirley F Page Harrell, Moultrie, GA; ed/AA Hillsboro Commun Col 1973; BSE Univ S Fla 1978; pa/Mech Engr Pullman Kellogg; Assoc Mem: Am Soc Heating, Refrigeration & Air Conditioning Engrs, Am Soc Mech Engrs; cp/Repub; r/Bapt; hon/1968 Reg Awd, Ford Future Scists Am Awds Prog.

HARRELL, FLYNN THOMAS oc/Administrator; b/Jun 25, 1934; h/3605 Old Lamplighters Rd, Columbia, SC 29206; ba/Columbia; m/Anne T; c/Elizabeth Anne, Flynn T Jr; p/Fred T and Irene W Harrell, Columbia; ed/BS Univ SC 1956; mil/AUS Inf 2 Yrs; pa/Asst to Exec Secy-Treas for Bus Affairs, Gen Bd SC Bapt Conv; Dir Nat Assn Accts; Dir Alston Wilkes Soc; Ch So Bapt Bus Ofcrs' Conf; cp/City of Columbia Planning Comm; VP USC Alumni Assn; Chm USC YMCA Bd Dirs; Pres The Luncheon Clb; r/1st Bapt Ch, Columbia: Deacon, Chm Sanctuary Bldg Com, Former Activs; hon/Algernon Sydney Sullivan Awd, USC.

HARRELL, HARDY MATTHEW oc/Retired; b/Oct 15, 1905; h/2228 Lake Shore Blvd, Jacksonville, FL 32210; m/Edna Mae Richardson; c/Hardy Jr, Edward, George; p/George Monroe and Willie Harrell (dec); ed/Bus Col; pa/Gulf Life Ins Co, J'ville 38 Yrs, Ret'd 1965 from Ofc of Corporate Secy

& Asst VP; Elected Exec Secy-Treas So Bapt Hosps Inc 1966-78 (Temporary Basis); Comm'd by Bd Dirs Affil'd Bapt Hosps Inc to write hist of hlth care sers; Bd Dirs: Bapt Hosp J'ville, Bapt Med Ctr J'ville, J'ville Hosp Ednl Prog, Affil'd Bapt Hosps Inc; cp/32° Scottish Rite Mason, Var Activs; J'ville C of C; J'ville Univ Coun; Stetson Univ Coun; Mem Stetson Assocs; r/So Bapt Ch: Mem, Deacon, Tchr Sr Men's Bible Class, SS Supt, Dir Bapt Yg People's Tng Union, Coms; Bd Mem Bapt Chd's Home, J'ville; Others; hon/Boss of Yr, Nat Secys Assn 1962-63, 1966-78; Dist'd Awd: Stetson Univ, Bethune Cookman Col, So Bapt Conv; Cits.

HARRIS, ARTHUR LEE oc/Businessman; b/Nov 12, 1940; h/2909 W Maple, Shreveport, LA 71109; ba/S'port; m/Minnie T; c/Jo Ann, Cynthia, Casundra Keidra, Shanna; p/Arthur Lee Harris (dec); Odessa Black (dec); pa/Restaurant & Grocery Store Owner & Mgr; r/Bapt; hon/W/W: La, S&SW.

HARRIS, BETSEY MATTHIS oc/Realtor; b/Sep 14, 1942; h/1362 10th St Pl NW, Hickory, NC 28601; c/David, Scott; p/J J and Sylvia P Matthis, Goldsboro, NC; pa/Realtors Nat Mktg Inst; NC Assn Realtors; Nat Assn Realtors; NC Cert'd Residentials Spec Chapt (Charter Mem); cp/Chm, Newcomers Task Force, Catawba Co C of C; United Fund; Catawba Co Med Aux; Adv Bd Mem, Bd Dirs, Bank of Granite; r/1st United Meth Ch: Adm Bd, 1st VP U Meth Wom, Chair, Completed Med Mission to Bolivia (S Am); hon/Grad of Realtors Inst, UNC-CH.

HARRIS, BEVERLY HOWARD oc/-Professor, Department Chairman; b/Aug 22, 1927; h/910 E Division, Bolivar, MO 65613; ba/Bolivar; m/Zorine Pruitt; c/Susan H Spurgeon, Steven, Joy; p/Howard K and Mattie B Harris, Bolivar; ed/AA SW Bapt Col 1947; BS SW Mo St Univ 1949; MA 1953, EdD 1963 Univ Mo-C; mil/AUS 1946-47, Squad Ldr, Expert Marksman w M-1 Rifle, Regimental Control Sgt, Camp Stoneman, Cal; pa/SW Bapt Col: Prof Math, Dept Chm, S'ship Coor; Former Acad Positions; Mem Vis Team to Re-eval El Dorado Sprgs HS (Mo) (N Ctl Assn Cols & Sec'dy Schs); Participant NSF Sum Inst Math, Univ Wis-M 1967; Phi Delta Kappa; Math Assn Am; cp/Past Pres Bolivar Tennis Assn; Mem Six Gallon Clb, ARC; Bd Mem Enterprises Unlimited Inc; Others; r/So Hills Bapt Ch: Mem, Ordained Deacon, SS Dir, Choir Mem, Ch Cabinet, Chm Money Counting Com; hon/Curator's Scholar, Univ Mo; Biogl Listings.

HARRIS, ELISABETH TAMLYN oc/-Psychiatric Social Worker; b/Aug 10, 1919; h/29 Mitchell Pl, Port Chester, NY 10573; ba/White Plains, NY; c/John; p/Walter I and Ethel Bishop Tamlyn (dec); ed/BA magna cum laude Wilson Col; MS Columbia Univ Sch Social Wk 1944; pa/Psychi Social Wkr NY Hosp-Cornell Med Ctr-Westchester Div; Former CoChm Pvt Pract Com Westchester Chapt Nat Assn Social Wkrs; Former Conslt to Parents Without Partners, W'chester Chapt; Nat Bd Mem Soc for Sci Study of Sex 1978-; Am Orthopsychi Assn; Acad Cert'd Social Wkrs; cp/Chm Com for Acad Freedom, Rye Neck (NY) Sch Dist; Former Dir Funeral Planning Soc of W'chester; r/Commun Unitarian Ch, White Plains; hon/Author Articles for Profl & Popular Pubs; Fellow, Soc

Clin Social Work-Psychotherapists.

HARRIS, ERNEST E oc/Professor; Director; b/Aug 29, 1914; h/21 Chestnut Dr, Hastings-on-Hudson, NY 10706; ba/New York, NY; m/Evelyn Marie; c/Rose Marie, Ernest E Jr; p/Walker F Harris (dec); Viola Gilmore Harris, Birmingham, AL; ed/AB Catawba Col 1936; MA 1940, EdD 1944 Tchrs Col Columbia Univ; pa/Columbia Univ (Tchrs Col): Prof Music, Dir Instrnl Support Sers; Frequent Appearances as Guest Conductor, Adjudicator, Lectr & Conductor Music Fests & Instrumental Music Clins & Wkshops; Former Nat Pres Am String Tchrs Assn; Exec Com Nat Music Coun; Province Gov Phi Mu Alpha; Phi Delta Kappa; MENC; Music Tchrs Nat Assn; Col Band Dirs Assn; Assn for Ednl Communs & Technol; Former Conslt to Dept of Ed, St of Hi; hon/Hon LittD, Catawba Col; Recipient Commend for Contbn to Artistic & Aesthetics Devel of Yth & Reps (Hi); Author: *Learning to Teach Through Playing-String Techniques and Pedagogy* & *Music Ed-Information Sources.*

HARRIS, JEAN W oc/Former Teacher; Homemaker; b/Mar 27, 1941; h/PO Box 582, Dunn, NC 28334; m/Oscar Nathan; c/Oscar N II, Shelia Carol; p/Junius Milton and Vida M Wood, Benson, NC; ed/BS Atl Christian Col; pa/Tchr 8 Yrs; NEA; NCEA; PTA: Mem, Advr Sch Newspaper & Bus Clbs; cp/Am Legion Aux; Dunn Jaycettes: Former 1st Lady, Held Every Ofc; Former CoWkr NC Heart Assn Fund Dr; Former Local Chm Dunn Area Fund Raising, NC Kidney Foun; Sponsor Harnett Co Reg Theatre; Harnett Co Yg Dems; Harnett Co Dem Wom; Others; r/Emmanuel Bapt Ch: Mem, Asst SS Tchr 3 Yrs; hon/Dunn Jaycettes: Jaycette of Yr 1970-71, 1974-75, Jaycette of Month 1975-76 (2), Sparkette of Yr Plaque 1976-77, Ser Awd, Plucked Hen Cert, Others; Var Hons Junn JCs; NC St Jaycettes: St Pres' Awd of Hon, Cert of Apprec, Cert of Recog, Others; Cert of Apprec, Harnett Co Yg Dems; Others.

HARRIS, JORDAN CLIFTON JR oc/Minister; Counselor; b/Sept 27, 1932; h/840 Armstrong St, Statesville, NC 28677; ba/S'ville; m/Leola Thompson; c/Rhonda L; p/Jordan C Harris Sr (dec); Elizabeth D Harris, Louisburg, NC; ed/AB; MDiv; DD; pa/Min 1st Bapt Ch, S'ville; Cnslr Mitchell Commun Col; Pastor New Shepherd Bapt Ch, Cooleemee, NC; Former Pastor: Symona Grove Bapt Ch, Oxford (NC), St John Bapt Ch, Aberdeen, Social Union Bapt Ch, Nashville, 1st Bapt Ch, Wadesboro; Mem Gen Bd, Exec Bd, Chm Com on Camp Devel; Dir Yth Bible Camp Wom's Conv; Bd Trustees Shaw Univ Divinity Sch; Former Chm Pastor's Conf Shaw Divinity Sch; Moderator Rowan Bapt Assn; Pres S'ville Min Assn; cp/Secy SMCD Meml Foun, S'ville; Bd Dirs NC Legal Aid Corp; Chm NAACP Legal Com; Appt'd (by Gov Hunt) to Citizens Affairs Coun of Gov's Ofc; Others; r/Bapt: Ordained Min 1953.

HARRIS, LANA JOAN oc/Photojournalist; b/Jul 14, 1947; ba/1211 Williams St NW, Atlanta, GA 30309; p/Joseph E Harris (dec); Billie Jane Harris, Jacksonville, FL; ed/BS Univ Fla 1969; pa/Nat Press Photogs Assn; Atlanta PPA; hon/Nom'd for Pulitzer Prize; Rep'd in Perm Collection, High Mus of Art (Atlanta).

HARRIS, LOUISE oc/Researcher; h/15 Jay St, Rumford, RI 02916; ba/Providence, RI; p/Samuel P and Faustine M Borden Harris (dec); ed/AB Brown Univ; Pvt Organ Study; pa/Reschr, Curator C A Stephens Col; Tchr, Recitalist of Organ & Piano 1928-42; Music Career 1930-50; Genealogy 1956-61, Reschr 1961-; Life Mem Am Guild of Organists; Smithsonian Assocs; Res Work of "Yth Companion"; IPA; cp/Am Heritage Soc; Nat Trust for Hist Preserv; Nat Wildlife; Hist Socs: Nat, E Providence; Wkg for Better Flag Laws & Correcting Author of Pledge of Allegiance for 1976, Writing Stories on Authorship of Pledge for Pub; Wn RI Civic Hist Soc; Brown Alumnae; 1st Fdr Med Sch at Brown Univ;

Elected to Corp of RI Hosp; Vol Wkr w Chd; r/Prot; Ch Organist; hon/Life Fellow: Intercont Biogl Assn, Intl Inst for Commun Sers; Life Patron, Intl Biogl Assn; Lib of Human Resources of Am Bicent Res Inst; Pub'd Author Num Books & Compiled Books of C A Stephens, Collection Brown Univ; Num Dipls, Certs of Merit, Medals, Plaques, Var England Dics & Hon Socs; Book of Honor; Commun Ldrs & Noteworthy Ams.

HARRIS, LOYD ERVIN oc/Dean & Professor Emeritus; b/Sept 21, 1900; h/2514 S Pickard Ave, Norman, OK 73069; m/Maurine Dill; c/Lorene H Reid, Ronald D; p/Howard L and Necie Harris (dec); ed/PhG; PhC; BS; MS; PhD; mil/AUS Col, Ret'd; pa/Ret'd;

Univ Okla: Dean Emeritus & Prof Emeritus (Pharm); Prof Emeritus Ohio St Univ; cp/Lions Clb Intl; r/Presb; hon/Beal Awd, Ohio St Pharm Assn; Dist'd Alumni Awd, Univ Okla Pharm Alumni; Phi Beta Kappa; Sigma Xi; Rho Chi.

HARRIS, MARTIN HARVEY oc/Aerospace Company Executive; b/Mar 14, 1932; h/2845 Summerfield Rd, Winter Park, FL 32792; ba/Orlando, FL; m/Patricia Ann Franklin; c/Lori Kathryn, Barbara Ann; p/Leo and Gertrude Harris (dec); ed/BAeronautical

Engrg NY Univ 1953; MS Univ So Cal 1973; mil/USAFR Col; pa/AF Assn: Nat Secy, Perm Nat Dir; Nat VP Am Def Preparedness Assn; cp/Trustee Aerospace Ed Foun; Orlando Area C of C; hon/Nat Man of Yr, AF Assn; Meritorious Achmt Awd, Martin Marietta; Patentee in field; Biogl Listings.

HARRIS, MARY BIERMAN oc/Professor; b/Feb 9, 1943; h/1719 Rita Dr NE, Albuquerque, NM 87106; ba/Albuquerque; m/Richard J; c/Jennifer M, Christopher R; p/Norman and Margaret Loeb Bierman, St Louis, MO; ed/BA Radcliffe; MA, PhD Stanford; pa/Prof Endl Founs Univ NM; Author Num Pubs; Reviewer Manuscripts for Jours; hon/Phi Beta Kappa; USPHS Traineeship.

HARRIS, MARY I oc/Teacher; Author; h/Box 51367, Tulsa, OK 74151; ba/Tulsa; p/(dec); ed/BA; MA; EdD; pa/Tchr Tulsa Public Schs; OEA; NEA; TCTA; Delta Kappa Gamma; Kappa Delta Pi; cp/Red Cross; Commun Chest; U Way; r/Meth: SS Tchr, Lay Pastor; hon/Tchrs Medal, Freedoms Foun; Ctl St Spch Awds; Others.

HARRIS, MORTON A oc/Attorney at Law; h/2854 Cromwell Dr, Columbus, GA 31906; ba/Columbus; m/Judye; c/Alvin,

Wendy, Tracy, Beth; p/Harriett B Wolpin, Columbus; ed/BBA summa cum laude Emory Univ 1956; LLB, JD 1959 Harvard Law Sch; pa/Atty, Firm Page Scrantom, Harris, McGlamry & Chapman, PC: Bd Dirs 1971-, Secy-Treas 1971-; Mng Atty 1975-; ABA: Sect Taxation, Com on Profl Ser Corps, Chm 1978-80, VChm 1976-78, Subcom Chm 1973-76; St Bar Ga; Pres Columbus Est Planning Coun 1973-74; Columbus Lwyrs Clb; Am Judic Soc; So Pension Conf; Small Bus Coun Am Inc, Bd Dirs; Lectr; cp/Past Pres Harvard Law Sch Assn Ga; VChm Bd of Ed Muscogee Co Sch Dist; Kiwanis Clb Gtr Columbus; Bd Dirs Bradley Ctr; SEn Reg Adv Bd ADL; Var Other Activs; r/Temple Israel: SS Tchr, SS Bd of Ed; Bd Trustees; hon/Dist'd Ser Awd, Outstg Yg Man of Yr 1966; Contbr to Var Pubs; Biogl Listings.

HARRIS, NANCY EDWARDS oc/Hospital Evening Supervisor; b/Jul 15, 1918; h/4705 Surry Pl, Alexandria, VA 22304; ba/Washington, DC; m/Foley White; c/Charles Edward, Dale Louis Harris; p/John Frederick Edwards (dec); Mary Maude Frank (dec); ed/RN; BSNE Cath Univ 1951; Grad Work: Cath Univ Am, Univ Va, Univ Md; pa/DC Gen Hosp: Evening Supvr, Chm Policy & Procedure Com, Chm Nsg Audit Com, RN Med Audit Com & Med Eval Com; Formerly Served in USPHS; Am Nurses' Assn; Coun Nsg Ser Admrs, ANA; Capital City Sch Nsg Alumnae

Assn: Pres, Treas; cp/Cub Scout Den Mother; DAR; Sons & Daughs of Pilgrims; St Pres US Daughs of 1812; Chd of Am Revolution: Sr Nat Registrar, Sr Nat Rec'g Secy, Hon Sr Nat VP; Parent Tchr Orgs: VP, Secy, Treas; U Daughs of Confed; Dir Chd of Confed, Wash DC; Assn for Preserv of Va Antiquities; No Neck Hist Soc, Warsaw, Va; Sr Nat Ofcrs' Clb CAR; Assn St Pres, US Daughs of 1812; Mem Alexandria Hosp Corp; r/Meth: Ch Sch Supt, Pres Ch Wom, Altar Guild, Ch Sch Tchr, Cnslr Yth Group, Dir Vacation Ch Schs, Cnslr Ch Camp; hon/1 of 25 Outstg Grads, Capital City Sch of Nsg (Alumnae Assn); DC Govt Employees Nat Public Hall of Fame; Num Biogl Listings.

HARRIS, PETRA J oc/Administrator; h/946 E 48 St, Chicago, IL 60615; ba/Chgo; p/Charles and Julia Harris (dec); ed/BE Chgo St 1949; MA DePaul 1955; EdD Nova Univ 76; pa/Admr Dept Pupil Pers & Spec Ed Chgo Public Schs; Gov CEC Exec Bd; AASA; AAMD; Phi Delta Kappa; NABSE; CATA; Delta Kappa Gamma; IASE; CCBD; CASE; NAPPA; NCAWE; WEF; cp/Pres Foun Excepl Chd; Adv Bd Opportunity Ctrs; Alpha Kappa Alpha; r/Christian Sci; hon/Wom of Yr 1964; Courtenay Ser Awd; Stratton Ser Awd.

HARRIS, POLLY ADAIR oc/Public Relations Executive; Alderman; b/Dec 18; h/6212 Papago, El Paso, TX 79905; ba/El Paso; m/Paul; p/M A and Lyllian A Elstein (dec); ed/AA K C Jr Col; BS Univ Mo-Kansas City; pa/Pres Harris & Harris Public Relats; cp/Elected to El Paso City Coun (2nd Wom); hon/Outstg Ad Person of Yr, Ad Fdn; Outstg Wom in Polits, Wom's Polit Caucus.

HARRIS, ROBERT L oc/Attorney; b/Mar 4, 1944; h/650 39th St, Richmond, CA 94805; ba/San Francisco, CA; c/Anthony, Regina; p/Benjamin and Lucy Harris; ed/AA; BA; JD; pa/Atty at Law Pacific Gas & Elect Co 1972-; Admitted to Cal St Bar 1972; Dep Probation

Ofcr Alameda Co Probation Dept 1965-69; Grader St Bar Exams, Cal St Bar 1973-; ABA; SF Bar Assn; Secy/Treas Exec Com of St Bar's Public Law Sect; Pres Charles Houston Bar Assn 1976-77; VP Nat Bar Assn; Fdr & Prin Orgr Cal Assn Black Lwyrs; cp/Bd Mem: SF Lwyrs Comm on Urban Affairs, Richmond, Hunter's Point & Salesian Boys Clbs; SF Jr C of C; World Affairs Coun No Cal; Former Chm Richmond City Planning Comm; Pres Wn Province Kappa Alpha Psi; Others; hon/Man of Yr, Berkeley Alumni Chapt Kappa Alpha Psi 1977; Top Yg Man 1975, Tex Col Alumni; Pub'd Author; Notable Ams; Intl W/W Commun Ser; Men of Achmt; Outstg Yg Men Am; W/W Among Black Ams.

HARRIS, RUTH BEALL oc/Professor; b/Jan 6, 1947; h/19336 Lanark, Reseda, CA 91335; ba/Los Angeles, CA; m/Philip E; p/F Wayne Beall (dec); Edythe Gerlach Beall, Middletown, OH; ed/RN; BA; BS (Biol); BS (Nsg); MS; CCRN; pa/Asst Clin Prof (Nsg Ed & Clin Specialization in Critical Care of Surg Patient) UCLA Sch of Nsg; St Rep to Lic'd Voc Nurse's Leag; ANA; Cal Nsg Assn; Alt St Rep to Cal Jt Pract Comm Rep'g Critical Care; Coun Adv'd Med Surg Nurse Practitioners, ANA; Am Heart Assn, Cardiovas Div; Wn Interst Comm on Higher Ed in Nsg; Nat Assn Critial Care Nsg; Alpha Tau Delta; Sigma Theta Tau; Tutor for St Bd Nurse Exam, Surg Nsg; Others; cp/Cert'd Instr in CPR, Am Heart Assn; ARC; Nat Leukemia Soc; Former Jefferson Co (Colo) Vol Probation Cnslr; r/Sherman Oaks Luth Ch: Yth Group Ldr 1977; hon/Hon Mem, Alpha Tau Delta; Recipient Grant, S'ships; Profl Pubs.

HARRIS, SHARON BIRDWELL oc/Singer; Writer; Teacher; Composer; b/Jan 29, 1948; h/904 Parkside Ct, Modesto, CA 95350; m/Dan R; c/Michael Daniel, Elizabeth Esther; p/Lester D and Esther E Birdwell, Modesto; ed/AA, BA Cal St Col Stanislaus; pa/Pt-Owner Rainbow Heart Cards; r/Assembly of God; hon/Pub'd Author; Currently Completing 1st Novel.

HARRIS, THOMAS (TOMMY) LEE oc/Industrial Engineer; b/Nov 13, 1941; h/6515 Marsh Ave, Huntsville, AL 35806; ba/Redstone Arsenal, AL; m/Lynn Marie Sharpless; c/Thomas Lee II, Johanna Lynn, Elizabeth Juanita, Margaret Pauletta; p/John Pearson Harris (dec); Bertha Viola Townsend Harris, H'ville; ed/AA Pensacola Jr Col 1967; BS Univ Ala-H 1973; pa/Indust Engr US Army Miradcom DRDMI-KB, Redstone Arsenal; Pres Continental Leag 1976; H'ville Sci Fiction Assn; The Franklin Mint Collectors Soc; Soc Chd's Book Writers; cp/Am Legion; Dem; Cand US Ho of Reps (8th Congl Dist Ala) 1970; Other Campaign Activs; r/Ch of Christ; hon/Lttrs of Commend: Cmdr AUS Missile Res & Devel Command, Senator Edward M Kennedy, Gov George C Wallace; Hon Lit Col Aide-de-Camp, Ala St Militia; Biogl Listings; Author *The Little Lady Wore a Glove*, 1976; Composer *Memory Lane*, 1966.

HARRIS, YVONNE J oc/Manager; b/Sept 15, 1942; h/508 Broad Ave, Englewood, NJ 07631; ba/New York, NY; m/Robert L; p/Albert and Mary Thomas; ed/BA CCNY 1970; MA New Sch for Social Res 1977; pa/Mgr Human Resource Devel Am Stock Exc; Tng Specialist Fed Resv Bk of NY 1972-76; Sr Tng Asst NY Life Ins Co, NYC 1969-72; Vis Prof Urban Leag's Black Exec Exc Prog; Am Soc for Tng & Devel; Am Soc for Pers Adm; Coun of Concerned Black Execs; cp/Coalition of 100 Black Wom; Past Pres Zeta Delta Phi; hon/Black Achievers Awd; W/W Am Wom; World W/W Wom.

HARRISON, ANNIE THELMA oc/Educator; b/Apr 24, 1923; h/5951 Conveyor St, Columbia, SC 29203; ba/Columbia; m/Willie M Sr; c/Latrecia Devonne, Willie M Jr; p/Lafayette J and Rozenia E McRae (dec); ed/AB Johnson C Smith Univ 1944; MA Columbia Univ 1958; pa/NCTE; Life Mem NEA; SC Ed Assn; Richland Co Tchrs #1 Assn; Columbia Rdg Coun; Richland Co Ed Assn: Bd Dirs, Internal Ofc Com, Budget

Com; cp/Poll Mgr Fairwald Precnt; Fdn Wom Org; Nat Coun Negro Wom; Nat Assn Univ Wom; Daughs of Isis Caira Ct #125; Golden Cir C C Johnson Consistory Assembly #1; r/Lebanon U Presb Ch, Ridgeway, SC: Mem, Chperson Christian Ed, Pres Loal U Presb Wom Org, VP Fairfield-McClelland Presb; Others; hon/Recog'd for 25 Yrs of Ser, Gamma Omega Chapt Alpha Kappa Alpha; Awd for Outstg Utilization of Instrnl TV of SC Dept of Ed; Nom for Human Relats Awd, Fairwald Mid Sch; Del to NEA Conv 1978; Others.

HARRISON, FRANK RUSSELL III oc/University Professor; b/Mar 11, 1935; h/310 Cedar Creek Dr, Athens, GA 30605; ba/Athens; m/Dorothy Louise Gordy; p/F R Harrison Jr, Jacksonville, FL; Annye Mae Blackwelder Harrison (dec); ed/BA Univ of S 1957; MA 1959, PhD 1961 Univ Va; pa/Univ Ga: Prof Phil 1972-, Coor Grad Studies Dept Phil 1971-76, Adm Intern to Provost 1973, Adm Asst for Grad Studies 1976-77, Assoc Prof 1966-72, Asst Prof 1962-66, Grad Fac 1966-, Hons Prog Fac 1968-; Vis Prof: Univ NC-CH (Sum) 1963, Emory Univ, Atlanta, Ga (Sum) 1965, Others; Am Guild of Scholars; Metaphysical Soc Am; Ga Phil Assn; So Soc for Phil & Psychol; Soc for Phil of Rel; Am Phil Assn; Am Soc for Value Inquiry; Am Assn for Advmt of Humanities; Other Former Mbrships; Var Edit Activs; r/Epis; hon/Phi Kappa Phi; Phi Sigma Tau; Outstg Edr in Am; Profl Pubs; Biogl Listings.

HARRISON, GEORGE BROOKS oc/Air Force Officer; b/Jul 30, 1940; h/42 Cinderella Ln, Fort Walton Beach, FL 32548; ba/Maxwell AFB, AL; m/Pennie Maria Jenkins; c/Taylor Leigh, Todd Henry, Tracy Elizabeth; p/William H Harrison, Greenville, SC; Mary O Harrison (dec); ed/BS USAF Acad; MBA w distn Univ Pa-W; Army Parachutist Sch; Sqdrn Ofcr Sch; Armed Forces Staff Col; Air Command & Staff Col; Air War Col; USAF Pilot Tng; mil/Col USAF; Former Cmdr 4485 Test Sqdrn; pa/Mem AF Assn; Am Ordnance Assn; Org Structure Conslt; cp/Quiet Birdmen; USAFA Assn of Grads; Beta Gamma Sigma; r/Bapt; hon/Dist Flying Cross; Meritorious Ser Medal w 2 OLC; Air Medal w 11 OLC; AF Commend Medal w 1 OLC; Vietnam Cross of Gallantry w Palm.

HARRISON, GEORGE LOUIS oc/Minister; Social Worker; b/Oct 24, 1928; h/7661 Lake Dr, Circle Pines, MN 55014; ba/Circle Pines; m/Francel Oliver (dec); c/Wayne, Emily; p/Hugh and Beth Whitehead Harrison, Circle Pines; ed/BA; BS; BD; pa/APGA; Am Rehab Cnslg Assn; Minn Corrections Assn; cp/Past Area Pres Minn Bible Col Alumni; r/Disciples of Christ; hon/Contbr Articles to *Christian Standard* Mag; Order of Arrow, BSA.

HARRISON, LEANNE KAY oc/Insurance Clerk; b/Nov 30, 1940; h/514 5th Ave SW, Independence, IA 50644; ba/Indep; m/James E; c/Trevor J; p/Leo Frank Fenner (dec); Minnie B Wells Fenner, Indep; pa/Ins Clerk People's Meml Hosp; cp/Bd Mem Wapsipinicon Mill Restoration Com; Charter Mem Indep Area Art Assn; Former Bd Mem C of C; Ia St Hist Soc; NE Ia Geneal Soc; Buchanan Co (Ia) Bicent Com; Buchanan Co Hist Soc & Geneal Soc; Editor "125 Yrs-Independence" (Hist Booklet); Secy Oakwood Cemetery Assn, Indep; Others; hon/Outstg Resident of Yr, Indep 1975; 5th Pl Mother of Yr 1975; Hereditary Reg of US; Outstg Yg Wom Am; Notable Ams.

HARRISON, SHIRLEY M oc/Teacher; Religious Leader; Actress; Lecturer; b/Aug 13; h/2840 Jefferson Ave, New Orleans, LA 70115; p/Joseph and Celia S Rosenberg, New Orleans; ed/BS 1952; MSW 1955; PhD 1965; Further Studies; pa/Edr in Parapsychol Delgado Col 1977; Parapsychol Univ NO Fall 1978; Dillard Univ 1971-76: Asst Prof Spch & Drama, Admr Dept, Play Dir, Cnslr to Students; Other Former Positions; Profl Lectr; AEA; SAG; AFTRA; Credits on Film incl: *Close Encounters of a Third Kind, The Deadly Tower, Maryanne, Hard Times, Madwoman* of *Chaillot*, Others; TV: *Movin' On, The Line of Duty*, Others; Var Off Broadway Appearances; Commls; Others; hon/Hon DD, Univ Spiritual Assn Marion Col; Phi Beta.

HARRISON, WILLIAM EARL oc/Geologist; b/Apr 7, 1942; h/624 Reed Ave, Norman, OK 73071; ba/Norman; m/Nancy Clare; c/William Scott, Joy Nicole; p/T O Harrison, Crockett, TX; ed/BS Lamar Tech 1966; MS Univ Okla 1968; PhD LSU 1976; pa/Am Assn Petrol Geol; Geochem Soc; Assn Prof Geol Sci; Sigma Xi.

HARRISON, WINNIE M oc/Teacher; Homemaker; b/Jan 17, 1894; h/216 Ponce De Leon, Spartanburg, SC 29302; m/Julius; ed/Grad Bapt Acad 1913; Spec Studies; mil/USAF WWII: Chaplain's Asst, Air Transport Command, Palm Springs, Cal & White Horse, Canada; pa/Current Pt-time Tchr of Bible; Tchr Black Missions 1st Presb Ch, S'burg 4 Yrs; Tchr Mexican Mission,

Dallas, Tex; Supt Ch Vac Bible Sch Sev Sums; Tchr Bible in Poor Dists, Dallas 1 Yr; Com Mem Past Nat Pres' S'ship Fund; Mem-at-large SC Fdn Music Clbs; Life Mem Nat Fdn Music Clbs; Pres Aeolian & Jubal Music Clbs; r/1st Presb Ch: SS Tchr, Organist; hon/PhD, Colo St Christian Col; Dipl, Bd of Woms Work, Presb Ch US Montreat (NC); Awd of Merit, Nat Fdn Music Clbs; Charter Donor Hosp'd Vets Awd; Biogl Listings.

HARRISS, C(LEMENT) LOWELL oc/Educator; Consultant; b/Aug 2, 1912; h/14 Plateau Cir, Bronxville, NY 10708; ba/NYC; m/Agnes M; c/Patricia, Lowell, Martha, Brian; p/Riley Harriss (dec); Alice Hunt Harriss, Fremont, NE; ed/BS summa cum laude Harvard; PhD Columbia Univ; mil/USAF Capt 1943-46; pa/Prof Ec Columbia Univ 1938-; Ec Conslt Tax Foun Inc; Assoc Lincoln Inst Land Policy; Former Conslt Num Orgs; Pres Nat Tax Assn-Tax Inst Am; VP Intl Inst Public Fin; Former Bd John C Lincoln Foun; Adv Bd Am Enterprise Inst; Metro Ec Assn; Am Assn Univ Profs; Num Other Profl Assns; cp/Clbs: Fac, Bronxville Field, Princeton; hon/Phi Beta Kappa; Dist'd Ser Awd, Grad Fac Soc; Lambda Alpha Awd; Intl Assoc Assessing Ofcrs; Intl Inst Public Fin; Pub'd Author.

HARROLD, WILLIAM EUGENE oc/Educator; Writer; b/Jun 24, 1936; h/1982 N Prospect 2A, Milwaukee, WI 53202; ba/M'kee; p/William and Helen Mason Harrold; ed/BA Wake Forest Univ 1959; MA 1967, PhD 1971 Univ NC-CH; pa/Prof Univ Wis; MLA; MMLA; MHRA; Browning: Soc, Inst; hon/NC Poetry Coun Awd 1973.

HARSHAW, JACK RAYMOND oc/Editor; b/Oct 23, 1927; h/951 Wendy Ln, Carthage, MO 64836; ba/C'age; m/Betty; p/John and Mary Harshaw, Creston, IA; ed/BJ Univ Mo 1953; mil/AUS 1946-47 & 1950-51; pa/City Editor *The C'age Press*; Sigma Delta Chi Soc Profl Journalists; cp/Rotary Clb; r/Bapt Ch; hon/Cert Awd, Mo Press Assn; Certs Var Civic Orgs.

HARSHBARGER, J ARLENE oc/Counselor; b/Aug 8, 1935; h/6305 Windwood Dr, Kokomo, IN 46901; ba/Kokomo; m/George; c/Tim, Cindy; p/Edwin and Enid Record, Michigantown, IN; ed/BSHE; MSEd; pa/Guid

Cnslr; Former Home Ec Tchr; NEA; ISTA; NCTA; IPGA; Delta Kappa Gamma; cp/Bd YWCA; Yth Com; Open Horizons; 4H Ldr 10 Yrs; Past Pres Clinton Co Crippled Chds Soc; r/Prot; 1st Congreg.

HART, AGNES oc/Artist; Art Instructor; h/Maverick Rd, Rt 1, Box 671, Woodstock, NY; ba/New York, NY; m/Josef Presser (dec); p/Edward J Hart; Adelina M Dauphinais; pa/Tchr Art Students Leag of NY; Solo Exhbns incl: NY, Woodstock, Coral Gables (Fla); Group Exhbns incl: Metro Mus of Art, Butler Art Inst, Pa Acad, Bklyn Mus, Phila Mus; Woodstock Artists Assn; ASCA NY; Am Soc Contemp Artists; hon/Yaddo Resident; Kunmoshi Awd; Other Awds: ASCA, WAA.

HART, ELEANORE HAYS oc/Realtor; b/Jun 4, 1931; h/319 Hallsborough Dr, Pittsburgh, PA 15238; ba/Pgh; m/John M; c/Lynne J Reed, J David; ed/Grad Realtors Inst; pa/Pres Hays Real Est; Instr: Polley Inst, Duquesne Univ, Hall Inst Real Est; Elects Realty Assocs; Nat Assn Realtors; Realtors Nat Mktg Inst; Pa Assn Realtors; Pa Assn Notaries; cp/Gtr Pgh C of C Bd Dirs; Fox Chapel Assn; r/N F'ship (Nondenom): Bible Tchr, Spkr; hon/W/W: Am, Fin & Indust.

HART, ELIZABETH JOHNSON oc/Professor; b/May 11, 1937; h/150 Meadow Lake Dr, Columbia, SC 29203; ba/Columbia; m/Marion L; c/Sanquinetta, Donadrian; p/Charlie Julius and Rosanna G

Johnson (dec); ed/BA Benedict Col; MA Univ NC-CH; pa/Prof Eng Benedict Col; NCTE; Phi Delta Kappa; SCCTE; cp/Chd's Bur SC; r/Bapt; hon/Dist'd Fac Awd, Benedict Col; IPA; Alpha Kappa Mu; Author Num Articles & Reviews; Outstg Edr Am.

HART, RONALD CARY SR oc/Research Administrator; b/Feb 25, 1949; h/137 Bank St, Elkhart, IN 46514; ba/Elkhart; m/Deborah Froehlich; c/Michelle Naomi, Ronald Cary Jr; p/Robert Clyde and Mary Scott Hart, Memphis, TN; ed/BS Va Polytech Inst & St Univ; MS Univ Notre Dame; pa/Mgr Res Planning & Sers; Am Chem Soc; Soc Res Admrs; Am Mgmt Assn; AAAS; Systems Conslt Tech Pubs; cp/Vol BSA; Former UUFE Pledge Chm; Conservation Activs; hon/Phi Kappa Phi; Sigma Pi Sigma; Phi Eta Sigma; Eagle Scout; Notable Ams; DIB; Personalities W&MW; Other Biogl Listings.

HART, VALERIE O oc/Food Columnist; Importer; Teacher; Civic Leader; b/May 6, 1936; h/620 E Di Lido Dr, Di Lido Isl, Miami Beach, FL 33139; ba/Miami; m/Robert Fredric; c/Alexandra Caryn, Gregory Steven Alan, Katherine Ann; p/Royal A and Elsa Freeman Oppenheim, Detroit, MI; ed/Univ Mich; Sorbonne & Alliance Francaise (Paris, France); Cordon Bleu Cooking Sch (London, England); pa/Assoc'd w Husband's Wholesale Importing Furniture & Accessories Firm; Runs Valerie's Imports at Omni; Writer Gourmet Cooking Column "Val's Cooking Course", Appears Weekly in Pan-Ax Syndicated Papers; cp/Past Pres: Parents' Assn Ransom-Everglades Sch, Sponsors of Mus of Sci; Mem Orange Bowl Luncheon Com; Bd Trustees Mus of Sci; Former Mem Bd Dirs Am Cancer Soc; Bd Dirs Mar Dimes; Former Ldr Brownie Troops.

HARTE, JOSEPH MEAKIN oc/Clergyman; b/Jul 28, 1914; h/815 E Orangewood, Phoenix, AZ 85020; ba/Phoenix; m/Alice; c/Victoria, Judith, Joseph Jr; p/Charles Edward and Ruth Elizabeth Harte (dec); ed/AB; STM; DD; STD; Lic (Oxon); mil/TNG Maj; pa/Bishop of Ariz; Chm St Luke's Hosp Phoenix & Tuscon (Ariz); cp/Human Relats Comm Phoenix; Dir Gt Wn Bk & Trust; r/Epis; hon/Man of Yr, NCCJ 1973.

HARTGE, LAWRENCE C JR oc/Product Manager; b/Aug 1, 1948; h/4966 Calida Dr, San Jose, CA 95136; ba/Cupertino, CA; p/Lawrence C Sr and Henrietta E Hartge, Omaha, NE; ed/BS Purdue Univ 1971; MS Krannert Grad Sch Mgmt (Purdue) 1972; pa/Hewlett-Packard Co: Prod Mgr Distributed Processing Prods 1976-, Prog Dir Satellite Communs Experimt Proj Prelude

1974-76, Sales Devel Mgr Canada & Wn US 1972-74; Other Former Positions; Assn for Computing Machinery; Lectr/Spkr: Am Inst Indust Engrs, Am Prodn & Inventory Control Soc, Australian Computer Soc, Canadian Info Processing Soc, IEEE, Others; hon/Pub'd Author; Personalities W&MW; Notable Ams; Intl W/W Commun Ser; Others.

HARTKE, VANCE oc/Legislator; Attorney; b/May 31, 1919; ba/Washington, DC; m/Martha Tiernan; c/Seven; ed/AB Evansville Col; JD Ind Univ; pa/Mem US Senate 1958-; Coms Served incl: Fin, Commerce, DC Com, Com on Employmt Probs, Others; Del to Atl Cong, NATO Parliamentns Conf; Other Activs; Former Appt'd Dep Prosecutor 1950; cp/Former Mayor E'ville; Del Dem Nat Conv 1960; Former Chm & VChm Dem Senatorial Campaign Com; Exc Clb; JCs; Charter Mem Wabash Val Assn; Others; r/St Paul's Luth Ch E'ville & Falls Ch, Va; Luth Layman's Leag; hon/Life Mem, JCs; Man & Boy Awd, Wash Boys Clbs; Friend of Small Bus Awd, Nat Retail Druggists; Dist'd Alumni Awd, Tau Kappa Alpha.

HARTLAGE, LAWRENCE CLIFTON oc/Professor; b/May 11, 1934; h/2705 Bellevue, Augusta, GA 30909; ba/Augusta; m/Patricia Hughes; c/Mary Beth; p/Clifton P and Mary Louise Hartlage, Coquina Key, FL; ed/BS; MA; PhD; pa/Prof Neurol Med Col Ga; Pres Nat Acad Neuropsychol 1978-79; r/Rom Cath; hon/Fellow, Am Psychol Assn.

HARTLING, MARJORIE-ANNE oc/Executive Director; b/Sept 5, 1934; h/2014 Woodglen Crescent, Ottawa, Ontario Canada K1J 6G4; ba/Ottawa; m/Robie; c/Janet, J Robie, Kathleen, Jo-Anne, Judith, June, Andrea, John; p/Edgar A and Margaret E Reid, Chilliwack, BC Canada; pa/Nat Anti-Poverty Org Exec Dir 1973, Orgr & 1/Pres 1971-73; Pres Nat PLURA (Inter-Ch Assn to Promote Social Justice in Canada); Bd Dirs Public Interest Advocacy Centre 1977-; Mem Working Unit on Social Issues, Div Mission in Canada U Ch of Canada 1979-; Orgr & Pres Fed'd Anti-Poverty Groups BC 1969; cp/-Former Mem: Consumers' Assn Canada Regulated Industs Policy Bd, Canadian Consumer Coun, Nat Adv Coun on Vol Action, Nat Coun on Wel, Adv Com of Consumers (Standards Coun Canada); r/U Ch of Canada.

HARTMANN, M CLARE oc/Sister of

Religious Order; Teacher, Librarian; b/Jul 3, 1909; h/Box 85, Hays, MT 59527; ba/Hays; p/Jacob William and Emma Sodoma Hartmann (dec); ed/BA; ME; pa/Entered Order Sch Sisters of St Francis 1927; Am Lib Assn; Nat Sci Assn; Mont Lib Assn; Mont Media Assn; cp/Ecology & Hlth Progs; NAm Indian Leag; r/Cath; hon/1 of 5 Top Runner Ups, Mont Outstg Biol Tchr Awd 1972; Recipient Wings (Hon CoPilot), Wn Airlines; Monetary Awd for Ldrship in Ecology Prog; HS Valedictorian; Adopted into Gros Ventre Tribe (as Speaks Holy); Biogl Listings.

HARTWIG, CHARLES WALTER oc/-College Professor; b/Dec 15, 1941; h/PO Drawer U, State University, AR 72467; ba/St Univ, AR; m/Mary Steen; c/Karin Beata, Markus Daniel; p/Hellmut A and Beata Erickson Hartwig, Carbondale, IL; ed/BA So Ill Univ 1964; MA 1968, PhD 1975 Univ Ky; pa/Asst Prof Polit Sci Ark St Univ-J; Ark Polit Sci Assn: Pres-elect, VP, Prog Chm; Am & So Polit Sci Assns; AAUP; Policy Studies Assn; Intl Devel Assn; African Studies Assn; Others; cp/US Peace Corps Vol (Monrovia, Liberia) 1965-67; r/Meth; hon/Sev Grad & Undergrad F'ships & S'ships.

HARUTUNIAN, JOHN MARTIN oc/-Graduate Student; b/Aug 29, 1948; h/355 Newtonville Ave, Newtonville, MA 02160; p/John and Karmille Harutunian, N'ville; ed/BM Wheaton Col 1969; Grad Study Harvard Univ 1969-70; MA Univ Pa 1975; Doct Student UCLA 1975-; mil/AUS 1970-73, Bandsman; pa/Piano Soloist w Boston Pops Orch 1965; Perf'd Own Composition *Fantasy-Gavotte* at Yth Concerts w Boston Symph Orch 1966; Current Tchg Assoc UCLA; r/Presb; hon/Paderewski Medal.

HARVEY, ELEANOR THORNTON MOSS oc/Retired Social Worker; Research Worker; Writer; b/Dec 17, 1904; h/Ireland St, W Chesterfield, MA 01084; m/Benson Heale; c/Eleanor H Tejirian (Mrs Edward J); p/James and Eleanor Thornton Moss (dec); ed/BA Wellesley Col; MS Wn Resv Univ; MA Univ Mass; pa/Caseworker Assoc'd Charities, Cleveland (Ohio) & Philadelphia Fam Soc; Missionary & Med Social Wkr No Luzon, Philippians & St Luke's Hosp, Manila; Field Wkr & Exec Dept Christian Social Relats Diocese Wn Mass; Acad Cert'd Social Wkrs; Nat Assn Social Wkrs, Former Secy Pioneer Val Chapt; cp/Local & St Bds Mass Soc for Prevention of Cruelty to Chd; Bd Prot Yth Ctr, Belchertown; Former VP & Secy Worthington Hlth Ctr; Easthampton Wom's Clb; Mass Fdn BPW Clbs; Others; r/Epis; hon/Whiteman Awd for Ser to Chd, Mass Soc for Prevention of Cruelty to Chd; Wom of Yr Awd, St BPW Clb; Commun Ldr Am.

HARVEY, HAROLD MICHAEL oc/Public Safety Officer; b/Jul 10, 1951 (dec Jan 26, 1978); h/289 Edgewood Cr, Woodruff, SC 29388; m/Susan P; c/Kathleen Ann; p/-William Harold and Thelma B Harvey, Woodruff; pa/Former Public Safety Ofcr (Police Ofcr-Fireman), City of Aiken, SC; Former Dir Helping Hands Inc (Home for Neglected, Abandoned & Abused Chd), Aiken; Former Rock Musician; cp/Former Mem: SC JCs, Sertoma Clb; r/Bapt Ch: Former Yth Wkr; hon/Man of Yr 1975, Aiken Co; Dist'd Ser Awd, JCs; 1 of 3 Outstg Yg Men SC; SC Firefighter's Assn Hall of Fame 1978.

HARVEY, RAYMOND C oc/Educator; b/Dec 14, 1934; h/2360 Hackberry Ln, Birmingham, LA 35226; ba/B'ham; m/Mary; c/Mary Grace, Raymond C III; p/Raymond C Sr and Eula Cromwell Harvey; p/BA Baylor Univ; BD SWn Sem; MS, PhD E Tex St Univ; pa/Edr Sanford Univ; APA; APGA; Phi Delta Kappa; cp/VP Rotary; Mason; Shriner; r/Bapt; hon/Outstg Tchr, Sch of Ed 1973; Friendliest Prof, Student Body.

HARVIE, RICHARD EUGENE oc/Staff Engineering Technician; b/Sept 29, 1943; h/35873 Burning Tree, Newark, CA 94560; m/L Elaine Gilderoy; c/Kenneth Brian, Douglas James, Michael Eugene; p/Eugene T Harvie (dec); Geraldine P Lyman; ed/AA

Ohlone Col; pa/SHARE Inc: Group Libn, Co Installation Rep; U Airlines Mgmt Clb; Lectr Indust Automation Groups; Numerical Control Soc: Past Pres, Past Secy, Past Treas; Former Advr San Quentin Prison; Former Mem San Francisco Interline Clb; Former Tech Advr San Mateo Col; cp/Mem PTA; BSA: Den Ldr, Com Ldr, Asst Scoutsmaster, Tng Staff, Merit Badge Advr, Former Activs; r/Prot; hon/Awds of Merit, U Airlines (2); PTA Fdrs Day Awd, Lincoln Sch; BSA: Dist Awd of Merit, Cubmaster Awd, Cert of Ser, Others; Profl Pubs; Biogl Listings.

HARZ, FRANCES MARIE KIRKLAND oc/Department Director; b/Oct 29, 1926; h/207 Jeffry Ranch Pl, PO Box 489, Clayton, CA 94517; ba/Concord, CA; m/Raymond Frank; c/Diane R H Hoerig; c/Elijah Erps and Mamie Allison Kirkland, Alameda, CA;

ed/Att'd Univ Cal-B 1971-77; pa/Dir Data Processing Dept Nav Weapons Sta; Am Mgmt Assn; Data Processing Mgmt Assn; Conslt USN Dept, Dept Def, Diablo Val Col, Pleasant Hill, Cal; Others; r/Presb; hon/US Navy Dept: Outstg Achmt Commend, Penny Pincher's Awd.

HASBARGEN, ARTHUR oc/Educator; b/Apr 20, 1925; h/813 Orchard Dr, Macomb, IL 61455; ba/Macomb; m/Lorayne; c/James, Janet, Karen, Nancy; p/Arthur E Hasbargen (dec); Zelpha Spence Hasbargen, Kankakee, IL; ed/BS w high hons NIU 1949; MA MSU 1950; EdD Univ Ill 1969; mil/USAAF 1943-46; pa/Edr Dept Spec Ed Wn Ill Univ; APGA; NVGA; CEC; AAMD; cp/Kiwanis; Var Adv Groups; r/Luth; hon/USOE Fellow; Kappa Delta Pi; Phi Delta Kappa.

HASKIN, DOROTHY CLARK oc/Organization President; Writer; b/Mar 19, 1905; h/2573 Glen Green, Hollywood, CA 90068; ba/Burbank, CA; m/Roy A (dec); p/William Clark (dec); Emma Evelyn Howard (dec); ed/Grad Biola Col 1938; pa/Spkr; Writing; Pres Charitable Org; cp/Mem RSVP; r/Hollywood Epis Ch; hon/Hon'd by Korean Govt.

HASKINS, SUE ANN GROVES oc/-Management Information Systems Analyst; b/Feb 23, 1943; h/11511 Wembley Rd, Los Alamitos, CA 90720; ba/Long Beach, CA; m/Corrinne Michelle, Erinn Nicole; p/Clide Groves, Summersville, WV; Gratia Bailey Groves, Laguna Hills, CA; ed/BA Scripps

Col; pa/Mgmt Info Systems Analyst Sr McDonnell-Douglas Corp, LB; Conslt to Airlines: Sydney, Melbourne, Auckland 1971; Spkr Airline Group Intl Fdn Opers Res Socs, Sydney 1977; cp/LB Philharm Jrs, Affil LA Philharm, Chperson Concert Arrangemts

Com; hon/Pi Mu Epsilon.

HASLAM, JAMES A III oc/Marketing Executive; b/Mar 9, 1954; h/1239 Forest Brook Rd, Knoxville, TN 37919; ba/K'ville; m/Susan Bagwell; p/James A Haslam II, K'ville; ed/BS Univ Tenn 1976; pa/VP Mktg Pilot Oil Corp; cp/Past Pres Knox Co Yg Repubs; Former St Chm Yth Com Tenn for Ford; Repub Exec Com; r/Epis: SS Tchr, Acolyte Master; hon/Man of Yr, UT 1976; Loan Exec of Yr, U Way 1977.

HASLEY, ROBERT NATHAN b/Apr 2, 1933; h/RD 8, Box 96, Hasley Lane, Greensburg, PA 15601; ba/Greensburg; m/Thelma Marie Cottrill; c/Deborah H Wallace, Vicky H Lentz, Roberta Nelle, James Paris, Jeffrey Robert; p/Nathan and Nellie Hasley (dec); mil/Ohio Nat Guard; cp/Ctl Westmoreland C of C; CB 13 Clb; IPA; Luxor Fire Dept; r/Prot; hon/W/W: Fin & Indust, E; Community Ldrs; Others.

HASSOUNA, FRED oc/Professor; b/Mar 26, 1918; h/31242 Flying Cloud Dr, Laguna Niguel, CA 92677; ba/Mission Viejo, CA; m/Verna Arlene Dotter; p/Amin S Hassouna (dec); Dawlat Hassouna, Alexandria, Egypt; ed/Dipls: Cairo Univ (Egypt), Univ Liverpool (England); MArch, MS Univ So Cal; pa/Saddleback Col: Prof Arch, Hd Dept Arch; Pres Cal Coun Arch Ed 1977; Liaison Com on Arch, Landscape Arch, Urban & Reg Planning in Higher Ed in Cal; Am Inst Archs; Am Inst Planners; Indust Tech Adv Bd Cal St Univ-Long Bch; Adv Com on Envir & Interior Design Univ Cal-Irvine; Lic'd Arch: Cal, Tex; hon/Fellow, Intl Inst Arts & Lttrs; Brit Coun F'ship; Num Biogl Listings.

HASTINGS, AGNES (AGGIE) MARY oc/Secretary, Stenographer, Library Clerk; b/Oct 11, 1922; h/613 Bainbridge St, Foster City, CA 94404; ba/San Francisco, CA; m/Donald; c/Donna Moreno, Don; p/Joseph Smith (dec); Sophie Meyer (dec); ed/BA Golden Gate Univ; Postgrad Studies: SF St Univ, San Jose St Univ, Col Notre Dame; pa/Secy-Stenographer-Lib Clerk CALTRANS (Dept Trans), SF; Outpatient Desk Sequoia Hosp, Redwood City, Cal; Former Mem Sigma Delta Chi; cp/Former Vol Wkr Travelers Aid; USO; Current Vol St Bonfice (SF Tenderloin Dist); Others; r/Cath; hon/W/W Am Wom; World W/W Wom.

HASTINGS, BAIRD oc/Musician; Conductor; Writer; Teacher; b/May 14, 1919; h/33 Greenwich Ave, New York, NY 10014; m/Louise L; p/Albert Baird Hastings, La Jolla, CA; Margaret Hastings; ed/AB; MA; PhD; mil/US Mil Intell 1942-46; pa/Conductor Mozart Fest 1960-; Guest Conductor: Dessoff Choirs, Hartford Symph, Am Recorder Soc, Holyoke, Others; Dir Instrumental Music Trinity Col, Hartford 1965-70; Asst Music Critic *Hartford Times* 1967-70; Guest Lectr: Harvard, NY Univ, Tufts, NY Public Lib, Others; Orch Libn The Juiliard Sch 1973-; hon/Fulbright F'ship; Tanglewood S'ship; Contbr 300+ Articles, Reviews & Translations to Arts Pubs; Biogl Listings.

HASTY, BEATRICE GIROUX JONES oc/Artist; Registered Real Estate Broker; h/2780 W Marion, Punta Gorda, FL 33950; m/Palmer G; c/2 Chd; ed/Edison Commun Col (Fla); Cont'g Studies Preparatory Law & Fine Arts; pa/Real Est Saleswom 1956-57; Self-employed Real Est Brokerage Bus 1959-70, Currently Ret'd; IPA; Leonardo de Vinci Centro Studie Scambi Internationali (Italy); Art Assns: SW Fla, Sarasota, Venice; Charlotte Co: Art Guild, Water Color Soc, Bd Realtors; Mem Opport House, Hendersonville, NC; H'ville Art Assn; Charter Mem & Past Pres Englewood (Fla) BPW Clbs; Orgr & Past Pres Sarasota Co Farm Bur Wom; cp/Former Chm E'wood C of C; Org'g Mem & 1st Pres Charlotte Co Friends of Auditorium; Former 4-H Clb Ldr; Former Secy & VP Dist 9 Fdn Wom's Clbs; Past Pres E'wood Mixed Repub Clb; Orgr & 1st Pres E'wood Repub Wom's Clb; Former Repub Com-wom, Precnt 9, Sarasota Co; hon/Num Art Awds; Wom of Yr, E'wood 1968; Art Shown in Num Exhbns

& Juried Shows; Intl Reg Profiles; Book of Honor.

HATCHER, JOSEPH CARROLL oc/-Chemical Engineer; b/Jan 15, 1939; h/4012 Goldstein Ln, Louisville, KY 40272; ba/L'ville; m/Rosemary Helen Shaw; c/James Carroll, Robert Lloyd, Christopher Lee; p/J C and Tressie Britt Hatcher, Glasgow, KY; ed/BSChE, MSChE Purdue Univ; pa/Am Inst Chem Engrs; cp/Gideons Intl; Repub Precnt Capt; MENSA; Scout Activs; r/Bapt; hon/Pershing Rifles Mil Hon; Tau Beta Pi; Omega Chi Epsilon; Eagle Scout.

HATCHETTE, EDWIN ERSDALE oc/Director of Treasury; b/Sept 2, 1944; h/PO Box 2472, St Thomas, VI 00801; ba/St Thomas; c/Efrain A, Ana Patricia; p/Antonio and Idalia Caiby Hatchette, St Thomas; ed/BA cum laude Inter Am Univ PR; mil/AUS 1965-67, Sp E-5 Instr/Bus & Pers Adm Sch; pa/Dir of Treas Govt of VI; MFO of USA & Canada; NA; AGA; VI Small Bus Org; Former Mem Bd Dirs, Chm Constitution Com; cp/Discussion Ldr Manpower Tng Conf; Water Isl Comm, VI & the Sea; CoChm Citizens Com; Past Pres Yg Dems; Others; r/Moravian; hon/USCG Aux Cert; Batallion Soldier of Month (Aug 1966); W/W in Govt.

HATFIELD, BENJAMIN FRANK oc/Public Utility Consultant; Professional Engineer; Retired Executive; Retired Colonel; b/Jul 31, 1906; h/3916 Land O' Lakes Dr NE, Atlanta, GA 30342; m/Ada Ella Hatcher; c/Ada J H Coleman (Mrs James E), Benjamin Frank Jr (dec); p/Henry and Kate Scholl Hatfield (dec); ed/BS (EE), BS (ME) Univ Tenn 1930; US Army Engr Sch, US Army Signal Corps Sch; mil/AUS 1930-66, Moved up Ranks to Col, Ret'd 1966; pa/VP A L Groce Assoc, Public Utility Conslts 1972-; Tech Mem Steinhauer, Hatfield & Good, Assocs, Public Utility Conslts 1971-; So Bell Telephone & Telegraph Co: Asst VP Co Hdqtrs 1953-71, Maintenance & Practs Engr Co Hdqtrs 1946-49, Others; Mem Bell Sys Regulatory Adv Panel for Regulatory Res 1969-71; Former Instr So Bell Engrg Ecs Courses; Lectr; Reg'd Profl Engr: Ga (& Former La); Num Other Profl Activs; Sr Mem IEEE; Am Inst Elect Engrs; Ga Arch & Engrg Soc; Life Mem, Telephone Pioneers Am; NC Indep Telephone Assn; Phi Kappa Phi; Tau Beta Pi; cp/Ga Easter Seal Soc; Former Secy-Treas SEn Shrine Band Assn; Yaarab Temple, Ancient Arabic Order of Nobles of the Mystic Shrine; Masons; Land O' Lakes Civic Clb; Shrine Bandmasters & Bandsmen Assn NAm; YMCA; Trumpet Player Yaarab Temple Shrine Band; Sustaining Mem Repub Nat Com; Sponsor Nat Repub Congl Com; Fdg Mem 2nd Amendmt Foun; Num Others; r/Grace U Meth Ch, Memphis, Tenn: Mem, Tchr Adult Classes, Com on Hist & Records, Lay Spkr, Ch Trustee, Bldrs Clb, Others; hon/Sev Mil Hons; Krusi Prize in Elect Engrg, Univ Tenn; Biogl Listings; Others.

HATFIELD, CORDELIA M oc/Paralegal; h/2521 Old Lake Shore Dr, St Joseph, MI 49085; m/Malcolm K (dec); c/Susan M, Malcolm K II; p/George H and Mary Firehammer (dec); pa/Current Paralegal w Law Firm; Register of Probate, Probate Ct, Berrien Co (Mich) 1944-57; cp/Ec Clb; IPA; Past Pres Valparaiso Univ Guild; Former Mem Wom's Hosp Assn; Vol Wkr Meml Hosp, St Joseph; r/Luth; hon/Recipient Awd for Selling War Bonds; W/W: MW, Am Wom; Nat Social Dir; Royal Blue Book.

HATHAWAY, WILLIAM DODD oc/-United States Congressman; b/Feb 21, 1924; h/80 Orchard St, Auburn, ME 04210; ba/-Washington, DC; m/Mary Lee; c/Fred William, Susan H Boydston; p/James F Hathaway, Bryn Mawr, PA; Charlotte D Hathaway (dec); ed/BA; LLD Harvard; mil/-USAAC 1943-46; pa/Atty; Asst Co Atty; St Liquor Comm Hearing Examr; cp/US Senator; Mem US Ho of Reps 1965-72; r/Epis; hon/Dist'd Ser Awd, NEA; 1st & 14th Amendmt Foun Awd; Annual Awd of Merit; Nat Assn Public & Cont'g Adult Ed, Rural Housing Awd.

HATHORN, SUZETTE FLOWERS oc/Graduate Teaching Assistant; b/Feb 20, 1948; h/2315 Lowell Rd, Gastonia, NC 28052; ba/Oxford, OH; c/Jeff Bumgarner; p/Amos and Grace Cherry Flowers, Gastonia; ed/BA; Grad Work; pa/Miami Univ: Grad Tchr Asst 1977-, Pt-time Secy 1977; Employed w Bus Ofc McCullough-Hyde Meml Hosp, Oxford 1975-77; Var Other Former Positions; cp/Miami Univ Precision Ice Skating Drill Team; r/Bapt; hon/Phi Beta Kappa; Phi Theta Kappa; Sigma Tau Delta; Dean's List; Commun Ldrs & Noteworthy Ams.

HATMAKER, CAROLYN L oc/Teacher; b/Feb 28, 1951; h/D-18 Rt 2, Jacksboro, TN 37757; ba/J'boro; p/Fred M and Lucille S Hatmaker, Caryville, TN; ed/BS; MS; pa/Tchr Campbell Co High; NCTE; Tenn Ed Assn; E Tenn Ed Assn; NEA; Secy Campbell Co Ed Assn; Del to Tenn Ed Assn Rep Assembly; Tchr Wel Com; cp/Cancer Dr; Mar Dimes; r/Meth; hon/Gamma Beta Phi (Var Ofcs Held); Mortar Bd; Phi Lambda Theta; Phi Kappa Phi; Recipient S'ships, F'ship; Recog for Sers as Cnslr, Am Inst Fgn Study; Noteworthy Commun Ldr Awd; Others.

HAUGE, GABRIEL oc/Executive; b/Mar 7, 1914; h/950 Park Ave, New York, NY 10028; ba/NYC; m/Helen L Resor; c/Ann Bayliss, Stephen, John, Barbara Thompson, Susan Lansdowne, Elizabeth Larsen, Caroline Clark; ed/AB Concordia Col 1935; MA 1938, PhD 1947 Harvard Univ; LLD: Concordia Col 1957, Muhlenberg Col 1959, Gettysburg Col 1960; LHD Pace Col 1969; LLD: Yale Univ 1978, Hampden-Sydney Col 1979; mil/USN 1942-46, Battleship, Pacific; pa/Chm of Bd 1971-79: Mfrs Hanover Corp, Mfrs Hanover Trust Co; Pres: Mfrs Hanover Trust Co 1963-71, Mfrs Hanover Corp 1969-71; VChm of Bd Mfrs Hanover Trust Co 1961-63; Other Former Positions; Assn Resv City Bkrs: Mem 1960-78, Pres 1976-77; Bus/Labor Wkg Group, NYC 1976-77; NY Clearing House Assn: Mem 1965-79, Pres 1977-79; Secy Treasury's Adv Com on Reform of Intl Monetary Sys 1973-75, 1977-; Former Adm Asst to Pres of US for Ec Affairs 1953-56; Spec Asst to Pres of US for Ec Affairs 1956-58; Former Mem US Coun on Fgn Ec Policy; Public Policy Com of The Advt'g Coun 1964-73; Dir or Trustee Var Corps & Cos; Other Profl Activs; cp/Former Mem: Bus Com for the Arts Inc, Juilliard Musical Foun; Com for Ec Devel; Treas Coun on Fgn Relats Inc; Salvation Army; UF Gtr NY; Norwegian-Am Hist Assn; Fed City Coun (Wash); Mem Var Clbs; hon/Louis C Wills Awd, Indust Home for Blind; Dodge Medallion, YMCA; Ayers Ldrship Awd, Stonier Grad Sch Bkg; Charles E Wilson Awd, Rel in Am Life; Reg Plan Assn Awd; Fam of Man Awd, Coun of Chs City of NY; Others.

HAUGH, RICHARD STANLEY oc/-Professor; Editor; Translator; b/May 4, 1942; h/PO Box 911, E Falmouth, MA 02536; m/Vera; c/Alexandra, Andrew, Peter; p/Victor and Marion Haugh, Lexington, MA; ed/BA; MA; PhD; pa/Fdr & Chm Bd Trustees Falmouth Acad 1977-; Vis Prof Ch Hist Rice Univ 1978-79; Assoc Prof Humanities Tuskegee Inst 1977-78; Nat Endowmt for Humanities' Postdoct "Fellow in Residence" (Medieval Hist) Harvard Univ 1976-77; Iona Col: Asst Prof Humanities 1975-76, Asst Prof Rel Studies, Adjunct in Classics 1971-75; Other Former Positions; Author Books & Articles; Var Edit Activs; r/Greek Orthodox; hon/Jessie Noyes S'ship; F'ship; Dir Am Scholars; Contemp Authors; Outstg Edrs Am; Intl W/W Commun Ser; W/W: Rel, E; Men of Achmt; Notable Ams; Commun Ldrs & Noteworthy Ams.

HAUN, FRANCES CONWAY (CONNIE) MALONEY oc/Retired Teacher; b/Jan 2, 1910; h/Green Hills, Rt 1, Box 69, Russellville, TN 37860; ba/Morristown, TN; m/Fred Burwin; c/Hugh Leslie, Frances Lavinia, Philip Maloney; p/Hugh Conway and Lena McCorkle Maloney (dec); ed/Salem Acad; BS E Tenn Univ 1933; MS Univ Tenn 1956; Mid St Univ 1971; NEA Writing Course NY 1969; Dipl Inst of Chds Lit 1973; Currently in Cont'g Ed Prog Univ Tenn; pa/E Tenn Ed Assn; TEA;

NEA; Former Supvr Hamblen Co Hot Lunches; Sherwood Elem Sch: Tchr 19 Yrs (Ret'd), Orgr, Coach 1st Girls Basketball Team; Author Var Pubs, Contbr to Newspapers; Wkshop Mid Tenn St Univ, Murfreesboro, Tenn; NSF Resource Elem Ser Prog, Oak Ridge, Tenn; Intl Aerospace Group, Mid St Univ incl'g 1974 Trip to Japan, New Zealand, Hong Kong, Australia, Figi Isls, Singapore, Bangkok & Others; Invited to Join IPA 1974, 75; cp/Charter Mem M'town Humane Soc; Meml Heart Chm; Nolachuckey Chapt DAR: Mem, Former Libn, Dir, Chm Am Indians; Samuel Doak Chapt DAR, Del Nat & Tenn St Meetings 1978; UDC M'town; Ladies Rdg Cir; Upland Terr Garden Clb M'town: Mem, Pres 1948-50, Var Ofcs; Yth Emer Sers (YES) Bd; Springvale Commun Clb; Hamblen Co: Histn, Assn Preserv Tenn Antiquities, Farm Bur Exec Bd Mem; Chm Woms Div So Sts Coop; Pres M'town-Hamblen Co Alumni Chapt ETSU 1970-72; ARC Swimming Instr; Heart Chm Hamblen E Tenn Div 1969; Public Spkr; M'town-Hamblen Co Bicent Comm; M'town-Hamblen Lib Bd; Dir Davy Crockett Tavern 1976-77; Elected Dir Rose Ctr Mus for 3 Yrs; Tenn Soc Poets; St, Local Dem Clbs; Hamblen Co Woms Dem Clb: Prog Chm, 2/VP; Hamblen Co Exec Com of Dem Party; r/1st U Meth Ch: Mem, Choir, Dir Chds Choir, Bible Sch, SS Tchr, VP Mae Baker SS Class, Dist Chm Holston Div; WSG: Mem, Pres 1967-69, Chm; Pres Guild II; Del: Holston Conf Sch Christian Missions Emory & Henry Col 1972, 1973 Assembly U Meth Wom Cinc, Ohio, 1978 Assembly UMW Louisville, Ky; hon/1st Runner-up First Lady of M'town Contest 1967, Nom 1970; E Tenn Heart Assn: Ldrship Awd, Ser Awd; St Del Nat DAR Conv Wash DC 1971, Nashville, Tenn 1973; Guest Spkr Awd 1967 JCs; Traveled Var European Countries; 2000 Wom Achmt; DIB; World W/W Wom; Outstg Alumnae Awd, ETSU; Intercont Biog Dir; Commun Ldrs Am; W/W Am Wom; Ser Awd (Engraved Silver Tray) Knoxville, Tenn Awds Banquet at Univ Tenn Student Ctr Bldg; Others.

HAUPTFUHRER, BARBARA BARNES oc/Corporate Director; b/Oct 11, 1928; h/1700 Old Welsh Rd, Huntingdon Valley, PA 19006; m/George J Jr; c/George J III, W Barnes; p/J Foster and Myrtle Preyer Barnes (dec); ed/BA w hons Wellesley Col; pa/Dir: Vanguard Group Investmt Cos, Gt Atl &

Pacific Tea Co (A & P), Gen Public Utilities Co, J Walter Thompson Co, Knight Ridder Newspapers Inc, The Marble Foun, Gtr Philadelphia Partnership, World Affairs Coun Phila; Trustee: Phila Saving Fund Soc, Wellesley Col, Com for Ec Devel, U Way SEn Pa; Var Former Activs; r/Luth.

HAUSEN, JUTTA oc/Mathematician; b/Jan 6, 1943; h/6351 Del Monte, Houston, TX 77057; ba/Houston; p/Harald W and Martha D Hausen, Frankfurt, Germany; ed/Dipl Math; PhD; pa/Prof Math Univ Houston; Assoc Mng Editor Houston J Math; hon/Post-doct F'ship, NM St Univ; Grants: NSF, Univ Houston; Contbr Num Articles to Profl Jours.

HAUXWELL, GERALD DEAN oc/Professional Chemical Engineer; b/Sept 24, 1935; h/2915 Ennismore Ct, Richmond, VA 23224; ba/Same; m/Ingrid M D Postner; p/Lawrence F Hauxwell (dec); Mildred E Hauxwell, McCook, NE; ed/AA; BS; MS; PhD; mil/-

USN Comm'd 1959; pa/Va & Nat Soc Profl Engrs; Am Inst Chem Engrs; cp/Pres Newberrytowne Assn; Polit Coms; r/Christian; Var Ch Coms; hon/Profl Cert'd Engr: Va, Oreg, Md; Sigma Tau; Alpha Chi Sigma; Phi Kappa Phi.

HAVELOS, SAM GEORGE oc/Restaurateur; Numismatist; Calligraphist; b/Dec 4, 1915; h/PO Drawer E, Blacksburg, VA 24060; ba/Same; m/Dina K Karageorge; p/George D Havelos (dec); Spyridoula G Kanavos, Athens, Greece; ed/Parkwood Bus Col 1961; Statesville Bus Col 1963; Zanerian Col Penmanship 1964; Addit Studies; pa/Mgr: Greeks Cellar (Restaurant), B'burg 1969-, Sam's Gourmet, Winston-Salem, NC 1965-69; Owner: Reynolda Manor Cafeteria, W-S 1961-64, Washington Restaurant, Wytheville, Va 1952-61; Others; Am Numismatic Assn; Am Philatelic Soc; Pres Cumberland & Robinson Cos Restaurant Assn 1950-51; Dir NC Restaurant Assn; cp/Red Cross; C of C; Nat Flag Foun; Nat Wildlife Fdn; Am Helenic Ed Progressive Assn; Ks of Thermopylae; Nat Trust for Hist Preserv; Smithsonian Inst; Nat Geographic Soc; Calhoun's Collectors Soc; Others; r/Greek Orthodox, Ch of N & S Am; hon/Cert of Meritorious Ser, Nat Soc SAR; W/W S&SW.

HAWES, MIRIAM LUCILLE oc/Librarian; b/Feb 24, 1919; h/Rt 2, New Concord, OH 43762; ba/Byesville, OH; p/Walter Hawes (dec); Margaret Hawes, New Concord; ed/BA Muskingum Col; Grad Study: Ohio Univ, Chgo Univ, Univ Wyo; pa/Libn Meadowbrook HS; NEA; OEA; Delta Kappa Gamma: VP 2 Yrs, Treas 2 Yrs; cp/Ohio Geneol Soc, St & Local; Former Trustee Guernsey Hist Soc; Former 4-H Clb Advr; Var Other Former Activs; r/Claysville Meth Ch: Secy.

HAWES, RALPH EDGAR oc/Executive; b/Dec 27, 1930; h/2644 San Andres Way, Claremont, CA 91711; ba/Pomona, CA; m/Solita-Anna; c/Ralpha Edgar III, Jon Jeffrey, Lynn Caprice; p/Ralph Edgar Sr and Gertha Mains Hawes, Hemet, CA; ed/BSEE Clarkson Col Technol 1952-55; MEngrg UCLA 1967-69; mil/AUS Signal Corp 1957; DMG; pa/Gen Dynamics, Pomona Div: VP, Gen Mgr; Am Inst Aeronautics & Astronautics; Am Def Preparedness Assn; Assn US Army; Am Mgmt Assn; cp/BSA, Mem Old Baldy Coun; W Coast Univ Indust Coun; Cal Poly Adv Bd Cal St; UCLA Dean's Coun; Galileo Soc-Harvey Mudd Col; r/Prot; hon/Pershing Rifles, Mil Hon; Eta Kappa Nu.

HAWK, GARY DEAN oc/Watercolor Artist; b/Dec 24, 1932; h/307 S Buckeye, Iola, KS 66749; ba/Same; m/Beverly Jeanine; c/Lora, Susan, Deborah H Smail; p/Orville and Nine Hawk, Iola; ed/Att'd: Ks St Univ, Ks City Art Inst; pa/Assoc'd w: Hallmark Cards (Ks City, Mo), Am Greeting (Cleveland, Ohio); Designed IMP Boats, Iola; Num One-Man Shows; Others; cp/Iola Lib Bd; Zoning Bd; Citizen's Action Comm; Bd Ed Iola; r/Bapt; hon/Gov's Artist, Ks; SWn Bell Telephone Contest Winner; Patrons Purchase Awd, KWS.

HAWKINS, JOSEPH KEY oc/Communications Company Executive; b/Aug 13, 1926; h/3873 Ingraham St, D-104, San Diego, CA 92109; ba/San Diego; c/Ann Patrick, Torrey Sue, Gale Britta; p/Joseph K Hawkins (dec); Helen E Hawkins, El Cajon, CA; ed/BS, MS Stanford Univ; JD Wn St Univ; mil/AUS 1946-48; pa/Lectr UCLA; Author Books on Computer Design & Info Sci; Editor Pattern Recog (Book) & Jour; Contbr to Num Profl Pubs; hon/Phi Beta Kappa; Am Jurisprudence Awd.

HAWKINS, LEONARD J oc/Systems Engineer; b/Oct 23, 1918; h/27860 Peppermill, Farmington Hills, MI 48018; ba/Troy, MI; m/Anniece; c/Carol Peters (Mrs R L), Edmund J; p/B Jay and Geraldine Hawkins, Ashtabula, OH; ed/Grad Intl Accts Soc 1954; Num Courses Data Processing Mgmt; Wkshops & Sems; mil/USN 1942-45, MMAC 1c; pa/Conslt to A Louis Supply Co

(for Computer Installation); Curric Advr & Instr: Lake Erie Tech Sch, Ashtabula Co Jt Voc Sch; Mem Com for Improvemt Devel & Expansion (Ashtabula Co Jt Voc-Ed); Featured Spkr; cp/Allocation Com U Appeal; Bd Dirs YM-YWCA; r/Prot; hon/Author Pub'd Articles; IPA; DIB; Commun Ldrs & Noteworthy Ams; Men of Achmt; W/W: Fin & Indust, Am, US.

HAWKINS, ROBERT A oc/College Administrator; b/Aug 21, 1924; h/3305 Providence Dr, Midland, TX 79703; ba/Midland; m/Nina Jo Milton; c/Paul Clark, Sheila Ann H Jordan; p/Lawrence R Hawkins (dec); Grace Lauer, Delta, BC, Canada; ed/BA 1948, MA 1967 Abilene Christian Univ; EdD

Tex Tech Univ; pa/Dir Guid Midland Col; Tchr Phil; Tex Pers Guid Assn; Jr Col Student Pers Assn Tex; cp/Midland Col Spkr's Bur; Mem Num Bds; Conslt; r/Translator & Pubr Bible Student's New Testament 1978; hon/Phi Kappa Phi; Alpha Chi; W/W: Rel, SW; Book of Honor; Personalities of S; DIB.

HAWKINS, SARAH MARGARETT oc/Hospital Advisor; b/Mar 9, 1915; h/6801 Alter St, Baltimore, MD 21207; p/James H and Barbara B Hawkins (dec); ed/RN; BS; pa/Ret'd Hosp Advr; Sigma Theta Tau; St Nurses Assn; Md Gen Nurses Alumni Assn; AWRT; MCEA; cp/Eng Spkg Union; Md Hist Soc; Alumni Assn Cath Univ Am; John Eager Howard Chapt NS DAR; r/Epis; hon/Freedoms Foun Awd; Nurse of Yr 1979, Md Gen Nurses Alumni Assn.

HAWLEY, ELIZABETH HOOVER oc/Executive Secretary; b/Feb 11, 1923; h/63 Quaker Ch Rd, Dover, NJ 07801; ba/Dover; m/Willard Hayden; p/Thomas E and Fidelis C Hoover (dec); ed/BS Geo Wash Univ 1948; LLB LaSalle Univ 1975; pa/Exec Secy ARRADCOM; Fed'ly Employed Wom; cp/Columbian Wom, Geo Wash Univ; Joseph Coolidge Chapt DAR; r/Epis; hon/Sev Fed Awds; Gold Star II w hons, Imperial Soc Tchrs of Dancing Inc; Intl W/W Intells; World W/W Wom; Notable Ams; Commun Ldrs & Noteworthy Ams.

HAWLEY, ROBERT PATRICK oc/Court Administrator; b/Dec 15, 1946; h/538 Seneca St, Harrisburg, PA 17110; ba/H'burg; m/Jhan L; c/Matthew, Michael; p/John R and Frances C Hawley, Camp Hill, PA; ed/AS HACC 1969; BA Lycoming 1971; MGA Univ Pa 1978; mil/AUS Enlisted 1966; USAR CPT 1978; Sch Qtrmaster Ofcr; Presently Completing Command & Gen Staff Col; pa/Admr Dauphin Co Ct; HS Govt Tchr 1971-76; Chm Local PSEA Leg & Polit Action Coms; Busman; cp/Elected Judge of Elections; Inspector of Elections; Assessor; Alt Del Repub Nat Conv; Cand City Coun; H'burg Optimist Clb; H'burg JCs; Post 1001 Am Legion; Others; r/Our Lady's Rom Cath Ch, H'burg: Lectr; hon/W/W: Am Jr Cols, Am Polits.

HAWLEY, WILLARD HAYDEN oc/Metallurgist; b/Dec 4, 1923; h/63 Quaker Church Rd, Dover, NJ 07801; ba/Dover; m/Elizabeth Hoover; p/Willard H and Louise J Hawley (dec); ed/BS Va Polytech Inst; MEng Yale Univ; mil/AUS 1943-46; pa/Metallurgist ARRADCOM; Am Soc for Testing & Mats: Com BO5, Com BO7; Am Soc for Metals; Am Inst Mining & Metall Engrs; AAAS; Yale Sci &

Engrg Assn; Reg'd Prof Engr: Wash DC, Mass; r/Epis; hon/30 Yr Ser Awd, US Govt; Gold Star I, The Imperial Soc Tchrs of Dancing Inc; DIB; Men of Achmt; W/W in E.

HAY, FRANCES T oc/College Administrator; b/Oct 13, 1917; h/6205 W 99th Terr, Overland Park, KS 66207; ba/Kansas City, KS; m/Hardy; c/Michael, Margaret, Roxanne; p/Frank J Rines (dec); Margaret Gill (dec); ed/JD New Eng Sch Law; Ctf Sch Naval Justice (Port Huenene, Cal); mil/USMC (WR) 1/Lt; Legal Ofcr, Adjutant; pa/Asst to Pres; Mem Bar; Conslt Ednl Planning, Nat Coun Indep Jr Cols; Nat Coun for Resource Devel; cp/Org'd Vol Prog St Joseph's Hosp Guild, Orange, Cal; Former Mem Mayor's Com for Capital Improvemts, KC; r/Cath; hon/LLB Magna Cum Laude.

HAY, GEORGE AUSTIN oc/Motion Picture Producer; Director; Actor; Artist; h/2022 Columbia Rd NW, Washington, DC 20009; ba/Wash DC; p/George and Mary Austin Hay; ed/BS, MLitt Univ Pgh; MA Columbia Univ; mil/AUS (S Pacific) Newscaster-Editor Inf & Ed, HQ 331 Div; pa/Actor 2 Yrs on Broadway; Prodr & Dir Off-Broadway Prodns; Appearances TV, Feature Pictures; Exhbns Paintings: Duncan Galleries (NY), Lincoln Ctr, Carnegie Inst, Am Painters in Paris; Art Works Rep'd in Lib of Cong & Metro Mus of Art; Fed Design Coun; Wash Film Coun; Am Fdn TV & Radio Artists; Screen Actors Guild; Am Artists Profl Leag; Nat Acad TV Arts & Scis; Arts Clb Wash (Trustee); Nat Press Clb; cp/Nat Trust for Hist Preserv; SAR; Inst for Bach Studies; Music Lib Assn; Shakespeare-Oxford Soc; Am Philatelic Soc; Cambria Co Hist Soc; Allied Artists; The Players; Others; hon/St Bartholomew's Silver Ldrship Awd; Jr Leag Loyal Ser Awd; Others.

HAY, RUSSELL EARL JR oc/Scientist; b/Jan 5, 1918; h/Rt 2, Box 314, Carthage, NC 28327; m/Patricia Aull; c/Nancy, Susan, Kathy; p/Russell E Hay Sr (dec); Harriet E Hay, Carthage; ed/AB; MS; PhD; mil/Corps of Engrs 1941-46; USAR 1946-71; LTC (Ret'd); pa/Ret'd; Agronomist-Plant Physiologist; Res Mgmt & Adm; Am Chem Soc; Am Soc Plant Physiologists; Am Soc Biol Sci; Nat Coun Univ Res Adm; Soil Sci Soc Am; cp/Precnt Chm Repubs; Mason; Scottish Rite; Shriner; Am Heart Assn; Grandview Height Bd of Hlth; Others; r/Presb: Ruling Elder; hon/Sigma Xi; Gamma Sigma Delta; Phi Sigma.

HAYASHI, TETSUMARO oc/University Professor; b/Mar 22, 1929; h/1405 N Kimberly ln, Muncie, IN 47304; ba/Muncie; m/Akiko Sakuratani; c/Richard Hideki; p/Shieko Honjyo Hayashi, Sakaide City, Japan; ed/BA; MA; MALS; PhD; pa/Prof Ball St Univ; Editor-in-Chief Steinbeck Qtrly; Pres Steinbeck Soc Am; Dir Intl Steinbeck Soc; cp/Dem; r/Buddhist; hon/Folger Fellow; Am Phil Fellow; Am Coun Learned Socs Fellow.

HAYES, ARTHUR C oc/Consultant; Legislator; b/Aug 24, 1918; h/2001 Oakland St, Ft Wayne, IN 46808; m/Miriam E (dec); c/Arthur C Jr, Bethany M, Gayle H Crosby; p/Walter F Hayes (dec); Marie P Hayes, Ft Wayne; ed/BS Ind Univ 1948; mil/WWII; Ret'd Maj Ind Guard Resv; cp/St Rep 1962-; Am Negro Emancipation Centennial Comm; Ind Sesquicentennial Comm; Am Revolution Bicent Comm; Ind Protection & Advocacy Ser Comm for Devel'ly Disabled; Others; r/Luth; hon/W/W: MW, Am Polits; Personalities W&MW; Royal Blue Book; DIB; Creative & Success Personalities; Intl W/W Commun Ser, 2000 Men Achmt; Fellow, IBA; Ky Col; Others.

HAYES, DEANNE oc/Librarian; b/Aug 31, 1937; h/Box 384, Hollis, OK 73550; p/L G Bell and Pauline Smollock; ed/Att'd Univ Idaho; Silver Wings Recipient SW Airline Sch, Los Angeles, Cal 1957; Cert Am Inst Bkg (LA) 1958; Assoc Art Wn Okla St Col 1977; Deg Lib Sci Oscar Rose Col 1979; Am Inst Fgn Study; pa/Clothing Model, House of Nine, LA; Airline Stewardess SW Airlines, LA 1956-57; Med Secy Horton Nsg Home, Nampa, Idaho

1959-60; Acct'g Dept Tandy Homes Inc, Tulsa, Okla 1960-63; Med Secy, Tulsa 1963-64; Owner & Operator Dee's Dept Store, Hollis 1966-68; Legal Secy Myers & Cummings Attys, Hollis 1970-73; Hd Libn Hollis Public Lib 1977-; Nat & Okla Assns Legal Secys; Am, Okla & SWn Lib Assns; Notary Public, St of Okla; cp/Univ Tulsa Law Wives, Secy; Chm Harmon Co Hist Assn; Okla Arts & Humanities Coun; Okla Image Prog; Treas Beta Sigma Phi; Nat Girl Scout Coun; Garden Clb; hon/Miss Nampa (Idaho) 1955; Miss Idaho Pageant 1955; Miss For Theater 1956; Outstg Newspaper Story 1955; Most Photogenic Awd 1956; Comm'd Hon Col, Gov Okla; Dean's & Pres's Hon Roll 1975-79; Biogl Listings; Pub'd Author.

HAYES, EDWARD JAMES oc/Priest; b/Dec 11, 1914; h/1961 Ernst Terr, Union, NJ 07083; p/James E and Teresa I Hayes; ed/BA Seton Hall Col 1938; BTh Immaculate Conception Sem 1941; pa/Ordained Priest 1941; Mt Carmel Ch, Lyndhurst, NJ: Pastor 1968-77, Pastor Emeritus 1977-; Assoc Pastor: St Thomas Aquinas Ch 1958-68, St Charles Borromeo's Ch, Newark, NJ 1948-58, Others; Asst Chaplain Newark Fire Dept 1948-; Visual Aid Res Dir Apostolate for Deaf, Newark 1945-76; Prof Med Ethics St Michael's Med Ctr, Newark 1959-61, All Souls Hosp, Morristown, NJ 1961-69; Charter Mem Senate of Priests, Newark 1967-68; cp/Mil Chaplains Assn USA; K of C 4th Deg; Prodr Rel Instnl Films 1941-49; Coauthor Med-Moral Books; hon/Contbr Articles to Rel Jours; Author: *Catholicism and Life* 1976, *Catholicism and Soc* 1975, *Confession Aid for Chd* 1959, Others.

HAYES, GAYNELLE HASSELMEIER oc/College Administrator; b/Feb 14, 1943; h/4811 Woodrow, Galveston, TX 77550; ba/Galveston; c/Anne-Marie; p/A Gale Sr and Nellie Hasselmeier, Galveston; ed/BA Lamar Univ 1965; MEd Univ Houston 1969; EdD Nova Univ 1977; pa/Coor Cnslg & Placemt Galveston Col; Jr Col Student Pers Assn Tex: Pres 1977-79, Secy-Treas 1977; Pres

Omicron Chapt Delta Kappa Gamma 1976-78; Tex Jr Col Tchrs Assn (Cnslg & Student Pers Sect): Chperson 1978-79, VChperson 1977-78; TPGA; APGA; TACUSPA; cp/Former Secy Pilot Clb Intl Galveston; Former VP Galveston Col Fac Coun; Galveston Col Spkrs Bur; Others; r/Cath; hon/Sponsor Phi Theta Kappa; Outstg Yg Wom Am; W/W S&SW; Commun Ldrs & Noteworthy Ams; White-Arrington S'ship, Alpha St S'ship Com Delta Kappa Gamma.

HAYES, HARROLD HENRY oc/Professional Engineer; b/Oct 17, 1907; h/PO Box 507, Custer, SD 57730; ba/Custer; m/-Caroline S; c/Peggy Jane, Donaline Louise; p/James Hayes (dec); Rosaline Tyler (dec); ed/BS; Completed Command & Gen Staff; mil/USAR Col; pa/Reg'd Profl Engr: Mich, Ill, Ohio; Nat Soc Profl Engrs; Soc Am Mil Engrs; cp/VFW; Res Ofc Assn; Mason; r/Christian; hon/Bronze Star; W/W in Engrg.

HAYES, JOHN MARION oc/Professor Emeritus; Consulting Structural Engineer; b/May 18, 1909; h/312 Highland Dr, W Lafayette, IN 47906; ba/Same; m/Coye Matilda Cunningham; c/Marian Sue H Jernigan; Julia Kathleen H Casey; p/(dec);

ed/BSCE Purdue Univ 1931; MS Univ Tenn 1944; CE Purdue Univ 1946; pa/Purdue Univ Prof Emeritus Structural Engrg, Prof 1958-75, Assoc Prof 1948-58; Dist Bridge Engr Ark, US Bur of Public Rds 1946-48; Other Former Positions; ASCE, Num Actives Var Sects; Nat Soc Profl Engrs; Am Concrete Inst; Am Welding Soc; Intl Soc for Bridge & Structural Engrg; AAAS; Soc for Experimtl Stress Analysis; Am Railway Engrg Assn; Sigma Xi; Others; cp/Lions Intl, Lafayette; r/1st U Meth Ch, W Lafayette: Mem Adm Bd 1971-, Former Pres Meth Men's Clb, Others; hon/Spec Cit Awd, AISC; Outstg Engrg Alumnus Awd, Univ Tenn-K; Hon Deg Mem Emeritus, Com 15, Am Railway Engrg Assn.

HAYES, KYLE oc/Attorney; b/Oct 4, 1905; ba/PO Box 1105, N Wilkesboro, NC 28659; m/Margaret Smithey; p/Charles C and Ida H Hayes (dec); ed/LLB Wake Forest Univ 1931; JD Wake Forest Univ 1970; mil/USMC WWII; pa/Admitted to Bar St of NC 1930; Gen Pract Law N W'boro 1931; Formed Partnership w brother (Clyde Hayes), Sr Mem Hayes & Hayes 1937-; Admitted to Pract All Cts; ABA; Fed, NC, Wilkes Co Bar Assns; NC

St Bar; Am Trial Lwyrs Assn; Pract'g Law Inst; Am Judic Soc; Mem Rules Making Com US Dist Ct for Mid Dist NC; Other Activs; cp/NC St Repub Exec Com; Past Pres: N W'boro Kiwanis Clb, W'boro BPM Clb; Oakwoods CC; Mason; Elk; Others; r/W'boro Bapt Ch: Deacon, Tchr Men's Bible Class; hon/Intl Reg W/W; 2000 Men Achmt; Commun Ldrs Am; W/W S&SW; NC Lives; Lib of Human Resources, Am Bicent Res Inst.

HAYES, MARGARET SMITHEY oc/Retail Department Store Executive; b/Aug 11, 1911; h/604 E Main St, Wilkesboro, NC 28697; ba/N W'boro; m/Raymond Kyle; p/Nikeard B Smithey (dec); Hattie Eudora Little Smithey, Charlotte, NC; ed/Lenoir Rhyne Col 1929-30; pa/Secy-Treas & Dir N B Smithey Stores Co Inc; cp/Bd Mem Old Wilkes Inc; OES, Former Worthy Matron; Repub; r/Meth; hon/Hon Life Mem, WSCS; W/W Am Wom.

HAYES, MARY MARGARET oc/Teacher; b/Feb 20, 1926; h/93 Fuller Pl, Irvington, NJ 07111; ba/I'ton; p/John Hayes (dec); Nora Murphy (dec); ed/BA Notre Dame Md; MA Seton Hall Univ; pa/Tchr Archbishop Walsh HS; NCTE; Nat Assn Tchrs Jour; r/Cath; hon/Outstg Ldr in Ed; Hon'd by UN & Merchant Marine for Students' Winning Essay Competitions; Poetry Pub'd; Recog'd for Ser on Eval'g Coms for Mid Atl Assn Cols & Schs.

HAYES, PAUL JAMES oc/Priest; b/Sept 26, 1922; h/111 S St, New Providence, NJ

07974; p/James Edward and Teresa Meyers Hayes (dec); ed/AB Seton Hall Univ 1944; Immaculate Conception Sem; pa/Ordained Rom Cath Priest 1948; Pastor: Our Lady of Peace 1975-, St Patrick's, Jersey City 1974-75 (Admr 1969-74); Communs Ofc, Archdiocese of Newark: Asst Dir 1957-65, Appt'd Dir 1965; Elevated to Papal Chamberlain by Pope Paul VI 1965; Pres, Interdenom Clergy Coun of New Providence & Berkeley Heights 1978; Author *Catholicism and Life* 1976; Others; hon/Notable Ams.

HAYES, PAUL WESLEY oc/Physician; b/Jan 27, 1911; h/610 N Noyes Blvd, St Joseph, MO 64506; ba/St Joseph; m/Dorothy E; c/Karen H Morgan; p/Oren W Hayes (dec); Jennie Maye Hayes, St Joseph; ed/BS 1933, MD 1936 Univ Neb; mil/AUS Comm'd Med Res Corps 1936; Served WWII (France); Pscyhi Ser Var Mil Hosps; Ret'd Col; Mil Decorations; pa/Clin Dir St Joseph St Hosp (Outpatient Psychi Clin) 1976-79; Psychiatrist: St Joseph Hosp 1961-79, Meth Med Ctr, St Joseph 1961-79; Pvt Pract Gen Psychi Thompson Brumm Knepper Clin, St Joseph 1961-76; Other Former Positions; AMA; Mo Wn Dist Med Assn; Mid-Continent, Titus Harris & Am Psychi Assns; Others; cp/AF&AM Scottish Rite; Am Legion; r/Meth; hon/Profl Pubs; W/W: Mo, MW.

HAYGOOD, CAROLYN MARIE oc/-Nurse; b/Mar 6, 1928; h/Seminoe Dam Rt, Sinclair, WY 82334; m/Raymond Leroy; c/Terry Lee, Allen Wesley; p/Alex H E and Hedwig M Witte Scholz (dec); ed/RN; pa/Sev Coms, Am Nurses Assn; 1st VP & Pres, Wyom Nurses Assn (Bd Dirs 1956-68); Exec Dir, Wyom Nurses Assn 1968-78; Wyom League for Nsg; NLN; Am Soc Assn Execs; hon/W/W Am Wom; Rec'd Sev Awds as Editor of *Wyoming Nurse*; Awds Contest, Am Jour of Nsg.

HAYMAN, MARLENE RHODES oc/Management Specialist; b/Dec 15, 1938; h/446 Banbury, Arlington Heights, IL 60005; ba/Chicago, IL; c/Edward Mark, Scott David; p/Edward W and Marjorie Jane Sheppard Rhodes; ed/BA Univ Mich 1960; MPH Univ Ill 1976; pa/Mgmt Specialist Legal Ser Corp; Tchr; Adm Ill Reg Med Prog; r/Presb; hon/Dist'd Ser Scroll, Ill Cong P's & T's.

HAYNES, KENNETH GEORGE oc/-Superintendent; b/Nov 30, 1924; h/12 Quintana Dr, Galveston, TX 77551; ba/Galveston; m/Margaret Conroy; c/-Kenneth Jr, Melinda, Christopher; p/Fletcher Johnson Haynes (dec); Vyola Mae Parker, Garland, TX; ed/BS Univ Tex 1947; MA Geo Wash Univ 1964; mil/USN 36 Yrs, Rear Admiral (Ret'd); pa/Supt Tex Maritime Acad; US Naval Inst; Univ Tex Ex-Students Assn; cp/Tex A&M Univ Alumni Assn; cp/Propeller Clb; Life Mem USN Leag; r/Moody Meml Meth Ch; hon/Def Superior Ser Legion of Merit; Bronze Star; Navy Commend Medal; W/W in Am.

HAZEL, ERIK RICHARD oc/Marketing Researcher; b/Dec 16, 1944; h/11945 Red Barn Ct, Florissant, MO 63053; ba/St Louis, MO; m/Cheryl Anne; c/Sara Anne; p/George A and Marthanne Hazel, Jamestown, NY; ed/BA Wittenberg Univ 1970; MA 1974; PhD Case Wn Resv Univ 1974; mil/AUS 1964-67; Mil

Advr Vietnam; pa/Mktg Reschr SWn Bell Telephone Co; Am Mktg Assn; Am Studies Assn; Am Film Inst; Phi Gamma Delta; cp/US Chess Fdn; Nat Wildlife Fdn; Dem Party; Conslt Cleveland (Ohio) Commun Cols; r/Nondenom; hon/Newbell Niles Puckett Awd, Outstg Grad 1974; Nat Am Studies Fac Fellow; W/W MW; Phi Delta Theta.

HAZLITT, HENRY oc/American Editor, Author; b/Nov 28, 1894; h/65 Drum Hill Rd, Wilton, CT 06897; m/Frances S Kanes; ed/CCNY; pa/The Freeman: Editor-in-Chief 1953, CoFdr & CoEditor (w John Chamberlain) 1950-52; Syndicated Columnist Los Angeles Times 1966-69; Var Former Edit Activs; Pubs incl: The Inflation Crisis: and How to Resolve It 1978, The Conquest of Poverty 1973, Man vs The Wel State 1969, The Founs of Morality 1964, 1972, Others; hon/Hon LittD, Grove City Col; Hon LLD, Bethany Col; Hon SScD, Universidad Francisco Marroquin (Guatemala).

HAZZARD, DON PHILIP oc/Musician; b/Sept 30, 1947; h/2825 S King, Honolulu, HI 96826; m/Claire S; p/Allen C and Rose E Hazzard, Egan, IL; ed/BME Univ Mich; BFA Ohio Univ; pa/Prin Trumpet Honolulu Symph; Instr Univ Hi; Free-lance Show; Soloist; hon/Finalist, Prague Spring Intl Solo Competition 1974; Soloist w NC, Mexico & Honolulu Symph.

HEADLEE, WILLIAM HUGH oc/Educator; Medical Parasitologist; Professor Emeritus; b/Jun 15, 1907; h/762 N Riley Ave, Indianapolis, IN 46201; m/Gabrielle Mills; c/Joan H Bowden (Mrs Charles B), Anne; p/Walter C and Nellie Ann A Headlee (dec); ed/AB Earlham Col 1929; MS Univ Ill 1933; PhD Tulane Univ 1935; pa/Ind Univ: Prof Parasitic Diseases Sch of Med 1943-77, Grad Sch 1953-77, Prof Emeritus 1977-; AARP, Emeritus Fellow: AAAS, Ind Acad Sci, Royal Soc Tropical Med & Hygiene (London); Emeritus Mem: AAUP, Am Soc Tropical Med

& Hygiene, Sigma Xi; Sr Inactive Mem Am Soc Parasitologists; Soc Ret'd Execs; Ret'd Profs Ind; Nat Ret'd Tchrs Assn; Others; cp/Nat Geographic Soc; Nat Assn Partners of Alliance; Alumni Assns; Mayor's Adv on Aging & the Aged; Ind Writers Guild; Num Others; r/All Souls Unitarian Ch, Indpls: Budget Com, Chm Denom Affairs Com; hon/Cert of Recog for Mbrship in Sigma Xi, Ind Univ Med Ctr Chapt; Recog'd & Commended, Comm on Aging St of Ind; The Older Ams Awd, St of Ind; Num Others.

HEADRICK, FLORA RUNNELS oc/Retired Registered Nurse; Public Health Nurse; b/Sept 4, 1919; h/1017 First Ave, Laurel, MS 39440; m/Belton Harris; c/Tina Suzanne H Carr; p/Willis J Runnels (dec); Levia J Byrd (dec); ed/RN St Vincent Sch Nsg; pa/Tchr Lic'd Pract Nurses Jones Co Jr Col, Ellisville, Miss 1954-55; Sch Nurse Laurel City Sch Sys 1966-67; Public Hlth Nurse, Miss St Bd Hlth 1952-73; Dist 8 Nurses Assn, Past Pres; cp/Docent Lauren Rogers Mus; Lung Assn; YWCA; SEAM; r/Bapt: Ch Sch Tchr, Organist, Pianist, Soloist; hon/Salute to a Lady Awd.

HEADSTROM, BIRGER RICHARD oc/Author; b/Feb 21, 1902; h/1144 Cornish St, Aiken, SC 29801; m/Ruth; c/John Richard; p/John Birger and Anna Headstrom; ed/Ret'd Tchr; Mus Curator; Newspaper

Columnist; cp/Former Town Entomologist; Former Mem Mun Tree Com & Mun Conservation Com; hon/Commun Ldrs & Noteworthy Ams.

HEALD, BRUCE DAY oc/Music Director; b/Jun 5, 1935; h/2 Peninsula Dr, Kennebunk, ME 04043; ba/Kennebunk; m/Helen Peaslee; c/William H Forrestall III, Craig, Eric Bentley, Allyson Key; p/Henry M and Muriel D Heald, Largo, FL; ed/AA; BS; mil/USMC; cp/Repub Clb; r/Prot; hon/Hons of Merit; 2000 Men Achmt; Others.

HEARD, ROWITA CHARLENE oc/Industrial Specialist; b/Oct 29, 1932; h/916 W Arizona St, Philadelphia, PA 9133; ba/Phila; m/Samuel Jr (dec); c/Marian E H Colon; p/Charles L Shaw (dec); Elizabeth C Shaw, Columbus, OH; ed/BA; pa/Indust Specialist Dept of Def; Pt-time Secy The Old York Rd Shopping Ctr Bus Assn & RonCor Enterprises; Var Former Positions; Fed Bus Assn; cp/Former Mem Assn for Study of Negro Life & Hist; Urban Leag; Former SEcy Columbia Cooperating Coun on Christian Ed, Columbia Br YMCA; Former Sponsor GSA; Others; r/U Meth: Cert'd Lay Disciple, Mbrship Secy, Retreat Ldr, Ch Sch Supt, Communion Steward, Others; hon/Mother of Yr, Mt Zion UM Ch Sch 1963; Cit of Apprec, Chapel of Four Chaplains; Lttrs of Commend; Plaques; Cert of Achmt, Phila Bd Ed, Def Indust Supply Ctr; Biogl Listings; Num Others.

HEATH, BARBARA J oc/Assistant Administrator; b/Aug 6, 1938; h/PO Box 402, Dayton, TN 37321; ba/Chattanooga, TN; m/John B; c/Perry, Richard, Scott, Steven; p/Edmund E and Esther C Faber, Chatta; ed/RN; BS Cand; pa/Asst Admr Diagnostic Hosp; Past Pres Tenn Soc Nsg Ser Dirs; Tenn Hosp Assn; Am Bus Wom's Assn; Dayton BPW Clb; Mem Tenn Hosp Assn Blue Ribbon Task Force; cp/OES; Cub Scout Ldr 6 Yrs; Merit Badge Cnslr BSA; Past Pres Dayton City Sch PTO; r/Bapt; hon/DAR Awd;Nat Hon Soc; Sr S'ship Awd, Nsg Sch; Boss of Yr, Tenn Val Chapt Am Bus Wom's Assn 1974; Wom of Yr, Dayton BPW Clb.

HEATH, CHARLES CHASTAIN oc/- Management Consultant; b/Sep 7, 1921; h/97-3 Edgemont Ave, Shelby, NC 28150; ba/Shelby; m/Doris; c/Janice Chuk, Brian Neal, Eric Scott; p/Connie Clifton and Keren Boyd Heath (dec); ed/Univ of NC-CH; mil/USMC 1942-46; pa/Pres, Heath & Assocs 1959-; Supt of Gass, City of Shelby 1954-59; Supt of Gas, Ill Power Co (Decatur, Ill) 1950-54; Mgr, Shelby Gas Inc (Shelbyville, Ill) 1946-49; Am & SEn Gas Assns; cp/Dir 10th Dist, Conservative Caucus 1976; Dir, NC Congl Clb; Ofcr & Bd Mem, NC Railroad Co; Charter Mem, NC Indust Devel Foun; Past Pres, Shelby Jr C of C; Dir, NC Conservative Union; r/Bapt; hon/Author: You Can Save America! (1972), The Golden Egg, The Goose & Us (1976); Geo Washington Medal of Hon; Nat 1st Pl Essay Awd, Freedoms Foun; Edit Awd, Gas Mag; Awd from Am Security Coun; Others.

HEATH, MILDRED oc/Retired Bank Executive; b/Sept 13, 1903; h/Box 362, Riggins, ID 83549; m/Ora Kendall (dec); c/Arnold F, Roger K, Muriel Swetson (Mrs Fred G); p/Ernest Mann and Jennie Isabelle Fisher Fletcher; pa/Woodsville (NH) Guaranty Savs Bk: Ret'd 1972, Asst Treas 1967-72, Bookkeeper & Stenographer 1921-29, 1966-72; Bookkeeper & Stenographer W'ville Nat Bk 1921-29; w Grafton Co Farm Bur, W'ville 1920-21; cp/Treas Bd Trustees Trust Funds Town Haverhill; Repub; OES, Treas Lodge; r/Meth: Charter Mem & Past Pres Meth Girls Clb; hon/Biogl Listings.

HEATON, JANE oc/Sales Director; b/Nov 23, 1931; h/20 Plaza Sq, Apt 1101, St Louis, MO 63103; ba/St Louis; p/Wilbur E Heaton (dec); Nina H Heaton, Columbia, MO; ed/BMusEd DePauw Univ; MRE Christian Theol Sem; pa/Dir Curric & Prog Sales Christian Bd of Pub; Assn Christian Ch

Edrs; Direct Mktg Clb St Louis; cp/Zontal Intl; r/Disciples of Christ: Ordained 1970; hon/Theta Phi; Dist'd Alumna Awd, Christian Theol Sem; W/W: Am Wom, Rel.

HEDIN, EDNA JENKS oc/Reading Specialist; b/Nov 15, 1924; h/1605 Sears, Artesia, NM 88210; ba/Artesia; m/Alvin Morris; c/John Alvin, Edward Morris, James Lee; p/Edward Lee Jenks, Tulsa, OK; Tressie Jackson Jenks (dec); ed/AA Ctl Col for Wom 1945; BMus Okla Bapt Univ 1948; MEd Tex Tech 1972; pa/Rdg Specialist Title I Prog, Artesia Public Schs; IRA; Delta Kappa Gamma; Phi Kappa Phi; Sigma Alpha Iota; Kappa Delta Pi; Nat Guild Piano Tchrs; NMEA; NEA; AEA; cp/Dem; r/1st Bapt Ch, Artesia: Mem, Organist; hon/W/W: Am Wom, World Musicians.

HEDLEY, KATHERINE HENBY oc/Volunteer; b/Aug 12, 1905; h/824 N Biltmore Dr, Clayton, MO 63105; m/William J; c/William H, Mary Anne Speer (dec); p/William H Henby (dec); Alvina Steinbreder (dec); ed/AB Washington Univ; cp/Pres Nat Coun St Garden Clbs Inc 1977-79; Var Vol Activs; r/Presb; hon/Phi Beta Kappa; Life Mbrship: Fed'd Garden Clbs Mo, Nat Coun St Garden Clbs; Wom of Achmt in Civic Ser, St Louis Globe Dem; Order of the Golden Climatron, Trustees Mo Botanical Garden; Gold Medal Egyptian Hort Soc UAR; Cert of Apprec, US Dept of St; Wom of Yr, Clayton 1974; W/W Am Wom; DIB; World W/W Wom.

HEDRICK, BANIUS C oc/Parole Agent; b/May 15, 1921; h/2010 Whittleey St, Flint, MI 48503; ba/Flint; m/Ann; c/Marcia Ann; p/Banius C and La Ursa S Hedrick (dec); ed/BS; mil/AUS Corps of Engrs 1943-46; pa/Parole Agt St of Mich Dept of Correction 1957-; Past Pres Chapt 25 Mich St Employees Assn; Bd Mem Nat Alliance Bus-men; cp/Urban Leag; UF, Chm Govt Sect; Flint Human Sers Planning Coun; Operation Opport; Past Pres Ctl Flint Optimist Clb; 1/VChm Genesee Co Commun Action Agy; Others; r/Bethel U Meth Ch: Mem, Chm Trustee Bd.

HEDRICK, HAROLD BURDETTE oc/Professor; b/May 11, 1924; h/902 Westover, Columbia, MO 65201; ba/Columbia; m/Virginia S; c/Thomas E, David A; p/Guy Fred and Laura Eva Hedrick (dec); ed/BS; MS; PhD; mil/USAF Capt; pa/Prof Food Sci Univ Mo; Am Meat Sci Assn; Am Soc Animal Sci; r/Meth; hon/Signal Ser Awd, Am Meat Sci Assn.

HEFFERNAN, THOMAS PATRICK CARROLL oc/Poet; b/Aug 19, 1939; h/413 Guildford Ave, Greensboro, NC 27401; ba/Jamestown, NC; p/Thomas C and Mary E S Heffernan, Boston, MA; ed/AB Boston Col 1961; MA Univ Manchester (England) 1963; pa/Writer in Residence Var Schs & Cols; Author 4 Books of Poems; MLA; COSMEP; Poetry Soc Am; Assoc'd Writing Progs; Am Com for Irish Studies; IASAIL; Vis Artist in Poetry Guilford Tech Inst; cp/Poetry Rdgs; Writing Wkshops; Lectrs; Others; r/Rom Cath; hon/Gordon Barber Meml Awd, Poetry Arts Agys; Dillard Awds, Poetry Soc Va; St Andrews Awd for Poetry; Crucible Awds for Poetry.

HEFLIN, HAROLD oc/County Administrator; b/Apr 4, 1920; h/625 Heflin Trail,

Beaver Dam, KY 42320; ba/Hartford, KY; m/Mary Gwen Washburn; c/Marsha Rafferty (Mrs Ed), Mary Anne Sumner (Mrs Stephen), Edward; p/E C and Carrie Barnard Heflin (dec); mil/USNR 4 Yrs; ca/Ohio Co Property Valuation Admr, St of Ky; PVA Assn Ky; Intl Assn Assessing Off; cp/Pres Ohio Co Shrine Clb; Rizpah Shrine; Master Beaver Dam Lodge #420 F&AM; Past Patron OES #37; Mem H'ford City Coun 6 Yrs; Past Pres Ohio Co Fish & Game Assn; Chm Ohio Co Mar Dimes; r/Meth; hon/Hon Ky Col; Ky Admiral; Hon Clerk Ky Ct of Appeals & Senator.

HEFNER, CHRISTIE ANN oc/Publishing Executive; b/Nov 8, 1952; ba/919 N Michigan Ave, Chicago, IL 60611; p/Hugh M Hefner, Los Angeles, CA; Mildred Williams, Northfield, IL; ed/BA summa cum laude Brandeis Univ 1974; pa/Mktg Adv Coun Am Mgmt Assn; Exec Opinion Panel Crain Chgo Bus; cp/Bd Trustees Chgo Mus Contemp Art; Nat Adv Bd Nat Wom's Polit Caucus; Pres Com ACLU; Fdr Chgo Network; Bd Playboy Foun; hon/Phi Beta Kappa; Brandeis Councillor/Pubr of Yr.

HEFNER, LILLIAN E LYNGE oc/Educator; b/Apr 3, 1921; h/Circle 30 Ranch, Rt 2, Box-A, Whitewright, TX 75491; ba/Denton, TX; m/Roy Allan; c/Milton Roberts, Dean Rhea, (Foster sons:) Guy E Blankenship, Gary L Blankenship; p/Oscar E Lynge (dec); Tommie Whisenaut Lynge, Allen, TX; ed/BA Baylor Univ; MA Univ Tex; Att'd: Tex Wom's Univ, N Tex St Univ; mil/USNR 1943-50; pa/Asst Prof Jour Tex Wom's Univ; Sec'dy Tchr; Pubs Advr; Nat Scholastic Orgs: Judge, Critic, Lectr, Writer; Dir Tex HS Press Assn 1970-; r/Bapt; hon/Phi Kappa Phi; Kappa Tau Alpha; CSPA Gold Key; ILPC Golden Quill; Newspaper Fund Fellow (Wall St Jour).

HEFNER, W G (BILL) oc/United States Legislator; b/Apr 11, 1930; h/Concord, NC 28025; ba/328 Cannon House Bldg, Washington, DC 20515; m/Nancy Hill; c/Stacye Hugh, Shelly; pa/Pres & Owner WRKB Radio, Kannapolis, NC; cp/Mem US Ho of Reps: Elected 94th, 95th & 96th Congs; Coms Served: Public Works & Trans, Vets Affairs (Chm VA Subcom on Ed, Tng & Employmt), Dem Steering & Policy; Mem Congl Textile Caucus; r/N Kannapolis Bapt Ch, Kannapolis.

HEGSTAD, ROLAND REX oc/Editor; b/Apr 7, 1926; h/2121 Sondra Ct, Silver Spring, MD 20904; ba/Washington, DC; m/Stella Marie Radke; c/Douglas Roland, Sheryl Marie H Clarke, Kimberly Marie; p/Philip Roland and Lydia Hegstad (dec); ed/BTh Walla Walla Col; MA Andrews Univ; pa/Editor *Liberty* Mag 1959-; Assoc Secy Intl Rel Liberty Assn (Wash DC) 1959-; Acting Editor *Insight* Wkly Mag for Adventist Yth 1971-72; Other Former Positions; Acad Adventist Mins; Assoc'd Ch Press; Ch-St Study Comm 1970-; Bd Higher Ed SDA 1973-; Mem Exec Com Gen Conf SDA; cp/Walla Walla Alumni Assn; Smithsonian Assocs; r/SDA: Ordained Min 1955; hon/Profl Pubs; Biogl Listings.

HEHL, LAMBERT LAWRENCE oc/-Attorney at Law; County Judge; b/Jul 22, 1924; h/46 Madonna Dr, Ft Thomas, KY 41075; ba/Newport, KY; m/Helyn; c/Susan Snyder, Barbara; p/Lambert Lawrence Sr and Martha Hehl (dec); ed/JD Chase Col Law No Ky Univ 1952; mil/USMC 1943-46, Pacific; pa/Mem Bischoff, Hehl & Howe Law Firm; Co Judge/Exec Campbell Co 1978-; Past Pres Campbell Co Bar Assn; Ky Bar Assn; Am Judic Soc; Past Pres Ky Magistrates & Commrs Assn; Pres Ky Co Judge/Exec Assn; cp/Former Mem Ky Senate; Former City Atty (Crestview, Ky); Past Pres: No Ky Area Plng Coun, No Ky Trans Adv Comm; Mem Ky St Ctl Dem Com; 1/VP No Ky Area Devel Dist; r/Cath; hon/Lifesaving Awd, VFW.

HEIER, DOROTHY RUTH oc/Musician; Educator; b/Oct 28, 1927; h/680 Ramapo Valley Rd, Oakland, NJ 07436; ba/Wayne, NJ; p/Charles L Heier (dec); Jessie R Heier,

Port Crane, NY; ed/BSM; MM; EdD; pa/Trumpeter (Soloist); Tchr William Paterson Col; Conductor; Pubs incl "Trumpet Variations and Trombone Variations"; cp/Choir Dir; r/Prot; hon/Nyack Hon Soc; St George S'ship; Pi Lambda Theta; Kappa Delta Pi.

HEILMAN, MARILYN PATTON MANGUM oc/Secondary School Art Teacher; b/Aug 31, 1925; h/5609 Pinellas Dr, Knoxville, TN; ba/K'ville; m/Walter Ritter Jr (dec); Walter Ritter III; p/Frank I Mangum (dec); Juanita S Emerson (dec); ed/BA; MA; Addt Studies; pa/Art, Hist & Humanities Tchr Bearden HS, K'ville 1958-78; Vis Lectr Art Ed E Tenn St Univ Sum 1971; Spec Instr Mod Dance Wake Forest Col 1957; Knox Co Ed Assn: 1958-63, Rep Assemblyman 1962-63; K'ville Ed Assn: 1963-, Rep Assemblyman 5 Terms, Leg Coun 1964, Social Com 5 Terms, Ad Hoc Internal Communs Com 1972-73, Safety Awareness Com 1977-78; E Tenn Ed Assn; Tenn Ed Assn; NEA; E Tenn Art Ed Assn: Chm 1964-67, Exec Coun 1967-68, Social Chm 1964-73; Tenn Art Ed Assn, Var Ofcs; Nat Art Ed Assn; SEn Arts Assn: SAA Sts Assembly 1971-73, Chm Div Sec'dy Art Tchrs 1973-75, Others; Am Crafts Coun; Intl Soc for Ed through Art; US Soc for Ed through Art; AAUW; cp/Former Mem Alumnae Coun Lindenwood Col; Former VP Am Mothers Com of Tenn; Former St CoChm Am Lung Assn Christmas Seals of Chd's Art; Others; r/Presb; hon/Awd for Contbn in Devel of *Evaluative Criteria* (5th Edition), Nat Study of Sch Eval; Awd for Outstg Contbns to Prof of Art Ed, Wn Reg Nat Art Ed Assn; Guest Spkr; Biogl Listings; Var Exhbns & Pubs.

HEIMLICH, HENRY JAY oc/Surgeon; b/Feb 3, 1920; h/17 Elmhurst Pl, Cincinnati, OH 45208; ba/Cinc; m/Jane; c/Philip, Peter, Janet, Elizabeth; p/Philip Heimlich Sr, Cinc; ed/MD; mil/USN Lt (SG); pa/Prof Adv'd Clin Scis Xavier Univ, Cinc 1977-; Dir Surg Jewish Hosp, Cinc 1969-77; Assoc Clin Prof Surg Univ Cinc Col of Med 1969-; Fellow: Am Col Surgs, Am Col Chest Physicians, Am Col Gastroenterology; Fdr Mem Soc Thoracic Surgs; AMA; Cinc Surg Soc; Sr Mem Ctl Surg Assn; Collegium Internationale Chirurgiae Digestivae; Am Gastrointerological Assn; Soc for Surg of Alimentary Tract; Other Profl Assns; cp/Past Pres Nat Cancer Foun; Fdr & Pres Dysphagia Foun; Others; hon/Sachs Awd for Outstg Achmt in Field of Med; Medaglione Di Bronzo Minerva, 4th Intl Fest of Med-Sci Films 1961; Pub'd Author; Others.

HEINEMANN, SOL oc/Physician; b/Dec 17, 1914; h/4252 Ridgecrest Dr, El Paso, TX 79902; ba/El Paso; m/Katherine A; c/Katherine H Taucher; p/Sol Heinemann (dec); Hattie Heinemann, Newport, AR; ed/BS Univ Ark 1935; MD Univ Tenn 1939; MS St Louis Univ 1950; mil/AUS Med Corp 1941-45; pa/Physician, Pvt Pract: St Louis (Mo) 1950-55, Carlsbad (NM) 1955-60, El Paso 1960-; Active Staff: Providence Meml Hosp, El Paso, Hotel Deiu Hosp, Sun Towers Hosp; Courtesy Staff: SWn Gen Hosp, Sierra Med Ctr, Eastwood Hosp; El Paso Co, Tex, NM Med Socs; AMA; S Ctl Sect Am Urological Assn; Am Urological Assn; Am Bd Urology; Fellow Am Col Surgs; Pan Am Med Assn Inc; cp/Past VP & Pres El Paso Archaeol Soc; Rotary Clb El Paso; Former Mem: El Paso Drive-A-Meal Coun, El Paso Co Bd Devel, Bd Dirs Fest Theatre; Nat Assn Arts & Lttrs, El Paso Chapt; Bd Dirs Carlsbad ARC, (Fdr Operation Res-Q); Instituto Inter-americano; Heritage Foun; Soc for Am Archaeol; Archaeol Inst Am; CEDAM of Mexico; CEDAM Intl; Others; r/Jewish; hon/Profl Pubs; W/W S&SW; Notable Ams.

HEINZEN, RAYMOND FRANK oc/-Farmer; Legislative Liaison Officer; b/May 11, 1918; h/Rt 5, Trout Dr, Marshfield, WI 54449; ba/Madison, WI; m/Reba; c/Anne Marie Fisher, Paul Ben; p/Jacob and Rosa Schuler Heinzen (dec); pa/Leg Liaison Ofcr Dept Public Instrn, Madison; cp/Former St Senator; St Voc Bd; Rotary Clb; Farm Bur; Ks of C; r/Rom Cath; hon/Outstg Yg Farmer, JC; Alpha Zeta; Wis Ed Leg of Yr 1971; Dist'd Ser Awd 1974.

HEISER, JOSEPH MILLER JR oc/Military Officer; Management Consultant; b/Jan 22, 1914; h/3486 Northshore Rd, Columbia, SC 29206; ba/Same; m/Edith Cox; c/Annette Ficker, Joel M, Joan C Weitzel; p/Joseph M Sr and Alma Maetze Heiser (dec); ed/MBA Univ Chgo; mil/AUS Lt Gen, Ret'd; Cmdg Gen 1st Logistical Command AUS (Vietnam) 1968-69; Enlisted as Pvt, Moved up Ranks 1942-68; pa/Govt Conslt w: Comptroller Gen, Secy of Def, Secy Gen NATO, Supreme Allied Cmdr Europe & US Army 1973-; Legistic Conslt w Other Govt Agys; Lectr Var Instns & Agys of Govt & Indust; Exec-in-Residency/Adjunct Prof Univs; Profl Conslt Pvt Indust; Dept Chief Staff Logistics, Dept of Army 1969-72; Am Mgmt Assn; Nat Security Indust Assn; Assn US Army; Dir Armed Forces Mgmt Coun; Bd Ofcr Am Def Preparedness Assn; VP Carolina Chapt Am Def Preparation Assn; Others; cp/Boys Clb Am; Alumni Clb Univ Chgo; Dir Nat Bd BSA; Bds Dirs Civic/Commun Clbs; r/Cath; hon/Hon Fellow, Soc Logistic Engrs (Bd Advrs).

HEISKELL, GAYLE BEVERLY oc/Physician; b/Mar 3, 1953; h/119 Pompano, Galveston, TX 77550; ba/Galveston; m/-Michael Porter; c/Marin Phenice; p/Chester A Beverly Jr, Avon Hill, MD; Theria Mae F Beverly, Tucson, AZ; ed/BS Baylor Univ; MD Univ Tex Med Br-G; pa/Phys Univ Tex Med Br; Galveston Co Med Soc; So Med Assn; AMA; cp/Galveston Co Dem Clb; NAACP; Galveston Co Bar Aux; r/St Paul's U Meth; hon/Miss Teenage Tucson 1971; Alpha Lambda Delta; Outstg Sr Wom, Baylor Univ; 2nd Runner-up Miss Waco Pageant 1973; Num S'ships; Others.

HEKTNER, VERNON E oc/College Dean; b/Oct 9, 1921; h/718 N 6, Wahpeton, ND 58075; ba/Wahpeton; m/Leona; c/Sonia, Arla, Kara, Joel; p/Joseph Hektner (dec); Mabel Huss Hektner, Wahpeton; ed/BA Concordia; MA Univ Colo; pa/Col Dean ND St Sch of Sci; Pres Richland Co Hist Soc 1948-54; Bd Dirs 1st Bk ND; cp/Former Mem Bd of Ed Wahpeton Sch Dist #37; r/Luth; hon/Life Mem, Kiwanis Intl.

HELGANZ, BEVERLY BUZHARDT oc/Staff Supervisor; b/Jun 7, 1941; h/5000 San Jose Blvd, Apt 77, Jacksonville, FL 32207; ba/J'ville; m/Charles F Jr (dec); p/M Owain Buzhardt, J'ville; Jeanne Crabb, Pacific Palisades, CA; ed/AA; BA; pa/Staff Supvr EEO (So Bell Telegraph & Telephone); Telephone Pioneers Am; Pilot Intl; Am Bus Wom's Assn; cp/Beta Sigma Phi; Zeta Tau Alpha; OES; J'ville Mus Arts & Scis; J'ville Panhellenic Assn; r/Meth; hon/Zeta Tau Alpha: Alumnae Cert of Merit, Hon Ring; Am Bus Wom's Assn: Merit Awd, Wom of Yr Awd; Girl of Yr Awd, Beta Sigma Phi.

HELGELAND, LES L oc/Executive Editor; b/Nov 5, 1919; h/1003 Mulberry, Yankton, SD 57078; ba/Yankton; m/Irma; c/Patricia, David, Deanna, Mary; p/Anna Helgeland, Sioux Falls, SD; mil/USAAC 1942-45; pa/Exec Editor Yankton Press & Dakotan; Past Pres SD AP Newspaper Assn; cp/Former SD Bicent Chm; r/Cath; hon/Sertoma Ser to Mankind Awd (SD); Newsman of Yr, SD 1976.

HELLER, MELVIN PAUL oc/Professor; Consultant; Lecturer; b/Feb 18, 1927; h/2234 Lake Ave, Wilmette, IL 60091; ba/Chicago, IL; m/Judith T O'Connell; c/Linda M Petersen; James M, Thomas M, John M; p/A T Heller, Chgo; Rose Heller (dec); ed/AB w hons 1948, MEd 1950 De Paul; EdD Loyola Univ 1959; mil/USN; pa/Prof Loyola Univ 1963-; Asst Dir Adm Res Dept Ednl Res Coun Gtr Cleveland 1962-63; Asst Supt & Curric Dir Ridgewood HS Dist 234, Norridge, Ill 1960-62; Conslt Nat Cath Ednl Assn & Num Sch Dists; Assoc Dir Adm Internship Prog, Nat Assn Sec'dy Sch Prins; Am Assn Sch Admrs; Assn for Supvn & Curric Devel; Delta Epsilon Sigma; Phi Delta Kappa; Zeta Tau; hon/Edr of Yr, Loyola Phi Delta Kappa Chapt 1976; Dist'd Alumni Awd, DePaul Univ; Pub'd Author; Biogl Listings.

HELLMAN, HAL oc/Free-lance Writer;

b/Sept 15, 1927; h/100 High St, Leonia, NJ 07605; ba/Same; m/Sheila Almer; c/Jill, Jennifer; p/Louis B and Anna Hellman (dec); ed/BA Hunter 1950; MA City Col 1955; MS Stevens Tech 1961; mil/AUS MC 1945-47; pa/Free-lance Sci Writer; Tech Info Mgr Gen Precision Inc 1956-66; Nat Assn Sci Writers; World Future Soc; AAAS; Books Pub'd incl: *Deadly Bugs and Killer Insects* 1978, *Understanding Physics* (Col Text w Coauthor) 1978, *Migration, Urbanization, and Fertility* 1976, *Technophobia: Getting Out of the Technology Trap* 1976, Others; Pub'd Articles & Booklets; r/Jewish.

HELLMUTH, GEORGE FRANCIS oc/Architect; b/Oct 5, 1907; h/5 Conway Ln, St Louis, MO 63124; ba/St Louis; m/Mildred Henning; c/George W, Nicholas M, Mary C, Theodore H, Daniel F; p/George W and Harriet F Hellmuth (dec); ed/BArch 1928, MArch 1930 Washington Univ; Dipl Ecole des Beaux Arts, Fontainebleau (France) 1931; mil/AUS Resv Corps 1930-33; pa/Chm of Bd: HOK-Intl Inc 1977-, Hellmuth, Obata &

Kassabaum Inc 1955-78; Prin Firm Hellmuth, Yamasaki & Leinweber (Archs), St Louis & Detroit 1949-55; Other Former Positions; Fellow Am Inst Architects; St Louis Chapt Am Inst Architects; Mo Coun & Soc Archs; Arch Assn London; The Fontainebleau Assn; Egypt-US Bus Coun; cp/Chm Landmarks & Urban Design Comm, City of St Louis 20 Yrs; Bd Dirs Downtown St Louis Inc 5 Yrs; r/Rom Cath; Assn Master Ks of Sovereign Mil Order of Malta USA; hon/1st Hon Awd, Am Inst Archs; Cit, Wash Univ; Cit, *Engrg News-Record*.

HELPERN, JOAN M G oc/Business Executive; Designer; Manufacturer; b/Oct 10, 1926; h/1010 Highland Dr, Cambridge, MA 02138; ba/New York, NY; m/David M; c/David M Jr, Elizabeth Joan; p/Edward Marshall (dec), Ethel Tilzer (dec); ed/BA Hunter 1947; MA Columbia 1948; Doct Studies Harvard Univ; pa/Author, Psychologist, Edr, Lectr, Dir Pupil Pers Progs: (1948-60) NYC Bd of Ed, Yeshiva Univ, Hunter Univ, (1960-68) Lexington (Mass) Public Schs, Lesley Col, Harvard; hon/Coty Am Fashion Designer Awd.

HEMBY, JAMES BENJAMIN JR oc/- Professor, Department Chairman; b/Mar 1, 1934; h/1605 Highland Dr, Wilson, NC 27893; ba/Wilson; m/Joan Edwards; c/James B III, Scott Edwards, Thomas Simmen; p/Mavis Parker Hemby, Ayden, NC; ed/AB; BD; MA; PhD; pa/Prof & Chm Dept Eng ACC; Assn Depts Eng; MLA; cp/Secy Wilson Kiwanis Clb; Wilson Co Sch Bd; Wilson Dem Party; r/Disciples of Christ; hon/Lilly Scholar, Duke Univ; W/W in SW; Other Biogl Listings.

HEMENWAY, ROBERT B oc/State Representative; b/Jul 24, 1934; h/128 Kantishna Way, Fairbanks, AK 99701; ba/Same; m/Ureatha Mildred; c/Tyronne, Julio, Jennifer, Betti Jo; p/Juanita Hemenway (dec); ed/BS; MA; BA; mil/AUS Spec 5; cp/C of C; Eagles; Masons; Odd Fellows; r/Mormon.

HENDERSON, CAROL MORNER oc/Assistant Dean; Associate Professor; b/Oct 12, 1941; h/2904 Starlit Dr W, Mobile, AL 36609; ba/Mobile; m/Joe B Jr; c/Alicia, Angela, Shannon; p/Lester Arthur Morner

(dec); Mildred Kindschi, Madison, WI; ed/BSN; MA; Doct Cand; pa/Univ S Ala Sch Nsg: Asst Dean, Assoc Prof; ANA; NLN; ALN: Past 1/VP, Subcom Chm; cp/Secy & Bd Mem U Cerebral Palsy Assn; Bd Mem Profl Home Hlth Care Sers PTA; r/Cath; hon/Nurse of Yr, Mobile Co 1977-78; Sigma Theta Tau; W/W Am Wom; Personalities of S; World W/W Wom.

HENDERSON, DONALD BLANTON oc/Attorney; Businessman; State Representative; b/Aug 25, 1949; h/139 Old Bridge Lake, Houston, TX 77069; ba/Houston; m/Marjory; p/Donald V and Marjory Blanton Henderson, Houston; ed/BA Univ Houston 1971; S Tex Col Law; pa/Tex Bar Assn; Assoc Adams, Adams & Blackburn (Attys-at-Law); VP Ctl Iron Works, Houston; cp/St Rep 1973-; Houston NW C of C; Houston C of C; Del St Constitutional Conv; r/St Christopher's Epis Ch; hon/Kappa Alpha Awd for Outstg Alumnus in St 1975; Num Meritorious Ser Awds from Var Orgs.

HENDERSON, DOUGLAS JAMES oc/Physicist; b/Jul 28, 1934; h/23454 Skyview Terr, Los Gatos, CA 95030; ba/San Jose, CA; m/Rose-Marie Steen-Nielssen; c/Barbara, Dianne, Sharon; p/Donald R Henderson (dec); Evelyn L Henderson, Vancouver, BC Canada; ed/PhD Utah; BA Univ BC; pa/Physicist IBM Res Lab 1969-; Prof Applied

Math & Physics Univ Waterloo (Canada) 1967-69; Other Former Positions; Am Chem Soc; Fellow: Am Inst Chemists, Am Phy Soc, Inst Physics; Canadian Assn Physicists; NY Acad Sci; Math Assn Am; Sigma Xi; Phi Kappa Phi; Sigma Pi Sigma; Var Edit Activs; r/Ch Jesus Christ LDS; hon/Outstg Res Contbn Awd, IBM; Recipient Var F'ships & S'ships; Johnathan Rogers Awd; Profl Pubs.

HENDERSON, JAMES H oc/Dentist; b/Jan 29, 1925; h/PO Box 866, New Iberia, LA 70560; ba/New Iberia; m/Mabel White; c/Eryn Janyce, Edithe Jeannell, James Henry Jr; p/James Henderson, Manson, NC; Sarah Evans Henderson (dec); ed/BS Hampton Inst 1948; DDS Meharry Med Col 1953; mil/AUS 1943-46, Aviation Cadet, Engr Airborne Inf; AUS Dental Corp 1952-55; USAR 1955-59; pa/Pvt Practitioner New Iberia 1957-; Staff Iberia Parish Hosp; Vis, Foun Hosp, Franklin, La; Past Pres Pelican St Dental Assn; Nat Dental Assn: Del & Reference Com; Acadiana, La, Chicago Dental Socs; Am Dental Assn; Acad Gen Dentistry; Fellow Royal Soc Hlth (Gt Britain); Bd Mem Nat Dental Assn Foun; cp/New Iberia Bicent Comm; Iberia Parish Rec & Playground Bd; La Comm on Human Relats, Rts & Responsibilities; Chm Iberia Paris ESAA & Bilingual-Bicult Ednl Com; Little Leag Baseball Coach; Boy Scout Comman; Life Mem Alpha Phi Alpha; Life Mem NAACP; 33° Mason; Shriner; Royal Vanders Social Clb; r/Mt Calvary Bapt Ch, New Iberia: Trustee Bd; hon/Beta Kappa Chi; Achmt Awd, Omega Psi Phi; Talheimer Awd, NAACP; Man of Yr Awd, Alpha Phi Alpha; La Beauticians Awd in Outstg Achmt in Civic, Rel & Improvemt to Mankind Everywhere; W/W S&SW; Men of Achmt; Notable Ams Bicent Era.

HENDERSON, JOHN BAXTER oc/College Professor; b/Feb 8, 1941; h/607 Bessemer Circle, Fayetteville, NC 28301; ba/F'ville; m/Gwendolyn Cowan; c/Joye Dvnene;

p/Baxter Henderson, Lexington, NC; Merlene Henderson, L'ton; ed/BA NC Ctl Univ 1963; MSW Atlanta Univ Sch Social Work 1971; Further Studies; pa/F'ville St Univ: Asst Prof Sociol Dept 1972-, Dir Public Relats & Sports Info Dir 1972-77; Univ Photog 1972-77; Social Wkr Dept Social Sers, Wilmington, NC 1964-66 & Winston-Salem, NC 1966-68; Coun on Social Work Ed; Am Assn for Higher Ed; AAUP; Intl Assn Schs Social Work; Profl Photogs Am Inc; r/Meth; hon/W/W S&SW; Outstg Yg Man Am.

HENDERSON, MORRIS oc/Administrator; b/Oct 31, 1926; h/St Louis, MO 63133; ba/5471 Dr Martin Luther King Dr, St Louis, MO 63112; m/Lowell Verniece Battle; c/Kenneth Morris, Carlton Eugene; ed/BA, MA Webster Col; Addit Studies; mil/1st Sgt WWII, Overseas Duty S Pacific; pa/Proj Dir St Louis Comprehensive Neighborhood Hlth Ctr Inc; Sports Editor: *St Louis Am Newspaper* & *St Louis Crusader Newspaper*; Former Dep Gen Mgr Human Devel Corp; Other Former Positions; Bd Dirs MW Assn Commun Hlth Ctrs; Mo Assn Hlth Sers Execs; St Louis Chapt Mo Assn Social Wel; Inner City Black Ath Assn; NASCO; Am Public Hlth Assn; Nat Assn Commun Hlth Ctrs; Nat Assn Hlth Sers Execs; Am Hosp Assn; Life Mem Alpha Phi Alpha; Am Acad Hlth Adm; Others; cp/NAACP St Louis Co Br; Metro Sickle Cell Anemia Assn; Former Mem Var Orgs; r/Ctl Bapt Ch: Bd Deacons, Bd Trustees, Bd of Ed; hon/Mound City Press Clb's Dist'd Public Ser Awd; Jr C of C Cit; Citizen of Week, Radio KATZ; Gov's Cert of Apprec; Commend, Black Nurses Assn; Other Hons & Commends; Biogl Listings.

HENDERSON, ROBBYE ROBINSON oc/Librarian; b/Nov 10, 1937; h/PO Box 42, MVSU, Itta Bena, MS 38941; ba/Itta Bena; c/Robreka Aljuria; p/Robert Robinson (dec); Aljuria Myers Robinson, Morton, MS; ed/BA; MSLS; PhD; pa/Libn Miss Val St Univ; MLA; AAUP; ALA; SEn Lib Assn; Phi Delta Kappa; cp/Am Astrological Assn; Miss Val St Univ Fac & Staff Progressive Wom's Clb; Alpha Kappa Alpha; Kappa Delta Pi; r/Bapt; hon/Cum Laude F'ship, Mellon-ACRL Internship Prog; Other F'ships.

HENDERSON, WILLIAM DONALD oc/Management; b/Jun 20, 1914; h/PO Box 164, Cleveland, GA 30528; ba/Same; m/Edythe Edwards; p/Thomas Ewell and Cordie Ethel Nelson Henderson (dec); ed/BS; pa/Elects Design, Bus Mgmt & Prop Land Surveys; hon/W/W S&SW.

HENDLEY, GRAHAM FISHER oc/Hospital Administration Officer; b/Jun 19, 1927; h/Winter Park, FL 32792; p/W Fisher and Margaret C Hendley (dec); ed/BS Univ SC; BS, MHA Med Col Va; mil/AUS 1954-56; USAR 1949-53; pa/Ret'd Hosp Admr Ofcr; Reg'd Pharmacist; Am Col Admrs; Am Hosp Assn; Am Pharm Assn; Band Ldr; Jazz Musician; cp/Rotary; Past Mem Lions; Life Mem Disabled Am Vets; Am Heart Assn, Ctl Fla Chapt; r/Meth; hon/Awd for Scholastic Achmt, Phi Delta Chi; S'ship; Rho Chi; Sigma Zeta; Kappa Sigma Kappa; Alpha Epsilon Delta; Biogl Listings.

HENDON, DONALD WAYNE oc/University Professor; Consultant; b/Jun 1, 1940; h/PO Box 659, Kingsville, TX 78363; ba/K'ville; m/Brenda Louise Bradford;

c/Travis, Natalie; p/Jesse M and Jennie M Hendon, San Antonio, TX; ed/BBA 1962, PhD 1971 Univ Tex-A; MBA Univ Cal-B 1964; mil/AUS 1963-64; USAR 1963-69; pa/Prof & Chm Mgmt-Mktg Dept Tex A&I Univ; Var Former Positions Univ Wyo; Former Assoc Prof Mktg Div Bus & Ec, Columbus Col, Columbus, Ga 1972-76; Former Tchr: Univ Tex-, Univ Nev-LV, Columbus Col; Vis Prof: Univ Australia (New South Wales Inst Technol in 1975 & Univ Melbourne 1972), Mexico (Instituto Tecnologico in Monterrey 1973); Conslt Sev Firms incl'g Am Mgmt Assn, Australian Assn Nat Advertisers, Australian Inst Mgmt, Colgate-Palmolive, Kodak, Lever & Kitchen, Singapore Inst Mgmt, Vision Pub'g Corp Manila in Philippines, & McDonald's Restaurants; Testified on Mktg Practs before Employees of Fed Trade Practs Comm & Bur of Stats in Australia, the Fed Trade Comm & Fed Communs Comm in US, & before Num Govtl Ofcls; Mem 18 Profl Assns incl'g Acad Intl Bus, Am Acad Advtg, Am Coun on Consumer Interests, Am Mktg Assn, Assn for Consumer Res, Am Psychol Assn, Intl Commun Assn & Market Res Soc of Australia; Reschr; Pub'd in Jours incl'g: Jour of Applied Psychol, Australian Jour of Mktg Res, Jour of Retailing, Tex Bus Review, B&T, Mexican World, The Bulletine, Others; Arbitrator for Better Bus Bur & Am Arbitration Assn; Jr Achmt, Minority Bus Conslts Task Force, & Public Policy Resources Panel of Am Mktg Assn; cp/JCs: Columbus Ad Clb; Others; hon/Alpha Delta Sigma; Delta Sigma Pi; Sigma Iota Epsilon; Div of Bus & Ec Awd for Outstg Perf & Competence in Res & Pub, Columbus Col 1973; Pub'd Author; Biogl Listings.

HENDREN, MERLYN CHURCHILL oc/Furniture Company Executive; b/Oct 16, 1926; h/3504 Hillcrest Dr, Boise, ID 83705; ba/Boise; m/Robert Lee Jr; c/Robert Lee IV, Anne Aleen; p/Herbert Winston Churchill, Gooding, ID; Annie Averett Churchill (dec); ed/Student Univ Idaho 1944-47; pa/CoOwner & VP Hendren's Inc; cp/Bd Dirs Idaho Law Foun; Former Chm Col Idaho Symposium; Past Pres Boise Coun on Aging; Former Mem Gov's Comm on Aging; Idaho Del to White House Conf on Aging 1961; Former Mem AAUW; Boise C of C; Boise Jr Leag; r/Epis; hon/Boise Outstg Wom 1960; Idaho Dist'd Citizen 1978.

HENDRICK, ZELWANDA oc/Teacher; b/Nov 28, 1925; h/3016 Westminster, Dallas, TX 75205; p/Lloyd Hendrick (dec); Viola McGuire Hendrick, Rusk, TX; ed/AA; BS; MA; pa/Ret'd Tchr Theatre-Fine Arts, Dallas Ind Sch Dist 13 Yrs; John Robert Powers Finishing Sch; Am Theatre Assn; cp/Daughs of Republic of Tex; OES; TSTA; STA; hon/Delta Kappa Gamma; AAUW; W/W Am Wom; Tex PTA Hon Lifetime Mbrship.

HENDRIX, DANIEL W oc/Educator; b/Oct 16, 1922; h/1549 Sixth St, West Palm Beach, FL 33401; m/Panchita; c/Gia, Piaget, Danielle; p/(dec); ed/BS magna cum laude Savannah St Col; MS Atlanta Univ; Addit Studies; mil/USN WWII, Steward Mate's Br; pa/Sr Instr Math Palm Bch Jr Col; Var Former Positions; Phi Beta Sigma: Past Nat Dir Bigger & Better Bus, Former Nat Dir Social Action; Delta Omicron Chapt Phi Theta Kappa; St Text Book Adoption Coun; cp/Palm Bch Co Job Opport Tng Coun: Exec Com, Chm Grievance Com; Adv Bd Mid-Co Med Ctr Inc; Exec Bd U Way Palm Bch Co; Wom's Polit Caucus, Local, St & Nat; Urban Leag Palm Bch Co Inc: Bd Dirs, Sustaining Mem; Sci Mus & Planetarium Palm Bch Co Inc: Pres, Bd Trustees, Pres Exec Com, Patron; Gold Coast Voter's Leag; Fla St Voter's Leag; Atl Mem Adm'g Bd Commun Action Coun Palm Bch Co; Others; r/Payne Chapel AME Ch: Chm Bd Trustees; hon/Outstg Edrs Am; Commun Ldrs & Noteworthy Ams; W/W Among Black Ams.

HENISCH, HEINZ KURT oc/Professor; b/Apr 21, 1922; h/346 W Hillcrest Ave, State College, PA 16801; ba/University Park, PA; m/Bridget Ann; p/Leo and Fanny Henisch (dec); ed/BS 1942; PhD 1949; DSc 1977;

pa/Pa St Univ: Prof Physics, Prof Hist of Photog; Editor & Fdr: Hist of Photography & Materials Res Bulletin; Corr'g Mem Deutsche Gesellschaft fur Photographie; hon/Fellow: Am Phy Soc, Royal Photo Soc Gt Britain, Inst Physics (London).

HENKIN, LOUIS oc/Professor; Attorney; Author; Consultant; b/Nov 11, 1917; h/460 Riverside Dr, New York, NY 10027; ba/NYC; m/Alice Barbara Hartman; c/Joshua, David, Daniel; p/Yoseph Elia Henkin (dec); Frieda R Kreindel (dec); ed/AB Yeshiva Col 1937; LLB Harvard Law Sch 1940; mil/AUS 1941-45, Silver Star; pa/Prof & CoDir Human Rts Ctr Columbia Univ; CoEditor-in-Chief Am Jour of Intl Law; Pres US Inst HR; Advr US Task Force Law of Sea; Advr Intl Project Ctr for Law & Social Policy; cp/Bd Trustees Cardozo Law Sch; Bd Dirs Lwyrs Com for Intl HR; r/Jewish; hon/DHL, Yeshiva Univ; Fellow, Am Acad Arts & Scis.

HENNEY, ROBERT LEE oc/Educator; b/Oct 16, 1933; h/3903 Bloomingdale Ave, Valparaiso, IN 46383; ba/Philadelphia, PA; m/Caroline A; c/Philip L, Linda K; p/George K Henney, Kendallville, IN; May W Henney (dec); ed/AB Drury Col; BD Christian Theol Sem; MA Butler Univ; PhD Ind Univ; pa/Pres: EMC Inst Inc, Ednl Diagnostic Sers Inc; Dir: Adult Ed Bd for Fundamental Ed, Literacy Ed Dept Corrections (St of Ind); Min Christian Ch, B'field; Adult Ed Assn; Am Correctional Assn; Bd Mem Nat Adv Com Model Demon Prog for Persons Who Are Hearing Impaired; IPA; cp/Scoutmaster 20 Yrs; Org'd Little Leag Baseball Leag; Est'd The New Readers Clin, Ind Reformatory; Designed Cooperative Steel Ed Prog; Est'd Papago Indian Mine Tng Inst; r/Disciples of Christ: Ordained Min; hon/Outstg Yg Edr, Jr C of C; W/W MW; Men of Achmt; Personalities W&MW; Profl Pubs.

HENRIKSON, ARTHUR ALLEN oc/Political Cartoonist; b/Jun 1, 1921; h/27 N Meyer Ct, Des Plaines, IL 60016; ba/Arlington Heights, IL; m/Lois Elizabeth Wessling; c/Diane E, Janet C, Michele C; p/Allen B and Florence E Henrikson (dec); ed/BS NWn Univ 1946; mil/USAF 1942-46, Medic, Capt MAC;

pa/Polit Cartoonist Daily Herald; Lectr in Cartooning 1953-; cp/Bd Mem Girls Scouts NW Cook Co Coun 8 Yrs; r/Des Plaines U Ch of Christ, 1st Congreg Ch: Past Moderator; hon/George Washington Hon Awds, Freedom Foun Val Forge (6).

HENRY, AARON E oc/Businessman; b/Jul 2, 1922; h/213 4th St, Clarksdale, PA 19141; ba/C'dale; m/Noelle Michael; c/Rebecca; ed/Grad Col Pharm Xavier Univ 1950; mil/Armed Sers US 1943-46; pa/Owner & Operator Fourth St Drug Store, C'dale; cp/NAACP: Orgr & Pres Coahoma Co Br, Pres Miss St Conf, Mem Nat Bd Dirs 1965-, Exec Com; Nat Bd Dirs: So Christian Ldrship Conf, So Reg Coun, The Medgar Evers Meml Fund Inc; Bd Dirs Miss Coun Human Relats; Chm Freedom Dem Party; Mem Dem Nat Com; Bd Dirs Mound Bayou (Miss) Commun Hosp; Fdr The Child Devel Group Miss; Bd Dirs: Miss Action for Progress, Coahoma Opports Inc; Iota Omicron Chapt Omega Psi; Chm: Nat Black Caucus on Aging, Nat Rural Housing Coalition, VChm Nat Rural Am Inc; Reg'd Lobbyist; Mem Adv Com Ret'd Sr Citizens Vol Prog, Coahoma Co (Miss);

CoChm Dem Party St of Miss; Num Other Civic Activs; r/Haven U Meth Ch: Mem, Former Lay Ldr & Chm Comm Christian Social Concerns; hon/Num Awds of Apprec for Ser: Ofc Ec Opport, Dept HEW; Hon HHD, Miss Bapt Theol Sem; W/W: Am, SE Am, Polits; Other Biogl Listings.

HENRY, EDWIN ROSCOE oc/Missionary; Pastor; Teacher; b/Mar 19, 1924; h/3052 Meredith, Indianapolis, IN 46201; ba/Cleveland, OH; m/Ruth Esther; c/Lawrence Edwin; p/Carl and Ethel May Henry (dec); mil/USN Sea Bees; pa/Bapt Bible Sch Windward Isls (WI): Fdr, Pres, Fac Mem; Pastor: Calvary Bapt Ch, Arnos Vale, St Vincent, Emmanuel Bapt Ch, S Rivers, St Vincent, Grace Bapt Ch, Mt Grennan, St Vincent; Pastor & Fdr Fellowship Bapt Ch, Prospect, St Vincent; Pres Bapt Mid-Missions, Windward Isls; r/Gen Assn Regular Bapt; hon/DIB; Intl W/W Commun Ser; 2000 Men Achmt; Dic Caribbean Biogs.

HENRY, JAMES A oc/Educational Administrator; Counselor; b/Dec 17, 1911; h/418 E Buford Ave, Forrest City, AR 72335; m/Oleevia C; c/James Marshall; p/Ray R and Eudora Belle Henry (dec); ed/BA; MA; mil/NG; pa/Ret'd; Life Mem & Past Pres: Ark, NE Ark Pers & Cnslrs Assns; IPA; Delta Kappa Pi; cp/Dem; Mem & Past Pres Forrest City Kiwanis Intl Clb; Past Lt Gov Kiwanis Intl-Mo-Ark Dist, Div 22; r/Meth: Past Pres Meth Men; Adult Ch Sch Tchr; Mem & Past VP Forrest City Gideons Camp; Ldr Zone 3-Ark Gideons Intl 1977-; hon/Personality of Week 1971; W/W S&SW; 2000 Men Achmt; Blue Book; Commun Ldrs Am; DIB: Nat Reg Prom Ams; Personalities of S.

HENSCHEL, BEVERLY JEAN SMITH oc/Industry-Congressional Liaison; b/Nov 1; h/12701 Epping Terr, Wheaton, MD 20906; ba/Washington, DC; c/Laura Jane, Karl Bruce, Lisa Margaret, Linda Jean; p/Theodore and Laura F Smith (dec); ed/BA Univ Wyom; MFA & EdD, Univ of Utah; pa/Congl Liaison, US Dept of Energy; Nat Fdn Press Wom (Press Credentials); Exhibited Original Art Work at Lib of Arts, Martin Luther King Meml Lib (Wash, DC) Aug 1980; r/Epis; hon/Featured in Fed Pub released to Fed Workers; Num Nat & Intl Awds.

HENSLER, MARY ELSIE oc/Homemaker; Former Teacher; b/Oct 29; h/605 Western Ave, Joliet, IL 60435; m/Harold D; p/Harry E Clinger (dec); Sylvia I Clinger; ed/BA Wittenberg Univ; Addit Studies Ohio St Univ; pa/Eng & Hist Tchr Cable (Ohio) HS; Eng & Drama Tchr Lewisburg (Ohio) HS; Travelling Tchr Piqua (Ohio) HS; Substitute Tchr Piqua Jr & Sr HSs; OEA; NEA; PTA; BPW, Piqua; AAUW: Bd Mem, Orgr Piqua Chapt, Publicity Chm Joliet Chapt, Others; cp/Gen Fdn Wom's Clbs, Num Ofcs & Activs Local, Co, Dist & St Levels; Mem Panhellenic Coun Will Co (Ill); OES; YWCA; King's Daughs & Sons Inc (Intl Order); Var Activs GSA; ARC, Will Co Chapt; Wel Coms; Former Orgr & Charter Mem Will Co Citizens for Action Traffic Safety; Sao Paulo-Ill Partners of Ams; Var Fund Drs; Others; r/1st Presb Ch, Joliet: Deaconess, Ch Nom'g Com, Former Activs; hon/Cert of Hon, Am Heritage Res Assn; Hon Mem, Newcomers' Alumnae Joliet; CARE Recog Pin; 25-Yr Mbrship-Ser Recog Pin, Trailways Girl Scout Coun USA; Cert of Recog, Sao Paulo Wom's Clb; Num Others; Biogl Listings.

HENSLEY, BETTY AUSTIN oc/Private Flute Teacher; Musician; b/Oct 12, 1923; h/4707 Looman, Wichita, KS 67220; ba/Same; m/Cline Douglas; c/Douglas A, William H, Lawrence A; p/Allen C Austin (dec); Ruth Cady Austin, Kansas City, MO; ed/BA Univ Ks 1944; pa/Owner-Perf Ethnic Collection "Flutes of the World" (Over 200 Instruments); Current Mem Friends Univ-Commun Symph Orch (20 Yrs); Univ Ks Alumni Bd; Mu Phi Epsilon Flute Quartet; Dienstag Woodwind Quartet; Mem Wichita Pan Pipers (Flute Duo) 1974-76; Nat Bd Mem Am Musical Instrument Soc 1975-; Bd Mem:

Yg Audiences Ks 1970-73, Musical Arts Ks Inc 1973-; Pres Wichita Musical Clb 1976-78; Mem George B Tack Meml Flute S'ship Com, Wichita 1966; Nat Flute Assn; Galpin Soc; Soc for Ethnomusicology; Soc for Asian Music; Var Local Music Clbs; cp/Nat Bd Mem Nat Neighbors 3 Yrs; Mem Human Resources Devel Adv Bd, Wichita 3 Yrs; Past 1/VP Med Soc Sedgwick Co (Ks) Aux; AAUW; Wom's Assn Wichita Symph Soc; Mid-Am All-Indian Ctr; Friends Wichita Art Mus; Others; r/1st Unitarian Ch, Wichita Trustees 1975-78; hon/Phi Beta Kappa; Iota Sigma Pi; Mu Phi Epsilon; Dist'd Ser Cit, City of Wichita; Contbn to Ks Day Bicent Parade of Am Music, Ks Fdn Music Clbs 1976; Profl Pubs & Recording.

HENSON, A MIRIAM MORGAN oc/-Research Assistant Professor; b/Nov 7, 1935; h/317 Reade Rd, Chapel Hill, NC 27514; ba/CH; m/O'Dell Williams; c/Phillip William; p/Bert Emerson Morgan (dec); Esther M Morgan, Lee's Summit, MO; ed/AB Park Col; MA Smith Col; PhD Yale Univ; pa/Res Asst Prof UNC Sch Med, Div Otolaryngology; Am Assoc Anat; Acoust Soc Am; S Soc Anat; hon/Grad Cum Laude; Sigma Xi; Fulbright Scholar.

HENSON, O'DELL WILLIAMS JR oc/Professor; b/Jan 11, 1934; h/317 Reade Dr, Chapel Hill, NC 27514; ba/CH; m/Miriam Morgan; c/Phillip William; p/O'Dell Williams and Natalie Smith Henson, Topeka, KS; ed/BA, MS Univ Ks; PhD Yale Univ; pa/Prof Dept Anatomy Univ NC-CH; Reschr.

HENTSCHEL, ALZA J STRATTON oc/Artist; b/Jul 2, 1911; h/147 Forest Ave, Lexington, KY 40508; ba/Same; m/William E (dec); p/Jess and Alza Proctor Stratton, Lexington, KY; ed/AB Univ Ky; Grad Work: Univ Ky, Univ Cincinnati, Cinc Art Acad; pa/Profl Artist, Designer, Ceramist; La Col; Cinc Art Acad; Mural Painter; Exhbns: France, England, S Am, Var US Museums; Art Del (w husband) to UN; r/Prot; hon/W/W Am Wom; World W/W Wom; World W/W Wom; DIB; Am Artists; Dic Am Artists; Var Exhbn Awds; Others.

HENZLIK, RAYMOND EUGENE oc/-Professor; b/Dec 26, 1926; h/3311 Somerset Dr, Muncie, IN 47304; ba/Muncie; m/Wilma Bartels; c/Randall E, Nancy Jo; p/William H Henzlik, Spring Hill, FL; Adeline Wolff, Sun City, AZ; ed/AA; BS; MS; PhD; mil/USN; pa/Prof Physiol & Hlth Sci Ball St Univ; Conslt in Physiol & Anatomy; Sci Pubs; cp/UF; YMCA; Kiwanis; r/Meth; hon/-S'ships, Univ Neb; NSF F'ships; Atomic Energy Comm Res Participation; Sigma Xi; Oak Ridge Assn Univ Grant; Phi Delta Kappa; Mensa.

HEPBURN, EILEEN HARKINS oc/-Educator; b/Oct 1, 1931; h/208 St George's Rd, Andmore, PA 19003; ba/Chester, PA; m/Austin Barry; c/Austin Barry Jr, Martin Hayes, Dorothy Morley, Douglas Perin; p/Thomas Francis Harkins (dec); Claire Martin Harkins, Andmore, PA; ed/BA 1953, MA 1970 Univ Pa; PhD Cand; pa/Instr Sociol Widener Col; r/Rom Cath.

HEPPENHEIMER, THOMAS ADOLPH oc/Author; Planetary Scientist; b/Jan 1, 1947; h/11040 Blue Allium Ave, Fountain Valley, CA 92708; ba/Palos Verdes Peninsula, CA; c/Laurie, Alex, Connie; p/Henry Gunther and Betty Lorraine Amitin Heppenheimer (dec); ed/BS 1967, MS 1968 Mich St Univ; PhD Univ Mich 1972; pa/CoFdr & VP Tech Forum for Advmt of Students in Sci & Tech 1971-73; VP KRG Inc 1978-; cp/Former Mem Co Com Ann Arbor (Mich) Dem Party; hon/Res F'ship Cal Inst Tech; Author *Colonies in Space*, Won Book-of-the-Month Clb Selection 1977; Dist'd Achmt Awd, Univ Mich.

HERBERTT, STANLEY oc/Dance Administrator; Choreographer; Lecturer; b/Apr 11, 1919; h/7548 Parkdale, St Louis, MO 63105; ba/St Louis; p/Sam W and Anna S Maltz (dec); ed/BEd Chicago Tchr's Col; Masters Nat Acad Ballet; Dance Tng; pa/Owner & Dir Ballet Arts Acad, St Louis 1951-79; Soloist & Choreographer Cain Park Sum Theatre, Cleveland, Ohio 1950-51; Soloist Other Ballets & Theatres; Fdr & Dir St Louis Civic Ballet 1959-; Lectr: St Joseph (Mo) Civic Ballet, Copper Coin Civic Ballet (Springfield, Ill), Nat Soc Arts & Lttrs (St Louis), Others; Dir Stix Baer & Fuller Dept Stores, Music Fashion Shows 7 Yrs; Choreographer: Musicals, Ballet Cos, Concerts, TV, Commls; Dance Masters Am; Assn Am Dance Cos; Am Dance Guild; Dance Edrs Am; Dance Concert Soc; IPA; cp/Former Mem Dance Com Mo St Coun on Arts (Appt'd by Gov); hon/Pub'd Articles; Maharishi Awd; Fontbonne Col Ed for the Arts; Biogl Listings.

HERBST, LAWRENCE ROBERT oc/Investment Advisor; Tax Consultant; Economist; b/Aug 8, 1946; h/Apt 2, 145 N Hamilton Dr, Beverly Hills, CA 90210; ba/New York, NY; p/Morton and Ruth I Cooper Herbst; ed/Att'd: UCLA 1966-67, Alexander Hamilton Bus Inst 1963; DD Missionaries of New Truth 1971; pa/w ABC-TV, Am Fdn Guards, Local I 1972-74; Investmt Advr, Fin Conslt, Fin Economist, Tax Conslt; Antejo Corp, Total Sound Records, Montrose (Cal) & Lawrence Herbst Records, Beverly Hills (Cal) 1975-; Owner Larry's Wn Supply; Broadcast Music Inc; Pres & Admr Lawrence Herbst Foun; Nat Acad TV Arts & Scis; LA Press Clb; Navy Leag US; Intl, Hollywood, Beverly Hills, LA Cs of C; cp/Pres' Assn; Nat Clb Assn; Epsilon Delta Chi; LA Ath Clb; hon/Author; W/W in W.

HERD, RICHARD MURLEN oc/Oral Maxillofacial Surgeon; b/Sept 16, 1922; h/6825 Creekside Ln, Indianapolis, IN 46220; ba/Indpls; m/Harriet Jean; c/Richard Murle Jr, Eric Alan, Dorothy Jean; p/Murlen and Mary Herd, Peru, IN; ed/AB; DDS; mil/AUS; USN; pa/Conslt Ind Univ; Pvt Pract; cp/BSA; Ednl Activs; r/Luth; hon/Citizen for Day, Indpls; Boy Scouts.

HERDER, THOMAS G oc/Assistant Professor Modern Languages; b/Oct 29, 1939; h/41 Elm St, Greenville, PA 16125; ed/BA; EdM; PhD; pa/Interpreter AUS 1951-53, Genesco, France 1974; Tchr Franklin & Edison, NJ Schs 1957-63; Instr: N Tex St Univ 1963-69, Pa St Univ 1969-72; Asst Prof & Chm Mod Langs Dept George Peabody Col, Nashville, Tenn 1972-75; Dept Langs (French Lit, German Lang) Thiel Col, Greenville, Pa 1975-; Mem Sev Profl & Acad Orgs incl'g: MLA, Am Assn Tchrs French (Chapt Pres 1966-68), Coun on World Affairs, Pi Delta Phi, Phi Delta Kappa; Luth Ch Am; Nat Def Ed Act, (NDEA) F'ship; Nom'd for Palmes Academiques; Pub'd Author; Biogl Listings.

HERMAN, JOHN ALLEN oc/Editor, Publisher; b/Apr 9, 1936; h/6192 65th St S, Cottage Grove, MN 55016; ba/Cottage Grove; m/Joan Elaine; c/Sarah Elizabeth, Andrew Allen; p/Herbert Allen and Mable Boyer Herman (dec); ed/Univ Minn; pa/Editor & Pubr *The Washington County Bulletin*; Pres Bulletin Pub'g Corp; Dep Registrar City of Cottage Grove; Minn & Nat Newspaper Assns; Minn Press Clb; Intl Soc Weekly Newspaper Editors; Minn Dep Reg Assn; CG C of C; cp/Cand for US Senate 1978; Conservative Caucus; Orgr Minn Voters Coalition; r/Presb; hon/St Americanism Awd, Minn VFW; W/W Upper MW.

HERMAN, MAX oc/Executive; b/Jul 1, 1914; h/3561 Valley Meadow Rd, Sherman Oaks, CA 91403; ba/Hollywood, CA; m/Ida; c/Marlene Seltzer, Barry A; p/Sam Herman (dec); Rose Herman, Sherman Oaks, CA; mil/USCG WWII; pa/Pres Musicians Union; Formerly Worked in Big Band Era & Studios; cp/Yth Projs & Labor Polit Activs; Los Angeles Co Fdn Labor; VP Hollywood Film Coun; r/Jewish; hon/City & Co Cult Awds.

HERMELEE, LAURENCE STEPHAN oc/Bank Executive; b/Dec 22, 1937; h/8540 SW 104th St, Miami, FL 33156; ba/Miami; m/Mary Beth Moore; c/Noelle, Harold, Rory; p/Harold B Hermelee (dec); Hermine Pallot; ed/BS Univ Pa; Grad NY Univ; mil/USAR

1960-66; pa/Exec VP Biscayne Fed Savs & Ln Assn; Instr Inst Fin Ed; Fin Mgrs Soc; Am Mgmt Assn; Pvt Fin Conslt'g; Audit & Acct'g Study Com Fla Savs & Ln Leag; cp/Com on Ecology & Beautification Arabian Horse Assn Fla; hon/Num Dist'd Ser Awds, Trade Orgs.

HERNANDEZ, AL (ALFREDO EUFRONIO GUILLERMO ANTONIO ORNEZ de) oc/Executive; Retired Military Officer; Wartime Secret Agent; Author; b/Jun 25, 1909; h/Las Vegas, NV; m/Maria Lachonas; c/Alana, Angela, Alfred, Rita; ed/Columbia Col, Radio-TV Acad, YMCA Inst, Pswar Sch, Espionage Courses; mil/1942, Exec Ofcr & Asst Expedition Cmdr, Secret Expedition in Enemy Territory; Mil Gov in Area of Occup; CO Pswar Univ, 6th Army; CO 306th Radio Bcst Propaganda Group & Advr & Coor Unconventional & Pswarfare Theatre Exercises 6th Army; Maj; Num Awds;

pa/Dance Dir Choreographer Hollywood; Prodr Far En Exposition, Manila, PI 1937; Prodr, Stage, Radio, Film W Coast 1939; Fac Mem Glickman Col Fine Arts, Chgo, Ill 1949, 1947, Wespac Import-Export Co, SF; Pubr *Movie News* Mag, H'wood; Constrn Engr Sloan Bldg, Beverly Hills 1950; Sch Dir TV-Radio Tng Sch; Inspector Admiral TV; VP Intl Film Fest Host Las Vegas 1966; Proj Ofcr Gravitics Rsch & Devel Corp; 1970-, VP Intl Resources, LV; cp/Ret'd Ofcrs Assn; Am Guild Variety Artists; Am Legion; VFW; hon/Pub'd Author; Author "Bahala Na", Documentary of Prep Wk to "I Shall Return" by MacArthur; Hist Link, Vol'd on Secret Mission ISRM; Biogl Listings.

HERNANDEZ, ALMA G oc/Educational Diagnostician; b/Mar 2, 1927; h/103 City St, San Antonio, TX 78204; ba/SA; m/Ernesto V; c/William Larry Carrera, Robert Gary Carrera; p/Eusebio Gavza (dec); Carolina S Gavza, SA; ed/AA; BS; MEd; pa/TSTA; APGA; CEC; Chd w LD; Tex Assn Ed Diagnosticians; cp/Dem; r/Cath; hon/Notable Ams; Personalities of S; W/W S&SW.

HERNANDEZ, CRUZ G oc/Producer Manager; b/May 3, 1942; h/217 Berkshire Ln, Fort Worth, TX 76134; ba/Garland, TX; m/Martha Ann; c/Cynthia Jo, Deanna Kay, Daniel Cruz; p/Benito Hernandez, San Benito, TX; Concepcion Hernandez (dec); ed/AAS, Food Mktg Cert Tarrant Co Jr Col; mil/AUS, Discharged E-4; pa/Produce Mgr Safeway Stores Inc; Real Est Agt; cp/Del Dem St Conv 1972, 74, 76, 78; Pres Elector 1976; Alt Del PTA Coun; r/S Park Bapt Ch: Mem; hon/W/W Am Polits.

HERNDON, JUDITH A oc/Lawyer; State Legislator; b/Jun 5, 1941; h/27 Elmwood Pl, Wheeling, WV 26003; ba/Wheeling; p/Richard G and Virginia H Herndon, Wheeling; ed/AB Duke Univ 1963; JD WVa Univ Col Law 1967; pa/WVa St, Ohio Co Bars; WVa & Am Bar Assns; cp/St Senator 1974-, Var Coms; Bd Dirs: WVa Tax Inst, Wesbanco, Wheeling Dollar Savings & Trust Co, Russell Nesbitt Home, The Good Zoo, Mt de Chantal Visitation Acad; r/Rom Cath; hon/Dist'd W Virginian, Gov Moore.

HERNDON, TERRY EUGENE oc/Educator; b/Feb 24, 1939; ba/1201 16th St NW, Washington, DC 20036; m/Mary Jeanne Gandolfi; c/Julie, Holly; p/Chester and Wilma Herndon, Russellville, KY; ed/BS 1961, MA 1964 Wayne St Univ; HHD Morehead St Univ 1974; pa/Chm Nat Foun for Improvemt of Ed; Mem Nat Coun for Chd & TV; Com on Nat Hlth Ins; cp/Assoc Dir, Dir UN Assn; Dir Coalition Am Public Employees; Chm Assn Div U Way; Coun on Hemispheric Affairs; r/Christian; hon/Dist'd Ser Awd, Mich Ed Assn; Outstg Citizens Awd, Lansing, Mich; Anthony Wayne Awd for Ldrship, Wayne St Univ.

HERREN, PETER HANS oc/Hotel Executive; b/Oct 8, 1927; h/10 W Lakeview Dr, Granby, CT 06035; ba/Jamaica, NY; m/Beryl; c/Rebecca, David; p/Hans Walter Herren (dec); ed/Dipl Hotel Mgmt; pa/Gen Mgr Hilton Inn, Jamaica; Am Mgmt Assn; Am Hotel & Motel Assn; NY St Hotel & Motel Assn; Hotel Sales Mgmt Assn (Intl); Dir Hotel Assn NYC; cp/Charter Pres JFK C of C; Past Pres JFK Rotary Clb; Mem Other Cs of C; 32° Mason; Knight Templar; Shriner; r/Presb; hon/Fellow, ABI; Waldorf-Astoria Dist'd Alumnus Awd; Biogl Listings.

HERRING, MICHAEL MORRIS oc/Mineral Development, Acquisition; b/Oct 15, 1922; h/4309 NW 61st Terr, Oklahoma City, OK 73112; ba/Same; m/Dorothy Eleene; p/Mike Eugene Herring (dec); Flossie Josephine Herring; mil/USAF WWII, B-17 Bombers; pa/Originator & Designer Businesses; Nat Write-ups, Commerce & Indust; Nat Soc Lit & Arts; cp/Assoc Mensa; Mastor Councilor DeMolay; Blue Lodge Mason 276; 32° Mason; Shriner; Beta Beta Beta; Kappa Alpha; Delta Psi Omega; Nat Amateur & Profl Champ Ath; r/Bapt; hon/Infantile Paralysis & Crippled Chd Awds; Hon Dep Sheriff; St of Okla: Hon Col Army, Hon Commodore Navy, Hon Admiral Fleet; Safety Awd in Mfg & Trans; Armed Forces Combat Commando Champ; Cits; N Atl Command Awd; US Nav Awd, Outstg Bus Man 8th Nav Dist; Biogl Listings.

HERRON, BETTIE JANE HOLLIS oc/School Librarian; b/Jun 2, 1930; h/Verde Village, Box 2632, Cottonwood, AZ 86326; ba/C'wood; m/Edgar Allison Jr; c/Hollis,

James Lee, Mark Edgar; p/James Floyd and Nevada Whiteside Hollis (dec); ed/BA Baylor Univ; MA No Ariz Univ; pa/NEA; AEA; CEA; ASLA (SLD); cp/Beta Sigma Phi; r/Meth.

HERSCHER, IRENAEUS JOSEPH oc/Clergyman; Librarian; Archivist; b/Mar 11, 1902; h/Box 66, St Bonaventure PO, NY 14778; ba/St Bonaventure; p/Jean Baptiste and Josephine Herscher (dec); ed/BA 1929, MA 1930 St Bonaventure Univ; STB Cath Univ 1931; MLS Columbia 1934; LittD (Hon Causa) 1969; pa/Chaplain St Jos Manor (Nsg Home); Art Curator; r/Rom Cath; hon/Cits: Canisius Col, Wn NY Cath Lib Conf.

HERSHEY, H GARLAND oc/Orthodontist; Teacher; Administrator; b/Nov 6, 1940; h/607 Shadylawn Rd, Chapel Hill, NC 27514; ba/Chapel Hill; m/Rae; c/Brooke, Dru Ann, Paige Marie; p/Howard Garland and Erna E Hershey, Iowa City, IA; ed/BA 1962; DDS 1965; MS 1971; mil/AUS 1965-68, Capt; pa/Univ NC Sch Dentistry: Prof Dept Ortho 1978-, Dir Grad Ed 1975-, Asst Dean Acad Affairs 1975-; Other Acad Positions; Staff NC Meml Hosp 1973-; Pvt Dental Ser 1971-; Am Dental Assn; Delta Sigma Delta; Intl Assn for Dental Res; Durham-Orange Co, 3rd Dist, NC

St Dental Socs; Am Assn Dental Schs; NC Ortho Alumni Assn; So Soc Orthodontists; AAAS; Sigma Xi; Am Soc Dentistry for Chd; Intl Assn Dentofacial Abnormalities; Charles H Tweed Foun; Others; cp/Former Boy Scout Merit Badge Cnslr; Other Activs BSA; Former Bd Govs, Ofcrs & Civilians Open Mess, Aschaffenburg, Germany; r/Prot; hon/Omicron Kappa Upsilon; Mem Tchg Staff, Charles H Tweed Foun; Mem Edward H Angle Soc Ortho; Lactona Awd; W/W: S&SW, NAm; Personalities of S; Others.

HERSHEY, PHILIP oc/Retired State Official; Retired College Teacher; b/Sept 1, 1913; h/4138 NW 88 Ave #206, Coral Springs, FL 33065; m/Faye; c/Edward, Nancy H Lord; p/Louis and Betty Hershey (dec); ed/AB Cornell Univ 1934; MS Col City NY 1937; pa/Current Pt-time Col Tchr (Math) & Adult Ctr Tchr (Numerical & Verbal Skills); Intl Assn Pers in Employmt Security; Math Assn Am; Judge Gtr Metro NY Math Fair; cp/Asst Editor Commun Newspaper; Pers Mgmt Conslt, Ser Corps Ret'd Execs; Mediator Citizen Dispute Settlemt Prog; hon/Recipient S'ship; Cit, Gov NY St for Proposing Method for Reducing Overpayments in St's Unemploymt Ins Prog; Cit of Merit in Recog of Devoted Ser, NY St Civil Ser Employees Assn.

HERSHMAN, JOANN OPPENHEIMER oc/Sales Executive; b/Sept 6, 1934; h/10311 Mohawk Rd, Leawood, KS 66206; ba/Same; c/Brent Lon, Adrian Ilene; p/Harry Oppenheimer (dec); Rebecca Oppenheimer, Kansas City, MO; ed/Tex St Col for Wom; BA Univ Mo 1958; pa/Pres JoAnn & Assocs Inc (Advt'g Specialty Cnslrs & Social/Comml Printing Brokers); Gtr Ks City C of C; Centurion Com (1 of Only 2 Wom); Intl Relats; cp/Alumni Bd Univ Mo-KC; Public Relats Chair Gtr Ks City Reg Comm on Status of Wom; Pres Mortar Bd Alumnae Gtr KC; Pres Sch Ed Alumni Assn; VP Wom's Am Org for Rehab Through Tng; Others; hon/Alumni Ser Awd, Univ Mo-KC; Outstg Yg Wom of Ks, Outstg Ams' Foun; Dist'd Ser Awd, Univ Mo-KC Alumni Assn; Queen of Univ Mo-KC; Recipient Sev Indust Sales Awds; Biogl Listings.

HERSLIP, LARRY oc/Farmer; b/Dec 30, 1945; h/Souris, ND 58783; ba/Same; m/Donna; c/Leslie, Dawndi, Sarah; p/Lawrence Herslip (dec); Luella Herslip, Kent, WA; mil/AUS; cp/St Legislator; r/Luth; hon/Outstg Yg Man Am.

HERZIG, SIEGFRIED (SIG) M oc/Screen & Television Writer; Playwright; b/Jul 25, 1897; h/11924 Montana Ave, Los Angeles, CA 90049; ba/Same; m/Betty; p/Leopold and Paula Herzig (dec); ed/Columbia Sch Jour 1919; mil/Communs WWI; pa/Coauthor Bwy Musical *Bloomer Girl*; Author Book *Around the World*, 40 Screenplays, Num TV Plays; Currently Writing Memoirs; Acad Motion Picture Arts & Scis; Writers Guild Am; Others; hon/Num Cits for Screenplays & Musical Plays.

HESS, EDWARD JORGEN oc/Librarian; Educator; b/Feb 18, 1925; h/517 N Vista Bonita Ave, Glendora, CA 91740; ba/Los Angeles, CA; p/Edward A and Luella B Nelson Hess; ed/BA; MA; MS; PhD; mil/AUS 1943-46; pa/Univ So Cal-LA: Asst Univ Libn for Public Sers 1976-, Asst Prof Sch Lib Sci 1970-76, Lectr 1969-70, (Pt-time) 1967-69; Other Positions; Cal Lib Assn: Chm Com on Alts to Fee Charging 1979, Councilor 1975-77, Others; Cal Corres for *The ALA Yrbook*, Pub'd by Am Lib Assn 1976; ALA; Am Soc for Info Sci; Assn Col & Res Libs; Gtr LA Chapt Cal Lib Assn; So Cal Tech Processes Group; Others; cp/Friends of Chinatown Lib; Wn Photo Collectors Assn; Nat Trust for Hist Preserv; Sierra Clb; Former Activs; r/Prot; hon/Beta Phi Mu; Kappa Delta Pi; Num Profl Pubs.

HESS, IRENE ROSE oc/Elementary School Principal; b/May 5, 1935; h/2813 Pioneer Ave, Cheyenne, WY 82001; ba/Cheyenne; p/Eugene Vernon and Margaret Rose Mantey Hess, Cheyenne; ed/BA Colo St

Col Ed 1962; MA Univ No Colo 1968; Addit Studies; pa/Prin: Rossman Elem Sch, Cheyenne 1977-78, Henderson Elem Sch (Cheyenne) 1975-77; Former Tchr; NEA: Life Mem, Wom's Caucus, Del (Atlantic City, Portland, Chicago); WEA: Helpmobile Demon Tchr, Helpmobile Planning Com, Del, Conv Planning Com; Pres Cheyenne Tchrs Ed Assn 1974-75; CTEA; ACEI; EKNE; ASCD; KKI; NCTA: Secy, Treas; Fdr's Life Mbrship, Univ No Colo Alumni Assn; Num Other Profl Activs; cp/C of C; Citizens Adv Com; PTA; PTO; Pres Laramie Co Rdg Coun; IRA; Girl Scout Ldr; Tchr Rep Sch Bd Meetings; Delta Kappa Gamma; Kappa Kappa Iota; Var Campaign Activs; Others; r/Ch & SS Sch; hon/Nom'd Rdg Tchr Yr 1974; Runner-up Outstg Yg Edr; S'ships; Num Biogl Listings.

HESS, PATRICIA ALICE oc/Nurse Educator; b/Apr 25, 1938; h/2815 Filbert St, San Francisco, CA 94123; ba/SF; p/Frederic and Anne Goldman Hess, Erie, PA; ed/BS Case Wn Resv Univ 1961; MS Univ Colo 1966; Certs; pa/SF St Univ: Assoc Prof 1978-, Asst Prof Dept Nsg 1970-78, Instr Dept Nsg

1967-70; Other Former Positions; Instr SF St Univ Ext, Gerontol Cert Prog 1975-; Instr Univ Cal Ext Courses by Newspaper 1979-; Gerontol Soc; Wn Gerontol Soc; Forum for Death Ed & Cnslg Inc; Am Nurses Assn 1967-76; Nat Leag for Nsg 1976-; hon/Sigma Theta Tau; Book of Yr Awd, Geriatric Nsg Catagory, *Am Jour Nsg* 1978; Profl Pubs.

HESTER, RUBY oc/Teacher; b/Aug 7, 1921; h/Rt 6, Box 94, Russellville, AL 35653; p/Grover Cleveland Hester (dec); Flossie B Hester, R'ville; ed/BS Florence St Univ 1943; MA George Peabody Col for Tchrs 1951; pa/3rd Grade Tchr R'ville City Schs 1946-; AEA; NEA; RTA; Alpha Upsilon Chapt Delta Kappa Gamma; cp/Dem; r/Meth; hon/Runner-up for Favorite Tchr of Ala; Intl W/W Commun Ser; DIB; 2000 Wom Achmt; Notable Ams Bicent Era; Commun Ldrs & Noteworthy Ams; Personalities of S; W/W in Ala; World W/W Wom.

HEURICH, BETTY ELEANOR oc/Association Executive; b/Sept 20, 1915; h/Lake Shore Dr E, Harbor Hill RR #1, Hebron, OH 43025; ba/Columbus, OH; m/Herbert H; c/Barbara Bayer (Mrs John F), Nancy H McConnell; p/Leo Adam and Hattie Hall Reeb (dec); pa/Conslt on Mtgs & Conv to Govs; Soc Assn Execs; Ohio Trade Assn Execs; Mng Editor Cemeterian Mag; cp/Bd Dirs Pauline Home for Aged; Col Meannerchor Swiss Clb; Child Conserv Leag; r/Epis; hon/W/W Am Wom.

HEYBL, LAURICE oc/Sister of Religious Order; Youth Consultant; b/Mar 21, 1930; h/1416 Cumming, Superior, WI 54880; ba/Duluth, MN; p/Jacob Heybl (dec); Gertrude Denfeld (dec); ed/BA Viterbo Col; MA Univ Wis-S; pa/Duluth Diocesan Yth Conslt; Secy Superior Diocesan Liturgical Comm; Rep for Superior Sisters Coun; Duluth Sisters Assn; r/Cath: Mem Franciscan Sisters of Perpetual Adoration, La Crosse (Wis).

HEYWARD, JOHN WESLEY JR oc/Minister; b/Nov 20, 1934; h/6949 Julian Ave, University City, MO 63130; ba/St Louis, MO; m/Dorothy Elizabeth; c/John Wesley III; p/John W Sr and Wilhelmena Wright Heyward (dec); ed/BA Claflin Col 1956; BD

1959, MDiv 1959 Gammon Theol Sem; DD Claflin Col 1976; mil/USAFR Chaplain, Maj; pa/Sr Min Union Meml U Meth Ch; Trustee Gammon Theol Sem; Mem Black Meth for Ch Renewal; Alpha Phi Alpha; Dir Visitation U Meth Div Chaplains 1971-76; cp/NAACP; 32° Mason; r/U Meth; hon/Meth Crusade Scholar; H D Bollinger S'ship; W/W Methodism; Personalities of S.

HEYWARD, JOSEPH EDWARD oc/College Administrator; b/Nov 17, 1941; h/PO Box 384, Florence, SC 29503; ba/Florence; m/Evelyn Sargent; c/Joseph Edward II, Ryan Christopher; p/John W and Wilhelmena W Heyward (dec); ed/BS; MA; mil/USAR; pa/Francis Marion Col: Dir Smith Col Ctr, Asst Dean Students, Instr Math 1974-, Acad Cnslr & Instr Math 1973-74; Prin Williams Jr HS, Florence Sch Dist I, Florence 1972-73; Other Former Positions; NEA; Nat & SC Assn Sec'dy Sch Prins; Florence Co Ed Assn; SC Assn Sch Admrs; Assn Col Unions (Intl); SC Col Pers Assn; Alpha Phi Alpha: Secy Delta Kappa Lambda Chapt 7 Yrs, St Exec Com, St Secy SC Reg, Del St Meetings, Exec Secy Alpha S, Others; cp/Bd Dirs Florence Boys Clbs Am; Bd Dirs Pee Dee Big Brothers Assn; Exec Com-man Florence Precnt #3; Mem Zoning Bd Adjustmt & Appeals, City of Florence; Florence Co Hist Comm; Former Assoc Mem Nat Coun Negro Wom Inc; NAACP; Others; r/Cumberland U Meth Ch: Yth Cnslr, Supt Studies, Com on Music, Work Area on Worship, Choir Dir; hon/Plaque of Apprec, Williams Jr HS; SC Alpha Man of Yr 1975; So Reg Grad Brother of Yr 1975; Cert of Apprec, Nat's Bicent; Dist'd Ser Awd, Alpha Phi Alpha; Outstg Yg Men Am; Awd of Apprec, McLeod Reg Med Ctr; Others.

HIAASEN, CARL ANDREAS oc/Lawyer; b/May 26, 1894; h/2417 NE 27th Ave, Fort Lauderdale, FL 33305; ba/Ft Lauderdale; m/Clara Landmark (dec); c/Kermit Odel (dec); p/Knute O and Mary Flaagen Hiaasen (dec); ed/JD Univ ND 1922; mil/AUS WWI, Machine Gun Ofcr; pa/Sr Mem McCune,

Hiaasen, Crum, Ferris & Gardner; Life Fellow Am Bar Foun; ABA; Bar Assn City NY; cp/Bd Dirs Pittsburgh Theol Sem; Univ Fla Pres' Coun; Com Chapel of Four Chaplains, Univ Philadelphia; r/Luth; hon/Order of Coif; Phi Delta Phi; Delta Sigma Rho; Contbr Articles to Legal Jours.

HIATT, DOUGLAS PIERCE oc/Architect; Interior Designer; b/Oct 8, 1946; ba/9701 Wilshire Blvd, Suite 710, Beverly Hills, CA 90212; p/Mr and Mrs O C Hiatt, Salinas, CA; ed/ASJD; BFA; BA; pa/Dir & Adv Hey Foun; Bd Dirs, Adv Giant Step; cp/Beverly Hills C of C; hon/Cupertino HS Hall of Fame 1978.

HIBBETT, EUGENE P oc/Teacher; b/Jul 17, 1932; h/482 White Ave, Henderson, TN 38340; ba/Henderson; m/Jacqueline; c/Lee, Lynn; p/Rufus G Hibbett, Florence, AL; ed/BA David Lipscomb 1955; MS Univ Ala 1958; MA 1962, PhD 1969 Univ Miss; mil/USNR MC 1949-57; pa/Freed-Hardeman Col: Tchr Chem 1958-, Chm Dept Phy Scis; Am Chem Soc; cp/Lions Clb; r/Ch of Christ: SS Tchr, Preacher.

HIBBS, RUTH STRAIGHT oc/Teacher; Artist; b/Mar 12, 1918; h/115 Chelsea Cir, Statesboro, GA 30458; ba/S'boro; m/Edwin Thompson; c/Michael, Stephen, Anne, Paul, Henry; p/Asa Edgar and Lovie Clifford

Straight, Yarrow, MO; ed/BS NE Mo St Univ; BA, MFA Univ Colo; pa/Tchr Fine Arts: NE Mo St Univ, Univ Colo, Cornell Univ; Tchr Watercolor & Crafts: Art Ctrs Ames (Ia) & S'boro; Presented Series of TV Progs on "Straw Sculpture", Ames; One-Wom Painting Exhibits: NE Mo St Univ, Univ Colo, Cornell Univ, Story City, Ia, S'boro; r/Presb Ch: Mem; hon/Author & Illustrator Book *Straw Sculpture: Techniques & Projects* 1974; Author Chapt "Raffia & Straw" for Time-Life Series, *Fam Creative Wkshop* 1975; Contbr Articles to Art & Craft Mags; Kappa Delta Pi; Delta Kappa Gamma; Nat Hon Soc; Paintings Exhibited Juried Shows; Acad Hons.

HICHENS, WALTER W oc/State Legislator; b/Mar 8, 1917; h/424 State Rd, Eliot, ME 03903; ba/Augusta, ME; m/Elmira B; c/Walter Jr, Jared, Mary, Janice, Judith, Kathy, Bethany; p/Walter G and Mary E Norton Hichens (dec); cp/St Senator; Former Selectman; Water Dist Dir; C of C; Maine Christian Civic Leag; r/Bapt: Pres Me Bapt Men; Past Pres Me Assn Gideons Intl; hon/Leg Contb'g Most to Better Living, Me Citizens; Certs of Apprec: Me Rt to Life Assn, Me Special Olympics; Life Mem, Me Frat Assn for Blind.

HICKEL, WALTER JOSEPH oc/Business Executive; b/Aug 18, 1919; h/1905 Loussac Dr, Anchorage, AK 99503; ba/Anchorage; m/Ermalee; c/Ted, Robert, Wally, Jack, Joe, Karl; p/Robert A and Emma P Hickel (dec); mil/AUS 1942-46, Civilian Aircraft Inspector; pa/Bd Mem: Rowan Cos Inc 1976-, Salk Inst 1972-; World Adv Coun Intl Design Sci Inst 1972-; AAAS, Com on Sci Freedom & Responsibility; cp/Gov of Alaska 1966-69; Secy of Interior 1969-70; Coun of Former Govs 1975-; Nat Citizens Communs Lobby; Fdr Mem John F Kennedy Ctr for Perf'g Arts; Life Trustee Nat Rec & Pk Assn; Nat Press Clb; Bd Regents Gonzaga Univ; Bd Dirs: Boys Clb Alaska, Wn Airlines; Mem Providence Hosp Adv Bd; Dir Coast Guard Acad Foun Inc; Alaska-Nippon Kai (Alaska-Japan Clb); Equestrian Order Holy Sepulchre; Charter Mem The Cousteau Soc; Ks of Sovereign Mil Order of Malta; Pioneers of Alaska; r/Alaskan of Yr 1969; Cert of Awd for Best Non-Fiction Book, Alaska Press Clb; Alaska Press Clb Hall of Fame; Nom'd for Pres as Favorite Son Cand from Alaska; Boss of Yr, Nat Secys Assn, Juneau, Alaska 1968, Anchorage, Alaska 1974; 10 Hon Degs; Others.

HICKMAN, HOYT LEON oc/Minister; b/May 22, 1927; h/2034 Castleman Dr, Nashville, TN 37215; ba/N'ville; m/Martha Whitmore; c/Peter, John, Stephen, Mary (dec); p/Leon E and Mayme Hoyt Hickman, Pittsburgh, PA; ed/AB Haverford Col 1950; MDiv Yale Univ 1953; STM Union Theol Sem 1954; DD Morningside Col 1978; mil/USN 1945-46, Seaman 1/c; pa/U Meth Min; Asst Gen Secy Bd of Discipleship U Meth Ch; cp/Dem; r/U Meth; hon/Phi Beta Kappa.

HICKMAN, KATHRYN THERESA oc/Graduate Assistant; b/Sept 28, 1956; h/513 Arlington, Lawton, OK 73501; ba/Wichita Falls, TX; p/Harold T and Genevieve K Hickman, Lawton; ed/BA cum laude Cameron Univ 1978; MM Cand, Grad Asst Music Dept MWn St Univ; pa/Mu Phi Epsilon; Pi Kappa Lambda; Phi Kappa Phi; cp/Former Camp Fire Girls Camp Cnslr; Rehearsal Accompanist & Mem Orch Lawton

Commun Theatre; r/Blessed Sacrament Cath Ch: Mem, Organist; hon/Camp Fire Girls Dist'd Ser Awd; Schubert Clb Music Theory Awd; S'ships; Nat Dean's List; W/W Am Cols & Univs.

HICKOK, LESLIE GEORGE oc/Assistant Professor; b/Jul 15, 1946; h/PO Box 2680, Mississippi State, MS 39762; ba/Miss St; m/Donna M; c/Christopher G; p/Harriet E Hickok, Glens Falls, NY; ed/BA; MS; PhD; pa/Asst Prof Botany Miss St Univ; Genetic & Chromosome Studies Tropical Ferns; Bot Soc Am; AAAS; Sigma Xi; Am Fern Soc; hon/Phi Kappa Phi; Pterid Sect Bot Soc Awd.

HICKS, EVA PAULINE oc/Teacher; Statistician; Librarian; b/Jun 28, 1900; h/Rt 1, Box 450, Andrews, NC 28901; p/Stephen and Alice Swanson Hicks (dec); pa/Ret'd; Tchr, Libn & Study Hall Supvr; Secy to Sch & Supt & Treas Sch Funds; Statistician Andrews Carnegie Lib; cp/Homemaker's Clb; WOC; Konnaheeta Clb; r/Presb; hon/Ribbons for Oil Paintings.

HICKS, WILLIAM TROTTER oc/Economist; b/Mar 15, 1907; h/Chapel Hills, Vicksburg, MS 39180; m/Za-Ida Moore; c/William Jr, Colquit Keeling, Beverly Ann; p/William Wooten Hicks (dec); Matilda Faith Trotter (dec); mil/AUS Corps of Engrs, Chief Ecs Br, Miss River Com (Ret'd); pa/Retired Economist; r/Epis.

HICKSON, CHARLESTINE DAWSON oc/College Administrator; b/Jul 24, 1938; h/1625 Magnolia Dr, Orangeburg, SC 29115; ba/O'burg; m/William F; c/Nina R, William Franklin III, George G O; p/Kemp Dawson, Seattle, WA; Ida V Dawson Blake, Chicago, IL; ed/BA; MEd; pa/Dir Spec Progs Claflin Col; Pres SC Coun Spec Progs; Exec Bd SEn Assn Ednl Opport; cp/Pres Palmetto Aux to Med, Dental & Pharm Assn; Delta Sigma Theta; r/St Luke Presb Ch.

HIEBERT, ELIZABETH BLAKE oc/Civic Worker; b/Jul 18, 1910; h/1517 Randolph, Topeka, KS 66604; m/Homer L (dec); c/Mrs John Beam, Mrs Don Wester, John Bittie, Henry L, David; p/Henry Seavey and Grace Riebeth Blake (dec); ed/BS Tex Univ; cp/Swimming Tchr Normal & Handicapped Persons; Bd Mem: YM, YW-Med Aux, PEO, DAR; DAC; Topeka Beautification; AAUW; Pen Wom; Cousteau; Topeka Sci Fair; Arthritis Foun; IPA; People to People; AARP, NRTA; NAMP; Others; r/Meth; hon/Hon Mem, Delta Kappa Gamma.

HIERS, GERALD LAMAR oc/Guidance Counselor; b/Apr 19, 1939; h/1030 Edgehill Rd, Apt 111, Charlotte, NC 28207; ba/Charlotte; c/Mark Christopher, Erin Kimberly; p/Rudolph V Hiers (dec); Thelma Hiers; ed/BS The Citadel; MEd UNC; PhD Walden Univ; pa/NEA; NCAE; APGA; NCPGA; Devised & Coor'd 1st Sch-wide Behavior Modification Prog Charlotte-Mecklenburg Public Schs & St of NC; Developed & Planned Story-Hour Prog for Pre-Schoolers; Var Other Profl Activs; cp/Kiwanis Clb Mecklenburg Co; RIF; JCs; Big Brothers Inc; Fdr & Dir W Islip Ski Clb; Fdr & Coor 1st Annual Yth Arts & Crafts Fest, Rock Hill (SC); Coor 1st Yth Employmt Ser, Rock Hill; r/Luth; hon/7 Awds in Art Shows, Long Isl (NY) 1969-74; W/W S&SW.

HIGGINBOTHAM, DORIS ROSS oc/Realtor; b/Jan 25, 1926; h/705 E 14th, Casper, WY 82601; ba/Casper; m/Robert Lee (dec); c/Rebecca Hegranes, Kristy Smith, Laurie Jones; p/Albert S and Viola Bumgarner Ross, Ada, OK; ed/BS E Ctl Univ; cp/Pres Higginbotham Realty Inc; Casper Bd Realtors; WBR; WAR; RPAC; WPAC; NARB; NIRB; cp/C of C; Trustee WPAC; r/1st Presb Ch: Deacon; hon/DIB; Notable Ams; Book of Honor.

HIGGINS, BARBARA oc/Sister of Religious Order; Youth Consultant; b/Jun 6, 1935; h/2405 W 5th St, Duluth, MN 55806; ba/Duluth; p/James Clinton and Genevieve

Higgins, Duluth; ed/BS Col St Scholastica; cp/Diocesan Yth Conslt; Dir HS Retreats; Lead & Coor Ldrship Tng; Recruit, Screen & Train Vol Staff; Coor & Ldr 6 Hr Twilights Out (in parishes); r/Cath: OSB.

HIGGINS, EARL BERNARD oc/College Professor; Counselor Educator; b/Dec 20, 1946; h/846 Dewey St, Auburn, AL 36830; ba/Auburn; m/LaValle Coleman; c/Earl Bernard Jr; p/Hazel Marie Higgins, Charleston, SC; ed/BS Claflin Col 1968; MEd SC St Col 1972; EdD Auburn Univ 1976; mil/AUS 1968-70; pa/Auburn Univ: Asst Prof Cnslr Ed 1976-, Instr Cnslr Ed Dept 1974-76, Grad Tchg Asst 1973-74; Cnslr SC St Col, Orangeburg 1971-72; Asst Dean Men Claflin Col 1970-71; Fam Hlth Asst Med Col SC, Charleston, SC 1968; cp/Rotary; Kappa Alpha Psi; r/St Michaels Cath Ch; hon/Phi Delta Kappa; Kappa Delta Pi.

HIGGINS, F EDWARD oc/Educator; b/Nov 29, 1935; h/7660 W 131 St, Palos Heights, IL 60463; ba/Country Club Hills, IL; p/Frank E and Mary Alyce Fahey Higgins, Palos Hgts; ed/BS; MA; MEd; EdD; pa/Tchr Hillcrest HS; Tchr Col St Francis; Lectr; Book

Reviewer; Brit Hist Assn; Am Cath Hist Assn; Ill Hist Soc; Ill & Nat CSS; NSSE; cp/St Alexander Sch Bd; r/Rom Cath; hon/Pi Gamma Mu; Brit Univ F'ship 1962; Fulbright Summer Fellow; Eng Speaking Union Fellow; BSA Awd Merit, Chgo Coun.

HIGGINS, LESTER EDWARD oc/Student; b/Jul 9, 1958; h/508 S H, Hugo, OK 74743; p/Lester and Florence Higgins, Hugo; ed/BS Cand; pa/Student Univ Okla; cp/Col Repubs; r/Ch of God; hon/Okla Hon Soc; Soc Dist'd Am HS Students; OSU Alumni Awd; Beta Sigma Phi S'ship.

HIGNITE, ROBERT E oc/Teacher; b/Oct 6, 1940; h/5119 Central, Indianapolis, IN 46205; ba/Indpls; c/Greg Alan; p/Earl E and Phyllis Hignite, Connersville, IN; ed/BS Ind St Univ 1961; MA Ball St Univ 1968; pa/Sec'dy Tchr Emmerich Manual HS 14 Yrs; Master Diving Instr Divers Supply Co; IIEA; IEA; ISTA; NEA; PADI; CMAS; Cousteau Soc; Oceanic Soc; Intl Oceanographic Foun; cp/YMCA; Past Pres Kiwanis; Luth Sch Bd; Div'g Coor BSA; Past Bd Mem MS; hon/BSA Eagle; St Underwater Photog Yr; Num Intl Awds Underwater Photog.

HILDEBRAND, VERNA L oc/Professor; b/Aug 17, 1924; h/724 Albert, E Lansing, MI 48823; ba/E Lansing; m/John R; c/Carol, Steve; p/Carrell E Butcher (dec); Florence Butcher, Dodge City, KS; ed/BS; MS; PhD; pa/Prof Fam & Child Scis Mich St Univ; Am Home Ecs Assn, Ofcr 1975-77; Nat Assn for Ed Yg Chd; AAUP; NEA; cp/NOW; LWV; hon/Author *Intro to Early Childhood Ed, Guiding Yg Chd, & A Workbook for Introduction to Early Childhood Ed.*

HILEMAN, SALLY JEAN SUGAR oc/-Director; Social Worker; b/Sept 5, 1929; h/4137 N Vecino Dr, #5, Covina, CA 91723; ba/Covina; c/Paul William, Jay Aaron; p/John A and Molly Naomi Aronovich Sugar (dec); ed/BS 1971, MSW 1973 Ariz St Univ; ACSW 1975; LCSW 1977; pa/Dir Clin Social Ser Intercommun Hosp; Psychi Social Worker; Pvt Pract Comprehensive Cnslg Ctr Inc; Profl Supvr Social Work Interns,

Marriage & Fam Cnslr Interns for St Lic'g; Field Instr Cal St Univ; Psychi Conslt: 2 Hosps, 3 Police Agys, Extended Care Facilities; Soc Hosp Social Work Dirs; Am Cancer Soc Oncology Social Workers; Human Sers Org Parliamentn; Nat Assn Social Workers; Nat Assn Clin Social Workers; cp/Secy Hospice E San Gabriel Val Inc; Bd Mem Handicapped Persons Resource Ctr; Bd Dirs E Val Free Clin; Profl Advr Desert Mtl Hlth Assn; r/Jewish; hon/W/W Am Wom.

HILES, WILLIAM GAYLE JR oc/College Administrator; b/Sept 2, 1945; h/1705 Cedar Ln, Nashville, TN 37212; ba/N'ville; p/William G and Virgie O Hiles, Lexington, KY; ed/AB Transylvania Col 1967; MA Univ Durham (England) 1968; pa/Dir Public Info George Peabody Col for Tchrs 1974-; Tenn Col Public Relats Assn; AAUP; Nat Coun Col

Pubs Advrs; Nat Sch Public Relats Assn; cp/Travelers Aid Bd Dirs; Tenn in Corrections, Chperson 1975-76; Tenn Spec Olympics: Pres, Bd Dirs 1977-79; r/Disciples of Christ: Ordained Min; hon/Franklin B Matchette Foun Awd for Excell in Undergrad Tchg; Rotary Foun Awd for Intl Understanding.

HILL, BOBBY L oc/Lawyer; b/Jul 24, 1941; h/Savannah, GA; c/Ashley Conrad; ed/BS cum laude Savannah St Col 1963; JD Howard Univ Sch of Law 1966; pa/Sr Partner Law Firm Hill, Jones & Assocs, Atlanta & Savannah; Cooperating Counsel NAACP Legal Def Fund Inc (NYC); Bd Dirs Nat Assembly for Social Policy & Devel (NYC); Yg Lwyrs & Crim Law Sects Ga & Am Bar Assns; Savannah Bar Assn; cp/Chatham Co Citizens' Adv Com on Commun Improvemt & Urban Renewal; Savannah Area C of C; St Adv Bd Am Civil Liberties Union; Adv Bd Ga Ser Ctr for Elected Ofcls; Adv Bd Exec Inns Am; Ga St Rep, House Dist 127, Var Coms; Var Former Activs; r/Bapt; hon/Awd for Outstg Achmt in Polits, Savannah St Col Nat Alumni Assn; Maj Richard Wright Awd for Continuous Sponsorship of Leg to Receive Human Suffering & Deprivation; Man of Yr, Beta Phi Lamba, Alpha Phi Alpha 1969-70; Dist'd Alumnus Awd, Student Bar Assn (Howard Univ Sch Law); Biogl Listings; Others.

HILL, CAROL oc/Assistant to President; h/388 State St, Brooklyn, NY 11217; ba/New York, NY; p/Preston Lewis Hill (dec); Melinda Cuillard Hill (dec); ed/BA cum laude; MS; pa/Asst to Pres NY Law Jour Seminars Press 1978-; Asst to Sr Prog Atty Pract'g Law Inst, NYC 1977-78; Adj Lectr John Jay Col Crim Justice 1973-77; Adj Lectr Kingsborough Commun Col, Bklyn 1972-73; Tchr, Announcer Tng Studios, NYC 1960-72; Other Former Positions; Spch Commun Assocs 1972-77; World Poets' Resource Ctr: Exec Dir 1973, Exec Secy 1971-72; En Centre, Poetry Soc (London): Exec Dir 1973, Exec Secy 1971-72, Secy 1968-71; IPA; Am Wom in Radio & TV; hon/Hon Doct Social Pedagogy in Arts, Gt China Arts Col 1973; Awd for Outstg Ser to Broadcast through Dedication to Excell & Cont'g Work in Broadcast Tng, Announcer Tng Studios; Crowned w Bicent Hons, IJ Poets Laureate Intl; W/W Am Wom; World W/W Wom; Commun Ldrs & Noteworthy Ams; 2000 Wom Achmt; Other Biogl Listings.

HILL, CONNIE VIRGINIA oc/Teacher; Department Head; b/Jun 26, 1950; h/2715 K,

Galveston, TX 77550; ba/Galveston; p/Rose Forcey, Galveston; ed/BA Tex So Univ; pa/Ctl Sch; Tchr, Hd Dept Fgn Langs, Advr Student Coun & Spanish Clb, Coor Extracurric Activs; NEA; TSTA; GEA; NATSP; cp/Big Brother-Big Sister; Sigma Gamma Rho-Basileus; Secy Black Ladies Distn; NAACP; r/1st Union Bapt Ch; hon/Sigma of Yr (Local); W/W Among Sigma (Nat); 1st Runner-up Tchr of Yr, Galveston; Num Ser Awds; RSVP Awd; Personalities of S.

HILL, DON ROBERT oc/Supervisor; b/Dec 17, 1942; h/303 E Third St, Del Rio, TX 78840; ba/Del Rio; m/Earline Sankey; c/Landon Ned, Jim Earl; p/Rivers W Hill (dec); Ora Davis Hill, Denver, CO; ed/BA Abilene Christian Univ 1964; Tex St Tchg

Cert Univ Tex 1968; pa/Supvr Unemploymt Opers, Tex Employmt Comm; Tex Public Employees Assn; Intl Assn Pers in Employmt Security; cp/BSA: Asst Cubmaster 2 Yrs, Den Ldr 2 Yrs; r/Ch of Christ.

HILL, EARLINE SANKEY oc/Supply Analyst; b/Jul 11, 1942; h/303 E Third, Del Rio, TX 78840; ba/Laughlin AFB, TX; m/Don R; c/Landon Ned, Jim Earl; p/Earl E and Nora S Sankey (dec); ed/BSEd Abilene Christian Col 1964; pa/Supply Analyst, Laughlin AFB; AFGE Local #1749; EEO Cnslr 1974-77; cp/Laughlin AFB Luncheon Clb; Cubscout Den Ldr; Cubscout Com Chm; Little Leag Baseball Refreshmt Com; r/Ch of Christ; hon/Kappa Delta Pi; Outstg Perf Rating.

HILL, ETHEL BROWN oc/Administrative Officer; b/Oct 30, 1932; h/5129 W Running Brook Rd, Columbia, MD 21044; ba/Baltimore, MD; m/Donald B; c/Donna Bernay, Terri Lynn; p/William L Sr and Ethel K Brown, Chester, PA; ed/BA Pa St Univ; MSS Bryn Mawr Col; pa/Adm Ofcr Social Security Adm, Bur Retiremt & Survivor's Ins; Equal Employmt Opport Cnslr Social Security Adm; Other Positions SSA; Hd Med Social Work Sers Adm Staff, Md St Med Assistance Prog; Social Wkr (Child Psychi) Sheppard-Pratt Hosp, Towson, Md; Admr & Supvr Adoption Ser, Del Co Child Care Ser, Media, Pa; Other Positions; Nat Asn Social Wkrs; Acad Cert'd Social Wkrs; Black Fam Life; cp/Pres & Charter Mem Pa St Chapter Alpha Kappa Alpha; Com of 100; LWV; NAACP; Nat Wom's Polit Caucus; Orgr & CoChperson Howard Co Coalition of Citizens Concerned About Proposed Boundary Changes; PTA Activs; 208 Public Adv Com Water Quality Control; Howard Co: Mtl Hlth Adv Com, Citizens Task Force on Crime Preven & Crim Justice; Others; r/St John's Bapt Ch: Public Relats Com; hon/Spkr, Roast Given in Hon of James Rouse, Developer Columbia; Featured in "Spkg of Wom", Balto Afro-Am; Del Countian of Month; Mortar Bd; Biogl Listings; Others.

HILL, FLOSSIE J oc/Assistant Professor; b/Jan 1; h/2408 Greenmount Dr, Albany, GA 31705; ba/Albany; m/James L; c/Deron, Toussaint; p/C Jackson, Brunswick, GA; E B Johnson, St Simon Isl, GA; ed/BS summa cum laude Ft Val St; MA Univ Ia-Ia City; pa/Asst Prof Albany St Col; NCTE; CCCC; IRA; Wil Lou Gray Rdg Coun; r/Urban Leag; NAACP; r/Prot; hon/Alpha Kappa Mu; Personalities of S; W/W Am Cols & Univs.

HILL, GEORGE B oc/Registered

Professional Mechanical Engineer; b/Feb 1, 1914; h/4610 Locust Lane, Salt Lake City, UT 84117; ba/Same; m/Thelma Irene Orman; c/Rust Jane Soper, Charles Philip; p/John Ensign Hill (dec); Ivy Blood Hill, Riverside, CA; ed/BSME Montana St Col 1935; pa/Pres & Owner Hill's Engrg (Celina, Ohio), (Mansfield, Ohio) & SLC 1954-; Pres & Dir, Newspaper Equipmt Co (SLC) 1972-; Pres & Dir, McGee & Hogan Machine Co (SLC) 1970-72; Instr Mgmt Classes, Utah Tech Col 1963-66; Other Former Positions; Reg'd Profl Mech Engr: Pa, Ohio, Utah; Chm Power Machinery Div, Am Soc Agri Engrs 1951-52; Chm Com to Standardize Baling Wire for Hay Balers, Farm Equipmt Inst 1951-52; Life Mem, Am Soc Mech Engrs; Life Mem, Am Soc Auto Engrs; Others; cp/Past Pres, Celina (Ohio) Lions Clb; Past Scoutmaster, BSA; r/LDS: 1st Cnslr in En States Mission & Gt Lakes Mission; Past Pres En Atlantic States Mission; Host on Temple Sq; SS Tchr; Others; hon/Holder 63 US Patents & Sev Canadian Patents; Tau Beta Pi; W/W: Commerce & Indust, Am, E, MW, W, Engrg, Ohio, Commun Ser, Others.

HILL, GERALD WAYNE oc/State Legislator; b/Jun 20, 1947; h/11,405 Spicewood Pkwy, Austin, TX 78750; ba/Austin; m/Donna; c/Carolee, Julie Ann; p/Clyde and Alta Mae Hill, Austin; ed/BS; pa/Austin Bd Realtors; cp/St Rep; Chm Mar Dimes; Boys Clb; r/Epis; hon/Outstg Yg Men Am.

HILL, JAMES LEE oc/Associate Professor; b/Dec 10, 1941; h/904-B College Dr, Albany, GA 31705; ba/Albany; m/Flo J; c/-Deron James, Toussaint LeMarc; p/Willie Lee and Vanilla Hill (dec); ed/BS; MA; PhD; pa/Assoc Prof Eng Albany St Col; AAUP; NCTE; CLA; CCCC; CAAS; ADE; AKM; cp/Bd Dirs Albany Urban Leag; r/AME Meth; hon/Atlanta Univ Fellow; NEH Sum Fellow; NEH Fellow, Univ Ia.

HILL, JAMES MARK oc/General Surgeon; b/Oct 7, 1918; h/1222 Dovecrest Rd, Memphis, TN 38134; p/Martin Luther and Lillian Addington Hill (dec); ed/BA 1940, MA 1942, BS 1945 Univ Miss; MD Jefferson Med Col Phila; mil/USNR MC 1955-57, Lt; pa/Ret'd Gen Surg; Pvt Pract Memphis 1954-74; Assoc Prof Surg Anatomy Univ Miss 1951-55; Surg Residency Bapt Meml Hosp, Memphis 1950-54; Other Former Positions; AMA; Am Col Surgs; Am Soc Abdominal Surgs; So & Tenn Med Assns; Memphis & Shelby Co Med Socs; Phi Chi; c/32° Mason; Am Orchid Soc; Mid-S Orchid Soc.

HILL, MALCOLM LANSDEN oc/Minister; College President; b/Jan 12, 1934; h/PO Box 532, Cookeville, TN 38501; ba/Same; m/Billie Ruth; c/David, Victor, Tammi; p/M L and Cecil Hill, Livingston, TN; ed/BA; LLD; pa/Pres Tenn Bible Col; r/Ch of Christ; hon/Pres Student Body, Freed-Hardeman Col.

HILL, MAY DAVIS oc/Museum Curator & Archivist; h/191 Baldwin Ln, Birmingham, MI 48009; ba/Ann Arbor, MI; m/William R Nolte; p/Marion Stuart and May Holmes Davis (dec); ed/BA; MA; BSLS Univ NC-CH; Further Studies Inst Fine Arts, NY Univ; pa/Mus Curator & Archivist Mich Hist Collections, Univ Mich-Ann Arbor; Vis Lectr & Res Curator Univ Mich; Asst Curator Prints & Drawings Phila Mus Art; Acting Curator Prints Art Mus, Princeton Univ; Curator Ackland Art Ctr, UNC-CH; Soc Am Archivists, Com on Aural & Graphic Records; Wom's Res Clb Univ Mich; VP NC Museums Coun; Secy NC St Art Soc; cp/Belgian Am Alumni Assn, Exec Com; hon/Phi Beta Kappa; Beta Phi Mu; S'ships; NY Univ, Belgian Am Ednl Foun, UNC.

HILL, MICHAEL EMMANUEL oc/Research Administrator; b/Apr 5, 1943; h/7120 S Ingleside, Chicago, IL 60619; ba/Chgo; m/Margarite Lewers; c/Michael Jr, Trisha, Tracy; p/Sidney Batson Hill (dec); Margaret Boyce, Baltimore, MD; ed/BS (EE);

BS (Computer Sci); mil/AUS Air Def Command, Sgt 1963, Field Engr; pa/Coauthor "Technol Transfer & Market Res: Essential Tools for Managing New Product Commercialization", Indust World 1978; cp/Guest Lectr Baltimore City Col 1978; r/Meth; hon/Nom'd for F'ship, Brit Interplanetary Soc; Public Ser Awd, Nat Space Inst; W/W MW.

HILL, SANDRA VERNICE oc/Auditor; Management Analyst; b/Sept 21, 1951; h/1884 Columbia Rd NW, #508, Washington, DC 20009; ba/Wash DC; p/Wellington A and Marie Wooden Hill, St Petersburg, VA; ed/AAS; BA; MPA; pa/Auditor-Mgmt Analyst US Gen Acct Ofc; Am Soc Public Adm; Acad Polit Sci; Intl City Mgmt Assn; ASPA; Polit Sci Assn; Com Wom in Public Adm; Yg Prof Forum; Nat Coun Career Wom; Toastmasters Intl AAUW; AAUP; cp/Nat Wom's Polit Caucus; Nat Wom's Party; r/Bapt; hon/Pi Alpha Alpha; Phi Delta Gamma; Phi Theta Kappa; Delta Psi Omega; Personalities of S.

HILL, WILHELMINA oc/Writer; Lecturer; Consultant; b/Aug 29, 1902; h/4000 Cathedral Ave, Washington, DC 20016; ba/Same; p/William E and Ida R Hill (dec); ed/BS; MA; EdD; mil/Supreme Command Area of Pacific; cp/Ret'd Prof Univ Denver; Social Scist US Ofc of Ed HEW 1949-72; cp/Soroptimist Intl; VP Chapt 100, AARP (Wash DC).

HILLDRUP, LUCILLE PENNEY oc/-Retired Educator, Businesswoman; b/Jul 17, 1909; h/PO Box 213, Fredericksburg, VA 22401; m/James Russell (dec); p/Eustace M and Ada Bruce Penney, Bowling Green, VA; ed/Grad FSTC; pa/Tchr; Prin; Hotel Owner-Operator; Col Aths; cp/Vol Red Cross; r/Bapt: Country Ch Organist; hon/Judged Best in Hobby Ceramics, Va St Show.

HILLER, ARTHUR GARFIN oc/Film Director; b/Nov 22, 1923; h/1218 Benedict Canon Dr, Beverly Hills, CA 90210; ba/Burbank, CA; m/Gwen; c/Henryk, Erica; p/Harry and Rose Hiller; ed/MA Univ Toronto; mil/Royal Canadian AF, Flying Ofcr; pa/Film Dir Burbank Studios; Bd Govs Acad Motion Picture Arts & Sci; Dirs Coun Dirs Guild Am; r/Jewish; hon/Best Dir Nom: DGA, AMPAS; Best Dir: Golden Globe, NY Fgn Press; Doct Laurate, Imperial Order Constantine; Others.

HILLERY, MARY JANE oc/Managing Editor; b/Sept 15, 1931; h/66 Willow Rd, Sudbury, MA 01776; ba/Acton, MA; c/Thomas; p/Donato Larato and Porzia Avellis, Boston, MA; ed/BS; mil/USN 1950-54, BuPers Washington, DC; USAR Maj, Liaison Ofcr to Mil Acad W Point 1975-; pa/Newspaper Mng Editor Beacon Pub'g Co; Mass Dept Secy Resv Ofcrs Assn US; Past Pres Boston Br Nat Leag Am Pen Wom; Past Pres Sudbury Ch Intl BPW Clbs; cp/Sudbury Sch Com; Var Town Appts; r/Christian; hon/Medal of Apprec, Intl Order DeMolay; Cert of Apprec, Def Civic Preparedness Agy, BSA; S'ship; Editor of Yr; Others.

HILTON, HARVEY LEE oc/Retired Realtor; b/Dec 7, 1888; h/38415 McKenzie Hwy, Springfield, OR 97477; m/Geraldine Lucille; p/Newton H and Surrilda Smith Hilton (dec); mil/Regular Army WWI; pa/Ret'd 1974; Owner Harvey L Hilton Realtor 1946-74; Real Est Bus, Eugene, Oreg 1938; w Ford Motor Co 1932-37; VP Pearl Novelties Co Inc, NYC 1921-32; Underwriter Oil Co 1920-21; Past Pres Eugene Realty Bd; Nat Assn Real Est Bds; cp/Past Cmdr Am Legion; Univ Oreg Alumni Assn; Dem; Mason; Shriner; Life Mem McKenzie River Lodge #195 AF&AM; Hon Mem Eugene Lions Clb; Perm Cont'g Mem Shriners Hosp for Crippled Chd; Others; r/Prot; hon/Hon Life Mem, St Assn Real Est Bds; W/W: W&MW, Fin & Indust, Commerce & Indust; DIB; IPA; Commun Ldrs Am; Personalities W&MW; 2000 Men Achmt.

HINDMAN, EDWARD EVANN II

oc/Research Meteorologist; b/Sept 26, 1942; h/536 Mary Ann, Ridgecrest, CA 93555; ba/China Lake, CA; m/Nancy Maxson; c/Kathryn Cecilia, Andrew Asa, Joseph Edward; p/Edward E and Josephine L Hindman, Powell Butte, OR; ed/BS Univ Utah 1965; MS Colo St Univ 1967; PhD Univ Wash 1975; pa/Res Meteorologist, Hd Atmospheric Interaction Sect, Atmospheric Applications Br NWC 1974-; Pt-time Instr Meteorol Cerro Coso Commun Col, R'crest 1978 (Spring); NWC Fellow Univ Washington, Seattle 1972-74; Other Former Positions; Soaring Soc Am; Am Meteorol Soc, Hampton Rds Chapt Secy 1970-71; Royal Meteorol Soc; Weather Modification Assn; Sigma Xi; Am Geophy Union; Mobile & Remote Monitoring Tech Coor'g Com, Air Pollution Control Assn; r/Grace Luth Ch, R'crest: Ch Coun 1976-78; hon/Dist'd Alumni Awd, Luth HS (Los Angeles, Cal); 1st Pl Slide Rule Paper Contest, Colo St Univ Student Engrg Pub; W/W in W; DIB; Men of Achmt; Num Profl Pubs; Others.

HINDSLEY, MARK HUBERT oc/Emeritus Director of Bands; Professor; b/Oct 18, 1905; h/1 Montclair Rd, Urbana, IL 61801; m/Helena Alberts; c/Harold, Marilyn Haynie, Robert; p/Orvah L and Goldie Warner Hindsley (dec); ed/AB 1925; AM 1927; Hon DMus Ind Univ 1972; mil/USAAF 1942-46, Capt to Lt Col, Music Ofcr AF Tng Command, 6 Months Fac Biarritz Am Univ (France); pa/Univ Ill: Asst Dir & Dir Bands, Assoc to Prof Music 1934-70, Dir & Prof Emeritus 1970-; Other Former Positions; Pres Col Band Nat Assn 1946-47; Pres Am Bandmasters Assn 1957-58; Sum Fac Other Cols & Univs; Reschr; Nat Band Assn; MENC: Edit Bd, Com Chm; Ill Music Edrs Assn; Am Soc Composers & Conductors; cp/Rotary Clb, Champaign; Ind Univ & Univ Ill Alumni Assns; Loyal Order Beaded Belts; Ind Soc Chgo; Others; r/1st U Meth Ch, Urbana; hon/Pi Kappa Lambda; Phi Beta Mu; Phi Mu Alpha; Cit of Merit, Univ Ill Foun; Fellow, Intl Inst Arts & Lttrs; Acad Wind & Percussion Arts, Nat Band Assn; Dist Ser to Music Awd, Kappa Kappa Psi; Goldman Awd, Am Sch Band Dirs Assn; Compositions & Concert Band Arrangemts Pub'd; Others.

HINEMAN, ANNA L oc/Secretary; h/725 Sportsman Ln, Kennett Sq, PA 19348; ba/Glen Mills, PA; m/Edwin S Sr (dec); c/Edwin S Jr, Suzanne Jenkins, Clifford O, Donald Charles and Martin Litz; p/George H and Florence Gibney Litz (dec); ed/Beacom Bus Col; pa/Secy Tri Co Supply Co (Lumber Bus); Oil & Watercolor Artist; Cert'd NAUI Scuba Diver; cp/Var Commun & Sch Activs; Com-wom 10 Yrs; hon/Num Awds for Paintings; 3 One-Man Shows; Paintings Rep'd in Pvt & Public Collections.

HINES, DONALD DEIBERT oc/Minister; b/Apr 10, 1925; h/4404 W 17th, Topeka, KS 66604; ba/Topeka; m/Thelma L; c/Gary G, Sandra L; p/Calvin Newton and A Ora Alpha Deibert Hines (dec); ed/BA York Col 1945; MDiv U Sem 1951; pa/U Meth Min; Dir Yth Work, Christian Ed Conf Prog; cp/Pres PTSA; Kiwanis; Mem Supt Adv Comm, Act BSA; r/U Meth; hon/Nat Hon Soc; W/W Am Col.

HINES, DOROTHY ANNE oc/Assistant Professor; b/Nov 20, 1925; h/904 Maple, Ruston, LA 71270; ba/Ruston; p/Silas H and Helen Stewart Hines; ed/BA La Tech Univ; MS Univ Ark; pa/Asst Prof Elem Ed A E Phillips Lab Sch, La Tech Univ; Past Pres N La Rdg Assn; Secy Caddo Tchrs Assn; r/Bapt; hon/ADK; KDPi; Mortar Bd.

HINES, DOROTHY LYNN oc/Manager; b/Nov 30, 1944; h/1882 E Carmen, Tempe, AZ 85283; ba/Phoenix, AZ; m/Eldridge D; p/Adam Pobar, Organ, NM; ed/BBA; pa/Mgr Fin Systems & Procedures; Nat Assn Accts; cp/Zeta Tau Alpha; r/Interdenom; hon/Motorola Exec Inst, Motorola Phoenix Adv Coun.

HINGSON, ROBERT ANDREW oc/-Physician; h/816 Grandview Ave, Pittsburg, PA 15211; ba/Pgh; m/Gussie D; c/Dickson

James, Roberta Ann, Andrew Tobian, Ralph Waldo, Luke Lockhart; p/Robert Andrew and Elloree Haynes Hingson (dec); ed/AB; MD; mil/USPHS: Asst Surg 1939-42, PA Asst Surg 1942-43, Surg 1943-50, Med Dir (Resv) 1965-; pa/Pres & Dir Brother's Brother Foun 1958-; Chm Action Com World Fdn Socs Anesthesiologists; Pres & Dir Anesthesia Ednl & Relief Foun; Trustee Rel Heritage Am 1968; Prof Anesthesiol Univ Pgh Schs Med & Dentistry 1968-73; Prof Public Hlth Pract Univ Pgh Grad Sch Public Hlth 1968-75; Dir Anesthesiol Magee-Wom's Hosp 1968-73; Fdr-Prof Anesthesia Wn Resv Univ Sch Med, Cleveland, Ohio 1951-68; Other Former Positions; Bd Dirs Am Assn Maternal & Infant Hlth 1957-68; Conslt; Guest Fac Mem; Fellow: Am Col Anesthesia, AMA, Fac Anesthesia Royal Col Surgs (England), Intl Col Anesthetists, Sigma Xi, Pi Kappa Alpha, Intl Col Surgs; r/Bapt: Deacon; hon/Cert of Med Merit, Republic of Honduras; Dist'd Ser Cit, Universitario de Caracad, Venezuela; Hon Mem, Col Med & Surg Costa Rica; Ser Cit, Cruz Roja Costarricense (Red Cross); Ch Civic Leag; Num Profl Pubs; Others.

HINKLE, BLANCHE ELIZABETH oc/Educational Administrator; b/May 29, 1918; h/Old Fields, WV 26845; ba/510 Ashby St, Moorefield, WV 26836; p/James O Hinkle, Old Fields; Mary Arnold Hinkle (dec); ed/BA Shepherd Col; MA WVa Univ; pa/Current Co Rdg Admr, WVa St Dept Ed Rdg Improvemt Prog; Gen Supvr Instn Hardy Co 1961-; Asst Prof Glenville St Col 1959-61; Former Classroom Tchr; Life Mem NEA; WVa & Hardy Co Ed Assns; Nat, St & Reg Assns for Supvn & Curric Devel; Reg Rdg Coun; Alpha Sigma Tau; Kappa Delta Pi; Delta Kappa Gamma; Pres Eta Chapt Delta Kappa Gamma; Var Other Ofcs; cp/Mem Var Local Orgs; r/Moorefield Ch of Brethren: Currently Moderator, Bd Chm, SS Tchr, Supt SS, Mem Bds; hon/Outstg Edr Am, Acad Am Edrs; Outstg Tchrs Exceptl Ed; W/W Sch Dist Ofcls.

HINNANT, OLLEN B oc/Lawyer, Assistant General Counsel; b/Jan 16, 1931; h/1 McDonough St, Montclair, NJ 07042; ba/Newark, NJ; m/Ella Marie Lilly; c/Denise, Greg, Cheryl; p/Ollen B Hinnant (dec); Grace Edmonds Hinnant, Lexington, KY; ed/BA Ky St; JD Univ Ky; Postgrad NYU; pa/Asst Gen Counsel Lane Dept Prudential Ins Co; Pvt Pract; Ky Bar 1955; NJ Bar 1963; US Supreme Ct Bar; Nat Bar Assn; ABA; NJ St Bar Assn; cp/VP Planned Parenthood Essex Co; Newark Fresh Air Fund; Milford Reservation; Newark Day Ctr; Newark YMWCA; r/Bapt; hon/Housing Awd, Union Devel Corp; Nat Dental Assn.

HINSON, JON oc/Legislator; b/Mar 16, 1942; ba/Washington, DC; p/Clifton and Lyndell Newman Hinson; ed/BA Univ Miss 1964; mil/USMC 1964-70; pa/US Capitol Page (for Cong-man John Bell Williams-Miss) 1959; Doorman US Ho of Reps 1967; Leg Asst to Miss Cong-man Charlie Griffin 1968; Adm Asst 1969; Adm Asst Cong-man Thad Cochran 1973-77; Elected to US Ho of Reps 4th Dist Miss 1978-; Mem House Com on Bkg, Fin & Urban Affairs, Ed & Labor Coms.

HINZ, RANDAL RICHARD oc/Artist; b/Aug 2, 1944; h/1425 Lakeside Dr 302, Oakland, CA 94612; p/Richard Hinz, San Jose, CA; Myrna Wilderson, San Jose; ed/Att'd Sheaffers Sch Design; pa/Num Shows; Included in 6 Art Museums; cp/Mem Oakland Mus; r/Cath; hon/Num Awds in Art & Creative Writing.

HIRAYAMA, TETSU oc/Teacher; b/Mar 1, 1923; h/1553 Thurston Ave, Honolulu, HI 96822; ba/Honolulu; m/Betsy T; c/Lynn A, Shirley S; p/George Takuzo and Taka Kido Hirayama (dec); ed/BA Andrews Univ; MA San Jose St Univ; MLS Univ Hi; pa/Nat Coun for Social Studies; IPA; Am Security Coun; r/SDA; hon/Personalities W&MW, DIB, W/W in W; Nat Social Dir.

HIRSCHBERG, BESSE BRYNA oc/Social Worker; b/Aug 12; h/2 Stuyvesant Oval, New York, NY 10009; ba/Same; p/Sigmund and Lottie Popik Hirschberg; ed/BA Hunter Col; Num Grad Studies; pa/NYC Dept Social Sers; Supvr Social Ser Casewkrs & Clerical Staff Bur Public Asst 1968-75, Supvr PREP & Conslt Div Employmt & Rehab (Anti-Poverty Proj) 1965-68, Dir Day Ctr Prog for Older Persons Bur Spec Sers 1965; Other Former Activs; Lectr; TV Appearances; Bus & Profl Chapt Am ORT; Pres Assn Supvrs NYC Dept Wel; NY Leag BPW: Chm Leg Com, 1st VP & Current Pres; Am Soc Psychodrama & Group Therapy; NAm Assn Alcoholism Progs; hon/Pub'd Author; W/W Am Wom; DIB; Intl W/W Commun Ser; Notable Ams Bicent Era; Commun Ldrs & Noteworthy Ams; World W/W Wom; Others.

HIRSHBERG, RUTH oc/Executive Director; b/Oct 11, 1925; h/402 E 42 St, Paterson, NJ 07504; ba/Paterson; m/Charles; c/Barbara, Diana; p/Samuel and Frances Dall (dec); pa/Exec Dir: Info/Spec Events Paterson, Sr Skills/Crafts/Boutiques Prog Passaic Co; Bd Mem Clin for Mtl Hlth Sers Passaic Co; Bd Mem & Past Pres Paterson Aux Daughs Miriam Home for Aged; Treas Great Falls Devel Corp; Paterson Coun on Aging; Passaic Co Com of Aged Providers; cp/Chm Gt Falls Fest 3rd Yr; Mem Falls Dist Boy Scout Adv Bd; Paterson Girls Clb Am; Paterson Residents Org; Temple Emanuel, Ort, Hadassah, Order of Goldent Chain, B'nai B'rith Wom; Var Former Activs; r/Jewish; hon/Recog Awd, Vet's Coun; Civic Awd, Paterson's Citizens Commun Devel; Dist'd Citizen Awd; Meritorious Awd Title I, Ctl Parent Coun.

HIRT, FRED DENIS oc/Executive Director; b/Sept 9, 1943; h/220 W San Marino Dr, Miami Beach, FL 33139; ba/Miami; c/Shari Jo, Jennifer; p/Rose Pitterman, Hollywood, FL; ed/MHA; BBA; pa/Exec Dir Miami Jewish Home & Hosp for Aged 1969-; Adm Surg Div Montefiore Hosp Med Ctr, Bronx, NY 1966-69; Bd Dirs Nat Assn Jewish Homes for Aging; Nsg Home & Leg Coms Fla Assn Homes of Aging; Clin Instr Barry Col; Instr: Fla Intl Univ Grad Sch, Univ Miami Grad Sch Bus; Fla Area Agy on Aging Inc; Spec Conslt Bd Ed, Progs on Gerontol; Mem Ho of Dels Am Assn of Homes for Aging; Fla Intl Univ Adv Hlth Com; Long-Term Planning Com Hlth Systems Agy S Fla; Am Col Nsg Home Admrs; Conslt Metro Dade Co Ad-Hoc Congregate Housing Com; Others; cp/Bd Dirs Tri-City Commun Assn; Miami-Dade Jr Col Adv Bd; Fla St Rep ANHA Reg III Day Care; Mem City of Miami NE Adv Com; U Way Activs; r/Jewish; hon/Pub'd Author.

HITCHENS, CHARLES NORWOOD oc/Artist; b/Oct 29, 1926; h/620 W Valley Rd, Strafford, PA 19087; ba/Strafford-Wayne, PA; p/Charles Hitchens (dec); Corrie Hitchens, Wayne, PA; ed/Att'd Univ of Ill & Pa Acad Fine & Applied Arts; pa/Am Fdn Arts; The Art Assn; IPA; cp/Smithsonian Instn; Nat Trust for Hist Preserv; Acad Polit & Social Sci; r/Bapt; hon/Intl W/W Intells; Notable Ams; Commun Ldrs & Noteworthy Ams; Other Biogl Listings.

HITCHCOCK, CARL D (BUCKY) oc/Minister; b/Jan 22, 1941; h/615 S McGregor, Carthage, MO 64836; ba/Carthage; m/Cindy; c/Ryan, Melissa; p/Carl D Hitchcock (dec); Capitola E Hitchcock; ed/BA; MDiv; DMin; mil/USN; pa/Pastoral Activs; Cnslg; cp/Lions Clb; r/So Bapt.

HITT, JANET RUSSELL oc/Aviation Safety Inspector; b/Jan 13, 1929; h/36647 Sugar Pine Ct, Newark, CA 94560; ba/Oakland, CA; m/William C Jr; c/William C III, David M; p/Edward A and Beatrice Burnell Russell, Rosemont, PA; ed/AA Stephens Col; pa/Fed Aviation Adm, Aviation Safety Inspector, Opers; Flight Instr & Charter Pilot: NJ, New Castle (Del), St Petersburg (Fla); Co Pilot Bellanca Aircraft Corp; Chief Pilot & Opers Mgr W Indies Airways, San Juan, PR; Flight Instr; Tng Specialist Fed Aviation Adm, Seattle Flight Standards Dist Ofc; Others; cp/Mem The Ninety Nines Inc; Soc Air Safety Investigators; Collie Clb Am Inc; Santa Clara Val Kennel Clb; r/Presb; hon/Flight Instr of Yr 1974, San Jose; Aviatrix of Yr, Santa Clara Ninety Nines.

HIXSON, ALLIE CORBIN oc/Educator; Women's Rights Activist; b/May 28, 1924; h/Rt 4, Bos 502, Greensburg, KY 42743; m/William Forrest; c/Mary Emma, Clarence Hervey, Walter Lawrence; p/Alfred B Corbin (dec); Emma Triplett Corbin, Columbia, KY; ed/BA Okla St Univ 1949; MA 1961, PhD 1969 Univ of Louisville; pa/Tchr of English & Humanities; Author of Book on Scottish Poetry; cp/Active in Wom's Orgs: Chrperson Ky Wom's Agenda Coalition, IWY Cont'g Com; r/Unitarian; hon/Phi Kappa Phi; Hon Mem, Delta Kappa Gamma; Fac Tchg Awd, AAUW.

HLAVINKA, ANTHONY CHARLES oc/Farmer; Professional Engineer; b/Sept 1, 1947; h/PO Box 27, East Bernard, TX 77435; ba/E Bernard; m/Phyllis Arlt; c/Brian Charles, Stephen Jacob, Thomas Frank; p/Frank C and Lillian Poessel Hlavinka, E Bernard; ed/BS Tex A&M Univ; pa/Reg'd Profl Engr Tex; Am Soc Profl Engrs; Tex Soc Profl Engrs; Am Soc Ag Engrs; cp/Tex Farmers Union: Co Pres & St Full Bd Dir; Ks of C; r/Cath; hon/W/W.

HOADE, JANE RICHTER oc/Attorney at Law; b/Jun 13, 1921; h/9301 SW 54th St, Miami, FL 33165; ba/Miami; c/James Donald, Joel Taylor; p/Otto George and Nannie Powell Richter; ed/BA Fla So Col 1942; JD Univ Miami Law Sch 1953; pa/Assoc'd w Firm Blackwell, Walker, Gray, Powers, Flick & Hoehl, Miami (Real Est Div) 1975-; Dade Co Title Status Atty for Lwyr's Title Guaranty Fund, Orlando, Fla 1973-75; Other Former Positions; Beta Theta Chapt Kappa Beta Pi; Soc Bar 1st Jud Circuit Fla 1955-58; Dade Co Bar Assn; Fla Bar; Nat & Fla Assns Wom Lwyrs; ABA; cp/Life Mem Intl Toastmistress Clbs; Nat Fdn BPW Clbs; Nat & Fla Assn Parliamentns; Zonta Intl; Former Capt CAP; IPA; r/Presb; hon/W/W Am Wom; World W/W Wom; Wom in Bus, NAm Edition; Intl W/W: Commun Ser, Intells; DIB; Commun Ldrs & Noteworthy Ams; Book of Honor.

HOAG, CHARLES RICHARD oc/Instructor; b/May 5, 1941; h/8250 Park Place Blvd #302, Houston, TX 77017; ba/LaMarque, TX; m/Lisbeth Joan; p/Charles Chandler Hoag, Port Arthur, TX; Evelyn Eager Hoag (dec); ed/BA Tex Wesleyan Col 1963; MA Univ Houston-Clear Lake 1978; pa/Instr Drama LaMarque HS; Tex St Tchr's Assn; NEA; Alpha Psi Omega; cp/Theatre Adv Bd Col of Mainland; r/St Paul's U Meth Ch, Houston: Mem; hon/LaMarque Edr of Yr 1977; Dir 1st Pl Univ Interscholastic Leag St, 4A One Act Play Competition 1977.

HOARD, YVONNE WALKER oc/Assistant Professor; Athletic Director; b/Nov 22, 1922; h/815 E Dunklin St, Jefferson City, MO 65101; ba/Jefferson City; m/Charles M; c/Adrienne, Charles Jr, Andrea; p/A M and Hauzie J Walker (dec); ed/BS Howard Univ; Masters Univ Mich-AA; pa/Lincoln Univ: Dir Wom's Aths, Asst Prof Hlth & PE, Liaison Ofcr Nat Yth Sports Prog; Coach Girls' Basketball Team Fla A&M Univ Lab HS; Other Former Positions; AAHPER; Ctl Dist Assn PE Col Wom; St Mbrship Chm Mo Assn HPER; Secy Mo Assn for Intercollegiate Aths for Wom; cp/Bd Dirs: Am Cancer Soc (Cole Co Div), Thomas Jefferson Lib Sys; Former Mem Bd Dirs: Jefferson City Fam YMCA, Jefferson City Wom's Bowling Assn; r/2nd Bapt Ch: Chperson Deaconess Bd.

HOARE, TYLER JAMES oc/Sculptor; Printmaker; Designer; b/Jun 5, 1940; h/30 Menlo Pl, Berkeley, CA 94707; ba/Albany, CA; m/Kathy Joyce; c/Janet Elaine; p/Melvin and Dorotha Hoare, Joplin, MO; ed/BFA Univ Ks 1963; pa/Instr Univ Cal-B 1973-74; Guest Lectr Var Ednl Insts & Civic Orgs; Num One Man Shows incl: Stuart Gallery (Berkeley, Cal) 1978, Spiva Art Ctr (Mo So St Col) 1977, Purdue Univ Gallery 1 (W Lafayette, Ind) 1976, Daly City Civic Ctr (Daly City, Cal) 1975, San Mateo Arts Coun

Sunshine Gallery (San Mateo, Cal) 1975, Others; Num Invitational & Juried Exhbns 1963-77 incl'g: (1977:) Univ Waterloo Art Gallery (Ontario, Canada), Reconstruction Art (Rotterdam, Holland), Chinese Junk (San Francisco Bay), Art Dept Visual Arts Bldg Univ Ga (Athens, Ga), Others, (1976:) New Reform Art Ctr (Aalst, Belgium), San Francisco Art Inst, Jesse Besser Mus (Alpena, Mi), Gardiner Art Gallery (Stillwater, Okla), Others, (1975:) Corres Art Exhibit Pierce Col (Cal), Oakland (Cal) Mus's Archives Cal Art, SF Art Fest, Num Others; SF Mus Art; SF Art Inst; Oakland Mus Assn; Ctr for Visual Arts (Oakland); Metal Arts Guild (SF); Nat Soc Lit & Arts; Los Angeles Print Soc; Richmond Art Ctr; Works Rep'd in: Atherton Gallery (Menlo Park, Cal) & ADI Gallery (SF); Guest Curator Ctr Gallery Univ Cal 1973, 74; hon/Age of Enlightmt Awd, T M Berkeley World Plan Ctr; 4th Annual Bay Area Graphics Competition, DeAnza Col; Jurors' Choice Awd, Westart Graphics '70; Merit Awd, 22nd Annual SF Art Fest; Pubs & Reviews; Others.

HOBBS, CECIL oc/Consultant; b/Apr 22, 1907; h/"Hobbs Knob", 5100 Backlick Rd, Annandale, VA 22003; ba/Same; m/Cecile; c/Mary Louise; p/John Alva and Mary Belva Whitten Hobbs (dec); ed/BA Univ Ill; BD, ThM Colgate-Rochester; pa/Lib of Cong: Hd So Sect 1958-72, Specialist on SE Asia 1943-58, Conslt; Exec Secy Conf on Am Lib Resources on So Asia 1957-60; Conslt Philippine Projs Subcom Am Lib Assn 1960-68; Survey SE Asian Collections Columbia Univ 1967; Mem PL 480 Team to Indonesia (Lib of Cong) 1963; Conslt on SE Asia Australian Nat Univ Lib, Canberra, Australia 1972-73; Pres Washington Oriental Clb 1950; cp/Exec Com Lib Friends, Annandale Lib; r/Meth Ch, A'dale; hon/Lib of Cong Awds: for Meritorious Ser, for Superior Achmt.

HOBBS, SONIA A B oc/Registered Nurse; b/Feb 3, 1945; h/6700 Cabot Dr, Nashville, TN 37209; ba/N'ville; m/George Ira (dec); c/Christopher Alan; p/Antonio R and Francisca A Blanco (dec); ed/BS; pa/RN Parkview Hosp; Am Assn Critical Care Nurses; Am Heart Assn; Mid Tenn Heart Assn; r/Rom Cath; hon/Timawa Scholar 1961-62.

HOBBY, WILLIAM PETTUS oc/Newspaper & Broadcast Executive; b/Jan 19, 1932; h/1506 S Blvd, Houston, TX 77006; ba/-Houston; m/Diana Poteat; c/Laura, Paul, Andrew, Katherine; p/William Pettus Hobby (dec); Oveta Culp Hobby, Houston; ed/BA Rice Univ 1953; mil/USN 1953-57, Lt (jg); pa/Mem & Ofcr Num Profl Orgs; cp/Lt Gov Tex 1973-; Mem Num Civic Orgs; r/Prot; hon/Outstg Yg Texan 1965.

HOCHBERG, FREDERICK GEORGE oc/Accountant; b/Jul 4, 1913; h/6760 Hillpark Dr, Los Angeles, CA 90068; ba/Burbank, CA; c/Frederick George, Ann; p/Frederick Joseph and Lottie A LeGendre Hochberg; ed/BA UCLA 1937; pa/Solar Engrg Co Inc: VP, Gen Mgr 1977-; VP Vicalton SA Mexico 1974-; VP & Gen Mgr Mo Hickory Corp 1972-74; William L Pereira Assocs, Planners, Archs, Engrs 1967-72; VP, Treas, Dir Bus Affairs; Other Former Positions; Soc Cal Accts; Mensa; Am Arbitration Assn Panel; LA C of C; Secy Avalon City Planning Com 1956-58; Other Profl Activs; cp/VChm Town Hall W; Dir & Pres LA Child Guid Clin;

Former Chm Friends of Avalon Foun; Former Mayor City of Avalon; Others; hon/Man of Yr, Catalina Isl 1956; Pub'd Author; W/W: W, Fin & Indust, World, Cal; DIB; 2000 Men Achmt; Blue Book.

HODGDON, SHIRLEY LAMSON oc/-Dental Hygienist; b/Sept 24, 1921; h/10 Kent St, Portsmouth, NH 03801; ba/P'mouth; m/Richard Wyman; c/Marilynn Levinson, William W, Clifton L; p/Everett C and Bessie R Halse Lamson (dec); ed/Reg'd Dental Hygienist; cp/Forsyth Alumni Assn; Former NH St Repub; NH Adv Coun Small Bus Adm; Former Regent DAR; Former Matron OES; Adv Bd Altrusa; St Chm Resolutions for NH Fed'd Repub Wom's Clb; P'mouth Fed'd Repub Wom's Clb; St Constitution Week Chm St DAR; Capt Cancer Dr P'mouth; DCW; Piscataqua Pioneers; Newington & P'mouth Hist Socs; P'mouth Garden Clb; Others; r/Congreg: Pres N Ch Coun 1977.

HODGENS, PAUL MORTON SR oc/Retired Hospital Administrator; b/Dec 18, 1925; h/311 Nixon St, Albertville, AL 35950; ba/Tupelo, MS; m/Grace Wilson; c/Lisa, Paul M Jr, John Bart; p/John C Hodgens (dec); Fannie Victoria Hodgens, Albertville, AL; ed/BS; mil/USN; pa/Am Col Hosp Admrs; Am Hosp Assn; cp/Civitans; r/Bapt; hon/Dist'd Ser, Am Nat Red Cross.

HODGES, LUTHER HARTWELL oc/Banker; Senatorial Candidate; b/Nov 19, 1936; h/534 Hempstead Pl, Charlotte, NC 28207; ba/Charlotte; m/Dorothy; c/Anne, Luther II; p/Luther Sr and Martha B Hodges (dec); ed/AB Univ NC; MBA Harvard; mil/USNR Lt; pa/Former Chm Bd NC Nat Bk; r/Epis; hon/Selected as 1 of Outstg Ldrs in US, *Time* Mag.

HODGIN, SIDNEY LaRUE oc/Merchant, Owner & Operator Sporting Goods Shop; b/Sept 8, 1926; h/1215 Bickett Rd, Sanford, NC 27330; ba/Sanford; p/John Henry and Clara Hinshaw Hodgin (dec); mil/AUS MC, Med Tech, Rank T-5, WWII; pa/Owner & Operator Sanford Rod & Gun Shop; Played Professionally, Blue Grass & Country & Wn Music; cp/Am Legion; Past Mem Kiwanis Clb; Vol "Uncle Sam" of NC during Bicent Celebration, Participating in 70 Events Across the St & Receiving Ext Recog for Contbn to Bicent; Appearances w Govs of NC & SC, Movie Stars, Polit Ldrs, Beauty Queens &

Other Dignataries; r/Prot; hon/Life Mem Clb of NC Govs "The Order of the Long Leaf Pines"; Meritorious Ser Awd; ATO Medal; Good Conduct Medal; WWII Victory Medal; 30-40 Plaques & Trophies for Participation in Bicent; Cert Apprec: NC Bicent Comm, Town of Troy; Resolution of Commend: Bd Commrs of Lee Co, Bd Alderman of City of Sanford; Tysinger's Photo of "Uncle Sam" in Nat Traveling Exhibit Titled "Best of the Bicent"; Lttrs of Apprec & Commend from Num Senators, Cong-men, Mins, Prins, Tchrs, Mayors & US Pres incl'g: Pres Ford, Pres Carter, Gov Holshouser, Lt Gov Hunt, Dir NC Bicent Comm, Senator Jesse Helms, US Rep James T Broyhill & Others; Recog'd in Num Newspapers Across St incl'g *Fayetteville Observer, The Sanford Herald, Greensboro Daily News, Durham Morning Herald, News & Observer* (Raleigh), UP & AP; Dist'd Citizenship Awd, Sanford C of C; 2 Photos of "Uncle Sam" included in Bicent Time Capsule to be Reopened by Tricentennial Com;

Mayor's Trophy at Bicent Parade in Winston-Salem; "Uncle Sam" Story Printed in Final Edition of "Bicent Times" 1976, Am Revolution Bicent Adm, Wash DC; Others.

HODNETT, JUDITH VERA oc/Registered Nurse; Clinical Nurse Specialist; b/Jan 23, 1947; h/RFD 1, White Plains, GA 30678; ba/Milledgeville, GA; p/James Pierce and Sibyl Bickers Hodnett, White Plains; ed/ADN Ga SWn Col 1968; BSN 1974, MSN 1975 Med Col Ga; pa/Ctl St Hosp, M'ville: Coor Nsg Ser Vets Div 1979-, Tng Prog Coor Dept Planning, Eval, Res & Tng 1978-79, Clin Specialist Dept Planning, Eval, Res & Tng 1975-78, Tng Prog Coor Dept Planning, Eval, Res & Tng 1978-; Other Former Positions; Am Nurses Assn; 14th Dist Ga Nurses Assn; Nat & Ga Assns Paraplegics; Conslt; cp/Greene Co Hist Soc; Dem; r/Christian; hon/W/W Am Wom; World W/W Wom.

HOEKSTRA, HAROLD DERK oc/-Aeronautical Engineer; b/Aug 18, 1902; h/253 N Columbus St, Arlington, VA 22203; ba/Same; m/Laura Barker; c/Elizabeth Keeley (Mrs William C), Thomas B, Ann Geis (Mrs Charles G), Dirk M; p/Dirk J and Grietje Zandt Hoekstra (dec); ed/BS Univ Mich 1929; pa/US Tech Advr Miles-Phoenix Ltd, Ashford, Kent, UK 1976; VP Engrg Flight Safety Foun 1970-72; Chief Engrg & Safety Div FA R&D 1961-70; CAA-FAA Flight Standards Aero Engr to Chief Proj Ofcr-Transports 1937-61; Other Former Positions; Fellow: Royal Aeronautical Soc, AIAA, Soc Automotive Engrs; Assoc Mem Aerospace Writers Assn; Soc Air Safety Investigators; Past Mem NASA Com on Aerodynamics; Aero Clb Wash; Other Profl Activs; cp/Army & Navy Clb; r/Meth; hon/Tau Beta Pi; Dist'd Alumnus Cit, Univ Mich; Legion of Merit; 8 Aviation Patents; Profl Pubs; Num Biogl Listings.

HOELSCHER, HAROLD E oc/University President; b/Sept 28, 1922; h/Am Univ Beirut, Beirut, Lebanon; ba/Same; m/Anna S; c/Lillian Anna Grothe, David S; p/Emil H and Lillian I Hoelscher, St Louis, MO; ed/BS Princeton; MS, PhD Washington Univ; pa/Am Univ Beirut: Pres 1977-, Tchr 1977-; Pres The Asian Inst Technol, Bangkok, Thailand 1973-75; Univ Pittsburgh: Prof-at-Large 1975-77, Prof on Leave 1972-75, Dir Space Res Coor Ctr 1967-70, Dean Sch Engrg 1965-72; Other Former Positions; Com on Public Engrg Policy Nat Acad Engrg; Mem & Chm Jt Com on Intl Activs Am Soc for Engrg Ed; Mem EAROPH, Comm for Planning in En Reg; Conslt; Reg'd Profl Engr: Ohio, Md; Hon Mem Fac Univ Madras (Madras, India); Bd Trustees Am Univ Cairo; Mem Danforth Foun, India Bd; Hon Trustee Technol Resources Inc (Cal); hon/Profl Pubs; LLD (Honoris Causa), Amherst Col.

HOENACK, PEG COURSE oc/Music Educator; b/Mar 6, 1916; h/8409 Seven Locks Rd, Bethesda, MD 20034; m/August; c/Stephen A, Judith H Schultz, Francis A, August Jeremy; p/Herbert Moore and Mary Hart Course; ed/BA magna cum laude Wash St Univ 1937; MMus Cath Univ Am 1972; pa/Music Conslt & Wkshop Clinician Montessori, Parochial & Public Schs 1967-; Lectr Elem Music Ed: Chautauqua (NY) Inst 1977, Trinity Col (Wash) 1977, George Mason Univ (Fairfax, Va) 1976, Am Univ 1972-74; Group Piano Instr Montgomery Co (Md) Public Schs 1960-70; Other Former Positions; Fdr 1967 & Dir Music for Yg Chd, Studios & Pub'g, Bethesda; Fdr Com for Music in Public Schs, Montgomery Co 1953; Intl Soc Music Ed; MENC; Md Music Edrs; Am Montessori Soc; Assn Childhood Ed Intl; Am Orff Schulwerk Assn; DC Fed'd Music Clbs; Washington Friday Morning Music Clb: Perf'g Mem, Violist; Phi Kappa Phi; Pi Lambda Theta; Psi Chi; Mu Phi Epsilon; cp/Podickory Yacht Clb; Former Mem Bd Dirs Concerned Citizens for Arts in Public Schs; Former Mem Steering Com Cult Arts in Schs, Montgomery Co; r/Presb; hon/Grantee, Rockefeller Foun; Ednl Profl Devel Act; Philip Stern Fam Fund; Contbr to Profl Jours; Author Music Textbooks, Others; W/W Am Wom.

HOFFER, JANICE ANN oc/College Administrator; b/Feb 13, 1934; h/1120 Williams, Adrian, MI 49221; ba/Adrian; c/Richard, Randal, Edward; p/Harry and Lena Hill, Sun City, AZ; ed/BA; MA; PhD; pa/Adrian Col: VP for Student Affairs 1977-, Dean Students, Dean Cont'g Ed, Dir Sum Sch 1975-77; Telecommuns Conslt Adrian Public Schs 1974-75; Other Former Positions; APGA; NASPA; ACUHO, Leg Issues Com 1979-80; Former Mem Bd Dirs Zonta Intl; Spch Assn Am; Former Mem: NEA, MEA, MASSP, NASSP; cp/Zeta Tau Alpha; Lenawee Co Fam Cnslg & Chd's Sers: Public Relats Com, Prog & Ser Com (Secy); Bd Dirs Croswell Opera House & Fine Arts Assn; r/Prot; hon/Kappa Delta Pi; Theta Alpha Pi; Delta Kappa Gamma; Zeta Tau Alpha; Outstg Jr of Yr Awd, Outstg Grad Trophy; Outstg Yg Wom Yr 1967; Profl Pubs; W/W: Am Wom, MW; DIB; World W/W Wom; Notable Ams.

HOFFMAN, ELISE oc/Administrator; Professor; b/Mar 10, 1922; h/609 Front St, Richmond, TX 77469; ba/Richmond; m/Billy C; c/Rosilyn H Overton, B Mazie H Peschel; p/James E and Laura Jack Foster Gay (dec); ed/BA Univ Houston; MEd Prairie View A&M Univ; Postgrad Studies; RN Hermann Hosp Sch Nsg; pa/Admr Tech Prog II, Col Prof; Dept Chm Alvin Commun Col (Tex); Dir Sc Voc Nur; Dir Sc Prof Nurses; Unit Dir Tex Dept Mtl Hlth & Mtl Retard; Mem & Lectr; NLN, ANA, AAUP; cp/Adv Com ARC; Girl Scout Ldr; Pres: PTA, Band Boosters; Dist Dep Pres Rebekah Lodge; Writer; r/St John's Meth Ch: Adm Bd, SS Tchr; hon/Life Mbrship, PTA; Intl W/W in Ed; W/W Am Wom.

HOFFMAN, GARLYN ODELL oc/Range Management Specialist; b/Sept 1, 1920; h/1013 James Pkwy, College Station, TX 77840; ba/Col Sta; m/Mary Jo; c/David G, Oliver J; p/Frank R and Ollie G Hoffman (dec); ed/Lt Col Ret'd, DFC; Air Medal; Purple Heart; 3 Theatres; pa/Ext Range Brush & Weed Control Specialist, Tex Agri Ext Ser TAMU; r/Presb; hon/Outstg Range Man; Superior Ser; Dist'd Fac Achmt.

HOFFMAN, HOWARD ALLAN oc/- Teacher; Minister; Musician; b/Jul 16, 1939; h/PO Box 1676, Orangeburg, SC 29115; ba/O'burg; p/Howard A and Jane P Hoffman, St Petersburg, FL; ed/BA magna cum laude; AM; Cert Ednl Media; pa/Tchr SC St Col; Am Min Assn; Spch Commun Assn; Am Forensic Assn; So Sts Spch Commun Assn; r/Christian: Min; hon/Nat Tchg Fellow; Grantee.

HOFFMAN, HOWARD TORRENS oc/Executive; b/Dec 30, 1923; h/5545 Stresemann, San Diego, CA 92122; ba/San Diego; m/Ruth Ann Gisela Koch; c/Howard Torrens, Jean Gisele, Glenn Kevin; p/Edmund Howard Hoffman (dec); Beulah Esther Hoffman, Wayzata, MN; ed/BSEE Ia St Univ 1950; MSEE 1972, PhD 1977 Thomas Univ; mil/AUS Ofc of Mil Govt for Germany (Berlin) 1943-46; pa/Reg'd Profl Engr; Pres Hoffman Assocs 1966-; Exec Dir H & R Assocs

1966-; Teledyne-Ryan, San Diego 1960-66: Div Mgr, Prog Dir, Ch Engr; Mgr Missile Systems Litton Industs, College Park, Md 1958-60; Other Former Positions; IEEE; Nat Soc Profl Engrs; AIAA; Armed Forces Communs & Elects Assn; Assn US Army; Nat Mgmt Assn; Am Mgmt Assn; IPA; cp/DAV; Univ City Civic Assn; r/Presb; hon/Patentee

in Field; Commun Ldr Awd; U Crusade Commun Ser Awd; Mil Decorations; Biogl Listings.

HOFFMAN, MARY ANN oc/University Professor; b/Mar 23, 1950; h/9125 Flower Ave, Silver Spring, MD 20901; ba/College Park, MD; m/Damon Silvers; p/Paul and Patricia Patrick Hoffman, St Cloud, MN; ed/BA Macalester Col; PhD Univ Minn; pa/Prof Dept Cnslg & Pers Univ Md; Am Psychol Assn; En Psychol Assn; cp/Dem; r/Prot; hon/Phi Beta Kappa; Univ Md Res Grant.

HOFFMAN, ROBERT J oc/Herbalist; Reflexologist; b/Apr 2, 1957; h/380 Oak Spring Rd, Paradise, CA 95969; ba/Paradise; p/H J Hoffman, Oroville, CA; Lucille I Amick, Paradise; ed/CH Dominian Herbal Col; MST E-W Col Hlth Pract; pa/Am Massage Therapist Assn; Commun Lectr on Hlth & Natural Healing; r/Oriental/Cath; Ordained in Ch of Antioch; hon/W/W in Am; Others.

HOFFMAN, RUTH IRENE oc/Professor; Laboratory Director; b/Mar 23, 1925; h/255 S Williams, Denver, CO 80209; ba/Denver; p/George H and Rosalie M Hoffman (dec); ed/BA, MA Univ Colo; EdD Univ Denver; pa/Univ Denver: Prof Math, Dir Math Lab; Nat Conslt Math Ed & Calculator & Computer Usage; Author Profl Books & Jour Articles; r/Cath; hon/Phi Beta Kappa; Outstg Edrs Am.

HOFFMANN, WILMA M oc/University Teacher; Teacher Supervisor & Researcher; b/Feb 27, 1925; h/342 Sauk Trail, Park Forest, IL 60466; ba/Chicago, IL; c/Gerhard C, William M; ed/PhD Loyola Univ; pa/Univ Ill-Cir Campus: Asst Prof Slavic Langs, In Charge of Tchr Ed Progs for Students of Russian & Polish; Former Tchg Positions incl: Elmhurst Col, NWn Univ, Loyola Univ, Chgo City HSs; MLA; ACTFL; AATSEEL; LACUS; Var Ofcs Held Ill AATSEEL; Others; Translator & Interpreter Var Govtl Agys; Tchg Sev NDEA Insts & Pharm Labs; Org'd Ethnic Sch for Gypsies; r/Rom Cath; hon/Pubs incl: *Chicago Area Ethnic Weekend Schs: Goals & Achievements* 1978, *Institutional Self-Study and Tenth Year Review–Univ Ill at Chgo Cir* 1978; Have Written German Scripts for Var Ednl Films; Other Pubs.

HOGAN, FANNIE BURRELL oc/Librarian; b/Apr 6, 1923; h/1981 Valley Ridge Dr SW, Atlanta, GA 30331; ba/Atlanta; m/Isaac N; c/Maria Monique, Erica Whipple Jones; p/Alexander Sr and Lorenze Nicholas Burrell (dec); ed/AB; MSLS; pa/Am Lib Assn; Ga Lib Assn; Metro-Lib Assn; cp/Past Pres: D M Therrell PTSA, Harper HS, M Agnes Jones Elem; Former Neighborhood Capt Heart Fund; r/Ben Hill U Meth Ch; hon/All Expense Paid Trip to Poland, Clark Col.

HOGAN, JUDY oc/Coordinator; b/May 27, 1937; h/300 Barclay Rd, Chapel Hill, NC 27514; ba/Same; c/Amy Fordham, Timothy Michael, Virginia Lynn; p/William R and Margaret R Stevenson, Maryville, TN; ed/BA cum laude Univ Okla; pa/Coor Home Grown Books (Review Proj); Pres COSMEP Inc 1975-78; Org'd Poetry Rdgs: Chapel Hill & Durham 1974-; Editor Hyperion Poetry Jour & Carolina Wren Press; Conslt Soundscape & WUNC Radio 1977-78; cp/Creative Writing Wkshop; r/Prot; hon/Woodrow Wilson Fellow; Phi Beta Kappa.

HOHF, JEROME CHALMERS oc/Surgeon; b/Jun 17, 1918; h/PO Box 3096, Victoria, TX 77901; ba/Victoria; m/Dorothy Grunewald; c/Judith Kay Lee, Jill Carol Davol; p/Julius Amos and Rose Olive Hohf (dec); ed/BA; MD; FACS; DABS; FASAS; mil/AUS MC WWII, AFWES PHC; pa/Former Conslt in Surg: VA Hosp & Foster AF Base Hosp; cp/32° Masons; Shriner; r/Meth.

HOISTAD, LOUISE MARIE CHARLOTTE oc/Businesswoman; b/Mar 23, 1915; h/2210 Midland Grove Rd, Apt 102, St Paul, MN

55113; m/Arthur Owen; c/Maredeth Searle, Jonathan, Karen, Gerald, Barbara Polland, Ronald, Charles; p/Albert Hohfeldt and Louise Marie Charlotte Potthoff Clark (dec); ed/Grad (RN) Univ Minn Sch Nsg 1939; pa/Night Supvr St Paul Nsg Home 1971; Sch Nurse, Alexandria, Minn 1942; Sch Nurse-Dietitian Snead Jr Col, Ala 1940-41; Vis Nurse St Paul 1939-40; cp/UF; Urban Coalition; Ctr Urban Encounter; r/U Meth Ch: US Del World Yth Conf, Amsterdam 1939; Lay Spkr; Pres Minn Coun Chs 1972-74; Pres Minn Sch of Missions 1974-76; Pres Ch Wom U Minn 1976-79; Others; hon/Hon Mem: Minn PTA, U Meth Wom.

HOKE, SHEILA WILDER oc/Library Director; b/Jul 15, 1928; h/817 N Kansas, Weatherford, OK 73096; ba/W'ford; m/Robert Edward (dec); c/Raymond Fellow, Philip Wilder; p/Herbert Bruce Wilder (dec); Virginia Wilder Dell, W'ford; ed/BA, BS Univ Ks; MLS Univ Wis-M; mil/(Civilian) Spec Sers Libs Germany; pa/Lib Dir SWn Okla St Univ Lib; Okla Lib Assn: Chm Univ & Col Div 1973, Chm LED 1976, Chm Tech Ser 1970; ALA; SWLA; OEA; NEA; cp/Ed Com W'ford C of C; Delta Kappa, Res Chm Lambda Chapt, St Res Com; AAUW; r/Bapt.

HOLCOMB, DOROTHY TURNER oc/Public Relations Executive; b/Jun 15, 1924; h/6525 Greenway Dr NE, Apt F-68, Roanoke, VA 24019; m/Wiley Bryant and Lena Gray Turner, Roanoke; ed/Cert NY Sch Interior Design; r/Eckist; hon/W/W Am Wom.

HOLCOMB, GERARD FRANK oc/Mortgage Banking Executive; b/Mar 18, 1936; h/751 Gleneagles Dr, Fort Washington, MD 20022; ba/Oxon Hill, MD; m/Betty J; c/Patrick Gerard, Patricia Ann; p/Gerard Holcomb; Mary Dalvagio; ed/Cath Univ; mil/USMC Hon Disch E6; pa/Pres & Chm of Bd John Hanson Ser Corp; Former VP John Hanson Savs & Ln Inc; Former VP (Mktg) US Ser Industs; Former Exec Dir Metro Washington Assn Plumbing, Heating & Cooling Contractors; Other Former Positions; US Savs & Ln Leag, Sec'dy Mortgage Market Com; Metro Wash Mortgage Bkrs Assn, Ethics & Grievance Com; No Va Home Bldrs Assn; Washington Bd Realtors; Prince George's Co Bd Realtors; Nat Assn Execs Clb; Other Activs; cp/Prince George's Co JCs: Past Dir, Pres, VP, Chm of Bd; Past St VP Md JCs; Prince George's Co Red Cross: Past Mem, Bd Dirs, Exec Com, Fundraising Chm; Del 2 Repub Nat Convs; Prince George's Co Repub Ctl Com; Campaign Activs; r/St Mary's Cath Ch; hon/Outstg Yg Man Am; Outstg Yg Man Prince George's Co; W/W Am Polits; Outstg Ser Awd; USMC Leag.

HOLCOMBE, CRESSIE EARL JR oc/Ceramic Engineer; b/Dec 18, 1945; h/1613 Blackwood Dr, Knoxville, TN 37919; ba/Oak Ridge, TN; m/Catherine Joselyn Brockman; p/Cressie Earl Sr and Blanche Elizabeth Keaton Holcombe (dec); ed/BS 1966, MS 1967 Clemson Univ; Postgrad Studies; pa/Ceramic Engr Union Carbide Nuclear Div; R&D on Refractory Mats; Am Ceramic Soc; Keramos; Tau Beta Pi; Sigma Xi; IPA; r/Bapt; hon/Col Hons Prog; 4 Col S'ships; Cabot Corp Indust F'ship; Contbr Articles to Profl Jours; US Patents.

HOLCOMBE, TROY LEON oc/Marine Geologist; b/Mar 8, 1940; h/Rt 1, Box 192A, Picayune, MS 39466; ba/NSTL Sta, MS; m/Janis Eileen O'Neal; c/Leigh Harold, Virginia Luce, Terry Estelle; p/Horace Cleveland Holcombe (dec); Nellie Estelle Holcombe, Cleburne, TX; ed/BA Hardin-Simmons Univ 1961; AM Univ Mo 1964; PhD Columbia Univ 1972; pa/Hd Geology Br NORDA; Sigma Xi; Geol Soc Am; Am Geophy Union; Am Assn Petrol Geologists; Participant Num Profl Wkshops; r/So Bapt; hon/Univ Mo: NSF Sum Fellow, Gregory Fellow; Columbia Univ: Higgins Fellow, Pres' Fellow; Author & Coauthor Profl Papers.

HOLDAWAY, GEORGE HARMER oc/Administrator; b/Oct 10, 1921; h/3861 Grove Ct, Palo Alto, CA 94303; ba/Moffett Field, CA; m/Lorna Lee; c/Sheryl Lee, Larry

Lee, Steven Lee, George Lee; p/Hugh and Pearl Harmer Holdaway (dec); ed/BS Univ Utah; Masters Stanford Univ; mil/USN 1944-46; pa/Chief Facilities Planning Ofc NASA Ames Res Ctr; Aerospace Res Engr; AIAA; cp/Exec Bd Mem BSA; Am Rt of Way Assn; Com for Scouting for Handicapped; r/LDS; hon/BSA Beaver Awd; NASA Spec Achmt & Group Achmt Awd.

HOLLAND, EARL STAFFORD oc/Accountant; h/PO Box 397, Tampa, FL; c/Earl Stafford Jr, Phyllis H Barton, Marianne H Stern; p/James Timothy and Ballie S Holland; ed/Att'd William & Mary Col, Elon Col, Univ Va; pa/Public Sch Tchr; Supvr Adult Ed; Real Est Broker; Acct, Franklin, Va; Co-Owner, Corporate Secy Powhatan Corp; Co-Owner & Corporate Secy Tidewater News, Franklin; Tax Dir Baker Equipmt Engrg Co, Richmond, Va; Broadcaster Var Va Radio Stas; Pvt Pract Acct'g, Tampa; Del to Inst Public Affairs Univ Va; Kappa Psi Nu; cp/Carrsville Ruritan Clb; Lt Gov Ruritan Nat; Charter Mem C'ville Commun Ctr; Instnl Rep BSA; Past Pres PTA; Kiwanis; Lafayett Yacht Clb; r/Epis Ch: Mem, SS Tchr, SS Supt; hon/W/W S&SW; DIB; Intl W/W Intells; Personalities of S.

HOLLAND, GENE (SCOTTY) GRIGSBY oc/Teacher, Artist; b/Jun 30, 1928; h/102 Ayers Cir, Summerville, SC 29483; m/George William; c/Shereta Lee Nieradka, Harvelyn Georgene, Alicia Hope; p/Edward and Virginia Lee Watson Grigsby (dec); ed/BA; pa/Elem Sch Tchr, Hillsborough Co (Fla) 1968-72; Clerk Fogarty Bros Moving & Transfer, Tampa & Miami, Fla 1954-57; News Reporter & Photo Bryan *Daily News*, Bryan, Tex 1952; Other Former Positions; cp/Fdr Mem & VP S'ville Inner Wheel; Flowerton Garden Clb; S'ville SPCA; S'ville Fam YWCA; Green Wave Band Boosters; SC Watercolor Soc; Charter Mem Intl Soc Artists; SC Hist Soc; Nat Trust for Hist Preserv; Nat Hist Soc; NEn Okla St Univ Alumni Assn; USF Alumni Assn; Fla Geneal Soc; Charleston Christian Wom's Clb; IPA; BPW; Delta Sigma Epsilon; S'ville Artists Guild; Var Former Activs, Tampa, Fla; r/Bethany Meth Ch, S'ville: Rec'g Secy UMW, Rec'g Secy S Spell Sub-Group; hon/Ribbons for Paintings; Personalities of S; Notable Ams Bicent Era; Commun Ldrs & Noteworthy Ams; Book of Honor; World W/W Wom; Intl W/W Intells, Commun Ldr.

HOLLAND, JOHN GORDON oc/Professional Engineer; b/Jun 13, 1948; h/3124 Dreeben Dr, Ft Worth, TX 76118; ba/Arlington, TX; m/Mary Kay; p/William T and Doris Berg Holland, Wauwatosa, WI; ed/BSME 1971, MBA 1975 Univ Wis-M; mil/AUS; pa/ASHRAE; NSPE; TSPE; hon/Personalities of S; W/W Fin & Indust.

HOLLAND, KEN oc/Member of Congress; b/Nov 24, 1934; ba/103 Cannon House Ofc Bldg, Washington, DC 20515; m/Diane; c/Lamar, Amy, Elizabeth; p/James A and Ruby B Holland, Gaffney, SC; ed/BA 1960, LLB 1963 Univ SC; mil/SC NG; USAR Sgt E-5, Hon Disch 1969; pa/Atty; SC Hwy Comm 1972-74; cp/Mem Cong; Former Chm Exec Com Kershaw Co Hosp Bd; Former St VP JCs; Former Mem Kiwanis; r/St John's Meth Ch, Rock Hill, SC; hon/Recipient Euphradian & James Patterson Hons in Oratory.

HOLLAND, RAY G L oc/Group Research Worker; Educator; b/Oct 30, 1931; h/57 Elgin St, Port Colborne, Ontario, Canada L3K 3J9; m/Mary Kennedy; c/1 Child; p/John and Mary Holland; ed/BCh, BM, MA Oxford Univ (England); MD; Residency in Psychi St Univ NY-Binghamton; mil/Royal Canadian Navy 1964-69, Lt Cmdr & Flight Surg; Mem Aircraft Accident Investigation Team; pa/Current Asst Clin Prof Psychi St Univ NY-Buffalo; Canadian Civil Rts Assn; Am Humanist Soc; hon/Commun Ldrs & Noteworthy Ams; Book of Honor; W/W in E.

HOLLAND, RUBY LOVE oc/Retired; b/Feb 21, 1904; h/1888 W 23rd St, Los Angeles, CA 90018; m/Louis L; p/Jesse E and Amie Douglas Sams (dec); ed/Prairie View

A&M Univ; pa/Former Tchr; Ret'd from Lockheed Aircraft; Panelist on Minority Relationships, Nat Assn Deans, Admrs & Cnslrs Conv 1978; Bd Dirs Normandie Christian Sch, LA; Assty Secy Commun Devel Adv Com; Mem Normandie-Adams Redevel Proj Area Com; Wom's Steering Com 10th Councilmatic Dist, LA; cp/Fdr Ladies Aux for Christian Ed; CoFdr Ctr for Wom's Studies Inc; Orgr Neighborhood Active Group; Initiated Black & White Interracial Communs Sems; Gtr Normandie Devel Adv Com; Assoc'd Wom Pepperdine Univ; Manual Arts Commun Adult Sch Adv Com; Beethoven Soc Am; Hon Mem Alpha Gamma; r/Figueroa Ch of Christ: Bible Sch Tchr, Other Sers; Tchr "Operation Concern"; hon/Achmt Cert, LA Unified Sch Dist Adult Ed Adv Coun; Trophy for Outstg Ldrship, Ladies Aux Christian Ed (Pres SWn Christian Col); Apprec Plaque, Ho of Reps; Apprec Cert, Mayor Tom Bradley; Lttr of Apprec, Gov Reagen; Others.

HOLLANDER, DORIS A oc/Psychologist; b/Oct 13, 1941; h/6330 Alexander, Clayton, MO 63105; ba/St Louis, MO; m/Jerrold Blumoff; c/Sam, Rebecca; p/Samuel Hollander (dec); Rose Heller, St Louis; ed/AB; MA w distn; PhD; pa/Pres Resource Devel Conslts 1979-; Asst Prof Webster Col 1979-80; Psychol Wom's Achmt Prog 1976-78; Pres Whole Food & Grain Depot Inc 1972-78; cp/Past VP & Prog Com Chperson Oak Park Commun Mtl Hlth Bd.

HOLLANDER, TONI ANN oc/Graphic Designer; b/Sept 26, 1945; ba/1880 Century Park E, Los Angeles, CA 90064; ed/BA 1966, MA 1968 UCLA; Cert of Studies University di Padova (Padova, Italy) 1964-65; pa/LA Advt'g Wom; Commun Arts Soc LA; Others; hon/Cert of Merit, LAAW; Art Ctr Col of Design Awd; Others.

HOLLEY, EDGAR MERRITT oc/Controller; b/575 Main St, New York, NY 10040; m/Mary Anne; c/Edgar Jr; p/Edgar M and Bernice Holley, Maywood, IL; ed/BA; MBA; mil/Sgt E-5; pa/Am Mgmt Assn; cp/Yale Clb; BSA; Little League; Voter Registration Poll Watcher; r/Bapt; hon/W/W Fin & Indust; Outstg Indust Achmt, YMCA of Gtr NY; DIB.

HOLLIDAY, JOSEPHINE CRAIN oc/Retired Executive Housekeeper; b/Oct 7, 1913; h/Rt 2, Box 214, Preston, MS 39354; m/L Hughey; p/Robert B Crain (dec); Nannie G Crain, Preston; ed/BS Miss St Col for Wom; pa/Ret'd, Exec Housekeeper Grand Hotels, Mobile, Ala 1972-73; Real Est Sales Byrd Cos, Birmingham, Ala 1971-74; Tng Dir Jack's Hamburgers Inc, B'ham 1970-71; Instr Hospitality Ed Voc Ed Dept, St of Ala 1966-70; Other Former Positions; Local, St & Nat Home Ecs Assns; Ala & Am Voc Assns; Nat Assn Realtors; Hotel-Motel Assn Am; Restaurant Assn Ala; Nat Restaurant Assn; cp/Pilot Clb Intl: Pres Local Clb, Gov Dist III, Chm Intl Mbrship Com; Rural & Urban Commun Devel Orgs; hon/Wom of Yr, Booneville, Miss 1955; Hon Citizen, New Orleans, La; Cert of Merit for Vol Activs: Cancer Progs, Mar Dimes, 4-H Clb Adv Coun, Hlth & Safety Progs; Biogl Listings; Pub'd Author.

HOLLIN, SHELBY W oc/Attorney; Counselor at Law; b/Jul 29, 1925; h/7710 Stage Coach, San Antonio, TX 78227; ba/SA; m/Martha Jane Fisch; c/Sheila K, Henry T, Richard G, Roberta E, Nathan W, Jacob C; p/Herbert and Maggie Hollin, Lynch, KY; ed/BBA St Mary's Univ; JD St Mary's Law Sch; mil/USAF 1/Lt (Ret'd); Maj USAFR; Grad Air War Col; pa/ABA; Tex & SA Bar Assns; Delta Theta Phi; cp/Life Mem ROA, DAV; VFW; r/Bapt; hon/Air Medal; AF Commend Medal w OLC; Outstg Perf Awd, USAF; W/W: Am Law, Tex.

HOLLINGER, ORA K oc/Principal; b/Jul 28, 1927; h/PO Box 1762, Hollywood, CA 33022; m/Evans; c/W Ray, Donna D Montgomery; p/Charles and Ora S Kennedy (dec); ed/BS; MS; pa/FASA; BAESP; NAESP; cp/NW Fed'd Wom's Clb; NAACP; Zeta Phi Beta; r/Meth; hon/HHD.

HOLLING-KAEMMERER, JANICE AVELLA oc/Film Editor/Writer; Executive; b/Sept 10, 1940; h/229 E 29th St, New York, NY 10016; ba/Same; m/Ron T; p/William Julian Holling, Scottsdale, AZ; Charlotte Frost Bublitz, Sycamore, IL; ed/BA 1972, MA 1973 Columbia Univ; Cert NY Univ Film Inst 1976; pa/Pres Holling Edit Sers, NYC 1976-; Writer *Time/Life* TV (Ecs) 1977; Asst Editor, Instnl Investor, NYC 1973-76; Art Reschr, Pvt Collector, NYC 1971-73; Ec Reschr Townsend-Greenspan & Co, NYC 1965-71; CoEditor "A New Approach to Advt'g Creativity"; hon/Jour Awd Nom, Univ Mo; W/W Am Wom; World W/W Wom; DIB.

HOLLOMON, J HERBERT oc/Educator; b/Mar 12, 1919; h/121 Carlton St, Brookline, MA 02146; ba/Cambridge, MA; m/Nancy Gade; c/Jonathan Bradford, James Martin, Duncan Twiford, Elizabeth Wheeler Vrugtman; p/John Herbert and Pearl Twiford Hollomon (dec); ed/BS 1940, ScD 1946 MIT; mil/AUS 1942-46, Maj; pa/MIT: Dir Ctr for Policy Alts 1972-, Prof Engrg 1963-, Japan Steel Indust Prof 1975-, Vis Prof Engrs 1972-73, Conslt to Pres & Provost 1970-72; Univ Okla: Pres 1968-70, Pres-Designate 1967-68; Other Former Positions; Am Soc for Metals: Fellow, Former Dir; Fellow: Metall Soc Am Inst Mines, Metall, & Petrol Engrs, AAAS, Am Phy Soc, Am Inst Chemists; Soc for Hist of Technol; Exec Coun 1972-74, Adv Coun 1968-71; Nat Acad Engrs: Fdg Mem 1964-, Com Mbrships; Num Adv Activs; Var Edit Positions; cp/Former Mem: Bd Univ Trustees Nelson Gallery (Kansas City, Mo), Bd Trustees St Okla TV Auth; Past Pres Mid-Am St Univs Assn; Mem Var Clbs; hon/Hon Degs; Sigma Xi; Fellow, Am Acad Arts & Scis; Fgn Mem, Royal Swedish Acad Engrg Scis; Hon Lectrs; Rosenhain Medal, Brit Inst Metals (1st Am Recipient) 1958; 10 Outstg Yg Men US, Nat Jr C of C; Num Profl Pubs; Others.

HOLLOWAY, EVELYN ANN oc/Food Service Instructor; Registered Dietitian; b/Mar 13, 1936; h/Rt 5, Box 98, Franklin Rd, Franklin, TN 37064; ba/Franklin; m/James F; c/Linda A, Russell L, Jon F, Laurie E; p/Paul Jackson (dec); Maxine Jackson Smith, Obion, TN; ed/BS; MA; pa/Food Sers Instr Yates Voc Ctr; Nashville Dist, Tenn, Nat Dietetic Assns; Am & N'ville Area Home Ecs Assns; NEA; Tenn & Williamson Co Ed Assns; r/Bapt; hon/Kappa Delta Pi; Kappa Delta Epsilon; Kappa O Phi.

HOLLOWAY, JAMES FRANKLIN oc/Department Chairman, Instructor; b/Dec 4, 1933; h/Rt 5, Box 98, Franklin Rd, Franklin, TN 37064; ba/Franklin; m/Evelyn A; c/Linda, Russell, Jon, Laurie; p/Ira L Holloway (dec); Lorene M Holloway, Ridgely, TN; ed/DEd; MAT; MAT; BS; mil/AUS; pa/Battle Ground Acad: Chm Sci Dept, Physics Instr; AAPT; Life Mem: NEA, NSTA; Tenn Ed Assn; r/Bapt; hon/Sigma Pi Sigma; Outstg Yg Men Am; Outstg Yg Male Tchr of Yr Awd.

HOLMAN, OTTILIE ANN oc/Employee Development Specialist; b/Aug 1, 1949; h/58-25 74 St, Elmhurst, NY 11373; ba/Flushing, NY; p/Edward Harry and Ellen T F Holman, Middle Village, NY; ed/BA 1979; pa/Career Cnslg; cp/Former Mem F'ship Profl Poets; r/Rom Cath; hon/Cert of Merit, L Mark Press; Fdr-Fellow, Intl Acad Poets.

HOLMES, BETTY JEAN oc/Library Assistant; b/Mar 6, 1929; h/911 N Mulberry, Abilene, KS 67410; ba/Abilene; p/Emery R Holmes (dec); Mrs Emery R Holmes, Abilene; ed/Cert Ks Lib Assn Bd for Vol Certn of Libns; pa/Lib Asst Abilene Public Lib; Ks Lib Assn; Mtn Plains Assn; Am Lib Assn; cp/Vol U Commun Fund Dr; Dickinson Co Hist Soc, Abilene; r/U Meth: Choir Mem 1978; hon/World W/W Wom; W/W in US.

HOLMES, CLIFTON oc/Automobile Salesman; State Legislator; Farmer; b/Sept 3, 1932; h/Rt 3, Box 238, Foxworth, MS 39483; ba/Columbia, MS; m/Ida Elizabeth B; c/Diane, Vickie, Clifton Jr, Carol, Milli; p/Herschel and Letha Smith Holmes, San Angelo, TX; ed/Att'd W Tex St Univ; mil/USAF, Ret'd S/Sgt; pa/Salesman

Columbia Motors; Ins Adj; cp/St Rep, Coms: Mil, Hlth, Bk, Utilities; Hist Soc; Optomist Clb; DAV; VFW; Dem Party; Southland Gospel Music; Pi Tau Chi; r/1st U Meth Ch, Columbia: Mem Ofcl Bd; hon/Cert of Recog, USAF; Rated 2nd Best in Miss Leg 1976; Personalities of S; W/W: Am Polits, Miss.

HOLMES, ROGER CURTIS oc/Attorney; b/May 10, 1942; h/933 McClatchy Way, Sacramento, CA 95818; ba/San Francisco, CA; p/Joseph Oliver and DeLia Lee Holmes; ed/BA; JD Univ Santa Clara Sch of Law; pa/Intl Atty; Cal Bar Assn; ABA; cp/African Am Assn; r/Moslem; hon/W/W W; Intl W/W Commun Ser; DIB.

HOLMES, THOMAS HALL oc/Educator; Psychiatrist; b/Sept 20, 1918; h/3023 NE 180 St, Seattle, WA 98155; ba/Seattle; m/Janet Lawrence; c/T Stephenson, Janet, Eleanor, Elizabeth; p/Thomas Hall and Elizabeth Stephenson Holmes, Weldon, NC; ed/AB Univ NC 1939; MD Cornell Med 1943; Postgrad Studies; mil/AUS MC 1944-47, Maj; pa/Univ Wash Sch Med: Prof Psychi 1958-, Assoc Prof 1953-58, Asst Prof 1950-53, Instr 1949-50; Clin Asst Vis Neuropsychiatrist Bellevue Hosp 1948-49; Hon Conslt'g Psychiatrist Royal Prince Alfred Hosp, Sydney, Australia 1971-; Att'g Staff: Univ Hosp 1959-, Seattle VA Hosp 1951-; Att'g Phys Harborview Med Ctr 1949-; AAAS; Charter Fellow Am Col Psychiatrists; Fellow Am Psychi Assn; AMA; Am Fdn for Clin Res; Am Public Hlth Assn; Am Psychosomatic Soc; Am Sociol Soc; Assn for Res in Nervous & Mtl Diseases; Wn Soc for Clin Res; Wn Sect Am Fdn for Clin Res; Psychi Res Soc; Sigma Xi; Other Profl Orgs; Adv Bd: Jour of Psychosomatic Res 1967-, Social Psychiatry 1969-; Conslt; Other Profl Activs; hon/"Dr Thomas Holmes Day", St Francis-Mayo Fam Pract Residency/Fam Hlth Ctr, La Crosse, Wis (Sept 19, 1977); Dist'd Lectr in Psychi, So Ill Univ Med; Spec Lectr'ships; Spec Awd; Med Student Grad'g Class 1972; Num Profl Pubs; Others.

HOLSTEIN, THEODORE D oc/Professor; b/Sept 18, 1915; h/345 20th St, Santa Monica, CA 90402; ba/Los Angeles, CA; m/Beverlee R; c/Lonna H Smith, Stuart A; p/Samuel and Ethel Stein Holstein (dec); ed/BS cum laude 1935, PhD 1940 NY Univ; MA Columbia 1936; pa/Prof Physics UCLA; Fellow AAAS; APS.

HOLSTI, OLE RUDOLF oc/Department Chairman; b/Aug 7, 1933; h/2439 Tilghman Cir, Chapel Hill, NC 27514; ba/Durham, NC; m/Ann Wood; c/Maija, Eric (dec); p/Rudolf Waldemar and Liisa Franssila Holsti (dec); ed/BA; MAT; PhD; mil/AUS, Resv & Active Duty; pa/Chm Dept Polit Sci Duke Univ; r/Prot.

HOLT, CAROL E oc/College Administrator; b/May 28, 1947; h/120 Elizabeth Ave, Morehead, KY 40351; ba/Morehead; m/-Charles E Jr; c/Kim Kaye, Charles E III; p/George W Peek (dec); Clarica Peek Earhart, Excelsior Springs, MO; ed/BA Ctl Mo St Univ 1968; Masters Morehead St Univ 1973; pa/Dir Placemt Sers Morehead St Univ; CPC; SCPA; ASCUS; APGA; NAWDAC; Ky Col Placemt Assn; Past Pres, Bd Dirs; cp/Former Ofcr; Morehead Wom's Clb, Univ Wom's Clb, LWV; r/Faith Presb Ch: U Campus Min Bd 1978-79; hon/Regents & BPW S'ships; W/W S&SW.

HOLT, MARJORIE SEAWELL oc/United States Legislator; b/Sept 17, 1920; ba/1510 Longworth House Ofc Bldg, Washington, DC 20515; m/Duncan M; c/Rachel Tschantre (Mrs Kenneth Hall), Edward, Victoria Stauffer (Mrs James); p/Edward R and Juanita F Sewell; ed/BA Jacksonville Univ 1945; JD Univ Fla 1949; pa/Admitted to: Fla Bar 1949, Md Bar 1962; Pract Law Annapolis, Md 1962; Clerk Anne Arundel Co Circuit Ct, Annapolis 1966-72; Am, Md, Anne Arundel Bar Assns; Phi Kappa Phi; Phi Delta Delta; cp/Mem 93rd-95th Congs, Md 4th Dist (US Ho of Reps); Var Com Mbrships; Former Supt

Elections, Anne Arundel Co; Del Repub Nat Conv 1968-76; Md Fdn Repub Wom; r/Presb; hon/Dist'd Alumni Awd, Univ Fla; Coauthor "Case Against the Reckless Cong", 1976.

HOLTKAMP, DORSEY EMIL oc/Medical Research Scientist; b/May 28, 1919; h/9464 Bluewing Terr, Cincinnati, OH 45241; ba/Cinc; m/Marianne Church Johnson (dec); 2nd Marie P Bahm Roberts; c/Kurt Lee, (Stepsons:) Charles Timothy Roberts, Michael John Roberts; p/Emil H and Caroline M Holtkamp; ed/AB 1945, MS 1949, PhD 1951 Univ Colo; pa/Group Dir Endocrine Clin Res Med Res Dept, Merrell-Nat Labs, Div of Richardson-Merrell Inc, Cinc 1970-; Hd Dept Endocrinology Wm S Merrell Co, Div Richardson-Merrell Inc, Cinc 1958-70; Endocrine-Metabolic Group Ldr Biochem Sect, Res & Devel Div, Smith, Kline, & French Labs, Philadelphia, Pa 1957-58; Other Former Positions; Fellow: AAAS, Am Inst Chemists; Am Assn for Lab Animal Sci; Am Chem Soc; Am Inst Biol Scis; Affil Mem AMA; Am Soc for Pharm & Experimtl Therapeutics; Am Soc Zoologists; Soc for Experimtl Biol & Med; Assoc Mem Cinc Acad Med; Other Profl Socs; hon/Dist'd Ldrs in Hlth Care; W/W: Am, World, Fin & Indust, MW, E; 2000 Men Achmt; The Wisdom Encyclopedia (Wisdom Hall of Fame); Nat Reg Prom Ams & Intl Notables; DIB; Other Biogl Listings.

HOLTZMAN, ELIZABETH oc/United States Representative; b/Aug 11, 1941; ba/1024 Longworth House Ofc Bldg, Washington, DC 20515; p/Sidney and Filia Holtzman; ed/AB magna cum laude Radcliffe Col 1962; JD Harvard Law Sch 1965; r/Jewish; hon/Ecology Awd, Brooklyn Friends of Clearwater; Faith & Humanity Awd, Nat Coun Jewish Wom; Trustees Dist'd Ser Awd, Fairleigh Dickinson Univ; Spirit of Achmt Awd, Albert Einstein Col Med Yeshiva Univ; Tribute Medallion, Bklyn Coalition for Soviet Jewry; Comm, Delta Sigma Theta Inc; Cert of Recog for Efforts on Behalf of Survival of Jewish People throughout World, Hudson Val Area Coun; Hon LLD, Regis Col (Weston, Mass); Citizen of Yr, B'nai B'rith Bronx Schoolmen's Lodge & Sch-wom's Chapt 1976; Other Hons.

HOLTZMAN, EVA SEAMAN oc/Postmaster; b/Jun 27, 1918; h/PO Box 43, Ridgeway, NC 27570; ba/Ridgeway; m/-Christian Fred Sr (dec); c/Christian Fred Jr, Reuben Glenn, George William, Claiborne Rufus; p/John Jacob and Ruth Champion Seaman (dec); ed/Att'd Dept Commun Col Mgmt Devel Prog; Postmaster Ridgeway 1957-; Nat Assn Postmasters USA; cp/-Philatelic Ofcr (Raleigh) Sectional Ctr; Orgr Ben Franklin Stamp Clb; Chm Social Ser Bd Warren Co; St Safety Chm Nat Ext Homemakers; Bd Dirs NC Easter Seal Soc for Crippled Chd & Adults; Cancer Bd, Secy Warren Co Unit; 4-H Ldr 28 Yrs; 1st Pres Ridgeway Commun Clb; r/St Paul Luth Ch: Mem 45 Yrs, SS Tchr, Ofcs Held LWWL, God's Blk Chm; hon/Postmaster of Yr, Nat Assn Postmasters USA 1972; Public Relats Awd & Trophy, NAPUS; Mother of Yr 1972; Others.

HOLYER, ERNA MARIA oc/Author, Artist, Teacher; b/Mar 15, 1925; h/1314 Rimrock Dr, San Jose, CA 95120; ba/Same; m/Gene W; p/Mathias and Anna Schretter (dec); ed/AA San Jose Evening Col 1964; pa/Tchr Creative & Nonfiction Writing San Jose Metro Adult Ed Prog 1968-; Author: The Southern Sea Otter 1975, Sigi's Fire Helmet 1975, Lone Brown Gull 1971, Song of Courage 1970, At the Forest's Edge 1969, Others; Contbr 60+ Mags & Newspapers; Var One-Wom Showings; Cal Writer's Clb; r/Christian; hon/Lefoli Awd for Excell in Adult Ed Instrn; Wom of Achmt Awd, San Jose Mercury-News; Art Awds.

HOLZUM, HELEN MARIE oc/Sister of Religious Order; Occupational Therapist; b/Mar 26, 1934; h/3544 Vista Ave, St Louis, MO 63104; ba/St Louis; p/Leo Holzum, Leopold, MO; Wilhelmina N Holzum (dec); ed/BS St Louis Univ 1959; Cert in OT

Washington Univ 1962; MS Sargent Col Boston Univ 1970; pa/Dir Rehab Sers St Louis Univ Hosp-Firmin Desloge 1975-; Adj Asst Prof Phy Therapy 1975; Instr: Acad Tchr 1970-75, Clin Experience 1965-; Supvr Phy Therapy & Occupl Therapy Cardinal Glennon Meml Hosp for Chd 1966-75; Other Former Positions; Am Phy Therapy Assn: Sect on Ed, Sect on Res, Secy on Adm; Am Occupl Therapy Assn; Mo Occupl Therapy Assn; Mo Pk & Rec; Nat Spinal Cord Injury Foun; Allied Hlth Profs, Arthritis Foun; cp/VP St Louis Univ Sch Nsg & Allied Hlth Profs Alumni Assn 1978-; Chm Public Relats Com Mo PTA; Former Mem Spkrs Bur Am Lung Assn En Mo; Others; r/Rom Cath: Mem Sisters of St Mary; hon/Awd in Apprec for Sers Rendered; Mo Arthritis Foun, Mem Bi-St Hemophilia Assn; Personalities W&MW; Book of Honor; W/W Am Wom; Commun Ldrs & Noteworthy Ams.

HOMBURGER, RICHARD H oc/Professor; b/Aug 15, 1914; h/2260 N Roosevelt, Wichita, KS 67220; ba/Wichita; m/Ursula Sinell; c/Ann Marie; p/Paul and Anna S Homburger (dec); ed/JD Univ Zurich 1937; MS Columbia Univ 1946; CPA WVa; pa/Prof Acct'g Wichita St Univ 1961-; Hd Dept Bus Adm WVa St Col 1946-56; Acad Acct'g Histns: VP 1975, Bd Trustees 1976-78; hon/Beta Gamma Sigma; Phi Kappa Phi; Outstg Edrs Am; W/W MW.

HOMER, FREDERIC D oc/Department Head; b/Jun 9, 1939; h/1315 Curtis, Laramie, WY 82070; ba/Laramie; m/Carole G; c/Scott, Marc, Laurie; p/Kip and Mildred Homer, Royal Palm Beach, FL; ed/AB Rutgers Univ; PhD Ind; mil/AUS 1961-62, 2/Lt; pa/Hd Polit Sci Dept Univ Wyo 1976-; Dir Adm of Justice Prog 1974!; Author Guns & Garlic, Myths & Realities of Organized Crime; cp/Bd Mem Laramie Yth Crisis Ctr; Former Dep Probation Ofcr Lafayette (Ind); hon/Book Listed as 1 of Outstg Books Pub'd by Acad Presses 1973-74, Am Scholar; Soc Listed Book as 1 of Best New Books for Review.

HOOBLER, RAYMOND LEIGH oc/-Executive; b/Aug 23, 1927; h/2359 Geranium, San Diego, CA 92109; ba/San Diego; m/E Joan; c/Cherly, Linda, Jeffrey; p/Harold Eugene and Thelma Lewish Hoobler (dec); ed/AA; MPA; mil/USNR; pa/Atlas Hotels Inc: VP Corporate Affairs, Dir Pers & Commun Sers 1975-; Instr Police Acad 1961-; Police Dept San Diego 1951-75: Chief 1971-75, Dep Chief 1970-71, Asst Chief 1970, Police Insp 1968-70, Police Capt 1965-68, Police Lt 1964-65, Police Sgt 1958-64, Patrolman 1951-58; Gov's Task Force for Safer Cal; Nat Steering Com Mun Police & Hwy Patrol Selection Project; Pres' Cabinet Nat Univ, San Diego; Peace Ofcrs Res Assn; Cal Peace Ofcrs Assn; Police Edrs Assn Cal; San Diego Peace Ofcrs Assn; Intl Assn Chiefs Police: Mem Exec Com, Leg & Crim Law & Procedures Com; cp/Past Pres Kiwanis; hon/W/W in W.

HOOD, ANN WALLACE oc/Registered Nurse; b/Jul 13, 1944; h/4514 Gilbert, Dallas, TX 75219; ba/Dallas; p/Allton Wardon and Susie Alice Harris Hood, Greenville, KY; ed/Dipl Nsg; BS; Grad Work: Baylor Univ, E Tex St Univ, Tex Wom's Univ; pa/Asst Dir Operating Room Baylor Univ Med Ctr; Assn Operating Room Nurses; r/So Bapt; hon/W/W Am Wom.

HOOD, BURREL SAMUEL III oc/-University Professor; b/Dec 14, 1943; h/411 Myrtle St, Starkville, MS 39759; ba/-Mississippi St, MS; m/Billie Lane Williams; c/Kelli Elizabeth; p/Chief B S and Rosemary Juel Hood, S'ville; ed/BS; MMusEd; EdD; mil/AUS; Army NG, Adm Pers Specialist; pa/Prof Music Ed Miss St; MENC; Nat Assn Col Wind & Percussion Instrs; Miss Music Edrs Assn; Assn Childhood Ed Intl; Miss Alliance for Arts Ed; MENC Res Soc; Music Conslt: Music Adjudicator; Phi Delta Kappa; Phi Kappa Phi; Phi Mu Alpha Sinfonia; cp/Masonic Lodge, Past Master; Knight Templar; Hamasa Shrine Temple; Hamasa Brass Band; S'ville Shrine Clb; Former JC; r/1st Bapt Ch, S'ville: Deacon, Chm Music Com, Chm Music Bldg Com, Bldg Steering

Com, Budget Com, Sanctuary Choir, Instrumental Music Coor; hon/Intl W/W Commun Ser; DIB; Intl W/W Music; Commun Ldrs & Noteworthy Ams; Book of Honor; Personalities of S; Men of Achmt.

HOOPER, VIRGINIA FITE oc/Homemaker; b/Sept 23, 1917; h/800 N 8th St, Columbus, MS 39701; m/James Fullerton III; c/Cynthia H Rood (Mrs Ralph E), James F IV, Ped Fite; p/Ped and Nell Brooks Fite (dec); cp/Meml Gifts Chm Lowndes Co Heart Assn; Lowndes Co Chowder & Marching Soc; Adv Bd: So Debutante Assn, Lowndes Coun on Aging; Bd Dirs: Lowndes Co Kidney Foun, Natchez Trace Assn; Nat Assn Parliamentns; Lowndes Co Hist Soc; Miss Hist Soc; Nat Trust; Former Repub Nat Com-wom; Nat Assns Jr Auxs; DAR; Magowah Gun & Hunt Clb; Wednesday Sewing Clb; Monday Bridge Clb; Others; r/Epis: Pres ECW St Paul's 1978-79; Altar Guild, Earline Robertson Guild, Yth Sponsor 1976-78; hon/GOP Wom of Yr, Miss 1969; Lowndes Co Wom of Yr 1972; Most Outstg Miss Alumnae Awd, Chi Omega.

HOOPES, ALICE ELIZABETH oc/Retired Supervising Social Case Worker; b/Jul 2, 1905; h/12923 Glenoaks Blvd, Sylmar, CA 91342; m/Adrian Greist (dec); p/Perry Nelson and Maud A Stetson Teeple (dec); ed/BA 1929; Grad Studies; pa/Fam Wel; Placemt of Spec Chd in Foster Homes; Placemt of Chd in Adoptive Homes; Tng Case Aides; Supvr Social Case Work LA Co DPSS; Others; Charter Mem Acad Cert'd Social Wkrs; NASW; CARSW; AARP; cp/Lung Assn; r/Unity; hon/Cert for 27 Yrs w LA Co; Gold Cert Mem Life Time, NASW & ACSW; Biogl Listings.

HOOTEN, ANN BRATRUD oc/Document Analyst; b/Jan 18, 1928; h/3806 W Calhoun Blvd, Minneaplis, MN 55410; ba/Mpls; m/Floyd; c/Susan Epperson Vater, Arthur Theodor, William Craig, Rebecca Ann; p/Arthur F Bratrud (dec); Harriet G Bratrud, Mpls; pa/Pvt Pract Document Analyst, Mpls 1958-; VP & Secy Edie Adams Cut & Curl Beauty Salons, Minn 1968-; Intl Assn for Identification; Ind Assn Document Examrs; BPW Clb; cp/Bd Dirs Maranatha Home for Aged; Edina CC; Others; hon/W/W MW.

HOPE, KATE JEFFREYS oc/Teacher; b/Nov 29, 1928; h/Rt 1, Box 79, Milton, NC 27305; m/Blanch, NC; m/Herbert L; c/Kathy LaVerne, Darrell LaSaine, Esselyn LaAnne; p/Essie and Maggie P Jeffreys (dec); ed/BS; MA; pa/NEA; CCEA; Zeta Phi Beta; Caswell Co Classroom Tchrs Assn; cp/High Rock PTA; Caswell Voters Leag; Boy Scout Ldr; Sr Citizen Advr; r/Macedonia AME Ch; High St & Haven Bapt Chs; hon/Tchr of Yr (Runnerup), Caswell Co 1977; Miss Alumni, Winston-Salem St Univ; Mother of Yr, Caswell Co 1976.

HOPE, THELMA PADDOCK oc/Artist; Writer; Poet; b/Nov 6, 1898; h/440 Santa Ana Ave, Newport Beach, CA 92663; m/Fredric Putnam (dec); c/Marcia Young, Fredric Paddock, Stephen Ackerman; p/Sherman and Elizabeth Ackerman Paddock (dec); ed/Chicago Art Inst; pa/Staff Artist MGM 7 Yrs; Tchr Col Adult Ed & Pvt Classes; 1st Portrait Comm, Rudolph Valentino (for Picture "Cobra"); Num Portraits, Murals; Zonta Intl; hon/1st & 3rd, Nat Leag Am Pen Wom (Cal); 1st Awd, All Cal Show (1923); Num Ribbon Awds.

HOPE, WALTER BARRINGTON oc/Professor; b/Aug 4, 1934; h/1319 44th Pl SE, Washington, DC 20019; ba/Wash DC; m/Beryl Kathlyn; c/Walter Jr, Lee, Juan; p/Aaron and Gladys Elizabeth Hope, Sparendaam, Guyana; ed/BA cum laude Howard Univ 1960; MA 1962, PhD 1977 Cath Univ Am; pa/Howard Univ: Prof Dept Geol & Geography, Instr & Lectr 1961-77, Chm Dept 1968-72, Exec Com 1968-71, Gen Ed Com Col Liberal Arts 1968-70; Lectr US Peace Corps Prog for Guyana 1966; Mem Num Profl Orgs;

Participant Sev Profl Meetings; Presented Papers; cp/Dept Keyman Campus Commun Chest; U Givers Fund; Campaign Activs; r/Presb Ch: Mem; hon/Gold Button, Guyana Weightlifting & Phy Cult Assn; Phi Alpha Theta; Pi Gamma Mu; Nat Scholastic Hon Socs; Ford Foun F'ship; NSF Grantee; W/W in Am; Pub'd Author.

HOPEWELL, HARRY LYNN oc/Telecommunications & Computer Systems; b/Dec 19, 1937; h/9105 Westerholme Way, Vienna, VA 22180; ba/Falls Church, VA; m/Leslie Ann Lindsay; c/Harry Lynn III, Frank Mathew; p/Harry Lynn Hopewell; Charlotte Ross Mathews; ed/AA Col William & Mary 1958; BA VPI 1961; MA Harvard 1968; pa/Sr Mem IEEE; Nat Chm IEEE Computer Soc; Tech Com on Computer Commun 1975-78; cp/Va Commerce: Bd Mem, VChm; Bd Dirs Va Soc for Preven of Blindness; r/Unitarian.

HOPKINS, MARGARET LAIL oc/College & University Librarian; b/Oct 19, 1910; h/2231 Colts Neck Rd, Apt 410, Reston, VA 22090; m/Garland Evans (dec); c/Nancy H Phillips, E C D, Peter Evans; p/David Arthur

and Hattie Hollie Lail (dec); ed/BA Scarritt Col; MSLS Cath Univ Am; pa/Life Mem: Va Lib Assn, Iranian Lib Assn; cp/Lib Conslt to Winchester-Frederick Co (Va) Hist Soc; r/Market St U Meth Ch, Winchester; hon/Fulbright Scholar (Iran).

HOPKINS, WILLIAM BARTON JR oc/Public Affairs Director; b/Nov 28, 1924; h/4420 Victory Ave, Minneapolis, MN 55412; ba/Golden Valley, MN; m/Rhea Joan; c/Ronald Gregory, William Jeffrey, Mary Elizabeth, Jonathan Barton; p/William Barton Hopkins (dec); Pansy M Ross, Baton Rouge, LA; ed/BA; mil/AUS Trans Corps, Water Div; pa/Public Affairs Dir Courage Ctr; Chm Tech Adv Com on Handicapped Minn St Dept Adm, St Bldg Code Div; CoChm Twin Cities Metro Transit Com for Disabled; Adv Com on Handicapped Minn St Dept Natural Resources, St Pks Div; Fdg Mem Nat Coun for Trans Disadvantaged; Bd Dirs Isls of Peace Foun; Nat & Minn Rehab Assns; Nat Ctr for Barrier Free Environment; Others; cp/Reg'd Lobbyist, St Minn Leg; Fdg Mem Sweetest Day Com; Mem & Past Pres Kiwanis Clb SW Mpls; Former Lt Gov Minn-Dakota Dist Kiwanis Intl; Mpls Lodge Loyal Order of Moose; r/So Bapt; hon/W/W in MW; Outstg Social Ser Wkr, St of Minn 1974.

HORAK, PENELOPE CATHERINE oc/Engineer/Administrator, Manager; h/5610 Katrine Ave, Downers Grove, IL 60515; ba/Batania, IL; p/Helene Catherine Kohes

(dec); ed/BS; MPA w highest hons; MPH w highest hons; Addit Studies; pa/Asst Div Dir Tech Sers, Fermilab; Pres Hinsdale BPW 1976-77; Intl Solar Energy Soc; Soc Logistic Engrs; AAUW; cp/Polit Cand (DuPage Co); Dem; hon/W/W MW; Personalities W&MW.

HORAN, CATHERINE ANNE oc/Doctoral Student; b/Sept 30, 1948; h/704 Sheridan Rd, Wilmette, IL 60091; p/Charles P and Julianna W Horan, Wilmette; ed/BA St

Xavier Col 1970; MMus 1971, PhD Cand 1976 NWn Univ; pa/Am Musicol Soc; Friends of Cast Iron Arch; Sigma Alpha Iota; cp/Smithsonian Assocs; r/Rom Cath; hon/Debut, NWn Univ; Tchg Certs.

HORAN, LINDA h/70th TRANS BN (AVIM), APO, NY 09028.

HORD, VIOLET CATHERINE McNEESE oc/Homemaker; Civic Worker; b/Dec 11, 1901; h/1219 S Box Elder, Casper, WY 82601; m/Charles Abner; c/Mary Violet H

Chopping, Charles William; p/Charles M and Rilla Magill McNeese (dec); ed/Att'd Univ Wyo 1920; cp/Past Pres Wyo St Hist Soc; Pres: Natrona Co Hist Soc, Am Legion Aux; r/Prot; hon/W/W: W, Am Wom.

HORKA, LORAYNE ANN oc/Physician; ba/Western-Jefferson Profl Group, 3111 S Wn Ave, Suite 202, Los Angeles, CA 90018; p/Lawrence and Hazel Cecilia DuHaime Horka, Whittier, CA; ed/BA Whittier Col 1961; MA Cal St Univ-LA 1964; LLB Blackstone Col Law 1971; Residency Roentgenology Glendale Chiropract Clin 1972-74; Addit Studies; pa/Est'd Own Clin 1977; Staff Phys: Manchester-Prairie Group 1974-77, Clin of Dr R Moscatel 1972-74; Instr Roentgenology LA Col Chiro 1973-74; Other Former Positions: Am Coun Wom Chiropractors; Am, Cal, LA Co Soc Chiropractic Assns; Am Chiropractic Coun on Roentgenology; Former Mem: Cal Tchrs Assn, PTA, El Rancho Ed Assn, Cal Coun on Adult Ed; cp/Sacred Heart of Mary Alumnae Assn; Whittier Col Alumni Assn; Conslt to Attys in Med-Legal Matters; r/Rom Cath; hon/Life Mem, Phi Delta Gamma; Fellow, St Andrew's Res Foun; Cit for Acad Achmt, Doct Prog; Others; Biogl Listings; Profl Pubs.

HORNADAY, WILLIAM H D oc/Minister; b/Apr 26; ba/3281 W 6th St, Los Angeles, CA 90020; m/Louise Clara Wright; c/William H D Hornaday III; p/William H D Sr and

Mary Leaming Hornaday (dec); ed/Hon DDiv, Rel Sci Inst; PhD Rel Sci Inst; Hon Master of Humanities, Cal State Col-LB; Hon DDiv, Whittier Col; pa/Min, Founder's Ch of Religious Science; Lectr; Granted Meth Ch Lay License to Preach at age 16; Missionary Study (Shanghai, China); Rel Study (Buddhism) in Japan; Conslt'd w Dr Albert Schweitzer (Lambarene, Africa); Theol Study w Karl Barth & Emil Brunner; Author: *Prayer for Universal Peace* (reprinted in 23 Langs), *Success Unlimited* (1955), *Life Everlasting* (1957), CoAuthor Others; Radio Broadcaster, "This Thing Called Life", daily prog on Los Angeles Sta KIEV (Armed Forces Radio Ser, Worldwide); Pacific Pioneer Broadcasters; cp/US Yacht Racing Union; Jonathan Clb (LA); Consistitory, Scottish Rite, Al Malaikah Shrine; Past Chm Bd Trustees, So Cal Chapt of Multiple Sclerosis Soc; Past Mem, Cal Adv Comm to US Com on Civil Rights (under Eisenhower & Kennedy); White House Conf on Hlth (appt'd by Pres Johnson); Bd Dirs: Cancer Prevention Soc (LA), Friendly House (for alcoholic wom), Intl Orphans Inc; r/Science of Mind; hon/Ser to Mankind Awd, Cal St Senate; Proclamation, City of LA; Humanitarian Awd, Albert Schweitzer Col (Switzerland); Freedoms Foun Awd; Terra Sancta, State Medal of Israel; Guest Chaplain, US Senate; Paul Harris F'ship, Rotary Intl; Others.

HORNBLASS, ALBERT oc/Medical Doctor; b/Jul 5, 1939; h/176 E 77th St, New York, NY 10021; ba/NYC; m/Bernice; c/David, Moshe; p/Maurice Hornblass (dec); Betty Hornblass, Brooklyn, NY; ed/BA; BRE; MD; mil/Chief Ophthal 71st Evacuation Hosp, Pleiku S Vietnam 1969-70; Kimbrough Army Hosp, Ft George Meade, Md 1970-71; pa/Ophthal Plastic Surg; Assoc Chief Ophthal Walter Reed Gen Hosp, Washington DC; cp/VP Bd Jewish Ed, NYC; Nat Cabinet UJH; Bd Dirs HIAS; r/Jewish; hon/Bronze Star; Medal of Hon; 1st Class, Vietnamese Govt; 3 Battle Ribbons; Vietnamese Campaign; 25 Anniv Alumni Grad of Yr, Hebrew Inst Boro Park; Warner Hoppins Awd, NY Acad Med (2); Others.

HORNE, ANNIE PEARL COOKE oc/-Civic Worker; b/Nov 2, 1918; h/1107 Anderson St, Wilson, NC 27893; m/Elmer Lee; c/Patricia H Smith, Elmer Lee, Doris H Pruitt, Hadie Cooke; p/Erastus and Pearl C Cooke; ed/Grad Wilson Tech Inst; pa/Saleslady J C Penny Co Inc, Wilson 1939-41; Horne Scale & Equipmt Co, Wilson: Secy 1942-77, VP 1942-; cp/Vol Wkr Wilson Meml Hosp; Former Vol Wilson Crisis Ctr; Former Cnslr Jr Garden Clb, Wilson; Org'd Jr Garden Clb for En NC Sch for Deaf; Lois Rainwater Ext Homemaker Clb (Wilson Co); Former Secy-Treas Dem Precnt #2, Wilson; Former Cub Scout Den Mother, Wilson; Albrusa Clb; Wilson Wom's Clb; BPW Clb; r/1st Christian Ch, Wilson: Deaconess 1965-69, Ofcr Friendship SS Class 1938-75; hon/Ser to Mankind Awd, Sertoma Clb; Green Band Awd, Wilson Dist Scouting Com; Silver Tray Awd, Wilson Wom's Clb; Merit Awds: Altrusa Clb, BPW Clb.

HORNSBY, J MARIE oc/Writer; b/Jul 21, 1927; h/Briarwood Ests, PO Box 2156, Gulfport, MS 39503; m/Thomas L; c/Wanda M; p/Mr and Mrs John L Baker, Gulfport; pa/Author & Lectr; 20 Works on Market incl'g: *The Recipe for Eternal Life;* Contb'g Editor Rel Page Reg Pub; Owner & Operator Honey in the Rock (Full Ser Bookstore); r/Bapt; hon/Lib Human Resources; DIB; World W/W Wom; W/W: Miss, Am Wom; Outstg Ams S; Commun Ldrs & Noteworthy Ams.

HORNSBY, J RUSSELL oc/Attorney; b/Jul 3, 1924; h/480 S Lake Sybelia Dr, Maitland, FL 32751; ba/Orlando, FL; c/Lawrence H, James Russell, Kevin Lee, Tonya Lisa, David Brandon, Richard Earl; p/Benjamin Franklin Hornsby (dec); Lillie Weiss Hornsby, Davenport, FL; ed/LLB; mil/USMC; pa/Fla Bar; Orange Co Bar; Am Bar; Acad Fla Trial Lwyrs; cp/Loyal Order of Moose; Legion of Moose; Am Legion; C of C;

Rolling Hills CC; r/Epis.

HOROVITZ, SAMUEL BERTRAM oc/Lawyer; Lecturer; Author; b/Nov 23, 1897; h/16 Shuman Cir, Newton, MA 02159; ba/Boston, MA; m/Evelyn M; c/Paul, David; p/Israel and Bessie Horovitz (dec); ed/AB 1920, JD 1922 Harvard; mil/WW I & II; pa/Prof Workmen's Compensation Suffolk Law Sch, Boston; World-Wide Lectr on Workman's Compensation; Author 15 Books; 50 Articles & Book Reviews; cp/Repub; VP Temple B'nai B'rith, Boston; r/Jewish; hon/Phi Beta Kappa; Harvard Pres Appointee to US Com on Workmen's Compensation.

HORTON, JANET E oc/Television Producer-Writer; Artist; b/Nov 4, 1930; h/3203 Prytania, New Orleans, LA 70115; ba/Same; m/Marvin D; c/James M, Anne Marie; p/Charles A and Eva Morton Hunt (dec); ed/BFA Univ Neb 1953; Grad Studies La St Univ 1975-77; pa/MEMO; Miss Art Assn; Rep'd by Two Plus Two, Ltd Art Gallery; cp/Bd Dirs Yg *Audiences;* Coor Media Trinity Epis; r/Epis; hon/Num Painting Awds incl'g 1st Awd, Cross-Tie Arts Competition, Cleveland, Miss; Scripted & Prod'd 200-Prog Series "Art for the Day", WMAA, Jackson, Miss (Voted to Receive Peabody Awd for Excell in Overall Prodn).

HORWICH, DIANA M DeWOLF HUBBARD oc/Executive; b/Sept 24, 1952; h/210 S Ft Harrison Ave, Clearwater, FL 33516; ba/New York, NY; m/Jonathan Lewis; c/Roanne Lee Marysue; p/L Ron and Marysue Hubbard; pa/Exec Mgmt Intly; cp/Social Reform in Govt & Ed; r/Scientology; hon/Var Scientology Awds; Keys to Long Beach (Cal); Var Royal Acad Hons in Arts (England).

HORWITZ, THOMAS ARTHUR oc/-Theatrical Make-Up Artist; Theatrical Lighting Engineer; Sculptor; b/Sept 7, 1906; h/7021 Environ Blvd, #415, Inverrary, Lauderhill, FL 33319; m/Selma S; c/Elinor H Stecker; p/Joseph and Fay Horwitz (dec); ed/BFA Mechs Inst; MA Univ Rochester; pa/Pres Mich Theatrical Light Co, Pontiac, Mich 1942-; Lectr on Art of Make-up for Spch & Drama Depts at Maj Cols & Univs; Dir Make-up for Large Outdoor Pageants & Spectacles incl'g: Railroads on Parade (NYC) 1939, Syracuse Jubilee 1937, Century of Progress (Rochester, NY) 1933, Tex Centennial 1933, A Century of Progress (Chicago, Ill) 1933-34; Acad Make-up Artists; Soc Restorative Make-up Artists; Pontiac Soc Artists; cp/Secy YMCA; Kappa Nu; Past Pres B'nai B'rith; Past Master Mason; Grotto; Elks; Shrine; Pythias; Toastmasters; Coun of Human Relats; Rotary; Illum Engrs; r/Jewish; hon/Num Awds for Sculpture; Exhbns of Work; Biogl Listings.

HOSMER, CRAIG oc/Energy Analyst; b/May 6, 1915; h/5024 Van Ness St NW, Washington, DC 20016; ba/Wash DC; m/Marian C; c/Craig L, Susan J; p/Chester C and Mary Craig Hosmer (dec); ed/AB Univ Cal-B 1937; JD Univ So Cal 1940; mil/USNR, Real Admiral (Ret'd); pa/Atty at Law; Writer & Spkr; Pres Am Nuclear Energy Coun 1975-78; Mem Bars: Cal, DC, US Supreme Ct; cp/Mem Cong (Cal) 1953-75; r/Prot; hon/Var Mil & Civil.

HOSTETLER, DAVID LEE oc/Sculptor; b/Dec 27, 1926; h/PO Box 989, Athens, OH 45701; ba/Athens; p/Melwood David and Grace Anna Penrod Hostetler (dec); ed/BS Ind Univ 1948; MFA Ohio Univ 1949; pa/Sculptor Am Wom Series; Ohio Arts Coun 1971; Vis Prof Woodcarving Coun Grove Sch Arts & Crafts, Missoula, Mont (Sum) 1976; Ohio Univ: Prof Sculpture 1967-77, Assoc Prof Sculpture 1961-66, Asst Prof Ceramics 1956-61, Instr Ceramics 1950-56; Other Former Tchg Positions; Num One-Man Exhbns incl: Swearingen & Haynie Gallery, Louisville, Ky 1977, Hambleton Gallery, Nantucket Isl, Mass 1977, Cedar Rapids Art Ctr, Cedar Rapids, Ia 1976, McCann-Wood Gallery, Lexington, Ky 1974, Num Others; Num Group Exhbns incl: Winter Group Exhbn Buyways Gallery, Sarasota, Fla 1976, 77, Ohio Artists & Craftsmen Invitational,

Massillon Mus, Massillon, Ohio 1976; Am Masters Exhbn Canterbury Sch Gallery, Ft Myers, Fla 1975; Num Others; Fdr Art Park 1969 (Experimt in Art & Envir, Athens, Ohio); Rep'd US in Expo '71, Montreal, Canada; Others; hon/Over 2 Dozen Art Awds; Public Collections incl: Milwaukee Mus Perm Collection, Mid Tenn St Univ, St Lawrence Univ, Solon Public Lib (Cleveland, Ohio), Ft Lauderdale Mus, Others; Elected to Exec Bd Kenneth Taylor Gallery, Nantucket, Mass 1974; Designe Ohio Arts Awd, Ohio Arts Coun 1971; DIB; W/W: MW, Am Art, Am; Others.

HOSTETLER, SHIRLEY ANN oc/High School Librarian; h/420 Sherman, Meyersdale, PA 15552; ba/Rockwood, PA; p/Carl E Hostetler (dec); Florence S Hostetler, Meyersdale; ed/BS; MS; pa/Libn Rockwood Area HS; NEA; PSEA; REA; Scholastic Quiz

Advr; Sr Class Advr; cp/Casselman Val Choral Soc; Maple Fest; r/Grace Brethren: SS Pianist, Ch Organist; hon/DIB; Intl W/W Commun Ser; Notable Ams; Commun Ldrs & Noteworthy Ams; W/W Sch Dist Ofcls.

HOUCHINS, JUNE FARLEY oc/Guidance Counselor; b/May 22, 1936; h/3106 Lynch St SW, Massillon, OH 44646; ba/Massillon; m/Thomas J; c/Lisa Michelle; p/Cyrus O Farley (dec); Lena B Vallentine, Canton, OH; ed/BS; MA; pa/Guid Cnslr; NEA; OEA; ECOEA; SCEA; TCTA; SCGA; NRTA; OSCA; OACAC; r/Bapt; hon/Kappa Omicron Phi; Outstg Yg Wom Am; Outstg Sec'dy Edrs; Notable Ams; W/W Am Wom; World W/W Wom.

HOUCK, LEWIS DANIEL JR oc/Economist; Educator; US Government Official; b/Jul 9, 1932; h/1111 Woodson Ave, Kensington, MD 20795; ba/Washington, DC; c/Marianne Jennifer, Leland Daniel; p/Lewis D and Mary D Houck, Princeton, NJ; ed/AB Princeton Univ 1955; MBA w distn 1964, PhD

1971 NY Univ; mil/USNR 1955-56, 1/Lt; pa/US Dept Agri, Wash DC: Project Ldr Ec Res Ser 1973-, Spec Conslt 1971-73; Ednl Projects Mgr Nat Assn Accts, NYC 1969-71; Instr NYU Grad Sch Bus, NYC 1966-69; Other Former Positions; Acad Polit Sci; IPA; Am Inst Mgmt; Am Acct'g Assn; Am Ec Assn; Am Acad Polit & Social Sci; Am Mktg Assn; AAAS; Others; cp/Former Campaign Activs; Princeton Clb Wash; r/Epis; hon/Ford Foun Fellow; Fdrs Day Awd, NYU; Fellow: ABI, IBA; Chm Mktg & Communs Sems, 4th Cong IBC (London, England) 1977; Biogl Listings.

HOUGHTON, NEAL DOYLE oc/Professor; b/May 8, 1895; h/2134 E Sixth St, Tucson, AZ 85719; ba/Tucson; m/Katherine; c/Neal Doyle, Virginia Mae Culhane, Charles William; p/William Dudley and Engeline Lawson Houghton (dec); ed/BS; MA; PhD; pa/Prof Polit Sci Univ Ariz 1928-; Prof Polit Sci NE Mo Tchrs Col 1925-28; Vis Prof: Univs Mo, Ill, Wash & Sask (Canada); Pres Wn Polit Sci Assn; Exec Coun Am Polit Sci Assn; Am Soc Intl Law; AAUP; cp/Mem & VChm Ariz Power Com 10 Yrs; r/Prot; hon/Carnegie F'ship; Tucson Trade Bur Fac Recog Awd, Outstg Ser Univ Ariz; Retiremt Awd, Univ Ariz; Annual Neal D Houghton S'ship Est'd at Univ Ariz 1972; Contbr to Profl Pubs; Biogl Listings.

HOULIHAN, BARBARA ETT oc/Manager; b/Sept 2, 1937; h/14321 Cherrywood Ln, Tustin, CA 92680; ba/Anaheim, CA; c/Elizabeth, Michael, Patricia; p/Alanzo and Claudia Bell; p/Mgr Maj Subcontracts Mgmt; Ofcr Nat Mgmt Assn; NCMA; AMA; Wom in Mgmt; Profl Wom in Mgmt; Tchr/Conslt Rockwell Intl; cp/Singer Irvine Master Chorale; Mem Benefit Com for New Orange Co Music Ctr; Mem UCI Coun for Devel of Contract Mgmt Courses; hon/Cert of Achmt, YWCA; Blue Book Am Heritage; Blue Book Orange Co; W/W Am Wom; World W/W Wom.

HOUSEAL, REUBEN ARTHUR oc/-Clergyman; Educator; Writer; b/Jan 6, 1910; h/132 S Erie St, PO Box 132, Mercer, PA 16137; m/1st Jennie Belle Hinkle (dec); 2nd Marguerite Edna Ruth Arnold; c/Reuben John, Elizabeth June (Mrs James Page Honecker), Lawrence Garrison; p/John Franklin and Beatrice Vervean Dellinger Houseal; ed/Grad Phila Col Bible & Evang Tchr Tng Assn 1932; AM Univ Pa 1935; Postgrad Reformed Epis Theol Sem 1934-37; ThD 1973, LLD 1974, PhD 1977 Clarksville Sch Theol; Hon MS Cit by Ency Britannica 1954; pa/Ordained Min 1940; Pastor: Bethany Commun Ch Dayton, Ohio 1937-40, Olive Br Congreg Ch St Louis, Mo 1941-45, Ctl Bapt Ch Erie, Pa 1950-57; CoFdr, VP, Acad Dean Calvary Sch Theol Mercer, Pa 1974-; Instnl Chaplain Mercer Co Bible Conf Spkr & Evangelistic Min 1967-; Writer *Weekly Meditation* Column 1960-; Fdr/Dir GospeLiteHouse of the Air 1942-57; Constituent Mem The York Gospel Ctr; Mem Exec Bd & Fac, Greensburg (Pa) Bible Inst 1960-71; cp/Life Mem Mercer Co Hist Soc; r/Indep Fundamental Chs Am, HQs Westchester, Ill; hon/Outstg Alumnus Awd Phila Col of Bible 1972; Cert Merit & Dist'd Achmt Cit, Life Fellow, Intl Biogl Assn 1976; Life Patron ABIRA; Ky Col; Pub'd Author: *Enoch's Monumental Masterpiece - The Great Pyramid of Gizeh, Halloween - Is It Christian or Pagan?, Why We Are Not Ecumenists, An Introduction to Evangelical Fundamental Christian Theology* (Textbook), Others; Biogl Listings.

HOUSEAL, RUTH ARNOLD oc/Retired Educator; Clergyman's Wife; b/Nov 23, 1904; h/132 S Erie St, PO Box 132, Mercer, PA 16137; m/Reuben Arthur; c/John Andrew Johnson, Marguerite Johnson (Mrs Donald E Redmond); p/Samuel B McAle and Mary Edna Williams Arnold; Dipl 1927, BS 1958 Slippery Rock St Col; MS Westminster Col 1963; Scofield-Grad Moody Bible Inst 1966; DRE 1973, Hon LHD 1974 Clarksville Sch Theol; pa/Ret'd Edr; Successfully Ed'd Exceptl Chd 1955-70; Classroom Tchr, Bldg Prin 1943-47; Classroom Tchr, Art Supvr 1924-33;

Life Mem Nat, Pa St Ed Assns; cp/Life Mem Mercer Co Hist Soc; r/Indep Fundamental Chs of Am, HQs at Westchester, Ill; hon/Life Patron ABIRA; Pub'd Author: *A Survey of Christian Education; Life Fellow Intl Biogl Assn; W/W Rel; DIB; Intl Reg Profiles; 1st Edition Intl Men & Wom of Distn; Book of Honor; Notable Ams; Commun Ldrs & Noteworthy Ams.*

HOUSEL, JAMES ROBERT oc/Library Director; h/PO Box 855, Ontario, CA 91761; ba/Ontario; m/Virginia; c/Lucille, Thomas, Marian; p/(dec); ed/BA Univ Wyo 1941; BSLS Univ Cal-B 1948; MSLS Univ So Cal 1971; mil/AUS 1941-46, ETO-USA; pa/Lib Dir-Adm Ontario City Lib 1959-; Hd Libn-Adm Monterey Park (Cal) Public Lib 1956-59; Dir-Adm 1st Reg Lib Miss 1952-56; Hd Libn Ellensburg (Wash) Public Lib 1950-52; Other Former Positions; Am & Cal Lib Assns; Inland Lib Sys; Public Lib Exec Assn So Cal; Chaffey HS Study Com; Fdr & Pres Cal Inst Parapsychol; Lib Assn (England); cp/Am Legion; Masons; Chaffey Communs Cult Ctr Bd; Pomona Val Writers' Clb; Cal Hist Soc; 1st Pres W End Symph Orch Assn; Ontario C of C; hon/Pub'd Papers; Men of Achmt; Commun Ldrs Am; Personalities W&MW; Royal Blue Book; 2000 Men Achmt; DIB; Dir Lib Conslts; Other Biogl Listings.

HOUSTON, CAROL S oc/Instructional Television Producer/Director; b/Jan 25, 1948; h/1873 Lincoln Ave, E Meadow, NY 11554; ba/Garden City, NY; m/Al; p/Milton Shulman (dec); Celia Saltzman, Brooklyn, NY; ed/MS Bklyn Col 1971; pa/Instrnl TV Prodr/Dir Nassau Commun Col; Nat Assn Ednl Broadcasters, Com Chm; cp/Vol Work in Commun; r/Jewish; hon/Alexander Lampart Awd; Appt'd Co-Editor Newslttr, *Broadcast Ed*, NAEB.

HOUSTON, HARRY ROLLINS b/Mar 2, 1928; h/2070 NE Oriole Way, Bremerton, WA 98310; ba/Bremerton; m/Bette-Jane G; c/Susan, James, Barbara; p/Howard R and Ethel E Houston; ed/MD Tufts Univ Med Sch 1955; mil/USN MC 31 Yrs, Ret'd Capt; pa/Obstetrician/Gynecologist; Chief Obs/Gyn Harrison Meml Hosp, B'ton; cp/CoPres N Kitsap Chapt Am Rhododendron Soc; r/Congreg.

HOUSTON, LILLIAN PEARL SCOTT oc/Instructor/Program Coordinator; b/Oct 24, 1946; h/1435 N Bois d'Arc, Tyler, TX 75702; ba/Marshall, TX; m/David R; p/Hosea Jr and Lula Mae Hampton Scott, Tyler; ed/BA Tex Col; MS ETSU; pa/Instr/Prog Coor Nsg Home Adm Wiley Col; Am Col Nsg Home Adm; Tex Nsg Home Assn; cp/Nat Caucus on Black Aged; Bd Mem Harrison Co Nsg Home, Marshall; r/Christian Meth Epis Ch; hon/Outstg Yg Wom Am; Men & Wom Distn; Personalities of S; W/W Among Black Ams.

HOUTMANN, JACQUES GEORGES oc/Music Director, Conductor; b/Mar 27, 1935; h/5303 Toddsbury Rd, Richmond, VA 23226; ba/Richmond; m/Yolaine; c/Helene, Marie-Virginie; p/Georges and Paule Houtmann, Mirecourt (France); ed/Licence in Conducting, Ecole Normale (Paris); Dipl Sta Coecilia (Roma); pa/Conductor in Europe, USA & SAm; cp/Rotary Intl; r/Cath; hon/DFA, Univ Richmond; 1st Prize, Mitropoulos Competition in Conducting (NY); 1st Prize, Conductor Competition (Besancon, France).

HOUTS, EARL oc/Realtor's Associate; b/Jun 29, 1912; h/105 Oak St, Slippery Rock, PA 16057; ba/Wexford, PA; m/Kathryn Neumeyer; c/Carol Anne Purich, Jamie Lynn Smith; p/D L and Emma Ashwill Houts (dec); ed/BEd; MM; DEd; mil/AGF 1943-46; cp/Grad Adv Com Slippery Rock Col; cp/Rotary Intl; r/Meth; hon/Ldrs in Ed; Outstg Edrs Am; DIB; Notable Ams Bicent Era; W/W; W/W in E; Notable Ams 1976-77.

HOWARD, JAMES TOMMY oc/Police Chaplain; b/Aug 6, 1948; h/4028 Foxe Basin Rd, Lexington, KY 40503; ba/Lexington; m/Margaret Noreen; c/Andrea Suzanne;

p/James Howard (dec); Edith Howard, P'ville; ed/BS En Ky Univ; mil/USAR; pa/Gospel Singer; Mem Min Assn; r/So Bapt; hon/Sev: Local Kiwanis Clbs, Lions Clb, Others.

HOWARD, JIM M oc/Vocational Agriculture Instructor; b/Nov 18, 1945; h/Rt 2, Box 174, Mt Vernon, MO 65712; ba/Mt Vernon; p/Merwyn and Lillian Shiermeyer Howard, Mt Vernon; ed/BS 1967, MEd 1973 Univ Mo-C; pa/Voc Agri Instr Mt Vernon R-5

Sch; MSTA; Past Pres CTA; AVA; MVA; NVATA; MVATA; Dist Pres Farm Bur; cp/C of C; MC for Applebutter Making Days; r/1st Christian Ch: Elder, Chm of Bd; hon/MVATA: Dist'd Ser, St Win Exc of Ideas; Farmer's Friend, Farm Bur; Mt Vernon Tchr of Yr.

HOWARD, JOHN MALONE oc/Professor; b/Aug 25, 1919; h/924 Francis Ave, Toledo, OH 43609; ba/Toledo; m/Nina Abernathy; c/John M, Robert F, Nina, George G, Susan E, Laura L; p/Fontaine Maury and Mary O'Brien Howard (dec); ed/BS; MD; mil/AUS MC 1951-53, Capt; Dir AUS Res Team in Korea; Legion of Merit; pa/Pres Am Trauma Soc; cp/Vol Surg in Algeria, Vietnam; r/Meth; hon/Dist'd Ser Awds: Am Trauma Soc, AMA.

HOWARD, MARTHA CUMMINS oc/-Associate Dean, Associate Professor; b/Mar 6, 1922; h/360 Mulberry St, Morgantown, WV 26505; ba/M'town; m/John W (dec); c/Thomas W; p/Charles Frank and Ella Ruby Allen Cummins (dec); ed/AB, AM Univ Mich; mil/USNR 1943-51, Lt (jg); pa/Ch Arts & Scis WVa Univ: Assoc Dean, Assoc Prof Eng; Past Pres WVa Assn Acad Deans; NCTE; SCMLA; Acad Adm; Delta Kappa Gamma; St Coor for Identification of Wom in Adm, ACE; cp/Chm Chd's Theater; M'town Ser Leag; Past Pres: WVa Coun Chd's Arts, M'town Wom's Music Clb; r/Prot; hon/Outstg Tchr Awd, Col Arts & Scis; Personalities of S; W/W: Am Scholars, Am Wom.

HOWARD, NOAH EUGENE oc/Banker; Farmer; Supervisor; Author; b/Jun 4, 1923; h/38 Hassler Mill Rd, Harriman, TN 37748; m/Melda Marie James; c/Nathan Eugene, Nancy Evone; p/Gilbert Herman and Lanora B Howard; mil/Att'd USN Trade Schs; USN 1941-45; pa/Union Carbide Nuclear Corp: Joined 1946, Currently Maintenance Supvr; Oak Ridge-Knoxville Chapt Soc Mfg Engrs; Conservationist Tenn Citizens for Wilderness Planning; Bd Dirs 1st Nat Bk & Trust Co, Rockwood, Tenn; cp/1 of Original Promotors & Advocator of Preserving Obed River

(Morgan Co) as Scenic River; SAR; Secy & Treas Am Bicent Comm (Roane Co); S Gate Lodge #569 F&AM Harriman; Past Pres S Harriman Ruritan Clb (Ruritan Nat); r/S Harriman Bapt Ch, Harriman: Bd Deacons, SS Tchr; hon/Author *War In Tenn, Ky & Ga* (Based on Civil War), Also Sev Articles on Obed River.

HOWARTH, PATRICIA HARRIET oc/Elementary School Teacher; b/Aug 17, 1949; h/31 Reid St, Sayreville, NJ 08872; ba/S'ville; p/Wilbur T and Margaret Grady Howarth, S'ville; ed/BA Ga Ct Col; pa/1st Grad Tchr Our Lady of Victories; Former 5th & 6th Grade Tchr Social Studies; NCEA; Math Curric Com Chm Primary Grades; cp/Parish Yth Act Org: Mem, Former Corr'g Secy; Dir Sch Folk Group; CYO: Former Advr, Dir Folk Group; Parish Bicent Float Com; Fac Advr Student Coun; Singer w "Amici Musicorum" (Jersey City); r/Rom Cath; hon/Delta Tau Kappa; Outstg Ldrs Elem & Sec'dy Ed; Commun Ldrs & Noteworthy Ams.

HOWE, EVELYN FREEMAN oc/Public School Teacher; b/Jan 11; h/219 Crestview Dr, Gaffney, SC 29340; m/Jack D; c/Andrew W, Angela J; p/D O and Janie B Freeman (dec); ed/BA Limestone Col; MAT Winthrop Col; pa/Past Pres Cherokee Co Ed Assn; Rep to Del Assembly; Bldg Rep to CCEA; Past Pres

Gaffney Br AAUW; cp/Concert Com; Past Pres: Jr Wom's Clb, Town & Gown; r/Limestone Presb: Circle Chm, Past Pres Wom of Ch; hon/People to People Goodwill Ambassador to Europe 1967; Recipient 1st Annual Awd for Ser to Commun, Limestone Col.

HOWE, JONATHAN THOMAS oc/-Attorney at Law; b/Dec 16, 1940; h/3845 Normandy Ln, Northbrook, IL 60062; ba/Chicago, IL; m/Lois H; c/Heather, Jonathan T Jr, Sara; p/Fred K and Rosalie C Howe; ed/BA w hons NWn Univ; JD w distn Duke Univ 1966; pa/Partner Jenner & Block, Chgo; Gen Pract 1966-; Mem Firm Exec Bd & Mgmt Com 1975-; Admitted to Pract: Supreme Ct Ill 1966-, US Dist Ct No Dist Ill 1966-, US Ct of Appeals 7th Circuit 1967-, DC Ct Appeals 1976-, US Supreme Ct 1970-, US Tax Ct 1968-; ABA: Chm Yg Lwyrs Sect, Mbrship Com, Ill 1967-71, Others; Var Positions Held Ill St & Chgo Bar Assns; DC Bar Assn; Am Judic Soc 1966-70; Legal Clb Chgo; Lectr-Author Ill Inst for Cont'g Legal Ed; Panelist ABA Nat Inst Antitrust Sect "The Enforcers" 1972; Mem Lwyrs Coun Am Soc Assn Execs; cp/Pres Bd of Ed Div No 27; Ill Assn Sch Bds; Pres & Bd Dirs Sch Mgmt Foun Ill; Nat Sch Bds Assn; Former Mem Exec Com Northfield Twp Repub Org; NWn Univ & Duke Univ Alumni Assns; Chgo Ath Assn; r/Village Presb Ch, Northbrook: Bd Deacons; hon/Profl Pubs; W/W: Am Law, MW; Notable Ams.

HOWE, LYMAN H III oc/Research Chemist; b/Nov 5, 1938; h/1241 Mountain Brook Cir, Signa Mountain, TN 37377; ba/Chattanooga, TN; m/Mary Louise Reinhart; c/Jennifer; p/Lyman Harold and Esther Madeline Howe (dec); ed/BS Duke Univ 1960; MS Emory Univ 1961; PhD Univ Tenn 1966; pa/Res Chemist TVA Div Envir Planning, Chatta; ASTM: D-19 Water Com Results Advr, Chm Voltammetry Task Group, D-22.03 Secy on Instrumentation for Atmospheres Com; Am Chem Soc; Nat Mgmt

Assn; AAAS; Torch Clb; r/Presb; hon/Personalities of S; DIB; Notable Ams; Men of Achmt; W/W S&SW; Book of Honor.

HOWE, WILLIAM E oc/Electronics Engineer; b/Jun 5, 1920; h/4940 Lowell St NW, Washington, DC 20016; m/Mary Louise H; c/William Clay, Eleanor Cameron, Robert Collins; p/Edmund G and Eleanor Louise White Howe (dec); ed/AB Yale; Cert Univ Ala; MS Georgetown; Nat War Col; mil/USNR Lcdr, Ret'd; Active Duty WWII; pa/Engrg & Sci Orgs; cp/Grand Jury Foreman (2 Times); Citizens Assn; r/Epis; hon/Dist'd Civilian Ser Awd, Dept of Navy.

HOWELL, HENRY GARLAND oc/Auto Electro Plating Line Operator; Evangelical Vocalist; b/Aug 31, 1920; h/3430 Floyd St, Ashland, KY 41101; ba/Huntington, WV; m/Audrey Louise Lemaster (dec); c/Carlin Sue H Wright, Gereda Myra H West; p/Henry and Ottie Bowling Howell, Glenwood, KY; ed/Att'd Mrs T M Chandler Studio of Music &

Voice; mil/AUS 1941-43, Pvt 1/C; Survivor of Pearl Harbor Attack; pa/Auto Electro Plating Line Operator, Houdaille Industries, Huntington, WVa, Ret'd 1978 after 29 Yrs Ser; Profl Evangel Vocalist, Ch & Radio; Featured in Rel Prog "Forward in Faith Meditation"; cp/Masonic Lodge 626, Willard; r/W Catlettsburg (Ky) U Meth Ch: Mem; hon/Ky Col & Comm'd Admiral by Commonwealth of Ky, Dept Natural Resources, 1969; Featured in Mass Media.

HOWLETT, PHYLLIS L oc/Assistant to Athletic Director; b/Oct 23, 1932; h/2605 Madison Ave, Des Moines, IA 50310; ba/Des Moines; m/Ronlin L Royer; c/Timothy A Howlett, Jane A Howlett; p/J Clarence and Mabel F Hickman, Indianola, IA; ed/BA

Simpson Col 1954; pa/Asst to Ath Dir for Men Drake Univ; Nat Assn Dirs Collegiate Aths; cp/Chair Ia Comm on Status of Wom; Former Nat Pres Assn Vol Burs Inc; Past Pres Ia Chd & Fam Sers.

HOWSER, JOHN WILLIAM oc/Surgeon; b/Dec 27, 1911; h/5 Oakbrook Clb Dr, Oakbrook, IL 60521; ba/Oak Park, IL; m/Lya Fulgenzi (dec); p/Reid Owen and Jessie Johnston Howser (dec); ed/BA Cornell Col 1933; BS 1934, BM 1936, MD 1937 NWn Univ; mil/AUS 1943, Capt; pa/W Suburban Hosp, Oak Park: Pres Staff 1970-71, Chm Past Surg Staff; Prof Surg Cook Co Grad Sch; Cook Co Hosp: Att'g Surg, Resident Surg 1936-42; cp/Bd Trustees: W Suburban Hosp, Cornell Col, Cook Co Grad Sch; r/Prot; hon/Fellow: Am Col Surgs, Chgo Surg Soc, Intl Col Surgs; Diplomate, Am Bd Surg.

HOYT, CLAREMONT EARL oc/Minister; b/Jun 24, 1908; h/50 N 32nd St, Newark, OH 43055; ba/Marion, OH; m/Margaret H; c/Carolyn A, Mary E Griffes, John A, Josephine E Bero, Margaret A Nasemann, David F; p/Arthur E Hoyt (dec); Flora B Hoyt, Huntington, WV; ed/BA Heidelberg Col; pa/SS Missionary, Am SS Union 1931-32, 1936-41; Min Am Bapt Chs: Ohio, NY & Mich 1941-74; Staff Min Ohio Bapt Conv 1974-77; Min-at-Large Am Bapt Chs USA; Interim Min Grand Prairie Bapt Ch, Marion; cp/Mayor Bethesda, Ohio 1943; Former Chaplain Nat Home Daughs of Am; Past Pres: Meigs Co Coun Christian Ed, Pomeroy (Ohio) Lions Clb; r/1st Bapt Ch, Granville, Ohio; hon/Nat Hon Soc; 25 Yr Ser Awd, Ohio Bapt Conv.

HOYT, STEPHEN LEE oc/Marriage & Family Counselor; b/Feb 24, 1947; h/2408 Auburn St #115, Lubbock, TX 79415; ba/Lubbock; m/LaRita; c/William T and Janet L Hoyt, Pittsburg, PA; ed/BA; MS; mil/AUS, Hon Disch 1971; pa/Marriage & Fam Cnslr Univ Cnsl'g Ctr, Tex Tech Univ; Am Assn for Marriage & Fam Therapy; Am Assn Sex Edrs, Cnslrs & Therapists; r/1st Christian Ch; hon/Phi Kappa Phi.

HRINKO, JEAN AYR oc/Teacher; b/Mar 20, 1923; h/3641 Troy Rd, Springfield, OH 45504; ba/S'field; m/Henry Peter; c/Daniel Dean; p/Benjamin Harrison and Inez Nora Gregory Wallace, S'field; ed/BS; Certs: Deaf Ed, LD, EMR; pa/Tchr of Hearing Impaired Chd; NEA; OEA; SEA; ACLD; CEC; Ohio Low Incidence Curric Com; Highland Sch Fac Counsel; cp/Mercy Hosp & Commun Hosp Guilds; Opera Guild; Quota Intl; S'field Art Assn; r/Prot; hon/Wom of Yr, Quota Intl; Tchr of Yr; Jennings Scholar.

HSI, EUGENE YU-TSENG oc/Professor; b/May 25, 1917; h/902 Cheryl Ave, Marshall, MN 56258; ba/Marshall; m/Siu-Tsun; c/Nancy Shi-Heng, Edward Shi-Ping; p/Teh-Feng and Chu-Siu Hsu Hsi (dec); ed/BS; MS; PhD; mil/Army Pharm Plantation (China)

1942-44; pa/Prof Biol; Dir Univ Herbarium & Greenhouse; cp/Participant Activs w Reg DNR & Park Bd Wkshops, Field Trips; hon/Nat Def Sci Awd for Discovery of Rubber Substitute in Szechuan, Chinese Govt.

HSU, JOHN CHEU-WANG oc/Energy Engineer; b/Sept 27, 1941; h/8441 Deepcliff Dr, Huntington Beach, CA 92646; ba/Redondo Beach, CA; m/Auxilia C; c/Leslie Dehgine, John Dehsaar; p/Yen-zing Hsu and Chen-ming Woo, Taiwan, China; ed/BS Nat Taiwan Univ 1963; MS 1967, MS 1971, PhD 1976 NC St Univ; mil/Chinese Air Force 1963-64, 2/Lt; pa/Project Engr Tech Staff TRW Inc 1978-; Sr Engr Carolina Power & Light Co, Raleigh, NC 1972-78; Res Asst Dept Nuclear Engrg NC St Univ, Raleigh 1970-72; Other Former Positions; r/Cath; hon/Num Profl Pubs; Dean's List (Col); W/W S&SW.

HSU, JOSEPH JEN-YUAN oc/Biomedical Scientist; International Financing Consultant; b/Mar 25, 1928; h/1500 Hornell Loop, Brooklyn, NY 11239; ba/New York, NY; m/Helen W; c/Ava, Hank, Bond; p/Wang-Chih Hsu and Ping-Heng Ling, Shanghai, PRC; ed/BS; MS; PhD; pa/R/D in Cancer & Cardiovas Diseases; cp/Bilingual Ed; r/Quaker; hon/W/W in E; Other Biogl Listings.

HSU, WYEN-YING oc/Composer; Performer; b/1909; h/440 N Madison Ave #117, Pasadena, CA 91101; ed/Yenching Univ (Peiping, China) 1930-33; Bach's Deg (Composition) Geo Peabody Col 1954; Master's Deg (Musicology) New Eng Conservatory 1958; pa/Tchr of Piano, Taiwan 1951-54; Num Concerts incl'g: Wom's Chamber Music Soc (Los Angeles), Chinese Cult Soc, Wom's Univ Clb; Works Broadcast over KUSC & KFAC in LA & WNYC in NYC; Cal Fdn Music Clbs: Former Mem Bd, Chm Adult Composition Contest, Chm Intl Music Relats; Bd Mem Nat Bd Music Nat Leag Am Pen Wom; St Chm Music NLAPW; hon/Num Awds & Prizes: Nat Fdn Music Clbs, Sigma Alpha Iota, Nat Leag Am Pen Wom, Manuscript Clb LA; Num Poetry Awds; Pub'd Author; Num Compositions; Book of Honor.

HUBBARD, HAMPTON oc/Urologist; b/May 19, 1923; h/102 Country Clb Cir, Clinton, NC 28328; ba/Clinton; m/Anne Holmes; c/Margaret Frost (Mrs R T Jr), John H, Elizabeth Cox (Mrs G R), Anne F, Mark T, M Kevin; p/Robert C and Florence A Hubbard (dec); ed/Cert Med UNC; MD Med Col Va; mil/USN MC 28 Yrs, Ret'd as Capt; pa/Pres Clinton Urologic Assocs; Chief Surg Sampson Co Meml Hosp 1979; Dir 3rd Dist Pvt Docts of Am; AUA; SESAUA; AMA; SMA; NC Med Soc; Affil Royal Soc Med; Am Assn Clin Urologists; Fellow Am Col Surgs; cp/Lions Clb; Repub; r/Rom Cath; hon/Decorations: Am Theater WWII, WWII Victory Medal, Nat Def Medal w 1 Star, Korean Ser Medal w 2 Stars, UN Medal, Meritorious Ser Medal.

HUBBARD, JERE oc/Homemaker; b/Sept 25, 1927; h/#1 Lazywood Ln, Rt 2, Midland, TX 79701; m/Walter C III; c/Clayton Walter, Craig Engle; p/Jerry B Clayton, Lovington, NM; Mary Clayton (dec); ed/BA Goucher Col 1949; pa/Writer Weekly Newspaper Commentary; cp/Wom's Aux Midland Meml

Hosp; Mem St Bd Tex Assn Hosp Aux; DAR, Col Theunis Dey Chapt: St Ofcr, Past St Chm, Past Chapt Regent; Jr Leag Am John Birch Soc; Local Comm for Commun Housing; Citizen Adv Comm to Meml Hosp; r/Prot; hon/Cit for Commun Ser, U Way.

HUBENAK, JOE A oc/Accountant; Tax Consultant; b/Jul 2, 1937; h/2635 Sequoia, Rosenberg, TX 77471; ba/R'berg; m/Sandra Lynn Taylor; c/Elizabeth Lynn, Joe Anthony, Michael Andres; p/John Joe Sr and Rose Marie Hubenak, Rosharon, TX; ed/AA Alvin Jr Col; BBA Univ Houston; mil/Tex Army NG 8 Yrs; pa/Owner Acct'g Firm Hubenak & Assocs; Farmer & Rancher; cp/VChm So Leg Conf Com on Agri & Rural Devel; Nat Conf St Legs; Tex Coastal & Marine Coun; Mem Tex Ho of Reps; Rosenberg-Richmond Area C of C; Past Pres Rosenberg Lions Clb; Ft Bend Co Farm Bur; KJT; SPJST; BSA; Ft Bend Assn for Retard Cit; Dir Ft Bend Co Mar Dimes; Lifetime Mem Ft Bend Co Stock Show & Rodeo; Ks of C; Am Cattle Breeders Hall of Fame; Chm Holy Rosary Cath Sch Bd; Others; r/Cath; hon/Hon'd as Citizen Who Contributed Most to Ed in Area, Tex St Tchrs Assn; Dist'd Leg Awd, Voc Agri Tchrs Assn; Outstg Rep, *The Texas Lawman;* Outstg Yg Men of S.

HUCKABY, THOMAS GERALD oc/- Congressman; b/Jul 19, 1941; h/PO Box 544, Ringgold, LA 71068; ba/Washington, DC; m/Sue Woodard; c/Michelle, Clay; p/-

Thomas Milton and Eva Toland Huckaby; ed/BS La St Univ 1963; MBA Ga St Univ 1968; pa/Mem 95th Cong, Com Mbrships: House Agri, House Interior & Insular Affairs; Mem Exec Com 95th Cong New Mems Caucus; Mem Rural Caucus; Dem Study Group; Dem Res Org; cp/La Farm Bur; N La Milk Prodrs Assn; La Cattlemen's Assn; Lions Clb; Former Boy Scout Master Ringgold Troop; r/Meth; hon/Peace Through Strength Medal, Am Security Coun.

HUCKENPAHLER, VICTORIA oc/- Dance Historian; b/Oct 7, 1945; h/2122 California St, Washington, DC 20008; m/James G; c/Bernard; pa/Author Pub'd Book *Ballerina,* 1978; Contbr Num Articles to: *Dance Mag* (NY) & *Danse Perspective* (Paris); Lectr: Georgetown Univ; Smithsonian Instn; r/Epis.

HUDLIN, GRACE ELIZABETH oc/- Manager; b/Oct 2, 1908; h/PO Box 127, Hulbert, OK 74441; ba/Hulbert; m/Bob; p/Thomas D and Delia Carter Edwards (dec); ed/BEd; MEd; Mgr's Cert; pa/Mgr Lake Reg Elect Cooperative Inc; Tchr, Supt of Co Schs; cp/Soroptimist Clb; C of C; Am Legion Aux; S-Clb Sponsor; Bd Dirs: CETA, Commun Action; r/Meth; hon/4-H Clb Awds; W/W Am Wom.

HUDNUT, WILLIAM H III oc/Mayor; b/Oct 17, 1932; h/722 Pine Dr, Indianapolis, IN 46260; ba/Indpls; m/Susan Greer; c/Michael, Laura, Timothy, Theodore, William IV; p/William H Jr and Elizabeth Allen Kilborne Hudnut, N Creek, NY; ed/Princeton 1954; Union Theol Sem 1957; pa/Former Dir Dept Public Affairs & Commun Ser Ind Ctl Univ; Mgmt Conslt to Sev Large Local Businesses; Former Mem Adv Bd Am Fdn Small Bus; cp/Mayor Indpls 1976-; Nat Leag Cities; US Conf Mayors; Ind Assn Cities & Towns; Exec Com Metro

Mayor's Caucus; Intergovtl Sci, Engrg & Technol Adv Panel; Ind 11th Dist Cong-man, 93rd Cong 1973-74; Bd Mem: Commun Ser Coun, Flanner House, Mlt Hlth Assn, Fam Ser Assn, BSA, YMCA, Christian Theol Sem; Bd Mem Public Safety; Mason; Downtown Kiwanis Clb; Moose Lodge #17; Antelope Clb; Columbia Clb; r/Min Presby Whitewater Val; 2nd Pres Ch, Indpls; Former Sr Min; Former Chs Served: Buffalo (NY) & Annapolis (Md); hon/Hon Degs, Hanover & Wabash Cols; "Watchdog of the Treasury" Awd; Recog'd by Nat Assn Mtl Hlth for Mtl Hlth Leg.

HUDSON, ELIZABETH DESMOND oc/Controller; b/Dec 17, 1941; h/5616 Fanshaw Ct, Virginia Beach, VA 23462; ba/Va Bch; p/Lawrence Boykin Jr and Willetta Smith Hudson (dec); ed/BS Univ So Miss 1965; Postgrad Work; pa/Ayers Insulating & Supply Co Inc: Controller, Corporate Secy/Treas 1975-, Acct 1973-75; Bus Mgr Summer Stock Co, Univ So Miss; Mbrship Secy & Bookkeeper Le Petit Theatre du Vieux Carre, New Orleans 1967-72; Bus Mgr Dance Guild Va Inc 1972-73; Acct King's Grant Acad Dance & Gymnastics, Va Bch 1978-; Tidewater Assn Credit Mgmt 1974-; cp/Former Girl Scout Ldr; Del Metro Arts Cong 1978-; Former Mem: Assn Am Dance Cos, Tidewater Arts Coun, Bd Dirs Actor's Theatre, Norfolk, Va, Others; Former Alt Mem Va Bch Comm Arts & Humanities; Other Civic Activs; r/Presb;

hon/Personalities of S; Commun Ldrs & Noteworthy Ams; W/W: Am Wom, S&SW.

HUDSON, GLADYS W oc/Director, Editor, Writer; b/Jul 23, 1926; h/3030 Lasker, Waco, TX 76707; ba/Waco; m/Jack W; c/Thomas E Jr Waden Jr, Andrew F Waden; p/Robert A Watts (dec); Gertrude Watts, Waco; ed/BA E Tex Bapt Col; MA Baylor Univ; pa/Dir Prod Devel Success Motivation Inst Inc; Am Mgmt Assn; Intl Transactional Assn; r/Bapt; hon/Compiler, *Paradise Lost: A Concordance,* An Elizabeth Barrett Browning Concordance.

HUDSON, JAMES JACKSON oc/Professor & Dean; b/Jan 19, 1919; h/721 N Ashwood, Fayetteville, AR 72701; ba/F'ville; m/Mabel Elizabeth; c/Karen H Grimes, Deborah H Glenn; p/Randolph Hudson (dec); Lillie Hudson, Charleston, AR; ed/BA, MA Univ Ark; PhD Univ Cal; mil/USAF WWII, Fighter Pilot; Ret'd as Lt Col; pa/Univ Ark-F: Grad Dean, Prof Hist; VP Conf So Grad Schs; r/Presb.

HUDSON, JOHN W oc/Professor; b/Mar 26, 1926; h/5524 N Quail Run Rd, Scottsdale, AZ 85253; ba/Scottsdale; m/Karen; c/Karen, Cynthia, Tommy, (Stepchd:) Ian Hammond, Stephanie Hammond; p/Alfred Lee Hudson (dec); Esther Mary Hudson, Ravenna, OH; ed/PhD; pa/Prof ASU; Marriage Cnslr; Past Pres Am Assn Marriage & Fam Cnslrs; cp/Bd Dirs Phoenix Ctr for the Blind; Ombudsman Com S'daie Sch Dist; hon/Grant Fellow, The Merrill Palmer Inst; Fellow: Am Assn Marriage & Fam Cnslrs, Am Acad Psychotherapists; Ernest Osborne, Tchr of Yr Awd 1976.

HUDSON, LEONARD LESTER oc/Administrator; b/Jul 23, 1910; h/5945 S Terry Joe Ave, Oklahoma City, OK 73129; ba/Okla City; m/Reba Porter; c/Robert L, Frank L; p/Harvey H and Laura Watson Hudson (dec); ed/AS; BS; MEd; DD; HD; DArts; PhD; pa/Park Admr; cp/Dem; r/Bapt; hon/Hon Doct; Life Mem, NEA, Am Assn for Higher Ed; Pi Sigma Alpha; Alpha Psi Omega; Alpha Sigma Chi; W/W: S&SW, Am Ed, Am; Other Biogl Listings.

HUDSON, MAXINE TAYLOR oc/Teacher; b/Aug 7, 1928; h/The Citadel, Charleston, SC 29409; ba/N Charleston, SC; m/Herschel C; c/Shera; p/L Rogers Taylor (dec); Mrs Glenn Taylor Fallaw, Columbia, SC; ed/BA; MA; pa/NEA; SCEA; Y-Teen & Jr Class Sponsor; NDEA Hist Inst; Inst for Polit Legal

Ed; cp/Girl Scout Ldr; Alpha Delta Kappa; Save Charleston Foun; En Star; r/Meth; hon/ROBIS Inst Participant; Taft Fellow (3 Times); Star Tchr, Nat Merit Finalist; 1st Wom Grad, The Citadel; Pub'd Author; Outstg Ldrs in Elem & Sec'dy Ed; Notable Ams; Personalities of S; Others.

HUDSON, ROY D oc/Executive; b/Jun 30, 1930; h/3745 Charter Pl, Ann Arbor, MI 48105; ba/Ann Arbor; m/Constance T; c/Hollye Lynne, David Kendall; p/J Roy and Everence L Hudson, Chattanooga, TN; ed/BA: MS; MA; PhD; LLD; mil/USAF 1948-52, S/Sgt; pa/VP Res Planning, Warner-Lambert/Parke-Davis Pharm Res Div 1977-; Pres Hampton Inst, Hampton, Va 1970-76; Brown Univ: Assoc Prof Med Scis 1969-70, Asst Prof & Assoc Dean Grad Sch 1968-69,

Asst Dean & Asst Prof 1966-68; Other Former Positions; AAAS; Sigma Xi; Am Soc for Pharm & Experimtl Therapeutics Inc; Am Men of Sci, The Phy & Biol Scis; Dept HEW Adv Com to Dir Nat Inst Hlth 1974-; Cong of US, Ofc Technol Panel on Applications of Sci & Technol 1976-; NY Acad Sci; Former Mem: Am Assn Higher Ed, Va Acad Sci, Coun Indep Cols Va (Richmond), Others; cp/NAACP; Former Mem Afro-Am Soc (Conn Col for Wom); Former Mem Adv Coun BSA; Other Civic Activs; r/Meth; hon/Hon LLD: Princeton Univ 1975, Lehigh Univ 1974; Outstg Civilian Ser Awd, Dept of Army; Ldrs in Ed; Elected to All-Time All-Livingston Ftball Team (Celebration of Centennial Yr of Ftball in US), Livingstone Col 1969; Dist'd Alumni Achmt Medallion, Livingstone Col; Danforth Foun Tchr; Mem Hon Socs; Profl Pubs.

HUDSON, SALLIE MARGARET GLADDEN oc/Bookkeeper; b/Jan 1, 1948; h/Rt 2, Box 528, Chester, SC 29706; ba/Great Falls, SC; m/Loren E Sr; c/Eugene, Keith; p/Jesse E and Mary B Gladden, Great Falls, SC; ed/Att'g York Tech Col; pa/Bookkeeper Gt Falls Bookkeeping & Tax Ser; Chester BPW Clb; Gt Falls Merchs Assn; cp/Former Jaycee-ette; Cand Chester Co Sch Bd; Chm Chester Co Mar Dimes; Ldr Cub Scout Pack 64 Den 1; r/1st Bapt Ch: Mem, SS Secy; hon/Jaycee-ette of Yr 1969, 70, 71, 72; Chester Dist'd Yg Wom 1974; Outstg Yg Wom Am; Hon'd at Gov Mansion for Mod Work.

HUDSON, WORTH McLANE oc/Educational Coordinator; b/Apr 22, 1935; h/-"McLane", Virgilina, VA 24598; ba/Halifax, VA; m/Shirla Griffin; c/Tyler McLane, Craven Franklin, Brandon Griffin, Tansel Marcus; p/Arthur F and Minnie B Hudson, Virgilina; ed/BS VPI&SU 1957; MEd Univ Va 1967; mil/USAR 1/Lt; pa/Coor Gifted-Talented Prog; Phi Kappa Phi; NEA; VEA; HEA; Phi Delta Kappa; cp/Parsons-Brace Art Assn; McLaugh Sch Fdn; Dir Meck Elect Coop; r/So Bapt: Deacon, Moderator Dan River Bapt Assn.

HUEBNER, DONALD FRANK oc/-Corporate Controller; b/Oct 24, 1925; h/1104 Linden Le, Mt Prospect, IL 60056; ba/-Chicago, IL; m/Nancy Minor Stearns; c/-Donald Frank Jr, Barry Carpenter, Orrin John, Scott Stearns, Christopher James, Heidi Jane, Rebecca McLean, Mary-Esther; p/Frank E Huebner (dec); Erna Gorges Huebner, New London, WI; ed/BBA w hons; mil/UNSR 1944-46; pa/Newcomen Soc NAm; Nat Assn Corporate Controllers; cp/Secy Bd Dirs Theater Arts Guild, Arlington Heights, Ill; r/Luth; hon/Beta Gamma Sigma.

HUEBNER, NANCY MINOR STEARNS oc/Educator; b/Jun 1, 1931; h/1104 Linden Ln, Mt Prospect, IL 60056; m/Donald Frank; c/Donald Frank Jr, Barry Carpenter, Orrin John, Scott Stearns, Christopher James, Heidi Jane, Rebecca McLean, Mary-Esther; p/Harry Carpenter Stearns (dec); Esther Minor Stearns, Hinsdale, IL; ed/BMus 1953, MMus 1972 NWn Univ; pa/MENC; NATS; ACDA; NEA; IEA; TAG; cp/Mayflower Soc; Secy NWn Univ Music Alumni Assn; r/Immanuel Luth Ch: Mem Ed Com; hon/Alpha Lambda Delta; Num Musical Awds; Nat Social Dir; World W/W Wom; DIB; Commun Ldrs & Noteworthy Ams; Notable Ams; Personalities W&MW.

HUEBNER, RICHARD ALLEN oc/-Executive Director; b/Jul 31, 1950; h/2700 Leeds Ln, Charlottesville, VA 22901; ba/-C'ville; m/Marsha Lawrence; c/Andela Carol, Holly Anne; p/Otto LeRoy Huebner (dec); Audrey Elizabeth Huebner, Racine, WI; ed/BBA Univ Wisc-Madison; pa/Exec Dir Kappa Sigma Frat; Am Soc Assn Execs; Frat Execs Assn; Assn Frat Advrs; IPA; cp/Dir C'ville-Albemarle JCs; r/St Mark's Luth Ch: Lay Catechist; hon/Outstg Yg Men Am; Notable Ams; W/W S&SW; Personalities S; Men Achmt.

HUEY, MARY EVELYN BLAGG oc/-University President; b/Jan 19, 1922; h/2801 Longfellow Ln, Denton, TX 76201; ba/-Denton; m/Griffin Burns; c/Henry Griffin; p/Henry Hurst and Melissa Evelyn Manning Blagg (dec); ed/BS, MA (2); PhD; pa/Pres Tex Wom's-Univ; Bd Dirs Assn Tex Cols & Univs 1977-79; Comm on Status of Wom in Higher Ed 1976-; cp/N Ctl Tex Coun Govts; Former 2nd VP U Way; r/1st Presb Ch, Denton; hon/Dist'd Alumna Awd, Tex Wom's Univ; Public Admr of Yr, N Tex Chapt AAPA; Outstg Wom of Tex Awd, Tex Div AAUW; Outstg Contbns to Ed, Iota Chapt Delta Kappa Gamma; Hon Mem, Soroptimist Intl.

HUFF, CHERRY LEE IRBY oc/Homemaker; b/Mar 23, 1924; h/2929 Cunningham Dr, Wichita Falls, TX 76308; m/William B; c/William Godwin; p/Raymond Guerry and Lila Sue Godwin Irby (dec); ed/Att'd Columbia Univ & CCNY; pa/Former Med Secy; cp/Wichita Falls Assn Retard Citizens; Am Cancer Soc; Coor Vol Sers Bethania Hosp; Advr TARS; Commun Coun; Exec Bd Spec Olympics; r/Bapt; hon/Wom of Yr, Am Bus Wom 1968-69; Vol of Yr, Am Cancer Soc 1976; Outstg Vol of Yr, Assn Retard Citizens 1976.

HUFF, IMA KEELING oc/Poet; Retired Teacher; b/Jan 13, 1910; h/Box 891, Henderson, TX 75652; ba/Henderson; m/G J (dec); c/Jasper, Ima Gene Thomas, Harold, Floyd, Margaret Ann Bee; p/William B and Ethel C Keeling (dec); ed/BS, MA Stephen F Austin Univ; pa/Tchr 24 Yrs incl'g: Mt Enterprise, Gary, Leverett's Chapel, Tatum, Henderson, NE Houston, Lockney, Kress;

Current Substitute Tchr W Rusk Consolidated Schs; Author 3 Books of Verse: *Shadows of Wings, Cherry-Ripe, Somewhere Violets*; Edited Poetry Corner; Helped Org Rusk Co Chapt Poetry Soc Tex; Tex St Tchrs Assn; Delta Kappa Gamma; r/Ch of Christ; hon/Intl W/W Poetry; Bronze Plaque for Dist'd Achmt in Poetry, IBC.

HUFF, NORMAN NELSON oc/Academic Instructor; Chairman; b/Apr 22, 1933; h/16823 Bear Valley Rd, Hesperia, CA 92345; ba/Victorville, CA; p/George Peabody Huff, San Diego, CA; Norma Rose Nelson, Warrington, FL; ed/AA; BS; MBA; mil/AUS; USN; USAF Comm'd Ofcr to Capt; 8 Yrs; pa/Victor Val Col: Instr, Chm Computer Sci & Info Systems 1967-; Systems Programmer & Conslt Mojave Water Agy 1973-78; Mgmt Info Conslt Pfizer Inc 1972; Other Profl Positions; Nat Adv Bd Am Security Coun; Charter Mem Nat Space Inst; Bd Dirs Cal Computing Consortium 1978; Treas & Affil Chm Cal Bus Ed Assn; Treas & Pres Inst Aeronautical Sci San Diego St Univ 1956, 57; Cal Tchrs Assn; cp/Am Legion; DAV; Life Mem Soaring Soc Am; Life Mem IBA; Rep Nat Com; r/Cath; hon/Instr of Yr, Victor Val Col 1968; F'ship Awd; Shooting Awd, VFW; Num Mil Awds; Ath Awds; Profl Pubs; Intl W/W: Intells, Commun Ser; DIB; Notable Ams; W/W: W, Am; Personalities W&MW; Men of Achmt; Intl Reg Profiles.

HUFF, OZZIE oc/Environmental Scientist; b/Mar 30, 1944; h/3501 Union Ave, Florence, AL 35660; ba/Muscle Shoals, AL; m/Vivian Foster; c/La Quedia Machelle,

Vanessa Renee; p/Emmitt Huff, Sprott, AL; Adelle Huff (dec); ed/BS; MS; pa/Envir Scist Tenn Val Auth; Am Chem Soc; Air Pollution Control Assn; Black Ednl Tutoring Assn; Phi Beta Sigma; cp/Minority Investmt Forum; r/Bapt; hon/Tchr of Yr; Best Student in Chem Awd; Grad Magna Cum Laude.

HUFFER, ELIZABETH LOUISE oc/-Minister, Writer, Teacher, Lecturer, Counsellor, Clairvoyant; b/Sept 25; h/505 Peace Grove Ln, Santa Barbara, CA 93105; ba/-Same; m/Richard Donn; c/Damon Richard; p/Charles Wesley Verge (dec); Josephine Mary Verge, Santa Barbara; ed/DDiv; DPsychol; pa/CoFdr Joy Foun (Rel/Ednl); r/Nondenom.

HUFFMAN, JAMES HUDSON oc/-Symphony Conductor; Teacher; b/Aug 28, 1929; h/3207 10th Ave N, Fort Dodge, IA 50501; ba/Ft Dodge; m/Georgann; c/James Michael, Laura Ann, Elizabeth Lee; p/Leroy Huffman, Moberly, MO; Mildred Lee Huffman (dec); ed/BS 1956; MA 1957; mil/USAF; pa/Ia Music Conductors; AF of Musicians; Am Symph Orch Leag; cp/Civic Concert Assn; Fine Arts Assn; r/Meth; hon/Eldon Jones Awd; Phi Mu Alpha.

HUFFMAN, JOHN WILLIAM oc/-Professor; b/Jul 21, 1932; h/Box 614, Clemson, SC 29631; ba/Clemson; m/Dana Alayne; c/Paul William, James Richard, George Robert, John Edward; p/John W Huffman, Pentwater, MI; Florence K Huffman, Lexington, KY; ed/BA NWn Univ 1954; AM 1956, PhD 1957 Harvard Univ; pa/Clemson Univ: Prof Chem 1967-, Assoc Prof 1962-67, Asst Prof 1960-62; Asst Prof Chem Ga Inst Tech 1957-60; r/Rom Cath; hon/NSF Fellow; NIH Career Devel Awd.

HUFFMAN, PHYLLIS oc/Administrative Assistant; b/Sept 19, 1937; h/1609 N Johnson, Arlington, VA 22201; ba/Washington, DC; c/Kelly John, Natalie Gae, Pauline Ann; p/Kenneth LaSalle and Ann Marie Johnston, Twin Falls, ID; pa/Adm Asst Elect Industs Foun; "People"-Profl Cnslr, Hypnotist, Writer; Public Spkr & Sem Ldr on "Death & Dying", "Reincarnation-Symbology-Wholistic

Hlth & Healing"; cp/Var Commun Activs; hon/Awds for Writing Excell; Humanitarian Recog, Indian Tribe; Gov's Meritorious Wage Increase for Outstg Ser to Idaho; Prose Writer of Yr, Boise, Idaho; Men & Wom of Distn in World; Intl W/W: Intells, Commun Ser; World W/W Wom; Book of Honor; Commun Ldrs & Noteworthy Ams; Others.

HUFFMAN, VIRGINIA M oc/College Professor; b/May 19, 1925; h/10 McIntosh Ln, RD #2, West Chester, PA 19380; ba/W Chester; m/John (dec); p/H Milford and Mary L Loop, Eldred, PA; ed/BS E Stroudsburg St Col 1947; MS Pa St Univ 1964; HSD Ind Univ 1969; pa/Assoc Prof Hlth Ed West Chester St Col; APHA; ASHA; SOPHE; AAHPER; PAHPER; PSEA; NEA; Public Sch Tchr; Sayre, Pa 1 Yr, Bradford Area Sch Dist 13 Yrs, Gettysburg Col 4 Yrs, WCSC 10 Yrs; cp/Bd Dirs ARC; r/Meth; hon/Pi Lambda Theta.

HUGGINS, JAMES BERNARD oc/-Assistant to Congressman; b/Jun 5, 1950; h/3010 Hemlock Ave, Parkersburg, WV 26101; ba/Washington, DC; p/Bernard A Huggins (dec); Evelyn W Huggins, P'burg; ed/AA P'burg Commun Col 1970; BA WVa Univ 1975; mil/USAF-CAP 2/Lt; Stationed w NATCAP Wing, Bolling AFB, Wash DC; pa/Asst to US Senate Majority Ldr Robert C Byrd; Sr Partner Georgetown Assocs (PR Firm); cp/Dir "Yth for Randolph", US Senate Campaign 1972; Dir WVa Campaign "Byrd for Pres" & "Byrd for US Senate" 1976; Mem & Former Ofcr WVa Soc Wash DC; WVU Alumni Assn, Nat Capital Area; Current Treas Nat Conf St Socs; Nat Com-man Yg Dems WVa; Alt Del to Dem Nat Conv 1976; r/Bapt; hon/Personalities of S; W/W in Polits.

HUGHES, ANNE F oc/Staff Services Assistant; b/Aug 8, 1934; h/2609 Hemlock Dr, San Angelo, TX 76901; ba/Carlsbad, TX; m/William Jerome Jr; c/Elizabeth Anne Roberson, Randal Lee Roberson, Robert Donald Roberson; p/Robert Melville and Mary E Huffman Finks, Christoval, TX; ed/Att'd Tex Tech, SMU; pa/Staff Sers Asst TDMHMR; Dir Arts & Crafts; Exec Dir Chimney House; Past Pres Tex Public Employees Assn; Chm San-Tex Credit Union; cp/Sustainer Jr Leag; r/Epis; hon/Cert of Accomplishmt, Tex Rehab Comm & Gov Dolph Brisco; Cert of Achmt, Ctr for Study of Human Resources, Univ Tex; Cert of Recog, TPEA.

HUGHES, EDWIN McCULLOC oc/-Minister; Teacher; Psychologist; b/Feb 22, 1911; h/205 N Grand, Searcy, AR 72143; m/Ruby Jo; c/Eddy Jo, Philip Edwin; p/Sugar Henry Hughes (dec); Epsie Allen McEachern (dec); ed/BA Harding Col 1937; MA Univ Ark 1942; EdD Denver Univ 1957; pa/Pvt Pract Psychol 1961-; Ark Bd Examrs in Psychol; Mem 1970-75, Exec Secy 1976-; Gov's Adv Coun Mtl Retard 1970; Clin Psychologist VA Hosp, N Little Rock, Ark 1960-77; Other Former Positions; APA; Ark Psychol Assn; Ark Soc Clin Hypnosis; Assn Mil Surgs US; Am Assn Suicidology; IPA; Phi Delta Kappa; cp/Searcy C of C; r/Ch of Christ; hon/Cert of Merit, Ark St; Book of Honor; Biogl Dir APA; DIB; Intl Reg Profiles; Men of Achmt; W/W S&SW; Personalities of S; Notable Ams; Commun Ldrs & Noteworthy Ams; Others.

HUGHES, IRENE F oc/Astrologer; Psychic; Columnist; Radio & TV Personality; h/Rt #1, Box #190 Stony Island Ave, Crete, IL 60417; ba/Chicago, IL; m/William J II; c/William III, Karen, Patricia, Kathleen; p/(dec); pa/Newspaper Columnist; Author 1 Book; Num Articles; Chgo Commerce & Indust; Spiritual Frontiers F'ship; Ancient Astronaut Soc; Chgo Press Clb; Nat Fdn Press Wom; r/Prot; hon/15 Awds in Jour.

HUGHES, JOHN oc/Editor & Manager; m/Libby Pockman; c/Wendy, Mark; pa/The Christian Sci Monitor: Editor & Mgr 1976-, Editor 1970-, Corres to Far E 1964-70, Asst Overseas News Editor 1962-64, Africa Corres 1955-61; Dir & Conslt News-Jour Co, Wilmington, Del 1975-78; Pres Own Co (Commun Newspapers in Mass); Mem Pulitzer Prize Adv Com; Judge Sigma Delta Chi Awds in Jour; Mem Selection Com Colby Col's Elijah Parish Lovejoy Awds in Jour; Adv Com World Press Inst; Am Soc Newspaper Editors: Dir, Pres; Mem 22-Man Delegation (ASNE) to People's Republic of China 1972; hon/Yankee Quill Awd, Sigma Delta Chi; Awd for Best Daily Newspaper or Wire Ser Reporting from Abroad, Overseas Press Clb; Pulitzer Prize for Intl Reporting; Neiman F'ship, Harvard Univ.

HUGHES, LINDA G oc/Marketing Director; b/Sept 6, 1942; h/6121-12 Shoup Ave, Woodland Hills, CA 91367; ba/Monica, CA; p/Walter Pierce, Fontara, CA; Indianola Pierce, Springville, AL; ed/BA UCLA; MBA Pepperdine Univ; pa/SMEA; Am Mktg Assn; cp/NOW; r/Prot; hon/Dun & Bradstreet: Outstg Mktg, Outstg Salesmanship.

HUGHES, MARGARET CLINE oc/Jan 28, 1903; h/1251 Topeka Blvd, Topeka, KS 66612; m/Daniel Shelton (dec); c/Patricia Jane H Bashor (dec), Margaret H Glazzard; p/Robert N and Margaret G White Burns (dec); ed/AA Stephen's Col 1923; Att'd: Warrensburg Tchrs Col, Washburn Univ; pa/Lectr; Substitute Tchr Topeka Public Schs; Pres The Three Arts of Topeka 1978-79; Exhibited in Gift Shops (Oil Miniatures & Landscapes, Water Color Flower Prints); cp/PEO: Past Chapt Pres, Former Treas Coop Bd; Stephen's Col Alumnae Assn; Girl Scouts: Former Art Cnslr, Coun Mem; PTA 12 Yrs; St Andrews Soc KC; r/Presb: Former Ch Cir Ldr.

HUGHES, MARGARET CYRENA oc/-Retired Association Executive; b/Jun 4; h/417 E Canedy St, Springfield, IL 62703; p/Thomas P and Elizabeth D Hughes (dec); ed/Att'd S'field Col, Univ Ill; pa/Ret'd Exec Lung Assn; Past Pres Ill Conf TB Execs; cp/Girl Scouts: Former Ldr, Bd Dirs; Past Pres Wom's Clb; Past Pres & Area Dir Zonta Clb; Secy S'field Safety Coun; RSVP; Bd Mem Sr Citizens Sangamon Co; r/Cath; Past Pres, Nat Bd Dirs (4 Yrs) Diocesan Coun Cath Wom; hon/Thanks Badge, GSA; Pro Ecclesia et Pontifice Medal, Holy Father.

HUGHES, PHILIP EDGCUMBE oc/-Clergyman; Professor; b/Apr 30, 1915; h/1565 Cherry Ln, Rydal, PA 19046; m/Margaret; c/Marion; p/Randolph William and Muriel Hughes (dec); ed/BA, MA, DLitt Univ Cape Town; BD Univ London; THD Australian Col Theol; Jagger Scholar, Laurence Prizeman in Classics, Greek Medallist UCT; pa/Anglican Clergyman; Theol Prof; Author, Editor & Translator Num Works; Public Lectr; Pastoral & Acad Appts: England, S Africa, Europe, USA; r/St John's Epis Ch, Huntingdon Val, Pa; hon/Outstg Edr Am.

HUGHES, ROBERT DALE oc/Executive Secretary-Treasurer; b/Aug 1, 1919; h/8255 N Sunnyside, Clovis, CA 93612; ba/Fresno, CA; m/Ruth Naomi Williams; c/John Orville, Peggy Jean, Robert Don; p/Robert Edward and Rachel Grace Johnson Hughes; ed/BA Ouachita Bapt Col; ThM SWn Bapt Theol Sem; DD (2) Cal Bapt Col & Ouachita Bapt Col; pa/Exec Secy-Treas So Bapt Gen Conv Cal 1966-; Pastor: 1st So Bapt Ch, Long

Beach, Cal 1958-66; Calvary So Bapt Ch (now 1st So Bapt Ch), Ventura, Cal 1948-58, Other Pastorates; SBC: Conv Base Model 1969-71, BSU Study Com 1968-70, Hosp Comm 1963-69, Others; SBC of Cal: Exec Bd 1948-50, 1951-54, 1957-61, 1962-66, Chm Exec Bd (Twice), Pres 1953-54, Others; cp/Kiwanis Clb, Ventura; r/So Bapt.

HUGHES, STACY E oc/Supervisor of Music; b/Jun 30, 1930; h/11 Alden Rd, Larchmont, NY 10530; m/Norma; c/Stephen, Leslie; p/Edward and Mary Hughes (dec); ed/BA, BM, MM, MA; Cert'd Doct Cand Columbia Univ; mil/Resv; pa/Asst Prin JHS 1976-; Other Ednl Positions; Pres NYC Music Tchrs Assn; NY St Rep Nat MENC Conv 1970; Adv Ednl Coun Metro Opera 1970-; Clin: NYS Music Tchrs Assn 1975, Mass St's 1st Humanities Prog 1973; Fac Manhattan Sch of Music, Pace Univ; Conslt; r/Cath; hon/Outstg Sec'dy Admr; W/W Ed & Intl Music.

HUGIN, ADOLPH CHARLES oc/Lawyer; Engineer; Inventor; Professor of Law; b/Mar 28, 1907; h/7602 Boulder St, N Springfield, VA 22151; ba/Washington, DC; p/Charles and Eugenie Vigny Hugin (dec); ed/BSEE Geo Wash Univ Engrg Sch 1928; MSEE MIT 1930; JD Georgetown Univ Law Sch 1934; LLM Harvard Univ Law Sch 1947; SJD Cath Univ Am Law Sch 1949; Certs; pa/Pvt Law Pract & Conslt'g Engr, Wash DC 1947-; Reg'd Elect & Mech Profl Engr, DC 1952-; Cath Univ Am Law Sch 1949-55; Vis Prof Law, Chm Law Sch Admissions Com; Admitted to Num Bars; Editor-in-Chief Am Patent Law Assn Bltn 1949-54; Other Former Positions; cp/ABA, Num Coms; Am Patent Law Assn; Delta Theta Phi; DC & Nat Profl Engrs Socs; Nat Ret'd Tchrs Assn; cp/Past Pres Diocese Arlington (Va) Ctl Coun, Nat Trustee Coun of US; Former Mem Schenectady (NY) Com BSA; N S'field Civic Assn; John Carroll Soc; Nocturnal Adoration Soc; r/Lector-Commentator St Michael's Parish, Annandale (Va); Former Mem St Margaret's Cath Ch Coun; Num Others; hon/Dietzen Prize, Machine Drawing, Geo Wash Univ; Cath Univ Am Law Sch: Aviation Prize, Radio Law Prize; W/W: Am Law, Rel, S&SW; Other Biogl Listings.

HUIBREGTSE, DORIS MARIE oc/Business Instructor; b/Nov 9, 1931; h/514 Scott Dr, Big Spring, TX 79720; ba/Big Spring; m/Harlan Howard; c/Robert Neil, Kenneth

Wayne; p/Leonard A Blanton (dec); Opal V Blanton, Mt Enterprise, TX; ed/BBA; MS; pa/Co Chm TBEA; TSTA; NBEA; NEA; TJCTA; AAUP; DKG; ABCA; cp/Lions Aux; r/Meth; hon/Dist 18 Bus Tchr of Yr 1976.

HUIBREGTSE, HARLAN HOWARD oc/School Principal; b/Nov 29, 1926; h/514 Scott Dr, Big Spring, TX 79720; ba/Big Spring; m/Doris M Blanton; c/Robert Neil, Kenneth Wayne; p/C L Huibregtse (dec); Esther Huibregtse, Premont, TX; ed/BS; MS; mil/AUS 1945-47; pa/Prin Goliad Mid Sch; Treas Bd Dirs Big Spring Ed Emp Fed Credit Union; TSTA; TEPSA; NEA; cp/VP Bd Dirs Boys Clb; Downtown Lions Clb; r/1st U Meth Ch: Adm Bd; hon/All Conf Basketball, A&I Univ 1950, 51.

HUIZENGA, CLARENCE JOHN oc/-Educational Specialist; b/May 9, 1935; h/15242 Weddington St, Van Nuys, CA 91411; ba/Los Angeles, CA; p/William E Huizenga (dec); Elizabeth Grit Huizenga, Hudsonville, MI; ed/BA Hope Col 1956; MS Carnegie Mellon Univ 1958; pa/Ednl Specialist UCLA Ext; Conslt to W Assoc Art Mus; Dir Mus Mgmt Inst; Am Ec Assn; Wn Ec Assn; Am Soc Tng & Devel; Mem & Past Fac Advr Alpha Upsilon Chapt Alpha Kappa Psi; r/Prot; hon/GSA-UCLA Outstg Tchr on Campus Awd 1972; Silver Ser Awd, Alpha Kappa Psi.

HULL, S LORAINE BOOS oc/Director & Teacher; b/Aug 5; ba/6757 Hollywood Blvd, Hollywood, CA 90028; c/Dianne Lee, Donald John; p/Myron Boos (dec); Vera Cleal Boos, West Bend, IA; ed/BFA; MA; PhD; pa/Dir & Tchr The Lee Strasberg Theatre Inst; Dir Actors Studio, Dirs-Writers Unit; Am Theatre Assn; Intl Del to Monaco & Sweden, Intl Theatre Confs & World Play Fest & Wkshop Ldr; Author Articles on Acting & Directing: Am Commun Theatre, Am Theatre Assn, Var Profl Pubs; Fdr & 1st Pres NAm Reg Theatre

Alliance; cp/Del 1976 Dem Nat Conv; hon/Winner Trophies & Plaques for Directing; 1st Pl Plays for St, Reg & Nat Groups; Author: *School-Community Drama & Strasberg's Method.*

HULLEY, CLAIR MONTROSE oc/Professor; b/Aug 27, 1925; h/11560 Deerfield Rd, Cincinnati, OH 45242; ba/Cinc; p/Clair M Hulley (dec); Vera A VonHagen Hulley, Cinc; ed/BS; ME; pa/Prof Engrg & Computer Graphic Sci Univ Cinc; ASME; ASEE; AAUP; cp/Sycamore-Symmes Civic Assn; hon/W/W; Engrg, Am, MW, Computer Res & Ed; Other Biogl Listings.

HULS, JAMES JOSEPH oc/Manufacturing Executive; b/Aug 27, 1941; h/240 N Pierce, Salem, SD 57058; ba/Salem; m/Patricia Delores; c/James Michael, Nancy Jo, Christopher John; p/Joe and Gladys Huls, Salem; ed/BSME SD St Univ 1964; mil/USAF 1964-68, Capt; pa/Exec Feterl Mfg Co; Conslt'g Engr; ASAE; ASME; Reg'd Profl Engr; cp/Post Cmdr Am Legion; Past Pres McCook CC; r/Cath: Mem Ch Bd, Lector, Min Euchirist; hon/Commun Ldrs & Noteworthy Ams; W/W MW.

HUME, JOHN CHANDLER oc/Professor; b/May 6, 1911; h/317 Tuscany Rd, Baltimore, MD 21210; ba/Baltimore; m/Amelia B; c/John C Jr, William P, Susan H Artes (Mrs Lawrence); p/(dec); ed/MD; Dr PH; mil/USPHS Comm'd Asst Surg 1942; Adv'd through grades to Med Dir 1956; Resigned 1961; USAFR MC 1962-71, Col; pa/The Johns Hopkins Univ Sch Hygiene & Public Hlth: Dean 1967-75, Prof Dept Hlth Sers Adm 1961-, Chm Dept Public Hlth Adm 1961-69; Chief Hlth Div Tech Cooperation Adm (Intl Coop Adm), New Delhi, India 1955-61; hon/Edward W Browning Achmt Awd for Preven of Dis; Hon Mem, Ind Public Hlth Assn; Venezuelan Soc Dermatology & Syphilology.

HUMENIK, FRANK JAMES oc/Associate Department Head; b/May 26, 1937; h/4008 Pepperton Dr, Raleigh, NC 27606; ba/Raleigh; m/Sue Anne; c/Kerry, David; p/Frank Joseph and Pauline Humenik, Cleveland, OH; ed/BSCE, MS, PhD Ohio St Univ; pa/Reg'd Profl Engr: Ohio, NC; Assoc Dept Hd in charge of Biol & Agri Engrg NC St

Univ; Conslt Agri Waste Mgmt & Envir Quality & Waste Treatmt Systems; Am Soc CE; Am Soc Agri Engrs; Water Pollution Control Fdn; Sigma Xi; Chi Epsilon; Author 50+ Res & Tech Articles; Chm Profl & Ser Coms; hon/Man of Yr to NC Agri, Progressive Farmer 1975; Dist'd Lectr, Auburn Univ; ASAE Gunlogson Countryside Engrg Awd.

HUMMEL, FRANCES COPE oc/Research Librarian; b/May 13, 1911; h/9627 Whiteacre Rd, Columbia, MD 21045; ba/Baltimore, MD; m/Ralph D (dec); c/Ralph D Jr (dec); p/Edge Taylor and Ella Mollison Cope (dec); ed/BS, MS Univ Mich; MSLS Columbia Univ; pa/Res Libn Alcolac Inc; Am Chem Soc, Wom's Com (Nat); Am Soc Info Sci; Treas Chesapeake Bay Chapt; Spec Libs Assn; r/Christian; hon/Phi Beta Kappa; Phi Kappa Phi; Iota Sigma Pi.

HUMMER, GLEN SHARP oc/Teacher, Coach; b/Feb 18, 1905; h/RR #8, Huntington, IN 46750; ba/H'ton; p/Rafe Hummer (dec); Fanny Isabelle Harris (dec); ed/BS Univ Ill

1931; MS Columbia Univ 1937; Grad Work Univ Wash 1932; mil/USN 1942-45; pa/H'ton Col: Assoc Prof PE, Swimming Coach; Phi Epsilon Kappa; Nat AAU Long Distance Swimming Chm; cp/1st Intr Nat Swim Meet, Santa Clara, Cal; C of C; Life Hon Mem Kiwanis; Mem Jr C of C; r/Presb; hon/Joseph G Rogers Awd; James Clard Awd; Ind AAU Apprec Cit; 1st Ind Swimming & Diving Coaches Awd; US Coach for European Trips; Hon'd by Japan.

HUMPHREY, LAWRENCE CEAPHUS oc/Mortgage Banking; b/Apr 4, 1931; h/9000 E Jefferson, Detroit, MI 48214; ba/Detroit; m/Bobbie J; c/Kevin R, Nikeeta L, Lawrence C Jr; p/Joe Ceaphus Humphrey (dec); Viola Rucker, Detroit; ed/EIT; mil/USAF; pa/Premier Mortgage Corp: Chief Operating Ofcr 1974-, Pres 1970-, Incorporator 1969; Fac Mem (Fin, Pt-time) Oakland Univ 1975-; Real Est Broker Grand Bahama Intl 1968-73; Opened Four Star Realty Inc 1964; Bd Dirs: Nat Bus Leag, Nat Housing Conf Inc; Minute-Man Com Mortgage Bkr Assn; Pres U Mortgage Bkrs Am; Chm Urban Affairs Com Mich Mortgage Bkrs Assn; Mem Consumer Credit; Former Chm Detroit Residential Housing for the Realtors; Appt'd to Fed Nat Mortgage Assn Adv Com 1976; cp/Former Mem Tech Constrn Com Detroit C of C; Chm Housing Com Cotillion Clb; hon/Broker of Month for US (Dec 1978), Nat Assn Real Est Brokers; Broker of Yr, Detroit Real Est Brokers 1968; 4 Cits, US Govt.

HUNDREDMARK, BERT A III oc/College Professor; b/Jul 10, 1944; h/Three Williams St, PO Box 146, Morrisville, NY 13408; ba/M'ville; p/Bert A Jr and Helen Wojniak Hundredmark, Batavia, NY; ed/AA SUNY; BS Rochester Inst Tech; pa/Prof SUNY; Nat Restaurant Assn; AAUP; NY Assn Jr Cols; Am Dietetic Assn; Coun on Hotel, Restaurant & Instnl Ed; cp/Area Ldr & Dir Am Cancer Soc; BSA Fund Raiser; Chm Town of Eaton Dem Com; M'ville Lodge #658 F&AM; Scottish Rite; AAONMS Utica; Moose; r/Rom Cath; Eucharist Min, St Joan of Arc Ch; hon/Chancellor's Awd for Excell in Tchg; Sarah Margaret Gillam Awd, Outstg Alumnus of RIT Food Adm Dept; Outstg Yg Man Am; W/W in Food Ser.

HUNNEWELL, GERALDINE GROSVENOR oc/Researcher in Early American History; Poet; Scholar; b/Aug 21, 1918; h/10799 Sherman Grove Ave, #39, Sunland, CA 91040; c/Larry Dennis, Richard Lynn; p/William Bennett and Lavinia Ruth Lay Grosvenor; pa/Pt-Owner Hunn Engrg Mfg; Am Fgn Ser 1967-76; Fgn Affairs 1966-67; Am Acad Arts & Scis 1964-65; World Affairs Coun, LA Chapt 1963-75; MIT 1975-76; Atlantic Coun US 1974-75, Previous Mbrship 1967-75; Am Public Hlth Assn; NATO; Inst World Affairs: USC, March AFB; UN, LA; Ensalen Inst; Viewpoints Inst; Carnegie Endowmt for Intl Conciliatory Peace; Cal Pan Am Assn; Pan Am Union; Cal Fdn Chaparall Poets; Santa Monica Writers Clb; Hollywood Pen Wom; Poets Haven; Franklin Mint: 3 Yr Mem, Gold Pin; LA Area ABMAC; Intl Soc for Gen Semantics (DATA); Univ Denver Sch Intl Studies (Africa); UCLA-Univ Ext Painters, Poets, Artists; Am Col of Arms; Am Forestry Assn; Propylean Soc; Nat Soc Arts & Lttrs; LA Chapt, Santa Monica Chapt; Fellow Royal Soc St George, England); Psychedelic Review; WAIF; Huntington Lib Rare Books Readers Clb; Augustan Soc; U Inventors & Scists; Pres Circle, LA; Am Judic Soc; Patroness: Libs, LA Ctl Lib, Morningside Park Lib; Acad Polit Sci, Columbia Univ; H S Truman Lib: Hon Fellow, Bronze Pres Medal; Hon, Inst for Intl Policy; Others; cp/Music Ctr Fdrs Circle; Hollywood Wilshire Symph; Cult Clb Cal; Save the Redwoods Leag; Chds Bapt Home So Cal; Num Geneal Socs; Variety Clb; Mayors Coun for Intl Visitors & Sister Cities; Nat Travel Clb; Sev Woms Clbs; Intl Soc Toastmistressess of Inglewood; Smithsonian Inst Fdrs Circle; US Olympic Soc; Hon Mem, Bronze Pin, Silver Medalist; Others; r/Prot; Evang Crusades Inc; hon/Hon Certs Recog & Apprec, U Inventors & Scists for Res in Fields of Nuclear Physics & Astro-Physical Deductions; Hon Cert: ASIL, APHA; Gold

Seal Cert, Hon, Acad Polit Sci, Columbia Univ; Am Biogl Inst; Notable Ams Bicent Era; Am Scholars; Town & Gown, USC; W/W: Am Wom, Cal; DIB; World W/W Wom; IPA; Others.

HUNT, HOWARD LEE oc/Pastor; b/Nov 29, 1948; h/4550 SE Flavel Dr, Portland, OR 97206; ba/Portland; m/Mary Serena Primrose; c/Serena Ann Hunt; p/Ralph E and Earline Jacobsen Hunt, Fresno, CA; ed/BA Fresno Pacific Col; MDiv/MRE Golden Gate Theol Sem; pa/Pastor Trinity U Ch of Christ 1977-; Interim Min Sonoma Val Christian Ch; Bd Christian Ed Col Commun Congreg Ch; Asst to Pastor Calvary Bapt Ch, Col Commun Congreg Ch; Others; Conf Del; Camp Cnslr; cp/Portland Area Steering Com Boycott of J P Stevens Prods; Treas Yth for Decency of Fresno, Cal; Former Dir Rescue Mission Sers Fresno Pacific Col; r/Boy's Aux Ldr Harvard Terr So Bapt Ch, Fresno; SS Tchr Harvard Terr, Tiburon Bapt Ch, Tiburon (Cal), Others; hon/Hoover High (Fresno); PTA S'ship Awd, Prins Ser Awd.

HUNT, JOHN DuBOIS oc/Aerospace Physiologist; b/Jun 23, 1926; h/504 4th St SW, Independence, IA 50644; c/JoAnne, Jill Marie, Denise Cecile, John II; p/John Levi and Vera DuBois Hunt (dec); ed/BA Coe Col; JD

Wn St Univ; mil/USMC 1944-46; USAF 1952-72; pa/Aerospace Med Assn; Aerospace Physiologist Soc; cp/St & Fed Polit Activs; hon/USAF Commend Medal; DFC & Air Medal w 5 OLCs.

HUNT, LULA MAI oc/Superintendent; b/Dec 4, 1919; h/222 Shevel Dr, Goodlettsville, TN 37072; ba/G'ville; m/James F; c/James F Jr, Judith Kay, Wayne S; p/William W and Malvina Elizabeth DeSheles (dec); pa/Supt Postal Opers, G'ville; Former Postmaster, Edenwold, Tenn; Former Ofcr-in-Charge US Post Ofc, Springfield, Tenn; cp/PTA: Secy, Treas, Pres; Dir 10th Dist Commun Chest; G'ville C of C: Secy, Bd Dirs, Treas; r/Rivergate Ch of Christ; hon/2 Superior Accomplishmt Awds US Postal Ser; Wom Pioneers in Postal Ser; Personalities of S; Notable Ams; Book of Honor; DIB.

HUNT, MARY ALICE oc/Associate Professor; b/Apr 14, 1928; h/1603 Kolopakin Nene, Tallahassee, FL 32301; ba/Tallahassee; p/Blair T Hunt (dec); Grace H Hunt, Tallahassee; ed/AB, MA Fla St Univ; PhD Ind Univ; pa/Assoc Prof Sch Lib Sci Fla St Univ; ALA; SELA; AALS; FAME; FLA; AECT; cp/Friends of Leon Co Lib Group; r/Presb; hon/Beta Phi Mu; Kappa Delta Pi; Pi Lambda Theta.

HUNTER, CAMERON KREG oc/Engineering Chief; b/Apr 2, 1956; h/Apt 18N, 5016 S Toledo, Tulsa, OK 74135; ba/Tulsa; p/Cameron Booth and Grade Ann Hunter, Fox, OK; ed/Univ Tulsa; Univ Okla; pa/Mech Engr Soc (Univ Okla 1976); cp/Fund Raiser Dem Party; r/Fox So Bapt Ch; hon/Bausch & Lombe Sci Awd; Outstg Teenagers Am; OSU Engrg S'ship.

HUNTER, CANNIE MAE oc/Educator; b/Jul 16, 1916; h/4626 30th St, Lubbock, TX 79410; c/2 Chd; p/Jesse and Alice Cox; ed/BS Mary Hardin Univ 1942; Grad Studies: Univ Tex, Baylor Univ, Univ Ariz, Univ San Diego, St Mary's Univ San Antonio, Tex Tech Univ, Stephen F Austin Univ; Participant Num Sems

& Wkshops in Ed; pa/Lubbock Public Schs:
Classroom Tchr Bilingual Ed Prog 1975-, Var
Assignmts 1954-74; Former Tchg Positions:
Belton (Tex) Schs, Galveston (Tex) Schs, Univ
Ariz, Phoenix Public Schs & Killeen (Tex)
Public Schs; VP Killeen Housing Corp 1954;
Pres CMC Corp, Lubbock & Killeen 1974; Nat
Assn for Supvn & Curric Devel; IPA; NEA;
Tex St Tchrs Assn; Assn for Childhood Ed;
Nat Assn for Bilingual Ed; AAUW; cp/Former
1st Aid Chm Lubbock Co ARC; hon/Outstg
Ser Awd, ARC; Tex Cert'd Profl Edrs Awd;
Contact Teleministry Intl Bronze Hon Roll;
Book of Honor.

HUNTER, ELIZABETH SHEALY oc/-
Executive State Department; b/Jan 2, 1924;
h/PO Box 325, Prosperity, SC 29127; ba/-
Columbia, SC; m/J Ray; c/Sheila, Karen; p/D
Malcolm and Ella Bedenbaugh Shealy (dec);
ed/AB Newberry Col; pa/Assoc Dir SC
Probation, Parole & Pardon Bd; Public Sch
Tchr; cp/Pres Newberry Co Assn for Retard
Citizens; Pres Reg Div St Assn for Retard
Citizens; Bd Mem Newberry Co Adult Activs
Ctr; Am Legion Aux: Chperson Jr Legion Aux
Activs, Mbrship Com; Pres William Lester
Chapt U Daughs Confed; Secy Ridge Dist U
Daugh of Confed; Treas Newberry Col Wom's
Leag; r/Grace Luth Ch, Prosperity: SS Supt,
Asst Adult Tchr, VP Wom of Ch; hon/Outstg
St Employee 1977.

HUNTER, JACQUELINE HERITEAU
oc/Author; Editor; b/Oct 12, 1925; h/1049
Park Ave, New York, NY 10028; ba/Same;
c/Krishna S Littledale, David S, Holly B;
p/Marcel and Piney Sutherland Heriteau;
pa/Author/Editor 20+ Books on Gardening
& Cooking.

HUNTER, J(AMES) PAUL oc/Professor;
Writer; Lecturer; b/Jun 29, 1934; h/1251
Fairview Rd NW, Atlanta, GA 30306;
ba/Atlanta; m/Kathryn Montgomery;
c/Debra, Lisa Marlene, Paul III, Anne; p/Paul
W Hunter, Erie, PA; Florence Irene Walmer
Hunter (dec); ed/AB Ind Ctl Col; MA Miami

Univ; PhD Rice Univ; pa/Prof & Chm Eng
Dept Emory Univ; Am Soc for 18th Century
Studies; Mod Lang Assn; cp/Ga Conservancy;
Ga Mtl Hlth Assn; hon/Guggenheim Fellow;
Pubs: *The Reluctant Pilgrim*, 1966, *Norton
Intro to Poetry*, 1973, *Norton Intro to Lit*,
1973, 77, *Occasional Form*, 1975.

HUNTER, LENA VIRGINIA oc/Farmer;
Community Leader; h/6040 Seward Rd,
Pfafftown, NC 27040; ba/Same; p/Cicero
Gilbert and Ada Doub Hunter, Pfafftown,
NC; ed/Assoc Bus Ed; pa/Acct Exec Blue
Cross & Blue Shield 1957-77; pa/Master Old
Richmond Grange; Ofcr NC St Grange; 7th
Deg Mem Nat Grange; Dir NC Grange Mutual
Ins Co; r/Pleasant Hill U Meth Ch: Music Dir,
Tchr, Mem Adm Bd; hon/Wom of Yr in Ser to
Agri 1955; NC Granger of Yr, Farmers &
Traders Life Ins Co 1972; W/W Am Wom,
S&SW; World W/W Wom.

HUNTER, RAMONA E oc/Student;
b/August 2, 1932; h/PO Box 2642, Sepulveda,
CA 91343; p/Ida Blythe, Tulsa, OK; ed/AA
Los Angeles Mission Col; hon/Dean's Honor
List; Special Awd for Helping Others, LAMC;
Justice of Supr Ct, LAMC; Emer Medical Tech
I Deg.

HUNTER, ROBERT E oc/Executive;
b/May 1, 1940; h/613 Maryland Ave NE,
Washington, DC 20002; ba/Wash DC;

p/Robert Hunter Jr; Inez E Hunter (dec);
ed/BA; PhD; pa/Nat Security Coun Staff; Dir
W European Relats; NSC; cp/Dem Party;
hon/Phi Beta Kappa.

HUNTER, WILLIAM A oc/Journalist;
Politician; b/Sept 27, 1953; h/Weathersfield,
VT 05156; ba/Ludlow, VT; p/Armstrong and
Edith Hunter, Perkinsville, VT; ed/BA Yale
Univ 1977; BA Oxford Univ 1979; pa/Pubr
The Black River Tribune, Ludlow; cp/Mem Vt
Ho of Reps; hon/Rhodes S'ship.

HUNTLEY, WILLIAM ROBERT oc/-
Administrative Librarian; b/Apr 7, 1928;
h/4215 Flam St, Camp Springs, MD 20022;
ba/Washington, DC; c/Teri Buff, Sheri Lynn;
p/John Frederick Huntley (dec); Dessie
Gertrude Buff Huntley, Rutherfordton, NC;
ed/AB Univ NC 1958; mil/AUS 1952-54;
DCANG 1956-62; pa/Adm Libn Lib of Cong;
Spec Libs Assn; cp/BPO Elk; Secy Kiwanis;
r/Prot; hon/Meritorious Ser Awd, LC; Cert of
Merit, Kiwanis.

HURD, PRISCILLA ALDEN PAYNE
oc/Writer; Civic Leader; b/Sept 26, 1919;
h/PO Box 398, Springtown, PA 18081;
m/George A Sr; c/2 Chd; ed/AA Finch Col
1940; BA Chicago Univ 1942; Grad NY Sch
Radio Technique 1943; MTheol 1948, DDiv
1971 Life Sci Col; pa/Free-lance Writer
Specializing in Travel; Author 2 Anthologies
& Book on Archaeol for Bklyn Mus, *Chasing
Cult with the Brooklyn Mus*; Prod'd & Dir'd
1st Weekly Radio Prog Lehigh Val for UN,
"UN Calling You"; cp/Pres Bd Trustees
Eisenhower Meml S'ship Foun; Bd Dirs
Madeira Sch; Assoc Mem Kirkland Col;
Trustee Assn Am Museums; Nat Adv Bd Am
Christian Col, Tulsa, Okla; Secy Bd Trustees
Allentown Art Mus; Pa Chm Friends of
Kennedy Ctr; Menninger Foun; IPA; Hist
Bethlehem; Accredited Press; Assoc Mem: Nat
Hist Soc, Smithsonian Instn; Nat Wildlife Fdn;
Former Mem Bd Dirs: Girls Clb Bethlehem, St
Lukes Hosp Ladies Aid Soc, Bethlehem Chapt
ARC, Commun Concert Assn, UF Drive;
Former Mem Am Wom's Vol Sers Chgo;
Former Pres Bd Trustees Bethlehem Rehab
Ctr; hon/Hon HHD, Mt Sinai Univ Ohio;
Alpha Psi Omega; Sigma Chapt Delta Psi; Phi
Beta Kappa; Recipient Cit for Outstg Work,
Gov of Ill; W/W Am Wom; Intl W/W:
Commun Ser, Intells; World W/W Wom;
DIB; Notable Ams; Commun Ldrs &
Noteworthy Ams; Others.

HURR, DORIS SMITH oc/Librarian;
b/Oct 18, 1949; h/2619 Huntington Rd,
Fayetteville, NC 28303; ba/F'ville; m/Steven
Arthur; p/Elbert William Smith; Doris
Holmes Smith, F'ville; ed/BA St Andrews
Presb Col; MLn Emory Univ; pa/Asst Dir
Cumberland Co Public Lib; Pres Cape Fear Lib
Assn 1977-78; NC, SEn, Am Lib Assns; Var
Coms; cp/Bd Mem F'ville Symph Orch; F'ville
Mus of Art; r/1st Presb Ch.

HURSH, JOHN RAY oc/Attorney at Law;
Rancher; b/Feb 16, 1943; h/Eight Mile Rd,
Riverton, WY 82501; ba/Riverton; m/Judith
Ann Lopez; c/Bryan Watkins; p/R Max and
Virginia L Hursh (dec); ed/BA 1965, JD 1968
Univ Wyo; mil/USMC 1968-72, Capt; pa/Pres
Hursh Agy Inc; Hamilton & Hursh, PC; Wyo
Bar Assn; Wyo Trial Lwyrs Assn; Am Trial
Lwyrs Assn; Wyo Stockgrowers Assn;
cp/Judiciary Com Wyo St Leg; Lions; Eagles;
Masons; Sigma Nu; r/Epis; hon/Biogl Listing.

HURST, GEORGE SAMUEL oc/Physi-
cist; b/Oct 13, 1927; h/103 Newark Ln, Oak
Ridge, TN 37830; ba/Oak Ridge; m/Betty
Partin; c/Donald Edward, Karen H Holbrook
(Mrs John); p/James H and Myrtle Wright
Hurst (dec); ed/AB; MS; PhD; pa/Physicist
Oak Ridge Nat Lab; 1 of Fdrs Scists & Engrs
for Appalachia (SEA); hon/Indust Res IR-100
Awd: for One-Atom Detector, The Elograph.

HURT, BILLY GREY oc/Minister; h/8
Breckinridge Ln, Frankfort, KY 40601;
ba/Frankfort; m/Scharlyene Harbison; c/Billy
Grey Jr, Robert Hal, Mark Harbison; p/Mr
and Mrs Wilburn H Hurt, Murray, KY;
ed/Grad Cumberland Col, Union Univ; PhD
So Sem; pa/Current Pastor 1st Bapt Ch,
Frankfort; Former Pastorates: Bethel Bapt Ch,
Humboldt (Tenn), Scotts Grove Bapt Ch,

Murray (Ky), 1st Bapt Ch, Benton (Ky), 1st
Bapt Ch, Independence (Mo), Immanuel Bapt
Ch, Paducah (Ky); Exec Bd Mem W Union
Assn; Ky Bapt Conv: Exec Bd, Fin Com;
Trustee Campbellsville Col; Chm Prog Com
Ky Bapt Pastor's Conf; Active Participant
Local Min Assns; Writer Adult Lessons Mats,
Bapt SS Bd; cp/Var Commun Activs; r/So
Bapt.

HUSER, CARL FRANK oc/Assistant
Professor; b/Sept 19, 1942; h/406 N Elgin,
Bolivar, MO 65613; ba/Bolivar; m/Carol
Kay; c/Cary Wayne, Cathryn Ann; p/Frank
and Evelyn Marie Huser, Lockwood, MO;
ed/AA; BS; MS; pa/Asst Prof Biol SW Bapt
Col; AAAS; Mo Acad Scis; Springfield Acad
Scis; Gtr Ozark Audubon Soc; cp/Cub Scout
Ldr; Spkr & Lectr; r/Bapt: Deacon; hon/Life
Beautiful Awd, SW Bapt Col; W/W in
Ecology.

HUSKETH, ALMA ORMOND oc/-
Librarian; b/Aug 17, 1918; h/Box 198, Brass-
field Rd, Creedmoor, NC 27522; ba/Creed-
moor; m/Edward Thomas Jr; c/E T III,
William Ormond, Craig Moss; p/William
Henry and Ella White Ormond (dec); ed/AB
UNC-G; MSLS UNC-CH; pa/Libn S Granville
HS; Bd Dirs RHT Lib, Oxford; NCAE; AG;
NCLA; NEA; cp/Dir SG CC; Wilton Grange;
r/U Meth: Ch Sch Supt, UMW Ofcr; hon/-
W/W Am Wom; Alpha Delta Kappa.

HUSSEIN, CARLESSIA AMANDA oc/-
Health Administrator; b/Sept 1, 1936; h/1510
S Bascom Ave #87, Campbell, CA 95008;
ba/San Jose, CA; c/Monica Suzanne; p/-
Nathan and Amanda Roberts Minor, Wash-
ington, DC; ed/RN Freedmen's Hosp Sch Nsg;
BS 1966, MS 1967 Univ Cal-San Francisco;
DrPH Univ Cal-Berkeley Sch Public Hlth
1977; pa/Exec Dir Hlth Systems Agy 1977;
Hlth Planner 1975-77; Assoc Dean Univ Cal-B
Sch Public Hlth 1972-73; Res Dir Hypertension
Study, Univ Cal-B 1974-77; hon/Public Hlth
Ser Grants (3 Yrs).

HUSSEINY, ABDO AHMED oc/Mana-
ger; b/Jul 7, 1936; h/2144 Ashmore Ct, Ames,
IA 50010; ba/Ames; m/Zeinab Sabri; p/-
Ahmed Husseiny and Fahima Sabbah, Egypt;
ed/PhD Univ Wis 1969; pa/Mgr Decision
Analysis & Adv'd Systems Div SAI; Chm
Ia/Neb Am Nuclear Soc 1977-78; hon/Cert of
Governance & Dist'd Sers Awd, Am Nuclear
Soc.

HUSTING, EDWARD LEE oc/Public
Health Consultant; Educator; b/Feb 25, 1939;
h/555 Pierce St, Albany, CA 94706;

ba/Albany; c/Sheila Renee; p/Francis Edward and Margaret Cole Hooting (dec); ed/BS; PhD; MPH; pa/Indep Conslt 1978-: Teknekron Inc (Berkeley), Systems Applications Inc (San Rafael); Lectr Hlth Sci Prog Cal St Univ-Hayward 1978-; Flow Resources Corp, San Rafael: Dir Hlth Sys Planning & Eval 1978, Mgr Hlth & Safety Progs 1977-78, Chief Occupl Hlth Progs 1976-77; Cal St Univ-H: Prof & Dir Hlth Scis Prog 1975-76; Other Former Positions; Fellow Royal Soc Tropical Med & Hygiene; Full Mem (Nat) Am Indust Hygiene Assn; Am Public Hlth Assn; Assn Tchrs Preven Med; Intl Epidemiological Assn; Nat Assn Envir Profls; Soc for Occupl & Envir Hlth; World Safety Org; Other Profl Orgs; cp/Mem Adv Bd Proseminar Inst, SF; hon/W/W: Hlth Care, W; DIB; Men of Achmt; Intl W/W in Commun Ser; Num Profl Pubs.

HUSTON, JEFFREY CHARLES oc/- Engineering Professor; b/Jan 30, 1951; h/108 Tenth Ave, Slater, IA 50244; ba/Ames, IA; m/Patricia Ann; p/Charles V Huston (dec); Pauline Huston, Johnstown, PA; ed/BS III Inst Technol; MS 1973, PhD 1975 WVa Univ; pa/Engrg Prof Ia St Univ; ASME; SESA; SAE; ASEE; r/U Ch of Christ; hon/Sigma Xi; W/W Among Students in Am Cols & Univs; WVa Univ Foun F'ship.

HUTCHINSON, BARBARA P oc/Tax Law Researcher/Author; b/Nov 5, 1926; h/4416 Alamo Dr, San Diego, CA 92115; ba/San Diego; c/Howard Jr, Harold; p/Moore Pelham (dec); Laura Lingenfelter, Mobile, AL; pa/Exec Trustee Estate Guardian Ednl Trust; Chief Lectr Citizens Ctroom Wkshop; Tax Specialist; cp/Reg'd Libertarian Party Mem; Rolando Commun Group; Cuyamaca Clb; Assn Concerned Taxpayers; r/Cath; hon/Good Citizen Awd, Parents & Taxpayers San Francisco; Sam Adams Awd, MENSA; Fierce Courage Awd.

HUTCHINSON, RICHARD CHARLES oc/Management Consultant; b/Dec 9, 1916; h/716 Shady Ln, Lakeland, FL 33803; ba/Lakeland; m/Mary Ellen; c/Judith Hodges; p/Charles B and Helen A Hutchinson (dec); ed/BS MIT 1937; MEA USF 1968; pa/Owner Richard C Hutchinson, PE 1970-; Indust Engrg Experience Var Industs; AIIE; NSPE; FES; IMI; r/Prot; hon/Outstg Indust Engr; VP AIIE 1974-76.

HUTH, ALLEN J oc/Legislative Council Research Assistant; b/Sept 13, 1955; h/1320 Willow St, Denver, CO 80220; ba/Denver; m/Terry A; c/Jason Allen, Ryan Joseph; p/Robert W and Janet R Huth, Colorado Springs, CO; ed/BA Univ No Colo 1977; pa/Student Govt Adm Asst, US 1975; Nat

Student Assn Del 1975; r/Christian, Calvary Temple; hon/Outstg Yg Men Am; W/W Am Cols & Univs.

HUTTON, JOHN E JR oc/Physician; b/1931; h/338A Infantry Terr, Presidio of San Francisco, CA 94129; ba/Presidio of SF; m/Barbara Joyce; c/John III, Wendy, James, Elizabeth; p/John Evans Hutton (dec); Antoinette Abbott Weech, Gainesville, FL; ed/BA Wesleyan Univ 1953; MD Geo Washington Univ Med Sch 1963; mil/USMC 1953-57, Capt; AUS MC 1963-, Col; pa/Letterman Army Med Ctr, Presidio of SF: Chief Gen Surg Ser 1975-, Asst Chief 1971-75, Chief Peripheral Vascular Surg 1971-; Asst Chief Peripheral Vascular Surg Walter Reed Army Med Ctr, Washington, DC 1970-71; Conslt; Other Former Positions; Diplomate: Am Bd Med Examrs, Am Bd Surg 1969; AMA; Fellow Am Col Surgs; SF Surg Soc; Intl Cardiovas Soc; Soc for Clin Vascular Surg; cp/Mbrship & Race Coms St Francis Yacht Clb; Contbr to Nat Yachting Mags; r/Epis; hon/Profl Pubs; Mil Decorations.

HUYCK, MARGARET HELLIE oc/- Educator; b/Apr 14, 1939; h/1718 E 55th St, Chicago, IL 60615; ba/Chgo; m/William Thomas; c/Elizabeth, Karen; p/Ole and Elizabeth L Hellie, Des Moines, IA; ed/AB Vassar Col; MA, PhD Univ Chgo; pa/Assoc Prof Psychol III Inst Technol 1975-; Guest Fac Sexual Attitude Recog Wkshops NWn Med Sch, Chgo 1973-; Vis Prof & Lectr; Res Conslt Dutch Sci Soc 1978; Scholar-in-Residence Norwegian Inst Gerontology, Oslo, Norway 1977-78; Other Profl Activs; Gerontological Soc; Nat Coun on Aging; APA; MW Psychol Assn; Am Sociol Assn; Res Adv Group Mayors Ofc for Sr Citizens & Handicapped, Chgo 1977-; Others; cp/Bd Dirs SE Chgo Comm; Former Parent Rep Bret Harte Public Elem Sch Ed Coun; Former Mem Bd Dirs Hyde Park Neighborhood Clb; Others; r/Prot; hon/NICHD Trainee in Adult Devel & Aging, Univ Chgo; Univ Fellow, Univ Chgo; Hon Mention, Woodrow Wilson F'ship; Other Acad Hons; Num Profl Pubs; Biogl Listings.

HYATT, GUY WILLIAM oc/Retired Educator; Writer; Theologian; b/May 27, 1913; h/Waterfront Dr, Pineland, FL 33945; ed/Grad Lindlawr Col, St Andrews Sem, Dequer Inst Res; pa/Ext Work in Nutritional Res; Fdr Am Bible Col; Nat Moderator Am Evang Christian Chs; Mem Royal Geographical Soc London; cp/Appt'd & Comm'd Col by Gov Finch (St of Miss) to Serve in Exec Dept as Aide de Camp to Gov's Staff; hon/7 Hon Degs for Cult Achmt.

HYDE, HAZEL MARGUERITE

oc/Educator; Local Historian; b/May 29, 1908; h/1518 Comanche Dr, Rockford, IL 61107; m/Harold Beardslee; p/Wilson S and Ida M Powell Mortimer; ed/BS Pittsburg St Univ Ks; MA NWn Univ; pa/Life Mem NEA; Rockford Hist Soc: Charter Mem, Charter Bd Mem, Past VP; Life Mem III St Hist Soc; Assoc Editor *Nuggets of History*; AAUW; Nat Preservation Trust; Nat Geneal Soc; Nat Audubon Soc; Sinnissippi Audubon Soc; Phi Alpha Theta; cp/DAR: Mem Rockford Chapt 38 Yrs, Former Chaplain, Spkrs Bur, Former Geneal Records Chm, St JAC Chm, Others; Patron Lyric Opera Chgo; Florentine Opera Guild Milwaukee (Wis); Metro Opera Guild NYC; Wednesday Afternoon Lit Group; Tinker Swiss Cottage Assn; Friend of Rockford Mus Ctr; Rockford Wom's Clb; Others; r/Meth; hon/Freedoms Foun; Credo Clb, Rockford's Lady of Distn; WWII Medal (Vol Work), DAR; Newton Farr Awd as Tchr of Yr, III Hist Soc.

HYDER, NANCY ELIZABETH oc/Student; b/May 22, 1958; h/407 Long Forest Cir, Anderson, SC 29621; ba/Due West, SC; p/A G Jr and Betty R Hyder, Anderson; ed/Att'g Erskine Col; cp/Intern for US Senator Strom Thurmond; r/Meth; hon/Dean's List; Omicron Delta Kappa; Erskine Scholar; Phi Beta Kappa; Others.

HYNDS, FRANCES JANE oc/Communications Consultant; Senior Lecturer; b/Oct 27, 1929; h/1033 Carol Dr, #107, Los Angeles, CA 90069; ba/LA; p/Loyd Orion and Hunter Elizabeth Hynds, Martin, TN; ed/BS McMurry Col; MA USC; pa/Sr Lectr Sch Jour Univ So Cal 1977-78; Communs Conslt to Bus & Indust, Commun & Profl Groups, Govt Agys & Ednl Instns 1975-; Owner Fran Hynds Public Relats, LA 1965-75; Acct Exec Joe Leighton & Assocs Inc, Hollywood, Cal 1956-65; Other Former Positions; Bd Mem Nat Public Relats Coun for Human Sers Inc 1968-73; Public Relats Soc Am, LA Chapt; Wom in Communs Inc, LA Chapt; cp/Nat Conf on Social Wel; Psi SEARCH; Orgr & Coor Cal Coalition for Equal Rts Amendmt (Wom in Communs Inc); Other Civic Activs; hon/Pub'd Author; W/W: Am Wom, W.

HYNES, GEORGE P oc/Retired Librarian; b/Mar 17, 1910; h/924 15th Ave N, Fort Dodge, IA 50501; m/Dorothy Ellen; c/- Wallace, Ronald, Constance, Kathleen, Renee; p/Leo and Emma Hynes (dec); ed/BS; Grad Work; pa/Public Libn; Author (Book on Boxing); cp/Boxing Coach; Ks of C; Lt Gov Moose; Pres Eagles; Lions; Rotary; Elks; Garden Clb; r/Cath; hon/Man of Yr, ND 1959, 60, Ia 1973.

I

I'ANSON, LAWRENCE WARREN oc/Chief Justice; b/Apr 21, 1907; h/214 W Rd, Portsmouth, VA 23701; ba/Portsmouth; m/May Frances Tuttle; c/Lawrence Warren, May Frances I Ramsey (Mrs Peter); p/James Thornton and Emma Warren I'Anson; ed/BA 1928, LLD 1964 Col William & Mary; LLB Univ Va 1931; pa/Admit'd Va Bar 1931; Pract'd Law Portsmouth 1931-41; Commonwlth's Atty 1938-41; Judge Ct of Hustings 1941-58; Supr Ct Va: Justice 1958-74, Chief Justice 1974-; Author *Handbook for Jurors*; Mem Bd Dirs Nat Ctr St Cts; Former Chm Va Ct Sys; Va Bar Assn; ABA; Inst Jud Adm; Former Dir Am Judic Soc; 2/VCh Exec Coun Conf Chief Justices; Others; cp/Pres Beazley Foun; Pres Foun Boys' Acad; Chm Bd Trustees Frederick Mil Acad; Commonwlth Clb; Harbor Clb; Dem Party; Mason; Knights Templar; Royal Order Jesters; Nat Sojourners; Exec Clb; Kiwanis; Others; r/Bapt; hon/Recipient Dist'd Ser Awd, Va Trial Lwyrs Assn; Lincoln Harley Awd, Am Judic Soc; Col William & Mary: Medallion, Cit Dist'd Ser; Univ Va Sesquicentennial Awd; Named 1st Citizen Portsmouth; Pi Kappa Alpha; Phi Alpha Delta; Flat Hat Clb Soc; Omicron Delta Kappa; W/W Am; Blue Book; Others.

IBOK, EFFIONG ETUKUDO oc/Educator; Researcher; b/Nov 4, 1952; p/Etukudo and Affiong Bassey Ibok, Nigeria; ed/BS; MA; pa/Tchr & Reschr Dept Chem Engrg, Princeton Univ Grad Col; Local, Regional & Nat Workshops Intl Politics; hon/Tau Beta Pi; Pi Epsilon Tau; Phi Eta Sigma; Phi Gamma Kappa; Biogl Listings.

IBRANYI, FRANCIS JOSEPH oc/Professor; b/Apr 30, 1901; h/Mt St Joseph, 670 Tower Hill Rd, Wakefield, RI 02879; ba/Wakefield; ed/BA; STD; PhD; pa/Prof Mt St Joseph Convent; Holds Weekly Confs Phil & Theol; Cnslr; cp/Intl Inst RI; r/Rom Cath; hon/Doctor Collegiatus; Papal Domestic Prelate; Fellow Intl Inst Commun Ser; Fellow Am Biogl Inst.

ICHORD, RICHARD H oc/US Congressman; b/Jun 27, 1926; h/116 W Main, Houston, MO 65483; ba/Washington, DC; m/Millicent; c/Richard III, Pamela Lee, Kyle; p/Richard Howard and Minda Ichord; ed/BS Mo Univ 1949; JD 1952; mil/USN Air Corps; pa/US Cong: Mem 87th-95th Congs; Mo Ho of Reps: Rep Tex Co 1953, Speaker 1959-60; City Atty Houston 1952; Mem Lay & Ichord Law Firm, Houston 1952-60; r/Bapt.

IDE, JUDITH H oc/Legal Secretary; b/Jul 31, 1943; h/PO Box 2, Wayland, MA 01778; ba/Boston, MA; p/Donald K and Dorothy L Ide, Wayland; ed/Chamberlayne Jr Col; cp/GOP St Com Wom; Secy & Dir Repubs for Middlesex Co; Del Repub Nat Conv 1976; r/Prot.

IGBOKWE, EMMANUEL CHUKWUEMEKA oc/Educator; b/Jan 18, 1941; h/5900 Enterprise, El Paso, TX 78912; m/Gwendolyn Mattie Capers; p/Aaron O Igbokwe (dec); Edna A Igbokwe, Enugu, Nigeria; ed/BS w Hons Univ Nigeria 1965; MS Mich St Univ 1967; PhD Queen's Univ (Canada) 1971; MD Univ Juarez (Mexico) 1981; pa/Rust Col: Hd Dept of Biol 1974-79, Chm Div of Sci 1978-79, Prof of Biol 1977-, Assoc Prof 1974-77, Asst Prof 1971-74; Post Doctl Res Assoc, Univ Notre Dame 1970-71; Res Investigator, Nat HLK Assn, Hypertension Grant 1978; Prin Res Investigator, MISIP, Nat Sci Foun Grant 1972-75; Other Former Positions; Am Soc Parasitology; AAAS; Am Genetic Assn; Canadian Genetic Soc; Miss Acad Sci; Contbr to Profl Jours; Participant in Profl Confs; Others; hon/Directory; Intl Union Physiol Sci.

IMBRECHT, CHARLES RICHARD oc/Attorney; Legislator; b/Feb 4, 1949; h/1079 Belfast Ln, Ventura, CA 93003; ba/Sacramento, CA; p/Earl Richard and Hazel Berg Imbrecht, Ventura; ed/BA Occidental Col; JD Loyola Univ; pa/Former Atty Advr Interstate Commerce Comm; Ventura & Am Bar Assns; cp/Ventura Downtown Lions Clb; JCs; Ventura & Oxnard C of C; Ventura Co Repub Ctl Com; hon/Sigma Alpha Epsilon; 2 Cits Outstg Perf, Fed Govt; Former Ritcher Nat Study Fellow; Former Argo Public Affairs Fellow.

IMHOFF, MYRTLE MARY ANN oc/Retired; b/Oct 7, 1910; h/Rancho San Joaquin Apts, 83 Promenade, Irvine, CA 92715; p/Clyde C Sr and Laura E Imhoff (dec); ed/BA Harris Tchrs Col; MA St Louis Univ; PhD Wash Univ & Col Univ; pa/Prof Ed Cal St Col-LA 1968-76; Prof Ed Cal St Col-F 1960-68; UNESCO Curric Expert & Advr, Min Ed Thailand 1959-60; Assoc Prof Cal St Col-LB 1953-60; Conslt Coronet Instrl Films 1969; Conslt Kindergarten In Espanol, Coun Mexican Am Affairs 1969; Other Positions; Author Num Articles Profl Jours; Am Psychol Assn: Div Ed Psychols, Div Tchg Psychol; Intl Coun Psychol; Am Acad Polit & Social Sci; AERA; Nat Soc Study Ed; Nat Assn Ed Yg Chd; NEA; IPA; Others; cp/Washington Univ & St Louis Univ Alumni Assns; Southland Water Com; World Affairs Coun Orange Co; Others; hon/McMillan S'ship; Heerman's F'ship; Jesse K Barr Hon F'ship; Kappa Delta Pi; Nat Register Prominent Ams; Nat Register Sci & Technol; Rec'd Plaque, Nat Register W/W; W/W Am Wom; DIB; Others.

INEZ, COLETTE oc/Poet; Teacher; b/Jun 23, 1931; h/5 W 86th St, New York, NY 10024; m/Saul Stadtmauer; ed/BA Hunter Col 1961; pa/Instr Poetry New Sch (NYC) 1973-; Former Positions: Workshop Instr St Univ NY-S, Instr & Poet-in-Residence Kalamazoo Col, Instr Cranbrook Writer's Conf, Others; Author: *Alive and Taking Names (1977), The Woman Who Loved Worms (1972)*; Pub'd Num Poems Anthologies; Conducted Seminars & Wkshops: Harvard Fac Clb,

Hunter Col, Tenn Poetry Circuit, Depauw Univ, Others; Book Reviewer: *Parnassus, Poetry in Review, Three Rivers Jour,* Others; CETA Artist Panelist; Poetry Soc Am; PEN Am Ctr; Others; r/Cath; hon/Grantee, Maryland Coun on Arts; Kreymborg Awd PSA; NY St CAPS F'ship; Nat Endowmt Arts F'ship; 1st Book Prize *The Woman Who Loved Worms*, Gt Lakes Cols Assn; Reedy Meml Awd PSA; Osgood Warren Awd, Poetry Soc New Eng; W/W: Am, World; Contemp Authors.

ING, CELINA S oc/Assistant Dean; b/-Sept 21, 1947; h/PO Box 60053, Sunnyvale, CA 94088; ba/Sacramento, CA; p/Albert Sau Yee and Nancy Ngan Chew Ing, Sunnyvale; ed/BA maxima cum laude Col Notre Dame 1972; MA 1973, Cand EdD Univ San Francisco; Addit Studies; pa/Asst Dean, Div Social Studies; Cal Assn Wom Deans & Cnslrs; Am Classical Leag; Am Hist Assn; Am Assn Hist Med; Acad Com, Wn Reg Consortium Cont'g Ed RNs; r/Rom Cath; hon/Regents; F'ship; Univ Cal-SF; Recipient Outstg Yg Wom Am; W/W Am Wom; Notable Ams; World W/W Wom; DIB; Others.

INGALLS, GEORGE LEWIS oc/Lawyer; b/Jun 7, 1914; h/38 Beethoven St, Binghamton, NY 13905; ba/Binghamton; m/Dorothy I; c/Bryan W, Robert G, John S, Janet E; p/Louis S Ingalls (dec); Ethel Gallup (dec); ed/BA cum laude Amherst Col 1935; LLB magna cum laude Syracuse Univ Col Law 1939; pa/Am, NY St & Broome Co Bar Assns; Power Authority St of NY 1967-; Mem NY Gen Assembly 1953-66: Maj Ldr 1961-64, Min Ldr 1965; cp/Former Chm Broome Co Rep Com; r/Congreg; hon/Phi Beta Kappa; Phi Kappa Phi; Justinian.

INGRAM, BETTY E oc/Executive; b/May 9, 1937; h/1780 Murray Hill Rd, Birmingham, AL 35209; ba/B'ham; m/Bill M; c/Bill M Jr, Phillip R, Jon B; p/James W Elam, B'ham; ed/BS Univ Tenn-K; pa/VP & Partner Bagwell/Ingram & Co Inc; Reporter & Wom's Editor Kingsport (Tenn) *Times-News* 1 Yr; Asst Dir Public Relats, Jefferson Co United Way 4 Yrs; ARC: Dir Public Relats (B'ham Area) 8 Yrs, Asst Mgr (Ala Div) 5 Yrs, Deputy Mgr 4 Yrs; Am Wom Radio & TV; Am Bus Wom's Assn; Am Mgmt Assn; B'ham Press Clb; Others; cp/Jr Wom's Com, B'ham Symph; Former Mem Jefferson Drug Abuse Coor'g Com; Jefferson Co Com Ed Opportunity; United Way Vol; Others; r/Shades Valley Luth Ch: Mem, SS Tchr; hon/Wom Yr, Am Bus Wom's Assn; Dist'd Yg Wom Awd, Jayceettes; Boss Yr Awd, ABWA; Photo Awds, United Way Am; W/W Am Wom; DIB; Others.

INGRAM, CHARLES DEAN oc/Librarian; b/Dec 29, 1928; h/1304 Lark, Rt 2, Weatherford, OK 73096; ba/Weatherford; p/Jim C Ingram (dec); Nan M Ingram, Weatherford; ed/BFA 1951, MFA 1963 Univ Okla; pa/Libn Al Harris Lib, SWn Okla St Univ; cp/Soc N Am Artists; r/Presb; hon/Beta Phi Mu.

INGRAM, ROBERT BRUCE oc/Lawyer; b/Jul 19, 1940; ba/4340 Redwood Hwy, Suite #133, San Rafael, CA 94903; m/Judith J; c/Stephanie, Ashley, Robert; p/Earl J and Francis F Ingram, Des Moines, IA; ed/BA Drake Univ 1962; JD Col William & Mary 1970; mil/USAF 1964-68; pa/Bd Dirs San Francisco Trial Lwyrs Assn; cp/Am Heart Assn: VP, Treas & Mem Bd Dirs (Marion Co Chapt); Bd Dirs Cal Heart Assn; r/Presb; hon/W/W Am Law; Intl Biogl Ctr.

INMAN, FRANKLIN P JR oc/Professor; b/Aug 2, 1937; h/707 Willmar St, Johnson City, TN 37601; ba/Johnson City; m/Barbara B; c/Jody Lin, J Walter; p/F P Inman Sr, Greensboro, NC; Aieleen S Inman, Sanford, NC; ed/BA 1959, PhD 1964 UNC-CH; pa/E Tenn St Univ: Prof & Chm Dept Biochem 1977-; Univ Ga: Prof Biochem & Microbiol 1975-77, Assoc Prof 1970-75, Asst Prof

1966-70; Gen Editor *Contemp Topics in Molecular Immunol* 1972-; Reschr; Other Positions; Am Assn Immunol; Am Soc Biol Chems; Am Soc Microbiol; Am Chem Soc; cp/JCs; Past Pres PTA; Former Bd Dirs Forest Hgts Pool Inc; r/Meth; hon/John M Morehead S'ship, UNC-CH; M G Michael Awd, Univ Ga; Am Cancer Soc Scholar; Am Men Sci; Personalities of S; Others.

INNIS, ROBERT WILLIAM oc/Associate Professor; b/Oct 23, 1919; h/307 Haskins St, Bowling Green, OH 43402; ba/Bowling Green; m/Evangeline S; c/Nela Rose; Patricia Ann; p/William J and Nela B Innis (dec); ed/BS; MS; EdD; mil/USAF 1943-46; pa/Assoc Prof Indust Ed & Technol, Bowling

Green St Univ 1960-; Asst Prof Air Sci, Mich St Univ 1953-56; Indust Ed Ctr, Mo St Col 1959-60; USAF Instr (Findlay, Ohio) 1960-68; Others; Am Indust Arts Assn; Nat Assn Indust Technol; Am Coun Indust Arts Tchr Ed; cp/32° Mason; r/Meth; hon/Pub'd Author.

INSELBERG, ALFRED oc/Professor; b/Oct 22, 1936; h/15 Mishol Arava, Beersheva, Israel; ba/Beersheva; Los Angeles, CA; m/Hadassa; c/Louisa, Dona; p/Valentino and Louisa Inselberg (dec); ed/BSc 1958, MSc 1956, PhD 1965 Univ Ill; pa/Assoc Prof Dept Math, Ben Gurion Univ of Negev; Sr Sci Staff Mem IBM; SIAM: Chm, Treas (So Cal Section); AMS; MAA; r/Jewish; hon/Sigma Chi; Work Math Model Displayed EXPO'70; Appeared *Time, Newsweek, US News & World Report,* Others; Corp Outstg Contbn Awd, IBM.

INYART, GENE oc/Writer; b/Jul 11, 1927; h/333 Lincoln Ave, Takoma Park, MD 20012; m/Stanley B Namovicz; c/Susan, Catherine, Matthew, Daniel; p/Ernest William and Pauline Martin Inyart, Charleston, IL; ed/BA Univ Mich 1949; MS Cath Univ Am 1963; pa/Author: *Tent Under the Spider Tree (1959), Chd's Ser in Public Libraries (1963), Susan & Martin (1965), Jenny (1966), Orange October (1968);* r/Rom Cath; hon/Franklin Watts Fiction Awd.

IPES, THOMAS PETER oc/Counselor; Minister; b/Feb 25, 1948; h/224 Concord Dr, Newburgh, IN 47630; ba/Newburgh; m/Mary Anne; c/Christine Marie, Melinda Joy; p/Thomas Peter Sr and Ruth Lydia Ipes, Virginia Beach, VA; ed/BA Columbia Union Col; MDiv Andrews Univ; DMin Lancaster Theol Sem; Addit Studies; pa/Marriage & Fam Cnslr, Christian Cnslg & Ed Ctr Inc; Ser'd Clinical Residency Progs: Wash (DC) Gen Hosp, Lancaster Gen Hosp, Others; Nat Alliance Fam Life Inc; AAMFC; Assn Christian Marriage Cnslrs; Nat Assn Christians Social Work; Am Assn Sex Edrs; Wn Assn Christian Psychol Studies; Others; r/SDA; hon/Rec'd Awd Outstg Contbns Field Marriage & Fam Enrichmt.

IRVINE, RAYMOND GERALD JR oc/Engineer; b/Mar 31, 1937; m/Elizabeth Ann Williams Bazemore; c/4; p/Raymond Gerald and Jane T Schenck Irvine; ed/BS w Hons, Norwich Univ 1959 (Gen Motors S'ship); Addit Studies; mil/AUS Signal Corps 1960-63; pa/Sr Engr, Wn Electric Co Inc (New York) 1978-; Electrical Power Engrg Conslt w Office in Suffern (NY); Staff Engr, IBM-Sterling Forest (NY) 1974-78; Proj Engr, Dubin-Mindell-Bloome (NYC) 1974; Other Positions; NY St Soc Profl Engrs; Nat Soc Profl Engrs (Energy Com); IEEE; Intl Assn Electrical Inspectors; Nat Fire Protection Assn; Illuminating Engrg Soc; Am Soc Heating, Refrigerating & Air Conditioning Engrs; Norwich Engrs Soc; Vols Intl Tech Asst; AEE; Others; Co-author, *NY St Energy Outlook (1976);* Contbr Articles Profl Jours; cp/Aircraft Owners & Pilots Assn; hon/Frederick Asher Spencer Prize in Electrical Engrg, Norwich Univ; Rec'd Outstg Ser Awd, Capital Dist Chapt NY St Soc Profl Engrs; Biogl Listings.

IRVINE, ROBERT BRUCE oc/Professional Engineer; b/May 9, 1939; h/4855 Alatar Dr, Woodland Hills, CA 91364; m/Judy E Caviedes; c/Julie, Chris;

p/John William and Pauline Kesheimer Irvine, Ashland, KY; ed/BSME Univ Ky 1961; MSME Univ So Cal 1968; Addit Studies; pa/Teledyne: Assoc Dir Inertial Engrg 1974-, Prog Mgr 1973-74; Former Proj Engr GFAE Flight Dirs Sys & Components; Other Positions; Pub'd Papers Profl Jours; Am Soc Mech Engrs; Am Inst Aeronautics & Astronautics; Inst Navigation; cp/Am Fdn Musicians; Repub Party; r/Presb; hon/Holds US Patent; W/W: Am, W.

IRVING, GEORGE W JR oc/Biochemist; Consultant; b/Nov 20, 1910; h/4836 Langdrum Ln, Chevy Chase, MD 20015; ba/Bethesda, MD; m/Frances Catherine Connell; c/George W III, Mary Constance I Patrick; p/George W Irving (dec); Adelaide Louise Butman Irving, Kensington, MD; ed/BS 1933, MA 1935, PhD 1939 George Washington Univ; pa/Life Scis Res Ofc Fdn Am Socs Exptl Biol: Res Assoc, Chm & Chief of Staff Com Reschrs FDA 1971-77, Conslt 1977-; ARS: Deputy Admr 1954, Assoc Admr 1964-65, Admr 1965-71; USDA: Asst Chief, Bur Agri & Indust Chem 1947-53, Reschr So Reg Res Lab 1942-44, Others; Lectr: George Wash Univ Med Sch 1947-53, USDA Grad Sch 1946-52; Author Num Articles & Papers; Public Trustee Nutrition Foun; Former Conslt Nat Grad Univ; Am Chem Soc; Chem Soc Wash; Fellow AAAS; Fellow Wash Acad Scis; Am Soc Biol Chems; Inst Food Technols; Others; r/Rom Cath; hon/Awd Sci Achmt Physical Scis, Wash Acad Scis; Co-Recipient Superior Ser Awd, Dist'd Ser Awd USDA; Rec'd Awds: Am Inst Chems, Am Leather Chems Assn; Alpha Chi Sigma.

ISHAM, QUENTIN DELBERT JR oc/-State Senator; Independent Insurance Agent; b/Apr 30, 1944; h/3231 W Devils Lake Rd, Lincoln City, OR 97367; ba/Lincoln City; m/Paulette; c/Shane Gordon, Shaun Lane; p/Quentin D and Leah S Isham, Aumsville, OR; ed/BS Weber St Col 1967; MA Col St Univ 1969; mil/AUS 1/Lt; pa/Nat Assn St Legs; Independent Ins Agents Assn; cp/Lions Clb; C of C; Dem Party Precinct Com-man; r/Unit.

ISRAEL, JEANNETTE NEMECEK oc/Human Geneticist; Pediatrician; Physician; b/Oct 20, 1944; ba/Chicago, IL; m/George; p/Joseph G and Jeannette Nemecek, Lagrange

Park, IL; ed/BS Univ Ill 1967; MD Chgo Med Sch 1971; pa/Hosp Affiliations: Pres St Lukes (Chgo), Maddenment Hlth (Hines, Ill), Hektoen Inst Med Res (Chgo), Univ Ill Hosp; AMA; Am Soc Human Genetics; Chgo Peds Soc; Am Soc Advmt Sci; Tissue Cult Assn; Others.

ISSARI, M ALI oc/Professor; b/Aug 13, 1924; h/4454 Seneca Dr, Okemos, MI 48864; ba/East Lansing, MI; m/Joan Aamodt; c/Sherri, Katayoun, Roxana; p/Abbas Issari (dec); Qamar Soltan Issari, Abadan, Iran; ed/BA Univ Tehran; MA, PhD Univ So Cal;

pa/Prof Mich St Univ; Motion Picture Prodr, Dir; Edr; Public Relats Conslt; r/Moslem; hon/Decorated by Govts: Iran, Jordan, Italy, Holland, Denmark, USA; Rec'd Decoration Pope John XXIII; Cine Sagle Awd.

ISSEL, RICHARD PHILLIP oc/Psychologist; b/Oct 7, 1938; h/5307 W Agatite, Chicago, IL 60630; ba/Chgo; p/John Phillip Issel (dec); Ann Frances Issel, Chgo; ed/BA; MS; PhD; pa/Sr Conslt Archdiocese Chgo; Sr Clinical Conslt: Ill St Psychi Inst, VA; Fac Mem: Mid Wn Sch Profl Psychol, St Mary Lake Sem; Pvt Pract; cp/Chgo Coun Foreign Relats; Chgo Symph Soc; Ethics Com, Canon Law Soc Am; r/Rom Cath; hon/Sigma Xi; Delta Epsilon Sigma; Cit Excel Tchg & Pract Psychol, Assn Chgo Priests.

IVERSON, JOHN W oc/Minister; Athletic Director; b/Dec 9, 1942; h/Po Box 10, Terrell, TX 75160; ba/Same; m/Patricia Mae; c/John Jr, Spencer Warren, Margaret Elizabeth, Ivan Rowan; p/John Willie Iverson; Gertrude Iverson, Jacksonville, FL; ed/AA; BS; pa/Track Coach; Athletic Instr; Min Ch of Christ; Tex Jo Co Tchrs Assn; Nat Jo Co Coaches Assn; hon/Tchr Yr; Outstg Yg Men Am; Outstg Edrs Am.

IZLAR, ROBERT LEE oc/Forester; b/Dec 5, 1949; h/Box 8750, Jackson, MS 39204; ba/Same; m/Janice Elaine; p/Durham Wright and Marion Odom Izlar, Waycross, GA; ed/BS; MS; MBA; mil/AUS 1/Lt Mil Police Corps; pa/Soc Am Foresters; Wildlife Soc; Am Soc Mammalogists; cp/SAR; SCV; MOOWW; MOOFUSA; MOSB; r/Epis; hon/Blue Key; Omicron Delta Kappa; Phi Kappa Phi; Xi Sigma Pi; Alpha Zeta; Gamma Sigma Delta; Alpha Phi Omega; Delta Tau Delta; Gridiron Secret Soc; Commun Ldrs & Noteworthy Ams; Notable Ams Bicent Era; Others.

J

JACKSON, B GORDON oc/Guidance Counselor; b/Jan 27,1936; h/Rt 3, Chipley, FL 32428; m/Barbara; p/Perry Jackson (dec); E'Thell Jackson, Graceville, FL; ed/MA; mil/AUS; pa/NEA; APGA; r/Meth; hon/Personalities of S; W/W S&SW.

JACKSON, BARBARA WILLIAMS oc/Educator; Museum Administrator; Black Culture Specialist; b/Feb 18, 1932; h/792 Columbus Ave, #11-A, New York, NY 10025; m/James Curtis; p/Elnora Williams Flake, Tuskegee Inst, AL; ed/BS Tuskegee Inst; MA NY Univ; PhD Syracuse Univ; pa/Mus Devel; Univ Tchr; cp/Vol, Devel Yth Cult Progs; r/Prot; hon/Grad Summa Cum Laude; Inst Scholar; Hon Soc; Ed Awd.

JACKSON, CHARLIE WILTON oc/Estate Planning Consultant; Political Activist; b/Feb 23, 1953 h/Rt 4, Tylertown, MS 39667; ba/Same; m/Josie Belinda; c/Thomas Jesse; p/Wilton Thomas and Martha Alfreda Jackson, Tylertown; ed/BS Univ So Miss;

pa/Pers Dirs Assn; HALV; TMLEA; USM Polit Soc; Chm Ins Com FS&L Prog; Former Dist Crim Just Comm; cp/JCs; Dem Party; Field Coor Jimmy Carter Campaign; Cand Public Ser Comm 1979; r/Tylertown Bapt Ch: Mem; hon/Dean's List, USM; Del 1976 Dem Caucas.

JACKSON, COLON RAY oc/City Manager; b/Feb 29, 1944; h/4303 Bridle Path, Marshall, TX 75670; ba/Marshall; m/Carolyn; c/Staci; p/H C Jackson (dec); Kathryn Jackson, Grand Saline, TX; ed/N Tex St Univ: MPA 1973-75, BBA 1966-68; AA Tyler Jr Col 1964-66; mil/AUS Lt; USAR Capt; Tex NG: Exec Ofc, Co Cmdr 1973-76;

pa/Mfg Supvr, Tex Instruments Inc 1966-73; E Tex City Mgmt Assn; Tex City Mgmt Assn; Intl City Mgmt Assn; Am Soc Public Adm, Texarkana Bd Dirs; cp/Editor Newslttr, Rotary Intl (Marshall); Bd Dirs C of C; MPA Adv Bd, E Tex St Univ-T; hon/Clarence E Riddley S'ship, Tex City Mgmt Assn 1974; Commend Medal, AUS 1970-72.

JACKSON, DOROTHY FLOYD oc/- Pharmacist; Businesswoman; Executive; b/Jan 11, 1932; h/2143 Daladier Dr, Rancho Palos Verder, CA 90274; ba/Los Angeles, CA; c/Erroll, Michael; p/Nathan Daniel Floyd (dec); Ora Anna Ellis Floyd, Mobile, AL; ed/BS Xavier Univ Louisiana 1955; PhD Univ Humanistic Studies 1979; Addit Studies: Ala St Col 1948-50, Los Angeles City Col 1967, UCLA 1976; pa/Reg'd Pharmacist: Tex, La, Cal; Pres Clotilda Intl; Am Pharm Assn; Nat

Assn Retail Druggists; Ctl Los Angeles Pharm Assn; Am Bridge Assn; Am Contract Bridge Leag; cp/Dem Party; Mem Cal Delegation Pres Carter's Inauguration; Fdr Ora A Floyd Foun; Harmonettes Bridge Clb; OES; NAACP; r/Sci of Mind Ch; hon/Gamma Phi Delta; Zeta Phi Beta; W/W: Intl Biog, Am; Others.

JACKSON, EARL J oc/Pastor; Radio Minister; Employment Interviewer; b/Mar 11, 1943; h/804 Gilbert St, Bowling Green, KY 42101; ba/Bowling Green; m/Barbara Faye Anderson; c/Earl Darelwin, Roderick Lamar; p/James C Jackson (dec); Keathryn C Jackson, Chattanooga, TN; ed/ThG; BTh; BA; MRE; MDiv; DDiv; pa/Ky St Employmt Interviewer; Ky Welfare Assn; cp/IAPES; PUSH; NAACP; BG Kiwanis Clb; Bd Dirs BG Big Brothers & Sisters Prog; Bd Dirs BG Boys' Clb; r/Missionary Bapt; hon/BG Alumni Kappa Alpha Psi.

JACKSON, EDGAR NEWMAN oc/- Clergyman; Adjunct Professor; b/Jul 8, 1910; h/34 Washington Rd, Corinth, VT 05039; ba/Same; m/Estelle Miller; c/Lois Estelle; p/Edgar Starkey and Abbie Eugenia Jackson (dec); ed/BA; STB; BDiv; MDiv; DDiv; mil/USAF WWII CC Capt; Tech Advr; Conslt; Crisis Psychologist Walter Reed Army Med Ctr; pa/Adj Prof Union Grad Sch; Conslt Sev Nat Bodies; Edit Advr Num Profl Jours; Lectr 14 Countries; cp/Hon Chaplain US Ho Reps; r/Meth; Ser'd Vatican Secretariate Distribution Relief Supplies WWII; hon/Author 24 Books; 18 Profl Book Clb Sels; Contbr 16 Learned Symposia; Other Ser Awds.

JACKSON, HARVEY L JR oc/Executive Director; Sales Manager; b/Oct 10, 1946; h/331 S Scottish St, Adrian MI 49221; ba/Clinton, MI; m/Elizabeth Shaw; c/Amy, Harvey III; p/Harvey L Sr and Marion Jackson, Adrian; ed/BA Adrian Col 1968; Masters; Addit Studies; pa/John Underwood Chev Olds Pont Inc: Mktg Mgr Sales, Exec Dir Fin & Ins 1975–; Ath Dir Siena Hgts Col 1973-75; PE Tchr Madison HS 1971-73; PE Tchr & Coach Onsted HS 1966-71; NEA; Mich Ed Assn; Nat Wrestling Coaches & Ofcls Assn; AAHPER; Mich HS Coaches & Ofcls Assn; cp/Exec Dir Lenawee Co Explorers Post BSA; r/United Meth Ch: Mem; hon/Commun Ldrs & Noteworthy Ams; W/W: Fin & Indust, Am, MW; Symbol of Outstg Sales Achmt, Pontiac Master Sales Guild; Hon'd for Achmt, Chevrolet Truck Sales Hon Clb; Others.

JACKSON, HERBERT CROSS oc/Professor; b/May 13, 1917; h/1927 Tomahawk Rd, Okemos, MI 48864; ba/E Lansing, MI; m/- Mary Carolyn London; c/Charlotte, Carolyn, Bruce, Stephen; p/John Henry and Sara Martha Jackson (dec); ed/BA; ThM; MA; PhD; pa/Mich St Univ: Prof Rel Studies & Asian Studies 1970–; Act'g Dir Asian Studies Ctr 1969, 76, 77; Res Secy Div Overseas Mins,

Nat Coun Chs of Christ 1961-66; Adj Prof Hist of Rels, Theol Sem NY City 1961-66; Intl Assn Hist Rels; Soc Asian & Comparative Phil; Intl Assn Buddhist Studies; Assn Asian Studies; Am Acad of Rel; Other Num Orgs; r/Am Bapt Chs USA; hon/Dir Am Scholars; Contemp Authors; Dir Am Brit Writers; W/W: Am Ed, E, Rel, S; Num Other Biogl Listings; Phi Epsilon; Recipient F'ship; Pub'd Author: MAN REACHES OUT TO GOD; Profl Articles.

JACKSON, LARRY DEAN oc/Minister;

b/Oct 9, 1943; h/1030 Fairway, Edinburg, TX 78539; ba/Edinburg; c/Kimberly, Brian; p/Leon D and Virgie M Jackson (dec); ed/BS 1965, MBA 1967 La Tech Univ; MDiv Austin Presb Theol Sem 1977; pa/Min Presb Ch; Min Relats Com Pastoral Care & Profl Devel; Instr Bus Adm Pan Am Univ; cp/Bd Mem Wom Together; Bd Mem Rotary Clb; r/Presb: Deacon, Elder; hon/Pres Austin Presb Sem Student Govt.

JACKSON, LINDA DUFF oc/Rate Analyst; Traffic Consultant; b/Feb 26, 1949; m/Phil Stacy (dec); p/Lawrence W and Wilma Hume Duff; ed/Ind Ctl Bus Col; Johnson Bible Col; Grad, Hotel Mgrs Sch & Mid Am Rate Sch; pa/Lo-Jac Traffic Ser Inc: Ednl Coor, Public Relats Ofcr, Rate Analyst, Secy-Treas, Bd Mem; Former Rate Analyst, Turner Trucking Co (Lebanon, Ind); Former Rate Analyst, Tex Cartage & Leeway Motor Freight (Dallas, Tex); Other Positions; IPA; Am Bus Wom's Assn (VP, Bd Mem); cp/Toastmasters Intl; Fdr, Phil Stacy Jackson Hist S'ship Awd, Univ Tex-T; Var Commun Activs; r/New Hope Christian Ch (Whitestown, Ind); hon/Biogl Listings.

JACKSON, MARION THOMAS oc/Minister; Building Constructor; b/Jul 24, 1945; h/PO Box 1585, N Wilkesboro, NC 28659; ba/Same; m/Sharon Davis; p/Pat Marion Jackson (dec); Louise Jackson, Dalton, GA; ed/BA; pa/Min SDA Ch; Bldg Constr; Currently Writing 2 Books; cp/Num Commun Activs; r/SDA; hon/I Dare You Awd; Personalities of S; Others.

JACKSON, MAYNARD HOLBROOK JR oc/Mayor; Attorney; b/Mar 23, 1938; m/Valerie Richardson; c/Elzabeth, Brooke, Maynard III; ed/BA Morehouse Col 1956; JD w Hons NC Ctl Univ Sch Law; pa/Former Gen Atty US Nat Labor Relats Bd; Former Mng Atty Neighborhood Law Ofc, Emory Commun Legal Sers Ctr; Fdr & Former Partner Jackson, Patterson, Parks & Franklin (Law Firm); Mayor Atlanta; Bd Dirs Nat Leag of Cities; Coor Exec Comm NCDM; Nat Chrperson Nat Gun Control Ctr; Num Orgs; cp/Nat VChm Ams for Dem Action; Chrperson Ga Assn Black Elected Ofcls; Nat Dem Party; So Conf Black Mayors; Others; r/Bapt; hon/Hon Bd Mem Am Cancer Soc; Hon Bd Mem Nat Conf Christians & Jews; Others.

JACKSON, MORRIS K oc/Educator; Anatomist; b/Nov 2, 1945; h/6126 Lovers Ln, Shreveport, LA 71105; ba/Shreveport; m/Sarah N Myers; p/George E and Evelyn E Jackson, Clifton, TX; ed/BS 1968, MS 1971 Baylor Univ; PhD Med Col Ga 1975; mil/Tex

Army NG; pa/Prof Dept Anatomy LSU Med Ctr; Contbr Profl Jours; Am Assn Anatomists; Soc for Neurosci; Soc for Study of Amphibians & Reptiles; AMA; hon/Beta Beta Beta; Omicron Delta Kappa; Sigma Xi; D Dwight Davis Awd in Vertebrate Morphol, Am Soc Zoologists 1971.

JACKSON, NARAH THELLIS oc/Registered Professional Nurse; b/Oct 5, 1908; h/1300 So Border, Weslaco, TX 78596; ba/Same; p/Richard Irving and Mamie Harwell Jackson (dec); ed/Dipl St Joseph Sch Nsg, (Memphis, Tenn); BS Univ Minn; MA Univ Chgo; pa/Former Instr Profl Nsg; Dir Film Chd Nsg; cp/ARC Vol; Var Activs, C of C; r/Presb; hon/S'ships: Univ Minn, St of Miss; W/W Am Wom; World W/W Wom; Personalities of S.

JACKSON, NORMAN ALLEN oc/Executive Director; b/Nov 16, 1929; h/Rt 6, Box 248, Quincy, FL 32351; ba/Tallahassee, FL; m/Lillie S; c/Deborah, Norma, Lena, Glynnis, Christina; p/Christine Saunders, Tampa, FL; ed/BS Tuskegge Inst; MA Mich St; PhD Fla St Univ; mil/AUS 1/Lt Inf; pa/Exec Dir Fla Comm Human Relats; Nat Assn Human Rights Workers; cp/NAACP; Former Mem Bd Dirs: St Cancer Soc, Apalachee Commun Mtl Hlth Ser Inc, Others; r/AME Meth; hon/Phi Delta Kappa; Dr Johnnie Ruth Clarke Meml Awd, Coun on Black Affairs (So Reg); Dist'd Ser Awd, 11th Epis Dist AME Ch; Apprec Awd, Gov's Coun Employmt of Handicapped; Others.

JACKSON, RUTH FRANCES oc/Medical Technologist; b/Jul 1, 1907; h/1400 Center St, Jacksonville, ILL 62650; ba/Jacksonville; m/Robert (dec); p/Frederick James and Alice Speed Comber (dec); ed/RN; Med Tech; AART; Med Tech (ASCP); pa/Passavant Area Hosp, J'ville: Staff Technologist 1977-, Nuclear Med Supvr 1972-77; Chief Tech Culbertson Meml Hosp, Rushville (Ill) 1957-72; Other Former Positions; Am Soc Med Tech; Schuyler Co Bus & Profl Clb; cp/Secy & Pres Schuyler Co Heart Assn; Schuyler Co Cancer Assn; r/Epis.

JACKSON, VONICLE BARNES oc/Elementary School Teacher; b/Jun 4, 1937; h/11354 Harbour Woods Rds, Jacksonville, FL 32225; ba/J'ville; m/J Sheldon; c/Randall Alan, Kevin Duane; p/Bessie Barnes,

Cottondale, FL; ed/BSEd; pa/2nd Grade Tchr; Rdg Coun Rep; Fac Rep PTA Bd; Accreditation Com; Read-a-Thon Rep; Nat Affil for Lit Adv; PTO; Others; cp/ARC Vol; Jr Garden Clb Sponsor; Harbour Civic Assn; Beacon Hills Garden Clb; r/Meth; hon/Duval Co Tchr Yr 1979; Fla Finalist Tchr Yr 1980; Hon Life Mem Fla Cong P's & T's.

JACKSON, W A DOUGLAS oc/Professor; b/Nov 25, 1923; h/18308 84th Pl W, Edmonds, WA 98020; ba/Seattle, WA; p/Joseph Walter Jackson (dec); Sara Justine Palmer (dec); ed/BA; MA; PhD; ATCM; LTCM; pa/Prof Geog Univ Wash; Lectr; Author; Pianist; r/Anglican.

JACKSON, WILMA oc/Writer; Editor; h/2018 Whittlesey St, Flint, MI 48503; ba/Flint; ed/BGS Univ Mich 1977; Cert (Urban Studies, Crim Just) Mich St Univ 1976; pa/Feature Writer & Columnist Sepia Mag; Columnist Hip Mag 1963-; Columnist Var Other Mags; Guest Lectr Creative Writing Univ Mich-F 1977; Pres Nat Assn Media Wom Inc, Flint Chapt; Nat Editor Newslttr NAMW; Pub'd Num Articles: "Star Treks", "Star O Scope", Others; Mem Working Press During Pres Carter's Inauguration; hon/Flint Writer's Clb: Top Columnist Awd, Top Writer's Awd (5); Fdr's Awd, Nat Assn Media Wom Inc 1977; Num Biogl Listings.

JACKSON, ZANE GRAY oc/Credit Counseling Director; b/Jan 12, 1927; h/500 Hearthside Dr, Winston-Salem, NC 27104; ba/W-S; m/Mary Reich; c/Julie Ann; p/Z D and Bertha W Jackson (dec); ed/Gen Bus; mil/USN; pa/Dir Consumer Credit Coun Ser 1st Union Nat Bk 1972-; Exec Com Nat Foun Consumer Credit Inc; NC Consumer Forum; Bd Dirs W-S Fin Assn; Bd Dirs NC Fin Assn; Adv Com DEEP Forsyth Co Schs; cp/Forsyth Tech Inst: Bd Trustees, Chm Policy Com, Ed Foun; r/Moravian Ch: Past Chm Fam Planning Com.

JACOBS, ALLAN DUANE oc/Professor; b/Sept 5, 1934; h/10 Gardner Ave, Dillon Plan, Lemont Furnace, PA 15456; ba/California, PA; m/Janice Pless; c/Kurt Douglas; p/Leland B and Beatrice Houghten Jacobs, Leonia, NJ; ed/BS En Mich Univ 1957;

MA Tchrs Col Columbia Univ 1961; EdD Wayne St Univ 1969; mil/USAR Ret'd Capt; pa/Prof Ed Cal St Col 1970-; Pub'd Author 3 Chd's Books; KSRA Newslttr Editor; PCTE Bd Mem; IRA; Cal Coun IRA; NCTE; Others; r/Meth; hon/Outstg Edr Am; Notable Ams.

JACOBS, AUGUSTA ADELE oc/Teacher; Business Executive; b/Nov 25, 1925; h/2840 N Hill Rd, Portsmouth, OH 45662; ba/Portsmouth; p/Jacob H Jacobs (dec); Rose L Jacobs, Portsmouth; ed/BSEd Univ Cinc; Grad Work Ohio St; pa/Bus Tchr Green HS; VP & Secy Eagle Coal & Iron Co; Coauthor Aids for Branch Adm; NEA; Ohio Ed Assn; Ohio Bus Tchrs Assn; Others; cp/Ladies Div C of C; Vol: ARC, Little Theatre; Capt United Way Drs; Others; r/Jewish; hon/Jour Bus Ed Awd, Univ Cinc; Ky Col; Kappa Delta Pi; Yrbook Dedication; Num Biogl Listings.

JACOBS, GORDON WALDEMAR oc/General Surgeon; Educator; b/May 30, 1933; h/1130 Harvard Rd, Piedmont, CA 94610; ba/Berkeley, CA; m/Lorraine Maria; c/Mary Lou, Melanie Ann, Kristen Clara; p/Rev Elmer W and /Clara E Jacobs, Charles City, IA; ed/BA 1955, MD 1958 Univ Ia; mil/AUS 1960-62, Med Corp, Capt, Europe;

pa/Gen Surg, Solo Pvt Pract, Berkeley & Oakland Staff, Alta Bates, Herrick, Peralta, Providence, Merritt, & Chd's Hosps; Instr Surg & Acting Chief Surg, Haile Selassie Univ Med Sch, Addis Ababa, Ethiopia 1973-74; Med Missionary, New Guinea 1966-69; AMA; Mass, Cal, Alameda-Contra Costa Co, Christian Med Socs; cp/Former Big Brother; Alumnus, Lahey Clin; Credentials Com Herrick Hosp, Berkeley; Toastmasters Intl; r/Trinity Luth Ch, Oakland: VP; hon/Diplomate, Am Bd Surg; Fellow, Intl Col Surgs & Am Col Emer Phys; W/W W; Men Achmt; Personalities of W&MW; Book of Hon; DIB; Intl W/W Commun Ser; IPA; Intl Reg Profiles.

JACOBS, HERB FRED oc/Retired; Union Committeeman; b/Nov 6, 1915; h/4363 Barham St, Detroit, MI; m/Marie (dec); c/Rita; p/William A Jacobs, Orlando, Fl; Margaret Jacobs, Detroit; ed/Mech Engrg; mil/USMM WWII; pa/Ret'd Chrysler Corp; Union Com-man Skilled Trades; World Champs Briggs-Beautyware; cp/AMVETs; Polit Del VAW; r/Luth; hon/Champs: Softball, Bowling, Basketball, Others.

JACOBSEN, ALBERT oc/Retired Commercial Artist; Writer; Painter; b/Jan 12, 1896; h/21 Lotus St, Westwood, NJ 07675; p/Albert and Ida Jacobsen (dec); pa/Pub'd Num Articles, Poems, Ink Drawings; r/Luth; hon/Num Nat Mag Awds; DIB.

JACOBSEN, WILLIAM DUTTON oc/Government Official; b/May 31, 1936; ba/New Cumberland, PA 17070; m/Renate Wilden; c/2; p/Emil John and Jean Dutton Jacbsen; ed/BA Univ Neb 1971; MS w Hons, Univ So Cal 1974; PhD Cand, Univ Pittsburgh; Vietnamese Lang 1971; Addit Studies; mil/AUS: Ser'd to Maj, Ret'd 1977; pa/Logistics Mgmt Spec, AUS Logistics Evaluation Agy 1978-; Asst Prof Mil Sci, Univ Pittsburgh 1974-77; Deputy Maintenance Ofcr (Germany) 1974; Other Positions; Am Assn Higher Ed; Nat Assn Pers Res; Am Defense Preparedness Assn (Secy); Soc of Logistics Engrs; Contbr Articles Profl Jours; cp/DAV; Mason; Advr BSA; Royal Arch Mason; Mil Order World Wars; Sojourners; Advr ROTC; Bd Mem, ROTC S'ships; Others; r/Epis; hon/Rec'd Commend Ribbon, Bronze Star Medal, Vietnamese Ordnance Badge, Meritorious Ser Medal, Vietnam Cross of Gallantry AUS; Hon Grad, Integrated Logistics Course; Hon Grad, Hist Workshop; Winner, Oratorical Contest, Am Legion; USA Lifesaving Commend; Hon'd by Vietnamese for Adv Duty; Biogl Listings.

JACOBSON, ALAN FRANK oc/Professor; Psychologist; b/Sept 19, 1947; h/8122 SW 103 St, Miami FL 33156; ba/Miami; m/Rose Frankel; c/Mark Howard, Brian Scott; p/Myer Jacobson (dec); Nellie Levin Jacobson, Portland ME; ed/BA Univ Miami 1969; MS 1971; PhD 1973; pa/Asst Prof Psychi Univ Miami; Pvt Pract Psychologist; Am Psychol Assn; Assn Advmt Behavior Therapy; Biofeedback Soc Am; Others; r/Jewish; hon/W/W S&SW; Personalities of S; Psi-Chi.

JACOBSON, ETHEL oc/Writer; Reviewer; Speaker; b/Nov 4; h/Star Rt 1, PO Box 172, Mammoth Lakes, CA 93546; ba/Fullerton, CA; m/Louis John; c/Dorcas Gould Salzman, Noel Hoyt Lamkin; p/(dec); pa/Reviewer: Chgo Tribune, St Louis Post-Dispatch, Santa Ana Register; Poet; Author 8 Books; So Cal Wom Press Clb; PEN Intl; Cal Writer's Guild; cp/Freedoms Foun Val Forge; Orange Co Philharm Soc; Fullerton Cult Ctr; hon/Will Strong Awd.

JACOBSON, MICHAEL H oc/Educational Administrator; h/4124 N Clarendon Ave, Chicago, IL 60613; ba/Chgo; p/Irving R and Bernice M Jacobson, Chgo; ed/BS Loyola Univ; LLD LaSalle Univ; MA NEn Ill Univ; PhD Sussex Col; pa/Chgo Bd Ed 1967-: Tchr, Cnslr, Assoc Prin; Grad Div Fac Nat Col Ed;

Pub'd Articles: "The Question of Acad Standards", "Achmt Test'g in the Chgo Schs", Others; APGA; Am Sch Cnslr Assn; Nat Org Legal Probs in Ed; cp/Chgo Bd Ed: Exploring Advr, Dist Explorer Chm, Asst Dist Commr; Alpha Phi Omega: Chapt Pres, Nat Alumni Com, Reg IV Alumni Rep; hon/Dr Humane Lttrs; Knight Cmdr Order of Sursum; BSA: Explorer Advr of Yr, Dist Awd of Merit; Psi Chi; Phi Delta Kappa; Alpha Phi Omega; Num Biogl Listings.

JACOBSON, SELMA MARIA oc/Curator; Archivist; b/Oct 10, 1906; h/5641 Warwick Ave, Chicago, IL 60634; ba/Chgo;

p/Albin A and Bertha T Jacobson (dec); ed/PhB; MA; pa/Curator & Archivist Swedish Pioneer Archives; Ret'd Tchr; Creator Swedish Archives; Dir Swedish-Am Mus; Ser'd 6 Yrs Conslt Chgo Schs; cp/Num Civic Affairs; r/Luth; hon/Citizen of Yr 1978; Royal Order Cmdr N Star; Royal Order Knights of Yasa; Num Biogl Listings.

JACQUES, MARY ELEANOR oc/Director Prayer Center; b/Jan 8, 1905; h/502 Halsey Ave, San Jose, CA 95128; m/Epifanio (dec); c/Imelda, Josephine J Curran, Rosalie J Villanueva, Frank, Perpetua J Clark, Richard, Edward; p/Jose Severino and Juanita Mascarenas Garcia (dec); pa/Dir Prayer Ctr; cp/Orgr for Pro-Life; Mem Legion of Mary (Past Pres); Chaperone for Amigos Anom (Santa Clara Univ Students); r/Rom Cath.

JAFFA, AILEEN RABY oc/Retired Librarian; Poet; Artist; b/Apr 26, 1900; h/1105 Wellesley Ave, Modesto, CA 95350; c/Lawrence Marvin, Joan Elizabeth (dec);

p/Myer Edward and Adele Solomons Jaffa (dec); ed/BA 1922, Cert of Libn'ship 1928 Univ Cal-B; pa/Ret'd 1962; Poet; Artist; Cal Writer's Clb; Cal St Poetry Soc; San Francisco Browning Soc; Nat Leag Am Pen Wom; Ctl Cal Art Leag; r/Judeo-Christian; hon/Theme Poem Cal Fdn Chaparral Poets 1970; Mason Sonnet 1972.

JAFFA, LAWRENCE MARVIN oc/Teacher; Minister; b/Aug 19, 1923; h/Casa Quixote, 1105 Wellesley, Modesto CA 95350; c/Thomas Emerson; p/Milton J Katzky; Aileen R Jaffa, Modesto; ed/BS Univ Cal-B 1944; MDiv Harvard 1949; mil/USNR (Ret'd);

pa/Social Sci Tchr Modesto City Schs 1972-; Instr Parapsychol; cp/Pres Modesto Men's Clb; Big Brothers; Cal Assn For Gifted; r/Unitarian; hon/Life Mem, Cal PTA; Life Mem, NEA; W/W W; Others.

JAHN, EDWARD LOUIS SR oc/Research Scientist; Technical Writer; b/Mar 11, 1915; h/PO Box 594, Mt Vernon, TX 75457; ba/Mt Vernon; m/Billie Jane Downing; c/James T (dec), Antoinette R, Thomas L, Edward L Jr, Janette E; p/James John and Antoinette Cecilia Pliska Jahn; ed/BA Wayne St Univ 1971; MS 1976, PhD Cand 1979 Tex St Univ; Addit Studies; mil/AUS Asst Quartermaster 1939-40, 2/Lt to Lt Col 1941-47; p/Res Scist (Computer Applications); Tech Writer & Rancher 1973-; Past Pres Dos Cabezas Inc (Res Foun) 1979; Publs: *Computer Usage in Ed, Psychopathol for Nsg Students, Commun Col Adm*; AAAS; Am Math Soc; cp/Ks of Pythias; hon/Croix de Guerre; Silver Star; China Liberation Medal; St of Mich Cit for Excell.

JAKEWAY, KEVIN W oc/Accounting Policy Analyst; b/May 31, 1955; h/17 Forbes Blvd, Eastchester, NY 10709; ba/Greenwich, CT; p/Philip E and Rita Anne Jakeway, E'chester; ed/BSBA; MBA; pa/Acctg Policy Analyst Amax Inc; cp/Georgetown Bar Assn; DC Repubs; r/Cath; hon/Fin Mgmt Hon Soc; Grad Summa Cum Laude.

JAMES, ADVERGUS DELL JR oc/Financial Aid Director; b/Sept 24, 1944; h/4734 Geneva Dr, Houston, TX 77066; ba/Prairie View, TX; m/Anna; p/Advergus D Sr and

Helen G James, Muskogee, OK; ed/BS Langston Univ; MS Okl St Univ; pa/Dir Student Fin Aid; Conslt St Student Fin Asst Prog; Basic Grant Tnr; Tex, SWn, Nat Assn Student Aid Ofcrs; cp/Prairie View Optimist Clb; BSA; Masonic Lodge; r/Bapt.

JAMES, ALLIX BLEDSOE oc/University President; b/Dec 17, 1922; h/1200 W Graham Rd, Richmond, VA 23220; ba/Richmond; m/Sue Nickens; c/Alvan Bosworth, Portia Veann p/Samuel Horace James Sr (dec); Tannie E James, Dallas, TX; ed/BA 1944, MDiv 1946 Va Union Univ; ThM 1949, ThD 1957 Union Theol Sem Va; pa/Va Union Univ: Pres 1970-, VP 1960-70, Dean Sch of Theol 1956-70, Others; Pres: Am Assn Theol Schs, Coun on Theol Ed (Am Bapt Conv), Clergy Assn Richmond; Other Profl Activs; Min Var Bapt Chs; Chm Univ Ctr Va; St Bd Ed; cp/Bd Dirs U Negro Col Fund; Bd Trustees Rich Meml Hosp; Bd Dirs Better Richmond Inc; Kiwanis Intl; Num Others; r/Moore St Bapt Ch, Rich: Mem; hon/LLD honoris causa, Univ Rich; Alpha Kappa Mu; W/W: Am, Am Ed, S&SW; Dir Am Schlrs; Citizen of Yr Awd: Richmond Urban Leag 1974, Omega Psi Phi 1972, Astoria Beneficial Clb 1971; Nat Brotherhood Awd, Nat Conf Christians & Jews; Others.

JAMES, MICHAEL LYNN oc/Director of Photography; b/Sept 24, 1946; h/107 Choctaw Dr, Searcy, AR 72143; ba/Searcy; m/Elizabeth Jane; c/Jennifer, Jeremy; p/Jesse R and Lona M James, Kennett, MO; ed/BS; mil/AUS Corps of Engrs 1/Lt; pa/Dir Photo Harding Col; Profl Photog Am; Profl Photog Ark; cp/Searcy Optimist Clb; r/Ch of Christ.

JAMES, SHAYLOR LORENZA oc/Musician; b/Aug 12, 1942; m/Barbara H; c/1; ed/BS Fla A&M Univ 1964; MMus 1973, PhD Cand Fla St Univ; Addit Studies; pa/Fla A&M Univ: Asst Prof Percussion Instruments, Dir Percussion Ensemble 1964-; Percussion Conslt, Clinician & Marching Band Adjudicator, Ala St Band Clinic 1965-66 & Ga St Band Clinic 1967; Lectr; Performer; Other Positions; Percussive Arts Soc; Nat Assn Col Wind & Percussion Instrs; AAUP; Col Mus Soc Inc; Composer: "Entrance Routines for Marching Band" (1972-73), "Accentuation, Snare Drum Solo" (1973-74), Others; hon/Rec'd Plaque & Meritorious Ser Awd, Seven-Up Co (St Louis, Mo); Winner Trophy as Dir Percussion Ensemble; White House Fellow Nom; Conducted Fla A&M Univ Percussion Ensemble & Perf'd w Wesley Foun Singers, *Ted Mack Amateur Hour*; Perf'd for United Nations Gen Assembly; Biogl Listings; Others.

JAMES, WILLIAM J oc/Professor; b/Sept 17, 1922; h/PO Box 45, Rolla, MO 65401; ba/Rolla; m/Arlene Carll; c/Varie J Lynch,

Candice J Metcalf; p/(dec); ed/BS; MS; PhD; mil/USAAC 1/Lt; pa/Prof Mats Res Univ Mo; Conslt & Pres Mead Chem Inc; Staff Mem Inst for Chem & Extractive Metall; Others; cp/Mem Tech Adv Com St Louis Reg Coun for Growth & Commerce; r/Unitarian; hon/Univ Mo-R: Outstg Tchr Awd (Cir K), Outstg Res Awd; Alumni Merit Awd; Others.

JAMIESON, ADDIE MAE oc/Church and Community Worker; b/May 9, 1919; h/PO Box 100, Ripley, MS 38663; ba/Same; p/Jesse Darnel and Frances Moore Jamieson (dec); ed/BA Blue Mtn Col 1943; MA Scarritt Col 1949; pa/Tchr Miss Public Schs 1939-47; Rural Worker: Fla Conf (Hosford) 1949-51, Branford (Fla) 1951-55; Coor Ga Coop Rural Work 1955-60; cp/Var Activs Ch & Commun 1972-; Hosp Aux; BPW Clb; Bd Dirs Wesley Foun NE Miss Jr Col 1978-; Others; r/United Meth: Deaconess, Diaconal Min; Chrperson Bd Diaconal Min 1976-80; Treas N Miss Conf Christian Edrs 1978; Num Others; hon/Wom of Achmt, Louisville (Miss) BPW Clb; Num Ch Hons.

JAMISON, SARA MOYNE oc/Professional Counselor; h/3818 N 43d Pl, Phoenix, AZ 85018; ba/Phoenix; m/Lloyd D; c/Kendall Owen, Nolya Augspunger, Jarrol Lloyd; p/Elmo L Tustin (dec); Etta Jane McKinney (dec); ed/BS, MS Ariz St Univ; pa/Cert'd Cnslr: Ariz, Cal; HS Cnslr West HS, Phoenix 19 Yrs; Other Former Positions; APGA (St Ofcr, St Del to Conv); St Ofcr Ariz Sch Cnslrs Assn; Orgr ANYTOWN; Nat Assn Sch Cnslrs: St Dir, Reg Dir; hon/Dist'd Ser Awd, NCCJ; Psi Chi; Ser Awd YWAC; W/W: W, Am Wom; World W/W Wom; Others.

JAMME, ALBERT JOSEPH oc/Research Professor; b/Jun 26, 1916; h/1624 21st St, Washington, DC 20009; ba/Wash DC; p/Alfred Jamme (dec); Albine Roulin (dec); ed/STD; Doct Oriental Phil & Hist; Lic'd Bibl St; mil/Underground Forces WWII Chaplain; r/Cath.

JAN, GEORGE P oc/Professor; b/Jan 6, 1925; h/2253 Goddard Rd, Toledo, OH 43606; ba/Toledo; m/Norma Y; c/Gregory, David, Daniel; p/Y M and T C Jan (dec); ed/BA; MA; PhD; pa/Univ Toledo: Prof Polit Sci, Chm Asian Studies Prog; Chm of Bd 2 Corps; Pub'd Author; Bd Mem Toledo Coun on World Affairs; hon/Phi Beta Kappa; Pi Sigma Alpha; Phi Kappa Phi; Recipient Num Res Grants; Num Biogl Listings.

JANI, SUBHASH NATWERLAL oc/-Professor; b/Feb 9, 1940; h/2043 W Adams St, Macomb, IL 61455; ba/Macomb; m/Linda Aylesworth; c/Shanti, Krishna, Jayshree, Raam; p/Natwerlal S and Chandrika N Jani, Indianapolis, IN; ed/OD Northampton City Univ 1961; MS Ind Univ 1967; MS 1969, PhD 1971 Purdue Univ; pa/Assoc Prof Spec Ed Wn Ill Univ 1974-; Pvt Pract Gen Optometry; Var Former Positions; Conslt Vision & LD; Pub'd Num Articles; Mem Intl ASP; Fellow AAO; ACCD; Num Others; cp/Life Mem Var Alumni Assns; r/Hindu; hon/Phi Delta Kappa; "Pick a Prof" Nom; Life Freeman City of London; Ky Col; Commun Ldrs & Noteworthy Ams; Others.

JANOSIK, STEVEN M oc/College Administrator; b/May 18, 1951; h/1070 Blue Hill Ave, Milton, MA 02186; ba/Milton; m/Rhoda C; p/James P and Midge L Janosik, Richmond, VA; ed/BS VPI & SU 1973; MEd Univ Ga 1975; pa/Curry Col: Lng Skills Conslt, Asst Dean of Students; NASPA; ACPA; APGA; ASGW; Regional Editor ACPA Newsltr; Others; cp/BSA Asst Scout Master; hon/W/W S&SE.

JANOWSKY, OSCAR I oc/Professor; Editor; Author; b/Jan 15, 1900; h/247-C Mayflower Way, Rossmoor, Jamesburg, NJ 08831; ba/New York, NY; m/Pauline Rubin; c/Sylvia, Melvin, Tamar; p/Aaron and Dinah Janowsky; ed/BSS CCNY 1921; MA 1922, PhD 1933 Columbia Univ; Hon DHL Jewish Theol Sem Am 1966; Hon DHL Hebrew Union Col 1967; pa/Prof Hist CCNY 1924-; Other Profl Activs; Pub'd Author: *Founs of Israel, The JWB Survey*, Others; Editor: *The Ed of*

Am Jewish Tchrs, The Am Jew; Edit Adv Bd Menorah Jour; VP Am Jewish Hist Soc; Am Hist Assn; AAUP; Others; cp/Exec Com Am Friends of Hebrew Univ; Others; r/Jewish; hon/Hadassah Awd; Frank L Weil Awd, JWB; Friedman Gold Medal Am Jewish Hist Soc; Others.

JARBOE, ROBERT NOLEN oc/Executive Director; b/Nov 19, 1947; h/1611 Idaho, Caldwell, ID 83605; ba/Nampa, ID; m/Janet; c/Christopher, Garic; p/Robert and Gladys Jarboe, Wilder, ID; ed/BA Col of Idaho; Cert Rehab Wkshop Adm Seattle Univ; MRA Univ

of SF; pa/Exec Dir Wn Idaho Tng Co Inc; Prog Dir Idaho Dept Hlth & Wel; Prog Dir Idaho St Sch & Hosp; Past Pres Assn Idaho Rehab Facilities; Conslt Negotiating Skills Seattle Univ 1977-78; Gov's Coun on Devel Disabilities 1978; Others; cp/Former Mem Bd Dirs: Civitan Clb, Meals on Wheels; r/Prot.

JASCOURT, HUGH DONALD oc/Attorney; b/Feb 25, 1935; h/7 Maplewood Ct, Greenbelt, MD 20770; ba/Same; m/Resa Zall; c/Stephen, Leigh; p/Jacquard A Jascourt (dec); Gladys M Jascourt, Upper Darby, PA; ed/BA Univ Pa 1956; JD Wayne St Univ Law Sch 1960; mil/AUS 1956-57; pa/Dir Public Employmt Relats Res Inst; Asst Solicitor Labor Relats, US Dept Interior; Labor Relats Editor Jour of Law & Ed; Prof Law Geo Wash Univ; Other Positions; ASPA; DC Bar; Others; cp/Bd Dirs Nat Jogging Assn; Former Pres Road Runners Clb Am; Started Run for Your Life Prog in Am; r/Mem Rel Sch Com of Congregs; hon/W/W Am Law; Outstg Young Man Awd; Outstg Vol Rec Ldr Awd; Others.

JASEK, DIANE MARTHA oc/Student; b/Jun 24, 1955; h/915 Vance St, Taylor, TX 76574; ba/Austin, TX; p/Edward T and Martha T Jasek, Taylor; ed/Student Univ Tex-A; cp/Del to Dem Nat Conv 1976; r/Rom Cath; hon/W/W Am Polits; Personalities of S; Yth Adv Coun; Goodwill Ambassador St Tex.

JASEN, MATTHEW J oc/Associate Judge; b/Dec 13, 1915; h/26 Pine Terrace, Orchard Park, NY 14127; ba/Buffalo, NY; Albany, NY; m/Grace Yungbluth Frauenheim; c/Peter, Mark, Christine J MacLeod (Mrs David K), Carol Ann; p/Joseph John and Celina Perlinski Jasinski (dec); ed/LLB; mil/AUS 1943-46, Capt; pa/Sr Assoc Judge NY Ct of Appeals; Am Law Inst; Nat Conf Appellate Judges; ABA; NY St Bar Assn; Am Judic Soc; Others; cp/Former Mem Coun Univ of Buffalo; Bishop's Bd Govs Buffalo Diocese; Ks of C; r/Rom Cath; hon/Dist'd Alumnus Awd, St Univ NY Sch of Law; NY St Trial Lawyers Assn Law Day Awd; Others.

JASPER, A WILLIAM oc/Department

Director; b/Jun 3, 1925; h/822 S Roosevelt Ave, Arlington Heights, IL 60005; ba/Park Ridge, IL; m/Dorothy Moore (dec); c/William Mark, Peggy Joy (dec); p/G Leonard and Jessie Lea Jasper (dec); ed/BSc; MSc; PhD; mil/ETO WWII; USAR Ret'd Maj; pa/Dir Poultry Dept Am Farm Bur Fdn; Past Pres USA Branch World's Poultry Sci Assn; Hon Past Pres World's Poultry Sci Assn; cp/Former Mem HS Bd Ed; r/Prot; hon/Am Poultry Indust Awd of Merit; Dist'd Alumnus, Ohio St Univ; Oth─

JASPER, MARTIN THEOPHILUS oc/-Educator; b/Feb 19, 1934; h/Box 155, Mississippi State, MS 39762; ba/Miss St; m/Mary Altha Ledbetter; c/Nellie, Alice, Martin, Mary, William; p/Thomas Theophilus and Alice Maie Norton Jasper (dec); ed/BS 1955, MS 1962 Miss St Univ; PhD Univ Ala 1967; Addit Studies; mil/AUS MSC 1956-57: Pres Comm 1956; Miss NG 1957-62; USAR 1962-65; pa/Miss St Univ Prof Mech Engrg 1975-; Chm Grad Prog Com; Contbr Profl & Tech Jours; Conslt to Govt & Indust; SME; ASME; cp/Kiwanis Clb; Chm Maj Emphasis Com for the Gtr Yrs; r/1st Bapt Ch Mathiston, Miss; Deacon, SS Tchr; hon/Pi Tau Sigma; Tau Beta Pi; NSF Fac Fellow; NASA Trnee; Others

JASPER, RUTH MOWBRAY oc/Interior Designer; Personal Property Appraiser; h/924 Pueo St, Honolulu, HI 96816; ba/Honolulu; m/(dec); c/Charles Richard, James Thomas;

p/Robert Thomas and Ava Watts Bradbrook Mowbray (dec); ed/BA Univ No Iowa; Interior Design Grad Chgo; pa/1st Pres Am Inst Interior Designers Honolulu; Illuminating Soc of Engrs; cp/Jr Leag; DAR Regent; Altrusa; r/Prot.

JAUTOKAS, VICTOR oc/Electronics Engineer; b/Nov 29, 1929; h/5859 S Whipple St, Chicago, IL 60629; ba/Chgo; m/Ruta;

c/Paul, Raminta; p/Zigmas and Emilia Jautokas (dec); ed/BSEE; mil/AUS 1951-53; pa/Editor-in-Chief Engrg World; Pub'd Tech Jours; IEEE; APCO; NSPE; Am Lithuanian Engr & Arch Soc; r/Rom Cath; hon/Lttrs of Apprec for Writing.

JAVELLAS, INA J oc/Mental Health Consultant; b/Jun 15, 1934; h/3447 SE 44th St, Apt #231, Del City, OK 73105; ba/Oklahoma City, OK; ed/BA 1956, MSW 1958 Univ Okla; pa/Chief Commun Mtl Hlth Planning & Devel, Dept Mtl Hlth (Okla); 1977-; Conslt: Dept HEW 1976-, Nat Inst Mtl Hlth 1972-; Coor Commun Mtl Hlth Div, Dept Mtl Hlth 1965-; Psychi Social Worker 1963-65; Social Work Supvr 1962-63; NIMH Conslt Core Adv Group; Editor Com Hlth & Social Work; Interagency Hlth Planning Data Task

Force; Nat Assn Social Wkrs; Acad Cert'd Social Wkrs; Others; cp/Active Dem Party; Okla Hlth & Wel Assn: Past Editor, Past Mem Bd Dirs, Past Conf Coor; AAUW (Coms); Univ Okla Alumni Assn; Others; hon/Outstg Yg Wom in Am 1965; Phi Mu Scholar; Social Worker Yr, Wn Okla Chapt NASW; NASW Ldrship Tng Prog; W/W: Am Wom, Govt; Others.

JAY, HILDA LEASE oc/Media Specialist; Teacher; b/Dec 29, 1921; h/Box F, Sandy Hook, CT 06482; ba/Ridgefield, CT; m/John; c/Margaret Ellen, Sarah Louise; p/Frank Lease (dec); Hilda Whitton Lease, Ridgefield; ed/BS Ind Univ 1945; MS Danbury St Col 1960; EdD NY Univ 1970; Addit Studies Univ Bridgeport;

pa/Conn Ed Media Assn: Past Pres, Mem Bd Certn Com; Assn Ed Communs & Technol; Conn Del to Affil Coun, Am Assn of Sch Libns; cp/Hon Coun Housatonic GSA Coun; r/Epis; hon/Kappa Delta Pi; Pi Lambda Theta; Conn Okoboji Conf.

JEAN, GABRIELLE LUCILLE oc/Sister of Religious Order; Nursing Home Administrator; b/Apr 8, 1924; h/975 Varnum Ave, Lowell, MA 01854; ba/Lowell; p/Alfred Jean (dec); Claudia Guillemette (dec); ed/BA Rivier Col 1954; MEd 1957, PhD 1961 Boston Col; pa/Admr D'Youville Manor Nsg Home 1976-;

House of Affirmation Inc 1974-76: Staff Psychol, Dir Psychol Testing, Dir Consltg Ctr, Dir Grad Studies Prog, Dir Res; Coor Psychol Dept Roger Williams Co (Bristol, RI) 1972-74; Bd Dirs Assn Mass Homes for Aging; Am Psychol Assn; APGA; Nat Geriatrics Soc; Other Assns; Pub'd Num Articles; Edited Shalom: Peace, 7 Others; cp/Mem Bd St Joseph's HS; Others; r/Rom Cath; VP Sisters of Charity Ottawa; hon/Commun Ldrs Am; W/W: E, Am Ed; Others.

JECKO, PERRY TIMOTHY oc/Actor;

Educator; Author; b/Jan 24, 1938; h/207 Inwood Ave, Upper Montclaire, NJ 07043; ba/Same; m/Mary Louis; c/Christopher, Nicholas; p/Perry Joseph and Cora Timothy Jecko, Bethesda, MD; ed/BA; MFA Yale Univ; mil/USNR Lt; pa/Perf'd on TV Drama *All My Children*; Perf'd 2 Off-Off Broadway Prodns: *Faces of O'Neil, The Friday Bench*; Sev Nat TV Commls; Am Fdn TV & Radio Artists; Screen Actors Guild; Ext Leave from Tchg (Arlington, VA); r/Epis.

JEFFERSON, MARGARET CORREAN oc/Professor; b/Aug 22, 1947; h/1409 Oneonta Knoll, S Pasedena, CA 91030; ba/Los Angeles, CA; p/Mae Jefferson, Milwalkee, WI; ed/BS Univ Dubuque 1969; MA Univ Colo 1971; PhD Univ Ariz 1977; pa/Asst Prof Biol; AAAS; Soc of Evolution; AGS; GSA; ANAS; cp/Vol Compton Sickle Cell Ed & Detection Ctr; r/Interdenom; hon/Nat Inst Hlth Grants: MBS, BRSG; Affirmative Action Grant; Dissertation of Yr Awd, Nat F'ship Foun.

JEFFERSON, MARIA BUSTOS oc/Retired Educator; Folklorist; b/May 19, 1912; h/1646 Elevado St, Los Angeles, CA 90026; c/Benjamin E Jr; p/Patricio Bustos Castellanos and Marta Vargas; ed/BA Occidental Col 1933; MA Cal St Univ-LA 1956; Folklore Deg Conservatorio Nacional de Musica 1947; pa/Pub'd Author: *Chd's Folk-Games & Folksongs of Mexico, Folksongs of San Nicola's de Ibarra*; Coauthor 6th Grade Spanish Guide for St of Cal; Mem Instnl Mats Evaluation Panel St Dept Ed 1975-77; Instr: Univ Nev 1961, Cal St Univ 1959-63, Others; Master Elem Tchr LA Unified Sch Dist 1956-77; Mem Sec'dy Elem Tchrs Org; LA Elem Schs Tchrs Assn; Others; cp/Former Asst to Exec Secy So Cal Coun Inter-Am Affairs; CoFdr & Treas LA Inter-Am Lib; Am Acad Polit & Social Sci; Assn Ret'd Tchrs; Others; r/Rom Cath; hon/Resolution Awd, City Coun LA; Medal Awd, LA Bd Ed; Hon'd by Mexican Embassy; Num Biogl Listings.

JEFFREDO, JOHN VICTOR oc/Business Executive; Engineer; b/Nov 5, 1927; h/4318 Palomar Dr, Fallbrook, CA 92028; ba/Fallbrook; c/Joyce J Ryder, Michael John, John Victor, Louise Victoria; p/John Edward Jeffredo (dec); Pauline Matilda Whitten Jeffredo, F'brook; ed/BSAE Cal Aeronaut Tech Inst 1948; AA Pasadena City Col 1951; Addit Studies: USC, Palomar Col; mil/AUS 1951-53; pa/Owner-Operator, Fdr Jeffredo Gunsight Co; Chief Engr Wn Designs; CoChm & Exec Dir, Bd Dirs Indian World Corp; Conslt Energy Scis Corp; Former Conslt ITT Canon & Pertec Corps; Former Chief Engr for Control Data Corp, Aerospace Div; cp/Mem NRA; Nat Hist Soc; Nat Wildlife Fdn; San Diego Zool Soc; Sierra Clb; hon/W/W: W, Fin & Indust; Intl W/W.

JENG, HELENE WU oc/Librarian; b/Jul 23, 1938; h/4108 Paran Rd, Randallstown, MD 21133; ba/Mt Wilson, MD; m/Bih-Jing; p/Shou-li Wu and Mei-Chi Huang, Taipei, Taiwan; ed/MLS; pa/Libn Mt Wilson St Hosp; Mem Md Hlth Scis Libns Assn; r/Christian; hon/W/W Am Wom.

JENKINS, ALMA RICE oc/Teacher; h/1718 W Pierson Rd, Flint, MI 48504; ba/Flint; m/Harold; c/Milous; p/Milton and Elderada Rice, Toccoa, GA; ed/BS; MA;

pa/Sev Profl Groups; r/Prot; hon/Student Tchg Awd; Tchr of Yr 1972; Recog'd for Starting Camp Fire Girls, Flint.

JENKINS, CLARA BARNES oc/Professor; h/920 Bridges St, Henderson, NC 27536; ba/Lawrenceville, VA; p/Stella G Barnes, Henderson; ed/BS Winston-Salem St Univ; MA NC Ctl Univ; EdD Univ Pittsburg; Addit Studies; pa/Prof St Paul's Col; AAUP; Nat Soc Study Ed; AAUW; NEA; Others; cp/- Notary Public St of NC; r/Prot; hon/Fac Fellow United Negro Col Fund; Rec'd Grant Am Bapt Conv; Cert Recog Univ Pittsburg; Num Biogl Listings.

JENKINS, DOROTHY DAVIS oc/Teacher; b/Jan 6; h/105 Oak Hill Cir, Lebanon, TN 37087; ba/Lebanon; m/William Ralph; c/- Claire J Mason (Mrs W R), William Jr, Linda J Williams (Mrs M D), Julie, Todd, Patrick, Dorothy; p/Harwell Goodwin and Lena Vail Davis, Birmingham, AL; ed/BA; MA; pa/- Tchr Cumberland Col; Assn Adult Edrs; Delta Kappa Gamma; cp/Dem Wom; Mem Bd Wilson Co Devel Ctr; r/Presb; hon/W/W Am Cols & Univs.

JENKINS, DOROTHY HARGROVE oc/Instructor; b/Dec 10, 1943; h/655 W Irving Park Rd, #5510, Chicago, IL 60613; ba/Chgo; m/Thomas Miller II; p/Jack Hargrove Sr (dec); Luella Hargrove, St Cuthbert, GA; ed/BS; MBE; pa/Instr Truman Col; NBEA; Am Bus Communs Assn; Ill Bus Tchrs Assn; cp/Bd Dirs Commun Action Comm, Heniold Neighborhood Sers Cincinnati; Conslt AFSCME Cinc; r/Bapt; hon/Outstg Yg Wom of Am.

JENKINS, EDWIN GARTH oc/Dean of Student Affairs; b/Oct 4, 1937; h/1705 E Minnesota Ave, Deland, FL 32720; ba/Deland; m/Elmarie Smith; c/Benjamin Hubert, Marie Eloise; p/Hubert Rogers Jenkins (dec); Eloise Snyder Jenkins, Fayetteville, NC; ed/BA Wake Forest Univ 1959; MEd 1965, EdD 1974 Auburn Univ;

mil/AUS 1960-63 Pers Ofcr, 1/LT; USAR 1963-65; Ala ANG 1975-78; pa/Dean Student Affairs Stetson Univ; Asst Dean Student Affairs Auburn Univ 1969-78; Exec Dir Pi Kappa Alpha 1967-69; Others; APGA; ACPA; SCPA (Pres 1976-77); NASPA; cp/Mtl Hlth Assn; Reg Crisis Ctr; Social Concers Coun; r/Bapt; Deacon, SS Tchr; hon/Army Commend Medal; Dist'd Ser SEITC Advr, Auburn Univ.

JENKINS, HAYS JR oc/Assistant District Attorney; b/Jun 14, 1949; h/17 Charleston Park Dr, #2605, Houston, TX 77025; ba/Houston; p/Hays Sr and Nelcena Jenkins, Ft Worth, TX; ed/BS Univ Houston 1972; JD Tex St Univ 1976; pa/Asst DA, Harris Co Dist Atty Ofc; Lic'd St of Tex 1977; ABA; Tex Bar Assn; Nat DAs Assn; Yg Dems; Phi Alpha Delta; r/Wheeler Ave Bapt Ch; hon/Pres Law Sch Class; Rec'd Earl Warren Legal Tng Prog S'ship; Others.

JENKINS, MARY ELIZABETH oc/Restaurant Operator; b/Jun 6, 1923; h/1708 St Duke, Beaufort, SC 29902; ba/Beaufort; m/Luther Charles; c/John, Frances Morrall, Charles L; p/Ottis William and Joanna Murray (dec); pa/Mgr Food Ser; cp/Pres AL Aux; Bd Dirs LWV; r/Bapt; hon/Howard Univ Org Devel Prog.

JENKINS, ROBERT WARLS JR oc/Scientist; b/Jun 12, 1936; h/105 Gun Club Rd, Richmond, VA 23221; ba/Richmond; m/Alma Rowe; c/Mark, R Brent, Hunter; p/Robert W Jenkins (dec); Catherine L Jenkins, Richmond; ed/BS VMI; MS Purdue;

PhD CWU; mil/AUS Active Duty 1960-63; USAR 1963-79 Lt Col; pa/Assoc Prin Sci Philip Morris Res Ctr; Am Chem Soc; Am Nuclear Soc; cp/Resv Ofcrs Assn; r/Epis; hon/Dist'd Achmt in Tobacco Sci Awd, Philip Morris; Mem Pres' Hundred; USAR Rifle Champ.

JENKINS, ROY L oc/Letter Carrier; b/Feb 29, 1921; h/1807 N 6th St, Orange, TX 77630; ba/Same; m/Wilma J; c/Evelyn J Briggs, Gwen, Roy L Jr; p/Earnest Jenkins (dec); Eunice Jenkins, Orange; ed/BA; mil/AUS Master Sgt; pa/POD Lttr Carrier; cp/EOOC; OCA; AMAC; r/Bapt: Deacon; hon/Commend, Gov of Tex.

JENKS, HALSEY DENTON oc/Petroleum Distributor; b/Sept 2, 1937; h/216 Hanover St, Concord, MI 49237; ba/Concord; p/Halsey Barnes and Rosha Leha Jenks, Concord; ed/BA Spring Arbor Col 1970; mil/AUS 1956-66; pa/Partner Wholesale & Retail Petro Distribution; cp/Pres Concord HS Alumni Assn; Village of Concord: Trustee, Mem Planning Bd, Cand Pres; Am Legion; Org Am Histns; hon/W/W MW; Notable Ams.

JENKS (MRS JORDAL), MARY ELLEN oc/Director Consumer Affairs and Services; b/Oct 4, 1933; h/6624 Dovre Dr, Edina, MN 55436; ba/Chaska, MN; m/Douglas R Jordal; c/Joyellyn, Jared, Juliette; p/Frank George Jenks (dec); Emma Augusta Jenks, Chippewa Falls, WI; ed/BS cum laude 1956, MS 1957 Univ Wis; pa/Dir Consumer Affairs & Sers, Green Giant Co; Consumer Affairs Com Grocery Mfrs Am; Am Wom in Radio & TV; Am Home Ecs Assn; Soc Consumer Affairs Profls Bus; Others; cp/Minn Soc Fine Arts; Wom's Assn Minn Symph Orch; r/Colonial Ch of Edina; hon/Phi Kappa Phi; W/W: MW, Am Wom; World W/W Wom; Others.

JENNINGS, JOHN J oc/Corporate President and Director; b/May 26, 1947; h/504 29th St, Orlando, FL 32805; m/Wendy Christina; p/Michael J and Catherine D Jennings (dec); ed/BS 1968, MBA 1970 St John's Univ; Addit Studies; pa/Dir: Univ Coun, Indust Waste Mgmt, Storybook Village Bus Conslt; Chm Citizens Action Adv Com; Chm Solid Waste Contractors Assn; Other Positions; Soc Adv pf Mgmt; Bus Adm Soc; Gov Com Adv Bd Small Bus Contractors Assn Ctl Fla; Seminole Co Bd Realtors; cp/Mem Smithsonian Inst; r/Cath; hon/Outstg Spkrs Awd; Hon Fellow Truman Inst.

JENNINGS, ROBERT WENDELL oc/Theatrical Public Relations Director; b/Mar 13, 1932; h/13423 Blossomheath Ln, Dallas, TX 75206; ba/Dallas; p/T L Jennings (dec); Ida Vallerie Mann Jennings, Dallas; mil/USNR 1950-58 2nd Class Petty Ofcr Med Corps; pa/Public Relats Dir Tex Assn Film/Tape Profls; Legit Theatre Conslt Peggy Taylor Talent Inc; Other Profl Activs; r/Epis.

JENSEN, FRED CHARLES oc/Research and Development Engineer; b/Jan 11, 1947; h/1607 Bell, Chagrin Falls, OH 44022; ba/Brookpark, OH; m/Barbara Elizebeth;

p/Hays Hamilton and Hedwig Elizebeth Jensen, Lyndhurst, OH; ed/BS Fla St Univ 1970; pa/Lic'd Profl Engr; CESPE: Bd Dirs 1974-, Pres 1978-79; Am Mgmt Assn; Am Soc for Metals; Am Nuclear Soc; Nat Soc Profl Engrs; Others; r/Cath; hon/Holder 2 US Patents.

JENSEN, HARRY ROBERT oc/Singer; b/Mar 10, 1921; h/1603 E Wellesley St, Spokane, WA 99207; ba/Same; m/Jo Ella Pitts; c/Betty, Katherine Jo, Bonnie Gay, Harry R II; p/James and Ruby Jensen (dec); ed/BMus; MRE SW Sem; mil/USN 1942-45; pa/Sacred Singer; Participaed Over 100 Revivals in NW; Perf'd Sacred Mus Concerts; Choir Clinics; Cnslr; cp/Pres PTSA; Yth Sports; hon/W/W Rel.

JENSEN, MARY DONNA oc/Assistant Professor; b/Dec 29, 1923; h/61 Harvard St, Pocatello, ID 83201; ba/Pocatello; m/Jay G; c/Jay G Jr, Mary J Steele; p/Evan E and Lillie Jones, Pocatello; ed/BA w High Hons; MA; Grad Study: Brigham Young Univ, Ohio St Univ; pa/Asst Prof Eng Idaho St Univ; MLA; RMMLA; Nat Endowmt for Humanities; CAP Com, S'ships & Awds Com Chm; AAUP; ICTE; cp/Var Commun Projs; r/Ch of Jesus Christ LDS; hon/NEW Scholar; "Not Goodbye", Short Story.

JENT, SUE ALLEN oc/Retired Public School Teacher and Administrator; b/Apr 4, 1916; h/Rt 2, Box 124, Madisonville, KY 42431; m/Crawford Lee Jent; p/Claude Bailey and Robbie Baker Allen (dec); ed/AA Bethel Col 1935; AB Oberlin Col & Oberlin Conserv 1939; MA 1959, EdS 1971 Wn Ky Univ; pa/KAST; IRA; ACE; KMEA; NEA; KCTE; KCTSS; CBE; Num Activs & Ofcs: ASCD, KEA, Others; cp/Farm Bur; Nat Fdn Mus Clbs; Commun Concerts Assn; Num Others; r/Missionary Bapt; hon/Ky Col; Duchess of Paducah; Phi Theta Kappa; Hon Citizen Glasgow (Ky); Num Biogl Listings; Others.

JEREMIAH, LESTER EARL oc/Research Scientist; b/Dec 9, 1941; h/Box 2043 Lacombe, Alberta TOC 1SO; ba/Lacombe; m/Virginia Dorothy; c/William Everett, Johanna Sue, John David; p/Everett Ray Jeremiah (dec); Lillian Rose Jeremiah, Walla Walla, WA; ed/BSc Wash St Univ 1965; MSc Univ Mo 1967; PhD Tex A&M Univ 1971;

pa/Res Scist Canada Agri Res Sta; Am Meat Sci Assn; Am Soc Animal Sci; Inst Food Tech; r/Christian; hon/Gamma Sigma Delta; Recipient Asst'ships; Num Biogl Listings.

JERNIGAN, NANCY FRANKLIN oc/Project Director; b/Apr 18, 1912; h/7306 Caillet St, Dallas, TX 75209; ba/Dallas; m/Willie; c/Michael, Joyce Franklin; p/(dec); ed/BA; MEd; pa/Proj Dir Wom in Commun Ser; Elem Tchr & Prin; Public Speaker; Pianist; cp/Mem Tex Col Nat Alumni; Bd Mem Adv'g Black Art & Writing; Job Corps; US Labor Dept; ARC; r/Meth: Pianist, Pres Bd Christian Ed; hon/Var Profl & Civic Awds.

JERNIGAN, RAWLIN CLEVELAND oc/General Engineer; b/Oct 13; h/1506 Glastonberry Rd, Maitland, FL 32751; ba/Washington, DC; m/Jo; c/Rawlin Jr, Jan, Jill, Paul, Timothy; p/Roy C and Nettie McClaran Jernigan (dec); ed/BS Tenn Tech Univ 1965; pa/Gov Tech Rep Martin Marietta (Orlando, Fla); Past Mem Optical Sys Group

Range Cmdrs Coun; Tenn Amateur Archeol Soc; Am Def Preparedness Assn; cp/Fredericksburg Civil War Roundtable; r/Past Min Ch of Christ: Buffalo Valley, New Ctr Grove (Tenn), Wiesbaden (Germany), Fredericksburg (Va).

JESSNER, LUCIE NEY oc/Psychiatrist; Psychoanalyst; b/Sept 15, 1896; h/3640 Appleton St NW, Washington, DC 20008; m/Fritz (dec); c/Anne, Eva J Sampson; p/Emanuel and Rosa Loewenhaar Ney (dec); ed/MD; PhD; pa/Prof Psychi Emerita Georgetown Univ Sch Med; Tng Analyst Wash Psychoanalytic Inst; r/Jewish.

JESSUP, BELVIN J oc/Minister; ba/High Point, NC, m/Arnetta McKee; c/Timothy Belvin, Benita Veloise, Belvin Jr; p/Rolen and Lula Jessup; ed/BS A&T St Univ 1968; MDiv Gammon ITC Theol Sem 1971; pa/Min Memorial U Meth Ch, High Pt 1974-; Past Positions: St Mark U Meth Ch (Charlotte)

1971-74, St Luke U Meth Ch (Asheboro) 1967-68, Others; Wn NC Conf: Chm Com Black Ch Devel, VChm Bd Ordained Min & Recruitmt, Secy Bd Inst of Homiletical Studies, Secy & Coor Wash Dr Improvemt Com (High Pt); Mem High Pt Min Alliance; cp/Mem Yth Needs Adv Com; hon/Sel'd to Travel w Ed Prog "The Living Word and World".

JESTICE, LOIS BURNEZ oc/Teacher; b/Oct 15, 1936; h/8266 Franklin-Madison Rd, Carlisle, OH 45005; ba/Carlisle; m/Dennie Lee; c/Lennie Dee, Lynda Lee; p/Granville P Kidd, Franklin, OH; Livia Clair Kidd (dec); ed/BSEd Miami Univ (Ohio); Student Masters Prog Univ Cinc; pa/IAC Tchr EMR Jr HS; Warren Co Spec Ed Curric Guide Com; cp/Miami Campus & Commun Chorale Mem; Music Dir Lebanon Correctional Inst Chapel Choir; r/1st Ch of God, Middleton, Ohio: Pianist; hon/St Tchr Grant Devel Reading Lang Arts Prog Jr High IAC.

JETT, CLARIBEL B oc/Artist; b/May 2, 1907; h/2223 Trescott Dr, Tallahassee, FL 32312; m/Robert S; c/Robert S II, W Lloyd, Elizabeth J Wyrick; p/William Lewis and Mary Cooke Brandon (dec); ed/LI 1928, BS 1932 John B Stetson Univ; Grad'd Famous Artists Sch 1970; pa/Self-employed Artist 1954-; Former Art Tchr: Flagler Bch 1928-29, Groveland (Fla) 1930-31, El Paso (Tex) 1932-33; Pvt Lessons Tallahassee 1954; Num Portraits & Paintings in Print and Public Display; Nat Leag Am Pen Wom; Fla Coun Mem Am Photo Artist Guild 1972; Art Div Chm Tallahassee Wom's Clb 1960-62; Others;

cp/DAR: VRegent, Registrar; Tallahassee Mus Guild; Nat Trust for Hist Preserv; Num Others; hon/Wom Yr 1960; Colonial Dames XVII Cent Hist Ser Awd; Dist'd Alumni Awd, Stetson Univ; Num Hist Art Presentations: Fla St Leg, Colonial Dames, Palm Vista Sch, Others; Painted Mich Art Train, Fine Arts Coun Fla.

JILANI, ATIQ A oc/Mechanical Engineer; b/Feb 1, 1948; h/PO Box 2461, Glen Ellyn, IL 60137; m/Khalida; p/Siddiq Ahmed and Nasima Jilani; ed/BE Karachi Univ 1969; MS Tuskegee Inst 1971; pa/Mgr Engrg, Sea Containers, Broadview, Ill 1978-; Prod Engr Borg-Warner Corp, Chicago, Ill 1974-78; Design Engr Lummus Indust, Columbus, Ga 1971-73; Other Positions; Contbr Articles Profl Jours; Charter Mem Assn Energy Engrs; ASME; Nat Soc Profl Engrs; ASAE; r/Muslim; hon/Holder 11 US & Intl Patents.

JIMENEZ-de-la-SOTA, RAFAEL oc/- Priest; b/Nov 12, 1922; h/237 Carlton Ave, Brooklyn, NY 11205; ba/Bklyn; m/Regla Garcia Vidal; c/George Phelps, Dorothy Virginia; p/Rafael Jimenez and Brigida De La Sota, Seville, Spain; ed/BA Jesuit Col; LTh; DD; mil/Spanish Army Chaplain; pa/Cnslr N V Peale T Ctr, NYC; Epis Priest; cp/Mem Long Isl Hist Soc; r/Epis; Vicar; Curator Trinity Ch of NY; hon/Order of Cross Jerusalem; Count of Sota-Lastra, Vatican.

JIMERSON, JAMES COMPERE SR oc/Toxicologist; b/Oct 10, 1936; h/1820 Fairhaven Dr, Indianapolis, IN 46229; ba/Indpls; m/Ina Sue Jones; c/Martha LeAnn, James Compere Jr; p/George Alexander and Lois Compere Jimerson, Corning, AR; ed/BA, BS Ouachita Bapt Col; pa/Toxicol Wishard Meml Hosp; Am Chem Soc; Soc Applied Spectroscopy; Am Acad Forensic Scis; Others; cp/BSA, Nat Eagle Scout Assn; Mason; Scottish Rite; VHF/UHF Radio Clb; r/So Bapt: Deacon, Ch Sch Supt; hon/BSA: Silver Beaver, Awd Merit; Man Yr 1976; NESA Silver Wreath Awd; ARRL Public Ser Awd.

JOB, KENNETH A oc/Professor; b/Feb 2, 1926; h/5 Navajo Trail, W Milford, NJ 07480; ba/Wayne, NJ; m/Amy Grace; c/Karen, Annamarie, Kenneth Jr; p/James and Marie Job (dec); ed/BS Jersey St Col; MA, EdD NY Univ; pa/Prof Social Studies Ed W Patterson Col; NJ Studies Coun; NJ Hist Comm Coms; Jerseymen Adv Coun; Pub'd Sev Articles & Books; cp/Local & Co Bicent Comms; Co Hist Trustee; Sch Conslt; Hobart Manor Restoration Com; hon/Fdrs Awd, NYU; Phi Delta Kappa; Kappa Delta Pi; NJ Hist Comm Awd.

JOBE, MADISON ALPHONSO JR oc/Company President; b/Feb 26, 1955; h/4407 Oneida, Pasadena, TX 77504; ba/Pasadena; m/Sandra Sue; c/James Benjamin; p/Madison A Sr and Evelyn Jobe, Pasadena; ed/Assocs Applied Sci; pa/Pres O'Malley's Inc; VP Whataburger Pasadena Inc; cp/Secy S Pasadena Rotary Clb; r/So Bapt; hon/W/W: Am Jr Cols, S&SW; Notable Ams; Outstg Yg Men Am.

JOCELYN, WAYNE LEWIS oc/Minister; b/Apr 8, 1939; h/Rt 4, Box 131, Elwood, IN 46036; m/Nadine; c/Brian, Ellen, Daniel (dec); p/Lewis Jocelyn (dec); Leone Smith

(dec); ed/BSL Johnson Bible Col; pa/Dir & Secy "Come Alive in Christ"; IPA; cp/Vol Fire Dept Leisure, Ind; r/Christian; hon/W/W Rel; DIB; Outstg Commun Ldrs; Notable Ams.

JODOCK, DARRELL HARLAND oc/Professor; Pastor; b/Aug 15, 1941; h/1425 Grantham St, St Paul, MN 55108; ba/St Paul; m/Janice Marie; c/Erik Thomas; p/Harry N Jodock (dec); Grace H Jodock, Northwood, ND; ed/BA summa cum laude St Olaf Col 1962; BD Luther Theol Sem 1966; PhD Yale Univ 1969; pa/Luther Theol Sem: Instr 1969-70, Asst Prof Ch Hist 1970-78; Grace Luth Ch: Asst Pastor, Chm Fac Affairs Com 1976-78; Am Acad Rel, Steering Com 19th Cent Theol Working Group 1976-; Translat'd *Luther and the Peasant's War*, 1972; Pub'd Sev Book Reviews Profl Jours; Soc Higher Values Ed; Am Soc Ch Hist; cp/Del St Polit Conv; Del Dist Polit Conv; Amnesty Intl; Bread for World; r/Prince Glory Luth Ch (ALC), Mpls, Minn: Past Treas, Past Mem Call Com, Past Mem Fin Comm, Past Instr; hon/Phi Beta Kappa; Danforth Grad Fellow; Num Biogl Listings.

JOE, YOUNG-CHOON CHARLES oc/Professor; b/Jan 23, 1936; h/1113 Chickering Pk Dr, Nashville, TN 37215; ba/N'ville; m/Hee-Mee Yoo; c/Jeannie, John, Jeffrey; p/Kyoung Hwan and Geel-Hwa Kim Joe, Korea; ed/MD; MS; pa/Prof Med

Meharry Med Col; Diplomate Am Bd Fam Pract; Fellow Am Acad Fam Phys; Fellow Am Soc Abdominal Surgs; Am Col Emer Phys; Assn Am Med Col; Soc Tchrs Fam Med; Pan Am Med Assn; cp/Advr Korean Commun Assn Mid-Tenn; r/Nashville Korean Ch: Ofcr; hon/Michael A Gorman Awd; AMA Phys Recog Awds.

JOFFE, EUNICE CLAIRE oc/Executive Director; b/Jul 1, 1933; h/353 Pk Ave, Highland Pk, IL 60035; ba/Chicago, IL; m/Jerome; c/Shari, Lora; p/Louis Gershman, Chgo; Mascha Tolchinove Gershman (dec); ed/BE Nat Col Ed 1953; Addit Studies; pa/Imagination Theater: Exec Dir 1975-, Exec Bd Pres 1975-76, Mem Bd 1977; Fdr & Dir Playmakers 1968-; Prodr, Creator, Dir Progs for Handicapped 1976-77; Dir & Tchr Chds Theater 1962-75; Author, Performer *The Magic Door*, CBS-TV 1961; Num Other Positions; Ill Chds Theater Assn; Chgo Alliance Perf'g Arts; Ill Dance Co Assn; cp/Conslt Arts & Handicapped Conf; Past Chm Cult Enrichmt Indian Trail PTA Bd; Past Bd Dirs Elm Pl Jr HS PTA; Others; r/Jewish; hon/Rec'd Grants: Ill Arts Coun, Comprehensive Employmt Tng Act, Continental Bk.

JOHN, ELIZABETH (BETTY) BEAMAN oc/Author; Artist; b/Oct 24, 1907; h/Vista del Rio, Green Valley, AZ 85614; m/Henry J (dec); p/Charles Worcester and Laura Zoe Bogue Beaman (dec); mil/ETO WWII, Ser'd 3 Yrs ARC, War Corres; pa/Liturgical Artist; Author Sev Books & Plays; Cntbr Num Mags;

Former Tchr Writing & Art incl'g Cuyahoga Commun Col (TriC); Former Artist-in-Residence, Sandoval Co, NM; One-Man Shows Var En Cities; IPA; Nat Leag Am Pen Wom; Nat Fdn Press Wom; Woms Overseas Ser Leag; Santa Fe Designer Craftsman; cp/CoFdr & Former Dir Camp Ho Mita Koda for Diabetic Chd, Geauga Co, Ohio; r/Epis Ch Wom; hon/Work Rep'd in Treasury Conventry Cathedral, England & 1st Christian Ch, Santa Fe, Cal; Local, Nat & Intl Awds; Num Biogl Listings.

JOHNN-ST JOHN, ALLISON NICHOLS oc/Writer; Poet; Author; Literary Consultant; Editor; h/Tarrytown, NY; New York City, NY; ba/PO Box 248 Radio City Station, NY 10019; p/G Allison and Mary D Nichols Johnn-St Johnn (dec); ed/BA; BSc; MA; PhD; pa/Former Prof Eng & French Lit; Author: *Lights Out?*, *Crystal Waters*, *Muffled Drums*, Num Others; Editor & Compiler *Singing Pens Anthology*; Others; Contbr Maj Nat & Intl Mags, Anthologies, Jours; Cosmosynthesis Leag; Intl Guild Contemp Bards; Work incl Num Anthologies; cp/Mem Exec Adv Coun Nat Reg Prom Ams; Am Bible Soc; hon/Nat Poetry Awds, NY World's Fair; Work Rep'd Harris Spec Collection, Brown Univ Lib (Providence, RI); Nom Nobel Prize Lit 1970; Num Achmt & Merit Awds; DIB; Intl W/W: World Wom, Poetry, Intellectuals; Others.

JOHNSON, ANNETTE R MACFARLANE oc/Budget Analyst; b/Aug 10, 1952; h/PO Box 5, Tremonton, UT 84337; ba/Brigham City, UT; m/Tracy L; p/Ted D and Lynette Gardner Macfarlane, Riverside, UT; ed/BFA Utah St Univ; pa/Budget Analyst Space Shuttle Fin Team, Thiokol Corp; BPW Clb

Utah Fdn Chapt Pres 1977-79; cp/LWV; Heritage Theatre; CoChm Am Party; Others; r/LDS: Drama & Speech Spec; hon/Golden Spike BPW: Wom Yr, Yg Careerist, Essay Winner; Ole Awd, Heritage Theatre; Acad Hons & Entrance S'ship USU; Others.

JOHNSON, BARBARA JEAN oc/Judge; b/Apr 9, 1932; ba/110 N Grand Ave, Los Angeles, CA 90012; m/Ronald Mayo; c/Belinda Sue; p/Clifford Clarence Barnhouse; Orma Cecile Boring; ed/BS; JD; pa/Adj Prof SWn Univ Law Sch; Lectr Univ So Cal Law Sch Advanced Profl Prog; CoEditor *Cal Mun Ct Bench Guide*; Exec Com LA Mun Ct; Bd Trustees: LA Co Bar Assn, Legion Lex; Pres: Cal Wom Lwyrs, LA Co Wom Lwyrs Assn.

JOHNSON, CHARLES BRUCE oc/Engineer; b/Aug 5, 1935; h/6521 Centerton Dr, Ft Wayne, IN 46815; ba/Ft Wayne; m/June Graham; c/Kimberly Jill, Kristen June; p/David H Johnson, Sioux City, IA; Alice K N A J Pillar, Seminole, FL; ed/BS Iowa St Univ 1957; MSEE 1963, PhD 1967 Univ Minn; mil/Air NG, Hon Discharge 1961; pa/Prin Engr, Electro-Optical Prods Div ITT Corp; Former Tchg Asst & Res Fellow Univ Minn; Former Instr Lawrence Inst Tech (Southfield, Mich); AAAS; Am Physical Soc; IEEE; Optical Soc Am & Soc Photo-Optical Instrumentation Engrs; Pub'd Num Articles Profl Jours; r/Meth; hon/Certs Recog, NASA; Holder 2 US Patents.

JOHNSON, CHARLIE JAMES oc/Minister; b/Sept 24, 1923; m/Mary Ellen Upton; c/2; p/Emory Moses and Ruth Belle T Johnson; ed/BA Morehouse Col 1956; BD

Morehouse Sch of Rel & Interdenominational Theol Ctr 1960; MDiv 1973; Doct Cand, Toledo Bible Col & Sem 1978; pa/Ordained to Min, Atlanta Bapt Assn & Mt Vernon Bapt Ch 1949; Pastor, New Hope Bapt Ch (Dalton, Ga) 1951-61; Presb of Holston (UPCUSA): Johnson City, Kingsport & Greeneville (Tenn) 1961-66; Presb of Union, Athens & Sweetwater (Tenn) 1966-; Sweetwater Min Assn; Weekly Columnist, *Daily Post-Athenian* (Athens, Tenn) 1967-69; cp/Former Mem, Mayor's Com on Human Relats; Former Mem Bd Dirs, McMinn Co Voc Sch; Former Mem Mtl Hlth Com; r/United Presb Ch USA; hon/Rec'd Mathalathian Awd (2), Morehouse Col; Rec'd Cit, Athens Kiwanis Clb; Biogl Listings.

JOHNSON, CURTIS WILLIAM oc/Physician; Ophthalmologist; b/Aug 10, 1942; h/1119 2nd Ave So, Clinton, IA 52732; ba/Clinton; m/Charlotte Ann; c/Jolene R, Brett W; p/Arthur W and Mildred E Johnson, Rockford, IL; ed/BA; MD; pa/Am Assn Ophthal; Diplomate Am Bd Ophthal; Diplomate Nat Bd Med Examrs; Am Acad Ophthal; cp/Rotary; C of C; Bd Dir Ecuminical Housing; r/Luth; hon/Phi Eta Sigma; Rec'd Grant NSF.

JOHNSON, DAVID BASCOMB oc/Instructor; Researcher; Administrator; b/Jan 11, 1940; h/3007 Diamond, Ames, IA 50010; ba/Ames; m/Sara Jane; c/Jennifer Lee, Willian Paul, Molly Kathryn; p/Paul B and Leota S Johnson, Garland, TX; ed/BSME, MSME Univ Tex; PhD Stanford; pa/Iowa St Univ Dept Engrg Sci & Mechs: Instr, Reschr, Admr; ASEE; ASME; SESA; SES; hon/NASA Summer Fac Fellow; Outstg Prof SMU; ASEE New Engrg Edr Awd, Iowa St.

JOHNSON, DAVID PITTMAN oc/Assistant Professor; b/Jul 29, 1936; h/Drawer CG, University AL 35486; ba/Univ AL; m/Linda June Russell; c/Michael David; p/Calvin Leonard and C Bernice Cagle Johnson, Jacks Creek, TN; ed/BS Huntington Col; MSW, DSW Tulane Univ; pa/Asst Prof Univ Ala Sch Social Work; Nat Assn Christians Social Work: Bd Mem, Pres Ala Chapt; Consltg Editor *The Paraclete*; cp/Mem Bd Govs Am Col Heraldry; r/Ch of Christ.

JOHNSON, EDDIE BERNICE oc/Executive; b/Dec 3, 1934; h/2107 Lanark, Dallas TX 75203; ba/Dallas; c/Dawrence Kirk; ed/BS Tex Christian Univ; MPA So Meth Univ; pa/Prin Reg Ofcl Dept HEW; Chief Psychi Nurse-Psychotherapist VA Hosp; Exec Asst Pers Div Nieman-Marcus; Conslt Zale Corp, Dept Urban Affairs; St Rep Dist 33-0, Tex Ho of Reps 1972-77; cp/Bd Trustees Dallas Alliance; Bd Mem Wom for Change Inc; Dallas Black C of C; NAACP; YWCA; LWV; Nat Coun Negro Wom (Past Pres); Dem Wom Dallas Co; Num Other Activs; r/St John Bapt Ch; hon/Civil Libertarian Yr Awd, Am Civil Liberties Union 1978; Nurse Yr, Tex Nurses Assn 1978; Outstg Citizen Yr, Omega Psi; Wom Yr: Black C of C 1973, Zeta Phi Beta 1973, Greyhound Corp 1972; Num Others.

JOHNSON, ELLIOTT A oc/Attorney; b/Feb 21, 1907; h/1831 Post Oak Pk Dr, Houston, TX 77027; ba/Houston; m/Katherine Ryckman; c/Nancy J Lucke, Glenn, Karen; p/John C and Sarah Knutson Johnson; ed/PhB Univ Chgo 1928; JD 1931; LLB S Tex Col 1937; Addit Studies; pa/Partner Johnson, Milligan & Donaho (Law Firm) 1968-; Admit'd Bar: Ill 1931, Tex 1937; Schlumberger Well Survey'g Corp: VP Fin, Treas, Gen Cnslr 1936-68; Other Former Positions; Bar Assns: Am, Tex, Houston; Phi Delta Theta; Alpha Kappa Psi; Other Activs; cp/Trustee Univ Houston Foun; Pres Bd Trustees Rosewood Gen Hosp; Past Chm Bd S Tex Col; Mason; Kiwanis Clb; Others; r/Presb.

JOHNSON, ELSIE oc/Superintendent; b/Jan 1, 1922; h/558 Lee, Glen Ellyn, IL 60137; ba/Carol Stream, IL; m/Robert D; c/Jeffrey Evan, Jay Eric; p/George and Carrie Ohlman Carlson; ed/BS Ill St Univ 1945; MS Univ Ill 1946; CAS 1969, Doct 1978 No Ill

Univ; pa/Supt Commun Consol Schs Dist 93, 1959-; Prin Cloverdale Sch TM Handicapped 1966-70; Former Tchr: Dist 93 (1957-59), Dist 41 (1954-56); Other Former Positions; DuPage Valley Div Elem Prins Assn: Secy-Treas, Pres; NEA; AASA; Ill Assn Sch Adm; Mem 5 PTAs; Other Activs; cp/Wheaton United Fund: Bd Mem, Pres; Envir Coun Carol Stream; Past Pres Glen Ellyn Countryside Garden Clb; Chm Salvation Army Ser Unit Carol Stream; hon/Dist'd Ser Awd, Carol Stream JCs; Ser & Achmt Awd, Wheaton Col; Profl Devel Awd, AASA Nat Acad Sch Execs; Rec'd S'ships; Others; Num Biogl Listings.

JOHNSON, EVELYN G oc/Homemaker; b/Nov 27, 1916; h/73061 Cabazon Peak Dr, Palm Desert, CA 92260; m/Gerald H; c/Harriet J Laird (Mrs John), Carl H, Edward G; p/Neil Harman and Carrie Lenora Robbins Graham (dec); ed/Cert Cal St Fdn Wom's Clbs 1973; Dipl Glendale Parliamentary Law Clb 1973; Cert Marina Del Ray Clb 1972; Addit Studies; pa/Avon Rep Burbank, Cal 1967-73; Donna's Frozen Foods (N Hollywood, Cal): Kitchen Supvr 1960-63, Asst Mgr 1963-66; cp/AUS Mothers & Wives Clb: Past Pres, VP, Chm Var Coms; Wom's Coun Burbank; Burbank Beautiful Inc; Burbank United Patriotic Org; Palm Desert Greens Assn; Num Other Orgs; Vol Activs; r/Prot; hon/Thank You Awd Cert, BSA; Certs Apprec, VA Hosp (Sepulveda, Cal); City of Burbank: Wom Yr Awd 1974, Civic Achmt Awd, Soc Wel Awd; Num Others.

JOHNSON, FIELDING HOLMES oc/- Consulting Engineer; b/Dec 15, 1934; h/961 Tifton Dr, Baton Rouge, LA 70815; ba/Baton Rouge; m/Mary Anna Jurgensen; c/Fielding

Jr, Stuart T H , Barton B, Margaret Kelley; p/Perry Mark and Oline Marie Judice Johnson, Baton Rouge; ed/BS La St Univ; mil/-USAF Capt (1956-70 Resv); pa/CEC/L Pres; AIChE; La Engrg Soc NSPE; cp/Rotary Clb; Dem Party; r/Cath.

JOHNSON, FLORENCE GIFFIN oc/- Retired; b/Apr 4, 1899; h/123 Medford Leas, Medford, NJ 08055; m/A Pemberton Johnson; p/Clarence Shepard and Elizabeth Burnside MacDonald Giffin; ed/BA St Lawrence Univ 1919; LHD 1973; Addit Studies; Clerk Chase Nat Bank 1919-21; Secy to Editor *Good Housekeeping Mag* 1921; Pers Spec Johns-Manville Corp (NYC) 1941-58; Other Past Positions; Compiler *Simon Giffin and His Descendants* 1971; NY Pers Mgmt Assn; Intl Assn Pers Wom; Others; cp/Trustee Emeritus St Lawrence Univ; New England Hist Geneal Soc; St Lawrence Co Hist Assn; Others; r/Prot Commun Ch, Medford Lakes: Mem; hon/- Delta Delta Delta.

JOHNSON, FRANCIS WILLARD oc/- Clergyman; b/Mar 13, 1920; h/606 Yorkshire Dr, Washington, IL 61571; ba/Wash; m/Ruth Marian Palm; c/Christine Louise J Speight, Roland Wayne; p/Aaron William Johnson (dec); Lettie Victoria Lindgren Johnson, Wenona, IL; ed/BA; BDiv; MDiv; Doct Min; pa/Sr Pastor St Mark's Luth Ch; Ill Synod (LCA): Dean Peoria Dist, Com of Deans; Pres Wash Min Assn; Bd Dirs Luth Home (Peoria, Ill); r/Luth Clergy of Gtr Peoria; hon/W/W: MW, Rel; Intl W/W Commun Ser.

JOHNSON, FRANKLYN ARTHUR

oc/Administrator; b/Nov 6, 1921; h/Barry College, 11300 NE 2nd Ave, Miami, FL 33161; ba/Same; c/Franklyn Arthur Jr, Terri J Cochran, Sandra J Fox; p/Robert Barnes and Olyve E Johnson (dec); ed/BA Rutgers; MA, PhD Harvard; mil/AUS 1st Inf Div 1942-45, 1/LT; pa/Barry Col: Asst to Pres, Foun Exec; Prof Adm Fla Atl Univ (Boca Raton); Fla Gov's Coun; Chm SEn Coun Founs; Trustee 4 Cols & Univs; r/Presb; hon/Hon Degs: Jacksonville Univ, Mt Senario Col, Flagler Col, Drury Col, Mo Valley Col.

JOHNSON, FREDERIC HENRY oc/Research Scholar; b/May 23, 1929; h/158 N Humphrey Ave, Oak Park, IL 60302; c/Gary Richard, Frederic Henry; p/Leonard W Johnson Sr (dec); Helene E Johnson, Oak Park; ed/BA 1948, MA 1950, PhD 1951 Cornell Univ; mil/Nav Air Corps WWII; pa/Res Scholar Neuroanatomy; Am Assn Anatomists; cp/Assoc Newberry Lib; Mem John Crerar Lib; hon/Alpha Kappa Kappa; Hon Mem Intl Peace Assn.

JOHNSON, FREDERICK DEAN oc/Food Consultant; b/Feb 27, 1911; h/4546 Shetland Ln, Houston, TX 77027; ba/Same; m/Haulwen Richey; c/Frederick D II, Mary H, Grace E; p/Harry H and Grace Cammarn Johnson (dec); ed/BA; pa/Am Chem Soc; Inst Food Technol; AAAS; cp/Former Dir Afton Oaks Civic Clb; Del Tex Repub Conv 1978; r/Presb: Ruling Elder; hon/Cit Nat Preservers Assn.

JOHNSON, GARY REID oc/University Administrator; b/Feb 23, 1934; h/PO Box 5430, Lubbock, TX 79417; ba/Lubbock; p/Ernest R and Sophrona E Johnson, Lubbock; ed/BM, MBA, MA Univ Mich; pa/Am Acad Med Admrs: Fellow, Tex St Dir, Reg VIII Bd Dirs 1975-; Acad Mgmt; Am Soc Public Adm; Nat Assn Col & Univ Bus Ofcrs; Am Acad Polit & Social Sci; AASA; Others; cp/SAR; Sons Confederate Vets; Soc Colonial Wars; hon/Tau Kappa Epsilon; Alpha Kappa Psi; Phi Mu Alpha; Kappa Kappa Psi; W/W: Am, W, S&SW, Fin & Indust; DIB; Others.

JOHNSON, GEORGE oc/Professor; b/Apr 6, 1926; h/410 Westwood Dr, Chapel Hill, NC 27514; ba/Chapel Hill; m/Marian; c/Sally Hope, George William, David Ritchie, Robert Hill; p/George Johnson (dec); Evelyn Hill (dec); ed/BS (Med) 1949; MD 1952; mil/AUS 1/st Lt (Inf) 1944-46; pa/UNC-CH Med Sch: Prof & Chief Div Vascular-Trauma-Transplantation Surg, Ad Hoc Com Oral Surg (MD Prog) 1977-, Search Com VChancellor Hlth Affairs 1976-, Ad Hoc Com Cancer Res Human Rights 1974-, Others; NC Meml Hosp: Primary Care Com 1978-, Operating Rm Com 1976-, Rehab Com 1964-, Others; Edit Bd *NC Med Jour*, 1974-; Edit Conslt *Jour of Trauma*, 1978-; AMA; AAUP; Am Col Surgs: Pres NC Chapt 1975, Bd Govs, Com Trauma, Others; NC Med Soc: Com Traffic Safety, Com Disaster & Emer Care, Others; Num Other Assns; cp/Rotary Clb; Bd Dirs Ctl Carolina Bk & Trust Co; Advr S Orange Co Rescue Squad; C of C; Others; r/Presb; hon/Roscoe B G Cowper Dit'd Prof Surg; Hon Mem New Hanover Meml Hosp Staff (Wilmington, NC); Fdr's Awd, NC Heart Assn; W/W Am; Phi Chi; Phi Beta Kappa; Phi Delta Theta.

JOHNSON, GORDON GILBERT oc/Vice President; Dean; b/Nov 19, 1919; h/6411 Squire Dr NE, Fridley, MN 55432; ba/St Paul, MN; m/Alta Borden; c/Gregg Alan, Gayle Ellen J Boyd; p/Gilbert O and Myrtle I Johnson, St Paul; ed/BA; BD; ThM; ThD;

mil/USN 1944-45; pa/Bethel Theol Sem: VP, Dean 1959-; Bapt World Alliance Gen Coun; Assn Profl Ed Min; Am Acad Homileticians; r/Bapt; hon/Moderator Bapt Gen Conf.

JOHNSON, GORDON GUSTAV oc/Professor; b/Jun 23, 1936; h/2010 Fairwind, Houston, TX 77062; ba/Houston; m/Nancy May; c/Cathy Lynn, Kim Marie, Carl Gustav, David Hjalmar; p/Gustav Hjalmar and Selma Marie Johnson; ed/BS; PhD; pa/Prof Math Univ Houston; Fdg Editor & Mng Editor *Houston Jour Math*; cp/Dir Clear Creek Basin Authority; hon/Fellow Oak Ridge Inst Nuclear Studies; Sr Assoc Nat Res Coun.

JOHNSON, GRACE MANCHESTER oc/Columnist; Free-Lance Writer; b/Mar 26, 1907; h/261 Harwood, Apt 509, Lebanon, MO 65536; m/Arvil Monroe (dec); c/Sarah Frances (dec); p/Solon Hayes and Nora Elizabeth Farris Manchester (dec); ed/BS SW Mo Univ; Grad Work Mo Univ-Kansas City; pa/Columnist *Lebanon Daily Record*; Former Tchr Mus & Eng Mo Public Schs; Pvt Instr Piano, Voice, Organ; Other Positions;

Author: *History of United Meth Ch of Lebanon, Touches of Grace*; Composer *Our Flag Fraternal*; Ozark Pen Writers Guild; NART; cp/OES; Laclede Co Hist Soc; Mo St Hist Assn; Nat Repub Wom Clb; Lebanon Commun Bettermt; Others; r/Meth; hon/Ret'd Ser Plaque, Lebanon Schs; Ser Placque 1st Meth Ch; Dist'd Ser Awd Intl Assn Rebekah Assemblies; Cert Apprec Lebanon Bicent Comm; Alt Repub Nat Conv 1972; Biogl Listings.

JOHNSON, HARVEY MARSHALL oc/Business Owner; b/Sept 20, 1920; h/37 Ash St SE, Calvert City, KY 42049; ba/Same; m/Eugenia Marie; c/Marietta Sue J Lambert; p/Earl Harvey and Myrtie Elizabeth Johnson, Fancy Farm, KY; ed/DMS Gupton-Jones Col Mortuary Sci; mil/AUS Inf WWII; pa/Owner Johnson & Lambert Funeral Home; NFDA-Ky; FDA; W Ky Dist FD Assn; cp/Lions Clb; Elks Lodge; Masonic Lodge; Am Legion; Dem Party; r/So Bapt Ch Calvert City; hon/One of Three Yg Men of Ky; JC Dist'd Ser Awd; Am Legion Baseball Awd; Lion Clb Pres Yr.

JOHNSON, HERMAN BLUITT oc/- Executive; b/Jul 28, 1925; h/2404 Lake Terrace, Sylacauga, AL 35150; ba/Sylacauga; m/Harriett Lucille Joiner; c/Judy Diane J Worrel (Mrs John D), Nancy Carol J Snockey, Barbara Lynn; p/Clark Albert and Gartrude Shivers Johnson; ed/BS Anderson Col 1948; pa/1st Fed Savs & Ln: Pres, Treas, Dir 1958-; Dir Investors Fidelity Life Ins Co; Mgr Godwin Radio & TV Co (Birmingham, Ala) 1954-58; Other Past Positions; cp/Local Bd Dirs BSA; Sylacauga Beautification Coun; C of C: Dir, Former VP; Kiwanis Clb; Former Trustee Warne So Col; Others; r/Ch of God: Mem, VChm, Trustee.

JOHNSON, IRIS MARIE oc/Teacher; b/Jul 6, 1939; h/Rt 1 Box 86R, Portales, NM 88130; ba/Portales; m/Jerry Lee; c/Tawnia D'eon, Shawnia Deanna, James Leonard W; p/James Merritt and Helan Lucille Gibson, Elida, NM; ed/BA; EdM; pa/Sec'dy Tchr 8th Grade NM & Am Hist; NM Del NEA; Portales Ed Assn: Secy, Treas; AAUW; Nat Coun Social Studies; NM Coun Social Studies;

Others; cp/CoChm Bicent Mini-Pageant; Mother Advr Intl Order Rainbow for Girls; r/Bapt; hon/Notable Ams; DIB.

JOHNSON, IRIS MERLE oc/Law Enforcement Officer; b/Jul 7, 1932; p/Beatrice Clark; ed/Grad Barrington Col 1964; Commun Col, Philadelphia 1976-78; pa/Fed Law Enforcemt Ofcr; Pastor; Tchr; Missionary; Prin Monrovia, Liberia (W Africa) 1965-74; Artist & Arch (AAS Deg, Commun Col); r/Holy Tabernacle of God Inc: Mem, Former Elder; hon/Biogl Listings.

JOHNSON, JACK D oc/Publisher; Artist Manager; b/May 24, 1928; h/1218 Carl Seyfert Dr, Brentwood, TN 37027; ba/Nashville, TN; m/Edith Hussey; c/William Carson, Lisa Elaine, David Tregg, Cherie Shannon; p/Elmer Carson Johnson (dec); Lily Bell Fielden Johnson, Knoxville, TN; ed/BSJ Univ Tenn-K 1958; mil/AUS 1954-56; pa/Pres Jack D Johnson Talent Inc 1964-; Pres Highball Mus Inc 1975-; Pres Lowball Mus Inc 1975-; Liberty Bk (Brentwood): Dir, Fdr, Mem Exec Com 1974-; Pres Chess Mus Inc 1964-75; Editor & Pubr *W Knoxville News* 1958-61; Personal Mgr: Charley Pride 1964-75, Ronnie Millsap 1973-79; Other Past Positions: Pres Nashville Assn Talent Dirs 1979-; Nat Assn Record'g Arts & Scis; Country Mus Assn; Broadcast Mus Inc; Others; cp/Intl Assn Fairs & Expositions; City Hope Foun; Nat Conf Christians & Jews; r/Presb; hon/Sigma Delta Chi; Record Prodr Yr, Country Mus Assn 1975; 11 Gold Records, RCA Records; Grammy Prodr Participation Awd, NARAS; Apprec Awd, USO: Far E Tour, Bob Hope Tour.

JOHNSON, JACK R oc/Executive; b/Sept 28, 1934; h/1185 N 29th, Humboldt, TN 38343; ba/Jackson, TN; m/Linda; c/Leigh Ann, Dawn, Marie, Stephen Ross, Robert Joseph; p/Joseph Odell and Nell F Johnson, Paducah, KY; ed/BBA; mil/USAF 4 Yrs; pa/Lambuth Col: Dir Planning & Res, Dir Computer Ctr; DPMA; ACM; cp/Lambuth Devel Coun; r/Cumberland Presb; hon/Medallions & Cert NASA; Intl W/W Commun Ser; Men Achmt; Notable Ams; Others.

JOHNSON, JEAN ATIONELL oc/Teacher; b/Jun 13, 1929; h/504 Eisenhower Cir, Portsmouth, VA 23701; ba/Portsmouth; m/Cornelius William; c/Cornelius W Jr, Archie L, Hereminia A, Washington A, Charles J, Bertha L; p/Eugene Saunders, Portsmouth; Ada G Spies (dec); ed/BA Vir Union Univ; Post-Grad Studies: Norfolk St

Col, Vir St Col, De Paul Univ; pa/Lang Arts Tchr 5th & 6th Grades; Lang Arts Coor; Mus Coor; Portsmouth Read'g Assn; Nat Assn Lang Arts; cp/Vir Union Univ Alumni Assn; Portsmouth Cath HS PTA; Commun Action Clb; YMCA; YWCA; Cystic Fibrosis Foun; Tidewater Heart Assn; r/Meth (Emanuel) AWE; hon/Personalities of S; Personalities Am.

JOHNSON, JERRY KENNETH II oc/Student; b/Nov 26, 1957; h/6061 Center Hwy, Nacogdoches, TX 75961; p/Jerry K and Joan Y Johnson, Nacogdoches; ed/Student Tex A & M Univ; pa/Nat Pres FFA; cp/Active Student Govt TAMU; Regl Yg Dems; r/Fredonia Hill Bapt Ch; hon/W/W Am HS

Students; Outstg Yg Men Am; Kiwanis Yth Ldrship Awd; Rotary Yth Awd.

JOHNSON, JOE DAVID oc/Minister; Psychologist; b/Apr 2, 1927; h/111 Shirley, Marshall, TX 75670; ba/Marshall; m/Doris Clyde; c/David, Wayne, Ray; p/Carl David and Lena Ruth Johnson (dec); ed/BS; MEd; PhD; mil/USN; pa/Am Psychol Assn; r/Bapt.

JOHNSON, JOHN M oc/Surgeon; b/Jan 5, 1938; h/319 E State, Phoenix, AZ 85020; ba/Phoenix; m/Jeanette; c/Lachelle, John; p/Chester Johnson (dec); Opal Johnson, Monticello, AR; ed/BS; MD; mil/AUS 1965-66; 1st Air Cav Div S Vietnam 1966-67; pa/Good Samaritan Hosp: Dir Peripheral Vascular Lab, Dir Vascular F'ship; Tchg Staff: St Joseph's Hosp, Maricopa Co Gen Hosp; Maricopa Co Med Soc; Fellow Am Col Surgs; SWn Surg Cong (Cnslr St of Ariz); AMA; Diplomate Am Bd Surg; Am Soc Artificial Internal Organs; Others; Num Articles Profl Jours; cp/Bd Dirs Ariz Kidney Foun; r/1st Christian Ch: Chm Bd Dirs; hon/Former Rotary 100; Commun Ldrs & Noteworthy Ams Awd; Outstg Sci Exhibit Awd, AMA; AUS: Air Medal, Bronze Star, Purple Heart, Med Combat Badge; W/W W; Intl W/W Commun Ser; Others.

JOHNSON, JOHNNY ALBERT oc/Professor; b/Mar 6, 1938; h/7802 La Roche Ln, Houston, TX 77036; ba/Houston; m/Betty Jean; c/Johnny Alden, Brenda Lynn; p/Walter Albert Johnson; Lillian Ann Johnson, Iowa City, IA; ed/AA Riverside City Col 1964; BS w Hons 1965, MA 1966, PhD 1968 Univ Cal; pa/Univ Houston: Dir Grad Studies (Math Dept) 1974-77, Math Prof; Assoc Mng Editor *Houston Journal of Math* 1974-; Am Math Soc; Math Assn Am; London Math Soc; Pi Mu Epsilon; hon/F'ship Nat Sci Foun; Res Grants Univ Houston.

JOHNSON, JOHNNY RAY oc/Professor; b/Dec 19, 1929; h/953 W Lakeview Dr, Baton Rouge, LA 70810; ba/Baton Rouge; m/Betty Moore; c/Todd Michael, John Fitzgerald, Shauna Renee; p/Dave E Johnson (dec); Bessie Morris Johnson, Chatham, LA; ed/BS (EE) Cum Laude La Tech Univ 1951; MS 1953, PhD 1959 Auburn Univ; mil/AUS 1954-56 (Sp-3); pa/Prof Elect Engrg La St Univ; IEEE; AAUP; La Engr Soc; Coauthor Sev Books incl'g *Basic Elect Circuit Sys* 1978; cp/Dem Party; Past Pres PTA; hon/Valedictorian Chatham HS; Phi Kappa Phi; Sigma Xi; Eta Kappa Nu; Tau Beta Pi; Pi Mu Epsilon; Am Men & Wom Sci; W/W S&SW; Notable Ams; Others.

JOHNSON, JOSEPHINE L oc/Associate Professor; Counselor; b/Sept 22, 1933; h/643 Meadow Dr, Macomb, IL 61455; ba/Macomb; m/Clarence William (dec); c/Christopher Anthony; p/Harold Leo Stevens (dec); Mary Cecile Stevens, Macomb; ed/BSEd 1955,

MSEd 1958 Wn Ill Univ; EdD Univ Wyom 1972; pa/Wn Ill Univ: Assoc Prof, Cnslr Ed Univ Cnslg Ctr; Author 25 Articles Profl Jours; Editor Bd Wyom Pers & Guide Jour; Presented Num St, Regl & Nat Conv Progs; APGA; ACPA; Nat Voc Guide Assn; NEA; Ill Ed Assn; AAUW; Others; r/Presb; hon/Delta Kappa Gamma; Phi Kappa Phi; Kappa Delta Pi; Wn Ill Univ: Alumni Achmt Awd, Pres Merit Awd.

JOHNSON, JOYCE oc/Sculptor; Art

Administrator; b/Jul 12, 1929; h/Box 756, Truro, MA 02666; ba/Same; p/Charles S Johnson (dec); Dorothy D Johnson; ed/Cert w Hons Sch Mus of Fine Arts 1962; Addit Studies; pa/Truro Ctr Arts: Dir 1972-, Instr Sculpture 1975-; Fdr 1972; Former Tchg Positions (Sculpture): Cape Cod Conservatory Mus & Art (Barnstable, Mass) 1968-77, Nauset Adult Ed (Orleans, Mass) 1963-68, Others; Fdr Nauset Sch Sculpture; Est'd Sculpture Studio (N Eastham, Mass) 1963; Prodn Asst Master Motion Picture Co (Boston, Mass) 1955-56; Other Former Positions; Hon VP Provincetown Art Assn & Museum; Trustee Lower Cape Arts Coun; Others; cp/Advr Wom's Hlth Clin; Mem Town Truro Fin Com; hon/Num One-Man & Group Shows; Work Sel'd for "Art in Transition" (100 Yrs Museum Sch); Recipient F'ship, Sch Museum Fine Arts.

JOHNSON, JUNE BEVERLY oc/Librarian; b/Oct 10, 1930; h/1506 Horseshoe Dr, Pueblo, CO 81001; ba/Pueblo; c/Deanna Kathleen, Marlena Babette; p/E Clifford and V Bernice Lombard, Pueblo; ed/AA Univ So Colo 1950; BA Univ No Colo 1952; MA Univ Denver 1960; pa/Libn; Media Spec; Colo Ed Media Assn; cp/Secy Clean Commun Comm; r/Meth; hon/Rec'd Malcolm Wyer S'ship, Univ Denver.

JOHNSON, LARRY W oc/Executive Director; ba/105 N Virginia Ave, Falls Church, VA 22046; m/Sondra Elizabeth Howard Baker; c/Elizabeth, Anne, John, Robert, Patricia, Larry, James; ed/AA Campbell Col 1958; BA UNC-ChH 1960; MEd NC St Univ 1965; pa/VICA: Exec Dir, Admr & Supvr Nat Org & Staff, Exec Ofcr Yth Devel Foun, Others 1965-; St Dept Public Instn: Asst St Supvr Trade & Indust Ed 1963-65, Asst St Dir Voc Ed 1963; Life Mem AVA; NASSTIE; NATIE; Am Soc Assn Execs; NCCVSO; Others; cp/Loudoun Co Voc Ed Adv Com; Former Clb Ldr Round Hill Elem Sch 4-H; Former Mem Va Bus Ed Com; r/St Peter's Epis Ch (Purcellville, Va); Mem; hon/US Del to Intl Org Promotion Voc Tng & Yth Competitions; Hon Citizen Tenn; Ark Traveler; Hon OKIE; Ky Col; Tex Admiral; W/W S&SW, Am, Others.

JOHNSON, LEWIS NEIL oc/Superintendent; b/Sept 4, 1940; h/5347 Greengate Dr, Groveport, OH 43125; ba/Groveport; m/Joyce Waybright; c/Michael Neil, Bryan Lewis; p/Charles M and Lillian B Johnson, Sand Fork, WV; ed/BS 1966, MA 1968 Miami Univ; EdD Ball St Univ 1973; mil/USN 1958-61; pa/Supt Groveport Madison Schs; Contbr Articles Profl Jours; Conslt St Dept Ed; AASA; BASA; cp/Former Mayor W Milton, Ohio; Dist Chm BSA; r/Meth; hon/Outstg Yg Edr.

JOHNSON (BICKNELL), MARJORIE RUTH oc/Teacher; b/Mar 22, 1938; h/1667 Calabazas Blvd, Santa Clara, CA 95051; ba/Santa Clara; m/Frank Emmett; c/-

Jeannette, Steve, Chris, Ami; p/Evan W and Clara Thomas, Nevada City, CA; ed/BA w Hons 1962, MA 1964 San Jose St Univ; pa/Sec'y Math Tchr Wilcox HS; *Fibonacci Qrtly* Jour: CoEditor 3 Yrs, Editor Bd 13 Yrs; Author Num Articles & 2 Books; r/Prot; hon/World Dir Math, Others.

JOHNSON (BURRELL), MARY ELIZ-

ABETH oc/Director; b/Mar 25, 1950; h/187 Bradley St, Chagrin Falls, OH 44022; ba/Beachwood OH; m/Timothy Harlan; c/Zachary Scott; p/David H Burrell III, Sarasota, FL; Nancy Blunt Burrell (dec); ed/BA; pa/Asst Dir Salvador Dali Mus; Lectr; Reschr.

JOHNSON, MARY LYNN MILLER oc/-Teacher; b/Mar 12, 1938; h/3004 Croydon, Denton, TX 76201; ba/Dallas, TX; m/James Jefferson Jr; c/Melinda J Casey, James Jefferson III; p/Emmitt Ray and Ladye Hortense Allison Miller, Dallas; ed/BS Univ Tex-EP; MS New Mex St Univ; PhD Penn St Univ; pa/Chem & Physics Tchr Hockaday Sch; Am Chem Soc; Combustion Inst; cp/Denton Area Art Leag; Denton Long Range Planning Com; r/Presb: Chm Chd's Christian Ed Com, SS Tchr; hon/Iota Sigma Pi; Alpha Chi; W/W Am Wom; DIB; Others.

JOHNSON, PHILIP M oc/Lawyer; b/Feb 22, 1940; h/Church Hill, So Woodstock, VT 05071; ba/Woodstock; m/Mary Carol; c/Charles T, Jennifer M, Melissa C; p/Philip E and Catherine M Johnson, Hanover, NH; ed/BA Colgate Univ 1963; LLB 1966, JD 1968 Union Univ; pa/Vt Bar Assn; Assn Trial Lwyrs Am; cp/Woodstock Town Moderator; Bd Dirs Woodstock Union HS; Dept Rec; Dir & VP Rotary Clb; r/Unit.

JOHNSON, PHYLLIS ANN oc/Associate Professor; b/May 30, 1944; h/2184 Pemberton Rd SW, Atlanta, GA 30331; ba/Atlanta; p/David and Edith Johnson, St Petersburg, FL; ed/RN Grady Meml Hosp 1965; BSN Med Col Ga 1969; MN Emory Univ 1970; PhD Ga St Univ 1977; pa/Ga St Univ: Dir Masters Prog Nsg 1977-, Instr, Asst Prof, Assoc Prof 1970-,

Other Positions; Grady Meml Hosp: Instr 1966-67, Staff Nurse 1965-66; Presented Num Papers; Am Nurses Assn; Ga St Nurses Assn; Advr So Assn Cols & Schs; Others; cp/Cnslt Head Start Progs; Conslt HS Cnslrs; NAACP; Others; r/Big Bethel AME Ch, Atlanta; hon/Sigma Theta Tau Res Awd; W/W S; Book Hon; Personalities Am.

JOHNSON, RALPH M oc/Dean; b/Apr 19, 1918; h/2044 N 13th E, Logan, UT 84321; ba/Logan; m/Genevieve Porter; c/Karen, Christian, Wilford; p/Ralph M and Millie G Johnson (dec); ed/BS Utah St Univ 1940; MS 1947, PhD 1948 Univ Wis; mil/AUS 1941-46: Maj Intell Dept; pa/Dean Col Sci, Utah St

Univ 1968-; Ohio St Univ: Dean Col Sci 1966-68, Dir Inst Nutrition & Food Tech 1963-66, Prof Physiol Chem & Pharmacol, Res Prof & Dir Res Labs 1959-63, Others; Asst

Prof Wayne St Univ 1951-59; Others; cp/Dir Cache C of C; Rotary Intl; Pres United Way Cache Valley; r/Ch of Jesus Christ LDS; hon/Contbr Num Articles Profl Jours; Am Men Sci; Outstg Edrs Am; Men Achmt; W/W Am.

JOHNSON, RAY ARVIN oc/Executive; b/May 2, 1920; h/2227 Platwood Rd, Minnetonka, MN 55343; ba/Litchfield, MN; m/Kay Meredith Durbahn; c/Sherry Kay, Diane Rosalind, Laura Faye; p/Walter David and Rosalind Hesser Johnson; ed/Iowa St Univ; Univ Minn; Addit Studies: William & Mary Col; mil/USN 1942-45; pa/Johnson Bros Corp: Partner 1941-, VP 1959-67, CoFdr & Mem Bd Dirs 1959-, Sr VP 1968-72, Chm Bd 1973-, Others; Assoc'd Gen Contractors Am: Equipmt Expense Com 1974-, Jt Task Force 1969-78; Assoc'd Gen Contractors Minn: Jt Task Force 1971-, Hwy Dir 1973-74, VP 1974, Others; cp/Mason; 32° Shriner; Zuhrah Scottish Rite; CoFdr & Mem Minn Moles; Former Commr City Minnetonka; Others; r/Minnetonka Luth Ch: Mem.

JOHNSON, RITA B oc/Teacher; b/Jul 19, 1933; ba/One Allen Ctr, Suite 3200, Houston, TX 77002; m/Stuart R; p/William Blaustein, LA; Anna Kasten (dec); ed/AA 1953, BA, MA 1963, EdD 1966 UCLA; pa/Sensitivity Tnr; Instrl Technol; Dir Hlth Instn Exchange 1976-;

UNC: Prof Fam Med 1973-76, Med Edr 1971-73; Coor RELCV 1969-71; Conslt Profl Bus Groups; Author; Speaker; cp/US Del 1st Intl Cong Social Psychol; US Del Venezuela; US Del People's Repub China; hon/Phi Beta Kappa; Hons Doctoral Exam UCLA; Grad'd Highest Hons UCLA 1956; Pi Lambda Theta; Helen Matthewson Awd, Alumni Awd UCLA.

JOHNSON, ROBERT EUGENE oc/-Professor; b/Dec 19, 1926; h/Rt 6, Box 224-Al, Murray, KY 42071; ba/Murray; m/Shirley Jean Teach; p/LeRoy C and Margaret Garrity Johnson (dec); ed/BS, MA Ohio St Univ; ABD Ind St Univ; mil/USN; pa/Murray St Univ: Prof, Theatre Dir, Designer Univ Theatre, Advr, Theatre Conslt; Prodr & Dir Over 80 Theatrical Prodns; cp/Commun Theatre Conslt; USCG Aux; r/Christian; hon/Alumni Awd MSU; Sigma Chi; Alpha Psi Omega.

JOHNSON, ROBERT LELAND oc/-Attorney; b/May 1, 1933; h/9751 Melody Dr, Northglenn, CO 80221; ba/Denver, CO; m/Pamela Gay Stearns; c/Mary Morris (dec), Anthony Morris; p/Albert E and Wilma N Charlesworth; ed/JD 1958, BA 1962 Univ Denver; Addit Studies; pa/Pvt Pract; Admit'd Bar: St of Col, Fed Dist Ct (Col), 10th Circuit Ct Appeals, Inter-St Commerce Comm, Supr Ct; Lectr for Bar Assns; Others; Num Profl Pubs; ABA; Am Judic Soc; Col Trial Lwyrs Assn; Denver Bar Assn: Var Coms; Col Bar Assn: Var Coms; Adams Co Bar Assn; cp/Col Press Assn; Col Soc SAR; Col Yale Assn; Elks; Moose; Nat Hist Soc; Nat SAR; Others; hon/Cert Merit, Univ Denver; Commun Ldr Am; Denver Opportunity Cert Merit; Patriot Medal, Col Soc SAR; W/W: Am Law, W, Fin & Indust, Col; Other Biogl Listings.

JOHNSON, ROGER ALAN oc/Professor; h/22 Leighton Rd, Wellesley, MA 02181; ba/Wellesley; m/Carol; c/Nils, Tina, Peter; p/Herman Johnson, Venice, FL; Florence

Mattson Johnson (dec); ed/BA; BD; ThD; pa/Prof Rel Wellesley Col; Author Sev Books & Articles; r/Luth.

JOHNSON, ROMAN E oc/Artist; b/Sept 4, 1917; h/802 Rosemore Ave, Columbus, OH 43213; ba/Columbus; m/Iona; ed/Studied 5 Yrs New York Art Student's Leag; Addit Studies Paris; pa/Still-life & Portrait Painter; Former Art Instr ARC; Num Exhbns incl'g Kenneth Taylor Gallery (Nantucket, Mass), Art Assn (Newport, RI), Nat Acad Arts & Design (NYC), Others; Life Mem Art Student's Leag; Am Artists Profl Leag; hon/Num Awds; Work in Perm Collections: Huntington Bank Gallery, Columbus Art Museum, Isabell Ridgeway Home, Schumacher Gallery-Capital Univ; Work in Num Pvt Collections.

JOHNSON, RUFUS WINFIELD oc/-Attorney; b/May 1, 1911; h/Rt 2, Box 220A, Prairie Grove, AR 72753; ba/Same; m/-Vaunda L; p/Charles L Sr and Margaret Smith Johnson (dec); ed/BA; LLB; mil/USAR Ret'd Lt Col; AUS Active Ser WWII; pa/Gen Pract; Cert'd Spec Crim Law; Conslt on Appeals; cp/Var Civil Rights & Consumer Rights Groups; 32° Mason; r/Bapt: SS Tchr; hon/AUS: CIB, Bronze Star, Purple Heart, Spec Cit; Others.

JOHNSON, SALLIE KATHRYN oc/-Psychometrist; h/555 Gayle St, Mobile, AL 36604; c/Carlee Richard III; ed/BA Spelman Col 1952; MA Atlanta Univ 1963; Addit Studies: NY Univ, Howard Univ; Ala St Univ; pa/Mobile Co Public Schs: Psychometrist 1968-, Guidance Cnslr 1963-68, Social Studies Tchr 1953-62; Mobile Co Ed Assn; Ala Ed Assn; NEA; APGA; Ala Pers & Guide Assn; AERA; AAUP; Others; cp/YWCA; Nat Coun Negro Wom; NAACP; Others; r/Ch Good Shepard (Epis): Mem, Elected Vestry; hon/Delta Sigma Theta; W/W Am Wom; Intl W/W; Personalities of S; Others.

JOHNSON, SELINA TETZLAFF oc/-Museologist; b/Sept 7, 1906; h/24 Hawthorne Terrace, Leonia, NJ 07605; ba/Same; m/H Herbert (dec); c/Jaqueline J Horvath (Mrs Donald), Frank Wheeler; p/John Victor Tetzlaff (dec); Augusta Bertha Seidel (dec); ed/BA cum laude Hunter Col 1925; MSEd CCNY 1954; PhD Ctr Human Relats Studies, NYU 1962; pa/Instr PE Hunter Col 1925-26; Instr Biol CCNY 1926-32; Photog & Illustrator Med Textbooks Harvard Univ Press; Author; Fdr & Dir Yth Mus Leonia 1950-56; Fdg Dir: Eng Neighborhood Hist Soc 1959-, N Jersey Opera Theater 1969-, Others; Editor *Gtr Light on Nantucket* 1973-; Fdg Assoc Nat Hist Soc; Others; hon/Silver Orchid Awd, NJ St Fdn Wom's Clbs; Phi Beta Kappa; Med Hon Soc; Others.

JOHNSON, TERENCE ELWYN oc/-Minister; b/Dec 24, 1938; h/2602 Glenwood Rd, Royal Oak, MI 48073; ba/Royal Oak; m/Joan Davis; c/Kimberly G, Kenneth Armand; p/Elwyn M Johnson (dec); Gathary Ward, Orlando, FL; ed/BA Fla St 1960; MA Peabody Col 1964; Post-Grad Studies: David Lipscomb Col, Crozen Theol Sem, Others; pa/Sr Min 1st Coun Ch 1974-; Assoc Min Plymouth Congreg Ch Minneapolis, Minn 1969-74; Min Valley Forge Ch of Christ King of Prussia, Penn 1966-69; cp/Royal Oak Arts Coun; Yth Asst Com; r/Keynote Spkr; Former Mem Exec Com Nat Assn Congreg Chs; hon/Del Intl Congreg Conf; Summer Pastoral Exchange Congreg Ch Penge, Eng; Others.

JOHNSON, THOMAS oc/Minister; b/Nov 14, 1924; h/PO Box 172, Waller, TX 77484; ba/Same; m/Jimmie Lee; c/Thomas Fitzgerald; p/(dec); ed/Cert Prairie View A&M Col 1950; mil/AUS 1943-46; pa/Pastor Bailey Chapel, Prairie View & Zion Temple COGIC; Resident Chaplain Drew Hall, Prairie View Univ; Fdr & Pubr *The King's Messenger*; Mem & Former Pres Min Alliance; St Treas Tex SW Jurid; cp/St Pres Yth 11 Yrs; hon/W/W Rel; Asiatic-Pacific Theater Ribbon; Victory Medal; Am Theater Ribbon; Others.

JOHNSON, VANNETTE WILLIAM oc/Professor; b/May 27, 1930; h/Box 123 UAPB, Pine Bluff, AR 71601; ba/Pine Bluff; m/Delois D; c/Juliette, Alberta, Melanie, Leontyne; p/Charlie and Laura Johnson (dec); ed/BA; MEd; EdD; pa/AAHPER; VP Ark Assn Hlth, PE, Rec; cp/J of P Dist 7; Commr Ark Coun Human Resources; Del Dem St Conv; r/Meth; hon/Ldrs in Ed; W/W Am Polits; Men Achmt.

JOHNSON, WILLARD LYON oc/Professor; Writer; b/May 30, 1939; h/4149 6th Ave #25, San Diego, CA 92103; ba/La Jolla, CA; p/Willard Lyon Sr and Marjorie E Johnson, San Diego; p/BA Oberlin Col; MA, PhD Univ Wis; pa/Prof UCSD Extension; Author *The Buddhist Rel*, Others; Lectr; hon/Phi Beta Kappa; Woodrow Wilson Fellow.

JOHNSON, WILLIAM H E oc/Professor; b/Sept 10, 1907; h/One Forbes Terrace, Pittsburgh, PA 15217; ba/Pittsburgh; m/Annette Fox; p/William George and Clara Eckart Johnson (dec); ed/BA, MA UNC; PhD Colombia Univ; mil/US Mil Intell (Civilian Ser) 1943-46; pa/Prof Emeritus Ed Univ Pittsburgh; Pres Intl Ed Soc; Pres Hist Ed Soc; Edit Staff Sev Pubs on USSR; hon/ACLS Fellow; USA-USSR Cult Exchange; Sr Fulbright Lectr, Yugoslavia.

JOHNSTON, BILLY GRAY oc/Preacher; Farmer; Inventor; b/Nov 30, 1931; h/Rt 2, Box 467, Dobson, NC 27017; ba/Same; m/Georgia Ella; c/Brenda Sue, Billy Jr; p/George and Allie Johnston (dec); Johnston & Son Tire: Fdr, Pres, Gen Mgr; Pres VA-CA Rabbit Breeders; Inventor: Tire Slising Machine, Hole & Spacer Machine; Evangelist; r/Bapt; hon/Personalities of S; Merit Awd, Intl Inventors.

JOHNSTON, EDWARD ELLIOTT oc/Executive; b/Jan 3, 1918; h/65 W 5th Ave, #221, San Mateo, CA 94402; ba/San Francisco, CA; m/Clare M; c/Janice J Regine, Karen; p/Leonard Edward Johnston, Erma Elliot Johnston, Jacksonville, IL; ed/AB 1939, LLD 1970 Ill Col; mil/USAF 1942-48 Pvt to Capt, 1951-52 Capt to Maj; pa/Exec VP Pacific Area Travel Assn 1976-; VP Hawaiian Ins & Guaranty Ltd 1966; Other Past Positions; Adv Bd Travel Indust Mgmt Sch, Univ Hawaii; Adv Coun Golden Gate Univ Travel Sch; Inst Cert'd Travel Agents; ASTA; ASAE; Others; cp/Former Secy Hawaii; Former Chm Hawaii St Bd Ec Devel; Former High Commr, Trust Territory Pacific Isls; Dir & Former Pres Easter Seal Soc; Hon Life Mem Ala Moana Kiwanis Clb; Pacific Clb; Others; r/Prot (Congreg); hon/Phi Beta Kappa.

JOHNSTON, LILLIAN BEATRICE oc/Consultant; b/Aug 7, 1910; h/538 W Vernon Ave, Phoenix, AZ 85003; ba/Same; m/Charles L (dec); c/Charles L Jr; p/Michael and Elizabeth Birkbeck Spinner (dec); ed/BA;

MA; EdD; Addit Studies; pa/Ed Conslt; cp/Mem Leg Com; r/Epis; hon/Awd for Devotion to Handicapped; Rec'd Plaque Pres Eisenhower; Num Ed Awds.

JOHNSTON, WILBUR LEE JR oc/Professor; b/Mar 2, 1943; h/922 Rolling Hills Cove, Wilmington, NC 28403; ba/Wilmington; m/Catherine Hohman; c/Daniel Lee, Rebecca Catherine; p/Wilbur Lee Sr and Ruth Bailey Johnston, Belhaven. NC; ed/BA

UNC-CH 1961; MA 1971, PhD 1973 UM-CP; pa/Prof Polit Sci; Am Polit Sci Assn; So Polit Sci Assn; NC Polit Sci Assn; cp/Rotary; Masons; Heart Fund City Chm; Dem Party; r/1st Christian Ch; hon/Phi Eta Sigma; Pi Sigma Alpha; Gamma Beta Phi.

JOHNSTON, WILLIAM JAMES oc/Business Owner; b/Apr 18, 1942; h/2126 Poleline Rd, Pocatello, ID 83201; ba/Pocatello; m/Karen Yvonne Sundrud; c/Kristine, Michael, Russell, Sheri, Suzanne, Eric, Greg; p/Peter Barbour Johnston Jr, Twin Falls, ID; Ruth E Brown Johnston; ed/BS Univ Idaho; MRE Brigham Young Univ; DRE ISU; pa/-Owner Remy-Johnston Real Estate Co Inc; Ed Com Bd Realtors; cp/Chm Bannock Co Repub Ctl Com; r/Ch of Jesus Christ LDS; hon/-Outstg Yg Men Am.

JONES, ALICE HANSON oc/Professor; Economist; b/Nov 7, 1904; h/404 Yorkshire Pl, Webster Groves, MO 63110; ba/St Louis, MO; m/Homer; c/Robert Hanson, Richard John, Douglas Coulthurst; p/Olof and Agatha M Tiegel Hanson (dec); ed/AB, MA Univ

Wash; PhD Univ Chgo; pa/Economist, US Labor Stats & Exec Ofc Pres 1934-48; Nat Accounts Review Com 1957; US Dept Agri 1958-61; Lectr Wash Univ (St Louis) 1963-77; Prof Emeritus Ec 1977-; Former VP Ec Hist Assn; Author *Am Colonial Wealth: Documents & Methods*, 1977; r/Congreg; hon/Phi Beta Kappa.

JONES, AVALENE CHUMBLEY oc/Analyst; b/Apr 4, 1934; h/32 Denton Blvd, Apt 15, Fort Walton Beach, FL 32548; ba/Columbus AFB, MS; m/James Therix; c/Steven W, Christi B, Alan B; p/Lewis W Chumbley (dec); Martha Catherine Roy Chumbley, Rantoul, IL; pa/Mgmt Analyst 14th Flying Tng Wing; Past Mem St Adv Bd Civil Air Patrol; cp/Mem & Ofcr Tupelo Chapt OES; Mem & Ofcr Tenn-Tom Toastmistress Clb; Past Pres & Mem Altrusa Clb; Adv Bd N Miss Kidney Disease Ctr; r/Ch of Christ; hon/DAR; Citizenship 1952; Hon EEO Awd; Dist'd Fed Wom's Awd USAF; Others.

JONES, BEULAH AGNES oc/Professor; Professional Lyric Soprano; Piano Accompanist; b/Apr 21, 1933; h/1601 New York Ave, Austin, TX 78702; ba/Austin; p/Leon Bonner (dec); Beulah Mabery B Thompson, Austin; ed/BA Prairie View A&M Univ; MA Tex So Univ; Doct Cand Univ Houston; pa/Huston-Tillotson Col: Chm FA Dept; Voice & Mus Ed Instr; Instr Public Schs 15 Yrs; Conslt Ch & Commun Choirs; cp/Vol Tutor for Deprived Chd; Vol Musician Ch Convs & Civic Confs; r/Ebenezer Bapt Ch (Austin): Choir Mem, Soloist; Song Ldr; Conslt; hon/Hon Vocal Recitals; E Austin Musicians Awd; F'ship Univ Houston; Others.

JONES, BRIAN KEITH oc/Minister; b/Apr 21, 1943; h/Rt 1, Box 177, Gatlinburg, TN 37738; ba/Gatlinburg; p/Cleo Herbert Jones (dec); Marion Schweitzer, Hobart, IN; ed/BS Mo St Univ 1965; MDiv Wartburg Theol Sem 1970; pa/Minister LCA; Reg Del Assn Chs; Synodical Social Min Bd; Supvr & Treas Christian Min Nat Parks; Resort Min Chaplain; cp/Nat Coun Commun Sers Foreign Visitors; Kiwanis; C of C; Knoxville Area Intl Coun; Am Field Ser; r/LCA; hon/Person-alities Am; Personalities of S; Commun Ldrs &

Noteworthy Ams; W/W Rel; Others.

JONES, CALVIN PAUL oc/Historian; b/Jun 13, 1934; h/RFD 2, Waddy, KY 40076; ba/Frankfort, KY; m/Stella Mae Wigginton; c/James Edwin, Leticia Gay, Melissa Ann; p/Russell E Jones (dec); Mary Agnes Livingston Jones, Frankfort; ed/BA 1955, PhD 1966 Univ Ky; MA En Ky Univ 1959; pa/Sr Histn & Res Analyst Ky Heritage Com; Prof Hist Pikeville Col 1959-62, 1964-68, 1970-75; Salem Col (W Va): Assoc Dean 2968-69, Dean 1969-70; cp/Mem Dem Party; Var Other Assns; r/Presb; hon/Haggin F'ship, Univ Ky; NDEA F'ship, Univ Neb.

JONES, CLARENCE KLOTZ oc/Investor; b/Sept 24, 1909; h/1775 Circle Dr, Reno, NV 89509; ba/Reno; m/Martha; c/Ann Mason, Charlotte J Markewitz; p/Lionel E and Kate Klotz Jones (dec); ed/BS Univ Nev-R 1931;

pa/Grand Master Gen, Convent Gen Knights York Cross; IEEE; Hon Inst Newspaper Controllers & Fin Ofcrs; cp/Washoe Co Citizens Adv Trans Com; Life Mem Repub Nat Com; r/Prot; hon/Dist'd Nevadan, Univ Nev-R.

JONES, DALE PASCHAL oc/Vice President; b/Oct 19, 1936; h/2721 Stagestand Rd, Duncan, OK 73533; ba/Duncan; m/Anita Ruth; c/Lee Anna, Leisa Raye; p/Ray Elgin Jones (dec); Alma Lee Jones, Mena, AR; ed/BS Ark Univ; mil/USAF 1/Lt; pa/Halliburton Sers: VP Fin, Treas; Am Inst CPAs; Adv Com

Indust & Govt; Inter Tax Subcom (Fed Tax Div); AICPA Gov'g Coun; Okla Soc CPA; Fin Exec Inst; Am Petro Inst; Intl Assn Drilling Contractors: Tax & Acctg Coms; AMA; Others; cp/Dir & Past Pres C of C; Duncan Reg Hosp: Chm Bd, Pres; Dir YMCA; Dir Rotary Intl; BPOE; Dir Okla Polit Action Com; Num Others; r/1st Bapt Ch, Duncan: Deacon; hon/Man of Yr, C of C.

JONES, DONALD COLLINS oc/Student; b/Sept 6, 1938; h/59 Springside Rd, Hendersonville, NC 28739; ba/Knoxville, TN; m/Patsy Farmer; c/William Kyle, Bradley Clifford; p/James Clifford Jones (dec); Catherine Baxter, Temple, GA; ed/AB Wofford (SC) 1961; MS Univ Tenn 1967; mil/AUS 1961-63; USAR 1976 Ret'd Maj; pa/Doct Cand Univ Tenn-K; r/Meth; cp/Lions Clb; hon/Commend Medal, AUS; Outstg Yg Man Am.

JONES, ELISE J oc/Physician; b/Jun 2, 1922; h/57 N Somerville, Memphis, TN 38104; ba/Same; p/Elmer H Jones (dec); Mary Ellen McKinnon Jones, Coldwater, MS;

ed/BA; BS; MD; pa/Pathol; Gen Pract 1951; r/Epis.

JONES, FRANK WARREN oc/Manager; b/Dec 4, 1922; h/5335 Nottingham Dr N, Saginaw, MI 48603; m/Martha A; c/Terry Lee, Dennis Warren, Shirley Kaye, Steven Allen, Connie Linn, Kenneth Stanley, Karl Curtis, (Stepchd); Gerald E, Michael A, Paula Elaine; p/Jason Wilson and Berta D Filson Jones (dec); ed/BS Kansas St Univ 1943; MS US Naval Postgrad Sch 1963; mil/USN 1944-46, 1951-70; pa/Township Mgr; Reg'd Profl Engr: Kan, Col; Chm Bd & Past Pres Tri-Cities Coun, Navy Leag US; Bd Dirs Branch 244 Fleet Resv Assn; Ret'd Ofcrs Assn; NCECOA; Nat Adv Bd, Am Security Coun; cp/Bd Dirs Saginaw Valley Rotary Clb; Orgr & VChm Can-Amera Games Inc; Mem & Past Chm Saginaw Co Policy Com; VFW; BSA; Others; r/Bapt; hon/Outstg Citizens Awd, VFW; USAF Commend Medal; USNR Medal; WWII Victory Medal; Expert Pistolman Medal; Nat Defense Medal; Others.

JONES, HATTIE ELIZABETH RUSSELL oc/Professor; b/Feb 18, 1932; h/605 Union St, Murfreesboro, NC 27855; ba/Murfreesboro; m/Robert Noble; p/Ervin Smith Russell, Bluefield, VA; Eula Burns Puckett Russell (dec); ed/BS Concord Col 1957; MEd VPI & St Univ 1964; pa/Prof Chowan Col; NC Bus Ed Assn; Delta Pi Epsilon; cp/OES; r/Bapt; hon/W/W Am Wom; Personalities of S; World W/W Wom; World W/W Wom Ed.

JONES, HELEN HINCKLEY oc/Writer; Teacher; b/Apr 12, 1903; h/1191 E Mendocino, Altadena, CA 91001; ba/Cincinnati, OH; m/Ivan Charles; c/Jacqueline Ballard, Samellyn Wood; p/Samuel E and Ida Lenore Hinckley; ed/BS summa cum laude, Brigham Young Univ; Addit Studies; pa/Tchr Writer's Digest Sch;

Author Num Books incl'g *The Mountains Are Mine, A Wall & Three Willows*; Pub'd Num Articles; Dir Pasadena Writers' Conf; Instr Sierra Writers' Camp; Author's Guild Inc; Cal Writers' Guild; PEN Intl; Wn Hist Assn; Others; r/Ch of Jesus Christ LDS; hon/Dist'd Ser Alumni Awd, Brigham Young Univ; Dist'd Ser Cert, Pasadena City Col; Dist'd Contbn Field Chd's Lit, So Cal Coun on Lit for Chd & Yg People; Hon Mem LA Wom's Press Clb; Hon Mem Pasadena Writers' Clb.

JONES, HENRY PHILIP oc/Automobile Dealer; b/May 4, 1899; h/205 Valley Dr, Americus, GA 31709; m/Louise McKenzie; c/Henry Philip, Camille (dec), William McKenzie (dec); p/Henry Philip and Catherine Whitehead Jones (dec); mil/SATC Ser, Mercer Univ; pa/Auto Dealer GM 43 Yrs; Past Pres

Ga Auto Dealers Assn; cp/Helped Organize Americus & Sumter Co Devel Corp; Past Bd Chm Sumter Co Commrs; Rep Sumter Co Commrs to Local Hosp Authority; Asst'd Organizing Local BSA; Former City Coun Mem; Past Pres Americus & Sumter C of C; Others; r/United Meth Ch: Mem, Steward, Former Trustee.

JONES, JAMES GRADY oc/Physician; b/Dec 19, 1933; h/3208 Ellsworth Dr, Greenville, NC 27834; ba/Greenville; c/James G Jr, Robert Glenn; p/A B and Nora Revels Jones; ed/AA Mars Hill Col 1953; BS Wake Forest Univ 1959; MD Bowman-Gray Sch Med 1959; Addit Studies; mil/USN 1960-62 1/Lt, Med Ofcr; pa/Fam Pract 1975-; East Carolina Univ Sch Med: Chm Dept Fam Pract 1976-, Dir Fam Pract Residency Prog (Pitt Meml Hosp) 1975-, Prof Fam Med 1975-, Assoc Clin Prof Fam Med 1972-75, Others; Pitt Meml Hosp: Active Staff, Chief Ser Dept Fam Pract, Dir Med Ed 1975-77; Other Past Positions; NC St Med Soc; NC Acad Fam Phys; AAFP; Pitt Co Med Soc; Onslow Co Med Soc; AMA; Other Assns; Author Articles Profl Jours; Lectr; cp/Past Pres Onslow Co Heart Assn; Past Pres Onslow Co Cerebral Palsy Fund; Jacksonville Kiwanis Clb; Past Div Chm United Fund (G'ville); Others; r/Oakmont Bapt Ch, G'ville: Mem; hon/W/W S&SW.

JONES, JAMES ROBERT oc/Professor; b/Dec 16, 1934; h/Private Rd, Rt 2, Mendham, NJ 07954; ba/Piscataway, NJ; m/Carol Ann; c/Michael, Francis, Leslie, Laurie Ann, Christopher; p/Harold E Jones, San Francisco, CA; Elenor Jones (dec); ed/BS Manhattan Col 1956; MD SUNY (Brooklyn) 1960; mil/AUS 1964-68 Maj Med Corps; pa/Prof & Chm Dept Ob-Gyn, Rutgers Med Sch; SUNY; Lectr 1977-, Prof 1977, Assoc Prof 1968-76; Conslt Num Hosps; Endocrine Soc; Am Col Ob-Gyn; Am Fertility Soc; NY Acad Sci; AAAS; Others; Num Pubs Profl Jours; r/Rom Cath; hon/Res Fellow, Univ Cal-SF; Rec'd Num Grants; William Hammond Awd, NY St Jour Med; Cert Am Bd Ob-Gyn; Hon Fellow Bklyn Gyn Soc; Alpha Omega Alpha.

JONES, JARL HAMILTON oc/Executive; b/Jan 9, 1939; h/4818 Ferncreek Ct, Arlington, TX 76017; ba/Arlington; m/Katherine Soles; c/Lance Stewart, Brett Hamilton, Stacey Elizabeth; p/Henry Stewart amd Sara Roddis Jones (dec); ed/BBA Univ Wis 1961; JD Univ Denver 1964; pa/PMC Corp: Pres, Commodity Brokerage Exec; cp/Past Pres Local Toastmaster's Clb; Repub Party; r/Epis; hon/W/W S&SW.

JONES, KATHLEEN ROBERTS oc/Teacher; b/Oct 17, 1927; h/Palmer, TN; ba/Laager, TN; c/John Wesley Jr; p/Henry A and Oda Roberts; ed/BS; MEd; pa/Tchr Swiss Meml Sch; NEA; TEA; TAPACE; GCEA; cp/OES; PTA; r/Prot; hon/Personalities of S; Intl Platform; Outstg Elem Tchrs Am; W/W Poetry.

JONES, KELSEY A oc/Professor; b/Jul 15, 1933; h/5427 Kansas Ave, NW, Washington, DC 20011; ba/Wash; m/Virginia Bethel Ford; c/Kelsey Jr, Cheryl J Campbell (Mrs Elvin), Eric Andre, Claude Anthony; ed/BA summa cum laude Miss Indust Col 1955; MDiv Garrett Theol Sem 1959; DDiv Miss Indust Col 1969; Addit Studies; pa/UDC: Assoc Prof Dept Crim Just, Chm Dept Social/Behavioral Scis 1977-78, Assoc Prof Social Scis 1972-77, Chm Sociol/Anthro Sub-Com; Inter-Met; Dir Baccalaureate Prog 1973-77, Staff Advr MDiv Cands; Visiting Lectr Black Hist, Fed City Col 1973-75; Min Celebration & Human Resources, Israel Metro & Christian Meth Epis Chs; Chm Bd Probation & Parole, St of Kansas 1965-70; Other Past Positions; Lectr; Pub'd Num Articles & Papers Profl Jours; Dir Higher Ed, Higher Achmt Assn; Past Mem Ed Com, Interfaith Metro Theol Ed Inc; Others; cp/CoOrgr & Past Pres 4CL (Omaha); Past Pres Bd Dirs Phyllis Wheatley Chd's Home; Former Conslt Summer Aide Prog, Naval Ordinance Lab; Alternate Nat Com-man Dem Party; Others; r/Christian Meth Epis Ch; hon/Alpha Phi Alpha; Commun Ldrs Am; Men Achmt; W/W: Black Am, Rel; Others.

JONES, KENNETH MAXWELL oc/-Administrator; b/Jan 2, 1922; h/Rosemont Green, 4152 Player Cir, Orlando, FL 32804; ba/Orlando; m/Margaret L; c/Kenneth L, Michael A, Heath Annette, Frederick W; p/Charles M Jones (dec); Thelma E Jones, Clearwater, FL; ed/BBA Marshall Col 1943; MA Stetson Univ 1960; Addit Studies; mil/USN 1942-43; pa/Dir Instrnl Mats Sers, Sch Bd Orange Co 1966-; Glenridge Jr HS

(Winter Park, Fla): Former Tchr, Dir Guide, Dean Boys; Pres Fla Assn Supvrs Media; Bd Dirs Fla Assn Instrnl Supvrs & Admrs; Am Lib Assn; Assn Ed Communs & Technol; Others; cp/Conslt Commun Resource Vol Prog; Winter Park JCs; Leg Com Improved Fund'g St Adopted Instrnl Mats; Former BSA Ldr; Others; r/Bapt: Deacon, Former SS Tchr, Former SS Supt; hon/Phi Delta Kappa; Author *War With The Seminoles*, 1975; Nat Inst Guid & Cnslg F'ship, Univ Ala; DIB; Intl W/W Intellectuals; Others.

JONES, KENNETH W oc/Director; b/May 12, 1941; h/4633 Plover Ln, Abilene, TX 79606; ba/Abilene; m/Glenda Lee; c/Kristin Gail, Katherine Lee; p/Kenneth and Anna May Jones (dec); ed/BA, MA Univ So Cal; PhD Univ Cal; MLS Univ Ala; pa/Dir Univ Libs, Hardin-Simmons Univ; Am Hist Assn; Org Am Histns; Tex Lib Assn; cp/Rotary Clb; r/Bapt; hon/Recipient Sev S'ships, Grants.

JONES, LETHA PARRIS oc/Retired Secretary; b/Jul 3, 1910; h/Rt 5, Box 578, Poplarville, MS 39470; m/Julian L (dec); p/T H and Martha H Parris (dec); ed/Jr Col Bus; pa/Ret'd 1977; Secy Commr James D Faughn (Hattiesburg) 1973-77; Exec Secy Mayor Hattiesburg 1969-73; Exec Secy SEn Am Life Ins Co 1954-68; Other Past Positions; Miss Fdn Bus & Profl Wom's Clbs: St & Local Ofcs; cp/Easter Seals; Salvation Army Adv Bd; Bd Dirs, Secy; Commun Concerts Assn Bd; Life Mem Hattiesburg Hist Soc; Others; r/Bapt: Clerk, Tchr, Pres WMU; hon/Commun Ldrs & Noteworthy Ams; Personalities of S; Intl Biogs; Royal Blue Book; W/W Am Wom.

JONES, LETHONEE ANGELA oc/-Professor; b/Jun 10, 1938; h/2226 So Westnedge Ave, Kalamazoo, MI 49008; ba/Kalamazoo; m/Leander Corbin; c/Angela Lynne, Leander Corbin Jr; p/Elbert Lewis Hendricks II (dec); Alma Bernice Jackson Hendricks Andrews, Cleveland, OH; ed/AB Wn Col Wom 1960; MSW Univ Ill 1969; PhD Union Grad Sch 1977; pa/Prof Social Work, Wn Mich Univ; Assn Black Social Workers; Coun Social Work Ed; Peace Corps Vol 1964-66; cp/Chgo Coun Foreign Relats; Glowing Embers Coun GSA; r/Prot; hon/Jessie Noyes Smith Fdn Negro Students; Walter Jackson Meml Fund, Wn Col Wom.

JONES, LILLIAN HOGAN oc/Disabled American Veteran; b/Mar 15, 1916; h/1918 13th St NW, Apt 5, Washington, DC 20009; ba/Same; c/James Thomas; p/John Thomas and Fannie Love Hogan (dec); ed/LLB; mil/Adjutant; pa/DAV Aux; VFW; Other Mil Assns; cp/Life Mem Acad Polit Sci; Life Mem Nat Coun Sr Citizens Inc; Model Cities Sr Ctr; Railway & Locomotive Hist Soc; RR Station Hist Soc; Columbia Hghts Commun Ownership Proj; r/Bapt; hon/Life Awd DAV; Notable Ams, Others.

JONES, LINDA LEE oc/Real Estate

Broker; b/Nov 9, 1947; h/1909 Thunderdino, Edmond, OK 73034; ba/Edmond; m/Gerald T; c/Robert R, Neil T; p/Elmer and Clara Neil; ed/BA; pa/Wom's Coun Realtors; Bd Realtors; r/Luth; hon/Listed Top Dollar Vol Read Estate Sales Nation, Realty World.

JONES, LOIS MONAHON oc/Professor; b/Apr 28, 1933; h/110 Cheek Rd, Nashville, TN 37205; ba/N'ville; m/Robert H; p/Harry Monahon (dec); Calma Case Monahon, Germantown, KY; ed/BA magna cum laude Georgetown Col; MA George Peabody Col Tchrs; Addit Studies; pa/Belmont Col: Asst Prof Ed 1973-, Instr 1970-73; George Peabody Col: Sub-Tchr Demo Sch 1966-70, Supvr 3rd Grade Demo Sch 1963-66; Other Positions; Mid Tenn Ed Assn; Life Mem NEA; Assn Tchr Edrs; Assn Supvn & Curric Devel; cp/Adelicia Acklen Wom's Clb: 1st VP, Pres; Tenn Botanical Gardens & Art Ctr; So Highland Handicraft Guild; r/1st Bapt Ch (N'ville): Mem, Dir 3rd Grade SS Dept, SS Coun; Eng Tutor Intl Students; Com Renovation of Ed Facilities; hon/Sigma Alpha Iota; Kappa Delta Pi; Delta Kappa Gamma Soc; W/W Among Students Am Univs & Cols; Others.

JONES, LOUIS WORTH oc/Retired; b/Jan 8, 1908; h/511 Verano Ct, San Mateo, CA 94402; m/Pauline Ernest; c/David Worth, Roger Louis, Ethan Ernest, Faye J Youngs, Arthur Carlyle; p/Ed C Jones (dec); Vida Jones Schaeffer; ed/Attended Wash Univ (St Louis); pa/Ret'd Mgmt Analyst USN Dept (San Francisco); Former Analyst Var Fed Govt Agys; Journalist; Social Critic; Nat Assn Intergroup Relats Ofcls; Wn Govtl Res Assn; ASPA; Editor *Lou Jones Newslttr* 1959-70; Fdr & Exec Dir Intergroup Relats Assn N Cal; cp/Mid-Peninsula Coun Civic Unity; Human Relats Clearinghouse (SF); r/Unit: Mem; hon/Mem Yr Awd, Unit Ch; Nat Hon Soc; W/W W; Mem Achmt; Commun Ldrs & Noteworthy Ams.

JONES, MARCUS EARL oc/Professor; b/Jan 7, 1943; h/1505 W Alabama St, Tallahassee, FL 32304; ba/Atlanta, GA; m/Diann; c/Anthony, Omar, Taisha, Malik, Samira, Malaika; p/George Leslie and Bernetta Jones, Decatur, IL; ed/BA 1965, PhD 1968 So Ill Univ; MA Chgo St Univ 1969;

pa/Asst Prof Geog Morris Brown Col; Assn Am Geog; African Studies Assn; Fla Soc Geog; cp/NAACP; SCLC; Urban Leag; Del 6th Pan Africa Cong; r/Non-Sectarian; hon/Rockefeller S'ship; Spec Doct F'ship.

JONES, MELVIN OWEN oc/Consultant; b/Oct 28, 1927; h/278 Evelyn Dr, Pleasant Hill, CA 94523; ba/Schaumburg, IL; m/Wanda Jean; c/Melvin Michael, Aletha

Jean, Wayne Mark, Brian Timothy, Martha Kay, Esther Nancy; p/Solen Kodie Jones (dec); Charlotte Lanora Jones, Martinez, CA; ed/Dipl Wn Bapt Bible Col; NW Bapt Sem; Addit Studies; mil/US Maritime Ser; AUS Trans Corps; pa/Wn & SWn SS Conslt; Conducted Christian Confs Over 150 Chs W & SW; Org'd Chs: Martinez, Antioch, Pleasant Hill; r/Bapt; hon/SS Conslt, Gen Assn Regular Bapt Chs.

JONES, MICHAEL A oc/Pastor; Assistant; ba/Rm 208, 165 Ctl Ave SW, Atlanta, GA 30303; ed/BA Ga St Univ 1965; BDiv Turner Theol Sem 1968; PhEd Am Univ (Wash, DC) 1970; MA Atlanta Univ 1973; Addit Studies; pa/Pastor Fedville Parish AME Ch; Spec Asst to Commr H D Dodson Rel Sers & Resources Com Fulton Co 1977-; Dir Boys' Affairs, Morris Brown Col 1970-76; Elem Tchr Atlanta Public Schs 1970-76; Nat Coun Deans & Registrars; GAE; cp/Bd Mem United Yth Adult Conf; SCLC; NAACP; YMCA; Christian Coun Atlanta; Ga Coun Chs; 1980 Clb Re-Elect Pres; Others; r/Meth.

JONES, MILDRED JOSEPHINE oc/Real Estate Broker; b/Jan 29, 1927; h/3024 Biltmore Ave, Montgomery, AL 36109; ba/Montgomery; p/Howard McFadden Jones (dec); Gladys Eulalah Carr, Montgomery; ed/Attended Howard Col; pa/NAR; Farm & Land Inst; Montgomery Bd Realtors; cp/Point Aquarius Country Clb; Nat Adv Bd Am Christian Col; r/Trinity Presb Ch (Montgomery): Mem; hon/Rec'd Num Sales Awds; Appointed Pres' Adv Com, Field Enterprises Ed Corp.

JONES, MYRTIS IDELLE oc/Retired; b/May 16, 1908; h/5608 Geyer Springs Rd; Little Rock, AR 72209; m/(dec); c/Jack Barham, Charles Ray, Mary Ann Scheie; William Robert, Johnathan Edward, Ethel Rachel Hubka, Paul David; p/Andrew Bryce and Ethel Hardwick Barham (dec); ed/BS;

MLS; pa/Former Libn: HS, Ark Sch Blind; Originator Orgnl Methods Libs Ser'g Blind Chd; CoAuthor *COMSTAC Standards for Sch Libs*; Author *AEVH Lib Cataloging Manual*; cp/Activs Dir Pulaski Co Coun on Aging; Ret'd Mem Sr Vol Prog; r/Prot; hon/Cit Outstg Ser, AAIB; Outstg Achmt Awd, COMSTAC; John Cotton Dana Lib Publicity Awd.

JONES, MYRTLE JONES oc/Teacher; b/Aug 22, 1913; m/R M (dec) c/3; p/George H and Mary E Jones; ed/BA Clark Col 1937; MA NYU 1961; pa/Asst Prof Eng, Floyd Jr Col (Rome, Ga); Nat Coun Tchrs of Eng; Ga Assn Edrs; NEA; Co-author, *England in Lit* (1973);

cp/Ga Coun on Human Relats; Nat Dem Com for Civil Rights; NAACP; Bd Dirs, Rome Area Coun for Arts; r/Mt Olive Bapt Ch; hon/Alpha Kappa Alpha; Rec'd John Hay F'ship; Biogl Listings; Others.

JONES, NELSON oc/Consultant; b/May 21, 1947; h/333 E Ontario, Chicago, IL 60611; ba/Niles, IL; c/Selene Tess, Nelson Jr, Manuel; p/George and Rosa Jones (dec); ed/BSBA; MBA; mil/ROTC; pa/Computer Conslt; Am Mktg Assn; Assn MBA Exec; Nat Spec Mech Assn; Writer WTTW-TV (Chgo); r/Non-Denom; hon/Mgmt Fellow; Boost Scholar.

JONES, PATRICIA oc/Senior Analyst; b/Mar 5, 1939; h/5907 Old Richmond Ave, Richmond, VA 23226; ba/Richmond; p/Mathew P and Sara C Jones, Brentwood, TN; ed/BS 1960, MA 1971 George Peabody Col Tchrs; Hon EdD 1974, Cand DBA US Univ Am; mil/USN 1959-66; USNR 1966-72; pa/Sr Analyst Sys Engrg Computer Co 1977-; Computer Sys Devel Supvr, Va St Police 1974-77; W VA Wesleyan Col: Asst Prof Math, Asst Coor Computer Based Mgmt 1974, Asst Dean Students & Dir Housing 1972-73; Other Past Positions; AAUP; AAUW; IPA; Am Soc Dist'd Citizens; cp/ARC Vol; r/So Bapt; hon/W/W: Am Wom, S&SW; Book Hon; Personalities of S; Notable Ams Bicent Era; Others.

JONES, RALPH E oc/Manager; b/May 15, 1927; h/361 Washington St, Norwood, MA 02062; ba/Westwood, MA; m/Norma Hazen; c/Nancy J Butler (Mrs William P); p/Ralph E and Maggie B Jones (dec); ed/AB cum laude 1950, MA 1951 Bucknell Univ; LLD Phil Col Osteopath Med 1968; mil/Penn NG 1969 Brigadier Gen; pa/Mgr Manpower Planning & Devel, Wm Underwood Co; Past Pres Penn Assn 2 Yr Cols; Am Soc Tng & Devel; r/Epis; hon/Phi Beta Kappa; Freedoms Fdn Medal.

JONES, RUBY AILEEN HIDAY oc/Newspaper Columnist; Author; Free-Lance Writer; b/Oct 29, 1908; h/Maplesteon Farm, RR 1, Box 53, Daleville, IN 47334; ba/Same; m/Harry Paul; c/James Dennis, David Meredith, Jon Stuart; p/James W and Ora Claude James Hiday (dec); ed/BA Earlham Col; pa/Author 19 Yrs *As I See It*; Wrote 18

Yrs Alexandria (Ind) *Times Tribune*; Wrote Var Travelogues Middletown (Ind) News; Pub'd *The Searching Wind*, 1964; Contb'd Num Articles Profl Jours, Mags, Rel Pubs; Former HS Tchr; cp/Repub Party; r/United Meth; hon/Poetry Awd, Poets Ind; Hoosier St Press Assn Awd; Rep'd Nat Poet Anthol; Foremost Wom Communs; Dist'd Citizens; Wom Achmt; W/W World Wom; Others.

JONES, SONDRA MICHELLE oc/Director; b/Sept 7, 1948; h/18 Hannum Dr, Apt 1A, Ardmore, PA 19003; ba/Chester, PA; p/Mary A Edwards, Baltimore, MD; ed/BA Morgan St; Cand Masters Temple Univ; pa/Dir 5th St Day Care Ctr; Delaware Valley Assn Ed Yg Chd; Nat Assn Ed Yg Chd; r/Epis; hon/S'ship Harvard Univ.

JONES, SUZANNE TAFFY oc/Writer; b/Sept 27, 1922; h/4852 Malibu Dr, Bloomfield Hills, MI 48013; m/Donald S;

c/Ronald, Laurie; p/Frank William Taft, Binghamton, NY; Villo Latcher Taft, Utica, NY; pa/Writer, Prodr, Dir Whistle-Stop Chd's Theatre Inc 1976-; Mem St Dunstan's Theatre; Dir Birmingham Chd's Theatre; Drama Tchr; Writer & Commentator *Show Window*, WNBF-TV; Dir Aquacades & Ballets Sidney Rec Ctr 1959-69; Other Former Positions; Contbr Num Jours & Mags; Editor *Book Wom*, Wom's Nat Book Assn; NAP; Others; cp/Bd Dirs Camp Brace Yth Ctr & Roberson Art Ctr; Others; r/Presb: Deacon, Secy.

JONES, THOMAS EVAN oc/Professor; Writer; Consultant; b/Apr 3, 1937; h/61 Horatio St, Apt 1F, New York, NY 10014; ba/NYC; p/Ernest E and Martha Hiemke Jones, San Jose, CA; ed/BA; MA (Theol); MA (Phil) Harvard Univ; PhD John Hopkins Univ; DSSc New Sch Social Res; mil/ROTC;

pa/Prof: New Sch Social Res, Polytechnic Inst NY; Conslt Indust Mgmt Inst (Teheran, Iran); Lectr; Presented Num Papers Profl Orgs; Currently Writing Book *Options For The Future*; Adv Bd NYC Chapt World Future Soc; hon/F'ships: Aspen Inst, Intl Inst Applied Sys Analysis; Rec'd Grant Oxford Univ; Finalist Essay Contest, Alternatives to Growth.

JONES, VERNON oc/Educator; b/Oct 13, 1897; h/267 Salisbury St, Worcester, MA 01609; ba/Worcester; m/Harriet C Marble (dec); c/Patty J Lovell, Nancy Clement Pearson; p/Frank A Jones (dec); Pattie A McLemore (dec); ed/BA, MA Univ Va 1920; MA 1924, PhD 1926 Columbia Univ; pa/Clark Univ: Orgr & Chm Dept Ed 1949-68, Prof & Chm Dept Psychol & Ed 1937-49, Assoc Prof Ed Psychol 1926-37, Ret'd 1968; Assoc Prof Ed Columbia Univ 1924-26; Conslt Pers Selection Norton Co 1968-77; Other Past Positions; Pub'd Sev Books, Num Articles; cp/Planning Com Nat Conf Citizenship; Others; r/Worcester 1st Bapt Ch: Mem, Bd Deacons, Ecumenical Com; hon/Phi Beta Kappa (1st Pres Clark Univ); Presented Key City Worcester; Notable Ams.

JONES, VIOLA oc/Businesswoman; b/Nov 11, 1911; h/Box 57, Leggett, TX; ba/Seven Oaks, TX; c/George Kenneth; p/George Washington and Betty Adeline Hopper; pa/Owner J & C Liquor Store, Shopping Ctrs, 6 Subdivisions (Apts), Real Estate Ofc, Motel, Restaurant, Beauty Shop, Cleaning Shop, Laundry Ser, Others; BPW Clb; cp/Mayor & Mun Judge, Seven Oaks; r/Meth; hon/Finalist, Torch Awd, BPW (Winner Dist 14).

JONES, W ALLAN JR oc/Executive; b/Dec 31, 1952; h/150 2nd St NW, Cleveland, TN 37311; ba/Cleveland; c/Courtney Elaine;

p/W A Sr and Virginia S Jones, Cleveland; pa/Pres Credit Bur, Credit Corp, Tenn Atl Corp; Dir ACB Tenn; cp/Repub Party; r/Meth; hon/St Ldrship Awd, ACB Tenn.

JONES, WALTER ALFRED oc/Retired; b/May 1, 1902; h/1801 16th St NW, #412, Washington, DC 20009; ba/Same; m/Pauline J; c/Walter A (dec), Arnold T, Reeves C (dec); Robert L, Lorenzo T; p/Walter Augusta and Mary Jane Green Jones (dec); mil/Sel Ser Comm, Air Raid Warden, Mil Police WWII; pa/Var Fed Ser Orgs & Activs; cp/DC Commr on Aging; r/Cath; hon/Papal Awd; Medallion Cir; Nat Cert Apprec; Archbishop's Medal; Cits from 3 US Pres & Mayor DC.

JONES, WALTER BEAMON oc/Congressman; b/Aug 19, 1913; h/PO Drawer 90, Farmville, NC 27828; ba/Washington, DC; m/Dot L; c/Dotdee Moye, Walter B Jr; p/George and Fannie Jones (dec); ed/BA NC St Univ; pa/Mem US Ho of Reps; cp/Lions Clb; Rotary; Masons; r/Bapt.

JONES, WORTH ROOSEVELT oc/- Professor; b/Mar 1, 1923; h/6896 Greenfield Dr, Cincinnati, OH 45224; ba/Cinc; m/Franca Luisa; c/William Paul; p/Arthur Glenn Jones (dec); Lettie E Jones, Hickory, NC; ed/BA; MA; EdD; mil/AUS 1943-46; Civilian Employee War Dept 1946-47; pa/Prof Cnslr Ed, Univ Cinc; Lic'd Psychol (Ohio); Mem Num Profl Assns; r/Prot; hon/Ky Col.

JONSSON, RICHARD EUGENE THOMAS oc/Instructor; b/Feb 10, 1935; h/1613 W Ball Rd, Apt 7, Anaheim, CA 92802; ba/Anaheim; p/John Eric Walter Johnson (dec); Anna Patricia McGrath Johnson; ed/BA Univ Ams (Mexico) 1960; MA NEn Univ 1973; Cert TESL Cal St Univ-F 1978; mil/USAF 1954-58; pa/Eng Instr; Contest Editor *Dragonfly Mag*; Author *Full Sails*, 1971; Critic; Contbr Num Mags; Poet; r/Rom Cath; hon/Bronze Med, Centro Studi e Scambi Internazionale (Rome); 1st Annual Harold G Henderson Awd, Haiku Soc Am.

JORDAN, BARBARA LESLIE oc/Poet; b/Sept 30, 1915; h/901 W El Caminito, Phoenix, AZ 85021; ba/Same; m/John Ingle Yellott; c/Philip Van Rensselaer Schuyler III, Richard Hanford Jr, (Stepchd): John H, Ann W; p/William Methven Leslie (dec); Maud

Prendergast (dec); pa/Author *Comfort the Dreamer*, *Web of Days*; Pub'd Num Articles; VP John Yellott Engrg Assocs Inc; Poetry Soc Am; NY Wom Poets; Nat Soc Arts & Lttrs (Val of Sun Branch); cp/Repub Party; Life Bd Mem San Pablo Home for Yth; r/All Sts Epis Ch, Phoenix; hon/World W/W Authors/Writers; W/W Am Wom; Intl W/W Poetry; DIB.

JORDAN, CARL RANKIN oc/Physician; Surgeon; Proctologist; b/Jul 24, 1924; h/1627 Mills B Ln Blvd, Savannah, GA 31405; ba/Savannah; m/Anne Knight; c/Carmen J Cox, Karen T, Harold K; p/Charles G and Elizabeth R Jordan (dec); ed/BS, MD Howard Univ; Addit Studies: Harvard Univ, Mayo Clin, Johns Hopkins Univ, Others; mil/AUS 1951-53 Capt; pa/Pvt Pract; Cert'd Diplomate Intl Bd Proctol; Fellow Am Soc Abdominal Surgs; Past Trustee & Secy Bd Trustees, Nat Med Assn; r/Rom Cath; hon/Phys' Recog Awd, AMA.

JORDAN, EDDIE JACK oc/Professor; Artist; b/Jul 27; h/5545 Congress Dr, New Orleans, LA 70126; ba/New Orleans; m/Gladys McDaniel; c/Eddie J Jr, Gregory Keith, LaKara Jovarn; p/Oscar and Arnesta Jordan, Oklahoma City, OK; ed/BA Langston Univ; MA Iowa Univ; MFA St Univ Iowa; MS 1974, Doct Art Ed 1975 Ind Univ; mil/95th Inf Bt Cpl; pa/So Univ New Orleans: Prof & Chm Art Dept; Assoc Prof Art Langston Univ 1960; Former Chm Art Dept Claflin Univ; Designed Art Depts SUNO & Allen Univ; 38 One-Man Shows; Exhbns: NY Arch Leag, Nat Sculpture Soc (NY), New Vistas Am Art (Wash, DC), Intl Print Show (Leipzig, Germany), Num Others; Bd Dirs Nat Conf Artists; Nat CoChm Nat Com Devel Art Negro Cols; Others; cp/Douglas HS Nat Reunion Com; Hon Mem Nat Black Sports Fdn; Others; r/Bethany Meth Ch (New Orleans): Mem, Adv Bd Chm; hon/Delta Phi Delta; 29 Works in Perm Collections incl'd Ind Univ Mus Art; 41 Local, Reg, & Nat Competition Art Awds; Rep'd in *Prints by Am Negro Artists*, *Black Museum*, *Black Dimensions Contemp Art*, Others; W/W: Am Art, Among Black Ams; Outstg Edrs Am; Others.

JORDAN, GARY BLAKE oc/Engineer; b/Feb 3, 1939; h/1012 Olmo Ct, San Jose, CA 95129; m/Gloria Jean Heppler; c/Gareth Kyle, Glynis Jerelle; p/Robert Leslie and Lois Evelyn Schildhammer Jordan, Dayton, OH; ed/Doct Elect Engrg Pacific So Univ; PhD Elect Engrg

Sussex Col; BSEE Ohio Univ; pa/Elect Engrg & Mktg; Armed Forces Communs & Elect Assn; AAAS; IEEE; Am Defense Preparedness Assn; Soc Tech Communs; Wash Acad Scis; US Naval Inst; Ohio Acad Sci; cp/Intl Amateur Radio Clb; Radio Soc Gt Brit; Am Radio Relay Leag; Assn Old Crows; hon/W/W W.

JORDAN, GRACE ELLEN oc/Teacher; b/Apr 30, 1928; h/11222 Kensington, Los Alamitos, CA 90720; ba/Carson, CA; m/John R; c/John R Jr, Ellen B, Patricia A; p/George

W and Grace A Hedge (dec); ed/BA, MA Cal St Univ-LB; Tchr S M White Jr HS; Read'g Conslt; United Tchrs LA; cp/Mem Commun Adv Com; Am Leg Aux; Subscriber LB Civic Light Opera; r/Rom Cath; hon/Grad'd Cum Laude; Phi Delta Kappa.

JORDAN, JAMES JACKSON oc/Architect; Engineer; b/Jan 7, 1926; h/5236 Overbrook Way, Sacramento, CA 95841; ba/McClellan AFB, CA; m/Louella; c/James Jr, Lyndon, Jonathan; p/George S and Esther Lee Jordan, Jet, OK; ed/BArch; BE; mil/USN 1943-45; pa/Arch & Engr McClellan AFB; NSPE; Cal Soc Profl Engrs; cp/Rotary;

r/Meth; hon/Nat Arch 2nd Medal; Merit Achmt, USAF.

JORDAN, JOHN R oc/Engineer; b/Feb 27, 1924; h/11222 Kensington, Los Alamitos, CA 90720; ba/Long Beach, CA; m/Grace Ellen; c/John R Jr, Ellen, Patricia; p/Vincent R Jordan (dec); Ruth Cheetham, Seal Bch, CA;

ed/Dipl Chem Rutgers Univ 1951; BA 1953, MBA 1954 Univ Miami; mil/AUS ETO 1942-45; pa/Supvr Gen Engr, Aerospace Engr & Scist NAVPRO/DAC; Am Soc Quality Control; Contbr Articles Profl Jours; cp/K of C; r/Rom Cath; hon/W/W W.

JORDAN, JOHN RICHARD JR oc/-Attorney; b/Jan 16, 1921; h/809 Westwood Dr, Raleigh, NC 27607; ba/Raleigh; m/-Patricia Exum Weaver; c/Ellen Meares, John Richard III; p/John Richard and Ina Love Mitchell Jordan (dec); ed/BA 1942, LLD 1948 Univ NC; pa/Senator NC Gen Assembly 1959, 61, 63; Mem Staff Atty Gen NC 1948-51; Bd Editors *NC Law Review;* Contbr Polit Articles; ABA; NC Bar Assn; Wake Co Bar Assn; Am Judic Soc; NC Acad Trial Lwyrs; Intl Bar Assn; cp/NC Comm Higher Ed Facilities; Bd Govs UNC; Trustee Ravenscroft Fdn; NC Rep Nat Com Support Public Schs; Num Activs Dem Party; Sphinx Clb; City Clb Raleigh; Torch Clb; Lions Clb; ARC; Bd Dirs NC Med Fdn; Bd Dirs St Capitol Fdn; Num Others; r/Bapt; hon/Pi Kappa Alpha; Phi Delta Phi; Raleigh Yg Man Yr; S'ship & Ldrship Awds, Phi Delta Phi; Tar Heel Week Polits & Govt; Dist'd Ser Awd, NC Public Hlth Assn; Gold Medal Awd, Am Cancer Soc; Others.

JORDAN, LAN oc/Psychotherapist; b/Apr 20, 1923; c/1; p/Charles Paul and Ora Lee Whatley Jackson; ed/BS Ill Inst Technol 1940; MA Univ Chgo 1944; Cert, William Alanson White Inst Psychi 1952; PhD Univ So Cal 1956; Addit Studies; pa/Pvt Pract: Los Angeles (Cal) 1952-62, Beverly Hills (Cal) 1962-; Conslt, Marriage & Fam Cnslg 1974-; Speaker & Lectr: CBS-TV (LA) 1969, Mt Sinai Hosp (LA) 1967, LA City Hlth Dept 1945-49; Psychi Social Worker (Bronx, NY) VA Hosp 1949-52; Other Positions; Cal Assn Marriage & Fam Cnslrs (Awd, Former Trustee); So Cal & Am Assns Marriage & Fam Cnslrs; LA Group Psychotherapy Assn; cp/Univ So Cal Alumni Assn; Menninger Foun; hon/Alpha Kappa Alpha; Alpha Kappa Delta; Biogl Listings.

JORDAN, ROBERT oc/Concert Pianist; b/May 2, 1940; h/305 W End Ave, New York, NY 10023; ba/Same; p/Ira Jordan, Chattanooga, TN; Mamie Jordan, Wilmington, DE; ed/BM Eastman Sch Mus 1962; MS Juilliard Sch Mus 1965; Addit

Studies; pa/Adj Lectr Bronx Commun Col 1972-; Soloist w Orchs incl'g Symph New World (NYC), Buffalo Philharm, Baltimore Symph, Others; Concert Appearances: NYC, Wash (DC), Philadelphia, Denver, Paris (France), Munich (Germany), Others; Bd Dirs Triad Presentations Inc; Pres Paris Inst Mus NY; hon/Comm'd Present New Composition World Premier Kennedy Ctr (Bicent Celebration); S'ships: Fulbright, Juilliard Sch Mus, Eastman Sch Mus; German Govt Grant; W/W Am; Outstg Yg Men Am; Others.

JORDAN, STELLO oc/Real Estate Manager; b/Dec 17, 1914; h/87-15 204 St, Hollis, NY 11423; m/Matilda C; p/Michael and Ida Jordan (dec); pa/Tech Communs; Mgr Real Estate & Real Estate Trusteeships; Bd Mem Fdn Section 213 Coops Inc; Past Pres Soc Tech Communs; cp/Bd Mem Concerned Citizens Creedmoor Inc; Coun Judges Am Inst Sci & Tech, City of NY; r/Rom Cath; hon/Assoc Fellow, Soc Tech Communs.

JORDAN, W A oc/Retired Farmer; b/Jul 9, 1902; h/Rt 2 Box 205, Tulia, TX 79088; m/Jenelle M; p/Charles George and Cora May Walker Jordan; hon/Personalities of S.

JORDAN, WILLIAM THOMAS oc/Editor; b/Oct 13, 1923; h/314 N Ave T, Clifton, TX 76634; ba/Clifton; m/Beverly Ann Frazier; p/William Thomas and Belle MacMaster Graham Jordan (dec); ed/BBA w Hons 1952, MBA 1958 NEn Univ; mil/AUS 1945-46; pa/Past Dir Nashville (Tenn) Advtg Fdn; cp/Bosque Co Rotary Clb; Rotary Clb of Brookfields; r/Epis.

JORDAN-COX, CARMEN ANTOINETTE oc/Administrator; b/Mar 19, 1950; h/1005 Marlau Dr, Baltimore, MD 21212; p/Carl R and Annie K Jordan, Savannah, GA; ed/BA; MEd; Cand PhD; pa/Col Admr; Am Assn Higher Ed; r/Cath; hon/W/W Black Ams; World W/W Wom; Notable Ams; W/W E.

JORGENSEN, CHARLES CONRAD oc/Engineering Psychologist; b/Feb 14, 1947; h/3221 El Morro, El Paso, TX 79904; ba/Ft Bliss, TX; m/Beverly Jean; p/Carther M Jorgensen (dec); Edith M Jorgensen, Sun City, AZ; ed/BA Ind Univ 1969; PhD Univ Col 1974; pa/Army Res Inst: Team Ldr 1978, Work Unit Ldr 1978, Sr Res Psychol 1977, Res Psychol 1975; Stats Instr Univ Col 1975; Res Fellow Carnegie Mellon Univ 1974; IEEE; Psychometric Soc; Mil Operations Res Soc; cp/Editorialist KCIK-TV (El Paso); Yth Ldr Bethel Assembly of God; r/Prot; hon/Post-Doct Fellow Carnegie Mellon Univ; Pre-Doct Fellow Univ Col; Nat Sci Scholar, Ind Univ; Nat Hon Soc.

JOSLEN, ROBERT A oc/Car Dealer; b/Jun 28, 1929; h/PO Box 961, Pagosa Springs, CO 81147; ba/Pagosa Springs; m/Eloime F; c/Robert Jr, Lisa, Nancy; p/Fred L Joslen (dec); Elsie A Joslen, Springfield, OR; ed/BS Anderson Col & Theol Sem 1952; MBA George Washington Univ 1966; mil/AUS 1946-48; pa/Chevrolet Dealer; cp/Fellow Am Col Hosp Admrs; Acad Hlth Care Conslts; Mich Hosp Assn: Former Mem Bd Trustees, Former Chm Unemploymt Compensation Com; Former Bd Trustees Group Hlth Ser Mich; Former Mem Bd Trustees Mich Osteopathic Hosp Assn; Kiwanis; Elks; hon/Annual Anniv Article Awd, Hosp Fin Mgmt Assn.

JOSLYN, GOLDA FISCHER oc/-Pediatrician; b/Mar 28, 1913; h/1317 Spruce St, Berkeley, CA; m/Maynard A; p/Joel and Esther Fischer (dec); ed/Univ Vienna 1933-38; Univ S Wales (Cardiff) 1938-40; MD Med Col St SC 1943; pa/Intern Jewish Hosp (Cincinnati, Ohio) 1943; Resident Babies Hosp (Philadelphia, Penn) 1944; Resident Queens Gen Hosp (NY) 1945; PrivPract 1945-; Priv Pract Pediatrics Berkeley, Maternal & Child Wel Clins (E Bay) 1946-58; Attended Clin Chds Hosp (Zurich) 1960; Mtl Retardation Clins, Contra-Costa Co 1972-; Staff Affiliations: Alameda Co Hosp, Herrick Gen Hosp, Chd's Hosp SF, Contra-Costa Co Hosp; Other Positions; AMA; Cal & Alameda-Contra-Costa Med Assns; E Bay Pediatric Soc; Am Med Woms Assn; Hon Mem Woms Med Assn Israel; Others; cp/Pioneer Wom; Vol Ped Work & Mtl Retardation w Underpriviledged; Former Cnslr Camp Judea; Am Friends Hebrew Univ; ZOA; Others; r/Jewish; hon/Pub'd Author; W/W Am Wom; Personalities W&MW.

JOY, CAROL MARIE oc/Librarian; b/May 10, 1944; h/1955 Garland St, Lakewood, CO 80215; ba/Denver, CO; m/Stanley Ray; p/Thomas Henry Briggs IV, Orefield, PA; Dorothy P Williams, Golden, CO; ed/BA 1966, MA 1969 Univ Denver; pa/Libn Auraria Libs; Col Lib Assn, Govt Documents Roundtable VChm 1977-; Col St Lib Com, Col Documents Depository Law;

Spec Libs Assn: Documentation Div Local Rep 1976, Chm Col Chapt Nom'g Com 1977, Other Coms; Am Lib Assn; AAUP; Pub'd Author; cp/Ladies of Rotary; Denver Concert Band: Former Secy, Libn, Mem Bd Dirs, Publicity Com; Adult Ed Coun Metro Denver; r/Lakewood United Meth Ch: Chancel Choir, Past Co-Chm; hon/Beta Phi Mu; Phi Sigma Iota; Tau Beta Sigma; Rec'd Grant Cent/Bicent Comm & Col Lib Assn.

JOYCE, EDWIN ANTHONY oc/Director; b/Feb 23, 1937; h/Rt 1, Box 180-H, Tallahassee, FL 32303; ba/Tallahassee; m/Mary Dale; c/Edwin Anthony III, William Christopher, (Stepchd): Katherine Woodberry, Helen Kimberly, Beth, Kelly Gray, Mary Carson; p/Edwin Anthony Joyce (dec); Leah Bell Gates Joyce, St Petersburg, FL; ed/BA Butler Univ 1959; MS AIUV Fla 1961; Addit Studies; pa/Fla Dept Natural Resources: Dir Div Marine Resources 1975-, Chief Bur Marine Sci & Technol 1972-75, Supvr Marine Res Lab 1968-72, Sr Fisheries Biol 1967-68, Other Positions (Fla Bd Conserv); Pub'd Num Articles Profl Jours; Nat Shellfisheries Assn; Bd Dirs Gulf & Caribbean Fisheries Inst; Bd Dirs Coastal Plains Ctr Marine Devel Sers;

Am Inst Fishery Res Biols; Others; cp/Fla Audubon Soc; Capital City Kiwanis Clb; hon/Sigma Xi; Rec'd Grad Tchg Asstship Univ Fla; Others.

JOYNER, CHRISTOPHER CLAYTON oc/Professor; b/May 16, 1948; h/1223 Knossos Dr, #9, Whitehall, PA 18052; ba/Allentown, PA; m/Nancy Douglas; p/Houston Clay Joyner (dec); Besse Sowers Joyner, Winter Park, FL; ed/AA Orlando Jr Col 1968; BA magna cum laude 1970, MA (Intl Relats) 1972, MA (Govt) 1973 Fla St Univ; PhD Univ Va 1977; pa/Asst Prof Intl Relats Muhlenberg Col 1973-77; Sr Editor *Va Jour Intl Law* 1973-77; Instr Fla St Univ 1972-73; Co-Dir Ctr Peace & Envir Studies FSU 1971-73; Am Polit Sci Assn; Am Soc Intl Law; Intl Studies Assn; NEn Polit Sci Assn; Others; Author: *Intl Law of the Sea & the Future of Deep Seabed Mining* (1976), *The Changing Intl Ec Order: Probs, Prospects, & Legal Implications* (1977), Others; Pub'd Num Articles Profl Jours; cp/Muhlenberg Col: Advr Model United Nations Conf Proj, Dir Forensics Prog; BSA; Others; r/Meth; hon/Phi Beta Kappa; Phi Kappa Phi; Phi Theta Kappa; Phi Alpha Theta; Omicron Delta Kappa; Pi Sigma Alpha; Raven Soc; Gold Key, FSU; W/W Students Am Univs & Cols; Intl W/W Commun Ser; Personalities of S.

JOYNER, DELORES W oc/Student; b/Sept 16, 1936; h/104 Avon Pl, Warner Robins, GA 31093; m/James P; c/Robin, Connie; p/John Paul and Mildred Wilson

Williams, Bonaire, GA; ed/BA; MS; Currently Studying Mus Weslyan Col; pa/NEA; AAUW; cp/Dem Party; r/Epis; hon/W/W Child Devels.

JOYNER, NANCY DOUGLAS oc/Administrator; b/Oct 28, 1945; h/1223 Knossos Dr, #9, Whitehall, PA 18052; ba/Allentown, PA; m/Christopher C; p/Walker M and Virgie P Douglas (dec); ed/BA SEn La Univ; MA,

PhD Fla St Univ; mil/USO Dir Vietnam 1970-71; pa/Cedar Crest Col: Dir Cont'g Ed, Dean Elderhostle; Nat 1st VP, AAUW & AAUW Ed Foun; r/Rom Cath; hon/Outstg Yg Wom Penn; W/W Am Wom; Mem 1st Arab-Am Dialogue Libya.

JUDSON, LORRAINE ANDERSON oc/Registered Nurse; b/Jun 26, 1946; h/13310 Dwyer Blvd, New Orleans, LA 70129; ba/New Orleans; m/Bruce Richard; c/Richard Charles, Cheryl Lynn; p/Morris Edison and Lillian Wesley Anderson, New Orleans; ed/RN Touro Inf Sch Nsg 1970; mil/USAF 2/Lt; pa/Conslt & Staff Nurse New Orleans

Hlth Dept; Am Nurses Assn; La Nurses Assn; New Orleans Dist Nurses Assn; r/Prot.

JUDY, WILLIAM LEE oc/Civil Engineer; b/May 10, 1946; h/824 Lyndhurst Rd, Waynesboro, VA 22980; ba/Waynesboro; m/Ellen Fowlkes; c/Ruth Ellen, Anna Marie; p/Kerlin O and Ruth N Judy, Harrisonburg,

VA; ed/BS W Va Univ 1968; MS Ohio St Univ 1973; pa/Prin Engr John McNair & Assoc 1978-; Engr Burgess & Niple Ltd (Columbus, Ohio) 1969-78; Profl Engr St of Ohio; NSPE; Va Soc Profl Engrs; Am Water Works Assn; Water Pollutions Control Fdn; r/Mem United Christian F'ship.

JUERGENSEN, HANS oc/Professor; Poet; b/Dec 17, 1919; h/7815 Pine Hill Dr, Tampa, FL 33617; ba/Tampa; m/Ilse; c/Claudia; p/(dec); ed/BA Upsala Col 1942; PhD Johns Hopkins Univ 1951; mil/Ser'd 1942-45; pa/Editor *Gryphon*, Univ S Fla; Contbg Editor *Poet Lore*, Others; Author 9 Books incl'g *Fla Mortgage* (1966), *From the Divide* (1970); Staff Mem SW Coast Writers' Conf 1975, 76, 78, 79; Mem Lit Panel Fla Arts Coun 1978-79; Pres Nat Fdn St Poetry Socs 1968-70; Others; cp/Former Chrperson Concerned Dems in Tampa Bay Area; ACLU; Conslt Tampa Arts Coun in Lit; r/Jewish; hon/Spec Awd; Phi Kappa Phi; Omicron Delta Kappa; Hon Mem Nat Pre-Med Hon Soc; Dist'd Tchr Yr USF; Outstg Prof Yr USF; Requested by Swedish Acad to Nominate Cands Nobel Prize in Lit 4 Yrs.

JUKKALA, PEGGY J oc/Director; b/Oct 17, 1934; h/509 2nd Ave NE, Jamestown, ND 58401; ba/Jamestown; m/Gerald W; c/Tara, Traci, Jeff; p/Dave and Lucile Botton, Phoenix, AZ; ed/BA; pa/Dir Home Hlth Agy; Supvr Surg Jamestown Hosp; cp/Lib Bd: Pres, St Trustee; Bd Fine Arts Assn; Bd Mtl Hlth Assn; Bd Sr Citizens; Bd Swim Assn; Bd Frontier Village; r/Presb; hon/Grad'd Cum Laude.

JULICH, DOROTHY LOUISE oc/Retired Government Worker; b/Jan 1, 1912; h/2510 Sherwood Dr, SE, Decatur, AL 35601; ba/Same; m/Jule M; c/William Lee Roberts, Paul M, Marvin M; p/Eugene E and Lillie P Stroup Milam (dec); ed/Grad Bus Univ of Okla City; Att'd Calhoun Jr Col, Univ of Ala Exts; pa/Exec Secy & Personal Secy to Succeeding Gen Ofcrs of US Army Ballistic Missile Command & US Missile Command (Redstone Arsenal, Huntsville, Ala), Ret'd 1971; Past Editor, Decatur *Free Press*; Writer of Geneology Column, Wom's Page; Compiled Brochure, "All About Decatur" for BPW Clb; Past Pres, Decatur Nat Secys Assn; cp/Compiled "Roster of Revolutionay Soldiers & Patriots in Ala" for DAR; Past Regent, Col John Robins Chapt DAR; Past Pres, Joe Wheeler Chapt U Daughs of Confederacy; Past Pres: Decala Toastmistress Clb, Col Walter Aston Chapt Colonial Dames XVII Cent; Past St Recording Secy, Colonial Dames XVII Cent; Daughs of Am Colonists; Wom's C of C; Tenn & Tenn Valley Geneological Socs; Norfolk (Va), E Tenn & Fayette Co (Tenn) Hist Socs; Watauga Assn Geneology; Altrusa; Others; r/Meth; hon/BPW Wom of Achmt; Toastmistress of the Yr 1964-65; Wom of Distn, Hartselle, Ala; Biogl Listings; Others.

JUMONVILLE, FELIX JOSEPH JR

oc/Professor; Business Owner; b/Nov 20, 1920; h/8816 Whitaker Ave, Sepulveda, CA 91343; ba/Northridge, CA; m/Mary Louise; c/Carol J Litchfield, Susan; p/Felix and Mabel Jumonville (dec); ed/BS; MS; EdD; mil/USCG; pa/Prof PE Cal St Univ-N; ACSUP; CAHPER; NAHPER; Owner-Broker Jumonvile Realty; San Fernando Val Bd Realtors; Cal Assn Realtors; Nat Assn Realtors; cp/Northridge C of C; r/Meth; hon/US Commend Medal.

JUNE, WILLA DEE oc/Retired; b/Sept 6, 1903; h/5436 A Lisette, St Louis, MO 63109; m/Milo; c/Thomas Edgar (dec); p/Edgar and Josephine Mitchell (dec); pa/Supvr Psychiatric Aides St of Maryland 35 Yrs; r/Prot; hon/Girl of Yr, Beta Sigma Phi; World W/W Wom; Personalities of S; Personalities of W&MW.

JUPIN, LAURA ROSE oc/Retired; h/1063 E McCord St, Centralia, IL 62801; m/Earl Cranston (dec); c/Sondra Rose J Gillice (Mrs James T), Lawrence Earl; p/Charles William and Alice Marshall Potter Rose (dec); ed/BS, MA Univ Ill; Addit Studies; pa/Tchr Mason City HS 4 Yrs; Centralia Schs: Dir Art 1948-72, Dir Art & Public Relats 1962-72; Free-Lance Art Judge; Tchr Adult Art Classes; NEA; Ill Ed Assn: Former Dir Public Relats, Former Mem Bd Dirs; Past Pres Ill Art Ed Assn; Nat Schs Public Relats; Ill & Nat Am Assn Sch Admrs; BPW; Life Mem Univ Ill Alumni Assn; cp/Centralia Cult Soc; Marion Co Wel Com Ill; Marion Co Chapt Cancer Soc; DAR; Marion Co Geneol & Hist Soc; r/1st Christian Ch Centralia: Mem; hon/Delta Kappa Gamma; Delta Zeta; Recipient Profl Ldr Awd, Centralia City Schs; Rec'd Plaque NEA; Rec'd Plaque Ill Art Ed Assn.

JUSTUS, IOLIENE oc/Secretary; b/Jan 22, 1920; h/1548 W Hedding St, San Jose, CA 95126; ba/San Jose; m/Calvin W (dec); c/Benson E; p/James W and Martha Meshwert Legg (dec); cp/Intl Toastmistress Clb; IPA;

Smithsonian Assocs; Nat Hist Soc; San Jose Museum Assn; Nat Wildlife Fdn; Assn Nat Archives; San Jose PAL All Stars; hon/Var Speech Awds, ITC; Notable Ams.

JUVANCIC, RICHARD WILLIAM oc/Medical Director; b/Nov 15, 1920; h/1537 Squaw Creek Dr, Girard, OH 44420; ba/Youngstown, OH; m/Rose Mary Volk; c/Judith Ann J Forde, Richard Jr, Janet Kay, Joyce Elizabeth; p/John Sr and Frances Knouse Juvancic, Girard; ed/BA Ohio Univ 1948; MD Univ Penn 1952; Addit Studies; mil/AUS 1942-45 Med Corps; pa/Prog Dir Fam Pract, Youngstown Hosp Assn 1978-; Med Dir Youngstown Dist, Youngstown Sheet & Tube

Co 1972-78; Dir Med Ed Trumbull Meml Hosp (Warren, Ohio) 1963-71; Other Former Positions; Author Sev Papers Ed; Ohio Acad Fam Pract; AAFP; AMA; Am Occupational Med Assn; Soc Tchrs Fam Med; Mahoning Co Med Soc; Others; cp/Var Civic Orgs; r/St Rose Rom Cath Ch (Girard): Mem Parish Coun, Chm Parish Life Com; hon/Ohio Phys of Yr, Gov's Com Employ'g Handicapped.

K

KADABA, PANKAJA KOOVELI oc/-Research Asscoiate; b/May 15, 1928; h/3411 Brookhaven Dr, Lexington, KY 40502; ba/-Lexington; m/Prasad; c/Lini; p/Subramani and Mangalamma (dec); ed/BSc; MSc; PhD Univ Delhi; pa/Res in Organic Chem; 1, 2, 3-Triazolines, Chem; Reaction Mechanisms & Synth fo Heterocyles; 1, 3-Cycloaddition Reactions; Role of Protic & Dipolar Aprotic Solvents; Res Assoc Brown Univ 1957-60; Assoc Prof Chem Morehead St Univ 1965-66; Christian Brothers Col 1966-68; Guest Scholar, Univ Ky 1954-55; Fulbright Fellow, Univ Wis 1953-54; Author Num Res Pubs Profl Jours; r/Hindu; hon/Sigma Xi Res Hon; Fulbright-Smith Mundt Fellow 1953-54; Visit'g Scist Univ Ljubljana, Yugoslavia.

KADABA, PRASANNA V oc/Engineer; Educator; b/Jul 4, 1931; h/2756 Carolyn Dr SE, Smyrna, GA 30080; ba/Atlanta, GA; m/Usha Rajgopal; c/Vaibhav; p/K V Iyengar (dec); K V Sharadamma, Bangalore, India; ed/BS (Mech) 1952; BS (Elect) 1954; MS 1956; PhD 1964; pa/Sr Res Engr, Borg Warner Res; Sr Res Scist, Westinghouse Elect Corp; Assoc Prof, Ga Inst Technol; ASME; ASHRAE; ASEE; cp/Chm Bd Dirs, India Am Culture Assn; r/Hindu; hon/Sigma Xi; Atlanta ASHRAE Engr.

KAFKA, MARIAN STERN oc/Physiologist; b/Mar 30, 1927; h/7834 Aberdeen Rd, Bethesda, MD 20014; ba/Bethesda; m/John S; c/David Egon, Paul Henry, Alexander Charles; p/Henry S Stern (dec); Adele L Stern, Richmond, VA; ed/BA Conn Col 1948; PhD Univ Chgo 1952; pa/Physiol, Nat Inst Mtl Hlth; Endocrine Soc; Physiol Soc; Soc Neurosci; Am Physiol Soc; AAAS; Chm Public Information Com, Federated Socs Exptl Biol; Public Information Com, APS; hon/Marie J Mergler Fellow; Phi Beta Kappa; Sigma Xi.

KAHLE, NAOMI RUTH oc/Secretary; b/Dec 8, 1927; h/Rt 1, Box 28, Kildare, OK 74642; ba/Blackwell, OK; m/Melvin F; c/Donna K Page (Mrs Gary), Ruth K Brown (Mrs Charles); p/Louie E and Ruth Lowry Hollingsworth (dec); pa/Secy to City Mgr; ABWA; cp/Precinct Chm Repubs; Judge Election Bd; r/Luth Ch-Mo Synod: Mem; hon/Wom Yr, ABWA; Local Awds.

KAHLER, WOODLAND oc/Retired; b/Feb 6, 1895; h/350 S Ocean Blvd, Palm Beach, FL 33480; m/Amy Lorton; p/Harry Adams and Beulah Pace Kahler (dec); ed/BA Yale Univ; mil/USAF WWI, 2/Lt; pa/Ret'd Writer; r/Cath; hon/Marquis of St Innocent; W/W Am.

KAHN, BRIAN V oc/Chairman; b/Jan 22, 1947; h/125 E Spain St, Sonoma, CA 95476; ba/Santa Rosa, CA; c/Brice; p/Albert E and Riette Kahn, Glen Ellen, CA; ed/BA Univ Cal-B 1969; JD Boalt Law Sch 1973; pa/Chm Sonoma Co Bd Supvrs; Co-Author *The Unholy Hymnal*, 1971; Author Sev Articles on Hunt'g & Conserv; Cal St Bar Assn; ABA; Cal St Bd Corrections; cp/NAACP; Commonwlth Clb; Big C Soc; Ducks Unltd; Trout Unltd; Boalt Hall Alumni Assn.

KAHN, JULIAN oc/Consultant; b/Aug 18, 1932; h/1227 Cambridge Ct, Highland Park, IL 60035; ba/Chicago, IL; m/Gerri; c/Marci, David, Sharon, Debbie, Cheryl, Lois, Lisa; p/Abraham Kahn (dec); Lillian Kahn; ed/BA Roosevelt Univ; mil/NG 6 Yrs; pa/Investor Contruction Profls 1978-; Exec Head Julian Kahn & Assocs; Pres Am Profl Conslts Ltd 1977-; Pres Doctors Aid Profl Asst Corp, Phys' Brokerage Ser 1974-; Owner Kahn's Stamps & Coins 1940-; Other Positions; Nat Assn Life Underwriters; Nat Assn Security Dealers; Chgo Assn Commerce & Indust; cp/Former Dir Bellwood C of C; Former Precinct Com-man Dem Party; VChm Deerfield Township Ctl Com; r/Jewish; hon/W/W: Midwest, World, Fin & Indust;

Commun Ldrs & Noteworthy Ams; Personalities Am; Intl W/W Commun Ser.

KAISER, BEVERLY A oc/Educator; h/1528 E Fox St, South Bend, IN 46613; ba/Niles, MI; m/John Kaiser; c/Bessie Nell, Ernestine Beverly, Bejamin Phillip Edward, John Jr; ed/BS cum laude Ind Univ 1957; MA Mich St Univ 1958; Addit Studies; pa/Dir Migrant Prog, St Dept Mich 2 Yrs; Wn Mich Univ: Asst Dir Summer Sch 1 yr, Dir Off-Campus Summer Sch 8 Yrs; Brandywine Public Sch Sys: Primary Tchr 6 Yrs, Intermediate Tchr 1 Yr, Prin 1960-66, Elem Supvr 1966-73, Coor 1973-76, Instr Adult Ed; Life Mem NEA; Mich Classroom Tchrs; Nat Ed Primary Assn; Trustee SWn Mich Intl Read'g Assn; AAUP; Others; cp/Heart Fund Com; Wom's Federated Clbs; Area Chm United Fund; Wom's Federated Clbs; Masonic Affiliations: En Star, Amaranth, White Shrine, Daughs of Nile; hon/Delta Kappa Gamma; Alpha Beta Epsilon; Rec'd Plaque, Reg V Mich Assn ELem Prins; World W/W Wom; Personalities W&MW; Commun Ldrs & Noteworthy Ams; Intl W/W Commun Ser; Others.

KAISER, WALTER CHRISTIAN JR oc/Professor; b/Apr 11, 1933; h/1150 Linden, Deerfield, IL 60015; ba/Deerfield; m/Margaret R Burk; c/Walter Christian III, Brian Addison, Kathleen Elise, Jonathan Kevin; p/Walter C Kaiser Jr (dec); Estelle E Jaworsky Kaiser; ed/BD Wheaton Grad Sch 1958; MA 1962, PhD 1973 Brandeis Univ; mil/ROTC; pa/Prof Semitic Langs & Old Testamt, Trinity Evangelical Div Sch; Soc Biblical Lit; Evangelical Theol Soc (Nat Pres 1977); Bd Mem Near E Archaeol Soc; cp/YMCA Bldg Fund Dr; r/Evangelical Free Ch Am; hon/Wheaton Col: Danforth Tchr Study Grant, Jr Tchr Yr, Scholastic Hon Soc; Staley Dist'd Scholar Lctr.

KAISTHA, KRISHAN KUMAR oc/Toxicologist; b/Apr 6, 1926; h/542 N Ashbury Ave, Bolingbrook, IL 60439; ba/Chicago, IL; m/Swarn L; c/ Anita K Mahajan, Vivek, Vinek; p/Mangat Ram Kaistha, Pradesh, India; Tara Devi Mahajan Kaistha (dec); ed/BS (Chem) 1947, BS (Pharm) w Hons 1951, MS 1955 Panjab Univ; PhD Univ Fla 1962; pa/Chief Toxicol, St Ill Dangerous Drugs Comm 1974-; Res Assoc

Dept Psychi, Univ Chgo 1969-75; Other Positions; Contbr Aritcles Profl Jours; Cert'd Forensic Toxicol, Am Bd Forensic Toxicol; Cert'd Clinical Chem, Nat Registry Clincial Chem; Am Acad Forensic Scis; Am Assn Clinical Chems; Am Acad Clinical Toxicol; Am Soc Pharm & Expmtl Therapeutics; hon/Rho Chi; Phi Kappa Phi; Rho Pi Phi; Lunsford-Richardson Awd; Gov's Ec Incentive Awd, St of Ill; Fellow NY Acad Scis.

KAKKIS, ALBERT oc/Neurologist; b/Sept 21, 1927; h/6398 Rochelle Ln, Long Beach, CA 90813; ba/Long Beach; m/Julia Metaxas; c/Joyce Ann, Emil Denis, Aris Jack, Jane Lillian; p/Emil and Elvira Benmayor Kakkis; ed/MD; mil/Greek Army; pa/Dir Neurol, St Mary's Med Ctr; Asst Clinical Prof UCLA; Dir Clinic Movemt & Paroxysmal Disorders; FAAN; FRSH; MACP; FRSM; hon/AMA Phys' Recog Awd.

KALES, ROBERT G oc/Industrialist; b/Mar 14, 1904; h/87 Cloverly Rd, Grosse Pte Farms, MI 48236; ba/Detroit, MI; m/Shirley M; c/Jane, Robert Gray, William Robert,

Anne Webster, David Wallin, John Gray, Nancy Davis; p/William Robert and Alice Gray Kales (dec); ed/BS MIT 1928; MBA Harvard Grad Sch 1933; mil/USN 1942-45; USNR 1963-66 Capt; pa/Pres & Dir Kales Kramer Investmt Co 1935-; Dir Independent Liberty Life Ins Co (Grand Rapids) 1966-; Dir Atlas Energy Corp 1978-; Others; cp/Mil Order WWs: Former St Cmdr (Detroit Chapt), Gen Staff & Former Cmdr-in-Chief (Nat); Navy Leag US: Former Treas, Dir, Secy, Pres; US Naval Sea Cadets; Detroit Power Squadron; r/Prot; hon/Naval Resv Medal; Am Campaign Medal; WWII Victory Medal; Navy & Marine Corps Medal; Naval Resv Medal w Star; Armed Forces Resv Medal; Order of Croix de Guerre; Order of Lafayette.

KALISKI, JUDITH PUTNAM oc/Clinical Psychologist; b/Aug 7, 1946; h/81 Beach St, Foxboro, MA 02035; ba/Norton, MA; m/Martin Edward; p/Allan Ray and Marion Witmer Putnam, Chagrin Falls, OH; ed/BA Wellesley Col 1968; MA 1971, PhD 1976 Univ RI; pa/Conslt Human Resource Inst 1976-; Instr Emmanuel Col Ext (Hingham, Mass) 1976; Clinical Asst, Psychol Clinic Univ RI 1973-74; Others; APA; AAAS; cp/NOW; Hadassah; r/Temple Israel of Sharon; hon/NIMH Fellow, Kent St Univ; W/W Am Wom; Intl W/W.

KAMACK, NANETTE TYSON oc/Social Worker; b/Aug 12; h/10411 8th Ave, Inglewood, CA 90303; ba/Los Angeles, CA; m/Bennie Lee; c/Bennie Lee, Richard Glen, Daryl Wayne; p/Willie E Tyson, Little Rock, AK; Ruthie Lee Stout (dec); ed/BA; pa/Social Worker LA Co; Woms Bus & Profl Soc; cp/NAACP; Chm LWV; OES; hon/Leta Phi Beta; W/W: Am Wom, Am Wom World, Bus & Fin.

KAMAR, ASTRID ELAINE oc/Executive; b/Nov 29, 1934; h/1757 Paseo Del Mar, Palos Verdes Estates, CA 90274; ba/Torrance, CA; m/Pascal M; c/Christopher, Jenny Lynn, Laurie Lynn; p/Ernest Wennermark (dec); Emmy Kraus Wennermark, Palm Springs, CA; ed/Grad'd Sawyer's Bus Sch 1953; pa/Exec VP Kamar Intl Inc; IPA; Catalyst Corp Bd Resource; cp/LA Chapt Val Orthopedic Hosp Com: Bd Dirs, Former Chm; r/Luth; hon/Intl Wom Yr.

KAMBACK, MARVIN CARL oc/Psychologist; b/Jul 15, 1939; h/627 Howell, Worland, WY 82401; c/Eliazbeth Farrell; p/Carl Melvin and Pauline Elizabeth Kamback, Yankton, SD; ed/BA 1961, MA 1962 Univ SD; PhD Vanderbilt Univ 1965; Addit Studies; pa/Cert'd Psychol Maryland; Dir & Psychol Washakie Mtl Hlth; Former Assoc Prof Psychi Inst, Univ Maryland Med Sch; Asst Prof Johns Hopkins Univ Sch Med, Dir Fams & Chd's Ctr 1974-78; Other Positions; Pub'd Num Articles Profl Jours; Soc Gen Sys Res; AAAS; Am Psychol Assn; Maryland Psychol Assn; cp/Rotary Intl; hon/NIMH Predoctoral F'ship; AM Wom & Men Sci; NIMH Postdoctoral F'ship; W/W E; Sigma Xi.

KAMII, CONSTANCE KAZUKO oc/Professor; b/Mar 14, 1931; h/1700 E 56th St, Chicago, IL 60637; ba/Chgo; p/Mark Yoshio Kamii (dec); Ruth Haruko Kamii, Los Angeles, CA; ed/BA cum laude Pomona Col 1953; MA 1955, PhD 1965 Univ Mich; pa/Prof & Reschr Col Ed, Univ Ill; Jt Appointmt w

Univ Ill & Univ Geneva 1973-; Author *Physical Knowledge in Preschool Ed,* 1978; Lectr; hon/Phi Beta Kappa.

KANAGAWA, ROBERT KIYOSHI oc/Rancher; Businessman; b/Sept 10, 1917; h/16156 E McKinley Ave, Sanger, CA 93657; m/Yukiye; c/3; p/Yasoichi T and Jitsuyo S Kanagawa; ed/BBA Ctl Cal Commercial Col; pa/Pres, Kanagawa Citrus Co 1965-; VP & Bd Dirs, Orange Cove Sanger Citrus Assn; Former Pres & Bd Mem, Sanger Citrus Assn; Others; cp/Sanger Japanese-Am Citizens Leag; Dist Gov, Ctl Cal Dist Coun Japanese-Am Citizens Leag; Dir, St Agnes Hosp; Chm, Valley Regional Occupational Prog; Rotary Intl; Comm Mem, Sanger Senior Citizens; Dir, 21st Dist Agri Assn; Exec Dir, Sequoia Coun BSA; Co-chm, Agri Museum Adv Com; Others; r/United Meth Ch: Former Trustee; hon/Man of Yr Awd, Sanger C of C 1968; Golden Apple Awd, Fresno Co Assn Sch Admrs; Biogl Listings.

KANDA, JANICE HUMPHREY oc/Interpreter; b/Apr 3, 1947; h/208 Carswell, Waco, TX 76705; ba/Waco; m/Masato; c/Kimberly, Kristina; p/C J and Ophelia Humphrey, Amarillo, TX; ed/AS 1970; BS 1971; pa/Interpreter Deaf, Tex St Tech Inst; r/Bapt.

KANDRAVY, JOHN oc/Lawyer; b/May 9, 1935; h/56 Monte Vista Ave, Ridgewood, NJ 07450; ba/Newark, NJ; ,/Alice Elizabeth Sullivan; c/Elizabeth Ann, Katherine Ann; p/Frank Kandravy, Garfield, NJ; Anna Chan Kandravy (dec); ed/BA Wesleyan Univ 1957; JD Columbia Univ 1960; mil/AUS 1960-61; pa/Partner Shanley & Fisher Esqs 1968-; Admit'd NJ Bar 1960; Admit'd DC Bar 1969; Admit'd Supr Ct Bar 1973; Mem: Am, NJ, Essex Co & DC Bar Assns; cp/VChm Ridgewood Zoning Bd; Trustee Palisades Cnslg Ctr; Secy & Trustee NJ Res Foun Mtl Hygiene; Others; r/Westside Presb Ch: Ruling Elder; hon/Recipient Edward John Noble Foun Ldrship Grant; W/W E.

KANEKO, RUTH Y oc/Pianist; b/Sept 12, 1937; h/7977 Pumpkin Ct, Cupertino, CA 95014; ba/Palo Alto, CA; m/Richard T; c/Jeffrey, Wendy; p/Albert S Kosakura, Berkeley, CA; Tomiko Kosakura; ed/BA Univ Cal-B; pa/Reschr Ed Gifted Yg; cp/Dir Concerts & S'ships.

KANG, KI DONG oc/Executive; b/Dec 9, 1934; h/633 Harrow Way, Sunnyvale, CA 94087; ba/Sunnyvale; m/Soonho; c/James, Nancy; p/Chong Moo Kang and Byung Soon Ham, Seoul, Korea; ed/BS Seoul Nat Univ 1957; MS, PhD 1962 Ohio St Univ; pa/KDK Intl Sales Corp: Fdr & Pres 1976-; Fdr & VP Overseas Operations, Integrated Circuits Intl Inc 1973-76; Fdr & Pres, Korea Semiconductor Inc 1973-76; Other Positions; IEEE; Electro-Chem Soc; cp/C of C; r/Bapt; hon/Export Contbn Awd, Technol Contbn Awd Republic of Korea; Holds Sev Patents.

KANTZER, KENNETH SEALER oc/-Teacher; b/Mar 29, 1917; h/1752 Spruce, Highland Park, IL 60035; ba/Deerfield, IL; m/Ruth Forbes; c/Mary Ruth K Wilkinson, Richard Forbes; p/Edwin F and Clara Sealer Kantzer (dec); ed/BA Ashland Col; MA Ohio St; MDiv, ThM Faith Sem; PhD Harvard; pa/Trinity Evangelical Div Sch: Dean, VP Academic Affairs, Tchr; Editor; Past Pres Evangelical Theol Soc; r/Evangelical Free Ch Am.

KAPACINSKAS, JOSEPH oc/Engineer; b/Oct 20, 1907; h/6811 S Maplewood Ave, Chicago, IL 60629; m/Marie Kulikauskas; c/Joseph Vytautas; p/George and Teofile Kapacinskas (dec); ed/BA Allied Inst Technol 1960; Tech Col Germany; pa/Burlington No RR 1951-72; Editor *Sandara,* 1973-76; Contbr Articles Lithuanian Newspaper; Author: *Siaubingos Dienos (Horrifying Days)* 1965, *Iseivio Dalia (Emigrant's Fate)* 1974, Others; Lithuanian Engrs & Archs Assn; Lithuanian Journalist Assn; AAAS; IPA; Am Soc Tool & Mfg Engrs; cp/Am Coun Chgo; r/Rom Cath.

KAPLAN, MURIEL SHEERR oc/Sculp-

tor; b/Aug 15, 1924; h/150 E 69th St, New York, NY 10021; ba/NYC; m/Murray; c/Janet K Belsky, James, S Jerrold, Amy; p/Maurice J Sheerr (dec); Lillian J Sheerr, Palm Beach, FL; ed/BA Cornell Univ; MFA Sarah Lawrence Col; pa/Art Conslt; Interior Designer; Exhbns: Brooklyn Museum, Bergen Co NJ Mus; Scupltors Guild; Allied Artists Am; Nat Assn Wom Artists; Co-Chm 1st Channel 13 Art Auction; Chm Brandeis Creative Arts Fest; cp/Fdn Jewish Philanthropies; Brandeis Woms Org Westchester; Chm Students Elect Johnson 1964; hon/Perm Collections: Portrait J F Kennedy (Israel), Portrait Busts Columbia Univ, Univ Tex, Brandeis Univ, Steel Sculpture Tarrytown (NY); Sculpture Awds: Allied Artists Am, Nat Assn Wom Artists, Catherine Lorillard Wolfe Clb.

KAPP, JOHN PAUL oc/Neurosurgeon; b/Feb 22, 1938; h/455 Bunkers Cove Rd, Panama City, FL 32401; ba/Panama City; m/Emily Lureese Evans; c/Paul Hardin, Emily Camille; p/Paul Homer and Jesse Katherine Vass Kapp, Galax, GA; ed/BS 1966, MD 1963 Duke Univ; PhD 1967; mil/AUS; pa/Pvt Pract 1972-; Neurosurg: Bay Meml Med Ctr 1972-, Gulf Coast Commun Hosp 1977-; Asst Prof Neurosurg, Univ Tenn 1971-72; Bd Dirs Fla Area I Foun Profl Standards 1978-; Pres & Mem Bd Dirs, Coast Res Foun 1978-; AMA; Tenn Med Assn; Fla Med Assn; Bay Co Med Assn; Cong Neurol Surgs; So Neurosurg Soc; Am Col Surgs; Others; Pub'd Num Articles Profl Jours; cp/Dem; r/Meth; hon/Res Awd, Am Acad Neurol Surg; Alpha Omega Alpha; Phi Beta Kappa; W/W S&SW; DIB; Directory Med Specs; Personalities Am; Others.

KAR, ANIL KRISHNA oc/Consulting Engineer; b/Jul 9, 1941; h/1038 Barbara Ct, N Bellmore, NY 11710; m/Parul Chakrabarti; p/Manoranjan and Nirmala Prova Kar; ed/BSCE Bangladesh Univ Engrg & Technol 1962; MSCE 1969, PhD 1971 Penn St Univ; pa/Consltg Engr 1973-; Sr Engr, Ebasco Sers Inc 1977-; Sr Engr, Gibbs & Hill Inc 1975-77; Other Positions; Guest Reviewer Engrg Pubs; Lectr; Guest Panelist, Nat & Intl Confs; Reg'd Profl Engr, Penn; Am Soc Civil Engrs (Coms); Intl Assn Shell & Spatial Structures; Com for Preparation of Standards for Khoa (Lightweight) Concrete, Pakistan Standards Inst 1965; Author Num Tech Papers & Reports; Others; hon/Rec'd Editor Awds, Dravo Corp (Pittsburgh, Penn); Nat & Intl S'ships for Study Engrg; Chi Epsilon; Biogl Listings.

KARAFYLLAKIS, ANTONIOS A oc/-Artist; b/Apr 17, 1908; h/3500 Dinwiddie St N, Arlington, VA 22207; ba/Washington, DC; m/Niki Antonios; c/Leonidas A, Michael A, Steven A; p/Leonidas A and Maria A Karafyllakis (dec); ed/Royal Acad Fine Arts (Greece); mil/Greek-Am Army; pa/Former Art Tchr; Former Pres Sch Fine Arts (Greece); Former Dir Sch Fine Arts (Rhodes); Exhbns: US, Greece, Australia, Mid E, Bahamas; Mem Royal Art Soc Australia; Num Others; cp/Cretans; Pandodekanisiens; Greek-Am Lobby Org; r/Greek Orthodox; hon/Averofion Prize for Nude Paint'g; Philadelphia Prize for Composition; Hotchin Prize; Outstg Achmt Awd, Rockledge Inst (S Norwalk, Conn); Trophy Awd, *The Washington Post*; Awds from Am Art Leag; Perm Collections: Calgoolie Public Mus (Australia), St Nicholas Greek Orthodox Ch

(Tarpin Springs), Nat Gallery Athens; Comm'd to Create Busts Robert Kennedy & Martin Luther King, Kennedy King Univ (Chgo); 2 Gold Medals; Hon Dipl, Greek Govt; Num Other Awds; Biogl Listings.

KARAMPELAS, NAPOLEON DIMETRIUS oc/Archpriest; h/239 W Ridge, Marquette, MI 49855; ba/Marquette; m/Panagoula Londos; c/Angelos, Peter; p/Dimetrios and Georgia Kalampokes Karampelas (dec); ed/Dipl

Ecclesiastical Theol Sch Corrinth (Greece); mil/Greek Inf; pa/Archpriest, Greek Orthodox Ch; Author Num Articles Human Rights; Hellenic Profl Assn Am; cp/Ecumenical Coun Marquette; Var Activs Human Rights; r/Greek Orthodox; hon/W/W Rel.

KARDOS, JAMES WESLEY oc/Counselor; b/Dec 26, 1931; h/1283 Westfield SW, North Canton, OH 44720; ba/Canton; m/Ruth; c/Christopher, Brad; p/James Emry Kardos (dec); Caroline M Kardos, Wooster, OH; ed/BA Col Wooster 1953; MA Kent St Univ 1963; mil/Ret'd Resv; pa/Rehab Cnslr, Ohio Bur Voc Rehab 1963-; Nat Rehab Cnslg Assn; Chm Nat Coun Consumer Mems; Nat Ctr Barrier-Free Envir; Am Coalition Citizens w Disabilities; Others; cp/Chm Trans Disadvantaged Com; Chm Stark Co Citizens Adv Coun; Stark Co Reg Planning Comm; Stark Co Employmt Handicapped Com; Comman BSA; r/Faith United Meth Ch: Tape Recorder & 3 Yr Discipleship Chm; hon/Fellow NRCA; Dist'd Ser Awd, NRCA.

KARESH, ANN BAMBERGER oc/Painter; Sculptor; b/Aug 26, 1933; h/6867 Golfcrest Dr 16, San Diego, CA 92119; ba/Same; c/Barbara M, Jae, Billy; p/Ludwig Bamberger (dec); Thea Bamberger, Charleston, SC; ed/Willesden Tech Col (London, England); Hornsey Col Art (London); pa/Studio Painter; Guild SC Artists: Pres 1966-67, VP 1965-66; Tchr Jewish Commun Ctr; Exhbn Com, Carolina Art Assn 1955-59; Exhbns: 18th Annual Nat Watercolor Exhbn (Jackson, Miss), Watercolor USA Nat Watercolor Exhbn, Soc 4 Arts Nat Exhbn (Palm Beach, Fla), Hunter Gallery Annual, Others; hon/Perm Collections: Columbia Mus Art, Gibbes Art Gallery, Home Fed Savs & Ln Assn, Num Pvt Collections; SC Craftsmen: Best in Metal, Best In Enamel; C C Fine Arts: 1st Prize Sculpture, Draw'g Prize, 1st Watercolor Prize; Num Others; W/W: Am Art, Am Wom; DIB; Others.

KARKALITS, OLIN CARROLL oc/Dean; b/May 31, 1916; h/1161 Bayouwood Dr, Lake

Charles, LA 70605; ba/Lake Charles; m/Barbara; c/Kay Ann, Karen Sue; p/O C and Mabel Patterson Karkalits (dec); pa/Dean Sch Engrg & Technol, McNeese St Univ; Consltg Engr; cp/United Appeal; Boys Village; r/Bapt.

KARL, DOROTHY THERESA oc/Teacher; b/Mar 27, 1917; h/Five Mile Rd, Allegany, NY 14706; ba/Allegany; p/Vincent E Karl (dec); Theresa A Gallets Karl, Allegany; ed/BS St Bonaventure Univ; Elem Cert Geneseo St Col; pa/Math Coor; Life Mem St Bonaventure Univ Alumni Assn; Nat Coun Tchrs Math; Assn Math Tchrs NY St; NYEA; NEA; Nat Ret'd Tchrs Assn; Am Assn Ret'd Persons; Allegany Ctl Sch Tchrs Assn; cp/Bartlett Country Clb; Wom's Golf Assn (Bartlett); r/Rom Cath; hon/Rec'd Nat Sci Foun Awd, Boston Col; W/W Biogl Record-Sch Dist Ofcls; Notable Ams; World W/W Wom; DIB.

KARN, GLORIA STOLL oc/Artist; Teacher; b/Nov 13, 1923; h/151 Louise Rd, Pittsburgh, PA 15237; m/Fred S Jr; c/Vera, Shari, Keith; p/Charles T Stoll (dec); Anne V Stoll, Pittsburgh; pa/Tchr Commun Col Allegheny Co; Exhbn Carnegie Inst Museum Art; r/Presb; hon/Purchase Awd: Carnegie Inst Museum Art, Brooklyn Museum.

KARNA, MAYA TOLANI oc/Physician; b/Oct 27, 1939; h/18617 Rolling Acres Way, Olney, MD 20832; ba/Washington, DC; m/Indersen P; c/Sujeet, Dev; p/Jivatram and Saraswati (dec); ed/BS; MB; pa/Attend'g Anesthesiol Chd's Hosp, Nat Med Ctr; Asst Prof Anesthesia, George Washington Univ; Am Soc Anesthesia; Md & DC Socs Anesthesia; Intl Anesthesia Res Soc; r/Hindu.

KAROHS, ERIKA MARGARETE oc/Professor; b/Jul 9, 1930; h/PO Box 1476, Pebble Beach, CA 93953; ba/Monterey, CA; c/Michael Erich Friedrich; p/Erich Schwabe (dec); Lina Schwabe, Ilmenau, Germany; ed/Staatsexamen Univ Jena (Germany); MA (Langs) 1964, MA (SS) 1966 Monterey Inst Foreign Studies; Addit Studies; Monterey Peninsula Col; Tchg German, Lectr Handwriting Analysis; Author German & Handwriting Analysis Textbooks; cp/Lectr Var Civic Orgs; r/Luth; hon/World W/W Wom; W/W; Am Wom, Graphol Worldwide; Notable Ams; Others.

KARUNAKARAN, KIZHAKEPAT PISHARATH oc/Surgeon; b/Feb 15, 1936; h/3508 Spicer Dr, Saginaw, MI 48603; ba/Saginaw; m/Lakshmi; c/Sreekala, Sreelekha; p/K P Chakrapani Pisharoty and Kochukutty Pisharasyar; ed/MD Madras

Univ 1958; FRCS Edinburgh UK 1966; Addit Studies; pa/Surg St Mary's Hosp; Fellow Surg, Tufts Univ Sch Med (Boston); Asst Prof Surg, Med Col India 1967-71; Consltg Surg, Lakshmi Hosp India 1967-70; Other Positions; Pub'd Articles Profl Jours; r/Hindu; hon/Col Merit Awds.

KASBERG, MICHAEL oc/Retired Educator; Songwriter; b/Oct 26, 1909; h/1115 Ch St, Redlands, CA 92373; ba/Redlands; m/Lois A McKillop; c/Michele L, Randal E; p/Jacob J and Lisa Papelpud Kasberg (dec); BA Dickinson St Col 1935; EdM Univ SD 1956; pa/Pub'd 14 Songs incl'g Is Jesus the Only One, Is God In or Is He Out?; Released 2

Albums; cp/Redlands YWCA; r/Non-Sectarian; hon/Rho Delta Kappa; DIB; W/W; Am Ed, Commun Ser; Creat & Success Personalities of World; Personalities W&MW; IPA.

KASDON, LAWRENCE M oc/Professor; b/Jul 26, 1918; h/13 W 13 St, Apt 7Gs, New York, NY 10011; ba/NYC; m/Nora Sauer (dec); p/David and Lillian Collins Kasdon (dec); ed/BA UCLA; MA, EdD Stanford Univ; mil/AUS Sgt; pa/Prof & Dir Lang-Read'g Ctr, Yeshiva Univ; AAUP; Col Read'g Assn; Am Ed Res Assn; Intl Read'g Assn; Others; cp/Secy Jobs For Yth; Bd Mem, Two Together; hon/Crossroads Key Awd; Fellow Nat Coun Res Eng.

KASHIKI, ELAINE GAYLE oc/Arts Administrator; b/Jun 23, 1948; ba/1308 S New Hampshire Ave, Los Angeles, CA 90006; p/Akira and Misako Kashiki, Riverside, CA; ed/Univ Cal-LA; pa/Inner City Cultural Ctr: Adm Dir 1977-, Asst Exec Dir 1969-77, Prog Dir 1974-76, Budget Analyst 1975-76, Other Positions; Appeared Plays: Art Who? 1973-76 (Inner City), Earthquake 1973 (Inner City), La Ronde 1973 (Inglewood Playhouse), Others; Light Designer Piano Bar, 1976 (Inner City); Asst Dir Langston Hughes Said, 1975 (Inner City); Others.

KASHIN, NICOLAI NICOLAEVICH oc/Tax Consultant; Writer; b/Feb 26, 1896; h/3235 Barnes Cir, Glendale, CA 91208; ba/Los Angeles, CA; m/Kathrine; c/George, Linda; p/Nicolai Vasilievich (dec); Maria Ivanovna (dec); ed/Baccalaureate, Finland; Grad Artillery Acad; mil/Russian Artillery Ofcr WWI; pa/Author 2 Vol Poem 1000 Yrs of Russia; r/Greek Orthodox; hon/Var War Decorations.

KASINDORF, BLANCHE RUTH oc/Principal; b/May 18, 1925; h/50 Kenelworth Pl, Brooklyn, NY 11210; ba/Bklyn; m/David; p/Samuel Robins (dec); Anna Block Robins, Bklyn; ed/BA; MA; Cand PhD; pa/Prin Day Elem Sch; Mem Var Profl Orgs; cp/Var Commun Activs; hon/W/W: Am Wom, E, Ed Res, Intl Commun Ser.

KASLOW, DAVID MARTIN oc/Musician; b/May 12, 1943; h/365 S Williams St, Denver, CO 80209; ba/Denver; m/Judith; c/Matthew, Katherine; p/Clifford and Florence Kaslow, Delray Beach, FL; ed/BM, MM Manhattan Sch Mus; mil/USN Band; pa/Instr Lamont Sch Mus, Denver Univ; Free-lance French Horn Player; Clinician; Lectr; cp/Ct Last Resort Mensa Soc; r/Jewish.

KASPARIAN, ALICE ELIZABETH oc/Professor; b/Feb 28; h/4324 Seton Rd, Irvine, CA 92715; ba/Costa Mesa, CA; p/Armenog and Christina Kasparian (dec); ed/BA; MA; pa/Prof Bus Ed, Orange Coast Col 1958-; Instr Bi-lingual Shorthand; Conslt

Bus & Indust; Lectr; Others; r/Armenian Orthodox; hon/Cit Outstg Achmt, Orange Coast Col Bd Trustees; Grand Prize Winner, Intl Gregg Shorthand Contest; Recipient S'ships; W/W Wom Ed.

KATHREN, RONALD L oc/Health Physicist; Educator; b/Jun 6, 1937; h/137 Spring, Richland, WA 99352; ba/Richland; m/Susan; c/Sally Beth, Daniel; p/Ben

Kathren, Los Angeles, CA; Sally Kathren (dec); ed/BS UCLA 1957; MS Pittsburgh 1962; pa/Affil Asst Prof, Univ Wash Jt Ctr Grad Study; Am Bd Hlth Physics Panel Examrs; Am Nat Standards Inst (Var Coms); Hlth Physics Soc; AAAS; Am Nuclear Soc; Am Assn Physicists Med; Author Num Sci Papers, Book Chapts, 3 Texts; Lic'd Profl Engr; Former Mem Oregon St Radiation Adv Com; hon/Elda E Anderson Awd; Diplomate Am Acad Envir Engrs; Diplomate Am Bd Hlth Physics.

KATONA, ANNA BARBARA oc/Professor; b/Jul 7, 1920; h/63 Rutledge Ave, Apt 31, Charleston, SC 29401; ba/Charleston; p/Joseph and Margit Kenyeres Katona (dec); ed/Tchr Dipl 1944, PhD 1959 Univ Debrecen;

Addit Studies; pa/Prof Eng, Col Charleston 1975-; Univ Debrecen: Chrperson Eng Dept 1970-74, Deputy Chrperson 1957-69; Eurpean Screen'g Com, Am Coun Learned Soc; r/1st Scots Presb Ch; hn/British Coun Scholar; Rec'd Ford Foun Grant; Rec'd ACLS Grant; Post-Doct Fellow Yale Univ.

KATZ, ANNETTE SARA oc/Journalist; b/Jan 25, 1948; h/7740 Camino Real, Miami, FL 33143; ba/Miami; m/Stephen; p/Harold and Jean Van Dam, W Palm Beach, FL; ed/BS; pa/Dir Communs; Wom in Communs; AFT; cp/Active Dem Party; r/Jewish; hon/-Suburban Jour Yr, Fla Sch Bell; Dist'd 1st Pl Feature Writ'g, Union Tchrs Press Assn; Dist'd Achmt Awd; W/W: Am Wom, SEn US; World W/W; Personalities of S.

KATZ, IRVING I oc/Administrator; b/Mar 31, 1907; h/16159 Oxley Rd, Apt 203, Southfield, MI 48075; ba/Birmingham, MI; m/Gail Peres; c/Nina Claire K Isaac (Mrs Lawrence A), Myrna K Adelman (Mrs Melvyn); p/Michael Leiser and Rebecca Deutsch Katz (dec); ed/Univ Cleveland; Addit Studies; pa/Admr Temple Beth El 1939-; Oheb Zedek Congreg (Cleveland, Ohio): Synagogue Admr, Ed Dir 1927-36; Admr Anshe Emeth Temple (Youngstown, Ohio) 1936-39; Author Beth El Story - With A Hist of the Jews in Mich Before 1850, The Jewish Soldier From Mich in the Civil War, Others; Contbr Articles Jewish Hist Profl Mags, Encys; Fdr & Hon Life Pres Nat Assn Temple Admrs; UAHC: Hon VP, Mem Exec Bd, Exec Com; Exec Bd Metro Detroit Fdn Reform Synagogues; NATA Exec Bd; Others; cp/Jewish Nat Fund; Allied Jewish Campaign; Jewish Commun Coun; Jewish Hist Soc Mich; Wayne St Univ Press; Others; r/Jewish; hon/Recipient Num Awds: UAHC, NATA, Hebrew Union Col-Jewish Inst Rel, Reform Jewish Appeal, Am Jewish Hist Soc, Others.

KATZ, JANE oc/Professor; b/Apr 16, 1943; h/400 2nd Ave, New York, NY 10010; ba/Bronx, NY; p/Leon and Dorothea Oberkovitz Katz, NYC; ed/BS CCNY 1963; MA NYU 1966; MEd Col Univ 1973; pa/Prof Hlth & PE, Bronx Commun Col; Fdg Orgr, Intl Yth Fest Games Israel; Chrperson Aging Com, US Swim Foun; Co-Chm Wom's Swim'g Com, US Com Sports for Israel; Masters Track & Field Assn; Masters Sports Assn; Profl Staff Cong; NYC Zone Hlth Ed Tchrs Assn; Intl Acad Aquatic Art; Am Alliance Hlth, PE & Rec; Others; cp/Vol ARC Fac Div Aquatic, First Aid & Small Crafts Sch; Asst'd Creat Amateur Ath Union Metro Masters Swim Team; Emanuel Midtown Yg Men's-Yg Wom's Hebrew Assn; East Midtown Plaza Hous'g Co-op Local Reporter; r/Jewish;

hon/Recipient CCNY Hall Fame Ath Awd; Amatuer Ath Union Metro Outstg Masters Swim'g Awd; 10 Yrs Ser Hon Awd, ARC; Intl Swim'g Hall Fame; Traineeship S'ship Adm Aging, Columbia Univ; Others.

KATZ, MENKE oc/Poet; Editor; Teacher; b/Apr 12, 1906; h/1321-55 St, Brooklyn, NY 11219; ba/Bklyn; m/Ruth Rivke Feldman; c/Troim Handler, Hirshe David; p/Hirshe David and Badane Katz; ed/Columbia Univ; Bklyn Col; Univ So Cal; pa/Editor-in-Chief *Bitterroot*; Author 11 Pub'd Books Poetry; Incl'd Num Anthologies; r/Jewish; hon/Stephen Vincent Benet Awd; Poet Lore Narrative Awd; Poet Lore Descriptive Poem Awd.

KATZ, MORRIS oc/Artist; b/Mar 5, 1932; h/406 6th Ave, New York, NY 10011; ba/Same; p/Marcus and Lea Morris; ed/Ulm, W Germany & Gunsburg: Studied w Hans Facler; Art Students Leag (NY); pa/Evansville Mus Arts & Scis (Ind); Jr Col Albany (NY); Butler Inst Am Art (Youngstown, Ohio); St Lawrence Univ Griffiths Art Ctr (Canton, NY); Univ Art Gallery, St Univ NY Binghamton; Exhbns: Instant Art Shows, More than 2000 Throughout the World; Nat Acad TV Arts & Scis; IPA; Am Guild Variety Artists; Intl Arts Guild (Monaco); r/Jewish; hon/Paintings Distributed Throughout World, incl'g Portrait of Pope Paul VI.

KATZ, RICHARD JON oc/Marketing Executive; b/Feb 26, 1932; h/243 Parkside Dr, Roslyn Heights, NY 11577; ba/New York, NY; m/Helene G; c/Robin Lee, Juli Beth, Jennifer Sue; p/Irving and Lillian Katz, NYC;

ed/AAS Bklyn City Col; mil/USAF 1951-55; pa/Advtg & Mktg Exec; Am Mgmt Clb; Pres' Clb; Intl Soc Audio Scists; Advtg Clb; Futurist Soc; Builders Inst; cp/E African Wildlife Assn; Smithsonian Inst; Audubon Soc; Lib Pres Papers; hon/Holds Sev Patents; Rec'd Num Awds for Advtg & Mktg.

KATZMAN, LOUISE BROOKS oc/Retired Social Worker; b/Mar 21, 1914; h/5545 Stanford Dr, Nashville, TN 37215; m/Herschel; c/Terry B, Cindy L, Brooks H; p/Louis H and Rachel Brooks (dec); ed/BA Vanderbilt Univ; Ma Wash Univ; Univ Tenn Sch Social Work; pa/Profl Social Worker 10 Yrs; Former WPA Adm Staff, Tenn Dept Public Wel; Dir Chd's Bur; ACSW; cp/ARC; Jewish Social Ser; Pres N'ville Mtl Assn; N'ville Drug Treatmt Ctr; Sunshine House-Residence for Alcoholic Wom; Coun Jewish Wom Home Convalescent Chd; Others; r/Jewish; hon/Clara Barton Awd, ARC; Cult Integrity Awd, Am Foun Sci Creat Intell.

KAUFMAN, DONALD DAVID oc/Businessman; b/Jan 10, 1933; h/609 Central Ave, Newton, KS 67114; m/Eleanor Wismer; c/Kendra Janean, Galen David, Nathan Dean; p/David Daniel Kaufman (dec); Hulda Graber Kaufman, Freeman, SD; ed/AA 1953; BA 1955; BD 1958; MDiv 1969; pa/Pastor; Writer on War Tax Alts; Author *What Belongs To Caesar?*, *The Tax Dilemma: Praying for Peace, Praying for War*; cp/Var Civic & Commun Activs; r/Anabapt; hon/Commun Ldrs & Noteworthy Ams; Personalities of W&MW.

KAUFMAN, GARY EDWARD oc/Biologist; b/Dec 16, 1947; h/241 Boyd Ave,

Elmhurst, IL 60126; ba/Chicago, IL; m/Jean Jefferson; p/Max and Yetta Rose Kaufman, Philadelphia, PA; ed/BS Drexel Inst Technol 1968; PhD Univ Rochester 1974; pa/Res Assoc Radiol, Univ Chgo; Res Assoc, Franklin McLean Meml Res Inst; Assoc Radiation Biol & Biophysics, Univ Rochester 1977-78; Post-Doct Fellow Nat Cancer Inst 1974-77; Num Pubs Effects Ionizing & Non-ionizing Radiation; Radiation Res Soc; AAAS; Conslt Hlth, Safety & Envir Issues; cp/Former Asst Scoutmanster, BSA; hon/Sigma Pi Sigma; Awd for Sci Exhn, Radiation Soc N Am; Travel Awd, Radiation Res Soc; Recipient Sev S'ships & F'ships.

KAUFMAN, IRENE MATHIAS oc/Principal; b/Jan 28, 1942; h/936 Fairway Dr, Waynesboro, VA 22980; ed/BA Mary Baldwin Col 1963; MEd Univ Va 1968; pa/Elem Sch Prin (Waynesboro) 1973-; Media Spec (Waynesboro) 1967-73; 1st Grade Tchr (Waynesboro) 1963-67; NEA (Life Mem); Va Ed Assn; Waynesboro Ed Assn; Former Pres, Dist G Elem Sch Prins' Assn; Nat Assn Elem Sch Prins; Va Assn Elem Sch Prins; cp/Former Pres & Secy, Ctl Va Chapt Credit Unions; Va Credit Union Leag (Leg & Liaison Com); Former Pres & Bd Mem, WPSE Credit Union; Adv Bd, Waynesboro Salvation Army; Past Pres, Staunton-Augusta Repub Wom's Clb; Augusta Co Repub Com (Secy); 6th Dist Repub Wom's Rep; Wayne Dist Repub Com; Del, Repub Nat Conv 1972; Others; hon/World W/W Wom; Intl W/W Intells; Others.

KAUFMAN, JEAN J MASON oc/Professor; b/Aug 11, 1938; h/241 Boyd Ave, Elmhurst, IL 60126; ba/Chicago, IL; m/Gary Edward; p/Glen Vernon Jefferson, Lincoln, NE; Marion Lee Jefferson, Pittsburgh, PA; ed/RN Columbia Hosp Sch Nsg 1960; BSN 1966, MEd 1970, PhD 1976 Univ Pittsburgh; Addit Studies; pa/Rush Univ Col Nsg: Assoc Prof, Chm Dept Pediatric Nsg 1978-; Univ Tex Sch Nsg: Asst Prof 1 Yr, Assoc Prof 4 Yrs 1973-78; Chd's Hosp Pittsburgh: Staff Nurse Med Unit, PRN Nurse, Inservice Ed Coor 1963-69; Other Positions; Editor Review Panel *Nsg Res*, 1977-; Pub'd Num Articles Profl Jours; ANA; NLN; AECT; PLRA; HEMA; TAET; Others; cp/Bermuda Beach Homeowner's Assn; Adv Com Meals on Wheels; LWV; Task Force Ctr Devel Hlth Policy St Tex; r/Christian; hon/Norman Linde Meml Awd; Robert Wood Johnson Fac F'ship; Mrs George Sands Meml Awd; Personalities Am; World W/W Wom; Others.

KAUFMANN, MARION KENNETH oc/Physician; b/Jun 6, 1926; h/933 N Elm St, Greenville, IL 62246; ba/Greenville; m/Stella Miriam Butcher; c/Kenneth W, Bruce G, Donald Alan, Gary Bryan, Stella L, Sheryl L, April Dawn; p/Albert W and Aldah Wynona Kaufmann, Logan, OH; ed/BA Greenville Col 1949; MD Univ Ill Sch Med 1953; mil/USAF 1944-46; pa/Chief of Staff Utlaut Meml Hosp; Pres Bond Co Med Soc; Del Ill St Med Soc; cp/Bd Mem Ctl Ill Conf FM Ch; Bd Mem G'ville Col Alumni Assn; r/Free Meth Ch (G'ville): Mem; hon/Rec'd Pres Awd, G'ville Col.

KAULILI, ALVINA NYE oc/Retired; b/Oct 20, 1918; h/3817 Kaimuki Ave, Honolulu, HI 96816; m/Lordie Olinoikalani; p/Henry Atkinson and Pearl Kekumano Nye (dec); ed/BM New England Conservatory

Mus; MA Columbia Univ; pa/Former Chm Mus Dept Public Schs; Mus Dir: Honolulu Commun Theatre, Chinese Dramatic Clb, McKinley Theatre Group, Honolulu Police Chord Group; Am Choral Dirs Assn; Hawaii Mus Edrs Assn; cp/St Foun Cult & Arts; Public Radio Authority; Am Classic Week; Daughs Hawaii; Hawaiian Hist Soc; r/Rom Cath; hon/Delta Kappa Gamma; Mu Phi Epsilon; Phi Lambda Theta; Pi Kappa Lambda; Tchr Yr Awd.

KAVANAUGH, ROBERT LEE oc/Executive; b/May 11, 1945; h/111 Monticello Dr, Monroe, LA 71203; ba/Dallas, TX; m/Toni Renee Miller; c/Jason; p/Jimmy Lee Kavanaugh, Monroe; Audrey Bearden Brooks, Pine Bluff, AR; ed/BA; pa/Indust Acct Exec Mgr; r/Bapt; hon/Inner Cir Awd & Dist'd Ser Awd, Motorola.

KAWAHARA, FRED KATSUMI oc/-Chemist; b/Feb 26, 1921; h/2530 Eight Mile Rd, Cincinnati, OH 45244; ba/Cinc; m/-Sumiko Hayami; c/Robert K, Kiku-S, Richard H; p/Kentard and Kikue Seo Kawahara (dec);

Kawahara (dec); ed/BS w Hons; PhD; pa/Envir Trace Analysis (Oils, Carcinogens); Am Chem Soc; AWWA; Am Inst Chems; r/Bapt; hon/Fellow AIC; Group Superior Ser Awd, BAIC; Pres Commend Awd; Men Achmt; DIB.

KAWATRA, MAHENDRA P oc/Educator; Researcher; b/Jun 22, 1935; h/10 Seagull Lane, Port Washington, NY 11050; ba/Brooklyn, NY; m/Ved; c/Anjali, Anita, Sandhaya; p/Behari L Kawatra (dec); Chanan D Kawatra; ed/BA; BS w Hons; MS; PhD; pa/Prof & Reschr in Physics, M Evers Col, CUNY 1971-; Doctl Fac Mem; Asst Prof, Fordham Univ 1966-71; Assoc Res Scist, NYU 1964-66; Lectr; Author over 50 Res Papers in Intl Profl Jours; Author, *Dynamical Aspects of Critical Phenomena*; cp/Trustee, Hindu Temple; Others; r/Hindu; hon/Fulbright Scholar; Smith-Mundt Scholar, MIT; Sev Merit Awds.

KAY, KASMIR STANLEY oc/Administrator; Educator; Consultant; b/Sept 15, 1918; h/704 W Bay View Dr, Biloxi, MS 39530; m/Beverly B; c/Sherryl B; p/William B Kay (dec); Margaret R Kay, Terryville, CT;

ed/BSC; MBA; MPA; DPA; mil/USAR Lt/Col; pa/AAUP; Am Soc Public Adm; cp/Reserv Ofcrs Assn; r/Cath; hon/Men Achmt; DIB; Personalities of S; W/W: Govt, S&SW.

KAYE, SHIRLEY POSKANZER oc/Executive; b/Jun 15, 1932; h/Box 94, New Scotland, NY 12127; ba/Miami Beach, FL; m/Jesse; c/Lori-Nan, Neil, Melanie; p/Louis Poskanzer (dec); Edna P Grosberg, Albany, NY; pa/Pres Coconuts Record'g Co; Day Camp Dir; Dancer; Theatre Prodr; cp/Public Relats Rep, GSA; Past Pres Aux NYS Med Soc; r/Jewish.

KAYE, WILLIAM MARK oc/Administrator; b/Jun 29, 1949; h/801 Cherry St, Philadelphia, PA 19107; ba/Same; p/Philip R and Leona H Kaye, Boca Raton, FL; ed/BA Wilkes Col; MS Syracuse Univ; pa/Dir Hous'g & Fin Aid, Penn Col Podiatric Med 1976-; Pvt Cnslr; Free-lance Conslt Pers Mgmt Var Firms; Dir Hous'g, Wn New England Col (Springfield, Mass) 1973-76; Other Positions; APGA; Assn Col Pers Admrs; Assn Col & Univ Hous'g Ofcrs; Nat Assn Student Pers Admrs; cp/Soc Hill Clb; Vesper Clb; r/Jewish; hon/Outstg Yg Men Am; W/W: E, Am Cols & Univs; Recipient Ser Awd, Wn New England Col.

KEARIN, ANITA M oc/Manager; b/Jul 24, 1924; h/River Plaza, Apt 4205, 405 N Wabash Ave, Chicago, IL 60611; ba/Chgo; p/Dennis A and Anne M Brophy Kearin (dec); ed/In-Ser Govt Spec Tng; pa/Mgr Fed Info Ctr, US Gen Sers Adm 1968-; Tax Technician, US Treas Dept (IRS) 1943-68; Other Positions; cp/Chgo Outdoor Art Leag; Chgo & Cook Co Wom's Clb; Loretto Hosp Wom's Aux; Chgo Boosters Leag; Others; r/Cath; hon/Superior Perf Awds; First Lady of Day, Radio Station WAIT; Pile of Gold Awd, Chgo Boosters Leag; 1000 Hour Clb Awd; Nom Outstg Fed Supvr; Nom Fed Wom's Awd.

KEATINGE, RICHARD HARTE oc/Lawyer; b/Dec 4, 1919; h/1141 S Orange Grove, Pasadena, CA 91105; ba/Los Angeles, CA; m/Betty West; c/Richard West, Daniel Wilson, Nancy Elizabeth K Tronick; ed/BA w Hons Univ Cal-B 1939; MA Harvard 1941; JD Georgetown Univ 1944; pa/Partner Reavis & McGrath Law Firm 1979-; Partner Keatinge, Pastor & Mintz Law Firm 1948-79; Spec Asst, Atty Gen St Cal 1964-68; Other Positions; Admit'd DC Bar 1944; Admit'd NY Bar 1945; Admit'd Cal Bar 1947; Admit'd Supr Ct Bar 1964; Cal Law Revision Com; Am Law Inst; Intl Bar Assn; St Bar Assn Cal; Am Judic Soc; Assn Bus & Trial Lawyers; Others; cp/Former Del Dem Nat Conv; Former Trustee Dem Assocs Inc; Others; r/Epis; hon/Phi Beta Kappa.

KEATON, HAZEL VICTORIA oc/Homemaker; b/Feb 12, 1890; h/33-N 5 St, San Jose, CA 95112; m/Richard T (dec); p/Nels Peter Johnson (dec); Anna Matilda Neilson (dec); hon/Commun Ldrs & Noteworthy Ams; DIB; Notable Ams; Personalities W&MW; Gold Oak Leaf Pin, Am War Mothers; Received Plaque, Pacific Neighbors Sister City Prog; Others.

KEDER, VIRKO oc/Engineer; b/Sept 20, 1930; h/6548 Kirn St, McLean, VA 22101; ba/McLean; m/Ellen; c/Tina; p/Jakob Keder (dec); Leida Keder, Philadelphia, PA; ed/BSEE 1955, MSEE 1956 Purdue Univ; pa/Sr Sys Engr, Mitre Corp; Sr Mem IEEE; Computer Soc; Aerospace & Elects Sys Soc; Armed Forces Communs & Elects Assn; cp/Estonian-Am Nat Coun; Washington Estonian Soc; r/Luth; hon/Sigma Xi; Tau Beta Pi; Eta Kappa Nu; Arnold Air Soc.

KEEFE, MILDRED JONES oc/Retired Educator; b/Aug 14, 1896; h/10 Pearl St, Mattapoisett, MA 02739; p/John Augustin and Eliza Sweat Jones Keefe (dec); ed/BS 1934, MA 1936 Boston Univ; pa/Boston Univ: Former Asst Prof FAs in Rel, Former Dir Mus & Drama; Greenbriar Col (W Va): Former Dir Dramatic Art, Former Dir FAs Dept; Poet; Fdr Creat Arts Fest W Va; United Poets Laureate Intl; Nat Leag Am Pen Wom; AAUW; cp/Repub Party; r/Fairhaven Unit Meml Ch: Mem, Chm Creat Arts Coun; hon/Pi Lambda Theta; Pi Gamma Mu; 2000 Wom Achmt; W/W: Poetry, Am Wom.

KEEFER, EVELYN MAE oc/Executive;

---

b/Mar 24, 1925; h/1620 Sunrise Ln, Ada, OK 74820; ba/Ada; m/Howard Eugene; c/Janice K Diamond, Paul Eugene; p/Louis Delbert Denney (dec); Lucy Jane Milde Denney, Ada; pa/Keefer Supply Co: Co-Owner, Treas, Secy; cp/Past Pres Tanti Study Clb; Past Pres Ada Coun Garden Clbs; Past Pres Jr HS PTA & Ada Coun PTA; Past Pres FAs Dept, Study Clb; r/So Bapt: Past Pres Wom's Missionary Union, Past Chm Cureent Missions, Past Pres SS Class; hon/World W/W Wom; W/W: S&SW, Am; Commun Ldrs & Noteworthy Ams; Ams Bicent Yr; Personalities of S.

KEELE, MARJORIE SUE oc/Pediatrician; b/Jun 27, 1921; h/12512 Croydon Cir, Dallas, TX 75230; ba/Denton, TX; m/Doman Kent; c/Roger, Randy (dec), Sheri; p/Grant Elmore and Willie Elmira Goodpasture Harshbarger, Pottsboro, TX; ed/BS; MS; MD; pa/Tex Wom's Univ Denton: Pediatrician; Pediatric Neurol; Prof Spec Ed; Num Orgs Involv'g Disabled Chd; cp/Repub Party; r/Ch of Christ; hon/Alpha Chi; Alpha Omega Alpha.

KEEN, MARIA ELIZABETH oc/Professor; b/Aug 19, 1918; h/608 S Edwin, Champaign, IL 61820; ba/Urbana, IL; p/Harold Fremont and Mary Eileen Honore Dillon Keen (dec); ed/AB Uni Chgo 1941; MA Univ Ill 1948; pa/Univ Ill: Asst Prof Eng as 2nd Lang, Univ Senate Com Student Eng, Col

Liberal Arts & Scis Com Acad Standards, ESL Dept Coms (Curric, Fin Aid, Search Com), Dept Affirmative Action Rep; AAUP; Nat Assn Wom Deans, Advrs & Cnslrs; Am Inst Biol Scis; cp/LWV; ERA Ill; Champaign Commun Devel Com; Humane Soc; People for Animals; Univ YWCA; r/Bapt; hon/Phi Kappa Epsilon; W/W Am Wom; DIB.

KEEPLER, MANUEL oc/Professor; b/Nov 4, 1944; h/Box 1656 SCSC, Orangeburg, SC 29117; ba/Orangeburg; m/Dannie Lee Horusby; c/Adriane Kapayl; p/Agustavus H Keepler, Atlanta, GA; Charssie Nobell Prothro Keepler (dec); ed/BS Morehouse Col 1965; MA Columbia Univ 1967; PhD Univ N

Mex 1973; pa/SCSC: Assoc Prof Math & Computer Sci, Curric Conslt, Chm Dept Math 1973-76; Pub'd Num Papers Random Evolutions & Numerical Math; Lectr; Mem Num Profl Assns; cp/Advr & Tournamt Dir, Chess Clb; r/Bahai; hon/Rec'd Woodrow Wilson F'ship; Other F'ships; Sev Awds for Excell Tchg; Sigma Xi.

KEESLING, KAREN R oc/Research Analyst; b/Jul 9, 1946; h/3504 Stoneybrae Dr, Falls Church, VA 22044; ba/Washington, DC; p/Paul W and Ruth S Keesling, AZ; ed/BA

1968, MA 1970 Ariz St Univ; JD Cand Georgetown Univ; pa/Res Analyst, Lib Cong; Falls Ch BPW Clb; Nat Assn Wom Deans, Admrs & Cnslrs; cp/WEAL; N Va Polit Caucus; Nat Fdn Repub Wom; hon/Outstg Yg Wom Am; Outstg Achmt Awd, ASU Alumni.

KEEVER, ROSALIE AUSMUS oc/Historian; Writer; h/7002 Stockton Dr, Knoxville, TN 37919; ba/Same; c/Dale W, John Ausmus; p/John Franklin and Matilda Walden Ausmus (dec); pa/Author *Some Pioneer Preachers & Teachers of Tenn*; Others; Tenn Wom's Press & Authors Clb; Past Histn Claiborne Co; Bd Dirs Assn Preserv of Tenn; Bd Knoxville Branch Am Pen Wom; Others; cp/Secy Vol Wom's Repub Clb; Mem John Sevier Meml Assn; Nat VP Tenn Nat Soc So Dames Am; DAR; Others; r/Meth; hon/Num Prizes Art; Pub Awds; Others.

KEIL, NORMA FERN oc/Retired Rancher; b/Sept 27, 1906; h/701 SILL, Conrad, MT 59425; ba/Same; m/John (dec); c/Edgar Rheinhardt, Daniel Dean, Stephen Max; p/Edgar A Elliott, Salina, KS; Mary Elliott; ed/Elem Tchr Cert; cp/Chm Horizon Lodge Inc; Bd Chm Pondera Coun on Aging; VChm Area III Coun, Dem Nat Com; r/Prot; hon/Mont Sr Citizen Yr; Personalities of W&MW; Commun Ldrs & Noteworthy Ams.

KEITH, GLADYS PAULINE SMITH oc/Retired; b/Nov 3, 1908; h/PO Box 165, Melbourne Beach, FL 32951; m/James Early (dec); c/Mary Lou K Whitt (Mrs James Finney), James Sanders (dec); p/William Thomas and Rena Adeline Denton Smith (dec); pa/Ret'd Real Estate Broker 1968; Lic'd Tenn Real Estate Comm 1955; Author "Love Divine", Other Poems; Nat Writers' Clb; IPA; cp/Former Mem Knoxville Wom's Clb; Former Mem K'ville Flower Clb; Former Mem: Knox Co Yg Dem Clb, Knox Co Dem Wom's Clb, K'ville Dem Wom's Clb, Others; Ser'd Hospitality Coms for: Adali Stevenson, John F Kennedy, Lyndon B Johnson; Appt'd White House Com, Former Tenn Gov Bufford Ellington; Num Other Activs; r/Meth Ch: Mem; hon/Rec'd Commend & Cert Merit, Am Song Fest Cal; Intl Register Profiles; Personalities of S.

KEITH, VIRGIE IRENE oc/Supervisor; b/Aug 28, 1922; h/1808 7th St, Radford, VA 24141; ba/Pulaski, VA; p/Greene T Keith (dec); Ocie A Keith, Radford; ed/BS cum laude, Marion Col 1953; MS VPI & St Univ 1958; EdD Univ Va-C 1970; Addit Studies; pa/Supvr Math & Coor Sci, Pulaski Co Schs 1972-; Adj Prof Math Ed, VPI & St Univ 1974; Instr Math & Math Ed, Univ Va Sch Gen Studies 1959-; Other Positions; Lectr; Va Ed Assn; NEA; Nat Coun Tchrs Math; Nat Assn Supvn & Curric Devel; Nat Coun Adm Wom Ed; IPA; Others; r/Wesleyan Meth Ch: Mem, SS Tchr, Missionary Cir, Pianist, Yth Dir; hon/Kappa Delta Pi; Phi Kappa Phi; Delta Kappa Gamma; World W/W Wom; W/W Am Wom; Outstg Edrs Am; DIB; Others.

KELL, JEAN MARIE oc/Antique Dealer; b/Sept 3, 1909; h/305 Front St, Beaufort, NC 28516; ba/Beaufort; m/Copeland; c/Copeland III, Dogald, R Geoffrey, Jean, Marie, Jerome, Rosalie; p/Walter R Bruyere (dec); Edith Owen (dec); pa/Reschr; Author 3 Chd's Books, 3 Hists, 1 Play; cp/Dir C of C; Fdr Carteret Co Hist Res Assn; Chm Bicent Comm (Carteret Co); r/Epis.

KELLAM, JEFFREY STANTON oc/Clergyman; b/Jun 30, 1944; h/10649 Red Queen Rd, Richmond, VA 23235; ba/Richmond; m/Joan Maisch; c/Wendy Michelle, James Scott; p/Harry Victor and Beverly Warfield Kellam, Raleigh, NC; ed/BA Westminster Col; MDiv Union Sem; pa/Prodr & Host, *Celebration Rock* (Syndicated Radio Prog); Field Staff Person for Media & Yth, Hanover Presb; Chm Chesterfield Yth Sers Task Force; cp/Res & Devel Com, United Way; Citizens Res Com Cable TV; r/Presb; hon/Gabriel Cit for Radio Prog, Nat Assn Cath Broadcasters; W/W Rel.

KELLEHER, PAMELA RUTH oc/Executive; b/Jan 29, 1949; h/1421 Pheasant Run Ct, Norman, OK 73069; ba/Norman; m/Michael D; c/Christopher Michael, Julie Ann; p/Morris D and Virginia R Hurst, El Reno, OK; ed/Attend'd SWn St Univ; pa/Pres Personalized Direct Mail; VP Robb, Kelleher & Assocs; cp/Damrosh Mus Clb; Assoc Campaign Mgr & Treas, Robb for US Cong Campaign; Pres Home Demo Clb; r/Presb; hon/Nat Hon Soc.

KELLER, ERNESTINE CHRISTY oc/Homemaker; Artist; b/Sept 15, 1921; h/4236 Shannon Dr, Fort Worth, TX 76116; ba/Same; m/John F; c/John Christy, Karyn Cristelle; p/Ernest Christy (dec); Hazel L Christy, Ft Worth; ed/Attend'd Tex Wesleyan Col, Tex Christian Univ; Master Flower Show Judge Cert; Pvt Art Study; pa/Lectr & Judge, Flower Arrang'g; Tex Fine Arts Assn; Spectra Art Clb; GD Art Assn; Ft Worth Coun Nat Accred'd Flower Show Judges; cp/Wom's Clb Ft Worth; Ft Worth Garden Clb; City Coun PTA; Former Cub Scout Mother; Former Camp Fire Mother; Others; r/Univ Christian Ch; hon/Hon Life Mem Tex PTA.

KELLER, SUZANNE oc/Sociologist; b/1929; h/59 Col Rd, Princeton, NJ 08540; ba/Princeton; ed/PhD Columbia Univ 1954; pa/Sociol, Princeton Univ; VP Am Sociol Assn; hon/Recipient Guggenheim S'ship; Recipient Fulbright S'ship.

KELLEY, BEVERLY GWYN oc/Officer; b/Jun 26, 1952; h/Rt 1, Box 4254, Bonita Springs, FL 33923; ba/Maui, HI; p/Thomas E and Lois G McLear, Bonita Springs; ed/BA;

mil/USCG; pa/Ofcr USCG; r/Prot; hon/1st Female Cmdg Ofcr of US Mil Vessel in Naval Hist.

KELLEY, CALLIE IMOJEAN oc/Counselor; b/Aug 7, 1932; h/Rt 2, Box 43, Kelley Rd, Greenwood, SC 29646; ba/Greenwood; c/Paula Elizabeth; p/A B Kelley, Greenwood; Jane Klaus, Greenwood; ed/AB Lander Col; MEd Clemson Univ; pa/Cnslr, Southside Jr HS; SC Advr Sci World Adv Bd Scholastic Mags Inc; Rep SC Asst Ctr Wrkshop Suspensions & Dropouts; Secy Commun Adv

Coun for SC Ed Fin Act; Rep Greenwood Co Ed Coun; Chm Fin Com Southside Jr HS; Nat Assn Sch Cnslrs; NEA; SC Ed Assn; AAUP; AAUW; Others; cp/Greenwood Co Mtl Hlth Assn; Drug & Alcohol Assn Comm; Nat Rehab Assn; Chm Heart Fund; Rep Commun Adv Coun; Others; r/Rock Presb Ch: Mem, SS Tchr, Yth Advr; hon/Tchr of Yr Conserv Ed; Dist 50 Tchr Yr; Outstg Sec'dy Edr Am; Delta Kappa Gamma.

KELLEY, ELBERT HOLLIS oc/Minister; b/Jan 10, 1926; h/7730 Irvington Ave, Dayton, OH 45415; ba/Dayton; m/Evelyn; c/Michael, Murray, Gregory; p/Allen Kelley, Columbus, GA; Lupah Kelley (dec); ed/BS Fla So Col; BA SEn Col; mil/USN; pa/Pres Gtr Dayton Assemblies of God; Secy & Treas W Ctl Section Assemblies of God; cp/Northridge Sch Steer'g Com; hon/W/W Rel.

KELLEY, LOUISE SALTER oc/Director; b/Aug 19, 1907; h/1724 Wrightsboro Rd, Augusta, GA 30904; ba/Augusta; m/George W Sr; c/George W Jr, Helen K Cleveland; p/James Blaine Salter (dec); Flewda Parker Salter, Augusta; ed/BA Ga St Col; MEd Univ Ga; Addit Studies; Richmond Co Schs; Proj Dir Right to Read & Coor Devel 1st Grade (1976-78), Read'g Coor (1966-76); Tchr Eng & Read'g, Tubman Jr HS (1960-66); Other Positions; Org'd CSRA Read'g Coun; Orgr Richmond Co Eng Coun; Org'd Tutorial Prog, Richmond Co Bd Ed; St Read'g Coun; St Adv Com, Ed Resources; Info Ctr & Clearinghouse; GDIS; ASCD; Others; r/Bapt; hon/Alpha Delta Kappa; Kappa Delta Pi; Outstg Ldrship & Ser Awd, Ga Coun Internation Read'g Assn.

KELLEY, ONETIA MAY oc/Artist; b/May 27, 1909; h/3417 Groman Ct NE, Albuquerque, NM 87110; ba/Same; m/David Otis; c/Onetia Jean K Leonard, Robert Otis,

p/Walter Thistle and Bessie Anna Currey Nettles (dec); ed/BA Univ So Cal; pa/HS Math Tchr 3½ Yrs; Painter Landscapes 40 Yrs; r/Ch of Christ; hon/Rec'd S'ship; Rec'd Num Art Awds.

KELLEY, RONALD D oc/Minister; b/Oct 4, 1941; h/2923 Ashton Rd, Sarasota, FL 33581; ba/Same; m/Sheila Mae Fites; p/Leo Clark Kelley (dec); Rose Adda Johnson Kelley, Wheatland, IN; ed/AS Vincennes Univ 1968; BA Lincoln Christian Col 1972; MA Lincoln Christian Sem 1976; Addit Studies; mil/USAF 1960-63; pa/Sr Min Sarasota Christian Ch; Acad Dean, Ohio Val Christian Col 1976-78; Secy Little Galilee Christian Camp; Author *Help! I'm Dying*, 1977; Conducted Travel Tours; Am Assn Christian Cnslrs; Fla Westcoast & St Min's Assn; Pres Minier Bus Assn; Lic'd HS Basketball Ofcl; r/Christian Ch: Mem; hon/Outstg Yg Men Am; W/W Rel.

KELLINGER, JOSEF MICHAEL oc/Professor; b/Oct 7, 1916; h/735 Philadelphia Ave, Chambersburg, PA 17201; ba/Chambersburg; m/Cesi; c/Ellie M, Pavla C; p/Andrew and Maria Kellinger (dec); ed/BA; MA; PhD; mil/Intell; pa/Prof German, Wilson Col; AATG; MLA; AAUP; r/Luth; hon/Recipient Christian R & Mary F Lindback Foun Awd for Dist'd Tchg.

KELLNER, DAVENA MAE oc/Professor; h/1701 Patricia Ave, Willow Grove, PA 19090; ba/Brynmawr, PA; m/Hugh L; c/Robert Hugh; p/Robert Pollock (dec); Ida B Pollock Smith, Ontario, Canada; ed/BA Univ Toronto; MA Villanova Univ; pa/Harcum Jr Col; Assoc Prof Eng; Chm Fac Affairs; AAUW; r/Prot; hon/Recipient Grants: Nat Endowmt Humanities, Newpaper Fund, Govt Jr Col England; W/W: Wom's Studies, Am Wom.

KELLNER, THEDA AILEEN oc/Librari-

an; Educator; b/Mar 3, 1919; h/1612 Independence Ct, Fort Collins, CO 80526; ba/Denver, CO; m/Harvey William; c/Judith Ann K Hancock; ed/BA Univ Colo 1940; MA Univ Denver 1959; pa/Conslt, Colo St Lib 1967-; Libn, La Junta (Colo) 1959-67; Other Positions; Contbr Articles Profl Jours; Am Lib Assn: Dir-at-Large, A-V Com, Exeptional Ser Awd Com, St/White House Conf Com; Colo Assn Sch Libns; Colo Ed Media Assn; Colo Consortium Law Libs; Colo Lib Assn; NEA; BPW; Others; cp/Colo Soc Prevention Blindness; Am Correctional Assn; hon/W/W: W, Am Wom; Intl W/W Commun Ser; DIB; Intl Scholars Dictionary; Others.

KELLY, CECILIA MARY oc/Dancer; b/Mar 10, 1922; h/Meadowland Farm, PO Box 171, Greenwood, LA 70133; ba/Same; m/Eugene Joseph; c/Eugene James, Chinta Monica; p/James Robert and Emily Monica Hewitt Ellis, Kent, England; pa/Guest Master Tchr, So Meth Univ (Dallas, Tex) 1966-67;

Artist-in-Residence, Shreveport Symphony Ballet 1974-75; Fdr & Dir: Twin City Civic Ballet (Monroe, La) 1970-, Shreveport Symphony Ballet 1966-72, Others; Nat Dance Chm, Nat Soc Arts & Lttrs 1978-; Other Positions; cp/Jr VP Ladies Aux VFW; Chm Save the Whale Com, La Soc Animal Protection Legislation; r/Rom Cath; hon/Gov Faubus Awd.

KELLY, DORIS LILLIAN oc/Educator; b/Oct 30, 1921; h/203 Loudon Rd, B-6, A-16, Concord, NH 03301; ba/Concord; p/Gilbert H and Lillian M Kelly (dec); ed/BS En Nazarene Col 1954; MBA Boston Univ 1959; mil/Wom's Army Corps 1942-52; pa/Prof & Head Bus Adm Dept, NH Tech Inst; r/Dist Missionary Treas; Missionary; Pres; Organist; SS Tchr; Auditor; Ch Bd; hon/Fellow Am Biogl Inst.

KELLY, HELEN S oc/Librarian; b/Jan 31, 1917; h/82 Euclid Ave, Riverside, RI 02915; ba/Providence, RI; m/George H; c/G Richard, Donald Paul; p/George Jr and Lille Eisenhauer Stikeman (dec); ed/BS (Bus Adm) Univ RI 1938; BS (Lib Sci) Carnegie Inst Technol 1941; pa/Libn & Asst Prof, URI; ALA; NELA; RILA; NETSL; NUEA; AAUP; r/Congreg; hon/Rec'd 1st RILA S'ship.

KELLY, MARGARET McLAURIN RICAUD oc/Retired Teacher; Poet; b/Mar 22, 1910; h/402 Fayetteville Ave, Bennetsville, SC 29512; p/Robert Barry and Lulu M Croclaud Ricaud (dec); ed/BA; Addit Studies; pa/Author *Jack & the Flying Saucer*, Other Chd's Stories; Author Num Poems incl'g "The Ricaud Fam"; Writer Features & News, SC Newspaper; Nat Soc Poets; Cert'd Geneol (Wash, DC); Nat Geneol Soc; cp/Mayflower

Soc; SC Hist Soc; Nat Geographic Soc; Col Dames XVII Cent; Nat Argumt Soc; Others; r/Meth; hon/Rec'd Humanitarian Awd for Poetry; Work Incl'd in *The Charleston Poetic Review*, *New Voices Am Poetry*, Others; Directory SC Writers; W/W Am Wom, S&SW; Writer's Dictionary; Others.

KELLY, MICHAEL JOHN oc/Executive; b/Jul 9, 1928; h/9210 Country Clb Rd, Woodstock, IL 60098; ba/Woodstock; m/Marietta F; c/Karen, Michael Shawn, Kimberly, Kevin, Brian; p/George A and Elizabeth K Kelly; ed/BS Mich St Univ 1949; mil/USAAF 1943-46; pa/Chm Bd: Kelco

Industs Inc, Flex-Weld Inc (Bartlett, Ill), Atl India Rubber Co (Chgo), Mogul Rubber Corp (Goshen, India), Technoflex (Mexico City, Mexico), CEDAM Intl, Others; Ec Clb Chgo; cp/Woodstock Opera Clb; Chgo Clb; Explorers Clb; Newcome Soc; Others; r/Rom Cath; hon/Rec'd Air Medal, USAAF; Psi Upsilon.

KELLY, ROBERT EMMETT oc/Physicist; b/Nov 26, 1929; h/Box 493, University, MS 38677; ba/University; m/Sarah Grace; c/Katelyn, Frank, Tara; p/Robert E Kelly (dec); Gladys Kelly, Cape Girardeau, MO; ed/BS; MS; PhD; mil/AUS 1954-56; pa/Physicist, Univ Miss; Am Geophysical Union; Conslt, Los Alamos & Lawrence Livermore Labs; cp/Am Fdn Mus & Symph Orchs; r/Meth; hon/Grad'd w Hons; Omicron Delta Kappa; Pi Mu Epsilon; Sigma Xi; Sigma Pi Sigma.

KELLY-GADOL, JOAN oc/Author; Professor; b/Mar 29, 1928; h/150 Claremont Ave, New York, NY 10027; ba/NYC; p/George V and Ruth Jacobsen Kelly; ed/BA summa cum laude, St John's Univ Col 1953; MA 1954, PhD 1963 Columbia Univ; pa/Prof Hist, CCNY; Instr Sarah Lawrence Col 1971-74; Visit'g Asst Prof, Columbia Univ 1963-64; Am Hist Assn; Renaissance Soc Am; Inst Res Hist; Others; Author *Universal Man of the Early Renaissance*, 1969, 73; Contbr Num Articles Profl Jours; hon/Recipient F'ships: Woodrow Wilson, Fulbright, Yale Univ, Columbia Univ, William Duryea, NYU, Kent (Nat Coun Rel Higher Ed), Danforth; Jr Fellow, Nat Foun Arts & Humanities; Others; W/W Am Wom; World W/W Wom Ed; Contemp Authors; Others.

KEMP, DOROTHY ELIZABETH oc/- Musician; b/Nov 23, 1926; h/4559 Hamilton Ave, Cincinnati, OH 45223; ba/Newport, KY; m/David H; p/Frederich W and Lula M B Walter, Cinc; ed/BS Col Conservatory Mus, Univ Cinc 1948; MA En Ky Univ 1949; Addit Studies; pa/Free-Lance Mus (French Horn,

Piano, Accordian) 1950-; Mus Tchr K-6, Newport Public Schs 1967-; Other Positions; Pub'd Brass Quartettes, Others; Am Fdn Mus; cp/Conductor Powel Crosley Jr YMCA Adult Symph Band; r/Prot; hon/Rec'd S'ships, En & Wn Ky Univs; Phi Beta Mus Frat; W/W Mus; DIB; Fellow Intl Biogl Assn.

KEMP, LAMAR ELLIOTT oc/Attorney; b/Dec 5, 1912; h/8000 Carey Pl, Oxon Hill, MD 20022; ba/Oxon Hill; c/Carolyn K Parker, Barbara K Gasque; p/Thomas Ardell and Rosalie Elliott Kemp (dec); ed/ABJ; MAG; LLB; mil/Civilian Employee Army, Navy, Air Force; pa/Ga, DC & Fed Bar Assns; APRA; SPA; PG & Md Bd Realtors; cp/Oxon Hill Dem Clb; Oxon Hill Rec Coun; Civic Cong SPGC; AARP; NARFE; r/Oxon Hill Meth Men's Ch; Former Pres; hon/Rotary Clb Hons S'ship, Univ Ga; Spec Citizens Awd, SPGC Civic Cong; Dedicated Vol Awd.

KEMPF, JANE E oc/Journalist; b/Sept 28, 1927; h/Rt 2, Box 438, Waterloo, IN 46793; ba/Auburn, IN; m/Peter; c/Peter Albert, Jan Michael, Richard Allen, Jeffery Val; p/Albert T and Alice Gaston Mullen, Coldwater, MI; pa/Columnist Auburn *Evening Star*; Hoosier St Press Assn; IPA; cp/Bd Mem, DeKalb Co Pre-Sch for Handicapped; Former Mem DeKalb Co Alcoholic Beverage Comm; Repub Party; r/Presb.

KENDRICK, DIANE PRISCILLA oc/Art Instructor; b/Feb 26, 1948; h/PO Box 81, Milton, NC 27305; ba/Danville, VA; p/James and Alice Kendrick, Greensboro. NC; ed/BS

East Carolina Univ 1971; MFA UNC-G 1976; pa/AAUP; SECAE; NAEA; Caswell Coun Arts & Hist; VP Weavers Guild; r/Rolling Roads Bapt Ch (G'boro); hon/Rec'd Tchrs Ser Awd; Rec'd Restoration Grant, St of NC.

KENDRO, RICHARD JOSEPH oc/Executive; b/Dec 15, 1931; h/3428-W Colette Ct, Mequon, WI 53092; ba/Milwaukee, WI; m/Barbara Ann Goedicke; c/Margo Elizabeth, Colby Elizabeth; p/Joseph Francis Kendro (dec); Anna Marie Kvasnick Kendro;

ed/BS; BA; mil/USAF 1951-55; pa/Cleaver-Brooks Div, Aqua-Chem Inc: Pres 1974-, Plant Mgr 1967-71, VP Mfg Water Tech Div 1971-73, Exec VP Water Tech Div 1973-74, Others; IPA; Indust Mgmt Clb; Am Boiler Mfrs Assn; Exhb'd Art Shows: Canton Art Inst, N Canton Art Gallery; cp/Former Scoutmaster BSA; St Michael's Men's Clb; Toastmaster Clb; hon/Named Pa Sports Hall Fame.

KENNEDY, D JAMES oc/Minister; b/Nov 3, 1930; h/2750 NE 58th St, Fort Lauderdale, FL 33308; ba/Ft Lauderdale; m/Anne Craig Lewis; c/Jennifer Lynn; p/George R Kennedy (dec); Ermine Kennedy, Tampa, FL; ed/BA Univ Tampa; MDiv cum laude, Columbia Theol Sem; MTh summa cum laude, Chgo Grad Sch Theol; DD Trinity Evangelical Sch; PhD NYU; pa/Sr Min, Coral Ridge Presb Ch; hon/Rec'd George Wash Hon Medal Awd, Freedom Foun Val Forge; W/W: Fla, Rel Am; DIB; Men Achmt; Others.

KENNEDY, M PATRICE oc/Principal; b/Sept 7, 1925; h/520 School St, Ness City, KS 67560; p/Joseph L Kennedy (dec); Bertha W W Kennedy, Eureka, KS; ed/BS; MS;

pa/Sister Rel Order; Prin & Tchr 7th & 8th Grades; KSTA; NCEA; NEA; cp/Works w Culturally Deprived Chd; Chd's Safety Patrol; Adult Advr; Voc Bible Sch; r/Cath; hon/Hon Chd's Safety Awd, St of NM.

KENNEDY, MARTIN TRAVIS oc/Clergyman; b/Dec 1, 1917; h/PO Box 825, Anton, TX 79313; ba/Anton; m/Bessie L; c/Peggy Ann K Peters, Martin T, Kirby K; p/Roscoe C Kennedy, Odessa, TX; Myrtle Lauderdale Kennedy (dec); ed/BS Okla Bapt Univ 1949; BD SWn Bapt Sem 1957; Addit Studies; mil/US Calvary 1938-41; USN 1942-45; USAF Maj 1960-; pa/Pastor Num Chs; Instr Bible & Homeletics, Grand Canyon Col 1958-62; Instr Sem Ext Ctr (Albuquerque, NM) 1974-76; Moderator Platte Val Bapt Assn; Secy Colo Pastor's Conf; Exec Bd, NM Bapt Conv; cp/Lion's Intl; Past Grand Master, IOOF NM; r/Bapt; hon/W/W Rel; Intl Dictionary Biography; Intl W/W Commun Ser.

KENNEY, ALAN oc/Supervisor; h/8 Central St, Somerville, MA 02143; ed/BS NEn Univ 1972; pa/Bradlees Co: Supvr Elect Register Prog 1973-, Asst Store Mgr 1973, Dept Mgr 1969-72; Am Mktg Assn; cp/Somerville Sch Com: Bd Mem, Chm Spec Ed Com; Nat Sch Bd Assn; Mass Assn Sch Coms; Smithsonian Inst; Gtr Boston Assn Retarded Citizens; Nat Trust Hist Preserv; Conservative Caucus; Coun Basic Ed; r/St Anthony's Ch; hon/Outstg Yg Men Am; W/W: E, Am; Men Achmt; DIB; Commun Ldrs & Noteworthy Ams.

KENNY, BETTIE ILENE oc/Artist; Author; Diamond-Point Engraver; b/Jun 5, 1931; ba/PO Box 30049, Seattle, WA 98103; m/Donald Keith; p/Lester Arthur and Ruby Doris Harmon Cruts, Spanaway, WA; ed/BA w Hons, Univ Wash; pa/Past Pres Wash St Chapt Nat Profl Artist Assn; IPA; PNAC; Psychol Forum; cp/Adv Bd, Good Shepherd Commun Ctr; NRTA; Coor for Seafair; r/Ecumenical; hon/Rec'd Lttrs Commend: Lawrence Welk, Gov Daniel Evans, Gov Dixie Lee Ray, Mayor Wes Uhlman, Paul Friedlander, Others; Rec'd Merit Awds, Boeing; Rec'd Paint'g Awds; W/W Wom; DIB; Intl W/W Arts & Antiques; Others.

KENT, BARBARA ELLEN oc/Professor; b/Aug 10, 1928; h/207 Santa Margarita, Menlo Park, CA 94025; ba/Palo Alto, CA; p/William J Kent (dec); Dorothy Simpson Kent, Dallas, TX; ed/BS; MA; pa/Stanford Univ Sch Med: Adj Prof, Clinical Coor, Phy Therapist; Am Phy Therapy Assn: Book Reviewer, Survey Team for Accreditation Profl Phy Therapy Progs, Ed Section; Soc Behavioral Kinesiology; Former Commr St

Exams Registration Phy Therapists, Cal Bd Med Examrs; Lectr; Conslt; Pub'd Num Articles Profl Jours; Other Activs; r/Epis; hon/Rec'd Nat Foun Tchg F'ship; Rec'd Golden Pen Awd; World W/W Wom Ed.

KENT, MARY LOU oc/State Representative; b/Oct 3, 1921; h/22 Spring Lake, Quincy, IL 62301; ba/Springfield, IL; m/Lawrence S; c/Curtis B, Roger H, Laura Auckley; p/Frank M and Myrtie Booth McFarland (dec); pa/Ill St Gen Assembly: Rep 48th Dist, Spokesman Exec Com (House), Appropriations Com, Trans Com; r/Meth.

KERANS, LAWRENCE CLINTON oc/Clergyman; b/Dec 8, 1904; h/Rt 5, Box 610, Monroe, LA 71203; m/Mable McClaurin; c/Robert H Colvard (Step-S); p/James Robertson and Jessie Prather Kerans (dec); ed/BA Centenary Col; MA Baylor Univ; Cert Pastoral Clinical Tng, LSU; mil/USAF;

pa/Pastor Num Cumberland Presb Chs Ill; Dir & Ldr: Ind, La & Tex Yth Camps; Author *The Four Books of Revelation*; cp/Com on Aging, C of C; Caddo Coun on Aging; r/Presb; hon/Alpha Chi; Chi Sigma Nu; Kappa Delta Pi; W/W Rel; Intl W/W Intellectuals.

KERESTAN, RICHARD MICHAEL oc/Music Educator; b/Apr 26, 1945; h/2706 Moeller Dr, Hamilton, OH 45014; ba/Hamilton; m/Kitty Wilde; c/Aaron R, Brian C; p/Michael and Anna B Kerestan, Cheswick, PA; ed/BMEd Morehead St Univ; pa/Ross Sr HS: Dir Mus & Bands, Coor Mus; Pvt Instrn; Conslt Butler Co (Ohio) Schs; Asst Instr, Morehead St Univ Bands 1968; Mus Camp Cnslr & Instr, Springdale HS 1964-65; Perf'd Mus Plays; NEA; Mus Edrs Nat Conf; Ohio Ed Assn; Ohio Mus Ed Assn; Nat Band Assn; Pub'd Articles Profl Jours; r/Luth; hon/Recipient Dist'd Alumni Awd, Morehead St Univ; 4 Awds for Bicent Concert Prog, Ohio St Bd Ed; Nat Arion Foun Awd for Mus; Men Achmt; Personalities W&MW; Others.

KERR, CATHERINE E BAILEY oc/Artist; b/Jul 4, 1928; h/1412 W Hendricks, Roswell, NM 88201; m/J K; c/2; p/A D and Lynn Marie Wilson Bailey; ed/BA Mason Col Mus & Fine Arts 1952; Art Students Leag (NYC) 1962; pa/Owner, Kerr Sch Art for Handicapped; Art Exhbns: Ligoa Duncan Gallery (NYC), Raymond Duncan Galleries (Paris, France), David's Gallery (Roswell), Security Nat Bank (Roswell), Num Others in US & Europe; Work in Perm Collections, US & Europe; Allied Artists WV; Luxemburg Museum, Paris; hon/Rec'd Awds, Assn Belgo-Hispanica; Las Palmas de Ora al Mierte Belgo Hispanico, Raymond Duncan Gallery; Prix du Centenaire Dipl & Medaille Ciencias Humanisticas Relaciones Dipl (Santo Domingo, Dominican Republic); Grand Prix Humanitaire, Luxemburg Mus de France; Intl Fest Paintings; Personalities of S.

KERR, CHARLES MACDONALD III oc/-Lecturer; b/Jul 3, 1912; h/Box 4033, New Orleans, LA 70178; m/Eleanor Carol Morris; c/Theresa Helen, Charles M IV; p/Charles M and Helen Marion Kerr (dec); ed/BBA; pa/Lectr Num Civic Orgs & Univs; r/Epis; hon/Man of Yr, La Goodwill; Rec'd Cit, War Dept; Others.

KERR, GRETCHEN H oc/Human Developmentalist; b/Jul 17, 1935; h/Rt 1, Swedesford Rd, North Wales, PA 19454; ba/Phila-

delphia, PA; m/Leland Green; p/Kenneth and Marguerite, Franklin, NC; ed/BA Fla St Univ 1957; MA Univ Plano 1975; pa/Study'g & Tchg Mental Devel; r/Soc of Friends; hon/-Rec'd Brazilian Gold Medal of Hon & Merit; Recipient British Star of Hope & Japanese Medallion.

KERR, MILDRED HOOVER oc/Teacher; b/Aug 31, 1919; h/21 D, E Georgia, Temple, OK 73568; ba/Temple; m/Wesley H; c/John W, Mary L; p/Willie E and Minnie C Hoover (dec); ed/AS; BS; Addit Studies; pa/Bus Ed Tchr, Temple HS; Yrbook Advr 15 Yrs; Career Cnslr 25 Yrs; 25 Yr Mem: NEA, OEA, TEA; Pres & Secy Cotton Co Unit, United Tchrs Profession; Del to OEA Assembly; Pres, VP, Secy Local TEA; Sch Coun: Bldg Rep, Chm Accountability, Chm Public Relats; cp/Pres & Secy Home Demon Clb; Fac Rep to C of C; r/1st Bapt Ch (Temple): Mem, SS Tchr, Advr Adult Lib Pubs; hon/Tchr Yr: Masonic Lodge, Cotton Co, Temple HS; Cand Okla Tchr Yr; Yrbook Dedication 2 Yrs; Aerospace Ed Awd; Outstg Sec'dy Tchr Am; Outstg Sec'dy & Elem Tchr Am; Personalities S; Intl W/W Commun Ser.

KESSLER, MINUETTA SHUMIATCHER oc/Concert Pianist; h/30 Hurley St, Belmont, MA 02178; ba/Same; m/Myer M; c/Ronald, Jean; p/Abraham Isaac and Luba Lubinskaya Shumiatcher; ed/Grad & Post-Grad Degs, Julliard Sch Mus; pa/Composer; Tchr; Author; Pres New England Pianoforte Tchrs Assn; VP Mass Mus Tchrs Assn; r/Jewish; hon/2 Canadian ASCAP Awds; Compostition Awd, Brooklyn Lib Mus; Rec'd Gold Key to City of Calgary.

KESSMAN, ALAN S oc/Executive; b/Sept 29, 1946; h/9039 N Karlov, Skokie, IL 60076; ba/Chicago, IL; m/Nancy; c/Erin Sherene; p/Herbert and Florence Kessman, Mt Vernon, NY; ed/BA; MBA; CPA; pa/Pres Rolm Corp; Am Mgmt Assn; Am Inst CPAs; NY St Soc CPAs; NAA; Pres' Clb; cp/C of C; United Way Fund Raiser; r/Jewish; hon/W/W E; Intl W/W; Others.

KESSNER, DANIEL AARON oc/Composer; b/Jun 3, 1946; h/10955 Cozycroft Ave, Chatsworth, CA 91311; ba/Northridge, CA; m/Dolly Eugenio; c/Darren Eugene, Demian Edward; p/William Kessner (dec); Dorothy B Saxe, Guerneville, CA; ed/BA cum laude 1967, MA 1968, PhD w Distinction 1971 Univ Cal-LA; pa/Assoc Prof Mus; Composer Num Works incl'g *Symph for Small Orch, Equali I,*

Wind Sculptures, Others; Nat & LA Chapt Pres, Nat Assn Composers; Secy & Treas, US West Coast Section Intl Soc Contemp Mus; r/Jewish; hon/Recipient Num Composition Awds: 11th Annual Contemp Mus Fest Competition (Ind St Unv), Cal St Univ Northridge Pres' Clb, Queen Marie-Jose Intl Composition Prize, Broadcast Mus Awds Student Composers, Others; Nom'd Pulitzer Prize *Strata*; Others.

KEYS, RAYMOND R oc/Lieutenant Colonel; b/Jun 10, 1929; h/421 Eagle Dr, Satellite Beach, FL 32937; ba/Patrick AFB, FL; m/Gloria P, c/Kimberly A, Sharon K, Karen L, Raymond R; p/Audra R Keys, St Petersburg, FL; ed/BSC Ohio Univ 1951; BSEE Okla St Univ 1962; MBA George Wash Univ 1965; Grad Squadron Ofcrs Sch 1958; Command & Staff Sch 1965 Air Univ; Grad

Indust Col Armed Forces 1974; mil/USAF Active duty; pa/Instr & Dir USAF Elect Schs; Spec Work Elects, Mechanics, Physics & Geology in Spain; US Elects Staff & Liaison Ofcr Canadian Govt; Prog Mgr USAF Res Satellites, Office Aerospace Res; Sci Prog Mgr USAF Tech Applicatons Ctr (Wash, DC & Patrick AFB); Chief Contract Mgr En Test Range; Contbr Articles Profl Jours; IEEE; cp/Dir Yth for Christ Interdenom Yth Choir; Chm Jr HS Adv Com; BSA Merit Badge Cnslr; Cub Scout Com; Others; r/Lay Speaker; Lay Ldr; Tchr; hon/Phi Delta Theta.

KHATENA, JOE oc/Professor; b/Oct 25, 1925; h/8 Tally Ho Dr, Starkville, MS 39759; ba/Mississippi State, MS; m/Nelly; c/Annette, Jacob Allan, Moshe, Serena; p/Jacob and Rachel Khatena (dec); ed/BA (2); MEd; PhD; pa/Prof & Head Dept Ed Psychol, Miss St Univ; Author Sev Books, Others; Editor Bd, *Gifted Child Qrtly*; Pres Nat Assn Gifted Chd; Fellow Am Psychol Assn; r/Jewish; hon/Recipient S'ships; Rec'd Univ Malaya Awd; Rec'd Marshall Univ Res Awd; Cert Recog, USOE Office Gifted.

KHIMCHIACHVILI, ROBERT von B oc/Executive; b/Feb 15, 1925; h/116 Ctl Park S, New York, NY 10019; c/George; p/Robert von Baden-von Badische and Princess Diane von B-Khimchiachvili; ed/MS; DD; PhD; mil/Bulgarian Army; pa/Pres Eurodollars Bk Ltd; cp/74th Grand Master Sovereign Mil & Hospitaler Order St John Jerusalem; Knights of Malta; Ofcl Seat the Hague; Kingdom Netherlands; r/Luth; hon/Rec'd 22 Decorations; Recipient Humanitarian Awd, Fairleigh-Dickinson Univ.

KHO, JAMES WANG oc/Professor; m/Joanne Jane; p/Eng-Too and Lour-Chii Kho, Sacramento, CA; ed/BA cum laude, MS, MBA, PhD Univ Wis; pa/Prof & Chm Dept Computer Sci, Cal St Univ-S; Conslt St of Cal; Pres Data Process'g Co; ACM; DPMA; SGSR; SCS; ORSA; UPE; Lectr; Pub'd Articles Profl Jours; Owner Import Bus; hon/Recipient Var Res Awds; Sigma Xi; Men & Wom Scist Am; Others.

KIENZLE, JOHN FRED oc/Teacher; b/Apr 1, 1945; h/Rt 1, Box 265, Nassau, NY 12123; ba/Castleton, NY; m/Patricia Catherine; p/Fred John Kienzle, Titusville, FL; Florence Mary Kienzle, Patchogue, NY; ed/BA w Hons, St UNiv NY 1967; MA w Hons, NY Univ 1969; PhD Princeton Univ;

pa/Instr Asian, African, Middle En Studies & Chief Media Ctr Technician, Maple Hill HS 1970-; Asst Near E Collection, NYU Lib 1967-69; Oriental Collection, Firestone Lib (Princeton Univ) 1969-70; Nat A-V Assn; Nat, NY & Capitol Dist Couns Social Studies; NY St Ednl Communs Assn; Middle E Inst; Others; cp/Ofcr Rensselaer Co Radio Civil Emer Ser; r/Rom Cath; hon/Recipient Awd, NY St Regent's Coun; Rec'd S'ships; W/W Sch Ofcls; DIB; Commun Ldrs & Noteworthy Ams; Notable Ams.

KIESELHORST, LOIS GENEVIEVE oc/Accountant; b/Feb 21, 1933; h/2556 N Avon, Roseville, MN 55113; ba/Minneapolis, MN; m/Henry Edward; c/Lory Ann, John Arthur; p/Arthur R and Genevieve Wiegele, Roseville; pa/Mgr Dan N Hansen & Assocs Inc (St Paul, Minn) 1967-75; Property Mgmt 1975-77; VP TYCON Mgmt Inc; Nat Soc

Public Accts; Minn Multi Hous'g Assn; cp/Bloomington C of C; IPA; r/Luth.

KIKO, PHILIP GEORGE oc/Legislative Assistant; b/Jul 16, 1951; h/126 N Brookside St, Arlington, VA 22201; ba/Washington,DC; m/Mary McKenzie; p/Willard LeRoy and Stella Jane Kiko, Malvern, OH; ed/BA; JD; pa/Legal Cnslr to Cong-man F James Sensenbrenner Jr; Mem US Dist Ct DC & US Circuit Ct DC; Va St Bar; DC Ct Appeals; cp/JCs; Prince George's Repub Clb; Arlington Co Repub Com; Crim Just Adv Coun, N Va Plan'g Dist Comm; r/Cath; hon/S'ship Team.

KILBERT, FLORENCE JANE oc/Teacher Counselor; b/Nov 1, 1925; h/2772 E 75th St, Chicago, IL 60649; ba/Chgo; m/Porter L (dec); c/Anthony Carlos; p/John M and Stella Green (dec); ed/RN Homer G Phillips Hosp (St Louis, Mo); BS Loyola Univ; MA Univ Chgo; Addit Studies; pa/Tchr Cnslr Bd

Examrs, Chgo Public Schs Bd Ed 1970-; Asst Prin, Jirka Sch (Chgo) 1958-70; Other Positions; Field Recruiter, Univ Chgo Grad Sch Ed; NEA; cp/Chgo Urban Leag; NAACP; Alumna Univ Chgo; Vol Ser, 1st Ch Rel Sci; r/1st Ch Rel Sci; hon/Cert Vol Ser, Coun Exceptional Chd; 10 Yr Ser Pin, ARC; Recog Awd, Univ Chgo; W/W Am Wom; Intl W/W Wom; Notable Ams.

KILLEEN, CATHERINE D oc/Professor; b/Aug 7, 1931; h/1092 Carnation Dr, New Milford, NJ 07646; ba/South Orange, NJ; p/Daniel J and Mary E Killeen (dec); ed/BA Caldwell Col Wom 1960; MA Seton Hall Univ 1969; MA Montclair St Col 1971; EdD Rutgers Univ 1977; Addit Studies; pa/Adj Prof Ed, Seton Hall Univ 1969-; Adj Prof Psychol, Montclair St Col 1977-; Consltg Clinical Psychol, Mt Carmel Hosp Alcoholism 1975-76; Other Positions; Pub'd Num Articles Profl Jours; AAUP; Am Psychol Assn; Nat Coun Eng Tchrs; Nat Coun Clergy on Alcoholism; NJ Psychol Assn; NJ Assn Sch Psychol; NJ Ed Assn; Nat Cath Ed Assn; Others; r/Rom Cath; hon/Kappa Delta Pi; Nat Inst Mtl Hlth Awd, Pomoca Mtl Hlth Complex; Rec'd Nat Sci Foun Grants: Rutgers Univ, St Peter's Col; Rec'd Nat Humanities Inst Grant, William & Mary Col; Others.

KILSDONK, ANN GABRIEL oc/Associate Professor; b/Jun 21, 1924; h/8500 Marygrove Dr, Detroit, MI 48221; ba/Detroit; p/Martin J Kilsdonk (dec); c/Catherine Sexton Kilsdonk, Birmingham, MI; ed/BS Marygrove Col 1945; MA Mich St Univ 1959; PhD Cand; Addit Studies; pa/Sister Rel Order; Marygrove Col: Chrperson Div Profl Studies 1976-, Coor Dept Human Ecology 1976-,

Assoc Prof Human Ecol 1972-, Chm Home Ec Dept 1968-71, Asst Prof Home Ec 1958-72, Curric Com, Acad Advr, Others; Other Past Positions; AHEA; MHEA; NCFR; MCFR; ACPTC; AAHE; HEEA; Others; Pub'd Articles; r/Mem Sisters, Servants of Immaculate Heart of Mary; hon/Iota Gamma Alpha; Omicron Nu; Grad'd cum laude; Rec'd AHEA Ellen H Richards F'ship; Rec'd MHEA Dean Dye S'ship; Recipient Shell Foun Grant; Others.

KIM, KEITH oc/Broker; b/Oct 11, 1935; h/1825 Sharon Pl, San Marino, CA 91108; ba/El Segundo, CA; m/Ann; c/Dominick, Glenn; p/Rinsuk Kim, Pasadena, CA; S E Chu (dec); ed/AA; BA; pa/Lic'd Customs Broker; Intl Freight Forwarder; cp/Lions Clb; r/Cath.

KIMBELL, MARION JOEL oc/Engineer; b/Sep 7, 1923; h/22324 Ralston St, Haywood, CA 94541; ba/Oakland, CA; m/Juliann Weidner; c/Nancy Haag, Susan, Candace; p/Mary McMillan, Houston, TX; ed/BS; MSCE; mil/AUS: Sgt, Med Dept; pa/Bldr w Kaiser Engrs; Reg'd Profl Engr; Control Sys Engr; Nuclear Engr; Instrument Soc of Am; cp/Moose Lodge of Castro Valley (Cal); Moose Legion; r/Christian; hon/W/W SW.

KIMBROUGH, ALYNDA KAY oc/Manager; b/Oct 14, 1937; h/Rt 5, Box 385, Amarillo, TX 79118; ba/Amarillo; m/-Richard; c/Rhonda Kay, Traci Lynn, Julie Nichole, Rochelle Renee; p/Hubert Edgar Hudspeth (dec); Maudie Mae Hudspeth, Amarillo; ed/Assoc Deg Bus Adm, Amarillo Jr Col; pa/Reg Mgr, Sarah Coventry Inc; cp/Canyon HS Booster Clb; r/Paramount Terrace Christian Ch; hon/Profl Awds.

KIMMITT, JOSEPH STANLEY oc/Secretary; b/Apr 5, 1918; h/6004 Copely Ln, McLean, VA 22101; ba/Washington, DC; m/Eunice L Wegener; c/Robert M, Kathleen A, Joseph H, Thomas P, Mark T, Mary P, Judy J; ed/BS Utah St Univ; Hon LLD Montana Col Mineral Sci & Technol; mil/AUS 1941-66; pa/Secy, US Senate; cp/Bd Trustees, Univ Montana Foun; r/Cath; hon/Rec'd Dist'd Ser Awd, Logan (Utah) JCs.

KING, ALGIN BRADDY oc/Dean; b/Jan 19, 1927; h/103 N Will Scarlet Ln, Williamsburg, VA 23185; ba/Newport News, VA; m/Joyce; c/Drucie, Martha; p/Dewey A and Elisabeth B King (dec); ed/AB Univ SC 1947; MS NYU 1953; PhD Ohio St Univ 1966; pa/Christopher Newport Col: Prof Mktg & Mgmt 1976-, Dean Sch Bus & Ecs 1979-, Dir Div Bus & Ecs 1977-79; Wn Carolina Univ: Prof Mktg 1974-76; Dean Sch Bus 1974-76; Other Positions; Co-Author: *Mgmt Perceptions* (1976), *The Sourcebook of Economics* (1973), Others; Pub'd Num Articles Profl Jours; Lectr; Former Conslt: US Civil Ser Comm, Nat Meml Park Inc, Law Firms, Others; Acad Mgmt; Am Inst Decision Scis; Am Mktg Assn; Exec Com, Atl Ec Soc; Intl Coun Small Business; So Mktg Assn; Mktg & Sales Exec Clb; cp/Rotary Clb; Queens Lake Country Clb; r/United Meth Ch; hon/Grad'd Cum Laude; Rec'd W T Grant S'ship; W/W: Authors & Journalists, World, Am; DIB; Personalities of S; Contemp Authors; Am Men Sci; Others.

KING, ALMA GEAN oc/Operator; b/May 18, 1954; ba/110 Hayes Ave, Jackson, TN 38301; m/Willis Jr; c/Tyrone, Jerome, Tywone, Juan; p/Dan Blockett; Gussie Lee Blockett, Jackson; pa/Operator Happy Hours Day Care Ctr; cp/Vol Tenn Dept Correction; r/Pentacostal; hon/Rec'd Child Care Awd, Union Univ.

KING, BARRETT TAYLOR oc/Reporter; b/Jul 1, 1947; h/1701 Hidden Hollow Ct, Conyers, GA 30207; ba/Atlanta, GA; m/Elizabeth Ann; c/Lisa Marie, Barrett T Jr; p/Charles C King Jr, Covington, GA; Sally Lambe King; ed/AB Univ Ga; mil/AUS; pa/Reporter, *Atlanta Constitution*; Outdoor Writer; Atlanta Press Clb; NE Ga Ad Clb; cp/Ga Conservancy; Sierra Clb; Am Cancer Soc; r/Rom Cath; hon/Rec'd Superior Broadcast Awd, Assoc'd Press.

KING, CARL STANLEY oc/Chaplain; b/Feb 9, 1934; h/PO Box 1949, Sierra Vista, AZ 85635; ba/Fort Huachuca, AZ; m/Harriette C; c/Elizabeth Carol, Patricia Leigh; p/C S and Vivian Kester King, Xenia, OH; ed/AB Lenoir Rhyne Col 1955; BD 1958, MDiv 1972 Luth Theol Sem; MA Long Isl Univ 1972; Addit Studies; mil/AUS Maj; pa/Chaplain, AUS; Instr Sociol, Cochise Col 1976-; Min Luth Ch Am; r/Luth; hon/Recipient Num Mil Hons: Bronze Star, Meritorious Ser Medal, Air Medal, Army Commend Medals, Nat Defence Ser Medal, Vietnam Campaign Ribbon (w 4 Stars), Armed Forces Reserv Medal; 3 Foreign Awds.

KING, CHARLES WILLIS oc/Consultant; b/Nov 17, 1935; h/15750 Daleport Cir, Dallas, TX 75248; ba/Dallas; m/Audrie Ann; c/Elizabeth Ann, Charles Byers; p/James Byers and Dorothy Louise King, Denton, MD; ed/BS Wash Col; MS Univ Pittsburgh; pa/Power Sys Analysis Conslt, Tex Am Bk; IEEE; Var Computer Orgs; r/Presb; hon/Grad'd Cum Laude; W/W S&SW; Personalities of S.

KING, DENNIS R oc/Executive; h/750 Beech Cir NW, Cleveland, TN 37311; ba/Cleveland; ed/BA Univ Cincinnati 1969; MS Cal St Univ 1973; pa/Hiwassee Mtl Hlth Ctr: Act'g Exec Dir 1978-, Dir Progs & Resource Devel Evaluation 1977-78, Psychol Examr & Coor Adult Sers 1973-77; Pvt Pract Psychol Examr 1973-; Instr, Cleveland St Commun Col 1975-; Others; Am Psychol Assn; Tenn Psychol Assn; Biofeedback Soc Am; Am Assn Sex Edrs, Cnslrs & Therapists; Tenn Assn Mgmt Human Sers; Pub'd Profl Articles; cp/Former Bd Mem, Child Shelter Inc; hon/W/W S&SW; DIB; Personalities Am; Personalities S; Notable Ams; Cleveland JCs Proj Chm Yr.

KING, EDWARD BEVERLY JR oc/-Executive; b/Aug 17, 1939; h/611 Oakdale Rd, Newark, DE 19713; ba/Austin, TX; p/Edward B Sr and Gladys Ruth Mae Johnson King; ed/BS; EdD; pa/Ednl Textbook Sales Exec, Steck-Vaughn Pub'g Co 1975-; Sr Assoc & Dir, Assn Am Pubrs (NYC) 1970-75; Presidential Asst, Hofstra Univ (Hempstead, NY) 1968-70; Others; NEA; cp/Am Negro Commemorative Soc; r/Bapt; hon/Recipient Dist'd Alumnus Yr Awd, Wilberforce Univ; New Career Opportunity Awd, Talladega Col; Cert Recog, Nat Alliance Bus Men; Incl'd in Books: *What Manner of Man* (Lerone Bennett), *Freedom Ride* (James Peck), Others; Men Achmt; W/W World; Outstg Yg Men Am; W/W Am; Alpha Phi Omega.

KING, ETHEL MARGUERITE oc/Professor; b/Jun 16, 1927; h/3620 6th St SW, Calgary, Alberta, Canada; ba/Calgary; p/Walter and Mildred Laura King (dec);

ed/BEd; MA; PhD; pa/Prof & Reschr Dept Curric & Instrn, Univ Calgary; cp/Altrusa Clb; r/Anglican; hon/Fellow Canadian Col Tchrs; Rec'd Provincial Achmt Awd.

KING, HELEN BLANCHE oc/Educator; b/May 21, 1919; h/2915 Casamia, Palmdale, CA 93550; p/George Edward and Carolyn Campbell King; ed/AS Weber St Col 1939; Normal Deg, Utah St Univ 1940; BA Cal St Col 1957; MA Northridge St Univ 1964; Addit Studies; pa/Tchr, Westside Union Sch Dist (Lancaster, Cal) 1954-; Tchr, Quartz Hill & Del Sur (Westside) Jr HSs 1955-63; Jr Col Gen Studies Instr 1964-66; Other Positions; Intl

Reading Assn; AAUW; Others; cp/Shows Tinka Samoyeds (Owns Pup'n Kitten Dog Lodge, Palmdale); Antelope Valley Kennel Clb; Samoyed Clb Wash St; So Cal Samoyed Clb; No Cal Samoyed Fanciers Inc; Samoyed Clb Am; Cal Sled Dog Assn; Northridge St Univ Alumni Assn; Antelope Val Commun Orch; Others; hon/Biogl Listings.

KING, JOHN QUILL TAYLOR oc/- President; b/Sept 25, 1921; h/2400 Givens Ave, Austin, TX 78722; ba/Austin; m/Marcet Hines; c/John Q Taylor Jr, Clinton Allen, Marjon K Christopher, Stuart Hines; p/John Q Taylor (dec); Alice King Johnson, Austin; ed/BA Fisk Univ; BS Huston-Tillotson Col; MS DePaul Univ; PhD Univ Tex-A; LLD SWn Univ; LLD St Edward's Univ; mil/AUS WWII; USAR; pa/Pres Huston-Tillotson Col; Math Writing Team, Pitman Pub'g Corp; Co-Author w Wife, 2 Books; cp/Austin Kiwanis Clb; Austin Civil Ser Comm; Statewide Hlth Coor'g Coun; Former Mem Gov's Com on Aging; r/Wesley United Meth Ch: Mem; hon/Rec'd Alumni Awds, Fisk Univ & H-T Col; Phi Beta Kappa.

KING, JOSEPH JERONE oc/Consultant; b/Sept 27, 1910; h/Ioka Beach-Hood Canal, 11655 Ioka Way NW, Silverdale, WA 98383; ba/Silverdale; m/Kathleen Martin; c/Sally K Thompson, Nikki K Ring, Cindy K Mullen; p/Joseph J and Alice E Halferty King (dec); ed/BA Stanford Univ; MA Duke Univ; mil/USAAF WWII; pa/Exec Conslt Public Affairs; cp/Profl Ed St Adv Coun; Dir Manpower; Public Ed Mgmt Survey; r/Prot; hon/Rec'd Dist'd Ser Awd, DAV; Outstg Ser Awd, Assn Wash Industs; Dist'd Ser Awd, Assn Wash Bus.

KING, JOYCE PAULINE oc/Assistant Professor; b/Dec 19, 1929; h/103 N Will Scarlet Ln, Williamsburg, VA 23185; ba/Norfolk, VA; m/Algin Braddy; c/Dan L, Marshall A, Mary Joanne; p/Paul Magnus Johnson (dec); Maud Emily Ross, Minneapolis, MN; ed/BS 1969, MS 1971 Utah St Univ; PhD Univ Minn 1973; pa/Old Dominion Univ: Asst Prof Mktg 1976-, Chm Dept Mktg 1977-, Co-Editor *Tidewater Economic Report* 1977-; Wn Carolina Univ: Asst Prof Mktg 1974-76, Act'g Head Dept Mktg 1977; Other Positions; Tech Advr Pub'd Monographs; Lectr; Bus Conslt; Pub'd Num Articles Profl Jours; Am Mktg Assn; So Mktg Assn; Intl Coun Small Bus; Atl Ec Soc; r/Epis; hon/Rec'd Utah St Univ Acad S'ship; World W/W Wom Ed; Commun Ldrs & Noteworthy Ams; Personalities S; Intl W/W Commun Ser.

KING, LAURA JANE ZEPERNICK oc/- Home Economist; b/Jan 19, 1947; h/14553 N River Rd, Pemberville, OH 43450; m/Bruce William; p/Richard D Zepernick (dec); Jessie F Brown Zepernick, Pemberville; ed/BA 1969, MEd 1976 Bowling Green St Univ; pa/- Economist & Former Co Ext Agent, Paulding Co; Ohio Home Ec Assn; AHEA; cp/OES;

Wood Co Hist Soc; Ohio Hist Soc; Paulding Co Hist Soc; Wood Co Geneal Soc; Ohio Geneal Soc; DAR: Former Chief Page Continental Cong, Former Asst Page; Others; r/Presb; hon/Theta Sigma Phi; Rec'd Cit Exceptional Ser, Bicent Comm Paulding Co; W/W Am Wom.

KING, LEROY H JR oc/Physician b/Sept 4, 1937; h/7610 Cape Cod Cir, Indianapolis, IN 46250; ba/Indpls; m/Carol Jane;

c/Stephen, Heather, Brandon, Carson, Travis; p/LeRoy H Sr and Goldia Fletcher King, Indpls; ed/BA Duke Univ 1959; MD Ind Univ Sch Med 1964; mil/AUS Med Corps 1969-71; pa/Co-Dir Renal Transplant Prog, Meth Hosp Ind 1971-; Pvt Pract Internal Med & Nephrology 1971-; Instr Ind Univ Sch Med 1968-69; Staff Phys Renal Dept, VA Hosp 1968-69; Other Positions; Cert'd Am Bd Internal Med 1971; Pub'd Num Articles Profl Jours; AMA; Am Heart Assn; Am Soc Nephrology; Intl Soc Nephrology; Am Fdn Clinical Res; Am Soc Internal Med; Nat Kidney Foun; Others; cp/Ind Univ Men's Clb; Patron Footlight Musicals; Indpls Chd's Museum; Indpls Museum Art; Ind Univ Alumni Assn; Others; r/E 91st St Christian Ch: Mem; hon/Beta Theta Pi; Nu Sigma Nu; Ky Col; Fellow Am Col Phys; Rec'd F'ship, Ind Univ Med Ctr Hosps; W/W MW.

KING, LIS oc/Counselor; h/30 Dundee Ct, Mahwah, NJ 07430; ba/New York, NY; m/Theodore A Pace; c/Dorte; p/C O Petersen, Roskilde, Denmark; Gerda Petersen (dec); ed/Grad Sch Fine Arts, Copenhagen; Grad L'Universita Per Stranieri, Perugia (Italy); pa/Public Relats Cnslr; Author; IPA; Nat Consumer Accounts; Contbr Num Mags; cp/Repub Party; r/Luth; hon/Rec'd United Nations Essay Awd; Am Embassy (Copenhagen) Awd; W/W Am; W/W World Wom; Others.

KING, MAE ELIZABETH oc/Retired Educator; b/Feb 4, 1908; h/826 So 14th, Richmond, IN 47374; p/Frank D and Winifred R King (dec); ed/AB Ind Univ 1931; BSLS Univ Ill 1943; pa/Asst Prof Lib Ser & Periodicals Libn, Ball St Univ 1957-74; Head Libn Sec'dy Schs, Richmond 1949-57; Dir Township HS, Jackson Co 1937-39; Other Positions; Past Pres, Muncie Branch AAUW; Past St Treas, Ind Sch Libns Assn; Former Secy-Treas, Ctl Section Sch Libns; cp/Bd Dirs, Friends Muncie Public Lib Inc; r/United Meth Ch; hon/Delta Kappa Gamma; F'ship AAUW.

KING, MARTIN LUTHER SR oc/Minister; ba/Atlanta, GA; m/Alberta Christine Williams (dec); c/Christine K Farris, Martin Luther Jr (dec), Alfred Daniel Williams (dec); p/James and Delia King (dec); ed/Attended Bryant Preparatory Inst; BTh Morehouse Col Sch Rel; pa/Pastor Emeritus, Ebenezer Bapt Ch; Lectr & Min Throughout US & World; cp/Bd Trustees: Atlanta Univ, Morehouse Col, Interdenom Theol Ctr, Morehouse Sch Rel ITC; Hon Pres, Martin Luther King Jr Ctr Social Change; Bd Mem Emeritus: Citizens Trust Bk Atlanta, Carrie Steele Pitts Home; Moderator Emeritus, Atlanta Missionary Bapt Assn; Bd Mem SCLC; r/Bapt; hon/Recipient Hon Degs: DDiv Morris Brown Col, HHD Wilberforce Univ, DLitt Univ Haiti, DDiv Morehouse Col, HHD Va Sem & Col, DDiv Allen Univ, HHD Bethune-Cookman Col, DDiv Berea Col; Clergyman Yr, Coun Christians & Jews; Order of Lion, Republic Senegal (W Africa); Others.

KINGERY, BERNARD TROY oc/Physicist; b/Jul 16, 1920; h/92 Oakridge Ave, Nutley, NJ 07110; ba/Newark, NJ; m/Catherine Murgia; c/Deborah Ann, Jacqueline; p/Thomas Eddie and Ruth Alma Trapnell Kingery (dec); ed/Dipl, Freeman Bus Col 1938; BS Ga So Col 1948; MA 1949, Profl Dipl 1951 Columbia Univ; Addit Studies; mil/USN 1942-46; pa/Asst Prof Physics, NJ Inst Technol 1952-; Instr Physics, Columbia

Univ 1957; Instr Physics, Orange Co Commun Col 1950-52; Other Positions; Am Assn Physics Tchrs; AASE; Past Mem AAUP; Past Mem Nat Sci Tchrs Assn; AAAS; Others; cp/Repub Party; r/Bapt; hon/Kappa Delta Pi; Sci Manpower Fellow, Columbia Univ; Am Men Sci; W/W E.

KINNEY, JAMES W oc/Minister; b/Nov 12, 1937; h/4004 E 8th St, Cheyenne, WY 82001; ba/Francis E Warren AFB, WY; m/Lois Bouknight; c/Martha Elizabeth, Gordon Andrew; p/Paul G Kinney (dec); Annie M Kinney, Burlington, NC; ed/AB Univ NC 1960; MDiv Luth Theol So Sem 1963;

mil/USAF Chaplain 1968-; pa/Mbrship Chm, Cheyenne Min Assn; Chaplain Assignmts: Wyom, Utah, Vietnam, Tex, Ark, Italy, Australia; r/Luth Ch Am; hon/Rec'd Bronze Star, Meritorious Ser Medal, Commend Medal w 2 Oak Leaf Clusters USAF.

KINNEY, MARGUERITE RODGERS oc/Nurse; b/Dec 2, 1939; h/5136 Selkirk Dr, Birminghan, AL 35243; ba/B'ham; m/Cecil David; c/Meredith DeMonbrun; p/John Wilson and Dorothy McCarron Rodgers, Tuscaloosa, AL; ed/BSN; MSN; DNSc; pa/Assoc Prof Nsg, Univ Ala Sch Nsg; Am Assn Critical Care Nurses; Secy (BD Dirs) 1976-78, Co-Chrperson Pub Com 1976-77, Chrperson Res Com 1977, Others; Editor Bd, *Jour of Critical Care* 1977-; ANA; ASNA; DNA; Am Heart Assn; Coun Cardiovascular Nsg; Ala Lung Assn; Nat Leag Nsg; Ala Acad Sci; Others; r/Epis; hon/Sigma Theta Tau; Omicron Delta Kappa; Rec'd Spec Nurse F'ship, Div of Nsg NIH; Rec'd Cert Merit, Ala Heart Assn; Outstg Yg Wom Am; W/W US; Wom of Day, Mobile.

KINNEY, WILLIAM LIGHT JR oc/- Publisher; b/Oct 26, 1933; h/508 E Main St, Bennettsville, SC 29512; ba/Bennettsville; m/Margaret Rene Pegues; c/Elisabeth Mayer, William Light III; p/William Light and Annie Laurie Mayer Kinney, B'ville; ed/BS Wofford Col; BA Univ SC; mil/AUS 1956-58; pa/*Marlboro Herald-Advocate*: Reporter 1958-59, Advtg Mgr 1959-60, Bus Mgr 1960-65, Mng Editor 1965-70, Editor & Pubr 1970-; Other Positions; Past Pres SC Press Assn; cp/Past Mem City Coun; Rotary Clb; JCs; Hist Soc; Others; r/Meth; hon/SC Yg Man Yr.

KINSLOW, MELLIE CRITTLE ENGRAM oc/Retired Music Teacher; b/Nov 20, 1908; b/3119 Stratford Dr, Macon, GA 31211; ba/Same; m/Jimmy Daniel; c/Mellie Engram Briggs; p/Walter W and Bessie Echols Crittle (dec); ed/MA Tchrs Col Columbia Univ; BA Ft Valley St Col; Typing & Shorthand Dipl Walker's Bus Sch; Mus Dipl Clemons Conservatory Mus; pa/Tchg; Ofc Work; Notary Public; Pianist; Sewing; Arts & Crafts; Organist; r/SDA; hon/49 Yr Tchg Awd, Bibb Co; 8 Yr Awd, Yth Camp; Life Profl Cert in Ed.

KINTNER, JANET IDE oc/Judge; b/Feb 25, 1944; ba/County Courthouse, 220 W Broadway, San Diego, CA 92101; m/Charles F; c/Zachary Ide; p/Herbert A and Marian G Ide, Tucson, AZ; ed/BA; JD; pa/Mun Ct Judge, San Diego Judicial Dist; Admit'd Cal St Bar 1968; Tchr Legal Courses; Bd Dirs San Diego Co Bar Assn 1973-76, VP 1976; Assoc Editor *Courts Commentary*; San Diego Adv

Com, St of Cal Wom's Cont; VChm Co Ad Hoc Com, Wom's Rehab; hon/W/W: Am Wom, Am Law, W; Notable Ams.

KINZER, DENNIS RAY oc/Minister; b/Jun 28, 1951; h/PO Box 233, Loyall, KY 40854; ba/Loyall; m/Hilda Sponaugle; c/Anita, David, James, Susan; p/John McKinley and Frances Earline Kinzer, Pinnacle, NC; ed/AB Johnson Bible Col; pa/Harlan (Ky) Area Min Assn; r/Christian Ch; Ch of Christ; hon/W/W Rel; Intl W/W Commun Ser.

KIRBY, CHARLES D II oc/Minister; b/Jun 27, 1930; h/1006 Iowa Ave, Lynn Haven, FL 32444; ba/Lynn Haven; m/Bapbara L; c/Lyle David, Kenneth W; p/Charles D Kirby, Hosston, LA; Rubye A Thrash, Vernon, TX; ed/Doct Optometry So Col Optometry 1949; BA 1955, MA 1956 New Orleans Bapt Theol Sem; pa/Min of Mus & Yth, 1st Bapt Ch; Dist Mus Dir, Fla Bapt Conv; So Bapt Conv; NW Fla Bapt Sing'g Men; Fla Bapt Ch Mus Conf; ASCAP Composer & Arranger Over 60 Works; r/So Bapt.

KIRBY, MAYME CLARK oc/Retired; b/Nov 15; h/4628 Ave S, Birmingham, AL 35208; m/H A (dec); c/Herbert Andrew Jr (dec); Mildred Naomi Kirby-Phillips; p/William Jackson and Willie A Conville Clark (dec); ed/Certs Radio Technol & Engr; Grad Theol; BA Howard Col (Samford Univ) 1955; pa/Sch Tchr 5 Yrs; Former Asst Bookkeeper & Admissions Clerk for 2 Hosps; Former Beauty Operator & Instr Beauty Col;

Inspector Radio Parts WWII; Former PO Clerk; Gov Clerk SS Adm 23 Yrs; Pub'd: Travelogue, (Booklet) "A Beautiful Dream of Peace", (Book) *Tapping Secrets in Silence*; cp/Taught Bible in Housing Proj 3 Yrs; Vol Positive Maturity; Tchr Writing Class Sr Citizens; Contbg Editor *Oscar Review* (Sr Citizens Paper); Orgr Nat Correspondence Prayer Group, Pubr Bulletin "World Hope"; r/Assembly; hon/Rec'd 2 Nat Liberty Awds; Cert Apprec, Positive Maturity; Bronze Plaque, DIB; World W/W Wom; Commun Ldrs & Noteworthy Ams.

KIRCHNER, JOHN HOWARD oc/Psychologist; b/Dec 28, 1933; h/2208 Forest Parkway, Muscatine, IA 52761; ba/-Muscatine; m/Nora I Kuehne; c/John D, Gregory Allen; p/John Howard Kirchner (dec); Anita G Smith Kirchner, Phoenix, AZ; ed/AB w Hons, Univ Ill 1955; MA 1956, MA 1968, PhD 1964 NWn Univ; mil/AUS Intell 1957-59; AUS Security Agy 1961-62; pa/Exec Dir, Gt River Mtl Hlth Ctr 1975-; Chief Psychol, Wood Co Mtl Hlth Clinic (Bowling Green, Ohio) 1971-75; Assoc Prof Psychol & Staff Psychol, Psychol Cnslg Ser (Ill St Univ) 1964-66; Other Positions; Pub'd Num Articles Profl Jours; Am Psychol Assn; Mid W Psychol Assn; Iowa Psychol Assn; Ill-Iowa Hlth Sys Agy; Review Team II, Mtl Hlth Subcom; Dist IX Core Com, Devel Disabilities; cp/Bd Mem Sheltered Workshop; Muscatine Chapt, Parents Without Partners; Muscatine Commun Hlth Assn; r/Presb; hon/Diplomate Clinical Psychol, Am Bd Profl Psychol; Phi Beta Kappa; Phi Delta Kappa; Delta Phi Alpha; Phi Eta Sigma.

KIRIAZIS, JAMES WILLIAM oc/Anthropologist; Professor; b/Mar 12, 1928; h/444 Westgate Blvd, Youngstown, OH 44515; ba/-

Youngstown; m/Isabel Fernandez; c/James A, Karen, Lisa, Laura; p/Wiliam Kiriazis, Warren, OH; Mary Kiriazis (dec); ed/AB Youngstown Univ; MSW La St Univ; MA, PhD Univ Pittsburgh; mil/AUS; pa/Youngstown Univ: Instr Sociol 1957-62, Prof Anthropol 1962-77, Chm Dept Sociol & Anthropol 1968-77, Med Sch Com & Curric Com 1968-76, Others; Pub'd Articles Profl Jours; Field Trips: Koskinou, Isl of Rhodes, Isls of Symii & Kalymnos (Aegean Sea); Apopointed Ohio Jt Mtl Hlth & Mtl Retardation Adv Comm, Ohio St Senate 1978; Lectr; Other Positions; Nt Ctl Sociol Assn; Am Anthrolpol Assn; cp/En Men's Soc; Pan Rhodian Apollo Soc Am; Co-Mgr, Harry Meshel St Senate Campaign; r/En Orthodox; hon/Rec'd Watson Dist'd Prof Awd, Youngstown Univ; Awd'd Grant, HEW; Man of Yr, EOMS; NDEA Fellow, Univ Pittsburgh; Am Men & Wom Sci; W/W MW.

KIRK, BARBARA ELLEN oc/Ceramic Instructor; b/Jul 16, 1938; h/7125 Old Polk City Rd, Lakeland, FL 33801; ba/Lakeland; m/D Lee; c/Debra, Michael, Shawn; p/William Audie Belew (dec); Norma Schlessman Belew, Burton, OH; ed/Cert Scuba Diving; Cert Ceramic Art; pa/Instr Beki's Big Top Ceramics; Clown; Puppeteer; Entertainer; cp/Vol Sheltered Work Shop; r/Crestview Bapt Ch; hon/Rec'd Blue Ribbons for Cooking & Ceramics.

KIRK, COLLEEN JEAN oc/Professor; b/Sept 7, 1918; h/2028 Wildridge Dr, Tallahassee, FL 32303; ba/Tallahassee; p/Bonum Lee Kirk (dec); Anna C Kirk, Tallahassee; ed/BS, MS Univ Ill; EdD Columbia Univ; pa/Prof Ed & Mus, Univ Ill

1945-70; Dir Mus, Wesley Meth Ch (Ill) 1947-70; Prof Mus, Fla St Univ 1970-; Conductor Fest Choruses; Workshop Clinician; Lectr; Pres, So Div Am Choral Dirs Assn; MENC; FMEA; FCMEA; FVA; hon/Pi Kappa Lambda; Sigma Alpha Iota; Kappa Delta Pi.

KIRK, SARA oc/Director; h/715 Red Oak Ln, Park Forest So, IL 60466; ba/Chicago, IL; m/(dec); c/Dawna; p/(dec); ed/MA; pa/Exec Dir, Chgo Advocates for Sub Reg V; Wom's Ad Clb; Am Mktg Assn; BPW; cp/S Suburban NOW; LWV; hon/W/W Am Wom.

KIRKHAM, M B oc/Assistant Professor; h/623 W University, #3-1, Stillwater, OK 74074; ba/Stillwater; p/Don and Mary Elizabeth Erwin Kirkham, Ames Iowa; ed/BA Wellesley Col; MS, PhD Univ Wis; pa/Asst Prof Agronomy, Okla St Univ; Reschr; Written Over 30 Pubs; hon/Wellesley Scholar; Rec'd Mary White Peterson Prize, Wellesley Col; Rec'd S'ship, Wellesley Col; Grad Fellow, Univ Wis; NDEA Fellow, Univ Wis; Post-Doct Fellow, Univ Wis; Summer Fac Fellow Envir Transport Div, Savannah River Lab (E I du Pont de Nemours & Co).

KIRKLAND-CASGRAIN, CLAIRE oc/-Judge; b/Sept 8; h/45 Northridge Rd, Ile Bizard, Quebec, Canada; ba/Montreal, Quebec; c/Lynne-Marie, Kirkland, Marc; p/Charles Aime Kirkland (dec); Rose A Demers, Ile Bizard; ed/BA McGill Univ 1947; Grad McGill Univ Law Sch 1950; pa/Judge, Quebec Provincial Ct 1973-; VP Minimum Wage Bd; Cerini & Jamieson Law Firm 1952; Mem Canadian & Montreal Bar Assns; cp/Mem

Quebec Leg: Min Transport, Min Tourism, Min Fish & Game, Min Cult Affairs; Fdr & Pres Canadian Chapt Intl Alliance Wom; Others; r/Rom Cath; hon/1st Wom Judge, Provincial Ct Quebec; 1st Wom Elected Quebec Leg; Rec'd Hon LLD, Moncton Univ; Honoris Causa, Glendon Col.

KISER, ELIZABETH QUINTER oc/-Recreation Therapist; b/Jul 14, 1953; h/Rt 4, Box 81, Lincolnton, NC 28092; ba/Dallas, NC; m/H Stephen; p/Alvin Senter Quinter (dec); Charlene L Quinter, Gastonia, NC; ed/BS cum laude, Univ Ga 1976; pa/Nat Therapeutic Rec Soc; NC Parks & Rec Soc; NC Spec Olympics; r/Meth.

KISSINGER, DOROTHY VALE oc/Resort Owner; b/Feb 20, 1916; h/3319 E McDowell Rd, Mesa, AZ 85203; ba/Mesa; m/John Raymond; c/Harvey S Durand, Stephen V Durand; p/Roy Ewing and Jess Dobson Vale (dec); ed/BA Beloit Col; Attended Univ Mich, Wayne St Univ, Chicago Conservatory; Bus & Pers Mgmt, Statler Hotels & Hay Assocs; pa/Co-Owner & Mgr, Sahuaro Lake Guest Ranch Resort 30 Yrs; Asst Mgr, St Clair Inn (Mich) 4 Yrs; Statler Hotels & Ford Motor Co 2 Yrs; Am Hotel Assn; Others; cp/Past Pres, Soroptimist Intl Ams; Appointed by Pres Ford, US Comm Intl Wom's Yr; Appointed by Pres Carter, Cont'g Com Decade Wom; Del Houston Wom's Conf; Pres' Com Handicapped; Nat Coun Wom; Mesa Commun Coun; C of C; Rel Comm ERA; Others; r/United Presb Ch; Mem, Ruling Elder, Others; hon/Phi Sigma Iota; Pi Beta Phi; Rec'd Cit Dist'd Ser, Beloit Col; Rec'd Ldrship Awds: Richard Nixon, Govs of Ariz, Cal, Nev, NM, Tex; Rec'd Awd AAUP; Intl Civic Ldrs; W/W Rel; Others.

KISTLER, DONALD D JR oc/Minister; b/Aug 6, 1923; h/PO Box 573, Kings Mountain, NC 28086; ba/Kings Mt; m/Shirley Annette; c/Chris Yancey, Tammie Clewis, Patricia, Donald, Michael; p/Donald and Hilda Yho Kistler (dec); mil/USN; pa/Min; Writer; Tchr; Lectr Bible; Conducted Tour Israel; cp/Kiwanis; hon/W/W Colo; Personalities S; Intl W/W.

KISTLER, ERNEST LOSSON oc/Mechanical Engineer; b/Oct 30, 1931; h/1515 Haven Lock, Houston, TX 77077; m/Dorothy Palmer; c/Ernest III, Linda, Steven; p/Ernest L Kistler Sr (dec); Angie Mae Smith Kistler, Coushatta, LA; ed/BS 1955, MS 1957 Univ Tex-A; PhD Rice Univ 1969; Addit Studies; mil/AUS Corps Engrs; pa/Pres Ernest L Kistler & Assocs Inc (Consltg Engrs Offshore Indust) 1978-; Chief Engr, R J Brown & Assocs 1976-78; Tex A&M Univ: Head Marine Sys Engr Prog, Assoc Prof Ocean Engrg, Civil Engrg & Marine Sci 1967-72; Other Positions; Author Over 30 Profl Papers & Reports; Reg'd Profl Engr Tex 1960; Editor Review Com, Soc Petro Engrs; Fdr Houston Sect, Marine Technol Soc; Soc Naval Archs & Marine Engrs; AIAA; Others; r/So Bapt; hon/Rec'd Best Sect & Best Sect Spec Events Awds, AIAA; BSA Order of Arrow; Rec'd NASA Apollo Achmt Awd; Dist'd Mil Grad, Univ Tex-A; DIB; Men Achmt; Personalities Am; W/W: S&SW, Tex, Aviation; Others.

KITCHEN, DENNIS LEE oc/Song Composer; Writer; b/Aug 27, 1946; h/114 Washington St, Princeton, WI 54968; ba/Princeton; m/Juanita Maria; c/Steven, Carlos, Tyler; p/Harvey J Kitchen, Del City, OK; Cynthia Ann Krupp, Milwaukee, WI; ed/BA, MS Univ Okla; mil/1968-69; cp/K of C; Rotary; Pistol Clb; Repub Party; Cand Ill Senate 1974; Cand Racine Co Coroner 1976; r/Rom Cath: Ch Treas; hon/Rec'd 1st Prize, Song Writers Assn Am; Good Citizen Awd, Evansville (Ill); Others.

KITTRELL, FLEMMIE P oc/Consultant; h/PO Box 1156, Gloucester, VA 23061; p/James Lee and Alice Mills Kittrell (dec); ed/BS Hampton Inst; MS, PhD Cornell Univ; Hon DHL Univ NC; pa/Conslt Home Ec; Res in Nutrition; Conslt Fam Devel; cp/Conslt

Dept Social Sers; r/United Meth; hon/Fulbright Prof to India; Rec'd Alumni Awd, Cornell Univ.

KLEBANOFF, PHILIP SAMUEL oc/Physicist; b/Jul 21, 1918; h/6412 Tone Dr, Bethesda, MD 20034; ba/Washington, DC; m/Angelyn E Calvo; c/Steven Michael, Susan Marian, Leonard Elliot; p/Morris and Celia Klebanoff (dec); ed/BS; pa/Sr Physicist (Fluid Dynamics), Nat Bur Standards; Editor Bd, *The Physics of Fluids* 1970-73; Am Physical Soc: VChm Exec Com (Div Fluids) 1968, Chm 1969, F'ship Com 1972-; Naval Sea Sys Hydromechanics Com; Assoc Fellow, Am Inst Aeronautics & Astronautics; Fellow, Am Physical Soc; Fellow, Wash Acad Scis; AAAS; Phil Soc Wash; Profl Pubs; Others; r/Jewish; hon/Rec'd Naval Ordnance Devel Awd; Rec'd Gold Medal, Dept Commerce.

KLEE, JAMES B oc/Professor; b/Aug 5, 1916; h/24 Forest Dr, Carrollton, GA 30117; ba/Same; m/Lucille H; c/Margaret Ann, Kathren Elizabeth; p/Charles Hunter and Anna Butt Klee (dec); ed/BS 1938, MA 1941, PhD 1943 Univ Mich; pa/Prof Psychol, West Ga Col; Am Psychol Assn; Assn Humanistic Psychol; Soc Existential Psychi & Psychol; r/Christian; hon/Phi Kappa Phi; Sigma Xi; Fulbright Hays Scholar India.

KLEE, LUCILLE HOLLJES oc/Professor; b/Dec 8, 1924; h/24 Forest Dr, Carrollton, GA 30117; ba/Carrollton; m/James Butt; c/Margaret Ann, Kathren Elizabeth; p/Henry Diedrich and Elizabeth Kennedy Holljes (dec); ed/AB 1946, MA 1947, PhD 1951 Bryn Mawr Col; pa/Assoc Prof Chem & Sci Ed, West Ga Col 1971-; Sci Curric Supvr, Douglas Co Bd Ed (Douglasville, Ga) 1969-70; Assoc Prof Chem, Lowell Univ (Mass) 1967-71; Conslt Sci Ed 1968-71; Editor MVESP Newslttr 1970-71; Other Positions; Author *Lab Text in Gen Chem* (1958, 60); Pub'd Articles Profl Jours; AAAS; Am Chem Soc; NSTA; Coun Elem Sch Sci Intl; Others; cp/Former Pres, Carrollton PTA; Past Bd Mem, Carroll Co LWV; Ga Conservancy Coms; Bd Ed; Ga Mtl Hlth Assn; DAR; hon/Sigma Xi; Outstg Achmt Human Sers; Outstg Ser Ecology.

KLEIN, BARRY TODD oc/Publisher; b/Dec 7, 1949; h/7001 Blvd E, Guttenberg, NJ 07093; ba/Rye, NY; p/Bernard and Betty Klein, Margate, FL; ed/BS NYU 1971; pa/Res Editor; Author: *Reference Encyclopedia of the American Indian, Reference Encyclopedia of American Psychology & Psychiatry, Bibliography of American Ethnology;* r/Jewish.

KLEIN, GEORGE oc/Director; b/Oct 8, 1935; h/2980 Barron, #47, Memphis, TN 38114; ba/Memphis; p/Morris Klein (dec); Bertha Klein, Memphis; ed/BS Memphis St Univ; pa/Dir Mktg & Public Relats, Mid S Fair (Libertyland Parks); Free-Lance Radio Announcer; Songwriter; cp/Goodfellows, Mile O Dimes Dir; Orgr Bong Show, Epilepsy Foun; r/Jewish; hon/Rec'd Memphis Mus Awd.

KLEIN, JAMES ALBERT oc/Executive; b/Aug 19, 1919; h/3122 So Everett Pl, Kennewick, WA 99336; ba/Richland, WA; m/Traute Rosemarie; c/Steven Chapin, Jonathan Winthrop, Geoffrey Downing; p/Gustav Klein (dec); Estella Ione Yarno Klein, Laguna Hills, CA; ed/BA Univ Wash 1942; Post-Grad Studies Univ Wis; mil/AUS Ret'd 1962; Attended Armed Forces Sch, Adv'd Inf Sch, Command & Gen Staff Col; pa/Utility Exec, Wash Public Power Supply Sys; Am Nuclear Soc; cp/Bd Dirs, Mid-Columbia Symph; Fulbright S'ship Com (Barcelona, Spain); r/Cath; hon/Legion of Merit; Rec'd Bronze Star.

KLEIN, KENNETH ROBERT oc/Symphony Conductor; b/Sept 5, 1939; h/110 S Swall Dr, Los Angeles, CA 90048; ba/Same; m/Leslie Marie; p/Samuel R and Hildegarde Klein, Beverly Hills, CA; ed/BM magna cum laude; pa/Debuts as Guest Conductor: Paris 1974, Moscow 1974, Vienna 1975, New York (Carnegie Hall) 1977, Geneva 1977, Montreux

Fest 1977, Rome 1979, Casals Fest 1977; Released Phonograph Record 1979; Mus Dir, Westside Symph (LA) 1963-68; Mus Dir (Guadalajara, Mexico) 1967-78; hon/Rec'd 1st Gold Medal for Cult Achmt Intl Relats, Mexican-Am Inst & City of Guadalajara; Ency Britannica; Phi Kappa Phi.

KLEIN, MARTIN JOHN HERMAN oc/Electronic Engineer; b/Feb 26, 1937; h/1247 June Rd, Huntingdon Valley, PA 19006; ba/Philadelphia, PA; p/Martin and Emma M V Klein; ed/AS Spring Garden Col; pa/Cert'd by Inst Cert of Engrg Technicians; IEEE; Am Soc Cert'd Engrg Technicians; Dela Val Bus Assn; Nat Bus Assn; cp/Repub Party: Sustaining Mem, Nat Congl Com; Frat Order Police; Contbr US Olympics; Past Deputy Constable, Abington Township Election Ser; Profl Magician: Entertain Charity Functions; Intl Brotherhood Magicians; hon/Rec'd Cit for Ser, Collier Pubg Co; Rec'd 1st Awd Essay Contest, NE Philadelphia Com Employmt Handicapped; Cert Apprec, Gen Elect Speakers Bur; Rec'd Lttrs Commen, Gen Elect Mgmt & US Govt; DIB; W/W E; Commun Ldrs & Noteworthy Ams; Others.

KLEIN, MILDRED LUCILLE oc/Music Teacher; b/Sept 19; h/3304 37th St, Lubbock, TX 79413; ba/Lubbock; p/Edward and Jessie K Hiatt Klein (dec); ed/BM; pa/Mus Edr; Pvt Piano & Organ Tchr; Pianist; Composer; Local, St & Nat Mus Assns; Nat Guild Piano Tchrs; Past Pres Tex Mus Tchrs Assn; Former Pres Federated Mus Clb; Former 1st VP Student Affiliate Div, Tex Mus Tchrs Assn; r/Christian Sci; hon/Tchr of Yr, St of Tex; Tchr of Yr, Lubbock.

KLEINBERG, PHILIP REUBEN oc/Educator; b/Jun 7, 1924; h/6526 Maryland Dr, Los Angeles, CA 90048; m/Irene Y; c/Eliot, David, Deborah; p/Samuel Dov and Mollie Kleinberg (dec); ed/AA LA City Col 1951; BA 1956, MA 1964 Cal St Univ; PhD Col Appllied Sci (England) 1973; DSc Free Epis Univ (Switzerland) 1973; PhD Accademia Teatina per le Scienze (Italy) 1977; mil/AUS; pa/Tchr, Supvr, Asst Prin & Admr: Paramount Unified Sch Dist, LA City Col, La Verne Col, Pepperdine Univ & So Cal Inst Grad Studies 1957-; NEA; Cal Tchrs Assn; Tchrs Assn Paramount; IPA; Intl Lang Soc; Pub'd Num Articles; cp/K of P; Dramatic Order Knights of Khorassan; hon/Rec'd Hon Ser Awd, Cal Cong Parents & Tchrs; Rec'd Acad Senate Pres Cit, W LA Col; Knighted Ritter, German Order Signum Fidei; DIB; Personalities W&MW; Commun Ldrs & Noteworthy Ams; Others.

KLEINER, JANELLYN PICKERING oc/Librarian; b/Sept 9, 1936; h/5357 Bennington Ave, Baton Rouge, LA 70808; ba/Baton Rouge; c/Mark Laurence; p/Herschel Laurence and Hester Perle Rutherford Pickering (dec); ed/BA 1958, MSLS 1965, MA 1974 La St Univ; Addit Studies; pa/La St Univ: Asst Libn, Head Interlib Sers Dept 1968-, Coor Ctr Res Libs Task Force 1977-, Chrperson Lib Fac Policy Com 1975-77, Advr Lib Public Relats 1965-73, Others; Account Copywriter, James Hundemen Advtg Agy; Crim Reporter, Baton Rouge *Morning Advocate* 1958-60; Pub'd Books incl'g *LNR: Numerical Register of Books in Louisiana Libs* (1977); Editor Profl Pubs; Contbr Profl Jours; Wom Communs; Assn Coop Lib Orgs; Am Lib Assn; SWn Lib Assn; La Lib Assn (Coms); LSU Wom's Fac Clb; Others; cp/Arts & Humanities Coun; BR Cancer Assn; BR Symph Aux; BR Press Clb; Others; r/Broadmoor Meth Ch; hon/Phi Kappa Phi; Beta Phi Mu; W/W Am Wom; Intl Registry Res & Innovation.

KLIMLEY, NANCY E oc/Civic Worker; h/3240 Lake Shore Dr, Chicago, IL 60657; m/Francis J; c/Cary K Malkin, Brooks; p/William P and Flora Sutherland Enzweiler (dec); ed/BA; cp/Pres, Wom's Bd Ill; Pres Chd's Home & Aid Soc; Bd Dirs: WSO, Boys Clb, Sponsor Parent Assn, Chgo Heart Assn; NWn Univ Settlmt; r/Cath; hon/Rec'd Golden Heart, Chgo Heart Assn; Rec'd Awds,

Ill Chd's Home & Aid Soc; Rec'd Awds, Crusade of Mercy & WTTW Ednl TV; One of 25 Outstg Wom Chgo Bicent Yr, C of C.

KLINE, LENORE MARIE oc/Registered Nurse; b/Nov 11, 1947; h/113 Holl Rd NE, North Canton, OH 44720; ba/Canton; p/Thomas I and Eleanor Graskemper Kline, Parma, OH; ed/MS; pa/Clinical Spec for Mtl Hlth Nsg; ANA; Nat Leag Nsg; Com Nsg Pract; r/Rom Cath; hon/W/W Am Wom.

KLINE, TEX RAY oc/Broadcast Engineer; b/Sept 14, 1938; h/972 W Reache St, Indianapolis, IN; c/Troy Ray, Tracy Renee, Terri Rae; p/Ray L Kline (dec); Berneice E Kline, Warren, IN; ed/Attended: USN Communs Tech Sch, Ind St Univ, DeVry Tech Inst, RCA Ser Schs. Others; mil/USN;

pa/Broadcast Engr, WRTV-TV 1974-; Chief Engr, Sound Stage 1971-75; WTTV-TV: Video Tape Engr, Tech Dir 1963-74; Owner & Operator, KMMS (A-V Firm); Other Positions; Soc Broadcast Engrs; Indpls Ad Clb; Indpls Press Clb; r/Prot; hon/Rec'd Awd, Citizens Forum Beautification; W/W W&MW; Men Achmt; DIB; Others.

KLINGENSMITH, DON JOSEPH oc/Retired Pastor; b/Apr 1, 1901; h/PO Box 613, Mandan, ND 58554; ba/Same; m/Thelma Hyde; c/M Joseph, Eunice V; p/George F and Dora Kincaid Klingensmith; ed/AB; MA; MDiv; pa/Ret'd Pastor; Translator, *Everyday Eng Version, New Testamt;* cp/St Chm & Nat Com-man, Nat Statesman Party; Cand, US Ho of Reps; Toastmaster; r/United Meth; hon/Hon Chief & Coun-man, Ponca Indians.

KLIPPSTATTER, KURT L oc/Music Director; b/Dec 17, 1934; h/12781 Southridge, Little Rock, AR 72207; ba/Little Rock; m/Mignon; p/Karl and Karoline Klippstatter (dec); ed/Attended Conservatory of Mus, Austria; pa/Guest Conductor in Europe, US & Mexico; Tchr Memphis St Univ 1975-76; Dir Orch Activs, Hartt Sch Mus (Univ Hartford) 1977-; r/Rom Cath; hon/Outstg Musician, Fdn Mus Clbs Ark.

KLISCH, KAREN oc/Associate Professor; b/Jun 12, 1941; h/1704 Dahlgren Rd, Middletown, MD 21769; ba/Frederick, MD; p/Roland and Marion Young Klisch, Ft Lauderdale, FL; ed/BS Fla St Univ 1962; MA 1966, Cand PhD Univ Maryland; pa/Assoc Prof & Dir Huntsinger Aquatic Ctr, Hood Col; AAUP; AAHPER; Am Col Sports Med; cp/NOW; Instr Water Safety: ARC, Am Heart Assn; hon/Phi Delta Pi.

KLOBE, MARTHA PATRICIA JANE oc/Associate Professor; State Extension Specialist; b/Sept 19, 1932; h/2023 Vine St, Columbia, MO 65201; ba/Columbia; p/George N and Harriet W Klobe (dec); ed/BS; MS; pa/Mo Home Ec Assn; Am Home Ec Assn; cp/Envir Arts Assn; Am Crafts Coun; r/Rom Cath; hon/Beta Sigma Phi; Omicron Nu; Gamma Sigma Delta; Epsilon Sigma Phi; Outstg Yg Wom Am; W/W Am Wom; World W/W Wom; W/W Wom Ed.

KLOPSTEG, PAUL ERNEST oc/Retired; b/May 30, 1889; h/3161C Alta Vista, Laguna Hills, CA 92653; m/Amanda; c/Marie K Graffis, Ruth K Reed, Irma (dec); p/(dec); ed/BS; MA; PhD; Hon ScD; mil/AUS; pa/Former Prof, NWn Univ; Past Pres Mfg Co; Past Chm Artificial Limbs Com, NAS-

NRC; Past Bd Mem, Com Weather Control; cp/Repub Nat Com; r/Prot; hon/Hon Life Mem, Physics Clb Chgo; Hon Mem, Am Meteorological Soc; Rec'd Oersted Awd & Robert A Millikan Lectr Awd, Am Assn Physics Tchrs; Hall of Fame, Am Archery Assn.

KLOZE, IDA IRIS oc/Attorney; h/4201 Cathedral Ave, Washington, DC 20016; p/Max and Bertha Kloze (dec); ed/AB, AAB George Wash Univ; LLB, LLD Maryland Univ; pa/Pvt Pract Trial Lwyr; Mem Md Bar Assn; Dept Labor, Fed Trade Comm US Govt; Nat Coun FBA; Others; hon/W/W Am Wom; Life Mem Nat Wom's Party.

KMETZ, DONALD WILLIAM oc/Teacher; Writer; b/Apr 30, 1937; h/15 Daisy Pl, Tenafly, NJ 07670; m/Gail; c/Seth, Kira; p/George and Anne Zemlansky Kmetz; ed/BA; MA.

KNAEBEL, JEFF oc/Mining Engineer; b/May 11, 1939; h/Box 81467, College, AK 99708; m/Ida Louise Deconcini; c/2; p/John B and Joy Knaebel; ed/Colo Sch Mines 1963; mil/USN; pa/Pres, Resource Assocs of Alaska Inc 1970-; VP Charles Bettisworth & Co 1976-; VP, Ocean Home Exploration Ltd 1977-; Am Inst Min'g Engrs; Soc Economic Geol; Canadian Inst Min'g Engrs; Am Inst Profl Geol Scis; Geol Soc Am; Author: *Min'g & Mineral Policy on the Public Domain, A Brief Guide to Land Selection for Economic Resources*; cp/Kiwanis; Salvation Army; BSA; hon/Rec'd D W Burton Awd; Navy Commend Medal w "V"; Navy Unit Cit; Men Achmt; Notable Ams.

KNAPP, MARY ELIZABETH oc/Assistant Professor; b/Nov 2, 1944; h/1416 N 53, Seattle, WA 98103; ba/Seattle; m/Richard Dean; c/Sara Jean, Aaron Davis; p/Aaron Dee Light, Mt Vernon, WA; Amy Reedy Light, Mt Vernon, WA; ed/BS; MS; pa/Univ Wash Sch Nsg: Asst Prof, Maternal Child Nsg 1975-, Instr & Sch Nurse Conslt, Exptl Unit 1971-75, Var Coms, Others; Psychi Staff Nurse, Langley Porter Neuropsychi Inst (San Francisco, Cal) 1967-68; Lectr; Pub'd Num Articles Profl Jours; Am Assn Mtl Deficiency; Others; cp/Vol Cnslr, Planned Parenthood; Former Mem Commun Adv Bd; Former Mem Sex Ed Com, WARC; Conslt Var Civic Groups; r/Unitarian; hon/Sigma Theta Tau; Phi Beta Kappa.

KNAUF, JANINE BERNICE oc/Assistant Professor; b/Apr 10, 1945; h/32 Magnolia Ave, Kearny, NJ 07032; ba/Newark, NJ; c/Christopher; p/William C and Ila M Hauss Knauf, Pittsford, NY; ed/BS MIT 1967; MBA Rutgers Univ 1971; PhD Cand Columbia Univ; pa/Asst Prof Inf Sys & Acctg; IPA; Am Acctg Assn; Am Wom's Soc CPAs; NY Soc CPAs; Soc Wom Engrs; Am Inst Aeronautics & Astronautics; hon/Rec'd Spec Medal Awd, Beta Gamma Sigma; Rec'd Puder & Puder Awd.

KNEPPER, EUGENE ARTHUR oc/Real Estate Broker; b/Oct 8, 1926; h/283 Tomahawk Trail SE, Cedar Rapids, IA 52403; ba/Cedar Rapids; m/Lanel; c/Kenton Todd, Kristin Rene; p/Arlie John Knepper (dec); May C Knepper, Riverside, CA; ed/BS Drake Univ; mil/USN; pa/Pres Commercial Investmt Div, Iowa Assn Realtors 1973; Nat

Assn Accts; Nat Assn Realtors; Real Estate Securities & Syndication Inst; Pres Consumer Credit Cnslg Ser, Cedar Rapids-Marion Area; Guest Lectr Var Schs & Cols; cp/Pres Oakhill-Jackson Outreach Fund Inc; Leg Com, Iowa Assn Realtors; Jt Com Bus & Ed Cedar Rapids; r/Meth; hon/Rec'd Storm Awd for "One Person's Fin Futrue - Yours!"; W/W: MW, Fin & Indust; DIB; Intl W/W Commun Ser; Others.

KNIGHT, GRANVILLE F oc/Physician; b/Oct 12, 1904; ba/15525 Pomerado Rd, Poway, CA 92064; m/Eileen Hillyer Bonner; c/Peter Granville, Sara; p/Frank Henry and Belle Brown Knight; ed/AB Dartmouth 1926; MD Columbia Univ 1930; mil/USN Med Ofcr 1967-69; pa/Pvt Pract, Allergy & Nutrition (Santa Monica, Cal) 1963-; Staff, Santa Monica Hosp & Bel Air Meml Hosp; Conslt, Westwood Hosp; Commr LA Co Med Milk Comm 1968-; Pres Price-Pottenger Nutrition Foun 1967-; *Jour of Applied Nutrition*: Editor-in-Chief 1964-67, Editor 1967-72; Fellow Am

Col Allergists; Intl Assn Allergists; Intl Col Applied Nutrition; Am Geriatrics Soc; Assn Am Phys & Surgs; AMA; LA Co Med Assn; Fellow San Diego Res Inst; Others; Author Num Articles Profl Jours; Lectr; cp/Pure Water Assn Am; SAR; Gen Soc Colonial Wars; Mayflower Soc; hon/Rec'd Cert Meritorious Ser, Cal Dental Assn; Rec'd Plaque Outstg Work w Vitamin C, Com World Hlth; Rec'd Plaque, Am Nutrition Soc; Cert Apprec, Cal Dental Assn; Cert Meritorious Ser, Opthalmologic & Otolaryngologic Allergy; Hon F'ship, Intl Col Applied Nutrition; Outstg Ser, Am Acad Applied Nutrition; Biogl Listings.

KNIGHT, JAMES WESLEY oc/Retired; b/Feb 6, 1879; h/Rt 3, Lillington, NC 27546; m/(dec); p/Archiebald and Nancy Thomas Knight (dec); pa/Former Farmer, Grocer, Carpenter; cp/Var Charity Contbns; r/Prot.

KNIGHT, KATHLEEN (KIT) MARIE oc/Writer; Editor; Publisher; b/Sept 21, 1952; h/PO Box 439, California, PA 15419; ba/Same; m/Arthur Winfield; c/Tiffany Carolyn; p/Basil and Helen Swerdi Duell, Ambridge, PA; ed/BA Cal St Col (Penn) 1975; pa/Pub'd Creative Works 30 Lit Mags; COSMEP; hon/Rec'd Grants, Coorg Coun Lit Mags; Rec'd Pushcart Prize, Best of Small Presses.

KNOEBEL, DANIEL McCLELLAN oc/Executive; b/Jan 16, 1928; h/911 Osceola Ave, Winter Park, FL 32789; ba/Orlando, FL; m/Dorothy Wilson; c/Norwood B, Sandra M, Steven M, Deborah; p/Edward Lott and Mary Susan James Knoebel (dec).

KNOWLES, THOMAS GEORGE oc/-Architect; b/Feb 17; h/2407 Hunter, Tyler, TX 75701; ba/Tyler; m/Dorothy G; c/Mark, Steven, Glenn; p/George L Knowles (dec); Mary Inez Knowles, Tyler; mil/USN 1945-47; pa/Am Inst Archs; cp/Kiwanis; BSA; Co Fair Bd; r/Bapt; hon/Rec'd Intl Design Awd, Stran Steel.

KNOWLTON, EDGAR COLBY JR oc/Professor; b/Sept 14, 1921; h/1026 Kalo Pl, Apt 403, Honolulu, HI 96826; ba/Honolulu; p/Edgar Colby Knowlton (dec); Mildred Mason Hunt Knowlton, Honolulu; ed/BA 1941, MA 1942 Harvard; PhD Stanford 1959; mil/USNR 1944-46, 1951-52; pa/Prof European Langs, Univ Hawaii; Bibliog Com, Modern Lang Assn Am; Oral Hist Adv Com, Hawaii Multi-Cult Ctr; cp/Former Mus Reviewer, *Honolulu Advertiser*; hon/Rec'd Translation Prize, Secretaria de Estado da Informacao e Turismo (Lisbon, Portugal); Rec'd 2 US Grants to Serve Visiting Lectr: Univ Malaya, Univ Ctl de Venezuela (Caracas).

KNOX, WILLIAM FRANKLIN oc/Minister; b/May 14, 1915; h/326 Washington St, Norwell, MA 02061; ba/Same; c/Betty Anne K Davis, Jean Lois K Marino; p/Cleveland James and Clara Bel Taylor Knox (dec); ed/BA; MA (2); EdD; mil/USAF Chaplain; pa/Cnslr; Author; Exec Secy Am Assn Clinical Cnslrs; Clinical Mem NAFL; AMHCA; Pilgrim Assocs, United Ch of Christ; cp/Pres Elect Kiwanis Clb; Bd Dirs Norwell C of C; r/United Ch of Christ: Min.

KNUDSON, MARTHA AILENE oc/Educator; Nurse; b/Dec 28, 1910; h/212 Clydesdale Trace, Louisville, KY 40223; m/Kenneth E; p/James P Taylor (dec); Alma G Taylor-Belk (dec); ed/BSN; MEd; mil/AUS Nurse Corps 4 Yrs; pa/Univ Ky Commun Col Sys: Assoc Prof, Instr & Chm Assoc Deg Nsg (Elizabethtown) 11 Yrs; Instr & Dir Nsg Ed Hosp Dipl Schs 9 Yrs; Appointed to Bd Nsg Ed & Nurse Registration 4 Yrs; Nsg Ser Admr & Supvr 8 Yrs; Gen Staff Nurse 8 Yrs & Sch Nurse 4 Yrs; Helped Organize Ky Hlth Sys Agy W; Nat Leag Nsg; ANA; Ky Nurses Assn (Coms); Ky Leag Nsg: VP, Bd Dirs, Public Affairs Com; Others; cp/March of Dimes; Kidney Foun; Heart Assn; Cancer Soc; Past Chm, Reg Hearing & Speech Ctr Coun; Vol ARC; Var Wom's Clbs; r/Bapt: SS Tchr; Wom's Activs; hon/Ky Col; Rec'd Spec Merit Awd, Ky Leag Nsg; World W/W Wom Ed; Outstg Edrs Am.

KOBRYN, ATANAS TARAS oc/Business Officer; b/Mar 8, 1928; h/48 Brandis Ave, Eltingville, SI, NY 10312; ba/Staten Island, NY; m/Kateryna Osadciw; c/Alexander Z; Maria-Luba, A Bohdan, A Ihor; p/Alexander Kobryn (dec); Kateryna Stecula Kobryn, Ukrainian, USSR; ed/BS Univ Buffalo 1959; MA Niagara Univ 1971; mil/AUS 1952-54; USAR 1954-77; pa/Chief Fiscal & Adm Ofcr; AMHA; Am Arbiters Assn; NAA; NASD; Others; cp/Am Legs; Kiwanis; Ukr Frat Assn; Ukr Nat Assn; UB Alumni; NU Alumni; Others; r/Ukrainian Cath; hon/Rec'd Cert Merit, NYS Ser Dept; W/W E; Ukrainians N Am.

KOCH, CHRISTINE HODGES oc/Interior Decorator; b/Dec 25, 1930; h/104 Lakeview Dr, Enterprise, AL 36330; ba/Enterprise; m/Owen Albert; c/Mark Thomas, Jeffery Owen, Victor Bruce, Valerie Candace; p/Burley and Martha Baggett Hodges, Cunningham, TN; ed/Studied Paint'g, Sculpture, Decorat'g 3 Yrs; cp/Histn, Fdn Garden Clb; Flower Lovers Garden Clb: Ways & Means Chm, Meml Garden Chm, S'ship Com; Bd Dirs, Altrusa Clb; Hist & Geneal Soc; Leukemia Soc Am; Heart Assn; Others; r/Bapt; hon/Wom of Yr 1977; Rec'd Awd of Merit, Bicent Com; Rec'd Awd Apprec, Leukemia Soc Am.

KOCH, MARY THERESE oc/Social Services Coordinator; b/Oct 28, 1924; h/4821 Westwood Rd, Kansas City, MO 64112; ba/Kansas City; p/Frank J Koch, Norfolk, NE; Elizabeth Brachle Koch (dec);

ed/Attended Col; pa/Sister Rel Order; Lic'd Nsg Home Admr; Fellow Am Col Nsg Home Admrs; Fellow Am Acad Med Admrs; cp/US Civil Defense Coun; r/Rom Cath: Rel Sisters Am Benedictine Fdn St Scholastica; hon/Rec'd Pfizer Awd Merit; Rec'd Awd Merit, Mid-Am Coun BSA.

KOCHANSKY-KATZ, ROSALIE oc/- Artist; Writer; b/Jan 18; h/311 W 24th St, New York, NY 10011; m/(dec); p/(dec); ed/BA Brooklyn Col; MA NYU; Addit Studies; pa/Fdr Lower Eastside Independent Artists 1955; Tchr Art & Visual Remedial Read'g, NYC Spec Ser & 600 Schs 1962-70; United Nations Hospitality Com Tutor 1969; Lectr Col Nat Coun Jewish Wom 1973; Sev One-Man & Group Shows: Contemp Arts Gallery, Newark Museum, Bicent Exhbn Hudson Guild, Others; Life Mem Art Students Leag; Artist Equity; Others; cp/Vol ARC; YMHA & YWHA Ed Evaluation Com; Foun Creat Commun; Public Relats & Fund Raising, Gotham Chapt UJA Art; Am-Israel Cult Foun; Jerusalem Hosp Rehab Physically Handicapped Chd; Commun Planning Com, Brooklyn Museum Art; Museum Modern Art; Pres' Com Ed Handicapped; Others; r/Jewish; hon/Rec'd 1st Prize, Washington Square Outdoor Show; Rec'd S'ship, NYU Art Sch; Rec'd Govt Awd Post-Grad Inst, Sec'dy Sch Ed Disadvantaged; W/W: E, Am Wom; Intl Scholars Directory; Intl W/W Commun Ser.

KOCHEN, MANFRED oc/Scientist; b/Jul 4, 1928; h/2026 Devonshire Rd, Ann Arbor, MI 48104; ba/Ann Arbor; m/Paula; c/David J, Mark N; p/Max Kochen (dec); Pepi Kochen, New York, NY; ed/BS MIT 1950; MA 1951, PhD 1955 Columbia Univ; pa/Univ Mich: Info Scist, Prof, Res Mathematician; Am Soc Info Sci; Am Math Soc; Am Phys Soc; r/Jewish; hon/Rec'd Post-Doct F'ship, Harvard Univ.

KOCKINOS, CONSTANTIN NEOPHYTOS oc/Physicist; b/Oct 14, 1926; h/2121 Creeden Ave, Mountain View, CA 94040; ba/San Jose, CA; c/Marc Demetrius; p/Demetrius Kockinos (dec); Irene Sovrani; ed/BA (Physics) 1950; BA (Math) 1954; MA w Hons 1956; PhD 1974; pa/San Jose St Univ:

Physicist, Math Reschr; Conslt; Lectr; Var Sci Contbns; cp/Peace Corps; Intl Univ; Preservation of Life on Earth; Others; r/Greek Orthodox; hon/W/W W; Men Achmt; Intl W/W Intellectuals; Intl Register Profiles; Notable Ams; Am Men & Wom Sci; Intl Men & Wom Distinction; Others.

KOEHLER, ISABEL WINIFRED oc/Poet; Artist; b/Feb 5, 1903; h/30 Fremont Ave, Everett, MA 02149; ba/Same; m/F Mills; c/Alden, Muriel Joyce; p/George Wallace and Mary Elizabeth Strout Goodwin (dec); pa/Lectr; Sev One-Man Art Shows; Author: *Quaderni di Poesia "Bouquets of Poems"* (1974), *Quaderni di Poesia "Masters of Modern Poetry", "Versified Variety"* (1978); Agnes Carr Writers Clb Boston (All Positions); New England Wom's Press Assn; Mass St Poetry Soc; Intl Poetry Soc; IPA; Nat Writers Clb; NY Poetry Forum Inc; Old Boston Soc Independent Artists; Everett Arts Assn; Others; r/Glendale United Meth Ch: Mem; hon/Appointed Intl Com, Centro Studi E Scambi Internazionali (Rome); Hon Rep, Accademia Internationali "Leonardo Da Vinci" (Rome); Rec'd Diploma Di Benemerenza, CSESI; Rec'd Cert Merit, Bd

Editors IBA; 20 Poems Placed Perm Archives of London; Rec'd Gold Medal, Accademia Internationali; Rec'd Gold & Silver Medals for *Albo D'Oro* & *Masters of Modern Poetry*; Others.

KOESTERS, MARY JUSTINA oc/Retired Teacher & Librarian; b/Mar 2, 1904; h/3265 St John Rd, Maria Stein, OH 45860; p/Bernard and Catherine Link Koesters (dec); ed/BS Univ Dayton 1941; MSLS Cath Univ Am 1953; pa/Sister Rel Order; Libn Maria Stein Retreat House Lib 1977-79; Libn Immaculata Lib 1968-77; Ctl Cath HS (Lafayette, Ind): Libn, Math & Eng Tchr 1963-68; St Mary HS (Phoenix, Ariz): Libn & Asst Prin 1960-63; Other Positions; Author; OLA; CLA; ALA; Com to Establish Elem Libs & Media Ctrs All Schs City of Lafayette; Others; r/Cath: Congreg Sisters Precious Blood (Dayton, Ohio); hon/Rec'd Awd for Super Lib Ser, Cath Men Am; Intl W/W Commun Ser; Intl W/W Wom; W/W Lib Ser; DIB.

KOESTLER, ISABEL oc/Chairman; b/May 23, 1907; h/75 Ctl Park West, New York, NY 10023; ba/NYC; m/Albion (dec); c/Anthony; p/Joseph and May Cohn (dec); ed/Attended Hunter Col; pa/Chm Actors' Fund Bazaar; Pres Assn Charitable Thrift Shops NY; r/Jewish; hon/Rec'd 2 Awds, Actors' Fund Am.

KOHN, MARY LOUISE BEATRICE oc/Registered Nurse; b/Jan 13, 1920; h/28099 Belcourt Rd, Cleveland, OH 44124; ba/Shaker Heights, OH; m/Howard D; c/Marcia R; p/Theophilus J and Mary K Schmitkons Gaehr (dec); ed/BA Col Wooster 1940; MN Wn Reserve Univ 1943; mil/AUS 1944-45; pa/Ofc Nurse 1952-72; Fac Mem, Frances Payne Bolton Sch Nsg (Wn Reserve Univ) 1948-51; Staff Nurse, Peter Bent Brigham Hosp (Boston, Mass) 1948; Other Positions; Wom's Aux Acad Med of Cleveland & Cuyahoga Co: Ofcr, Asst Editor *Cleveland Physician* 1967-72; ANA; Ohio Nurses Assn; Assn OR Nurses; Frances Payne Bolton Sch Nsg Alumni Assn; Fac Wives Clb, Case Wn Univ Sch Med; Others; Co-Author *Berry & Kohn's Intro Operating Room Technique*, 1955; cp/Cleveland Hlth Museum; Coun World Affairs; Orange Commun Arts Coun; Wom's Com, Cleveland Orch; Aux, PBS WVIZ-TV; Aux, Frederick Crawford Auto Museum; Cleveland Racquet Clb; Antique Auto Assn Am; r/Prot; hon/Nat Hon Soc.

KOLAWOLE, LAWRENCE COMPTON oc/Artist; b/Aug 20, 1931; h/357-B Scott St, San Francisco, CA 94117; ba/Same; m/Annie R Daniels; c/William Lawrence Compton II, Darius Straughter, T'schad Bonis; p/Sam and

Marie Savannah Compton (dec); ed/Cal Sch Fine Arts (SF); mil/USAF; pa/One-Man Shows: Mark Mus Der Stadt Witten (Germany), Galerie Ruf (Munchen), Galerie Dimitrios (Amsterdam), Others; Group Shows: USA Nat Shows SF Museum, Harbstsalon Hausder Kunst (Munich, Germany), Salon Int Art Actuel (Brussels), Intl Art Market Paint Show (Dusseldorf, Germany); Others; IPA; Visual Arts & Gallery Assn; Artist Equity; r/Prot; hon/Work Rep'd Perm Collections: Leinbach Mus Gallery (Munich), Stadt Witten Mus, Insel Film Gmb (Munich), SF Mus Modern Art, Oakland Mus, Others; W/W Am Art; Am Art Directory; Book of Hon; Intl Directory Art; Commun Ldrs & Noteworthy Ams; Others.

KOLB, FLORENCE ALICE oc/Businesswoman; b/Aug 22, 1928; h/1809 Juniper, Alamogordo, NM 88310; ba/Alamogordo; m/Arnold A; c/Maurita Carol K Autrey, Pamela M, Theone Denise K Oliver, Kimberly Kay, Nathan Howard, Sterling Arnold (dec);

p/Marvin and Mabel Dutton, Prairie City, SD; pa/Corporate Secy-Treas; Mgr; PEO; cp/C of C; Repub Wom; r/Grace United Meth Ch: Mem, Fin Bd, Chm Florence Cir; hon/Beta Sigma Phi; Valedictorian Lemmon HS; Girl of Yr, Beta Sigma Phi; Valentine Sweetheart, Beta Sigma Phi; Order of Rose.

KOLBER, JAMES S oc/Union Representative; b/Oct 19, 1949; h/136 Kantishna Way, Fairbanks, AK 99701; ba/Same; p/M L and S Kolber; ed/BS; MA; BA; cp/Softball; Basketball; Volleyball; r/Jewish; hon/Golden Gloves; Shoreline Tournamt; All Conf Football; Coach & Player of Yr; Others.

KOLIN, IRVING SEYMOUR oc/Physician; b/Feb 15, 1940; h/122 Variety Tree Cir, Altamonte Springs, FL 32701; ba/Orlando, FL; m/Rochelle Tinkelman; c/Lawrence, Marc; p/Jean Kolin, Brooklyn, NY; ed/MD; mil/USN Med Corps; pa/Chm Dept Psychi, Orlando Reg Med Ctr 1977-; Chief of Psychi, Orange Meml Hosp 1976-77; Med Dir, Orange Meml Hosp Comprehensive Commun Mtl Hlth Ctr 1972-; AMA; Fellow Am Psychi Assn; Am Acad Child Psychi; Fellow Am Orthopsychi Assn; Fla Med Assn; Fla Psychi Soc; Intl Assn Study Pain; Am Pain Soc; Others; cp/Rotary; Hemophilia Assn Ctl Fla; Mtl Hlth Assn Orange Co; r/Jewish; hon/Rec'd Recog Awd, AMA; W/W S&SE; DIB; Commun Ldrs & Noteworthy Ams; Personalities Am; Men Achmt; Personalities of S; Notable Ams; Others.

KOLOSVARY, EVA J oc/Artist; b/May 14, 1937; h/30211 Via Rivera, Rancho Palos Verdes, CA 90274; m/Paul; c/Judy; p/Alexander Stein, Los Angeles, CA; Anna Herczog, LA; ed/MA Cal St Univ-LB 1974; pa/Art Instr, Orange Coast Col; Exhbns US & Abroad; hon/Num Purchase Awds.

KOMOSA, ADAM ANTHONY oc/Retired Lieutenant Colonel, US Army; b/Aug 24, 1913; h/Circle 'K' Acres, Rt 1, Columbia, KY 42728; m/Naomi Evlyn; c/Kathrine Louise, Adam Anthony Jr; p/Simon and Catherine Komosa (dec); ed/AA Univ Fla 1960; BA 1962, MA Fla St Univ 1963; PhD InterAmerican Col 1967; mil/US Army 1932-58; pa/Instr, No Mich Univ 1968-78; Secy, Alpha Kappa Psi; Phi Alpha Theta; Phi

Kappa Phi; Soc of Wireless Pioneers; Am Assn Advmt of Slavic Studies; cp/Polish Am Hist Assn; Kosciuszko Foun; Rotary Intl; BPOE; Am Legion; Ret'd Ofcrs Assn; 82nd Airborne Div Assn; Airborne Cent Clb; r/Cath; hon/Silver Star Medal; Purple Heart; Bronze Star w OLC; Belgian Fouragerre; Korean Dist'd Mil Ser Medal; French Cherbourg Liberation Medal; Polish Guard Silver Wing; Others.

KONA, MARTHA M oc/Librarian; b/May 12; h/600 Third St, Wilmette, IL 60091; m/William; c/Olivia, Lindy Ann; p/Albert and Ann; ed/BA 1953, MALS 1958 Rosary Col; Addit Studies; pa/Rush Univ Lib: Asst Dir Tech Sers 1977-, Coor Cat & Multi Media 1967-77; Res Libn Chemurgy Dept, Ctl Soya 1965-67; Catalog Libn & Instr, Univ Ill 1958-63; Pub'd Bibliogs & Articles; AAUP; AAUW; Med Lib Assn; Hosp & Nsg Sch Libns MW; Ill A-V Assn; Ill Hlth Sci Media Assn; Others; r/Cath; hon/Pi Gamma Mu; Ordre Souverain et Militaire du Temple de Jerusalem; Sovereign Byzantine Order Lascaris Comnemus of Sts Constantine & Helen; Ordine Di Santa Agatha dei Paterno; Academia Internat de Ponzen Di Lettere, Scienze & Arti.

KONES, RICHARD J oc/Physician; b/Apr 8, 1941; ba/(Main Ofc) 356 Horseshoe Hill Rd, Pound Ridge, NY 10576; 305 Baronne St, 9th Floor New Orleans, LA 70112; 2710 Stemmons Freeway, Suite 305, Dallas TX 75207; 2070 NW 7th St, Miami, FL 33125; 1901 Old Middlefield Way, Suite 14, Mountainview, CA 94043; PO Box 1919, Bridgeport, CT 06601; m/Sandra Lee Morrissey; c/Kimberly, Robin (dec), Melanie, Sabrina; p/Joseph I and Ruth Winkler Murphy; ed/BS NYU 1960; NY St Regents Scholar 1958-60; Elected Del Am Chem Soc & Eshborn Scholar 1960 (Physiology); Recip Freshman Chem Achmt Awd 1958, NYU Dept Chem; Chem Engr & Lectr Postgrad Math Analysis; MD NYU Med Sch 1964; Arthritis & Rheumatism Foun Scholar; Recip Physiology Dept Res F'ships 1961-62 NYU; Fellow in Surgical Physiology NYU 1963; pa/Intern Med, Kings Co Hosp, Downstate Med Sch, Bklyn, NY 1964-65; Surg Res Bronx Mun Hosp, Albert Einstein Col of Med, Bronx, NY 1965-66; Internal Med Res, Lenox Hill Hosp, NYU Sch of Med, NYC 1966-68; Tchg Fellow in Cardiol & Dir Intensive/Coronary Care Units, Knickerbocker Hosp, NYC 1968-69; Fellow in Cardiol & Acting Chief Res, VA Hosp-Tulane Univ Sch of Med, New Orleans 1969-70; Instr in Internal Med, Tulane Univ Sch of Med 1969-71; USPHS Nat Heart Inst Res Fellow in Cardiol, Tulane Univ Sch of Med 1970-71; Asst Prof of Clin Med-Cardiol, NY Med Col, NYC 1971-76; Vis Physician, Sect of Cardiol, Tulane Univ Sch of Med 1974-; Assoc Clinical Prof Med (Cardiology), Mt Sinai Sch Med CUNY 1979-; Cardiol Conslt, Arthur C Logan Meml Hosp, NYC 1975-; Cardiol Conslt & Physician, NYU Med Ctr-Midtown Hosp, NYC 1976-; Cardiol Conslt & Physician, Park City Hosp/Yale New Haven Med Ctr, Bridgeport, Conn 1976-; Cardiol Conslt, Lefferts Gen Hosp, Bklyn, NY 1976-; Cardiol Conslt, Parkchester Gen Hosp, Park East Hosp, Park West Hosp, Commun Med Hosp, Kings Hwy Hosp, Flatbush Gen Hosp, Cabrini Hlth Care Ctr/Columbus-Italian Hosp, Med Arts Hosp, LeRoy Hosp, Madison Ave Hosp, Westchester Sq Hosp, Mt Eden Gen Hosp, Williamsburg Gen Hosp, All NYC; Mem: ACP, AHrtA, AHrtA Couns on Clin Cardiol, Basic Res, Cardiopulmonary Diseases, Thrombosis & Hemostasis, Circulation, ATS, AACT, AALM, NYCS, RSH (Fellow), Am Bd Internal Med & Nat Bd Med Examrs (Diplomate), NYTS, NYAS, ASZ, NYSSIM, AAPSS, ISHR, IUPAB, Nat Res Coun, SEBM, SMA, Musser Burch Soc (NO, La), APHA, AAAS, Am Soc for Internal Med, Am Fed for Clin Res, Am Cancer Soc, Am Chem Soc, Am Col Cardiol, (Fellow) Am Soc of Clin Pharm & Exptl Therapeutics, Am Med Writers Assn, Am Col of Emer Phyisicians, (Fdg Mem) Am Diabetes Assn, Am Lung Assn, Am Stat Assn, Am Inst of Biol Scis, AHA, APHA, Am Assn for Advmt of Med Instrumentation, Soc Gen Physiologists,

Laennec Soc, (AHA) Biophysical Soc, Soc for Exptl Bio & Med, Biomed Engrg Soc, Soc for Critical Care Med, Med Electronics & Data Soc, Audio Eng Soc, Intl Study Group for Res in Cardiac Metab, Microcirculatory Soc, Intl Soc on Thrombosis & Haemostasis, Intl Soc of Internal Med, Belgian Soc Cardiol, French Cardiol Soc, Intl Soc of Cardiol, Intl Diabetes Fed, Intl Union of Physiol Scis, US Bioenergetics Group, Am Physiological Soc, Charter Mem APS/AZS, Charter Mem Assoc, Am Soc for Bariatric Physicians (Hon), (Fellow) ACCP, Am Col of Chest Physicians, (Fellow) Royal Soc of Med, (Fellow) Royal Soc of Hlth, (Fellow) Am Col of Angiol, (Fellow) Am Col Clin Pharm, (Fellow) Am Geriatrics Soc, (Fellow) Intl Col of Angiol, (Fellow) Am Col of Cardiol, Assoc AMA; Conslt Editor: Chest 1973, 76, Current Prescribing 1976, Am Soc of Hosp Pharmacists, for Am Hosp Formulary Ser 1976-79; Author: *Cardiogenic Shock* (1974), *Glucose, Insulin, Potassium and the Heart* (1975); Co-Author: *Coronary Care Handbook* (w J H Phillips) 1979, *Inherited Diseases and the Heart* (w J H Phillips) 1979; Co-Editor: *Electrocardiography* (w J H Phillips) 1979, *Basic and Clin Pharm of the Heart* (w J H Phillips) 1979, *The Molecular and Ionic Basis of Myocardial Contractility* (1973), *Cardiovas Diseases, New Directions in Therapy*, in press; Editor, *Advances in Cardiol* (Annual Series of Vols 1979-); Medicolegal Conslt Tech Adv Ser for Attys; Cardiopulmonary Conslt Soc Sec Adm Bur of Disability Determinations; Conslt & Spec Examr Metropolitan Ins Co, Travelers Ins Cos, Penn Mutual Ins Co, Phoenix Mutual Ins Co, New England Life Ins Co, Mutual of Omaha, Northwestern Mutual Life Ins Co, Equitable Ins Co, Bankers Life Ins Co, Bankers Security Life Ins Co, Lincoln Nat Life Ins Co; Editor Conslt, Futura Pub Co, NY (Cardiol); Author of over 88 Sci Articles; Has Given Num Hon Lectrs at Med Schs; Ext Original Res Contbns on Basic Physiology; Noted Authority of Shock & Physiology; Pres, Commun Med Ofcs, Inc; cp/US Lawn & Tennis Assn; Am Mus Nat Hist; E African Wildlife Soc (Kenya); Nat Wildlife Fdn; Nat Geographic Soc; Am Med Tennis Assn; Tulane Med Alumni Assn; NYU Sch Med Alumni Assn; Albert Einstein Col Med Alumni Assn; hon/Cont'g Ed Awd, 1969, 71, 76, 78.

KONKEL, WILBUR STANTON oc/-Missionary; b/Sept 4, 1912; h/622 Oakdale Ave, Chicago, IL 60657; ba/Chgo; m/Arlene Kathrene; c/Olive K Cruver, Marjorie K Vorhees, Pamela K Aldstadt; p/Samuel M and

Clara May Simmonds Konkel (dec); ed/BA Alma White Col; Addit Studies; pa/Dir African Missions; Dir Pillar of Fire, West African Missions; cp/Lakeview Coun; r/Prot; Bishop for Am Missions; hon/NGS; Intl W/W; Others.

KONNER, JOAN WEINER oc/Producer; b/Feb 24, 1931; h/Snedens Landing, Palisades, NY 10964; ba/New York, NY; m/(dec); c/Rosemary, Catherine; p/Martin and Tillie Fraukel Weiner (dec); ed/BA Sarah Lawrence Col; MS Columbia Grad Sch Journalism; pa/Prodr, Writer, Dir WNET-TV; Newswom's Clb NY; Cath Broadcasters Assn; cp/Columbia Univ Exec Com Alumni Assn; Nat Coun Chs; hon/Sigma Delta Chi; Recipient 5 Emmys, Nat Acad of TV Arts & Scis; Rec'd Ohio St Awd (2); AP Broadcasters Awd (3); Atlanta Film Fest; Chgo Film Fest; NY Film Fest; Rec'd Alumni Awd, Columbia

Sch Journalism.

KONO, TOSHIHIKO oc/Concert Cellist; b/Nov 8, 1930; h/400 W 43rd St, New York, NY 10036; m/Libby; c/Miyo, Kaori; p/Zenshiro Kono (dec); Miyo Kono; ed/LLB Kyoto Univ 1953; Mannes Col of Mus; Stanford Univ; Berkshier Mus Ctr; pa/Intl Concert Soloist; Chamber Player; Symph Orch Mem: Asst Prin Cello w Kyoto Symph, New Orleans Philharm, Cellist w Am Symph, Prin Cello w Westchester Philharm; Resident Artist w Bar Harbor Fest; Bd Trustees, Am Symph Orch; IPA; cp/Intl Biogl Assn; hon/Rec'd Fromm F'ship; Rec'd Silver Medal & Dist'd Ser Awd; Others.

KONZAL, JOSEPH C oc/Sculptor; b/Nov 5, 1905; h/360 W 21st, New York, NY 10011; ba/NYC; m/Theresa Sherman; p/Frank A and Sylvia Baresh Konzal (dec); pa/One-Man Shows: Brata Gallery; Bertha Schaefer Gallery, Andre Zarre Gallery; Maj Exhbns: Museum Modern Art, Carnegie Intl, Galerie Claude Bernard (Paris), Whitney Mus of Am Art Annuals, NY World's Fair, Others; Num Works Pvt Collections; cp/Dem Party; hon/Rec'd Guggenheim F'ship; Num Works in Perm Collections: Whitney Museum, New Sch for Social Res, NJ St Mus, Tate Gallery (London), Storm King Art Ctr (Mountainville, NY), Canton Art Inst (Ohio).

KOO, ROBERT C J oc/Educator; b/Mar 20, 1921; h/2223 12th St NW, Winter Haven, FL 33880; ba/Lake Alfred, FL; m/Margaret Chung; c/Robert, Kenneth, Dennis; p/T Z and Ge Tseng Koo (dec); ed/BS Cornell Univ;

MS, PhD Univ Fla; pa/Inst Food & Agri Sci, Univ Fla: Reschr Citrus, Mineral Nutrition & Water Mgmt; cp/Rotary; Dem Party; r/Epis; hon/Rec'd Res Awd, Fla Fruit & Vegetable Assn; Rec'd Pres Gold Medal Awd; Hon Mem, Fla St Horticult Soc.

KOPPLEMAN, DOROTHY oc/Consultant; b/Jun 13, 1920; h/498 Broome St, New York, NY 10012; ba/NYC; c/Chaim, Ann; p/Harry and May; pa/Painter; Writer; Tchr; Pres Aesthetic Realism Foun Inc; Aesthetic Realism Conslt w The Kindest Art Painter; hon/Rec'd Tiffany Grant for Painting.

KORDUS, HENRY oc/Landscape Architect; b/Apr 20, 1922; h/12787 Ramona Ave, Chino, CA 91710; ba/Pomona, CA; m/Juanita; c/Maria Elizabeth, Marcela Natasha; p/Michal and Jadwiga Kordus (dec); ed/BS St Col (Warsaw, Poland) 1944; MS 1951, PhD 1972 Univ Agri (Warsaw); MA Warsaw Univ 1957; pa/Planning Conslt, Pvt Pract 1964-; Prof Landscape Arch, Cal St Polytechnic Univ 1964-; Landscape Designs: Ft Mohove Indian Reservation Redevelopmt Plan (Needles, Cal), Ctl Park (Warsaw), Others; Author: *Org of Envir Tchg in Relation to Contemp Probs* (1972, 77), *The Rationale for Interdisciplinary Studies* (1972), Others; Pub'd Num Profl Papers; Lectr; Other Positions; Am Soc Landscape Archs; Hon Soc Agri; Gamma Sigma Delta; r/Cath; hon/Rec'd Medals: Krzyz Walecznych, Krzyz Armii Krajowej, Medal Wojska; Rec'd S'ships: Univ Agri (Poland), NYU; Rec'd Grants: Kosciuszko Foun, Bur Cult Affairs (US St Dept); Rec'd Cert Apprec, City of Chino; Rec'd Cert Merit, City of Montclair; Rec'd Lttrs Apprec from Var Schs, Cols, Dirs, Pubrs, Others; W/W W; Men Achmt; Notable Ams; DIB; Commun Ldrs & Noteworthy Ams.

KORN, ELIZABETH P oc/Artist; h/1 Marine View Plaza, 4th Hudson, Box 20C, Hoboken, NJ 07030; m/Arthur (Dec); ed/Mus Fine & Applied Arts, Masterclass (Berlin, Germany); Columbia Univ; New Sch of Social Res; Inst Fine Arts (NYU); Art Students Leag; pa/Artist in Residence & Visiting Scholar (Govt Grants), Emory & Henry Col (Va), King Col (Bristol, Tenn); Prof & Chm Art Dept & Artist in Residence, Drew Univ; One-Man Shows: Roko Gall (NYC); Theol Sem (Drew Univ), Univ Ctr (Drew Univ), Cornell Univ; Group Shows: Commun Ctr (Gall, NYC), Gala Art Exhibit (Dept Interior, Wash, DC); 200 Portraits & Sketches of Famous Physicists, Niels Bohr Lib, Am Inst Phys, Others; Author: *At Home w Chd, Skippy's Fam, Portraits of Famous Physicists;* Mem Var Socs & Assns; hon/Rec'd Grumbacher Awd; Works incl'd: Archives Am Art, Smithsonian Inst.

KORSHAK, MARGIE oc/Executive; b/Feb, 17, 1939; h/1014 Elmridge Dr, Glencoe, IL 60022; ba/Chicago, IL; m/Theodore Ruwitch; c/Susan, Steve; p/Marshall and Edith Sloane Korshak; ed/Attended Univ Colo, Univ Chgo; pa/Pres Margie Korshak Assocs, Inc; Public Relats & Advtg for Shubert Org Inc, Nederlander Org, Arnie's, Others; Publicity Clb of Chgo; cp/Bd Dirs, Chgo Heart Assn; r/Jewish.

KORTE, ADELE D J oc/Psychologist; b/Dec 21, 1922; h/4092 Haven St, St Louis, MO 63116; ba/St Louis; p/Arthur F Korte (dec); ed/MA; pa/Dist Sch Psychologist; Nat Assn Sch Psychol; r/Luth; hon/Kappa Delta Pi.

KOSKOFF, THEODORE I oc/Attorney; b/Jun 23, 1913; h/17 Bonnie Brook Rd, Westport, CT 07880; ba/Bridgeport, CT; m/Dorothy; c/Michael, Elizabeth, Susan K Glazer; p/Israel and Hattie Koskoff; ed/LLB Boston Univ Sch of Law; pa/Atty Koskoff, Koskoff & Bieder (Law Firm); Admit'd to Cts: Conn Superior & Supr Cts, US Dis Ct (So Dist NY), US Dist Ct (Conn), US Supr Ct, Others;

Mem: Am, Conn, Bridgeport & Fed Bar Assns; Assn Trial Lwyrs Am; AJS; Conn Trial Lwyrs Assn; Nat Assn Crim Defense Lwyrs; Lifetime Fellow, Am Trial Lwyrs Foun; Fdr & Chm, Nat Bd Trial Advocacy; Other Assns & Positions; Pub'd Num Articles Profl Jours: "Quest for a Fair Trial," *Trial Mag* (Jan/Feb 1971), "The Lang of Persuasion," *Litigation Mag* (Aug 1977), Others; r/Jewish; hon/Rec'd Silver Shingle Awd for Dist'd Ser Legal Profession, Boston Univ Law Sch.

KOSLOVSKY, ITZIK oc/Editor; b/Dec 2, 1898; h/387 Grand St, New York, NY 10002; p/Moishe and Frima Koslovsky (dec); pa/Editor *Bnai Yiddish Mag;* Author *Cross Currents,* (Play); Secy Bnai Yiddish Org; r/Jewish; hon/Rec'd Awd, Bnai Brith.

KOSMACH, FRANK P oc/Retired; b/Nov 19, 1893; h/180 Isle of Venice, Ft Lauderdale, FL 33301; m/Clare L; p/Anton and Katarina Kosmach (dec); mil/WWI; pa/Chm Emeritus, St Paul Fed (Chgo); Savs & Ln; cp/Past Dir Oak Park Hosp, Others; r/Rom Cath; hon/Man of Yr, Ill Coun Savs & Ln.

KOSTEM, CELAL NIZAMETTIN oc/- Professor; b/Feb 8, 1939; h/3520 Chippendale Cir, Bethlehem, PA 18017; ba/Bethlehem; m/Kathy Michele; p/Naki Kostem (dec);

Suada Kostem, Istanbul, Turkey; ed/BS 1960, MS 1961 Istanbul Tech Univ; PhD Univ Ariz 1966; mil/Turkish Land Forces Command 1961-63; TLFC-NATO Active Reserv; pa/Lehigh Univ: Prof 1978, Assoc Prof 1972-78, Asst Prof 1968-72, Post-Doct Res Assoc 1966-68, Chm Computer-Sys Group (Fritz Lab) 1968-78; Conslt Var Engrg Firms & Orgs; Instr & Analyst, Nuclear Protective Design & Construction; Seismic, Wind & Fire Engrg; AAAS; ACI; ASCE; IABSE; IASS; LVASCE; NSPE; PSDE; Others; hon/Sigma Xi; Chi Epsilon; Fulbright Fellow (3).

KOULOGEORGE, PATRICIA ANDREA oc/Student; b/May 9, 1956; h/4019 Crestwood, Northbrook, IL 60062; p/James and Mary Koulogeorge, Northbrook; ed/BS NWn Univ; pa/Grad Student; Urban Planning Dept Data Analyst; Mktg Res Asst; Sociol Dept Res Asst; Secretarial Work; Child Care; cp/NWn Univ: Big Sister-Big Brother Prog, Col Repub Clb, Publicity Com, Others; Northfield Township Yg Repubs; Asst Coor John Edward Porter for Cong Campaign; Others; r/Greek Orthodox; hon/Rec'd Outstg Sr Awd, NWn Univ; Rec'd Outstg Achmt Awd, Panhellenic-IFC; Rec'd Outstg Ser Awd, NWn Univ.

KOUSSA, HAROLD ALAN oc/Engineer; b/Jun 20, 1947; h/73 Childs Rd, E Hampton, CT 06424; ba/Farmington, CT; m/Marsha Lynn Leidenis; p/Harold A and June John Koussa, Narragansett, RI; ed/BSES Univ Rhode Island; MBA Univ Hartford; MS Rensselaer Polytechnic Inst; pa/Sr Staff Nuclear Engr, Am Nuclear Insurers 1977-; Reactor Engr, Conn Yankee Atomic Power Co 1969-77; Am Nuclear Soc; Assn MBA Execs; Am Nuclear Standards Inst; Failure & Incident Report Review Com; r/Congregl; hon/W/W E.

KOUW, WILLY ALEXANDER oc/Professor; b/Dec 20, 1932; ed/BA McMaster Univ (Canada) 1961; PhD Univ Tex 1965; Addit Studies; pa/Pvt Pract Clinical Psychologist (San Antonio, Tex) 1967-; Clinical Asst Prof, Dept Psychi, Univ Tex Med Sch 1968-; Fac Coor, Fielding Inst (Santa Barbara, Cal); Other Positions; Am Psychol Assn; Bexar Co Clinical Psychol Assn; Tex Assn Chd w LDs; Intl Transactional Analysis Assn; Lic'd Psychol, Tex St Bd Examrs Psychols; Lic'd Social Psychotherapist, Tex St Bd Examrs Social Psychotherapy; Lectr; Reschr; Pub'd Num Articles Profl Jours: hon/Am Men Sci; W/W S&SW; DIB; Men Achmt; Nat Register Hlth Ser Providers Psychol.

KOVACH, KENNETH JULIUS oc/Sociologist; b/Aug 26, 1941; h/3035 Ripley Rd, Cleveland, OH 44120; ba/Cleveland; m/Mary Ann Catherine; c/Juliana Catherine; p/Julius Stephen and Catherine Bittner Kovach, Parma, OH; ed/BA 1967, MA 1973 Case Wn Reserv Univ; BD St Vladimir Orthodox Theol Sem 1969; Addit Studies; pa/Dir Cleveland Urban Mus Proj, Ohio Hist Soc; Conslt Nat Comm on Neighborhoods; Former Dir Public Affairs Dept, Cleveland Area Arts Coun; Others; Am Sociol Assn; Intl Sociol Assn; Nat Ethnic Studies Assembly; cp/Fdg Trustee & First Pres, Buckeye Woodland Commun Cong; Bd Dirs, City Clb of Cleveland; Adv Coun, Wn Reserv Area Agy on Aging; Admissions Com & Ldrship Com, United Way Sers; Commun Spec Gtr Cleveland Proj; Others; r/St Theodosius Cathedral, Orthodox

Ch Am: Mem, Choir Master; hon/Omicron Delta Kappa; Alpha Kappa Delta; Rec'd Nat Sci Foun Grad F'ship; Rec'd World Coun Chs Ecumenical F'ship; Certs Apprec; W/W Rel; Commun Ldrs & Noteworthy Ams; Others.

KOVALCHUK, FEODOR SAWA oc/- Archpriest; b/Mar 5, 1924; h/727 Miller Ave, Youngstown, OH 44502; ba/Same; m/Anna Korewik; c/Sergius, Basilissa, Natalia; p/Sawa John Kovalchuk (dec); Rose Boryk Kovalchuk, Masury, OH; ed/BA St Vladimir Theol Sem; MA; pa/Exec Secy, Patriarchal Parishes of Russian Orthodox Ch USA; Editor *One Church;* Translator; Author; Instr Lang & Hist; AATEEL; Ohio Acad Hist; r/Orthodox Cath; hon/Mitred Archpriest; Nat Slavic Hon Soc (Dobro Slovo).

KOVALENKO, VIRGIL NICHOLAS oc/Consultant; Educator; b/Nov 20, 1934; h/Salt Lake City, UT 84117; ba/USAF Academy, CO; m/Lela Joyce Musick; c/Nicholas Virgil, Michael Virgil, Lisa, David Virgil, Kanya; p/Nicolai Nicolaiyvich Kovalenko (dec); Ruth Clawson, Laguna Beach, CA; ed/AA Orange Coast Col 1960; BA Brigham Young Univ 1962; MA Universidad Interamericana (San German, Puerto Rico) 1969; PhD Univ Utah 1974; mil/USN 1953-61; USAF 1962-; pa/LDS Cadet Inst Instr; USAF Acad: Asst Prof Spanish, Chm Spanish 1976-78; Instr Eng & Criminology 1971-72; Public Relats Writer 1960-61; Newpaper Editor 1954-56, 1961-62; Other Positions; cp/Former Planning Commr OCC; BSA: Explorer Advr, Former Mem Intl Div, Others; Former Prog Features Staff, Explorer Olympics; Former Dir Colo Springs Spanish Choir; Mormon Hist Assn; Smithsonian Assoc; Nat Geographic Soc; Ret'd Ofcrs Assn; Others; r/Ch of Jesus Christ LDS; hon/Phi Delta Kappa; Sigma Delta Chi; Rec'd Gold Ldrship Key; Rec'd Jr Leag Spanish Awd; Eagle Scout w Bronze Palm; Silver Awd Explorer; Nat Hon Soc; Dist'd Mil Grad; Dist'd Grad, USAF/AFIT; Explorer Tng Awd; USAF Good Citizen Awd; USAF Commend Medal; Rec'd Bronze Star; Vietnamese Cross of Gallentry; Vietnamese Hon Medal (1st Class); S Vietnam Plaque of Hon; Others.

KOWALSKI, CASH JOHN oc/Vice President; b/Apr 9, 1942; h/Westview Rd, Morrisville, NY 13408; ba/Morrisville; m/Luba Johanna; c/Joey, Matthew, Peter; p/Peter and Bernadine Kowalski, Warners, NY; ed/BS SUNY; MA, EdS Wn Ky Univ; EdD; pa/VP Acad Affairs, SUNY 1977-; Asst Dir, Univ Ky 1974-77; Assoc Editor *Psychol Jour of Human Behavior;* NAGC; KACE; KPGA; Author *The Impact of College on Students;* cp/VP Rotary Clb; Treas N Am Assn; Bd Dirs, Gifted Chd; Others; r/Cath; hon/Rec'd Fac Awd Profl Ldrship; Ky Col.

KOZELKA, TRESSIE MASOCCO oc/- Retired Teacher & Counselor; b/Nov 16, 1908; h/2520 W Davis Cir, Peoria, IL 61604; m/Robert T; p/Angelo and Antonietta Licini Masocco (dec); ed/BS Eureka Col; MA Univ Chgo; Addit Studies; pa/Cnslr Peoria HS 1969-71; Cnslr W Sr HS (Rockford) 1958-69; Bradley Univ: Critic Tchr 1947-57, Tchr 1947-48; Other Positions; Ill Guid & Pers Assn: St Prog Chm 1961-62, VP 1962-63; Others; cp/Former Trustee Eureka Col; Former Case Aide for Ill Emer Relief Comm (Fulton Co); Former Cnslr Girls' Camp; Former Mem St Hlth Curric Com; Others; r/Prot; hon/Pi Kappa Delta; Pi Lambda Theta; Rec'd Alumni Awd of Merit, Eureka Col; Notable Ams; World W/W Wom; W/W Am Wom; DIB; Others.

KRANTZ, MARILYN oc/Editor; Poet; Journalist; b/Jan 31, 1927; h/1383 Kimberly Dr, Philadelphia, PA 19151; m/Barney; c/Jane K Silverbrook (Mrs Fred), Charles, Martin, Kathy; p/Samuel and Ethel Rosenthal Rosen, Philadelphia; ed/BS Temple Univ 1948; pa/Penn Poetry Soc; Pres Phil Folkshuln; Pres M E Kalish Folkshul; cp/Fdn Jewish Agencies: Com Jewish Ed, Wom's Coun Bd (Correspond'g Secy); Bd Mem, Jewish Nat Fund of Phil; r/Jewish; hon/1st Prize Poetry, Phil Regional Writers' Conf; Rec'd Ser Awd,

Lamberton Home & Sch Assn.

KRASIC, LJUBO oc/Director; b/Mar 18, 1938; h/4851 S Drexel Blvd, Chicago, IL 60615; ba/Same; p/Pero Krasic (dec); Stana Dugandzic, Croatia; ed/BC (Classics) 1958, BC (Philosophy) 1964 Sarajevo; STM Zagreb 1967; Master Sociol, Rome 1973 (All summa cum laude); pa/Dir Croatian Ethnic Inst Inc; Secy Gen Croatian Schs of USA, Canada & Australia; Spec Res Prog on Immigrants from Yugoslavia to Switzerland 1977-; Rel Profile on Croatians in USA & Canada 1975-; Telephone Data-Rad, Res Prog (NY, Chgo) 1974-; Catechet for Students, Univ Mostar (Yugoslavia) 1976; Pastoral Mission Canada 1975-76; Others; Author *Kleine Auslaender* (1972), Others; Editor: *Intl Migration Review* 1974-, *Migration Today* 1974-, Others; Croatian Cath Union; Am Sociol Assn; Intl Sociol Assn; Am Acad Polit & Social Sci; Others; cp/Fellow Am Biogl Inst; Nat Archives; Montana Hist Assn; r/Cath: Franciscan Order, Ordained Priest; hon/Rec'd Pontificia Commissione per la Pastorale del Turismo e delle Migrazioni for Res; Others.

KRASNER, WILLIAM oc/Writer; b/Jun 8, 1917; h/538 Berwyn Ave, Berwyn, PA 19312; m/Juanita Frances; c/David E, Daniel A, Lawrence S, James N; p/Samuel and Braine Krasner (dec); ed/BS Columbia Univ 1948; mil/AAF Meteorologist 1942-46; pa/Pub'd 4 Novels, 1 Non-Fiction, Num Articles; cp/Var Commun & Civic Activs; r/Hebrew; hon/Rec'd Grant, Nat Inst Arts & Lttrs.

KRATZ, ELIZABETH ELLEN oc/Retired Minister; b/Jan 6, 1902; h/78 A Waterside Ln, Clinton, CT 06413; m/(dec); c/Phyllis K Hall, David G, Charles R, James S; p/Robert and Ellen Gordon Orr (dec); ed/AA Oregon Normal Sch; pa/Former Tchr Oregon Schs; Dir Christian Wom's F'ship (N Cal-Nev); VP Christian Ch of N Cal-Nev; Exec Min, Christian Ch N Cal-Nev; Exec Dir N Cal Coun Chs; r/Disciples of Christ.

KRATZ, MILDRED SANDS oc/Artist; h/Maple Gardens, Pottstown, PA 19464; ba/Exton, PA; c/Melinda Lou, Melissa Ann; p/Stanley and Ann Elizabeth Sands (dec); pa/Mem 12 Art Socs; Lectr; Exhibits Nat Museums; Fdr Art Guild Pottstown; cp/Pres Doe Clb; Pottstown Hosp Jr Aux; r/Prot; hon/Rec'd 5 Gold Medals, Art Mats Clb & Nat Acad (NYC); Rec'd 60 Other Awds for Art; Rec'd Penn Senatorial Cit.

KRAUS, MOZELLE BIGELOW oc/Clinical Psychologist; b/Sept 29, 1929; ba/1660 L St, NW, Suite 212, Washington, DC 20036; m/Russell Warren; p/Raymond DeMar Bigelow (dec), Henrietta DeWitte Bigelow, Bethesda, MD; ed/BS Wilson Tchrs Col 1952; MS George Washington Univ 1954; EdD Am Univ 1965; pa/Pvt Pract Psychotherapist; Assoc Prof Psychol, George Washington Univ 1965-; Profl Lectr, Dept Human Relats, US Dept Agri Grad Sch 1964-; Res Asst/Res Assoc to the Late Dr Leonard Carmichael (Former Secy Smithsonian Inst & VP Res Nat Geographic Soc) 1956-71; Guest Lectr Profl Orgs; Contbr Num Articles Profl Jours; Author Bi-monthly Column Maryland Newpaper; Am Psychol Assn; DC Psychol Assn; Intl Assn Cnslg Agencies; AAAS; Am Assn Outpatient Psychi Ctrs Am; Am Orthopsychi Assn; cp/Lectr PTA, DAR Groups & Equal Employmt Groups; r/Epis; hon/Psi Chi; Kappa Delta Epsilon; Phi Delta

Gamma; Sigma Xi; Nat Register of Providers Hlth Sers Psychol; Book of Honor; Edit Advy Bd, ABI; W/W: Am Wom, E; Am Men Sci; Commun Ldrs Am; Notable Ams; Others.

KRAUS, PANSY DAEGLING oc/Editor; b/Sept 21, 1916; h/6127 Mohler, San Diego, CA 92120; ba/San Diego; p/Arthur David Daegling Sr, San Diego; Elsie Pardee Daegling (dec); ed/AA San Bernadino Val Jr Col 1938; FGA Gemmological Assn Gt Brit 1960; GG Gemological Inst Am 1966; pa/Editor *The*

Lapidary Jour; Instr Classes Gemology; F'ship Gemmological Assn Gt Brit; Mineralogical Soc Am; Accred'd Gemologists Assn; Hon Mem San Diego Mineral & Gem Soc; Life Mem Gemological Soc San Diego; r/Prot; hon/Epsilon Sigma Alpha; W/W Am Wom; World W/W Wom; Intl Register Profiles; Book of Honor; Commun Ldrs & Noteworthy Ams; Others.

KRAUSE, LLOYD THOMAS oc/Musician; b/Feb 23, 1920; h/3479 Harding Ave, Honolulu, HI 96816; ba/Honolulu; m/Erma Lois Privat; c/Kathleen (Mrs Joseph K Hirata), Darryl L, Harlan A; p/Jacob Krause (dec); Sophy M Krause, Honolulu; ed/Dipl USN Sch Mus 1939; BA San Diego St Col 1948; Profl Tchg Cert Univ Hawaii 1962; mil/USN; pa/Ret'd Mus Tchr, Dept Ed; Mus Libn-Arranger, Honolulu Symph Soc; Composer; Conductor; Former Bandmaster Royal Hawaiian Band; Life Mem, Musicians' Assn; r/Christian Ch; hon/Rec'd Good Conduct Medal, Univ; City Coun Resolution Commend for Work as Royal Hawaiian Bandmaster; Rec'd Var Plaques & Trophies.

KREAGER, DAVID J oc/Attorney; b/Apr 28, 1929; h/1245 Nottingham Ln, Beaumont, TX 77706; ba/Beaumont; m/Ann Fleetwood; c/David Jay III, Michael Lee, Cameron, Heather, Gretchen, Paige; p/David J Kreager, San Angelo, TX; Ethel Mae Kreager, Houston, TX; ed/BA Tex A&M Univ; SJD Univ Tex; pa/Dir St Bar of Tex 1963-76; Chm Tex Bar Foun 1978-79; Trial Attys of Am; cp/Beaumont Civil Ser Comm; Beaumont Rotary Clb; r/Presb; hon/Outstg Law Student; Phi Delta Phi; Others.

KREDA, SALLIE B oc/Public Relations; b/Mar 8, 1929; h/345 E 56th, New York, NY 10022; ba/Same; m/Seymour (dec); c/Kathy, Karen, Helvi; p/Edwin and Frances Peters (dec).

KROKER, BRUNO ERNEST KURT oc/Journalist; b/158 Magnolia Ave, Tenafly, NJ 07670; ba/New York, NY; m/Linda; c/Kevin Olaf; p/George E and Anna Kroker

(dec); pa/Press Ofcr, World Coun Chs 1974-; Correspondent UPI (Manilla) 1949; Correspondent *Evening Post* (Shanghai) 1947-49; China Press 1945-47; Editor *China Jour* 1937-41; Reporter *Peking Chronicle* 1936-37; Royal Asiatic Soc (N China Branch); Overseas Press Clb; cp/Nat Coun Chs; Christian Rural Overseas Prog; Nat Rel Public Relats Coun; r/Riverside Ch (NYC): Mem.

KROPF, JOAN R oc/Museum Director; b/Aug 4, 1949; h/Grantwood Dr, Parma, OH 44134; ba/Beachwood, OH; p/Joseph Kropf, Euclid, OH; Irene Kropf; pa/Photographer.

KRUPP, GUINEVERE ANN oc/Piano Teacher; b/Jul 6, 1930; h/1712 Cresthill, Royal Oak, MI 48073; m/Norman C; c/Sharon, Nathan, Rachael; p/Herbert P and Anna M Dorn, St Louis, MO; ed/BM; pa/Royal Oak Musicale; Mich Mus Tchrs Assn; Nat Mus Tchrs Assn; Fdn Mus Clbs; cp/YWCA; Former Ldr GSA; Royal Oak Arts Coun; r/Luth; hon/Sigma Alpha Iota; Outstg Contbr to Yth in Mus; Rec'd Sword of Hon, SAI; Rec'd Awds: GSA, Band Boosters.

KRYSIAK, JOSEPH EDWARD oc/-Mechanical Engineer; b/Jan 13, 1937; h/8990 Billings Rd, Willoughby, OH 44094; ba/-Solon, OH; p/Edward Aloysious Krysiak (dec); Anna Margaret Molinski Krysiak,

Willoughby; ed/BS 1964, MS 1973 Univ Dayton; pa/Am Soc Metals; Math Assn Am; cp/K of C; r/Rom Cath; hon/Holds 6 US Patents; Rec'd Invention Awds, USAF; Outstg Lab Awd; W/W MW; Men Achmt.

KSIAZEK, MARILYNN C oc/Nutrition Consultant; b/Mar 15, 1950; h/302 Cleveland St, Olyphant, PA 18447; p/Francis and Madelyn Delores Ksiazek; ed/BS 1972, MS 1979 Marywood Col; Addit Studies; pa/Pvt Pract Nutrition Conslt 1979-; Conslt, Visiting Nurse Assn/Home Hlth Maintenance Org 1979-; Developing Ednl Guide for Dietitians to use in Treatmt of Obesity & Engaging Behavioral Modification Techniques 1979-; Other Positions; Am, Pennsylvanian & NE Penn Dietetic Assns; Am Dietetic Assn Consltg Nutritionists Spec Group; NE Penn Jour Clb; Nutrition Today Soc; One of First Dietitians NE Penn to Voluntarily Promote Nutrition Ed for Diabetes Mgmt through Free Public Ed Classes; cp/Nat Kidney Foun; Nat, Penn Affiliate & NE Penn Chapt, Am Diabetes Assn; Keystone Chapt, Am Heart Assn; NE Penn Hemodialysis Assn; r/Rom Cath; hon/Mgr of Month & Cert of Apprec, Custom Food Mgmt Sys (Kingston, Penn); Rec'd Outstg Dietitian Awd, Am Diabetes Assn NE Penn; Biogl Listings.

KUBY, CARL JOSEPH JR oc/Minister; b/Nov 5, 1944; h/11309 Chicamauga Tr SE, Huntsville, AL 35803; ba/Huntsville; m/Patricia Ann; c/Kathryn Amelia; p/Carl J Sr and Lydia A Kuby, New Orleans, LA; ed/BA La Col; MRE, EdS, EdD New Orleans Bapt Theol Sem; pa/Min Ed, So Bapt Conv; So Bapt Rel Ed Assn; SEn Bapt Rel Ed Assn; Ala Bapt Assn of Rel Ed Workers; r/So Bapt Conv (Nashville, Tenn); hon/W/W Rel.

KUCINGIS, JOHN ANTHONY oc/Catholic Priest; b/Dec 23, 1908; h/2718 St George St, Los Angeles, CA 90027; ba/Same;

p/Steponas and Barbora Gecas Kucingis, Lithuania; ed/Theological Sch (Telsiai, Lithuania); Cath Univ (Milan, Italy); mil/Former Chaplain Lithuanian Army; pa/Prof Jr Col Telsiai; Pastor St Caimir's Lithuanian Ch (LA); Rel Ldr; r/Rom Cath; hon/Right Rev Monsignor by Pope Paul VI.

KUCSERA, ABBIE KENT oc/Author; Editor; b/Mar 14, 1916; h/45 Seminole Trail, Whispering Pines, FL 32039; ba/Georgetown, FL; m/Carl Coleman; c/Lorraine Joan, Carl Walter; p/Walter Green and Marion Ella Szekrak-Miller Kent; ed/Attend'd Detroit Inst Technol 1954; pa/Journalist, Editor *Pontiac (Mich) Press* 1947-57; Mng Editor *Inter-Lake News,* Walled Lake (Mich) Bur 1959-61; Promotion & Publicity Writer, City of Sunrise (Fla) 1961-62; Writer & Editor *On-the-Go Mag* (Ft Lauderdale, Fla) 1963; Copywriter Fla Advtg Inc (Ft Lauderdale) 1963; Author: *Prize Winning Watercolors* (1964), *Best of Show, Flower Arrangemts* (1964); Editor (as Jan Malcolm) *Hell Turned Wrong Side Out* 1965-66; r/Bapt; hon/Recipient Apprec Cert, Palm Beach Co Bar Assn; Poet laureate, SE Fla Dairy Assn.

KUEKER, JOHN DAVID oc/Pastor; b/Apr 2, 1933; h/Rt 1, Box 144, Burton, TX 77835; ba/Same; m/Jean Kleinecke; c/Jo Lynne, Joy Annette; p/Robert Kueker (dec); Mary Kueker, Cuero, TX; ed/BS SW Tex Univ 1960; BD 1965, MTh 1974 Wartburg Univ; mil/USAF 4 Yrs; Tex NG 7 Yrs; pa/Pastor St Paul Luth Ch; Dist Stewardship Task Force; Challenge of Generations (LSST), Task Force Capt; Dist Coms 1967-70; Dist Coun 1972-74; Dean, Brenham Deanery 1977-79; Advr to Conf Yth 1966-70, 1976-78; cp/Lions Clb; BSA: Cub Master, Dist Commr; Nat Rifle Assn; Tex St Rifle Assn; Burton Booster Clb; r/Luth; hon/Arrowhead for Scout'g Commr; FHA (Area III) Awd Recog.

KUGLER, IDA CAROLYN oc/Educator; b/Dec 22, 1905; h/1124 Dionne, St Paul, MN 55113; ba/Same; m/William John; p/Herman Grunke (dec); Petrine Pedersen; ed/AA St Cloud St Univ 1930; BS 1941, MA 1956 Univ Minn; PhD Walden Univ 1972; pa/Ed Dir & Registrar, Musical Instrument Museum 1974-; Instr Eng to Chinese Immigrants 1965-; Instr St Paul Public Schs 1965-74; Pioneer'g Prin, Aiyepe HS (Aiyepe-Ijebu, Wn St Nigeria) 1961-65; Other Positions; Author *A Music Museum, An Ednl Resource* & *The Role of a Musical Museum;* Editor HS Curric, Ansar Ud Deen Schs (Lagos, Nigeria); Oriental Inst, Chgo Univ; Nat Ret'd Tchrs Assn; St Paul Ret'd Tchrs Assn; cp/Repub Nat Com; Nat Adv Bd; Am Security Coun; Interamerican Soc OAS; Fdr Ctr Intl Security Studies; IPA;

r/Rom Cath; St Rose of Lima Ch (St Paul); hon/DIB; Intl W/W Commun Ser; World W/W Wom; Intl Register Profiles; Book of Hon; Others.

KUHNER, SUSAN MARY oc/Psychologist; b/Aug 16, 1947; h/803 Annan Terrace, Los Angeles, CA 90042; ba/Hollywood, CA; p/Arthur and Mary A Franklin Kuhner, Cleveland, OH; ed/BA Case Wn Reserv Univ; MA, PhD Univ Portland; pa/Asst Exec Dir, LA Gay Commun Sers Ctr 1977-; Bd Mem Alcohol Ctr for Wom 1975-76; Bd Mem New AGE; Lic'd Clinical Psychol; Pub'd Poetry & Articles *Lesbian Tide Mag;* cp/ACLU Gay Rights Chapt; NOW; LA Wom's Bldg; Hollywood Human Sers Proj; Fdn Preservation So Womanhood; So Poverty Law Ctr; Lincoln Repub Clb.

KULKARNI, HEMANT oc/Professor; b/Nov 25, 1916; h/1510 E, 1100 N, Logan, UT 84321; ba/Logan; m/Snehaprabha; c/Ravi, Teja, Jaya, Pramod; p/Balvantrao (dec); Laxmibai, Nipani, India; ed/PhD Univ Utah 1962; pa/Prof Eng, Utah St Univ; Pres S Asian Literary Assn (MLA Group) 1977-79; Editor *South Asian Review;* Author: *Morning Dew* (Poems) 1977, *Welding Flame* (Poems) 1977, Others; Modern Lang Assn Am; r/Hindu; hon/Poems incl'd in Anthologies: *Utah Sings, Prize Poems, The Society Poetry Book,* Others; Rec'd Fulbright Awd; Fav Tchr Awd, Univ Utah; Phi Kappa Phi; Rec'd James C Miller Awd for Excell Poetry, Utah St Poetry Soc & Utah St Inst Fine Arts; Rec'd Humanist of Yr Awd, Col of Humanities, Arts, & Social Scis (Utah St Univ); Others.

KUNCE, JAMES FRANKLIN oc/Minister; b/Jun 30, 1920; h/511 Howland, Emerson, IA 51533; ba/Emerson; m/Frances Ayres; c/Genna Lou K Vanous, Douglas Bradley; p/Ray Homer and Charlotte Isabelle Pyle Kunce (dec); ed/AB, ThM; mil/AUS; pa/Lic'd Fam Cnslr; Ordained Min, Am Bapt Chs USA 1944; Min Coun: Regional & Area Ordination Rep; cp/Masonic Lodge; Commun Clb; r/Am Bapt Ch USA; hon/Rec'd Recog for Dedicated Ser to Chd's Bapt Homes So Cal; Pastor Ch of Yr, Nebraska Bapt Conv; Others.

KUNITZ, SHARON LEE oc/Assistant Editor; b/Jan 24, 1955; h/513 Dickey Rd, Grand Prairie, TX 75051; ba/Grand Prairie; p/Lee H and Dorothy Jean Kunitz, Sherman, TX; ed/BA Stephen F Austin St Univ 1977; pa/Asst Editor *Grand Prairie Daily News;* Soc Profl Journalists; cp/GP C of C; Yth Com; Steer'g Com, Big Brother-Big Sister Org; r/1st United Meth Ch (Sherman); hon/Rec'd Cert of Merit, Tex St Tchrs Assn Sch Bell Awds.

KUNTZ, ROSALIE LOIS oc/Insurance Agent; b/Sept 20, 1924; h/PO Box 3147, Pasadena, TX 77501; ba/Pasadena; m/Gerald J; c/Kyle J, Rita A, Linda J; p/William Sr and Rose Mae Savarino (dec); ed/Attended Bus Col; pa/Co-owner Kuntz Ins Agy; Gen Agent, Ky Ctl Life Ins Co; Adv Dir, Pasadena Nat Bk 1974-78; Dir & Public Ser Chm, Pasadena Assn Life Underwriters; Tex Assn Life Underwriters; Wom Ldrs Round Table NALU; Exec Bd 1977-78, Editor Newslttr 1978; Others; cp/Orgr St Pius V Ath Prog & Ath Booster Clb; Past Secy Bd Ed, Diocese of Galveston-Houston; Dir C of C 8 Yrs; Dir Soroptimist Intl; Dir Tex Soc Prevention of Blindness; Past Dir (Pasadena) Am Heart Assn; Dir S Houston C of C; Com Nat

Olympic Girls Volleyball Team; Others; r/St Pius V Ch: Fin Com, Parish Coun; hon/Pasadena Citizen of Yr 1968; Rec'd Dist'd Ser Awd, Pasadena JCs; Nat Sales Achmt Awd; Rec'd Nat Hons, NALU Conv; Rec'd Ky Ctl Awds.

KUNZ, McKAY HEBER oc/Pharmacist; Teacher; b/Nov 15, 1923; h/975 E, 1175 S #3, Kaysville, UT 84037; ba/Bountiful, UT; m/Velma Mae Fagan; c/Jeffrey, Bryan (dec), Warren, (Stepchd): William, Nora (Mrs Manuel Jr) Reyes, Bruce, Ricky, David; p/Heber Christian and Marie Clark Kunz, Bern, ID; ed/BS Idaho St Univ 1945; BA 1952, MA 1962 Brigham Young Univ; pa/Pharmacist, Mountain View Pharm 1965-77; Chandler Drug (Clearfield) 1969-76;

Tchr 5th Grade Sci & Math, Lyman (Wyom) Elem Sch 1974-77; Physics Tchr, Clearfield HS 1962-63; Other Positions; Helped Operate Sabin Oral Polio Vaccine Clinics, Utah St Med Assn; Helped Intermountain Indian Sch: Tchr, Bus Driver; Author: Utah Pharm Assn; Utah Ed Assn; San Juan Ed Assn; Davis Ed Assn; Utah Farm Bur Assn; NEA; Montpelier Nat & Slide Rule Clb; Intermountain Sch Sci Hobby Clb; Others; cp/Ordeal Mem, Oala Ishadalakalish Lodge (Order of Arrow); Ordeal Mem, Tu Cubin Noonie Lodge (Order of Arrow); Repub Party; Former Utah Nat Parks Coun Com-man; BSA Scoutmaster; Others; r/Ch of Jesus Christ LDS: Mem, Former Missionary; SS Tchr, Others; hon/Rec'd Awd Yg Men's Mutual Improvemt Assn LDS Ch; Participant, Utah Pharm Assn Seminar; Others.

KURAU, WARREN PETER oc/Professor; b/Aug 16, 1952; h/50 Travis St, Torrington, CT 06790; ba/Colleg, MO; p/Sheldon C and Ruth A Kurau, Torrington; ed/BM Eastman Sch Mus 1974; Cert Adv'd Studies, Guildhall Sch Mus & Drama 1975; Assoc Dipl, Royal Col Mus 1975; MA Univ Conn 1977; pa/Asst Prof Mus, Univ Mo-C; Rochester Philharm, Syracuse Symph; Rochester Chamber Orch; Colo Philharm; London Flori Legion; Mo Arts Quintet; Mo Symph Soc Chamber Orch; Intl Horn Soc; MENC; r/Meth; hon/Pi Kappa Lambda; ITT Intl F'ship; W/W Mus; 3rd Place Winner, Heldenleben Intl Horn Competition.

KURIGER, FRANK JOSEPH JR oc/Pastor; b/Jun 11, 1924; h/141 S Reed Rd, Grafton, OH 44044; ba/Grafton; m/Emma Pauline Tingle; c/Connie K Rucker, Frank Forrest, Aleda Kathleen, Howard Timothy, Stephen Kyle, Walter & Rozella; p/Frank J Sr and Georgie Ann Kuriger (dec); ed/BA; MDiv; ThD; mil/USNR; pa/Min; Assnl Clerk 17 Yrs; r/So Bapt; hon/Clerk of Distinction, So Bapt Conv; Others.

KURJAKOVIC-BOGUNOVICH, MIRA oc/Research Chemist; b/Sept 20, 1924; h/432 Atwood St, Pittsburgh, PA 15213; c/2; p/Kata and Ilija Bogunovich; ed/BS Univ Zagreb (Yugoslavia) 1955; pa/Res Chem, US Dept Energy (Bruceton Res Ctr) 1976-; Inst Metall (Sisak, Yugoslavia) 1956-69; Am Chem Div, Am Chem Soc; Contbr Articles Profl Jours; hon/Commun Ldrs & Noteworthy Ams.

KURK, ANNA JEAN oc/Purchasing Agent; b/Apr 7, 1927; h/PO Box 851, Graham, TX 76046; ba/Graham; p/Fred M

Kurk (dec); Pearl T Kurk, Graham; ed/Cert Public Relats Course; pa/Purchasing Agent, City of Graham; cp/Past Pres Graham Credit Wom's Clb; r/United Meth Ch.

KURTZ, FREDA W oc/Research Analyst; b/Nov 23, 1919; h/4341 Wallington Dr, Dayton, OH 45440; m/Carroll T; c/Nancy K Haynes, Russell C; p/Fred and Maude M Witherow (dec); ed/BS NE Mo St Univ; MA Univ Ky; pa/Wright-Patterson AFB: Operations Res Analyst, Instr Ecs & Mgmt; Federally Employed Wom Inc (Nat Treas); Pres, Dayton Chapt Am Statistical Assn; Exec Bd, Life Cycle Cost Task Group JSDE for Inertial Sys; Operations Res Soc Am; r/Bapt; hon/Rec'd 2 Sustained Superior Perf Ratings, Civil Ser; Nom'd Profl Employee of Yr; Nom'd Patricia Keyes Glass Awd.

KURTZ, S JAMES oc/Composer; b/Feb 8, 1934; ba/Harrisonburg, VA 22807; ed/BA Washington Sq Col 1955; MA Grad Sch Arts & Sci (NYU) 1960; PhD Univ Iowa; Pvt Clarinet Study, Simeon Bellison 1946-53; Composition Study w Philip James; pa/Mus Dept, James Madison Univ: Prof Mus & Instrumental Coor 1965-, Chamber Arts Wind Quintet; Clarinetist w: Metro Museum Orch, Little Orch, Firestone TV Orch, Others 1953-65; Composer: *Suite for Three Clarinets*, *Three Impressions for Two Clarinets*, *Notturno for Clarinet or Flute and Piano*, Others; Nat Assn Col Wind & Percussion Instrs; hon/Winner, Marion Bauer Composer's Contest; Rec'd James Madison Univ Res Grant for Wind Mus Res En Europe; Intl W/W Mus; Men Achmt; Personalities of S; DIB.

KURZ, ALBERT LESLIE oc/Clergyman; Author; b/Jan 6, 1933; h/2 Lisa Ct, Pekin, IL 61554; ba/Pekin; m/Karla Lynn Kelsey; c/David, Robert, Peggy, Cathy, Jonathan, p/Walter C Kurz (dec); Bertha C Kurz, Dixon, IL; ed/BA Wheaton Col 1958; Grad Study: Trinity Evangelical Div Sch 1964-65, Winona Lake Sch Theol 1966, Univ Denver 1967-68; DD Hindustan Bible Inst & Col (India) 1978; Addit Studies; pa/Pastor 1st Bapt Ch (Pekin) 1973-; Pastor Belcaro Evangelical Free Ch (Denver) 1967-73; Christian Ed Conslt,

Evangelical Free Ch Am 1970-73; Missionary: Ill, Wis, Minn, Mich, 31 Foreign Countries, Others 1960-; Weekly Radio Broadcast 1968-72; Author: *Let Christ Take You Beyond Discouragemt* (1975), "How to Become A Better Person" (Booklet) 1974; Pub'd Articles Christian Jours; Pres' Adv Coun, Conserv Bapt Theol Sem (Denver) 1974-; Bd Mem, Conserv Bapt Assn Am; VP Ill Conserv Bapt F'ship 1976-; Others; cp/Trustee, Judson Col (Elgin, Ill); r/So Bapt; hon/Grad Magna Cum Laude, Moody Bible Inst; W/W: Colo, Rel; DIB; Commun Ldrs & Noteworthy Ams; Others.

KURZWEG, ULRICH HERMANN

oc/Professor; b/Sept 16, 1936; h/8407 NW 4th Pl, Gainesville, FL 32601; ba/Gainesville; m/Sophia; c/Tina; p/Hermann Herbert and Erna Michealis Kurzweg, Silver Spring, MD; ed/BS Univ Md 1958; MA 1960, PhD Princeton Univ; pa/Prof Engrg Scis, Univ Fla-G; Reschr Applied Math & Fluid Mechanics; r/Luth; hon/Woodrow Wilson Fellow; Rec'd Fulbright Grant; Rec'd Sigma Tau Awd for Excell Engrg Tchg.

KUSHNER, DAVID ZAKERI oc/Musician; b/Dec 22, 1935; h/2215 NW 21st Ave, Gainesville, FL 32605; ba/Gainesville; m/Rebecca Ann Stefan; c/Jonthan Moses, Joshua Sanford, Jeremy Avram, Jason Daniel; p/Nathan and Rita Forgatsh Kushner, Palm Beach, FL; ed/BM Boston Univ; MM Univ Cinc; PhD Univ Mich; pa/Dept Mus, Univ Fla-G: Prof (Doct Res Stat), Lectr & Recitalist, USA & Europe; Chm Bd Dirs, Am Liszt Soc; Life Mem Mus Tchrs Nat Assn; "Recitals in Schs" Series (w Wife); Visiting Prof Mus, Florence (Italy) Study Ctr 1975; Book & Music Reviewer; Fla St Mus Tchrs Assn; Gainesville Mus Tchrs Assn; Nat Musicology Soc; cp/City of Gainesville Cult Comm; B'nai Israel Cong; Chm Ed Com, Bd Dirs; hon/Nat Mus Coun People-to-People Del to Czechoslovakia, Hungary, Poland, Austria & W Germany: Performed at Chopin Birthplace; Rec'd Res Grants, Univ Fla Humanities Coun; Critical Pubs Listed in *Repertoire International de Litterature Musicale*; Intl W/W Mus; DIB; W/W Am; Men Achmt; Nat Register Prominent Ams; Commun Ldrs Am.

KUTCHINSKY, LEIGH ELENA oc/Epidemiologist; b/Aug 4, 1947; h/5771 E 112th Ave, Northglenn, CO 80233; ba/Wheatridge, CO; c/Buddy, Yaakov; ed/BA; BS; MPh; PhD; MD; pa/Asst Prof; HEW Reschr, Communicable Diseases; Lamaze Instr; APHA; AMWA; CPHA; MCHR; cp/Adams Co Wom's Caucus; Adams Co Dems; r/Jewish; hon/Phi Beta Kappa; Alpha Gamma Sigma; W/W: Am Wom, Hlth Care; World W/W Wom; Public Hlth Fellow; Cal St Fellow; Cal St Scholar; Univ Cal Regents Fellow; Valedictorian, Univ Cal-B; Berkeley Hon Soc; Rec'd Alameda-Contra Costa Med Soc S'ship; Others.

KUTGER, JOSEPH PETER oc/Researcher; b/May 26, 1917; h/474 N Cherry St, Tulare, CA 93274; ba/Tulare; m/Samuella Sue Bailey; c/JoAnne K Opie, April Ruth; p/Joseph A and Elizabeth Baust Kutger (dec); ed/BA; MA; PhD; mil/USAF 1941-61; pa/Pvt Reschr; Operations Res Symposia; cp/Former Speechwriter St Repub Com; Contbr Articles Mil & Polit Jours; Sponsor Vietnamese Refugee Fam (Boat People); r/Free Thinker; hon/Rec'd 13 US Mil Awds & Decorations; Rec'd St Dept Medal; Rec'd 4 Decorations,

Govt S Vietnam (incl'g Order of Merit).

KUZMAK, LUBOMYR I oc/General & Vascular Surgeon; b/Aug 2, 1931; ba/657 Irvington Ave, Newark, NJ 07106; m/Roxanne A Smishkewych; c/Roxolana; p/Wolodymyr and Lidia Litynsky Kuzmak (dec); ed/MD Med Acad (Lodz, Poland); DSc Silesian Acad Med (Katowice, Poland); pa/Med Pract Spec, Vascular Surg; Affiliated w St Barnabas Med Ctr (Livingston) & Irvington Gen Hosp 1971-; Chief Resident Vascular & Gen Surg, Barnabas Med Ctr 1966-71; Silesian Acad Med (Bytom, Poland): Gen Surg, Head Div, Assoc Prof 1961-65; Other Positions; Diplomate Polish Bd Gen Surg; AMA; Ukrainian Med Assn N Am; NJ Med Soc; Essex Co Med Assn; Contbr Articles Profl Jours; cp/Ukrainian Inst Am; r/Ukrainian Cath; hon/Rec'd AMA Recog Awd.

KUZNIAR, ZOFINA oc/Artist; b/Jun 20, 1923; h/2416 N Harding Ave, Chicago, IL 60647; ba/Same; m/Peter; c/Emilyna, Edmund; p/Vincent Arendarczyk (dec); Marianna Gabrys (dec); ed/Attended UCLA; Pvt Art Study w Pierie Kuss; pa/Oil Portrait Painter; Operator-Owner, Zofina's Oil Portrait Studio 29 Yrs; Exhibited Works E & W Coasts; hon/Work Rep'd at Glouster Art Inst; Pvt Collections USA & Europe.

KWIE, WILLIAM WIE LIAM oc/Chemical Engineer; Chemist; b/Jan 7, 1931; h/4122 Beran Dr, Houston, TX 77045; ba/Bellaire, TX; p/Teck Kwie (dec); Noes Tan, Singapore; ed/BS BIT 1955; MA 1958, PhD 1962 Univ Tex-A; pa/ACS (Secy-Treas WF-D Sect 1979); AAUP; Okla Anthropol Soc; ASTM; cp/Dem Party; r/Dutch Prot; hon/Phi Lambda Upsilon; Rec'd R A Welch Foun F'ships; Rec'd US Govt Grant.

KWIK, CHRISTINE IRENE oc/Physician; b/Sept 12, 1939; h/8303 Tulpehocken Ave, Elkins Park, PA 19117; m/(dec); c/Christine T, Catherine L; p/Karl and Leonarda Kostek,

Cracow, Poland; ed/MD; pa/Dir Emer Dept, J F Kennedy Meml Hosp; r/Rom Cath; hon/Grad'd w Hons, Med Acad Cracow.

KYRIAZIS, ANDREAS P oc/Physician; b/Jan 19, 1932; h/508 Williamsburg Rd, Cincinnati, OH 45215; ba/Cinc; m/Katherine; c/Joanna-Christina; p/Panayiotis and Christina (dec); ed/MD Nat Kapodistrian Univ (Athens, Greece) 1957; DSc Univ Thessaloniki (Greece) 1961; PhD Univ Thomas Jefferson Univ 1968; mil/Med Ofcr Greek Army; pa/Asst Prof Pathology & Reschr in Cancer, Univ Cinc; Mem Var Profl Assns; Contbr Num Articles Profl Jours; r/Greek Orthodox; hon/Seymour Comman Fellow, Univ Chgo.

L

LAABS, ERNST A oc/Clergyman; b/Sept 28, 1915; h/140 Orchard Ln, Napoleon, OH 43545; ba/Napoleon; m/Irma J; c/Claire Schwiebert; p/H H and Marie Laabs, Mayville, WI; ed/BTh; pa/Pastoral Advr:

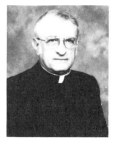

Ohio Dist LLL, NW Ohio Zone LLL; Bd Dirs: Luth Wel Coun Ohio, Luth Social Sers NW Ohio; r/Luth; hon/W/W; Servus Ecclesiae Christi.

LaBELLE, DONALD JOSEPH oc/Public Administrator; Professor; b/Sept 8, 1942; h/151 Cotillion Rd, Fort Worth, TX 76134; ba/Ft Worth; m/Sharon Kay Popp; c/Todd Alan, Renee Kathleen; p/James LaBelle Jr, Kansas City, MO; Grace Hilland Smith LaBelle (dec); ed/BA 1966, MA 1973 Ks Univ; mil/USAF 1966-71, Spec Ground Elects Ofcr, Served to Capt; pa/Public Admr City of Ft

Worth; Adj Prof Tex Christian Univ; Intl City Mgmt Assn; Am Public Works Assn; KUCIMATS; cp/Toastmasters Intl; Project Team Ldr Ft Worth Keep Am Beautiful Prog; r/1st Presb Ch Ft Worth: Ruling Elder 1979-81, Chm Opers Com 1979, Budget Chm 1977, Nom'g Com 1978; hon/Outstg Unit of AF 1968, 70; Mun Fin Ofcrs Assn Awd for Budget Innovation, City of Ft Worth; Recog'd for Local Govt Innovation, Nat Comm for Productivity.

LABRAM, CALE DEANE oc/Managing Editor; b/Aug 14, 1939; h/709 Versailles Dr SE, Huntsville, AL 35803; ba/H'ville; m/Frank H; c/F Eric, Frederic B, Marc E; p/Kenneth George Lang (dec); Dorothy L Carpenter Lang, Aurora, CO; ed/Att'd Baldwin-Wallace Col; Cert Famous Artist Schs; pa/Mng Editor *The Advertiser* (NW Commun Paper); Free-lance Artist; Secy Software Mgmt Anal Div, USA SAFSEA, White Sands Missile Range, NM 1971-72; Secy Corps of Engrs, WSMR, NM 1970-71; Secy, Fin Ofcr, Ft Greely, Alaska 1969-70; cp/Past Mother Advr Order of Rainbow for Girls; OES; BSA Merit Badge Cnslr (10 Badges); PTA; H'ville Commun Chorus: Exec Bd Mem, Public Relats Chm, Chorus Mem; Past Halma Mem; Past Pres & Past Corr Secy Port Clinton Artists Clb; r/Latham U Meth Ch: Soloist, Choir, UMW, Cir Chm 1976-77; Christian Woms Clb Bible Studies Guide; hon/IPA; Intl W/W: Intells, Commun Ser; Commun Ldrs Am; Gold Book Ldg Am Fams; World W/W Wom; Notable Ams Bicent Era; Personalities of S.

LACEY, V DUANE oc/Health Executive; Hospital Consultant; b/Nov 11, 1932; h/7913 Patriot Dr, Annandale, VA 22003; ba/Washington, DC; m/Joan; c/Lauren Joan; p/John Vearl Lacey (dec); Rose Leah Lacey, College Place, WA; ed/BA; MA; mil/AUS MC 1953-54; pa/VP & Mgr Hlth Facility Constrn; Hosp Conslt AHS, Wash DC; Am Col Hosp Admrs; Intl Hosp Fdn; Am Soc for Public Adm; Soc for Intl Devel; Am Soc Intl Law; Am Hosp Assn; Am Reg Radiol Technologists; Am Soc Allied Hlth Professions; Nat Assn for Hosp Devel; Am Assn for Hosp Planning; Am Soc Res Admrs; Am Soc Planning Ofcls; Assn Wn Hosps; Hlth Devices Com Am Nat Standards Inst; Other Profl Orgs; cp/Merch Brokers Exc (London); Nat Fgn Trade Coun (NY); r/Rom Cath; hon/Notable Ams; DIB; Men of Achmt; Intl W/W Intells; Book of Honor; W/W in E; Intl W/W Commun Ser.

LACEY, WALTER H oc/Retired; Records Management-Microfilm Systems Analyst; b/Sept 16, 1910; h/623 W 5th St, Apt 110, Los Angeles, CA 90017; c/Karen Dorothy; ed/Cert, Creative Ed Foun (Buffalo, NY); mil/AUS WWII (3 Yrs); pa/Title Ins & Trust Co, LA 1928-75: Real Est Ofcr, Mgr Microfilm & Records Mgmt, Public Relats Systems Analyst; Am Records Mgmt Assn, LA Chapt: Charter Mem 1955, Pres, Other Ofcs; Assn Intl Documentalists (Paris, France); Fdn Intl Documentalists (Hague, Holland); Soc Am Archivists; Soc Cal Archivists; Intl Coun on Archives (Paris, France) 1976; hon/Contbr Articles to Num Trade Mags; Records Mgr of Yr 1966; Hon Mem, Space Assn USA; Hon Mem Other Assns (USA & Europe).

LACK, SYLVIA ANNE oc/Medical Director; b/Jun 1, 1944; h/58 Lyon St, New Haven, CT 06511; ba/New Haven; p/Brian and Doreen Minter Lack, Leighton Buzzard, Beds, England; ed/BM; BSurg; pa/Med Dir The Conn Hospice 1973-; (Reduced Schedule) Resident Internal Med St Mary's Hosp, Waterbury, Conn 1977-; Hosp Fellow Yale-New Haven Hosp 1973-77; Med Ofcr St Christopher's Hospice & St Joseph's Hospice, London 1971-73; House Ofcr Opthalmol St Bartholomew's Hosp, London 1970-71; House Phys Gen Med Whipps Cross Hosp, London 1970; House Surg Gen Surg Whipps Cross Hosp, London 1969; r/1st Meth Ch, New Haven; hon/Assoc Ofcr Order of St John of Jerusalem.

LACKEY, GUY ANNADALE oc/Emeritus Professor of Education; b/Jul 23, 1891; h/326 S Stallard, Stillwater, OK 74074; m/Wylma Blackey (dec); c/Virginia Bernice L-Mathews, Woodard Harwell, Guy Annadale Jr; p/-Benjamin Franklin and Mary Ella Harwell Lackey (dec); ed/BA; MA; PhD; mil/USAAC 1942-43, Civilian Tchr; pa/Tchr, Admr, Prof 1910-79; cp/Dem Party; Num Orgs; r/Presb: Elder; Unitarian; hon/Phi Beta Kappa; Phi Kappa Phi; Kappa Delta Pi; Phi Delta Kappa; Pi Gamma Mu; Psi Chi; W/W Am Ed; Ldrs in Ed; Personalities of S; DIB; Royal Blue Book; Successful & Creative Personalities; Hon Col on Gov's Staff (Okla); Others.

LACKEY, MARILYN LOUISE oc/College Administrator; b/Aug 1, 1935; h/PO Box 76, Athens, WV 24712; ba/Athens; c/Michael David, William Lawrence; p/Earl and Louise Wood, Bluefield, WV; ed/BS in Ed Concord Col 1959; MS Va Polytech Inst & St Univ 1963; pa/Dir Col Relats Concord Col; Concord Col Foun Inc: Secy, Bd Dirs; cp/Exec Secy/Dir Concord Col Alumni Assn; Mem Town of Athens-Concord Col Liaison Com; r/Presb; hon/Alumnus of Yr, Concord Col 1976.

LA COSTA GONZALES, CARLOS E oc/Teacher; Lawyer; b/May 24, 1933; h/Cond Villas Del Mar, Oeste, Ph-D, Isla Verde, PA 00913; ba/Santurce, PR; p/Carlos La Costa Calaf (dec); Maria L Visa Gonzalez Echenique (dec); ed/AB 1955, MBA 1957 Cornell Univ; JD Univ PR 1960; pa/Univ Sacred Heart: Prof Bus & Law 1970, Hd Ecs Dept 1960-66, Hd Social Sci Dept 1966-68, Student Advr 1975-78, Univ Adm Coun

1975-77, Univ Acad Coun 1977-; Fdg Mem Museo De Santos; Alpha Kappa Psi; Law Pract (Pt-time) 1976-; r/Cath; hon/Num Tchg Awds.

LaCOUR, VIVIENNE oc/Controller; Secretary-Treasurer; b/Jun 16, 1940; h/8527 Winding Way, Fair Oaks, CA 95826; ba/Sacramento, CA; m/Ambris Jr; c/Degina Rene, Ronald Keith, Carlton Boyd, Alicia Maria; p/Edwindo and Inez Tidvell (dec); ed/BBA Univ Mass; pa/Am Bus Wom; cp/Soroptimist Intl; Life Mem: NAACP, Nat Coun Negro Wom; Kosmos Civic Clb Inc; r/Cath; hon/W/W Am Wom; Sacramento 10 Best Dressed Wom 1978-79.

LACY, BARBARA oc/Educator; Media Specialist; b/Jan 19, 1930; h/1206 Glacier Ave SE, Washington, DC 20027; ba/Wash DC; m/(dec); c/John Edwin Isom Jr, Michael G Isom, Steve C Isom, Harold, Linda; ed/BS; Grad Study; pa/Am Lib Assn; cp/Repub Party; Hillside Civic Assn; r/Meth.

LAD, PRAKASH, SHRIPAD oc/Civil Engineer; b/Sept 7, 1940; h/2008 Claremont, Springfield, IL 62703; ba/S'field; m/Nilima; c/Ashvin; p/Shripad Narayan and Sumitra Lad (dec); ed/MS Utah St Univ; pa/Am Soc Civil Engrs; cp/Am Forestry Assn, Washington, DC; r/Hindu.

LAFFIN, SHIRLEY ELEANOR oc/-Comptroller; Machine Operator; b/Jul 29, 1935; h/Bridge St, Hillsboro, NH 03244; ba/H'boro; m/Thomas W; c/Lester Belloir Jr, George Belloir, Ray, Colleen; p/Harold E and Anna M Greenwood Duefield; pa/Comptroller Communs Systems Ctr; Machine Operator GT&E Sylvania; IPA; hon/Lic'd Comml Operator.

LaFON, JOHN WALTER oc/Environmental and Water Resource Engineer; b/Feb 11, 1937; h/102 Williamsburg Pl, Franklin, TN 37064; ba/Nashville, TN; m/Sandra D; c/Pamela Louise, John Walter Jr; p/James Earl and Gladys Martha LaFon, Norman, OK; ed/BS 1959, MS 1963 Univ Okla; mil/AUS 1959-62, Med Ser Corps; USPHS 1964-66; pa/Envir & Water Resource Engr Corps of Engrs; Ky-Tenn Water Pollution Control Assn; r/Forest Hills Bapt Ch: SS Dir, Deacon; hon/Men of Achmt; W/W S&SW.

LAGOW, RICHARD J oc/Associate Professor; Researcher; b/Aug 16, 1945; ba/Austin, TX; ed/BA 1967, PhD 1969 Rice Univ; pa/Assoc Prof Dept Chem Univ Tex-A 1976-; Asst Prof Dept Chem MIT 1970-75; Instr Dept Chem Rice Univ, Houston, Tex 1967-69; Var Chem Res; hon/NSF Postdoct F'ship; Alfred P Sloan Fellow; Num Profl Pubs; Patentee.

LA HARRY, NORMAN oc/Pharmacist; b/Apr 10, 1930; h/601 E 32nd St, Chicago, IL; c/La Joy; ed/BS Tougaloo Col; Att'd: Howard Univ Grad Sch, Xavier Univ Col Pharm, Tex So Univ, Univ Ill Col Pharm; mil/AUS 1951-53, US & Europe; pa/Norman's Pharm, Chgo 1969-; Westside Pharm, Chgo 1965-; Norman's Pharm Ida Mae Scott Hosp, Chgo 1969; Indep Pharm 1961-63; Am Acad Gen Practioners-Pharm; Past Del at Large Nat Pharm Assn; Am Pharm Assn; Nat Assn Retail Druggists; Fellow Am Col Apothecaries; Chm of Bd Chgo Pharmacists Assn; Ill Acad Preceptors in Pharm; Pres 20th

Century Pharmacists Investmt Clb; Spkrs Bur for Div of Narcotic Control; cp/Fdr & Pres Norman La Harry S'ship Golf Classic; Jt Action in Commun Ser; Past Asst Cub Scout Master; Chgo Urban Leag; Bd Dirs Daniel Hale Williams Meml Hlth Foun; Sno Gophers Ski Clb; Comprehensive Neighborhood Hlth Sers Prog; Mid S Hlth Planning Org Bd; NAACP; Ill St Rifle Assn; r/St James Cath Ch: Mem, Former Bd Mem; hon/Chi Delta Mu Frat Outstg Achmt Awd; Pharmacist of Yr Awd 1974; Humanitarian Awd, Wyeth Labs; Achmt Awds as Pres of Nat Pharm Assn: Tougaloo Col, Mound Bayou HS, Am Col Apothecaries; Century Clb Awd, Tex So Univ; Devoted Ser Awd, Ill Pharm Assn; Guest Spkr, Tex So Univ Silver Anniv 1972; Others.

LAHIRI, SUBRATA oc/Professor; b/Feb 28, 1932; h/530 Lakeridge, Fayetteville, AR 72701; ba/F'ville; m/Betty Ann; c/Sabrina Ann, Kiron Lal; p/Kiron Lal Lahiri (dec); Annapurna Lahiri; ed/BFA; MS; MFA; pa/Prof Univ Ark; Intl'ly Known Sculptor; Num Sculptors Rep'd in Var Countries; r/Hindu; hon/2 US Patents; Mich Sculptor of Yr 1977; Num Govt & Pvt Hons, Awds & Collections.

LAING, BETTY JEAN oc/Hospital Administrator; b/Jan 29, 1925; h/2807 52nd, Lubbock, TX 79413; ba/Lubbock; m/R W (dec); c/John Leslie, Mary Lou L Munnecke, Jo Ann; p/E G Sanders (dec); Lettie Emily Cook Sanders, Amarillo, TX; ed/RN NW Tex Hosp Sch Nsg; BA Univ Redlands; mil/Nsg Cadet Student 1944-46; pa/Dir Inser St Mary of the Plains Hosp; Am Hosp Assn; Tex Hosp Ednl Assn; Am Heart Assn; Fac Mem Lubbock Country Assn of Inser Edrs; HOPEC; r/Presb; hon/World W/W Wom; W/W: HS, Am Wom.

LAIR, HELEN M oc/Artist; Poet; Free-lance Writer; b/Jan 2, 1918; h/1202 Mourer St, New Castle, IN 47362; ba/Same; m/Marvin; c/Michael Lucas, Joan Krueckeberg; p/Harry Humphrey (dec); Loma Humphrey, New Castle; cp/Pres: Art Assn, Raintree Writers; Prog Chm Art Guild; Treas New Castle Poetry; r/Cath; hon/Nat & Intl Poetry Awds; Short Story Awd, Hibiscus Press; St Poetry Awds, Fed'd Poetry.

LAKELA, OLGA oc/Retired Educator; b/Mar 11, 1890; h/Congregational House, Rm #513, 2855 Gulf to Bay Blvd, Clearwater, FL 33519; p/Joseph Korhonen and Mantba Charlotte K Lakela (dec); ed/BA Univ Minn; MS 1921; PhD 1924; Hon DS 1974; pa/Ret'd from Univ Minn-Duluth 1958; Writer of Tropical Flora of Fla, Univ S Fla-Tampa; r/Luth; hon/Wall of Fame, World's Fair (NY) 1940, as 1 of 5000 Fgn Born Ams.

LAMAR, CARL FLETCHER oc/Profes-sor; b/Oct 7, 1914; h/357 Glendover Rd, Lexington, KY 40503; ba/Lexington; m/Ruby Miller; c/Don Miller, Denis Carl (dec), Carla Jane; p/Edmund Newman and Hallie Fletcher Lamar, Hawesville, KY; ed/BS Wn Ky Univ 1937; MS 1949, PhD 1957 Univ Ky; mil/USMC 1942-56, Maj; pa/Prof Voc Ed Univ Ky 1968-; Asst Supt Voc Ed, St Dept Ed Ky 1967-76; Dir Res Voc Ed Ky 1965-67; Other Former Positions; Ky Farm Bur Fdn: Mem, St Bd Dirs 1967-76; Nat Assn St Dirs Voc Ed; So Assn Cols & Schs, Comm of Occupl Ed Instns; Am Voc Assn; Am Assn Sch Admrs; NEA; Gamma Sigma Delta; Iota Lambda Sigma; Am Assn Tchr Edrs in Agri: Charter Mem, Treas 1967; Am Voc Ed Res Assn; Others; cp/UF Dr, Former Team Capt Univ Ky; Agri Ed Mag Book Review Editor; Wn Ky Univ Alumni Assn; Univ Ky Alumni Assn; Ky Hist Assn; Adv Coun for Innovative Devel Ctr Ky Manpower Devel Inc; Dem; r/Calvary Bapt Ch, Lexington, Ky: Mem, Tchr Adult Men's Crusader SS Class, Usher, Pres Barraca Bus Men's Bible Class, Former Activs; hon/Ky Admiral; Hon Am Farmer Awd; Outstg Alumnus Awd, Gamma Sigma Delta; La Col; Hon Ky Future Homemakers Am Awd; AVA: Outstg Ser Awd for Dist'd Ldrship, Outstg Dedication Awd; Outstg Edr Awd, Acad Am Edrs; Num Others.

LAMB, CHARLES WILLIAM JR oc/-Professor; b/Oct 17, 1944; h/2008 Angelina Cir, College Station, TX 77840; ba/Col Sta; m/Sharon L; c/Christine Louise, Jennifer Jeanne; p/Charles W Sr and Jeanne A Lamb, Vandalia, OH; ed/AS Sinclair Commun Col 1964; BS Miami Univ 1966; MBA Wright St

Univ 1970; DBA Kent St Univ 1974; mil/AUS 1967-69; pa/Prof Mktg Dept Mktg Tex A&M Univ; Am, So, SWn Mktg Assns; Acad Mktg Sci; Advr Collegiate Mktg Assn; cp/DAV; Mil Order of Purple Heart; Secy House Corp, Delta Tau Delta; r/Prot; hon/Purple Heart (2); Outstg Yg Men Am.

LAMB, LAWRENCE WEBSTER oc/-Inventory Control Supervisor; b/Dec 11, 1919; h/Box 2916, Stateline, NY 89449; ba/Stateline; m/Alice; c/Benjamin Howard

and Geneva Mae Lamb (dec); ed/La Salle Univ; mil/Air Trans & Supply Ofcrs Adm; pa/Inventory Control, Wholesale & Liquor Supvr; cp/C of C; VFW; Dem Ctl Com; CAP; r/Meth; hon/Mil Type Only Parachutist.

LAMBRIGHT, CAROLINA GALE oc/Professor; b/May 15, 1931; h/Rt 5, Box 79 WW, Mobile, AL 36608; ba/Mobile; p/Clyde Smith and Daisy Peacock Lambright, Mobile; ed/BS Mary Washington Col; MEd, EdD Univ Va; pa/Prof Spec Ed Univ S Ala; Tchr Exceptl Chd; Instr Var Former Univs incl'g: Univ Miss, Univ Va, Univ Tex, Others; Prog Devel Tchr

Ed; Diagnostic Progs for Handicapped; Past Pres Ala Fdn Coun for Exceptl Chd; Com Mem AAUW; cp/Quota Clb; r/Bapt: SS Tchr for Handicapped; hon/Author Manuals & Chapts on Spec Ed Techniques; Nat Hon Soc; Ser Awd, Reg XIII Ser Ctr of Tex; Truman Pierce Awd, CEC (Auburn Univ); Edr of Yr, Mobile Assn for Retarded Citizens.

LAMBRO, PHILLIP oc/Composer; Conductor; Pianist; b/Sept 2, 1935; h/1888 Century Park E (10), Century City, CA 90067;

p/Pascal and Mary Lapery Lambro; ed/Att'd Music Acad of West 1955; mil/AUS Inf; pa/Piano Debut Pianist's Fair Symph Hall, Boston 1952; Composer & Conductor Films, Documentaries incl'g: *Energy On The Move*, *Mineral King*; Compositions incl: *Miraflores* (for string orch), *Dance Barbaro* (for percussion), *Two Pictures* (for soprano & orch), *Toccata* (for piano), Others; Compositions Perf'd by: Leopold Stokowski, Phila Orch, Rochester Philharm, Balto, Indpls, Miami & Okla City Symphs & Others in US, Europe, SAm, Orient; ASCAP; Composers & Lyricists Guild Am; Tau Kappa Epsilon; cp/NH Wildlife Fdn; US Tennis Assn; NATO Tennis Team 1958-59; hon/Awd for Best Music for *Mineral King*, Nat Bd Rev; Biogl Listings.

LAMKIN, SELMA H oc/Financial Management; Author; Educator; b/Mar 29, 1925; h/698 River St, Mattapan, MA 02126; ba/Same; m/Sherman A (dec); c/Barry D, Deborah L, Leonard; p/Irving Hoffman (dec); Julia Hoffman, Mattapan; ed/Hebrew Tchrs Col; Bentley Col; pa/CPA; Tchr Courses in Acctg & Money Mgmt: Graham Jr Col, NEn

Univ, Cambridge YWCA; Treas Wom Entrepenuers; cp/Cambridge YWCA; Fin Chair Ofc of Chd-Child Abuse Com; Bd Mem Hlth Commun Planning Coun Gtr Boston; LWV Boston; Mass Feminist Credit Union; Mass Wom's Polit Caucus; r/Jewish; hon/Author: *Money Mgmt & Investmt*, *Acct'g: Self-Instrn Manual & Small Bus Success Manual*; W/W Am Wom.

LAMONT, FRANCES (PEG) STILES oc/State Senator; Real Estate; Farming; b/Jun 10, 1914; h/"Meadowlark" Rt 1, Aberdeen, SD 57401; ba/Aberdeen; m/William M (dec); c/William Stiles, Nancy, Peggy L Lauver (Mrs G L), Frederick; p/Frederick B and Frances Kenney Stiles (dec); ed/BA, MA Univ Wis; cp/SD St Senator 1974-78; Jt Appropriations Com, Hlth & Wel Com; SD Adv Coun on Aging; Bd Mem, Past Chm; SD Com on Status of Wom: Former Mem, VChm; AAUW: St Pres 1959-61, Nat Trustee Ednl Foun 1971-75; Bd Dirs Nat Trust for Hist Preserv; Former Mem Nat Bd Nat Assn Mtl Hlth; Del Nat Wom's Conf (Houston) 1977; Pres Dacotah Prairie Mus; Pres Brown Co Hist Soc; r/St Mark's Epis Ch, Aberdeen: Mem; hon/Aberdeen 1st Lady Awd 1954; Sertoma Ser to Mankind Awd; St Mother of Yr 1974; Nat Cit for Civic Work, Am Mothers Com Inc; Runner-up Nat Mother of Yr; Dist'd Ser Awd, Univ Wis Alumni; Dist'd Ser in Hist Presv, Dacotah St Col Awd; St Awd for Ser, SD St Mtl Hlth Assn; Bicent Awd for Hist Preserv, SD St Hist Soc; Ser Awd, Foster Grandparent Project; Leg Awd, Uppermost Kidney Foun.

LA MONTAINE, JOHN oc/Composer; ed/Studied under: Stella Roberts, Bernard Rogers, Howard Hanson, Nadia Boulanger; pa/Celestist & Pianist w NBC Symph (under Arturo Toscanini) 1950-54; Comm'd by Ford Foun to Compose Work for Nat Symph Orch ("Concerto for Piano & Orch") 1958; Wrote 1st Work Ever to be Comm'd in Hon of Pres Inauguration, "From Sea to Shining Sea", Perf'd by Nat Symph at Inaugural Concert for Pres & Mrs John F Kennedy 1961; Composer-in-Residence Am Acad, Rome 1962; Vis Prof Composition Var Univs incl'g Eastman Sch Music; Other Compositions incl: "Birds of

Paradise", "Missa Naturae", "Wilderness Jour", "Novellis, Novellis" (1st Opera of "Christmas Trilogy"), Others; hon/Eastman Sch Dist'd Alumni Awd; Guggenheim F'ships (2); Comms from Ford Foun & Koussevitsky Foun; Pulitzer Prize for "Concerto for Piano & Orch" 1959; Won Rheta Sosland Chamber Music Competition w String Quartet, opus 16, 1960; Num Others.

LAMPO, STEPHEN FREDERICK oc/-Attorney; b/Dec 18, 1941; h/Rt #3, Neosho, MO 64850; ba/Neosho; c/Jeremy Dennis, Katherine Marie; p/Lewis Maxwell and Elinor Louise Lampo, Neosho; ed/BS; JD; mil/-USMC; pa/Prosecuting Atty Newton Co (Mo); Mo Bar Assn; Mo Prosecuting Attys Assn; cp/Bd Mem Rotary Clb; Neosho Rec Dept; r/Meth; hon/Purple Heart; Bronze Star; Silver Star; Outstg Yg Man.

LAMPP, BARRETT MAURICE oc/Pastor, Minister; b/Nov 7, 1933; h/3520 W Howard, Visalia, CA 93277; ba/Visalia; m/Connie Mac Groves; c/La Cynda Ann, Brent Denver; p/Mildredge Denver and Billie G Lampp, Lithia; ed/BA; MDiv; Further Studies; mil/Served in Korea, 3rd Med Tk Bn,

24th Inf Div, Commo Chief (Sgt), Hon Discharge 1962; pa/So Bapt Pastor, Evangelist, Musician, Conf Ldr; Treas Visalia Mins F'ship 1977-78; Exec Bd So Bapt Gen Conv Cal, 4 Yrs Conf Ldr; cp/Pilot Com; Law in a Free Soc, Marin Co; Teen-Beat Comm, Marin City; Marin Crisis Unit-Suicide Preven; Tulare Co Chaplaincy; r/So Bapt; hon/Merit Awds for Mil Ser, Civic & Denom Ser.

LANCASTER, F WILFRID oc/Professor; b/Sept 4, 1933; h/1807 Cindy Lynn, Urbana, IL 61801; m/Maria Cesaria; c/Miriam, Owen, Jude, Aaron; p/Frederick and Mary Violet Lancaster (dec); ed/Assoc Lib Assn, Newcastle-Upon-Tyne Sch Libn'ship (England) 1954; Fellow Lib Assn Gt Britain 1969; pa/Univ Ill-U: Prof Lib Sci Grad Sch Lib Sci 1972-, Assoc Prof Lib Sci, Dir Prog in Biomed Libn'ship Grad Sch Lib Sci 1970-72; Dir Info Retrieval Sers Westat Res Inc, Bethesda, Md 1969-70; Info Systems Specialist Nat Lib Med, Bethesda 1965-68; Other Former Positions; Am Soc for Info Sci; Brit Lib Assn; Mem Panel on Info Scis Technol Com on Sci & Tech Info (COSATI) of Fed Coun for Sci & Technol 1966-67; Conslt; Edit Adv Bd Jour Res Commun Studies; Edit Advr Adv'd Technol/Libs Newslttr, Knowledge Indust Pubs Inc 1973-; Participant Num Confs; Vis Lectr Var Univs; Vis Prof Instituto Brasileiro de Informacao em Ciencia e Tecnologia (IBICT) 1975, 77, 78; Other Profl Activs; r/St Patrick's Cath Ch, Urbana; hon/Num Profl Pubs; Rec'd Best Paper Awd for "MEDLARS: Report on the Eval of its Operating Efficiency", Am Soc for Info Sci 1969; Ralph Shaw Awd for Outstg Contbn to Lit Lib Sci 1978; Awd for Best Book of Yr on Info Sci, Am Soc for Info Sci 1970, 75; Phi Kappa Phi; Fulbright Tchg Fellow; Postdoct F'ship, Norwegian Coun for Sci & Indust Res.

LANCIANO, CLAUDE OLWEN JR b/Jun 12, 1922; h/Lands End Farm, Box 370, Rt 3, Gloucester, VA 23061.

LAND, GEORGE THOMAS LOCK oc/Research Company Executive; Author; Educator; b/Feb 27, 1933; h/27 Henry St, Southampton, NY 11968; ba/New York, NY;

c/Robert E, Thomas G, Patrick A; p/George Thomas Lock and Mary Elizabeth Land; ed/Student Millsaps Col 1952-54, Univ Veracruz (Mexico) 1957-59; PhD Sussex Col Technol (England) 1973; DSc Max Planck Inst (Germany) 1977; pa/Chm, Partner Turtle Bay Inst, NYC 1971-; Prof Mankato St Col 1973-74; Mem Fac Edison Elect Grad Mgmt Inst 1972-; Pres Hal Roach Studios, NY 1969-71; Chief Exec, Chm Innotek Corp, NYC 1969-71; Dir Motivation Scis Inc, Creative Alts Inc, Conslt-in-Residence Social Systems Inc, Chapel Hill, NC, Chd's Hosp, Nat Med Ctr, Washington, Agape Clin Jamestown 1974; Lectr Var Ednl Instns; AAAS; Soc Gen Systems Res; Am Soc Cybernetics; Creative Ed Foun; Acad Parapsychol & Med; IPA; Author's Guild; Author's Leag Am; Oceanic Soc; Other Profl Activs; cp/Mem Var Clbs; hon/Commun Ldrs Am Awd, ABI; Fellow NY Acad Scis; Contbr Profl Jours & Gen Mags; Author: Creative Alts & Decision Making, 1974, Grow or Die: The Unifying Prin of Transformation, 1973, Others; Biogl Listings.

LAND, ROBERT DONALD oc/Management Consultant; b/Feb 16, 1926; h/111 Cambridge Blvd, Pleasant Ridge, MI 48069; ba/Southfield, MI; c/Brian Robert, Diane Elizabeth, Susan Jane; p/Allan Reginald and Beatrice Beryl Land (dec); ed/BA Univ

Toronto 1948; Cert'd Profl Bus Conslt 1971; mil/Royal Canadian Navy 1944-46; pa/Pres & Dir: PM Detroit Inc, Pract Mgmt Assocs Ltd; Sr VP & Dir Black & Skaggs Assocs Inc; r/Epis, St Joseph's Ch: Vestryman 1956-59; hon/Past Trustee Inst Cert'd Profl Bus Conslts; Past Dir Soc Profl Bus Conslts.

LANDERS, NEWLIN J oc/Contractor; Businessman; b/Jul 10, 1906; h/905 Landers Ln, Landers, CA 92284; m/Vernette Trosper; c/Larry, Marlin; p/DeLoy Landers (dec); Pearl Paige; pa/Howard Hughes' Multi-Color Lab; Hughes Devel Co; Paramount Motion Picture Studios; Fdr Landers' Machine Shop; Owner Selwyn-Landers Valve Co; Owner Havasu Landing, Needles, Cal; Fdr Commun of Landers, Landers Air Strip; Contractor Installation Tanks & Water Sys; cp/Hon Mem Landers' Vol Fire Dept; Donator: Land for Fire Sta, Land for Homestead Val Woms Clb, Bldg for Landers' PO; hon/Hon Mem Moose Lodge; Bus-man of Week, KJST Radio Sta; Plaque & Badge for 13 Rangers; Book of Honor; DIB; Intl W/W Commun Ser; Intl Register Profiles; Men Achmt; W/W: Fin & Indust, W, Cal; Commun Ldrs & Noteworthy Ams; Personalities W&MW; Notable Ams.

LANDERS, VERNETTE TROSPER oc/Retired School Counselor; Author; b/May

3, 1912; h/PO Box 3188, Landers, CA 92284; ba/Landers; m/Newlin; c/Larry, Marlin; p/Fred Trosper (dec); LaVerne Trosper, Escondido, CA; ed/AB; MA; EdD; pa/Tchr Sec'dy Schs, Montebello 22 Yrs; Prof Long Beach City Col 1 Yr; Prof Los Angeles St Col 1 Yr; Dean Girls 29 Palms High 5 Yrs; Dist Cnslr Morongo Sch Dist 8 Yrs; Pres Montebello BPW Clb; cp/Pres Hablamos Toastmistress; Secy Landers Vol Fire Dept; VP & Secy Landers Assn; hon/Soroptimist of Yr 1967; Creativity Recog Awd 1972; Intl W/W in Poetry; Biogl Listings.

LANDGARTEN, HELEN oc/Educator; b/Mar 4, 1921; h/2427 Arbutus Dr, Los Angeles, CA 90049; ba/LA; m/Nathan; c/Aleda Siccardi, Marc; ed/BFA; MA; pa/Coor Art Psychotherapy Fam Child Dept Psychi, Thalians Commun Mtl Hlth Ctr, Cedars-Sinai Med Ctr 1967-; Immaculate Heart Col: Assoc Prof, Dir Art Therapy Master's Deg Prog; Fac Wright Inst; Past Advr Jt Comm for Accreditation of Child Psychi Facilities in US; Wkshops: US, Europe, SAm, S Africa; 1st Pres So Cal Art Therapy Assn; Bd Mem Am Art Therapy Assn; Num TV Appearances; Num Paper Presentations; hon/Hon Lie Mem: Am Art Therapy Assn, So Cal Art Therapy Assn; Fellow Am Soc Psychopathol of Expression; W/W Am Wom; World W/W Wom in Ed.

LANDMAN, GEORGINA B oc/Attorney; h/3241 S Troost, Tulsa, OK 74105; ba/Tulsa; c/Nathaniel Martin; p/August Swarz (dec); ed/BA; JD; MA; LLM; pa/Atty Williams, Landman & Savage 1978-; Tulsa Co Bar Assn: Exec Com, Chm Pubs Com, Land Use Planning Com, Title Lwyrs Assn; Okla Bar Assn, Prepaid Legal Sers Com; ABA; Fed Energy Bar Assn; Intl Fdn Wom Lwyrs; cp/Bd Mem Tulsa Metro Area Citizens Crime Comm; hon/Pub'd Frequently in Profl Jours; Presented Tech Paper, Assises Internationales de l'Environment, Paris, France 1976; Boettcher Foun Judicial Clerkship 1968-69 (1st Wom); Intl Law Awd for Yr 1969-70 (1st Wom); John C Gage Hons F'ship, Univ Mo-Ks City Sch Law.

LANDRON VILLAMIL, JOSE MANUEL oc/Assistant Director; b/Feb 4, 1936; h/44 St 707 Fairview, Rio Piedras, PR 00926; ba/Caguas, PR; m/Judith A Baralt; c/Lindy Aurora, Blanca Alexandra; p/Jose Landron Oliveras and Blanca R Villamil (dec); ed/BS Clemson Univ 1963; Indust Engrg Univ PR; pa/Asst Dir Pers Audio & Capacitors Divs, Matsushita Elect of PR Inc 1975-; Dir Indust Relats Gulf & Wn Caguas, PR 1974; Dir Adm ITT Aetna Corp, Hato Rey, PR 1973-74; Other Former Positions; Am Soc Pers Adm; Profl Soc for Accident Preven PR; Engrs Soc for Accident Preven; cp/Rotary Clb; Campaign Dir Caguas Reg Red Cross; r/Cath; hon/Awd of Merit, UF; Cit, Jr Achmt PR; Employer's Rep for Yr, Secy of Ed PR 1972; W/W S&SW; Pub'd Author.

LANDWEHR, ARTHUR J oc/Minister; b/Mar 8, 1934; h/310 Church St, Evanston, IL 60201; ba/Evanston; m/Avonna Lee; c/Arthur J III, Andrea Lea; p/Arthur J and Alice B Landwehr, Northbrook, IL; ed/BA Drake Univ 1956; pa/U Meth Min; Chm Com on Acad Affairs; VChm Bd Trustees Garrett-Evang Theol Sem; cp/Chgo Conf on Rel & Race; Gen Bd Ch Fdn Gtr Chgo; r/U Meth; hon/Commend from Pope Paul VI & World Coun of Chs for Fdg Ecumenical Insights, 1st Post Vatican II Lay Ecumenical Prog in US.

LANE, IRENE ELISABETH oc/Department Sales Manager; b/Aug 31, 1952; h/6019 S Clayton, Littleton, CO 80121; ba/Denver, CO; p/James Leo and Patricia O Lane, Coronado, CA; ed/BS magna cum laude Metro St Col 1974; pa/May D & F Denver Co: Dept Sales Mgr 1977-, Asst Buyer 1976-77, Selling Supvr 1975-76; Phi Chi Theta; Nat Editor The IRIS, Nat Mag PCT; VP Denver Alumnae Chapt PCT; Jr Exec Clb, May D & F; r/Cath; hon/Colo S'ship Awd; Nat Key Awd, Phi Chi Theta.

LANE, L QUENTIN oc/College President;

b/Nov 22, 1934; h/1211 Greenwood Trail NW, Cleveland, TN 37311; ba/Cleve; m/Clara D; c/M Darlene; p/(dec); ed/BS Mid Tenn St Univ 1954; MA Geo Peabody Col for Tchrs 1959; EdD Univ Tenn 1973; mil/AUS Med Lab Specialist 1957-58; pa/Cleve St Commun Col: Pres 1978-, Dean Acad Affairs 1973, 78, Dir Res 1971-73, Dir Cont'g Ed 1971; Exec Dir Chattanooga Model Cities Prog 1969-71; Dir Staff Pers Sers Chatta Public Schs 1967-69; Other Former Positions; Past Pres: TEA Dept Higher Ed, E Tenn Ed Assn; Mem Orthopaedic Phys' Asst Adv Com, Chatta St Tech Commun Col; Bd Trustees: Cleve St Commun Col Foun, Mid Tenn St Univ Foun, E Ridge Commun Hosp; NEA; Tenn Ed Assn; Cleve St Commun Col Ed Assn; Coor Area 7B Phi Delta Kappa; Others; cp/Ga-Tenn Reg Hlth Comm; Cleve Rotary Clb; Adv Bd U Way Cleve/Bradley Co; r/1st Bapt Ch, Cleve: Mem; hon/DIB; W/W: Am Univs & Cols, Am Ed; Outstg Edrs Am; Personalities of S.

LANE, STANLEY GWIN oc/Clergyman; State Correctional Chaplain; b/Aug 20, 1925; h/2313 Black Rd, Joliet, IL 60435; ba/Joliet; m/Betty Lou Voight; c/Jerry Gwin, Sydney Lloyd, David Alan, Linda Ruth; p/Lloyd J and Nellie J H Atkinson Lane (dec); ed/BA Neb Wesleyan Univ; Mdiv Garrett Evang Theol Sem; Further Studies in Clin Pastoral Ed; mil/USAAF 1944-46, 44th Field Arty Bn, Instr Field Arty Sch, Ft Sill, Okla; pa/St Correct Chaplain Ill Yth Ctr; Ill St Assn Chaplains; Am Correc Chaplains Assn, Cert'd; Am Prot Hosp Assn: Cert'd, Fellow Col Chaplains); Convenor/Secy Juvenile Chaplain Dept Corrects; Others; cp/Exec Com, CoChm Yth Comm; Commun Ser Coun; hon/Hon Life Mem, PTA; DIB; Commun Ldrs & Noteworthy Ams; W/W; Article Pub'd in Jour APHA.

LANG, FRANZ oc/Sister of Religious Order; b/Sept 7, 1921; h/11300 NE Second Ave, Miami, FL 33161; ba/Miami; p/Andrew Lang (dec); Elizabeth Lang, Detroit, MI; ed/BA Siena Hgts Col; MA Univ Mich; mil/USAAF 1942-45, USAFR 1946-50; pa/Dir Lib Sers Barry Col, Miami 1970-; Hd Libn St Dominic Col, St Charles, Ill 1963-70; Asst Libn Siena Hgts Col, Adrian, Mich 1962-63; Other Former Positions; Conslt; ALA; Am Assn Col & Res Libs; AAUA; Cath Lib Assn: Pres-elect 1977-79, Pres 1979-81; Dade Co Lib Assn; Fla Assn Univ Admrs; Fla Chapt Cath Lib Assn; Fla Assn SEn Lib Assn; Others; cp/Gov's Conf on Lib & Info Sers, Reg 12 1977-78; Mem NETWORK; Common Cause; Former Activs; r/Cath: Affil'd w Sisters of St Dominic, Congreg of The Most Holy Rosary, Adrian; hon/Cert of Merit, City of St Charles, Ill Human Relats Coun; W/W Am Wom; Pub'd in Profl Jours.

LANG, JAMES DeVORE JR oc/Real Estate Investment Executive; b/Apr 29, 1941; h/531 Fairway Dr, PO Box 1521, Novato, CA 94947; ba/Novato; m/Barbara Jo Drury; c/Kathrena, Teresa, Christina, Angela; p/James DeVore Lang (dec); Margaret Van Oosbree Lang, Santa Rose, CA; ed/BS USAF Acad 1963; MBA Pepperdine Univ 1978; mil/USAF 1963-68, Capt, Pilot; 7 Air Medals; AF Commend Medal; pa/Intl Assn Fin Planners: Mem 1971-, Nat Pres 1973-74, Chm 1974-75; Former Dir & Pres Ins Corp; Fin Forum Am: Reg Dir & Cert'd Instr 1968; Rep & W Coast VP MW Investmt Co 1969; CoFounded Own Investmt Co; cp/Intl Platform Spkr's Assn; Rotary Clb Novato, Paul Harris Fellow Rotary Intl; USAF Acad &

Pepperdine Univ Alumni Assns; C of C Novato; Aircraft Owner's & Pilot's Assn; r/Presb Ch Novato: Elder, Chm Fin Com; Exec Sem Campus Crusade for Christ Arrowhead Sprgs; Lay Inst for Evang, Campus Crusade for Christ, Arrowhead Sprgs; Ecumenical Housing Assn Marin; hon/Cert'd Fin Planner.

LANG, JOVIAN PETER oc/Priest; Professor; Librarian; Liturgist; Speech Therapist; b/Jun 2, 1919; h/3945 Jerusalem Ave, Seaford, NY 11783; ba/Jamaica, NY; p/Peter and Margaret Lang (dec); ed/MA; MSLS; pa/Prof, Libn Div Lib & Info Sci St John's Univ; Am, NY & Cath Lib Assns; cp/K of C; r/Rom Cath: Priest; hon/Cert of Hon, Fla Coun on Stuttering; Beta Phi Mu.

LANG, MARY P oc/Professor; b/Mar 18, 1923; h/2107 E North St, Greenville, SC 29607; ba/G'ville; m/Robert L Sr (dec); c/Lynda L Wagner, Edwardean L Rexroad, Dawn L Salle, Robert L Jr; p/Russell and Zora Lee Plummer (dec); ed/BA 1952, MA 1955 Bob Jones Univ; Bob Jones Univ: Prof Eng & Bus 1953-78, Dormitory Supvr 1952-61; Secy Ind 1942-47; cp/Former Girl Scout Ldr; r/Indep Bapt: Former SS Tchr, Jr Yg Peoples Ldr; hon/Personality List, BJU Yrbook; Personalities of S.

LANG, MAUD ORA oc/Retired Home Economist, Staff Member; b/Dec 10, 1911; h/R2, Richland, IN 47634; p/Curran R and Lue Tallie Lewright Lang (dec); ed/AB 1933, BS 1941 Ind St Univ; pa/Home Economist Purdue Univ & Warrick Co Ext Ser, Boonville, Ind 1941-74; Tchr Home Ecs, PE & Biol Luce

Twp HS 1933-41; Ind Ext Agts Assn; Pres Ind Ext Agts Home Economists 1954; Nat Ext Agts Assn, Epsilon Sigma Phi; Ind & Home Ecs Assn; Ret'd Tchrs Assn; Ind Univ Alumni; BPW Assn; cp/AARP; Ret'd Public Employees Ind; Ind Acad Sci; Sr Citizens Coun on Aging; ARC; Ind Farm Bur; Garden Clb; Pres Warrick Hosp Aux; r/Meth; hon/Nat Awd, Nat Assn Home Economists; 30 Yr Cert, Dept Agri.

LANGE, ADELINE ROSE oc/Assistant Director Nursing Service; b/Oct 21, 1935; h/3 Emery St, Iselin, NJ 08830; ba/Perth Amboy, NJ; m/Robert; c/Robert Jr, Cathy, Donna, Mark; p/John Michalczyk (dec); Sophy P Michalczyk, Dickson City, PA; ed/BA Jersey City St Col; MA Seton Hall Univ; MBA Cand Fairleigh Dickinson Univ; pa/Asst Dir Nsg Ser Perth Amboy Gen Hosp; Am Nurses' Assn; NJ St Nurses' Assn: Corr Secy Dist #4, CoChperson Leg Com Dist #4; r/Rom Cath.

LANGENBRUCH THEODOR oc/Uni-

versity Professor; b/Oct 12, 1940; h/2741 Tryon Pl NE, Atlanta, GA 30319; ba/Atlanta; m/Linda; c/Danielle Meredith, Andrea Helen; p/Theodor and Mechthild Langenbruch, Wuppertal-1, Germany; ed/MA 1966, PhD 1969 Univ Hamburg (Germany); pa/Assoc Prof Mod Langs Ga Tech; Lectr & Conf Contbns; r/Covenant Presb Ch, Atlanta: Mem, Ruling Elder; hon/Sev S'ships; Author Book *Dialectical Humor in Hermann Kant's Novel DIE AULA; A Study in Contemp E German Lit*, 1975; Sev Articles Pub'd.

LANGER, ELIEZER oc/Rabbi; b/Dec 3, 1946; h/4855 College Ave, San Diego, CA 92115; ba/San Diego; m/Lucy; c/Shoshana, Elisheva, Yaakov; p/Moses and Zmira K Langer, San Francisco, CA; ed/BA, MA Yeshiva Univ; Ordination Rabbi Isaac Ellhanan Theol Sem; pa/Rabbinical Coun Am; VP RIETS Alumni; cp/Chaplain Grossmont Hosp; r/Jewish; hon/Semicha F'ship; St of Israel Bonds; Ks of Pythias.

LANGER, SANDRA LOIS oc/Art Historian/Critic: Modern & Contemporary; b/Dec 18, 1941; h/3300 Heyward St, Columbia, SC 29205; ba/Columbia; p/Moe and Doris Langer, Coral Gables, FL; ed/BA; MA; PhD; pa/Asst Prof Art Hist/Criticism Univ SC 1978-; Grad Prog Goddard Univ Field Fac 1976-78; Columnist Art Criticism *Miami Mag* 1974-75; Asst Prof Fla Intl Univ 1973-78; Other Former Positions; NY Hist Soc; Col Art Assn Am; Soc Aesthetics & Criticism; Nat Trust for Hist Preserv; Coalition Wom's Art Orgs; Wom's Caucus for Art; SEn Col Art Conf; Nat Wom's Studies Assn; SEn Wom's Caucus for Art; Victorian Soc; Lectr; Competition Judge; Edit Activs; Com & Task Force Mem; Contb'g Editor *Contemp Art SE*; Poet; cp/Var Cult Activs; hon/Phi Kappa Phi; Num Profl Pubs.

LANGLOIS, AIMEE oc/Speech/Language Pathologist; b/Jun 7, 1945; h/99 Corona Apt 601, Denver, CO 80218; ba/Denver; p/Paul and Suzanne Fortier Langlois, Montreal, Canada; ed/BA 1965; MA 1967; EdD 1975; pa/Speech Pathologist Porter Meml Hosp, Denver 1978; Asst Prof Spch Pathol Dept Commun Disorders & Spch Sci Univ Colo, Boulder 1975-; Var Former Positions; ASHA, Cert of Clin Competence in Spch Pathol 1972; NY St Spch & Hearing Assn; Aphasia Study Group NY; AAUP; Colo Spch & Hearing Assn; Biofeedback Soc Am; Jour Reviewer; Reschr; Others; r/Rom Cath; hon/-Traineeship F'ship; Profl Pubs.

LANGSTON, DEWEY FRANCIS oc/-Assistant Dean Admissions; b/Jul 17, 1920; h/1500 W 17th Ln, Portales, NM 88130; ba/-Portales; m/Dessie D Rierson; c/Jackie Frances, Judy Kaye; p/(dec); ed/BA En NM Univ 1943; MEd Springfield Col 1948; Postdoct Studies Stanford Univ 1956; mil/NM St Guard 1942-43 (Resv Duty); USMC 1942-43, Comm'd 2/Lt 1943, Pacific Theater Opers 1944-45, Ret'd 1962, Capt; Purple Heart; AUS 1962, Capt, Lt Col 1968, Cmdr 4153 Resv Co, Portales 1965-68, Ret'd Lt Col 1971; pa/En NM Univ (ENMU): Asst Dean Admissions 1977-, Affirmative Action Ofcr 1977-, Asst to Grad Dean 1975-76, Dir Intercollegiate Aths 1970-74, Chm Div Hlth, PE & Rec 1970-75, Varsity Track Coach 1951-56, Hd Profl PE Prog 1967-71, Prof Hlth & PE 1957-, Assoc Prof 1953-57, Asst Prof 1951-53, Vis Prof PE Sum 1951; Other Former Positions; Life Fellow AAHPER; F'ship Christian Aths; Fac Senate ENMU (Past Mem); Life Mem NEA; Past Pres NM Assn Hlth, PE & Rec; Fellow Am Col Sports Med; Bd Govs AAHPER 1977-79; Past Pres ENMU Chapt NEA 1976-77; VP Am Sch & Commun Safety Assn 1976-; Chm Adv Panel on Comms, Phi Delta Kappa; Others; cp/Past Pres NM Coun on Yth Fitness; Ks Templar NM; Masons; VFW; Past Mem Bd Dirs Portales Campfire Girls; Shriner; Past Worthy Patron OES NM; Am Legion; C of C; Past Pres Portales Rotary Clb; Former Dist Gov Rotary Intl, Dist 552; Life Mem Am Rifle Assn; Antique Auto Clb Am; Sports Philatelist Intl; Past Chm Roosevelt Co Red Cross; Chm Portales Armory Bd, NM NG;

BSA; Past Gen Fund Chm Roosevelt Co UF; Num Others; r/1st Bapt Ch, Portales: SS Tchr, Deacon; hon/Paul Harris Awd, Portales Rotary Clb; Dist'd Ser Awd, ENMU; Past Mem Gov's Citizens Adv Com on Yth Fitness; Top Merit Prof 1959; Hon Awds: SWD, AAHPER, NM AHPER; Phi Kappa Phi; Sigma Delta Psi; Num Biogl Listings; Profl Pubs; Others.

LANGSTON, JUDY ANN oc/Photographer; b/Jan 1, 1950; h/1122 Kemman Ave, LaGrange Park, IL 60525; ba/Chicago, IL; p/John S and Marcella R Langston, LaGrange;

ed/BA; MA; MS; pa/Photog Nat Insts Hlth 1976; Var Group & One-Wom Photo Shows; hon/Awd Winner, MidStates Indust Photogs' Assn; Ill Inst Technol & Lydia Bates S'ship Awd Recipient.

LANIER, T WAYNE oc/Dentist; b/Sept 19, 1932; h/RR#1, Box 1147, Greenwood, AR 72936; ba/Ft Smith, AR; m/Helen Barnes; c/Lance Littleton, Tara Kaay; ed/BS Univ Ark 1958; DDS Wash Univ Sch Dental Med 1962; mil/USN Aviation Elects Technician 1951-54; Current Cmdr USNR Dental Corps; pa/Pvt Pract Gen Dentistry, Ft Smith 1962-; Pres-elect Ark St Dental Assn 1979; Pres Am Assn Dental Editors 1974; Editor Ark Dental Jour 1965-75; Fellow Am Col Dentists; Past Pres: Ark Unit Am Soc Dentistry for Chd, Ft Smith Dental Soc, Tau Chapt Xi Psi Phi; Dental Hlth Conslt City of Ft Smith 1965-70; cp/Ark Ednl TV Comm; Bd Trustees Westark Commun Col; Exec Bd Wn Ark Coun BSA; Former Commun Advr Jr Leag Ft Smith; Former Mem Bd Trustees Ft Smith Public Lib; Former Dir Ft Smith C of C; Former Mem: St Adv Bd Ark Arthritis Foun, Bd Dirs 4-H Foun Sebastian Co, Bd Dirs Bost Sch for Limited Chd; Others; hon/W/W S&SW; DIB; Personalities of S.

LANOUETTE, ETTA MAY oc/Real Estate Broker; b/Jan 25, 1930; h/900 Fuchsia, Oxnard, CA 93030; ba/Oxnard; m/Raymond F; c/Ronald, Randal, Craig, Linda; p/Robert Edward Hill (dec); Alma Fraysher (dec); ed/Col 2 Yrs; pa/Pres Etta Lanouette Realty Inc; Treas Oxnard Harbor Bd Realtors; cp/Chm Bus Ed Adv Bd Oxnard Unified HS Dist; Polit Ed Com Repub Cal St Ctl Com; Ventura Co Yth Chm; r/Presb: Wom's Assn Social Concerns Chm; hon/W/W: Am Wom, Bus Wom; World W/W Wom.

LANTZ, ALMA E oc/Research Psychologist; b/Apr 28, 1946; h/3451 E Asbury, Denver, CO 80210; ba/Denver; m/Joseph Halpern; p/John Edward and Ruth Cox Lantz, Atlanta, GA; ed/BA 1968, MA 1969 Univ Denver; PhD Rutgers Univ 1972; pa/Res Psychologist Denver Res Inst, Univ Denver; APA, Var Divs; Colo Psychol Assn; Am Wom in Psychol; AAAS; Sigma Xi; Human Factors Soc; Am Ednl Res Assn; Am Wom in Sci; Conslt; cp/Denver Dem Wom's Caucus: Treas, VP, Bd Mem; NOW; WEAL; NWPC; Dem Com-person; r/Meth; hon/NASA F'ship; Ford F'ship (2); Dean's List; Biogl Listings; Profl Pubs.

LANTZ, EVERETT D oc/University Administrator; b/Oct 10, 1912; h/1614 Garfield, Laramie, WY 82070; ba/Laramie; m/Elizabeth M Stratton; c/Phillip Edward, Keith William, George Everett, Barbara Elizabeth; p/John M and Emma O Lantz (dec);

ed/BA 1936, MA 1939 Univ Wyo; EdD Univ Cal 1954; mil/USN; pa/Univ Wyo: Asst to Pres for Instrn & Res, Fac 1936-; Exec Secy Wyo Coun for Chd & Yth; Pres Am Ednl Studies Assn 1970-71; Nat Standing Com of 7 Nat Socs Concerned w Ed 1969-72; Exec Secy Rock Mtn Found Ed Assn 1965-76; Wyo Ed Coun 1968-70; Gov's Comm on Ed 1964; Past Pres Wyo Cong P's & T's 1963-64; Hist of Ed Soc; Phil of Ed Soc; John Dewey Soc; Nat Assn Ed Profs; Delta Tau Kappa; Kappa Delta Pi; Phi Delta Kappa; Comparative & Intl Ed Soc; Am Acad Polit Sci; Wyo Ed Assn; NEA; AAUP; Others; cp/Del White House Confs on Chd 1970, Yth 1971; Secy-Treas Twin Rivers Cabin Owners Assn; Bd Mem Nat Coun for Accreditation Tchr Ed; Pres Nat Coun St Coms for Chd & Yth; r/Epis; hon/Hon Life Mem: Nat Wrestling Coaches Assn, Wyo Cong P's & T's; George Duke Humphrey Dist'd Fac Awd; Helms Foun Hall of Fame; Outstg Fac Awd, Alpha Kappa Psi, Univ Wyo; Kiwanis Outstg Citizen Awd; Profl Pubs; Biogl Listings; Others.

LAPOSKY, BEN FRANCIS oc/Commercial Artist; b/Sept 30, 1914; h/301 S 6th St, Cherokee, IA 51012; ba/Cherokee; p/Peter Paul and Leona A Laposky (dec); mil/Sgt 43rd Div Hq, G-3 Sec, WWII, WIA, Rendove, Sols 1943; pa/Oscillographic Designer (Elect Abstractions in US & Abroad); 125 One-Man Shows & 95 Group Shows incl: US Info Agy (France) 1956, Inst Contemp Art (London) 1969, Computer Art (Hannover, Germany) 1969-, Computer Graphics (NY) 1976, Others; Var Profl Pubs; cp/Treas Sanford Mus Assn, Cherokee; r/Rom Cath; hon/NY Dirs Clb Medal.

LA PRAD, QUENTIN CHARLES oc/Executive; b/Sept 16, 1922; h/600 Hicks Rd, Nashville, TN 37221; ba/N'ville; m/Sybil Jane Johnson; c/Stephen Charles, Philip Gregory, Robert Louis, Jeanine Suzanne, Michele Marie, Quentin Edward (dec); p/Louis Ligouri and Susanna A S La Prad (dec); ed/BS USMA W Point 1945; MSEE Ga Tech 1953; MS Vanderbilt 1973; mil/AUS 1945-53, 2/Lt; Ret'd LTC 1965; pa/Chief Constrn Sect Div Water Quality Control, Dept Public Hlth; St Dir Needs Survey 1973, 74, 76, 78; Apollo Prog 1965-70; PE Tex & Tenn; AWWA; WPCF; NSPE; Conslt APP Reg Coun 1975-; cp/Mensa; Isaac Walton; Nat Wildlife Fdn; Pres Bellevue Civitan; Chm Bellevue Civic Coun; r/St Henry's Cath Ch: Ks of C; hon/Army Commend; EPA F'ship to Vanderbilt.

LARDE, ENRIQUE ROBERTO oc/-Insurance Executive; b/Feb 7, 1934; h/80 King's Ct, Apt 601, Condado, PR 00911; ba/Old San Juan, PR; m/Ida Maria Hess (dec); p/Enrique Rafael Larde-Arthez and Marina Bellegarrigue de Larde, Woodside, NY; ed/BA Columbia Col 1956; MGA Intl Graphoanalysis Soc 1965; mil/AUS 1957-59;

pa/Supt Intl Div The Continental Ins Co, NY 1970-72; Dir & Treas S Continental Ins Agy Inc 1972-; Dir & Exec VP Corporacion Insular de Seguros 1973-; Dir & Secy Asociacion de Companias de Seguros Incorporadas en PR 1975-77, Dir & 1/VP 1977-; Adv Com Ins Sers Ofcs PR 1977-; Ins Inst PR 1975-; r/Rom Cath.

LARIMORE, LEON oc/Minister; b/Jul 22, 1911; h/1041 Eastern Pkwy, Louisville, KY 40217; ba/L'ville; m/Blanche Lile; c/Marjorie

Broady; p/William C and Myrtie D Isenberg Larimore (dec); ed/AB 1949; MDiv 1973; DD 1962; pa/Pastor 3rd Ave Bapt Ch, L'ville 1957-; Field Supvr Boyce Bible Sch, S Bapt Theol Sem 1976-; Ky Bapt Conv: Adm Comm 1972-73, St Bd 1972-73, VP 1965; Dir Bapt Homes for Elderly 1962-77; Trustee Wigginton Home for Men 1967-77; Long Run Bapt Assn: Pres Exec Bd 1971-72, Moderator 1971-72; Other Profl Activs; cp/Former Chm Hart Co Unit Am Cancer Soc; Former Mem Ec Security Wel Com; Former Dir S Ctl Rural Telephone Coop; Mason; Scottish Rite; Shriner 1978; r/So Bapt; hon/Ky Col; Ky Admiral; Dist'd Ser Awd, Am Cancer Soc; Num Biogl Listings.

LARISEY, MARIAN LAURA M oc/-Instructor; b/Jul 30, 1947; h/1435 Riverfront Dr, Charleston, SC 29407; ba/C'ton; c/-Angela Marie; p/Loring Lee Myers (dec); Leila Myers, Dillon, SC; ed/BSN Med Col SC 1969; MSEd So Ill Univ-E 1975; pa/Med Univ SC: Instr Nsg Col Nsg, Instr Staff Devel 1973-75, Instr Lab Prog 1970-72, Staff Nurse 1969; ANA; NLN; SCPGA; r/Epis.

LARSON, EVA HILBORG oc/Assistant Professor; b/Oct 7, 1912; h/3000 N Grant, Springfield, MO 65802; ba/S'field; p/Albert E and Caroline Dokken Larson (dec); ed/BS Moorhead St Tchrs Col; BA Ctl Bible Col; BA Evang Col; pa/Asst Prof Ctl Bible Col; Tchr 48 Yrs, 14 Yrs Public Schs, 34 Yrs Ctl Bible Col; Beta Mu Chapt Delta Kappa Gamma, Delta St (Mo); Rec'g Secy 1976-78, Pres 1978-80; AAUW; AAUP; r/Assemblies of God; hon/Contbr Var Jours & Pubs; W/W: Am Ed, Am Wom; World W/W Wom in Ed.

LARSON, LARRY GALE oc/Executive; b/Aug 26, 1931; h/10971 Meads, Orange, CA 92669; ba/Irvine, CA; m/Dolores Jean Albrecht; c/Larry G Jr, Gregory Alan, Dawn Marie Blair; p/Hardy Larson, Fontanelle, IA; Dorothy Marie Dybdahl, Minneapolis, MN; ed/BEE Univ Minn 1959; Postgrad Work Univ Cal 1959-61; mil/USAF 1950-54; pa/Pres & Chief Exec Ofcr EOCOM Corp, Irvine 1969-; Dir Progs Textron Inc, Dalmo Victor Co, Belmont, Cal 1968-69; Group Mgr Honeywell Inc, Mpls 1962-68; Other Former Positions; Conslt 1959-; Acoustical Soc Am; Optical Soc Am; Am Inst Physics; Am Inst Aeronautics & Astronautics; Am Geophy Union; AAAS; Optical Soc Am; IEEE; Soc Photo-Optical Instrumentation Engrs; Soc for Applied Spectroscopy; Graphic Arts Tech Foun Inc; cp/Univ Minn Alumni Assn; Wn Elect Mfrs Assn; Gtr Irvine Indust Leag; Am Security Coun; Am Def Preparedness Assn; Repub Party; Chm Nat UN Day Com; r/Luth; hon/Cert of Apprec, 1976 Pollution Engrg Cong; Good Conduct Medal; Strategic Air Command Air Crew Mem of Month; Profl Pubs.

LARSON, WALTER RAMEY oc/-Electronics Executive; b/Mar 14, 1918; h/Stone Rd, Hampstead, NH 03841; ba/-Garden Grove, CA; m/Harriet A; c/Linda Anne Stover; p/Walter A and Jessie M Larson

(dec); ed/BS Cal Inst Technol; mil/USAFR, Ret'd Lt Col; pa/Pres L Z Enterprises Inc; cp/Former Chm Cal Tech Alumni Fund Dr, N Orange Co; r/Congreg; hon/Sr Pilot, USAF.

LARY, EUGENE oc/Attorney; b/Nov 28, 1906; h/7039 San Pedro #905, San Antonio,

TX 78216; ba/Same; c/Victor, Diane L deDios Martinez (Mrs Juan), Sharon L Ehrhardt (Mrs David); ed/LLD Universidad Autonoma de Puebla (Mexico) 1964; Addit Studies; pa/Pvt Pract Law: Dallas 1937-70, San Antonio 1971-; Former Mun Ct Judge, City of University Park; Intl, Am, Tex Bar Assns; Tex Police Assn; Contbr Articles Profl Jours; Others; r/Unity Ch of San Antonio; hon/Order Aztec Eagle (Mexico); La Cruz Laureada, La Orden Mexicana del Derecho y La Cultura; Rec'd Homenaje de Simpatia Awd, La Associacion Nacional de Abogados; Rec'd 50 Yr Awd, St Bar of Tex; Biogl Listings.

LASBURY, LEAH B oc/Realtor; Painter; Community Leader; b/Apr 1, 1915; h/PO Box 777, Englewood, FL 33533; ba/E'wood; m/Clyde P; c/Cherick Pitchford, Dana Cleveland, Leah Jr; p/J E and Nelhia A Bartlett (dec); ed/BA Rollins Col; BS; pa/Org E'wood Bd Realtors; Org BPW; cp/Dir & Past Pres E'wood Lib; E'wood Teen Clb; Dir Sarasota Co Goals Coun; Past Pres E'wood C of C; Dir Sarasota Co Lib Adv Bd; Past VP Ringling Mus; 1/Pres E'wood Wom Taxpayers Leag; Carter Mem Venice Yacht Clb; DAR; Others; r/Prot; hon/Patriots Awds: E'wood, Sarasota Co (Fla); W/W: Am Wom, Fin & Indust; World W/W Wom; DIB; 2000 Wom Achmt; Intl W/W Commun Ser; Others.

LASH, ANDRÉ DUANE oc/College Music Instructor; b/May 18, 1947; h/408½ McIntosh, Vidalia, GA 30474; ba/Mt Vernon, GA; p/Eugene L Lash; Mildred B VanSant, Coffeyville, KS; ed/BME; MM; AAGO;

mil/AUS 3 Yrs, 371st Army Band; pa/Music Instr Brewton-Parker Col; Am Guild Organists; Am Musicological Soc; Am Music S'ship Assn; So Bapt Ch Music Conf; r/Bapt: Organist, SS Tchr; hon/Personalities of S; Outstg Yg Man Am.

LASHLEY, VIRGINIA STEPHENSON oc/Educator; b/Nov 12, 1924; h/1240 San Marino Ave, San Marino, CA 91108; ba/Glendale, CA; m/Richard H; c/Kenneth W Hughes, Linda Hughes Tindall, Robert H, Lisa, Diane; p/Herman H Stephenson (dec); Edith W Stephenson, Sun City, AZ; ed/BA; MA; pa/Glendale Col; Chm Bus Div, Coor Computing Ctr; Dir & Corporate Secy Rose of Happiness, Montessori Schs Am; Pres San Gabriel Valley Data Processing Mgmt Assn; Treas San Gabriel Assn for Systems Mgmt; AAUP; Am Fdn Tchrs; Cal Fdn Tchrs; Nat Soc Programmed Instrn; Cal Ednl Computing Consortium; NCTM; Others; r/Congreg; hon/Phi Beta Kappa; Pi Mu Epsilon; Phi Alpha Theta; Delta Phi Upsilon; Fellow, John Randolph & Dora Haynes Foun; NSF Grant; Others.

LA SOR, WILLIAM SANFORD oc/- Clergyman; Professor; b/Oct 25, 1911; h/1790 E Loma Alta Dr, Altadena, CA 91001; ba/- Pasadena, CA; m/Elizabeth Granger Vaughan; c/William Sanford Jr, Elizabeth Ann, Frederick Eugene Vaughan, Susanne Marie; p/William Allan and Sara Lewis La Sor (dec); ed/AB; MA; ThB; ThM; PhD; ThD; mil/- USNR Ret'd Chaplain, Cmdr; pa/Prof Old Testament Fuller Theol Sem 1949-; Pres Bd Tokyo Evang Ctr 1958-; VP SACO 1972-73; Mil Chaplains Assn: 1972 Nat Conv Com Chm, Pres So Cal Chapt 1967-69; Vis Prof & Lectr Var Ednl Instns; Hon Lectr Am Sch Oriental Res (Jerusalem) 1956-57; Am Schs

Oriental Res; Intl Org Old Testament Scholars; Nat Assn Profs Hebrew; Soc Biblical Lit & Exegesis; Soc Old Testament Scholars (Gt Britain); Inst for Biblical Res; r/Presb: Former Pastor; hon/Author Pubs incl'g: *Dead Sea Scrolls and the New Testament* 1972, *Church Alive!* 1972, *Commentary on 1-11 Kings* 1970, Others; Biogl Listings.

LAST, SONDRA CAROLE oc/Legislative Aide; b/Nov 6, 1932; h/1250 NE 206th St, Miami, FL 33179; ba/N Miami Bch; c/Mikel Eve Renner; p/Irving B Last (dec); Lynn F Last, Miami; ed/BA; SB; MA; pa/Campaign Mgr, Leg Aide for St Rep Gwen Margolis 1974-; Editor & Pubr *Wom's Almanac*, Miami 1978-; Acad Cnslg, Col Bd Preparation Courses, CLEP Preparation Courses (Irvin W Katz), Miami Bch, Fla 1969-74; Gen Mgr Mirror Poster Printing Inc, Miami 1967-69;

Other Former Positions; cp/Public Affairs Com YWCA; N Miami Bch Comm on Status of Wom; Dade Co Wom's Rts Day Activs 1977; Wom's Equality Action Leag; Concerned Dems; Chm Issues Com Dem Clb N Dade; ACLU; Wom's Com of 100; Wom Artists It's Time, Miami; Advr Folio Soc (London, England); NOW: Former Mem Bd, Former Mem Polit Endorsemt Com, Past Pres, Others; Var Former Activs; r/Hebrew; hon/Outstg Achmt, Nat Coun Jewish Wom; Trail Blaser Awd, Fed'ly Employed Wom Inc; Susan B Anthony Awd, NOW; "Sondra C Last" Proclamation, City N Miami Bch.

LATHAM, WILLIAM PETERS oc/- Composer/Educator; b/Jan 4, 1917; h/1815 Southridge Dr, Denton, TX 76201; ba/- Denton; m/Joan Seyler; c/Leslie Virginia, William Peters Jr, Carol Jean Seyler (Mrs Robert I); p/Lawrence L and Eugenia Peters Latham (dec); ed/BS MusEd Univ Cinc; BMus, MMus Col Music Cincinnati; PhD Eastman Sch Music; mil/AUS 1942-46, 2/Lt; pa/Sch Music N Tex St Univ 1965-: Dir Grad Studies Music, Prof Composition, Dist'd Prof Music;

Prof Theory & Composition Univ No Ia 1946-65; Composer Num Works, Sev Pub'd; Perf'd throughout US, Canada, Europe, Japan; Orch Works Perf'd by: Cinc Symph, Eastman-Rochester Philharm, Dallas Symph, St Louis Symph, Radio Orchs (Brussels, Belgium, Hilversum, Holland); r/Epis; hon/Dist'd Prof Music; Bd Regents N Tex St Univ 1978; Baker's Biogl Dic Musicians; W/W: Am Ed, Am; Personalities S; ASCAP Biogl Dic; DIB; Contemp Am Composers: Biogl Dic; World W/W Musicians; Outstg Edrs Am; Men of Achmt; Others.

LATHROP, GERTRUDE ADAMS oc/-

Laboratory Director; Chief Chemist; b/Apr 28, 1921; h/301 Mountain St, Black Mountain, NC 28711; ba/Old Fort, NC; p/William Barrows and Lena Abigail Adams Lathrop (dec); ed/BS Univ Conn 1944; MA 1953, PhD 1955 Tex Wom's Univ; pa/Old Fort Finishing Plant, Div U Merch: Chief Chemist, Lab Dir 1979-; Lab & Warranty Mgr Automotive Div Collins & Aikman Corp 1964-78; Res Chemist UM Res Ctr, Langley, SC 1963-64; Other Former Positions; Am Chem Soc; Am Assn Textile Chemists & Colorists: Sect Treas, VChm, Res Chm Palmetto Sect 1957-64, Charles H Stone S'ship Mem & Com Chm 1974-79 Piedmont Sect; Iota Sigma Pi; Nat Fdn BPW Clbs Inc; NC FBPWC Inc: Pres Albemarle (NC) Chapt 1974, 76, Chm Foun Com Asheville Chapt 1979-; r/U Congreg Ch, Norwich, Conn: Mem; hon/Sch Valedictorian; Career Wom of Yr, Albemarle BPW Clb 1979; Coauthor "Today's Man-Made Fibers" (Supplement to Today's Clothing).

LATIMER, FRED HOLLIS oc/Educator; b/Feb 21, 1921; h/1429 Wreyhill Dr, Hurst, TX 76053; ba/Hurst; m/Emma Jean Fletcher; c/George Henry; p/James Aurelus and (Stepmother:) Thelma Banister Latimer, Houston, TX; Rosa Paralee Mitchell (dec); ed/BS; MBA; mil/USAF; pa/Tarrant Co Jr Col, NE Campus 1967-: Assoc Prof, Chm Data Processing; Lee Col 1957-67: Bus Tchr, Chm Bus Div; D J Fletcher Produce 1948-53: Acct, Asst Mgr; Other Former Positions; Coauthor *Col Typewriting, Bus Ed Handbook for Tex*; TBEA; TJCTA; TAEDS: Prog Chm 1969, Bd Dirs 1971-77; AEDS; TJCTA: Chm Bus Sect, Data Processing Sect; Prog Chm SABE 1968; Cert'd Data Processor; cp/Mem & Past Pres Kings Men (Gospel Singing Group), Recorded 2 Records; Former Mem Computer Users Conf Planning Com E Tex St Univ; Mem Tex Ed Agy Task Force for Planning Annual Work Shop, Tex Data Processing Tchrs; Alpha Theta Chapt Delta Pi Epsilon; Mason; r/Bapt: Deacon; hon/Asst'ships: Stephen F Austin St Univ, Data Processing Sum Sch Colo St Univ.

LATTS, LEATRICE LYNNE oc/Attorney at Law; Certified Public Accountant; b/Aug 28, 1938; h/1591 Virginia Rd, San Marino, CA 91108; ba/Pasadena, CA; m/Elliott E; c/Leslie Alicia, Mara Gwynne, Justin Seth; p/Samuel and Myrtle Gordon Posner (dec); ed/JD UClA 1967; BA Woodbury Univ 1962; CPA Cert 1969; pa/Pvt Pract Law; Appt'd Judge Pro Tem of Los Angeles Small Claims Ct 1978-79; Appt'd to Panel Arbitrators, Am Arbitration Assn 1975-; Cal St Bar: Examr Disciplinary Com 1977-78, Com on Unauthorized Pract Law 1977-78, 1978-79, Exec Com Tax Sect 1975; Cal Wom Lwyrs: Bd Govs 1976-78 (Appt'd), Bd Govs 1978-80 (Elected); LA Co Bar Assn: Com on Cont'g Ed 1977-78, 1978-79, Credit Union Com 1978-79; Bd Dirs Am Soc Wom Accts 1978-79; Bd Dirs Nat BPW Clb LA 1978-79; Treas LA Chapt Nat Assn Wom Bus Owners 1978-79; Others; cp/Bd Dirs Pasadena Planned Parenthood; Panelist-Lectr; Guest Spkr; Instr UCLA Ext Bus Courses; hon/Hon Tchg Cert, LA Unified Sch Dist; W/W in W.

LATZ, ROBERT oc/Attorney; b/Jul 15, 1930; h/6850 Harold Ave, Minneapolis, MN 55427; ba/Mpls; m/Carolyn; c/Ronald, Martin, Michael, Shari Lynn; p/(dec); ed/BSL 1952, LLB 1954 Univ Minn; mil/USNR 1950-52; pa/Admitted to Minn Bar 1954; Asst Atty Gen St of Minn 1955-58; Partner Sachs,

Latz & Kirshbaum, Mpls 1960-; Regent Univ Minn 1975-; Nat Panel Arbitrators Am Arbitration Assn; ABA, Sects on Labor Relats & Antitrust Law; Am Soc Law & Med; Am Trial Lwyrs Assn; Delta Sigma Rho; Sigma Alpha Mu; cp/Nat Comm Anti-Defamation Leag; Former Chm Mpls Urban Coalition Action Coun; Ofcr & Dir Gtr Mpls Metro Housing Corp; Del Dem Party Nat Convs 1960, 64; Former Chm Dem Farmer Labor Party Convs; r/Jewish.

LAUER, FRANCES LOUISE PEACOCK oc/Educator; b/Feb 20, 1942; h/4263 Mt Castle Ave, San Diego, CA 92117; ba/Same; m/Ralph E Jr; c/AnnaLisa, Ralph Edward III; p/Eldred Giles and Robert Shanks Peacock, Spokane, WA; ed/BA Univ Wash 1964; MA Pa St Univ 1970; pa/Conslt Ice Arena W Inc; IPA; APGA; Am Col Pers Assn; Assn Humanistic Ed & Devel; US Figure Skating Assn; Inventor Insta-shelf; cp/PTA; Early Childhood Ed; Soc Mayflower Descendants; Experimt in Intl Living; Former Mem Citizens Adv Com Mid-City Sr Day House; Former Asst Ldr Camp Fire Girls; r/Prot; hon/Phi Beta Kappa; Delta Phi Alpha; Sigma Tau Delta; Guest Figure Skating Soloist, Pa St Ice Revue 1966; W/W W; Personalities W&MW; Intl W/W Commun Ser.

LAUGHLIN, JOAN MARIE oc/Associate Professor; b/Sept 11, 1940; h/827 Indian Hills Dr, Lincoln, NE 68520; ba/Lincoln; p/Matthew John Laughlin (dec); Helen Frances Roscoe Laughlin, Imogene, IA; ed/BS Col St Mary; MS Ia St Univ; PhD Pa St Univ; pa/Assoc Prof Textiles; Am Home Ecs Assn: Bd Dirs, Chm Cols & Univs Sect; Pres Assn Col Profs Textiles & Clothing; Am Soc for Testing & Mats; Am Assn Textile Chemists & Colorists; AAAS; cp/Neb St Geneal Soc; hon/Sigma Xi; Sigma Delta Epsilon; AHEA Foun F'ship; Omicron Nu; Phi Upsilon Omicron; Gamma Sigma Delta; Sigma Phi Sigma; Sigma Tau Delta.

LAUGHLIN, JOY JUDGE oc/Retired Naturalist; b/Mar 14, 1904; h/1044 Pamona, Walla Walla, WA 99362; m/Ruth I Hug; c/Awanna L Kalal, Lorraine L Longacre; p/Clarence Clyde Laughlin (dec); Fannie Josephine Meserve (dec); ed/Att'd: Linfield Col, Oreg St & Wash St Univs; mil/USMC 3 Yrs; pa/Ret'd Dir Ft Walla Walla Mus Complex; Instr Public Schs 6 Yrs; Owner Laughlins Craftshop 10 Yrs; Author Dr J W Meserve Fam Hist Translation of "The Secret Doctrine"; cp/Dir NA Lily Soc 3 Yrs; Former Sgt Police Dept; Past Pres Camera & Cinema Clb; Hist Soc; Mens Garden Clb; Reg, VP The Theosophical Soc; r/Unitarian-Theosophist; hon/Dist'd Marksman Gold Medal; Bronze Medal, Mens Garden Clbs; Wash St Gen; Pub'd Author.

LAUGHLIN, MILDRED KNIGHT oc/Associate Professor; b/Mar 23, 1922; h/19 Green Mountain Dr, Iowa City, IA 52240; ba/Ia City; m/William A; c/Debra Jean L Warren, Barbara Joan; p/Henry and Anna Knight (dec); ed/AB Ft Hays St Univ; MA Wichita St Univ; MLS, PhD Univ Okla;

pa/Assoc Prof Sch Lib Sci Univ Ia; Editor: *Lng Today* Column "Action Activs" & *Rdg for Yg People: The Great Plains*; ALA; ILA; AECT; IEMA; KEA; Chm AASL/*Encyclopedia Britannica* Sch Media Ctr of Yr Awd Com 1976; r/Luth; hon/W/W Among Students in Am Cols & Univs; Beta Phi Mu.

LaVELLE, FAITH WILSON oc/Associate Professor; b/Mar 14, 1921; h/642 Highland Ave, Elmhurst, IL 60126; ba/Maywood, IL; m/Arthur; c/Audrey Anne; p/Theodore H Wilson, Penney Farms, FL; Faith H Wilson (dec); ed/BA, MA Mt Holyoke Col; PhD Johns Hopkins Univ; pa/Loyola Univ Med Ctr: Assoc Prof Anatomy, Admissions Com; Reschr; cp/Nat Pres Camp Fire Girls Inc; r/Prot; hon/Res Grant, USPHS; Medal of Hon, Mt Holyoke Col Alumnae; Sev Tchg Awds; Camp Fire Gulick Awd.

LAW, RALPH AREGOOD oc/Division Manager, Chief Chemist; b/Nov 20, 1927; h/1934 Rambling Ridge Ln, Carrollton, TX 75007; ba/Dallas, TX; m/Frances Adair; c/David Bruce, Leslie Claire Krieger, Brian Duncan; p/Ralph Aregood Law (dec); Frances Louise Law, Little Rock, AR; ed/BA Univ

Ark; mil/USN Air Corps 1946-48; pa/Ecology Audits Inc, Dallas: Div Mgr, Chief Chemist Water Sers; Am Chem Soc; Water Pollution Control Fdn; Okla Water Resources Bd Certn; Tex Air Control Bd, Certn Visible Emissions; Contb'g Author "Subsurface Geology"; cp/Repub; r/Epis; hon/ATO Silver Cir Awd; W/W S&SW; Personalities of S.

LAWRENCE, GLADYS WILKINSON oc/Association Executive; b/May 30, 1904; h/10467 Sunset Blvd, Bel Air, Los Angeles, CA 90024; m/Paul William Sr (dec); c/Paul William Jr; p/Richard and Sarah Rees Wilkinson; ed/BA Univ Nebraska; cp/Fdr, Nat Charity League; Nat Flower Guild; Footlighters; Life Mem: Social Ser Aux, Good Shepherd Guild, St Anne's Guild; CoFdr, Las Benevolas of Assit League; Patroness of Am Debutante Ball in Vienna, Austria; Costume Coun, LA Co Museum of Art; Past Pres: Wom's Breakfast Clb, Univ of Nebraska Alumni, LA Chapt Gamma Phi Beta; Former VP, Delta Omicron; Dun & Bradstreet's Millionaires of Am; Others; r/Epis; hon/Hon Ky Colonel; Admiral of Gt Navy of Nebraska; W/W: Cal, Am Wom, E, Geneology, LA, NAm Authors, Commerce & Indust, Others.

LAWRENCE, JAYE A oc/Artist; b/Jan 8, 1939; h/2097 Valley View Blvd, El Cajon, CA 92021; ba/Same; m/Les; c/Laurie L; p/Harvey L and Mina Kirk Ackman, Scottsdale, AZ; ed/BFA; MFA; pa/Allied Craftsmen San Diego; Am Crafts Coun; Num Exhbns incl: Objets En Cuir, USA, Galerie Coach Bag, Paris France 1978, Allied Craftsmen San Diego Exhbn, San Diego Univ Art Gallery 1978, The Gt Am Hort, Mus Contemp Crafts, New York City 1978, San Diego Fine Arts Mus 1977, Others; Group Shows incl: Spectrum Gallery (San Diego) 1977, Am Craftsmen Gallery (NYC) 1975, SWn Col (Chula Visa, Cal) 1973, Others; One-Person Shows: Grossmont Col (El Cajon) 1976, Limner Gallery (Scottsdale, Ariz) 1975, Palomar Col (San Marcos, Cal) 1974, Others; r/Unitarian; hon/Rep'd in Public Collections: Yuma Fine Arts Assn (Yuma, Ariz), Ariz St Univ Art Dept Collection (Tempe, Ariz), Pacific Luth Univ Collection (Tacoma, Wash).

LAWRENCE, REGGIE RAY oc/Bank Executive; b/Feb 7, 1947; h/Kencindot St, McKenzie, TN 38201; ba/McKenzie, TN; m/Susan Marie; c/Benjamin Todd; p/Barney Joseph Lawrence (dec); Wynona Elizabeth Lawrence, McKenzie; ed/Att'd Tenn Yg Bkrs Sch,

Vanderbilt Univ; mil/USANG 1966-67; pa/Asst VP Bk McLemoresville; cp/Coun City McKenzie; Co Commr Carroll Co; Local & St JCs; Pres' Clb, Tenn JCs; r/Bapt; hon/Tenn JCs: Top Reg VP 1974-75, Top Nat Dir 1976-77.

LAWS, MILAS TIMOTHY (TIM) oc/- Drivers License Examiner II; b/Apr 21, 1944; h/Rt 1, Box 58A, Boone, NC 28607; ba/- Boone; m/Frances Louise Townsend; c/- Angela Joice; p/Joe Donley Sr and Helen

Blanche Benfield Laws, Hickory; ed/Att'd Catawba Val Tech Sch; H&R Block; pa/NC St Drivers Lic'g Prog: Examr II 1978-, Examr I 1973-78 (Gastonia); Gen Elect Co, Hickory: Factory Helper, Coil Winder, Tank Fabricator; cp/Dem; r/Bapt; hon/Lttr of Apprec for Helping Cut Costs Drivers Ser Sect St Govt, Gov Jim Hunt.

LAWSON, THEODORE EARL oc/- Executive Director; b/Apr 29, 1941; h/4403 Bilboa Dr, Austin, TX 78759; ba/Austin; m/Nancy Sue Wilson; c/Michael L, Larry D, Kristin L, Jay E, F L Rick Mellish, D Scott Mellish, Clarissa Renee Mellish; p/Earl L and Vera M Heitschmidt Lawson, Ashland, OR; ed/BA Univ Ks 1963; MST Portland St Univ

1970; mil/USAFR 1963-65, Maj; pa/Exec Dir Tex Dental Assn; Former Exec Dir Spokane Co Med Soc; Am Assn Med Soc Execs; Am Soc Assn Execs; Wash Soc Assn Execs; Spokane Public Relats Coun; Wash St Public Hlth Assn; cp/Bd Dirs Spokane Hlth; Govt Affairs Com, Spokane Area C of C; r/Unity Ch of Truth; hon/Geo Wash Freedom's Foun Medal; AF Commend Medal.

LAWSON, VERNA REBECCA oc/Educator; b/Apr 7, 1943; h/335 Lantana Rd, Crossville, TN 38555; ba/Daytona Beach, FL; p/Hoarce Freeman Lawson (dec); Zera Currie Lawson, Crossville; ed/BS; MS; PhD; Cert German Goethe Inst (Luneburg, Germany); pa/Chm Div Sci & Math Bethune-Cookman Col; ASPP; AIBS; AAAS; ASHS; Weed Sci Soc; Torrey Botanical Soc; ISHS; AAUP; CAST; cp/Smithsonian Inst; r/Bapt; hon/Beta Beta Beta; Sigma Xi.

LAY, FRANCES BALLARD oc/Author; Free-lance Writer; b/Feb 23, 1919; h/PO Box 64, Summersville, KY 42782; ba/Same; c/Denise, Mark A; p/Charles Levans and Olive Thornhill Ballard (dec); ed/Cert Interior Design; pa/Reg Animal Breeder; Exhibitor; cp/Charter Mem SPCA; Vol Red Cross; Ret'd Ofcl C of C; PTA; Cert, Spec Awd Bible Study & Achmt; hon/Awds: C of C, BCA; Spec Awd in Field of Writing; Others.

LAY, MARY ALICE oc/College Administrator; b/Apr 23, 1939; h/242 Cumberland Ave, Barbourville, KY 40906; ba/B'ville; ed/BS; MS; Adv'd Studies Ind Univ & Univ SD; pa/Union Col: Dir Alumni, Dir Home Ecs Prog; Am & Ky Home Ecs Assns; AAUW; Delta Kappa Gamma; Kappa Delta Pi; Phi Upsilon Omicron; cp/DAR; Knox Co Hosp Aux; Repub; r/U Meth: Lay Delegate to Ky Conf; hon/DAR: Ky Outstg Jr Mem, Outstg Jr Mem E Ctl Reg; Outstg Yg Wom Am; Personalities S; Nat Reg Prom Ams; World W/W Wom.

LAYMAN, JOHN WHITNEY oc/- Accountant; b/Oct 21, 1947; h/224 Parker Heights, Waynesboro, VA 22980; ba/- Staunton, VA; p/Minor A and Lois A Layman, W'boro; ed/BS Va Polytech & St Univ; mil/USN Petty Ofcr; pa/Acct Smith's Transfer Corp; Delta Sigma Pi; Nat Assn Accts; cp/JCs: Chapt Ofcr, Dist Ofcr, Va JCs;

Moose; Elks; Repub Party; MC Miss Crimora Ruritan Pageant 1979; r/Main St Meth Ch, W'boro; hon/1 of 6 Outstg St Dirs, Va JCs; JCs: Outstg Mem Dist & Reg, Outstg Dir Dist & Reg, 1 of 10 Most Activs Local Chapt, Recog'd for Outstg Ser to Reg, Dir Yr Local Chapt 1976-77, Chapt JC of Month.

LAZAROW, ARTHUR oc/Radio Station Executive; b/Mar 3, 1927; h/PO Box 673, Gloucester, VA 23061; ba/Same; m/Joan R Daniels; c/Arthur Jr, Susan Ruth, Linda Lee; p/Joseph and Sophie Lazarow (dec); ed/BA 1950, MA 1956 Wayne St Univ; mil/AUS 1945-46; pa/Pres & Gen Mgr Radio Sta WDDY; Dir: Bk West Point, 1st Settlers Bk, Old Dominion Eye Bk; Chm Bd Rappahannock Commun Col; cp/Pres Gloucester C of C; Past Dist Gov Lions Intl; Past Gov Ruritan Nat; r/Cath.

LEACOCK, INGRID CARMEN oc/Freelance Journalist; b/Apr 23, 1947; h/2130 Broadway, New York, NY 10023; ba/NYC; c/Stephen; p/James and Elizabeth Razack, NYC; ed/BA w hons CCNY; MA Cand New Sch for Social Res; pa/Tchr Guyana (NY); Poet; Broadcaster; Corres Archdiocese NY 1966-68; Asst Editor Newslttr Intl Ctr (NY) 1972-74; Assoc Mem ASCAP; Bd Dirs Visual Individs U; r/Cath; hon/IBC; World W/W Wom.

LEAF, ALBERT L oc/Professor; b/May 16, 1928; ba/SUNY Col Envir Sci & Forestry, Syracuse, NY 13210; m/Wilma Lorraine Parker; p/Aaron and Dora Leaf; ed/BS Univ Wash-S 1950; MForestry 1952; PhD Univ Wis-M 1957; mil/USN AF V-5 Prog, 1 Yr; pa/SUNY Col Envir Sci & Forestry: Current Prof Forest Soil Sci & Proj Ldr; Fac Exc Scholar 1974-; Vis Prof Tokyo Univ Agri & Technol 1972-73; Invited Lectr: Tottori Univ, Kyushu Univ, Nippon Univ, Forest Fertilization Soc Japan; Lectr Univ Toronto & Univ Col Dublin (Ireland); Mem 5-Person Team US Foresters Invited to Turkey 1977; AAAS; Soil Sci Soc Am; Sigma Xi; Soils Comman US Forest Ser Pinchot Consortium; Phi Sigma; Xi Sigma Pi; CoChm Soils Resource Subcom, Forest Resource Com, NE Reg Long Range Nat Resources Res Planning Task Force USDA; Invited Participant Num Nat & Intl Congs devoted to forestry & related fields; hon/Pub'd Author; Num Biogl Listings.

LEAHY, MIRIAM KRAMER

oc/Homemaker; Volunteer; b/Nov 6, 1891; h/3325 Garfield St, Washington, DC 20008; m/(dec); p/Thomas B and Luanna C Kramer, Wash DC; cp/Vol ARC, Georgetown Univ Hosp; r/Epis; hon/Hon LLD, G'town Univ; Cit, ARC.

LEASK, BARBARA GLENN WALLACE oc/School Teacher; b/Oct 7, 1925; h/2907 Christmas Tree Ln, Bakersfield, CA 93306; m/Richard H; c/Jerelyn L Harrington, Larry, Wally; p/Joel Glenn and Doris C Wallace, B'field; ed/AA; BA; MA; PhD; pa/Wingland Sch: Chm Christmas Prog Standard Sch Dist, Chm Freedom Foun Scrapbook 1973-76, Dir Glee Clb Standard Sch, Bldg Rep 2 Yrs, Kern

Co Textbook Com 2 Yrs; Pres AAUW 1977-78; Standard Sch Dist Tchrs Assn: 1/VP & Pres Elect 1977-78; NEA; CAl Tchr's Assn; IRA; cp/Assoc Mem Assistance Leag; Wom's Chapt Freedoms Foun Val Forge, Kern Co Chapt; YWCA; Wom's Clb Bakersfield: Life Mem, Bd Mem, Chmships; Symph Assocs Kern Co Philharm Assn; OES: Past Pres, Past Matron; B'field Col Alumni Assn; Others; r/1st Presb Ch; hon/Tchrs Medal, Freedoms Foun Val Forge; Outstg Elem Tchr Am Awd; Profl of Yr Awd, Standard Sch Dist 1973-74; Intl W/W Commun Ser; World W/W Wom; Notable Ams; W/W Am Wom.

LEASURE, BETTY JEAN oc/Homemaker; b/July 11, 1925; h/552 Kappel St, New Martinsvle, WV 26155; m/John Frank; p/Francis Marion and Susan Olive Blake Cross (dec); ed/Att'd West Liberty St Col & WV No Commun Col; pa/Former Glass Etcher; Poet; Author: "Summer Theme", "Christmas Theme", "Thanksgiving Theme", "St Patrick's Day" (all poems); Contbr to World Treasury of Gt Poems, The Gen Poem Book, Pageants of Poetry, Best Loved Contemp Poems in World Poetry; Essayist; Author, Betty's Gems (1980); Stella Woodall Poetry Soc; Gtr Nat Soc of Poets Inc; cp/Var Civic Activs; r/Ch of Nazarene: Christian Ser Tng; SS Tchr; Others; hon/Cert of Bible Memorization Awd; Consecrated Ser Awd; World W/W Wom; DDA; Commun Ldrs Am; Others.

LEATHERBURY, JOHN RAYMOND JR oc/Electrical Engineer; b/Jun 22, 1942; h/2420 College Ave, Ft Worth, TX 76110; ba/Ft Worth; p/John R and Hester Hoffecker Leatherbury, Ft Worth; ed/BSEE Univ Tex 1965; mil/USMC; pa/IEEE; cp/Arts Coun Ft Worth Art Mus; Friends of Alec; Secy EE Class 1965 UT; Former Mem Coun Sectors; r/St John's Epis Ch: Vestryman, Lay Reader, SS Tchr; hon/Mem David W Leatherbury S'ship Com.

LEAVER, VINCENT WAYNE oc/Minister, Director; b/Aug 21, 1947; h/1426 NW 83rd Terr, Miami, FL 33147; ba/Miami; m/Diane; c/Meredith; p/Vincent Hill Leaver (dec); Doris Eddins Leaver, Birmingham, AL; ed/BA; MDiv; PhD Cand; pa/Current Pastor Sellers Meml U Meth Ch, Miami; Min to Yth, Assoc Pastor & Pastor of Chs in Ala, Ga, Md & Fla 1967-77; Meth Chaplain Univ Tampa 1970-71; Lic'd to Preach 1964; Miami Dist Coun Mins: Mem 1976, Chperson 1977, Agenda Bldg Task Force, Res Com 1976-77; Bd Mem Miami Dist Urban Mins 1976-77; Tchg Del US Cong on Evang, Minneapolis,

Minn 1969; Other Tchg Activs; Assn for Clin Pastoral Ed; cp/Ams for Dem Action; Acad Polit Sci; Acad Polit & Social Sci; Common Cause; US-China Peoples Friendship Assn; Pres Clb Nat Dem Party; Former Dir Sellers Day Care Ctr; Bd Mem Northside Neighborhood Fam, Miami; Var Former Activs; r/U Meth; hon/W/W: Rel, S; Notable Ams Bicent Era; Men of Achmt.

LEAVITT, GLADYS G oc/Bank Executive; b/Oct 2, 1920; h/1454 W Flournoy, Chicago, IL 60607; ba/Chgo; m/Alex E; c/Stanley S, Adrienne R Stevens; p/Benjamin and Dora Ziff Levinson (dec); pa/VP Nat Republic Bk; cp/Pres Adv Bd Ill Hosp Sch for Crippled Chd; Bd Mem Cabrini Hosp Guild; Bd Mem Near W Side Adv Bd; Mem Gail Ditore Hotchkins Foun; Others; hon/Accountability Awd, Chronicle Newspaper; Hon Awd, Columbus-Cuneo-Cabrini Hosp; Awd, Ill St Hosp Sch for Crippled Chd; W/W Am Wom.

LeBLANC, VERA ADORE oc/Registered Nurse; Teacher Coordinator; b/Apr 17, 1929; h/1517 Franklin Ave, Nederland, TX 77627; ba/Nederland; m/Carl Nelson; c/Vicki Anne, Danny Michael, Greg Alan, Matthew Wayne, Terry Joseph; p/Clyde Floyd and Vera Alletta

Langworthy (dec); ed/RN; BS; pa/Tex Nurses Assn; Am Nurses Assn; Tex St Tchrs Assn; NEA; Tex Classroom Tchrs Assn; cp/Phi Sigma Alpha; YMCA; Little Leag; Jr Ftball Leag; Bd Mem Mar Dimes; Jefferson Co Teen Advr; r/Rom Cath; hon/Valedictorian, St Mary's Sch Nsg 1950; W/W Am Wom; World W/W Wom.

LeCOMPTE, PEGGY LEWIS oc/Teacher; h/212 Bunker Hill Rd, Belleville, IL 62221; ba/E St Louis, IL; m/Larry Ferdinand Sr; c/Larry F Jr; p/Obadiah Sr and Winnie L Lewis, St Louis; ed/BS; Masters Cand; pa/Tchr of Gifted, Lang Arts, Dept Hd; NCTE; Ill Coun Tchrs Eng; Metro-E Eng Tchrs Assn; Lang Arts Textbook Eval Com 1976; Ill St Eval Team 1975-76; Cont'g Editor Spectrum Newspaper, Dist 189; Crusader Newspaper: Columnist, Soc Edito.; cp/Public Relats Chperson Soc Ethnic & Spec Ser; Rec'g Secy Bd Dirs E St Louis Br NAACP; Corr Secy Bd Dirs St Clair Co Comprehensive Mtl Hlth Ctr; Pres: E St Louis Chapt Jack & Jill Am Inc, Bd Dirs Boys' Clb E St Louis; Corr Secy E St Louis Urban Leag Guild; Mem St Commun Col Adv Bd; 1/VP, Charter Mem Metro-E Lioness Clb; Alpha Kappa Alpha: Reg Dir, Past Pres Delta Delta Omega Chapt, Mem Bd Dirs; Others; r/Wesley-Bethel U Meth Ch: Mem, Choir, Hlth & Wel Com, Public Relats Com; Pres Bd Dirs Metro-E U Meth Coun; hon/Outstg Ser Awd, E St Louis Br NAACP; Citizen of Week

Awds: Radio Sta WRTH & KKSS; Dist'd Citizen Awd, Rep Wyvetter Younge; Tchr of Yr, Zeta Phi Beta 1977; Commun Ser Awd, Wom of Essence; Others.

LeCROY, RUTH BROOKS oc/Writer; Christian Science Practitioner; h/1601 W 8, Little Rock, AR 72202; p/Joshua King and Rosa Ella Thomson LeCroy (dec); r/Christian Scist; hon/Var Biogl Listings.

LEDFORD, HORACE B oc/Administrator; b/Nov 22, 1931; h/1214 Brookwood Rd, Shelby, NC 28150; ba/Shelby; m/Shirley Pritchard; c/Lisa Kaye; p/C W and Claudie Ledford; ed/Grad Howard's Bus Col; Gardner-Webb Col; Wake Forest Univ; mil/USN 1950-54; Good Conduct Medal; Navy Unit Commend Medal; UN Ser Medal; Nat Def Medal; Korean Pres Unit Cit; Others; pa/Dover Textiles 1963-: Dir Indust Relats, Tng & Placemt Dir, Pers Dir; Sales Promotion Dir Colgate-Palmolive Co 1959-63; Am Soc Pers Admrs; Am Soc Tng Dirs; NC Pers Assn; Nat Assn Mfrs; Am Mgmt Assn; Alpha Kappa Psi; Phi Theta Phi; Charter Pres Cleveland Indust Relat's Assn; cp/Dir Shelby Rotary Clb; Toastmaster Intl Clb; VFW; Dir Blue Ridge Safety Conf; Dir UF; Pres Cleveland Co Heart Assn; Bd Dirs NC Heart Assn; Com on Civil Def; Dir Boys' Clb Am; Dir & Pres CODAP; Dir: ARC, Am Cancer Soc; Panel Mem Bur Nat Affairs Wash; r/Ross Grove Bapt Ch; hon/Toastmaster of Yr; Cleve Co Heart Assn: Fdrs Awd, Bronze Medallion, Silver Engraved Medallion; W/W: S&SW, Fin & Indust; DIB.

LEDFORD, KENNETH AVERY oc/-Personnel Manager; b/Sept 29, 1946; h/PO Box 262, Polkville, NC 28136; ba/Lawndale, NC; m/Janet Pruitt; c/Michael Kenneth; p/Fred Arthur and Mary McNeilly Ledford, Casar, NC; ed/AA Gardner Webb Col 1966; BS Wn Carolina Univ 1968; Addit Studies; mil/AUS 1968-70, Served in Vietnam 11 Months; Sev Mil Decorations; pa/Pers Mgr Cleveland Mills Co; Cleve Co Indust Relats Assn; Past Mem Am Soc for Pers Admrs; cp/Bd Dirs Cleve Co Chapt Am Cancer Soc; Bd Dirs Cleve Co Chapt ARC; Bd Dirs Upper Cleve Co C of C; Former Chm Upper Cleve Co Water Sys Project; Former Chm Bd Dirs Upper Cleve Area Needs; Mem Reg C Manpower Adv Com; VChm Polkville Dem Precnt; Lawndale Lions Clb: Mem, Past Pres, Treas; Former Boy Scout Com-man; Others; r/Lawndale Bapt Ch: Mem, Past Chm Bd Deacons, Past Brotherhood Pres, Past SS Supt, Former Adult SS Dir; Assn Royal Ambassador (RA) Dir Kings Mtn Bapt Assn 1975-; NC RA Com 1977-78; NC Bapt Mens & Brotherhood Fin Com 1979; hon/John L Stickley Awd; Ser Awd, NC Assn for Blind; Outstg White Cane Chm; Cleve Co Citizen of Yr 1978 (1st); Outstg Yg Men Am; Outstg CARE Com Chm; Cert of Merit, Am Cancer Soc; W/W S&SW.

LEE, ANNA MARIE oc/Realtor; Mortgage Broker; b/Aug 8, 1936; h/418 El Greco Dr, Brandon, FL 33511; ba/Brandon; m/James Winston; c/William D, Thomas A, Elizabeth A, Marilyn E; p/Joseph Anthony and Elizabeth Marcano, Brandon, FL; ed/Att'd: St Mary's Univ 1957-58, Hillsborough Commun Col 1972-73; Grad Realtor's Inst 1975; mil/USAF 1954-56; pa/Lectr Real Est Sems, Brandon & Tampa; Served on ReState Panels, Tampa; Fal BPW Assn; Fla Mortgage Brokers Assn; Nat Home Bldrs Assn; Tampa & Nat Bd Realtors; cp/Co Comm; St House & Senate Campaigns; St Gov's Campaign; Dem Party; r/Rom Cath; hon/W/W Am Wom.

LEE, FELICIA S W oc/Librarian; b/Oct 19, 1938; h/6138 Bent Tree, Charlotte, NC 28212; ba/Charlotte; m/Thomas A; c/Heidi; p/Felix and Muriel Schroetel, Anderson, SC; ed/BS Univ Me 1960; MS La St Univ 1962; pa/Libn Rohn Univ; Am Lib Assn; Spec Libs Assn; NC Lib Assn; Metrolina Lib Assn.

LEE, RICHARD GEORGE oc/Evangelist; b/Jul 1, 1946; h/PO Box 20789, Atlanta, GA 30320; ba/Same; m/Judith Starr; c/Christopher Jason, Tonya Elizabeth; p/W B

and Ongie Hitt Lee, Conley, GA; ed/BA Mercer Univ; MDiv Luther Rice Sem; pa/So Bapt Evangelist 1978-; Fdr, Pres Richard G Lee Evang Assn Inc; Pastor New Hope Bapt Ch 1974-78; r/So Bapt.

LEEDS, SYLVIA C oc/Director Financial Development; b/Aug 21, 1926; h/290 Bal Bay Dr, Bal Harbour, FL 33154; m/William (dec); c/3 Sons; p/Max and Kate Meisner Zuckerman; ed/BA Bklyn Col 1946; MA Univ Del 1968; PhD Courses Queens Col 1968; Case Wn Resv Univ 1969-70; pa/Ursuline Col: Asst Prof Dept Commun Arts 1970, Acting Dept Chm 1970-71, Dept Chm 1971-73, Public Relats Dir 1973-74, Dir Fin Devel 1974-76; Dir Fin Devel Cleveland (Ohio) YWCA 1976-79; Nat Patron Phi Beta; AAUW; AAUW; Coun World Affairs; cp/Gov Nelson Rockefeller's Coun for Wom; Parents Assn PS 199, Pres; hon/World W/W Wom; Book of Honor; Notable Ams.

LEEDY, DWIGHT ADRIAN oc/Science Teacher; b/Apr 7, 1947; h/21 Union St, Gorham, NH 03581; ba/Berlin, NH; p/William N and Emily L Leedy, Berea, OH; ed/BS Baldwin-Wallace Col; MS Univ Vt; pa/Sci Tchr Berlin Jr HS 1973-; Staff Devel Com; Vt Inst Natural Scis; Ohio Forestry Assn; Nat Audubon Soc; Nat Wildlife Fdn; cp/BSA: Dist Com, Merit Badge Cnslr; r/Disciples of Christ; hon/Grad Tchg F'ship, Univ Vt; NSF Undergrad Res Participation F'ship; Other F'ships; Jr Conservationist of Ohio 1965, Ohio Forestry Assn; Eagle Scout, BSA; DIB; Intl Reg Profiles; Commun Ldrs & Noteworthy Ams; Book of Honor; Intl W/W: Intells, Commun Ser; Men of Achmt.

LEETE-SPAULDING, HELEN AMES oc/Financial Planner, Insurance; b/Mar 3, 1913; h/PO Box 1623, 1619 Greenland Dr, Murfreesboro, TN 37130; m/Eugene F Voit (dec); 2nd Albert Edward Carpenter; c/2 Chd; p/Theodore Coomes Leete; George Olive Marr Ames Leete Spaulding; ed/Att'd Univ Mo 1951, Hunter Col NYC 1960; Addit Studies; pa/Agt w 4 Investmt Cos in Palm Bch & Ofc Mgr 1 Area Zone 1966-71; Exec In-Charge Pers B Ray Robbins Co (Investmts), NYC 1959-60; w Radio Sta WCAX, Burlington, Vt 1944 & Petrometal Co, Long Isl City, NY 1942-43; Other Profl Activs; cp/Fdr & Past Pres Forgotten Generation Inc, NYC; Soc Mayflower Descendents; Jr Leag; Soc Four Arts & Flagler Mus; Former Mem IPA; hon/Author: Self Help Plan (Forgotten Generation), Presented Plan to Govt of India 1961 & to US Lib of Cong & Others, Preceded Peace Corps; Other Pubs; DIB; Foremost Wom in Communs; Notable Ams Bicent Era; World W/W Wom; Others.

LEFFT, JOSEPH DANIEL oc/Educator; b/Jan 8, 1936; h/2113 Chestnut St, Orangeburg, SC 29115; ba/Holly Hill, SC; m/Winifred G; c/Joseph R, Joyce, Charmaine; p/Joseph E and Emily Lefft, St Stephen, SC; ed/BS, MEd; Further Studies Geo Wash Univ; mil/Former Maj, Resvs; pa/Elem Sch Prin; SC Ed Assn; NEA; cp/Master Mason; r/Trinity U Meth Ch: Mem; hon/Bronze Star; Army Commend Medal.

LEHL, MABEL BOWMAN oc/Administrator; b/Aug 6, 1917; h/346 N Cammann, Coos Bay, OR 97420; ba/Coos Bay; m/George Peter; c/Phyllis Brostrom (Mrs Glenn W), Harvey C Golbek, Leslie P Golbek Jr, Dorothy Myers, Louise Robb (Mrs Kenneth R); p/Ben Franklin and Dycie Ellen Bowmen (dec); ed/Assoc SWn Oreg Commun Col 1965; BS 1968, MEd 1970, MS 1971 Univ Oreg; pa/Dir Ed Eval Ctr, Coos Co Intermediate Ed Dist 1976-; Tchr-Cnslr Emotionally Disturbed Sec'dy 1971-75; Tchr Jr HS 1969-70; N Bend BP Clb; cp/Bay Area Soroptimists; r/1st Presb Ch, N Bend, Oreg; hon/Scholastic Awd, SWOC.

LEHMAN, HYLA BEROEN oc/Educator; Performing Artist; h/4347 Eaglemere Ct SE, Cedar Rapids, IA 52403; m/Fredrick B; c/Rolfe Beroen, Rhea Helene; p/Lewis B and Helene Hagen Beroen (dec); ed/BSE w hons Drake Univ; MA Univ Ia; Addit Studies;

pa/Fac Theatre Arts Coe Col, Cedar Rapids; Former Mem Fac Eng & Drama Alexandria (Va) & Des Moines (Ia); Phi Mu Gamma: Nat Pres, Nat Alumni Dir; AAUW: St Pres Ia Div, St Arts Chm; Perf'g Artist Dance Theatre Hemispheres; Perfs incl: Elizabethan Twelfth Night, Nutcracker, Chidambaram Karanas, Stations of the Cross, Others; cp/Curric Com Public Schs; Chm Linn Co Chapt Am Cancer Soc; hon/Dist'd Alum Awd, Waldorf Col; Kappa Delta Pi; Phi Theta Kappa.

LEHMAN, LEONARD oc/Assistant Commissioner; b/Jul 5, 1927; h/5008 Alta Vista Rd, Bethesda, MD 20014; ba/Washington, DC; m/Imogene; c/Jeffrey, Toby, Amy, Zachary; p/Samuel and Marcy Lehman (dec); ed/BA Cornell Univ 1949; JD Yale Law Sch 1952; pa/Asst Commr, Regulations & Rulings US Customs Ser; ABA; Fed Bar Assn; Am Judic Soc; cp/B'nai B'rith; r/Jewish; hon/Phi Beta Kappa; Phi Kappa Phi; Yal Law Jour; Meritorious Ser Awd, US Treas Dept; Customs Hon Awd; Others.

LEHRHOFF, IRWIN oc/Licensed Psychologist; Licensed Speech Pathologist; b/Jun 4, 1929; h/3627 Cody Rd, Sherman Oaks, CA 91403; ba/Beverly Hills, CA; m/Barbara; c/Terri, Debra, Howard, Steven; p/Carl and Esther Lehrhoff, Miami Beach, FL; ed/MA 1949; PhD 1954; pa/Pvt Pract, Pres Irwin Lehrhoff, PhD & Assocs 1954-78; Dir Dept Commun Disorders Harbor Gen Hosp, Torrance, Cal 1955-58; Dir Dept Commun Disorders Chds Hosp, Los Angeles, Cal 1950-55; Adv Bd Am Acad Child Psychi; Reiss-Davis Chd Study Ctr; Am Acad Pvt Pract Spch Pathol & Audiol; Dir, Nat Pres 1974-78; Am Assn Marriage & Fam Cnslrs; Fellow Am Orthopsychi Assn; APA; AAAS; Cal Psychol Assn; Cal Spch Pathologists & Audiologists in Pvt Prac; ASHA; NY Acad Sci; Intl Soc Mtl Hlth; Others; cp/Dist Attys Adv Coun; Thalians Pres's Clb: Fdr, Chm; Thalians Commun Mtl Hlth Ctr, Cedars-Sinai Mtl Ctr; Others; r/Jewish; hon/Profl Pubs; Contbr to Num Med & Profl Jours; Am Men of Sci; W/W: Am Ed, W; Ldrs in Am Sci; Nat Reg Prom Ams & Intl Notables; Personalities W&MW; DIB; Intl W/W Commun Ser; Royal Blue Book; Others.

LEIDIG, MELVIN DWIGHT oc/Minister; Counselor; Social Worker; b/Aug 3, 1925; h/1939 Third St SE, Canton, OH 44707; ba/Same; m/Lois Gisel; c/Shari Jean, Debra Anne; p/Reuben G and Emily M Leidig (dec); ed/AA; ThB; BS; MA; pa/Pastor: 1st Mennonite Ch, Canton 1974-, Moorepark Mennonite Ch, Three Rivers (Mich) 1972-74, Grace Chapel, Saginaw (Mich) 1955-72; Cnslr Dept Labor, Battle Creek, Mich 1970-72; Social Wkr: Starr Commonwealth for Boys,

Albion, Mich 1972-73, Jenkins Rehab Ctr, Kalamazoo 1974; Nat Assn Social Wkrs; Christian Assn Psychol Studies; APGA; Nat Assn Christians in Social Work; Nat Chaplains Assn; Mtl Hlth Profls; Alpha Psi Omega; Assn Christian Marriage Cnslrs; cp/Former Mem Mayor's Task Force on Crime & Task Force Stark Tech Col; Former Mem Adv Com Sch Supts; r/Mennonite Ch; hon/Commun Ldrs & Noteworthy Ams; W/W: Rel, MW; Intl W/W Commun Ser; DIB.

LEIFERMAN, SILVIA WEINER oc/Artist, Sculptor, Collector of Objects d'Art, Designer of Jewelry, Civic Worker; h/Standard Clb Suite 812, 3205 Plymouth Ct, Chgo, IL 60604; m/Irwin Hamilton; p/Annah Caplan Weiner; ed/Univ Chgo 1960-61; Ext Study Design & Painting; Chgo, Mexico, Rome, Madrid & Provincetown, Mass; pa/Corp Activs: Active Accessories by Silvia, Chgo 1964, Silvia & Irwin H Leiferman Foun (VP & Secy), Leiferman Investmt Corp (VP & Secy); Orig & Orgr of Num Charitable & Social Events w Many Chmships & CoChmships; Art Inst Chgo (Life Mem); IPA; Am Fdn Arts; Artists Equity Assn Inc, Chgo & Miami; Intl Coun Mus; Patron & Mem Miami Art Ctr; Gtr Miami Cult Art Ctr; Lowe Art Mus; Ft Lauderdale Mus Arts; Life Fellow Royal Soc Arts & Scis; Life Mem Miami Mus Mod Art; Num Painting Exhbns, 1-Wom & Group Shows; Art Work Shown in Var Media; Works Rep'd in Pvt Collections; cp/Former Bd Mem: Nathan Goldblatt Soc Cancer Res (Life Mem,Trusteeship), George & Ann Portes Cancer Preven Ctr Chgo Inc, Mt Sinai Hosp, N Shore Wom Aux of Mary Lawrence Jewish Chd's Bur; Bd Mem: Nat Coun Jewish Wom, Fox River Sanitorium, Temple Sholom, Brandeis Univ (Life Mem), Edgewater Hosp, Org Rehab & Tng, Charter Mem Wom's Div Hebrew Univ Chgo; Charter Mem Sponsor Clb WPBT Channel 2, Miami; 1st Annual Cult Conf Chgo; Wom's Div: Edgewater Hosp, Hebrew Univ; Mem Nat Bd Govs Bonds for Israel; Miami Bch Opera Guild; Donor: Gift Shop & 7th Floor Reception Room Edgewater Hosp, Conf Room Mary Lawrence Jewish Chd'd Bur, Yeshiva Univ NYC, Michael Reese Hosp, Miami Heart Inst, BSA; Patron of the Arts; Social Clbs: Westview CC, Intl, Boyer, Whitehall, Key, Covenant, Standard, Green Acres CC, Bryn Mawr CC; Num Other Civic Activs; hon/2000 Wom Achmt, 1st Edition Dedication & Pub'd w Her Memoirs, 1969; Nat Reg Prom Ams & Intl Notables; W/W: Art in Am, World, Am, Fin & Indust, Am Wom, World Jewry, Commerce & Indust, Arts & Antiques, Intl Bus-men, US, Israel, Also Spec Jubilee Issue; Nat Social Dir; Ill Lives; Am Honorarium; Israeli Honorarium; Royal Blue Book; Personalities of: S, W&MW; Bd Govs Lib W/W, Marquis W/W Inc; DIB (Merit Awd); Book of Honor; Lib Cong Achmt Recog Recog Inst; Presented Key to 5 Metro Cities of Miami & Surrounding Cos; 1st Israel Bond Cit; For Dist'd Ser w Insignia of Her Majesty Queen Elizabeth II, Cambridge, England; St Israel Achmt Awd, Chgo; Recog for Ldrship & Achmt from Secy Treas St Israel, Wom of Valor Awd; Cotillion Fdr's Awd, Chgo; "Pro Mundi Beneficio" Gold Medal, Brazilian Acad Humanities 1976; Silver Medal, Intl W/W Art & Antiques; Num Other Awds & Hons.

LEIMAN, ROBERT W oc/Assistant to Principal; h/3030 S Harrison St, Ft Wayne, IN 46807; ba/Ft Wayne; m/Ellen; c/Ronald, Mary Ellen, Sandy Sue, Debbie; p/William J Leiman (dec); Neva Leiman, Mansfield, OH; ed/BS; MEd; mil/AUS 3½ Yrs, Sgt; pa/Asst to Prin Wayne HS; Life Mem NEA; Phi Delta Kappa; cp/Mason; Jr Optimist Ldr; Toastmaster; Cert'd Profl Parliamentn; r/Presb: Elder; hon/Dist'd Toastmaster; Dist'd Awd, JCs; Outstg Nat Chm, US JCs; Others.

LEIN, CHARLES D oc/University President; b/Nov 2, 1941; h/1028 Valley View Dr, Vermillion, SD 57069; ba/Vermillion; m/Susan; c/Kent, Keith, Steven, Greg; p/H D Lein (dec); Willa Lein, Rapid City, SD; ed/BS Augustana Col; MS, EdD Univ Wyo; pa/Univ SD, Vermillion: Pres, Prof Mgmt Sch Bus 1977-, (Pres Univ SD-Springfield) 1977-; Prof & Dean Sch Bus Boise St Univ, Boise 1973-77; Assoc Prof Bus & Chm Dept Bus Adm Weber St Col, Ogden, Utah 1970-73; Other Former Positions; Bd Mem: Black Hills Playhouse Corp (Univ SD), Bd Trustees Univ Mid-Am (Lincoln, Neb), The Karl E Mundt Hist & Ednl Foun (Madison, SD), SD Shrine to Music Foun (Univ SD); Chm N Ctl Conf of Presidents 1978-79; Chm SD Bd Regents Coun Presidents 1978-79; Lay Rep Public Broadcasting Ser, Washington, DC; Mem Small Bus Adm Reg VIII, Sioux Falls Adv Coun 1978-80; Idaho Coun on Ec Ed; AAUA; Acad Mgmt; Sales & Mktg Execs Boise; Am Assembly Collegiate Schs Bus; VChm, Nat Com on Fac Devel;

Num Others; cp/Rotary Clb Boise; Pi Sigma Epsilon; Hillcrest CC; r/Luth; hon/Phi Delta Kappa; Blue Key; Pres Awd, JCs; Nom Tchr of Yr, Mont St Univ 1969-70; Outstg Tchr Awd, Weber St Col 1972; Idaho Edr of Yr 1974-75; Civic Awd, Alpha Kappa Psi; Alumni Achmt Awd, Augustana Col; Intl Men Achmt; Personalities W&MW; Num Others.

LEININGER, HAZEL LUCILLE oc/-Homemaker; Typist; b/Jul 22, 1922; h/PO Box 1325, Longmont, CO 80501; m/Henry B; c/James D, Marlene J (dec); p/James L Simmons (dec); Pearl E Simmons, Longmont:

cp/4-H Ldr 24 Yrs; Campfire Ldr 5 Yrs; Ext Homemakers Editor 6 Yrs; Past Co Pres 5 Yrs; Boulder Co Fair Bd 18 Yrs; Fair Bd Secy 4 Yrs; Adv Bd Ext Ser; hon/Hon'd for Ldrship; Cited for Outstg Commun Ser; Ext Homemaker of Yr 1976, Colo.

LEINONEN, ELLEN A oc/Assistant Professor; b/Oct 15, 1912; h/303 Lexington, Ann Arbor, MI 48105; ba/Ann Arbor; p/Matt and Maria Leinonen (dec); ed/BS w distn; MS; PhD; pa/Univ Mich Med Sch: Asst Prof Anatomy 1971-, Asst Prof Sch Dentistry 1965-, Instr Dentistry 1949-62; NY Acad Scis; Am Assn Anatomists; Fellow Am Inst Chemists; Wom's Res Clb Mich; AAAS; AAUP; Nat & Mich St Dental Hygienists Assns; Smithsonian Instn; cp/Zonta Intl, Former Mem Exec Bd; BPW Clb; r/Luth; hon/Legro Res S'ship, Sch Dentistry Univ Mich; Pi Lambda Theta; Sigma Phi Alpha, Nu Chapt; Sigma Delta Epsilon, Theta Chapt; Sigma Xi; Num Profl Pubs; World W/W Wom; Commun Ldrs & Noteworthy Ams; Intl Scholars Dir; W/W Am Wom; Am Men & Wom Sci.

LEIPPRANDT, MARY MITIN oc/Writer; Composer; Poet; Musician; b/Apr 23; h/3864 N Sturm Rd, Pigeon, MI 48755; ba/Pigeon; m/John Carl; c/Esther, Thomas, Martin, Karen, Patricia; p/Walter and Jane Mitin, Bay Port, MI; cp/Write & Perf Progs for Charities, Chs & Civic & Patriotic Activs; r/Meth; hon/Intl Reg Profiles; Intl W/W Poetry.

LEISKE, ROBERT WARREN oc/Clergyman; b/Jul 9, 1931; h/10849 Ridge Spring Dr, Dallas, TX 75218; ba/Dallas; m/Elizabeth Ann Forsberg-Leiske; c/Vicky Kay L-Tandy, Cynthia Lucille, Wendy Rachelle; p/A A and Mae Rachel Leiske, Dallas; ed/BS; pa/Corp Exec; Nat TV Personality; r/SDA.

LEITCH, ALMA oc/Revenue Commissioner; b/Nov 24, 1926; h/511 Hanover St, Fredericksburg, VA 22401; ba/F'burg; p/-Maurice Andrew Doggett and Nora May Spicer Leitch (dec); ed/Att'd Univ Va, Va Polytech Inst & St Univ, Johy Tyler Commun Col, Va Dept Taxation; pa/Commr of Revenue, F'burg 1970-; Dep Commr Revenue, F'burg 1946-69; Mem Subcom Commonwealth Va Revenue Resources & Ec Comm 1978; Va Adv Leg Coun 1977-78; BPW Clb: Former Exec Com Mem; Commrs Revenue Assn Va: Pres 1979-80, Leg-Exec Com; Intl Assn Assessing Ofcrs; Leag No Va Commrs Revenue; Va Assn Assessing Ofcrs, Chm Arrangmts Com; Va Assn Local Exec Constitutional Ofcrs, Exec Com; Dir-at-Large Va Govtl Employees Assn Inc; cp/Ednl & Public Relats Com Hist F'burg Foun Inc; Past Secy-Treas F'burg Coun of Garden Clbs;

Mbrship Chm Altrusa Intl Inc; ARC; U Way; r/Prot; hon/Citizenship Awd, F'burg Area C of C; Awd for Outstg Ser, Rappahannock U Way; Awd for Outstg Ldrship, ARC; Mary B Benoit Awd for Contb'g Most to Clb, Ann Page Garden Clb.

LEITNER, STANLEY ALLEN oc/Chairman of Board; b/Sept 11, 1938; h/1593 Foxham, Chesterfield, MO 63017; ba/C'field; m/Janet Sherman; c/Stacy; p/Perry O Leitner (dec); Ruth A Leitner, St Louis, MO; ed/BA Univ Bordeaux; mil/AUS 1955-58; pa/Chm of Bd Weapons Corp Am; Author Book *Last Chance to Live*; r/Prot; hon/Most Humorous Bus-man of Yr, Humor Soc Am 1977.

LeKASHMAN, CAROL ANN oc/Banker; b/Mar 29, 1952; h/201 E 17th St, Apt 30E, New York, NY 10003; ba/NYC; p/Raymond and Beatrice Burke LeKashman, Westport, CT; ed/BA Wellesley 1973; MBA Wharton 1975; pa/Citibank: Current Strategic Planning Proj Mgr, Opers Mgr 1978, Staff Ofcr 1977, Prodn Analyst/Trainee 1976; Conslt/Mkt Res Gen Cable Co & Chesebrough-Ponds, Greenwich, Conn 1975-76; Other Former Positions; Nat Assn Bank Wom; Nat Assn MBAs; Nat Assn Female Execs; cp/Kent Alumnae Assn; Univ Pa Alumnae Assn; MENSA; Mem Clbs; r/St Bartholomew's Epis Ch: Stewardship Com; hon/Cum Laude Soc; Nat Merit S'ship Finalist; Thomas Talbot Seeley Prize for Excell in Classical Greek.

LEKUS, DIANA ROSE oc/Librarian; b/Feb 5, 1948; h/215 E Main St, Apt 1B, Somerville, NJ 08876; p/Max and Eleanor Lekus, Hewlett, NJ; ed/BA Emerson Col; MLS Univ Pittsburgh 1970; cp/Friends NY Public Lib; cp/NOW; Nat Ctr for Wom in Perf'g & Media Arts; r/Jewish; hon/W/W Am Wom; World W/W Wom; Sr Editor *Am Book Pub'g Record* 1974.

LEMKE, ARTHUR ATHNIEL oc/Hydraulic & Environmental Engineer; b/Feb 26, 1913; h/3329 Noyes St, Evanston, IL 60201; m/Rosalie Lyga; p/Frederick William and Ruth Wilhelmina Hauser Lemke (dec); ed/BSCE 1934, MSCE 1935, CE 1946 Univ Wis; pa/Ret'd 1978; FMC Corp, Chicago & Itasca, Ill: Sr Proj Engr, Patent Liaison & Conslt 1972-78, Suprvr Process Engrg 1964-72, Mgr 1952-64, Asst Mgr Application Engr, Sewage Equipmt Engrg Dept 1948-52; Other Former Positions; Fellow Am Soc Civil Engrs; Diplomate, Am Acad Envir Engrs; Water Pollution Control Fdn; Intl Assn for Hydraulic Res; r/1st U Meth Ch, Evanston; hon/Phi Eta Sigma; Chi Epsilon; Contbr to Num Profl Pubs; Patentee in field of Envir Engrg.

LENNOX, MARJORIE ELIZABETH oc/Equal Opportunity Specialist; b/Sept 10, 1938; h/722 J E George Blvd, Omaha, NE 68132; ba/Omaha; p/George B Lennox (dec); Viola R Lennox, Omaha; ed/BS; MS; pa/Equal Opport Specialist US Dept HUD; Am Soc Polit & Social Scis; Am Soc for Public Adm; cp/Nat Urban Leag; Am Civil Liberties Union; Omaha Chapt Links Inc; NAACP; r/Epis; hon/W/W Am Wom.

LENNOX, WILLIAM R oc/Professor; b/Feb 9, 1912; h/Oxford House 205, 415 S Oxford, Los Angeles, CA 90020; ba/LA; m/Agnes Lozano; c/Susan Agnes, William Smalley, Andrew Malcolm, Martha Marguerita; p/Robert and Agnes McGlynn Lennox (dec); ed/BS; MA; MA; MIA; PhD Univ Oriental Studies 1979; mil/USN Capt, Ret'd Submarine Cmdr; pa/Prof Engrg & Psychol Emeritus; LA City Col: Prof Psychol, Prof Engrg, Assoc Prof Engrg; Asst Prof Engrg Cal St Univ; Ret'd from Fgn Ser Standard Oil Co (now EXXON); Pres Marriage, Fam & Child Cnslrs San Gabriel Val; Lic'd Life & Casualty Ins Rep Cal; Reg'd Rep Nat Assn Security Dealers; Chm Inst Theol Literacy; Chief Advr Polytech Ed & Coor Tech Tchr Tng Prog, W Pakistan; Mgr ELECTREITSBEDRIJF ELECTRA, Aruba, NWI; Conslt Aruba Gas Supply Co; Fin Advr Firma John G Eman (Aruba Bk); Num Other Profl Activs; cp/Bd Dirs Nishi Hongwanji,

Little Tokyo (LA); Chm Hollywood Japanese Cult Inst; Fdr Adult Lit Prog, Karachi, Pakistan; CoFdr Boystown & Girlstown; r/Buddhist; Pres Hollywood Japanese Buddhist Ch; hon/Outstg Engrg Prof, So Cal 1957; Dist'd Fgn Ser, Okla St Univ; 18 Mil & Naval Medals.

LENT, JOHN ANTHONY oc/Professor; b/Sept 8, 1936; h/669 Ferne Blvd, Drexel Hill, PA 19026; ba/Philadelphia, PA; m/Martha L; c/Laura M, Andrea H, John V, Lisa K, Shahnon A; p/John and Rose Lent, E Millsboro, PA; ed/BSJ cum laude 1958; MS summa cum laude 1960; PhD 1972; Addit Studies; pa/Prof Communs Temple Univ; 1st Coor Mass Communs Universiti Sains Malaysia, Penang 1972-74; Lectr, Participant Nat & Intl Confs & Sems: Malaysia, Singapore, India, Thailand, Laos; Acad Positions Held at Cols & Univs in: WVa, Wis, Wyo, NY, Ia; Malaysia/Singapore/Brunei Studies Group, Assn for Asian Studies: Fdr, Chm 1976-, Est'd Newslttr Berita 1975, Editor; Spkr & Present Papers Num Profl Confs; Author 8 Books, 9 Monographs, 3 A-V Presentations, 120+ Articles; hon/8 S'ships; Mem Hon Socs; Biogl Listings.

LESKO, LEONARD HENRY oc/Professor; b/Aug 14, 1938; h/PO Box 4705, Berkeley, CA 94704; ba/Berkeley; m/Barbara Switalski; p/Matthew Edward Lesko (dec); Josephine B Lesko, Chicago, IL; ed/AB Loyola 1961; AM 1964; PhD Univ Chgo 1969; pa/Univ Cal: Prof Egyptology Dept Near En Studies 1977-, Assoc Prof 1972-77, Asst Prof 1968-72, Acting Asst Prof 1967-68, Chm Grad Prof Ancient Hist & Archaeol 1977- (Sum), Chm Dept 1975-77, Others; Pres San Francisco Br Archaeol Inst Am 1976-78; Nom'g Com Wn Br Am Oriental Soc 1975-77; Bd Govs Am Res Ctr in Egypt 1973-76; hon/Humanities Res F'ship, Univ Cal; Nat Endowmt for Humanities Proj Grant; Awd for Computer-Oriented Res in Humanities, Am Coun Learned Socs; Others; Num Profl Pubs.

LESKOW, OLIVE oc/Teacher; b/Jun 25, 1919; h/234 W Forty-Ninth, Gary, IN 46408; ba/Gary; p/Julian and Antonina H Leskow (dec); ed/AB Ball St Univ 1941; MA Univ Minn 1947; pa/Tchr Lew Wallace HS; NCTM

Rep 1969-; Ind Coun Tchrs Math: Editor Newslttr 1951-54, Bd Dirs 1948-51; AAUW; Gary Area Coun Tchrs Math; r/St Mary's Russian Orthodox Ch; hon/Sigma Zeta; W/W Wom; Ldrs Am; Author Webster Transparency Series 1968.

LESTER, WILLIAM M oc/Attorney at Law; b/Dec 31, 1895; h/2503 Henry St, Augusta, GA 30904; ba/Augusta; m/Elizabeth M Miles (dec); c/William M Jr, James L; p/W Marcus and Hattie B Connelley Lester; ed/LB Atlanta Law Sch 1920; mil/Vet WWI; pa/Admitted to Ga Bar 1920; Law Pract Augusta 1920-; Spec Asst to US Atty Gen 1943-47; Dir Tax Revision Comm St of Ga 1947-51; Asst St Revenue Commr Ga Until 1952; ABA; St Bar Ga; Delta Theta Phi; cp/Former Mem: City Coun Augusta, Ga Gen Assembly, St Senator; Past Pres: Ga Jr C of C, Ga Exc Clb, Augusta Exc Clb; Masonic Order; Augusta City Planning Comm; r/U Meth Ch: Mem; hon/Pubs incl: Ga Revenue Laws 1948, Comparison of St Revenue Systems 1949;

Commun Ldrs & Noteworthy Ams; Hist of Ga.

LE TOURNEAU, RICHARD HOWARD oc/College President; b/Jan 3, 1925; h/NL-21 Lake Cherokee, Longview, TX 75603; ba/Longview; m/Louise Jensen; c/Robert Gilmore II, Caleb Roy, Linda L Garcia, Liela L Redding; p/Robert Gilmore LeTourneau (dec); Evelyn LeTourneau, Longview; ed/BS, MS Tex A&M; PhD Okla St Univ; mil/AUS WWII, S/Sgt Army Engrs, Pacific Theater; pa/Pres LeTourneau Col; SAE; AIIE; ASEE; cp/Former Commr Tex Indust Comm; r/Christian; Missionary Alliance, Intl Bd Mgrs; hon/Tau Beta Pi; Alpha Pi Mu; Phi Kappa Phi; Sigma Xi.

LEVI, HENRY THOMAS oc/Gemologist; b/May 5, 1941; h/103 Prospect St, Nanticoke, PA 18634; ba/Allentown, PA; m/Cathy Ann Ellsworth; p/Henry Louis and Elinor Stigora Levi, Nanticoke, PA; ed/BS Franklin Pierce Col 1966; Grad Canadian Jewellers Inst 1976; Dipl, Gemnol Asssn of Gt Britain 1977; pa/Mgr Ser Merchandise, Musselmans Jewelers; Owner, Gemologist, Levi Jewelers 1977-; Sales Mgr, Pomeroys Co (Wilkes-Barre, Pa) 1973-75; Other Former Positions; Gemological Assn Gt Britain; Canadian Gemological Assn; Gemological Assn of Australia; Rhodesian Gem & Mineral Soc; Jewelers Vigilance Com, Retail Jewelers Am; Editor, Lapidary Jour (1977), Canadian Gemologist (1977), Jewellery World (1977); r/Jewish; hon/Men of Achmt.

LEVI, MICHAEL MENAHEM oc/Physician; b/Feb 19, 1929; h/30 Waterside Plaza, New York, NY 10010; ba/Brooklyn, NY; m/Sharon McAdam; p/Moric and Lenka Levi, Jerusalem, Israel; ed/BA Gymnasium (Yugoslavia) 1947; MS Univ of Lausanne (Switzerland) 1953; MD 1957, PhD Univ of Geneva (Switzerland) 1958; pa/Clin Asst Prof Ob-Gyn, SUNY 1977-; Att'g Phys, Bapt Hosp (Bklyn) 1977-; Med Dir, Ob-Gyn Assocs (Bklyn) 1971-; Conslt: Addiction Res & Treatmt Ctr, Med Editor of Springer & Verlag (Pubrs); Pub'd Author: NY Acad Scis; Fellow, Am Col Ob-Gyn; NY Gynecological Soc; Fellow Intl Col Surg; AAAS; Fellow Am Inst Chemists; Pan Am Med Soc; Royal Soc Hlth; hon/Josiah Macy Jr Res Fellow; F'ship, Columbia Col of Phys & Surgs, Columbia Univ Dept of Ob-Gyn; Awd for Sci Thesis, World Hlth Org; Best Sci Paper, 3rd Pan Am Cytology Cong; Foun Prize Thesis, Am Assn Ob-Gyn; Diplomate, Am Bd Ob-Gyn; Biogl Listings.

LEVIN, A LEO oc/Lawyer; Educator; b/Jan 9, 1919; h/1713 S St, Washington, DC 20009; ba/Wash DC; m/Doris; c/Allan David, Jay Keva Michael; p/Issachar Levin (dec); Minerva H Levin; ed/BA Yeshiva Univ; JD Univ Pa; mil/USAAF 1942-46, 1/Lt; pa/Dir Fed Judicial Ctr; Lectr on Judicial Adm; Prof Law Univ Pa; Author Var Legal Works; cp/Former Chm St (Pa) Leg Reapport Comm; r/Orthodox Jew; hon/Dist'd Ser Awd, Univ Pa Law Sch; Hon LLB, Yeshiva.

LEVIN, LAWRENCE LEE oc/Publisher; b/Dec 16, 1928; h/4463 Meadowlark Ln, Santa Barbara, CA 93105; ba/Santa Barbara; m/Rita Ellen; p/M Jastrow and Alexandra Lee Levin, Baltimore, MD; ed/BA Wn Resv Univ 1962; MA 1963; PhD Univ Wis 1969; pa/Univ Lectr; Sr Editor, Pubr; cp/Violinist Santa Barbara Orch; hon/Nat Endowmt for Humanities Grant.

LEVIN, SHEILA E oc/Program Assistant; b/Dec 7, 1945; h/PO Box 264, Patton, CA 92369; ba/Patton; p/Hershel Levin (dec); Harriett Freedman Levin, St Joseph, MO; ed/BA 1967, MS 1975 Univ Mo-C; pa/Prog Asst Patton St Hosp (Penal Code Prog); Nat Therapeutic Rec Soc; Nat Rec & Park Assn; Soc for Pk & Rec Edrs; Reg'd Therapeutic Rec Specialist; Var St Coms in field of Hosp Systems; r/Judaism; hon/W/W Am Wom; Personalities of W&MW; World W/W Wom.

LEVINE, HERNAND EUGENE oc/-

Financier; b/Sept 25, 1929; h/5837 E University Blvd, Dallas, TX 75206; m/Harriet-Honey Zarow; c/Karen-Ann, Michael-David; p/Maximilian David and Isabela Salgar Y Roldan Levine; ed/BBA Univ Ariz; MBA 1948; ScD Univ Buenos Aires 1953; PhD Cambridge Col (England) 1965; pa/VP Fin M P Crum Co, Dallas 1974-78; Dir Perlou Industs, New Orleans, Banco Comercial y Industriales, SA, Mexico; Sr Exec VP Lehigh Val Industs, NYC 1968-73; Sr Partner H Eugene Levine & Assocs, CPAs & Intl Conslts, New Orleans 1964-68; Other Former Positions; Fin Execs Inst; Acad Profl Mgmt Conslts; Nat Assn Accts; Soc Royal Chartered Accts (UK); cp/Dallas C of C; Former Mem: La Devel Comm, New Orleans Parish Planning Comm; Dir 1st La Nat Life Ins Co; Son Confed Vets; Mem Clbs.

LEVY, BATIA GOODMAN oc/Occupational Therapist; b/Apr 15, 1925; h/619 Sheridan Rd, Evanston, IL 60202; ba/Chicago, IL; c/Jonathan A, Ruth A, Naomi A; p/Leon and Leah Goodman (dec); ed/Reg'd Occupl Therapist; Tchr's Dipl; Master's Cand; pa/Fac Curric Occupl Therapy Univ Ill; Fam Therapy Wkshops; Sr Citizens Progs; r/Jewish; hon/W/W Am Wom; Featured in Home for Life, Documentary on Gerentology.

LEWIS, CHARLES BADY oc/Teacher, Missionary; b/Sept 20, 1913; h/N Union St, PO Box 53, Natchez, MS 39120; ba/Natchez; p/Irving J and Elizabeth Lewis, Daimcount Ville, LA; ed/AB Leland Col 1944; BD 1947; ThM; DD; pa/Missionary Tchrs Assn; Nat Assn Adult Edrs; cp/Natchez Bus & Civic Leag; r/Bapt; hon/W/W: Am Ed, Rel, Black Am.

LEWIS, CHARLTON SCOTT oc/Civil Engineer; Transportation Planner; b/Dec 22, 1948; h/1501 Ruritan Rd NE, Roanoke, VA 24012; ba/Roanoke; m/Paulette G; c/Stephanie, Lorinda, Anna; p/Earnest Lewis (dec); Ann T Moore, Alma, GA; ed/BCE Ga Inst Technol; MS Univ Cal-B; pa/Civil Engr US Forest Ser; Assoc Mem Am Soc Civil Engrs; r/Ch of God; hon/W/W in Govt.

LEWIS, DI ANN BARTEE oc/Educator; b/May 2, 1941; h/221 Carol Ln, Oxford, MS 38655; ba/Oxford; m/Harvey Shelton; c/Brian, Lauri, Heather; p/Rex Bartee, Brookhaven, MS; Catherine Barteen, Baton Rouge, LA; ed/BS, MEd, PhD Miss St Univ; pa/Dir Psychol Dept N Miss Retard Ctr; Pres Miss Assn for Gifted & Talented; Am Psychol Assn; CEC; cp/Former Mem Pilot Clb; r/Meth: Chm Comm on Ed 1978-; hon/Biogs of Sch Admrs; Personalities of S; World W/W Wom; NDEA F'ship; Grad Cum Laude.

LEWIS, GLADYS SHERMAN oc/Freelance Writer; Nurse; b/Mar 20, 1933; h/3620 Ridgehaven Dr, Midwest City, OK 73110; ba/MC; m/Wilbur Curtis; c/Karen Kay, Mark David, Leanne Gwynneth, Cristen Sue; p/Andrew Sherman, Wynnewood, OK; Minnie Sherman, Oklahoma City, OK; ed/RN; BA; pa/Okla & Am Nurses Assn; Okla Co Med Aux; Okla Med Aux; Wom's Aux Am Col Surgs; Wom's Aux Intl Col Surgs; Okla Co Mtl Hlth Assn; Contbr to Profl Pubs; cp/Dem Party; AAUW; OK-ERA Coalition; Nat Rel Com ERA; Evang Wom's Caucus; Okla Wom's Polit Caucus; NOW; r/1st Bapt Ch, MC: Mem, Bible Tchr, Conf Ldr; Med Missionary (w husband) S Am 10 Yrs; Bd Trustees SWn Bapt Theol Sem; Mem Com on Order of Bus, So Bapt Conv 1979-81; hon/MC Pilot Clb's Wom of Yr 1979; W/W: Am Wom, MC; Personalities of S; World W/W Wom; Intl W/W Intells.

LEWIS, GOLDA oc/Artist; Consultant; Pioneer Hand-Papermaker; h/31 Union Sq W, New York, NY 10013; ba/NYC; ed/Art Studies: (Painting) Hans Hofmann, Jack Tworkov, (Sculpture) Robert Laurent, (Papermaking) Douglas Howell, (Woodblock) Seong Moy; pa/Casts Own Paper, Making Paper in Lab 1961-; Devel Process for Making Paper on Unsized Canvas 1968; Paper Conslt Wildcliff Mus, New Rochelle, NY; Lectr: Am Fdn Arts Prog at Benedicta Arts Ctr Gallery &

Sch, Col of St Benedict 1974, Marymount Col 1972; 1-Wom Exhbns: Univ Wis-Milwaukee 1976, Alonzo Gallery NCY 1974 & 71, Peter M David Gallery Mpls, Minn 1974, Benedicta Arts Ctr Gallery 1974 & 67, Ct Gallery Copenhagen, Denmark 1970, Other NYC Galleries; Group Exhbns: Gallery K Wash DC 1979, San Francisco Mus Art 1978, William Rockhill Nelson Gallery Atkins Mus Art Kansas City, Mo 1978, Nat Collection Fine Arts Smithsonian 1977, Mus Mod Art NYC 1976, Fla Atl Univ 1976, St Peters Col Art Gallery 1976, Joseloff Gallery Univ Hartford 1975, Kresge Art Ctr Galleries 1957-, Others; Collections: Ciba-Geigy Chem Co Ardsley, NY, Founs of Paper Hist Haarlem, Holland, Paper Mus Helsinki, Finland, Brit Paper Mus London, UK, Canadian Paper Mus Montreal, Denmark, Norway, Israel, Num Other Nat & Intl Instns; hon/Pub'd Author; Subject of Num Pub'd Articles & Reviews; W/W: Am Wom, Am Art, Art & Antiques; DIB.

LEWIS, LORAINE RUTH oc/Teacher; b/Jul 22, 1921; h/1914 Highland Dr, Prosser, WA 99350; ba/Prosser; m/Jesse Dale; c/Nancy Loraine, Dale Delbert, Paul Jeffrey; p/Perrie Benjamin Galbreath (dec); Hazel Bentley Galbreath, Prosser; ed/BSacred Lit; BS; pa/Tchr Title I Migrant, Kgn through 2nd Grades; Pvt Music Tchr; NEA; Wash, Prosser

Ed Assns; r/Ch of Nazarene: Mem, Pianist/Organist, Choir Dir, Chm Music Com; hon/W/W: Child Devel Profls, Am Wom; World W/W Wom; DIB; Intl W/W: Commun Ser, Intells; Notable Ams; Commun Ldrs & Noteworthy Ams; Personalities W&MW; Book of Honor; Outstg Wom Linotype Operator, BPW Org; Most Outstg Wom, Prosser Ch Nazarene; Feature Story in *Record-Bltn* (For Biogl Listings).

LEWIS, POLLY MERIWETHER oc/Urban Planning; b/Aug 16, 1949; h/2945 Katherine Valley Rd, Decatur, GA 30032; ba/Decatur; m/Joseph B; c/Barry; p/Virgil and Viola Meriwether, Clarksville, TN; ed/BS Ga St Univ; pa/Am Soc Public Admrs; Conf Minority Public Admrs; cp/Katherine Val Civic Assn; Alpha Kappa Alpha; NCNW; NAACP; VP Snapfinger Sch; Exec Com Dem Party DeKalb; r/Gtr Travelers Res Bapt Ch: Mem, SS Supt Presch Div, VChm Wom's Coun.

LEWIS, WILLIAM CHESLEY JR oc/Lawyer; b/Oct 29, 1912; h/807 Milestone Dr, Silver Spring, MD 20904; p/William Chesley Sr and Nelle Wyrick Lewis (dec); ed/AB, JD Univ Okla; MBA Harvard; LLM SEn Univ; mil/USAF Ret'd Maj Gen; Also AUS, USN; Rising through Ranks from Army Pvt to Cmdr in Navy, Lt Col Army; Dist'd Ser Medal, AF; Legion of Merit, Navy; Meritorious Ser Medal, Army; Jt Ser Commend Medal, Jt Chiefs of Staff; #2 Ranking Ofcr AFR time of retiremt; Grad Indust Col Armed Forces w highest grade in hist of instn; Air War Col high distn; Nat War Col; Nav War Col; pa/Vis Prof Sev Univs & Cols; Fac Mem Nat War Col; r/Presb; hon/Editor *Declaration of Conscience*, 1972; Press Clb Awd for Best Reporting on Fgn Affairs; Others.

LEWIS, WINDERLEAN SMITH oc/Librarian; b/Oct 19, 1933; h/PO Box 339, Natchitoches, LA 71457; c/Mark La John, Ollie Mae; p/Shelby Smith (dec); Earnestine Smith, Robeline, LA; ed/BS; MEd; Addit

Studies; pa/Profl & Local Writing; cp/Am Legion Aux, Post #518; Hibiscus Garden Clb; r/Asbury U Meth; hon/Outstg Wom of Yr.

LIBACKYJ, ANFIR oc/Physical Scientist; University Professor; Theologian; b/Sept 8, 1926; h/84-22, 107 Ave, Jamaica, NY 11417; p/Serhij and Kateryna Slowinskyj Libackyj (dec); ed/MS Liege Univ 1954; PhD Poly Inst Brooklyn 1965; MDiv Union 1977; r/En Orthodox.

LICHTENSTADTER, ILSE oc/Professor Emeritus; b/Sept 10, 1907; h/14 Concord Ave, Cambridge, MA 02138; ba/Cambridge; p/Jacob and Flora Levi Lichtenstadter (dec); ed/PhD 1931; DPhil 1937; pa/Harvard Univ: Lectr Arabic, Dept Near En Langs & Lits, Ctr for Mid En Studies 1960-, Emeritus 1974; Lectr Hist & Civilization Near & Mid E, Rutgers St

Univ, New Brunswick, NJ 1959; Lectr Islamic Cult Area Studies Prog, Grad Sch Arts & Scis NY Univ 1953-59; Other Former Positions; Prof Emerita Univ Frankfurt am Main (Germany) 1974; Am Oriental Soc; NY Oriental Clb: Past VP, Past Pres; MESA; r/Jewish; hon/Num Profl Pubs; Fulbright-Hays Travel Awd for Travel in India & Pakistan.

LIEBE, RUTH DOROTHY oc/Homemaker; Civic Leader; b/Feb 8, 1905; h/7209 Interlaaken Dr SW, Tacoma, WA 98499; m/Harold E (dec); c/Carol Ann l Nortz, Richard Hamilton; p/Loren Hamilton and Mary E Hamilton Slade (dec); ed/Oreg St Univ; cp/4-H Clb Ldr; Pierce Co Rec Chm; Started Cub Scout Prog, Lakes Dist; Dep Commr Tacoma Girl Scout Coun; Started Hot Lunch Prog, Clover Park Sch Dist 400; Lakewood Rep Original Pierce Co Lib Bd; Pres Ofcrs Wives Clb; ARADCOM: Tchr Craft Classes; CoFdr Mtl Hlth Clin, Lakes Dist; Ed Com Lakewood Unlimited; Chm Ed Survey Lakewood Tomorrow; Pres Junia Todd Hallen Book Clb; Mem Ida S Baillie Orthopedic Guild 6 Yrs; Num Others; r/Presb: SS Tchr, Primary Dept Supt, Choir Mem; hon/Num Certs of Apprec.

LIEBRENZ, MARILYN LOUISE oc/Management Consultant; b/Aug 3, 1944; h/-280 Durand, E Lansing, MI 48823; ba/E Lansing; p/Allan F and Emma Tohms Liebrenz, Mound, MN; ed/BA Wheaton Col 1966; MA

Mich St Univ 1973; PhD Cand 1979; pa/Prog Coor Managerial Corres Course Mich St Univ; Former Prof Bus Adm Alma Col; Am Mktg Assn; Acad Intl Bus; Acad Mgmt; r/Prot.

LIEBSON, ALICE RUTH oc/Politician; b/Oct 2, 1950; h/112 Maplewood Ave, W Hartford, CT 06119; p/Sidney and Jeannette Burman Liebson, Stamford; cp/Adv Bd Project Thrust; St Steering Com, Common Cause; Past Pres Yg Dems Stamford; Justice of Peace; Exec Bds: AAUW, LWV, Dem Wom; Del 1978 Dem Nat Conf; Chief Aide Ella Grasso Re-election Com; Exec Aide Conn Comm on Housing; r/Jewish; hon/Pres Carter's Talent Bank of Wom; Ky Col; Conn Gen Assembly Resolution for Dedicated Public Ser.

LIGGETT, DELMAS E oc/President Chemical Corporation; b/Feb 19, 1907; h/411 Dayton Rd, Champlin, MN 55316; p/Enoch and Lula L Liggett, King City, MO; ed/BA Wn Masters Univ Mo; mil/WWII, 3½ Yrs Ser; pa/Ret'd; cp/Mpls Ath Clb; AARP, Local; Nat Geographic Soc; Nat Wildlife Fdn; Nat Audubon Soc; Sierra Clb; Smithsonian Assn; r/Prot.

LIGGETT, DELMORE oc/Bible Instructor; Retired Educator; b/May 19, 1906; h/PO Box 35, RD1, Rising Sun, IN 43070; p/Harvey Liggett (dec); Lydia Hannah Liggett; ed/BS; PsD; MsD; DD; FIBA; FWA; mil/ROTC, 1/Sgt; pa/Tchr, Prin; Conslt: ISTA, NEA, World Field Res 1972-; Am Psychiatrical Assn; IPA; Org of Am Sts; Fdg Mem Nat Hist Soc; Trustee BonDurant Agape Min 1972-; cp/Former Assoc Mem

Smithsonian Instn; UN Assn; Mus Natural Hist; Century Clb, LA; Secy New Rising Sun Cemetery; r/U Meth Ch: Trustee, SS Supt, Organist, Pianist, Bible Tchr; hon/Cert of Apprec, Nat Police Ofcrs Assn; Hon Mem, Nat Assn Taylor Univ Alumni Assn; W/W: Am, MW; Intl W/W; Commun Ser, Intells; Men of Achmt; DIB; Notable Ams Bicent Era; Commun & Noteworthy Ams; Personalities W&MW; Others.

LIGGETT, FRANCES J oc/Editor, Gerontologist; b/Oct 9, 1946; h/4741 S Country Clb Wy, Tempe, AZ 85282; ba/Mesa, AZ; p/Cloyd E Liggett, Mishawaka, IN; Lois R Hall, Niles, MI; ed/BA Mich St Univ 1968; MSW Cand Ariz St Univ; pa/Secy Treas ASU Student Gerontology Soc; Wom in Communs; Wn Gerontology Soc; cp/Val of the Sun Hospice Assn; Bd Dirs Ctl Ariz Hlth Sys Agy; r/Unitarian-Universalist; hon/1st Pl Awd, Ariz Press Wom Competition 1973 for Newspaper 2000-5000 Category.

LIGHTFOOT, HARRIETT ANNA GRIMM oc/Concert Soprano; b/Dec 7, 1897; h/1155 Lake Miriam Dr, Lakeland, FL 33803; m/Edwin N (dec); c/Edwin N, Brodale L Ehlert; p/Ernest Anthony and Emile D Grimm (dec); ed/Univ Ill; Am Conservatory Music; cp/Pres Wom's Clbs; Chm Num Orgs; Vol w Seminole Indians; Flower Show Judge; Lectr; hon/Wom of Yr; Fla Mother of Yr; Top Awds for Paintings; Top Awds for Poetry, Wis; Excell Hon, Wis Theatre Guild for Playwriting.

LIGHTSEY, VIRGINIA ANN oc/Children's Librarian; b/Nov 17, 1948; h/2116 Maple St, Pine Bluff, AR 71603; ba/Pine Bluff; p/Virgle and Gladys V Lightsey, Pine Bluff; ed/BS Henderson St Univ; pa/Chd's Libn Pine Bluff & Jefferson Co Public Lib; Ark Lib Assn; VChm Public Lib Div; r/2nd Bapt Ch.

LIKINS, WILLIAM HENRY oc/College &

University Administrator; b/Feb 7, 1931; h/1062 Oram Dr, Adrian, MI 49221; ba/Adrian; m/Martha Ann Grant; c/Jeanne Marie, William Henry Jr, David Scott; p/William H and Katherine H Likins, Louisville, KY; ed/AB; MDiv; ThD; PhD; Addit Studies; pa/VP for Devel Adrian Col 1979-; Exec Dir Comm on Higher Ed, & Ky U Meth Higher Ed Foun Inc 1976-77; U Meth Ch: Assoc Dir Black Col Fund 1974-76, Dir Min Enlistmt 1967-74; Sr Pastor Fisk Meml Meth Ch, Natick, Mass 1962-67; Other Former Positions; L'ville Annual Conf, U Meth Ch; Phi Delta Kappa; Am Assn for Higher Ed; APGA; Former Mem: Am Col Pers Assn, Assn for Clin Pastoral Ed, Ctr for Study of Dem Instns, Insts Rel & Hlth, Nat Voc Guid Assn, Soc for Sci Study of Rel, World Future Soc, Others; Conslt; Lectr; Del to Nat & Intl Meetings of Rel Orgs 1958-; Other Profl Activs; cp/Chaired Num Coms, Bd, Agys for Instnl & Commun Devel 1957-; Former Chaplain Worcester (Mass) Police Dept; Former Chm Friends for Edgehill, Nashville, Tenn; r/U Meth: Min; hon/Orme M Miller Fellow, Emory Univ; Commun Ldrs & Noteworthy Ams; Notable Ams; W/W: US, Meth Ch; DIB; Personalities of S; Others.

LILLY, JAMES ALEXANDER oc/Executive; b/Sept 1, 1918; h/3001 S Roosevelt, #17, Boise, ID; ba/Boise; c/James Alexander, Pamela, Robert Clifton, Anne Martha; p/Clifford A Lilly (dec); Eva Acre Dinwiddie Lilly, Bluefield, WV; ed/BSME Va Poly Inst & St Univ 1940; pa/Exec VP & Dir Morrison-Knudsen Co Inc; Pres & CEO M-K Nat Corp; VP & Dir Canadian Rescon Ltd, No Wn Dredging Co, Ltd, No Constrn Co Ltd, High Rock Mining Co Ltd, Emkay Fin Co Inc; Dir Intl Engrg Co Inc; Alaska Pipeline Bldrs Assn; AAAS; Am Inst Chem Engrs; Am Inst Constructors; Am Nuclear Soc; ASCE; ASME; Am Underground-Space Assn; Assn Energy Engrs; Assn US Army; Brit Tunnelling Soc; IEEE; Intl Technol Inst; Soc Am Mil Engrs; Soc Mining Engrs AIME; Sunsat Energy Coun; Dir NYC Gen Contractors Assn; cp/Beavers: Dir, Mem Prog & Noms Com; Moles: Dir, Mem Fin Com; r/St Michael's Epis Ch; hon/Air Medal w OLCs; DFC w Stars.

LINCOLN-SMITH, DOROTHY A oc/-Singer; Professor of Voice; b/May 3, 1936; h/3228 E San Miguel Pl, Paradise Valley, AZ 85253; m/Harvey K Smith; c/Kerstan, Lisa; p/Harold Ashbacher, Waukon, IA; Louise Scharping Ashbacher (dec); ed/EdD; MMus; BMus; pa/Solo Appearances w: Phoenix & Detroit Symphs, Scottsdale Commun Orch 1977, Yg Audiences of Ariz 1977, Bach & Madrigal Soc 1977, Others; Operatic Roles Perf'd incl: Constanza *The Abduction from the Seraglio* (Mozart), Marie *The Bartered Bride* (Smetana), Josephine *HMS Pinafore* (Gilbert & Sullivan), Others; Var Operatic Roles Coached; Sev Solo Perfs w Orchs; Num Solo Oratorio Perfs; Ariz Opera Assn; Phoenix Music Theatre; Nat Assn Tchrs of Singing; Nat Soc Arts & Lttrs; Am Choral Dirs Assn; Soloist on Tour w Phoenix Boys Choir to Europe, En US, Cal; r/Epis.

LIND, VIIU SARAL oc/Veterinarian; b/Apr 15, 1910; h/346 State St, Marion, NC 28752; ba/Same; m/Harry (dec); c/Thomas Carl, Mary; p/Karl and Ebba Saral (dec); ed/DVM; Dr Small Animal Surg; pa/Owner-Operator Small Animal Clin; cp/Scouting; Public Spkg; r/Luth; hon/Thanks Badge, GSA; Americanism Awd, DAR.

LINDAHL, LORRAINE ELSIE oc/-Communications Director, Editor; b/Jan 20, 1921; h/4904 Park Ave S, Minneapolis, MN 554117; ba/Mpls; m/Murlin Seward; c/David Mark, Marcia Gail, Sandra Jean; p/Edward James and Emma Christine Griffith, Williston, ND; ed/BA cum laude; pa/Ctl Luth Ch, Mpls: Communs Dir, Editor *Spirit of Central*; Adm Asst to Dir Edit Div, Augsburg Pub'g House, Mpls 1960-73; Editor *Nat Battery News*, Employee Pub Gould Nat Battery Co, St Paul, Minn 1945-46; Other Former Positions; Wom in Communs Inc; Minn Indust Editors' Assn; Cult & Arts Com Gtr Mpls C of C; Contbr to Var Org Pubs Locally; 1st Editor *Oslo Hi-Lites*, Sons of Norway 1950's; r/Luth; hon/Mortar Bd; W/W Am Wom; Intl W/W Intells; DIB; Personalities W&MW.

LINDHOLM, HELGE WALDEMAR oc/-Retired Patrolman; b/Nov 21, 1906; h/14281 S Academy Ave, Kingsburg, CA 93631; ba/-K'burg; m/Evelyn Ingabritt; c/James Henning, Sharon Ann; p/Claus Henning and Esther C Nilsson Lindholm (dec); pa/Patrolman & Chief of Police 22½ Yrs; cp/C of C; Masons; Charter Mem K'burg Hist Soc; Assoc Mem Nat Trust for Hist Preserv; r/K'burg Evang Covenant Ch; hon/Patentee; Cert of Recog, W/W in Fresno (Cal).

LINDNER, GAYLE LEE oc/Instructional Site Coordinator; b/Mar 20, 1953; h/4063 Heathersage, Houston, TX 77084; ba/Houston; ed/BSEd; pa/Site Instrnl Coor Houston Indep Sch Dist; Cashier K-Mart Dept Store, Houston 1977; Waterfront Instr San Jacinto Girl Scouts 1977 (Sum); Other Former Positions; Tex Rec & Pk Soc; Tex St Tchrs Assn; AAPER; cp/Civic Assn; hon/Contbr to Var Profl Pubs; Stella P Ross Medal Outstg Eng Student 1972; Baylorian Lit Awd, Editors Awd; World W/W Wom; Intl W/W Poetry; Others.

LINDSAY, HENRY E H oc/Acting Director; b/Mar 28, 1933; h/1212 W Oxford St, Philadelphia, PA 19122; ba/Phila; m/Rubye C; c/Traci Pamela; p/Crawford B and Rachel Darden Lindsay, Nashville, TN; ed/MD; DSc; pa/Acting Dir C H S P Med Ctr; Hypnotist; r/Bapt; hon/Var.

LINDSAY, JON STEPHEN oc/County Judge; b/Dec 4, 1938; h/19951 Kuykendahl, Spring, TX 77379; ba/Houston, TX; m/Tonita Lee Davis; c/Steven Vaughn, Leslie Jon, Larry James; p/James Jonathan Lindsay (dec); Constance Evans Lindsay, Santa Fe, NM; ed/BS NM St Univ 1959; mil/USAF 3 Yrs, Capt; pa/Co Judge Harris Co 1974-; Civil Engr; Chm Harris Co Juv Bd; Chm Policy Adv Com Multimodal Trans Planning, Gulf Coast St Planning Reg; VChm Conf Urban Cos; Bd

Dirs: Tex Assn Cos, Harris Co Flood Control Dist; Exec Com Houston-Galveston Area Coun; Tex Adv Comm on Intergovtl Relats; Harris Co Bail Bond Bd; Others; cp/Bd Dirs: Spring Creek YMCA, Houston Symph; Former Dir: NW Rotary Clb, Houston JCs; Downtown YMCA Yth Coun; Exec Com U Way Tex Gulf Coast; Adv Bd Teen Challenge; Bd Trustees Blood Ctr; Others; r/Tomball U Meth Ch: Mem.

LINDSEY, O RUSSELL oc/President Insurance Agency; b/Oct 20, 1915; h/1121 Third Ave, Laurel, MS 39440; ba/Laurel; m/Margaret Murphey; c/Mary Margaret,

Robbie Louise; p/Will Lindsey (dec); Beulah Lindsey, Laurel; ed/BA Univ Miss; mil/USN WWII Lt; pa/Pres Graves, Lindsey & McLaurin Inc (Ins Agy); Dir 1st Nat Bk, Laurel; cp/Pres: Laurel Rotary Clb, Laurel C of C; Chm Var Coms; Chm Laurel Airport Bd; Chm Laurel Planning Comm; r/1st Bapt Ch, Laurel; hon/Outstg Citizens Awd, City of Laurel.

LINE, JAMES V oc/Minister; b/Jan 30, 1945; h/765 Patton St, Newark, OH 43055; ba/Newark; c/Eric Vincent; p/Paul V and Lucille F Line, Mesa, AZ; pa/Pres En Ctl Ohio Dist Min Assn 1977-78; Mem Newark Evang Min Assn; r/Nazarene; hon/Lancaster Ch Growth Awd; Personalities W&MW; DIB; Commun Ldrs & Noteworthy Ams; Men of Achmt; IPA; Notable Ams; Others.

LINGENFELSER, ANGELUS JOSEPH oc/Clergyman; b/Aug 30, 1909; h/1503 Kansas Ave, Atchison, KS 66002; ba/Same; p/Max and Josephine Bonaly Lingenfelser (dec); ed/AB, BS St Benedict's Col; pa/Ordained Rom Cath Priest 1936; Pastor, Sacred Heart Ch (St Louis, St James); Former Pastorates; Prof of Math & Bus Mgr, St Benedict's Col; cp/Bd Mem, Ks St Water Resources; Bd Mem, Ks St Hist Soc; Pres, Atchison Co Hist Soc, r/Cath; hon/Hon Mem, Atchison Co Soil Conserv; FFA Stamp Collection Awd; Instr in War Effort.

LINK, AMELIA GWIN oc/Income Tax Accountant; h/Rt 1, Box 74, Verona, VA 24482; ba/Same; m/John Paul; c/John Daniel, Suzanne Gwin; p/William Tell Gwin (dec); Maude Roberts Gwin, Verona; pa/Nat Soc Public Accts; cp/Repub Party; Augusta Expo; Augusta Co Farm Bur Fdn: Secy-Treas, Bd Dirs; r/U Meth: Active Mem; hon/Ser Awd, Augusta Co Farm Bur Fdn; W/W Am Wom.

LINKER, DOROTHY INSLEY oc/Homemaker; Retired Librarian; b/Sept 12, 1913; h/Athens, GA; m/Robert W (dec); c/Thomas Polk, Dorothy Waddell Linker Sander; p/Levin Irving and Sadie Bell Waddell Insley (dec); ed/BA 1935, BS UNC-CH1941; pa/Former Asst Law Libn, Univ of NC Law Sch; Former Asst Libn in Order Dept, UNC Lib; Mem & Fdr of Chapel Hill (NC) Sch of Art Guild (ser'd as 1st Pres); cp/Athens Garden Clb, Pres Garden Clb Coun; DAR; Geneal Socs of Ga & Md; r/Epis: Wom's Aux, Choir Mem; hon/W/W: Am, Ga; World W/W Wom; DIB; Personalities of S; Others.

LINVILLE, NANNIE LOU BROCK oc/Teacher; b/Feb 15, 1930; h/R4, Box 360, Berea, KY 40403; ba/Berea; m/Robert Moss; c/Larry Edward; p/Curgie Lew and Minnie Maness Brock, Mt Vernon, KY; ed/BS; MA EKU; pa/Tchr Spec Ed (EMH), Berea Indep, Madison Co 1977-; Tchr EMH Jr HS Rockcastle Co 1973-79; CEC; KEA; NEA; BEA; cp/Charter Mem Rockcastle Chapt DAR; r/Scaffold Cane Bapt: Mem.

LIPOVICH, GEORGE JAY II oc/General Manager; b/Jun 8, 1948; h/107 Gold Thorn Way, Sterling, VA 22170; ba/McLean, VA; m/Bobbie Gay; c/Erin Lee, Katie Alice; p/G J Sr and Ruth Lee Lipovich, Columbus, OH; ed/BS Ohio St Univ 1971; pa/Inventor Meas Soc Bur; CMG; CDE; cp/BSA: Former Scoutmaster, Unit Comm; r/Mormon; hon/Hon Mem Fac, Dept Def Computer Inst; Pres' Awd 1975; W/W.

LIPPERT, CATHERINE BETH oc/- Associate Curator; b/Feb 8, 1947; h/751 Fairway Dr, Indianapolis, IN 46260; ba/Indpls; m/Charles B Jr; p/Robert Lippert, Chicago, IL; Pearl Lippert, Skokie, IL; ed/BA Univ Wis; MA Univ Mich; pa/Assoc Curator Decorative Arts Indpls Mus of Art 1974-; Instr Art Hist: Avila Col, Kansas City (Mo) 1973, Univ Mich 1970; Curatorial Asst Univ Mich Mus of Art 1969-71; Exhbns incl: Indpls Mus Art 1977, 76, 75, William Rockhill Nelson Gallery Art-Mary Atkins Mus Fine Arts 1972, Others; Am Assn Museums; Decorative Arts Trust; Victorian Soc Am; Decorative Arts Chapt Soc Arch Histns; Am Ceramics Cir; Royal Oak Foun; MW Art Hist Soc; Intl Coun Museums; hon/Harry M Grier Meml S'ship, Attingham Sum Sch Trust, Attingham (England); For Foun F'ship; Grad Res F'ship, Smithsonian Instn; Anna O Smith Tuition F'ship, Univ Mich; Phi Beta Kappa; Woodrow Wilson Fellow; Other Acad Hons; Profl Pubs; World W/W Wom; DIB.

LIPPITT, ELIZABETH CHARLOTTE oc/Free-lance Writer; h/2414 Pacific Ave, San Francisco, CA 94115; p/Sidney G and Stella Lippitt (dec); ed/Mills Col; Univ Cal; pa/Writer for 80 Papers (20 Yrs); Pub'd in: *Shreveport Jour, Miami Herald, St Louis Globe-Dem, Jackson News, Union Leader, Orlando Centinel, Phoenix Republic, Tampa Tribune, Birmingham Post Herald, Montgomery Advertiser, Ark Dem, St Petersburg Indep, Houston Chronicle, Chicago Tribune, Utah Indep,* Num Others; Writer & Perf Own Satirical Monologues; Popular Singer; IPA; cp/Metro Clb; Olympic Clb; Nat Adv Bd Am Security Coun; Commonwealth Clb; Nat RR Passengers; Nat Trust for Hist Preserv; Defenders Wildlife; Am Conservative Union; Wilderness Soc; Friends of Animals; Chd's Village; Amvets; Others; hon/Cong of Freedom Awd for Articles on Nat Affairs (8); Book of Honor; w/W: W, Cal, Am Wom; World W/W Wom; DIB; Intl W/W Commun Ser; Blue Book; *Talent* Mag (IPA); Others.

LIPPMAN, ALFRED oc/Chemical Engineer; b/Mar 13, 1908; h/4613 Purdue Dr, Metaire, LA 70003; ba/New Orleans, LA; m/Alyse Crum; c/Alfred Sol, Darryl Rock, Tanya L Murray (Mrs Ray); p/Alfred and Belle Levy Lippman (dec); ed/BEng; pa/Reg'd Profl Chm Engr; Am Inst Chem Engrs; Am Inst Mining, Metall & Petrol Engrs; Nat Soc Profl Engrs; Am Chem Soc; Am Ceramic Soc; cp/Former Mem Lions; Rotary; Dist Boy Scout Com; r/Jewish; hon/Tau Beta Pi; Fellow, Am Ceramic Soc.

LIPSCHITZ, CHAIM URI oc/Rabbi; b/Aug 10, 1912; h/225 Keap St, Brooklyn, NY 11211; ba/Bklyn; m/Rivka Rachel Bernstein; c/Beatrice Beer, Bina Esther Seitler, Sarah Stefansky, Ziona Katzman; p/Moshe Lipschitz (dec); Chaye Lichtman Lipschitz, Bnai Brak, Israel; ed/Hon DDiv: St Andrews Col (London, England) 1959, Philaethia Col (Windsor, Ontario, Canada) 1965; pa/Mem Intl Com Tvuno, Jerusalem, Israel 1977; Pres Agudath Bais Veyelepole, Jerusalem (Pub'd House for Hebrew & Classical Works) 1973; VP Res & Projs Yeshiva Torah Vodaath & Mesivta, Bklyn 1968-; VP Torah Haadam Inst Inc (Res & Pubs Encyclopedia Jewish Social Knowledge of Torah) 1967-; Assoc Editor *The Jewish Press* 1960-; Rabbi Congreg Ohev Sholom, Bklyn 1950-61; Other Former Positions; NY St Fin Aid Admr's Assn; Am Assn for Higher Ed; IPA; Intl Conf Weekly Newspaper Editors; Presidium Mem Metro Bd Orthodox Rabbis 1961; Num Others; cp/Treas Yeshiva Chai Olom, Jerusalem; Chm Bd Govs Girls Col Israel; Advr for Jewish Affairs Fairfield Univ, Fairfield, Conn; Others; r/Jewish; hon/Appt'd Editor in Chief *Encyclopedia of Orthodox Biogs* 1977; Holocaust Lib at Mesivta Torah Vodaath Named "The Chaim U Lipschitz Holocaust Lib" 1975; Selective Ser Sys Meritorious Ser Awd & Gold Medal, Col Paul Akst (NY Dir); Featured in 1st Rel Article in *Am Way* 1970; Biogl Listings; Profl Pubs; Others.

LIPSCOMB, PEGGY ELAINE oc/Pharmacist; Real Estate Broker; b/Jul 27,

1924; h/446 Woodland Cir, Clear Lakes Village, Quitman, TX 75783; ed/BBA So Meth Univ 1945; MA E Tex St Univ 1951; BS (Pharm) Univ Tex 1959; Addit Studies; pa/Assoc Realtor Fletcher's Realtors, Dallas, Tex 1963-; Pharmacist & Owner Lipscomb Pharm 1964-; Pharmacist 1959-63; HS Tchr, Dallas 1951-55; Kappa Epsilon; Beta Sigma Phi; BPW Clb; Others; hon/Hon PhD, Colo Christian Co 1974; Biogl Listings.

LIPSTATE, EUGENE J oc/Geologist; b/Dec 6, 1927; h/401 Shelly Dr, Lafayette, LA 70503; ba/Lafayette; m/JoAnn Davis; c/James M, Betsy Ann; p/Phillip H and Gertrude Faber Lipstate (dec); ed/BS Univ Tex; mil/USAF 1/Lt; pa/VP NW Oil Co; Pres E J Lipstate Inc; Dir Lipstate Creative Sers; Tri-Limited (Real Est Devel); AAPG; Lafayette Geol Soc; Gulf Coast Geol Soc; cp/Repub Party; r/Jewish.

LIPTON, LENNY oc/Filmmaker; Writer; Inventor; b/May 18, 1940; h/236 Water St, Point Richmond, CA 94801; ba/Same; m/Diane J; c/Chloe M; p/Sam Lipton (dec); Carrie Saposnik; ed/AB Cornell Univ; pa/Soc Motion Picture & TV Engrs; ASACP; r/Jewish; hon/Awds San Francisco Intl Film Fests 1966, 68; Awds: Cal Arts Coun, Am Film Inst, Nat Endowmt for Arts.

LITKENHAUS, RAYMOND ARTHUR oc/Manufacturer's Representative; b/Jan 26, 1920; h/8230 Presidential Dr, Jacksonville, FL 32216; ba/J'ville; m/Cornelia Virginia; c/Jaimi Delphine; p/Arthur Bernard and Elsie Kathryn Litkenhaus, Victoria, BC, Canada; ed/BS; mil/Royal Canadian Navy 1941-46, Lt Cmdr; pa/Pres R A Litkenhaus & Assocs Inc,

J'ville 1953-; VP Pan Arabian Co; Real Est Broker; Engr Elliot Co, Pittsburgh 1950-52; Conslt Engrs, Toronto 1947-49; Others; Am Water Works Assn; Fla Pollution Control Assn; Assn Profl Engrs; Geologists & Geophysicists Alta; Lambda Chi Alpha; cp/J'ville C of C, Chm Intl Fin Sem; Dem; River Clb; Deerwood Clb; Masons; Shriners; Kiwanis; Others; r/Presb Ch: Elder; hon/W/W S&SW.

LITTLE, ANNE SHARPE oc/Administrator; b/Sept 28, 1939; h/130 Tudor Ave, River Ridge, New Orleans, LA 70123; ba/-Destrehan, LA; m/A Rush; c/A Rush II; p/C M and Helen Trahan Sharpe, Houston, TX; ed/Univ Houston Fine Arts; La Travel Promotion Agy; Nat Trust for Hist Preserv; cp/Nat Ofcr Alpha Chi Omega; Pres Alpha Omicron; Conclave Kappa Kappa Iota; Les Dames de Destrehan, Mem 1st Bd; River Rd Hist Soc; r/Rom Cath; St Matthew: Mem; Choir St Charles; hon/Key to City, NO; World W/W Wom; DIB; Commun Ldrs & Noteworthy Ams; Personalities of S; Intl W/W Commun Ser.

LITTLE, DAINTY MARGO RICH-ARDSON oc/Career Counselor; Employee Development Specialist; b/May 22, 1942; h/19323 DuBarry Dr, Brookeville, MD 20729; ba/Washington, DC; m/Charles Perry; p/Lester Franklin and Ester Mae Edwards Richardson; ed/AA Univ Fla; BS, MA Univ Md; pa/Cnslr & CoInstr Geo Wash Univ 1977-; Voc Conslt/Employee Devel Specialist US Dept Labor 1976-; Indep Conslt US Dept Agri Grad Sch 1975-76; Adm Asst US Dept Commerce 1969-73; Other Former Positions;

APGA; Md Pers & Guid Assn; Am Soc for Tng & Devel, DC Chapt; Soc Advmt for Mgmt; Phi Chi Theta: Pres Wash Alumnae Chapt, Pres Collegiate Chapt, Nat Councillor; Student Adv Bd Career Devel Ctr; cp/Chm Greenbriar Civic Assn; r/Prot; hon/RSA Traineeship; Govt Quality Step Increases & Cash Awds; W/W Am Wom; Pub'd Author.

LITTLE, FLORENCE HERBERT oc/- Teacher; b/Jul 7, 1911; h/1093 Belle Terre Dr, La Place, LA 70068; m/Alfred Lamond (dec); c/Alan Rush, Barbara Joan L Votaw; p/- Charles Arthur and Bertha Schlachter Herbert (dec); ed/BA; MSE; pa/Ret'd Tchr; Kappa Kappa Iota; Mu Phi Epsilon; ABWA; NEA; ISEA; DMEA; cp/River Parish Fam CB Clb; r/Presb.

LITTLE, JAMES EARL oc/Vocational Administrator; b/May 8, 1930; h/735 N 41st St, East St Louis, IL 62205; ba/E St Louis; m/Dorothy Robinson; c/Janessa, Jennise, Cheryl, James, Darwin Stanley; p/Jefferson and Pauline Little, E St Louis; ed/BS; MS; Cert Voc Curric; mil/CPL Co Medic; pa/Dist 189

Dir Voc & Career Ed; Ill Voc Ed Assn; Charter Mem Am Assn Career Ed; Spec Conslt to US Ofc of Ed; Conslt Ill Ofc of Ed; cp/Adv Bd Mem E St Louis CETA; r/U Meth: Lay Ldr, Lay Spkr; hon/Supt Awd for Curric Devel; Voc Staff Awd for Outstg Work in Voc Ed; Alpha Phi Alpha; Phi Delta Kappa; Pub'd Author.

LITTLE, MARY E oc/Librarian; b/Jun 22, 1916; h/111 S Spring St, R#4, Sparta, TN 38583; ba/Sparta; m/Joe Perr; c/Joe Jr, Mary Elizabeth L Evans; p/Dallas Carmichael England (dec); Althea Alcorn England, Sparta; ed/BS; MA; MSL; pa/Dir Caney Fork Reg Lib 1957-; Classroom Tchr Eng 1938-57; Chm MTES 1951-52; Pres Tenn Lib Assn 1978-79; Bd Mem: SELA; ALA 1978-79; cp/Former Bd Mem Tenn Cong P's & T's; Pres Gen Alumni Assn Tenn Tech Univ; r/Ch of Christ; hon/Life Mem: Tenn Cong P's & T's, Nat Cong P's & T's, NEA; Pi Gamma Mu; W/W: Am Wom, S&SW, Ed; Nat Social Dir.

LIU, DAVID TA-CHING oc/Librarian; Writer; b/Dec 6, 1936; h/PO Box 954, Pharr, TX 78577; ba/Pharr; m/Agnette; c/Nadine, Austin; p/Mr and Mrs Chung-Ling Liu, Taipei, Taiwan; ed/BA; MALS; pa/Book Reviewer *Lib Jour*; Chm Mbrship Com CALA 1978-79; Completed 2 Lib Bldgs for Acad & Public Libs, Mich & Tex; cp/Former Reg Dir Chinese Cult Assn; Former Chm Intl Yth Projects, Rotary Clb Escanaba, Mich; Former Secy-Treas Rotary Clb, Pharr.

LIU, HENRY oc/Professor; b/Jun 3, 1936;

h/2001 Rose Dr, Columbia, MO 65201; ba/Columbia; m/Dou-Mei; c/Jerry B, Jason C; p/Yen Huai and Bardina Liu, Taipei, Taiwan; ed/PhD Colo St Univ 1966; pa/Prof Civil Engrg Univ Mo; Chm Aerodynamics Com Am Soc Civil Engrs.

LIVESAY, GEORGE BENTON JR oc/Chaplain; b/Jan 11, 1949; h/3282 Phoenix Way, Merced, CA 95340; ba/Castle AFB, CA; m/Martha Kay Jones; p/George Benton and Mildred Faye Strange Livesay, La Mesa, CA; ed/BA 1973; MA 1974; PhD Bob Jones Univ 1977; mil/USAF Capt, Chaplain 1977-; AUS 1967-70; USAR 1977, 1/Lt; pa/Min, Cnslr,

Guest Preacher & Lectr 1970-; CoFdr Yth Work "Life in Action" 1976; cp/Pi Kappa Alpha: Former Treas, Past Pres; Vol Wkr Orphanage (Korea) 1968-70; Former Korea Sum Camp Cnslr; Sum Missionary Team to Mexico 1966; Former Mem Gospel Quartet; Others; r/Indep Bapt: Ordained Mt Calvary Bapt Ch, Greenville, SC 1977; hon/Outstg Yg Men Am; AUS Commend Medal; AUS Chaplain Sch Hon Grad; Commandant's Trophy.

LIVESAY, RICHARD WYMAN oc/Diagnostic Radiologist; Physician; b/Jun 11, 1943; h/4341 Mt Helix Highlands Dr, La Mesa, CA 92041; ba/El Cajon, CA; m/Linda Lee; c/Shaunna Marie, Richard Russell; p/Jackson E and Jean E Livesay, Flint, MI; ed/MD Univ Mich Med Sch 1968; mil/USNR LCDR; pa/AMA; CMA; SDCMS; ACR; CRS; SDRS; RSNA; Prof, Chm Radiation Safety Comm, ECUH; r/Fletcher Hills Presb Ch, La Mesa; hon/Outstg Yg Am; W/W in W.

LIVINGSTON, GEORGE HERBERT oc/Minister; Professor; b/Jul 27, 1916; h/502 Bellevue Ext, Wilmore, KY 40390; ba/Wilmore; m/Maria Saarloos; c/Burton George, Nellie Marie Kester (Mrs Ralph), David Herbert; p/George W and Clara Lutheria Baker Livingston (dec); ed/AB; BD; PhD; pa/Prof Old Testament; Lectr; r/Free Meth Ch NAm: Ordained Min; hon/Outstg Edrs Am; Dist'd Ser Awd, Asbury Theol Sem.

LIVINGSTON, VON E oc/Attorney; b/Dec 10, 1903; h/5219 Hickory Ln, Fort Wayne, IN 46825; m/Katharine T; c/Katharine Evans, Mary Moore, Martha McCoy; p/Warren Frank and Katharine Bridger Livingston (dec); ed/BA magna cum laude Knox Col 1925; JD Univ Chicago 1928; pa/Sr Partner Law Firm Livingston, Dildine, Haynie & Yoder 1965-; Partner Campbell, Livingston, Teeple & Dildine 1945-65; Gen Counsel Ind Ser Corp, Ft Wayne 4 Yrs; Former Partner Other Law Firms; Ind Supreme Ct Comm of Character & Fitness; ΛΒΛ, Com Public Utility Law; Ind Bar Assn, Com Adm Law; Am Judic Soc; Dir: Peoples Trust Bk & Fin Inc, Mktg Enterprises Inc, Petrusco Realty Inc; cp/Ind Soc Chgo, Scabbard & Blade; Newcomen Soc; 32° Mason; Past Pres & Dir Ft Wayne Rotary & Quest Clbs; Ft Wayne C of C: Former Dir, Exec Com Mem; Past Pres & Dir Ft Wayne Charity Horse Show Assn; Repub Party; r/Ft Wayne Plymouth Congreg Ch: Past Mem Bd Deacons & Bd Trustees; hon/Former Hon Ind Asst Atty Gen, IPA; Phi Beta Kappa; Phi Alpha Delta; Sigma Delta Chi; Fellow, Ind Inst Technol; Knox Col Ambassador; Mem DePauw Univ Nat Bequests Com; Commun Ldrs & Noteworthy Ams; W/W: US, MW; Notable Ams; Intl W/W Intells.

LLOYD, CORRINE AVIS oc/Microbiologist; b/May 15, 1943; h/6212 Bixby Ave, Affton, MO 63123; ba/Clayton, MO; p/J Howard and Pearl R Lloyd, Affton, MO; ed/BS 1965, Postgrad Studies 1966-, St Louis Univ; pa/Asst Instr Med Tech St Louis Univ 1966-77; Microbiologist St Louis Co Hosp 1973-78; Chief Micro Med Tech Cardinal Glennon Hosp for Chd, St Louis 1965-73; cp/St Louis Univ Alumni Coun; St Louis Univ Nsg Alumni: Former Mem Bd Dirs, Past VP; r/Affton Presb: Deacon, Elder, Christian Edr; hon/Pres Sports Awd for Swimming 1975; Ret'd Microbiologist, ASM; Reg'd Med Tech, ASCP.

LLOYD, THEODORE REES oc/Associate Professor; Coach; b/Jun 20, 1934; h/43 Harding Dr, Searcy, AR 72143; ba/Searcy; m/Marcelene; c/Rees, Melissa; p/Dwight E and Ruby R Lloyd; ed/BA Harding Col; MS Univ Miss; pa/Harding Col: Assoc Prof PE, Track & Cross Country Coach; AAHPER; Ark Track Coaches Assn, Past Charter Pres; Pres NAIA Track Coaches Assn; VP Ark AAU; cp/Optimist Clb; r/Ch of Christ: Deacon; hon/Hd Nat Coach Panama 1969-70; Coach of US Team to Brazil 1974.

LLOYD-WAYNE, LETHA MEMORIE oc/Singer; Pianist; Music Instructor; b/Jun 5, 1912; h/3237 Meadowbrook Dr, Concord, CA 94520; m/Earl A Wayne; c/E Anthony; p/James Carlton and Maybelle Eva McAuley Lloyd; ed/Juilliard Music Sch; San Francisco St Col; Mills Col; Univ Cal-B; cp/NATS; SF Music Tchrs; Nat Coun Met Opera; Asst Dir Jr Aux, Pacific Musical Soc; cp/SF Symph Foun; Others; r/Christian Sci; hon/Winner SF Opera Merola Sch; Voice Scholar to Mills Col; Frieda Scholar in SF; Paul Steindorf Voice Scholar, Oakland.

LO, HANG HSIN oc/Researcher; b/Feb 22, 1937; h/20 Old Still Rd, Woodbridge, CT 06525; ba/Trumbull, CT; m/Pallas M Sun; c/Serena C, Elliot H; p/Chu Tsai Lo and Jane Chiao Wang; ed/BS; MS; PhD; pa/Res & Devel Mgr, Res Labs, Chesebrough-Ponds Inc; Tech Supvn; Analytical Instrumentation; Computer Applications; Regulatory Affairs; hon/Res F'ships; Phi Lambda Upsilon; MIT Faculty Clb.

LOBB, MARGARET E oc/Professor; b/Mar 19, 1899; h/40 Lenox Rd, Berkeley, CA 94707; p/William Henry and Emily Ellen Lobb (dec); ed/BTh; BA; MA; DD; pa/Patton Bible Col: Prof Christian Ed, Chperson Profl Div 1975-, Acad Dean, Prof Rel Ed 1970-; Pacific Sch Rel, Cal: Assoc Prof Rel Ed 1950-69, Instr Rel Ed 1950-69; Vis Prof: Seiwa Col for Christian Wkrs (Japan) 1964, Union Theol Sem (Philippines) 1965, Meth Theol Sch (Sarawak) 1965; Other Former Positions: No Cal & Nev Coun Chs: Chm Chd's Comm 1946, 47, 48, Chm Adult Comm, Chm Dept Christian Ed; Nat Adult Ed Assn; Rel Ed Assn; Assn Sem Profs in Practical Fields; Creative Activity Wkshop, Am Bapt Assembly (Wis), Dir 1947-49; World Christian Ed Inst: Dir Creative Activs, Rel Exhibit, Toronto, Canada 1950, Others; Upsilon Chapt Delta Kappa Gamma; Other Orgs; r/Am Bapt: Var Ch Positions Held; hon/Hon'd for Contbn to Christian Ed, 21st Intl SS Conv (Ia) 1947; DDiv; World W/W Wom; DIB; Creative & Successful Personalities; 2000 Wom Achmt; Personalities W&MW.

LoBOVES, JANET MARGARET oc/-Photographic Marketing Specialist; b/Mar 11, 1950; h/115 Sixth St, Ridgefield Park, NJ 07660; ba/New York, NY; p/Rudolph C and Margaret C LoBoves, R'field; ed/BA Ithaca Col 1972; pa/Photo Mktg Specialist Osawa & Co (USA); Nat Press Photogs' Assn; NJ Press Photogs' Assn; hon/Hon Mention, NJ Press Photogs' Assn Competition 1977; Hon Mention, Bergen Commun Mus Competition 1976.

LOCKETT, ALLAN NEIL oc/Counselor; b/Aug 30, 1950; h/1733 Pasadena Dr, Abilene, TX 79601; ba/Abilene; p/Tom and Lenora M Lockett (dec); ed/BA Prairie View

Univ 1972; MEd Abilene Christian Univ 1975; pa/HS Cnslr; NEA; APTA; TSTA; TCTA; Pres-elect BCPGA; r/Bapt; hon/W/W S&SW.

LOCKHART, GEORGE III oc/-Ophthalmologist; b/Aug 1, 1924; h/3151 Perry Dr, Canton, OH 44708; ba/Canton; m/Mary Ann Mearig; c/George IV, Constance Chesebrough, Virginia Meeks; p/George Jr and Helen Grauch Lockhart (dec); ed/MD; mil/USAMC Capt; pa/Canton Eye Ctr; Cleveland Ophthal Soc; Diplomate Am Bd Ophthal; Fellow, Am Col Surg; cp/Lions Clb, Canton; r/St Mark's Epis Ch, Canton.

LOCKHART, JAMES LEMUEL oc/Salesman; b/Jun 27, 1929; h/709 Serene Dr, Charleston, WV 25311; ba/C'ton; m/Flora Janet Taylor; c/Gerry James, Bruce Alan, Marie Frances; p/Owen Weaver and Marie Archer Lockhart, C'ton; mil/USAF S/Sgt; pa/Salesman Economy Marine Sales; Sales Rep for Bona Alan Tannery 1978-79; Owner-Operator Lockhart Printing Co, C'ton 1971-77; Mgr Am Handicrafts Co, C'ton 1962-70; Mgr Tandy Leather Co, C'ton 1959-78, Ret'd 1978; Salesman Quality Press Printing Co, C'ton 1959; Salesman Rose City Printing Co, C'ton 1956-59; cp/Kanawha Co CD Div, Capt USCG Aux; Repub; r/Prot; hon/Lifetime Hon Mem, Future Home Makers Am; Awds of Merit: WVa Voc Assn, WVa Indust Arts Assn.

LOCKHART, VERDREE oc/State Education Consultant; b/Oct 21, 1924; h/2964 Peek Rd NW, Atlanta, GA 30318; ba/Atlanta; m/Louise H; c/Verdree II, Vera Louise, Fernandez, Abigail; p/Fred D Sr and Minnie Bell R Lockhart (dec); ed/BS Tuskegee Inst; MA, PhD Atlanta Univ; mil/AUS Master Sgt; pa/NEA; Am Voc Assn; APGA; cp/Treas NW Coun Clbs; Atlanta Br NAACP; Trustee Atlanta Univ; BSA: Bd Mem, Asst Coun Commr; r/Union Missionary Bapt Ch: Mem Bd Deacons, Chm Yth Ldrship Devel Coun; hon/Outstg Ser to Ed Awd, Ga Tchrs & Ed Assn; Silver Beaver Awd, Atlanta Area Coun BSA; Dist'd Ser to Guid & Cnslg Awd, Dept Guid Ga Tchrs & Ed Assn; Noticeable Achmt & Dist'd Ser Awd, Atlanta Univ Nat Alumni Assn; St of Ga Faithful Ser Cert; Awds of Merit: Eta Lambda Chapt Alpha Phi Alpha, SEn Reg Tuskegee Inst Nat Alumni Assn.

LOCKLAIR, DAN STEVEN oc/Musician; Composer; b/Binghamton, NY; m/-Suzanne A; p/Archie Greer and Hester Helms Locklair, Charlotte, NC; ed/BM cum laude Mars Hill Col 1971; SMM Sch Sacred Music Union Theol Sem 1973; Addit Studies; pa/Binghamton Dean Syracuse Diocese's Organist Tng Prog 1974-; Organist-Choirmaster 1st Presb Ch, B'ton 1973-; Pt-time Lectr Music Hartwick Col, Oneonta, NY 1973-74; Organist-Choirmaster Our Savior's Luth Ch, Glen Head, Long Isl, NY 1971-73;

Other Former Positions; ASCAP; Am Guild Organists; MENC; Col Music Soc; r/Prot; hon/Pubs incl: "O God of Earth & Altar", (Anthem) 1977, "Triptych for Manuals", (Organ) 1976, "Prayer of Supplication & Thanksgiving" (Anthem for Choir & Organ) 1975, Others; Winner 1st Prize Nat Composition Contest, DC Chapt AGO 1972; Winner Utley Fletcher Slip Organ Competition; Winner St-wide MTNA Organ Competition NC 1970; Crisp Medal for Most Outstg Music Student, Mars Hill Col; Intl W/W Music.

LOCKWOOD, BARBARA J oc/Nurse Administrator; b/Aug 23, 1948; h/5571 S Lowell Blvd, Littleton, CO 80123; ba/Denver, CO; m/Mark R; p/Ernest B Jordan (dec); Christa B Jordan, Aurora, CO; ed/BS 1970, MS 1973 Univ Colo; Cert'd Critical Care Nurse Practioner, Am Col Surgs; pa/St Anthony Hosp Sys, Denver: Mgr Critical Care Sers 1976-, Flight Nurse Supvr 1975-76, Flight Nurse 1973-75; Med Pers Pool, Denver 1973;

Staff RN Denver Gen Hosp 1970-72; Var Tchg Activs; Colo Nurses Assn 1970-76; Am Assn Critical Care Nurses 1974-; Nat Leag for Nsg 1976-; cp/Former Vol RN Comitis Crisis Ctr, Aurora, Colo; r/Luth; hon/Sigma Theta Tau, Alpha Kappa Chapt; W/W Am Wom; Contb'g Author of Chapt on Flight Nsg, "New Horizons: Flight Nsg", *Critical Care Nsg* 2nd Edition 1977.

LODHI, M A K oc/Professor; ba/- Lubbock, TX 79409; ed/BSc w hons 1952, MS 1956 Univ Karachi (Pakistan); DIC Imperial Col Univ London 1960; PhD Univ London 1963; pa/Tex Tech Univ: Prof 1973-, Assoc Prof 1969-73, Asst Prof 1963-69; Guest Scist PINSTECH, Pakistan Atomic Energy Comm, Rawalpindi 1973 (Spring); Guest Prof: Univ Darmstadt (W Germany) 1971 (Spring), Univ Frankfurt (W Germany) 1970 (Fall); Other Vis Activs; Conslt; Fellow Physical Soc (UK); NY Acad Scis; AAUP; Am Astronautical Soc; Sigma Xi; Sigma Pi Sigma; Inst Physics (UK); All Pakistan Math Soc; Num Profl Pubs.

LOEB, BARBARA SNYDER oc/Market-ing Executive; b/Oct 12, 1947; h/1985 Gasper Dr, Oakland, CA 94611; ba/Oakland; m/Michael J; p/Morris and Annabelle M Snyder, Columbus, OH; ed/BA Cornell Univ 1969; MBA Stanford Univ 1977; pa/Mktg Exec Clorox Co; cp/Stanford Alumni Assn; r/Jewish; hon/Top 10% Stanford MBA Class 1977; Mortar Bd; Alpha Lambda Delta; Tau Beta Sigma; Others.

LOEFFLER, DAN THEODORE oc/- Publisher; Computer & Direct Mail & Pro-duction Consultant; b/Jan 21, 1952; h/PO Box 15064, Sacramento, CA 95813; ba/San Diego, CA; m/Linda; c/Jonathan, Laura Lee, Mark, Suzanne; p/Ted and Mary Loeffler, San Diego; ed/Grad Univac Ed Inst San Diego; Addit Courses; pa/Pres & Prin Share Holder Prodn House Corp 1972-; Pubr *The Church News* (Newspaper) 1975-; Dir Prodn & Data Processing Computer Caging Corp Sacra-mento 1977-; Exec Dir Law & Order Campaign Com Sacramento 1976-77; Pubr Christian Bus Dir 1975-78; Other Former Positions;

cp/Kiwanis Intl; r/Christian; hon/W/W in Cal.

LOENING, SARA LARKIN oc/Author; b/Dec 9, 1896; h/PO Box 905, Southampton, NY 11968; m/Albert Palmer (dec); c/Albert Palmer Jr; p/Adrian Hoffman and Katherine Bache Satterthwaite Larkin; cp/Trustee St Hilda's & St Hugh's Sch, NYC; VChm Suffolk Co Chapt ARC; Chm St John's First Monday Clb; Chm & Fdr Biblical Garden, Cathedral St John the Divine; r/Epis; St John's Ch, Southampton: Vestry; hon/Dame Am Order St John of Jerusalem; Medaille de La Reconnaissance par Le govt Francais.

LOESCH, LARRY CHARLES oc/Associ-ate Professor; b/Jul 11, 1945; h/7817 SW 1st Pl, Gainesville, FL 32611; ba/G'ville; m/Barbara M; c/Jane, Tracy, Julie, Stacey; p/William O Loesch (dec); Katherine H Loesch, Fairview Pk, OH; ed/BSEd 1967, MEd 1970, PhD 1973 Kt St Univ; pa/Assoc Prof Cnslr Ed Univ Fla-G 1973-; Grad Tchg Asst Kent St Univ 1972-73; Sch Cnslr Kent St Univ Lab Sch 1971-72; Computer Programmer Campus Sportswear Co, Cleveland, Ohio 1970-71; Other Former Positions; APGA; AMEG; NVGA; ACES; AERA; EPGA; FAMEG; FACES; ASCA; FASCA; Phi Delta Kappa; Var Univ Coms; Var Ed Conslts; cp/Kiwanis Clb; r/U Congreg Ch; hon/Dist'd Ser Awd, Fla Assn for Cnslr Ed & Supvn; W/W SE; Num Profl Pubs; Others.

LOEWENSTEIN, GEORG W oc/Medical Consultant; Instructor; Director; b/Apr 18, 1890; h/880 Mandalay Ave, #522, Clearwater Beach, FL 33515; ba/Same; m/Fohauua S Sabath; c/Peter Lansing (dec), Ruth Gallagher; ed/MD; Spec Courses: Hygiene, Tropical Med, Preventive Med; mil/WW I 40 Mos; pa/Med Dir; Prof Berlin Acad Postgrad Med Tng; Dir Public Hlth & Yth Wel; Hlth Ofcr; Med Conslt; MD 57 Yrs; Fellow: Royal Soc Hlth, AAAS; Charter Mem, Fellow Emeritus Am Col Sportsmed; Corr Mem Berlink Med Soc; Life Mem Fla Public Hlth Assn; Am Acad Fam Physicians: Life Charter Mem, Fellow; cp/Pres UNA Clearwater, Peace Medal; Dir & Hon Pres, IFA Paris, France; Rotarian; Shrine; Musicologist, Richey Symph Soc; Num Books & Papers; Fellow Am Public Hlth; Fellow Emeritus AAAI; ARC Vol 52 Yrs; hon/Cert of Commend, USA Pres; Am Medal, DAR; Sertoma Ser to Mankind Awd; Hon Awd Clearwater Jr Woms Assn; Commun Ser Awd, Fla Acad Fam Physicians; Gold MD Dipl, Univ Berlin 1973; Pres Sport Awd 1978; Awd for 12 Yrs as Musicologist, Richey Symph Soc; Personalities of S.

LOFTUS, DARLENE JOYCE oc/Savings & Loan Branch Manager; b/Mar 20, 1932; h/Hancock & Porter Sts, Clifton, IL 60927; ba/Clifton; c/Danny, Michelle, Steven; p/Lloyd J and Esther Dubois, St Anne, IL;

pa/Br Mgr Iroquois Fed Savs & Ln, Clifton; Kankakee Co Realtors; Kankakee Co Home Bldrs; E Clt Ill Coun Savs & Ln; Iroquois Co Realtors; cp/Clifton's Wom's Clb; r/Meth; hon/W/W: MW, Am Wom, Am.

LOFTUS, JOHN RICHARD oc/College Administrator; b/Jan 14, 1921; h/5820 Porsche Rd, Jacksonville, FL 32210; ba/J'ville;

m/Estelle Vivian; c/John Richard Jr; p/John Rinehart and Marie R Loftus (dec); ed/BS Fla St Univ 1963; MEd 1967, AMEd 1970 Univ Miss; mil/USN, Ret'd 22 Yrs; Pres Unit Cit; pa/Fla Jr Col: Campus Evening Admr 1975-78, Dean 1970-75, Dir Indust Ed 1968-70; HS Tchr/Dept Chm 1963-68; Chm Col Credit Appeal Com 1977-78; AVA; FVA; Epsilon Pi Tau; cp/Fleet Resv Assn; En Star; Mason; Scottish Rite; Shrine; BSA: Asst Scoutmaster, Troop Com Chm 7 Yrs, Order of Arrow, Former Star; r/Meth; hon/Outstg Awd, Nat Assn Homebldrs.

LOGAN, CATHERINE ROSE oc/- Professor; b/Apr 2, 1939; h/Rt #2, Cleveland, GA 30528; ba/Cleve; p/Harry Rollins Logan (dec); Flora McPhail Logan, Asheville, NC; ed/BA Furman Univ; MChMusic So Sem; Grad Study Fla St Univ; pa/Prof Voice & Music Hist Truett-McConnell Col; NATS; Sigma Alpha Iota; VP Ga Bapt Ch Music Conf; r/Bethlehem Bapt Ch, Clarkesville, Ga: Choir Dir; hon/Outstg Yg Wom Am; Outstg Edrs Am.

LOGAN, LESLIE CELESTE oc/Research Microbiologist; b/Jan 9, 1916; h/1315 Wesley Rd NW, Atlanta, GA 30327; ba/Atlanta; m/John Roy; p/Walter W Cauthen (dec); Betsie Clementine T Cauthen, Buchanan, GA; ed/BS Univ Ga; pa/Sigma Xi; Am Soc Microbiol; Contbr Articles to Profl Jours; r/Bapt; hon/Spec Achmt Awd, USPHS; Sustained High Quality Perf Awd.

LOGAN, RALPH HOWARD JR oc/Instructor; b/May 10, 1943; h/5645 MacGregor, Ft Worth, TX 76148; ba/Dallas, TX; m/Sandra M; c/Raymond; p/Ralph Sr and Mary Jo Logan, Kansas City, MO; ed/BS Univ ND 1965; MA Univ Tex-A 1968; mil/USAF; pa/Instr Chem & Phy Sci El Centro Col 1972-; So Bapt Col: Tchr Chem, Phy Sci & Math 1970-72, Dean of Men 1 Yr; Tchr Freshman & Sophomore Chem Laredo Jr Col 1968-70; Am Chem Soc; Tex Jr Col Tchrs Assn; IPA; Tex Acad Scis; AAAS; AAUP; Participant Profl Wkshops; r/Interdenom: Bus Min, Choir Mem; hon/F'ship, NSF Col Tchrs Res Prog; Outstg Tchr Am 1975; Presented Num Papers; Pub'd Sev Articles in field.

LOGAN, ROBERT ALLEN oc/Computer Programmer; b/Nov 17, 1934; h/3301 Catalina, Austin, TX 78741; ba/Austin; m/Mary Lou Smith; m/Robin Ann, Laura Marie; p/Louis James and Iris Allen Logan, Houston, TX; ed/BS Baylor Univ 1956; MBA Univ Tex 1968; mil/USN 1960-63, Lt (jg); pa/Computer Programmer VA; Data Processing Mgmt Assn; cp/Treas S Austin Neighborhoods E; r/Bapt.

LOGAN, THOMAS WILSON STEARLY SR oc/Clergyman; b/Mar 19, 1912; h/46 Lincoln Ave, Yeadon, PA 19050; ba/Philadelphia, PA; m/Hermione Hill; c/Thomas W S Jr; p/John Richard Sr and Mary Harbison Logan (dec); ed/AB Lincoln Univ 1935; STM Phila Div Sch 1941; pa/Diocesan Coun Pa; Trustee Cathedral Chapt; Former Dean W Phila; cp/Life Mem NAACP; Fdr Afro-Am Mus; 33° Mason, Past Grand Master Prince Hall Masons; Past Hon Exalted Ruler Elkdom; r/Epis: Rector; hon/Negro Col Fund Awd; DeMolay Consistory Awd; Phila Tribune Charities Awd; City of Phila Awd; Pa St Gov Shepp Awd.

LOGEL, ANNIE WHEELER oc/Librarian; h/4018 E Crestview Dr NW, Huntsville, AL 35805; ba/Redstone Arsenal, AL; m/Alan Stahler Jr (dec); c/Barbara Ann Darnell (Mrs Tom A), Susan Wheeler Jones (Mrs Bill Jr); p/Charles Conrad Wheeler (dec); Lillie James Wheeler, Tuscumbia, AL; ed/Larimore Col 1934-35; Florence St Col 1956; Univ Utah 1957; pa/Libn Redstone Sci Info Ctr; Spec Libs Assn: Mem 1952-, Pres 1974-75, VP 1973-74, Chm Dir Proj 1974, Dir 1969-70, 64-65, Other Ofcs; Ala Lib Assn: Chm Col, Univ & Spec Libs Div 1967-68, VChm 1966-67, Secy Col, Univ & Spec Libs Div 1965-66, Other Ofcs; cp/Former Trustee Huntsville Public Lib; Former Bd Mem Friends Lib H'ville; Bd Mem H'ville Commun Concert Assn; r/1st Bapt Ch,

H'ville: Ch Libn 1955-, Mem Sanctuary Choir 1951-, SS Dept Supt 1950-67; hon/Oratorical Contest Winner, N Ala; Others.

LOHRER, ALICE oc/Professor Emerita; h/6033 N Sheridan, Apt 28J, Chicago, IL 60660; p/Richard Hugo Schultz (dec); Mary Nyman (dec); ed/PhB; BSLS; AM; pa/Prof Emerita Grad Sch Lib Scis Univ Ill; Pres Ill Lib Assn; Pres Ill Assn HS Libns; Pres Beta Phi Mu; r/Congreg; hon/Num Profl Pubs; Fulbright Lectr: Thailand, Iran; Rockefeller Grant; USOE Res Grant; Nat & Intl Awds.

LOISEAUX, PIERRE ROLAND oc/-Professor; b/Apr 10, 1925; h/18 Meadow-brook, Davis, CA 95616; ba/Davis; m/Helen H; c/David, Kendall, Susan, Shelley; p/-Roland L Loiseaux (dec); Dorothea L Washburn, Orleans, MA; ed/LLB Boston Univ 1950; LCM NY Univ 1951; mil/AUS 1943-46; pa/Univ Cal Law Sch: Prof Law, Dean 1974-78; ABA; Mass Bar; Nat Bkry Conf; Comm Law Leag; Personal Fin Corp; cp/Conslt to Nat Comm on US Bankruptcy Laws 1973; r/Prot; hon/Fulbright Lectr, Denmark 1964-65.

LONDON, HERBERT I oc/Dean; Professor; Writer; h/2 Washington Sq Village, New York, NY 10012; ba/NYC; m/Vicki; c/Staci, Nancy; p/Jack London (dec); Esta London, Deerfield Beach, FL; ed/BA; MA; PhD; pa/NY Univ: Dean, Prof; Am Hist Assn; Pop Cult Assn; cp/COnslt Hudson Inst; CBS TV Prog; r/Jewish; hon/Fulbright Awd.

LONDON, JANICE B oc/Business Education Teacher; b/Jun 12, 1929; h/1002 S McDonald, Stillwater, OK 74074; ba/Stillwater; m/Merlin E; c/Terry E, Robert P; p/Harry Klingman, Binger, OK; Lillian Meiers, Ames, OK; ed/BS; MS; pa/Bus Ed Tchr Col Bus Adm Okla St Univ; Delta Pi Epsilon; OBEA; NBEA; Mtn-Plains BEA; SW Adm Sers Assn; Am Bus Commun Assn; cp/Commun Chest; Lib Bd; r/Bapt.

LONDON, KURT L oc/Professor Emeritus; b/Sept 12, 1900; h/710 Christine Dr, Palo Alto, CA 94303; m/Jean Louise; p/Maurice and Betty London (dec); ed/PhD; mil/USAR Lt Col, Ret'd; pa/Prof Emeritus intl Affairs; Res & Writing: Editing Soviet Anthology; r/Unitarian; hon/Cert of Merit w Distn, US Govt.

LONG, BEATRICE POWELL (pen name Bee Bacherig Long) oc/Former Credit Manager; Insurance Agent; Secretary; b/Oct 8, 1907; h/103 Eastland Dr, Memphis, TN 38111; m/Benjamin James; p/John Edgar and Susan E Byars Powell (dec); ed/Bowling Green Bus Univ; Univ Tenn-M; pa/Past Pres Memphis Chapt Credit Wom Int; Past Pres Poetry Soc Tenn; cp/Gray Lady VA Hosp 10 Yrs; r/Cath; hon/Author 2 Books of Poetry: *Reflections* 1964 & *Where Treasures Lie* 1967; Hon VP, Centro Studi e Scambi; Others.

LONG, EULA KENNEDY oc/Free-lance Journalist; b/Sept 25, 1891; h/371 Albemarle SW, Roanoke, VA 24016; m/Frank M; c/James, Eulalee Anderson, Lewis, Edith Schisler; p/James L Kennedy; Janice Wallace; ed/BA; Grad Okla Univ; pa/Writer Articles & Chd's Stories for Mags; Author 7 Books in Portuguese (1 in 10 Editions, 1 in 8); hon/Acad Wom Writers, Portu-Alegre, Brazil; Acad Writers, Brazil; R-M, W C Cit.

LONG, LEWIS M K oc/Psychologist; b/Nov 19, 1923; h/816 Eden Ct, Alexandria, VA 22308; ba/Rockville, MD; m/(dec); c/Mark A D, Susan A, David L H, Stephen S D; p/F M Long (dec); Eula K Long, Roanoke, VA; ed/AB; BS; MA; MS; PhD; mil/USN 1943-46; pa/Am Sociol Assn; Am Psychol Assn; DC Psychol Assn; cp/VP Bd Mt Vernon Commun Mtl Hlth Ctr; r/Unitarian; hon/Charles Smith Scholar Awd, Harvard Univ.

LONG, MATTIE LEE RUTH oc/Telephone Company Administrator; b/Jan 12, 1948; h/1948 Caldwell St, Saginaw, MI 48601;

ba/Saginaw; p/Cleveland Cooper (dec); Ruby Mae Burnell, Saginaw; ed/AA Delta Col 1967; BBA Saginaw Val St Col 1973; MA Ctl Mich Univ 1979; pa/Alpha Beta Kappa; AAUW; cp/NAACP; Pres Yg Ladies Christian Coun; Dem; r/Pentecostal, Ch of God in Christ; hon/Blain S'ship Fund.

LONG, MONA PYBAS oc/Homemaker; Civic Leader; b/Jun 24, 1933; h/Box 549, Garber, OK 73738; m/Ed; c/Donna, Dave, Steve, Stacia; p/J B and Ethel Pybas, Pauls Valley, OK; ed/BA Okla St 1956; MS Phillips Univ 1979; pa/Cert'd Modeling Instr; Substitute Tchr; cp/OSU Alumni Assn; Nat Queen Chm Am Polled Hereford Assn; Enid Commun Theatre: Pres, Bd Mem 8 Yrs; Phillips Univ Foun Fine Arts: Pres 2 Yrs, Mem 6 Yrs; Garber Band Boosters; Dir Miss Garber Pageant 8 Yrs; VChm Nat Poll-ettes; Dir "Top Ten" 2 Yrs; Others; r/Garber U Meth: Choir Dir, Pianist, Organist, Worship Chm, Coun on Mins, Adm Bd, Pres WSCS, Soloist; hon/Okla Mother of Yr; Outstg Grad, Dorothy Carnegie Course.

LONG, SHIRLEY DOBBINS oc/General Contractor; Designer; Real Estate Broker; Purchasing Agent; Public Relations; Professional Speaker; b/Feb 5, 1943; h/PO Box 19123, Guilford Col Sta, Greensboro, NC 27410; m/(dec); p/Matt Dobbins (dec); Louiva Davis Dobbins, G'boro; ed/BS UNC; Univ Mich Sch Design; pa/Shirley D Long, Bldrs Inc; Designs By Shirley; NC Lic'g Bd for Gen Contractors; Profl Bldr; NC Real Est Bd; Land Devel; Designer, Res Inst Am Mgmt; r/Meth; hon/Design Awd; Patent Pending for Invention; W/W S&SW; Other Biogl Listings.

LONGORIA, EARLENE MOORMAN oc/Attorney; b/Mar 22, 1925; h/PO Box 182, Edinburg, TX 78539; ba/Same; m/Raul L; c/Samuel Glenn, Janiece Maxene, Roy Alan, Martha Elaine, Cecilia Joyce; p/Earl C and Fint Winters Claitor Moorman, Pharr, TX; ed/BBA w hons Univ Tex 1949; pa/Hidalgo Co Bar Assn; Tex St Bar Assn; cp/Tex Senate Wives Clb; r/St Jude's Cath Ch: Mem.

LONNEKER, ArLEEN PATTERSON oc/Owner & Manager; b/Apr 26, 1940; h/610 S Palouse, Walla Walla, WA 99362; m/Robert Frederick; c/3 Chd; p/William Edgar and Marietta McCanse Patterson; ed/Att'd: Weaver Sch Real Est, Metro Mus Art, Moody Bible Inst; pa/Operates Indian Trail Ranches, Pomeroy, Wash; Owner & Mgr Ken-A-Lan Land Enterprises, Spokane, Wash; Maj Stockholder & Secy-Treas Lonneker Farms Inc, Walla Walla; Walla Walla Co, Wash St & Nat Assns Wheat Growers; Past Pres Pomeroy Delta Clb; cp/Advr Wash Ec Bur Info; Dir Wash St Repub Assembly; Exec Bd Mem Wash St Repub Com; Advr: Nat Com for Survival of Free Cong, Am Security Coun; Past Ofcr Global Circumnavigators Travelogue Presentation Soc; Fam Life Dir Walla Walla Wom's Christian Union; Rep 5th Congl Dist Repub Clb; Del Wash St Repub Convs; Var Former Activs; hon/Former Wheat Queen Chm; FFA Sweetheart; Cruise Queen, Franca C Cruises, Genoa, Italy; Hon Citizen, Rotorua, New Zealand; Pub'd Author; Book of Honor; Notable Ams.

LONSFORD, FLORENCE HUTCHINSON oc/Artist; Designer; b/Jan 7, 1914; h/311 E 72nd St, New York, NY 10021; ba/Brooklyn, NY; m/Graydon Lee (dec); p/Frank Edwin and Jennie Cecelia Pugh (dec); ed/BS Purdue Univ; MA Hunter Col; Nat Acad Fine Arts; Art Students League; John Herron Art Inst of Ind Univ; pa/Painter, Sculptor, Lithographer; Paintings sold by Lord & Taylor; Gallery Affiliations: Hoosier Salon (Indpls, Ind), Marcoleo (NYC), Gallery One (Ann Arbor, Mich); Artists Equity; Intl Soc Artists; Artists Space, Am Artists Profl League; Cooperstown Art Assn; cp/Salmagundi Clb of NY; Art Editor, *The Key*, Pub of Kappa Kappa Gamma; r/Presb; hon/Graphics Reviewed in *La Revue Moderne* (Paris); Prix d'honneur, Exposition Intercontinentale, Monaco; Exhibited Deauville & Cannes (France); Prized in Group Shows: Ky, Va, Ind, Ill, Ohio, NY Conn, Mass; Named Outstg Art Edr, NY Sch

Art; League Awd, Metro Museum; Pub'd Author; World W/W Artists.

LOOKER, ANTONIA HANSELL oc/Free-lance Fiction Writer; Poet; h/Hillhouse, Lakemont, GA 30552; ba/Same; m/Earle (dec); c/James Ross Macdonald; p/Andrew Jackson and Elise Compton Hansell (dec); pa/Former Med & Psychi Case Wkr; Dir Psychi Soc Ser Lenox Hill Hosp, NYC; Med & Psychi Work AIEA Nav Hosp (Hi); Free-lance Writer 1947-; cp/Lake Rabun Assn; ARC Vol Nav Hosp WWII; r/Epis; hon/Anthologized, Poetry Soc Ga.

LÓPEZ, ANA MARÍA oc/Instructor; b/Jan 19, 1930; h/PO Box 2681, Mississippi State, MS 39762; ba/Miss St; m/Mariano; c/Candido, Teddy; p/Candido Hernandez, Madrid, Spain; Justiniana Perez (dec); ed/Licentiate Univ Madrid 1969; MA 1974, PhD 1978 SUNY-B; pa/Instr Spanish Lang & Spanish-Am Lit Miss St; cp/Fac Advr Intl Wom's Clb, Miss St Univ; r/Cath; hon/Author Num Articles in Profl Jours.

LÓPEZ, MARIANO oc/Associate Professor; b/Sept 11, 1931; h/PO Box 2681, Mississippi State, MS 39762; ba/Miss St; m/Ana Maria; c/Candido, Teddy; p/Mariano Lopez, Segovia, Spain; Anastasia Sanz (dec); ed/LST Univ Salamanca (Spain) 1956; MA 1969, PhD 1974 SUNY-B; pa/Assoc Prof Spanish Miss St Univ; AAUP; MLA; AATSP; Others; cp/Former Social, Cult & Relf Work in PR & w Hispanic Population in Buffalo, NY; r/Rom Cath; hon/Grant, City of Paris (France); Author Num Articles in Nat & Intl Profl Jours.

LOPEZ, MIGUEL oc/Planner/Scheduler; b/Oct 24, 1949; h/102 Linnville, Port Lavaca, TX 77979; ba/Port Lavaca; m/Hortencia V; c/Anna Valeria; p/Olayo Lopez, Port Lavaca, TX; Maria Elena B Lopez, Falfurrias, TX; ed/Del Mar Col 1968-69; Tex A&I Univ 1969-72; pa/Planner/Scheduler Brown & Root Inc; Tex Press Assn 1972-74; Nat Fdn Amateur Softball Assn Umpires 1975-79; cp/Past VP LULAC; Past Pres JCs; Former U Citizen Leag Mem; r/Our Lady of the Gulf Cath Ch; hon/Outstg Yg Men Am; Outstg UCL Mem; JC of Yr 1974; 2nd Pl, TICPA Newspaper Column Awd; 1966 Cross Country St Championship.

LORD, GAYLE KAY oc/Classroom Teacher; b/Mar 9, 1949; h/620 S Beech, Casper, WY 82601; ba/Casper; p/James E and Ruth S Lord, Greeley, CO; ed/BA; MA; pa/Current Tchr 3rd Grade, Crest Hill Elem Sch; Former 8th Grade Rdg Tchr, Casper 1 Yr; Former 4th Grade Tchr, McCook, Neb 5½ Yrs; Natrona Co Classroom Tchrs Ed Assn; Wyo Ed Assn; NEA; Involved in Pilot Sch Prog for Gifted; Former Mem: McCook Ed Assn, Neb St Ed Assn, Sch Dist Exec Bd McCook, Other Former Activs; r/Meth.

LORD, MARGARET PLUNKETT oc/Consultant; h/2139 Wyoming Ave NW, Washington, DC 20008; ba/Same; m/Charles Edwin; c/Mrs Roger Kelly Brown, Sarah, Charles E Jr, William P; p/William Caldwell Plunkett (dec); Eleanore Kennedy Plunkett, Fairfield, CT; ed/Vassar Col; Hartford Sch Music; pa/Fdr Lord Assocs (Public Relats & Communs Conslt'g) 1976-78; Conslt Downtown Coun-Knox Foun, Hartford, Conn 1974-76; Free-lance Writer; New England Coun Public Affairs Roundtable, Energy Com; Gtr Hartford C of C Congl Clb; cp/VChm Bd Nat Urban Leag; Conn Housing Investmt Fund: Bd Mem, Exec Com, VP, Secy; Bd Mem Conn Trust for Hist Preserv; Pres Urban Leag Gtr Hartford; VP Brotherhood Alcoholic Treatmt Ctr; Allocations Com Panel U Way Gtr Hartford; Nom'g Com Camp Fire Girls; Original Simsbury Bd Chd's Sers Conn; Others; r/Congreg; hon/W/W Am Wom.

LORD, RUTH S oc/Teacher; b/Nov 21, 1927; h/2722 50th Ave, Greeley, CO 80631; ba/Greeley; m/James E; c/James E Jr, Gayle K; p/Jake and Katherine E Steving (dec); ed/BA. MA Univ N Colo; pa/Tchr, Unit Ldr;

Past Secy Greeley Tchrs Assn; Colo Ed Assn; NEA; IRA; Coun for Social Studies; cp/Greeley Knife & Fork Clb; r/Meth; hon/S'ship; Kappa Delta Pi; Alpha Delta Kappa; World W/W Wom.

LOUGHEED, JACQUELINE ISOBEL oc/University Professor; b/Nov 24, 1931; h/4468 Sashabaw, Drayton Plains, MI 48020; ba/Rochester, MI; p/John Clarence and Susan M Ramsay Lougheed, Leamington, Ontario, Canada; ed/BS 1953; MS 1957; EdD 1968; pa/Oakland Univ; Prof 1968-, Dir Tchr Corps (US Ofc of Ed) 1969-; Dir Sch Crime Preven US Ofc Juv Justice Delinq Preven 1976-78; Tchr Detroit Schs & St Clair-Lakeview Schs 1953-61; Admr Detroit Schs 1961-68; r/Presb; hon/Alpha Delta Kappa; Pi Lambda Theta; Mu Phi Epsilon; World W/W Wom in Ed; World W/W Wom; W/W Am.

LOUI, BEATRICE LAN QUE oc/Education Consultant; b/Jun 18, 1907; h/1562 Kanaliu St, Honolulu, HI 96816; ba/Same; p/Heong Poo and Shiu Shee Loui (dec); ed/BA; MA; pa/Conslt Assessmt & Eval Ednl Projects 1973-; Hi St Dept Ed: Specialist in Testing 1964-72, Dir Testing & Measuremt 1960-64; Cnslr Univ Cal 1956; Other Former Positions; Hi Ed Assn; Nat Coun Measuremt in Ed; APGA; Nat Coun Measuremt in Ed; Dirs St Testing Progs; Pi Lambda Theta; Delta Kappa Gamma; Pi Gamma Mu; cp/Pres Assn Chinese Univ Wom; Secy Altrusa Intl; Hi Chinese Hist Ctr; Vol Wkr Honolulu Acad Arts; r/Congreg; hon/Num Profl Pubs; W/W Am Wom; 2000 Wom Achmt; Commun Ldrs Am; DIB; W/W W; World W/W Wom; Creative & Success Personalities.

LOUIS, ENID oc/Registered Nurse; b/Sept 21, 1921; h/199-04 115th Ave, St Albans, NY 11412; ba/Jackson Heights, NY; m/Noel; c/Conan, Anthony, Patricia, Lynette; p/Lucien and Alice Hernandez, Trinidad, WI; ed/RN; pa/Var Nsg Activs; r/Rom Cath; hon/W/W Am Wom.

LOUNSBERRY, ROBERT HORACE oc/State Secretary of Agriculture; b/Jun 22, 1918; h/RR, McCallsburg, IA 50154; ba/Des Moines, IA; m/Muriel; c/William, Beth, Janet, Paul, Steven; p/Horace Charles and Alice Mae Elmore Lounsberry (dec); ed/BA; mil/USAF 1942-45; pa/la Secy Agri; Farmer; Pres: MASDA 1976-77, MIATCO 1975-76; Grain & Feed Tech Adv Com; Nat Meat & Poultry Inspection Adv Com; Des Moines Area Comun Col Agribus Adv Com; Former Mem la Sheep & Wool Growers Assn; la Cattlemen's Assn; Am Nat Cattlemen's Assn; Story Co Swine Prodrs Assn; Story Co Cattlemen's Assn; cp/Bd Mem Ia Public Sch Sys 19 Yrs; Chm Story Co Bd Ed 2 Yrs; Pres Local PTA 2 Yrs; ASCS Com-man 3 Yrs; Story Co Repub Party Chm 5 Yrs; Am Legion: Local Post Cmdr 2 Yrs, Former Nat Exec Com-man, Others; Masonic Lodge; Des Moines Consistory; Gtr Des Moines C of C; Resv Ofcr's Assn US; Other Activs; r/M'burg Presb Ch: Ordained Elder, Chm Trustees, SS Tchr; hon/Life Hon Mem, Davis Co Sheep Prodrs; W/W Univs & Cols; Mil Decorations.

LOVE, DOROTHY BRYAN oc/Accountant; Comptroller; b/Sept 2, 1923; h/PO Box 1238, Reidsville, NC 27320; ba/R'ville; m/John Daniel Sr; c/John Daniel Jr, Anne Docia L Stutts; p/William E and Docia C Bryan, Bladenboro, NC; ed/Grad Campbell Jr Col; pa/Partner, CoMgr Hitching Post Antique & Gift Shop, R'ville 1969-; Acct: Love Car Wash, Eden, NC 1970-, Love Rentals, Eden 1972-, Love & Lovelace Bldrs, R'ville 1968-; Notary Public Rockingham Co (NC) 1965-; Beech Mtn (NC) Property Owners Assn Banner Elk; cp/Secy R'ville City Beautification Comm; R'ham Co Hist Soc; R'ville Jr Ser Leag R'ham Co; Farm Bur; Garden Clbs NC; Former Dist Secy; Dem; Mem Var Clbs; r/Bapt; hon/W/W Am Wom.

LOVE, HOWARD L oc/Agency Executive; b/Dec 8, 1942; h/6509 Sherry Dr, Little Rock, AR 72204; ba/Little Rock; m/Carol A; c/Howard L Jr, Netra Lashawn;

p/John M Love (dec); Willie Mae Love Pointer; ed/BA; Master's; pa/Exec Com Nat Urban Leag Coun Exec Dirs; Pres So Reg Exec Dirs Coun; cp/Ldrship Roundtable; Ark Black Caucus; NAACP; r/U Meth; hon/Distn in Field; Bapt Pastors Conf Layman of Yr 1977; Dist'd Ser & Awds of Recog: City of Little Rock, Hope Inc, GYST House.

LOVE, ROSALIE STOCKS oc/Writer; Retired School Teacher; b/Oct 31, 1913; h/PO Box 430, Norphlet, AR 71759; m/Fred E; c/David Edward (dec), Gerry Beth, Joe Fred; p/Carl Lee and Ora Hayes Stocks (dec); ed/BSE So St Col 1960; Cert Famous Writers Sch 1972; pa/Tchr: 1st Grade (Norphlet) 1967-75, 4th & 5th Grades Union Sch (El Dorado) 1959-67, Kgn 1st Bapt Ch (El Dorado) 1953-59, Piano 1934-51; NEA; Ark Ed Assn; Past Pres: Union Co Tchrs Assn, Norphlet Ed Assn; Histn Union Co Ret'd Tchrs Assn; Delta Kappa Gamma, Var Ofcs; Nat Leag Am Pen Wom: Br Treas, Secy, Pres; Poets Roundtable Ark; Ozark Writers & Artists Guild; cp/PTA; Local Civic Clb; r/Norphlet Bapt Ch: Pianist, Organist, Tchr, Ldr Var Ednl Depts; Conf Ldr Tng Union Dept, Ark Bapt St Conv 1952-57; Curric Writer Presch Mats, Bapt SS Bd, Nashville, Tenn 1954-; Fac Mem Conv Conf Ctrs: Ridgecrest (NC), Glorieta (NM); hon/Dean's List; 1st Pl Awds for Writing, Ark Fest Arts 1977.

LOVE, RUSSELL JACQUES oc/University Professor; Speech & Language Pathologist; b/Jan 11, 1931; h/162 Lelawood Circle, Nashville, TN 37209; ba/N'ville; m/Barbara Williams; c/Steven, Gregory; p/Abraham Issac Love (dec); Olive K Love, N'ville; ed/BS 1953, MA 1954, PhD 1962 NWn Univ; pa/Vanderbilt Univ: Assoc Prof Spch & Lang Pathol 1970-, Asst Prof 1967-70; Spch Conslt Bill Wilkerson Hearing & Spch Ctr 1967-; DePaul Univ, Chicago, Ill: Assoc Prof Spec Ed 1964-67, Coor Prog Spch Pathol; Other Former Positions; Pres Tenn Spch & Hearing Assn 1973-74; Leg Councilor ASHA 1973; Tenn Bd Examrs Spch Pathol & Audiol 1974-78; Spch Conslt VA Hosps: N'ville 1973-, Murfreesboro 1975-; Edit Conslt; cp/St Profl Adv Com U Cerebral Palsy Assn; Bd Trust Cloverbottom Devel Ctr; Mayor's Adv Com on Handicapped, N'ville; Nat Adv Com for An Accessible Envir; hon/Alpha Chi Omega; W/W: SE, Med Scis.

LOVEJOY, DALLAS LANDON oc/Land Surveyor; b/Jul 29, 1936; h/1245½ Pike St, Milton, WV 25541; ba/Milton; m/Elizabeth

Ann; p/Aaron and Thelma Lovejoy, Palermo, WV; ed/LLS; cp/Mason; Shriner; r/Prot; hon/Personalities of S; W/W.

LOVELADY, JOE RENDER oc/Minister; b/Aug 25, 1930; h/6730 Manchester, New Orleans, LA 70126; ba/NO; m/Betty; c/Joe Render Jr; p/Neely L and Fronie Calloway Lovelady (dec); ed/BA; MDiv; MTh; DMin; mil/USAF 1948-53; pa/NO Bapt Assn: Chm Fin Com, Adm Com; Nom'g Com La Bapt Conv; cp/Pres Kiwanis Clb NO; r/So Bapt; hon/Clergyman of Yr 1971; Hon St Senator; 2 Mayoralty Certs of Merit.

LOVERIDGE, DELLA L oc/Teacher; Educator; b/Aug 9, 1904; h/2336 S 3rd E, Salt Lake City, UT 84115; ba/Same; m/(dec); c/Max Elmer; p/Larenzo Lisonbee and Sarah Petersen; ed/Brigham Young Univ; pa/Tchr,

Latter Day Saints Bus Col; Owner & Operator, College of Beauty Culture, Hollywood Col of Adv'd Hair Styling; Editor & Pubr, Utah St Beauticians Mag; BPW 25 Yrs; cp/Ser'd Utah St Legislature 16 Yrs; Nat, St, Co & City Level in Dem Party; Ofcr, Nat Order Wom Legislators; Leg Coun Charter Pres, Dem Wom's Clb; Appt'd to St Com for Higher Ed; Chm Num Legislative Coms; White House Conf on Aging; Others; r/LDS; hon/Hon Life Mem, Deaf Org; 1st Wom to Ser Utah St Legis Coun; Mother of Yr, Lady Lions; Bus Wom of Yr, BPW; Others.

LOVETT, EVELYN JOYCE MILLER STALLINGS oc/Teacher; Reading Specialist; b/Dec 2, 1925; h/Star Rt, Box 47, Clovis, NM 88101; ba/Clovis; m/Roy C; c/Anna C Stallings Taylor, William W Stallings, Evelyn J Stallings, Don, Vickie L Range, Terry, Tim; p/Wesley Braxton and Martha Julia Wade Miller (dec); ed/BS; MA; Addit Studies; pa/Rdg Specialist Clovis Mun Schs; AAUW; NM Nat Ed Assn; IRA; CEC; Assn Chd w LD; Orton Soc; Conslt to Carver Clovis Public Lib; Conducted Num Wkshops; Presentations: Annual Rdg Confs (ENMU, Portales, NM), IRA Convs; Other Profl Activs; r/So Bapt; hon/Pub'd Author; DIB; World W/W Wom; W/W: Child Devel Profls, Am Wom; Intl W/W: Commun Ser, Intells; Personalities W&MW; Intl Reg Profiles.

LOVINGER, WARREN CONRAD oc/University President; b/Jul 29, 1915; h/518 S Holden, Warrensburg, MO 64093; ba/W'burg; m/Dorothy Blackburn; c/Patricia Mae L Schutjer, Wilma Jeanne L Peters, Warren C Jr; p/Wilbur G Lovinger (dec); Ruth K H Lovinger Patterson, Great Falls, MT; ed/BA, MA Univ Mont; EdD Columbia Univ; mil/USNR; pa/Pres Ctl Mo St Univ; Am Assn Cols for Tchr Ed: Pres 1963-64, Exec Com 1956-60, 62-66, Eval Criteria Com 1966-70, Rep to Intl Coun on Ed for Tchg (Paris, France) 1964, Others; Am Assn St Cols & Univs: Del to Republic of China 1976, Del to People's Republic of China 1975, Pres 1974-75, Bd Dirs 1969-77, Others; Am Coun on Ed; Exec Com Mo Assn Cols & Univs 1970-71; Mo Wn Col Conslt; Nat Coun on Accreditation of Tchr Ed: Coor'g Bd 1966-72, Chm Visitation & Appraisal Com 1960-62; NEA; Coun on Public Higher Ed for Mo: Pres 1973-74, Bd Dirs 1972-74; Synod Com on U Presb Cols Mo; Others; cp/W'burg C of C, Former Mem Bd Dirs; Past Pres Rotary Clb; hon/Phi Delta Kappa; Kappa Delta Pi; Phi Kappa Phi; Silver Beaver, BSA.

LOVVORN, MARTIN CRAFT oc/Banker; b/Apr 15, 1928; h/3820 W Bay Circle, Dallas, TX 75214; ba/Richardson, TX; m/Mary Carolyn Goodman; c/Janet, Mark, Linda, Laurie; p/Ben H and Floyd Craft Lovvorn; ed/BBA So Meth Univ 1948; pa/Chm of Bd & Pres: 1st Nat Bk, Richardson 1964-, Dynamerica Corp, Dallas 1969-, Am Nat Bk Garland (Tex), Lovvorn-Davison Inc, Prudential Bldrs Inc; Chm of Bd: Lewisville (Tex) Nat Bk 1963-65, Tex Nat Bk, Dallas 1965-74, Baluco Minerals Inc, Baco Inc, Mr Dobbs Enterprises Inc, Truitt Packing & Export Co; Dir: Branch Properities Inc, Buckner Park Inc, Buckner Ests Inc, Buckner Comml Inc, Buckner Indsl Inc, Spring Val Properties Inc, Mercantile Security Life Ins Co; cp/Bd Dirs Tex Bapt Foun; r/1st Bapt Ch, Dallas: Chm Bd Deacons, Corporate Pres; hon/Biogl Listings.

LOWE, WARREN oc/Research Chemist; b/Jun 4, 1922; h/5619 Jordan Ave, El Cerrito, CA 94530; ba/San Francisco, CA; m/Caroline; p/Lung Lowe (dec); Yee Shee Lowe; ed/BS w highest hons Univ Cal-B; mil/Manhattan Project w AUS Corps & US Atomic Energy Comm; pa/Sr Res Assoc in Chem; Sigma Xi; Am Chem Soc; AAAS; Sci Res Soc Am; Am Inst Chemists; cp/YMCA; El Sobrante Boys' Clb; Nat Bd Missions; Adv Com Mt Hermon Assn; Tung Sen Tong Benevolent Assn; r/Pres: Elder, Pres Missions Dept, Commr to Nat Gen Assembly & Pacific Presb Meetings; hon/Fellow, Am Inst Chemists; Patentee in Chem Fields; Contbr

Articles to Profl Jours.

LOWERY, JOHN STEWART oc/Special Insurance Representative; b/Apr 28, 1953; h/PO Box 433, Lincolnton, NC 28092; ba/L'ton; m/Kathy Lynn; c/Jennifer Lynn; p/Jimmy Lee Lowery, Gastonia, NC; Shirley Williams Lowery, Gastonia; ed/Att'd Gaston Col; pa/Spec Rep Jefferson Standard Life Ins Co 1978-; Leasing Mgr & Salesman Abernethy Chev-Olds, L'ton 1977-78; Free-lance Photog CBS Sports & Car & Track Prodns 1975-77; Other Former Positions; Nat Assn & Lincoln Co Life Underwriters Assn; cp/Dir Lincoln Co Heart Assn; Lincoln Co Red Cross Chapt:

Blood Prog Chm, Dir; Publicity Chm Lincoln Co Bicent Celebration; Chm Rec Com C of C; Reg Dir NC JCs; r/Holy Cross Luth Ch: Fin & Budget Chm; hon/JCs: Clint Dunagan Meml Awd (US), Most Outstg #1 Dist Dir (US & NC), Fast Start Awd (NC), Top Ten Outstg Mem USA, Others; Heart Assn: Fdrs Awd NC, NC Pres' Awd, Achm Recog Awd (NC); Jefferson Standard Life Ins Co: Fast Start Awd Winner, Awd of Excell; Awd for Excell in Photog, Freedom Foun Val Forge; Biogl Listings.

LOWN, WILFORD FRANKLIN oc/- Administrator; b/Feb 13, 1920; h/2809 Brad Ln, Manhattan, KS 66502; ba/Manhattan; m/Nadine; c/Linda L Grover, Carol L Moyer; p/Robert C and Bessie Hall Lown (dec); ed/AB; MS; EdS; LittD; DD; pa/Adm Christian Higher Ed; Past Pres NAm Christian Conv; VP Ks Christian Conv; r/Christian Ch: Mem; hon/Phi Kappa Phi; Phi Delta Kappa; MCC Dist'd Alumnus Awd.

LOWRY, BERNICE GERTRUDE oc/- Occupational Therapist; b/Apr 3, 1922; h/200 George Wallace Dr, Apt 3, Pearl, MS 39208; ba/Jackson, MS; p/Riley W and Junie Rucker Lowry (dec); ed/BS Miss St Univ; MA Geo Peabody Col; Cert Occupl Therapy Wash Univ; pa/Occupl Therapist VA Med Ctr; Miss & Am Occupl Therapy Assns; BPW Clb; AAUW; r/Bapt.

LOWRY, K PATRICIA oc/University Professor; Lecturer; b/Apr 29, 1927; h/Lowry Ln, Rt 3, Box 143-2, Huntsville, TX 77340; ba/H'ville; m/S Douglas; c/Patricia Marjorie, Fredrick Robert Hugh; p/Robert Paul and Kathleen Cleola Fleming Heilman Beardsley; ed/BA 1951, MA 1964, EdD 1968 Ball St Univ; pa/Assoc Prof Dept Ed Sam Houston St Univ 1971-; SHSU Hons & Awds Comm; Pubs incl: Poetry, Curric Manuals, Handbooks, Kgn Parents' Guide; Public Sch Tch 1951-65; Judge Nat Poetry Soc; NEA; IRA: Chapt Pres, St Spkr; Tex Assn for Improvemt of Rdg; Gtr

Houston Area Rdg Coun; Tex Assn Profs Rdg; Early Rdg Res Coun; cp/Delta Sigma Theta; NOW; Quality of Life; OES; PTA; BPW; Audubon; Former Girl Scout Ldr; Camp Fire Girls Ldr; 4-H Ldr; Others; r/Christian Sci: Mem, Sponsor Col Org, Exec Bd Dirs, Field Rep, SS Tchr; hon/Kappa Delta Pi; Phi Delta Kappa; Outstg Alumnus Awd, Ball St Univ; Dist'd Achmt Awd; Notable Ams; World W/W Wom; W/W in Poetry; Personalities of S.

LOWRY, MARY ANN oc/English Professor; b/Nov 2, 1927; h/2764 Lexington Ave NW, Warren, OH 44485; ba/Warren; p/A Lawrence Strabley (dec); Violet E Remalia Strabley, Warren; ed/BS summa cum laude Youngstown St Univ 1965; MA, ABD Kent St Univ 1967-68; pa/Mod Lang Assn; AAUP; Col Eng Assn; MW Mod Lang Assn; NCTE; Eng Assn Ohio; AAUW; Alpha Gamma Sigma; Kappa Delta Pi; Phi Kappa Phi; cp/Charter Mem Quota Clb Intl Inc, Trumbull Val, Ohio; Our Lady of Walsingham, Y'town Chapt; r/Christ Epis Ch, Warren: Worship Comm, Art Com; hon/George M Wilcox Awd for Outstg Tchg; Hon Mention Awd, Ohio's "Poet's Finest" Contest 1978.

LUAHIWA, JUDITH BAGWELL oc/Estate Planner; Insurance Executive; b/Sept 7, 1941; h/1992 Severn Rd, Grosse Pointe Woods, MI 48236; c/1 Son; p/Paul Douglas and Edith Harriet Clark Bagwell; ed/Att'd Stephens Col 1959-60, Mich St Univ 1960, Univ Hi 1961-; pa/Casualty & Life Ins Agt; cp/Metro Detroit Mar Dimes; Former Mem Nom'g Com Bd Dirs Detroit Chapt GSA; Grosse Pointe Symph Wom's Com; Metro Grand Opera Assn; Cranbrook Acad Arts & Mus; Grosse Pointe Theatre; Fdrs Soc Detroit Inst Arts; Smithsonian Inst Fdrs Cir; Friends Detroit Lib; Assistance Leags NE Guid Ctrs & Bon Secours Hosp; Mich Humane Soc; Precnt Del 14th Congl Dist; r/People's Ch, E Lansing (Mich); hon/Book of Honor; Notable Ams Bicent Era; Mich Social Reg; Nat Social Dir; Social Secy; Commun Ldrs & Noteworthy Ams.

LUCAS, GEORGETTA MARIE SNELL oc/Teacher; Artist; b/Jul 25, 1920; h/9702 W Washington St, Indianapolis, IN 46231; ba/Indpls; m/Joseph William; c/Corleen Anita Underwood, Thomas Joseph, Joetta Jeanne Allgood; p/Ernest Clermont Snell (dec); Sally McIntyre Snell, Harmony, IN; ed/BS; MS; pa/Artist; Lectr; Tchr; Paintings in Num Schs, Lodges & Chs; r/Meth; hon/Silver Awd, 1st Pl Intl Platform Art Exhibit 1978.

LUCAS, WILLIAM R oc/Government Executive; b/Mar 1, 1922; h/6805 Criner Rd SE, Huntsville, AL 35802; ba/Marshall Space Flight Ctr, AL; m/Polly Torti; c/Donna Jeanne, William R Jr, Michael Lee; p/William S and Dona Ray Lucas (dec); ed/BS Memphis St Univ; MS, PhD Vanderbilt Univ; mil/USN 1943-46; pa/Fellow: AIAA, Am Soc for Metals, Am Astronautical Soc; Am Chem Soc; Sigma Xi; Nat Acad Engrs; cp/Trustee Mobile Col, Mobile (Ala); r/1st Bapt Ch, H'ville: Deacon; hon/Exceptl Sci Achmt Medals, NASA (3); Dist'd Ser Medal, NASA; AIAA: Hermann Oberth Awd, Holger N Toftoy Awd; Hon DHL, Mobile Col.

LUCIDO, JOSEPH L oc/Thoracic Surgeon; b/Mar 19, 1911; h/6 Bellenive Acres, St Louis, MO 63121; m/Ines; c/John Joseph, Donna Angeline; p/Joseph Sr and Angela Lucido (dec); ed/BS; MD; FACS; mil/USAF Lt Col; pa/Conslt; Active Staff St Louis Univ Med Ctr; St Mary's; Others; Clin Prof Surg St Louis Univ Sch Med; r/Cath; hon/Alpha Omega Alpha; Cert'd: Am Bd Surg, Am Bd Thoracic Surg.

LUDWIG, RAY WOODROW oc/Educator; b/Jun 10, 1941; h/PO Box 550, Moorefield, WV 26836; ba/M'field; p/Branson G Ludwig (dec); Nerva L Ludwig, Rio, WV; ed/AB Shepherd Col 1964; AM 1966, MA 1972 WVa Univ; pa/Edr M'field HS; Hardy Co Schs: Eng Tchr 1976-, Dir Sec'dy Ed, Coor Spec Projs 1969-76; Reg II WVa Curric

Improvemt Ctr Math Specialist 1968-69; Other Former Positions; WVa Ed Assn, Del; NEA: Del, Local Ed Assn, VP HC Classroom Tchrs Assn; Classroom Tchrs Assn Pres; ASCD; cp/Past Mem, Pres, VP: Sperrys Run Yth F'ship, Cir K Clb, Student Christian Assn; Past Treas Kappa Delta Pi; Cohongoroota: Former Editor, Asst Editor; Nat Geographic Soc; Am Mus for Natural Hist; Nat Hist Soc; 4-H Clb; r/U Meth; hon/W/W: Students in Am Univs & Cols, Sch Dist Ofcls; Circle K Man of Yr, Kiwanis Clb, Col Br 1964; Hon Farmers Deg; Citizenship Awd, Am Legion; M'field Examr Jour Awd; Shepherd Cols 1st Cohongoroota Awd; Nat Hon Soc; Outstg Yg Men Am; Personalities of S; Notable Ams; Commun Ldrs & Noteworthy Ams; DIB; Intl W/W Commun Ser; Men of Achmt.

LUDWIG, RUBY BALLARD oc/Learning Disability Teacher, School Psychometrist; b/Sept 18, 1913; h/R-1 Lake Rd One B-547, Grove, OK 74344; ba/Grove; p/Archable L and Cynthia E Gladney Ballard (dec); ed/BA 1970; MS 1972; Addit Studies; pa/CEC; cp/Okla Fed Indian Wom: Rec Secy 1964-66, 2/VP 1966-68; Del Commun Cherokee Indian Org; Ariz St Univ Alumni Assn; Grove Dem Wom's Clb; OES; Nat Assn Mature People; Okla Indian Rts Assn; Okla Hist Soc; Alquerque Haskell Alumni Assn; r/Christian Ch; hon/Outstg Tchrs in Exceptl Ed; W/W Child Devel Profls; Notable Ams; Personalities of S; Commun Ldrs & Noteworthy Ams; World W/W Wom; Book of Honor; Cert of Apprec, Ariz St Univ Alumni.

LUING, GARY A oc/University Administrator; b/Apr 24, 1937; h/9550 NW 42 Ct, Coral Springs, FL 33065; ba/Boca Raton, FL; m/Sherry Lea; c/Heather; p/Dwight O and Marjorie Mae Luing, Marshalltown, IA; ed/BS cum laude Stetson Univ; MAS Univ Ill; mil/Fin Corps 1/Lt; pa/Dean Sch of Bus Fla Atl Univ; Editor, Fla Cert'd Public Acct; cp/Chm Palm Bch Co Trans Com; r/Bapt; hon/Dist'd Ser Awd, Fla Accts Assn.

LUKAS, GAZE ELMER oc/Accountant, Appraiser; b/Nov 9, 1907; h/719 Lori Dr #19-210, Palm Springs, FL 33461; ba/Same; m/Frances Adelaide Lyman; c/Victor Thomas; p/Victor and Theresa Dinzenberger Lukas (dec); ed/BS 1930, MS 1933, JD 1956 Univ Ill (w hons); CPA, Ill 1930; mil/AUS 1942-45, Capt to Maj; ETO 1 Battle Star, Bronze Star Medal; pa/Acct & Appraiser Oriental Art & Antiques, Palm Bch Co; Partner Tuscan Ct Orientalia, Urbana, Ill 1964-68; Vis Prof Acctg Fla Tech Univ, Orlando 1968-70; Vis Prof Acctg Fla Atl Univ, Boca Raton 1971-72; Partner Paul M Green & Assoc, Bus Ed Conslts, Champaign, Ill 1955-68; Other Former Positions; Ill CPA Soc; Am Inst CPAs; Alpha Kappa Psi; Phi Delta Phi; Appraisers Assn Am; cp/Former Mem Co Audit Adv Bd Ill; r/Christian; hon/Public Ser Awd, St of Ill; Meritorious Civilian Ser Awd, QM Gen; Beta Alpha Psi; Beta Gamma Sigma; Pi Kappa Phi; Order of Coif; Profl Pubs.

LUKAS, RICHARD ANTHONY oc/Music Teacher; Free-lance Musician; Private Investigator; b/141 Park Pl, Pompton Lakes, NJ 07442; ba/Wayne, NJ; m/Carol C; c/Marie Christine, Sophia Jean; p/Milton and Ann Lukas, Union, NJ; ed/BA; MA; pa/Trumpet: Columbia Symph Orch, Linden Symph Orch,

Summit Symph Orch, Others; Lead & Jazz Trumpet: Andy Wells Orch, Lynn Oliver Orch; Ldr Dick Lukas Quartet; Pvt Investigator D R Capello Assn; r/Cath; hon/Contbr to Music Jours; Pub incl *Original Music for the Jr HS Band*, 1971.

LUM, JEAN L J oc/Professor; b/Sept 5, 1938; ba/Honolulu, HI 96822; p/Yee Nung and Pui Ki Young Lum, Honolulu; ed/BS; MS; MA; PhD; pa/Univ Hi-Manoa: Instr to Prof Dept Profl Nsg 1961–, Dept Chm 1973–76; Proj CoDir Analysis & Planning for Improved Distribution of Nsg Pers & Sers Prog, Wn Interst Comm for Higher Ed, Boulder, Colo 1977; Extramural Assoc, Extramural Assocs Prog Div Res Grants, Nat Insts Hlth 1978–79; Conslt; ANA; ANA Coun Nurse Reschrs; Fdg Mem Wn Soc for Res in Nsg; Nat Leag for Nsg; Am Sociol Assn; Adv Bd Wn Jour for Nsg Res; Pacific Sociol Assn; Assn for Wom in Sci; Hi Public Hlth Assn; Nurses' Coalition for Action in Polits; Exec Com Ethnic Nurses for Advmt of Hlth Care; cp/Child & Fam Ser; Univ Hi Foun; r/Epis; hon/Alpha Kappa Delta; Sigma Theta Tau; Mortar Bd; Phi Kappa Phi; Delta Kappa Gamma; Fellow, Am Acad Nsg.

LUM, PAUL P oc/Writer; Business Partner; b/Feb 10, 1923; h/2899 SE Division St, Portland, OR 97202; p/Mr and Mrs Hing Lum (dec); ed/BA 1945; pa/Partner Wor Chung Co; Advt'g Mgr Walnut Cafe 1972-73; Writer; AAAS; Former: IPA, ASPA, APSA; cp/Exec Com Chinese Considated Benevolent Assn; Pres Portland Lum Fam Soc; hon/Pub'd Author; DIB; Men of Achmt; W/W: W, Fin & Indust; Royal Blue Book; Commun Ldrs & Noteworthy Ams.

LUMICAO, BENJAMIN GUIAB oc/-Physician; b/Mar 15, 1936; h/2629 Kingston Dr, Northbrook, IL 60062; ba/Chicago, IL; m/Felicitas Evangelista; c/Benjamin Jr, Robert Felicisimo; p/Tomas Lumicao and Josefina Guiab, Philippines; ed/MD; pa/AMA; Am Med Soc; Ill Med Soc; r/Rom Cath.

LUMPKIN, THOMAS RILEY oc/Physician; Assistant Dean; b/Jan 4, 1926; h/#2 Ridgeland, Tuscaloosa, AL 35401; ba/University, AL; m/Jean Perry; c/Leah, Ry, Mary Lyman, Cliff; p/William Clifford Lumpkin; Harriet Graham Riley Lumpkin, Tuskegee, AL; ed/MD 1958; mil/AUS MC; pa/Fam Med; Asst Dean for Cont'g Med Ed; Bd Dirs AAFP; cp/Tuscaloosa Rotary Clb; Advr Med Explorers Post; r/Meth; hon/Charter Diplomate, ABFP; St Advr AAMA.

LUNA, DAVID G oc/County Commissioner; Businessman; b/Nov 6, 1948; h/Box 283, Brackettville, TX 78832; ba/Same; m/Julia; c/Yvonne Michele, Vivian; p/-Rodolfo Luna (dec); Barbarita Luna, B'ville; mil/AUS Paratrooper 8 Yrs; Combat Tour in Vietnam; S/Sgt; pa/Chm of Bd Peso Inc; cp/Co Commr; Actively involved w: Mexican Am Rts, Civil Rts, Polits, Voters Registration for Mexican Ams, Ec Devel; r/Cath; hon/Mil Decorations incl: Combat Inf-mans Badge, Silver Star, Bronze Star, Parachute Wings, Good Conduct Medal, Army Commend Medal, Vietnam Ser Medal, Vietnam Commend Medal, 82d Airborne Div Dist'd Trooper Awd; 8 Certs of Merit, 82d Airborne Div; Outstg Post Cmdr, VFW (US).

LUNARDINI, ROBERT CHRISTOPHER oc/Consulting Civil Engineer; b/Feb 18, 1933; h/3747 Crane Blvd, Jackson, MS 39216; ba/Jackson; m/Susan Haywood; c/Karen Ann, Robert C Jr, William, Kathy, Vicki, Maria, Thomas, Michael, John; p/Virgil J Lunardini (dec); Christine Lunardini, Chicopee, MA; ed/BS Mich Tech; MS Univ Mich; mil/AUS Corps of Engrs 1/Lt; pa/Owner So Consluts Inc; PE: Miss, Ala, La, Ill; ASCE; SAME; MES; AWWA; WPCF; cp/Mass Arts; Miss Ballet; Jackson C of C; r/Cath; hon/Fellow, ASCE; W/W in S.

LUNDQUIST, CARL HENRY oc/College & Seminary President; b/Nov 16, 1916; h/1900 N Asbury Ave, St Paul, MN 55112; ba/St Paul; m/Nancy Zimmermann; c/Carole L Spickelmier (Mrs James), Eugene Truett, Jill L Anderson (Mrs James), Susan Elizabeth; p/Henry and Esther G Lundquist (dec); ed/BA; BD; ThM; DD; ThD; pa/Bethel Col & Sem: Pres 1954, Pres-elect & Acting Dean 1953-54, Prof of Preaching (Sem); Pastor Elim Bapt Ch, Chicago, Ill 1943-53; Am Assn Higher Ed; Adv Bd Am Behavioral Sci Tng Labs; Assn for Profl Ed of Min; Assn Sem Profs in Pract Fields; Bapt Gen Conf: Moderator, Exec Coun, Trustees, Bd Bible Sch & Yth, Bd Home Missions; Bapt Hosp Fund; Pres Nat Assn Evangelicals; NEA; Pi Kappa Delta; Minn Coun Chs; Bd Advrs Interdenom Cont'g Ed Prog for Clergy in Minn; Other Profl Activs; cp/Exec Com US Cong on Evang; St Paul C of C; Rotary Clb St Paul; Bd Dirs YMCA St Paul; Others; r/Calvary Bapt Ch, Roseville, Minn: Mem 1953–; hon/Commun Ldrs & Noteworthy Ams; DIB; Personalities W&MW; Royal Blue Book; Ldrs in Ed; Intl W/W Commun Ser; Men of Achmt; Others.

LUNDSTROM, JEAN LOUISE oc/-Administrator; b/Aug 5, 1935; h/23951 Leeward Dr, Laguna Niguel, CA 92677; ba/-Laguna Hills, CA; m/Gene E; c/Stuart; p/Floyd C and Lois Tucker; ed/BS Cal St Univ-F; pa/Admr & Dir Saddleback Commun Hosp Home Hlth Agy 1972–; Charge Nurse John F Kennedy Meml Hosp, Stratford, NY 1966-67, 1968–; Cal Assn Hlth Sers at Home; Am Public Hlth Assn; cp/Laguna Niguel Woms Clb; Orange Co Coun on Aging; Acad Polit Sci; r/Prot; hon/Outstg Mothers March Ser Awd; St Awd in Communs Radio, TV & Motion Pictures Cal Fdn Wom's Clbs; W/W Am Wom.

LUTER, YVONNE MARIE-LOUISE oc/Journalist; b/Feb 26, 1928; h/1185 Park Ave, New York, NY 10028; ba/NYC; p/Ernest Spiegelberg (dec); Marie-Louise Spiegelberg, NYC; ed/BA Bryn Mawr Col 1949; MA Columbia Univ 1958; r/Prot.

LUTTRULL, RONALD RAY oc/Electronics Manufacturing Company Executive; b/Aug 9, 1936; h/2724 Aspen, Plano, TX 75075; ba/Richardson, TX; m/Jo Ann Ollar;

c/Lisa Renee, Jeffrey Todd; p/Loyd Jacob and Bessie Madlen Barker Luttrull, Bartlesville, OK; ed/BSIE Okla St Univ; MBA SMU; mil/-AUS 1959-61, 1/Lt; pa/Nat Mgmt Assn; cp/YMCA, Indian Guides; PSA; r/Bapt; hon/W/W; Cert'd Profl Mgr.

LUTZ, PAUL EUGENE oc/Professor; b/Jun 25, 1934; h/5408 Ainsworth Dr, Greensboro, NC 27410; ba/G'boro; m/Patricia Moss; c/Carol Susan; p/C E Lutz (dec); Mrs C E Lutz, China Grove, NC; ed/AB Lenoir-Rhyne; MS Univ Miami; PhD Univ NC; pa/Prof Biol Univ NC-G; Reschr; Author 50+ Pubs; r/Luth Ch in Am: Active; hon/Alumni Tchg Excell Awd; Outstg Edr Awd; Dist'd Ser Cit.

LUTZ, RAYMOND PRICE oc/Professor; b/Feb 27, 1935; h/10275 Hollow Way, Dallas, TX 75229; ba/Richardson, TX; m/Nancy Cole; p/Raymond P Lutz (dec); Sibyl H Lutz, New Boston, TX; ed/BS; MBA Univ NM; PhD Ia St Univ; pa/Prof Mgmt Univ Tex-Dallas; VP Indust & Mgmt Am Inst Indust Engrs;

cp/Selection Bd Inventors Hall of Fame; r/Presb; hon/Fellow: Am Inst Indust Engrs, AAAS; Sigma Xi.

LUTZKER, EDYTHE oc/Historian; Writer; Researcher; Free-lance; b/Jun 25, 1904; h/201 W 89th St, New York, NY 10024; ba/Same; m/Philip; c/Michael Arnold, Arthur Samuel, Paul William; p/Solomon and Sophia Levine (dec); ed/BA CCNY 1954; MA Columbia Univ 1959; pa/Res Asst to Prof Edward Rosen (Histn of Sci in Renaissance) CCNY 1952-55; Var Res Projs; Author: *Wom Gain a Place in Med* 1969, *Edith Pechey-Phipson, MD (1845-1908), The Story of England's and India's Foremost Pioneering Wom Doctor* 1973; AAAS; Am Assn for Hist of Med; Am Hist Assn; Am Soc for Microbiol; Fawcett Soc (London); Hist of Sci Soc; Social Hist Med (London); Societe Internationale d'Histoire de la Medecine; Judaica Hist Philatelic Soc; cp/LWV; Pres City-Wide & St-Wide Child Care Ctr Parents Assn; r/Humanist; hon/Fellow, Royal Soc Med; Key Participant Platinum Jubilee of Haffkine Inst (Bombay) 1974; Grantee: Am Philosophical Soc, Nat Lib of Med, Nat Insts Hlth of DHEW.

LUZARRAGA, MARLENE KATHRYN oc/Medical Bacteriologist; b/Apr 8, 1933; h/8608 Hickory Thicket Pl, Baltimore, MD 21236; ba/Balto; m/Artemio Soriano; c/Arthur John, Maria Louise; p/Harry Riley and Mary Baker Bowen, Balto; ed/Grad Johns Hopkins Univ Dept Pathol Tng Prog in Med Bacteriol 1952; pa/Johns Hopkins Univ Sch Med: Bacteriologist (Div Comparative Med) 1976, Res Technician (Dept Infectious Diseases 1964-76, Lectr (Sch of Nsg) 1957-60; Other Former Positions; Local & Nat Brs Am Soc for Microbiol; Jacques Cousteau Soc; AAAS; cp/Assoc Mem Am Mus Natural Hist; Smithsonian Assoc; Past Pres PTA; Vol Wkr Rec Coun; Commun Improvemt Assns; hon/Awd in Recog of Vol Ser to Local Elem Schs (Sci Proj Demon Lectures Given); W/W Am Wom; Pub'd Author.

LYDA, HAP oc/Professor; b/Dec 25, 1932; h/1012 Circle Ln, Bedford, TX 76021; ba/Ft Worth, TX; m/Julia Whiteman; c/Marc, Jay, Lance; p/Thomas and Martha Greuneich Lyda (dec); ed/BTh; MDiv; MA; PhD; pa/Prof Phil & Rel Tarrant Co Jr Col; Am Acad Rel; Am Soc Ch Hist; SWn Phil Soc; AAUP; Tex Jr Col Tchrs Assn; Soc for Hlth & Human Values; Inst on Rel in Age of Sci; Matchette Consortium of Philosophers; World Futures Soc; cp/CoEditor *Jour of Expression*; Fdg Partner Crim Justice Press; YMCA; Kiwanis; Common Cause; hon/Mandelia Awd; Ofburne F'ship.

LYELLS, RUBY E STUTTS oc/Businesswoman; Executive; h/1116 Montgomery St, Jackson, MS 39203; m/Meredith Jerry (dec); p/T F and Rossie Cowan Stutts (dec); ed/BS Alcorn St Univ; BSLS Hampton Inst; MA Chicago Univ; pa/Co-Owner, Mgr MLS Ser Co Drug Store 1959-69; Exec Dir Miss St Coun on Human Relats 1955-59; Libn Carver & Col Park Brs Jackson Mun Lib 1951-55; Other Former Positions; NEA; Nat Negro BPW Clbs; IPA; Miss Tchrs Assn-NEA (now Miss Assn Edrs-NEA); Miss Lib Assn; cp/Lady Sabena Clb-Understanding Through Travel; Life Mem: Nat Assn Colored Wom's Clbs, NAACP, Nat Coun Negro Wom; Smithsonian Instn Assocs; L Q C Lamar Soc; Pres Miss Chapt Nat Assn Landowners; Miss Wom's Cabinet for Public Affairs; Mississippians for Ednl TV; Miss Wildlife Fdn; Bd Mem Miss Consumers Assn; Miss Common Cause; Urban Leag; LWV; Pres Jacksonians for Public Ed; Opera Guild (Jackson); Num Others; r/Christian Sci; hon/Fellow, Intl Inst Commun Ldrs; Num Profl Pubs; Commun Ser Awd, Miss Indep Beauticians Assn; Cit for Public Ser, Univ Chgo Alumni Assn; Awd for Dist'd Ser & Outstg Ldrship, Hampton Inst; Gov's Cert of Apprec for Civic & Commun Endeavors; Nat Coun Negro Wom "Mary McLeod Bethune" Centennial Cert of Apprec; Outstg Ldrship Awd, Miss Black Ldrship Conf; Others.

LYLE, MARY EMMA MALONEY

oc/Teacher; b/Oct 19, 1917; h/107 Rankin Dr, Greeneville, TN 37743; m/Robert A III (dec); p/Hugh Conway and Lena McCorkle Maloney (dec); ed/BS 1940; MA George Peabody Col 1952; pa/Ret'd 1979, Tchr 1st Grade E View Sch, G'ville; Life Mem PTA; NEA; Round Pacific Tour 1974; cp/DAR; Regent 1970-72, Nolachuckey Chapt Gold Hon Roll, Del to Continental, Chaplain Nolachuckey Chapt; CAR: Sr Pres Robert Sevier Soc, St, Nat & Life Promoter; r/Christ U Meth Ch: Exec Bd Mem, Chd's Choir Dir, Chm Comm on Missions; hon/WSCS Ch Pin; Delta Kappa Gamma, Psi Chapt Key; Others.

LYMAN, JANICE KAY oc/Psychiatric Social Worker; b/Jan 3, 1945; h/210 Jackson, Macon, MO 63552; ba/Kirksville, MO; p/John Thomas Lyman (dec); Lorene Nisbeth Lyman, Macon; ed/BA, MA NE Mo St Univ; pa/APGA; r/Disciples of Christ; hon/Rel Ed S'ship, Culver-Stockton.

LYMAN, RUTH ANN oc/Psychologist; Mental Health Administrator; b/Feb 2, 1948; h/3228 Highland Dr, Birmingham, AL 35205; ba/B'ham; m/Robert Dennis; p/Oren E and Frances U Frerking, Florence, AL; ed/BS 1969, MA 1972, PhD 1973 Univ Ala; Addit Studies, Certs; pa/Dir Bur Mtl Hlth & Dir Wn Mtl Hlth Ctr, Jefferson Co Dept Hlth, B'ham 1975-; Chief Mtl Hlth Sect & Clin Psychologist Univ Hlth Ser, Col Commun Hlth Sers, Univ Ala-T 1973-75; Assoc Resource Design & Devel Corp, Univ (Ala) & NYC 1973-78; Other Profl Activs; APA; Ala Coun Mtl Hlth/Mtl Retard Dirs Inc; Ala Acad Neurol & Psychi; Assn Lic'd Psychologists Ala; SEn Psychol Assn; Am & Ala Public Hlth Assns; Assn Mtl Hlth Admrs; Others; Var Presentations; Mem Bds & Coms; r/Meth; hon/Num Profl Pubs; Reg Finalist, Pres' White House F'ship; Fellow, Ala Dept Mtl Hlth; Martin S Wallach Awd, Dept Psychi, Univ NC Sch Med; Outstg Yg Career Wom Awd, Tuscaloosa (Ala) BPW Clb 1975; Biogl Listings.

LYNCH, BENJAMIN LEO oc/Educator; College Dean; Oral Surgeon; b/Dec 29, 1923; h/509 S Happy Hollow Blvd, Omaha, NE 68106; ba/Omaha; m/Colleen D Cook; c/Kathleen, Mary Beth, Patrick, George, Martha, Estelle; p/William Patrick and Mary (Rauber) Lynch; ed/BSD 1945, DDS 1947, AM 1953 Creighton Univ; MSD NWn Univ 1954; pa/Creighton Univ: Coor Dental Sch Grad & Postgrad Progs 1967-, Prof Oral Surg 1957-, Dir Oral Surg Dept 1954-67, Assoc Prof Oral Surg & Dir Dept Oral Surg 1954-55, Dean Sch Dentistry 1954-61, Others; Staff Appts incl: Archbishop Bergan-Mercy Hosp, Bishop Clarkson Hosp, Chd's Meml Hosp, Luth Med Ctr, Neb Meth Hosp, St Joseph's Hosp; Conslt to VA Hosp, Omaha; Diplomate Am Bd Oral Surgs, Neb Blue Cross Bd Dirs (Exec Com); Am Dental Assn; Am Soc Oral Surgs; Neb Soc Oral Surgs: CoFdr 1957, Pres 1961; MW Soc Oral Surgs; Neb Dental Assn, Num Positions; Fellow Am Col Dentists; Delta Sigma Delta; Fdg Mem Am Col Oral-Maxillofacial Surgs 1975; Fdr & 1/Pres Neb Dental Soc Anesthesiol; Num Other Profl Activs; cp/Optimists Clb; YMCA; Fdg Mem Apollonia Clb; hon/Nom Outstg Yg Man of Yr Omaha 1951, 52, 57; Omicron Kappa Upsilon; Alpha Sigma Nu; Pub'd Author; W/W: Am, MW, Am Ed, Am Dentistry; Commun Ldrs & Noteworthy Ams; Intl W/W Commun Ser; Personalities W&MW; DIB; Others.

LYNCH, WILLIAM EDWARD oc/General Family Counselor; b/May 17, 1930; h/8705 SW 137 Ave, Miami, FL 33183; ba/Coral Gables, FL; m/Barbara; c/Eileen, Kevin, Barbara, Jeannine; p/William T and Mable A Lynch (dec); ed/BA; MA; STL; SSL; pa/Lectr; Author; r/Rom Cath.

LYNCH, WILLIAM WRIGHT JR oc/Real Estate Developer; b/Aug 26, 1936; h/3604 Haynie Ave, Dallas, TX 75205; ba/Dallas; m/Sandra; c/Mary Margaret, Katherine; p/William W and Martha Hirsch Lynch, Dallas; ed/BS Ariz Univ 1959; MBA Stanford Univ 1962; mil/AUS 1959-60; pa/Pres Ins Bldg Corp, Dallas 1965-; Secy & Dir Cimarron Properties Corp 1972-; Dir: Llano Inc, Broadmoor Properties Inc, NM Elec Ser Co, Hobbs Gas Co, Ins Bldg Corp; Pres & Dir Argus Realty Corp; cp/Former Mem: Dallas Civic Music, Ednl Opports Inc, Dallas Symph Orch; r/Epis; hon/Blue Key; Tau Beta Pi; Pi Mu Epsilon.

LYND, JAMES PAUL oc/Executive Director; b/Jan 16, 1928; h/PO Box 31, Gotha, FL 32734; ba/Winter Park, FL; m/Ann W; c/Lonnie, Robin; p/Ben H Lynd (dec); Frances L, Orlando, FL; ed/BLS; MLS; DCE; mil/USN; pa/Exec Dir Lynd Cnslg Ctr; Assn Christian Marriage Fam Cnslrs; Assn Christian Mtl Hlth; cp/Sertoma; 32° Mason; Shriner; r/Christian; hon/Awds: Ser to Mankind, Zeus, Layman of Yr, Dist'd Ser.

LYNDE, JOSEPH ERNEST (TIMBERJACK JOE) oc/Trapper, Outdoorsman, Mountain Man; b/Mar 8, 1911; h/Bear Hole 621, Dubois, WY 82513; m/Marian Hoffer; p/Isaac Worthy and Winnifred Ethel McCawlley Lynde; pa/Former Rancher, Farmer; Diseased Timber Contractor US Forest Ser; Trapper, Tanner, Dubois; Movie Appearance *Golden Eagle, Silver Eagle*; Star TV Prog, Cody, Wyo; Guest Appearance w Dog Tuffy in Num Wn & Rodeo Shows throughout US; Nat Geog Soc; Nat Rifle Assn; Nat Muzzel Loaders Assn; cp/Elk; Eagle; Active DuBois Pony Express Revival, Local Bicent Planning; hon/Blood Brother John Johnston (Jeremiah Johnston), Participant in Reburial in Mtn Site; 1st Pl, Los Angeles Intl Sports Show; Named Hon Chief Arapahoe Indians, Crow Indians; Contbr to Record Album, Jim Bridges & Seekers of the Fleece; Biogl Listings.

LYNN, SARA GAW oc/Assistant Professor; b/Nov 28, 1923; h/PO Box 66, Cookeville, TN 38501; m/Sam H; c/Sandra Joyce; p/(dec); ed/MA; pa/Tenn Tech Univ; Asst Prof, Alumni Placemt & Devel Com, Ath Com, Judiciary Selective Com Assoc'd Student Body, Panhellenic Coun, Others; Life Mem NEA; Guid Chm TEA 1970-71; APGA; ASCA; AACES, Secy 1971-72; TAWDC; Pres CPGA 1971-72; AAUW; Delta Kappa Gamma: 1/Pres Alpha Upsilon Chapt 1963, Profl Affairs Chm 1970-72; Fac CoSponsor Kappa Delta Pi; So Assn Cnslr Ed & Supvn; Fac Advr Mortar Bd & Phi Mu; hon/S'ship Awd, Delta Kappa Gamma; IPA; Outstg Fac Awd, Tenn Tech Univ; Phi Delta Kappa; Kappa Delta Pi; World W/W Wom in Ed; W/W S&SW; DIB; W/W Am Wom; 2000 Wom Achmt; Others.

LYONS, DAN oc/Editor; b/Aug 13, 1920; h/4135 E 46th St, Tulsa, OK 74135; ba/Tulsa; m/Mary; c/Ashling, Daniel; p/Patrick and Alice Lyons; ed/MA (Phil); MA (Sociol); STL; pa/Editor *Christian Crusade Weekly* 1975-; Contb'g Editor *Human Events* 1971; Fdr Twin Circle Pub'g Co (New York City) 1967; Fdr Radio Talk Show "Sound Off", KWEN (Tulsa) 1978; Host "Twin Circle Headline", 30-minute Weekly TV Show; Fdr Asian Spkrs Bur 1965; Current Events Columnist for *Our Sunday Visitor* 1964-67; Other Former Positions; Author or Coauthor 6 Books incl'g *Vietnam Crisis*; Num Articles or Columns; r/Rom Cath; hon/Recipient 19 Awds.

LYONS, GEORGE W C oc/Minister; Educator; b/Aug 20, 1923; h/1206 W 89th St,

Los Angeles, CA 90044; ba/Same; m/Delores S; c/JoAnne C, George W C Jr; p/Coleman and Emily E Lyons (dec); ed/AB; DD; PhD; mil/USAAF WWII; pa/CTA; NEA; CEA; cp/Omega; Mason; LA Policy Clergy Coun; Lyons Rel & Personal Cnslt'g Clin; r/Mystic; hon/W/W Among Black Ams; Notable Ams; Good Conduct Medal, AUS.

LYONS, JAMES FELTON oc/Attorney; b/Sept 28, 1938; h/207 Grant St, Bonners Ferry, ID; ba/Bonners; m/Lynne; c/James, John, Benjamin; p/A L Lyons (dec); Shirley Lyons, Lewiston, ID; ed/AB Stanford 1960; JD Univ Idaho 1968; mil/USAF Maj; Grad US Army Command & Gen Staff Col; pa/Assoc & Partner Nixon, Nixon, Lyons & Bell 1968-; Pres Kaniksu Assocs 1975-; Kaniksu Title Co Inc: Pres 1969-75, Former VP, Secy & Treas; Dir Schweitzer Inc (Ski Resort) 1975-; Spec Asst Atty Gen, Public Hlth Dist #1 1971-78; Prosecuting Atty Boundary Co (Idaho) 1971-73; Justice Ct Judge Moscow, Idaho 1966-68; cp/St Com-man, Dem Party; Spokane Clb (Spokane, Wash); Empire Clb (Spokane); Pres Boundary Co Hist Soc; r/Epis; hon/Nathan Burkan Copyright Law Competition, 1st Prize, Univ Idaho 1968.

LYONS, JERRY L oc/Engineer; Author; Lecturer; Executive; Professor; b/Apr 2, 1939; h/7535 Harlan Walk, St Louis, MO 63123; p/Ferd H and Edna T Lyons; ed/BSME Okla Inst of Tech; pa/Pres Yankee Ingenuity Inc Res & Devel Ctr, St Louis; Adj Prof Bradley Univ; Chm Mo Registration Com Soc Mfg Engrs; Intl Cert Com SME; St Louis Soc of SME Chapt 17: Chm-elect 1978-79, Chm Ed Com, Chm Profl Devel, Registration & Cert Com; ASME; NSPE; MSPE; Sr Mem: ISA, SME; Corporate Mem St Louis Engrs Clb; Com-man Am Security Coun; Former Proj Engr Essex Cryogenics 1964-73, Harris Mfg Co Inc; Former Mgr Engrg Res, Chemetron Corp 1973-77; Reg'd Profl Engr; Cert'd Mfg Engr in Product Design; Written 4 Books, Num Articles, Tech Books; Com-man on Pressure Ratings for Nat Fluid Power Assn, ANSI; ASME: Sr Com-man of OAC Com, VChm 3 Intl Conf; Hd Num Sems; Instr in Fluid Controls, Wis & Wash Univs Ext Div; Profl Assns; Designed pilots flight control stick for Am's 2 newest aircraft, the McDonnell-Douglas F-15 Eagle & B-1 Bomber by NAm Rockwell; r/Luth; hon/St Louis Engrs Clb Awd of Merit; St Louis Chapt 17 & Reg V of SME: Profl Devel Awd, Pres Awd; DIB; W/W: MW, Engrg.

LYONS, SARAH PEARL MATHILDA oc/Librarian; b/Aug 31, 1938; h/2940 S Steele, Denver, CO 80210; ba/Denver; p/Samuel Henry Lyons (dec); Anna D Lyons, Indiana, PA; ed/BS; MRE; MA; pa/Am Theol Lib Assn; Christian Libns' F'ship; r/Bapt.

LYONS, SHARON LYNN oc/Educational Consultant; College Instructor; b/Jul 11, 1946; h/3412 Pinehurst, Plano, TX 75075; c/Michael Patrick; p/Robert Charvoz, Dallas, TX; Dottie Burkley, Dallas; ed/BS; MEd; pa/Instr Child Devel Eastfield Col, Mesquite, Tex 1977-; Instr Hurst-Euless-Bedford Schs, Bedford, Tex 1968-75; Other Former Tchg Positions; Ed Conslt Collin Co Co-op Spec Dept Human Resources, Dallas 1977-; Wkshop Presenter Dallas Assn Ed of Yg Chd 1978-; Others; Bd Dirs HEB Assn Retard Chd; 3/VP Assn Chd LD; So Assn for Chd Under Six; Dallas, Tex Assns Yg Chd; NEA; Tex St Tchrs Assn; Tex Assn Chd LD; IRA; PTA Tex; Am Assn Fam Therapist; Intl Transactional Analysis Assn; Other Profl Activs; cp/2/VP Wilshire PTA; Org'd Drug Wkshop; hon/Ser Pin Awd, Wilshire PTA; Tchr of Yr Awd 1971-72; S'ships; Pub'd Author.

LYSER-SHOUBY, KATHERINE M oc/Professor; b/May 11, 1933; ba/Box 1030, Hunter Col CUNY, New York, NY 10021; m/Elli Shouby; p/Charles R and Anita S Lyser; ed/BA; MA; PhD; pa/Prof Biol Scis Hunter Col; Res; hon/Res Grants: NIH, CUNY, U Cerebral Palsy.

M

MA, CHEN-LUAN oc/Professor; b/Aug 18, 1912; h/12700 Tomanet Trail, Austin, TX 78758; ba/Austin; m/Sharon Y Shang; c/Jannie, Amy, Doris (Mrs Peter Chang), Douglas, Danny; p/Sheng San Ma and Wang Shih (dec); ed/BA Nat Peking Normal Univ 1938; MA San Francisco St Univ 1950; EdD NYU 1955; mil/Instr Ctl Army Sch; pa/Prof & Head Dept HPER, Huston-Tillotson Col 1967-; AAHPER; So Dist Assn AAHPER; Tex Assn HPER; Others; Author *A Proposed Curric for the Profl Preparation for PE*, 1955; cp/Former Unit Dir YMCA Camp (NYC); Former Group Worker, NYC Yth Bd; Grand Jury Assn Travis Co (Tex); Others; r/Univ Meth Ch: Former Mem Adm Bd; hon/Univ Hon Scholar NYU; Outstg First Aid Instr ARC; Most Outstg Fac Mem Huston-Tillotson Col; Outstg Edr Am; Outstg Contbns to Students, Field Corrective Therapy; Personalities of S; Notable Ams & Noteworthy Ams; Others.

MAA, PETER SHENG-SHYONG oc/Chemical Engineer; b/Apr 25, 1942; h/3708 Autumn Ln, Baytown, TX 77521; ba/Baytown; m/Carol Yen; c/Edward F T, Victor F J; p/Kuen-chen and Tsai-fong Maa, Taipei, Taiwan; ed/BS Nat Taiwan Univ 1964; MS Kansas St Univ 1968; PhD W Va Univ

1971; pa/Exxon Res & Engrg Co: Sr Staff Engr 1978-, Sr Res Engr 1976-78, Res Engr 1974-76; Res Assoc, Inst Mining & Minerals Res (Univ Ky) 1972-74; Res Engr, Dept Chem Engrg (W Va Univ) 1971-72; AICHE; ACS; hon/Holds 4 US Patents; Omega Chi Epsilon, Phi Lambda Upsilon.

MAAS, THELMA MAXINE oc/Artist; b/Jul 21, 1923; h/4680 Paradise Dr, Tiburon, CA 94920; ba/Same; c/Patricia Ann, Kent Donald; p/Frank L Ellingwood (dec); Virginia J Wade, Port Alberni, BC, Canada; pa/Exhibited Num Shows; Marin Soc Artists: Correspond'g Secy, Coun, Hostess, Chm, Ed Chm; Chm Life Drawing Workshop; Soc Wn Artists; r/Prot; hon/Accepted by Benjamin Franklin Mint (Penn) as One of Most Outstg 200 Marine Artists in Am; Rec'd Num Awds for Oil Paintings.

MAASS, VERA SONJA oc/Psychologist; b/Jul 6, 1931; h/PO Box 923, Richmond, IN 47374; m/Joachim A; p/Willy and Wally E Keck; ed/BA Monmouth Col 1971; MA Lehigh Univ 1977; PhD Univ Mo-KC 1978; pa/Psychol-Therapist, Dunn Mtl Hlth Ctr Inc (Richmond) 1976-; Developer & Conductor Workshops in Rational Behavior Therapy, Assertion Tng, Decision Making, Others; VP, Vitatronics Inc (Wall, NJ) 1969-; Workshops & Presentations, Nat & Intl Confs; Res Asst, Univ Mo-KC 1974-76; Other Positions; APGA; Nat Coun on Fam Relats; Intl Assn Applied Psychol; hon/Life Mem, Psi Chi; Book of Hon; Others.

MABE, DAVID LINWOOD oc/Electronics Technician; b/Mar 22, 1941; h/Rt 2, Box 68B, Lynchburg, VA 24501; ba/Lynchburg; m/Erika Gaertig; c/Thomas Linwood, Michael David; p/Robert Homer and Nellie EuJean Collins-Mabe, Patrick Springs, VA; ed/Grad Danville Tech Inst 1962; Student Ctl Va Col 1972-; pa/General Electric Co: Test

Sys Maint C & M Engrg Labs 1976-, Digital Equipmt Spec 1974-76, Foreman/Spec MASTR II Assembly 1972-74, Tech Ldr Calibration Labs 1968-72, Others; cp/Local Repub Campaign Com; Base Cmdr, Va Commun Alert Patrol; AOPA; NRA; Smithsonian Assn; Nat Geographic Soc; r/Bapt: SS Tchr, WOL Ldr; hon/GE Awds: 10 & 15 Yr Ser Awds, Microwave Design, Transistor Design, Quality Control, Others; US Patent Application.

MABIRE, KENNETH EARL oc/Insurance Agent; b/Jan 8, 1946; h/9801 Baymeadows Rd, Suite 56, Jacksonville, FL 32216; ba/Winter Park, FL; m/Erica Frazier; p/Daniel Edward and Lora Lee Hollingsworth Mabire, Pensacola, FL; ed/BS Univ W Fla; MS Rollins Col; pa/Fin & Ins Agent; Bk Mktg Assn; Fla Bankers Assn; cp/Rotary Clb; J'ville C of C; r/Meth.

MABON, EDITH M oc/Professor; b/Jan 29, 1923; h/PO Box 472, Morrisville, NY 13408; ba/Morrisville; m/Robert G; p/Jr Arthur and Ruth Beck Mummery (dec); ed/BS; MS; pa/Prof & Div Chm Home Ec, NYS Agri & Tech Col; Am Dietetic Assn; Nat Rest Assn; Am Sch Food Ser; Conslt Am Coun Ed; cp/OES; r/Presb; hon/Pres Sigma Chapt, Delta Kappa Gamma; W/W Am Wom.

McABEE, ALVIN AIKEN oc/Nurseryman; b/May 10, 1931; h/Rt 1, Roebuck, SC 29376; ba/Roebuck; m/Jean Miller; c/Debbi M Clark, Vicky, Ricky; p/Wilford and Annie Faye Strange McAbee, Roebuck; ed/Grad Cecil's Bus Col (Spartanburg, SC); mil/USAF 1951-55 Active Duty; pa/Nurseryman, Roebuck Greenhouses; SC Nurserymen's Assn; So Nurserymen's Assn; r/Bethlehem Bapt Ch: Former Deacon; hon/Rec'd Good Conduct Medal & Overseas Medal, USAF; Won 2nd Pl Awd Sales Competition, Carolina Div.

McAFEE, IVAN PAUL JR oc/Chaplain; b/May 8, 1930; h/13105 Parkview Ave NE, Albuquerque, NM 87123; ba/Albuquerque; m/Shirley Naomi Anderson; c/Trudy M Hadden, Karen M Johnson, I Paul III, Julie; p/Ivan P Sr and Gladys W McAfee, Roswell, NM; ed/Independent Study w Rockmont Col 1971; Dipl, Conserv Bapt Theol Sem 1973; ETTA Tchrs Dipl 1973; pa/Lic'd Bapt Min 1970; Ordained 1973; Pres, Exec Dir & Chaplain, Light & Liberty Mins Inc 1976-; Jail Chaplain, Albuquerque/Bernalillo Co Dept Correction & Detention 1976-; Vol Chaplain, Albuquerque Police Dept 1974-; Writer, Prodr & Broadcaster of Daily Radio Prog, "Light & Liberty" 1977-; Editor "Inside News" (Qtrly) 1977-; Columnist "Chaplain's Corner", *Corrections Comments* 1977-; Other Positions; Pres NM Instnl Chaplains' Assn; Am Prot Corr Chaplains' Assn; Am Corr Chaplains' Assn; Am Corr Assn; NM Corr Assn; Intl Conf Police Chaplains; Evangelical Min Assn; IPA; Others; cp/Rotary; r/Bapt; hon/W/W Rel; Intl Men Achmt; DIB; Intl W/W Commun Ser; Notable Ams; Others.

McALISTER, JAMES DOUGLAS oc/Community Development Specialist; b/Jan 15; h/1304 Greendale Dr, Blacksburg, VA 24060; ba/Blacksburg; m/Patsy Darline; c/Sean Douglas, Kimberly Dawn; p/William Russell and Mary Myers McAlister, Lynchburg, VA; ed/BS, MA E Tenn St Univ; EdD Univ Ga; pa/Assoc Prof, Va Polytechnic Inst & St Univ; Pres, Va Commun Devel Soc 1978-79; Co-Chm, Va Rec & Park Soc; Nat Rec Spec Workshop; Nat Commun Devel Soc; cp/Former Chm, Blacksburg Town Coun's Rec Adv Authority; Bd Dirs, Blacksburg United Fund; Rotary Clb; VPI&SU Campus United Fund; Others; hon/One of Ten Outstg Yg Men Am, Nat C of C; Rec'd Doct F'ship, Ga Power Co; Hon Col Aide-de-Camp, Gov Jimmy Carter; Rec'd NASA Res F'ship; Pres' Coun, Gamma Theta Upsilon; Rec'd Res Grant, Tenn Val Authority; Others.

McALLISTER, BERNICE JACKLYN LYONS oc/Professor; b/Sept 5, 1916; h/426 Camaritas Dr, Diamond Bar, CA 91765; ba/- Alta Loma, CA; m/James A; c/Bruce Hugh,

John Milton; p/Elbert Luton Lyons (dec); Lulu Marie Lyons, Diamond Bar; ed/AA Long Beach City Col 1935; BA Scripps Col for Wom 1937; MA 1940, EdD 1967 Leland Stanford Univ; pa/Chaffey Col: Prof Anthropol, Archaeol & Psychol 1965-; Cal Wn Univ: Assoc Prof Anthropol, Phil & Rel 1957-59, 1962-64; Conslt'g & Asst'g Archaeol, San Bernardino Co Museum & Univ Cal-R 1973-; Rep'd Calico Archaeol Excavation, Sabbatical Around-the-World Travel 1974; Other Positions; Lectr; Author *Edrs' Traditional & Emergent Values*; Contbr Articles Profl Jours; Am Anthropol Assn; Cal Tchrs Assn; AAUP; cp/San Bernardino Co Museum Assn; Garden Clb Am; Wom's Clb Am; San Diego Yacht Clb; Others; r/Christian; hon/Rec'd Anthropol & Ed Tchr F'ships, Stanford Univ; Rec'd Scripps Col Hons Awd; Rec'd Long Beach City Col Hon Awd; Others.

McANALLY-MILLER, VIRGINIA F oc/Writer; Social Worker; b/Sept 2, 1913; h/1236 Michigan Ave, Naples, FL 33940; m/Maurice E (dec); c/2; p/James Virgil Stewart and Mayme Frances Vickers; ed/Col, 2 Yrs; Working on Career, Journalist Am; Author: *The Goat Herder's Wife, He Touched Me, A Spawn on the Devil*; cp/Political Issues Worker, Conservative Causes; Repub Clbs of Naples & Collier Co; Pres, SW Fla Fed Repub Wom's Clb; N Naples Civic Assn; DAR; hon/Most Courageous Wom Collier Co (for Battle Against Almost Complete Paralysis from Polio); Ky Col; Jefferson Davis Awd; Biogl Listings.

McANINCH, ROBERT D oc/Associate Professor; b/May 21, 1942; h/Bert Combs Dr, Prestonsburg, KY 41653; ba/Prestonsburg; m/Linda Strawdrman; c/Robert Michael, Christopher Funkhouser; p/Robert and Dorothy McAninch, Wheeling, WV; ed/BA W Liberty St Col 1969; MA W Va Univ 1970; MA Morehead St Univ 1977; PhD Cand Univ Hawaii; mil/AUS 1962-65; pa/Assoc Prof Govt & Phil, Univ Ky-P; Am Polit Sci Assn; Ky Phil Assn; Am Assn Cols & Jr Cols; cp/Population Res Bur; VP Ctr for Hous'g & Socio-Ec Options; VP Calico Corner Inc; Prog Devel Adv Bd, En Ky Hlth Sys Agy; r/Meth-Bapt; hon/Decorated for Outstg Ser to Kingdom of Belgium; Gt Tchr Awd; Ky Col.

McAULEY, VAN ALFON oc/Mathematician; b/Aug 28, 1926; h/3529 Rosedale Dr, Huntsville, AL 35810; ba/Huntsville; p/Stephen Floyd and Floree Cox McAuley, Greenville, SC; ed/BA UNC 1951; Post Grad Studies, Univ Ala 1956, 60-63; mil/AUS 1944-46; pa/Marshall Space Flight Ctr (NASA): Aerospace Mathematician, Physicist; Contbr Articles Profl Jours; cp/Dem Party; r/Bapt; hon/Holds US Patents in Control Sys; Rec'd NASA, Apollo & Skylab Recog Awds; Rec'd Outstg Perf Awds; Others.

McBROOM, RUBY CUREINGTON oc/Homemaker; b/Dec 21, 1918; h/Rt 1, Box 81, Trout, LA 71371; m/Haskell L (dec); c/Charles Michael, Jennifer Susan, Mary M Wright; p/Aaron G Cureington (dec); Mary Smith Cureington, Trout; r/Bapt; hon/Rec'd Gertrude B Saucier Humerous Poem Awd.

McCALEB, ANN CHILD oc/Voice Teacher; Singer; b/Oct 20 1931; h/5746 N 19th St, Phoenix, AZ 85016; ba/Same; m/Thomas Bruce; c/Peter Graham, Michael Miller; p/Kenneth Edgar and Justine McDonald Child (dec); ed/BA ASU 1955; Addit Studies San Diego St Univ, Univ of Ariz, ASU; pa/Voice Fac Mem, Glendale Commun Col & Phoenix Col; Pvt Studio; Robert Shaw Collegiate Chorale; Soloist w Phoenix Symph, Phoenix Pops, Flagstaff Summer Fest Orch, Bach & Madrigal Soc, Phoenix Summer Opera, Ariz Opera Assn, ASU Symph; Dir Chd's Choirs, Cross Roads Meth Ch; Nat Assn Tchrs of Singing: Chm Student Aud, Ariz Chapt Pres; Nat Soc Arts & Lttrs: Music Chm, Valley of Sum Chapt; cp/Secy Alumni, Sigma Alpha Iota; Monday Morning Musicale; TTT Soc; r/Trinity Epis Cath, Cross Roads Meth Ch: Soloist; hon/1st Runner-up Met Audition.

McCALLION, WILLIAM J oc/Clergyman; b/Aug 7, 1923; h/PO Drawer G, Des Allemands, LA 70030; ba/Same; p/Edward J and Rose Ann Smith McCallion; ed/Marist Sem (Longhorn, Pa) 1941-43; AA St Joseph's Col (Covington, La) 1943-45; Post Grad Studies LSU 1963-64; pa/Ordained Priest 1948; Pastor, St Gertrude Ch 1973-; Pastor, Annunziata Ch (Houma, La) 1969-73; Chm, St Charles Parish Rec Assn; Asst Dir, Archdiocesan CYO; Archbishop's Adv Bd; Other Positions; cp/Life Mem, KC Sacred Heart Ath Assn; Life Mem, St Raphael Ath Assn; Pres Catfish Fest; Chaplain Des Allemands Fire Dept; Hon St Senator; Col on Gov's Staff; r/Cath; hon/Rec'd Ray Mock Awd; W/W Rel; Commun Ldrs & Noteworthy Ams.

McCARLEY, CAROLYN JOSEPHINE oc/Businesswoman; b/Oct 16, 1919; h/102 Wildwood, Harlingen, TX 78550; ba/Harlingen; m/Clint Weldon; c/Clint Weldon Jr, Philip Allen, Charles Aubra, Kelvyn Joe; p/Charles Burnell Spence (dec); Marguerite Gerdina Schoenbohm Spence, Kingsville, TX; ed/BA Tex A&I Univ 1942; Grad Study, Univ Guadalajara 1944; pa/Co-owner Carolyn's Shoe Store; Former Tchr Eng & Spanish: Gregory, Harlingen, Kingsville & Falfurrias (Tex); cp/City, Val, Dist & St Fdn Wom's Clbs: Former Pres (City), Former Pres (Dist), Former Secy, S'ship Com, Chm, Intl Hostess & Gerontology (St), Prog Chm, Hospitality, Cult Affairs, Others (Val), Others; Rio Grande Val Hist Museum Assn; Bd Dirs, Fam Emer Asst; Zonta: Num Activs & Coms; r/Presb: Ruling Elder, SS Tchr, Others; hon/Rec'd Cit, Tex Fine Arts Comm; Outstg Fdn Clbwom, Rio Grande Val Fdn Wom's Clbs; W/W: Am, Am Wom, S&SW; DIB; Personalities of S; Others.

McCARROLL, STEPHEN JAMES oc/Professional Photographer; b/Oct 18; h/1238 Bush St, San Diego, CA 92103; ba/Same; p/Sylvester McCarroll (dec); Mildred Ryckman, Stockton, CA; ed/Brooks Inst Photog; pa/Am Soc Mag Photogs; Profl Photogs Am; cp/Save Our Heritage Org; r/Prot; Hon/One Yr Exhbn Hang Gliding

Photog, Nat Aerospace Mus, Smithsonian Inst; Contb'd Photog to Best Selling HG Manual, The Flyingest Flying; Rec'd Num Awds For Cover & Inside Photog, Psychol Today; Rec'd 13 Awd Credits w Profl Photogs Am; Rec'd 24 Communs Arts Awds, San Diego; Others.

McCARTHY, ELEANOR EDITH oc/Assistant Director Nursing; b/Jun 12, 1933; h/Star Rt 2, Box 70, Hibbing, MN 55746; ba/Hibbing; m/Robert J; p/John A and Elna L Dahl Ruona, Hibbing; ed/Dipl Minn Sch Bus 1952; ASRN Hibbing Commun Col 1967; Cert Food Ser Supvn, Am Dietetic Assn 1969; Adm Cert, Univ Minn 1974; pa/Asst Dir Nsg & Asst Admr; Am Col Nsg Home Admrs; Minn Assn Hlth Care Facilities; Minn Nurses' Assn; Hosp Inst Ednl Food Ser Supvr; NLN; ANA; Others; cp/BPW; Hibbing St Jr Col Alumni Assn; Hibbing Area Voc Inst Adv Com; Nat Assn Retarded Chd; Minn Assn Retarded Chd; No Lites Snowmobile Clb; r/Luth; hon/W/W Am Wom; Notable Ams; Others.

McCARTHY, MARY FRANCES oc/College President; b/Jul 25, 1916; ba/Boston, MA 02115; p/Charles J McCarthy (dec); Elizabeth

Weeks McCarthy, West Springfield, MA; ed/BA Trinity Col 1937; MA Cath Univ Am 1938; PhD Johns Hopkins Univ 1961; pa/-Sister of Rel Order; Pres, Emmanuel Col 1975-; Trinity Col: Instr, Asst Prof, Assoc Prof, Prof German & Russian 1957-75; Orgr & Dir, Trinity Col Study-Travel Prog for German & Prog for German Tchrs of Eng; Lectr; Reschr; Modern Lang Assn; Medieval Acad Am; ACE; AAU; AICUM; AAUW; NCEA; Contbr Articles Profl Jours; Currently Writing Book; r/Rom Cath: Sisters of Notre Dame de Namur; hon/Fulbright Travel Awd & F'ship, Deutscher Akademischer Austauschdienst; NDEA F'ship; Nat Screen'g Com, Fulbright-Hays Awds to Germany; Rec'd Sr F'ship, NEH; Others.

McCARTHY, MARY THERESA oc/Professor; b/Aug 13, 1927; h/313 Brooklyn Bd, Sea Girt, NJ 08750; ba/Lakewood, NJ; p/Charles J and Winifred Murphy McCarthy (dec); ed/BA Georgian Ct Col 1957; MA Laval Univ (Quebec) 1965; PhD Rutgers Univ 1973; pa/Sister of Rel Order; Prof French, Georgian Ct Col 1959-; Writer; Translator; Reader of Adv'd Placemt French Tests, Ednl Test'g Ser (NJ); Prog Chm, Alliance Francais Ocean Co; r/Rom Cath: Sisters of Mercy; hon/Fulbright Scholar, Univ Paris; Nat Endowmt for Humanities Fellow, Univ Chgo.

McCASLIN, LEON H oc/Attorney; b/Oct 3, 1931; h/1096 Briar Ln, Yuba City, CA 95991; ba/Yuba City; m/Diana; c/Robyn, Lynn, Marcus, David, Teddy; p/Robert O and Gladys M McCaslin, Olivehurst, CA; ed/BS 1956; LLB 1960; Addit Studies; mil/USN 1948-54; pa/Admit'd Cal Bar 1968; Pvt Law Pract (Yuba City) 1968; Deputy Dist Atty, Yuba Co 1970-74; Cal-Farm Ins Co (Yuba City) 1959-68; Am Arbitration Assn; Yuba-Sutter Bar Assn; Am Judicature Soc; Superior Cal Claims Assn; cp/Former Mem, Yuba-Sutter Dem Ctl Com; Former Treas Buttes Area Chapt BSA; r/Prot; hon/Rec'd Cert, Dept Yth Authority, St of Cal Inst Juvenile Control.

McCAWLEY, ELTON LEEMAN oc/-Professor; b/Jan 1915; h/210 NE Laurelhurst, Portland, OR 97232; ba/Portland; m/L Annette; c/Douglas F, Melinda M Godbey; p/Arthur T and Lavernia S McCawley (dec); ed/BA; MS; PhD; mil/OSRD; pa/Prof Pharm, Univ Oregon Hlth Scis Ctr; Pres Wn Pharm Soc; Am Soc Pharm; Oregon Med Assn; Am Fdn Clinical Res; Pres Bd Dirs, Portland Ctr Hearing & Speech; Chm Oregon Methadone Treatmt Prog; cp/St Welfare Comm; r/Prot; hon/Post Doct Fellow, Intl Cancer Res Fdn; Others.

McCLAIN, CHARLES J oc/University President; b/Sept 1, 1931; h/706 S Halliburton, Kirksville, MO 63501; ba/Kirksville; m/Norma; c/Anita M Kinkeade, Melanie M Brown; p/John F McClain (dec); Hazel McClain, Potosi, MO; ed/BSE; MA; EdD; pa/Pres, NE Mo St Univ; Profl Conslt: Public Sch Dists, Cols & Univs; Mo St Com on Acctg Methods & Auditing Standards; cp/Mo Hist Records Adv Bd; Bd Dirs, NE Mo Hlth & Wel Coun; Mid-Mo Hlth Consortium; Corp Assembly of Blue Cross; r/Meth; hon/Rec'd Cit Medal, Col of Ed (Univ Mo); Rec'd Outstg Alumnus Awd, SW Mo St Univ.

McCLANAHAN, BEULAH CHRISTINE oc/Supervisor; b/Dec 25, 1914; h/941 Phillips St, Apt #1, Jacksonville, FL 32207; ba/Jacksonville; p/John F and Anna Perry McClanahan (dec); pa/Office Supvr, Bapt Book Store; Nat Leag Am Pen Wom; IPA; Nat Writers' Clb; Pub'd Author; Contbr Articles Mags & Jours; cp/Nat Hist Soc; Dem Party; r/Southside Bapt Ch (J'ville); hon/Speaker for IPA; Helping to Construct Chs in Nigeria & Tanzania (Africa).

McCLANAHAN, LOUISE ANN oc/Teacher; b/Oct 18; h/Box 276, Kimball, WV 24853; ba/Northfork, WV; m/Leonard; p/Saunders Lee Manson (dec); Laura C Manson, Keystone, WV; ed/BS W Va St Col; Grad Studies: Fisk Univ, Syracuse Univ;

pa/Sec'dy Tchr Bus Ed, Northfork HS; McDowell Co ACT; McDowell Co CEA; W Va Ed Assn; So Bus Ed Assn; Nat Bus Ed Assn; FBLA; Adj Fac Mem, Bluefield St Col; W Va Bus Ed Assn; Others; cp/NAACP; Nat Coun Negro Wom; Links of So W Va; McDowell Ma-So-Lit Clb; Del Assembly W Va; IPA; r/Scott St Missionary (Bluefield): Mem; hon/W/W Am Wom; DIB; Personalities of Am; Personalities of S; Intl W/W Commun Ser; Rec'd Lola M Parker Awd, Denver, Colo.

McCLELLAND, GOLDA PAGE oc/Minister; b/Jul 8, 1939; h/107 Perry Dr, Goldsboro, NC 27530; ba/Same; m/George; c/Carlton Lee, Sara Elizabeth; p/Allen Linwood Page, Slater, MO; Goldie Nita Page (dec); ed/BA magna cum laude, Mo Val Col 1961; MRE Lexington Theol Sem 1970; pa/Wayne Co Min Assn; Mt Olive Min Assn; Chaplain of Pilot Clb; Milcreek Dist Yth Advr; cp/Wayne Co CCE; Vol Nurse ARC; Woodmen of World; Life Mem, Nat Order Gregg Artists; ACCE; r/Disciples of Christ; hon/Sigma Tau Delta; Pi Gamma Mu; Rec'd ESTARL & DAR S'ships; Outstg Sr Awd; Personalities of S; DIB; W/W Commun Ser.

McCLINTOCK, BETTIE LOU oc/Physician; b/Apr 21, 1930; h/1412 E Ridge Dr, Clovis, NM 88101; ba/Clovis; m/Hoyt Mingus; c/Joe, Mike, Roy, Marsha; p/Joseph Lyndon and Nannie Cross Reed Brown, Pine Bluff, AR; ed/BS; MD; pa/Pediatrician, McClintock Pediatric Clinic; Staff Mem: Clovis Meml & Cannon AFB Hosps; Micro Med Lab; Dist Hlth Dir; Civil Ser Pediatrician; Curry Co Med Soc; NM Med Soc; AMA; NM Pediatric Soc; Fellow Am Acad Pediatrics; IPA; cp/Soroptomist Intl Bus Wom's Ser Clb; AAUW; r/Bapt: Nursery Com; hon/W/W Am Wom; Personalities of W&MW; Commun Ldrs & Noteworthy Ams; World W/W Wom; DIB; Nat Social Directory.

McCLOUD, SUSAN EVANS oc/Writer; b/Jul 28, 1945; h/588 E Ctr St, Provo, UT 84601; ba/Same; m/James Wylie; c/Heather,Jennifer, Jared, Rebeccah, Morag; p/Preston D Evans, Salt Lake City, UT; Dorothy England, Murray, UT; pa/Screenwriter: The Great Brain at the Acad (Movie), John Baker's Last Race (Movie), Others; Prod'd Series of Filmstrips for use by LDS Sems; Lyracist: "Cry to the Wind"

(Recorded by Jimmy Rogers 1977), "This is My Day", Others; Prog Outline, Brigham Young Univ's Intl Yg Ambassadors's Prog; Pub'd Poetry; Feature Writer, Dixon Evening Telegraph (Ill) 1967-70; Others; cp/Hostess & Tour Guide, Restored Beehive House (Salt Lake City); r/LDS (Mormon); hon/Intl W/W Poetry; Intl W/W Intellectuals; Personalities of W&MW; Book of Hon; Intl Anthology World Poets.

McCLUNG, NORVEL MALCOLM oc/Professor; b/Jun 9, 1916; h/2701 Varsity Pl, Tampa, FL 33612; pa/Univ Mem F (dec); c/Charles F, Margaret L, Ralph A, Susan E; p/Virgil E McClung (dec); Mary Anderson McClung, Webster Springs, WV; ed/BA Glenville St Col; MS, PhD Univ Mich; mil/USNR 1941-45; pa/Prof Biol, Univ So Fla; Reschr; r/Prot; hon/Phi Kappa Phi; Sigma Xi; Phi Sigma; Rec'd Purple Heart, Navy & Marine Medals; Rec'd Fulbright Res Awd.

McCLURE, ENOS SWAIN oc/Engineer;

b/Jun 12, 1918; h/#83 W Sherwood Dr, St Louis, MO 63114; ba/St Louis; m/Ruby-Ellen Featheringill; p/Enos J and Nellie E Freeland McClure (dec); ed/BS Bradley Univ 1952; mil/USN 1943-45; pa/Sr Design Engr, McDonnell-Douglas Aircraft Corp; MAC Mgmt Assn: Past Pres, Toastmasters; cp/Ferguson Lions' Clb; hon/Psi Alpha Lambda; Rec'd 25 Yr Hon Emblem, McDonnell-Douglas Corp.

McCLURE, MICHAEL WAYNE oc/Chemist; b/Nov 15, 1950; h/Rt 2, Princeton, KY 42445; ba/Hopkinsville, KY; p/Earnest Mack and Mary Frances McClure, Princeton; ed/BS Murray St Univ 1972; pa/Murray St Univ Vet Diagnostic & Res Ctr: Chem & Toxicology Chief; AAAS; Am Chem Soc; Soc Envir Geochem & Hlth; r/Ogden Meml United Meth Ch: Yth F'ship Ldr, SS Tchr.

McCLURE, RUBY-ELLEN oc/Free-lance Writer; Violinist; b/Jul 3, 1920; h/83 W Sherwood Dr, St Louis, MO 63114; m/Enos Swain; p/William N and Theren D Orndorff Featheringill (dec); ed/Brown's Bus Col; pa/Journalist; Tchr Violin; Guest Speaker; Music Study Clb; Past Pres 5th Dist Mo Fdn Mus Clbs: Crusade for Strings, Most Mus Fam Mo; IPA; cp/20th Cent Art Clb; hon/1 of 50 IPA Personalities to Preview Report, "Russia As I Saw It"; Others.

McCOMBS, SHERWIN oc/Chiropractor; b/Jan 27, 1934; h/1808 Thome Dr, Sterling, IL 61081; ba/Sterling; m/Rita; c/Kim, Kelly, Jeff, Terry; p/Vernon McCombs, Sterling; Helen McCombs (dec); ed/DC; mil/USN; pa/Intl Chiropractic Assn: Prairie St Chiropractic Assn; Whiteside Co Chiropractic Assn; cp/Sterling C of C & Indust; r/Prot; hon/Intl Chiropractic Hon Soc.

McCOMBS, SOLOMON oc/Artist; b/May 17, 1913; h/4311 E 58th Pl, Tulsa, OK 74135; ba/Same; m/Margarita Sauer; p/James and Ella McCombs; pa/Am Indian Artist; cp/V-Chief, Creek Nation of Okla; Speaker of Ho; Intertribal Coun (Chaplain); r/Bapt; hon/Rec'd Waite Phillips Trophy, Spec Indian Artists' Awd; Rec'd Shield Awd; Rec'd Master Artist Awd; Rec'd Okmulgee Cult Foun Awd; Bronze Medallion Awd; Recipient, US St Dept's Intl Exchange Ser: Toured Mid E, Africa, India & Burma.

McCONN, JAMES J oc/Mayor; h/Houston, TX; ba/Houston; m/Margie; c/Jim Jr, Mike, Kevin, Melissa, Terry, Andy; ed/Notre Dame Univ; pa/Mayor of Houston 1978-; City Coun-man (Dist C) 1971-75; Homebldg & Bldg Supply Co Over 30 Yrs; Gtr Houston Builders Assn: Past Pres, St & Nat Leg Coms; Nat Assn Homebuilders; Nat Hous'g Ctr Bd Trustees; Tex Assn Builders Leg Com; Others; cp/Baseball Coach: Pony Leag, Little Leag & Am Legion; Other Civic Activs; hon/Coach: World Champion Karl Young Pony Leag, World Champion NW Colt Team & St Champion St Thomas Am Legion Team; Builder of Yr (Houston).

McCONNELL, DOROTHY F oc/-Consultant; b/Sept 4, 1924; h/2810 Del Norte, Temple, TX 76501; ba/Same; m/Fredrick E; c/Lester E, R Fraiser, O Elizabeth; p/Albert R and Norma Statzer Fraiser (dec); ed/BA; MEd; EdD; mil/USN; pa/Dissertation Conslt; Ret'd Col Prof; NEA; TSTA; NAWDAC; TAWDAC; NCAWE; cp/Friends of Lane for US Cong; OES; Friends of Lib; City Fdn Wom's Clbs; r/SS Tchr; Ch Wom; hon/Alpha Delta Kappa; Delta Kappa Gamma; Am Soc Dist'd Citizens; Rec'd Awd Exceptional Achmt, Bd Trustees Mary Hardin-Baylor Col; Dist'd Ldrship to Girls & Wom; Belle of Brazos; St of Tex; Hon Citizen of Ireland.

McCORD, CHARLES EDWARD oc/Architect; b/Aug 18, 1934; h/PO Box 127, Dutton, AL 35744; ba/Same; m/R Janette; c/Paula Fay, Donna Lynn, Mary Alison; p/James Richard McCord Jr (dec); Mrs Z T Houser Jr, Perry, GA; pa/Reg'd Arch, NCARB; Assn Energy Engrs; Am Inst Archs; cp/C of C; r/Prot.

McCORD, JAMES RICHARD III oc/Mathematical & Chemical Engineer; b/Sept 2, 1932; h/PO Box 61, Norristown, GA 30447; ba/Chamblee, GA; m/Louise France Manning; c/Neil Alexander, Stuart James, Valerie France, Kent Richard; p/(Step-father) Zachariah Thigpen Jr and Neilie Mae Sumner McCord Houser, Perry, GA; ed/BS Ga Inst Technol 1955; MS 1959, PhD 1961 MIT; mil/Col ROTC; pa/Am Inst Chem Engrs; Am Math Soc; cp/Repub Party; BSA; r/Anglican Meth: Key Meml Foun Inc; hon/Phi Lambda Upsilon; Phi Kappa Phi; Tau Beta Pi; hon/Rec'd Cert Apprec, Repub Nat Com; W/W S&SW; DIB.

McCORMACK, FRANK A oc/Osteo-pathic Physician; b/Mar 12, 1916; h/Rt 3, Box 259, Murphysboro, IL 62966; ba/Malden, MO; m/Majorie H; p/Cass Q and Oma Bush McCormack (dec); ed/BS So Ill Univ; DO Kansas City Col Osteopath Med; pa/Am Osteopath Assn; Mo Osteopath Assn; cp/IPA; r/Prot.

McCORMICK, JOSEPH FRANCIS oc/Engineer; b/Sep 7, 1933; h/N Quaker Hill Rd, Pawling, NY 12564; m/Mary Anne; c/Patricia, Jeanmarie, Michael, Joseph Jr, James; p/Frank P and Margaret McCormick, Hanson, MA; ed/BSME Lowel Technol Inst; mil/AUS 1953-55; pa/Nat Mgmt Assn; Am Fluid Power Soc; cp/Past Chm, Yg Dems; E Fishkill Hist Soc; Pawling Rec Assn; r/Rom Cath; hon/W/W; Men Achmt; DIB.

McCORMICK, MICHAEL PATRICK oc/Physicist; b/Nov 23, 1940; h/1 Neff Dr, Hampton, VA 23669; ba/Hampton; m/Judy Moyer; c/Lynn Ann, Michael Patrick; p/Arthur John and Mary Ann McCormick (dec); ed/BA; MA; PhD; mil/Ser'd to Capt; pa/Physicist, NASA-LRC; GARP-JOC (Aerosols & Climate): Optical Soc Am; Working Group, Shuttle Lidar; cp/Chm Bldg Adv Coun, S P Langley Sch; Gen Alumni Assn, W & J Col; r/Christian; hon/Outstg Sr Ath, W & J Col; Rec'd Group Achmt Awds, NASA.

McCORMICK, WILLIAM EDWARD oc/Executive; b/Feb 9, 1912; h/419 Dorchester Rd, Akron, OH 44320; ba/Akron; m/Goldie S; c/John F, Kirk W; p/George H McCormick (dec); Nellie C Mingle McCormick, Centre Hall, PA; ed/BS 1933, MS 1934 Penn St Univ; mil/US Public Hlth Ser Comm Corps 1943-46; pa/Mng Dir, Am Indust Hygiene Assn 1973-; Mgr Envir

Control, B F Goodrich Co (Akron) 1970-73; Other Positions; Secy, Soc Toxicol; Nat Safety Coun; Chlorine Inst; Mfg Chems Assn; Former Mem Adv Com Heat Stress, US Dept Labor; Am Indust Hygiene Assn; Am Chem Soc; AAAS; Indust Hygiene Roundtable; Pub'd Num Articles Profl Jours; cp/Akron City Clb; Formerly Active BSA; Repub Party; r/Epis; 32° Mason; Shriner.

McCOTTER, CHARLES KENNEDY JR oc/Attorney; b/Oct 29, 1946; h/3503 Windsor Dr, New Bern, NC 28560; ba/New Bern; m/Patricia Byrum; c/Virginia Byrum, Patricia Dunn; p/Charles Kennedy and Lucy Dunn McCotter, New Bern; ed/BS, JD Univ NC; pa/Am, NC & Craven Co Bar Assns; cp/JCs; C of C; r/Christ Epis Ch (NB): Vestry; hon/US Magistrate.

McCOUL, VICKY JEAN oc/Free-lance Writer; b/Jan 24, 1947; h/2950 C-2, So Col St, Arlington, VA 22206; ba/Wash, DC; p/Alfred J McCoul (dec); Grace Dill McCoul, San Francisco, CA; ed/BA Univ Cal-SB; mil/USAF 1974-: 2/Lt 1974, 1/Lt 1976; pa/Contbr Articles Newspaper, Mags, Jours, Others; Nat Writers' Clb; cp/Am Civil Liberties Union; Civil Rights Activs; NOW; hon/Hon Soc; Cal S'ship Fdn; Dean's List.

McCOY, ALMO N oc/Banker; b/Jul 31, 1912; h/PO Box 954, Reidsville, NC 27320; m/Narviar Walker; p/Almo N and Ida McCoy (dec); ed/BS, MA A&T St Univ; pa/Ret'd Voc-Agri Instr; NEA; Orgr & Bd Dirs, Greensboro Nat Bank 1971-; Num Assns; cp/BSA; Rockingham Co Fund Inc; NAACP; Adv Coun Rockingham Co Unit, NC Dept Correction (by Gov James B Hunt Jr); r/1st Christian Ch: Bd Dirs, Mem; hon/Rec'd Cit, Sigma of Yr; Rec'd Num Other Commun & Sch Ser Awds.

McCOY, NARVIAR WALKER oc/Librarian; Educator; h/PO Box 954, Reidsville, NC 27320; m/A N McCoy; p/S C Walker (dec); Loretta Jane Reives, Durham, NC; ed/BS Win-Sal Univ 1941; MLS NC Ctl Univ 1958; pa/Contbr Poetry Var Jours & Books; Assn Chdhood Ed Intl; Negro BPW

Clb; Advr, YABPWC (Rockingham Co); NC Soc Poets; Bd Dirs, Reidsville Public Lib; cp/LWV; Dem Wom's Org; r/Bethel AME Ch: Steward, Pastor's Aid, Conf Worker; hon/Rec'd Plaque for Commun Ser & Achmt, Reidsville Bd Ed; Biogl Listings.

McCRANEY, WILLARD KARY oc/Pub-lic Accountant; b/Aug 4, 1904; h/1804 S Sneed St, Tyler, TX 75701; m/Bland E; c/Bobby M Campbell; p/John H and Mattie E Williams McCraney; ed/BA La Salle Ext Univ; pa/Past Pres Tex Public Accts; Assoc'd Sch Bus Ofcls & Tex Assn Sch Bus Ofcls; Nat Soc Public Accts By-Laws Com, Asst St Dir; Contb'g Author "Port Folio of Acctg Sys for Small & Medium Sized Bus"; cp/Past Pres Exec Clb; r/Bapt: Deacon, SS Tchr, BTU Dir, Past Pres (La) Big Creek BTU Conv, Past Pres NE BTU Conv; hon/Hon Citizen of Houston; Others.

McCRAW, RONALD KENT oc/-Psychometrist; b/Dec 6, 1947; h/902 Linder-wood, TX 77520; p/Leon F and Lorna Mae Bailey McCraw, Baytown, TX; ed/BA w Hons, Univ Tex-A 1970; MA Univ Tex-G (Med Branch); Cand PhD Univ S Fla; pa/Psychometrist, Hillsborough Commun Mtl Hlth Ctr 1978-; Resident Clinical Psychol, Univ Tex Hlth Sci Ctr (San Antonio) 1977-78; Grad Asst, Fla Mtl Hlth Inst (Tampa) 1975-76; Res Technician, Univ Tex-G 1972-74; Fellow, Am Orthopsychi Assn; AAAS; Am Public Hlth Assn; Am Assn Sex Edrs, Cnslrs & Therapists; Assoc Mem, SWn & Am Psychol Assns; Film Reviewer, Sci Books & Films; Contbr Articles Profl Jours; cp/Univ Tex Ex-students Assn; r/Grace United Met Ch (Bayton): Mem; hon/Psi Chi; Sigma Xi; W/W S&SW; DIB; Chevalier Awd, Order of DeMolay.

McCRAY, ROBERT DEWEY oc/Pastor; b/Jul 5, 1932; h/Oakwood Dr, Dandridge, TN 37725; ba/Dandridge; m/Rebekah Anne; c/Angela Denise; p/Ross Dewey McCray

(dec); Ona Mae Davis McCray, Bristol, TN; ed/BA magna cum laude, Carson-Newman Col 1954; MDiv So Bapt Theol Sem 1957; pa/Pastor, 1st Bapt Ch; Tenn Bapt Conv: Exec Bd Trustees, Com on Coms; Pres, Min Assns Rockwood & Dandridge; Moderator, Jefferson Co Bapt Assn; E T Bapt Hist Soc; cp/Carson-Newman Col: Bd Trustees, Adv Bd, Bd Govs of Torchbearers Clb, Exec Co Alumni Assn; Commun Col Coun; Bd Dirs, Jefferson Co Humanities Coun; JCHS Voc Adv Com; r/So Bapt: Ser'd on Staffs Bristol, Crossville, Rockwood & Dandridge; hon/W/W: Am Cols & Univs, Rel; Commun Ldrs & Noteworthy Ams; DIB; Intl W/W Commun Ser; Rec'd Num Dist'd Ser Awds.

McCREATH, WILLIAM CALLAN oc/Artist; b/Jan 2, 1934; h/208 Montclair Ave, Upper Montclair, NJ 07043; ba/Montclair; m/Ethel E (dec); p/Mrs M McCreath, Girvan, Scotland; ed/BFA Univ Manitoba (Canada); MFA Cranbrook Acad Art (Mich); pa/Prof & Chm Dept Fine Arts, Montclair St Col; Art Exhbns; Workshops; Seminars; r/Christian; hon/Rec'd Carl Milles S'ship, Cranbrook Acad Art; Rec'd 2 Grants to NJ Coun Arts; Rep to World Crafts Coun Conf (Kyoto, Japan); Work Rep'd Public & Pvt Collections; Winner Sev Prizes for Sculpture, Ceramics & Prints.

McCUBBIN, NICHOLAS DAVID oc/Attorney; b/Jul 1, 1941; h/1831 Cantrill Dr, Lexington, KY 40505; ba/Winchester, KY; m/June Delaine; c/Natalie Delaine; p/N B and Ethel McCubbin, Lexington; ed/BS Univ Ky 1963; MDiv So Bapt Theol Sem 1968; JD Univ Louisville Law Sch 1971; pa/Ky & Am Bar Assns; Assn Trial Lwyrs Am; Ky Assn Trial Attys; Am Judicature Soc; Christian Legal Soc; Admit'd to Pract Law: Ky Ct Appeals, US Dist Ct (En & Wn Dists Ky), US Tax Ct, US Ct Claims, US Customs Ct, US Ct Customs &

Patent Appeals, US Supr Ct, Ky Supr Ct, Fayette Circuit Ct, Others; cp/Rotary Intl; Ky Hist Soc; Ky Assn Mtl Hlth; Ky Easter Seal Soc; Precinct Chm, Ky Dem Party; Others; r/Trinity Bapt Ch: Ch Sch Tchr, Fin Com, Budget Com, Constitution Com; hon/Hon Ky Col; Hon Ga Col; Hon Tenn Col; Hon NC Tarheel; Hon Tex Citizen; Hon Louisville Citizen; Hon Ky Commr Agri; Hon Wyom Cowboy; Hon Okla Citizen; Rec'd Hon ND Intl Peace Cit; Hon Col Ky St Police; DIB; Book of Hon; Intl W/W Commun Ser; W/W Am Law; Num Others.

McCULLOUGH, CONSTANCE MARY oc/Lecturer; b/Jan 15, 1912; h/1925 Cactus Ct #4, Walnut Creek, CA 94595; p/John Simeon and George Babette Mayer McCullough (dec); ed/AB; MS; PhD; pa/Prof Emeritus, San Francisco St Univ; Editor Advr, *Reading Res*

Qtrly; Conslt; Author; Past Pres Intl Reading Assn, Nat Conf on Res in Eng, Reading Hall of Fame; r/Prot; hon/Intl Reading Assn: Cit of Merit, Intl Cit; Rec'd Marcus Foster Meml Awd, Cal Reading Assn.

McCULLOUGH, JOHN PHILLIP oc/Educator; Consultant; b/Feb 2, 1945; h/42 Dogwood Dr, Triadelphia, WV 26059; m/Barbara Elaine Carley; c/Carley Jo; p/Phillip McCullough (dec); Lucile McCullough, Atlanta, IL; ed/BS 1967, MS 1968 Ill St Univ; PhD Univ ND 1971; CDE 1972; CBE 1973; CAM 1974; APD 1977; pa/W Liberty St Col: Chm Dept Mgmt & Adm Sys 1974-, Prof Mgmt 1974-, Assoc Prof Mgmt 1972-74, Asst Prof Bus 1971-72; Lectr Bus, W Va Univ 1972-; Adj Prof Bus, Wheeling Col 1972-; Independent Mgmt Conslt 1971-; Other Positions; Nat Chm, Soc Humanistic Mgmt; Nat Dir, Nat Bus Hon Soc; Dir Spec Interest Group, Cert'd Bus Edrs; Others; cp/VP Fed Credit Union, W Liberty St Col; Rep, W Va Bd Regents Adv Coun of Fac; hon/Delta Mu Delta; Delta Pi Epsilon; Delta Tau Kappa; Phi Gamma Nu; Phi Theta Pi; Pi Gamma Mu; Pi Omega Pi; Omicron Delta Epsilon; Rec'd Outstg Grad Student Awd, Ill St Univ; Rec'd Harris-Casals Foun Acad Achmt Awd; Rec'd Ill Ctl Col Fac Recog Awd; Rec'd S'ship Awd, Cath Bus Ed Assn; United Fund Commun Ser Awd; AFL-CIO Commun Ser Cit; NBHS Excell in Tchg Awd; Others; Biogl Listings.

McCURDY, MARTHA ELIZABETH (BETTY) oc/Director; b/Jul 27, 1946; h/303 Chalfont Dr, Athens, GA 30606; ba/Elberton, GA; p/Gyp and Ruth Mitcham McCurdy, Warm Springs, CA; ed/BA Tift Col; MEd Auburn Univ; PhD Univ Ga; pa/Dir Mtl Retardation Ctr; APGA; Mtl Hlth Cnslrs Assn; Nat Rehab Cnslg Assn; Assn Retarded Citizens; Regional VP, Ctr Dirs Assns Ga; Reschr; Pub'd Sev Articles Profl Jours; cp/Former Co-Chm, Athens Area Dimensions for New Decade; VP Tift Alumnae Chapt (Athens); Orgr Devel Home for Mentally Retarded Wom (Elberton); Tchr Communs Skills Area Chs; r/So Bapt; hon/W/W S&SW; Outstg Wom Am; Personalities of S; Kappa Delta Pi; Betty McCurdy Day, Tift Col; Hon Miss Ga, Rehab Ctr; Rec'd Rehab Cnslg Grant, Auburn Univ; Rec'd FTA S'ship.

McDANIEL, ELIZABETH L oc/Psychologist; h/8933 Willmon Way, San Antonio, TX 78239; m/(dec); p/(dec); ed/Doct; pa/Prof.

McDANIEL, JAN L oc/Piano Instructor; b/Jun 18, 1957; h/522 Montague St, Nocona, TX 76255; ba/Nocona; m/Len E; p/William A McDaniel (dec); Jenice McDaniel, Nocona; ed/Cand BM Mid Wn St Univ; pa/Pvt Piano Instr; Nat Guild Piano Tchrs; Mus Edrs Nat Conf; r/Grace Ch (Wichita Falls); hon/Clark Scholar; Huff Scholar; Theodore Presser Scholar.

McDANNALD, CLYDE ELLIOTT oc/Executive; b/Jun 29, 1925; h/57 Canterbury Ln, Wilton, CT 06897; m/Virginia Washington; c/Leslie Ann, Clyde Jr, Bruce Robert, Bonnie Washington, Brian Christopher, Laura Leigh; p/Clyde E McDannald (dec); Evelyn Tunison Morgan, New York, NY; ed/BA, MBA Columbia Univ; mil/1942-45; pa/Pres, H H Pott Distillers Ltd; Nat Assn Mfg; Am Mgmt Assn; Nat Fin Com; NY St Indust Devel Com; cp/Dem Party; r/Presb; hon/Rec'd Air Medal; Rec'd Ser Cross.

McDONALD, JOHN WILLIAM (JACK) oc/Educator; b/Sept 1, 1936; h/10521 Stella St, Oakland, CA 94605; ba/Oakland; m/Jane; c/John D, Kevin J; p/John T and Mary C McDonald, Manchester, NH; ed/BA Univ NH 1963; MA San Francisco St Univ 1967; DTM 1977; pa/Pres, Speaking Dynamics; Tchr, Oakland Unified Sch Dist 1968-; Oakland Ed Assn; Cal Tchrs Assn; NEA; cp/Cand, Alameda Co Bd Ed; Lt Gov, Toastmasters Intl (Dist 57); Cal Coun Exceptional Chd; Former Scoutmaster, BSA; Former Instr, ARC; Former Trustee, Italian Cath Fdn; Former Trustee, St Teresa's Haven (SF); Others; r/Rom Cath; hon/Rec'd Dist'd Toastmaster Awd.

McDONALD, MARIANNE oc/Classicist; b/Jan 2, 1937; h/Box 929, Rancho Santa Fe, CA 92087; m/Torajiro Mori; c/5; p/Eugene and Inez McDonald; ed/BA magna cum laude, Bryn Mawr Col 1958; MA Univ Chgo 1960; PhD Univ Cal-I 1975; pa/Current Res Appointmt w TLG Pubs, Univ Cal-I; Instr Dept Classics, Univ Cal-I 1975-79; Reschr; Author: *A Semilemmatized Concordance to Euripides' Alcestis* (1977), *A Semilemmatized Concordance to Euripides' Cyclops* (1978), Others; Contbr Articles Profl Jours; hon/Am Registry Series; Personalities of S.

McDONALD, THERESA BEATRICE PIERCE oc/Counselor; Teacher; b/Apr 11, 1929; h/9810 S Calumet Ave, Chicago, IL 60628; m/Ollie; p/Leonard C Pierce (dec); Ernestine Morris Templeton, Chgo; ed/-Tougaloo Col 1946-47; Roosevelt Univ 1954-56, 1959-62, 1964; Univ Chgo, Indust Relats Ctr 1963-64; pa/Author Poetry; Guest Speaker, Radio & TV Progs; Supvr, US Postal Ser 1963-70; Vets' Benefits Cnslr, VA Regional Office (Chgo) 1973-77; White House Regional Conf 1961; cp/Vol Rep, Liberty Bapt Ch &

Am Legion Aux, VA West Side Hosp; Former Pres Am Legion; OES: Worthy Matron, 1974 Debonettes Matrons Clb, Marschniel Clb, Others; r/Liberty Bapt Ch: Public Relats Staff, VP Sr Usher Bd, Pres Wom's Guild, Others; Instr, Cong Christian Ed; Others; hon/Rec'd Outstg Dedicated Ser Awds, Am Legion; Rec'd 25 Yr Ser Awd, US Govt; Perf Awd, VA Regional Office; Merit Cit, Vets' Group, WWII; Superior Accomplishmt Awd, Post Office Dept; Cert Apprec, VA West Side Hosp; Nat Cit Meritorious Ser, Am Legion Aux; Biogl Listings.

McDONALD, WILLIAM LINDSEY oc/Management Staff Planner; b/Jun 7, 1927; h/2207 Berry Ave, Florence, AL 35630; ba/Tennessee Valley, AL; m/Dorothy Carter; c/Nancy M Buttram (Mrs Marvin), Suzannah M McClellan (Mrs Mark); p/William Ervin McDonald, Florence; Pauline Lindsey McDonald (dec); ed/BS Univ N Ala; Grad AUS Command & Gen Staff Col; Col of Armed Forces; mil/USAR; WWII & Korean War; pa/Mgmt Staff Planner, Nat Fertilizer Devel Ctr; Author *Paths in the Briar Patch* (1979); Histn; Newspaper Journalist; cp/Chm, Florence Hist Bd; Advr, Hist Comm; Past Pres, Local Hist Socs; r/United Meth; hon/Rec'd Awd of Merit, Ala Hist Comm; W/W: Ala, S&SW; Personalities of S.

McDONNELL, LOIS EDDY oc/Assistant Professor; h/123 Parker St, Carlisle, PA 17013; ba/Shippensburg, PA; m/Fred V (dec); c/Mary M Harris, Milton Eddy; p/Milton Walker and Rebecca Reiley Eddy (dec); ed/BA Dickinson Col; MA Tchr Col, Columbia Univ; pa/Asst Prof, Shippensburg St Col; Tchr Carlisle Area Schs; Tchr Rowland Sch Yg Chd; Author: *Stevie's Other Eyes* (1962), *Susan Comes Through the Fire* (1969); Pub'd Units & Articles; r/United Meth.

McDONNELL, M GERALDINE oc/Administrator; Professor; b/Mar 20, 1920; h/2300 Adeline Dr, Burlingame, CA 94010; ba/San Francisco, CA; p/Michael J and Elizabeth A Moran McDonnell (dec); ed/BA; BS; MS; EdD; pa/Sister of Rel Order; Univ SF: Dean Sch Nsg, Prof; St Mary's Hosp: OR Supvr, Tchr & Nsg Ser Dir; Hlth Adv Bd,

Sisters of Mercy; AAUP; AAUD; Cath Hosp Assn; Nat Leag Nsg; r/Cath: Sisters of Mercy; hon/Rec'd Henry Clay Hall Awd, USF; Sigma Theta Tau; Alpha Sigma Nu.

McDOWALL, MARY RUTH WOODS oc/Teacher; b/Oct 14, 1914; h/4131 Oaklawn Dr, Jackson, MS 39206; m/John Kennedy Jr; c/Mary M Varnell, Frances Ozella; p/James Lucius and Etha Ozella Sherer Woods (dec); ed/BS Livngston Col 1942; MEd Miss Col

1971; pa/Elem Tchr, Boyd Sch; Nat & Miss Ed Assns; PTA; Former Mem, Assn Childhood Ed (Var Positions); r/Presb: Wom's Gideon Aux Intl; hon/Alpha Delta Kappa; Personalities of S; W/W Am Wom; World W/W Wom; DIB; Commun Ldrs & Noteworthy Ams.

McDOWELL, JOSLIN DAVID oc/Author; Lecturer; b/Aug 17, 1939; h/1212 Navaho Trail, Richardson, TX 75080; ba/Richardson; m/Dorothy Ann; c/Kelly Nae-Ann, Sean Joslin; p/Wilmont and Edith McDowell (dec); ed/BA Wheaton Col; MDiv Talbot Theol Sem; r/Christian; hon/Kappa Tau Epsilon; Rec'd Lyman Strauss Speaker of Yr Awd; Rec'd Dist'd Ser Awd.

MACEBUH, SANDY oc/Writer; Playwrite; b/Jul 21, 1950; h/927 Norwood Ave, Toledo, OH 43607; ba/Same; p/J Walter Carroll (dec); Mae H Carroll, Silver Spring, MD; ed/BA; MA; pa/Tutor & Instr, Toledo Univ; Writing Poetry Anthology; Perf'd Works on TV (Mid Wn Sts); Perf'd Univs & Orgs MW; Created & Produced Radio Prog, Bowling Green St Univ 1977; Head Public Relats & Publicity, Third World Theatre (BG, Ohio); Fdr, Black Inspiration; Others; cp/Var Human Rights Activs; Worked w Disadvantaged Communities; r/Cath; hon/Omega Phi Si; Poet Laureate, *The Communicator*; Whole NW Region Hon Chm, Black Arts Fest (Hayward, Cal).

McELWAIN, JOHN ALLEN oc/Executive; b/Jul 7, 1901; h/714 S Washington St, Hinsdale, IL 60521; ba/Chicago, IL; m/Jane McKenna; c/Edward Frank, John Allen IV, Phyllis M Forward (Mrs Richard); p/Frank McElwain (dec); Bertha Thompson McElwain; pa/Pres, John A McElwain Co (Printers & Mailers); cp/Pres & Trustee, Hinsdale Sanitary Dist; Bd Control, Ill Assn Sanitary Dists; r/Epis; hon/Constrn John A McElwain Regional Water Reclamation Facility.

McEWEN, COLIN ELLIS oc/Educator; b/Aug 10, 1904; h/Pacific Plaza Towers, 1431 Ocean Ave, Santa Monica, CA 90401; ba/Los Angeles, CA; p/Robert and Martha S Ellis McEwen; ed/Phoenix Col 1923-25; Univ Cal 1927-28; BA Univ Ariz 1930; Post Grad Studies; pa/Former Pres & Dir, Colin McEwen HS & Elem Sch; Tchr: Long's Sch (Hollywood, Cal) 1946-47, Brawley Public Schs & Colin McEwen Schs (Hollywood) 1946-48; Prin, Nehalem Val HS (Oregon) 1943-45; Maricopa Co (Ariz): Social Worker, Psychometrist, Juv Ct, Probation Dept, Exam'g Bd 1933-39; Other Positions; Mem Num Assns & Orgs; hon/W/W: Man Ed, W, Cal, Am; Men Achmt; DIB; Commun Ldrs & Noteworthy Ams; Intl Registry W/W; Others.

McFARLIN, BARBARA ANN oc/Educator; b/Oct 4; h/635 N Fisher, Kennewick, WA 99336; c/James Daniel; ed/BA, MA Tex

Christian Univ; pa/Foreign Lang Tchrs Assn; Pasco Ed Assn; WEA; NEA; cp/Pres, Kennewick Repub Wom's Clb; r/1st Christian Ch (Disciples of Christ): Pianist, Vocalist, Deacon, SS Tchr.

McGAVOCK, POLLY P oc/Real Estate Broker; b/Feb 7, 1904; h/314 Kent Rd, Charlottesville, VA 22903; ba/Charlottesville; c/Shirley M McConnell; p/Flor S and Shirlie Tucker Pollitt; ed/BA Randolph Macon Wom's Col; pa/Nat Real Estate Appraisers; C'ville & Albermarle Real Estate Bds; Nat & Va Assns Realtors; Intl Real Estate Fdn, Nat Inst Real Estate Brokers; Nat Inst Farm & Land Brokers; Nat Assn Real Estate Bds; IPA; cp/C of C; Bd Mem ARC; C'ville Albermarle Child Wel Assn; Commun Chest Campaign; Am Cancer Soc; Assoc Univ Va Lib; r/Epis; hon/Rec'd Most Ethical Realtor Awd; Del for US to XXIth Cong, Intl Real Estate Fdn (Dublin, Ireland); 2000 Wom Achmt.

McGEE, GALE W oc/Ambassador; b/Mar 17, 1915; m/Loraine Baker; c/Four; ed/BA Neb St Tchrs Col 1936; PhD Univ Chicago 1947; Addit Studies; pa/Ambassador OAS 1979-; US Senate 1958-79: Senator Wyom, Appropriations Com, Foreign Relats Com (Chm, Wn Hemisphere Sub-com); Univ Wyom: Former Prof Hist & Latin Am Hist, Former Chm Inst Intl Affairs; Former Instr: Neb Wesleyan Col, Iowa St Univ, Notre Dame Univ; Coun Foreign Relats: Participated Confs Sponsored by Bilderberg Conf, Ditchley Foun, Anglo-Am African Group, Brookings Instn, Johns Hopkins Univ; Accompanied Secy St Kissinger to Panama (Negotiating Canal Treaty); Accompanied Pres Carter Panama (Signing of Treaty); Conf Foreign Mins Latin Am; Guest Speaker; Contbr Articles Profl Jours; hon/Article Chosen for Inclusion, 75th Anniv Edition *South Atlantic Qtrly*.

McGEE, TIMOTHY WILLIAM oc/Social Worker; Psychoanalyst; b/Nov 5, 1945; h/Two Adrian Ave, Bronx, NY 10463; ba/New York, NY; p/James Edward and Norah Elizabeth Russell McGee; ed/BA St Johns Univ 1972; MSW Fordham Univ 1974; Cert in Psychoanalytic Psychotherapy, Washington Sq Inst 1977; Doctl Cand, Columbia Univ; mil/USAF 1965-68; pa/Psychi Technician, Jacobi Hosp (NYC) 1968-69; Commun Mtl Hlth Assoc, St Vicent's Hosp (NYC) 1969-74; Dir of Clin Sers, Assn for Help of Retarded Chd (NYC) 1974-77; Dir of Yth Sers, Stanley Isaacs Neighborhood Ctr (NYC) 1977-78; Pvt Pract Psychotherapy 1977-; Adj Prof, Fordham Univ 1977-; Adm Asst, Jacobi Hosp 1978-; Nat Accreditation Assn Psychoanalysis; Acad Cert'd Social Workers; Soc Clin Social Workers for Psychotherapy; cp/Dem Party; r/Cath; hon/USAF Commend Medal; Bronze Star Medal; NIMH Awd.

McGEEVER, MARGARET E oc/Professor; b/Aug 11, 1918; h/Rt 4, Charleston, IL 61920; ba/Charleston; m/John F (dec); c/Kathleen (dec), Kelly; p/Charles David Cook (dec); Maude Ruth Freeman Cook; ed/BS Ohio Univ 1940; MS UCLA 1952; EdD 1959; pa/Prof Ecs, En Ill Univ; Tchr Eng & Sci; Fac Supvr; cp/Bd Dirs, Big Brothers & Big Sisters; r/Ch of Jesus Christ LDS; hon/Kappa Omicron Phi; Omicron Nu; Phi Upsilon Omicron; Phi Lambda Theta; Commun Ldrs & Noteworthy Ams.

McGEHEE, ALFRED ZACHARY oc/-Attorney; b/Jul 9, 1942; h/Rt 5, Box 149, N Enfield, ME; ba/Lincoln; m/June W Savage; c/Mary, John and Jack; p/Daniel and Denise McGehee (dec); ed/BS, Univ Maine-Orono; JD, Univ Maine-Portland; pa/Atty at Law, Pvt Pract, 1970-; ABA; MBA; Am Jud Soc; Supreme Ct Bar Assn; Am Trial Lwyrs Assn; Univ Maine Alumni Assn; cp/C of C; Lions Clb; Rotary Clb; US Nature Conservancy; United Fund; YMCA; Pilot Clb Intl; Platform Assn; Smithsonian Assocs; r/United Meth: Administrative Com, Choir Dir, SS Tchr; hon/1 of 10 Outstg Yg Men, Lincoln; Num Biogl Listings.

McGEHEE, H COLEMAN JR oc/Bishop; b/Jul 7, 1923; h/749 Henley Dr, Birmingham,

MI 48008; ba/Detroit, MI; m/June Stewart; c/Lesley, Alexander, Coleman, Donald, Cary; p/Harry C and Anne Lee Cheatwood McGehee, Richmond, VA; ed/BS; MDiv; JD; DD; mil/AUS 1943-46; pa/Bishop, Epis Diocese Mich; Asst Atty Gen, St of Va 1951-54; Va Bar Assn; US Supr Ct; cp/Bd Dirs, Detroit Ec Clb; r/Epis.

McGILL, DENNIS W oc/Attorney; b/Oct 2, 1941; h/5763 38th St, Lubbock, TX 79401; ba/Lubbock; m/Beverly; c/Julie Kay, Shelley Dee, Richard Brandon; p/Dennis L McGill (dec); Doris McGee Moss, Dallas, TX; ed/BS; LLB; mil/AUS; pa/Am, Tex, Lubbock Co & Lubbock Co Jr Bar Assns; S Plains Trial Lwyrs Assn; Tex Crim Defense Lwyrs Assn; Tex Trial Lwyrs Assn; Admit'd to Pract: All Tex Cts, US Supr Ct, US Dist Ct (Nn Dist Tex), 5th Circuit Ct Appeals, 10th Circuit Ct Appeals; cp/Bd Dirs, Lubbock Meals on Wheels Inc; Bd Dirs, ARC; Bd Dirs, Lubbock Juv Rehab Ctr Inc; Bd Dirs, Lubbock Coun Camp Fire Girls; Lubbock JCs; Tex JCs; Bd Dirs, Lubbock Fam Sers Assn; Ranch HQs Assn; United Fund; YMCA Fund Raiser; Bd Dirs, March of Dimes; Others; r/St Paul's Epis Ch: Mem, Yth Activs Sponsor; hon/1 of 5 Outstg Yg Texans; Outstg Yg Man of Lubbock; JCs Intl Senator; Order of DeMolay Legion of Hon; Others; Biogl Listings.

McGINTY, HELEN oc/Loan Assistant; b/Aug 15, 1915; h/229 Peachtree Hills Ave NE, #E, Atlanta, GA 30305; ba/Atlanta; p/Newton Elliott and Susie Veazey McGinty (dec); ed/BA Shorter Col 1936; MS Univ Ga 1943; Addit Studies; pa/US Dept Hous'g & Urban Devel: Clerk Typist, Pers Clerk, Loan Asst 1975-; Data Transcriber, IRS (Chamblee, Ga) 1974-75; Math Tchr: Cobb Co Schs 1973-74, Atlanta City Schs 1971-73; Other Positions; NEA; Ga Ed Assn; Atlanta Ed Assn; Acad Parliamentary Procedures; Am Inst Parliamentarians; AAUW; Nat Assn Parliamentarians; Others; cp/Atlanta Wom's Clb; Pilot Clb Intl; LWV; Others; r/Bapt; hon/Most Traveled Tchr Ga; 1 of 10 Most Traveled Tchrs US; Rec'd Spec Achmt Awd, US Dept HUD Pers; Alpha Delta Kappa; Delta Kappa Gamma; Kappa Kappa Iota; Biogl Listings.

McGLYNN, BETTY LOCHRIE HOAG oc/Art Historian; b/Apr 28, 1914; h/1708 Lexington Ave, San Mateo, CA 94402; ba/Same; m/Thomas A; c/Peter, Robert, Jane H Brown; p/Arthur J Lochrie (dec); Elizabeth Lochrie, Ventura, CA; ed/BA Stanford Univ 1936; MA Univ So Cal 1967; pa/So Cal Reschr, Archives Am Art 1964-67; Res Dir, Carmel Art Mus 1967-69; Dir, Triton Mus (Santa Clara) 1970; Archivist & Editor Monthly Jour; San Mateo Co Hist Assn Mus 1971-75; Tchr Art Ext, Monterey Peninsula Col 1970; Instr, San Jose City Col 1968-70; Monterey Peninsula Arts Coun; Chinese Hist Soc; Author *World of DeNeale Morgan*; r/Epis.

McGOWAN, MARJORIE FRANCES oc/Attorney; b/Feb 16, 1937; h/12951 Asbury Park, Detroit, MI 48227; p/Austin and Cassie McGowan (dec); ed/BS; LLB; LLM; pa/Atty, Holy Trinity Free Legal Clinic; r/Repub Party; r/Rom Cath; hon/1st Black Wom to Hold Position of Asst Legal Advr to Gov of Mich; Outstg Working Wom of Yr, Ctl Bus Dist of Detroit 1960; Cit'd for Outstg Ser as Asst Prosecuting Atty of Wayne Co, Wom's Aux Mich Fed'd Dem Clbs; Cit'd for Outstg Effort in Adm of Extradition Process, Nat Assn Extradition Ofcls; Rec'd Plaque, Asst Secy for Hous'g Mgmt; Rec'd Commend, Pres Clemency Bd; Num Lttrs Commend, Var Govt Agencies; Biogl Listings; Pub'd Author.

McGOWAN-SASS, BRENDA KATHLEEN oc/Psychologist; b/May 23, 1939; h/15115 Venetian Way, Morgan Hill, CA 95037; ba/San Jose, CA; m/Robert Carl; c/Taryn Elizabeth; p/Thomas Patrick McGowan (dec); Katherine Regan McGowan, Winchester, MA; ed/BA 1962, MS 1965, PhD 1967 Univ Mass; pa/Psychol, Santa Clara Co Hlth Dept, Mtl Hlth Div; Author Chapt, "The Hippocampus & Hormonal Cyclicity" in *The Hippocampus* (1975); Pub'd Articles Profl Jours.

McGUIRE, JENNIE RAE oc/Executive; b/Apr 2, 1953; h/745 South East Ave, Oak Park, IL 60304; ba/Chicago, IL; p/William and Marilyn McGuire, Oak Park; ed/AA; pa/Pres & Owner, McGuire Inc (Ct Report'g Agy); Former Pres & Co-owner, Morrissy & McGuire (Cert'd Shorthand Reporters); r/Cath.

McGUIRE, MARY LYNN oc/Assistant Coordinator; b/Apr 28, 1949; h/1875 N Burling St, Chicago, IL 60614; ba/Chgo; p/William Dennis and Marilyn R McGuire, Oak Park, IL; ed/BA Loretto Heights Col 1971; MA Cand De Paul Univ; pa/Chgo Park Dist: Asst Coor Spec Rec Activs & Sr Citizens Progs (Jr Citizens' Awds Banquet & S'ship Prog, Arbor Day Poster & Essay Contest, Coho Fishing Derby, Arts in Park, Sr Citizens' Picnic, Sr Citizens' Talent Show, Others), Supvr Dist Sr Citizens' Ctrs; Ed & Rec Com of Mayor's Office for Sr Citizens & Handicapped; Adv Com, Sr Citizens' Fitness Progs (Orgr Sr Citizens' Fitness Fun Fest); Mayor's Office Sr Citizens & Handicapped Hall of Fame Selection Com; Metro Chgo Forum on Aging; cp/Lincoln Park Zoological Soc; Grant Park Concerts Soc; r/Cath; hon/Nat Hon Soc.

MACHEN, ROY WALTER oc/Consulting Engineer; b/Jul 5, 1906; h/Rt 2, Box 130 A, Olive Hill, KY 41164; ba/Same; m/Estha Omega Slone; c/Patricia M Jordan, Russell W, Mary M Caviness, Roy W II, Elizabeth M Greenhill; p/Harvey Lee and Mary Jane Marshall Machen (dec); ed/BA magna cum laude, Okla City Univ 1927; MA Hardeman St Univ 1965; ThD Clarksville Sch Theol 1956; DD 1958; DRE 1959; DMin 1978; Post Grad (Newspaper Fund Fellow) Marquette Univ 1966; mil/Okla NG; pa/Reg'd Profl Engr Tex; Natural Gas Plant & Refinery Chemist 1927-35; Constrn Engr & Operations Supt, Natural Gas & Petro Refineries 1935-48; Warehouse & Motor Trans Supt Sulphur Co 1950-59; Owner & Pres Sulphuric Engrg (Hydrological Conslt'g Engr) 1948; Former Mem: NEA, OEA, WOEA; Lectr & Visiting Prof Bible Studies, Clarksville Sch Theol 1957-; Former Free-Lance Writer Profl Jours; Author Notes on the Book of Colossians, Research Paper Manual; Composer; Others; cp/Former ARC First Aid Instr; Former BSA Scoutmaster; Others; r/VP Repent or Perish Gospel Mins; hon/BSA Awds: Scoutmaster's Key, Gold & Silver Palms, Silver Beaver Awd, Others; Ky Col; Profl Awds.

MACHIONE, MARGHERITA FRANCES oc/Professor; b/Feb 19, 1922; h/Villa Walsh, Morristown, NJ 07960; ba/Madison, NJ; p/(dec); ed/BA Georgian Ct Col; MA, PhD Columbia Univ; pa/Sister of Pal Order; Prof Italian, Col of Arts & Scis, Farleigh Dickinson Univ; Dir NDEA & FDU Italian Insts; Former Pres Walsh Col; Press AAIS; Exec Coun AIHA; Lectr US & Abroad; Author: L'imagine Tesa (1960), 20th Cent Italian Poetry (1974), Clemente Rebora, Others; Contbr Articles Profl Jours; Am Italian Assn; Modern Lang Assn; AAUP; Others; cp/Grad Fac Alumni, Columbia Univ; NJ Hist Records Comm; United Nations Assn; r/Rom Cath; Hist Tchrs of St Lucy Filippini; hon/Giuseppe Garibaldi Scholar, Columbia Univ; Rec'd NDEA Grant, Univ Ky; Fulbright Scholar, Univ Rome; Rec'd Cert of Merit, FDU Evening Coun; Rec'd AMITA Achmt Awd Ed; Recipient FDU Res Grants; Wom of Yr; W/W: Am Wom, Authors & Journalists, Am Col & Univ Adm, Am, E; DIB; Intl W/W Commun Ser; Others.

MACHORRO, MARGARET OZUNA oc/Broker; b/Jun 20, 1935; h/9841 La Docena Ln, Pico Rivera, CA 90280; ba/S Gate, CA; c/Lorelei Ann M Garcia, Robert A Moreno; p/Santos Machorro (dec); Lorenza Machorro, Pico Rivera; ed/Mgmt & Adm 1975; Real Estate Pract & Law 1969; pa/Real Estate Broker & Owner; Bd Realtors; cp/C of C; r/Cath; hon/W/W Am Wom.

McILHANY, STERLING FISHER oc/Writer; b/Apr 12, 1930; h/52 Morton St, New York, NY 10014; ba/Same; p/William Wallace McIlhany, Long Beach, CA; ed/BFA

w Hons, Univ Tex 1953; pa/Pres, Art Horizons Inc; Author 4 Books; Pub'd Num Articles; r/Christian; hon/Rec'd Nat Awd to Tour European Art Ctrs; Rec'd Rotary Intl F'ship for 1 Yr Study, Accademia delle Belle Art (Rome).

McILVAIN, TERRY MARK oc/Minister of Youth; b/Apr 14, 1950 h/8044 E Gilbert, Wichita, KS 67207; ba/Wichita; m/Ginger; p/T J and Maxine McIlvain, Hennessey, OK; ed/BA Wichita St Univ; pa/Yth Evangelism Staff, Kan-Neb Conv So Bapt 1975-; Super Summer Progs, K-NCSB; Yth Evangelism Ldrship Conf, K-NCSB 1978; Kan City Metro Bible Conf 1977; Sedwick Bapt Assn (Yth Conslt) 1976; Nat Yth Evangelism Ldrship Conf 1975; Others; Pub'd Articles Profl Jours; r/So Bapt; hon/Personalities of W&MW; W/W Rel; Outstg Yg Men Am; Rec'd Spec Cit, Okla St Senate; Rec'd Spec Tchr Cit, Okla Bapt Gen Conv; Ambassador of Goodwill, St of Okla & Gov David Hall.

McILVEENE, CHARLES STEELE oc/Minister; b/Feb 11, 1928; h/1305 Woodland Dr, Lufkin, TX 75901; ba/Lufkin; m/Betty Fahlberg; c/Carol Ann M Lemmond, Mary Beth, Scott; p/Bonnie Leonard and Lillian Owen McIlveene (dec); ed/BA Hardin-Simmons Col; BD, MRE SWn Sem; pa/Former VP, La Bapt Conv; cp/Former Trustee, La Col; Trustee ETBC; Former Dir Exec Bd, LBC; Dir Exec Bd, BGCT; Ser'd Var Coms, St & Nat Convs; Rotary Clb; Dir Angelina Div, Am Heart Assn; Lufkin C of C; r/So Bapt; hon/W/W Rel.

McINTEER, JIM BILL oc/Minister; b/Jun 16, 1921; h/1100 Belvedere Dr, Nashville, TN 37204; ba/Nashville; m/Betty Bergner; c/MariLynn, Mark; ed/David Lipscomb Col; Harding Col; pa/Min, West End Ch of Christ 1956-; Editor-in-Chief, 20th Cent Christian; Staff Writer, Bible Herald (Parkersburg, WV); Secy, Christian Pubs Inc; Adv Bd, Royal Pubrs Inc (Johnson City, Tenn); Past Pres Bd Dirs, Foun for Christian Ed; Author: The Tiny Tots Bible Reader, Reviving the Gospel Meeting, Crisis in the Am Fam, Others; Other Positions; cp/Bd Dirs, Potter Chd's Home (Bowling Green, Ky); Dir, Fanning Orphan Sch Bd; SAR; West End Civitan Clb; Past Pres David Lipscomb Col Alumni Assn; Bd Dirs, Tenn Lung Assn; r/Ch of Christ; hon/Rec'd Dist'd Alumnus Awd, Harding Col.

McINTURFF, ERNEST ROBERT oc/Aerospace Engineer; b/Feb 28, 1936; h/1417 Audmar Dr, McLean, VA 22101; ba/Charlottesville, VA; p/Ernest Raymond McInturff; Elva Whitehurst McInturff, McLean; ed/BS Univ Va 1959; Addit Studies; mil/USN 1960-68; pa/Aerospace Engr, Fed Aviation Adm (Wash, DC) 1959-64; Res Spec, Dept Army (Wash) 1964-67; Aerospace Engr, Dept Army 1967-71; Supvr Aerospace Engr, Dept Army (C'ville) 1971-; Interagy Bd, US Civil Ser Examrs; Am Inst Aeronautics & Astronautics; Am Defense Preparedness Assn; r/Columbia Bapt Ch (Falls Ch, Va); hon/Rec'd Outstg Perf Awd, Dept Army; Rec'd Am Legion Student Awd; Rec'd Fed Campaign Keyman Awd.

MACIUSZKO, JERZY (GEORGE) J oc/Professor; b/Jul 15, 1913; h/133 Sunset Dr, Berea, OH 44017; ba/Berea; m/Kathleen Lynn; c/Christina Olga; p/Bonifacy and Aleksandra Maciuszko (dec); ed/MA Univ Warsaw; MS, PhD Case Wn Reserv Univ; pa/Baldwin-Wallace Col: Prof Emeritus 1978-, Prof & Lib Dir 1974-78; Chm Div Slavic & Modern Langs, Alliance Col (Cambridge Springs, Penn) 1973-74; Other Positions; Co-author (w Dr Walter Smietana) An Exploratory Survey of the Accreditation and Certification of Polish Lang Tchg in the US (1970); Author The Polish Short Story in English (1968); Book Reviewer for Books Abroad, 1957-; Conslt; Contbr Articles Profl Jours; Am Assn Advmt Slavic Studies; Am Lib Assn; Am Assn Tchrs Slavic & E European Langs; Assn Advmt Polish Studies; Assn Polish Writers Abroad; Assn Polish Univ Profs & Lectrs Abroad; Modern Lang Assn; Others; cp/Polish Am Hist Assn; Rowfant Clb Cleveland; r/Luth; hon/Rec'd Kosciuszko

Foun Annual Dissertation Awd; Rec'd Hilbert T Ficken Awd, Baldwin-Wallace Col; Contemp Authors; DIB; W/W MW; Intl Scholars Directory; Outstg Edrs Am.

MACK, ARLENE oc/Administrator; b/Nov 26, 1932; h/716 Washington St, Bismarck, ND 58501; ba/Bismarck; m/Thorval; c/Richard, Cindy; p/George and Selma Hedman, Scranton, ND; ed/Dipl Bismarck Hosp Sch Nsg 1954; BS Mary Col 1972; Cert Patient Care Adm, Univ Minn 1977; pa/Patient Care Admr; Lectr: Minot St Col, Bismarck Hosp Sch Nsg, Others; Credentials Com, ANA; Coun Nsg Ser Facilitators; ND St Nurses Assn; Am Hosp Assn; Nat Leag Nsg; ND Occupational Therapy Assn; SHCC (Gov Appointed); Steer'g Com, St/White House Conf Handicapped; Others; cp/BPW: Luther Leag; Quota Clb; YMCA; Conslt: ND March of Dimes, United Tribes Aide Tng Prog, Vocational Nurses Aide Prog (Bismarck HS & Jr Col); Others; r/Luth; hon/Submitted & Received Contbn March of Dimes for High Risk Nursery Dept; Outstg Yg Wom Am; W/W Am Wom; Fellow Am Acad Nsg.

MACK, BRENDA LEE oc/Executive; b/Mar 24, 1940; h/PO Box 5942, Los Angeles, CA 90055; ba/LA; c/Kevin Anthony; p/William James and Virginia Julia Pickett Palmer (dec); ed/AA; Cand BA; mil/US Wom's Army Corps 1960-61; pa/Transportation Facilities Exec; Secy Bus Facilities; cp/Ombudsman; hon/Num Hon Coms; W/W Am Wom; Others.

McKAIG, PATRICIA LYN oc/Teacher; b/Jul 22, 1949; h/Rt 1, Box 313, Logansport, IN; p/Edward E and Elizabeth J McKaig, Logansport; ed/BA 1971, MS 1979 Purdue Univ; Tchr Cert, Cleveland St Univ 1974; pa/Elem Sch Tchr; Tchr-Cnslr, Outdoor Ed Prog; 4th Grade & Mus Tchr (Lakewood, Ohio) 2 Yrs; 5th & 6th Grade Tchr (Logansport) Pioneer Sch Sys; NEA; cp/VISTA Vol; Girls 4-H Clb Ldr; r/Webb Chapel UMC: Mem, SS Tchr & Ed Chm, Past Yth Group Sponsor; hon/Rec'd Outstg Rec Student Awd, Purdue Univ; Rec'd Nat 4-H Clb Cong S'ship.

MacKAY, ERIC GEORGE oc/Executive; b/Aug 19, 1918; h/7525 W Treasure Dr, Miami Beach, FL 33141; ba/Same; m/Kathleen; c/David Clive, Eric Jr, Heather, Robin, Ian; p/William MacKay (dec); Jean MacKay, Berwick-on-Tweed, England; ed/BS Aberdeen Univ; mil/Brit Navy; pa/Pres, MacKay Corp; Propeller Clb; Marine Conslt; VP Eagle Marine of Miami; cp/Turf Clb; Racquet Clb; r/Presb; hon/Personalities of S; Notable Ams; Fellow, Intl Biogl Assn.

McKAY, GEORGE WILLIAM oc/Conservationist; b/Mar 18, 1933; h/Rt 1, Box 137, Pelahatchie, MS 39145; ba/Jackson, MS; c/George William Jr; p/M H McKay (dec); Gladys C McKay, Pelahatchie; ed/Police Sci; mil/USN; pa/Wildlife Conserv Ofcr; Miss Law Enforcemt Ofcrs & FBI Nat Assns; cp/Mason; Scottish Rite; Shriner; r/Prot; hon/Ofcr of Yr: Shikar Safari 1976, Wildlife Fdn 1977.

McKAY, GWENDOLYN SICKLES oc/Retired; b/Aug 18, 1912; h/513 W Storey, Midland, TX 79701; c/Martha Gwen M Evans, Irene (dec); p/Frank Phillip and Mary Prescilla Rochester Sickles (dec); ed/RN Meml Hosp Sch Nsg 1937; Addit Studies; mil/AUS Nurse Corps 1940-48; pa/Midland Meml Hosp 1959-79: Dir Nurses 7 Yrs, Head Nurse (Nursery) 10 Yrs, Others; Chg Nurse Nursery, Robert B Green Hosp (San Antonio) 1955-58; Other Positions; Tex Nurses' Assn: Former Leg Chrperson, 2/VP, Pres; cp/Recruit'g Chrperson, Midland ARC; Adv Bd: Local HS, Odessa Col, Howard Col; r/Meth; hon/Nurse of Yr, Midland Meml Hosp 1972; Rec'd 40 Yr Ser Awd, ARC; W/W Am Wom.

MacKAY, JOHN ALEXANDER oc/Retired Clergyman; b/May 17, 1889; h/Meadow Lakes, Apt 39-09, Hightstown, NJ 08520;

m/Jane Logan Wells; c/Isobel Elizabeth, Duncan Alexander Duff, Elena Florence, Ruth; p/Duncan and Isabella Macdonald Mackay, Inverness, Scotland; ed/Dipl, Ctr Hist Studies (Madrid, Spain) 1916; BD Princeton Theol Sem 1915; MA Aberdeen Univ 1912; pa/Fdr & Prin, Anglo-Peruvian Col (Now San Andres) Lima, Peru 1917-25; Prof Metaphysics, San Marcos Univ (Lima) 1924-25; Lectr Latin Am Univs Sponsored by YMCA 1926-32; Secy S Am & Africa Bd of Foreign Missions 1932-36; Pres & Prof Ecumenics, Princeton Theol Sem 1936-59; Chm, Intl Missionary Coun 1948-58; Chm World Presb Alliance 1954-59; r/United Presb Ch USA; hon/Rec'd Upper Room Cit; Rec'd Palmas Magisteriales, Peruvian Govt; Others.

MacKAY, KATHLEEN IRIS oc/Professor; Executive; b/Nov 17, 1926; h/7525 W Treasure Dr, Miami Beach, FL 33141; ba/Same; m/Eric; c/Michael, Ian; p/Charles and Cora Simon (dec); ed/BA Grove City Col; MA Univ Okla; pa/Secy-Treas, MacKay Corp; Pilot Clb; Intl Propeller Clb; r/Presb; hon/W/W Am Wom; Intl Blue Book; World W/W Wom; Fellow Intl Biogl Assn.

McKAY, LAWRENCE BRIAN oc/Marketing Consultant; b/Feb 19, 1924; h/4141 N Braeswood, #8, Houston, TX 77025; ba/Same; m/Lola Merle; p/William Leo and Lillian McKay, New York, NY; ed/BA; mil/USAF WWII; pa/Am Mktg Assn; cp/Repub Nat Com; Nat Adv Bd, Am Security Coun; r/St Phillip's Ch (Houston); hon/Mem Arista; Rec'd Victory Medal, Asiatic-Pacific & Am Theatre Campaign Medals, Good Conduct Medal, WWII.

McKEE, JOHN WALTER oc/Public Relations Director; b/Jun 7, 1926; h/1530 Willemoore Ave, Springfield, IL 62704; ba/Springfield; m/June Marian Meers; c/Jennifer Ann, Jeffrey Meers; p/Clifford Edwin and Zelda Goodjohn Jones McKee (dec); ed/George Wash Univ, Univ Ill; mil/USNR WWII; pa/PR Dir, Taxpayers' Fdn of Ill; cp/Former Yg Repub Nat Com-man; Mid W Yg Repub Chm & Dir; Yg Repub Nat Fdn; Jr C of C; Jr Chamber Intl; Past Pres, Boys' Clbs; Chm, Heart of Am Awd Com (Boys' Clbs); Rees Carillon Soc; Former Pres, Cosmopolitan Clb; Aid to Retarded Citizens; Others; r/Westminster Presb Ch: Elder, Trustee, Deacon, Former Clerk Of Session; hon/Rec'd Bronze Keystone & Medallion, BCA.

McKEE, TIMOTHY GENE oc/Administrator; b/Apr 27, 1945; h/6107 W 74th St. Los Angeles, CA 90045; m/Judith Rae; c/Dana Cheryl; p/Earl R and Nadine Sowder McKee, Denison, TX; ed/BA Okla Christian Col 1967; MA 1970, MS 1978 Pepperdine Univ; MA Loyola Univ 1971; PhD Cal Grad Sch Theol 1973; PhD Cand, Grace Sch Theol; EdD Cand, Pepperdine Univ; pa/VP & Admr, World

Mission Inst; Fdr & Chm, Admr's Assn; Accreditation Com, Assn Christian Schs Intl; Nat Assn Christian Sch Admrs; Christian Fin Exec Assn; cp/Ctr for Law & Rel Freedom; Bd Ed, Pioneer Christian Schs So Cal; r/Westchester Ch of Christ: Deacon, Ednl Dir; hon/Outstg Yg Men Am; W/W Rel; Personalities of W&MW; Men Achmt.

McKEEL, MARION ELIZABETH oc/Artist; b/May 8, 1919; h/Still Waters, 54A

Shadow Ln, Whispering Pines, NC 28327; m/James Cook III; c/Marion M Fogler, Lynn M Casjuk, James Forrest; p/Lloyd Ranson and Florence Marion Harper Terwilliger, Dayton, WA; ed/BA Scripps Col 1941; Grad Studies: Claremont Univ Grad Sch 1941, Penn Acad Fine Arts 1942, Colo Col 1944; pa/Art Curric Chm, Thornbury Elem Sch 1964; Home Studio Yth Classes 1964-67; Yth Classes, Chester Co Art Ctr 1967-72; Art Instr, Dela Co Prison (Broadmeadows) 1972-74; Nat Leag Am Pen Wom; Art Exhibit Judge; Lectr; cp/Exec Bd, Chester Co Coun Addictive Diseases; Bd Mem, Witae House; Bd Mem, Main Line Coun on Alcohol & Drug Abuse; Wom's Div, Dela Val Coun on Alcoholism; r/Dilworthtown United Presb Ch; hon/Rec'd Commend in Field Awd, Scripps Col; Rec'd F'ship, Penn Acad Fine Arts; One-person Shows: Lancaster CCAA, Westchester St Univ, Others; Work in Pvt Collections; Comms; Biogl Listings.

McKEMIE, ISABELLE McKENZIE oc/Homemaker; h/PO Box 187, Sylacauga, AL 35150; m/William Joel; c/William Joel Jr (dec); p/John Marvin and Mary Isabelle Dixon McKenzie; ed/AB Randolph Macon Wom's Col; Att'd Emory Univ; cp/John Piney Oden Chapt UDC; Sylacauga Chapt DAR; Horse Shoe Bend Chapt, DAC; Thomas Johnson Chapt NS Col Dames XVII Cent; NS Magna Charta Dames; Most Noble Order of Knights of Garter; Plantagenet Soc; Sov Col Soc Am of Royal Desc; Col Order of the Crown; Huguenot Soc; Matron's Study Clb; Cherokee Garden Clb; Am Camellia Soc; Mignon Bridge Clb; Sylacauga Art Leag (Charter Mem & 1st Pres); Fellow, Intl Biogl Assn; Charter Mem, Sylacauga Beautification Comm; Sylacauga Coun of Arts & Humanities; Talladega Co Hist Soc; hon/Kappa Alpha Theta; World W/W Wom; W/W Intells; Others.

MacKENZIE, MALCOLM LEWIS oc/Executive; b/Jan 19, 1926; h/108 Southwick Dr, Wilmington, DE 19810; ba/Wilmington; m/Barbara Lee Webb; c/David, Ellen; p/William Forbes Mackenzie (dec); Grace Lewis Mackenzie, South Duxbury, MA; ed/BA Brown Univ 1951; Attended RI Sch Design, Phillips Acad; mil/USMM; Grad'd Maine Maritime Acad; pa/Pres Malcolm L Mackenzie & Assocs 1966-; VP Daily Ser 1965; Head Mktg Dept, Grey & Rogers Adv (Phila) 1964; Dir Composite Structures Inc; Dir Am Prestige Arts; Advtg Col Delaware; Delaware Press Clb; Others; cp/Bd Dirs, Dela Safety Coun; Sister Cities of Wilmington; Freedom Intl; Kiwanis Clb; Pres Windy Bush Civic Assn; Dela Hope Com; Gtr Wilmington Devel Coun; BSA; Repub Party; Gov's Com on Hous'g; Others; r/Aldersgate United Meth Ch: Fdr, Missions Com; hon/Delta Upsilon; Order of Merit & Woodbadge, BSA; Rec'd Kiwanis Cert Apprec.

MACKEY, R ELIZABETH (BETTY) oc/Associate Professor; b/Sept 30, 1918; h/Box 86, 225 W Taylor St, Mount Victory, OH 43340; ba/Bowling Green, OH; m/Gage R; c/Linda M Buroker (Mrs Walter), Sue M Burrey (Mrs Richard), Betsy, Carol; p/Paul E and Fern McColley Schutzberg (dec); ed/BS; MS; RD; pa/Assoc Prof Food & Nutrition, Bowling Green St Univ; Reg'd Dietician; Secy, Ohio Nutrition Coun; Adv Com, Ohio Sch Food Ser; AAUW; Num Other Profl Activs; cp/DAR; Repub Wom; r/Meth; hon/Delta Kappa Gamma; Pi Kappa Delta; Kappa Delta Pi; Hon Fac; Hon FHA Mem; Biogl Listings.

McKIG, ELOISE (BILLIE) oc/Dental Hygienist; b/Nov 29, 1926; h/4851 W Alder Dr, San Diego, CA 92116; ba/San Diego; m/Robert (dec); c/Monica, Susan, (Stepdaugh:) Jennifer; p/Mark E Olson (dec); Hazel Staley Littler, Algona, IA; ed/RDH; pa/Wom's Aux Dental Soc; So Cal Dental Hygiene Assn; Am Dental Hygienists Assn; cp/OES; r/Presb; hon/W/W: Am, Cal; Others.

McKINLEY, JIMMIE JOE oc/Executive;

b/Jul 23, 1934; h/PO Box 2106, Longview, TX 75601; ba/Same; p/Joseph Crofford McKinley (dec); Velma Anne Barnett McKinley, Longview; ed/BA Univ Tex; MLS Univ Ky; pa/Asst Libn, Bethel Col (McKenzie, Tenn) 1961-63; Reference Libn 1966-70; Act'g Head Libn 1970-71; Owner-Mgr, Longview Book Co 1974-; cp/Bd Dirs, ARC; Longview Piney Woods Chapt; Bd Trustees, Bethel Col; r/1st Cumberland Presb Ch: Mem.

McKNIGHT, HARRY F oc/Director; b/Oct 11, 1931; h/PO Box 3348, Valley View Acres, Laredo, TX 78041; ba/Laredo; m/Alice Akins; c/Margaret Edith, Evelyn Marie; p/C D Sr and Marguerite P McKnight (dec); ed/BA Springhill Col; MA Tulane Univ; PhB St Anselm's (Rome, Italy); Doct Cand, Univ Tex; pa/Dir & Lectr, Silva Mind Control Intl Inc; Author *Silva Mind Control Through Psychorientology*; r/Cath; hon/Valedictorian.

McKNIGHT, LENORE RAVIN oc/Psychiatrist; b/May 15, 1943; h/3441 Echo Springs Rd, Lafayette, CA 94549; ba/Walnut Creek, CA; m/Robert L; p/Abe and Rose Ravin, Denver, CO; ed/BA Univ Col 1965; MD Univ Cal-SF 1969; Internship, Chd's Hosp (San Francisco) 1969-70; Residency, UCSF 1970-73; pa/Asst Clinical Instr Child Psychi, UCSF; Pvt Pract Child Psychi; Am Acad Child Psychi; Am Psychi Assn; No Cal Psychi Soc; Am Med Wom's Assn; cp/Tnr Arabian Horses; Intl Arabian Horse Assn; Desert Wind Arabian Horse Assn; hon/Rec'd F'ship, Intl Inst Ed; Rec'd Grant, Nat Inst Hlth; W/W Am Wom; World W/W Wom; Diplomate, Am Bd Psychi & Neurol.

McKUEN, ROD oc/Poet; Composer; Author; Singer; Classical Composer; b/Apr 29, 1933; h/PO Box G, Beverly Hills, CA 90213; ba/Los Angeles, CA; oc/Composer: *Seasons in the Sun, Love's Been Good to Me, If You Go Away, Jean, A Boy Named Charlie Brown*, Num Others; Classical Compositions: *Concerto for Four Harpsichords, Symph No 1, Adagio for Harp & Strings*, Others; Comms: *Concerto No 3 for Piano & Orch* (Ballet), *The Plains of My Country* (25th Anniv London Royal Philharm Orch), Others; Film Scores: *The Prime of Miss Jean Brodie* (1969), *A Boy Named Charlie Brown* (1970), *The Borrowers* (1973) Others; Author: *Stanyan St & Other Sorrows* (1966), *Listen to the Warm* (1967), *The McKuen Omnibus* (1975) Num Others; Pres: Stanyan Records, Discus Records, New Gramophone Soc, Mr Kelly Prodns, Cheval Books, Rod McKuen Enterprises, Others; VP, Tamarack Books; ASCAP; Writers Guild; AFTRA; AGVA; Nat Acad Record'g Arts & Scis; Bd Dirs, Market Theatre (Johannesburg, S Africa); Modern Poetry Assn; cp/Bd Dirs, Am Nat Theatre Ballet; Animal Concern; Adv Bd, Intl Ed; Fund for Animals; hon/Nom Pulitzer Prize Classical Mus, *The City*; Rec'd Acad Awd, *Jean & A Boy Named Charlie Brown*; Rec'd Grande Prix du Disc (Paris); Rec'd Golden Globe Awd; *Motion Picture Daily* Awd; Winner Grammy Awd, *Lonesome Cities*; Freedoms Foun Awd; Man of Yr, Menniger Foun 1975; Entertainer of Yr, LA Shriners' Clb 1975; Winner Emmy Awd, *Say Goodbye & Hello Again*; Others.

McLAFFERTY, DEE HARTMANN oc/Teacher; h/1587 Tolly Ganley St NW, Dogwood Garden Clb, Orangeburg, SC 29115; m/Charles Lowry; c/Ardith M Zander, Karen Dee, Charles L Jr, Kevin Paul; p/Henry J and Ottilie Truebenbach Hartmann; ed/BSc Univ Neb; Grad Studies, Wn Ky Univ; pa/Tchr Chd w LDs 1975-; Tchr, A G Parrish HS (Selma, Ala) 1967-68; A B Dick Co (Niles, Ill) 1950-51; Tchr, Franklin-Simpson HS (Franklin, Ky) 1949-50; cp/Dogwood Garden Clb; Bd Dirs, Orangeburg Fest of Arts; Orangeburg Mus Clb; Bd Dirs, Orangeburg Attention Home; Treas, Maude Schiffley Chapt SPCA; Charity Leag of Selma; Orangeburg Country Clb; Tarantella Clb; Others; r/Orangeburg Luth Ch; hon/Hon Ala Admiral; Hon Ala Col.

McLAUCHLIN, BEATRICE HALL oc/Piano & Theory Teacher; b/May 22, 1896;

h/5100 Sharon Rd, Charlotte, NC 28210; ba/Same; m/Hugh Currie; c/Thomas Neill, Josephine M Crenshaw, Beatrice Wells (dec), John William; p/Thomas Newberry and Lucy Rankin Abernathy Hall, Morresville, NC; ed/BM Flora Macdonald Col 1918; pa/Cert'd Piano & Theory Tchr, NCMTA 1959; Tchr Piano, Flora Macdonald Col 1917-18; Raeford Public Sch 1918-21; Pvt Tchr; Raeford 1929-51, Charlotte 1967-76; Judge, Jr Fest Nat Fdn Mus Clbs; Orgr & Dir, Raeford Commun Chorus; Nat & NC Mus Edrs Assn; Mus Tchrs Nat Assn; NC Mus Tchrs Assn; Nat Guild Piano Tchrs; Charlotte Piano Tchrs Forum; Orgr Chaminade Mus Clb; Charlotte Mus Clb; Queen City Mus Clb; cp/El Viernes Book Clb; United Daughs Confederacy; DAR; Charlotte Chapt, Eng Speaking Union; Adv Bd, Flora Macdonald Col; Adv Bd Peace Col; Adv Bd, Presb Jr Col; Dem Party; Others; r/Convenant Presb Ch: Tchr, Others; Presb Survey; Christian Observer; Presb Wom; Contbr Articles Rel Jours; hon/Life Mem Past Pres Assembly, Nat Fdn Mus Clb; Life Mem Wom of Ch: Raeford Ch & Fayetteville Presb; Rec'd Cert Outstg Ser Trustee, Presb Jr Col; Silver Awd & Cit, Raeford Wom of Ch; Gold Awd & Cit, Chaminade Mus Clb; NC Merit Mother; W/W Am Wom; Intl W/W Mus; Personalities of S; Others.

McLAUGHLIN, GLEN oc/Executive; b/Dec 21, 1934; h/20264 Ljepava Dr, Saratoga, CA 95070; ba/Cupertino, CA; m/Ellen Marr Schnake; c/Helen Elizabeth, Glen Wallace; p/Champe and Mattie Bet Jenkins McLaughlin, Shawnee, OK; ed/BBA Univ Okla 1956; MBA Harvard Univ 1964; mil/USAF 1956-62; pa/VP Fin, Four-Phase Sys Inc; Pres, Four-Phase Fin Inc; Fin Execs Inst; Planning Execs Inst; Nat Assn Accts; cp/Pres & Bd Dirs, Jr Achmt; Guarantor, Civic Light Opera; Eng Speaking Union; Commonwealth Clb; r/Bapt; hon/Rec'd Gold Letzeiser Medal as Most Outstg Univ Sr Man.

McLAUGHLIN, JERRY LOREN oc/Professor; b/Oct 14, 1939; h/2940 State Rd, 26 W, W Lafayette, IN 47906; ba/Lafayette; m/Frances Jeanette; c/Angie Lee, Andrew Todd; p/Ralph Todd and Rosella McLaughlin, Coldwater, MI; ed/BS 1961, MS 1963, PhD 1965 Univ Mich; pa/Prof Pharmacognosy, Dept Med, Purdue Univ; Am Soc Pharmacog; Am Pharm Assn; AAAS; Others; r/Prot; hon/Rho Chi; Phi Lambda Upsilon; Phi Kappa Phi; Sigma Xi; Rec'd Grants; Others.

McLEAN, STEPHEN ALDERMAN oc/Land Owner; b/May 28, 1919; ba/N Main St, Wagram, NC 28369; p/Allan and Ella Alderman McLean, Wagram; ed/BS Davidson Col 1940; mil/USNR WWII; pa/Pres, Wagram Bus Com; cp/Precinct Chm; r/Presb: Deacon, Elder, Others; hon/Rec'd Commend; Others.

McLEAN, RUTH ANN oc/Guidance Counselor; h/80 Lakeshore W, Lake Quivira, Kansas City, KS 66106; ba/Kansas City; m/John Thomas (dec); c/Sally Hart, Robert Bruce, Joan M Davies (Mrs James); p/George Hoff Sr and Anna Mehew Price Irvin (dec); ed/BSEd, MA Ohio Univ; MEd, EdS Univ Kansas; pa/Guid Cnslr: J C Harmon HS 1975-, W Jr HS (Ks City) 1974-75; Elem Guid Cnslr, Ks City 1966-74; Former Tchr, Water Safety Instr & Waterfront Dir; Former Dir Pvt Nursery Sch; Adv Coun, Wy Co Assn Child LDs; Life Mem NEA; Pres Shawnee Tchrs Assn; ASCA: Nat Del, Speaker, Awds Chm; Ks PGA: Exec Bd, Coms; Ks Chm APGA, Govt Relats Capitol Hill Visits; Author; cp/Adv Coun Donnelly Col; hon/Rec'd Jefferson Medallion Awd, Am Inst Public Ser & WDAF Radio-TV; Cnslr of Yr of Am Ed Week, Bunche Chapt Student Action For Ed; Cnslr of Yr 1972; Fulbright Scholar; Delta Kappa Gamma; Others.

McLENDON, DOROTHY oc/Psychologist; b/Feb 20, 1918; h/100 Memorial Dr, Cambridge, MA 02142; ba/Brookline, MA; m/Hiram James; c/Hiram J Jr; p/J Newton and Dora Ryall Fullenwider (dec); ed/BA; MA; EdD; pa/Sch Psychol; Am Psychol Assn; NEA; Mass Sch Psychol; cp/LWV; r/Prot;

hon/Diplomate, Am Assn Profl Psychols.

MacLENNAN, BERYCE W oc/Psychologist; b/Mar 14, 1920; h/6307 Crathie Lane, Bethesda, MD 20016; ba/Rockville, MD; m/John Duncan (dec); p/William Mellis (dec); Beatrice MacRae Mellis; ed/BS w Hons; LSE; PhD; pa/Prof of Psychol & Cnslg, Md Univ 1967-69; Prof, Geo Washington Univ 1974-; Clin & Commun Psychologist; Group Therapist (NYC) 1950-58; Group Therapist (Wash, DC) 1959-63; Dir & Assoc Prof, Yth Tng Ctr, Howard Univ 1963-66; NIMH Regl Mtl Hlth Adm 1974-75; Asst Dir, GAO of DC 1976-; VP Compliance, Federally Employed Wom 1980; Bd Mem, AGPA 1962-; Planned Parenthood Bd 1968-72; MHA Adv Bd 1967-; Others; cp/ADA; So Md Sailing Assn; hon/Vol Awds, DC Psychol Assn & PG City Mtl Hlth Assn; Superior Performance Awd, NIMH; Fellow: AGPA, APA, AOA; Biogl Listings; Others.

MacLEOD, MARION A oc/Author; Lecturer; h/2717 Florida Blvd, #523, Delray Beach, FL 33444; ba/Same; m/Glenn; c/Dianne Marion; p/John Wesley and Agnes Hadessah Zealand McLean (dec); ed/Attended: Cleveland Col, Boston Univ, Harvard Univ, Others; pa/Author's Guild; Nat Leag Am Pen Wom; Boston Author's Clb; Vermont Poetry Soc; Profl Wom's Clb Boston; Boston Author's Clb; Others; cp/Commr, Mass Gov's Comm on Adoption & Foster Care; Fdr, Adoption Assn Mass; Co-Dir, Delray Beach Police, Fire & Rescue CB Monitors; Bd Dirs, Chd's Home Soc Fla; Crisis Line; Secy Delray Beach Repub Clb; Others; r/Ch of the Palm (Congreg); hon/Rec'd Annual Awd, New England Home for Little Wanderers; Rose Awd, *Jewish Advocate*; Portrait of Month, *United Ch Herald*; Biogl Listings.

McLERON, LEE MARIE oc/Homemaker; b/Jul 17, 1927; h/S 2320 Jefferson, Spokane, WA 99203; m/Roy Edwin; c/Merrilie M Shipman, Michael Roy; p/Albert Cox, BC, Canada; Marie Cox, BC, Canada; ed/BS Univ Buffalo; Accred'd Flower Show Judge & Landscape Design Critic; cp/Wash Cong PTA: Sustain'g Mem, St Conv Chm, Bd Mgrs; Past Pres, Spokane Coun PTA; Past Pres, Spokane Flower Designers Guild; Past Pres, Inland Empire Garden Study Clb; Wash St Fdn Garden Clbs; Former Advtg Editor, Smoke Signals (Garden Clb Pub); Assoc'd Garden Clbs of Spokane; United Way; March of Dimes; Camp Fire Girls; Sch Vol Aide; Spokane Chd's Theatre; Bd Trustees, Gtr Spokane Mus & Allied Arts Fest; Spokane Symph Wom's Assn; Lewis & Clark Mus Boosters; Others; r/Meth; hon/Life Mem Golden Acorn, Spokane Coun PTA; Book of Recog, Wash St Fdn Garden Clbs; Wom of Yr, Assoc'd Garden Clbs of Spokane 1974; Book of Hon; Men & Wom Distinction; Notable Ams; World W/W Wom; Commun Ldrs & Noteworthy Ams; Others.

McLEVIE, ELAINE MARIANNE oc/Administrator; b/Jul 25, 1932; h/2440 Maddux Ave, El Cajon, CA 92021; ba/El Cajon; m/John Gilwell; c/Anne Jeanette, Karen Elaine, Lynne Diana; p/Geoffrey W and Mona Foote, Taupo, New Zealand; ed/BA, MA Victoria Univ; PhD Mich St Univ; pa/Grossmont Col: Admr, Fac Senate Pres 1976-78, Dean Communs Arts 1978; Exec Com, Acad Senate of Cal Commun Cols; cp/Heartland Creat Commun Assn; r/Epis; hon/Rec'd Silver Medallion, Royal Life Sav'g Soc; Notable Ams.

McLEVIE, JOHN GILWELL oc/Professor; b/Nov 2, 1929; h/2440 Maddux Ave, El Cajon, CA 92021; ba/San Diego, CA; m/Elaine Marianne; c/Anne Jeanette, Karen Elaine, Lynne Diana; p/Edward Mitchell McLevie (dec); Gwendoline Mary McLevie, Willington, New Zealand; ed/BA 1955, Dipl Ed 1957, MA 1956 Victoria Univ; PhD Mich St Univ; pa/Col of Ed, San Diego St Univ: Prof Ed, Chm Dept Sec'dy Ed 1978; Chief of Party, Ed Team in Brazilian Min of Ed 1973-76; Prof Ed 1976; Asst/Assoc Prof 1970-76; Lectr Univ Hong Kong 1963-68; cp/Former VP Citizens

Adv Com, El Cajon Val Sch Dist; r/Epis; hon/Outstg Edrs Am; Intl Bibliog Ed; Personalities of W&MW; Notable Ams.

MacLIN, MELVIN MARLO oc/Dentist; b/Feb 7, 1929; h/8149 S St, Lawrence Ave, Chicago, IL 60619; ba/Chgo; c/Richard, David, Melvin II, Melanye; p/Richard Sidney Maclin (dec); Carrie Maclin, Chgo; ed/BS 1956, DDS 1958 Univ Ill; mil/AUS 1951-53; pa/Pvt Pract Dentistry; ADA; Ill St Dental Soc; Chgo Dental Soc; Nat Dental Assn & Lincoln Dental Soc; Independent Dental Org;

Others; cp/Chgo Urban Leag; Life Mem NAACP; Life Mem Tenn Univ Alumni; Life Mem Univ Ill Alumni Assn; Am Coun YMCA; Adv Coun, Univ Ill; Mid Wn Social Clb; Others; r/Holy Cross Immanuel Epis Ch: Mem; hon/Beta Kappa Chi; Rec'd S'ship, Fayette Co Tchrs Assn; Dist'd Alumni TSU; Merit Awd, Chgo Chapt TSC; W/W: MW, Black Am; Notable Ams; Personalities of S; Others.

McLURE, GAIL THOMAS oc/Program Coordinator; b/Sept 1, 1935; h/Rt 6, River Heights, Iowa City, IA 52240; ba/Iowa City; m/John W; c/David P, John R; p/Omer E and Cora S Thomas, Cullman, AL; ed/BA Univ Ala 1957; MEd Univ Ill 1965; PhD Univ Iowa 1973; Tchg Cert Kansas St Univ 1959; Iowa Supt's Cert 1975; pa/Iowa Regents Univs: Interinstitutional Prog Coor, Ext & Cont'g Ed Progs 1977-, Interinstitutional BLS Com 1977-, Prog'g & Delivery Com 1977-, Public Info & Prog Awareness Com 1977-; Task Force on Assessmt of Exptl Lng, Iowa Coor'g Com for Cont'g Ed 1978-; Plan'g Coor, Study on Postsec'dy Plan'g for Nontraditional Learners in Iowa (Higher Ed Facilities Comm); Am Col Test'g Prog, Res Psychol: Assessmt Sers Dept & Devel Res Dept 1975, Test Devel Dept 1974-75, Devel Res Dept 1975-76; Tchg Asst Div of Sec'dy Ed, Univ Iowa 1971-72; Other Positions; Nat Assn Public Cont'g & Adult Ed; Nat Univ Ext Assn; Am Psychol Assn; Iowa Assn Lifelong Lng; Contbr Num Articles Profl Jours; Lectr; r/Unit Universalist; hon/Phi Beta Kappa; Phi Delta Kappa; Pi Lambda Theta; World W/W Wom; W/W MW.

MacMAHAN, HORACE ARTHUR JR oc/Professor; b/Aug 13, 1928; h/1303 Collegewood Dr, Ypsilanti, MI 48197; ba/Ypsilanti; m/Marcia Jeanne; c/Kerri; p/Horace Arthur Sr and Anne Louise MacMahan (dec); ed/BA; MSEd; EdD; mil/US Submarine Ser 1947-49; pa/Prof Geog & Geol, En Mich Univ; Author: *Stereogram Book of Contours, Investigating the Dynamic Earth*, Others; Contbr Articles Profl Jours; r/Prot.

McMAHAN, JOHN JULIA oc/Retired Teacher; b/Sept 1, 1911; h/2501 Chaparral St, Las Cruces, NM 88001; p/John and Annis Binnion McMahan (dec); ed/BS E Tex St Univ; MA Geo Peabody Col for Tchrs; pa/Assn Childhood Ed Intl; US Nat Com OMEP; NRTA; Las Cruces RTA; cp/Las Cruces Com on Aging; Dona Ava Co Repub Election (Com Mem, Poll Clerk); Vol Income Tax Aide Worker; r/Presb; hon/Delta Kappa Gamma; DIB; W/W Commun Ser; W/W: Wom, NM.

McMAHAN, REBECCA SUE oc/Student; b/Aug 13, 1957; h/1700 Fawn Ct, Loveland, OH 45140; p/Robert T and Gail D McMahan, Loveland; ed/BA Kent St Univ 1979; pa/Intern, US Sen John Warner 1979; Summer

Clerk Asst, Shaw, Pittman, Potts & Trowbridge 1978; Summer Intern, Ohio Dept Trans 1977; Receptionist, Mike Albert Leasing Inc 1973-75; cp/Repub Nat Com: Nat Field Rep, Col Repub Nat Com; Vol, Bollinger for Coun; Campus Chrperson, Pres Ford Com; Yth Vol, Repub Nat Conv; Vol, Gradison for US Cong; Ohio Leag of Col Repub Clbs; Others; r/Presb; hon/Delta Gamma; Rho Lambda; S'ship Nom, Omicron Delta Kappa; W/W Students Am Cols & Univs.

McMILLAN, MAE FRANCES oc/Child Psychiatrist; b/May 12, 1936; h/4114 Cornell St, Houston, TX 77022; ba/Houston; p/Ben III, Michael, Joseph, John Emeka Udeh; p/Ben S Sr and Annie M Walker McMillan, Houston; ed/BS; MD; pa/Dir Therapeutic Nursery, Tex Res Inst of Mtl Scis; Clinical Assoc Prof, Univ Tex Med Sch (Houston); Assoc Prof, Baylor Col Med; Others; cp/Dem Party; Others; r/United Meth Epis Ch; hon/Adj Prof, Tex Wom's Univ; Outstg Wom of Yr, YWCA 1979; Others.

McMILLIAN, FREDRINA TOLBERT oc/Music Teacher; b/Sept 20, 1936; h/1927 Lorick Ave, Columbia, SC 29203; m/Charles L; c/Charla Tolbert, Charles Leon II; p/Fred William and Helen Grant Tolbert, Mt Pleasant, SC; ed/BM; MM; pa/Public Sch Mus Tchr; Pvt Voice Tchr; Nat Assn Tchrs of Sing'g; MENC; SCMEA; r/Anglo-Cath; hon/Rec'd Awds for Vol Work: Multiple Sclerosis, Muscular Dystrophy, Cancer, Heart Fund; Delta Sigma Theta.

McMILLIAN, MARIE Y oc/Draftsperson; Judge; Justice of the Peace; b/Oct 26, 1926; h/Rt 1, Box 196, Huntsville, TX 77340; m/James Dean; c/3; p/Anderson E and Edna Manly Yates; ed/Sam Houston St Tchrs Col 1943-47; Tex A&M Univ 1971; Lamar Univ 1972; SW Tex St Univ 1973-76; pa/VP & Secy-Treas, McMillian Constrn Co 1964-72; Secy, Treas & Bd Dirs, Pine Prairie Water Supply Corp 1969-76; Ednl Adv & Leg Coms, Tex J of P & Constables Assn; Tex Rural Water Supply Assn; W Tex J of P Assn; ABA; cp/Rural Commun Chm: United Fund, March of Dimes & Am Cancer Soc; Adult Ldr, 4-H Clb of Am & GSA; OES; r/Bapt; hon/Alpha Phi Sigma; Biogl Listings.

McMILLON, RAYMOND CECIL JR oc/Dentist; b/Aug 21, 1943; h/1901 Lonlipman Ct, Louisville, KY 40207; ba/Louisville; m/Carol Crush; c/Jennifer Lynn, Wendy Raye; p/Raymond C McMillon (dec); Evelyn Bernice McMillon, San Antonio, TX; ed/BS Baylor Univ 1966; DMD Univ Louisville 1972; mil/AUS Dental Corps; pa/Am Dental Soc; Ky Dental Assn; Louisville Dental Soc; Am Orthodontic Soc; Intl Col of Oral Implantologists; Am Endodontic Dental Soc; Conslt, Ky Sch for Blind; cp/Pres Bd Dirs, Chance Sch Inc; r/Cath; hon/Rec'd Commend Medal, AUS.

McMULLEN, LINDA ADDILENE ROYSTER oc/Adolescent Counselor; b/Oct 20, 1945; h/Rt 2, Box 166, Hartsville, SC 29550; ba/Darlington, SC; m/James Clayton; c/Linda Jean; p/Floyd Robertson and Elma Hall Royster, Macon, GA; ed/BA Emory Univ 1967; MS Univ Bridgeport 1976; pa/APGA; AAUW; Intl Transactional Analysis Assn; SCPGA; Assn for Specs in Group Work; Darlington Co Human Sers Assn; Am Sch Cnslr Assn; cp/Emory Univ Alumni Assn; Laubach Supplies Chrperson for Hartsville; r/St Luke's United Meth Ch (Hartsville): Mem; hon/Outstg Yg Wom Am; Outstg Sec'dy Edrs Am; Westmoreland (NY) HS Yrbook Dedication; W/W S&SW; Personalities of S; DIB; Kappa Delta.

McMURRY, CLAUDIA PAULINE oc/Speech Pathologist; b/Feb 7, 1952; h/610 Belmont, Box 272, Dumas, TX 79029; ba/Same; m/David Lynn; p/Gordon N and Jean V Herr, Moundridge, KS; ed/BA cum laude 1974, MA 1975 Wichita St Univ; pa/Cert'd Speech & Lang Pathol; Am Speech, Lang & Hear'g Assn; Tex Speech & Hear'g

Assn; Panhandle Regional Speech & Hear'g Assn; Tex St Tchrs Assn; Tex Profl Edrs; AAUW; cp/Water Safety Instr, ARC; Speech Therapist DISD (Public Schs); r/1st United Meth Ch (Dumas): Mem; hon/Selected to Study Univ Salzburg (Austria), Ohio Wesleyan Univ; Sigma Tau Sigma; Rec'd Ideal Active Awd, Hastings Coll; Ks St Speech & Hear'g Assn Conv Speaker; Multi-Discipline Cleft Palate Team; Others.

McNABB, TALMADGE FORD oc/Retired Chaplain; b/Mar 22, 1924; h/1 Springfield Rd, Rt 1, Box 21, Pemberton, NJ 08068; ba/Same; m/Pirkko Marjotta; c/Darlene Roberta, Marla Dawn, Valerie Anne, Lisa Rhea, Marcus Duane; p/Robert Pierce and Dora Isabelle Bailey McNabb (dec); ed/BA 1947, ThB 1949 SWn Col; BS Birmingham So Col 1952; MA Univ Ala 1957; mil/AUS Corps of Engrs 1943-46; Chaplain: AUS Gen Hosp (El Paso, Tex) 1971-72, Germany 1970-71, Ft Dix (NJ) 1967-69, Ft Knox (Ky) 1961-66, Korea 1954-55, Others, Ret'd 1972; pa/Tchr: El Paso & Ysleta Public Sch Dists 1972-73, Woodbury (NJ) Jr-Sr HS 1973-74, Hamilton Sch Dist (Trenton, NJ) 1974-75; Ordained Min 1950; Pastor Chs Ala; Contbr Articles Rel Jours; cp/Worked w War Orphans & Adoption Progs Korea & France; Speaker Var Civic Clbs & Vets' Orgs; Former Yth Dir; r/Prot; hon/Rec'd Commend Medal w 2 Oak Leaf Clusters & Meritorious Ser Medal, AUS; Selected by AUS to Study Inst Rel (Tex Med Ctr); W/W Rel.

MACNAIR, SANDRA oc/Teacher; b/Dec 2, 1938; h/87 Coronado Dr, Newington, CT 06111; ba/New Britain, CT; p/George E and Gertrude E Macnair, Newton, MA; ed/BS; MS (2); pa/AAHPER; AAUP.

McNEILLY, JUANITA R oc/Assistant Director; b/4834 Warm Springs, Houston, TX 77035; ba/Houston; m/D G Roy Sr; c/D G Roy Jr; p/Henrietta Assee-Leepack, Trinidad, West Indies; ed/BA; MEd; Tchg Cert; Conslr Cert; pa/Univ Houston: Asst Dir Progs for Minority Engrg Students, Acad Cnslr; Social & Fin Cnslg; Former Ed Ofcr; cp/Toastmasters Intl; Willowbend Civic Clb; Westbury PTD; r/Rom Cath; hon/Rec'd Winifred Garrison Awd Excell in Latin, Univ Houston; Intl Student Honor Roll, Univ Houston; Gamma Epsilon Sigma.

MACON, MYRA FAYE oc/Assistant Professor; b/Sept 29, 1937; h/3006 Hillmont Dr, Oxford, MS 38655; ba/University, MS; p/Thomas Howard Macon, Calhoun City, MS; Reba Edwards Macon (dec); ed/Dipl Holmes Jr Col 1957; BSE Delta St Univ 1959; MA La St Univ 1965; EdD Miss St Univ 1977; Addit Studies; pa/Univ Miss: Asst Prof, Grad Sch Lib Info Sci 1971-, Act'g Chrperson Dept Lib Sci 1972-73; Lib Supvr, Cuyahoga Falls Schs 1965-71; Other Positions; Conducted Num Workshops for Sch Libns; Conslt Public Schs; Chrperson, Gov's Conf on Libs; Miss Lib Assn; SEn Lib Assn; Am Assn Sch Libns; Am Lib Assn; Miss Assn Media Edrs; Others; r/Bapt; hon/Phi Delta Kappa; Kappa Delta Phi; Beta Phi Mu; W/W: Lib Sci, Am Wom; Personalities of S.

McPHAUL, LONNIE RICHARD b/Jun 6, 1903; h/Box 992, Freer, TX 78357; m/Georgia B; c/Gracie Mae M Storms, Helen M Carter; p/Jesse and Mary McPhaul (dec); cp/C of C; Credit Union; r/Pentecost; hon/Rec'd Pen Plaque, Brush Co Bank.

McREAVY JOHN MORGAN oc/Retired; b/May 2, 1908; h/96 Laurel St, #8, San Carlos, CA 94070; ba/Same; c/Jean M Bolton; p/Charles Everett and Nellie Morgan McReavy (dec); mil/AUS WWII; pa/Former Journeyman & Revenue Ofcr, US Treas Dept (Los Angeles); Former Justice of Peace (Fairhope, Ala); Past Secy & Public Relats, Ala Taxpayers; Former Newpaper Columnist; Author: *Cave of the Candles, Makah* (Epic Narrative of Am Indian), *Whale Hunters*; Poetry Soc Am; cp/Olympia Yacht Clb; r/Cath; hon/Rec'd Num Prizes for Pubs; Best

of Best, Cal Fdn of Chaparral Poets; Others.

McREYNOLDS, NEIL LAWRENCE oc/Manager; b/Jul 27, 1934; h/14312 SE 45th St, Bellevue, WA 98006; ba/Seattle, WA; m/Nancy; c/Christopher, Bonnie; p/Dorr E and Margaret McReynolds, Edmonds, WA; ed/BA Univ Wash; Addit Studies; pa/ITT Corp: NW Regional Mgr, Public Relats & Civic Affairs; Accred'd by Public Relats Soc Am; Soc Profl Journalists; Lectr; cp/VP Seatle C of C; Wash St Intl Trade Fair & Seattle Ctr Foun; Bd Mem, Rotary Clb; Bd Mem, Overlake Hosp; r/Epis: Lic'd Layreader; hon/Rec'd 30 St & Nat Jour Awds; Bellevue Area's Citizen of Yr 1963; 1 of 3 Outstg Yg Men, St of Wash.

McWILLIAMS, MARGARET EDGAR oc/Professor; b/May 26, 1929; h/1916 N Gilbert, Fullerton, CA 92633; ba/Los Angeles, CA; m/Donald A; c/Roger, Kathleen; p/Alvin R and Mildred L Edgar; ed/BS 1951, MS 1953 Iowa St Univ; PhD Oregon St Univ 1968; pa/Prof Food & Nutrition, Cal St Univ-LA; Author 10 Textbooks; Gtr LA & Orange Co Nutrition Couns; Adv Coms, Home Ec Depts 4 Commun Cols; hon/Rec'd Profl Achmt Awd Home Ec, Iowa St Univ; Outstg Prof, Cal St Univ; Rec'd Centennial Alumni Awd, Iowa St Univ.

MADDIGAN, RUTH JEAN oc/Economist; b/Jun 23, 1952; h/822 E 7th St, Auburn, IN 47606; ba/Same; p/Richard Joseph and Barbara Ford Maddigan, Auburn; ed/Att'd Purdue Univ, Univ Cal-B; pa/Ind Univ-B: Res Asst Sch of Bus 1977, Assoc Instr 1976-77; Res Asst, Sch Public & Envir Affairs, Ind Univ-FW; Mng Editor, *DeKalb Record-Herald* (Butler, Ind) 1974; Res in Ecs, Fed Reserv Bank (San Francisco); Editor Directory Wom Attys US; Other Positions; cp/Humane Soc; Ind Crim Justice Planning Agy Task Force (DeKalb Co); Izaak Walton Leag; Animal Wel Leag; Costeau Soc; Pres' (J Carter) Clb; Others; r/Luth Ch: Mem; hon/Rec'd Amoco F'ship, Ind Univ-B; Wall St Jour Student Achmt Awd; Hons Cert, Purdue Univ; Dept Cit, Dept Ecs Univ Cal-B; Phi Beta Kappa; World W/W Wom; Book of Hon; Intl W/W Commun Ser; Others.

MADDOX, IRENE NEWCOMB oc/Flute Soloist; b/Jun 29, 1940; h/4508 Carriage Dr, Charlotte, NC 28205; m/Robert L III; c/Robirene, Melisande; p/J S and Gail B Newcomb, Haskell, TX; ed/BA; MME N Tex St Univ; pa/Flute Tchr; Perf'd Duo w Doug James; Prin Flutist, Charlotte Summer Pops; Pres Charlotte Flute Clb; Bd Mem, Charlotte Pops; NFA; Mus Pub'd by So Mus Co; cp/Bd Mem Spirit Sq; r/Presb.

MADDOX, ROBERT LEE JR oc/-Speechwriter; b/Apr 14, 1937; h/7718 Jansen Dr, Springfield, VA 22152; ba/Washington, DC; m/Linda C; c/Andy, Ben, Elizabeth; p/Robert L Maddox Sr (dec); Virginia C Maddox, Decatur, GA; ed/BA Baylor Univ; BD SWn Bapt Sem; STD Emory Univ; pa/-Speechwriter for Pres Jimmy Carter; cp/Trustee Tift Col; Moderator, Gordon Bapt Assn; VP Ga Coun on Moral & Civic Concerns; Chaplain, Calhoun City Govt; Bd Dirs, Vol Action Ctr (Calhoun); Chm ARC Blood Prog (Gordon Co); r/Bapt Min, So Bapt Conv; hon/Biogl Listings.

MADEIRA, DASHIELL LIVINGSTON oc/Retired Admiral; b/Dec 19, 1897; h/3810 Atlantic Ave, Virginia Beach, VA 23451; ba/Virginia Beach; m/Elizabeth Ambrose; c/Edward, Mrs Seymour B Reich; p/Easton Earle Madeira (dec); Marie Louise Ireland Madeira; ed/BS US Naval Acad; mil/USN: Ser'd All Ranks; pa/USN: Chief of Staff, Commandant 3rd Naval Dist 1949-51, Asst Chief of Staff for Logistics & Mobilization, Staff Cmdr En Sea Frontier 1947-49, Num Other Positions 1917-51; Investmt Dealer 1951-63; cp/Descendants of the Signers of Declaration of Independence; Soc of Lords of Manors; Soc Colonial Wars; Huguenot Soc; Univ Clb; Others; r/Epis; hon/Combat Legion of Merit; Gold Star; Silver Life-Saving Medal of Hon; French Medal of Hon; Others.

MADIGAN, EDWARD R oc/Congressman; b/Jan 13, 1936; h/404 Fifth St, Lincoln, IL 62656; ba/Washington, DC; m/Evelyn; c/Kim, Kellie, Mary; p/Theresa Madigan, Lincoln; ed/Bus Deg, DHL Lincoln Col; LLD Milliken Univ; pa/US Congressman, 21st Ill Dist; cp/K of C; Eagles; Elks; r/Cath.

MADRID, VIOLA L oc/Assistant Superintendent; b/Jan 4, 1941; h/Box 48, El Rito, NM 87530; ba/El Rito; m/Joseph David; c/Katrina, Gabriel, Joseph Johnny, Raymond; p/Bonifacio Hererra, Salt Lake City, UT; Evangelina Lopez, El Rito; ed/BA 1968; MA 1975; EdD 1977; pa/Asst Supt & Dir Instrn, Ojo Caliente Indian Sch Dist; Tchr Tnr; r/Cath; hon/Rec'd F'ship, USOE; Ednl Profl Devel Awd (3), Okla St Univ.

MADRY-TAYLOR, JACQUELYN YVONNE oc/Administrator; b/Sept 27, 1945; h/5800 Quantrell Ave, Alexandria, VA 22312; ba/Annandale, VA; m/Harvey Lee; p/Arthur C and Janie C Madry, Jacksonville, FL; ed/BA Fisk Univ; MA Ohio St Univ; EdD Univ Fla; pa/Dean for Instrnl Sers; Am Assn Higher Ed; AAUW; Nat Coun Instrnl Admrs; r/St Stephens AME Ch; hon/Phi Delta Kappa; Omicron Delta Kappa; Pi Lambda Theta; Alpha Kappa Alpha; Rec'd Tchr-Student Humanitarian Awd, B'nai B'rith; Personalities of S; Outstg Yg Wom Am.

MAGARGAL, LARRY E oc/Ophthalmologist; b/Jun 14, 1941; h/Morelton Manor, 9601 Milnor St, Philadelphia, PA 19114; m/Helga O; c/3; p/Rodney N and Caroline Magargal; ed/BA w Hons, Temple Univ 1965; MD w Hons, Temple Med Sch 1969; mil/AUS VA Hosp 1972; pa/Ophthalmol, Wills Eye Hosp (Phila); Conslt Retina Diseases; Co-dir, Retina Vascular Ser, Wills Eye Hosp; AMA; PMS; PCMS; AIOLS; ACS (Fellow); AAOO (Fellow); PAOO; Author Profl Papers & Textbook Chapts; r/Prot; hon/PMA F'ship; PMS F'ship; Eli Lilly Awd; Retina Fellow, Wills Eye Hosp; Commun Ldrs & Noteworthy Ams.

MAGEE, THOMAS ESTON JR oc/Minister; Educator; b/Aug 9, 1947; h/Rt 3, Box 223, DeRidder, LA 70634; m/Linda Ruth Lewis; p/T E Sr and Doris G Magee, DeRidder; ed/McNeese St Univ 1966-69; ThB Tex Bible Col 1972; pa/Asst Pastor, United Pentecostal Ch (Pasadena, Tex) 1969-72; Tex Bible Col: Dean of Wom 1970-71, Instr 1970-72; Evangelist Var UP Chs; Pastor, United Pentecostal Ch (Ragley, La) 1977-; Sectl Yth Dir, La Dist U Pentecostal Ch 1979-; Others; cp/Colonel on Gov Edward's Staff 1975-; hon/W/W Rel; Intl W/W Commun Ser; Men Achmt.

MAGINNIS, IVA-ANNE oc/Tax Consultant; h/53 Elm St, Worcester, MA 01609; m/John J; p/William and Addie Sampson Appleyard (dec); ed/BA Vassar Col; Post Grad Work: Boston Univ, Pace & Pace, Berlitz Sch of Langs; pa/Mgr Tax Dept, Charles H Tenney & Co (Boston, Mass); Owner I A Appleyard-Tax Conslt; New England St Tax Ofcls Assn; Others; cp/Worcester Vassar Clb; Boston Vassar Clb;

Alliance Francaise; Mass Soc Mayflower Descendents; DAR; Gov Bradford Compact; Others; r/Unit; hon/1st Wom to Pract Before IRS.

MAGINNIS, JOHN JOSEPH oc/Retired; h/53 Elm St, Worcester, MA 01609; m/Iva-Anne Appleyard; p/Patrick J and Bridie M Maginnis (dec); ed/BS Univ Mass; Hon LLD; Addit Studies; mil/WWI: Inf AEF; WWII: 101st Airborne Div, Mil Gov, US Deputy Cmdr Berlin; pa/Former Dir US Shelter Prog (Wash, DC); Former Dir Mass Civil Defense; Former Bd Mgrs, Paul Revere Ins Co (Worcester); Former VP Claflin-Sumner Co (Worcester); Former Fac Mem, Univ Mass; Author *Mil Govt Jour - Normandy to Berlin,*

1971; cp/Trustee Univ Mass; Worcester Rotary Clb; Trustee Public Lib; USO; Salvation Army; Mil Order Foreign Wars; Mil Govt Assn; D Day Normandy F'ship; Intl Wine & Food Soc; VFW; Others; r/Unit; hon/Canadian Legion; French Legion of Hon Assn; Hon Citizen, Carentan (Normandy, France); Hon Citizen, Charleville-Mezieres (Ardennes, France); Hon Citizen, Mons (Hainaut, Belgium); Rec'd Stadt Berlin Gold Freedom Bell; Rec'd Victory Medal (Battle Star); German Occupation Medal; French 1918 Medal; Rec'd Bronze Star; French Croix de Guerres; Others.

MAGNUSON, WARREN G oc/Senator; b/Apr 12, 1905; h/Seattle, WA 98104; ba/Washington, DC; m/Jermaine Elliot Peralta; c/Juanita Peralta M Garrison (Mrs Donald); ed/Attended Univ ND 1923, ND St Univ 1924, JD Univ Wash-S 1929; Hon LLD: Gonzaga Univ 1966, Seattle Univ 1967, St Martin's Col 1967, Gallaudet Col 1972, Univ Alaska 1973; Hon Doct Public Adm, Univ Puget Sound 1967; Doct Polit Sci, Univ Pacific 1970; mil/USN; pa/US Senator 1944-: 3rd Overall Ranking Mem, Chm Commerce Com, Rank'g Mem Appropriations Com (Chm Subcom Labor, Hlth, Ed & Wel; Public Works; Others), Rank'g Mem Budget Com, Rank'g Mem Dem Policy Com, Former Chm Dem Senatorial Campaign Com; Led 1st Congl Delegation to Mainland China 1973; Leg: Nat Cancer Inst, Magnuson-Moss Warranty Act, Nat Sci Foun, Public Accommodations Sect of Civil Rights Act 1964, Ednl TV Facilities Act, Corporation for Public Broadcasting, Flammable Fabrics Act, Agy Consumer Advocacy, Hwy Safety Act, AMTRAK, Num Consumer Bills, Nat Hlth Ser Corps, Ports & Waterways Act, Clean Air Act, Tax Reduction Act, Others; Co-Author *The Dark Side of the Marketplace* (1968), *How Much for Hlth?* (1974); US Rep 1937-44; Atty, King Co (Wash) 1934-36; Others; r/Luth; hon/Rec'd Dist'd Ser Awd, Am Col Cardiol; Man of Yr, Nat Fisheries Inst 1964; Life Fellow, Intl Oceanographic Foun; Rec'd Excalibur Awd, Nat Motor Vehicle Adv Coun; Rec'd Wright Bros Awd, NAA; Admiral of the Ocean Sea Awd, AOTOS; Maritime Man of Yr, Maritime Press Assn 1955; Rec'd Awds, Nat Defense Trans Assn; World Trade Awd, Metro Bd of Trade; Albert Lasker Awd for Public Hlth Ser; Others.

MAHAN, JACK LEE JR oc/Behavioral Scientist; Businessman; b/Oct 2, 1941; h/1982 Craigmore Ave, Escondido, CA 92027; ba/Same; m/Ronna C Ward; p/Jack L Mahan

Sr (dec); Jane V Mahan, Escondido; ed/AA Palomar Col 1961; BA 1964, MA 1966 San Diego St Univ; PhD US Intl Univ 1970; MBA (2) Nat Univ 1978; pa/Pres Jack L Mahan Jr & Assocs Real Estate; Pres MAYO Constrn Inc; Secy-Treas, Mahan Custom Homes Inc; Instr, Cal Sch Profl Psychol (San Diego) 1977-; Instr Psychol, Palomar Col 1975-; Escondido City Plan'g Comm 1975-; San Diego Mayor's Task Force On Urban Design 1975-; Owner & Exec VP, JAMACO Commun Developers 1971-73; Conslt; Lectr; Other Positions; Contbr Num Articles Profl Jours; Am Psychol Assn; Am Inst of Archs; Envir Design Res Assn; Assn for Study of Man-Envir Relats; Cal Real Estate Assn; World Future Soc; Others; cp/Bd Dirs, Escondido Regional Arts Coun; Fdr, Escondido Beautiful Com; Advr, Cal Dept Trans; Escondido Civic Concourse Task Force; UN Assn US; San Diego Zoological Soc; Others; hon/Rec'd Lttr Commend, FAO HQs (Rome, Italy); Rec'd Edwin T Olson S'ship, Nat Col Student Foun; Rec'd Spec Awd, Am Inst Archs; Rec'd Urban Plan'g Awd, Am Inst Planners; W/W: W, Am; Others.

MAHESHWARI, PREM NARAIN oc/Radiation Physicist; b/May 21, 1939; h/2761 Woolery Dr, Jacksonville, FL 32211; ba/Jacksonville; m/Pushpa; c/Archana, Mukul; p/Motilal and Choti Devi, India; ed/MSc; MS; PhD; mil/1954-55; pa/Reschr Radiation, Bapt Med Ctr; Pub'd Num Articles Profl Jours; Presented Num Papers & Lectures to Profl Groups; cp/VP Indian Cult Assn (Jacksonville); r/Hindu.

MAHLER, MARY LEE oc/Nurse's Aide; b/Oct 28, 1911; h/Rt 2, Box 399, Four Oaks, NC 27524; m/John R Jr (dec); c/James R (dec), Peggy M Hill; p/Joseph Elam Lee (dec); Willie C Lee, Four Oaks; ed/Dipl, Johnston Tech

Inst; pa/Nurse's Aide, Johnston Meml Hosp; Former Florist; Former Sewing Machine Operator; Former CETA Employee; r/Blackmon's Grove Bapt Ch: Pianist 30 Yrs.

MAHONEY, MARY JANE oc/Wildlife Rehabilitation; b/Dec 15, 1948; h/3102 Jim Lee, Tallahassee, FL 32301; ba/Tallahassee; p/Charles A and Mary F Mahoney, Friendswood, TX; pa/Fed & St Lic'd Wildlife Rehabilitator; Fdr & Pres, St Francis of Assisi Wildlife Assn Inc; Head of Only Org Providing Humane Sers to All Wildlife; r/Cath; hon/Intl Recog.

MAHOOD, VIOLETA TANNER oc/Retired Journalist; h/625 Earl Garrett, Apt 102, Kerrville, TX 78028; m/Robert F (Dec); c/Betty M McClellan, Robert H, Margaret M Wendeborn; p/Joseph R and Viola Davenport Tanner (dec); pa/Journalist *Stamford Ldr* (7 Yrs) & *Stamford Am* (25 Yrs); Assoc Editor; Public Relats Dept, Hardin-Simmons Univ 2 Yrs; Journalist *Record-News* (Wichita Falls) 1 Yr; Wom's Editor *Perryton Herald* 16 Yrs; Past Pres Tex Press Wom; Mem Nat Wom's Press; Past Secy-Treas W Tex Press Assn; r/1st Bapt Ch; hon/Rec'd Num Journalistic Awds; Wom of Yr, Stamford Ser & Perryton BPW Clbs.

MAIER, CHARLES ROBERT oc/Plant Pathologist; b/Oct 9, 1928; ba/Wayne, NE 68787; m/Barbara Jeanne Miller; c/Thomas Orin, Timothy Ivan, Pamela Ann; p/Harry Maier; Rachel Louise Rafter Maier (dec); ed/BS 1953, MS 1955 Emporia St Univ; PhD Oregon St Univ; mil/AUS 1950-53; pa/Prof

Biol, Wayne St Col 1968-; Res Prof, Univ Neb-L (Summers 1972-78); Res Plant Pathologist, NM St Univ 1958-68; Other Positions; Am Phytopath Soc; Am Mycol Soc; Cotton Disease Coun; Kansas Acad Sci; Oregon Acad Sci; Nat Sci Tchrs Assn; Nat Assn Biol Tchrs; Assn Mid W Col Biol Profs; St Ed Assn; NEA; cp/Wayne Lion's Clb; Dir, Wayne Co Hist Soc; Wayne Co Bicent Comm; VFW; Dem Party; r/Luth Ch: Voters' Assembly, Duo Clb, Campus Min Com; hon/Lambda Delta Lambda; Beta Beta Beta; Sigma Xi; Phi Kappa Phi; Awd'd Fac Res Grant, Wayne St Foun; Named Curator, Wayne St Arboretum; W/W: W&SW, Agri, MW; Am Men Sci; Men Achmt; Others.

MAILE, CARLTON ARTHUR oc/-Professor; b/Sept 29, 1937; h/1627 Russett Ln, Sycamore, IL 60178; ba/DeKalb, IL; m/Lois Anna; c/Cameron James; p/Carl Robert Maile (dec); Pauline Emma Maile, Lawton, MI; ed/BS, MA Univ Mich; PhD Univ Ga; pa/-Prof Mktg, N Ill Univ; Intl Mktg Conlt w Clients in US, Canada, Latin Am; Currently Writing 2 Books; Contbr Num Articles Profl Jours; Session Chm, SW Mktg Assn (Dallas, Tex) 1978; Discussant, Am Inst for Decision Scis (St Louis) 1978; cp/Guest Lectr Num Ednl & Civic Orgs; r/Meth; hon/DIB; Sigma Iota Epsilon; Beta Gamma Sigma.

MAISH, JAMES IVAN oc/Psychologist; b/Mar 24, 1946; h/713 Woodgate Ct, Augusta, GA 30909; ba/Augusta; m/Anne; c/Jonathon, Rhett; p/James T and D Pauline Maish, Frankfort, IN; ed/BA; MA; PhD; pa/Pvt Pract Psychol; Lic'd Applied Psychol, St of Ga; Am Psychol Assn; SEn Psychol Assn; Ga Psychol Assn; CSRA Psychol Assn; Assn Advmt Psychol; Nat Assn Disability Examrs; Nat Register Hlth Ser Providers; Conslt, Lenwood VA Hosp; Rep ECGHSA to St Hlth Planning Com, Ga Psychol Assn; cp/Optimist Clb; Nat Repub Clb; r/Presb; hon/Rector Scholar; Beta Beta Beta; Psi Chi; W/W: Am, S&SW; Personalities of S; DIB; Men of Hon; Men Achmt.

MAKANSI, MUNZER oc/Chemical Engineer; b/Dec 23, 1923; h/106 Stratford Way, Signal Mountain, TN 37377; ba/Chattanooga, TN; m/Nellie May; c/Delal, Antar, Jason, Tarek; p/Ismail and Amina Khudari Makansi (dec); ed/BSc w Hons, Fouad-I Univ (Cairo, Egypt) 1947; MA Columbia Univ 1950; MS 1951; Doct of Engrg Sci 1957; pa/Tchr, Alma-Amoun HS (Aleppo) 1947-49; Dupont Co: (Wilmington, Dela) 1954-66, Supvr Res & Devel (Chattanooga) 1966-; RESA; NY Acad Sci; Author *Periodic Classification of Chemical Elements* (1949); cp/Assn Arab-Am Univ Grads; hon/Sigma Xi; Phi Lambda Upsilon; Patentee.

MAKAR, NADIA EISSA oc/Chairman; b/Oct 7, 1938; h/410 Fairmont Ave, Jersey City, NJ 07306; ba/Jersey City; m/Boshra Halim; c/Ralph, Roger; p/Michel and Yvonne Issa, Montreal, Canada; ed/BA; pa/Chm Sci Dept; Nat Sci Tchrs Assn; NJ Sci Supvrs Assn; Am Chem Soc; NJ Sci Tchrs Assn; NJ Sci Supvrs Assn; Assn Ed Tchrs Sci; NY Acad Sci; NJ Acad Sci; Intl Sci Com; AAAS; Coun Basic Ed; IPA; cp/World Poets Resource Ctr. Bd Dirs, Chm HS Sect Annual Fest, Editor; Life Fellow, Intercontinental Biogl Assn; United Poets Intl; BPW; hon/Outstg Sec'dy Edr Am (Nat Winner); Rec'd Nichols Awd, Am Chem Soc; Rec'd Awd, Mfg Chems Assn;

Hudson Co Wom Achmt; Nat Edr Awd; Reec'd Medal of Excell Tchg Chem; Highest Order of Merit; Rec'd S'ship Moscow Univ; Num Others.

MAKK, AMERICO IMRE oc/Artist; b/Aug 24, 1927; h/1515 Laukahi St, Honolulu, HI 96821; ba/Same; m/Eva H; c/Americo B; p/Pal and Katalina Samodai Makk; pa/Prof Fine Arts Acad; Num One-Man & Group Shows; Chm & VP Sev Nat & Intl Art Exhibits; r/Cath; hon/Num Nat & Intl Art Awds.

MAKK, EVA HOLUSA oc/Artist; h/1515 Laukahi St, Honolulu, HI 96821; ba/Same; m/Americo; c/Americo B; p/Bert Alan Holusa, Honolulu; Julie Ribenyi Holusa (dec);

pa/Prof Fine Arts Acad; Num One-Man & Group Shows; Chm Sev Nat & Intl Art Exhibits; r/Rom Cath; hon/Rec'd Num Nat & Intl Art Awds.

MAKKAI, ADAM oc/Linguist; b/Dec 16, 1935; h/360 MacLaren Ln, Lake Bluff, IL 60044; ba/Chicago, IL; m/Valerie Becker; c/Sylvia, Rebecca Rose; p/John D and Rozsa Igadcz; ed/BA cum laude, Harvard Univ 1958; MA 1962, PhD 1965 Yale Univ; pa/Univ Ill Chgo Cir: Prof Linguistics 1974-, Assoc Prof Linguistics 1969-74, Asst Prof Linguistics 1967-69; Independent Reschr, Idiomaticity, Translation Theory & Lexicography; Assoc Editor *SILTA*; Editor-in-Chief *ForLing*; Dir, Jupiter Press; LACUS/ALCEU: Chm Bd, Exec Dir, Dir Pubs; Other Positions; Linguistic Soc Am; Modern Lang Assn; Author *Idiom Structure in English* (1972); Editor: *A Dictionary of Space English* (1973), *Toward a Theory of Context in Linguistics & Lit* (1975), Others; Contbr Num Articles Profl Jours; Lectr Profl Orgs; cp/Pres & Fdr, Zolton Kodaly Hungarian Cult Soc; r/Hungarian Reformed Presb; hon/Rec'd LOEB Fund, Harvard; Rec'd Ford Foun Foreign Area Tng F'ship; Univ Wilson F'ship, Yale; Jr Sterling F'ship, Yale; Rec'd Paderewski Foun & Intl Devel Foun Travel Grant; Dissertation Grant, Am Coun Learned Socs; Rec'd Nat Sci Foun Post Doct Res Grant, Rand Corp.

MALBON, JANICE CROTTS oc/Assistant Director; b/Aug 26, 1950; h/PO Box 573, Starkville, MS 39759; ba/Mississippi State, MS; m/Michael J; p/Porter and Carrie Blount Crotts, Savannah, TN; ed/BS, MS Univ Tenn; pa/Cert'd Profl Secy; Asst Dir Purchasing; Pres, Miss Div Nat Secys Assn 1977-78;

cp/Starkville C of C; Bd Dirs, Oktibbeha Gen Hosp; Bd Dirs, Am Cancer Soc; r/Bapt; hon/Miss Secy of Yr 1978; Starkville BPW Yg Careerist 1974; Grad'd Summa Cum Laude; Commun Ldrs & Noteworthy Ams; W/W Am

Wom; Others.

MALIK, RAYMOND HOWARD oc/Scientist; b/Feb 4, 1933; h/PO Box 3194, Chicago, IL 60654; ba/Chgo; p/John Z Malik, Antelias, Lebanon; Clarice R Malik (dec); ed/BA; BS; MS; PhD; pa/Supvr Arabian Am Oil Co (Beirut, Lebanon) 1952-54; Prof, Head World Trade Progs, Ctl YMCA Commun Col (Chgo) 1966-74; Pres Malik Intl Enterprises Ltd 1959-; Treas Am Mgmt Assn; VP Am Ec Assn; Import Clbs US; Pres Intl Trade Clb; IEEE; Inventor Selectric Typing Elements &

Mechanism; Pioneer Devel Interplanetary Communs Sys; Inventor Cir of Sound Concept of Sound Propogation; Introduced Modular Concept Color TV; Introduced Cancer Detector (Gamma Ray); cp/Scout Master; Independent Dem; r/Orthodox Christian; hon/Fulbright Scholar; Meth Ch Scholar; So Ill Univ Fellow; Phi Beta Kappa; Sigma Xi; Delta Rho; Beta Gamma Sigma; Alpha Phi Omega; W/W: Am, Fin & Indust; DIB; Personalities of W&MW; Others.

MALLARD, ELIZABETH KEITH oc/Retired Teacher & Librarian; b/Sept 15, 1915; h/Box 37, Topsail Beach, NC 28445; m/Steve Hodges; c/Merle Graham M Morris, Patsy Keith M Braxton; p/William Herbert and Mayme Cameron Keith (dec); ed/AB; Cert Lib Sci; pa/Bd Dirs, NCAE; NCHLA; Pres Local & Dist NCAE; Others; cp/Pace; Past Matron, OES; Bd Govs, Emma Anderson Meml Chapel; r/Wallace Presb Ch; hon/Merit Mother; Dist'd Ed Awd, NCAE.

MALLOY, MARTHA REUSS oc/-Administrator; b/Oct 2, 1942; h/248 S Ashbrook Cir, Ft Mitchell, KY 41017; ba/-Cincinnati, OH; c/Melissa Lynn; p/Carl W and Ruth O Reuss, Cinc; ed/BA Denison Univ; MA Ohio St Univ; pa/Univ Cinc: Asst Dir Career Planning & Placemt 1976-, Asst Dean Student Devel 1975-76, Coor Univ Orientation; N Ky Univ: Dir Career Sers Ctr 1970-75, Instr Psychol, Affirmative Action Coor; Other Positions; Assn Wom Admrs; Assn Mid-Level Admrs; Advr Mortar Bd; So Col Placemt Assn; Ky Col Placemt Assn; hon/Phi Beta Kappa; Omicron Delta Kappa; W/W Am Wom; Personalities of S.

MALOLA, MARY E oc/Teacher; b/May 25, 1923; h/4422 S 10th St, Terre Haute, IN 47802; ba/Terre Haute; m/Mousa; c/Ann I M Phillips, Hane M; p/John C Work (dec); Irene Work, Evansville, IN; ed/AB; MA; pa/Life Mem NEA; Profl Devel Com, ISTA; PR Chm, UCTA; St Roster Experts in Lang Arts; AAUW; Regional Judge, Nat Coun Tchrs of Eng Writing Competition; St Conf Instrn;

Others; cp/Ladies Soc; r/St George Orthodox Ch: SS Tchr; hon/Gov's Roster Outstg Wom; Delta Kappa Gamma; Works Pub'd *Nat Poetry Anthology*; Biogl Listings.

MALONE, JOHN IRVIN oc/Pediatrician; b/Oct 10, 1941; h/7005 Whittier, Tampa, FL 33617; ba/Tampa; m/Gloria J; c/John I Jr, Michael Albert, Jennifer Amy; ed/BS Penn St Univ 1963; MD Univ Penn 1967; pa/Assoc Prof Pediatrics, Univ S Fla 1976-; Co-Dir, Fla Camp for Chd & Yth w Diabetes 1973-; Dir, Suncoast Regional Diabetes Prog 1976-; Staff Affiliations: Philadelphia Gen Hosp 1971, Tampa Gen Hosp 1972, All Chd's Hosp 1973; Other Positions: Lic'd by: St of Penn, Am Bd of Pediatrics, St of Fla, Am Acad Pediatrics, Am Bd Pediatric Endocrinology; AAAS; Am Diabetes Assn; Lawson Wilkins Pediatric Endocrine Soc; So Soc Pediatric Res; Am Fdn Clinical Res; Soc Pediatric Res; Contbr Num Articles Profl Jours; hon/Rec'd Baldwin Lucke Meml Prize for Med Student Res.

MALONE, JUNE C oc/Principal; b/Jul 18, 1916; h/5815 Sherbourne Dr, Los Angeles, CA 90056; ba/LA; m/Herbert F (dec); c/Judith L M Carl, Joan M Snyder, Herbert F; p/George W and Bessie M Peters Culler (dec); ed/AA LA City Col; BA, MA Cal St Univ-LA; Doct Cand Claremont Grad Sch; pa/Elem Sch Prin; AESA; ACSA; NAESP; NCAWE; EDUCARE; Nat Ret'd Tchrs Assn; LA City Music Assn; Venice-Mar Vista Coor'g Coun; Smithsonian Inst; Jacques Cousteau Soc; IPA; LA Zoo Assn; r/Knox Presb Ch: Mem; hon/Life Mem Cal S'ship Assn; Grad'd Magna Cum Laude; Hon Life Mbrship, PTA; Outstg Music Student, LACC; W/W Am Wom; Notable Ams; World W/W Wom; DIB; Intl W/W Commun Ser.

MALONEY, FLORENCE CECELIA oc/Supervisor; b/Apr 23, 1926; h/43-34 192 St, Auburndale, NY 11358; ba/Holbrook, NY; p/David Christopher and Catherine Cecelia Maloney; ed/BBA; MS; EdD; pa/Elem Curric Supvr, Sachem Ctl Sch Dist; Past Pres Gregg Shorthand Tchrs Assn; NAESP; ASCD; SAANYS; cp/Am Security Coun; Nat Repub Clb; NY Conserv Clb; r/Rom Cath: Cenacle Retreat Leag, Conf Christian Doctrine; hon/Delta Kappa Gamma; Phi Delta Kappa; Delta Pi Epsilon.

MALOOF, JOYCE MORGAN oc/-Automobile Dealer; b/May 28, 1928; h/5715 Green Island Dr, Columbus, GA 31904; ba/Columbus; m/Harold M (dec); c/Harold M Jr; p/Wheeler Austin and Catherine Geeslin Morgan, Coleman, GA; ed/Ga St Univ 1945; Piedmont Sch Nsg 1945; pa/Nurse Piedmont Hosp Sch Nsg (Atlanta) 1945; Patterson Hosp (Cuthbert) 1947; Maloof Motor Co Inc 1955-: Owner & Pres 1965-; Ins Agent, Moore Ins Co (Atlanta) 1975-; Toyota Dealer Coun Rep 1979-80; Used Car Dealers Assn; New Car Dealers Assn; Nat Bus Mgmt Clb; Nat Automobile Dealers Assn of Ga; Independent Automobile Dealers Assn; Am Bus Wom's Assn; Bus Wom's Clb; Others; cp/Bldg Com Hilton Terrace Bapt Ch; C of C; Better Bus Bur; Green Isl Country Clb; Big Eddy Clb; Pers Review Bd, City of Columbus; r/Bapt; hon/W/W S&SE; Personalities of S; Book of Hon; Others.

MANAHAN, MANNY CELESTINO oc/Accountant; b/Apr 6, 1935; h/2022 Judah St, San Francisco, CA 94122; p/Pastor Manahan & Maria Santos Manahan; ed/BBA Univ E (Manilla, Philippines) 1963; MBA Golden Gate Univ 1969; pa/Sole Owner Acctg & Tax Ser (SF) 1974-; Part-time Instr on Spec Assignmt, IRS Tng Ctr 1974-75; Appointed Notary Public of Cal, City & Co of SF 1977; Other Positions; Am Acctg Assn; Taxpreparers Assn Cal; SF Commun Col Dist Fdn of Tchrs; Philippine Inst Cert'd Public Accts; Nat Soc Public Accts; Filipino Accts Assn-Cal (Former Pres); Former Assoc Mem, Soc Cal Accts (SF Chapt); Others; cp/Golden Gate Univ Alumni Assn; Men's Clb, St Anne's of Sunset Parish; Intl Ctr-Marin; Assn for Hope; SF Heart Assn; Others; hon/Cert Apprec, SF Chapt Soc Cal Accts; One Of 7

Noms for 1975 Dist'd Ser Awd, Filipino-Am JCs; Biogl Listings.

MANAZIR, FLORA MARY oc/-Homemaker; b/Sept 26; h/39 Glendower Rd, Roslindale, MA 02131; ba/Same; m/Tawfik; c/Theodore, Charles Howard; p/George and Catherine Sabino (dec); ed/BA NWn Col (Tulsa); pa/Chief Exec Ofcr & Pres, Wayside Mfg Co Inc 1950-70; c/OES: Former Worthy Matron, Former Grand Matron; Order of White Shrine of Jerusalem: Former Worthy High Priestess Siloam Shrine, Former Supr Chm Obituary Com; Dist Chm Mbrship Com, Bethany Shrine; Order of Amaranth: Former Royal Matron, Former Grand Royal Matron; Order of Rebekahs; Chief Ofcr, Miss Amaranth Fund for Nsg Students; Amaranth Diabetic Foun; United Fund Worker; Sponsor Syrian Child Wel Camp; r/Prot; hon/Rec'd Awd for Meritorious Ser, ARC; Supr Hons, White Shrine; Others.

MANDERS, KARL LEE oc/Physician; b/Jan 21, 1927; h/5845 High Fall Rd, Indianapolis, IN 46226; ba/Indpls; m/Ann Lorraine; c/Maidena, Karlanna; p/David Bert Manders (dec); Frances Edna Manders, New York, NY; ed/MD; mil/USN 1952-54; pa/Pvt Pract, Neurosurg; Med Dir, Commun Hosp Rehab Ctr for Pain; Coroner, Marion Co; Am Soc Cryosurg; Am Soc Contemp Med & Surg; AMA; Cong Neurol Surg; Intl Assn Study of Pain; NY Acad Sci; Undersea Med Soc; Ctl Neurosurg Soc; Others; r/Unit; hon/Fellow, Am Col Surg; Fellow, Am Col Angiology; Fellow, Am Psychosomatic Soc; Diplomat, Nat Bd Med Examrs; Others.

MANEES, MARTHA J oc/Retired Teacher; b/Jun 18, 1908; h/8300 Linda Ln, Little Rock, AR 72207; m/Edward O (dec); p/Paul B and Necie S Jefferson (dec); ed/BA; pa/Tchr HS Eng 40 Yrs; Book Reviewer; cp/Bd Mem, Florence Crittenton Home; Aux, Ark Chd's Hosp; Ark Art Ctr; YWCA; Others; r/Winfield Meth Ch: Bd Mem, Pres Meth Wom, SS Tchr; hon/Life Mem: PTA, United Meth Wom.

MANESS, DORIS KAY oc/Student; b/Aug 22, 1955; h/15-D Indian Lake, Northport, AL 35476; p/Hiram Fulton Jr and Juanita Laura Maness, Alpharetta, GA; ed/BA Judson Col; Cand MA; pa/Ala Assn Speech Tchrs; Assn of Ventriloquists; cp/Relief Parent, Tuscaloosa Shelter & Group Home; Pres, Tuscaloosa Judson Alumnae Chapt; r/Bapt; hon/W/W: Am Cols & Univs, Rel, Am Wom; Personalities of S; DIB; Intl W/W Commun Ser; Commun Ldrs & Noteworthy Ams; Notable Ams; Rec'd Best Actress Awd, Judson Col Players.

MANGIERI, ROBERT PAUL oc/Insurance Consultant; b/May 20, 1941; h/82-60 116th St, Kew Gardens, NY 11418; ba/New York, NY; p/Frank and Augustine Mangieri, Kew Gardens; ed/BA (2); mil/USMC; pa/-Author *The Pictorical Hist of Richmond Hill, Kew Gardens, Woodhaven, Ozone Park*; cp/Exec Secy, Commun Planning Bd #9; Chm Public Relats, USMC S'ship Foun; Former Pres Queensboro Yg Repubs Assn; Native New Yorkers' Hist Assn; Others; r/Cath: Chm Civic & Polit Com; hon/NY St Hon Fire Chief.

MANKA, DAN PAUL oc/Consultant; b/May 2, 1914; h/1109 Lancaster Ave, Pittsburgh, PA 15218; m/Louise Ann Wunderlich; c/Paul D, Timothy E, John W, Dan P Jr; p/John Emil and Gizela Mary Bella Manka; ed/BS Valparaiso Univ 1936; Grad Study, Carnegie-Mellon Univ; pa/Lic'd Profl Chem; Sr Res Chem & Conslt, Jones & Laughlin Steel Corp 1941-; Lectr Cols & HSs; Chem, Koppers Co (Pittsburgh) 1936-41; Contbr Articles Profl Jours; Am Chem Soc; Fellow, Am Inst Chems; Publicity Chm, P'burgh Conf Analytical Chem & Applied Spectroscopy; En States Blast Furnace & Coke Oven Assn; Instrmt Soc Am; Others; cp/Former Troop Com & Review Bd Mem, BSA; Regents Sq Parents Assn; Valparaiso Univ Alumni; Acad Arts & Scis; Nat Audubon Soc & Audubon Soc Wn Penn; Nat & Intl Wildlife Assn; r/First Trinity Luth Ch: Chm, Elder; hon/Patentee; Instrnl Staff, 36th

Appalachian Gas Measuremt Short Course; Invited Speaker, 4th Intl Conf on Analytical Chem (Univ Birmingham, England); W/W E; DIB; Men Achmt; Others.

MANKA, WALTER RALPH III oc/Executive; b/May 22, 1942; h/Rt 2, Hwy 76 W, Clayton, GA 30525; ba/Franklin, NC; m/Glendia Rae; p/Walter R II and Mildred Manka (dec); mil/AUS: Mil Police; pa/Co-owner, Macon Graphics; r/Prot; hon/Ky Col.

MANN, JAMES ROBERT oc/Attorney; b/Apr 27, 1920; h/118 W Mountain View Ave, Greenville, SC 29609; ba/Washington, DC; m/Virginia Brunson; c/James Robert Jr, David Brunson, William Walker, Virginia Brunson; p/A C and Nina G Mann (dec); ed/BA The Citadel 1941; Juris Doct magna cum laude, Univ SC 1947; mil/AUS 1941-46;

USAR; pa/US Ho of Reps 1969-; Former Mem SC Ho of Reps; Atty 1963-68; Circuit Solicitor, 13th Judicial Circuit SC 1953-63; cp/Alston Wilkes Soc; Am Legion; BPO Elks; Greenville Shrine Clb; VFW; AFM; Hejaz Temple; Reserv Ofcrs Assn Am; Nat Coun, BSA; r/Bapt; hon/Participant, Annual Chief Justice Earl Warren Conf; Bicent Conf on US Constitution; Hon LLD, The Citadel.

MANNING, FERDINAND L oc/-Consultant; b/Oct 1, 1925; h/130 W 67th St, Apt 24D, New York, NY 10023; ba/Same; c/Jill A M Stockman, Patricia Larue, James Williams; p/George C Manning (dec); Blanche L Manning, Fort Wayne, IN; ed/BA Tulane Univ 1948; MFA Yale Univ 1951; mil/AUS 1943-44; USNR 1944-45; pa/Pres & Bd Chm, Lyteman Inc; Contbg Editor *Lighting Dimensions*; Bd Dirs, Martha Stuart Communs; Instr, Fairfield Univ Grad Sch Ed 1969; Instr Am Theatre Wing 1956-57; Lighting Conslt: Pres Nixon, Pres Carter.

MANNING, WALTER SCOTT oc/Professor; b/Oct 4, 1912; h/405 Walton E, College Station, TX 77840; ba/Same; m/Eleanor; c/Sharon Frances, Walter Scott Jr, Robert Kenneth; p/(dec); ed/MBA Tex Univ; pa/Prof Emeritus Acctg, Tex A&M Univ; Pract'g CPA; Am Inst CPAs; Am Acctg Assn; AAUP; cp/B-CS C of C; Kiwanis; r/Christian; hon/Alpha Chi; Beta Alpha Psi; Beta Gamma Sigma; Knight York Cross of Hon.

MANOGUE, HELEN SMITH oc/-Businesswoman; b/Dec 14, 1931; h/610 River St, Hoboken, NJ 07030; ba/Newark, NJ; m/Joseph F; c/J Mark, Stephen, Philip; p/William C and Tereas Wulftange Smith, Hoboken; ed/BA summa cum laude, Rutgers Univ 1975; pa/Prog Ofcr, NJ Mortgage Fin Agy; cp/Trustee, Assn NJ Envir Comms; Dir, Ctl NJ Lung Assn; Chrperson & Fdr, Hoboken Envir Com; Co-dir & Fdr, Waterfront Coalition of Hudson & Bergen; Past Mem NJ Solid Waste Adv Coun; Past Mem, Liberty St Park Study & Planning Comm; Coun on Future NJ; hon/Phi Beta Kappa; Jersey Jour Wom Achmt.

MANOR, FILOMENA ROBERTA oc/Dietitian; b/Jul 6, 1926; h/307 Yoakum Parkway, Apt 1104, Alexandria, VA 22304; ba/Washington, DC; p/G Robert and Mary Carmina S Fusco, Riverside, CA; ed/BS Russell Sage Col 1948; MS Ohio St Univ 1960; Addit Studies; mil/USAF 1950-; pa/Chief Med Food Ser Div & Dir Internship, Malcolm Grow USAF Med Ctr (Andrews AFB, Wash) 1970-;

Office of Surg Gen, USAF HQs: Assoc Chief Dietetics/Nutrition Biomed Sci Corps, Conslt to Surg Gen, Staff Advr Wom in Ser, Rep to Food & Nutrition Bd of Nat Res Coun 1972-; Chm, Interagy Com Food Ser for Fed Hosps 1978-; Chm Food Ser & DOD Space Planning Panel, DOD Mgmt Evaluation Com 1974-; Other Positions; Reg'd by Am Dietetic Assn; Aerospace Med Assn; Assn Mil Surgs of US; hon/Rec'd USAF Commend Medal; Rec'd Meritorious Ser Medal; Rec'd McLester Awd, AMSUS; Rec'd Dist'd Alumna Awd, Ohio St Univ; W/W: Students Am Cols & Univs, E; Commun Ldrs & Noteworthy Ams; DIB; World W/W Wom; Others.

MANSKE, CHARLES LOUIS oc/College President; b/Oct 20, 1932; h/14782 Elm Ave, Irvine, CA 92714; ba/Irvine; m/Barbara M; c/David Charles, Christine Joy, Noel Ruth; p/Charles Louis Manske (dec); Loma Estella Manske, Costa Mesa, CA; ed/MA Wash Univ 1958; MDiv Concordia Sem 1958; PhD Univ So Cal-LA 1979; pa/Fdg Pres, Christ Col of Irvine (Affiliated w Luth Ch-Mo Synod); Luth Campus Min, Univ So Cal 1958-73; Rel Public Relats Coun; r/Luth Ch-Mo Synod: Pastor; hon/Recipient Commend Resolutions for Outstg Civic Ser: Mayor of LA, LA City Coun, LA Co Bd Suprvs & Cal St Assembly.

MAPLES, EVELYN LUCILLE oc/Editor; Author; b/Feb 7, 1919; h/16216 E Sea St, Independence, MO 64050; ba/Independence; m/William E; c/Norman, Billi Jo M Short, Matthew; p/Thomas Sherman and Bertie Josephine Dalby Palmer (dec); pa/Author *The Many Selves of Ann-Elizabeth*; Guest Lectr Schs & Cols on Poetry Writing for Chd; Mo Writers Guild; cp/Commun Assn for Arts; Neighborhood Coun; Good Govt Leag; r/Ch of Jesus Christ LDS; hon/Rec'd Awd for *The Many Selves of Ann-Elizabeth*, Mid Wn Books Competition; W/W Am Wom; Others.

MARBURY, RITCHEY McGUIRE III oc/Engineer; b/May 18, 1938; h/2549 Green Valley Ln, Albany, GA 31707; ba/Pocatello, ID; m/Fonda Gayle Starnes; c/Mary Kathryn, Ritchey IV; p/Ritchey McGuire Marbury Jr, Albany; Shirley Kathryn Van Houten Marbury (dec); ed/BS, MS Ga Tech; mil/AUS; pa/Pres Idaho Pacatello Mission for Ch of Jesus Christ LDS; Past Pres Marbury Engrg Co; Past Pres Marbury, Ritter, Scott & Turner Engrs; ASCE; ACEC; St Dir CEC; St Dir SAMSOG; Others; cp/Rotary; Pres Lake Park PTA; r/Ch of Jesus Christ LDS: Dist Pres, Branch Pres; hon/Phi Kappa Phi.

MARCH, KATHERINE B oc/Homemaker; b/Mar 16, 1910; h/Acacia Lumberton Manor, Bldg 4 Apt 0, Lumberton, NJ 08048; ba/Same; m/Hugo; c/Owen B, John (dec); p/Nickolas Burmann Sr (dec); Katherine Burmann, Bronx, NY; pa/Former Newspaper Correspondent; cp/Former Publicity Chm, Am Legion Aux; r/Prot; hon/Poet Laureate, Stella Woodall Poetry Soc; Rec'd Civic Awd, *Inky Trails Mag*; Rec'd Num Awds of Merit.

MARCHETTI, JEAN WOOLLEY oc/Educator; b/Dec 19, 1938; h/1210 Plato Ave, Orlando, FL 32809; m/Alfred; c/6; p/Charles Jackson & Margaret Hinson Woolley; ed/BS 1973, MA 1978 Rollins Col; pa/Tchr, Thacker Ave Elem Sch (Kissimmee, Fla) 1972-; Tchr, St John Vianney (Orlando) 1971-73; St Teresa Sch (Titusville, Fla) 1970-71; Other Positions; PTO; Osceola Classroom Tchrs Assn; NEA; Notary Public Assn; APGA; cp/Smithsonian Inst; r/St John Vianney Rom Cath Ch; hon/W/W S&SW; Personalities of S; Others.

MARCOM, ORVAL WELDON oc/Judge; b/Jan 2, 1908; h/101 San Jacinto, Levelland, TX 79336; ba/Levelland; m/Laura Lucille Latimer; c/Patsy M Methvin (Mrs W R), George Weldon, Marilyn M Wham (Mrs Robert F); p/George Ralph and Hattie Jones Marcom (dec); ed/BA; MA; EdD Tex Tech Univ; pa/Judge of Hockley Co 1978-; San Jacinto Col (Pasadena, Tex): Acad Dean 1961-67, Acad VP 1967-74; Supt Schs Levelland 1947-61; Prin, Tchr 1928-47; Tex St Tchrs Assn; NEA; cp/C of C; Mason; Rotary; hon/Phi Delta Kappa.

MARDELL-CZUDNOWSKI, CAROL D oc/Professor; b/Nov 30, 1935; h/6 Jennifer Ln, DeKalb, IL 60115; ba/DeKalb; m/Moshe M; c/Benjamin, Dina, Ruth; p/Albert and Lee Goldstein, Chicago, IL; ed/BS Univ Ill; MA Univ Chgo; PhD NWn Univ; pa/Prof Spec Ed, No Ill Univ; Co-author of DIAL (Devel Indicators for the Assessmt of Learning); r/Jewish; hon/Phi Kappa Phi; Phi Delta Kappa; Alpha Lambda Delta; Kappa Delta Pi; Pi Lambda Theta; W/W MW.

MARDIS, ELMA HUBBARD oc/Assistant Professor; b/Jul 16, 1932; h/2324 Bridgeport Dr, Memphis, TN 38114; ba/-Memphis; m/William C; c/Marlah Hubbard; p/Walter L Hubbard Sr (dec); Edith Scott Hubbard, Memphis; ed/BS; MEd; EdD; pa/-Univ Tenn: Asst Prof, Coor Bur Ednl Res & Ser (W Tenn Ctr); VChm Plan Z Desegregation Review Com, Memphis City Schs; Assn Supvn & Curric Devel; Tenn Assn Supvn & Curric Devel; Am Ednl Res Assn; Mid S Ednl Res Assn; Nat Coalition of Title I Parents;

Coun Basic Ed; Nat Alliance Black Sch Edrs; Tenn Math Tchrs Assn; cp/Chm Bd Dirs, Jessie Mahan Day Care Ctr; Secy Bd Dirs, Porter Leath Chd's Ctr; Memphis Conf Rotary Clb; Bd Dirs, Wife Abuse Crisis Ser Ctr; Fund for Needy Chd; NAACP; People United to Save Humanity; Others; r/2nd Congreg Ch: Supt of SS; hon/Pi Delta Kappa; Kappa Delta Pi; Phi Delta Kappa; Outstg Edr; Basileus of Yr, Alpha Kappa Alpha; Outstg Wom, Shelby Co; Hon Wom in Field of Work, Memphis Area C of C; Outstg Grad, LeMoyne Owen Col.

MARELLI, JOHN VINCENT oc/Astronomer; b/Dec 26, 1943; h/42 Chestnut St, Charlestown, MA 02129; ba/Same; p/Carlo and Luisa Balaschi Marelli (dec); pa/British Interplanetary Soc; AAAS; Astronomical Soc Pacific; Royal Astronomical Soc of Canada; Intl Soc Gen Relativity & Gravitation; Astronomical League; ALPO; Org'g Local Br of British Interplanetary Soc; Pubr & Editor of Mag, *Space Reports*; Est'g Astronomical Data Bank for use of En, Wn & Third World Nations.

MARGOLIS, GWEN oc/State Legislator; b/Oct 4, 1934; h/13105 Biscayne Bay Dr, Keystone Island #5, N Miami, FL 33161; ba/Miami Beach; m/Allan; c/Edward, Ira, Karen, Robin; p/Joe and Rose Liedman, N Miami Beach; pa/Fla Ho of Reps 1974-; Chrperson Ad Valorem Subcom Fin & Tax, Tourism & Ec Devel, Standards & Conduct Coms 1976-, Chm Select Com Nuclear Power, Chm Dade Co Leg Del; Realtor; S Fla Planning & Zoning Assn; Wom's Coun Realtors; Bd Dirs N Miami Beach C of C; cp/Ser'd Num City Bds; Fla Anti-Defamation Leag; N Dade Wom's Polit Caucus; Dir Dade Co Girl Scouts; r/Jewish; hon/Rec'd Humanitarian of Yr Awd, City of Hope; Outstg Wom in Polits, BPW Assn; W/W: Fin & Indust, Am Wom; World W/W Wom.

MARGOLIUS, HANS oc/Librarian; b/Sept 12, 1902; h/1506 SW 23 St, Miami, FL 33145; m/Edith Metzger; p/Alexander and Bianka Margolius; ed/PhD Univ Hamburg; pa/Author: *Werte und Wege* (1977), *Das Gute im Menschen* (1969), *Values of Life* (1971), Others; r/Jewish.

MARINEL, INNA (dec); oc/Lawyer; Harpist; Librarian; b/Oct 6, 1899 to Oct 10,

1979; p/Adolf Gutman and Cecile Zolotnitzky Marinel (dec); ed/Moscow St Univ Law Sch 1919; Am Lib Sch (Paris); Ecole Normale de Musique (Paris); Ecole du Louvre (Paris); pa/Perf'd over 40 Concerts in France & Europe; Came to USA 1941; Ref & Res Libn, French Embassy (Wash, DC) 1943-48; Legal Indexer, United Nations (NYC) 1949-63; Fac Mem, NYU 1963-65; Resumed Concert Activs in US w Var Orchs at Carnegie Hall, Lincoln Ctr, Others; Pub, *Index to Intl Treaty Series*, Vols 1-IV; Contbr to Profl Jours; Fdr, Am Harp Soc; Intl Law Assn; Spec Lib Assn; r/Jewish; hon/Bronze Medal, "Offerte par le Comite du Festival Israelien de Harpe".

MARINO, VINCENT JOSEPH oc/Priest; b/Nov 22, 1947; h/436 Wildwood Ave, #1, Verona, PA 15147; ba/Same; p/Vincent J Sr and Catherine Agnich Marino, Verona; ed/BA cum laude, Duquesne Univ 1969; Cert, Pontifical Inst Christian Archaeology (Rome) 1972; STB cum laude, Pontifical Gregorian Univ 1972; MSW Cath Univ Am 1979;

pa/Ordained Priest 1974; Assoc Pastor, St Mary's Ch (Pittsburgh) 1978; Assoc Pastor, St Pius X Ch (P'burgh) 1977; Instr Cont'g Christian Devel Prog, Diocese of P'burgh 1975-77; Chaplain, Rosalia Manor for Unwed Mothers (P'burgh) 1975-77; Other Positions; Lectr; r/Rom Cath; hon/W/W Rel; Notable Ams; DIB.

MARK, MARILYN oc/Artist; b/Aug 7, 1930; h/2261 Ocean Ave, Brooklyn, NY 11229; ba/Same; m/Herbert Murray; c/Tippy Blu; p/Nathan M and Henriette Valensky Sabetsky, Bklyn; pa/Mgr Public Relats, Nat Art Mus of Sport (NYC); Co-Fdr & Pres, Visual Individualists United; Nat Leag Am Pen Wom: NY St Pres, Nat Chrwom for Publicity & Public Relats, Others; Bd Mem, Burr Artists; Public Relats Dir, Eleanor Gay Gallery Foun; Group Shows: Nat Art Mus of Sport, Grand Palais on the Champs Elysees (Paris, France), Nat Arts Clb (NYC), Museum Moderne Art (Paris), Metro Mus Art (NYC),

Num Others; 3-Wom Show, Nat Art Mus of Sport; Artists Equity Assn NY; Les Surindependants Artistes Assn (Paris); Societes Des Artistes De France; Life Mem, Gallery of Art, Nat Art Mus of Sport; Art Sales & Rental Gallery; Raymond Duncan Galleries; Intl Wom's Art Fest; Wom's Interart Ctr; Others; cp/Assn Belgo-Hispanica; hon/Work incl'd in Perm Collections: Nat Art Mus of Sport, Raymond Duncan Galleries-Mus (Paris), Du Musee Des Beaux Arts (Montbard, France); Work incl'd Over 100 Pvt Collections; 5 One-Wom Shows US; Outstg Bklyn Wom, NOW; Outstg Ldrship Recog, Artists Leag of Bklyn; Rec'd Cit & Gold

Medal, Academia De Ciencas Humanisticas Y Relaciones; Rec'd Global Awd, Brussels C of C; Rec'd Bronze Medal, Raymond Duncan Centennial; Num Other Art Awds; W/W: Am Wom, Am, Am Art; Notable Ams; DIB; Other Biogl Listings.

MARKEWICH, MAURICE ELISH oc/Physician; Musician; b/Aug 6, 1936; h/Bacon Hill, Mt Pleasant, NY 10570; ba/New York, NY; m/Linda; c/Jennifer, Melissa; p/Arthur and May Markewich, NYC; ed/AB; MSSW; MD; Cert'd Psychoanalyst; mil/AUS 1960-61; pa/Clinical Instr Psychi, Mt Sinai Sch of Med (CUNY) 1973-; Psychi, Beth Israel Med Ctr 1973-; Staff Mem, Gracie Sq Hosp (NY) 1973; Other Positions; Jazz Musician; Albums: *New Designs in Jazz w the Reese Markewich Quintet, This is It*; Perf'd w: Chuck Mangione, Duke Ellington Sextet, Scott La Faro, Others; Cornell Univ Big Red Band; USAR Band; AUS TV; SUNY Albany Jazz Fest; Others; Author *Inside Outside: Substitute Harmony in Modern Jazz & Pop Music*, Others; Am Psychi Assn; Med Soc Co of NY; Nat Assn Social Workers; Acad Cert'd Social Workers; Soc Clinical Social Workers; Others; r/Jewish; hon/Winner Nat Intercollegiate Jazz Contest; Winner NY Jazz Critics' New Star Combo Contest; Rec'd Stephen Jewett Awd, NY Med Col.

MARKLEY, BLANCH LUCIEL oc/Interior Designer; h/5210 S Dixie, Lima, OH 45806; ba/Lima; m/Merritt M; p/Frank C and Emma Rouge Frisbie (dec); ed/Interior Design, Fine Art, Higher Acctg; pa/Owner Blanch L Markley Shoppe (Interior Design); Lectr; cp/Better Bus Bur; Shawnee Country Clb; C of C; r/Prot.

MARKLEY, LAURA ANN oc/Music Teacher; b/Nov 9, 1942; h/509 Chickadee, #C, Little Rock, AR 72205; ba/Mabelvale, AR; p/Howard Wesley Markley (dec); Sallie Ann Price Markley, Booneville, AR; ed/BA Hendrix Col; pa/Choral Mus Tchr, Mabelvale Jr HS (Pulaski Co Sch Dist); NEA; AEA; Ark Choral Dir Assn; Am CDA; Pulaski Assn Classroom Tchrs; Bach Soc Gtr Little Rock; r/Booneville United Meth Ch: Mem; hon/Mu Phi Epsilon; Outstg Tchrs Am; Commun Ldrs & Noteworthy Ams; Notable Ams Bicent Era.

MARKLEY, ROGER BRUCE oc/Accountant; b/Feb 25, 1921; h/Rt 3, Box 20, Nashville, IN 47448; ba/Nashville; m/Betty June Sheffer; c/Jeffrey Bruce, Patrice Faye, Rodney Lee; p/Herman R and Beaulah May Markley (dec); ed/BA; Grad Command Sch USAF; Addit Studies: mil/USAF 23 Yrs; pa/CPA; Mgr Apt Complex; Bd Dirs 4 Corps; Instr Acctg; St & Nat CPA Assns; cp/Reserv Ofcrs Assn US; r/Meth: Trustee; hon/Rec'd Air Medal (3); Purple Heart; ETO Awds; Rec'd Press Cit; Am Legion Hon Awd; Ind Berlin Crisis Awd.

MARKS, HENRY S oc/Educational Consultant; b/May 26, 1933; h/405 Homewood Dr SW, Huntsville, AL 35801; ba/Huntsville; m/Marsha Kass; c/Barbara Carol; p/Benjamin Edwin and Florence Hirsh Marks (dec); ed/BBA, MA Univ Miami; pa/Editor *Huntsville Hist Qtrly & Hist Huntsville Qtrly*; Author 4 Books, 55 Articles, Num Book Reviews; PCAS; ASNA; cp/Rotary Clb; Dem Party; Pres, Huntsville Jewish Commun Coun; r/Jewish; hon/W/W S&SW; DIB; Dir Am Scholars; Others.

MARKS, MARSHA KASS oc/Professor; b/May 6, 1935; h/405 Homewood Dr SW, Huntsville, AL 35801; ba/Normal, AL; m/Henry S; c/Barbara Carol; p/Aaron Kass (dec); Edith M Kass, Atlanta, GA; ed/MA; pa/Asst Prof Hist, Ala A&M Univ; Am Hist Assn; Popular Cult Assn; Am Studies Assn; Hakluyt Soc; So Hist Assn; Ala Hist Assn; OAH; Huntsville Hist Soc; Assn Social & Behavioral Scis; cp/Rotayann; Hadassah; Huntsville Mus Assn; r/Jewish; hon/Phi Beta Kappa; Phi Alpha Theta; W/W Am Cols & Univs.

MARKUS, ANTHONY BUD oc/Landscape Architect; b/May 19, 1931; h/4243 Fruitville Rd, Sarasota, FL 33580; ba/Same; m/Dolores; c/Louis, Neal, Anthony; p/Louis and Catherine Markus, NJ; ed/Rutgers Univ; mil/DFC Korea; pa/Conslt & Designer for Sev Noted Persons; r/Cath; hon/Rec'd 4 Bronze Stars; Rec'd Silver Star; Rec'd Nat & St Awds.

MARKWORTH, ALAN JOHN oc/Physicist; b/Jul 13, 1937; h/1679 Cambridge Blvd, Columbus, OH 43212; ba/Columbus; m/- Margaret Gordon Raines; c/Sharon Marie, David John, Caroline Marie; p/Henry John Markworth (dec); Helene Marie Eleonore Dopmeyer Markworth, Lakewood, OH; ed/- BSc w Hons, Case Inst Technol; MSc, PhD Ohio St Univ; pa/Prin Physicist Metal Sci Sect, Columbus Labs; Am Inst Mining, Metall & Petro Engrs; Am Assn Physics Tchrs; cp/Former Foster Parent, Franklin Co Chd's Sers; r/First Commun Ch (Columbus): Mem; hon/Sigma Pi Sigma; Sigma Xi.

MARON, MILFORD ALVIN oc/Judge; b/Jan 21, 1926; h/6245 Matilija Ave, Van Nuys, CA 91401; ba/Los Angeles, CA; m/Esther Kass; c/Melissa Allison, Adam Curtis, (Stepchd:) Steven Alan, Dean Eran; p/Martin and Anna Maron (dec); ed/BA 1949, MA 1953, LLB 1954, LLM 1958 Univ So Cal-LA; mil/AUS 1944-46; pa/Adm Law Judge, St Office of Adm Hearings 1963-; Trial Cnslr: St

Div Labor Law Enforcemt 1960-63, Fed Securities & Exchange Comm 1957-60; Cal Deputy of Corps 1956-57; Contbr Num Articles Profl Jours; Admit'd Cal Bar, US Ct Appeals (9th Dist), US Dist Ct (So Dist Cal) 1955; Admit'd US Supr Ct 1959; Past Mem Am & LA Co Bar Assns; Past Mem LA Lwyrs' Clb; hon/Rec'd Good Conduct Medal & Victory Medal, AUS; W/W Am Law; DIB; Men Achmt.

MARQUIS, GERALDINE M oc/Educator; h/814 N 16th St, Fort Dodge, IA 50501; ba/Ft Dodge; m/Forrest W; c/Robert W; p/(dec); ed/BA; MS; pa/NEA; ISEA; FDEA; ACEI; NAEYC; OMEP; FDACE; cp/Nat TTT Soc; r/Meth; hon/Rec'd Am Legion S'ship Awd; Rec'd PTA S'ship; Outstg Elem Tchr Nom.

MARRETT, MICHAEL McFARLENE oc/Clergyman; b/Oct 7, 1935; h/185 Stimson Rd, New Haven, CT 06511; ba/New Haven; m/Melicent Anabel Roye; p/Kenneth Louis Marrett (dec); Ivy Lynmae Marrett, Jamaica, W Indies; ed/AMIET; MDiv; STM; BA; MS; pa/Priest Assn of Holy Cross; Confrat of Blessed Sacrament; Co-fdr Assn Black Clergy of New Haven; cp/Bd Mem Urban Leag; hon/Phi Delta Kappa; W/W Rel.

MARSH, BETTIE JEAN oc/Deputy Attorney; b/Sept 27, 1941; h/1540 Country Hills Dr, Ogden, UT 84403; ba/Salt Lake City, UT; m/William Dale; c/Bradley Trent, Stacy Leigh; p/Loranzo and Imogene Neaves McJunkin, Ponca City, OK; ed/BS; JD; pa/Deputy Atty, Salt Lake Co 1977-; Admit'd Wis Bar 1967, Fed Dist Ct for En Dist Wis Bar 1967, Utah St Bar 1971; Law Reform Coor (Milwaukee, Wis) & Legal Sers Prog 1967-69; Asst Res Dir, Nat Legal Aid & Defender Assn (Am Bar Ctr, Chgo) 1969-70; Asst Atty Gen Utah 1974-77; Weber Co Legal Sers Prog; cp/Bd Dirs, Weber Basin Mtl Hlth Assn; Utah St Mtl Hlth Assn; r/Presb; hon/Russell Sage Fellow.

MARSH, GWENDOLEN oc/Concert Pianist; b/Mar 17, 1908; h/1120 E 44 St, Kansas City, MO 64110; ba/Same; p/Charles W and Myrtle Wolven Marsh (dec); ed/Attended Kansas City Conservatory 1921-27; pa/Master Classes Critic for *Musical Ldr Mag*; Judge Nat Guild of Piano Tchrs; Mus Clb; Federated Mus Tchrs; r/Christian Ch Kansas City: Mem; hon/Rec'd Outstg Composer Awd, Mo Fdn Mus Tchrs.

MARSH, KENNETH STANLEY oc/Chief Engineer; b/May 17, 1925; h/990 McCosh St, Hanover, PA 17331; ba/Hanover; m/Jeanne Carol Fink; c/Andrew Kenneth; p/Cecil Stanley and Lucy Marsh (dec); ed/King's Col; Royal Air Force Col; Street Technical Inst; mil/Royal Air Force Pilot 1944-49 & 1951; pa/Chief Engr, The Hanover Shoe Inc 1964-; Chief Tng Ofcr, C & J Clark Ltd 1953-64; Asst Prodn Mgr 1951-53; Sr Industl Engr 1959-61; Author/Editor of Tng Manuals for Shoemakers, Industl Engrs, Prodn Controllers, Craft Apprentices, Others; Contbr to Profl Jours; Sr Mem, Am Inst of Industl Egrs; Assn Energy Engrs; Am Soc Heating, Refrigerating & Air Conditioning Engrs; Am Mgmt Assn; Others; cp/VP York-Adams Area Coun BSA; Past Mem Nat Coun, British Boot & Shoe Instn; Am Security Coun; Citizens Adv Coun, Hanover Sch Dist; Others; r/Epis; hon/Reg'd Profl Engr in Pa, WV; Fellow, British Boot & Shoe Instn; W/W; Men of Achmt; W/W Technol Today.

MARSH, MILTON RUDOLPH WILLIAM oc/Educator; Composer; Arranger; b/Sept 29, 1945; h/PO Box 635, Astor Station, Boston, MA 02123; m/Doreen Johnson; c/2; p/Inspector & Mrs Milton Marsh Sr; ed/London Certs Ed, Berkeley Inst (Pembroke, Bermuda); BMEd Berklee Col Mus 1969; MMus, New England Conservatory Mus 1971; pa/Conslt, Nat Ctr Afro-Am Artists (Roxbury, Mass) 1970-71; Asst Prof & Dir Afro-Am Mus Studies, St Univ NY-B 1973-77; Other Positions; Extensive Show Engagemnts w Internationally Known Artists & Num Appearances as Featured Artist incl'g "Fest of New England Composers, Past & Present," & "Weekend of Contemp Jazz"; Composer: *Poems for Saxophone Quartet, Psychic Impulses, Gamaka*, Others; Contbr Articles Profl Jours; Col Mus Soc; AAUP; Recorded *Monism*, Perf'd by Himself; Extensive Travels; hon/Book of Hon.

MARSHALL, HELEN E oc/Retired Teacher; b/Oct 25, 1898; h/1109 Fairlawn Ct #6, Walnut Creek, CA 94595; p/David Conwell and Laura Catherine Agnes Souter Marshall (dec); ed/AB Col of Emporia; MA Univ Chgo; PhD Duke Univ; pa/Former Instr, Ill St Univ; cp/LWV; Salvation Army Adv Bd; r/Christian Sci; hon/Delta Kappa Gamma; Career Wom of Yr, BPW 1961.

MARSHALL, IRA BRUCE oc/Corporate Law Officer; b/Nov 10, 1947; h/750 Stierlin Rd #51, Mountain View, CA 94043; ba/Palo Alto, CA; p/Henry Marshall (dec); Lillian Tabak, Mountain View; ed/BA; PhB; pa/Chief Exec Ofcr, Intl Common Law Exchange Soc 1974-; Legal Asst Danaher, Gunn & Klynn (Law Firm) 1973-74; Legal Asst, Commun Legal Sers of Santa Clara Co 1972-73; Editor-in-Chief *Common Law Lwyr*; Mng Editor *Transnational Immigration Law Reporter*; Res Asst for Prof Paul Smoker on Nuclear Power Plant Accidents on Lake Mich; Res on Vietnam w Assoc Law Prof Anthony D'Amato; Other Profl Positions; Proposals: Implementation Plan for Australian-Am Legal Exchange Prog 1972-73, Legal Aid & Legal Ser Visual Aid Grant 1976, Others; Contbr Num Articles Profl Jours; Pres, Intl Common Law Exchange Soc; Intl Bar Assn; Lwyr's Com for Civil Rights Under Law; Canadian Bar Assn; Intl Legal Aid Assn; Nat Legal Aid & Defender Assn; Law Soc of England; r/Jewish; hon/Ford Foun Grantee, Intl Common Law Exchange Soc; Rec'd Highest Acad Achmt Awd, NWn Univ; Rec'd S'ship to Pract'g Law Inst, Legal Rights of Mentally Handicapped; W/W Fin & Indust; Others.

PERSONALITIES OF AMERICA

331

MARSHALL, JOHN DAVID oc/Librarian; Author; b/Sept 7, 1928; h/802 E Main, Riviera Apt 34, Murfreesboro, TN 37130; ba/Murfreesboro; p/Maxwell Cole Marshall (dec); Emma W Marshall, McKenzie, TN; ed/BA Bethel Col 1950; MA Fla St Univ 1951; pa/Univ Bibliographer & Assoc Prof, Middle Tenn St Univ Lib 1976-; Author: Books in Your Life (1959), A Fable of Tomorrow's Library (1965), Others; Editor: Of, By and For Libns (1960, 74), Mark Hopkins' Log & Other Essays of Louis Shores (1964), Others; Contbr Ency Americana, Others; Am Lib Hist Round Table; Am Lib Assn; Assn Col & Res Libs; Hon Mbrship Chm, SEn Lib Assn; Tenn Lib Assn; Others; r/Cumberland Presb; hon/Beta Phi Mu; Phi Kappa Phi; W/W: S&SE, Lib Ser; Contemp Authors; Intl Scholars Directory; Personalities of S.

MARSHALL, O B oc/Commissioner; b/Nov 17, 1919; h/5906 Westmore Dr, Jackson, MS 39206; ba/Jackson; m/Roma D Walton; c/Victor Barron, Michael Walton; p/Harbert Davis Marshall, Louisville, MS; Elizabeth Barron Marshall (dec); mil/CWO, ANG Ret'd; pa/Commr of Savs Assns, St of Miss; Jackson Mortgage Lenders Assn; Jackson Mortgage Sers Assn; Past Dir & Leg Chm, Miss Savs & Ln Coun; cp/C of C; Active in UGF; r/Bapt.

MARSHALL, SHARON GERALDINE oc/Student; pa/Law Student, George Wash Univ; Student Senator; Student Div, ABA; Black Am Law Student Assn; cp/Chrperson, Min Coun (SGA, Clemson Univ); Treas, Student Leag for Black Identity; Yg Dems; NAACP; Others; hon/Hon Grad, Clemson Univ; Sigma Tau Epsilon; Mu Beta Psi; Kappa Beta Phi.

MARSTON, JOSEPH G LANAUX JR oc/Retired; b/Jul 13, 1919; h/339 Park Ave, Mobile, AL 36609; m/Rose Marie Smith; c/Joseph L III, Clifton Henry, Leila M Sanford (Mrs Gordon U), Christopher A, Rose Marie M Fogarty (Mrs Bernard A Jr), Patrick J, Nicholas S, Herferd F; p/Joseph G Lanaux Marston (dec); Emily Page Hereford Marston, Mobile; ed/Attended Spring Hill Col, Univ Ala, Auburn Univ; mil/USMS WWII; pa/Former Dir, Cath Cemetary of Mobile; Former Admr, Cath Hous'g of Mobile; Pres Nat Assn of Holy Name Soc 1975-77; Chm NATC Adv Bd; Pres, Diocesan Pastoral Coun (Mobile) 1974-75; Pres Mobile Dist Cath Bd Ed 1973-74; Past Pres, "Conscience, Mobile"; Past Pres, Mobile Dist Holy Name Union; Former Mem Bd Dirs, Assn Ala Cemeteries; Num Other Orgs & Positions; Contbr Articles Profl Jours; cp/Former Radiological Defense Ofcr, Mobile Co Civil Defense; Former Chm, Disaster Preparedness & Relief Com (ARC); Nat Cath Disaster Relief Com; K of C; Mobile Cath Men's Breakfast Clb; IPA; Fdg Fellow, Intl Inst Commun Ser; Former Mem, Mobile C of C; Sons of Confederate Vets; Num Others; r/Corpus Christi Cath Ch; hon/Rec'd Enemy Action Ribbon, Pacific Theatre Ribbon, Atlantic Theatre Ribbon & Mediterranean Ribbon USMS; Rec'd Verlelli Gold Medal & Cit, NAHNS; Humanity Medal, ARC; Dedicated Ser Awd, Mobile Chapt ARC; Rel Lay Ldr Awd, Mobile Jr C of C; Humanitarian Awd, Assn Ala Cemeteries; Rec'd Medalion Cir Awd, NAHNS (Chgo); Rec'd Bene Merenti Gold Medal & Dipl, Pope Paul VI; Silver Awd, Am Petro Inst; Num Others.

MARTIN, ANNA MIRIAM WENGER oc/Retired Registered Nurse; b/May 4, 1914; h/413 Massachusetts Ave #3, Boston, MA 02118; c/Carol Ann, Joan Louise; p/Eli D and Anna Louisa S Wenger (dec); ed/RN; cp/Mid E Inst (Wash, DC); Active in Var Mid E Peace Activs; r/Unit; hon/W/W Am Wom; Intl W/W Wom; Notable Ams.

MARTIN, CHARLES ALLEN oc/Research Manager; b/Apr 3, 1938; h/16884 Renwick, Livonia, MI 48154; ba/Walled Lake, MI; m/Jeanette Bienko; c/Jacqueline Marie, Christopher Charles; p/Joseph Allen Martin (dec); Anna L Martin, Detroit, MI; ed/BS, MS (2) Wayne St Univ; pa/Product Res Mgr, Ex-Cell-O Aerospace Devel Ctr; Chm Mich Sect Am Inst Aeronautics & Astronautics 1977-79;

Soc Automotive Engrs; Am Soc Mech Engrs; pa/Livonia Sch Bd Adv Com; YMCA; r/St Colette Ch, Livonia.

MARTIN, CLARENCE E III oc/Delegate; b/Jul 24, 1946; h/Martinsburg, WV; p/Clarence E and Catherine Silver Martin; ed/Mercersburg Acad; AB Univ Ariz; JD Cath Univ Sch of Law; pa/Former Asst Counsel, Interstate & Foreign Commerce Com (US Ho of Reps); Former Trial Atty, US Dept of

Justice; W Va Ho of Delegates Coms: Constitutional Revision, Ed, Govt Org (VChm), Polit Subdivs, Jt Exec Com on Energy, Majority Caucas; Bd Dirs W VA Legal Sers Plan; VP W Va Yg Dems; W Va, DC, Am & Fed Bar Assns; hon/Beta Theta Pi; Rec'd Am Jurisprudence Scholastic Achmt Awd; Rec'd Cert of Merit, ARC.

MARTIN, COLA ALLEN oc/Retired Army Officer; b/Jan 9, 1929; h/631 Madisonville St, Princeton, KY 42445; ba/Jasper, AL; m/Lois F; c/Gary Allan, Pamela Ann; p/Cola S and Wilma A Martin, Warner Robins, GA; mil/US Army 1948-; Tuba Player 256th Army Ground Force Band; 3rd Inf Div during Korean War (Hon Mem Greek Army); Drum Major & Tuba Soloist for 3rd Army Band (Ft McPherson, Ga); Tuba Instr at Navy Sch of Music (Wash, DC); Made Warrant Ofcr 1958; Commanded 4th Army Band Tng Sch (Ft Chaffee, Ark), 30th Army Band (Munich, Germany), Full-time Band (Ft Benjamin Harrison, Indiana); Commanded 296th Army Band (Camp Zama, Japan) 1966-69; Staff Bands Ofcr & Commanding Ofcr, 3rd Army Band; Org'd US Army Forces Command Band (Ft McPherson); Perf'd for Presidents Truman, Eisenhower, Johnson, Nixon & Carter, Queen Elizabeth, Prince Phillip, Prime Minister of Bavaria, Astronauts John Glen & Pete Conrad, Num Others; Ret'd 1974 as Chief Warrant Ofcr; cp/Past Master: Capitol View Lodge #640 (Atlanta, Ga), Furstenfeldbruck Lodge #851 (Munich, Germany); Past Dist Grand Master, So Dist of Bavaria (Germany); Past Pres, Ft Benjamin Harrison Chapt of Nat Sojourners; Heroes of '76; Past Mem, Princeton Kiwanis Clb; Others; r/1st Christian Ch (P'ton): Min of Music, Ch Bd, Choir Dir, Others; hon/Commended by Secy of Army, Bo Calloway & US Chief of Staff, Gen Creighton Abrahms; Legion of Merit; Army Commend Medal w 2 OLC; Good Conduct Medal; Korean Sers Medal w 4 Bronze Stars; United Nations Medal; Others.

MARTIN, DALE ALISON oc/Professor; b/May 4, 1941; h/3325 Allendale Pl, Montgomery, AL 36111; ba/Montgomery; m/Blanche Waters; c/Alyssa; p/Ted C and Omie Lee Frith Martin, Montgomery; ed/BS

cum laude; MS; PhD; pa/Prof & Chm Dept Cnslg & Psychol, Troy St Univ; Am Psychol Assn; Am Pers & Guid Assn; Nat Vocational Guild Assn; Ala PGA; Ala Psychol Assn; r/First Bapt Ch (Montgomery): Deacon, SS Tchr, Secy, Bd Dirs; hon/Phi Delta Kappa; Rec'd Alpha Epsilon Delta S'ship; Omicron Delta Kappa.

MARTIN, DAVID EDWARD oc/Physiologist; b/Oct 1, 1939; h/510 Coventry Rd, Stone House, Decatur, GA 30340; ba/Atlanta; p/Edward Henry and Lillie Luckman Martin, Owen, WI; ed/BS 1961, MS 1967, PhD 1970 Univ Wis; pa/Physiologist, Col of Allied Hlth, Ga St Univ; Author 30 Sci Pubs in Reproductive Biol & Sports Med; Lectr; cp/Nat Ofcr Ath Union; r/Prot; hon/Dist'd Prof.

MARTIN, EVERETT S (BUNNY) oc/Entertainer; h/1720 N Beal, Belton, TX 76513; m/Mary Etta Lawrence; c/Trae, Cory; p/Mr and Mrs Everett S Martin Sr; ed/BS Howard Payne Col 1960; pa/Magician; Juggler; Folk Singer; Perf'd w: Roger Miller, Ethel Waters, Others; Guest Billy Graham Crusade; Filmed Spec for CBS w Art Linkletter & Dale Evans; Others; Former Disk Jockey (Brownwood, Tex); Former Min of Yth Ed & Rec (Oklahoma City, Okla); Former Assoc Dir Col Affairs, Mary Hardin-Baylor Col (Belton); Other Positions; Intl Brotherhood of Magicians; Tex Assn Magicians; IPA; r/Guest on 700 Clb; Guest on PTL Network; Others; hon/Yo-Yo Champion of World; Outstg Yg Men Am; FCA; Personalities of S; Commun Ldrs & Noteworthy Ams; Subject of Film, "Bunny Martin - Work & Life Style"; Others.

MARTIN, HARVEY T JR oc/Provost; b/Jul 18, 1924; h/8801 Thunderbird Dr, Pensacola, FL 32504; ba/Pensacola; m/Esther Lee; c/Michael T, Lory Lee; p/Harvey T Sr and Mildred S Martin, Rutland, VT; ed/BA Middlebury Col 1950; MS 1952, PhD 1957 Wash St Univ; mil/USAF 1942-46; pa/Provost of Omega Col, Univ W Fla; AAAS; Fla Psychol Assn; Fla PGA; Am Psychol Assn; Fla Sch Psychol Assn; cp/Former Dir, NW Fla Speech & Hear'g Assn; Former Mem C of C; Airport Adv Com; hon/Psi Chi; Outstg Edrs Am; Personalities of S; Am Men Sci; W/W S&SW.

MARTIN, HENRY LAWRENCE oc/-Chaplain; b/Oct 25, 1925; h/9514 Meadow Grove Ct, Burke, VA 22015; ba/Norfolk, VA; m/Carolyn Taylor; c/Timothy Lawrence, Lisa Carol; p/William Hardy Martin (dec); Rose Ella Johnson Martin, Clinton, TN; ed/AB maga cum laude, Carson-Newman Col; MDiv

New Orleans Bapt Theol Sem 1953; ThM So Bapt Theol Sem 1955; DMin McCormick Theol Sem 1976; mil/USN 1944-46; Chaplain 1967-; pa/Pastor Chs in Ky, Tenn & Conn 1955-77; Pub Num Articles Secular, Rel & Mil Pubs; cp/Rotary Intl; Optimist Clb; r/So Bapt; hon/Tenn Col; W/W Rel; Rec'd Commend Medal, USN; Other Mil Awds.

MARTIN, JAMES GRUBBS oc/Congressman; b/Dec 11, 1935; h/Box 638, Davidson, NC 28036; ba/Washington, DC; m/Dorothy McAulay; c/James Jr, Emily, Benson; p/Arthur M and Mary Grubbs Martin, Columbia, SC; ed/BS Davidson 1957; PhD Princeton 1960; pa/Assoc Prof Chem, Davidson Col 1960-72; Com of Ways &

Means, US Ho of Reps 1975-; VP Nat Assn Regional NC Del 1968 Repub Conv; Metrolina Coun of Govts; r/Presb; hon/Danforth Fellow; Beta Theta Pi.

MARTIN, LOIS E oc/Teacher; b/Jan 1, 1914; h/641 Westwood Dr, Abilene, TX 79603; ba/Abilene; m/H Gebhard (dec); c/Jois M Ross, Kenneth Gebhard; p/John Washington Baker (dec); Eliza E Moore Baker, Itsaca, TX; ed/BS 1940, MS 1942, EdD 1964 N Tex St Univ; pa/Instr HSU; AAUP; APA; TPGA; NEA; TSTA; AHEAD; AAUW; TPA; Tex Soc Col Tchrs Ed; ASEA; TATE; Univ Wom; r/Bapt; hon/Rec'd Dist'd Alumni Awd; Citizen of Day; Hometown Honoree; Delta Kappa Gamma.

MARTIN, MARGARET ALLISON oc/Teacher; Writer; Illustrator; Executive; b/Apr 15, 1954; h/PO Box 27610, Los Angeles, CA 90027; ba/LA; m/Ernest Joseph Terrance; c/Mars; p/Ivan and Patricia Manning; ed/AB; HRS; HDC; pa/Dir Fam Ser

Ctr; Fdr & Exec Dir, Pregnancy & Natural Childbirth Ed Ctr; Secy Intl Hlth Org; Pres Fast Flow Survey Sers; cp/Exec Dir, Hollywood Yth Theatre; r/Scientology; hon/Kha Khan.

MARTIN, MELVIN D oc/Farmer; Businessman; b/Feb 1, 1930; h/Rt 5, 232 Campbellsville, KY 42718; ba/Same; m/Reba Lee; c/Peggy Ann M Caulk, Stephen D, Janet Lee; p/Cloyd and Amelia Martin, Greensburg, KY; ed/Agri; mil/USAF; pa/Agri Supvr Working w Dairy Belt & Hog Farmers; Local Farm Mgr; cp/Am Legion; Dem Activs; r/Bapt; hon/-Rec'd JCs & Am Legion Awds; Notable Ams; Intl W/W.

MARTIN, NORMA QUIGGLE oc/Realtor; b/Jan 2, 1915; h/1700 Vamo Dr, Sarasota, FL 33581; ba/Same; m/John R; c/Douglas C, David Q; p/Carl and Anna Burke Quiggle (dec); ed/Grad Realtor's Inst; pa/Corp Secy,

Fla Assn Realtors 1978; Gov for Nat Assn Realtors Wom's Coun 1977-78; Former Pres Fla Assn Realtors Wom's Coun; Former Bd Mem, Sarasota Bd Realtors; hon/Presb Ch US: Deacon, Elder; hon/Rec'd Realtor of Yr Awd, Sarasota Chapt Wom's Coun Realtors; Wom of Yr, Fla Wom's Coun Realtors; Rec'd Omega Tau Rho Nat Awd in Real Estate.

MARTIN, PATRICIA MILES oc/Writer; h/910 Bromfield Rd, San Mateo, CA 94402; m/Edward R; p/Thomas Jefferson and Nelle Miles (dec); pa/Author 91 Pub'd Books for Chd; Some Works Written Under Pseudonym "Miska Miles"; hon/Rec'd Newbury Hon for *Annie and the Old One*.

MARTIN, PHILIP JOE oc/Geophysicist; b/Jul 26, 1934; h/PO Box 393, Oklahoma City, OK 73101; ba/Oklahoma City; m/Shelia Ann Redd (div); c/Michael Brent, Kimberly Annette, Susan Yvette; ed/BS Univ Okla 1958; BS 1958; mil/AUS 1958; pa/Geol Trainee, Shell Oil Co (OC) 1956-58; Geophysical Engr, Mobil Oil Co (Dallas, Tex) 1959-60; Geophysicist & Mathematician, Texaco Inc (Bellaire, Tex) 1960-68; Sci Analyst, Skelly Oil Co (Tulsa, Okla) 1968-75; Data Processing Conslt, Sperry Rand Corp (Tulsa) 1975-77; Proj Geophysicist, Gulf Oil Exploration & Prodn Co (OC) 1977-; Pres, Home Computer Prods Inc; Soc Exploration Geophysicists; Geophysics Soc of OC; OC Geol Soc; IPA; cp/Univ Okla Alumni Assn; Repub Party; hon/Biogl Listings.

MARTIN, RICHARD FRED oc/Recruiter; b/Nov 24, 1947; h/300 Pecore, Houston, TX 77009; ba/Houston; p/H Clayton Martin (dec); Dorothy Martin, El Paso, TX; ed/BSM Gulf Coast Bible Col 1971; pa/Public Relats & Recruiter, Gulf Coast Bible Col; Instr Vocal & Instrumental Mus; Advr Var Classes & Clbs; Mus Workshop Ldr; cp/Pres NM St Yth F'ship 4 Yrs; Del to Intl Yth Planning Coun; r/Houston 1st Ch of God: Assoc Pastor, Min Mus, Mus Evangelist, Revival & Conf Speaker, Yth Ldr, Bd Christian Ed, SS Tchr; hon/Nat Hon Soc; Rec'd Kiwanis Citizenship Awd; Outstg Alumnus, Gulf Coast Bible Col.

MARTIN, ROBERT LEO oc/Professor; b/Jul 6, 1929; h/PO Box 579, Alva, OK 73717; ba/Alva; m/Mary Jo; c/Robert L Jr, Dana Caroline M Golbek (Mrs Larry); p/Leo Howell Martin (dec); Mabelle Anna Martin, Pueblo, CO; ed/BS 1951, MS 1956 Kansas St Tchrs' Col; Addit Studies Okla St Univ; pa/Asst Prof Speech & Drama, NW Okla St Univ-A; cp/Dir, Actor & Past Pres, Alva Commun Theatre Inc; Dir & Narrator Outdoor Christmas Pageant, Little Sahara St Park; Past Dist Deputy Grand Exalted Ruler; BPO Elks; Past St VP, Okla Elks Assn; Past Pres Rotary Clb; Bd Dirs UF; Co Chm Okla Heart Fund; Others; r/Presb: Bd Trustees, Deacon; hon/Rec'd Arts & Humanities Coun Awd For Theatre; Rec'd Acting Awds, Commun Theatre; Rec'd Awd, Okla Heart Assn; DIB; Personalities of S; Intl W/W Intellectuals.

MARTIN, RUTH M oc/Nurse; b/Oct 10, 1926; h/3032 Belair Dr, Bowie, MD 29715; ba/Washington, DC; p/Clarence R Martin (dec); Erma L Martin, Havertown, PA; ed/BSN, MEd Univ Cinc; pa/Nurse, D C Gen Hosp; Num Coms, Am Nurses Assn; Asst'd w Filming of Gerontalogy Series, *Am Jour of Nsg*; Secy Local Chapt, Nat League for Nsg; Prince George's Commun Col Adv Bd on Nsg Prog: Pract Nsg Prog Adv Bd, Margaret Murray Washington Voc Sch; Adv Com, Cath Univ of Am Sch of Nsg (Master's Prog in Nsg Adm) 1981-; cp/Bowie Boys' & Girls' Clb; Bowie Civic Assn; Smithsonian Assoc; Am Assn Ret'd Persons; Univ of Cinc Alumni Assn; r/Presb: Deacon, Var Coms; hon/Sigma Theta Tau; W/W E; Commun Ldrs of Am.

MARTINEK, ROBERT GEORGE oc/Clinical Biochemist; b/Nov 25, 1919; h/4736 N Tripp Ave, Chicago, IL 60630; ba/Chgo; m/Lydia Mildred Chab; p/Anton and Agnes Martinek (dec); ed/BS (Pharm) 1941, BS (Med) 1945, MS 1943 Univ Ill; PhD

Univ So Cal 1954; mil/AUS WWII & Korean War; pa/Chief Lab Impr Sect, Ill Dept Public Hlth 1965-; Biochem, Chgo Bd Hlth 1962-65; Chief of Biochem, Ia Meth Hosp 1958-62; Sr Prof Assoc in Biochem, Butterworth Hosp 1956-58; Bd Dirs, Lab-Line Instruments Inc; Res Chem, Mead Johnson & Co; AMA; Life Mem AAAS; Assoc Editor *Jour Am Med Technol*; Editor Conslt *Med Electronics*; Am Pharm Assn; Nat Geog Soc; AIER; Subcom Temp Meas, Area Com Intruments, NCCLS; Clin Chem Adv Bd, Ctr Disease Control, USPHS; Lectr Dept Preven Med Com Hlth, Col Med, Univ Ill; hon/Fellow, Am Inst Chem; Accred'd Profl Chem, AIC; Accred'd Clin Chem, AACC; Cert'd Am Bd Bioanalysis; Rho Chi; Sigma Xi; Phi Kappa Phi.

MARX, GARY D oc/Director; b/Nov 28, 1938; h/1831 Toyon Way, Vienna, VA 22180; m/Judy; c/John, Daniel; p/Harvey and Lucille Stemple Marx, Iroquois, SD; ed/BA Univ SD; pa/Dir Communs, Jefferson Co Public Schs (Colo); Cnslt Nat Sch Public Relats Assn; Fac Mem Nat Sch Bds Acad; Author *Radio: Your Publics Are Listening* & *Get the Message*; Tchr Communs Univ Neb-L, Univ Neb-O & Creighton Univ; Owner & VP Radio Station KOAK (Red Oak, Iowa); Newscaster, Announcer & Prodr-Dir WOW Radio & TV (Omaha); Other Positions; Am Assn Sch Admrs; CASE; Others; cp/Omaha Parks & Rec Bd: Omaha Urban Growth Policy Com; Chm Keystone Commun Task Force; Co-Chm UCC Task Force on World Hunger; Chm, Pres Gerald Ford Birth Site Time Capsule Com; Bd Dirs West Coun of Gtr Omaha C of C; Others; r/Congreg Lakewood United Ch of Christ: Mem; hon/One of Ten Outstg Yg Men of Omaha; Outstg Yg Men of Am; Rec'd Neb Ldrship Awd; Rec'd Am Cancer Soc Awds; Dist'd Ser Awd, Neb Sch Public Relats Assn; RAB Commercial Awd for Writing & Announcing; Rec'd Num Pub Awds; Others.

MASON, ARETHA H oc/Occupational Therapist; b/Jul 24, 1925; h/3172 Espanola Dr, Sarasota, FL 33579; m/James Frederick; c/2; p/Ernest and Pearl Van Core Hammond; ed/BS Wn Mich Univ 1948; OT Dipl, Sch Occupational Therapy 1948; Addit Studies; pa/Occupational Therapy Conslt, Hillhaven Nsg Homes (Sarasota & Venice, Fla) 1968-; St OT Rep for Dept HEW & Nsg Home Assn Prog for Improvemt & Guidelines; Pvt Pract OT & Neurol Disfunction (Sarasota) 1965-67; Other Positions; AAUW; Fla OT Assn; Am OT Assn; Others; cp/Co Golden City Wom's Clb; Panhellenic Assn Coun on Aging; Nat Trust for Hist Preserv; Former Mem, Dem Clb; r/Congreg Ch: Outreach Com; hon/W/W Am; World W/W Wom; Others.

MASON, CLIFFORD GENE oc/Retired Pastor; b/Oct 20, 1937; h/2208 Glen Haven Dr, Dothan, AL 36301; ba/Same; m/Barbara Adams; c/Sharon M Traylor, Barry Gene, Timothy James; p/L D and Gladys Nix Mason, Oneonta, AL; ed/Dipl Bapt Bible Inst;

BA La Col; mil/AUS 1954-55; pa/Moderator of Assn; cp/Masonic Lodge; OES; City Councilman (Hillsboro, Ala); r/So Bapt; hon/Eta Sigma Phi; Alpha Mu Gamma; Grad'd Cum Laude; Rural Pastor of Yr; W/W Rel; IPA; Others.

MASON, DEAN TOWLE oc/Physician; b/Sept 20, 1932; h/3015 Country Clb Dr, El Macero, CA 95618; ba/Davis, CA;

m/Maureen O'Brien; c/Kathleen, Alison; p/Ira J and Florence Towle Mason, Bethesda, MD; ed/BA 1954, MD 1958 Duke Univ; mil/US Public Hlth Ser 1961-63; pa/Chm Cardiovascular Med, Univ Cal-D; Past Pres, Am Col of Cardiology; Past Pres, Wn Soc for Clinical Res; Conslt: Nat Inst of Hlth, NASA, AMA, Nat Sci Foun, VA, Others; Editor Bd: Am Jour Cardiology, Catheterization & Cardiovascular Diagnosis, Others; Editor Clinical Cardiology; Author 7 Books & Over 600 Profl Aritcles; Am Bd Internal Med Cardiovascular Diseases; Am Soc Clinical Investigation; Fellow: Am Col Phys, Am Heart Assn, Am Physiol Soc, Am Pharm & Therapeutics Soc, Am Col Chest Phys, Am Fdn Clinical Res, NY Acad Scis, Royal Soc Med (London), Intl Soc Heart Res, Num Others; r/Presb; hon/Rec'd Am Therapeutic Soc Res Awd; Rec'd Expmtl Therapeutics Awd, Am Soc Pharm; Rec'd Humanitarian Awd, US State Dept; Rec'd Skylab Achmt Awd, NASA; Others.

MASON, DOROTHY ALLISON oc/Retired Teacher; b/Apr 20, 1905; h/3C Victoria Dr, Canterbury Gardens, Coldwater, MI 49036; c/Anne M Byron, Janet M Uhl, Sally M Hiatt; p/Robert G and Mabel S Allison (dec); ed/BA, MA Univ Mich; pa/AAUW; AARP; Christian Bus & Profl Clb; cp/Univ Mich Clb; r/Epis; hon/Rec'd Golden Pen Awd, Univ Mich; Intl W/W Poetry; Alumna Emeritus, Univ Mich.

MASON, ERNEST JR oc/Mortician; b/Apr 22, 1939; h/605 Rolling Acres, Madisonville, KY 42431; ba/Madisonville; m/Cynthia Palmer; c/Lori Anne, Scott Palmer; p/Ernest Mason Sr (dec); Mayme Starks Mason, Madisonville; mil/AUS & USAR; pa/Mgr Mason & Son's Funeral Home; Bd Dirs, St Funeral Dirs Assn; cp/Madisonville JCs; C of C; r/E View Bapt Ch: Deacon; hon/Rec'd Cert of Recog for Outstg Civic & Commun Sers; First Black Man to Win Primary Election in Madisonville.

MASON, LUCILE GERTRUDE oc/Director; b/Aug 1, 1925; h/142 N Mountain Ave, Montclair, NJ 07042; ba/New York, NY; p/Mayne Seguine and Rachel Entorf Mason (dec); ed/AB Smith Col 1947; MA (2) NYC; pa/Dir Devel, Ethical Cult Schs (Fund Raising, Public Relats, Alumni Affairs); Past Pres Am Wom Radio & TV; Am Soc Fund Raising Execs; Public Relats Soc Am; cp/BPW's Com, Henrietta Livermore Sch of Politics; Wom's Nat Repub Clb; Bd Cnslrs, Smith Col; Others.

MASON, MADELINE oc/Poet; Author; b/Jan 24, 1913; h/22 E 29th St, New York, NY 10016; m/Malcolm Forbes McKesson; p/Jacob and Maud Frederica Mason Manheim; ed/Student of Pvt Tutors, US & Abroad; Pvt Piano & Composition Study; pa/Poet-in-Residence, Shenandoah Col (Winchester, Va) & Dellbrook Ctr for Adv'd Studies (Riverton, Va) 1969-76; Poetry Workshops & Lectures throughout US & England; First Am to give Fest Address before Scottish Assn for Speaking Verse at Edinburgh Fest; Author: Hill Fragments (1925), Riding for Tex (1936), The Challengers (1975), Others; Contbr Nat Mags; Syndicated Columnist; Inventor of Mason Sonnet, First Presented Lib of Cong 1956; Exhbn of Poetry & Prose, Harvard Univ; Works in Collection of 20th Cent Am Poets, Lockwood Meml Lib; Composers, Authors & Artists Am; Poetry Soc Am (VP, Exec Bd); Authors Leag Wom's Aux; Pen & Brush; Nat

Leag Am Pen Wom; Wom's Press; Others; cp/NY Jr Leag; NY Philharm Soc; NY Wom's Bible Soc; hon/Edna St Vincent Millay Awd & Dipl for Intl Distinction, Centro Studi E Scambi Internazionali; Intl Awd of Hon & Dipl, Intl Coun Ldrs & Scholars; Diamond Jubilee Awd, Nat Leag Am Pen Wom; Biogl Listings.

MASSENGILL, ELLEN WEBB oc/Librarian, Teacher; b/Mar 6, 1932; h/510 W 6th St, Littlefield, TX 79339; ba/Littlefield; p/Lester L Massengill (dec); Bessie Massengill, Littlefield; ed/BS 1953, MS 1959 Tex Tech Univ; MLS N Tex St Univ 1969; pa/Libn, Littlefield Jr HS 1973-; Tchr Home Ec (L'field) 1971-73; Libn, Odessa HS (Odessa, Tex) 1969-71; Other Positions; NM St Tchrs Assn; Tex St Tchrs Assn; NEA; Am Home Ec Assn; Tex Home Ec Assn; Tex Classroom Tchrs Assn; Am Voc Assn; Tex Lib Assn; Seminole Curric Coun: Bldg Rep, Secy; FHA: Num Positions; Am Lib Assn; Others; cp/Yg Wom's Aux: Pres, Secy, VP, Cnslr, Dir, Others; Wom's Missionary Soc; PTA; Co-ldr GSA; Accompanist, Yg Musician Choir; Pianist for Hospitality House (Convalescent Home); Others; r/First Bapt Ch: Pianist, Organist, SS Class Pres, Choir, Others; hon/Phi Kappa Phi; Panhellenic Awd; Forum Awd; Rec'd Borden Co Home Ec S'ship; Rec'd Grad F'ship Lib Sci, N Tex St Univ; Alpha Chi; Rec'd Alpha Lambda Delta Sr Awd; Phi Upsilon Omicron; Rec'd Cit, YWA; Rec'd Num Awds, So Bapt Conv; DIB; Intl W/W Commun Ser; IPA; Others.

MASSEY, DONALD WAYNE oc/Executive; b/Mar 7, 1938; h/Massland Farm, Rt 7, Box 43, Charlottesville, VA 22901; ba/Charlottesville; m/Violet Sue McIlvain; c/Kimberly Shan, Donn Krichele, Leon Dale; p/Gordon Davis Massey (dec); Lucille Alma Massey; ed/Atended Univ Hawaii, Univ Ky; mil/USMC 1957-60; pa/Pres Micrographics II; Owner Massland Farm Thoroughbred Horse Breeding; Nat Microfilm Assn; Va Microfilm Assn; cp/Pres Workshop V for Handicapped; r/Grace Epis Ch (Cismont, Va); hon/Ky Col; Rec'd Pioneer Awd, Va Micro Assn; Rec'd Fellow Awd, Va Micro Assn; Others.

MASSEY, HAL oc/Dean; b/Apr 10, 1921; h/50 Ave E, Big Coppitt Key, Key West, FL 33040; ba/Key West; m/Marie Jennings; p/John Madison and Alberta Keith Massey (dec); ed/BS w Hons 1953, MEd 1955 Univ Fla; EdD Univ Md 1965; mil/AUS Corps of Engrs 1943-46; pa/Dean, Fla Keys Commun Col 1974-; Daytona Bch Commun Col: Dir 1962-67, VP Acad Affairs 1967-74; Asst Prof, NC St Univ 1957-58; Univ Fla: Asst Prof 1955-57, 1958-62; Fla Assn Commun Cols; Am Voc Assn; Fla Voc Assn; r/Meth; hon/Phi Delta Kappa; Phi Kappa Phi; Rec'd Dist'd Ser Awd, Daytona Bch Commun Col; Phi Theta Kappa; Biogl Listings.

MASSMAN, VIRGIL FRANK oc/Librarian; b/Jul 19, 1929; h/3411 Vivian Ave, St Paul, MN 55112; ba/St Paul; m/Nancy; c/Donna, Ruth, Sara; p/Anton and Christine Massman (dec); ed/BA St John's Univ 1957; MA (Eng) 1960, MA (Lib Sci) 1960 Univ Minn; PhD Univ Mich 1970; Addit Studies; mil/AUS 1953-55; pa/Exec Dir, James Jerome Hill Reference Lib 1971-; Univ SD: Dir Libs, 1966-71, Assoc Prof Eng, 1965-66, Coms; Other Positions; Conslt: Dakota Wesleyan Univ, Huron Col Lib, Mt Marty Col Lib, Others; Pub'd Articles Profl Jours; AAUP; Am Lib Assn; Minn Lib Assn; Former Pres, SD Lib Assn; Former Mem, Minn St Lib Adv Coun; Others; cp/Minn Hist Assn; SD Hist Assn; r/Cath; hon/Rec'd S'ship (Minn); Rec'd F'ship, Univ Mich; Others.

MASSO, GONZALEZ GILDO oc/Executive; b/Dec 8, 1926; h/Munoz Rivera St 158, San Lorenzo, PR 00754; ba/Caguas, PR; m/Carmen G Aponte; c/Gildo, Carmen; p/Rafael Masso Vazquez and Francisca Gonzalez Padin (dec); ed/Bus Adm; pa/Pres Masso Enterprises: Caguas Lumber Yard Inc, Ferreteria Masso Inc, Fabrica de Bloques Masso Inc & Lorenzo Devel Corp; Bd Dirs, Banco Ctl & Economias; cp/Rotary Clb; Lion's Clb; Casino de Puerto Rico; Casa

Espana; Bankers Clb; r/Cath: Pres Cursillos de Cristiandad; hon/Bus Man of Yr, Puerto Rico C of C.

MASSOD, MARY FATETTE oc/Clinical Chemist; b/Oct 30, 1921; h/338 N Warren Ave, Brockton, MA 02401; ba/Brockton; p/Bolis T and Mary Nessralla Massod (dec); ed/BS Tufts Univ 1945; pa/Chemist, Brockton Hosp; Am Assn Clinical Chem; Am Assn Med Technol; Mass Assn Med Technol; Royal Soc Hlth (London); AAAS; cp/Lebanon Am Nat Clb (Aux); r/Cath; hon/Rec'd 20 Awds, Mass Assn Med Technol; Mass Med Technologist of Yr 1968; W/W Am Wom; World W/W Wom; DIB.

MASTERS, ROGER D oc/Professor; b/Jun 8, 1933; h/Dogford Rd, Etna, NH 03750; ba/Hanover, NH; m/Judith R; c/Seth J, William A, Katherine R; p/Maurice Masters (dec); S Grace Masters; ed/AB summa cum laude, Harvard Univ 1955; MA 1948, PhD 1961 Univ Chgo; mil/AUS 1955-57; pa/Prof Dept of Govt, Dartmouth Col; Author: The Polit Phil of Rousseau (1968), The Nation is Burdened (1967); Editor: Rousseau's First & Second Discourses, Rousseau's Social Contract; Chm Editor Bd, "Biol & Social Life Sect", Social Sci Info; Cult Attache, US Embassy (Paris, France) 1969-71; hon/Guggenheim Fellow; Fellow Inst of Soc, Ethics & Life Scis.

MASTERSON, MARY EILEEN oc/Ministry Team Member; b/Jan 13, 1913; h/115 N 4th St, Decatur, IN 46733; ba/Decatur; p/William M and Rosella Carlson Masterson (dec); ed/Rel Tchr's Cert; pa/Sister Rel Order; Team Mem, Spanish Pastoral Min; Rel Instr w Adults & Chd; cp/St Action Com for Migrants; Third World Bd Mem; Nat Migrant Wkr Com; E Coast Migrant Projs Bd; r/Rom Cath: Sister; hon/W/W Rel.

MASTERSON, THOMAS ROBERT oc/Consultant; b/Sept 17, 1915; h/873 N Superior Ave, Decatur, GA 30033; ba/Atlanta, GA; m/Dorothy J; c/Katherine Irene, Judith Amanda, Miriam A; p/Peter A and Isobel Woods Masterson (dec); ed/PhB 1946, MBA 1948, PhD 1956 Univ Chgo; mil/USAF 1940-45; pa/Mgmt Conslt; Prof Sch Bus Adm, Emory Univ; Author 4 Books & Pub'd 30 Articles Profl Jours; Am Soc Pers Adm; Acad Mgmt; Am Mgmt Assn; AAUP; So Mgmt Assn; Ga Conservancy; Exec Ofcr, Ctr for Corp Policy & Dir (Emory Univ); Bd Dirs: Mandabach & Simms Inc, Others; cp/C of C; hon/Rec'd Num Dist'd Ser Awds.

MATHER, ROGER FREDERICK oc/Researcher; b/May 27, 1917; h/308 4th Ave, Iowa City, IA 52240; ba/Iowa City; m/Betty Bang; c/Arielle Diane, Christopher Richard; p/Richard and Marie L G C A Mather (dec); ed/BA w Hons, MA Cambridge Univ (England); MSc Mass Inst Technol; pa/Reschr & Mus Instr, Iowa City Sch of Music; Contbr Num Articles Profl Jours; Currently Writing Sev Books; Mem Num Mus, Sci & Engrg Assns; r/Epis.

MATHEWS, HENRY JAMES oc/Dentist; b/Oct 9, 1915; h/4618 Clausen, Western Springs, IL 60558; ba/Chicago, IL; m/Floretta Esther; c/Beth Ann, Jeanne Kay, James Henry; p/Christopher and Emily Mathews (dec); ed/DD; mil/Maj Dental Corps; pa/Am Dental Assn; Ill St Dental Soc; Chgo Dental Soc; cp/Wn Springs Hist Soc; Luth Layman's Leag; Bd of Control, Concordia Col; r/Luth; hon/Fellow Am Col Dentists; Fellow Odoutographic Soc Chgo.

MATHEWS, JAMES R oc/Minister; b/Nov 8, 1942; h/4½ M, Vanderbilt Hill, Juncau, AK 99802; ba/Juncau; m/Gloria Jean; c/Jeffry Douglas, Tonya Annette, Thomas Rowden; p/Jesse J and Abbie R Mathews, Kirbyville, TX; ed/BS E Tex Bapt Col; MDiv SWn Bapt Theol Sem; pa/Bd Mem Var Bapt Agencies; Exec Bd, Alaska Bapt Conv; cp/Leg Chaplain; r/So Bapt; hon/W/W Rel; Commun Ldrs & Noteworthy Ams.

MATHEWSON, HUGH SPALDING

oc/Physician; Educator; b/Sept 20, 1921; h/6523 Overbrook Rd, Shawnee Mission, KS 66208; m/Hazel; c/5; p/Walter Eldridge and Jenny L Jones Mathewson; ed/BA; MD; mil/USNR; pa/Univ Kansas Med Ctr: Prof Anesthesiology, Med Dir Respiratory Therapy; Dir Anesthesia, Kansas City Gen Hosp; Head Sect of Anesthesia, St Luke's Hosp (Kansas City); Mo Soc Anesthesiols; Kansas Soc Anesthesiols (Past Pres); Author: *Structural Forms of Anesthetic Compounds, Respiratory Therapy in Critical Care, Pharmacol for Respiratory Therapists*, Others; cp/Kansas City Museum; hon/Rec'd Bird Literary Prize; Phi Beta Kappa; Sigma Xi; Biogl Listings.

MATHISEN, HELEN ALICE oc/Retired; b/Mar 27, 1915; h/Box 391, Loma Linda, CA 92354; m/Maurice Earl; p/John and Inga Kobler (dec); ed/BS Pacific Union Col 1937; Former Tchr & Secy Preparatory Schs (7 Yrs); Ser'd as Secy to 4 Pres, Pacific Union Col (16 Yrs); Secy Dean of Sch of Nsg, Loma Linda Univ 1963-1979; cp/City Planning Comm, Loma Linda; Tuesday Evening Ladies Clb; Loma Linda Wom's Bus & Profl Clb; Loma Linda Wom's Clb; Secy, Bd Dirs, Loma Linda Credit Union; Pacific Union Col Alumni Assn; Author *Grade Point Average Index*; r/SDA: Secy & Supt, Sabbath Sch; hon/Commun Ldrs & Noteworthy Ams; Notable Ams; World W/W Wom; Book of Hon; DIB; Others.

MATSON, LARRY JAMES oc/Consultant; b/Feb 15, 1944; h/222 Deckbar Ave, Apt 127, New Orleans, LA 70121; ba/New Orleans; c/Amy Lynne; p/Leonard P Matson, Hacienda Hghts, CA; Marilyn M Matson (dec); ed/Aerospace Engrg, Auburn Univ; mil/AUS 1969-71; pa/Broadcasting Conslt; Sportscaster; cp/Cystic Fibrosis Foun; r/Meth; hon/Sigma Delta Chi; Best Play-by-Play Ala; Rec'd AP Radio/TV Awd.

MATSON, VIRGINIA F oc/Educator; b/Aug 25, 1914; h/950 N St Mary's Rd, Libertyville, IL 60048; ba/Lake Forest, IL; m/Edward J; c/Karin M Renfer (Mrs Rudolf A Jr), Sara M Drake (Mrs Carl B III), E Robert, Lawrence D, David O; p/Axel George and Mae D Freebers (dec); ed/BA Univ Ky; MA NWn Univ; pa/Pres Grove Sch; Treas, Ill Coun for Exceptional Chd; cp/Dem; r/Quaker: Lake Forest Soc of Friends; hon/Rec'd Friends of Lit Novel Awd; Rec'd Chgo "I Will" Awd; Humanitarian of Yr, Ill Wom's Aux Med Soc.

MATTHEWS, ELSIE C SPEARS oc/Legal Researcher; Writer; b/Aug 8, 1901; h/926 Sandstone Dr, Bartlesville, OK 74003; m/Thomas A (dec); ed/Thomas A II, Byron Stewart; p/Byron A and Catharine Clark Spears (dec); ed/BA Wheaton Col 1923; NWn Univ Law Sch 1922-24; pa/Asst Compiler Codes of Ordinances, Ill 1928-70; Compiler of Digests of Ill Statutes 1928-70; Asst Editor "Current Mun Probs" 1959-76; Asst Author Mun Ordinances 1959-; Asst Compiler Supplements to Mun Ordinances 1960-; cp/Chm, Conserv & Multiple Use of Public Lands; Rocky Mountain & Fdn Gem & Mineral Socs Inc; Am Fdn Gem & Mineral Socs: Conserv & Public Relats Com; Johnny Horizon Prog; r/Presb; hon/Rec'd Plaque for Anti-Litter Work; Rec'd Plaque Apprec, Osage Hills Gem & Mineral Soc; Rec'd Commend, Am Fdn & Rocky Mountain Gem & Mineral Socs; Rec'd Bronze Medallion for Commun Ser; Fellow, Intl Biogl Soc; Fellow, Am Biogl Soc; 2000 Wom Achmt; W/W Commun Ser; Personalities of S; Others.

MATTHEWS, EVAN JAN oc/Puppeteer; b/Apr 2, 1954; h/1241 Goodwin Rd NE, Atlanta, GA 30324; ba/Same; m/Gary McCoy; p/Zane A Williams, Simpsonville, SC; Polly H Neal, Atlanta; ed/BA; pa/SEn Puppet Guild; Puppeteers of Am; hon/Shared UNIMA Awd for Excell in Art of Puppetry; Personalities of S; W/W Am HS Drama.

MATTHEWS, HENRY JAMES oc/Counselor; b/Dec 13, 1905; h/455 SW 16th Ave, #B8, Miami, FL 33135; ba/Miami; m/Hilda Milagro Valle; c/Stephson Manuel Lopez;

p/Hendricus Jacobus Suiker and Johanna Petronella Schoenmaker, Holland; ed/MA Salem St Col 1964; pa/Ordained Priest 1934; Conslr for Elderly; Reschr Gerontology; cp/Intl Liaison for Peace & Human Rights; r/Rom Cath.

MATTHEWS, MYRETA JULIA oc/Retired Teacher; b/Apr 30, 1903; h/PO Box 127, Liberty Hill, TX 78642; p/Joseph Neely and Emma Marrs Matthews (dec); ed/BS SW Tex Univ 1934; MEd Univ Tex-A 1943; pa/Primary Tchr (1st Grade) 48 Yrs, Tex Public Schs; Rancher; cp/DAR; OES; Secy Local Civic Assn; Lib Bd; Cult Affairs Coun; Chm, Williamson Co Hist Comm; r/United Meth Ch (Austin, Tex); hon/Delta Kappa Gamma; Rec'd John Ben Shepperd Awd; Outstg Co Chm, San Antonio (Tex).

MATTOX, JAMES ALBON oc/Congressman; b/Aug 29, 1943; h/1100 Valencia, Dallas, TX 75223; ba/Dallas; p/Norman Mattox, Dallas; Mary Mattox (dec); ed/BS magna cum laude, Baylor Univ 1965; Juris Doct, So Meth Univ Sch of Law 1968; pa/US Ho of Reps: Rep 5th Dist, Elected 1976 (Com Assignments: Banking, Fin & Urban Affairs; Budget Com; Fin Insts Supvn; Coinage & Hist Preserv; Task Force on Nat Security; Others), Re-elected 1978; Tex St Ho of Reps: 1972, Re-elected 1974; Atty Crowder, Mattox & Morris (Law Firm), Est'd 1970; Former Asst DA, Dallas Co 1968-70; Congl Intern in Office of Earle Cabell, Summer 1967; Other Positions: Dallas, St of Tex Bar Assns; Admit'd to US Supr Ct, US Ct of Appeals (5th Circuit), US Dist Ct, Nn & Wn Tex Dists; Tex Trial Lwyrs Assn; Tex Crim Lwyrs Assn; cp/Former Dem Precinct Chm; Del to Dallas Co Dem Conv; Campaign Worker: Mgr for Judge Robert Hughes 1968; Former Del to 16th Dist Senatorial & St Dem Convs; r/E Grand Bapt Ch (Dallas): Mem, Pres SS Class, Former SS Dir, Christian Life Com; hon/Rec'd Leg of Yr Awd, Dallas Co Wom's Polit Caucus; Outstg Freshman Rep, Tex Intercol Students' Assn; One of Ten Best Legs, *Tex Monthly Mag*; Rec'd Wall St Jour Awd; Rec'd Alpha Kappa Psi S'ship Key; Alpha Chi; Beta Gamma Sigma; Omicron Delta Kappa; Rec'd Jackson Hughes S'ship; Rec'd Humble Oil & Refining Co S'ship; Others.

MATTY, RICHARD P oc/State Legislator; b/Sept 16, 1932; h/Crivitz, WI 54114; ba/Madison, WI; m/Sandra Borman; c/Paul, David, Shelly, Rhonda, Mike, Scott, Kerry; p/Paul Matykowski, Crivitz; mil/USAF 4 Yrs; pa/Ser'g 3rd Term on Gov's Coun on Hwy Safety (VChm), Gen Assembly's Trans, Veterans & Mil Affairs Coms, Com on Third Reading; Owner & Operator Small Bus 23 Yrs;

Marinette Co Coroner 5 Yrs; cp/Past VChm, Wis Conserv Cong; Past Pres, Crivitz Rec Assn; Past Pres, NE Wis Conserv Coun; Past Cmdr, Amvets Post 68; Am Legion; VFW; Elks Clb; Lion's Clb; Former Scoutmaster BSA; Num Sportsmen's Clbs; Hon Mem, Marinette JCs; r/St Mary's Cath Ch (Crivitz).

MATUSIK, WALTER MICHAEL oc/Principal; b/Sept 27, 1923; h/4331 Ivy St, E Chicago, IN 46312; ba/E Chgo; m/Dorothy L; c/Denise, Mark, Sharon; p/John Matusik (dec); Stephanie Matusik, Highland, IN; ed/BA; MA; Ed Spec; mil/AUS; pa/Prin, Joseph L Block Jr HS 1967-; Prin, Carrie Gosch Elem Sch 1958-67; Prin, James Garfield Sch

1955-58; Other Positions; Proj Supvr, E Chgo Public Schs 1966-67: "Parenthood in a Free Nation" (Survey Proj); Co-author *Reading Activs in the Primary Grades* (1962); NEA; Nat Elem & Sec'dy Sch Prin Assn; Others; cp/Cmdr Am Legion; Lion's Clb; Elks; Moose; PTA; Others; r/Rom Cath; hon/Outstg Sch Admr; Rec'd Am Legion Dist'd Ser Awd; Rec'd Purple Heart; Rec'd French Croix de Guerre; Others.

MAUGHAN, MEREDITH GAIL oc/Reading Specialist; b/Oct 17, 1935; h/1451 Creekside Dr, #2089, Walnut Creek, CA 94596; ba/Lafayette, CA; p/Alexander R Maughan, Modesto, CA; Marion Cross Maughan (dec); ed/AA, BA Cal St Univ-SJ; MA Stanford Univ; pa/Intl, Cal & Contra Costa Reading Assns; Reading Specs of Cal; NEA; CTA; Local Tchrs' Orgs; Assn for Supvn & Curric Devel; cp/Oakland Museum Assn; Var Alumni Assns; hon/Phi Kappa Phi; Kappa Delta Pi; Pi Lambda Theta; Alpha Delta Kappa; Rec'd PTA Life Mem Ser Awd; DIB; Personalities of W&MW; Others.

MAULDIN, JEAN oc/Executive; b/Aug 16, 1923; h/102 E 45th St, Savannah, GA 31405; ba/Santa Ana, CA; c/William Timothy III, Bruce Patrick; p/James Wiley and Lena Leora Crain Humphries, Northridge, CA; ed/BS Hardin Simmons Univ 1943; MS Univ So Cal 1961; Addit Studies; pa/Pres, Stardust Aviation Inc 1962-77; Pres Mauldin & Staff, Public Relats 1958-77; Author: *The Consummate Barnstormer* (1962), *The Daredevil Clown* (1963), Others; Am Mgmt Assn; cp/Dem Party of Ga; Am Cancer Crusade Cal; Treas, Dem Alternative; Newport Beach Dem Clb; E Orange Co Dem Clb; LA Dem Wom's Forum; Ga Dem Wom's Fdn; Cal St Ctl Com; Orange Co Dem Ctl Com; Del Wn Sts Dem Conv; Del Cal Dem Conv; Del Cal Dem Coun Convs; Del Law of the Sea; Del Dem Nat Conv; Friends of Santa Ana McFadden Public Libs; Others; r/Epis; hon/Mu Phi Epsilon; Others.

MAUPIN, BENITA M oc/Interpreter; b/Sept 7, 1934; h/4339 E Ruth Pl, Orange, CA 92669; m/Charles L; c/Thomas J, Linda L M Brown; p/Arthur J and Letha M Grider, Orange; pa/Interpreter for the Deaf; Nat Registry of Interpreters for the Deaf; So Cal Registry of Interpreters for the Deaf; CCIA; Gtr LA Coun on Deafness; r/Prot; hon/Certs from NRID; W/W Am Wom.

MAURER, MICHELE LYNNE oc/Supervisor; b/Jun 10, 1948; h/12005 King Rd, Roswell, GA 30075; Rocky Hill, CT; ba/Hartford, CT; p/Ralph C and Evelyn M Maurer, Roswell; ed/BA cum laude 1970, MS 1972 Univ Ga; Cert in Gen Ins, Ins Inst Am 1976; Addit Studies; pa/Commercial Multiperil Ins Supvr, Aetna Ins Co; Cert'd Property & Casualty Ins; Am Mktg Assn; Mariners' Clb; Others; cp/Roswell Hist Soc; r/Roswell Presb Ch: Mem; hon/Pi Delta Phi; Outstg Yg Wom; W/W S&SW; Personalities of S; DIB.

MAUST, EZMA M COBB oc/Music Teacher; b/Jan 29, 1914; h/5714 Academy Dr, Paradise, CA 95969; ba/Same; m/Paul C; c/Delores Jean M Jones, Patricia Ann M Hibben, Carol Lee M Scheve; Lana Elaine M Bennett, Paul C Jr; p/Omer Cobb (dec); Myrtle A Bingham, Paradise; ed/AA Butte Col; BA Chgo St Univ; Dipl Sherwood Mus Sch; Addit Studies; pa/Piano, Organ, Harmony & Theory Instr; Tchr 25 Yrs; Nat Guild Piano Tchrs; cp/Former PTA Pres; r/Bapt: Dir Yth Choir, Pianist, Organist, Choir Mem; hon/Rec'd Cert, Nat Guild Piano Tchrs; Hon Roll, NGPT.

MAXSON, HARMON DAVID oc/Lawyer; b/Feb 4, 1927; h/3108 Parkway, Cheverly, MD 21785; ba/Washington, DC; m/Marcia Grace; c/Susan, Stanley, Harley; p/Frank and Otilda Marie Maxson (dec); ed/BA; BCL; JD; mil/AUS; USN; pa/Chm Indian Law Com, Fed Bar Assn; Justice, PAD Law Frat; cp/Pres Cheverly Masonic Lodge; Bd Dirs, Ariz St Soc; r/Seneca Indian; hon/Rec'd Num Outstg Ser Awds.

MAXWELL, ROBERT E oc/Judge; b/Mar 15, 1924; h/PO Box 1818, Elkins, WV 26241; ba/Elkins; m/Ann G; c/Mary Ann M Durland, Carol Lynn, Ellen L, Earl W; p/Earl L and Nellie E Maxwell (dec); ed/Attended Davis & Elkins Col; LLB W Va Univ; mil/Air Transport Command; pa/US Dist Judge, Nn Dist of W Va; Chm Budget Com, Judicial Conf US; Fac Mem, Fed Judicial Ctr; r/Cath; hon/Rec'd Dist'd Ser Awd, D & E Col.

MAXWELL, STANLEY FIELDING oc/Sovereign Grand Commander; b/Apr 27, 1910; h/365 Haverhill St, Reading, MA 01876; ba/Lexington, MA; m/Dorothy R; c/Stanley F Jr, Allen R; p/James M and Alice C Maxwell (dec); ed/BA; pa/33° Masons: Sovereign Grand Cmdr (Supr Coun), Intl Supr Coun (Order of DeMolay) 1975-, Exec Com George Wash Masonic Nat Meml Assn, Former Exec Secy Supr Coun, Former Sovereign Grand Inspector Gen, Former High Priest, Others; Quincy Mkt Cold Storage & Warehouse Co (Boston, Mass) 1929-45; Office Mgr, United Farmers of New England Inc 1945-65; cp/Bay St Conclave; Red Cross of Constantine (Past Sovereign); Hon Mem, Canada's Grand Imperial Conclave; Former Secy-Gen, Societas Rosicrucuiana; Royal Order of Scotland; Nat Sojourners; High Twelve Intl; Aleppo Temple; Former Mem Bd Govs, Shrine Burns Inst; Hon Trustee Ill Masonic Med Ctr; Former Trustee of Cemeteries; Capital Expenditures Planning Com, Town of Reading; Rationing Bd WWII; r/Prot; hon/Rec'd Hon Legion of Hon Deg, DeMolay Foun; Hon Mem Supr Couns (Masons): Dominican Republic, England, Chile, Panama, France, Others; Rec'd Benjamin Hurd & Paul Revere Medals, Grand Royal Arch Chapt Masons; Rec'd Henry Price Medal, Grand Lodge of Mass; Rec'd Philip C Tucker Awd, Grand Lodge of Vermont; Rec'd Christopher Champlin Medal, Grand Lodge of RI; Others.

MAY, JOHN C oc/Professor; b/Dec 20, 1944; h/2603 Berkshire Rd, Augusta, GA 30904; ba/Augusta; m/Millicent A Crockett, Slidell, LA; ed/BA cum laude, 1967, MA 1969, PhD 1971 LSU; mil/Col ROTC; pa/Asst Prof German; Var Col Coms; Pub'd Poetry Sev Jours;

Translations of German Poetry; Am Poetry Soc; Modern Lang Assn; AATG; cp/Narration for C of C; Merit Badge Cnslr, BSA; Vol ARC; hon/Phi Eta Sigma; Delta Phi Alpha; Mu Sigma Rho; Phi Kappa Phi; Finalist, J B White Lit Competition.

MAY, JUDY GAIL oc/Counselor; Writer; b/Sept 5, 1943; h/E 1 Hillside Ct, Highlands, NJ 07732; ba/Matawan, NJ; m/Dean E; p/Casimir and Elizabeth Nesterowicz Rozwat, Palatine, IL; ed/Loyola Univ; Rome, Italy; pa/Pres & Dir, May Communs Inc 1976-; Acct Dir, Infoplan Intl Public Relats (NYC) 1973-76; Other Positions; Author: *Scuba Divers' Guide to Underwater Ventures* (1973); Co-author *Great Diving - 1* (1974); Pub'd Syndicated Column; Contbr Articles Mags & Jours; cp/Envir Chm, NJ Coun Diving Clbs; Underwater & Indust Photog; Lectr on Marine Life; r/Cath; hon/W/W Am Wom.

MAY, MARION LOUISE oc/Supervisor; b/Apr 26, 1937; h/957 W Montana, Chicago, IL 60614; ba/Chgo; m/Philip L; c/Trina L; p/Kylie F Bovee (dec); Frances M Bovee, Ithaca, MI; ed/BS En Mich Univ 1959; Post Grad Studies, Wn Mich Univ; pa/Reg'd

Occupational Therapist; Physical/Occupational Therapist IV: Supvr OT, Ill Chd's Hosp Sch 1976-; Physical Rehab Therapist II: Student Coor, Ill Chd's Hosp Sch 1973-76; Occupational Therapist, Kalamazoo Public Schs (Mich) 1966-72; Conslt Perceptual Devel, St Charles Public Schs (Mich) 1965-66; Pvt Pract OT, Saginaw (Mich) 1964-66; Other Positions; Chgo Area Coun OT Dirs; Am OT Assn; Ill OT Assn; Conslt, United CP of Chgo; cp/Nat Assn Riding for Handicapped; Friends of Handicapped; r/Prot; hon/W/W Am Wom.

MAYNARD, KENNETH DELANO oc/Minister; b/Aug 30, 1914; h/Rt 4, Box 32 A, Sylvester, GA 31791; ba/Sylvester; m/Kathleen Henning; c/Gregory Owen, Mignon; p/Lorenza Dow and Nancy Maynard (dec); ed/Freed-Hardeman Col; pa/Ordained Min 1946; Supt, Tenn Chd's Home; cp/Civitan Clb; Am Cancer Soc; Parent Adv Coun; r/Ch of Christ; hon/WOW; Commend Ser Awd; Pres' Awd; Intl Civitan.

MAYNOR, HAL W JR oc/Retired Engineer; b/Oct 5, 1917; h/518 Cary Dr, Auburn, AL 36830; m/Marjorie Baker; c/Sandra M Averhart, Susan Lynne, Hal W III; p/Hal W Sr and Ophelia Hill Maynor (dec); ed/BS 1944, MS 1947, PhD 1954 Univ Ky; mil/WWII; pa/Auburn Univ: Prof Emeritus (Dept Mech Engrg) 1978, Prof 1959-78; Assoc Prof Mining & Metall Engrg, Univ Ky 1957-59; Res Engr, Gen Electric Co (Louisville, Ky) 1954-57; Res: "Devel of Technique to Determine Fracture Toughness of Sheet Steel in Short Transverse Dir" (AUS Missile Command) 1970-71, Proj Ldr "Investigation of Mechanisms of Failure of High-Strength Materials" (AUS Missile Command) 1959-66, Others; Conslt: Morris Trucking Co (Anniston, Ala) 1968, Hand & Arendall (Law Firm) 1968, Hobbs & Copeland (Law Firm) 1969, Others; Other Positions; Contbr Num Articles Profl Jours; Ala Acad Sci; NY Acad Sci; Ky Acad Sci; Am Soc Metals; AIMMPE; ASEE; Ala Soc Profl Engrs; Nat Soc Profl Engrs; Sci Res Soc Am; Others; cp/Former Mem Kiwanis; Former Mem Bd Dirs, Auburn Univ Fed Credit Union; Former Bd Mem, Friends of Auburn Lib; Others; r/Village Christian Ch (Auburn): Bd Dirs; hon/Rec'd 6 Bronze Stars & 1 Silver Star; Rec'd Commends: Univ Ky Alumni Assn & AUS Missile Command; Awd'd Medal for Ser'g 2nd World Metall Cong; Rec'd Cert of Merit, DIB; Rec'd Grant, Am Soc for Testing & Materials; Rec'd Dipl for Dist'd Achmt, 2000 Men Achmt; Rec'd Cert Recog for Engrg Res & Reviews; Others.

MAYOL, PEDRO MAGDIEL oc/Physician; b/Jan 22, 1933; h/H-16, Villa Caparra, PR 00657; ba/Bayamon, PR; m/Nohemi Urdaz; c/Nancy, Rebecca, Sandra Nohemi, Magdiel; p/Bartolo Mayol Arroyo and Ana Rita Serrano, Hato Rey, PR; ed/BS; MD; mil/USAR 1955-57; US Public Hlth Ser 1962-63; pa/Asst Prof Pediatrics, Puerto Rico Sch of Med; Med Dir Pediatric Pulmonary Ctr, Univ Puerto Rico; Chief of Pediatrics, San Pablo Hosp; cp/Past VP Rotary Clb; Dir Puerto Rico Lung Assn; r/Prot; hon/Rec'd Nestle Awd for Pediatrics; Rec'd Chest Medal, PR Lung Assn; Others.

MAYS, LARRY WESLEY oc/Professor; b/Feb 2, 1948; h/8703 Sparta Ln, Round Rock, TX 78664; ba/Austin, TX; m/Marge; p/Fred W and Lola M Mays, Pittsfield, IL; ed/BS 1970, MS 1971 Univ Mo; PhD Univ Ill 1975; mil/AUS 1970-73; pa/Asst Prof Civil Engrg, Univ Tex-A; Am Soc Civil Engrs; Am Geophysical Union; Am Water Resources Assn; Pub'd Articles Profl Jours; cp/Trumpet Player, Austin Civic Wind Ensemble; hon/Chi Epsilon; Sigma Xi; Outstg Yg Men Am; W/W S&SW.

MAYSILLES, ELIZABETH oc/Educator; h/155 E 77th St, New York, NY 10021; p/Evers and Rose (dec); ed/BA; MA; Cand PhD; pa/Instr Speech Communs; Radio Announcer; Conducted Own Prog; cp/Telephone Cnslr; IPA; UN Inst NYU;

r/Christian; hon/Alpha Psi Omega; Kappa Delta Pi; Rec'd Bodman S'ship, NYU; W/W Am Wom; World W/W Wom.

MAZELAUSKAS, M GABRIELLE oc/Educator; b/Feb 2, 1906; h/Grove & McRobert Rd, Pittsburgh, PA 15234; ba/Same; p/Anthony and Mary Katauskas Mazelauskas (dec); ed/BS; MSc; PhD; pa/Sister of Rel Order; Tchr in Sec'dy Schs of Pa, Conn & Mich 51 Yrs; Prin in Pa, Conn & Mich Schs; Lectr, Duquesne Univ Ext Courses; Diocesan Sch Bd; Nat Biol Tchrs Assn: Dir-at-Large 1963-65, Nat Chm Cath Schs Mbrship Com, VP 1966, Past Mem Edit Staff of ABT, Others; Nat Sci Tchrs Assn: Nom'g Com, Adv Cm "Vistas in Sci" Future Scists, Others; Pgh Diocesan Sci & Math Assn: VP, Past Chm Biol Sect, Editor, Others; VP, Allegheny Inst for Environmental Studies; AAAS; Pa Jr Acad Sci: Dir Reg 7 1947, St Dir 1970, Pres, Others; Var Profl Pubs; Others; cp/Interagy Coun on Smoking & Hlth; r/Rom Cath: Sisters of St Francis; hon/Cits from Buhl Planetarium Sci Fair, Pa Jr Acad; Cert of Merit, Spectropscopy Soc of Pgh; Kevin Burns Cit for Excel in Sci Tchg; Nom Outstg Biol Tchr; Ford Future Scists Awd; Cits from Gov of Pa & St Dept; Ser Awd, Pa Sci Tchrs; Hon Mem, Nat Biol Tchrs Assn of Boston; Others.

MBIRIKA, SIR ABUKUSE V E P oc/Fraternal Executive; b/May 15, 1935; h/382 Ctl Park W, New York, NY 10025; ba/NYC; m/Gloria; c/Andayi, Ayieta, Abukuse III; p/Peter Andayi Mbirika (dec); Naomi Mbirika, Kenya, E Africa; ed/BA;

MA; PhD; pa/Secy of State, Knights of Malta; Prof of Higher Ed; Diplomat; cp/Chm Bd African Universal Inc; r/Prot; hon/Knight of Grand Cross; Knight of Justice; Rec'd Cert Achmt; Men Achmt; Others.

MEAD, FRANK W oc/Entomologist; b/Jun 11, 1922; h/2035 NE 6th Terrace, Gainesville, FL 32601; ba/Gainesville; m/Eileen C; c/David H, Gregory S; p/A D Mead, Columbus, OH; ed/BS 1949, MS 1949 Ohio St Univ; PhD NC St Univ 1968; mil/AUS Med Dept 1943-46; pa/Entomologist, Fla Dept Agri; St Survey Entomol; Adj Prof, Univ Fla; Secy, Fla Entomol Soc; Exec

Com SE Branch, Entomol Soc Am; Soc Sys Zoologists; Am Mosquito Control Assn; Fla Ant-Mosquito Assn; Nat & Fla Audubon Socs; Fla Ornithological Soc; Entomol Soc Wash; Others; cp/Steer'g Com, Regional Blood Bank; Alachua Hist Soc; SAR; Bd Dirs, Alachua Awds Com; Others; r/Presb; hon/Rec'd Cert Apprec, Fla Entomol Soc; Sigma Xi; Gamma Sigma Delta; Registry Profl Entomologists.

MEADOR, BEN FRANKLIN JR oc/Executive; b/Apr 12, 1939; h/4012 Paraguay, Pasadena, TX 77504; ba/Pasadena; m/Dolores; c/Melinda, Trey; p/B F and Reba Meador, Houston, TX; ed/BBA Lamar Univ 1962; pa/Pres, Meador-Brady Pers Sers Inc & Meador-Brady Assocs; VP Pasadena Honda Dealership; Nat Employmt Assn; Tex Pvt Employmt Assn; Houston & Nat Assns Temporary Sers; Nat Fdn Independent Bus; cp/Bd Dirs, Pasadena Nat Bank; Bd Dirs, C of C; Rotary Clb; r/Meth.

MEADOR, LENORA MELISSA oc/Retired Teacher; b/Aug 31, 1904; h/Rt 2, Box 141, Belton, TX 76513; m/(dec); c/Mona LeVonne; p/William Henry and Nancy Ida McKamie (dec); ed/BA; MEd; pa/Ret'd Admr; Tex Execs; Assn Childhood Ed; Ret'd Tchrs Assn; Intl Reading Assn; Others; cp/Var Clbs & Activs; r/Meth; hon/Life Mem PTA; Rec'd Plaque, Dickson Sch (Temple, Tex); Rec'd Cert of Hon, Am Heritage; Boss of Yr, Am Bus Wom's Assn.

MEAGHER, CHARLES FRANKLIN oc/Executive; b/Nov 25, 1925; h/PO Box 124, Prospect, TN 38477; ba/Prospect; m/June Elizabeth Jones; c/Vicki Jo, Charles Lee, David Jonathan, Beth Carol, Nancy Jean, Ellen Lee; p/Arch and Winnie Wayne Webster (dec); ed/BS; mil/USN 1944-46; pa/Engrg Co Exec; Pilot, Aircraft & Power Mech; Profl Engr; Am Rocket Soc; EAA; r/Prot: Born Again; hon/Biogl Listing.

MEANS, WILLERMA FRAZIER oc/Librarian; b/Apr 23; PO Box 606, St George, SC 29477; m/Paul Allen; p/Patrick and Cora Lee Cohen Frazier, St George; ed/BS SC St Col 1968; MS Univ Ill 1969; pa/Media Spec, St George Elem Sch 1973-; Eng Tchr, Williams Meml Adult Sch 1973-75; Reading Tchr, Williams Meml Sch 1973-74; Nat Lib Med (Bethesda, Md): Adm Libn 1970, Lib Assoc 1969-70; Gov's Conf on Libs; Regional Planning Com; SCEA Fed Lobbying Team; ITV Regional Adv Coun; Intl Reading Assn; SCASL; AECT of SC; NEA; SCEA; Others; cp/DRE; Assn for Study Afro-Am Life & Hist; UTP; SC Chd's Book Awds Com; St George Elem & Williams Meml Schs PTA; Sch Fin Adv Coun; PACE; Leg Chrperson; Others; r/Fine Bapt'd Holiness; hon/Rec'd Lib Sci Awd; Rec'd USPHS F'ship; Outstg Dist Worker, FBH Ch; Alpha Gamma.

MEEKER, DUANE oc/Engineer; b/May 12, 1940; h/Rt 2, Box 157, Logansport, IN 46947; ba/Same; m/Kay Ann Purdy; c/Karen Sue, Barbara Lynn, James Edward, Janet Lee; p/C Eldo and Florence Meeker, Logansport; ed/BS Purdue Univ 1966; MIT 1964; pa/Reg'd Profl Engr, St of Ind; Owner & Chief Engr, Meeker Agri Conslts; Farmer (Clinton Township); Ind Sect, Am Soc Agri Engrs: Past Pres, VP & Secy-Treas; Ind Soc Profl Engrs; Nat Soc Profl Engrs; Top Farmer of Am Assn; Profl Farmers Am; Cass Co Beef Cattle Assn: Bd Dirs, VP; Farm Bur; Others; Author Profl Articles; cp/Clinton Township Vol Fire Dept; Purdue Agri Alumni Assn; Rotary: Bd Dirs, Com Chm; Cass Co Crop & Livestock Improvemt Assn: Bd Dirs, Past Pres, Others; Mason; Scottish Rite; Others; r/Webb Chapel United Meth Ch: Camp Coor, Adult Coor, Lay Ldr, Adm Bd, Lay Speaker, SS Tchr, Pastor-Parrish Com; hon/Cass Co, Ind & Nat Outstg Yg Farmer; W/W; Commun Ldrs & Noteworthy Ams; Deputy St Fire Marshall; Others.

MEEKS, ELSIE M oc/Retired Medical Record Administrator; b/Jun 8, 1917; h/3635 College Ave #46, San Diego, CA 92115; m/Leslie Cadillace Sr (dec); c/2; p/Downey Brown and Maude Goodwin; ed/AA E Los Angeles Jr Col; Nat Cert as Reg'd Record Admr; pa/Former Asst Med Records Dir, Martin Luther King Hosp (LA); Former Tchr Med Records (Part-time), LA City Unified Sch Dist; cp/Magella C Mars Unit #752, Am Legion Aux; Vol Worker, W LA Veterans Ctr, Brentwood & Wadsworth Hosp; Myasthenia Gravis Foun; Regal Dames Aux for Myasthenia Gravis; Ctr for Wom's Studies Inc; Cub Scout Den Mother; LA Clb of Nat

Assn Negro BPW Clbs; Anthurium Social & Charity Clb; Wom at Work Groups; Vol Kairos Yth House; Active Mbrship Drives for Urban Leag, NAACP & YWCA; Others; r/Ch of Christ: Bible Sch Tchr, Yth Com, Visitation Team, Vacation Bible Sch Worker; Mem Missionary Tean From Normandie Ch of Christ to Georgetown, Guyana; hon/Rec'd Ser Pin, VA; Den Mother's Awd & Instr Tng Cert, BSA; Basic & Adv'd Tchr Tng Cert, Bible Tchrs Normandie Ch of Christ; Sojourner Truth Plaque, Nat Assn Negro BPW Clbs; 20-Yr Pin, Myasthenia Gravis Foun (Cal Chapt); Cert Apprec, Normandie Christian Sch; Biogl Listings.

MEFFERD, ROY B JR oc/Researcher; Educator; b/Sep 22, 1920; h/823 Longview Dr, Sugar Land, TX 77478; ba/Houston, TX; m/Mary Louise Key; c/Marsha Ellen Steele, Roy Scott; p/Roy B Sr and Delfa Russell Mefferd (dec); ed/BS 1940; MS; PhD 1951; mil/Ret'd Col, USAR; pa/Dir, Psychi & Psychosomatic Res Lab, VA Medical Ctr 1959-; Prof Physiology, Baylor Col of Med 1959-; Adj Prof Psychol, Grad Sch, Univ of Houston 1977-; Adj Prof Behavioral Scis, Univ Tex Sch of Public Hlth; Pres, Birkman-Mefferd Res Foun 1972-; cp/BSA 10 yrs; FFA Lone Star Farmer; Former Voc Agri Tchr; hon/Rosalie B Hite Fellow in Cancer Res, Univ Tex; Damon Runyon Fellow in Cancer Res; Author over 225 Sci Pubs.

MEGILL, VIRGIL GLEN JR oc/Clergyman; b/Feb 28, 1924; h/83 S Courtland St, E Stroudsburg, PA 18301; ba/E Stroudsburg; m/Ruth Elizabeth Armstrong; c/Virgil G III, Margaret Faith, Caroline Beth; p/V Glen and Rosie Madge Olney Megill, Hutchinson, KS; ed/BA; MDiv; MA; pa/Key 73 Nat Mass Media Dir 1972-74; cp/Temporary Chm, Commun Action Coun (Ephrata); r/United Meth.

MEHLINGER, KERMIT THORPE oc/Psychiatrist; b/Jun 17, 1918; h/5555 S Everett, Chicago, IL 60637; ba/Chgo; m/Lillian; c/Diane M Craig, Bonnie M Threatte, Renee M Mitchell, Jill; p/Eugene and Bonita Mehlinger (dec); ed/BA Oberlin Col; MD Howard Univ; mil/Air Corps & Inf, WWII; pa/Assoc Prof Clinical Psych, Rush Med Sch; Prof Communs, Columbia Col; Chm Hlth Care Com, Chgo Med Soc; cp/Bd Mem, Gateway Houses Incorp; r/Prot; hon/Rec'd Cit for Hlth Care to Poor, AMA; Fellow, Am Psych Assn.

MEHTA, VED PARKASH oc/Writer; b/Mar 21, 1934; ba/25 W 43rd St, New York, NY 10036; p/Amolak Ram and Shanti Devi Mehra Mehta; ed/BA Pomona Col 1956; BA Balliol Col 1959; MA Harvard Univ 1961; pa/Staff Writer, *The New Yorker* 1961-; Author: *Face to Face* (1957), *Walking the Indian Streets* (1960), *Fly and the Fly-Bottle* (1963), *The New Theologian* (1965), *Delinquent Chacha* (1967), *The New India* (1978), Others; Author Num Mag Articles & Stories; hon/Phi Beta Kappa; Rec'd Harvard Prize F'ship & Guggenheim F'ship; Ford Foun Travel & Study Grantee; Rec'd Hon DLitt, Pomona Col.

MEIER, WILLIAM HENRY oc/Lawyer; b/Dec 23, 1904; h/305 N Tower Ave, Minden, NE 68959; ba/Minden; m/Mabel; c/William E, Joel F, Sarah M Peterson; p/Otto W and Mary G Bothwell Meier (dec); ed/BA Univ Neb 1926; JD 1930; pa/Gen Pract Law 1930-; City Atty (Minden) 1973-; Kearney Co Atty 1959-67; Asst US Atty 1942-44; Atty, Fed Land Bank (Omaha, Neb) 1933-36; Spec Agent FBI 1930-32; Neb St Bar Assn: Ho of Dels, Former Pres Gen Pract Sect, Former Chm Co Law Lib Com; cp/Former Mem Neb St Leg; Former Pres, Minden C of C; Former Scoutmaster, BSA; hon/Rec'd Congl Selective Ser Medal; Minden's Man of Yr 1950; Lions' Dist Gov.

MEINDERS, HILDRED McCANTS oc/Attorney; b/Jan 27, 1908; h/West Rt, Davis, OK 73030; ba/Same; m/Wesley H; c/Janet M Charalampous, Don W, Ann M Heaton, Mary M Johnson; p/James Franklin

and Maude Putnam McCants (dec); ed/BS Okla Col for Wom; Grad, John B Ogden Law Sch; pa/Co Atty of Garvin Co (Okla) 3 Terms; Okla St and Garvin Co Bar Assns; cp/Former Leg Chm, AAUW; Study Clbs; ARC; GSA; St PTA Bd; Pres Local PTAs; Wynnewood, Woodland & Yukon; r/United Meth.

MEINDERS, WESLEY H oc/Flood Control Specialist; b/Apr 14, 1914; h/West Rt, Davis, OK 73030; ba/Pauls Valley, OK; m/Hildred McCants; c/Janet M Charalampous, Don W, Anne M Heaton, Mary M Johnson; p/Harry H and Rosella Meinders (dec); ed/BS Okla A&M; Grad, John B Ogden Law Sch; pa/Okla St & Garvin Co Bar Assns; cp/Kiwanis; Former Sch Bd Mem; BSA; r/United Meth.

MEISELMAN, E ANNE oc/Legislative Researcher; Political Strategist; b/Mar 9, 1950; h/1600 Mason Hill Dr, Alexandria, VA 22307; ba/Washington, DC; p/Sumner and Bernice Meiselman, Alexandria; ed/BA cum laude; MA Cand, George Wash Univ; pa/10 Yrs Experience Staff, US Senate & US Ho of Reps; Free-lance Author, Radio & TV; White House Conslt; Advr, Secy Transportation; US Rep, Nat & Intl Confs; Nat Press Clb; Public Relats Soc Am; Senate Press Assn; r/Epis; hon/Notable Ams; Wom in Govt; W/W Am Cols & Univs.

MELANCON, DONALD oc/Principal; b/Nov 12, 1939; h/Rt 3, Box 30, St Anne, IL 60964; ba/Kankakee, IL; m/Hortense F; c/Douglas Louis, Girard James; p/Louis Melancon (dec); Amy Melancon Star, Franklin, LA; ed/BS So Univ (Baton Rouge, La) 1963; MS Univ Ill 1971; PhD Univ Ill-Champaign-Urbana 1976; Addit Studies; pa/Prin, Benjamin Franklin Mid Grade Ctr 1973-; Ctl Office Admr, Dir Titles IV & 45 Progs 1971; Psychol Cnslr, Kankakee Sch Dist #111 1970; Other Positions; Participant Workshops; Guest Lectr; Designed Weekly TV Show, *The Human Relations Forum*, Channel 6 (Kankakee); Author 2 Title VII Commun Projs for Remedial Reading & Math, Kankakee Co; Conslt: YMCA, Pembroke Consolidated Sch Dist, St Anne HS, Others; Planning Com, Ill Coun Ednl Sers; Tchr Evaluation Com, Kankakee Sch Dist #111; Former Chm, Sch-Commun Com for N Ctl Assn Field Testing; Advr, Supt's Student Adv Com; Bd Mem, St Anne Commun HS Dist; Appointed by Gov Walker to Serve Region 8K Com for CETA; Contbr Articles Profl Jours; NEA; Am Psychol Assn; Ill Assn Sch Bds; Kankakee Co Admrs Assn; Others; cp/Bd Mem, Old Fair Park Day Care Ctr; Bd Mem, Threshold Drug Abuse Prog; Bd Mem, YMCA Ext Prog; Cub Scout Master; Am Humanist Assn; Univ Ill Alumni Assn; Others; r/Cath; hon/Rec'd Ebony Esteem Awd Commun Ser; Bicent Declaration, Ser to Cub Scouting; Awd of Merit, Urban/Rural Sch Prog; Gov's St Univ Recog Awd for Urban Tchr Prog; W/W Among Black Ams.

MELGAR, JULIO oc/Mechanical Engineer; b/Jul 4, 1922; h/6108 Menger Ave, Dallas, TX 75227; ba/Fort Worth, TX; p/Lorenzo and Maria Melgar (dec); ed/BME Univ Detroit; mil/USMAC; pa/Bd Govs, Am Soc Heating, Refrigeration & Air Conditioning Engrs; Tex Soc Profl Engrs; ASME; cp/Bd Dirs, Ft Worth Opera Assn; Rep, Metroplex Rec Coun; Rep, Fed Bus Assn; Fed Aviation Clb; Ft Worth Humane Soc; r/Cath; hon/DIB; W/W S&SW; Men Achmt; Outstg Contbn Handball, City of Ft Worth; High Score Bd of Regents Exam in Spanish, St of NY; Spanish Surnamed Am in Sci & Engrg.

MELTON, C ALAN oc/Campus Minister; b/Mar 21, 1953; h/150 N Jane St, Apt 3, Louisville, KY 40206; ba/Louisville; m/Kathy Bridges; p/Ira B Sr and Mildred Drummond Melton, Pine Lake, GA; ed/BA Univ Ga 1975; MDiv So Bapt Theol Sem (Louisville) 1979; pa/Campus Min, Univ Ky 1979-; Campus Min, Spalding Col 1977-79; Dir, Camp Amigo for Underprivileged Chd (Charlotte, NC) 1976; Min of Yth, St John's Bapt Ch (Charlotte) 1975-76; Supply Preacher: Ga, NC, SC, Ky 1975-79; Past Pres, Ga Clb So

Sem; Past Pres, Univ Ga Bapt Student Union; Other Positions; Ordained, Pine Lake Bapt Ch 1978; Lic'd Min 1974; cp/Nat Coun Fam Relats; Nat Staff, FCA; r/Bapt; hon/Rec'd Clyde T Francisco Preaching Awd, So Sem; Outstg Yg Layman of Yr, Athens (Ga) JCs 1973.

MELTON, IRA B SR oc/Business Executive; b/Dec 21, 1918; h/613 Dogwood Rd, Pine Lake, GA 30072; m/Mildred Drummond; c/Ira B Jr, Donna M Benson, Timothy LaRue, Charles Alan, Kathleen M Stephens; mil/US Inf WWII; pa/VP & Dir: Consolidated Conslts Inc, CCI Funds Inc, CCI Realty Inc; Owner, Ira B Melton Enterprises; Pres, Melton-McKinney Inc; VP, Mortgage Investmts Inc; VP & Treas, Spec Tng Inst Inc; VP & Dir, Peachstone Devel Corp; Dir, Shallowford Arms Inc; Austin Realty Co; Partner, Warren 1-20 Assn; Lic'd Securities & Real Estate Rep; Am Soc Sanitary Engrs; Others; cp/Former Judge, Mun Ct; Former Coun-man & Mayor, Pine Lake; Ser'd on Staffs: Gov Marvin Griffin, Gov Jimmy Carter; Dir, DeKalb C of C; DeKalb Zoning Appeals Bd; DeKalb Co Bd Registrars; Former Deputy Sheriff, DeKalb Co; DeKalb Grand Jury Assn; Ga Peace Ofcrs Assn; Bd of Policy of Liberty Lobby (Wash, DC); Past Pres, Pine Lake Lions Clb & Civic Clb; Past Scoutmaster; Past Pres & Hon Life Mem, Atlanta Metro Masters Plumbers Assn; IPA; Others; r/Pine Lake Bapt Ch: Mem, Former Choir Dir, Former Chm Bd Trustees, Deacon; hon/Rec'd 2 Bronze Battle Stars ETQ Europe; W/W Ga; DIB; Intl W/W Intellectuals; W/W Commun Ser; Notable Ams; Others.

MELVIN, MARY LEE oc/Assistant in Aquatics; b/May 6, 1937; h/Box 185, Rt 2, Federalsburg, MD 21632; p/H G Pedrick Jr, Pedricktown, NJ; Mrs W Perry Messick, Federalsburg, MD; ed/AA Chesapeake Col 1980; pa/Asst in Aquatics, Benedictine Sch for Excptl Chd 1980-; hon/BSA: Den Ldrs Tng Awd, Scouters Tng Awd, Water Safety Instr (Cert'd); W/W Am Cols & Univs; John T Harrison Awd as Outstg Grad, Chesapeake Col.

MENAGH, HARRY BERESFORD oc/College Dean; b/Mar 29, 1918; h/16 Hunter Pl, Staten Island, NY 10301; ba/Staten Isl; m/Margaret Hannah; c/Maureen P, Philip S, Hardy B; p/Henry William and Mary Bateman Menagh (dec); ed/BA, BS Bowling Green Univ 1947; MA Univ So Cal 1949; PhD Univ Denver 1962; mil/USN WWII; pa/Dean of Fac, Wagner Col 1977-; Dean Col of Fine Arts, St Cloud St Univ 1972-77; Pres, Beresford Assocs (Wash, DC) 1969-72; Exec Dir, Am Ednl Theatre Assn 1966-69; Nat Com-man, Edrs' ad hoc Com on Copyright Law 1966-69; Pres, Minn Alliance for Arts Ed 1973-76; Dir & Moderator, Intl Confs on Arts Ed: Quito, Lima, Buenos Aires, Rio de Janeiro, Brasilia & Caracas (1977) & Canton, Peking, Shanghai & Nanking (1978); Others; cp/Former Nat Com-man, VP Humphrey's Com on Yth Summer Opportunites; Former Mem Bd Dirs, L'Enfant Plaza Merchants Assn; Former Dir Devel Projs, Wolf Trap Nat Park Foun (Wash, DC); Former Chm of Bd, Ctl Minn Commun Arts Ctr; Ldr, People-to-People Citizen Ambassador Prog; Others; hon/Eli Lilly Foun Fellow in Indian Studies; Rec'd Purdue Res Foun Grant; Rec'd Entertainmt Prog Spec Apprec Awd, AUS; Del Intl Conf Arts Ed: Romania 1975, Poland 1977; Phi Kappa Phi; Kappa Delta Pi; Phi Delta Kappa; Theta Alpha Phi.

MENDELSON, SOL oc/Scientific Researcher; Professor; b/Oct 10, 1926; h/446 W 25th St, New York, NY 10001; p/David C and Frieda Cohen Mendelson; ed/BS cum laude CCNY; MS 1957, PhD 1961 Columbia Univ; pa/Current Res in Physical Behavior Crystalline Materials & Scholarly Endeavors; Made Significant Discoveries in Mech Behavior of Solids, Epitaxial Growth of Semiconductor Films & Theory of Mechs for Diffusionless Phase Transformations; Prof Physics & Engrg, Baruch Col CCNY; Sr Scist, Bendix Res Labs (Southfield, Mich) 1967-68; Other Positions; Am Physical Soc; Am Soc

Metals; Metall Soc AIME; Materials Res Soc; NY Acad Scis; Am Assn Physics Tchrs; AAAS; Fdn Am Scist; Contbr Num Articles Profl Jours; hon/Sigma Xi; Tau Beta Pi; Pi Tau Sigma; Biogl Listings.

MENDEZ, FÉLIX G oc/Pharmacist; Public Relations Consultant; b/Jul 31, 1932; h/PO Box 2114, San Juan, PR 00936; ba/San Juan; m/Antonia Gonzalez; c/Felix Antonio, Mercedes, Rosa Margarita, Francisco Javier, Marife; p/Ledo Edelmiro Mendez and I Soto; ed/Univ Puerto Rico; Am Univ; Cornell Univ; mil/AUS 2/Lt; pa/Past Pres, Casa de Lares; Public Relats Soc Puerto Rico; cp/Casino de Puerto Rico; r/Cath: Advr to Better Movemt, Advr to Cardinal Apoute; hon/Most Dist'd Mem, Alpha Beta Chi.

MENENDEZ-MONROIG, JOSE M oc/Attorney; b/Jun 22, 1917; h/54 Krug St, Santurce, PR 00911; ba/Santurce; m/Lyda Cortada; c/Jose A, Michele Marie; p/Albert S Menendez and Agustina Monroig (dec); ed/BA 1939, LLB 1941 Univ Puerto Rico; mil/Ser'd to Capt 1941-46; pa/Colegio de Abogados de Puerto Rico; Am Bar Assn; Assoc Atty, Public Ser Comm 1946; Adjudicator, VA 1947; Mem Martinez-Alvarez, Fernandez-Paoli, Menendez-Monroig, Menendez-Cortada & Lefranc-Romero (Law Firm); cp/Former Senator, PR Senate; Past Minority Ldr; Former Secy Gen, New Progressive Party; Pres, Forward Statehood PR 51st; VP & Bd Dirs, PR Telephone Co; r/Cath; hon/Rec'd Caribbean & Pacific Theatre Medals.

MERCATANTE, ANTHONY STEPHEN oc/Psychotherapist; Author; b/Jan 29, 1940; h/15 Abingdon Sq, New York, NY 10014; p/Carmela La Tempa; ed/BA; PhD; pa/Author: *The Illustrated Ency of World Mythology*; *Who's Who in Egyptian Mythology*; *Good and Evil: Mythology & Folklore*; *Who's Who in Medieval Folklore & Mythology*; *The Magic Garden: Myths & Folklore of Flowers, Plants, Trees & Herbs*; *Zoo of the Gods: Animals in Myth, Legend & Fable*; Editor, *The Harper Book of Christian Poetry*; Pvt Pract Psychotherapist; Radio & TV Appearances; Dir, Mythos Ctr in NY; r/Anglican.

MERCER, JAMES LEE oc/Manager; b/Nov 7, 1936; h/1119 Aurora Ct, Dunwoody, GA 30338; ba/Atlanta, GA; m/Carolyn Prince; c/Tara Lee, James Lee Jr; p/Fred Elmo Mercer Sr (dec); Ora Lee Davidson Mercer, Sayre, OK; ed/BS 1964, MBA 1966 Univ Nev; mil/USN 1955-59; pa/Gen Mgr, Battelle So Operations; AIIE; ICMA; ASPA; Technol Transfer Soc; cp/Atlanta Rotary Clb; r/Prot; hon/Rec'd 2 Awds & Key to City, Raleigh (NC) City Coun; Rec'd George C Franklin Awd, NC Leag of Municipalities.

MERCHANT, VASANT V oc/Professor; b/Sept 11, 1933; h/1436 N Evergreen, Flagstaff, AZ 86001; ba/Flagstaff; p/Vallabhdas Permanand Merchant (dec); Ratanbai Vallabhdas Merchant, Bombay, India; ed/BA w Hons; TD; MA w Hons; LLB; PhD; pa/Prof & Ednl Conslt, Nn Ariz Univ; Nat Soc for Study of Ed; Other Profl Orgs; Writer; Poet; Lectr, US & Abroad; cp/Pres-Elect, Ariz Humanities Assn; Pilot Intl; hon/Phi Kappa Phi; Rec'd Wisdom Soc Awd; Outstg Achmt Awd, Pres' Com on Employmt of Handicapped; Outstg Fac Wom of Yr, Nn Ariz Univ 1977; Others.

MERGELE, HARRIETTE GANT oc/Psychologist; b/Oct 2, 1930; h/9423 Saddle Trail, San Antonio, TX 78255; ba/San Antonio; m/John Byrd; c/John B Jr, Monique Elene; p/John Edward Gant, Shelbyville, TN; Glennie L Gant, Rockledge, GA; ed/BS Univ Ga; MEd Trinity Univ (San Antonio); pa/Assoc Sch Psychol; Bexar Co & Tex St Psychol Assns; cp/Chm, Nat Mothers' Clb; Dir, Nat Devel; Dist Adminae Dir; r/1st Bapt Ch (Leon Springs, Tex): Mem, Choir, Chm Nominating Com, Dir Vacation Bible Sch; hon/Delta Kappa Gamma; Phi Mu; Others.

MERRICK, MARY JAMES oc/Elementary Principal; b/Oct 28, 1918; h/1019-18 Ave, So Grand Forks, ND 58201; ba/Grand Forks; p/Joseph Merrick (dec); Mary R Merrick, Breckenridge, MN; ed/BS; MS; pa/Sister of Rel Order; ND Dept Elem Sch Prins; NEA Exec Com, Elem Dept; Nat Cath Ed Assn; Bishops Coun, Diocese of Fargo; Diocesan Bd of Ed; Holy Fam Sch Bd; Parish Coun; r/Cath: Mem, Sister of St Francis of Immaculate Heart of Mary; hon/Commun Ldrs & Noteworthy Ams; W/W: Rel, Among Elem Sch Prins; DIB; Intl W/W Commun Ser.

MERRICK, ROBERT GRAFF oc/Banker; b/Nov 18, 1895; h/201 Woodbrook Ln, Baltimore, MD 21212; ba/Baltimore; m/Anne McEvoy (dec); c/Robert G Jr, Anne M Pinkard (Mrs Walter D); p/Samuel Kemp and Mary Charlton Graff Merrick (dec); ed/BA John Hopkins Univ 1917; PhD 1922; mil/WWI; pa/Former Pres, Chm of Bd & Chief Exec Ofcr, Equitable Trust Co; Former Chm, Baltimore Revenue Authority; cp/Former Pres, Baltimore Museum of Art; Trustee, Johns Hopkins Univ; SAR; Soc of Cincinnati; r/Epis; hon/Beta Theta Pi.

MERRICKS, DAVID LEE oc/Director; b/Jun 17, 1934; h/Rt 1, Box 70B, Brookneal, VA 24528; ba/Lynchburg, VA; m/Yes; c/3; ed/BA Lynchburg Col 1961; MEd 1969, AGS 1971 Univ Va-Ch; EdD Univ Fla-G 1972; pa/Dir Multihandicapped Habilitation Ctr, Lynchburg Tng Sch & Hosp 1978-; Assoc Prof & Coor Spec Ed, Sch of Ed, Univ Tenn-Ch 1975-78; Asst Prof & Coor Spec Ed, Dept Ed Psychol, Meml Univ Newfoundland (St John's, Newfoundland, Canada) 1972-75; Ednl Evaluator, Univ Va: Div Field Sers (Sch of Ed) & Bur Ednl Res; Conslt & Investigator, Va Consortium on Crime Prevention & Law Enforcemt; Mem-at-Large Adv Com on Spec Ed, Undergrad & Grad Progs, Atlantic Inst Ed (Halifax, Nova Scotia); Tenn Gov's Com on Employmt of Handicapped; Chrperson, SE Tenn White House Conf on Handicapped; Field Reader, HEW-BEH Handicapped Early Childhood Ed Div (Wash, DC); Other Positions; Am Assn Mtl Deficiency; Atlantic Assn for Cerebral Palsy; Coun for Diagnostic Sers; Coun for Exceptional Chd; Div Mtl Retardation; Fac Advr, Student Coun for Exceptional Chd; Tchr Ed Div; Past Pres, Tenn Fdn AAMC; Del Nat CEC Conv; Senate Com of Ednl TV; Reschr; Author, *Where the Action Is: Teaching Exceptional Chd* (1973); Contbr Num Articles Profl Jours; hon/Rec'd Grants: Univ Chattanooga Foun (2), HEW-BEH (7); Rec'd 4 F'ships, HEW-BEH; Jefferson Soc; Rec'd Certs Apprec: Minister of Hlth for Canada, Canadian Mtl Hlth Assn, Newfoundland Mtl Hlth Assn, Ray Blaxton (Gov Tenn); Others.

MERRILL, GIRLDINE FALLON oc/Primitive Artist; b/Sept 18, 1920; h/1018 Maple Dr, Windsor, CA 95492; ba/Same; m/Robin; c/Mardi Kelley, Beverly Ann M La Font; p/James O Williamson (dec); Willie Lee Smith, Santa Rosa, CA; ed/St Tchr Cert in Primitive Art; pa/Exhbns: De Young Mus, Cal St Fair, Las Vegas Nat Art Roundup, Others; Comm'd Work; Nat Leag Am Pen Wom; Intl Soc Artists; cp/Num Benefit Exhbns; r/Christian; hon/Rec'd Num Awds for Art.

MERRILL, JANET LOUISE oc/Professor; b/Aug 20, 1937; h/9314 Waterview Rd, Dallas, TX 75218; ba/Dallas; m/Eugene H; c/Sonya Leigh; p/Harland Virgil and Irma Edna McConnell Hippensteel (dec); ed/EdD Columbia Univ; MA Univ Notre Dame; BS Bob Jones Univ; pa/Prof, So Meth Univ; Mem Num Profl Orgs; r/Bapt; hon/Grad'd Magna Cum Laude; Fac Coor of 2nd Pl Winner, Gen Motors Bus Understanding Prog.

MERRITT, DOREATHA FROST oc/Counselor; b/Aug 18, 1942; h/925 2nd Ave, Smithfield, NC 27577; ba/Smithfield; c/Phyllis, Timothy, Michelle, Calvin, Roy Jr; p/Kalip Sr and Bertha Frost, Valdosta, GA; ed/LaSalle Univ; E Carolina Univ; Fayetteville St Univ; NC Ctl Univ; pa/Gen Sers & Cert'd Hous'g Cnslr, Johnston-Lee Commun Action 1969-; Vol Social Worker, Johnston-Lee Commun Action 1967-69; Self-employed

Interior Decorator 1963-67; NC Commun Action Assn; Nat Fdn Hous'g Cnslrs; Johnston Co Concerned Citizens Assn; cp/NAACP; r/African Meth Epis Zionist; hon/Rec'd Num Merit Awds, Commun Sers Adm.

MERRITT, GARRY ALLAN oc/Community School Coordinator; b/Oct 13, 1950; h/7200 Powers Ave, #8, Jacksonville, FL 32217; ba/Jacksonville; p/Carlin H S Merritt, J'ville; Audrey B Washington, Alameda, CA; ed/BA Morgan St Univ 1972; Grad Studies, Univ Pittsburgh 1972-73; pa/Duval Assn for Commun Ed; Fla Assn Commun Ed; cp/Gateway Civitan Clb; J'ville Urban Leag Bd; Operation RESPECT; r/Mt Zion AME Ch; hon/Rec'd Commun Ser Awd, J'ville Headstart.

MERRITT, GEORGE WILLIAM oc/Minister; b/Aug 17, 1944; h/204 Martin, Enterprise, AL 36330; ba/Enterprise; m/Wanda Fay Gonce; c/Laura Kay, Diana Fay, Maria Gay, Franklin Brown; p/J F Jr and Louise Green Merritt, Decherd, TN; pa/Min, Col Ave Ch of Christ; Daily Rel Broadcasts; Weekly Newspaper Columnist; Cnslr; Contbr Articles Profl Jours; Author, *Truth for Today*; Former Radio Announcer, News Dir & News Editor for Newspaper; cp/ARC: Dir & Past Blood Chm; Past Pres, PTA; Vol 4-H Ldr; Chaplain, Soil Conserv Dist; Num Adv Bds; Narrations for AUS & Agri Ext Ser; Others; r/Ch of Christ; hon/Nat 4-H Winner; Rec'd News & Journalism Awds: AP, Tenn Press Assn, Ala Press Assn; Outstg Yg Rel Ldr, Enterprise JCs; Nom Man of Yr, Enterprise.

MERRITT, PEGGY F oc/Director; b/Sept 7, 1944; h/5 Kingston Ave, Belmont, NC 28012; ba/Belmont; m/L James; c/Patrick, Kevin; p/(dec); ed/BS; BA; Addit Studies; pa/Dir Placemt, Sacred Heart Col; Col Placemt Assn; Nat Assn Social Workers; cp/Chm & Bd Dirs, Gaston Coun Dept Social Sers; r/Bapt.

MERRITT, ROSE BILLINGSLEY oc/Social Worker; b/May 10, 1936; h/12 E 86th St #1428, New York, NY 10028; ba/New York; c/William Paul; p/Harold J Billingsley (dec); Rose Sladack Billingsley, Pasadena, CA; ed/BA Golden Gate Univ 1978; pa/Fin Wom's Clb of San Francisco; Am Bankers Assn; Pres, Colo Assn Chd w LDs 1972; Secy, Cal Assn Neurologically Handicapped Chd 1968-69; Vol Classroom & 1 to 1 Asst Prog, Grand Co (Colo) 1970-71 (Proposed, Coor'd & Implemented the Prog); r/Choral Dir Var Secular & Rel Groups; hon/World W/W Wom.

MESIC, HARRY RANDOLPH oc/Instructor; b/Dec 30, 1935; h/3103 Hartnett Blvd, Isle of Palms, SC 29451; ba/Charleston, SC; m/Harriet Lee Bey; c/Catherine Denise, Daniel Douglas; p/Harry Underwood Mesic, Hampton, VA; Evelyn Mae Hamaker Mesic (dec); ed/BS Univ Richmond; mil/USMC 1959-60; pa/Instr Med Technol, VA Hosp; Instr Allied Hlth & Med, Univ SC; Am Soc Clinical Pathologists; cp/Former Pack Master & Webelo Ldr, BSA; Former Chm, Bd Dirs & Sr Advisor, GSA; CPR Instr, ARC & Heart Assn; Short Term Missionary to Puerto Cabezas (Nicarauga); r/New Life Ministry: Life Mem, Tchr, Deacon; hon/Outstg Student Awd, Am Chem Soc.

MESNEY, DOROTHY TAYLOR oc/Musician; b/Sept 15, 1926; h/324 Manor Rd, Douglaston, NY 11363; ba/Same; m/Peter Michael; c/Douglas Taylor, Kathryn Muriel, Barbara Jennifer; p/Franklin and Kathryn Ross Munro Taylor, Brooklyn, NY; ed/BA; pa/Singer; Pianist; Performer; Tchr; Fdr & Dir, Concerts for Chd; r/Prot; hon/Recording Artist, Folkways Records.

METCALF, GERTRUDE ROTHENBERGER oc/Retired; b/Sept 9, 1907; h/17 Orchard Ln, Audubon, Norristown, PA 19403; m/Charles O (dec); c/Lucy M Ennis (Mrs George); p/Issac S and Mabel Rothensdadt Rothenberger (dec); ed/BA Ursinus Col; MS Drexel Univ; pa/Former Head Sch Libn & Dir Media Ctr;

PSEA; NEA; ALA; PLA; BPW Clb; AAUW; r/United Ch of Christ; hon/Rec'd Student Coun Awd for Contbn of Interest to Students.

METZ, M JEAN oc/Assistant Professor; b/Jul 13, 1945; h/1006 Stoneybrook Trail, Fairborn, OH 45324; ba/Dayton, OH; p/John Anderson and Jean Baker Ekers, Columbus, OH; ed/BFA; MA; ABD; pa/Asst Prof Communicative Arts; Dir Forensics; Coor Ohio Fellows; Free-lance Conslt; Chrperson, CSSA Commun Col Group; Chrperson, SCA Commun Col Sect; Nat Coun, AFA; OFA; SCAO.

MEYER, WALTER oc/Professor; b/Jan 19, 1932; h/206 Devine Ct, Columbia, MO 65201; ba/Columbia; m/Jacqueline; c/Kim, Holt, Leah, Suzannah; p/Walter Meyer; Ruth Meyer Freitag; ed/BChE 1956, MChE 1957 Syracuse Univ; PhD Oregon St Univ 1964; pa/Prof & Chm Nuclear Engrg Dept, Univ Mo; Conslt: NE Utilities Co, Wisc Elect Power Co, Boeing Co, Argonne Nat Lab, Fed Trade Comm, Gen Physics Corp, Kerr McGee, Ga Pacific Co, EG&G Idaho Inc; cp/Columbia LWV; No on Proposition J Com; Kansas Gov's Nuclear Energy Coun; r/Congreg Ch: Deacon, Yth Ldr; hon/Rec'd Am Nuclear Soc Spec Awd for Public Info; Fellow ANS; Rec'd ANS Cert Governance.

MHLABA, SONDLO L oc/Negotiator; b/Mar 15, 1943; h/211 W Springfield St, Boston, MA 02118; ba/Boston; m/Helen J; c/'Meleni N; p/Mnene S Mhlaba and Nabo Ncube, Bulawayo, Rhodesia; ed/BS; MEd; pa/Former Math Tchr, Northfield Hermon Sch (Mass); Started Own Sch for Disadvantaged Chd (Leominster); Former Regional Dir, Commun Action Agy; VISTA Supvr; Contbr Articles Profl Jours; Author: Loeb Fellow in Adv'd Envir Affairs, Harvard Univ; Statewide Adv Com on Transportation Coor; cp/Bd Dirs, Robert F Kennedy Action Corps; Exec Mem, Zimbabwe African Peoples Union in N Am; hon/Men Achmt; Outstg Yg Men Am; Intl Register Profiles; Others.

MICHAELS, PEARL DOROTHY oc/Educator; b/Aug 18, 1936; ba/New York, NY; m/James Peter; p/John Blissak; ed/BA 1958, MS 1962; pa/Tchr, NYC Public Schs 1958-; Common Brs in Day Elem Sch; Tchr of English as 2nd Lang; DES; MLA; TESOL; Life Fellow Intl Acad Poets; Author Bilingual French-English & Spanish-English Workbooks, Linguistic Readers & Companion Peewee Cards; cp/Reg'd Dem; Life Mem: Am Cause, NY Hist Soc, Nat Wildlife Fdn, Soc for Intl Numismatics; Life Mem, IBA; r/Am Orthodox Ch; hon/Men & Wom Distn; Intl W/W Intells; World W/W Wom; Intl Authors & Writers W/W; Intl W/W Poetry; DIB.

MICHAELSEN, SHIRLEY ANN oc/Coordinator; b/Dec 24, 1919; h/621 Union St, Cheney, WA 99004; ba/Spokane, WA; m/Robert L; c/Dianne M Dilling, Gail M Nelson; p/Frederick H and Bertha Roberts McCroskey (dec); ed/BA Univ Wash; MA Whitworth Univ 1978; pa/Spokane Commun Col: Coor Wom's Cont'g Ed Progs (Dist 17) 1976-, Coor Woms Activs 1970-76, Speech Communs Tchr 1968-70; Wash St Adv Com, St Bd Commun Col Ed & Homemakers' Com of Gov's Wom's Coun; Forums Moderator, 22 Bus-Ed Forums, Wash Bicent Traveling Fest; Speaker's Bur, Commun Col Dist 17; Guest Facilitator Var Cols; Steer'g Com, Wash St Wom Progrs Assn; Former Bd Mem, Nat Assn Wom Deans, Admrs & Cnslrs; cp/Speakers Bur, Spokane C of C; YWCA Res & Devel Com; r/United Ch of Christ; hon/Dist'd Speech Tchr's Awd, Wash St Speech Assn; Nom, 1 of 15 Outstg Wom Contbg to Other Wom; Dist'd Citizen of Week, KSPO; Others.

MICHNA, MARIENKA (MARY) oc/Concert Pianist; b/Dec 17, 1910; h/Hotel Ansonia, Broadway & 73, New York, NY 10023; p/Lawrence and Maria G Michna; ed/Julius Hartt Sch of Mus (Hartford, Conn); pa/Fac Mem, Julius Hartt Sch 1938-47; NY Debut, Piano Soloist 1944; Num Solo Concerts, Hartford & Univ Mo-KC; Operatic Coach, Metro Opera 1967-; Asst Conductor,

Conn Opera 1970-75; Asst Conductor, Brooklyn Opera 1960-68; Performance as Pianist at Whitehouse & Conducted Marine Orch for Reception for Haile Selassie 1973; Tours Through US & Canada as Piano Soloist & Accompanist; hon/Rec'd Muza Tatier, Slovak-Am Cult Ctr (NY); Outstg Wom-Mus of Slovak Heritage; Rec'd Cert Outstg Achmt, Julius Hartt Sch Mus; Biogl Listings.

MICKE, MARILYN oc/Superintendent; b/Jun 11, 1918; h/518 N 24th Ave W, Duluth, MN 55806; ba/Duluth; p/Theodore and Jennie Verbeten Micke (dec); ed/BS; ME; pa/Sister Rel Order; Supt Schs, Diocese of Duluth; Tchr; cp/United Way; UNICEF; CEF; City Wide-City Pride; Admr, Operation Aware Crime Prevention Prog; r/Rom Cath; hon/Rec'd Cert, Tchr Perceiver Spec; W/W: Rel, Biog Record, Wom; DIB; Notable Ams; Commun Ldrs & Noteworthy Ams; Personalities of W&MW.

MICKEL, HUBERT SHELDON oc/Neurologist; b/Aug 27, 1937; h/Leverett House G-107, Cambridge, MA 02138; ba/Boston, MA; c/Paul David, Deborah Elizabeth, Pamela Marie; p/Ralph A and Lillian Burkett Mickel, Alum Bank, PA; ed/BS summa cum laude, En Nazarene Col 1958; MD Harvard Med Sch 1962; Sch of Aerospace Med; mil/USAF MC 1968-70; pa/Neurologist Dept Neurol, Chd's Hosp Med Ctr; Pre-Med Advr, Leverett House (Harvard Col); Asst Clinical Prof Neurol, Harvard Med Sch; Hon Res Assoc Dept Chem, Harvard Univ; hon/Am Men & Wom Sci; Intl W/W Commun Ser; Outstg Yg Men Am; W/W E; Intl W/W Intellectuals; Others.

MIETHE, TERRY LEE oc/Educator; Administrator; b/Aug 26, 1948; h/3178 Florinda St, Pomona, CA 91767; m/Beverly Jo; c/John-Hayden; p/Billy and Rosemary Miethe, Ladoga, IN; ed/BA cum laude, Lincoln Christian Col 1970; MA cum laude, Trinity Evangelical Div Sch 1973; MDiv McCormick Theol Sem 1973; PhD St Louis Univ 1976; pa/Adj Prof Phil of Rel, Fuller Theol Sem 1978; Assoc Prof Theol & Phil, Pacific Christian Col 1977-78; St Louis Univ: Asst Prof Dept Theol Studies 1976-77, Asst Dir Univ Hons Prog 1975-76, Profl Lectr Phil 1975-76; Other Positions; Dist Adv Com, Claremont (Ga) Christian Sch; V-Chrperson Sch Site Coun, Mt View Sch (Claremont); Nat Assn Student Pers Admrs; Evangelical Phil Soc; Soc Biblical Lit; Am Acad Rel; Evangelical Theol Soc; Am Phil Assn; r/Christian; hon/Phi Beta Kappa; Phi Alpha Theta; Psi Chi; Eta Sigma Phi; Alpha Sigma Nu; Rec'd Pearl Denham Miller S'ship; McCormick Theol Sem S'ship; St Louis Univ F'ship; US Govt Finalist, Fulbright F'ship; Biogl Listings.

MIGRDICHAN, VARTKES oc/Chemist; b/Oct 8, 1893; h/51 Connecticut Ave, Greenwich, CT 06830; ba/Stanford, CT; p/Migrdich and Araxie Mardirussian (dec); ed/BA Cornell Univ; PhD; pa/Chem, Am Cyanamid Co Res Lab; Author; cp/Var Activs; r/Christian.

MIKUS, JOSEPH A oc/Professor Emeritus; b/Jul 3, 1909; h/3619 Alton Pl NW, Washington, DC 20008; m/Renee M Perreal; c/Isabelle; p/Joseph and Christine Mikus (dec); ed/MCL George Wash Univ Law Sch; JD Univ Bratislava; pa/Prof Emeritus Hist & Polit Sci; Author Books in Slovak, French & English; cp/Defense of Human, Rel & Polit Rights; r/Rom Cath; hon/Delta Theta Kappa.

MILANDER, HENRY MARTIN oc/College President; b/Apr 17, 1939; h/5145 NW El Camino Blvd, Bremerton, WA 98310; ba/Bremerton; m/Joan M; c/Martin H, Beth A; p/Martin and Margaret Milander, Northampton, PA; ed/BS; MA; EdS; EdD; pa/Pres, Olympic Col 1972-; VP Acad Affairs, Lorain Co Commun Col (Elyria, Ohio) 1969-72; Dean Instrnl Progs & Sers, Dir of E Campus, Belleville Area Col 1968-69; Other Positions; Nat Coun for Accred of Tchr Ed Evaluation Team; Adv Com, Cosmetology Accred'g Comm; Am Assn Higher Ed; Am Assn Commun & Jr Cols; AAUA; Wash Assn

Commun Cols; AASA; Am Tech Ed Assn; Others; Contbr Num Articles Profl Jours; cp/Bremerton Ctl Lions Clb; Bremerton Area C of C; Kitsap Co United Way; Bd Dirs, Puget Sound Naval Base Assn; Bd Dirs, Kitsap Co Hlth Planning Coun; City Beautification Com; USN Leag; Bd Dirs, Cardio Pulmonary Res Inst; Others; r/Luth; hon/Kappa Delta Pi; Phi Delta Kappa; Rec'd Commun Ser Awd; W/W MW; Outstg Edrs Am; DIB; Men Achmt; Others.

MILBURN, THERESA HOLTZCLAW oc/Retired; b/Jul 24, 1914; h/Rt 2, Harmon Hgts, Danville, KY 40422; m/William Isaac; c/Theresa M Sallee; p/Walter S and Ophelia Walker Holtzclaw (dec); ed/BA Georgetown Col; MA; Attended Univ Ky-L; pa/Tchr Kgn-HS 40 Yrs; NEA; NRTA; AARP; cp/Former Mem AAUW & BPW; r/Bapt; hon/World Travels: Spain, Egypt, Moroco, Holy Land, Greek Islands, Others.

MILBURN, WILLIAM ISAAC oc/Banker; b/Mar 15, 1914; h/Rt 2, Harmon Hgts, Danville, KY 40422; m/Theresa Holtzclaw; c/Theresa M Sallee; p/John and Pearl Sparrow Milburn (dec); ed/Bus Deg, Campbellsville Col; mil/AUS 1943-45; pa/Old Bank (Perryville, Ky): Banker 1933-76, VP 1966-75, Dir 1960-76; Ret'd 1976; cp/Ch Commun Dr; Former Secy Boyle Sch Bd; r/Bapt (Perryville): Cemetery Bd; hon/Ky Col.

MILFORD, MURRAY HUDSON oc/-Professor; b/Sept 29, 1934; h/3606 Tanglewood Dr, Bryan, TX 77801; ba/College Station, TX; m/Marsha Ann Rasmussen; c/Rebecca Ione, Murray Daniel; p/Murray Lane Milford (dec); Vivian Ione Milford, Honey Grove, TX; ed/BS 1955, MS 1959 Tex A&M Univ; PhD Univ Wisc 1962; mil/USAR 1955-57; pa/Tex A&M Univ: Prof Dept Soil & Crop Scis 1974-, Assoc Prof 1968-74; Cornell Univ: Assoc Prof Dept Agronomy 1968, Asst Prof 1963-68; Other Positions; Author, *Introduction to Soils & Soil Sci - Lab Exercises* (1970, 75); r/Christian-Presb; hon/Alpha Zeta; Phi Kappa Phi; Gamma Sigma Delta; Sigma Xi; Fellow, AAAS; JC of Yr (Ithaca, NY) 1964; Prof of Merit, Col of Agri, Tex A&M Univ; Fac Dist'd Achmt Awd; Dist'd Ser Awd & Lawrence Sullivan Ross Awd for Outstg Ser, Meml Student Ctr; Agronomic Resident Ed Awd, Am Soc Agronomy; Biogl Listings.

MILLARD, VIVIAN TURNER oc/Poet; b/Apr 18, 1888; h/PO Box 338, Yarnell, AZ 85362; ba/Same; m/Dell E (dec); p/Rollin J and Mary Heathcote Turner (dec); pa/Former Post Office Clerk, Stenographer & Bank Teller (Los Angeles, Cal); cp/Former Treas, Stark Co (ND); r/Christian; hon/Book of Hon; Commun Ldrs & Noteworthy Ams; Personalities of W&MW; Others.

MILLER, ALBERT RAYMOND oc/Physician; b/Feb 27, 1921; h/8698 W 108th Pl, Overland Park, KS 66212; ba/Overland Park; c/Jeffrey Jon, Timothy Douglas; p/Ananias P and Emma Jane Miller (dec); ed/BA Goshen Col 1945; DO Kansas City Col Osteopathic Med 1960; Addit Studies: Ind Univ, Ball St Univ, Butler Univ, Am Col Gymnastic Union, Tex Tech; pa/Gen Pract Phys & Surg; Former Tchr & Coach; Fdr & Chm, Ks-Mo Ath Injury Sem & Workshop 1971-78; Instr KCC of Osteopath Med 1962-63; Phys: KC Chiefs Football Clb 1963-78 & World Cup Tennis 1977-78; Bd Dirs & Mbrship Com, Am Osteopath Col of Sports Med; Ks Osteopath Med Assn; Am Osteopath Col of Gen Pract; E-Ctl Ks Osteopath Assn; Nat Ath Tnrs Assn; Assoc Mem, Lakeside Hosp; Lectr; Reschr; Others; cp/Pres Local Chapt, High-12 Intl; Cnslr, Hoosier Boys St; Mason; r/Presb; hon/Holds US Patent.

MILLER, CAROL MILLER oc/Executive; Music Educator; b/Feb 18, 1931; h/Shorefront Park, S Norwalk, CT 06854; ba/Norwalk; m/Robert B; p/Charles Edward Miller (dec); Gladys Ilene Miller, Winnetka, IL; ed/BME 1953, MMus 1954 NWn Univ; pa/VP & Dir, Trade Routes Inc 1968-; VP & Dir, Sealanes

Intl Inc (Chicago, Ill) 1958-68; Dir Instrumental Mus, Ill & Chgo Schs 1954-61; 1st Flutist, W Suburban Symph Orch (Cook Co, Ill) 1956-58; Other Positions; cp/Repub Party; En Packard Clb; Viking Yacht Clb; Former Pres, Ladies' Aux; r/Presb; hon/Rec'd 3 Achmt Awds & S'ship, Phi Beta; Nat Awd for Flute & Piano Composition, "Confusion"; S'ship to Mus Camp; W/W: Am Wom, E; Intl W/W Mus & Musician's Directory; Notable Ams; DIB; Others.

MILLER, CARRIE EULAH oc/Minister; h/Oronogo, MO 66769; ba/Redfield, KS; p/Charles Willis and Emma Jane Fuller Miller (dec); ed/BS; MA; PhD; pa/Min, United Meth Ch; Assoc Mem, Ks E Conf, UMC; S Ctl United Meth Deaconess Assn; Am Psychol Assn; r/United Meth.

MILLER, DOROTHEA WELSH oc/Director; b/Sept 7, 1904; h/204 N G St, Wellington, KS 67152; ba/Wellington; m/(dec); p/Burt Watson and Lila Fossey Welsh (dec); ed/BSLS George Peabody Univ 1943; pa/Dir, Chisholm Trail Museum 1971-; Reference Libn: Wichita Univ 1943-46, Boeing Aviation Co (Wichita) 1946; Head Libn, SWn Col (Winfield) 1947-48; Former HS Tchr; NEA; ALA; AAUP; cp/GSA Ldr 15 Yrs; Fed'd Wom's Clbs; Soroptimist Intl; r/Meth; hon/Best Eng Tchr in Ks 1934; W/W; W&MW; Am Wom; DIB.

MILLER, EARL BEAUFORD oc/Artist; b/Sept 19, 1930; h/5026 22nd Ave, #1, Seattle, WA 98105; ba/Seattle; c/Joseph Dale, Hugh Stephen, Pringl Lee; ed/Roosevelt Univ 1950; Inst Design, Ill Inst Technol 1951-52; Pratt Inst (Bklyn, NY) 1954-56; Bklyn Mus of Art 1956; Art Students Leag (NY) 1957; Akademie der Bildenden Kunste (Munich, Germany) 1963; pa/Assoc Prof Art, Univ Wash; Exhbns: Assoc'd Am (NY), Galarie L55 (Paris, France), Genesis Gallery Ltd (NY, London), Kiku Gallery Fine Arts (Seattle), Mus Art (Univ Oregon), Source Gallery (San Francisco, Cal), Others; hon/Work in Perm Collections: Chase Manhattan Bank (NY), City of Seattle, Henry Art Gallery (Univ Wash), IBM (NY), Jamaica Nat Gallery, De Centre National D'Art Et De Culture (George Pompidou Archives, Paris), Mus Modern Art (NY), Others; Nom'd for Awd in Painting, Nat Inst of Arts & Lttrs; 2nd Prize, Seattle Art Comm; Prize Winner, "Original Editions 1978", Oregon Arts Coun; Others.

MILLER, ELIZABETH LOUISE oc/Administrator; b/May 12, 1930; h/9101 Cedar Ave, S Bloomington, MN 55420; ba/Same; m/Robert A (dec); c/Pamela M Boswinkel; p/Cecil C Noecker (dec); Carolyn Windon Noecker, Pensacola, FL; pa/Contractor; Writer; Hypnotist; cp/Repub Party; Polit Writings; r/Meth.

MILLER, FANNIE ROLL oc/Retired Educator; b/Mar 23, 1906; h/7719 Jasen Dr, Springfield, VA 22152; m/William Peoples (dec); c/Frances M Barnett (Mrs Robert Alan), Janet M Crooks (Mrs H Robert); p/Edward Francis Roll (dec); Louisa Caroline Roll Chambers; ed/Grad Univ Buffalo 1927; NY St Col Grad Life Cert; Tchg Cert, Beaver Col; Addit Studies: pa/Tchr (Lewiston, NY): Eng, Ancient, Medieval & Am Hist; Tchr Buffalo Sch Sys; Tchr, St Basil Acad (Philadelphia, Penn); Ret'd 1970; Pub'd Poetry: *Child Life, Jack & Jill, Dew Drops*; Writer; Traveller; Reschr, Works of G K Chesterton; Publicity Chm NY Branch, Nat Leag Am Pen Wom; Phila Branch, NLAPW: Histn, Treas; Nat & Penn Couns for Social Studies; Phila Eng Tchrs Assn; Others; cp/World Affairs Clb; Evaluating Com, Mid Atlantic Sts; hon/Rec'd Scroll of Recog, Chrysostom Chapt Quill & Scroll, St Basil Acad.

MILLER, FRANCES FOX oc/Administrator; b/Mar 23, 1928; h/420 S College Ave, Muncie, IN 47303; ba/Muncie; m/Guy N; c/Marlene M Greenwalt, Norman; p/Clarence E and Minnie Carolina Mier Fox (dec); ed/BS, MS Univ Mich; EdD Ind Univ; pa/Pres, Fraunce Enterprises Inc; Educator; Writer & Pubr; Lectr; Nat Press Clb; Wom in Communs; cp/2 Gubernataurial Elections; 1

Congl Election; Others; r/1st United Presb Ch; hon/Chi Omega; Phi Delta Kappa; S'ship to Toronto, Canada; Wall St Jour F'ship to Univ Mich; Others.

MILLER, GREGORY FRANCIS oc/-Physician; Psychiatrist; Psychoanalyst; b/-Mar 15, 1943; h/PO Box 75, Old Westbury, NY 11568; ba/Same; p/Samuel H and Marguerite Mezzacapo Miller; ed/PT Kellberg Inst Physical Therapy 1960; MD Instituto Politecnico Nacional (Mexico City) 1972; Student Fellow, S'ship SISM, Giovanetti-Giordano Inst Nephrology, Universita delgi Studi di Pisa (Italy) 1970; Clinical Clerkship, Harvard Med Sch, Peter Bent Brigham Hosp 1971; Neurosurgical Tng, N Staffordshire Royal Infirmary (Stoke-on-Trent, Gt Brit) 1971; Alcoholic Rehab Ctr, Secy of Public Hlth & Wel (Mexico City) Psychi Tng 1969; II Pan-Am Course Diabetes Mellitus, Harvard Med Sch, Joslin Diabetes Foun & Universidad Nacional Autonoma de Mexico 1972; Post Grad Studies: Guy's Hosp (London, England), Denver Gen Hosp (Univ Colo), Others; DD St Stephan's Sem (NM) 1975; pa/Phys & Psychi, Inst for Study Psychoanalysis, Rel & Reality Therapy; Worked w: Prof Dr David Contreras (Fray Bernadino de Alvarez Psychi Hosp, Mexico City), Gomez-Tagle (Nat Inst Neurol & Nervous Diseases, Mexico City); Rep'd Mexico, World Gen Assembly, Intl Fdn Med Students Assn (Berlin, Germany) 1969; Co-Pres, Nat Med Student Assn Mexico; AAAS; NY Acad Scis; Assn Mil Surgs US; Brit Post Grad Med Fdn; Fellow, Intl Cong Phys & Surgs; MPH, Braintridge Univ; Fellow, Royal Soc of Tropical Med; Fellow, Am Col of Angiology; Former Conslt, Cath Charities, Men of Achmt; Author Books on Biochem & Pharmacol; Others; cp/Assoc, Smithsonian Inst; Lt/Col, Aide de Camp Gov's Staff (St of Ga) & Hon Lt/Col Gov's Staff (St of Ala); DAV; r/Order of St Stephan; hon/Alicia Fernandez de Lara Awd; Hon Citizen Boys Town, Neb; Others.

MILLER, IDA MAE GOOD oc/Librarian; b/Mar 25, 1919; h/525 E Main St, Plainfield, IN 46168; ba/Indianapolis, IN; m/John Chester; c/Susan M Carter (Mrs John E), Julia Christina, David Alan, Carl Edward; p/Irbv J and Mabel Iota Rivir Good (dec); ed/BA; BLS; BMus; mil/WAAC & WAC WWII; pa/Lib Cataloger; Am Lib Assn; Ind Lib Assn; Friend of Plainfield Lib; cp/Ind Hist Soc; Hendricks Co Hist Soc; Guilford Township Hist Soc; Japan-Am Soc Ind; Hymn Soc Am; r/Soc of Friends (Quaker).

MILLER, J D oc/Maintenance Manager; b/Jan 14, 1931; h/1491 Hilltop St, Albemarle, NC 28001; ba/Charlotte, NC; m/Blanche Page; c/Joy Darlene; p/Mumpford C and Nellie Almond Miller, Albemarle; mil/1952-54; pa/Maintenance Mgr, Collins & Aikman Corp; cp/Dem Party; r/Bapt.

MILLER, JOHN EDWARD oc/Life Insurance Salesman; b/Sept 23, 1946; ba/174 W Comstock Ave, Winter Park, FL 32789; m/Rebecca H; c/Christie S, Tracie L, (Stepdaugh:) Wendy J; p/B Dean and Ruth I Miller; ed/AA, AS St Petersburg Jr Col; mil/USAF; pa/Rep, Mass Mutual Life Ins Co 1978-; Owner-Operator John E Miller Agy 1977-; Agent, Integon Life Ins Co 1976-77; Store Mgr, Radio Shack Corp 1971-76; cp/Winter Park JCs: Former Chm of Bd, Former Pres, Former Dir; Winter Park C of C; Former Dir, Big Brothers of Orlando; Former Chm Pres' Clb, Fla JCs; r/Prot; hon/Quartermaster Sea Explorer; Eagle Scout; Outstg Yth of Pinellas Co (Fla); JC of Month.

MILLER, L T JR oc/Executive; b/Nov 13, 1914; h/3103 Eastover Dr, Odessa, TX 79762; m/Grace; c/Samuel Clifton, Steve, Janis Ann; p/Luther T Sr and Estelle Franklin Miller (dec); ed/BBA 1936, MBA 1937 Tex Christian Univ; Addit Studies, Univ Cal-LA; pa/McVean & Barlow Inc: Chm of Bd Dirs & Pres 1973-, Former VP, Former Secy-Treas, Former Comptroller 1953-73; Conslt, Cert'd Life Underwriters; Owner, L T Miller CPA Firm (Ft Worth, Abilene & Midland) 1947-51;

Former Fac Mem, McMurray Col (Abilene); Partner w Patterson, Leatherwood & Miller CPAs (Ft Worth) 1943-47; Tex Christian Univ: Prof 1935-41, Asst to Dir Evening Sch 1935-41, Act'g Dir Sch of Bus 1941; Tex Soc CPAs; Am Inst Accts; St & Nat Socs Ins Mgrs; Nat Assn Cost Accts; cp/Past Pres & Secy-Treas, Indust Foun Permian Basin; IPA; hon/Rec'd Spec Awd Outstg Achmt, Odessa C of C; 2 Awds Outstg Ser, Indust Foun Permian Basin; Biogl Listings.

MILLER, LAVERNE G oc/Registered Professional Nurse; b/May 4, 1922; h/525 W Jackson Blvd, Oak Park, IL 60304; m/Edward J Jr; c/1; p/Fredrick Helmuth and Ida Marie Brand Flueckiger; ed/RN Rush-Presb-St Luke's Sch Nsg; BS Col of St Francis; pa/Staff Mem: Rush-Presb-St Luke Complex, Oak Park Hosp, W Suburban Hosp; Ser'd as Staff Nurse, Charge Nurse, Supvr & Head Nurse; Co-ldr Sem on Cancer, Am Cancer Soc; ANA; Ill Nurses Assn; Am Critical Care Nurses Assn; Chgo Coun Cath Nurses Assn (Bd Dirs); Oak Park Hosp Wom's Aux; cp/Vol Worker, ARC Blood Donor Dr & Am Cancer Soc; Col of St Francis Alumni Assn; R-P-SL Sch Nsg Alumni Assn; Fenwick HS Mothers' Clb; United Swiss Soc; Swiss Benevolent Soc; Swiss Ladies Benefit Soc; Former Cub Scout Den Mother; Repub Leag Voters; Others; r/St Vincent Ferrer Ch & Guild of Tabernacle; hon/Rec'd Cit Outstg Ser, R-P-SL Med Staff; Biogl Listings.

MILLER, MARGARET FAYE oc/Music Educator; b/Feb 16, 1930; h/52 Stanford Ave, Pueblo, CO 81005; ba/Same; m/Arthur W; c/David Michael, Melody Ann; p/Kermit and Ruby Knudsen, Fremont, NE; ed/BSEd; MA; pa/Performer, Pueblo Symph Orch; Colo St Mus Tchrs Assn; Nat Mus Tchrs Assn; Nat Guild Piano Tchrs; Pueblo Area Mus Tchrs; r/King of Kings Luth Ch (Pueblo); hon/Kappa Delta Pi; Certs from Nat & Colo St Mus Tchrs Assns.

MILLER, MARY JEANNETTE oc/Records Management Consultant; b/Sept 24, 1912; ba/600 5th St, NW, Washington, DC 20013; m/Cecil (dec); c/Cecil Jr, Ferdi Agusto, Sylvenia; p/John William and David Evangeline Hill Sims (dec); ed/Howard Univ 1929-30; Univ Ill 1943-45; Dept Agri Grad Sch 1957-59; Univ Md 1975; pa/Conslt AID; Pub'd 6 Textbooks; Bd Real Estate; Pubr Monthly Newslttr; Others; cp/Bechtel Assn; Bd Dirs Embassy Clb (Seoul Korea); Ret'd US Foreign Ser; Others; r/Cath; hon/Zeta Phi Beta; World Travels; Others.

MILLER, MICHAEL DOUGLASS oc/Farm Broadcaster; b/Dec 21, 1953; h/PO Box 264, Charlottesville, VA 22902; ba/Earlysville, VA; m/Karen Lee Nielsen; p/Douglass Harrison and Helen Gibson Miller, Keswick, VA; ed/Woodberry Forest

Sch; VMI; pa/1 of 127 Voting Mems, Nat Assn Farm Broadcasters; cp/Chm Public Relats Com, JCs; Fin Chm, Monticello Dist BSA; r/Bapt; hon/Nat Merit Awd; Eagle Scout; Rec'd Commend, Va NG; Sev Commends, Multiple Sclerosis Soc.

MILLER, ROBERT J oc/Poet; b/Jun 12, 1918; h/Hwy 60, Box 13, Plainview, AR 72857; p/Homer Cleo Miller, Little Rock, AR; Matilda Alice Dalton (dec); ed/AA Hendrix Col; BS St Tchrs Col (Now UCA) 1941;

mil/GI; pa/Author: *Freely Remembered* (1972), *Rustique* (1947), *Weird Balk* (1964), *To Span the Seasons* (1977); Contbr Profl Jours & Anthologies; Am Poets F'ship Soc; Fla St Poetry Soc Inc; Nat Soc Poets Inc; Resident Poet, MacDowell Colony (Peterborough, NH) 1941; cp/Ark Sheriffs' Assn; hon/Cit Dist'd Achmt, Intl Register Profiles.

MILLER, RUTH M H oc/Physician; Educator; b/Jul 12; h/161 Johnson St, Somerset, MA 02726; ba/Same; p/Carl Frederick and Helen Adelaide K Miller (dec); ed/Rosary Col 1936-38; BA Univ Wisc 1941; MD Univ Wisc Med Sch 1945; PhD Belin Univ 1958; MA 1972, PhD 1975 NWn Univ; Addit Studies; mil/AUS Med Corps 1951-55: Comm'd as Capt, 4th Wom to Enter Active Duty as Med Ofcr Korean War; USAR 1955-; pa/Bd Qualified Neurologist; Pvt Pract Phys: Avon Park (Fla) 1949-51, Fall River (Mass) 1959-66, Somerset 1966-; Clinical Dir Med & Surg, NM St Hosp (1 Yr); Ward Ofcr Psychi Ser, Brockton VA Hosp (6 Months); USAR Med Instr (15 Yrs); Clinical Instr, City of NY Dept Hosps (3 Yrs) Other Positions; Contbr Articles Profl Jours; Fellow: Am Col Angiology, Intl Col Angiology; Am Geriatrics Soc, Royal Soc Hlth, Acad Psychosomatic Med, Am Col Emer Phys; Reserv Ofcrs Assn; Assn Mil Surgs; Am Med Wom's Assn; AMA; cp/OES; Order of White Shrine of Jerusalem; Order of Amaranth; Coun Wom's Clbs; Mass Citizens' Rights Assn; AAUW; Univ Wisc & Rosary Col Alumni Assns; Mass Coun Public Justice; LWV; Humane Soc; Others; r/Prot; hon/Alpha Epsilon Iota; Phi Sigma Soc; Psi Chi; W/W: Am Wom, E, Mass, US; World W/W Wom; Intl W/W Commun Ldrs; DIB; Lib Human Resources; Others.

MILLS, FREDERICK VAN FLEET oc/University Administrator; Professor of Art; b/Jun 5, 1925; h/Rt 4, Rustic Acres, Bloomington, IL 61701; ba/Normal, IL; m/Lois Jean; c/Mark Steven, Michael Sherwood, Mollie Sue, Merre Shannon, Randall, Susan, Todd; p/Fred W Mills (dec); Juanita Ellen Mills, Watseka, IL; ed/BS Ohio St Univ 1949; MS 1951, EdD 1956 Ind Univ; mil/USAR Ret'd Maj; pa/Admr & Prof Art, Ill St Univ; Col Art Assn; Bd Dirs, Nat Art Ed Assn; Res Com, Nat Assn Schs Art; Bd Dirs & Res Editor, Nat Coun Art Admrs; Pres, Wn Art Assn; Pres, Ill Task Force Arts Ed; Pres, Ind Art Ed Assn; Editor: *Wn Arts Bulletin & NCAA Res & Info Bulletin*; Author: *Status of Visual Arts in Higher Ed* (1976), *The Adm of Visual Arts* (1977), *Issues in the Adm of Visual Arts* (1978), *Politics And/Of the Visual Arts* (1979); r/Meth.

MILLS, WILLIAM A oc/Certified Public Accountant; b/Apr 7, 1910; h/802 E 41st St, Savannah, GA 31401; m/Ruth H Waters (dec); p/Oscar Lee and Willie Mae Griffin Mills; ed/BS Univ Ga-Athens 1934; Passed CPA Exams 1934; mil/Fiscal Div, Ordnance Dept; pa/Mem M H Barnes & Co CPAs (Savannah) 1934-43; Partner, M H Barnes & Co 1947-73 (Firm Name Changed to Barnes, Askew, Mills & Co 1947; Merged w Haskins & Sells 1961); Ret'd 1973; Ga Soc CPAs; Am Inst CPAs Inc; Estate Planning Coun (Savannah Chapt); Nat Assn Accts; cp/Kiwanis Clb; Chatham Clb; Ga Hist Soc; hon/Beta Gamma Sigma; Phi Kappa Phi; Beta Alpha Psi; Biogl Listings.

MIMS, THOMAS JEROME oc/Insurance Executive; b/Dec 12, 1899; h/Knollwood Dr, Greenville, SC 29607; ba/G'ville; m/Valma Gillespie; c/T J Jr, G Frank; p/L and Rebecca White Mims (dec); ed/BA Furman Univ; pa/Canal Ins Co: VP & Secy 1942-48, Pres & Dir 1948-; Mgr, William R Timmons Agy 1933-; VP, Century-Lincoln Mercury; Past Pres, G'ville Assn Ins Agents; Former Chm Ins Com & Past Dir, Motor Transportation Assn; Past Pres, Assn SC Property & Casualty Ins Cos Inc; Chm Mbrship Com, Truck & Heavy Equipmt Claims Coun; Other Positions; Local, St & Nat Assns Ins Agents; Am Mgmt Assn; Pres' Assn; Pres' Coun, Am Inst Mgmt; Others; cp/Rotary Clb; Past Pres, G'ville Little Theatre; Past Dir, Metro Arts Coun; Palmetto Clb; Summit Clb; Elks; Past Pres,

United Way; Adv Bd, Furman Univ; Others; r/First Bapt Ch (G'ville): Mem, Former Pres Men's Bible Class, Former Mem Fin Com; hon/Hon Roll, Furman Univ; Bd Govs, Intl Ins Seminar; Boss of Yr, G'ville JCs 1964 & G'ville Assn Ins Wom 1966; Rec'd Marquis Awd, Am Inst Mgmt; W/W: SC, Ins, Fin & Indust; DIB; Others.

MIN, FRANK K oc/Plastic Engineer; b/Mar 29, 1915; h/2915 Lavoha Pl, Honolulu, HI 96813; ba/Honolulu; m/Elaine Nam; c/Donna M Shiroma, Dwight F; p/Euikyong Min (dec); Sarah Y Min, Honolulu; ed/NYU; Univ Hawaii; mil/1941-45; pa/Pres, Min Plastics & Supply Inc; Conslt; cp/Honolulu Civitan Clb; Bd Dirs, Honolulu C of C; Pres, Korean C of C; r/Prot; hon/Intl Civitan Awd; ROHM & HAAS Awd.

MINER, LORINE VERNA oc/Director of Placement; b/Jun 26, 1925; h/112 N College, Webb City, MO 64870; ba/Joplin, MO; m/Lawrence L; c/Patricia M Fisher (Mrs Marion), Robert S, David L; p/Guy and Cora Spencer, Asbury, MO; ed/BS; MS; pa/Dir Placemt, Mo So St Col; Mo St Tchrs Assn; Nat Bus Ed Assn; Rocky Mountain Col Placemt Assn; MW Col Placemt Assn; Adv Coun, St Dept Ed; cp/Soroptomist Clb; Webb City BPW Clb; r/Prot; hon/Delta Kappa Gamma; Outstg Edr Yr 1971; BPWC Wom of Yr 1978; World W/W Wom; DIB; Notable Ams Bicent Era.

MINTO, GEORGE DENNIS oc/Logistics Engineering Manager; b/Jun 15, 1941; h/3900 LeJune Ave, Titusville, FL 32780; ba/Orlando, FL; m/Charlotte J; c/Tanya L, Heidi K; p/George and Katherine L Minto, Butler, PA; ed/Assoc Elect Engrg; pa/Former Ofcr Soc, Logistics Engrs; Am Defense Preparedness Assn; cp/Martin Marietta Mgmt Clb; Assn Realtors Fla; r/Cath; hon/W/W S&SW; DIB; Personalities of S.

MIODUSZEWSKI, THOMAS PHILLIP oc/Design Engineer; b/Nov 22, 1950; h/18940 Tireman, Detroit, MI 48228; ba/Dearborn, MI; p/Chester and Anne Mioduszewski; ed/BSEE Univ Mich 1973; MBA Univ Detroit 1978; pa/Elect Product Design Engr, Ford Motor Co; Engrg Soc Detroit; Soc Automotive Engrs; Fisher Body Craftsman Guild; Dearborn Campus Engrs; r/St Peter & St Paul Cath Ch (Detroit): Mem; hon/Mich Competitive S'ship; Engrg Internship, Univ Mich; BSA Parvuli Dei Awd; Others.

MIR de CID, MARGARITA oc/Associate Professor; b/Nov 11, 1926; h/162 W 13th St, Apt 36, New York, NY 10011; ba/Brooklyn, NY; m/Leopoldo Cid-Hurtado; p/Antonio Mir (dec); Margarita Busquets, Mallorca; ed/Summa Cum Laude: BS, MA, MEd, EdD; pa/Assoc Prof in Charge of Bilingual Student Tchr Practicum, Undergrad Bilingual Tchr Tng Prog, Bklyn Col CUNY 1972-; Deputy, Sch Gen Studies CUNY 1974-75; Univ Sacred Heart (Puerto Rico); Chrperson Dept Ed 1971, Devel'd Career-Ladder Prog Elem Sch Tchrs; Former Elem Sch Tchr, Sec'dy Sch Tchr, Cnslr, Asst Prin, Prin, Supvr & Supt of Schs (Puerto Rico); Curric Spec; Conducts Workshops; Lectr; Author, *Hacia Una Identidad Hispanoamericana* (1977); r/Cath; hon/Hon of Merits Awd, WNJU-TV (NJ); Cert of Merit, Assn Puerto Rico & Hispanic Culture; Rec'd Plaque, NE Conf Tchg of Foreign Langs.

MIRENBURG, BARRY LEONARD oc/-Artist; Designer; Publisher; b/Feb 16, 1952; ba/413 City Island Ave, New York, NY 10064; p/Fred and Mildred Solomon Mirenburg; ed/Rhode Isl Sch Design; Fordham Univ; Mercy Col; Cooper Union (Sch of Art & Arch); pa/Graphic Designer, Num Fortune 500 Cos; Pres & Pubr, Barlenmir House (Pub'g Co) 1970-; Pres & Creat Dir, Barlenmir House of Graphics 1970-; Pres, Barlenmir House Theatres Inc 1972-; Pres & Dir, Barlenmir House Foun on Arts 1972-; Pres & Owner, City Isl Theatre 1972-; Design Conslt: Catalyst Press 1977-, Croton Review 1977-; Conslt, E Coast Writers Inc 1976-; Advr, Leg Adv Com NY 1975-; Designed & Illustrated Num Books Poetry & Art; Pub'd & Anthologized Num Books Art & Lit; Others; Copyright Soc USA; Am Inst Graphic Arts; Croton-Coun-on-Arts; Am Assn Pubrs; cp/Mensa; Metro Mus Art; Mus Modern Art; Nat Jogging Assn; Pres' Coun Fitness & Ath Achmt; r/Jewish; hon/Awd Excell in Advtg & Graphic Design, NY Art & Design; Finalist, Best Poster in USA, *Print Mag*; Rec'd Awds, Am Inst Graphic Arts; Rec'd Awd Designed Poster, Metro Mus Art; Rec'd Awds, Innovative Designs & Concepts for Book Covers; W/W Illustration; All About the Illustrator; DIB; Men Achmt; Others.

MISHRA, BIPIN BIHARI oc/Engineer; b/Jan 9 1946; h/1053 S Memphis, Aurora, CO 80012; ba/Denver, CO; m/Bessie Sue; p/Braja Bihari and Anna Poorna Mishra, India; ed/BT; MS; pa/Elect Engr; Sr Mem, Instrument Soc Am; IEEE; Reg'd Profl Engr; r/Hindu; hon/Best Tech Paper, WWID-ISA.

MITCHELL, BARBARA JEAN oc/Elementary School Principal; b/Mar 22, 1933; h/2231 E 67th St, Chicago, IL 60649; ba/Chgo; c/Leon Ellis, Brian DeWitt; p/C B and Hilda Ellis, Chgo; ed/BEd Chgo Tchrs Col 1952; MA Roosevelt Univ 1955; pa/Tchr 1952-62; Asst Prin 1963-72; Prin 1972-; Nat Coun Adm Wom Ed; Chgo Prins' Assn; r/Epis; hon/Phi Delta Kappa; Dist'd Ser Mem Scroll, Ill Cong Parents & Tchrs; Cert Recog, Park Manor Commun Coun.

MITCHELL, GREGORY JEROME oc/-Law Student; b/Oct 15, 1958; h/1153 21st St, Newport News, VA 23607; p/James R and Ruth C Mitchell, Newport News; ed/AA; Cont'g Ed for Law Deg; pa/Peer Cnslr; VP, SGA; cp/Hampton Yth Coun; hon/Phi Theta Kappa; W/W Am HS & Jr Cols; Others.

MITCHELL, JERRY DON oc/Consulting Psychologist; b/Dec 24, 1940; h/1303 N 4th, Alpine, TX 79830; ba/Same; m/Margaret Cloean Walker; c/Brent, Melissa; p/Wilbur Robert Mitchell (dec); Mary Lena Ray, Grandbury, TX; ed/BA 1963; MEd 1970; EdD 1974; mil/AUS 1966-69; pa/APA; APGA; TPA; TPGA; cp/Ser'd as J of P, Coleman, Tex; r/Presb; hon/Kappa Delta Pi; Psi Chi; W/W S&SW.

MITCHELL, JOSEPHINE A oc/Dietician; b/Sept 11, 1934; h/530 Montclaire SE, Albuquerque, NM 87108; ba/Albuquerque; m/James E; c/Barry James, Richard Stephen; p/Dick B Friesen (dec); Eva M Friesen, Hooker, OK; ed/BS 1960, MS 1962, Internship 1961 Okla St Univ; pa/Dir Food Sers, Lovelace Med Ctr; Am Dietetic Assn; Am Soc Hosp Food Ser Admrs; NM Dietetic Assn; cp/Albuquerque TVI Culinary Arts Adv Bd; Adv Bd, Albuquerque Public Schs Hlth Occupations; r/Prot; hon/Outstg Yg Wom Am; W/W W.

MITCHELL, LAWRENCE DU-WAYNE oc/Physician; b/Feb 23, 1925; h/Rt 2, Box 35, Huntsville, TX 77340; ba/Anderson, TX; m/Ethel Clark; c/Michael Warren, Melissa Ann; p/Edward Preston and Martha Alma Mitchell, Huntsville, TX; ed/BBA; BA; MA; MD; FRSH; mil/USNR 1943-46 WWII; pa/AMA; Tex Med Assn & Fdn; Fellow, Royal Soc of Hlth; Medic Alert Foun; Nat Acupuncture Res Soc; Intl Acad Preventive Med; cp/Tex Farm Bur; r/Ch of Christ; hon/Author, *An Approach to the Problem of Alcoholism on the Basis of Altered Cell Metabolism; Cert of Proficiency in Basic Sci*; TDC Awd; Phi Chi.

MITCHELL, MARION FAULKNER oc/-Retired Librarian; b/Jan 1, 1914; h/705 16th Ave E, Cordele, GA 31015; m/George Thomas; c/George Thomas Jr, Robert Norris; p/Robert Hunter Faulkner (dec); Louise Wicker Norris (dec); mil/Armed Ser Forces 1944-45; pa/BPW; cp/Cordele Wom's Clb; Cordele Garden Clb; Pilot Intl; Garden Clb

Ga; Crisp Co Registrar; Voter Registrars Assn Ga; Crisp Co Hist Soc; Hosp Aux; Ga Wildlife Assn; r/Meth; Pres United Meth Wom; hon/First Wom Clerk, Crisp Co Grand Jury; First Forewom of Yr, Crisp Co 1963; Wom of Yr, BPW 1972; Sweepstakes Awd, BPW Hobby & Art Show; Art Awds; Den Mother Awd; Others.

MITCHELL, MELVIN JAMES oc/Minister; b/Feb 29, 1904; h/1628 Granville St, Columbus, OH 43203; ba/Columbus; m/-Katherin T; c/Melvin Thomas, Beverly Ann, William James (dec); Mary Jane, R Nathaniel; p/Steven and Mary Stewart (dec); ed/PhD 1974; pa/Pastor, Pilgrim Bapt Ch Over 36 Yrs; CLASP Bd; Ofcr, Ohio Mins' Conf; Ofcr, Columbus Bapt Min Alliance; Pres Ohio Bapt St Conv Inc 3 Yrs; Treas, Columbus Pastors' Alliance; Ofcr, Ohio Bapt St Conv Inc; Ofcr, Nat Bapt Conv Inc; Ofcr, Nat Bapt BTU & SS Cong; Past Pres, Mt Calvary Bapt Assn; Others; cp/Fdr, Columbus Area Devel & Tng Sch; Fdr, Boys' Own Yth Shelter Inc (3 Homes); Pres, Model Neighborhood Assembly; Mayor's Adv Bd; Citizens' Progressive Org; Mid-Ohio Hlth Planning Fdn; Grand Master, St John's Masonic Lodge; r/Bapt; hon/Rec'd Recog Awds, WCOL (Father of Week & Most Influential Black Man Columbus); Rec'd Rel Achmt Awd, Gay St Bapt Ch; Awd Recog, St Leg of Ohio; Others.

MITCHELL, ROY DeVOY oc/Management Engineer; b/Sept 11, 1922; h/324 Valley Vista Dr, Jackson, MS 39211; ba/Jackson; m/Jane Caroline Gibson; c/Michael, Marilyn, Martha, Stewart, Nancy; p/Watson W and Marie Stewart Mitchell; ed/BS Okla St Univ 1948; MS 1950; BIM Auburn Univ 1960; mil/USNR 1943-46; pa/Metro Devel Office, HUD: Area Engr 1971-72, Chief Arch & Engrg 1972-75, Chief Prog Planning & Support Branch 1975, Dir Arch Branch 1975-; Field Engr, HHFA Commun Facilities Adm (Atlanta & Jackson) 1963-71; Constrn Army Balistic Missile Agy (Huntsville, Ala) 1957-58; Auburn Res Foun (NASA) 1963; Others; Reg'd Profl Engr: Ala, Miss; Ctl Miss Fed Pers Adv Coun; Nat Soc Profl Engrs; Am Soc Engrg Ed; Miss Soc Profl Engrs; Nat Assn Govt Engrs; Jackson Fdn Execs Assn; cp/Ctl Miss Safety Coun; Am Water Works Assn; River Hills Clb; Univ Clb; r/Meth: Trustee, Former Bd Mem; hon/Iota Lambda Sigma; Commend Outstg Achmt, Dept HUD.

MITCHELL, WAYNE LEE oc/Educator; Social Worker; b/Mar 25, 1937; h/PO Box 61, Phoenix, AZ 85001; ba/Phoenix; p/Albert C Mitchell (dec); Elizabeth Nagle Mitchell, Phoenix; ed/BA Univ Redlands 1959; MSW Ariz St Univ 1970; EdD 1979; mil/USCG; pa/Profl Social Worker Var Co, St & Fed Agencies 1962-70; Bur Indian Affairs (Phoenix) 1970-77; US Public Hlth Ser 1977-; Bd Dirs, Phoenix Indian Commun Sch 1973-; Bd Dirs, Phoenix Indian Ctr 1974-; Phoenix

Area Hlth Adv Bd 1975; Commun Behavioral Mtl Hlth Bd 1976; Lectr; Nat Cong Am Indians; Nat Assn Social Workers; Am Orthopsychi Assn; cp/NAACP; Dem Party; r/Congreg; hon/Phi Delta Kappa; Chi Sigma Chi; Kappa Delta Pi; W/W W; Intl W/W Commun Ser; Personalities of W&MW; DIB; Others.

MITRA, GOPAL C oc/Artist; Educator; b/Nov 1 1928; h/12530 Cedar Dr, Edinboro, PA 16412; m/Reba; c/2; p/Shyama Das and Panchanani Mitra; ed/Intermediate of Arts, Patna Univ (India) 1948; Dipl Fine Arts, Govt Sch Arts & Crafts (India) 1953; MFA 1963, PhD 1967 Univ Minn; pa/Prof Art & Non-Wn Art Hist, Edinboro St Col 1969-; Assoc Prof, Chgo St Unvi 1967-69; Visiting Artist, Lectr; Others; Num Solo Exhbns Throughout World; Over 500 Works Pvt & Public Collections; Dir, Moni-Mela Patna Branch; Dir Mitra Ctr (Patna); Interior Decorator, Roy's Studio (Calcutta); Author: *Art & Aesthetics, Art in Ed, The Himalayan Art*; Phil E&W; Intl Soc Comparative Study Civilization; Am Assn Asian Studies; Am Soc Aesthetics; Am Assn St Cols & Univs; Num Lit & Art Orgs; hon/Num Res Grants; Num Awds & Purchase Prizes Art Work; Titled Master Tchr, Worthington Sch Sys; Biogl Listings.

MITTEN, LOUIS OTTO oc/Retired Pastor; b/Jul 18, 1915; h/PO Box 2389, Rapid City, SD 57709; ba/Same; m/Gladys Marie Gabehart; c/Donald L, Janet M Beatty (Mrs Donald K), Carol M Anderson (Mrs Edwin G); p/Grenville L Mitten (dec); Vera V Mitten, Sunbury, PA; ed/BS Anderson Col 1958; Addit Studies: Adams St Col, Univ N Colo, Black Hills St Col; pa/Ordained to Min, Ch of God (Anderson, Ind) 1960; Pastor: Toppenish (Wash) 1958-64, Minot (ND) 1965-66, Springfield (Colo) 1966-73, Rapid City 1973-76; Tchr & Dir Adult Literacy Classes, LARK Foun (Toppenish) 1959-63; Good Samaritan F'ship; Hosp Chaplains; Springfield Min F'ship; Ordination & Credentials Com, Colo Mins Ch of God; Dept Yth Camps, Colo Conf Ch of God; SD Bd Ch Ed, Ch of God; Christian Edrs United; AARP; Others; Constbr Articles Profl Jours; r/Ch of God; hon/W/W Rel; Commun Ldrs & Noteworthy Ams; Personalities W&MW.

MLOTT, SYLVESTER ROMAN oc/Clinical Psychologist; b/Dec 17, 1925; h/745 Creekside Dr, Mt Pleasant, SC 29464; ba/Charleston, SC; m/Yvonne Dunaway; c/Brent A, Bruce W; p/Roman and Mary Margaret Haber Mlott (dec); ed/BS; MA; PhD Univ Miss 1964; mil/USAF 1944-46; pa/-Conslt Var Govt & St Agencies; Reschr: Renal Dialysis, Heart Attack, Personality Correlates of Individuals in Var Job Categories; Am, SC, SEn & Charleston Psychol Assns; Nat Assn Voc Rehab; r/Rom Cath; hon/W/W S&SW; Personalities S; DIB; Men Achmt; Am Men & Wom Sci; Intl W/W Commun Sers.

MOBERLEY, CONNIE M oc/Photographer; b/Jul 5, 1947; h/215 Asbury, Houston, TX 77007; ba/Same; p/O R and Doris Bell Moberley, Matagorda, TX; ed/BS Sam Houston St Univ 1969; Addit Studies; pa/Sam Houston St Univ: Former Lab Asst, Former Photo Prodn Employee; Former Lectr, Univ Hawaii; Photog, John Mason Photog (Houston); Independent Photo Work; Work Exhibited: Fashion Inst Technol (NY), APA Intl Exhbn Photog (Japan), John Fitzsimmons & Co (Houston), Canon Gallery (San Francisco, Cal), Pace Gallery (Briarcliff, NY), Tex Wom's Photog Show (Dallas, Tex), V Nemir Gallery (Galveston, Tex); Ofcr, Local Chapt ASMP; cp/ERA Supporter; hon/Work Rep'd in Book, *Wom Photograph Men*; Color Portfolio Pub'd in *Peterson's Photographic Mag* (Dec, 1978); Others.

MOBLEY, HERBERT BROOKS oc/Retired Minister; b/Jun 18, 1909; h/PO Box 165, Summit Station, PA 17979; m/Catherine Bieber; p/Herbert M and Parrie Brooks Mobley; ed/DD Faith Theol Sem 1968; Penn St Univ; Wn Reserv Univ; Grad, Auburn Christian Col 1929; pa/Ordained Min 1934; Pastorates: Emmanuel United Ch of Christ (Minersville, Penn), St Peters (Frackville,

Penn), St Mark's UCC (Summit Station) 1977-79; Interim Pastor, St Mark's (Brown's) UCC 1977-; Dir Reading-Berks Chapt, Nat Conf Christians & Jews; Other Positions; Pres St Clair Ministerium; Bd Dirs, Minersville Clergy Assn; Lectr; cp/Rotary Clb; Dir, Schuylkil Mtl Hlth Assn; 4-H Clb; Mem Ofcl Bd, AAA of Schuylkil Co; Camp Cnslr, Modern Woodmen Am; Others; r/United Ch of Christ; hon/Rec'd Cit for Pastoral Ser, United Ch of Christ (Annual Conf); Recog for 40th Yr Since Ordination; Cit for Dist'd Ser, Penn SE Conf UCC; Biogl Listings.

MOFFETT, HENRY CLAY NICK oc/- Floraculturist; b/Nov 30, 1908; h/Rt 11, Box 125Q, Ft Myers, FL 33908; m/Dorothy D (dec); c/Betty M Terres; p/Charles C and Melissa Moffett (dec); mil/Cryptographer, Pacific Theatre WWII; pa/Propagator New Varieties Gladiolus; Co-Originator 24 Varieties Gladiolus; TV & Radio Commentator on Gladiolus Culture (NY & NJ) Sev Yrs; Lectr; Dir & Judge, All Am Gladiolus Selections; Former VP, The Most Co (Public Relations); Former Tax Commr, Gloucester Co (NJ); Others Positions; Past Chm, Gloucester Co Ec Stabilization Bd; Past Horticult Conslt, Gloucester Co 4-H Clb; Past Pres, NJ Gladiolus Soc; Past Auditor, N Am Gladiolus Coun; Others; cp/Past Pres: Woodbury Rotary Clb, Gloucester Co Holy Name Soc, St Patrick's Holy Name Soc, Woodbury Men's Cath Clb, Woodbury Repub Clb; Former VP, Metro VA (NJ); Former Repub Campaign Mgr (Gloucester Co); Others; r/Cath; hon/Hon Mem: Royal Brit Horticult Soc, New Zealand Gladiolus Soc, Canadian Gladiolus Soc; Hon Citizen, Lubbock (Tex); Gold Medal Awd, N Am Gladiolus Coun; Man of Yr, Gloucester Co 4-H; Commun Ser Awd, City of Woodbury; Outstg Ser Awd, Woodbury Rotary Clb.

MOHAMMED, M HAMDI ABDELHAKIM oc/Professor; b/May 10, 1940; h/3236 SW 62nd Ln, Gainesville, FL 32601; ba/Gainesville; m/Assma Abdelwahab; c/Karim, Eman; p/Abdelhakim Mohammed El-Tahawi and Enayat Abdelhakim Abdelsamad, Egypt; ed/DDS; MScD; PhD; pa/Prof & Chm Dept Dental Biomaterials, Univ Fla-G; Fellow Royal Soc Hlth; Fellow Intl Col Oral Implantology; Intl & Am Assns Dental Res; r/Moslem; hon/Medal Sci Achmt, Egypt.

MOHANTY, SANTOSH KUMAR oc/- Physician & Surgeon; b/Jun 29, 1936; h/2313 Scott Dr, Dublin, GA 31021; ba/Dublin; m/Carolyn I; c/Chaiya Rebecca, Jawahar Kennedy; p/Pravat K and Puspalata Mohanty, India; ed/BS Utkal Univ (Orissa, India) 1954; MBBS, SCB Med Col (Orissa) 1960; mil/Indian Air Force; USAR; pa/Chief Surg Ser, VA Med Ctr (Dublin) 1978-; USAR Hosp (Hamilton AFB, Cal) 1977-; VA Med Ctr (Reno, Nev): Staff Surg, Dir Respiratory Therapy 1972-78; Clinical Asst Prof Surg, Sch of Med Scis (Univ Nev) 1974-79; Other Positions; Diplomate, Am Bd Surg 1969; Diplomate, Bd Thoracic Surg; Lic'd Pract Med: NJ, NY, Penn, Ohio, Ill, Cal; Steering Com, Broncho-Esophagology, Col Chest Physicians; Fellow, Am Col Surgs; AMA; Am Soc Clinical Hypnosis; Contbr Articles Profl Jours; cp/Instr Basic & Adv'd Cardio-Pulminary Resuscitaion, Am Heart Assn & ARC; r/Hindu & Christian.

MOHD, MAQSOOD AHMED oc/Computer Controls Systems Engineer; b/Mar 4, 1952; h/420 E Lindsey, Norman, OK 73069; ba/Oklahoma City, OK; m/Anwar Sultana; p/Mohd Osman and Masooma Begum, Hyderabad, India; ed/BEECE; MSEE; pa/AAAS; IEEE; Computer Clb for Hobbyists; cp/Social Work; r/Islam; hon/Gold Medals; S'ships; Prizes; Distinctions.

MOHR, G ROBERT oc/Professor; b/Feb 15, 1922; h/247 Brookline Ave, Daytona Beach, FL 32018; ba/Daytona Beach; m/Wilma L; c/Robert K, Deborah M Foster, Loretta M Ruess; p/Leon H Mohr (dec); Adella I Dye, Winter Haven, FL; ed/BS, MA Unvi Iowa; mil/USCG 1941-45; pa/Prof Fin &

Area Coor Bus Adm, Bethune-Cookman Col; Jacksonville Soc Fin Analysts; Fellow, Fin Analyst Fdn; AIDS; r/Unit: Treas Unitarian Soc Ormand Beach; hon/Rec'd Ecs-in-Action F'ship; Alpha Iota Delta; Others.

MOIR, GERTRUDE M FISHER oc/Artist; b/Feb 15, 1896; h/45090 Namoku St, Kaneohe, HI 98744; m/John Troup Jr; c/John Troup III, Mrs George G Mason; p/Henry Clay and Lillian Metz Fisher; ed/Phila Acad Fine Arts; Penn Acad Mus; Cornell Univ; Bates Col; BA Univ Cal 1943; EdM Univ Hawaii 1945; pa/Prin Iao HS to Retirement 1961; Paintings Sold Through Gumps, Rust Craft & Grassman Moody; Wrote Radio Script, "Intl Mail Bag", Sunset Mag", "Reader's Digest"; Former Piano & Hula Tchr; Social Editor Garden Island; 1st Aid Instr & Mobile Unit WWII; Standardized ARC Tests Copyright & Patent Donated to ARC; Co-Chm, Hi Bd War Records, U of H Archives, Wrote Lahaina Part in WWII for U of H, Evacuation Comm WWII; Former Concert Pianist; cp/OPA Com, Co-Fdr Maui Public Lib; Worthy Matron OES; Charter Mem, Kauai Mus Clb, Maui Wom's Clb (Wrote Constit & 1st Sect), Lahaina Art & Cult Ctr, Friends of Lahaina Restoration; Sponsor, Hawaii Loa Col; Dir YWCA; VP Hawaii PTA;

Maui Hist Soc; Hui Manu; Outdoor Cir; Pres, Koloa Wom's Clb; Lahaina Wom's Clb; hon/Author, *Ancient Hawaiian Hulas*; Author, Book on Art; Publishing pictorial album *Hawaii's Flowers* now at museums, art acedmy, stores; One-woman Show exhibiting 192 Paintings (Oils, Pastels, Watercolors); Awds, Hons & S'ships All Schs; Gold Medal Dancing Acad; Nat Hon Soc; Phi Kappa Phi; Del, White House Cnslg Conf; Del & Page, OES Triennial as Worthy Matron; Grand Prize Art: Maui Co Fair, W Maui Fair, Hon Art Acad; Life Master ACBL; Life Hon Mem: Hi Ed Assn, Maui Ed Assn, Hi Civic Clb; Letters Commend: Cmdg Gen Pac Area for Art Work, Prime Min W Samoa for Ed Help under Kennedy's People to People Prog; Del to 1st Indep Celebration W Samoa; Guest of Embassy at Sukarno's Cult Asia-Africa Conf 1965; Collaborated w Porteus in "Blow Not the Trumpet" (WWII); Gold Medal Award for Art, Accademia Italia Delle Arte in Italy; Contemporary European Artists, 1980; World W/W Wom; Cornell Alumni News & Men & Wom Hi; W/W: Maui Co, Hi; Blue Book Hi; Wom Hi; Social Directory USA; DIB; Nat Directory; Others.

MOIR, JOHN TROUP JR oc/Retired; Plantation Manager; b/May 23, 1894; h/45090 Namoku St, Kaneohe, HI 96744; m/Gertrude M E Fisher; c/John T III, Mrs George G Mason; p/John T and Louisa Silver Moir (dec); mil/Lt/Col 1st Bat Maui Vols for Def W Maui; pa/Ret'd 1952; Mgr: Koloa Sugar Co, Pioneer Mill Co; Pres, Lahaina Lt & Power Co; Maui Planters' Assn; Hi Technologist, HSPA, PM Supvr; Bldr War Observation Posts, Sighting Instrumts, Shoulder Stocks to Convert Pistols to Rifles; cp/Mgr, Maui Rifle Team; Nat & Hi Rifle Assns; Citizens' Com Right to Keep & Bear Arms; Sponsor, Gun Owners Am; Smithsonian Assn; Bur Govtl Res; Gov's Ec Com; Intl Oceanographic Foun; Chm Dist Police; Am Fdn Police; Disaster Coun, Civil Def, Alien Interment Bd, Past Chm YMCA; BSA; Past Pres Kauai C of C; PM Ath Clb; Maui Co Fair & Racing Assn; Trustee Alex Settlement; Charter Mem: Lahaina Art & Cult

Ctr, Lahaina Restoration; Chm Kauai Co Repub Party; Humane Soc Hi; Big Game Fishing Clb; Am Yachtsman Assn; Hui Manu; Cornell Ath Clb; Savage Clb; Quill & Dagger, Maalaeo Boat Clb; Pres W Maui Boat Clb; Cornell Tower Clb; Capt Kauai Polo Team, Punahou Century Clb; Sponsor Hi Loa Col; Conservative Caucus; Nat Right to Work Com; Accuracy in Media; Adv Bd Am Security Coun; AARP; Cousteau Soc; Nat Trust Hist Preserv; 2nd Amendment Foun, Heritage Foun; Others; r/Koloa Union Ch: Deacon, Chm Lgr Parish Plan; hon/Am Police Hall of Fame; Hon Life Mem, Maui Hi Civic Clb; Expert Rifle Men's Awd, Meritorious Ser Ribbon, WWII; Bldrs of Hi; Men Hi; Koa Malu, Pan Pac W/W; DIB; Blue Book of Hi; Soc Dir Hi; Men Achmt; W/W: Trans & Communs, USA; Nat Cyclopedia Am Biog; Hon Soc Am.

MOLINA, MARIA TERESA oc/Social Worker; b/Feb 26, 1932; h/2956 Staunton Rd, Huntington, WV 25702; m/Rafael E; c/Louis,

Maria Teresa, Manuel, Rafael Jr; p/Manuel Rodriguez (dec); Teresa F Rodriguez, Huntington; ed/BSW; cp/Civic Ldr; Lectr; r/Cath.

MOLLENHAUER, BERNHARD oc/- Writer; b/Oct 23, 1902; h/3614 Third Ave, San Diego, CA 92103; ba/Same; m/Tekla Van Norman; p/Bernhard (Well-known Violinist) and Frances Burton (Violinist) Mollenhauer (dec); ed/Isis Conservatory Mus (Point Loma, Cal) 1923-36; Correspondence Courses, Univ Cal; Hon PhD; pa/Contbr Scholarly Jours; Scholar of Phil, Parapsychol & Greek Hist; Author Articles: "Horizons of the Western Mind", *Hibbert Jour* (1952), "The Polit Phil of William E Hocking", *Jour of Royal Phil Soc of Glasgow* (1971), Others; Contb'd Essay to *Radhakrishnan Souvenir Vol* (1964); Other Contbns to: *World Affairs Interpreter*, *The Quest for Peace* (1945), *B L Atreya Souvenir Vol*, Others; Reviewer for *Books Abroad* 1950-70; Others; Am Soc Psychical Res; Metaphysical Soc Am; Hegel Soc Am; Royal Phil Soc Glasgow; Canadian Phil Soc; Life Fellow, Intl Inst Arts & Lttrs (Switzerland); Recording Secy, San Diego Browning Soc 1976; hon/Rec'd Cert Merit, Intl Soc World Adventurers & DIB; W/W Am; Directory Am Scholars; Others.

MONTGOMERY, ELEANOR MOORE oc/Author; Editor; Painter; Poet; b/Nov 19; h/875 Fifth Ave, New York, NY 10021; ba/Same; m/A Moore (dec); p/(dec); ed/BA Univ Chgo; pa/Assoc Fashion Editor, *Vogue Mag* 15 Yrs; Former Radio Script Writer; Book of Paintings Currently in Progress; Art Exhbns: Fest Intl de Peinture ed d'Art Graphico-Plastique de St Germain des Pres 1974 & 1975, Salon de Thouet (Thouars, France) 1974, 43eme Grand Salon des Surindependants (Paris, France), Parrish Art Mus (Southampton, Long Isl, NY), New Sch Social Res & Old York Clb (NY) 1975; Poetry Pub'd England, Am & South India; Pres, Foun World Ed Inc; cp/Dame, Order St John of Jerusalem, Knights of Malta (Am Ecumenical Branch); Pres, Sri Aurobindo Intl Ctr; Old York Clb; Meadow & Southampton Clbs; r/Universal; hon/One-man Show & Laureat, Galeries Raymond Duncan (Paris); 2 Paintings Shown Bicent Issue, *Artists/USA*; Awd'd Las Palmas de Oro al Merito Belgo-Hispanica, Sponsored by Queen Fabiola; Rec'd Medaille d'Argent pour sers rendus aux Arts, Grand

Prix Humanitaire de France; Dipl Meritisimos de Academia de Ciencias Humanisticas y Relaciones (Republica Dominicana); Humanitarian Awd, Becton Soc, Farleigh Dickinson Univ (Rutherford, NJ).

MONTGOMERY, GILLESPIE V oc/-Congressman; b/Aug 5, 1920; h/PO Box 5618, Meridian, MS 39301; ba/Washington, DC; p/Gillespie Montgomery (dec); Emily Tims, Jackson, MS; ed/BS Miss St Univ; mil/USAR Brigadier Gen; Miss NG Former Brigadier Gen; Ser'd Over 30 Yrs WWII & Korea; pa/US Ho of Reps (Third Dist, Miss) 1966-; House Veterans Affairs Com (Chm Compensation, Pension & Ins Subcom & Hosps Subcom), House Armed Sers Com (Pers Subcom & Intelligence & Mil Application Nuclear Energy Subcom), Chm House Select Com US Involvemt SE Asia 1970, Chm House Select Com Missing Persons SE Asia 1975-76, Now Ser'g 6th Term; Visited Hanoi for Woodcock Comm 1977; Former Owner & Operator, Montgomery Ins Agy; Former VP, Gtr Miss Life Ins Co (Meridian); Elected Miss St Senate 1956-66; cp/VFW; Am Legion; Shriner; Mason; Scottish Rite; Past Pres Miss Heart Assn; Miss St Alumni Assn; Miss NG Assn; Former Mem, Miss Agri & Indust Bd; r/Epis Ch: Mem; hon/Rec'd Legion Merit, Bronze Star for Valor, Commend Medal, WWII European Theatre Ribbon USAR; Miss Magnolia Cross Awd; Cert Merit, ARC; Dist'd Ser Medal, NG Assn US; Mississippian of Yr, Miss Broadcasters Assn; Gov's Outstg Mississippian Awd; Dist'd Ser Cit, Reserv Ofcrs Assn US; Spec Awd, NG Assn US; Others.

MONTGOMERY, RICHARD MATTERN oc/Retired Air Force Officer; Company Director; b/Dec 15, 1911; h/PO Box 93, Longboat Key, FL 33548; m/Anne Johnson Young; c/Nancy, Richard M Jr, Thomas; p/Charles W Sr and Eva Mattern Montgomery; ed/BS US Mil Acad 1933; Student Flying Tng Ctr (San Antonio, Tex) 1933-34; AC Tech Tng Sch 1937-38; Air War Col 1946-47; mil/AUS Cmdr 2/Lt 1933, Adv'd through Grades to Lt/Gen 1962; Chief Insp, Test Pilot Panama Air Depot (France Field, CZ) 1935-37; Assigned Chanute Field (Ill) 1937-38; Flying Instr, Flight & Stage Cmdr, Randolf Field (Tex) 1938-42; Dir Flying Tng, Army Air Field (Enid, Okla) 1942; Cmdr Army Air Field (Independence, Kan) 1943; Chief Individual Tng Div Office Asst, Chief Air Staff Tng (Pentagon, Wash, DC) 1943-44; Cmdr 383d Bomb Wing 1944-45; Mem Jt

Strategic Plans & Operations Group HQs, Far East Command (Tokyo, Japan) 1947-48; Cmdr 51st Jet Fighter Wing, Naha AFB (Okinawa) 1948-49; Dep Cmdr 97th Bomb Wing, Biggs AFB (El Paso, Tex) 1949-51; Dep Chief Staff HQs, Strategic Air Command (Omaha, Neb) 1951-52, Chief of Staff 1952-56; Dep Cmdr 2d Air Force (Guam, MI) 1958-59; Asst V-Chief of Staff HQs USAF (Wash, DC) 1959-62; V-Cmdr-in-Chief USAF, Europe 1962-66; Ret'd 1966; pa/Dir, Gen Sers Life Ins Co (Wash) 1968-; Freedoms Foun Valley Forge (Penn): Exec VP Dered 1967-68, Regional VP 1968-76, Coun Trustees 1976-; cp/Former Commr, Town of Longboat Key; Order of Daedalions; Air Force Assn; Repub Party; 32° Mason; Shriner; Scottish Rite; r/United Meth; hon/Decorated DSM w Oak Leaf Cluster, Army & Air Force; Legion of Merit w Oak Leaf Cluster; Army Commend Medal w 2 Oak Leaf Clusters; Silver Beaver Awd, BSA; Silver

Antelope Awd; Gold Medal Humanitarian Awd, Penn St Univ.

MONTGOMERY, ROYCE LEE oc/Associate Professor; h/728 Shadylawn Ct, Chapel Hill, NC 27514; ba/Chapel Hill; m/Jane Hansford; c/Todd, Scott, Jill; p/E L and Jimmie Montgomery, Montgomery, WV; ed/BA Univ Va 1955; MS 1961, PhD W VA Univ; mil/AUS 1/Lt 1955-57; pa/Assoc Prof Anatomy, Univ NC-CH; Am Assn Anatomists; r/Epis; hon/Dist'd Tchg Awd.

MONTIE, IRENE C oc/Statistician; h/5411 Old Temple Hill Rd, Washington, DC 20301; ba/Wash; m/Walter G; c/Michael, Thomas, John, Kitty, Suzanne; p/Michael E and Catherine M Curran; ed/AA (2); BA, BS; MA (2); PhD; pa/Statistician, Dept Energy;

Tech Writer; Speaker; Analyst; Reschr; cp/Polit Campaigner & Fund Raiser; r/Cath; hon/Sev Outstg & Dist'd Ser Awds, US Census Bur; Grad'd Summa Cum Laude; W/W World Wom; Other Biogl Listings.

MOOMAW, G DUNBAR oc/Poet; Philosopher; b/Oct 4, 1949; h/PO Box 232, Dahlgren, VA 22448; ba/Dahlgren; p/Gilbert F Moomaw (dec); Frederica H Moomaw, Dahlgren; pa/Author 4 Volumes Poetry incl'g *Thoughts of Innocence & Romantic Gems from the Soul of a Romanticist*; Author Posters Featuring: "The Ten Commandments of Equality", "Loveatude", Others; Author Num Leaflets incl'g: "Abundant Love Is. . .", "An Idealist's Creed", "Success Transmutation", Others; Contbr Num Works Mags & Anthologies; Nat Writers Clb; NY Poetry Forum; Thomas Jefferson Inst for Study of Rel Freedoms; r/Truth Seeker; hon/Phi Theta Pi; Rec'd Awds for Poetry; Intl W/W Poetry; Intl W/W Intellectuals; Personalities of S; Men Achmt.

MOON, WILLIE MARGARET oc/Retired; b/Sept 11, 1913; h/1235 Ben Lora Ln, San Benito, TX 78586; m/David Daniel (dec); c/William David, James Daniel, Thomas Lynn; p/William Wilkins and Mattie Maggie Andrews (dec); pa/Writer of Poetry; hon/Recommended to Stella Woodall Poetry Soc.

MOORE, CHARLES AUGUST JR oc/Clinical Psychologist; b/Feb 22, 1944; h/12514 Camino Emparrado, San Diego, CA 92128; ba/Chula Vista, CA; p/Charles August and Bernadine G Newlun Moore, Grants Pass, OR; ed/BS Lewis & Clark Col 1965; MA 1967, PhD 1972 Univ Colo; pa/Clinical & Consltg Psychologist in Cont'g Care, San Diego Co Mtl Hlth Sers 1974-, (Intern Tng & Selection

Com 1977-); Clinical Psychologist, Individual Pract (Chula Vista) 1978-; Psychologist Info & Referral Ser; Dir Intern Tng & Clinical Psychologist, Rural Clinics (Reno, Nev) 1972; Cnslr & Prog Supvr, Ctr for Student Life Progs & Studies, Univ Colo 1971-72; Other Positions; Public Employees Assn; Acad San Diego Psychologists: Exec Bd, Newslttr Editor, Conv Prog Com 1976; Doct Dissertation Com, US Intl Univ 1975-76; Guest Lectr; cp/Univ City Commun Coun.

MOORE, CHARLES LEE oc/Special Education Teacher; b/Jul 24, 1949; h/415 S Franklin, Kirksville, MO 63501; ba/Kirksville; p/Cecil E Moore (dec); Inis A Moore, Yale, IA; ed/BSE NE Mo St Univ 1971; pa/Spec Ed Tchr, Trainable Level Prog, Kirksville R-III Schs; Treas, Kirksville MNEA; NEA; Mo St Tchrs Assn; K'ville Comm Tchrs Assn; Region II Coun for Devel Disabilites; cp/Am Iris Soc; K'ville Chapt Mo Citizens for Life; Travellers Commun Theatre; r/Ch of Christ (Ottumwa, Iowa); hon/W/W Child Devel Profs; Personalities of W&MW; Commun Ldrs & Noteworthy Ams; Notable Ams; DIB; Men Achmt.

MOORE, COLLEEN N oc/Piano & Voice Teacher; b/Oct 2, 1928; h/803 Westlake Dr, Austin, TX 78746; ba/Same; m/Doyle H; c/Frosty, Robin, Sherry M Waldrop (Mrs Jack); p/Herbert Bohn (dec); Alice Bohn, Austin; ed/Attended Univ Tex; pa/Pvt Piano & Voice Tchr; Secy, Austin Dist Mus Tchrs; Nat Piano Guild; cp/Wom's Symph Leag; Austin Wom's Clb; Wednesday Morning Mus Clb; r/Presb; hon/W/W Am Wom; Rec'd Plaque Appec, Austin Symph Orch.

MOORE, DALTON JR oc/Petroleum Engineer; b/Mar 25, 1918; h/4965 Waldemar Dr, Abilene, TX 79605; m/Janey Twila Culpepper; c/3; p/Dalton and Anne Y Moore; ed/Dipl Tarleton St Univ 1938; BS Tex A&M Univ 1942; Dipl US Army Command & Gen Staff Col 1945; mil/AUS 1940-46; pa/Field Engr, Gulf Oil Corp 1946; Dist Engr, Chicago Corp 1947-48, Chief Reservoir Engr 1949; Mgr Burdell Oil Corp (NYC & Snyder, Tex) 1950-52; Mgr, Wimberly Field Unit 1953-55; Profl Petro Conslt (Abilene) 1956-; Pres Dalton Moore Engrg Co 1957-67, First Oil Co 1960-67, Second Oil Co 1960-72, Petro Engrs Operating Co 1967-; Evaluation Engr for Investment Bankers Corp 1968-, Investment Bankers Oil Co Inc 1968-; Am Inst Mining, Metall & Petro Engrs; cp/Former Pres, Sweetwater (Tex) Jr C of C; Former Precinct Chm, Taylor Co Dem Com; Former Mem Bd Dirs, Taylor Co Chapt ARC; hon/Eagle Scout, BSA; Num Mil Awds; Commun Ldrs & Noteworthy Ams; W/W S&SW.

MOORE, DAN TYLER oc/Writer; Director; b/Feb 1, 1908; h/2564 Berkshire Rd, Cleveland Hghts, OH 44106; ba/Same; m/Elizabeth Valley Oakes; c/Luvean M Owens, Elizabeth O Thorton, Harriet Clements, Dan Tyler III; p/Dan T and Luvean Jones Butler Moore (dec); ed/BS Yale Univ 1931; mil/AUS 1942-44; pa/Dir Gen, IPA 1965-; Editor, *Talent Mag*; Pres, Middle E Co & China Co (Cleveland) 1946-48; Chief of Counter Intell Mid E, Office of Strategic Sers 1943-44; Author: *Cloak and Cipher* (1962), *The Terrible Game* (1957), *Wolves, Widows & Orphans* (1966), *Lecturing for Profit* (1967); Contbr Num Articles Profl Jours & Contbr Stories Popular Mags US, England, Others; cp/Former Pres, Gtr Cleveland Muscular Dystrophy Assn; Former Exec Com Mem, Cuyahoga Co Dem Party; Former Ohio Fed Jury Commr; Former Trustee, Cleveland Mus Natural Hist; Bd Dirs, Near E Rehab Ctr; Near E Col Assn; Karamu Theatre; Rowfant Clb; Union Clb; Tavern Clb; Hangar Clb; Metro Clb (Wash, DC); Yale Clb (NYC); r/Epis; hon/Rec'd Artillery Medallion, Order St Barbara; "Best Adventure Speech Being Given in US" Awd; Teen Age Book Awd.

MOORE, DORIS ELIZABETH oc/Student; b/June 19, 1929; h/3130 Nine Mile Rd, Richmond, VA 23223; chd/3; ed/AA, AAS, AS J Sargeant Reynolds Commun Col 1980; hon/Cert of Achmt, R-CAP Head Start Prog;

Ldrship Awd, J Sargeant Reynolds Commun Col.

MOORE, DOYLE H oc/Contractor; b/Dec 25, 1928; h/803 Westlake Dr, Austin, TX 78746; ba/Austin; m/Colleen; c/Frosty, Robin, Sherry M Waldrop; p/Doyle E and Helen Moore, Austin; ed/BA Tex A&M Univ 1951; mil/USAF 1951-53; pa/Fiberglass Contractor; Am Gen Contractors; Nat Assn Heat & Frost Asbestos; cp/Former Little Leag Coach; Pres & Life Mem, Optimist Clb; Planning & Zoning Bd, City of Westlake Hills; Scottish Rite; Ben Hur; Past Pres, Austin HS Booster Clb; Pres, Westlake Chapparal Clb; r/Presb; hon/Fdr, Jr Leag Football, Westlake Hills; Park Named in his Hon.

MOORE, ELIZABETH T oc/Homemaker; Genealogical Researcher; b/Aug 27, 1907; h/1214 8th Ave, Tuscaloosa, AL 35401; m/Lewis Reynolds (dec); c/1; p/Edward Eugene and Bonita Parker Todd; cp/Clubwom, AFCW; GFCW; ASPS; NFSPS; IBC; r/Presb; hon/Rec'd AFWC Creat Writing Awd; Commun Ldrs & Noteworthy Ams; World W/W Wom; Intl W/W Poetry.

MOORE, HERSHELL EDWARD WAYNE oc/Evangelist; Director; b/Nov 17, 1941; h/PO Box 8011, Springfield, MO 65801; ba/Springfield; m/Olevia Sue; p/Dewey and Gracie Emaline Moore (dec); ed/Ark Sch for Blind; Ark Tech Univ; BA Tex Tech Univ 1967; r/Ordained Min, Assemblies of God; Distbr Free Lit in Braille & Recorded Form to Legally Blind throughout US & Canada; Dir, Assemblies of God Lib for the Blind; Coor Ministries for the Blind; Speaker & Lectr; Fdr, Springfield Chapt Nat Fdn of the Blind; Author Currently Writing Novel; cp/Host Lions Clb; r/Assembly of God; hon/W/W Rel; Intl W/W Commun Ser; Personalities of W&MW; Men Achmt; DIB; Others.

MOORE, JAMES KENNETH SR oc/Computer Scientist; b/Oct 3, 1943; h/12345 Coleraine Ct, Reston, VA 22091; ba/Reston; m/Cherie Faye Meyer; c/James Kenneth Jr, Aimee Catherine, David Michael; p/James T and Hassie C Moore, Franklin, KY; ed/BEEE Vanderbilt Univ 1965; Post Grad Studies: Univ Md, Va Tech; mil/USN 1965-73; pa/Computer Scist, Defense Communs Agy 1975-; Electronic Engr, Nat Security Agy (Ft Meade, Md) 1970-75; Electronic Engr, Naval Security Group (Ft Meade) 1968-70; IEEE; AMA; Armed Forces Communs & Electronics Assn; Naval Reserv Assn; Authored & CoAuthored Num Tech Papers; cp/Reston JCs; Repub Party; r/Vienna Presb Ch (Vienna, Va); Mem; hon/Rec'd Navy Achmt Medal; Num Mil Decorations; Outstg Perf Awd; W/W S&SW.

MOORE, LORENA LAUTERBACH oc/Executive; b/Dec 26, 1934; h/600 Wishart Cir, Richmond, VA 23229; ba/Richmond; m/Benjamin Franklin; c/Montgomery, Keith, Robin, Pamela; p/Fred Vincent Lauterbach (dec); Viola Allen Lauterbach, Richmond; ed/Attended Va Commonwealth Univ; pa/Pres, Lauterbach Electric Co Inc; Bd Mem, Adm Mgmt Soc; Nat Assn Accts; Am Soc Pers Adm; cp/Past Pres, West Hampton PTA; r/Epis: Past Pres Wom of Ch; hon/W/W Am Wom; Intl W/W; Personalities of S.

MOORE, PHYLLIS JEANETTE TILBURY CLARK oc/Library Director; Writer; b/Jan 31, 1927; h/1151-C Park Ave, Alameda, CA 94501; ba/Alameda; m/R Scott Wellington; p/John Oscar Clark, Binghamton, NY; Galdys Jeanette Tilbury Clark Shadduck, Bing-hamton; ed/BA; MS; MA; LittD; PhD; pa/Conslt; Author: *Command Performance* (1960), *Mission Accomplished* (1962), *Beneath the Sea* (1974); cp/DAR; BPW; Defenders of Wildlife; r/Presb; hon/Rec'd Elliott Howell Reed Meml Awd; USAREUR Awds: Tournament of Plays Awd, Best Actress, Best Original Writing for Stage; Arts & Lttrs Awd, Univ Md; Intl Commun Ser Awd; DIB; Others.

MOORE, RUBY JOHNSON oc/Executive Housekeeper; b/Dec 3, 1924; h/401 E H St,

Erwin, NC 28339; ba/Erwin; m/Earl R; c/John W, Kathy J; p/John H and Myrtie G Johnson (dec); ed/Cert'd Exec Housekeeper; pa/Exec Housekeeper, Good Hope Hosp Inc; Ole North St, Nat Exec Housekeeping Assn; r/First Bapt Ch: Missionary.

MOORE, THADELUA JO oc/Teacher; Librarian; Minister; b/Jan 28, 1928; h/424 Brookfield Dr, Apt 104, Fairfield, OH 45014; ba/Fairfield; p/Elsie Moore, Denton, TX; Eula Moore, Royse City, TX; ed/BA; MLS; pa/Ordained Min; Yth Dir; Mus Dir; Asst Pastor; Tchr; Evangelist; Libn; r/Assemblies of God.

MOOREHEAD, GEORGE A oc/Physician; b/Apr 5, 1917; h/PO Box 3668, Charlotte Amalie, St Thomas, VI 00801; m/Ilse-Maria Schwarz; p/George A and Beatrice Eleanore La Frank Moorehead (dec); ed/BS; MD; pa/Pharmacist; Asst Physician, Nat Inst Public Hlth (Oslo, Norway) & Oslo Emer Med Ctr 1967; Res Dir & Conslt VI Law Enforcemt Comm, Task Force on Alcoholism & Narcotics 1969-71; Exec Dir (Insular) VI Comm on Alcoholism & Narcotics, Dept Hlth (St Thomas) 1971-; Profl Assns; Contbr Papers on Drugs & Narcotic Probs (Local, Nat, Intl); r/Frederick Luth Ch (St Thomas): Usher; VChm Luth Social Soc VI; hon/Biogl Listings.

MOORHEAD, ROLANDE ANNETTE oc/Professional Artist; b/Sept 24, 1937; h/PO Box 8692, Ft Lauderdale, FL 33310; ba/Same; m/Elliott Swift III; c/Edward Marc, Rolande Elliott, Remy Bruce; p/Remy Jean Reverdy (dec); Andree Marcelle Lavollee Reverdy, France; ed/Col Technique (Nice, France); pa/Painter Oils & Watercolors; Group Shows: St Coleman Cath Ch (Pompano Beach, Fla) 1971, Ocean Clb Art Gallery (Ft Lauderdale) 1971-72, Gold Coast Spring Art Fest 1972-73, Parker Playhouse (Ft Lauderdale) 1973, Boca Raton C of C Art Show 1973, Pier 66 Art Gallery 1973, Jackie Gleason Environ Art Fest 1974, Nova Sch Art Exhibit & Art Demo 1975, Intl Salon Biarritz, France (Best in Show) 1977, Intl Salon (Paris, France) 1977, Others; Lauderdale-by-the-Sea Art Guild: VP 1972-74, Chm Exhibit Com 1972-75; Broward Art Guild; Delray Beach Art Guild; Boca Raton Ctr for Arts; Fla Leag Arts; Gold Coast Watercolor Soc; cp/Alliance Francaise de Dade Co (Former Treas & Bd Mem); Nat Assoc Smithsonian Inst; hon/One-man Shows: Galerie du Palais des Fetes (Perigueux, France) 1978, Galerie Vallombreuse (Biarritz) 1978, St Basil Cath Orthodox Ch (N Miami Beach, Fla) 1977, Ft Lauderdale C of C 1976, Coral Spring Bank 1976, Pan Am Bank of Broward Co 1974-76, Pier 66 Art Gallery 1972, 74, 76, Ocean Clb Art Gallery 1971-74, Others; Comm'd for Paintings: St Front Cathedral (Perigueux) & St Sacerdoce Cathedral (Sarlat, France); Perm Collections: DAV HQs (Wash, DC), Ft Lauderdale City Hall; Spec Bicent Painting "Remember" Exhibited throughout Fla; Feature Article on Background in Art, *Fiesta* (Jan 1973); W/W Am; Personalities of S; Artists/USA; DIB; Others.

MORAHAN, DANIEL MICHAEL KEVIN oc/Writer; Manpower Economist; b/Aug 15, 1940; h/4005-74th Pl, Bellemead, Hyattsville, MD 20784; p/John Joseph and Eileen Alice McKeown Morahan; ed/AA 1962; BBA George Wash Univ 1965; Strategic Mgmt, NYU; Computer Learning Ctr (Fairfax, Va) 1974; mil/AUS Civilian Ofcr 1973-74; pa/Current Mgmt Conslt, Pers & Indust Relats/Public Relats; Chm & Pres functioning as Mgmt Conslt, Res Writer & Labor Economist (in matters of Defense, Pers, Polits, etc) M-Metra Ltd Enterprises 1973-; Writer-Editor, Adjutant Gen's Office (Wrote & Edited Army Regulations, Others) 1972-73; Classifier, Army Gen Staff, Civilian Pers Office 1968-72; Economist, Bur Labor Statistics (US Dept Labor) 1967-68; Manpower Advr, Manpower Adm, US Dept Labor 1965-67; Exec Coun, Am Inst Mgmt; Assn MBA Execs; IPA; Author, *Acad Wom: The Ed of Tomorrow's Mil Ofcrs (Wom in Ldrship Roles)*; hon/Am Registry Series.

MORALES, RAUL oc/Physician; b/Feb 5, 1931; h/42 Anderson Ave, Englewood Cliffs, NJ; ba/Yonkers, NY; m/Blanca; c/Alice, Albert; p/Antonio and Valeria Morales, Havana, Cuba; ed/Univ Havana Med Sch; Addit Studies; pa/Lic'd to Pract: Miss, NY, NJ; Am Bd Fam Pract 1971; r/Cath; hon/Fellow: Westchester Acad of Med, Am Acad Fam Physicians; AMA Phys' Recog Awd; Res Fellow, Inst Applied Biology; Subject incl'd in *The Best Doctors in Am*; Biogl Listings.

MORAN, ANN ELIZABETH oc/Supervisor; b/Jul 13; h/Rt 11, Franklin, TN 37064; ba/Franklin; p/James Walker and Emma Mai Fly Moran (dec); ed/BS Middle Tenn St Univ; BLS, MA Peabody Col; pa/Supvr Lib & Instrnl Materials; United Tchr Profs; ALA; TLA; Mid-St Lib; cp/Williamson Co Heart Coun; Former Chm, Mid Tenn Heart Assn Campaign; BPW; Williamson Co Hist Soc; Wom's Nat Book Assn; r/Ch of Christ; hon/Delta Kappa Gamma; Wom of Yr, McMinnville BPW; Others.

MORGADO, SADIE DAWN oc/Director/Coordinator; b/Oct 30, 1932; h/1241 S 50th St, Birmingham, AL 35222; ba/B'ham; m/Nelson; c/Alton; p/Clara Rice Cooper, B'ham; ed/BA Univ Ala 1977; pa/Dir-Coor, Jefferson Co Civil Defense; Lic'd to Handle Radioactive Materials, Atomic Energy Comm; Real Estate Broker, St of Ala; Tchr License, St of Ala; Ala Civil Defense Assn; US Civil Defense Coun; Am Security Coun; cp/B'ham BPW; Gen Employees' Credit Union (City of B'ham); Wom Employees Assn; B'ham Assn City Employees; Rep to City of B'ham Pension Bd; Bd Dirs, Mtl Hlth Assn; Bd Dirs, Vol Bur Gtr B'ham; LWV; r/Bapt; hon/Rec'd Nat Med Self-Help Humanitarian Awd, Dept HEW; Hlth Dept St Apprec Awd; Lttr Commend, Gov Lurleen Wallace; Certs Commend: Mayor George G Seibels, Chief of Police Jamie Moore, Ala St PTA, Ala NG, Ala St Civil Defense Dir, Ala St Fair Authority, J Carroll Chambers (Jefferson Co Hlth Ofcr), Sertoma Clb & Kiwanis Clb; Biogl Listings.

MORGAN, BARBARA ANN oc/Real Estate Broker; b/Dec 27, 1937; h/703 Bullock Ave, Lexington, KY 40508; ba/Lexington; c/John H Gilliam II; p/Lester J and Gladys New Morgan, Owenton, KY; pa/Owner Real Estate Firm; Nat Bd Realtors; Ky Bd Realtors; Former Mem Bd Dirs, Lexington Bd Realtors; cp/Past Pres, Wom's Coun; r/Bapt.

MORGAN, HAROLD CLIFFORD oc/Psychiatrist; b/Aug 26, 1936; h/1305 Westminster Dr, Columbia, SC 29204; ba/Columbia; p/Guerry W Morgan (dec); Evelyn Hughes Morgan, Buford, GA; ed/BA Emory Univ 1958; MD Med Col Ga 1962; mil/USAR; pa/Pvt Pract Gen & Forensic Psychi; Conslt: Dept HEW, SC Law Enforcenmt Div, SC Dept Mtl Hlth, Middlesex Superior Ct; Instr Psychi, Harvard Med Sch; Chief Psychi, SC Bapt Hosp 1975; Secy SC Dist Branch, Am Psychi Assn; Fellow Forensic Psychi, Harvard Univ; Pub'd Articles; cp/Columbia Mus Fest; Columbia Mus Art; Town Theatre; United Way Vol; r/Trinity Epis Cathedral: Mem, Comm on Min Diocese of Upper SC.

MORGAN, J DERALD oc/Electrical Engineer; b/Mar 15, 1939; h/Rt 4, Box 112 Rolla, MO 65401; ba/Rolla; m/Elizabeth June; c/Laura Elizabeth, Kimberly Ann, Rebecca Ruth, Johnnie Derald; p/Johnnie Baber and Avis Ruth Morgan, Rolla; ed/BSEE La Tech Univ 1962; MSEE Univ Mo-R 1965; PhD Ariz St Univ 1968; pa/Dept Chm & Prof Elect Engrg, Univ Mo-R; Reg'd Profl Engr Mo; IEEE: Sr Mem, Power Soc Power Sys Engrg Com, Intl Practs Subcom, Ed Com, PES Power Sys Engrg Standards Com, PES Ed Com, Others; Engr's Clb St Louis; NSPE; MSPE; MW Power Symposium Adv Bd (VP 1973-74); Student Fac Attendance Com, Am Power Conf; Univ Soc Rep Com, Am Power Conf; Tech Com & US Nat Com, World Energy Conf; Assoc Editor Gen Systems, *Electric Power Systems Res Jour*; cp/Dist Chm & Former Scoutmaster, BSA; Cir K Clb;

r/United Meth Ch: Mem, Adm Bd, Bd Dirs United Mins Higher Ed, VP Bd Adm, Former Pres Bd Trustees, Others; hon/Beta Clb; Tau Beta Pi; Eta Kappa Nu; Sigma Xi; Phi Kappa Phi; Omicron Delta Kappa; Rec'd Scouters Awd, Key Awd & Awd Merit, BSA; Kappa Sigma S'ship Ldrship Awd; Rec'd T H Harris S'ship; Outstg Freshman Engrg Student, La Tech Univ; Outstg Sophomore Elect Engrg Student, La Tech Univ; Intl Assn for Exchange of Students for Tech Experience, Sponsored by Engrs Jt Coun Am; Selected to Make One-month Scientific Visitation to Romania, Nat Acad Sci; Am Men & Wom Sci; Intl Scholars Directory; Outstg Yg Men Am; W/W Mo Ed; DIB; Others.

MORGAN, JAMES EMEROUS oc/Sales Manager; b/Apr 1, 1917; h/2106 Marbury Dr, District Hghts, MD 20028; ba/Washington, DC; m/Una Lorraine Cole; c/James Emerous Jr, Susan Camille, Steven Cole; p/George Emerous Morgan (dec); Mabel Elizabeth Bock; ed/Penn St; Univ Md; mil/USAF 1942-45, Capt; cp/Pres Kiwanis; Pres PTA; Pres Retail Div, C of C; Exec Com & Indust Rep, BSA; Mgmt Com, YMCA; Adv Bd, Salvation Army; DHTA Amateur Theatre; r/Dist Hghts Presb Ch: Elder, Pres Men's Clb, Skipper Mariners, Choir; hon/Rec'd Dist'd Flying Cross w Cluster; Air Medal w 5 Clusters; Pres' Cit (Unit); VIP Awd, BSA; Gen Hershey Dist'd Ser Awd; Dist'd Ser Awd, GSA; Dist'd Ser Awd, Distributive Ed, Arlington Schs (Va); Dist'd Ser Awd, Rec Coun, Prince George's Co (Md).

MORGAN, JAMES LELAND oc/Researcher; b/Nov 9, 1914; h/2205 Nantucket Dr, Houston, TX 77057; m/Blanche Therese Williams; c/1 son, 1 daugh; ed/BS 1953, MS 1955 Univ of Okla-Norman; pa/Palynologist, Res Div, Humble Oil & Refining Co (Houston) 1955-64; Palynologist, Esso Prod Res Co (Houston) 1964-74; Pathologist, Exxon Prod Res Co 1974-; Author, *Spores of McAlester Coal* (1955), Others; Contbr Articles to Profl Jours; Am Assn of Stratigraphic Palynols; Am Assn Petro Geols; Soc of Econ Paleontols & Minerals; Paleontol Soc; Sigma Xi; Sigma Gamma Epsilon; hon/3 Ser Medals & Bronze Star for each of 3 Mil Campaigns; Biogl Listings.

MORGAN, ROY L oc/Government Consultant; b/Nov 14, 1908; h/1720 W 28th Sunset Island #1, Miami Beach, FL 33140; ba/Washington, DC; m/Rosamond Woodruff; c/Richard W; p/Henry Clay and Elizabeth Aitken Morgan (dec); ed/BS 1930, LLB 1933, JD 1972 Univ Va; pa/Admit'd Va Bar 1932, NC Bar 1941, Japan Bar 1951; Atty Dept Agri 1933; Spec Agent FBI 1934-45; Pvt Pract (Greensboro, NC) 1945-47, 50; Assoc Prosecutor War Criminals, Intl Tribunal (Tokyo, Japan) 1946; Legal Advr & Counsel, Ford Motor Co (Japan) 1950-54; Am Advr,Min Japan 1955-56; Chief Justice, US Civil Adm Appellate Ct for Far East 1956-60; Spec Asst to Secy Commerce 1960-61, Dir Office Field Sers 1961-67; Conslt to US Govt, Advr Intl Trade w Japan; Head US Govt Trade Missions to Japan 1962, 68; Editor Bd, *Va Law Review* 1931-33; Contbr Articles Profl Jours; cp/Mason; Rotary Clb; Execs Clb; Pres' Clb; Explorers; Active BSA; United Givers; Chm, Am Cancer Soc; Former Mem, Greensboro City Coun; Former Mem Bd Dirs, Elizabeth Saunders Home (Tokyo); Fdr, Mt Sinai Med Ctr (Miami Beach); r/Bapt; hon/Am VP, Am C of C in Tokyo; Sigma Chi; Phi Alpha Delta; Others.

MORGENSTERN, DONALD EARL oc/Certified Public Accountant; b/Feb 14, 1938; h/1041 Driftwood St, Corona, CA 91720; ba/Rialto, CA; c/Douglas, Dirk, Dean, Derek; p/Howard W Morgenstern, Riverside, CA; Margaret E Wilson Mock, Corona; ed/AA Mt San Antonio 1967; BA Cal St Univ-F 1969; mil/USMC 1955-59; pa/Self-employed CPA; Instr, Chaffey Col; AICPA; Am Acct Assn; Soc Cal Accts; Cal Soc CPAs; cp/BPOE; r/Prot.

MORGENTHALER, HELEN MARIE oc/Manufacturer; Importer; Designer; b/Apr

9; h/1730 W Dr, San Marino, CA 91108; ba/Same; p/Albert Mitchell and Clara Mattes Morgenthaler (dec); ed/Miss Orton's Sch for Girls (Pasadena, Cal); USC; pa/Designer Flora Appliques & Secy, Pioneer Wall Paper Co (Los Angeles, Cal) 1940-49; Pres Clara Somers Co (Mfgrs Designer Resort Wear) 1950-59; Pres, Morgenthaler Co (Mfgrs, Designers, Importers of Oriental Hand-Painted Wall Murals, Silk Wall Coverings; Factories in Seoul, Korea, Shimizu, Japan, Hong Kong) 1960-; cp/Asst Leag So Cal (Chm, Gift Shop Display); Fdr, Pasadena Guild Chd's Hosp; Chm Thrift Shop; Chm Doll Fair, Chd's Hosp; Fdr (Life), LA Orphanage Guild; Patroness, Athenaeum of Cal Inst Tech; Cal Hist Soc; Resources Coun Am; Town Hall of Cal; LA World Affairs Coun; Balboa Bay Clb; Others; hon/W/W: Am Wom, Fin & Indust, W; World W/W Wom; DIB; Intl Register Profiles; Others.

MORIAL, ERNEST NATHAN oc/Mayor; b/Oct 9, 1929; h/1101 Harrison Ave, New Orleans, LA 70122; ba/New Orleans; m/Sybil H; c/Julie C, Marc H, Jacques, Cheri, Monique; p/Walter E and Leonie Moore Morial (dec); ed/BS 1951, LLD Honoris Causa 1978 Xavier Univ; JD La St Univ Law Sch 1954; Grad Nat Col Juv Justice, Univ Nev; mil/AUS Intell Corps 1954-56; pa/Mayor New Orleans, Elected 1978 (First Black Elected Mayor NO); 4th Circuit Ct Appeals (First Black Elected to this Ct) 1974-77; Juv Ct (First Black to Serve) 1970-73; La St Ho of Reps (First Black Since Reconstruction) 1967-70; Law Pract w A P Tureaud 1954-65; Former Lectr Ins & Bus Adm, Xavier Univ; Former Lectr Juv Law, Tulane Univ Law Sch; Former Instr Bus Adm, So Univ NO; Other Positions; US Conf Mayors: Adv Bd Urban Hlth Care Financing Prog, Urban Ecs Standing Com, Resolutions Com; ABA; Bd Dirs, La Mun Assn; Steer'g Com, Nat Urban Coalition; Nat Urban Conserv Task Force, Nat Leag Cities; Gov's St Manpower Sers Coun; Former Mem, La Comm on Law Enforcemt; Fdr & 1st Pres, NO Legal Asst Corp; Crim Just Coor'g Coun; Am Trial Lwyrs Assn; Ho of Dels, La St Bar Assn; Louis A Martinent Legal Soc; Fdr Judicial Coun, Nat Bar Assn; Num Others; cp/NAACP (Former Pres NO Chapt); Bd Govs, Tulane Univ Med Ctr; Bd Trustees, Xavier Univ; Former Mem Bd Dirs, Loyola Univ; Bd Dirs, Total Commun Action; Bd Mem, La Voter Ed Proj; Nat Advocate, Knights of Peter Claver; Bd Dirs, Ctr for Interracial Coun for Bus Opportunity; United Fund Agy Relats Com; Others; r/Cath; hon/Named by Pres John F Kennedy as Fdr Mem Lwyrs' Com for Civil Rights Under Law; First Black Del to Dem Conv 1968; Fellow Inst Politics, John F Kennedy Sch Govt (Harvard Univ); Named 1 of 100 Most Influential Black Ams, *Ebony Mag*; W/W: Am Politics, S&SW, Am; Outstg Yg Men Am.

MORING, FELIX CLEVELAND oc/-Attorney; b/Jun 9, 1941; h/1101 Collier Rd NW, Atlanta, GA 30318; ba/Atlanta; p/Joel J and Johnie Winge Moring, Soperton, GA; ed/BA 1963, Grad Study Sch of Law, Emory Univ; MA 1971, JD 1973 Univ Tenn-K; mil/USMC Active Duty Vietnam; USMCR Maj, Asst Chief Staff; pa/Gen Pract Atty; Instr Law, John Marshall Law Sch (Atlanta); Adj Instr, DeKalb Commun Col (Decatur, Ga); Supr Ct & Ct Appeals Ga; 5th Circuit Ct Appeals & Fed Dist Ct; US Tax Ct; US Supr Ct; Atlanta, Ga & Am Bar Assns; Am Soc Judicature; Am Intl Law Soc; cp/Atlanta Com Foreign Relats; Atlanta C of C; Atlanta Hist Soc; Ga C of C; Ga Forestry Assn; High Mus Art; Marine Corps Reserv Ofcrs' Assn; Atlanta Arts Alliance; Atlanta City Forum; Kiwanis; Others; r/First Presb Ch Atlanta; hon/Sigma Alpha Epsilon; Pi Sigma Alpha; Phi Delta Phi; Outstg Atlantans; W/W S&SW; Personalities of S & Am; DIB; Men Achmt; Book of Hon; Best Lwyrs Am.

MORLANG, BARBARA BLAUVELT oc/Nutritionist; h/1314 Peters Creek Rd NW, Suite 130, Roanoke, VA 24017; ba/Roanoke; ed/BS Brigham Young Univ 1960; MS Columbia Univ 1964; PhD Univ Mass 1969; Internship, Yale-New Haven Commun Hosp 1961; pa/St Nutrition Conslt, Va St Hlth Dept

1970-; Part-time Conslt, Commun Nutrition Inst (Wash, DC) 1973-74; Dir & Nutritionist, Springfield Dairy Coun (Mass) 1965-66; Nutrition Conslt, Bur Nutrition, NYC Hlth Dept 1964-65; Other Positions; Roanoke, Va & Am Dietetic Assns; Va Home Ec Assn; Am Home Ec Assn; Am Public Hlth Assn; Va Coun on Hlth & Med Care; Botanical Soc Am; Jt Pubs: *The Budget Watcher's Cookbook*, *Adapting Food Intake to Individual Needs*; Conducted Nutrition Survey of 5th & 6th Grade Students (Roanoke); cp/Adult Activs Coun Roanoke Valley; hon/Sigma Xi; Phi Sigma; Omicron Nu; Nat Hon Soc; Outstg Citizens Awd, Adult Activs Coun; Dist'd Dietitian, St of Va.

MOROZ, MYCHAJLO oc/Artist; b/Jul 7 1904; h/76 Coursen Pl, Staten Island, NY 10304; m/Irene; c/Ihor; p/Ilia Moroz and Paraskevia Mandiw (dec); ed/Attended Art Sch (Lviv, Ukraine) 1923-28; Conservatoire Nat des Arts et Metiers (Paris, France) & Academie Julian (Paris) 1928-29; pa/Profl Artist-Painter (Landscapes & Portraits) 1928-; Asst Prof Drawing & Painting, Ukrainian Art Sch (Lviv) 1927-35; Pvt Lessons Europe & USA 1930-78; Author Num Articles About Painters' Works in Var Langs; r/Cath; hon/Silver Cup, Locust Val (NJ); Prix de Paris, Galeries Raymond Duncan; Most Artistic Christmas Card Prize, Syracuse (NY).

MORRIS, BERNARD NEWTH oc/Minister; Writer; Administrator; b/Nov 11, 1919; h/18 Townley Dr, Burnt Hills, NY 12027; ba/Scotia, NY; m/Lorraine Weiderhold; c/Faith Ann, Bernard N Jr, Hope Louise, Grace Miriam; p/George and Virgina Calahoun Morris (dec); ed/BA En Bapt Col 1953; STB 1954, STM 1973 Temple Univ; ThB; mil/USN 1953-61 Chaplain; pa/Min, 1st Bapt Ch (Schenectady, NY); Adm Dir, Schuyler Co Older Am Vol Prog; Pres, Bapt Retiremt Ctr; Instr, Elmira Col 1975; Other Positions; Author: *Harmony of Words* (1965), *Harmony of Truth* (1972), *Harmony of Sermons* (1973), *Harmony of Hope* (1974); Contbr Articles Profl Jours; Am Col Nsg Home Admrs; St & Nat Bapt Mins Assns; Capital Area Bapt Assn of NY St; Maj Poets of Am; Writers Guild; Others; cp/Kiwanis; Avon Soc; Regional Human Sers Comm; Others; r/Bapt; hon/Rec'd Gold Medal for Poetry; Poems Pub'd Sev Anthologies; Other Poetry Awds; Nat Musical Awd; St 7 Nat Awds for Trumpet Playing; Biogl Listings.

MORRIS, EUGENE oc/Mayor; Real Estate & Insurance Businessman; b/Sept 27, 1918; h/234 Riverview Dr, Forest City, IA 50436; ba/Forest City; m/Helen Eloise McCart; c/Elgin Eugene; p/William Harley and Ethel Enright Morris (dec); ed/LaSalle Bus Sch 1937-38; mil/Iowa NG 1950-51; pa/Mayor, Forest City 1976-; Owner, Morris Ins & Realty Co 1950-; J of P 1954-59; Worked Parts Dept, Forest City Motor Co 1949-50; Ins Inspector, Grinnell Mutual Re-ins Co 1947-49;

Other Positions; St & Nat Assn Realtors; St & Nat Independent Ins Agents' Assns; St & Nat Profl Ins Agents' Assns; NW Iowa Leag Muns; Hancock Co, Iowa & Winnebago Co Conf Bds; Others; cp/Forest City Lions Clb (Lions Intl): Former Dist Gov, Gavel Clb, Past Pres, Others; Forest City C of C; IOOF Lodge; Dir, Forest City Devel Corp; Former Chm, Winnebago Co Red Cross; Former Chm, N Iowa Area GSA; Past Pres, FC Little Theatre; Beauty Pageant Judge; Coin Show Judge; Dir,

Minn Org Numismatics; Ctl Sts & Am Numismatics Assns; Clarion Collectors; Wayne & Winnebago Hist Socs; Orgr, Adventure Lands of Am & N Iowa Mus; Num Others; r/United Meth Ch: Mem; hon/Rec'd 1st & Only Past Pres' Awd, Forest City Coin Clb; Am Numismatic Assn Individual Nat Awd; Lions Intl: Mr Lion Awd, 3 Ext Awds, Key of Nations, Dist Gov Apprec Awds, Quarter Cent Awd, Hon Roll, Life Mbrship, Old Monarch, Others; Apprec Awds, St & Nat Numismatic Assns; Winner Over 200 Trophies & Ribbons at Coin Shows; Featured in Article, "Meet Your Businessman", *Forest City Summit Newspaper*; W/W MW; Personalities of W&MW; Intl W/W Commun Ser; Others.

MORRIS, HARRIET JONES oc/Lecturer; Instructor; b/Oct 29, 1929; h/4045 N 41st St, Arlington, VA 22207; ba/Same; m/David D; p/J P Jones (dec); Martha L Jones DePriest, Arlington; ed/Attended St Mary's Univ (San Antonio, Tex); pa/Free-lance Instr & Lectr; Created, Devel'd & Presented Progs & Lectures on Profl Devel & Applied Personal Growth Nat, St & Local Levels (Leading Bus Firms; Orgs; Govt Agencies; Ednl Insts) 1955-78; Instr, Strayer Col (Wash, DC) 1959-78; Guest Instr, WRC/NBC-TV 1960-63; cp/Wrote, Devel'd & Activated Hist Prog, Fairfax Co Public Sch Sys (Va); Created, Devel'd & Taught Tng Prog for Blind Chd (Wash, DC); Created, Devel'd & Activated Applied Personal Devel Prog, Sch for Blind Chd (China); Personal Contbn to Yth Guidance; r/Prot; hon/Num Lttrs Apprec.

MORRIS, IDA TOTH oc/Executive; b/Jul 5, 1923; h/1202 E Tyler, Harlingen, TX 78550; ba/Same; m/James Claxon; c/Ray Claxon; p/Geza Toth (dec); Margaret Marosi Toth, Detroit, MI; pa/Owner, Media Matters (Public Relats Firm) & The Writing Place; Creative Writing Instr, Tex St Tech Inst 1977-78; Wom's Editor, *Valley Morning Star* 1972; Exec Secy, Steel Ser Ctr Inst (Cleveland, Ohio) 1963-64; Owner & Fdr, Morris Co (Resume Ser) 1960-61; Office Mgr, Wheeler-Becker Archs (Detroit) 1955-60; Res Coun Am; Valley By-Liners; Christian Writers' Leag (VP & Newslttr Editor 1976-78); Wom's Assn Freedom of Press; cp/Former Asst Admr, Lynn Hosp (Lincoln Park, Mich); Cameron Co Comm on Status of Wom; Brownsville Wom's Polit Caucus; Valley Wom's Polit Caucus; Public Speaker on Wom's Rights.

MORRIS, IRVING oc/Teacher; b/Mar 31, 1927; h/21-15 34th Ave (2-D) LIC, New York, NY 11106; ba/NYC; m/Joan A; c/David C; p/Herman Morris (dec); Celia Morris, Brooklyn, NY; ed/BA Bklyn Col; MLS Columbia Univ; mil/AUS 1945-47; pa/Tchr & Sch Lib Media Spec, Brandeis HS; Active Tchr Union Movemt; Var Profl Activs; cp/Var Orgs; r/Jewish; hon/Rec'd Num Commend Certs; Num Biogl Listings.

MORRIS, R EDWIN oc/Minister; b/Jun 30, 1941; h/Rt 11, 108 Davis Dr, Greenville, SC 29611; ba/Greenville; m/LaVoylyn C; c/Marla Lyn, Ralph Edwin Jr; S U Sr and Louise B Morris, Greenville; ed/BA; BTh; Addit Studies; mil/USMC 4 Yrs; pa/Min, Assembly of God; Fdr & Pres, Life Tabernacle Pentecostal Bible Inst 1972-; SC Notary Public; PFNA; SC Dist By-Law Revision Com; Dist Constitution Revision Com, Assembly of God; Others; cp/Dem Del to G'ville Co Conv 1976; W G'ville Commun Action; r/Assembly of God; hon/Civitan Clb Apprec Awd; Order of Broom; SC Pastor Apprec Awds; YWCA Missions Awd; W/W Rel; Personalities of S; Commun Ldrs & Noteworthy Ams; DIB; Men Achmt; Others.

MORRIS, ROGER DALE oc/Artist; b/Feb 23, 1947; h/PO Box 183, Carrsville, KY 42030; ba/Marion, KY; p/Guy Robert Morris (dec); Corena Irby Morris, Carrsville; pa/Teller, Gary Nat Bank (Gary, Ind) 1965-70; Asst Cashier, Peoples Bank 1971-; Free-lance Artist 1975-; Intl Soc Artists; hon/Winner 1st Pl & 2nd Pl, Art Instrn Schs Competition (Mpls, Minn); W/W S&SW; Artists/USA.

MORRIS, VISTA LORENE oc/Retired Teacher; b/Nov 27, 1908; h/PO Box 501, Owensboro, KY 42301; p/Lorenzo Elisha and Rena Pulliam Morris (dec); ed/BA; pa/Pres, Ky Coun Tchrs of Eng 1958-59, Achmt Awds Com 1958-74; r/Meth; hon/Past Pres, Ky Delta Kappa Gamma Soc; Outstg Tchr Am, Am Acad Edrs.

MORRISEY, ROBERT BREWSTER oc/- Publisher; b/May 2, 1926; h/8778 Caminito Abrazo, La Jolla, CA 92037; ba/San Diego, CA; m/Mary Jane; c/Kathleen, Michele; p/James Robert and Helen Brewster Morrisey (dec); mil/USMC 1943-67; War Correspondent Korea 1953-54; pa/Chief News Bur, Teledyne Ryan Aero (San Diego) 1968, Mgr Public Relats & Communs 1969-77, Cons 1977-; Writer, Lectr & Edr on Subject of Wine; Fdr & Chm, The Wine Group 1976-; Pubr, *The Wine Spectator* 1976-; Author Weekly

Newspaper Column,"Pleasures of Wine", *San Diego Evening Tribune* 1972-78; Dir & Instr Adv'd Wine Courses, Univ San Diego 1976-; Judge: Los Angeles Co Fair, 1st All-Am Wine Competition & Intl Wine & Cheese Fest; Public Relats Soc Am; Bus & Profl Advertisers Assn; Aviation/Space Writers Assn; SD Indust Advertisers; SD Press; Soc Wine Edrs; Univeral Order of Knights of Vine (Master Knight); Chevalier, Les Amis du Vin; Compagnon de Bordeaux, Le Grand Counseil de Bordeaux; N Coast Prestige Wine Soc; So Cal Wine Writers; Napa Val Wine Lib; Others; cp/Marine Corps Assn; San Diego C of C; r/Prot.

MORRISON, FRANCINE REESE oc/- Gospel Singer; Evangelist; b/Aug 16, 1935; h/928 E Bowie St, Ft Worth, TX 76104; ba/Ft Worth; m/Jury; c/Luwilda Diane; p/Dewey Reese, Wichita Falls, TX; Luvenia Eugenia Flemings Bostic (dec); ed/DD Sch Intl Deliverance Ch Inc (Dallas, Tex) 1975; Hon Doct Sacred Mus, Union Bapt Theol Sem (Houston, Tex) 1966; pa/Ordained by Rev W V Grant, Souls Harbor Ch (Dallas); Num Appearances as Soloist in US, Mexico, Europe, Russia & The Holy Land; Guest Soloist Fed'd Choirs of Austin 1963 (Presented w Plaque from St John Regular Bapt Assn); Sang at First Annual All Singing Mus Fest, Will Rogers Meml Auditorium; Guest Soloist, St Stephens Bapt Ch (Presented w Key to City of Kansas City & Made Hon Citizen); Soloist, Swearing-in Ceremony, Mayor Ft Worth (Woodie Woods); Others; cp/C of C Comperson; r/Interdenom, Interracial, Pentecostal; hon/First Black Am to Sing for Tex Gov's Inauguration (Gov John B Connally); First Soloist to Sing in Astrodome (Houston); First Black Female Newsmaker of Yr, Ft Worth Press Clb; Rec'd Florence B Brooks Wom of Yr Awd; Name Chosen for Inclusion in Lunar Bible (for 2nd Alan Bean Trip to Moon); Others; Biogl Listings.

MORRISON, FRANCIS SECREST oc/Professor; b/Jul 29, 1931; h/771 Belhaven, Jackson, MS 39216; ba/Jackson; m/Dorothy Daniels; c/Francis, Thomas, Kenneth; p/Clifton B Morrison (dec); Marie Blanche L Morrison, Biloxi, MS; ed/BS w Hons, Miss St Univ 1954; MD Univ Miss Sch Med 1959; Addit Studies; mil/USN 1965-69; pa/Univ Miss Sch Med: Asst Prof Med, Dir Div Hematology & Instr Clinical Lab Sci 1969-70, Assoc Prof Med, Dir Div Hematol & Instr Clinical Lab Sci 1970-76, Fac Grad Sch Med 1971-, Dir Div Hematol & Oncology 1976,

Attend'g Phys 1969, Dir Univ Hosp Blood Bank 1974; Coms: Clinical Cancer Com (Chm), Cancer Res Adv Com (Chm), Exec Com of Univ Hosp Staff, Transfusion Com, Pres UMC Assocs, Ad Hoc Com Income Evaluation, Anatomy Search Com, VA Ctr Clinical Res Review Panel, Others; Other Positions; Lic'd, Miss & Mass; Fellow, Am Col Phys; Am Col Chest Phys; Am Fdn Clinical Res; Am Soc Hematol; Intl Soc Hematol; Am Assn Blood Banks (Coms); Intl Soc Blood Transfusion; Am Soc Nuclear Med; Soc for Cryobiology; AMA; NY Acad Sci; Am Soc Internal Med; Miss St Med Assn; Ctl Med Soc; Jackson Acad Med; Miss Foun Med Care; World Fdn Hemophilia; Am Assn Cancer Res; AAUP; IPA; Num Others; Contbr Num Articles Profl Jours, Pub'd Abstracts; cp/Bd Dirs & Exec Com, Miss Div Am Cancer Soc; Adv Com for Hemophilia Prog, Miss St Bd Hlth; Exec Dir, Miss Regional Blood Ctr; Blood Procurement Com, Jackson Hinds Hosp; Commun Disaster Plan; Gov's Coun on Aging; Am Blood Comm; Others; r/St Joseph HS Assn; Chm, Ctl Regional Meeting for Diocesan Planning; Others; hon/Dean's & Pres's List Scholars, Miss St Univ; Former Pres Sch Sci, Miss St Univ; Phi Kappa Phi; Omicron Delta Kappa; Sigma Xi; Best Clinical Fac Mem (Elected by Students); Res Fellow, Blood Res Lab, Tufts New England Med Ctr (Boston, Mass); Rec'd Num Res Grants; Others.

MORSE, JEAN ALSTON oc/Psychologist; b/Jul 12, 1931; h/3249 Ramsgate Rd, Augusta, GA 30909; ba/Augusta; m/Paul Kenneth; c/David Thomas, Steven John, Mark Andrew; p/Edgar Alston (dec); Opal Alston, Royal Oak, MI; ed/BA cum laude, En Mich Univ 1965; MA Univ Mich 1969; PhD Univ Ga 1972; pa/Ednl Psychol & Assoc Prof

Ednl Res & Devel, Med Col of Ga; APA; AERA; CEC; NLN-GLN; NAACOG; cp/Bd Advrs, Lynndale Sch; ICEA; r/Holy Cross Presb Ch (Evans, Ga); hon/Phi Delta Kappa; Rec'd Tng Grants & F'ships; Outstg Edr, Augusta Col; Tchr of Yr (Sch of Nsg); Other Awds; Biogl Listings.

MORSE, SAMUEL ALTON oc/Corporate Director; b/Feb 24, 1943; h/3620 Cross Bend Rd, Plano, TX 75023; ba/Dallas, TX; m/Neville Janice Stromquist; c/Joshua Dean, Jeremy Scott; p/S A and Dorothy Mae Morse, Woodlands, TX; ed/BS Abilene Christian Univ 1966; MS Trinity Univ 1971; MBA St Mary's Univ 1973; Doct Bus Adm, Ind Nn Univ 1974; Doct Cand, Univ Tex Sch Public Hlth; Addit Study & Tng; mil/USAFR 1965-; pa/Dir Mgmt Sys, Am Medicorp Inc 1978-; Assoc Hosp Dir, Hermann Hosp (Houston, Tex) 1977-78; Adm Asst, Office of Pres, En Div Am Medicorp (Atlanta, Ga) 1977; Exec

Dir, Daytona Beach Commun Hosp (Fla) 1974-77; Instr: Trinity Univ, San Antonio Col, Univ Tex 1971-; Asst Adj Prof, Ind Nn Univ & Stetson Univ 1971-; Preceptor: Hlth Care Adm (Trinity Univ), Hosp Adm (Wash Univ & Univ Fla), Hlth Sers Adm (Univ Houston), Hlth Care Adm (Tex Wom's Col) 1974-; Other Positions; Am Col Hosp Admrs; Am Hosp Assn; Fellow, Am Acad Med Admrs; Am Public Hlth Assn; Fellow, Soc Public Hlth Edrs; Assn Mil Surgs; Fellow, Royal Soc Hlth; Assn MBA Execs; Tex Hosp Assn; Reserv Ofcrs Assn; Air Force Assn; Others; Contbr Articles Profl Jours; Lectr; cp/Editor, *Kaleidoscope*, Trinity Univ Hlth Care Adm Alumni Assn; Notary Public, Bexar Co (Tex); Chm Yth Com, SE Kiwanis (Houston); Chm Jr Dirs Com, Gtr Metro Houston Area YMCAs; Pres Jr Ofcrs Coun, 37 Aeromedical Evacuation Group (Mac Dill AFB, Fla); Bd Mem: Daytona Beach Commun Col, Embry Riddle Aeronautical Univ, Boy's Clb (Daytona Beach), YMCA (Daytona Beach), Mus Arts & Scis (Daytona Beach), Volusia Assn Retarded Citizens, Am Heart Assn; JCs; Num Others; r/Westbury Ch of Christ (Houston): Song Ldr; hon/Mil Awds: Nat Defense Medal, Pres Unit Cit w Oak Leaf Cluster, Air Force Outstg Unit Awd w 2 Oak Leaf Clusters, Small Arms Marksmanship Awd w Bronze Star, Air Force Longevity Awd w Oak Leaf Cluster, Armed Forces Reserv Medal; Daytona Beach JCs: Outstg JC of Mon, Pres' Cit, Speak Up Awd, Spoke Awd & Spark Plug Awd; Paul Gross First Annual Public Relats Awd; BSA: Eagle Scout, Bronze Palm, Silver Palm, Gold Palm, Order of Arrow, Others; Outstg Yg Men Am; Personalities of S; Notable Ams; DIB; W/W Hlth Care; Commun Ldrs & Noteworthy Ams; Men Achmt; Book of Hon; Fellow, Am Biogl Inst; Others.

MOSAK, HAROLD H oc/Clinical Psychologist; b/Oct 29, 1921; h/3650 Crain, Skokie, IL 60076; ba/Chicago, IL; m/Birdie; c/Derin, Lisa, Neal; p/Nathan and Lena Mosak; ed/BA 1953, PhD 1950 Univ Chgo; mil/USAAF 1943-46; pa/Chm Bd Dirs, Alfred Adler Inst; r/Jewish; hon/Phi Beta Kappa; Sigma Xi; Psi Chi.

MOSCRIPT, DOROTHA MARGUERITE oc/Librarian; b/May 10, 1913; h/305 E Windsor, Box 700, Arkansas City, KS 67005; ba/Ark City; m/(dec); c/William Otis, James Tracy; p/Robert Herr and Gracie Ann Yoder (dec); pa/Libn, Windsor Ct Lib; Newspaper Reporter; Bookkeeper; Acct; cp/Scouts; 4-H Clb; r/Meth; hon/Rec'd Awd for 25 Yrs Ser, 4-H Clb & 15 Yrs as Libn.

MOSELEY, ROBERT CARTER oc/- Minister; b/Aug 29, 1948; h/407 Franklin Ave, Moberly, MO 65270; ba/Moberly; n/Leta B; c/Kendall Carter, Sheri Lee, Michael Robert; p/Robert L Moseley, Rothville, MO; Julia A Moseley (dec); ed/AA, ThB Hannibal-LaGrange Col; BS Univ Mo; mil/USAF; pa/Pastor, N Park Bapt Ch; Royal Ambassador Dir; Past Camp Dir, Mt Pleasant Bapt Assn; Mt Pleasant Bapt Assn Ch Tng Dir; Mt Pleasant & Tri-Mission Bapt Bd; Asst Moderator, Tri-Mission Bapt Bd; Vacation Bible Sch Staff; Moberly & Randolph Co Min Alliance; Conslt Brotherhood Dept, Mo Bapt Conv; Growth Conslt Ch Tng Dept, Mo Bapt Conv; cp/Chm Commun Ser Com for Moberly, Mo All Cert'd Cities Prog; Past Chm Selection & Interview Com, Randolph Co Big-Brother/Big-Sister Prog; Former Pee-wee Baseball Mgr; Precinct Chm, Am Cancer Soc Master, Moberly Pioneer Grange #2241; Asst Steward, Mo St Grange; 9th Congl Dist Agri Com; Randolph Co Mtl Hlth Assn; r/Bapt; hon/Phi Kappa Theta; FFA: St Farmer Deg & Am Farmer Deg; Mo Grange Yg Couple of Yr; Outstg Yg Men Am; W/W Rel; Personalities of W&MW; Intl W/W Commun Ser; Notable Ams; Others.

MOSES, JAMES ANTHONY JR oc/Clinical Neuropsychologist; b/Feb 25, 1947; h/177 Westlawn Ave, Daly City, CA 94015; ba/Palo Alto, CA; p/James A Sr and Lucille M Moses; ed/BA magna cum laude, San Francisco St Univ 1968; MS San Jose St Univ 1970; MA 1971, PhD 1974 Univ Colo-B; pa/Stanford Univ Sch Mec: Clinical Asst Prof Psychi 1978-,

Clinical Instr 1975-78; Palo Alto VA Hosp: Coor Psychol Assessmt Unit 1976-, Staff Clinical Neuropsychol 1974-, Level IV Intern 1973-74 (Also, SF Ft Miley Hosp); Other Positions: Lic'd Psychol, Cal 1975; Am Psychol Assn; Wn Psychol Assn; Soc Personality Assessmt; Stanford Univ Clinical Fac Assn; Others; Contbr Articles Profl Jours; cp/Chevalier, Intl Supr Coun Order of DeMolay; 2° Black Belt, Zen Budo Kai Martial Arts Soc; 1° Black Belt, Zen Bie Butoku Kai Martial Arts Soc; r/Prot; hon/Life Mem, Cal S'ship Fdn; Psi Chi; Rec'd Meritorious Ser Medal, Order DeMolay; George Hendry S'ship Awd; USPHS Intermediate Level Predoct Fellow, Univ Colo; Outstg Vol Sers Awd, Palo Alto VA Hosp; Biogl Listings.

MOSLEY, MARY MAC H oc/Librarian; b/Nov 11, 1926; h/Lyons Bridge Rd, Cave Spring, GA 30124; ba/Rome, GA; c/Samuel A Jr, Pamela Ann, James Irwin; p/William M and Mary Caldwell Howell, Rome; ed/BS Auburn Univ; MLS Emory Univ; pa/Libn, Shorter Col; Am, SE, Ga & Coosa Val Lib Assns; AAUW (Pres Rome Chapt 1973-75); cp/ARC; March of Dimes; Cave Spring Hist Assn; r/Disciples of Christ; hon/Delta Kappa Gamma.

MOSLEY, MAXINE V oc/Professor; b/Feb 27, 1928; h/Queen City, MO 63561; m/Raymond J (dec); c/Linda M Knight, Brenda Jo M Henry, Anita Rae; p/Abner Hamilton Ellsworth (dec); Anna Partin Ellsworth, Novinger, MO; ed/BSEd NE Mo Univ; MA Univ Mo-C; pa/Prof Eng; Ser'd Num Local, Dist, St & Nat Coms; Author, *Devel'g Composition Skills*; cp/GSA; r/United Meth Ch; hon/Rec'd Regents S'ship; World W/W Wom; W/W Wom Ed; Personalities of W&MW; Directory Am Scholars; Am Biogl Assn.

MOSS, FRANCES P oc/Teacher; b/Apr 8, 1940; h/1303 First Ave SW, Decatur, AL 35601; ba/Decatur; p/William A Moss I, Oxford, AL; Ada Nichols Moss (dec); ed/BMus Jacksonville St Univ; MMus, PhD Univ Ala; Addit Studies; pa/Head Dept Mus, Calhoun Commun Col; Conductor, Choral Fests & Competitions; Pub'd Composer; Ala Mus Edrs Assn (Twice Pres); Ala Vocal Assn (Twice Pres); Mus Edrs Nat Conf; Ala Jr & Commun Col Assn; r/Bellview Bapt Ch (Decatur): Mus Dir; hon/Delta Kappa Gamma; Kappa Delta Pi; Pi Kappa Lambda; Delta Omicron; Hon Conductor Ala All-St Choruses, Ala Vocal Assn; Recog'd by St of Ala Hist Comm; Outstg Yg Wom Am; Intl W/W Mus; Personalities of S.

MOSS, ROBERT SHERIFFS oc/Lawyer; b/Jul 15, 1908; h/8521 Doter Dr, Waynewood, Alexandria, VA 22308; ba/Washington, DC; m/Bernice M Pfeifer; c/Marilyn, Karen; p/Roy M and Cornelia M Sheriffs Moss; ed/BS NWn Univ 1929; JD Univ Wis 1932; LLM Georgetown Univ 1964; pa/Partner w Firm of Sullivan, Beauregard, Clarkson, Moss, Brown & Johnson 1976-; Prin Atty, Robert Sheriffs Moss & Assocs, Chartered 1971-76; Pvt Pract (Milwaukee, Wis) 1932-43, (Wash, DC) 1947-; Admitted to Wis Bar, DC Bar, US Supreme Ct Bar; Am (Num Ofcs, Coms), Wis, Fed (Nat Coun 1968-69, 71-72) Bar Assns; Bar Assn DC: Chm Taxation Com 1954-55, Steering Com Sect Govt Contracts, Chm Adm Law Sect 1975-76, Dir 1975-76); Pub'd Author; Others; cp/Bd Govs, Nat Grad Univ; Pres, Milwaukee YMCA Toastmasters Clb; Army & Navy Clbs; Others; hon/Phi Delta Phi; Others.

MOSS, TOMMYE ATKINSON oc/- Homemaker; b/Nov 8, 1894; h/PO Box 3229, Odessa, TX 79760; m/William Paul (dec); c/Betty M Dean (Mrs Charles A), William Paul Jr; p/Everett Buchanan and Minnie Weaver Atkinson (dec); ed/BA Tift Col 1917; cp/Orgr First Wom's Clb Odessa (1st Pres); 1rst Pres, Odessa PTA; Past Pres, Odessa Book Clb; Past Pres, 9th Dist Tex Fdn Mus Clbs; St Pres, Tex Fdn Mus Clbs; Bd Mem, Nat Fdn Mus Clbs; Hon Life Mem, Odessa Civic Concert Bd; Hon Mem, Odessa Symph Guild; Hon Mem, Jr Ser Leag; Patron, Bd of Gt SW; Contbr, Midland-Odessa Symph &

Chorale; Donations: 100 Books to Univ Tex Permian Basin, Husband's Law Books to Tex Tech Univ, Organ to Tex Tech, Freedom Fountain to Floyd Gwen Park, Authentic Shakespearean Theatre, LBJ Meml Grove on Potomac; United Fund; YMCA; Negro Boys Clb; Sheriff's Posse; Org for Blind; Salvation Army; Am Cancer Soc; r/Bapt: Ser'd on Bldg Com, SS Secy, Pres Wom's Missonary Union, Dist Pres, St Bd Mem; hon/Rec'd 3 Annual S'ships Mus Sch, Tex Tech Univ; S'ship, Baylor Univ; Odessa First Lady 1955; Grand Lady of Symph, Symph Bd; Outstg Ldrship Awd in Mus Ed; Rec'd Plaque, Bd Dirs Odessa Symph Assn; Rec'd Plaque, Odessa Arts & Humanities Coun; Cert Apprec, Salvation Army Bd; W/W Am Wom.

MOTTER, ROBERTA LEE oc/Director; b/Mar 8, 1936; h/6881 Brian Michael Ct, Springfield, VA 22153; ba/Arlington, VA; c/Edwin, Lori, Lisa; p/Donald D and Florence B Reed; pa/GS 13 Prog Analyst, Gen Ser Adm (Crystal City, Va) 1980-; Dir Adm Sers, St of NY Ins Dept Liquidation Bur 1975-80; Pers Dir & Ofc Mgr, Summit Ins Co of NY (Houston, Tex) 1974-75; Conversion Specialist, Accts Payable, Medenco Inc (Houston) 1973-74; Other Former Positions; NY Purchasing Mgmt Soc; Am Soc Pers Admrs; Am Mgmt Soc; Bd Dirs, Adm Mgmt Soc of Washington (DC); Purchasing Mgmt Assn; IPA; Contbr to Var Tech Manuals; Others; cp/Bd Dirs, Lincoln Commun Ctr (Short Hills); Dem Clb; Inaugural Activs as Mem of Labor Com 1981; Hawaii St Soc; r/Cath; hon/Beta Sigma Phi; Wom of Yr, Beta Sigma Phi; Recog'd as Purchasing Profl, NY Purchasing Mgmt Assn; Featured in *NY Metro Mag*; Commun Ldrs & Noteworthy Ams.

MOUNGOVAN, JULIA LONGFELLOW oc/Retired Teacher; b/Apr 20, 1902; h/243 W Bush St, Fort Bragg, CA 95437; ba/Same; m/Thomas O (dec); c/Gayle Ethel M Bulger; p/George Albert and Eva Tibbit Longfellow (dec); ed/BA 1924, MA 1925 Univ Cal-B; Grad Studies; pa/HS Tchr: Los Molinos (Cal) 1925-26, Princeton (Cal) 1926-29, Daville (Cal) 1929-32, Others; Agent Mutual Life Ins (NY) 1950-70; Elem Tchr (Ft Bragg) 1958-68; Lectr: Univ Cal Workshop (Mendocino) 1968, Sonoma St Ext 1969-71; Part-time Instr Hist, Ft Bragg Branch Col of Redwoods; Author: *The Henry Beeson Story, The Potter Valley Story, Vignettes of Mendocino Co;* Co-author w Husband, *Where There's a Will, There's a Way;* Co-Author: *Logging w Ox Teams, Saga of Little River,* Others; Editor: Mendocino Co Hist Soc Newsltter (1962-), *Lore of Coast* (1964), *Tales of Mendocino Co* (1965), Others; Nat, St & Local Ret'd Tchrs Assns; cp/Past Pres, Mendocino Co Hist Soc; Regional VP Cal Conf Hist Socs; Chm Nn Cal & So Oregon Symposium, Conf Cal Hist Socs; Past Pres Mendocino Coast Repub Wom's Assn; Del Nat Fdn Repub Wom Conv; Co Ctl Com, Repub Party; Hon Mem, PTA; Exec Secy & Ser to Mil Fams, ARC; Others; r/Presb; hon/Delta Kappa Gamma; Bay Named in Hon, Mendocino Co Mus; DIB; Commun Ldrs & Noteworthy Ams; W/W: Commun Ser, US; Personalities of W&MW.

MOUNTAIN, CLIFTON FLETCHER oc/Professor; b/Apr 15, 1924; h/1612 S Blvd, Houston, TX 77006; ba/Houston; m/Marilyn Isabelle Tapper; c/Karen Lockery, Clifton F Jr, Jeffrey Richardson; p/Ira Fletcher Mountain (dec); Mary Elizabeth Stone, Copperas Cove, TX; ed/BA Harvard Univ 1946; MD Boston Univ 1954; mil/USNR 1942-46; S&SW PTO Operations; pa/Prof Surg; Chief Sect Thoracic Surg, M D Anderson Hosp; Am Jt Com on Cancer Staging & End Results Reporting; USA-Japan Sci Mission on Lung Cancer 1975-; USA-USSR Sci Mission on Lung Cancer 1974-; Mike Hogg Visiting Lectr, South Am 1967; hon/Sigma Xi; Rec'd Postdoct S'ship, Univ Chgo; Rec'd Kelsey-Leary Res Awd.

MOVSKY, MYRON B oc/Clergyman; b/Aug 21, 1917; h/3061 Reed Ave #C, Cheyenne, WY 82001; ba/Cheyenne; m/Hadassah H; c/Margaret M Mayer, David S; p/Philip and Rose G Movsky (dec); ed/BA; MA; DD; mil/Chaplain, Army Spec'd Tng

Prog & VA Hosp; pa/Rabbi: Mt Sinai Congreg (Cheyenne) 1977-, Congreg Am Echod (Waukegan, Ill) 1969-76, Others; Instr Theol, Holy Child HS 1972-75, Laramie Co Commun Col, Others; Lectr; Editor, *Partners in Prayer*; Contbg Editor, *Fship in Prayer*; Chaplain: Kalamazoo St Hosp (Mich), VA Hosp (Battle Creek, Mich), Lima St Hosp (Ohio); Past Pres, Lima Lodge B'nai B'rith; Past Pres, Torch Clb Intl; BD Mem: Nat Conf Christians & Jews, United Jewish Appeal; Min Alliance; Coun Human Relats; Assn Mtl Hosp Chaplains; Rabbinical Assn Am; Rabbinical Comm Ill; Fdg Mem, Assn Clinical Pastoral Ed Inc; Zionist Org Am; Chgo Bd Rabbis; cp/Former VP, Optimist Clb; Former VP, Big Brothers (Kalamazoo); Bd Mem: Nat Coun Jt Distribution Comm, Taylor House (Half-way Ho), Citizens' Assn Kalamazoo St Hosp; Bd Govs, St of Israel Bonds; NAACP; Jewish Pub Soc; Jewish Hist Soc; Waukegan Exchange Clb; r/Jewish; hon/Rec'd Medal, Prime Min Israel; W/W: Ill, World Jewry; Am Jews -Their Lives & Achmts; Israel Honorarium Vol; Personalities of W&MW.

MOWDY, AL oc/Carpenter (Disabled); b/Apr 27, 1938; h/PO Box 53, Durant, OK 74701; ba/Durant; c/Cheryl Kay, David Allen, Lisa Carol, James Aaron; p/Arvin Allen Mowdy (dec); Oma Mowdy, Lewisville, TX.

MOZINGO, MARGARET JOHNSON oc/Homemaker; h/126 Oak St, Darlington, SC 29532; c/Thomas Aladdin, Margaret Brock; p/Olin Thomas Johnson (dec); Mary Evelyn Johnson, Florence, SC; ed/Univ Ga; Univ SC; cp/Am Cancer Soc; Heart Fund; r/Presb; hon/Notable Ams; Personalities of S; DIB.

MSCICHOWSKI, LOIS I oc/Insurance Executive; b/Nov 24, 1935; h/8401 SW Frances Ave, Vancouver, WA 98664; m/Peter A; c/1; p/Edward and Evelyn Davidson Morrison; pa/Ins Clerk, Gross Wilson Ins Agy 1955-57; Ins Secy-bookkeeper, Reed Paulson Ins Agy 1957-58; Office Mgr, Asst Secy & Agent, Don Biggs & Assocs Inc 1958-; Ins Wom SW Wash; cp/Soroptimist Intl; Ctl City Task Force; Block Grant Task Force Com; Adv Com, Clark Col; hon/Ins Wom of Yr, Ins Wom SW Wash; Soroptimist of Yr; Book of Hon; W/W Am Wom; World W/W Wom; Men & Wom Distinction; DIB.

MUELLER, WILLIAM FEGLEY oc/-Clergyman; b/Jan 19, 1936; h/Rt 1, Box 243 H, Churchville, VA 24421; ba/Same; m/Patty Ann; c/Kurt, Elizabeth M Nunery (Mrs Randy Jr), Steven, James, Cheryln; p/Lewis J and Mildred Mueller, Morristown, TN; ed/AB; BD; MDiv; FIBA; mil/Va Army NG, Maj;

pa/Pastor, Luth Ch; Luth Human Relats Assn Am; ROA; LHRA; cp/Smithsonian Assoc; Cousteau Soc; United Nations Assn; r/Luth; hon/Chaplain of Four Chaplains Legion of Hon; Num Biogl Listings.

MÜLLER, GENE ALAN oc/Latin-American Scholar; b/Jan 10, 1943; h/10523 Eaglestone Way, El Paso,TX 79925; ba/El Paso; c/Michelle Nicole; p/Ludwig Frederick Muller (dec); Erma Gorin Muller, Grand Island, NE; ed/BA cum laude, Midland Luth Col 1965; Ma 1969, ABD 1970 Univ Kansas-L; Addit Studies; pa/El Paso Commun Col: Instr Hist 1974-, Hist Discipline Coor 1975-76, Co-reschr w Edward J Silva, Study Abroad Advr (Office Intl Student Sers) 1979-, Dir Dept Hist & Fam Hist Proj 1975-, Others; Part-time Instr, Park Col (Ft Bliss, Tex) 1978-; Asst Prof Hist, Kansas St Univ (Ft Hays) 1973-74; Other Positions; Editor Bd, *The Kansas Latinamericanist*, Univ Kansas-Ctr of Latin Am Studies (Lawrence) 1972-73; Participant, Univ Tex-A Inst Latin Am Studies Cult Confs 1978; Panelist, NAFSA Conf 1978; Proj Reviewer, Nat Endowmt for Humanities 1978-; Book Reviewer; Contbr Num Articles Profl Jours; Presents Workshops; Lectr; Author Textbook Chapts; Am Hist Assn; Am & Cath Hist Assns; Latin Am Studies Assn; Conf on Latin Am Hist; Rocky Mountain Coun Latin Am Studies; MW Assn Latin Am Studies; AAUP; Others; r/Good Shepherd Luth Ch (El Paso): Coun Mem, Luth Brotherhood, Aid Assn for Luths; hon/Announcer, El Paso Commun Col Graduation Ceremonies 1979; Rec'd S'ship, NYU in Spain; Hon S'ship, Midland Col; Fulbright-Hays F'ship, Nat Univ Tucuman (Argentina); Rec'd NDFL Title VI F'ship, Univ Kansas; OAS F'ship to Guatemala; Blue Key Nat Hon Frat; Best Supporting Actor Awd, Midland Col Drama; Nom'd Tex Piper Tchg Awd, EPCC Fac; Spec Listing, Inst Latin Am Studies (Univ Tex-A); Directory Am Scholars; Others.

MULLER, JANET SLOANE oc/Writer; Editor; b/May 19, 1948; h/114 High St, Middletown, CT 06457; ba/Middletown; p/Henry and Barbara Muller, E Hampton, CT; ed/BA Goucher Col; MA Univ Penn; pa/Editor, *Alumni Record*, Wesleyan Univ 1979-; Freelance Poet; Author Short Stories; Pub'd in US & Abroad; Editor, *Ofcl Associated Press Almanac* 1974 & 1975; Asst Editor, Rodale *Synonym Finder*; Editor of Chd's Ency, Dictionary of Sports Personalities Nicknames; Conn Assn Profl Communicators; r/Congregl; hon/Phi Beta Kappa; BA cum laude; Isabelle Kellogg Thomas Awd in English.

MULLINS, EDWARD WADE JR oc/Lawyer; b/Jan 17, 1936; h/1413 Milford Rd, Columbia, SC 29206; ba/Columbia; m/Andrea Robertson; c/Edward Wade III, Andrew Robertson; p/Edward W and Katherine Clarke Mullins; ed/BS 1957, LLB cum laude, JD 1959 Univ SC; mil/USAF 1960-61; pa/Admit'd SC Bar 1959; Assoc &

Partner Nelson, Mullins, Grier & Scarborough (Law Firm); Other Previous Firms; Am, SC & Richland Bar Assns; Fed Ins Coun (Regional VP); Def Res Inst (Regional VP); SC Def Attys Assn (Pres 1973); Am Judicature Soc; cp/Past Chm Bd, Columbia Area Mtl Hlth Ctr; Past Pres, Richland Sertoma Clb; Former Pres, Tarentilla Clb; Dir & VP, Wildewood Country Clb; Columbia Cotillion; hon/Phi Delta Phi;

Kappa Alpha Order; Kappa Sigma Kappa; Omicron Delta Kappa.

MUMFORD, PATRICK WAYNE oc/-Executive; b/Oct 10, 1944; h/303 Brentwood Ln, Rt 3, Advance, NC 27006; ba/Winston-Salem, NC; m/Sudie Bland; p/Herman Wayne and Frances James Mumford, New Bern, NC; ed/BS E Carolina Univ 1966; JD Univ Tenn 1972; mil/USAF 1966-70; USAFR 1973-78; pa/Title Ins Co Exec; NC St Bar; NC, Tenn & Am Bar Assns; Forsyth Co Jr Bar (Past Secy); Forsyth Co Real Estate Bar (Past VP); cp/Stratford Sertoma Clb; W-S C of C; Ambassadors Clb; r/Clemmons United Meth Ch: Tchr Bible Study Class; hon/Rec'd Mayor's Merit Awd, City of Knoxville (Tenn); Num Mil Awds; W/W S&SW.

MUNDAHL, FRANCES MAE oc/Teacher; b/May 26, 1913; h/221-Second St, Madison, MN 56256; ba/Madison; m/Orvin; p/Joseph B and Jessie Belle Rademacher, Madison; ed/BS; pa/Spec Class Tchr, Madison Elem Sch (Dist 377); Staff Mem &

Recorder, Child Study Com 1974-78; Bd Dirs, Day Activs Ctr 1960-74; Assn Retarded Citizens; r/United Ch of Christ (Madison); hon/Tchr of Yr: Madison Elem Sch 1974 & Madison Public Schs 1977-78; Notable Ams.

MUNDY, ELLA MAE oc/Broker; b/Aug 16, 1933; h/Rt 1, Box 272, Hopkinsville, KY 42240; ba/Hopkinsville; m/James D; c/Ronald Kent, Kimberly Ann; p/Henry F and Rosie P Hargrove, Pembroke, KY; pa/Assoc Broker, Bilt Rite Realty; Dir & Mbrship Chm, Hopkinsville Bd Realtors; cp/United Way Campaign Worker; Hon Life Mem, Jennie Stuart Hosp Aux; hon/Assoc Realtor of Yr, Hopkinsville Bd Realtors.

MUNGER, ELIZABETH MACK oc/Retired Teacher; b/Jul 28, 1906; h/500 Marquette Trail, Michigan City, IN 46360; m/Robert C (dec); c/Gilbert Ridgway Hitchcock, John Lathrop Hitchcock; p/Joseph Lathrop and Robert C Smith Mack (dec); ed/BS Univ Ill 1928; MA NWn Univ 1943; Media Spec, Purdue Univ 1967; pa/Author, *Mich City's First 100 Yrs*; AAUW; cp/Org Pres, Eunice Mather Williams Colony (NSNEW); 1st VP, Ind Soc Colonial Dames XVII Cent; Pres Ind St Soc US Daughs 1812; Nat Chm (Defense), Wom Descendants Ancient & Hon Artillery Co; Past Regent Abijah, Bigelow Chapt DAR; Gen Soc; Mayflower Descendants; Nat Soc Huguenot Descendants; Nat Soc Dames Ct of Hon; Descendants Colonial Govs; Daughs of Fdrs & Patriots; Order Crown of Charlemagne;

Magna Charta Dames; Sons & Daughs of Pilgrims; Past Pres, Mich City Hist Soc; Trustee, NW Ind Geneol Soc; Conn Soc Genealogists; Pilgrim Soc; Nat Archives Assoc; Num Others; r/Alliance New Ch Wom; hon/Hall of Fame, Mich City Area Schs; Nom, LaPorte Co Wom of Yr; Delta Kappa Gamma.

MUNROE, BARBARA oc/Retired; b/-Sept 17, 1920; h/61 Broad Reach, No Weymouth, MA 02191; p/Charles Munroe (dec); Beatrice Mae Bassett Munroe, No Weymouth; ed/Grad Mass Gen Hosp Sch Nsg 1942; Grad Boston Sch Occupational Therapy 1948; mil/-USN; CDR MSC 34 Yrs; pa/ANA; Am OT Assn; Assn Mil Surgs; r/Prot; hon/Rec'd Commend Awd, Cert of Merit & Maj Louis Livingston Seaman Prize, USN; Awd for Article, "Rehab of Upper Extremity Traumatic Amputee", Mil Med.

MUNTER, PAMELA OSBORNE oc/Psychotherapist; b/Mar 27, 1943; h/18060 SW Salix Ridge, Aloha, OR 97005; ba/Portland, OR; ed/BA Univ Cal-B 1964; MA (2), Cal St Univ 1966, 69; Certs, Univ Neb Sch Alcohol Studies 1971 & Reproductive Biol Res Foun (Masters & Johnson) 1975; PhD Univ Neb 1972; Addit Studies; pa/Portland St Univ: Assoc Prof Psychol 1976-, Asst Prof 1973-76; Pvt Pract Psychotherapist (Beaverton, Oregon) 1973-; Univ Neb: Lectr 1970-71, Omaha VA Hosp 1971-72, Lincoln's VA Hosp 1970-71, Psychol Consltg Ctr 1969-70, Others; Other Positions; Conslt: Rockwood Sch Dist, Psychol Clinic, Crisis Intervention Ctr, Wom's Union at Portland St Univ, Albertina Kerr Child Ctr, Others; Lic'd Psychol, Neb & Oregon; Reschr; Pub'd Num Book Reviews & Profl Articles; Bd Dirs: Oregon Grad Sch Profl Psychol & NW Film Study Ctr; Am Psychol Assn; Assn Humanistic Psychol; Wn Psychol Assn; Oregon Psychol Assn; Oregon Acad Profl Psychols (Fdg Editor, The Oregon Psychologist); Portland Psychol Assn; Soc Personality Assessmt; Am Soc Clinical Hypnosis; Assn Wom Psychol; hon/W/W: Am Wom, W, Am; World W/W Wom; DIB; Notable Ams; Am Men & Wom Sci; Intl W/W Intellectuals; Others.

MURDOCK, DARYL LYNN oc/Artist; b/Oct 10, 1939; h/200 E 80th Terrace, Kansas City, MO 64114; ba/Same; m/John William; c/Zachary Jay; p/Hans L Jorgensen, Seattle, WA; Toby Keller Jorgensen, Fayetteville, AR; ed/BFA Univ Ark; pa/Profl Artist; Assn Sci-Fi Artists; Gtr Kansas City Art Assn; Kansas City Artist Coalition; Nat Leag Am Pem Wom; r/Christian; hon/Winner 2nd Pl in Show & 2 Purchase Awds, Spira Art Ctr Competition; Best of Show, Am Pen Wom St Art Show.

MURDOCK, PERCY oc/Administrator; b/Dec 26, 1935; h/3616 Trendley Ave, E St Louis, IL 62207; ba/St Louis; c/Angela D; p/John and Canary Murdock, St Louis; ed/BS Jackson St Univ 1958; MS (2) Bradley Univ 1965, 72; Civil Def Cert; Addit Studies; pa/Sch Adm to Col Prof; Participant NDEA 1968 (1 of 24 Choosen); AAUP; Am & Ill Fdn Tchrs; Am & Ill Voc Assns; cp/BSA; Bradley Grad Ind Ed Clb (Past Pres); L M & M Clb (Pres & Fdr); Shuqualakian Clb (Pres & Fdr); Square Deal Lodge; Heroines of Jericho; Others; hon/W/W Among Black Ams; Men Achmt; Notable Ams; Commun Ldrs & Noteworthy Ams.

MURILLO-ROHDE, ILDAURA M oc/-Professor Nursing; h/12044 7th Ave NW, Seattle, WA 98177; ba/Seattle; m/Erling; p/Amalio and Ana Etanislaa Diaz de Murillo (dec); ed/BS 1951, MA 1953, MEd 1969 Tchrs Col (Columbia Univ); PhD NYU 1971; pa/Prof & Assoc Dean Sch Nsg, Univ Wash; Assoc Prof & Psychi Coor, CUNY, Hostos Commun Col 1972-76; Other Positions; ANA; Commr Human Rights 1976-80; Am Assn Marriage & Fam Cnslrs; Pres Nat Assn Spanish-Speaking Surnamed Nurses 1976-; Bd Dirs, Nat Coalition Hispanic Mtl Hlth & Human Serv Org 1976-; Bd Dirs, King Co Hlth Plan'g Coun (Seattle) 1977-80; Conslt Hlth Resources Adm, HEW 1978; Fellow: Am Acad

Nsg 1974, Am Orthopsychi Assn 1973-, Am Assn Marriage & Fam Cnslrs 1975, Intl Inst Commun Sers 1975; Nat Leag Nsg; Wash Assn Marriage & Fam Cnslrs; Orgr, COSSMHO 1st Wash St Hispanic Conf on Hlth & Human Sers; Profl Adv Bd, Save-A-Marriage 1976-; Manuscript Review Panelist, Nsg Res 1974; Editor Bd, Cancer Nsg: An Intl Jour 1977-79; Other Orgs & Assns; Author Num Articles Profl Jours & Books; cp/Bd Dirs, Intl House; Riverside Dems; r/Prot; hon/Sigma Theta Tau; Cand, Mary Mahoney Awd (ANA); W/W: Am Wom, E, Hlth Care, W; World W/W Wom; Outstg Profls Human Sers; Commun Ldrs & Noteworthy Ams; DIB; Intl W/W Intellectuals; Nat Directory Hispanic Profls in Mtl Hlth & Human Sers; Nat Directory Specs in Psychi-Mtl Hlth Nsg; Others.

MURPHY, FREDERICK A oc/Professor Microbiology; b/Jun 14, 1934; h/1116 Ponderosa Dr, Ft Collins, CO 80521; ba/Ft Collins; m/Irene M; c/Frederick III, William, John, Terence; p/Frederick A Murphy (dec); Louise A Murphy, Islip, NY; ed/BS; DVM; PhD; mil/AUS; US Public Hlth Ser Cmdr; pa/Assoc Dean & Prof Microbiol, Col Veterinary Med & Biomed Scis (Colo St Univ); Hon Fellow Dept Microbiol, John Curtin Sch Med Res (Australian Nat Univ) 1970-71; Chief Viropathology Unit, Ctr for Disease Control (Atlanta, Ga) 1964-72; Other Positions; VChm Virology Sect, Intl Assn Microbiol Socs 1978-82); Prog Chm, 5th Intl Cong for Virology (Paris) 1978-81; VP, Intl Comparative Virology Org 1978-; Bd Mem, WHO/FAO Comparative Virology Prog 1975-; Chm Exec'e Coun (1974-75), Exec Coun Mem (1972-76) & Mem Am Com on Arthropod-Borne Viruses 1965-; Conslt, Viral Diseases Progs, WHO; Assoc Editor, Virology; Editor Bd: Intervirology, Archives of Virology, Jour Med Virology; Infectious Disease Soc Am; Am Assn Immunologists; Am Soc Microbiol; Soc Exptl Biol & Med; Am Veterinary Med Assn; Electron Microscopy Soc Am; Am Soc Tropical Med & Hygiene; AAAS; Others; Author 138 Papers & Book Chapts; r/Rom Cath; hon/Sigma Xi.

MURPHY, HERTA ALBRECHT oc/College Educator; b/Jul 26; h/422 Summit Ave E, Seattle, WA 98102; ba/Seattle; m/Eugene Arthur; c/Jeanette Darlene; p/Joseph and Hedy Albrecht (dec); ed/BBA cum laude, MA Univ Wash-S; Grad Studies: UNnv So Cal-LA, Armstrong Col Bus Adm (Berkeley), George Wash Univ (Wash, DC); pa/Univ Wash: Lectr, Asst Prof, Assoc & Full Prof 1946-74, Prof Emeritus; Prof, Am Savs & Ln Inst's Sch for Exec Devel 1960-65; Asst & Assoc Prof, Univ Alaska 1943-46; Other Positions; Lectr Num Bus Agencies & Orgs; Editor "Over the Teacups" Sect, The Angelos; Reviewer Books & Manuscripts: Prentice Hall, Wadsworth, McGraw-Hill; Contbr Articles Profl Jours & Mags; Co-author: Effective Bus Communs (1972, 76), Instr's Manual to Accompany EBC (1972, 76), Savs Assn Lttrs (1974), Others; Former NW Regional VP, Chm & Speaker, Am Bus Communs Assn; Seattle Branch Pres, Nat Leag Am Pen Wom; Past St Mbrship Chm, Nat Bus Tchrs Assn; Asst Treas, Wash St Inter-Instnl Comm Higher Ed Employees; Others; cp/Fac Wom's Clb, Univ Wash; Pres' Forum; Univ Wash Fac Retiremt Assn; Chm, Capitol Hill Commun Ser Comm; r/St Patrick's Cath Ch; hon/Fellow, Am Bus Communs Assn; Finalist, Dist'd Tchr Awd, Univ Wash; Seattle & King Co Conv & Visitors Bur Awd; Matrix Table; Jury of Authorities, Bus Communs; Phi Beta Kappa; Kappa Delta; Beta Gamma Sigma; Gamma Alpha Chi; Commun Ldrs & Noteworthy Ams; World W/W Wom; Intl Authors & Writers W/W; W/W: Am Wom, W, Pac Coast; Personalities of W&MW; Others.

MURPHY, JERRY JOHN oc/Lawyer; b/Mar 28, 1942; h/23 Middlesex, Brentwood, MO 63144; ba/Clayton, MO; m/Judy Ossenfort; c/Scott Michael, Molly Anne, Andrew Christopher, Jerry John Jr, Timothy Patrick; p/Forrest and Virginia Weber Murphy (dec); ed/BA Univ Notre Dame 1964; JD St Louis Univ 1968; LLM Wash Univ 1976; pa/Admit'd Mo Bar 1968, US Supr Ct Bar

1974; Asst Circuit Atty (St Louis) 1968-70; Asst US Atty En Dist Mo (St Louis) 1970-74; Spec Atty in Charge of St Louis Office of Drug Abuse Law Enforcemt 1972-74; Individual Pract (Clayton) 1974-; Spec Conslt, White House Coun (Wash, DC) 1974-75; Spec Conslt, US Dept Justice Drug Enforcemt Adm 1975; Instr, St Louis Univ Sch Law 1974; ABA; Mo Bar Assn; Bar Assn Metro St Louis; St Louis Co Bar Assn; Mo Trial Lwyrs Assn; St Louis Lwyrs Assn; cp/St Louis Estate Planning Coun; Bd Dirs, Legal Aid Soc; Bd Dirs Magdala Foun; Bd Mem, Immacolata Sch; r/Rom Cath; hon/Rec'd Spec Act Awd, Assn Fed Investigators; Narcotic Law Enforcemt Awd, US Dept Justice; Awd of Merit, St Louis Metro Bar Assn.

MURPHY, JOHN B oc/College Administrator; b/Jun 8, 1919; h/722 Candleglo Dr, San Antonio, TX 78239; ba/San Antonio; m/Edwina King; c/John Edwin; p/Patrick H Murphy (dec); Hazel Pearl Murphy, Austin, TX; ed/BS w Hons, Prairie View A&M Col 1943; MS Kansas St Univ 1946; PhD Univ Tex 1959; Addit Studies; pa/Former Tchr Voc Agri (Yoakum, Tex); Former Tchr Sci, Kealing Jr HS (Austin); Former Co Agri Agent (Austin Co, Tex); Prof & Chm Div Plant Scis, NC

A&T St Univ 10 Yrs; Prairie View A&M Col: Div Ed Staff 1959-69, Dir Tchr Ed & Cert Ofcr, Chm Ed Dept 1966-69; Dean, St Philip's Col 1969-; Author Profl Papers & Reports; Tex Jr Col Instrnl Admrs; Am Assn Commun Jr Cols; Assoc Mem, Tex Public Commun/Jr Col Assn; Tex Jr Col Tchrs Assn; Others; cp/Prairie View Alumni Assn (Former Exec Secy); r/Prot; hon/Phi Delta Kappa; Phi Theta Kappa; Alpha Phi Alpha; Rec'd Nat F'ship Awds, Alpha Phi Alpha & So Ed Foun.

MURPHY, NATALIE OWEN oc/Insurance Agent; b/Oct 21, 1918; h/5013 Ave O, Galveston, TX 77550; ba/Galveston; m/T N Owen (dec); Ethel L Owen, Galveston, TX; ed/CPIW; Bus Certs; pa/Past Pres, all Local Ins Groups; Past Pres, Fdn of Ins Wom of Tex (var coms); cp/Work on State Leg Coms for FLWT; Ins Com, City of Galveston; Traffic Comm; Others; r/Bapt: Choir, Tng, Yth Activs; ho/CPIW Awd; Others.

MURPHY, POLLY LEWIS oc/Teacher; b/Aug 21, 1915; h/111 NE Fullerton St, Lawton, OK 73501; ba/Geronimo, OK; m/Benjamin Vinson (dec); c/Mary M Still (Mrs David L), Kathleen M Rankin (Mrs Johnnie); p/Hugh Henry and Mabel Stuart Lewis (dec); ed/BA magna cum laude, Univ Sci & Arts of Okla 1969; pa/Tchr Eng, Spanish & Speech; HS Libn; Am Assn Tchrs Spanish & Portuguese; NEA; OEA; ACTFL; Soc Honaria Hispanica (Chapt Sponsor); Others; cp/SD Hist Soc; DAR; GSA 28 Yrs AAUW; Detroit Soc Geneal Res; Life Mem, Magna Charta Dames; SW Okla, Mass & Conn Geneal Socs; Pilgrim Soc; Higher Ed Alumni Coun Okla; Life Mem & Past Pres, Alumni Assn USAO; Inst Gt Plains; Others; r/Epis; hon/Hypatia Hon Soc, Okla Col Lib Arts; Top Ten Students; Nat Partners of Am Cert; Alumni Hall of Fame, Univ Sci & Arts; Univ Hon Roll, Okla Col; Rec'd Statuette, Plaque & Other Awds, GSA; Adult Selectee to Our Chalet (Switzerland); Others.

MURPHY, WINIFRED LEE oc/Producer; Writer; Director; b/Aug 6, 1931; h/43 Fowler

Ct, San Rafael, CA 94903; ba/San Rafael; m/Owen J; c/Dana Catherine, Megan Elisabeth; p/John J and Ida Drady Schmale (dec); ed/AA San Francisco City Col; BA San Francisco St Univ; pa/Co-fdr, Marin Writer's Group; Columnist & Feature Writer, Marin Suburban Newspapers 1964-; Prodr & Dir, KQED-TV 1954-73; Free-lance 1973-; cp/Bd Dirs, Inner Light Foun; r/Rom Cath; hon/Rec'd Ohio St Awd for Prog Series, *Once Upon a Japanese Time* (for PBS Network); Rec'd Emmy Awd for Documentary, *Vasectomy: Male Sterilization* (for KQED & PBS).

MURRAY, JULS MAREE oc/Writer; b/Nov 13; h/3106 SE 56th St, #2, Portland, OR 97206; p/Rod and Marie Murray, K Falls, OR; ed/BA; MA; Cand PhD; pa/Writers' Conf of W; Keynote Lectr, Portland Public Schs; hon/Dalby Hon Mention for "The Art is Art".

MURRAY, PHILIP ALLEN oc/School Psychologist; b/Aug 23, 1950; h/4125 Ralph Rd, Petersburg, VA 23803; ba/Colonial Heights, VA; p/Elton L Jr and Edith C Murray, Petersburg; ed/BA Univ Va; MS Radford Univ; EdD VPI; pa/APA; VPA; NASP; VASP (Pres-Elect); cp/Bd Dirs, Kiwanis Clb; r/Bapt; hon/Phi Sigma; Phi Eta Sigma; Phi Kappa Phi.

MURRAY, ROCHELLE ANN oc/Librarian; b/Dec 14, 1936; h/407 E 30th St, Davenport, IA 52803; ba/Davenport; p/Walter Raymond and Lila Murray, Davenport; ed/BA Marycrest Col; MA Univ Wis; Chd's Libn, Davenport Public Lib;

Am Lib Assn; Iowa Lib Assn; cp/Reading Chm, Brotherhood Reading Prog for Christians & Jews; r/Luth; hon/Beta Phi Mu; Kappa Gamm Pi; Alpha Delta Kappa; Rec'd Outstg Yg People's Awd.

MURRAY, VINCENT D oc/Director; b/Mar 3, 1947; h/734 Shorter Terrace NW, Atlanta, GA 30318; ba/Atlanta; m/Renee Camille; p/Warren Taylor Murray (dec); Carloyn Faye Ward Murray, Atlanta; ed/BA Morehouse Col 1969; MA Univ Ga 1971; PhD Boston Univ 1975; pa/Dir Cnslg Ctr & Asst Prof Depts Psychol & Ed, Morehouse Col; Atlanta Univ: Instr Dept Spec Ed 1977, Part-time Instr Depts Spec Ed & Psychol Sers 1976-77; Master Tchr (Spec in Spec Ed & Behavioral Therapist), Hayden Goodwill Inn for Boys 1974-75; Mtl Hlth Worker (Boston, Mass) 1973; Other Positions; Lic'd Marriage & Fam Cnslr, St of Ga 1978; Atlanta Univ Student Pers Assn; APGA: Assn Measuremt & Evaluation in Guid, Assn Non-White Concern in Pers Guid, Am Col Pers Assn; Coun Exceptional Chd: Coun for Chd w Behavior Disorders, Div for Chd w LDs; Am Assn Higher Ed; Ga Col Pers Assn; Assn Black Psychols; Nat Org on Legal Probs in Ed; cp/NAACP; Lectr to Parents & Tchrs of Learning Disabled Yth; Attended Summer Encampment for Citizenship (San Juan, Puerto Rico); r/Epis; hon/Rec'd Ser Awd, Morehouse Col Psychol Dept; Rec'd Alpha Gamma Delta S'ship on Behalf of Nat Easter Seal Soc; Awd'd Grad Asst'ship (Boston Univ); Rec'd Commun Sers Awd, WBS Radio Station (Atlanta); Phi Delta Kappa; Pi Lambda Theta.

MUSGRAVE, RAY SIGLER oc/Psychologist; b/Feb 3, 1911; h/Rt 7, Box 193A,

Hattiesburg, MS 39401; ba/Hattiesburg; m/Anna Phair; c/Rae Ann M Lambert (Mrs C S Jr); p/P Z and Mary Maude Sigler Musgrave (dec); ed/BA Bethany Col 1933; MA Ohio Wesleyan Univ 1935; Clinical Internship, Mooseheart Lab for Child Res 1934; PhD Syracuse Univ 1937; Addit Studies; mil/AUS Comm'd Psychol & Pers Conslt 1942-46; pa/Univ So Miss: Prof & Head Dept Psychi 1956-75, Dist'd Prof Psychol 1975-78, Emeritus Dist'd Prof 1978; Tex Wom's Univ (Denton, Tex): Prof & Head Psychi Dept, Dir Student Pers Sers 1954-56; Res Assoc, Psychol Corp 1935-60; Conslt St Bd Ed, Guid & Cnslg Spec Ed 1956-74; Other Positions; Miss St Bd Psychol Examrs (2 Terms); Contbr Articles Profl Jours; Presented Papers Profl Socs; Currently Writing *Hist of Psychol*; Fellow, Am Psychol Assn; Past Pres, Miss Psychol Assn; APGA; Regional Psychol Assns; cp/Kiwanis Clb; Past Pres, Little Theatre; BSA; r/Meth; hon/Sigma Xi; Kappa Phi Kappa; Biog in Hon, *Ray S Musgrave: A Biog of a Dedicated Edr*, by M Vujnovich 1976; Rec'd Achmt & Ser Awd in Sci, Bethany Col Alumni; Outstg Contbn to Psychol Awd, Miss Psychol Assn; Biogl Directory of Am Psychol Assn; Am men Sci; W/W S&SW; Others.

MUSGROVE, ZULA HYCHE oc/Retired Postmistress; b/Jul 22, 1924; h/Drawer 9, Cordova, AL 35550; m/L Frank; c/Brenda J Tillman; p/Fred F and Bertie Tuggle Hyche, Cordova, AL; pa/Postmistress in Cordova 35 Yrs; cp/Var Commun Activs; Hist Interests in Walker Co; r/Bapt; hon/Rec'd Gold Watch at Ret'mt.

MUSIC, EDWARD C oc/Company Executive; b/May 12, 1924; h/341 S Lake Dr, Prestonsburg, KY 41653; m/Thelma Keith; c/2; p/Sam K and Nora Davis Music; ed/Attended Mayo Voc Sch; pa/Purchased & Operated C H Smith Motor Co (Prestonsburg) 1949-53; Org'd B & D Motor Co & Music-Colvin Motor Co 1956; Car Dealer for Edsel 1957, Chevrolet 1958 & Buick 1959; Pres:Archer-Music Enterprises, Music-Carter-Hughes Chevrolet-Buick Inc, Music Motor Co Inc, C & M Leasing Co Inc, Mountain Parkway Chair Lift Inc, Jesse James Enterprises Inc & Music Enterprises Inc; Chm, Prestonsburg Indust Foun; Prestonsburg Indust Coun (Chm of Bd Dirs); cp/VChm, Highland Regional Med Ctr; Prestonsburg Kiwanis Clb; Appointed by Gov Julian Carroll of Ky to Tourism Com for Ky; hon/Outstg Citizen Awd, Prestonsburg C of C; W/W Ky; Personalities of S; Book of Hon.

MYERS, DONALD MILO oc/Director; b/Oct 7, 1935; h/3313 W Sevilla Cir, Tampa, FL 33609; ba/Tampa; p/Cloyd and Elsie Baker Myers, Tampa; ed/BS; MS; mil/AUS 1/Lt; pa/Dir, AAA World Wide Travel; Nat Tour Brokers Assn; En Airlines Travel Agent Adv Bd; Pac Area Travel Assn; Suncoast Travel Indust; SKAL; African Travel Assn; Cer't Travel Cnslr; cp/Ball St Univ Alumni Assn; r/Christian Ch; hon/W/W Am Cols & Univs; Rec'd Num Airline & Other Travel Indust Awds; Blue Key Awd; Commun Ldrs & Noteworthy Ams.

MYERS, HECTOR FRANKLIN oc/Assistant Professor; b/Aug 20, 1945; h/735 N Eucalyptus #25, Inglewood, CA 90302; ba/Los Angeles, CA; m/Iris G; c/Ebony Maisha, Henry Carn III; p/Milton G Myers, Panama; Adela Gikes Myers (dec); ed/BA 1969; MA 1971; PhD 1974; pa/Asst Prof Psychol, UCLA; Dir Res, Faxon Res & Devel Ctr; Mtl Hlth Conslt; Psychotherapist; Reschr; cp/Lectr to Commun Groups; hon/Rec'd Achmt Awd; BA cum laude; Phi Theta Kappa; W/W Am Cols.

MYERS, JOANNE oc/Magazine Publisher; b/Jul 7, 1941; h/2900 NE 24th Ct, Ft Lauderdale, FL 33305; ba/Ft Lauderdale; c/-Deborah Lynne; p/Charles and Clara Kissel; ed/BA NYU 1963; pa/Pubr & Fdr, *Broward Life Mag*; VP, Ft Lauderdale Advtg Fdn; So Fla S&L Mktg Soc; r/Jewish; hon/Wom of Yr 1978, Wom in Communs; Outstg Yg Wom Am; W/W.

MYERS, JOHN PHILIP oc/Social Work Educator; b/Sept 10, 1936; h/56-52 195th St, Flushing, NY 11365; ba/New York, NY; m/Barbara Yohe; c/Keith Alan, Mark Leslie; p/Leroy H and Pauline S Myers, York, PA; ed/BM Univ Miami (Fla); MSW Univ Pittsburgh; pa/Acad Cert'd Social Workers; Nat Assn Social Workers; Nat Conf on Social Wel; Am Orthopsychi Assn; Others; cp/Bd Mem, NY Hlth Sys Agy E; r/Friend Unitarian-Universalist Ch; hon/Outstg Edr of Am; Dean's Outstg Ser Awd, Univ Ky; Ula Faust Ser Awd, Dist 15 Ky Wel Assn; Sparkplug Awd, JCs; Ky Col; Others.

MYERS, MARY PELL oc/Poet; b/Jul 8, 1920; h/University Ave, Morgantown, WV 26505; ba/Same; m/Raymond A; c/Raymond A II; p/Frank and Grace Field Pell (dec); ed/Attended Morgantown Bus Col; Agent's Lic, Ins Agy Sch (Keyser, W VA); pa/Secy-Treas, Morgantown Chpt W VA Poetry Soc; Author: *Poetic Bits & Pieces* (Poems, Short Stories & Epigrams 1972), *My Sentiments* (Poems & Epigrams 1976); r/Christian & Missionary Alliance Ch: Mem, Wom's Missionary Prayer F'ship; hon/1st Pl Awd for Poem, "Winter Woods", & 2nd Pl Awd, Lula M Cady Meml Contest; 1st Hon Mention, Oscar DuBois Contest.

MYERS, ROCHELLE GRUSKIN oc/Educator; b/Jun 9, 1926; h/3827 California St, San Francisco, CA 94118; ba/Same; p/Morris and Julia Taus Gruskin (dec); ed/BA 1963, MA, MS 1967, Gen Sec'dy Credential 1963, Spec Ed Credential 1969 SF St Col; Addit Studies; pa/Fdr-Dir, Creativity Unlimited Enterprises 1977-; Fdr-Dir, Getting Clear & Getting Clear Tng Inst 1976-; Fdr-Dir, Art & Growth Studio 1971-; SF St Univ: Lectr Dept Rec & Leisure Studies (Part-time) 1973-77, Asst Prof Dept Spec Ed (Part-time) 1968-73; Dir Vol Sers, Chd's Hosp (SF) 1973-75; Other Positions; Panelist Parental Neurol, Univ Cal-SF Med Ctr; Annual Meeting, Am Assn Mtl Deficiency; Bd Dirs, Rec Ctr for Handicapped Inc; Coun for Exceptional Chd; Cal Assn Neurol Handicapped Chd; Day Care Com; Speakers Bur, SF St Univ; SF Coor'g Coun on Mtl Retardation; Com on Childhood Mtl Hlth, SF Assn Mtl Hlth; Chm Prog Adv Coun, Rec Ctr for Handicapped Inc; Assn Humanistic Psychol, Inst Humanistic Med; Others; Lectr; Conducts Workshops; Pub'd Articles Profl Jours; cp/Vol Sers: SF St Univ Student Hlth Sers, Group Ldr for Foreign Born Adults (Intl Inst), Tchr Frederick Burk Sch (SF), Mt Zion Hosp, Jewish Commun Ctr (New Haven, Conn), Edgewood Home, Others; r/Jewish; hon/Rec'd S'ships to Kenyon Col (Gambier, Ohio) & NY Col of Mus; Dean's List, SF St Col; Rec'd Joseph P Kennedy Jr Foun S'ship; Rec'd Awd, SF-2nd Dist, Cal Cong Parents & Tchrs.

MYERS, SAMUEL LLOYD SR oc/Executive Director; b/Apr 18, 1919; h/3608 Baskerville Dr, Mitchellville, MD 20716; ba/Washington, DC; m/Marion R; c/Yvette M May, Samuel L Jr, Tama M Clark; p/David Elkanah and Edith Reid Myers (dec); ed/BA Morgan St Col 1940; MA Boston Univ 1942; MA 1948, PhD 1949 Harvard Univ; Post Grad Studies: Univ Penn, Foreign Ser Inst; mil/AUS 1942-46; pa/Nat Assn for Equal Opportunity in Higher Ed: Exec Dir 1977-, VP Bd Dirs 1975-77; Pres, Bowie St Col 1967-77; Comm on Higher Ed, Middle Sts Assn Cols & Schs 1976-; Nat Ed Adv Com, Consumers Union 1976-; Advr Regional Integration & Trade, Bur of Inter-Am Affairs (US Dept of St) 1963-67; Assoc Prof, Prof & Chm Div Social Scis, Morgan St Col 1950-63; Bd Dirs, Am Assn St Cols & Univs 1976-77; Gov's Task Force on Desegregation of Higher Ed 1974; Past Pres, Md Assn Higher Ed; Num Others; Author Series of Booklets Distributed by Baltimore Urban Leag 1964 (Later Used as Basis for Anti-poverty Prog, Baltimore); Del Col & Univ Pres to: India 1971, People's Republic of China 1975, Pakistan 1973, Nigeria 1973, Others; cp/Former Mem, Gov's Comm on Prevailing Wage Law in Md; Helped Organize Morgan St Col Grad Sch; Former Mem, St S'ship Bd of Md; Others; r/Meth;

hon/Cited by Baltimore Urban Leag for Booklet Series; BA w Highest Hons, Morgan St Univ; Hon LLD, Morgan St Col; Outstg Citizen of Yr, Bowie (Md); Alumnus of Yr, Morgan St Univ; Grad Asst, Boston Univ; Res Fellow & Rosenwald Fellow, Harvard Univ; Alpha Kappa Mu; Rec'd Pacific Theatre Ribbon, AUS.

MYHRE, TRYGVE CHATHAM oc/Product Engineer; b/May 1, 1937; h/100 Greenbriar Ln, Oak Ridge, TN 37830; ba/Oak Ridge; m/Elizabeth Halsted; c/Elise, Glen Scott, Kari; p/Roy Ernest Myhre (dec); Dorothea Constance Chatham Tanney (dec); ed/BME; MME; pa/Product Engr, Y-12 Plant; Am Soc Metals; Nat Soc Profl Engrs; Tenn Soc Profl Engrs; cp/Proj Concern, Walk-for-Mankind; r/Prot; hon/W/W S&SW.

MYRICK, FRED LEE JR oc/Executive Director; b/Sept 24, 1946; h/4282 Roswell Rd, Apt E-2, Atlanta, GA 30342; ba/Atlanta; p/Fred L Myrick Sr (dec); Molly Hatfield, Weatherford, TX; ed/BBA 1969, MBA 1970, PhD 1972 Univ Tex; pa/Exec Dir, Mktg Info Ser; Am Mktg Assn; Am Psychol Assn; So Mktg Assn; cp/Bd Dirs, Am Trauma Soc; r/Universal; hon/Beta Gamma Sigma; Sigma Iota Epsilon; Omicron Delta Epsilon.

N

NADON, JOHN DOUGLAS oc/Scenery, Costume & Lighting Designer; b/Apr 2, 1952; h/3157 Warner Blvd #2, Burbank, CA 91506; ba/New York, NY; c/Joseph Donald Nadon, Galveston, TX; Nancy Ann Ward (dec); ed/Cert'd Theatre Design Allan Hancock Col; pa/Free-lance Designer "Xenon" Discotheque 1978; Theatrical Conslt (Design) & Sales Mgr Litelab Corp-W 1977; Prof Design & Guest Artist in Residence Grand Val St Cols, Perf'g Arts Ctr, Allendale, Mich 1976-77; Guest Designer Opera Assn Wn Mich & U Stage, Grand Rapids, Mich 1976-77; Resident Designer Santa Rosa Jr Col 1973-76; Designed 100+ Profl, Col Resident & Commun Theatre Prodns incl'g: Ballet, Opera, Mod Dance, Drama, Musical Comedy; hon/Hons Entrance, Cal St Col-Stanislaus; W/W MW; Notable Ams; DIB.

NAGY, BARTHOLOMEW STEPHEN oc/Professor; Scientist; b/May 11, 1927; h/245 Greenock Dr, Tucson, AZ 85704; ba/Lois Anne Brach; c/Erika Anne, Yvonne Maria; p/Stephen Nagy (dec); Mary Mueller Nagy, Budapest, Hungary; ed/BS Peter Pazmany Univ (Budapest) 1948; MA Columbia Univ 1953; PhD Pa St Univ 1953; pa/Univ Ariz: Prof Geoscis, Chief Scist Lab of Organic Geochem; Univ Cal-San Diego: Assoc Res Geochemist 1965-68, Vis Assoc Prof 1963-65; Assoc Prof Fordham Univ 1957-65; Hd Geophy Res Cities Ser Oil Co 1955-57; Other Former Positions; Mem Adv Bd Lunar Sci Inst, Houston, Tex 1972; Chm Geol Scis Div NY Acad Scis 1960-62; Councilor Geochem Soc 1960-63; r/Rom Cath; hon/1 of 4 Mng Editor Jour Precambrian Res 1972; Prin Investigator Apollo Missions 11.

NAGY, GABOR oc/Film Producer; Director; Writer; b/Aug 21, 1936; h/2007 N Hobart Blvd, Los Angeles, CA 90027; ba/LA; m/Erika M; c/Anthony M; p/Gabor Nagy; Ilona Nagy, Romania; ed/BS Univ So Cal; pa/Dirs Guild Am W Inc; r/Presb; hon/Oscar Nom; 20+ Nat & Intl Film Awds.

NAKAMA, CHRISTIAN S oc/Health Executive; Gerontologist; b/Nov 19, 1922; h/2056 Okika Pl, Honolulu, HI 96822; ba/Honolulu; m/Yoshinae Naeko Majikina; c/Eleanor Riko, Clifford Sei; p/Saburo and Tsuru Murayama Nakama (dec); ed/BA Univ Hi 1949; MA Loyola Univ Chgo 1951; MS Harvard Univ 1952; Postgrad Studies; mil/AUS 1941-45, 442nd Inf Regimental Combat Team; Instr US Army Censorship Sch; pa/Exec Bd Kalihi-Palama Walk in Hlth Clin; Nat Assn Social Wkrs, Hi Chapt; AFL-CIO AFSME Local 152, Hi Chapt; NARFE, Hi

Chapt 311; Harvard Clb Hi; Univ Hi Alumni Assn; Hi Public Hlth Assn; Fellow Am Sch Hlth Assn; cp/Gov's Adv Coun on Hosps & Med Facilities; Mayor's Coun on Urban Renewal Adv Com; Adv Bd Sr Citizen's Ctr; Dep Chm Mayor's Meml Day Ser Prog Com; Exec Dir Vet's Assn Hi, Oahu Hlth Coun Inc, Hi Cancer Soc Inc, Honolulu Comm on Aging; Shelter Mgr Ofc Civil Def; Mil Intell Ser Vets of PTO; Secy, Past Pres; Nat Task Force on Social & Public Wel Needs of Asian-Ams; r/Rom Cath; Mem Sacred Heart Maryknoll Parish, Honolulu; hon/Dist'd Cit, Japan Ret'd Civil Ser Assn; Outstg Employee of Yr, City &

Co of Honolulu; Grad F'ships; Ctl Hall of Fame, Honolulu; W/W in Hi; Others.

NAKARAI, TOYOZO W oc/Professor; b/May 16, 1898; h/Rt 4, Box 240, Elizabethton, TN 37643; m/Frances A; c/Charles F T, Frederick Leroy; p/Tosui and Wakae Nakarai (dec); ed/AB Kokugakuin Univ 1920; AB 1924, AM 1925 Butler Univ; PhD Univ Mich 1930; Postdoct Studies; pa/Hon'd Prof Emmanuel Sch of Rel, Milligan

Col; Past Pres: MW Br Soc Biblical Lit, Nat Assn Profs of Hebrew; Author Books & Articles; Edit Activs; Others; r/Christian; hon/Phi Kappa Phi; Theta Phi; Eta Beta Rho; Holcomb Prize; Baxter Foun Awd; B'rith Abraham Medal & Scroll; Histadrut Ivrit Cit; Cit S'ship & Merit, Nat Assn Profs Hebrew; Hon'd Min Christian Ch; Others.

NASH, EDWARD MERL oc/Executive; b/Aug 28, 1927; h/2711 Floral Trail, Long Beach, Michigan City, IN 46360; ba/Grant Park, IL; m/Shirley A; c/Dennis M, Barry A, Kathleen M, Cynthia A; p/Aubrey J and Lena M Phillips Nash; mil/AUS 1945-47; pa/VP The Triangle Corp; Pres Container Div; Am Inst Indust Engrs; Indust Mgmt Assn.

NATH, SUNIL B oc/Public Administrator; Researcher; Planner; b/Mar 31, 1937; h/432 Victory Garden Dr, Tallahassee, FL 32301; ba/Tallahassee; m/Abha R; c/Subrata, Sunita, Lipika; p/Sarat Chandra and Sarada Devi Nath; ed/BA Inst Rural Higher Ed (Sriniketan, W Bengal) 1960; MA Agra Univ 1964; PhD Cand Fla St Univ; pa/St of Fla Dept Offender Rehab, Tallahassee: Planner & Evaluator/Reschr 1976-, Dir Planning & Eval 1974-76, Dir Res & Statistics 1973-74; Prof Dir & Adm Asst Fla Parole & Probation Intensive Projs, St of Fla 1971-73; Other Former Positions; Am Judic Soc; Am, Fla & So Sts Correctional Assns; Am & So Sociol Assns; Am Acad Polit & Social Scis; IPA; Nat & Fla Couns on Crime & Delinq; Assn for Correctional Res & Statistics; Intl Howard Leag for Penal Reform (England); Am Soc for Public Adm; Participant & Contbr to Sev Nat & Intl Profl Confs; CoDir Fla Conf on Eval Res; Others; cp/Dem; Cub Scouts; Former Mem Planning Group Gov's Adult Corrections Reform Plan; Intl Clb; r/Hindu; hon/Contbr Articles to Profl Jours; W/W S&SW; Notable Ams; Book of Honor; DIB.

NAVIA, JUAN oc/Senior Scientist; b/Jan 16, 1927; h/629 Lexington Rd, Birmingham, AL 35216; ba/B'ham; m/Josefina B; c/Betty, Anna, Juan, Carlos; p/Juan and Hortensia Navia, Miami, FL; ed/BS; MS; PhD; pa/Univ Ala-B: Sr Scist Inst Dental Res, Prof Dentistry, Comparative Med, Biochem & Nutrition Scis, Dir Nutrition & Food Scis Div, Dir Res Tng (Sch Dentistry); Var Former Acad Positions; Conslt; AAAS; Am Chem Soc; Am Inst Nutrition; Am Inst Chemists; Am Soc for Microbiol; Inst Food Technologists; Intl Assn for Dental Res; NY Acad Scis; Charter Mem Soc for Envir Geochem & Hlth; Soc for Experimtl Biol & Med; Var Res Activs; hon/Hon Mem, Omicron Kappa Upsilon; Phi Lambda Upsilon; Sigma Xi; Fellow, Royal Soc Hlth; San Esteban Conde de Canongo Awd; Acad Scis, Habana, Cuba; Biogl Listings; Num Profl Pubs.

NAVRATIL, ROBERT NORMAN oc/Attorney; b/Dec 27, 1928; h/2038 Eckles Dr, Maryville, TN 37801; ba/M'ville;

m/Nancy Jane Naylor; b/Rebecca Carol N Walker, Joseph Naylor, Angela Jane; p/John R Navratil, Van Nuys, CA; Ida W Navratil (dec); ed/AB cum laude M'ville Col 1954; JD Univ Chgo 1957; mil/USAF 1947-50; pa/Mem Ho of Dels, Tenn Bar Assn; cp/Coun-man, City of M'ville; r/Presb: Elder; hon/S'ship, Univ Chgo Law Sch.

NAYLOR, GEORGE LEROY oc/Lawyer; b/May 11, 1915; h/Rt 7, Box 437-G, Pensacola, FL 32506; ba/Barrington, IL; m/Maxine Lewis; c/Georgia Price (Mrs Ralph E), Rose Hammer (Mrs Glenn B), George LeRoy II; p/Joseph F and Josephine Wood Naylor; ed/JD Univ San Francisco 1953; mil/AUS WWII; pa/Pvt Law Pract; VP &

Secy IUMMSW, CIO, Dist 2; Examr, Asst Mgr So Pacific Co; cp/Carrier Mem & Chm Nat Railroad Adjustmt Bd, Village Atty Fox River Val Gardens; r/LDS; hon/Author: Underground At Bingham Canyon, Choice Morsels in Tax and Property Law, Defending Carriers Before the NRAB, NRAB Pract Manual.

NAYLOR, PLEAS COLEMAN oc/Realtor; b/Nov 22, 1914; h/327 Clubhill Dr, San Antonio, TX 78228; ba/San Antonio; m/Ellen W; c/Ruth Schraedley, Ellen Ferne Mooney, Patty Martin, Chester A Slimp III; p/Pleas Coleman and Beulah Pettus Naylor (dec); ed/Att'd Univ Tex; mil/AUS WWII; pa/Pres & Chief Adm Ofcr Naylor Realty Inc; Trustee SW Res Inst; Soc Indust Realtors; Accredited Farm & Land Broker Farm & Land Inst; Cert'd Property Mgr Inst Real Est Mgmt; Intl Real Est Fdn; Nat Assn Realtors; Tex Assn Realtors; SA Bd Realtors; Mem & Chm Tex Real Est Comm; cp/1978 Jerry Lewis Labor Day MD Assn, SW Tex Telethon Com; Ec Devel Coun Steering Com; SA C of C Urban Affairs Coun Steering Com; Gov's Coun Advrs; Masonic Orders; Others; hon/Hon LLD, Univ Tex-SA; Realtor of Yr: Tex Assn Realtors, SA Bd Realtors; Biogl Listings.

NEAL, TIMMIE ANN oc/Assistant Registrar; b/Apr 18, 1942; h/601 4th St, Hempstead, TX 77445; ba/Prairie View A&M, Houston, TX; ed/BS Prairie View A&M Univ 1979; hon/Alpha Kappa Mu; Pi Omega Pi; Alpha Mu Gamma.

NEEPER, RALPH ARNOLD oc/Computer Programmer; b/Sep 29, 1940; h/13530 Delaney Rd, Woodbridge, VA 22193; ba/Ft Belvoir, VA; m/Nancy Diane; c/Rachel Claudine, Jennifer Alice; p/Guy Enoch and Alice Elizabeth Arnold Neeper, Toledo, OH; ed/BS 1963, MS Purdue Univ 1972; mil/LEDC 1976, USAC & GS 1978; pa/Software Spec, Defense Mapping Sch; Assn for Computing Machinery; AAAS; Washington Area Operations Res Coun; Am Defense Preparedness Assn; Mensa; cp/Gideon's Intl: Meml Bible Rep, Public Relats E Camp, Zone Ldr; r/Epiphany Luth Ch: Lorton Liturgy Com, Outreach Com; h/Pi Mu Epsilon; LTFTT; Suggestion Awds; W/W: Computers & Data Processing, MW; Commun Ldrs & Noteworthy Ams.

NEFF, CLARENCE E oc/Bank Executive; State Legislator; Farmer; Businessman; b/Aug 3, 1909; h/Box 368, Stronghurst, IL 61480; ba/Same; m/Elaine Droste; c/Janice N Hamilton, Charles Edward; p/Jesse James and Elizabeth Feirira Neff (dec); ed/EE; CE; pa/Pres Bk of Stronhurst; cp/Chm Henderson

Co Repub Ctl Com; Elks; Masons; Shrine; Warren Co YMCA; r/Bethel Luth Ch, S'hurst; hon/Dist'd Ser Awd, Tri-St Univ, Angola, Ind.

NEFF, ROBERT LEE SR oc/Assistant Principal; b/Jun 1, 1931; h/5201 Yorktown Rd, Knoxville, TN 37920; ba/K'ville; m/Elizabeth E; c/Robert Lee, Jayne Elizabeth, Patti Ann; p/Herbert Preston Neff Sr (dec); Wanda Roth Neff, K'ville; ed/BS 1954, MS 1958, Addit Studies Univ Tenn; mil/AUS 1954-56; pa/Asst Prin South-Young High 1969-; Teacher & Coach (Ftball, Basketball, Track, Cross Country) 1956-69; Mem St Track Com TSSAA 1965-78; KEA; ETEA; TEA; NASSP; TSSPA; cp/CoFdr K'ville Track Clb 1961; r/Meridan Bapt Ch: SS Tchr 1957-77; hon/Outstg Ser Awd, KTC; Tchr of Yr, City Sch Sys 1965.

NEIBURG, GLADYS EUDAS oc/Homemaker; b/Jul 29, 1898; h/41 Federal St, St Albans, VT 05478; p/Louis M and Lena Press Neiburg (dec); ed/BA Univ Vermont 1949; r/Jewish.

NEIDERT, KALO EDWARD oc/University Professor; b/Sept 1, 1918; h/2300 Balsam St, Reno, NV 89509; ba/Reno; m/Stella Vest; c/Edward, Karl, David, Wayne, Margaret; p/Edward R Neidert, St James, MO; Margaret Kinsey Neidert (dec); ed/BSBA w hons, MSBA Wash Univ; Postgrad Studies Univ Minn; pa/Prof Col Bus Adm Univ Nev 1962-; Asst Prof; Gustavus Adolphus Col, Univ Tex, Univ Miss; Instr Univ Minn; r/Presb; hon/Beta Gamma Sigma; Beta Alpha Psi; BSA: Scouter's Key, Dist Awd of Merit.

NEIGHBORS, JOYCE LaRUE oc/Secretary; b/Aug 11, 1927; h/901 Noccalula Dr, Gadsden, AL 35901; ba/Gadsden; p/Aubrey A and Inez Whitley Neighbors, Lineville, AL; ed/Bus Mgmt Intl Corr Schs 1960; Anniston Bus Col 1956; pa/Secy Life Ins Co Ala; Secy to Edward M Almond (Lt Gen, USA, Ret'd) 1955-77; Secy W M Longshore (Gen Agt, Life of Ala) 1957-77; Exec Secy Anniston-Calhoun Co Assn Life Underwriters 1972-77; Nat Secys Assn (Intl): Anniston Chapt 1959-74, Chapt Ofcs & Secy Ala Div 1963-65; cp/Gen John H Forney Hist Soc: Secy, Bd Mem; Eagle Forum; STOP ERA; Calhoun Co Unit Am Cancer Soc: Former Bd Mem, Past Pres; Pilot Clb Anniston; Former Secy Ala Dist Pilot Intl; Anniston Bicent Comm; Chm Christmas Seal Campaign; Dir E Ala Dist, Ala TB & Respiratory Dis Assn; r/Bellevue Bapt Ch, Gadsden: Mem; hon/DAR Good Citizenship Awd; Pilot of Yr 1963; Dist'd Ser Awd, Gen John H Forney Hist Soc 1970.

NEIL, JESSIE M oc/Financial Executive; b/Oct 20, 1927; h/310 Hermosa St, S Pasadena, CA 91030; m/Edmund R; c/Edmund R II, Jessica R, Neil, R William; p/(dec); ed/BS Univ So Cal; pa/Chief Fin Ofcr, So Counties Escrow 1958-; Pres, Futuramic Homes Inc 1956-68; Treas, Reliance Bldg Corp 1951-68; Pres, Barrett Devel Corp Inc 1951-70; Sales Dir, Washington Sq Bldg Corp 1950-52; Dir of Design, Leland Gardens Bldg Corp 1950-56; Assoc Mem, Am Inst Mgmt; cp/Past Fdr, VP & Pres, Cardiac League, Guild of Huntington Meml Hosp; Past VP & Recording Secy, San Marino League; Past Pres & VP, Docent Coun Pasadena Mus of Modern Art; Opera Assocs of Metro Opera; Fdrs of Los Angeles Music Ctr; World Affairs Coun; IPA; Life Mem, Arcadia Meth Hosp

Aux; Others; hon/Pasadena Arts Coun Graphics Awd; 1 of 10 Best Dressed Wom in So Cal; Eve Awd; W/W: Am Wom, W, Cal; World W/W Wom; Others.

NELLER, ARTHUR AUGUSTUS JR oc/Textile Executive; b/Feb 28, 1937; h/PO Box 13111, 610 Myers Ln, Greensboro, NC 27408; ba/G'boro; m/Barbara Eichham; c/Mary Victoria, Anne Markel; p/Arthur A

Neller (dec); Phrieda P Neller, G'boro; ed/BS UNC-CH; mil/USNR 1959-64, Ensign; pa/Mem The Thread Inst; cp/Dem; r/Epis; hon/W/W S&SW.

NELSON, CHARLES LAMAR oc/Guidance Counselor; Author; b/Jun 9, 1917; h/PO Box 57, Caledonia, MS 39740; ba/Caledonia; m/Lena Reaves; c/Timothy Lamar; p/Charles Robert Nelson (dec); Willie Aline Welch Nelson, Caledonia; ed/BA 1946, MA 1947 Univ Miss; S'ship in Earth Sci Shorter Col 1967; S'ship Cnsl'g & Guid Auburn Univ 1957; mil/USN WWII, Pharmacist Mate 2nd Class, S Pacific; pa/Guid Cnslr Caledonia HS; Top Area Mgr (Miss) World Book & Childcraft Encyclopedias, Chicago, Ill 1959; NEA; Miss Assn Edrs; Lowndes Co Assn Edrs; PTO; Miss Pers & Guid Assn; Treas Miss Poetry Soc 1964-65; CoFdr Natchez Poetry Soc (Natchez,

Miss; cp/Former Prog Chm Natchez Exc Clb (Natchez, Miss); Former Registrar Selective Ser Comm, Lowndes Co (Miss); Former Local Chm Voc Rehab Div Lowndes Co; r/Ch of Christ; hon/Chm Annual Conv IPA, Wash DC 1973; Pub'd Author; Contbr Poems to: Nat Poetry Anthology, Mid-Century Prose & Verse, Miss Poetry Anthology, Others; Num Articles in Newspapers & Mags; Author 4 Books: Our Neighbor, William Faulkner 1977, A Chain That Breaks A Man 1975, William Faulkner: The Anchorite of Rowan Oak 1973, The Marble Urn 1941; DIB; W/W S&SW; Personalities of S; Bibliog Miss Authors (Univ Miss).

NELSON, JEAN ANN oc/Anesthesia; b/Jul 15, 1921; h/61 Sycamore St, Macungie, PA 18062; ba/Allentown, PA; m/Milton F; c/Pamela Basmadjian, Wendy Lampe, James F; p/George J Young (dec); Edna Kislingbury (dec); ed/RN; CRNA; Att'g Cedar Crest Col; pa/AANA, Trustee; cp/Past Pres: Lehigh Co Fdn Wom's Clbs, Wom's Clb Macungie; World Hunger Com; GSA: Troop Orgr, Former Ldr; Allentown Music; Altrusa Intl; St Hosp Coun for Chd; Coun-wom (2 Terms); Upper Milford Coun Repub Wom: Mem, Leg Chair; Jt Planning Com Lehigh-N Hampton Cos; Mid-Cos Repub Coun; r/Luth: SS Tchr, Ch Choir, Past Pres Luth Ch Wom (Macungie Chapt); hon/2 Certs of Profl Excell.

NELSON, RALPH ERWIN oc/Professional Land Planner; Community Planning Consultant; b/Jul 30, 1946; h/4611 30th St W, Bradenton, FL; ba/Bradenton; m/Elarie; c/Anne; p/Vernon and Astrid Nelson, Wheaton, IL; ed/BS McPherson Col; Masters Cand Univ S Fla; pa/Profl Land Planner R E Nelson Inc; Assoc Mem Am Inst Planners; Am Soc Planning Ofcls; cp/Repub; r/So Bapt; hon/W/W S&SW.

NESBIT, PHYLLIS SCHNEIDER oc/District Judge; b/Sept 21, 1919; h/PO Box 447, Daphne, AL 36526; ba/Bay Minette, AL; m/Peter Nicholas; p/Vernon Lee and Irma Mae Biddle Schneider (dec); ed/BS; LLB; JD; pa/Dist Judge Baldwin Co (Ala); Ala Wom

Lwyrs Assn; Nat Assn Wom Lwyrs; Judic Soc; Coun Juv Judges; Ala Assn Dist Judges; Nat Coun Juv Judges; BPW Clb; cp/Jt Leg Coun Ala; Baldwin Co Mtl Hlth Assn; r/Indep Meth; hon/Wom of Achmt, Dist I BPW Clb.

NeSMITH, VERA C oc/Retired Executive Secretary; b/Oct 24, 1917; h/1912 Weber St, Orlando, FL 32803; m/J Vernon (dec); c/Patricia E, John S, James E; p/Ernest H and Edith E Cox (dec); ed/Dipl Orlando Secyl Sch; Cert Orlando Jr Col; pa/Secy, Dept of Hlth & Rehab Sers, Voc Rehab Prog 1938-80; Am Assn Med Assts: Prog Chm Nat Conv 1962-63, Secy-Treas 1966-67, Charter Mem & Pres (Orange Co Chapt) 1959-61, Chm By-Laws Com (Fla St Soc), Parliamentn (Orange Co Chapt); Fla Assn Rehab Secys: Rec'g Secy, Parliamentn, Chaplain; SE Regional Assn Rehab Secys: Bd Mem, Pres, Charter Mem, Parliamentn, Installing Ofcr; Instr through Univ of Tenn (Handbook Com); Intl Biogl Assn; r/Broadway U Meth Ch; hon/Fla Rehab Assn Cit; Outstg Mem of Yr, Orange Co AAMA 1965; Med Asst of Yr, Fla St Soc AAMA 1965; Others.

NESTI, RICHARD PIERRE oc/Orthopedic Surgeon; b/Jan 23, 1933; h/1815 Shelburne Rd, S Burlington, VT 05401; ba/B'ton; m/Frances; c/Edmund, Leon; p/Pierre Leon Nesti (dec); Belle Nesti; ed/AB Columbia 1954; MD 1961; mil/AUS, Atomic Test Site Mercury, Nev; pa/Chief Orthopedic Surg Fanny Allen Hosp; cp/Lectr; r/Cath; hon/Am's 1st Oceanographic Surg Scist.

NEUENSCHWANDER, JOYCE EVONNE oc/Teacher; b/Jan 7, 1932; h/1619 Cedar Pl, Olathe, KS 66061; ba/Kansas City, KS; m/Dwight Edward; c/Dwight Edward Jr, Nancy Lynette Chandanais; p/Evert and Edna Striegel (dec); ed/BMus; MMusEd; pa/Tchr; Supvr; Admr; r/Prot; hon/W/W: Wom Edrs, Am Wom; Notable Ams.

NEUSNER, JACOB oc/University Professor; b/Jul 28, 1932; h/70 Vassar Ave, Providence, RI 02906; ba/Providence; m/Suzanne Richter; c/Samuel, Eli, Noam, Margalit; ed/AB magna cum laude Harvard Col 1954; MHL Jewish Theol Sem Am 1960; PhD Columbia Univ 1960; Addit Studies; pa/Dept Rel Studies Brown Univ: Prof Rel Studies, Ungerleider Dist'd Scholar of Judaic Studies 1975-, Prof Rel Studies 1968-75; Dartmouth Col: Assoc Prof Rel 1966-68, Asst Prof 1964-66; Other Former Positions; Chm Sect on Hist of Judaism Am Acad Rel 1979-81; Mem Nat Coun on Humanities 1978-; Bd Advrs Ancient Biblical Manuscript Ctr Lib,

Sch of Theol (Claremont) 1978-; Contb'g Editor *Moment* 1977-; Bd Conslts *Rel Traditions* 1977-; Other Edit Activs; Pres The Max Richter Foun 1969-; Fellow Am Acad for Jewish Res 1972-; Num Vis Prof'ships, Lectures; Life Mem Am Oriental Soc; Fellow Royal Asiatic Soc (London); Soc Biblical Lit; Am Hist Assn; Assn for Jewish Studies; Elected Mem Am Soc for Study of Rel; Phi Beta Kappa; hon/Num Pubs; AM Ad Eundem, Brown Univ; Univ Medal for Excell, Columbia Univ; LHD, Univ Chgo; Recipient S'ships & F'ships.

NEVEL, EVA MARY oc/Teacher; b/Aug 13, 1924; h/Box 1, Pa Ave RD2, Binghamton, NY 13903; ba/B'ton; p/Ralph E Nevel (dec); Eva Myrtle Hinchman, B'ton; ed/BE cum laude Cortland St Tchrs Col 1945; BME 1951, MM 1960 Syracuse Univ; Addit Studies; pa/Tchr Vocal Music Jr HS & Elem Sch, City Sch Dist, B'ton 1945-; Tchr Grades 4, 6; NEA; MENC; NYEA; B'ton Tchrs Assn: Pres, Var Other Ofcs; Pres Intl ACE 1956; Del to NYS Tchr Retiremt Sys 1965-66; cp/Choral Soc; r/Park Ave Bapt Ch: Ch Clerk, Trustee, Bible Sch Tchr, Choir Mem, Var Other Activs; Min of Music W Windsor Bapt Ch 1962-73; hon/Delta Kappa Gamma, Beta Iota Chapt; Kappa Delta Pi, Cortland Chapt; Intl W/W: Intells, Music, Commun Ser; Intl Reg Profiles; Notable Ams; Commun Ldrs & Noteworthy Ams; IPA; DIB.

NEVILLE, GENEVIEVE JEWEL oc/Tennis Clerk; b/Oct 21, 1915; h/51 Rowan Rd, White Sulphur Springs, WV 24986; m/George Edward; p/Joseph Leonard Dean Sr (dec); Bessie Ann Alderman (dec); ed/Ext Courses Concord Col; pa/Tennis Clerk Greenbrier Hotel; cp/Greenbriar Co Dem Exec Com; Past Pres Greenmitt Garden Clb; 2/VP White Sulphur Wom's Clb; Trustee Greenbriar Co Yth Camp; Dir Ron-Sul-Lew Chapt Izaak Walton Leag; r/Meth; hon/Flower Show Awds incl: 3 Sweepstake Awds, 3 Tri-Colo Awds, Awd of Distn (All at WVa St Fair), 1st Pl Flower Arranging, WVa Wom's St Conv.

NEVILLE, LAURINE oc/Sister of Religious Order; Educator; b/Aug 11, 1901; h/Maria Hall, Adrian, MI 49221; p/William J and Robinetta Allan Neville (dec); ed/BA; MA; PhD; LittD; pa/Tchr, Admr; cp/Var

Social Work w Spanish-Spkg People; r/Cath: Mem Dominican Order of Rel Wom; hon/Cit & Medal for Cult, Ec Uplift of Spanish Spkg People in Area, Archdiocese Detroit.

NEVILLE, ROBERT CUMMINGS oc/Philosopher, Theologian; b/May 1, 1939; h/49 Harbor Cir, Centerport, NY 11721; ba/Stony Brook, NY; m/Elizabeth E; c/Gwendolyn (dec), Naomi, Leonora; p/Richard P Neville (dec); Rose C Neville, Mt View, CA; ed/BA; MA; PhD; pa/Chm Prog in Rel Studies SUNY-SB; Author; APA; MSA; SSPP; NHTDG; r/U Meth: Min; hon/Chancellor's Awd for Excell in Tchg.

NEWBERN, CAPTOLA D oc/Educator; b/Sept 22, 1902; ba/United Theol Sem, 1810 Harvard Blvd, Dayton, OH 45406; m/Samuel H (dec); p/John W and Arnetta E Dent; ed/Tchr Tng Cert 1923, BS cum laude 1925 Paine Col; BMus Talladega Col 1937; MSSW 1942, EdD 1954 Columbia Univ; Addit Studies; pa/(Former) Lincoln Meml Univ: Prof Social Work, Dir Undergrad Social Work Ed; (Former) Lane Col: Chperson, Prof Rel & Phil,

Orgr/Dir Vesper Choir, Instr/Cnslr/Coor Undergrad Social Wel Ed Prog; (Former) Lambuth Col: CoDir w Chperson Dept Sociol & Fam Devel; (Former) Paine Col: Hd Music Dept, HS Dept Instr; (Former) Talladega Col: Dir Col-Commun Ext Prog; (Former) Howard Univ, Instr Commun Org; (Former) Albany St Col, Asst Prof Eng; Past Pres Harrogate (Tenn) Br AAUW; Pi Lambda Theta; Columbia Univ Acad Sci; Rel Ed Assn; Nat Adv Bd Am Security Coun; IPA; cp/Life Mem NAACP; Former Chaplain Lincoln Meml Univ Lincoln Dames; r/Christian Meth Epis Ch & AME Ch: Active; Nat Coun Chs Comm on Faith & Order; hon/Num Cits, Trophies, Scrolls, Plaques & Certs in Apprec & Recog of Sers Rendered to Prof, Commun & Chs; Cit, US War Dept for Outstg Ser as 1st Negro Wom Appt'd Employee Cnslr at Pentagon; Testimonial Dinner in her hon following her sers as Exec Dir of Plainfield (NJ) YWCA; Columbia Univ Tchrs Col Highlight Hon; Book of Honor; DIB; W/W Am Ed; 2000 Wom Achmt.

NEWBY, CHARLES DAVID oc/Executive; b/Dec 15, 1953; h/1517 Byrd Dr, Fort Worth, TX 76114; ba/Ft Worth; p/Milas Edward and Ruth Laverne Newby, Ft Worth; ed/BBA; pa/Exec VP Greenfield Sales Co; IGA; ASIA; Am Mgmt Assn; cp/Nat Right to Work Com; r/Ch of Christ; hon/W/W S&SW.

NEWELL, ROBERT CHARLES oc/Minister; b/Jun 25, 1918; h/645 Bending Bough Dr, Webster, NY 14580; ba/Rochester, NY; m/Bettemae VanDussen; c/Tamara Leigh, Kent Denison, Scott Denison, Brad Denison; ed/Albert Bulkley and Anna Brandt Newell; ed/AB Hastings Col; BD, MD Colgate Rochester Div Sch; pa/Min Bapt Temple, Rochester; Mem Bapt Mins' Coun NY St 1978-; Monroe Bapt Assn: Dir Hispanic Mins 1978-, Chm Dept Min 1971-, Exec Com 1969-; Clergy Occupl Devel & Employmt Project: Bd Mgrs 1976-77, Pres 1976-77, VP 1975-76; Bd Trustees Cleveland Bapt Assn 1961-68, 1946-60; Others; cp/Bd Dirs Rochester Humane Soc; VP U Kidney Assn Rochester; Var Former Activs; r/Bapt; hon/Dist'd Ser Awd, Cleve Bapt Assn; Pub'd Author; W/W: Am Cols & Univs, Ohio, MW, Rel; Notable Ams.

NEWMAN, BARBARA MAE oc/Teacher; b/Jul 16, 1932; h/1918 Bruner St, Rockford, IL 61103; ba/Rockford; p/Greene Adam and Emma Lorene Fields Newman, R'ford; ed/BS No Ill Univ 1973; pa/Tchr Itinerant, Blind & Partially Sighted; CEC; Assn for Ed Visually Handicapped; cp/St Bernadette Choir, Rockford Diocesan Chorale, Rockford Literacy; r/Rom Cath; hon/Wom of Yr, Forest City Chapt Am Bus Wom's Assn 1966.

NEWMAN, JAMES SAMUEL oc/Department Supervisor; b/Sept 25, 1922; h/410 Glover St, Hendersonville, NC 28739; ba/H'ville; m/Kate Miller; c/Jerry F, Jama R Johnston; p/S O and L A Newman, Seymour, TX; ed/BS Univ Tenn 1951; mil/AUS; pa/AIChE; ACS; AATCC; cp/Adv Com Am Security Coun; VFW; Am Legion; Mason; WOW; r/Bapt; hon/Man of Yr, Henderson Co Com Dev; Civil Preparedness Commend; Cert of Apprec, US Dept Agri.

NEWMAN, LINDA ELAINE oc/Transportation Coordinator; b/Oct 10, 1948; h/9641 Courthouse Rd, Vienna, VA 22180; ba/Washington, DC; p/Charles A and Beatrice C Newman, Vienna; ed/BA; cp/Alpha Kappa Alpha; NAACP; r/Rom Cath; hon/Cert of Apprec for Homecoming 1976, Spch & Hearing Hon Soc.

NEWTON, PATRICIA A oc/Physician, Psychiatrist; b/Aug 11, 1946; ba/4940 Audubon Ave, Renard Hosp, St Louis, MO 63150; p/McKinley and Bernice Newton, Little Rock, AR; ed/BS Univ Ark-PB 1967; MA Geo Peabody Col 1969; MD Wash Univ Sch Med 1975; pa/Washington Univ Med Sch 1975-; Chief Resident Group 1978-79, Clin Instr, Asst Prog Dir "Sum Bridging Prog" 1971 (Sum);

Res Asst Dept Commun Med St Louis Univ Med Sch 1970 (Sum); Microbiologist I Tenn Public Hlth Dept, Nashville, Tenn 1969-70; Other Former Positions; Mem Quality Control Com The Ctr for Fam Mtl Hlth, City of St Louis; Bd Trustees Al Akhbar Insts Sci & Technol; Chperson Com on Residents En Mo Psychi Soc 1978-79; Chm "Task Force on Psychi Sers to Med Students" Am Psychi Assn; Am Med Wom's Assn; Advr & Conslt Psychi Sers Republic of Guyana, SAm; Conslt; Others; cp/Advr & Conslt *Black Radio Exclusive* Mag; Past Mem Pres's Task Force on African & Third World Affairs; Profl Adv Com St Louis St Hosp Yth Ctr; All Japan Karate Fdn; Intl Karate Fdn; r/Meth; hon/Outstg Yg Wom in Am; Del to 1st Caribbean Conf of Psychi, San Juan, PR 1976; Fellow, Am Psychi Assn, Nat Insts Mtl Hlth; Fgn Study Awd, Nat Coun Minority Hlth Inc; Others.

NGUYEN, VIETSON VAN oc/Mathematician; b/Apr 7, 1952; h/3600 N Lake Shore Dr, Apt 2306, Chicago, IL 60613; ba/Chgo; m/Stavroula F Matsoukas; p/Nguyen Van Hai and C T T N Ha Lanh, Guyana; ed/BS cum laude Univ Wis-Stevens Point 1973; pa/Mathematician Dept Math Univ Chgo (on leave); Am Math Soc 1974-; Math Assn Am 1977-; cp/Shedd Aquarium Soc; Intl Oceanographic Foun; hon/Life Fellow IBA.

NIBLICK, GERNA DEAN oc/Pharmacy Supportive Person; Actress; b/Mar 31, 1924; h/125 Harrison Rd SE, Winter Haven, FL 33880; ba/Lake Wales, FL; m/Clarence; c/Gern DeVogel, David, Reed, Jon (dec), Kim N Swindall; p/Gern H and Mary Wilhelm Johnson (dec); ed/Guy Bates Post Sch Drama 1941; pa/Pharm Supportive Person Lake Wales Hosp; Commun Theatre Actress: Ohio, Ind, Fla; cp/Repub Wom's Clb; Lady Elks; Band Parents Assn; r/Rom Cath; hon/26 Acting Awds for Best Actress & Supporting Actress, Van Wert Civic Theatre (Van Wert, Ohio); Anthony Awd for Best Actress, Ft Wayne Perf'g Arts (Ft Wayne, Ind) 1974; Best Actress Awds: Ohio-OCTA Competition (Columbus, Ohio) 1975, NW Reg Ohio OCTA Competition 1977.

NICHOLAS, ROSE CATHERINE DAVIS oc/Independent Oil Producer; b/Apr 22, 1921; h/PO Box 730, Brenham, TX 77833; ba/Same; m/James W (dec); p/Calvin P Davis, Austin, TX; Alma Brau Davis (dec); ed/Von Kalow Sch Stenography; Blinn Col; Lic'd Hairdresser & Cosmetologist, St of Tex; pa/Tex Indep Prodrs & Royalty Owners Assn; cp/Assoc Mem Fortnightly Clb Brenham; Tex Fdn Wom's Clbs; Past Pres St Jude Hosp Aux, Brenham; r/St Paul Luth Ch of Rehburg, Burton, Tex; hon/Placed in Var Art Contest; 1st Pl 1974-75 Yrbook, Tex Fdn Wom's Clbs; Personalities of S.

NICHOLLS, JAMES HAROLD oc/Clergyman; Broadcast Consultant; Lobbyist; b/Mar 27, 1923; h/Rt 1, Box 620 A, Sumner, WA 98390; ba/Washington, DC; m/Merlyn Alfreda; c/Terrill James, Geoffrey Harold, Lauralee Louise; p/Robert James Nicholls (dec); Laura A Nicholls, Vancouver, BC, Canada; pa/Nat Press Clb; Evangelist Grace Gospel Missions 1940-44; Ordained to Min Apostolic Ch of Pentecost 1944; Pastor Full Gospel Ctr, Ft William, Ontario, Canada 1944-46; Evangelist, Editor, Pubr Christian Books, Orgr Mins & Lay Persons Sems,

Devel'd Mass Invasion Tech Used by Every Home Crusades Worldwide 1946-53; Assoc Pastor Evangelistic Tabernacle, Vancouver 1953-59; Pastor Ctl Bible Ch, Longview, Wash 1965-73; Pres Am Assn Broadcasters 1971-75; Chm Nat Com for Truth & Justice 1972-73; Exec Dir Freedom Def Coun 1973-75; Secy Grace Gospel Evang Assn Intl 1962-75; hon/Outstg Naturalized Citizen Awd, Tacoma Pierce Co Americanization Coun; Cit for Meritorious Ser by Edward B Rhodes Post #2 Am Legion, Tacoma; Dist'd Citizen Awd, St of Wash; Cit of Apprec, Am Legion 4th Dist, Wash; Key to City of Tacoma & Proclamation of Jim Nicholls Day; Spec Recog by Senator Warren Magnuson; Spec Recog by Senator Henry M Jackson; Cert of Participation by Paul H Johns Post #202 Am Legion, Tacoma; Tacoma City Coun Cit; Am Legion Awd of Merit, Edward B Rhodes Post #2; Dist'd Ser Awd, St Conv, Amvets, Dept of Wash; Public Ser Awd, Am Assn Ret'd Persons & Nat Ret'd Tchrs Assn; W/W: W, Am, Indust & Bus; Intl Biog Dic; Commun Ldrs & Noteworthy Ams.

NICHOLS, THOMAS S oc/Business Executive; b/May 8, 1909; h/PO Box 253, Owings Mills, MD 21117; m/Tatiana Mckenna (dec); c/2 Chd; ed/Univ Pa; Temple Univ; mil/Var Capacities during WWII incl'g Conslt to US Chem Bur & US Dept Meml Harriman Mission to London 1943; Chm Sullphuric Acid Operating Comm (War Prodn Bd) & Served as Mem Tech Indep Intell Comm; pa/Former Pres & Dir Mathieson Chem Corp; Pres Olin Mathieson Chem Chorp (merger of Mathieson Chem Corp & Olin Corp), Elected Chm 1957-63, Chm Exec Com 1963-74, Dir & Mem Exec Com 1974-; Former Mem Bd Govs NY Stock Exc; Former Pres/Dir Thomas S Nichols Foun, Owings Mills; Life Trustee Applied Physics Lab, Johns Hopkins Univ; Trustee Olin Corp Charitable Trust & Logistics Mgmt Inst; cp/Bd Trustees Md Hist Soc; hon/Personalities of S; Book of Honor.

NICKOLS, JOHN oc/Author; Child Psychologist; Psycho-Educational Case Management; b/May 27, 1926; h/2220 Reddfield Dr, Falls Church, VA 22043; ba/Same; c/Patrice Ann, Zana Alizabeth, Liese Ellaine, Kurt Allen; p/John Erwin and Nora Destamony Harrison Nickols (dec); ed/BA, MA, PhD Univ Denver; Postdoct Studies; mil/USN 1944-46; USPHS 1962-68; pa/Pract Clin Psychol; Conslt in Human Resource Analysis; Diplomate Am Bd Examrs in Profl Psychol; cp/Bd Advrs DC Area Clin, Pvt Sch & Parent Groups; hon/Psi Chi; Delta Epsilon; 40+ Profl & Sci Pubs; Life Mem, Nat Rifle Assn Am; 20+ Copyrights; Creative & Successful Personalities; Commun Ldrs Am; Others.

NICOL, MARJORIE CARMICHAEL oc/- Psychological Evaluator; b/Jan 6, 1932; h/89 Linden St, Millburn, NJ 07041; ba/Montclair, NJ; p/Norman Carmichael and Ethel Sarah Siviter Nicol, Waterbury, CT; ed/AB 1942, MS Upsala Col 1978; pa/Psychol Evaluator, F L Merritt Inc; Creator, "Nicol Index", Personality Instrument used in Career Guid & Upsala Col; APGA; Am Voc Assn; cp/Pres, Montclair Rehab Org for Handicapped; Fdr, Metro Opera Co at Lincoln Ctr; r/Prot.

NIEDZIELSKI, HENRYK ZYGMUNT oc/Educator; b/Mar 30, 1931; h/419 Keoniana #904, Honolulu, HI 96815; ba/Honolulu; m/Krystyna; c/Henry Jr, Daniel, Robert, Anna-Pia; p/Sigismond Niedzielski, Troyes, France; Anna Pelik; ed/PhB Univ Dijon 1954; BA; MA; PhD Univ Conn 1964; mil/French Armored Cavalry 1951-53; pa/Univ Hi: Assoc Prof French, Chm 1966-72, Prof French Linguistics 1972-; cp/Past Pres Fam Ed Ctrs Hi; Dir Alliance Francaise; r/Cath; hon/Dist'd Commun Ser Awd, Honolulu; NDEA F'ship; Fulbright Lectureship.

NIEMEYER, GROVER CHARLES oc/Educator; Scholar in Film History; b/Jan 29, 1913; h/1616 18 NW, Washington, DC 20009; ba/College Park, MD; p/Grover

Cleveland and Eloise Knox Niemeyer (dec); ed/BA magna cum laude DePauw Univ 1933; MA NWn Univ 1935; PhD Yale Drama Sch 1942; pa/Broadway Actor, Appearances incl: *Mother, Left Turn, Searching for the Sun, Swing Your Lady, Red Harvest, Golden Boy, The Cradle Will Rock* 1935-39; Prof Theatre & Film: Ohio Univ 1941-43, Tex Wom's Univ 1943-44, Carnegie Inst Tech (Pitts) 1944-45; Univ Md, Col Pk: Prof Dept Commun Arts & Theatre 1945-, Prof Film Studies 1957-, Created Current Undergrad, Grad Curric in Dramatic Art, Co-Est'd Univ Theatre; Film Conslt to Pres' Coun on Arts, Am Film Inst; Dir 14 Dramatic Prodns; Spch Commun Assn; AAUP; Am Film Inst; Phi Beta Kappa; Nat Collegiate Players; hon/Edward Rector Scholar, DePauw Univ; Margaret Noble Lee Prize for Public Spkg, Am Coun on Ed; *Old Line* Mag Awd for Best Dramatic Dir, Best Prodn, *Antigone* 1958, *Medea* 1959-60; Pub'd Author; Contbr Articles to Theatrical & Film Mags; Others.

NIFFENEGGER, JAMES ALBERT oc/Ophthalmologist; b/Sept 5, 1934; h/321 Hume St NE, North Canton, OH 44720; ba/Canton, OH; m/Joyce; c/Catherine Ann, John Harley; p/John Niffenegger (dec); Hildegard Niffenegger, Top of the World Clearwater, FL; ed/BA; MS; MD; mil/USAF; pa/Sr Att'g Staff Aultman Hosp 1973-; Courtesy Staff: Timken Mercy Hosp 1966-, Massillon City Hosp 1973-; Aultman Hosp: Pres 1976, Secy 1974; Pres Hosp Bur Ctl Stark Co 1973-75; Am Acad Ophthal & Otolaryngol; AMA; Ohio St Med Soc; Am Assn Ophthal; Contact Lens Assn Ophthalmologists; Cleve Ophthal Soc; Am Col Surgs; Am Intraocular Implant Soc; Others; cp/Chm Ctl Stark Co U Way Res Com; Trustee Canton Med Ed Foun; Bd Trustees Eight Co Hlth Planning & Devel Coun; Exec Bd U Way Ctl Stark Co Hlth Foun Trustee; r/Meth; hon/Alpha Omega Alpha.

NIKOLAI, LORRAINE C oc/Homemaker; Saleswoman; Writer; b/Feb 20, 1910; h/701 Humboldt Ave, Wausau, WI 54401; m/Jacob N; c/Mary C Zimmerman, Judith A Goralski; p/Theodore and Catherine Goeden (dec); ed/Dale Carnegie Course in Public Spkg; pa/Current Saleswom Indust Aid for the Blind of Milwaukee (Wis); Former Saleswom Avon Co; Active Mem Wausau Writers' Clb 23 Yrs; Wausau Reg Writers' Assn; Contbr to: *New World Poets, Bouquet of Roses, Quaderni Di Poesia, Wausau Daily Herald, Masters of Mod Poetry, Quaderni Di*

Poesia, Others; cp/Secy N Ctl Tech Inst Homemakers' Clb Wausau; Ldrships: GSA, VFW; Repub Wom's Aux; Awd Chm Cancer, Heart, & MS Annual Fund-Raising Drives Wausau; Treas Wausau Key Proj; Others; r/St Michael's Cath Parish: Mem, Chwom Queen of Peace Group Seven; hon/Fdr-Fellow Intl Acad Poets (Cambridge, England); Cert, Centro Studi E Scambi Internazionalli for Poem "Christmas Joy" 1976; Cert of Ofcl Recog, Bicent Com Marathon Co; Num Biogl Listings; Others.

NIMMONS, BILLY TRUETT oc/Minister; b/811 Atkinson Dr, Dalton, GA 30720; ba/Dalton; m/Joanne Ball; c/Rhonda, Truett, Deborah; p/Lindsey Nimmons, Chattanooga, TN; ed/BA Baylor Univ; MRE SWn Bapt Theol Sem; pa/Pastor 1st Bapt Ch, Dalton; Guest Spkr Yth Retreats & Banquets; Ldr Confs Bapt SS Bd & Local Confs; N Ga Bapt

Assn Exec Com; cp/Kiwanis; r/Bapt; hon/W/W in Rel.

NIXON, JOHN WILLIAM oc/Dentist; ba/1728 20th St W, Birmingham, AL 35218; ed/DDS Meharry Med Col 1951; Fist Univ 1946-47; Bethune Cookman Col 1939-42; pa/U Ser Assocs Inc, B'ham 1975-: Chm of Bd, Pres, Chief Exec Ofcr; Assoc Clin Instr UAB Sch Dentistry (Appt'd) 1974; Pres & Chief Exec Ofcr Hayes Intl Corp, B'ham 1971-; Dental Surg (Pvt Pract) 1952-71; Appt'd Mem Nat Adv Dental Res Coun Nat Inst Hlth 1976; cp/Exec Com Citizen's Adv Com; Operation New Birmingham's Exec Com of Commun Affairs; Nat Assoc Smithsonian Instn; Am Issues Forum Adv Coun Univ Ala, Tuscaloosa; Former Mem: B'ham Com on Fgn Relats, Adv Bd to Sch of Social Work (Univ Ala); Bd Dirs Ala Chapt LQC Lamar Soc; Nat Chm Nat Pvt Resources Adv Com, US Ofc of Ec Opportunity 1972; B'ham Manpower Area Planning Coun; Chm B'ham Red Cross, Extended Commun Sers Com; Num Others; Actor; Roles Played incl: "Joe" in *Show Boat*, "Othello" in *Othello*, "Senator" in *How, Now, Dow Jones*, Others; hon/Dist'd Ser Awd, U Negro Col Fund; Hon LLD, Daniel Payne Col; Outstg Ser Awd, Lawson St Jr Col; Outstg Commun Ser Awd, B'ham Area Chapt ARC; NAACP Pres' Awd, Ensley-Pratt City NAACP Br; Outstg Commun Ser Awd, B'ham Housing Auth; Man of Yr B'ham, Yg Men's Bus Clb 1970; Pub'd Author; Intl W/W Commun Ser; W/W Hon Soc Am; W/W US; Ldrs of Black Am; DIB; Personalities of S; Others.

NOBES, LEON D oc/Assistant Professor; b/Apr 9, 1911; h/2033 Crozier Ave, Muskegon, MI 49441; ed/BA 1964, MA 1966 Wn Mich Univ; mil/Mich St Troops 1943-46, Inf Capt; Public Relats Dir Muskegon Co Def Coun WWII; pa/Asst Prof Commun Arts & Scis Wn Mich Univ 1966-; Tchr Muskegon HS 1965; Civilian Employee USN Dept 1952-57: Supv Prodn Specialist, Prodn Engrg Div Supvr; Dir Priorities Continental Aviation & Engrg Corp, Muskegon 1944-46; Nat Adv Bd Am Security Coun; Fdr Ctr for Intl Security Studies, Boston, Va; Am Acad Polit & Social Sci; Mich Spch Assn; Phi Theta Kappa; Phi Rho Pi; Delta Psi Omega; Theta Alpha Phi; Kappa Delta Pi; Pi Gamma Mu; Alpha Kappa Psi; cp/Nat Rifle Assn; US Senatorial Clb; US Nav Inst; Life Mem Lovell Moore Lodge No 182, Muskegon; Ancient Accepted Scottish Rite, Grand Rapids, Mich; Shriner; Humane Soc, Muskegon; hon/Certs: Metall Tng, Navy Contract Law, Supvy Devel Tng (Navy Dept); Cert for Adv'd Statistical Quality Control, Am Soc Quality Control; W/W MW; 2000 Men Achmt; Men of Achmt; DIB.

NOBLE, ALMA NEASE oc/Retired Teacher; b/Jun 16, 1901; h/301 W Tenth Ave, Huntington, WV 25701; ba/H'ton; p/John Myron and Inez Brown Noble (dec); ed/AB Wittenberg Col; AM Columbia Univ; PhD Ohio St Univ; AM Wn Resv Univ; pa/Morris Harvey Col, Charleston, WVa: Acting Hd Fgn Lang Dept 1970-72, Assoc Prof French 1969-72; Marshall Univ, H'ton: Prof Emerita 1973, Assoc Prof French 1945-69, Hd French Dept 1943-64, Asst Prof 1943-45, Asst Prof French & Latin 1941-43; Other Former Positions; Mod Lang Assn Am; Nat Ret'd Tchrs Assn; Nat Fdn Mod Lang Tchg; Am Assn Tchrs of French; Am Guild Organists; Eta Sigma Phi; Pi Delta Phi; Delta Kappa

Gamma; r/Presb; hon/Plaque for 25 Yrs of Dist'd Ser, Marshall Univ; Wittenberg Alumna Cit; Cert of Meritorious Ser, Morris Harvey Col; Plaque for Interest in Commun, New Vienna Bus Assn.

NOBLE, FRANCES ELIZABETH oc/-Educator; Author; b/Sep 3, 1903; h/2915 NE Center Ave, Ft Lauderdale, FL 33308; p/George William and Clara Louise Lane Noble (dec); ed/BA cum laude Northwestern Univ 1924, MA 1926, PhD 1945; pa/Prof & Hd Lang Sect, Wn Mich Univ; Delta Kappa Gamma; Alpha Phi; Alliance Francaise; AATF; Author, *Destiny's Daughter* (1980); hon/Phi Beta Kappa; Palmes Academiques, French Govt.

NOBLE, GEORGE WASHINGTON oc/Landscape Architect; b/Nov 18, 1933; h/5075 Emery Dr, Reno, NV 89506; ba/Reno; m/Nalma Lee; c/Daniel Alan, Craig Edward, Rodney Scott, Lori Anne; p/Daniel Alfonzo Noble (dec); Pearl Lewis Noble, Norwich, NY; ed/BS Syracuse Univ 1960; Postgrad Studies: Univ Nev-R, Wn Nev Commun Col; mil/AUS Signal Corps 1953-55, Corporal; pa/Landscape Architect Toiyable Nat Forest, US Forest Ser; Reg'd Landscape Architect: Nev, Utah, Idaho; Am Soc Landscape Architects; Soc Am Foresters; Soc for Range Mgmt; Assn Envir Planners; Nev Rec & Pk Soc; cp/Pres Eagle Assn, Nev Area Coun of BSA; Alpha Phi Omega; Washoe Co Civil Def Staff; Nev Envir Ednl Coun; Life Mem Reno Civic Chorus; r/Bapt Ch: Deacon; hon/NY St Regents Scholar; Nat Hon Soc; Eagle Scout w Palms; Outstg Perf Awd, US Dept Agri, Forest Ser; Fellow: ABI,IBA; W/W in W; Notable Ams; Commun Ldrs & Noteworthy Ams; Book of Honor.

NOBLE, JAMES VAN PETTEN oc/Lawyer; b/Apr 4, 1922; h/615 E Barcelona Rd, Santa Fe, NM 87501; m/Sara Jane Crail; c/James Van Petten, Sara Ann, Charles Fulton; p/Merrill Emmett and Martha Van Petten Noble; ed/Att'd Univ NM 1940-43; LLB, JD Univ Colo 1949; mil/USAAF 1943-45, 2/Lt; AUS 1942-43; pa/Spec Asst Atty Gen St Hwy Dept, NM 1970-; Chief Counsel & Dir Merc Investmt Corp 1970-; St of NM: Asst

Atty Gen 1968-70, 1963-68; Atty, Las Vegas 1958-60; Other Former Positions; Dir Las Vegas Portland Cement Co; Mem Com Rules for Crim Procedures & Instrns NM Supr Ct; NM Bar Coms Real Property, Land Titles; Am, NM, San Miguel Co Bar Assns; cp/Exec Com, Bd Dirs NM Soc Crippled Chd; Mayor's Santa Fe Action Airport Com; Bd Dirs Las Vegas Commun TV Inc, Las Vegas Devel Corp; Jr C of C; hon/Author (w Ben S Galland), *Re-statement of the Laws of Corps*; Biogl Listings.

NOBLE, WESTON HENRY oc/Professor; b/Nov 30, 1922; h/602 Mound, Decorah, IA 52101; ba/Decorah; p/Merwin and Ruth Noble, Riceville, IA; ed/BA Luther Col 1943; MM Univ Mich 1953; Addit Studies; mil/AUS 1943-46, Am & European Theaters; pa/Luther Col: Prof Music, Chm Dept Music 1953-73, Dir Music Activs 1973-, Dir Nordic Choir 1948-, Dir Concert Band 1948-73; HS Tchr, LuVerne, Ia 1946-48; MENC; Ia Music Edrs; Ia Bandmasters Assn; Col & Univ Bandmasters Assn, St Chm Ia 1961-63; Col Music Soc; Music Tchrs Nat Assn, St VP 1961-63; Charter Mem Am Choral Dirs Assn 1958; Am

Bandmasters Assn; Conducted Fests 34 Sts & Canada; Dir 10 St All-St Bands, Sev All-St Choruses; Dir Num Band & Choral Tours; Adjudicant Intl Fest Three Cities (Vienna, Budapest, Prague) 1973, 74; Band Conslt & Guest Dir Assn for Intl Cult Exc, Vienna, Austria 1978, 79; Num Other Profl Activs; hon/MAC Awd Gov'g Bd; Adv Bd Sch Musician Dir & Tchr Mag; Hon Mem: Phi Mu Alpha Sinfonia Frat, Grand Chapt Kappa Kappa Psi; Sch of Music Achmt Awd, Univ Tulsa; 1 of 10 Most Outstg Music Dirs in US, Sch Musician Mag 1972; Num Biogl Listings; Profl Pubs.

NOEL, MARK GERARD oc/Manufacturing Executive; b/Mar 13, 1942; h/2910 Westmoreland Dr, Birmingham, AL 35223; ba/B'ham; m/Milner Smith; c/Mark McDowell, Martha Milner; p/Noah McDowell; Sarah Collins McDowell, Greenville, SC; ed/BA Wofford Col 1964; mil/AUS 1964-66, Capt Adjutant Gen Corps; pa/Pres The Kesler Co Inc; Owner, Chm of Bd Noel Mfg Corp; So Prods Assn; B'ham Bd Realtors; cp/Dir Mtn Brook Swim & Tennis Clb; Dir Metro-Kiwanis Clb; r/Epis, Ch of the Advent, B'ham; hon/Personalities of S; DIB; W/W S&SW.

NOGUERAS RIVERA, NICOLAS oc/Educator; b/Sept 10, 1902; h/173 Taft St, Santurce, PR 00911; ba/San Juan, PR; m/Berta; c/Nicolas Jr, Rosa Maria N Gonzales (Mrs Jose Ramon); ed/Certn Elem Ed Univ PR 1920; Elem Eng Tchr's Cert 1926; Att'd Labor Ed Inst 1935; pa/Tchr Public Schs PR 1920-35; Pres Protective Labor Union, Cayey 1931; Lectr Dept Labor 1935; Secy-Treas Fed Labor Union, San Juan 1936; Secy-Treas PR Fed Fdn of Labor 1936-52; Pres Fac & Agri Labor Coun PR 1938-41; Orgr & Pres Round Table Conf on Sugar Indust Probs 1943-44; Pioneer & Exec Secy 1st Statehood Cong PR 1943; Drafter Labor Unity Charter 1945; Pres Prog & Constitution Comm, 1st InterAm Labor Conf; Cong for Plebiscitary Action 1959-60; Bd Dirs PR Tchrs Assn; Am Security Coun; IPA; Pub'd: *Prospects of the Univ Reorg* 1942, *Collective Bargaining in the Sugar Indust of PR* 1956; Editor *Forty Years of Labor Activs*; Fdr & Dir Monthly Paper *Salario*; Composer 2 Waltzes; cp/Former Mem RP Ho of Reps; Former Mem Bd Appeals, Selective Ser Sys; Mem Apprenticeship Coun PR; Fellow IBA; hon/Spec Cert of Apprec, 5th Anniv of Signing of Selective Ser Act; Certs of Apprec: Former Presidents Roosevelt, Truman, Eisenhower, Kennedy, Johnson, Nixon, Gen Hershey (Dir Selective Ser); Former Gov Luis A Ferre, Col Manuel F Silverio (PR Selective Ser Dir); Medal & Insignia of Selective Ser Sys US; Meritorious Ser Awd; Biogl Listings.

NOLAN, DAVID BRIAN oc/Political Journalist; Law Student; b/Jan 1, 1951; h/8414 Orion Ave, Sepulveda, CA 91343; p/John J and Mary Jane Donnelly Nolan, Arlinton, VA; ed/BA Duke Univ 1943; MPA Am Univ 1975; JD Univ San Fernando Val Col of Law 1978; pa/Student Mem LA Co Bar; Reporter "Human Events" 1972; Political Columnist & Contbr to: *Duke Chronicle*, *Harvard Crimson*, *Stanford Daily*; Congl Intern 1971; cp/Cal Yg Repubs; Cal Repub Assembly; Alt Del to Repub Nat Conv 1972; hon/Nat Student Reg; W/W in Am Polits; IPA; DIB.

NOLEN, MILTON WAYNE oc/Minister; b/Apr 11, 1937; h/1070 Coronado Dr, Redlands, CA 92373; ba/Redlands; m/Jacqueline; c/Michael Wayne, Kimberly Ann, Jeffrey Craig, Kristen Leigh; p/Grover Cleveland Nolen (dec); Beulah Nolen, Redlands; ed/BA Cal Bapt Col; MDiv Golden Gate Bapt Sem; mil/USAF 1955-63; pa/St Exec Bd; Past Pres Local Nat Evang Assn; Pres Redlands Min Assn; cp/Bd Dirs U Way; Bd Corp Plymouth Village Retiremt Ctr; r/So Bapt; hon/Personalities of W&MW; Notable Ams; Men of Achmt; W/W in Rel.

NONG oc/Artist; b/Oct 10, 1930; h/999 Green St, No 2701, San Francisco, CA 94133; ed/LLB; mil/AUS; USAF; pa/Painter-Sculptor; Major One-Man Exhbns incl: Nat

Mus Mod Art (Seoul, Korea) 1975, SF Zoological Garden (SF) 1975, Shinsegye Gallery (Seoul) 1971, Nihonbashi Gallery (Tokyo, Japan) 1971, Nat Mus Hist (Taipei, Taiwan) 1971, Galerie Vallombreuse (Biarritz, France) 1970, Others; Maj Group Exhbns incl: Galerie Hexagramme (Paris, France) 1975, SF Mus of Art 1972, Taipei Provincial Mus 1971, Nat Sculpture Soc (Lever House, NYC) 1971, Galerie Des Champs Elysees (Paris) 1971, Maison de la Culture du Havre (Le Havre, France) 1970, Others; Num Perm Collections incl: Tetro Museo (Figueras, Spain), Security Pacific Nat Bk (SF), IBM (San Mateo, Cal), Kook Min Col (Seoul), Chd's Ctr (Seoul), The Dong-a Ilbo (Oriental Daily News, Seoul), Sato Kogyo Co Ltd (Tokyo), Security Nat Bk (Walnut Creek, Cal), Num Others; cp/SF-Seoul Sister Cit Com Mem; hon/Lttr of Apprec, Min of Cult & Info, Republic of Korea.

NOONE, JOHN THOMAS oc/Catholic Priest; b/Dec 29, 1941; h/1102½ E Beach Blvd, Long Beach, MS 39560; ba/Gulfport, MS; p/John Noone, Roscommon, Ireland; Delia Kelly, Roscommon; ed/Ordained Priest; MSW; pa/Dir Cath Social Sers, Gulfport; r/Cath.

NORFLEET, ALMETA FAYE oc/Registered Nurse; b/Jul 27, 1934; h/3405 E 66 Pl, Tulsa, OK 74136; ba/Tulsa; m/Edward K; c/Steven Wayne, Bryan Scott Farless; p/Rutherford A and Hazel A Hays, Vinita, OK; ed/Hillcrest Med Ctr Sch Nsg 1956; pa/RN St Johns Hosp; Am Nurses Assn; Okla Nurses Assn, Dist No 2; Del to ONA; Am Assn Neurosurg Nurses: Past Treas, Bd Dirs; cp/Bd Dirs RN Commun Vols; Tulsa Woms Philharm Soc; Aux Tulsa Co Med Aux; r/Bapt.

NORFOLK, GLENN DALE oc/Baptist Minister; Senate Chaplain; b/Oct 22, 1932; h/Perry Dr, Holts Summit, MO 65043; ba/Holts Summit; m/Barbara Jean; c/Dennis Dale, Lori Lynn; p/Herman Norfolk (dec);

Edna Keck, Hannibal, MO; ed/AA; BA; BD; MEd; pa/Bapt Min; VP Hannibal LaGrange Col; Radio Spkr; Sem Ext Tchr; Mem Ctl Mo Mission Bd; cp/Chaplain Mo Senate; r/So Bapt.

NORMAN, JOHN EDWARD oc/Petroleum Landman; b/May 22, 1922; h/2710 S Jay St, Denver, CO 80227; ba/Denver; m/Hope Sabin; p/John Thomas, Gerould Winthrop, Nancy E McConnell, Susan G Heare, Douglas Edward; p/J Edward and Ella Warren Norman (dec); ed/BSBA 1949; MBA Univ Denver 1972; mil/AUS 1942-45, 1st Cavalry Div; pa/Am, Wyo, Denver Assns Petrol Landmen;

Rocky Mtn Oil & Gas Assn; cp/Former Precnt Com-man Repub; r/Epis: Choir, Vestry, Deanery, Conv Del; hon/Outstg Local Pubs Chm, Am Assn Petrol Landmen.

NORMAN, PATRICIA J BROWNSON oc/Journalist; b/Jul 6, 1930; h/814 Woodside Ave SE, N Canton, OH; m/Ralph Edward Sr; c/Ralph E Jr, Pamela Shoup, Mary Kay, Nancy, William T, Janet Fashbaugh, Linda, Amy, Barbara; p/William T and Mildred Corson Brownson, Baldwin, MI; ed/AB Univ Mich; pa/Reporter Akron *Beacon Jour*; Wom in Communs; Ohio Press Wom; Ohio Newspaper Wom; Sigma Delta Chi; cp/Alpha Xi Delta Alumnae; Former Mem N Canton Jr Wom's Clb; Former Repub Poll Wkr; r/Cath; hon/Nat & St Awds, Ohio Press Wom & Ohio Newspaper Wom.

NORRIS, RUBY LEE oc/Creative Writing Consultant; b/Dec 16, 1915; h/2422 Grove Ave, Richmond, VA 23220; ba/Richmond; m/Vernon W; c/Vernon W Jr; p/Squire Rogers and Ruby Hall Norris (dec); ed/BS, Master in Humanities; pa/Creative Writing Specialist Henrico Co Humanities Ctr, Title IV-C Proj, Henrico Co Schs 1976-; Richmond Humanities Ctr, Richmond City Schs: Humanities Specialist, Coor Poetry-in-the-Schs Richmond 1974-75; Coor Poetry-in-the-Schs Var Cos, Richmond Intercult Ctr for Humanities, Title IV-C Proj; Other Former

Positions; NCTE: Mem 1978-79, Poetry Wkshop on Composition (Spring) 1978, Spkr Annual Conv 1958, 61; Va Assn Tchrs Eng, Var Ofcs & Activs; Columbia Scholastic Press Assn; Nat Scholastic Press Assn; So Interscholastic Press Assn; Va HS Leag; Nat Assn for Humanities Ed; Va Ed Assn; Delta Kappa Gamma; Other Profl Activs; r/Grace & Holy Trinity Epis Ch: Mem Child Care Ctr Bd Dirs 1975-77, Altar Guild 1970-77, Conslt to Dir Christian Ed 1973-75, Chm Bd Christian Ed 1974; Yth Ldr St Matthews Epis Ch 1966; Others; hon/Lit Travel Grant, NEA; Dist'd Ser Awd, So Interscholastic Press Assn Wash & Lee Univ; Cert of Merit, Va Assn Tchrs Eng; Pub'd Author.

NORTHCROSS-WALKER, DAVID AARON oc/Counselor, Director; b/Nov 20, 1947; h/122 N 19th, Apt D, Frederick, OK 73542; ba/Frederick; m/Lela May N-W; c/Angela Francis Elizabeth Walker; p/Aaron Eugene and Betty Jean Walker, Presidio of SF, CA; ed/BA E Ctl Univ; mil/Okla Army NG; USAFR; USAF; pa/Cnslr & Dir Turning Point Inc; APGA; Okla Assn Yth Sers; Okla Jt Coun Chds Sers; r/Baha'i Faith.

NORTHROP, MONROE oc/Attorney; b/Jan 1, 1931; h/4722 Waring, Houston, TX 77027; ba/Houston; m/Jane; c/Ronald Viator Jr; p/(dec); ed/BBA 1953, LLB 1954 Univ Tex; mil/AUS Counter Intell Corps 1955-57; pa/Fellow Tex Bar Foun; r/Epis.

NORTHUP, WILLIAM CARLTON oc/Management Analyst; b/Dec 1, 1930; h/24 Williamsburg, Evanston, IL 60203; m/Sharon Joan; c/Richard Carlton, Karen Frances; p/Lansford Lionel and Elsie Rebecca Northup, Columbia, MO; ed/BS; MBA; pa/Mgmt Analyst, Fin Systems; HFMA; AMA; ASA; MAA; AMBAE; Credit Com Mizzou Employees; Fed Credit Union; cp/Optimist Intl; Secy-Treas JCs; Teen Auto Clb; Nat Bd Advrs Am Security Coun; Spec Advr to Gov

of Mo for Printing & Pub'g; Pack Com Chm CSA; Delta Sigma Pi; Vol Probation Ofcr Boone Co Juv Ct; Columbia Civic Orch; Bonne Terre Civic Orch; Univ Singers; Univ Mo Men's Glee Clb; SPEBSPSA: Var Ofcs; Others; r/Bapt: SS Tchr, Yth Dir, Choir Dir; hon/1st Runner-up, Open Competition, MBA Fin Cands, Univ Mo-Columbia 1974.

NORTON, DOROTHA OLIVER oc/Associate Professor; b/Jul 25, 1937; h/528 Poplar, Kenton, TN 38233; ba/Martin, TN; m/Robert Marion; c/Robbie Jean, Robert Marion II; p/Lacey and Pearl Cunningham Oliver, Kenton, TN; ed/BA Union Univ; MA Memphis St; MA Murray St; pa/Univ Tenn: Assoc Prof Communs 1978-, Instr 1966-70; Kenton HS, Kenton: Tchr Eng & Shorthand, Guid Cnslr 1958-66; Other Former Positions; Phi Kappa Phi; Spch Commun Assn; Rel, So, Tenn Spch Commun Assns; NEA; Poetry Soc

Tenn; AAUP; Tenn Phil Assn; S Atl Mod Lang Assn; Num Profl Activs; cp/Pres-elect Dist VIII Tenn Fdn Wom's Clbs; Kenton Wom's Clb II, Tenn Fdn Wom's Clbs, Var Ofcs, Activs; Past VP Kenton PTO; Former Room Mother 3rd Grade, Kenton Sch; Others; r/1st Bapt Ch, Kenton: Dir Pre-sch II 1970-78, Co-Dir Mission Friends 1973-78, Tchg Asst to Pastor (Wkly Tchrs' Tng Sessions) 1977-78; Certn of Commend, Poetry Soc Tenn; Wom of Yr Awd 1973, Dist'd Ser Awds Banquet, Kenton JCs & Kenton Jaycettes; Phi Kappa Phi; Var Acad Hons; Biogl Listings.

NORWOOD, JAMES MADISON III oc/Clergyman; b/Oct 30, 1948; h/3127 Columbine, Denver, CO 80205; m/Wanda Jean Burnett; c/Danielle Eleanor, Adrienne Marie, James Madison IV, Jaqueline Monae; p/James Madison Norwood Jr, San Francisco, CA; Audrey E Norwood, Salina, KS; ed/AB Ks Wesleyan Univ; MRE Iliff Sch Theol; pa/Min Music & SS Supt Zion Temple Ch, Denver; r/Pentecostal; hon/W/W in Am.

NOWACKI, WALENTY oc/Chemical Engineer; Editor; b/Jan 26, 1906; h/67-34 Austin St, Forest hills, NY 11375; ba/NYC; m/Halina K Nowacki; p/Marcin and Jozefa Lyczka Nowacki (dec); ed/MS; pa/Editor for Abstracting, U Engrg Ctr, Abstracting & Indexing for Sci & Tech Info; r/Rom Cath; hon/Author Books & Articles on Polit Matters; Dist'd Cross (Poland).

NOWELS-LLOYD, DIANA MARIE oc/Elementary School Teacher; b/May 16, 1941; h/600 McKelvey Ave, Bakersfield, CA 93308; ba/B'field; m/Berlun Britt Lloyd; c/DeLynne Marie, Erin Lee; p/Clyde Wesley Nowels (dec); LaVera Marie Nowels-Price, B'field; ed/AA B'field Col; BA magna cum laude Fresno Univ; MS Cal Luth Col; pa/Mbrship Chperson Cal Tchr Assn; NEA; AAUW; PTA; r/Meth; hon/Recipient Mid-Career S'ship for Ed, Cal PTA; Lttr of Commend for Help w Hard-of-Hearing Students, Kern Co Supt of Schs; Hon Cert, Val Forge (Freedom Foun Book); Outstg Grad Awd, DAR & VFW; Others.

NOWOTNY, ERHARD PETER oc/Realtor, Life Insurance Agent; b/Feb 28, 1905; h/660 Laurel Ln, New Braunfels, TX 78130; ba/Same; m/Frances Dial; c/Beth, Frances Ferguson; p/Peter Jr and Emilie Linnartz Nowotny (dec); ed/BS Tex A&M Univ 1926; mil/Field Artillery Reserves 1926-32; US Air

Corps 1942-46, Maj; pa/Pres New Braunfels Bd of Realtors, 4 Yrs; VP, Dir Tex REA; Tex Ins Bd Zone Chm; cp/Pres C of C; Dem Co Chm, 9 Yrs; New Braunfels Lions Clb: Past Pres, Tailtwister 9 Yrs; Past Pres: Jr C of C, New Braunfels Optimist Clb, New Braunfels & Guadalupe Valley Shrine Clbs; Past Master, Local Masonic Lodge; Former Exalted Ruler, New Braunfels Elks Lodge #2279, 2 Terms; New Braunfels Bd Ed: Secy, VP, 6 Yr Ser; Comal Co Commun Fund: Past Pres, 1st Dr Chm; Chm: Bd of Equalization NBISB, Comal Co Salvation Army Com, Comal Co US Savings Bond Com, Law Enforcement Com for City of New Braunfels for 5 Yrs; r/U Ch of Christ: Mem Coun 9 Yrs, Pres 5 Yrs; hon/C of C Hall of Honor 1968; HS Silver Unicorn 1967; Tex Jr C of C: Outstg St VP 1937-38, Outstg Achmt Awd 1937-38; New Braunfels JC Life Mbrship 1965; Optimists Intl Life Mbrship 1966; New Braunfels Elks Lodge #2279 Life Mbrship 1976; Outstg Achmt Awd, Comal Co Commun Fund 1954; Minute Man Awd, US Treasury Dept for Patriotic Ser 1978; Salvation Army Special Awd for Ser 1966; Num Biogl Listings.

NUCKELS, ROBERT (BOBBY) LEE oc/Community Relations Officer; b/Jul 4, 1932; h/Wesgate, Alleghany County, VA; ba/Box 47, Iron Gate, VA 24448; pa/Commun Relats Ofcr, SJAC, BSA; Yth Lecturing to More Than 1,000,000 Students NW USA Auspices Antrim Bur, Subject Drug Abuse & "How to Survive Teenage Yrs"; Radio Prog Dir; Sum Camp Dir; Prog Dir; Chaplain; Mem IBM; Use of Magic & Ventriloquism in Yth Work; Pictured w "Goober" (Sidekick for 20 Yrs); hon/Scouting Awd of Merit; Va Elk's Masinter Awd; Others.

NUGENT, DONALD YORK oc/Photographer; Artist; Lecturer; Inventor; b/Apr 24, 1939; h/12414 Parknoll Ave, Baton Rouge, LA 70816; ba/Baton Rouge; p/Leroy Homer Nugent (dec); Elma Anne Schroeder (dec); ed/BS La St Univ 1967; mil/AUS Chem Corps 1961-64; pa/Dir Photo Sch of Geosci, La St

Univ; cp/Dem Party; Past Pres Apt Renters Assn of Middleway & Establishmt Apts; ; r/Meth Ch: Mem; hon/Mayorality Awd, City of New Orleans (La); Silver Bowl for Excell in Profl Photo, Photo Coun of La; Hon Awd for Univ Photo, Univ Profl Photogs Assn; Blue Ribbon Awd, Photo Coun La.

NUMANO, ALLEN STANISLAUS MOTOYUKI (pen name A L A Corenanda) oc/Writer, Translator, Violinist, Industrial-Designer, Pioneer in "Mentalogy"; b/Nov 3, 1908; h/PO Box 2442, Honolulu, HI 96804; p/Hidekazu and Sadako Magamitsu Numano (dec); ed/St Josephs Col (Ceylon); Worcester Col (England); Royal Col of Music (England); Studied w Prof Achille Rivarde; pa/Former Sr Examr Translator at GHQ (SCAP) Tokyo, under Gen MacArthur 1945-47, also at US-Japanese Jt Venture Co, Pfizer Taito Co, Ltd, Tokyo 1955-68; Violin Recital w White Russian Pianist, Prof S Maklezoff, at Royal Col Hall, Colombo 1940 in Aid of British Red Cross; Currently Gives Short Progs on Violin; "Black & White" Artist, Exhibiting at 55th Annual Art Exhbn of Ceylon Soc of Arts, Colombo 1952; Tchr Eng Composition at Intl Div of Sophia Univ, Tokyo 1967-68; Pub'd "The Violin & Violin Playing" 1940; Translated & Pub'd L P Lochner's "Fritz

Kreisler", 1959, Maymie R Krythe's "All About Christmas", 1962, "Fairbanks-Morse Opposed Piston Engine Instrns 3800 D81/8", 1964, Num Tech Items from Japanese into Eng; Pending Pub of Own Writing "Music & Reminiscenses" 2 Pub'd Articles; Completed Film Script; Assoc Mem Soc of Authors, London; Fellow Inst of Linguists, London; Translators Assn, London; Hi Coun for Cult & the Arts, Hi; Nat Mem Smithsonian Inst, Wash DC; Am Translators Assn, USA; Assn of Honolulu Artist, Honolulu, Hi; r/Cath; hon/Men of Achmt; Authors & Writers W/W; Intl Register of Profiles, Pub'd by Intl Biogl Ctr, Cambridge, England.

NYDICK, DAVID oc/School Superintendent; College Professor; Syndicated Columnist; b/Feb 10, 1929; h/22 Lesley Dr,

Syosset, NY 11791; ba/Jericho, NY; m/Gilda; c/Leslie, Jay; p/Irving and Minnie Nydick, Queens, NY; ed/BA; MA; PD; mil/AUS; pa/Supt of Schs Jericho Public Schs; Ed Writers Assn; Am Assn Sch Adm; cp/Pres: E Plains Mtl Hlth Ctr, NY Univ Ed Alumni Assn; hon/Ed Awd, Nat Conf Christians & Jews.

NYE, BERNARD CARL oc/Assistant Vocational Director; b/Nov 25, 1927; h/315 E Dunedin Rd, Columbus, OH 43214; ba/Columbus; m/Nancy Ann; c/Vicki Lynn, Linda Lee, Patricia Ann, Terri Jo, Steven Alan, Melanie Sue, Michael Scott, Brian Douglas, James Andrew; p/Bernard H Nye, Columbus; ed/BS, PhD Ohio St Univ; MS Bowling Green St Univ; mil/AUS 1946-47; pa/Asst Voc Dir Distributive Ed (DE) St Dept

of Ed (Ohio); Pres Nat Assn St Supvrs of DE 1965-68; Past VP Am Voc Assn; Current Mem AVA, OVA; r/No Broadway Meth Ch: Mem; hon/Grad Cum Laude, Ohio St Univ; Men of Achmt; W/W Am Ed; W/W Hon Soc Am; Others.

NYUN-HAN, NORMAN oc/Professor; b/May 23, 1921; h/1250 Bel Air Dr, Santa Barbara, CA 93105; ba/Santa Barbara; m/Emma; c/Darryl, Maureen N Franssen, Christine; p/Ba Han and Daw Thein Lwin (dec); ed/BA; PhD; Barrister-at-Law (London, England); pa/Westmont Col: Prof Polit Sci & Intl Studies, Pre-Law Advr; cp/Advr Japanese Am Citizens' Leag SB; Participant Nat & St Election Campaigns; r/Christian; Tchr Adult Bible Class (Ch); hon/Hon Citizen, City of Winnipeg, Manitoba, Canada.

O

OAKES, HERBERT C oc/Business Executive; b/Nov 17, 1927; h/1736 Milford, Houston, TX 77098; ba/Houston; c/Bailie, Herbert Jr; p/Herbert Oakes, Edmond, OK; Loraine Oakes, Houston; ed/BS Univ Okla 1950; MBA Harvard 1955; mil/USN Lt jg; r/Meth.

OAKLAND, SAM-ADOLF SJURSEN oc/Professor; b/Mar 17, 1934; ba/Portland St Univ, Portland, OR 97207; m/Sara McKim; c/Steven, Sasha; p/Sjur Andreassen and Ada Patterson Oakland, Norway; ed/AB 1961, MA 1963 Mich St Univ; Cert Lit Edinburgh Univ 1962; mil/USN Korean Theatre 1951-55; pa/Portland St Univ: Assoc Prof Eng & Chm Scandinavian Studies Com 1974-, Asst Prof 1967-74; Apulais Profesori Wkrs Inst, Finland 1966-67; Asst Prof En Wash Univ 1964-66; Fellow: Am Acad Rome, Strindberg Mus; AAUP; cp/Clk Bicycle Lobby Oreg; Oreg Envir Coun; Multnomah Co WN Quadrant; Bd & Treas Oreg Chapt Am-Scandinavian Foun; Strindberg Soc; Baltic Studies Assn; Soc Advmt Scandinavian Studies; hon/Lobbyist of Yr, Oreg Leg; NDEA Title IV F'ship Comparative Lit; Fulbright Finland 1966; Fulbright Rome 1974; Portland St Univ Foun Travel Grant Yugoslavia.

OAKS, DALLIN HARRIS oc/Administrator; b/Aug 12, 1932; h/Pres Home, Brigham Yg Univ Campus, Provo, UT 84602; ba/-Provo; m/June Dixon; c/Sharmon, Cheri, Lloyd, Dallin, TruAnn, Jenny; p/Lloyd Oaks (dec); Stella Oaks, Provo; ed/BA w High Hons BYU 1954; JD cum laude & Order of Coif Univ Chicago Law Sch 1957; mil/Utah

NG 1949-54; Ill NG 1954-57; USAR 1957-60; pa/Pres BYU; ABA; Fellow Am Bar Foun; Am Law Inst; Pres Am Assn Pres' Indep Cols & Univs; Dir Nat Assn Indep Cols & Univs; cp/Dir Public Broadcasting Ser; Bd Trustees Intermtn Hlth Care; r/Ch of Jesus Christ Latter-Day Sts.

OBERHAUSER, JOSEPH FRANCIS oc/Computer Management; b/May 26, 1947; h/8631 Fairhaven #109-14, San Antonio, TX 7829; ba/SA; p/Francis and Marie Oberhauser, Toledo, OH; ed/BSBA cum laude Bowling Green St Univ 1974; MBA Univ Minn 1976; CDP Inst Cert Computer Profls; mil/AUS Sgt 1965-68; pa/Bus Data Processing Mgmt; Phi Kappa Phi; Fdg Mem & Chapt VP Delta Sigma Pi; r/Rom Cath; hon/Vietnam Ser Medal; W/W S&SW.

OBERLE, GEORGE HURLEY oc/Director; Professor; b/Sept 21, 1930; h/4808 Country Clb Ct, Stillwater, OK 74074; ba/S'water; m/Marie; c/Douglas, Teresa; p/George and Margaret Oberle, Indianapolis, IN; ed/AB Earlham Col 1952; MS Butler Univ 1956; PED Indiana Univ 1969; mil/USAR 6 Yrs; pa/Prof & Dir Sch Hlth, PE & Leisure Scis Okla St Univ 1974-; Prof & Chm Dept HYER & Aths Chgo St Univ 1971-74; Ind St Univ: Asst Dean Sch HPER, Assoc Prof PE, Coor Grad Assts 1962-71; City Supvr Hlth & PE and City Dir Aths Marion Public Schs 1960-62; Other Past Positions; Conslt Num Univs; Officiating Mbrships Num Col Confs & Assns; Ind Intercollegiate Coaches Assn; Ind St Tchrs Assn; Ind Interagy Res Coun; Phi Delta Kappa; Phi Epsilon Kappa; NAIA; NEA;

OAHPER; IAPHER: Past Bd Dirs, Past Pres, Intl Relats Com, Okla Leg Com; MW Dist AAPHER: Past VP Gen Div, Past VP PE, Former Ind Rep Bd Dirs, Num Coms; Nat AAPHER: Former Del Rep Assembly, PEPI Chgo Area Coor, PEPI Nat Task Force; Num Wkshops & Convs; cp/Past Bd Dirs: Richmond YMCA, Marion Boys Clbs Am, Pilgrims Inn Inc, Shoe-Inns Am, Play-Co Inc; r/Prot; hon/Earlham Cols Hall Ath Fame; Hoosier Col Conf Baseball Coach of Yr; Ind Assn HPER Awd; Am Assn HPR Commend; Ill Assn HPER Commend; Chgo Dist IAPHER Spec Commend; Ext Res; Pub'd Author; Num Biogl Listings.

O'BRIEN, CHARLES RICHARD oc/Director; b/Nov 10, 1934; h/1334 Parkview Dr, Macomb, IL 61455; ba/Macomb; p/Charles O'Brien (dec); Dorothy DeBesse O'Brien Johnson, Pocasset, MA; ed/BA 1956, MA 1960 St Johns Col; MS N Dakota St Univ 1960; EdD Univ Wyo 1972; mil/USNR 1962-72; pa/Dir Univ Cnslg Ctr Wn Ill Univ; Lectr Num Univs & Cols; APA; APGA; ACPA; IGPA; AMCHA; N Ctl Assn Cnslr Edrs & Supvrs; r/Rom Cath; hon/Cert Recog, IGPA; Pres Merit Awd, Wn Ill Univ; EPDA F'ship, Univ Wyo; Pub'd Author.

O'BRIEN, ELIZABETH JONES oc/Photographer; b/1903; h/315 Oakland Ave, Waukesha, WI 53186; ba/Same; m/Warren Sylvester; c/Dean; ed/Att'd Eastman Sch Photo; pa/With Husband Operated 2 Camera Shops, 1 32 Yrs & A Studio 18 Yrs; Ext Travel Attending Sems & Convs Photo USA; Wis Div

Master Photo-Finishers Am; Est'd 1928, Secy, VP & Pres 1930; cp/Orgr & Past VP Palettiers; Former Mem & CoFdr Milwaukee Astronomical Soc; Est'd Waukesha Kettle Moraine Geol Soc 1965; Reorg'd Milwaukee Wis Canoe Clb; Chapt 55 En Star; hon/50 Yrs Ser, En Star; Designated "Voyageur", Canadian Govt 1967; W/W Intells Intl.

O'BRIEN, FRANCIS TUCKER oc/Consultant; b/Jan 19, 1928; h/431 San Elijo St, San Diego, CA 92106; m/Gwyneth Jean Smith; c/Ronald Stewart, Arthur Douglas, Peter Francis, Carolyn Elizabeth, Rosemary Anne; p/Francis T and Gwyneth J O'Brien, Crescenta, CA; ed/BA; MDCM; mil/AUS 1946-47; pa/Gen Med Pract in Conslt Role; Geneological Activs; r/Cath; hon/Dictionary of Intl Biography.

O'BRIEN, KERAN oc/Researcher; b/Nov 5, 1931; h/30 Dover Terr, Monsey, NY 10952; ba/New York, NY; m/Barbara Hope Zwickel; c/David Keran, Judith; p/Raymond Keran O'Brien (dec); Mary Elizabeth O'Brien, River Vale, NJ; ed/BS Fordham Univ 1953; pa/Am Nuclear Soc; Am Physical Soc; Radiation Res Soc; Chm, Divisional Hons & Awds Com, ANS 1979; Charter Mem, USDOE Adv Panel on Accelerator Radiation Safety 1965-70 & 1977-; Contbr Num Articles to Profl Jours; Guest Lectr, Ettore Majorana Ctr (Trapani, Sicily) 1978; Reschr of Radiation & Radioactivity in Human Envir, Space & Atmosphere from a Theoretical View; hon/Am Nuclear Soc Divisional Outstg Ser Awd.

O'BRIEN, PAMELA RENEE oc/Social Services; b/Apr 4, 1950; h/5020 S Lake Shore Dr, Chicago, IL 60615; ba/Chgo; p/Raymond O'Brien Jr, Lutz, FL; Geraldine O'Brien Farmer, Chgo; ed/BA; MA 1978; mil/Crim

Spec 910 Mil Intell/Spec 5; pa/Social Sers Coor Dept Human Resources; Assoc Editor & Mng Editor *News-Clarion Newspaper*; cp/Exec Dir Timothy C Evans Yth Foun; Public Relats Spec Alderman Timothy C Evans; CoChrperson Woms Aux; Pres & Treas Yg Dem Org 4th Ward; Exec Bd 4th Ward Regular Dem Org; Dem Wom Chgo; Intl Toastmasters Am; r/Cath; Altar & Rosary Sodality/Corpus Christi; hon/Lions Intl Ser Awd; Debs Ser Leag Ser Awd; Timothy C Evans Yth Foun Spec Awd.

O'BRIEN, WARREN SYLVESTER oc/Photographer; b/Mar 24, 1898; h/315 Oakland Ave, Waukesha, WI 53186; ba/Same; m/Elizabeth Jones; c/Dean; p/Daniel and Emily Carlstedt O'Brien (dec); ed/Profl Photo Certs; mil/WW-I Corp Ofcrs Tng; WW-II Vol; Helped Est CAP Aux USAF Capt 1948-66; pa/Qualified 24 Brs Photo incl'g Aerial, Circuit, Indust, Movies, Others; Opened 1st Camera Shop 1921 Oper'd 32 Yrs; Oper'd E Ave Studio 18 Yrs; Oper'd 18 Brs Comml & Indust Photo; 20,000 Prints &

40,000 Negatives Mus Waukesha Co Heritage; Produced Motion Picture *Transit Mercury Sun* 1953; Profl Photogs Am; Profl Photos Assn Wis; Nat Aeronautic Assn; Nat Fdn Small Bus; cp/Bd Dirs & Orgr Milwaukee Astronom Soc; Seal Aths Clb ; Past Pres & Fdr Waukesha Aviation Clb 1929; Am Legion; Waukesha Kiwanis Clb; Wis Soc Ornithology Inc; Kettle-Moraine Geol Soc; Wilderness Soc; Num Others; r/Presb; hon/Holder 120 Certs, Plaques, Trophies & Appts incl'g: Cert Merit Dist'd Ser DIB, Cert Outstg Asst CAP Waukesha Co Composite Squadron, Plaque Outstg Achmt Histn Waukesha Aviation Clb, Spec Plaque PPA Inc; Appt'd Sr Observer CAP Nat Hdqtrs.

O'CONNOR, HELENE ALLEN oc/Educator; b/Dec 4, 1917; h/360 E 49th Ave, Eugene, OR 97405; ba/Eugene; m/John; c/Megan Allen; p/Challis and Bethel McKenzie Allen (dec); ed/BS; pa/Elem Sch Tchr; NEA; OEA; EEA; VChm Oreg Tchr Standards & Practs Comm; r/Presb; hon/World W/W Am Wom.

O'CONNOR, JOHN JOSEPH oc/Surgeon; b/Jun 19, 1941; h/5101 Westport Rd, Chevy Chase, MD 20015; ba/Washington, DC; m/Patricia Hunt; c/Erin Eileen; p/William R and Ernestine G O'Connor, Buffalo, NY; ed/BA 1962, MD Univ Buffalo 1966; pa/Asst Instr Surg, SUNY-Buffalo; Instr Surg, Georgetown Univ; Asst Prof Surg, George Washington Univ; Chm, Dept Colon & Rectal Surg, Columbia Hosp for Wom; Cnslr, So Med Assn; Contbr Articles to Profl Jours; Am Col Surgs; Intl Col Surgs; Diplomate: Nat Bd Med Examrs, Am Bd Colon & Rectal Surg, Intl Bd Proctology; Am Soc Rectal Surgs; Intl Acad Proctology; AMA; Fellow, Royal Soc Med (London); Treas, Gtr Metro Surg Colonoscopy Soc; Dir, Proctology Res Foun; Dir & Secy/Treas, Intestinal & Rectal Surg Assn; cp/Com Chm, Am Cancer Soc; r/Cath; hon/Hermance Awd, Am Proctology Soc; Display Awd, DC Med Soc.

O'CONNOR, MARY CATHERINE oc/-Librarian; h/193 Earl St, Kingston, Ontario, Canada K7L 2H5; ba/Kingston; p/Fergus O'Connor (dec); Frances Keating (dec); ed/BA Queens; BLS Univ Toronto; pa/Chief Libn Nat Defence Col Canada & Canadian Land Forces Command & Staff Col; SLA; OLA;

cp/Bd Kingston Public Lib; r/Rom Cath; hon/Queen Elizabeth II's Silver Jubilee Medal; Pub'd Author; Hon Grad Nat Defence Col.

O'DELL, V EDWIN oc/General Contractor; b/Dec 23, 1932; h/Hermosa Dr, Pulaski, VA 24301; ba/Pulaski; m/Leora Sweat; c/Tami, Richard; p/Harry and Eunice Parks O'Dell, Pulaski; ed/WVa Bus Col; pa/Pres: Edwin O'Dell & Co, O'Dell Fuels Ltd, Tam-Rik Coal Co; cp/Repub; r/Rom Cath; hon/-W/W S&SW; Personalities S.

O'DELL, WILLIAM GEORGE oc/Minister; b/Nov 8, 1921; h/2709 W Pine, Enid, OK 73701; ba/Enid; m/Wanda Jane Willcoxon; c/Billy, Mary Egger (Mrs Vernon), Debra Bacino (Mrs Mike), Helen Cleveland (Mrs Rick); p/Hubert and Faith Smith O'Dell (dec); ed/BS magna cum laude Wayland Bapt Col; mil/AUS 1943-46; pa/Pres Sedgwick Co; Bapt Min; Bapt Pastors Conf; Recording Secy Ks-Neb Conv So Bapts; Moderator George Truett Meml Bapt Assn & S Ctl Bapt Assn; cp/Commun Betterment Assn; r/1st Bapt Ch, Enid; hon/Meritorious Ser Awd, Ks-Neb Conv So Bapt.

ODOM, ROY HARRIS oc/Executive; b/Oct 14, 1906; h/558 Nelson Dr, Baton Rouge, LA 70808; ba/BR; c/Roy, William, Elsa; p/George and Mary Deaton Odom; pa/Exec Public Relats Soc Am 1969-; Owner Gulf South Adv Agy 1946-; Tech Reports Editor St La Dept Public Works 1939-52; Steel Advtg Assn Intl; Intl Assn Bus Communicators; cp/Prog Dir La Forestry Comm 1952-74; VP Leag Am Wheelmen 1970-75; Pres: La Bicycle Assn 1975-, BR Bicycle Clb 1969-75, La Info Reps 1971; Chm Housing & Hlth SubCom Rural Devel Com; Mason; r/Prot; hon/50 Yr Cert, Masonic Order.

O'DONNELL, DAVID RICHARDSON oc/Civil Engineer; b/Jun 2, 1937; h/PO Box 784, Sheboygan, WI 53081; ba/Sheboygan; c/Irene, Derek; p/Herbert and Elizabeth Minerva O'Donnell, Sacramento, CA; ed/-BSCE Univ Idaho; mil/AUS; pa/ASCE; Ill Soc Profl Engrs; Am Water Works Assn; Lic'd Engr: Delaware, Ind, Ill, Ia, NJ & Pa; cp/Dir Chapt Parents Without Partners; r/Christian; hon/W/W MW.

O'DONNELL, PATRICK ALBERT oc/-Administrator; b/Mar 17, 1934; h/66 Via Cheparro, Greenbrae, CA 94904; ba/San Francisco, CA; m/Elizabeth; c/Kevin, Theresa, John, Terrence; p/Mary O'Donnell, SF; ed/BA 1955, MA 1961 SF St Univ; EdD Stanford Univ 1969; mil/USAF 1955-58; pa/Prof & Chm Dept Spec Ed SF St Univ; Spkr & Conslt Num Profl Orgs; Former: Dir Instrn San Anselmo, Res Asst Stanford Univ, Dir Pre-Sch & Primary Ed Mtn View, Elem Sch Prin Mtn View; St Curric Com CESAA; Early Childhood Com CASCD; Assn Supvn & Curric Devel; Am Ednl Res Assn; NEA; Cal Tchrs Assn; Pres Cal Assn Profs Spec Ed; Coun Exceptl Chd; Am Assn Ed Severely & Profoundly Handicapped; Secy & Treas Higher Ed Consortium; Phi Delta Kappa; cp/Profl Devel Com Cal St Dept Ed; Panel Experts Bur Ed Handicapped US Ofc Ed; Adv Bd Christina B Cameon Sch Physically Handicapped; SFSU: Bd Inst Res Exceptionality, Cabinet Sch Ed, Steering Com Mainstreaming Proj; Pres Marin Swim Leag; Num Other Civic Assns; r/Rom Cath; hon/Pub'd Author; Num Biogl Listings.

O'DONOGHUE, DON H oc/Orthopaedic Surgeon; b/Nov 13, 1901; h/1403 Glenwood, Oklahoma City, OK 73116; ba/OC; m/Ragnhild (dec); c/Donald; p/James O'Donoghue; Janet Fairburn; ed/BS, MD 1926, Hon DS Univ Ia Med Sch; FACS 1933; pa/Prof Emeritus & Chm Emeritus Orthopaedic Dept Okla Med Sch; Dir Sports Med; Orthopaedic Conslt OU & OSU; cp/Dir YMCA; Trustee U Fund; Participant Num Civic Activs; r/Epis; hon/Okla Hall of Fame; Dist'd Ser Awd OU & IU; NATA Pres' Challenge Awd; AOSSM Outstg Contbr Sports Med; Okla Acad Univ Fellows; Pub'd Author.

OGILVIE, MARGARET PRUETT oc/Counselor; b/Jan 8, 1922; h/240 Snead Dr, PO Box 1522, Fairfield Glade, TN 38555; ba/Same; m/Frederick; c/Ida O Haines, James; p/William and Ida Houk Pruett (dec); ed/BA Baylor Univ 1943; MEd Hardin Simmons Univ 1968; pa/Pvt Personal & Marital Cnlsr; Tchr Tex 1943-44; Tchr Cal, Alaska & Germany 1953-66; Guid Cnslr Columbia, SC & Clarksville, Tenn; APGA; Exec Bd & Public Affairs Tenn Mtl Hlth Assn; cp/Dir Crossville Mtl Hlth; DAR; B&PW Clb; Chm Red Cross Vols; Pres Woms Golf Assn; Parliamentarian FG Woms Clb; r/FG Bapt Ch: Mem, Choir Dir, Organist; hon/Pi Gamma Mu; W/W S&SW; Personalities S; Num Certs Apprec Civic Participation; Var Golf & Bowling Awds.

O'GWYNN, OLIVE LILLIAN oc/Educator; b/Jul 2, 1902; h/137 Tuscaloosa St, Mobile, AL 36607; p/John and Martha Andrews O'Gwynn (dec); ed/Grad Troy St Univ; pa/Tchr Glendale Sch Mobile Sch Sys 1921-71; cp/Secy PTA 10 Yrs; r/Jr SS Tchr; hon/Kappa Delta Pi; Christian of Yr 1960; Tchr of Yr, Mobile Co Tchrs Assn; Ser Medal Ala 7th, Birmingham Paper; Lifetime Mbrship Awd, PTA.

OH, KONG TATT oc/Educator; b/Jun 12, 1944; h/71 Poland Manor, Poland, OH 44514; ba/Youngstown, OH; m/Gim Saik; c/Kean Theng, Phaik Mae; p/Soon Guan and Eng Lean Oh, Penang, Malaysia; ed/BS; MB; pa/Asst Prof Opthalmol, NEn Ohio Univ Col of Med; Fellow: Am Col Surg, Am Acad Ophthalmol; Am Med Assn; Ohio Med Assn; Mahoning Co Med Soc; cp/Chm, Poland Bahai Group; r/Bahai.

O'HARE, JOHN MICHAEL oc/Educator; Calligrapher; b/Apr 20, 1940; h/407 Kearney, Atchison, KS 66002; ba/Atchison; m/Miriam Perkins; c/Kieran, Sean; p/John and Catherine Honick O'Hare, Ks City, KS; ed/BA Conception Sem; MA Marquette Univ; Addit Studies; pa/Tchr Rel Studies Benedictine Col; Assn Asian Studies; Soc Italic Handwriting; Soc Calligraphy; Cit & Design Comms Var Rel, Ednl & Nat Bus Orgs; cp/F'ship Reconciliation; Bd Dirs Atchison Art Assn; r/Treas Parish Coun; Adult Ed; CCD Coms; hon/S'ship Marquette; F'ship Fordham; Res F'ship Inst Ecumenical & Cult Res; Grant Inst E Asia.

OHL, RONALD EDWARD oc/Administrator; b/May 30, 1936; h/10 Roxbury Pl, Glen Rock, NJ 07452; ba/Rutherford, NJ; m/Joan Eschenbach; p/Howard and Ella Ohl, Bradenton Bch, FL; ed/BA Amherst Col 1958; MA Columbia Univ 1960; MDiv Union Theol Sem 1964; PhD Cand Univ Pa; pa/Fairleigh Dickinson Univ: Pres' Asst 1976-, Acting Chm Relats Div Univ Resources & Public Affairs 1975-76, Conslt Ofc Univ Resources & Public Affairs 1975; Dean Student Affairs & Instr Ed Colo Col 1968-74; Spec Asst to Dean Men Temple Univ 1967-68; Asst Dean Students & Asst Prof Hist Elmhurst Col 1964-67; Cnslr Grad Students & Head Resident Columbia Univ 1960-62; Comparative Ed Soc; Am Assn Higher Ed; APGA; AAUA; Review Team Onondaga Commun Col, Planning Com Nat Assembly VI; Nat Assn Student Pers Admrs: Governance Com, NASPA Foun Com; cp/Conslt SWn Col & Univ Cal-R 1973; Colo Outward Bound Sch 1969-70; Former Student Asst Yth Ctr & Drug Addiction Ctr Judson Meml Ch; Past Chief Admr Yg Am Artists Prog; Phi Gamma Delta; r/U Ch of Christ; hon/Yg Am Artists Dirs Awd, US Embassy; Blue Key Awd Outstg Ser, Colo Col; Edward Poole Lay F'ship Awd; Rockefeller Brothers Fellow; Pub'd Author.

OLAH, SUSAN ROSE oc/Artist; b/Jun 14, 1947; h/37 Haultain Cres, Regina, Sask S4S4B4, Canada; p/Joseph and Emma Olah, Regina, Sask S4S4B4; ed/Cert Attainment Grad Art Instrn Sch 1969; pa/Exhibited 1 Wom Shows: Galerie Vallombreuse 1977, Galerie Mouffe 1977, Gallery Roof 1973; Wascana Hosp: Art & Talent Evaluator 1970-72, Art Tchr 1969-72; hon/Recipient Awds Regina Enhbn 1960; Minneapolis Awd

Painting 1967; W/W: Am Wom, W, World Wom, Intl Intells; Dic Intl Biog.

OLDHAM, HENRY NEVEL oc/Engineer; b/Apr 29, 1943; h/8801 Willow Hills Dr SE, Huntsville, AL 35802; ba/Redstone Arsenal, AL; m/Wynn Hamilton; c/John; p/Arthur and Florrie Oldham (dec); ed/BS Univ Ga; BAE Ga Tech; MAE Univ Va; mil/AUS: Active Duty 1968-71, Resv Maj Ordnance Corps, Active Resv 87th Maneuver Area Command; pa/Aerospace Engrg AUS Missile R&D Command; Comml Pilot Airplane Single & Multi-Engine Land; AIAA: Assoc Dir, Treas; IEEE; Aircraft Owners & Pilots Assn; Ala Solar Energy Assn; Assn AUS; Resv Ofcrs Assn; Phi Mu Alpha; cp/H'ville JCs: Dir, VP, Pres, Chm Bd; H'ville/Madison Co C of C: Armed Forces Com, Dir; H'ville/Madison Co Indust Devel Assn; Dir N Ala Kidney Foun; VP Civic Clb Coun; Dir Ala Vols Corrections; r/Val U Meth Ch: Adm Bd, SS Tchr, Pianist; hon/Phi Eta Sigma; Outstg JC Spkr Ala; 1 of 5 Outstg 1st Yr JCs Ala; 1 of 3 Outstg Sustaining JCs Ala; Outstg H'ville JC; JCs Intl Senatorship; AUS Missile Command: Outstg Perf Rating, Cert Achmt; Nat Sci Foun Traineeship.

OLDHAM, HOWELL G oc/Administrator; b/Jan 31, 1925; h/803 13th St, Gothenburg, NE 69138; ba/G'burg; m/Mary Ann; c/Jack, Suzanne O Gallaghen, Jeffrey, Gregg; p/Jack and Mildred Oldham (dec); ed/AS Am Col 1948; BA Hastings Col 1950; MM 1958, EdD 1966 Univ Neb-L; mil/632nd AAF Band Perrin Field Sherman; pa/Supt G'burg Public Schs; AASA; NCSA; ASBDA; CNMA; Phi Delta Kappa; Phi Theta Kappa; cp/Kiwanis; G'burg C of C; Am Leg; Elks; G'burg Ser Clb; r/Prot; hon/Rotary Awd Outstg Tchg; IDEA F'ships; Danforth/NASE F'ship; MENC/USOE Ldrship Inst Behavioral Objectives.

O'LEARY, WILLIAM COLDEN JR oc/Psychologist; Educator; b/Mar 9, 1941; h/Rt 1 Hereford Farm Rd, Evans, GA 30809; ba/Augusta, GA; m/Bonnie Tyner; c/William III, Ronald, David; p/William Sr and Julia Chapman O'Leary, Savannah, GA; ed/BA Columbia Bible Col 1965; MDiv Trinity Divinity Sch 1968; MEd Univ Ga 1972; PhD Univ SC 1974; pa/Psychologist VA Hosp Augusta 1971-; Pvt Pract Psychol N Augusta; Adj Fac Augusta Col; Papers Presented Num Cols: Am, Ga, SC & SEn Psychol Assn; SEn Behaviour Therapy Assn; Nat Reg Hlth Ser Providers Psychol; Intl Assn Pers Employment Security; Phi Delta Kappa; cp/VP Lions Clb; Employment Handicapped: Mayors Com 1976-, Del Pres Com; r/Bapt: Deacon, SS Tchr; hon/Recipient Dirs Commend 1976; W/W S&SW; Dic Intl Biog.

OLIVER, C JR oc/Professor; b/Dec 3, 1915; h/727 NW 19th St, Gainesville, FL 32603; ba/G'ville; p/Clifton and Laura Pearl Oliver, Amarillo, TX; ed/BA, MA Tex Technol Univ; mil/AUS 2nd Lt; pa/Assoc Prof Mgmt Col Bus Adm Univ Fl; Conslt Num Bus Firms & Govtl Agys; Nat Panel Am Arbitration Assn; Acad Mgmt; AMA; Am Soc Tng Dirs; Nat Coun Small Bus Mgmt; ASPA; AEA; AAA; Nat Assn Purchasing Agts; Nat Football Foun & Hall of Fame; Alpha Chi; Pi Sigma Alpha; Kappa Kappa Psi; Pi Gamma Mu; Alpha Kappa; Alpha Tau Omega; cp/Fla Com Manpower; Chm Suggestion Com St Fla Merit Sys; Dir Indust Communs Coun; F Clb Ath Assn Univ Fla; Elks; Kiwanis; Am Legion;

Fla Blue Key; r/Bapt; hon/Recog'd Contbn: Alpha Kappa Psi, Fla Bkg Assn, Fla Purchasing Assn; Commun Ldr 1968 & 1971-73; 3 F'ships Am Ec Foun; W/W; S&SW, Intl Commun Ser, Intl, Hon Soc; Am Men & Wom Sci; Dic Intl Biog; Royal Blue Book; Nat Social Dir; Dir Ednl Specs; Personalities S.

OLIVER, DeLORIS HAM oc/Educator; b/Dec 23, 1939; h/Rt 5 Box 213, Spartanburg, SC 29301; ba/S'burg; m/Edwin; c/Pamela; p/J H Ham (dec); Eliza Pringle Ham, Sumter, SC; ed/BS, MEd SC St Col; Addit Studies; pa/Tchr Educable Mentable Handicapped Chd; CEC; NEA; NCNW; AAUW; ARC; MRDD Bd; NAACP; cp/Mtl Hlth Assn; Mtl Retardation Coun; Past Nat Pres Pharm Aux; Jack & Jill Am; Past Pres Lambda Chapt Guys & Dolls; Alpha Kappa Alpha; r/Epis Ch of Epiphany; hon/AKA: Ldrship Awd 1977, Outstg Ldrship 1976; Notable Ams.

OLIVER, JUDITH A oc/Professor; b/Mar 6, 1939; h/120 Deerfield Dr, Wexford, PA 15090; p/Woodrow and Marian Oliver; ed/BA cum laude S'ship Ursuline Col 1961; MA F'ship Niagara Univ 1963; Postgrad Studies; pa/Craft Dept Head & Unit Ldr Camp Christopher Summers 1959-61; Proctor Nurses Residence Niagara Univ 1961-62; Tchr Eng & Bus Grades 9-11 Villa Angela Acad 1962-64; Claims Correspondent US Steel Corp 1964-65; Robert Morris Col: Assoc Prof Humanities 1976-, Asst Prof 1969-75, Instr 1965-68, Chperson Bicent Art Work Search Com, Pres Fdn Tchrs, Secy Humanities Dept, VP Fac Senate, Num Coms; Nat Coun Tchrs Eng; Participant Art Exhibits: 2nd Annual Alumnae Art Show, Art Show & Fair, Pgh Nat Bank, Carnegie Inst Art, Others; cp/Acad Selection Com 25th Congl Dist; r/Rom Cath; hon/Winner Pittsburgh Nat Bank Awd; Num Ribbons Pgh Rose Soc Rose Shows; Nom'd Outstg Yg Wom Am Prog, RMC; S'ship Case Wn Resv Univ; Pub'd Author; Commun Ldrs Am.

OLKOWSKI, ZBIGNIEW L oc/Educator; Physician; b/Nov 24, 1938; h/Villa "Sadyba" 1018 McConnell Dr, Decatur, GA 30033; ba/Atlanta, GA; m/Krystyna Nardelli; p/Joseph and Jane Olkowski, Poland; ed/MD; ScD; pa/Radiation Oncologist; Emory Univ Sch Med: Prof Radiol/Radiobiol, Asst Prof Immunology, Dir Lab Tumor Biol & Clin Immunology; Fellow: Royal Microscopical Soc, Intl Acad Cytology, Kosciuszko Foun; r/Rom Cath; hon/Pub'd Author.

OLOFFSON, WERNER OLAF oc/-Consultant; Artist; b/Jun 21, 1905; h/35-33 83rd St, Jackson Hts, NY 11372; ba/Same; p/Walter and Margot Oloffson (dec); ed/Pract Aviation Cert NYU; pa/Tech Purchasing Accts Pan Am-Grace Airways 1931-37; Profl Ser Dir & Export Mgr Wyeth Labs 1938-45; VP Copy Chief & Sci Dir Med Div Ted Bates & Co 1962-; Conslt Field; Exhibited 1 Man Shows Painting: Hamburg 1957, Monte Carlo 1959, NYC 1960-61 & 74; Exhibited Num Group Shows incl'g Jury Shows: NYC 1942-, Phila 1961-; Am Watercolor Soc; Am Artists Profl Leag; NJ Painters & Sculptors Soc; Nat Soc Lit & Arts; Intl Oceanographic Foun; cp/Queens Co Crim Grand Jury; Advtg Clb; Salmagundi Clb; r/Agnostic; hon/Awds Jury Art Shows; W/W E.

OLSEN, MARTHA BROWN oc/Administrator; b/Jun 6, 1948; h/5025 Hillsboro Rd 7H, Nashville, TN 37215; ba/N'ville; m/Robert Joseph; p/Raymond and Mary Brown, Cookeville, TN; ed/BS Tenn Technol Univ 1970; Dipl Ed Univ Wn Australia 1971; Addit Studies; pa/Asst Commr Revenue Opers Tenn Dept Revenue; Univ Tenn N'ville: Former Exec Asst to Chancellor, Dir Devel & Alumni Relats, Asst Dir Admissions & Records; Former Admissions Cnslr Tenn Technol Univ; Kappa Delta Pi; Mu Phi Epsilon; SAHPER; So Assn Col Registrars & Admissions Ofcrs; Coun Advmt & Support Ed; AAUW; cp/Tampa Bay Alumnae Assn; Yg Execs Coun N'ville City Bank & Trust; N'ville Bar Aux; Soc Gifts Chm Middle Tenn Heart Assn; Chm Gov Lamar Alexanders

Inaugural Activs; U Way Allocations Com; Commun Response Com N'ville Acad Med; r/Disciples Christ; Vine St Christian Ch: Sponsor, Christian Yth F'ship; hon/Outstg Grad, Tenn Technol Univ; Phi Kappa Phi; Mortar Bd Woms Hon Soc; Rotary Grad Fellow Australia; Outstg Yg Wom Am 1971, 72, 74, 76 & 78; W/W Students Am Cols & Univs; Personalities S.

OLSON, DONALD GEORGE oc/Management; b/May 16, 1941; h/10265 E Evans, Denver, CO 80231; ba/Denver; c/Todd; p/George and Ellen Olson, Minot, ND; ed/BS; MS; Cert Data Processing; pa/Mgmt Mtn Bell 1977-; Dir Data Processing Nat Assessmt Ednl Progress 1974-77; Data Processing Mgr Los Alamos Sci Lab 1969-74; Asst Dir Computer Ctr & Asst Prof ND St Univ 1966-69; Analyst/Programmer Bur Reclamation 1963-66; ACM; AAAS; Past Chapt Pres DPMA; Reg'd Profl Engr; cp/Little Leag Baseball Mgr; r/Presb.

OLSON, GERALD WALTER oc/Professor; b/Mar 22, 1932; h/1878 Slaterville Rd, Ithaca, NY 14850; ba/Ithaca; m/Mary Lee Gruber; c/Bradford, David, Eric; p/Walter Olson, Gothenburg, NE; Mabel Olson (dec); ed/BS 1954, MS 1959 Univ Neb; PhD Univ Wis 1962; mil/AUS Artillery; pa/Soil Technologist & Assoc Prof Soil Sci Resource Dept Agronomy Cornell Univ 1962-; Conslt Soil Conserv Auth St Victoria, Australia 1976; Vis Soil Scist Environmtl Geol Sect Univ Ks 1973; Sr Conslt FAO of UN Rome & Iran 1972; Conslt Planning & Engrg Firms Use Soil Surveys Specific Purposes; Conslt Australia, Philippines, Honduras & Others; Adv Bd *Environmtl Geol Digest*; Author Approx 150 Soil Survey & Soil Survey Interpretation Reports & Articles; Am Soc Agronomy; Soil Sci Soc Am; Intl & British Soc Soil Sci; Gamma Sigma Delta; Sigma Xi; Soil Conserv Am; Assn Am Geographers; Conf Latin Am Geographers; Intl Platform Assn; cp/Cornell Panel 10 Fac Advise Environmtl Impact Statement Assessmt; AF&AM; r/Meth; hon/Spec Reg, Ks Geol Survey; Fellow AAAS; Epsilon Sigma Phi; Num Biogl Listings.

OLSON, HAROLD ROY oc/Manufacturing Company Executive; b/Apr 8, 1928; h/12 Stony Point Rd, Westport, CT 06880; ba/New York, NY; m/Angela Davis Hennesay; p/Roy A and Sara Calla Margarita Carlson Olson; ed/BA Mich St Univ 1950; mil/AUS; pa/Mail Clerk, McCann Erickson Co (NYC) 1950, 52-53; Book Promotion Specialist & Mgr of Mag Promotion, McGraw-Hill (NYC) 1953-56; Mgr Mag Promotion, Reinhold Pubg Co (NYC) 1956-58; Space Salesman, McCall Corp (NYC) 1959-60; Pres, Visual Identity Inc (NYC) 1960-68; Mktg Rep, Honeywell Info Sys Inc (NYC) 1969-; hon/Biogl Listings.

OLSON, ROBERT WILLIAM oc/Counselor; b/Mar 5, 1930; h/252 168th Ave SE, Bellevue, WA 98008; m/Seiko Itoyama; c/Troy, Dean, Trina; p/Milton and Lenore Stillman Olson, Bellevue; ed/BS George Williams Col; MA Univ Chicago; Addit Studies; mil/AUS 1953-56; pa/Partner Silfvast & Olson Cnslr Firm 1975-; Jr HS Cnslr Fed Way 1975-; Coor Title III Ed Ctr 1973-75; Jr HS Cnslr Mercer Isl 1967-73; Coor Spec In-Ser Cnslr Courses Univ Wash & Ctl Wash St Col 1969-72; Employment Cnslr Joliet & Chgo Hts 1965-67; HS Cnslr Lockport 1963-67; Jr HS Cnslr Rockford 1959-63; Elem Sch Tchr Matteson 1956-59; cp/Prog Dir WSPGA St Conv 1973; Pres KCSGA 1972; Personal Inventory Cnslg Procedure, Team Cnslg & Contractual Fam Cnslg.

O'MALLEY, WILLIAM JOSEPH oc/Association Executive; b/Oct 27, 1915; m/Wini Shaw; p/William and Alice O'Malley; pa/Owner Orange & Lemon Grove Pauma Val; Treas Hellinger-Nederlander Assn (Theatres); Stage Employer & Moving Picture Operator US & Canada; Backer Several Musical Shows; Sgt Arms Local 751 Intl Alliance Theatrical; Bd Dirs Cath Actors Guild Am; Actors Fund Am; Adv Bd Ziegfeld

Clb; Bd Dirs Inst Am Musicals Inc; Nat Adv Bd Am Security Coun; cp/Will Rogers Hosp Fund; Assn Help Retarded Chd; hon/K of Malta, St Patrick Cathedral; Awd Apprec, St Benedicts Col; DIB; Commun Ldrs & Noteworthy Ams; Notable Ams.

O'NEAL, MARY LOIS oc/Educator; b/Jul 29, 1930; h/2321 Diana Dr, Sherman, TX 75090; ba/Denison, TX; m/Kenneth; p/John and Myrtle Abicht Dalton (dec); ed/BA Austin Col; MEd SEn St Univ; pa/Art Instr Grayson Co Col; Lic'd Preach; Delta Kappa

Gamma; cp/Denison Arts & Crafts Soc; Sherman Art Leag; Spkr Am Fdn Woms Clb; Altrusa; Camp Fire Girls; r/Key Meml U Meth Ch: Adm Bd, Chperson Coun Mins, Ch Sch Tchr; UMW; Local Pastor; hon/Wom Achmt, AAUW; Life Mbrship WSG.

O'NEAL, ROBERT P oc/Lieutenant Colonel USMC; b/Sept 20, 1912; h/Rt 1 Pine Knoll Shores, Morehead City, NC 28557; ba/FM Flant, Staff AWSS, Norfolk, VA; m/Nancy Monroe; c/Robert, Nancy Arthur, Patricia Colyer, Peggy Perry; p/Aimee Ford O'Neal, Santa Monica, CA; ed/BA 1935, MA 1936 Occidental Col; Grad Var Trade & Profl Schs; pa/w USMC 1944-: Aerospace Engr, Devel'd F4B, A4, F14 Aircraft; Ofcr & Instr Trade Maths USN Apprentice Sch Cherry Point 1946; Proj Admr & Plant Engr 1950-52; Prod Control Ofcr 1952; Asst Prodn Ofcr Dept MCAS Cherry Point 1952-; Aircraft Maintenance Ofcr MAG-13, H&MS 13, 1st MAW, Vietnam 1969-70; Currently Staff AWSS Norfolk, VA A/C Maintenance Ofcr; Pres PKS; Other Past Positions; AIAA; ACS; AAAS; SAME; Am Ordnance Assn; cp/Marine Corps Aviation Assn; Fleet Resv Assn; VFW; r/Pres Neuse Forrest Soc; hon/Delta Upsilon; Fellow Intercont Biog Assn; 19 Mil Cits incl'g: Bronze Star, Navy Lttr Commend, Navy Univ Cit; Pub'd Author; Num Biogl Listings.

O'NEILL, JOSEPH IGNATIUS JR oc/Executive; b/Oct 1, 1914; h/22 Oaklawn Park, Midland, TX 79701; ba/Midland; m/Mary Eaton; c/Helen Schwab (Mrs Charles), Joseph III, Kevin, Michael; p/Joseph and Helen Byrne O'Neill (dec); ed/BS Notre Dame; Addit Studies; pa/Indep Oil Operator & Investor Joseph I O'Neill Jr Oil Properties 1948-; Sales Mgr Van Waters & Rogers Inc 1946-48; Spec Agt FBI 1942-46; Spec Agt Home Ins Co 1939-42; Adv Com & Dir Am Petro Inst; Tex Mid-Continent Oil & Gas Assn; Bd Trustees Permian Basin Petro Assn; Indep Petro Assn Am; cp/Past Pres Midland Meml Hosp; Notre Dame: Alumni Assn, Bd Lay Trustees, Law Coun; Citizens Coun Scott & White Meml Hosp; K of C; UN Day Com; hon/Silver Anniversary All-Am, Sports Illustrated; Men Achmt Tex.

ONGWELA, GADO APPOLLO oc/-Teacher; b/Apr 16, 1946; h/Garland D7, Berrien Springs, MI 49103; ba/Same; m/Grace Hully; c/Jimmy; p/Lukio and Hildah Ongwela, Kenya; ed/BA India 1971; MA Andrews Univ 1977; Addit Studies, pa/Kanyamafwa: Secy, Sch Tchr; Nyabola: VPrin, Student Advr, Tchr; r/Seventh-Day Adventist; hon/-Intl Men Achmt.

ONUFROCK, RICHARD SHADE oc/Pharmacist; b/Jul 5, 1934; h/PO Box 457, Ganado, AZ 86505; ba/Same; m/Karen Larson; c/Richard, Amy; p/Frank Onufrock (dec); Mildred Onufrock, Colorado Springs,

CO; ed/BS Univ Colo 1961; pa/Pharmacist: Sage Meml Hosp Pharm Navajo Nation Hlth Foun 1977-, St Joseph Hosp Pharm 1976-77, Aley Drug Co; Comml Artist Illustrations: Univ Colo, Jour Pharm *Pharm Nurses;* Fine Art Exhibits: Colo Springs Fine Arts Ctr, Gilpin Co Art Assn, 1st Nat Space Art Show; Am Soc Hosp Pharmacists; Am Pharm Assn; Acad Pharm Pract; Phi Delta Chi; cp/Adjunct Instr Navajo Alcoholism Tng Prog 1978; Vol Fireman & Co Lt Ganado Fire Dept; CPR Basic Life Support Instr Am Heart Assn; Com BSA; Precnt Com-man Dem Party; Delta Sigma Phi; r/Epis.

OREM, REGINALD CALVERT oc/Consultant; Author; Lecturer; b/Jul 24, 1931; h/5225 Palco Pl, Col Park, MD 20740; ba/CP; m/Edith Freund; c/John, Thomas, Jessica; p/Reginald and Hazel Robinson Orem, Cambridge, MD; ed/Dipl McDonogh Sch; BA 1953, MEd 1957 Univ Md; pa/Former Public & Pvt Sch Tchr; Former Staff Tng Improvemt Conslt Indust, Govt & Ed; Profl Assoc w Planning Res Inc; Conslt AVCO Ec Sys Corp; Assoc Editor *Nat Montessori Reporter;* Author: *Devel Vision For Lifelong Lng 1977, Montessori Her Method & Movemt: What You Need To Know 1974, Montessori Today*

1971, Others; CoAuthor: Prescription For Chd w Lng Disabilities 1977, Am Montessori Manual 1970, Chds House Parent-Tchr Guide Montessori 1970, Others; Adv Editor Chds House Mag; Montessori Lectr; cp/Proj Dir Forest Haven & Grants Spec w DC Bur Yth Sers; r/Wesleyan; hon/9 F'ships & Acad Grants; Phi Kappa Phi; Montessori Commemorative Gold Medal; Optometric Ext Prog Foun; Montessorian of Yr 1972; Contemp Authors; W/W E; Compendium Persons Eminence Field Exceptl Chd; DIB; Men Achmt; Intl W/W Commun Ser; Writers Dir; Notable Ams.

ORGANIST, DONNA MARIE oc/Geologist; b/Dec 29, 1929; h/14 Ritter Ln, Newark, DE 19711; ba/Newark; m/Richard Henry; c/Gale; p/William and Pearl Harstick Builte (dec); ed/BA Augustana Col; Postgrad Studies; pa/Reg'd Profl Geologist; Partner DM Organist Petrographic Lab; Geol Soc Am; AAAS; Phila Geol Soc; Sigma Xi; cp/Past Pres Leag Wom Voters; Treas NOW; hon/Pub'd Author.

ORLAND, HENRY oc/Composer; Conductor; Professor; Writer; b/Apr 23, 1918; h/21 Bon Price, St Louis-Olivette, MO 63132; ba/St Louis-Ferguson, MO; p/Theodore Orland (dec); Hedwig Weill (dec); ed/BMus; MMus; PhD; mil/AUS Liaison Ofcr European Theatre WW-II; pa/Prof Music & Chm Dept; Literary Critic; Conductor Symph

Orch & Chorusus; hon/Pi Kappa Lambda; AUS: Purple Heart, 5 Campaign Stars; Delius Prize Composition; Chicago Music Critics Awd Composition; MacDowell Foun Fellow; Fromm Foun Fellow.

ORLICH, MARGARET ROBERTA oc/Educator; Writer; Speaker; b/Feb 27, 1917; h/421 Anderson Rd, Duluth, MN 55811; m/Eli; p/Henry and Anna Westerman Carlson (dec); ed/BS; MA; Doct Cand; pa/Instr Col St Scholastica; Former HS Prin: Wrenshall, Hermantown; Rep US Edr World Tours & Confs; Nat Pres Nat Coun Pres; Lake Superior Prins Org: Mem 8 Yrs, Secy; Am Fdn Tchrs: Local VP, Exec Bd; NEA: Nat Curric Com, Local Ofcr, Deg St Level; AAUW: Mem Duluth Clb, Chm Sev Coms, Bd, Lectr, Chm 8 Yrs, Others; Alpha Delta Kappa: Past Grand Pres World Org, N Ctl Reg VP Nat Level, Editor NC Newslttr, St & Local Pres, Orgr 28 Chapts, Spkrs Bur, Gen Chm Num Confs, Others; Num Other Profl Assns; cp/BPW Clb: Past Pres Duluth Clb, Sev Chmships, Parliamentn Duluth Clb, St World Affairs Chm, Sev Newslttrs, Radio & TV Appearances, Lectr, Others; UN Hd of Lakes Chapt: Fdr, Chm Mayors Com UN 4 Yrs, Spkrs Bur, Lectr, Radio & TV Appearances, Others; PTA: Past Pres Hermantown, Dist Conf Chm, Prog Chm 15 Yrs, Leg Chm Ctl HS PTSA; Duluth Hts Commun Clb: Sponsor Brownie Troop, Coms, Others; Past Pres Anderson Rose Garden Clb; Coun YWCA: Life Mem, Pers Com; Ed & Beautification Coms Woms Inst; HOLWAC: Orgr, Bd Dirs, Pres; Exec Bd: Leag Wom Voters, St Louis Co Hist Soc, Duluth Woms Clb; Orgr Duluth Playhouse; Sponsor: Hong Kong Orphan 4 Yrs, Greek Foster Fam, Others; ARC; Other Vol Civic Activs; r/Bethel Luth Ch: Mem, Estarl Chm 2 Yrs, Others; hon/Nat Awd AAU Nations; Dist'd Civil Ser Awd 3 Yrs; UN F'ship Awd, Nat Fdn Bus & Profl Wom; UN Peace Awd; Outstg Ser Intl Affairs, St BPW; Plaque Ser Handicapped; Ser Yth, YMCA; Ser Pin, ARC; IPA; DIB; Finalist Duluth Hall Fame.

ORR, JOHN BERK oc/Professor; b/Apr 1, 1933; h/3702 Fenley Dr, Los Alamitos, CA 90720; ba/Los Angeles, CA; m/Thelma; c/Steven, John; p/Robert Orr (dec); Esther Orr, Seal Bch, CA; ed/BA Univ NM; BD San Francisco Theol Sem 1958; MA 1963, PhD 1965 Yale Univ; pa/Univ So Cal: CoDir Curric Devel Proj Humanities Div 1974-, Dir Sch Rel 1970-, Tansey Chair Christian Ethics Sch Rel 1975-, Prof Social Ethics 1975-, Assoc Prof Sch Rel 1968-75, Asst Prof Sch Rel 1967-68; Tex A&M Univ: Chm Dept Phil 1965-67, Asst Prof Phil 1964-66; Am Acad Rel; Am Soc Christian Ethics; Soc Sci Study Rel; Phi Kappa Phi; Conslt: U Auto Wkrs, US Senate Com Ed, Num Others; Dir Res Proj Inter-Cult Ed SW Ednl Devel Lab; Sr Fellow Inst Urban Ecology; Nat Bd Conslts Nat Endowment Humanities; cp/Bd Dirs Victor Gruen Ctr; Chm Comm USC Ctr Futures Res; UCLA: Bd Dirs Humanities & Wom Proj, Bd Dirs Humanities & Urban Crisis Proj, Adv Com Humanities & Public Issues; r/U Presb Ch: Res Conslt & Writer Ofc Ch & Soc, Res Conslt Gen Assembly, Adv Com Ch & Ec Life, Gen Assembly Task Force Quality Am Cities; hon/Num Grants; Pub'd Author.

ORR, PAUL G oc/Administrator; b/Dec 29, 1928; h/30 Arcadia Dr, Tuscaloosa, AL 35401; ba/Univ; m/Edwina Elrod; c/Paul Jr, Dawson, Caryl; ed/BS 1951, MEd 1956 N Tex St; PhD Mich St 1964; pa/Univ Ala: Prof Ednl

Adm & Higher Ed 1964-, Dean Col Ed 1966-, Univ Coun 1967-74, Grad Coun 1969-72, Coun Dean, Num Coms; Res Assoc Mich St Univ 1963-64; Supt Schs Am Sch Foun Mexico 3½ Yrs; Conslt: BESE/PPE, TVA, Others; Num Other Former Positions; Pub'd Author: Books, Monographs, Articles; So Assn Cols & Schs: Com Latin Am Relats, Chm Com Intl Relats; Instnl Rep & Com Intl Relats Am Assn Cols Tchr Ed; UPEP Prog Study Comm Undergrad Ed & Ed Tchrs 1972-; Nat Adv Comms Tchr Exc (Fulbright-Hayes) 1973-75; Bd Trustees Intl Coun Ed Tchg 1974-; Am & Ala Assns Sch Admrs; Assn Supvn & Curric Devel; hon/Cert SEn Ed Lab; Dipl Recog San Carlos Guatemala; Phi Delta Kappa; W/W.

ORTIZ de la RENTA, FRANCISCO A oc/Consultant; b/Feb 17, 1944; h/3621 Albemarle St NW, Wash, DC 20008; ba/Same; p/Francisco Ortiz de la Renta, Hato Rey, Puerto Rico; Aurea Roca-Mattei, HR; ed/MPA, BA Univ PR; MA Cath Univ Am; pa/Am Assn Public Adm; Am Polit Sci Assn; S Atl Mod Langs Assn; Soc Intl Devel; Nat Conf Social Wel; Nat Trust Hist Preserv; APHA; cp/Florentia Publishers; Casa de Espana; Casa de PR; Circulo de PR; Del Cong Hispanic Orgs; r/Cath; hon/S'ship Univ PR; E M de Hostos; E&M Compos del toro Foun Awd; Commun Ldrs & Noteworthy Am Awd; W/W Latin Ams Wash-Bicent Ed; Puertorican Personalities Today.

ORYSHKEVICH, ROMAN SVIATOSLAV oc/Physiatrist; Dentist; Scientist; Educator; b/Aug 5, 1928; h/1819 N 78th Ct, Elmwood Park, IL 60635; ba/Chicago, IL; m/Oksana Lishchynsky; c/Marta, Mark, Alexandra; p/Simeon Oryshkevich, Olesko; Caroline Deneshchuk Oryshkevich, Ukrainian Soviet Republic; ed/MD 1953, DDS 1952, Med & Dental Schs Heidelberg Univ; PhD cum laude Rupert-Charles Univ 1955; pa/VA W Side Med Ctr: Clin Exec Bd 1970-, Ednl Com 1974-, Quality Assurance Com 1974, Chm Med Rehab Bd, Asst Chief Amputee Clin, Chm In-Patient Amputee Clin, Others; Ed Dir & Coor

Univ Ill Affil'd Hosps Integrated Residency Prog Phy Med & Rehab 1974-; Assoc Clin Prof Dept Phy Med & Rehab Univ Ill Abraham Lincoln Ctr 1975-; Pres & Bd Dirs Ukrainian Med Assn NAm Ill Chapt 1977-; Ill Soc Phy Med & Rehab: Exec Bd Dir, Secy-Treas 1977-78, VP & Pres 1978-79; Fdr Ukrainian World Med Mus & UWMM Assn 1977; CoFdr & 1st Exec Secy Sci & Res World Fdn Ukrainian Med Assns; Diplomate Am Bd Phy Med & Rehab; Fellow: Am Acad PM & Rehab 1978-79, Chgo Soc PM & Rehab 1978-79; Num Other Profl Assns; r/Ukrainian-Cath; hon/W/W MW.

ORZE, HELENE WLADZIA oc/Writer; b/May 20, 1909; h/757 Alameda Ave, Youngstown, OH 44510; m/Alexander; c/Gloria Skica (Mrs Daniel), Sandra Copich (Mrs William), Diana Dul (Mrs Edward), Yolanda Madden (Mrs Michael); p/Jan Osowiecki (dec); Stanislawa Pulawska (dec); pa/Writer 38 Polish Folklore Tales *A World Remembered;* Lectr; Translator Polish; cp/Polish Art Clb; PAHA; Koscurszho Foun; CAAA; PNA; r/St Casimirs Cath Ch.

OSBORN, PRIME F III oc/Attorney; b/Jul 31, 1915; m/Grace Hambrick; c/2; p/Prime Jr and Anne Osborne (dec); ed/JD Univ Ala 1939; Grad Army Command & Gen Staff Sch; mil/AUS Lt Col Pacific Theatre

1941-46; Current Reservist Ofc Emer Trans; pa/Asst Atty Gen St Ala; Commerce Atty Gulf, Mobile & Ohio RR; Pres & Chief Exec Ofcr: Louisville & Nashville RR Co, Seabd Coast Line RR Co, Seabd Coast Line RR Industs; Dir: 1st Nat Bank, 1st Ky Trust Co, Ethyl Corp, Seabd Coast Line Industs; Exec Com & VP So Sts Indust Coun; So Acad Lttrs, Arts & Scis; Adv Bd Am Security Coun; cp/VP Univ Ala Nat Alumni Assn; Rotary; BSA: Pres N Fla Coun, Reg Exec Com, Chm Reg 6; C of C: Dir & Past Pres Gtr Jacksonville Area, Dir Gtr Louisville Area; Dir U Fund J'ville & L'ville; Nat Adv Coun Yg Ams Freedom; Adv Coun Spirit 76 Foun; Chm Nat Adv Coun Salvation Army; Trustee Prot Epis Theol Sem; Bd Vistors Berry Col; Deans Adv Coun Purdue Univ; Bd Overseers & Dir Sweetbriar Col; Dir & Trustee Epis HS; Deerwood & River Clbs; L'ville Country Clb; Omicron Delta Kappa; Beta Gamma Sigma; r/Prot Epis Ch: Vestryman, Sr Warden, House Deps Gen Conv, Nat Exec Coun; hon/Man of Yr, J'ville 1962; Man of S 1978; Awd Merit, Ala Bar Assn; BSA: Silver Beaver 1965, Silver Antelope 1967, Silver Buffalo 1972; Bicent Brotherhood Awd, Nat Conf Christians & Jews; LLD Deg 1970; Num Biogl Listings.

OSBORNE, BERNICE DARLAND oc/Artist; b/Oct 31,1941; h/413 Andrew Jackson Trl, Gulf Breeze, FL 32561; ba/Same; m/Frank; c/Donna, David, Mark; p/(dec); ed/Att'd Pensacola Jr Col & Univ W Fla; pa/Est'd Wkshop Bus 1975; Tchg Fac Pensacola Mus Art; Reg & Nat Exhbns; So Watercolor Soc: Newlttr Editor, Dir Wkshop, Bd; Fla & Ky Watercolor Socs; Sustaining Assoc Allied Artist Inc Am; r/Bapt; hon/Best

Show Awd, Fine Arts Mus of S; Gtr Gulf Coast Arts Fest: 1st Awd Mixed Media 1978, 4th Awd Watercolor 1978, Purchase Awd 1978, 1st & 2nd Awd Mixed Media 1977, 4th Awd Watercolor 1977, 1st Awd Watercolor 1976; Cordova Fest Fine Arts: 2nd & 4th Awd Watercolor 1978, Best of Show Awd 1977 & 1976; Best of Show Awd, 1st Fed Annual Arts Show 1978; 3 Judges Choice Awds, Art Public Places; Profl Wom Pensacola; Personalities Am.

OSBORNE, JOHN RANDOLPH oc/Administrator; b/Jul 15, 1936; h/Norwood Acres, Berea, KY 40403; ba/Berea; m/Jane; c/Roger, Sarah; p/Roy and Ressie Oaks Osborne (dec); ed/AB; BD; MA; mil/USAR Capt Chaplain 10 Yrs; pa/Spec Asst to Pres

Berea Col; Nat Assn Col & Univ Chaplains; Nat Inst Campus Min; Am Schs Oriental Res; Soc Biblical Lit; cp/Berea Bd Ed; Former Police Judge; r/Prot; hon/Grants: Ford Fdn, Danforth Fdn, Hebrew Union Col.

OSLER, EDITH PETRIE BROWN oc/Physician; b/Jun 7, 1900; h/835 E Cooper St, Tucson, AZ 85719; ba/Tucson; m/Howard Ray; c/Margaret Fleming (Mrs John), William Brown; p/William and Hattie Shontz Petrie (dec); ed/BS w hons Westminster Col 1923; MD w distns George Washington Univ 1927; DH 1963; FAAFP; pa/Staff Christian Meml Hosp Pakistan 1971-; Tumu Tumu Hosp Kenya 1972; Orgr & Admr Measles Immunization Prog Kenya 1971; Carl Hayden Commun Hosp 1970; Pima Co Hosp So Ariz Mtl Hlth Ctr 1969-70; Staff Sage Meml Hosp 1968-69; Phys & Field Rep Joint Comm Accreditation Hosps 1964-68, Num Other Past Positions; Contbr Articles Med Jours; Fellow Acad Psychosomatic Med; Assn Am Phys & Surgs; Am Phys Art Assn; AMA; Am Med Woms Assn; Am Acad Fam Pract; Ariz Acad Gen Pract; George Washinton U Med Soc; Am Heart Assn; Cleveland Acad Med; World & Ohio Med Assns; Christian Med Soc; Med Woms Intl Assn; Intl Platform Assn; cp/C'land Ctr Alcoholism; Governing Bd Woms Hosp C'land; Bedford Hist Soc; C'land Mus Art; C'land Hlth Mus; Zonta Intl; r/U Presb; hon/Recipient Alumni Achmt Awd, Westminster Col Alumni Assn.

OSMER, DENNIS oc/Color Research; b/Jun 25, 1947; ba/c/o CIBA-GEIGY Corp, Sawmill River Rd, Ardsley, NY 10502; m/Donna May; c/Eric; p/William and Grace Osmer, Paramus, NJ; ed/BA FDU; pa/Mgr Colorimetry Lab Pigment Dept CIBA-GEIGY Corp 1974-; Former Position Spectrophotometry Crompton & Knowles

Corp; Lectr US & Canada; Num Presentations & Sems; Inter-Soc Color Coun; Optical Soc Am; Colour Group; NY Soc Coatings Technol; Soc Plastics Engrs; hon/DCMA Awd 1977; CAD Awd 1978; Pub'd Author; W/W E; Noteworthy Ams.

OSTERHAUS, LEO B oc/Professor; Dean; b/Jan 19, 1920; h/8307 Tecumsen Dr, Austin, TX 78753; ba/Austin; m/Edna; c/Susan, Annette; p/Bernard and Carolyn Osterhaus (dec); ed/BS Ks St Univ; MS

Trinity Univ; PhD Univ Tex-A; mil/AUS Lt Col Med Ser Corps; pa/Prof & Dean Ctr Bus Adm Univ Tex-A; Conslt Bus, Hosps & Govt; r/Cath; hon/Gilbreth Mgmt Awd; Outstg Edr Am 1972 & 1975; Sigma Iota Epsilon.

OSTERKAMP, DALENE M oc/Professor; Artist; b/Dec 1, 1932; h/Box 387, Glennville, CA 93226; ba/Same; m/Donald Edwin (dec); p/James and Bernice Simmons, Davenport, IA; ed/MA; pa/Prof Bakersfield Col; Lectr Univ Cal Ext; 13 One-Wom Exhibts & Num Nat & Intl Juried Exhbns; Cal Printmaking Soc; hon/Recipient Num Art Awds incl'g:

CCAC S'ship, SJSU F'ship, AAUW Awd.

OSTLUND, LEONARD ALEXANDER oc/Professor; b/Jul 1, 1910; h/Rt 6 Box 83, Athens, OH 45701; ba/Athens; m/Anna-Lisa; p/Charles and Bertha Ostlund (dec); ed/BA Colgate Univ 1948; MEd Clark Univ; PhD Ks Univ 1953; mil/USN Y 2/C Secy & Interpreter 1944-46; pa/Prof Guid & Cnlsg Ohio Univ; Cnslg, Res, Translating & Abstracting: 741 Psychol Abstracts; Am Psychol Assn; Cert'd Rehab Cnslr; Lic'd Psychologist; hon/Phi Beta Kappa; Nat Register Htlh Providers Psychol.

OSTROM, CYRUS WARREN oc/Electrical Engineer; b/Dec 3, 1900; h/4816 Pullmane Ave NE, Seattle, WA 98105; ba/Seattle; m/Faith; c/Patricia Stoddard; p/Chas and Cristine Ostrom (dec); ed/BS Univ Wash 1922; pa/Pres & EE Consolidated Electric Corp; Pres C Kirk Hillman Co; Control Sys Oceanography; Mining Power Sys; AIEE; Num Tech Groups; hon/Holder Num Patents.

O'TOOLE, EDWARD THOMAS oc/Microbiologist; Educator; b/Jul 7, 1933; h/1811 Thornton Ridge Rd, Riderwood, MD 21139; ba/R'wood; m/Edith Helen Stimson; c/Shirley Hope, Edward, Eugene; p/Edward Sr and Margaret Dorsey O'Toole, Baltimore, MD; ed/BS; MS; ScM; PhD; RM & SM (AAM); CT (ASCP); mil/AUS Med Ser 1956-58; pa/Am Assn Contamination Control; Am Chem Soc; Soap & Detergent Assn; Soc Cosmetic Chems; Toilet Goods Assn; Royal Soc Hlth; Am & Md Socs Med Technols; Am Soc Clin Pathologists; Am Soc Cytology; AAAS; Am Inst Biol Sci; Num Coms Md Br Am Soc Microbiol; cp/Boy Scout Testing Cnslr; Firearms Safety Cnslr; r/Rom Cath; hon/KKA; Nat Register: Sci & Tech Pers, Microbiologists Am Acad Microbiol.

OTTAWAY, LOIS MARIE oc/Public Relations Specialist; b/Oct 9, 1931; ba/News Ser, Wheaton Col, Wheaton, IL 60187; p/Albert and Clare Ottaway, Viola, KS; ed/BS Ks St Univ; MA St Univ Ia; pa/Contbg Editor The Other Side; Recording Secy

Suburban Press Clb Chicago; Former Pres, VP, Secy & Bd Ill Col Relats Conf; CASE & Evangelical Press Assn; cp/Vol PACE Cook Co Jail; Minority Student Affairs Com Wheaton Col; r/Indep Prot; Deacon LaSalle St Ch, Chgo; hon/Vol of Yr, PACE; Phi Kappa Phi.

OVERBY, GEORGE ROBERT oc/Administrator; b/Jul 21, 1923; p/T E Sr and Virginia Overby; ed/BA 1951, PhD 1966 Fla St Univ; MEd 1959, Spec Ed 1963 Univ Fla; mil/USN Vol Aviator WW-II; pa/Pres Freedom Univ 1974-; Lectr & Conslt Ednl Levels; Former Life Ins Underwriter & Mgr; Headmaster and Tchr Elem & Sec'dy Schs; Prof & Dept Chm Higher Ed; Univ Profs Acad Order Inc: CoFdr Spec Ohio Com, Univ Campus Rep, Chm Nat Com Textbooks & Lit; Former Pres Christian Enterprises; Editor Christian Ed; Fdr & Pres Intl Assn Christian Ed; Fdr Ctr Intl Security Studies Am Security Coun Ed Foun; Author; Editor; Scholar; Am Assn Higher Ed; Kappa Delta Pi; Phi Delta Kappa; NEA; AASA; NAESP; ASC; Nat Coun Social Studies & Assn Supvn & Curric Devel; cp/Bd: BSA, Am Security Coun, Citizens Decent Lit; r/Bd: Christian & Missionary Alliance Ch, Faith Bible Ch, Lords Ch, Child Evang, Christian Boys Clb, Christian Enterprises Inc; hon/Pres

Unit Cit, USN; US Nav Aviation Mus; Fellow: Intercont Biogl Assn, Intl Inst Commun Ser; Intl Biogl Assn; 3 Hon Degs; Num Ser & Ldrship Awds; Num Biogl Listings.

OVERHOLSER, J HOMER H oc/Consultant; Executive; b/Jun 18, 1914; h/4961 Palomar Dr, Tarzana, CA 91356; ba/Woodland Hills, CA; m/Marian Lee; c/James, Sharyl; p/Alden and Nora Liscilla Overholser (dec); ed/Att'd Wittenberg Col & UCLA; pa/Chm Bd & Chief Adm Ofcr Lyricard Corp Am Inc 1978-; Chm Bd & Exec VP Nat Golf Media Inc 1977-; Chm Bd & Pres Nat Golf Products Inc 1977-; Chm Bd & Pres Alphatec Intl Inc 1977-; Pres Brush Away Vending Corp 1976-77; Num Other Past Positions; Bus Partnerships: Contemporary Films 1972-75, Wonder Palms Devel Co 1971-74, Hotel Devel Co 1970-74, Fullerton Hilton Inn 1968-84, Others; Reg'd Cal Profl Engr; Inst Aero Scis; Am Ordnance Assn; ASME; AIM; Am Helicopter Soc; Chm Fuel

Valve Com SAE; Am Soc Air Affairs; Am Soc Air Affairs; AF Assn; Assn AUS; cp/Intl Platform Assn; Repub Party; N Hollywood & Aviation Com Los Angeles C of C; Indust Chm LA Co March of Dimes; Lakeside & Braemar Golf Clbs; Free & Accepted Masons; Lodge Perfection; Al Malaikah & Woodland Hills Shrine Clbs; LA Co Mus Art; Chm Bd Govs San Fernando Wine & Food Soc; Nat Voter Adv Bd Am Security Coun; LA World Affairs Coun; SAR; Ky Cols; r/Prot; hon/Freedom Season Pioneer Awd, WH C of C; Cert Apprec Nat Foun Infantile Paralysis; 2,000,000 Mile Clb, U Airlines; Yg Ams Freedom Awd; Cert Merit Dist'd Ser Bus Devel; Holder Num Patents; Pub'd Author; Num Biogl Listings.

OVERHOLSER, RONALD LEE oc/Actor; b/Jun 25, 1942; h/5104 Hawaiian Terrace, Cincinnati, OH 445223; p/James and Jewel

Overholser; ed/Att'd Num Cols & Univs; pa/Scriptural Character Impressionist; Actor Num Bible Characters incl'g: Messiah, Paul of Tarsus, 12 Disciples & Others in Var Schs, Chs & Cols; Designed 14 Costumes for Protrayals; Narrator "The Good Life" NAm Christian Convs Cinc Riverfront Stadium 1972; hon/Intl Platform Conv Talent Previws; Nat Assn Smithsonian Inst 1974-76.

OVERMAN, FRANCES HENSON oc/Writer; b/Mar 9, 1913; h/107 E Vanderbilt Dr, Oak Ridge, TN 37830; ba/Same; c/Ted Jr, Ann O Creger; p/John and Ida Belle Koon Henson (dec); ed/BA Murray St Univ 1937; Addit Studies; pa/Free Lance Writer; Intl Platform Assn; Fellow Intercontinental Biogl Assn; Intl Com Fine Arts Sect Centro Studi E Scambi Internazionali; Acadamia "Leonardo Da Vinci" Roma; Adv Bd Marquis Biogl Lib Soc; cp/Leag Wom Voters; Bd Var Playhouses & Music and Art Assns; Ldr Y-Teens YWCA; Den Mother BSA; Ldr GSA; PTA; Var Sch Affairs; r/Mem 1st Bapt Ch, OR; hon/Tau Kappa Alpha; Num Dist'd Ser Awds; Num Biogl Listings.

OVERTON, EDWIN DEAN oc/Minister; Educator; b/Dec 2, 1939; h/223 S Ave K, Portales, NM 88130; ba/Same; p/William Overton (dec); Georgia Beryl Overton, Beaver, OK; ed/BT; MA; mil/Army Resv; pa/Campus Min; Instr Rel & Phil; Mission Ldr Proj Challenge; Am Assn Col Profs; Intl

Platform Assn; cp/Pres Beaver Alumni Assn; Commun Forum; St Dir JCs; Portales Tennis Assn; Chm March of Dimes; Repub Party; r/Christian Ch; hon/W/W: Rel, Intl Commun Ser, Intl Intells; Men Achmt; DIB; Intl Register Profiles; Num Other Biogl Listings.

OWEN, DOLORES BULLOCK oc/Librarian; h/218 Antigua Dr, Lafayette, LA 70503; ba/Lafayette; m/Travis; c/Alexandra, Gabrielle, Monique; p/Andrew and Dolores Nicholls Bullock (dec); ed/BA 1954; MS 1968; pa/Libn SW La; Am, La & SW Lib Assns; Documents Com Soc SW Archivists; Author: *Abstracts & Indexes Sci & Technol, Am Guide British Social Sci Resources*; cp/Lafayette Little Theater; r/Unitarian.

OWEN, LILLIAN ECHOLS oc/Nurse; b/Sept 18, 1912; h/1507 W 23rd, Pine Bluff, AR 71603; m/(dec); c/William Jr, Claudette, Sharon Camp; p/(dec); ed/BS; mil/Cadet Nurse 1943-45; pa/Ret'd Reg'd Nurse; ANA;

NLN; cp/Pilot Intl; r/Bapt; hon/Nursing Hall of Fame, ASNA; W/W Am Wom; Commun Ldrs & Noteworthy Ams.

OWEN, JEANNINE DOLORES oc/Clinical Psychologist; b/Jul 27, 1932; h/1925 Glatt Dr, Arnold, MO 63010; ba/St Louis, MO; p/Willis Owen (dec); Dorothy Owen, Arnold; ed/BS; PhD; pa/Am & Pres Mo Psychol Assn; Pres Soc St Louis Psychologists; St Louis Pers & Guid Assn; Assn Wom Psychol; Inst Rational Living; cp/Zonta Intl; NOW.

OWENS, ANDREA SHIRLEY oc/Educator; b/Aug 22, 1943; h/127 Palmetto Pkwy, Belton, SC 29627; ba/Same; m/C Douglas; c/Kerri; p/John and Hattie Timms Shirley, Belton; ed/AA Anderson Col; BA cum laude Lee Col; pa/Pvt Piano & Organ Tchr; Adjudicator Am Col Musicians; Ednl Conslt Nat Keyboard Arts Assn; r/Prot; hon/Acad Music Awd, Lee Col; DIB; Intl W/W Music.

OWENS, HILDA FAYE oc/Professor; Administrator; b/Mar 23, 1939; h/32B Landmark Dr, Columbia, SC 29210; ba/C'bia; p/Floyd and Essie Gay Owens (dec); ed/BS 1961, MAE 1965 East Carolina Univ; PhD Fla St Univ 1973; Addit Studies; pa/Assoc Prof Higher Ed & Student Pers Sers Adm Univ SC 1977-; Dean Students & Professor Mount Olive Col 1973-77; Coor Student Affairs St Univ Sys Fla 1971-73; Mount Olive Col: Dir Cnslg Sers & Prof 1966-71, Cnslr Wom 1965-66; Jr HS Tchr Math & Sci New Bern City Schs 1960-62; Conslt Ednl Related Orgs 1971-; Spkr Var Civic, Ch, Ed & Yth Confs 1955-; Num Wkshops Student & Profl Devel 1963-; Am Assn Higher Ed; Nat Student Devel Coun; Am & SC Pers & Guid Assns; Nat & Treas SC Couns Adm Wom Ed; Am, SC & So

Col Pers Adms; Nat Assn Student Pers Adm: Edit Bd *Naspa* Jour, Prog Planning Adv Com 1979 Nat Conv, Prog Com 1977 Nat Conv, Chm Res & Prog Devel Com Reg III; cp/Bus & Profl Woms Clb Inc: Nat Fdn Del 1976 & 1977 Convs, NC Fdn Bd Dir & Num Other Positions, Mount Olive Charter Pres; Exec Bd Tuscarora Coun BSA 1975-; So Wayne Co Clb; U Way; Cancer Soc; Heart Fund; Cerebral Palsy Fund; Dem Party; Var Polit Activs Local Govt; r/Bapt; Num Ch Progs & Orgs; hon/Outstg Bus & Profl Wom of Yr Awd, Mount Olive 1976; Nat Semi-Finalist, White House Fellows Prog; EPDA Jr Col Adm Awd, Fla St Univ; Fellow: Gen Electric Univ Louisville, NDEA Fla St Univ, Z Smith Reynolds Wn Carolina Univ; Pub'd Author; Num Biogl Listings.

P

PAFFENBARGER, GEORGE CORBLY oc/Dental Research; b/Nov 3, 1902; h/17300 White Ground Rd, Boyds, MD 20720; ba/Washington, DC; m/Rachel Ada Appleman; c/George C Jr, Gretchen Minners, Anne; p/A W and Ida P Seal Paffenbarger (dec); ed/DDS; mil/USNR (Ret'd), RADM; pa/Sr Res Assoc (from Am Dental Assn Hlth Foun) at Nat Bur of Standards; Pres Wm J Gies Foun for Advmt of Dentistry; r/Prot; hon/Hon DS: Georgetown Univ Sch Dentistry, Col of Med & Dentistry NJ, Nihon Univ (Tokyo, Japan); Fellow: Am Col of Dentists, AAAS; Fgn Acad Correspondent, Acad Med Sci (Cordoba, Argentina) 1976; Hollenback Meml Prize, Acad of Operative Dentistry; Awd for Outstg Achmts in Mats for Operative Dentistry, Acad Operative Dentistry; Intl Miller Prize, Fdn Dentaire Internationale; Hon Mbrships: Royal Soc Med London (Sect Odontology), Am Acad of Hist of Dentistry, Carl O Boucher Prosthodontic Conf, Am Dental Assn, Others; Awd for Res in Prosthodontics, Intl Assn for Dental Res; Fauchard Gold Medal, Pierre Fauchard Acad; Outstg Xi Psi Phi Alumnus of Yr 1967; Golden Plate Awd, Am Acad of Achmt; Phi Sigma; Omicron Kappa Upsilon; Sigma Xi; Num Others.

PAGE-STOCKS, BARBARA ANN oc/- Free-lance Artist; b/Sept 14, 1931; h/8903 Mastin Dr, Overland Park, KS 66212; ba/Same; m/Leroy J Stocks; c/Leanne, Christine, Laura, Lisa, Leslie; p/Paul Edward Page, Dallas, TX; Gertrude M Hoppers Page-Berch, Las Vegas, NV; ed/AAB; BS; BA; pa/Tchr Fine Art: Johnson Co Pk & Rec 1975-78, YWCA 1975-78, Mission Studio 1969-71; Tchr Art Grades 4-8 1966-68; Nat Leag Am Pen Wom, Kansas City (Mo) Br; Ks Watercolor Soc; KC Artist Coalition; Graphic Soc NY; AAUW; Photo Soc Am; Tri-Co Art Leag; Photog's Exhibitor Assn KC; Intl Soc Artists; So & MW Watercolor Socs; Gtr KC Art Assn; Num One-Wom Shows incl: Johnson Co Lib 1979, Univ Ks Lib Regents Ctr Dec 1978-Jan 1979, The Brass Boot 1978, Jewish Commun Ctr Contemp Gallery, Margery & Joseph Lichtor Gallery 1978, Plaza Bk & Trust 1977, Others; Group Shows incl: Randall Jesse Poetry & Art Exhibit 1977-78, Overland Pk Show 1977, Plaza Hilton Hotel 1974, 75, 76, 77, Johnson Co Nat Bk (NLAPW) 1978, Woms City Clb Annual-NLAPW 1977-78, Others; Galleries: The Art Works, Hank Smith Gallery, Compair Lapain; Paintings Rep'd in Sev Sts & Waterford, Ireland; cp/Lifetime Mem YWCA; Wom's Caucus on Art; Past Pres & VP Nat Alumnae Assn, Benediction Col; Former Secy MSSC KC Alumna Assn; r/Cath; hon/Artist of Month Awds: Tri-Co (Watercolor) Sept 1978, Tri-Co (Mixed Media) Jul 1978, GKCAA Feb 1975; 1 of 10 Best Paintings in Show Awd, Oak Park 1978; Awd, Garden Centre Assn & KC Garden Clb; Awd, Santa Fe Trail Blazers; Dir 1st Crown Ctr Multi-Media Forum Art Show 1974; Others.

PAISNER, CLAIRE V oc/Editor; Publicist; b/Apr 10, 1933; h/138-17 78 Rd, New York City, NY 11367; c/Renee, Cathy; p/Philip and Hilda Paisner, Newton, MA; ed/BA w hons Cornell; MA Harvard; hon/Phi Beta Kappa; 11 Jour Prizes, Lincoln Univ & Nat Newspaper Pubrs Assn (for Articles Pub'd in *The New York Voice* 1969-76).

PALLADINO, MADALINE oc/Attorney; b/May 5, 1924; h/226 N 27th St, Allentown, PA 18104; ba/Allentown; p/Joseph Palladino (dec); Angelena Palladino, A'town; ed/AB Univ Pa; JD Columbia Univ Sch of Law; pa/Pvt Pract Law 1949-; Asst Dist Atty Lehigh Co 1960-64; Asst City Solicitor, A'town 1952-56; Solicitor: To Register of Wills 1965-, To Recorder of Deeds 1952; Nat Panel Am Arbitration Assn; Lehigh Co Bar Assn: Bd Dirs, Exec Com, Secy-Treas 1958-61, Chm Lehigh Co Law Jour 1977-; Chm Public Relats Com Pa Bar Assn 1964-68; ABA; Pa Bar Assn, Chm & Past Secy-Treas Conf of Co Legal Jour Ofcrs; Civil Procedural Rules Com Supreme Ct Pa; Past Pres: A'town Br AAUW, A'town Quota Clb; cp/Past Pres: Lehigh Co Chapt ARC, Lehigh Co Repub Wom, Girls Clb A'town; Bd Dirs Blue Cross Lehigh Val; Pres' Coun A'town Col of St Francis de Sales; Commun Adv Com LWV; A'town Wom's Clb Legal Counsel; Exec Com Lehigh Co Repub Com; Pres Adv Bd Pa St Univ, A'town Campus; Others; r/Cath; hon/W/W Am Wom.

PALLASCH, THOMAS JOHN oc/Professor, Department Chairman; Peridontist; b/Jun 15, 1936; h/1410 Royal Blvd, Glendale, CA 91207; ba/Los Angeles, CA; Burbank, CA; m/Christine Peterson; c/Brian, Jennifer, Robert; ed/MS, Cert Proficiency (Periodontics) Univ Wash-Seattle; DDS Marquette Univ Sch Dentistry 1960; mil/USN Dental Corps 1960-64, Lt; pa/Pvt Dental Pract (Periodontics), Burbank 1968-; Univ So Cal Sch Dentistry, LA: Assoc Prof Pharm & Periodontics, Chm Dept Pharm 1969-, Dir Pain & Anxiety Control Prog 1972-75, Dir Oral Biol Grad Prog 1969-72, Asst Prof Pharm & Periodontics, Chm Dept Pharm 1967-69; Conslt; Am Acad Periodontology; AAAS; Am Assn Dental Schs; Am Dental Assn; Am Dental Soc Anesthesiol; Assn Pharm & Therapeutic Tchrs in Dentistry; Delta Sigma Delta; Cal Soc Periodontists; Cal Dental Assn; Glendale Acad Dentist; Other Profl Orgs & Activs; hon/Omicron Kappa Upsilon, Zeta Chapt; Intl W/W: Commun Ser, Intells; DIB; Lib of Human Resources; Quest's W/W 1975, Dist'd Citizens of NAm; W/W: Hlth Care, Cal, W; Commun Ldrs & Noteworthy Ams; Notable Ams; Men of Achmt; Profl Pubs; Grantee, Dept HEW.

PALMATIER, ANNA CURRAN oc/- Academic Dean; Teacher; b/Jan 15, 1930; h/PO Box 31245, Washington, DC 20031; m/(dec); c/Carol, Nanette, Thomas, Claire; p/Michael E and Catherine K Curran (dec); ed/BS Upper Ia Univ 1976; BA Pratt Inst; MBS Ctl Mich Univ 1978; pa/Acad Dean Temple Bus Col; Assn of Indep Cols & Schs; NEA; Upper Ia Univ PATH, Mbrship Com; cp/Smithsonian Inst; Former Chperson Heart Fund Area; r/Cath; hon/Grad w Hons.

PALMER, ARNOLD DANIEL oc/Professional Golfer; b/Sept 10, 1929; h/PO Box 52, Youngstown, PA 15696; ba/Same; m/Winifred Walzer; c/Margaret Anne Reintgen (Mrs Douglas), Amy Lyn Saunders (Mrs Robert Leroy III); p/Mildred J Palmer (dec); Doris L Palmer, Latrobe, PA; mil/USCG; pa/Pres Arnold Palmer Enterprises, Div Nat Broadcasting Co; Bd Dirs ProGroup Inc, Chattanooga,Tenn; Pres Arnold Palmer Cadillac, Charlotte, NC; Pres & Owner Latrobe CC, Latrobe; Pres & Pt-Owner Bay Hill Clb & Lodge, Orlando, Fla; Bus Assoc Ironwood CC, Palm Desert, Cal; Bd Dirs Latrobe Area Hosp; Other Profl Positions; Profl Golfers Assn Am; Laurel Val Golf Clb, Ligonier (Pa); Rolling Rock Clb, Ligonier; Duquesne Clb, Pittsburgh (Pa); Oakmont CC, Oakmont (Pa); Others; r/Presb; hon/PGA Tour Victories incl: Bob Hope Desert Classic 1973, 71, 68; Citrus Invitational 1971; Westchester Team Champ 1971; PGA Nat Team Champ 1970; Heritage Classic & Danny Thomas Diplomat Classic 1969; Kemper Open 1968; Thunderbird Classic, Am Golf Classic, Tucson Open & LA Open 1967, Num Others; Hon LLD, Wake Forest Univ; Hon HHD, Thiel Col; PGA Player of Yr 1960, 62; Charter Inductee, World Golf Hall of Fame (Pinehurst, NC); Inductee, Am Golf Hall of Fame (Foxburg, Pa); Bob Jones Awd, US Golf Assn; William D Richardson & Charles Bartlett Awds, Golf Writers Assn Am; Gold Tee Awd, Metro NY Golf Writers Assn; Man of Silver Era, *Golf Digest*; Mem US Ryder Cup Team 1961, 63, 65, 67, 71, 73 (Capt 1963-75); Arthur J Rooney Awd, Cath Yth Assn; Sportsman of Yr, *Sports Illustrated* 1960; Author 5 Golf Books; Others.

PALMER, FORREST CHARLES
oc/Professor; b/Oct 17, 1924; h/60 E Weaver Ave, Harrisonburg, VA 22801; ba/H'burg; m/Lois Mae Davis; c/Forrest C Jr, Beth Elaine, Janet Lorrayne; p/Forrest B Palmer (dec); Marie F Palmer, Beloit, WI; ed/BA Valparaiso Univ 1948; BSLS 1949, MSLS 1953 Geo Peabody Col; mil/AUS Signal Corps 1943-46; pa/Prof Lib Sci Madison Meml Univ, James Madison Univ; Pres Va Lib Assn 1969-70; SEn Lib Assn: Exec Bd, Treas 1974-76; Am Lib Assn Com on Instrn in Use of Libs 1977-79; cp/Precnt Capt & Mem City Repub Com; r/Presb: Ruling Elder; hon/Pi Gamma Mu; Beta Phi Mu; Alpha Beta Alpha; Golden Triangle Awd, YMCA; Outstg Lib Sci Student Awd, Geo Peabody Col.

PALMER, JEANNETTE URSULA oc/- Instructor; b/Jun 21, 1941; h/1242 N Selva, Dallas, TX 75218; ba/Mesquite, TX; c/Michelle; p/E J Jaruszewski (dec); Jeannette Wilkon Jaruszewski, Tucson, AZ; ed/BA Salve Regina Col 1963; Masters (Rehab) Univ Ariz 1971; Addit Studies; pa/Instr/Prog Dir Eastfield Col, Mesquite 1973-; Asst Dir/Cnslr Proj for Multiple Handicapped Deaf Goodwill Rehab Ctr, Winston-Salem, NC 1972-73; Conslt to Def Attys 1971-72; Adj Prof Sch Allied Hlth SWn Med Sch Univ Tex 1975; Invited Observer 1st World Conf on Deaf/Blindness (NY) Fall 1977; TRCA; NRCA; NRA; ADARA; TCADARA; CEASD; RID; NCTRID; TSID; Lic'd Social Psychotherapist, Tex; CRC, Nat Rehab Assn; Other Profl Activs; r/Cath; hon/F'ship, Rehab Sers Adm; Phi Delta Kappa; W/W Am Wom; Profl Pubs.

PALMER, JOHN DAVID oc/Professor, Program Head; b/Jan 25, 1936; h/8310 Athenian, Universal City, TX 78148; ba/San Antonio, TX; m/Robin; c/John David Jr, Elizabeth McMillian; p/Cary D and Helen M Palmer, Austin, TX; ed/BS NWn Univ 1958; PhD Univ Tex-A 1965; mil/USNR Supply Corps, Cmdr; pa/Our Lady of the Lake Univ San Antonio: Prof Polit Sci, Hd Public Adm Prog; Book Review Editor *Hlth Adm Qtrly* 1976-78; Tchr Polit Sci & Public Adm: Univ SC 1965-68, Univ Su 1968-76, E Tex St Univ-Texarkana 1976-78; Conslt: Tex Home Nsg Assn, Autumn Hills Nsg Homes Houston, US Armed Forces Command, US Civil Ser Comm, La Chapt Intl Pers Mgmt Assn, Others; CoEditor *Natural Resources, Envir & Lifestyles* (Monograph); Pubs Com Intl Pers Mgmt Assn; Public Adm NASPAA Fellow, US Dept Housing & Urban Devel in Ofc of Pers 1971-72; VP Sam Houston Chapt Am Soc for Public Adm; Secy SA Chapt Am Soc for Tng & Devel; cp/Chperson Univ Relats Com & Mem Planning Coun, Our Lady of Lake Univ; Mem Var Couns Gtr SA C of C; Former Mem Bd Dirs Texarkana Oaklawn Rotary Clb; r/Meth; hon/Cert of Apprec, Mayor & City Coun Texarkana; Certs of Merit, Chief of Naval Opers; "Live Wire Awd" for Outstg Commun Ser, *Columbia Record*; Outstg Yg Men Am; Ldrship Atlanta; Spec Cert of Achmt, US Dept Housing & Urban Devel; Commun Ldrs & Noteworthy Ams; Intl W/W Commun Ser; Personalities of S; Notable Ams Bicent Era; Centurian Awd, Chief of Naval Opers; DIB; W/W S&SW.

PALMER, RALPH THOMAS oc/Division Chairman; b/Mar 18, 1926; h/1820 Sequoin Dr, Tyler, TX 75703; ba/Hawkins, TX; m/Mary Maxine Jones; c/Angella Marie, Carol Celeste; p/Olaf Gideon and Dorothy Louetta Palmer (dec); ed/AB 1948, MDiv 1950 Tex Christian Univ; MS Yale Univ 1952; DMin Phillips Univ 1973; mil/USNR 1944-45; pa/Chm Div Scis & Math Jarvis Christian Col; r/Disciples of Christ.

PALMER, RAYNOR W oc/Motivational Trainer; b/Mar 19, 1936; h/6875 E Iliff, Denver, CO 80224; ba/Denver; m/Lorraine; p/Raynor Palmer Sr, Dover, NH; Leah Langlois, Dover; mil/AUS; pa/Motivational Tnr-Self Devel; Fdr Universal Secrets of Achmt, "Success Clb"; Create A Success Habit! Prog.

PALMER, ROBERT GERALD oc/Professor; b/May 25, 1936; h/30 Steven Ct,

Macomb, IL 61455; ba/Macomb; m/Doris Leah Denton; c/Wesley, Robert Jr, Virginia Denise; p/Albert Gerald and Leona M Palmer, Phillips, WI; ed/BS, MS Univ Tenn; PhD Ia St Univ; pa/Prof Dept Agri Wn Ill Univ; VP & Treas Key Agri Sers Inc; cp/Kiwanis, Macomb; r/Prot; hon/Borden Awd S'ship; Ser Awd, Sect III Ill Chapt Soil Conserv Soc Am.

PALMER, STEPHEN DONALD oc/Pediatrician; b/Mar 30, 1924; h/Hyden, KY; ba/Frontier Nursing Ser, Hyden, KY 41749; c/Kathryn Love, James Gordon, Stephen Leon, Anne Caldwell; p/Leon Carlos and Lala Keith Caldwell Palmer (dec); ed/BA Univ S; MD Med Col Ala; mil/USNR; pa/Med Dir Frontier Nsg Ser 1979-; Former Clin Assoc Prof Pediatrics Univ Ala-Birmingham; Pvt Pract Pediatrics; Chd's Hosp, B'ham: Past Pres Staff, Bd Trustees; Chief of Pediatrics: Brookwood Hosp, B'ham, Salvation Army Home & Hosp, B'ham; r/Epis; hon/Phi Beta Kappa; Omicron Delta Kappa; Alpha Omega Alpha.

PALMS, JOHN M oc/Scientist; Educator; Dean; b/Jun 6, 1935; h/334 Durand Falls, Decatur, GA 30030; ba/Atlanta, GA; m/Norma Cannon; c/John Jr, Danielle, Lee; p/Peter J Palms (dec); Mimi D Palms, Dunedin, FL; ed/BS; MS; PhD; mil/USAF 1958-62, USAFR 1962-70, 2/Lt, 1/Lt, Capt; pa/Emory Univ: Dean Col Arts & Scis, Prof Physics, Assoc Prof Radiol Dept 1974-, Prof Physics & Chm Dept Physics 1973-74, Chm & Assoc Prof Dept Physics, Assoc Prof Radiol Dept Sch of Med 1969-73, Assoc Prof 1968-73, Asst Prof 1966-68; Other Former Positions; Am Phy Soc; Am Assn Physics Tchrs; Sigma Xi; Sigma Pi Sigma; IEEE; Am Nuclear Soc; Soc Nuclear Med; AAAS; Hlth Physics Soc; Am Conf Acad Deans; Conslt; Other Profl Activs; cp/Adv Com to Bd Visitors The Citadel, Charleston, SC; r/Cath; hon/Num Profl Pubs; Phi Beta Kappa; Omicron Delta Kappa; World W/W in Sci; Am Men of Sci; Am Men & Wom of Sci; W/W: Am, S&SW; Var Col Hons.

PALUMBO, LOUIS ALEXANDER oc/Clergyman; b/Nov 24, 1919; h/c/o Mrs Joseph Lepizzera, 5 Beckwith St, Cranston, RI 02910; p/(dec); ed/AB; MA; PhD; BS; MS; DSc; LLD; DD; DTh; Over 100 Other Earned Doct Degs maxima cum laude; pa/Reg'd Embalmer 1946-; Pres Evang Bible Sem & Col, Italian Br; VDean Thomas Alva Edison Col, Palm Beach, Fla; Intl Bd Dirs Ohio Christian Col; Bd Regents Sussex Col Technol; OMC, Cal: Pres Intl Bd Dirs, Col Comm, Prof Theol,

Phil, Anatomy & Other Natural Scis; Nat Soc Psychol Cnslrs; Gamma Xi Epsilon; Conducted Res Work in Fields of Sci, Natural & Supernatural, Ecology & Nsg Ed; Clin Psychotherapist, Palm Beach (Diplomat); r/Cath; hon/Knight Grand Cross, Order of St John of Jerusalem; Grand Ofcl, Mil Order of St Bridget, Sweden; Knight Cmdr, Thomas Alva Edison Col; Dean & Knight Cmdr, Order of St John Jerusalem; Hon Pin for Free Humanitarian Ser, RI Hosp, Providence; Hon Right Reverend, Thomas Alva Edison Col; Num Hon Degs; Author Num Pubs in Fields of Theol, Phil, Supernatural & Natural Scis; Biogl Listings; Others.

PAMILLA, JEANNE ROSE oc/Orthoped-

ic Surgeon; b/Apr 2; h/320 E 57 St, New York City, NY 10022; ba/NYC; p/Salvatore Charles and Josephine DiGregorio Pamilla, Glendale, NY; ed/BS; MD; pa/Asst Att'g Ortho Surg Hosp for Spec Surg & NY Hosp, Cornell Med Ctr; Conslt NYC Dept Hlth, Bur for Handicapped Chd; r/Rom Cath; hon/Physicians' Recog Awd; Fellow, Am Acad for Cerebral Palsy; Diplomate, Am Acad Ortho Surgs.

PAMOJA, IMANI oc/Writer; Teacher; b/Feb 3, 1947; h/Box 41453, Dallas, TX 75241; ba/Dallas; m/Duane J Thomas; c/Hisani, Idris, Aisha, Jamila; p/Aron Malone (dec); Carrie E Malone, Dallas; pa/Tchr Bishop Col; CoDir Uhuru Cult Devel Ctr; Creative Writing Instr Mus of African-Am Life & Cult 1979; Dir Cult Enrichmt Arts Prog 1978; Tex Poetry Soc; Contb'g Editor *Premise* Mag 1979; cp/Vols in Ser to Am (VISTA); hon/1st Pl Essay Contest, Bishop Col; Silver Medal, Intl W/W in Poetry; Writers Dir; Personalities of S; SCAM.

PAMPLIN, ROBERT BOISSEAU JR oc/Executive in Business & Agriculture; b/Sept 3, 1941; h/3131 W View Ct, Lake Oswego, OR 97034; ba/Same; m/Marilyn; c/Amy Louise, Anne Boisseau; p/Robert Boisseau and Katherine Reese Pamplin, Portland, OR; ed/BS (Bus Adm) 1964, BS (Acct'g) 1965, BS (Ecs) 1966 Lewis & Clark Col; MBA 1968, MEd 1975 Univ Portland; MCL Wn Conservative Bapt Sem 1978; DBA Cal Wn Univ 1975; pa/Pres R B Pamplin Corp, Portland, Oreg; Chm of Bd & Pres: Columbia Empire Farms Inc (Lake Oswego, Oreg), Twelve Oaks Farms Inc (Lake Oswego); Appt'd to Nat Adv Coun on Voc Ed (by Pres Ford) 1975; Appt'd to Oreg St S'ship Comm (by Gov McCall) 1974-; Exec Mem Acad of Mgmt 1973-; Var Former Activs; cp/Trustee Riverview Cemetery Assn; Rewards Review Com, City of Portland; Bd of Overseers Lewis & Clark Col; Bd Regents Univ Portland; Former Activs; hon/Delta Epsilon Sigma; Hon Degs; Small Bus Adm Awd for Outstg Perf as Mem of Winning Small Bus Inst Conslt'g Team 1974-75: Dist Winner, Reg Winner, Nat Runner-up; Dist'd & Exceptl Ser Cit, Alpha Kappa Psi; Student Achmt Awd in Ecs, *Wall St Jour*; Awd for Extraordinary Ser to Dept of Bus Adm & Col of Liberal Arts, Lewis & Clark Col; DIB; W/W in W; Outstg Yg Men Am; Dist'd Alumni, Lewis & Clark Col; AF ROTC Dist'd Ser Awd, USAF; Profl Pubs.

PAN, HUO-HSI oc/Educator; b/Nov 11, 1918; h/76 Edgars Ln, Hastings-on-Hudson, NY 10706; ba/Brooklyn, NY; m/Chao; c/Lillian Yi, Nina Mai; p/Bai-Ming and Won-Ching Chen Pan (dec); ed/BSME Nat SW Assoc Univ (China) 1943; MS Tex A&M 1949; MS Ks St 1950; PhD Univ Cal-B 1954; pa/Prof Mech & Aerospace Engrg Polytech Inst NY 1973-; Asst Prof to Prof Applied Mechanics NY Univ 1957-73; Asst Prof: Univ Ill 1955-57, Univ Toledo 1954-55; Reviewer Applied Mech Rev; ASME; AIAA; Am Acad Mechanics; Soc Indust & Applied Math; Soc Engrg Sci; AAUP; Sigma Xi; Phi Kappa Phi; Others; hon/NSF & NASA Res Grantee; Num Pubs in Profl & Sci Jours.

PANAJOTOVIC, ELENA MARIA oc/Librarian; b/May 24, 1941; h/1615 Crest Dr, Los Angeles, CA 90035; m/Ilija; c/Eric, Sonja; p/Werner and Lutte Kahn; ed/BA Occidental Col; MLS UCLA; pa/Libn.

PANTELL, PHYLLIS ROSS oc/Writer; Editor; Community Relations; Public Relations; b/Nov 18, 1929; h/1466 S Mississippi Riv Blvd, St Paul, MN 55116; m/Robert E; c/Timothy Figge, Theresa Figge, Jill Figge, Julia Figge, John Figge; p/John Ross (dec); Mary Allen Paulson, St Paul; ed/BA Cand Macalester Col; pa/Twin City Coun for Hosp Public Relats; Public Relats Soc Am; Intl Assn Bus Communicators; Minn Press Clb; cp/CoFdr Hereditary & Acquired Neurol Disabilities (HAND Inc); Original Bd Face to Face Crisis Interven Ctr; hon/W/W Am Wom; World W/W Wom.

PAPASAN, MAVOUR RUTH oc/Elementary Teacher; b/Sept 15, 1914; h/Rt 1, Etta, MS 38627; ba/Myrtle, MS; m/Robert Wayne (dec); c/Bobby, Larry, Ruth Stroud; p/Huelet S and Eula M Gafford, Etta; ed/BAE, MMA Univ Miss; Am Col Music; pa/Local, St & Nat Tchrs Orgs; Song Writer; cp/Writer Wkly Column *New Albany Gazette*; Repub Party Activs; r/Salem U Meth Ch: Pianist, Ed Bd, Adult Bible Tchr, Lay Mem to Annual Conf, Del; hon/Outstg Tchr, W Union; Outstg Elem Tchrs Am; Intl W/W in Music.

PAPPAS, NEVA J (pen name Neva Jay) oc/Writer; b/Feb 1, 1917; h/Rt 1, Box C 29, Mammoth Spring, AR 72554; c/Jack J, Ricardo R Lerma, Victor P Lerma, Audrey R Lerma; p/Harrison Flansburg (dec); LaVerne Fuller Flansburg, Alma, MI; ed/Dipl Costume Designing Woodbury Col; r/Presb; hon/Num Awds for Poetry; Poems Read Over: KMOX (St Louis, Mo), WCKY (Cincinnati, Ohio), WHPL-WEFG (Winchester, Va) & in Monticello, Ark.

PAPPER, EMANUEL M oc/Medical Doctor; Educator; b/Jul 12, 1915; h/640 NE 98th St, Miami Shores, FL 33138; ba/Miami, FL; m/Patricia M; c/Barbara Ellen Lupatkin, Richard Nelson; p/Max and Lillian Weitzner Papper; ed/AB Columbia 1935; MD NY Univ 1938; mil/AUS MC 1942-46, Maj; Chief Sect on Anes, Torney Dibble & Walter Reed Hosps; pa/Univ Miami 1969-: VP Med Affairs, Dean, Prof Anesthesiol; Francis Delafield Hosp 1951-69: Dir Anesthesiol, Vis Anesthesiologist; Other Former Positions; Fellow Fac Anesthesiologists Royal Col Surgs, Royal Soc Med; NY Acad Med; Am Surg Assn; Am Soc Anesthesiologists, Pres 1967-68; NY St Soc Anesthesiologists, Past Pres; NRC; Am Col Anesthesiologists; Am Soc Pharm & Experimtl Therapeutics; AMA; NY Acad Scis; NY Co Med Soc; Am, NY Socs Anesthesiologists; AAAS; Am Assn Thoracic Surg; Harvey Soc Am Soc Clin Investigation; Am Thoracic Soc; Assn Univ Anesthetists; CoFdr, 1/Pres; Pan Am Med Assn; Assn Anaesthestists Gt Brit & Ireland; Other Profl Activs; hon/Silver Medal, City of Paris; Diplomate, Am Bd Anesthesiol; Phi Beta Kappa; Sigma Xi; Alpha Omega Alpha; Author Sci Papers Pub'd in Var Med Jours, 3 Textbooks; W/W in Am; Est'd Annual Lectureships in his hon, Columbia Univ & UCLA; Hon Pres European Cong of Anes (Paris, France) 1978; Hon Mem, European Acad Anes (Paris); Others.

PARCH, JOSEPH RAYMOND oc/Gas Distribution Engineer; b/Mar 1, 1930; h/6501 Sherborn, Parma Heights, OH 44130; ba/Cleveland, OH; m/Ruth Anne; c/Roberta A, Andrea L; p/Joseph C and Josephine K Parch, Bedford, OH; ed/BME 1952, MEngrg 1973 Univ Louisville; mil/USN 1952-55, Lt (jg); USNR 1955-68, Lt; pa/Gas Distribution Engr E Ohio Gas; Cleve Engrg Soc, Chm Public Utilities Div 1974-75; ASME; Profl Engr Ohio 1962; cp/SW Music Assn, Former Treas; Parma Fathersingers; Fdr & Past Pres E Ohio Toastmasters Clb; r/Rom Cath; hon/Pub'd Author.

PARHAM, DOROTHY I oc/Kindergarten Teacher; b/Apr 2, 1935; h/Rt 1, Dyersburg, TN 39024; p/Bertie Owen, Memphis, TN; ed/BS Lambuth Col 1974; MEd, Memphis St Univ.

PARHAM, GLADYS BOLT oc/Park Technician; b/Jun 10, 1906; h/1411 W St SE, Washington, DC 20020; ba/Wash DC; m/Peter J (dec); c/Martha, Percy, Peter, Betty, Johnnie, Curtis; p/William Robert and Annie C Young, Warrington, NC; pa/Technician Nat Capital Pk Ser, Frederick Douglass Home 1965-78; Food Ser Spec Diets Andrews AFB, Malcomb Graw Hosp 1959-65; Food Ser on Spec Diets Walter Reed Army Med Ctr 1945-59; cp/Ldr Cub Scouts; Caretaker Frederick Douglass Home, Frederick Douglass Meml & Hist Assn Inc; Red Cir Missionary Soc Ldr; r/Bethlehem Bapt Ch: Mem, Pres E B Delaney Missionary Soc, Chm,

Trustee Bd 1971-77, Orgr Boy Scout Troop; Pres DC Bapt Conv 1969-73; Chm Fund of Renewal Com Progressive Bapt Conv 1975; hon/Commend for Meritorious Civilian Ser, Dept of War 1946; Outstg Ser to Frederick Douglass Home, Anacostia Bus & Profl Assn; Outstg Perf in Human Ser, Nat Task Force for Sr Citizens; Outstg Citizen Awd for Ser to Ed, Mission Moten Ednl Opport Ctr; Awd for Faithful Ser on Bd Trustees, Bethlehem Bapt Ch.

PARHAM, RUBY INEZ McCOLLUM oc/Retired Teacher; b/Nov 4, 1914; h/215 S College, Tahlequah, OK 74464; m/Rufus K McCollum (dec); 2nd Jewell A Parham; c/Bill, Donal, Garry, Anne Garrett; p/Ola Thomas and Bursha Bell Culver Myers (dec); ed/BS 1940; Master of Tchg 1955; Grad Palmer Writer's Sch in Non-Fiction 1973; pa/Ret'd;

Tchr Eng Dept Westville Jr & Sr HS, Tahlequah; OEA; NEA; Kappa Kappa Iota; Delta Kappa Gamma; cp/Precnt Wkr; Election Clerk; Worthy Matron OES; Past Pres Rebekah Lodge; r/So Bapt; 1st Bapt Ch, Tahlequah: Mem; hon/W/W: Am Wom, S; DIB; Dir Ednl Specialists; Featured in Newspaper.

PARHAM, WILLIAM HAROLD oc/Administrator; Executive; b/Jan 5, 1924; h/3946 McGirts Blvd, Jacksonville, FL 32210; ba/J'ville; m/Mary L Copeland; c/Mary, Will Jr; p/Mr J R Parham Sr (dec); Mrs J R Parham Sr, J'ville; ed/AB John B Stetson Univ 1949; Grad Armed Forces Info Sch 1951; DHA (Honoris Causa) Univ Fla 1974; mil/AUS Active Duty 1943-46, 1951-52; 2 Battle Stars WWII & Korean War; Other Medals & Cits; pa/Atty-in-Fact Fla Phy Ins 1976-; Secy-Treas Fla Med Foun 1976-; Chm Bd Profl Ins Mgmt Co 1975-; Asst Treas Fla Med Polit Action Com 1975-; Dir & Secy-Treas Alpendorf Inc 1973-; Pres FLAMEDCO Inc 1972-; Dir SE 1st Bk J'ville 1963-; Fla Med Assn Inc 1949-; Exec VP 1958; Exec VP Fla Med Foun 1958-; Chm Bd Dirs Harlan-Med Inc 1972-76; Other Former Activs; Pres: Am Assn Med Soc Execs 1968-69, Profl Conv Mgmt Assn 1968-71; Assoc Mem So Med Assn; Affil Mem AMA; Fla & Am Soc Assn Execs; Fla Assn Life & Casualty Underwriters; cp/Fla Yacht Clb; Ye Mystic Revellers; Univ Clb J'ville; River Clb; Ponte Vedra Clb; r/Ortega Meth Ch; hon/W/W S&SW.

PARK, CYNTHIA oc/Sociologist; Educator; Art Consultant; b/Feb 7, 1925; h/59 Trumbull St, New Haven, CT 06510; ba/New Haven; p/Robert Hirum Park, Cape Cod, MA; Miriam Nelson Park, Pembroke, MA; ed/BA New Sch Social Res; MS Ferkauf Grad Sch Ed, Yeshiva Univ; MA Hunter Col, CUNY; PhD Cand; pa/Asst Prof Sociol; Cert'd Sec'dy Social Studies Tchr; Am Sociol Assn; En Sociol Soc; AAUP; Am Fdn Musicians; cp/Polit Party Activs; Vol Cnslr & Tutor to Disadvantaged in Arts; r/Prot; hon/Grants-in-Aide, Job S'ships, Nat Def Student Loan; Fulbright Awd for Grad Study in Finland, Helsinki Univ; Others.

PARK, MARY CATHRYNE oc/College Professor; b/Jun 18, 1918; h/450 Norwood St, Merritt Island, FL 32952; ba/Cocoa, FL; p/J Theodore and Lucie C Park; ed/AB w hons; AM; PhD; pa/Brevard Commun Col: Prof Eng 1960-, Prof Humanities & Hist, Chm Div Social Scis; Assoc Prof Eng Fla So Col,

Lakeland, Fla 1955-60; Assoc Prof Eng Stetson Univ, DeLand, Fla 1952-55; Other Former Positions; Life Mem Mod Lang Assn; AAUW: Fdr & Pres Salisbury (NC) Chapt, Liaison Ofcr Fla So Col; Del Co (Pa) Inst Sci; Am Studies Assn; Chm S Atl Mod Lang Assn 1955, 58; Eng Spkg Union; SEn Am Studies Assn; Higher Ed Dept, Fla Ed Assn; Fla Acad of Sci; Fla Tchrs of Hist; Fla Anthropol Soc; Pres Indian River Anthropol Soc 1969; Appt'd to Gov's Comm on Hist 1968-; Dir Shelton Col Cont'g Ed, Cape May, NJ 1978; Exec Secy Assn Cols, Intl Accreditation Agy, Intl Coun Christian Chs 1978; Dir OEDP Com, Brevard Co Ec Devel Adm Projs & Funds; Conslt; Other Profl Activs; cp/Alpha Gamma Delta; DAR, Regent Col Arthur Erwin Chapt; Am Cancer Soc: Pres Brevard Co, Dir Fla Cancer Soc; Spkr Brevard Commun Col Spkrs' Bur; Budget & Fin Com Brevard Co UF; Charter Mem & Dir Brevard Co YMCA; Dir Coun on Aging, Brevard Co; Pianist: Cocoa Kiwanis Clb, Rockledge Kiwanis Clb, Cocoa Rotary Clb; Others; r/1st U Meth Ch, Cocoa: Ofcl Bd, Lic'd to Preach; hon/Dist'd Ser Awd, Am Cancer Soc; Sigma Tau Delta; Pi Gamma Mu; Alpha Psi Omega; Sigma Pi Alpha; Alpha Theta Chapt Delta Kappa Gamma; Biogl Listings; Others.

PARK, VIRGINIA R oc/Teacher of Dentistry; b/Jul 27, 1920; h/1081 Beverly Rd, Jenkintown, PA 19046; ba/Philadelphia, PA; c/Todd Park Merolla, Richard Park Merolla; p/Matthew Park Jr (dec); Caroline R Rich, Phila; ed/DDS Univ Pa Sch Dental Med 1942; pa/Univ Pa Sch Dental Med: Asst Prof Restorative Dentistry, Tchr 1951-, Dir Course for Dental Assts 1956-69; Vis Dentist Babies' Hosp Phila 1951-58; Asst Dentist Chd's Hosp Phila 1952; Active Med Staff Chd's Heart Hosp Phila 1963-; Pres Assn Am Wom Dentists 1970-71; Univ Pa Wom's Dental Soc: Fdr 1952, Pres 1963-67; Pres Pa Assn Dental Surgs 1973-74; Intl Assn for Dental Res, Dental Mats Group; Acad Stomatology; Univ Pa Wom's Fac Clb; AAUP; Pvt Pract Royersford, Pa 1942-46; cp/Spkr: HSs, PTA Meetings, Local Orgs; r/Epis; hon/Omicron Kappa Upsilon, Eta Chapt; Author A Textbook for Dental Assts, 1966 (2nd Edition 1975); Fellow, Intl Col Dentists.

PARKE, SCOTT JAMES oc/Student; b/Mar 26, 1958; h/529 Minette Ln, Chicago Heights, IL 60411; p/David J Jr and Eleanor E Parke, Chgo Hgts; ed/Att'g En Ill Univ; cp/En Ill: Swim Team Mem 1976-77, Tennis Team Mem 1978-79; Sr Life Saving & Water Safety Cert'd, Cert'd Lifeguard 1976; Progressive Swimming Instr Park Forest Aqua Ctr 1977, 78, 79; Other Activs; r/Luth; hon/Outstg Sr Ath in Swimming & Tennis, Bloom Twp HS; Park Forest YMCA Aqua Ctr: Trophy (Swim Team Mem), Outstg Swimmer, High Point Scorer; Swim Meet Medals, Des Plaines Val Conf 1976; 5th Pl & 2nd Pl, Ribbon Almost Anything Goes Team Competition (1978, 79).

PARKER, BOOTS LEE FARTHING HIXSON oc/Hostess; Model; Restaurateur; Humanitarian; Philanthropist; b/Dec 25, 1929; h/7421 Daniel Webster Dr, Orlando, FL 32807; Box 246, Boone, NC 28607; ba/Titusville, FL; m/Paul Hixson (dec); 2nd W Dale Parker; p/Lula Farthing; ed/Att'd Ohio St Univ; pa/Former Chief Cashier Firestone's U Trading Co & Ofcl Hostess Firestone Intl, Monrovia, Liberia (W Africa); Formerly Assoc'd w M O'Neil Co, Akron, Ohio; Former Employee: Holiday Inns Am, F W Woolworth's, Ronnie's (Orlando); Pres Multiple Sers (Mgmt Conslt, Public Relats & Pub'g Firm, Wholesale Retail Supplier of Many Doll Prods); cp/Royal Oak Golf & CC; Other CC Mbrships; Benevolent & Patriotic Order of Does; NY Vets Police Assn; Fla Frat Order of Police; Va Sheriffs Assn; Former Mem Dem Exec Com; hon/Intl Humanitarian Awd, London, England; Dist'd Ser Awd, Fla Sheriffs Assn; Hon Col, Ala St Militia; Hon Navy Recruiter, US Navy Dept; Personalities of S; Nat Social Dir; World W/W Wom; Notable Ams Bicent Era; DIB.

PARKER, CLYDE J oc/Semi-Retired; Insurance Agent; Public Relations & Advertising; b/Mar 26, 1908; h/Rt 11, Box 206B, Crossville, TN 38555; ba/Same; m/Clara Brewer; c/Marlyn Ann, Janet Clara; p/Aaron Vernon and Fannie Zoe Parker (dec); ed/Att'd Var Cols & Univs; pa/Highland Fed Savs & Ln Assn, C'ville: Dir, Exec VP 1961-77; Ins Bus, Stone Broker, C'ville 1954-61; Assoc'd w Ideal Furniture Co, C'ville 1946-54; Owner Cumberland Cleaners, C'ville; Other Former Positions; cp/Mayor C'ville 1951-52; Bd Dirs Cumberland Clin Foun; Cumberland Co Chapt CCARC; UF; Hilltoppers Inc; Janet C Clark Meml Home for Retard Men; Kiwanis: Past Pres, Lt Gov Ky & Tenn, Dist Div IV; Fairfield Glade CC; Good Neighbor Clb; Masons; Past Patron OES; r/1st U Meth Ch: Trustee, SS Dept Activs, Choir, Chancel Hand Bell Group; hon/Outstg Pres, Kiwanis; Apprec Cert, C'ville Lodge 483 Masons; Achmt Awd, Cumberland Co Cancer Crusade; Grand Cross of Colors Deg, OES.

PARKER, DOROTHY oc/Commissioner; b/Jan 30, 1916; h/1600 S Joyce St, Arlington, VA 22202; ba/Washington, DC; m/Benjamin M; p/Bernard Johnson and Clara Landsman Botwen (dec); ed/BA Barnard Col 1936; JD Columbia Law Sch 1938; pa/Commr US Parole Comm (Appt'd by Pres Ford) 1976-; Minority Coun US Senate Com on Judiciary, Subcom on Refugees & Escapees 1974-76; Minority Counsel US Senate Com on Judiciary, Subcom on Constitutional Amendmts 1970-74; Other Former Positions; Admitted to Bar St of NY; Bars: Supr Ct US, US Cts of Appeals 2nd Circuit & DC, US Ct of Claims, US Dist Ct for DC.

PARKER, E CAMILLE KILLIAN oc/Ophthalmologist, Physician, Surgeon; b/Jun 28, 1918; h/2500 E Broadway, Logansport, IN 46947; ba/L'port; m/Francis W Jr; c/Paul Killian, Clyde Killian; p/John Vincent Hill, Findlay, OH; Myrtle Kagy Hill (dec); ed/MD; pa/Fellow Am Acad Ophthal & Otolaryngol; Charter Mem Soc Eye Surgs; Ind St Med Assn; Ind Acad Ophthal & Otolaryngol; AMA; Mtl Guid Bd 1967-69; Diplomate Am Bd Ophthal; Meml Hosp Med Staff Secy 1959; Pres Cass Co Med Soc 1971; Chm Cont'g Med Ed Prog & Lib, Cass Co Med Soc & Staff Meml Hosp; VP Acad Ophthal 1978; Pres Ind Acad Ophthal 1979-80; cp/Past Pres L'port Coun for Public Schs; Leg Affairs Com C of C; Repub Woms Clb; r/Meth: Chm Social Concern 1963-65, Ofcl Bd 1961-65; hon/Ser Awd, Culver Mil Acad; Physicians Recog Awd, AMA.

PARKER, JACK DuPREE oc/Gynecologist; b/Sept 28, 1904; h/4 Harvest Ln, Greenville, SC 29601; ba/G'ville; m/Anne; c/Kitty, Noel; p/William Harrison and Anna B DuPree Parker (dec); ed/BS; MD; pa/Gynecologist: G'ville Hosp Sys, St Francis Hosp; r/Epis; hon/Diplomate, Am Bd Ob/Gyn; Fdg Fellow: Am Col Ob/Gyn, S Atl Assn Ob/Gyn; Fellow Am Col Surg.

PARKER, JACQUELYN SUSAN oc/Aeronautical Engineer; b/Jul 4, 1960; h/4605 NASA Rd 1 #4-308, Seabrook, TX 77586; p/William Dale and Boots Lee Farthing Parker; ed/BS Math, BS Computer Sci Fla Tech Univ; Art, Drama & Music Studies w Elem Tchr, NYC; Used sign lang at age 7; pa/1 of 5 Va Students to Produce, Film & Edit a Motion Picture for that St; Tchrs Aide; Ext Travel: US, Mexico, Canada, Europe, Bahamas; Active in Efforts to Achieve Career as an Astronaut; Currently working w NASA, LBJ Space Ctr, Houston, Tex; cp/CAP; Rec'd Pilots Lic 1977; Nat Space Inst; Mensa Intl; Reads Music, Plays 2 Instruments; Expert Swimmer & Diver, Horsewom; Water & Snow Skier; hon/Deans List; Cert Merit in Ed, Cambridge, England 1976; Mensa Register; Notable Ams Bicent Era; Intercont Biogs; DIB; Nat Social Dir.

PARKER, JAMES LEE FITZGERALD oc/Visiting Teacher; School Social Worker; b/Jan 25, 1949; h/Rt 4, Box 1-AA, Hillsville,

VA 24343; ba/Galax, VA; m/Rita Cox; c/George, Christina; p/Lee T F Parker (dec); Kitty S Parker Smith, Vienna, VA; ed/BA 1971, MA 1975 VPI&SU; mil/USAR Capt, Asst Trans Ofcr; Va Corps of Cadets; pa/Galax, Va, Nat Ed Assns; cp/BSA, Eagle Scout; Toastmasters Clb; Lions Clb; Yg Dems; JCs; r/Meth: Ch Choir Dir; hon/Post-grad Ednl Cert; Mil Lttrs of Commend; AUS Field Arty & Trans Certs; Expert Rifleman; Nat Def & Army Achmt Medal.

PARKER, LOISLEE M oc/Teacher; b/May 14, 1929; h/1601 S Shade Ave, Sarasota, FL 33579; m/L L; c/2 Chd; p/Oran and Grace Cutler; ed/BS; MEd; pa/Elem Tchr & Hlth Coor; St Pres Kappa Kappa Iota 1975-77; Kappa Nat Public Relats Bd; SC Tchrs Assn 1975-77; Grade Level Chm 1974-77; Kappa St Conv Chm 1975; Kappa St Bd 1977-78; cp/Bd Dirs Coun on Aging; Former Mem Co Report Card Revision Com; r/Prot; hon/Kappa Tchr of Yr; Dist'd Ctl Mich Univ Alumni Recog Awd; Given Cherokee Indian name by Ho-Chee-Nee, "Indian Princess"; Outstg Elem Tchr Am; Meritorious Ser to Mankind Awd; Reg Tchr Awd; 1961 Tchr Awd for Achmt & Improving Ed through Use of TV; Red Cross Recog Cert; CMU Alumni Ambassador; Personalities of S; DIB; W/W Among Am Edrs.

PARKER, NANCY B oc/Student; b/Dec 30, 1944; h/4805 Deeson Rd, Lakeland, FL 33805; p/Homer N Parker, Lakeland, FL; ed/AA Hillsborough Commun Col; hon/Phi Theta Kappa; National Dean's List; HCC Dean's List.

PARKER, PHYLLIS HEPBURN oc/Social Worker; b/Aug 1, 1948; h/5454 Copley Sq Rd, Grand Blanc, MI 481139; m/Eugene Sr; c/Eugene Jr, Patrick; p/Spencer Sr and Fannie Johnson Hepburn, Petersburg, VA; ed/BA; MA; pa/Mem Alcoholism Spec Interest Com, APGA; Am Rehab Cnslg Assn; Reviewer APGA Jour; Rape Crisis Cnslr; r/Prot; hon/Lttr of Commend; Outstg Achmt Awds; W/W S&SW.

PARKER, ROBERT MILES oc/Artist; Author; b/Aug 22, 1939; h/1929 Front St, San Diego, CA 92101; ba/San Diego; p/Robert Miles Parker (dec); Helen Elizabeth Treakle Parker Bratton, San Diego; ed/AB Col William & Mary 1961; MA San Diego St Univ 1963; pa/Profl Artist, Restoration & Design Conslt 1974-; Author & Artist Book *Images of Am* 1979; Art Therapist Commun Mtl Hlth

Day Treatmt Ctr 1970-74; Art Instr SD Commun Cols 1967-70; Instr Eng & Art Carlsbad Jr High, Chm Art Dept 1964-66; cp/Art Guild of Fine Arts Gallery: Mem, Former VP; Fdr & 1/Pres Save Our Heritage Org, San Diego; Victorian Soc Am; Nat Trust for Hist Preserv; Uptown Planners, San Diego; hon/Cert of Recog, Co Bd Supvrs (Co San Diego); One Man Shows incl: Mont Hist Soc (Helena, Mont), Dahl Fine Arts Ctr (Rapid City, SD), Orr's Gallery (San Diego), Brown Studio (New York City).

PARKER, THOMAS (TIM) LYLES oc/Criminal Justice Teacher; b/Oct 3, 1924; h/3807 Bethel, Houston, TX 77002; ba/Houston; m/Clara M; c/Thomas Jr, Duane, Jim, Diane; p/Timothy McCuen and Mary Parker (dec); ed/LLB, JD 1957 S Tex Col

of Law; mil/USN 1943-45, Pacific; 3 Battle Stars; pa/Crim Justice Tchr Madison Sr HS, Houston; US Marshal (Dep), So Dist Tex 1978 (Ret'd); Crim Def Investigator, Harris Co Dist Atty's Ofc 1954-57; Houston Police 1948-54; Previously Employed by 200+ Houston Attys & 22 Judges; 31 Yrs in Field of Crim Justice; r/Prot; hon/Recommended by 31 US Senators as Dir of FBI 1977; Hon'd for Dedicated Ser to Justice Dept, US Atty Gen.

PARKER, WALLACE O'NEIL oc/Director; b/Oct 4, 1931; h/3750 Gurley Rd, Jacksonville, FL 32211; ba/J'ville; m/Annie Fay Morton; c/Neil, Donna Lynn, Suzanne Leigh; p/Robert E Lee Parker, Hubert, NC; Essie Marie Holland Parker (dec); ed/BS NC St Col 1959; MS NC St Univ 1965; mil/AUS 1952-54, PFC; pa/Res Dir Fla Pub'g Co 1972-; Res Dir J'ville Area C of C 1965-75; Res Planner Div Commun Planning NC Dept Conservation & Devel's Div of Commun Planning; Dir Info & Public Relats NC Farm Bur Fdn 1960-62; Fdr & Pres J'ville Area Res Assn 1966-68; Pres Fla Crown Coun C of C 1967-68; Pres Am C of C Reschrs Assn 1971-72; Chm Task Force on Ins & Sts & Hwys 1977-78; Bd Mem J'ville Advt'g Fdn; Secy-Treas J'ville Bus Devel Corp 1977-78; Bd Mem J'ville Area C of C 1974-77; cp/YMCA; Deerwood Clb; Former Chm Envir-Ec Interface Team Com of 100; Past Pres NC St Univ Alumni Assn of NE Fla; r/St Paul Meth Ch: Mem, Pres Foun 1978, 79, Chm Bd 1974, 75, Chm Coun on Mins 1972, 73, Others.

PARKER, WALTER RALEIGH JR oc/Professor, Department Chairman; b/Jan 25, 1930; h/Box 474, Woodland, NC 27897; 238 Cokey Rd Extension, Fairview Farms, Rocky Mount, NC 27801; ba/Wilson, NC; p/Walter R Sr and Mary Ella C Parker, Woodland; ed/BS Wake Forest Univ; MA E Carolina Univ; MEd Univ NC; PhD UNC; Addit Studies NCSU & E Carolina Univ; pa/Atlantic Christian Col: Psychol Prof, Chm Dept; En NC Psychol Assn; Am Guid Assn; NC Guid Assn; Assoc Dir & Dir Col Cnsl'g Prog; cp/Hope, Murfreesboro, Northampton Co & Wilson Hist Assns; Securities Limited; Sponsor: Psychol Clb, Civitan Clb; Spec Dir Multiple Sclerosis (MS) Fund Raising Dr; Bd Trustees Triangle Chapt Nat MS Soc; Bd Trustees Devel Eval Ctr, Pres Dist L; r/Woodland Bapt Ch: Mem; hon/Devel'd New Deg Prog in Psychol at Atlantic Christian Col; Phi Delta Kappa; Kappa Alpha; Grad Tchg Fellow, UNC-CH; Reschr & Coauthor Book *Teenage Drop Out*; Spec Scholastic Awd to Attend Grad Sch; W/W S&SE; Outstg Edrs Am.

PARKER, WILLIAM DALE oc/Executive; Humanitarian; b/Apr 13, 1925; h/724 Jamestown Dr, Winter Park, FL 32792; Deck Hill, Boone, NC 28607; ba/Titusville, FL; m/Frances Ross Jennings (dec); 2nd Boots Lee Farthing; c/Frances Lea, Elizabeth Dale, Kim Carolyn, Penny Jo Ann, Jacquelyn Susan; p/Otis Durie and Eva Estelle Dempsey Parker (dec); ed/Grad Col Wm & Mary 1949, Intl Corr Schs (IE) 1956, Univ Del 1959, Cal Wn Univ 1963, Univ Cal-SD 1964, Stetson Univ 1969; (Hon) DSc James Balmes Univ 1968; PhD Fla Inst 1970; (Hon) DD Univ Life 1971; mil/USCG WWII; pa/Engr & Dir Salaried Pers & PR, Gen Motors Corp 1949-60; Dir Intl Inst Human Relats, La Jolla, Cal 1964-;

Aerospace Scist, Mgmt Specialist, Gemini & Expmts Prog Ofc, NASA, Houston 1964-67; Cape Kennedy 1967-69; Mfg Engr & Lectr, Gen Dynamics/Astronautics, San Diego 1961-64; Fam & Marriage Cnslr, Titusville, Fla & Boone, NC 1969-; Dir & VP in Charge of Franchising, Am & Intl Model Fests & Spangler TV Inc, NYC 1969-73; Chm Bd, Travel Intl Inc 1971-74; Mayor Monroe Park, Del 1951; Fdr Indust Mgmt Clb of Newark, Del 1952; Pres NFFE Local 1575, 1968; Former Columnist, Intl Mag Writer, & Asst Editor; Former Prodr TV & Radio Shows; Art Collector; Edit Adv Bd, Am Biogl Inst; Other Former Profl Positions & Assn Mbrships; cp/Fdr Monroe Park Civil Def Org; Former Dir: New Castle Co Civil Def Coun, Del St Civil Def Warden Div, Del St Evacuation Comm, Boys & Girls Aid Soc & Marcy Manor Sch, San Diego; Former Chm & Pres, Del Am Legion Child Wel Com, Del, Md & Penn Tri-St Hosp Comm, Del St Safety Coun; Num Frat Orgs; Bd Advrs, Salvation Army; Alumni Assns; Mem SAR (Fla Soc); Former Mem Dem Exec Com; Life Mem: Am Legion, Nat Space Inst, Portsmouth BPOE Lodge #82; Num Others; hon/Designer Astronaut Celestial Navigation Tng Ctr Medallion & Owner Worlds Largest Collection of Space Artifacts on Display at Col of Wm & Mary, Williamsburg, Va; Designed Medallions for All Maj Profl Sports Teams in USA 1975; Placed One-half Billion in Investmts in 1976; Keys to Cities: Wilmington (Del), T'ville & Miami (Fla); Del Outstg Yg Man of Yr 1956; Del Vol Silver Awd 1957; GM Mgmt Awd; NASA Gemini Prog Group Achmt; Intl Dist'd Ser to Humanity 1969; Nat Spch Awd, Nat Dept Am Legion, St Louis, Mo 1959; Hon Sheriff, Portsmouth 1976; Ext Biogl Listings; Author of *The Philosophy of Genius* (1971) and *Gutless America* (1973) which influenced many Federal legislative changes in society; Num Other Cits & Recog.

PARKMAN, JAMES N oc/Association Director; b/Dec 14, 1931; h/400 Sassafras Rd, Roswell, GA 30076; ba/Atlanta, GA; m/Hazel W Wilkinson; p/Gertrude Hollingsworth, Atlanta; mil/USN 1951-55; pa/Exec VP Ga Bus & Indust Assn 1968-; Indust Relats Dir Anaconda Aluminum Co 1960-67; Gen Mgr & Pt Owner Macon Venetian Blind & Awning Co 1959-60; Adm Asst Ga Forestry Comm 1954-59; Com Chm Am Soc Assn Execs; VP Am Soc Pers Adm; Cert'd Assn Exec; Mgmt Rep Ga Employmt & Tng Coun; Past Pres Ga Soc Assn Execs; NIC: Wkrs Compensation Adv Com, Unemploymt Compensation Adv Com; Former VChm Nat Alliance Bus-men; Sev Other Profl Activs; cp/VChm Ga Heart Assn; Mgmt Rep Ga Dept Labor Adv Coun; VChm Gov's Prayer Breakfast; Past Chm Indust Relations Com COSMA; Trustee Intl Dietary Foun; Others; r/Prot; hon/Outstg Assn Exec Ga; W/W S&SW.

PARKS, AGATHA E oc/Staff Assistant; b/Jul 21, 1922; h/612 Beechmont Rd, Lexington, KY 40502; ba/L'ton; m/James Richard; c/Susan Ann Williams, Deborah Lynn, Shelagh Gayle Wells, James Richard Jr, Duke Allen; p/John Homer and Alma Farris English, L'ton; pa/Staff Asst to VP for Med Ctr Univ Ky; Mem Blue Grass Chapt Nat Secys Assn; Past Pres Am BPW Assn; cp/Mar Dimes; Heart Fund; r/Meth; hon/Notable Ams; Ky Col; Girl of Yr, Beta Sigma Phi.

PARKS, JACKELEE A oc/Certified Shorthand Reporter; Registered Profl Reporter; Business Owner; h/Astro Sta, Box 20393, Houston, TX 77030; c/Joel David; p/Herbert Frank and Dorothy L Anthonise (dec); ed/Univ Houston; pa/Owner & Operator PARKS REPORTING 1962-; Exec Secy Atl Refining & J Ray McDermott Co 1961; Ins Investigator Intl Ser Ins Co 1960; Exec Secy Pan Am Ins Co 1958-60; Profl Singer/Dancer Joyce Roland Dancers 1957-58; Singer/Dancer Theatre Inc (Amateur Group) 1956-57; Other Profl Positions; Nat, Tex, Houston Shorthand Reporters Assns; IPA; cp/Ecumenical Soc Psychorientology; Holistic Hlth Assn; Cousteau Soc NY; Gulf Coast Fencing Assn.

PARKS, JAMES HAYS oc/Opera Performer; Associate Professor; b/Aug 25, 1943; h/1606 18th Ave, East Moline, IL 61244; ba/Moline, IL; p/James A and Julia Etta Parks, Topeka, KS; ed/BMus; MMus; pa/Assoc Prof Music; Fdr/Artistic Dir Genesius Guild Opera Theatre; St Paul Opera Co; Min of Music St James Luth; Staff Dir Playcrafters Inc; Soloist St George Greek Orthodox; r/Epis; hon/Intl W/W in Music; W/W: Am Cols & Univs, MW; Outstg Edr Am.

PARKS, SHERMAN A oc/Judge; b/May 15, 1924; h/314 Taylor, Topeka, KS 66604; ba/Topeka; m/Alberta Lewis; c/Sherman A Jr; p/James and Rosa Drane Parks (dec); ed/BBA Washburn Univ 1949; LLB 1955, JD 1970 Washburn Univ Sch Law; mil/USN 1943-46, Yeoman 1st Class; pa/Judge Ct of Appeals Ks; Admitted to Pract Law: Supr Ct Ks, US Dist Ct Ks, 10th Judicial Circuit & US Supr Ct; cp/Former Chm & Mem Bd Regents Washburn Univ; Bd Dirs YMCA; Former Mem Adv Bd St Francis Hosp, Bd Govs Washburn Law Sch; r/Prot; hon/Omega Psi Phi, Man of Yr 1978.

PARLEE, NORMAN ALLEN DEVINE oc/Professor; Engineer; b/Mar 23, 1915; h/12145 Edgecliff Pl, Los Altos Hills, CA 94022; ba/Stanford, CA; ed/BS, MS Dalhousie Univ; PhD McGill Univ; Postdoct Study Cambridge Univ; pa/Prof Extractive Metall Stanford Univ 1962- Prof Metall Engrg Purdue Univ 1952-62; Dominion Steel Corp: Asst Dir Metall & Res 1951-52, Dir Res & Devel 1946-51, Asst Chief Metallurgist 1941-46, Res Metallurgist 1939-41 (Canada); Fellow: Chem Inst Canada, Am Inst Chem; Reg'd Profl Engr: Cal, Nova Scotia, Canada; AAUP; Sigma Xi; Am Soc for Engrg Ed; NS Inst Sci; Canadian Inst Mining & Metall; Am Soc for Metals; Am Inst Metall Engrs; Conslt; hon/NRC F'ships; H G Fraser Prize in Chem; Martin Murphy Prize for Engrg Inst Canada; F'ship, NSF; Num Profl Pubs.

PARLOTZ, ROBERT DAVID oc/College Professor; Minister; b/May 30, 1944; h/PO Box 6102, Bellevue, WA 98008; ba/Kirkland, WA; m/Barbara Ellyn; c/David Bryan, Tonya Renee; p/Mirko E Parlotz, Troy, MI; Marcella I Anderson, Concord, CA; ed/BS Bethany Bible Col 1966; MA Cand Wheaton Col 1968; MDiv 1972, DMin 1973 Tex Christian Univ; Parkland Meml Hosp, Dallas, Tex: Internship Basic Clin Pastoral Ed 1972, Internship Adv'd Clin Pastoral Ed 1972-73, Residency Supvy Clin Pastoral Ed 1973-74; pa/NW Col: Prof, Dir Cnslg Sers, Chm Cnslg Com; Dir Ref-Co Info & Referral Ofc: Trinity Val Mtl Hlth Mtl Retard Auth, Dallas Co Mtl Hlth & Mtl Retard Ctr, Ft Worth St Sch Tex Dept MHMR 1976-77; Calvary Evang Temple, Ft Worth 1974-77; Fdr & Exec Dir, Social Psychotherapist Pastoral Consultation & Cnslg Ser; Campus Min Tex Christian Univ, Ft Worth 1971-77; Assoc Pastor; Sem S Assembly of God, Ft Worth 1969-71, Bethel Temple, Oak Park, Ill 1968; Mem 6 Yrs Campus Mins Com N Tex Dist Coun Assemblies of God; Lic'd Social Psychotherapist St of Tex; Ordained Gen Coun Assemblies of God; Am Acad Rel; Evang Theol Soc; Assn for Clin Pastoral Ed; Acad Pastoral Cnslrs; Assn Mtl Hlth Clergy; Foun Thanatology (NY); Tarrant Co (Tex) Assn Marriage & Fam Cnslrs; Dallas Alliance for Employmt of Handicapped; Profls Working w Devel Disabled Persons (Dallas); Ft Worth Assn for Retard Citizens; Tarrant Co: Mtl Hlth Assn, Soc for Autistic Chd; Nat Soc for Autistic Chd; cp/Adv Com Airport Chaplaincy, Seattle-Tacoma Intl Airport; Mem Existing Resources Task Force, Trinity Val MHMR Auth, Tarrant Co; r/Assemblies of God.

PARMER, OPAL E oc/Psychologist; Teacher; b/Feb 15, 1920; h/4034 Pegg Ave, Columbus, OH 43214; ba/Columbus; m/Robert LeRoy; p/George Roy and Mary Alice Belchar (dec); ed/BA; MEd Temple Univ; Grad Study: Ohio No, Toledo Univ, Ohio St; pa/Am Psychol Assn; Local Assns in Field; NEA; Others; r/Prot; hon/Hon'd for Ser to Psychol

& Ed; World W/W Wom; W/W Am Wom.

PARR, FRANK ROBERT oc/Science Writer; b/Oct 7, 1922; h/1213 NW 38th St, Oklahoma City, OK 73118; ba/Okla City; m/Barbara Ann Wheelock; c/Charles, Barbara, Felicia, Brad, Brian; p/Claude Albert and Thelma Miller Parr (dec); ed/AA; BA; MA; DD; DComl Sci; mil/AUS; USAF; WWII & Korea; pa/Aviation/Space Writers Assn; Inst Navigation; cp/Repub St Com; US Olympic Soc; r/Epis; hon/Alpha Sigma Lambda; Am Mensa Soc.

PARRAMORE, JOSEPH VERNON JR oc/Budget Analyst; b/May 1, 1947; h/2811 Nepal Dr, Tallahassee, FL 32303; ba/Talla; m/Patricia Tankersley; c/Joseph Michael; p/Joseph Vernan and Jamie Cottingham Parramore, Talla; ed/AA Talla Commun Col; BS Fla St Univ; mil/USM 1970-71; cp/Talla JCs; r/Bapt; hon/Chevaliar Deg, Order of DeMolay.

PARROTT, BARBARA MARIE oc/Geophysicist; b/Jun 6, 1940; h/5237 Woodlawn Pl, Bellaire, TX 77401; ba/Houston, TX; p/John B Parrott (dec); Vera J Parrott, El Paso, TX; ed/BA 1962; pa/Soc Exploration Geophysicists; Houston Geophy Soc; r/Bapt.

PARSON, HAZEL SNIPES oc/Mayor; b/Aug 12, 1937; h/Rt 2, Box 7, Ridgeville, SC 29472; ba/R'ville; m/Murray (dec); c/Glenford, Deborah, Edna, Alice, Murray Adolphus, Mark Avery; p/Charlie and Edna Davis Snipes, R'ville; ed/Tchr's Aide; cp/Mayor, R'ville; r/AME; hon/Certs: Consumer Ed, Indiv Instrn.

PARSONS, DONALD JAMES oc/Bishop; b/Mar 22, 1922; h/3900 Hawthorne Pl, Peoria, IL 61616; ba/Peoria; m/Mary Russell; c/Mary, Rebecca, Bradford; p/Earl and Helen Drabble Parsons (dec); ed/BA; BD; ThM; ThD; pa/Bishop Diocese of Quincy (Epis); Dean & Pres Nashotah House 1963-73; r/Epis; hon/Hon DDiv, Div Sch (Philadelphia); DCL, Nashotah House; Author 3 Volumes.

PARSONS, GUS LEE oc/Fire Department Captain; b/Mar 15, 1925; h/403 Lakeside Rd, Hot Springs, AR 71901; ba/Hot Springs; m/Edna Ruth Evans; c/Philip Lee, Stephen Marvin; p/Newman L and Lillie Henthorne Parsons (dec); mil/USN 1943-46, 3rd Class Petty Ofcr; pa/Hot Springs Fire Dept: Fire Fighter to Capt, Secy, Treas, Chaplain, Mem Efficiency Bd, Grievance Com, Pension Bd; Chaplain Ark Fire Fighters Assn; cp/BSA: Wood Badge Scoutmaster, Brotherhood Mem Wazhazee Lodge Order of Arrow, Scoutmaster, Troop Com-man, Former Asst Scoutmaster, Ouachita Area Coun Camporee, Patrol Dad, Nat BSA Jamboree 1977; Bd Govs Malvern Rd Property Owners' Assn; r/Pentecostal Ch of Hot Springs: Mem, Music Dir, Yth Ldr, SS Tchr, Chm Bldg Fund Com, Deacon, Chm Bd Deacons; hon/BSA: Wood Badge w Beads, Lake Ouachita Dist Awd of Merit.

PARSONS, JAMES MONROE oc/Medical Doctor; b/Dec 15, 1931; h/3250 Fell Rd, Melbourne, FL 32901; ba/Melbourne; m/Diane Buck; c/Jay Marck, Melanie Renee, Walter Cox III, Olin Keene, Jennifer Diane; p/Walter Cox Parsons (dec); Hazel Conner Parsons, Kissimmee, FL; ed/MD Univ Tenn-M 1961; mil/USN 1951-54; pa/Doct, Psychi; Med Staff Wuesthoff Meml Hosp, Rockledge, Fla; Assn Am Physicians & Surgs; Acad Orthomolecular Psychi; Intl Col Applied Nutrition; Pres Sci Info & Ed Coun of Physicians Inc; Pres Pro Media Inc; r/Prot.

PARTHASARATHI, MANAVASI NARASIMHAN oc/Manager of Development; b/Jan 13, 1924; h/47 Whittier St, Hartsdale, NY 10530; ba/New York, NY; m/Lakshmi; c/Arvind, Arjun, Aanand; p/M K Narsimachari (dec); Janakiammal (dec); ed/BS (Physics); BS (Metall); MS; PhD; pa/Mgr Devel Intl Lead Zinc Res Org; Fellow:

Am Soc for Metals, Instn of Metallurgists (London); hon/Winner Gold Medals, Indian Inst of Metall; F'ship, Num Learned Socs.

PARTRIDGE, LLOYD D oc/Professor; Editor; h/3061 Dumbarton, Memphis, TN 38128; ba/Memphis; m/Jean M Rutledge; c/L Donald, David L, Gayle Kneller; p/Bert James Partridge; Marian Rice Partridge, Cazenovia, NY; ed/BS; MS; PhD; mil/AUS 1944-46; pa/Prof Physiol Univ Tenn-M; Assoc Editor Jour; Reschr; Profl Pubs.

PASSWATER, RICHARD ALBERT oc/Biochemist; Author; b/Oct 13, 1937; h/529 Southview Ave, Silver Spring, MD 20904; ba/Same; m/Barbara Gayhart; c/Richard Alan, Micheal Eric; p/Stanley Leroy Passwater (dec); Mabel King Passwater, Wilmington, PA; ed/BS Univ Del 1959; PhD Bernadean Univ 1976; pa/Adv Bd & Fac Union Univ, Los Angeles, Cal 1978-; Adv Bd Am Nutritional Guid Ctrs, Va Bch, Va 1978-; Corporate Dir Am Gen Enterprises, Minneapolis, Minn 1969-78; Prod Mgr Am Instrument Co, Silver Spring 1965-78; Dir Res Am Gerontological Res Labs Inc, Rockville, Md 1969-75; Washington Rep Inst Nutritional Res, Woodland Hills, Cal; Dir Applications Lab Am Inst Co, Silver Spring 1966-70; Other Former Positions; Am Chem Soc; Am Acad Preven Med; Gerontology Soc; Am Geriatric Soc; Am Aging Assn; Soc Applied Spect; ASTM; Conslt Solgar Co Inc, NY 1977-; Editor *Fluorescence News* 1966-77; Edit Bd: VIM Newslttr (Inst Nutritional Res), Nutritional Perspectives Am Chiro Assn; cp/Former Cubmaster; hon/Nom Awd, Am Chem Soc; W/W in E; Nom Lasker Awd; Pub'd Author.

PASTERNAK, EUGENIA oc/Institutional Administrator; b/Jan 8, 1919; h/130 Humbercrest Blvd, Toronot, Ontario, Canada; ba/Toronto; m/Eugene; p/(dec); ed/Profl Admr; pa/Gerontol Soc; Canadian Gerontol Soc; cp/Ukrainian Pensioners Clb; Canadian Nat Exhbns, Arts, Crafts & Hobbies; r/Greek-Cath; hon/Medal & Scroll, Ukrainian Canadian Com; Life Dir, Ukrainian Home for Aged; Medal & Scroll, Ukrainian Free Cossacs; Life Fellow, IBA.

PASTINE, MAUREEN DIANE oc/Librarian; b/Nov 21, 1944; h/905 W Washington, Champaign, IL 61820; ba/Urbana, IL; m/Jerry J; p/Gerhard Hillman (dec); Ada Hillman, Ogallah, KS; ed/AB; MLS; pa/Libn Undergrad Lib Univ Ill; Am Lib Assn; Ill Lib Assn; AAUP; hon/Beta Phi Mu.

PASTOR, LUCILLE E oc/Accountant; Artist; Author; b/Sept 7, 1920; h/94 Ledgeside Ave, Waterbury, CT 06708; ba/Same; p/Thomas Pastor, W'bury; Fannie Russo Pastor (dec); ed/Univ Conn 1953-56; Univ Bridgeport 1957; Paier Sch of Art 1966-67; pa/Owner Lucille E Pastor Co, W'burg 1968-78; Bkkeeper Allies Airco Sers, W'burg 1970; Secy-Bkkeeper W'bury Truck Ser 1966-70; Bkkeeper-Acct W'bury Clb 1960-63; Other Former Positions; Artists & Writers Conn Inc: Chm Exhibits 1965-69, 1/VP 1961-62; BPW Clb, W'bury: Mbrship Chm 1968-75, Corr Secy 1965, 2/VP 1963-64; Hospitality Chm Public Relats Soc Am 1964 (Conn Val Chapt); Var Positions W'bury Arts Coun; Washington Art Assn; Guilford Art Leag; Meriden Arts & Crafts Assn; Torrington Artist Assn; Conn Classic Arts Assn; Naugatuck Art Leag; Nat Soc Fine Arts, Miami (Fla) 1977; r/Cath; hon/Author Book of Poetry *Versatile Poetry*; Num Prizes for Paintings; Contest Judge; Others.

PATE, RACHEL B oc/Student; b/Nov 13, 1943; h/120 Goldenwood Dr, Brandon, FL 33511; ed/Hillsborough Commun Col; cp/Pres, Alpha Gamma Theta Chapt, Phi Theta Kappa 1978-79; hon/Outstg Yg Wom Am; National Dean's List; W/W Am Cols & Univs; Outstg Student, HCC-Plant City Campus; Harry S Truman Nat S'ship Semifinalist; Blue Key Awd Semi-finalist, Univ of Fla.

PATE, WILLIAM WILSON oc/Real Estate Owner; b/Aug 17, 1900; h/R#2, Greenville, SC 29602; ba/G'ville; m/Alethea Fennell; c/William Wilson Jr, Wallace Fennell; p/William Walter and Willie McElwee Pate (dec); pa/Owner Real Est; r/Meth.

PATERSON, LOIS STONE oc/Artist; Retired Teacher; Dietitian; b/Sept 6, 1909; h/7724 Elgar St, Springfield, VA 22151; m/Roy Mackenzie; c/Roy M Jr, George Hamilton Gordon; p/Charles Stone (dec); Rose E Doble Stone, Springfield; ed/BS Col Wm & Mary 1931; Grad Studies: Univ Maine 1937, Univ Va 1954-63, 64-, Am Univ 1967; pa/Watercolor Artist 1971-78; Elem Tchr Fairfax Co (Va) Schs 1954-70; Home Ec Tchr NNHS, Newport News, Va 1937-39; Other Former Positions; Va Ed Assn; NEA; AAUW; Fairfax Ed Assn; cp/Chi Omega; Nat Leag Am Pen Wom; Fairfax Co Coun of Arts; S'field Art Guild; Resident Assoc Smithsonian; r/Bapt; hon/3 Awds in Fairfax Area Shows; One-Man Show (Watercolor), Fairfax 1975; Others.

PATTERSON, EDWIN oc/Minister; Accountant; b/Sept 6, 1921; h/Box 486, Andalusia, AL 36420; ba/Andalusia; m/Margaret Hall; p/Walter L and Kate A Patterson, Andalusia; mil/USAAF 1942-45;

pa/Acct Ben Williams Equipmt Co Inc, Andalusia 1962-; Pastor Harmony Bapt Ch, Andalusia 1967-; r/So Bapt; hon/IPA; Men of Achmt; Personalities of S; Notable Ams; W/W Rel; Intl W/W Commun Ser; Commun Ldrs & Noteworthy Ams.

PATTERSON, ESTHER FLEMING oc/- Retired Teacher; b/Feb 17, 1902; h/36 Robin Hood Cir, Winston-Salem, NC 27106; m/- Glenn (dec); c/Leon Fleming, Ellen P Boose; p/Leon C and Daisy R Fleming (dec); ed/BA; pa/Ret'd Tchr W-S Co Schs; HS Glee Clbs; r/Mt Tabor U Meth Ch: Ch Sch Tchr, Chd's Choral Groups; hon/25 Yr Awd for Tchg; Art Exhbns.

PATTERSON, JAMES N oc/Physician; Pathologist; b/Feb 15, 1902; h/900 Golfview Ave, Tampa, FL 33609; ba/Tampa; m/Viola; c/Joseph R; p/Joseph S and Catherine Nelson Patterson (dec); ed/BS Bucknell Univ 1924; BM 1928, MD 1929 Univ Cinc Col Med; MS 1932 Univ Cinc Grad Sch; mil/USAAF 1942-46, Maj to Lt Col; pa/Clin Prof of Pathol, Univ S Fla Col Med 1973-; Conslt, Patterson Coleman Labs 1970-; Pvt Pract 1946-64; Chief Lab Ser, AAF Reg Hosp Lab, Orlando, Fla 1942-46; Asst St Hlth Ofcr 1941-42; Dir Bur Labs, Fla St Bd of Hlth 1938-42; Chief Lab Ser, Kennon Durham TB Hosp, Cinc, Ohio 1936-38; Pathologist to Coroner, Hamilton Co, Ohio 1931-35; Attending Pathologist, Cinc Gen Hosp 1931-38; Prof & Hd Dept Pathol, Eclectic Med Col 1932-34; Univ Cinc Col Med: Asst in Pathol 1929-31, Instr 1931-34, Asst Prof 1934-38; Staff Mem: Centro Asturiano Hosp, Tampa, Centro Espanol Hosp, Tampa, Citrus Meml Hosp, Inverness, Fla, Commun Hosp of New Port Richey, Fla, DeSoto Meml Hosp, Arcadia, Fla, Hillsborough Co Hosp, Tampa, Jackson Meml Hosp, Dade City, St Joseph Hosp, Tampa, Tampa Gen Hosp, Tarpon Sprgs Gen Hosp, Tarpon Sprgs, Fla, Univ Commun Hosp, Tampa, West Pasco Hosp, New Port Richey, Wood G Pierce Meml Hosp, Arcadia; Pres, Fla Soc Pathologists 1949; Fla Assn Blood Banks: Past Pres, Past Secy;

Hillsborough Co Med Assn: Past Pres, Past Secy, Past Chm Bd Trustees, Others; Am Bd Pathol: Pres 1966, Life Trustee 1967-, VP 1965; Col Am Pathologists; Pvt Practioners of Pathol Foun; Tampa Res Foun; SW Fla Blood Banks; Am Soc Clin Pathologists; Am Assn Blood Banks; Am Soc Hematology; Intl Soc Hematology; AMA; Fla Med Assn; Intl Acad Pathol; Others; cp/SW Fla Blood Bank (Med Dir Emeritus); Hon Life Mem, Am Cancer Soc; Wm Bucknell Clb, Bucknell Univ; McMickin Soc, Univ Cinc; Boys Clb of Tampa; Tampa C of C; UF; Commun Chest; Hillsborough Co Heart & TB Assns; Tampa Rotary Clb; Palmu Ceiu Golf & CC; Univ Cinc Pres's Clb; Others; r/St Andrews Epis Ch; hon/Awd'd Plaque for 25 yrs Ser by Franciscian Sisters, St Joseph's Hosp 1974; Awd'd Plaque in Apprec for 18 yrs Ser as Med Dir, SW Fla Blood Bank 1968; Pvt Practioner of Yr Awd, Am Pathol Foun 1968; Cert of Apprec, Fla Med Assn 1967; W/W in S&SW; Comm'd Admiral, Tex Navy.

PATTERSON, NOBLE FESTUS oc/Editor; Business Owner; b/Jan 17, 1924; h/PO Box 7481, Fort Worth, TX 76111; ba/Ft Worth; m/Emily Ellene; c/Marcene Herrick (Mrs James), Rita Orbison (Mrs Steve), Nancy Fowler (Mrs Tom), Lee Ann McKee (Mrs Tom); p/(dec); ed/Att'd Freed-Hardeman Col;

Abilene Christian Univ; Tex Christian Univ; pa/Editor *Christian Jour*; Owner Jour Tchr Supply (Local Retail & Nat-wide Mail Order); Tex Underwriters Assn; Grad Realtor Inst; Real Est Fin; r/Ch of Christ; hon/W/W in Tex.

PATTERSON, RICKEY LEE oc/Pastor; b/Sept 24, 1952; h/11311 SW 200 St #310-D, Miami, FL 33157; ba/Miami; m/Sharon R; p/William I Patterson, New Castle, IN; Wanda Marhoefer, Naples, FL; ed/BA Ind

Univ; MBA Univ Miami; pa/Pastor Jesus Student's F'ship Inc; Bible Tchr; Evangelist; Radio Spkr; cp/Pershing Rifles Mil Frat; Sigma Pi; Audubon Soc; r/Full-Gospel; hon/IU Hon Student; W/W.

PATTERSON, VIRGINIA G oc/Social Worker; Day Care Director (for Elderly); b/Feb 21, 1917; h/1709 Sherwood Ln, Nashville, TN 37216; ba/N'ville; m/F Woodall; c/Judith P Murphy; p/Marsh and Lena G Goodwin (dec); ed/BA Geo Peabody Col; MSW Univ Tenn Sch Social Work; pa/NASW; Nat Gerontological Soc; Tenn Fdn of Aging; Prog Com Coun Commun Sers; cp/GSA, Camp Dir; Am Camping Assn; Past Pres PTA; Repub; r/Meth: Pres UMW; hon/Pi Gamma Mu; Notable Ams; Thanks

Badge, Cumberland Val Girl Scout Coun; W/W: Am Wom, S&SW; World W/W Wom.

PATTON, CELESTEL HIGHTOWER oc/Associate Professor; b/Jul 14, 1912; h/4934 Echo Ave, Dallas, TX 75215; ba/Baton Rouge, LA; m/Ural L; p/Felix and Martha Hightower (dec); ed/BS; MA; MA; DH;

pa/Assoc Prof So Univ; APHA; ADHA; AAHPER; Tex Dental Hygiene Assn; Dallas Dental Hygiene Group; AAUP; AAUW; Tex Public Hlth Assn; SWn Sociol Soc; cp/Commun Chest; Repub; r/Warren Ave Christian Ch; hon/Pres & Alumni Awds, Meharry Med Col for Sers in Commun.

PAUL, BANI oc/Librarian; b/Sept 21, 1944; h/110 Fieldtree Ct, Jackson, MS 39212; ba/Lorman, MS; m/Madhabendra Prasad; c/Leena, Moushumi; p/N K and U R Paul, Calcutta, India; ed/MSLS Univ Miss; BSLS, BA, MA Gauhati Univ; pa/Hd Cataloging Libn Alcorn St Univ Lib; ALA; MLA; Consortium Lib Automation; cp/Var Activs; GSA, BSA; r/Hinduism; hon/Var Merit S'ships.

PAUL, GRACE oc/Retired; Free-lance Writer; Volunteer; b/Mar 12, 1908; h/705 N Main, Temple, TX 76501; p/David and Myrtle Helen Brewer Paul (dec); mil/Woms Army Corp 1944-46; pa/Author *Your Future in Med Technol-A Short Course in Skilled Supvn*; Med Technologist 1930-; Plant Quarantine Inspector 1948-51; Social Security Adm 1956-71; Contbr to Envir Engr's Handbook; cp/RSVP Vol w Yth Sers Bur & Cult Activs Ctr; Contbr to Books on Early Times in Bell Co; r/Presb; hon/Winner Poster Contest, Am Soc Med Technologists 1953; Writing Contests; Outstg Vol.

PAUL, MADHABENDRA PRASAD oc/Professor; b/Jan 1, 1937; h/110 Fieldtree Ct, Jackson, MS 39212; ba/Lorman, MS; m/Bani; c/Leena, Moushumi; p/Radhika Prasad and Hemanta Bala Paul (dec); ed/PhD Univ Fla; pa/Prof Elects Alcorn St Univ; IEEE; AGU; AAPT; Sigma Xi; MAS; MAP; cp/Activs: BSA, GSA; r/Hinduism; hon/Hons w Distn (Physics); Merit S'ships.

PAVELKA, ELAINE BLANCHE oc/- Mathematics Professor; b/Feb 4; h/1900 Euclid Ave, Berwyn, IL 60402; ba/Cicero, IL; p/Frank Joseph Pavelka (dec); Mildred Bohumila Seidl, Berwyn; ed/BA, MS NWn Univ; PhD Univ Ill; pa/Math Prof Morton Col; Am Ednl Res Assn; Am Math Assn 2-Yr Cols; Am Math Soc; Am Mensa Limited; Assn

for Wom in Math; Canadian Soc for Hist & Phil of Math; Ga Ctr for Study of Lng & Tchg Math; Ill Coun Tchrs Math; Ill Math Assn Commun Cols; Intertel; Math Assn Am; Math Action Group; Soc for Indust & Applied Math; Others; cp/NWn Univ & Univ Ill Alumni Assns; hon/Pi Mu Epsilon; Sigma Delta Epsilon; Invited Spkr 3rd Intl Cong on Math Ed, Karlsruhe, Germany 1976; Biogl Listings.

PAWLIKOWSKI, JOHN THADDEUS oc/Professor, Priest; b/Nov 2, 1940; h/4836 S Wolf Rd, Western Springs, IL 60558; ba/Chicago, IL; p/Thaddeus Pawlikowski (dec); Anna Pawlikowski, Chgo; ed/AB Loyola Univ; Ordination St Mary of the Lake Sem; PhD Univ Chgo; pa/ADA; CALC; Nat Cath Theol Union; Mem Secretariat for Cath-Jewish Relats of Nat Conf Cath Bishops; r/Cath: Mem Order of Servites; hon/Interfaith Awd, Am Jewish Com; Fdrs' Cit, Nat Cath Conf for Inter-racial Justice.

PAXTON, FAY MURRAY oc/Retired; b/May 23, 1889; h/602 Quapaw Ave, Hot Springs, AR 71901; p/Jacob M and Frendly D Murray (dec); pa/Ret'd; Hot Sprgs BPW; cp/Pres: Hot Sprgs Shrine Clb Aux, Thinkers Clb, Salvation Army Aux; r/Epis; hon/Gold Medal, Col Contest; Notable Ams.

PAYNE, EMILY CLEMENT oc/Librarian; b/Oct 10, 1920; h/Rt 6, Larkwood Dr, Rome, GA 30161; ba/Rome; m/Albert S; c/Le Ann Strom, William L; p/William M and Leona L David Clement (dec); ed/AB; ML; DASL; pa/Tri-Co Reg Lib, Rome: Dir 1965-, Acting Dir 1964-65, Chd & Yg People's Libn 1959-64; Instr Rome Off-Campus Ctr Univ Ga Sys 1965-68; Other Former Positions; Floyd Co & Ga Assns Edrs; Atlanta Hist Soc; Coosa Val, Ga, Am Lib Assns; Adv Com Mem Ga Coun Public Libs 1976; Lib Adv Coun Chm St Dept of Ed, Lib Sers Constrn Act; IPA Mem AAUW 1968-69; Conslt Media Panel Nat Foun on Arts & Humanities 1977; Gov's Conf on Libs; Adv Com on Public Libs Mem St Supt Schs; Cherokee BPW Clb: VP, Leg Com, Prog Chm, Steering Com; cp/Former Prog Chm Floyd Co Farm Bur; Former Mem Steering Com Rome Civic Ctr Com; Rome-Floyd Clean Commun Comm; Floyd Co Dem Assn; Past VP Wom's Leag Dem Party Floyd Co; Var Positions Rome Area C of C; r/Bapt; hon/Wom of Yr Nom 1973, 74; Biogl Listings.

PAYNE, SANDRA GLENDA oc/Hospital Administrator; b/Nov 17, 1949; h/Rt 3, Box 120, Gretna, VA 24557; ba/Same; ed/Cert Acct'g & Jr Exec, Danville Commun Col;

pa/Billing Supvr Meml Hosp, D'ville; cp/YMCA; r/Cherrystone Bapt Ch; hon/W/W Among Black Ams; World W/W Wom; Notable Ams; Personalities of S.

PEARCE, CHARLES WELLINGTON oc/Cardiovascular & Thoracic Surgeon; b/Nov 2, 1927; h/1662 State St, New Orleans, LA 70118; ba/NO; m/Dorothy D; c/John Y, Charles W Jr, Andrew F, Margaret E; p/Francis Marion and Fanny Chamberlain Pearce (dec); ed/MD Cornell 1953; mil/AUS 188th Parachute Inf Regimt 1946-48; pa/Tulane Univ: Clin Assoc Prof Surg 1969-, Hd Sect Cardiovas & Thoracic Surg 1967-69, Assoc Prog Surg 1962-66, Other Acad Positions; Vis Surg Charity Hosp, NO; Conslt in Surg: Huey P Long Charity Hosp (Pineville, La), Lallie Kemp Charity Hosp (Independence,

La), VA Hosp (Alexandria, La); Staff Mem: Touro Infirmary, So Bapt Hosp, Mercy Hosp, Hotel Dieu, E Jefferson Gen Hosp; Fellow: Am Col Surgs, Am Col Cardiol, Am Col Chest Physicians; Am Assn for Thoracic Surg; Am Heart Assn; NO Surg Soc; Soc for Vascular Surg; Intl Cardiovas Soc; Intl Soc Surg; Num Others; cp/Gov La Soc Mayflower Descendents; SAR; Bd Govs NO Opera House Assn; Fgn Relats Assn; La Landmark Soc; Sponsor NO Mus of Art; Others; r/Presb; Alpha Omega Alpha; Est'd Investigator, Am Heart Assn; Awd of Honor, Wisdom Soc; Biogl Listings; Pub'd Author.

PEARCE, DOROTHY DeLORENZO oc/-Civic Worker; b/Mar 22, 1927; h/1662 State St, New Orleans, LA 70118; m/Charles W; c/John Y, Charles W Jr, Andrew F, Margaret E; p/Andrew DeLorenzo (dec); Margaret Robilotti (dec); ed/BA Barnard Col Columbia Univ 1947; pa/Exec Res Libn Shell Chem Co, Houston (Tex) & New York (NY) 1955-57; Res Asst to Dr George Papanicolaou, Cornell Med Col, NYC 1950-55; Others; cp/Friends of the Cabildo; Sponsor NO Mus of Art; Valencia Mother's Aux; Former Mem Bd Dirs Vis Nurses Assn; La Landmark Soc; Fgn Relats Assn; AAUW; NO Garden Soc; Orleans Parish Med Soc Wom's Aux; Sara Mayo Hosp Guild: Mem, Former Mem Bd Dirs, Former Chm Hospitality Com; Mercy Hosp Wom's Aux: Mem, Past Pres, Bd Dirs; Fund Raising Com Hotel Dieu Wom's Aux; Crippled Chd's Hosp Guild; DePaul Hosp Wom's Aux; NO Symph Previews; Num Others; r/Rom Cath; hon/Biogl Listings; Key to City NO for Outstg Ser.

PEARCE, MARY McCALLUM oc/Artist, Painter; b/Feb 17, 1906; h/5400 Ocean Blvd, Apt 141, Sarasota, FL 33581; m/Clarence A; c/Mary Pearce Robinson (Mrs William B), Thomas McCallum; p/Archibald and Mabel M McCallum (dec); ed/AB Oberlin Col; Addit Study Cleveland Inst Art; pa/Exhibitor;

Demonstrator; r/Presb; hon/Best Wom Artists, Ohio Watercolor Soc; Columbus Gallery Fine Arts: Bush Meml Awd, Wolf Awd; Littlehouse Awd, Ala Watercolor Soc; Var Awds Nat Leag Am Penwom; Merit Awd, Sarasota Art Assn; Others.

PEACHEY, CHRISTINE oc/Librarian's Assistant; b/Nov 21, 1915; h/139A Meadowbrook Ln, Magnolia, AR 71753; c/2 Chd; ed/SW Tech Inst (Br of So Ark Univ); pa/Resource Spkr Jr HS 1974; cp/Commun Vol Wkr; Current Pres Ext Homemakers Clb; Pres Ext Homemakers Co Coun; Org'd Pine Val Ext Homemakers Clb; Welcome Wagon Intl Clb; hon/Apprec Cert, Ark Heart Assn; Art of Food Preserv Awd, Kerr Glass Mfg Corp & Bernardin Inc; Wom of Yr, Ext Homemakers Clb 1975 (Runner-up 1976); Life Patron ABIRA.

PEARMAN, REGINALD A oc/College Professor; b/Aug 8, 1918; h/200 Fort Meade Rd, #1203, Laurel, MD 20810; ba/Bowie, MD; m/Barbara A; c/Reginald Jr, Jocelyn R; p/Reginald J and Louise I Pearman (dec); ed/BS; MEd; mil/AUS WWII, Europe; pa/Prof Hlth Ed Bowie St Col; Fellow AAHPER; ASA; APHA; Nat Pk & Rec Soc; cp/Omega Psi Phi; Dem; Commun Activs; r/Cath; hon/Cert for Meritorious Ser, St of

Md; DIB; Men of Achmt; Personalities of S; Intl W/W Intells.

PEARSON, JIM BERRY oc/College Dean; b/Jan 3, 1924; h/915 Sherman Dr, Denton, TX 76201; ba/Denton; m/Mary; c/Jim Jr, Terry; ed/BA 1947, MA 1949 NTSU; PhD Univ Tex 1955; mil/AUS 1943-46; pa/N Tex St Univ: Prof Hist 1971-, Dean Col Arts & Scis 1973-, Univ Tex-A: Asst VP for Acad Affairs 1970-71, Asst Dean Col Arts & Scis 1962-66, Assoc Prof Hist & Ed, Others; Org Am Histns Com on Status of Hist in Schs 1974-; Tex Ed Agy, Com on Confluence of Cults 1972-; Exec Bd Tex Col & Univ Am Bicent Com 1971-; SWn Social Sci Assn, Former Chm'ships; Chm Tex St Hist Assn Com on Tchg 1969-72; Assoc Ctr for Hist of Ed 1968-; Adv Editor: Tex Coun Jour 1968-, Social Sci Qtrly 1964-; Book Review Editor SWn Hist Qtrly 1969-72; Num Other Profl Activs; cp/Kiwanis; YMCA; World Neighbors Inc; Toastmaster's Clb Inc; Scholia; Austin's Com on Human Relats; Sponsor Univ Tex-A Alpha Phi Omega Chapt; r/Sev Meth Chs: Bd Stewards, Chm Var Comms, Tchr; Wesley Foun Exec Bd, Austin & Arlington; hon/Dist'd Ser Awd, Coun of Chief St Sch Ofcrs (Salt Lake City Conf); Outstg Tchr Awd, Univ Tex Student Assembly 1964; Profl Pubs; Biogl Listings.

PEARSON, NORMAN oc/Town Planner; Land Economist; Political Scientist; b/Oct 24, 1928; h/PO Box 5362, Sta A, London, Ontario, Canada N6A 4L6; m/Gerda Josefine Reidl; p/Joseph and Mary Pearson; ed/BA w hons Univ Durham (UK) 1951; PhD Intl Inst for Adv'd Studies 1979; mil/Royal AF-NATO-RCAF 1951-52, Flying Ofcr, GD/Nav (Aircrew); Flying Ofcr GD/Nav (Aircrew) RAF Vol Resv; pa/Conslt to Stanley Urban Dist Coun on Devel of Ctl Area, UK 1946-47; Planning Asst Accrington Town Plan & Bedford Co Planning Survey, Univ Durham Planning Team (UK) 1947-49; Planning Asst Messrs Allen & Mattocks, Conslt'g Planners & Landscape Designers & Architects (UK) 1949-51; Adm Asst Scottish Div Nat Coal Bd, Scotland (UK) 1951-52; Planning Asst London Co Coun (UK) 1953-54; Planner Ctl Mortgage & Housing Corp, Ottawa 1954-55 Planning Analyst, City of Toronto Planning Bd 1955-56; Dir Planning, Hamilton-Wentworth Planning Area Bd 1956-59; Dir Planning for Burlington & Suburban Area Planning Bd & Commr Planning for Town of Burlington (Ontario) 1959-62; Profl Conslt'g Pract as Planner 1962-; Pres Tanfield Enterprises Ltd 1976-; Num Acad Positions; Mem Social Scis, Ec & Legal Aspects (Standing Com), Res Adv Bd of Intl Jt Comm (Canadian Univs Rep) 1972-76; Edit Bd Intl Assn for Gt Lakes Res Jour of Gt Lakes Res 1973-; Canadian VP Gt Lakes Tomorrow 1976-77; New Communs & Large-Scale Devel Coun, Urban Land Inst (USA) 1979-; Life Fellow: Royal Ec Soc, IBA, Am Geographical Soc, Atl Ec Assn; Life Mem US Com for Monetary Res & Ed; Lambda Alpha; Fdr Mem Brit Sociol Assn; Fellow Royal Town Planning Inst (UK); Canadian Inst Planners; Am Inst Cert'd Planners; Canadian Assn Cert'd Planning Technicians; Other Profl Orgs; hon/Pres's Prize, Royal Town Meeting Inst (UK); Profl Pubs; Biogl Listings.

PECKHAM, WILLIAM HENRY III oc/Horse Farm Owner & Breeder; Real Estate; b/Mar 11, 1929; h/2929 Paris Pike, Lexington, KY 40511; ba/Same; m/Mary Elizabeth Sparks; c/William Henry IV, Joan Olive, Harriett Carlton, Elizabeth Ann, Mary Lou; p/Rufus Walter Peckham (dec); Frances Mary Jackson (dec); pa/Breeder & Owner Thoroughbreds; Pres & Gen Mgr Commonwealth Race Course, Louisville, Ky 1977, 78; Pres Quarter Horse Racing Guild 1965-67; Owner W End Lumber Co, Houston, Tex until 1968; cp/Mem Houston CC; Bd Dirs Lexington CC; Blue Grass: Boys Ranch, Land & Nature Trust, Trust for Hist Presv; r/Mt Hored Presb Ch: Elder.

PECKWAS, EDWARD ALAN oc/Executive; b/May 1, 1942; h/6640 W Archer Ave, Chicago, IL 60638; ba/Same; m/Jane Ann; c/Kimberly Marie, Dawn Marie, Amanda Jane Ann; p/Edward Michael and Yarmilla H

Peckwas, Chgo; ed/Assoc Commerce Hannibal La Grance Col; pa/Pres & Chm of Bd KCNS Inc; Nat Assn Ed of Yg Chd; Free-lance Conslt Pres-Sch Ed; Pre-Sch Owners Ill; NEA; Ill Ed Assn; cp/Fdr & Pres Polish Geneal Soc; Bd Dirs Polish Mus Am; Author; Lectr; r/Rom Cath; hon/HERO Awd, Chgo Bd Ed; Num Dist'd Ser Awds.

PECKWAS, JANE ANN BINGAMAN oc/Educator; Secretary-Treasurer; b/Feb 26, 1945; h/6640 W Archer Ave, Chicago, IL 60638; ba/Same; m/Edward Alan; c/Kimberly Marie, Dawn Marie, Amanda Jane Ann; p/Harry Byron and Marian J P Bingaman (dec); ed/BEd Chgo St Univ 1965; pa/Secy-Treas, Bd Dirs KCNS Inc; Free-lance Conslt Pre-Sch Ed; Pre-Sch Owners Ill; NEA; Ill Ed Assn; cp/Past Pres Ladies Aux Polish Mus; Polish Mus Am: Bd Dirs, Past VP; DAR: Chgo Chapt, Jr Mbrship Com; Girl Scout Master; r/Rom Cath; hon/Nat Hons Soc; Tchr of Yr, PTA 1969; Num Dist'd Ser Awds.

PEDRONE, DINO J oc/Minister; b/Feb 26, 1945; h/600 Miller St, Chambersburg, PA 17201; ba/C'burg; m/Roberta Dee; c/JoAnna Ruth; p/Fred Pedrone (dec); Bertha Pedrone, C'burg; ed/ThB; ThD; pa/Pres Cumberland Val Christian Sch; Pastor The Open Door Ch; Exec Bd Trinity Bapt Col, Jacksonville, Fla; Exec Cooperating Bd Sword of the Lord; r/Indep Bapt; hon/Intl W/W; Outstg Yg Men Am; Commun Ldrs & Noteworthy Ams; Notable Ams.

PEEL, VALERIE STOVALL oc/Retired Licensed Registered Nurse; b/Oct 2, 1912; h/PO Box 696, Montgomery, TX 77356; m/Thomas Jefferson; c/Mary E P Lee, Robert Harold, Sarah Anne P Mabry; p/William Eugene and Ada Ann Williams Stovall (dec); ed/Grad St Joseph Sch Nsg; Postgrad Geo Peabody Col; pa/Ret'd Lic'd Reg'd Nurse, Field of Hlth Ed, St of Tex; Tex St Tchrs Assn;

Staff Mem Med & Surg Nsg; Supvn Nsg Staff Huntsville, Tex; Sch Nsg, N'ville Indep Sch Dist; Supvr Hlth Ed, Montgomery Co Schs 25 Yrs; Com That Org'd San Jacinto Area TB Assn; cp/DAR; St Dem Exec Com Wom to Rep Dist 5; Daughs of Republic of Tex; Montgomery PTO; Blue Bell Garden Clb; Montgomery Hist Soc; Bd Ed Mont Sch Dist; Tex St Hist Soc; Mont Co Soc for Perf'g Arts; Fayette Co Heriage Mus Leag (La Grange, Tex); r/1st Bapt Ch, Mont: Mem; hon/Grandmother of Yr: CAR, Gen Andrew Lewis Soc (Chd of Am Revol).

PEER, GARY G oc/Assistant Dean; b/Nov 14, 1940; h/4152 E 47th St, Tulsa, OK 74135; ba/Tulsa; m/Beverly; c/Teresa, Mike,

Duke; p/Glenn and Genevieve Peer, Spring Hill, KS; ed/BA Washburn Univ 1963; MS Emporia St Univ 1967; EdD Ind Univ 1971; pa/Univ Tulsa 1972-: Asst Dean Col Ed 1976-, Chm Div Profl Studies in Ed 1975-76, Asst to Dean for Certn 1974-75, Assoc Prof Ed 1974-, Asst Prof Ed 1972-74; Vis Prof Ed Ind Univ 1971-72; Other Former Positions; ASCD; Br Coun Mem, MW APGA 1976-79; ACES; RMERA; PDK; NEA; OEA; APGA; OATE; OPGA; OACES; hon/Nom'd for Profl Devel Awd, APGA; Dist'd Ser Awd, Okla Pers & Guid Assn; EPDA F'ship Awd, Ind Univ; Num Profl Pubs; Outstg Yg Men Am; W/W S&SW; Others.

PEGRAM, ELIAS H JR oc/Clothing Retailer; b/Feb 1, 1948; h/2614 Confederate Dr, Wilmington, NC 28403; ba/W'ton; p/Lucille R Pegram, W'ton; ed/AA; BA; Grad Study; mil/USAF 4 Yrs; pa/Self-employed, Clothing Retailer: The Haberdasher, The Cotton Exchange, W'ton; Local Govt Task Force, C of C; cp/Cand NC St Ho of Reps; Pres New Hanover Co Heart Assn; CoChm NH Co Human Relats Month; r/Myrtle Grove Presb Ch: Mem; hon/Outstg Yg Men Am.

PELLERIN, MARY ANN oc/Assistant Professor; b/Nov 23, 1934; h/228 Morningside Dr E, Bristol, CT 06010; ba/New Britain, CT; p/Jesse L and Cora E Pellerin, Lebanon, NH; ed/BEd Keene Tchrs Col 1956; MS Ctl Conn St Col 1963; DMin Christian Intl 1976; pa/Asst Prof & Media Specialist; Life Mem NEA; CEA; CCSC Fac Assn; AAUP; CEMA; cp/Pres Gtr Bristol Conf of Congregs; r/Bristol Bapt Ch: Mem, Deacon, Secy Bd, SS Tchr, Secy Sunshine Cir; Camp Cnslr; Dir; hon/Curved Bar Awd, GSA.

PELLOW, RITA BOLL oc/Clinical & School Psychologist; b/Nov 15, 1925; h/105 Oak Park Pl, Pittsburgh, PA 15243; ba/Pgh; m/James A; c/James III, Michael, David, Lisa; p/Raymond A Boll (dec); Stella Henson Boll, Pgh; ed/BS; MS; PhD Univ Pgh; pa/Pgh, Pa & Am Psychol Assns; Coun for Nat Register of Hlth Ser Providers in Psychol; hon/Phi Beta Kappa; Sigma Xi.

PEMBERTON, JANETTE E oc/Educator; h/4404 Sunflower Dr, Rockville, MD 20853; m/S Macpherson; pa/Cath Univ: Instr 1975-78, Chm Afro-Am Com 1976-77; IPA; cp/Pres's Clb; r/Sligo SDA Ch, Takoma Pk, Md: Hospitality Hostess; hon/Nat Tchg Fellow, Bovine St Col; Tchg Awds, CUA; Men & Wom of Distn; World W/W Wom in Ed; Intl W/W Intells; World W/W Wom; Others.

PEMBERTON, S MacPHERSON oc/Historian; Policy Analyst; h/4404 Sunflower Dr, Rockville, MD 20853; ba/Washington, DC; m/Janette Emelda; p/Abraham E and Rachael Adelaide Pemberton, St Kitts, West Indies; ed/BA, MA, PhD Univ Cal-B; pa/Current Reschr & Policy Analyst Bur Higher & Cont'g Ed, US Dept HEW; Policy Analyst Ofc of Asst Secy for Ed (HEW) 1977-78; Liaison Rep for Prog Eval Bur of Postsec'dy Ed, US Ofc of Ed, Wash DC 1976-77; Sr Reschr Nat Inst Ed, HEW 1973-76; Other Former Positions; Mem Adv Panel for Statistical Analysis Group in Ed Proj, Nat Ctr for Ed Statistics; Asst Secy for Ed Rep to Nat Coun on Ednl Res 1978; Mem NIE Equality of Ednl Opport Com 1974-75; Dep Commr for Higher Ed Rep to Fed Adv Coun on St Statistics 1977; Nat Inst Ed Rep to NIE-Puerto Rico Conf (San Juan) 1973; Other Profl Activs; r/SDA; hon/Fulbright S'ship; Canadian Govt S'ship; Phi Beta Kappa; IPA; Buhl Foun Res Grant, Univ Pgh; Dissertation Awd, Univ Cal-B; Other Acad Hons; Profl Pubs.

PENDELL, ELMER oc/Author; Retired Professor; b/Jul 28, 1894; h/c/o Mrs James E Griffin, 4002 Old Mill Rd, Alexandria, VA 22309; m/Lucille Hunt; c/Martha Jane Griffin (Mrs James); p/George Grant and Ida May Harris Pendell (dec); ed/LLB Geo Wash Univ 1917; BS Univ Oreg 1921; MA Univ Chicago 1923; PhD Cornell Univ 1929; mil/2/Lt 1917-19, 1/Lt 1918; pa/Instr & Prof: Univ Ark, Cornell Univ, Pa St Undergrad Ctrs, Baldwin-Wallace Col, Jacksonville St (Ala)

Col; hon/Dist'd Ser Cross; Legion of Valor; Author: *Why Civilizations Self-Destruct* 1977, *Sex Versus Civilization* 1967, *Population on the Loose* 1951, *Human Breeding and Survival* 1947, *Population Roads to Peace or War* 1945.

PENDER, POLLARD EUGENE oc/Controller; b/Feb 5, 1931; h/8342 Southmeadow Cir, Dallas, TX 75231; ba/Dallas; m/Lynelle George; c/Jeffrey Scott, Gary Warren; p/Ralph Pender, Bossier City, LA; Annie Penny (dec); ed/Att'd: NWn St Col 1948-50,

Centenary Col 1950-52; pa/Controller The Southland Corp; Am Inst CPAs (La); Tex Soc CPAs; cp/Former Mem: Airmen's Assn, Bd Dirs Better Bus Bur, Mtl Hlth Ctr; UF; Former Keyman QBs, Pres Ark-la-Tex; r/Epis; hon/Amelia Earhart Awd.

PENDERGRASS, PRESLEY WADE oc/College Dean; b/Dec 28, 1934; h/731 N Polk Dr, Oakland City, IN 47660; ba/Oakland City; m/Paula Ann Belcher; c/Kimberley Anne, Shannon Dawn; p/Theodore R and Elsie Barclay Pendergrass, Scottsboro, AL; ed/BA Samford Univ; MDiv, ThM So Bapt Theol Sem; MEd, EdD Univ Fla; pa/Dean Acad Affairs Oakland City Col 1978-; Pikeville Col, Pikeville, Ky: Chperson Div Human Devel 1976-78, Prof Ed & Psychol 1973-78, Assoc Prof 1971-73; Mid-Appalachian Tchr Ed Prog: Prog Devel Specialist 1977-78, Dir 1973-77; Other Former Positions; Former Bd Dirs: Mid-S Tchr Corps Network (Nashville, Tenn), SEn Tchr Corps Network, Big Sandy Commun Action Agy (P'ville); Conslt; AAUA; AAUP; AESA; ASCD; ATE; Phi Delta Kappa; Other Profl Activs; cp/Kiwanis Clb; r/1st Bapt Ch, Oakland City; hon/Apprec Plaque, Bd Dirs Mid-S Tchr Corps Network; Nom'd by Pres for ACE Acad Adm Internship; Personalities of S; W/W Intl Biog; Profl Pubs.

PENDLETON, ROGER LEE oc/Professional Civil Engineer; b/Mar 2, 1923; h/8909 Cromwell Dr, Springfield, VA 22151; ba/Reston, VA; m/Velda LaVerne Brown; p/Patricia Lee; p/Raymond Fowles and Lulu Myrtle Miller Pendleton (dec); ed/BS Univ Me; Grad Work: Geo Wash Univ, Va Polytech Inst; mil/USAR Colonel; Vet WWII, Korea; Current Resv Assignmt, Dep Asst Chief Engrs, Ofc Chief of Engrs; pa/Civil Engr Def Communs Agy, Command & Control Tech Ctr; Past Pres Va Soc Profl Engrs; Reg'd Profl Engrs; Fellow ASCE; Past St Ofcr Va Assn Professions; cp/Past Pres S'field Kiwanis Clb; Repub; Mason; Shriner; Jester; Past Ofcr Resv Ofcrs Assn; r/Epis; hon/Var Awds: ROA, Engrg Socs, Mil Ser; Dist'd Ser Awd, Va Soc Profl Engrs.

PENDLEY, PATRICIA ELLIS oc/Administrative Assistant; b/Dec 30, 1944; h/11601 W 75th Terr, Apt 10, Shawnee, KS 66214; ba/Kansas City, KS; c/Kevin; p/Durward M and Nola Ellis, Commerce, OK; ed/AA; BA; MS; PhD; pa/Adm Asst Turner USD #202, Ks City 1978-; Grad Tchg Asst Ks St Univ-Manhattan 1977-78; Elem Prin, Aurora, Mo 1973-77; Classroom Tchr, Oswego, Ks 1970-73; Other Former Positions; Am Ednl Res Assn; Nat Commun Ed Assn; Phi Delta Kappa; Ks Assn Sch Admrs; Ks Sch Public Relats Assn; Prog Chm AAUW 1975; Kappa Kappa Iota: Pres 1976, Secy-Treas 1974; SW Dist Prins' Assn: Pres 1976, VP 1975; Pres Oswego Tchrs' Assn 1973; r/Ch of Christ; hon/Outstg Yg Wom Am; W/W Mo Ed; Dean's Perm Hon Roll, Wichita St Univ; Recipient "Mickey Mantle Col S'ship".

PENN, WINONA ELIZABETH oc/Homemaker; b/Dec 27, 1929; h/13189 Huntercreek Ridge Rd, St Louis, MO 63131; m/Thomas Wilson; p/Ewell Winfred Coleman (dec); Hazel E C Coleman, Dowdy, AR; ed/BS Univ Ark; MS Univ Wyo; pa/Mo, Am Home Ecs Assns; Am, Mo Voc Assns; Mo St Tchrs Assn; Chm Curric Com Univ City Public Schs; St Louis Tchrs Assn; Local Commun Tchrs Assn; cp/Garden Clbs; Indep & Lawrence Co Ar Geneal Socs; Ark & St Louis Geneal Socs; r/So Bapt: SS Tchr, Pianist; hon/Krogor S'ship, Univ Ark; ADK; Others.

PENNINGTON, LILLIAN BOYER oc/-Retired School Teacher; Artist; b/Apr 2, 1904; h/900 Saturn Dr, Colorado Springs, CO 80906; m/R Corbin; c/Corbin Jr; p/Lynn Hutchinson and Eva Liggett Boyer (dec); ed/Grad Shippensburg St Col 1926; pa/Tchg,

Writing, Painting; Nat Leag Am Pen Wom, Pikes Peak Br; cp/Altrusa Clb; Wom's Forum; DAR; 2 Star PSA; r/Meth; hon/Dist'd Alumnus Awd, S'burg St Col; Num Art Awds; Awd for "What is a Pen Wom?"; NLAPW: Biennal Awd, Others.

PENNOYER, CECILY oc/Art Researcher; b/Jun 18, 1928; h/Duck Pond Rd, Locust Valley, Long Island, NY 11560; ba/New York, NY; m/Paul G Jr; c/Jennifer, Deirdre, Paul, Sheldon, William; p/Warwick Henderson (dec); Elizabeth Davidson, Essex, MA; ed/BA Post Col; PhD Cand NY Univ; Addit Studies; pa/Secy & Bd Dirs Intl Foun for Art Res, NYC; Bd Dirs Glen Cove Coun of Arts; Mem Fdg Bd Hulton House Lectures, C W Post Col, Greenvale, NY.

PEPPER, HENRY CORNELIUS oc/College Teacher; b/Jan 10, 1901; h/2525

Lynwood Dr, Cape Girardeau, MO 63701; ba/Lillin, IL; m/Mary Elizabeth; c/Henria Paula; p/Jesse James and Mary M Pepper (dec); ed/AB 1922; AM 1924; Grad Work; PhD Univ Ia 1932; pa/Tchr: Shawnee Col 1970-, SE Mo St Univ 1968-70, Oglethorpe Col, Atlanta, Ga 1968 (Spring); Ga St Univ, Atlanta: Prof Public Adm & Dept Chm 1951-58, Prof Ecs 1958-68, Dir Undergrad Prog in Hosp Adm 1952-64; Other Former Positions; Am Polit Sci Assn; AAUP; Alpha Kappa Psi; cp/Nat Geog Soc; Nat Wildlife Assn; Natural Hist Soc; Audubon Soc; Smithsonian Assocs; Ctr for Study of Dem Instns; Pi Gamma Mu; Mason; Shriner; Kiwanis; Others; r/Prot; hon/Bronze Plaque for Outstg Contbn to Hosp Adm; Commun Ldrs & Noteworthy Ams; Men Achmt; DIB; W/W Am Ed; Dir Am Scholars; Am Men of Sci; Others.

PERKINS, DAVID WILLIAM oc/Minister; b/Sept 16, 1944; h/235 S Fifth St, Williamsburg, KY 40769; ba/W'burg; m/Nancy Pruett; c/Benjamin David; p/William and Ruth Carter Perkins, Oakdale, LA; ed/BS NE La Univ; ThM, ThD New Orleans Bapt Theol Sem; pa/Pastor 1st Bapt Ch, W'burg 1976-; Student Pastorates La & Miss 1965-76; Trustee Ky Bapt Bd Child Care 1978-80; Adj Tchr New Testament NO Bapt Theol Sem 1973-76; Trustee SE Ky Bapt Hosp 1976-; Soc Biblical Lit; Adv Com Home Bible Study, So Bapt Conv 1979-80; Current Chm Mt Zion Bapt Assn Missions Com; Other Denom Positions; cp/Mem Pers Com Sr Citizens W'burg; Adv Com Nsg Dept, Cumberland Col (W'burg); r/So Bapt; hon/Author Bible Study Mats, SS Bd (SBC) & Periodical Articles; Acad S'ship, NE La Univ.

PERKINS, KENNETH WARREN oc/Art Laboratory Director; b/Mar 3, 1927; h/PO Box 396, Elon Col, NC 27244; ba/Burlington, NC; m/Margaret Southard; c/Virginia, Susan, David; p/L Warren and Gladys Bell Perkins, B'ton; ed/BA; MS; PhD; mil/AUS 1946-47; pa/Dir Art Labs Carolina Biol Supply Co; AAAS; Assn SEn Biologists; Soc Plastics Engrs; AIBS; Assn SEn Parasitologists; Am Soc Zoologists; hon/Sigma Xi.

PERLBERG, WILLIAM oc/Executive; b/Jul 30, 1933; ba/700 S Fourth St, Harrison, NJ 07029; m/Muriel; c/Mark, Elyssa; p/Samuel and Pearl Pulver Perlberg; ed/BS City Col NY 1954; Grad Studies Univ City NY 1960-63; mil/AUS 1954-56; pa/VP Res & Devel; Chem Specialties Mfrs Assn; Am Chem Soc; Air Pollution Control Assn; r/Judaism; hon/Holder 5 Patents in Chem, Engrg, Related Fields; Author & Lectr on Topics of Bus Adm, Res & Devel, Disinfection, Aerosols & Pollution.

PERLIK, CHARLES ANDREW JR oc/Labor Union President; b/Nov 13, 1923; h/2407 Barbour Rd, Falls Ch, VA 22043; ba/Washington, DC; m/Marion Ford; c/Paul, Lesley, Stephen; p/Charles A Perlik, Vienna, VA; Theresa Anna Perlik, Vienna; ed/BSJ 1949, MSJ 1950 NWn; mil/USAF 1943-46, 3½ Yrs, WWII, 1/Lt; pa/VChm NA Intl Fdn Journalists; Secy-Treas Mellett Fund for a Free & Responsible Press; Sigma Delta Chi; cp/-Steering Com Nat Urban Coalition; r/Unitarian.

PERLMAN, EILEEN ELEANOR oc/Investor (Self-employed); b/Oct 31, 1935; h/6401 Cellini St, Coral Gables, FL 33146; c/3 Chd; p/Bennett Viggo and Eleanor Lucille Christensen; ed/NWn Univ 1954; Patricia Stevens Modeling Sch; Liberty Bapt Col 1978-80; pa/CoFdr Lum's Inc (Restaurant Chain); cp/Protect Our Chd; Anti-ERA Campaign Wkr; Wom for Responsible Leg & Polit Action, S Fla Chapt; Active in Floridians Against Casino Takeover; US Lawn Tennis Assn; US Figure Skating Assn; Am Bridge Clb; Am Security Coun, Nat Adv Bd; Sustaining Mem Repub Nat Com; Philip Crane for Pres; r/Granada Presb Ch: Chm Visitation 1973-75, Cir Chm 1978-80; Bd Dirs Christian Wom's Clb, S Fla Chapt; Interfaith Com Against

Blasphemy; Christian Broadcasting Co "700" Clb; Personalities of S.

PERRAM, STEVEN WILLIAM oc/Executive; b/Jul 25, 1951; h/7211 Creek Crest Dr, Houston, TX 77095; ba/Houston; p/Peter M and Lorraine E Perram, Houston; ed/BS cum laude 1973, MBA magna cum laude 1974 USC; pa/Pres The People Power Assn Inc (Distributors of Aloessence Cosmetics); VP Fin Seer Industs Inc (Nev) 1978; Dir Mktg Stewart W Coast Title Co, Los Angeles, Cal 1977; Securities Analyst Reynolds Securities Inc, LA 1975; VP & CoFdr World Sports Mgmt Inc, LA 1971; Other Former Positions; So Cal Motion Picture Coun; So Cal Solar Energy Soc; cp/Mem Key Clb Intl; Rotary Clb LA; Toastmasters; hon/Dist'd Alumni Awd, USC; Dist'd Bus Achmt, LA.

PERRITT, HENRY HARDY oc/Educational Consultant; Insurance Broker; Farmer; b/Jun 13, 1918; h/Lake Tyler Rd, Rt 1, Whitehouse, TX 75791; ba/Same; m/-Margaret Floyd; c/H H Jr, Margaret P Davis; p/F S and Blanche Bagley Perritt (dec); ed/BA 1938, MA 1942 La St Univ; PhD Univ Fla 1954; mil/USNR, Cmdr Ret'd, WWII, Korean; pa/Real Est Investor; Raises Horses; Human Relats Advr Public Schs, Little Rock; Chm Div Humanities Miles Col, Birmingham, Ala 1962-(on leave); Pres B'ham Univ Sch 1959-62; Assoc Prof Univ Ala 1956-59; Asst Prof Univ Fla 1954-56; Asst Prof Univ Va 1946-53; Instr La St Univ 1942; HS Tchr Miss & La 1938-41; Instr Adult Classes La, Va, DC, Ala & Ark 1939-; Moderator "Know Your News" Ala ETV Network 1960-62; Prof Linguistics Wichita, Ks St Univ Sum 1966; cp/UF; Kiwanis; K of P; r/Unitarian & Meth; hon/Phi Kappa Phi; Kappa Phi Kappa; Tau Kappa Alpha; W/W: S&SW, Am Ed; DIB; Dir Am Scholars; Commun Ldrs Am; Personalities of S; Fulbright Lectr Brazil 1964; Conslt-Lectr Binational Ctr Sems for Eng Tchrs Rio de Janiero & Fortaleza, Brazil 1964; Pres So Spch Assn 1958-59; Res Grants; Univ Ala 1957-59, Richmond, Va Area Univ Ctr 1950; Grad Fellow Univ Fla 1952-54; Pub'd Author Num Works.

PERRY, CHARLES W oc/Military Chaplain; b/Jul 25, 1948; h/828-A Nevada Oval, Plattsburgh AFB, NY 12903; ba/Plattsburgh AFB; m/Joyce Marie Sumners; c/Christopher Warren; p/Collin Wade Perry Jr, Birmingham, AL; Belle Ray Perry, Louisville, KY; ed/BA cum laude 1970; MDiv 1974; DMin Cand; mil/USAFR 1973-77; Active Duty 1977-; USAF Chaplain; pa/ACPE; Inst Soc, Ethics & Life Scis; cp/JCs; Boy Scout Ldr; CAP Ldr; Vol Instr Heart Assn; r/U Meth: Clergyman; Ala-W Fla Conf; hon/Former Eagle Scout; Order of Arrow, BSA; W/W in Rel; Awd of Honor, Md Heart Assn.

PERRY, REGINALD CARMAN oc/Professor Emeritus; b/Aug 15, 1903; h/110 S Beech St, Apt 2, Pine Bluff, AR 71601; p/William and Mary Horwood Perry (dec); ed/BA Mt Allison Univ 1930; BD Victoria Univ 1935; MA 1936, PhD 1945 Toronto Univ; Postdoct Studies; pa/Prof Emeritus Humanities & Phil Univ Ark-PB; Am, Ark Phil Assns; Ark & Nat Ret'd Tchrs Assns; Former Mem: AAUP, IPA; cp/Meth; hon/Hon Mem, Ark Sheriffs' Assn; Plaques for Outstg Ser to Ed, Intl Clb (UAPB); Pub'd Author.

PERRYMAN, BRUCE CLARK oc/Insurance; Rancher; b/Jan 28, 1939; h/404 S 18th, Worland, WY 82401; ba/Worland; m/Sharon Lynn Lungren; c/Kimberly Jo, Bruce Homer; p/Homer F and Phyllis Coltharp White Perryman, Murray, UT; ed/BA (Bus Ad) 1965; BA (Ed) 1966; MS 1966; Addit Studies; mil/USAF 1958-62; p/Phi Delta Kappa; AMA; AASA; Life Mem NEA; AVA; AVERA; NALU; cp/Masonic Lodge 32°; Elks; Repub; Civitan Intl; r/Luth; hon/Phi Delta Kappa; Outstg Edr Am; Ftball NYLIC top Clb Qualifier; W/W Fin & Indust; W/W W.

PERSCH, RUTH LUCILLE KELLY oc/Parliamentarian; Retired Teacher; b/Nov 3, 1892; h/Room 377, Menger Hotel, 204 Alamo Plaza, San Antonio, TX 78295; m/Albert Adolph Persch; p/Patrick H and Emily Elizabeth Short Kelly; ed/AA; BS; MS; MEd; cp/Nat Adv Bd Am Security Coun; hon/Hons: Tex Fine Arts Com, Univ So Cal Pres's Cir; AAUW Gift Name; Notable Ams.

PESKE, PATRIC O oc/Psychologist; b/Sept 21, 1942; h/PO Box 7149, Flint, MI 48507; ba/Same; m/Nancy; c/Arthur Z Aleksandor; p/R Wilhelm Peske, Arkon, OH; E Michele Bordeaux, Akron; ed/BA; MA; pa/Psychologist: Human Devel, Lng & Pathol; Profl Pract; Nat & Intl Lectr'g, Res & Writing; Bd Dirs ACLU; IPA; cp/Guest Lectr Var Commun Groups; hon/7 Awds for Original Res; W/W MW; Intl Men of Achmt; Others.

PETERS, ELMER SYLVESTER oc/Investments; b/Feb 27, 1923; h/7667 E 45th St N, Wichita, KS 67220; ba/Wichita; m/Mary L; c/John Charles, Elmer Jr, David Lee, Cecilia Marie; p/(dec); mil/Vet WWII; pa/Sedgwick Co Commr 1963-75; Sedgwick Co Comm Bd Chm 1964, 68, 71; Dir Nat Assn Cos 1969-74; Dir Govt Res Corp, Topeka, Ks 1970-75; Dir Nat Reg Couns Govt, Washington, DC 1969-74; Appt'd to Ks Adv Coun on Inter-Govtl Relats 1973-77; Mem 12-man St-wide Wel Policy Com for Co Commrs 1970-71; Pres Local Govt Res Corp, Leag Ks Municipalities 1968; Chm Sedgwick Co Pers Bd 1968-72; cp/Cath Social Sers: Chm, Former Dir; Former Dir Ks Nat Jr Livestock Show; Former Chm Sedgwick Co Repub Ctl Com; Former 4th Dist Dir Ks Day; Former Chm Sedgwick Co Bd for Social Wel; Former Judge Freedoms Foun at Val Forge (Pa); r/Cath; hon/W/W: MW, Gtr Wichita; Cit of Apprec, Lions; Hon Life Mem, Wichita C of C; 1st Intl Cosmopolitan of Yr for US, Canada & Mexico.

PETERS, GEORGE THOMAS oc/University Professor; b/Nov 24, 1930; h/2804 Turtle Creek, Jonesboro, AR 72401; ba/State Univ, AR; m/Mary Helen; c/Jennifer, Gregory, Douglas; p/Emery Thomas and Opal Peters, Poplar Bluff, MO; ed/BSE; MSE; EdD; mil/AUS; pa/APGA; ACES; NVGA; NEA; Num St & Reg Affils; cp/Benevolent & Protective Order of Elks; r/Meth; hon/Men Achmt; DIB; Intl W/W Commun Ser; Notable Ams; Commun Ldrs & Noteworthy Ams; Ldrs in Ed; Personalities of S; W/W: Child Devel Profls, S&SW, MW.

PETERSEN, GARY MICHAEL oc/Executive, Resource Recovery/Recycling; b/Nov 23, 1947; h/605 Swarthmore Ave, Pacific Palisades, CA 90272; ba/Pacific Palisades; m/Alexandra; c/Samantha Kate; p/S E and Kathleen Petersen, Los Angeles, CA; pa/Fdr

Cal Resource Recovery Assn; Recycling Conslt; Market Analysis & Res; cp/Recycling Progs for Schs, Bus, Chs, Civic Groups; Lobbying Leg for Funding Recycling Progs; hon/Cal Com for Resource Recovery Recycling Awd; Humane Awd; Cits: City & Co of LA.

PETERSON, BARBARA ANN BENNETT oc/History Instructor; b/Sept 6, 1942; h/1341 Laukahi St, Honolulu, HI 96821;

ba/Honolulu; m/Frank Lynn; p/George W and Hope H Bennett, Portland, OR; ed/BA, BS Oreg St Univ; PhD Univ Hi 1978; pa/Hist Instr Univ Hi; Hawaiian Hist Assn; Hi Com for Hist & Humanities; Edit Bd CCSA 1977; cp/Honolulu Symph; Honolulu Acad Arts; Heart & Cancer Fund Drs; Fund Raiser Stanford Alumni Assn; r/Prot; hon/Fulbright Scholar to Japan; Phi Kappa Phi; Outstg Sr Wom, Oreg St Univ; Outstg Edrs Am.

PETERSON, DAVID LAWRENCE oc/Manufacturing Methods Engineer; b/Apr 25, 1923; h/811 E Ruth Ave, Phoenix, AZ 85020; ba/Phoenix; m/Bertie L Wicker (dec); Donna L; p/David and Alma Haglund Peterson (dec); ed/ME; Mech Design'g Engr; Cert'd Mfg Engr; pa/Mfg Methods Engr Sperry; Soc Mfg Engrs; Computer & Automated Sys Assn; Phoenix Adv Com Phoenix Elec Mfg Conf & Exhibits; r/Presb: Ruling Elder on Session, Worship Com, Communion Dir, Coor Our Pairs & Spares Social Group, Pres & Alt Instr Adult Bible Class; hon/Soc Mfg Engrs: Ser Awd, Past Chm's Gavel; Men Achmt; DIB; W/W in W.

PETERSON, EULAH LEANA oc/Assistant Professor; b/Nov 30, 1948; h/PO Box 84, Mound Bayou, MS 38762; ba/Itta Bena, MS; p/Isaac M Peterson Sr (dec); Eldra H Peterson, Mound Bayou; ed/BA cum laude; MEd; PhD; pa/Asst Prof Spec Ed & Elem Ed Miss Val St Univ; CEC; cp/Mound Bayou Civic Clb Inc; Alpha Kappa Alpha; r/1st Bapt Ch, Mound Bayou: Mem; hon/Alpha Kappa Mu; Kappa Delta Pi; W/W Among Students in Am Univs & Cols; Outstg Yg Wom in Am Nom; Mound Bayou Hall of Fame Inductee.

PETERSON, FREDRICK ALVIN oc/Professor; Author; Lecturer; b/Jun 23, 1920; h/15 Elizabeth St, Buckhannon, WV 26201; ba/Buckhannon; m/(dec); c/Claudia, Fredrick; p/(dec); ed/BA; MA; ABD Ind Univ 1973; DD 1975; mil/Served 1942-45; European Theatre SHAEF & USFET, M/Sgt, 3 Battle Stars; pa/WVa Wesleyan Col: Prof Anthropol, Dir Latin Am Studies; Author: 7 Books, 60 Articles; Explorer Lacandon Jungle; Fellow Am Anthropol Assn; r/Luth; hon/Outstg Tchr Am Awd (2); Merit Tchg Awds; Omicron Kappa Delta; Pi Gamma Mu; Fellow Instituto Interamericano.

PETERSON, JAMES NEAL oc/Pharmaceutical Representative; b/Apr 24, 1951; h/189-8 Merrimac Trail, Williamsburg, VA 23185; ba/Same; p/John A and Elgie A Peterson, Clinton, NC; ed/AA Chowan Col 1971; BS 1975; MA E Carolina Univ 1978; pa/Pharm Rep USV Labs; Profl Sales Rep 1978; CoDir Admissions 1977; Assoc Dir Admissions 1976; Hd Tennis Coach E Carolina Univ 1976; Va Pharm Assn 1978; cp/Murfreesboro (NC) JCs; r/1st Bapt; hon/Outstg Yg Men Am; W/W S&SE.

PETERSON, WILLIAM DAVID oc/College Administrator, Counselor, Educator; b/Oct 20, 1942; h/W808 Rolland Ave, Spokane, WA 99218; ba/Spokane; m/-Kathleen Parrish; c/Kerstin Swan; p/David William Peterson (dec); Esther Swan Peterson, Santa Barbara, CA; ed/BA Wheaton Col 1964; MA 1965, PhD 1972 Mich St Univ; pa/Whitworth Col, Spokane: VP for Student Life & Dir Student Devel 1975-; Asst Prof Ed Purdue Univ 1971-75; Mich St Univ: Asst Dir Grad Ed & Res, Ofc Dean of Students 1970-71, Asst Dir Fin Aids 1968-70; Other Former Positions; Am Assn for Higher Ed; Assn for Study of Higher Ed; Am Col Pers Assn; APGA; Am Assn Christian Cnslrs; Am Assn Sex Edrs, Cnslrs & Therapists; Christian Assn for Student Affairs; Nat Assn Student Pers Admrs; NW Col Pers Assn; Christian Assn for Psychol Studies; Assn for Creative Change; Profl Conslt; Edit Bd Activs; cp/Conslt & Spkr Parents Without Partners & Parenting Cooperatives; r/Presb; hon/Ldrs in Ed; DIB; W/W W; Outstg Yg Man Am.

PETHEL, DOROTHY LORENE oc/Nursing Instructor; Marriage, Family & Child Counselor; b/Aug 15, 1927; h/8150

Chipwood Way, Orangevale, CA 95662; ba/Rocklin, CA; m/James Worth; c/Darlene Kapelewski, Glenda Seawel, Craig; p/William Jennings and Ruby Coral Hooe (dec); ed/AA San Bernardino Val Col; AA Riverside City Col; BS Los Angeles St Col; MS Cal St Univ; PhD Cal Nat Open Univ; pa/Nsg Instr Sierra Col; Pvt Pract Cnsl'g; Am & Cal Nurses' Assns; Cal Tchrs Assn; Nat Orthopedic Nurses' Assn; Golden W Orthopedic Group; Cal Voc Nurse Edrs; r/Holy Fam Cath Ch; hon/Author: *A Comparison of Two Approaches to Planning Instrn on Drug Abuse* & Periodicals.

PETILLO, JOHN JOSEPH oc/Deputy Director; b/Mar 19, 1947; h/91 Washington St, Newark, NJ 07102; ba/Newark; p/Jerry and Geraldine Petillo, Newark; ed/MA Seton Hall Univ; Profl Dipl Fordham Univ; MDiv Darlington Sch Theol; PhD Fordham Univ; MPA Rutgers Univ; pa/Dep Dir Cath Commun Sers; Fieldwork Bd Fordham Sch Social Sci; Chd's Com NJ Mtl Hlth Planning Com; Asst to Pres Seton Hall Univ; r/Rom Cath.

PETRY, JAMES WESLEY oc/Executive; b/Jun 16, 1938; h/Rt 1, Box 92, Stephenson, VA 22656; ba/Winchester, VA; m/Hazel Bryant; c/Scott David, Julie Elizabeth; p/Maurice D and Robertine P Petry, Verona, VA; pa/VP Sales & Mktg; Past Pres Shenandoah Traffic Clb; Hagerstown Traffic Clb; Sales & Mktg Coun ATA; cp/Past Pres Exc Clb Winchester; r/1st U Meth Ch, Winchester: Adm Bd.

PETTIT, ANNE oc/Professor; b/Feb 14, 1924; h/4501 N Wheeling, Muncie, IN 47304; ba/Muncie; c/Margaret Anne Dutcher, John Edward; ed/BS 1945, MS 1951 MacMurray Col; PhD Laurance Univ 1974; Addit Studies; pa/Ball St Univ 1974-: Coor Spec PE, Coor Elem Sch PE, Elem Sch Specialist, Coor Instrnl Devel, Conslt for Handicapped; Asst Prof Univ Ill 1969-72; Supvr-Instr NW Mo St Col 1968-69; Dir Hlth, PE & Driver Ed Rosary HS, Aurora, Ill 1964-69; Dir Hlth & PE Madonna HS 1957-64; Other Former Profl Positions; ASP; Charter Mem TAASP; ADIS; ACM-SIGCUE; AAAA; Local Pres Wom's Intl Bowling Cong; Ind Ladies Golf Assn; Wn Golf Assn; US Golf Assn; Laban Art of Movemt Guild (England); U Cerebral Palsy Ind: Adv Bd, Chm PE & Rec Com; Spec PE Conslt Univ Ill; Bd Dirs Hope Foun; Bd Dirs Hope Ctr; New Hope Foun Ill Div: Bd Dirs Secy, Prog Chm; Ill Assn for Cerebral Palsy: Adv Bd, Pres Five Rivers Area; IRA; WAPECW; MAPECW; CAPECW; MAHPER; MSTA; IEA; ADTSEA; AAUP; Conslt; Num Other Profl Activs; cp/GSA; Nat Travel Assn; Nat & Ctl Ski Assns; Ill Archery Assn; Num Vol Activs; r/Reorg'd Ch LDS; hon/Life Mem: Phi Nu, Alpha Sigma Nu, Phi Lambda Pi, Phi Epsilon Kappa; Spec Merit Salary Supplemt, Ball St Univ; Hon'd for Outstg Activs to Aid Cerebral Palsied, U Cerebral Palsy of Ind Inc; Bailey Scholar, Univ Ill; Qtr Century Awd for Tchg, Ill Assn HPER; Recog'd by Prime Min Kenyatta (Kenya, E Africa) for "Ambassadorship" to Kenya; Cit of Commun Ser Awd, U Commun Sers Awd (Aurora, Ill); Var Ser Awds; Num Hon Life Mbrships; Num Biogl Listings; Pubs; Others.

PETTIT, KATHERINE DENSHAW oc/Librarian; b/May 22, 1925; h/8443 Hidden Meadow, San Antonio, TX 78230; ba/San Antonio; m/George Sr (dec); c/Kim Moreau, Georgeanne, George Jr; p/Moreau E Denshaw, Marshall, TX; Rose K Denshaw (dec); ed/BA; MSLS; pa/Libn Trinity Univ; ALA; TLA; NLA; BLA; ANA; TNA; AAUP; CLENE; cp/Am Heart Assn; r/Rom Cath; hon/World W/W Wom in Ed.

PFEIFFER, DAVID GRAHAM oc/University Professor; b/May 13, 1934; h/17 Corey Rd, Brookline, MA 02146; ba/Boston, MA; m/Marguerite; c/Clifford, Katherine, Carol; p/David C and Ruth D Pfeiffer, Dallas, TX; ed/BA 1956, MA 1963 Univ Tex-A; MDiv Epis Theol Sem of SW 1960; PhD Univ Rochester 1975; pa/Chperson & Assoc Prof Public Mgmt

& Adm Suffolk Univ; Num Adv Bds & Couns; Spkr Var Profl Orgs; cp/Mass St Dir White House Conf on Handicapped Indivs.

PFIESTER, RALPH GERALD oc/Librarian; b/Mar 31, 1934; h/PO Box 1647, Paradise, CA 95969; ba/Paradise; p/George Samuel and Flossie Josephine Pfiester, Ft Lauderdale, FL; ed/BA; MS; BD; MTheol; pa/Libn Paradise HS; Life Mem NEA; Cal Tchrs' Assn; Am Lib Assn; cp/Secy Veritas Foun; r/Presb; hon/S'ship, McCormick Theol Sem.

PHELPS, EDNA MAE oc/Homemaker; Politician; b/Jun 12, 1920; h/RR #1, Seminole, OK 74868; m/Joe; c/Ronald Jerome, Joelton Mark; p/W H and Nedda Hough, Seminole; ed/BA Okla St Univ; Grad Studies Okla Univ; cp/Dem Nat Com-wom (Okla); Past Pres: Okla Fdn Dem Wom, Seminole Co Dem Wom's Clb; Okla Mem Dem Nat Charter Comm; Del Dem Nat Conv 1968, 72, 76; Del Dem Nat Mid-Term Conf 1974-78; Former Precnt Chm Seminole Co; r/Presb; hon/1st Wom Named to Okla St Election Bd (Elected Chm 1969-76).

PHELPS, WAYNE ARNITA oc/Homemaker; Civic Worker; b/Aug 26, 1919; h/1448 Steven Dr, Birmingham, AL 35226; m/Sam Perry; c/Janice P Dukes, Lynn P Kelley; p/William Edward Bynum (dec); Clara B Bynum, B'ham; ed/AB B'ham-So Col 1941; cp/2/VP 3rd Dist Ala Fdn Wom's Clbs; Past VP Hoover Homeowner's Assn; Former Mem Adv Coun Commun Schs, Berry Area; Past Pres: Birch Tree Garden Clb, W Haven Garden Clb, 5th Dist Ala Sch Bd Assn, Intra St Parlimentary Unit, B'ham Bd Ed; Bd Dirs Spain Rehab Wom's Com; Former Mem: Hlth Coun B'ham-Jefferson Coun, Tuscaloosa Field Adv Coun, SEn Ednl Lab, Bd B'ham Chapt ARC; Delta Zeta; Secy Ala St Assn Parliamentns; Others; r/Beverly Meth: Adm Bd, Supt Yth Dept 1963-71, Pres Wom's Soc Christian Ser 1962-64; hon/Wom of Yr, Delta Zeta (B'ham) 1964; Life Mem: Ala Cong PTA, Nat Cong PTA.

PHIBBS, PHILIP MONFORD oc/Private University President; b/Oct 2, 1931; h/3500 N 18th St, Tacoma, WA 98406; ba/Tacoma; m/Gwen Willis; c/Kathleen, Jennifer, Diana; p/Clifford and Dorothy Wright Phibbs, Gardiner, WA; ed/BA; MA; PhD; mil/USAF; pa/Pres Univ Puget Sound; Govt Intern; Congl Fellow; Prof Polit Sci; Pacific Sci Ctr Foun; Trustee Tacoma Art Mus; r/Prot; hon/Rotary Foun Fellow; Edward Hillman Fellow; Fulbright Grant; Phi Beta Kappa; Phi Kappa Ohi; Pi Sigma Alpha; Phi Kappa Delta.

PHILIPS, WALLACE MERRITT JR oc/Ophthalmologist; b/Sept 21, 1941; h/452 Fletcher Pl, Winter Park, FL 32789; ba/Orlando, FL; m/Carolee O; c/Stephen Todd, Mark Wallace; p/Wallace M Sr and Jane Elizabeth Philips, Sanford, FL; ed/BS Davidson Col 1963; MD Emory Univ Sch Med 1967; mil/USN Lt Cmdr, Chief Opthalmol Ser Nav Hosp, Charleston, SC 1973-74; pa/Staff Orlando Reg Med Ctr; Exec Com Orange Co Med Soc; Fla Med Assn; Am Acad Ophthal & Otolaryngol; Am Intra-ocular Implant Soc; Fla Soc Ophthal; Ctl Fla Ophthal Soc; cp/John Young Mus Mem; Repub; r/Epis; hon/Alpha Omega Alpha; W/W S&SW.

PHILLIPS, CHANDLER ALLEN oc/Physician; Educator; b/Dec 21, 1942; h/4310 K Springcreek, Dayton, OH 45405; ba/Dayton; p/Chandler Arza Phillips (dec); Ann Lloyd Phillips, La Canada, CA; ed/AB Stanford 1965; MD Univ Cal 1969; PE Cal 1974; mil/USAF 1970-72, Capt MC; SEA; pa/Wright St Univ: Asst Prof, Prog Mgr Biomed Engrg, Conslt in Med Dayton VA Ctr (Ohio); hon/Commend Medal, USAF; AMA Physicians Recog Awd.

PHILLIPS, KAREN ANN oc/Musician; Radio Producer; Composer; Recording Artist; b/Oct 29, 1942; ba/25th Floor, Municipal Bldg, Ctr & Chambers Sts, New York, NY 10004; ed/Yale Univ Sum Sch, Norfolk, Conn 1964; Curtis Inst Music, Phila, Pa 1964-65; BM w distn Eastman Sch Music 1964; Postgrad Dipl Juilliard Sch Music 1967; pa/Nat Endowmt Fund, Sears-Roebuck Foun Affil Artist w Perf'g Arts Coun of LA Music Ctr 1969-71, w Worcester Arts Assn, Mass 1971-72; Spec Progs Recorded for US & Fgn Radio Broadcasts; Lectr, Concert Artist for Cols, Univs, Sororities, Frats, Guilds, Clbs; Guest Artist Lincoln Ctr Chamber Music Soc (2); Solo Recitals: Metro Mus of Art, NYC, Paris Mus of Mod Art, Strasbourg Conservatory, BBC Radio, Kennedy Ctr for Nat Music Coun's Bicent Parade of Am Music, Tex Day Perf of Composition, Sev Univs, Others; Soloist: Mus Mod Art (NY), Rockefeller Inst (NY), London's Queen Elizabeth Hall & Purcell Rm & Round House for London Proms, BBC & Helsinki & NY Philharm Orchs, Theater Fenice, Venice, Others; Solo & Chamber Music: Liederkrantz Soc, The Bohemians (NY Music Clb); Tchr: New Col, Sarasota, Fla, Univ Hi (Artist-in-Residence), Quebec Conservatory, Quebec, Canada, Riverdale Sch of Music, Bronx, NY, Merrywood Sch of Music, Lenox, Mass; Sev Recordings, Comp Perfs; Bd Dirs: NY Fdn Music Clbs, Am Landmark Fest; Adv Bd Merrywood Music Sch Inc; Profl Pubs; Pub'd Poetry, Gt Brit; Nat Acad Recording Arts & Scis; Am Wom Composers Inc; ASCAP; Other Profl Assns; 13 Recordings; c/Secy Democracy for Stockholders Inc, NYC; Hostess OVERTURE TO WOM Radio Series, WNYC AM Radio; Staff 92nd St YMCA; r/Bapt; hon/DIB; W/W Music; Outstg Yg Wom Am; Ency Mod Music; Book of Honor; Intl W/W Intells; Intl Reg Profiles; Num Reviews & Features; Intl House Living S'ship, NYC; Juilliard; Elsie & Walter Naumberg Awd, S'ship; NeCollins Fund, NY Univ; HS Acad, Sports, & Music Awds; Others.

PHILLIPS, MARELL KNOTT oc/Elementary Teacher; b/Oct 26, 1922; h/35 Severance Cir Dr, Cleveland Heights, OH 44118; ba/Cleveland; m/Hiawatha (dec); p/John Sidney and Madeline Davidson Knott (dec); ed/BA, MA Case Wn Reserv Univ; Addit Studies; pa/Tchr, Bolton Sch; Phi Delta Kappa; Assn of English; cp/Phillis Wheatley Assn (YWCA); r/Cory U Meth Ch; hon/Tchr of Yr 1971, 73, 76; Phillis Wheatley Merit Awd; Martha Holden Jennings Foun Tchr Ldrship.

PHILLIPS, MARJORIE oc/Artist; b/Oct 25, 1974; h/2101 Foxhall Rd NW, Washington, DC 20007; m/Duncan (dec); c/Laughlin, Mary Marjorie; p/Chas Ernest and Alice Beal Acker (dec); pa/Dir Emeritus Phillips Collection (Mus) 1966-78; Var Exhbns of Paintings; r/Epis; hon/Awd of Merit (w husband), Pa Mus; Hon Deg, Smith Col 1973; Author.

PHILLIPS, MICHAEL JOSEPH oc/Poet; Literary Critic; College Teacher; b/Mar 2, 1937; h/5840 Washington Blvd, Indianapolis, IN 46220; ba/Indpls; p/Bernice Hollibaugh, Indpls; ed/BA Wabash; MA, PhD Ind Univ-B; Addit Studies; pa/Tchr Adv'd Creative Writing Poetry Free Univ Indpls; Pub'd 600+ Poems, 30 Books; hon/Phi Beta Kappa; Purdue Alumni S'ship; Ind Univ Grant; Vis Fellow, Harvard Univ.

PHILLIPS, WILLIAM HENRY oc/Civil Engineer; b/Jul 21, 1945; h/103 Cherokee Garden, Frankfort, KY 40601; ba/Frankfort; p/Jack C Phillips (dec); Martha W Phillips, Monticello, KY; ed/BSCE; MSCE; mil/USMC 1/Lt; pa/Civil Engr Ky DOT; Div Mats; ASCE; NSPE; KSPE; KATE; r/Prot; hon/Chi Epsilon; Tau Beta Pi.

PHILLIPS, WINFRED MARSHALL oc/Professor; b/Oct 7, 1940; h/924 W Fairmount, State College, PA 16801; ba/Univ Pk, PA; m/Lynda; c/Stephen, Sean; p/Claude Marshall Phillips, Richmond, VA; Gladys Barden Phillips (dec); ed/BSME; MAE; DSc; pa/Pa St Univ: Prof Aerospace Engrg Artificial Heart Res Lab, Interdisciplinary Prog Com on Bioengrg 1971- (Grad Sch),

Bioengrg Subcom on Grad Course Prog 1975-, Rank & Tenure Com Dept Aerospace Engrg 1978-79, Res Com Col Engrg 1978-79; Ctl Pa Secy ASME: Exec Com 1978-79, Chm Hons & Awds Com 1978-79; Chm Elect Mid Atl Sect Am Soc for Engrg Ed 1978-79; Acting Chm Intercol Prog Bioengrg 1978-79; Chm ASTM, Est'g Task Force on Med Device Standards, Blood Pumps 1978-; Annual Conf Com ASEE 1977-80; Bd Dirs Am Heart Assn, Ctl Pa

Chapt 1974-81; Am Phy Soc (Fluid Mechanics Div); Assoc Fellow Am Inst for Aeronautics & Astronautics; AAAS; Am Soc for Artificial Internal Organs; Intl Soc Biorheology; NY Acad Scis; Others; cp/Adv Com Explorer Scouts, BSA; r/Prot; hon/Sigma Xi; Pi Tau Sigma; NSF Traineeship, Univ Va; Dow Awd, Outstg Yg Fac Mem; Sigma Gamma Tau; Res Career Devel Awd, USPHS; Outstg Advr Awd, Pa St Univ Engrg Soc; Biogl Listings; Others.

PHILLIPS-SILVERNAIL, LESLIE J oc/-Administrative Manager; b/Apr 18, 1950; h/606-1 Woodside Sierra, Sacramento, CA 95825; ba/Davis, CA; p/Joe B Phillips; Dorothea Little, Colorado Springs, CO; ed/Att'd Univ Cal-D 1968-70; mil/USAR; pa/Univ Cal-D: Adm Mgr Cardiovas Med, Ad Hoc Com on Status of Wom on Campus, Affirmative Action Group, Adm Mgmt Group; hon/S'ships & Awds; Life Mem, Cal S'ship Fdn; Bk of Am Awd for Social Scis; Spec Commemorative Awd, Am Col Cardiol; World W/W Wom; Personalities W&MW; Commun Ldrs & Noteworthy Ams; DIB; Intl W/W Intells.

PHILPOTT, EMALEE ISOLA EWING oc/Librarian; Media Specialist; b/Dec 19, 1921; h/PO Box 233, Duncan, AZ 85534; m/Earl Russell; ed/AB Col Wm & Mary 1942; Geo Wash Univ 1945-47; MEd Univ Ariz 1955; pa/Chief Libn Engrg Res & Devel Labs, Ft Belvoir, Va 1948-50; Tchr Spanish, Hist & Social Studies Duncan Union HS (Ariz) 1950-52; Libn & Tchr Eng Pima Public Schs (Ariz) 1952-55; Libn Thatcher HS (Ariz) 1955-; Jr Partner Philpott & Son (Wholesale Distributors), Duncan 1950-; Past Pres ALSA; Ariz Adv Coun on Libs; AAUW; ALA; Ariz Assn for A-V Ed; Beta Sigma Phi; cp/St Leg Com; hon/World W/W Wom; Life Fellow ABIRA.

PICKEL, CONRAD L oc/Stained Glass Designer, Manufacturer, Artist; b/Feb 10, 1906; h/500 SW 16th St, Boynton Beach, FL 33435; ba/Boynton Bch; m/Joan; c/R Paul, Erma P Obermayr; p/Konrad and Kathrine Pickel (dec); ed/Grad Art Acad (Munich, Germany); Master's Deg Franz Mayer Studio (Munich); pa/Liturgical Art Design; Painter; hon/Intl Recog.

PICKETT, JOSEPH C oc/Arts Administrator; b/Jul 19, 1943; h/1503 Ski Lodge, Montgomery, AL 36117; ba/Montgomery; p/-Orlie W Pickett (dec); Wilda D Pickett, Montgomery; ed/BS; BSEd; MACT; MPA; EdS; mil/USCGR, Lt (Jg), Adm Ofcr; pa/Arts Admr Ala St Coun on Arts & Humanities; Phi Delta Kappa; Kappa Delta Pi; Am Soc for Public Adm; cp/Singletons; Former Kiwanis; Former Bd Dirs Big Brothers; r/Meth: Career Singles Class; hon/Dist'd Ser, Delta Chi; Pi Sigma Alpha; W/W S&SW; Personalities of S.

PIERSOL, EDNA WAGNER oc/Artist; b/Feb 9, 1931; h/12905 Sunnybrook Dr, Prospect, KY 40059; ba/Same; m/Fay L; p/Eric, Kurt; p/Arthur E Wagner (dec); Ruth Wagner, Prospect; ed/Att'd Art Inst Pgh; pa/Tchr: Art Ctr Assn Louisville 1974-, Ivy Sch Profl Art (Substitute), 1st UP Commun House, Artists & Craftsmen's Guild 1962-71, Arts & Crafts Ctr Pgh 1960's; Solo Shows incl: J B Speed Art Mus 1978, Upstairs at the Train Sta (Anchorage, Ky), Gallery of The Different Drummer (Ft Myers Bch, Fla), WHAS Gallery (L'ville), Millsop Ctr (Weirton, WVa), Irwin Inn (Ontario, Canada), Others; Num Invitational & Competitive Exhbns incl: M-W Watercolor Soc Exhbn 1978, Allied Artists Am Nat Acad Gallery (NY) 1977, Ky Wom Artists Univ Ky 1977, So Watercolor Soc Annual 1977 (Cheekwood, Nashville, Tenn), Cinc Art Clb "Viewpoint" 1975, 76; Others; Rep'd in Var Collections incl'g: Ky St Pks Comm, Butler Inst Am Art (Youngstown, Ohio), Mt Lebanon Public Schs (Pa), Mellon Bk (Pgh), Citizen's Fidelity (L'ville), Others; Bd Dirs Arts & Crafts Ctr Pgh 1970-73; Exhibiting Mem Assoc'd Artists Pgh; Pres Pgh Watercolor Soc 1971-74; Bd Dirs Art Ctr Assn L'ville 1975-76; Lexington (Ky) Art Leag; Exhibiting Mem So Watercolor Soc; Nat Leag Am Pen Wom; Lecture Demonstration Bur Am Soc Artists (Chgo, Ill); Charter Mem Ky Watercolor Soc; r/Christian; hon/DIB; World W/W Wom.

PIERSON, J O oc/Executive Director; b/Nov 6, 1937; h/325 Crossfield Dr, Knoxville, TN 37920; ba/K'ville; m/Norma; c/Rebecca Lynn, Rachel Adell, Erika Leigh; p/Bascom and Georgia Pierson, Fall Branch, TN; ed/BA Milligan Col 1959; MA Univ Tenn 1962; pa/Exec Dir E Tenn Chd's Rehab Ctr; Lectr Spec Ed Milligan Col, Tenn; Conslt in Spec Ed Standard Pub'g Co, Cincinnati, Ohio; Tenn Hearing & Spch Assn; Knox Co Hlth Coun; CEC; Assoc Mem Am Acad Cerebral Palsy; Am Assn Mtl Deficiency; cp/Kiwanis Clb K'ville; U Planning Coun Gtr K'ville; r/Woodlawn Christian Ch: Mem, Supvr Spec SS Prog; hon/Author *Dynamic Ideas for the Christian Ed of the Handicapped* & Qrtly Articles to *KEY to Christian Ed*; HS Valedictorian; Milligan Col: Fac Awd (Outstg Sr), Dist'd Alumnus.

PIGMAN, GLADYS HARGREAVES oc/Materials Engineer; h/316-0 Sharon Way, Jamesburg, NJ 08831; ba/Same; m/Ward; p/Leon A and Essie B Hargreaves, Pearson, GA; ed/BS 1935, MS 1941 Univ Ga; pa/Pres Apollo Solar Energy Corp 1977-; Nav Air Mats Lab: Mats Engr 1970-, Res Chemist 1960-70, Textile Technologist 1956-60; Other Former Positions; Fellow AAAS; Am Phy Soc; Am Chem Soc: Mbrship Com 1969-73, Chm Intl Relats Com 1969-71, Cand for Councilor 1974-76, Others; Sigma Delta Epsilon: Pres 1980-81, Pres-elect 1979-80, VP 1978-79, Others; NY Microscopical Soc; Photo Soc Am; Fellow Am Inst Chemists; hon/Profl Pubs; Am Men & Wom Sci; Am Chem Soc Cit Index.

PIKAART, LEN oc/Professor; b/Jan 4, 1933; h/27 Utah Pl, Athens, OH 45701; ba/Athens; m/Constance Headapohl; c/Leonard Frederick, William Edward, Lori Janette, Lucinda Corinne; p/Leonard Gascoigne Pikaart (dec); Janette Hendrick Pikaart, Chatham, NJ; ed/BA w distn 1959, MEd 1960, DEd 1963 Univ Va; mil/AUS 1956-58, Sgt (Arty); pa/R L Morton Prof Math Ed Ohio Univ; Var Former Positions; Ga Coun

Tchrs Math, Past Pres; Chm CONTTAC Com Math Assn Am 1977-78; NCTM; OCTM; Ohio Coun Tchrs Math, SE Ohio Dir 1978-81; Phi Delta Kappa, Coor Area 79-Ga 1969-70; Spec Interest Group for Res in Math Ed, AERA; Conslt; cp/Athens Kiwanis Clb: 2/VP, Former Mem Bd Dirs; Athens Co Unit Am Cancer Soc; r/Epis; hon/Postdoct Fellow, Tri-Univ Proj in Math Ed, NYU; Directed Prog for which Univ Ga Rec'd 1967 Dist'd Achmt Awd for Excell in Tchr Ed, Am Assn Cols for Tchr Ed; Profl Pubs.

PILSON, SUSAN C M oc/Speech & Language Pathologist; b/Jul 1, 1947; h/8356 Halls Ferry Rd, St Louis, MO 63147; ba/Waterloo, IL; m/Thomas R; p/Charles C and Lucille H Marsanick, St Louis; ed/BS 1973, MS 1974 So Ill Univ-E; pa/Spch & Lang Pathologist Waterloo Commun Unit Sch Dist 1974-; ASHA; Mo, SWn Ill Spch & Hearing Assn; Spch & Hearing Assn Gtr St Louis; NEA; Ill Ed Assn; Treas Waterloo Classroom Tchr Assn 1978; cp/Waterloo PTA; Baden Improvemt Assn; r/Northminster Presb Ch: Choir, Former Deacon, SS Tchr; hon/Cert of Clin Competence, ASHA; World W/W Wom; Men & Wom Distn; W/W: Child Devel Profls, MW, Am Wom.

PINION, RICHARD LEWIS oc/Insurance Company Executive; b/Sept 7, 1947; h/3159 Norfolk Ln, Falls Church, VA 22042; ba/Arlington, VA; m/Maryruth Anne Chevalier; p/Jack Andrew and Eleanor Hampton Whitacre Pinion; ed/AA Hagerstown Jr Col 1968; BS Am Univ 1970; MBA 1973; pa/Mgr Bk-Agt Prog 1st Nat Bk Washington 1973-74; Sponsored Mktg Mgr Aetna Life & Casualty, Arlington 1974-; Am Mktg Assn; Assn Masters Bus Adm; Life Underwriters Polit Action Com Century Clb; Gen Agts & Mgrs Conf NALU, Intl Pers Mgmt Assn; Nat Assn Life Underwriters; Million Dollar Round Table; cp/Smithsonian Assn; Wolf Trap Assn; hon/Nat Sales Achmt Awd, Nat Assn Life Underwriters; Sales Mgmt Forum Awd, Aetna Life & Casualty; Biogl Listings.

PIPER, HENRY BURTON oc/Nuclear Engineer; b/Dec 8, 1931; h/Rt 4, Box 293, Kingston, TN 37763; ba/Oak Ridge, TN; m/Dorothy Sue Gregory; c/Brenda Kay (dec), Henry Burton Jr, Allen Brent; p/Henry H Piper (dec), Hinda L Burton Piper, Atlanta, GA; ed/BE cum laude Vanderbilt Univ; Oak Ridge Sch Reactor Technol; mil/USN 1951-55; pa/Clinch River Breeder Reactor Proj: Mgr Safety, Lic'g, Risk Mgmt 1976-79, Tech Dir

Risk Assessmt 1975-77; Tech Staff Proj Mgmt Corp 1973-75; Mgmt/Tech Staff Nuclear Safety Info Ctr 1967-73; Experimtl Staff Molten Salt Reactor Experimt 1964-67; Other Former Positions; Cert'd Profl Engr Tenn; Tenn & Nat Socs Profl Engrs; Am Nuclear Soc; Conslt; Writer; Lectr; cp/Vol Tchr; Former Scoutmaster; r/Ch of Christ: Bible Tchr, Song Dir; hon/Tau Beta Pi; Dept of Energy Outstg Achmt; Scouter's Key.

PITTMAN, BENNY RAY oc/Lumber & Wood Products Broker; b/Aug 6; h/335 W Court St, Rutherfordton, NC 28139; ba/R'ton; m/Carletta W; c/Timothy; p/Howard J and Mary A Pittman, R'ton; ed/BS NCSU 1971; pa/Nat Assn Accts; Nat Hardwood Lbr Assn; cp/Lodge #91, AF&AM; r/St Francis Epis Ch,

F'ton; hon/Nat Salesman of Yr, Northrop Data Systems 1975, 76.

PITTMAN, FLOYD E oc/Minister; b/Apr 5, 1914; h/1305 Harbison Ave, Nat City, CA 92050; ba/San Diego, CA; m/Corrinne B; p/Albert Sidney and Sara Gertrude Pittman (dec); ed/DDiv; pa/SD So Bapt Pastors Conf; cp/Rotary Clb, Nat City; Election Bd; r/So Bapt; hon/W/W Rel; Personalities W&MW.

PITTMAN, JIM PAUL oc/Pastor; Director; h/305 Raymond, San Francisco, CA 24134; cp/Dir Yth Ctr; Fdr-Dir, Sr Citizen's Alert Prog; Mtl Hlth Bd; Mayor's Manpower Bd; Intl Students Cnslr; Night Min for Coun of Chs; Diversion Yth Cnslt; Pres, SQUIRES (Inmates Prog); hon/W/W: Am Cols & Univs, Rel.

PLATT, DAVID D oc/Principal; b/Jun 5, 1934; h/3004 Tonawanda Dr, Fort Wayne, IN 46815; ba/Ft Wayne; m/Patsy L; c/Michael, Jay, Robin; p/Hershel D and Pascaline S Platt, Ft Wayne; ed/BME; MM; DEd; mil/USAF Capt; pa/Prin FWCS Ed Ctr 1977-78; Asst Prin R Nelson Snider HS, Ft Wayne 1975-77, 1972-74; Grad Asst Dept Ednl Adm & Supvn 1974-75; Assoc Fac Ind Univ-Purdue Univ-Ft Wayne 1967-72; Other Former Positions; Mem Ind St Music Ed Coun 1969-71; Conslt:

Madison Commun Schs (Madison, Ind) 1972, Ft Wayne Commun Schs (Music) 1970-72, Others; Mem Conslt'g Team Dr James McElhinney, Ball St Univ 1975; Pres Ind Music Edrs Assn 1975-76; Phi Delta Kappa; Phi Mu Alpha; Kappa Kappa Psi; Other Profl Activs; r/Presb; hon/Experienced Tchr Fellow in Humanities, Univ Mich; Edna Furnough S'ship for Grad Study, Ball St Univ; Pi Kappa Lambda; Pub'd Author.

PLATT, THOMAS COLLIER oc/District Judge; b/May 29, 1925; h/448 W Neck Rd, Lloyd Harbor, Huntington, NY 11473; ba/Brooklyn, NY; m/Ann Byrd Symington; c/Ann Byrd, Charles Collier, Thomas C III, Elizabeth Louise; p/Collier and Louise Lusk Platt, Syosset, NY; ed/BA Yale Col 1947; LLB Yale Law Sch 1950; mil/USNR 1943-46; pa/Judge US Dist Ct, En Dist NY; cp/Former Suffolk Co Repub Com-man; Alt Del Repub Nat Conv 1964, 68, 72; Del Repub St Conv 1966; r/Epis.

PLATT, W GERALD oc/Professor; Director; b/Feb 12, 1947; h/1421 Livorna, Alamo, CA 94507; ba/San Francisco, CA; m/Cathleen Ireland; p/William G and Myriam B Platt, St Clair, MI; ed/BS cum laude Mich St; MBA Wayne St; MA, PhD Ohio St; pa/SF St Univ: Prof Fin, Dir MBA Public Fin Mgmt Prog; Am Statistical Assn; Wn Fin Assn; Mun Fin Ofcrs Assn; Sr Conslt on Hlth Policy Res, Pracon Inc.

PLEWINSKI, GUSTAW LUDWIK oc/- Physician; Diplomate in Surgery & Phlebology; b/Feb 14, 1925; h/10 Waterside Plaza, Apt 33A, New York, NY 10010; m/Teresa M Sauer; c/2 Chd; p/Marian R and Janina H Kaminski Plewinski; ed/Diplomate Sch Polit Scis & African Studies Warsaw Univ; MD; PhD; mil/Polish Underground Home Army & Warsaw Uprising 1944; pa/Pract'g Phys, NYC; FPCS; FACA; Mem Num Am & Fgn Sci Socs; hon/Home Army Cross; Phys's Recog Awds, AMA; Pioneer Mod Non-

Operative Treatmt of Varicose Veins in US; Commun Ldrs & Noteworthy Ams.

PLEWINSKI, TERESA M oc/Physician; h/10 Waterside Plaza, Apt 33A, New York, NY 10010; m/Gustaw L; c/2 Chd; p/Gustaw and Jadwiga Bedynska Sauer; ed/MD Wroclaw & Warsaw Med Sch 1951; PhD 1966; Diplomate in Pediatrics, Pediatric Surg, Internal Med, Fam Pract; pa/Resident, Att'g Phys Cabrini Med Ctr, NYC 1969-; Att'g in Pediatrics Bedzin Chd's Hosp 1951-52; Att'g in Pediatrics & Pediatric Surg Gliwice City Hosp 1952-57; Dep Surg-in-Chief Chd's Surg Hosp, Warsaw 1957-67; Hd Pediatrics & Pediatric Surg Reg Hosp, Ho, Ghana, W Africa 1968; Med Soc Co & St NY; AMA; Polish Med Alliance; ACP; NY Co, St & Am Socs Internal Med; NY Cardiol Soc; NY & Am Heart Assns; NY Co Hlth Ser Review Org; FPCS; FAAFP; FACP; Am Acad Fam Physicians; Coun for Thrombosis; NY Acad Scis; Am Med Wom's Assn; Am Geriatric Soc; hon/Phys's Recog Awds, AMA; Profl Pubs; Book of Honor; Commun Ldrs & Noteworthy Ams.

PLUMB, FORREST LEO oc/Minister; b/Jun 15, 1930; h/22421 Carlysle, Deaborn, MI 48124; ba/Dearborn; m/Darlene B; c/Susan, Theodore, Kelly; p/Floyd N and Mildred K Plumb, Toledo, OH; ed/BTh; pa/Min, Evangelist Christian & Missionary Alliance Ch; Pastor: G'ville (Ohio) 1973-, Columbus (Ohio) 1967-73, Painesville (Ohio) 1958-67, Weirton (WVa 1955-58); Crusade

Song Ldr; Choir Dir; Chd's Dir Beulah Bch 7 Yrs; Dist Dir Bible Quizzing; Pres & Chm Darke Co Evang Crusade; Secy Beulah Bch CE Com; Darke Co Chs in Action Com; cp/C of C; Repub Men's Clb; Chaplain: Concord Fire Dept 7 Yrs, Lake Co (Ohio) Firemen's Assn 6 Yrs; r/Christian; hon/W/W in Rel; Life Mbrship, Concord Fire Dept; Awd for Ser as Chaplain, Lake Co Firemen's Assn.

PLYLER, BONNIE D oc/Teacher; b/Nov 25, 1945; h/Rt 1, Box 187, Parrish, AL 35580; ba/Jasper, AL; p/George W Plyler (dec); Lorene Wheeler Plyler, Parrish; ed/BS, Masters Univ Ala; pa/6th Grade Tchr Jasper Mid Sch; AAUW; Delta Kappa Gamma; BPW Clb; cp/Concerned Citizens; Jaycettes; Crafts Instr Indian Creek Camp; r/Ch of Christ; hon/Nom Outstg Wom Am; Wom of Achmt, BPW Clb.

POINTEK, ALBERT JOSEPH oc/Administrative Contracting Officer; b/May 28, 1932; h/4171 Felters Rd, Binghamton, NY 13903; ba/Johnson City, NY; m/Patricia Ann George; c/John, Mary Ann; p/Albert W and Anna Chorba Pointek, Swoyersville, PA; ed/BS; pa/Nat Assn Accts; NCMA; cp/Treas Kopernik Soc Broome Co; Bd Dirs Binghamton US Employees Fed Credit Union; r/Rom Cath; hon/Cert'd Profl Contracts Mgr, NCMA.

POLIS, HARRY JOHN oc/Chief of Police; b/Aug 16, 1947; h/5908 St Moritz Dr #101, Temple Hills, MD; ba/Forest Heights, MD; m/Vicki Lee Smith; c/John, Robert, Laurene; p/John Harry Polis (dec); Lake Ella Polis, Oxon Hill, MD; ed/AA w hons Prince Georges Col; pa/Chief of Police Forest Heights Police Dept; VP-Elect Md Chiefs of Police Assn; cp/Pres Optimist Clb Eastover; r/Cath; hon/J Edgar Hoover Meml Awd.

POLLACK, ROBERT HARVEY oc/Professor; Director; b/Jun 26, 1927; h/190 Gatewood Place, Athens, GA 30606; ba/-Athens; m/Martha Katz; c/Jonathon, Lance, Scott; p/Solomon Pollack (dec); Bertha Levy Pollack, Athens; ed/BS; MA; PhD; mil/AUS 1945-46; pa/Univ Ga: Prof Psychol 1969-, Dir Grad Tng 1978-, Chm PhD Prog Experimtl Psychol 1970-78; Prog Supvr Experimtl Psychol Dept Res, Inst for Juv Res, Chicago, Ill 1967-69; Other Former Positions; Am Assn Sex Edrs, Cnslrs & Therapists; Fellow APA; Fellow AAAS; Australian Psychol Soc; Psychonomic Soc; Fellow Intl Coun Psychologists; Soc for Res in Child Devel; En Psychol Assn; So Soc for Phil & Psychol; Gerontological Soc; Mem NICHD Site Visit Com to Review Prog Proj Grant Proposal at Geo Peabody Col 1972; Reference Panel *Science* 1969-; Conslt'g Editor: *Psychonomic Sci* 1972, *Memory & Cognition* 1973-77; APA Vis Scist Tenn Wesleyan Col (Mar) 1972; Bd Edit Conslts *Perceptual-Cognitive Devel* 1967; Other Profl Activs; hon/Sigma Xi; Awd for Significant Res Contbn, Univ Ga; Num Profl Pubs; Recipient F'ships, Grant; Biogl Listings.

POLLARD, JOSEPH KIERAN oc/Priest, Communicator; b/Jan 4, 1937; h/311 N Raymond Ave, Pasadena, CA 91103; ba/Los Angeles, CA; p/Joseph Pollard Sr (dec); Elizabeth J Pollard; ed/STB Lateran Univ Rome; MA Loyola-Marymount Univ LA; STLict Lateran Univ; STD Angelicum Univ Rome; pa/Dir Dept Communs Archdiocese LA; Pres LA Senate of Priests; r/Rom Cath; hon/Named Chaplain of His Holiness, the Pope, April 1978.

POLLARD, WILLIAM FRANCIS III oc/Church Administrator, Foundation Director, Theologic Essayist, Youth Rehabilitation Counselor; b/Nov 12, 1954; h/Rt 5, Box 246-3, Rocky Mount, VA 24151; ba/Same; m/Cynthia D Cook; p/William F Jr and Dorothy O Pollard, Williamsburg, VA; ed/AAAS Blue Ridge Commun Col 1977; Profl Cert w hons USI 1975; pa/Fdr & Presiding Ofcr Judaic Christian Orthodox Ch; Chm Bd Dirs Judaic Christian Res Foun Ltd 1977-80; Orgr Judaic Christian Devel Org 1979; Secy Va Col Press Assn 1977; Treas Literary Soc Am 1977; cp/Mem Negotiating Com Nat Union Hosp & Hlth Care Employees, Div RWDSU, AFL-CIO Dist 1199E; r/Orthodox Cath; hon/Author: *Articles of Faith* 1978, *Articles of Adm* 1978, Others; Cert of Achmt, USI; Cert of Awd, BRCC.

POLLEI, PAUL CANNON oc/Professor; b/May 9, 1936; h/525 E 2875 N, Provo, UT 84601; ba/Provo; m/Norene Barrus; c/Emilie, Mark; p/Eric C Pollei (dec); Emily C Pollei, Salt Lake City, UT; ed/BM Univ Utah; MM Eastman Sch Music; PhD Fla St Univ; pa/Prof Band Brigham Yg Univ; Recitalist; Lectr; Tchr; Author; Mem Nat Piano Foun Ednl Adv Bd; Dir BYU Sum Piano Fest & Gina Bachauer Intl Piano Competition; Former VP Utah Music Tchrs Assn; Perf'd Recitals in Num Sts, Canada, Europe, Japan; Guest Fac Mem Var Cols & Univs in US; CMS; MTNA; Mem Other Nat Orgs; r/Mormon Ch: Bishop; hon/Tchr of Yr, Music Tchrs Nat Assn; World W/W Musicians.

POLLEY, ELIZABETH MARIE oc/Art Journalist; Art Consultant; b/May 9, 1908; h/112 Lain Dr, Vallejo, CA 94590; m/Raymond W (dec); c/1; p/William Russell and Elizabeth Marie Menard Patterson; ed/BA Univ Cal 1928; Postgrad Studies: Mills Col 1949, Cal Col Arts & Crafts 1951; MA Univ Guadalajara 1954; MFA; pa/Art Editor & Critic Gibson Pubs, Vallejo 1946-74; Instr Vallejo Unified Sch Dist 1947-65; Art Critic: *Artforum* Mag, San Francisco 1962-66, *San Francisco* Mag 1974-76; Owner, Dir & Instr Channel Artists, Vallejo 1971-; Current Lectr on Art Subjects; Publicity Public Relats Dir Richmond (Cal) Art Ctr; Fdr & Pres (4) Artists Leag Vallejo; NEA; Oakland Art Mus; SF Art Mus; SF Fine Art Mus; Cal Ret'd Tchrs Assn; Others; cp/Vallejo Hist Mus: Bd Trustees, Chm Docent Coun; Chm Decorations Com Soroptimists Intl; Former Mem Vallejo Cult Activs Comm; Navy Leag; hon/Navy-Army

Awd; Recipient Cits: Am Artists Profl Leag, City of Vallejo, City Vallejo Beautification Comm; Recipient Var Paintings Awds; Pub'd Author; Intl W/W Intells; DIB; Notable Ams; Commun Ldrs & Noteworthy Ams.

POLLITT, GERTRUDE oc/Clinical Social Worker; Psychotherapist; b/Sept 12, 1919; h/481 Oakdale Ave, Glencoe, IL 60022; ba/Same; m/Erwin P (dec); p/Julius and Sidonie B Stein (dec); ed/MA; pa/Acad of Cert'd Social Wkrs; Pvt Pract, Psychotherapist, Chd, Adolescents & Adults; cp/Mem Exec Com Winnetka ORT; r/Jewish; hon/Child Wel Leag of Am Record Exhibit; Fellow: Ill Soc for Clin Social Work, Am Orthopsychi Assn; Commun Ldrs & Noteworthy Ams.

POLYDOROFF, SUSAN WILLS oc/Dental Hygienist; b/Dec 12, 1941; h/4904 Morning Glory Ct, Rockville, MD 20853; ba/Chevy Chase, MD; m/Theodore; c/Christopher, Stephen, Elise, Michael; p/James T and Martha S Wills, R'ville; ed/BS Univ Ind 1962, Cert'd Dental Hygienist; pa/Pres Md St Dental Hygienists Assn; Pres So Md Dental Hygienists Assn; Secy Md Dental Hygienists Assn; cp/Coach Wheaton Boys Clb Soccer Assn; hon/Hon Fdr, Md St Dental Hygienists Assn; Class E Lic, Fdn Internationale de Ftball Assn.

POMERANTZ, LOUIS oc/Conservator of Works of Art; b/Sept 26, 1919; h/6300 Johnsburg Rd, Spring Grove, IL 60081; ba/Same; m/Elisabeth Catherina; c/Carrie Johanna, Lonnie Roberta; p/Jacob and Gussie Pomerantz (dec); ed/Att'd: Institut Royal du Patrimoine Artistique (Brussels, Belgium), Ctl Lab Belgium Museums, Art Students Leag (NYC); Pvt Studies; mil/AUS 1941-45, N African & European Theatres; pa/Conservator Dept Paintings & Sculptures Art Inst Chicago 1956-61; Indep Pract 1961; Conslt Conservator: Milwaukee (Wis) Art Ctr 1958-76, Nat Gallery Canada 1961, George F Harding Mus (Chgo) 1965-68, Ia Mus Art (Ia City) 1973-; St Hist Soc Ia 1973-; Conslt Mus Contemp Art (Chgo) 1976; Field Mus Conservator Anthropol Dept Gamelan Restoration Proj 1977; Conslt SITES, Smithsonian Inst, Washington, DC 1977; Vis Expert: Detroit Inst Arts Conserv Dept 1977, Cooperstown Grad Progs in Conserv (C'town, NY) 1977; Num Other Profl Positions & Activs; Fellow: Intl Inst for Conserv of Hist & Artistic Works, Am Inst for Conserv; Fdg Mem IIC-Am Group; Am Assn Museums; ICOM; MW Museums Conf; Com Positions; r/Unitarian; hon/Profl Pubs; DIB; Intl W/W Art & Antiques; Commun Ldrs & Noteworthy Ams; W/W: Am, Am Art, MW.

PONT, JOHN oc/Director of Athletics; b/Nov 13, 1927; h/2520 Sheridan Rd, Evanston, IL 60201; ba/E'ton; m/Sandra; c/John Wilson, Jennifer Ann, Jeffrey David; p/Bautista and Susie Pont (dec); ed/BS, MS Miami Univ; mil/USN Submarine Ser; pa/Dir Athletics NWn Univ; Am Ftball Coaches Assn: Chm Ethics Com, Recruiting Com;

NCAA, Recruiting Com; Nat Assn Col Dirs Assn; cp/Bd Dirs MS; Pres' Coun Phy Fitness; Chm: Easter Seals, Cancer Crusade; Repub; r/Rom Cath; hon/Coach of Yr Ftball, Coaches Assn & Ftball Writers; Significant Sig, Omicron Delta Kappa; Blue Key; Phi Epsilon Kappa.

POOLE, MARJORIE HARTMAN oc/-Homemaker; b/May 28, 1910; h/708 Londonderry Dr, Findlay, OH 45840; m/Robert Mason; p/Morse Emmitt and Jessie Borough Hartman (dec); ed/BS Wittenberg Univ; pa/Tchr Ohio Elem Schs 1934-43; Tchr Whittier Elem Sch 1946-50; cp/Vol Repub Nat Hdqtrs, Washington, DC (during Eisenhower, Nixon Campaign); ARC Rec Wkr WWII;

NSDAR: Prog Chm, Public Relats; Public Relats NSUSD of 1812; NS Colonial Dames XVIIth Century: Chaplain, Public Relats; DAR Ohio Ofcrs Clb; Ohio St Geneal Soc; Hancock Co Geneal Soc; Clan Sutherland Soc Am; Fellow IBA; IPA; Var Former Activs; r/U Meth; hon/St & Nat Awds, DAR Regent; 3 Nat Awds for Prog'g DAR Yrbooks.

POPE, MYRA JOE oc/Elementary School Teacher; b/Dec 10, 1930; h/15113 Lotus Dr, Cleveland, OH 44128; ba/Cleve; m/Kermit R; c/Betty; p/James Wilson (dec); Maggie Wilson, Cleve; ed/BA 1953, MEd 1956, Cert to Teach Mtly Retard 1956, Univ Pittsburgh; pa/Tchr 26 Yrs; Current Tchr Harvey Rice Elem Sch; Tchr Grades 1 to 12: Herron Hill, Mayflower, Wooldridge, Harvey Rice; NEn Ohio Tchrs Assn; Assn for Childhood Ed; Gtr Cleve Coun Tchrs Eng; Cleve Tchrs Credit Union; cp/Urban Leag; Open House Prog Chm Martin Luther King Jr Prog, Career Day Prog Chm, PTA Fashion Show Chm, Wooldridge Sch Newspaper Sponsor; Others; Delta Sigma Theta; Miles Playfield St Clb; NAACP; r/St Paul U Meth Ch: Mem, Rec'g Secy Sr Usher Bd; hon/Martha Holden Jennings Scholar; Martha Holden Jennings Cash Awd; Outstg Elem Tchr Am Awd; Outstg Ldrs in Elem & Sec'dy Ed.

POPESCU-JUDETZ, EUGENIA oc/Ethnomusicologist; Choreographer; b/Sept 9, 1925; h/700 Forbes Ave, Pittsburgh, PA 15219; m/Gh (dec); p/Avel and Florica Marinescu (dec); ed/Univ Bucharest (Romania); pa/Dancer Performer 1944-54; Choreographer & Tchr w Profl Companies; Folk Dance Tchr 1949-70; Fac Mem Duquesne Univ Tamburitzans Inst Folk Arts 1973-; TV Choreographer; Author: Books, Monographs, Articles on Mid E Music, Arts & Folk Dance; r/Cath; hon/Intl 1st Prize of Dance, Prague 1950; High Orders of Romani for Cult Merits.

POPOVIC, DEYAN N oc/Physician; b/Mar 27, 1949; h/223 E Pearson St, #1702, Chicago, IL 60611; ba/Glen Ellyn, IL; m/Christine Ann; p/Nenad D and Tatyana V Popovic, Dewitt, NY; ed/BA magna cum laude Syracuse Univ 1969; MD SUNY 1972; pa/Phys: Facial Plastic & Reconstructive Surg,

Otorhinolaryneology; Chgo Med Soc; ISMS; AMA; Am Col Emer Physicians; Others; Reschr; cp/Centurion Clb of Deafness Res Foun; Adler Planetarium (Chgo); hon/Profl Pubs; Alpha Epsilon Delta; Phi Beta Kappa; Men Achmt.

POPPEL, SETH RAPHAEL oc/Executive; b/Mar 17, 1944; h/38 Range Dr, Merrick, NY 11566; ba/New York, NY; m/Danine; c/Clarysa, Jared, Stacy; p/Frank M Poppel (dec); Fannie A Poppel, Merrick; ed/BS magna cum laude LIU 1965; MBA Columbia 1967; pa/VP Corporate Planning; hon/Beta Gamma Sigma; Omega Epsilon; Psi Chi; Claire F Adler Awd; DuPont F'ship.

PORTEN, LAURENCE oc/Orthopedist; CPO Emeritus Practitioner; b/Mar 22, 1894; h/172 Lido Dr, St Petersburg Beach, FL 33706; m/Saskia; c/Edith McDade, Hedi Dolanch; p/Hans and Walburga Portenkirchner (dec); ed/Bach Deg; 2 Masters; mil/4 Yr Ser WWI; pa/Deutsche Orthopaedische Werke: Shop Foreman (Manheim, Germany) 1918-21, Br Mgr (Konstanz, Germany) 1922-29; Deutsche Orthop Werke (Berlin, Germany): Res Work & Instr 1929-32, Invention Suction Socket Leg 1932-33; Mgr Orthop Shop, Chattanooga, Tenn 1937-44; Est'd Own Shop, Pittsburgh, Pa 1944; Lectr & Guide Suction Socket Sch in Coor w Nat Res Coun & VA (Pgh) 1948-49; Dipl "Emeritus Practitioner", Am Bd for Certn; Am Acad Orthopedists & Prosthetists; Am Orthop & Prosth Assn; Other Profl Activs; hon/DIB; "Golden Masters Lttr, Hausham, Bavaria, Germany (Birthplace); Hon Mem, Bavarian Orthopedic Assn; Dist'd Ser Cross, Pres German Republic; Bronce Plaquette, C of Trade, Konstanz; Notable Ams Bicent Era; Personalities of S; Men Achmt; IBA Yrbook; 2000 Men Achmt; Others.

PORTER, DARWIN FRED oc/Author; b/Sept 13, 1937; h/75 St Marks Pl, Staten Island, NY 10301; p/Numie Porter (dec); Hazel Porter Triplett, Key West, FL; ed/BA Univ Miami 1959; pa/Editor-Author: Arthur Frommer Inc & Frommer/Pasmantier Pub'g Corp 1964-78; VP Haggart House, NYC

1961-63; Bur Chief *The Miami Herald*, Miami, Fla 1959-60; Pubs incl: (Novels:) *Butterflies in Heat* 1976, *Marika* 1977, (Screenplay:) "Chemical Transfer, Union Carbide", Others; IPA; cp/Smithsonian Assn; hon/Silver Awd, Intl Film & TV Fest NY.

PORTER, GARLAND BURNS oc/Retired Publisher & Editor of Trade Magazines; b/Jun 3, 1897; h/69 Mobile Ave, Atlanta, GA 30305; m/Margaret McFarland; p/Polly P Sewell (Mrs Hugo), Garland Jr, David, Joseph, (Stepchd:) William W Tracy, Margaret Tracy; p/William and Letitia Cockerham Porter (dec); ed/USMC WWI, 2/Lt; pa/Fdr Porter Pub'g Co; Editor-Owner So Markets/Media 1970 (Sold); Former So Mgr Hearst Adv Ser; Former City Ed W-S Jour; Former Dir NC St News/Advt'g Bur; r/Prot; hon/Declaration of Apprec, Am Adv Fdn; Mem Coun Judges; Am Advt'g Hall of Fame; Hunter Lee Harris Meml; Hons in Lang & Lit, UNC.

PORTER, LEONARD oc/Family Therapist; b/May 19, 1945; h/Rt 3, Box 141, St Anne, IL 60964; ba/Evergreen Park, IL; m/Evelyn; c/Duwarn Verdis, Jarmar Myron; p/Issac and Evandres Porter, Marvell, AR; ed/BA Ark Bapt Col; MA Govs St Univ; PhD

Union Grad Sch 1979; mil/AUS 1968-70, Vietnam; pa/Dir Sers & Tng Coor MW Fam Resources Assocs Ltd 1977-; Pvt Contract w Ill St Dept Chd & Fam Ser, Kankakee Field Ofc 1977-78; Dir Tng The Depot 1973-77; Other Former Positions; Big-Brothers Metro Chgo; Commun Adv Bd Michael Reese Hosp & Med Ctr, Psychi Clin; cp/VP Chgo Chapt Col Alumni; Urban Leag; r/Mt Calvary MB Ch, St Anne, Ill: Deacon; hon/Bronze Star; Good Conduct; Combat Inf Badge; Vietnam Ser Medal; Pub'd Author.

PORTER, MILTON CLYDE oc/Retired Educator; b/Aug 22, 1912; h/3258 S Adrian Hwy, Adrian, MI 49221; m/Margaret Lorenz; c/Nancy P Thompson (Mrs J Martin); p/Clyde B Porter, Blissfield, MI; Laura Sayler Porter (dec); ed/AB Mich St Normal; MA Univ Mich-Ann Arbor; Grad Work; pa/Supt

Emeritus Lenawee Schs; In Ed 47 Yrs, Supt 35 Yrs; Life Mem: NEA, MEA; Mem Comparative Ed; Past Mem Mich Ed Assn Bd; Fdr, Mem Lenawee Co Fam Cnsl'g Assn; cp/Bd Mem Salvation Army; Exc Clb; Maurice Spear Probate Ct Campus & Sch; Past Mem & Chm Huron Val Child Guid Ctr; Past Mem Goodwill Adv Bd; r/Meth Ch: Mem; hon/The Milton C Porter Ed Ctr Named in his honor; Hon DHumanities, Adrian Col; Pub'd Author.

PORTER, PARA WRIGHT oc/Educational Diagnostician; b/Jan 14, 1915; h/1616 S 9th, Waco, TX 76706; m/Andrew Washington; c/Drue Anelle P Burt, James Patrick; p/James Thomas and Margaret Jane Wells Wright (dec); ed/BS, MS N Tex St Univ; PhD Baylor Univ 1960; pa/Supvr Spec Ed McLennan Co Schs, Waco 1972-; Supt Bosqueville Indep Sch Dist, Waco 1971-72; Baylor Univ, Waco 1966-71: Asst Prof Ed, Supvr Student Tchg; E Tex St Univ, Commerce, Tex 1962-66: Asst Prof Ed, Supvr Student Tchg; La Col, Pineville, La 1961-62: Dir Student Tchg, Assoc Prof Ed; Supvr Hill Co Schs, Hillsboro, Tex 1949-51; Other Former Positions; IPA; Kappa Delta Pi; Delta Kappa Gamma; Tex St Tchrs Assn; Tex Assn for Childhood Ed; Assn for Childhood Ed Intl; CEC; Var Assnl Activs & Positions; r/Bapt; hon/Profl Pubs; Num Biogl Listings.

PORTER, WILLIAM HOWARD JR oc/College Physics Instructor; b/Dec 25, 1941; h/1045 Park Dr, Hillsboro, TX 76645; ba/H'boro; m/Ryta; c/David, Darren; p/Howard and Erdene Porter, Greenville, TX; ed/BS 1965, MS 1968 E Tex St; pa/Physics Instr Hill Jr Col; Tex Jr Col Tchrs Assn; Am

Assn Physics Tchrs; r/1st Bapt Ch, H'boro: Mem, SS Dept Dir; hon/F'ship, NSF; Energy Res & Devel Adm.

POSNER, JON S oc/Broker; b/Sep 20, 1943; h/989 E Broadway, Woodmere, NY 11598; ba/New York, NY; m/Jo-Anne; p/Hyman and Rosaline Posner, Lauderhill, FL; ed/BA magna cum laude Princeton Univ 1965; pa/Intl Mortgage Broker providing Fin'g & Syndication for Developers; cp/Woodmere Clb; Dem Party; Univ Clb; r/Hebrew; hon/Nat Hon Soc.

POSY, CARL JEFFREY oc/Assistant Professor; b/Oct 15, 1944; h/5914 Douglas St, Pittsburgh, PA 15217; ba/Pgh; m/Phyllis M; c/Kenneth Bezalel, Michelle Tmima; p/Manuel and Frances Hendel Posy; ed/BA Yale Col 1966; PhD Yale Univ 1971; pa/Asst Prof Philosophy Univ Pgh; Am Phil Assn; Phil of Sci Assn; Assn for Symbolic Logic; Abstractor Bibliog of Phil; Referee: Am Phil Qtrly, Jour of Phil Logic, Phil of Sci, Phil Studies; Participant Var Confs & Symposia; Author Articles in Phil & Logical Jours; cp/Bd Ed Hillel Acad Pgh; hon/Grant, Ctr for Phil of Sci; F'ship for Indep Study & Res, Nat Endowmt for Humanities; Other F'ships, S'ships.

POSZ, ALBERT CONRAD oc/Educator; Public Speaker; b/Sept 11, 1921; h/9307 W 23rd St, St Louis Park, MN 55426; ba/Minneapolis, MN; m/Marie G Fjelstad; c/Carl Conrad, Sylvia Marie; p/Albert Daniel and Mary Etta Gaylord Posz (dec); ed/BS Winona St Col; MS St Univ Ia; EdD Mich St

Univ; pa/Art Instrn Schs; Profl Public Spkr; Mem Res & Ednl Standards Com, Nat Home Study Coun; Minn Adv Comm for Pvt Bus, Trade & Corres Schs; Staff Spkr Nat Mgmt Assn; r/Westwood Luth Ch: Mem, Former Coun Mem, Stewardship Comm, Ed Com, Music & Fine Arts Com; hon/Dist'd Ser Awd, Nat Home Study Coun.

POTNIK, CARL DAVID oc/Entertainment Businessman; b/Aug 2, 1941; ba/1540 Broadway, Suite 300, New York, NY 10036; p/Henry and Phoebe Ann Potnik, Levittown, PA; ed/BA Temple Univ; r/Jewish; hon/Outstg Scholar/Athlete, Temple Univ; Temple Univ Open & Competitive S'ship; W/W E.

POTTHOFF, JEROME J oc/Executive; b/Nov 28, 1931; h/400 Paul Ave, San Francisco, CA 94124; ba/SF; m/Jeanne; p/Theodor J Potthoff, Carroll, IA; Margaret A Potthoff (dec); mil/USN; pa/Pres; SF Ad Clb; Composite Can & Tube Inst; cp/Olympic Clb; r/Cath.

POTTS, DONALD RALPH oc/Professor, Writer; b/Jun 10, 1930; h/702 Ambassador, Marshall, TX 75670; m/N Jeanne Daugherty; c/Cynthia Diane, Donald M; p/B Sedwick Potts (dec); Ethel D Potts, Dellwood, MO; ed/AA; BA; BD; MDiv; ThD; pa/Mem Coms Bapt Gen Conv Tex; Christian Ed Comm; Bapt Hosp Bd; cp/Pres Rotary Clb Groves; Groves Min Alliance; Lawton-Ft Sill Min Alliance; r/So Bapt; hon/Nat Hon Soc; St Louis Sci Fair Awd.

POTTS, NANCY D oc/Marriage, Family

& Divorce Therapist; b/Dec 21, 1947; h/3111 W Creek Clb Dr, Missouri City, TX 77459; ba/Houston, TX; m/Lloyd L; p/Sidney Boyd and Katie Sue McDonald Needham, Houston; ed/BA; MEd; EdD; pa/Bourne & Potts Marriage & Fam Conslts 1977-; Cnslr, Conslt, Wkshop Devel; Cnslr The Ctr for Cnslg 1975-76; Cnslr & Prog Conslt S Main Bapt Ch 1974-75; Other Former Positions; AAMFT; APGA; TPGA; ASCA; AMEG; AOA; cp/LWV; Wom's Polit Caucus; Col Wom's Clb; AAUW; Vol Crisis Cnslg at Crisis Hotline; r/Bapt; hon/Pub'd Author; W/W S&SW.

POU, EMILY QUINN oc/College Dean; b/Nov 3, 1928; h/379 Sandstone Dr, Athens, GA 30605; ba/Athens; m/John William; c/John, Connie Yellowmoon, David Michael Quinn; p/Leonard B and Thelma Jennings Hotchkiss (dec); ed/BS; MS; PhD; pa/Dean Col Home Ecs Univ Ga 1971-; NC St Univ: Prof Ed & St Ldr Tng 1967-71, Assoc Prof & St Ldr Tng 1964-67; Fellow & Res Asst Univ Wis 1961-63; Other Former Positions; Mem Exec Bd Assn Admrs Home Ecs; So Assn Admrs Home Ecs; Ga Univ Sys Adv Coun Com on Home Es; Ga Univ Coun Exec Com, Univ Ga; Gamma Sigma Delta; Univ Ga Coun on Gerontol; Ga Nutrition Coun; Ga Home Ecs Assn; Public Policy Comm, Assn Admrs Home Ecs; Var Past Profl Activs; r/Cath; hon/Delta Kappa Gamma; Omicron Nu; Phi Upsilon Omicron; Dist'd Ser Awd, Ag Hill Coun; Land Bk & Credit Bk Awd, Fed Land Bk of Columbia & Fed Intermed Credit Bk Columbia; Friend of Ext in Home Ecs Awd, Ga Cooperative Ext Ser; Hon Mem, Alpha Zeta; Acad of Outstg Tchrs, NC St Univ; Others.

POU, JOHN WILLIAM oc/Assistant Director; b/Jul 8, 1917; h/379 Sandstone Dr, Athens, GA 30605; ba/Athens; m/Emily Quinn; c/John Jr, David, Connie; p/W C Pou (dec); Mary Pou Hendley, Statesville, NC; ed/BS; MS; PhD; mil/USAR, Lt Col, Ret'd; pa/Asst Dir Cooperative Ext Ser Univ Ga; VP & Hd Agribus Ofc NE Reg, Wachovia Bk & Trust Co, NA; Dir Cooperative Ext Ser Univ Ariz; Prof & Hd Dept Animal Indust NC St Univ; Prof & Hd Dairy Dept Univ Md; Mem & VP Bd Trustees NC St Univ; Indust Devel Coun Ga C of C; Past Pres: Assn Agri Bkrs, Coastal Plain Planning & Devel Comm, G'ville C of C & Merchs Assn, NC Soc Farm Mgrs & Rural Appraisers; Former Chm: Agri Com NC St Bkrs' Assn, So Div Am Dairy Sci Assn, Others; cp/Past Pres: Pitt Co UF, Pitt Co Mtl Hlth Assn, G'ville Rotary Clb; Former Chm: En Lung Assn Christmas Seal Campaign, Bd Dirs NC St Univ YMCA, Bond Campaign for New Pitt Co Meml Hosp; Others; Rotary; Farm House; Alpha Zeta; Golden Chain; Alpha Tau Alpha; Gamma Sigma Delta; Phi Kappa Phi; r/Bapt: Former Chm Bd Deacons; hon/Dist'd Alumni Awd, Sch Agri & Life Scis NC St Univ; Spokesman of Yr Awd, Chevron Chem Co & Farm Chems Mag 1974; G'ville Citizen of Yr 1970; Pres's Key Awd, G'ville C of C & Merchs Assn; Book of Golden Deeds Awd; Outstg Ser Awd, Future Farmers Am; Outstg Citizenship Awd, Pitt Co UF; Biogl Listings; Others.

POWELL, ANICE CARPENTER oc/Librarian; b/Dec 2, 1928; h/Box 387, Sunflower, MS 38778; ba/Indianola, MS; m/Robert Wainwright; c/Penelope Elizabeth, Deborah Alma; p/Horace Aubrey and Celeste Brian Carpenter (dec); ed/BS; MLS; pa/Dir Sunflower Co Lib; Miss, SEn, Am Lib Assns; Chm S Delta Dist Miss Gov's Lib Conf; LSCA Adv Bd, Miss Lib Comm; Miss Lib Assn: Leg Com, Fed Relats Coor, Var Former Positions; r/Meth.

POWELL, CHARLES EDWIN oc/Public Health Sanitarian; b/Jan 12, 1940; h/420 Buckhorn Rd, Goldsboro, NC 27530; ba/G'boro; m/Juanita Hinson; c/Charles Edwin Jr, William Kevin; p/William Alexander Powell (dec); Thelma Gore Powell, Clinton, NC; ed/Grad Presb Jr Col 1960; BSPH Univ NC 1963; MSPH UNC Sch Public Hlth 1978; Addit Studies; pa/Wayne Co Hlth

Dept, G'boro: Sanitarian Supvr 1977-, Asst Sanitarian Supvr 1972-76, Sanitarian II 1966-72; Sanitarian I Onslow Co Hlth Dept, Jacksonville, NC 1964-66; Sanitarian I New Hanover Co Hlth Dept, Wilmington, NC 1963-64; NC Public Hlth Assn: Gov'g Coun & Current Pres Envir Hlth Sect (VP 1979, Secy-Treas 1978), Secy En Dist 1968, VChm En Dist 1969, Chm En Dist 1970, Exec Com Envir Hlth Sect 1970, Auditing Com 1975-76, Fin Com 1974-75, Profl Devel Com 1975-76-77; SEn Dist Envir Hlth Sect, NCPHA: Chm 1970, VChm 1969, Secy-Treas 1968; Reg'd Sanitarian in NC; Secy-Treas Envir Hlth Supvrs Conf 1973; Nat Envir Hlth Assn; Wayne Co Land Use Planning Study Com 1977; Envir Mgmt & Adm Com, Envir Mgmt Sect, Nat Envir Hlth Assn 1976-77; Ex-Officio Mem Wayne Co Planning Bd 1976-; cp/Water & Sewer Sign-Up Com; Mem Third Century Singers (Commun Chorus); Former Scoutmaster Local Commun Boy Scout Troop; Former Cub Scout Den Ldr (Local); Former Coaching & Assisting Love Meml Commun Park Little Leag Ftball & Baseball; Formerly Active Love Meml Commun Park Adult Rec Prog; Former Mem JCs; Mem & Chm Brogden (Public) Schs Adv Coun; r/Love Meml Bapt Ch: Mem, SS Tchr 1971-74, Deacon 1972-74, Ch Choir 1970-74, RA, Yth Ldr 1970-72; hon/Sanitarian of Yr, SEn Dist Envir Hlth Sect, NCPHA 1977; Spoke Awd, JCs; Regimental Cmdrs Orderly, Ft Jackson Army Base (Twice); Phi Theta Kappa; Other Scholastic Hons; Eagle Scout, BSA; Personalities of S; Intl W/W Commun Ser; Intl Men of Achmt.

POWELL, DONNIE MELVIN oc/Engomologist; b/Apr 4, 1930; h/906 S 36th Ave, Yakima, WA 98902; ba/Yakima; m/Willa Dene; c/D Michael; p/William Samuel and Melvie Powell (dec); ed/BS 1956, MS 1958 Univ Ark; Wash St Univ 1968-70; mil/AUS 1951-53; pa/Res Entomologist USDA-ARSEA; ESA; Kan ESA; Wash St ES; OPEDA; cp/Past Pres Yakima USDA Clb; r/So Bapt: Deacon.

POWELL, RICHARD KEITH oc/Educator; Librarian; Church Worker; b/Sept 18, 1928; h/116 Grove St, Berrien Springs, MI 49103; ba/Berrien Springs; p/Chester Don Powell (dec); Selma Christine Powell, Berrien Sprgs; ed/BS; MA; Ma; DEd; pa/Andrews Univ, Berrien Sprgs: Current Asst Libn, Asst Prof Ed, Dir Tchg Mats Ctr; Instnl TV Coor Neb Ednl TV Coun for Higher Ed & Union Col, Lincoln, Neb; Alta Vista Sch, San Jose, Cal: Tchr, Asst Prin, Libn; Tchr-Prin (Upper Grades) Salinas-Monterey Union Sch, Salinas, Cal; Tchr-Prin (Grades 3-5, 6-8, 1, 2) Burlingame SDA Sch, Burlingame, Cal; Other Former Positions; Mich Assn for Media in Ed; Mich Assn for Supvn & Curric Devel; Rural Ed Assn; Assn for Ednl Commun & Technol; Mich Acad Sci, Arts & Lttrs; cp/Pres Local Chapt Mich Singles, Berrien Sprgs; Past Pres Coterie Clb, Mtn View, Cal; r/SDA: Missionary, Deacon (Pioneer Meml Ch); hon/S'ship to Pacific Union Col, Inst for Sci Study for Preven of Alcoholism; Profl Pubs; DIB; W/W MW; Men of Achmt; Intl W/W Commun Ser; Others.

POWELL, RUSSELL FRANCIS oc/Strategy Simulator; b/Aug 19, 1944; h/5820 John Ave, Long Beach, CA 90805; ba/Long Bch; m/Donna Rae Abell; c/Sherry Lee, Malinda May, Tina Rae; p/Russell LeBaron and

Florence Delores Israel Powell, Des Moines, IA; pa/Pres Intl Gamers Assn 1978-; Chm Exec Com 1974-78; Sales Rep Avalon Hill Co, Baltimore 1973-74; Spartan Intl Inc: Pres (Bellflower, Cal) 1970-74, Chm Bd Dirs 1970-74; cp/Long Bch Area C of C; Vol Ser Local Govt; US Nav Inst; Nat Hist Soc; Oceanic Soc; Smithsonian Soc; r/Ch of Christ, Long Bch; hon/Strategy Simulations Hall of Fame & Archives Recog; Spartan of Yr 1970-71; Vol Ser Awd, Long Bch; Ldrship Awd, Monarch Printing Co, Baltimore; US Nav Champ; US Armor Champ; Others.

POWELL, RUTH HILL REID oc/Teacher; b/May 25, 1920; h/507 Mack Dr, Valdosta, GA 31601; ba/Valdosta, GA; m/Frank Dewey Jr (dec); c/Anthony Frank, Janice Ruth, (Stepchd:) Melissa D Day, Mac H Dethlefsen; p/Robert Roberson and Ruth Hill Reid (dec); ed/AB Wesleyan Col 1942; MEd Valdosta St Col 1975; pa/Tchr 8th Grade Chem & Earth Sci Valdosta Jr HS; NEA; GAE; VAE; GSTA; VFTCU; cp/Elks Aidmore Aux; OES; Chaperone Action Trav'lers; Bloodmobile Wkr; Planning & Devel'g Fern Trails in McKey Park; r/Park Ave U Meth Ch: Mem, Former Mem Bd Stewards, Former SS Tchr & Yth Wkr; hon/Elks Sweetheart 1967; 2nd Runner-up 1st Lady Lowndes Co, Valdosta Bicent Contest; Valdosta Wom of Yr, Elks Aidmore Aux 1977; Elks Aidmore Aux named Emer Fund in her hon; VHJS Yrbook Dedn 1975; Spec "Newsmakers" Article on her, *Valdosta Daily Times*; Personalities of S.

POWELL, WILLA DENE oc/Teacher; b/Sept 21, 1933; h/906 S 36th Ave, Yakima, WA 98902; ba/Ellensburg, WA; m/Donnie M; c/D Michael; p/Victor L and Ada Powell, Hatfield, AR; ed/BSHE Univ Ark 1959; MEd Ctl Wash Univ 1974; pa/Tchr Home & Fam Life Ed Ctl Wash Univ; AVA; Life Mem: WVA, NEA, WEA, YEA; Past Treas ADK; Secy Alpha Delta Kappa; r/So Bapt: SS Tchr; hon/Cert of Merit, Coord Coun for Occpl Ed.

POWER, PAUL WAYNE oc/Minister; b/Jan 17, 1945; h/2415 Fallingtree Dr, San Jose, CA 95131; ba/Milpitas, CA; m/Judy Jennalea Johnson; c/tiffani LeWayne, Tisha Linette; p/Paul Elton and Roma Pearl Power,

Liberty, MO; ed/BA; MRE; mil/AUS 1963-66, Kirchgoens, Germany; pa/Min of Ed Park Victoria Bapt Ch; Wn Rel Ed Assn; cp/Brooktree Sch, Commun Coun; r/So Bapt.

POWERS, GEORGIA M oc/State Senator; b/Oct 29; h/733 Cecil Ave, Louisville, KY 40211; m/James Lewis; c/William F Davis, Cheryl Campbell, Carlton, Deborrah Rattle;

p/Ben G Montgomery, L'ville; Frances Montgomery (dec); cp/Chm Labor & Ind Comm; Secy Dem Caucus; NAACP; Urban Leag; YWCA; r/Prot; hon/Wom of Yr Awd, Ky Wom's Coalition 1978.

PRADIER, JANICE MARIE oc/Counselor; b/Feb 3, 1950; h/Box 163, APO, NY 09240; ba/Same; m/Jerome M; p/Virgil J and Iva Young Anderson, Griffin, GA; ed/BA HRI; MRC; pa/APA; APGA; NRA; NRCA; AMEG; ARCA; Kappa Delta Pi; ASURCA; Vol Cnslg-Alcoholism; Vol Casework-Child Abuse; cp/HOPE Coun; Basewide Chd's Events Com; Ofcrs Wives Clb; Child Advocacy Com; r/Rom Cath; hon/W/W S&SW; Personalities of S.

PRADIER, JEROME MARTIN oc/Air Force Pilot; Social Actions Officer; b/Nov 1, 1947; h/PO Box 163, APO, NY 09240; ba/APO; m/Janice Marie Anderson; p/Frank T Pradier (dec); Effie C Pradier, Columbus, OH; ed/BA St Joseph's Sem; mil/USAF 1972-; B-52 Pilot 1973-76; Currently Social Actions Ofcr; cp/Fdr "The Joyful Spirit" (Gospel Music Group); Edit Conslt *Freeing the Spirit* Mag, Nat Ofc Black Caths; Author USAF

Human Relats Ed Sems; cp/Former Blytheville AFB, AR Spkrs Bur; San Vito Air Sta, Italy Spkrs Bur; Pres Brindisi Province Italy HOPE Coun; r/Rom Cath; hon/Outstg Instr in 8th AF, SAC; 1 of 5 Outstg Yg Men in Strategic Air Command, SAC; Outstg Social Actions Ofc of Yr Awd, SAC & AF 1977; Kappa Delta Pi; W/W S&SW; Personalities of S; Men of Achmt.

PRATHER, MELVIN oc/Public Relations & Advertising Executive; b/Aug 3, 1947; h/1429 E 6th #8, Big Spring, TX 79720; ba/Big Spring; p/Roy Prather, Saltillo, TX; Alice Marie Prather, Mt Vernon, TX; ed/BJ Univ Tex-A; mil/USAF 1965-69, S/Sgt; pa/Advt'g & Info Ofcr Citizens Fed Credit Union; Tex Public Relats Assn; Public Relats Soc Am; Sev Profl Sems; cp/C of C; Howard Co Christmas Lighting Contest, USAF Acad Falconaires Show Band, Chm Army Forces Command Band, Big Spring Arts & Crafts Fest, Chm Arts & Crafts Com, Ambassador Big Spring, Others; Bd Dirs: Westside Commun Ctr, Westside Day Care Ctr; Former Chm U Way Metro Gifts Div; Former Mem Base-Commun Coun Century Clb; AF Assn; Former CoChm Webb Olympic Com, Webb AFB; Num Others; hon/Man of Yr, Big Spring JCs 1978; Outstg Yg Men Am; 2nd Pl Class A, Tex Credit Unions' Newslttr Awd; Big Spring-Howard Co Bicent Awd; Mayor's Commend Awd; Roll of Hon Awd, Fam Cnslg Ctr; Others.

PRATT, SAMUEL B oc/Dermatologist; b/Mar 26, 1940; h/Rt 6, Box 303, Inman, SC 29349; ba/Spartanburg, SC; m/Eva; c/Suzanne Louise, Samuel Pressly, David William, Isabel Laurens; p/S B and Louise P Pratt, Charleston Heights, SC; ed/AB; MD Med Univ SC 1966; Univ Va Med Ctr, Charlottesville, Va: Co-Chief Resident in Dermatol 1971-72, Asst Resident Dermatology 1969-71; mil/USNR 1967-69, Lt; Clin Instr Dept Dermatol Univ NC-CH, NC 1978-79; AMA; SC Med Assn; Dermatology Foun; Treas S'burg Co Med Soc 1978; Am Soc for Dermatol Surg; S'burg Gen Hosp: Secy Div

Dermatol, Dept Med, Patient Care Com; Piedmont Dermatol Soc SC: Secy 1973-78, Pres 1979; Mary Black Meml Hosp: Secy Div Dermatol Dept Med, Secy of Staff 1976; SC Med Care Foun; Fellow Am Acad Dermatol; r/S'burg Assoc Reformed Presb Ch: Ruling Elder 1974, Bldg Fund Chm 1974-; hon/Phys' Recog Awd, AMA; Sertoma Awd for Outstg Pre-Med S'ship; Garnet Cir; Mosley S'ship Awd; Algernon Sydney Sullivan Awd, Erskine Col; W/W Am Cols & Univs.

PRATT, WILLIAM DEVAUGHN o/Physician; b/May 17, 1941; h/213 W Dixie St, London, KY 40741; ba/London; m/Peggy; c/Michael, Mark, Elizabeth; p/H Devaughn Pratt (dec); Frances Crawford Pratt, Lexington, KY; ed/AB Centre Col Ky 1963; MD Univ Ky Col Med 1967; pa/Phys Proj Review of Cumberland Val Sub-Area Dist Hlth Coun, E Ky Hlth Sys Agy; KAFP; AAFP; KMA; AMA; cp/Kiwanis Clb; Phys' Search Com for Doctors of London-Laurel Co; r/Presb.

PREJEAN, L WAYNE oc/Fire Chief; b/Dec 14, 1941; h/419 Acorn Dr, Lafayette, LA 70507; ba/Lafayette; m/Judy L; c/Dwayne, Shawnee; p/Percy Prejean (dec); Mildred Prejean; ed/Grad Fire Adm Inst, LSU; mil/USNR 8 Yrs; pa/Fire Chief Lafayette Fire Dept; Pres La Fire Chiefs Assn; 2/VP Intl Assn Fire Chiefs; cp/Bd Dirs: BSA, Beavers, Red Cross; r/Nondenom; hon/Silver Beaver Awd, BSA; Var Life Saving Awds; Ser to Mankind, Sertoma; Ser Awd, JCs.

PRENDERGAST, GWEN DIANA oc/-Artist; Photographer; Conservator; b/Jul 31, 1926; h/546 Catalina Blvd, San Diego, CA 92106; m/Robert A; c/Stephen, Michael; p/Thomas Morley Harvey (dec); Evelyn Elisabeth Harvey, San Diego; pa/Artist: Sculptress, Comml Artist, Portrait Painter; Free-lance Artist 1962-77; Comml Artist: Yg's Art Studio 1957, Phillips-Ramsey Advt'g Agy 1955-57; Studio of the Cliffs 1946-55: Painter, Retoucher, Darkroom Lab Technician, Photog; Other Former Positions; Creative Works incl: Constrn of Replica of Baptismal Font (Majallorca, Spain, Surg Photo & Med Illustration for Neurosurg 1975-76, Design & Constrn of Scale Working Model of Fountain w Pump (San Diego) 1976-77, Others; Mem of Team Comm'd to Restore Trans Mural & Explorer II Mural in Ford Bldg for New Aerospace Mus (Balboa Park, San Diego); r/Rom Cath.

PRENTICE, STEWART WEBSTER oc/-Traffic Director; b/May 4, 1919; h/800 Circle Ave, Forest Park, IL 60130; ba/Chicago, IL; c/(Foster:) Robert, Carol, Debra, Cindy; p/Robert James and Grace Lombard Prentice (dec); mil/AUS WWII, 1/Lt; pa/Railroad Traffic Dir; Delta Nu Alpha Alumnae; Col Adv'd Traffic; Assoc'd Traffic Clbs Am; Experimtl Aviation Assn; r/Congreg; hon/W/W Am.

PRESCOTT, PATSY oc/Missionary; Gospel Singer; Speaker; b/Dec 3, 1919; h/307 N Main St, Athens, PA 18810; c/Ronald R Noll; p/Lewis Stellwagen (dec); Esther Myers (dec); pa/Singer-Composer; Radio-TV-Records; KASA Radio Prog Dir; cp/Entertainer USP Clbs 1942-45; r/Prot.

PREVOZNIK, STEPHEN J oc/Anesthesiologist; b/Jun 21, 1929; h/474 Fairfax Rd, Drexel Hill, PA 19026; ba/Philadelphia, PA; m/Rita Kellett; c/M Therese, Stephen J Jr, John Cyril, Michael Edward, Margaret Anne, Rita Marie, Thomas William, Jean Marie; p/John G Prevoznik (dec); Mary F Prevoznik, Mt Penn, PA; ed/RN; BS; MD; pa/Hosp Univ Pa: Prof Anesthesia, Dir Clin Activs; Exec Coun Assn Univ Anesthetists; Chm Sect on Clin Care Am Soc Anesthesiologists; r/Cath.

PREWITT, JUDITH MARTHA oc/-Mathematician; b/Oct 16, 1935; h/8008 Aberdeen Rd, Bethesda, MD 20014; ba/-Bethesda; c/David Joshua; p/Charles Shimansky (dec); Rebecca Shimansky, Brooklyn, NY; ed/BA w high hons Swarthmore Col 1957; MA Univ Penn 1959; PhD Univ Uppsala

(Sweden) 1978; pa/Mathematician Nat Insts of Hlth, Bethesda; Editor, Jours, Num Pubs on Computers in Med; IEEE; BES; MAA; AMS; SIAM; IAC; Sigma Xi; hon/Phi Beta Kappa; Sigma Xi; USPHS, F'ships & S'ships; Vis Scist, Uppsala Univ.

PRICE, BETH D oc/Free-lance Artist; Student; b/Jun 12, 1951; h/405 Sunset Terr, Amarillo, TX 79106; ba/Same; c/G Mason; p/Frank Meadows and Cloe Grammer

Wheeler, Amarillo; ed/Cand Deg Comml Art 1980; cp/Palo Duro Hand Weavers Guild; China Painters Guild; r/Trinity Luth Ch, Amarillo: Mem; hon/Sev Awds in Art & Aths.

PRICE, DAVID LEE oc/Administrative Aide; b/Jan 11, 1934; h/8705 Curtis Ave, Alexandria, VA 22309; ba/Alex; m/Eva W; c/David Jr, Scott Alfred; p/Mildred Price, Newport News, VA; ed/BS; MEd; MEd & Addit; mil/AUS Police Corps 1953-55; pa/Adm Aide Glagow Int Sch; OEA; MOA; POS; DOIB; WWSS; Who WNA; r/Bapt: Deacon, Sr Usher, Tally Clerk; hon/Kappa Delta Pi; Phi Delta Kappa; Other Hon Socs.

PRICE, EARNEST JR oc/College Professor; b/Mar 6, 1919; h/4402 Oak Hollow Dr, High Point, NC 27260; ba/High Point; m/Catherine Upchurch; c/Catherine P Laube; p/Earnest and Vivian Jordan Price, Ellisville, MS; ed/BS Miss St Univ; MA Columbia Univ; Grad Study; mil/AUS MC 1942-43; pa/Dist'd Lectr & Chm Human Relats Dept High Point

Col 1977-; Nat Bd YMCA's, New York, NY; Dep Dir Pers Sers 1969-77, Dir Student & Yg Adult Sers 1969, Assoc Dir Col & Univ Dept 1961-68; Other Former Positions; Trustee Am Humanics Inc; AAUP; Assn Profl Dirs YMCA's; Former Mem Am Mgmt Assn; cp/-Former Rotarian; Kiwanian; Former Pres Commun Chest, Glen Ridge, NJ; Common Cause; Dem Party; r/U Ch of Christ: Min, Chm Num Bds & Coms; Mem Glen Ridge Congreg Ch; hon/Omicron Delta Kappa; Personalities of S.

PRICE, ROBERT W oc/Engineering Company Executive; b/Nov 2, 1914; h/5746 E Burns St, Tucson, AZ 85711; ba/Tucson; m/Jane C; c/John, Ann, Gail; p/W Clyde and Edna MacDonald Price (dec); ed/Profl Engr Mines Colo Sch Mines 1935; mil/AUS Engrs 1935-56, Lt Col CE Ret'd Resv; pa/Mtn Sts Mineral Enterprises Inc, Tucson: Current Sr VP, Dir 1975-, Exec Engr 1970-75; Mtn Sts Engrs Inc, Tucson 1975-78: Exec VP, Gen Mgr; Proj Mgr Parsons Jurden Corp, New York, NY

1965-70; Mining Engr Arthur G McKee Co, San Francisco, Cal 1964-65; Other Former Positions; Reg'd Profl Engr: Colo, Cal; AIME; Mining & Metall Soc Am; NM Mining Assn; Mining Clb SW; r/Prot; hon/Tau Beta Pi; W/W W; Men of Achmt; Personalities W&MW.

PRICE, RUTH PUGH oc/Retired Educator; b/Dec 23, 1903; h/15009 Shadowood Dr, Monroe, MI 48161; m/Raymond A (dec); c/Doris Jean P Greiner; p/Walter E and L Maude Neudorfer Pugh (dec); ed/BEd 1941, MA 1948 Univ Toledo; Addit Studies; pa/-Tchr Lincoln Jr HS 16 Yrs; Elem Prin 10 Yrs; St

Mary Acad 4 Yrs; AAUW; Past Pres BPW; Local, St & Nat Ret'd Tchrs; Past Pres Local Ret'd Tchrs; cp/Monroe Co Hist Soc: Life Mem, Treas; Vol Work; r/Past Pres St Paul's U Ch Wom; Tchr Adult Bible Class Tchr; Past Pres Monroe Coun Chs; hon/Pi Gamma Mu; Phi Alpha Theta; Fulbright Awd.

PRICHARD, THORA INEZ oc/Secretary; b/Dec 25, 1908; h/100-104 SE Choctaw, Bartlesville, OK 74003; m/Cliff B (dec); c/1 Daugh, 1 Son; p/Andrew M and Eliza Anne Sanders; ed/Bus Adm; mil/Chief Pers & Payroll (Civilian) Ordnance Dept; pa/Ret'd Pastor's Secy 1st Bapt Ch, B'ville; cp/Am Cancer Soc; Pilot Clb; Other Commun Activs; hon/Personalities of S.

PRIEST, HELEN RUBYOR oc/Homemaker; b/Nov 4; h/101 Mulberry Dr, Hartford, KY 42347; m/Whayne; c/Whayne Jr, Adrienne McGaw; p/Sidney and Margaret Rubyor (dec); ed/BA; pa/Editor *Ky Keynote*; Bd Dirs NFMC; cp/VChm Nat Music Week; r/U Meth: Adm Bd; hon/Ky Col.

PRIESTLEY, VIOLET ARTA oc/Filmstrips Producer; b/Dec 14; h/3033 Aloma, Wichita, KS 67211; ba/Wichita; p/William E and Vina Kate Priestley (dec); ed/BS Ks St Univ; MA Emporia St Univ; pa/Prodr Color Sound Filmstrips; Nat A-V Assn; Assn Media Prodrs; Intl Quorum Motion Picture Prodrs; Assn for Ed & Commun & Technol; AAUW; cp/Book Coterie; r/Hillside Christian Ch; hon/Grand Awd, Intl Film & TV Fest NY; Var Other Awds.

PRIMM, BOB BRUNER oc/Teacher; b/Jun 30, 1948; h/515 Glenview Dr, Jasper, AL 35501; ba/Parrish, AL; p/John W Primm (dec); Beatrice B Gambrell, Jasper; ed/AS Walker Col 1968; BA Jacksonville St Univ 1973; MA Univ Ala 1977; pa/5th Grade Tchr Parrish Elem Sch; Walker Co Ed Assn; PTA; r/Ch of Christ.

PRINCE, ARTHUR HESSEL oc/Teacher; b/Aug 30, 1938; h/1446 Snowden Ave, Memphis, TN 38107; p/Philip R Prince (dec); Rebecca R Prince, Memphis, TN; ed/BA; MA; pa/Tchr Philosophy Mem St Univ, Univ Tenn Ctr for Hlth Scis; Tchr DeNeuville Heights Sch

for Girls; Am Phil Assn; Introduced Phil in Memphis City Schs, Mini Class Prog; cp/Memphis St Univ Alumni Assn, Class Agt; hon/Lttr from Pres of US; DIB; Intl W/W Commun Ser; Men Achmt; IPA; Hon Sgt-at-Arms Tenn Ho of Reps; Other Biogl Listings.

PRIVETT, A REX oc/Rancher; Politician; b/May 28, 1924; h/2300 Westwood Dr, Norman, OK 73069; m/Patricia Ann Nichols; c/Deborah P Fletcher, Rex, Patricia; p/Arnold Loyde and Claudia Muriel Privett (dec); ed/BA Okla St Univ; mil/AUS Engrs WWII, Technician; Battle Campaign Ribbons; Good Conduct Medal; pa/Past Pres Okla Cattlemen's Assn, Pawnee Co; cp/Pawnee Co C of C; Am Legion; Will Rogers; Coun BSA; Mem Okla Ho of Reps 16 Yrs, Spkr of House 6 Yrs; St Corp Commr 6 Yr Term (1972); r/Meth Ch: Chm Adm Bd, Fin Com; hon/Okla Ambassadors Corps; Hon Chief of Pawnees, Given Pawnee Name "Bucks-Pa-Hut Pawnee-Hasharo".

PROBBER, LLOYD oc/Financial Consultant; b/Apr 26, 1929; h/136 E 56th St, New York, NY 10022; ba/NYC; c/Judith, Shelley, Helene, Marc; p/Joseph Probber; Edna Kessler Probber, NYC; ed/CLU; CPCU; mil/AUS 1952-54; pa/Nat Assn Life Underwriters; Soc Chartered Life Underwriters; Nat Assn Security Dealers; Reg'd Investmt Advr; Commodity Futures Trade Comm; r/Jewish; hon/Million Dollar Round Table, Life Mem; Vanguard Awd, New England Life.

PROGAR, DOROTHY RUTH oc/Library Administrator; b/Sept 14, 1924; h/1800 Trinity, Waco, TX 76710; ba/Waco; m/Walter L; c/James Scott; p/George Thomas Watkins (dec); Florence Scott Watkins, Waco; ed/BA Baylor Univ; Mich St Univ; Tex Woms Univ; pa/Dir Libs; Lib Assns: Tex, Am, SWn; cp/Advt'g Clb Waco; McLennan Co Hist Survey Comm; YWCA; ARC Water Safety Instr; r/Bapt; hon/Nat Hon Soc; Profl Articles; 1st Wom City Dept (Hd).

PROPST, E ALLEN oc/Retired Professional Pilot Aircraft Agriculture Field Adv; b/Jan 11, 1926; h/253 SE Scravel Hill Rd, Albany, OR 97321; c/Richard Lee, Ronald Dean; p/Elmer E and Eva Anna Probst, Albany; mil/Aviation Cadet Mil Police & Security; pa/Aerial Pesticide Application & Timber Protection Fire Control; cp/Cand for

Gov of Oreg; Author Documents, Memorando Nat Security; r/Prot; hon/4 Bronze Battle Stars, Pres Cit, Air Medal, Good Conduct; IPA; Civilian Awds incl'g Dist'd Ser Awd; Personalities W&MW; Commun Ldrs & Noteworthy Ams.

PRYOR, GEORGE WALTER JR oc/- Counselor; b/Feb 20, 1937; h/Rt #2, Douglas, GA 31533; ba/Douglas; p/George W Sr and Valeria L Pryor, Brunswick, GA; ed/BA Morehouse Col 1960; MA Atlanta Univ 1969; Addt Studies; pa/Cnslr: Coffee HS 1972-79, Coffee Jr HS 1969-72, Fair St Elem Sch, Gainesville (Ga) 1964-69; Cnslr Coor CEETA Sum Prog Slash Pine Commun Action Agy, Waycross, Ga 1978 (Sum); Adm Coor Coffee Co Schs 1976-78; Other Former Positions; Ga Assn Edrs, Coffee Co Unit: Polit Action for Ed Com Chm 1973-76, Unit VP 1979-80, Leg Com Chm 1976-77, Fac Rep Coffee High 1977-78;

NEA; S Ga Col Basic Issues, Douglas: Mem, Book Reviewer 1972-79; Coffee Co Schs' Guid & Testing Com, Douglas, Recorder 1971-72, 1974-75; Ga Sch Cnslrs Assn: Dist VIII Presiding Chm, St Bd Dirs 1972-73; Ga Tchr & Ed Assn, Hall Co Unit: VP 1967-69, Pres-elect 1969-70; cp/Var Positions Mtl Hlth Assn Ga; BSA; Am Legion, Dept Ga; Fund Raiser ALSAC, Douglas; Dist VIII Citizens Adv Coun; r/Gaines Chapel AME Ch, Douglas: Dir Public Relats 1973-75, Bd Stewards 1973-75, 76-77, 78-79, Cub Master Pack 781 1970-71; hon/Dist Awd of Merit, Alapaha Area Coun of Yellor Pine Dist; Certs of Commend: Coffee Co Assn Edrs, Douglas & Coffee Co Commun Progressive Clb, AME Ch, Nat Assn Mtl Hlth, Coffee Co Mtl Hlth Assn; Recipient Grant; Yrbook Dedication for Outstg Ser, Coffee Jr HS 1971; Biogl Listings; Profl Pubs; Others.

PRYOR, SHEPHERD GREEN III oc/Lawyer; Professional Engineer; Sales Representative; b/Jun 27, 1919; h/135 Spalding Dr NE, Atlanta, GA 30328; ba/Same; m/Lenora Standifer; c/Sandra P Clarkson, Shepherd IV, Robert, Patty P Smith, Alan, Susan; p/Shepherd G Jr and Jeffie Persons Pryor

(dec); ed/BAE Ga Inst Technol; JD Woodrow Wilson Col Law; mil/USAF 1942-45; USAFR 1942-56, Capt, Pilot; pa/Reg'd Profl Engr Ga; Mem: St Bar Ga, US Dist Ct, Ct of Appeals, 5th Dist, US Supr Ct Bars; cp/Past Pres Loring Hgts Civic Assn; Current Precnt VChm; Del to Fulton Co Repub Party Conv; r/Meth.

PTASZKOWSKI, STANLEY EDWARD JR oc/Civil Engineer; b/Jun 11, 1943; h/12916 Greenway Chase Ct, Houston, TX 77072;

ba/Houston; p/Stanley Edward and Elsie Helena Ptaszkowski, Middle Village, NY; ed/AAS 1967; BS 1975; pa/Civil Engr Brown & Root Inc; Am Inst Aeronautics & Astronautics; Am Soc Civil Engrs; r/Luth.

PUCKETT, DOROTHY WILLIFORD oc/Counselor; b/Aug 10, 1940; h/Rt 1, Box 66-B, Oxford, NC 27565; ba/Creedmoor, NC; m/Carl Leland Jr; c/Carleen, Elainie Anne (dec), John Banks (dec); p/Percy E Williford, Oxford; Hettie Adcock Averette Williford (dec); ed/AA; BS; MEd; pa/APGA; NCPGA; Nat Voc Guid Assn; NCVGA; NEA; NC Assn Edrs; Triangle Chapt NCPGA; cp/OES; r/Enon Bapt Ch: Mem.

PUCKETT, RUBY P oc/Hospital Administrator; b/Nov 26, 1932; h/Rt 3, Box 108 B-2, Gainesville, FL 32601; ba/G'ville; m/Larry W; c/Laurel Lynn, Hollie Kristina; p/John Franklin Parker (dec); Ethel V Short Tuggle, Palmerdale, AL; ed/BS 1954; RD 1955; MA 1976; pa/Dir Food & Nutrition Sers Shands Tchg Hosp 1974-; Dir Dietetics (Hosp): G'ville 1968-74, Eustis (Fla) 1963-68, Knoxville (Tenn) 1961-63; Other Former Positions; Am Dietetic Assn: Teller's Com 1975, 76, Ed for Supportive Pers 1975-, Sect on Ed Preparation 1975-, Task Force for Adm Dietetics 1974-, Others; Fla Dietetic Assn: Editor *Orange Blossom* 1974-, Exec Bd 1965-, Others; Var Ofcs G'ville Dietetic Assn; SEn Hosp Conf for Dietitians; Field Agy Nutrition; Nutrition Ed Soc; Am Soc Hosp Food Ser Admrs; Nutrition Sect Fla Coun on Aging: Adv Bd, Secy, Chm 1974-; Other Profl Activs; cp/U Way; Compentency Com HIEFSS; Com on Animal Prods Nat Res Coun Adv Bd on Mil Pers Supplies; N Ctl Fla Hlth Planning Coun; Others; r/LDS: Mem; hon/Copher Awd, Am Dietetic Assn (Nom'd); IFMA's Silver Plate Awd Recipient, Intl Gold & Silver Plate Soc; Recog'd as 1 of 50 Wom Top Mgrs, *Instns & Volume Feeding* 1977; Fellow Royal Soc Hlth; IPA; Num Biogl Listings; Profl Pubs.

PUGH, JESSIE TRUMAN oc/Pastor; Professor; b/Oct 28, 1923; h/1500 Tangelwood, Odessa, TX 79760; ba/Odessa; m/Bessie Byrl; c/Datha, Names Terry,

Nathan; p/Jessie True Lonzer and Lucy Sanderson Pugh (dec); ed/BTh; DDiv; pa/Pastor 1st U Pentecostal Ch, Odessa; Pres Wn Apostolic Bible Col, Stockton, Cal; r/U Pentecostal; hon/IPA; W/W in Rel.

PUGH, JULIAN FRANKLIN oc/Marketing Executive; b/Sept 22, 1938; h/26214 Hwy 75, Spring, TX 77373; ba/Houston, TX; m/Sharon D Braswell; c/Julian F II, Shawnna D, Steven Craig; p/Jack Thomas and Lora

Virginia Smith Pugh, Conroe, TX; pa/Gtr Houston Bldrs Assn; Tex Assn Bldrs; Nat Assn Home Bldrs; Sales & Mktg Coun; Author *How to Invest in Real Est* 1972; r/Ch of Christ; hon/1 of Top 10 Mktg Men in Nation 1977; W/W S&SW.

PUH, CHIUNG oc/Professor; h/3420 Belden Dr NE, Minneapolis, MN 55418; m/J S Lee; p/Tze-Chian Puh and Wu-shie Sen; ed/PhD; pa/Current Prof Dept Physiol Med Sch, Univ Minn; Sigma Xi; Iota Sigma Pi; Am Physiol Soc; AAAS; NY Acad Sci; hon/F'ships; Est'd Investigator Am Heart Assn; Personalities W&MW; Notable Ams.

PULVARI, CHARLES F oc/Professor Emeritus; b/ Jul 19, 1907; h/2014 Taylor St, Washington, DC 20018; ba/Wash DC; ed/Dip Engrg Royal Hungarian Univ Tech Scis (Budapest) 1929; pa/Cath Univ Am: Prof 1953-, Res Prof; Lectr Postgrad Univ Tech Scis (Budapest) 1943-49; Fdr Pulvari Electrophy Lab, Budapest 1943-49; Fellow IEEE; Life Mem NY Acad Scis; Sigma Xi; Tau Beta Pi; hon/DAR Americanism Medal; Pub'd Author; Patentee in Field; DIB.

PURCELL, GEORGE RICHARD oc/Federal Employee; b/May 4, 1921; h/1 Gregory Pkwy, Syracuse, NY 13214; m/Mary Sutter; p/George Thomas Purcell (dec); Katherine Eagan Purcell; ed/BS Niagara Univ 1947; mil/AUS 1943-46, ETO, 97th Gen Hosp, MC; cp/Fdr & Pres Syracuse Chapt Cath Med Mission Bd 1973-76; Rep 1976-; r/Rom Cath; hon/DIB; Notable Ams; W/W Rel; Men Achmt; Comun Ldrs & Noteworthy Ams; IWWCS; Intl W/W Intells; NYS War Ser S'ship.

PURKEY, ROGER FRANKLIN oc/Certified Public Accountant; b/May 18, 1949; h/Rt 1, Box 646-K, Morristown, TN 37814; ba/M'town; m/Delores Bales; c/Deedra Ann, Jessica Yvonne; p/W Brown and Willie Belle Carter Purkey, M'town; ed/BS Tenn Technol Univ; pa/Past Pres Exc Clb M'town; Dir 1st Tenn Bk M'town; Am Soc CPAs; Tenn Soc CPAs; r/Bapt; hon/Phi Kappa Phi; Sigma Iota Epsilon; Fac S'ship, Sch Bus Adm; Alpha Kappa Psi S'ship Key; Grad w highest acad achmt, Sch Bus Adm 1971; Nashville Chapt Nat Acct'g Assn Awd for Proficiency in Study of Acct'g; Recipient Exchangeite, 1976.

PURVIS, MARY BELLE oc/Chemist; b/Jun 12, 1932; h/426 W Main St, Greeneville, TN 37743; ba/G'ville; p/Silas Wayne Sr and Malcena Elizabeth Purvis, G'ville; ed/BA, Tchrs Cert Tusculum Col; MA E Tenn St Univ; pa/Chem Lab Asst Tusculum Col 1951-53; Bill Collector (Self-Employed) 1954-59; Bkkeeper (Self-Employed) 1956-65; Organic Lab Instr E Tenn St Univ 1958-59; Chem Lit Resch (Self-Employed) 1959-; Pvt Res 1965-; Free-lance Writer 1950-; Am Chem Soc; cp/Nat Soc DAR, Nolachuckey Chapt: Libn 1978-80, Histn 1975-78, Registrar 1972-75, CAR CoChm 1970-78, Regent 1964-66; Tenn Soc DAR: Personal Page to Tenn St Regents at Nat Cong 1954-57, 1966-68, Page to Chaplain Gen 1955, 56; Chd of Am Revolution: Sr Pres Robert Sevier Soc 1970-77, Tenn St, Nat & Life Promoter, Mem "300" Clb; Nat Soc So Dames Am, Rec'g Secy Tenn Sco 1967-70; Intl Fdn Univ Wom; AAUW; Nat Soc Dames Ct of Honor, Memphis Soc; E Tenn Hist Soc; Greene Co Hist Soc; Geneal Clb Am; Nat Hist Soc; Tenn Fdn Wom's Clbs; Wash Co Chapt Assn for Preserv of Tenn Antiquities; IPA; Nat Fdn Press Wom; Tenn Wom's Press & Authors Clb; OES; Sierra Clb; Nat Travel Clb; Am Mus Natural Hist; Num Others; r/1st Presb Ch USA: Wom Assn Pres 1962-64, Ch Choir 21 Yrs, Former SS Tchr; hon/Nat Soc DAR Awds incl'g: 1965 Nat Outstg Jr, 1965 SEn Div Outstg Jr, 1965 Tenn Outstg Jr, Outstg Clb Wom of Yr, Union Temple Home Demonstration Clb 9164; Sr Student Awd, Am Chem Soc; Pub'd Author; Num Biogl Listings.

PURVIS, ROBERT CRAIG III oc/Coach, History Teacher; b/Jan 26, 1952; h/906

Wenasoga Rd, Corinth, MS 38834; ba/Glen, MS; m/Peggy Cheryl; p/Robert Craig Jr and Kathleen Joan Purvis, Corinth; ed/BS Miss St Univ; cp/BSA; Corinth City Pk Rules Com; r/W Corinth Bapt: Mem, Deacon, SS Tchr; hon/Student's Coach Awd: Ftball, Track; Var Coaching Champ's; Sev Ath Awds.

PYLES, LORAN RAY oc/Director; b/Jun 22, 1934; h/4000 S West Ave, Sioux Falls, SD 57105; ba/Sioux Falls; m/Sally W; c/Daniel L, David A, Stephen H, Mark D; p/Albert I and Helen B Pyles, Hamilton, OH; ed/Miami Univ Ohio; Mo Val Col; Asbury Col; Yth for Christ Dirs Sch; En Ky Univ; Morehead St Univ; Graham Bible Col; Univ Ga; pa/Dir Glory House (Halfway House for Men), Sioux Falls 1977-; Adj Instr Sioux Falls Col, Augustana Col 1978-; Pastor Laurel Springs Bapt Ch, Maribe, Ky 1972-77; Chief Cnslr Frenchburg Correctional Facility, F'burg (Ky) 1970-77; Other Former Positions; Lic'd Social Wkr Ky; Am, So Sts, Ctl Sts Correctl Assns; Nat, Ky Couns on Crime & Delinq; Va Coun on Social Wel; Wolfe Co Min Assn; Moderator Red River Assn So Bapts; VChm Menifee Co Min Assn; Sioux Falls: Min Assn, Evang Assn; Inter-Agy Sioux Falls; Allied Hlth Agys Sioux Falls; cp/BSA; Var Activs; Chaplain: JCs, Kiwanis Clb, Civitan Clb, Optimist Clb (also Pres); Yg Dems Clb; Bd Dirs: Powell Co for Mtly Retard, Mtn Maternal Hlth Leag; VChm Menifee Co Dry Leag; r/So Bapt; hon/Good Govt Awd, JCs (Bristol, Va-Tenn); Ky Bur of Corrections Awd.

Q

QADIR, SYED M A oc/Chemist; b/Jul 12, 1943; h/4712 Green Field Ctr, Lake Charles, LA 70605; ba/LC; m/Rafia; c/Shabnum; p/Syed and Saghira Sajjad (dec);

ed/BSc hons; MSc; pa/Chemist PPG Industs; Fellow Am Inst Chemists; Am Chem Soc; cp/Sustaining Mem Repub Nat Party; r/Islam; hon/DIB; Men Achmt; W/W S&SW.

QUALLS, MARSHALL DAVID oc/Educator; b/Dec 23, 1950; h/3107 Atkinson #213, Killeen, TX 76541; ba/Ft Hood, TX; p/Gene and Dee Qualls, Euless, TX; ed/AA TCJC; BS ETSU; MEd Tex Woms Univ; Doct Cand N Tex St Univ; pa/Occupl Invest Tchr Smith Mid Sch; Tex Voc Tech Assn; Phi Delta Kappa; Am Voc Assn; APGA; cp/Killeen C of

C Ed Com; Big Thicket Assn; r/Bapt; hon/Outstg Student Behavioral Scis; Dean & Hon Lists; W/W S&SW.

QUIGG, DOROTHY QUAY oc/Librarian; h/3515 N Washington Blvd, Arlington, VA 22201; ba/Wash, DC; p/Quay and Ella Atherton Quigg (dec); ed/BA Wn St Univ 1941; MS Cath Univ Am 1954; pa/Chief Cataloging Sect HUD Lib 1957-; Nav Ordnance Lab Lib 1955-57; Lib Congress 1943-55; Libn & Tchr Eng Rutherford HS 1941-43; Editor *New Serial Titles*; cp/VRegent DAR; r/Bapt.

QUIMBY, MYRON JAY oc/Author; Lecturer; b/Jun 17, 1922; h/1461 52nd Ave N, St Petersburg, FL 33703; ba/SP; c/Pamela Cushnie, Myron Jr, Martha Aumond; p/Myron Sr and Martha Eller Quimby (dec); ed/AB; mil/AUS Pattons 3rd Army ETO & ASA Ethiopia 1941-59; pa/Author: Num Books, Articles; cp/Former Pres & VP St Pete Writers Clb; Repub; r/Prot; hon/7 Ser Medals; 5 Battle Stars, WW-II; French Croix de Guerre; W/W S&SW; Contemporary Authors.

QUINN, JOSEPH EARL oc/Sheriff; b/Jun 14, 1932; h/PO Box 214, Caroleen, NC 28019; ba/Rutherfordton, NC; m/Frances; c/Joseph Jr, Richard; p/Earl Quinn (dec); Pearl Biggerstaff Quinn, Caroleen; ed/AA; Addit Studies; mil/USAF S/Sgt Germany; pa/Dep Sheriff; Lt Juv Ofcr; NC Juv Ofcrs Assn; cp/Piedmont Ruritan Clb; Am Legion; Bd Dirs Yth House; Task Force Yth Study Comm; r/Bapt; hon/Intermediate & Adv'd Law

Enforcement Certs, NC Dept Crim Justice; Personalities S.

QUISENBERRY, JOHN HENRY oc/Professor; b/Jun 25, 1907; h/1006 Puryear Dr, Col Sta, TX 77840; ba/CS; m/Pearl Buzy; c/Alex, Judith Terry (Mrs William); p/Walter and Nancy Quisenberry (dec); ed/BS w hons Tex A&M Col 1931; MS 1933, PhD 1937 Univ Ill; Addit Studies; pa/Dept Poultry Sci Tex A&M Univ: Prof & Dept Head 1946-72, Prof Emeritus 1972-; Assoc Prof & Head Dept Poultry Sci Univ Hi 1945-46; A&M Col of Tex: Assoc Prof Animal Husbandry 1944-45, Assoc Prof Genetics 1936-44; Res Asst Poultry & Animal Genetics Univ Ill 1931-36; Num Consltships; Poultry Res Survey Coms: Univ

Mo, NH, NC & So Reg Poultry Task Force; Pres & Chm Exec Com Poultry Sci Assn; Soc Experimental Biol & Med; Worlds Poultry Sci Assn; Tex & NY Acads Sci; AAAS; SAE; Tex Assn Col Tchrs; Pres AAUP; Genetics Soc Am; Am Genetic Assn; Am Inst Biol Scis; Soc Study Reproduction; Tex Poultry Improvemt Assn; Bd Dirs Tex Poultry Fdn; Tex Allied Poultry Assn; Tex Turkey Fdn; Am Soc Naturalists; AARP; Bd Dirs NRTA; Pres & Bd Dirs Am Poultry Hist Soc; cp/Pres Kiwanis Clb; Bryan-Col Sta C of C; Aggie Clb; Brazos Co A&M Clb; BSA; r/Bapt; hon/Fac Dist'd Achmt Awd Res; Dist'd Ser Awd, MSC; Golden Feather Awd, Tex Poultry Fdn; Gamma Sigma Delta Dist'd Ser Awd; Pres: Sigma Xi, Phi Kappa Phi; Gamma Sigma Delta; Phi Kappa Epsilon; Phi Sigma; Alpha Zeta; Gamma Alpha; Phi Tau Sigma; Pub'd Author; Num Biogl Listings.

R

RADLER, LOUIS oc/Executive; b/Jul 29, 1931; h/Mills Ln, Weston, CT 06430; ba/Fairfield, CT; m/Harriet Weisburg (dec); c/Lauren, Jeffrey, Allyson; p/Benjamin Radler (dec); Hattie Radler, Forest Hills, NY; ed/BS Univ Bridgeport; Addit Studies; mil/AUS 1953-55; pa/Pres: Chessco Industs Inc 1965-, Chem Specs Sales Corp 1962-; Gen Partner Rec Ventures Inc; Past Dir: Am Fidelity Fire Ins, Am Plan & Am Ins Co; cp/Bd Dirs Alumni Assn U Bapt; Newcomen Soc; Yg Pres Org; r/Jewish.

RAFTOPOULOS, DEMETRIOS DIONYSIOS oc/Professor; b/May 30, 1926; h/-3703 Cherrywood Ln, Toledo, OH 43615; ba/-Toledo; m/Eugenia; p/Dionysios Raftopoulos (dec); Mary-Elen Raftopoulos, Ventnor, NJ; ed/BSCE PMC Cols 1959; MSCE Univ Dela 1963; PhD Pa St Univ 1966; mil/Greek Army; pa/Prof Mech Engrg Univ Toledo 1967-73 & 1974-; Vis Prof Athens Nat Tech Univ 1973-74; Grad Asst & Res Asst Pa St Univ 1964-66; Instr PMC Cols 1961-64; St Hwy Engr Dela St Hwy Dept 1959-61; Field Supvr Costas Papadakis Engrg Consltg Co 1945-49; Engr Conslt; Reg'd Engr: Pa, Ohio & NJ; ASEE; ASCE; ASME; AAM; cp/Triangle Clb; r/Greek Orthodox; hon/Sigma Xi; Pi Tau Sigma; Phi Kappa Phi; Tau Beta Pi; Num NSF Grants; Ford Found Grant; Pub'd Author; Num Biogl Listings.

RAGAN, MARLEEN CLAIRE oc/-Editor, Executive; b/Jun 15, 1958; h/Rt 4 Box 39, Wake Forest, NC 27587; p/Charles Carlton and Louise Hilton Ragan; ed/BA Wn Carolina Univ; Attending NCSU; pa/Editor, American Biographical Institute, 1981-; Receptionist, Solid Sounds, 1977-81 (summers); Pres, Ragan Enterprises; VP, Ragan Corp; Wn Carolina Univ Alumni Assn; Joyner Soc; Female Execs Assn of Wake Co; Exec Com, Wake Forest C of C, Women's Ext; Nat, NC & Wake Forest Bds Female Execs; AMA; cp/NAACP; Wake Co Humane Soc; Public Policy Res; Youth Cnslr, Wake Forest U Meth Ch; AIAA; Soc Civil War Histns; Early Am Soc; Nat Hist Soc; Nat Geog Soc; Audubon Soc; Smithsonian Assocs; Nat Archives Assn; Costeau Soc; US Nature Conservancy; Wake Co Literacy Assn; NC DAR; NC Victorian Soc; Num Others; r/Meth; hon/Num Biogl Listings.

RAGAN, SEABORN BRYANT TIMMONS oc/Marketing Executive; b/Apr 28, 1929; h/13502 Barry Knoll, Houston, TX 77079; m/Sandra; c/2; p/Alexander and Ela Timmons Ragan; ed/Emory Univ; Univ Ga-A; AB Ga St Col; mil/USAR 1948-60; pa/Advtg, Sales Promotion, Mdse & Dealer Devel Gulf Oil 1956; Korea Oil Corp: Advr Mktg & Opers 1967-69, Rep Dir & CEO Heung Kuk Sang-Sa 1969-71; VP Mktg Korea Oil 1971-73; Dist Mgr Philadelphia Dist Gulf Oil 1973-76; GOCUS: Proj Mgr New Prods & New Bus Devel 1976-, Coor Survey Res; Nat, Tex & Houston Bds Realtors; AMA; cp/Assoc Am Enterprise Inst Public Policy Res; Am C of C Korea; USO Cnslr; Soc Arch Histns; Early Am Soc; Nat Hist Soc; Nat Geog Soc; Audubon Soc; Smithsonian Assocs; Nat Archives Assn; Costeau Soc; Wilchester Clb; Pres Wilchester Adult Chapt Am Field Serv; Nat & Ga SAR; Tex Victorian Soc; Num Others; r/Epis; hon/Num Biogl Listings.

RAGLE, KAREN LOUISE oc/Teacher; b/Nov 8, 1935; h/37 Carlson Ct, San Anselmo, CA 94960; ba/SA; m/James Walton; p/Kenneth Lesan, Sequim, WA; Gertrude Harvey, Seattle, WA; ed/BA; MA; pa/Tchr Wade Thomas Sch; NEA; CTA; IRA; CRA; Intl Platform Assn; r/Presb; Ambassadorships Hong Kong & Phillipines Through Presb Ch; hon/W/W: Child Devel Profls, Wom Am; Notable Ams.

RAHIMTOOLA, SHAHBUDIN H

oc/Physician; Professor; b/Oct 17, 1931; h/2810 SW Scenic Dr, Portland, OR 97225; ba/P'land; m/Shameem; c/Aly, Nadia; p/Hooseinally (dec); Kulsum, Karachi, Pakistan; ed/MB, BS Univ Karachi 1954; MRCP Edinburgh 1963; FRCP 1972; pa/Conslt Cardiology Madigan Gen Army Hosp 1972-; Dir Res Div Cardiology Univ Oreg Hlth Scis Ctr 1973-; Prof Med Univ Oreg 1972-; CoDir Dept Adult Cardiology Cook Co Hosp 1969-72; Assoc Prof Med Abraham Lincoln Sch Med Univ Ill 1969-72; Res Asst Dept Med Royal Postgrad Med Sch & Hammersmith Hosp 1967-69; CoDir Cardiac Lab Mayo Clin 1965-66; AHA; Am Col Chest Phys; Royal Soc Med; Am Col Cardiology; FACP; AAAS; AAUP; British & Pakistan Med Assns; British Cardiac Soc; r/Moslem; hon/Alpha Omega Alpha; Recipient Num Awds; F'ships: Mayo, Minn Heart Assn; Fulbright S'ship; Pub'd Author; Personalities W&MW; W/W W; Men Achmt; DIB.

RAIFORD, ERNEST LEE oc/Director; b/Feb 16, 1905; h/1010 Benbow Rd, Greensboro, NC 27406; ba/Same; m/Blanche Marie Reynolds; c/Jo Anne R Hinton, Roger, Linda R Fowler; p/Ernest and Nannie Tillery Raiford (dec); ed/BS Howard Univ; Addit Studies; mil/ORC Lt; pa/Gen Dir Bloodworth St YMCA Raleigh 1946-77; Fdr Jesse Moorland Br YMCA Greensboro 1932; Nat Assn Profl YMCA Dirs; Nat Task Force Strengthening YMCA; r/U Meth Ch: Lay Ldr; hon/Merit Citizenship Awd, St Augustine Col; Citizen of Yr, Raleigh Commun Rel Comm.

RAINES, LAWRENCE WESLEY oc/Educator; Coach; b/Mar 13, 1951; h/129 Wellington Dr, McDonough, GA 30253; ba/McDonough; m/Doris; c/Wes; p/Rudolph and Mary Rose Raines, Prattville, AL;

ed/BS/MBY Univ Ala 1973; pa/Sci Tchr; Head Football Coach; F'ship Christian Aths; SEAIS Coaches Assn; r/1st Bapt Ch, McDonough: Mem, SS Tchr, Usher, Yth Wkr; hon/SEAIS Reg 2A Coach of Yr.

RAKESTRAW, GARY RAY oc/Educator; b/Jul 12, 1952; h/Two Twin Lakes Rd, Beaufort, SC 29902; ba/Beaufort; p/W R and Beatrice Rakestraw, Bluefield, WV; ed/AS Bluefield Col; BM Carson-Newman Col; pa/Music Tchr Beaufort Co Schs; Organist Bapt Ch Beaufort; Am Guild Organists; Music Edrs Nat Conf; Phi Mu Alpha; cp/Organ Hist Soc; hon/AGO Ser Playing Cert.

RAMBAUSKE, WERNER ROBERT oc/Consultant; b/Mar 18, 1911; h/170 Action St, Carlisle, MA 01741; ba/Bedford, MA; m/Hedy Maria; c/Alexander (dec), Elizabeth,

Mary Anne; p/Emanuel and Minna Rambauske (dec); ed/MS Abitur; pa/Conslt & Prin Physicist & Engr Raytheon Co; Dir Phys Labs Germany; Physicist Wright-Patterson AFB; Prof Physics Univ Dayton; r/Rom Cath; hon/Outstg Inventor: WPAFB, Raytheon; Outstg Prof Univ Dayton.

RAMETTA, C S oc/Physician; b/Oct 5, 1945; h/61 California Ave, Middletown, NY 10940; ba/Middletown; m/Mary; c/Thomas, Rachel, Benjamin, Robert; p/Sebastian and Lucy Rametta, Orange, NJ; ed/BA cum laude, Seton Hall Univ 1967; MD Georgetown Univ 1971; pa/Staff Physician: Kimbrough Army Hosp (Ft Meade, Md) 1974-76, (Asst Att'g) Horton Meml Hosp 1976-; Occupl Hlth Physician 1974-76; Fed Med Examr 1974-76; Chief, Dept of Clinics 1975-76; Bd Dirs, Am Cancer Soc; Fac Mem, Am Heart Assn Adv'd Cardiac Life Support Prog; Diplomate: Nat Bd Med Examrs, Am Bd Internal Med; Am Col Physicians; Am Soc Internal Med; AMA; Am Soc Mil Surgs; Fellow: Am Col Angiology, Am Col Utilization Review Physicians, Intl Col Angiology; Am Soc Law & Med; Am Geriatrics Soc; Others; r/Cath; hon/Alpha Epsilon Delta; Delta Epsilon Sigma; Alpha Omega Alpha; Tchr of Yr 1974.

RAMIREZ, PAUL MICHAEL oc/Neuropsychological Investigator; Educational Specialist; b/May 15, 1951; h/37-72 102nd St, Corona, NY 11368; ba/Brooklyn, NY; p/Paul Sr and Freda Ramirez, Corona; ed/BA Herbert H Lehman Col of CUNY 1973; MA NYU 1976; MA CCNY 1980; MPhil; pa/Instr, Downstate Med Ctr; Ednl Conslt; Intl Neuropsychol Soc; NY Acad Scis; Intl Reading Assn; Orgr & Chm Neuropsychol Issues in Reading Disabilities, Spec Interest Group of Intl Reading Assn; AAAS; Editor, *Jour of Ednl Neuropsychology*; Contbr to Profl Jours; hon/NSF Fellow.

RAMIREZ-RIVERA, JOSÉ oc/Doctor; b/Jun 26, 1929; h/Andalucia #67, Mayaguez, Puerto Rico 00708; ba/Mayaguez; m/Leila Suner; c/Frederico, Steven, Sally, Juliette, Natasha, Leila; p/Jesus Ramirez and Nieves Rivera, Mayaguez; ed/MD; pa/Doct Med; Prof Med Univ PR; Chief Med Mayaguez Med Ctr; Dir Wn Consortium Med Ed; Dir Rincon Rural Hlth Initiative Proj; Dir Clin Invests & Ed Wn Hlth Reg; cp/Pro-Arte; Mayaguez Swimming; Tennis Clb; r/Cath; hon/A Blaine Brower Travelling Scholar, Am Col Physicians.

RAMOV, EDWARD SAMUEL oc/Educator; b/Jul 16, 1936; h/1321 Levick St, Philadelphia, PA 19111; ba/Phila; p/Leonard and Mamie Ramov, Phila; ed/BS 1958, MEd 1961 Temple Univ; pa/Tchr Math: Washington High, Phila Public Sch Sys 26 Yrs, Jewish Rel Schs 1961-73; cp/Jewish Def Leag: Pres NE Chapt 1968-73, Exec Dir Pa 1974-; Yg Israel Oxford Cir: Pres 1968-75, Chm Bd 1975-; hon/Legion Merit Awd, 4 Chaplains Assn; Recipient Num Grants, Nat Sci Foun; W/W Rel; Book Hon; Personalities Am.

RAMSEY, ELLIOTT oc/Foreman; b/Dec 6, 1922; h/#5 Cir C, Orange, TX 77630; ba/Orange; m/Emogene Musgrove; c/Michael, Sharon R Jarvis, Steven; p/John Ramsey (dec);

Annie Ramsey, Merryville, LA; mil/Marines 3rd Div 9th Regiment 1942-45; pa/Prodn Foreman Dupont Co; cp/Commdr VFW; Yth Baseball & Football; Scouts; City Govt & Sch Activs; r/N Orange Bapt Ch.

RAMSEY, IRA CLAYTON oc/Treasurer-Controller; b/May 13, 1931; h/780 Wesley Oak Rd NW, Atlanta, GA 30328; ba/Atla; m/Marianne; c/Clayton, Robin; p/James Sr and Ruth Treadaway Ramsey, Quitman, GA; ed/BBA Univ Ga; LLB Atla Law Sch; mil/AUS 1954-56; pa/Treas-Controller Plantation Pipe Line Co; r/Bapt.

RAMSEY, VICTOR EUGENE oc/Clergyman; b/Feb 2, 1926; h/116 E Jones St, Williamsville, IL 62693; ba/W'ville; m/Margaret Annette Cook; c/Victor II, Brian; p/Preston Ramsey (dec); ed/Edith Houser Ramsey, Chicago, IL; ed/BA DePauw Univ 1950; MDiv Christian Theol Sem 1956; pa/Min Appts: Elkhart U Meth Chs W'ville 1978-, Trivoli U Meth Chs Hanna City 1974-78, Anchor U Meth Chs Sibley 1969-74, U Ch Woodhull 1969, Clover Chapel Meth Chs & Oscoe Commun Ch Woodhull 1967-69, Dir Public Relats Meth Sunset Home Quincy 1966-67; Num Other Min Positions; Peoria Area Min Assn: Pres, Chrperson, Task Force Christian Unity, 2/VP, Media Coor; Past Pres Gibson City Area Min Assn; Ctl Ill Conf: Bd Ch & Soc, Com Gen Wel, Com VChrperson, Com Memoirs; Bd Hosps & Homes Ctl Ill Conf Meth Ch; Coor *Evening Meditation* 1977-; Prodr *Christmas Is A Warm Fuzzy* 1977; Other Profl Activs; cp/CoFdr, Bd Dirs & Treas Bi-Partisan Citizens Assn; BSA; DePauw Univ Mens Hall Alumni Assn; Editor *The Hallman*, Secy-Treas; Bd Dirs Ford Co Assn Mtl Hlth; Chm Com Promotion & Public Ed Ford Co Mtl Hlth Referendum; Lions Clb: Pres Sibley Clb 1971-72, Dist 1-K Govs Cabinet & Zone Chm 1972-73; VFW; Am Legion; r/NW Ind Conf The Meth Ch: Admitted on Trial Ordained Deacon 1952, Admitted Full Connection Ordained Elder 1956; Transferred Ctl Ill Conf 1966; hon/Theta Phi; Ford Co Assn Mtl Hlth: 1st Outstg Mem Awd, 2 Ser Recog Awds; "Yen for News" Cert, Ind Area Meth Ch; BSA: Scouters Key Illowa Coun, Cert Apprec WD Boyce Coun; Nom'd Fellow Intl Platform Assn; Num Biogl Listings.

RANAHAN, SANDI MANNING oc/Public Relations; b/Sept 9, 1929; h/8750 E McDowell Rd, Scottsdale, AZ 85257; ba/Same; c/Barbara Durand, Susan; p/John Manning (dec); Mary Manning, Morris Plains, NJ; ed/AA w distns; BA summa cum laude; pa/Freelance Public Relats; Grad Asst Sociol Ariz St Univ; Maricopa Mtl Hlth Assn; Am & Pacific Sociol Assns; Wn Gerontological Assn; cp/Vol Spkrs Bur; Commun Coun; Alphamega Life Support Adv Bd; Fam Living Conf; Mesa Chds Theater; Friends of Fam; Mortar Bd Alumnae; hon/Phi Beta Kappa; Phi Kappa Phi; Alpha Kappa Delta; W/W Am Col; DIB; Commun Ldrs & Noteworthy Ams.

RANCOUR, JOANN SUE oc/Registered Nurse; b/Nov 10, 1939; h/205 Denison Ave, Elyria, OH 44035; m/Richard Lee; c/2; p/Joseph and Anna Donich Sokol; ed/CRN; Cert'd Generalist Practitioner; Psychi & Mtl Hlth Nsg Pract; pa/Head Nurse; ANA; Nat Leag Nsg; N Am Soc Adlerian Psychol; cp/Menninger Foun; Treas Alfred Adler Inst Cleveland; r/Cath; hon/W/W Am Wom; Commun Ldrs & Noteworthy Ams.

RAND, NANCY GERALDINE oc/Executive; Writer; b/Jan 10, 1924; h/2091 Fish Hatchery Rd, Grants Pass, OR 97526; ba/Same; m/Homer Charles; c/Loletta Garrison, Sandra Francisconi, Alana Wheeler; p/Guy Wetherbee (dec); Buena Minto Wetherbee, GP; pa/Pres Dog Tng Ctr; Dir & Past Pres Doberman Pinscher Clb So Oreg; Dir Rogue Val Kennel Clb; Judge Dog Puppy Tng Advr; Dog Devel Com OSU; Jackson Co Dog Tng Clb; Ldr Josephine Co Dog Clbs; cp/Jose Co Ext Adv Coun; 4-H Ldr; Jose Co Hist Soc; Past Worthy Matron OES; r/U Meth; hon/Nat 4-H Ldrs Recog; JCs Outstg Wom of Yr Awd; Silver Awd, Bethel 13 Intl Order Jobs Daughs; Ser Cit, OSU; Ser Awd, Rogue Val Kennel Clb.

RANDALL, EUDORA PATRICIA oc/Nurse; b/Jan 23, 1930; h/37 Forest Pk, Portland, ME 04101; ba/Yarmouth, ME;

p/Lewis Randall (dec); Emily Sanborn Randall, Winthrop, ME; ed/Grad Augusta Gen Hosp Sch Nsg 1951; BS 1960, MS 1965 Boston Univ; pa/Sr CHS Nurse Supvr Commun Hlth Ser Inc 1978-; Public Hlth Nsg Dir Dept Hlth City P'land 1973-78; Supvr & Conslt Dept Hlth & Wel St Me 1956-73; USVAC 1952-55; ANA; NLN; AAUW; APHA; Royal Soc Hlth; Me St Nurses Assn: Treas Ctl Dist, Dir Bd Dist 04, Cont'g Ed Com; cp/Tutor Literary Vols Inc; Treas Altrusa Clb; Num Adv Coms Hlth & Wel Orgs; r/Bapt; JH Advr Num Bapt Chs 8 Yrs.

RANDALL, GERALD ROBERT oc/Executive; b/May 27, 1936; h/29 Elaine Rd, Milford, CT 06460; ba/Syracuse, NY; p/Samuel Randall, Middletown, NY; Florence Boyce Randall, Milford; mil/AUS 1959-61; pa/Pres Record & Pubg Co; ASCAP; cp/Repub; r/Meth.

RANEY, RICHARD BEVERLY oc/Professor; b/Jul 21, 1906; h/Box 2467, Chapel Hill, NC; ba/CH; m/Carolyn Haldane Fuller; c/Richard Jr, Thomas Fuller; p/Richard and Kate Denson Raney (dec); ed/BA Univ NC 1926; MD Harvard Univ 1930; mil/Asst Surg US Public Hlth Ser Resv 1943; pa/Assoc Instr & Asst Prof Orthopaedic Surg Duke Univ 1937-52; Prof & Chm Orthop Surg NC Meml Hosp & Univ NC Med Sch 1952-67; Chm Bd Trustees *Jour Bone & Jt Surg* 1962-65; VP Am Acad Orthop Surgs 1961-62; Med Soc: Pres Durham-Orange Co 1962, NC; Am Col Surgs; Ga Orthop Soc; Num Other Profl Assns; cp/Trustee Olivia Raney Lib; Bd Trustees Wake Co Libs Sys; Former Exec Com NC Symph; r/Epis; hon/NC Govs Awd; Phys of Yr 1964; Pub'd Author.

RANGEL, CARLOS ENRIQUE oc/Consultant; Lecturer; b/Jan 18, 1928; h/1523 Port Royal, Lexington, KY 40504; ba/L'ton; m/Maria Begonia; c/Carlos Edvardo, Esmeralola, Roberto, Maria Teresa, Mike; p/Nicolas Rangel (dec); Carmen Rodriquez (dec); ed/MBA; pa/IBM; Mgmt Conslt; Lectr Transylvania Univ; cp/Chm Sisters Cities; Partners Am; Ky Col; Secy ASID; r/Cath; hon/IBM: Outstg Contbn, 3 Times Worldwide Sales Ldr.

RANGOS, JOHN G b/Jul 27, 1929; h/78 Locksley Dr, Pittsburgh, PA 15235; ba/Monroeville, PA; m/Patricia A; c/John Jr, Alexander William; p/Gust Rangos (dec); Anna Rangos, Monroeville, PA; mil/AUS 1951-54; pa/Bd Dirs, Craig House Technoma; Nat Comm, UNA 1977; Pioneered Maj Tech & Operational Advancements in Environ Area (Sewage Sludge Disposal, Disposal Sites, Resource Recovery Sys from Complex Wastes); cp/Chm Fund-raising, UNICEF (Pgh); Past Mem, Pa Corp Ch; Bd Dirs, Holy Cross Sem Theol, Clergy-Laity Co (NY); r/Greek Orthodox.

RANIVILLE, FRANCIS OLIVER oc/Industrial Belting & Mill Supply Employee; b/Oct 19, 1920; h/2350 4 Mile Rd NE, Grand Rapids, MI 49505; pa/Gen Worker Raniville Co & Ton-Tex Corp 30 Yrs; Poet; Composer 165 Hymns & 500 Sonnets incl'g: *Gods Loving Heart at Christmas, Our Christ Came Down From Heaven Above;* Rep Centro Studi d Scambi Intl; Hymn Soc Am; World Poets Resource Ctr Inc; hon/DLibA, Repub China; M Rel Lit, Pakistan; Sonnet Awd w Gold Medal, Intl Poets Shrine; World Belles Lettres Awd, Dr E R Trimble; Dr Div Lit & Dr Lit Arts, Poet Laureate Winning Hymn "God of Nations Whose Eternal Light" & Am Poet w Bicent Distn, Dr Amado Yuzo; Pub'd Author.

RANKIN, KATHLEEN ELIZABETH MURPHY oc/Homemaker; b/Nov 14, 1949; h/491 Selfridge, Peterson AFB, CO 80916; m/Johnnie; c/Jonathan Vinson, Daevid Hurley; p/Benjamin Murphy (dec); Polly Murphy, Lawton, OK; ed/BS Okla St Univ 1976; cp/Coor Nat Sudden Infant Death Syndrome Foun; DAR; La Leche Leag: Ldr, Dist Relactation Res Ldr, Chapt Libn; Orgr Peterson AFB Babysitting Co-op; Colo Parents for Chd; GSA: Ldr, Secy, Mem 22 Yrs; Vol ARC; r/Epis: Former Bible Sch Tchr, Choir;

hon/Psi Chi; Alpha Lambda Delta; Cert Apprec: Pond Barracks, Ofcrs Wives Clb.

RANSOM, JAY ELLIS oc/Author; b/Apr 12, 1914; h/1821 E 9th St, The Dalles, OR 97058; ba/Same; m/Wilhelmina Johanna Buitelaar; c/Jay, Alix-Gay DeVito (Mrs Leroy), Scott, Lisa, Stuart; p/Jay and Lucy Adams Ransom (dec); ed/BA hons Univ Wash 1935; Addit Studies; pa/Exec Dir Aleutian-Bering Sea Expeditions Res Lib W Am Inst Exploration; Univ Mich Res Asst & Asst Dir 5th Archeological Expedition Aleutians 1954; Free-Lance Photog 1932-; Sr Tech Writer & Editor Hercules Powder Co 1962; Chief Proposals Writer & Supvr Pubs Am Electronics 1959-60; Ret'd Conslt; Num Other Past Positions; Author 1962-: *High Tension, Ariz Gem Trls, Petrified Forest Trls, Rock-Hunters Range Guide, Fossils Am, Gems & Minerals Am,* Others; Features Num Mags & Jours incl'g: Writers Digest, Better Homes & Gardens, Field & Stream, Mans Life; Am Anthropological Assn; Am Folklore Soc; Intl Soc Am Linguistics; Inst Radio Engrs; Pi Gamma Mu; Phi Delta Kappa; Am Forestry Assn; cp/Secy Assoc'd C of Cs Siskiyou Co; Nominal Repub; r/Presb; hon/Denominated Wash & Oreg St Author; Res Grant Am Coun Learned Socs.

RANSOM, RAYMOND LINCOLN oc/Director; b/Jan 10, 1916; h/1404 Quarterman St, Waycross, GA 31501; ba/Same; m/Altomease; c/Raymond Jr, Gloria, Annette, James; p/Oscar and Dranna Ransom (dec); ed/AB Claflin Univ 1942; MS SC Grad Sch 1956; mil/AUS S/Sgt 1942; pa/Assoc Dir Rec Waycross-Ware Co Rec Dept 1969-; Prin & Asst Prin Num Schs 1949-68; Nat Cong Parents & Tchrs; NEA; Ga Tchrs & Ed Assns; Prin Sec'dy Schs & Cols; Nat Rec Assn; Phi Beta Sigma; cp/NAACP; Pres Waycross HS Parents & Tchrs Assn; Chm Minority Bd; Secy Su Union Annual & Gen Confs; Pres Northside Commun Clb; Chm Participation Com Bicent & Ware Co Sesquicentennial; ARC Bd; Adv Com Waycrosss & Ware Co Bds Ed; Commdr Am Legion; Keystone Voters; Civics Leag; Chm Cancer Crusade; March of Dimes; Heart Fund; Pres & Past Secy Waycross Mens Criterion Clb; r/Big Bethel Free Will Bapt Ch: Mem, Asst Tchr Mens Bible Class, Fin Secy; hon/George Washington Carver HS Indust Arts & DCT Awd; Britannica Soc Awd; Cert Merit, Ga Rec & Park Soc; Hon Deg New Farmers Am; AUS: 3 Battle Ribbons, Expert Markman; Num Biogl Listings.

RAO, DESIRAJU BHAVANARAYANA oc/Scientist; Professor; b/Dec 8, 1936; h/3520 Charter Pl, Ann Arbor, MI 48105; ba/AA; m/D Umadevi; c/D Pramila, D Kavitha; p/D Sreeramulu and D Hanumayamma Rao, India; ed/BSc 1956, MSc 1959 Andhra Univ; MS 1962, PhD 1965 Univ Chicago; pa/Res Scist & Head Phy Limnology & Meteorology Group Great Lakes Envir Res Lab 1975-; Adjunct Prof Limnology & Meteorology Univ Mich 1975-; Ctr Great Lakes Studies Univ Wisc-Milwaukee: Prof Dept Energetics 1972-76, Vis Assoc Prof Dept Physics 1971-72, Univ Senate, Div Exec Com Nat Scis Div, Grad Prog Com Col Engrg; Num Other Past Positions; Conslt: Canada Centre 1971, Marine Envir Data Ser 1974; Sigma Xi; Am Meteorological Soc; Am Soc Limnology & Oceanography; Intl Water Resources Assn; r/Hindu; hon/Postdoct Fellow Nat Ctr

Atmospheric Res Boulder; Res Scholar Indian Nav Phy Lab; Num Biogl Listings; Pub'd Author.

RAPHAEL, CARL S oc/Management; b/Apr 23, 1943; h/1705 LaRue Ln, Warrington, PA 18976; ba/Princeton, NJ; m/Ellen Gibson; c/Larissa, Heather; p/Harold and Ruth Raphael, Uniondale, NY; ed/BS; MA; MBA; pa/Mktg Mgmt E R Squibb & Sons Inc; Squibb Mgmt Assn; cp/Union Co Consumer Affairs Adv Com Chm; Warrington Ambulance Corps; r/Jewish; hon/NY St Regents S'ship; W/W E; DIB.

RAPPAPORT, HAROLD oc/Engineer; b/Feb 10, 1920; h/8662 SW 154 Cir Pl, Miami, FL 33193; ba/Coral Gables, FL; m/Berta; c/Paul, Jill; p/Louis and Rebecca Rappaport (dec); ed/BSCE cum laude NEn Univ 1950; mil/AUS 1942-44; pa/Structural Engr & Specifications Analyst; NSPE; FES; PEPP; ASTU; CSI; MENSA; Reg'd Profl Engr Mass; Lectr Univ Miami & Fla Intl Univ; Panel Arbitrators Am Arbitration Assn; r/Conservative Judaism; hon/Recipient Nat Awd, Lincoln ARC Welding Soc Competition; W/W S&SW.

RASBURY, AVERY GUINN oc/Accountant; Consultant; b/Dec 18, 1923; h/1608 S Gessner Rd, Houston, TX 77063; ba/Houston; m/Linda Loo; c/Sandra Cleveland; p/William Rasbury (dec); Annie Lynn Rasbury, Ft Worth, TX; ed/BBA N Tex St Univ 1950; mil/USMC 1941-47; pa/Exec Asst J Robert Neal 1953-; Controller G H Hart Co Inc 1978-79; Pres & Gen Mgr Multi-Fab Inc 1974-78; Exec VP & Gen Mgr West-Jet Aviation 1969-74; Bldg Mgr J Robert Neal Bldg 1953-69; Num Other Past Positions; cp/N Tex St Univ Alumni Assn; Optimist Intl; Pres, Area Lt Gov & Secy-Treas Civitan Intl; Houston Livestock Show & Rodeo; Las Vegas Country Clb; r/Rice Temple Bapt Ch, Houston: Chm, Bd Deacons; hon/Outstg Clb Pres, Civic Intl; Civitan of Yr 1963; Outstg Civic Ldrship Awd; AUS: Pres Unit Cit, Am Def Medal, Victory Medal, Asiatic-Pacific Campaign Medal, Others; Num Biogl Listings.

RASHMIR, ROSE LILLIAN oc/Consultant; b/Dec 20, 1899; h/The Penthouse, 101 Ocean Ave, Santa Monica, CA 90402; m/Meyer (dec); c/Lewis, Mark (dec); p/Louis Lapides (dec); Fruma Starobin Lapides Rickles (dec); ed/Att'd Num Univs; pa/Ret'd Direct Mail Mktg Conslt 1968-69; Res Dir & Dir Tr Mkt Compilation & Res Bur 1948-68; Sr Tr Jem Elect Co 1922-43; Author *Population Mobility;* Contbr Num Jours; Treas Direct Mail Clb; LA Woms Advtg Assn; Am Advtg Fdn; DM Advtg Assn; cp/Chm Census Comm; LA C of C; Pres Jewish Comm Ctr; Chm Price Panel Ratio Bd Div USO; Dir Coun Civic Unity; VP Un of SM; Exec Com Mankind Ctr; Gov Warrens Comm Leg Yth & Chd; Treas Leag Wom Voters; Prog Chm Coun Intl Rels; Chm Russian War Relief S New Eng; Chm Friends Leo G Rigler Cancer & Cardiovascular Res UCLA; Chm Bd Dirs Inst Preven Destructive Behaviors & Suicide Preven Ctr; hon/Pub'd Author.

RATHBONE, PERRY TOWNSEND oc/Director; b/Jul 3, 1911; h/151 Coolidge Hill, Cambridge, MA 02138; ba/New York, NY; m/Euretta de Cosson; c/Peter, Eliza, Belinda; p/Howard and Beatrice Connely Rathbone; ed/AB Harvard 1933; Addit Studies; mil/USNR Lt Commdr 1942-45; pa/Mus Dir: Christies Intl 1977-, Christies USA 1973-77; Mus Fine Arts: Dir Emeritus 1972-, Dir 1955-72; Dir: City Art Mus 1940-55, Masterpieces Art NY Worlds Fair; Num Other Past Positions; Advr Num Profl Orgs; Am Assn Mus; Assn Art Mus Dirs; Am Acad Arts & Scis; cp/Trustee: Am Fdn Arts, Mus Fine Arts, Assn Art Mus Dirs, New Eng Conservatory Music, Intl Exhbns Foun, Opera Co Boston, Cosmopolitan Art Foun, Royal Oak Foun; St Louis Round Table Assn; Mass Hist Soc; Colonial Soc; Royal Art Soc; Century Assn; Somerset; Other Civic Assns; r/Epis; Vestryman; hon/Phi Beta Kappa; Chevalier de la Legion d'Honneur; Pub'd Author; Num Hon Degs.

RATLIFF, FRANCES ANNE oc/Educator; b/May 17, 1935; h/Huntington Bch, CA 92646; ba/2501 Harbor Blvd, Costa Mesa, CA 92626; c/Lisa; p/Arthur and Ann Cornelia Swartzendruber (dec); ed/BA Upland Col 1957; MS Cal St Univ 1975; pa/Fairview Hosp 1959-: Classroom Tchr Mtlly Retarded & Orthopedically Handicapped 1959-70, Coor Tchr 1971-79, Coor Adult Spec Ed Ser 1979, In-Ser Tng Instr 1971-79; Facilitator TV Course Coastline Commun Col 1977-79; Orange Coast Col Ext 1974-75; Cal St Univ Ext 1972-75; Edr Mtlly Retared Pacific Hosp 1957-59; Guest Lectr Num Cols; Contbg Editor; cp/Bahari Troupe 1978-; r/Presb Ch of Covenant, CM: Mem; hon/Phi Kappa Phi; Pub'd Author.

RATLIFF, GERALD LEE oc/Professor; b/Oct 23, 1944; h/10 Edgewood Terrace, Upper Mountclair, NJ 00743; ba/UM; p/Frank and Peggy Donisi, Middletown, OH; ed/BA magna cum laude Georgetown 1967; MA Cincinnati 1970; PhD Bowling Green Univ 1975; pa/Prof Dept Spch-Theatre Montclair St Col 1975-; Tchg Fellow Bowling Green Univ 1972-75; Instr Glenville St Col 1970-72; Asst Cinc 1969-70; Feature Writer *Herald-Ldr;* Reviewer *Theatre Hist/Criticism;* Dir Num Univ Prodns; VP Res Intl Arts Assn; Am Theatre Assn; Spch Communs Assn: ERIC Coor, Sts Adv Coun; Spch-Theatre Assn NJ; cp/USA Rep *Inscape;* Lyceum Assn; r/Bapt; hon/Promethean Lamp Prize; Poetry Cong Achmt Awd; La Plume Prize; Am Poetry Cong Achmt Awd; W B Jones Meml Awd; El Camino Poets Awd; Hist Preserv Am Awd; Sigma Tau Delta; Phi Kappa Phi; Alpha Phi Gamma; Phi Alpha Theta; Alpha Psi Omega; Pi Kappa Delta; Intl Platform Assn; Fellow Intl Biogl Centre; Pub'd Author; Num Biogl Listings.

RAUCH, MARSHALL ARTHUR oc/-Executive; b/Feb 2, 1923; h/1121 Scotch Dr, Gastonia, NC; m/Jeanne Girard; c/John, Ingrid, Marc, Peter, Stephanie; p/Nathan and Tillie Rauch; ed/Att'd Duke Univ; mil/Inf Overseas European Theater WW-II; pa/Chm Bd, Pres & Dir Rauch Industs Inc; Dir & Treas E P Press Inc; Dir: Majestic Ins Fin Corp, Plastivac Corp; cp/NC Senate: VChm Appropriations, Chm Intergovt Relats, Chm St Govt, VChm Fin, Chm Law Enforcemt & Crime Control, Chm Fin, VChm Mfg, Labor & Commerce; NC Adv Budget Comm; Sports Facility Comm; City Gastonia: Mayor Pro Tem, City Coun-man; Other Polit Activs; Dir: Gastonia C of C, Gaston Skills, Salvation Army Boys Clb, U Fund, Gaston Boys Clb,

Carolinas AAU, Gaston Mus Nat Hist, Planned Parenthood & World Population, YMCA, Commun Action Inc, Tuberculosis Assn; VP & Dir Commun Concert Assn; Bd Advrs Gardner Webb Col; Big Brother; Conslt Comm Pioneer Girl Scout Coun; Num Other Civic Assns; r/Pres: Temple Emanuel, Frank Goldberg Lodge B'Nai B'Rith; Chm Gaston Jewish Wel Fund; Dir NC U Jewish Appeal Cabinet; Nat Coun Am Jewish Joint Dist Com; Bd Govs NC Jewish Home Aged; hon/Man of Yr: Gastonia Jr C of C, NC Hlth Dept, Gaston Co Omega Psi Phi, Red Shields Boys Clb, Jr Woms Clb; Nat Rec Cit, Nat Rec Assn; Nat Coun Christians & Jews Brotherhood Awd; Combat Inf Medal; W/W: S&SW, World Jewry; Leading Men US.

RAULT, JOSEPH MATTHEW JR oc/Real

Estate Developer; Independent Oil Producer; b/Feb 24, 1926; h/611 Northline, Metairie, LA 70005; ba/New Orleans, LA; m/Bonnie Mossler; c/Joseph III, Katherine, (Stepchd, Clements:) Miles, Evelyn C Cahoon, Bonnie, Edward, Marilyn, Robert; p/Joseph Rault (dec); Calista Morgan Rault, Metairie; ed/BS MIT 1948; LLB Tulane Law Sch 1950; mil/USN Ensign to Lt (jg) 1943; 2nd Law Dept 1947; Lt 1953; pa/Pres & Owner: Rault Petro Corp 1962-, Lamplighter Clb Inc 1967-, Lake Hillsdale Estates Inc 1970-, Domed Stadium Hotel Inc 1972-, LH Inn Inc (Holiday Inn) 1973-; Owner Rault Ctr 1972-; Fgn Oil Prodn: Pres Rault Petro Corp Venezuela, Construction-Otila, SA Mexico; Pt-Owner Oakbrook Vil 1972-; Terriberry, Rault, Carroll, Martinez & Yancey Law Firm 1951-59; Am Petro Inst; 1963 Del Frankfort World Petro Cong; Am & La St Bar Assns; Indep Petro Assn Am; NO Assn Bldg Owners & Mgrs Inc; Real Est Inst; Apt Owners Assn; cp/Bd Dirs: Cancer Assn; C of C NO Area, Sugar Bowl; Gen Chm 25th Anniv Campaign US Savs Bond; Chm NO RR Terminal Bd; Citys Rep NO Union Passenger Terminal; Coor Rapid Transit Sys; Miss River: Rd Comm, Pkway Comm; Sts-Items Chds Football Fund; Fin & Govs Com for Domed Stadium; CoChm Lions Crippled Chds Camp; Cult Attractions Fund Exec Com; Gen Chm Leukemia Soc Am.

RAVAL, PINAKIN M oc/Physician; b/Oct 1, 1943; h/79 Gwen Lake Blvd, Lake City, FL 32055; ba/LC; m/Mayuri; c/Sunali, Suhani, Sheel; p/Manubhai and Sharda Raval; ed/MD; pa/Med Pract; Med Ed; Asst Clin Prof Univ Mo; Fellow Am Col Angiology; cp/Commun Hlth Ser; r/Hindu.

RAVOIRA, JAMES oc/Artist; b/Sept 4, 1933; h/138 Bull St, Charleston, SC 29401; ba/Same; m/LaWanda; c/James, Karen R Strange; p/James Ravoira (dec); Josephine Ravoira, Weirton, WV; ed/BA W Liberty St Col 1962; MA 1966, MFA 1977 Kent St Univ; pa/Asst Prof Art: Univ SC/Coastal Carolina Col 1974-77, Citadel 1971-74; Art Instr Thronton Commun Col 1969-70; Art Dept Head & Asst Prof Indian River Commun Col 1967-69; Art Instr Warren City Schs 1962-67; Num Exhbns incl'g: Lynn Kottler Galleries, Palm Bch Art Galleries, Trumbull Art Guild, Park Forest Ill Art Fest, SC Art Comm Invitational; Mem: Trumbull Art Guild, Wash Art Gallery; hon/Eleanor D Caldwell Awd; Carnegie Lib Awd; Huntington Galleries Annual Awd; Num Artist Pubs; Biogl Listings.

READ, NELDA JOYCE oc/Educator; b/Jan 14, 1940; h/Rt 2, Comanche, OK 73529; ba/Duncan, OK; m/Joseph Stephen; c/Joy, Joseph Jr, Janeene; p/Jess and Carrie

McFatridge, Duncan; ed/BS; pa/Tchr Grades 5-7; Nat Coun Tchrs English; Okla & Nat Ed Assns; r/Bapt; Pianist & Organist; Yth Ch Ldr; hon/St Winner DAC Essay Contest.

RECCORD, ROBERT EUGENE oc/-Director; b/Sept 26, 1951; h/569 E McNab Rd, Box 23820, Ft Lauderdale, FL 33307; ba/-Atlanta, GA; m/Cheryl Ann; c/Christina; p/Estel and Ruth Reccord, Evansville, IN; ed/BA Ind Univ; MDiv, DMin SWn Bapt Theol Sem; pa/Dir Witness Tng Home Mission Bd So Bapt Conv; Preacher Crusade-Seoul, Korea; Author & Editor; r/So Bapt; hon/W/W Rel; Outstg Yg Men Am.

RECTOR, ROBERT LEE oc/Accountant; Consultant; b/Jun 16, 1943; ba/23 So Walton Ave, Tarpon Springs, FL 33589; c/Courtney, Drew, Egan; p/Hilden and Lois Hickok Rector, Palm Harbor, FL; ed/BS Kent St Univ; MS St Univ NY; pa/Public Spkr; Spec Fac Num Univs; Am Inst Prof Conslts; Nat Soc Public Accts; Inst Mgmt Scists; Acad Mgmt; r/Prot; hon/Beta Gamma Sigma; W/W S&SW; Student Asst'ship.

REDD, VIVIAN CORTEZZA b/Sep 18, 1934; h/2301 S Jefferson Davis Hwy #1316, Arlington, VA 22202; ba/Washington, DC; p/Minerva M D Redd (dec); pa/Federally Employed Wom's Legis Com 1971-72; Patent & Trademark Ofc Legal Asst Rep (Local 2600) 1973-75, EEO Com 1970-72, EEO Cnslr 1971-76, VP Com for Wom 1978-, Com for Black Concerns 1979; Com for Improving the Quality of the Work Experience Inc 1979-; Intl Pers Mgmt Assn 1973-76; Federally Employed Wom 1969-72; cp/United Negro Col Fund; NAACP; Legal Defense & Ed Fund; Am Civil Liberties Union; CoOrgr & Fdr, US Dept of Commerce Com for Wom; Nat Adv Bd, Am Security Coun; Past Mem: World Law Fund, World Assn World Federalists, United Nations Assn of USA, Am Acad Polit & Social Sci, Radio of Free Asia, Common Cause, Others; hon/US Patent & Trademark Ofc: Superior Perf Awd, Spec Achmt Awd, Lttrs Commend; Cert Apprec, Radio Free Asia; Cert Apprec, US Dept Commerce; Fdr's Cert & Spec Recog, Am Security Coun; Biogl Listings; Others.

REDDIN, OPAL LAURENE oc/Professor; Ordained Minister; b/Apr 23, 1921; h/1025 Van Couver, Springfield, MO 65803; ba/S'field; m/Thomas Wesley; c/Naomi Brewer (Mrs Tom), Joy Neubauer (Mrs Richard), Michael; p/Walter Smith (dec); Addie Smith, Russellville, AR; ed/BA Little Rock Univ; MA SW Mo St Univ; MA Assemblies God Grad Sch; pa/Asst Prof Bible & Eng Ctl Bible Col; Spkr Num St Ch Convs; Ed Com Ark Assemblies of God; cp/Spkr Woms Clbs; Heart Fund; Gov Adv Bd St Cols & Univs; r/Assemblies of God; hon/S'ship Ark Polytechnic Col; World W/W Wom Ed; W/W Rel; DIB.

REDMAN, J JAMES oc/Supervisor; Professor; b/May 19, 1919; h/1403 W 3rd Ave, Apt A, Columbus, OH 43212; ba/C'bus; p/James and Marcia Toops Redman (dec); pa/Bliss Col: Tchr, Coach, Ath Dir, Dir Ofc Public Info; Dep Auditor Franklin Co Auditors Ofc; Lyricist; Real Est Appraiser; Former Editor; AAUP; Ohio Bus Tchrs Assn; Past Pres Verse Writers Guild Ohio; Ohio Poetry Soc; Ohio Poetry Day Assn; Ohio Commun Theatre Assn; cp/Coach Nat Bus Col Championship Basketball Teams 1970-71 & 1971-72; Franklin Co Employees Rec Assn; Tabulator Franklin Co Bd Elections; Repub Ctl Com; Repub Exec Com; Buckeye Repub Clb; Repub Mens Org; Capital City Yg Repub Clb; Jr Fair Bd; Execs Clb; Leukemia Soc Am; Bucyrus Little Theatre; C'bus Players Clb; C'bus Jets Boosters Clb; Dapper Dan Clb; Ky Col; Agonis Clb; Jacques Clb; Moose; K of P; Big Brothers Assn; Coun Exploring Div BSA; 4-H Ldr; F'ship Christian Aths; r/Meth; Former SS Secy & Tchr; Vacation Ch Sch Tchr; Chm Ch Auditing Com; hon/Buckeye Intercollegiate Conf Hall of Fame; Bus Col Coach of World 3 Yrs; Agonis Clb Awd; Sideliners Awd Excell; Ser Awd, Ohio Poetry Soc; Nom Best Tchr Am; Nom Capital Univ Alumni Achmt Awd; St 4-H Alumni Awd; Pub'd Author; Num Biogl Listings.

REDMOND, JOHN DURHAM oc/Director; b/Jun 5, 1948; h/4008 Tifton Dr, Columbus, GA 31907; ba/C'bus; m/Patricia Ann Tate; ba/John, Brandi; p/Melvin Jr and Beebe Redmond, C'bus; ed/AS 1968, BS 1970, MBA 1977 C'bus Col; MBA Ga St Univ 1975; mil/AUS 1970-72; pa/Dir Actuarial-Underwriting; Inst Internal Auditors; MENSA; Sigma Pi; r/St Andrews U Meth Ch, C'bus: Mem, Bd, Chm Fin Com; hon/Num Biogl Listings.

REED, DALE CHARLES oc/Management; b/Aug 22, 1948; h/4015 Pineridge Dr,

Lilburn, GA 30247; ba/Lithonia, GA; m/Gayle Irene Ponto; c/Dustin, Lindsey; p/Dale and Barbara Thurman Reed, Arlington, VA; ed/BA Trinity Col; pa/Mfg Mgmt Rogers Corp; AMA; Bus & Indust Assn; Am MENSA; cp/Alpha Chi Rho; Dir Friends Trinity Rowing; r/Epis.

REED, DENNIS LEE oc/Director; b/Feb 17, 1946; h/744 Marlee Dr, Rocky Mount, NC 27801; ba/RM; m/Armelia Doris; c/Alicia, Trillia; p/Harry Sr and Alice Reed, Morristown, TN; ed/AA M'town Col; BA Carson Newman Col; pa/Exec Dir Boys Clb RM; Boys Clb Am Profl Assn; cp/RM C of C; Twin Co JCs; r/Prot; hon/S'ship M'town Col; Outstg Yg Men Am; W/W: NC, Am, S&SW; Men Achmt; DIB.

REED, KATHLYN LOUISE oc/Occupational Therapy Educator; b/Jun 2, 1940; h/800 Rolling Green, Oklahoma City, OK 73132; ba/OC; p/Herbert Reed, OC; ed/BS Univ Ks 1964; MA Wn Mich Univ 1966; PhD Univ Wash 1973; pa/Temp Supvr Occupl Therapy Vis Nurse Assn 1964; Staff Occupl Therapist Ks Univ Med Ctr 1964-65; Instr Univ Wash 1967-70; Res Assoc Child Devel Ctr 1972-73; Chm Dept Occupl Therapy Univ Okla 1973-; Conslt Dept HEW Public Hlth Grant Ohio St Univ 1970-71; Am & Okla Occupl Therapy Assns; CEC; Am Public Hlth Assn; Am Assn Mtl Deficiency; cp/Telephone Wkr & Cnslr Open Door Clin 1968-72; Exec Bd & CoChm Citizens Bd Seattle Mtl Hlth Ctr 1970-72; hon/Elmer H Wilds Awd, Wn Mich Univ; NIH Grant Am Occupl Therapy Assn 1972-73.

REED, ROBERT DE HART oc/Chemical Engineer; b/May 2, 1905; h/4192 S Troost Pl, Tulsa, OK 74105; ba/Tulsa; m/Iva Dodd; c/Alyce R Bryant, Michael; p/Robert and Gertrude De Hart Reed (dec); ed/ScD; pa/VP Engrg John Zink Co; Adjunct Prof Univ Tulsa; AICE; cp/Engrs Clb Tulsa; r/Presb; hon/Inventor of Yr, Okla Bar Assn; Hall of Fame, Univ Tulsa; Tau Beta Pi; Engr of Mo, Engrs Clb Tulsa; Inventor 360 USA & Fgn Patents; Num Biogl Listings.

REEDER, CLARENCE CHARLES oc/Minister; b/Feb 12, 1909; h/122 S Col St, Myerstown, PA 17067; m/Marian Irene Kramer; p/David and Hattie Willet Reeder; ed/Nat Bible Inst 1934; Addit Studies; pa/Ordained Min Evang Congl Ch 1939; Pastored Congs En Pa: Trinity, Mount Joy 1936, St Pauls, Reamstown 1941, Kemble Park, Philadelphia 1946, Trinity, Royerford 1952, Bethany, Allentown 1954, St Pauls, York 1961; Pubr Evang Congl Ch Pub'g House M'town & Bethany; Gen Mgr of Evang Congl Ch Ctr M'town 1975; Chaplain Retirement Vil Evang Congl Ch M'town 1977; r/Secy Ch Ext Soc 1942; Ch Ext: Secy Bd 1954, Treas Bd 1973; Stat: En Conf 1953-57, Gen Conf 1958; Secy NE India Gen Mission 1962-77; Secy-Treas Coun Ch Expansion 1974; Treas Gen Conf Evang Congl Ch 1977-78; hon/W/W Rel; DIB; Men Achmt; Notable Ams; Commun Ldrs & Noteworthy Ams; Intl W/W Intells; Book Hon; Personalities Am.

REEDER, JAMES ARTHUR oc/Attorney; Broadcast Executive; b/Jun 29, 1933; h/419 Janie Ln, Shreveport, LA 71106; ba/S'port; m/Mary Leone Guthrie; c/Mary, James Jr, Elizabeth; p/James Reeder (dec); Grace Britt, S'port; ed/BA cum laude Washington & Lee 1955; LLB Univ Tex Law Sch 1960; JDS La St Univ Law Sch 1961; mil/AUS Ofcr 1955-57; pa/Am, La & Tex Bar Assns; Dir ABC Contemp Radio Network Affils Adv Bd; cp/Pres Holiday in Dixie 1972; Pres Goodwill Industs 1972; Spec Projs Staff Conslt US Senator J Bennett Johnston La; r/Cath; hon/Outstg Yg Man S'port 1968; La Outstg Yg Man 1968; Outstg Yg Lwyr La 1969; Boy Scout "Scouter of Yr" Awd 1965.

REEL, RITA M oc/Educator; b/Aug 4, 1917; h/9728 Davies Rd, Lake Stevens, WA 98258; p/Winnfield Reel (dec); Wanda Reel, LS; ed/BS Ind Univ; MS Univ Colo; pa/Ret'd Instr Everett HS & Everett Commun Col; Author Ednl Wkbooks: *File & Find, Secretarial*

Careers; Nat, Wash St & Pres Wn Wash Bus Ed Assns; Am & Secy/Treas Wash Voc Assns; r/Rom Cath; hon/Ford Foun Awd.

REES, PAUL KLEIN oc/Author; Educator; b/Jun 10, 1902; h/345 Centenary Dr, Baton Rouge, LA 70808; ba/Same; m/Mary Boone; c/Paul, Charles; p/John and Josephine Klein Rees (dec); ed/AB SWn Univ; MA Tex Univ; pa/Prof Emeritus Math LSU; Author: *Plane Trigonometry, Col Algebra, Analytic Geometry, Intermediate Algebra, Math Fin, Trigonometry, College Algebra Trigonometry & Analytic Geometry, Calculus/Analytic Geometry*; Num Res Articles "Transforms Fuchsian Groups"; Am Math Soc; MAA: Chm SWn Sect, Chm La-Miss Sect, Sect Gov; cp/VChm BR Garden Clb; r/U Meth: VChm Adm Bd 1976; hon/Omicron Delta Kappa; Awd Merit, Alumnae Assn SWn.

REEVA, MONA R oc/Social Worker; Consultant; b/Sept 29, 1935; h/541 Vistamont, Berkeley, CA 94708; c/Daniel, Nicole, Joshua Albertson; p/Leon and Edith Greenberg, Van Nuys, CA; ed/BA Brooklyn Col 1957; MSW San Diego St Univ 1971; MPH Univ Cal-B 1976; pa/Pvt Psychotherapy Pract; Hlth & Mtl Hlth Conslt; Lic'd Clin Social Wkr; Guest Lectr Num Orgs; Group Facilitator: UC Berkeley Haste St House 1975-76, UCLA 1971; NASW; APHA; cp/Bd Dirs Bay Area Consumers Hlth Inc; Prog Com Merritt Col; Pers Com Consumers Coop Berkeley; hon/Pub'd Author.

REFIOR, EVERETT LEE oc/Labor Economist; b/Jan 23, 1919; h/205 N Fremont St, Whitewater, WI 53190; ba/W'water; m/Marie Culp; c/Gene, Wendell, Paul, Donna; p/Fred and Daisy Gardner Refior (dec); ed/BA summa cum laude La Wesleyan Col 1942; MA Univ Chicago 1955; PhD Univ Ia 1962; mil/AUS Med Technician US & England 1943-46; pa/Univ Wis: Prof Ec 1964-, Ec Dept Chm 1966-75, Assoc Prof 1962-64, Asst Prof 1955-62; Assoc Prof Ec Simpson Col 1952-54; Instr Ia Wesleyan Col 1947-50; Am & MW Ec Assns; Adv Bd Wis Chapt Indust Relats Res Assn; SANE; Fdn Am Scists; Am Civil Liberties Union; Wis Fdn Tchrs; cp/World Federalists USA: Fdr W'water Chapt, Pres 1960-68 & 1976-78, Nat Exec Coun, Pres MW Reg 1969-71 & 1975-, Del World Cong World Federalists Ottawa, Brussels & Paris; Del World Constituent Assembly; UN Assn: Govs Comm, VP Walworth Co; Dem Precnt Com-man 1966-; Chm Walworth Co Dem Party; VChm 1st Congl Dist Dem Party; St Dem Platform Com; r/U Meth: Lay Spkr; Wis Conf Bd Ch & Soc; Janesville Dist Dir Christian Social Concerns; Bd Dirs Wis Prot Leg Coun; hon/Donnellson HS Valedictorian; Order Artus, Univ Ia; W/W: MW, Am.

REGAN, CARROLL ROBERT oc/Publisher; b/Jul 3, 1926; h/4 Caledonia, Tallulah, LA 71282; ba/Tallulah; m/Carol Adams; c/William, Robert; p/Alva and Georgie Johnson Regan (dec); ed/BA LSU; mil/USN; pa/Pubr *The Madison Jour*; Past Pres La Press Assn; cp/Govs Priorities for Future Com; Past Pres Madison Parish C of C; Chm Madison Parish Hosp Bd Trustees; r/Bapt; hon/La Ec Devel Awd.

REGENSBURGER, EDITH R oc/Psychologist; b/Aug 10, 1922; h/753 James St, Syracuse, NY 13203; ba/Same; m/William; p/Morris Greenwald (dec); Florence Greenwald, Syracuse; ed/BA magna cum laude 1943, PhD 1968 Syracuse Univ; pa/Pvt Pract Clin & Conslt Psychol 1950-; Admr & Supvr Spec Ed Progs Bd Coop Ednl Sers Onondaga & Madison Cos 1959-; Syracuse Univ: Vis Lectr 1968-71, Instr Dept Spec Ed 1957, Clin Psychologist 1947-50; Dir Frank C McCarthy Sch Retarded Chd 1954-59; Clin Psychologist Cerebral Palsy Clin 1948-59; Social Wkr Home Ser Dept ARC Chapts 1943-46; Am, NY St & Ctl NY Psychol Assns; Am Assn Mtl Deficiency; Coun Exceptl Chd; cp/Commr Ed Syracuse Public Schs; Councilor-at-Large Syracuse Common Coun; Bd Dirs: Consolidated Industs Gtr Syracuse, Ctl NY Assn Hearing Impaired; Ldrship Tng

Com Vol Ctr; Metro Aquatics Adv Bd; Profl Adv Bd Assn Retarded Chd; Other Civic Assns; hon/Phi Beta Kappa; Psi Chi; Wom Achmt Ed, Syracuse Fdn Woms Clbs & Syracuse Post-Standard; W/W: Am Wom, E; DIB; Valedictorian Ctl HS; Pub'd Author.

REGENSTEINER, ELSE oc/Professor; Author; Lecturer; b/Apr 21, 1906; h/1416 E 55th St, Chicago, IL 60615; ba/Same; m/Bertold; c/Mrs Helga Sinaiko; p/Ludwig Friedsam (dec); Hilda Bachhofer, Carmel, CA; ed/Tchrs Deg Deutsche Frauenschule; Att'd Num Univs; pa/Prof Emeritus Art Inst Chgo 1945-71; Author: *The Art Weaving, Weaver's Study Course-Ideas & Techniques*; Textile Designer; Dir Handweavers Guild Am; Conslt Am Farm Sch; Fellow Am Crafts Coun; r/Jewish; hon/Num Textile Design Awds.

REICH, MINNA LERICH oc/Sculptor; b/Jun 18, 1919; h/116 Hollands Gove Ln, Washington, IL 61571; ba/Same; m/Gerald; c/Steven, Linda; p/Oscar and Sarah Rothman Lerich (dec); ed/BFA Manhattanville Col 1972; MA Bradley Univ 1975; pa/Art Instr:

Bradley Univ 1973, Ill Ctl Col 1973-77; Num Profl Exhbns; r/Jewish; Mem Anshai Emeth Reformed Temple; hon/Galesburg, Ill Civic Art Ctr Awd 1974; Ill Arts Coun Purchase Awd, Govs St Univ.

REICHEL, AARON ISRAEL oc/Editor; Rabbi; b/Jan 30, 1950; h/230 W 79th St, New York, NY 10024; ba/Englewood Cliffs, NJ; p/Asher and Josephine Reichel, NY; ed/BA 1971, MA 1974 Yeshiva Univ; JD Fordham Univ 1976; Ordination Rabbinical Sem 1975; pa/Legal Editor Prentice-Hall; Currently Completing 2-Volume Biog Herbert S Goldstein; Adv Com Court Adm Appellate Div Supreme Ct NY St 1st & 2nd Depts Legal Staff 1975-76; Environ Protection Bur Ofc Atty Gen St NY Legal Staff 1975; Law Clk Ofc Abraham J Hirschsprung Esq 1975; Editor-in-Chief *Yeshiva Col Alumni Bultn* 1974-; The *Authentic Voice*: Editor-in-Chief 1973, Columnist 1973-75; cp/Comm Law & Public Affairs; Exec Com Yeshiva Col Alumni; Resolutions Com Union Orthodox Jewish Congregs Am; Yth Com Am Jewish Cong; Nat Pres Yavneh Nat Rel Jewish Students Assn; Fdr & 1st Chm Student Com Orthodox Org Pres; r/Jewish; Ex Officio Am Zionist Yth Coun; Recipient Num S'ships.

REICHLE, FREDERICK A oc/Professor; Surgeon; b/Apr 20, 1935; h/771 Easton Rd, Warrington, PA 18976; ba/Philadelphia, PA; p/Albert and Ernestine Reichle, W'ton; ed/BA summa cum laude 1957, MD 1961, MS 1961, MS 1966 Temple Univ; Internship Abington

Meml Hosp 1962; Residency Temple Univ Hosp 1966; pa/Prof Surg & Chief Peripheral Vascular Surg Temple Univ Sch Med; Temple Univ Hlth Scis Ctr: Lab Animal Resources Com 1974-, Res Com 1976-79, Sub-com Nat Bds Part II 1978; Surg Temple Univ Hosp 1966-; Assoc Att'g Surg: Epis Hosp, St Marys Hosp, St Christophers Hosp Chd; Conslt: Vets Hosp, Germantown Dispensary & Hosp; Participant Num Profl Meetings; Fellow Col Physicians Phila; Am Surg Assn; Soc Univ Surgs; AMA; Pa Med Soc; Assn Acad Surg; NY Acad Scis; AAAS; Am Fed Clin Res; Nat Assn Professions; Am Gastroenterological Assn; Am Col Surgs; Phila Acad Surg; Phi Tho Sigma; Natl Soc Thrombosis & Haemostasis; Nat Kidney Foun; Soc Surg Alimentary Tract; Am Diabetes Assn; Gerontological Assn; cp/Heart Assn SEn Pa; Surg Biol Clb; Am Aging Assn; r/Prot; hon/Temple Univ: Nathan Ln Awd, Col Lib Arts Grad Awd, Student Res Awd; Phila Acad Surg: Gross Essay Prize, Surg Residents Res Paper Awd; Recipient Est'd Investigatorship Grant AHA; AMA F'ship; Omega Alpha; Sigma Xi; Pub'd Author.

REIDENBACH, ALBERT JAMES oc/Engineer; b/Feb 8, 1941; h/23041 La Granja Dr, Valencia, CA 91355; ba/Same; m/Raquel Simone; c/Alex, Alana; p/Robert and Dorthey Jewel Reidenbach, Jackson, MI; ed/Att'd: Univ Md, El Camino Col, Col Canyons & Alexander Hamilton Inst; mil/USAF 1959-63; pa/VP M&J & Assocs, Conslt Engrs 1976-; Num Sems; Soc Mfg Engrs; VChm Computer & Automated Sys Assn; Robot Inst Am; cp/Ednl Adv Com Santa Monica Col; Repub; r/Christian; hon/1st Devel & Publish Good Mfg Practs Manuals; 1 of First Devel Workmanship Standards; SME Pres Clb; W/W: Am, W; Intl Biogl Centre; Pub'd Author.

REIFLER, HENRIETTA oc/Librarian; b/Jul 29, 1917; h/NE 435 Oak #2, Pullman, WA 99163; m/Erwin (dec); c/5; p/Mendel Brown and Annie Horowitz; ed/BA London Univ; BA, MA, MLS Univ Wash-S; pa/Libn Wash St Univ Lib; Contbr *Index Reviews Bibliogl Pubs*; *Wash Lib Assn*; cp/WLA Woms Caucus; *Wash Wom U*; r/Jewish; hon/Phi Beta Kappa; *Commun Ldrs & Noteworthy Ams*.

REINHARDT, SIEGFRIED GERHARD oc/Artist; Poet; b/July 31, 1925; h/635 Craigwoods Dr, Kirkwood, MO 63122; ed/AB Washington Univ 1950; mil/AUS 1944-46: Art Editor Public Relats Ofc, Correspondent Shanghai Edition *The Stars & Stripes*; pa/Artist-in-Residence So Ill Univ 1950-54 & 1968-69; Fac Sch Fine Arts Wash Univ 1955-70; Designer & Executer Stained Glass Windows Emil Frei Inc 1948-; Currently Designer Furn & Textiles and Executer Murals; Num Pvt & Public Exhbns; Works: "Man of Sorrows", Rand-McNally Mural, 2 Mosaic Murals Concordia Sr Col, Mosaic Triptych Jefferson Nat Expansion Meml Mus, 11 Lithographs Encyclopdaedia Britannicas Propaedia; Fdr Acad Profl Artists; Contbr Num Profl & Lay Mags; Composer Mag *Arch*; hon/Life Mag Recog; Awd 1st Intl Exhbn Sacred Art; Wash Univ Alumni Cit; AFD London Inst Applied Res; DHL Occidental Univ St Louis; Doct Fine Arts & Humanities Concordia Sem; W/W Am; Book Hon.

REINL, HARRY CHARLES oc/Economist; b/Nov 13, 1932; h/1111 Arlington Blvd M-521, Arlington, VA 22209; ba/Same; p/Carl and Angela Plass Reinl (dec); ed/BS Fordham Univ 1953; MA George Washington Univ 1968; mil/AUS 1st Lt ORDC Korea 1953-55; pa/Labor Economist Fed Civil Sers; Spec Lttrs US Senate; cp/Repub Nat Com; George Washington Univ: Alumni Assn, Univ Devel; Assoc Nat Archives; Am Security Coun; Hon Mem Bd of Trustees & Sponsor, Am Police Hall of Fame; Hon Trustee, Am Police Acad (Both 1979); Mem, Am Film Inst; Smithsonian Instn; r/Rom Cath; hon/Life Mem Repub Nat Com & Repub Party US; Cert Commend, Exec Bd Nat Repub Congl Com; 1979 Spec Recog Awd, Ctr Intl Security Studies; Nat Def Ser Med 1955; 1976 Ofcl

Commemorative Medal, Repub Nat Com; Commun Ldrs Am; Personalities S; Notable Ams; 2000 Men Achmt; IBA Yrbook; Commun Ldrs Va; W/W: S&SW, E; Intl W/W Commun Ser; Nat Social Dir.

REISDORF, SHIRLEY CARMAN oc/Instructor; b/Apr 11, 1933; h/392 Collins Dr, Pittsburgh, PA 15235; m/Bartholomew George; c/Bart, Sharon, James; p/Benjamin Carman, Minneapolis, MN; Helen Hester Stone Carman, Pgh; pa/Swimming Instr Normal & Handicapped; r/Presb; hon/W/W: Am Wom, E, Worlds Wom, Intl Commun Ser; Notable Ams.

REMICK, ROBERT MERRICK oc/Financial Services Executive; b/May 8, 1924; h/116 Ctl Park S, New York City, NY 10019; ba/NYC; c/Lee, Scot, Lynn; p/Robert and Mary Moore Remick (dec); ed/BS NYU 1952; CLU Am Col Life Underwriters 1952; mil/USNR 1942-45; pa/Pres Income Planning Assocs Ltd; Bd Chm Computer Income Planning Corp; Million Dollar Round Table; Am Soc Pension Actuaries; Am Acad Actuaries; NY Soc Security Analysts; Nat Assn Security Dealers; Am Pension Conf; Nat Assn Life Underwriters.

RENDE, GIANDOMENICO oc/Advisor; b/Feb 6, 1936; h/45 Via Barranca, Greenbrae, CA 94904; ba/San Francisco, CA; m/Kathleen; c/Roberto, John, Giuliana; p/Salvatore and Lucrefia Rende, Rome, Italy; ed/PhD; Cert Bus Adm; pa/Commodity Trading Advr; Dir Commodity Clb SF; r/Cath.

RENICK, PATRICIA ANN oc/Professor; b/Jan 26, 1932; h/343 Probasco St, Cincinnati, OH 45220; ba/Cinc; p/Helen Renick, Tampa, FL; ed/BS Fla St Univ 1954; MA 1968, MFA 1969 Ohio St Univ; pa/Assoc Prof Fine Art Dept Univ Cinc; Solo Exhbns Cinc Art Mus & Contemp Arts Ctr; Exhibited 27 Invited & Juried Shows S&MW; Org'd & Directed Traveling Exhbn 14 Cinc Artists; Secured 7 Grants & Pvt Contbns Benefiting 20 Artists; Published Articles: *Am Jour Optometry, Archives Am Acad Optometry & Studies Att Ed*; hon/Corbett Awd; Bowan/Rankan Art Apprec Awd; Awd Exhbn, Cinc Art Mus; W/W Am Art; Personalities W&MW.

RENTFRO, ETHEL CHILTON oc/Book Reviewer; b/Feb 13, 1933; h/1312 Canterbury Ct, Dallas, TX 75208; ba/Same; m/John; c/John, James, Joe; p/Albert Chilton (dec); Mrs Albert Chilton, Marlin, TX; ed/BS SWn Univ 1953; pa/1st Grade Tchr Irving 1953-55; 2nd Grade Tchr Tyler Public Schs 1955-56; cp/Alpha Delta Pi; Planned Parenthood; Waco-Wichita Falls; Symph Bd; YMCA Bd; r/Meth; hon/Delta Kappa Gamma; Mary Mann Richardson Awd; Personalities S.

REPLOGLE, ELEANOR oc/Rug & Tapestry Restoration; b/Jan 14, 1909; h/6821 Brookside Rd, Kansas City, MO 64113; m/Fahy (dec); c/Ronald, Richard, Charles; p/John Taminosian (dec); Ellen Cook (dec); pa/Oriental Rug Conslt & Appraiser; cp/Woms C of C; Friends Art; PEO Sisterhood; Kings Daughs & Sons; r/Prot; Ldr Cir 1 Country Clb Christian Ch 3 Yrs; hon/"Happiest Married Couple" Cit, Minneapolis Aquatennial; Chosen Restore Tapestries Helen Spencer Mus Art.

RESCH, GERALD WILLIAM oc/Electronic Engineer; Manufacturing Consultant; b/Jul 10, 1938; h/1317 Castle Ave, Anaheim, CA 92802; ba/Urbine, CA; m/Mamie Boling Go; p/Gerald and Esther Van Tuyl Resch; ed/AA Graceland Col 1959; BSEE Ia St Univ 1963; Addit Studies; mil/AUS Lt Col; USMC; pa/Dir of Operation & Dir of Pers, Convergence corp (Urbine & El Paso, Tex) 1979-; Electronic Mgr, ITT Jabsco Prodns 1977-79; Electronic Mfg Conslt 1976-77; Dir Opers Ednl Data Sys 1975-76; Head Electronic Substaining Engrg Compucorp 1973-75; Asst Chief Engr Bergmaster Houdaille Inc 1973; Electronic Designer DNC Controls Actron Industs Inc 1971-73; Instr USMC Missile

Electronics Sch 1968-69; Head New Eng Air Def Missile Mentor Sys 1967-68; Conslt US Missile Bases USA & Republic Korea 1963-70; Num Other Positions; IEEE; cp/APICS; Pres, Coun of Ski Clbs, So Cal; Extended Bd Mem, Far West Ski Assn, Div USSA; Coached Girls Volleyball Team 1st Pl USVBA Reg 8 1971 & 4th Pl USVB Nats 1973; Liahona & Phileion F'ships; Repub; r/Mem Reorg'd Ch of Jesus Christ Latter Day Sts; hon/Num Slalom Ski & Volleyball Trophies; Assisted Design & Manufacture Vegreville Pysanka Monument, Supvr of Company's Emmy Awd for Tech Advmt in TV Indust; Pub'd Author; W/W W; DIB; Men Achmt.

RESTIANO, RICHARD ANGELO oc/Entrepreneur; b/May 9, 1948; h/10 Merriam Pl, Bronxville, NY 10708; ba/Mt Vernon, NY; m/Vincenza; c/Alessandra, Richard Jr, Claudia; p/Angelo and Michelina Restiano, MV; ed/BS; pa/Bd Dirs Westchester Profl Photogs Assn; cp/Lions Clb; C of C; Jr Achmt Advr; r/Rom Cath; hon/W/W E; Commun Ldrs Noteworthy Ams.

REUL, GEORGE JOHN JR oc/Cardiovascular Surgeon; b/Apr 19, 1937; h/11603 Applewood Ln, Houston, TX 77024; ba/Houston; m/Kay Ross; c/George III, Ross, David, Darren; p/George Sr and Anne Reul, Milwaukee, WI; ed/BS; MD; MS; mil/AUS Capt 1966-68; pa/Fellow: Am Col Cardiology, Intl Col Angiology, Am Col Chest Physicians; Am, Tex & Harris Co Med Assns; SWn Surgical Cong; Intl Cardiovascular Soc; Soc Vascular Surgs; Soc Thoracic Surg; Am Assn Thoracic Surg; Wn Surg Assn; So Thoracic Surg Soc; Houston Surg Soc; Houston Cardiology Soc; Am Heart Assn; Alpha Omega Alpha; cp/C of C; r/Cath.

REX, LONNIE ROYCE oc/Religious Organization Executive; b/May 11, 1928; h/2300 Riverside Dr, Tulsa, OK 74114; ba/Tulsa; m/Betty Louise Sorrells; c/Royce, Patricia, Debra; p/Robert and Lennie Gilcrease Rex; ed/BMus Okla City Univ 1950; DD Am Bible Inst 1970; pa/Gen Mgr Christian Crusade 1969-; Bus Mgr T L Osborn Found 1957-69; Advt Mgr Oral Roberts Evangelistic Assn 1955-57; Phi Mu Alpha; Contbr Articles Rel Jours; cp/Lepers of World Inc; Medix Intl Inc; Dir Commun Bank & Trust Co; r/Gen Bd Adm Pentecostal Holiness Ch 1973; Secy-Treas Am Christian Col 1970-74; David Livingstone Missionary Found; Secy-Treas 1970, VChm Philippines 1976, Secy-Treas Asia 1975, Dir India 1977; Secy-Treas Ch of Christian Crusade 1969; hon/Meritorious Ser Awd, Korean Christian Crusade; W/W Rel.

REYMAN, MARIA LANDOLFI oc/Educator; Lecturer; b/Nov 4, 1917; h/4 Hughes Ln, New Hartford, NY 13413; p/Thomas and Frances Landolfi; ed/BA Keuka Col 1940; MA Syracuse Univ 1950; Addit Studies; pa/Dept Head and Instr French & Eng Westmoreland Ctl Sch 1943-44; Lyons Falls HS 1944-45: Head French Dept, Instr French & Eng Lit; Instr Eng Proctor HS 1946-47; Instr Utica Free Acad: Eng 1947-, Italian 1949-53; Pioneer Team Tchg Adult Evening Classes Hamilton Col 1965-66; CoDir Sch Gifted Students Summers 1956-58; AAHP; NEA; Utica Tchrs Assn; UN Assn USA; AAUW; cp/Del White House Conf Ed 1955; Com Promote Inter-Commun Interests Hist Socs; Bd Dirs U Way; Bd Advrs Am Security Coun; OES; hon/Keuka Col: Gold Pin Awd, 1st Prize Art Exhibit, Profl Achmt Awd; Bronze Medal, Columbia Univ; Commun Ldrs & Noteworthy Ams; World W/W Wom.

REYNOLDS, JUDY LaCOE oc/Realtor; Property Manager; b/Dec 3, 1938; h/10740 Hewitt Rd, Brooklyn, MI 49230; ba/Jackson, MI; m/William; c/Danny, Michael, Cindy, Troy, Michele; p/Max Donovan (dec); Iva Farary Donovan, Inverness, FL; ed/GRI Mich St Univ Real Est Inst 1973; RAM Univ Mich; CPM; pa/Realtor Property Mgr McDevitt

Realty Inc 1966-; Guest Spkr Jackson Sch Vols; Realtor Spkrs Bur; Mich Assn Realtors: Public Relats Com, Bicent Com, Make Am Better Com, VChm Public Relats; Nat Inst Real Est Bds; R-Pac; Jackson Bd Realtors; Woms Coun Realtors: Pres Jackson Co Chapt 1971, 72 & 78, St VP 1978, CoChm Budget & Fin, Nom Com, Dist VP, Corresponding Secy; cp/Bus & Profl Woms Clb; Bd Dirs Jackson March of Dimes; Vol Mothers Marcher Muscular Dystrophy; Secy & Dir BPW; Jackson Co Vol "Meals on Wheels"; Mercy Hosp Aux; Real Est Alumni Mich; Aglow F'ship Intl; r/U Brethren Ch; hon/W/W Am Wom; Jackson Chapt Woms Coun Realtors: 1972 Realtor Assoc of Yr, Wom of Yr 1972 & 1977.

RHIGER, SULA MARIE oc/Stenographer; b/Jun 27, 1893; h/1004 Main St, Canon City, CO 81212; p/Thomas and Mildred Haynes Patterson (dec); ed/Grad Draughons Bus Col; mil/USN 2 Yrs; pa/Ret'd Stenographic Work USNRF; cp/VP SE Dist Col Fdn Woms Clb; Histn: Am Legion Aux, Twenty & Four; 8/40 Pikes Peak Salon; Repub Party; r/Disciples of Christ; Mem 1st Christian Ch, CC; hon/Colo Fdn Woms Clbs: Picture, Num Hons.

RHODIG, RUSSEL DELMER oc/School Principal; b/Mar 25, 1934; h/685 E York Way, Sparks, NV 89431; ba/Reno, NV; m/Phyllis Ruth; p/Mary Rhodig, LaGrande, OR; ed/BS; MS; mil/Army Resv 1st Lt; pa/NEA; NSEA; Nat Elem Prin Assn; Washoe Co Adm Assn; cp/Elks Lodge; Bd Dirs Nev Wildlife Fdn; Pres Sparks Traffic Survival Sch; PTA; r/Prot; hon/W/W W; Personalities W&MW; Notable Ams.

RICE, FREDERICK ANDERS HUDSON oc/Professor; b/Feb 19, 1917; h/8005 Carita Ct, Bethesda, MD 20034; ba/Washington, DC; m/Margaret MacKenzie Carson; p/Frederick Rice (dec); Karen Brebde (dec); ed/BA 1937, MSc 1945 Dalhousie Univ; PhD Ohio St Univ 1948; pa/Prof Chem Am Univ 1963-; Staff Army Material Command 1962-63; Chief Res Br Ofc Qtrmaster Gen AUS 1959-62; US Nav Propellant Plant: Chief Fund Processes Div 1957-59, Assoc Chief Chem Div 1955-57, Chief High Polymer Sect 1954-55; Asst Prof Microbiol John Hopkins Univ Sch Hygiene & Public Hlth 1948-54; Sci Master Kings Col; hon/Recipient Sr Fulbright Awd, London Sch Hygiene Trop Med; NIH Career Res Awd; Hillebrand Prize, Wash Chem Soc.

RICE, RONALD LEE oc/Real Estate Specialist; b/Nov 28, 1951; h/7771 Euclid Way, Springfield, VA 22153; m/Shannon Lea Weir; c/Ryan; p/Lloyd Jr and Ruth Harris Rice, Norfolk, VA; ed/BS Old Dominion Univ 1973; MBA George Washington Univ 1975; pa/Real Est Specialist: Gen Sers Adm 1977-, Nav Facilities Engrg Command 1975-77; AMA; Assn Fed Appraisers; Nat Assn Review Appraisers; cp/Old Dominion Univ & George Washington Univ Alumni Assns; r/Meth; hon/Num Outstg Performance & Achmt Awds.

RICH, ISADORE ALEXANDER oc/-Counselor; Instructor; h/Box 148, Frankfort, KY 40601; ba/Same; p/Lydia Rich, Montgomery, AL; ed/BS 1967, MEd 1970 Ala St Univ; Addit Studies; pa/Ky St Univ: Cnlsr & Instr Dept Ed and Eng 1973-, Ad Hoc Com Retention, Ad Hoc Com Self-Study, Ath Booster Clb Com, Chm Miss KSU Coronation Com, Chm Mr Green & Gold Pageant, Cnslr Transfer Students, Advr Pan Hellenic Coun, Others; Resident Hall Cnslr Ala St Univ 1970; Cnslr Stillman Col 1971-72; Tchr Eng Oglethrope Consolidated HS 1967; Editor Univ Cnlsg Ctr Newsletter; APGA; Alpha Phi Alpha; Alpha Phi Omega; Phi Delta Kappa; cp/Actor Diners Playhouse; Announcer Ky St Univ Marching Band; r/Epis; hon/Tchr of Yr, Public Sch Ga; Dist'd Ser Awd, Stillman Col; Man Achmt Awd, Delta Sigma Theta; W/W S&SW; Pub'd Author.

RICHARDSON, DELROY McCOY

oc/Counsel; b/Jun 26, 1938; h/6318 Hannon Ct, San Diego, CA 92117; ba/SD; m/Greta; c/Gayle, Monique; p/Roy Richardson, Chicago, IL; Goldie Roberti, Fort Scott, KS; ed/BA Univ Cal-LA 1962; JD Univ SD Sch Law 1969; MBA Nat Univ 1975; mil/USNR Lt Commdr Judge Advocate Gen Corps; pa/Asst Gen Counsel SD Gas & Elect Co; Cal Assn Black Lwyrs; Nat, Am, Cal St & SD Co Bar Assns; Am Arbitration Assn; Navy Leag of US; Nav Resv Assn; cp/Indust Relats Res Assn; NAACP; Pres Rotary Clb; Urban Leag; Funds Comm; Combined Arts & Ed Coun SD Co; Participant SD Commun Ldrship Devel Prog; r/Cath; hon/Dist'd Alumnus Awd, Univ SD Sch Law; Finalist Outstg Yg Man, Jr C of C; Ldrship Awd, Nav Resv Ofcrs Assn.

RICHARDSON, JAMES MILTON oc/Bishop; b/Jan 8, 1913; h/14 Shadowlawn Cir, Houston, TX 77005; ba/Houston; m/Eugenia Preston Brooks; c/James, Eugenia B Nash (Mrs James), Joan Doty (Mrs James), Preston; p/James and Pallie Stewart Richardson (dec); ed/AB Univ Ga 1934; BD 1936, MA 1942 Emory; LLD John Marshall Law Sch 1961, DD Epis Theol Sem 1960; Addit Studies; pa/Bishop Epis Diocese Tex; Chm Bd & Pension Fund Epis Theol Sem SW; Pres St Lukes Epis Hosp; Chm Bd St Stephens Epis Sch; Trustee Epis Radio-TV Foun & Baylor Col Med; r/Epis.

RICHARDSON, JOSEPH L oc/Manager; b/Apr 23, 1940; h/11505 22nd Ave S, Burnsville, MN 55337; ba/Bloomington, MN; m/Jacqueline; p/Joseph Richardson, Ks City, MO; Genevieve Richardson, Ks City, MO; ed/BA; mil/AUS Capt 1964-68; pa/Mgr Tng & Devel.

RICHARDSON, MILDRED COPELIN oc/Teacher; Librarian; b/Feb 14, 1909; h/Rt 1 Box 30, Upton, KY 42784; m/Leonard; p/Wallace and Arabelle Smith Copelin (dec); ed/BS Wn Ky St Tchrs Col 1950; MLS Nazareth Col 1963; pa/Ret'd Elem Sch Tchr & Libn 38 Yrs Ser; Ctl Lib Processing Ofc Jefferson Co Public Schs: Supvr Operations 1968-72, Libn 1965-67; Itinerant Libn Dixie, Greenwood & Sanders Schs 1961-64; Tchr: Val Elem Sch 1958-60, Fairdale Sch Jefferson Co 1953-54 & 56, Upton Sch 1949-52, 55 & 57, Sonora Schs 1947-48, Clarkson Sch 1945-46,

Millerstown Rural Sch 1932-33 & 37-42, Cherry Sprgs Rural Sch 1936, Big Clifton Sch 1931; Hart Co Bd Ed: Walnut Grove Rural Sch 1929, Watkins Bend Rural Sch 1930; Typist Dental Clin Ofc; Typist Tng Lit & Reproduction; AARP; Ky AV Assn; Nat, Ky & Hardin Co Ret'd Tchrs Assns; cp/Hist Socs: Ky, So, Hart Co & Grayson Co; PTA; Upton Bicent Com; 4-H Clb Ldr Grayson & Hardin Cos; Secy-Treas Upton Homemakers Clb; r/Upton Bapt Ch: WMU Dir, Libn Frances Keith Meml Lib, Child Care Rep, SS Outreach Ldr, Hist Com, Nom'g Com, Tchr Vacation Bible Sch; New Ch Study Course Credit Issued SS BD So Bapt Conv; Dipls: Christian Devel, Prog & Adm Sers, Adv'd Dipl Christian Ldrship; OES #74; hon/2000 Wom Achmt; DIB; Personalities S; Notable Ams Bicent Era; W/W Am Wom.

RICHMOND, JOHN oc/Attorney-at-Law; b/Dec 10, 1907; h/1611 Bonita Ave, Berkeley, CA 94709; ba/Same; p/Samuel and Sarah Stein Richmond (dec); ed/BS 1928, MS 1934 Univ Cal-B; LLB Oakland Col Law 1942;

mil/USAAF WW-II 1942-45; pa/Atty Richmond Enterprises; Fed, Am, Cal St, Berkeley-Albany & Alameda Co Bar Assns; Supreme Ct Hist Soc; Nat Lwyrs Clb; cp/Commdr VFW; U Vets Coun Berkeley; CoChm Lincoln & Washington Patriotic Prog; Chm City Berkeley; Gen Meml Sers, Aquatic Park Meml Sers; Free & Accepted Masons; hon/PhD Hamilton St Univ 1973; Att'd Balliol Col Under Sponsorship USAAF; Num Biogl Listings.

RICHMOND, QUINTON B oc/Public Accountant; Minister; b/Mar 7, 1924; h/1860 Nacoma Pl, Ketterino, OH 45420; ba/Dayton, OH; m/Patricia; c/Carolyn, Larry, Ronald; p/Calvin and Nora Garten Richmond (dec); ed/BA; THB Salutatorian & Hon Roll; mil/USN 1942-44; pa/Enrolled to Pract IRS; Govt Ofcl Contract Negotiator/Price Analyst; Pres & Chm S Ohio Profl Ser Co; Del Nat Soc Public Accts; Public Accts Soc Ohio; cp/Intl Platform Assn; r/Prot; Ordained Min & Evangelist 1950-65; Composer Songs: *Accept Christ Today, Please God Help Me, If You Miss Heaven You'll Miss Everything*; hon/Cert Merit Achmt, Small Bus; Accreditation Coun Acctancy; W/W MW.

RICHTER, ALICE EVE oc/Dentist; b/May 24, 1942; h/PO Box 1901, Jackson, WY 83001; ba/Same; p/Paul and Alice Richter, Sun City, AZ; ed/BS; DDS; pa/Assoc Prof Operative Dentistry Loyola Dental Sch; Am, Ill & Wyo Dental Assns; Am Wom Dentists; Sorority Wom Dentists; Profl & Bus Woms Assn; Beta Sigma Phi; r/Cath; hon/1st Dentist DAVEA Dental Clin, DuPage Co, Ill.

RICKER, NORMAN HURD oc/Professor; b/Oct 11, 1896; h/501 Terrace Pl, Norman, OK 73069; ba/Norman; m/Sallie Lee; c/Florence, Norman Jr, Sallie Lee; p/John and Julia Shaw Ricker (dec); ed/BA w hons 1916; MA 1917; PhD 1920; mil/USA Air Ser WW-I; pa/Prof Emeritus Physics Univ Okla; Res Physicist; Soc Exploration Geophysicists; Geophysical Soc Tulsa; r/Epis; hon/Reginald Fessenden Medal 1977; Nav Ordnance Devel Awd; Dist'd Alumnus Awd, Rice Univ 1978.

RIDGELY, JOSEPHINE JONES oc/Nurse; b/Jan 19, 1920; h/Howell St, Dawson, PA 15428; ba/Uniontown, PA; m/Paul Cromwell (dec); p/Joseph William and Rosa Eleanor Manigault Jones (dec); ed/RN Harlem Hosp; BS NYU; MLttr, Univ Pgh; pa/Nat Assn Colored Grad Nurses; Assn Operating Room Nurses of Wn Pa: Pres Pa/WV Chapt 1963-67; ANA; Pa Nurses Assn; Chi Eta Phi; cp/Nat Coun Negro Wom; Life Mem, Gold Nat Coun Negro Wom; r/St Paul African Meth Epis Ch: Organist; hon/Yrbook Dedication, Montefiore Hosp; Plaque for Outstg Commun Ser, SDA Ch; W/W E; DIB.

RIEDLINGER, MARILYN WOOD oc/Director; b/Nov 24, 1926; h/2752 Spring Val Rd, Lancaster, PA 17601; ba/Same; m/Louis Jr; p/Norvell Wood, Eureka, MO; Dorothy Wood, Clayton, MO; ed/Att'd Wash Univ; pa/Public Relats Dir Eldorado Corp; Author *Fund Raising is Fundamental*; cp/Pilot Clb: Public Relats Area Ldr, Past Pres Lancaster; Friends Lib; Child Devel Ctr; Lancaster Hist Soc; Andrew Ellicott Pa Chapt Lewis & Clark Trl Assn; Pa Assn Wom Hwy Safety Ldrs; r/1st U Meth Ch, Lancaster; hon/George Washington Medal, Freedoms Foun.

RIEG, DANIEL JOSEPH oc/Lawyer; Pharmacist; b/Jul 2, 1945; h/122 Southgate Dr, Morrow, OH 45152; ba/W Chester, OH; c/Karen; ed/JD; BSPharm; MSEd; ASME; pa/Gen Pract Law & Legal Consultation Hlth Care & Related Fields; cp/Union Township C of C; r/Cath; hon/Rho Chi.

RIEMER, LEROY ERWIN oc/Minister; b/Apr 7, 1944; h/PO Box A, 107 Washington, Sutherland, IA 51058; ba/Sutherland; p/Erwin and Gertrude Radue Riemer, Mequon, WI; ed/BA Concordia Sr Col 1966; MDiv Concordia Sem 1970; pa/Min: Bethel Luth Ch-Mo Synod Sutherland 1970-, Faith Luth Ch Orange City 1971-74, Pilgrim Luth Ch Quimby 1976-77; Cherokee Circuit: Pastoral Advr Luth Laymens Leag 1970-, Public Relats Advr 1971-, Stewardship Advr 1978-; Ia Dist W Public Relats Com 1972-; Bd Govs Camp Okoboji 1974-; Bd Dirs Luth Fam Ser Ia 1974-; Pastoral Advr Luth Fam Ser Aux 1974-; Guest Missioner Minn N Dist LC-MS 1975-; cp/Sutherland: Chm Am Revolution Bicent Com, Comml Clb, Ruritan, Mins; Intl Luth Laymens Leag; Concordia Century Clb; Concordia Hist Inst Assn; r/Luth Ch, Mo Synod.

RIES, EDWARD RICHARD oc/Executive; Petroleum Geologist; b/Sept 18, 1918; h/6009 Royal Crest Dr, Dallas, TX 75230; ba/Dallas; m/Maria Wipfler; c/Rosemary Zellmer (Mrs Daniel), Victoria Jennings (Mrs James III); p/August Ries, Freeman, SD; Mary Graber Ries (dec); ed/AB magna cum laude Univ SD 1941; MS Univ Okla 1943; PhD Univ Okla 1951; mil/AUS European Theater (Intell) 1944-46; pa/Mobile Oil Corp Dallas: Sr Reg Explorationist, Reg Geol Group 1975-, Sr Reg Explorationist Asia-Pacific 1973-75, Reg Explorationist E&SE Asia 1971-73; Geol Advr Europe & Far E Mobile Oil Corp 1965-71; Geol Advr Far E, Africa & Oceania Mobile Petro Co 1962-65; Geol Advr Far E & Africa Standard Vac Oil Co 1959-62; Other Former Positions; Participant Geol Field Excursions Num Countries; Assoc Editor Am Assn Petro Geologists 1976-69; Vis Lectr: NYU 1965-70, Calcutta Univ 1952-53; NY Acad Scis; AAAS; Soc Exploration Geophysicists; Am Geological Inst; Geological Soc Am; Am Assn Am Geologists; Contbr Num Sci Articles, Spec Papers & Reports Profl Pubs; Pub'd Author; cp/Nat Adv Bd Am Security Coun; Heritage Foun; Nat Org Mbrships incl'g: Am Legion, Nat Audubon Soc, Smithsonian Instn; r/Mennonite; hon/Phi Beta Kappa; Sigma Gamma Epsilon; Phi Sigma; Sev F'ships; Num Biogl Listings.

RIGG, MARGARET R oc/Visual Artist; Educator; Publisher; b/Dec 14, 1929; h/2960-58th Ave S, St Petersburg, FL 33712; ba/SP; c/Barbara Russ-Cho, Ruth Pettis, Dianne Paddison-Rigg; p/Carl and Ruth Massey Rigg, SP; ed/BA Fla St Univ 1951; MA Presb Sch Christian Ed 1955; Addit Studies; pa/Prof Visual Art Eckerd Col; Soc Scribes & Illuminators; Intl Soc Wom Calligraphers; AAUP; ACUL; ASAUN; FOR; 2 CBS-TV News Shows *My Calligraphy* 1970 & 72; 1 Wom Exhbn Korea; cp/Bd: SCEF, SOC; Resources Highlander Folk Ctr; Comm 75 Asian Woms Cols & Univs; r/U Meth Ch; Presb Bi-Nat Ser; hon/Fulbright-Hays Sr Res Grant; Stone Lectr, Princeton Sem.

RIGGS, DONALD EUGENE oc/Director; b/Sept 10, 1931; h/R #7 Val Springs, Warsaw, IN 46580; ba/Winona Lake, IN; m/Iris Jean; c/Karla, Kathy R Sorenson; p/Elmer and Marlene Riggs, Bloomington, IN; ed/AB; STD; PhD; pa/Dir Communs World Headqtrs Free Meth Ch; Ordained Min; cp/Kiwanis; Exc; r/Prot; Free Meth Ch; hon/W/W Am Cols & Univs.

RIGGS, KARL A JR oc/Consultant; Professor; b/Aug 12, 1929; h/109 Grand Ridge Dr, Starkville, MS 39759; ba/Miss St, MS; m/Patricia Ann Hartrick; c/George, Kathryn R Keen, Linda; p/Karl Riggs, Whitestone, Long Isl, NY; Marjorie Urquhart Riggs, Columbus, GA; ed/BS w hons 1951, MS 1952 Mich St Univ; PhD Ia St Univ 1956;

pa/Assoc Prof Miss St; Geologic Conslt; Abstractor Mineralogical Abstracts; NW Mining Assn; cp/C of C; Kiwanis; Repub; r/U Meth Ch; Gideons; hon/Num Biogl Listings.

RIGGSBY, DUTCHIE SELLERS oc/Educator; b/Oct 26, 1940; h/2214 Coventry Dr, Columbus, GA 31904; ba/C'bus; m/Ernest; c/Lyn-Dee; p/Malcolm and Celia Sellers, Montgomery, AL; ed/BS, MS Troy St Univ; EdD Auburn Univ; pa/Assoc Prof Instrnl Media C'bus Col; Assn Ed Communs & Technol; Ga Assn Instrnl Technol; Other Profl Orgs; cp/Dir Internal Aerospace Ed SE Reg Staff CAP; r/Bapt; hon/Star Awd, Nat Sci Tchrs Assn; Cert Merit, Aviations Mfgrs & Distributors Assn; PDK; KDP.

RIGGSBY, ERNEST DUWARD oc/Professor; b/Jun 12,1925; h/2214 Coventry Dr, Columbus, GA 31904; ba/C'bus; m/Dutchie Sellers; c/Lyn-Dee; p/Mrs Ann Durham, C'bus; ed/BS; BA; MA; EdS; EdD; mil/USAFR Col; pa/Prof C'bus Col; Fellow AAAS; cp/C'bus Execs Clb; hon/Hall Hon Am Soc Aerospace; Ford Scholar; Kettering Fellow.

RIGNEY, ROBERT BUFORD oc/Administrator; b/May 1, 1926; h/1101 Cajon St, Redlands, CA 92415; ba/San Bernardino, CA; m/Lowenda Mae; c/Michael, Jeffrey; p/Harold and Nellie Buford Rigney; ed/BA Stanford Univ; Addit Studies; mil/11th Airborne 1944-45; pa/SB Co Govt: Admr Envir Improvement Agy 1973-, Chm Cal Seismic Safety Comm 1975-, Exec Ofcr Local Agy Formation Comm 1966-73, Adm Analyst & Spec Dists Coor; Nat Assn Co Ofcrs; Com Nat Resources & Envir Adm Am Soc Public Adm; cp/Cal Inland Empire Coun; Bd Dirs Arrowhead U Fund; Pres Redlands Round Table; E Clampus Vitas; Redlands Horticultural Soc; Grayback Boy Scout Coun; SB Co Mus Assn; Rotary Clb; Bd Dirs Lighthouse of Blind; r/Prot; 1st Presb Ch: Elder, Chm Bd Trustees, Bldg & Fin Coms; Legal Comm Synod S Cal U Presb Ch; hon/Phi Alpha Theta; Phi Kappa Delta; Silver Beaver Awd, BSA; Commun Ser Ct; USA Nat Achmt Awds, NACo; Pub'd Author.

RILEY, MILES O'BRIEN oc/Catholic Priest; Director; b/Aug 31, 1937; h/3321-16th St, San Francisco, CA 94114; ba/SF; p/William and Francis Riley, Atherton, CA; ed/BA magna cum laude St Josephs Col 1958; STB St Patricks Sem 1960; STL Gregorian Univ 1964; Dir & Fdr & Dir: Archdiocesan Communs Ctr 1970-76, Teenagers For Action 1968-70; Assoc Pastor: St Pauls 1968-70, St Raphaels 1964-68, St Bartholomews 1964; Filmmaker 6 Musical Comedies & 7 Ednl Films; Num Radio & TV Progs; Author 4 Books: Songwriter; VEEP: UNDA-USA Nat Cath Broadcasters, Nat Syndicators Assn; cp/Chm Communs Comm; Sev Orch Bands 12 Yrs; Num Bds & Coms Civic Orgs; r/Rom Cath; hon/3 NATAS Local Emmy Awds; 10 Nat Gabriel Awds; Num Biogl Listings.

RING, LARRY RICHARD oc/Manager; b/Oct 28, 1946; h/43 Montclair Rd, Oak Ridge, TN 37830; ba/OR; m/Nicke Carpino; c/Denise, Kristen; p/Marshall and Nettie Ring, Youngstown, OH; ed/BS; pa/Mgr Lockheed OR Engrg Ctr; Energy & Envir Res & Engrg Apollo Space Prog; cp/Nat Mgmt Assn; JCs; C of C; r/Meth; hon/Dean's List Univ Fla; Outstg Yg Men Am; W/W S&SW; Personalities S; Men Achmt.

RINGROSE, JOSEPH STEPHEN
oc/Executive Director; b/Feb 29, 1936; h/749 Dubanski Dr, San Jose, CA 95123; ba/Sunnyvale, CA; m/Barbara Ann; c/Katrina, Kristina; p/Alan & Esther Ringrose, Waltham, MA; ed/BS w hons Boston Univ 1962; MBA SJ St Univ 1968; mil/USAF 1953-57; pa/Exec Dir Sunnyvale Med Clin 1977-; City SJ 1971-77; Bus Mgr SJ-Santa Clara Water Pollution Control Plant, City Pers Ofcr, Bus Mgr Dept Public Works, Budget Suprv City Mgrs Dept; Pers Ofcr SC Co 1970-71; Asst City Mgr 1967-70; Pers, Budget & Sr Budget Analyst 1964-67; Claim Rep Aetna Casualty & Surety Co 1962-64; Med Group & Intl City Mgrs Assns; IPMA; cp/Mun Fin Ofcrs Assn; Commonwealth Clb SF; Kenna Clb Univ SC; r/Agnostic.

RINGSDORF, WARREN MARSHALL JR
oc/Dental Educator; b/May 2, 1930; ba/Dept Oral Med Univ Ala, Univ Sta, Birmingham, AL 35294; m/Doris; c/2; p/W M and Mary Ringsdorf; ed/MS; DMD; pa/Tchr Univ Ala-B; Nutritional Reschr; Author 5 Books & 350 Pub'd Sci Articles; cp/Bd Dirs Teen Challenge; St Annes Home Alcoholic Wom; r/World-Wide Jewish Missions; hon/Notable Ams.

RITTER, OLIVE MAI oc/Music Teacher; b/Jun 29, 1900; h/207 W 10th St, Concordia, KS 66901; ba/Same; p/Horace and Clothilda Matthews Ritter, Selden, KS; ed/BMus Bethany Col 1931; pa/Pvt Piano Tchr; Judge Piano Auditions; Nat & Ks Music Tchrs Assns; cp/Concordia Music Clb; Chm Piano Guild Ctr Concordia; Active Nat, St & Local Levels Repub Party; r/U Meth; hon/Nat Piano Guild Hall of Fame.

RIVARD, ROBERT COOPER oc/Pianist; Teacher; b/Sept 7, 1945; h/11585 N Harrell's Ferry Rd, Bldg 25, Apt 1, Baton Rouge, LA 70816; p/Adrien Arthur Rivard (dec); Ruth Lounsberry Rivard Karger, De Funiak Springs, FL; ed/BM Fla St Univ 1967; MM La St Univ 1970; Doc Mus Arts LSU 1980; pa/Perf'd Sonata Recitals w Prof Louis R Ferraro 1972-76; hon/3.8 GPA Grad Sch.

RIVENBARK, REMBERT REGINALD
oc/Corporate Executive; b/Sept 9, 1912; h/114 Trent Shores Dr, New Bern, NC 28560; ba/NB; m/Marie Barbour; c/Rembert Jr, William, Patricia Pate (Mrs Dewey); p/Reginald Rivenbark (dec); Kathleen Fussell Rivenbark, Goldsboro, NC; pa/Chm Bd, Sr VP & Dir Barbour Boat Works Inc; Chm Bd & Pres Marine Trading Corp; Past Dir Ocean Scallops Inc; Past Pres & Dir Am Boat Bldrs Assn; Am Ordnance Assn; AMA; NC Wildlife Assn; Dir NC Fisheries Assn; US C of C; cp/Mason; Shriner; Elk; Rotarian; E Carolina Yacht Clb; NB Golf & Country Clb; r/Adm Bd U Meth Ch.

RIVERA, NICOLAS NOGUERAS
oc/Educator; b/Sept 10, 1902; h/173 Taft St, Santurce, Puerto Rico 00911; m/Berta; c/2; ed/Elem Tchr Cert Univ PR 1920; Elem Eng Tchr Cert 1926; Labor Ed Inst 1935; pa/Tchr PR Public Schs 1920-35; Pres Protective Labor Union Cayey 1931; Lectr Dept Labor 1935; Secy-Treas Fed Labor Union, San Juan 1936; PR Free Fdn Labor: Pres 1951-, Secy-Treas 1936-52; Pres Factory & Agri Labor Coun PR 1938-41; Bd Appeals Selective Sys 1942-70; Orgr & Pres Round Table Conf Sugar Indust Probs 1943-44; Pioneer & Exec Secy 1st Statehood Cong PR 1943; Drafter Labor Unity Charter 1945; Pres Prog & Constitution Comm 1st InterAm Labor Conf, Lima, Peru 1948; Orgr & Pres Cong Plesbicitary Action 1959-60; Author: *Prospects of Union Reorg 1942, Collective Bargaining in Sugar Indust PR 1956*; Editor *40 Yrs Labor Activs*; Fdr & Dir Mthly Paper Salario 1966; Composer 2 Waltzes; cp/House Reps PR 1932-36; Am Security Coun; Apprenticeship Coun PR; Intl Platform Assn; hon/Selective Ser Sys US: Medal WW-II, Cert Apprec, Medal & Insignia; Awds: Franklin D Roosevelt, Harry S Truman, Dwight D Eisenhower, John F Kennedy, Lyndon B Johnson & Richard Nixon; Fellow Intl Biogl Assn; Num Biogl Listings.

RIVES, JAMES HENRY oc/Civil Engineer; b/Nov 11, 1905; h/4450 James Dr, Chattanooga, TN 37416; m/Mabel Hemphill (dec); c/James Jr, Robert; p/Robert and Rose Lewis Rives (dec); ed/BS Univ Ala; mil/USNR Lt CEC SW Pacific Area WW-II 1943-45; pa/Ret'd CE; US Dept St: Chief Engrg Adv & CoDir Ec Mission Ethiopia 1957-60, Chief Engrg Advr US Ec Mission Jordan 1955-57, Acting Country Dir & Chief Engrg Advr Republic Liberia 1947-52; Instr Univ Tenn 1946-47; Engr Design Dept TVA 1933-47; ASCE; Capstone Engrs Soc; AAAS; cp/Num Civic Coms City C'nooga; r/Epis; hon/Commends: US TVA 1947, Republic Liberia & US 1952, Birmingham Mus Art; Theta Chi; Theta Nu Epsilon; W/W: Am, Commerce & Indust.

RIVKIN, ELLIS oc/Professor; Lecturer; Author; b/Sept 7, 1918; h/7610 Reading Rd, Cincinnati, OH 45237; ba/Cinc; m/Zelda Zafren; c/Roslyn Weinberger, Sharon Kilburn; p/Moses and Beatrice Leibowitz Rivkin (dec); ed/BA w hons 1941, PhD John Hopkins; BHL Baltimore Hebrew Col; pa/Vis Prof: So Meth Univ 1977, Univ Utah 1973, Antioch Col 1963; Hebrew Union Col-Jewish Inst Rel: Asst Prof 1949-51, Assoc Prof 1951-53, Prof Jewish Hist 1953-, Adolph S Ochs Prof Jewish Hist 1965; Instr Jewish Hist Gratz Col 1946-49; r/Jewish; hon/Phi Beta Kappa; Simon Guggenheim Fellow; Grants: Am Coun Learned Socs, Am Philosophic Soc; Joseph Rosenblatt Lectureship, Univ Utah; W/W; PhD Baltimore Hebrew Col.

RIZK, JOSEF SALEEM oc/Electrical Engineer; b/Mar 24, 1917; h/3903 Cove, St Johns Rd, Jacksonville, FL 32211; ba/J'ville; m/Mary; c/Melinda; p/Saleem and Wadeeha Rizk (dec); ed/BEE; mil/USNR Ensign Lt Commdr; pa/Reg'd Profl Engr; Am Mil Engrs; Fla Engrg Soc; NSPE; r/Rom Cath; hon/W/W; Intl Biog; Am Lives.

ROADEN, ARLISS LLOYD oc/Administrator; b/Sept 27, 1930; h/1155 N Dixie Ave, Walton House, Cookeville, TN 38501; ba/C'ville; m/Mary Etta Mitchell; c/Janice Skelton, Sharon; p/Johnie and Ethel Killian Roaden, Corbin, KY; ed/BA; MS; EdD; mil/AUS Signal Corps 1951-53; pa/Univ Pres Tenn Technol Univ; Chm Bd Govs Phi Delta

Kappa Foun; Pres Tenn Col Assn; Consultant; cp/Rotarian; Lion; r/Bapt; hon/Am Legion S'ship Awd; Dist'd Alumnus Designee, Cumberland Col; Dist'd Ser Awd, Ohio St Chapt Phi Delta Kappa; Centennial Medallion Dist'd Fac & Alumni, Ohio St Univ; Pub'd Author.

ROADS, LEO FRANKLIN JR oc/Insurance Executive; b/May 18, 1933; h/6907 Mormon Bridge Rd, Omaha, NE 68152; ba/Omaha; m/Margie Luegean Prentice; c/David, Susan, Karen, Christina; p/Leo Roads Sr (dec); Merita Brooks Roads, Wichita, KS; ed/BBA Wichita St Univ; mil/AUS; pa/CoChm Reimbursement Tech Adv Group Hlth Care Fin Adm, Baltimore; r/Bishop Omaha 1st Ward, Ch of Jesus Christ Latter-Day Sts; hon/CPA Cert.

ROBBINS, ARTHUR FREEMAN oc/- Minister; b/Sept 25, 1919; h/718 J Pl, Chula Vista, CA 92010; ba/CV; m/Esther Violet; c/Kathleen, William, Shirley; p/Arthur and

Bertha Robbins; ed/DDiv; mil/Army; pa/Intl Bd Evang China F'ship; cp/Pres San Diego Bible Col; r/Bapt; hon/W/W Rel; Intercontinental Biogl Assn.

ROBBINS, DOROTHY BRADSHAW
oc/Administrative Assistant; h/1620 Fuller St NW, Washington, DC 20009; m/William and Flora Porterfield Bradshaw (dec); pa/Adm Asst Div Cost Ascertainment PO Dept; cp/Past Pres: Capital BPW Clb, Toastmistress Clb, Sgrt Jasper Am Legion Aux; Am Penwom; r/Meth; hon/Gold Card, C of C; Bus Wom of Yr, Capital BPW Clb.

ROBBINS, JAMES TATE oc/Manufacturers Agent; b/Feb 12, 1945; h/4124 Ridgeway Ln, Knoxville, TN 37919; ba/Knoxville; m/Martha Walker; c/Walker, Elizabeth; p/Frank and Margaret Williams Robbins, Signal Mtn, TN; ed/AB; mil/AUS 1st Lt Ordnance Corp; pa/ASHRAE; cp/Concord Yacht Clb; W Knoxville Sertoma Clb; Mtn City Clb; r/Ch St Meth Ch; hon/W/W.

ROBBINS, LINDA S oc/Counselor Educator; b/Oct 27, 1943; h/196 Sycamore Ln, Athens, GA 30605; p/Norton and Helen Robbins, Greensboro, NC; ed/BS w hons & distns Univ Ill 1972; MEd 1973, PhD Cand Univ Ga; pa/Cnslr Action Inc 1978-; Human Relats Tnr Univ Ga 1975-77; Correctional Cnslr Athens Adjustment Ctr 1975; Prog Asst Ga Retardation Ctr 1974-75; Tchr Eng 1966-79; APGA; APA; ASSECT; cp/CPR Instr; hon/Citizen Action Awd, Ga Dept Corrections & Offender Rehab.

ROBBINS, SHEILA CALDWELL oc/- Principal; b/Jun 6, 1936; h/20 Paseo Margarita, Camarillo, CA 93010; ba/Simi Val, CA; m/Harry Pat; c/Martha, David, Pamela, Russell; p/Alfred Caldwell (dec); Ivy Johnson Caldwell, Sepulveda, CA; ed/BA BYU; MA Cal St Univ-N; pa/Elem Asst Prin; Intl & Cal Reading Assns; Cal Assn Sch Adm; SV Mgmt Assn; Delta Kappa Gamma; cp/Adv Bds Cal Luth Col & CSUN; Local & Area PTA Bds; Var St Ed Coms; r/Latter-Day Sts; hon/S'ship BYU; Golden Gleaner.

ROBERTS, ANNYE PEARL-HARDY SPROWL oc/School Social Worker; b/Jan 7, 1932; h/441 S 21st, Saginaw, MI 48601; ba/Saginaw; m/Ben Barton; c/Charles Sprowl, Cedric Sprowl, Iris S Owens, Darrell Sprowl; p/Charlie Hardy (dec); Delsie King Hardy, Montgomery, AL; ed/BS; pa/Nat Assn Social Wkrs; Mich Sch Social Wkrs; Nat, St & Local Ed Assns; Conslt & Lectr; cp/Saginaw Civic Ctr Bd; Nom'g Com YWCA; St Dir Zeta Phi Beta; r/African Meth; Commun Affairs Dept Cath Diocese; hon/Profl Awd, Saginaw BPW; Wom of Yr, Zeta Phi Beta.

ROBERTS, CHARLES TRUITT
oc/Minister; b/Mar 31, 1930; h/Rt 2, 2 Oriole Dr, Starkville, MS 39759; ba/S'ville; m/Mary; c/Patsy, Stephanie; p/George Roberts, Baldwyn, MS; Gladys Roberts (dec); ed/BMus; MChMus; pa/Min Music: 1st Bapt Ch S'ville 1973-, Jefferson Ave Bapt Ch 1969-73, Ardmore Bapt Ch Memphis 1963-69; MENC; ACDA; Choristers Guild; cp/Ch Music Conf FBC; 1st VP Miss Bapt Conv;

Kiwanis Clb; C of C; Asst Dir S'ville Symph Chorus; r/So Bapt; hon/W/W Rel.

ROBERTS, DENNIS WILLIAM oc/Public Relations; b/Jan 7, 1943; h/1709 Hiawatha NE, Albuquerque, NM 87112; ba/Albuque; p/William and Florence Roberts, Albque; ed/BA Univ NM 1968; pa/Soc Profl Journalists; Public Relats Soc Am; Am Soc Assn Execs; cp/Toastmasters Intl; U Way; Dem; r/Luth; hon/Public Relats Achmt Awd, Assn Gen Contractors; Dist'd Dist Awd, Toastmasters Intl.

ROBERTS, GERTRUD oc/Musician; Composer; b/Aug 23, 1906; h/4723 Moa St, Honolulu, HI 96816; m/Joyce; c/Michael, Marcia; p/Adolph and Anna Kloetzer Kuenzel (dec); ed/BA Univ Minn 1928; Addit Studies; pa/Concert Harpsichordist; Concerts Tours 1964 & 1966-78; "Premiere Record" Released 1979; Pub'd Works: *Chaconne for Harpsichord, Rondo-Hommage to Couperin, 12 Time-Gardens*; Num Compositions incl'g: Petite Suite, Triptych, Das Kleine Buch der

Bilder, Fantasy Atter Psalm 150; Num Chd Pieces Harpsichord & Compositions Manuscript; Nat Soc Arts & Lttrs; Nat Assn Composers & Conductors; Am Music Ctr; Nat Guild Piano Tchrs; Past Pres Pen Wom Am; AAUW; Sigma Alpha Iota; Alpha Gamma Delta; cp/Fdr & Pres: Fritz Hart Foun, Jean Charlot Foun; H'lulu: Commun Theatre, Piano Tchrs Assn, Chamber Music Soc, Morning Music Clb, Acad Arts, Bishop Mus; hon/Nat Guild Piano Tchrs Hall Fame; Most Dist'd Citizen 1975 Arts, Alpha Gamma Delta; Num Biogl Listings.

ROBERTS, HEYWARD DELAIN oc/Minister; b/Nov 12, 1933; h/Rt 2, Murray, KY 42071; ba/Same; m/Wanda; c/John, Sarai; p/Eucle and Thelma Roberts, Walnut Benton, KY; mil/1954-56; pa/Min Bapt; Pastored 4 Chs Since 1960; r/Bapt; hon/W/W: Rel, Ky; DIB.

ROBERTS, JEANETTE L oc/Director; b/Nov 9, 1920; h/528 S 8th St, Mayfield, KY 42066; ba/M'field; m/Eugene Sr; c/Eugene Jr; p/Horace Luther Sr (dec); Lillian Luther, M'field; pa/Exec Dir ARC 1956-; cp/Past Pres: Am Legion Aux, M'field Coun Clb Wom; Past Recording Secy BPW Clb; Bd Sr Citizens;

Inter-Agy Coun; Resource Devel Com; OES; Band Parents Clb; Secy U Way; Wayfarers; Nat Campers; Hikers Assn; Past Den Mother BSA; r/1st Bapt Ch, M'field: Mem, Tchr & Dir Dept SS, Rel Ed Com; hon/Wom of Yr, Graves Co Yg Dem Clb; 1st Lady of Yr, Beta Sigma.

ROBERTS, LOUISE VENABLE oc/Writer; b/Aug 17, 1944; h/1111 Army Navy Dr #C-1203, Arlington, VA 22202; ba/McLean, VA; p/John Roberts (dec); Frances Lancaster Roberts, Ashland, VA; ed/BA Brenau Col 1966; pa/Sr Tech Writer Adv'd Technol Inc; Soc Tech Communs; r/Meth; hon/W/W Am Wom.

ROBERTS, MARY ANNETTE oc/Freelance Artist; b/Mar 29; h/257 E Hill Dr, San Bernardino, CA 92404; m/Gordon Jr; c/Jon, Jonna, Richard; p/Theodore Van Loon (dec); Julia Tooker, SB; pa/Creative Art Works Num Mags incl'g Pen Wom; Num Exhbns Art Gallerys So Cal; Nat Leag Am Pen Wom; Histn Traditional Artists Am; cp/Fine Arts Inst SB Co Mus; SB Art Assn; r/Prot; hon/Recipient Awd Stationery Design, Nat Leag Am Pen Wom.

ROBERTS, MARY BELLE oc/Social Worker; b/Sept 27, 1923; h/PO Box 340955, Coral Gables, FL; ba/Miami; p/Joseph Roberts (dec); Inez Roberts, Silver Springs, MD; ed/BS, MSW Univ Mich; Addit Studies; pa/Social Wkr U Fam & Chds Sers Inc; Fellow Royal Soc Hlth; NASW; ACSW; NCSW; Cert'd Social Wkr St Md; Clin Reg NASW; cp/Past Pres Altrusa Clb Miami Inc; Chm Combined Classified Woms Ser Clbs; r/Christian; hon/Phi Kappa Phi; W/W Am Wom; Yg Adults Ser Com Persistence Awd, Yg Adults S Fla; Cert Apprec, YWCA; Pub'd Author.

ROBERTS, PHYLLIS VREELAND oc/Community Leader; b/Jan 8, 1925; h/8516 Crestview Dr, Fairfax, VA 22031; m/James Benton; c/Cameron Riddle, Mary Lauriston, James Jr; p/Walling Vreeland (dec); Dorothy Hawley Vreeland, Spring Lake, NC; ed/BA cum laude Univ NC-G; pa/Tchr Eng & Hist HS; Nat Assn Parliamentarians; AAUW; cp/Conserv Coun Va; Dist Pres VFWC; IFAW; NPCA; NWF; GFWC: Nat Safety Chm, Pres SEn Reg; Woms Clbs: Pres Pine Ridge & Jefferson Vil, Secy Gen Fdn, Va Fdn; Cousteau Soc; Audubon Soc; Friends Animals; Defenders Wildlife; Scout Ldr; Pres PTA; r/Epis: Vestry, Pres Ch Wom, Altar Guild, Yth Group Advr, Ch Hospitality Chm, Ed and Prayer & Worship Coms; Ch Wom U; hon/Phi Beta Kappa; Alpha Kappa Delta; Sigma Delta Pi.

ROBERTS, THELMA AMEINETTA oc/Teacher; Musician; b/Sept 19, 1903; h/332 1st St, Slatington, PA 18080; ba/Same; p/John and Ella Roberts (dec); ed/Grad Ithaca Col; pa/Tchr Piano Ithaca Col 2 Yrs; Organist & Pianist; Choir Dir; cp/Symph Wom Allentown; Symph Orch; r/St Johns Luth Ch, Slatington.

ROBERTSON, RALPH BYRON oc/Attorney-at-Law; b/Sept 4, 1943; h/1124 W Ave, Richmond, VA 23220; ba/Richmond; m/Susan Swanson; c/Linda; p/Reece and Elsie Robertson; ed/BA Va Mil Inst; MA Duke; JD Univ Va; pa/Trial Lwyrs Am; Crim Bar Assn; cp/Bd Team Progress Muscular Dystrophy Assn; r/Bapt; hon/Phi Delta Phi.

ROBESON, LILLYAN ROSE oc/Administrative Secretary; b/Aug 14, 1907; h/3632 E Behymer Ave, Clovis, CA 93612; ba/Same; m/Harvey; p/David and Grace Moyle (dec); Foster-Mother: Beatrice Simons, Norfolk, CT; mil/Air-WAC CBI Theatre WW-II; pa/CoOwner Robeson Ranch; Ret'd Sr Adm Secy US Ct Appeals 9th Circuit; Substitute Judicial Secy 5th Dist Ct Appeals St Cal; Chief Reporter War Crimes Trials China 1945-46; cp/Soroptimist Intl; Dir Dist 4 SWn Reg Am Inc, Pres Fresno Inc; U Celebral Palsy: Treas, Exec Com, Bd Dirs; hon/U Celebral Palsy: Vol of Yr Awd, Cert; Vol Awd, Fresno Co; China War Ser Meml, Republic China; Fellow Am Biogl Inst.

ROBICHAUD, PHYLLIS ISABEL oc/Artist; b/1915; h/1053 Lenox Cir, New Port Richey, FL 33552; ed/Grad Tutorial Col 1932; Addit Art Studies; pa/Tchr Art: Currently

Pasco-Hernando Commun Col NPR, NPR Rec Dept 1969-77, Other Insts Wel Ltd; Num 1-Person Shows & Exhbns; Creative Works: 6 Murals, 32 Hist Scenes Am Bicent; Nat Leag Am Pen Wom; cp/Algoma Art Soc; Jamaican Contemp Artists Assn; W Pasco Art Guild; Fla Fine Arts Guild; hon/Cert Merit: T Eaton Co, Bicent Paintings; Plaque Fla Bicycle Motor Cross Assn; Num Art Awds Var Countries; Num Biogl Listings.

ROBINETT, LESLIE WHITE oc/Civic Leader; b/Jun 13, 1909; h/3704 Country Clb Cir, Fort Worth, TX 76109; m/Ewell Jennings; c/Leslie Perryman (Mrs Wynne), John; p/Henry and Corrine Belle White (dec); cp/Bds: Fort Worth Symph Leag, Tex Christian Univ Fine Arts Guild, Opera Guild, Woms Clb, Van Cliburn Piano Competition; r/Broadway Bapt Ch.

ROBINETT, PATRICIA MILDRED oc/Nurse; b/Nov 21, 1933; h/9104 W 70 Terrace, Merriam, KS 66204; ba/Leavenworth, KS; c/Mark, Margaret, Sandra, Michelle; p/Walter and Mary Dackson (dec);

ed/BSN Avila Col 1974; MN Univ Ks 1979; pa/Psychiatric Clin Nurse Spec VA Ctr; Am Nurses Assn; Soc Nsg; Sigma Theta Tau; cp/Johnson Co Mtl Hlth Assn; r/Christian; hon/W/W: Am Wom, World Wom.

ROBINETTE, JOSEPH ALLEN oc/Teacher; Playwright; b/Feb 8, 1939; h/Box 11, Richwood, NJ 08074; ba/Glassboro, NJ; m/Helen; c/John, Anne, Michael, Christopher; p/Paul and Willie Merle Robinette, Jasper, GA; ed/BA 1960; MA 1966; PhD 1972; pa/Tchr Glassboro St Col; Author 17 Plays & Musicals; Drama Critic & Director; Chds Theatre Spec; ATA; CTAA; SCA; r/Prot; hon/Recipient Nat Playwriting Awd.

ROBINSON, CHARLYNN CHAMBERLIN oc/Psychologist; b/Feb 10, 1950; h/5268 Seaton Dr, Dunwood, GA 30338; ba/Atlanta, GA; m/Edward Jr; c/Edward; p/John Chamberlin, Chgo; ed/BS; MA; PhD; pa/Devel Psychologist Emory Univ; APA; Assn Black Psychologists; Soc Res Child Devel; IBW; GPA; cp/NAACP; Urban Leag; hon/Ford Foun S'ship; Lords Chesterfield; Homecoming Queen, Univ Ill; W/W.

ROBINSON, CHRISTINE HINCKLEY oc/Author; Lecturer; Teacher; Interior Decorator; b/May 11, 1908; h/670 E 3 Fountains Dr, #169, Murray, UT 84107; m/Oliver Preston; c/Miriam, Bruce, Christine; p/Bryant and Christine Johnson Hinckley (dec); ed/Att'd Brigham Yg Univ, NY Univ, Oxford Univ, UK; pa/Dir Ch Latter Day Sts Relief Soc Orgs Wn Europe 1964-67; Head Hist Interior Restorations St Utah 1961-63 and Nauvoo, Ill 1963 & 1967-69; Owner Christine H Robinson Interiors 1948-64; Publs: *Successful Retail Salesmanship 1942, Living Truths 1964, Inspirational Truths 1970, Biblical Sites in Holy Land 1963, Israels Bible Lands 1973, Christs Eternal Gospel 1976*; Contbr Num Mags; Bd Dirs Intl Relief Soc Org; Bd Dirs Dental Sers Assn; cp/Pres & VP Utah Div Intl Travelers Aid; Bd Dirs & Chm Wel Div Utah Commun Wel Sers; VP Utah Div Intl Crusade Freedom; hon/Silver Bowl & Plaque, Intl Relief Soc; Merit Hon Plaque, Travelers Aid; Joseph F Smith Fam Living Awd Outstg Couple, BYU.

ROBINSON, CLAYTON DAVID oc/- Reverend; b/Oct 30, 1955; h/715 Lake St, Huntington Bch, CA 92648; m/Kimberly Ann Cole; p/Gary and Gay Guilmette Robinson, HB; ed/BA magna cum laude So Cal Col 1975; MA summa cum laude Azusa Pacific Col 1976; MDiv summa cum laude Fuller Theol Sem 1978; Addit Studies; pa/Pastoral Staff & Admr Ch by the Sea, HB 1975-; Pastor Charge Yth Min 1979-; Dir & Instr Sch Bible Col 1980-; Orange Co Yth Dir 1973-79; SW Dist Missions Coun 1977-; Guest Lectr: So Cal Col 1977-, Azusa Pacific Col 1977-78; Camp Spkr Camps Cedar Crest & Pacific Pines 1977-; Author: *Revelation, Antichrist, Christology of Revelation, Baptism in Holy Spirit*; cp/Advr Woms Aglow; So Cal Col & Azusa Pacific Col Alumni; Rec Dir HB Rec Dept; Min Vietnamese Refugees 1976; hon/Pres S'ship Awd, So Cal Col; Orange Co Yth Dirs Awd; Num Biogl Listings.

ROBINSON, EDWARD ARLEN oc/- Professor; b/Jun 13, 1933; h/3340 Emerson, Evanston, IL 60203; ba/Chicago, IL; m/- Lavada Hill; c/Edward, Arlen; p/Joseph and Thelma Robinson (dec); ed/BA Howard Univ 1959; MAT Univ Chgo 1970; PhD NWn Univ 1974; mil/AUS 1953-55; pa/Assoc Prof Dept Sec'dy Ed NEn Ill Univ; Instr Eng & Drama and Chm Eng Dept Harlan HS 12 Yrs; Former Fac Afro-Am Lit Lake Forest Col; HS Eng Supvr Chgo Bd Ed; Conslt Num Sch Sys Metro Chgo Areas; Tchr-Host 30 TV Progs Afro-Am Hist & Cult *Like It Was: Black Men Am*; NCTE; AFT; Delta Kappa; Conf Eng Ed; Author: *Afro-Am Drama Ed: An Instrnl Strategy, NC Eng Bltn*; Consltg Editor: *Spch-Communs: Mod Approach, Voices of Man Series*; cp/Evanston YMCA; NAACP; Oper Push; Walker Sch PTA; r/Park Manor Congreg Ch, Chgo; hon/F'ships: Experienced Tchr, Ford Foun Grad.

ROBINSON, GARY GARTH oc/Pastor; Missionary Evangelist; b/Sept 9, 1932; h/20421 Ravenwood Ln, Huntington Bch, CA 92646; ba/HB; m/Gay Elizabeth Clara Guilmette; c/Joy Thornton, Clayton; p/Clayton Robinson, Monrovia, CA; Iola Griffith Robinson (dec); ed/AA Orange Coast Col 1966; BA 1968, MA 1970 Long Bch St Univ; BTh Life Bible Col 1954; PhD Cand Golden St Univ; pa/Pastor Ch by the Sea, HB 1960-; SW Dist Evangelist 1958-60; Pastor Perris 1955-58; Assoc Pastor Monrovia 1954-55; Missionary-Evangelist 42 Countries 1965-; Rel TV & Radio Broadcasting; Conf Spkr; cp/Fdr & Dir R&R Enterprises; Intl Platform Assn; CoFdr Breath Life F'ship; Advr Fountain Vly Woms Aglow; Tour Dir; Secy HB Mins Assn; Life Alumni Assn; Exec Mgmt Sems; r/Ordained Intl Ch Foursquare Gospel 1954; Intl Christian Ed Coor 1975-; Intl SS Com 1975-; Exec Coun & Bldg Com Intl Ch Foursquare Gospel 1975-; Coms: Ins, Ordination, Bldg & Planning 1974-76; Dist Coor 1972-75; hon/Phi Kappa Phi; Intl Awd Outstg Achmt SS; Pub'd Author; Num Biogl Listings; Inventor Choco Game; CoInventor Paper Wheeler.

ROBINSON, GAY ELIZABETH CLARA oc/Teacher; Author; Lecturer; b/Aug 13, 1933; h/20421 Ravenwood Ln, Huntington Bch, CA 92646; ba/HB; m/Gary Garth; c/Joy Thornton, Clayton; p/Theodore Guilmette (dec); Elizabeth Majher Guilmette, Newhall, CA; ed/AA Orange Coast Col 1966; BA 1968, MA 1970 Cal St Univ; PhD Cand Golden St Univ; pa/Dir Christian Ed & Assoc Pastor Perris 1955-58; SW Dist Secy & Evangelist 1960-76; Pastoral Staff Ch by the Sea 1960-; Missionary Evangelist 1965-; Instr Irvine Col 1976-78; U Foursquare Wom SW Dist: Secy 1955-58, Div Rep 1954-58 & 1960-62, Publicity & Promotion Chm 1966-72, Prog Chm 1962 & 1972-79; Advr Agape Ingathering 1978-; Ldr & Tchr Bible Groups 1978-; Lectr 40 Countries; Radio Broadcaster Breath of Life; cp/Tour Dir; Jr Woms Clbs; Past Secy Temple City, Arcadia; Repub Woms Com; Life Alumni Assn; Exec Mgmt Sems; Fdr Breath of Life Min; hon/Outstg Bus Student, LA C of C; Intl Awd SS Achmt; Awd Longest Ser Ofcr SW Dist, U Foursquare Wom; S'ships: Pepperdine Univ, Chapman Floating Col Seas; Pub'd Author; Num Biogl Listings.

ROBINSON, JAMES WILLIAM oc/Professor; b/Jul 12, 1923; h/375 Amherst Dr, Baton Rouge, LA 70808; ba/BR; m/Winifred Nixon; c/James, Linda, Sandra Hendrix; p/James and Eva Robinson (dec); ed/BS w hons; PhD; DSc; mil/RAF 1942-45; pa/Prof Chem Dept LSU; Editor: *Handbook of Spectroscopy, Spectroscopy Lettr*; r/Epis; hon/Guggenheim Fellow; La Chem Awd, AIC.

ROBINSON, NANCY MARGARET oc/Educational Researcher; Consultant; b/Jun 21, 1949; h/Condo Emajagua/Calle Emajagua 4B/9, Santurce, Puerto Rico 00913; ba/Santurce; m/David Earl; p/Charles and Margaret Neumann, Larchmont, NY; ed/BA 1973; BA w hons 1974; MA w hons 1977; PhD Cand 1979; pa/Ednl Conslt Univ PR; Res Assoc Ind Univ; Dir Lng Disabilities San Juan Sch; Mainstreaming & Res Com Intl Reading Assn; Australian Reading Assn; Coun Exceptl Chd; Assn Lng Disabilities; Pvt Pilots Assn; cp/Wkshops Parents of Handicapped; Commun Ser Parental Ed; r/Presb; hon/Australian Commonwealth Res Awd; Intl Reading Res F'ship; Pub'd Author.

ROBINSON, OLIVER PRESTON oc/Author; Educator; Publishing Company Executive; b/Jun 25, 1903; h/15670 Lakeforest Dr, Sun City, AZ 85151; m/Christine Hinckley; c/Miriam, Bruce, Christine; p/James and Romina Chaffin Robinson (dec); ed/AB Brigham Yg Univ 1928; MS, DCS NYU 1928-35; pa/Gen Mgr Deseret News Press 1967-73; Pres Brit Mission Ch Jesus Christ Latter-Day Sts 1964-67; Gen Mgr Deseret News Pub Co 1950-64; Asst Dir War Tng Ctr, Head Dept Mktg & Dir Bur Mdse Ser Univ Utah 1947-50; Charge Mktg Instrn Nat Inst Credit 1935-46; Dir & Chm Bd Promised Lands Pubs; Spec Conslt Hardware Furniture, Dept & Jewelry Stores; Num Other Past Positions; Author or CoAuthor Books incl'g: *How to Est & Operate A Retail Shop* 1952, *Retail Store Org & Oper* 1956, *The Dead Sea Scrolls & Original Christianity* 1958, *Successful Retail Salesmanship* 1966, *Challenge of Scrolls* 1963, *Biblical Sites in Holy Land* 1963, *Israels Bible Lands* 1973, *Christs Eternal Gospel* 1976; Printing Industs Am Computer Assn; Alpha Kappa Psi; Eta Mu Pi; Phi Kappa Phi; cp/Pres Yth Tobacco Action Com; Rotary; Timpenogus; r/Mem Ch of Jesus Christ Latter-Day Sts; hon/Recipient Nat Allstate Crusade Am Awd; BYU: Fam Living Awd, Dist'd Ser Medal; Outstg Civilian Ser Medal & Cit, AUS; Merit Hon Awd, Univ Utah.

ROBINSON, PATRICIA ISABELL oc/Nurse; b/May 14, 1947; h/c/o J F Shea Co, PO Box 343, Heber City, UT 84032; ba/Same; p/Monroe and Isabell Tuck Robinson, Lovell, WY; ed/AS Mesa Col 1967; pa/Indust Nurse J F Shea Co Inc; Asst Head Nurse Oncology Unit & Adm Asst Patient Care Ser Providence Med Ctr 1973-79; Charge Nurse: Sacred Heart Hosp 1971-73, Ivinson Meml Hosp 1969-71; Supvr Fairbanks Commun Hosp 1967-69; Oncology Nsg Assn; cp/Spkr Am Cancer Soc; hon/W/W Am Wom.

ROBINSON, RALPH ROLLIN oc/Physician; b/Jul 7, 1913; h/322 Englewood Rd, Middlesboro, KY 40965; ba/M'boro; m/Mona Rae McGraw; c/Kim, Mark, Nancy, Ralph Jr, Rachel; p/Walter Robinson Sr (dec); Mary Inslee, Nashville, TN; ed/BE Okla St Univ 1935; MD Univ Wash Sch Med 1951; pa/Solo Pract Gynecologist; Med Pract: Pineville Commun Hosp 1963-, Claiborne Co Hosp 1963-, M'boro Commun Hosp 1963-, Swedish Hosp 1959-63, Miners Meml Hosp 1955-59; Tchg Positions: Ky St-Wide Fam Planning Proj, M'boro Appalachian Hosp, St Elizabeth Hosp, Num Labs; Participant: Maternal & Infant Care Proj Bell Co, M&I Clins, Pan-Am Med Assns 42nd Annual Cong, 5th Nat Cong Iranian Gynecologists & Obs; Conslt Num Profl Orgs; Paper Presentations; Diplomate Am Bd Ob-Gyn; Am Col: Surgs, Ob-Gyns; Wash St & Bell Co Med Socs; Seattle Profl Engrs Soc; Seattle Gynecological Soc; Pan-Pacific Surg Assn; Pan-Am & So Med Assns; Am Soc Abdominal Surgs; World Population Coun; r/Deacon 1st Presb Ch,

M'boro; hon/Inventor: Intra-Uterine Birth Control, Currette Device, Intra-Uterine U Stem Pessary, Disposal Shoe Cover, Intrauterine Device Inserter, Rotating Wing Aircraft, Shielded Intrauterine Device; Num Biogl Listings.

ROBINSON, RENAULT A oc/Director; b/Sept 8, 1942; h/7639 S Luella, Chicago, IL 60649; ba/Chgo, IL; m/Annette Richardson; c/Renault Jr, Brian, Kivu, Kobie; p/Robert Robinson (dec); Mabel Stevens Robinson; ed/MA Roosevelt Univ; pa/Exec Dir Afro-Am Patrolmen's Leag; Secy-Treas Leag Improve Commun; Nat Info Ofcr Nat Black Police Assn; Chgo Forum; Com Fgn & Domestic Affairs; Concerned Com Police Reform; Am Soc Criminology; Meeting Planners Intl; r/Cath; hon/Recog Awd: Cath Interracial Coun Chgo 1969, NIU-Black Arts Fest 1971, Leag Martin 1974; Civil Liberties Awd, Ill Div Am Civil Liberties Union; 1 of 10 Men of Yr, Chgo JCs; Humanitarian Awd, Yth for Christ Choir; Malcolm X Col: Cert Brotherhood, Cert Merit, Phi Beta Lambda Achmt Awd; Black Olympics Com Awd; Cert Awd, Search for Truth; NABSW Awds 1974-75; Ser Awds: Westside Christian Parish 1974, BSPA 1975, Paul J Hall Boys Clb 1975, Newspaper Guild 1976, Black SPEAR 1974; 3rd Annual Dr M L King Jr Awd, Suburban Chapt SCLC 1975; Awd Merit, Eternal Flames Prodn Inc 1975; I Am My Brothers Keeper, Policemen For A Better Gary 1975; Achmt Awds: Charles Douglas & Co, Minority Alliance Group, Black Student Psychol Assn; AABS Awd Excell; Humanitarian Ser Awd, Ctr for New Horizons Inc; Apprec Awds: The Guardians, Kiwanis Clb; Affirmative Action Awd, Breadbasket Comml Assn; Public Ser Awd, Cook Co Bar Assn.

ROBINSON, RICHARD HARDEN oc/- Municipal Judge; b/Mar 30, 1918; h/PO Box 2538, Palm Springs, CA 92263; ba/PS; c/- Richard Jr, Patricia, Pamela; p/William and Lillyan Green Robinson (dec); mil/USMC 1943-45; pa/Cal Judges Assn; cp/VP Boys Clb PS; Rotary; r/Prot.

ROCHOWICZ, JOHN ANTHONY JR oc/Teacher; b/Mar 20, 1950; h/41 Columbia Ave, SCM, Reading, PA 19606; ba/Same; p/John Sr and Sara Jane Rochowicz, Reading; ed/BS 1972, Sec'dy Tchg Cert 1975 Albright Col; MS Lehigh Univ 1974; pa/Math Tchr; MAA; cp/Alpha Phi Omega; r/Rom Cath; St Catharine Siena Ch, Mt Penn, Pa.

RODDEN, DONNA STRICKLAND oc/Mayor; b/Aug 10, 1926; h/327 W Bank St, Albion, NY 14411; ba/Albion; c/Roberta R Tundermann (Mrs Leonard), Ellen Capurso (Mrs Alphonse); p/Burroughs Strickland (dec); Mildred MacDuffie Strickland, Albion; ed/BS Syracuse Univ 1946; MS SUNY-B 1962; pa/Mayor Vil Albion 1973-; Lib Media Spec Albion Sch 1956-; TV Dir Cayton Inc 1950-56; Editor Lyndonville Enterprise 1948-50; r/Bapt; hon/Cit Pres Nixon; Wom in Govt Awd, Leag Wom Voters; Wom Who Changed World Awd, Nat Org Wom; Dist'd Ser Awd, GSA; CG Aux Cert.

RODENBURG, CARL E oc/Dentist; h/635 Versailles Dr SE, Huntsville, AL 35803; m/Helena Kumme (dec); c/3; ed/AB Univ Pa 1955; DDS Columbia Univ Sch Dental & Oral Surg 1961; Addit Studies; mil/AUS Dental Corps 1st Lt to Lt Col; Positions incl'd: Asst & Clin Chief, Supply & Property Book Ofcr, Asst Dental Surg-Yukon Command, Cmdg Ofcr 47th Med Dept, 8th Army Conslt Fixed Prosthodontics & Area III Coor; pa/Lectr Num Profl Assns; Am Dental Assn; Fdn Dentaire Internationale; 38th Parallel Dental Soc; Korean Mil Med Assn; Assn AUS; cp/ARC: Vol Ser 13 Yrs, Instr/Tnr 1st Aid, Dir Stay Fit Prog, Reg Safety Sers Chm US Forces Korea; Commodore Longfellow Soc; Nat Polar Bear Clb; Nat Rifle Assn; Nat Ski Patrol Sys; Pres Birch Hill Ski Clb; Radio Emer Assoc'd Citizens Teams; Fort Bragg Ser Team Parents Assn; AF&AM; Ancient & Accepted Scottish Rite Masons; Fayetteville York Rite; K Templar; Sudan Temple

AAONMS; Order Amaranth; OES; Heroes 76 Cornelius Harnett Camp; hon/Psi Omega; Theta Xi; ARC: 2500 Vol Hours Cert, Ser Medal; Awds of Merit for Lifesaving; Cert Apprec Yth Activs, Fort Bragg; Num Ser Awds, Ancient & Acccepted Scottish Rite Masons; Book Hon; W/W S&SW; Men Achmt.

RODENRYS, JOHN J oc/Businessman; Educator; b/May 17, 1944; h/4436 Caminito Fuente, San Diego, CA 92116; ba/SD; m/Barbara Myers; p/Peter and Annie McHugh Rodenrys, Centerport, NY; ed/BS Rensselaer Polytechnic Inst 1966; MS US Intl Univ 1969; pa/Pres & Ch Bd Med Data Sys Inc; Fac & Dir Fin Dimensions: SD Ext Univ Cal, SDSU Sch Bus; Am Prodn & Inventory Soc: Past VP Ed & Res, Past Dir Cont'g Ed; cp/Old Globe Theatre; SD Co Heart Assn; C of C; Zool Soc; Aztec Ath Foun; Alpha Tau Omega; hon/Recog Cert, APICS 1974 & 75.

RODGERS, WILLIAM HARRY SR oc/Engineer; b/Apr 11, 1916; h/716 E Main, Glasgow, KY 42141; ba/Glasgow; m/Annie Kathryn Dilley; c/Willian Jr; p/William Rodgers (dec); Mary Drake Rodgers, Wichita, KS; ed/Sch Elect Engrg Univ Ark 1935-37; Joplin Bus Col 1937-38; Grad Air Conditioning Tng Corp 1950; pa/Facility Engr Glasgow St ICF/SNF 1976-78; Hosp Engr Dist 6 St Tuberculosis & Respiratory Disease Hosp 1965-76; Owner & Operator W H Rodgers Plumbing & Heating Co; Other Past Positions; Nat, Am & Ky Socs Hosp Engrs; SEn Assn Hosp Engrs; Refrigeration Ser Engrs; cp/Chm Safety Com and Adm & Opers Com Glasgow Dept Human Resources; BSA; Rotary Clb; Barren Co Wildlife Conserv Clb; Qtrback Clb; Band Boosters; Aux Police; Mason; Shriner; OES; Order White Shrine; Order Amaranth; Dem; r/Presb: Ordained Deacon & Elder; hon/Ky Col; Ky Admiral; BSA: Eagle Scout Awd, Silver Beaver, Dist Merit Awd, God & Country Awd, Order Arrow, Chief Fire Bldrs, Scouters Awd, Scoutmaster Key; Cal Rogers Awd; Sportmans of Yr Awd; Num Masonic Hons; Num Biogl Listings.

RODKIEWICZ, CZESLAW MATEUSZ oc/Engineer; ba/Dept Mech Engrg, Univ Alberta, Edmonton, Alberta, Canada; m/Krystyna Lukasiewicz; ed/Dip Ing Polish Univ Col; MSc Univ Ill; PhD Cleveland Case Inst Technol; Grad Artillery Acad Zambrow; mil/Polish Home Army; Polish II Corps; pa/Prof Dept Mech Engr Univ Alberta 1958-; Engrg Div Atomic Energy Canada Ltd 1960; Eng Lab Nat Res Coun 1959; Staff Ryerson Inst Technol 1955; Tech Asst Dowty Equipment Ltd 1954; Res Engr Eng Elect Co; Lectr Num Profl Meetings & Orgs; NY Acad Scis; Am & Canadian SME; Sigma Xi; Profl Engr Ontario; Adv Coun & Chm 1st World Tribology Conf Indian Inst Technol Madras; Chm Nat Canadian Cong Applied Mechs; Polish Combatants Assn; Canadian-Polish Socs; cp/Alberta Water Resources Ctr; Engrg Fac Coun Com Univ Alberta; Bd Dirs Ctl & E European Studies Soc Alberta; Chm Com SESEM Day Care Centre; Edmonton Flying Clb; CEESSA: Chm Resolutions Com, Res & Acad Adv Com; hon/Gold Decoration Outstg Ser Commun, Polish Canadian Cong Alberta; Recipient Grant AAF; Pub'd Author; Num Biogl Listings.

RODRIGUEZ, BEATRIZ MARTA oc/Director; b/Apr 21, 1937; h/60 W 11 St Apt 7, Hialeah, FL 33010; ba/Miami, FL; p/Pedro Rodriguez (dec); Elena Borras Rodriguez, Miami; ed/Grad Orbon Conservatory Music 1959; BST Regina Virginum Col 1966; BSEd magna cum laude Medaille Col 1972; MS Barry Col 1975; PhD Cand Univ Miami; pa/Tchr: Lestonac Elem Sch 1958-59, Apostolado HS 1959-67, St Mary of Sorrows Jr HS 1967-68 & 70-71, St Matthews Jr HS 1968-70; Rel Coor Loyola Sch 1971-72; Asst Prin, Guid Cnslr & Dir Student Activs Curley HS 1977-; APGA; Regina Pi; cp/Dem; Num Vol Activs; r/Rom Cath; Develp Personality Progs Rel Commun; Coor Spanish Spkg Sisters Archdiocese; Del Sister Coun; Coor Rel Instr Team; hon/Recipient Awds Fields Music, Theology, Ed & Cnslg; Num Biogl Listings.

RODRIGUEZ, JOHN ALBERT oc/EEO Specialist; b/May 6, 1941; h/4211 Clark #4, Kansas City, MO 64111; ba/KC; c/Jason; p/Samuel and Anita Rodriguez, Dodge City, KS; ed/BAEd; MAEd; Spec Ed; mil/USAR; pa/Equal Employmt & Tng Ed; cp/Human Rts Comm; Sch Bd; r/Rom Cath.

RODRIGUEZ, JOHNNY GOMEZ oc/Accountant; b/May 15, 1945; h/612 Ave C, Sinton, TX 78387; ba/Sinton; p/Gregorio Rodriguez (dec); Josefa Gomez Rodriguez, Sinton; ed/AA; BBA; mil/USAF S/Sgt 1967-71; pa/Notary Public; Assn Chicano Accts; cp/Ams Lib Action; LULAC; r/Rom Cath; hon/S'ship Del Mar Col 1965-66.

RODRIGUEZ, MARTA ELENA oc/- Coordinator; b/Nov 21, 1934; h/427 NW 24 St, Miami, FL 33137; ba/Miami; p/Pedro Rodriguez (dec); Elena Borras Rodriguez, Miami; ed/BEd cum laude Univ Miami; MA Univ No Colo; Att'd Univ Villanova 1957-59; Grad Sch Cathechesis & Biblical Studies Archdiocese Havana; pa/Miami Dade Commun Col: Coor Bilingual Bicult Voc Prog, Psychol Instr; Past Tchr: Bible Studies & French Baldor & Lestonnac Acads, Miami HS, Carrollton, Miami Pvt Sch; Orgr Peer Conslg & Student-Parent Interaction Progs; Writer & Broadcaster Radio Progs Radio Free Cuba 1962-63; cp/Fdr Movimiento de Recuperacion Revolucionaria; Exec Coun Rosa Mistica Univ Sodality 1955-: Dir Biblical Studies, Newspaper Editor, Coor Social Work, Employmt Ser; Del Intl Cong Cath Students 1959; Del Intl Cong Cath Edrs 1964; cp/Active Bilingual Ed & Cuban-Am Acculturation Progs; Social Work; r/Rom Cath; hon/Tchr & Cnslr of Yr; Valedictorian Acad Sacred Heart Mary.

ROEMER, WILLIAM NICHOLAS oc/Scientist; Researcher; b/Feb 8, 1925; h/2150 Smallhouse Rd, Bowling Green, KY 42101; ba/Same; p/William Roemer (dec); Catherine Bosler Roemer; ed/Att'd BG Bus Univ; pa/FIBA Cambridge; Self-Employed: Agri Chems, Chem, Plastic & Mech Engrg, Res & Dev Var Types; cp/C of C; K of C; European Weed Soc; Ky Col; r/Cath; hon/Otho Chem Spokesman Yr Awd 1977-78; Top Farmers Am Assn Awd; CAST Awd; MA Cambridge; Pub'd Author; Fellow Intl Biogl Assn.

ROEPER, GEORGE A oc/Headmaster; b/Sept 7, 1910; h/7400 Franklin Rd, Box 693, Franklin, MI 48025; ba/Bloomfield Hills, MI; m/Anne Marie; c/Thomas, Peter, Karen R Larmon; p/George and Anna Roeper (dec); ed/EdD; PdD; pa/ASCD; Comparative Ed Soc Elem Sch Prins; r/Luth; hon/DD En Mich Univ.

ROESEL, CATHERINE ELIZABETH oc/Professor; b/Feb 6, 1920; h/2722 Cherry Ln, Augusta, GA 30909; ba/Augusta; p/Albert Roesel (dec); Ruth Stelling Roesel, Augusta; ed/BA Vanderbilt Univ 1941; PhD Washington Univ 1951; pa/Prof Dept Cell & Molecular Biol Med Col Ga; Author Immunology: A Self-Instrnl Approach; AAUW; NY & Ga Acad Scis; Canadian Soc Immunology; Reticuloendothelial Soc; Am Soc Microbiol; Am Tissue Cult Assn; Am Soc Tropical Med & Hygiene; AAAS; Delta Kappa Gamma; cp/Augusta Kennel Clb; Am & GA Boxer Clbs; r/Mem Evang Luth Ch of Resurrection; hon/Recipient Carnegie Inst of Wash F'ship; Phi Beta Kappa; Sigma Xi.

ROETSCHKE, RONALD CLAY oc/Oil & Gas Producer; Oil Field Pipe Dealer; b/Mar 18, 1934; h/1609 N Garfield, Midland, TX 79701; ba/Midland; m/Elizabeth; c/Martha Rice, Ramona Lindsey, Drucilla Morren; p/Augusta Jr and Susan Roetschke, Val Mills, TX; ed/BS Tex A&M Univ; pa/Nat Fdn Indep Bus; Soc Plastic Engrs; Petro Basin; Petro Assn; cp/Repub Nat Com; Am Security Coun; r/Luth; hon/W/W: MW, S&SW; DIB; Men Achmt.

ROETTGER, DORYE oc/Musician; Author; Lecturer; h/3809 DeLongpre Ave, Los Angeles, CA 90027; ed/BMus Univ Ext Conservatory 1955; PhD Univ En Fla 1972; Addit Studies; pa/Gen Adm Conslt & Ofc Mgmt Warner Sutton & Warner Law Firm; Public Relats Conslt: LA Co Dept Parks & Rec, N Am Corr Schs, Nat Sys Corp; Musicologist Conslt & Lectr Profl Orgs & Demos; Editor Indep News Bur; Syndicated Columnist "Bridging Cult Gap"; Journalist Num Other Publs; Instr Chamber Music Immaculate Heart Col; Profl Oboist Perfs incl'g: Concerts, Theatres, Opera, Films; Am Musicological Soc; Cal Mus Edrs Assn; Nat Assn Music Therapy; cp/Fdr Fest Players Cal; Chm Dept Ed Cal Fdn Music Clbs; Chm S'ship Com PIRATES; Leg Com Chm Cal Music Coun; Steering Com Commun Resource Unit LA City Schs Vol Prog; Fine Arts Chm Exploring Div LA Coun BSA; LA St Scene Fest Com; Intl Platform Assn; AFM; OES; hon/Meritorious Public Ser, Cal St Assembly; Cert Apprec, LA City Coun; Merit Awd, LA Co Bd Suprvrs; Cit: Congl Record, Proj Head Start, LA City Schs Vol Prog, Nat Fdn Music Clbs, LA Mayors Ofc & Vol Action Coun; Num Biogl Listings.

ROGERS, A ROBERT oc/Administrator; b/Sept 9, 1927; h/1965 Pine View Dr, Kent, OH 44240; ba/Kent; m/Rhoda Page; c/Mark; p/Amos and Ethel Lutes Rogers (dec); ed/BA Univ NB; MA Univ Toronto; PhD Univ Mich;

pa/Dean Sch Lib Sci Kent St Univ; Am, Ohio & Canadian Lib Assns; r/U Meth Ch, Kent: Comm Ed, Adm Bd; hon/Libn of Yr, Ohio Lib Assn.

ROGERS, GAYLE oc/Author; Teacher; b/May 17, 1923; h/207 Dickenson Ave, Newbury Park, CA 91320; m/Jack Bullington; c/2; p/Manley and Gladyce Horton Rogers; ed/Gen Sec'dy; pa/Tchr 26 Yrs; Author: The 2nd Kiss, Nakoas Wom; r/Ch Self-Realization; hon/Contemp Authors Am; W/W Am Wom; World W/W Wom; Commun Ldrs & Noteworthy Ams.

ROGERS, GIFFORD E oc/Consulting Engineer; b/May 22, 1920; h/%515 N Grace, Grand Isl, NE 68801; m/Edna Marjorie Mull; c/4; p/Frederick and Beulah Crabtree Rogers; ed/BSCE Univ Neb 1943; MSCE Purdue Univ 1948; pa/VP & Gen Mgr PRC Engrg Conslts Inc; Res Mgr WS/WS Proj, Lampung, Sumatra, Indonesia; NSPE; ASPA; AMA; Diplomate Am Acad Envir Engrs; Fellow ASCE; Profl Engr Neb 1951; cp/Chm Fin Com BSA; hon/Sigma Xi; Dipl of Hon, Guatemala; Am Registry Series; Notable Ams.

ROGERS, HERBERT FRANCIS oc/Educator; Minister; b/Mar 12, 1911; h/756 Havenridge Dr, Conyers, GA 30207; ba/Atlanta, GA; m/Mary Louise Rhoton; c/Karen Daniel, Janine Harris; p/Edwin Rogers; Evelyn Schettenhelm; ed/BA 1946, MTh 1949, PhD 1951 Univ So Cal; pa/Edr & Chm Dept Rel & Phil Clark Col; cp/Optimist Clb; r/Grace U Meth Ch; Min Mem Pacific SW Conf; hon/Commun Ldrs & Noteworthy Ams; Notable Ams.

ROGERS, LORENE LANE oc/Adminis- trator; Professor; b/Apr 3, 1914; h/4 Nob Hill Cir, Austin, TX 78746; ba/Austin; m/Burl Gordon (dec); p/Mort and Jessie Lane (dec); ed/BA N Tex St Col 1934; MA 1946, PhD 1948 Univ Tex; pa/Univ Tex: Pres 1975-, VP 1971-74, Assoc Dean Grad Sch 1964-71, Prof Nutrition 1962-, Lectr Chem 1961-63, Res Scist Clayton Foun Biochem Inst 1950-64; AAAS;

ACS; AIC; AIN; Am Soc Human Genetics; Am Coun Ed; Intl T&T; Nat Assn St Univs & Land-Grant Cols; Nat Sci Foun; Alpha Lambda Delta; Iota Sigma Pi; Omicron Delta Kappa; Phi Kappa Phi; Sigma Xi; cp/SW Tex Public Broadcasting Coun; Bd Vis Air Univ Maxwell AFB; Adv Bd KTBC-TV; Bd Dirs: Gulf St Utilities, Texaco Inc; Adv Com Tex Leg Conf; Adv Coun Austin Symph; Eng Spkg Union; Open Forum; hon/Univ Tex: Students Assn Tchg Excell Awd, Eli Lilly Postdoct Fellow, Parke & Davis Predoct Fellow, Dist'd Alumnus Awd; Outstg Wom of Yr: Austin Statesmen 1960 & 71, Wom Communs 1974; Wom Agents Change Awd, AAUW; Dist'd Alumnus Awd, N Tex St Univ; DSc Oakland Univ 1972; DLaw Austin Col 1977; Num Biogl Listings.

ROGERS, MARY VIRGINIA oc/Gastrointestinal Clinical Specialist; b/Nov 1, 1938; h/4317 Burgundy Rd, Memphis, TN 38111; p/Leonard and Mary Rogers; ed/RN St Joseph Hosp Sch Nsg 1959; BSN 1977, MS 1979 Univ Tenn-M; pa/Gastrointestinal Clin Spec & Bus Mgr Pvt Phys 1979-; Phys Asst, Trustee & Bus Mgr Pvt Phys 1972-79; Head Nurse Pvt Phys Ofc 1965-72; St Joseph Hosp: Head Nurse Med/Surg Unit 1961-65; Head Nurse Emer Room 1960, Staff Nurse 1959-60; cp/Memphis Metro Opera; Mid-S Opera Guild; r/Epis; hon/Nat Beta Clb; Commun Ldrs Am.

ROHRER, WILLIAM GLEN oc/Consultant; b/Jul 28, 1916; h/PO Box 16, Redlands, CA 92373; ba/Same; m/Lillian Mae Akins; p/(dec); ed/AS Marion Mil Inst 1937; BA Univ Redlands 1942; Addit Studies; pa/Conslt Space Sci & Aerospace Ed: Riverside Flight Acad, Cal-Brown Flight Acad, N Am Aircraft Div, Republic Aviation Co, Atomics Intl; Staff Scist Res & Adv'd Devel Div Avco 1962-63; Sr Res Scist N Am Aviation Co 1960-61; Prin Astrophysicist Republic Aviation Corp 1958-60; Other Past Positions; Num Profl

Orgs incl'g: Cal Aerospace Ed Assn, Am Astronautical Soc, Astronomical Soc Pacific; Pub'd Author Approx 100 Tech Papers & Reports US, England, Germany & Republic China; cp/Former Dep Sheriff R'side Sheriffs Resv Corp; Former Group Tng & Opers Ofcr CAP; Bd Govs Edison Tech Col; R'side Co Civil Def Coun; Govs Spec Aviation Com Liaison Com Higher Ed; Cal Aviation Adv Com; r/Prot; hon/Astronautische Gesellschaft der DDR 1965; Intl Platform Assn; Intercontinental Biogl Assn; Hon Socs; Num Biogl Listings.

ROHRKASTE, DONALD WAYNE oc/Educator; Minister; b/Mar 26, 1935; h/1121 Maple Ave, Niagara Falls, NY 14305; ba/NF; m/Beatrice Baker; p/Roy Rohrkaste (dec); Gladys Walters Rohrkaste, Pittsburgh, PA; ed/BA Univ Pgh; MDiv Bangor Theol Sem; EdM Univ Buffalo; SLD En Neb Christian Col; pa/Eng Tchr; Pastor: Currently 1st Congreg Ch U Ch of Christ NF, Guys Mills Congreg Ch & Park Congreg Ch Meadville, Corinth Meth Ch Corinth; Spkr Num Sers & Orgs; Chm Radio Broadcast Coun Chs & Min Assn; cp/Chaplain Alcoholic Anonymous Group; NF Coun Chs; Cnslr: 1st Presb Boys Clb Pgh, Calvary Epis Camp; Participant Love Loaf & Foster Child Projs; Kiwanis Intl; Intl Platform Assn; Chm Phi Theta; Kappa Phi Kappa; Beta Tau; r/Prot; Congreg; Mt Wash Commun Ch: Choir, Trustee, Adult Supt Ch

Sch, Pres Pilgrim F'ship; hon/Outstg Yg Man Am; Outstg Sec'dy Edr Am; W/W Rel; Commun Ldrs & Noteworthy Ams; Intl Men Achmt; Intl Dic Biogs; DDiv Am Div Sch; Doc Lttrs & Laws Clarksville Sch Theol; Pub'd Author.

ROLLINS, DAVID T oc/Rehabilitation Consultant; b/Apr 27, 1935; h/7112 SE 27th Ave, Portland, OR 97202; ba/P'land; m/Ellie; c/Lynn, Jason, Scott; ed/BS Univ ND 1964; MS Canisius Col Buffalo 1965; PhD Univ Oreg Med Sch 1971; mil/AUS Pers Info & Ed Spec 1957-61; pa/Pres & Chief Operational Ofcr Rehab Consltg Sers Corp 1976-; Hlth Care & Rehab Conslt Pvt Pract 1972-76; Head Aural Rehab Sers P'land Ctr Univ Oreg Med Sch 1971-72; Other Former Positions; APHA; APGA; ARCA; ASHA; NRA; NRCA; Nat Assn Disability Examiners; Voc Eval & Work Adjustment Assn; cp/P'land Knife & Fork Clb; Intl Clb Hilton; hon/HEW S'ship; VRA & NIH F'ships; NY St Res Grant; Num Biogl Listings.

ROLSTON, MARGARET ELIZABETH oc/Realtor & Insurance Agent; b/Mar 10, 1910; h/804 Shannon Ln, Kirksville, MO 63501; m/Howard (dec); c/James, Ann Barlow; p/Marvin and Beryl Florea; ed/BS NE Mo St Univ 1932; pa/Partner & CoOwner Rolston & Rolston Realty & Ins; Tchr 2 Yrs; Orgr & 1st Pres St Chapt Woms Coun Real Est; Dir Mo St Real Est Assn; Nat, Mo & Pres NE Ctl Bd Realtors; cp/Bd Dirs & VP NE Mo Hlth & Wel Coun Inc; Adv Com "Child Devel Prog" N Mo St Univ; Chrperson K'ville Home

Show; Bd Trustees K'ville Col Osteopathic Med; Bd Govs K'ville Osteopathic Hosp; Dir C of C; Bd Adjustments City K'ville; Pres Adair Co PTA; Dir & Secy ARC; Orgr Red Cross Gray Lady Prog; Dir Cerebral Palsy Bd; Sojourners Clb; OES; El Kadir Jewels; Intl Platform Assn; Phi Kappa Sigma; Omega Tau Rho; Repub Party; r/Mem Christian Ch; hon/Fellow: Intl Inst Commun Sers, Intercontinental Biogl Assn; Num Biogl Listings.

ROMAIN, MARGARET A oc/Public Accountant; b/Jan 1, 1940; h/125 Koehler Dr, Sharpsville, PA 16150; ba/Sharon, PA; m/Joseph; c/Lucretia, Kimberly, Annette; p/Peter and Susie Murcko Kutcher; ed/Profl Certs; pa/Owner & Partner: Romain-Pendel Ofc Rental 1976-, R-P Computer Sers 1976-; Partner Public Acctg Romain-Pendel & Assocs 1976-; Self-Employed Public Acctg 1970-76; Num Other Past Positions; St Bd Dirs & Secy Pa Soc Public Accts; Asst St Dir Nat Soc Public Accts; Pa & Exec Dir St Pa Nat Assns Enrolled Agts; cp/Saddlemates Saddle Clb; Baldwin Organ Clb; Chwom Chds Pet Parade Sharpsville Centennial; 4-H Ldr S'ville Charmettes; Repub; r/St Johns Epis Ch: Asst Treas, Exec Bd Epis Chwom; hon/1st Runner-Up Queens Contest, S'ville Centennial; Ser Awd, Pa Assn Enrolled Agts; Num Biogl Listings.

ROMAN de JESUS, JOSE C oc/Anesthesiologist; h/K-22 Riverside, San German, Puerto Rico 00753; ba/Mayaguez, PR; m/Elizabeth; c/Jose, Rosa, Carlos, Maria, Ernesto; p/Jose Roman Rios, Margarita, Cabo Rojo; Candida Rosa de Jesus, Margarita, Cabo Rojo; ed/MD; BS; pa/Fdr & Chief Dept Anesthesiology Hosp de la Concepcion 1962-74; Ret'd Mem Hosp Bella Vista

Mayaguez Med Ctr; Lectr & Writer Sci & Polit Topics; cp/Puerto Rican Socialist Party; hon/W/W S; Personalities S.

ROMERO-BARCELÓ, CARLOS ANTONIO oc/Governor; b/Sept 4, 1932; h/La Fortaleza, San Juan, Puerto Rico 00901; ba/Same; m/Kate Donnelly de Romero; c/Juan, Melinda, Carlos, Andres; p/Antonio Romero-Moreno (dec); Josefina Barcelo-Bird, SJ; ed/BA Yale 1953; LLB Univ PR 1956; pa/Gov PR 1977-; Mayor SJ 1969-77; Nat & So Govs Assns; Pres Nat Leag Cities; cp/Pres New Progressive Party 1974-; r/Rom Cath; hon/JCs Outstg Yg Man of Yr 1968; James J & Jane Hoey Awd, Cath Interracial Coun NY; LLD Univ Bridgeport.

ROMINE, JOANNE BARBARA oc/-Handwriting Analyst; b/Jul 28, 1932; ba/PO Box 6482, Modesto, CA 95355; c/Deborah Sinclair (Mrs Richard), David, Diane Miller (Mrs Kenneth) (dec); Doug, Daniel, Denise; p/Ellis Penny; Josephine Elliot Porter, Modesto; pa/Handwriting Analyst 1959-; Marriage Cnslr 1960-; Lectr & Tchr 1964-; Syndicated Newspaper Columnist 1964-; Conslt Psychs & Psychologists 1969-; Personal Analyst Phyllis Diller, Robert Goulet & Other Notables 1972-; Fdr Intl Inst Handwriting Analysis; Intl Platform Assn; r/Latter Day St; Mormon; hon/Ygs Poetry Awd; W/W: Am, World.

ROMO, OSCAR I oc/Minister; Denominational Executive; b/Jan 29, 1929; h/2895 Delcourt Dr, Decatur, GA 30033; ba/Atlanta, GA; m/Zoe Harmon; c/Nelson, Miriam; p/Jose Romo (dec); Concepcion Romo; ed/BA Howard Payne Col; BD SWn Bapt Theol Sem; mil/AUS Chaplain; pa/Pastor: Brady, Tex 1948-51, Littlefield, Tex 1951-52, Iglesia Bautista Buena Voluntad, Ft Worth, Tex 1953-56; Assoc Lang Missions Dept Bapt Gen Conv Tex 1956-65; Home Mission Bd Atlanta: Asst Secy Lang Missions Dept 1965-70, Dir Lang Missions Dept 1971-; Adj Prof: MWn

Bapt Theol Sem, Golden Gate Bapt Theol Sem; Contbr Var Denom Pubs; Editor Spanish Edition *The Bapt Standard*; Dir'd 1st St-Wide Latin Am Kgn Wkshop 1964; Planned & Conducted: 1st Bapt Yth Cong, 1st Catalytic Ch Growth Conf 1966; Devel'd "Self-Support Achmt Guide" to Lead Chs Become Self-Supporting; Christian Ed Comm SBC; Ext Work Missions Other Countries; r/So Bapt; hon/DDiv Cal Bapt Col 1976; DHL Linda Vista Bapt Col 1975.

RONEY, ALICE MANN oc/Poet; b/Dec 6, 1926; h/1105 Georgina Ave, Santa Monica, CA 90402; ed/AA SMC 1946; BA UCLA 1950; pa/Tech Writer Hughes Aircraft Co 1949-52;

Corr'g Secy Ebell Jrs, Ebell Los Angeles 1958-59; Chm Ebell Jr Blind Recording 1959-63; Libn St Augustine Epis Day Sch 1961-68; Altar Guild Dir St Augustine-by-the-Sea Epis Ch 1969-71; Treas Epis Chwom Diocese LA 1970-73; Pres Cal Chapt PEO 1976-; Author: *Those Treasured Moments, Seeds of Love, Psalms for My Lord*; Contbr Poetry Jours & Anthologies; hon/Ebell Jr Ser Awd, Ebell of LA; Recog Ebell Jrs; Cerit Merit: Major Poets Chapt, Am Poets F'ship Soc; Intl W/W Poetry; World W/W Wom; DIB; Intl Register Profiles.

ROPER, JOHN WARREN oc/Minister; b/May 19, 1943; h/802 W 8th St, Tifton, GA 31794; ba/Tifton; m/Jane Roberta Johnson; c/Nathaniel, Christopher; p/Harley and Ellen Passmore Roper, Topton, NC; ed/BA; MDiv; pa/Bapt Min; Pastorates Va, NC & Ga; cp/Chaplain Civitan Clb; r/Bapt; So Bapt Conv; hon/W/W: NC, Rel.

ROPER, ROBERTA JOHNSON oc/Registered Nurse; b/Nov 6, 1942; h/802 W 8th St, Tifton, GA 31794; m/John; c/Nathaniel, Christopher; p/Robert and Jane Fluker Johnson (dec); ed/RN Ga Bapt Hosp Sch Nsg; BS Tift Col; pa/Currently Head Infection Control Tift Gen Hosp; Instr: RN Sch Nsg Berry Col, Floyd Hosp; Dir Nsg Granville Hosp; r/Bapt.

ROPP, RONALD DAVID oc/Chaplain; Pastoral Counselor; b/Aug 19, 1936; h/R #8, Box 73-A, Normal, IL 61761; ba/Bloomington, IN; m/Martha Jo Emerick; c/Martin, Jon; p/Peter and Anna Kropf Ropp, Normal; ed/BS; MDiv; DRel; pa/Chaplain &

Cnslr Mennonite Hosp; Fellow & Secy Am Col Chaplains; Assn Clin Pastoral Ed; cp/Bd Trustees Bluffton Col; Bd Mtl Hlth Ctr; Bd Ctr Human Resources; r/VP Hlth & Wel Com Mennonite Ch; Past Pres Mennonite Chaplains Assn; hon/Num Biogl Listings.

ROPPOLO, JOHN WAYNE oc/Administrator; b/Apr 1, 1939; h/3227 Grantwood, Dallas, TX 75229; ba/Dallas; m/Marilyn Royce; c/Robin, Joseph, John, Mary; p/Mrs J L Seyler, Waco, TX; ed/BA Baylor Univ 1961; Postgrad Studies; pa/VP Commun Relats St Paul Hosp 1971-; Am Col Hosp Admrs; Tex & Am Hosp Assns; Past Pres Tex Soc Hosp Public Relats; Am Soc Hosp PR Dirs; PR Soc Am; cp/Past Pres: Diocese of Dallas Bd Ed, St Monica Home & Sch Assn; PR Com Dallas Hosp Coun; Pres Tex Conf Cath Hlth Facilities; 500 Inc; Bd Dirs: Chapel Downs Commun Ctr, Dallas Co Chapt Am Heart Assn; Adv Com & PR Chm Ldrship Dallas; Bd

Dirs & Exec Com Cath Charities; Adv Com HS Hlth Profls; Hlth Achmt Com Goals for Dallas; Citizens Safety Adv Com; r/Rom Cath.

ROSE, ALLEN oc/Show Promoter; Master Wood Craftsman; b/Apr 7, 1928; h/Rt 4, Box 347, Picayune, MS 39466; m/Dana Lee; c/Richard, Steven, Patrica, Lee; p/L R Rose (dec); Irna Rose, Isabel, KS; mil/NG 7 Yrs; pa/Active 5 Art Leags; cp/Cub Scout Ldr; Preserve Am Heritage; r/Bapt.

ROSE, AUBERT V JR oc/Baptist Evangelist; b/Apr 5, 1926; h/5935 Bluebonnet Cir, Col Park, GA 30349; ba/Same; m/Katheren; c/Ann, Esther, Sarah; p/Aubert Rose Sr; Sophia Rose, Benton, KY 42025; ed/BS 1954; BB 1955; mil/AUS 1944-46;

pa/Pres & Fdr Ch Renewal Crusades Inc; Revival & Conf Spkr; Ordained Min So Bapt Conv Chs 26 Yrs; Former Public Sch Tchr; cp/Moderator Bapt Assns; VP Bapt St Conv; Bds St & So Bapt Convs; r/Mem 1st Bapt Ch, Col Park, Ga; Affil'd: Atlanta Bapt Assn, Ga Bapt Conv, So Bapt Conv; hon/HS Valedictorian 1943.

ROSELL, ANTOINETTE FRASER oc/School Counselor; b/Sept 18, 1926; h/4200 Rimrock Rd, Billings, MT 59102; ba/Billings; m/Earl Leonard Jr; c/Erleen R Royden, Earl III, Rene; p/Robert Fraser (dec); Rosabel Walter Fraser, Billings; ed/BA Univ Mont 1948; Dipl Univ Oslo 1951; MA Columbia Univ Tchrs Col 1952; pa/Asst Prin & Dean Girls Billings Sr HS 1967-73; Sch Cnslr Lincoln Jr HS 1965-67 & 1973-; Cnslr Yth Guid Coun Billings 1958-59 & 1961-64; Dir Student Activs En Mont Col 1954-56; Dean Girls Missoula Co

HS 1950-51; Senator Dist #7 Mont Pers & Guid Assn; Past Pres Delta Kappa Gamma; Nat Order Wom Legs; cp/Mont House Reps 1957-58 & 1961-64; Senate 1967-76; Asst Minority Ldr 1975-76; Mont Coor Com Intl Woms Yr; Nat Adv Coun Ec Opport; Zonta Intl; Bus & Profl Wom; Daus of Nile; DAR; Am Legion Aux; r/Presb; hon/Wom of Yr; 1 of 3 1957, Billings 1967, Mont 1967.

ROSEN, DORAH STERNE oc/Civic Leader; b/Nov 3, 1933; h/3225 Carlisle Rd, Birmingham, AL 35213; m/Lawrence; c/Dorah, Allan, Jacob; p/Mervyn Sterne; Dorah Heyman Sterne, B'ham; ed/BA Oberlin Col; cp/B'ham Planning Comm 1972-77; CoChm Com Land Use Plan, Zoning Adv Com; 1st VP & Bd Camp Fire Yth; NCJW; AAUW; LWV; Urban Leag; Nat & Local Dem Party; r/Reform Jewish; hon/Nom'd B'ham Wom of Yr.

ROSENBERG, ALEX J oc/Executive; b/May 25, 1919; h/3 E 69 St, New York, NY; ba/NY; m/Carole; c/Lawrence, Andrew; p/Israel and Lena Rosenberg; ed/Att'd Albright Col 1935-37 & Sch of Philadelphia Mus Art 1937-40; mil/USAAF 2nd Lt 1943-45; pa/Pres: Transworld Art Inc, Alex Rosenberg Gallery & Alba Editions; Gen Partner: Rostin Assocs 1970-, Lakewood Plaza Assocs 1973-; VP & Dir Starfax Corp 1968-70; Pres & Dir: BFC-CATV Corp 1966-71, Modern Cable Corp 1966-71; Num Other Past Positions; Lectr Parsons Sch Design; Art Appraiser; Bd: Artists Rts Today, Assn Artist-Run Galleries; cp/Dem Dist Ldr 1964-74; Dem St Com-man 1970-73; NY Co Dem Exec Com 1964-74; Del Dem Nat Conv 1968 & 72; NDC Coor NY Co 1969; Other Polit Positions; Trustee: Guttman Inst, Givat Haviva, New Lincoln Sch, Stephen Wise Free Synagogue; VP & Dir W Side C of C; SANE: Dir Nat Bd, Dir NY Coun; Commun Planning Bd; Dir Lower W Side Anti-Poverty Bd; Bd Nat Emer Civil Liberties Comm; Lincoln Ctr Commun Coun; So Elections Fund; Friends Wel Rts Org; r/Stephen Wise Free Synagogue; hon/Best Graphic Pubr, Grenchan Triennial; Israel Prize; Pub'd Author.

ROSENBLUM, HAROLD oc/Electronics Engineer; b/Mar 30, 1918; h/1310 Webster St, Orlando, FL 32804; ba/Kissimmee, FL; m/Hannah Berenice; c/Lawrence, Susan, Ira; p/Joseph Rosenblum (dec); Sadie Rosenblum, Danbury, CT; ed/BCHE Cooper Union 1943; MEE NYU 1951; mil/USN Elect Tech Mate 3/C 1945-46; pa/Dir Tech Sales Applied Devices Corp 1977-; Conslt Num Cos 1974-77; Nav Tng Equipment Ctr 1954-74: Deputy Dir Engrg, Head Sys Engrg Dept, Asst Tech Dir, Head Aerospace Sys Tnr Dept; Head Radar Sys Design Group & Elect Engr NY Nav Shipyard 1941-54; IEEE; NY Acad Scis; Sigma Xi; Sci Res Soc Am; cp/Pres PTA; r/Jewish; Bd Trustees Temple Israel; CoChm Cath/Jewish Dialogue Gtr Orlando; Vol Tchr: Inst Jewish Life, Hebraica HS; Congreg Ohev Shalom: Bd Trustees, Chm Rel & Ed Coms, Vol Tchr Rel Sch; hon/Superior Accomplishment Awds 1960, 63 & 64, USN.

ROSENWALD, CELIA KAY oc/Singer; Administrator; b/Jul 3, 1944; h/15, Grosvenor Gardens, London N.W. 2 England; ba/London W.1 England; p/Monte Rosenwald (dec); Marian Rosewald, Amarillo, TX; ed/LTCL; ARCM; pa/Personal Asst to Dir Studies Trinity Col Music; Tchr/Lectr; Soloist Opera Singer Major Concert Halls London; Fellow Trinity Col; cp/PEO; r/Epis; hon/Recipient Ricordi Opera Prize; Elisabeth Schumann Lieder Prize.

ROSET, WILFRED LAURIER oc/Chaplain; b/Jan 10, 1927; h/103 Madison St, Anaconda, MT 59711; ba/Warm Springs, MT; m/Leila Margaret MacIntosh; c/Grant, Gayle, Gregory; p/Bent Roset (dec); Eline Roset, Regina, Sask, Canada; ed/BTh Wn Bible Col & Sem 1949; Cert Univ Utah 1967 & 69; pa/Chaplain WS St Hosp 1968-; Pastored Chs: Morden, Manitoba; Powers Lake, ND; New Eng, ND; Wolf Point, Mont; Anaconda, Mont; Secy ND Evang SS Assn 1956-62; St Yth Pres ND Dist Assemblies God 1953-58; ND Youngest Presbyter 1953; AMHC; hon/W/W Rel.

ROSS, BECKY ANNE oc/Ballet Dancer; b/Mar 31, 1949; h/352 Maple Terrace, Pittsburgh, PA 15211; ba/Pgh; p/H D and Evelyn Ross, Winter Park, FL; pa/Ballet Dancer Pgh Ballet Theater; Dancer 4 European Ballet Cos 1970-77; Soloist Geneva & Nat Ballets; Toured Europe, Canada & S Am; r/Presb; hon/Acclaim *London Times* Up and Coming Yg Soloist.

ROSS, CHARLOTTE PACK oc/Executive Director; b/Oct 21, 1931; h/445 Virginia Ave, San Mateo, CA 94402; ba/Burlingame, CA; c/Beverly, Sandra; p/Joseph Pack (dec); Rose Pack, Shawnee Mission, KS; ed/Att'd Univ Okla 1949-52 & New Sch Social Res 1952-53; pa/Exec Dir Suicide Preven & Crisis

Ctr SM Co; Editor *Newslink* Bultn AAS 1975-76; Edit Bd *Suicide & Life-Threatening Behavior*; Secy & Bd Dirs Am Assn Suicidology; Intl Assn Suicide Preven; Am & Cal Public Hlth Assns; Pres Assn U Way Agy Execs; cp/Reg Selection Panel Pres Comm White House F'ship 1975-78; Revenue Sharing Comm; Chm Spec Progs Suicidology Univ Cal Sch Med; Comprehensive Hlth Planning Coun; VP & Bd Dirs Belmont Hills Neuropsychi Ctr Adolescent Foun; r/Jewish; hon/Outstg Ser Awd; Commun Achmt Awd; NIMH and Cal Dept Hlth Grants; Pub'd Author; W/W Am Wom; Intl W/W World; Personalities W&MW.

ROSS, MARY JANE oc/Accountant; Comptroller; b/Mar 7, 1906; h/222 E Water St, Rockland, MA 02370; ba/Same; p/Alexander and Jane Kirkpatrick Ross (dec); ed/AA Fisher Jr Col 1931; BA NWn Col 1978; pa/Ret'd Bus Exec 46 Yrs; cp/Mass Repub Clb; Royal Matron Order Amaranth; Past Worthy High Priestess & Treas Order White Shrine Jerusalem; Past Matron, Secy & Treas OES; Deg Pocahontas; Girl Scout Troop Work Lt 10 Yrs; r/Clerk Quincy Point Congreg Ch 1944-54; hon/Jervis B Webb Co Awd; 50 Yr Mbrship Pins OES & WSJ; Hon Mem Palestine Shrine.

ROSS, SUE G oc/Art Instructor; b/Mar 19, 1924; h/Box 450 Rt 2, Ashland, KY 41101; m/Lloyd; c/Bridgett Harding, Jo Anna Sturgill; p/Arthur and Samantha Greene (dec); ed/A'land Bus Col; pa/Tchr Art A'land Commun Col Br Univ Ky; 1 Man Show Ky Fair; Collections: Ky Govs Mansion, Num Art Galleries Ky; cp/A'land Art Gallery; Ky Creative Art; r/Bapt; hon/Ky Wom Artist 1977; 1 of Top 3 Artists Ky.

ROSSELLI, CHARLES ANTHONY oc/- Engineer; b/Sep 13, 1945; h/69 Mt Vernon St, Somerville, MA 02145; ba/Boston, MA; m/Marsha Elaine Read; p/Anthony C Rosselli (dec); Eleanor J Gaumond Rosselli; ed/AS Wentworth Inst 1965; BS 1969, MS NEn Univ 1974; Doctl Candidate, Tufts Univ; pa/Assoc Prof Civil Engrg, Wentworth Inst of Technol 1970-; Conslt'g Engr, Civil & Environ Engrg 1976-; Field & Lab Engr, Golder-Gass Assn Conslt'g Engrs 1965-70; Cert'd Fallout Shelter Analyst, US Govt; Am Soc Civil Engrs; Boston Soc Civil Engrs: Var Coms; Am Soc Engrg Ed; Soc Am Mil Engrs; New England Water Pollution Control Assn Inc; New England Water Works Assn; AAAS; cp/Public Lib of City of Somerville Bd Trustees; Minute Man Reg Tech HS Instrumentation Adv Bd; Environ Protection Devel Panel, Mario Umana Magnet Sch (Boston); Notary Public; hon/ASEE Dow Chem Outstg Yg Fac Awd; Tau Alpha Pi Curric & Res Grant; EPA Stipend Recipient; HEW Grant; Biogl Listings.

ROSZELL, CALVERT THEODORE JR oc/Attorney; b/Mar 30, 1924; h/1840 Blairmore Ct, Lexington, KY; ba/L'ton; m/Nancy; c/Calvert III, Stephen, Kathryn; p/Calvert Sr and Besse Byrd Roszell (dec); ed/LLB Univ Ky 1948; mil/95th Inf Div WW-II; pa/Adjunct Prof Col Law Univ Ky 1956-; cp/Co Judge Pro Tem 1956-61; Pres: L'ton Rotary Clb, Blue Grass Coun, Boy Scouts; ARC; r/Meth; hon/Outstg Yg Man Fayette Co, Jr C of C 1959; Silver Beaver, Boy Scouts; 95th Inf Div: Combat Inf Badge, Bronze Star,

FTO w/5 Battle Stars; W/W: S&SW, Am Law.

ROTH, FREDERIC HULL oc/Public Accountant; b/Feb 20, 1914; h/20661 Avalon Dr, Rocky River, OH 44116; ba/Cleveland, OH; m/Emmy Alice Braun; c/Frederic Jr, Robert; p/Stanley and Myrtle Hull Roth (dec); ed/AB Wooster Col 1935; MBA Harvard 1937; pa/CPA: Ohio 1942, La 1963, Va 1968, NC 1971; Started w Scovell, Wellington & Co 1939, Partner 1952; Merged w Lybrand, Ross Brothers & Montgomery 1962, Partner Coopers & Lybrand 1973; C'land Chapt OSCPA: Treas, VP, Past Pres, Dir, Chm Var Coms; OSCPA: Past Dir, Past VP, Chm Var Coms, Past Pres-Elect, Past Pres; Former Coun Am Inst CPAs; Past Bd Govs Inst Internal Auditors; NAA; AIM; cp/Past Dir & Treas Rotary Clb; Yacht Clb: Past Treas, Past Dir, Rear Commodore, Past VCommodore, Past Commodore; Intl Order Blue Gavel: Former CYC Chapt Secy Treas, Past Pres; Dist

9 IOBG: Past Secy, Past Treas, Past Pres, Past En VP, 3/VP, 2/VP 1978; Play House: Former Dir & Treas, Past Dir, Past Fin Com; Nat Adv Bd Am Security Coun; SAR; Al Koran Shrine; Newcomen Soc N Am; Intl Platform Assn; Harvard Bus Sch Clb; C of C; Union Clb; Westwood Country Clb; Others; r/Rocky River U Meth Ch; hon/W/W: Am, Ohio, NW, Fin & Indust, World, US; Ohio Lives; Nat Reg Prom Ams & Intl Notable; Intl Yrbook & Statemens W/W; 2000 Men Achmt; Nat Cyclopedia Am Biog; DIB; Intercont Biogl Assn; Intl W/W: Commun Ser, Intells; Men Achmt; Intl Reg W/W; Outstg Ams; Intl Reg Profiles; Notable Ams Bicent Era; Ency Proud Bicent Am; Lib Human Resources; Quest-W/W; C'land Blue Book; Blue Book; Royal Blue Book; Nat Soc Dir; Soc Reg; Personalities W&MW; Book Hon.

ROTHMAN, BARRY KENNETH oc/- Lawyer; b/Jun 12, 1942; ba/9200 Sunset Blvd, Los Angeles, CA 90069; c/Mathew; p/- Abraham Rothman; Lilliam Leiblein; ed/BA Univ Cal-LA 1965; JD SWn Univ 1970; pa/- Admitted Cal Bar & US Dist Ct Bar 1970; Am & LA Co Bar Assns; St Bar Cal; r/Jewish.

ROUGHTON, WILLIAM WESLEY oc/- Clergyman; b/Mar 24, 1925; h/2200 7 St N, St Petersburg, FL 33704; ba/SP; m/Lounettee McCullough; c/Kenneth, Philip, Mrs Judith Rustin; p/William Roughton (dec); Easter Bell, Sandersville, GA; ed/BA, DD Asbury Col; BD Asbury Theol Sem; pa/Sr Pastor Christ U Meth Ch, SP; cp/Kiwanis Intl Foun; r/U Meth; hon/Man of Yr, Delray Bch 1977.

ROUSE, ERNEST PHILIP oc/Entomologist; b/Aug 5, 1913; h/849 Kelly, Fayetteville, AR 72701; ba/F'ville; m/Marie May Shaffer; c/George, Joe; p/Ernest and Mary Arminda Rouse (dec); ed/BSA, MS Univ Ark; mil/USN; pa/Entomologist Univ Ark; Entomol Soc Am; Ks Entomol Soc; Ark Acad Sci; Alpha Lambda Tau; Gamma Sigma Delta; cp/Dem; SAR; Master Mason Pine Bluff Lodge 69; r/Presb; hon/3 USN Medals 1940; Entomol Hon Soc Outstg Achmt 1956.

ROUTON, JUDITH DIANE oc/Representative; b/Dec 16, 1952; h/Heritage Hills Trailer Park, Jonesboro, AR 72401; ba/J'boro; p/P C and Lola Watts Routon, Marmaduke, AR; ed/BA Ark St Univ; pa/Reg Rep

Commun Sers Div Ark Mtl Retardation Devel Disabilities Sers; Dept Human Sers Reg Ser Team, Interagy Coun, Am Assn Mtl Deficiency; cp/Woms Aux VFW; r/Ch of Christ; hon/Personalities S; DIB.

ROW, EDNA BERNIECE oc/Community Leader; b/Aug 4, 1924; h/178 Azalea Dr, Grants Pass, OR 97526; m/James William; c/William, Kari; p/William and Edna Fox Cauble (dec); ed/Att'g Rogue Commun Col; cp/Oreg Lit Inc; Chm Josephine Co Zoning & Planning Comms; Chm Blood Prog ARC 10 Yrs; Pres & St Chm PTA; Pres: Repub Wom, Art Leag, Rotaryann; Josephine Co Dist Budget Com; Chm Rogue Commun Col Budget Com; Boy Scouts; Girl Scouts; Commun Concert; U Way; VChm Heart Fund; Precnt Com-wom; r/Meth; hon/Dist'd Ser Awd, Josephine Co Sch Dist; Wom of Yr, JCs Awd; ARC Vol of Yr.

ROWE, IRIS GUIDER oc/Teacher; h/2708 Fillmore, El Paso, TX 79930; c/1; p/William and Lula Belle Guider; ed/BS Tenn Polytechnic Univ; Addit Studies; pa/Instr Bus Adm EP Public Schs & Commun Col; NEA; Nat & Intl Bus Ed Assns; Tex St, Classroom & Tran Pecos Tchrs Assns; cp/Former Secy & Pledge Chm Alpha Delta Kappa; Beta Sigma Phi; Intl Toastmistress Clb; hon/EP Tchr of Yr, Pilot Clb; Outstg Ser Instrn Cit, US Govt; Commun Ldrs & Noteworthy Ams; Book Hon; World W/W Wom; W/W Tex Ed.

ROY, ELSIJANE TRIMBLE oc/Judge; b/Apr 2, 1916; h/1101 Riviera Apts, 3700 Cantrell, Little Rock, AR 72202; ba/LR; c/James Jr; p/Thomas Trimble (dec); Elsie Walls Trimble, Lonoke, AR; ed/JD Univ Ark-F 1939; pa/Admitted Ark Bar 1939; Firm Reid, Evrard & Roy 1947-54; Roy & Roy 1954-63; Atty Ark Revenue Dept 1939-64; Law Clk Ark Supreme Ct 1963-65; Judge Pulaski Ct Circuit Ct 1966; Asst Atty Gen St Ark 1967; Sr Law Clk US Dist Ct 1968-74; Assoc Justice Ark Supreme Ct 1975-; Nat, Ark & LR Assns Wom Lwyrs; Ark & Pulaski Co Bar Assns; AAUW; cp/Univ Ark Alumni Assn; Med Adv Com Univ Ark Med Ctr 1952-54; Chm Com Ark Constnl Comm 1967-68; Com-wom Dem Party 16th Jud Dist 1940-42; VChm Ark Dem St Com 1946-48; PEO; Chm Omega; r/1st Bapt Ch, Lonoke; hon/John L McClellan Senate Delta Theta Phi; Delta Kappa Gamma; Altrusa Wom of Yr Ark 1976; Outstg Appellate Judge, Ark Trial Lwyrs; Num Biogl Listings.

ROYAL, ROBERT CURTIS oc/Clergyman; b/Oct 23, 1951; h/304 Electric Ave, Rochester, NY 14613; ba/Rochester; m/Lucinda Avery; c/Elizabeth Avery; p/Robert Royal, New York City, NY; Virginia Naomi Royal, New Milford, NJ; ed/BA; MDiv; pa/Chaplain Supvr Rochester Inst Technol; Interim Pastor 1st Spanish Bapt Ch; Pastor Rochester Bapt Ch; Conslt Urban Min RCBNM; GRBA: Chm Missions Com, Moderator; Bur Bus Mgmt; Missiology; Gtr Rochester Assn Evang; Maplewood Clergy Assn; cp/Alumni VP SEn Bapt Theol Sem; Meek Food Shelter; Bd Maplewood Photo Clb; Maplewood Continuum; r/So Bapt; hon/Prophets Acad.

ROYCE, ROSEMARY T oc/Nurse; b/Jan 2, 1941; h/209 Holly Hill Rd, Murfreesboro, NC 27855; ba/Ahoskie, NC; m/Philip; c/Jon, Karen; p/Charles and Mary Thomas, Gulfport, FL; ed/AA; FNP ECU; pa/Fam Nurse Practitioner Roanoke-Chowan Mtl Hlth Ctr; Past Chm Fam Planning Adv Cnslr; Therapist; Lectr; cp/Chaplain Melrose Woms Clb; Pres Chowan Wom & Wives Clb; Orgr Vol Nurses Aid Prog Teenage Girls; r/SS Tchr; Pres SS Class; Yth Prog; hon/Citizen of Week, R-C News Herald; Valuable Employee, R-C Hlth Ser; Phi Theta Kappa.

RUANE, RICHARD JAMES oc/Environmental Engineer; b/Feb 2, 1942; h/9313 Royal Shadows Dr, Chattanooga, TN 37421; ba/C'nooga; m/Nancy Kay Langford; c/Ary, James; p/Francis Martin (dec); Ary Davis Ruane, San Antonio, TX; ed/BS 1966, MS 1970 Univ Tex-A; pa/Res Com Water

Pollution Control Fdn; Intl Assn Water Pollution Res; ASCE; Intl Assn Hydraulics Res; NMA; r/Epis; hon/Tau Beta Pi; Chi Epsilon.

RUBLY, GRANT RUSSELL oc/Engineer; b/Jun 7, 1906; h/PO Box 154, Malvern, AR 72104; m/Lucille Alyce Pickering; c/John, Grant, Elizabeth Sills (Mrs Chas), Carl, Sharon Tilley (Mrs William); p/Carl and Louise Sump Rubly (dec); ed/BS 1928, MA 1939 Case Wn Resv Univ; pa/Chief Engr Miami Copper Co 1928-44; Resident Engr San Manuel Copper Corp Superior 1945-47; Engr Oreg St Hwy Dept 1947-48; Chief Engr & Mine Supt Magnet Cove Barium Corp 1948-50; US Bur Mines & Basic Refractories Gabbs 1950-51; Reynolds Mining Corp: Asst Chief Mine Engr 1951-56, Sr Staff Asst 1956-58, Sr Staff Asst 1958-71; Consltg Engr 1971-74; Am Inst Mining Engrs; Fellow AAAS; cp/Eminent Prior Albert Pike Priory #20 K of York Cross of Hon; Past: Master Rockport Lodge #58 A&FM, High Priest Malvern Chapt #100, Royal Arch Masons, Thrice Illustrious Master Solomon Coun #46, Royal & Selected Masters, Eminent Cmdr Trinity Commandery #33 Deg Mason Ancient & Accepted Scottish Rite, So Juris; Asst Orgr DeMolay in Malvern; Past Rainbow Dad; r/1st U Meth Ch; hon/Phi Kappa Tau; Theta Tau; Sigma Xi; Pub'd Author; Personalities S; W/W: S&SW, Ark; DIB; IPA; Men Achmt; Intl W/W Commun Ser; Fellow Intercont Biogl Assn; Notable Ams; Book Hon; Others.

RUBLY, LUCILLE A PICKERING oc/Stenographer; b/Nov 23, 1903; h/PO Box 154, Malvern, AR 72104; m/Grant; c/John, Grant, Carl, Elizabeth Sills (Mrs Charles), Sharon Tilley (Mrs William); p/Arthur and Ella Deggin Pickering; ed/Att'd YWCA Comml Sch & Cleveland Preparatory Sch; pa/Former Stenographer: Garfield, McGregor & Baldwin, Atty Philip White, Atty Edward Alexander, Canfield Oil Co, Num Others; cp/Interpreter Displaced Polish; Chaplain Intl Social Order Beauceants; Past Rainbow Mother; Band Mother; r/1st U Meth Ch; Cir Chm WSCS 2 Yrs; hon/Grand Cross Color, Intl Rainbow Girls; Fellow Book Hon; World W/W Wom; Commun Ldrs & Noteworthy Ams; ABIRA.

RUDENBERG, FRANK HERMANN oc/Neurophysiologist; Environmentalist; Teacher; b/Dec 4, 1927; h/3327 Ave Q½, Galveston, TX 77550; ba/G'ston; c/George, Eric, Peter, Karen; p/Reinhold Rudenberg (dec); Lily Rudenberg, Belmont, MA; ed/SB cum laude Harvard Univ 1949; SM S'ship 1951, PhD 1954 Univ Chicago; pa/Univ Tex Med Br: Assoc Prof Dept Physiol & Biophysics Sch Med & Fac Grad Sch Biomed Scis 1962-, Assoc Prof Sch Allied Hlth Scis 1976-, Asst Prof Dept Physiol & Biophysics & Fac Grad Sch Biomed Scis 1958-62; Instr & Asst Prof Dept Physiol & Pharm Mich St Univ 1954-58; Tchg Asst Dept Physiol Univ Chgo 1952-53; Conslt SW Res Inst: Med Instrumentation 1967-, Biomed Application Team NASA Contract 1967-73; Participant Num Wkshops & Confs; AAAS; Chm Com Adm Affairs AAUP; AIBS; Aerospace Technol Subcom Standards Com Assn Advmt Med Instrumentation; Biophy Soc; Neuroelectric Soc; Tex & NY Acads Scis; Soc Exptl Biol & Med; Soc Neurosci; Tex Soc Electron Microscopy; Sigma Xi; cp/Chm Univ Chgo Alumni; Sci Inc: Bd Dirs, Chm Resource Com, VChm Exec Com; Marine Affairs Coun; Cand City Coun; VChm Oil & Gas Master Plan

Com; Mayors Anti-Litter Com; G'ston Co Cult Arts Coun; Friends Rosenberg Lib; Hist Foun; SOS; Sierra Clb; Leag Wom Voters; r/Epis; hon/Atomic Energy Comm: Summer F'ship Marine Biol Lab, Predoct Fellow Univ Chgo & Marine Biol Lab; Pub'd Author; Num Biogl Listings.

RuDUSKY, BASIL MICHAEL oc/Physician; b/Jul 27, 1933; h/7 Pinetree Rd, Mountaintop, PA 18707; ba/Wilkes-Barre, PA; m/Bernadine; c/Daryl, Bryan; c/Michael and Ann RuDusky; ed/BA Va Mil Inst 1955; MD Univ Pgh 1959; mil/AUS Med Corp, Capt 1960-62; pa/Conslt (Internal Med & Cardiol): Retreat St Hosp, Armed Forces Examining Ser; Sr Conslt, Dept of Hlth & Wel, Social Security Sect; Conslitg Physician, Metropolitan Ins Co of Am; Att'g Physician in Internal Med & Cardiol: Mercy Hosp 1966-, Wilkes-Barre Gen Hosp 1966-; Dir, NE Cardiovascular Clin & Res Inst (WB); Pvt Pract 1966-; Contbr to Profl Pubs; Diplomate, Am Bd Internal Med; Fellow: Am Col Angiology, Am Col Physicians, Am Col Cardiol, Am Col Chest Physicians, Am Geriatrics Soc; Assn Mil Surgs of US; AMA; Nu Sigma Nu; Nat Panel for Heart Disease; Dist'd Grad, VMI; Lincoln Foun S'ship; Hons Achmt Awd, Am Col Angiology & Purdue Frederick Co.

RUIZ, ALDELMO oc/Missions Director; Civil Engineer; b/Jun 12, 1923; h/Box 299, Yauco, Puerto Rico 00768; ba/APO Miami 34002; m/Mary Lonardelli; c/Michael, Stella; p/Hipolito Ruiz Ramos; Mercedes Santiago de Ruiz; ed/BS 1949, MS 1950 Va Polytech Inst; Mgmt Course Completed RDL 1952; Postgrad Work Univ Va Ext & Geo Wash Univ; Studies Fgn Ser Inst 1969; Grad Indust Col Armed Forces 1971-72;; mil/1/Sgt Adm Duties 1942-45; pa/Reg'd Profl Engr: Del, Md, DC, Mass, PR; Grad Fellow Va Polytech Inst 1949-50; Designer Engr Wash Suburban Sanitary Comm 1950-51; Engr Res & Devel Labs and Sanitary & Proj Engr Ft Belvoir 1952-55; Chief Civil, Sanitary & Mech Engrg Depts and Asst Mgr & Tech Coor Far E Div Arch-Engrg Firm, Wash DC, Okinawa, Philippines & Taiwan 1955-58; Pres & Owner Conslitg Engrg Firm, Santurce, PR 1958-62; Chief Engr (AID), Dept St, Taiz Yemen 1962-64; Dir Water Supply & Envir Sanitation Dept, Yemen Arab Republic 1964-66; Devel Ofcr Sana Yemen 1966-67; Chief Engrg Advr USAID, Kabul, Afghanistan 1967-68; Gen Engrg Ofcr 1968-71; Inter-reg Engrg Coor, AID, Wash DC 1971-72; AID Affairs Ofcr, USAID, Yemen 1973-74; AID Rep 1974-75, Missions Dir 1974-77; Mission Dir El Salvador 1978-; Designer & Constructor Kennedy Meml Water Sys; Num Nat & Intl Profl Assns incl'g Am Soc CE, Am Water Works Assn, Colegio de Ingenieros Arquitectos y Agrimensures de PR, NSPE, USICID, Others; cp/Bd Dirs: Sana Intl Sch Yemen, Mill Creek Pk Citizens Assn; Lions Intl; r/Rom Cath; hon/Fellow Intercont Biogl Assn; Dist'd Awd, Agy Intl Devel; Cert Yemen Arab Republic; Contbr Num Articles Var Profl Jours; Num Biogl Listings.

RUMMERFIELD, WALTER GLEN oc/Clergyman; Administrator; b/Nov 14, 1911; h/17865 Adelanto Rd, Box 220, Adelanto, CA 92301; ba/Adelanto; m/Marie Mercedes; c/Judith, Michael; p/Walter and Clara Zora Bachman Rummerfield (dec); ed/BS W Tex St 1946-56; Cramwell Res Inst 1956; MSD, PsD, DD, Phil Col Univ Truth 1957; PhD City Temple Sch Rel 1967; DBA Cal Christian Col 1973; STD 1973, JDC 1974 CC & CTSR Univ Inst Ecumenical Study & Res; mil/USNR 1943-45; Navy FC Gunnery Schs GS-9; pa/Pres Cal Christian Univ & Ch Corp; Archishop Wn Reg Ecumenical Mvt World Peace; cp/Nat & St Repub Party; Legion; VFW; DAV; r/Christian Ch; hon/USNR: Purple Heart, Ship Unit Cit; Sir Knight; Ecumenical Noble; Dist.

RUSHTON, WILLIAM JAMES oc/Life Insurance Executive; b/Jul 10, 1900; h/2848 Balmoral Rd, Birmingham, AL 35223; ba/B'ham; m/Elizabeth Perry (dec); c/William III, James; p/James and Willis Roberts

Rushton (dec); ed/BS Washington & Lee Univ 1921; HHD SWn-Memphis 1959; mil/AUS: Col WW-II, Civilian Chief B'ham Ordnance Dist 1946-61; pa/B'ham Ice & Cold Storage Co: Asst Mgr 1922-27, VP 1927-32, Pres 1932-38, VChm Bd & Secy 1938-57; Protective Life Ins Co: Pres 1937-67, Chm Bd 1967-76, Dir 1927-; Adv Bd Investmt Co Am; Chm Bd Franklin Coal Mining Co 1927-42; Dir: Moore-Handley Hardware Co 1948-63, 1st Nat Bank B'ham 1927-73, Ala Power Co 1937-70, Gulf, Mobile & Ohio RR Co 1940-72, Ill Ctl Gulf RR 1972-74; Am Ordnance Assn; Nat Assn Ice Industs; Nat Assn Refrigerated Warehouses; Am Warehouses Assn; Life Ins Assn Am; Hlth Ins Assn Am; Am Life Conv; Inst Life Ins; Assn Industs Ala; Beta Gamma Sigma; Beta Theta Pi; Omicron Delta Kappa; Delta Sigma Rho; cp/Rotary; Pres & Dir B'ham Coun BSA; Nat Citizens Com U Commun Campaigns Am; B'ham Commun Chest: Past Dir, VP, Exec Com, Pres; Trustee: So Res Inst, B'ham Mus Art, Chds Hosp, Agnes Scott Col; Bd Dirs: YMCA, Salvation Army; Mtn Brook; B'ham Country; Downtown; Redstone; Chaparrall; r/Presb: Elder, Deacon, Chm Trustees, Bd Annuities; hon/AUS: Legion Merit, Recipient Num Cits; Ala Acad Hon.

RUSKAMP, JOHN ARTHUR JR oc/Educator; Administrator; b/Nov 21, 1948; h/8345 S Kostner, Chicago, IL 60652; ba/Chgo; p/John Sr and Mildred Ruskamp, Chgo; ed/BS 1970, MEd 1976, Doct Cand Loyola-C 1978; mil/USN: Tng Ofcr USS Constellation CVA-64, Army-Navy Acad Maths Instr; pa/Phi Delta Kappa; Alpha Chi Sigma; AASA; AAAS; ACS; NSTA; Am Mensa Ltd; Assn Sch Bus Ofcls; cp/VFW; SAR; r/Pres Holy Trinity Luth Ch, Joliet; hon/WATVAR; Dist'd Edr Awd, Emil Hirsch HS; USN: Lttr Commend, Pres Unit Cit, Vietnam Ser Medal, Vietnam Campaign Medal.

RUSSELL, CHRISTOPHER THOMAS oc/Geophysicist; b/May 9, 1943; h/3930 Mandeville Canyon Rd, Los Angeles, CA 90049; ba/LS; m/Arlene Ann; c/Jennifer, Danielle; p/Thomas Russell (dec); Teresa Mary Russell, White Rock, British Columbia; ed/BSc Univ Toronto 1964; PhD Univ Cal-LA 1968; pa/Geophysicist Inst Geophysics Univ Cal-LA; Am Geophy Union; US Nat Com & Chm Working Group Active Expts Intl Union Radio Sci; Div Planetary Sci Am Astronom Soc; AAAS; NASA Space Sci Adv Com; VChm Working Group Auroral Oval Intl Assn Geomagnetism & Aeronomy; hon/Macelwane Awd, Am Geophy Union; NASA: Interdisciplinary Scist of Galileo, Prin Investigatorship of Intl Sun-Earth Explorer & Pioneer Venus Orbiter.

RUSSELL, JANALYNN oc/Student; b/Jun 13, 1958; h/680 Cactus, Bridge City, TX 77611; ba/Huntsville, TX; p/Roger and Peggy Russell, BC; r/Bapt; hon/Alpha Chi; Pi Mu Epsilon; Orange Keys; Deans List & Perfect Scholastic Average Commend 4 Semesters; Major of Mo 1978; Volleyball S'ship; Nom'd W/W Students Am Cols & Univs.

RUSSELL, PHEBE GALE oc/Executive; b/Dec 23, 1910; h/5101 River Rd Apt 918, Wash, DC 20016; m/Frank (dec); c/Morgan, Gale R Holberton; p/George and Marian Hyde Gale (dec); pa/Owner TV Cable Cos Appalachia, Norton & Big Stone Gap, Va 1962-71; Pres: Ellensburg TV Corp 1961-68, PGR Enterprises 1962-70; VP Radio Sta WICO 1958-62; Publicity Dir NBC 1929-39; cp/Woms Bd George Washington Univ Hosp; DAR; Mayflower Soc; Huguenot Soc; Intl Platform Assn; Nepal Soc US; Md Golf Assn; Daus Cinc; Congl Country Clb; Kenwood Garden Clb; r/Epis.

RUSSELL, VICKI ROSEANN oc/School Teacher; b/Sept 15, 1953; h/PO Box 411, Humble, TX 77338; p/Harry and Bennice Russell; ed/BAT; pa/Tex St Tchrs Assn; NEA; cp/Poetry Socs Houston & Tex; Local & St Polit Campaign Wkr; r/So Bapt; hon/1st Runner-up & Talent Awd, Miss Humble; 2nd Runner-up, Miss Montgomery Co; Nat Hon

Soc; Commun Ldrs & Noteworthy Ams; Intl W/W Poetry.

RUTHERFORD, JAMES WILLIAM oc/Mayor; b/Apr 23, 1925; h/1713 Chelsea Cir, Flint, MI 48503; ba/Flint; m/Betty Merrill; c/Maria R Atchison, Michelle, Michael & James; p/Harry and Isabelle Rutherford (dec); ed/AA Flint Commun Jr Col 1958; BS 1960, MS 1964 Mich St Univ; mil/USN; pa/Flint Police Dept 1948: Det 1953, Det Sgt 1955, Det Lt 1961, Det City Mgr 1963, Police Insp 1965, Chief Police 1967; Instr Crim Invest Mich St Univ 1964; Vis Instr Manatee Jr Col 1970; Fdr 1st Mich Jr Col Police Prog; Coor'd Saginaw Val Law Enforcemt Ofcrs Sch; Devel'd Reg Police Acad Recruit Tng; Bd Dirs Mich Assn Chiefs Police; Author Num Police Jour Articles; Conslt: Am Assn Jr Cols, Mich Law Enforcemt Tng Coun, Others; cp/Mayor City Flint 1975-; Citizens Coun Improved Ed Flint; Bd Commrs Govs Ofc Crim Justice Prog; Former VChm Local Manpower Devel Tng Coun; Exec Com Flint Area Conf Inc; River Front Adv Com; Bd Dirs Flint Area Tourist & Conv Coun; US Conf Mayors; Mich Mutual Leag; Downtown Devel Authority; Flint Ec Devel Comm; Chm Citizens Crime Comm; Old Newsboys; Ldrship Flint; CETA Consortium; FEAT; Others; r/Prot; hon/Named 1 of 10 Outstg Police Ofcrs US, Intl Assn Chiefs Police Conv, IACP Parade Mag; Reverence Law Awd, Mich Frat Order Eagles; Golden Deeds Awd, Flint Exc Clb; Gideons Civic Awd; J Edgar Hoover Meml Awd; Pi Alpha; Phi Kappa Phi; W/W: MW, Govt; Men Achmt; DIB; Others.

RUTHERFORD, JOHN ELMER JR oc/Engineer; Teacher; Writer; b/Sept 3, 1941; h/1005 N Shore Rd #5, Rio Grande, NJ 08242; c/Kimberly, Kenneth; p/John Sr and Shirley Campbell Rutherford, RG; ed/BE Vanderbilt Univ 1971; MA Glassboro St Col 1975; Dipl Nav Preparatory Sch 1967; Grad Navy Electronics Sch 1960 & 62; mil/USN Electronics Tech Aviation 1959-70; pa/Substitute Tchr: Dorothy Elem, Handmaidens Elem; Electronics Design & Repair Plough Inc; Author Books Poetry: *Jean, Poetry Is, An Acrostics Aperture, Sea Scribblers, Seagulls Shadow, Cure For Indigestion*, Num Others; cp/Cape May Co Art Leag; Stella Woodall Poetry Soc; hon/USN: Sailor of Mo Awd, 2 Good Conduct Medals, Nav Enlisted Sci Ed Prog, Aircrew Wings Patrol Squadron 5; 2nd Prize, Rhode Island Poetry Soc.

RUTLEDGE, VARIAN PALMER oc/-Teacher; b/Dec 30, 1913; m/Morton Edgar; c/Morton Jr; p/John Palmer (dec); Sallie Gause Palmer, Plant City, FL; ed/BS Fla So Col 1950; MEd Univ Fla-G 1955; Postgrad Studies; pa/Tchr Chd Specific Lng Disabilities Winston Sch; Fla So Col Macdille AFB 9 Yrs:

Instr, Lib & Eval Coms, Cochaired "The Chds Book Fair", Orgr & Dir Audio-Visual Materials & Techniques Conf, Advr, Fac Advr Kappa Delta & Alpha Omicron Pi; Author: *Teenagers, As A Man Thinks*; Num Articles & Poems Pub'd Profl Mags; Nat & Fla Hist Socs; NEA; AAUW; Nat Acad Sci; Assn Chd Lng Disabilities; Intl Rdg Assn; Assn Childhood Ed Intl; cp/Wom Responsible Leg; Pol Co Dem Woms Clb: Pres 1974-76, Constit Revision Com; Capt PC Voting Precnt; Dist 38 Dem Com-wom; Nat & Lake Reg Audubon Soc; Fla Naturalist; BPW; PTA; Classroom Tchr Rep Park Ed Assn; Lakeland Classroom Tchrs; Coun Exceptl Chd; Sponsor & Advr Jr Acad Sci; Coor Coun Woms Orgs; Publicity Chm Citrus Tea; Garden Clb; Sponsor Jr Garden Clb; Lakeland Symph Orch Assn; Symph Guild; r/1st Bapt Ch, PC: Choir, Yth Cnslr, Del Summer Mission Studies; hon/Kappa Delta Pi; Pi Gamma Mu; Alpha Omicron Pi; Alpha Delta Kappa; Winner Vocal Div, Fla St Music Fest; Blue Key, Univ Fla; 30 Yr Pin, ARC; Cert Apprec: FFA, ARC.

RUZICKA, MARY FRANCES oc/Educator; Psychologist; b/Dec 4, 1943; h/12 Northview Terr, Maplewood, NJ 07040; ba/Springfield, NJ; p/Francis F and Margaret K Ruzicka, Madison, WI; ed/BA cum laude; MA; PhD; pa/Prof, Seton Hall Univ; Pvt Pract Psychol; Mgmt Conslt; Contbr Num Articles to Profl Jours; cp/Civic Spkr; r/Rom Cath; hon/W/W E; Outstg Yg Wom Am; DIB; Others.

RYAN, HERBERT F oc/Lawyer; b/Aug 10, 1931; h/1013 78 St, Brooklyn, NY 11228; p/(dec); ed/BA 1953, JD 1978 St John Col; pa/Pt-time Prof; 1st Deputy City Clerk, NYC; hon/W/W Am Cols & Univs; Freedom Foun Essay Awd.

RYAN, NANCY WILHELMSON oc/Educator; b/Feb 21, 1948; h/PO Box #82, Waseca, MN 56093; ba/Waseca; m/Michael James; p/Bernard and Ruth Wilhelmson, Skokie, IL; ed/BS Ia St Univ 1970; MS Univ Ill 1972; pa/Instr & Coor Mdse Prog Home & Fam Sers Div Univ Minn; Meier & Frank Co: Home Economist Fabric Dept 1976-77, Mdse

Internship Market Res 1975; Oreg St Univ: Participant Col & Univ Tchg Wkshop 1974-75, Instr Dept Clothing, Textile & Related Arts 1972-76; Univ Ill: Textile Res Asst 1971-72, Tchg Asst 1970-71; Am Home Ec Assn; Pi Sigma Epsilon; r/1st Evang Free Ch of Chicago; hon/Omicron Nu; Ldrship S'ship, Ctl Col.

RYAN, ROBERT DALE oc/Professor; Administrator; b/Apr 9, 1931; h/912-24th Ave N, St Cloud, MN 56301; ba/SC;

m/Barbara Ellen; c/Cynthia, Sara; p/Wallace Ryan (dec); Hulda Nelson Ryan, Norfolk, NE; ed/BA 1955; MA 1957; EdD 1964; mil/AUS 1952-54; pa/Prof & Chperson Dept Technol SCSU 1962-; Dean Students Commun Col Alpena, Mich 1959; Univ Minn-D 1957: Instr Math & Engrg Graphics, Univ Senate, Curric Com, Grad Coun, Chancellors Task Force, Gen Ed; NEA; ASME; ASEE; World Future Soc; cp/Assn Smithsonian; Energy Comm; r/Salem Luth: Ch Bd; hon/W/W: Am, Am Ed, Computer Ed, Commun Ser; Ldrs Ed; Outstg Edrs Am.

RYBAR, VALERIAN STUX oc/Executive; b/1929; h/16 Sutton Place, New York City, NY 10022; ba/NYC; p/Geza and Vilma Stux-Rybar (dec); ed/Matura Theresianum, Vienna; pa/Pres Valerian S Rybar Inc; Architect; Interior Designer; r/Prot.

RYDER, GEORGIA ATKINS oc/Professor; b/Jan 30, 1924; h/5551 Brookville Rd, Norfolk, VA 23502; ba/Norfolk; m/Noah (dec); c/Olive, Malcolm, Aleta; p/Benjamin Sr and Mary Carter Atkins (dec); ed/BS summa cum laude Hampton Inst; MMus Univ Mich; PhD NYU; pa/Prof Music Norfolk St Col; Lectr; Conductor; Accompanist; Adjudicator; cp/Bd: Norfolk Symph Orch, Greene Chorale; Norfolk Comm Arts & Humanities; Com Improvemt Ed; r/Am Bapt; hon/Fdrs Day Awd Outstg Sch Achmt, NYU; Achmt Awd, NCIE; Num Biogl Listings.

RYDER, WILLIAM HENDERSON oc/Professor; b/Apr 4, 1936; h/2704 79th Ave, Baton Rouge, LA 70807; ba/BR; m/Exyie Chambliss; c/Shauna, Samara; p/Walker and Naomi Ryder, New Bern, NC; ed/BS 1957; MM 1959; PhD 1970; pa/Prof Music So Univ; MENC; LMEA; NACWPI; cp/Bd Dirs: YMCA, BR Symph; r/Epis; hon/Alpha Kappa Mu.

RYE, SVEN oc/Author; Journalist; Editor; b/Feb 26, 1906; h/3906 Franklin Ave, Hollywood, CA 90027; ba/Same; p/Arnold and Caroline Rye, Randers, Denmark; ed/Att'd Univ Denmark, Sorbonne, Alliance Francais & Univ Berlin; mil/Danish Army; Danish Underground; pa/Newspaper Correspondent Paris, London, Vienna, Rome, Berlin, Stockholm, NY & Los Angeles; VConslt for Denmark at LA 1951-62; Pres Hollywood Fgn Press Assn 1963; Author 2 Novels & 400 Songs Pub'd Europe; r/Luth; hon/K Order of Dannebrog, Queen Margrethe II Denmark 1976; DLit Trinity So Bible Col & Sem 1960; Decorated Danish Nat Tourist Ofc, Copenhagen; Galathea Medal, Denmark.

RZEMINSKI, PETER JOSEPH oc/Personnel Administrator; b/Apr 19, 1947; h/13417 S Medina Dr, Orland Park, IL 60462; ba/Blue Isl, IL; m/Dorothy Morowczynski; c/Peter II, Stacey; p/Casmir Rzeminski, Chicago, IL; Bertha Rudisill Rzeminski (dec); ed/BS Univ Ill 1973; MBA De Paul Univ 1976; mil/AUS 1967-72; USAR Major 1972-; pa/ASPA; ASHPA; Chgo Hosp Pers Mgmt Assn; Ill Soc Human Resource Adm Hlth Care; SW Area Hosp & Sisters St Mary Pers Dirs Assns; Prog Com Yg Admrs Chgo; Hosp Mgmt Sys Soc; Resv Ofcrs Assn; cp/Sauk Area Career Adv Com 1974-76; r/Rom Cath; hon/Mil Decorations: Dist'd Flying Cross, Bronze Star Medal, Air Medal, Purple Heart, Army Commend Medal, Vietnam Campaign, Vietnam Cross Gallantry w/Palm.

S

SAARI, DOROTHY REYNOLDS oc/Personnel Director; b/Aug 1, 1937; h/1402 Verna, Jasper, TX 75951; ba/Jasper, TX; m/Harold J; c/Conya J; p/Royston H and Vivian B Reynolds; pa/Pers Dir, Owens-Illinois Wood Prods; cp/Gov, Tex Dist Pilot Clb Intl; r/Meth.

SABLATASH, MIKE oc/Communications Engineer; Applied Mathematician; Research Scientist; b/Sept 30, 1935; h/16 Bradgate Dr, Ottawa, Ontario, Canada K2G 0R6; m/Sophie (dec); c/3 Chd; p/Fred and Katryna Sablatash; ed/BSEE 1957, MSEE 1964 Univ Manitoba; PhD Univ Wis-M 1968; pa/Dept Communs Govt of Canada: Current Res Scist III, Hd Local Data Distribution, Directorate of Data Systems & Networks Res & Devel, Technol & Systems Br; Sr Analyst & Mathematician Energy Models Div Nat Energy Bd 1974-76; Sr Analyst & Mathematician Math Prog'g Div Opers Res Br, Nat Energy Bd 1972-74; Asst Prof Elect Engrg Univ Toronto 1968-72; Pt-time Tchg Asst Dept Elect Engrg Univ Wis 1965-68; Mem Consociates Conslt'g Group Univ Toronto 1968-72; Other Former Positions; Assn Profl Engrs Province Ontario; IEEE; AAAS; Sigma Xi; NY Acad Scis, Ottawa Chapt; Am Statistical Assn; Profl Inst Public Ser Canada; cp/Briargreen Commun Assn; Canadian Cancer Soc; U Appeal; Canadian Heart Fund; r/1st Unitarian Congreg Ottawa; hon/Pub'd Author; Biogl Listings.

SACHS, WILLIAM oc/Motion Picture Director; Writer; Producer; b/Oct 16, 1942; h/3409 Camino De La Cumbre, Sherman Oaks, CA 91423; ba/Same; m/Margaret; p/Milton Sachs (dec); Ann Sachs, Montvale, NJ; ed/Grad London Film Sch; mil/USAF 1962-65; pa/Dir-Writer-Prodr Motion Picture *There Is No 13* 1974; Dir-Writer-Editor Film

The Force Beyond 1976; Dir & Writer *The Incredible Melting Man* 1977; Dir & Writer *Van Nuys Blvd* 1979; hon/Films have won 25+ Awds at Fests incl'g: Marienbad, Oberhausen, Buenos Aires, Edinburgh, Southampton, Chicago, NY Film Fest & Forbidden Film Fest (London).

SACHTLEBEN, CARL HENRY oc/Librarian; b/Jun 24, 1919; h/Rt 4, Box 508, Paw Paw, MI 49079; ba/Kalamazoo, MI; m/Helen E; c/Carl R, Paul L, John R, Philip S, Anita M; p/Albert Sachtleben (dec); Eleonora Sachtleben, St Louis, MO; ed/AB; BSLS; MA; mil/Maj TC (Ret'd Resv); pa/Dir Libs Wn Mich Univ; ALA; ACRL; MLA; Mich Lib Consortium; Luth Acad for S'ship; cp/Kalamazoo Rotary Clb; Dem; r/Luth; hon/Beta Phi Mu.

SADEH, WILLY ZEEV oc/Professor; b/Oct 13, 1932; h/2020 Brookwood Dr, Ft Collins, CO 80525; ba/Ft Collins; m/Esther; c/Eligar, Tidhar; p/Eliezer and Tova Sadeh (dec); ed/BS; MS; PhD; pa/Prof Engrg Colo St Univ; Assoc Fellow AIAA; Sigma Xi; Tau Beta Pi; ASME; APCA; ASCE; AAAS; ASEE; AAUP; Soc Engrg Sci; cp/Past Pres Moore Sch PTO; r/Jewish; hon/NASA Cert of Apprec; Vernon Dishman Meml Awd, CSU.

ST CHARLES, PAUL W oc/Priest; b/Jun 23, 1938; h/1303 E Reelfoot Ave, Union City, TN 38261; ba/Union City; p/Paul F St Charles (dec); Rose Dattilo St Charles, Nashville, TN; ed/BA; STB; pa/Priest Immaculate

Conception Ch; Obion Co Min Assn; Priest Coun, Memphis; cp/Com Mem Obion Co Yth Org; r/Rom Cath: Priest; hon/St George Emblem; Farmer Chaplain Tenn K of C; K of C Nat Ch Activ Awd.

ST CLAIR, CHARLES WILLARD oc/Retired; b/Jan 24, 1901; h/1247 SE 7th Ct, Deerfield Beach, FL 33441; 91 Chatfield Dr, Painesville, OH 44077; m/Edna N; c/Julia S Graham; p/Charles Willard Sr and Elizabeth Maude St Clair (dec); ed/BSIE; mil/SATC;

pa/Exec Secy-Treas Gyro Intl 22 Yrs; Sales Mgr Steam Equipmt Div, Coe Mfg Co, P'ville 19 Yrs; cp/Chm Heart Assn; Campaign Mgr UF Campaign; Mem P'ville City Coun 7½ Yrs; r/U Meth Ch; hon/Intl Pres Gyro Intl; Gyro Honor Key; Gyro Merit Awd; UF Awd of Merit.

SAKHADEO, SHRIHARI S oc/Pediatrician; Pediatric Hematologist; Oncologist; b/Sept 20, 1938; h/54 Ivy Ln, Petersburg, VA 23803; m/Jotsna; c/2 Chd; ed/Grad w highest hons Fergusson Col & B J Med Col (Poona, India); Internship Duke Univ; Residency Duke Univ & Univ Tenn Med Sch-M; pa/Petersburg Gen Hosp, P'burg: Current Att'g Pediatrician, Pediatric Hematologist & Oncologist; Asst Prof Pediatrics & Pediatric Hematol & Oncology Med Col Va, Richmond 1977-; Current Chief Public Hlth Clin Va St Hlth Dept, P'burg; Att'g Pediatrician, Pediatric Hematologist & Oncologist Yonkers Gen Hosp, St Joseph's Hosp & Montefiore Hosp & Med Ctr 1974-76; Other Former Positions; Var Panel Activs; hon/L W Digg's Meritorious Ser Medal, Nat Sickle Cell Res Foun Inc; Sev Awds, Med Soc Va; Phys's Recog Awd & Others, AMA; Pub'd Author; Biogl Listings.

SALES, AMOS PAUL oc/Educator; b/Nov 6, 1941; h/2634 E Manchester, Tucson, AZ 85721; m/Catherine; c/Christopher Paul, Clinton Samuel; p/Sam and Mamie Dorene Sales, Bogota, TX; ed/BS 1965, MS Univ of Ariz-Tucson 1967; EdD Univ Fla 1971; pa/Asst Prof, Rehab Ctr, Col of Ed, Univ of Ariz 1973-; Dir of Prog, Nat Rehab Assn (Wash, DC) 1976-77; Acting Exec Dir, Nat Rehab Assn 1977; Conslt, In-Ser Tng Ofc, Ariz Div of Voc Rehab 1976-; Rehab Adv Com to Commr, Rehab Sers Adm, Dept of HEW; Staff, Nat Coun on Rehab Ed; Bd Dirs, Pacific Region, NRA 1977-; APGA; Am Rehab Cnslg

Assn; Ariz Rehab Assn; Am Psychol Assn; Nat Rehab Admrs Assn; Cert'd Psychologist, St of Ariz 1975-; Cert'd Rehab Cnslr, CRCC 1975-; Contbr Num Articles to Profl Jours; Others; cp/Past Mem Bd Dirs, Traditional Indian Alliance (Tucson); Past Mem Adv Com, So Ariz Mtl Hlth CEO Prog; Chm, United Way Com on Visually Impaired & Commun Sers Com; Past Mem Bd Dirs, Rehab & Work Adjustment Ctr; hon/Selected as 1 of 10 Rehab Edrs to Serve as Site Surveyors, Comm on Rehab Ed; W F Faulkes Awd, NRA; Cert of Commend, Tucson United Way; Nat Cit, NRA; Ariz Regional Veterans Adm Cnslg Grant; Outstg Edr Awd; Cert Apprec, Nat Rehab Cnslg Assn; Num Others.

SALIBA, SELMA G oc/Public Utility Specialist; b/Jan 15, 1952; h/904 Manor Rd, #201, Alexandria, VA 22305; ba/Washington, DC; p/Charles Saliba (dec); Stella Mae Saliba, Montgomery, AL; ed/BS 1974, MBA 1975 Univ Ala; pa/Public Utility Specialist Dept Energy; Former Sr Asst Mgr & Acting Mgr Household Fin Corp, W Fla Reg 3 Yrs; Assn MBA Execs; Am Bus Wom's Assn; AAUW; cp/Univ Ala Nat Alumni Assn; r/Ch of Christ; hon/Wom's Hons Prog, Univ Ala; Assoc'd Wom Students Judiciary Com, Univ Ala.

SALIMI, MOSTAFA oc/Cardiologist; b/Dec 6, 1939; h/28 Dartmouth Rd, Wayne, NJ 07470; ba/Clifton, NJ; m/Manizheh Ghaem-Panah; c/Parisa, Atoosa; p/Abbas and Zeinab Salimi, Wayne, NJ; ed/MD Tehran Univ Med Sch 1964; Att'd George Washington Univ; mil/Iranian Army Ofcr 1964-65; pa/Pvt Pract Cardiol; Am Col Med; Diplomate, Am Bd Internal Med & Am Bd Cardiovascular Diseases; r/Islam; hon/Fellow, Am Col Cardiol.

SALISBURY, FRANK B oc/Professor; Plant Physiologist; b/Aug 3, 1926; h/2020 Country Estates, N Logan, UT; ba/Logan, UT; m/L Marilyn Olson; c/5 Sons, 2 Daughs; ed/BS, MA Univ Utah; PhD Cal Inst Technol; pa/Utah St Univ: Prof Botany 1968-, Prof Plant Physiol 1966-, Prof Plant Physiol & Hd Plant Sci 1966-70; NSF Postdoct Fellow, Tubingen, Germany & Innsbruck, Austria 1962-63; Tech Rep in Plant Physiol, US Atomic Energy Comm, Germantown, Md 1973-74; Other Former Positions; Am Soc Plant Physiologists; Am Inst Biogl Scis; Fellow AAAS; Former Conslt Aerial Phenomena Res Org; Former Mem Bd Dirs Nat Investigations Com on Aerial Phenomena; Botanical Soc Am; Ecological Soc Am; Phi Kappa Phi; Sigma Xi; Utah Acad Arts, Lttrs & Scis; Wn Soc Naturalists; Var Res Activs; r/LDS; hon/Author 5 Books, Coauthor 3 Books, Num Articles.

SALISBURY, JANE JEFFORD oc/Professor; b/Jan 10, 1947; h/415 W Ash, Piqua, OH 45356; ba/Dayton, OH; m/Alvin B Jr; p/Richard D and Glendyl B Jefford, Greenfield, IN; ed/BA Univ Evansville 1969; MS 1972, HSD 1977 Ind Univ; Addit Studies; pa/Prof Ed Wright St Univ; Prof Hlth Ed Davis & Elkins Col, Elkins, WVa; Tchr Hlth & PE Columbus Sr HS, Columbus, Ind; AAHPER; Assn for Advmt Hlth Ed; Nat Assn for Sport & PE; MW Assn HPER; Am Sch Hlth Assn; Phi Delta Kappa; Conslt for Curric in Hlth Ed; cp/Adv Com for Drug Abuse, Ind & WVa; Kisler Proj Drug Abuse; Greene Co (Ohio) Hypertension Com; Com for Med Manpower (WVa); Others; r/Prot; hon/Boettiger Grant; Acad S'ship; Delta Theta Tau Res Grant.

SALLQUIST, GARY A oc/Chartered Life Underwriter; b/Jul 7, 1938; h/10033 Fieldcrest Dr, Omaha, NE 68114; ba/Omaha; m/Joyce; c/Susan, Steven; p/Hal T and Freda C Sallquist, Omaha; ed/BA w distn; Chartered Life Underwriter; mil/AUS; pa/Pres Sallquist Wilkinson Inc (Ins Est Planning Firm); Am Soc Chartered Life Underwriters; Million Dollar Round Table: Life & Qualifying Mem; NALU; OALU; Other Profl Activs; cp/Neb JCs: Neb St Mbrship Chm, St Chm for Ldrship in Action Prog; Creighton St Joseph Meml Hosp:

Bd Dirs, Long Range Planning Com, Constrn Sub-Com; Omaha Tomorrow Prog, Chm Hlth & Social Sers Com; Chm Curric Com Ldrship Omaha Prog; Univ Neb Foun Adv Com; Pres Univ Neb Omaha Alumni Assn; Pres Omaha JCs; Others; r/Presb; hon/Outstg Alumnus Awd, Univ Neb-O; 1 of 10 Outstg Yg Men, Omaha (7 Times).

SALOM, FRANCINE oc/Assistant Principal; b/Oct 10, 1930; h/2372 E 26 St, Brooklyn, NY 11229; ba/Bklyn; m/(dec); c/Ira Louis, Mark Hal, Claire Sarah; p/Morris and Clara Schranz Gratz (dec); ed/BA, MA, DD Bklyn Col; pa/Asst Prin South Shore HS; Adj Prof Psychol Long Isl Univ; Pres NY Biol Chms Assn; Am Soc Psychosomatic Dentistry & Med; Soc for Sci Study of Sex; cp/Mensa, Coor; r/Jewish; hon/Envir Sci Awd, Wom's Press Clb.

SALT, ALBERT ALEXANDER oc/Executive; b/Jul 14, 1920; h/PO Box 68, Cove City, NC 28523; ba/Cove City; m/Gertrude Essig; c/Gary Craig, Alger Dean; p/Albert Edward and Elizabeth Glass Salt (dec); ed/BS Univ Ga; MS (Forestry) Yale Univ; mil/AUS Capt, Ret'd; pa/Pres Salt Wood Prods Inc; Phi Beta Kappa; Xi Sigma Pi; Alpha Zeta; AWPB; AWPI; SAF; FPRS; cp/Dem Precnt Chm; Co Lib Bd; Bd Dirs Br Bkg & Trust Co, Trenton, NC; r/Prot; hon/Silver Star; Pres Cit; Govs Awd; Hon PhD, Univ Ga.

SALTER, MARILYN BURKE oc/Educator; Consultant; b/Aug 9, 1937; h/1708 Coronado Dr, Champaign, IL 61820; ba/Urbana, IL; c/Carolyn Diane, Roy Dan; p/Jenie Lee Jr and Joyce Gross Burke, Hobbs, NM; ed/BS, MS En NM Univ (ENMU); Cand Adv'd Cert Deg Ednl Adm Univ Ill; pa/Coor Reg Hearing Impaired Progs E Ctl Ill 1972-; Ill Admrs Spec Ed; Conf Am Instrs Deaf; Ill Tchrs Hearing Impaired; Film Evaluator

Captioned Films for Deaf, Rochester, NM 1975-78; Tchr/Ldr People to People HS Ambassador Prog to Europe 1976; Proj Dir/Supv'g Tchr Deaf-Blind Dept St of Oreg Spec Schs Div, Oreg Bd Ed 1970-72; Spec Schs Ed Assn: Org'g VP 1970, Pres 1971; Guest Lectr; cp/Vol: w Aged, Yth Hockey, Local Campaign in City Election; Former Mem Sch Commun Coun, Salem, Oreg; Past Pres McKinley Fgn Lang Assn (Salem) & Salem PTA; Others; hon/Outstg Yg Edr, Salem; Human Rts Awd, Oreg Ed Assn, B'nai B'rith; W/W Am Wom; World W/W Wom; Medallion for Ser Above & Beyond, Parents Clb Oreg; Recog Awd, Tchrs of Hearing Impaired Progs, Champaign.

SALVARY, STANLEY C W oc/Professor;

b/Nov 21, 1937; h/262 Westcroft Rd, Beaconsfield, Quebec, Canada; c/Montreal, Quebec; m/Veronica Rodriguez; c/Sharlene, Susan, Lisa, Roxanne, Keisha; ed/AAS 1962, BS cum laude 1965 Bklyn Col; MBA Long Isl Univ 1969; PhD NY Univ 1977; CPA Univ St NY 1968; pa/Assoc Prof Concordia Univ 1978-; Asst Prof Baruch Col 1976-78; Lectr Baruch Col, CUNY 1970-76; CPA Conslt 1970-77; Pres & Mng Dir Salvary & Daniels Inc 1970; Var Other Former Positions; Am Inst CPAs; NY St Soc CPAs; Am Acct'g Assn; Acct'g Res Assn; Am Ec Assn; Fin Mgmt Assn; C W Post Tax Inst; IPA; Taxation w Rep; Other Profl Activs; r/Cath; hon/Alpha Sigma Lambda; Richard Littlefield Meml Awd; W/W E; Notable Ams Bicent Era; DIB; Men of Achmt; Notable Ams; Commun Ldrs & Noteworthy Ams.

SALZMAN, BARNETT SEYMOUR oc/Physician; Psychiatrist; b/Feb 15, 1939; ba/1314 S King, Suite 722, Honolulu, HI 96814; m/Sandra Christian; c/Rachel Star, Sunshine Noel; ed/BA Hunter Col 1960; MD Univ Buffalo Sch Med 1965; pa/Current Pvt Pract Psychi, Hauula, Hi; Med Staff Queen's Med Ctr Castle Hosp; Med Advr Hlth Sers Escondido Union Sch Dist 1975-77; Radio Broadcaster " Barnett Salzman, MD, Mind & Soul'' 1975-77; Med Advr Intl Acad Biol Med, Phoenix 1975-77; Pvt Pract Psychi, Escondido, Cal 1975-77; Other Former Positions; AMA; Am Psychi Assn; Fellow Royal Soc Hlth; r/Ch Jesus Christ LDS, Escondido: Min 1975-77; hon/Physicians Recog Awd, AMA; Biogl Listings.

SANCHEZ, MARIA N oc/School Teacher; Reading Supervisor; b/Jul 22, 1929; h/114 Aguirre, Rio Grande City, TX 78582; ba/Rio Grande City; m/Joe R Sr; c/Joe Jr, Juan, Fred, David, Eddy, Jonell, Mary Jo; p/Juan and Dolores S Solis (dec); ed/BS; MEd; pa/Tchr & Rdg Supvr Ringgold Intermed Sch; Tex St Tchrs Assn; NEA; CTA; AAUW; cp/Dem Wom's Org; r/Cath: Current Lector; hon/Life Mem, PTA; IPA; Presenter, Atlanta (Ga) IRA (on individ'd instrn); Personalities of S.

SANDERLIN, EVA MAY SLOVER oc/Teacher, Librarian; b/Oct 18, 1924; h/Box 188, Knippa, TX 78870; ba/Knippa; m/Allen C; c/Judith Peggy S Beloat, Ted Allen, Claudia Ann; p/Leo Lloyd Slover (dec); Annie May Holmes Slover, Rio Frio, TX; ed/BA Mary Hardin-Baylor; MEd Our Lady of the Lake; Grad Study Sul Ross Univ; pa/Tchr-Libn Knippa ISD; Tex St Tchrs Assn; TAET; WICI; Tex Press Wom; cp/Knippa PTA; Knippa Commun Bldrs; Am Legion Aux; r/Prot; hon/Writing Awds, Tex Press Wom Commun Contest & SW Tex Jr Col Creative Writing Contest.

SANDERS, FRANCES BEYER oc/Court Reporter; b/Jun 11, 1923; h/PO Box 2340, Juneau, AK 99803; m/James C; c/3 Chd; p/Henry F and Wilma B Beyer; ed/Mason City Jr Col 1942-43; Merchant Marine Ct Reporting Sch (NYC) 1944; Temple Univ 1945-46; mil/USCG 1943-45; pa/Ct Reporter USCG, Tampa, Fla 1944-46; Free-lance Ct Reporter, Tampa 1947-48; HS & Adult Ed Tchr, Southport, NC 1953-54; Ofc Mgr, Yaupon Bch, NC 1954-59; Legal Secy, Juneau, Alaska 1959-62; Asst Secy Alaska Senate, Juneau 1962; Free-lance Ct Reporter operating Taku Reporters, Juneau 1962-; Nat Shorthand Reporters Assn; cp/Grant Chm Gtr Juneau Arts & Humanities Coun; Wom of the Moose;

OES; hon/Cit for Outstg Perf of Duty, USCG; Popular Awd, Art Show in Southport 1955; Biogl Listings.

SANDERS, SAMUEL oc/University Professor; Concert Pianist; b/Jun 27, 1937; h/473 W End Ave, New York, NY 10024; ba/Same; m/Rhoda Ross; c/Sophie; p/Irving Sanders (dec); Molly Sanders, NYC; ed/BS Hunter Col 1959; MS Juilliard Sch Music 1961; pa/Assoc Prof SUNY-Purchase 1972-; The Juilliard Sch (Tchr Vocal Lit Courses) 1964-; Tchr Vol Lit Sarah Lawrence Col 1971-72; Tchr Piano Univ Mass-Amherst 1968-69; Other Tchg & Lecture Positions; Recorded Var Record Cos incl'g: Columbia, EMI-Angel, RCA Red Seal, Vanguard, Musical Heritage Soc, Melodia, Desto, Others; Concerts Perf'd: NAm, Europe, Soviet Union, Japan, Philippines; Participant Num Maj Musical Fests incl: Marlboro Fest (Vt), Meadowbrook Fest (Mich), Mostly Mozart Fest Avery Fisher Hall (NYC), Caramoor Fest (NY), Others; Musical Adv Bd Pro Musicis Foun; hon/Phi Beta Kappa; Top Prize Accompanying in Tschaikowsky Intl Competition, Moscow 1966; Mem Hunter Col Hall of Fame; Best Record of Yr Awd (w Robert White, Tenor) 1976, Stereo Review 1976.

SANDERS, WALTER MacDONALD III oc/Sanitary Engineer; b/Dec 5, 1930; h/195 Xavier Dr, Athens, GA 30606; ba/Athens; m/Emily Joyce; c/Walter M IV, Emily Graham, Albert Brian, Stephen Craig; p/Walter M Sanders II (dec); Mary Minerva Easley Sanders, Athens; ed/BS; MS; PhD; mil/USAF Med Ser Corps 1953-55, Res San

Engr; pa/Assoc Dir Water Quality Res Athens Envir Res Lab; Am Soc Civil Engrs; AAAS; Sigma Xi; Res Assoc & Mem Grad Fac Ecology, Univ Ga; Adj Prof Clemson Univ; cp/Athens W Rotary Clb; r/Friendship Presb Clb; hon/Outstg Yg Men Am; W/W SE; DIB.

SANDRAPATY, RAMACHANDRA RAO oc/Professor; Professional Engineer; b/Feb 15, 1942; h/2688 Lakeside Dr NE, Orangeburg, SC 29115; ba/O'burg; m/Kalyani Kumari; c/Ravichandra Kumar, Kiran Kumar; p/Venkata Subbarao and Annapoornamma

Sandrapaty (dec); ed/BS w hons; ME; MSME; PhD; PE; pa/Prof Mech Engrg SC St Col; ASME; APCA; ASEE; cp/Indo-Am Clb, USC; O'burg Intl Clb; r/Hindu; hon/Postmatriculation Merit Scholar; Jr Res Fellow; Notable Ams Bicent Era; DIB; Men Achmt; Others.

SANFORD, G MARSHALL oc/Teacher; b/Sept 1, 1944; h/27 Turney Rd, Redding Ridge, CT 06876; ba/Norwalk, CT; p/Earle G Sanford (dec); Violet Rae Sanford, Redding

Ridge; ed/BA Grove City Col; MSEd Univ Bridgeport; pa/Tchr Norwalk HS; NEA; CEA; NTA: Past Pres, 1/VP, Rep Assembly Del; Charter Mem UB PDK; cp/Redding JCs; Secy Zoning Comm; Vol Danbury Hosp; Pres Antique Fire Apparatus Clb; r/Christ Epis Ch, RR; hon/PDK; Commun Ldrs & Noteworthy Ams; JC of Month 1977; Nat Social Sci Hon Soc.

SANFORD, PAUL EVERETT oc/Professor; b/Jan 14, 1917; h/343 N 14th St, Manhattan, KS 66502; ba/Manhattan; m/Helen Louise; c/Paula Louise Schubert, Patricia Kathleen Banning, Carolyn Ruth; p/Charles and Ina Sanford (dec); ed/BS; MS;

PhD; mil/AUS: ETO, PTO; pa/Prof Dept Animal Scis Ks St Univ; Univ Tchg & Res in Poultry Sci & Nutrition; cp/Manhattan C of C; Precnt Com-person, Repubs; r/Presb; hon/E Walter Morrison Awd; Gamma Sigma Delta Sr Fac Awd of Merit; Fellow, AAAS; Hon Mem, Broiler Soc Japan.

SANGER, ISAAC JACOB oc/Retired Artist; b/Jan 8, 1899; h/3610 Riviera St, Marlow Heights, Temple Heights, MD 20031; m/Marjorie Graybill (dec); p/Samuel Abraham Sanger (dec); Rebecca E Bowman (dec); ed/BS Tchrs Col Columbia Univ; Grad Work Sch Painting & Sculpture Columbia Univ & Art Students Leag; mil/USAF WWII; pa/Printmaker; Painter; Graphic Artist HEW, USPHS; r/Ch of Brethren, Wash DC; hon/Prints Rep'd in Var Collections incl'g: NY Public Lib, Newark Mus, San Diego Fine Arts Gallery, Nat Collection Fine Arts, Lib of Cong, Metro Mus, Wesleyan Univ, Princeton Univ, Univ Wis; Cit for Outstg Achmt in Graphic Arts, Bridgewater Col, B'water (Va); Wood Engraving Included in Smithsonian's Traveling Exhbn of Am Prints from Wood; Others.

SANSAVER, JAMES LEROY oc/Lawyer; Staff Assistant; b/Jan 13, 1935; h/3124 Glen Carlyn Rd, Falls Church, VA 22041; ba/Washington, DC; m/Kathleen Elaine Willis; c/Michael J, Cynthia M, Alexa T, Christopher J; p/Roy L and Mary Agnes Azure Sansaver, Wolf Point, MT; ed/BA 1957, JD 1961 Univ Mont; mil/Mont St Militia; pa/Staff Asst to Asst Secy of Interior for Indian Affairs, US Dept Interior; Legal Conslt on Native Am Rts on Natural Resources & Indian Water Rts to Var Am Indian Orgs incl'g: Native Am Natural Resource Devel Fdn 1973-76, Mont InterTribal Policy Bd 1973-75, Nat Cong Am Indians 1972-73, Others; Mont Bar Assn; Am Indian Bar Assn; Phi Delta Phi; Admitted to Pract: Supr Ct Mont, Dist Cts & Fed Dist Cts Mont; Dept Interior Task Force on Reorg of Bur of Indian Affairs; r/Rom Cath; Mem Christian F'ships; hon/Carroll Col Acad Scholar; Ft Peck Fellow; Bancroft-Whitney Awd for Adm Law; F'ship in Public Mgmt, US Civil Ser Comm.

SARAFIAN, ARMEN oc/University President; b/Mar 5, 1920; h/1950 Third St, La Verne, CA 91750; ba/Same; m/Margaret; c/William, Winston, Norman, Joy, Madeline; p/Kevork and Lucy Sarafian (dec); ed/AB; MA; PhD; LLD; pa/Pres Univ La Verne Col & Univ La Verne 1976-; Pres Pasadena City Col & Supt Pasadena Area Commun Col Dist 1965-76; Adm Dean for Instr Pasadena City Col 1959-65; Coor Sec'dy & Jr Col Ed

Pasadena City Schs 1951-59; Other Former Positions; Conslt to Bus, Indust & Govt; Mem Mgmt Team Univ Alaska St-wide Sys 1977-78; Dir Mgmt Reorg Conn Sys Reg Commun Cols 1974-75; Policy Bd Gt Plains Nat Institutional TV Lib 1975; Others; cp/Bd Dirs La Verne C of C; Past Pres: New Century Clb Pasadena, Cal Conservation Clb; Fdr & Adult Advr Pasadena Area Yth Coun; Fdr & Mem Exec Com Pasadena Hall of Sci Proj; Hon Adv Bd Pasadena Area Chapt ARC; Native Sons of Golden West; Arcadia Coor'g Coun; Pasadena Hist Soc; Patron Pasadena Area Mexican-Am S'ship Com; S Pasadena Oneonta Clb; Others; r/Ch of Brethren; hon/Dist'd Commun Ser Awd, Pasadena Ed Assn; Conserv Merit Awd, Cal Conserv Coun; Hon Life Mem, Pasadena Coun P's & T's; Citizen of Day Awd, Sierra Madre City Coun; Spec Recog Awd, Phi Delta Kappa; Biogl Listings; Num Others.

SARAFIAN, SYLVIA ANNETTE oc/Computer Scientist; b/Jun 16, 1931; h/13856 Bora Bora Way #1051, Marina Del Rey, CA 90291; ba/Marina Del Rey; p/Antranig Arakel Sarafian (dec); Elizabeth Zorian Sarafian, Newton Highlands, MA; ed/BA Mt Holyoke Col; pa/Author: *Compufarm* (Cost Analysis Computer Sys for Agri), *Aurora* (Computerized Agri Acct'g Prog); Coauthor *Safe* (Unemploymt Ins Cost Control & Wkr Utilization Sys); cp/Assoc Mem Repub St Ctl Com of Cal; Cal Wom for Agri; Appalachian Mtn Clb; r/Armenian Apostolic; hon/W/W in W.

SARTOR, CAROLYN DENISE oc/Program Executive; b/Jun 27, 1946; h/10815 Wrightwood Ln, Studio City, CA 91604; ba/Los Angeles, CA; m/Luther Hamilton Jr; c/Luther Hamilton III, Candice Dara; p/Herman James and Vivian Marie Clayborn, LA; ed/BA Cal St Univ-LA 1968; MA Columbia 1974; pa/Prog Exec Chd's Prog CBS Entertainmt Div, LA 1978-; KNXT, LA 1976-78; Prodr Var Shows, Assoc Prodr, Reschr, Prodn Asst; Tchr Adult Ed, Grades K-6 LA Bd Ed 1971-76; Other Former Positions; cp/Chd's Hosp; CoProdr U High Blood Pressure Foun Telethon; Nat Urban Leag Assn; Am Cancer Soc; "Friend" Golden St Mutual S'ship Foun; Broadcast Mem Com on Chd's TV; Wom on Target; NAACP, LA Chapt.

SASSIN, CAROL ANN oc/Assistant Professor; b/Oct 28, 1942; h/1601 Schley St, Wharton, TX 77488; ba/Beaumont, TX; p/Victor John ans Judith Marie Manofsky Sassin, Wharton; ed/BBA 1964, MBA 1970 Sam Houston St Univ; pa/Asst Prof Ofc Adm Lamar Univ 1977-79; Edr Odessa Col, Odessa, Tex 1971-77, Houston Indep Sch Dist,

Houston, Tex 1970-71; Other Former Positions; Tex Bus Ed Assn; Tex Pers & Guid Assn; APGA; AAUW; Delta Sigma Pi; cp/Lamar Univ Wom's Clb; r/Cath; hon/Pi Omega Pi, Hon Grad; Dean's List; Nat Hon Soc; Phi Chi Theta; Outstg Yg Wom Am; W/W: Tex, Wom in Ed.

SASSO, RUTH MARYANN oc/Associate Professor; b/Dec 9, 1928; h/86C Falls Terrace, Oakville, CT 06779; ba/Waterbury, CT; p/Nicholas and Mildred Sasso, Bridgeport, CT; ed/BS, MA; pa/Assoc Prof Mattatuck Commun Col; Coor Early Childhood Ed & Dir Mattatuck Early Childhood Lab Sch; Conslt Early Childhood Progs; Com Mem; Book Reviewer; Field Sponsor Hd Start

Supplimentory Tng Prog; r/Cath; hon/W/W: Am Wom, Intells, E.

SATCHIDANANDA, SRI SWAMI oc/Monk; b/Dec 22, 1914; h/PO Box 108, Pomfret Center, CT 06259; ba/Same; pa/Author; Lectr; Spiritual Guide; Cnslr; cp/Ecumenical & Spiritual Ldr; r/Universal, Integral Yoga; hon/Martin Buber Awd for Outstg Ser to Humanity; Hon Title & Position of Fellow, Col Human Scis, Intl Inst Integral Human Scis.

SATTERFIELD, G HOWARD oc/Doctor of Medicine, Obstetrics & Gynecology; h/PO Box 6043, Greenville, NC 27834; ba/Same; m/Joyce O; c/Karen Joyce, Debra Kay, George Howard III, Lisa Ann, Diane Lynn, (Stepson:) Bruce Koonce; ed/BS NC St Univ 1954; MD Duke Univ Sch Med 1957; pa/E Carolina Univ Med Sch: Clin Asst Prof, Vis Instr Sch Nsg 1971-; Ob/Gyn Cancer Conslt Pitt Co Hlth Dept 1973-76; Pitt Co Meml Hosp, G'ville: Chm Dept Ob/Gyn 1974, 75, Att'g Staff 1971-; Pvt Pract, G'ville 1971-; Var Former Positions; Am Col Ob/Gyn; Am Col Surgs; Am Fertility Soc; Baynard-Carter Ob/Gyn Soc; Am Assn Gynecologic Laparscopies; Royal Soc Med; Pan Am Med Assn; Other Profl Orgs; hon/W/W: NC, S&SW; NC Lives; Others.

SATTERFIELD, JOHN ROBERTS JR oc/College President; b/Dec 4, 1921; h/193 Longview Rd, Staten Island, NY 10301; ba/Staten Isl; m/Carolyn Talley; c/John R III, Kenneth Scott, Keith Charles, Jean Council; p/John Roberts Satterfield (dec); Elise Council Satterfield, Martinsville, VA; ed/BA; MM; MA; PhD; mil/USAAF 1942-45, Capt; Bronze Star; 2 Pres Cits; 7 Campaign Medals; European Theatre Opers; Melville Soc; pa/Pres Wagner Col; Author 5 Books, Num Articles, Reviews, Short Stories, Music; cp/Bd Dirs Staten Isl Col of C; r/Meth; U Meth City Soc; hon/Composer's Awd, NC Symph Soc; Harbison Awd for Dist'd Tchg, Danforth Foun.

SAUER, MARY LOUISE oc/Homemaker; b/Jun 26, 1923; h/830 W 58 Terr, Kansas City, MO 64113; m/Gordon Chenoweth; c/Elisabeth Ruth, Gordon Chenoweth, Margaret Louise, Amy Kietter Doyle;

p/Maurice E Steinhilber (dec); Katherine Barber, Cleveland Hgts, OH; ed/NWn Univ; pa/Am Guild Organists; Mu Phi Epsilon; cp/Pro Am; DAR; r/Presb; hon/Intl Reg Profiles; Notable Ams Bicent Era; Commun Ldrs & Noteworthy Ams; Vols in Ed, Ks City.

SAVITSKY, HELEN oc/Geneticist; h/-1003 Bay Wood Pl, Salinas, CA 93901; ba/-Salinas; p/Ivan Haretshko (dec); Anastasia

Degtjareva (dec); ed/PhD; pa/Geneticist US Dept Agri; Res in Genetics & Breeding; Pubs; Participant Sci Confs; r/Greek Orthodox; hon/Meritorious Ser Awd, Am Soc Sugar Beet Technol; Superior Ser Awd, US Dept Agri; Awd of Merit, Netherland's Res Inst Sugar Indust.

SAXENA, VINOD KUMAR oc/Research Associate Professor; b/May 23, 1944; h/4159 Persimmon Pl, Salt Lake City, UT 84107; ba/SLC; m/Indra; p/Kishoir L and Uma Saxena, Agra, India; ed/BS 1961, MS 1968 Agra Univ (India); PhD Univ Rajasthan (Jaipur, India); pa/Res Assoc Prof Meteorol Univ Utah 1977-; Cloud Physicist & Lectr Physics Univ Denver (Colo) 1971-77; Postdoct Fellow Univ Mo-Rolla 1968-71; Am Meteorol Soc; Am Geophys Union; r/Hindu; hon/Merit Scholar; Sigma Xi; Num Res Grants; Profl Pubs; Biogl Listings.

SCALLY, MARY ANTHONY oc/Sister of Religious Order; Librarian; h/1420 N St NW, Washington, DC 20005; ba/Wash DC; p/Robert Emmitt and Agnes Lillian Sanner Scally (dec); ed/AB St Mary of Woods Col; ABLS Rosary Col; Postgrad Studies; pa/Libn Assn for Study of Afro-Am Life & Hist; Ofcr Mgr & Nat Exec Dir Friendship House, Chicago, Ill 1970-73; Lib Staff Xavier Univ, New Orleans, La 1969-70; Libn Pensacola Cath HS, Pensacola, Fla 1958-69; Tchr-Libn HSs Va & Ga 1954-58; Other Former Positions; Nat & Local Ofcs Cath Lib Assn; Am Lib Assn; r/Cath: Mem Sisters of Mercy, Baltimore Province; hon/NAACP, Pensacola, Fla for Activs as Adult Advr in Yth Coun; Author: *Negro Cath Writers* 1945, *Walking Proud, the Story of Carter G Woodson* 1978.

SCARBOROUGH, CURTISS CLINTON oc/Editor; Columnist; Humorist; Short Story Writer; b/Dec 10, 1935; h/2476 Buttonwood Ct, Florissant, MO 63031; ba/St Louis, MO; m/Ruth Ann Jent; c/Karol Ruth, Keith Curtiss; p/Curtis Clinton Scarborough (dec); Jane Scarborough Rednour, Carterville, IL; ed/BA So Ill Univ 1956; BCM, MRE SWn Bapt Theol Sem 1959; MA Evang Col 1962; LittD

Stanton Col 1976; mil/USAFR 1953-55; pa/Editor *The Christian Citizen*; Assoc Dir & Pubr Christian Civic Foun; VP & Sr Editor Clarion Pub'g Co; Nat Writer's Clb; cp/Nat Chaplain Resv Law Ofcrs Assn Am; IPA; Smithsonian Instn; r/Parker Rd Bapt Ch, Florissant: Mem; Ordained So Bapt Min; hon/W/W Rel; Personalities W&MW; Commun Ldrs & Noteworthy Ams; Men of Distn; Intl W/W Commun Ser.

SCARBOROUGH, MARY JOANNA oc/Organist; Choir Director; b/Jun 22, 1932; h/727 Seneca Dr, Horseheads, NY 14845; ba/Elmira, NY; m/George F; c/George C, Carol E, Charles J; p/William Arthur Clark (dec); Mrs T F Turman, Pensacola, FL; ed/BMus; pa/Trinity Epis Ch: Organist, Choir Dir; Group Piano Instr; Radio Commentator; Music Ed Tchr; Judge Nat Guild Piano Tchrs; Am Guild Organists; Nat Music Tchrs Assn: VP, Prog Chm; cp/Pres Outstg Yg Ams Inc; St Dir Nat Teen-Ager Pageant; Prog Chm Matinee Musicale Clb; Commun Concert; Fortnightly Clb; Little Theatre; r/So Bapt; hon/Hon Roll, Am Col Musicians; Personalities of S; DIB; World W/W; Wom, Music; Commun Ldrs & Noteworthy Ams; Others.

SCARLETT, DOROTHY GLADYS oc/- Museum Director; b/Mar 7, 1909; h/PO Box 275, Harper, KS 67058; ba/Harper; m/Floyd M; c/Sandra J Beem; p/(dec); pa/Dir Harper City Hist Mus; Ks Watercolor Soc; cp/Pres Harper City Hist Soc; r/Meth; hon/Citizen of Yr 1949.

SCHABBEL, HELEN CAROL oc/Retired Educator; h/Rt 4, Box 323, South Haven, MI 49090; p/Arnold and Emilie Schabbel; ed/BA, Perm Life Tchg Cert in Sec'dy Ed Wn Mich Univ 1935; MA Univ Mich 1958; Addit Studies; pa/Tchr Mich Schs 37 Yrs, Sec'dy Schs of Evart, St Louis, S Haven, Ann Arbor, Benton Harbor & Fennville; Ret'd 1974; Involved in Basic Hlth Res as Recipient of Psychic Energy 1956-; Life Mem Pi Lambda Theta; Mich Ed Assn; NEA; AAUW; Ret'd Tchrs Assn; hon/Life Fellow, IBA; Pub'd Author; Biogl Listings.

SCHAFF, ROBERT ADAIR oc/Executive; b/May 27, 1937; h/One Horse Ln, Gainesville, TX 76240; ba/G'ville; m/Dorothy Stams; c/Allison, Stacy, Christy; p/Byron H Schaff (dec); Louise Sullivan Schaff, Shreveport, La; ed/Univ Okla; Centenary Col La; Grad Univ Houston, Inst Org Mgmt 1964; Deg Computer Sci Rutherford Col 1969; Cert'd, Reg'd C of C Exec 1974; pa/Exec VP G'ville Area C of C; TIDC; SIDC; Indust Developers Ark; TCCM; E & W Tex Cs of C; CCMSAET; CCEAWT; Past Dir N Tex Comm; Past Pres Gulf Coast C of C Mgrs

Assn; Past VP Red River Val Assn; Others; cp/Rotary Clb; BSA: VChm Frontier Trails Dist Longhorn Coun, Past VChm Chisholm Trail Dist, Longhorn Coun; Past Dir Lewisville Chapt Am Cancer Soc; Past Exec VP Shreveport Jr C of C & Spoke Awd Winner; Others; r/1st Presb Ch: Mem; hon/Citizen of Month, Lewisville, Tex (Apr 1975); Order of Arrow, BSA; Personalities of S.

SCHAFFNER, WINNIE MAE FULLERTON oc/Teacher; h/832 S 57th St, Birmingham, AL 35212; m/Henry W; pa/Fdr, Dir & Owner Day Nursery & Kgn; hon/Notable Ams Bicent Era.

SCHALLER, JEROME D oc/Manager Government Relations; b/Jun 27, 1925; h/12804 Hammonton Rd, Silver Spring, MD 20904; ba/Washington, DC; m/Helen M; c/Stephanie, Sandra; p/David A and Gertrude Schaller (dec); ed/BA St Thomas Col; mil/USAAC, Sgt; pa/Mgr Govt Relats Fed Govt Sers, 3M Co; Former Public Relats Conslt Fairmont Co; Former Asst to Advt'g Mgr Weyerhaeurser Sales Co; Other Former Positions; Intl Public Relats Assn; Intl & Am Assns Polit Conslts; Pres, Bd Dirs JACS Inc; cp/George Town Clb; Nat Capital Dem Clb; Capitol Hill Clb; Nat Press Clb; St Paul Ath Clb; r/Cath.

SCHANKMAN, SIDNEY oc/Music Educator; Musician; b/May 16, 1919; h/74-10 35th Ave, Jackson Heights, NY 11372; ba/Flushing, NY; m/Estelle; p/Jack and Anna Schankman, St Louis, MO; ed/Dipl Juilliard Sch Music; BS, MA Tchrs Col Columbia Univ; pa/AUS; pa/Tech Dir Manhattan Borough-Wide Salute to Music Prog; Conductor: Manhattan Borough-Wide Band, Manhattan-E Commun Band, Queens Borough-Wide Orch; Coor Music Borough Queens; Dir Queens

Instrumental Ctr, Salute to Music Prog; Asst Examr Music Lics, NYC; Dir Orch & Chamber Music Ensembles, Buck's Rock Work Camp; Chm Music NY St Sch Music Assn; Exec Coun Mem NY St Sch Music Assn; Nat Orch Assn; Nat Band Assn: Nat Assn Jazz Edrs; Assoc'd Musicians Gtr NY; Phi Mu Alpha; r/Jewish; hon/Intl W/W Music; Notable Ams.

SCHARLEMANN, HERBERT KARL oc/Minister; b/Aug 5, 1927; h/N Broadway, Hoffman, IL 62250; ba/Hoffman; m/Elizabeth Mae Fahrmann; c/LizBeth, Timothy, Nancy, Daniel, James, Mary, Benjamin; p/Ernst Karl Scharlemann, Chattanooga, TN; Johanna Harre (dec); ed/BA; BD; STM; DMin; pa/Min

Trinity Luth Ch, Hoffman; Chm So Ill Dist LC-MS-Worship Com; Staff Mem Kaskaskia Col, Centralia, Ill; Pres Centralia Area Min Alliance 2 Terms; Luth Human Relats Assn; cp/Past Pres Lion's Clb; Valparaiso Univ Century Clb; r/Luth; hon/Luth Acad for S'ship: Mem, Awd.

SCHARLEMANN, MARTIN HENRY oc/Professor; b/Dec 28, 1910; h/17 Seminary Terrace N, St Louis, MO 63105; ba/St Louis; m/Dorothy Hoyer; c/Edith Louise Rehbein, Ernst Theodor, Martin George, John Paul; p/Ernst K Scharlemann, Chattanooga, TN; Johanna Harre Scharlemann (dec); ed/MDiv; MA; PhD; ThD; mil/USAF Brigadier Gen, Ret'd Chaplain; pa/Prof Theol Concordia Sem; Theol Res & Writing; Tng Future Clergy; cp/Pres Clayton Rotary Clb; Chaplain Am Legion; r/Luth; hon/Air Univ Awd; St Martin of Tours (Silver) Medallion; Outstg Edr Am; Ky Col.

SCHAUBEL, HOWARD JAMES oc/Medical Doctor; Orthopaedic Surgeon; h/32 Gordon Dr, Big Pine Key, FL 33043; ba/BPK; m/Marjorie Moody; c/Candice Edwards (Mrs James), Jan Timmons (Mrs Robert C, Wendy Dickinson (Mrs Henry), Gayle Sue Klooster (Mrs Gary); p/Charles T and Gen Slager Schaubel; ed/AB; MD; mil/USAR MC, Maj (Ret'd); pa/Emeritus Staff (Conslt Ortho Dept) Butterworth Hosp, Grand Rapids, Mich 1973-; Conslt Ortho Surg: N Ottawa Commun Hosp, Grand Haven, Mich 1946-73, Upper Keys Commun Hosp, Plantation Key, Fla 1977-78, Ferguson Hosp, Grand Rapids 1978; Ortho Conslt Saladin Shrine Clin for Crippled Chd, Grand Rapids 1978; Sr Att'g Ortho Surg, Fla Keys 1973-78; Chief of Surg Fishermans Hosp 1974-76; Other Former Positions; Monroe Co Med Soc (Fla): Mem, Secy-Treas 1974, Pres 1976; Fla & Am Med Assns; Ottawa Co Med Soc; Other Med Socs; Diplomate Am Bd Ortho Surg; Fellow: Am Acad Ortho Surgs, Intl Col Surgs; En, Fla, Piedmont Ortho Soc; Fellow Am Fracture Assn; cp/F&AM; 32° Mason; Shriner; Rotary Intl; Bd Dirs Camp Blodgett U Commun Fund; r/Congreg; hon/Galens, Dist'd Alumni Awd, Grand Rapids Jr Col; Dist'd Ser Awd, Monroe Co Med Soc; Dist'd Ser Awd, U Commun Fund, Grand Rapids; Dist'd Ser Awd, Saladin Shrine; Others; Pub'd Author.

SCHAUER, WILLIAM CHARLES BLASE oc/Director; Clergyman; b/Mar 23, 1921; h/1752 Camino Corrales, Santa Fe, NM 87501; ba/Same; p/John J Schauer (dec); Julia Columbo (dec); ed/BA; MA; MDiv; mil/Served 1942-43; pa/Dir Liturgy in Santa Fe; Fdr Liturgy, the Las Cruces Experimt;

r/Rom Cath: Priest, Mem Dominican Order; hon/Nat Newman Ednl Awd.

SCHAUSS, ALEXANDER GEORGE oc/Criminologist; Biobehavioral Scientist; b/Jul 20, 1948; h/630 Maywood Ln, Fircrest, WA 98466; m/Sharon Lee; c/Frank and Anna Schauss, Jamaica, NY; ed/BA 1970, MA 1972 Univ NM; pa/Current Corrections Tng Ofcr Wash St Crim Justice Tng Comm; Adj Dir Acad for Biobehavioral Scis, Inst for Advmt of Knowledge & Sci, City Col, Seattle, Wash; Former Probation Dir Co Adult Probation Sers; St Asst Admr Yth Sers, St of SD; Others; Acad Crim Justice Sers; Am Soc Crim; Am

Orthopsychi Assn; Am Correctl Assn; Am Assn Correctl Psychologists; Am Assn Correctl Tng Pers; Other Profl Activs; cp/Former Conf Moderator 1st Conf on Domestic Violence, Tacoma, Wash; Former Chm Pierce Co Law & Justice Corrections Com; Former Mem Gov's Com on NM Crim Justice Standards & Goals; Bd Mem Wellness of Wash; Others; hon/Commun Ser Ldrship Awds; Sandia & Eldorado HSs; Mayor of NY Cit; Am Legion of Honor Awd for Commun Ser; APGA Assn Public Offender Cnsl'g Assn Awd; Biogl Listings; Others.

SCHEER, WILBERT E oc/Editorial & Research Assistant; Educator; b/Feb 8, 1909; h/804 Austin Ave, Park Ridge, IL 60068; m/Erna E Blumenschein (dec); c/Arlene Tharp, Stephany Oestreich; ed/NWn Univ; Medill Sch Jour; Univ: Ill, Chgo; Wash & Jefferson Col 1943; mil/Served WWII, Pers Technician Skilled (290); pa/Blue Cross-Blue Shield, Chicago, Ill: Edit & Res Asst 1969-74 (Ret'd 1974), Dir Pers 1951-69; Pers Dir Ill Agri Assn 1946-51; Ofc Mgr & Asst Opers Mgr McKesson & Robbins, Chgo 1928-46; Mem MENSA; Dartnell Adm Execs Res Panel 1970; Former Mem: Ofc Adm Edit Adv Coun (Toronto), Ill Pvt Bus Schs St Bd; Fac Mem: NWn Univ 1967-, Univ Chgo 1961, 62, 63, Maine Twp HS 1958-66, Ctl YMCA 1956-66; Guest Lectr; Other Profl Activs; hon/Feature "Meet Your Neighbor", *Park Ridge Herald* 1952; Cited "Luths You Must Meet" in *The Luth Witness* 1964; Dist'd Edr Awd & Plaque, Delta Mu Delta; Pub'd Author; Biogl Listings.

SCHELLER, ZBIGNIEW oc/Physician; b/Apr 7, 1941; h/11874 Lake Shore Pl, North Palm Beach, FL 33408; ba/Palm Beach Gardens, FL; m/Anna Maria; p/Zygfryd Scheller (dec); Helena Scheller, Gdansk,

Poland; ed/MD Univ Gdansk 1966; pa/Chief Pathol & Dir Labs Palm Bch Gardens Hosp; Med Dir Diagnostic Lab Inc, N Palm Bch; cp/Polish Inst Arts & Scis in Am; r/Rom

Cath; hon/Awds, AMA; Awd, Am Soc Clin Pathologists.

SCHERER, LEE RICHARD oc/Manager; b/Sept 20, 1919; h/550-10 Diplomat Apts, Cocoa Beach, FL; ba/Kennedy Space Ctr, FL; c/Candace, William, Michael, Tracy; p/(dec); ed/BS (Aero Engrg); BS (Marine Engrg); MS; mil/USN 25 Yrs, Ret'd Capt; pa/Mgr Kennedy Space Ctr; r/Prot; hon/NASA: Exceptl Ser, Exceptl Sci Achmt, Dist'd Ser.

SCHERLE, PHYLLIS JOYCE RUSHING oc/Assistant Professor; b/Apr 18, 1929; h/140 Woodcrest Dr, N Fork, Martinsville, IN 46151; ba/Indianapolis, IN; m/Kenneth E; c/Marla, Darla Crone, Carole S Baker; p/Orval A Rushing, Minneola, FL; Ernestine H Rushing, Pinckneyville. IL; ed/BS cum

laude 1957, MA 1958 So Ill Univ; pa/Asst Prof Eng; Past Pres Ind Col Eng Assn; Editor *The Associator* ICEA Jour 1973-; MW MLA; Mod Lang Assn; Reg Editor Col Eng Assn; hon/Betty Rhodes Meml S'ship; Thelma Louise Kellog S'ship; DIB; World W/W Wom in Ed; W/W Am Wom; World W/W Wom.

SCHILLER, JOHN A oc/Teacher; b/Jun 17, 1923; h/1217 Wheeler S, Tacoma, WA 98444; ba/Tacoma; m/Aleen B Linhardt; c/Paul Omar, Samuel Robert; p/Johann Carl Schiller (dec); Adele Schiller, Lincoln, NE; ed/BA; MA; PhD; pa/Pacific Luth Univ: Prof Sociol & Social Wel 1967-, Assoc Prof 1965, Asst Prof 1958, Chm Dept Sociol 1956-71, Chm Div Social Scis 1969-76, Mem Provost Coun 1969-76, Chm Provost Coun 1975-76, Dir Grad Progs Div Social Scis 1977-, Regency Prof 1976-77; Mem Var Coms; Prot Chaplain Beatrice St Home, Beatrice, Neb 1951-56; Prot Chaplain Good Samaritan Hosp, Sterling, Colo 1947-49; Other Min Positions; Am & Pacific Sociol Assns; Nat Coun on Fam Relats; Coun on Social Work Ed; Nat Conf on Social Wel; Wn Social Scis Assn; Other Profl Activs; cp/Bd Dirs Growth Policy Assn; Conslt Area Agy on Aging; Mem Commun Devel Com Tacoma C of C; Pierce Co Growth Policy Org; Var Activs St & Nat Levels; r/Luth; hon/Vis Scholar, Dept Sociol & Fam Study Ctr Univ Minn; Am Luth Ch Growth Awd; Shalom Res Grant; Luth Brotherhood Fac F'ship; Profl Pubs; Biogl Listings; Others.

SCHIRRIPA, DENNIS JAMES oc/Dentist; b/Dec 30, 1945; h/2700 Amelia Dr, Broadview Heights, OH 44141; ba/Medina, OH; p/Joseph Schirripa (dec); Norma Schirripa, Cleveland, OH; ed/BS John Carroll Univ 1970; DDC CWRU 1974; pa/Am Dental Assn; Psi Omega; cp/Kiwanis Intl; Am Cancer Soc, Chm; John Carroll Univ, Admissions Cnslr; r/Rom Cath; hon/Frat Achmt Awd; Biogl Listings.

SCHLANG, JOSEPH oc/Real Estate; Investments; Cultural Films Owner & Distributor; b/Feb 11, 1911; h/35 E 84 St, New York, NY 10028; 44 Cocoanut Row, Palm Beach, FL 33480; ba/NYC; m/Bernice S; c/Stuart A; p/Alexander and Blanch Schlang (dec); ed/BCS; pa/Chm of Bd Schlang Bros & Co (Real Est) 1932-79; LTD Partner, Kalb Voorhis & Co, NY Stock Exc 1950-; Pres Opera Presentations Inc (Cult Films); Pres Schlang Foun; Broad St Foun; Joseph Schlang Foun; Prodr Radio Show "100 More Ways to Improve NYC"; cp/Chair Bus Com for Arts (Fla); r/Jewish; hon/Albert Einstein Fdr; 1st Patron & Fdr Patron Prog; Cert of Merit,

Mayor NYC; Others.

SCHLERT, MARY ESTHER oc/Sister of Religious Order; Teacher; Administrator; Free-lance Writer; b/Aug 13, 1908; h/Mercy Convent, 129 Roseberry St, Phillipsburg, NJ 08865; ba/P'burg; p/Alfred A and Elizabeth M Stehlin Schlert (dec); ed/BS, MA Univ Notre Dame; Addit Studies; pa/Tchr P'burg Cath HS; Tchr Jr & Sr HS 1943-69; Dir Social Wel & Day Care Ctr, Mt Carmel Guild, Trenton, NJ 1969-78; cp/Adv Coun NJ Hist Soc for Students; Student Coun Advr; Student Mag & Newspaper Advr; r/Rom Cath; Mem Sisters of Mercy of NJ; hon/Num Profl & Civic Assns; Sev Local Civic Awds.

SCHMIDT, CLETUS J oc/Court Clerk; b/Mar 21, 1924; h/2022 N 3rd St, Bismarck, ND 58501; ba/Bismarck; m/Gertrude J; c/Gerald T, William J, Dona M, Patricia A, Carol S; p/Jacob N Schmidt (dec); Eva L Schmidt, Richmond, CA; ed/BS Minot St Col; mil/USN Seabees 1943-46; pa/Clerk Dist Ct Morton Co, Mandan (ND) 1947-62; Dep Clerk US Dist Ct in charge of div ofc, Bismarck 1962-69; Clerk US Dist Ct Dist ND 1969-; US Commr 1964-70; Admitted to ND St Bar 1967; Mem Fac in Conduct'g Var Sems for Fed Judicial Ctr 1972-76; St Bar Assn ND; Pres Burleigh Co Bar Assn 1975-76; Fed Ct Clerks Assn Pres 1974-75; Bd Dirs 1975-; cp/Am Legion; Elks; Moose; Ks of C; r/Cath; hon/Outstg Yg Man, Mandan JCs.

SCHMIDT, JOHN LOUIS oc/Clergyman; b/May 30, 1933; h/641 Lakeview Ave, Jamestown, NY 14701; ba/J'town; m/Alice Wagner; c/Bradford Jon, Alison Kay, Peter Godfrey; p/Ralph P Schmidt (dec); J Elizabeth Schmidt, Burghill, OH; ed/AB; BD; DMin; ThM; STD; pa/Pres Bd Trustees Presb Homes

WNY; Pres's Coun Pittsburgh Theol Sem; Presb Conf on the Arts; Presb Coun on Aging; cp/J'town Sch Bd; Leg Chautauqua Co Leg; Planning Coun Chautauqua Co; r/Presb; hon/Centennial Chaplain, Chautauqua Instn; World Coun Scholar, Univ Basel (Switzerland).

SCHMIDT, MARK OTTO oc/Student; b/Jul 31, 1956; h/RD #3, Box 393D, Leechburg, PA 15656; p/Andrew W and Elsie M Schmidt, Leechburg, PA; ed/BS (Physics); BS (Math) magna cum laude Bethany Col 1978; MBA Univ Rochester 1980; cp/Varsity Track; Beta Theta Pi; Kappa Mu Epsilon; hon/Gamma Sigma Kappa; Distn Math & Physics, Bethany Col; W/W; W H Cramblet Awd; J S V Allen Awd.

SCHMIDT, SANDRA ESTRELLA SALGUERO oc/Professor; b/Oct 15, 1949;

h/V-22 Juan Ramos St, Urb Sta Paula, Guaynabo, PR 00657; ba/Caguas, PR; m/Kenneth P; c/Kenneth Alexander, Veronica Estelle; p/Alejandro Salguero (dec); Estrella Roura-Salguero, Guaynabo, PR; ed/BA magna cum laude Univ PR 1971; MA Ctl Mich Univ 1973; pa/Eng Prof; TESOL of PR; Mem Acad Bd Colegio Universitario del Turabo; r/Evang-Wesleyan; hon/W/W S&SW.

SCHMIDT, WAYNE WILLIAM oc/Museum Administrator; b/Mar 31, 1945; h/155 Harbor Dr, Unit 302, Chicago, IL 60602; ba/Chgo; p/Walter and Gloria Schmidt, Chgo; ed/BA w hons 1971; MA Cand NISU 1979; mil/USNR 1963-65; pa/Combined Gt Lakes Navy Assn: Dir 1974-, Treas 1976-78; VP Hist Nav Ships of NAm 1977-79; cp/Sgt at Arms Cook Co Yg Repubs; Past Secy Ill Repub St Nationalities Coun; Former Mem Standing Rules Com Repub St Conv; r/All Saints Polish Nat Cath Ch, Chgo; hon/MW Col Repub of Yr 1968.

SCHMUCKER, RUBY ELVY oc/Psychiatric Registered Nurse, Supervisor, Nurse Educator; b/Nov 17, 1923; h/4214 Bellwood Dr NW, Canton, OH 44708; ba/Massillon, OH; m/Nelson; c/Gary, David, Barbara, Steven; p/Walter Ladrach (dec); Carrie Ladrach, Sugarcreek, OH; ed/RN Aultman Hosp Sch Nsg (Canton); BSN magna cum

laude 1970, MS 1973 Univ Akron; pa/Psychi Nurse Supvr Geriatric Ctr Massillon St Hosp, Massillon 1977-; Instr Nsg Div Nsg Ed Chd's Hosp, Akron 1976-77; Instr Nsg Col Nsg Univ Akron 1974-76; Other Former Positions; Nat Leag for Nsg; Secy Steering Com Ohio Leag for Nsg; Am Nurses Assn; Ohio Nurses Assn, Stark Carrol Dist, Nom'g Com; APGA; Am Col Pers Assn; cp/Var Ofcs Aultman Hosp Alumni Assn; ARC, Canton Chapt; Conslt; Former Hlth Chm Avondale Sch PTA, Canton; r/Trinity U Ch of Christ, Canton; hon/Alpha Sigma Lambda.

SCHNEIDER, MARJORIE LOUISE oc/Attorney at Law; b/Jun 29, 1923; h/2676 Springer Rd Apt #26, Galesburg, IL 61401; ba/G'burg; c/Karl Jeffry; p/Viola A Lersch, G'burg; ed/BS Univ Ill 1945; pa/Admitted to Ill Bar 1946; Pvt Pract Champaign, Ill 1946-47; Pvt Pract, G'burg 1948-; AAUW; Ill, Knox Co Bar Assns; Delta Delta Delta; cp/Altrusa; Jr Wom's Clb; Former Dem Co Chwom Knox Co; Former Mem St Spkrs Bur; Alt Ill Del at Large Nat Conv 1956; Past Dir YWCA; LWV; C of C; Others; hon/W/W: Am Wom, MW, Commerce & Indust; DIB; Royal Blue Book; Ill Lives; Others.

SCHNELLER, RAYMOND JOHN oc/Engineering Consultant; b/Nov 10, 1916;

h/875 Wilson's Lake Ln, Hot Springs, AR 71901; ba/Hot Springs; m/Helen Catherine Passineau; c/John, Mary Lou, George; p/Frederick and Louise Schneller (dec); ed/BS Univ Ala 1939; mil/AUS Corps of Engrs, Maj; pa/Fellow Am Soc Civil Engrs; Assoc Am Inst Planners; cp/Hot Springs Sertoma Clb; Elks Lodge; r/Rom Cath; hon/Sertoma Gem Awd; Nat Ser Awd, DAV.

SCHOETTLER, ELLOUISE D oc/Artist-Teacher; b/Jul 14, 1936; h/9112 Brierly Rd, Chevy Chase, MD 20015; m/James A; c/James Jr, Karen L, Robin A; p/Robert B and Louise K Diggle, Charlotte, NC; ed/BA Dunbarton Col of Holy Cross 1972; MFA Am Univ 1976; pa/Initiated Courses Montgomery Col Commun Sers, Takoma Park, Md 1977-; Var Art Ednl Activs Cynthia Warner Sch, Takoma Park 1972-77; Lectures: Mint Mus Art, Charlotte, NC, Am Univ, Washington, DC; Coalition Wom's Art Orgs: Exec Dir 1978-, Dir Wash Ofc 1977-78; Coor Wom's ARTSPACE, Intl Wom's Yr Conf, Houston, Tex 1977; Wash Wom's Arts Ctr, Wash DC: Exec Dir 1978-, Dir Exhbns 1977-78, CoDir Exhbns 1976-77; One-Person Shows: Blaine Wilson Gallery (Fresno, Cal) 1977, Lorenz Gallery (Bethesda, Md) 1977, Johns Hopkins Ctr (Bologna, Italy) 1977, Others; Group Shows incl: John Hopkins Univ (Baltimore, Md) 1979, Folger Shakespeare Lib (Wash DC) 1979, Wash Wom Arts Ctr 1979, 77, Mint Mus Art (Charlotte) 1977, Others; Rep'd in Collections incl'g: Johns Hopkins Univ, Chevy Chase (Md) Lib; Nat Col Art Assn; Nat Wom's Caucus for Art; Nat Coalition Wom's Art Orgs; Artists Equity, Wash DC; Wash Wom's Arts Ctr, Wash DC; cp/Appt'd Public Mem Ed & Cult Task Force, The Pres's Nat Adv Com on Wom; r/Rom Cath; hon/Pub'd Author; Kappa Gamma Phi; Wash Artist of Month, Lorenz Gallery (Bethesda) 1977.

SCHOOLCRAFT, VICTORIA LYNN oc/Assistant Professor; May 5, 1943; h/4022 NW 34th St, Oklahoma City, OK 73112; ba/OKC; p/R A and Barbara W Schoolcraft, San Antonio, TX; ed/BSN Univ Okla 1966; MSN Univ Tex 1971; pa/Univ Okla Col Nsg: Asst Prof 1972-, Course Coor 1973-, Com Mem, Advsr Student Assn 1975-; Task Force on Wom in Univ; Caucus for Men in Nsg; Am Nurses Assn; Bd Dirs Okla Nurses Assn 1974-75; Bd Dirs Dist Nurses Assn 1974-78; ARC Nurse; Participant Intl Coun Nurses Cong 1977; Conslt; Writer; cp/CoFdr Okla Co Rape Crisis Ctr; Equal Rts Coalition; Nat Wom's Polit Caucus; Former Dem Precnt Chair; Okla Wom's Ctr: CoFdr, Former VP Bd Dirs; Public Spkr; hon/Sigma Theta Tau; Outstg Edrs Am; AMOCO Foun Awd for Superior Tchg; Dist Nurse of Yr 1974, 77; Okla St Nurse of Yr 1977.

SCHREYER, EDWARD RICHARD oc/Governor General; b/Dec 21, 1935; ba/Govt House, Residence Du Gouverneur General, Ottawa, Canada; m/Lily; c/Lisa, Karmel, Jason, Toban; p/John and Elizabeth Schreyer; ed/BA; BEd; MA; St John's Col; Univ Manitoba; mil/Canadian Ofcr Tng Corps, Royal Canadian Armoured Corps, 2/Lt 1954-56; pa/Prof Polit Sci & Intl Relats St Paul's Col, Univ Manitoba 1962-65; cp/Gov General & Cmdr-in-Chief Canada 1979-; Premier Manitoba 1969, 73; Ldr Opposition Manitoba Leg 1977; MP for Selkirk 1968; House of Commons for Springfield 1965; Ldr New Dem Party, Manitoba 1969; Others; Commonwealth Parliamentary Assn; Interparliamentary Union; hon/Vanier Awd as Outstg Yg Canadian 1975.

SCHROEDER, LEONARD W oc/Chiropractic Physician; b/Jun 10, 1921; h/6601 West North Ave, Oak Park, IL 60302; ba/Oak Park; m/Elaine; p/Paul C and Anna Schroeder (dec); ed/DC; mil/AUS MC; 4 Battle Stars; Good Conduct Medal; Unit Cit Medal; pa/Team Phys: Nat Roller Derby, Luther North HS, Hornets Ftball Team (Chicago Pk Dist); Asst Tnr Chgo Cardinals Ftball Clb, Nat Ftball Leag; Org'd Coun on Sports Injuries, Am Chiro Assn; Pres Coun on Sports Injuries; Fellow Intl Col Chiro; Am Col Sports Med; Ill Chiro Soc: Bd Dirs, Chm Bd,

Conv Chm, Ed Com; Nat Col Alumni Assn: Mem, Conv Chm, Fund Raising Com, Fac Mem; Nat Ath Tnrs Assn; cp/Charles Roth Am Legion Post 692; BSA; Precnt Com-man Repub Party; r/St Paul's Luth Ch: Mem, Sch Bd, Ch Secy, Usher & Hd Usher, Pres Walther Leag, Zone Pres Walther Leag, Conv for Intl Walther Leag; hon/Hon Mem: Chi Rho Sigma, Delta Tau Alpha; Fellow Intl Col Chiro; Personalities W&MW; W/W in MW; Men of Achmt; Ser Awd, Luther North HS.

SCHUETZ, GORDON WILLIAM oc/Minister; b/Aug 21, 1933; h/105 Geo Wash Way, Richland, WA 99352; ba/Richland; m/Esther Lillian; c/Renae

Lyndelle, Yvonne Denise Harding; p/William Schuetz, Amisk, Alberta, Canada; Lillian Schuetz (dec); ed/Hon BTh 1978; cp/Police Chaplain; r/Christian; hon/W/W: W, Am, Others.

SCHUETZENDUEBEL, WOLFRAM GERHARD oc/Engineer; b/Feb 17, 1932; h/15405 E Monmouth Pl, Aurora, CO 80015; m/Ingeborg Jutta Lesch; p/G E Schuetzenduebel, Kaiserslautern, Germany; K Schuetzenduebel (dec); ed/BSME 1956; MSME 1958; MS 1958; DSc 1979; pa/Dir Utilities, Pittsburg & Midway Coal Mining Co 1979-; Gen Atomic Co (San Diego, Cal) 1968-79: Sr Staff Spec on Ft St Vrain Proj, Mgr Tech Sers Steam Generator Prog, Sect Ldr, Proj Mgr, Staff Conslt, Others; Sr Res & Devel Engr, Combustion Engrg Inc (Windsor, Conn) 1961-68; Other Former Positions; Reg'd Profl Engr: Germany & Cal; Accre'd Corrosion Spec, Nat Assn Corrosion Engrs; US Correspondent to German Pubs: *Energie*, *Waerme*, *Energy Developments*; CoAuthor, *Nuclear Steam Generators*; Assn German Profl Engrs; German Atomic Forum; Num Coms, ASME; Am Nuclear Soc; Sea Horse Inst, F L LaQue Corrosion Lab; Others; hon/W/W: W, Am, Cal, Commun Ser; Am Sci Registry; Intl W/W Intells; Other Biogl Listings.

SCHULTZ, CLARA PECK oc/Teacher; Author; Lecturer; b/May 21, 1921; h/8815 Hummingbird Ave, Fountain Valley, CA 92708; m/John Edward Sr; c/John, Pamela, Catherine; p/Maurice Emanuel, Grantville, PA; Catherine Buseck Peck (dec); ed/RDH; BS; MA; pa/Tchr Ftn Val Elem Sch Dist, Ftn Val 1966-; Vis Lectr: Chapman Col 1969, 70, Rocky Mtn Col 1977; Free-lance Lectr; Freelance Workshops; Juv Editor *Poet's Nook* 1977; Other Profl Activs; NEA; Cal Ed Assn; Ftn Val Ed: Bldg Rep 18 Yrs, Num Chm'ships; Ftn Val Writer's Wkshop: Fdr 1972, Pres 1972-80; Fdr Ftn Val Br Nat Leag Am Pen Wom; Pres Orange Co Br Nat Leag Am Pen Wom; Nat Leag Am Pen Wom, Var Activs; cp/Ftn Val Friends of Lib; Ftn Val Hist Soc; Ftn Val Commun Theatre; Ftn Val Chapt AAUW; Bd Govs Literary Hall of Fame, Huntington Beach, Cal; OES; Chi Omega; hon/Num Prizes for Poetry, Short Stories; Ftn Val Poet Laureate 1976; Ftn Val City Plaque for Ser to City; WHO Awd for Ser to Ed, Ftn Val Ed Assn; Hon Life Mem, PTO; Wom of Achmt, Nat Leag Am Pen Wom; Nom'd Ftn Val Citizen of Yr 1976, 77, 78, 79; Biogl Listings; Others.

SCHULZ, VICTOR ARTHUR oc/Minister; b/Feb 5, 1943; h/3296 W 74th Pl,

Merrilville, IN 46410; ba/E Chicago, IN 46312; m/Elsa Esparcia; c/Ronald Arthur, Leroy Edgard; p/Lucas John and Maria Medida Schulz, Alem, Misiones Argentina; ed/BA; MDiv; DDiv; pa/Conslt Public Relats & Jour; Author: *Happiness in the Home* 1967, *Flight 657 to Jerusalem* 1976; Profl Tours to Holy Land; cp/Past Pres Spanish-Am Assn; r/SDA; hon/Hon Citizen, New Orleans; Personalities W&MW; W/W Rel.

SCHUMACHER, FREDERICK JOHN oc/Minister; b/Mar 8, 1939; h/79 Greenridge Ave, White Plains, NY 10605; ba/White Plains; m/Joyce Elaine Morris; c/Frederick Eugene, John Frederick, Joy Elaine; p/Friedrich and Elizabeth P Schumacher, St Toms River, NJ; ed/BS Univ Okla 1961; MDiv Luth Sch Theol Chgo 1964; STM NY Theol Sem 1972; DMin Princeton Theol Sem 1978;

pa/Min St Matthew's Luth Ch; VChperson Luth Ch in Am Conslt'g Com on Aging; Exec Bd Metro NY Synod LCA; cp/Chaplain: White Plains Police & Fire Depts, Nsg Home & Extended Care Facility White Plains (also Bd Mem); Mem Nat Assn Eagle Scouts; r/Luth; hon/Order of Arrow; Pioneer Friendship Awd, U Cerebral Palsy Westchester; Samuel Trexler S'ship.

SCHUSKY, ERNEST L oc/Professor; b/Oct 13, 1931; h/412 Willowbrook, Collinsville, IL 62234; ba/Edwardsville, IL; m/Mary Sue; c/Read Eric, Mark Elliott; p/Ernest L Schusky (dec); Leona Schusky, Portsmouth, OH; ed/AB Miami Univ; MA, PhD Univ Chgo; mil/AUS 1954-55; pa/Prof Anthropol So Ill Univ; Fellow Am Anthropol Assn; Royal Anthropol Inst; Coor Behavioral Sci Prog; Author: *The Forgotten Sioux, The Study of Cult Anthropol, Introducing Cult*; hon/Fulbright Awd for Study in India 1964.

SCHUYLER, JANE oc/College Professor; Art Historian; Author; b/Nov 2, 1943; h/35-37 78th St, Jackson Heights, NY 11372; ba/Jamaica, NY; p/Frank J and Helen Oberhofer Schuyler, Jackson Heights; ed/BA Queens Col 1965; MA Hunter Col 1967; PhD

Columbia Univ 1972; pa/Prof York Col CUNY; Art Hist Lectures NY Cult Ctr & Hofstra; Author *Florentine Busts* 1976; cp/Dem; Dem Co Comm, 11th Election Dist, 35th Assembly Dist, Queens; r/Rom Cath; hon/Sum Travel & Res Grant, Columbia Univ; W/W Am Wom.

SCHWALB, SUSAN AMELIA oc/Artist; b/Feb 26, 1944; h/233 E 21 St, New York, NY 10010; p/Morris and Evelyn C Schwalb, NYC; ed/BFA Carnegie Mellon Univ; pa/Guest Lectr 1973-78: Cooper Union (NYC), Temple

Univ (Philadelphia, Pa), Douglass Col, Rutgers Univ (NJ), Art Tours NY, Loyola Univ (Chicago, Ill); Vis Artist NEn Ill Univ, Chgo 1978; Vis Artist Artists-in-the-Schs, NY Foun for the Arts 1978-79; Instr Kean Col NU, Union 1978-79; Asst Art Dir Holt, Rinehart & Winston Inc 1967-68; Book Jacket Designer Dell Pub'g Co 1965-67; Free-lance Graphic Designer 1968-; Fdg Exec Com Coalition Wom's Art Orgs 1977; Arts Del NY St to Intl Wom's Yr Conv, Houston, Tex (Chair Arts Caucus) 1977; Exec Adv Bd Wom's Caucus for Art, NY Chapt 1978; Art Dir Var Pubs; Group Exhbns incl: (1978:) One Hundred Dollar Gallery (NYC), Weatherspoon Art Gallery (Univ NC-G), Franklin & Marshall Col (Lancaster, Pa), (1977) Just Above Mid-Town Gallery (NYC), (1976) Wesbroadway Gallery (NYC), Others; Solo Exhbns incl: Loyola Univ, Chgo 1978, Douglass Col, New Brunswick, NJ 1977, The Open Mind Gallery, NYC 1974; Rep'd in Var Public Collections; Others; cp/Appt'd to Cont'g Com Intl Wom's Yr Conv 1978, Arts Rep to White House Conf; hon/Profl Pubs; Biogl Listings; Recipient F'ships & Grants.

SCHWAN, LeROY BERNARD oc/Director Art Education; b/Dec 8, 1932; ba/1444 Maine St, Quincy, IL 62301; c/David A, Mark J, William R, Catherine L, Maria E; p/Joseph L and Dorothy E Schwan, Star Prairie, WI; ed/BS 1958, MEd 1960 Univ Minn; mil/AUS Signal Corps 1954-56; pa/Dir Art Ed Quincy Public Schs; NAEA; PDK; Ill Art Ed Assn; cp/Quincy Art Clb; Past Mem Bd Dirs Quincy Soc Fine Arts; Former Ldr BSA; hon/Comm'd to Paint Large Mural in Lobby of Gem City Col Sum 1977; Cert of Accomplishmt, Secy of Army; Purchase Awd, MacNider Mus, Mason City, Ia; Num Other Art Awds & One-Man Art Shows; Author Book of Poetry *Portrait of Jean*; Intl W/W Commun Ser; Men of Achmt; DIB; Notable Ams Bicent Era; Commun Ldrs & Noteworthy Ams; Personalities W&MW; Nat Social Dir; Others.

SCHWARTZ, BARBARA DIANE oc/Attorney; b/Jul 30, 1937; ba/300 Ainsley Bldg, Miami, FL 33132; m/Kenneth Goldwich; c/David Scott, Lee Stewart, Mark Steven, Michael Craig; p/Samuel E and Ruth Greenfield Schwartz, Miami Beach, FL; ed/BA; JD; pa/Asst US Atty; Fla & Fed Bars; Nat Assn Wom Lwyrs; Fla Assn Wom Lwyrs; r/Hebrew; hon/Dept Justice Spec Awd; W/W Am Wom.

SCHWARTZ, JEROME L oc/Health Care Research; b/Jun 13, 1924; h/746 Hawthorn Ln, Davis, CA 95616; m/JoAnn Jordan; c/Judy, Jay Jordan; p/Jack and Mary Schwartz (dec); ed/BBA; MBA; MPH; DrPH; mil/AUS 1943-46; pa/Conslt Nat Cancer Inst; Tobacco & Cancer Com Am Cancer Soc; r/Jewish; hon/Phi Eta Sigma; Delta Omega.

SCHWARTZ, JOSEPH oc/Merchant; h/4818 Sherman, Galveston, TX 77550; ba/Galveston; m/Ida Anne (dec); c/Louis, Aaron, Steven, Ronnie, Phyllis Ruth Milstein; p/Simcha and Rachil Schwartz; ed/Koveno (Yeshiva), Hebrew Col; pa/Buyer, Mgr Mens & Woms Apparel; Owner Schwartz's Inc (Ladies Ready-to-Wear Apparel); Galveston C of C; Dir Am Bk; Nat Fdn Indep Bus; Nat Small Bus Assn; cp/Mem 50 Clb; Bd Mem Galveston Co Jewish Wel Commun Coun; Consumer Credit Assn Tex; Galveston Coun Cult Arts Coun; Nat Coun Christians & Jews;

Vol U Way; r/Congreg Beth Jacob & Temple B'nai Israel: Mem; hon/Hon'd w Testimonial Dinner, Congreg Beth Jacob; Cert of Awd, Galveston C of C; Featured in Newspaper.

SCHWARZOTT, WILHELM oc/Concert Pianist; Chamber Music Performer; b/Dec 14, 1914; h/1882-11th Ave, San Francisco, CA 94122; c/Tone, Jan; p/Karl and Maria Radax Schwarzott; ed/Cert Vienna Acad 1938; Dipl Royal Music Conservatory (Oslo, Norway) 1939; MA Equivalent Univ Denver 1957; Addit Studies; mil/Norwegian Army; pa/Dir & Prof Klaveracademiet, Olso, Norway 1950-55; Prof & Hd Piano Dept Univ Denver, Denver, Colo 1957-61; Prof & Hd Piano Dept Cal St Polytech Univ, San Luis Obispo, Cal 1961-63; Fac Mem San Francisco Conservatory Music 1963-67; Lectr in Music Univ Cal Ext-SF Campus 1966-; Fac Mem & Adjudicator Am Col Musicians 1959-; Fac Mem SF Music & Arts Inst 1967-; Concert Pianist, Soloist & Chamber Music Performer: Europe 1935-, US 1957-; Mem Oslo Chamber Trio 15 Yrs; Perfs w Sibelius String Quartet & Other Chamber Music Ensembles Europe & US; Num Perfs for European Broadcasting Corps & Am Ednl TV; Artist Soc (Oslo, Norway) 1953; Pacific Musical Soc; Denver & SF Musicians Assns; Fellow IBA; IPA; Current Dir Cal Music Tchrs Assn, SF Br (Pres 1975-77); hon/Book of Honor; 2000 Men Achmt; Dir of IPA; Personalities W&MW; Commun Ldrs Am; IBA Yrbook & Biogl Dir; DIB; Other Biogl Listings.

SCHWENDEMAN, JOSEPH RAYMOND oc/Professor; b/May 11, 1897; h/3512 Greentree Rd, Lexington, KY 40502; ba/L'ton; m/Eithnea O'Donnell; c/Mary Elaine, Marion, Gerald, Joseph Jr Francis, Elizabeth Ann; p/Frank and Margaret Tornes Schwendeman, Waterford, OH; ed/BS Ohio

Univ 1926; MA 1927, PhD 1941 Clark Univ; mil/USAAC WWII 1943-44 (Instr); Drafted WWI; pa/Instr Univ Minn 1927-28; Chm Dept Geography Minn St Col 1928-44; Chm Dept Geography Univ Ky 1944-67; Emeritus-Dist'd Prof Geography En Ky Univ, Richmond, Ky 1967; cp/Kiwanis, Lexington; r/Rom Cath; hon/Mem UN Sci Conf; Hons Cit, Assn Am Geographers.

SCIALABBA, ELMERINDA CACCAVO oc/Physician; b/Jul 12, 1933; h/920 Belvidere Ave, Plainfield, NJ 07060; ba/P'field; m/Dominick A; c/Fred Anthony, Damian Angelo, Marion Alexia; p/Nicholas James and Gilda Caccavo, Brooklyn, NY; ed/BS St John's Univ 1955; MD Wom's Med Col Pa 1959; pa/Pvt Pract Child Devel & Child Neurol; Sch Conslt in Pediatric Neurol, Elizabeth (NJ), Old Bridge (NJ), N P'field (NJ) & Watchung (NJ); Med Dir Union Co Cerebral Palsy Ctr 1978; Woodbridge St Sch (W'bridge, NJ): Med Dir 1966-68, Staff Phys 1965-66; Other Former Positions; Conslt'g Staff in Pediatric Neurol Cerebral Palsy Leag Union Co 1972-; Clin Instr Pediatrics NJ Col Med & Dentistry, Newark, NJ 1966-; Courtesy Staff Pediatric Dept Raritan Val Hosp 1965-; Other Hosp & Med Staff Appts; Fellow Am Acad Pediatrics; AMA; NJ & Union Co Med Socs; Am Med Wom's Assn; Am Assn Mtl Deficiency; P'field Area Med Assn: Treas 1975, Secy 1976, 2/VP 1977, 1/VP 1978; Alumnae Assn Wom's Med Col Pa; r/Rom Cath; hon/Dir Med Specialists; W/W: Am Wom, E; Intl W/W Commun Ser; Commun Ldrs & Noteworthy Ams; World W/W Wom; DIB.

SCOLLAY, PATRICIA ANN oc/University Professor; b/Apr 10, 1944; h/4609 Kensington, San Diego, CA 92116; ba/San Diego; p/Loren P Scollay (dec); Edith A Scollay, San Bernardino, CA; ed/AB Univ Cal-B 1966; MA 1968, PhD 1970 Univ Cal-D; pa/SDSU: Asst Prof Psychol & Anthropol 1974-, Lectr 1972-74; Former Acad Positions; Animal Behavior Soc; Am Assn Phy Anthropologists; AAAS; Intl Primatological Soc; SWn Anthropol Assn; Am Anthropol Soc; San Diego Zool Soc, Var Coms; Var Res Activs; hon/Outstg Yg Wom Am; NIH Grants; Papers Presented; Profl Pubs.

SCOTT, CHARLOTTE LAWANA oc/-School Teacher; b/Aug 25, 1929; h/PO Box 391, Tracy City, TN 37387; ba/Same; c/Paula Juana Mott; p/Charles Wesley and Maxie Milla Cleek Adams (dec); ed/BS; MEd; mil/-US WAC 2 Yrs; pa/Nat Tchrs Assn; Tenn Ed Assn; Grundy Co-Tchr's Assn; cp/Var Civic Activs; Dem; r/Meth, Bapt, Ch Activs; hon/-Dean's List; Dist'd Student & Hon Roll, MTSU-M.

SCOTT, GLEN D oc/Retired; b/May 25, 1908; h/2416 Valley Ave, Marion, IN 46952;

ba/Marion; m/Delores E; c/Dan E, Marilyn R Huber; p/John R and Sadie E Scott, Landers, IN; pa/Carpenter; r/Meth.

SCOTT, JOHN EDWARD oc/Librarian; b/Aug 12, 1920; h/PO Box 303, Institute, WV 25112; ba/Institute; m/Dorris; c/Patricia, Clifford, Martha; p/John E and Martha H

Scott (dec); ed/AB; BLS; MSLS; mil/USN 1942-45; pa/Libn WVa St Col; WVa Lib Assn; Am Lib Assn; Treas SEn Lib Assn; cp/Alpha Phi Alpha; r/St Paul AME Ch: Mem; hon/Cert of Merit, WVa Lib Assn.

SCOTT, KATHRYN (KATHY) LOUISE oc/Homemaker; b/Dec 8, 1931; h/15345 SW Bull Mtn Rd, Tigard, OR 97223; m/Edward M; c/5 Chd; p/Albert S and Eleanor A Hague; ed/BS Nsg; cp/Mem Tigard Sch Bd, Former Chm; Oreg Sch Bds Assn: Former Bd Dirs, Leg Com Chm, 2/VP; Nat Sch Bds Assn: Former Fed Relats Network, Del 1979, Former Task Force Mem; Past Pres Parents' Clb Pacific Univ; Former Vol/Area Dir U Good Neighbors; Host Parent Rotary Exc Student & Partners of Ams Student 1976, 79; r/Cath; hon/Co-editor (w husband) *Crim Rehab-Within & Without the Walls*; Tigard Lay Edr of Yr 1974; Tigard C of C Dist'd Ser Awd; Merit Mother for Am Mothers Com Inc, (Oreg) 1979; Commun Ldrs & Noteworthy Ams.

SCOTT, SHERRY JONES oc/Mayor; b/Dec 26, 1936; h/1104 Euclid Ave, Waycross, GA 31501; ba/Waycross; m/Sam P; c/Gregory, Kelly, Drew; p/William Sherard Jones (dec); Mrs Glenn C Allen, Vicksburg, MS; pa/Ga Mun Assn; Mem Mun Govt Comm; Secy SE Ga Assn Co & City Ofcls; cp/Pres U Way; Bd Dirs YMCA; Bd Mem C of C; Devel Auth; r/Cath.

SCOTT, WILTON C oc/Educator; b/Aug 29, 1921; h/1520 Chevy Chase Rd, Savannah, GA 31401; m/Lillian Shank; c/2 Daughs; p/Curtis and Mary Scott; ed/Grad Xavier Univ 1940; MA 1953, 6th Yr Specialist Dipl 1956 NY Univ; Addit Studies; mil/AUS Dept, Civilian Specialist Employee, Rations Ofcr & Cnslr; pa/Ret'd Dean for Extended Sers Savannah St Col; NEA; Am Col Public Relats; Adult Ed Assn USA; ASSA; cp/Bd Dirs YMCA; hon/Meritorious Ser Awd in Communs, So Reg Press Inst; Local & Nat YMCA Awds; Golden Crown Cert, Columbia Univ; Outstg Edr Yr Awd 1974-75; Dist'd Mag Advr Awd; Dipl of Honor for Commun Ser; Silver Jubilee Alumnus Awd, Xavier Univ; Cert of Apprec as Pubs Advr, So Univs Student Govt Assn; Fellow IBA; Cited for Accomplishmts, Senator Herman Talmadge during 85th Cong; Recipient 100% Right Clb's Recog, Dignity, & Worthy Among All Men Awd 1967; Biogl Listings.

SCRIBA, JOELYN A oc/Associate Professor; b/May 3, 1943; h/405-6 4th Ave NE, Jamestown, ND 58401; ba/J'town; m/Robert; p/Manfred and Anna Bymoen, New Rockford, ND; ed/BSN; MN; pa/Assoc Prof; Adv Coun Hlth Occup Proj HOPE, ND Nsg Consortium; ANA; NDSN; Am Acad Nsg; ND Lung Assn; cp/Num Spkg Engagemts; r/Luth: Ch Coun Com; hon/Hon Recog Awd, ND Nurses Assn; Charter Fellow Acad Nsg; Outstg Yg Edr; Outstg Yg Wom; W/W; Delta Kappa Gamma.

SEALE, MARGARET R oc/Composer; Teacher; Vocalist; Producer; b/Apr 20, 1915; h/4674 Franklin Ave, New Orleans, LA 70122; ba/Same; m/Clifton (dec); c/Clifton, Joy Ruth, Robert H; p/James Andrew Lamb (dec); Edna Lee Phillips (dec); ed/BChMus;

MChMus New Orleans Bapt Theol Sem; pa/Pres Marsile Music Co; Pres The Big Parade Co Inc; Pres La Fdn Music Clbs 1975-76; cp/LWV; C of C Aux; NO Conv & Tourist Comm; Am Bus Wom's Assn; r/Bapt; hon/Wom of Yr; ABWA Les Amis Ch 1978.

SEARS, WILLIAM JOHN oc/Aerospace Physiologist; b/Apr 13, 1931; h/309 Driftwind, San Antonio, TX 78239; ba/Brooks AFB, TX; m/Orpha Mae; c/Michael F, Cheryl A, John L, Patricia L; p/Chester Newman, Hedrick, IA; Mildred Newman (dec); ed/BS; MS; PhD; mil/USAF Col, BSC-Current Active Duty; pa/Aerospace Physiologist USAF Sch Aerospace; Mgmt Res & Devel; cp/Pres Bd Dirs Randolph/Brooks Fed Credit Union; r/Presb; hon/Assoc Fellow, ASMA; Alfred Hitchcock Awd Excell in Physiol; Meritorious Ser Awd w OLC; 1st Pl, Sci Awd.

SEBASTIANELLI, MARIO JOSEPH oc/Physician; Educator; b/Sep 14, 1935; h/176 Constitution Ave, Jessup, PA 18434; ba/Dunmore, PA; m/Prisca (dec); p/Carlo

and Antoinette Sebastianelli, Jessup, PA; ed/BS Univ Scranton 1958; MD Jefferson Med Col 1962; mil/USNR Lt, MC 1963-65; pa/Clin Assoc Prof of Med, Hahnemann Med Col 1977-; Prof of Nephrology, Kings Col (Wilkes-Barre) 1976-; Lectr in Fam & Commun Med, Hershey Med Ctr 1975-76; Pvt Pract Nephrology & Internal Med 1971-; Intl Soc Nephrology; Nat Kidney Foun; Am Med Assn; Am Col Internal Med; Am Fdn for Clin Res; Am Soc Artificial Internal Organs; Gov's Renal Disease Adv Com 1973-76; Bd Dirs: Hemodialysis Assn & Home Hlth Maintenance Org (Lackawanna Co) 1973-75, Am Cancer Soc (Lackawanna Unit) 1976-77, Scranton Lackawanna Human Devel Agy 1977-, Am Diabetes Assn (NE Pa Chapt) 1979-; Nephrologist Coor, Reg Kidney Harvesting Team; Tech Review Com of Gtr Delaware Valley Reg Med Prog 1973-74; N Ctl Reg Pres, Pa Soc Internal Med 1974-; Staff Mem: Moses Taylor Hosp, Mercy Hosp, Commun Med Ctr, Scranton St Gen Hosp (all Scranton), Mid-Valley Hosp (Peckville), St Joseph's & Carbondale Gen Hosp, Hahnemann Hosp; cp/Am Legion; Elks, K of C; r/Rom Cath; hon/Alpha Omega Alpha; Commun Testimonial for Pioneering Efforts in Hemodialysis Sers; F'ships: Am Col Physicians, Am Col Angiology; Num Biogl Listings; Others.

SEDDON, LISA RUTH oc/Art Historian; Executive; Publisher; b/Apr 13, 1950; h/5215 W 120th St Apt #4, Inglewood, CA 90304; ba/Pacific Grove, CA; c/Christopher Todd; p/Robert Lawrence and Alva Lee Wakefield Patton, Pacific Grove; ed/BA UCLA; Grad Studies; pa/Art Histn; Corp Chm of Bd & Pres; Pub'g Agent; Pub'g & Promoting Related to peace in 21st Century; Rep Alva Lee Mgmt Sers; Art Hist Specialist Archeol Res Teams w Concentration in Agaean Sea Area; Writer; Others; r/Meth.

SEEGALL, MANFRED ISMAR LUDWIG oc/Physicist; Research Scientist; b/Dec 23, 1929; h/8735 Blue Lake Dr, San Diego, CA 92119; ba/San Diego; p/Leonhard Seegall (dec); Vera Antonie Seegall, San Diego; ed/BS magna cum laude Loyola Col 1957; MS Brown Univ 1960; PhDC Stuttgart Tech Univ 1962-65; pa/Res Conslt Energy Res & Pollution Control 1974-; Tchr Physics, Statistics & Algebra to Col Students & Sec'dy Sch Tchrs; Prin Engr on Res Projs; Sr Res Engr Solar Div Int Harv Co, San Diego 1967-73; Instr Math San Diego City Col 1966; Res Scist Max Planck Inst, Stuttgart 1962-65; Other Former Positions; r/Rom Cath; hon/Hon Citizen, Father Flanagan's Boy's Town; Susan Murphy Gold Medal for Class Standing, Loyola Col; McTavish Gold Medal in Physics, Loyola Col; Contbr Articles to Tech Jours & Dept of Def Reports; Holder US Patents in Field.

SEEGER, CHARLES RONALD oc/Professor; b/Jan 31, 1931; h/630 Ironwood Dr, Bowling Green, KY 42101; ba/Bowling Green; m/Barbara Ashley; c/Leslie Ethel, Julie Ann; p/(dec); ed/BS Ohio St Univ; MS Geo Wash Univ; PhD Univ Pgh; mil/USNR; NROTC; USN Ofcr 4 Yrs; pa/Prof Geol & Geophysics Wn Ky Univ; Sci Res & Pubs; r/Unitarian; hon/Sigma Xi; Num Res F'ships.

SEETS, ETHEL B oc/Retired Teacher; b/Mar 30, 1909; h/Rt 3, Box 296, Humboldt, TN 38343; p/(dec); ed/BS; MS; pa/TEA; NRTA; AARP; cp/Tenn Voters Coun; r/Meth; hon/Bd Christian Ed Plaque, Alpha Kappa Mu; Meritorious Awd for Ednl Sers; AKA Soror of Yr 1970.

SEGEL, KENNETH IAN oc/Rabbi; b/Mar 16, 1942; h/4313 Cleary Ave, Metairie, La 70002; ba/Metairie; m/Sandra Goodman; c/Bree Arlyn; p/David and Ethel Wernick Segel; ed/BA; BHL; MAHL; PhD; pa/Weekly Radio Prog; Pub'd Num Articles; Prof Our Lady of Holy Cross Col; CCAR; Am Reform Zionist Assn; Soc Biblical Lit; Am Jewish Hist Soc; cp/Archbishop's Com for Commun Cooperation; New Orleans Commun Relats

Coun; Morality in Media; Inst for Human Understanding; r/Bd Mem Rel Ed Assn Am; Rabbi Cong Gates of Prayer, Metairie; Bd Dirs Israel Bonds So Reg; Orgr Metairie Clergy Coun; Secy Rabbinical Coun NO; Bd Mem NO Comm on Jewish Ed; hon/Delivered Opening Prayer before US Senate 1973, & US Ho of Reps 1972; Rabbi Lovis Mann S'ship.

SEGER, ROBERT MORSE oc/Librarian; b/Dec 16, 1926; h/2343 Cleveland St, Clinton, IA 52732; ba/Clinton; m/Lois; c/Ellen, Janet,

Nancy; p/Earl Fenton and Ruth Morse Seger, Lakeland, FL; ed/BA; AMLS; mil/AUS; pa/Am & Ia Lib Assns; cp/Kiwanis Clb; r/Prot.

SEHGAL, ROBERT oc/Scientist; b/Dec 25, 1927; h/3505 Leland St, Chevy Chase, MD 20015; ba/Falls Church, VA; m/Ellen; c/Evan David, Jeffrey Bruce; p/S D and Mimi Sehgal, Chevy Chase; ed/BS Punjab Univ (Pakistan) 1946; BS Univ Mich 1951; NY Univ 1952; pa/Scist AUS Operational Test & Eval Agy 1973-; Tech Advr AUS Mat Command, Wash 1969-73; Conslt Space Sys NASA, Wash 1965-69; Other Former Positions; Am Inst Aeronautics & Astronautics: Fellow, Tech Com on Missile Systems; Intl Aero Scis; Sigma Xi; r/Jewish; hon/Contbr Articles to Profl Jours; W/W: S&SW, Govt, E; DIB.

SEIBEL, GEORGE HENRY JR oc/Quality Assurance Specialist; b/Apr 21, 1921; h/Box 96-C-36 Rt #1, Oakridge Ests, Eastaboga, AL 36260; m/Estelle Lucille Gulley; c/Lorita Joeann, Georgeania Marie, Clifford George, Henry Curtis; p/George Henry Seibel (dec); Marie Sophia Johnson Seibel, Belleville, IL; ed/USAFI: Univ Ill, Univ Omaha; Att'd Univ Alaska & Univ NM; Att'd Var Mil Schs; mil/USAF T/Sgt (Ret'd); pa/Chief Instr USAAC Drivers Sch; Aircraft Intercept Controller Instr; Elect Counter-measures Instr; Conslt; USAF Detachmt Cmdr; Ch Flight Opers Elect-Countermeasure; Elect Intell Analysis, Specialist; Other Profl Positions; Life Mem Pearl Harbor Survivors Assn; Am Def Preparedness Assn; Nat Adv Bd Am Security Bd; USAF Sgts Assn; Am Inst Aeronautics & Astronautics; Am Fdn Govt Employee's; cp/Smithsonian Assocs; Nat Geog Soc; Nat Hist Soc; Early Am Soc; r/Nondenom; hon/Var Inventions; Composer; Lttrs Apprec & Fin Awd, USAF & AUS; Awd & Ceremonial Dinner for Assistance to People of Korea, Repub of Korea; Lttrs Apprec: Cmdr Concord Nav Sta, Ala Sheriff's Assn, Cmdr 2nd Coast Guard Dist, Dept Civilian Aviation, Repub of Costa Rica; Lttr Commend, Errol L des Santos, Colonial Secy Port of Spain (Trinidad).

SEIFERT, RALPH HAMMOND oc/Insurance Agent; b/Mar 27, 1928; h/Old Maple St, Mansfield, MA 02048; ba/Mansfield; m/Sandra Charles; c/Mitchel Grant, Susan Leslie, Arthur Radford, Melissa Louise; ed/BA Brown Univ 1950; mil/USN 1950-70; pa/Pres, New England Security Ins Agy Inc 1970-; Pres, Fin Security Corp 1970-; Partner w Herbert E King Agy (M'field) 1957-70; Other Former Positions; cp/Former Moderator, Town of M'field; Downtown Devel Comm; Bd of Investment & Bd Trustees, Attleboro Savs Bank; Chm M'field Devel Comm; Bd Dirs, CSF of Am; Trustee, Rumford Hist Assn; Treas, Brown Univ Assn of Class Presidents & Secys; Others; hon/Man of Yr, M'field JCs 1960; Outstg Achmt Awd, Brown Univ

Annual Fund; Ser to Yth Awd, CSF of M'field; Biogl Listings; Others.

SEILER, CHARLOTTE WOODY oc/Retired Educator; b/Jan 20, 1915; h/5002 Sturgeon Creek Pkwy, Midland, MI 48640; m/Wallace Urban; c/Patricia Anne Bootzin, Janet Alice; p/Clark Woody (dec); Lois M Long Woody, Thornton, IN; ed/AA Ind St Univ 1933; BA Univ Mich 1941; MA Ctl Mich 1968; pa/Delta Col: Ret'd from Eng Div, Orgr & Dir Puppeteers 1972-77; AAUW; IRA; Am Lib Assn; Mich Lib Assn; cp/Midland Art Assn; Treas Friends of Grace A Dow Meml Lib; Panhellenic; Midland Garden Clb; Seed & Sod; Tuesday Review; Chi Omega; r/Presb; hon/Pi Lambda Theta.

SEIPOS, ANDREW G oc/Manufacturing Company Executive; b/Feb 6, 1918; h/650 NE 31 St, Miami, FL 33137; ba/Miami; m/Mary Ann Doutrich; c/Lee Brooke Lawrence, Andrew G Jr, Thomas J; p/Andrew and Theresa Seipos (dec); ed/Att'd NY Univ, Cooper Union Schs Arch; pa/Coun on Furn Engrg & Res; NAFM; NABM; NWPCA; ISES; SCCF; cp/Mem Heart Assn Miami; r/Prot; hon/Challenger Awd, NAFM.

SEITZINGER, MARY LOU oc/Banker; Locksmith; Security Consultant; b/Mar 12, 1928; h/Triple Horseshoe Ranch, 6226 Taylor Rd, Blacklick, OH 43004; m/John R; c/John C, Christine E, Mark P; p/John F and Christine McLean Baumer (dec); ed/Grad Am Inst Bkg 1976; Att'd: Columbus Tech, Bkg & Fin Technol, Capital Univ; pa/Owner Lock Doc Security Co; Bkg Experience: Pa, NY, NJ, Tex, Alaska, Ohio; Am Soc Wom Accts, Columbus Chapt #16: Ed & Leg Chm, Bd Dirs 1976-78; Columbus BPW Clb: Pres 1973-75, Bd Dirs 1975-78; IPA; Phoenix House/Choices

for Victims of Domestic Violence, Columbus, Bd Dirs 1977-79; cp/Former Secy Am Legion Aux Franklin Unit #1; Toastmasters Intl, Dist 40 Sect Ohio, Ind, WVa, Ky; Ohio Wn Horse Assn: Past Pres, Life Mem; Beta Sigma Phi; Former 1/VP Wom's Repub Clb Ohio Inc; Former Asst Presiding Partner Buckeye Investmt Clb Columbus BPW; Intl Wom's Yr Com Columbus; Ohio Comm on Status of Wom; Wirenius Unit Ohio St Assn Parliamentns of NAP Inc; Notary Public St of Ohio; Others; r/E Side Grace Brethren Ch, Blacklick: Dir Public Info 1977-79; hon/US Observer to BPW Cong of Americas, Mexico City, Mexico 1975; Civilian Dist'd Visitor from Rickenbacker AFB (Ohio) to 8th AF Hdqtrs, Strategic Air Command, Barksdale AFB (La) 1975; Wom of Yr, Beta Sigma Phi; Biogl Listings.

SELBY, HUBERT JR oc/Writer; b/Jul 23, 1928; h/236 Riverside Ave, Riverside, CT 06878; m/Suzanne; c/Rachel, William; p/Hubert and Adalin Selby, Brooklyn, NY; mil/Merchant Seaman; pa/Writer.

SELBY, JOHN MARSHALL oc/Health Physicist; b/Apr 2, 1932; h/5504 W Umatilla, Kennewick, WA 99336; ba/Richland, WA; m/Gwen Silker; c/Greg, Lori, Kevin; p/Walter E and Mildred W Selby, Manhattan, KS; ed/BS Ks St Univ; mil/US Chem Corps, 1/Lt; pa/Vis Lectr in Radiation Protection Harvard Univ Sch Public Hlth 1977; Conslt to Adv Com on Reactor Safeguards, Envir Subcom Meeting 1977; Radiation Adv Com Wash St Radiation Control Prog 1979; US Rep

Intl Electrotech Comm 1977; US Rep Intl Standards Org 1976; Am Nat Standards Inst; Chm Instrmentation Sect Hlth Physics Soc Standards Com; Guest Lectr Berkeley; cp/Little Leag Coach Kennewick; Scoutmaster Troop 126 Kennewick; Former Chm Fin for Kennewick Sch Bd Campaign; Mem Fin Com Kennewick Sch Dist; Chm Spkr's Bur Kennewick Sch Levy Campaign; Others; r/U Prot Ch, Richland (Meth); hon/H H King Chem S'ship, Ks St Univ; S'ship in Piano; Merck Chem Co Col Sr Awd; Phi Lambda Upsilon; Phi Kappa Phi Freshman Awd; Cert'd Am Bd Hlth Physics; Scouters Key.

SELIGMAN, BERNARD oc/Physician; b/Aug 25, 1898; h/1818 Newkirk Ave, Brooklyn, NY 11226; ba/Bklyn; m/Edith; c/Stephen J; p/Jacob and Esther Levy Seligman (dec); ed/MD; pa/Med Staff Jewish Hosp 1928-: Attd'g 1956-69, Conslt 1969-; King Co Hosp: Conslt 1968-, Endocrine, Med & Cardiol 1931-40; Attd'g Phys Hebrew Convalescent Home 1939-47; Courtesy Staff Long Isl Col Hosp 1935-46; Tchg Assignmts incl: Downstate Med Ctr 1948-69, Long Isl Med Col 1935-39; AMA; Med Soc Co of Kings; Exec Com NY Endocrinological Soc 1935-69; Mem Var Res Socs; NY Diabetes Assn; Assn for Study of Internal Secretions (Emeritus); Fellow: Am Col Physicians, Royal Soc for Promotion of Hlth; Intl Soc Internal Med; NY Acad Scis; Am Heart Assn; NYC Public Hlth Assn; Past Pres Assoc Staff Jewish Sanitarium & Hosp for Chronic Diseases; Former VP Prospect Park Jewish Ctr; Pres Doctors Clb Bklyn; Num Others; cp/Smithsonian Inst; Chatauqua Art Assn; Judge NYC Sci Fairs; NY Physicians Art Clb; Others; r/Hebrew; hon/Biogl Listings; Profl Pubs.

SELKINGHAUS, WALTER EUGENE oc/Mechanical/Nuclear Engineer; b/Sept 11, 1911; h/Box 9, Supply, NC 28462; m/Jeanne Douglass; c/George Clifford, Charles William, Christine Louise, Bonnie Jeanne; p/George William and Louisa Selkinghaus (dec); ed/BS Newark Col Engrg; MME NC St Univ; pa/Lic'd Stationary Engr: NYC, St of

NJ; Lic'd Prof Engr NJ; Text Engr Wright Aero Corp; Metallurgist Titeflex Metal Hose Co; Assoc Prof Mech Engrg NC St Univ; Power Plant Supt Carolina P & L 1951-76; Am Nuclear Soc; AAAS; cp/Pres Lion's Clb; BSA Cnslr; Brunswick Co Art Assn: Pres, Treas; r/Luth, Rosicrucian; hon/Pi Tau Sigma; W/W: NC, S&SE.

SELLE, ELAINE LOUISE BABCOCK oc/Publisher; b/Dec 3, 1925; h/7 Claflin Cir, Hanover, NH 03755; ba/Hanover; c/Dorothy Foskin, Steven Foskin; p/Herbert Bruce Babcock (dec); Constance Lytle Babcock,

Sarasota, FL; ed/BA Wellesley; MS Boston Univ; pa/Pubr Dartmouth Printing Co; Public Relats Soc Am; Dir Soc for Tech Commun; Soc for Scholarly Pub'g; Dir AAUW; cp/Trustee Montshire Mus Sci; r/Epis; hon/Tchg Fellow, Boston Univ.

SELLERS, FRED COURT oc/Corporate Secretary; Certified Public Accountant; b/Jan 19, 1924; h/11601 Green Oaks St, Houston, TX 77024; ba/Houston; m/Ray Vina Aucoin; c/Fred Court, Sharon Ann; p/James Henry and Etta Court Sellers; ed/Univ Houston 1940-43; mil/USAAF 1943-46; pa/Corporate Secy: Postive Feed Inc, Sealy (Tex), NW Assocs, Houston; Self-Employed, Houston 1959-; Sr Acct U Gas Corp, Houston 1941-59; Am Inst CPAs; Tex Soc CPAs; Houston Chapt Tex Soc CPAs; Pres Harris Co Yth S'ship Fund; cp/Optimist Clb, Past VP; Rotary Clb; r/Bapt: Deacon; hon/Key Man Awd, Jr C of C 1948.

SEMAAN, KHALIL IBRAHIM HANNA oc/Educator; b/Mar 6, 1920; h/713 Country Clb Rd, Binghamton, NY 13903; ba/B'ton; m/Aline Elofson; c/Jan Jeffery, Johan Nicholas, Ingrid Emily Theresa; p/Ibrahim Hanna and Martha Elias Khoury Semaan; ed/BSL Georgetown Univ 1954; MA Columbia Univ 1955; PhD 1959; mil/French & Free French Armies 1939-45; Syrian Army 1945-50; pa/St Univ NY-B'ton: Mem Fac 1965-, Prof Arabic 1970-, Dir Arabic Studies 1965-75; Dir Mediterranean Studies Royal Univ (Malta) 1975-76; Vis Scholar Columbia Univ Tchrs Col 1964-65; Dir Afro-Asian Res Inst, Stockholm, Sweden 1962-64; Reschr; Other Former Positions; Am Oriental Soc; Mid E Study Assn NAm; Am Assn Tchrs Arabic; Fdr Arab-Am U Grads; Georgetown Arabic Clb; St Univ NY-B Arabic Cir; hon/Pub'd Author; Biogl Listings.

SEMONES, JO ANN oc/Assistant Regional Director; b/Oct 28, 1945; h/525 Trinidad Ln, Foster City, CA 94404; ba/San Francisco, CA; p/George W and Grace M Semones, Sepulveda, CA; ed/BJ Cal St Univ-N Grad Work Am Univ; MPA Golden Gate Univ; Doct Cand; pa/US Small Bus Adm: Reg Dir for Public Affairs & Communs, Former Public Info Specialist (Wash DC Ctl Ofc); Former Press Secy to So Cal Cong-man; Former Newspaper Reporter/Photog *San*

Fernando Val Sun; Lectr; Bd Dirs Nat Assn Govt Communicators; Dir Fed Exec Bd Public Affairs Com; Dir Am Soc Public Admr's Reg Conf Publicity Com; Commonwealth Clb; Intl Assn Bus Communicators; Wom in Advt'g; Wom in Communs; SF Press Clb; SF Publicity Clb; Fed Exec Bd Consumer Rep Com; r/Cath; hon/Hon'd for Outstg Achmt: IBC, ABI, USN Recruiting Ser, Val Press Clb, Combined Fed Campaign, Fed Exec Bd; Biogl Listings; Pub'd Author.

SENSAT, LLOYD LESTER oc/Art Specialist; b/Oct 20, 1944; h/2024 Burgundy, New Orleans, LA 70116; p/Lloyd Lester Sensat Sr; Marcella Stagg Sensat, Crowley, LA; ed/BA Univ SWn La 1967; Certn Art Ed McNeese St Univ 1973; MEdnl Supvn La St Univ 1975; mil/USAF, Sqdrn Illustrator, Security Police 1967-71; pa/Art Specialist St Charles Parish Sch Bd; Graphic Artist The Faubourg Marigny Corp; Exhbns incl: La Photo Salon, Old St Capitol (Baton Rouge, La) 1974, 1st Acadia Parish Bicent Assembly (Crowley) 1975, Invitational Art Exhbn

Diversity Gallery (New Orleans) 1977, Contemp Arts Ctr (NO) 1978, Faubourg Marigny Artists Lorenzo Bergen Gallery (NO) 1978, La Exhbn Chd's Art (Homeplace Proj) N Tex St Univ (Denton, Tex) 1978; Editor *The Rising Sun*, Newslttr La Art Ed Assn 1976-77; Profl Pubs; La Art Ed Assn: Dist Chm 1976-77, Pres 1977, Exec Coun 1978-; Nat Art Ed Assn: St Assembly Del Nat Conv 1977, 1978; La Tchrs Assn; La Alliance for Arts Ed; La Landmarks Soc; Faubourg Marigny Improvemt Assn: Bd Mem 1976-77, VP 1977-78; cp/Preservation Resource Ctr Save Our Cemeteries; Num Comms; r/Cath; hon/Tchr Incentive Awd for Art, St Charles Parish La Tchrs Assn; LAEA Outstg Tchr for Yth Art Month 1972-75.

SERENYI, PETER oc/Educator; b/Jan 13, 1931; h/79 Greenough St, Brookline, MA 02146; ba/Boston, MA; m/Agnes Kertesz; c/Peter, Denis; p/Nicholas Serenyi (dec); Emma Josika Serenyi, W Hartford, CT; ed/AB cum laude, Dartmouth Col 1957; MA Yale Univ 1958; PhD Washington Univ 1968; mil/AUS; pa/Instr, Dept of Art, NEn Univ 1968-; Former Instr: Amherst Col 1961-64, Smith Col 1962-63, Univ of Pa 1964-66, Boston Univ (Visiting Chapt): VP 1977-78, Pres 1978-79, Dir 1979-; Soc Preserv of New England Antiquities; Victorian Soc of Am; Assoc Mem, Boston Soc Archs; Mass Com for Preserv of Arch Records; Org'd 1st Traveling Exhbn of Contemp Arch in India; Others; cp/Fulbright Alumni Assn; r/Rom Cath; hon/NEH Grant; Am Phil Soc Grant; Graham Foun Grant; Fulbright Sr Res Grant to India; W N Cohen S'ship, Dartmouth Col; H M Boies F'ship, Yale Univ; Univ F'ship, Washington Univ.

SESSIONS, ANNIE CLAIRE AVERETT oc/Homemaker; b/Aug 6, 1927; h/Rt 1, Box 114, Samson, AL 36477; ba/Same; m/-Bowden; c/Annette S Davis, Amelia S Rhoades, Anita S Grimes; p/Marion Iasiah and Carrie Belva Crews Averett, Samson, AL; cp/Info Chm, Wom's Comm, Coffee Co Farm Bur; St Dir, Ala Cowbelles; Gov's Staff for Gov George Wallace 1971-75; Pres, Coffee Co Coun Home Demonstration Clbs; Ldr, 4-H; Chm, March of Dimes Dr; Others; r/Fairview Bapt Ch (Samson): Bible Sch Tchr & Dir, Secy & Treas, SS Tchr, Others; hon/Grand Prize Winner, Nat Peanut Fest Recipe Contest; Coffee Co Beef Cook-off Winner; Awd in Music Reading; Others.

SETO, EDWARD LEUNG oc/Licensed Real Estate Broker; b/May 27, 1933; h/351 11th Ave, San Francisco, CA 94118; ba/SF; m/Jean Wong; c/John; p/Ming and Yen Chee W Seto; ed/BSc Chinese Univ Hong Kong; pa/SF Bd Realtors; cp/Lions Clb; Repub Nat Com; Am Cause; Nat Adv Bd; C of C; Others; r/Christian; hon/Long Ser Medal, Queen Elizabeth II, 1961.

SETTLES, CARL E oc/Counseling Psychologist; b/Jul 23, 1948; h/Box 2148, Prairie View, TX 77445; ba/Prairie View; m/Carol Ann Hadnot; c/Carl Jr, Corey Tremayne; p/Paul S and Lena Epps Settles (dec); ed/BS 1970, MEd 1971 Prairie View A&M Univ; PhD Univ Tex-Austin 1976; pa/Prairie View A&M Univ: Cnslg Psychologist, Assoc Dir Cnslg Ser

1976-, Acting Asst to Dir Cnslg Ctr 1975-76; Guest Lectr w Cont'g Ed Univ Houston (Tex) 1976; Clin Internship VA Hosp, Houston 1975-76; Res & Cnslg Intern Tex Yth Coun, Austin 1975; Tchg Asst Dept Ed Psychol Univ Tex-A 1973-75; Other Former Positions; Conslt Coors Tng Inst, Cincinnati, Ohio 1978; Org'd & Chaired Symposium to Tex Psychol Assn Conv, Dallas (Tex) 1978; Pres Phi Delta Kappa, Prairie A&M Univ 1978; Prairie View Alumni Chapt Polemarch, Kappa Alpha Psi 1978-79; Res to Fgn Students Advrs Conf, Tex So Univ, Houston 1977; Tex Psychol Assn; Tex Acad Sci, Sam Houston St Univ; APGA; SWn Social Sci Assn, Houston; Former Mem: Tex Classroom Tchrs Assn, Austin Assn Tchrs Inc; cp/Past Secy Hempstead Prairie View Lions Clb; r/Ch of Christ; hon/Recipient S'ships, F'ships; Outstg Col Aths, Pub'd in *Outstg Col Aths of Am* 1970; T K Lawless Awd, Prairie View A&M Univ 1970; Biogl Listings; Profl Pubs; Others.

SEVCIK, LUDOVIT oc/Physician; b/Mar 17, 1933; h/12 Park Blvd, Scarsdale, NY 10583; ba/Yonkers, NY; m/Maria; c/Patrick, Doris, Beatrice; p/Rudolf and Maria Sevcik, Czechoslovakia; ed/MD; pa/Dir Dept Anesthesiol & Resp Care; ASA; NYSSA; AMA; NYSMS; IASP; APA; r/Rom Cath; hon/Fellow, ACA; Diplomate, ABA; Recog, AMA.

SEWARD, ESTELLE BEALE oc/Educator; b/Jun 1, 1901; h/Warrosquoacke-on-the-Pagan, 506 Jordan Ave, Smithfield, VA 23430; p/William and Chrisana Beale; ed/AA Va Intermont Col 1920; Bach, Masters Univ Va; Addit Studies; mil/USN, Probationary Ensign WWII (Vol); Lt Cmdr (Ret'd) Bethesda Nav Hosp, Bethesda, Md; Num Other Activs; pa/Tchr Math, Set Up Guid Progs: Smithfield

HS, Isle of Wight Co (Va) 1953-54, Front Royal HS, Warren Co (Va) 1948-49; Tchr Math & Eng Suffolk HS, Suffolk, Va 1927-42; Other Tchg Positions; IPA; BPW Clb (Local, St & Nat); Var Orgs for Tchrs; AAUW; cp/Smithsonian Inst; Am Legion; Ret'd Ofcrs Clb; Archeol Soc Va; Chi Omega; Art Clb (Suffolk); Choral Clb (Suffolk); Org'd Isle of Wight Co Hist Soc; r/Smithfield Bapt Ch, S'field: Started SS Class for Yg Wom, Supt Jr Dept SS; hon/W/W: S&SW, Am Wom; DIB; Personalities of S; 2000 Wom Achmt; World W/W Wom; Intl W/W Intells; Others.

SEXAUER, ARWIN F B GARELLICK oc/Poet; ba/Music Mission Inc, Cherry Tree Hill, E Montpelier, VT 05651; m/Howard T; c/Dawn-Linnie Bashaw Mennucci, Alson Charles Bashaw; p/Linnie A and Alson B

Fletcher (dec); pa/Hd Libn, Kellogg-Hubbard Lib 1974-76, Asst Libn 1966-73; Society Reporter, *Times-Argus* 1964-65; Freelance Reporter 1934-; CoFdr Music Mission; Radio/Theatre Monologist 1939-53; Dance/Theatre, TV & Lecture Appearances; Author, *Remembered Winds* (1963); Poetry in 21 Book Collections incl'g *Premier Poets*; ASCAP; World Poetry Soc; Stella Woodall Poetry Soc; Cal Fdn Chaparral Poets; Ina Coolbrith Poetry Cir (San Francisco); IPA; Others; cp/IOOF; Past VP, 4-H St Coun; Trustee-at-Large, 4-H Camp Ingalls; Past Chaplain, Dept of Disabled Am Veterans Aux; Past Pres, PTA; Others; r/Meth; hon/Fellow, Centro Studi E Scambi Internazionale, Accademia Leonardo Da Vinci (Dipl di benemerenza, Titular Mem, Laureate Awd); Hon Life Fellow, Anglo-Am Acad; Dist'd Ser Cit for Poetry, World Poetry Soc; Life Fellow, Intl Acad Poets; Hon DLitt, World Univ; Fellow, Am Biogl Inst; 3 Geo Washington Awds; Sylvia Auxier Meml Awd; World Peace Awd for Poetry; Num Others.

SHACKELFORD, ROBERT PAISLEY JR oc/Funeral Director; b/Jul 17, 1931; h/610 N Church, Savannah, TN 38372; ba/Savannah; m/Bobbie Rogers; c/Lisa, Robert Paisley III; p/Robert Paisley Sr and Kathryn Hall Shackelford (dec); ed/BA Vanderbilt 1952; Deg of Mortuary Sci Gupton's Sch Mortuary Sci 1955; pa/Orgr & Past Dir Tenn Ambulance Ser Assn; Flying Funeral Dirs Assn; Nat Funeral Dirs Assn; Nat Selected Morticians; Past Pres Tenn Funeral Dirs Assn; Nat Fdn Indep Bus; Pres: Shackelford Corp, S'ford Funeral Dirs of Savannah Inc, S'ford Funeral Dirs Selmer Inc, Memorial Gardens Hardin Co; Chm Leg Com TFDA; cp/Rotary: Charter Mem, Past Pres; C of C: Past Pres, Orgr; Shriner; 32° Mason; Fdr & Past Pres Hardin U Givers Org; Past Mem Tenn Emerg Med Ser Adv Coun; Former Chm Savannah Utility Comm; Past Pres Hardin Co Ctl High Band Boosters; Var Bd Mbrships; r/Ch of Christ, Savannah: Deacon; hon/Rotary Paul Harris Fellow; Yg Man of Yr, JCs; Outstg Citizen Awd, WOW.

SHADDEAU, DONNA MAY LIVINGS oc/Clinical Chemistry Technologist; b/Dec 16, 1947; h/5055 Saratoga Ave Apt 4, San Diego, CA 92107; ba/San Diego; m/David H; p/James Clinton Livings (dec); Helen Hollis Livings, Fairfax, VA; ed/BS Roanoke Col 1971; pa/Nat Reg in Clin Chem; Am Assn for Clin Chem; r/Presb; hon/Roanoke Col Jr Scholar, Sr Scholar; Freshman Chem Awd, Chem Rubber Co; W/W Am Wom.

SHAFER, WILMA CLARE COX oc/Professor; b/Apr 6, 1916; h/2621 Oak Hill Rd, Evansville, IN 47711; ba/E'ville; m/Ivan J; c/John A, David B (dec); p/Alfred Bruce and Lillian Collins Cox (dec); ed/BA Univ E'ville 1951; MA 1958, EdD 1962 Ind Univ; pa/Univ E'ville: Prof Ed, Dir Early & Elem Ed; Overseas Comparative Ed Tour Dir; Pi Lambda Theta: Nat Pres 1973-77, Nat VP 1969-73; St Pres Ind AAUW 1971-73; Ind ACE 1959-61; Ind ATE 1968-69; cp/Univ Theatre Soc; E'ville Philharm Guild; Mus Guild; Willard Lib; r/Oak Hill Presb Ch, E'ville Mem; hon/Alumni Achmt Awd, Univ E'ville; Best Prof Awd; Delta Kappa Gamma.

SHAFFER, DALE EUGENE oc/Library Consultant; Writer; Director; b/Apr 17, 1929; h/437 Jennings Ave, Salem, OH 44460; ba/Salem; p/William Shaffer (dec); Florence

Erma Gibbons (dec); ed/BS, MALS KSU; MA OSU; mil/USAF; pa/Lib Conslt/Pubr (Self-employed) 1971-; Lib Dir Capital U, Columbus, Ohio 1968-71; Hd Libn Ocean Co Col, Toms River, NJ 1965-67; Chief Libn, Hd Lib Sci Dept Glenville St Col (WVa) 1963-65; Other Former Positions; Pub'd 14 Books on Libn'ship & Ed incl'g: *The Maturity of Librarianship as a Profession, A Handbook of Lib Ideas*, Others; ALA; Soc for Advmt of Mgmt; Contbr Num Articles to Ednl Jours; Invented Sha-Frame Sys; Conslt for Bldg 3 New Col Libs; r/1st Christian Ch, Salem: Est'd "Erma Shaffer Choir Fund"; hon/Grad Cum Laude, KSU 1955; Est'd: "Peterson Lib Awd" (Glenville St Col) & "William Shaffer Lib Awd" (Ocean Co Col).

SHAFFER, FRANCES ANNETTE oc/- Director; b/Sept 22, 1945; h/2315 W Gordon, Albany, GA; ba/Albany; m/Thomas; p/Sam Jenkins, Dayton, OH; Myrtice Jenkins (dec); ed/BA; pa/Dir Project SAVE; Notary Public; Model; Nurses Asst; cp/Dem Party; r/AME; hon/Lttr of Commend; Citizens Awd; Lt Col, Aide De Camp, Gov's Staff.

SHAFFER, MA LUISA C de oc/Teacher Associate; b/Mar 20, 1915; h/1060 Ivy Ln, San Antonio, TX 78209; ba/San Antonio; m/Lyman H (dec); c/Frank, Corona, Ma Luisa S Gonzales, Julia S Hemon, Robert L, George E; p/Juan Manuel and Julia G de Corona (dec); ed/MA IWC; MAIFAL; BA OLLU; pa/Lang Tchr UTSA; Alamo Lang Assn; AATSP; Alliance Francaise; Delta Kappa Gamma; cp/Coun of Intl Relats; SA Conserv Soc; r/Cath; Cath Daughs of Am; hon/IFAL: 1st Pedagogie, 2nd Fr Enonomy, 3rd Stylistics.

SHAH, DINESH OCHHAVLAL oc/- Professor; b/May 31, 1938; h/1410 NW 30th St, Gainesville, FL 32605; ba/G'ville; m/- Suvarna D; c/Bijal, Prerak; p/Ochhavlal M Shah (dec); Shardaben O Shah, G'ville; ed/PhD Columbia Univ; pa/Prof Chem Engrg Dept Univ Fla; ACS; AIChE; SPE; ASEE; ASA; FSA; r/Hinduism; hon/Excell in Tchg Awd; Pres' Scholar Awd; Outstg Ser Awd, Univ Fla; Best Paper Trophy, Intl Chem & Tech Cong.

SHAH, NANDKUMAR S oc/Chief of Laboratory; Educator; b/May 6, 1928; h/2600 Quail Hollow Ln, West Columbia, SC 29169; ba/Columbia, SC; m/Neeta; c/Anita; p/Shankarlal H and Parvatiben S Shah (dec); ed/BS; BSc (Hon); MS; PhD; pa/Chief Ensor Res Lab Wm S Hall Psychi Inst; USC Sch Med: Res Prof Dept Neuropsychi, Adj Prof Dept Pharm; Am Soc for Pharm & Experimtl Therapeutics; Intl Soc for Neurochem; Am Soc for Neurochem; Div Drug Metabolism, Am Soc for Pharm & Experimtl Therapeutics; Soc Biol Psychi; Assn Physiologists & Pharmacologists India; Mem Edit Bd Ind Jour Physiol & Pharm 1970-; Adv Coun Assn Physiologists & Pharmacologists India 1970; Mem Ad Hoc Com NASA Biomed Res Prog in Space 1976-; r/Hindu; hon/Recipient Awd to Present Paper at 7th Intl Cong of Pharm (Paris, France 1978), Am Soc for Pharm & Experimtl Therapeutics; Adj Dist'd Prof Col Pharm Univ SC 1970-; Intl Dir Investigators in Psychopharm; Others.

SHAH, SWARUPCHAND, MOHANLAL oc/Professor; b/Dec 30, 1905; h/417 Columbia Ave, Lexington, KY 40508; ba/Lexington; m/Mafat Devi; c/Kanti Lal;

p/Mohan Lal D and Chuni Behn Shah (dec); ed/MA; PhD (London); DLitt; pa/Prof Dept Math Univ Ky-L'ton; Assoc Editor Intl Jour Math & Math Scis; r/Jainism; hon/Dist'd Prof Awd, Univ Ky; Alumni Res Awd for Outstg Res.

SHAH, VINOD M oc/Engineer; Motel Owner; b/Nov 7, 1938; h/Fulton Plaza Motor Inn, Hwy 45 & 51, Fulton, KY 42041; ba/Dyersburg, TN; m/Eka; c/Ruta, Tapan, Dipa; p/Madhavlal and Champaben Shah, Bombay, India; ed/BSCE; MS; pa/Owner: Fulton Plaza Motor Inn (Fulton, Ky) & Budget Motel (D'burg, Tenn); Am Soc Civil Engrs; Am Cong on Surveying & Mapping; Water Pollution Control Fdn; Formerly Assoc'd w Conslt'g Firms (Civil & Envir Fields) in NY & Conn; cp/Var Fund Drives for Commun Events; r/Hindu; hon/Featured in Newspaper Articles.

SHAKE, J(AMES) CURTIS oc/Teacher; b/Mar 27, 1918; h/1029 Westcott St, Syracuse, NY 13210; ba/Syracuse; m/Cornelia Hughes; c/James Curtis Jr, Thomas Hughes; p/Clarence Arthur and Clara Yunker Shake (dec); ed/BM DePauw Univ; MM Eastman Sch Music; PhD Syracuse Univ; pa/SU Sch Music: Acting Dean, Tchr Crouse Col; Dean Local Chapt Am Guild Organists; Providence Gov Phi Mu Alpha; Pi Kappa Lambda: Fdr, 1st Pres; c/U Way, Var Positions; BSA; r/St Alban's Epis Ch: Organist, Choirmaster.

SHALLCROSS, VIRGINIA CARTER oc/Farmer; b/Nov 7, 1910; h/"Heavenly Acres", New Park, PA 17352; m/Preston; p/Henry Le Roy and Virginia Johnson Carter, Baltimore, MD; mil/Wom's Land Army; pa/Actress; Milk Tester; Farmer; cp/Am Law Enforcemt Assn; r/U Meth: SS Supt; hon/Cert of Merit for Dist'd Ser; Del-at-Large Police Conf.

SHALOWITZ, ERWIN EMMANUEL oc/Civil Engineer; b/Feb 13, 1924; h/5603 Huntington Pkwy, Bethesda, MD 20014; ba/Washington, DC; m/Elaine Langerman; c/Ann Janet, Aliza Beth, Jonathan Avram; p/Aaron Louis Shalowitz (dec); Pearl Bessie Myer Shalowitz, Wash DC; ed/BCE; MA (Public Adm); mil/USNR, Engrg Ofcr, Cmdg Ofcr of Destroyer; pa/Gen Sers Adm (GSA), Wash DC 1959-: Chief Contracting Procedures (Bldg Design & Constrn Procuremt Policy), Chief Mgmt Info, Mem Interagy Com on Housing Res & Bldg Technol Sponsored by Pres' Ofc of Sci & Technol, Chm GSA Bldg Eval Com, Chief Res Br & Lectr on Engrg Res & Systems Topics, Proj Mgr for Bldg Systems (1st Public Bldgs Ser Proj Mgr), Spec Asst for Protective Constrn Progs & Emer Planning Ofcr-GSA Devel of Unique Underground Ctr & Lectr on Protective Constrn Topics; Conslts Br Waterfront Structures, Specialist, Constrn Mgmt Engr for Airfield Facilities, Chief Structural Res Engr, Proj Ofcr & Tech Advr for Atomic Tests, Hd of Def Res Sect & in chg at HQs Level of Prog Resulting in Devel of Atomic Blast Simulator, Mem Navy's Spec Weapons Effects Test Planning Group, Lectr on Atomic Def Topics, Dept of Navy, Wash DC 1948-59; cp/Commun Drs; PTA; Yth Ldr; r/Jewish; hon/Sigma Tau; Selected by Navy Dept, US Civil Ser Comm & Interdeptl Com on Career Devel Progs for 1st Fed Jr Mgmt Intern Prog 1950; F'ship in Public Mgmt; Cert as Reg'd Profl Engr 1952; Pi Sigma Alpha, Nat Polit Sci Hon; Spec Distn in Master's Deg Comprehensive Exam Areas; Selected for Roster of Key Navy Sci & Engrg Pers; Fellow, Am Soc Civil Engrs; Fellow, ABI; Spec Commend Ser Awd, GSA; Appt'd by Admr of GSA to Nat Eval Bd on Arch-Engr Selections; Outstg in Perf at GSA; W/W: S&SW, Am, World; Personalities of S; DIB; Men Achmt; Intl W/W Commun Ser; Nat Reg Prom Ams & Intl Notables; Commun Ldrs & Noteworthy Ams; Notable Ams; W/W Govt; W/W Am Jewry; W/W World Jewry; W/W Technol Today; Contbr of Arts to Mags & Other Profl Jours.

SHANNON, DALE E oc/District Judge; Special Lecturer; Lawyer; b/Feb 8, 1916; h/1427 W Mountain Ave, Fort Collins, CO 80521; m/Arlene G; c/James E, Joan S; p/Ray

P Shannon (dec); Winnie B Shannon, Hiawatha, KS; ed/JD Ks Univ Sch Law 1938; mil/Vet WWII, 1/Lt; Judge Advocate Gen's Ofc; pa/Ret'd Dist Judge; Spec Lectr & Spkr John Brown Univ, Siloam Springs, Ark; Past Pres Colo Dist Judges' Assn; Larimer Co, Colo & Am Bar Assns; cp/Past Pres Ft Collins Lions Clb; Poudre-Thompson Knife & Fork Clb; Former Chm Larimer Co Repubs; r/Meth; hon/Commun Bldr Awd, Ft Collins Ser Clb.

SHANNON, K ANN oc/Director; Performance; Producer; b/Dec 16, 1952; h/402 Jordan Dr, Redlands, CA 92373; p/Leo W and Marjorie C Shannon, Redlands; ed/BFA Cal Inst Arts 1975; pa/Prodr/Dir LA Feminist Theatre; Fdg Trustee LA Wom in Theatre; cp/Wom's Bldg; Wom's Resource Ctr; hon/Dir of Yr, LA Theatre Alliance 1978; Others.

SHANNON, ROBERT F oc/Physician, Psychiatrist; b/Apr 15, 1933; h/1611 Mt Drive, Little Rock, AR 72207; ba/Little Rock; m/Lyra Carolyn Fugler; c/Shawn, Scott, (Stepsons:) Jeffrey Conaway, Timothy Conaway; p/Karr Shannon (dec); Ollie Ellen Fudge Shannon Smith, Tulsa, OK; ed/BSM; MD; mil/AUS 1961-63, Capt; Chief Psychi Womack Army Hosp, Ft Bragg, NC; pa/Prof & Hd Div Gen Psychi, Dir Residency Tng, Dept Psychi & Behavior Sci, Col Med, Univ Ark Med Sci Campus; Fellow, Am Psychi Assn; Diplomate Am Bd Psychi & Neurol Inc; Co, St & Am Med Assns; Pres Ark Psychi Soc 1970-71.

SHAPERE, DUDLEY oc/Professor; Author; Lecturer; b/May 27, 1928; h/11200 Buckwood Ln, Rockville, MD 20852; ba/College Park, MD; m/Hannah Hardgrave; c/Elizabeth, Alfred, Catherine; p/Dudley Shapere (dec); Corinne Perl, Brownsville, TX; ed/BA, MA, PhD Harvard; mil/AUS 1950-52; pa/Prof Dept Phil Univ Md-CP 1975-; Previous Tchg Appts: Ohio St Univ 1957-60,

Univ Chgo 1960-72, Univ Ill 1972-75; Am Philosophical Assn; Phil of Sci Assn; Hist of Sci Soc; AAAS; Am Psychol Assn; Edit Bd Mbrships: *Philosophy of Sci, Jour for Hist & Philosophy of Sci*; Conslt; hon/Quantrell Awd for Excell in Undergrad Tchg, Univ Chgo 1968; Sigma Xi Nat Bicent Lectr; Mem The Inst for Adv'd Study, Princeton, NJ 1978-79; Fellow, AAAS; Dist'd Scholar-Tchr Awd, Univ Md; Biogl Listings; Pub'd Author.

SHAPEY, RALPH oc/Composer; Conductor; Professor; b/Mar 12, 1921; ba/5835 S University, Chicago, IL 60637; c/Max K; p/Max and Lillian Paul Shapey; ed/Violin & Composition Studies; mil/AUS 1942-45; pa/Univ Chgo 1964-: Prof Music, Music Dir Contemp Chamber Players; Formerly Assoc'd w Univ Pa 1963-64;

Conductor: (1964:) Fromm Foun Concerts (NYC, Chgo, LA), Chgo Symph Orch, London Symph Orch, Buffalo Symph Orch, (1962:) Fromm Foun Concert (NYC) Prog, Wolpe, Shapey & Berger, Others; Composer Num Musical Works; r/Jewish; hon/Woglun Fd Awd 1978; Nuremberg Recording Awd; Arts & Lttrs Awd; William & Noma Copley Foun Awd; Other Awds for Compositions; Biogl Listings.

SHAPIRO, LYNN IRENE oc/Psychologist; b/Aug 10, 1945; h/9 Newton St, Cambridge, MA 02139; p/Leo and Esther Shapiro, Alexandria, VA; ed/BA Univ Wis 1967; MAT Antioch Grad Sch 1971; MA Antioch Grad Sch 1976; pa/Dir CPCS Cnslg Ctr Univ Mass-Boston; Mem Greenhouse Inc, Cambridge; cp/Mem & CoDir Mandala Folk Dance Ensemble.

SHAPIRO, SUSAN H oc/Retailer, Interior Designer; b/Aug 27, 1943; h/40 Wickham Rd, East Hills, NY 11577; m/Lee; c/Christopher Morrow; p/Sam and Roslyn Polsky; ed/BA Syracuse Univ 1964; MA NY Univ 1965; pa/Current Pres: Trio Designs Inc 1975-, Apricot Designs Inc 1977-, Trio Designs of Roslyn 1978-; Dir'd Total Renovation & Design of Pediatric Dental Bldg; Tchr, NYC Public Schs 1964-66; Past Pres, Susan H Shapiro Antiques & Interiors; Interior Designer: Wallpaper Place 1974-75, Bagatelle Assocs 1972-73; Provisional Mem Am Soc Interior Designers; Assn Envir Designers; cp/Past Nat Field Secy, Alpha Epsilon Phi; VP, LWV; VP, Norgate Civic Assn; Chrperson, Roslyn Schs Budget Adv Comm; hon/Wom of Yr, Hadassah; W/W in E; Am Registry Series; Commun Ldrs Am.

SHAPTON, WILLIAM ROBERT oc/- Professor; b/Jun 25, 1941; h/506 Riddle Rd, Cincinnati, OH 45231; ba/Cinc; m/Patricia; c/Heather Lee, William Sargent; p/Lee and Ruth Shapton, Charlevoix, MI; ed/BS 1962,

MS 1963 Mich St Univ; PhD Univ Cinc 1968; pa/Prof Univ Cinc; Chm Cinc Sect ASME; SAE; Nat Chm Student Act SAE; r/Meth; hon/Brodie Fellow; Teetor Awd.

SHARLAND, TERESA C oc/Psychiatric Social Worker; b/Jan 26, 1941; ba/2355 Delta Rd, Bay City, MI 48706; m/Michael F; c/Jill, Beth, Michael; p/Joseph and Pauline Loeb Hauger; ed/BS; BA; MSW; pa/NASW; Nat Foster Parents Assn; Marriage Cnslg; Fdr & CoDir Pvt Out-Patient Clin; r/Rom Cath.

SHAW, ANNE P oc/Librarian; b/Feb 14, 1935; h/170 Ten Rod Rd, N Kingstown, RI 02852; ba/Providence, RI; c/Sarah E, Martha A; p/Carl and Anna Gorlich, New York, NY; ed/BA Hunter Col; MLS Univ RI; pa/Libn RI Dept St Lib Sers; Am Lib Assn; New England Lib Network Task Group on Document; r/Epis; hon/Phi Beta Kappa.

SHAW, ELIZABETH CHRISTINE FOX oc/Teacher; b/Oct 17, 1914; h/47 Whitethorne Ave, Columbus, OH 43223; ba/Columbus; m/Charles L (dec); c/Rowita Charlene S Heard, Regina Musetta S Green; p/William and Lottie Fox (dec); ed/BS (Bus Ed), BS (Social Group Work) 1952, MA 1975 OSU; MEd; MTh; DD Univ En Fla; mil/Civilian, Army Pers-Resv, Active Civilian

Depts 1954-62; pa/Bus & Ofc Career Ed Tchr; Ohio & Columbus Bus Edrs; OSU Alpha Xi; Pi Omega Pi; Ed Col EdLum; Social Sch & OSU Alumnae; Nat Assn Broadcasters; cp/Hilltop Civic & Commun & Ch Couns; Repub Clbs; Past VP UN Chapt; r/Hilltop U Meth Ch: Asst Min to 5 Pastors, Coor Fam Life, Former Spiritual Life Ldr Ch Wom U; hon/Good Neighbor; Mother of Yr; Citizen Jour 1 of 10 Outstg Wom; Omega Psi Phi; Mu Iota; Human Relats Scroll; Others.

SHAW, MILDRED HART oc/Journalist; b/Jun 27, 1909; h/2778 Patterson Rd, Grand Junction, CO 81501; ba/Same; m/J Earl; c/James Scott; p/William Lee and Parl Barker Hart; ed/Att'd Univ Wash 1927-30; pa/Soc Editor *The Daily Sentinel*, Grand Junction 1935-40; Book Editor 1974-; Chief Edit Writer 1956-72; Edit Page Editor 1970-72; cp/Former Mem Mesa Co Art Ctr Bd; Former Dir Jr Gt Books Prog for Sch Dist 51; Former Mem Exec Bd Com for Gifted Chd; hon/W/W Am Wom.

SHAWSTAD, RAYMOND VERNON oc/Computer Specialist; b/Mar 17, 1931; h/PO Box 551, Van Nuys, CA 91408; ed/San Bernardino Val Col 1964-65; Cert'd Data Processor 1965; W Coast Univ 1960-62; Profl Designation in Systems & Procedures UCLA 1971; Liberal Inst Natural Sci & Technol 1973-; mil/Ia NG 1948-57; USAR to 1963, 1/Lt Inf; pa/Sunkist Growers Inc: Sr Systems Programmer 1975-, Programmer & Internal Info Systems Conslt 1965-75; Conslt & Tchr in field Public & Pvt Schs & Sch Sers 1961-63; San Bernardino Co, Cal 1958-64: Control Clerk, Tabulating Equipmt Operator, Data Processing Technician; Other Former Positions; Assn for Computing Machinery, San Fernando Val Chapt, Spec Interest Groups for Software Engrg & Bus Data Processing, VChm Arrowhead Chapt 1961-62; Data Processing Mgmt Assn; Assn for Systems Mgmt, San Gabriel Val Chapt: Treas 1971-72, Secy 1972-73, Dir 1973-74; Assn for Systems Mgmt, Arrowhead Chapt, Ed Chm 1968-70; hon/Profl Pubs; Notable Ams; W/W in W.

SHAY, JOSEPH LEO oc/Researcher; b/Mar 12, 1942; h/24 Longview Dr, Holmdel, NJ 07733; ba/Holmdel; m/Marbeth; c/Joseph, Mary Elizabeth; p/Joseph L and Shirley M Shay, Albany, NY; ed/BEE Manhattan Col 1963; MS 1964, PhD Stanford Univ 1967; pa/Bell Labs 1967-: Appt'd Hd Solid State Device Physics Res Dept 1974-; Reschr in Optical Properties of Semiconductors; CoAuthor w J H Wernick, *Ternary Chalcopyrite Semiconductors: Growth, Electronic Properties & Applications*; Am Physical Soc; Electrochemical Soc; NJ Solar Adv Coun; Solar Resource Group of Nat Acad Scis Com on Nuclear & Alternate Energy Sys; Exec Com of Energy Technol Group, Electrochemical Soc; cp/Holmdel First Aid & Rescue Squad; Marlboro 1st Aid & Rescue Squad (Charter Mem); hon/NSF F'ship, Stanford Univ; Manhattan Col: Ellen S Rooney S'ship; NY St Regents S'ship, K of C S'ship.

SHEARD, KEVIN oc/Professor; b/Jan 30, 1916; h/4152 W 49th St, Cleveland, OH 44144; ba/Cleve; m/Ruth L; c/Wenda Jane, Sarah Anne, Elizabeth Margaret, Catherine Frances, Martha Joan, Bonniejean Meyer; p/Alec Michael and Frances Cox Sheard (dec); ed/BA Williams Col 1947; MS 1949; MBA Xavier 1955; JD Loyola-Chicago; mil/Pvt to Maj CAC 1939 (NYNG) to 1959 (USAR); pa/Prof Law Cleve St Univ; hon/Pubs incl: *Acad Heraldry in Am, Acad Dress & Insignia of the World's Univs*, Law Review Articles.

SHEEDER, WILLIAM B oc/University Administrator; b/Jan 21, 1938; h/8335 SW 72 Ave-316, Miami, FL 33143; ba/Coral Gables, FL; c/Lynn Suzanne, Traci JoAnn; p/Fred T and Amy F Sheeder, Elmira, NY; ed/BA; MA; pa/Univ Miami-CG: Dean Students, Asst VP for Student Affairs; Assn Col Unions-Intl: 1967-, Enrichmt Chm & Co-Host Dir 1975 Conf; Nat Assn Student Pers Admrs; Am Assn for Higher Ed; Conslt Centre for Experiential Lng & Living Inc 1976; Nat Orientation Dirs'

Assn; APGA; Intl Assn Auditorium Mgrs; Wesley Foun Bd Dirs, Dade Co (Fla); Treas 1971-73, Chm 1973-77, Mem 1971-; Work Area on Higher Ed & Campus Min Fla Conf Coun on Mins of U Meth Ch 1976-; Omicron Delta Kappa; Omega; Phi Mu Alpha; Zeta Beta Tau Adj Brother; r/Meth; hon/Phi Delta Kappa; Sigma Alpha; Phi Kappa Epsilon, Outstg Admr Awd (Univ Miami); Univ Miami 1972 Homecoming Dedication for Contbns to Student Devel; Ohio Univ: Fac Fellows Cit, Fac Hon Roll; Profl Pubs; Biogl Listings.

SHEILS, GEORGE ARTHUR oc/Clergyman; b/Nov 3, 1917; h/313 Sheriff Ave, Oskaloosa, IA 52577; ba/Oskaloosa; m/Doris T; c/Ruth Ethel S Jackson, JoAnn S Bell; p/George Arthur and Ethel Reed Sheils (dec);

ed/BA Hamline Univ; MDiv Boston Univ Sch Theol; pa/Pres Ia Bd Pensions, UMC; cp/Rotary Clb; UF Chm; r/U Meth Ch; hon/Alpha Kappa Delta; DD, Ia Wesleyan Col.

SHELEY, VERNITA LOREE oc/School Director; b/Jan 19, 1930; h/PO Box 127, San Bruno, CA 94066; ba/San Bruno; m/Donald Benjamin; c/Leighton Grant, Cabot Layne, Karlton Blair; p/Carl Ely Persing (dec); Zelna

Beulah Stokes Persing, Colma, CA; ed/Bethany Col; pa/Highlands Pre-Sch & Acad; Fdr 1966, Dir; r/Interdenom; Ch of the Highlands: Organist 1959-; hon/W/W Am.

SHELTON, JOEL EDWARD oc/Clinical Psychologist; Business Executive; b/Feb 7, 1928; h/PO Box 1298, Chico, CA 95927; ba/Oroville, CA; m/Maybelle Platzek; c/Sophia; p/John Granvil and Rosalma Fahy Ervin Shelton; ed/AB Chico St Col 1951; MA Ohio St Univ 1958; PhD 1960; mil/AUS 1945-46, AGD; pa/Butte Co Mtl Hlth, Chico: Clin Psychologist 1970-, Dir Consltn, Ed &

Commun Sers 1974-; Clin Psychologist El Dorado Co Mtl Hlth, Placerville, Cal 1968-70; Other Former Positions; Advr to Pres Protaca Industs, Chico 1974-; Exec Secy Protaca Agri Res 1974-; Assoc Ecology House 1974-; VP Moore-Shelton-Buckler Inc 1977-; Am, Wn Psychol Assns; hon/Biogl Listings.

SHELTON, JUNE POLLET oc/Educator; b/Jun 30, 1923; h/216 Oxford Ln, Longview, TX 75601; ba/Kilgore, TX; m/Theodore McQuown; c/Robert Byron, Kathleen Louise; p/Michael Simon Sr and Clemence Leona Pollet (dec); ed/BS Loyola Univ 1945; MS Tex Wom's Univ 1963; Addit Studies: Univ Tex, Tulane Univ, E Tex St Univ, Stephan F Austin Univ; pa/Instr Biology, Kilgore Jr Col; Am Soc Med Technologists; Tex Jr Col Tchrs Assn; Alpha Delta Kappa (Pres Theta Chapt 1978-80); Past Pres, Longview Br AAUW; Reg'd Med Technologist; Dir Med Lab in Hosp, Pvt Clin; cp/Gov's Coun on Wom & Legis Comm; Longview Civic Music Assn; Vocal Perfs w NO Opera & Shreveport Opera; Den Mother, BSA; Past Pres & Secy, PTA; Others; r/Cath; hon/Outstg Wom, AAUW; Nom'd Tchr of Yr (twice); Prog & Ednl Chm, Am Bus Wom of Am; Personalities of S; Soprano Winner, New Orleans Opera Auditions.

SHELTON, RAYMOND FRYAR oc/Chief of Police; h/2233 May Dr, Burlington, NC 27215; ba/B'ton; m/Carlene Wolfe; c/Alan, Kenny, Wanda; ed/Assoc Deg Police Sci w hons; BA w hons; MS Cand; Att'd Elon Col & A&T Univ; pa/B'ton Police Dept: Chief of Police 1978-, Former Police Ofcr, Spec Investigator, Desk Sgt, Line Sgt, Patrol Sgt, Patrol Lt, Yth Bur Cmdr; Pt-time Instr Dept Commun Cols & Salemburg Acad; Past Pres Alamance Co Law Enforcemt Assn; Past Pres B'ton Police Clb; NC Juv Ofcrs Assn; Intl Assn Juv Ofcrs; NC Police Exec Ofcrs Assn; Intl Assn Chiefs of Police; Alamance Co Law Enforcemt Execs Assn; cp/Former Mem Sertoma Clb; Bd Mem & Secy Campus Christian F'ship, Univ Chapel Hill; Master Mason; Treas Bula Lodge 409 AF&AM; Curric Devel Com S'burg Acad; U Way Drive; Commun Coun; Yth Needs Task Force, Alamance Co Commrs; Advr to Vols to Ct Prog; Local Com Mem Easter Seal Soc for Crippled Chd & Adults NC; Others; r/B'ton Ch of Christ; Mem, Yth Dir; hon/Police Ofcr of Yr, B'ton JCs 1966; Cert in Law Enforcemt, St NC Dept Justice; Cert'd Police Instr 1973, NC Crim Justice Tng & Standards Coun; Lynn Swanson Ward, Intl Juv Ofcrs Assn; Pubs.

SHELVER, JANET oc/Educational Administrator; h/2216 S Wn Ave, Sioux Falls, SD; ba/Sioux Falls; m/Raymond H; p/Maynard and Viola Werner (dec); ed/EdD; pa/Dir Ednl Ser Ctr; Cnslr; Career Ed Specialist; Dir Post-Sec'dy EPDA Proj, Voc Sch; hon/Notable Ams.

SHEPHARD, LENESE IVORY oc/Retired Teacher; Librarian; b/Nov 9, 1914; h/1046 E 51 St, Los Angeles, CA 90011; ba/LA; m/Isaac (dec); p/Felix and Edna Jones Ivory (dec); ed/BA; Grad Work; pa/Pt-time Libn; Tchr, 2 Yrs in Germany (Tchg Army Chd); Var Tchr's Clbs & Assns; cp/YWCA; Sr Citizens; r/Bapt.

SHEPPARD, RONALD JOHN oc/Planning Executive; b/Apr 13, 1939; h/19521 Burlington Dr, Detroit, MI 48203; ba/Warren, MI; m/Shirley Gaddler; c/Jeffrey, Mark; p/Lester and Louise Sheppard, New Rochelle, NY; ed/BS; MS; PhD; MBA; pa/Planning Exec Gen Motors; Ec Clb Detroit; Bd Dirs Prod Devel & Mgmt Assn; Bd Dirs Acct'g Aid Soc; cp/Rotary Intl; Bd Dirs Montessori Sch, Rochester, NY; r/Presb; hon/F'ships; K B Weissman Meml Awd.

SHEPPERD, WALTER ROBERT oc/Psychologist; b/Jan 13, 1950; h/16514 E Bails Pl, Aurora, CO 80012; ba/Lowry AFB, CO; m/Karin Elizabeth; c/Nicoletta Tatjana Carolina, Gordon Alexander Bo; p/Guy Jerry

Shepperd, El Paso, TX; Willie Eugene Shepperd, Roswell, NM; ed/PhD; mil/AUS 1968-72; pa/Psychologist Mtl Hlth Clin; Am Soc for Tng & Devel; APGA; cp/Substance Abuse Conslt Retraining Sq, Lowry AFB; hon/Intl Commun Ser Awd; Biogl Listings.

SHERMAN, EDNA SCHULTZ oc/Writer; b/Jul 27, 1907; h/840 Warren Way, Palo Alto, CA 94303; ba/Same; m/Roy V; c/John Roger, Julia S Payne, Patricia S Popper; p/George J and Helen Pope Schultz (dec); ed/BA w distn Univ Akron; Addit Studies Univ Cal; pa/Cal Writers; Am Assn Pen Wom; Nat Writers Clb; cp/Past Pres Akron LWV; Pres Univ Akron Fac Wives; r/Prot; hon/Cert of Apprec, Mayor & City Coun of Akron; Lit Awds; Personalities of W&MW.

SHERMAN, FRANCES BUCK oc/Professional Artist; b/Jan 30; h/4331 San Jose Ln, Jacksonville, FL 32207; ba/Same; m/W Scott Jr; c/Thomas M Frasier Jr, Harry B Frasier, Gregory Scott, Carolyn S Foley; p/Harry Catlett Jr and Elizabeth F Buck (dec); pa/Poet; Photog; Num One-Man Shows; Art Exhibits incl: Va Mus Fine Arts (Richmond, Va), Mint Mus Art (Charlotte, NC), Isaac Delgado Mus Art (New Orleans, La), Fla Fdn Art Mus (DeBary, Fla), Jacksonville Mus Arts & Scis (J'ville, Fla), Alonzo Art Gallery (New York, NY 5-Man Show), Latin Qtr Gallery (Tampa, Fla), Swan Coach House Gallery (Atlanta, Ga), Others; Pub'd Poet & Lyricist: Melody of the Muse, Yrbook of Mod Poetry, Lyrical Voices, Ofcl Centennial Hymn of Avalon (Pa), Others; Nat Leag Am Pen Wom: J'ville Br Pres 1974-76, Fla St VP 1974-76; Am Artists Profl Leag Inc; Fla St Poetry Soc; IPA; Arts Assembly J'ville; J'ville Art Mus; Nat Writers Clb Inc; cp/Var Art Demonstrations; Lectr; Hostess J'ville Arts Assembly for Arts Fest; Poetry Contest Judge, Sponsored by Indep Life Ins Co; Repub Campaign Activs 1976; r/Epis; hon/Outstg Patriot, Patriots of Am Revolution; Cert of Recog, Bicent Comm J'ville; Fellow, IBA; Num Awds for Art, Poetry & Photo.

SHERROD, PHILIP oc/Artist; b/Oct 12, 1935; h/41 W 24 St, New York, NY 10010; ed/BS 1957, BFA 1959 Okla St Univ; Att'd Arts Students Leag 1962-64; pa/Tchr Painting: Summit Art Ctr (NJ) 1977-78, Morristown Art Assn (NJ) 1973-74, Taos, NM 1959-62; Asst in Painting Art Students Leag (NY) 1964; Others; Num Exhbns incl: Bronx Mus (Bronx, NY) 1980, Bernard Baruch Col (NYC) 1979, Oakland Univ R B Bakers Collection (Rochester, Mich) 1979, Allen Stone Gallery (1-Man Show NYC) 1980, Peekskill Mus (Peekskill, NY) 1979, Ladycliff Col (Highland Falls, NYC) 1979, Summit Art Ctr 1977, Bayonne Jewish Commun Ctr (NJ) 1977, Num Others 1966-80; Rep'd in Collections: Tulane Univ Mus (New Orleans, La), Everhart Mus (Scranton, Pa), Almsford House Fine Arts Ctr (Anderson, Ind), ABC, Barry Diller (Pres Paramount Picture Prodns), Num Pvt Collections; Participant Panel Discussions; hon/Creative Artists Public Ser Prog (NYC) Grant; Childe Hassam Purchase Awd; Am Acad Arts & Lttrs; Fdn Arts & Lttrs S'ship; 1st Awds for Graphics, Pottery & Drawing, Okla St Univ 1959; Biogl Listings.

SHIELDS, RUBY oc/Hospital Administrator; b/May 7, 1936; h/716 Gelston Pl, El Cerrito, CA 94530; ba/El Cerrito; m/William M; c/Willie Jr, Gary; p/Clotiel Mixon, Oakland, CA; ed/BA; MA; PhD; cp/Adv Bd Mem: Salvation Army, Ombudsman; Southside Dem Clb; Consumer Bd E Bay Chapt Hlth Facilities; Former Mem Peer Review E Bay Nsg Home Assn; Rotary Ann; Broadcast Music Inc; Broadcast Com Corinthian (COGIC); Preceptor St of Cal, Admr; r/Prot.

SHIFFMAN, MAX oc/Mathematician; Professor; b/Oct 30, 1914; h/16913 Meekland Ave #7, Hayward, CA 94541; ba/Hayward; c/Bernard, David; p/Nathan and Eva K Shiffman (dec); ed/BS cum laude CCNY; MS 1936, PhD 1938 NY Univ; mil/Civilian Activs:

Mathematician NY Univ (US Ofc Nav Res & US Ofc Sci Res & Devel) 1942-45; Mathematician: Rand Corp, Santa Monica 1951, Geo Wash Univ 1958-60 (Def USA); Aided USA in Cuban Crisis 1962, 63; Others; pa/Prof Math Cal St Univ-H; Mem Var Math Socs (US); Res Pure & Applied Math; cp/Fdr Peace & Freedom Party 1966-68; Cal Repub Leag; Var Activs for Underprivileged Groups; hon/Blumenthal Fellow, NY Univ; Awd of Merit, USN; Var Plaques & Dipls for Dist'd Achmt; DIB; Men Achmt; Commun Ldrs & Noteworthy Ams; Personalities W&MW; Intl W/W Intells; Notable Ams; W/W W; Am Men & Wom Sci; Intl Scholars Dir.

SHIPLEY, L EARLE oc/Executive; b/Aug 1, 1916; h/21 Alida Ct, Oakland, CA 94602; ba/Oakland; m/E Geraldine; c/Thomas Allen, Rebecca Sue Woodward; p/L Earl

Shipley (dec); Adelia Pointer Douma (dec); ed/BA Linfield Col; MA Univ Pa; pa/VP Am Bapt Homes Foun of W; Devel Ofcr (Fund Raising); Min; cp/IPA; r/Am Bapt; hon/DD, Linfield Col.

SHIPP, VICTOR RAY oc/Retired Corporation President; b/Nov 22, 1921; h/625 NW 19th St, Oklahoma City, OK 73103; m/Wilma; c/Donua Ann Kratschmann, Linda Lou Butler, Donald Ray; p/Ray and Pauline Ballensky Shipp (dec); mil/AUS, USAAC WWII, 2/Lt, 1/Lt, Capt; Flight Ofcr; USAFR 2/Lt, 1/Lt, Ret'd 1963; Air Medal; Dist'd Flying Cross; WWII Victory Medal; pa/Vic Shipp Typography Inc 1961-73; Fdr, Ret'd 1973; Former Mgmt Conslt'g Engr: Greenville, SC & Wichita Falls, Tex; Gen Mgr SWn Press, Ft Smith, Ark 1954-59; Former Prodn Engr So Cal Newspaper Prodn Com; Former Sales

Engr Am Type Fdrs Inc; Fdr Victor R Shipp Co, Printers of Distn 1945-49; Developer & Sole Owner Star Printing Co, Okla City (until 1942); Former Model Newspapers, Mags & TV; Former Mem: Ctl Okla Indust Editors, Intl Assn Bus Communicators, Okla City Advt'g Clb, Okla City Art Dirs Clb; Okla City Better Bus Bur; Am Advt'g Fdn; Okla City C of C; Printing Indust of Am; Former Secy Creative Printers Am; Pubr Ad Galley 10 Yrs; cp/Am Legion; Resv Ofcrs Assn; r/Prot; hon/Self-Advt'g Mat Former Winner Nat 6th Pl Awd; Var Awds in Advt'g & Communs Fields.

SHIRK, FRANK CHARLES oc/Librarian; b/Apr 2, 1917; h/111 Country Clb Dr, Blacksburg, VA 24060; ba/B'burg; m/Mildred Rockwell; c/David, Linda S Wood (Mrs Henry Jr); p/(dec); ed/BA Rutgers Univ; BSLS Drexel Univ; mil/AUS Inf 1941-45; pa/Libn VPI&SU Lib; Va Lib Assn; Spec Libs Assn; cp/Rotarian; Commun Fdn; hon/Mensa Soc.

SHIRLEY, FEHL LORAYNE oc/Professor; b/Nov 28, 1918; h/8811 Canoga Ave, Canoga Park, CA 91304; ba/Northridge, CA; p/Mr and Mrs Fehl J Shirley, Canoga Park; ed/BA 1943; MA 1955; PhD 1966; pa/Prof Cal St Univ-N; Assn Childhood Ed Intl; IRA; NCTE; cp/Chperson Confs on Rdg & Multicult Ed; r/Congreg; hon/NDEA Inst in Rdg; Outstg Ser Awd, San Fernando Val Rdg Coun.

SHIRLEY, OLLYE BROWN oc/Administrator; b/Jan 10, 1934; h/114 California Pl, Jackson, MS 39213; ba/Jackson; m/Aaron; c/Kevin, Terrence, Christal, Erin; p/Walter G Brown (dec); Mrs Wilbert Brown, Mound Bayou, MS; ed/BA; MEd; EdS; pa/So Reg Admr Chd's TV Wkshop; Capitol Area, Miss & Am Pers & Guid Assns; cp/Bd Trustees Jackson Separate Sch Dist; Chperson Hinds Co Dem Exec Com; Delta Sigma Theta; r/Meth; hon/Polemarch Awd, Kappa Alpha Psi; W/W S&SW; Miss's Black Wom.

SHIVELY, MAX EDWARD oc/Educator; b/Jul 17, 1943; h/1438 N Meridian Rd, Apt 1, Tallahassee, FL 32303; ba/Tallahassee; m/Phyllis Ruth Reger; p/Marshall Shively (dec); Martha J Rousey Shively, Anderson, IN; ed/BS, MA Ball St Univ; PhD Cand Ohio Univ; pa/Asst Prof of Journalism, Fla A&M Univ, Tallahassee; Alpha Phi Gamma; Assn for Ed in Jour; Jour Alumni Assn of Ball St Univ; Kappa Tau Alpha; Nat Coun of Pub Advrs; Phi Delta Kappa; Soc of Profl Journalists, Sigma Delta Chi; Owner Pvt Lincolniana Collection (acclaimed 1 of finest collections concerning Abraham Lincoln in South); Author of Articles & Reviews on Pres Lincoln Appearing in 125+ Pubs throughout US & Australia; Abraham Lincoln Assn of Springfield, Ill; Pres Ind Collegiate Press Assn 1966-67; cp/Ind Yth Temperance Coun (Life Mem & Past Treas); Philadelphia Clb; Nat Yth Temperance Coun (Life Mem); Fla Heritage Foun; Lincoln F'ship of Wis; Tallahassee Hist Soc; r/1st Ch of Christian Scientist, Boston, Mass; 1st Ch of Christian Scientist, Athens, Ohio: Bd Dirs; hon/Ser Cit Awd from Nat Yth Temperance Coun; Dist'd Ser to Jour 1967, Sigma Delta Chi's Outstg Male Grad in Jour 1967, Outstg Jr Male in Jour 1966, Others; Named Hon Son of Ind by Gov Bowen 1976; Comm'd Ky Col by Gov Carroll 1976; Made an Hon Citizen of Ill by Gov Walker 1976; Made a Tenn Col Aide de Camp by Gov Blanton 1976.

SHOEBOTHAM, ANN WHITE oc/Real Estate Broker; b/May 17, 1938; h/7601 Beluche Dr, Galveston, TX 77551; ba/Galveston; m/Dennis R; c/Troy H, Todd E; p/Arnold J White, Frederic, WI; Maeta Anna Simon, Reno, NV; ed/Real Est Inst Tex; RE Inst Hi; pa/VChperson MLS Exec 1976-77, 1977-78; Gal Bd Realtors; cp/Former Cub Scout Den Mother; Former Secy & Editor Troop 897, Hayward, Cal; Coast Guard Ofcrs' Wives Clb, Galveston Chapt; r/Luth; hon/Miss Lincoln Co (Mont) 1954-55.

SHOEMAKER, FERN CATHERINE BEATY oc/Retired School Teacher, Principal; b/Jul 25, 1901; h/RR #2, Box 64, Lebanon, IN 46052; ba/Same; m/Russell E (dec); c/Janet Kathleen S Dulhanty; p/William Riley and Mary Louisa Beaty (dec); ed/BS, MS Butler Univ; pa/Sch Tchr 36 Yrs, Prin 9 Yrs, Ret'd Active Tchg 1970; Substitute Tchr Lebanon Commun Schs & Pvt Tutoring 3 Yrs; Mem & Ofcr Num Ednl Orgs; Orgr Boone Co Ret'd

Tchrs Assn; BPW Clb; AAUW; Beta Epsilon Chapt Delta Kappa Gamma; Mem Nat Election Bd BPW Fdn 1965; Mem St Bd BPW St Fdn 3 Yrs; Mem St Bd Delta Kappa Gamma 2 Yrs; cp/Vol: Witham Meml Hosp, Red Cross, Gray Ladies; Var Commun Drives; 4-H Ldr 6 Yrs; Friendly City Garden Clb; Florentine Clb; Boone Co Hist Soc; Hoosier D D's; Home Ext Clb; Former Mem Election Bd Dem Party; r/Mts Run Regular Bapt Ch: Mem 1914-, SS Tchr 1914-74, Ch Clerk, Ch Treas, Ldr Yg People's Group, VBS Dir Sev Yrs, Charter Mem Ch Wom's Group (Willing Wkrs); hon/NSF Grant Recipient; Pub'd Author; Ind Lives; Personalities W&MW; DIB; World W/W Wom.

SHONKWILER, JOHN A oc/Executive Director; b/Jul 7, 1942; h/7267 Macbeth Dr, Dublin, OH 43017; ba/Worthington, OH; m/Francine; c/John Clifton, Tracie Lauren; p/Clifton and Frances Shonkwiler, Westerville, OH; ed/Att'd Ohio St Univ; pa/Exec Dir St EMS Adv Coun; Past Pres & Charter Mem Dublin C of C; cp/Spec Dep Sheriff, Dep Registrar, Exec Com-man Franklin Co Trustees; Perry Twp Trustee; Repub Ctl Com-man; Franklin Co: Disaster Ser Comm, Bd Zoning Appeals; r/Meth.

SHORTER, LOUISE R oc/Assistant Cashier; b/Jan 30, 1927; h/1222 Commerce St #1904, Dallas, TX 75202; pa/Asst Cashier, Dallas Intl Bank; cp/Grass-roots Lobbyist; Contb'd Article, Leg Workshop, Gen Session VI, 65th Annual Intl Consumer Credit Conf (Boston, Mass) 1977.

SHOULBERG, HARRY oc/Artist; Painter; Serigrapher; b/Oct 25, 1903; h/223 W 21st St, New York, NY 10011; ba/NYC; c/Ted; p/Max and Tessie Shoulberg; ba/Rep'd in Perm Collections of Instns & Museums incl'g: Metro Mus, Denver Mus, San Francisco Mus, Ain Harod Mus, Tel Aviv Mus, Norfolk Mus, Butler Inst Am Art, Carnegie Inst, NY St Univ, Univ Wis, Univ Oreg, US St Dept, Brooks Meml Gallery, NJ St Col; hon/Purchase Prize, Milwaukee Art Inst; Tanner Prize, Am Color Print Soc; 1st Prize, Guild Hall.

SHOULDERS, HARLAN ROBERT oc/Artist; Photographer; Landscape Designer; b/Dec 25, 1954; h/215 W Dallas, Palestine, TX 75801; ba/Palestine; p/Robert L and

Therese Shoulders, Palestine; ed/Landscape Arch Deg Cand; mil/USN 4 Yrs; pa/Free-lance Artist; Photog; cp/Photog for Local Brochures & Mags; r/So Bapt; hon/Eagle Scout; Art Awds.

SHRIVASTAVA, KRISHNA KUMAR oc/Urban Designer; b/Oct 11, 1948; h/120 Sandstone Dr #10, Beckley, WV 25801; ba/Beckley; p/Mathura P and Leela Devi Schrivastava, Jabalpur, India; ed/BArch Univ Roorkee (India); MArch Ohio St Univ; pa/Am Planning Assn; Assoc Mem Inst Trans Engrg; Assoc Indian Inst Architects; Profl Affil WVa Soc Architects; Reg'd Architect India; cp/Intl Affairs in Conjunction w Delta Kappa Gamma & Jr Wom's Clb Beckley; r/Hindu; hon/Gen Knowledge Prize, Delhi Public Sch, New Delhi.

SHUMWAY, JAMES McBRIDE oc/Attorney; b/Aug 6, 1921; h/19 Willotta, Suisun, CA 94585; ba/Fairfield, CA; m/Hedwig

Maria; c/James M Jr, Ralph S; p/Dorice Dwight and Marcella McBride Shumway (dec); ed/BS Univ Ill; JD Stanford Univ; mil/USN, Carrier Combat Pilot WWII (S Pacific); Navy Cross; Silver Star; 2 Dist'd Flying Crosses; Cmdr Ret'd Resv; pa/Pract'g Atty; Former Chm Cal Alcoholic Beverage Control Appeals Bd; Former Mem Cal Unemploymt Ins Appeals Bd; Former Asst Admr Hlth & Wel Agy, St of Cal; St Bar Cal; Pres-elect & Dir Dist Atty's Assn Cal; Dir Nat Assn Co Civil Attys; Pt-time Prof San Francisco St Col Grad Sch; Lectr Golden Gate Univ; cp/Co Counsel Solano Co 11 Yrs; Former St Chm Civil Law Inst; Former Mem Law Review Comm for Admendmt of Ed Code Cal; Mem St-wide Study Workmen's Compensation Probs; Legal Adv Com Co Supvrs Assn Cal; hon/W/W: Am Law, Am Polits, W; Notable Ams; Commun Ldrs & Noteworthy Ams; Book of Honor; DIB; Men Achmt; Intl W/W Intells.

SICOTTE, GRACE DARLING D oc/-Community Resources Director; b/Nov 17, 1922; h/2825 Farragut A 201, Butte, MT 59701; ba/Butte; c/Joseph E, Nancy S Cassidy (Mrs Frank), Charles D; p/Dot R Dement (dec); Dollie Mae Butler (dec); ed/Portland Univ; Mont St Univ; pa/Commun Resources Dir; Butte Silver Bow Sheriff Dept; Dir YMCA; BPW; cp/Dep Dir Civil Def; Bd Dirs Red Cross; Mont Ambassador; Mtl Hlth Assn; Dir Mont St Wom's Network (Dir); Toast-mistress; Soroptimist; OES; r/Meth; hon/-Woms Achmt Awd, BPW; Queen of Olym-pics, YMCA; Nat Secy of Yr, NSA; Outstg Commun Ser Awd; Apprec Awd, US 6th Army Rec Dist; Num Study Grants; Wom of yr; Others.

SIDWELL, DEREK oc/Engineer; b/Jun 9, 1934; h/6023 Darkwood Dr, Houston, TX 77088; ba/Houston; m/George Anne; c/Jane Catherine, Timothy John, Peter Kirk;

p/Herbert Walter and Elsie May Sidwell, Southampton, England; ed/BS; mil/Royal AF; pa/ISA; Author Num Tech Papers; cp/S Tex Yth Soccer Assn; r/Ch of England; hon/Holder Num Patents.

SIEGENDORF, ARDEN M oc/Circuit Judge; b/1938; h/Coconut Grove, FL; m/Rebecca Lyle; c/Stacey; ed/Grad Bus Sch Univ Miami 1960; JD Univ Miami Law Sch 1963; pa/Appt'd Spec Asst Leg Div Ofc Atty Gen 1963; Asst Atty Gen Fla 1965, In Charge of S Fla Reg Ofc 1967-71; Appt'd to Miami City Comm 1971; Appt'd Judge Dade Co Small Claims Ct 1971; Elected Judge Co Ct 1972; Judge Circuit Ct 1974-; Inter-Am, Am, Fla & Dade Bar Assns; Am Judic Soc; Fla Bd

Bar Examrs 1970-71; VP Fla Conf Co Ct Judges 1973-74; Tchr Trial & Appellate Pract Miami-Dade Commun Col; Guest Lectr; Chm Bench-Media Relats Com 11th Judicial Circuit; Mem Judicial Compensation Com Fla Conf Circuit Judges; Chm Judges' Spkrs Bur 1977; cp/Past Pres Downtown Miami Optimist Clb; Former VP Tiger Bay Clb; Exec Com Reg Bd Anti-Defamation Leag B'nai B'rith; Tourist Action Com Miami-Dade C of C; Elks Lodge; Former Chm Adv Bd Comprehensive Offender Rehab Prog; Mem Judicial Comm (which planned Fla's Participation in Bicent Celebration) 1975-76; Dem Exec Com; Past Pres Yg Dem Clbs; hon/Ky Col; Outstg PAD Alumni Awd, Univ Miami Law Sch; Biogl Listings; Profl Pubs.

SIEGENTHALER, KENNETH EUGENE oc/Laser Physicist; Military Officer; b/Mar 10, 1939; h/575 Sun Hills Dr, Colorado Springs, CO 80908; ba/US Air Acad, CO; m/Phyllis Josephine Wood; c/John Paul; p/Paul and Ruth Siegenthaler, Elgin, MN; ed/BS West Point 1961; BS Univ Utah; MS 1973, PhD 1976 AF Inst Technol (Ohio); mil/USAF Lt Col; Dep Dir Directorate of Chem Scis Frank J Seiler Res Lab, USAF Acad 1977-; AF Mats Lab, Wright-Patterson AFB (Ohio); Asst Chief Electromagnetic Mats 1977, Acting Chief Analytical Br 1976-77, Staff Laser Devel Engr 1975-76; Laser Res Engr Aerospace Res Lab, Wright-Patterson AFB 1974-75; Other Positions; Moved up ranks from 2/Lt to Lt Col; Served in Vietnam; Air Medal w 2 OLC; AF Commend Medal w 2 OLC; pa/Am Soc for Mass Spectrometry; Sigma Pi Sigma; Tau Beta Pi; r/Village Seven Reformed Presb Ch, Colo Springs: Mem.

SIERRA, ANGELL O de la oc/Biophysi-cist; Educator; Writer; b/Feb 28, 1932; ba/Box 2060, UPR-Cayey, Cayey, PR 00633; m/Judith Ann Sheffer-La Valle; c/3 Sons, 2 Daughs; ed/BS Univ PR; MS CUNY; PhD St John's Univ; Addit Studies; pa/Former Res Assoc Experimtl Surg Cornell Univ (NY); Former Biophysicist Sloan Kettering Inst (Cornell Univ); Res Analyst Smithsonian Inst (Washington, DC); Res Chemist Dept Def Armed Forces, Radiobiol Res Inst; Prof Biophysics Georgetown Univ Med Sch, Wash DC; Univ PR: Vis Prof Fac Med, Chm Fac Natural Scis (Cayey); NY Acad Scis; Biophy Soc; Radiation Res Soc; Pres Conslt'g Bd Technol & Voc Tng, Cayey; Lectr; Var Other Profl Activs; cp/Fdr Org to Promote Perf'g Arts; hon/Author Num Pubs & Papers in field; Recipient Num Awds; Personalities of S; Intl W/W Commun Ser; W/W Am.

SILBER, MARK B oc/Corporate Psych-ologist; b/Sept 26, 1932; h/215 W Orchard, Arlington Heights, IL 60005; ba/Chicago, IL; m/Elizabeth Rose; c/Christy Lynn, Julie Ann; p/Harry M and Grace V Silber (dec); ed/-Undergrad Deg Univ Wis; Master's, Doct Deg Ohio St Univ; mil/USAF Strategic Air Command, Capt, Combat Flying Ofcr; pa/Sr VP Hume-Silber Assocs Ltd, Hosp Conslt'g Firm (Chgo); Assoc Prof Grad Sch Ill Inst Technol; Former Psychologist Lockheed Aircraft; Former Corporate Dir Mgmt Devel G D Searle & Upjohn Pharmaceuticals; Acad Positions: Univ Cal, Wn Mich Univ, Loyola Univ Chgo; Past Pres Indust Psychol Assn Chgo; Fdg Mem Chgo Org Devel Assn; Hosp Conslt; Reg'd Psychologist: Ill, Wis; Lic'd Conslt'g Psychologist Mich; Prog Spkr Canadian Col Hlth Ser Execs & Am Hosp Assn 8 Yrs; ACHA 8 Yrs; Bd Trustee Edr; Advr to Hosp Mgrs; Others; r/Luth; hon/Author *Managerial Perf & Promotability: The Making of an Executive*; Rated #1 Spkr, Cong Mbrship; Biogl Listings.

SILLIMAN, BENJAMIN DeWAYNE oc/Lawyer; b/Sept 10, 1945; h/245 25th St Dr SE, Cedar Rapids, IA 52403; ba/Cedar Rapids; m/Hannah Faye Nelson; p/Arthur Benjamin and Nella Whitbeck Silliman, Boone, IA; ed/BA Coe Col 1917; Law St Univ 1923; mil/WWI Arty; WWII 45 Months JAGD Prosecution Nurnberg Trial; pa/Past Pres Linn Co Bar Assn; Leg Ia St Bar Assn; cp/Past Cmdr Hanford Post Am Legion; Past Chm

Linn Co Repubs; r/1st Presb Ch, Cedar Rapids; hon/Bronze Star; AUS Meritorious Ser, WWI & WWII.

SILLS, GREGORY D oc/School Ad-ministrator; b/Mar 2, 1950; h/PO Box 212, Weldon, AR 72177; ba/Newport, AR; m/-Wanda L; c/Brian Keith, Phillip Lawrence; p/Fusel and Marie Sills, Weldon; ed/AA; BA; pa/Asst Dir White River Voc Tech Sch; Appt'd to Commun Adv Bd Ark Ednl TV Network; cp/Newport JCs; Newport Urban Leag; Alderman for City of Weldon; Ark Mun Leag; r/Ch of Christ; hon/Outstg JC of Yr, Newport JCs 1973-74.

SILVA, JOSE ANGEL oc/Maintenance Control Superintendent; b/Mar 19, 1930; h/PO Box 308, Marion, TX 78124; ba/Randolph AFB, TX; m/Ofilia Espinoza; c/Anna Cristina; p/Alejandro Silva Sr, Alice, TX; Apolonia Perez Silva (dec); pa/Non-comm'd Ofcr Acad; Sr Non-comm'd Ofcr Acad; USAF, Maintenance Control Supt Randolph AFB; r/Cath; hon/Dist'd Flying Cross; 6 Air Medals; Jt Ser Commend Medal; AF: Commend Medal, Outstg Unit Medal, Good Conduct Medal, Longevity Ser Awd; Army Good Conduct Medal; Nat Def Ser Medal; Vietnam Ser Medal; Small Arms Expert Marksmanship Ribbon.

SILVA, VALERIANO oc/Mechanic; b/Apr 6, 1911; h/1601 Taft St, Brownsville, TX 78521; ba/B'ville; m/Sofia T; c/Florence

Sulava, Santiago, Magdalena Gomez, Valeriano Jr, Guadalupe, Angie S Navarro, Mateo; p/Mateo and Ma del Jesus D Silva (dec); r/Cath, Christ the King Ch.

SILVAROLI, NICHOLAS J oc/University Administrator; b/Dec 4, 1930; h/955 E Southern #137, Tempe, AZ 85283; ba/Tempe; c/Diane, Christine, Pamela; p/Nicholas Silvaroli (dec); Caroline Silvaroli, Buffalo, NY; ed/BS; MA; EdD; pa/Ariz St Univ: Tchr Grad & Undergrad 1963-, Dir Rdg Ed 1963-, Dir Migrant Tchr Insts 1970-; Dir Ariz Migrant Child Ednl Lab, St Ariz 1971-; Dir SW Reg Conf, Phoenix, Ariz 1975-; Dir Annual ASU Rdg Conf 1969-; Vis Lectr Var Univs & Cols; Conslt; Spkr; Tchr 6th Grade Elem Sch, Williamsville, NY 1956-60; NCRE; IRA; NEA; AEA; Gamma Chapt Phi Delta Kappa; NSSE; Ariz St Rdg Coun; Adv Bd Mem Comm for Tchr Preparation & Lic'g 1973-; Other Profl Activs; hon/Recipient Grants; Profl Pubs.

SIMECK, CLYDE FREDERICK oc/Farm-er; Lecturer; Minister; b/Aug 16, 1915; h/PO Box 711, Somerset, KY 42501; c/Paul Clyde, Sibyl Elaine Stout; p/Charles and Annie S Simeck (dec); ed/2 Hon Docts (Agri & Div);

pa/Lectr; Preacher; Tobacco Farmer; cp/Cand for Commr of Agri; r/Indep: Min; hon/Hon Lttr, Mrs Nixon; Num Biogl Listings.

SIMKO, JAN oc/Professor; b/Oct 30, 1920; h/1337 Pennsylvania Ave SE, Washington, DC 20003; c/Jan, Vladimir; p/Simon Simko (dec); Terezia Simkova, Czechoslovakia; ed/MPhil Univ London 1967; PhD Univ Bratislava 1944; mil/Basic Tng 1946; pa/Tchr HS 1942-, Col 1945-; External Examr Critical Langs Prog Kent St Univ (Ohio) 1975-; Instr Slovak Fgn Ser Inst, Wash DC 1974; Prof Eng Rio Grande Col (Ohio) 1968-75; Other Acad Positions; Mod Lang Assn Am; Nat Travel Clb; Former Mem: Col Eng Assn, Medieval Acad Am, Renaissance Soc Am, IPA, Cir Mod Philologists; Num Pubs; r/Cath; hon/Brit Coun Grant, Univ London; F'ship, Folger Shakespear Lib, Wash DC & Canadian Govt; Book of Honor; Personalities of S; Intl W/W Intells; Notable Ams; Others.

SIMMONS, DAWN LANGLEY oc/Writer; b/Oct 16, 1937; h/390 Main, Catskill, NY 12414; ba/Same; m/John-Paul; c/Natasha Manigault Paul, Barry Stanley Maurice (Stepson); p/Stringer Davis (dec); Dame Margaret Rutherford; pa/Art Tchr St Patrick's Elem Sch, Catskill; r/Epis.

SIMMONS, JEWELL PHILLIPS oc/-Retired; b/Apr 10, 1898; h/207 W Harding, Greenwood, MS 38930; m/Jesse Eugene (dec); c/Jesse Eugene Jr, Sara Elizabeth Morgan, Dorothy Kimbrough; p/Virgil Leroy and Sebie Lenora Ware Phillips (dec); ed/BS Delta St Col 1951; MEd Univ Miss 1956; pa/Tchr: Water Valley (Miss) 1920, Senatoria (Miss) 1919, Leflore Co HS 1943-63; Miss Edn Assn 1943-63; NEA 1943-63; MFMC 1965-80 (Rec'g Secy 4 Yrs); AAUW; AARP; cp/Past Pres: Wom's Clb of Itta Bena (Miss), Itta Bena PTA, BPW, Matinee Musical, Others; Former Sponsor FHA; Others; r/Bapt: SS Tchr, SS Supt, Choir; hon/Rep'd Music Clb in Queen's Court, Leflore Co Centennial; Yrbook Dedication 1963; Ret'mt Awds.

SIMON, DAVID RICHARD oc/Physician; Educator; b/Nov 17, 1942; ba/201 N Univ Dr, Plantation, FL 33324; m/Andrea Carlo; c/Geoffrey L, Elizabeth A, Michelle L, Stephanie R; p/Hyman L Simon (dec); Betty S Simon, Surfside, FL; ed/AA Univ Fla; BS, MS, PhD, MD Univ Miami; mil/USNR, Cmdr MC; pa/Clin Assoc Prof Anatomy Univ Miami Med Sch; Fac Lancaster Course in Ophthalmol; Pvt Pract Ophthalmol; hon/1st Person to Simultaneously Receive MD & PhD Degs, Univ Miami; Sigma Xi; Epsilon Tau Lambda; Kappa Delta Awd; Am Col Orthopedic Surgs; Cert'd, Am Bd Ophthalmol; Fellow, Am Acad Ophthalmol & Otolaryngol; Biogl Listings.

SIMONINI, DAVID MICHAEL oc/Attorney; b/Jan 15, 1948; h/25 Luzanne Cir, San Anselmo, CA 94960; ba/San Rafael, CA; m/Susan Virginia; c/Clinton Michael, Jeanne Virginia; p/Aldo Joseph Simonini (dec); Lola Anita Simonini, Fairfax, CA; ed/BA; JD; pa/Cal St Bar; ABA; CTLA; ATLA; Alameda & Marin Bar Assns; cp/Marin Co Bd Appeals; r/Rom Cath; hon/W/W Am Law.

SIMPKINS, MARK ADELBERT oc/Executive; b/Sept 15, 1950; h/2644 Verona Cir, Salt Lake City, UT 84117; ba/SLC; p/Robert W Simpkins, SLC; Ramona Foulger Simpkins (dec); ed/BA (Intl Relats) 1975, BA (Hist) 1975 Brigham Yg Univ; MEd Univ Utah 1978; pa/Pres Intl Trade & World-Wide Mktg Co; Num Talk Show Appearances: Europe, US, Mid E, Africa; Ofcl Mem US Curr Dev Prog to Egypt 1977; Crim Res Asst J R Clark Law Sch; Others; r/Ch Jesus Christ LDS: Missionary in Africa; hon/Author *Child Support: Getting It!*; Phi Theta Delta; Gamma Theta Upsilon; Ofcl Guest to Israel 1973; Receiver of the Flag, 20 Countries Rep'd.

SIMPSON, ERVIN PETER YOUNG oc/Ordained Minister; Retired Professor;

b/May 13, 1911; h/Box 82, Alderson Broaddus Col, Philippi, WV 26416; m/Lillian Eileen Andrew; p/Donald McEwen, John Martin; p/Thomas Simpson (dec); Clara Glass McEwen (dec); ed/Dip Theol New Zealand Bapt Theol Col 1936; BA 1947, MA 1st Class Hons 1948 Univ New Zealand; BD 1950, ThM w distn 1950, ThD 1952 Berkeley Bapt Div Sch; pa/Interim Pastor Bapt Temple, Fairmont, WVa 1977; Prof Hist Alderson Broaddus Col 1969-77, Ret'd 1977; Sr Lectr Hist Massey Univ, Palmerston N, New Zealand 1967-69; Prof Ch Hist Grad Theol Union, Berkeley, Cal 1962-67; Other Former Positions; cp/Grand Prelate Grand Commandery Ks Templar of St Cal (Twice); r/Bapt Union New Zealand: Ordained; Transferred to Am Bapt Chs; hon/Fulbright Scholar; Fac Fellow, Am Assn Theol Schs; Fellow: Royal Anthropol Inst Gt Brit, Soc Antiquarians Scotland; Profl Pubs.

SIMPSON, GWEN-HOLLY oc/Professor; h/1001 La Cadena, Arcadia, CA 91006; ba/San Marino, CA; m/Albert Miller (dec); c/Pamela S L'Heureux; p/Alexander Curt Von Holly (dec); Kathlyn Madge MacDonald (dec); ed/BA; MA; PhD; pa/Prof Intl Univ LA; Edr: Marywood Sch, Univ San Diego, Pasadena City Schs, Intl Univ; Guest Instr England & France; Profl Edrs Cal; ISI; Other Profl Orgs; cp/Repub; r/Rom Cath; hon/Flynn Foun Awd; Intl W/W Intells; Others.

SIMPSON, JACK BENJAMIN oc/-Investments; b/Oct 30, 1937; h/68 Isla Bahia Dr, Fort Lauderdale, FL 33316; ba/-Indianapolis, IN; m/Clara Winona Walden; c/Janet Lazann, Richard Benjamin, Randall

Walden, Angela Elizabeth; p/Benjamin Harrison and Verda Mae Woods Simpson, Tompkinsville, KY; ed/Med Technol Wn Ky Univ; pa/Am Soc Med Technologist; Am Soc Clin Pathologist; Ind Soc Med Technologist; Royal Soc Hlth (London, England); r/Bapt; hon/Ky Col.

SIMPSON, MARSHALL WAYNE oc/Clergyman; b/Feb 7, 1918; h/569 Lake Thunderbird Dr, Putnam, IL 61560; ba/Henry, IL; m/E Berniece Smith; c/William, Barbara Marti, Margaret Selburg, Mary Anne Logan, Deborah Carlson, Timothy; p/Clifford Hill Simpson (dec); Edna Josephson Simpson, Alexis, IL; ed/BS Monmouth Col 1940; Dipl McCormich Sem 1943; DDiv Millikin Univ 1975; pa/Pastor Henry-LaPrairie U Presb Parish, Henry & Sparland, Ill 1964-; Previous Pastorates: Mich, Ind & Peoria, Ill; Moderator: Muncie Presby 1954, Synod Ill 1965-66, Peoria Presby 1969, Synod Lincoln Trails 1973-74; cp/Rotary Intl; Past Pres Henry Clb; r/U Presb Ch USA; hon/Awd'd 10 Freedom Foun Medals & Certs; Moderatorial Nom to 186th Gen Assembly, U Presb Ch USA 1974; Biogl Listings.

SIMPSON, WADE BLAND oc/Oil & Gas Producer; b/Sept 11, 1937; h/2604 Nasworthy Dr, San Angelo, TX 76901; ba/San Angelo; p/James B Simpson, San Angelo; Modesta G Stokes, Big Spring, TX; ed/BA; BS; mil/USAF; pa/Partner & Co-Owner: Simpson-Mann Oil Prodrs, MWA Oil & Gas, Simaco Ctr; VP Modesta's Inc; Secy-Treas San Angelo Geol Soc; Dir Permian Basin Petrol Assn; W Tex Oil & Gas Assn; Tex Indep Prodrs & Royalty Owners Assn; W Tex Geol Soc; Indep Landman's Assn; Am Assn Petrol Landmen; cp/Bd Mem San Angelo Arthritis

Foun; Bd Mem Concho Val Coun Boy Scouts; r/Emmanuel Epis Ch: Vestry Mem, Fin Chm, II Century Trust Trustee, Chm Fiscal Adv Com, Lay Rdr, Chm Bldg Com; hon/W/W S&SW.

SINDERS, MARY GALLEY oc/Administrator; b/Feb 12, 1920; h/1718 Windsor Pl, Louisville, KY 40204; ba/L'ville; m/John W; c/Mary Kathryn McDonald, John W Jr; p/William G and Lillian Marsden Galley (dec); ed/AA Clifton Jr Col; LLB St Mary's Law Sch;

mil/USNR WAVES; pa/Dir VA Reg Ofc; Atty, Admitted to Pract Ill & SC; cp/Preselect Fed Exec Assn; Mem Steering Com En Ky Task Force to Study Housing Needs; Past Chm LWV St Com for Constitutional Revision; Chm 1978 Combined Fed Campaign for L'ville Area; hon/Ky Col; Admiral Ky Fleet; Hon Citizen, L'ville; Awd for Outstg Ser, Non-Comm'd Ofcrs Assn; Cert of Apprec, Cmdg Gen Ft Knox (Ky).

SING, ERIC JOHN oc/Assistant Professor; b/Oct 9, 1936; h/162 E Ontario, Chicago, IL 60611; ba/Chgo; p/Walter M and Lilly Singh, Agra, India; ed/PhD; pa/Asst Prof Dept Ob/Gyn NWn Univ Med Sch, Chgo; Reschr; cp/Mem Repub Nat Com; r/Epis; hon/Cert in Recog of Outstg Contbn to Advmt of Sci & Technol, Am Chem Soc.

SINGER, JEANNE WALSH oc/Composer; Pianist; Educator; b/Aug 4, 1924; h/64 Stuart Pl, Manhasset, NY 11030; ba/Same; m/Richard G (dec); Richard V; p/H Vandervoort and Helen Loucks Walsh, Richmond, VT; ed/BA magna cum laude Barnard Col 1944; Artist Dipl Nat Guild Piano Tchrs; pa/Composed 50+ Works; Perfs Own Music in Public Concerts, Radio, TV; Concert Pianist, Solo & w Chamber Groups; Public Lectr; Pvt Tchr; Nat Music Chm Nat Leag Am Pen Wom; VP CAAA; Bd Dirs: Am Wom Composers Inc, Commun Concerts Gt Nk; Music Bd N Shore Commun Arts Ctr; ASCAP; Am Music Ctr; LWC; hon/Phi Beta Kappa; Recipient Grants; 20+ Nat Awds; Biogl Listings; Pub'd Works.

SINGH, TARA oc/Consulting Environmental Engineer; b/Sept 3, 1937; h/1502 Gingerwood Ct, Vienna, VA 22180; ba/McLean, VA; m/Pritam K Ubee; c/Robbie, Paul; p/S Santa and Bhagwant K Singh, Khanna, Pb, India; ed/BS Ohio Univ 1965; MS Univ Mo 1966; PhD Ill Inst Technol 1972; pa/Assoc & Chief Envir Engrg Div H D Nottingham & Assoc (Div of Lyon Assoc) 1973-; Mgr Envir Engrg Dept HOH Assoc, Chgo 1971-72; Instr Ill Inst Technol, Chgo 1970; Proj Engr, Cosoer, Townsend & Assoc, Chgo 1968-70; Other Former Positions; Fellow Am Soc Civil Engrs; Water Pollution Control; Water Pollution Control Fdn; Diplomate Am Acad Envir Engrs; AAAS; Var Ofcs Held; cp/Fdg Pres GSE Alumni Assn; r/Sikhism; hon/Res F'ship, Univ Mo; Tchg F'ship, IIT; Awd of Merit, Pollution Engrg; Vienna Yth Soccer Leag Awd; Pub'd Author.

SINGLETARY, LILLIAN DARLINGTON oc/Physicist; b/Dec 29, 1937; h/32759 Seagate Dr, Rancho Palos Verdes, CA 90274; ba/Redondo Bch, CA; m/John Boon; p/John Cox Darlington (dec); Mary D Roller, Rancho Palos Verdes; ed/BS; PhD; pa/Physicist TRW

Systems Group; APS; IEEE; Sigma Xi; cp/Sierra Clb; Wilderness Soc; r/Meth.

SIROONI, ALICE A oc/Pianist; Teacher; h/120 Schenck Ave, Great Neck, Long Isl, NY 11021; ba/Same; p/Ardshir and Aroose Vartanian Sirooni; ed/Postgrad Juilliard Sch Music; Pvt Studies; pa/Fac Mem Nat Guild Piano Tchrs; Assoc'd Music Tchrs Leag Piano Tchrs Cong; Recitals: Carnegi Recital Hall,

Town Hall, Others; Concert Tours, Radio; Concert Classics Recordings; Contbr *Tech Control for the Mod Pianist;* cp/Pub'd Compositions; "Rondo" Selected Judges Choice in *Piano Qtrly;* Awd of Merit, Nat Fdn Music Clbs; Hall of Fame, Nat Guild Piano Tchrs; Intl W/W in Music.

SISK, KATHERN IVOUS oc/Broadcasting Executive; b/Nov 18, 1936; h/PO Box 587, Fulton, MS 38843; ba/Fulton; m/Olvie E; p/Herman D and Minnie Lee Sizemore Thompson, Guin, AL; ed/BS (Art) 1959, BS (Ec) 1959 Univ N Ala; pa/Co-Propr Radio Stas: WVSA Vernon, Ala 1967-, WFTO Fulton 1968-, WEPA Eupora, Miss 1973-, WKNG Tallapoosa, Ga 1975-, WFTA Fulton 1976-, WEXA Eupora 1977-, WKEA Scottsboro, Ala 1978-; Ext Home Agt Coop Ext Ser, USDA 1959-67; cp/Bd Dirs: Itawamba Co Cancer Soc, Itawamba Co Fair Assn, (Nat) Gospel Music Assn & Hall of Fame 1975-76; Pres: S Fulton Homemakers Clb 1973-75, Fulton Civic Clb 1976-77, Dist III Miss Fed'd Wom's Clb 1978-79 (1/VP 76-77); Past VP Itawamba Co Retard Assn; Itawamba Co Bicent Com 1975-76; Chm Itawamba Co Progs 1977-78: Preven of Blindness, Cystic Fibrosis; Secy Itawamba Co Chapt Miss Lung Assn 1974-76; Sponsor Fulton Juniorettes 1977-78; Itawamba Co Orgs: Co Hosp Aux, Arts Coun, Friends of Lib, Am Legion Aux; Chm Miss Itawamba Beauty Pageant 1972-76; Univ N Ala Alumni Assn; Ldr GSA 1969-70, 4-H 1970-71; r/Ch of Christ: SS Tchr; hon/Vol Activist St of Miss 1977; Miss Fed'd Wom's Clb Pres's Report Awd 1977; Biogl Listings.

SISON, RAMON CANLAS oc/Physician-Surgeon; b/Aug 4, 1929; h/200 S Linden Dr, Beverly Hills, CA 90212; ba/Panorama City, CA; m/Rosario F; c/Renato, Reuven, Rebecca; p/Salustiano Serrano Sison (dec); Florentina Canlas Sison, Philippines; ed/AA; MD; mil/ANG MC 1978-, Lt Col; pa/Dir Labs Ill St Hosp, Jacksonville, Ill 1963-69; Coroner's Pathologist Morgan Co (Ill) 1963-69; Pathologist: So Cal Perm Med Group, Los Angeles (Cal) 1969-, St Mary Mercy Hosp, Gary (Ind) 1961-63; Var Hosps Chicago (Ill) 1960-61; Fellow: Col Am Pathologists, Am Soc Clin Pathologists; LA Soc Pathologists; Assn Philippine Pract'g Physicians in Am; Pres Philippine Med Sco So Cal Inc; Assn Mil Surgs US; MENSA; Var Dramatical Activs; cp/Screen Actors Guild; NG Assn Cal; Past Pres: U Filipino-Am Assembly So Cal Inc & Univ Philippines Alumni Assn So Cal Inc; r/Cath; hon/W/W: Med Specialists, W, Am.

SKAALEGAARD, HANS MARTIN oc/- Marine Artist; Lecturer; Art Gallery Owner-Director; b/Feb 7, 1924; h/25197 Canyon Dr, Carmel, CA 93923; ba/Carmel; m/Mignon Diana; c/Karen Solveig; p/Ole Johanes

Skaalegaard (dec); Johanna Elisa Skaalegaard Faroe Isls, Europe; mil/Served on Merch Ships during WWII; pa/Owner, Dir Skaalegaard Square-Rigger Art Gallery, Carmel; Mem Intl Acad Lit, Arts & Sci, Tommaso Campanella (Rome, Italy); Dir Allen Knight Maritime Mus; cp/Cult Dir Sons of Norway Lodge #112; Dir Navy Leag; Hist & Art Assn; r/Luth; hon/Silver & Gold Medal, Title Master Painter, Acad Arts & Lttrs & Scists (Rome).

SKIDMORE, JAMES ALBERT JR oc/- Executive; b/Jun 30, 1932; h/177 Sutton Dr, Berkeley Heights, NJ 07922; ba/Moorestown, NJ; m/PeggyAnn; c/Jacqueline Sue, James A III; p/James A Sr and (Stepmother) Agnes Skidmore, Belmar, NJ; Frances W Barker (dec); ed/BA Muhlenberg Col; mil/USMC; pa/Sci Mgmt Corp: Chm, Pres 1972-, Chief Exec 1975-; Handy Assocs: Pres & Chief Exec Ofcr 1971, VP 1969; Other Former Positions; Dir: The Coca-Cola Bottling Co of NY Inc (Hackensack, NJ), Franklin St Bk (Somerset, NJ), Newark Brush & Danline Mfg Co (Kenilworth, NJ), Granite St Machine Co (Manchester, NH); Yg Pres' Org, NJ Chapt; Bd Govs Alpha Tau Omega Foun, Champaign, Ill; Adv Bd Small Bus Adm; Ec Social Comm UN; Other Profl Activs, Current & Past; cp/Adv Trustee Bd Trustees Brick Twp Hosp Inc; Exec Bd Watchung Area Coun (NJ) BSA; Former Chm NJ Mar Dimes; Ec Devel Com Burlington Co; Past Pres Proj Concern, San Diego (Cal); Former Mem Citizens' Adv Bd on Yth Opport; Nat Coun Crime & Delinq; Past Treas JCI; Others; r/Luth; hon/Trinidad-Tobago Awd, Prime Min of Ireland 1970; 1st Ambassador Awd to NJ JC; Intl Understanding Awd, City of Brussels, Belgium; George Washington Medal Awd of Hon, Freedom Foun; 1 of 5 Outstg Yg Men, NJ 1965; 1 of Am's 10 Outstg Yg Men 1969; Order of St John, Queen of England; Featured in Num Pubs; Biogl Listings.

SKILES, JACQUELINE DEAN oc/Arts Administrator; Artist; Sociologist; b/Mar 31, 1937; h/236 W 27th St, 13 Floor, New York, NY 10001; ba/NYC; p/Coy E Skiles (dec); Vernetta B Skiles, St Louis, MO; ed/BFA; MA; MA; PhD Cand New Sch for Social Res; pa/Arts Admr Creative Wom's Collective; Bd Mem Wom in the Arts Foun; Wom's Caucus for Art; cp/Wom's City Clb; NOW; r/U Meth Ch; hon/Outstg Yg Wom of Yr; W/W Am Wom.

SKINNER, WALTER NATHANIEL oc/Physician; b/Oct 23, 1933; h/4400 Belclaire Ave, Dallas, TX 75205; ba/Dallas; m/Judith Ann; c/Walter N III; p/Walter N Skinner (dec); Nina Burns Skinner, Dallas; ed/BS; MD; mil/USAR; pa/Pract Internal Med; r/Presb; hon/Phi Beta Kappa; Alpha Omega Alpha; Fellow, Am Col Physicians.

SKIPWORTH, ELDON ROBERT (SKIP) oc/Farmer, Rancher; Self-Employed Businessman (Semi-Retired); b/Apr 26, 1906; h/Rt One, Argyle, TX 76226; ba/Dallas, TX; m/Faye Marcille; c/Dorothy June Buchanan, Helen Joyce Coston; ed/Att'd Tex A&M Col; Hills Bus Col; La Salle Law Sch; pa/Owner Furniture & Appliance Bus, Dallas 1950-75; Raises Angus Cattle on Ranch; Assoc'd w Small Bus Loan Adm 1948-49; US Dept Agri (Wash DC, St Louis, Mo, Ft Worth & Dallas, Tex) 1931-46: Reg Chief of Loan & Collection Div (Reg), Asst Reg Farm & Ranch Mgmt

Chief, Dist Supvr, Co Supvr, Asst Co Supvr; Other Former Positions; Denton Co Farm Bur: Past Pres, Dir, Chm Coms; Past Dir Denton Co Livestock Assn; Tex Cowboy Reunion Inc: Dir, Past Pres; Life Mem Am Angus Assn, St Joseph, Mo; Charter Mem Tex Angus Assn; Tex Poultry Assn; Other Profl Activs; cp/Indep Order Odd Fellows, Denton; BSA; r/Calvary Evang Temple, Ft Worth: Mem, Visitation, Bd Dirs, Var Activs.

SKOLL, SERGIUS R oc/Author; Professor; b/Jul 5, 1925; ba/PO Box 965, Orangevale, CA 95622; p/Rudolph and Anastasia Romanoff Skoll; ed/Doct honoris causa; mil/Liaison Ofcr WWII; pa/Prof Applied Arts; Fine Art Conslt; cp/Free-lance Journalist, Charge d'Affairs; r/Greek Orthodox; hon/Var Merit Awds, USA & Europe.

SLACK, FLORENCE K oc/Teacher; h/9 Farrand Dr, Parsippany, NJ 07054; ba/Brooklyn, NY; c/Brenda; p/Philip and Mae Kantor; ed/BA; MS; MA; pa/Tchr Bus Ed Ft Hamilton HS; Bus Ed Assn (Pitman); IPA; Am Res Ctr in Egypt Assn; hon/Hons Registry; W/W in E; Dist'd Achmt Plaque, IBA; Commun Ldrs Am; Notable Ams.

SLEDD, GERTRUDE LEE oc/Retired Teacher; b/Jul 20, 1890; h/233 E Green, Danville, KY 40422; p/Burry and Jane Spillman; ed/BS Wilberforce Univ; EdM Univ Cinc; pa/Ret'd Tchr, D'ville City Schs; Nat Tchrs, Phi Delta Kappa; cp/Treas CWU D'ville; Secy Exec Bd KACW Inc; r/AME Ch; hon/Clb Wom of Distn; Best Essay on Africa, Wilberforce Univ; Others.

SLETAGER, JANICE RAE oc/Communications Executive; b/Jan 7, 1933; h/1902 Mahan Ave, Richland, WA 99352; ba/Richland; c/Gregory Neil, Chris Andrew; p/Julius Marion and Laura Mae Foote Scherbacher (dec); ed/BA summa cum laude 1966, MA summa cum laude 1972 Wash Univ; pa/Battelle, Pacific NW Labs: Mgr Communs Dept 1978-, Mgr Tech Editing/Writing 1972-78, Supvr Tech Writing

1971, Sr Tech Editor 1970, Tech Editor 1967-69; En Wash Univ: Instr Eng 1967, Tchg Fellow Eng 1966-67, Geol Res Asst 1966; Other Former Positions; Am Mgmt Assn; Mod Lang Assn; Geol Soc Am; Soc Tech Commun; Delta Gamma; cp/Tri-Cities Conv Bur: Former Bd Trustees, Former Exec Bd, Former Advt'g Chm; hon/Kappa Delta Pi; Fellow, ABI; Battelle Loaned Exec, Active U Way; Grad Coun F'ship, EWU; Biogl Listings; Others.

SLIWINSKI, MITCHELL STANLEY oc/Mechanical Engineer; b/Dec 17, 1907; h/1831 N Van Ness Ave #8, Los Angeles, CA 90028; m/Kristina; c/Christopher, John (dec); ed/Franciszek and Weronica Hiller Sliwinski (dec); ed/Dipl St Aeronautic Col Warsaw; Dipl Mech Engrg Univ London (UK) 1948; mil/RAF 1941-44; pa/Conslt & Reschr Field of Aviation; Mem Eval Panel Satellite Proposal 1966-67; Tech Adv Panel on Gemini Stability Improvemt Prog 1964-67; Tech Staff Aerospace Corp, El Segundo 1961-69; Other Former Positions; Am Inst Aeronautics & Astronautics; cp/Polish-Am Cong; Polish AF Vet Assn; Former Exec Treas Polish Vet WWII; Repub; r/Rom Cath; hon/Patriots of Am Bicent Meml Plate; Sev Cits.

SLOAN, EDITH BARKSDALE oc/Commissioner; b/Nov 29, 1938; h/1639 Primrose Rd NW, Washington, DC 20012; ba/Wash DC; m/E Ned; c/Douglass Ned, Reuben Crawford; p/Odell Martin Barksdale (dec); Elizabeth Watts Barksdale, New York, NY; ed/BA; JD; pa/Commr Consumer Prod Safety Comm; cp/Del: Nat Black Ec Caucus 1975, World Conf on Peace Through Law (Abidjan, Ivory Coast) 1973, Intl Wom's Yr Tribunal (Mexico City, Mexico) 1975; Moderator Public Affairs Spec, WRC-TV 1975; r/Epis; hon/Awd for Contbns to Poor Wkg Wom, Nat Com on Household Employmt; Outstg Black Wom in US, *Black Enterprise Mag*; Spec Recog for Contbns to Labor Standards, Nat Consumers Leag; Adam Clayton Powell Awd, Congl Black Caucus; Sustained Superior Perf Awd, US Comm on Civil Rts; Eleanor Roosevelt Human Relats Intern F'ship.

SMALL, ROSEMARY oc/Musician; University Instructor; b/Nov 2, 1943; h/1021 Asylum Ave, Hartford, CT 06105; ba/Same; p/M C and Mabelle W Small (dec); ed/BS cum laude Weber St Col 1965; MA Wash St Univ 1970; DMA Cand Hartt Col Music; pa/Instr Music: Wash St Univ 1970-71, Tex A&I Univ 1971-77; Vis Instr Music Keene St Col 1976-; Percussionist Corpus Christi Symph Orch 1971-75; Free-lance Percussionist, Clinician, Recitalist; Hartford Musicians Assn; Percussive Arts Soc; hon/Weber St Col: Instrumental Music Awd, Outstg Musician Awd; Phi Kappa Phi; Intl W/W Music; World W/W Wom in Ed; Intl Reg Profiles; Commun Ldrs & Noteworthy Ams.

SMEDVIG, EGIL oc/Educator; b/Nov 22, 1922; h/12550 9th Ave NW, Seattle, WA 98177; m/Kristin; c/Jodene, Rolf, Siri; ed/BA, MA, PhD Studies Univ Wash; mil/AUS Band, Performer, Composer & Arranger 1942-45; pa/Instrumental Music Dir Seattle Public Schs: Thomson Jr HS (Dept Chm) 1964-78, Lincoln HS 1957-63, Marshall Jr HS 1951-56; Sum Music Dir: Seattle Public Schs (Hd Tchr) 1977, Shoreline Public Schs (Warm Bch Music Camp), Univ Wash (Music Inst); Profl Musician: Ldr Dance Bands & Combos, Record Albums, 1st Clarinetist & Libn Oakland Symph, Saxophone Soloist Thalia Symph; MENC; AFT; AFM; ARS; METRO; WSPTA; hon/Soloist in Debussy "Rhapsody for Saxophone & Orch" 1965; Golden Acorn Awd, WSPTA; Fine Arts Awd, Rites of Spring Fest 1972; Adjudicator & Guest Conductor for Fests, Contest & Music Groups throughout US; Original Composition for Symph Orch "Jubilation" Received Thalia Awd; Intl W/W in Music & Musicians' Dir; Pubs.

SMELKINSON, MARSHA ELLEN oc/Public Relations, Advertising; b/Dec 29, 1948; h/8 Merion Ct, Hilton Head Island, SC 29928; ba/Hilton Hd Isl; p/Isidore and Florence Smelkinson, Baltimore, MD; ed/BS magna cum laude Syracuse Univ 1970; r/Jewish.

SMETAK, LARRY ANTHONY oc/Educator; b/Oct 20, 1945; h/10th & Birch St, Douglas, WY 82633; m/Vera Mae Cook; c/Laurie Ann, Mark, Mike; p/Andrew J and Garnet Smetak, Phillips, WI; ed/BA Pillsbury Bible Col 1968; MDiv cum laude Ctl Bapt Sem 1972; ThD summa cum laude Toledo Bible Col 1978; pa/Tchr Calvary Christian Sch; Pastor 1972-78; Assn Activs: Exec Comm 1973, Resolutions Comm 1974-75, Missions Comm 1976-78; cp/Repub Precnt Chm; Former Chm Sch Adv Com; r/Calvary Bapt: SS Tchr; hon/Var Scholastic Awds; Christian Ed S'ship; Author SS Lessons for Minn Bapt Assn; Contbr to Profl Pubs.

SMILEY, GERTRUDE C oc/Reading Consultant; b/Jul 5, 1919; h/898 Goff Ave NE, Orangeburg, SC 29115; ba/O'burg; m/Wilmon D; c/Wilmon LaVerane, Brenda Joyce; p/Nathaniel and Effie M Cobb, Reesville, SC; ed/BS; MA; pa/Rdg/Lang Arts Tchr; NEA; SCEA; Edista Rdg Coun; IRA; cp/NAACP; Rec'g Secy Daughs of Elks; r/Piney Grove Bapt Ch: Secy; hon/Mother of Yr 1976, 77; Outstg Tchrs Awd.

SMITH, ALLIE MAITLAND oc/Research Scientist; b/Jun 9, 1934; h/1714 Country Clb Dr, Tullahoma, TN 37388; ba/Arnold AF Sta, TN; m/Sarah Louise Whitlock; c/Sara Leianne, Hollis Duval, Meredith Lorren; p/Allie McCoy Smith (dec); Emma Wright Smith, Tabor City, NC; ed/BS cum laude 1956, MS 1961, PhD 1966 NC St Univ; pa/Res Scist ARO Inc 1966-; Adj Prof Univ Tenn-Tullahoma 1966-, Knoxville 1974; Asst Prof (Ext), Raleigh 1961-62; Instr NC St Univ 1958-60; Other Former Positions; Am Inst Aeros & Astronautics: Assoc Fellow, Chm Thermophysics Tech Com 1976-, Session Chm 11th Aerospace Sci Meeting 1973, Chm Conf w ASME 1974, 78, Energy Activs Task Force 1976-, Assoc Editor Jour 1975-, Others; Am Soc Engrg Ed, Long Range Planning Com 1975-; AAUP; ASME; NY Acad Scis; Sigma Xi; Phi Kappa Phi; Tau Beta Pi; Pi Tau Sigma; cp/Dem; r/Bapt; hon/Author *Fundamentals of Silicon Integrated Device Technol, Vol I: Oxidation, Diffusion & Epitaxy* 1967; Contbr Articles to Profl Jours; Other Pubs.

SMITH, BERNARD J oc/Consulting Engineer; b/Aug 29, 1900; h/1446 Day Valley Rd, Aptos, CA 95003; ba/Aptos; m/(dec); c/Bernard, Sarah Ann, Maureen, Una Eileen, Aislin Therese, Thos E, Joan Pauline, John Philip; p/Thomas Joseph and Sara Anne Crum Smith (dec); ed/BEng w hons; MEng; pa/Staff Engr San Fran Bay Conserv & Devel Comm, Conslt to Comm; Chief San Fran Bay Sect, US Corps Engrs, San Fran Dist, SF, Cal; Asst Reg Rep & Reg Economist, Nat Housing Agy, Reg VIII, Dallas, Tex; Acting St Dir & St Planning Engr, Public Works Reserve, Tex; Dir Res & Pers, City Ft Worth, Tex; Engr Examr, Public Works Adm, Ft Worth; City Mgr, Baytown, Tex; Designing Engr, Humble Oil & Refining Co, Baytown; Asst Engr Alexander Poeter, Conslt'g Engr, NYC, NY; Underground

Conduit Engr, NY & NJ Tel Co & Ohio Bell Tel Co; Field Engr Underpinning & Foun Co, NY; Conslt'g Engr & Conslt'g Economist; Acad Lectr, So Meth Univ; Profl Engr: Cal, NJ, Tex; Public Surveyor Tex; Fellow Am Soc Civil Engrs; Profl Orgs; Former VP SWn Sts Water Co; Guest Lectr on Town Devel, Ala Polytech Inst; Guest Panelist, Annual Radio Conf, Univ Okla, Norman; Pi Gamma Mu; Am Soc CE Com on City Planning Tng for Civil Engrs; Bd Govs Dallas Fed Ref Exc; Resources Group Supporting Gov Reagan's Task Force on Trans, Charged w Solving Trans Prob in Cal; Water Comm, Co Santa Cruz, Cal; Projs: Irrigation, Flood Control, Reclamation, Bldgs, Water Supply & Distrib Sys, Sewers & Sewerage Sys, Power & Light Plants, Seawall, Swimming Pool, Gas Sys; Investigations: Engrg Tidal Regimen, Pollution, Sewerage, Waterworks, Irrigation, Urban Devel; Num Reports, Papers, Ct Testimony; Num Spchs on Profl or Related Topics; cp/Pres Irish Lit & Hist Soc of SF; hon/W/W: Engrg, S&SW, W; World W/W Commerce & Indust; Ldrs in Am Sci; Am Men of Sci; Who Knows & What.

SMITH, CALEB VIRGIL oc/Clergyman; b/Sept 23, 1909; h/1737 W 6th, Mesa, AZ 85201; ba/Mesa; m/Lela D; p/(dec); pa/-Pastor, Missionary, Bible Teacher; r/Assembly of God; hon/W/W: NM, USA.

SMITH, CATHLEEN MICHAELE oc/Registered Nurse; b/Jun 23, 1946; h/Rt 4, Box 244, Searcy, AR 72143; ba/Searcy; m/James H; p/Charles W and Lenora A

Goddard, E Liverpool, OH; ed/Nsg Dipl; BSN Univ SC; MN Emory Univ; Doct Prog Student George Peabody; pa/Chm Baccalaureate Nsg Prog Harding Col; 1/VP Ark St Nsg Assn; Am Nurses Assn; Nat Leag for Nsg; Am Public Hlth Assn; r/Ch of Christ: Active Mem; hon/Sigma Theta Tau; Kellogg Fellow; Outstg Am.

SMITH, C(HARLES) FOSTER oc/Certified Public Accountant; b/Nov 14, 1919; h/3400 N Kings Hwy, Myrtle Beach, SC 29577; ba/Myrtle Bch; m/Sarah Fore; c/Sarah Dianne, Rebecca Elaine, Caroline Virginia; p/Wade H Smith (dec); ed/BS Univ SC 1940; mil/Pacific Theatre WWII; pa/Am Inst CPAs; SC Assn CPAs: Secy-Treas, VP, Pres 1959-60; SC Bd CPA Examrs 1969, Predessor of Bd Accountancy; SC Bd Accountancy: Mem 1969-75, Chm 1971-74; Dir Peoples Nat Bk, Conway, SC 1959-69; Citizens & So Nat Bk, Myrtle Bch 1969-; cp/Past Pres: Myrtle Bch Civitan Clb, Horry Co Hist Soc; Dir The Coastal Ednl Foun; Former Councilor-at-Large Univ SC Alumni Assn; r/1st Meth Ch: Chm Adm Bd, SS Tchr; Bd Pensions, SC Conf; hon/Phi Beta Kappa; Omicron Delta Kappa; W/W: Among Students in Am Univs & Cols, SC, S&SW; Ser to Profession Awd, SC Assn CPAs.

SMITH, DAVID E oc/Physician; b/Feb 7, 1939; h/321 Crestmont Dr, San Francisco, CA 94131; ba/SF; m/Alice DeSwarte; c/Julia, Suzanne, Carolyn, Elen; p/Elvin and Dorothy Smith (dec); ed/MD; MS; pa/Fdr & Med Dir Haight Ashbury Free Med Clin; Pres Yth Projs Inc, SF; Assoc Prin Investigator SF Polydrug Proj, SF; Assoc Clin Prof Toxicology Univ Cal Med Ctr-SF; Assoc Clin Prof Behavioral Pharm Univ Nev Med Sch, Reno, Nev; Hon Lectr Dept Med Addiction Res Foun Clin Inst, Toronto, Canada; Nat Free Clin Coun: Fdr, Former Pres, Current Chperson; Conslt SF Gen Hosp Dept Psychi 1966-; Courtesy Staff SF Psychi Hosp 1973-; Chperson Nat Drug Abuse Con 1977, SF; Fdr & CoEditor *Jour of Psychedelic Drugs*; Conslt; SF Med Soc; Cal Med Assn, Chm Res Task Force Cal Interagy Coun on Drug Abuse; AMA, Conslt on Drug Abuse; Phi Beta Kappa; Sigma Xi; FASEB; Am Public Hlth Assn, Mtl Hlth Sect; Charter Mem Am Acad Clin Toxicol; Cal Soc for Treatmt of Alcoholism & Other Drug Dependencies: Charter Mem, Chm Edit Com; Var Edit Activs; cp/Mem Gov's Adv Panel on Narcotics & Drug Abuse 1977; Alcoholism & Drug Abuse for Dem Nat Platform 1976; Var Campaign Activs; hon/Examr 10 Most Dist'd Awd, 16th Annual SF; Chancellor's Awd for Commun Ser, Univ Cal-SF; Cal Jr Col Alumnus of Yr 1969; SAMA Res Awd; Bordon Res Awd; Survey of Anesthesiol Res; Num Pubs.

SMITH, DELPHIA FRAZIER oc/Writer, Poet, Painter, Sculptress, Carver, Musician, Singer, Speaker, Exhibitor, Collector, Humanitarian, Crossword Puzzle Constructor; b/Apr 24, 1921; h/202 9th St, Mammoth Spring, AR 72554; ba/Same; m/Clyde L; c/Janice Elaine Lancaster, Shirley Jean Dunn; p/Sidney and Lora Frazier; ed/Dipl Newspaper Inst Am; Dipl US Sch Music; Num Courses in Langs, Music, Painting, Art Apprec, Shorthand, Nsg & Self Help; pa/Author 35 Books incl: *Along Life's Way* 1961, *Tapestry of Life, Profiles and Footprints, So Swift the Night, Winged Thoughts* 1972, *Daffodils in the Snow, Patches & Ruffels, To Catch a Dream* 1973, *Into Each Heart, Craft of Tears, Distant Drums, Brocade and Denim, Bright Remnants, Song of the Wind, Out of the Mist, Finger of Life,* Ill, *Senryu, Voice of Images & Imprints,* Ill Haiku, *Before the Dawn, Vapors of Thought, Splintered Prisms,* Ill Haiku, *Ribbons of Thought,* Ill *Senryu, Parade of Life, Haiku & Senryu, Nat Carvers Mus, Awd Winning Poems, A Song to Sing* 1975, *Search for Tomorrow, The Hungry Heart* 1976, *Voice of the Dove, Shrunk or Sunk, Veil of Peace, Moon Sparks, We, The Women;* Books Used in Schs & Cols, Housed in Archives, Hall of Poets, Lib of Cong, Museums & Most Am Presidents or their Fams & World Ldrs in their Public or Pvt Libs (Rec'd Tokens of their

Apprec); Book have been read on TV & Complete Books Read w Certs; Sculpts, Paints & Carves Most Mats, Wood Burning in Color, Ceramics, Decoupage & Many Crafts; Appears on TV & Spkg Engagemts doing Rdgs, Interviews, Panels, Exhibiting Art & Books; Exhibited at I Templari Gallery, San Felice Circoco, Italy 1972; Contract w Ldg Greeting Card Co; TV Writer; Rep: World Poetry Soc, Centro Studi E Scambi, Italy, Nat Carvers Mus (Patron, Exhibiting Mem & Staff Writer); Life Mem Soc of Lit Designates Intl, Given Title "Danae"; Fdr, Fellow Intl Poetry Soc; Collectors Guild, LTD; Leonardo Da Vinci Acad; Poets Cong; Sculpture Collectors Limited; SW Mo Mus Inc; Kindness Clb; World of Creative Thinkers; Smithsonian Assocs Intl; Am F'ship Soc; Maj Poets; Whittlers & Carvers; IPA w Gold Pin; Adv Bd: Am Security Coun w Silver Pin, Am Biog Inst w Plaque; Citizens for Decent Lit; Recorded 2 Songs; Pub'd Worldwide since Young Age in Anthologies incl'g: Poet (Dist'd Ser Cit), Clover Collection (2 Intl Awds), Cultura Clb SS Crose (2 Silver Medals), Yrbook of Mod Poetry, Pagent of Poetry, Alltime Favorite Poetry, Cajun Press (2 Cash Awds), New & Better Poetry, Leonardo Da Vinci Acad (3 Gold Medals), Centro Studi E Scambi Intl (1 Gold Medal), The Intl (Janie Spellmon Awd, Gold Loving Cup Trophy & Oil Portrait), Maj Poets Chapt (3 Awds), Am Narrative (Num Dipls, Certs, Medals, Ribbons & Cash Awds); r/Ch of Christ: Active Mem; hon/MENSA; Personalities S; W/W: Poetry, Am Wom, Authors; World W/W Wom; Notable Ams Bicent Era; Writers Dir; W/W CSSI; DIB; Intl Reg Profiles.

SMITH, DOCK G JR oc/Lawyer; b/May 20, 1935; h/PO Box 955, 310 Frye St, Robbins, NC 27325; ba/Robbins; m/Peggy S; c/Dock III, Douglas, Sandra, Daniel; p/Dock G Smith (dec); Helen G R Smith, Norfolk, VA; ed/BS E Carolina Univ 1957; JD Univ NC 1960; pa/Town Atty 1964-79; NC Bar Assn; Moore Co Bar Assn; Trial Lwyrs Assn; cp/Pres Robbins Lions Clb; Past Pres: Robbins JCs, Robbins Merchs Assn; r/Meth.

SMITH, DORETTA FRENNA oc/Professional Artist; Teacher; b/Jul 23, 1924; h/1334 Richlands Hwy, Jacksonville, NC 28540; ba/Same; m/William Jessie; c/Frank A, George R, Rose Mary, William P, Anna Maria, Edward S, John Paul, Michael A; p/Antonio Frenna (dec); Antonietta Demel (dec); ed/Att'd Var Profl Schs, Univs; pa/Tchr Coastal Carolina Commun Col, J'ville; Tchr Pvt Classes Pvt Studio; Mem & Exhibitor S John Art Gallery, Wilmington, NC; Am Bus Woms Assn; Mem Var Art Socs; r/Rom Cath: Cath Daughs Am; hon/Cross of Merit for Ldrship; Num Art Awds; Certs for Commun Activs.

SMITH, DOROTHY LASSETER oc/Educator; b/Sept 5, 1910; h/1051 Frazier St, Apt EZ, Roswell, GA 30075; m/William Spencer (dec); c/Dorothy L S Fidler (Mrs Paul P), Diana Spencer S Highsmith (Mrs Robert Sparks); p/Zadoc Wilder and Ava Sutton Lasseter, Rochele, GA; ed/AB Tift Col; Postgrad Studies S Ga Col; pa/Secy Fed Mutual Ins Co, Atlanta; Tchr: Coffee Co Schs, Fulton Co Schs; Fulton Co & Coffee Co Ed Assns, Rep to Ga Ed Assn; Ga Ed Assn; NEA; cp/Atlanta Music Clb; Atlanta Music Clb Guild; Former Orgr & Dir GSA; Var Red Cross Activs; Pres: Douglas PTA, Douglas Garden Clb, Music Clb (College Park, Ga); r/Bapt Ch, Douglas: Soloist (Choir), SS Dept Ldr; 1st Bapt Ch, Atlanta; hon/Pub'd Author; Nom Douglas Wom of Yr.

SMITH, GLORIA FELECIA oc/Real Estate Broker; b/Sept 2, 1927; h/Rt 4, Box 332, The Dalles, OR 97058; ba/Mosier, OR; m/Walter R; c/Terry L Knipe Quinn, Steven G, Antoinette S, Janet H S Mundt; p/Guy and Sylvia E Pierce Healey (dec); pa/Owner Ranch & Rec Land Realtors; St, Local & Nat Realtors Bds; St & Nat Farm & Land Inst; cp/Secy Mosier Adv Com to Wasco Co Planning Adm; IPA; r/Prot; hon/Personalities W&MW; W/W Am Wom; Intl W/W; Commun Ldrs &

Noteworthy Ams.

SMITH, HELEN BREKKE oc/Retired School Teacher; Homemaker; b/Mar 7, 1907; h/1521-22 Ave, Longview, WA 98632; m/Reginald A A; c/Dale R I, Jean S Thornsbury; p/Lars Olesen and Kristianne Marie Fosnes Brekke (dec); ed/AB Whitman Col; pa/Tchr: Roslyn & Longview (Wash), Grangeville (Idaho) 1927-70, Havana (Cuba) 1946-47; Cowlitz Co AAUW; cp/Past Pres Evergreen Area Girl Scouts; Badoura Clb; Daughs of Niles; Longview Garden Clb; Ofcr Longview Repub Wom; Am Legion Aux; r/Longview Commun Ch; hon/Outstg Citizen Awd, Longview 23 Clb; Named S'ship Grant, Cowlitz Co AAUW.

SMITH, JANE LYNETTE oc/Visiting Teacher; b/Jul 17, 1939; h/108 Ferdinand St, Lockport, LA 70374; ba/Thibodaux, LA; p/Jacob Urban and Rhoda Hildegarde Guy Smith (dec); ed/BA; MEd; Ed Spec; pa/Home-Sch Visitor, Vis Tchr; Secy Lafourche Tchrs Inc; Pres L'port Friends of Lib; cp/Del to St Dem Conv; VP Lafourche Parish Friends of Lib; r/Cath; hon/W/W S&SW.

SMITH, JANET FAY oc/Administrator; b/Dec 27, 1948; h/119 Woodland Dr, Rutherfordton, NC 28139; ba/Spindale, NC; p/James R and Addie L Smith, Cumberland Furnace, TN; ed/BS; MA; PhD Cand; pa/Admr Isothermal Commun Col; AAHPER; NCACCIA; NCAHPER; NCISC: Exec Com 1971-72, Pres 1972-73; NDA; USTA; AAWCJC; NCATAECE; Liaison Wom in Higher Ed in NC; cp/Lynn Tanner Dancer Co; Dancers Unlimited; Sch Vol Prog; r/Presb; hon/Phi Delta Kappa; Grad Asst'ship, APSU & Geo Peabody Col; Outstg Yg Wom Am; World W/W Wom in Ed; W/W NC.

SMITH, JOHN GETTYS oc/Public Relations Consultant; b/Nov 24, 1932; h/Sea Pines Plantation, Hilton Head, SC 29928; ba/Hilton Hd Isl; m/Nelle Elliott McCants; c/John Gettys, Spencer McCants, Ora Elliott; p/Clyde B and Ora Gettys Smith; ed/AB USC 1956; mil/AUS 1954-56; pa/Tchr York HS 1956-57; w York Co Hlth Dept 1958-59; York Bur Chief Rock Hill (SC) Herald 1963; VP Public Relats Sea Pines Co 1963-64, VP Public Relats, Commun Devel Hilton Hd Isl 1964-74; VP Sea Pines Investmt Inc 1969-; Pres: Colibogue Properties 1971-, Harbour Ventures Inc 1971-; Pres John Gettys Smith, Public Relats Conslt; Fdr: York Mus Assn 1956, York Co Meml Mus 1958; Dir Annual Tour York Homes; Charter Mem York Co Hist Soc; Artists' Guild York; Chester, Lancaster Cos (SC), SC, Hilton Hd Isl, Beaufort Co Cs of C; Hugenot Soc; Hilton Hd Isl Homebldrs' Assn; Sigma Nu; Kappa Pi; cp/Mem SC Travel Coun; Mem Steering Com Hist Beaufort Foun; Var Golf Tournamts; Var Clbs; r/Epis: Vestryman; hon/Recipient Discover Am Travel Org Awds; Awd, Coun Reg Travel Execs; W/W Fin & Indust.

SMITH, JOHNNY EUGENE oc/Educator; b/Apr 22, 1947; h/16332 I H 35 N, Schertz, TX 78154; m/Martha Ann Martens; c/2 Chd; p/Wiley M Smith; Jeana M Griffin; ed/BA SW Tex St Univ 1970; Cert'd Voc-Indust Tex A&M Univ 1974; pa/Hd Instr Bldg Trades Gary Job Corps Ctr, San Marcos,TX; Conslt Tex Ednl Agy; Pres Local 4034 Tex Fdn Tchrs; AFT; AFL-CIO; cp/IBA; r/Meth; hon/Coauthor Voc Student Resource Manual

for Tex Public Schs 1973; W/W: Ed, S&SW; Personalities S.

SMITH, LAURA LEE WHITELY WEISBRODT oc/Professor Emeritus; b/Jul 16, 1903; h/1707 Slaterville Rd, Ithaca, NY 14850; ba/Ithaca; m/Ora; c/James Stanley, Sarah Jane S Burton (Mrs J H); p/Ferdinand W and Addie Markley Weisbrodt (dec); ed/BS 1925; MS 1927; PhD 1930; pa/Prof Emeritus Cornell Univ; Conslt; Writer; r/Unitarian; hon/Biogl Listings.

SMITH, MARY DEMETRIA oc/Sister of Religious Order; Registered Nurse; Missionary Nun; Midwife; b/Aug 7, 1932; h/702 Berkley Rd, Indianapolis, IN; ba/Uganda, E Africa;

p/Archie J and Bettie Will Crafton Smith, Indpls; ed/SRN; SCM; pa/Missionary Nun Uganda, E Africa 14 Yrs; Missionary Algeria, N Africa 1 Yr; r/Rom Cath: Sister; hon/Hon'd for Christian Ldrship.

SMITH, MARY ISABELLE oc/Operator Rental Property; Music Teacher; b/Oct 5, 1905; h/310 High St, Trenton, TN 38382; ba/Same; p/Leslie Warren and Mary Davis Smith (dec); ed/BS Peabody Col; pa/Operator Rental Property; Ret'd Classroom; Mem NGPT; Secy & Pres Music Clb; r/Presb Ch: Former Choir Mem, Fund Raising Com 3 Yrs; Other Activs; hon/Hall of Fame, Nat Hon Roll, NGPT; Intl W/W Music; World W/W Wom; Notable Ams.

SMITH, MERRETT T oc/Master Craftsman Portrait Photographer; b/May 14, 1926; h/2016 Kerwood Ave, Los Angeles, CA 90025; ba/LA; m/Gail; c/Theresa, Joy, Kathy, Jerry, Susie, Sandy, Richie; p/Ray Garfield and Luella Tuckett Smith (dec); mil/USN 1944-47 (Photog); pa/Mgr & Owner Portrait Studio, Salt Lake City 20 Yrs; Current Owner Studio, LA; Tchr W Coast Sch, Santa Barbara; Past Pres PPW Cal; Spkr Var St Convs; cp/Trustee: W Coast Sch, Brooks Inst, Santa Barbara; r/Mormon; hon/Subjects of Photos incl: Gov Ronald Reagan, Senator Robert Dole, Martha Mitchell, Pres Richard Nixon, Colonel Sanders, Yousef Karsh, Var Mayors, Other Ldg Personalities.

SMITH, NELSON HENRY oc/Minister; b/Aug 23, 1930; h/917 Goldwire Pl SW, Birmingham, AL 35211; ba/B'ham; m/Lessie M; c/Beverly, Monica, Nelson B, Costance Coleman; p/Nelson H Smith Sr (dec); Lillie A Smith, Mobile, AL; ed/AB Selma Univ; pa/Past Pres Progressive Nat Bapt Conv Inc; Pres B'ham Chapt So Christian Ldrship Conf;

r/Bapt; hon/DDiv: B'ham Bapt Bible Col 1969, Selma Univ, Temple Col & Sem.

SMITH, NORVEL E oc/Construction Company Executive; b/Mar 17, 1901; h/1514 N 21st St, Kansas City, KS 66102; m/Wilhelmina Bright; p/Archie Webb and Hannah Sarah Bright Smith; ed/Att'd Finley Engrg Col; pa/Current Pres Universal Constrn Co, Ks City; cp/Dir Ks St Blind Assn; r/Zion U Ch of Christ: Former Mem Bd Trustees; hon/Recipient "E" Awd, During WWII; Book of Honor; Personalities W&MW.

SMITH, PAUL ABRAHAM oc/Executive; b/Dec 11, 1912; h/3327 Blossom St, Columbia, SC 29205; ba/Columbia; m/Elizabeth P; c/Paul A Jr, Jane S Staton; p/James Adger and Lulie Jane Durham Smith, Easley, SC; ed/BS; pa/VP & Dir: Oliver Motor Co, Oliver Leasing Inc, Motor Parts Co; cp/Columbia Rotary Clb; r/Bapt: Deacon; hon/AMS Merit Awd.

SMITH, PAULINE GILES oc/Homemaker; b/Feb 10, 1912; h/411 Bayou Oaks Dr, Monroe, LA 71203; m/J Paul (dec); c/Janice Paula S Dowden; p/John William and Brooksie Spencer Giles (dec); pa/Beautician 1932-36; Buyer-Cashier Grocery Bus 1950-52; Mgr Hosiery Dept (Dept Store); Sales Person Palace Dept Store; cp/Monroe Art Assn; Monroe Garden Clb; Magnolia Study Clb; Am Mothers Comm Inc; Am Cancer Soc, La Div Inc; r/U Meth Ch; hon/Personalities of S; Commun Ldrs & Noteworthy Ams; World W/W Wom.

SMITH, ROBERT J oc/Administrator; b/Jul 8, 1936; h/1431 Third St, Apt #24, Sacramento, CA 95814; ed/BS John Carroll Univ, MA Claremont Col; Addit Studies; pa/Cal St Ec Opport Ofc: Planning Dir, Local Govt Coor, Staff Sers Mgr I; Planning Admr Pasadena Commun Sers Comm; Exec Dir Ctr for Commun Change; Exec Asst Los Angeles Co Ofc of Assessor; Tchr Don Bosco Tech HS & Col; Others; Am Soc Planning Ofcls; Sect on Human Resources Adm Am Soc Public Adm; Social Planning Com Cal/Nev Commun Action Exec Dirs & Bd Chpersons Assn; Coun Urban Ec Devel; cp/Past Chm City of Ontario Commun Relats Comm; World Future Soc; W End Drug Abuse Control Coor'g Coun; Cal Assn Human Rts Orgs; hon/Pub'd Author: W/W: W, US, Am; Intl Dic W/W; Notable Ams; Commun Ldrs & Noteworthy Ams; Personalities W&MW.

SMITH, ROBERT LEE oc/Clerk, Carrier; b/Dec 2, 1943; h/101 Rupolo, St Paris, OH 43072; ba/Urbana, OH; m/Becky Marie; c/Amy Lee, Robert Todd, Jason Christopher; p/Joseph James and Elnora Ruth Smith, Urbana; mil/USN; cp/Urbana & St Paris JCs; r/Nazarene; hon/Var.

SMITH, SAMUEL (SAM) J oc/City Councilman; b/Jul 21, 1922; h/1814 31st Ave, Seattle, WA 98122; ba/Seattle; m/Marion King; c/A Carl, Anthony E, Donald C, Ronald C, Stephen K II, Amelia; p/Stephen K Smith (dec); Berniece Smith Bailey, Grambling, LA; ed/BSS Seattle Univ 1951; BA Univ Wash; mil/Warrant Ofcr JG 1943-46; cp/St Rep 5 Terms; Coun-man 3 Terms; r/Bapt.

SMITH, STANLEY G oc/Research Scientist; b/Aug 11, 1939; h/1809 Garfield St, Oxford, MS 38655; ba/University, MS; m/Virginia; c/Scott, Suzanne, Jean Mary, Vicki Lynn; p/Stanley P and Vivian Smith; ed/BA; MA; PhD; pa/Res Scist Dept Pharm Univ Miss; Lectr US Dept Justice; Chm Psychol Div Miss Acad Sci; APA; Eurp Brain, Behavior Soc.

SMITH, TRAVIS I SR oc/Retired; b/Oct 7, 1895; h/#5 1717 Briar Ln, Wharton, TX 77488; m/(dec); c/Travis I Jr; mil/Signal Corps WW I 19 Mos (Sgt Maj), Entertained Troops as Piano Player (Nightly); cp/Succeeding Armistice Org'd Band & Toured France Entertaining Var Groups, Band

Returned to US & Played Broadway 3 Wks; Formed Dance Bands 1920s; Composer approx 25 Pieces of Music; Among 1st to Adapt Home Recordings (Paper Discs for Overseas-later became light metal); During WW II formed CAP of 3 different Battalions, Trained w assistants 541 Pilots for AF; Tennis Player since 1905, Currently Playing in Nat Tournaments in US & Mexico, Played in 75-Yr-Old Contest at Wimbledon 1977, Has Ranked #4 in Nation & Ranked in 1st 10 every year for the past 6 or 8 Yrs; Rated in 1st 10, 17 Yrs in Singles & Doubles in Tex & 9 Yrs in USA; Ext Travel US, Mexico & England; Collector of Tennis Items incl'g 60+ Antique Rackets, Books dating from early 1940s, Records of Famous Players & Famous Tournaments all of which is intended to go into a Tennis Hall of Fame; Owned & Operated a Tire, Appliance & Sporting Goods Business; r/Meth; hon/Winner Over 200 Tennis Trophies & Medals; 50 Yr Pins from Am Legion, Masonry, Shrine, Mexico's Admiration Cup 1976; Pres Sports Awd for Tennis (at age 84).

SMITH, TROY ALVIN oc/Professional Engineering; b/Jul 4, 1922; h/2406 Bonita Dr SW, Huntsville, AL 35801; ba/Redstone Arsenal, AL; p/Wade Hampton and Mabel Lindsey Smith (dec); ed/BCE Univ Va 1948; MSE 1952, PhD 1970 Univ Mich; mil/USN 1942-46; pa/Profl Engrg US Army Missile R&D Command; Profl Engr: Va, Ala; Soc Am Mil Engrs; Sigma Xi; Author Tech Pubs; Contbr to Tech Jours; hon/Secy Amry Res & Study F'ship, Univ Mich.

SMITH, VALENTINE JOY oc/Student; b/Aug 12, 1929; h/PO Box 33, Tonkawa, OK 74653; ba/Same; m/Ross John Primeaux; c/Jeffrey Clyde Austin; p/Ira B Haad (dec); Pauline Goldie Pyle Haag, Tonkawa; ed/Undergrad Student No Okla Col; Fdr & Pres LOVE Inc (Non-profit Org); Owner & Mgr Gibson Girls; cp/Ponca City Art Assn; hon/Dean's Hon Roll, No Okla Col; Pub'd Author.

SMITH, VINCENT L III oc/Music Teacher; Musician; b/Mar 15, 1947; ba/PO Box 2061, Daytona Bch, FL 32015; ed/BS Fla A&M Univ; mil/AUS 2 Yrs, 80th Army Band & Americal Div Band; pa/Arranger & Composer; FMEA; NAJE; NARAS; MENC; Kappa Kappa Psi; hon/Army Commend Medal w OLC; BCC Men's Senate Awd; Delta Beta Chapt Alpha Phi Alphi, Instr of Yr 1978.

SMITH, WARREN THOMAS oc/Clergyman; Educator; b/Oct 20, 1923; h/3460 Hemphill St, College Park, GA 30337; ba/Atlanta, GA; m/Barbara Sullards; c/James Warren; p/Warren T and Lola May Jones Smith (dec); ed/BA; BD; PhD; DD; pa/Asst

Prof Ch Hist Interdenom Theol Ctr; Am Soc Ch Hist; Wesley Hist Soc; Am Hist Assn; Assoc Editor *The Jour of the Interdenom Theol Ctr*; r/U Meth Ch, N Ga Conf: Mem; hon/Author: *Thomas Coke, Foreign Minister of Methodism, Heralds of Christ, At Christmas, Preludes, Georgia, Methodism, The Am Revolution.*

SMITH, WAYNE DELARMIE oc/Veterinarian; Farmer; b/Jan 22, 1928; h/Rt 3, Milan, MO 63556; ba/Winigan, MO; m/Evelyn Young; p/Frank D and Sylvia J Smith, Greencastle, MO; ed/BS; MEd; DVM;

pa/MVMA; AVMA; cp/Judge; r/Bapt; hon/Book of Honor; W/W.

SMITHERMAN, CHARLETON K oc/School Administrator; b/Jul 11, 1918; h/2011 Ray Ave, Caldwell, ID 83605; ba/Caldwell; m/Lois L; c/Ken, Jacque, Joy, David; p/David F and Lida K Smitherman, Haviland, KS; ed/BA Pacific Col; MEd Linfield Col; Adm Deg Col Idaho; pa/PDK; NEA; IASA; NAESP; Past Pres Idaho Elem Sch Prins Assn; cp/Kiwanis Clb; r/Quaker; hon/Hon Life Mem, PTA; W/W Am Ed.

SMITHERMAN, GUY VERNON oc/Retired Chief of Police; b/May 26, 1922; h/PO Box 14, East Bend, NC 27018; ba/Same; c/Charles Vernon, Kimber Grant, Michael Dean; p/Carlie Neal and Tennie Mae Speer Smitherman (dec); ed/Law Enforcemt Ofcrs Tng Sch 1947, 56; Basic Law Enforcemt Cert 1975; mil/AUS 1942-43; pa/Ret'd Chief of Police Town E Bend; Dep Sheriff, Constable, Chief of Police, E Bend Ruritan Nat; Am Law Enforcemt Ofcrs Assn; NC Police Execs Assn; NC Assn Chiefs of Police; NC Ret'd Peace Ofcrs Assn; cp/Am Legion Post 336, E Bend; r/Meth, E Bend; hon/Am Police Hall of Fame; Town of E Bend Apprec, Order of Long Leaf Pine of NC by Gov Holhouser for Assistance in Bridge Tragedy; Cert in Apprec for Assistance in Capturing Murder Suspect, Forsyth Sheriffs Dept.

SMOLER, ELEANOR C oc/Artist; Apr 30, 1910; h/132 Longview Ave, Leonia, NJ 07605; ba/Same; m/Morris; c/Arthur; pa/Painter; Textile Craftsperson; Mod Arts Guild; NJ Designer Craftsman; r/Jewish.

SNEADE, DANIEL CARSON oc/Assistant Executive Secretary; b/Sept 5, 1948; h/3200 Holly Ave, Colonial Heights, VA 23834; ba/Richmond, VA; m/Nancy Kolb; c/Amy Elizabeth; p/Raymond C and Ella Daniel Sneade, Colonial Heights; ed/BS Va St Col; pa/Asst Exec Secy Va Gasoline Retailers Assn; ICMA; IPMA; NACA; ASPA; VACA; VAM; VSAE; cp/Colonial Hgts Sch Bd: Mem, Trustee; Kiwanis Intl; Colonial Hgts Kiwanis Clb: Bd Dirs, Secy, July 4th Chm; ARC; Southside Area Chapt ARC: Bd Dirs, Chapt Blood Chm of Yr; Chm Colonial Hgts Bloodmobile; US JCs; Colonial Hgts JCs; Va St Fireman's Assn; Leg Com Southside Fireman's Assn; Bus Chm Am Cancer Soc & Am Heart Assn; Va Farm Bur Fdn; Tri-Cities YMCA; Tussing Elem Sch PTO; Exec Dir Pres of US Dinner Com; Dem Party Va, VChm 36th House Leg Dist Com; Other Polit Activs; r/Epis; hon/Local Kiwanian of Yr 1975; Commun Ldrs & Noteworthy Ams; Personalities of S; W/W Am Polits; Outstg Yg Man Am.

SNELL, PATRICIA POLDERVAART oc/Law Librarian; b/Apr 11, 1943; h/464 S Sherbourne Dr, Los Angeles, CA 90048; ba/Los Angeles; m/Charles Eliot; p/Arie Poldervaart (dec); Edna Poldervaart, Albuquerque, NM; ed/BA Univ NM 1965; MS Univ So Cal 1966; pa/Law Libn LA Co Law Lib; Am Lib Assn; Am Assn Law Libs; So Cal Assn Law Libs; cp/Lib Conslt to Lits; Ch Libn Var Chs; r/Presb; hon/S'ship, SWn Lib Assn; Pi Lambda Theta; Phi Alpha Theta.

SNIDER, RUTH A oc/Elementary Counselor; b/Jan 7, 1930; h/2428 Chattesworth Ln, Louisville, KY 40222; ba/L'ville; m/Arnold W; c/Yvonne Marie Price, Ray Wills, Mark Alan; p/Ellis Orrell Atkinson (dec); Fanola Miller Atkinson, Shelbyville, KY; ed/BS 1965, MEd 1970 Spalding Col; Att'd Wn Univ; pa/Guid Cnslr Jefferson Co Public Schs 1966-; Tchr: Jefferson Co (Ky) 1964-66, Louisville City Schs 1956-57, Public Schs Finchville (Ky) 1949-50; Past Pres Ky Elem Sch Cnslrs 1975-76; VP Elem Ky Sch Cnslrs Assn 1978-79; Del to Nat Elem Cnslrs Conv 1973, 75, 76, 77, 78, 79; Del to APGA Conv & 1977 Mem Ky Pers & Guid Assn; APGA; Am Sch Cnslrs Assn; Jefferson Co Cnslrs Assn; Ky Sch Cnslrs Assn; Ky

Elem/Mid Sch Cnslrs Assn; Prestonia & Klondike Elem Schs PTA; r/Bapt.

SNIPES, FELIX EARL oc/Minister; Evangelist; Magician; Entertainer; b/Dec 20, 1933; h/2338 Henderson Mill Ct, Atlanta, GA 30345; ba/Lubbock, TX; m/Patsy Ann Chambers; c/Larry, Teresa, Stanley; p/Ottis Lawrence Sr and Mariarle Underwood Snipes, Jackson, MS; ed/BA Miss Col 1957; pa/Former Pastor, Ch Staff Mem; Music Dir & Crusade Coor Wayne Bristow & Outreach Evang Inc; Profl Magical Entertainer; cp/Civic Clb Spkr & Entertainer; r/Bapt; hon/Awds: Num Sports, Spch & Drama, Rel, Civic, Profl Magic Orgs.

SNIPES, LAWRENCE PAUL oc/Businessman; b/Mar 27; h/2338 Henderson Mill Ct, Atlanta, GA 30345; ba/Same; p/F E and Patsy C Snipes; pa/Fast Food Indust, Baskin-Robbins Ice Cream Chain; cp/Civic & Commun Activs; r/1st Bapt Ch, Atlanta; hon/Var Sch, Commun & Rel Awds.

SNODDERLY, LOUISE DAVIS oc/Librarian; b/Feb 1, 1925; h/Rt 3, Box 165, Strawberry Plains, TN 37871; m/Charles Hugh; c/Lynn Jerome; p/Charles Benjamin and Grace C Davis, Strawberry Plains; ed/BS; MS; pa/Libn Carson-Newman Col; cp/Elected Jefferson Co Sch Commr 1974-; r/Bapt.

SNOW, HELEN FOSTER oc/Author; Researcher; Certified Genealogist; Researcher; h/148 Mungertown Rd, Madison, CT 06443; m/(dec); p/John Moody and Hannah Davis Foster (dec); pa/Pub'd Books incl: *Inside Red China* 1977, *The Chinese Communists: Sketches & Autobiographies of the Old Guard* 1972, *Song of Ariran* 1973, *Totemism, The Tao-T'ieh & The Chinese Ritual Bronzes* 1978,

Others; Var Collected Works; cp/Repub; Var Civic Groups; r/Prot; hon/Intl Scholars' Dir; Dir Brit & Am Writers; Writer's Dir; Am Authors Today; World W/W Wom; DIB; 2000 Wom Achmt; Nat Social Dir; Contemp Authors; W/W Am Wom; Foremost Wom in Communs; Commun Ldrs Am; Nat Social Dir; Others.

SNYDER, GLADYS REID oc/Pension Consultant; b/Apr 12, 1918; h/2790 E 3000 S, Salt Lake City, UT 84109; ba/SLC; m/Hugh Alfred; c/Sharon Kamerath (Mrs David E), Clyde Reid, Barbara Colton (Mrs John Phillip), Ronald Hugh, Steven Wayne, Kenneth Clair; p/Royal Shields Reid (dec); Marcia Porter Reid, Logan, UT; pa/Income Investmt Plans 1968-72; Prin, Chm, Pres; Pension Conslt 1965-; Wn Pensions Assocs: VP, Secy 1974-; cp/Voting Dist Chm, Repub; SL Coun Wom; PTA Ofcr; Vol Activs; r/LDS; hon/W/W Am Wom; DIB; World W/W Wom; Awd for Wkg w Yth Group, 15 Yrs.

SNYDER, MARJORIE SIMS oc/Professor; University Administrator; b/Oct 25, 1923; h/2704 Bramble, Monroe, LA 71201; ba/Monroe; m/J B (dec); c/Jerome Smith, Michael Henry; p/Smith I and Orga Munsey Sims (dec); ed/BA 1944, BS 1954, MA 1958, EdD 1962 Peabody Col; pa/NE La Univ: Prof Ed, Dir Rdg Lab; Chperson Clin Div Col Rdg Assn; Advr to Intl Students; cp/Red Cross; r/1st U Meth Ch.

SNYDER, MERLE L oc/Electrical, Industrial Engineer; b/Mar 21, 1917; h/100 Lincoln, Derby, KS 67037; ba/Mulvane, KS; m/Paula M; c/Jeanne Ann Breckenridge, Kent E; p/Don R Snyder; Florence Snyder (dec); ed/Profl Lic'd Elect Engr; mil/USN; pa/Pres Plastics Machinery Res; E E Conslt; Pres 5-B Plastics Inc; VP Wichita Plastics Inc; Chm Bd Dirs Milmerco Inc; Other Profl Positions; cp/Zone Chm 17SW, Intl Lions; r/So Bapt.

SNYDER, MYRA C oc/Assistant Dean; b/Jun 26, 1942; h/50 Halkin Ln, Berkeley, CA 94708; ba/San Francisco, CA; p/Ralph J and Catherine L Snyder, Pittsburgh, PA; ed/BS;

MS; EdD; pa/Univ SF: Asst Dean 1977-, Assoc Prof 1976-, Fac Coor 1976-77, Asst Prof 1974-77; Other Acad Positions; Am Nurses Assn; AAUA; Assn Am High Ed; cp/LWV; Wom's Polit Caucus; r/Cath; hon/Outstg Tchr, by Students 1978.

SNYDER, ROBERT MARTIN oc/Farmer; b/Sept 6, 1912; h/Noah Snyder Farm, Lahmansville, WV 26731; ba/Same; m/Gail Hiser; c/Rebecca S Peters, Margaret S Bensenhaver, Shirley S Williams, Robert M Jr; p/Noah Webster and Maggie Varner Snyder,

Lahmansville; ed/BS WVa Univ; mil/USNR Lt; pa/US Govt Agriculturist & Admr 36 Yrs; cp/Comm on Aging; Mus Comm; Nature Conservancy; Lt Gov Kiwanis; r/Prot; hon/W/W: Am, World; 35 Yr Ser Plaque, St Dept.

SODERSTROM, DOROTHY MARIE oc/Planner; b/Jun 8, 1921; h/1122 E 8th St, The Dalles, OR 97058; ba/The Dalles; c/Mary Louise Claycomb, Mike; p/Frank J Kargl, The Dalles; pa/Wasco Co (Oreg): Planner, Zoning Admr, Subdiv Admr; cp/Adv Bd Co-Owned Nsg Home & The Dalles Emblem Clb #406; Adv Bd Aerie Aux; r/Cath.

SOL, CARLOS DAVID oc/Minister; b/Oct 19, 1941; h/3706 Tilden St, Laredo, TX 78040; ba/Laredo; m/Edna; c/Nellie Opelia, Edith, Eunice, Carlos David Jr; p/Lauro and Ofelia Luna de Sol, Mexico City, Mexico; ed/BA Latin Am Sem (San Antonio, Tex); mil/Sgt 1959; pa/Min Ch of Nazarene, Laredo; Dir: Dist Commun 1976-78, Min Studies 1975-76; Secy Latin Am Dist 1976-78; Pastor Ch of Nazarene, Corpus Christi, Tex 1968-74; Ordained to Min 1968; Other Former Pastorates; Secy Latin Am Min Assn 1975-76; Tchr Nazarene Bible Inst, NYC 1975-76; Pres Spanish Dist E Nazarene Yg People's Soc (NYC) 1965-66; cp/Former Coor Oeo Commun Ctr, Corpus Christi; Former Dir Kelsey Meml Comm Sers, Corpus Christi; r/Ch of Nazarene; hon/W/W Rel.

SOLBERG, RUELL FLOYD JR oc/Research and Development Engineer; b/Jul 27, 1939; h/5906 Forest Grove, San Antonio, TX 78240; ba/San Antonio; m/Laquetta Jane Massey; c/Chandra Dawn, Marla Gaye; p/Ruel F and Ruby Mae Rogstad Solberg, Cranfills Gap, TX; ed/BS 1962, MA 1967 Univ Tex-A; MBA Trinity Univ 1977; mil/AUS; pa/Am Soc for Metals; Am Soc for Mech Engrs, (San Antonio Sect:) Nominator Gen Awds Com, Nat Chm Recruitmt for Hons & Awds, Reg X, Prog Com; Nat Soc Profl Engrs; Consumer Prods Tech Interest Group, Human Factors Soc; Other Profl Assns; Reg'd Profl Engr; Contbr to Profl & Tech Meetings & Pubs; cp/Norwegian-Am Mus; Leon Val Crime Preven Assn; Charter Mem Norwegian Soc Tex; Vesterheim Geneal Ctr; Oak Hills Terr Elem Sch Helping Hand Prog; Norwegian-Am Hist Assn; Pres Bronstad-Rogstad Reunion; Charter Mem Nordland Heritage Foun; Friends of NW Commun Lib; r/Hope Luth Ch: Chm Min Eval Task Force, Parish Ed Com, Lector, Communion Asst, Usher; hon/Theta Pi Epsilon; Pi Tau Sigma; Tau Beta Pi; Howell S'ship; Sigma Xi; Sigma Iota Epsilon; Charles E Balleisen Awd, San Antonio Sect Am Soc Mech Engrs; Patentee in field; Biogl Listings.

SOLBRIG, INGEBORG HILDEGARD oc/University Professor; b/Jul 31, 1923; h/228 S Summit St B2, Iowa City, IA 52240; ba/Ia City; p/Reinhold Johannes Solbrig, Germany; Hildegard Marianne Ferchland-Solbrig (dec); ed/BA summa cum laude; MA; PhD Stanford Univ 1969; pa/Prof Dept German Univ Ia; Intl Assn Germanistic Studies; Mod Lang Assn Am; Am Assn Tchrs German; Am Coun for Study of Austrian Lit; Am Comparative Lit

Assn; Am Soc for Study of German Lit of 16th & 17th Centuries; Goethe-Gesellschaft; Deutsche Schiller-Gesellschaft; Mem Univ Senate; hon/Ky Col; 1974 Gold Medal, Hammer-Purgstall Soc (Austria); Sev Res Grants & F'ships, US & Austria; Author *Hammer-Purgstall und Goethe* 1973; Prin Editor *Rilke Heute* 1975; Other Pubs.

SOLCZANYK, ANDRIJ DARIAN oc/-Electrical Engineer; b/Jul 8, 1923; h/26 Wyncroft Dr, Media, PA 19063; m/Irena Chuchra; p/Wolodymyr Solczanyk (dec); Maria Solczanyk, Media; ed/BS 1961, MSEE 1967 Drexel Univ; pa/Electronic Engr in Instrumentation 1961-67; Electrical Engr 1967-; Ukrainian Engrs' Soc Am; cp/VP Ukrainian Philatelic & Numismatic Soc; Ukrainian Hist Assn; Ukrainian Journalists Assn Am; Am Philatelic Soc; Am Topical Assn; Collectors of Rel on Stamps; Fine Arts Philatelists; Sammlergilde St Gabriel; Exhibitor Philatelic Exhbns: NOJEX, SEPAD,

BALPEX, SESCAL, SOJEX; r/Ukrainian Rite Cath; hon/Acad Achmt Awd; George W Childs Drexel Hon S'ship Awd; Alpha Sigma Lambda; Dean's List; Num Silver & Bronze Awds at Var Philatelic Exhbns.

SOLDINI, JOHN LOUIS oc/Teacher; Union Representative; b/Nov 7, 1935; h/51 Van Brunt St, Staten Island, NY 10312; ba/SI; m/Dina; c/Donna, David, Michelle; p/Bernard and Mary Soldini, SI; mil/USN; pa/Exec Bd U Fdn Tchrs; cp/Del Dem Nat Conv 1968, 72; VChm NY St New Dem Coalition; r/Rom Cath; hon/Phi Beta Kappa; Mensa Soc.

SOLOVY, ELLEN BRANSKY oc/Artist; b/Sept 14, 1926; h/467 High Point Dr, Peoria, IL 61614; ba/Same; m/Joseph Sheldon; c/Susan Margaret, Linda Anne Frakes, Karen Lee; p/David Wolf and Frieda Tarletz Bransky, Peoria; ed/PhB, BS Univ Chicago; pa/Painter; One-Person Shows incl: Peoria Art Guild, Bradley Univ Grad Sch (Peoria), Howard A Heller Gallery (Peoria), Phillips, Swager Assocs (Peoria), Lakeview Ctr for Arts & Scis (Peoria), Caterpillar Tractor Co (E Peoria); Group Shows incl: Joy Horwich Gallery (Chgo), YWCA Gallery (Peoria), GALEX TEN Galesburg Civic Art Ctr (Galesburg, Ill), 28th Ill Invitational Ill St Mus (Springfield, Ill), Others; Rep'd in Perm Collections incl'g: Bloomington (Ill) Fed Savs & Loan, Bradley Univ Grad Sch, Lakeview Ctr for Arts & Scis, G'burg Civic Art Ctr; cp/Peoria Human Relats Comm; r/Jewish; hon/Spec Purchase Awd, GALEX 5; Meml Awd, GALEX XI; Other Art Awds.

SOMERVILLE, HAZEL DORIS oc/Homemaker; b/Sept 30, 1929; h/1713 Douglas, Midland, TX 79701; m/J Keith; c/Bea Lea; p/Dillard E and Pearl Alma Babb (dec); ed/BA; pa/Former Asst Petr Engr Humble Oil & Refining Co, McCamey Prodn Dept; Bookkeeper for Husband's Bus; cp/Bd Dirs YMCA Hlth Clb; Tejas Garden Clb: Mem 22 Yrs, Treas 4 Yrs, Rec'g Secy, 3/Vice, 2/Vice, 1/Vice & Pres 3 Yrs, Bd Dirs Lancaster Garden

Ctr; 1/VP W Tex Iris Soc; Nat'ly Accredited Flower Show Judge; 1/VP Tex Garden Clbs; Dist Garden Clb: Publicity Press Book Chm 4 Yrs, Flower Show & Flower Show Schedule Chm, Yrbook Chm, Rec'g Secy, 1/Vice Dir & Dir, ACE Civic Concern Chm; Past Pres Midland Study Clb; Former Treas & Secy James Bowie Elem PTA; Former Public Relats Chm Midland HS PTA; Other Civic Activs; r/1st Christian Ch, Midland: Mem, Christian Wom's F'ship.

SONNEMANN, NELL BATTLE BOOKER oc/Artist; Professor; b/Aug 19, 1918; h/4718 Cumberland Ave, Chevy Chase, MD 20015; ba/Washington, DC; p/John Manning and Nell Lewis Battle Booker (dec); ed/AB 1938, MA 1940 Univ NC-CH 1938; MFA Cath Univ Am 1959; pa/Assoc Prof Dept Art Cath Univ Am 1959-; Sr Reschr & Staff Guest Royal Col of Art, Sch Textile Design (London) 1973; Participating Mem Wkly Sems on Popular Cult Conducted by Smithsonian Inst 1969-70; 6 One-Person Shows incl: Arts Consortium (Cincinnati, Ohio) 1977, Univ S (Sewanee, Tenn) 1972, George Thomas Hunt Art Gallery (Chattanooga, Tenn) 1972, Morehead Planetarium (Univ NC-CH) 1970; 2 & 3-Person Shows Fisk Univ 1972, 67; Exhibited Num Nat Exhibts, Competitive & Invitational; Comms incl 2 Tapestries for

Shrine of Most Blessed Sacrament (Wash DC) 1976, 3 Tapestries 1977; Illustrator: *Jane Eyre* 1946, *Wuthering Heights* 1947, *The Scarlet Letter* 1947, *Baby Book: A Handbook for Parents* 1947; Var Cartoons, Covers & Illustrations for *Integrity Mag* 1948-51; cp/Lectr on Liturgical Art to DC Civic, Ednl & Rel Groups; Guest Lectr on Art & Ed Nat Jesuit Art Inst, Santa Clara Univ (Cal); r/Rom Cath; hon/1st Prize Arts Exhibit, Nat Interfaith Conf on Rel & Arch (Boston); Purchase Prize, Art Students' Leag (NYC); Phi Beta Kappa; Other Art Awds.

SORDINAS, AUGUSTUS oc/Archaeologist; b/Jan 10, 1927; h/1224 Briarwood, Memphis, TN 38111; ba/Memphis; m/Sally Morrell; c/Antiope Joan, Elizabeth Anne, Anne Frances, Emily Augusta; p/John Baptist Sordinas (dec); Antiope Boikou (dec); ed/BS cum laude Georgetown Univ 1957; MA 1962, PhD 1968 Harvard Univ; mil/Greek Army Resv Ofcr, Class 1948; pa/Prof Anthropol Memphis St Univ 1967-; Tutor Cult Anthropol Harvard Univ 1967; Assoc Mem Am Sch

Classical Studies 1964-66; Asst Prof Anthropol Col Wm & Mary 1964; Mem Archaeol Expedition by Harvard Univ at Abri Pataud, Dordogne, France 1961-64; Anthropol Fieldwork Ghana 1959-60; Archaeol & Ethnographic Expeditions in: Sahara (N Africa), Dalmatian Coast (Yugoslavia), Corsica, Ireland, Mexico, Saudi Arabia; Sev Articles in Profl Jours & Monographs in Archaeol & Mat Cult Studies; Fellow: Am Anthropol Assn, Royal Anthropol Inst Gt Britain & Ireland; hon/Hon Fellow, Ionian Acad (Athens, Greece).

SORRELLS, FRANK DOUGLAS oc/- Professional Engineer; b/May 14, 1931; h/5516 Timbercrest Trail, Knoxville, TN 37919; ba/Alma M; c/Desiree G; p/Ralph P and Ila B Sorrells, Seneca, SC; ed/BSME, MS Univ Tenn; mil/USAF 1950-54; pa/Profl Engr w 22 Yrs Experience in Concept & Devel of New or Improved Mfg Process or Prods; Nat & Tenn Socs Profl Engrs; Am Soc Mech Engrs; Am Soc Testing & Mats; Sr Mem Plastics Engrs; r/Luth; hon/Pi Tau Sigma; Patentee 12 Times in field; Tech Papers Related to Devel Projs.

SOTO-MUNOZ, MANUEL oc/Painter; b/Jan 20, 1913; h/1605 Indo St, El Cerezal, Rio Piedras, PR 00926; m/Clara Hernandez; c/1 Son; p/Manuel Soto and Elisa Munoz; ed/Art Students Leag NY; mil/AUS WWII; pa/Art Dir *La Milagrosa* Mag, PR 1955-60; Art Instr Ext Div Univ PR 1962-64; Tchr Pvt Art Classes in Own Studio; Participant Group Shows: NY 1955, 57, La Cienega-Los Angeles

(Cal) 1968, LA 1970; One-Man Shows incl: Ateneo de PR, Casa de Espana, Galeria Las Americas, City hall of Bayamon, Univ PR Ext Div Gallery & Dorado del Mar Hotel (all in PR); Works in Pvt Collections: PR, Cal, NY, SAm; Artists Equity Assn; Life Mem Art Students Leag; Intl Art Assn; Long Bch Art Assn (NY); hon/Awd of Merit, Fla So Col Intl Exhbn for Painting "Landscape of Bronx Park"; Book of Honor; Notable Ams.

SOUTHERLAND, RANDY oc/Teacher; b/Aug 14, 1951; h/Box 86, Loco, OK 73442; ba/Comanche, OK; p/D L and Wanda Rhea Southerland, Loco, OK; ed/BS; Masters; pa/Eng & Music Tchr Meridian Sch; Okla Ed Assn; NEA; Classroom Tchrs Assn; Stephens Co Ed Assn; Okla Sch Cnslrs Assn; Okla Pers & Guid Assn; Reg IV Pers & Guid Assn; So

Dist Guid Assn; cp/Ldr 4-H Clb; Mem Red Red Rose; Meridian & VP Meridian PTA; Chm Exec Com Stephens Co OEA; cp/Pianist Sr Citizens Bicent Prog; Others; r/Immanuel Bapt Ch, Duncan, Okla: Organist; Loco Bapt Ch, Loco: Organist, Vocalist, Pianist; hon/Comanche Sch Sys's Tchr of Yr 1978-79; Stephens Co Tchr of Yr 1978-79; Outstg Yg Men Am; W/W Am Cols & Univs.

SOUTHWARD, BERNARD MORRISON JR oc/Counselor; Administrator; b/Nov 22, 1944; h/22 South Ave, Beacon, NY 12508; ba/Stormville, NY; p/B M Sr and Lucille T Southward, Augusta, GA; ed/BA Augusta Col, Univ of Ga; AM Columbia Univ; pa/Correction Cnslr: Clinton Correctl Facility 1973-74, Green Haven Correctl Facility 1974-77; Sr Correctl Cnslr, Green Haven 1977-; Adv Bd, SUNY-Plattsburgh 1973-74; Conslt: Dutchess Commun Col HEOP Prison Prog, Intl Key Wom, Project Build, Think Tank Inc; CoDeveloper, Honor Housing Concept 1976; Contb'd to Devel of "Role & Duties of Correction Cnslr" 1976; Public Offenders Cnslg Assn; APGA; Nat Assn Black Social Workers; cp/Advr, Green Haven Artists Collective; NAACP; Smithsonian Inst; Assoc Mem, Museum of Natural Hist; r/Bapt; hon/W/W E; Men Achmt; Commun Ldrs & Noteworthy Ams.

SOWERWINE, ELBERT ORLA JR oc/Professional Engineer; Planner/Rancher; Private Consultant; b/Mar 15, 1915; h/Broken H Ranch, Wapiti, WY 82450; ba/Wapiti; Nicaragua; m/Norma B; c/Sue-Ann S Jacobson, Sandra S Montgomery, Elbert III, John Frederick, Avril Ruth, Albaro Francisco, Octavio Evans, Zaida Margarita; p/Elbert Orla Sowerwine (dec); Margaret Alice Evans (dec); ed/BChem, ChEng Cornell Univ; mil/CMTC; 2/Lt Coast Arty Resvs; pa/Res & Devel Socony-Vacuum Oil Co Inc, Paulsboro (NJ) 5½ Yrs; Prodn Supvr Merck & Co Inc, Elkton (Va) 1¼ Yrs; Prodn Mgmt US Indust Chems Inc, Newark (NJ) 3¼ Yrs; Proj Engr Plant Design Wigton-Abbott Corp, Newark (NJ) & Cody (Wyo) 7 Yrs; Pvt Res & Conslt'g Engrg, Cody 9 Yrs; Dir Govt Planning Mont St Planning Bd, Helena (Mont) 1¾ Yrs; Pvt Conslt Engrg, Managua (Nicaragua), Hdqtrs 14 Yrs; Cert'd US Nat Bur Engrg Reg; Mem Exec Bd Mo Basin Res & Devel Coun; Am Inst Chem Engrs; Fellow Am Inst Chemists; Former Mem Mont Chapt Am Inst Planners & Chemurgic Coun; Nicaraguan Assn Engrs & Architects; Profl Mem Am Soc Planning Ofcls; Other Profl Activs; cp/Former Ldr & Commr Boy Scouts (NJ); Former Sch Bd

Ofcl (Wyo); Del to Co Sch Bds Assn; Lions Intl; Rotary Intl; Var Civic Coms; r/Congreg; Luth; hon/Delta Sigma Phi; Cit for Design of Plough Inc (Plant at Memphis), US Nat Indust Coun; Who Knows & What; W/W Fin & Indust; Men Achmt; Profl Pubs.

SOYARS, CRYSTINE YATES oc/Retired Teacher; b/Feb 2, 1904; h/3600 Dartmouth Ln, Nashville, TN 37215; m/Aubrey F; p/Walter E and Mary Ell Pack Yates (dec); ed/BS 1935, MA 1955 Geo Peabody Col; AB Trevecca Nazarene Col 1965; pa/Ret'd Public Sch Tchr; Trevecca Nazarene Col: In Charge of Alumni Ofc 1965-75, Liaison Between Adm & Alumni, Asst Editor & Writer Alumni Assn Mag, Exec

Secy Alumni Assn; Treas Elem Tchrs N'ville; NEA; Tenn Ed Assn; Delta Chapt ADK: Charter Mem, Corres Secy 3 Yrs, Chaplain; Nat, St, Reg & Local Assns for Ret'd Tchrs; cp/Jr Red Cross 20 Yrs; U Givers; Civil Def; r/Ch of Nazarene: SS Tchr/Supvr 37 Yrs; hon/SS Tchr of Yr 1962; "T" Awd, Trevecca Alumni Assn; Author: *Trevecca Missionaries-Past & Present* 1976, *The Thomas M Pack Clan* 1977; Phi Delta Lambda; Contbr Articles to Jours, Rel Periodicals, & *Sch Arts Mag*; Num Cits & Other Awds.

SPAETH, SHIRLEY TURNER oc/Homemaker; b/Jul 4, 1920; h/1904 Rivershore Rd, Elizabeth City, NC 27909; m/Walter; c/Walter MacNeille, Douglas Grant, Michael Turner; p/Ulysses Grant Turner (dec); Harriett Rollins Turner, Marlette, MI; ed/RN 1942; RNA Grace Hosp Sch Anesthesia 1947; mil/AUS Nurses Corp 1943-46, 1/Lt, Asst Hd Nurse Boca Raton Hosp; pa/Staff Nurse Henry Ford Hosp (Detroit, Mich); Anesthesia Staff: Grace Hosp (Detroit), Duke Hosp; cp/DAR: Var Chapt Ofcs, Coms, St Chm'ships, Others; Descendents Mayflower Soc NC: Orgr NE Colony 1974, Lt Gov, St

Secy; Nat Soc Dames of Magna Charta; Plantagenet Soc; Colonial Order of the Crown; NC Soc Colonial Dames XVII Century; USS NC Battleship Comm; Precnt VDir Dem Party; St Med Aux; PTA: Classroom Rep Many Yrs, Jr HS PTA, Secy, Pres; PTA Coun: VP, Pres; Var Activs Bicent Com; NC Geneol Soc; NC Lit & Hist Soc; NC Arts Coun; NC Mus; Elizabeth City Music Clb; Albemarle Choral Soc; Mus of Albemarle; Friends of Lib; Pasquotank Hist Soc; Former Mem Elizabeth City Human Relats Com; r/Cann Meml Presb Ch, Elizabeth City: Mem, Asst SS Tchr; hon/Bicent Awds: DAR, Elizabeth City; Girl Scout Hidden Heroine Awd.

SPARKS, CHARLES E oc/Pastor; b/Jul 29, 1941; h/Rt #2, Robbins, NC 27325; ba/Same; m/Phyllis Jean; c/Charles Edward Jr, Phillip Keith; p/Edgar and Annie Sparks, Moulton, AL; ed/BA magna cum laude Tenn

Temple Col 1973; MDiv w highest hons Temple Theol Sem 1976; mil/NG 1960-66; pa/Pastor Acorn Ridge Bapt Ch; r/Bapt; hon/Personalities of S.

SPARKS, MARIE CATHERINE oc/Librarian; b/Jun 13, 1951; h/728 NW 118 St, Oklahoma City, OK 73114; ba/Okla City; p/Melvin and Clara Kohlenberg, Republic, OH; ed/BA Ohio No Univ 1972; MLS 1974, MPH 1980 Univ Okla; pa/Serials Acquisitions Libn Univ Okla Hlth Sers Ctr Lib 1973-; Asst Prof Dept Med Lib Sci Univ Okla Col of Hlth; Med Lib Assn; Okla Hlth Scis Lib Assn; Okla Lib Assn; Tau Beta Sigma; Okla Soc on Aging; Okla Dept Libs Adv Bd, Conversion of Okla Union List of Serials to OCLC; Gerontol Subject Specialist 1977-; cp/Ad Hoc Com on Mtl Hlth Protective Sers Task Force, Okla Areawide Aging Agy; r/Bapt Temple: SS Tchr; hon/Beta Phi Mu; Beta Beta Beta; Ohio No Univ: Getty Scholar, Outstg Sr Biol Maj; W/W Among Col & Univ Students; Grade 1 Cert'd Libn, Med Lib Assn.

SPEAR, RUBY LOUISE oc/Teacher; b/Aug 13; h/410 Sixth St, Lawrenceburg, TN 38464; ba/L'burg; p/Lewis Ester Spear (dec); Ruthie Mae Grisham Spear, L'burg; ed/AB Trevecca Nazarene Col; MA Mid Tenn St Univ; pa/HS Eng Tchr; TEA; MNEA; LCEA; NEA; Delta Kappa Gamma; cp/Dem Party; r/Ch of Nazarene; hon/Notable Ams; World W/W Wom.

SPEER, ALLEN PAUL oc/College Instructor; b/Sept 4, 1951; h/Box 537, Banner Elk, NC 28604; p/Paul Speer Jr; Frieda Hinshaw; ed/BS, MA Appalachian St Univ; pa/Current Tchr Hist & Polit Sci Lees McRae Col; Former Tchr: Surry Commun Col, East Bend Elem Sch, Boonville Elem Sch; r/Bapt; hon/Author 2 Pub'd Poems, "Man on the Porch" 1978, "Aunt Nellie" 1979; Commun Ldrs Am; Outstg Yg Men Am.

SPEESE, JAMES STANLEY oc/Minister; Military Chaplain; Educator; Writer; b/Nov 24, 1911; h/900 Whitewater Ct, Altamonte Springs, FL 32701; m/Mary Florence Giddings; c/James, Carolyn, Shelley; p/August Friar and Elizabeth Erna Speese (dec); ed/BA Gordon Col 1940; MA Univ NH 1943; BD Gordon-Conwell Sem 1946; ThD Burton Sem 1960; Grad Doct Studies; mil/USAF Chaplain, Lt Col (Ret'd), EAD 1943-47, 1950-58, Resv Assignmts 1947-50,

1958-71; Resv Staff Chaplain; pa/Hd Dept Hist & Polit Sci Col of Emporia (Ks) 1968-71; Prof World Affairs Fla So Col, McCoy Br 1976-; Interim Pastor Covenant Presb Ch Sanford (Fla) 1978-; Assoc Pastor St Pauls Presb, Orlando (Fla) 1976-78; Ret'd as Pastor Woodland Heights Presb Ch, Springfield (Mo) 1976; Has Pastored Chs in NH, Mass, Wis, Ohio, Ill, Mich & Mo; cp/AFA Assn; Resv Ofcrs Assn; TROA; Mil Chaplains Assn; VFW; Smithsonian Instn; Am Legion; r/John Calvin Union Presby Snyod Mid-Am: Mem; hon/Phi Alpha Chi; 10 Freedoms Foun Awds for Writings & Sermons; Biogl Listings; Profl Pubs.

SPEIGNER, WILLIAM HENRY JR oc/Interpreter for Deaf; Carpenter; Welder; b/Oct 22, 1929; h/426 N John St, Orlando, FL 32811; c/Louis Pedro, Melvin Lee, Jaime Gilbert Vildosola, Pamela Chirstine Clayton, Roy Bruce Clayton III; p/William H and Sallie Mae King Speigner (dec); mil/AUS 1950-52, S/Sgt; pa/Interpreter for Deaf; r/Indep Bapt.

SPEIR, KENNETH G oc/Attorney; b/Jun 22, 1908; h/809 Main, PO Box 546, Newton, KS 67114; m/Helen (dec); c/3 Chd; p/John and Bessie Guinty Speir; ed/JD; mil/USMCR Lt Col (Ret'd); pa/Gen Counsel Acra-Plant Inc & 1st Fed Savs & Ln Assn, Newton; Co Atty, Harvey Co (Ks) 1939-41; Judge 9th Judicial Dist (Ks) 1941-44; r/Luth; hon/Notable Ams.

SPELTS, RICHARD E JR oc/Banker; Builder; b/Jan 1, 1919; h/2203 W Charles St, Grand Island, NE 68801; ba/Grand Isl; m/Dorothy Tipton; c/Connie S Brouillette, Susan S Richardson; p/R E Sr and Flo R Spelts, Grand Isl; ed/AB Hastings Col; BS Univ Neb; mil/USN WWII, Lt (jg); pa/Pres: 1st Nat Bk Grand Isl, U Bank Sers Co, Grand Isl; Chm Bkshares of Neb Inc, Grand Isl: 1st Nat Bk Grand Isl, 1st Savings Co Grand Isl, 1st Savs Co Hastings; Ofcr & Dir: Spelts of Neb Inc, Grand Isl, Spelts-Schultz Lumber Co, Grand Isl, Mid-Am Co, Grand Isl, Spelts Lumber Co, Kearney (Neb), Spelts-Swanson Implement Co, Kearney; Dir: M E I Corp, Minneapolis (Minn), NWn Public Ser Co, Huron (SD), Bus Devel Corp Neb, Lincoln (Neb); cp/Chm Golden Age Village, Hall Co Housing Auth; Dir & Past Pres: St Francis Medical Ctr, Neb Assn Commerce & Indust, Gtr Grand Isl Devel Corp; Dir: Univ Neb Foun, Grand Isl Charitable Foun; Trustee Grand Isl Indust Foun; Mem Nat Coun BSA; Var Polit Activs; r/Presb Ch: Elder; hon/Wisdom Awd of Honor, Wisdom Soc; Commun Ser Awd, KMMJ Radio; Awd, Am Cancer Soc; Mr Grand Isl Awd 1963; Silver Beaver Awd, BSA; Dist'd Ser Awd, Neb

Repub Party; Alumni Ser Awd, Univ Neb; US JCs Dist'd Ser Awd; Biogl Listings.

SPENCE, FLOYD DAVIDSON oc/Congressman; b/Apr 9, 1928; h/PO Box 815, Lexington, SC 29072; ba/Washington, DC; m/Lula Hancock Drake (dec); c/David, Zach, Benjamin, Caldwell; p/James Wilson Spence (dec); Addie Lucas Spence, Lexington; ed/BA; JD; mil/USNR Capt; pa/Atty at Law; Callison & Spence, W Columbia, SC; Lexington Co, SC & Am Bar Assns; US Supr Ct Bar; cp/Elected to US Cong 1970, Mem Var Coms; Former Mem SC Ho of Reps, SC St Senate; cp/Farm Bur; Former Dir W Columbia-Cayce C of C; BSA: Former Dist Chm, Former Scoutmaster, Exec Bd SC Coun, Silver Beaver Awd; 1st Pres Lexington Co Hist Soc; Am Legion; VFW; Resv Ofcrs Assn; Navy Leag; Nav Resv Assn; F'ship Christian Aths; Charter Mem Univ SC Assn Ltterman; r/St Peter's Luth Ch: Mem, Ch Coun, Adult SS Tchr; hon/W/W: Am, Am Polits.

SPENCE, LEONA CORDELL oc/Retired Educator; b/Aug 30, 1908; h/121 Stroud Ave, El Dorado, AR 71730; m/William Tyler; c/Zada Trull Watkins (Mrs Wayne), Frederick Hardeman Trull; p/John Hardeman and Zada Moore Cordell; ed/BA La St Univ; MA Columbia Tchrs Col; pa/Ret'd Tchr El Dorado Public Schs; Art Supvr 1953-54; Sum Replacemt Art Dept, So St Univ 1954, 55, Henderson Univ 1953; Pres Alpha Chapt Delta Kappa Gamma 1960-61; Pres AAUW; cp/El Dorado Art Leag: Charter Mem, Former 1/Pres: Past Pres: Kirkwood Newcomer's Clb

(Kirkwood, Mo), Oak Val Garden Clb (Frontenac, Mo), S Ark Audubon Soc; DAR: Former Regent Rosamond Chapt, Former Gen Chm, Ark St Conf 1977; DAR St Chm for CAR; Sr St Pres Nat Soc Chd of Am Revolution; Pres Union Co Chapt Ark Pioneer Assn; Ark St Chm Nat Pubs Fed'd Garden Clbs; Liaison Rep for S Ark Pres Con; r/1st Presb Ch: Former SS Dept Supt, Tchr, VBA Sch Dir, Christmas Decoration Com; hon/Invited to Show Photos at S Ark Arts Ctr Mar 1977; Produced Winning Slides, Audubon Contests; Wom of Yr Awd 1977.

SPENCER, AIDA BESANCON oc/Minister; b/Jan 2, 1947; h/G-4 Seminary Village, Louisville, KY 40207; m/William David; p/Heinrich Frederick Julius and Aida Guzman Besancon; ed/BA; MDiv; ThM; pa/Evang Theol Soc 1974-; Evangels for Social Action 1976-; Conf on Christianity & Lit 1978-; Evang Wom's Caucus 1976-; cp/Bd Mem John Witherspoon Inst; Former Bd Mem Model Cities in Plainfield (NJ); Rel Com ERA; r/U Presb Ch USA; hon/Outstg Ser, Alpha Omega Commun Theol Sch; Outstg Yg Wom Am; W/W in Rel; Commun Awd, Trenton St Prison; Samuel Robinson Foun Prize; Dean's List, Douglass Col.

SPENCER, CHAUNCEY EDWARD oc/Public Affairs Director; b/Nov 6, 1906; h/1306 Tierce St, Lynchburg, VA 24501; ba/L'burg; m/Anna Mae; c/Edward Alexander II, Carol Ann, Michael Stephan, LuJuan Stephanie, Chauncey Edward II, Joel Banister, Shaun Suzan; p/Edward Alexander and Anne Banister Spencer, L'burg; ed/AB; AE; BA; mil/AUS & USAF 1941-45; pa/Public Affairs Dir WLVA Radio; Pers Mgmt; Law Enforcemt; City Adm; cp/Tuskegee Airman

Inc; Conf of Cities; Nat Airmens Assn; LAFOIC; NAACP; Urban Leag; r/Congreg; hon/US Dept of Army & USAF Decoration for Exceptl Ser; Air Mat Command Ser Awd, USAF; Am GI Forum Cert of Recog, San Bernardino, Cal; Exceptl Ser Commend, City of San Bernardino; Exceptl Perf Awd, Negro Airman Inst, Detroit, Mich Chapt; Pioneer Awd, Nat Tuskegee Airmen Inc; Hon Mem Awd, AF ROTC.

SPENCER, WILLIAM DAVID oc/Minister; b/Nov 13, 1947; h/G-4 Seminary Village, Louisville, KY 40207; m/Aida Dina Besancon; p/William Day Jr and Helen Catherine Collis Spencer, N Plainfield, NJ; ed/BA; MDiv; ThM; pa/Conf on Christianity & Lit 1976-;

Evang Theol Soc 1974-; cp/Bd Dirs John Witherspoon Inst 1977-; Campus Christian Foun; r/U Presb Ch USA; hon/"In Apprec" Awd, Alpha Omega Commun Theol Sch; Samuel Robinson Foun Prize, Princeton Theol Sem; Nancy Higginson Dore Prize, Rutgers Univ; W/W in Rel.

SPERBER, DANIEL oc/Professor; b/May 8, 1930; h/1 Taylor Ln, Troy, NY 12180; ba/Troy; m/Ora; c/Ron Emanuel; p/Emanuel Sperber (dec); Nelly Sperber, Troy; ed/MSc; MA; PhD; mil/Israeli AF Capt; pa/Prof Physics RPI; Reschr; r/Jewish; hon/Fellow, Am Physical Soc.

SPERLINE, ELIZABETH STARR oc/Executive; b/Dec 16; pa/6840 E Sunnyvale Rd, Paradise Valley, AZ 85253; ba/Phoenix; c/Donald Arthur, Jean Marie, Victoria Elizabeth, Marcella Kathleen; p/Horace Homer; Hazel Starr Van Meter; ed/BA; MBA; pa/Pres: R T C Printing, AAM Graphics, Reflect-o-Screen, SWn Rehab & Cnslg Ctr, Bus Technol Corp, Ameribanc Shares; Treas Interim Corp; cp/Former Spec Conslt Ariz to Ofc Ec Opport; Former Mem: White House Conf Food, Nutrition & Hlth, Pers's Comm on Pers Interchange, Repub St Ctl Com, Electoral Col, Bd Cal Indian Ed Assn; Past Pres Cal Yg Repubs; BPW's Fed'd Clb; Huntington Park C of C; Fdg Bd Downey Rehab Hosp Aux; Friends San Antonio Reg Lib; Others; hon/1st Pl Awd, Cal-Am-Fed'd Woms Clb; Outstg Ser to Democracy Awd, Anaheim Yg Repubs.

SPERRY, SALLY BAXTER oc/Researcher; Educational Publisher; b/Jul 10, 1914; h/PO Box 202, Galt, CA 95632; p/John A and Lillian M Sperry (dec); ed/BA; MA; Life Credential; mil/Tchr & Writer Dept Army Command, AUS 1951-53; pa/Wom's Editor *Utah* Mag 1937-38; Tchr USA, Ryukyus Islands 1951; Writer Staff I&E, USA, Ryukyus 1952-53; Tchr USN, Philippine Isls 1956; Tchr Sacramento Co 1958; Asst Dir Public Relats Cal Redwood Assn, San Francisco 1963; Cnslr St Dept Rehab 1966-67; Propriet Covenant & Laurel Hill Presses, Galt 1967-; cp/Nat Trust for Hist Presv; Secy Dry Creek Antiquarian Soc; Chm Galt Property Owners Coun; hon/Psi Chi; Prize Lit Achmt, Browning Soc; Awd Lit Achmt, Sacramento Reg Arts Assn; Gold Medal, St of Cal; Commend as Dir Galt Bicent, Pres Ford; Author 36 Pub'd Books.

SPIKES, JESSE JAMES oc/Attorney; b/May 17, 1950; h/224 Milton Ave SE, Atlanta, GA 30315; ba/Atlanta; p/Robert Lee and Nellie Maude Spikes, McDonough, GA;

ed/BA magna cum laude Dartmouth 1972; BA Univ Col Oxford Univ 1974; JD Harvard 1977; hon/Phi Beta Kappa; Rhodes S'ship.

SPILLANE, JOHN H oc/Clergyman; Retired Surgeon; b/Sept 5, 1911; h/11931 Bajada Rd, San Diego, CA 92128; m/Margaret Mary Ruddy (dec); c/Margaret Mary Roberts, Catherine Elizabeth Brown, John H Jr, Thomas M, Anthony J, Patrick D; p/John H Spillane (dec); Elizabeth M Hammill (dec);

ed/BA cum laude 1931; MD 1934, MS 1934 Univ Colo; mil/AUS Med Res Corps 1937-46, Active Duty 1941-46, Regular Army 1946, Ret'd 1962; pa/Summit Co (Ohio), Ohio St Med Assns; AMA; FACS; FRS; cp/Past Pres Ft Knox Reg PTA; Former Med Advr Far E Coun BSA; r/Rom Cath: Ordained Perm Deacon 1972; hon/Advocate, Diocesean Tribunal, Diocese of San Diego; Diplomate, Nat Bd Med Exam; Am Bd Surg.

SPILLER, ELLEN BRUBAKER oc/Instructor; b/Jul 17, 1932; h/211 Rue Orleans, Baytown, TX 77520; ba/B'town; m/Sam C; c/Katherine Quesney, Georgianna; p/George Nunley Brubaker (dec); Lou Greathouse Brubaker, San Marcos, TX; ed/BJ Univ Tex; MA Univ Houston; Addit Studies; pa/Eng Instr Lee Col; AAUP; TJCTA; CCTE; Wom in Communs; Var Col Coms; r/All Saints Epis Ch, B'town: Altar Guild; hon/T R Larsen S'ship, Univ Tex.

SPINKS, WILLIAM HERSCHEL oc/Retired School Superintendent; b/Apr 20, 1917; h/Box 112, McAllen, TX 78501; m/Lillie Loreda Mahand; c/William Phillip, Brenda Joyce, Phyllis Carol; p/Bertha Spinks, Greenville, TX; ed/BS E Tex St Univ; MA Tex A&I Univ; mil/AUS 1941-45, Europe; pa/St Admrs Nat Assn; Other Profl Assns; r/Bapt: SS Tchr 18 Yrs; hon/Outstg Edr Tex; Outstg Edr in S; Book of Honor; DIB; Intl W/W: Commun Ser, Intells; Commun Ldrs & Noteworthy Ams; Notable Ams; Other Biogl Listings.

SPIVACK, HENRY ARCHER oc/Life Insurance Company Executive; b/Apr 15, 1919; h/1522 45th St, Brooklyn, NY 11219; ba/New York, NY; m/Sadie Babe Meiseles; c/Ian Jeffrey, Paula Janis; p/Jacob and Pauline Schwartz Spivack; ed/CCNY 1936-42; Am Col at Bryn Mawr 1962-65; mil/USN 1943-46; pa/Comptroller, Daniel Jones Inc (NYC) 1947-59; Field Underwriter, Union Ctr Life Ins Co (NYC) 1959-, Mgr Programming Dept 1966-69, Assoc Mgr 1977-; Penchant Dir, Bing & Co (NYC) 1975-77; Employee Benefit Plan Conslt; Instr NY St Ins Dept, C W Post Col of Long Island Univ; Chartered Life Underwriter; Life Underwriters Assn of NY; Am Soc Chartered Life Underwriter (Chm NY Chapt Pension Sect, Chm Profl Liaison Com); Am Soc Pension Actuaries; Pensioneers at C W Post Col; C W Post Col Tax Inst & Fin Planning Inst; Practicing Law Inst; Gtr NY Brokers Assn; Contbr Articles to Profl Jours; cp/K of P (Life Mem, Past Dep Grand Chancellor of NY St); hon/Author of 1st Maj Defense of Pension Reform Law (ERISA), Pub'd in *NY Times*, Read into Congl Record; Biogl Listings.

SPRADLIN-HANSON, FRANCES oc/Industrial Specialist; h/2301 S Jefferson Davis Hwy, 821, Arlington, VA 22202; ba/Washington, DC; m/S H Hanson (dec); p/(dec); ed/Am Univ; Geo Wash Univ; pa/Indust Specialist (Shipbldg) Dept of Navy, NAVSEA 1973-; Mem NAVSEA Equal Employmt Opport Com, Fed Wom's Prog Com, Upward Mobility Panel, EEO Coor & Cnslr at Large 1973-74; Pres No Va Chapt Fed'ly Employed Wom Inc 1977-78; Mem Exec Com DC Metro Reg Fed'ly Employed Wom Inc; Chapt Rep Nat Rep Com, Fed'ly Employed Wom Inc; Am Mgmt Assn; Nat Assn Ret'd Fed Employees; Am Assn Ret'd Persons; cp/Toastmistress Intl; Ret'd Ofcrs Assn; Soc Mil Widows; hon/2 Cits, Outstg Ser to EEO Progs, NAVSEA; Outstg & Dedicated Ser Awd, NOVA FEW; FEW Nat Chapt Achmt Awd; Lttr of Apprec, Combined Fed Campaign, U Givers; Nom, DC Metro FEW Merit Awd.

SPRINGER, WILLIAM LEE oc/Attorney at Law; b/Apr 12, 1909; h/900 W Park Ave, Champaign, IL 61820; m/Elsie Mattis; c/Katherine Curtis Hickey, Ann Tucker McKnight, Georgia Mattis Finger; p/Otha L and Daisy E Springer (dec); ed/AB DePauw Univ 1931; LLB Univ Ill 1935; mil/USN 1942-45; pa/Began Law Pract Champaign 1936; St's Atty Champaign Co 1940-42; Co Judge Champaign Co 1946-50; Appt'd Mem Fed Power Comm 1973-75; Del to Intl Conf on Liquified Natural Gal (Algeria) 1974; Appt'd to Fed Election Comm 1976-77; cp/Mem Congress 1950-1972; Num Com Activs; Del to 1st US-Mexico Interparliamentary Conf, Guadalajara, Mexico 1961; Del Other Confs; hon/Author 1st Fed Power Comm Opinion on Coal Gasification, Author Var Leg.

SPRUCE, FRANCES BLYTHE oc/Manager Marketing Services; b/May 4, 1927; h/4518 Drummond Ave, Chevy Chase, MD 20015; p/Samuel Stewart and Nell Anderson Spruce; ed/AA Mt Vernon Jr Col 1947; BA Geo Wash Univ 1950; Pvt Art Studies; pa/Mgr Mktg Sers Group Hosp Inc; Actor, Dir & Stage Mgr "Cross Roads" Theater 2 Seasons; Coor 1966 Bal Boheme; Montgomery Players: Dir 16 Plays, VP, Publicity Cir, Mem Play Selection & Nom'g Com; Dir 15 Plays Arts Clb Wash; Interviewer Drama Groups Wkly Radio Progs WASH-FM 2 Yrs; Judge No Va One Act Play Tournament & Montgomery Teen Contest & Forensic Contest, Montgomery Co HSs; Kensington Players; Players Intl; Brit Embassy Players; Brit Commonwealth Soc NAm; Pres Wash Theater Alliance; cp/Pi Beta Phi; Past Pres DC Alumnae Clb; hon/Pub'd Works; Commun Ldrs & Noteworthy Ams.

SPURLOCK, LASSENA CLARK oc/-Realtor; b/Dec 12; h/567 1st St NW, Hickory, NC 28601; ba/Hickory; m/Albert T; c/Clark Guin, Lassena Jan S Rowe; p/Edward Eugene and Lucinda Childers Clark (dec); ed/Att'd: UNC-G, UNC-CH; pa/Hickory Catawba Val Bd Realtors; cp/C of C; r/U Ch of Christ.

SRIVASTAVA, JAYA NIDHI oc/Professor; b/Jun 20, 1933; h/1318 Hillside Dr, Ft Collins, CO 80521; ba/Ft Collins; p/Mahabir Prasad Srivastava; Madhuri Srivastava (dec); ed/Proficiency in Germany 1953, Master's Deg 1954 Univ Lucknow; Statistician's Dipl Indian Statistical Inst (Calcutta) 1958; PhD Univ NC-CH; pa/Colo St Univ: Prof Dept Statistics, Dir Intl Confs in Combinatorical Math 1971, 78, Statistical Design & Linear Models 1973, Editor; Former or Current Mem Edit Bds Var Jours; Fdr & Editor Jour

Statistical Planning & Inference; Mem Num Profl Orgs; VP Forum for Interdisciplinary Math; Pres Indian Soc Agri Statistics; Invited Lectr Profl Orgs & Univs Worldwide; cp/IPA; hon/Pub'd Author; Recipient Prize (w K Kishen), Jour Indian Soc of Agri Statistics for Excell in Res; Fellow: Am Statistical Assn, Inst Math Statistics; Elected Mem, Intl Statistical Instn.

STAFFANSON, RUTH C oc/Office Manager; b/Jan 5, 1905; h/456 SE Roberts, Gresham, OR 97030; ba/Portland, OR; m/Joseph W (dec); p/Lewis William Dexfer and Sarah B Hickey McKeel (dec); pa/Barlow Tollgate Chapt Am Bus Woms Assn; r/Prot; hon/Dale Carnegie; W/W Wom; Others.

STAHL, DANIEL L oc/Sales Technician; Student; b/Oct 23, 1955; h/121 E Highland Ave, Ravenna, OH 44266; ba/Akron, OH; m/Roberta Huffman; p/Frederick L and Rita Bey Stahl, Piqua, OH; ed/Att'g Kent St Univ; Univ Cinc; cp/Chm Ohio Leag Col Repub Clbs; Orgr & Fdr Portage Co Repub Men's Clb 1979; Former NE Reg Coor Yg Ohioans for Pres Ford; Former Chm Kent St Univ Col Repub Clb; Former Cand: St Rep Ohio House Dist #62, Kent City Coun-at-Large; Former Adm Asst Kent Interhall Coun; Others; r/Immaculate Conception Rom Cath Ch; hon/Outstg Yg Men Am; Outstg Col Repub of Ohio; James Brown Meml S'ship Awd; Gilbert Shaw Sci Awd; MVP Cross Country, Piqua, Ohio.

STAKER, ERNEST VERNON oc/Agronomist; b/Jul 31, 1900; h/1634 Sylvester Rd, Lakeland, FL 33803; m/Frankie K; c/Francis Dale, James Douglas; p/James Benjamin and Elizabeth Fechser Staker (dec); ed/BA; MA; PhD; mil/Student Army Tng Corps 1918-19; pa/Asst Prof Agronomy Dept Cornell Univ

1929-45; Assoc Prof Agronomy Dept Univ Neb 1945-48, 1950-52; Agri Chemist & Agronomist USAID 1953-71 (Asia); cp/Former Secy Lakeland S Rotary Clb; r/Meth; hon/Travelling F'ship, Cornell Univ; USAID Meritorious Honor Awd for Outstg Ser in Afghanistan.

STALLINGS, R W oc/Clergyman; h/Rt 8, Box 86, Sumter, SC 29150; m/Mary Allen; c/1 Daugh, 1 Son; ed/AB Morris Col; Att'd: Union Theol Sem, Columbia Univ; pa/Pastor: Mt Zion Bapt Ch 1946-, New Bethel Bapt Ch 9 Yrs, Antioch Bapt Ch 2 Yrs, Taw Caw Bapt Ch 2 Yrs, Pearson Welcome Bapt Ch 15 Yrs; Pres Dist Conv 30 Yrs; Moderator Black River Assn; Morris Col: Field Dir, Trustee.

STALLWORTH, CHARLES D oc/Vista Worker; Retired Principal; b/Nov 22, 1906; h/PO Box 216, Chatom, AL 36518; m/Annie H; c/2 Chd; p/Lewis I Sr and Lydie E Stallworth; ed/BS, MEd; pa/Life Mem Ala Ed Assn; Past Pres: Wash Co & Monroe Co Tchrs Assns; Pres Dist IX PTA; ADC; MPC; r/Bapt; hon/Commun Ldrs & Noteworthy Ams.

STAMENKOVIC, HRISTA oc/City Official; b/Jul 17, 1917; h/4426 12th St, Riverside, CA 92501; ba/Riverside; m/Nada Petrovic; c/Suzanna Petrovic (Mrs Miodrag), Vera; p/David and Kata Bozilovic Stamendovic; ed/BS 1940, MS 1956 Belgrade Univ; pa/Engr Dept Public Works Bldg Div

R'side 1969-; Res Engr U Concrete Pipe Corp, Baldwin Park, Cal 1969; Res Engr Rockwin Prestressed Concrete Corp, Santa Fe Springs, Cal 1968; Am Pipe & Constrn Co, South Gate, Cal: Design, Quality Control Engr 1966-67, Lab Engr 1965-67; Other Former Positions; Session Chm Intl Conf Mech Behavor of Mats (Kyoto, Japan) 1971; Am Concrete Inst; Am Prestressed Concrete Inst; ASCE; Am Acad Mechanics; Intl Union Testing & Res Labs for Mats & Structures; Concrete Soc Gt Britain; hon/Inventor Method for Preven Fatigue Failure; Patentee in field; Contbr Articles to Profl Jours; W/W in World.

STAMM, ANN WAIDELICH oc/Systems Analyst Project Leader; b/Jan 31, 1947; h/10 Thornton Rd, Worcester, MA 01606; ba/Worcester; p/James R and Elizabeth M Waidelich, Naugatuck, CT; ed/BA Gettysburg Col; pa/Systems Analyst Proj Ldr Thom McAn: Data Processing Mgmt Assn; Assn Wom in Computing; Former Mem Pension Com St Mutual Life Assurance Co; cp/MENSA; Worcester Com on Fgn Relats; Former Sch Vol; Exec Com U Way Ctl Mass; Chperson Affirmative Action Compliance Com, U Way; Worcester Chapt NOW; Others; hon/Psi Chi; Pi Lambda Theta.

STANLEY, CHARLES RICHARD oc/-Retired Proofreader; b/Mar 28, 1902; h/-1408 Quarrier St, Charleston, WV 25301; p/-Charles E and Lennie J Stanley (dec); pa/-Proofreader *Charleston Daily Mail* approx 50 Yrs (Ret'd Feb 1977); cp/1st Dem Pres of Jr Repub (elected 1921); Old Lone Scouts of Am: Past Mem, Orgr Redbird Tribe & Pubr of Tribe Paper *The Kanawha Chief* (selected Best Tribe Paper by Lone Scout Mag); Orgr Girls' Clb serving as Ldr approx 30 Yrs; Pubr of Girls' Mag *The Girls' Friend* 15 Yrs, Pub'd as Ofcl Mag for Local & Corr Brs of Clb he Org'd, 1st as Rainbow Girls' Hiking & Camping Clb, later renamed Iris Girls' Hiking & Camping Clb; Prodr 2 Amateur Clb Movies for Girls' Clb; Home in Loudendale served as Playground & Playroom for Neighborhood Chd; Plans in progress for resumption of Girls' Clb & Mag incl'g Sum Camp & Dude Ranch; r/Presb Ch: Deacon Sev Yrs; Meth Ch: Exhorter Sev Yrs; Asst Supt Local Presb Mission; Tchr Jr Girls' Class in Local Mission 15 Yrs; Tchr Jr Girls' Classes Meth & Presb VBSs; Chd's Evangelist in Num Local Chs of Sev Denoms; hon/Commun Ldrs & Noteworthy Ams.

STANLEY, FRANCES KNIFFUN oc/-Concert Pianist; Educator; Lecturer; b/-Nov 9; h/Stanley Apts, Flossmoor Rd, Flossmoor, IL 60422; m/George Hamilton; c/Carmen S Eyramya; p/Benjamin Franklin and Eunice Besancon Kniffin (dec); ed/Cleve Inst Music; Columbia Univ; Boston Conservatory Music; Pvt Studies; pa/Own Radio Progs: Stas WHK, WADC, WFJC, WBBM, WMAQ; TV Stas WBKB, CBS; Adjudicator Var Socs & Contests; Pres & Tchr Stanley Music Studios; Bd Dirs & Past Pres: Chgo Artists' Assn, Music Study Clb Chgo, Chgo Hgts Symph Orch; Former VP Lyric Opera Chgo Suburban Chapt; Fac Mem: Nat Guild Piano Tchrs, Am Col Musicians; IPA; Intl Soc for Contemp Music; Soc Am Musicians; Chgo Symph Soc, Charter Mem; Chgo Wom's Musical Clb; Nat Fdn Music Clbs; Am Symph Orch Leag Inc; Piano Tchrs Cong NY Inc; cp/Chm Cerebral Palsy Fund Drives; Bd Dirs: Fam Ser & Mtl Hlth Ctr Aux, Jones Meml Commun Ctr; Flossmoor Wom's Clb; Book Clb; Garden Clb; LWV; Nat Fdn Repub Wom; Chautauqua (NY) Wom's Clb; Smithsonian Nat Assocs; r/Flossmoor Commun Ch; hon/Hon Life Mem: Zoltan Kodaly Acad & Inst, Music Study Clb Chgo, Chgo Hgts Symph Orch Bd Dirs; Congratulatory Lttr for Outstg Commun Ser, US Cong-man Derwinski; Cit for Outstg Humanitarian Ser, U Cerebral Palsy; Fellow, IBA; Designated "Ambassador of Good Will" to IBC Conf (London), by Chgo Mayor Michael A Bilandic; Biogl Listings.

STANLEY, GARLAND MAURICE oc/-Administrator; b/Dec 24, 1946; h/1907 71st St, Lubbock, TX 79413; ba/Lubbock; m/-Maurice Suzette; c/Jared Maurice; p/Kermit

Garland and Linda Lucille Stanley, Lubbock; ed/BA Tex Tech Univ 1970; MPA N Tex St Univ 1976; mil/AUS 902d Mil Intell Gp 1971-74; pa/Dir Spec Projs MBFA Foun; Est'g Halfway Houses for Mtly Retard; Pres Local Chapt Tex Public Employees Assn; cp/Yg Dems; JCs; r/1st Christian; hon/Commend Medal, AUS.

STANLEY, KERMIT RAY oc/Mailer; b/Aug 25, 1950; h/4115 27th, Lubbock, TX 79410; ba/Lubbock; m/Ava Renee; p/Kermit Garland and Linda Lucille, Lubbock; pa/Mailer Lubbock-Avalanch Jour; r/1st Christian.

STANLEY, PAUL L oc/Marriage & Family Counselor; b/Apr 2, 1925; h/9119 Wolverton, Ventura, CA 93003; ba/Oxnard, CA; m/Lois; c/Mark A, Phillip A; p/L G Stanley Sr (dec); Bertha Stanley, Clifton Forge, VA; ed/AB Marshall Univ; BD SWn Bapt Theol Sem; MA Univ No Colo; PhD Cal Grad Sch Theol; mil/Chaplain, Ret'd Lt Col; pa/Clin Mem AAMFT; NAFL; AASECT; APGA; CAPS; cp/Mason; Shriners; Repub; r/So Bapt; hon/W/W in W.

STAPLETON, KATHY J oc/Teacher; b/Sept 24, 1951; h/Rt 4, Box 552, Grayson, KY 41143; p/Joe E Stapleton, Grayson;

Norma Jean Dawson Stapleton, Grayson; ed/BA 1973, MA 1975 Morehead St Univ; pa/NEA; KEA; APGA; ACES; ASCA; KPGA; KSCA; AVA; ASCD; hon/W/W SW; Personalities of S; DIB; Notable Ams.

STARBARD, BARBARA EARL oc/Shoe Manufacturer; b/Oct 19, 1913; h/222 E Water St, Rockland, MA 02370; ba/Rockland; p/Ralph B Starbard, Rockland; Edna E Starbard (dec); ed/BS 1977, BS 1978, MA 1979 NWn Col; mil/AUS, WAAC, WAC 1943-46; pa/Shoe Mfr E T Wright; Brotherhood of Shoe & Allied Crafts, Brockton, Mass; cp/OES; Order of White Shrine of Jerusalem; Repub; r/U Ch of Christ, Rockland; hon/WAAC Ribbon; Good Conduct Medal; Am Theater Medal; Victory Medal.

STARNES, PAUL M oc/Educator; Legislator; b/Dec 31, 1934; h/4004 Patton Dr, Chattanooga, TX 37412; ba/Chatta; m/Mary Grace Feezell; p/James Albert and Helen H Starnes, Chatta; p/BA Tenn Wesleyan Col 1957; MEd Univ Chatta 1961; pa/Hamilton Co Dept Ed, Chatta: Asst to Supt & Bd Info Ofcr 1977-, Commun Relats Ofcr 1974-77, Coor Spec Projs 1969-71; Asst Prin E Ridge Jr HS, Chatta 1971-74; Dean Students Hiwassee Col, Madisonville, Tenn 1964-69; Other Former Positions; Chm Govt Liason Com Lookout Pers Guid Assn 1977-78; Pres: Tenn Sch Public Relats Assn 1977-78, E Tenn Ed Assn 1976-77; Hamilton Co Ed Assn; Lookout Schoolmasters; NEA; Nat Assn Sec'dy Sch Prins; Phi Delta Kappa; Chatta Chapt Public Relats Soc Am; Tenn Assn Sch Admrs; Tenn Ed Assn; Tenn Pers Guid Assn; Others; cp/Former Mem Allocations Panel UF Gtr Chatta Area; Former Leg Chm Hamilton Co Coun PTA; Appalachian Reg Arthritis Ctr Foun: Past Pres, Former Bd Dirs; Former Mem: Chatta CAMPS Exec Com, Child Devel Assn Tenn, Tenn Assn Chd Under Six, Chatta Chapt IRA, Num Others; BSA: Former Coun Chm, Ticket Com, Scout Exposition, Other Couns & Coms; Kiwanis Intl: Former Ky-Tenn Dist Chm Bldr Clbs, Former Ky-Tenn Dist Coor Yth Sers, Former Lt Gov Div III, Others;

Mem 88th, 89, 90th Gen Assemblies, Tenn St Ho of Reps; r/McFarland U Meth Ch: Mem, Tchr Yg Adults Ch Sch Class, Tchr HS Jrs & Sr Ch Sch Class, Pastor-Parish Com, Lay Ldr, Lay Del to Annual Conf, Other Activs; hon/East Ridge Outstg Citizen Awd; Outstg Man of Yr, Monroe Co 1963; JCs: Most Outstg Yg Men E Ridge, Tenn's Most Outstg Yg Tchr, E Ridge Most Outstg Tchr; Biogl Listings.

STARNES, WILLIAM HERBERT oc/Research Chemist; b/Dec 2, 1934; h/123-E Jerome St, Roselle Park, NJ 07204; ba/Murray Hill, NJ; p/W H Starnes Sr (dec); Edna O Starnes, Gate City, VA; ed/BS w hons Va Polytech Inst 1955; PhD Ga Inst Technol 1960; pa/Mem Tech Staff Bell Telephone Labs, Murray Hill 1973-; Res Assoc & Instr Dept Chem Univ Tex-A 1971-73; Baytown Res & Devel Div, Esso Res & Engrg Co, Baytown, Tex: Res Assoc 1967-71, Res Specialist 1965-67, Sr Res Chemist 1962-65, Sect Hd

1964, Res Chemist 1960-62; Am Chem Soc: Bd Dirs SEn Tex Sect 1970, Presiding Ofcr Nat & Reg Meetings, Local Sect Com Chm, Spkrs Bur, Div Polymer Chem 1976-; Vis Scist Tex Acad Scis 1964-67; hon/Fellow, AAAS; Life Fellow, Am Inst Chemists; Profl Progress Awd, Soc Profl Chemists & Engrs, Baytown; M A Ferst Doct Res Awd, Sigma Xi, Ga Inst Technol Chapt; Phi Lambda Upsilon; Phi Kappa Phi; Sigma Xi; NSF Predoct Fellow; USPHS Fellow; Sev Scholastic Awds; Contbr Articles to Sci Jours & Books; Biogl Listings.

STATMAN, JAN B oc/Artist; Art Instructor; Writer; h/27 Country Pl, Longview, TX 75601; m/Max; c/Charles-Barry, Louis Craig, Sherry-Michelle; p/Saul and Sylvia Rose Berliner, Dallas, TX; ed/BA Hunter Col; pa/Works Owned by Museums in Italy & Spain; Rep'd in Collections Across USA, Israel & Iran; Columnist: Longview News 1965-70, Longview Post 1970-77; cp/Past VP Longview LWV; r/Jewish; hon/Outstg Yg Wom Am, Fuller & Dees; Wom of Achmt, Dist 9 Tex Press Wom.

STATON, KNOFEL L oc/Professor; Author; b/Jun 8, 1934; h/Rt 1, Box 308, Joplin, MO 64801; ba/Joplin; m/Julia; c/Randall, Rena, Rhonda, Rachael; p/Glen Staton (dec); Ethel Schofield, Fairfield, IL; ed/BA; MDiv; mil/USAF; pa/Min; Prof; Soc Biblical Lit; Evang Theol Soc; Author 16

Books; cp/Exec Com PTA; Exec Com NALL; Chaplaincy Endorsemt Comm; Bd Advrs Emmanuel Sch Rel; Nat Textbook Com; r/Christian Ch; hon/Restoration Awd, DIB; Men of Achmt; W/W in Rel.

STAUDER, PAUL WENZEL oc/Roman Catholic Priest; School & Church Photographer; TV Film Producer; b/Apr 12, 1921; h/Old St Henrys Cath Rectory, IL 62201; ba/E St Louis, IL; p/Raymond L Stauder (dec); Elizabeth H Bachinger (dec); ed/BA; pa/Pastor & Trustee Old St Henrys Rom Cath Ch; Photog So Ill Cath Schs & Chs; Prodr 3 TV Films: Three Crosses on the Mohawk, The US NW Legacy, You Are a Priest Forever; Pastor: Immaculate

Conception Parish (Bridgeport) 1969-71, St Anthonys Parish (Lively Grove, Ill) 1963-69, Others; Am Fdn TV & Radio Artists Union, St Louis; Nat Acad TV Arts & Scis, St Louis; Free-lance Photo, Diocese of Belleville (Ill); Other Profl Activs; r/Rom Cath; hon/Spec Gold Medal of St Peter & Paul, Pope Paul VI; Cert of Merit for Dist'd Ser, IBC; Notable Ams; W/W in Rel; DIB; Men of Achmt.

STAUFFACHER, DEAN WORTHING oc/Sales Executive; b/Jan 11, 1910; h/177 Braybrook Dr SE, Cedar Rapids, IA 52403; ba/Cedar Rapids; m/Barbara Bloomhall; c/Stevan C, Scott Marr; p/Charles Henry and Madge Ruth Worthing Stauffacher (dec); ed/BA Case Wn Resv Univ 1933; JD Univ Ia Col Law 1934; mil/AUS 1943-46, S Pacific Theatre; Capt CMP; 4 Battle Stars; AUS Commend Medal; Philippine Mil Merit Medal;

pa/Diamond V Mills Inc: Pres 1974-, Sales Mgr 1950-, VP, Dir & Secy 1947, Salesman 1946; Nat Feed Ingredients Assn: Mem 1949-79, Dir 1954-68, Pres 1960-61; Cedar Rapids & US Cs of C; Repub Party; Rotary Intl; Masonic Lodge; Cedar Rapids CC; r/U Meth Ch; hon/Nat Feed Ingredients Assn: Dist'd Ser Awd, Spec Ser Awd.

STAVE, BRUCE MARTIN oc/Professor; b/May 17, 1937; h/200 Broad Way, Coventry, CT 06238; ba/Storrs, CT; m/Sondra Astor; c/Channing M L; p/Bernard R Stave, New York, NY; Mildred S Stave (dec); ed/AB 1959, MA 1961 Columbia Univ;

PhD Univ Pittsburgh 1966; pa/Prof Hist Univ Conn; Am Hist Assn; Org Am Histns; New England Hist Assn; Oral Hist Assn; New Eng Assn Oral Hist, Exec Bd 1978-80; Imm Hist Soc; Social Sci Hist Soc; cp/Bd Dirs Conn Civil Liberties Union; Secy-Treas NEn Conn CLU; Former Mem Coventry Sewer Auth; hon/Author Books incl'g: *The Making of Urban Hist* 1977, *Socialism & The Cities* 1975, *The Discontented Soc* 1972, *Urban Bosses, Reformers & Progressive Rerormers* 1972, *The New Deal & The Last Hurrah* 1970; Fulbright Prof, New Zealand, Australia, Philippines 1977, India 1968-69; Nat Endowmt for Humanities Fellow; Harvey Kantor Meml Awd for Significant Work in Oral Hist.

STEELE, JAMES E oc/Supervisor of Music; h/1001 Gates Ave, Apt 7B, Norfolk, VA 23507; p/James Edward and Blanche M Steele; ed/BS Col Wm & Mary 1961; MEd Temple Univ 1972; EdD Nova Univ 1976; Addit Studies: Mozarteum Acad Music (Salzburg, Austria), Univ London (England), Reid Sch Music of Univ Edinburgh (Scotland), Col Preceptors (London); Further Studies; pa/Piccoloist Norfolk Symph Orch 1951-73; Min Music Calvin Presb Ch, Norfolk 1962-; Hampton City Schs: Dir Choral Music 1960-65, Supvr Music Ed 1965-; Dir Hampton All-City Fest Music 1970-; Guest Flute Soloist for Music Tchrs of Gt Britain 1962; Nat, Va & Hampton Ed Assns; Hampton Instrnl Supvrs Assn; Tidewater Reg Supvrs; Va Assn Music Ed Admrs; Va Music Edrs Assn; MENC; Va Choral Dirs; Va Band & Orch Dirs Assn; Va String Tchrs Assn; Elem Sect Va Music Edrs Assn; Local 125 Am Fdn Musicians; IRA: Hampton Assn for Arts & Humanities; hon/Recipient Eagle, Ranger, Silver, Gold & Country & Order of Arrow Awds, BSA; Cert of Commend for Decade of Cult Sers to Peninsula Commun; Pub'd Works; Biogl Listings.

STEELE, ROBERT MILLER oc/Chemist; Teacher; X-Ray Diffraction Analyst; b/Apr 8, 1921; h/1517 Ebenezer Rd, Knoxville, TN 37922; m/Lou P; c/Kenneth M, Luanne S; p/Kenneth E Steele (dec); Ruth M Steele, Fresno, CA; ed/BS; pa/Ret'd; Assoc'd w Union Carbide Corp, Nuclear Div, Oak Ridge Nat Lab, Oak Ridge, Tenn 1946-, Metallurgist in X-Ray Diffraction Group of Metals & Ceramics Div 1950-; Chemist & Physicist X-Ray Diffraction Group Gaseous Diffusion Plant 1946-50; Other Former Positions; Am Chem Soc; AAAS; Am Crystallograpic Assn; cp/Former BSA Scoutmaster; r/Epis.

STEHLING, KURT RICHARD oc/Physicist; b/Sept 19, 1919; h/3310 Coquelin Terr, Chevy Chase, MD 20015; ba/Rockville, MD; m/Helen N Bauer; c/Wendy-Joan, Andrew A; p/William and Erna Stehling (dec); ed/BA; MA; ScD; mil/Canadian Armoured Corps 1942-46; pa/Chief Scist NOAA; Deep Ocean Cosmic Ray Studies; Sci Ballooning; cp/Citizen's Assn; Zoning Com; Others; r/Congreg; hon/Galbraith Awd; Montgolfier Awd; Others.

STEIN, DAVID ERIC oc/Military Captain; Physicist; b/Jan 15, 1950; h/4331 S Bend Cir E, Jacksonville, FL 32207; ba/Cecil Field NAS, Jacksonville; ed/BS w high hons 1971, MS 1977 Univ Fla; Doct Cand; mil/AUS Comm'd 1971, Active Duty 1977-, Interser Transfer to USAF 1979-, Current Capt, Res & Devel; Physics Instr, Ford Fellow, Res Asst 1971-76; Am Phy Soc; Am Assn Physics Tchrs; AAAS; AF Assn; IPA; Soc Am Mil Engrs; cp/-Smithsonian Assocs; r/Nondenom; hon/-Phi Beta Kappa; Omicron Delta Kappa; Phi Kappa Phi; Fla Blue Key; Sigma Pi Sigma.

STEIN, HILTON LARRY oc/Lawyer; Educator; b/May 5, 1946; h/Rt 1, Box 395, Hamburg, NJ; ba/Riverdale, NJ; c/Seth, Stephanie; p/Sid Stein, Parsippany, NJ; Shirley Stein (dec); ed/BA 1969, JD Univ Akron 1972; pa/Staff Mem, *Akron Law Review* 1970-72; Guest Lectr, Fairleigh Dickinson Univ 1973-75; NJ Bar Assn; Am Trial Lwyrs Assn; Am Bar Assn; Prosecutor

for Twps of Pequannock 1975-, West Milford 1975-, Borough of Riverdale 1976-; cp/Planning Res Technician, Dist 4, Comprehensive Law Enforcement Plan; Former Editor-in-Chief, *Arete;* Past Mem Bd Trustees, Jersey Battered Wives Assn; r/Jewish; hon/W/W Am Law; Commun Ldrs & Noteworthy Ams.

STEINBERG, DORA ELLEN oc/Library Consultant; Retired Teacher; b/Mar 31, 1906; h/176, Newburg, MO 65550; m/Roy D; c/David Lee; p/John Jacob and Dora Delashmit Brown (dec); ed/BS; MS (Ed);

MSLS; pa/Tchr, Libn, Conslt, Ency Brit Assoc; St & Nat Sch & Lib Assns; r/So Bapt; hon/R R Bowker's Dir; Other Biogl Listings.

STEINBURG, CHARLES LOUIS oc/-Professor; Artist; b/May 23, 1930; h/218 Cambridge Dr, Normal, IL 61761; ba/Normal; m/Joan Davis; c/Richard Louis, Jennifer Lynn; p/Paul L Steinburg (dec); Ann Dobbs Steinburg; ed/BS, MS, Addit Grad Work; mil/USN; pa/Prof Art Ill St Univ; Num Exhbns; One-Man Shows & Exhibits incl: Bicent Art Ctr & Mus (Paris, Ill) 1978, Ill St Bk (Normal, Ill) 1976, Ill St Univ Hovey Hall

Adm Bldg 1975, Unitarian Ch (Bloomington, Ill) 1975; Other Exhbns incl: McLean Co Arts Coun Holiday Exhibit (B'ton) 1978, 79, Peoria (Ill) Art Fest 1978, Galex '78, Galesburg Civic Art Ctr (G'burg, Ill) 1978, Num Others Through 1951; r/Presb; hon/Hon Mention: Peoria Art Fest 1978, McLean Co (B'ton) Bicent Art Exhbn 1976, Ill St Fair Profl Art Exhibit (Springfield, Ill) 1972; Other Art Awds.

STEINE, LYON oc/Medical Director; b/Feb 3, 1903; h/1585 Bainbridge Ln, Roswell, GA 30075; ba/Atlanta, GA; m/Hazel; c/Janet Petrecca, Ellen Milner, Michael, Lynette; p/Maurice Bertie and Tillie Lesser Steine (dec); ed/BS; MD; CM; mil/AUS 1942-45, Capt Med Corps; ETO Ward Ofcr; Others; pa/Pvt Solo Gen Pract Val Stream, Long Isl, NY 1932-73; Med Dir Hyland Donor Ctr, Atlanta Div Baxter-Travenol 1973-; Former Mem Adv Coun to NY Senate Com on Hlth; Former Staff Mem: Franklin Gen Hosp (Val Stream), Doctors Hosp (Freeport), S Nassau Communs Hosp (Oceanside); Fellow Royal Soc Hlth; Charter Fellow: Am Acad Fam Phys, Nassau Acad Med; NY St Med Soc; Nassau Co Med Soc; NY St & Nassau Co Acad Fam Phys; Nassau Phys Guild; Former Mem Var Profl Orgs; cp/Am Security Coun; hon/Alpha Omega Alpha; Winner M&R Awd; Guest Spkr Induction Dinner, Alpha Epsilon Delta Nat Preclin Hon Sor, NY Epsilon Chapt 1964; Selected as Rep Am Fam Doct 1971, Guid

Assocs, Pleasantville (NY), Ednl Div of Assoc'd Press; Contbr Num Papers to Med Lit.

STEINER, NANCY MILLER oc/Professor; b/Jun 6, 1930; h/2901 S Fillmore Way, Denver, CO 80210; ba/Denver; m/Jay A; c/Sally R, Susan J, Robert L; p/Philip and Ruchiel S Miller (dec); ed/BA 1951, MA 1967 Univ Denver; PhD Univ Colo 1977; pa/Metro St Col: Instr 1969, Asst Prof 1971, Assoc Prof 1978, Fac Senate, Treas Fac Assn; Var Profl

Orgs; cp/Anti-Defamation Leag; B'nai B'rith Chperson Denver Bd; Exec Com Nat Commun Ser Comm; Cath-Jewish Relationships Com; Gov's Appt to Colo Career Info Ser; Bd Dirs Allied Jewish Fdn; r/Jewish; Nom'g Com Congreg Emanuel; hon/Kappa Delta Pi; Cert of Awd, Allied Jewish Fdn; Personalities W&MW.

STENNIS, EARLENE JANETTE oc/-Teacher; b/Jun 16, 1934; h/1018 W Third Ave, Pine Bluff, AR 71601; c/Rudolph Jr, Anita, Cynthia; p/Fred and Classie Chislomn Griffith, Cynthia; AR; ed/BA Univ Ark-PB; pa/Polit Sci Tchr Watson Chapel HS, Pine Bluff; NEA; Ark, Watson Chapel Ed Assns; Former Mem Pine Bluff HS Ecs Adv Coun; Former Feature Writer *Ark Dispatch;* cp/Bd Dirs LWV; Past Pres Alpha Upsilon Chapt Iota Phi Lambda; Bd Mem Ednl Talent Search

Prog Univ Ark-PB; VP Helping Hand; Past Secy Pine Bluff Better Govt Assn; Jefferson Co Chapt ARC; Offender Adjustmt Resources Inc; Nat Fam Opinion Poll Panel; Vol Col Recruiter; Jefferson Co ARC Disaster Actions Team; r/1st Missionary Bapt Ch: Mem; hon/Outstg Jefferson Co Citizen; U Col Wom Outstg Black Wom Pub; Recipient Awds, ARC; Watson Chapel HS: Outstg Tchr, Tchr of Month (Apr 1974); Citizen for a Day, Radio Sta KOTN (Apr 26, 1978, Apr 12, 1974 & Jun 28, 1972); Others.

STENNIS, JOHN CORNELIUS oc/United States Congressman; b/Aug 3, 1901; h/DeKalb, MS 39328; ba/Room 205 Russell Senate Ofc Bldg, Washington, DC 20510; m/Coy; c/Margaret J S Womble, John Hampton; p/Hampton Howell and Cornelia Adams Stennis (dec); ed/BS Miss St Univ 1923; LLB Univ Va Law Sch 1928; LLD: Millsaps Col 1957, Univ Wyo 1962, Miss Col 1969, Belhaven Col 1972; pa/ABA, Miss Bar Assn; Elected Dist Prosecuting Atty, 16th Judicial Dist 1931, 35; Appt'd Circuit Judge 1937, Elected 1938, 42, 46; Phi Beta Kappa; Phi Alpha Delta; Alpha Chi Rho; cp/Elected US Senator 1947, 52, 58, 64, 70, 76; Chm Armed Sers Com, Mem Appropriations Com;

Mason; Lion; Former Mem Miss Ho of Reps; r/Presb.

STERN, AARON oc/Author; Educator; Lecturer; b/May 20, 1918; h/2485 NE 214 St, North Miami Beach, FL 33180; m/Bella; c/David, Edith; p/David and Helen Stern

(dec); ed/Univ Warsaw; Brooklyn Col; Columbia Univ; pa/Univ Lectures, Res; HEW Conslt; hon/Resolutions: City of Miami, Fla St Leg, Dade Co; Nom'd for Pulitzer Prize, Nobel Prize.

STERN, DORIS L oc/Attorney; Executive; ba/9107 Wilshire Blvd, Beverly Hills, CA 90210; c/Nancy, Elizabeth; p/Sam Lisitz, Long Beach, CA; Anna Shaffer Lisitz (dec); pa/Atty; VP Assoc Coun Gibraltar Savs & Ln Assn, Beverly Hills.

STERN, ELLEN oc/Occupational Therapist; Assistant Professor; b/Sept 6, 1948; h/1017 Stevens Creek Rd, J-196, Augusta, GA 30907; ba/Augusta; p/Hirsh and Evelyne Stern, Brooklyn, NY; ed/BS 1970; MHE 1978; pa/Asst Prof Med Col Ga; Am Occupl Therapy Assn; DCOTA; r/Jewish; hon/Alpha Eta, Grad Mem 1977.

STEVENS, GENEVIEVE JOHNSON oc/Teacher; b/May 10, 1934; h/6315 S Mayfield Ln, Mechanicsville, VA 23111; ba/Richmond; VA; m/Robert L Jr; c/Myra Gail, Tamara Lynn, Lori Sue; p/Ernest L and Ella Ellis Johnson, Bakersville, NC; ed/BS 1956, MA 1958 Wn Carolina Univ; Addit Studies; pa/Tchr Talented & Gifted Henrico Co Schs; Henrico Ed Assn; Va Ed Assn; NEA; Va Assn for Ed of Gifted; cp/Chickahominy Wom's Clb, Hlth & Mtl Hlth Ch; r/Presb: Yth Ldr, hon/Tchr of Yr 1978, Henrico Co.

STEVENS, MARY COGGIN oc/Music Teacher; b/Jul 22, 1918; h/Box 97, Front St, Lovingston, VA 22949; ba/Same; m/William Terry Jr; c/Debbie Truett Speilman; p/Carl Numa Coggin (dec); Swanna Ethel Lowclermilk Coggin; ed/BS Appalachian St Tchrs Col; pa/Eng & Hist Tchr, Meadows of

Dan, Va 1943; Vis Tchr Nelson Co 1948; 3rd Grade Tchr Fleetwood Sch, Nelson Co 1955; Spec Ed Tchr, Lynchburg, Va 1961-63; Piano Tchr, Meadow of Dan 1943; Piano Tchr, M of Dan & L'ton 1948, L'ton 1949-79; BPW Clb 1964-79; Pres Nelson BPW Clb 1979; r/St Stephens Bapt Ch: Choir Dir 1965-76, Writer & Dir Ch Christmas Plays.

STEVENS, MYRTLE CHANDLER oc/-Educator; b/Mar 16, 1925; h/Rt 1, Gracemont, OK 73042; m/Garland; c/2 Chd; p/-William and Molissie Chandler; ed/BS w hons

Okla Col for Wom 1959; MS Okla Univ 1966; Grad Work SWn Okla St Univ, Ctl St Univ, Tex Woms Univ; pa/Voc Home Ecs Tchr: Gracemont 1959-64, Ninnekah 1964-66, Riverside Boarding Sch, Anadarko 1966-67, Eakly 1967-79; Sponsor: for FHA, Yg Homemakers Okla, Pep Clb, Sr Class, Yth for Christ, 4-H Clb, Yrbook; Mem Com Developing Home Ecs Curric for Okla; Sub-Dist Advr FHA; Tchr Cnslr; Former St Pres: Yg Homemakers Okla, Future Homemakers Okla; Secy Okla Home Ecs Assn; Secy Home Ecs Div OHEA; Del to AVA; USAO Alumni Assn; SWn Okla St Univ Eval Team; NEA; Okla Voc Assn; Am Voc Assn; Beta Beta Conclave-Kappa Kappa Iota; Caddo Co Ed Assn; Okla Ed Assn; Okla & Am Home Ecs Assn; AAUW; Alpha Lambda Delta; Pi Gamma Mu; Others; r/Assembly of God Ch: Christ Ambassador Pres, SS Tchr; hon/Cert for Outstg Ser to Red Cross; Caddo Co Tchr of Yr 1972; Okla Home Ecs Tchr of Yr 1976; Pub'd Works; Biogl Listings.

STEVENSON, HENRY MILLER oc/-Research Fellow; Professor Emeritus; b/Feb 25, 1914; h/905 Briarcliffe Rd, Tallahassee, FL 32308; ba/Tallahassee; m/Rosa Belle Ard; c/Nell Sanders, Ernest, Henry Jr, James; p/Henry Munn and Mayme Gene Fuller Stevenson (dec); ed/AB; MS; PhD; pa/Res Fellow Ornithol Tall Timbers Res Sta; Prof Emeritus Fla St Univ; Am Ornithologists' Union; Wilson & Ga Ornithol Socs; Charter Mem: Ala & Fla Ornithol Socs; Former Mem Other Biol & Ornithol Socs; Editor: Fla Field Naturalist 1973-75, Audubon Field Notes (Fla Reg) 1953-; Reviewer Occasional Books on Birds; Spkr Profl Meetings; r/Meth; hon/Pub'd Author; Res Grants: Fla St Univ, USPHS; Am Men of Sci; DIB; Elective Mem, Am Ornith Union.

STEWARD, GEORGE EDMOND oc/Minister; b/Jul 29, 1906; h/940 E Ramsey, Ft Worth, TX 76104; ba/Ft Worth; m/Ella; c/Ruby May Flowers; p/George Edmond and Annie Lane Steward (dec); pa/Min Eastland St Ch of Christ 24 Yrs; SWn Christian Col, Terrell, Tex: Fdr, Bd Trustees, Pres Living Endowmt, Tchr Wkshop for Mins; Evangelist Radio Prog "The Voice of Truth" 24 Yrs; r/Ch of Christ; hon/EFWI Mins' Union Achmt Awd; Recog Awd, SWn Christian Col; Recog Trophy, Lake Como Ch of Christ; Author Book Our Pulpit; Author Record of Sermons.

STEWART, ARTHUR VAN oc/Dentist; Educator; Administrator; Researcher; b/Jul 25, 1938; h/6101 Tidewater Ct, Prospect, KY 40059; ba/Louisville, KY; m/Jacqueline Elaine Fischer; c/Mark Van, Jeffery Fischer, Laura Kristin; p/Arthur Sharpe Stewart, Clymer, PA; Doris Mildred Simpson (dec); ed/BS; MEd; DMD; PhD; pa/Univ L'ville Sch Dentistry: Asst Dean, Prof; cp/Cub Scout Pack Master; hon/Omicron Kappa Upsilon; Kappa Kappa Psi; Fellow, Am Col Dentists; Dean's Awd; Dist'd Alumni Awd.

STEWART, LOUIS ALVIN oc/Court Superintendent; b/Feb 28, 1928; h/2515 S Congress Ave, Austin, TX 78704; ba/Same; m/Della Polly Laqua; c/Debra Gayle, Louis Jr; p/George Stewart (dec); Albina Stewart, Flatonia, TX; ed/BA Tex A&M Univ; MA Sam Houston St Univ; mil/USAF; pa/Supt Travis Co Juv Ct; Chm Tex Inst on Chd & Yth; Pres Tex Juv Detention Assn; cp/Pres St Ignatius & Holy Cross HS; r/Cath.

STEWART, MARY ESTELLA SLEDD oc/Instructor; Assistant Professor; b/Jun 4, 1915; h/PO Box 418, Gallatin, TN 37066; ba/Gallatin; m/R A (dec); c/Roy Edward; p/William C and Lydia Mae Skinner Sledd; ed/AB 1935, MA Fisk Univ; EdS Geo Peabody Col; Doct Prog; pa/Vol St Commun Col: Instr, Asst Prof Eng Emeritus, Afro-Am Lit; Life Mem: NEA, Phi Delta Kappa; TEA; NRTA; NCTE; CLA; AAUW; AAUP; SEn Juris Hist Soc; cp/Gallatin C of C; NAACP; Sumner Co Minority Bicent Prog; r/Key-Stewart U Meth Ch: UMW, Moderator Christian Social Involvemt Tenn Conf; hon/Ky Col; Tenn Col; Outstg Cit, Phi Delta Kappa; Mary Stewart Day, Mary E Stewart Chapt OES; AKA Awds.

STEWART, ORA PATE oc/Author; Poet; Lecturer; Composer; b/Aug 23, 1910; h/383 E, 1980 N, Provo, UT 84601; m/Robert W; c/Sharon S Nielson, Robert W Jr, Janet S Geary, Allen Paul, David Grant, Glenda (dec), Wendell J; p/Ezra G and Ada Sharp Pate (dec); ed/Att'd: Brigham Yg Univ, Univ Utah; pa/Author 24 Pub'd Books, 34 Pub'd Songs; Books incl: Pages From the Book of Eve, I Talk About My Children, Brown Leaves Turning, Tender Apples, The Singing Kings, This Is the Land, Mopey the Mop, Gleanings, Others; Tchr Poetry & Creative Writing; Past Pres NLAPW, Hollywood Br; Bd Dirs Composers Guild; ASCAP; NLAPW; Past Pres: Leag Utah Writers (Utah Val), Utah Poets (Provo Chapt); Prog Lectr w Nat Artist & Lecture Ser 1953-; Other Profl Activs; cp/Hon Life Mem, Cal St PTA; Past Pres Mutual Improvemt Assn, Cal; r/LDS; hon/Dist'd Ser Awd, BYU Alumni; Hon DHL, Univ Free Asia; Hon DLitt World Univ Roundtable; World Laureate of Perf'g Arts w Golden Laurel Crown 1977; Gold Medal, Intl Poetry.

STEWART, ORO ROZELLA oc/Photographer; Businesswoman; b/Jul 8, 1917; h/1008 A St, Anchorage, AK 99501; ba/Anchorage; m/Ivan; p/Joseph Allen and Oro Rozella Overholtzer Holaday (dec); ed/BE Oreg St Col; pa/Owner Photo Store & Jade Mine; Instr TV Sch Photo; Master Photo Dealers Assn; Profl Photogs Alaska; cp/Pres Chugach Gem & Mineral Soc; Mem Tourist Com C of C; Alaska Miners Assn; Alaska Geol Soc; Tropical Fish Clb; Scottish Clb; Zonta; hon/Recipient Awds, Gem & Mineral Shows; Rep'd "Wom at Work" for Alaska; Var Photo Awds.

STICKNEY, KENNETH ARTHUR oc/Retired Minister; b/Mar 20, 1914; h/PO Box 437B, Holland, MI 49423; m/Marie Sietsema; c/Carol Marie, Arthur James II, Judith Maatman (Mrs Jerry); p/Arthur James and Cora Jane Tindall Stickney (dec); ed/Dipl Moody Bible Inst; AB Hope Col 1946; BD Alfred Univ Sch Theol 1949; Att'd New Brunswick Theol Sem 1946-48; mil/AUS 1952-53 (Korean Conflict) Chaplain; Chaplain CAP; pa/Pastor 1947-, incl'g: Piscataway Seventh Day Bapt Ch, New Market, NJ 1947-50, Rockville Seventh Day Bapt & I H Pikinton Seventh Day Bapt (RI) 1950-52, South Shore Bapt Ch, Holland 1962-66; Conducts Sers in Rest Homes, Jails, Rescue Missions; Assists at Holland City Mission; cp/Nat Assn Retard Citizens; Ottawa Co Assn Retard Citizens; AARP; Salvation Army; Friends Unlimited, Muskegon, Mich; r/Calvary Bapt Ch, Holland: Mem; hon/W/W in Rel; DIB; Personalities of W&MW; Men of Achmt.

STILLMAN, ALEXANDER oc/Finance Executive; b/Sept 29, 1911; h/Box 254, Penny Rd, Barrington, IL 60010; ba/B'ton; m/(dec); c/Peter; p/James Alexander Stillman; Anne Urquhart Potter; ed/AB, Masters, PhD Harvard; Art Inst Chgo; mil/USN Pilot; pa/Trusts (Banks); Pediatrician; r/Epis; hon/Rhodes Scholar; Others.

STILWELL, WILLIAM EARLE III oc/Psychologist; Educator; b/Jul 28, 1936; h/1919 Williamsburg Rd, Lexington, KY 40504; ba/L'ton; m/Doris N; c/Jane Belen, William E IV; p/William E Stilwell Jr (dec); Frances H Stilwell, Cincinnati, OH; ed/AB Dartmouth 1958; MS San Jose 1966; PhD Stanford 1969; mil/USNR-R Cmdr; pa/Edr Dept Ednl Psychol Col Ed Univ Ky-L'ton; AERA; APA; APGA; cp/Stanford Alumni Assn; Resv Ofcrs Assn; r/Epis; hon/Phi Delta Kappa; Psi Chi.

STIMM, TRUDY W oc/Executive; b/Sept 6, 1937; h/15 E 36 St, New York, NY 10016; ba/NYC; p/Fritz Hermann and Emma Hilda Bantle Stimm; ed/Att'd Col for Bus & Adm, Stuttgart, Univ Cal-Berkeley Ext; pa/Herder & Herder Inc, NYC: Controller 1968-72, Mgr Fgn Lang Dept, Specialist Fgn Lang Book Imports 1961-; Controller & Treas Stein &

Day Inc, NYC 1972-73; VP & Controller Seabury Press Inc, NYC 1973-; r/Cath; hon/Biogl Listings.

STIMSON, RICHARD ALDEN oc/-Assistant Professor; Management Consultant; b/Jan 18, 1923; h/900 Sixth St, High Point, NC 27262; ba/High Point; m/Joan D; c/Richard E F; p/Frank Giles Stimson (dec); Susie Alden Brown Stimson, High Point; ed/BA Yale 1943; MSM Fla Intl Univ 1976; mil/AGC-USAR Maj (Ret'd); Sgt in Europe during WWII; pa/Asst Prof E N Phillips Sch Bus Adm High Point Col; Mgmt Conslt to Corps; AAUP; cp/Former VP Dist 13 Bd Ed, Valley Stream, NY; r/Unitarian; hon/Silver Anvil; Vanguard Awd; Gold Image Awd; Dean's List & Orations, Yale.

STOCK, MARY-JULE SCHRAUFNAGEL oc/Counselor, Clinical Psychologist; b/Dec 14, 1927; h/12856 Big Bend Blvd, Kirkwood, MO 63122; ba/St Louis, MO; m/Bernard Joseph; p/Michael and Mary Catherine Ruby Schraufnagel (dec); ed/BA Col St Scholastica 1959; MEd Xavier Univ 1965; PhD St Louis

Univ 1969; pa/Clin Psychologist VA Hosp, St Louis 1971-; Res Assoc Mo Inst Psychi, St Louis, Dept Univ Mo Med Sch, Columbia (Mo) 1970-71; Dir Cnslg Fontbonne Col, Clayton (Mo) 1968-70; Other Former Positions; Former Conslt; APA; Mo Psychol Assn; Former Mem Bd Dirs St Louis Pers & Guid Assn; cp/St Louis Bach Soc Chorus; r/St Peter's Cath Ch, Kirkwood: Choir Mem .

STOCKTON, BARBARA MARSHALL oc/Center Director; b/Oct 19, 1923; h/6430 7th St NW, Washington, DC 20012; ed/BS 1951, MS 1955 Howard Univ; Wash Sch Psychi; Postgrad Studies; Certs; pa/Clerk w US Dept Def 1948-55; Analytical Statistician Med Statistics Div Surg Gen's Ofc, US Army Dept Def 1955-57; Psychol Intern Crownsville St Hosp (Md) 1957-59; Sch Psychologist Child & Yth Study Div Pupil Pers Sers 1959-65; Clin Psychologist: Rdg Clin, DC Public Schs 1965, Child & Yth Study Div 1965-67; Ctr Dir Dept Pupil Pers Sers, Ctr III, DC Public Schs 1967-; Delta Sigma Theta: Charter Pres 1972-74, Golden Life Mem; CEC: Bd Govs DC 1972-75, Pres Fdn No 524 1970-71, Pres Charter No 49; Epilepsy Foun Am, Bd Dirs DC Chapt; DC Mtl Hlth Assn: Bd Pres, Bd Dirs, Chm Spec Projs; APA; DC Psychol Assn; Nat Assn Sch Psychologists; Am Assn for Mtl Deficiency; Am Acad Polit & Social Scis; cp/Vol Wkr Wom's Com of Nat Symph; hon/1st in Psychol, Wom's Leag, Howard Univ 1951; Meritorious Civilian Awd, Surg Gen's Ofc, US Dept Def; Outstg Achmt Awd, DC Fdn No 524 CEC; Symposia Spec Cert, Univ Seville (Spain); Biogl Listings.

STOCKTON, JOHN DAVID oc/Mining Engineer; b/May 6, 1932; h/9536 E Calle Eunice, Tucson, AZ 85715; ba/Tucson; m/Patricia Mae Arnold; c/Tamara Anne, Christel Lynne, Scott David; p/Dean B Sr and Sarah Adeline Howard Stockton (dec); ed/Engr Mines Colo Sch Mines 1956; mil/USAR Corps of Engrs, Capt; pa/Am Inst Mining, Metall & Petrol Engrs; cp/GOP; r/Prot.

STOCKTON, RODNEY MAURICE JR oc/Chief Executive, Scientist; b/Feb 3, 1913; h/750 NW 38th St, Ft Lauderdale, FL 33309; c/Denise Twinkle; p/Rodney M Sr and Mae Z Stockton, Ft Lauderdale; ed/Asbury Col 2

Yrs; DS Ft Lauderdale Col; mil/Liaison QMC, Chgo, Ill, Maj Christianson War Food Adm, Wash DC; pa/Public Utilities Comm Lab Inc: Fdr, Past Pres, Former Chm of Bd, Chief Exec Ofcr (Life Contract); Currently Involved in Ext Med Res (Recog by Fed Govt); Cosmetics, Toiletry & Fragrance Assn; cp/Pres Com Employmt of Handicapped; Govs Com Handicapped; C of C; Fla St, Ft Lauderdale; Ft Lauderdale Univ Adv Bd of 100; Life Mem Fla Sheriffs Boys Ranch; Aerospace Med Assn; Am Security Coun; Nat Adv Coun Bd; Franklin Mint Collectors Soc; Past Mem, Broward Co Bicent Comm; r/Christ Meth Ch; hon/Wisdom Awd 1970; Fellow, Pres Coun Am Inst Mgmt; Hon Ky Col; Presented Gold Key by Miami Bch Mayor; Presented Large Key for Outstg Med Res by Mayor of Metro Dade Co (Fla); Hon PhD Hamilton St Univ 1973; 1st to Stabelize Fresh Gel in High Concentrates of Rare Tropical Aloe Vera Plant, Giving it a 2-7 Yr Shelf Life in Medications & Cosmetics for Mkg Nat'ly & Intl'ly; 2000 Men Achmt; W/W S&SW; DIB; World W/W Fin & Indust; Royal Blue Book; Nat Social Reg; Ft Lauderdale Social Reg of 400; Personalities of S; Intercont Biogl Assn; IPA; Am W/W; Blue Book; Commun Ldrs & Noteworthy Ams.

STODGHILL, PATSY ANN oc/Poet; Educator; b/Feb 1, 1935; h/1424 Highland Rd, Dallas, TX 75218; m/Donald R; c/Steven H, Sheri Sue; p/William Curtis Hall (dec); Emma Lou Lofland, Dallas, TX; ed/BS N Tex St Univ 1956; MA Univ Tex-A 1958; pa/Tchr Dallas Indep Sch Dist 1957-60, 61-65, 76-; Lectr So Meth Univ Cont'g Ed Prog 1977-; Pres Poetry Soc Tex; Nat Fdn St Poetry Socs Inc, St Pres

Bd 1976-; U Poets Laureate Intl; Intl Poetry Soc; World Poetry Soc; Delta Kappa Gamma; Fine Arts Soc Tex; Tex Assn Creative Writing Tchrs; Pen Wom; Avalon Poets; r/Bapt; hon/Poet Laureate Tex 1978-79; Nortex Press Book Pub Awd for *Mirrored Images*; Var Awds, Nat Fdn St Poetry Socs; World Poetry Awds; Num Pubs; Biogl Listings; Others.

STOESSEL, CAROLE JEAN oc/Physician; Pianist; Dealer in Antique Dolls; b/Jul 14, 1936; h/329 S Fulton St, Salisbury, NC 28144; ba/Same; m/Alexander W; p/Frank William and India Aldredge Stoessel, Salisbury; ed/AB magna cum laude Catawba Col; MD Bowman Gray Sch Med, Wake Forest Univ; pa/Dealer Antique Dolls 1977-; Substitute Phys Rowan Co Chapt ARC Bloodmobile Unit, Rowan Co (NC) 1972-75; Resident Fellow Dept Microbiol Columbia-Presby Med Ctr, New York, NY 1964-65; Intern Pathol Columbia-Presb Med Ctr 1963-64; Lic'd to Pract Med NC St Bd Med Examrs 1963; Concert Pianist Recitals 1950-59, 1971-75; Var TV & Radio Appearances 1950-55; cp/Hist Salisbury Foun Inc: Charter Mem, Bd Trustees, Exec Com; Residents of Old Salisbury: Bd Dirs, VP; Mem Rowan Co Dem Wom; r/St John's Ev Luth Ch: Mem; hon/Valedictorian Class 1954, Boyden HS (Salisbury); Dean's List, Catawba Col; Reynolds Scholar Bowman Gray Sch Med; Var Articles Pub'd in Med Jours; Biogl Listings.

STOFFERAHN, KENNETH DARRELL oc/Public Utilities Commissioner; b/Apr 5, 1934; h/1009 S Arthur, Pierre, SD 57501; ba/Pierre; m/Diane Claire; c/Michael, Stacey, Stuart, Steven; p/Edward H and Ida

M Stofferahn (dec); ed/BS SDSU 1957; mil/SD ANG, USAFR 1957-63; pa/Public Utilities Commr 1978-; r/Luth.

STOKES, VERNON L oc/Educator; Senior Engineering Technician; b/Nov 11, 1913; h/2609 Black Oak Ln, Arlington, TX 76012; ba/Ft Worth, TX; m/Dorothy W; c/Jennifer S McDowell; p/(dec); ed/BGE Univ Neb-O; MEd Tex Wesleyan; EdD N Tex St

Univ; mil/USAF Ret'd; pa/Tarrant Co Jr Col: Prof, Chm Engrg Technol; Past Chm: N Tex ASM, N Tex ASNT, Nat Edr Div ASNT; Phi Delta Kappa; ASM; ASNT; ASEE; ASCET; ASTM; cp/Past Pres A'ton, Tex St Tch Assn; r/Meth; hon/Tutorial Cit Awd, ASNT; Author Col Texts.

STOLL, BELLA oc/Writer; Artist; h/276 Rodney Ave, Buffalo, NY 14214; m/Clifford; c/Regina, Rosalie, Clifford Jr, Donald, Raymond; ed/BA Univ Buffalo 1964; pa/Trade Journalist Nat-wide Trade Agy (NYC) 1955-58; HS Tchr Buffalo Public Schs 1965-66; Portrait Artist Niagara Falls Blvd Mall 1970-72; Article Writer *Current Biog Mag* 1970; Wkly Columnist "Around Our Towns" *Am-Ton Jour*, Amherst, NY 1974-75; Lectr; Paintings Exhibited at Georgetown Gallery, Williamsville, NY 1975 (Apr & May); Tchr Water-Color Techniques Buffalo YWCA 1977-78; AAUW; Nat Leag Am Pen Wom, W NY Br; MENSA; W'ville Soc Artists; cp/Former Lectr LWV, Buffalo Br.

STONE, ELAINE MURRAY oc/Author; Composer; Clubwoman; Realtor; b/Jan 22, 1922; h/1945 Pineapple Ave, Melbourne, FL 32935; m/F Courtney; c/Catherine Rayburn (Mrs Robert), Pamela Webb (Mrs Don E), Victoria Francis; p/H Murray-Jacoby (dec); Catherine Murray-Jacoby, Palm Beach, FL; ed/Dipl NY Col Music 1943; Licentiate Trinity Col Music 1947; Fla Inst Technol; pa/Author:

Taming of the Tongue, Love One Another, Uganda: Fire and Blood, Melbourne Bicent Book, Others; Num Articles; Org'g Pres Cape Canaveral Br Nat Leag Am Pen Wom; Wom in Communs; ASCAP; Melbourne Bd Realtors; cp/Fla St Chm Music Nat Soc DAR; Bd Dirs Brevard Symph; Diocesan Bd Promotion, Diocese S Fla; r/Holy Trinity Epis Ch, Melbourne; hon/5 Plaques at Top Salesperson, Engle Realty Inc; 1st Pl in Photo-Jour, Fla St Penwom; Others.

STONE, IDELLA PURNELL oc/Writer; Poet; b/Apr 1, 1901; h/321 E Grandview Ave, Sierra Madre, CA 91024; ba/Same; m/Remington (dec); c/Remington, Marjorie Osborn; p/George Edward Purnell (dec); Idella Bragy (dec); ed/BA Univ Cal 1922; Dipls; pa/CoFdr Dianetics & Scientology; Fdg

Editor *Palms*, Poetry Mag 1923-30; Pub'd 10 Chd's Books, 2 Sci Anthols, 1 Mexican Cookbook; Other Profl Activs; cp/Var Polit Activs; r/Christian; hon/Most Outstg Guest, Univ Tex; Others.

STONE, IVY GOLDHAMER oc/Artist; b/Jul 2, 1917; h/1 Bratenahl Pl, Cleveland, OH 44108; ba/Cleve; m/Walter B; c/Marvin Elliot, Nancy Ellen; p/Joseph Goldhamer, Florence Goldhamer (dec); pa/Painter; Tchr Adv Painting; r/Jewish; hon/Exhibits incl: Intl Park Fest Art (Cleve), Art Show Phila Acad Fine Art, Corcoran Gallery Art (Wash DC), Invitational W C Art Show, Art Inst Chgo, Reg Butler Art Inst (Youngstown); Num Shows at Cleve Mus of Art.

STONE, LETTIE IRENE SNIDER oc/Retired School Teacher; b/Apr 8, 1911; h/505 E South St, PO Box 276, Talladega, AL 35160; m/Louie M; c/Lettie Sylvia S Boder; p/Robert O and Susan Edna Hannon Snider, Rockford; ed/Grad Troy Univ; pa/Ret'd; Tchr Talladega Co & Ala St Sch for the Blind; Past

Pres Local & Co PTA; Past Pres Talladega BPW Clb; cp/Vol Local Red Cross; U Way; Other Civic Drives; Dem Party; r/U Meth: Pres Anniston Dist Wom's Soc Christian Ser, Mem Bd N Ala Conf Meth Ch, Tchr Adult SS Class 25 Yrs.

STONECIPHER, KENNETH GENE oc/Organist; Free-lance Musician; Director; b/Feb 9, 1954; h/Box 1158 SAU, Magnolia, AR 71753; ba/Same; p/Tyra and Pearl Stonecipher, Magnolia; ed/BSE So Ark Univ; pa/Dir SAU Recruiting Group; Sum Stock Theatre 1974, 75, 76; Role of Don Pasquale in Comic Opera *Don Pasquale* Shreveport Symph; Studio Work, Russelville & Little Rock (Ark) & Shreveport (La); Tech Dir & Choreographer; Miss Magnolia, Miss Stephens, Miss So Ark Univ Pageants, SAU's Annual "Best of Broadway" Musical Revue 5 Yrs; Original Musical Adaptation, Scored Entire Musical Based on Book *Charlotte's Web*; Other Profl Activs; cp/Music Coor Joe Woodward for Gov Campaign; r/Asbury U Meth Ch; hon/Best Supporting Actor 1979, 75; Best Actor 1977; Outstg Technician Awd, SAU Theatre 1973.

STORZ, LESTER GILBERT oc/Pastor; Teacher; Former Overseas Missionary; Writer; b/Jul 17, 1921; h/1061 Dolores Ln, Fallon, NV 89406; m/Mabel Dorain; c/Donald, Edwin, Donna Burske; p/William F Storz (dec); Minnie Caroline Waltemathe-Storz (dec); ed/BA; MA; ThD; Addit Studies; pa/Missionary Vietnam 1945-59; Vietnam Mission Pres 1951-59; Fdr & Bd Chm Saigon Adventist Hosp 1953-59; Opened New

Mission Work, Montaignard Tribe (Vietnam) 1952-56; Began 1st Rel Prot Radio Broadcasts (Vietnam) 1952; Chm Dept Theol Mtn View Col, Philippines 1959-62; Chm Num Sch Bds & Pub'g House Bd; Pastor: Oreg, Cal, Nev 1962-; Pres Min Assns 3 Cities; Conduct Num "Five-Day Plans to Stop Smoking"; r/SDA: Min; hon/Hon Mem, Kiwanis; Contbr Articles to Var Mags; Biogl Listings.

STOTT, KENHELM WELBURN JR oc/Zoologist, Explorer, Author; Research Associate; b/Aug 27, 1920; h/2410 Albatross St, Apt 1, San Diego, CA 92101; p/Kenhelm Welburn Sr and Dorothy Cranston Stott (dec); ed/BA; pa/Res Assoc Zool Soc SD; Fellow London Zool Soc; Edit Bd *Explorers Jour*; Former Gen Curator San Diego Zoo; Smithsonian Res Collaborator for Sci Expeditions; Fellow Explorer Clb; Fellow Royal Geographical Soc; hon/Cit of Merit, Explorers Clb; Hon Trustee, Martin & Osa Johnson Safari Mus; Pers Cit, Dalai Lama.

STOUT, MARY KATHRYN oc/University Administrator; h/356 E 4450 N, Provo, UT 84601; ba/Provo; p/Clair LeRoy and Ivis Parrish Stout, N Hollywood, CA; ed/BA magna cum laude, MA summa cum laude Brigham Yg Univ; pa/Brigham Yg Univ Sch Mgmt: Asst Dir Prog for Study of Orgs & Free Enterprise 1978-, Res Asst Prog for Study of Orgs & Free Enterprise 1977-78; Conslt/Intern Wheelabrator Frye Inc, Hampton, NH Sum 1977; Reschr: MJB Assocs 1977-78, Skaggs Cos Inc 1977; Other Former Positions; BYU Mgmt Soc; Org Behavior Admissions Com; cp/Metro Mus Art (NYC); Utah Heritage Foun; Former Mem Relief Soc Gen Bd Ad Hoc Com on Sports, Phy Fitness & Rec; Others; r/LDS; hon/Mem Var Hons Socs; CASE Awd; Recipient S'ships; Outstg Yg Wom Am; 1st Pl Winner-Feature Writing, Rocky Mtn Collegiate Press Assn; Dean's Lists.

STOVER, IVA CLEMMONS CHILDERS oc/Retired; Teacher; Poet; b/Mar 27, 1894; h/3810 S 10 Ave, Birmingham, AL 35222; m/Hayden P Childers Jr (dec); 2nd Glen H (dec); c/Martha C McLaurine; p/James M and Martha Kelly Clemmons (dec); ed/Wheeler Bus Col; Athens Col; B'ham So Col; Howard Col; NC St Univ; pa/Tchr: Wheeler Bus Col, Jefferson Co Public Schs; Pers Dir Nat Yth Adm; Supv'g Rep in field, US Civil Ser Com; Ofc Mgr Camp Fire Girls; Housemother Fla St Univ; cp/Exec Bd Jefferson Co (Ala) Soc Crippled Chd & Adults; Exec Bd & Former Editor Newslttr Univ Ala Hosp Aux; Adv Coun RSVP; Past Pres B'ham Quill Clb; Past Treas Nat Leag Am Pen Wom; Past Pres Chatelaine Study Clb; Ala St Poetry Soc; Tenn St Poetry Soc; Jefferson Co TV & Radio Coun; B'ham Chapt Alpha Delta Pi; r/Prot; hon/1st Prize Inspirational Poem, Ala Writers Conclave Contest 1975; Alumnae Cert of Honor, B'ham Chapt Alpha Delta Pi; Ala Poet of Yr 1976; Silver Bell Awd, B'ham Chapt Quota Intl; Others; Pub'd Works.

STRAIN, ROBERT F oc/Minister; b/Jul 28, 1930; h/10902 N Armenia Ave, Tampa, FL 33612; m/Retha Fern; c/Randall F, Teresa Kay; p/Omer C and Kathryn B Strain, Colfax, IN; ed/BA Ky Christian Col; Addit Studies; mil/Ser 1952-53, Korea, 73rd Tank Battalion; pa/VP Christian Film Lib NEn Ohio; cp/Kiwanis Clb; r/Christian; hon/Contbr to Rel Pubs & Jours; IPA; W/W in Rel; Personalities W&MW.

STRANDELL, MARJATTA oc/Administrator; b/Apr 17, 1933; h/14 N Kenosha Dr, Madison, WI 53705; ba/Madison; ed/MSME; BBA; pa/Dir Human Resource Planning & Devel, Wis Power & Light Co; Sr Mem Am Assn Cost Engrs; Soc Wom Engrs; Profl Engrs, Oreg & Wis St Chapts; Advr on Productivity at St & Fed Levels; hon/Author Sev Profl Pubs & Papers Presented at Nat & Intl Meetings; Woms Book of World Records & Achmt; W/W in W; Intl W/W: Commun Ser, Public Affairs; DIB; Personalities W&MW; Am Men & Wom Sci.

STRANG, PETER MacDONALD oc/-Textile Research Consultant; b/Feb 20, 1896; h/31 Laurel Dr, Needham, MA 02192; m/-Muriel Howland (dec); p/James and Catherine Wright Strang (dec); ed/BS MIT 1918; US Nav War Col 1940-55; Addit Studies; mil/USNR 1939-55, Cmdr; pa/Textile Res Conslt, Semi-Ret'd 1960-; Textile Res Conslt Whitin Machine Works, Whitinsville, Mass 1948-60; Res Assoc Inst Textile Technol, Charlottesville, Va 1945-48; Proj Orgr Div Indust Cooperation, MIT 1933-39; Other Former Positions; CoDeveloper (w Lawrence M Keeler) of Method of Spinning Fibres in Rotating Vortex of Water; AAAS; NY Acad Scis; Am Assn Textile Chemists & Colorists; Intl Textile Assn (Switzerland); Acad Polit Sci Columbia Univ; Affil Am Assn for Textile Technologists Inc; Am Acad Polit & Social Sci; cp/Smithsonian Assocs; Frat Blue Lodge, Newtonville, Mass 55 Yrs; Scottish Rite 32° Deg Lodge; Aleppo Temple Shrine, Boston, Mass 54 Yrs; hon/Author Num Articles on Text.le Technol; Patentee in Textile Field; Biogl Listings.

STRANGE, THURMAN RAY oc/Minister; b/Sept 20, 1942; h/424 Dolphin, Gulf Breeze, FL 32561; ba/Gulf Breeze; m/Connie; c/Rick, Michael, Timothy; m/Clifford and Ollie Strange, Prairie City, IL; ed/AS; BA; MS; pa/Min Evangel Ch-Assemblies of God; Cnslr; Christian Cnslg Sem Min; cp/Red Cross; Mtl Hlth; r/Assemblies of God; hon/W/W: Am, Rel.

STRATON, ANDREW CHARLES oc/Financial Planner; b/Jul 26, 1923; h/164 Touisset Point Rd, Warren, RI 02885; ba/Warren; m/Olympia R; c/Daniel, Walter (dec), Alexandra, Lawrence; p/Charles A Straton (dec); Olympia J Rioux, Warren, RI; ed/AB Univ Cal; MS George Washington Univ; mil/USN (Ret'd): Cmdr, Naval Aviator 1943-73; Sales Staff, Conn Gen Life Ins Co (Providence, RI) 1974-76; Fin Planner, En Fin Sers 1977-79; Nat Assn Life Underwriters 1974-79; Intl Assn Fin Planners 1976-79; Recruiting Dist Asst Coun (Providence) 1976-79; Ret'd Ofcrs Assn 1973-79; Rep of US Mil Adv to SEATO 1965-69; Assoc Prof of Naval Sci, Brown Univ 1970-72; cp/Past Ldr, BSA (Karamursel, Turkey); Former Dir Little League Baseball; Past Pres & VP, Barrington (RI) Lions Clb; Former Mem Bd Dirs, Brown Navy Clb; Past Mem, Corvair Soc of Am; Others; r/Russian Orthodox; hon/Navy Commend Medal; Merit Ser Medal, United Nations Ser Medal; Nat Ser Medal; Victory Medal, WWII; Am Area Campaign Ribbon; Intl Lions Clb 100% Pres Awd; Biogl Listings.

STRAUB, NELLIE CORA oc/Retired; b/Dec 20, 1898; h/PO Box 8621 Waikiki, Honolulu, HI 96815; m/Frederick Guy; c/Evelyn Elizabeth S Savage; p/William

Nathaniel Perry; Mattie Marcy Gregory; ed/Col Commerce, Univ Ill; pa/NY Times, Reo Motor Car Co; cp/DAR; LWV; r/Meth; hon/2000 Wom Achmt.

STRAYER, VERNON JOHN oc/Corporation Manager; b/Feb 7, 1917; h/RD 4, Export, PA; ba/E Pittsburgh, PA; m/Betty M Fisher; c/Timothy J, Steven J, Douglas J, Bradley J, Kim J; p/Forest R and Elma E Fyock Strayer, Johnstown, PA; ed/BS Juniata Col 1946; mil/USAF 1942-45, Air Intell; pa/Spec Agt, FBI 1946-52; Supvr Pers & Labor Relats, E I DuPont (Louisville, Ky) 1952-55; Pers Dir, Y

& N Railroad (Youngstown, Ohio) 1955-62; Supvr, Pers Claims/Safety Tng, Union Railroad (Pgh) 1962-; Am Soc Safety Engrs 1977-79; Soc Former FBI Agts; cp/Franklin Twp Commr; Past Supt of Franklin Twp Police Dept; r/Presb: Deacon, Supt of SS Sch; hon/W/W E.

STREFF, JOHN D oc/Manufacturer's Representative; b/Feb 15, 1927; h/2058 Butternut Ln, Northbrook, IL 60062; ba/Chicago, IL; m/Denise; c/Denise, Monique; p/Harold P and Monica Streff (dec); ed/Att'd Univ Wis; mil/USN 2½ Yrs; pa/Profl Mfrs' Reps: Past Pres, Current Chm of Bd; Pres Mfrs' Reps Paint Supplies; cp/Chm Bd Fullerton Ave Assn Inc; Former Chm Ill Bronze Rep Panel; Lectr Cerebral Palsy; Others; r/Cath; hon/Rep of Yr, Ill Bronze Paint Co & C H Tripp Co 2 Yrs; Rep of Yr, Num Other Factories Over 12 Yrs.

STREITFELD, SHIRLEY oc/Library Assistant; b/Jul 27, 1926; h/1776 James Ave, Sea Beach Towers, Miami Beach, FL 33139; ba/Miami, FL; p/David Streitfeld (dec); Rose L Streitfeld, Miami Bch; pa/Lib Asst II Miami-Dade Public Lib; Mem Task Force Am Lib Assn: Past Pres Dade Co Lib Assn; Past Exec

Dir & PR Fla Lib Assn; Lib Adv Com, Past Pres Staff Assn Miami-Dade Public Lib; cp/Reg'd Lobbyist, Tallahassee, Fla; Clerk in Charge of Election Precnt; Pres, Treas Corp; r/Jewish; hon/Cit for Outstg Ser to City of Miami; Citizen of Day, Radio Sta WRIZ; Lib Front-Liner, Wilson Bltn Selection.

STRICKLAND, THOMAS JOSEPH oc/Artist; Painter; b/Dec 28, 1932; h/2598 Taluga Dr, Miami, FL 33133; ba/Same; m/Debrah J Ponn; p/Charles Edward Strickland (dec); Clementine McMillian, Miami; mil/AUS 1953-55; pa/30 One-Man Shows; Work Rep'd in 500+ Pvt & Public Collections; Contbr Articles to Mags; TV Guest Appearances; Pastel Soc Am; Miami Palette Clb; cp/Grove House, Hollywood Art Mus; r/Cath; hon/Top Awds in Num Exhbns; W/W: World, Am, Am Art, S&SE.

STRICKLER, PAUL EDWIN oc/Executive; b/Apr 23, 1916; h/R# 3, Decatur, IN 46733; ba/Decatur; m/Kathryn Pyle; c/Cassandra Sanderson, Paula Fuller, Deborah Lee, Cynthia; p/C Gilbert and Golda Shoaf Strickler (dec); pa/Pres: Adams Co Trailer Sales Inc, Strickler Investmts Inc; Chm Bd Decatur Bk & Trust Co; Past VP Ind Mobile Home Assn Bd Govs; cp/Pres City Decatur Ec Devel Comm; Indust Devel Com Decatur C of C; Bd Trustees: Anderson Col, Exec Com Anderson Col; Adv Bd Huntington House; Optimist Clb; Bluffton C of C; Charter Mem Anderson Col BPM Clb; Bd Mem Citizens No Bk, Elkhart (Ind); r/Decatur Ch of God: Bd Trustees; hon/Sales Awds: Vindale Corp (Brookville, Ohio), Horizon Mobile Homes (Portland, Ind), Detroiter Inc (Alma, Mich), Boise Cascade (Bourbon, Ind).

STRICKS, MAX oc/Financial Executive; h/10955 SW 122nd Ct, Miami, FL 33186; ba/Key Biscayne, FL; m/Bernice; c/Mark, Rochelle; p/Joseph and Rachael Stricks (dec); ed/BBA; MBA; mil/AUS; pa/Nat Assn Accts; Am Acct'g Assn; Nat Panel Am Arbitration Assn; r/Hebrew; hon/DIB; Personalities of S; Men of Achmt; W/W S&SW; Others.

STROMAN, SAMUEL DAVID oc/Assistant Professor; b/Dec 18, 1924; h/PO Box 1601, SC St Col, Orangeburg, SC 29117; ba/Same; m/Cleo Ables; c/Sandra D, Sherolyn D, Synthia D, Samuel D II; p/Moses Clay and Clara Beatrice Stroman (dec); ed/AB; MA; MS; PhD; mil/AUS 1950-76, Ret'd Col Regular Army; Enlisted Ser AUS 1941-45, Pvt to 1/Sgt; Sr Advr & Sr Inf Tng Advr Vietnamese Inf Sch (Vietnam) 1966-67; Inspector Gen US Army Crim Investigation Command, Wash DC 1972-73; pa/Asst Prof Dept Behavior Scis SC St Col 1976-; APGA; SC Pers & Guid Assn; Assn for Cnslr Ed & Supvn; SC Sch Cnslr Assn; SC Assn for Non-White Concerns in Pers & Guid; Edit Bd: *Ed Mag* & *Jour of Instrnl Psychol*; Bd Dirs

Vasquez Assocs, Ednl Res & Conslt'g Firm; Chair Symposium on "Sci Process of Decision-Making", 81st Annual Conv APA, Montreal (Canada) 1973; cp/Free & Accepted Mason; r/Prot; hon/Num Certs of Achmt & Commends; Num Mil Decorations incl'g: Legion of Merit w OLC, Parachutist Badge, Gen Staff Identification Badge, Meritorious Ser Medal w OLC, Good Conduct Medal, WWII Victory Medal, Vietnam Campaign Medal, Others; Outstg Col Tchr Awd, SC St Col Chapt Phi Delta Kappa; Awd for Outstg Sers, O'burg Alumni Chapt Kappa Alpha Psi; Army ROTC Hall of Fame, SCSC; Achmt Awd, SEn Province Kappa Alpha Psi; Mem Hon Socs; Biogl Listings; Others.

STROME, CLOYCE P A oc/Medical Research Biologist; b/Oct 7, 1917; h/7612 E YZ Ave, Vicksburg, MI 49097; ba/Rockville, MD; m/Margaret H; p/Walter E Strome (dec); Lona P Strome, V'burg; ed/Undergrad Studies Wn Mich Univ; mil/USN 1942-62; pa/Med Res Biologist NN Med Ctr, Nav Med Res, Bethesda (Md) 1962-76; Hd Dept Malariology Am Foun for Biol Res, R'ville 1976-; r/Prot; hon/Navy Combat Awd; Secy of Navy Achmt Awd; Num Civil Ser Awds; Num Sci Pubs.

STRONG, BLONDELL M oc/Librarian; h/2569 Stone Dr, Ann Arbor, MI 48105; ba/Ann Arbor; c/Stanford, Jeff Bertram; p/Jeff McDonald (dec); Bertha Mae McDonald, Ft Pierce, FL; ed/BS w distn; MSLS; Doct Cand; pa/Libn Sch Lib Sci Univ

Mich; Med Lib Assn; ALA; Am Assn Lib Schs; Tenn Lib Assn; cp/Bd Mem Logan Sch PTO; Ann Arbor PTO Coun; Staff Mem Commun Newslttr, UM Northwood V Housing; r/Presb; hon/Kappa Delta Pi; Beta Phi Mu; Outstg Ser Awd, Meharry-Hubbard Credit Union, Nashville, Tenn.

STROTHOFF, CARL FREDERICK oc/-

Real Estate; Rancher; b/Jan 2, 1927; h/Rt 10, Box 631, Tyler, TX 75707; ba/Same; m/Norma Jeanette; c/Kimberly Kaye, Michale David; p/Joseph Jr and Birdie Mae Strothoff (dec); mil/USM 1941-45; AUS 1946-50; pa/Self-employed Real Est; Tex Cattleman's Assn; Tex Ranger; cp/Dem Cand Co Commr; Kiwanis; Ks of C; VFW; Frat Order Eagles; Secy Pearl Harbor Survivors Assn; Life Mem Nat Rifle Assn; r/Cath; hon/Purple Heart; Bronze Star; Pres Cit.

STROUBE, WILLIAM BRYAN JR oc/Research Chemist; b/Oct 29, 1951; h/40 Fence Line Dr, Gaithersburg, MD 20760; ba/Washington, DC; m/Katharine Ann Kaiser; p/William Bryan Sr and Tillie Larkins Stroube, Princeton, KY; ed/AS Univ Ky-H

1971; BS Murray St Univ 1973; PhD Univ Ky-Lexington 1977; pa/Res Chemist US Food & Drug Adm; Am Chem Soc; Am Nuclear Soc; AAAS; Meteoritical Soc; r/Disciples of Christ; hon/Author Sev Pubs in Sci Fields.

STUEBER, GUSTAV oc/Consulting Engineer; b/Dec 25, 1909; h/720 E McMurray Rd, McMurray, PA 15317; m/Gertrude M Niere (dec); c/Loretta Maria, Gertrude S Eysel, Eric Gustav; p/Joseph and Maria Ross Stueber; ed/Univ Madison, Cologne, Germany; pa/Reg'd Profl Engr: Pa, Ohio, Ia, Mo, Ind, Tenn, NC, RI; Am Soc CE; Pres 1964-65 Wash Co Chapt Pa Soc Profl Engrs;

Nat Soc Profl Engrs; Nat Soc Conslt'g Engrs (Charter mem Pgh Sect); Life Mem Soc Civil Engrs; IPA; cp/Former Mem Ct of Common Pleas Wash Co, 27th Jud Dist; Charter Mem Sci Sem, Counsels Yg People Toward Their Chosen Profession; Former Mem Peters Twp Zoning Com; r/Ctr Presb Ch: Mem, Former Trustee; hon/Mem Pgh Constrn Indust Hall of Fame; Num Pubs; Intl W/W Commun Ser; DIB; Commun Ldrs & Noteworthy Ams.

STURIALE, GLORY oc/College Dean; b/Jul 26, 1924; h/999 Green St, No 1605, San Francisco, CA 94133; ba/Berkeley, CA; p/Nicholas and Rena B Sturiale (dec); ed/BA Univ Cal-B 1948; MS Trinity Univ 1953; MA Mills Col 1957; JD St Mary's Univ Law 1973; Addit Studies; mil/USAF, Comm'd Ofcr 1950-72, Ret'd Lt Col; Var Profl Positions; pa/Dean for Student Affairs Cal Sch Profl Psychol, Berkeley 1978-; Instr Intro Psychol: Trinity Univ (Tex) 1952, Univ Md 1957-59; Instr Applied Human Relats UCLA 1960; Atty-Advr Bur Hearings & Appeals Social Security Adm, HEW 1975-76; Trial Pract, Briefing Atty, Gen Pract, Pvt Pract 1976-77; St Bar Tex; ABA; Lic'd Psychologist: Cal, Tex;

hon/Phi Delta Phi; Am Juris Awds; Mem John F Harlan Soc; Pub'd Author; W/W: Am Wom, S&SW, W; Notable Ams; World W/W Wom; Intl W/W Intells; Book of Honor; Personalities W&MW.

SUÁREZ, MANUEL L oc/University Professor; b/Nov 8, 1945; h/2215 Lakeland Dr, Johnson City, TN 37601; m/Cynthia R; c/Laurentino, Cristina; p/Laurentino Suarez, Miami Beach, FL; Aida Suarez; ed/BA; MA; PhD; Postdoct Studies Univ Ga; pa/Prof E Tenn St Univ; MLA; SAMLA; SHA; AAUP; TFLTA; AATSP; cp/Lions Clb; r/Presb; hon/Bloomfield Col S'ship Key; NEH Grantee; ETSU Res Grant; Others.

SUBASIC, FRANK J oc/General Manager; b/Nov 26, 1940; h/Rt 4, Grove Heights, Berkeley Springs, WV 25411; ba/Hancock, MD; m/Patricia Ann; c/Frank, Scott, Shawn, Stephen, Kelly Jo; p/Michael Edwin Subasic (dec); Helen Ojnowski Walkowski, Pittsburgh, PA; ed/Grad Ed Inst Pgh; Att'd: Pgh Tech Inst, Univ Pgh Night Sch, Corning Commun Col; pa/Gen Mgr Fleetwood Enterprises, Prowler Indust of Md, Hancock 1974-; Gen Mgr Fleetwood Co, Wilderness Indust Ind, Frankfort 1972-74; Mgr Tng Prowler Indust Md, Hancock 1972; Gen Mgr Gichner Mobile Systems Div Union Corp, Berkeley Springs, WVa 1970-72; Asst Chief Indust Engrg Howes Leather Co, Boston 1968-70; Other Former Positions; Pres Hagerstown (Md) Chapt SPEBSQSA; cp/Soc for Barbershop Quartets; Repub; Pres Berkeley Springs Little Leag; Bd Dirs Hancock Hlth Care Corp; r/Rom Cath; hon/DIB; W/W S&SW.

SUELFLOW, AUGUST R oc/Institute Director; Educator; b/Sept 5, 1922; h/7249 Northmoor, St Louis, MO 63105; ba/St Louis; m/Gladys I Gierach; c/August Mark, Kathryn Lynn; p/August Henry and Selma Kressin Suelflow; ed/BD 1946, STM 1947 Concordia Sem (St Louis, Mo); DD Concordia Sem (Springfield, Ill) 1967; pa/Dir Concordia Hist Inst Dept Archives & Hist, Luth Ch-Mo Synod 1948-; Asst Curator Concordia Hist Inst, St Louis, Mo 1946-48; Concordia Sem, St Louis: Guest Lectr 1952-69, 74, Adj Prof 1975-, Chm Hist Theol Dept 1975-; Asst Pastor: Luth

Memorial, Richmond Heights, Mo 1948-56, Mt Olive, St Louis 1958-75; Archivist: Wn Dist LCMS 1948-66, Mo Dist LCMS 1966-; Instr Wash Univ, St Louis 1967-; Luth Hist Conf: Charter Mem, VP 1962-64, Pres 1964-68; Soc Am Archivists: Chm Rel Archives Com 1958-62, 64-77, Coun Mem 1962-64; Sem Archivist Concordia Sem, St Louis 1976-; Am Microform Acad Trustee 1962-75; Am Records Mgmt Assn 1969-72; Luth Soc for Worship; Music & the Arts; Luth Acad for S'ship; Am Assn Museums; Nat Trust for Hist Preserv; Org Am Histns; Other Profl Activs; r/Luth; hon/Fellow, SAA; Cert'd Genealogist, Bd Certn Genealogists; Sister M Claude Lane Awd; Pubs; Biogl Listings.

SULLIVAN, JESSIE PAULINE oc/Freelance Writer; b/Apr 18, 1922; h/4825 Westwood Rd, Kansas City, MO 64112; m/George Dennis; c/George Michael, Elizabeth Kathleen Stous, Robert Dennis; p/Dalton Levi Way (dec); Lillian Eldora

Dawson, Olathe, KS; ed/AA 1965; pa/Chd's Ch Specialist & Lectr; Author: *Exciting Object Lessons & Ideas for Chd's Sermons* 1970, *Chd's Ch Progs* 1973 (also pub'd as *Object Lessons & Stories for the Chd's Ch* 1974), *Michael's Discovery* 1975, *The New Christian's Guidebook* 1977, *Puppet Scripts for Chd's Ch* 1978; Contbr Articles & Stories to Ch Pubs; cp/Nat Village Ch Bd Mem, Lee's Summit, Mo; Bd Mem Nat Gerimed Hosp & Gerontol Ctr, Lee's Summit; r/Wornall Rd Bapt Ch, Ks City: Mem, Former SS Tchr, Past Tng Union Dir, Past Yth Dir, Chd's Ch Dir; Org'd Chd's Chs in Bapt Chs, Ks City: Calvary, Covenant, Broadway, Wornall Rd; Other Activs; hon/Hon Fellow, Harry S Truman Lib Inst.

SULLIVANT, BRYAN STERLING oc/Executive; b/Jun 13, 1955; h/921 Kearney St, Denver, CO 80220; ba/Denver; m/Janice; p/Sterling and Francis Sullivant, Denver; ed/BA Westminster Col; pa/Pres High Country Aquatics Inc; Pres Rocky Mt Swim Leag; cp/Pres Denver Co Yg Repubs; Intern: Senator Dole, Lt Gov Phelps; Staff Senator Plock; r/Presb; hon/Alpha Psi Omega; Phi Kappa Psi; Outstg Ldrship Awd; W/W Among Am Cols & Univs.

SUMMER, CAROL ROCHELLE oc/Publisher; Executive Editor; b/Apr 28, 1937; h/5509 Stansbury Ave, Van Nuys, CA 91401; ba/N Hollywood, CA; m/Gene Calvin Webster; c/Mark, Mitchell, Julie; p/Harry and Sophie Kaufman Cohen, San Francisco, CA; pa/Wn Pubs Assn; Am Trauma Assn; cp/Am Civil Liberties Union; hon/MAGGIE Awd for Best Med Pub, Wn Pubs Assn; Num Edit & Graphic Awds.

SUMMERS, GRACE STILLWELL oc/- Composer; Piano Teacher; Pianist; b/Jul 19, 1908; h/614 Elm St Ext, Ithaca, NY 14850; ba/Ithaca; m/Leonard Leroy (dec); c/Phyllis Jean, Barbara Jane Lamb; p/Elmer Clarence Stillwell (dec); Mamie B White Stillwell Chambers (dec); pa/Tchr Piano & Theory 53 Yrs; Fac Mem Nat Guild Piano Tchrs; Composer; Performer; cp/Fdr Ithaca Music Clb; Tompkins Co Jr Music Clbs; Bd Mem NY Fdn Music Clbs; r/St Pauls U Meth Ch; hon/S'ships, Ithaca Col; Sigma Alpha Iota; Hall of Fame Awd, NGPT; Winner 22 Parade of Am Music Awds; NFMC.

SUMMERS, KATHRYN J oc/Professor; Administrator; b/Jul 1, 1934; h/280 Peninsula Ave, San Francisco, CA 94134; ba/SF; m/Gene C Sr; c/Cynthia Y, Ayana M, Gene Jr, April T; p/William and Magdalene Jenkins, SF; ed/BS; MS; Post-Master Cert; mil/ANC, Former Maj; pa/City Col SF: Full Prof Nsg, Coor Wom's Re-entry to Ed Prog; Pres Bay Area Black Nurses Assn 1975; cp/Bd Mem SF Altrusa Clb; Former Mem Bd Dirs Ambulatory Hlth Care; Intl Toastmistress; Dem; r/Cath; hon/Vietnam Ser Awd; Merit Awd, Dept Ed & Tng.

SUMMERS, SALLY W oc/Elementary School Teacher; b/Jun 6, 1915; h/157 Combs St, Hazard, KY 41701; ba/Avawam, KY; m/James B (dec); c/James Lewis, John Hunter, Janet Irene, Margaret Jean; p/Granville Williams (dec); Mary Patterson (dec); ed/BA; pa/UKREA, Del; KEA, Del; PCEA; NEA; cp/Alcoholic Adv Com Mem; KEPAC Mem; r/Bapt: SS, Pre-Sch Dir; hon/Outstg Elem Tchr Am; Personalities of S.

SUMMIT, CAMILLIA W oc/Interior Designer; b/Jan 5, 1917; ba/PO Box 15503, West Palm Beach, FL 33406; c/Janet Barbara S Judson; p/Rudolph Carl and Jenny Schoenfeld Wollner (dec); ed/NY Univ; Parsons Sch Interior Design; pa/Former Dir Interior Design Studio, Ft Lauderdale; Owner Carriage Trade Interiors, Palm Bch; Radio & TV Appearances; Nat Home Fashions Leag: VP Ed, VP Mbrship & Hospitality; Contb'd to *House Beautiful, Town & Country, Arch Digest, Decorator Mag*, Others; hon/Recipient Awds for Best Models in NY, Conn, Miami; World W/W Wom; Personalities of S.

SUMNER, WILLIAM EDWARD oc/Minister; b/Oct 4, 1930; h/2713-D Kingman St, Metairie, LA 70002; ba/New Orleans, LA; m/Wilma Zachary; c/Cynthia Lea; p/John Weldon Sumner, Hammond, IN; Annie Whitaker, Franklin, NC; ed/AA Brevard Jr Col 1966; BA Carson-Newman Col 1968; ThM New Orleans Bapt Theol Sem 1971; Dipl Clin Pastoral Ed E Tenn Bapt Hosp; Further Clin Pastoral Ed SE La Hosp; mil/USAF 1950-54; pa/Dir Yth & Fam Sers Bapt Assn Gtr NO; Pastor: Airline Bapt Ch, Metairie, Cross Anchor Bapt Chapel,

Greeneville (Tenn); So Bapt Social Sers Assn; Past Pres Pastor's Conf Bapt Assn Gtr NO; Chm Coor'g Com on Sr Adult min Gtr NO Fdn Chs; cp/Chaplain CAP; Chm Clergy Com of Com on Alcoholism & Drug Abuse, U Way; Chm La Coun Race Tract Chaplaincy Am Inc; r/So Bapt Ch: Min 1963-, Ordained Deacon, Active Layman Local Ch; hon/Blue Key Nat Hon Frat; W/W Rel; Hon Conch (Citizen), Key West, Fla.

SUMRELL, GENE oc/Research Chemist; b/Oct 7, 1919; h/PO Box 24037, New Orleans, LA 70184; ba/New Orleans; p/Joe B Sumrell, Chandler Heights, AZ; Dixie Hughes Sumrell (dec); ed/BA En NM Univ 1942; BS 1947, MS 1948 Univ NM; PhD Univ Cal-B 1951; mil/AUS 1942-46, Pvt to S/Sgt; pa/Res Chemist So Reg Res Ctr, US Dept Agri, NO; Mem Num Profl Sci Socs; Active Pubr Sci Articles in Res Jours; r/Nondenom; hon/Patentee; Phi Kappa Phi; Sigma Xi.

SUN, TERESA CHI-CHING oc/Lecturer; Writer; Organization Executive; b/Dec 24, 1931; h/28717 Trailriders Dr, Rancho Palos Verdes, CA 90274; c/2 Chd; p/Yu-Tzu Lee and Hsin-Chin Wang; pa/Spkr on Chinese Cult & Chinese New Year Customs, Alhambra City Sch Dist Tchrs' Wkshop 1978; Att'd Meeting Chinese Lang Tchrs Assn, New Orleans, La 1977; Chperson Non-Spanish Lang Com Nat Adv Coun on Bilingual Ed 1977-78; Standing Com Mem The Asian Studies on Pacific Coast 1977-80; Prog Chperson China Soc So Cal 1978-79; Rep'd Nat Adv Coun on Bilingual Ed at 1976 Cal Bilingual Ed Conf; Mem Chinese Component Adv Com, Asian Am Bilingual Mat Devel Ctr, Berkeley, Cal 1976; So Cal China Colloquium 1974-; Sem Mem Ctr of Chinese Studies, Univ Cal-B 1974-; Att'd Conf on Tchg Eng to Spkrs of Vietnamese 1975; Rep'd Nat Adv Coun on Bilingual Ed at Meeting Sponsored by Ctr of Applied Linguistics Working w Nat Ctr for Ednl Statistics in Developing Measure of Eng Proficiency, SF; Conslt at 1st Planning Conf of Asian Am Bilingual Mats Devel Ctr, Berkeley 1975; Pres China Soc So Cal 1975-78; Secy Chinese Collegiate Colleagues of So Cal 1975-76; Ed Advr So Cal Coun Chinese Schs 1977-; Others; hon/Author Num Profl Papers Presented at Confs; Commun Ldrs Am.

SUNG, EUGENE Y C oc/Professional Appraiser; Consultant; b/Oct 10, 1915; h/198-51 Foothill Ave, Holliswood, NY 11423; ba/Same; m/Joyce; c/Victor, Michael, Roger, Stephen, Timothy, Anthony, Eugene Jr; p/Charles and Mary Sung (dec); ed/BA Univ Shanghai (China) 1937; pa/Profl Appraiser & Conslt of Chinese Arts & Antiques; Appraisers Assn Am, NYC: Dir, Mbrship Com; Guest Curator Oriental Arts Collection, St John's Univ (NY); Sr Mem Am Soc Appraisers; r/Rom Cath; hon/Ednl Contbn Awd, Am Soc Appraisers; Awd of

Profl Designation of ASA, Am Soc Appraisers.

SURBER, JOE ROBERT oc/School Psychologist; b/Apr 11, 1942; h/1308 DeSoto, Ponca City, OK 74601; ba/Ponca City; m/Jo Del N; c/Robert Brian, Karrie Jo; p/Hugh R Sr and Odema Surber, Pawhuska, OK; ed/BS Neb St Univ 1964; MS 1969, EdD 1974 OSU;

mil/USAR, S/Sgt; pa/Dir Spec Sers; Nat Assn Sch Psychol; APGA; cp/Bd Dirs Red Cross; Lion's Clb; Okla EHA-B Adv Panel; r/Presb Ch: Ruling Elder; hon/Outstg Yg Ams; 3 Outstg Yg Oklahoman's 1976; DIB; Notable Ams; W/W S&SW.

SUTHERLAND, WILLIAM ANDERSON oc/Lawyer; b/Oct 4, 1896; h/2101 Connecticut Ave NW, Washington, DC 20006; 300 W Peachtree St NE, Atlanta, GA 30308; ba/Wash DC; Atlanta; m/Sarah Hall; c/Mary Johnston Strong (Mrs Robert L), Margaret Copeland Coleman (Mrs James E Jr), Sarah Hall Stoner (Mrs Frank R III); p/Phocion Leonides and Jannis Mattox Sutherland; ed/AB Univ Va 1914; LLB Harvard 1917; AM Univ Wis 1919; mil/OTC, WWI; pa/Sr Partner Firm Sutherland, Asbill & Brennan & Predessor Firms 1924-; Law Pract Atlanta & Wash DC 1921-; Atty & Examr Fed Trade Comm, Wash DC 1919-20; Admitted to DC Bar 1919, Ga Bar 1921; Gen Solicitor TVA 1933-34; Am Bar Endowmt; Bd Dirs 1949-74, Secy 1963-67, VP 1967-69, Pres 1969-71, Bd Dirs Emeritus 1974-; ABA: Fed Taxation Com 1935-39, Taxation Sect Coun 1939-44, VChm 1944-46, Chm 1946-48, Ho of Dels 1951-54, 56-71; Past Pres Nat Tax Assn; Ga St, Atlanta, Fed, DC Bar Assns; Lwyrs Clb; cp/Mem Var Clbs; hon/Andrew Wallington Cordian Fellow; Fellow Am Bar Foun, Awd for Dist'd Ser to Legal Profession; W/W in Am.

SUTTON, EDMONDE D oc/Businesswoman in Advertising & Public Relations; h/5314 Lisa Ave, Lakeland, FL 33803; ba/Same; m/Earl W; p/Jean L and Andree L Duberos (dec); ed/Master's Deg (Langs); Grad Dale Carnegie; Grad Bus Law; Other Studies; pa/Owner Coml Art Ser 1978-; Polk Advt'g Fdn: Mem, Bd Dirs, Past Pres; cp/Wom's Guild; Vol Var Orgs; r/Cath, Mem Ch of the Resurrection, Lakeland; hon/Silver Medal Awd, Am Advt'g Fdn; Ad Wom of Yr; DIB; W/W S&SW; Notable Ams Bicent Era.

SVETLOVA, MARINA oc/Choreographer; Ballerina; Educator; b/May 3, 1922; h/Dorset, VT 05251; p/Max and Tamara Andreleff Hartman; ed/Pvt Studies; pa/Debut Paris Opera 1932; Baby Ballerina Original Ballet Russe de Monte Carlo 1934-41: Guest Ballerina Ballet Theatre, Met Opera Tour 1942; Prima Ballerina Met Opera Co (NYC) 1943-50, NYC Opera 1950-52; Own Concert Group Under Mgmt Columbia Artists Mgmt 1944-58, Nat Artists Corp 1958-69; Ballet Tours in US 1944-, Far East 1953, Mid E 1954, Europe 1955, 59, SAm 1962; Guest Ballerina London's Fest Ballet 1953, Teatro dell Opera, Rome 1953, Nat Opera, Stockholm 1955, Suomi Opera, Helsinki, Finland 1956, Het Nederland Ballet, Holland 1954, Cork Irish Ballet 1955, Paris Opera Comique 1958, London Palladium 1959-60; Appeared in Var Classical Ballets, Others; Choreographer Dallas Civic Opera 1964-67, Seattle Opera 1961-62, Houston Opera 1965, Ks City Perf'g Arts Foun 1965-67, Ft Worth Opera 1967-; Ballet Dir So Vt Art Ctr, Manchester 1959-65; Dir Svetlova Dance Ctr, Dorset 1963-; Prof Ballet Ind Univ, Bloomington 1969-; Chm Ballet Dept 1969-; Am Guild Mus Artists, Dir 1943; Nat Soc Arts & Lttrs; Choreographer Articles on Theatre, Choreography & Ballet Works to Newspapers & Var Mags; W/W Am Wom.

SVILAND, MARY ANN P oc/Clinical Psychologist; b/Jul 1, 1937; h/24021 Victory Blvd, Canoga Park, CA 91307; ba/Canoga Park; c/Laura, Gregory; p/Slavko John and Ann Rose Boldin Petrich, Canoga Park; ed/BS Univ Wis-M 1959; MA Cal St Univ-N 1967; PhD Univ So Cal 1971; pa/Clin Psychologist Pvt Pract; Asst Prof Dept Psychol Cal St Univ-N; Radio Prog "Be Good to Yourself", KCSN-

FM; Acad, Med & Mgmt Conslt; Am, Wn, Cal St, Los Angeles Co & San Fernando Val Psychol Assns; Exec Com Soc for Sci Study of Sex, Wn Reg; Bd Mem Ctr for Sex Res, CSUN; AASECT; hon/Sr Hons, Univ Wis; NIH Grant; Nat Inst Mtl Hlth Grant; W/W Am Wom; World W/W Wom; Personalities W&MW.

SWAEBE, RICHARD oc/Diamond & Precious Gem Dealer; b/Dec 4, 1938; ba/Ainsley Suite 1500 14 NE 1st Ave, Miami, FL 33132; m/Lily Kalkstein; c/Theodore Aaron, Daniela; p/Leslie and Rosa Landau Swaebe; mil/AUS 1956-59; pa/Pres & Chm Diamond Sales Co, Miami 1963-; Chm Bd Jewelers Co Fin Co; Conslt Diamond & Precious Gem Index, Smithsonian Inst Dept Mineral Sci; Diamond Dealer Assn; Diamond Trade Assn; Jewelers Security Alliance; Jewelers Trade; cp/Ocean Power Boat Racing Assn; Exec Bd Fla Reg Anti-Defamation Leag; Repub; r/Jewish; hon/Biogl Listings.

SWAIN, JAMES O oc/Educator; b/Dec 31, 1896; h/414 Forest Park Blvd, Carlton Towers, Knoxville, TN 37919; m/Nancy Jane Cox; c/James Maurice, Juan Robert; p/Ashbell Willard and Laetitia Lambert Swain; ed/AB 1921, AM 1923 Ind Univ; PhD Univ Ill 1932; Addit Studies; mil/AUS CE 1918-19; pa/Vis Prof: Univ Ky 1964-, Maryville Col 1966, Roanoke Col 1967, Lee Col 1969-70; Exec Secy Mtn Interstate Fgn Lang Conf 1963-64; Guest Lectr Univ Madrid Sum 1958, Maracaibo, Venezuela 1959; Guest Lectr Am Lit Univ Chile Sum Session 1952; Guest Dir Sum Langs Sch Wn Colo Col 1937; Prof & Chm Dept Romance Langs Univ Tenn 1937-58; Mich St Col: Mem Fac 1931-37, Asst Prof Mod Langs 1935-37; Mod Lang Assn Am,

Sect Ofcr Var Times; Ctl, So Sts, S Atl Mod Lang Assns; Am Assn Tchrs Spanish; Am Assn Tchrs French; Am Assn Tchrs Italian; Institute de Literature IBeroamericana; Sigma Delta Pi; r/Meth: Deacon; hon/Pub'd Author; W/W S&SW.

SWAMY, MAYASANDRA NANJUNDIAH SRIKANTA oc/University Dean; b/Apr 7, 1935; ba/Dept Engrg Concordia Univ, Montreal, Quebec, Canada H3G 1M8; m/Married; c/3 Chd; ed/BS w hons Univ Mysore (India) 1954; DIIS Indian Inst Sci (Bangalore) 1957; MS 1960, PhD 1963 Univ Saskatchewan (Canada); pa/Govt of India Scist Indian Inst of Technol, Madras 1963-64; Asst Prof Math Univ Saskatchewan 1964-65; Asst, Assoc & Prof Elect Engrg Nova Scotia Tech Col, Halifax 1965-68; Prof Elect Engrg Sir George Williams Univ, Montreal 1968-69; Prof Elect Engrg Univ Calgary 1969-70; Concordia Univ (formerly Sir Geo Williams): Prof & Chm Elect Engrg 1970-77, Dean Engrg 1977-; VP Circuits & Systems Soc IEEE 1976; Prog Chm IEEE Intl Symposium on Circuit Theory, Toronto 1973; Dir Math Sub-com Am Assn for Engrg Ed 1973-75; Fellow, IBA; cp/Intl Students' Clb, Univ Saskatchewan: Former Secy, Past Pres; Former Gen Secy India-Canada Assn, Saskatoon; Pres Bharatiya Sangeeta Sangam, Montreal; hon/Num Pubs; Biogl Listings.

SWANNACK, CHERYL oc/Artist; b/Dec 30, 1946; h/2119 Estrella, Los Angeles, CA 90007; ba/Same; p/Guy and Billie Jo Cox

Swannack, Las Cruces, NM; ed/BS; BFA; MFA; CFS; pa/Documentary & Phil Artist; cp/Dir Resource Ctr & Wom's Bldg; hon/Num Drawing & Sculpture Awds.

SWANSON, DAVID H oc/Administrator; h/6406 Olympic Ave, Madison, WI 53705; m/Married; c/2 Sons; ed/BA St Cloud St Col 1953; MA Univ Minn 1955; Cert'd Property & Casualty Underwriter; mil/USAF 1951-52; Admr Wis Div Bus Devel Sers, Madison 1976-; Dir Group Res Dept US Automobile Assn, San Antonio, Tex 1973-76; Div Mgr Deal Devel Co, New Orleans, La 1972-73; Dir New Orleans Ec Devel Coun, NO 1970-72; Dir Ec Devel & Res la So Utilities Co, Centerville, la 1963-60; Others; Wis Ec Devel Assn; Am Indust Devel Coun; Gt Lakes Area Devel Coun; Nat Assn St Devel Agys; Soc Ins Res, 1975 Wkshop Chm; Nat Assn Bus Economists; MENSA; Pres & Owner Lantern Corp; Adv Coun Bus Devel Ctr Univ Wis; Spec Conslt to Wis Commr of Ins; cp/Past Pres Toastmasters; hon/Profl Pubs; W/W: Fin & Indust, S, MW; Royal Blue Book; Others.

SWANSON, ROBERT LAWRENCE oc/Administrator; b/Oct 11, 1938; h/30 Erland Rd, Stony Brook, NY 11790; ba/Rockville, MD; m/Dana Lamont; c/Lawrence Daniel, Michael Nathan; p/Lawrence Wilbur and Hazel Graves Swanson, Kensington, MD; ed/BS Lehigh Univ 1960; MS 1965, PhD 1971 Oreg St Univ; pa/Dir Ofc of Marine Pollution Assessment, Nat Oceanic & Atmospheric Adm; ASCE; AAAS; MTS; ASP; cp/Former Cubmaster Pack 18, Stony Brook; r/Presb; hon/Silver Medal, US Dept Commerce; NOAA Awd for Prog Adm & Mgmt.

SWANSON, ROGER FULTON oc/Engineer; b/Oct 12, 1930; h/3208 Wood Ave, Burtonsville, MD 20730; ba/Washington, DC; m/Orchid T; c/Corinne, Sandra, Annette Christine, Craig Fulton; p/Elmer Fulton Swanson (dec); Beulah Mae Swanson, Hyattsville, MD; ed/BSIE Iowa St Univ 1961; Public Adm, Univ of Va 1973; mil/USAF 1950-54 (Japan); pa/Staff Mem, Veterans Adm, Dept of Med & Surg, Mgmt Sys 1967-69, Engrg Ser 1969-68, Bldg Mgmt Ser 1968-; Staff, US Continental Army, Maintenance Engr (Aberdeen, Md) 1965-67, Mgmt Sys Devel; Staff Mem, US Army Weapons Command (Rock Island, Ill) 1964-65; Other Former Positions; Engrg Mgmt Info Sys; Biomedical Engrg Prog Devel; Energy Conserv Prog Devel; HEW Seminars; Assn for Advmt of Medical Instrumentation; cp/VP Francis Scott Key PTA; r/Luth: Choir Mem; hon/W/W E; Men of Achmt.

SWARTOUT, BRUCE EDWIN oc/Energy Storage Executive; b/Mar 6, 1917; h/30821 Palm Hill Dr, San Juan Capistrano, CA 92693; ba/Irvine, CA; m/Violet; c/Mila Joy, Cynthia; p/Clifford Harlan Swartout (dec); Ruby Pease, Spokane, WA; pa/Pres, US Flywheels Inc; SAMPE; Real Estate Broker; cp/Pres, C of C; Jr C of C of Spokane; r/Meth; hon/Dow Dirstine Meml Awd; United Nations Commend.

SWARTHOUT, WALTER EMMET oc/- Public Safety Consultant; b/Mar 1, 1902; h/Box 21262, San Jose, CA 95151; m/Nha Thi Bui; c/Patricia Ann, Mary Alice, Walter Emmet Jr, William Charles, Anthony Emmet; p/William Allen Swarthout (dec); Lena Alma Nichols (dec); ed/BE No Ill St Univ; MA Univ Chgo; mil/AUS Ordnance Corps 1946-55, Med Corps 1941-46, Lt Col Ret'd; pa/Public Safety Advr AID, Dept St, Wash DC 1960-68; Advr: to Turkish Chief of Ordnance (Ankara), Laos Nat Police (Vientiane), Vietnamese Nat Police (Saigon); Prin Emerson Sch, Maywood, Ill 1930-41; Instr Scouting Ldrship No Ill St Tchrs Col, De Kalb, Ill 1927-30; Other Former

Positions; cp/Past Pres NISTC Alumni Assn; Eta Chapt Alpha Phi Omega; Lions Clb, Maywood; Huntsville Chapt ROA; Peninsula Ret'd Ofcrs Clb, Moffett Field, Cal; Cmdr Mil Order World Wars, Moffett Field; Cabinet Secy Treas Lions Intl Dist 1A; BSA: Scoutmaster, Dist Commr, Coun Explorer Chm, Dir'd Boy Scout Groups to 2 World Jamborees in England & Holland; hon/Police Hon Medal, Vietnamese Nat Police; Cert of Merit, Vietnamese Govt; Medal for Viet-Nam Ser, Dept of St; Rockefeller Foun Fellow in Study of Radio in Schs.

SWARTZ, CHRISTIAN LeFEVRE oc/- Lawyer; Artist; b/Aug 14, 1915; h/1900 S Eads St, Apt 908, Arlington, VA 22202; ba/Washington, DC; c/Christian Arthur, James Vanderbilt; p/Christian I and Anna F Swartz (dec); ed/BS Wharton Sch-Univ Pa; LLB Temple Univ; LLM Geo Wash Univ; mil/USNR Lt, Nav Aviator, Ret'd; pa/Ret'd Navy Ofc of Gen Coun; Gen Pvt Pract & Patent Law; DC Bar Assn; Fed Bar Assn; cp/Corinthian Yacht Clb; Capital Yacht Clb; US Power Sqdrn; Capitol Hill Clb; Ofcrs Mess AAFB; Pa St Soc: Past Pres, Bd Mem; Past Pres Lyon Village Citizens Assn; No Va Carvers; Am Shipcarvers Guild; Commun Arts Coun Arlington; Nat Trust for Hist Preserv; Others; r/Epis; hon/Var Art Awds.

SWARTZ, JANET A MAULE oc/College Lecturer; b/Jan 1, 1948; h/65 N Yorktown Rd, Macomb, IL 61455; m/Stanley L; c/Philip Hemming; p/David P and Lucille H Johnson Maule, Rocky River, OH; ed/BS Findlay Col 1970; MEd Bowling Green St Univ 1976; pa/Lectr Child Devel Carl Sandburg Col, Carthage, Ill; APGA; Am Sch Cnslr Assn; Assn Humanistic Psychol; AAUW; hon/Phi Delta Kappa.

SWEARINGEN, JOHN NEAFUS oc/- Accountant; b/Nov 30, 1920; h/303 W First St, Long Beach, MS 39560; ba/Same; m/- Fannie Mae Pearce; c/Adrian L Hester (Stepson); p/John N and Lizzie M Swearingen (dec); ed/BA Ctl Cal Col 1952; mil/AUS 1942-45; pa/Nat Assn Accts; Nat Soc Public Accts; S Miss Est Planning Coun; cp/Cand Public Ser Comm 1979; r/Meth; hon/W/W S&SW.

SWEETEN, JOHN MARBROOKS JR oc/Agricultural Engineer; b/Jan 11, 1944; h/1804 Leona, College Station, TX 77840; ba/Col Sta; m/Mary Claire Kinney; c/Jessica Lynn, Patrick Kinney; p/John Marbrooks and Johnnie Rachael Johnson Sweeten, Rocksprings, TX; ed/BS Tex Tech Univ 1965; MS 1967, PhD 1969 Okla St Univ; mil/USPHS 1969-71, Sanitary Engr & Lt Cmdr; pa/Ext Agri Engr-Waste Mgmt Tex A&M Univ 1972-; Sanitary Engr US Envir Protection Agy 1970-71; Tech Advr Envir Mgmt Com, Nat Cattlemen's Assn; Chm Odor Regulation Com Tex Air Control Bd; Am Soc Agri Engrs: Chm Food Processing Waste Subcom, Chm Envir Quality Coor'g Com; Exec Secy Indust/Ext Livestock Envir Sci Com; Air Pollution Control Assn; Conslt; Cattle Feeder & Rancher; cp/Brazos Val Yth Soccer Assn; r/1st Presb Ch, Bryan, Tex: Deacon; hon/1977 Yg Engr of Yr, Brazos Chapt Tex Soc Profl Engrs; Superior Ser Awd, Tex Agri Ext Ser; ASAE Paper Awd 1970.

SWEITZER, HARRY PHILLIPS oc/- Clergyman; b/Jul 30, 1916; h/1392 Wasatch Dr, Salt Lake City, UT 84108; ba/SLC; m/Margaret C; c/Paul, Mary, Jean; p/- Benjamin H and Agnes L Sweitzer (dec); ed/- BA, MDiv, DD; pa/Presb Min; Moderator Synod ND, St Paul, Pembina; Pres Bd Trustees Presby Utah; cp/Dir Bush Foun; Salt Lake Kiwanis Clb; Utah Alcohol Foun; Bonneville Knife & Fork Clb; Salt Lake Co Mtl Hlth Bd; YMCA; Salvation Army; r/Presb.

SWIDLER, LEONARD oc/Educator; b/Jan 6, 1929; m/Arlene Anderson; c/Carmel, Eva Marie; ed/BA St Norbert's Col 1950; MA Marquette Univ 1955; STL Univ Tubingen (Germany) 1959; PhD Univ Wis 1961; Addit Studies; pa/Prof Rel Dept Temple Univ 1966-; Guest Prof Cath Theol Fac & Prot Theol Fac Univ Tubingen 1972-73; ACUIIS Sum Sch Univ Graz (Austria) 1972, 73; Prof Duquesne Univ 1960-66; Other Tchg Positions; Com for Responsible Election of Pope 1978-; Assoc Dir Graymoor Ecumenical Inst, Atonement Fathers, Garrison, NY 1977-; Acad Coun Nat Inst on the Holocaust 1977-; Adv Com Secretariat for Cath-Jewish Relats of Nat Conf Cath Bishops 1977-; Com on Christian Ecumenism of Cardinal's Comm on Human Relats (Phila) 1971-72, Chperson 1975-; Phila Task Force on Wom in Rel 1970-; St Joan's Intl Alliance 1970-; Bd Dirs Emmaus House (NYC) 1966-; Num Others; hon/LLD, LaSalle Col; Num Profl Pubs; Recipient Grants.

SWIECICKA-ZIEMIANEK, MARIA oc/University Professor; h/RR #1, Glenwood Dr, Washington Crossing, PA 18977; ba/Philadelphia, PA; m/Janusz B Zienianek; c/Margaret A; p/George S and Frances Swiecicki, Collingswood, NJ; ed/PhD Univ Pa 1971; pa/Prof Temple Univ; Polish Inst Arts & Scis in Am: Mem Coun, Chm Phila Chapt; Exec Coun Polish Am Hist Assn; cp/CoChm Temple Ethnic Fests Acts I & II 1975, 77; Mem Temple Univ Bicent Com; Lectr; r/Rom Cath; hon/The Kosciuszko Foun Doct Dissertation Awd; Study Leave, Temple Univ; Pub'd Author.

SWIGGETT, HAL oc/Writer; Photographer; b/Jul 22, 1921; h/539 Roslyn, San Antonio, TX 78204; ba/Same; m/Wilma; c/Gerald, Vernon; p/Otho B and Mildred S Swiggett (dec); mil/USAF WWII; pa/Life Mem Nat Rifle Assn; Life Mem Tex St Rifle

Assn; Past Dir Outdoor Writers Assn Am; Past Pres Tex Outdoor Writers Assn; Past Pres Wildlife Unlimited; Ducks Unlimited; cp/Repub; r/Palm Hgts Bapt Ch: Deacon, SS Dir, Music Dir, Treas; hon/Top Ten Outstg Am Handgunner Awds 1973, 75, 78; Sev Photo & Writing Awds.

SWINK, ESTHER ELAINE COSTA oc/Teacher; Librarian; b/Jul 21, 1947; h/273 Clovernook Dr, Nashville, TN 37210; m/Jeffery Wayne; p/Jerry G and Viola Mae Costa, Nashville; ed/AB cum laude Trevecca Nazarene Col 1969; MLS Geo Peabody Col for Tchrs 1976; pa/Tenn Ed Assn; NEA; Metro N'ville Ed Assn: Pres 1977-78; Exec Bd Mem

1973-78; cp/Former Chperson N'ville Edr's Polit Action Com; Lobbying for Ed Interests; Dem Wom's Clb; r/Blakemore Ch of Nazarene: Mem, Pianist, SS Tchr; hon/W/W Am Cols & Univs; Outstg Yg Wom Am; Phi Delta Kappa; Phi Delta Lambda.

SWOBODA, JOSEPH STEPHEN oc/- Counselor; Consultant; b/Sept 12, 1947; h/- 1018 S 35th, Lincoln, NE 68510; ba/Lincoln; m/Mary Frances; p/Joseph S Swoboda (dec); Evalena T Swoboda, Schuyler, NE; ed/BA, MA Univ Neb-L; pa/Cnslr/Conslt Child Guid Ctr; APGA; AMCHA; Assn AAMFT; Neb AMFT; Neb MHCA; cp/Mem Vol Bur Cabinet; Social Sers Chair Vol Bur; Citizens Coalition for Preven Child Abuse & Neglect; Former Parent's Anonymous Sponsor; Mem Child Protective Sers Agy Com.

SYFRETT, MARY KATHRYN oc/Teacher; b/Aug 27, 1948; h/Rt 5, Box 274, Chipley, FL 32428; ba/Chipley; m/Paul; c/David, Laura; p/Larry Betts (dec); Jeanne Betts, Chipley; ed/AA; BS; MS; pa/Tchr Kate Smith Elem Sch; WCEA; FEA; NEA; cp/WHARC; r/Meth; hon/Mu Alpha Theta; Phi Theta Kappa; Kappa Delta Pi; World W/W Wom; Notable Ams; Personalities of S; Commun Ldrs & Noteworthy Ams; W/W Child Devel Profls; Others.

SYKES, RUBY LEE BROWN oc/Dentist; Educator; b/Aug 27, 1948; h/r5, Box 274, CA 90028; m/Hulbert S (dec); ed/DDS Univ So Cal 1928; pa/Ret'd 1964; Pvt Dental Pract 1929-64; Dental Asst, Secy, Treas, Bkkeeper, Buyer & Gen Mgr of Ofc, Ariz; Instr USC

Dental Col 1941-43; Instr Postgrad Dental Courses 1928-40 & Nutritional Course Univ So Cal 1929; Charter Mem & 1/VP Dental Acad of Applied Nutrition 1930-35; Am Dental Assn; 1/Pres Theta Chapt Upsilon Alpha Nat Dental Sorority; AARP; Others; cp/Am Wom Pacific Coast; Century Clb USC; 1/VP Daughs of Confed; Charter Mem El Birch White Shrine; OES: Worthy Matron, Grand Rep to Pa, La & Ga, Others; hon/Nat Dental Key, OKU for Scholastic Achmt; 50 Yr Awd Pin, OES 1970; World W/W Wom; Fellow IBA; DIB; Intl Reg Profiles.

SYKORA, SYLVIA ESTHER oc/Retired; b/Apr 21, 1898; h/1157 River Rd, Windom, MN 56101; m/Frank (dec); c/Charlotte S Viranovick, Harley, Richard, Merle H, Donna S Grahn, Lucy S Madison; p/William W and Ella D Peterson Hunter (dec); pa/Editor Cottonwood Co Hist 1870-1970; Farm Bur; cp/4-H; Sr Citizen Hist Soc; Dem; r/Bapt: Var Ch Activs; hon/Silver Plate as Curator for 30 Yrs in Hist Soc.

SZEGHO, EMERIC oc/Retired Educator; b/Sept 10, 1907; h/215 Ross Ave, Cambridge Springs, PA 16403; ed/License at Law Univ Cernauti (Rumania) 1938; Doct Juris Universi Univ Cluj (Rumania) 1947; Dipl as Atty-at-Law Rumanian Bar Assn (Bucharest) 1941; pa/Pract'g Atty-at-Law & Jurisconslt, Timisoara, Sibiu, Rumania 1941-60; Prof Alliance Col, Cambridge Sprgs 1966-73, Currently Ret'd w Awd of Tenure; Emeritus Mem AUP; Am Security Coun, Mem Coun's Nat Adv Bd; Am Security Coun Ed Foun (formerly Inst for Am Strategy); Fdg Mem US Senatorial Clb; IPA; Fellow IBA; r/U Presb Ch, Cambridge Sprgs; hon/Pub'd Author; Biogl Listings.

SZEMBORSKI, ELEANOR oc/Teacher; b/Sept 30, 1925; h/294 Maryland Ave, Paterson, NJ 07503; ba/Paterson; p/Jerome Szemborski (dec); Lottie P Szemborski, Paterson; ed/BA cum laude Carlow Col 1959; MA William Paterson Col 1968; Doct Student Fordham Univ; pa/NEA; NJEA; PEA; Fordham Univ Sch Adm Assn; Phi Delta Kappa; Pi Lambda Theta: Treas Beta Chi Chapt 1976-77, Pres Beta Chi Chapt 1977-; r/Cath; St Brendan's Parish Coun: Past Pres & Mem.

SZILASSY, SANDOR oc/College Administrator; b/Apr 9, 1921; h/14 Polaris Rd, Turnersville, NJ 08012; ba/Glassboro, NJ; p/Sandor Sr and Jolan Fenyves Szilassy (dec); ed/LLD; MA; pa/Dir Savitz Lng Resource Ctr Glassboro St Col; Pres-elect Tri-St Col Lib Cooperative; Pres S Jersey Col Lib Coop & Lib Sci & Bibliog Div Hung Cong; Past Pres Coun NJ St Col & Univ Libns; hon/Gold Medal, Arpad Acad; Phi Alpha Theta; Author Book, Papers, Articles & Book Chapts.

T

TABOR, CURTIS HAROLD JR oc/-Minister; Librarian; b/Jul 3, 1936; h/154 Kelly Ln, Thonotosassa, FL 33592; ba/Columbus, MS; m/Dorothy M Corbin; c/Timothy Mark, John Michael; p/Curtis H Sr and Gertrude

Olive Casey Tabor, Tampa, FL; ed/AA; BA; MA; MDiv; MLS; Cand DMin; pa/Vol Archaeol Excavations, Tell Gezer (Israel) 1969; cp/Nacogdoches (Tex) Baseball Leag; Cub Scouts; SAR; r/Ch of Christ; hon/Eta Beta Rho; Beta Phi Mu; Scouters Key.

TADLOCK, LILA CLEMENTA oc/Retired Teacher; b/Jan 13, 1903; h/Box 334, Bonham, TX 75418; m/William Lawton; c/Theodore Gamaliel (dec); p/Edward T and Martha Frances Swindell (dec); ed/BS, MS E Tex St Univ; pa/3rd VP, Fannin Co RTA; Treas, Tex RTA; Nat Fdn Poetry Socs; Acad Am Poets; cp/Repub Clb; Triple L Clb; Woodmen of World; Bonham Wom's Clb; WOC; r/Presb; hon/Rec'd Poetry & Civic Awds.

TAFFE, BETTY JO oc/Public Official; b/Nov 19, 1942; h/Quincy Rd, Rumney, NH 03266; ba/Concord, NH; m/William J; c/Daniel David, Michael Andrew; p/Albert J Miller; Elizabeth Ottey Miller, Malvern, PA; ed/BA summa cum laude, Juniata Col (Penn) 1964; MAT Univ Chgo 1968; pa/NH St Ho of Reps 1976-: House Ed Com 1976-, VChm 1978-; Grafton Co Exec Com 1976-, Clerk 1978-; cp/Chm Rumney Sch Bd; Bd Mem, Lakes Region Mtl Hlth Ctr; r/Christian.

TAGGART, MARION EWING oc/Retired; b/Jan 21, 1902; h/717 S Columbia Ave, Los Angeles, CA 90017; p/Francis William and Nancy Van Buren F Taggart; ed/BS Ctl Mo St Univ; MA Columbia Univ; pa/Tchr: Mo 1921-23, Altoona (Penn) HS 1924-25, S Barbara (Cal) Jr HS 1925-55; Dorgus Corp (Beverly Hills, Cal), Ret'd 1966; Contbr Articles Profl Jours; cp/Masonic Affiliation; Nom Repub Party Gen Election 1972; r/Ch of Christ & Fdr's United Ch of Sci (Both in LA): Mem; hon/Past Pres Rho Chapt, Kappa Delta Pi; Former Mem, Phi Delta Kappa; Alpha Epsilon.

TAHIR, ASH H oc/Physician; b/Sept 16, h/7061 Mayo Blvd, New Orleans, LA 70126; ba/Same; m/Dixie Ann; c/Lisa, Michael; p/Zia Mohd Khan and Mumtaz Begum, Pakistan; ed/BSc; MBBS; MRCP; FRCP; pa/Am Soc Anesthesiol; Intl Anesthesiol Res Soc; La Soc Anesthesiol; Others; r/Islam; hon/AMA Physicians' Recog Awd; Personalities of S.

TALLEY-MORRIS, NEVA BENNETT oc/Lawyer; b/Aug 12, 1909; h/101 N State St, Little Rock, AR 72201; ba/Little Rock; m/Cecil C Talley (dec); Joseph H Morris (dec); p/John W Bennett (dec); Erma R Bennett, Judsonia, AR; ed/BA magna cum laude, Ouachita Univ 1930; MEd Univ Tex 1938; Pvt Law Study; mil/AUS Ordnance Inspector; US Civil Ser 1942-46; pa/Chm Fam Law Sect, ABA 1970; Pres Nat Assn Wom Lwyrs 1956-57; Pres Ark Assn Wom Lwyrs 1950-51; Fellow, Ark Bar Assn; Fellow & Mem Bd Govs, Am Acad Matrimonial Lwyrs 1968-; World Assn Lwyrs; Author: *Fam Law Pract &*

Procedure (1973), *Appellate Civil Pract & Procedure* (1975); cp/Mem World Peace Delegation; r/2nd Bapt Ch (Little Rock); hon/Dist'd Ser Awd, Ark Bar Foun; Lwyr-Citizen Awd, Ark Bar Assn; Ldrship in Legal Profession Spec Awd, Ark Wom Lwyrs Assn; Dist'd Ser Awd, Nat Assn Wom Lwyrs.

TAN, OWEN T oc/Professor; b/Aug 30, 1931; h/649 Rodney Dr, Baton Rouge, LA 70808; ba/Baton Rouge; m/Martha G Liem; c/Joyce Yolanthe, Edward H, Cindy Liliane; p/Eng T Tan (dec); Lan H Tan; ed/BS 1953, MS 1955 Technol Fac Bandung (Indonesia); PhD Eindhoven Univ Technol (Netherlands) 1961; pa/La St Univ: Full Prof Elect Engrg 1978-, Assoc Prof 1972-78, Asst Prof 1966-72, Grad Fac, Grad Studies Com, Student Adv'g Com, Dept Power Group Coor; Bandung Inst

Technol: Sr Lectr Elect Engrg 1964-66, Lectr 1962-64; Indusrs: Willem Smit & Co (Rotterdam, The Netherlands), Siemens Schuckert (Erlangen, West Germany), R & D Engr 1956-62; IEEE; Royal Inst Engrs (Holland); r/Presb Ch; hon/Eta Kappa Nu; Am Men & Wom Sci; DIB; Intl W/W Commun Ser; Men Achmt; Book of Hon; Commun Ldrs & Noteworthy Ams; W/W S&SW; Personalities of S.

TANAKA, HISAKO oc/Instructor; h/-1118 Waterloo St, #8, Los Angeles, CA 90026; ba/University Park, PA; p/(dec); ed/BA Univ Chgo; MA Univ Cal-B; Cand PhD Univ Tokyo (Japan); pa/Instr Japanese Lang & Lit Prog, Penn St Univ; Lectr; Writer; Translator; hon/Alpha Gamma Sigma; Cal Hon Soc; Phi Theta; 1st Prize Essay Contest, *LA Japanese Daily News*; Others.

TANAKA, THOMAS V C oc/Legislator; b/Aug 7, 1940; h/PO Box 1258, Agana, Guam 96910; ba/Agana; m/Jane C; c/Stephen, Thomas, Jo Ann, Joyce, Gary, Eugene; p/Thomas S and Josephina C Tanaka, Agana; ed/BA; pa/Speaker, 15th Guam Legislature; Chm Com on Fin & Taxation 1974-78; r/Cath.

TANGEMAN, DELBERT RAY oc/Minister; b/May 19, 1933; h/100 Oakridge St, Spartanburg, SC 29301; ba/Spartanburg; m/Betty; c/Daniel, Nathan, Edsel; p/Linus Tangeman (dec); Esther McCain Spicer, Celina, OH; ed/ThB; mil/USN; pa/Pastor, Park Hills Ch of God 11 Yrs; Held All Offices in SC Assembly of Ch of God incl'g St Chm; cp/Lions Clb; Past Pres, PTA; r/Ch of God (Anderson, Ind) Affiliate.

TANNER, BILLY CHARLES oc/Investor; b/Jul 27, 1935; h/303 Crescent Dr, Hartselle, AL 33640; ba/Hartselle; m/Frances Leah; c/Terry Charles, Billy Renea; p/Orville Wright and Mabel Nettie Tanner, Hartselle; ed/BS Univ Ala; mil/AUS 1958; pa/Pres, Tanner Cos; cp/Pres Rotary Clb; Commerce Exec Soc, Univ Ala; N Ala Mgr: Gov George C Wallace for Gov 1970 & Bill Bailey for Gov 1978; r/Bapt; hon/Personalities of S; Notable Ams; W/W S&SW; Other Biogl Listings; Lambda Chi Alpha.

TANNER, JACK GENE oc/Insurance Agent; b/Mar 7, 1940; h/14 High Ridge Rd, Long Valley, NJ 07853; ba/Morristown, NJ; m/June Rita Sheehan; c/Craig Andrew; p/Ira John and Arlene Harper Tanner; ed/BS St John's Univ 1977; LLB LaSalle Univ; MBA Col of Insurance; mil/USN 1958-62, Hon

Discharge; pa/VChm, Excess Bonds Reinsurance Assn; cp/Repub Party; r/Mormon, Ch of Jesus Christ of LDS; hon/Sr Pilot Cit, Nat Pilot Assn (Wash, DC).

TANZLER, HANS GEARHART JR oc/Attorney; b/Mar 11, 1927; h/2701 Cove View Dr S, Jacksonville, FL 32217; ba/Jacksonville; m/Mercedes Woodard; c/Hans G III; p/Dorette W Tanzler; ed/BA; JD; mil/1945-46; Recalled 1962 (Cuban Missile Crisis); Air Intell Ofcr; p/Pract'd w Firm, Tanzler & Maddox; Former Asst St Atty; Named Gen St Coun, Fla St Bd Hlth 1961; Appointed Judge Crim Ct of Record by Gov Ferris Bryant 1962; Current Pract w Boyer, Tanzler, Blackburn & Boyer (Law Firm); cp/Former Mayor Commr, City of Jacksonville; Former Mayor of Consolidated City of J'ville (Duval Co), Twice Re-elected; Cand Gov Fla 1979; Former Pres, Nat Leag of Cities of US; Former Pres, Fla Leag of Cities; Testified Before US Senate Coms; Confs w Pres Gerald R Ford; r/Bapt; hon/Fla Blue Key Hon Ldrship Soc; Rec'd Ath S'ship.

TARNAWSKY, OSTAP E M oc/Writer; Educator; Librarian; b/May 3, 1917; h/6509 Lawnton Ave, Philadelphia, PA 19126; ba/Philadelphia; m/Marta; c/Mark M, Maxim D; p/David and Xenia Tarnawsky (dec); ed/Civil Engrg Dipl 1947; MSLC 1962; PhD 1974; PhD 1976; pa/Author 4 Books Poetry, 4 Books Essays & Short Stories; Intl PEN; Pres Ukrainian Writers Assn; cp/Exec Dir, United Ukrainian Am Relief Com; hon/Rec'd Sev Awds for Short Stories.

TARPLEY, THOMAS MARVIN JR oc/Health Scientist; b/Apr 23, 1934; h/7115 Ridgewood Ave, Chevy Chase, MD 20015; ba/Bethesda, MD; m/Patricia Ann Newman; p/Tim Tarpley (dec); Laura B Tarpley, Albany, CA; ed/DDS 1961; MS 1973; MA 1978; mil/AUS 1954-57; USPHS 1961-; pa/Hlth Scist Admr; Oral Pathologist; Dentist; ADA; AAOP; Conslt, US Naval Dental Ctr; Assoc Clinical Prof Pathology; cp/Sponsor, DC Humane Soc; r/Prot; hon/Rec'd Mosby Awd; W/W E; Phi Delta Kappa.

TARSON, HERBERT HARVEY oc/-University Vice President; b/Aug 28, 1910; h/-4611 Denwood Rd, La Mesa, CA 92041; ba/-San Diego, CA; m/Lynne Barnett; c/Stephen Glenn; p/Harry and Elizabeth Miller Tarson (dec); ed/PhD US Intl Univ; mil/USAF; pa/Fellow, San Diego Bio-Med Inst; cp/World Affairs Coun; hon/Rec'd Bronze Star Medal w Oak Leaf Cluster & Air Force Commend Medal w 2 Oak Leaf Clusters.

TARTOUE, CASSIE EUGENIA oc/Poet; Writer; b/Jun 9, 1931; h/Apt 311, Hotel Moscow, Moscow, ID 83843; m/Pierre (dec); p/Earl Dixson (dec); Elizabeth Dixson, Moscow; pa/Author 12 Books in Series & *Pallette and Palate* (Cookbook in 2 Editions); Writer Newspaper Column, "Gems"; Pub'd Articles, Poems & Stories in Mags; Some Poems Reproduced on Radio & TV; r/St Mary's Cath Ch (Moscow); hon/Rec'd Editors & Critics Awd; Awds from Readers' Votes; Peace & Brotherhood Awd.

TARWATER, ELLA FLOYD oc/Retired; b/Dec 3, 1894; h/Rt 5, Sevierville, TN 37862; m/Millard E; c/Ruth T Thomas (Mrs James A), Wilda T Parrott (Mrs Quinton), Doris T Phelps (Mrs Bill), Rosemary T Starnes (Mrs Bill M), Altha T Wager (Mrs Harold); p/Richard B and Adelene Keeble Floyd (dec); ed/BS Univ Tenn-K; pa/Ret'd Tchr & Prin; Guard, Alcoa WWII; E Tenn Ed Assn; Tenn Ed Assn; cp/Am Hemerocallis Soc; Whites Home Dem Clb; Past Regent, Spencer Clack Chapt, DAR; r/Pleasant Hill United Meth Ch (Sevierville); hon/Rec'd Cent Farm-Fam Land Heritage Cert of Hon, St of Tenn; Lttr Congratulations, Gov Frank Clement (on Retirement after 50 Yrs Ser).

TASSINARI, SILVIO JOHN oc/Radiochemist; b/Jun 2, 1922; h/47 Moriches Rd, Nissequogue, St James, NY 11780; ba/Northport, NY; m/Lorraine Murtha;

c/Patricia Jeanne, Barbara Lynne; p/Ceasar A Tassinari (dec); Adrean Tassinari, Hialeah, FL; ed/BS 1943, MS 1947 St Michael's Col; PhD Intl Univ 1949; mil/USNR 1945-72; pa/Radiochem in Nuclear Med, VA Med Ctr; Reg'd Nuclear Med Technol; Conslt, Nuclear Med & Radiation Protection; Devel'd Many New Procedures in Diagnostic Nuclear Med; Profl Assns; r/Rom Cath; hon/W/W E; Commun Ldrs & Noteworthy Ams; Men Achmt; DIB.

TATE, MERZE oc/Educator; Author; b/Feb 6, 1905; h/1314 Perry St NE, Washington, DC 20017; ba/Same; p/Charles Emmet and Myrtle K Lett Tate (dec); ed/BA, MA BLitt, PhD Radcliffe Col & Harvard Univ; 4 Hon PhDs; pa/Prof Hist Emeritus, Howard Univ; Speaker Num Hist & Polit Sci Confs; Foun Wn Mich Univ; Adv Com on Black Wom Oral Hist, Radcliffe Col; Author: *The Disarmament Illusion* (1942, 70), *The US & Armaments* (1948), *The US & the Hawaiian Kingdom* (1965), Others; r/Rom Cath; hon/S'ship & Hon Student, Wn Mich Univ; Rec'd 3rd Alpha Kappa Alpha Foreign F'ship; First Am Negro to Receive Higher Res Deg, Oxford Univ; Julius Rosenwald F'ship, Radcliffe Col; Rec'd Nat Urban Leag Outstg Achmt Awd; Fulbright Lectr in India; Radcliffe Col Alumnae Assn Grad Chapt Medal for Dist'd Profl Ser; Wn Mich Univ Dist'd Alumna Awd; Mich's Isabella Co's Most Dist'd Citizen; Am Coun of Learned Socs Res Grant; Rec'd Grant, *Wash Evening Star*; Rockefeller Foun Res Grant; Rec'd Sev Howard Univ Res Grants; Endowed Merze Tate F'ship, Radcliffe Col; Pi Gamma Mu; Phi Beta Kappa; Biogl Listings.

TAUSSIG, WALTER oc/Associate Conductor; b/Feb 9, 1908; h/320 Riverside Dr, #14G, New York, NY 10025; m/-Lore; c/Lynn; p/Joesph and Paula Taussig (dec); ed/Dipl as Conductor, Hochschule fur Music, Vienna; pa/Assoc Conductor, Metro Opera, Lincoln Ctr; Musical Staff, Ealzburg Fest (Austria); Recording w Polydor; hon/Fulbright Exchange Prof in Tokyo; Hon Title of Prof, Austrian Govt.

TAUTENHAHN, GUNTHER oc/Composer; b/Dec 22, 1938; h/1534 3rd St, Manhattan Beach, CA 90266; ed/Studied Composition NY; pa/Author: *The Importance of One* (1971), *Controlled Expressionism* (1976), *Fiber Movemts* (1978); Compositions: *Numeric Serenade, Brass Quintet, Concerto for D-Bass & Orch, Double Concerto for French Horn & Trumpet w Orch*, Others; Other Widely Unpub'd Works; Compositions Widely Perf'd Radio; Inventor, Clock Face Whereby Chd Can Learn to Tell Note Values & Time; ASCAP; ASUC; NACUSA; ICA; AMC; hon/W/W: Mus, Cal, W, Am, Intellectuals; ASCAP Directory & Symph Catalog; AMC Catalog; Chamber Mus Catalog; Directory New Mus; Contemp Am Composers; Men Achmt; Intl Register Profiles; DIB; Others.

TAVITIAN, HENRY O oc/Psychiatrist; b/Mar 13, 1934; h/90-45 56 Ave, Elmhurst, NY 11373; ba/Bronx, NY; p/Mrs Armeno Mavi Tavitian, Elmhurst; ed/MD 1960; Esquire 1968; pa/Sect Chief Dept Psychi, VA Med Ctr; Diplomate, Am Bd Psychi & Neurol; Nat Ofcr, NAVAP; Pres, Bronx Branch, Am Psychi Assn 1975-77; r/Armenian Orthodox; hon/Grad w Highest Hons, Med Sch; Fellow,

Am Psychi Assn; Rec'd Plaque for Dist'd & Extraordinary Ser, Gtr NY Conf on Soviet Jewry.

TAXELL, SOPHIE oc/Artist; h/729 Cooper St, Puntagorda, FL 33950; p/Peter Mykra and Lyydia Kauhanen, Finland; pa/Group Shows, Charlotte Co Art Guild 1974, 76-79; One-person Shows: Helsinki (Finland), Wash (DC), Annapolis (Md), Bethesda (Md), Chevy Chase (Md); r/Tomas; hon/Rec'd Awds: Finnish Nat Acad Art, City of Helsinki, Finnish Artist Soc, Charlotte Co Art Guild; Others.

TAYLOR, ALAN J oc/Author; Radio Station Manager; h/1 Union St, Dover-Foxcroft, ME 04426; p/James S and Gerry D Taylor, Dover-Foxcroft; pa/Mgr Film Cos; Writer Books for Crown Pubs; Contbr Articles; Designed New Radio Format; r/Meth; hon/Num Awds.

TAYLOR, CURTIS L oc/Superintendent; b/Oct 8, 1929; h/828 10½ St SW, Rochester, MN 55901; ba/Rochester; m/Barbara Nottleson; c/Kim T Jordan, Wendy, Thomas; p/Herbert C Taylor (dec); Emily Taylor, WI; ed/BS Univ Wis; mil/USN 1948-49; pa/Supt Parks & Rec; Nat Coun Mem, Nat Rec & Park Assn 1971; Adv Coun, Gt Lakes Park & Rec 1970-71; Minn Rec & Park Assn: Pres 1971,

VP 1970, Var Coms; So Minn Rec & Park Assn; Gov's Adv Com on Rec & Leisure Time 1962-65; Contbr Articles Mags & Jours; cp/Former Pres, Gamehaven Coun BSA; Former Mem Bd Dirs, United Way; Bd Dirs & Com Chm, Kiwanis Clb; Pers Com, YMCA; r/Gloria Dei Luth Ch: Chm Bldg Fund Appeal; Zumbro Luth Ch: Past Pres & VP; hon/W/W MW; Rec'd Sportsmanship Awd & Recog'd, YMCA; Rec'd Awd Outstg Ser, Minn Rec & Park Assn; Cert Recog, C of C.

TAYLOR, ERNEST AUSTIN JR oc/-Engineer; b/Jan 18, 1918; h/2202 Cleveland Ave SW, Decatur, AL 35601; ba/Decatur;

m/Charleen Morgan; c/Rachel T Clay (Mrs Harold), Charles Ernest; p/Ernest A Taylor Sr (dec); Alma Robinson Taylor, Tampa, FL; ed/BEE Ga Inst Technol 1948; mil/USNR; pa/Sr Spec, Devel Engr; Reg'd Profl Engr; NSPE; Fluid Power Soc; cp/Former Scoutmaster, BSA; Bd Dirs, Intl Bible Col (Florence, Ala); r/Hatton Ch of Christ; Ednl Dir.

TAYLOR, GERRY MAILAND oc/Library Administrator; b/Jul 7, 1913; h/1206 W Country Clb Terrace, Jonesboro, AR 72401; ba/State University, AR; m/Myra; p/Everett B and Amy Taylor (dec); ed/Dipl, Farmington St Tchrs Col 1932; BA cum laude 1951, MA w Hons 1952 Baylor Univ; MLS Univ Tex 1955; mil/Sgt Artillery 5 Yrs WWII; pa/Head Libn,

Ark St Univ; Am Lib Assn; Ark Lib Assn, (Past Pres Col & Univ Div); NE Ark Lib Assn (Past Pres); Contbr Articles Profl Jours; cp/32° Mason; Past Pres, NE Ark Shrine Clb; Past Eminent Cmdr, Ivanhoe Commandery 18; r/So Bapt: Deacon, SS Tchr, Dir Outreach; hon/Phi Delta Kappa (Newslttr Editor); Others.

TAYLOR, HORACE MELVIN oc/Retired Clergyman; b/May 25, 1908; h/1422 Elm St, Lebanon, PA 17042; ba/Same; m/Grace Evelyn Newton; c/Donald C, Paul F, Elizabeth A; p/Arthur F and Grace M Churchill Taylor (dec); ed/ThB Gordon Col; ThM Evangelical Sem; mil/AUS 16 Yrs Active Duty, 11 Yrs Reserv; 1/Lt Chaplain to Full Col; Ret'd 1968; pa/Ordained Am Bapt Clergyman; Capital Fund Dir, Am Bapt Home Misson Soc 1957-73; Since Retirement, Ser'g as Supply Pastor, Evangelical Congreg Denom; Mil Chaplains Assn; Assn AUS; Reserv Ofcrs Assn; Ret'd Ofcrs Assn; cp/Fellow, Royal Geographical Soc; Mil Order World Wars; Nat Assn Uniformed Sers; Nat Wildlife Fdn; r/Am Bapt; hon/Rec'd Plaque for 16 Yrs Ser, Am Bapt Home Mission Soc; Asiatic-Pacific Ribbon; 2 Battle Stars; Bronze Arrow; Am Defense Medal; German Occupation Medal w Aeroplane; Medal for Humane Action; WWII Victory Medal; Nat Defense Medal; Reserv Medal w Hour Glass; Philipine Liberation Medal w 1 Battle Star, Pres Cit & Independence Ribbon; W/W Rel; DIB; Men Achmt; Intl W/W Intellectuals; Notable Ams; Commun Ldrs & Noteworthy Ams.

TAYLOR, JOHN CALVIN oc/Dentist; Missionary; b/Jul 22, 1914; h/110 Highland Ave, Herminie, PA 15637; ba/N Huntingdon, PA; m/Adah Boggs; c/Sarah Elizabeth, Margaret Louise, Virginia Alden, John Calvin VII, Frederick Christian, Adah Alison, Carla Sue; p/John C Sr and Elizabeth S Taylor (dec); ed/BS Muskingum Col 1937; BD Reformed

Presb Theol Sem 1939; DDS Pittsburgh Univ 1949; Addit Studies; mil/Vol Reserv WWII; pa/Missionary & Supt, Roorkee (India) 1943-45; Pastor Fairview Ch (Industry, Penn), Moderator Reformed Presb Denom 1946-47; Presb Bd Home Missions (Tyre), Supt & Pastor Integrated Ch 1947-52; Dir Dental Clinic Meth Mission Hosp (Bareli, India) 1954-55; Fdr & Dir, Landour Hosp Dental Clinic 1955-59; Operated 5 Pvt Practs; Now in Dental Pract; Evangelical Preacher; Sci & Theol Lectr; Tchr & Tnr, Clinical Dentistry; Photographer; Cont'g Ed in Dentistry Courses 1973-; Acad Gen Dentistry 1975; Asian Rep, Missionary Dentist Inc 1953-; Am Dental Soc; Christian Dental Soc; Dentare Intl; Author: *Wildlife in India's Tiger Kingdom*; Currently Writing Rel Book; Ser'd Winters India, Worldwide Dental Hlth Ser Inc 1972-; Began Work Liberia (Africa) 1976-77; Built Oral Clinic Hosp (Dehra Dun, India) 1977-78; Bd Dirs, Missionary Dentist Inc & Worldwide Dental Hlth Ser; Others; cp/Rotary Intl; Life Mem, Wildlife Preserv Soc of India; Lectr Civic Groups; Politic Rallies; Others; r/Evangelical Christian, Reformed Presb; hon/Medalist for Long Distance Running; Varsity Football M Sweater; 4 Yr Varsity M Clb Blanket; Track Medal; Var Hons for Lectures & Clinical Demos; W/W: E, N Am; DIB; Men Achmt; Reformed Presb Archives; Intl W/W Intellectuals; Others.

TAYLOR, JOSEPH THOMAS oc/Administrator; b/Feb 11, 1913; h/300 W Fall Creek Parkway, Indianapolis, IN 46208; ba/Indpls; m/Hertha Ward; c/Bruce Thomas, Judith Fay, Joel Herbert; p/Joseph T Taylor (dec); Willie Wells, St Louis, IL; ed/BA 1936, MA 1937 Univ Ill; PhD Ind Univ 1952; LLD Berkeley Univ 1969; mil/AUS 1942-46; pa/Am Assn Higher Ed; Nat Conf of Acad Deans; cp/Bd Mem & Trustee, YMCA; Urban Leag; United Way; Fam Ser Assn; New Hope of Ind; r/United Meth; hon/NCCJ Man of Yr; Ind Jefferson Awd; B'nai B'rith Man of Yr.

TAYLOR, LISA oc/Museum Director; b/Jan 8, 1933; h/1115 Fifth Ave, New York, NY 10028; ba/NYC; m/Bertrand L III; c/Lauren Elise, Bertrand Lindsay; ed/Hon PhD, Pasrons Sch Design; pa/Dir, Cooper-Hewitt Mus, Smithsonian Inst's Nat Mus of

Design; hon/Rec'd Thomas Jefferson Awd; Bronze Apple Awd; Smithsonian's Exceptional Ser Awd; Am Legion Medal of Hon; Johns Hopkins YMCA Awd; Finalist, Trailblazer of Yr; Nom, *Ladies Home Jour* Wom of Yr.

TAYLOR, RUSSEL REID oc/Educator; b/Sept 9, 1917; h/71 Bryam Shore Rd, Greenwich, CT 06830; ba/Same; m/Kathleen T; c/Deborah T Souki, Cynthia T Kane; p/Howard W Taylor, Ontario, Canada; ed/BS; MBA; DBA; mil/Royal Canadian Naval Vol Reserv, Ret'd Lt/Cmdr; pa/Asst Prof Col of New Rochelle, Sch of Arts & Scis; Dir Minnetonka Corp, Russel Taylor Inc, Am Liquid Trust; With Annis Furs Inc 1938-43, Pres 1954-61; Author: *The Fir Indust* (1948) & *How to Buy a Fur Coat* (1950); Others; cp/Former Bd Mem ARC; Former Chm Coat & Suitry Div, Am Cancer Soc; Chm & Dir Planning, Cooper Inst Neuroscis (St Barnabas Hosp, NY); Bd Dirs, Jr Achmt, Greenwich; Urban Leag NYC; r/Unit.

TAYLOR, WESLEY DANIEL oc/Mental Health Specialist; b/Jul 14, 1945; h/1605 20th NE, Salem, OR 97303; ba/Salem; m/Melinda Croghan; c/Jocelyn; p/Daniel E and Thelma

M Taylor, Seattle, WA; ed/BA Willamette Univ 1967; MA Claremont Grad Sch 1970; DMN Sch of Theol, Claremont 1971; pa/Dir, Sunny Oaks Tng Ctr; Pres Marion Co Mtl Hlth Bd 1976-77; Conslt, Mtl Hlth Assocs of NW; Author 3 Books; Contbr Articles Profl Jours; cp/Past Pres, Oregon Assn Citizens; r/United Meth Ch: Ordained Min; hon/W/W Rel; Intl W/W Commun Ser; Intl W/W Intellectuals; Outstg Yg Men Am.

TEEGARDEN, MAUDE BOGGS oc/-Librarian; b/Aug 5, 1935; h/Germantown, KY 41044; ba/Brooksville, KY; m/Hal Sr; c/Hal Jr; p/Robert Bruce Boggs (dec); Ardella Meadows Boggs, Germantown; ed/BA; MEd; pa/Elem Sch Libn; Ky Ed Assn; Ky Lib Assn; NEA; NKSMA; cp/Ky Fdn Wom's Clb; Town & Country Wom's Clb; Local Clb; r/Meth.

TELLEEN, JUDY GERTRUDE JOHNSON oc/Educator; b/Dec 13, 1942; h/1941 N Vermont St, Arlington, VA 22207; m/David Roger; c/Karin, Kirstin, Erik; p/Kurt Theodore and Gertrude Lillian Lockwood Johnson; ed/BA Lawrence Col 1964; MA 1967, PhD 1970 Univ Mich; pa/HS Eng Tchr (Mich) 1964-67; Spec Asst to VP Student Affairs, Univ Mich 1967-68; Pvt Pract Guid & Cnslg (West Berlin) 1971-72, Arlington 1973-; APGA; Am Col Pers Assn; Assn Cnslrs Ed & Supvn; Nat Voc Guid Assn; Am Sch Cnslr Assn; Author: *A Predictive Model of the Cumulative Academic Achmt of Grad Students from India* (1970) & *Guid Factors Influencing Indian Students to Attend Univ Mich* (1971); cp/Former Wel Chm German-Am Wom's Clb (West Berlin); Former Rel Ednl Coun, Unit Ch (Arlington) & Chm Ednl Adv Div; r/Unit; hon/Doct Res Grantee, Univ Mich; Pi Lambda Theta; Pi Beta Phi; Phi Kappa Phi.

TEVIS, BETTY W oc/Director; b/Apr 7, 1929; h/9620 Bryson Dr, Dallas, TX 75238; ba/Dallas; c/Kathleen Ann, Cynthia Louise, Thomas Wayne, Mary Lynn; p/Jerry and Dorothy W Wertheimer (dec); ed/BA; BS;MA; PhD; pa/Chief, Heart Hlth Ed & Yg, Nat Ctr Am Heart Assn; Former Coor Div Hlth Ed, Tex Tech Univ; Num Offices & Coms: AAHE, ASHA, TPHA, TAHPER; Presented Res Profl Meetings; ACS; AHA; ALA; Tel-Med; Host TV Show, " What in Hlth is Going On"; r/Meth; hon/Rec'd Bryant Meml Awd, TPHA; Hon Awd, TAHPER; Elect Media Awd, THA; Other Local Awds.

THIERER, JUDITH ANN oc/Registered Nurse; b/Feb 14, 1938; h/620 NW 36 Ave, Rochester, MN 55901; ba/Rochester; m/Robert Gordon; c/Mark Alan, Lisa Sue; p/Wallace Young (dec); Edith Stella Young, Traer, IA; ed/RN; pa/Rochester Meth Hosp: Critical-care Edr 1977-, Nsg Course Dir 1969-77; Coronary Care In-ser & ICCU Charge Nurse, Allen Meml Hosp (Waterloo, Iowa) 1967-69; Staff Nurse Ob-Gyn 1966-67; Fac Mem, AACN Nat Tchr Inst 1975-78; Invited Lectr, Am Heart Assn Sci Session 1975; AACN Bd Dirs 1975-; Minn Bd Nsg Task Force on Implementation of Mandatory Cont'g Ed 1975-; Minn Heart Assn Com on Implementation of Cardiovas Nsg Standards 1976-; Editor Bd, *Heart & Lung, Jour of Critical Care*; Other Positions; Minn & Am Nurses Assns; Coun Cardiovas Nsg, Am Heart Assn; Am Assn Critical-Care Nurses; Past Mem, Soc Heart Assn Profl Staff; Contbr Articles Profl Jours; Num Profls Presentations & Lectrs; Others; r/Presb; hon/Pres, Am Assn Critical-Care Nurses.

THOM, ROBERT T ANDERSON oc/Missionary; b/Feb 28, 1915; h/PO Box 32362, Louisville, KY 40232; ba/Same; m/Valerie Wales; c/Drummond, Lionel, Roy, Elaine, David, Robert, Bernard, Leonard, Robyn; p/Alexander James and Maria Thom (dec); ed/Cape Tech Col; mil/Naval Forces WWII; pa/Charismatic Missionary to 5 Continents; Author 40 Books incl'g *The New Wine is Better, Making Known His Deeds, The Holy Spirit & The Name*; hon/Mil Awds: African Star, Italy Star, 1939/45 Star, War Medal, SA Medal, Efficiency Medal, Others; W/W Am; Contemp Authors; Best Seller

Authors; Others.

THOMA, SHIRLEY CHRISTOFF oc/Retired; b/Mar 27, 1931; h/4553 Norwin Rd, Pittsburgh, PA 15236; ba/Same; c/Robert E, Jeffrey Christoff, John Marshall, Peggy Ann, Jennifer Shirley; p/Emory E Christoff (dec); Mildred Bizub Christoff, P'burgh; ed/Robert Morris Col; Univ P'burgh; pa/Ret'd Controller, Easter Seal Soc Allegheny Co; cp/Incorporating Office of Credit Union for Hlth Agencies (P'burgh); Chm, Brentwood Heart Fund; Brentwood Civic Clb; Dem Party; P'burgh Purchasing Assn; r/Rom Cath.

THOMAS, ANDREW CHRISTIE oc/-Associate Professor; b/Apr 26, 1936; h/TTU Box 5141, Cookeville, TN 38501; ba/Same; m/Peggy Ann; p/Christie A Thomas (dec); Alice Thomas, Beverly, MA; ed/BS; MSEd; MS; EdD; mil/USAR Maj Med Corps; pa/-Assoc Prof Dept Ed Psychi & Cnslg, Tex Tech Univ; Coor, Jackson Co Assessmt Prog; Cnslt, AUS Office Deputy Chief of Staff (ROTC S'ship Prog); AERA; MASP; APGA; TEA; NEA; r/Greek Orthodox; hon/Phi Delta Kappa; Rec'd Fed F'ship; Personalities of S; Others.

THOMAS, GARNETT JETT oc/Administrative Officer; Chief Accountant; b/Jul 27, 1920; h/72 Ridge Dr, Rt 1, Starkville, MS 39759; ba/Mississippi State, MS; m/Katherine Gardner; p/Pinkney Madison and Ethel Drinkard Thomas (dec); ed/BS Lambuth Col; MS Miss St Univ; mil/USN 4 Yrs, Lt (jg); pa/Adm Ofcr & Chief Acct, Miss Agri & Forestry Experiment Sta, Miss St Univ; Nat & Am Assns of Accts; Assn of Govt Accts; So Assn Agri Scists; cp/Former VChm, Starkville Civic Coor'g Coun; Chm, Col of Agri & Expt Sta Commun Fund Dr; Chm, Univ Cancer Fund Dr; C of C; Farm Bur; Adv Bd, Nat Bank of Commerce of Miss; Rotarian 1952-, current Gov Dist 682, Rotary Intl; r/United Meth Ch: Conf Bd of Pensions, Del N Miss Annual Conf, Chm Adm Bd, Cert'd Lay Spkr, Lay Ldr.

THOMAS, JESS oc/Opera Singer; b/Aug 4, 1927; h/PO Box 662, Tiburon, CA 94920; m/Violeta; c/Victor, Jess David, Lisa Bet; p/Charles Thomas (dec); Ellen Best, Rapid City, SD; ed/BA Neb Univ; MA Stanford Univ; pa/Dramatic Tenor & Heldentenor; Resident Mem: San Francisco Opera, Metro Opera (NY), Staatsoper (Vienna); Perfs: Salzburg Fest (Vienna Staatsoper, Austria), Milan La Scala (Venice, Italy), Moscow Bolshoi (USSR), Others; Former Sch Psychol; r/Christian Scist; hon/Rec'd Bavarian & Austrian Kammersanger; Richard Wagner Medallion; SF Opera Medallion; Biogl Listings.

THOMAS, JONATHAN GRIFFEN oc/Minister; b/Dec 31, 1927; h/Rt 2, Oakland, MS 38948; ba/Charleston, MS; m/Elizabeth Hill; c/Rita, Danny Ray; p/Jonathan Thomas; Ida Beck Thomas, Grenada, MS; ed/GED; mil/1950-52 Sgt/Maj; pa/Min, Friendship E Bapt Ch (Charleston); cp/Lions Clb; r/So Bapt; hon/W/W Rel; Commun Ldrs & Noteworthy Ams.

THOMAS, LeROY DAVID oc/Professor; b/Jun 29, 1907; h/13011 N 19th Pl, Phoenix, AZ 85022; ba/Phoenix; m/Adrianna Rotier (dec); Lucille Clink; c/Betty T Winters,

Martha T Leech, Martin David, Billie C Mason, Charles Clink, Joyce C Ayers, Charlene C Graham; p/Irvin Leonard and Margaret Harrel Thomas; ed/Grad Denver Bible Inst 1931; BSEd Kansas St Univ 1938; DD Linda Vista Bapt Sem 1958; Addit Studies; pa/Ordained to Gospel Min 1934; Pastorates: Circuit Pastor (4 Chs) 1932-34, Kincaid Meml Bapt Ch (Girard, Ks) 1934-36, 1st Bapt Ch (Douglas, Az) 1937-44, Palmcroft Bapt Ch (Phoenix) 1944-69; Assoc Prof Bible, SWn Bapt Bible Col 1961-75, Prof Bible & Pastoral Studies 1976-; Fdg Bd Mem, Az Bible Inst; Fdg Bd Mem, SWn Bapt Bible Col; Bible Conf Speaker; r/Conservative Bapt; hon/VP Az Bapt Conv (2 Terms); Pres, Evangelical Mins; Learning Ctr Dedication, SBB Col.

THOMAS, MILDRED oc/Retired; b/Sept 28, 1901; h/PO Box 251, Penney Farms, FL 32079; m/John Sanders; p/Frank A and Jennie Macomber Thomas (dec); ed/BSEd; BMus; EdM; pa/Tchr 1st Grade: Longfellow Sch (Sanford, Maine) 1923-27, Lincoln Sch (Winchester, Mass) 1927-47; Reading Suvpr: Barrington (RI) 1947-48, Abington (Mass) 1948-51; Demo Tchr, St Tchrs Col (Gorham,

Maine) 1951-53; Eng & Read'g Tchr, Westbrook Col (Portland, Maine) 1953-54; Supvr Read'g, Hampton (NH) 1953-56; Sub Tchr, Winter Park & Orlando (Fla) 1956-69; Author Articles Ed, Travel & Poetry; Composer Music; Nat Leag Am Pen Wom; r/Christian Sci; hon/World W/W Wom; DIB; Maine Composers & Their Mus.

THOMAS, PATRICK ALOYSIUS oc/-Professor; b/Mar 16, 1936; h/c/o J Naveja, 645 Barrette St, Apt 1G, Bronx, NY 10474; ba/Louisville, KY; p/Harrison and Olga Desbrosses Thomas; ed/BS cum laude, Manhattan Col 1959; MA St John's Univ 1961; PhD SUNY-Buffalo 1971; pa/Prof, Univ Louisville; Fdr, Intl Courtly Lit Soc; Co-fdr, Medieval Assn of MW; Fdr: Tristania, Perspectives on Contemp Lit; r/Rom Cath; hon/Rec'd Tchg F'ship, NY St Regents Col; Epsilon Sigma Pi; Delta Phi Alpha; Rec'd Post Doct F'ship to Medieval & Renaissance Inst, Duke Univ.

THOMAS, WADE HAMILTON oc/-Accountant; b/May 12, 1922; m/Mary Katherine Scruggs; c/Michelle L, Korda, Renee, Wade, Karl, Harrison, Kenneth, George, Rex, Axel; p/Harrison Spurgeon and Lealer Bandy Thomas; ed/BS w Distinction, Tenn A&I Univ 1949; Addit Studies; mil/AAF, Ofcr WWII; pa/Fac Mem, So Tng Inst (Nashville) 1947-51; Soc Ordinary Rep, Universal Life Ins Co (Memphis, Tenn) 1951-52; Gen Clerk, US Post Office (N'ville) 1953-63; Partner Drake & Thomas (N'ville)

1954-60; Owner W H Thomas Public Acct 1973-; Other Positions; Asheville (NC) Fed Exec Assn; Nat Assn Ret'd Fed Employees; Nat Soc Public Accts; Asheville Bd Realtors; Others; cp/Former Coun Mem, Asheville Civic Ctr; Tenn A&I St Univ Alumni Assn; W Asheville Civic Commun; Asheville Optimist Clb; Others; r/Rom Cath; hon/Rec'd Golden Anniv Cit, Tenn A&I St Univ; US Post Office Superior Accomplishmt Awd; GSA Spec Accomplishmt Awd; Dist'd Ser Awd, Omega Psi Phi; Others.

THOMAS, WALTER SCOTT oc/Minister; b/Apr 2, 1950; h/3708 Oak Ave, Baltimore, MD 21207; ba/Baltimore; m/Patricia Grace; p/Calvin V Sr and L Elizabeth Thomas, Baltimore; ed/BS Univ Md 1971; MDiv cum laude, Howard Univ 1976; DD Va Sem 1977; pa/Pastor, New Psalmist

Bapt Ch; Prof New Testament, Va Sem & Col Ext of Baltimore; Past Mem Bd Dirs, OIC; r/Bapt; hon/Most Progressive & Innovative Pastor Awd, Bapt Clergy of Baltimore; Rec'd W O Carrington Awd for Min, Howard Univ.

THOMAS, WILLIAM VICTOR oc/-Company Executive; b/Feb 7, 1918; h/1518-G Pearl St, Alameda, CA 94501; m/Vena Shaw; c/4; p/Charles and Lorraine F Thomas; ed/-Grad, Merrit Bus Col; Passed Cal Hwy Patrol Exam; pa/Roofing Contractor Over 37 Yrs; Owner & Supvr, W Thomas Roofing Co; Former Master Driller, United Engrg Co; Former Master Rigger, Pacific Bridge Co; Inventor Naval Port-hole Jig (1942) & Spec Hand Soap; Cal St Contractors Assn; Others; cp/Initiator, Good Neighbor Prog (to Combat Crime); St Chm, Good Neighbor Prog Cal (for Order of Eagles); Intl Footprinter Assn; Pres, S Alameda Chapt Kiwanis; Diamond Improvemt Clb; Blue Lodge, Scottish Rite; Elks; Bd Dirs, ARC; Peace Builders Inc; Bd Dirs, Vote '76; W Alameda Bus Assn; Bd Dirs, E Alameda Bus Assn; C of C; Legion of Hon; Alameda Boys Clb; Alameda Ath Assn; Navy Leag US; Shriner; Adv Bd BSA; VP, Alameda Hist Soc; Others; r/Universal Life Ch; hon/Rec'd 2 Cits for Devel'g Good Neighbor Prog, St of Cal; Eagle & Gt Eagle Awds, Fraternal Order of Eagles; Holder Num Ath Records; Biogl Listings.

THOMEN, PHYLLIS ANN oc/Dental Hygienist; b/Jul 30, 1931; h/206 N Pine, Gardner, KS 66030; ba/Gardner; m/Robert K; c/Shirley, Robert, Sue; p/Robert M Riley (dec); Lavern W Riley, Kansas City, KS; ed/BA Baker Univ 1953; BS Univ Mo-KC 1973; pa/Am Dental Hygienists Assn; Ks Dental Hygienists Assn; Johnson Co Hygienists; Past Chm Bd, Univ Mo-KC Dental Hygienists Alumni Assn; cp/Pres & Precinct Com-wom, Gardner City Coun; Past Pres 2nd Dist, Ks Fdn Wom's Clbs; Past Secy Bd, Johnson Co Mtl Hlth Assn; r/Epis; hon/Rec'd Commun Ser Awd, Gtr Ks City Dental Hygienists Assn; Outstg Yg Wom Am.

THOMPSON, ANDREW BOYD JR oc/Executive; b/Mar 30, 1930; h/4353 Amherst Rd, Montgomery, AL 36116; ba/Montgomery; m/Laura June Guy; c/Guy Bradly, Eric Keipp; p/Andrew B Sr and Frieda S Thompson, Montgomery; mil/AUS 1953, Korean Combat; USAR Lt/Col; pa/VP, Gen Mgr & Editor, Nat Photo Pricing Ser Inc; Photo Mktg Assn Intl; Photographic Mfgrs & Distributors Assn; Reserv Ofcrs Assn; cp/Friends of Epilepsy; Past Pres, Past VP,

Secy, Bd Dirs; r/Normandale United Meth Ch: Mem; hon/Gen Gorgas Scholar, Auburn Univ; W/W S&SW; Personalities of S; DIB; Notable Ams; Men Achmt.

THOMPSON, BRENT DRUIEN oc/Commercial Banker; b/Oct 4, 1930; h/PO Box 25, Cadiz, KY 42211; ba/Cadiz; m/Dorothy Spencer; c/Rise Carol (dec), John Mark; p/Veachil I Thompson (dec); Lucille H Thompson, Center, KY; ed/BS 1950, MSEd 1958 Univ Ky-L; mil/USAFR Col; Admissions Cnslr, USAF Acad (Colo); pa/Chm & Pres, Trigg Co Farmers Bank; Tchr Voc Agri, Ky

Public Schs 1950-57; Former Agri Rep; Cert'd Commercial Lender; Am Bankers Assn; Ky Adv Bd, US Small Bus Adm; cp/Past Pres, Rotary Clb; Dir, Ky C of C; Past Bd Mem, Pennyroyal Regional Mtl Hlth, MR Bd; Adv Bd, Audubon Coun, BSA; Adv Bd, GSA; Univ Ky-L Alumni Assn; Cadiz Housing Authority; r/Cadiz Bapt Ch: Mem, Deacon, Former SS Tchr & Supt; Past Dir, Ky Bapt Foun; hon/Outstg Reservist Awd, USAF Acad (Colo); Hon Ky Farmer Deg, Ky Assn FFA.

THOMPSON, DONNIS HAZEL oc/-Athletic Director; b/Apr 1, 1934; h/46-337 Kahuhipa St, Kaneohe, HI 96744; ba/-Honolulu, HI; p/John William and Katherine Redmond Thompson; ed/BS; MS; EdD; pa/-Wom's Ath Dir, Univ Hawaii; Workshop Ldr, Track & Field; Chrperson, Wom's Track & Field Com, Nat Intercol Aths 1972-; Nat Chrperson Nat Assn Girls & Wom's Sports Track & Field Com, Am Assn Hlth, PE & Rec; Nat VChrperson Wom's Track & Field Com, Amateur Ath Union 1968-; Chrperson Wom's Cross Country Com, AIA 1974-; Head Coach, USA Wom's Track & Field Team's Competition w Russia & Poland 1962; Head Coach, Univ Wom Athletes Competition Rome 1975; Author: Wom's Track & Field (1969), Modern Track & Field for Girls & Wom (1971), Prentice-Hall Activs Handbook (1973); Pub'd Num Articles Profl Jours; cp/St Commr on Civil Rights; r/Rom Cath; hon/Female Edr Yr, Univ Nn Colo Alumni Assn; Rec'd Dist'd Ser Awd, Hawaiian Ath Union; Feature Article for Excell, Cal Physical Ed & Rec Jour; Dist'd Ser Awd, Hawaii St Am Assn Hlth, PE & Rec; Hawaii St Leg Passed Spec Resolution Commend for Devel'g Ath Prog, Univ Hawaii; Coaching Accomplishmts: 2 World Record Holders, 10 Nat AAU Champions, 9 Olympic Participants, 6 Am Record Holders, Others.

THOMPSON, DOROTHY McELRATH oc/Homemaker; b/Apr 21, 1922; h/626 Prospect, Fort Morgan, CO 80701; m/Kenneth George; c/Kenneth George Jr, Randall Lee; p/Lee Herbert and Lucy P

Cogburn McElrath, Wiggins, CO; pa/Collector Antiques; cp/Hosp Aux Ofcr; Asst Var Fund Drives; r/United Meth: Chm Supportive Commun Coor, United Meth Wom.

THOMPSON, ESTHER LEE oc/Editor; b/Apr 7, 1919; h/200 W Chandler, Fort Worth, TX 76111; ba/Same; m/George (dec); p/C Nelson and Christi Miller Spencer Johnson (dec); ed/Attended SMU & Tarrunt Co Jr Col; pa/Fdr, Pres & Bd Chm, Galaxy of Verses Lit Foun; r/Bapt: SS Tchr; hon/Poet-Pubr of Yr; Intl Poet Laureate; Lyrie Awd, Poetry Soc Tex.

THOMPSON, HERBERT ERNEST oc/- Business Owner; b/Sept 9, 1923; h/14009 N 42 Ave, Phoenix, AZ 85023; ba/Phoenix; m/- Patricia Elaine; c/Debra Lynn T Rauch, Robert Steven; p/Walter and Louise E Thompson (dec); mil/USAAF Capt & Pilot; pa/Owner Machine Shop; r/Prot; hon/W/W: W, Fin & Indust; Men Achmt; DIB; Commun Ldrs & Noteworthy Ams.

THOMPSON, JESSE JACKSON oc/Pro-fessor; b/Jul 26, 1919; h/13282 Cedar St, Westminster, CA 92683; ba/Long Beach, CA; m/Clara Roy; c/Lyle Blair, Carolrae T Addison (Mrs William P), Jon Royal; p/Lewis Elmer and Lucy Jane Hamilton Thompson (dec); ed/BA; MSEd; PhD; mil/AUS 1941-46; pa/Prof Communicative Disorders, Speech Pathology & Audiology; Bd Dirs, Long Beach Lung Assn 1975-78; Profl Adv Bd, Speech & Lang Devel Ctr (Buena Park); Profl Adv Bd, Long Beach Inst Socioanalysis; r/Prot; hon/AUS Medal of Merit; Hon Life Mbrship, Cal PTA; Phi Kappa Phi Lectr, Cal St Univ-LB.

THOMPSON, ROSCOE MULLINS oc/- Attorney; b/Jul 12, 1915; h/1725 Stark Ave, Columbus, GA 31906; ba/Columbus; m/- Mary Barr; c/Carol T Hodge, Cathy T McCosh, Alice T Hanson; p/Clarence A and Mary Mullins Thompson (dec); mil/USAF 1942-46; pa/Admit'd to Pract: Supr Ct Ga, US

Supr Ct; Former Asst Atty Gen, St of Ga; City Atty, Columbus; ABA; St Bar of Ga; Past Pres, Columbus Lwyrs Clb; cp/Former Mem, Ga St Ho of Reps; Past Pres, Columbus Jr C of C; Past Pres, Columbus Lions Clb; Am Legion; Dem Party of Ga; r/St Luke United Meth Ch: Chm Bd, Local, Dist & Conf Activs.

THOMSON, JOHN ANSEL ARMSTRONG oc/Biochemist; Sociologist; Nutritionist; b/Nov 23, 1911; ba/North Hollywood, CA; m/June Anna Mae Hummel; c/Sheryl Linn, Patricia Diane, Robert Royce; p/John Russell and Florence Antisdel Thomson (dec); ed/AA Pasadena Jr Col 1935; BA cum laude, Univ So Cal 1957; Bach Garden Sci (Hon), Cal Polytech St Univ 1961; mil/War Manpower Comm WWII 1943-44; pa/Owner & Pres, Vitamin Inst; Originator & Owner Over 100 Chem Prods, Formulas & Over 30 Trademarks; 3 Inventions Bought & Used (Classified AA-1 Priority), US Govt for Nat Defense WWII; Originator, Aquasol (1940) & Auzon Crystals (1950), Believed to Be Most Pure Multiple Vitamins for Humans; Contbr Articles Profl Jours; Soc Nutrition Ed; Am Inst Biol Scis; AAAS; Intl Soc Horticultural Sci; Am Horticultural Soc; Nat Nutritional Foods Assn; Nat Hlth Fdn; Am Nutrition Soc;

Huxley Inst Biosocial Res; Envir Defense Fund; Cal St Florists Assn; Cal Landscape Contractors Assn; Am Assn Nurserymen; Others; cp/Former Activs Chm, 10th Olympiad Olympic Games Intl Relats Com, World Coun of Yth; Former Mem, Cal Repub St Ctl Com; BSA: Nat Explorer Del Conf, Former Tng Chm, Former Scoutmaster, Former Public Relats Chm, Others; Former Coach, YMCA; Past BD Mem, Civic Res Leag Am; Past Chm, Allied Yth Coun; Past Pres, Hoover Victory Clb; ARC; Former St Organizing Com, Yg Repubs Cal; Friends of Earth; Am Physical Fitness Inst; LA World Affairs Coun; Sierra Clb; Soc Col Wars; Alumni Assn, Univ So Cal; Others; r/First United Meth Ch (N Hollywood): Past Cnslr Col Group, Past Mem Comm on Ed, Past Comm on Mbrship & Evangelism, Comm on Ch & Soc, Others; hon/Rec'd Sci Indust Gold Medal, SF Intl Exposition, Ofcl World's Fair; Outstg Sr Awd, BSA; Civic Ser Awd, St of Cal; Benjamin Franklin Essay Awd, DAR; Labor Essay Awd, Pasadena Labor Coun; Yorktown Essay Awd; Competitive Fest Awds; So Cal Inter-scholastic Cross-country Championship Team Mem Awd; Scouter's Awd & Wood Badge, BSA; Others.

THORMAN, LILLIAN JOAN GRUCCIO oc/Counsellor at Law; b/Jan 30, 1927; h/63 Sheffield Pl, Vincentown, NJ 08088; ba/Medford, NJ; m/William Harrington Taylor; p/Joseph and Millie Gruccio (dec); ed/AA; LLB; LLD; pa/Atty & Cnslr at Law of NJ; Admit'd US Supr Ct 1960; Admit'd NJ Bar 1952; US Dist Ct, Dist of NJ 1952; Partner Frank C Propert, Esquire (Camden, NJ) 1952-55; Legal Dept, Campbell Soup Co (Camden) 1955; Assoc, Lewis & Hutchinson (Camden) 1956-61; Self-employed Sole Practitioner (Pennsauken, NJ) 1961-73, Medford 1973-; Camden Co Bar Assn; ABA; NJ St Bar Assn; Burlington Co Bar Assn; Camden City Juv Conf Com; cp/Bd Dirs, Camden Co Hlth & Wel Coun; Bd Dirs, YWCA; United Fund; Rutgers Univ Law Sch Alumni Assn; Zonta Clb Gtr Camden; BPW: Past VP, Leg Com, Correspond'g Secy, Others; LeisureTowne Civic Leag; Burlington Co GSA Coun; Others; r/Bapt; hon/Commun Ldrs & Noteworthy Ams; DIB; Nat Register Prominent Ams; Nat Social Directory; W/W: Am Wom, Commerce & Indust, E, Fin & Indust; Wom Lwyrs US; Others.

THORNTON, JOY LEAH oc/Counselor; b/Sept 9, 1953; h/10131 Crailet Dr, Huntington Beach, CA 92646; ba/Huntington Beach; m/Gale Robert; p/Gary Garth and Gay Elizabeth Robinson, Huntington Beach; ed/BA So Cal Col 1975; MA Azusa Pacific Col 1976; pa/Dir Cnslg & Adm Asst, Ch by the Sea; Breath of Life Bible Instr 1977-78; Guest Lectr 1973-; Instr, Irvine Col of Bus 1976-77; Intl GA Dir 1973-77; SW Dist GA Aux Dir 1973-; Author, "Wom & Their Rights", Today Mag (Feb 1976); cp/Yg Repubs; Instr, Rec Dept; r/Ch by the Sea; hon/1st & 3rd Pl Awds, Tenn Walking Horse Class, LA Co Fair.

THORP, DOROTHY F oc/Civic Worker; b/Feb 22, 1922; h/1000 Tulip St, Johnson City, TN 37601; m/Nathan; c/Richard, Barbara, Julian & Valerie; p/Julius and Ruth Switgall (dec); ed/BA Geo Peabody Col; MA Columbia Univ; Addit Studies; pa/Tchr; cp/Preservation of SEn Region Bd Anti-Defamation Leag, B'nai B'rith; Chm & Fdr, Friends of Johnson City Commun Theatre;

Chm Beautification Com & Mem Ednl & Nominating Coms, Wom's Div C of C; Patron, Com for Tenn Perf'g Arts; Patron, Johnson City Symph Orch; Wednesday Morning Mus Clb; Secy of Foun & Corporate Aid, Steed Col; B'nai Sholom Congreg Sisterhood; Former Chm Intl Relats Com, AAUW; Past Regional Chm, United Way & March of Dimes; Former Campaign Mgr, Dem Wom's Div for Estes Kefauver; Past Chm Ednl Dept, Monday Clb; Others; r/Jewish; hon/W/W: Am Wom, S&SW, US; World W/W Commerce & Indust; Commun Ldrs & Noteworthy Ams; DIB; Nat Social Directory; Others.

THRALL, RICHARD CAMERON JR oc/Television Executive; b/Nov 13, 1929; ba/Cincinnati, OH; m/Shirley Annette Sturgeon; c/Vallerie, Laurie Jo, James; p/Richard C Sr and Pauline Taylor Thrall, Columbus, OH; ed/BA Miami Univ 1951; mil/USNR 1951; pa/Exec VP, Multimedia Prog Prods Inc; VP TV Program'g, Multimedia Broadcast'g Co; Nat Acad TV Arts & Scis (Bd Govs); Nat Assn TV Prog Execs; TV Prog Conf; cp/Ruth Lyons Chd's Christmas Fund (Trustee); Ye Merrie Players; Assoc, Smithsonian Inst; Former Europe Nat Safety Coun; hon/Alpha Epsilon Rho; Ky Col; Emmy Winner; Lamp of Knowledge; Others.

THURMAN, ARTHUR ODELL oc/- Educator; h/2438 W Paseo Blvd, Kansas City, MO 64108; ba/Kansas City; m/Leona Poun-cey; p/Albert G and Alice Thurman, Chil-licothe, MO; ed/BS; MS; EdD; pa/Admr, Ks City Sch Dist; Local Adm Ednl Socs; Author, The Negro in Cal Before 1890; cp/Past Pres, Hosts Lions Intl; Fdr, Lincoln Gardens African-Am Hist & Cult Museum Foun Inc; r/Prot; hon/Rec'd Cert Accomplishmt, Adult Basic Ed Inc; Kappa Delta Pi; Pi Gamma Mu; Kappa Chapt, Phi Delta Kappa.

THURMAN, LEONA POUNCEY oc/- Attorney; h/2438 W Paseo Blvd, Kansas City, MO 64108; ba/Ks City; m/A Odell; p/James Simeon and Walsie Parker Hendrix (dec); ed/BA Lincoln Univ 1947; LLB Howard Univ 1949; pa/Nat, Am & SW Bar Assns; cp/- Charter Mem, World Peace through Rule of Law; Univ Wom; AUS War Col; r/Bapt; hon/Pres' Blue Ribbon Defense Panel.

TIEMEYER, HOPE JOHNSON oc/- Executive, b/May 20, 1908; h/2786 Little Dry Run Rd, Cincinnati, OH 45244; ba/Cinc; m/Edwin H (dec); c/Ann T Lewin (Mrs Gustav Jr), Edwin Hougton (dec); p/Edward Tibbens and Fannie Burton Meyers Johnson (dec); ed/BA Univ Cinc; pa/Pres, Mail Way Advtg Co 1955-; Dir AAUW 1963-64; cp/Pres Cinc Chapt, Freedoms Foun Valley Forge; Local Exec Com & Intl Relats Com, Zonta Intl; Sr Nat Hon Pres & Parliamentarian, Chd of Am Revolution; Advr, Bd of Social Hlth Assn; United Appeal Campaign; Wom's Com, Cinc Symph Orch; Art, Tour & Travel Coms, Cinc Clb; Music & Tea Room Coms, Cinc Wom's Clb; Life Mem, Craft Shop for Handicapped; Fed'd Garden Clbs Ohio; Cinc Com, English Speaking Union; Sigma Nu Mothers Clb; Past Pres & VP, Univ Cinc Parents Clb; IPA; Others; r/Presb; hon/Hon Life Mem, Ohio St & Nat Cong Parents & Tchrs; Hon St Pres, Ohio Soc Chd Am Revolution; Chi Delta Phi; Rec'd Jonathan Moore Cit & Awd for Ser to

Yth; Hon Life Mem, Cinc Social Hlth Bd; Nat Assn Parliamentarians; Citizenship Medal, SAR; Others.

TILL, SANDRA L oc/Program Coordinator; b/Aug 7, 1934; h/1045 S Main, Box 617, Canton, IL 61520; ba/Canton; m/Farrell; c/Roger, Victor, Kelly; p/Claude and Beatrice Cooper Heathcock, Decatur, IL; ed/BA Harding Col; MS So Ill Univ; Addit Studies: SE Mo St, Alliance Francaise, Ark St Univ, Wn Ill Univ, Others; pa/Prog Coor, Canton Commun Workshop & Tng Ctr 1974-; Tchr & Dept Chm, Canton Sr HS 9 Yrs; Tchr PE & Hlth, Gallup Jr HS (New Mexico) 2 Yrs; Missionary to France 5 Yrs; Others; Canton Ed Assn

(Publicity Chm & Bldg Rep); Ill Ed Assn; NEA; Ill Coaches' Assn; Ill & Nat Assns Hlth, PE & Rec; Ill & Nat Rehab Assns; Voc Evaluation & Work Adjustmt Assn (St Bd Dirs & Mbrship Chm); AAUW; cp/Bluebird Ldr, Camp Fire Girls; YWCA Vol Instr; St Softball Tournamt Com; City Softball Coaches' Assn; City Tennis Tournamt Leag; Skirts & Shirts Square Dance Clb; Ill Polit Action Group; Canton Fed'd BPW; Fulton Co Social Sers Coun (Secy-Treas); Fulton Co Hlth Fair Com; Ctl Ill Spec Olympic Com; Others; hon/-Dean's Hon Student; 1st Runner-up, JC Yg Tchr of Yr Contest; Others.

TILLINGHAST, META IONE oc/Career Volunteer; ba/Alexandria, VA; m/F William; c/Anne T Riley (Mrs Robert); p/Ralph Vincent and Florence Virginia MacDonald Muldoon (dec); ed/Leland Powers Sch of Spoken Word; pa/Repertory Art Theatre; cp/Pres Wom's Clbs: Ten Hills (Baltimore, Md) & Glyndon; Pres, Talbot Co Wom's Clb; Sr Chm, Jr Garden Clb; Chm, Co Flower Mart; Conslt, Local GSA; Baltimore Co Read'g Chm for Homemakers; Dir, Ch Plays for Fund Raising; Organized: Civilian Defense Shelters, ARC Workshop & Canteen; Baltimore Co Chm, United Fund; Organized Spec Co Bloodmobile; Vol Field Conslt; En Area Adv Coun; ARC: Bd Dirs (Baltimore Chapt), Chapt Chm (Queen Anne's Co), Md St Fund Chm, Delmarva Div Conf, Md St Liaison Rep, Nat Bd Govs, Others; Num Other Activs; r/Epis; hon/ARC Vol of Yr, St of Md; Rec'd Awd for TV Prog Series on Am Heritage, Gen Fdn Wom's Clbs; Rec'd 30 Yr Ser Awd, ARC; W/W Am Wom; World W/W Wom; Others.

TILLMAN, DONALD C oc/City Engineer; b/Aug 1, 1924; h/14694 Deervale Pl, Sherman Oaks, CA 91403; ba/Los Angeles, CA; m/Doris Last; c/Donald C Jr; p/Peter Joseph and Edith Tillman; ed/BS, MS Cal Inst Technol; pa/USN; ba/City Engr, City of LA; APWA; ASCE; WPCF; ITE; Reg'd Profl, Civil & Traffic Engr; cp/YMCA; City Employees Retiremt Sys; r/Prot; hon/Engr of Yr Awd, San Fernando Val Engrs' Coun; Man of Yr, *Am City & Co Mag;* Top 10 Public Works Ofcls, APWA.

TILLMAN, JUNE TORRISON oc/Music Teacher; b/Jun 11, 1917; h/2300 NW 7th Ave, Wilton Manors, FL 33311; ba/Same; m/Jean Paul; c/Paula T Rosenkoetter (Mrs John S); p/Odvin Olai and Anne Johanne Andersen Torrison (dec); ed/BA Macalester Col; Addit Studies: Univ Minn, MacPhail & Gmun; pa/Former HS & Jr Col Tchr; Ch Musician USA & Japan 1935-; Independent Mus Tchr USA, Germany & Japan 1953-; Cert'd by:

MTNA, FSMTA, Am Col Musicians, Fla Dept Ed for Jr Cols; Choral Mus & Book Reviewer, *Am Mus Tchr Mag;* MTNA IMTF Nat Chm Studio Policies Com 1975-77; Fla St MTA Conv Chm 1978; Life Mem, NFMC; cp/AGO; NGPT; OES; Life Mem, Boys Clb's Wom's Div; Ft Lauderdale Symph Orch; Others; r/Luth: 9 Yrs Ser Moravian Ch (Original Choral Music on File, Moravian Archives NC); hon/Phi Beta; Rec'd Phi Beta Bracelet & Scroll for Ser.

TILY, STEPHEN BROMLEY III oc/Administrator; b/Jul 7, 1937; h/Churchill Dr, Berwyn, PA 19312; ba/Wilmington, DE; m/Janet Walz; c/Deborah Powell, Stephen B, James C III; p/Stephen B III and Edith H S Tily, Ardmore, PA; ed/BA Washington & Jefferson Col 1960; Temple Sch of Law 1962-63; mil/USAR QMC Capt 1960-61; pa/Pres & Dir, Delaware Charter Guarantee & Trust Co; Lectr; Guest Spkr; Fin Analysts of Wilmington Inc; Intl Foun of Employee Benefit Plans; Tchr, Am Inst Banking (Valley Forge Chapt).

TIMBRELL, CHARLES oc/Concert Pianist; b/May 5, 1942; h/1824 Wyoming Ave NW, Washington, DC 20009; ba/Same; p/Charles W and Miriam Cooke Timbrell, Hackettstown, NJ; ed/BM Oberlin Univ 1964; MM Univ Mich 1967; Grad Study, Conservatorio di Santa Cecilia (Rome, Italy) 1967-69; DMA Univ Md 1976; Pvt Study w: Emil Danenberg, Benning Dexter, Stewart Gordon, Guido Agosti; pa/Prof Piano: Howard Univ 1977-, Am Univ 1975-; Num Recitals US & Europe; European & World Premieres of Am Music; Record'g Artist, Vatican Radio; Author Num Articles & Reviews: *Music & Lttrs, Piano Qtrly, Am Music Tchr, Opera News, Washington Post;* Am Musicological Soc; Bd Dirs, Wash Mus Tchrs Assn 1975-; Ofcr & Chm Public Relats, Am Liszt Soc 1979-; Bd Dirs, Friday Morning Mus Clb; hon/Rec'd Haskell Prize in Piano, Oberlin; Rec'd Albert Lockwood Piano Prize; Phi Kappa Phi.

TIMMONS, EVELYN DEERING oc/-Pharmacist; b/Sept 29, 1926; h/5302 N 69th Pl, Paradise Valley, AZ 85253; ba/Phoenix, AZ; c/Roderick D, Steven P; p/Claude Elliot and Evelyn Allen Gooch Deering; ed/BS cum laude, Univ Colo 1948; pa/Chief Pharmacist, Meml Hosp (Phoenix) 1950-54; Med Lit Res Libn, Hoffman-LaRoche (Nutley, NJ) 1956-57; Mgr Profl Pharmacies Inc (Phoenix) 1968-72; Owner & Mgr, Mountain View Pharmacy 1972-; Pres, Ariz Apothecaries Inc 1976-; Am & Ariz Socs Hosp Pharm; Am, Ariz & Maricopa Co Pharm Assns; hon/Rec'd Awd for TV Prog Series on Am Soc; Contbr Articles Profl Jours; cp/Past Mem Platform Com St of Ariz, Nat Repub Conv; Past Asst Secy, Yg Repub Nat Fdn; Active Repub Coms; Am Aircraft Owners & Pilots Assn; Nat Assn Reg'd Parliamentarians; hon/Outstg Yg Repub of Yr, Nat Fdn Yg Repubs; Dist'd Public Ser Awds, Maricopa Co Med Soc; Outstg Pharmacist of Yr, Ariz Pharm Assn; Fellow, Am Col Apothecaries.

TINGLEY, DONALD FRED oc/Historian; b/Mar 13, 1922; h/98 Harrison Ave, Charleston, IL 61920; ba/Charleston; m/Eleanor Jeanne Cress; c/Elizabeth Catherine; p/James Fred and Ruth McDonald Tingley, Marshall, IL; ed/BS En Ill Univ 1947; MA 1968; PhD Univ Ill 1952; mil/USN 1943-46; pa/En Ill Univ: Prof Hist 1953-, Chm Fac Senate, Univ Coun on Acad Affairs; Res Editor, Ill St Hist Lib 1952-53; Author Books, Articles & Reviews Hist & Ednl Subjects; cp/Former Dem Precinct Com-man; Active Campaigns of Senator Eugene McCarthy & George McGovern; r/Meth; hon/Dist'd Fac Awd, En Ill Univ; Dist'd Am Edr & Man of Yr Awd.

TINSLEY-BROWN, BETTY ANN oc/Advisor; h/1907 Owens Dr, Bloomington, IL 61701; ba/Normal, IL; m/Forrest Edwin (dec); c/Joanne Kelley B Chacon (Mrs Carlos), Thomas Edwin, Richard Scott (dec);

p/William Franklin and Anna Kelley-Tinsley (dec); ed/BA Iowa Wesleyan Col; MA Ill St Univ; pa/Ill St Univ: Fin Aid Advr, Chm Work-Study Session & Resolutions Com, Intl Guide Com; MW Assn Student Employmt Adm; Treas, Ill Col Pers Assn 1976-77; cp/Pres, Normal Altrusa Clb; Lincoln Clb; r/2nd Presb Ch: Mem, Choir; hon/Kappa Delta Pi; Alpha Psi Omega; United Airlines Suggestion Awd; World W/W Wom; Personalities of W&MW; Intl W/W Commun Ser; Commun Ldrs & Noteworthy Ams; Others.

TIPPETT, JOHN THOMAS oc/Minister; b/Sept 17, 1920; h/1531 Spalding Rd, Savannah, GA 31406; ba/Savannah; m/Elise Dorsey; c/Thomas Henning, James Thomas; p/John Thomas Tippett Sr (dec); Ollie Hill Tippett, Macon, GA; ed/BA 1951, Hon DDD 1973 Mercer Univ; Hon LLD Atlanta Law Sch 1962; Addit Studies; pa/Pastor: Calvary Bapt Temple 1959-, Southside Bapt Ch (Spartanburg, SC) 1957-59, Tabernacle Bapt Ch (Carrollton, Ga) 1947-57, Others; Moderator, Carroll Co & Savannah Bapt Assns; So Bapt SS Bd; Pres, Savannah Prot Min Assn; Chm, Ga Bapt Conv Exec Com; Plans & Policies Com, So Bapt Conv SS Bd;

Bd Dirs & Contbr, *The Christian Index;* Editor: *Carroll Co Georgian* (1951-57), *Bldg Trades Jour* (1967-); Speaker, So Bapt Conv & St Conv Evangelistic Crusades & Confs; Conducted 2-week Revival Assignmt in Alaska; Led 2 Groups to Europe & Holy Land; Others; cp/Trustee: N Greenville Bapt Jr Col, Norman Bapt Jr Col; Co-pres, PTA (Carrollton); Lions Clb; Civitan Clb; Assoc Trustee, Candler Gen Hosp (Savannah); Chatham Co Nsg Home Authority; r/So Bapt; hon/Rec'd Commend, Ga Ho of Reps; W/W Rel.

TOBIAS, DONNA R oc/Assistant Professor; b/Sept 13, 1937; h/318 Ashburn, Robstown, TX 78380; ba/Kingsville, TX; m/-William Vern; p/Lois Wick, San Antonio, TX; ed/BSEd; MA (2); Cand PhD; pa/Tex A&I Univ: Asst Prof, Dir Debate, Dir Readers

Theatre; Charter Pres, S Tex Speech Communs Assn; Tex & So Speech Communs Assn; Tex Assn Col Tchrs; AAUW; r/Ch of Christ; hon/Pi Kappa Delta; Top 10 Profs, A&I Univ; Phi Kappa Phi; W/W Am Cols & Univs; World W/W Wom.

TODD, VIVIAN EDMISTON oc/Consultant; b/Feb 18; h/1873 Stearnlee Ave, Long Beach, CA 90815; m/Leonard Chrisman; c/David L, Philip C, Susan Mariko; p/Robert L and Sue Macracken Edmiston (dec); ed/BS,

MS Univ Idaho; PhD Univ Chgo; pa/Visit'g Lectr, Cal St Univ; CurricSpec, Supvr Command Allied Powers (GHQ, Tokyo); Assoc Ednl Supvr Res, NY St Dept Ed; Conslt: Cols & Univs St of NY, Nat Comm Tchr Ed; Res Assoc, Tchrs Col (Columbia Univ); Asst to Dr Ralph W Tyler, Univ Chgo; Classroom & Demo Tchr; Author: *The Yrs Before Sch: Guiding Preschool Chd* (1977), *The Aide in Early Childhood Ed* (1973), *Elem Tchr's Guide to Working w Parents* (1969); Contbr Articles Profl Jours; Others; cp/Cal Leg Roundtable; Zonta Intl; Others; hon/Sigma Xi; Pi Lambda Theta; Kappa Delta Pi; PedD, Univ Idaho.

TOLIVER, RAYMOND FREDERICK oc/Author; Historian; Aviator; b/Nov 16, 1914; h/5286 Lindley Ave, Encino, CA 91316; ba/Same; m/Jennie Sue Miller; c/Suzanne, Nancy Rae, Janet Mary; p/Francis LeRoy Toliver, Ft Collins, CO; Hattie Lorena Lowe Toliver (dec); mil/USAF 18 Yrs, Ret'd Col; pa/Author: *Fighter Aces* (1965), *Horrido!* (1968), *Blond Knight of Germany* (1970), *Fighter Aces of the Luftwaffe* (1977), *The Interrogator* (1978); r/Prot; hon/Top Awd for Best Non-fiction Book on Aviation, Aviation Space Writers Assn.

TOLLE, EUGENIA M VENNER oc/- Counselor; b/Mar 26, 1924; h/128 4th Ave E, Cresco, IA 52136; m/Gene L; p/Steve and Mary Venner, Breda, IA; ed/AA Ottumwa Hgts Col 1943; BS Maycrest Col 1945; MA Ark St Univ 1976; Addit Studies; pa/Cnslr: Howard-Winneshiek Commun Schs, Crestwood Jr-Sr HS 7 Yrs, Westbrook HS (Minn) 3 Yrs; Tchr: Perry HS (Iowa) 13 Yrs, Bayard HS (Iowa) 1 Yr, Scranton HS (Iowa) 5 Yrs, Others; Prog Participant, Howard Co Mtl Hlth; HWEA; ISEA; NEA; IPGA; SW Minn Guid Assn; Ark Cnslrs Assn; NOLPE; Others; cp/Howard Co Assn Retarded Chd; Commun Involvemt Com; Telephone Crisis Line; Tri-Co Coun of Alcohol & Drugs; Death & Dying Seminar; Chaired Class for Area 1, "Fam Living in a Single Parent Home"; Others; r/Cath.

TOLLESON, SHERWELL KLAWYN oc/Professor; b/Mar 19, 1935; h/Rt 5, Box 310, Cookeville, TN 38501; ba/Cookeville; m/Barbara Ann McCreless; c/Andrea Jon, Klawyn Seth, Thomas Avery; p/Alvin Roy and Lessie Sue Avery Tolleson (dec); ed/BS, MA, PhD Univ Ala; pa/TTU: Prof Ednl Psychol & Cnslr Ed, Chm Student Affairs Com; Editorial Bd, Ednl Catalyst; Conslt Var Pvt & Public Agencies; Others; cp/Citizens Adv Bd, Dept Human Sers; r/Meth; hon/Rec'd NDEA F'ship; Phi Delta Kappa; Kappa Delta Pi.

TOMAN, KURT oc/Scientist; b/Aug 11, 1921; h/85 Tobey Rd, Belmont, MA 02178; ba/Bedford, MA; m/Ludmila; c/Katherine, Nicholas, Marina; p/Karl and Paula Hradil Toman (dec); ed/MS; PhD; pa/Scist

(RADC/EEP) Hanscom AFB; Ionospheric Radio Propagation; Chm IEEE Wave Propagation Standards Com; cp/Pres, Austro-Am Assn Boston; hon/NAS/NRC Del to Gen Assembly, Intl Union Radio Sci; Patent Awd; Invention & Sustained Superior Perf Awds.

TONNESEN, STANLEY T oc/Research Scientist; b/Feb 2, 1935; h/17 Green Dr, E Hanover, NJ 07936; ba/Summit, NJ; m/Marion Olsen; c/Janet, David, Kevin; p/Magne Tonnesen, Holly Hill, FL; Alma

Hansen Tonnesen (dec); ed/BA NYU 1956; mil/USAF 1956-60; pa/Res Scist, Ciba Geigy Corp (Behavioral Pharmacol, Endocrinol, Cardiovascular Fields) 1960-; Bd Dirs, Christian Res Inst (Anaheim, Cal) 1968-; Am Sci Affiliation; cp/Bd Dirs, Dover Christian Nsg Home; Bd Dirs, Normanoch Assn Inc (Chm, Public Affairs Com); Pres, Culver Lake Men's Clb; r/Christ Union Chapel (Culver Lake, NJ): Pres; Calvary Evangelical Free Ch (Essex Fells, NJ): Elder, Choir, SS Tchr, Var Coms; hon/W/W E; Commun Ldrs & Noteworthy Ams; Notable Ams; DIB.

TOOKE, FLORENCE L oc/Assistant Professor; b/Jun 11, 1935; h/1301 Greenwood, Kalamazoo, MI 49007; ba/Kalamazoo; p/William G and Helen Coffey Tooke; ed/BS; MS; Addit Studies; pa/Asst Prof Home Ec, Wn Mich Univ; Co-Chrperson, Microwave

Seminar Food Indust (Chicago, Ill); Intl Microwave Power Inst & Cooking Appliance Sect (Var Coms); Assn Home Appliance Mfrs; Chm Consumer Info, Am Soc for Test'g & Materials; Consumer Ed Com, Vacuum Cleaners Study; College Edrs of Home Equipmt (Editor Newslttr); Intl Electrotech Comm for Intl Microwave Standards; hon/Gamma Phi; Sigma Phi Omega (Advr); W/W Wom Ed.

TORBERT, C C JR oc/Chief Justice; b/Aug 31, 1929; h/711, Opelika, AL 36801; ba/Montgomery, AL; m/Gene Hurt; c/Mary Dixon, Gene Shealy, Clement Clay III; p/Clement C and Lynda Meadows Torbert, Opelika; ed/BS Auburn Univ; LLB Univ Ala Law Sch; mil/USAF Capt; pa/Chief Justice, Supr Ct Ala; Lee Co Bar Assn (Past Pres) 1954-; Ala St Bar Assn 1954-, Bd Bar Commrs 1972-77; ABA: Judicial Adm Div 1977-, Appellate Judges Conf 1977-, Sect on Banking Corp & Bus Law 1970-76; Am Judicature Soc; Citizens' Conf on Ala St Cts 1966-70; Adv Comm, Implementation of Judicial Article 1973-75; Chm, Judicial Conf 1977-; Chm Perm Study Comm on Ala's Judicial Sys 1977-; Bd Mem, Ala Criminal Justice Info Sys 1977-; Conf Chief Justices: Com on Admission to Bar & Legal Ed, Com to Study Electronic & Photographic Coverage of Cts, Fed-St Relats Com 1977-; Ala Rep, Coun of St Ct Reps 1977-; Supvr Bd, Ala Law Enforcemt Planning Agy 1977-; Safety Coor'g Com 1977-; Ala Law Sch Foun; Exec Com, Ala Law Inst; cp/Kiwanis; r/Meth; hon/Outstg Freshman Legislator Awd, Capitol Press Corps; Most Effective Senator Awd.

TORDOFF, HARRY SLOCUM oc/Writer; b/Jun 28, 1905; h/272 Mayfield Ave, Cranston, RI 02920; m/Etna Louise Smith; p/Mark Sr and Melissa Ann Darling Tordoff

(dec); ed/Electronics Trade Sch; pa/Ret'd Electrical Inspector, City of Cranston; Writer, Poetry & Fiction; United Amateur Press; Nat Amateur Press; Columnist, *Poets on Parade;* Others; r/Epis; hon/Rec'd Plaque for Article, Freedoms Foun; Others.

TORRES-AYBAR, FRANCISCO G oc/- Pediatrician; b/Jul 12, 1934; h/A26 Jacaranda, Ponce, PR 00731; ba/Ponce; m/Elga; c/Elga, Jo Ann Marie; p/Francisco J Torres and Maria

Aybar; ed/BS; MD; pa/Prof & Chm Dept Pediatrics, Cath Univ Puerto Rico (Sch of Med); r/Cath.

TORRES-DELGADO, R oc/Assistant Professor; b/Jun 10, 1947; h/P O Box 21550, University Station, San Juan, PR 00931; ba/San Juan; p/Angel-Rene Torres-Lugo and Eva-Angelina Delgado-Pasapera; ed/BA Univ Puerto Rico 1969; MA Middlebury Col 1970; PhD Pacific-So Univ 1977; pa/Asst Prof Fine

Arts, Univ PR-Rio Piedras; AATI; AATF; AATSP; cp/Metro Mus Art; Mus Natural Hist; r/Rom Cath; hon/BA magna cum laude; Rec'd S'ships, Princeton Univ; Rec'd Bolivar Pagan Lit Prize, Inst PR Lit; Pontificia Academia Tiberina.

TOUTORSKY, BASIL P oc/Pianist; Composer; Educator; b/Jan 10, 1896; ba/Toutorsky Acad Music, 1720-16th St NW, Washington, DC 20009; ed/Pvt Tutors; Music Studies at Age Four; Violin Studies at Age Ten; Grad, Novotcherkask Gymnasya & Novotcherkask Mus Col; Moscow Conservatory Mus; LLB Moscow Imperial Lycee-Univ Tsarevitch Nicholas 1916; LLM Imperial Univ Moscow 1916; mil/Midshipman Naval Ser WWI; Cmdr-in-Chief Black Sea Fleet; Grad Naval Acad for Midshipmen of Fleet (Petrograd) 1917; White Army & Navy, Ret'd 1920; pa/Concert Tours Mexico, Canada, Europe & US; Fdr & Dir, Toutorsky Studio-Salon & Acad of Mus (Los Angeles); Dir Toutorsky Acad Mus 1936-; Head Piano Dept, Chevy Chase Col 1943-50; Judge Num Competitions; Considered Authoritative Interpreter of Chopin & the Russian Composers; DC Chapt, Nat Assn Am Composers & Conductors (VP); Washington Perf'g Arts Soc; IPA; Author: *Musical Devel of Russia* (1931), *Nationalism in Music* (1952), *Chords & Discords*, Others; Contbr Num Articles on Russian Music; cp/Organizer Benefit Performances & Lectr Series; Mil Order World Wars; Am Mus Natural Hist; Smithsonian Museum Assn; hon/Fellow, Intl Biogl Assn; Doct Mus, Am Intl Acad; Diplome de Medaille d'Or Compagnie Theatrale Philanthropique (France); Grand Prix Humanitaire de Belgique, Chevalier de Grand Croix; Biogl Listings.

TOWER, JOHN GOODWIN oc/US Senator; b/Sept 29, 1925; h/Wichita Falls, TX; ba/Washington, DC; m/Lilla Burt Cummings; c/Penelope, Marian, Jeanne; p/Joe Z and Beryl Goodwin Tower; ed/BA SWn Univ; MA SMU; LLD Howard Payne Col, Alfred Univ; mil/USNR; USN WWII; pa/US Senate: Chm Senate Repub Policy Com, Senate Armed Sers Com, Senate Com on Banking, Housing & Urban Affairs, Senate Ethics Com; cp/Bd Dirs, Wichita Falls Symph Orch; Trustee, So Meth Univ; Kiwanis Clb; 32° Mason (Shriner); r/Meth; hon/Hon LLD, SWn Univ; Kappa Sigma.

TOWLES, BETTY LORRAINE COX oc/Librarian; b/Oct 7, 1943; h/1822 Warwick, Garland, TX 75042; ba/Dallas, TX; m/Charles Clifford; c/Amy Jo; p/Arthur Ludene Cox, Jenks, OK; Erma Marie Greenhalgh Willey, Walnut Creek, CA; ed/BA, MLS Brigham Young Univ; Addit Studies: Univ Salzburg (Austria), N Tex St Univ, E Tex St Univ, Tex Wom's Univ; pa/Richland Commun Col: Libn & Instr 1972-, Fac Assn (Pres 1978-79, Secy 1972-73), Fac Hearing Com 1972-73, Commun Sers Adv Com 1976-77; Libn Res Div, Campbell Taggart Assoc'd Bakeries (Dallas) 1967-69; Student Messenger, Am Lib Assn 1972; Employmt Rep, Tex Lib Assn 1974; Planning & Devel Com (Chrperson), Dallas Co Lib Assn 1974-75; Dallas Ward Libn 1967-68; Garland 2nd Ward: Relief Soc Bd 1976-77; Cult Refinement Instr 1976-77; Soc Am Archivists; Archives Assocs (US Nat Archives); Tex Jr Col Tchrs Assn; Dallas Commun Col Fac Assn; cp/Dallas Geneal Soc; Assn Mormon Lttrs; Dem Party; r/Ch of Jesus Christ LDS; hon/Rec'd Heath Meml Awd; Biogl Directory Libns; W/W Am Wom; DIB; Intl W/W Commun Ser.

TOWLES, CHARLES CLIFFORD oc/Supervisor; b/May 6, 1943 h/1822 Warwick, Garland, TX 75042; ba/Richardson, TX; m/-Lorraine; c/Amy Jo; p/Ditz Clifford and Kathleen Towles; ed/AS; BS; mil/USAF; pa/-Receiving Supvr, Univ Tex-D; Amatuer Softball Assn Umpire 1970-; Umpire Tournaments incl'g Men's Regional Fast Pitch, Ladies Class A & Open Class Nat Tournaments; Am Inst Baking; cp/Former Scoutmaster, BSA; Dem Party; r/Ch of Jesus Christ LDS: Elder, SS Tchr, Ward Clerk; hon/Good Conduct Medal; Vietnam Ser Ribbon; NDCC-G2; Col Student Del AIB Conv; Outstg Airman; All Airforce Baseball (1st Team).

TRABULSI, RICHARD JOSEPH JR oc/Attorney; b/Aug 12, 1945; h/2307 Briarmead, Houston, TX 77057; ba/Houston; m/Diane Evans; c/Blake Evans, Genevieve Paige; p/Richard J Sr and Genevieve Jamail Trabulsi, Houston; ed/BA; JD; pa/Tex Bar Assn; cp/Houston C of C; Houston Area Coor, Carter for Pres Campaign 1976; r/Rom Cath.

TRACK, GERHARD oc/Music Director; b/Sept 17, 1934; h/130 Baylor, Pueblo, CO 81005; ba/Same; m/Micaela Maiahrt; c/Wolfgang, Alexander; p/Ernst Track, Austria; Kaethe Track, Austria; ed/BS, MS, MM Acad Mus & Perf'g Arts & Tchr Tng Col (Vienna, Austria); pa/Conductor; Composer; Dir: Vienna Boys Choir, St John's Symph Orch (Minn), Metro Yth Symph (Minn), Pueblo Symph Orch; Intl Guest Conductor; Pueblo Symph Assn; r/Rom Cath; hon/1st Prize, 16th & 19th Intl Mus Eisteddfod (Llangollen, Wales); 1st Prize, Austrian St Radio Network Composition; Golden Hon Cross, Republic of Austria; Num Others.

TRACY, LOUISE oc/Founder & President; b/Jul 31; h/700 S Beverly Glen Blvd, Los Angeles, CA 90024; ba/LA; m/Spencer (dec); c/John Ten Broeck, Louise Treadwell; p/Alline Wetmore and Bright Smith Treadwell (dec); ed/Hon Degs: DS NWn Univ 1951, DHL Univ So Cal 1953, DLA Lake Erie Col 1955, DHL Mac Murray Col 1956, DLitt Gallaudet Col 1966, DHL Whitworth Col 1974, DHL Ripon Col 1976; pa/John Tracy

Clinic: Fdr, Pres Bd Dirs & Dir-in-Charge 1943-74, Fdr Pres 1974-; Nat Adv Coun on Voc Rehab (Appointed by Secy M B Folsom, Dept HEW) 1956-60; Neurol & Sensory Disease Ser Adv Com, Dept HEW 1963; Nat Adv Bd, Nat Tech Inst for Deaf (Appointed by Secy John W Garner, Dept HEW) 1965-66; Pres' Task Force on Physically Handicapped (Appointed by Pres Richard M Nixon) 1969-70; Hon Mem, Am Orthopsychi Assn; Hon Mem Bd Dirs, Alexander Graham Bell Assn for Deaf; r/Epis; hon/Penn Ambassador; 6th Annual Awd, Save the Chd Fdn (NYC); 1st Humanitarian of Yr Awd, AID-United Givers; Dist'd Ser Awd, Conf of Execs of Am Schs for Deaf; Nat Wom of World Awd, Intl Orphans Inc; Medal of Hon, Nat Soc DAR; Awd of Hon, Am Acad Opthalmology & Otolaryngology; Father Flanagan Awd for Ser to Yth, Boys Town (Neb); Humanitarian Awd, Nat Aux AMVETS; Dist'd Ser Awd, Am Speech & Hearing Assn.

TRACY, MARILYN LOUISE oc/Speech Pathologist; b/Mar 11, 1933; h/Rt 131, St George, ME 04857; p/Joseph F and Janice Swain Tracy; ed/BS 1955, MA 1960 Univ Utah; Addit Studies: Bklyn Col 1965-67, Columbia Univ 1968-69; pa/Tchr, Salt Lake City Sch Dist 1955-56; Speech Therapist, Utah Soc Crippled Chd & Adults (Salt Lake City) 1957-59; Speech & Hearing Therapist 1960-65; Dir Speech & Hearing Dept, Menorah Home & Hosp for Aged, Infirm (Bklyn) 1965-69; Tchr Speech Improvemt, Speech Improvemt Bur (NYC Schs) 1967; Lectr LIU 1967-68; Asst Dir Mtl Retardation Ctr (Flower & 5th Ave Hosps, NYC) 1968-69; Dir Speech & Hearing Sers, Pine Tree Soc Crippled Chd & Adults (Bath, Maine) 1969-71; Speech Pathologist, Rockland

(Maine) Sch Dist 1971-75; Pvt Pract Pathol 1975-; Speech Pathol, Maine St Prison 1971-; Secy, Willey's Cornol Assocs; Confs for Speech & Lang; Guest Lectr Lang Disorders, Open Door Proj (Hancock Co, Maine) 1973-; Instr Speech Pathol, Univ Maine 1972-; Pupil Evaluation Team, Sch Adm Dist (Rockland) 1974-75; Maine Gov's Com on Leg for Exceptional Chd 1970-; Hlth Adv Com, Headstart (Knox Co, Maine), Penobscot Bay (Maine) Med Ctr Task Force on Exceptional Chd 1974-75; Com for Devel of Hearing Progsfor Pre-sch Age Chd, Maine Dept Hlth & Wel 1969-71; Utah St Normal Scholar 1951-55; Cert'd Tchr, Maine; Cert'd Speech Pathol, Psychol (Maine); Cert Clinical Competence, Am Speech & Hearing Assn; NEA, Am & Maine Speech & Hearing Assns; Amway Gold Direct Distributor 1978-; cp/Dem Party; Knox Co Better Homes Inc (Treas, Bd Dirs); hon/Sigma Alpha Eta; Phi Alpha Tau; Notable Ams; World W/W Wom; W/W Am Wom; Intl W/W Intellectuals.

TRAINA, ROBERT ANGELO oc/Professor; b/Aug 27, 1921; h/505 Bellevue Ave, Wilmore, KY 40390; ba/Wilmore; m/Jane Odell; c/Robert Edward, Janis Ann, Judith Arlene; p/Angelo Traina and Argia Giovannoni (dec); ed/BA; STB; STM; PhD; pa/Prof English Bible, Asbury Theol Sem; Soc Biblical Lit; Am Acad Rel; Nat Assn Profs Hebrew; r/United Meth Ch: Ordained Min; hon/Alumnus of Yr, Seattle Pacific Univ; F'ship Grant, Am Assn Theol Schs; Theta Phi.

TRAINOR, RUTH F oc/Teacher; b/Feb 22, 1938; h/107 Fairfield St, Fayetteville, NY 13066; ba/Camillus, NY; m/Phillip J; c/Leslie,

Michael, Greg; p/A Gradnauer, Tappan, NY; U Gradnauer (dec); ed/BS; MA; pa/Tchr for the Deaf; Interpreter; Evaluator Captioned Films; Com on Handicapped, Conf Exec Am Inst Deaf; r/Unit.

TRAMONTANA, JOSEPH SCAFFIDE oc/Draftsman; b/Aug 18, 1912; h/2526 Chapel Way, Tampa, FL 33618; ba/Tampa; m/Nadean Weeks; c/Marie T Clark, David Cono, Jonadean T Gonzalez, Virginia T Campoamor, Joseph Weeks, Emily Weeks, Eugene Weeks, Frederick Weeks; p/Cono and Maria Scaffide Tramontana (dec); ed/Univ Fla Col of Engrg & Drawing; mil/USCG; pa/Engrg Aeronautical Draftsman, Geodetic Survey Charts Div Engr; Notary Public, Tax Return Ser 30 Yrs; cp/US Power Squadron; Dem Party; Latin Am Fiesta Assn Tour of Spain, Portugal & Morocco (Rep'g US); r/Cath; hon/25 Yr Pin, US Power Squadron; Krewe of Sant' Yago Debutante Presentation of Emily Tramontana (Daugh).

TRAYLOR, JOSEPHINE Z oc/Department Head; b/Jun 22, 1925; h/216 Westmoreland SE, Huntsville, AL 35081; ba/Huntsville; m/Orba F; c/Joseph M, Robert F, John C; p/Joseph and Martha Khoury Zananiri (dec); ed/BA Univ Mo 1950; MA Middlebury Col 1952; PhD Cand NYU; pa/Chrperson Dept Modern Foreign Langs, Univ Ala; Lang Advr, Marshall Space Flight Ctr & AUS Missile Command (Huntsville); Past Pres, Alliance Francaise; cp/Rotaryann; r/Cath; hon/Exxon Grant, Dartmouth Col; Res Grant, Univ Ala; Mention Tres Hon, Univ Paris (France).

TRAYLOR, ORBA F oc/Consulting Economist; b/Jun 16, 1910; h/216 Westmoreland, Huntsville, AL 35801; ba/Huntsville; m/Josephine Z; c/Joseph M, Robert F, John C; p/Eddie Ewing and Dillie Stuart Traylor (dec); ed/JD NWn Univ 1936; PhD Univ Ky 1948; mil/Ret'd Lt/Col; pa/Adj Prof, Ala A&M Univ; Editor Bd, Public Adm Review; cp/Former Commr Fin, St of Ky; r/Bapt; hon/W/W Am.

TREADWELL, HUBERT THOMAS III oc/Student; b/Mar 2, 1953; h/5000 Allen Genoa Rd, Pasadena, TX 77504; ba/Houston, TX; m/Pamela Jane; c/Leonard Dustin; p/Hubert Thomas and Joan Lake Treadwell, Jacksonville, TX; ed/AS; AD; Student Anesthesia, Harris Co Hosp Dist; pa/Former Dept Head Surg Ser, Nacagdoches Meml Hosp (Tex); pa/Former Mem, Am Heart Assn; r/Meth; hon/Ath Awds.

TREECE, CORDELLA LOUISE oc/Artist; Musician; b/Mar 11, 1917; h/PO Box 1211, 606 Arvern Dr, Altamonte Springs, FL 32701; m/Robert Earl; c/Thomas Zane, Susan Clarissa T Grabner; p/Thomas H Weisenborn (dec); Clarissa Weisenborn, Rawson, OH; ed/Defiance Col; Toledo Mus of Art (Equivalent of MA); pa/Instr Art, Toledo

Univ; Pres, Toledo Artists' Clb 1966-77; Secy Toledo Fdn Art, Toledo Mus Art 1965-75; Instr Art 1940-; cp/Gov IPA; Bd Trustees, Maitland Art Assn; r/Meth; hon/Toledo Fdn Art Awd, Toledo Mus Art; IPA Awds; Best of Show Orlando, Lake Eola Arts & Crafts Fest; Firsts at Apopka & Pine Hills Art Fest; More Than 100 Art Awds; Over 20 One-man Shows.

TREIRAT, EDUARD oc/Engineer; b/May 25, 1912; h/238 N 19th St, Kenilworth, NJ 07033; ba/Springfield, NJ; m/Maimo Phabo; p/Mihkel and Marie Treirat (dec); ed/1st Class Engrg Dipl, Marine Col (Tallinn Estonia) 1942; BS Fairleigh Dickinson Univ 1957; Addit Studies: Baltic Univ (Hamburg, Germany), Stevens Inst of Technol, Cooper Union Engrg Col; pa/Sr Staff Engr, Valcor Engrg Corp 1976-; Bd Dirs, Gen Valve Co (Hanover, NJ) 1972-; Chief Design Engr, Walter Kidde & Co (Belleville, NJ) 1971-76, Asst Chief Design Engr 1965-70, Engrg Supvr 1960-65, Design Engr 1956-60; Lectr, Navigation & Marine Engrg Sch (Flensburg, Germany) 1947-49; Other Former Positions; Design & Devel of Control Valves for Nuclear Power Plants; Inventor; cp/Estonian Relief Com Inc; NY Estonian Students Soc of US; Am Security Coun Adv Bd; Fairleigh Dickinson Alumni Assn; r/Luth; hon/Phi Omega Epsilon.

TREMBLAY, JEAN-LOUIS oc/Retired Professor; b/Nov 22, 1906; h/1601 Blvd de L'Entente, Quebec, PQ, Canada G1S 2V3; ba/Quebec; m/Therese Dulac; c/Adrienne,

Jacques; p/Joseph and Georgianna Tremblay (dec); ed/BA 1927; BS 1931; PhD 1935; pa/Laval Univ: Fdr, Part-time Lectr & Ret'd Prof; r/Cath; hon/Rec'd Medal, Lt Gov; Royal Soc Canada; Others.

TREVINO, ESTELLA L oc/Executive Director; b/Aug 6, 1922; h/1014 S 14th, Edinburg, TX 78539; ba/Edinburg; m/Jose Luis; c/Chiqui T Guerra; p/Jack Sr and Estella Palacios Lane, Edinburg; ed/McAllen Bus Col; Holtry's Beauty Col; Pan Am Col; Spec Tng Courses; pa/Exec Dir, Hous'g Authority City of Edinburg; Hotel Auditor 1965-72; J of P (Hidalgo Co) 1959-64; Bus Owner 1940-58;

Tex Hous'g Assn: Past Pres, Treas & Secy; Past Pres & Treas, Hous'g Assn Val Employees; BPW: Pres, Former VP & Treas; Bd Dirs, Rio Grande Val Devel Coun; Past Pres, J of P & Constables Assn; Bd Dirs, Tex NAHRO; cp/Past Treas, LWV; Past Pres, Hidalgo Co Dem Wom; Past Pres, Sacred Heart Cath Mothers' Clb; Past Secy, Cancer Bd; Past VP Hosp Aux; Gov's Com on Aging; Alternate, Amigos del Valle Bd; Hidalgo Co Hist Soc; Bd Mem, Hidalgo Co Cancer Bd; hon/Hous'g Dir of Yr, HAVE; Commun Ctr Named in Hon.

TREVINO, LEE BUCK oc/Professional Golfer; b/Dec 1, 1939; h/11737 St Michaels, Dallas, TX 75230; ba/Dallas; m/Claudia Ann Fenley; c/Lesley Ann, Tony Lee, Troy Liana; p/Juanita Barrett (dec); ed/Hon BS, Lincoln Col; mil/USMC 1957-60; pa/Golfer Num Tournaments: US Open, World Cup, Tournament of Champions, Dunlop Intl,

British Open, Coral Springs Open, Danny Thomas Open, Bing Crosby Nat Pro-Am, Kemper Open, Num Others; PGA of Am; cp/Nat Multiple Sclerosis Soc Sports Com; Pres' Conf on Physical Fitness & Sports; Established Caddy S'ship, Singapore; Dir El Paso Boys' Clb; Helped Establish Cancer Radiation Treatmt Ctr; Donations to Orphanages, St Jude's Hosp, Others; Free Golf Exhbns for Armed Sers, Chd's Hosps, March of Dimes, Others; Rotary Clb (Dallas); r/Cath; hon/Golf Rookie of Yr 1967; El Paso Ath of Yr 1967,68; El Paso Press Headliner of Yr 1968; Monthly Awd, Hickok Awd; Grand Marshal, Sun Carnival Parade; Hon Chm, Trans-Pecos Christmas Seal Campaign; Parade Chm, El Paso Easter Seal Parade; W/W Am; Top Money Winner, Ofcl PGA Tournaments; Vardon Trophy Winner; Tex Pro Ath of Yr; Nat Christmas Seal Sports Ambassador; PGA Player of Yr 1971; *Golf Mag* Player of Yr 1971; Sportsman of Yr, *Sports Illustrated* 1971; Intl Sports Personality of Yr; AP Press Male Ath of Yr; Annual Hickok Belt Awd; Gold Tee Awd; Tex Hall of Fame; Tex Golf Hall of Fame; Num Others.

TRICE, ETHEL WILLIAMSON oc/-Inspector; b/Oct 15, 1920; h/506 Hedge Row, Brandon, FL 33511; ba/Tampa, FL; c/Barbara Jean T Stephenson, James H, Richard A, Robert W; p/Thomas J and Mattie L Williamson (dec); pa/Ordained Min; USPA Press Assn; ILPA Press Assn; cp/Works w Alcohol & Drug Progs; r/World Bibleway F'ship; hon/W/W: Am Wom, World; Book of Hon; Commun Ldrs & Noteworthy Ams; Rec'd Howard McCartney Jour Awd; Others.

TRIGG, CHRISTINE ELIZABETH oc/Manager; b/Oct 23, 1928; h/10 Goldsmith Ave, Newark, NJ 07112; ba/Cranford, NJ; m/Raleigh J; c/Shearon T Drakeford, (Stepchd); Ida, Iris T Barrow; p/Samuel McDonald (dec); Julia Baum Frasier, Camden, SC; ed/BS Allen Univ; pa/Former Tchr: Rober Small HS (Beaufort, SC), Mather Sch (Beaufort), Clearview HS (Easley, SC), A L Corbett HS (Wagner, SC), US Dependent Sch (Landshut, Germany); J B Williams Co (20 Yrs): Former Adm Asst Customer Ser Div, Customer Ser Mgr; NAUW; Zonta Intl; cp/Nat Coun Negro Wom; Kenneth Gibson Civic Assn; Prince Hall OES; Nat Pan-Hellenic Coun; r/Clinton Meml AME Zion Ch: VP Conf Workers, Pres Choral Guild, Bd Trustees, Sunday Order of Worship; hon/Wom Achmt; NE Region Dir, Sigma Gamma Rho; W/W Am Wom; World W/W Wom; Notable Ams.

TRIMMER, HARVEY W JR oc/Counselor; b/Jun 15, 1930; h/1524 Pinto Ct, Carson City, NV 89701; ba/Carson City; m/Judith; c/Rick, Edward, Douglas; p/Harvey W Trimmer Sr, Trenton, NJ; Anna C Trinner (dec); ed/BA; MA; MEd; Addit Studies; mil/USNCB; pa/Chief Cnslg & Spec Sers, Nevada Employmt Security Dept; Inst Adv'd Study in Rational Psychotherapy; APGA; Nn Nevada PGA; Nat Employmt Cnslrs Assn; Nevada PGA; Clark Co Cnslg, PGA; hon/Rec'd Res Awd, Nat Employmt Cnslrs Assn; USES Individual Commend; W/W: E,W; Personalities of W&MW; Men Distinction.

TROMBLEY, CHARLES CYPRIAN oc/-Minister; Educator; b/Aug 24, 1928; h/293 W Ithica, Broken Arrow, OK 74012; ba/Broken

Arrow; m/Gladys; c/David, Darlene, Deborah, Deanna; p/Carroll Cyprian and Beulah Bradshaw Trombley (dec); ed/ThG; mil/-ISCG; pa/Exec Secy, Gospel Crusades Inc (Sarasota, Fla) 1961-63; Editor, *The Expositor* 1960-; Instr, Trinity Bible Col 1972; Dir Gospel Light Telecast (Ottumwa, Iowa) 1970-72; Dir Way Out Drug Rehab Prog (Tulsa, Okla) 1972-74; Lectr: FGBMFI, CBMC, Aglow, Var Cols, Others; Author: *Visitation, The Key to Ch Growth, Kicked Out of the Kingdom, Guilty as Charged, Bible Answers for the Jehovah's Witnesses*, Others; Contbr Articles Rel Jours; TV Guest; Dir & Fdr, CTMI Mins; Weekly TV Moderator, *Testimony Time* (from Clarksburg, W Va); r/Bapt.

TROTTER, JESSE L SR oc/Minister; b/July 15, 1925; h/1702 Weed St, Ocean Springs, MS 39564; m/Semora L; c/Jesse, Melvin, Marvin, Leroy (dec), Barbara, Patricia, Valeria, Jacquelyn; p/Elijah Sr and Arcola Trotter (dec); ed/AA; BA; DD; BD; STD; LLD; Addit Studies; pa/Public Sch Tchr 1958-71; Proj Dir, Harrison Co Headstart 1967-71; Other Positions; NEA; Miss Tchrs Assn; Chaplain, 6th Dist Tchrs Assn; Others; cp/St & Nat Confs on Wel; IPA; Intl Biogl Ctr; NAACP; Alpha Phi Alpha; r/Bapt; hon/Pub'd Author; Men of Achmt; W/W: Am, S&SW; DIB; Others.

TRUDINGER, L PAUL oc/Professor; Theologian; b/May 5, 1930; h/3380 N Dickerson St, Arlington, VA 22207; ba/Alexandria, VA; m/Kathleen Binks-Williams; c/Philip, Ashleigh, Bronwen, Heather-Mary; p/Ronald and Lina Mathilde Trudinger (dec): ed/BA. BMus, MEd Johns

Hopkins Univ; STM, ThD Boston; LTCL, Dipl Ed London; pa/Author 4 Books, Over 40 Scholarly Articles; Composer Hymns Rel; Royal Sch of Ch Mus; Curric Coms, Local Schs; r/Congreg: Ordained Min.

TRUESDELL, JERRY LYNN oc/Artist; Teacher; b/Oct 22, 1936; h/1916 24th Ave, Greeley, CO 80631; ba/Greeley; p/O M and Ethel M Truesdell, Johnstown, CO; ed/BA Hastings Col 1961; MA Colo St Univ 1964; Addit Studies; mil/USAR; pa/West HS: Art Instr & Chm Dept Fine Arts, Indust Arts & Home Ec 1965-; Art Instr, Heath Jr HS & Greeley Public Schs 1964-65; Intern, Office Nat Art Ed Assn 1978; Pvt Lessons, Aims Commun Col & Workshops Univ Colo; Colo Chm, Yth Art Month; Nat Art Ed Assn: Bd Dirs 1973-75, Nat Chm Sec'dy Div 1973-75, Chm Wn Regional Art Assn Div 1969-71, Others; Past Pres, Art Assn Weld Co; Colo Art Ed Assn; Greeley Tchrs Assn; NEA; Nat Assn for Supvn & Curric Devel; Lectr; Juror;

High Plains Art Exhibit, Colo Artists Exhibit, Others; 2-man Show, 1st Nat Bank (Greeley) 1969; Artists & Their Students Show, Weld Co Gen Hosp 1975; Artists Invitational, James A Michener Lib, Univ Nn Colo 1978; Author & Contbg Author: *Art Guide for the Fremont Public Schs* (1963), *Art Education: Senior HS* (1969); Editor Art Books; Owner & Mgr, Max'ims Art Gallery (Greeley) 1971-75; Others; r/Presb; hon/Cert Merit in Jewelry Design, Hastings Col Student Exhbn; Best of Show & Hon Mention, AAUW Exhibit; Cert Commend, Crayon, Watercolor & Crafts Inst.

TRUMBULL, ROBERT OLIVER oc/Foreign Correspondent; b/May 26, 1912; h/431 Nahua St, Apt 1107, Honolulu, HI 96815; ba/Same; m/Jean M; c/Suzanne, Joan, Stephanie; p/Oliver M and Sydney F Trumbull (dec); pa/Reporter, *Honolulu Advtr* 1933-35; City Editor 1935-43; War Correspondent, *NY Times* 1943-45, Covering 4 Combat Landings & 13 Naval Engagemts in Pacific Theatre; Foreign Correspondent & Bur Chief, NY

Times in Asia, Canada & Pacific Area 1945-; Contbr Num Articles on Asian & Pacific Subjects; Former Mem, U E Ednl Foun (India & Japan); Overseas Press Clb Am & Num Foreign Press Clbs; Author: *The Raft* (Book of Month Clb Selection 1942), *As I See India, Paradise in Trust, Nine Who Survived Hiroshima & Nagasaki, The Scrutable East* (Best Book on Foreign Affairs 1964, Overseas Press Clb); Editor, *This Is Communist China*; hon/USN Commend & Theatre Ribbon; Better Understanding Awd, English-Speaking Union; Others.

TSCHATSCHULA, MARVIN EDWARD oc/Clergyman; b/Dec 30, 1929; h/1226 E Common, New Braunfels, TX 78130; ba/New Braunfels; m/Renita Efird; c/Mark Allen, Elizabeth Anne; p/(dec); ed/AA; BA; MDiv; DD; mil/USAR Staff Chaplain, Maj; pa/Cnslr; Chm, Tex Dist Ch Extension Bd; cp/Chm, Parks & Rec Bd; Indust Coun; Lions Clb; Repub Party; r/Luth-Mo Synod; hon/W/W; Tex, Rel; Personalities of S; Notable Ams Bicent Era; Others.

TSCHIRKI, ROBERT DEAN oc/Superintendent; b/Aug 31, 1937; h/104 Krestwood Dr, Burnsville, MN 55337; ba/Burnsville; m/Joan; c/Rhonda, Lona, Christopher; p/Chris and Mildred Tschirki, Forest City, IA; ed/BA Univ Nn Iowa 1958; MA Univ Iowa 1964; PhD Iowa St Univ 1972; pa/Supt of Schs 1975-; Supt Schs (Newton, Iowa) 1973-75; Asst Supt Sec'dy Ed (Marshalltown, Iowa) 1968-73; Other Positions; St Acad Ldr, NASE 1977-78; Key-Line Dir, Minn Assn Sch Admrs 1977-; Chrperson, "Conflict Mgmt" Clinic, AASA Nat Conv 1977; Adv Coun, Col St Thomas 1976-; Panelist, "Curric Probs in Small Dists", AASA Nat Conv 1975; Am Assn Sch Admrs; Nat Sch Public Relats Assn; Nat Org Legal Probs Ed; Conf Com & Exec Devel Com, Minn Assn Sch Admrs; Others; r/Epis; hon/World Devel Seminar 2 Yrs; Outstg Yg Edr; Danforth/NASE Fellow; W/W MW; Ldrs Am Sec'dy Ed; Men Achmt; Personalities of W&MW.

TSO, RAYMOND H oc/Employee Relations Officer; b/Oct 14, 1934; h/PO Box 1714, Shiprock, NM 87420; m/Dorothy Rose;

c/Montgomery, Rhonda, Salina, Christopher Ray (dec); p/Chester H Tso (dec); Cora C Begay, Shiprock; pa/Spec Pers Mgmt, USPHS Agy; cp/Assoc, Smithsonian Inst; Rodeo Clb; Basketball Clb; r/Prot; hon/Col Aide-de-Camp NM; Commun Ldrs & Noteworthy Ams; Commun Ldrs Am; Intl W/W Commun Ser; Intl Biogl Assn.

TUCK, WILLIAM POWELL oc/Associate Professor; b/Oct 30, 1934; h/2322 Thornhill Rd, Louisville, KY 40222; ba/Louisville; m/Emily Campbell; c/Catherine Mae, William Powell III; p/Hillard Witt and Elsie Mae Tuck, Lynchburg, VA; ed/AA Bluefield Jr Col; BA, DD Univ Richmond; BD, ThM SEn Bapt Theol Sem; ThD New Orleans Bapt Theol Sem; pa/Assoc Prof Christian Preaching, So Bapt Theol Sem; Pastor: 1st Bapt Ch (Bristol, Va) 1969-78, Harrisonburg Bapt Ch (Va) 1966-69, Others; Adj Prof, Va Intermont Col 1973-78; Prog Chm, Bapt Gen Assn Va 1971-72; Pres Gtr Bristol Min Assn

1972-73; Lectr, Univ Richmond Pastor's Sch 1973; Annual Preacher, Lebanon Bapt Assn; Workshop Ldr Va Bapt Student, Music & Christian Life Confs; Pastor Advr, Madison Col BSU 1966-69; Others; Author: *Facing Grief & Death, Knowing God: Rel Knowledge in the Theol of John Baillie*; Editor, *The Struggle for Mean'g*; Contbr Articles Rel Jours; cp/Former Mem Bd Dirs, Bristol Boys Clb; Past Mem, Dist Com Sequoyah Coun BSA; Past Mem Bd Dirs, YMCA; Former Mem, Drug & Sex Com Bristol Public Schs; Rotary Clb; Past Chm, Inter-racial & Interdenom Washington St Sch Sys; Ser'd Gov's Spec Ed Res Com; Others; r/Bapt; hon/Man & Boy Awd, Bristol Boys Clb; Phi Theta Kappa; Kappa Delta Pi; Grad F'ship, New Orleans Bapt Theol Sem; Am Acad Rel; Am Acad Homiletics; Men Achmt; W/W Rel; Intl W/W Commun Ser; Others.

TUCKER, C DeLORES oc/Civil Rights Worker; b/Oct 4, 1927; h/6700 Lincoln Dr, Philadelphia, PA 19119; ba/Same; m/William L; p/Whitfield Nottage, Phila; Captilda Nottage (dec); ed/Hon LLD Villa Maria Col & Morris Col; pa/Secy of St, Commonwealth of Penn 1971-77 (Highest Ranking Black Wom in St Govt US); First Black/Female Mem, Phila Zoning Bd; Former Pres, C DeLores Tucker Assocs (Public Relats Firm); cp/Cand Lt/Gov Penn 1978; Participated w Dr Martin Luther King Jr in Selma-Montgomery March; Del White House Conf on Civil Rights; Fdg Mem, Nat Wom's Polit Caucus; Co-fdr, Nat Black Wom's Polit Caucus; Past VChm, Penn Dem St Com; Nat VP Fdn Dem Wom; Nat Dem Com; Nat Bd NAACP Spec Contbn Fund; Bd Mem, Commonwealth Med Col Penn; Nat

Secy, Nat Bd Dirs PUSH; Links, Inc; Bd Dirs, New Sch Music; BPW; Messiah Col Bd Assocs; Others; r/Prot; hon/1 of 100 Most Influential Black Ams, *Ebony Mag*; Nom Wom of Yr, *Ladies Home Jour*; Commun Ser Awd, Quaker City Chapt B'nai B'rith; Wom of Yr, Nat Assn TV & Radio Artists; Rec'd Nat Elks Awd; Achmt Awd, Nat Assn Real Estate Brokers; Freedom Fund Awd, NAACP; OIC Achmt Awd; Martin Luther King Awd, Phila Trade Unions Coun; Hon Mem, Alpha Kappa Alpha; Num Others.

TUCKER, WANDA HALL oc/Editor; b/Feb 6, 1921; ba/Pasadena, CA; m/Frank R; c/Frank Jr, Nancy I; p/Frank W and Hazel Smith Hall (dec); ed/AA Citrus Col; pa/Mng Editor, *Star-News*; Soc Profl Journalists; Gtr LA Press Clb; cp/Former Ofcr, Soroptomists; PTA; Coor'g Coun, Pasadena Opportunity Improvemt Comm; r/Prot; hon/Wom of Yr, Pasadena Wom's Civic Leag; Num Writing Awds.

TUFTS, MARY ANN oc/Secretary; b/Oct 18, 1924; h/Rt 1, Box 1310, Dallas, TX 75224; ba/Dallas; m/John F Sr; c/Mary Frances T Smiley, John F Jr; p/Albert Fakes and Gussie Mae Sewell Wilkes (dec); ed/N Tex Tchrs Col; pa/Secy & Dir, Tufts & Son Vet Prods & Supplies Co; cp/Wom's Aux, Meth Hosp; Duncanville Book Review Clb; DAR; r/First Christian Ch (Duncanville): SS Tchr; hon/Vol of Yr, Meth Hosp; Wom of Month, Citizens Nat Bank (Dallas); W/W Am Wom.

TULIS, ALLEN JOSEPH oc/Chemical Engineer; b/Jan 28, 1929; h/174 N Country Clb Dr, Addison, IL 60101; ba/Chicago, IL; m/Elinore Cathaline Maass; p/Anton and Antoinette Drtilek Tulis, Berwyn, IL; ed/BS (2), MS Ill Inst Technol; mil/AUS 1951-52; pa/Sr Chem Engr, IIT Res Inst; Contbr Articles Profl Jours; AICHE; AIAA; ACS; ADPA; cp/Air Force Assn; Combustion Inst; Nat Adv Bd, Am Security Coun; r/Rom Cath.

TUMA, JUNE M oc/Psychologist; b/Jun 22, 1934; h/3917 Ave P½, Galveston, TX 77550; ba/Galveston; p/Harry and Mary Tuma, Alexandria, LA; ed/BA, MA, PhD La St Univ; pa/Clinical Child Psychol; APA; AOA; AAPSC; AAUP; hon/Phi Kappa Phi; Diplomate, Am Bd Profl Psychols.

TURNBACH, MARIE oc/Hospital Consultant; b/Mar 6, 1930; h/423 W Broad St, Hazleton, PA 18201; ba/Omaha, NE; p/William M Turnbach (dec); Marie Guckavan Turnbach, Hazleton; ed/BA cum laude, Misericordia Col 1952; MA Cath Univ 1955; MPA Univ Pittsburgh 1975; pa/Sister Rel Order; Col Misericordia: Chm & Asst Prof Sociol Dept 1969-73, Instr Social Scis 1952-73, Coms; Chm & Tchr Social Studies, St Gabriel HS 1968-69; Admr, Mercy Ctr 1972-73; Fac Advr, Ec Devel Coun, NEn Penn Yth Ldrship Prog 1971-72; Conslt, United Sers Agy 1972; Office Commun Affairs, Diocese of Harrisburg; Univ Pittsburgh: Judicial Bd 1974, Grad Sch Intl Affairs Student Govt Com 1973-74; Conslt: Franciscan Sisters, Sisters of Holy Names, Sisters of Mercy; Contbr Articles Profl Jours; Am Soc Public Adm, NAWR; Mercy Action Foun; Diocesan Speakers' Bur; Am Sociol Assn; Coun on Social Work Ed; En Sociol Assn; AAUP; Network; Interagency Conf; Num Other Activs; cp/Exec Dir, Com for Charter-Fall; Shelter Mgr for Flood Evacuees; Pres' Task Force on Aging; United Way; Former Shelter Coor, ARC; Cerebral

Palsy & Crippled Chd's Assn; Community Chest; Polit Campaigns; World Future Soc; Am Inst Parliamentarians; Common Cause; Public Citizen Inc; Commun Sers Penn; LWV; Others; r/Rom Cath, Sisters of Mercy; Chrperson Steer'g Com, Chrperson Task Force on Wom, Others; hon/Kappa Gamma Pi; Rec'd Cath Charities S'ship; Intl Studies Inst Awd; Tchr of Yr; NSF S'ship; East/West Ctr S'ship; Nat Endowmt for Humanities; EDPA S'ship; Carnegie Foun F'ship; Outstg Edrs Am; Others.

TURNER, ARTHUR EDWARD oc/- Administrator; b/Jan 31, 1931; h/4608 Arbor Dr, Midland, MI 48604; ba/Midland; m/- Johann May Jordan; c/Steven Arthur, Michael Scott, Kathryn Jo; p/Alvin S and Grace E Champlain Turner; ed/BS Alma Col 1952; MEd Wayne St Univ 1954; Addit Studies; pa/Northwood Inst: Co-fdr (w Dr R Gary Stauffer) 1959, First Pres & Trustee 1959-74, Chm Col, Chief Exec Ofcr & Trustee 1974-78, Chm Bd Trustees 1978-, Founded Ext Ctrs South America & Europe; Alma Col: Admissions Cnslr 1953-59, Dir Admissions & Alumni Relats 1953-59; cp/Midland Rotary Clb; Detroit Clb; Midland Country Clb; Midland Music Foun; Little Theatre Guild; Midland Symph; Poinciani Clb (Palm Beach, Fla); Mem at Large, Nat Coun BSA; 32° & 33° Mason; Bay City Scottish Rite Bodies; r/Meml Presb Ch (Midland): Mem; hon/Alpha Psi Omega; Phi Phi Alpha; Hon HHD, Colegio Americano (Quito, Ecuador); Hon LLD, Ashland Col (Ohio); Decoration of 1st Class, Govt of Ecuador for Devel of Ed; 1 of 10 Outstg Yg Men Am 1965; People of Peru Awd; Silliman Scholar; F'ship Hall Named in Hon, Eastminister Presb Ch (Alma); W/W: Am, MW, World; Commun Ldrs & Noteworthy Ams; Men Achmt; Others.

TURNER, BETTY LUCRETIA oc/Teacher; b/Jan 15, 1926; h/Box 81, Mulberry, FL 33860; ba/Mulberry; p/Chris Turner (dec); Myrtle F Turner, Mulberry; ed/BS Fla So Col; MEd Univ Miss; pa/3rd Grade Tchr, Mulberry Elem Sch; PEA; FEA; NEA; cp/Lakeland Little Theatre; Winter Haven Commun Theatre; Lakeland Symph Orch; r/Prot; hon/Var Awds.

TURNER, CLAYTON DUANE oc/Artist; Writer; b/Sept 17, 1935; h/5707 E Jensen, Fresno, CA 93725; ba/Same; p/Levi M and Jewell Turner, Fresno; pa/Painter Depicting Old W & Rural Life (Oils, Watercolors, Chalk, Acrylics, Inks); Paints Using Mouth & Feet; Works Featured 1978 Gt Wn Savs & Ln Calendar, *Calif Heartland* (Anthol of Writings About Cal's Gt Ctl Val, Pub'd by Capra Press); Works in Pvt Collections; Intl Exhibits; Intl Assn Mouth & Foot Paint'g Artists; Pub'd Short Stories; cp/Travels as Rep of All Disabled People; r/Prot; hon/Num Awds for Art in Open Competitions; Rec'd Life Achmt Awd, Soc of Illustrators; Paintings Reproduced & Distributed Throughout World by Assn Mouth & Foot Paint'g Artists, Vaduz Leichtenstein.

TURNER, DONALD HUNTER oc/Advertising Agency Executive; b/Jan 13, 1933; h/854 Van Buren St, Baldwin Harbor, NY; ba/Toronto, Ontario, Canada; m/Janice Canterella; c/Darren Bradford, Denise Starr; p/James Shortt Turner (dec); Gladys Marian Jean Hunter (dec); ed/Hunter Col 1951-53; Sch of Visual Arts 1955-57; mil/AUS 1953-55; pa/W J Walter Thompson Co Inc 1957; Artist, Adpix (NYC) 1958; Art Dir, Writer & TV Prodr, Morse Intl (NYC) 1959-66; Creative Supvr, Marschalle Co (NYC) 1966-68; Pres, Creative Dir, Don Turner & Partners Inc (NYC) 1968-71; VP & Assoc Creative Dir, Brandwynne Div of Benton/Bowles (NYC) 1971-73; Creative Group Hd, Kenyon & Eckhardt (NYC) 1973-74; Creative Dir, Doubleday Advtg Inc (NYC) 1974-77; Exec VP, Dir of Creative Sers & Prin Mem Bd Dirs, Michel/Cather Inc 197-79; Exec VP, Dir of Creative Sers & Partner, Fergo-Graff Inc (NYC) 1979-; Fine Arts Painter, 10 Maj Works 1967-; Illustrator Chd's Books; Am Film Inst; Others; cp/Created Campaign & Worked w Mayor John Lindsay's Ofc to Keep NYC Parks

Clean; r/Presb; hon/Judge for "Clio" Awds, Nat Acad TV Arts & Scis; IPA; Nom'd as 1 of Top 100 Creative People in Country, Nat Ad Day/USA Survey; Alpha Delta Tau; Best Teller Awd, Bus Press of Am; Effie Awds, Am Mktg Assn; W/W E; Others.

TURNER, GLADYS T oc/Social Work Administrator; b/Sept 16, 1935; h/1107 Lexington Ave, Dayton, OH 45407; ba/Dayton; m/Frederick M Finney; p/Willis J and Mary Bluford Turner, Pine Bluff, AR; ed/BA Univ Ark-Pine Bluff; MSW Atlanta Univ; pa/Social Work Admr, Dayton W Commun Mtl Hlth Ctr; Adj Asst Prof Sociol, Anthropol & Social Work, Wright St Univ 1970-76; Adj Asst Prof, Park Col 1974-75; Nat Assn Social Workers; Soc for Hosp Social Worker Dirs ANA; Acad Cert'd Social Workers; r/Presb; hon/Social Worker of Yr, Miami Val (Ohio) Unit Nat Assn Social Workers; W/W Am Wom.

TURNER, HERMAN NATHANIEL oc/Educator; Mathematician; b/Nov 6, 1925; h/4709 Lee Ave, St Louis, MO 62115; ba/St Louis; m/Helen Lorraine Quarles; c/Anthony Cabot, Mark Courtney, Herman Nathaniel III, Erik Alexander; p/Herman Nathaniel and Rosie Mae Williams Turner; ed/BS Bradley Univ 1951; Addit Studies; mil/USMC 1944-46; pa/Cartographic Photogrammetric Aide, Aeronaut Chart & Info Ctr (St Louis) 1953-54; Math, White Sands Proving Ground, Flight Determination Lab (Las Cruces, NM) 1954-55; Tchr Math: Vaux Jr HS & Stoddart-Fleisher Jr HS (Phila, Penn) 1956-59, Wash Sr HS (Caruthersville, Mo) 1961-62, United Township HS (E Moline, Ill) 1965-66, NW HS (St Louis) 1968-; St Tchr Cert Mo, Ill, Penn, NJ & NY; Am Math Soc; Math Assn Am; Am Fdn Tchrs; cp/Kiwanis; Dem Party; r/Presb; hon/Cert Apprec, Kiwanis; Cert of Merit, MOA; Student Apprec Awds, NW HS; Personalities of W&MW; Intl W/W Intellectuals; Commun Ldrs & Noteworthy Ams; Others.

TURNER, LYNN WARREN oc/Retired Educator; b/Jul 7, 1906; h/211 W Seminary Ave, Bloomington, IL 61701; ba/Bloomington; m/Vera Kathryn Arbogast; c/Veralyn Kinzer; p/Ira Burton and Sylvia Warren Turner (dec); ed/BA magna cum laude, Ind Ctl Univ; MA Ind Univ; PhD Harvard Univ; pa/HS Tchr 1930-34; Prof Hist, Monmouth Col (Ill) 1936-47; Dir Ind War Hist Comm & Assoc Prof, Ind Univ 1947-58; Pres Otterbein Col 1958-71 (Ret'd, Now Pres Emeritus); Author, *William Plumer of New Hampshire*; Contbr Hist Articles Mags & Jours; Editor: *The Histn* (Phi Alpha Theta), *Historical Messenger*; r/United Meth Ch; Histn & Archivist Ctl Ill Conf; hon/LLD Ind Ctl Univ; LHD Ohio Nn Univ; DLitt, Findlay Col; Past Nat Pres, Phi Alpha Theta.

TURNER, NAOMI COCKE oc/Retired; b/Dec 19, 1903; h/19 Village Ln, Arlington, MA 02174; m/Clair E (dec); c/Mary Frances T Bonk, Frederick Clair; p/William A and Brownie Rees Cocke; ed/BA Univ Tex 1925; MEd Harvard Univ 1930; pa/Res Assoc,

Forsyth Dental Infirmary for Chd 1944-57; Res Assoc Dental Public Hlth, Harvard Sch Public Hlth (Boston, Mass) 1954-60; Pub'd 30 Res Papers; Contbr Chapt, " The Oxidation-Reduction Potentials of Saliva", *Coronary Heart Disease in Yg Adults* (by Gertler-White 1954); Am Public Hlth Assn; Royal Soc Hlth; Intl Assn Dental Res; Fellow AAAS; cp/DAR; PEO; hon/Phi Mu; Sigma Xi.

TURNER, REX ALLWIN JR oc/Dean; Teacher; Minister; b/Dec 8, 1945; h/245 Tensaw Dr, Montgomery, AL 36117; ba/Montgomery; m/Barbara Parker; c/Michael Clark, April Laina; p/Rex A Sr and Opal Shipp Turner, Montgomery; ed/BA Ala Christian Col 1967; BS 1970, MS 1972 Troy St Univ; MA 1976. MTh 1978 Ala Christian Sch

Rel; EdD Univ Ala 1977; pa/Bookstore Mgr 1964-74; Prof Hist, Ala Christian Col 1973-74; Ala Christian Sch Rel: Prof Bible, Hist & Speech 1975-, Dean Students & Pers Affairs 1975-; Author Booklet, "The Caesars & Their Relationship w God's People"; cp/Lions Clb; r/Ch of Christ: Serd as Min Mt Olive, Ozark, Clanton & Butler Hill Chs of Christ; hon/Men Achmt; Phi Delta Kappa.

TURNER, RUTH ELAINE oc/Librarian; b/Jul 28, 1922; h/261 S 300 W, Kaysville, UT 84037; ba/Ogden, UT; p/Walter Scott and Mabel Ella Holt Turner (dec); ed/BS cum laude, Weber St Col 1965; MLS Brigham Young Univ 1969; pa/Weber St Col: Fac Senate 1973-76, Acad Freedom & Tenure

Com, Gen Ed Com, Profl Equity Com, Commun Ser Com, Orientation Com, *Utah Libs* Pub Coun Bd UEA; 1st VP, Ogden AAUW; GODORT ALA Const & By-Laws Com; Asst Coor & Coor GODORT ULA; cp/AAUW Leg Com for ERA; Coalition Utah ERA; r/LDS; hon/Lambda Iota Tau; Beta Phi Mu.

TURNER, VERA ARBOGAST oc/Retired Music Educator; b/Aug 13, 1907; h/211 W Seminary Ave, Bloomington, IL 61701; ba/Bloomington; m/Lynn Warren; c/Veralyn A Kinzer, Sylvia (dec), Ian Bruce; p/W H and Alta Menry Biehl Arbogast (dec); ed/BA summa cum laude 1927, BMus 1929 Ind Ctl Univ; MA Ind Univ 1956; pa/Mus Supvr & Conslt, Hendricks Co (Ind), Warren Co (Ill), Bloomigton; Bd Dirs. Ohio Fdn Mus Clbs

1964-, St Pres 1968-71; Bd Dirs, Ill Fdn Mus Clbs 1971-; Bd Dirs Rep'g Ill, Nat Fdn Mus Clbs 1978-; Editor: *Ohio Music Clb News* (1971-75) & *IFMC Mus Notes* (1975-); Assoc Editor, *Hist Messenger* (1974-); MENC; NEA; cp/Past Pres, Ch Wom United; Lectr on Travels to Civic Groups; Num Positions, Var Ch Wom's Groups; First Lady Otterbein Col (While Husband was Pres); Past Mem AAUW, BPW & LWV; Others; r/United Meth; hon/Delta Omicron; Delta Kappa Gamma; Otterbein Wom of Yr; Valiant Wom, Bloomington-Normal Ch Wom United.

TURPEN, MICHAEL CRAIG oc/District Attorney; b/Nov 10, 1949; h/2602 Rutherford, Muskogee, OK 74401; ba/Muskogee; p/Wallace Kendall Turpen (dec); Marjory Turpen, Owasso, OK; ed/BSEd, JD Univ Tulsa; pa/Muskogee Police Legal Advr 1975; Muskogee Co Asst DA 1976; Muskogee Co Chief Prosecutor & 1st Asst DA 1977; Adj Prof Bus Law, NEn Okla St Univ 1977; Adj Prof Am Govt & Crim Law, Connors St Col 1977; Okla Bar Assn: Chm Spec Corrections Com, St Chm Vols in Corrections Prog, Cont'g Legal Ed Speaker on Crim Law; ABA; Public Info Chm & Past Secy, Muskogee Co Bar Assn; Okla DA's Assn: Bd Dirs, Chm Com on Proposed Code of Evidence, Frequent Speaker St Trials Tactics Seminars; Okla Spec Leg Com on Crim Justice Sys; Frat Order Police; Pub'd Article, *Barrister*; Pub'd "Police Prosecutor Tng Manual" for Nat DA's Assn; cp/Rotary Clb; JCs; Bd Dirs & Coach, Green Country Girls Softball Assn; Muskogee HS Booster Clb; Coach, Knothole Leag Boys Baseball; Tulsa Univ Alumni Assn & Hurricane Clb; r/Cumberland Presb Ch; hon/Outstg Yg Lwyr, Okla Bar Assn; Rec'd Mayor's Commend Outstg Ser to City of Muskogee; Addressed Nat DA's Assn Annual Conf; Gave Commencement Address, Muskogee HS, Ft Gibson HS & Connors St Col.

TURTON, ROBERT STRAKER III oc/Minister; Teacher; Social Worker; b/Jul 12, 1937; h/Bethany, 144-146 Stockton St, Hightstown, NJ 08520; ba/Hightstown; m/Sandra H Bross; c/Francis William (dec), Robert Straker IV, Elisabeth Anne, Michael Stefan; p/Robert Straker Jr and Grace E Byer Turton, Hightstown; ed/Attended: Reformed Epis Theol Sem (Phila, Penn), Alma White Col, Zarephath Bible Sem (NJ); Grad'd BSc 1957, BSd 1960; mil/USAF Aux, Chaplain; Am Rescue Workers; pa/Pastor Gospel Mission Chapels; Pres Bd Trustees & Supt, Gospel Mission Corps; Tchr Public & Ch-related Schs; Broadcaster, Pillar of Fire Radio Stations; Intl Union Gospel Missions; Nat Assn Evangelicals; Others; r/Non-denom Evangelical Christian, Pillar of Fire Ch;

hon/W/W Rel; Commun Ldrs & Noteworthy Ams; DIB.

TURTON, SANDRA H BROSS oc/- Registered Nurse; Teacher; b/Aug 25, 1946; h/Bethany, 144-146 Stockton St, Hightstown, NJ 08520; ba/Hightstown; m/Robert S III; c/Francis William (dec), Robert Straker IV, Elisabeth Anne, Michael Stefan; p/Floyd Donald and Henrietta Tunison Bross, North Brunswick, NJ; ed/RN Helene Fuld Sch Nsg; En Pilgrim Col; Zarephath Bible Sem; mil/USAF Aux, Asst Med Corps Ofcr; pa/- Nurse, The Elms (Cranbury, NJ); Tchr, Heritage Acad (Windsor, NJ); Asst Christian Min Activs; Intl Union Gospel Missions; Brevet Lt, Am Rescue Workers; Wom's Christian Temperance Union; Assoc Mem, Pillar of Fire Soc; Wesleyan; r/Non-denom Christian.

TUTEUR, MURIEL FRIEDMAN oc/- Director; b/May 17, 1922; h/1355 W Estes, Chicago, IL 60626; ba/Chgo; m/Charles Anthony; c/Judith T Stechert, Peter Zachary; p/Morris and Jeanette Hirschenbein Friedman (dec); ed/BA Univ Chgo 1943; Masters Prog 1975; pa/Exec Dir, Amalgamated Child Day Care & Hlth Ctr; St of Ill Dept Chd & Fam Sers: Adv Com on Day Care, Chrperson Standards Review Subcom; Task Force on Salaries, Chgo Assn Ed Yg Chd; Nat & Ill Assns Ed Yg Chd; Day Care & Child Devel Assn Am; Day Care Crisis Coun Metro Chgo; Bd Dirs, Harper Square Child Care Ctr; Child Care Spec, Child Care Seminar Coalition Labor Union Wom; Pre-sch Adv Com, Chgo St Univ; Guest Lectr: Univ Chgo, Univ Ill & Oakton Commun Col; cp/- Pres Chgo Chapt, Coalition Labor Union Wom; Nat Exec Bd, Coalition Labor Union Wom; Adv Com, Midwest Wom's Ctr; Amalgamated Cloth'g & Textile Workers Union; r/Jewish.

TWADDLE, MELVIN LAWRENCE oc/Superintendent; b/May 30, 1928; h/PO Box 143, California, MO 65018; ba/California; m/Carol J; c/Michael, Terri, Tracy, (Stepchd:) Teresa, Tamara, Tonia; p/William H and Catherine Bayles Twaddle (dec); ed/BS NW Mo St Univ 1954; MA Univ Colo 1955; EdD Univ Mo 1976; mil/USAF 1946-48; pa/Tchr, Kinsley HS (Kansas) 1954-56; Supt of Schs (Mo): Clearmont 1956-58, Rosendale 1958-63, Fairfax 1963-65, Albany 1965-71, Calif 1971-; cp/Past Pres, Kiwanis; r/Christian Ch; hon/Boss of Yr in Albany 1969.

TWIGGS, DORIS DAVIS oc/Teacher; b/Dec 6, 1946; h/1221 Wimbee Dr, Charleston, SC 29407; ba/N Charleston;

m/George W; p/Emmett and Lucille Davis, N Charleston; ed/BSEd Paine Col 1968; pa/Elem Tchr; NEA; SCEA; CCEA; cp/Fdr & Dir, Pilgrim Bapt Pre-sch Prog; Com Chm, Omega-Quettes; r/Bapt: SS Tchr, Var Coms; hon/Remount Elem Tchr of Yr; Finalist, Charleston Co Tchr of Yr.

TYLER, CAROLYN SMITH oc/Librarian; b/Jan 30, 1923; h/1100 Eastminster Dr, Columbia, SC 29204; ba/Columbia; m/Josie Lee Jr; c/Josie Lee III; p/Marvin Henry Smith Sr (dec); Emmie Frank Waller Smith, Columbia; ed/BA Ga St Col for Wom 1942; BLS Emory Univ 1945; pa/Ed Libn, Thomas Cooper Lib, Univ SC; SC & Am Lib Assns; cp/AAUW; r/Meth.

TYSON, JOHN CAIUS III oc/Judge; b/Oct 7, 1926; h/3114 Jasmine Rd, Montgomery, AL 36111; ba/Montgomery; m/Mae Martin Bryant; c/Mary Harmon, Marc John; p/John Caius Tyson Jr, Montgomery; Virginia Bragg Smith Tyson (dec); ed/BS 1948, LLB 1951 Univ Ala; mil/USCG 1944-46; USCGR 1947-52; pa/Judge, Ala Ct Crim Appeals 1972-76; Presiding Judge 1976-77; Judge 1977-; Admit'd to Ala Bar 1951; Law Pract (Montgomery) 1951-59; Asst Atty Gen, St of Ala 1959-71; Lectr Univ Ala 1961-71; cp/Bd Dirs, YMCA; Soc Pioneers of Montgomery; Am Legion; Shriner; Kiwanis; C of C; Dem Party; r/Epis: Vestryman.

TYSON, TONY ANGELUS oc/Manager Trainee; b/Aug 29, 1955; h/1040 Shive Ln, Bowling Green, KY 42101; ba/Bowling Green; p/Napoleon B Tyson Sr, Winterville, NC; Mary Hunter Tyson, Greenville, NC; ed/BS NC A&T St Univ; pa/Mgr Trainee, Wickes Corp; cp/Bd Trustees, NC A&T St Univ; NC Assn Student Govts; Others; r/New Bethel Bapt Ch (BG); hon/W/W Among Students Am Univs & Cols; Kappa Man of Yr, Most Outstg Kappa for Highest Achmts & Alumni Awd for Outstg Sers, Kappa Alpha Psi.

U

UCHIN, ROBERT ALLEN oc/Dentist; b/Apr 19, 1933; h/1500 SW 15th Ave, Fort Lauderdale, FL 33312; ba/Ft Lauderdale & Plantation, FL; m/Marlene; c/Andrew, Richard, Carol; ed/Franklin & Marshall Col 1951-53; DDS 1957, Cert Endodontics 1960 Temple Univ Sch Dentistry; mil/USAF 1957-59; pa/Gen Pract Dentistry 1957-60; Endodontic Pract 1960-; Conslt: VA Hosp (Miami, Fla) 1968-, VA Ctl Office 1972-; Dir Endodontic Residency, VA Hosp 1972-; CoChm Oral Diagnosis & Pres, Broward Co Dental Res Clinic 1978-; Clinical Instr: Univ Penn Sch Dentistry 1973-, Univ Fla Sch Dentistry 1970-; Gtr Miami & So Endodontic Study Groups; Past Pres, Fla Assn Endodontists; West Broward Dental Study Group; Broward Co Dental Soc; Del, Fla St Dental Soc; Am Dental Assn; Conslt Coun Dental Ed, Hosp Dental Ser & Comm of Accred; NY Acad Scis; Fdg Mem & Past Chm Exec Com, Am Inst Oral Scis; Intl Assn Dental Res; Fdn Dentaire Intl; AAAS; Am Assn Dental Schs; AAUP; Asst'g Adv Com, Broward Commun Col; Hlth Ser Aide Adv Com, Sch Bd of Broward Co; Lectr Confs & Workshops; Pub'd Articles Profl Jours; Book Reviewer; Other Activs & Positions; cp/Former Cub Master & Sustain'g Mem Chm, BSA; Past Dir, Ft Lauderdale Mus of Arts; Past Mem Bd Trustees, Vanguard Sch (Haverford, Penn); Fdg Mem & Past Chm Bd Dirs, Vanguard Sch (Ft Lauderdale); Dir, Landmark Nat Bank of W Broward; Temple Emanu-El Reform Congreg; hon/Diplomate, Am Bd Endodontics; Fellow: Am Assn Endodontists, Am Col Dentistry, Intl Col Dentistry.

UHLAND, RUTH ELLEN oc/Educator; b/May 4, 1925; h/158 G St, Brawley, CA 92227; p/William and Ruth Uhland (dec); ed/AA Mira Costa Col; BA San Diego St Univ; Addit Studies; pa/IRA Rep for Schs; cp/Life Mem, Cooper Ornithol Soc; Sierra Clb; Audubon Soc; Var Fund Raising Campaigns; Desert Sect VP & Pres, BPW; Past Pres, Venture Clb; Heart Assn; IU Museum; Repub Party; r/Bapt; hon/Ecology Awd & Ser Awd, Browley BPW.

UHLIG, GEORGE ERNEST oc/Administrator; b/Dec 29, 1933; h/1207 Vendome W, Mobile, AL 36609; ba/Mobile; m/Nancy Hall; c/Piper; p/George E Uhlig Sr (dec); Evangeline Basler Uhlig, Hooper, NE; ed/BS 1955, MEd 1959, EdD 1963 Univ Nebraska; Addit Studies; mil/AUS 1955-57; pa/Univ S Ala: Prof Ednl Ldrship & Dean Col Ed 1976-, Prof Sport Sci & Res, Chancellor US Sports Acad 1975-; VP Operations & Sr Res Scist, Vasquez Assocs Ltd (Milwaukee, Wis) 1972-76; Exec Editor: Jour of Instrnl Psychology (1973-) & Jour of Sport Behavior (1978-); Pub Com, Assn for Cnslr Edrs & Supvrs (1967-71); Chm Gov's Com of Ed Tng, Statewide Plan'g Voc Rehab 1967-68; Editor Bd: Col Student Survey: A Jour Pertain'g to Col Students & Ed: Converg'g Trends; Cnslt: Fund for Improvemt of Post Sec'dy Ed, High Coun for Yth & Sport, EDUPLAN (Venezuela Min of Ed), Exec Sys Corp & Ednl Sys Corp (Wash, DC), Dept Defense (US Armed Forces Inst), Others; Am Psychol Assn; Am Assn Sch Admrs; Am Ednl Res Assn; APGA; Nat Soc Col Tchrs Ed; Soc for Irreproducible Results; Others; cp/Past Chm & VChm, United Fund Drive; Mobile C of C; hon/Phi Kappa Phi; Phi Delta Kappa.

ULMER, WILLIAM DOUGLAS oc/Social Service Administrator; b/Oct 3, 1950; h/2005 Vine St, Chattanooga, TN 37404; ba/Chattanooga; p/David E and Ethel M Ulmer, Chattanooga; ed/BA Morehouse Col; MA Univ Pittsburgh; Addit Studies; pa/Am Public Hlth Assn; Nat Assn Commun Hlth Ctrs; Nat Assn Social Workers; cp/NAACP; r/Bapt; hon/Omega Phi Phi; Alpha Kappa Delta.

ULMOS, GUILLERMO ENRIQUE oc/Physician; b/Jan 25, 1937; h/Calle I D-21, Ciudad Universitaria, Rio Piedras, PR 00926; ba/Rio Piedras; m/Carmen Leticia Rodriguez Torres; c/Lilia M, Guillermo Enrique, Jose Manuel, Guillermo Eduardo, Jazmina Leticia; p/Eduardo J Ulmos and Dominga Maltez (dec); ed/MD; pa/Intern, Atlantic City Hosp 1967-68; Resident Surg, Univ Dist Hosp Med Ctr (Rio Piedras) 1968-73; Fellow, Cancer Surg 1963-74; Attend'g Phys, ER PR Med Ctr 1974-75; Attend'g Phys Surg Dept, Hosp Indust 1975-; r/Born Again Christian; hon/Doctor en Medicina y Cirugia hon, Universidad Nacional Autonomade Nicaragua.

ULREY, EVAN oc/Professor; b/Aug 25, 1922; h/914 E Marhes, Searcy, AR 72143; ba/Searcy; m/Betty Thornton; c/Rebecca Ann, Bonnie Beth, Robert Evan; p/A Melvin

and Mary Robinson Ulrey (dec); ed/BA; MA; PhD; pa/Prof & Chm Dept Speech, Harding Col; Ark, So & Nat Speech Communs Assns; r/Ch of Christ: Min 30 Yrs; hon/Dist'd Tchr Awd, Harding Col; Past Nat Pres, Pi Kappa Delta.

ULTAN, LLOYD oc/Educator; Historian; b/Feb 28, 1938; h/91 Van Cortlandt Ave W, Bronx, NY 10463; ba/Same; p/Louis and Sophie Ultan, Bronx, NY; ed/BA Hunter Col 1959; MA Columbia Univ 1960; pa/Assoc Prof of Hist, Edward Williams Col of Fairleigh Dickinson Univ; Editor-in-Chief, Bronx Co Historical Soc Jour; Pres, Bronx Co Hist Soc 1971-76; Author, The Beautiful Bronx 1920-1950 (1970); cp/Past Gen Secy, Bronx Civic League; Past Mem Bd Dirs, Bronx Coun on Arts; Past Pres, Bronx Day Comm; Past Mem Prog Guidelines Com, NYC Dept of Cultural Affairs; hon/Phi Alpha Theta; Alpha Chi Alpha; Sigma Lambda; Thomas Hunter Awd; Univ of Wis Non-Resident S'ship; NY St Regents Tchg F'ship; College Alumni Hall of Fame; NEH Res Grant; W/W E.

UNDERWOOD, ROBERT CHARLES oc/Justice; b/Oct 27, 1915; h/#11 Kent Dr, Normal, IL 61761; ba/Bloomington, IL; m/Dorothy Roy; c/Susan U Barcalow (Mrs John C III); p/Marion L and Edith L Frazee Underwood (dec); ed/BA Ill Wesleyan Univ 1937; LLB Univ Ill Col Law 1939; pa/Admit'd Ill Bar 1939; Pvt Pract (Bloomington) 1939-46; City Atty (Normal); Asst St Atty (McLean Co) 1942-46; Judge Co Ct of McLean Co 1946-62; Justice, Supr Ct Ill 1962-; Chief Justice Supr Ct Ill 1969-75; McLean Co, Ill & Am Bar Assns; Past Mem, Conf Chief Justices; Dir, Am Judicature Soc; Inst Judicial Adm; Ill Co & Probate Judges Assn (Held Every Office); Author Num Articles Profl Jours; cp/Bloomington Consistory; Rotary Intl; Kiwanis; Past VChm, Ill Comm on Chd; Former Mem Bd Trustees, Ill Wesleyan Univ; Former Mem Bd Dirs, McLean Co Mtl Hlth Ctr; Chm Bd Higher Ed Com to Survey Legal Ed Needs Ill; Others; r/First Meth Ch (Normal): Lay Ldr, Bd Mem, Others; hon/Fellow, Penn Mason Juv Ct Inst; Rec'd Dist'd Ser Awd & Good Govt Awd, US Jr C of C; Ill Wel Assn Annual Cit; Outstg Citizen Awd, Normal C of C; 33° Mason; Cert Outstg Achmt, Univ Ill Col Law; Hon Degs: Loyola Univ, Ill Wesleyan Univ & Eureka Col; Am Law Inst; Annual Dist'd Ser Awd, Ill Scottish Rite; Significant Sig Awd; Awd of Merit, Ill St

Bar Assn; Biogl Listings.

UNFER, BEULAH M oc/Retired Technical Photographer & Teacher; b/Jun 12, 1902; h/308 W John St, Champaign, IL 61820; m/Louis Sr; c/Louis Jr, Edna Mae; p/Angus and Minnie Whisler Teskey (dec); ed/Univ Iowa; Univ Ill; cp/Nat VP, Am Legion Aux; Past Dept Pres, Ill Civil Preparedness; Ill Wom's Traffic Safety; VP, Champaign Wom's Clb; BPW; Mem Over 30 Yrs & Past Matron, OES; Univ Ill Wives; Wom of Moose; Acad Friendship; Deputy Rep, Danville VA Med Ctr; r/Meth; hon/Commun Ldrs & Noteworthy Ams.

UNGER, WILLIAM ERNST oc/Professor Art; b/Jul 30, 1914; h/1009 S Lewis St, Kirksville, MO 63501; ba/Kirksville; m/Hedwig M; p/Theodor William and Ernestine Von Unger (dec); ed/BSE; MFA;

European Doct Arts; pa/Free-lance Artist; Prof, NE Mo St Univ; MSTA; NEA; cp/Rotary; r/Rom Cath; hon/Prix de Rouce; Num 1st Awds & Hons for Art.

UPDEGROVE, PAT FORD oc/Library Coordinator; b/Dec 12, 1925; h/111 Seaside Ln, Texas City, TX 77590; ba/Tex City; m/Robert C; c/Glen Ray; p/George Winslow and Esther Jane Wickey Ford (dec); ed/BA Col Wm & Mary; MA Univ Houston; pa/Lib Coor, Tex City Independent Sch Dist; Chm, Tex Assn Sch Libns 1976-77; Tex St Tchrs Assn; Tex Lib Assn; Tex Classroom Tchrs Assn; AAUW; Am Lib Assn; cp/Galveston & Tex Hist Founs; r/Presb: Elder; hon/Hon Life Mem, Tex Cong Ps & Ts; Delta Kappa Gamma.

URSCHLER, FRIEDRICH KARL oc/Physician; b/Aug 26, 1927; h/143 Colonial Dr, New Port Richey, FL 33552; ba/New Port Richey; m/Judith Ann Sheets; c/Mark; p/Karl and Helene Mann Urschler (dec); ed/Karl Franzens Univ Sch Med (Graz, Austria) 1952; Internships: Swedish Hosp (Seattle, Wash) 1954-56, Res Pathol Grant Hosp (Columbus,

Ohio), Surg Laundeskrankenhaus Hosp (Furstenfeld, Austria), Miami Val Hosp (Dayton, Ohio), Radiol Ohio St Univ 1965-66; pa/Pvt Pract (Columbus) 1957-69 & NPR 1969-; Staff Mem Sev Hosps; Life Mem, Am Med Soc; Diplomate, Am Acad Fam Phys; AMA; Fla Assn Fam Phys; Am Geriatrics Soc; cp/Elks; hon/Appointed Consulate Phys by Consulate Gen Fed Repub Germany (Atlanta, Ga).

V

VACHÉ, CLAUDE CHARLES oc/Bishop; b/Aug 4, 1926; h/6603 Caroline St, Norfolk, VA 23505; ba/Norfolk; p/Jean Andre Vache (dec); Edith Fitzwilson Vache, Richmond, VA; ed/BA; MDiv; DD; mil/USN WWII; pa/Epis Bishop, Diocese of So Va 1978-; St Michael's (Bon Air, Va): Deacon, Priest-in-charge, Rector 1952-57; Rector, Trinity Ch (Portsmouth, Va) 1957-76; Bishop Coadjtuor, Diocese So Va 1976-; cp/Theophilus Clb; ARC; Hous'g, Hlth & Wel Plan'g (Portsmouth); United Fund; C of C; Humane Soc; Sr Citizens Activs Plan'g & First Bd STOP (SEn Tidewater Opportunity Prog); Pres, Tidewater Regional Hlth Plan'g Coun; Hous'g Bd Appeals; Chm, Task Force on Aging; Chm, Portsmouth Mayor's Sr Citizens Comm; r/Epis; hon/Phi Beta Kappa; Yg Man of Yr, Chesterfield Co (Va) & Portsmouth.

VACHON, LOUIS-ALBERT oc/Auxiliary Bishop; b/Feb 4, 1912; h/2, Rue Port-Dauphin, CP 459, Haute-Ville, Quebec, PQ G1R 4R6; ba/Quebec; p/Napoleon and Alexandrine Gilbert Vachon (dec); ed/BA 1934, PhD 1947 Laval Univ; ThD St-Thomas Aquinas (Rome) 1949; pa/Laval Univ: Prof Phil 1941-47, Prof Theol 1949-55, Rector 1960-72; Aux Bishop Quebec 1977-; Past Pres, Conf of Rectors & Prins Quebec Univs; Past Pres, Assn Univs & Cols Canada; Canadian Theol Soc; Cath Theol Soc Am; cp/Adm Bd, Intl Fdn Cath Univs; Adm Bd, Commonwealth Univ; r/Cath; hon/Fellow, Royal Soc Canada; Rec'd Hon Degs 11 Univs; Companion of Order of Canada; Gloire de l'Escolle (Univ Laval).

VADEN, NORMA JEAN oc/Nursing Technician; b/Sept 26, 1941; h/841 S 8th St, Nashville, TN 38206; c/Kimberly Patrice, Gregory Lawrence, Verdia Alean, Jonathan Randolph, Gwanyca Lenise; p/Major Davis (dec); Rosanna Tate, Alton, IL; ed/So Ill Univ; cp/St ure Tenn Dept Human Resources: 1st VChm Tenn St Social Sers Adv Coun, Davidson Co Adv Coun & Citizens Adv Com Davidson Co; Metro Devel & Hous'g Agy: Pres James A Cayce Residents Assn & Steer'g Com, Coun of Pres; Mayor's Office Commun Sers: Adv Com Urban Camps & Yth Patrol Adv Com; r/Mt Pisgah Bapt Ch.

VALACH, MIROSLAV oc/Research Director; b/Sept 12, 1926; h/13220 N 7th Dr, Phoenix, AZ 85029; ba/Phoenix; m/Zdena; c/Paul; p/Jan Valach, Czechoslovakia; Milada Seitzova (dec); ed/MEMA Inst Technol (Prague, Czechoslovakia) 1951; PhD Czech Acad Scis 1958; r/Prot.

VALENT, HENRY oc/Attorney; b/Jul 21, 1915; h/2575 Old Corning Rd, Watkins Glen, NY; ba/Watkins Glen; m/Joan; c/Joseph A, Oscar B, Albert W, Henry W, Nellie M; p/Joseph and Nellie Valent (dec); ed/AB; LLB; mil/Lt Col Inf; pa/Gen Pract Atty 1938-; Dir: Schuyler Hosp Inc, Glen Bank & Trust Co, Hi-Speed Checkweighs Co of Ithaca (NY); Pres & Dir, Watkins Glen Grand Prix Corp; cp/Past Cmdr, Am Legion; Past Mem Com on Profl Standards, NY Bar Assn; r/Cath; hon/Author: Wisdom Hall of Fame; W/W Commun Ser; World W/W; DIB.

VALLELY, ANNE ELIZABETH oc/Instr; b/Aug 2, 1942; h/100 Memorial Dr, Cambridge, MA 02142; ba/Boston, MA; m/Michael Petrucello; p/John P and Dorothy Gray Vallely; ed/BA cum laude Regis Col; MEd Suffolk Univ; pa/Chrperson Dept Retail'g, Newbury Jr Col; Fashion Group; Fashion Assocs New England; Bus Tchrs Assn; En Bus Tchrs Assn; hon/Outstg Tchr Awd, Sr Class Newbury Jr Col 1978; Dist'd Ser Awd, Students Dept Retail'g; W/W Wom Ed.

van APPLEDORN, E RUTH oc/Professor; b/Dec 19, 1918; h/5120 Norwood St, Duluth, MN 55804; ba/Duluth; p/John and Elizabeth Rinck van Appledorn (dec); ed/BM

Oberlin Col 1940; MM Mich St Univ 1942; pa/Univ Minn-D: Began Full-time Tchg Mus Theory & Piano 1947, Student Advr, Established (w James Smith) 1st Preparatory Div, Currently Prof Mus, Com on Coms, Sch of Fine Arts Curric Com, Others; Conducts Classes & Lectrs on Parapsychol; Duluth Mus Tchrs Assn; Col Mus Soc, SUNY-Binghampton; Am Soc Psychical Res Inc (NY); Psychical Res Foun Inc (NC); Parapsychol Assn NC; AAUP; cp/Matinee Musicale; r/Pilgrim Congreg Ch, United Ch of Christ; hon/Mu Phi Epsilon; Outstg Edr Am; 2 Univ Tchg Cits; Rec'd Medal for Bicent Res, Mayor of Duluth.

VANCE, HUBERT R oc/Administrator; b/Nov 27, 1941; h/51 Emery, Harrisonburg, VA 22801; ba/Harrisonburg; m/Sandra B; c/Shannon Heather, Megan Lizabeth; p/Mildred B Vance, Johnson City, TN; ed/BS, MA E Tenn St Univ; PhD Ohio St Univ 1973;

pa/Adm Dir Child Devel Clinic, James Madison Univ; SEn & Am Psychol Assns; Nat Assn Sch Psychol: Coun for Chd, Conslt St Dept Ed; Pub'd Over 60 Res Articles; Editor Bd, PITS; cp/Elks; r/Presb; hon/EPDA Fellow, Ohio St Univ; W/W S&SW; Men Achmt; Personalities of S; Notable Ams.

van der POEL, CORNELIUS JOHANNES oc/Director; b/Sept 19, 1921; h/933 Illinois Ave, Stevens Point, WI 54481; ba/Stevens Point; p/Jacobus van der Poel and Laurentia van der Geest (dec); ed/BA (Wert, Netherlands); MSEd Iona Col (NY); MA (Gemert, Netherlands); pa/Dir Dept Pastoral Care, St Michael's Hosp 1978-; Ordained Priest w Holy Ghost Fathers (Netherlands) 1947; Tchr Canon Law & Moral Theol (Morogoro, Tanzania) 1948-54; Tchr Rel Scis (Bagamoyo, Tanzania) 1955-59; Pastor Tanzania 1959-62; Tchr Moral Theol & Canon Law, St Mary's Sem (Norwalk, Conn) 1962-69; Co-dir Clinical Mtl Hlth Tng Prog (La Crosse, Wis) 1970-74; Visiting Res Prof, Univ Guam 1973; Dir Fam Life Office, Archdiocese of Detroit (Mich) 1974-78; Others; Author: The Search for Human Values (1971), Rel Life: A Risk of Love (1972), Integration of Human Values (1977); Contbr Articles Profl Jours; r/Rom Cath.

VanGILDER, MARVIN LEE oc/Journalist; b/Sept 24, 1926; h/1514 S Main St, Carthage, MO 64836; ba/Carthage; m/Irene; c/Paula V Burford (Mrs Craig), Linda V England, Leesa V Robinson (Mrs Mark), Carla, Chris; p/J T VanGilder (dec); Opal Lucietta, Lamar, MO; ed/BM Drury Col 1948; pa/The Carthage Press: Ct Reporter 1960-61, Feature Editor 1961-63, City Editor 1963-69, Photog Dir 1969-70, Histn, Editor Writer, Rel Writer & Mus Critic 1970-; Profl Musician w US Orgs & Individual Dance Orchs Mo & Okla 1941-46; Former Mus Supvr Mo Public Schs; Former Pastor; Other Positions; Author: The Story of Barton Co, Mo's Cradle of Fame (1972), Images (1976), Jasper City, Hometown USA (1976); Carthage Mus Clb; Past Mem: Am Fdn Mus, NEA, Mo St Tchrs Assn, Piano Guild, Others; cp/Carthage Repub City Com; Nat Hist Soc; Lions Clb; Chm, Carthage Historic Sites Comm; Carthage Min Alliance; C of C; Histn & Corp Reg'd Agent, En Jasper Co Hist Soc; St Hist Soc Mo; Others; r/Presb Ch: Elder, Lay Min; hon/Mo Rural Electrification Coops Essay Prize; Edgel

Oratorical Prize; Hoover Awd for Outstg Musicianship; 1st Pl Radio Stringer, Mo Bur AP; Best Editor Awd & Best Use of Local Pictures, Mo Press Assn; Certs, Am Fdn Mus Clbs; Prin Awd, Freedoms Foun Val Forge; Others; Biogl Listings.

VAN GRONINGEN, GERARD oc/Professor; b/Mar 25, 1921; h/102 Rankin Cove, Clinton, MS 39056; ba/Jackson, MS; m/Harriet Stuitje; c/Betty V Westendorp (Mrs H), Gerard Jr, Jay H, John P, Willis O, Beverly Grace, David T, Charles N; p/Henry and

Jennie Mesman Van Groningen, Ripon, CA; ed/BA; BD; ThM; MA; PhD; Cand ThD; mil/Motor Sgt Field Arty; pa/Prof & Chm, Dept New Testament; Pastorates; r/Christian Reformed Ch; hon/W/W Rel; Commun Ldrs & Noteworthy Ams; Men & Wom Achmt; Others.

VAN HAGAN, CHARLES EDWARD oc/Consultant; b/Jul 12, 1914; h/4010-1G Calle Sonora Oeste, Laguna Hills, CA 92653; ba/Same; m/Lorraine Margaret; c/Constance Jean V Walker, Stephanie Ann V Landau; p/Leslie F and Ethel Caine Van Hagan (dec); ed/BS Univ Wis 1936; Cert Engrg, Yale Univ 1941; pa/Conslt Tech Communs 1977-; Naval Weapons Ctr (Formerly Naval Ordnance Test Station), China Lake: Asst Tech Dir Info & Head Tech Info Dept 1971-77, Head Pub'g Div 1954-72, Head Editor Branch 1952-54, Sr Tech Editor 1950-52; Tchr Tech Writing: UCLA, UCSB, USC, Bakersfield Col, Twelfth Civil Ser Region, Var Naval Labs, Govt Labs 1950-; Other Positions; Author, Report Writers' Handbook 1961; Reg'd Profl Engr; Fdg Mem, Tech Pub'g Soc (Past VP & Dir); Soc for Tech Communs: Fellow 1970-, Dir 1971-75, Asst to Pres for Profl Activs 1973-75; Col of Fellows, Inst Advmt Engrg; Interlab Com Editors & Pubrs, West Coast Navy Labs 1956-71; cp/Maturango Mus Indian Wells Val (Life Mem, Past Trustee & Dir Pubs); Former Dir, Rotary Clb; r/St Michael's Epis Ch (Ridgecrest, Cal): Former Vestryman; hon/Rec'd Navy Meritorious Civilian Ser Awd; Equal Opportunity Awd, Naval Weapons Ctr.

VAN LANDINGHAM, EUGENIA PATTERSON oc/Retired; b/Sept 16, 1905; h/903 Main St, PO Box 456, Tarboro, NC 27886; m/Joseph Wilson; p/Robert Lee and Margaret Cowan Patterson (dec); ed/BS Flora MacDonald Col; pa/Asst Home Ec Instr, Flora MacDonald Col (Red Springs, NC) 1 Yr; Tchr Home Ec & Sci, Presb Orphanage (Borium Springs, NC) 3 Yrs; Co Home Demo Agent, Wash Co & Plymouth (NC) Over 3 Yrs; Dist Home Mgmt Supvr, Resettlemt Adm (Raleigh, NC) 2 Yrs; Co Home Ec Ext Agent, Edgecombe Co (NC) 1937-71; Past Chm, Co Nutrition Com; NC Assn Ext Home Economists; Past Councilor So Region, Nat Home Demo Agents Assn; NC Home Ecs Ext Assn: Past Pres, Chm Res Com, Leg Com, Others; cp/Past Bd Mem, Edgecombe Gen Hosp; Former Chm Wom's Div, Savs Bond Prog; Past VP Coastal Plain Heart Assn; Ser'd Nat Com, 4-H Clb; Dem Party; Secy Coastal Plain Area Devel Assn; Past CoChm, ARC Bloodmobile; Cancer Campaign; Ser'd as Co CoChm, Muscular Distrophy Prog & Multisclerosis Com; Sers for Mentally & Physically Handicapped; Edgecombe Co Mtl Hlth Assn; NC Symph; Tar River Lung Assn; Num Others; r/Howard Meml Presb Ch (Tarboro): Mem, Chm Bus Wom's Cir; hon/Dist'd Ser Awd, Nat Assn Home Ec Agents & NC Farm Bur; Wom of Yr,

Progressive Farmer 1953; Rec'd Awd, US Dept Agri; Cert Recog, Nat Coun Epsilon Sigma Phi; Loan Fund Established in Hon at E Carolina Univ by Edgecombe Co Home Demo Clb Wom; Home Ec Ctr Named in Hon, E Carolina Univ; Others.

VANN, DAVID JOHNSON oc/Mayor; b/Aug 10, 1928; h/4201 Cliff Rd, Birmingham, AL 35222; ba/B'ham; m/Lillian Foscue; c/Lillian Ruth, Michael Lee; p/Clyde and Ruth Johnson Vann (dec); ed/LLB 1950; LLM 1953; mil/AUS 1946-48; Counter Intell Ofcr 1951-53; pa/Mayor, City of B'ham; Ala, B'ham & Am Bar Assns; cp/YMBC; Lions Clb; K of P; DAC; r/Highland Meth Ch; hon/Farrah Order of Jurisprudence.

VAN PLEW, WRIGHT HENRY oc/Clergyman; b/Mar 24, 1915; h/41 Thornapple Dr, Battle Creek, MI 49017; ba/Battle Creek; m/Thelma Francis Robinson; c/Philip Wright, David Charles; p/James Wright and Anna Fredericka Van Plew (dec); ed/Dipl, Moody Bible Inst 1939; Wheaton Col 1942-44; pa/Ordained Min, Grace Bible Ch (Elmhurst, Ill) 1942; Pastor: Sunnyvale Chapel (Pontiac, Mich) 1945-49, Open Bible Ch

(Grand Rapids, Mich) 1956-59, S Side Bible Ch (Battle Creek) 1976-; Independent Bible Mission (Comstock, Mich): Co-fdr & Pres 1952-59, Field Dir 1959-67; Field Dir, Bible Ch Mission (So Cal) 1967-76; Independent Fundamental Chs Am: Nat Rep Ch Ext Coun 1975-, Trustee Nat Exec Com 1947-50 & 1962-67, Pres Mich Region 3 Terms, Chm Nat Pubs Com 1973-, Others; Editor: *The Tie* (1976-) & *The Voice Mag* (1975-); Former Bd Mem, Mich Child Evangelism F'ship; r/Waterford Commun Ch (Mich): Mem.

VAN PUFFELEN, JOHN HERMAN oc/Instructor; b/Nov 26, 1920; h/Bradley, WV 25818; ba/Bradley; m/Gertrude F; c/Darlene Kay, David John, Richard Alan; p/John Van Puffelen, Grand Rapids, MI; Lena Van Puffelen (dec); ed/BS; MDiv; MLS; pa/Instr & Libn, Appalachian Bible Col; Pastor; r/Independent.

VAN RENSSELAER, LILLIE oc/Homemaker; b/May 12, 1912; h/PO Box 333, Locust Valley, NY 11560; m/Stephen; c/Stephen Jr; p/Loraine Langstroth, Centerport, NY; Sue Hall Langstroth (dec); ed/Univ Cal-B; Kunstqueweber Schule (Vienna); cp/Sponsor Var Charity Events; Fund Raiser, ARC; r/Epis Ch.

VANZANT, JIMMIE LOU oc/Homemaker; b/Mar 30, 1936; h/4705 Dodd, Corpus Christi, TX 78415; m/Jimme Lee; c/Joey Thomas, Jerrel Lee; p/Ivan and Nellie Cooper,

Del City, OK; ed/Del Mar Col; cp/Instr Parliamentary Procedure 2 Yrs; Past Mem, Hosp Vol Aux; Past Assoc Yth Dir; Past Pres, Local WMU; Cub Scout Ldr & Tnr; Christian Wom's Clb; Pres Dist 16, PTA; r/So Bapt; hon/Life Mem, Tex PTA; Rec'd Ser Awds, PTA.

VARNER, CHARLEEN LaVERN McCLANAHAN oc/Administrator; b/Aug 28, 1931; h/Main PO Box 1009, Topeka, KS 66601; ba/Same; m/Robert Bernard; p/Roy Calvin McClanahan, Carthage, MO; Lela Ruhama Smith McClanahan (dec); ed/BS Pittsburg St Univ (Ks); MS Univ Ark; PhD Tex Wom's Univ; pla/Ednl Admr & Conslt'g Dietitian; Am Dietetics Assn; r/Meth; hon/Delta Kappa Gamma; Kappa Kappa Iota; Phi Upsilon Omicron; Rec'd Res Grant, NASA.

VARNER, NELLIE M oc/Associate Dean & Professor; b/Aug 27, 1935; h/9140 Schaefer Rd, Detroit, MI 48228; ba/Ann Arbor, MI; p/Tommie Varner, Detroit; Essie Varner (dec); ed/BS; MA; PhD; pa/Univ Mich: Spec Asst to Dean Col Lit, Sci & Arts 1968-70, Fac Assoc, Ctr for Russian & En European Studies 1968-, Asst Prof Politic Sci 1968-, Dir Affirmative Aciton Progs 1972-75, Assoc Dean, Rackham Sch Grad Studies 1976-; Res Fellow, Harvard Univ Ctr for Intl Affairs 1970-71; Res Assoc, Harvard Univ Russian Res Ctr 1970-71; Tchr, Detroit Public Schs 1959-64; VP & Secy, The Precision Group (Real Estate Corp) 1976-; Strather & Assocs (Subsidiary of Precision Group): VP 1976-, VP & Secy Adjust'g Div Inc 1976-; Chm Real Estate Adv Bd, Dept Lic'g & Regulation (St of Mich) 1978-; Sales Assoc, Real Estate One (Firm) 1971-75; Adv Com for Minority Progs Sci Ed, Nat Sci Foun; Exec Bd Wayne St Univ, Univ Mich Inst Gerontology; Comm Wom in Higher Ed, Am Coun Ed; Adv Com Intl Affairs, Univ Mich; Others; cp/Senate Adv Com St Relats, Unvi Mich; Former Chrperson Equal Opportunity Com, Nat Assn St Univs & Land Grant Cols; Past Mem, HEW Title I St Adv Coun to Bd Ed (St of Mich); Former Conslt: Dept HUD & Proj for Acad Affirmative Action Tng, Intl Assn Ofcl Human Rights Agencies; Del, Wayne Co Dem Conv; Campaign Worker; Others; r/Bapt; hon/Rec'd Cit, Mayor Jerome P Cavanagh (City of Detroit); Selected 1 of Top 100 Ldrs Higher Ed, *Change Mag* & Am Coun Ed; Rec'd Res Grants: Carnegie Endowment for Intl Peace & Ctr for Russian & En European Studies (Univ Mich); Res F'ship, Social Sci Res Coun; Wilton Park F'ship; CIC Grant for Field Study USSR; NDFA F'ship; Tchr F'ship; Pi Sigma Alpha; Phi Kappa Phi; Detroit Wom Prins' Clb S'ship; Florence Sweeney S'ship; Hons Convocation 3 Yrs, Wayne St Univ; Biogl Listings.

VASS, LARRY IVAN oc/Dentist; b/Aug 18, 1946; h/360 Arrowhead Trail, Christiansburg, VA 24073; ba/Christiansburg; m/Patricia Branscome; c/Melanie Dawn; p/Carbin P and Violett M Vass, Hillsville, VA; ed/BS Va Tech 1967; DDS Med Col, Va Sch Dentistry 1972; Internship, St Agnes Hosp (Baltimore, Md); pa/Math & Physics Tchr, New River Commun Col (Redford, Va) 1967-68; Author, "Treatmt of Misunderstood Facial & Ear Pain", *Jour Dental Pract*; Cert'd Oral Implantologist; Am Inst Hypnosis; cp/C of C; r/Bapt; hon/Delta Sigma Delta; W/W S&SW; DIB; Men Achmt; Personalities of S.

VAUGHAN, JOHN NOLEN oc/Minister; b/Nov 23, 1941; h/2116 McKeller Hills Ave, Memphis, TN 38116; ba/Memphis; m/Joanne Wooten; c/Johnna Noel, John Nathan; p/Nolen Lewis Vaughan and Montez Cannon Herring; ed/BA Memphis St Univ 1964; MDiv SWn Bapt Theol Sem (Ranked Top 5th in Class) 1967; Addit Studies; pa/Asst Pastor: Westridge Bapt Ch (Euless, Tex) 1964-67, Hunter St Bapt Ch (B'ham, Ala) 1967-69, Trinity Bapt Ch (Memphis) 1973-77, E Park Bapt Ch (Memphis) 1977-; Pastor, Univ Bapt Ch (Iowa City, Iowa) 1969-73; Other Positions; Ordained 1962; Conslt Adults, Tenn Bapt Conv SS Dept 1975-; Shelby Bapt Assn: Conslt Adults 1975-, SS Plan'g Com,

Bapt Student Union Com, Prison F'ship Care Com, Others; Assn Rel Ldrs; Assn Evangelicals; Iowa Bapt Assn: Mo Loan Fund Com, Publicity Chm; Advr, Billy Graham Crusades 1965, 78; Speaker for Local, St & Nat Rel Confs; Contbr Articles Profl Jours; cp/Apt Owners' & Mgrs' Assn (Dallas-Ft Worth); Optimists Intl; r/Bapt; hon/Sigma Alpha Epsilon; W/W: Rel, S&SW; Men Achmt; DIB; Men & Wom Distinction; Personalities of S; Notable Ams.

VAUGHN, MARY oc/Executive; b/Apr 20, 1930; h/8442-81 Via Sonoma Ave, La Jolla, CA 92037; ba/San Diego, CA; p/Grover Webster and Vivian Lenora Dorman; ed/B'ham Bus Col 1952; Howard Col 1959; Univ Ala 1960, 62; Balboa Intermediate Care Facility (San Diego) 1969-76; Cert Therapeutic Activs Tng, Grossmont Adult Sch 1975; PhD; pa/Owner, Pres, Treas Balboa Manor Inc & Balboa Manor Hlth Facility 1974-76; Cert'd Nsg Home Admr; Am Hlth Care Assn; Am Col Nsg Home Advrs; Am & Cal Nsg Home Assns; cp/Pres, Top O'The Beach Condominium; Past Charter Pres, B'ham (Ala) Quota Clb; Past Lt/Gov 8th Dist Quota Intl; Supt Adv Com to Jim Bates (4th Dist Supt San Diego Co); Notary Public; Com of 100, San Diego Klee Wyk Soc; San Diego Opera; BPW Clb; San Diego Mus Natural Hist; San Diego Mus of Man; Nat Notary Assn; Dem Party; r/Meth; hon/Rec'd Safety Awd, Indust Indemnity; Cert Apprec, Jim Bates.

VAUGHN, PEARL HENDERSON oc/Retired; h/PO Drawer-V, Grambling, LA 71245; c/Roy Orlando Jr, p/Cicero C and Fannie Strickland Henderson (dec); ed/BS w Hons 1956, MS 1957 Univ Tenn A&I St Univ; Addit Studies; pa/Tchr Public & Pvt Schs (Chattanooga, Tenn) 12 Yrs; Tenn A&I St Univ 1957-60: Asst Prof PE & Rec, Profl Cnslr, Asst Dean Wom, Rec Dir, Others; Assoc Prof, LeMoyne Col 1960-62; Grambling St Univ 1962-77: Asst Prof PE & Rec, Rec Coor Dept Hlth, PE & Rec, Co-Advr Rec Majors Curric,

Coms, Ret'd 1977; NRPA; APRS; LRPA; AAHPER; LAHPER; AAUP; Rec Coor, Town Hall of Grambling & Rec Exec, Playground Prog 1978; cp/Ldr, Pelican Coun GSA; Pres, NE La Branch Mtl Hlth Assn; Am Forestry Assn; Am Camping Assn; BSA; LWV; Others; r/Lewis Temple CME Ch (Grambling): Rec Coor, VP Bd Christian Ed; hon/Rec'd Spec Cit, Metro Rec Ath Assn (Chattanooga); Alpha Kappa Mu; 1 of Am's Ldrs; Nom Outstg Adm & Ldrship Rec, NRPA; Pearl H Vaughn Apprec Weekend Observance, Alumni Assn Grambling St Univ; W/W: Am Wom, Students Am Cols & Univs; Personalities of S.

VÁZQUEZ-SANTANDER, JÓSE ENRIQUE oc/Minister; b/Jul 24, 1978; h/2109 Parkdale Ave, Glenside, PA 19038; ba/Philadelphia, PA; m/Maria de los Angeles (Gonzalez-Sotolongo); c/Maria Amparo, Jose Enrique; p/Jose Alfredo Vazquez and Amparo de la Caridad (Santander-Fonseca) (dec); ed/Havana Bapt Theol Sem 1927; pa/Pastor: First Bapt Ch (Camajuani, Cuba) 1927-35, First Bapt Ch (Pinar del Rio, Cuba) 1935-67, First Bapt Ch (Phila) 1968-; Began So Bapts' Spanish Bapt Work 1968; Pres, Asociacion de Pastores Bautistas de la Convencion Bautista de Cuba Occidental 1947-48; r/Bapt; hon/Hon Pin for 25 Yrs Ser, Convencion Bautista de Cuba Occidental; Gran Logia de

Cuba, Premio a la Constancia for 25 Yrs Ser as Mason; Plaques for 50 Yrs Ser, Bapt Pastorates.

VEALE, WARREN LORNE oc/Scientist; b/Mar 13, 1943; h/622 Varsity Estates Crescent, Calgary, Alberta, Canada T3B 3C3; ba/Calgary; m/Maureen Eola; c/Pamela Margaret, Jeffrey Lorne; p/Lorne E and Loletta Veale, Canada; ed/BSc Univ Mantioba 1964; MS 1968, PhD 1970 Purdue Univ; pa/Univ Calgary: Asst Prof Div Med Physiol & Fac Med 1970-72, Assoc Prof 1972-76, Assoc Dean Res 1974-, Prof 1976-; Assoc Editor, *Pharmacol, Biochem & Behavior* 1973-; Editor Adv Bd, *Progress in Neuropsychopharm* 1976-; Med Res Coun Canada: Core Com for Prog Grants 1978-,

Chm Studentship Com 1978-; Res Com, Alberta Provincial Cancer Hosps 1978-; Foothills Hosp, Res & Devel Com 1974-; Bd Dirs, Alberta Chd's Hosp Res Ctr 1976-; Com on Res & Grad Studies, Assn Canadian Med Cols; Coun Mem, Canadian Physiol Soc; AAAS; MWn Psychol Assn; Canadian Physiol Soc; NY Acad Scis; Am Physiol Soc; Collegium Internationale Neuro-psychopharmacolicum; Soc for Neurosci; Author Num Sci Papers; Editor 2 Books; r/Prot; hon/Hon Soc, Brandon Univ; Sigma Xi.

VEATCH, PRUDENCE MELVINA oc/Retired Teacher; b/Aug 28, 1906; h/100 Stahl Rd, Getzvill, NY 14068; p/Henry Clay and Prudence Bessie Higgins Veatch (dec); ed/BA Wellesley Col 1929; MA Yale Univ 1931; pa/Former Eng Tchr; NY St Tchrs Assn; Buffalo HS Tchrs Assn; UNY Branch Buffalo Pen Wom; Buffalo Poetry Soc; NY Assn Pen Wom; Former Histn, Secy & Life Mem Buffalo Branch, Nat Leag Am Pen Wom; Former Publicity Chm, Nat Hon & Profl Assn Wom Ed; Del Buffalo Tchrs Assn; Pub'd Poetry & Essays; cp/Fund Raiser, Cancer Soc & Commun Chest; Bd Mem, Frontier Clb Repub Wom (Editor & Writer Newslttr, 'Frontierama'); Del Wn NY Summer Conf & Nat Repub Com; r/Ctl Park United Meth Ch; Tchr Adult Bible Seminars, Tri-L Class; hon/Rec'd Hons for Poetry & Essays; Biogl Listings.

VEGA, BENJAMIN URBIZO oc/Judge; b/Jan 18, 1916; ba/Los Angeles, CA; p/Benjamin Urbizo Sr and Catalina Tablas Vega; ed/BA Univ So Cal 1938; LLB Univ Cal Law Sch & Pacific Coast Univ 1941; mil/USAF 1942-45; pa/Judge, E LA Mun Ct 1966-; Admit'd Pract Cal 1947, US Dist Ct for So Dist Cal 1947, Bd Immigration Appeals 1948, US Supr Ct 1958; Legal Pract (LA) 1947-51; Deputy Dist Atty, LA Co 1951-66;

Blackstonian Pre-legal Scholastic Soc; Conf Cal Judges & Mun Ct Judges' Assn; Former Mem, Am Judicature Soc; Lwyrs Clb LA; Inglewood, E LA-Montebello, Inter-Am & Am Bar Assns; cp/Dem Party; Former Mem, Gov's Adv Com on Chd & Yth; Bd Dirs, LA-Mexico City Sister City Com; Former Mem Bd Dirs, Yth Opportunities Foun; r/Cath; hon/Pres, Pi Sigma Alpha; Rec'd Outstg Ser Awd & Dist'd Ser Awd, LA Mayor Sam Yorty.

VELAMOOR, SESHADRI RAJAGOPAL oc/Director; b/Jun 9, 1944; h/7458 W Mercer Way, Mercer Island, WA 98040; ba/Sea, WA; m/Shobana Rangaswamy; c/Gautam Rangaraj, Priya Arati; p/P V and Vedavalli Rajagopal, India; ed/BS; MS; MBA; pa/Dir Materials, Cx Corp; Secy & Prog Chm, Portland Chapt AIIE 1971-73; r/Hindu; hon/1st Gold Medal, Rotary Clb; Order of Ski-U-Mah, Univ Minn.

VELARDO, JOSEPH THOMAS oc/Endocrinologist; b/Jan 27, 1923; h/607 E Wilson Rd, Old Grove E, Lombard, IL 60148; m/Forresta M Monica (dec); p/Michael A and Antoinette Iacullo Velardo (dec); ed/BA Univ Nn Colo 1948; MS Miami Univ (Ohio) 1949; PhD Harvard Univ 1952; mil/USAAF WWII; pa/Harvard Univ: Tchg Fellow to Assoc Endocrinol, Biol, Surg, Gynecol & Pathol 1949-55; Asst Prof Anatomy & Endocrinol, Yale Univ Med Sch 1955-61; Prof & Chm Anatomy, NY Med Col 1961-62; Dir, Inst for Human Reproduction (Cleveland) 1962-67; Prof Biol & Endocrinol, John Carroll Univ 1962-67; Head Res, St Ann Hosp 1964-67; Stritch Sch Med; Prof Anatomy & Endocrinol 1967-, Chm Dept 1967-73; Fellow, NY Acad Scis; Fellow AAAS; Am Assn Anatomists; Gerontol Soc; Am Soc Zoologists; Am Physiol Soc; Assn Anatomy Chm; Endocrine Soc; Soc Endocrinol (Gt Brit); Soc Exptl Biol & Med; Am Fertility Soc; Others; r/Rom Cath; hon/Rec'd Num Titles Vol Distinction; Kappa Delta Pi; Phi Sigma; Gamma Alpha; Sigma Xi; Alpha Epsilon Delta; Phi Beta Pi; Rubin Awd, Harvard Med Sch; Lederle Med Fac Awd, Yale & Harvard Univs; 1 of 10 Outstg Yg Men, NJ St C of C; Hon Citizen, Sao Paulo, Brazil.

VELLEMAN, RUTH ANN oc/Librarian; b/Apr 12, 1921; h/15 Cliffway, Port Washington, NY 11050; ba/Albertson, NY; m/Morilz; c/Paul, Daniel, David; p/Joseph C Saltman (dec); Celia Saltman, Roslyn, NY; ed/BA Smith Col 1942; MS Palmer Grad Lib Sch, Long Isl Univ 1965; pa/Head Libn, Human Resources Sch 1963-; Lectr, Workshop Ldr & Conslt Var Seminars on Lib Sers for Handicapped; Adj Asst Prof, Palmer Grad Lib Sch; Pub'd Num Articles Profl Jours; Am Lib Assn; APGA; LSCA Commr's Adv Com NY St Ed Dept, Bur Lib Devel; Med Lib Assn; Nassau-Suffolk Sch Lib Assn; Lib Com, Pres' Com on Employmt Handicapped; hon/W/W Am Wom.

VENABLE, JOSEPHINE DOTT oc/Registered Nurse; b/May 31, 1934; h/1222 Newbern Rd, Pulaski, VA 24301; ba/Pulaski; m/Wilburn Eugene; c/Joseph Eugene; p/Effort Wayne Jr and Opal Phillips Akers, Pulaski; ed/Dipl, Pulaski Hosp Sch of Nsg; pa/Asst Dir Nsg Sers, Pulaski Commun Hosp; Secy, Adm Nsg Staff; Chm Policy, Procedure & Job Description Com; Instr CPR; Past Mem, Va Lung Assn Nurse Adv Coun; Writer; Artist; Tutor Eng Grammar & Composition for Col Students; hon/Employee of Month; Thomas F First Awd; Employee of Yr 1977; Personalities of S.

VENDITTO, JAMES JOSEPH oc/Sales Engineer; b/Nov 13, 1951; h/1220 Bank & Trust Tower, Corpus Christi, TX 78477; ba/New Orleans, LA; m/Ann R; c/Vincent James, Joseph Ryan; p/Vincenzio R and Maria Nichola Venditto, Irvington, NY; ed/BS; pa/Reg'd Profl Engr, St of Tex; Regional Ser Sales Engr, Halliburton Sers; Am Inst Chem Engrs; Soc Petro Engrs; Am Petro Engrs; Nat & Tex Socs Profl Engrs; cp/Repub Party; Pinewood Country Clb; r/Cath; hon/2 Papers Pub'd, Soc Petro Engrs.

VICKERS, MOZELLE CARVER oc/-Professor; b/Mar 5, 1927; h/500 E Anderson, Austin, TX 78752; c/Mark Graham, Susan V Haas; p/Isaiah Thomas Carver, Durham, NC; Sadie Ball Carver (dec); ed/BA, MA TCU; PhD Univ Tex; pa/Col Prof; Admr; Writer; Nat Leag Am Pen Wom; Nat Poetry Soc; Dir, Writers' & Drama Groups; Poetry Pub'd Num Jours & Mags; r/Christian Disciples Ch; hon/HS Valedictorian; W/W: Am Wom, Poetry; World W/W Wom; Intl Biogl Soc.

VICKERS, ROBERT CLEMONS oc/Artist; b/Oct 9, 1924; h/73 W 21st St, Holland, MI 49423; ba/Holland; m/Judith Ann; c/Sherrill Elyse, Judson K, Katherine Elizabeth; p/John H Vickers (dec); Ruth C Vickers, Piffard, NY; ed/BA St Univ Col (NY) 1947; MA Columbia Univ 1949; Ecole des Beaux Arts (Fontainebleau, France) 1949; Academie Julian (Paris, France) 1950; Ohio St Univ 1952-53; pa/Hope Col: Prof Art 1974-, Assoc Prof & Chm Art Dept 1969-73; Visiting Prof African Art, Ctl St Univ 1968; Assoc Prof Art Hist & Fine Arts, Ohio Univ 1967-69; Conslt, Dr Alvin Wolfe (Prof Anthropol, Wash Univ); Conslt Primitive Art Textbooks, McGraw-Hill Pub'g Co; Conslt on WPA Murals, Gen Sers Adm Fed Govt; African Tribal Art Lecture Series, Gt Lakes Cols Assn 1970; Fellow, Royal Anthropol Inst; Col Art Assn Am; Group Shows: Fisher Gallery (Muskegon, Mich) 1975, Gallery One (Ann Arbor, Mich) 1977, Gilman Galleries (Chgo, Ill) 1971-75, Galleria Schneider (Rome, Italy) 1964, Others; Nat Invitational Shows: Art/USA '58 (NY), Am Art of Our Time (Provincetown, Mass) 1961, Bon Marche Nat Gallery (Seattle, Wash) 1963, Watercolor/USA '66 (St Louis, Mo), Contemp Am Artists in Italy (Milan) 1977, Others; r/Epis; hon/OWU Fac Grants; Kress Foun Fac F'ship; GLCA Grant; US Govt Grant; Hope Col Summer Res Grant, M J Wilson Fund; Reviews & Biogl Listings: *Prize-Winning Oil Paintings, Valigia Diplomatica, La Revue Moderne, Arts Mag, NY Times, Herald Tribune, Columbus Dispatch, Midland Daily News, TV Reviews,* Others; Dist'd Alumni Awd, St Univ NY; First Prize, Battle Creek 100th Cent Exhbn; Purchase Awds: Watercolor/USA, Otterbein Col, Capital Univ, Dayton Art Inst; Thomas Potts Purchase Awd & Louis Shepherd Hengst Meml Prize, Columbus Gallery Fine Arts; Others; Works in Perm Collections: Mexican-N Am Inst for Cult Relats (Mexico City), Museo Civico (Vicenza, Italy), Rockefeller Inst (NY), Galerie Jean Royere (Paris), Galleria Schneider (Rome), Vincent Price Collection (LA), IBM Collection, Marathon Oil Co Collection, Num Others; One-man Shows: Bi-Nat Inst (Guadalajara, Monterrey & Mexico City), Highland Gallery (Cinc, Ohio), Galerie Jean Royere, Galerie Intl (NY), USIS Gallery (Milan), Museo Civico, Northwood Inst Gallery (Midland), Num Others.

VICKREY, JAMES F JR o/Administrator; b/Feb 6, 1942; h/Flowerhill, Montevallo, AL 35115; ba/Montevallo; m/Suzanne; c/John Robert; p/Mrs F G Murray, Montgomery, AL; ed/BA 1964, MA 1965 Auburn Univ; PhD Fla St Univ 1972; Cert Inst for Ednl Mgmt, Harvard Univ 1974; Addit Studies; pa/Pres, Univ Montevallo 1977-; Exec Asst to Chancellor & Dir Public Affairs, St Univ Sys Fla 1975-77; Asst to Pres & Dir Univ Relats, Univ S Fla 1971-75; Adm Asst to Exec VP, Fla St Univ 1970-71; Instr & Dir Forensics, Auburn Univ 1965-68; Author Num Articles Profl Jours; Communs Conslt; Former Mem Nat Freedom of Speech Comm, Speech Communs Assn; Nat Govt Relats Com, Coun for Advmt & Support Ed; Am Assn St Cols & Univs; Others; cp/Speaker Civic Orgs; Tampa C of C; Auburn Alumni Clb; Downtown Redevel Com; Ednl Com, Fine Arts Coun; Others; r/Bapt; hon/Exceptional Achmt Awd, Coun for Advmt & Support Ed; Univ Fellow, Fla St Univ; Doct Hons Seminar Participant, Speech Communs Assn; Phi Delta Phi; Awd, S Allen Edgar F'ship; Alegernon Sydney Sullivan Awd, Auburn Univ; Phi Kappa Phi; Omicron Delta Kappa; Others.

VICTOR, BARRY ALAN oc/Artist; b/May 11, 1949; h/3 Mansion Dr, Hyde Park, NY 12538; ba/Same; m/Diana R Digrandi; p/Louis and Evelyn Victor, Rochester, NY; ed/AA; BS; MFA; pa/Owner of B A Victor Art Gallery; Painter, Sculptor, Ceramicist; 1-Man Shows in Paris (France) & Rome (Italy) 1980, Other European Countries 1981; cp/Hyde Park C of C; r/Jewish; hon/Num Gold Medals & Awds for Art; Work Rep'd in Num Collections in US & Europe; Artist/USA; W/W E; Others.

VILLALÓN, MANUEL FELIPE oc/Certified Public Accountant; b/Apr 10, 1944; h/Condominio Park Plaza, Apt 1005, Isla Verde, PR 00913; ba/Hato Rey, PR; m/Josefa Cristina Brito; c/Manuel Felipe II, Cristina Maria; p/Jose Manuel and Hortensia Silva de Villalon, Winston-Salem, NC; ed/BS, MS

Wharton Col; JD Harvard Law Sch; pa/Atty; Colegio de CPA de Puerto Rico; AICPA St Leg Area 5 Plan'g Subcom; ABA; Spec Advr Tax Reform Col, Area of Puerto Rico Excise Taxes; r/Rom Cath; hon/Joseph Wharton Scholar; Fellow, Org Am Sts; Spec Awd for Outstg Contbns, Colegio de CPA de PR.

VILLOT-CHRISTINE, VIGNOLA oc/-Supervisor; Teacher; b/Aug 2, 1950; h/850 E 17th St, Apt 4c, Brooklyn, NY 11230; ba/Bklyn; m/Luis E; c/Rachel M; p/Louis and Josephine Vignola, Union, NJ; ed/BS; pa/Suprv Cardio-Pulmonary Lab, Downstate Med Ctr; Res Scist; AALAS; NY St Soc Cardio-Pul Technol; Cert'd Cardio-Pul Resusitationist; r/Cath; hon/Dean's List.

VINING, PEGGY CAUDLE oc/Child Supervisor; Teacher; b/Mar 4, 1929; h/6817 Gingerbread Ln, Little Rock, AR 72204; ba/Little Rock; m/Donald D; c/Suzanne V Kunkel, Kathy, Vicky V Crawley, Donny Jr, Cheri; p/C R and Winnie Moore Caudle, Eudora, AR; ed/BS Univ Ark; Elem Cert, Union Univ; pa/Tchr, Univ Ark Chd's Ctr; Free-lance Writer; Poetry Pub'd Num Anthologies & Jours; Ark Assn Early Childhood Ed; NTRE; So Assn Chd Under Six;

VP, Poets Roundtable Ark; Okla & Tenn Poetry Socs; Nat Fdn St Poetry Socs; Bd Mem, Ozark Creative Writers; Ark Writers Conf; Lit Chm, Ark Arts Fest; Ark Authors; Composers & Artists Soc; cp/Univ Wom's Clb; r/Bapt; hon/Mem of Yr, Poets Roundtable 1976; Rec'd Awd for Outstg Ser to Fine Arts Ark; Winner, Sybil Nash Abrams Awd for Poetry.

VIRGIN, HERBERT W oc/Orthopedic Surgeon; b/Oct 12. 1906; h/3635 St Gaudens

Rd, Coconut Grove, Miami, FL 33133; ba/Miami; m/Frances True; c/Herbert W III, Charles Edward, Frances V Pierce; p/Herbert W and Isabella Goff Virgin (dec); ed/BA, MB, MD NWn Univ; mil/USNR; pa/Chief of Staff, Mercy Hosp (Miami) 1965; Doctors Hosp; One of Fdrs, Profl Football Team Physicians Assn; Team Physician: Miami Dolphins (Football), Ft Lauderdale Strikers (Soccer), Miami Orioles (Baseball), World Jai Alai (Miami & Ft Pierce, Fla); Dilpomate, Am Bd Ortho Surgs; Fellow, Am & Intl Col Surgs; Fellow, Acad Ortho Surgs; Fdr, Fla Ortho Soc; Am Fracture Assn; AMA; Fla & Dade Co Med Assns; r/Bapt; hon/NWn Univ 1st Nat Alumni Awd for Commun Ser.

VIZCARRA, GINORIS oc/Attorney; b/Feb 7, 1934; h/Garden Meadows B-9, Garden Hills, Guaynabo, PR 00657; ba/Santurce, PR; m/Carlos Lopez-Lay; c/Carlitos, Ginorita, Gloriana; p/Salvador Vizcarra (dec); Edelmira Castellon, Hato Rey, PR; ed/BA Bennington Col 1954; LLB Yale Univ Law Sch 1957; Addit Studies; pa/Admit'd Pract Supr Ct Puerto Rico 1958, Dist Ct for Dist PR, US Ct Appeals for 1st Circuit Ct & US Supr Ct; Pvt Pract w Var Attys, w Husband 1967-73; Lectr Labor Leg, Univ Puerto Rico 1960-61; Law Clerk to Justice Emilio S Belaval, Supr Ct PR 1958-61; Others; Co-author (w Sarah Torres Peralta), *Digest of Adm & Judicial Decisions Issued Under the Puerto Rico Labor Relats Law* (1960); Pub'd Articles Profl Jours; Mem Bd Bar Examrs, Appointed by Supr Ct PR 1975-77; Editors Comm, PR Bar Assn Jour 1962; Others; cp/Former Secy Yale Clb PR; Past Pres, Regent & Secy Bd Dirs, Colegio Puertorriqueno de Ninas; Former Advr, Infantile Paralisis PR; Past Trustee, Fam Inst; hon/Outstg Yg Wom Am

VLACHOS, ESTELLA MARIA oc/-Accountant; Controller; b/Oct 24, 1939; h/-PO Box 6094, Anaheim, CA 92806; ba/Fullerton, CA; m/Emanuel James; p/Rudolph John Carlson (dec); Estelle S Carlson, Costa Mesa, CA; ed/AA; pa/Soc Cal Accts; Nat Taxpreparers Assn; Am Soc Wom Accts; Nat Soc Public Accts; r/Greek Orthodox: Ch Parish Coun Mem & Treas; hon/W/W: Am Wom, Fin & Indust, Intellectuals; World W/W Wom; Notable Ams; Book of Hon; Personalities of W&MW; Commun Ldrs & Noteworthy Ams.

VLAHOS, GEORGE EFTHYMIOS oc/Associate Professor; b/Jun 18, 1936; h/8305 Woodgrove Dr, Centerville, OH 45459; ba/Dayton, OH; p/Efthymios Georgios Vlahos, Centerville; Maria E Vlahos (dec); ed/BS Univ Ill 1964; MS So Ill Univ 1967; PhD Univ Nn Colo 1974; Addit Studies; mil/NATO Forces in Europe; pa/Eureka Col: Assoc Prof & Dept Head 1974-, Statistical Conslt, Chm Coun on Coms, Admissions & Acad Status Com, Fac Status Com, Acad Affairs Com, Com for Plan'g & Budgeting, Curric & Statistical Conslt UPWARD BOUND, Others; Part-time Instr Data Processing, Bus Statistics & Math, Ill Ctl Col 1976-; Tchg & Res Fellow, Univ Nn Colo 1972-74; Real Estate Broker, Home View Realty 1976-; Other Positions; Speaker, Confs & Workshops; Contbr Articles Profl Jours; Am Statistical Assn; Math Assn Am; Am Ed Res Assn; Am Inst for Decision Sci; Intl Coun Ed for Tchg; Ill & Nat Coun Tchrs Math; AAUP; hon/Pi Mu Epsilon; Sigma Zeta; Rec'd Hons, Greek Min Ed & Univ Ill; Rec'd Sev

S'ships & F'ships; Men Achmt; W/W Mid-West; Am Hellenic W/W Bus & Professions; W/W Greek Origin Higher Ed; Personalities of W&MW.

VOGELE, DOROTHY DIXON oc/Freelance Writer; h/22 President Way, Belleville, IL 62223; m/Alfred C (dec); c/David Dixon Beamon; p/Adlai Stevenson and Mathilda M Dixon (dec); ed/Attended Wash Univ (St

Louis, Mo); pa/Author 3 Books, Num Articles & Christian Fiction; Pres Cahokia Val Branch, Nat Leag Am Pen Wom; cp/Past Grand Ofcr OES; r/Bapt; hon/Miss So Ill; Nom, Outstg Govt Employee Adm Category.

VOLZ, PAUL ALBERT oc/Professor; b/Mar 26, 1936; h/Ann Arbor, MI; ba/Ypsilanti, MI; p/Albert Carl and Frieda Clara Volz, Ann Arbor; ed/BA; MS; PhD; pa/Prof Mycology, Plant Pathol & Biospace Technol, En Mich Univ; Mich Acad Sci; Intl Soc Human & Animal Mycol; Med Mycol Soc

Ams; Am Fern Soc; Assn for Tropical Biol; NY Acad Sci; AIBS; AAAS; ASM; Mycological Soc Am; Am Phytopath Soc; Am Security Coun Ed Foun; IPA; cp/Am Acad Polit & Social Sci; Ctr for Study of Presidency; r/United Ch of Christ; hon/Tri Beta; Sigma Xi; Res Awds from Var Sci Socs.

VOOK, RICHARD WERNER oc/Educator; b/Aug 2, 1929; h/Rt 1, Box 322, Nedrow, NY 13120; ba/Syracuse, NY; m/Julia Deskins; c/Katherine Julia, Elizabeth Anna, Richard Stuart, Frederick Werner; p/Fred L and Hedwig A Vook, DeBary, FL; ed/BA; MS; PhD; pa/Prof Materials Sci, Syracuse Univ; Author 65 Res Pubs; Am Physical Soc; Am Vacuum Soc; Electron Microscope Soc Am; Metall Soc AIME; r/Luth; hon/Phi Beta Kappa; Sigma Xi; Pi Mu Epsilon.

VOOBUS, ARTHUR oc/Professor; b/Apr

28, 1909; h/230 S Euclid Ave, Oak Park, IL 60302; ba/Chicago, IL; m/Ilse Luksep; c/Ruth, Eti; p/Karl Ed Voobus (dec); Linda Helene Voobus, Oak Park; ed/Cand BTh, ThM, DTh; pa/Manuscript Res in Syrian Orient; Discoverer of Unkown Manuscript Sources; Author 64 Books & 300 Articles in Intl Scholarly Jours; cp/Antibolshevik Bloc of Nations; r/Evangelical Luth; hon/Intl Acad Scis & Lttrs; Royal Acad Belgium; F'ships: J S Guggenheim Meml Foun, Am Coun Learned Socs; Am Phil Soc, Nat Endowmt for Humanities; 40 Lead'g Intl Scholars Pub'd *A Tribute to Arthur Voobus: Studies in Early Christian Lit & Its Environment, Primarily in the Syrian East* (1977).

VOZZA, EVELYN MARKERT oc/- Managing Editor; b/Sept 26, 1931; h/178 Kinderka mack Rd, Westwood, NJ 07675; ba/Park Ridge, NJ; m/Joseph L; c/Mary Ann Markert, Ruth Ellen Markert; p/Nicholas and Theresa Schiotis Garifalos, Westwood; ed/AA Averett Col 1951; Grad Donovan Bus Col 1953; pa/Assoc Editor, Pascack Pubs (Park Ridge) 1966-73; Columnist & Mng Editor, *The Distaff Side* 1973-; NJ Press Assn; cp/1st VP Gtr Pascack Val C of C; LWV; NOW; Pres, Wash Twp Jr Wom's Clb; OES; r/Greek Orthodox; hon/Rec'd 2nd Pl Awd, Wom's Interest Writing, NJ Press Assn; YWCA Tribute to Wom & Indust Awd.

W

WACKENHUT, GEORGE R oc/Executive; b/Sept 3, 1919; h/20 Casuarina Concourse, Cables Estates, FL 33143; ba/Coral Gables, FL; m/Ruth; c/Richard, Jan; p/William H and Frances M Hogan Wackenhut (dec); ed/BS Univ Hi; MEd John Hopkins Univ; mil/AUS; pa/Pres & Chm of Bd The Wackenhut Corp; Am Soc for Indust Security; Soc Former Spec Agts of FBI; r/Christian Scist; hon/Cert'd Protection Profl Awd, Am Soc for Indust Security; Vigilant Patriot Awd, All-Am Conf to Combat Communisum; George Washington Hon Medal, Freedoms Foun Val Forge.

WACKERNAGEL, HANS BEAT oc/Astronomer; b/Aug 31, 1931; h/2939 Country Clb Dr, Colorado Springs, CO 80909; ba/Peterson AFB, CO; m/Irene Everalda Chavez; c/Barbara Elisabeth, Jacob Laurenz, William Beat, Patricia Ruth; p/Karl Heinrich Wackernagel (dec); Georgine Hagenbach Wackernagel, Basel, Switzerland; ed/Dr phil II Univ Basel; mil/Heavy Howitzers Swiss Army; pa/Hq NORAD, Peterson AFB: Physicist 1978-, Mathematician 1975-78; Opers Res Analyst 2nd Communs Sqdrn, Buckley ANGB, Colo 1975; Computer Specialist Hq NORAD, Ent AFB 1973-75; Lectr Celestial Mechanics Univ Colo 1965-70; Other Former Positions; Life Mem: Astronomical Soc Basel, Swiss Astronomical Soc; Am Astronomical Soc; Fellow British Interplanetary Soc; cp/Colo Sprgs Racquet Clb: Former Dir, Past VP; r/E U Meth Ch: Pres Meth Men 1972-75, Chm Coun on Mins 1976-79; hon/Sustained Superior Perf, Civil Ser; Outstg Perf Awd, Civil Ser.

WADDELL, ROBERT MALCOLM oc/Retired Industrial Economist; b/May 12, 1909; h/6836 Westhill Dr SW, Olympia, WA 98502; m/Leora Rafter Warne; c/Tedder Douglas; p/John Henry and Elizabeth Douglas MacArthur Waddell (dec); ed/Undergrad Studies Univ Pa, Wharton Sch Fin; BS Univ Ky Col of Commerce; pa/Ret'd 1978; Conslt'g Engrg Economist Wash Metro Area Transit

Auth, DeLeuw, Cather & Co, Wash DC 1970-78; Sr Indust Economist Nat Planning Assn, Wash DC 1962-70; Planning Supt & Sr Statiscian duPont Co, Wilmington, Del 1952-62; Other Former Positions; cp/Chm Eagle Scout Exam'g Bd, BSA; r/Presb; hon/BSA: Eagle Scout, Dist'd Scout; Beta Gamma Sigma; Recog'd as creator of MIOS, a modular input output system.

WADE, DOROTHY R oc/Piano Teacher; b/Nov 4, 1928; h/6121 Coralite St, Long Beach, CA 90808; m/Harry B; c/Deborah J Kopp; p/James Edward Rutherford (dec); Leola Lillian Rutherford, Long Beach; ed/Att'd Pasadena Col, Long Bch City Col, Ext Classes Biola Col; pa/Piano Tchr (in home); Play Marimba for Chs & Clbs; r/Grace Brethren Ch, Long Bch: Mem; hon/Nat Guild Hall of Fame; Intl W/W in Music.

WADE, EUGENE HOWARD oc/Educator, Department Head; b/Dec 10, 1943; h/910 15th Ave S, Nashville, TN 37212; ba/Franklin, TN; p/Jesse and Margaret R Wade (dec); ed/BS, MA TSU; pa/Dept Hd Bus Franklin HS; Williamson Co Ed Assn: Past

Pres, Past Chm Profl Rts & Responsibilities, Chm Leg Com; Mem Profl Negotiation Team Williamson Co Schs; Mid Tenn, Tenn, Nat Ed Assns; Nat Assn Bus Tchrs; cp/NAACP; Urban Leag; Davidson Co Indep Polit Coun; r/Ebenezer Missionary Bapt Ch: Mem, Supt SS, Tchr Intermed Boys, Dir Yg People's Activs; Exec Dir MW Missionary Bapt Yth Conf; hon/Pi Omega Pi.

WADE, GERALDINE ELIZABETH oc/Educational Counselor; b/Jan 13, 1929; h/3700 S Anderson Rd, Choctaw, OK 73020; ba/Midwest City, OK; c/Christopher L Kerns, Stephen M Kerns; p/John Reed and Mildred Virginia Mobley Raymer; ed/BS 1950, MEd 1963 Univ Okla; pa/Tchr Eng & French Midwest City Sch Sys 1959-64; Cnslr: Mid-Del Sch Sys (Midwest City) 1964-, Carl Albert Jr

HS 1971-; Oscar Rose Jr Col, Midwest City: (Pt-time) Admissions Cnslr, Evening Asst to Registrar, Psychol Tchr 1975-; APGA; Okla Pers & Guid Assn; NEA; Okla Ed Assn; Assn Classroom Tchrs; cp/MW City C of C; Univ Okla Alumni Assn; Dem; r/Meth; hon/Recipient Grant; Author *Occupl Info: Focus on Guid*; W/W S&SW; DIB.

WADIA, MANECK S oc/Author; Professor; Entrepreneur; Management Consultant; b/Oct 22, 1931; h/1660 Luneta, Del Mar, CA 92014; ba/Same; m/Harriet Fern; c/Sara Jean, Mark Sorab; p/Sorabji Rattanji and Manijeh Wadia; ed/BA; MA; MBA; PhD;

mil/Conslt to Armed Forces; pa/Bd Govs, Cal Pacific Univ; Conslt to: Home Fed Savs & Loan, Sugar Bowl Resort, Solar, Convair, General Dynamics, San Diego Sch Dist, San Diego Police Dept, San Diego Fire Dept, IRS; r/Zoarastrian; hon/Ford Foun F'ship; Hon Awd, Acad of Mgmt.

WAGER, SCOTT THOMAS oc/National Sales Director; b/Oct 17, 1948; h/1715 Madsen Ct, Wheaton, IL 60187; ba/Westchester, IL; m/Patricia; c/Carrianne; p/Roy E and Diane R Wager, Des Plaines, IL; ed/AA Col Dupage; Att'd Wis St; pa/NMA; CADEM; SMME; cp/Pres Col DuPage Alumni Assn; r/Cath; hon/W/W Am Jr Cols.

WAGNER, JIMMY WAYNE oc/College Professor; b/Dec 1, 1946; h/1015 S Main, Boliver, MO 65613; ba/Boliver; m/Brenda R; c/Carolyn Lynn, Brittany Blaire; p/J W and Mary Blanche Wagner, Boliver; ed/BA; MA; PhD; pa/Prof SWBC; AAUP; cp/Common Cause; r/So Bapt; hon/Outstg Yg Men Am; W/W in Rel; DIB; Personalities W&MW.

WAGNER, JOSEPH CRIDER oc/University Administrator; b/Feb 19, 1907; h/629 Forest Ave, Muncie, IN 47304; ba/Same; m/Geraldine B; c/Joene W Henning; p/Arthur A and Grace E Wagner (dec); ed/AB; MA; LLD; pa/VP Emeritus Ball St Univ; Bd Trustees Ind St Tchrs' Retiremt Fund; Pres Ind Schoolmen's Clb 1949; Supt Schs Hartford City & Crawfordsville (Ind) 11 Yrs; Past Pres Del Co Ret'd Tchrs Assn; cp/Bd Dirs Muncie

YMCA; U Way Del Co; Past Pres Hartford City Rotary Clb; Pres Bd Trustees: U Meth Meml Home (Warren, Ind), Muncie Mission; Mem Gen Bd Ed U Meth Ch, Nashville, Tenn; hon/"Benny" Awd for Dedicated Ldrship to Ball St Univ; Named a Sagamore of Wabash, Gov Ind 1976; Hon Mem Tau Kappa Alpha; Delta Pi Epsilon; Phi Delta Kappa; Earhart Fellow Univ Mich; IPA.

WAGNER, LOUIS EDWARD oc/Executive; b/Mar 12, 1937; h/8 Eltham Dr, Eggertsville, NY 14226; ba/Niagara Falls, NY; m/Mary Fitzgerald; c/Maribeth, Thomas; p/Louis E Sr and Lucille Olson Wagner, Hamburg, NY; ed/BS, MBA SUNY; pa/Pres & Fdr, Chem-Trol Pollution Sers Inc 1969-76; Fdr, NEWCO Chem Waste Sys Inc 1976-; Plant Mgr, Amercoat Corp (Mfrs of Indust Coatings & Adhesives) 1965-69; Chm, Water Comm of Elma Comm for Conserv of Environment; Environmental Activs Coun; Nat Air Pollution Control Assn; NY St Conserv Coun; Assoc Industs of NYS; Am Nat Standards Inst Inc; Am Forestry Assn; Lectr on Treatment of Chem Wastes: Inventor; Contbr to Profl Jours; Others; cp/Buffalo (NY) C of C; Lancaster Country Clb; Conserv Clb; Others; r/Rom Cath; ho/W/W: Ecology, E, Fin & Indust; Other Biogl Listings.

WAINWRIGHT, MARY LEE SELLERS oc/Teacher; Composer; b/Apr 24, 1913; h/1519 Dewey St, Hollywood, FL 33020; m/N D Jr (dec); c/1 Daugh; p/Samuel Joseph and Martha Ellen Sellers; ed/Att'd Stetson Univ; pa/Tchr of Democracy for US Govt; Composer; Singer; Pianist; Concert Lectr; Bd Mem Am Security Coun, Wash DC; Pres's Action Com; Coun for Inter-Am Security; ASCAP, Hon Mem; Pres Hollywood Chapt Nat Fdn Music Clbs 1974-76, 1976-77; Leg Chm Fla Foun Music Clbs; Recent Compositions incl: "The New Spirit Lives" 1976, "You Are My Inspiration" 1977, "The Touch of His Hand" 1979; cp/Pres's Clb Hon James E Carter of Dem Nat Com; Com to Restore US Constitution; Sustaining Mem Repub Nat Com; New Spirit '76 Foun; Active in Security & Intell Fund, Christian Anti-Communism Crusade & Am Police Hall of Fame; Adv Bd Am Police Hall of Fame & Mus; r/1st Bapt Ch, H'wood: Choir Mem, Pianist, Bible Tchr; hon/Inducted into Songwriters Hall of Fame; Nat Awd, Gold Star & Double Blue & Gold Ribbons in Parade of Am Music for Concert Theme & Song "The New Spirit Lives", Nat Fdn Music Clbs & ASCAP; Name Chosen for Lib of Human Resources of Am Heritage Res Assn during 1976 Bicent Celebration; Bicent Signet Ring, New Spirit of '76 Foun; Elected "Patriot of the Am Bicent", US Commemorative Gallery; Biogl Listings; Others.

WAITE, SARAH FRANCES oc/Retired Substitute Teacher; h/4249 S Lincoln, Englewood, CO; m/William T (dec); c/William, Sally L Bridgeman; p/Charles D

McBride (dec); Mrs R M Minshall (dec); ed/AB De Pauw Univ 1929; pa/Ret'd Substitute Tchr Arapahoe Co; Sponsor Pep Squad Montrose HS (Colo) 1934-35; cp/Vol for Var Drives; r/St James Presb Ch; hon/Order of Golden Rose, Delta Zeta.

WALD, EDWIN PRESCOTT oc/Civil Engineer; b/Jul 23, 1920; h/230 N Valencia St, Alhambra, CA 91801; ba/Alhambra; c/Stephen, Suzanne Montgomery (Mrs Blaine), Diane Larson (Mrs Al), Kathleen Boyum (Mrs Larry); p/George Gustav and Edith Percy Wald; ed/BS Cal Inst Tech 1941; pa/Asst Civil Engr, City of Alhambra 1964-; Designer Cal Inst Tech's Jet Propulsion Lab, Pasadena 1956-61; Draftsman & Designer N Am Aviation Inc, El Segundo, Cal 1941-53; Loftsman Consol Aircraft Co, San Diego 1940; Fellow Leakey Foun; Mem Lindbergh Foun; Fauna Soc; ASCE; Am Forestry Assn; cp/AF Assn; Epigraphic Soc; Repub; r/Epis; hon/Profl Pubs.

WALDEN, KATHRYN C oc/Community Worker; b/Apr 5, 1910; h/PO Box 86, Headland, AL 36345; m/Arthur Durward (dec); c/David C, Gwendolyn Hand; p/Marvin and Lula Mixon Carroll (dec); ed/BS Ala Col (now Univ Montevallo) 1931; Art Studies Univ Ala 2 Yrs; Addit Studies; cp/Set up S'ship Foun at Univ Montevallo for Outstg HS Grads in Home Ecs from 3 Cos in Ala (Henry, Dale & Houston); Donates Gifts to Cols & Univs in US & Abroad; Ext Travel incl: Scotland, Ireland, England, France, Holland, Italy, Germany, Switzerland, Egypt, Greece, Lebanon, Jordan, Syria, Israel, Spain, Portugal, Hungary, Austria, Russia, Poland, Turkey, Norway, Sweden, Denmark, Finland, Africa, Japan, China, Thailand, Malaya & Korea; DAR; Study Clb; Homemakers Clb; Hist Soc Henry Co; r/Ext Work in Local Ch & Dist & Conf Divs of Meth Ch; hon/Book of Honor.

WALDHEIM, KURT oc/Secretary-General of United Nations; b/Dec 21, 1918; ba/UN, New York, NY 10017; m/Elisabeth Ritschel; c/Liselotte, Gerhard, Christa; p/Walter Waldheim; Josefine Petrasch; ed/JD; LLD; pa/Secy-Gen of UN; hon/Var Hon Degs.

WALKER, C R JR oc/Behavioral Scientist; Administrator; h/248 Boyer St, Dayton, OH 45407; ba/Dayton; m/Lillian Hughes; c/C R III, Ferieda, Bernice, Anton; p/C R and MC Walker, Nassau, NP, Bahamas; ed/PhD; PhD; SD; pa/Pres & Fdr Walker Res Inst; Dep Dir Montgomery Co Wel Dept; Former Coor Diagnostic & Treatmt Sers, Dayton Human Rehab Ctr; Exec Dir Trans-Am Ctr for Urban Affairs; Adj Prof Union Experimental Cols & Univs, Union Grad Sch; Commun Resource Fac Univ Without Walls; Dir-Conslt YES Prog; Mgmt Conslt; Ec Conslt; Author 5 Pub'd Books & Num Articles; AAUP; Soc of Criminol; AAAS; IPA; Am Judic Soc; Nat Ctr of Humanistic Ed; Intl Acad Criminol; Other Profl Orgs; cp/Var Interests in: Mtl Hlth, Urban Affairs, Intl Affairs, Local, City & St Govt, Others; r/Ch of England; hon/Man of Yr, ARSA; Var Biogl Listings.

WALKER, EUNICE ARNAUD oc/Writer; h/205 James Thurber St, Falls Church, VA 22046; m/William Roy Little; c/Diane Leigh W Smith, Carole Cecile W Baker; p/Emile and Pauline Barriquand Arnaud (dec); ed/BA; Grad Work; pa/Nat Press Clb; Nat Leag Am Pen Wom; Nat Fdn Press Wom; Nat Archives; cp/Smithsonian Assocs; Mem Pres's Clb; Nat Dem Party; Var Campaign Activs; r/Epis; hon/Nat Prize & Features, Awd'd by Agri Editors; Lttrs of Commend.

WALKER, LUCILE HILL oc/Homemaker; Civic Worker; Lecturer; b/Feb 2, 1900; h/704 W 11th St, Plainview, TX 79072; m/Julius Waring (dec); c/Julius Waring Jr; p/Daniel Chapman and Alma Amerial Hill (dec); ed/BS Tex Wom's Univ; mil/Dollar-a-Yr Wom WWII, Dir Tex Schs-at-War Prog WWII; pa/HS Sci Tchr; Ed *Tex Clubwoman*; Profl Parliamentn; Lectr for Miscellaneous Civic Groups; Book Reviewer, Wom's Study

Groups; cp/Orgr & Fdr Mary McCoy Baines Chapt DAR; Wom's Clb Plainview; AAUW, P'view Br; Hale Co Hist Comm; Chm Num Coms & Comms at Local Level incl'g: UF, YMCA, Salvation Army, Wayland Bapt Col Drs; Chm Hale Co Dem Party; VChm Tex Tidelands Comm; Tex Interracial Relats Comm; Tex Tech Univ Adult Ed Com; Tex Dem Exec Com; Del to 1960 Dem Nat Conv; Past Pres Tex Fdn Wom's Clb; r/Presb: Music Dir 19 Yrs, SS Tchr 43 Yrs, Sr Ch Advr; hon/Life Mem, Tex Fdn Wom's Clbs; Dist'd Ser Awds: Wayland Bapt Col, Llano Estacado Mus, UF Tex, W Tex St Univ, Salvation Army, Gen Fdn Wom's Clbs; Ser Medal, US Treasury; 1960 Citizen-of-Yr Plainview Awd; Key to City of Los Angeles; Key to Ks City Awds.

WALKER, MARGARET PHILLIPS oc/Teacher; College Professor; b/Jul 29, 1905; h/Rt 3, Box 134, Denton, TX 76201; m/Philip Whitman; c/Katherine, L'Jon; p/W L and Belle Farmer Phillips (dec); ed/BA Baylor Col 1926; MA Univ Tex 1945; pa/Ret'd; AAUW; Delta Kappa Gamma; NT Univ Wom; Classroom Tchr, Prin, Cnslr; Asst Prof Ed: TWU, NTSU; r/Meth; hon/Outstg Ex Student, Blooming Grove HS; Biogl Listings.

WALKER, WILLIAM HOOD oc/Ironworker; b/May 17, 1903; h/803 Lincoln Ave, Talladega, AL 35160; m/Edna Lorene Matson; p/Clem Agusta and Mary Etta Walker (dec); pa/Structural Ironworker 50 Yrs; r/Prot; hon/Personalities of S.

WALKINSHAW, LAWRENCE HARVEY oc/Retired Dentist; b/Feb 25, 1904; h/1145 Scenic Dr, N Muskegon, MI 49445; m/Clara May Cartland; c/James Richard Walkinshaw, Wendy Anne Schake; p/Beatson Charles and Eva Maria Grinnell Walkinshaw (dec); ed/DDS; pa/Pres SW Mich Dental Soc

1945-46; cp/Past Pres: Battle Creek Lions Clb, Wilson Ornithol Soc, Ridge Audubon Soc (Lake Wales, Fla); Former Secy Am Ornithol Union; r/Meth; hon/Hon'd by: Detroit Audubon Soc, Mich Acad Scis, US Fish & Wildlife Ser.

WALKO, MARY ANN oc/Assistant Dean of Students; b/Jan 1, 1938; h/1581 Cooper Rd, Scotch Plains, NJ 07076; ba/Union, NJ; m/Michael; c/Michael Edward; p/Mary L Murray, Scotch Plains; ed/BA, MA Kean Col NJ; EdD Cand Rutgers Univ; Addit Studies; Certs held: Elem Prin, Dental Nsg, Small Bus Adm for Tng in Bus; pa/Asst Dean of Students Kean Col of NJ; HERS-MID-Atl, Assn of St Col Admrs; Nat Orientation Dirs Assn; Convenor Career Advmt for Profl Wom in

Higher Ed 1978-79; Nat Assn for Wom Deans, Admrs & Cnslrs; Chaired Com for Self-Eval of Progs & Facilities for Handicapped; Started Intl Student Adv Com Kean Col; Coor Intl Student Orientation, Kean Col; Others; cp/Mem Gran Centurions, Clark, NJ; Campaign Assistance for 12th Congl Dist, Union Co; Others; hon/Kappa Delta Pi; Nat Sci Def S'ship; S'ship at Kean; Hon'd by Alumni Assn; Commun Ldrs & Noteworthy Ams.

WALLACE, GEORGE JOHN oc/Professor Emeritus; b/Dec 9, 1906; h/Rt 1, Box 1638, Grayling, MI 49738; ba/Same; m/Martha; c/Sylvia W McGrath, Mya W Connor; p/James Moses and Florence Ida Richardson Wallace (dec); ed/AB 1932, MA 1933, PhD 1936 Univ Mich; ScD CMU 1970; pa/Prof Emeritus Zoology Mich St Univ; Var Profl Socs; Writer; r/Meth; hon/Cits, Plaques: Detroit Aud Soc, Mich Aud Soc; Hon Deg.

WALLACE, GLENN WALKER oc/Symphony Founder; b/May 19; h/2520 Walker Ln, Salt Lake City, UT 84117; m/John M; c/John M Jr, Mathew Walker; p/Mathew H and Agelena A Walker (dec); ed/Grad Winsor Sch, Boston; Hon HHD: Westminster Col, Col of En Utah, Univ Utah; cp/Fdr & Past Pres Utah Symph; Fdr & Pres Ballet West; Fdr Civic Music; Francisco Clb, San Fran; Hon Mem, Altrusa Intl; Bd Mem Am Security Coun; r/Congreg; hon/Hon Phi Beta Kappa; Bronze Minute Man, Utah NG; Grand Cross Dame Knightly Order St Brigitte, Venerable Order St John of Jerusalem, Salt Lake Coun of Wom, Hall of Fame Awd for Outstg Commun Ldrship in Arts; AAUW Awd for Outstg Contbn to Arts.

WALLACE, J B oc/Police Chief; b/Feb 16, 1930; h/942B Simpson Terr, Bedford, TX 76021; ba/Bedford; m/Karen J; c/J B Jr, Larry, Lynn, (Stepchd:) Joe Allen, Mike Allen; p/Elmer W and Rushie Wallace, Ft Worth, TX; ed/AS Police Sci; Adv'd Cert Tex Comm Law Enforcemt; mil/M/Sgt 2nd Inf Div, Korean War; pa/Pres Tarrant Co Police Ofcr Assn; Intl Police Chief Assn; Tex Police Chief Assn; N Tex Police Chief Assn; cp/C of C; HEB; BSA; Little Baseball & Ftball; r/Bapt; hon/W/W in Tex; Personalities of S.

WALLACE, JOAN S ba/USDA, 14th & Independence, Rm 212E, Washington, DC 20050.

WALLACE, JOHN FRANCIS III oc/Missionary, Teacher, Minister; b/Aug 4, 1956; h/7704-D College Cir, Ft Worth, TX 76118; ba/Ft Worth; p/John F Jr and Patricia McCabe Wallace, La Mesa, CA; ed/BS Bethany Bible Col; MA Cand Tex Christian Univ; pa/Bethany Bible Col, Santa Cruz, Cal: Tchg Asst 1977-78, Dir Intl Missions 1976-77; Intl Correspondence Inst. Author A-V

Supplemt to *Intro to Anthropol* 1977, Brussels, Belgium; CAMA Cnslg & Music Evang: Cal, Oreg, Nev 1976; Instr Biblical Lit Far E Adv'd Sch Theol, Manila, Philippines 1978; Prof Theol Bethel Bible Inst, Manila 1978; Missionary Evangelist in: Europe, SAm, Asia, US 1977-78; Phi Delta Kappa; SWn Social Sci Assn; cp/ARC; First Aid; r/Assemblies of God: Lic'd Clergy; hon/Cal Scholastic Fdn; Music Conservatory Hon F'ship; W/W Am Cols & Univs.

WALLER, DAVID THOMAS oc/Minister; b/Feb 14, 1950; h/580 NE 3rd St, Lake Butler, FL 32054; ba/Lake Butler; m/Darlene Louise Snyder; c/Deanna Louise; p/Jesse Emmett and Gladys Hill Waller, Macon, GA; ed/AB Pfeiffer Col 1972; MDiv Emory 1975; pa/Min 1st U Meth Ch, Fla Conf 1977-80; Assoc 1st UMC, Miami 1975-77; Ordinations: Deacon 1973, Elder 1977, Fla Conf; Secy Dist Coun on Mins (Lake Butler); Columnist w *Union Co Times*; Dist Dir Ecumenical & Interrel Concerns (Lake Butler); (Miami:) Dist Coun on Mins, Mem Mercy Hosp Pastoral Care Adv Bd; cp/Bd Dirs Rotary Clb, Lake Butler; 2 Yr Comml Solicitor for Am Cancer Soc (Lake Butler); Publicity Chperson Mar Dimes Superwalk 1979, Lake Butler; Chaplain Goodwill Industs, Miami; Mem 3rd Century Bicent Com "City Under One God", Miami; r/U Meth; hon/Outstg Sr (Col); DIB.

WALSH, NANCY LEE BALLARD oc/Librarian; b/Aug 25, 1927; h/4306 S 8th St, Arlington, VA 22204; ba/Washington, DC; m/W Michael; p/Henderson Suter Ballard, Bedford; Ethel Blanche Davis Ballard (dec); ed/BA James Madison Univ; pa/Libn Nat Def Univ (Ft McNair); Am Lib Assn; DC Lib Assn; Spec Libs Assn, Ch Mil Div 1976; cp/Beta Sigma Phi; DAR; UD; r/Epis; hon/Gen Elect F'ship for Math Tchrs.

WALSTON, GEORGE STANCILL oc/Radio Station General Manager; b/Nov 21, 1913; h/Rt 2, Clinton, NC 28328; ba/Clinton; m/Melba Warner; c/Betty Jo Wright (Mrs Thomas T), Anne Peterson (Mrs Daniel J), Kathy Dowdy (Mrs John); p/George S and Lenora Neal Walston (dec); mil/ARC Field Dir WWII; pa/Gen Mgr Radio Stas WRRZ & WRRZ-FM; Bd Dirs: NC Leag Municipalities, NC Assn Broadcasters; cp/Former Mayor City of Clinton; Pres: Clinton 100 Com, Clinton C of C, Clinton Kiwanis Clb, Sampson Shrine Clb, Clinton Improvemt Soc; Chm Sampson Co Planning Bd; Sampson Co Bd Hlth; Bd Dirs Cape Fear Bk & Trust, Clinton; r/1st U Meth Ch: Ofcl Bd, Pres Meth Men; hon/Man of Yr, Clinton C of C 1977; Sev Dist'd Ser Awds.

WAN, RICHARD T C oc/Physician; b/Apr 3, 1936; h/Thomas St, Morgantown, KY 42261; ba/M'town; c/Julia, Everett; p/Henry and Doris Wan, Bowling Green, KY; ed/Rotating Internship 1960-61; Internal Med Residency 1961-62; Sr Internship 1962-63; Residency & F'ship of Pediatrics 1963-66; pa/KMA; AMA; Tri-Co Med Soc; Ky Hlth Dept; cp/Lions Clb; Repub; r/Bapt.

WANDERMAN, RICHARD GORDON oc/Physician; Pediatrician; b/Apr 17, 1943; h/6748 Meadow Oak Pl, Memphis, TN 38138; ba/Memphis; c/Richard Gordon Jr, Gregory Lloyd; p/Herman L Wanderman (dec); Helen C W Schneider, New York, NY; ed/BA Wn Resv Univ 1965; MD SUNY-Downst Med Ctr 1969; pa/Fellow Am Acad Pediatrics; Clin Assoc Prof Pediatrics Univ Tenn; Soc for Adolescent Med, Mem Com on Sch & Col Hlth; cp/Former Chm: St Sch Hlth Task Force (WVa), Parent Adv Coun to Hd Start in 4 Counties (WVa); r/Jewish; hon/W/W S&SW; Men of Achmt; DIB.

WARD, DONALD MAXWELL oc/Dentist; b/Dec 21, 1917; h/3548 Doncaster Ct S, Apt B-8, Saginaw, MI 48603; ba/Saginaw; c/Jaquelyn Wygmans, Wendy List, Cindy

Wickham, Bradley, Wayne; p/Harold B Ward (dec); Gertrude R Ward, Midland, MI; ed/BA; DDS; mil/USNR Dental Corps WWII; pa/Saginaw Co Dental Soc: Past Pres, Secy, Treas; Var Com Chm'ships Saginaw Val Dental Soc; Am Dental Assn; Saginaw Hosp Cleft Palate Team; Mich Assn Professions; cp/Trustee & Past Secy Saginaw Twp Bd of Ed; Past Secy Saginaw Little Theatre; Elks; Knife & Fork Clb Bd Dirs; Saginaw Ski Clb; r/Presb; hon/Hon Life Mem, Am Cleft Palate Assn; Mem 1959 Good Will Tour Team to Soviet Union & Czechoslovakia; Life Mem: Delta Sigma Delta, Mich Union, Elks, ASA.

WARD, ROSIE GRAHAM oc/Educator; Interpreter for the Deaf; b/Jun 25, 1925; h/5156 Gault St, Jackson, MS 39209; ba/Jackson; m/Willis; c/Stephenson, James, Willis, Tyrone, Excell, Stanley; p/Johnny Graham (dec); Lucille Scott Graham, Edwards, MS; ed/BS; pa/MRID; MSDEA; Miss Sch for Deaf; Con, Am Instrs for the Deaf; cp/NAACP; Medgar Evers St Deaf Assn; Royal Maid (Blind); r/Bapt; Gtr Northside Bapt Ch Missionary Soc; hon/OETA; MAE; W/W Am Wom; Personalities of S; Book of Honor; DIB.

WARD, THOMAS VINCENT oc/Engineer; b/Dec 10, 1938; h/100 Grandview Ave, Apt 12D, Quincy, MA 02170; ba/Boston, MA; p/Thomas F and Hanna Ward (dec); ed/BS 1962; Postgrad Studies Portia Law Sch; pa/ASME; Am Mgmt Assn; AWWA; NSPE; MSPE; Proj Mgr, C T Main Inc 1973-; Engrg Supvr, Bechtel Corp 1969-73; Lead Mech Engr, Stone & Webster Engrg Corp 1962-69; Sr Mech Designer, St Regis Paper Co 1960-62; Mech Designer, Computer Control Corp 1958-60; cp/Mensa; Past V Commodore, Sailing Clb; hon/Math Awd; W/W E; DIB; Others.

WARD, VICTORIA FRANCINE oc/Educator; b/May 12, 1951; h/1623 Murdoch Rd, Philadelphia, PA 19150; ba/Phila; p/John and C Margaret Covington, Philadelphia, PA; ed/AS Commun Col of Phila 1971; BS w Hons, Penn St Univ 1972; MEd, Antioch Univ 1977; pa/Pa Sch Cnslrs Assn; Pers & Guid Assn of Gtr Phila; Pa Sch Guid Assn; APGA; Wom in Ed; BPW Clb; cp/Past CoChrperson Career Ed Com, Delta Sigma Theta; Urban League; r/Bethlehem Presb Ch: Trustee; hon/Trophies & Plaques for Coaching Girls Cheerleading Squad, Holy Trinity Bethlehem Presb Ch; W/W: Am Cols & Univs, E; Am Registry; Other Biogl Listings.

WARE, EUNICE LETIRIA oc/Retired Teacher; b/Jun 29, 1895; h/310 W Avalon, Longview, TX 75602; p/John Alsen and Horace B Flanagan Ware (dec); ed/BA 1916, MA 1928, PhD 1936 Univ Tex; pa/Hd Eng Dept Le Tourneau Col, Longview 1961-63; E Tex Bapt Col, Marshall: Hd Eng Dept, Chm Div Rel & Social Studies 1954-61, 1963-67; Eng Tchr: Longview Sr HS 1938-52, Stephen F Austin St Tchr's Col, Nacodoches, Tex 1928-30; Other Former Positions: S Ctl Mod Lang Assn; Longview: Fine Arts Clb, Music Clb, C of C; Fdn Wom's Clbs; Sustaining Mem Ex-Student's Assn, Univ Tex; Assoc Smithsonian Instn; Nat Trust for Hist Preserv; Nat Hist Soc; Magna Carta Dames; Ams of Royal Descent; Plantagenet Soc; Descendents of Ks of Order of Garter; DAR; Daughs of Am Colonies; Colonial Order of the Crown; Pres Daughs of Republic of Tex; Histn U Daughs of Confed; r/Bapt.

WARE, LARRY GORDON oc/College Professor; b/Feb 14, 1944; h/Rt 1, Box 418, Bolivar, MO 65613; ba/Bolivar; m/Donna Gayle; c/Natalie D'Ann; p/Maurice L and Rubye J Ware, Memphis, TN; ed/BA Hardin-Simmons Univ 1967; MRE 1971, EdD 1978 SWn Bapt Theol Sem; mil/AUS 1967-69, 1/Lt; pa/Asst Prof Rel Ed SW Bapt Col 1975-; Min Ed & Adm Wedgwood Bapt Ch, Ft Worth, Tex 1969-75; So Bapt Rel Ed Assn; Pres Mo Bapt Rel Ed Assn 1977-79; Advr to Local Chapt Alpha Chi; Mem Var Coms; Assn Profs & Reschrs in Rel Ed; r/1st Bapt Ch, Bolivar: Ch Tng Dir; hon/Outstg Yg Men Am.

WARMSLEY, ERNESTINE LAURA oc/Social Worker; b/Feb 20, 1930; h/1533 Giese King Ln, St Louis, MO 63147; ba/St Louis; p/Ernest Walker; Laura Walker, St Louis; ed/BA; Postgrad Work; MSW; Cert Pract Nsg; pa/Writer; Pubr; Fdr of Proj Commun Outreach; Assn Black Social Wkrs; cp/Pres Homer Phillips Hosp Aux; Mem Foster Parents Assoc'd; r/Prot; hon/W/W in Rel.

WARNER, JOSEPHINE G oc/Former Broadway Star, Pianist, Singer; b/1910; h/70-17 168 St, Flushing, NY 11365; c/Dolores, Marie; p/(dec); pa/Former Broadway Pianist; r/Christian.

WARREN, MARIE HALEY oc/Bottling Company Executive; b/Aug 18, 1915; h/617 S Lee St, Americus, GA 31709; c/Vernon Haley, Kathryn Jackson W Powell, Lillian Marie; p/William Banks and Vernon Shelley Haley; ed/AB cum laude Wesleyan Col 1936; pa/Mgr Moultrie Coca-Cola Bottling Co (Ga) 1942-45; Tifton Coca-Cola Bottling Co (Ga): Secy, Dir 1943-45, VP 1977-; VP & Dir Americus Coca-Cola Bottling Co (Ga) 1951-; The Albany Coca-Cola Bottling Co (Ga): Treas & Dir 1971-77, VP, Dir 1977-; Bainbridge Coca-Cola Bottling Co (Ga): Secy-Treas 1971-77, VP, Dir 1977-; VP: Pelham Coca-Cola Bottling Co (Ga), Fitzgerald Coca-Cola Bottling Co (Ga), Cordele Coca-Cola Bottling Co (Ga) 1977-; cp/Host Victory Parade of Spotlight Bands, Spence Field, Moultrie 1944; Hon Mem & Former Treas Jr Ser Leag, Americus; Former Ldr Blue Bird Group, Camp Fire Girls, Americus; r/Meth; hon/Recipient Accolade of Apprec Plaque, Americus & Sumter Co C of C.

WARSHAVSKY, BELLE oc/Reading Specialist; b/Apr 14, 1917; h/35 Cooper Dr, Great Neck, NY 11023; ba/Plainview, NY; m/Henry; c/Beth Sachs, Barry Alyn Benes; p/Morris and Sarah Bennett; ed/BBA St Johns Univ 1940; MSEd Hofstra Univ 1957; Profl

Dipl Rdg 1965; PhD Walden Univ 1975; pa/Adj Queenboro Commun Col; VP NEA; Spkr NYS Rdg Assn; Dir Sum Rdg Prog; AAUW; cp/Civic Assn; PCT; Former Girl Scout Ldr; r/Temple Israel; hon/PTA Ser Awd; W/W: E, Am Wom; DIB; World W/W Wom.

WARTHEN, JOHN EDWARD oc/Leasing Executive; b/May 8, 1922; h/2475 Viking, Las Vegas, NV 89121; ba/Las Vegas; m/Norma Hansen; c/Russel Edward, John Merrill, Judy, Linda, Carla, Lauri, Mark Edward (dec); p/Mark Tew Warthen (dec); Emma Simkins Warthen; mil/AUS Engrs 1943-44; pa/Pres & Owner New Automobile Dealership; Americanism Ednl Leag; Nev St Chm Dealer Election Action Com; Citizens for Pvt Enterprise: Mem, CoChm Dist 13; Coun Mem Nat Indep Bus Fdn; cp/Mem Coun for Inter-Am Activs; Nev Devel Auth; Dist Chm Fin Snow's Canyon BSA; Dist Dir Freemen Inst; Former City Commr; Former Mem: Kiwanis, Rotary; Trustee & Treas LDS Br Geneal Lib; CoFdr Ctr for Intl Securities Studies; Nev Chapt SAR; Life Mem IBA (England); r/LDS Ch: Ordained Bishop; hon/Silver Bond Awd, Gen Motors.

WASHBURN, PAUL ARTHUR oc/Clergyman; b/Mar 31, 1911; h/413 E Parkway, Wheaton, IL 60187; ba/Chicago, IL; m/Kathryn Elizabeth; c/Mary Kathryn Smith, Jane Ann Eigenbrodt, Fredrick Paul, John Arthur; ed/BA N Ctl Col; BD Garrett Evang-Theol Sem; DD Ind Ctl Col; DCL Westmal Col; LHD N Ctl Col; DD Wiley Col; pa/Bishop U Meth Ch; r/U Meth; hon/St George's Gold Medal Awd.

WASHINGTON, CHARLES LLOYD oc/Ordained Clergyman; b/Jun 25, 1928; h/704 5th St, Natchitoches, LA 71457; ba/Natch; m/Bertha Baldwin; c/Jeanetta, Charles Jr, Kenneth Wayne; p/W M Washington, Corinth, MS; Beatrice Olive Washington (dec); ed/Adv'd Cert Gifted Child; 30 Grad Hours Over 3 Masters Degs; BS Univ Ill; mil/AUS Resv Ofcr, Ret'd 26 Yrs 3 Months Ser; pa/Pastor: Asbury U Meth Ch, Williams Chapel UMC, St Mark UMC; Other Profl Positions incl: Tchr, Hd Coach, Ath Dir, Asst Prin, Tchr Rep, Tax Conslt; Natch Area Min Alliance; U Mins for Higher Ed, NWn St Univ, Natch; Mem Alexandria Dist U Meth Ch, La Conf; cp/Am Legion; Grand Inspectus Gen 33° & Last Deg Ancient Accepted Scottish Rite Masonry, Prince Hall Affil; Ishmael Temple #154, Prince Hall Shriners; Pride of Baton Rouge Royal Arch Masons #202; r/U Meth; hon/Pub'd Author; Hon Grad (MS) So Univ; Prince Hall Shriner of Yr 1972.

WASHINGTON, WILLIAM ELBERT oc/Attorney at Law; b/Nov 5, 1925; h/9801 S Parnell Ave, Chicago, IL 60628; ba/Chgo; m/Vercye; c/Willinda K, Verrita L; p/W M Washington, Corinth; Beatrice Olive Washington (dec); ed/JD DePaul Univ Law Sch 1952; mil/USN WWII; pa/Cook Co Bar Assn; Chgo Bar Assn; Am Trial Lwyrs Assn; Am Judic Soc; cp/NAACP; Urban Leag; 17th Ward Dem Org; r/Prot; hon/Num Dist'd Ser & Hon Awds.

WATERS, JOHN W oc/University Professor; b/Feb 5, 1936; h/704 Park Dr NE, Atlanta, GA 30306; ba/Atlanta; p/Henry and Mary A Randall Waters; ed/BA Fisk Univ 1957; STB cum laude 1967, PhD 1970 Boston Univ; mil/AUS 1960-63; pa/Univ Detroit: Assoc Prof 1970-76, Dir Ctr for Black Studies 1971-75; Assoc Prof Old Testament Interdenom Theol Ctr, Atlanta Univ 1976-; Adj Prof Hebrew Life & Cult Sem Without Walls, Shaw Univ 1975; Instr: Sch Theol Boston Univ 1969-70, Physics & Basic Sci L J Price HS, Atlanta 1963-64; Admr Army Ed Ctr, Ulm, W Germany 1960-63; Other Former Positions; AAUP; Am Humanist Assn; Am Acad Rel; Soc Biblical Lit; cp/Bd Dirs SE Mich Reg Ethnic Heritage Studies Ctr; Black-Polish Conf Gtr Detroit; r/Am Bapt; hon/Rockefeller Doct F'ship in Rel; Nat F'ship Fund Fellow; Frank D Howard F'ship, Boston Univ; Dist'd Lectr, Inst for Christian Thought, John Courtney Murray Ctr, Port Huron, Mich; Others.

WATERS, RAYMOND WOOLSEY oc/Company Executive; Criminologist; b/Sept 8, 1924; h/20 Carmel Ave, Salinas, CA 93901; m/Rowena Kimzey-Cohan; p/Robert Wesley Waters Sr; Myrtle Dora Woolsey Prickett; ed/BS Univ Wis; LLB Chgo Law Sch; MS Geo Wash Univ; Command & Gen Staff Col; mil/USAAC 1940-45; Police 1945-50; Mil Police Corp 1950-57; pa/Criminologist 1958-73; Exec VP: Oceanview Cablevision 1973-77, Hudson-Cohan Pub'g & Communs Co 1973-; Pres: KTMR Enterprises Inc, Foun for Human Achmt 1976-; Reg'd Polled Hereford Breeder & Land Developer 1977-; cp/Hot Springs CC (Hot Sprgs, Ark); Carmel Val Racquet Clb (Carmel Val, Cal); Kiwanis; Elk Lodge; hon/Silver Star; Bronze Star; Dist'd Flying Cross w Cluster; Air Medal w 16 Clusters; Purple Heart; Croix de Gurre w Palm; Pilots Badge; Combat Infantryman's Badge; Army Commend Medal; Pub'd Author.

WATERS, ROWENA JOYCE KIMZEY-COHAN oc/Television/Cable Television

Executive; Land Developer; b/Dec 15, 1931; h/20 Carmel Ave, Salinas, CA 93901; m/Raymond W; p/Joseph Wood and Jalina Jane Thomas Kimzey; ed/Henderson St Univ 1948; pa/Adm Asst to Pres Salinas Broadcasting Corp & Successor Corp, Ctl Cal Communs Corp, Salinas 1951-71, Dir & Secy-Treas 1951-71; Pres: Ocean View Cablevision Inc, Seaside (Cal) 1970-77, Hudson-Cohan Pub'g & Communs Co (Salinas) 1970-; VP KTMR Enterprises Inc, Magnet Cove (Ark) 1978-; cp/Former Treas Salinas Val Meml Hosp Aux; Dir Ark Easter Seal Soc; Trustee York Sch, Monterey, Cal; Carmel Val Racquet Clb; Hot Springs CC (Hot Sprgs, Ark); Life Mem Monterey Hist Soc; Life Mem Intl New Thought Alliance; hon/Spec Citizens Awd, Marina, Cal; Coveted Butterfly Awd, Pacific Grove, Cal.

WATKINS, ALBERT BURROW JR oc/Retired Public School Educator; b/Jan 6, 1916; h/2504 Central Dr, Big Spring, TX 79720; m/Susie Kathryn Gullion; c/Albert B III, James Paul (dec), Edward Philip; p/Albert Burrow and Ella Kathleen Halbert Watkins

(dec); ed/BS; BBA; MEd; mil/AUS 1941-45; pa/Pres Grand Prairie Local Unit TSTA 1952-53; Phi Delta Kappa 1953; cp/Fin Com Big Spring Local "Texans for Tower"; Editor Newslttr of Geneal Soc Big Spring; VP Ed Criddle Nat Hon Hist Soc; NTSU Jr Acad Sci; r/14th & Main St Ch of Christ.

WATSON, JERRY D oc/Minister; b/Jan 11, 1935; h/4415 Damsen Ln, Visalia, CA 93277; ba/Visalia; m/Betty L; c/Kathy Ann, Gary Don; p/John W Watson (dec); Vera M Watson, Sulphur, OK; ed/Pacific Bible Col; Cal Christian Col; pa/Ordained to Min 1960; Pastor: Neighborhood Free Will Bapt (FWB) Ch, Goshen, Cal 1961-64; Calwa Ch, Fresno, Cal 1965-66, Goshen Ch, Visalia 1966-74, 1st Ch 1974-; Moderator Ctr Assn 1964-65; Exec Bd 1963-74; Mission Bd 1970-74; Exec Bd So Assn 1974-75; cp/Former Activs Little Leag; Former Dir Yth Camp Activs; r/Free Will Bapt; hon/W/W in Rel; Personalities W&MW; Pubs.

WAUNEKA, ANNIE DODGE oc/Navajo Tribal Councilwoman; b/Apr 10, 1910; h/PO Box 629, Ganado, AZ 86505; ba/Window Rock, AZ; m/George; c/Georgiann Pluumer, Irma Bluehouse, Laurcita Cohoe, Franklin, Sally, Henry, (Adopted Son) Lawrence C Huerta; p/Henry Chee Dodge; pa/Navajo Tribal Coun-wom, Dist #17, Klagetoh Precnt (1st Wom Elected to Coun 1951); Chm Navajo Tribal Coun's Hlth Com 1951-63; US Surg Gen's Adv Com on Indian Hlth 1956-62; CoChm Hlth Com, Navajo Tribal Coun 1968-78; Appt'd "Hlth Envoy" for Navajo People 1973; Mem Adv Com Navajo Tribal Coun; Navajo Area Indian Hlth Bd; cp/Navajo Nation Sch Bd Assn; Navajo Hlth Auth's Bd Commrs; Navajo Tribal Utility Auth; Wide Ruins/Klagetoh Clin Com; Chm "Sch for Me" Inc Bd Dirs; Mem Wide Ruins/Klagetoh Grazing Com; Local Hlth Progs on Hlth Probs & Progs; Lectr; Proj Concern (Intl); Nat & Wn TBC Assn; Am Public Hlth Assn; GSA; NM Cancer Control; Nat Ctr for Hlth Ed; Proj Hope; Bd Mem Nat Indian Hlth Bd; Pres' Comm on Intl Wom's Yr 1975-76; r/Cath; hon/Recog of Support & Inspiration for Navajo Profls; Dine Bii Profl Assn; Awd in Recog of Cont'g Humanitian Ser for Betterment of Life for Native Ams, Nat Assn for Human Devel; Silver Cup Awd. TB

Control; Awd, Am Hosp Assn (Chgo); Wom of Yr Awd for Work in Ed 1976; Outstg Ldrship, Support & Dedication Across the Country, Nat Commun Hlth Reps; Manuelito Begay Dist'd Hlth Ser Awd, Navajo Nation Hlth Assn; Num Other Awds & Hons.

WEATHERS, LENA JANE oc/Professional Counselor; b/Sept 5, 1930; h/737 N 40th St, E St Louis, IL 62205; ba/E St Louis; m/Henri H; c/Shelley Bredette, Alicia Montrece, Lena Janene, Henri IV, Edward Eugene, Fre; p/Edward Knight, St Paul, MN; Ethel Cushman, E St Louis; ed/BA Fisk Univ; BS SIU; PhD Cand St Louis Univ; pa/Dir Profl Cnslg Sers; cp/Campaign Mgr, St Rep W Young; r/CME; hon/Outstg Commun Ldr, Mayor of City 1969; Outstg Black Ldr, Urban Leag; Outstg Mother 1977.

WEATON, GEORGE FREDERIC oc/Mining Engineer; Researcher; Teacher; b/Aug 19, 1911; h/3117 Edgewood Ave S, Minneapolis, MN 55426; ba/Mpls; m/Wylea S (dec); c/Brenda Louis Whittaker, Janet Martha Johnson; p/George Frederic Weaton Sr (dec); Gertrude Crowell (dec); ed/BS; Engr of Mines; mil/USN 1943-53, Lt; pa/Tchr Univ Minn; Reg'd Profl Engr: Colo, Mo, Minn; Soc Mining Engrs of AIME; cp/Taxpayers Assn; Ariz Small Mine Opers; cp/Taxpayers Assn; r/St George's Epis: Lay Rdr, Vestry; hon/Public Ser & Good Citizenship Awd, Minn Taconite Comm; Ser & Achmt Awd, Minn Sect AIME; Mbrship Awd, Soc Mining Engrs.

WEATHON, FERDINAND FRANK oc/Archivist; Professor; Researcher; b/May 6, 1959; h/894 S Peabody Ln, Keacuck, IA 52110; m/Isabella Georgette Tarantella; c/Martha, George, Roger, Thomas, James, Benjamin; p/Boris Stephen and Natasha Carmichael Weathon; ed/BS, magna cum laude, Princeton Univ; mil/USN 1943-63, Ret'd Major; pa/Archivist, Keacuck Public Library, 1971-; Visiting Asst Prof,Univ Iowa; Researcher; ALA; ILA; Keacuck Assn of Univ Profs; Interfaith Comm against Blasphemy; Soc of Ednl Res; AAUP; cp/SAR; Keacuck Literacy Comm; Taxpayers Assn of Keacuck; C of C; r/St Peter's Epis: Lay Rdr; hon/Public Ser & Good Citizenship Awds, Outstg Ldr in Keacuck, Keacuck Literacy Assn; Num Biogl Listings.

WEAVER, ELVIN PAUL oc/Pastor; b/Oct 13, 1912; h/70673 Co Rd 11, R 1, Nappanee, IN 46550; ba/Same; m/Eleanor Carter; c/Nelda W Sollenberger, Bruce H, (Stepsons:) E James Carter, David L Carter, Leonard J Carter; p/M J and Fanny Ritchey Weaver (dec); ed/AB Elizabethtown Col; BD

Bethany Sem; pa/Gen Bd Ch of the Brethren 1951-57, 72-78; Ind Coun Chs: Bd Dirs 1948-78, Leg Counsel 1948-; Nat Coun Chs, Assembly Detroit & Dallas; Missionary Nigeria 1939-44; cp/Chm Ind IMPACT; r/Ch of Brethren: Min 1932-.

WEAVER, RICHARD DONALD oc/Clergyman, Educator; b/Mar 25, 1926; h/654 E Fourth St, Hobart, IN 46342; ba/Hobart; p/Robert Raymond Weaver (dec); Ada Viola Holz Weaver, Hobart; ed/BS St Louis Univ 1949; MDiv Garrett Theol Sem 1952; MA Scarrett Col 1979; Addit Studies; mil/AUS 1944-46. ETO, 99th Inf Div;

pa/Min: 1st U Meth Ch, Hobart 1973-, Ind Harbor U Meth Ch, E Chicago (Ind) 1958-73, Centenary Meth Ch, Veedersburg (Ind) 1953-58, Lizton & Salem Meth Chs, Lizton (Ind) & Boone Co (Ind) 1951-53; Lectr Theol Calumet Col, Hammond, Ind 1967-; AAUP; Am Soc Ch Hist; Assn for Sociol of Rel; Hymn Soc Am; Insts Rel & Hlth; Rel Ed Assn US & Canada; Rel Res Assn; Soc for Sci Study of Rel; cp/Adv Coun Consumer's Credit Cnslg NW Ind, John Wesley Corp; Bd Dirs: Lake Area U Way, Referral & Emer Ser, Ind U Meth Chd's Home Inc; r/U Meth: Ordained 1952; hon/Theol Prize, Garrett Theol Sem; Commun Ldrship Awd, Twin City Commun Sers.

WEAVER, RITA MARGARET oc/Reporter; b/Oct 28, 1925; h/330 E 52nd St, New York, NY 10022; m/Robert A (dec); c/Richard L N, Michael Cameron; p/(dec); ed/BA; Grad Work Lady Margaret Hall, Oxford (England); pa/Nat Soc Arts & Lttrs, Ways & Means Chm on Nat Bd 1976-78; Empire St Chapt NSAL: Pres 1978-80, 2/VP 1976-78, Rec'g Secy 1974-78, Chm Public Relats & Publicity, Career Awds Dinner Chm; Eleanor Gay Lee Gallery Foun: Ways & Means CoChm 1977, Mbrship Chm 1978; r/Christ Ch (Meth), NY; hon/Rec'd Medal for Classical Piano Competition; Rec'd St-Wide Spch Awd.

WEBB, MICHAEL RICHARD oc/Accounting Manager; Financial Reporting; b/Jan 10, 1949; h/7514 Adams, Darien, IL 60559; ba/Chicago, IL; m/Diane G; b/Natalie Kay; p/B Richard and Alice Mary Peterson Webb, American Fork, UT; ed/BS, BA Brigham Yg Univ; mil/USAR Capt; pa/Am Inst CPAs; Ill CPA Soc; cp/Var Activs Local Polits; r/LDS; hon/Phi Kappa Phi; Beta Gamma Sigma; Grad Cum Laude; Kemper Scholar.

WEBB, ROZANA oc/Poet; Writer; Teacher; Lecturer; b/Mar 31, 1908; h/PO Box 467, Visalia, CA 93279; m/Ernest (dec); c/1 Daugh; p/William Donaldson and Aubrey Leota Amelia Hill Sprigg; ed/Pvt Studies; pa/Instr Creative Writing; Orgr Poetry Wkshops; Free-lance Artist, Painting in Oil, Mixed Media & Black & White; Has done Covers for Var Lit Mags; Nat Writers; Centro Studi E Scambi Internazionali; IPA; Cal Chapparral Poets; San Joaquin Val Authors & Artists; cp/Tulare Co Hist Soc; Tulare Co Cotton Wives; Sequoia Geneal Soc; OES; Wom's Clb; hon/Silver Trophy, S & W; Golden Pegasus, Cal Chapparral Poets; Author 6 Poetry Books incl'g: The 13th Man, The Moonsoon Breeds, Eternal the Flow, The Coffee Break, The Way, The Ghost Walkers; Contbr 200+ Poems to Lit Mags; Book of Honor; Notable Ams.

WEBER, FRANK E oc/Periodontist; b/Aug 30, 1932; ba/NW Med Ctr, 3500 Lafayette Rd, Indianapolis, IN 46222; c/Gregory K, Frank K II; p/Frank H Weber (dec); Elizabeth A Weber; ed/BA 1954, DDM 1962 Univ Louisville; Masters Univ Ky 1955; mil/Grad USAF Pilot Tng (Jet) 1956; Instr Pilot USAF 1956-58; pa/Pvt Pract Periodontics & Gen Dentistry 1964-; Grad Asst Periodontics Ind Univ Sch Dentistry 1962-64; Res S'ship US Public Hlth & Damon Runyon Cancer Res Grants 1959-62; Life Ins Underwriter 1958-60; Am & Ind Dental Assns; Indpls Dist Dental Soc; Fellow Royal Soc Hlth 1972; Acad Gen Dentistry; Am Endodontic

Soc; IPA; Nat Fdn Indep Bus; Life Mem: Sigma Phi Epsilon, Delta Sigma Delta; cp/Am Legion; Nat Reg; Worthy Master (Former), Demolay; hon/Phi Kappa Phi; Omicron Kappa Upsilon; Phi Delta; Beta Delta; Omicron Delta Kappa; Awd of Merit, Acad Oral Med; 3rd Awd, Student Clinicians of Am Dental Assn; Res S'ship, Univ L'ville; Profl Pubs; Biogl Listings.

WEBER, IRWIN JACK oc/Systems Analyst; Management Consultant; b/Mar 14, 1933; h/3402 Gage Pl, San Diego, CA 92106; ba/Same; m/Sheila K; c/Michele J, Robert L; ed/BEE 1954, MEE 1956 Polytech Inst Bklyn; MBA Univ Santa Clara 1965; PhD US Int Univ 1978; pa/Sr Mem IEEE; AIEE; hon/Navy Commend for Satellite Commun Experimts.

WEBER, SHEILA K oc/Library Administrator; h/3402 Gage Pl, San Diego, CA 92106; ba/Bakersfield, CA; m/Irwin J; c/Michele, Robert; ed/BS; MLS; PhD; pa/Asst Libn for Spec Projs Cal St Col; Tchr Chd's Lit & Dramatic Play, Child Devel N Orange Col, Fullerton 1974-; Tchr Chd's Lit Santa Ana Col, Santa Ana 1975-78; Other Former Tchg Positions; Lib Conslt Long Beach Unified Sch Dist, Long Bch 1972-74; Other Profl Positions; Am & Cal Lib Assns; Cal Assn Sch Libns; NEA; Cal Tchrs Assn; hon/Selected as 1 of 12 People in US to Participate in Futuristic Chd's Lib at NY World's Fair 1964 (by Am Lib Assn); DIB; W/W: Lib Ser, Am Wom.

WEBSTER, BURNICE HOYLE oc/-Thoracologist & Physician; b/Mar 3, 1910; h/2325 Volley Brook Rd, Nashville, TN 37215; ba/N'ville; m/Georgia Fogleman; c/Brenda Kathryn Hamilton (Mrs James A III), Phillip Hoyle, Adrienne Elise; p/Thomas J and Martha Ann Melton Webster (dec); ed/BA magna cum laude, MD Vanderbilt Univ; PhD Fla Res Inst; DSC, STD, BD; Hon Degs: DLitt, DHL, LLD, DD, DCE; mil/Dir USPHS; Chm: Med Selective Ser for Tenn, Nat Security Agy for Tenn; Ofcrs' Resv Assn; pa/Specializing in Internal Med & Thoracology; Res in Diseases of Chest, Mutations Following Multiple Animal Passages, & Parasitic Diseases; 50+ Papers Pub'd in Sci Jours; Num Appearances on Progs, Nat & Intl; Nat Acad of Med; Tenn St Med Assn; Am Thoracic Soc; Tenn Lung Assn; N'ville Soc of Internal Med; cp/Master Mason, 32° Scottish Rite Mason, Royal Arch Mason, Royal & Select Mason; Order of Elks; Order of Immaculate; K of Hon; Prior to the Priory of Franklin of Royal Yugoslavian Hospitaller Order of St John of Jerusalem; Soc of SAR; Andrew Jackson Tenn Chapt, Nat Chapt, Pres, Nat Trustee; Dep Pres Gen, Nat Soc of Sons of Colonial Wars; Cmdr-in-Chief, Sons of Conf Vets (2 Terms); Cmdr Gen John Hunt Morgan Chapt, Order of Stars & Bars; Pres & Chm Bd of Regents, Holy Trinity Col; r/So Epis Ch: Prelate; hon/F'ships: Am Col of Chest Phys, Am Col of Angiol, Am Gerontol Soc, Am Geriatric Soc, Royal Soc Hlth; Phi Beta Kappa; Alpha Omega Alpha; Phi Beta Pi; Silver Stethoscope Awd; Dist'd Phys & Thoracologist Awd; Wisdom Awd of Hon; Lib of Bicent Awd; So Heritage Awd; J Edgar Hoover Awd; Colonels of Y, Ala & Ga; Num Biogl Listings.

WEBSTER, ERNEST WESLEY oc/Concert Accordionist; Music Teacher; Conductor; Composer; b/Oct 30, 1932; ba/Webster Sch of Music, 1232 SW 31 Ave, Fort Lauderdale, FL 33312; m/Arlene Waite; c/Elizabeth Anne, Victoria Christina; p/Melvin Harold and Nora Mae Webster, New Johnsonville, TN; ed/NWn Sch; Univ Ariz; Moody Bible Inst; pa/Accordionist: Radio Stas KPHO & KOOL (Phoenix, Arix) 1948, 49, Paul Brown Min of the Air Prog & Phoenix Yth for Christ Broadcasts (KPHO) 1949-51; Sacred Music Concerts, Chicago, Ill 1951-53; Webster Sch of Music: Owner, Dir 1959-; Mem Music Fac Broward Commun Col 1974-; Mem Pt-time Music Fac Barry Col, Miami, Fla 1976-; Pt-time Music Fac Mem Fla Atl Univ 1976-; Starred in Ednl Films Prod'd by Instrnl TV Sta (Ft Lauderdale), Conducting Webster Accordion Symphonette; Other Film

Appearances; Presenter Accordion Wkshops: Accordion Tchrs' Guild Intl, Music Tchrs' Nat Assn, Broward Co Music Tchrs' Assn; Judge ATG US Accordion Champ'ship Contest Chgo 1969, St Louis (Mo) 1973; Judge Canadian Nat Accordion Champ'ship Contest, Toronto (Canada) 1970; 1st Nat Chm MTNA Accordion Subject Area Sect 1972-75; Accordion Tchrs' Guild Intl: Mem, 1/VP 1973-75; Fla St Music Tchrs' Assn: Mem, Pres Dist 6 1972-74; Broward Co Music Tchrs' Assn: Mem, Pres 1967-69; NFMC; Compositions incl: "Fugue in G" (Accordion Trio) 1975, "In The Meadow Green" (Voice & Piano) 1970, "Isle of Venice" & "Sleep Walkers" (Solo Accordion) 1968, Others; Recordings incl "Webster Accordion Symphonette", Prod'd by Gulfstream Records (Ernest Webster, Conductor); Other Profl Activs; hon/Winner Fla St Most Outstg Perf'g Accordion Orch (Conductor Webster Accordion Symphonette), 1963-71; Pubs; Biogl Listings.

WEDDING, ERLING SOLHEIM oc/Physician; Pathologist; b/May 29, 1908; h/203 Hudson Dr, Sault Ste Marie, MI 49783; ba/same; m/Gertrude M; c/William R, Dorothy Ann Glover; p/R H and Synnove Wedding (dec); ed/BA Univ Utah 1932; MD Louisville Med Sch 1940; mil/Capt MC Bd of Hlth Lab; pa/Pathologist & Dir Clin Labs War Meml Hosp, Sault Ste Marie 1962-70; Mem Dept Pathol & Nuclear Med Plummer Meml Public Hosp, Sault Ste Marie, Ontario,

Canada 1969; Conslt to 507th USAF Hosp, Kincheloe Air Base (Mich) 1962-; Clin Asst Prof Pathol St Univ NY, Kings Co Hosp, Brooklyn 1956-61; Clin Asst Internal Med SUNY, Kings Co Hosp 1948-55; Other Former Positions; AMA; Diplomate Panam Med Assn, Sect Pathol; Fellow: Am Col Pathologists, Am Col Clin Pathologists; Nat Assn Med Examrs; Soc Nuclear Med; Am Acad Forensic Scis; US Canadian Div Intl Acad Pathol; Am Col Nuclear Physicians; Other Profl Assns; Mem Com on Establishmt of St-wide Med Examr Sys for St of Mich 1968-71; Other Profl Activs; r/LDS; hon/Commend, US Surg Gen for Pub; Exhibits, Papers Pub'd.

WEEDON, WILLIAM STONE oc/University Professor; b/Jul 5, 1908; h/Box 3492, University Sta, Charlottesville, VA 22903; ba/C'ville; m/Elizabeth Bayard; c/Ellen Bayard (dec), Mary W Pollock, Elizabeth Bayard, Jennifer W Phillips; p/William S and Mary C Weedon (dec); ed/BS 1929; MS 1931; MA 1933; PhD 1936; MA 1962; mil/USN 1942-46 & 1950-52, Ret'd Rank of Capt 1968; pa/Univ Va: Asst in Math, Instr in Phil to Prof & Chm of Corcoran Dept of Philosophy, Resigned to Accept William Griffin Professor of Phil (Wesleyan Univ) 1968, Univ Prof of Phil 1963, Prof Emeritus 1979-; Vis'g Prof, Wesleyan Univ (Austin, Tex); Exec Com, Am Phil Soc; Pres, So Soc Phil & Psychol; Pres, Va Phil Assn; Pres, Va Humanities Conf; Coun Mem, Metaphysical Soc of Am; Chm of Bd, Virginia Qtrly Review; Mem Var Edit Bds; Others; cp/Bd Mem, C'ville-Albemarle SPCA; Chm of Bd, Va Metalcrafters; Chm of Bd, Sprigg Lane Investment Corp; Pres, Ellen Bayard Weedon Foun; Others; r/Epis; hon/Phi Beta Kappa; Omicron Delta Kappa; Raven Awd, Raven Soc; Dist'd Prof Awd; Algernon Sydney Sullivan Awd; Others.

WEHRER, CHARLES S oc/Educator;

Management Training Consultant; b/Jul 13, 1914; h/2932 S 93rd Plaza, Omaha, NE; ba/Same; p/Charles C and Ella A Siecke Wehrer (dec); ed/BA; MA; LHD; PhD Cand; mil/USAF 1941-45; Pvt to Maj; Bronze Star; Soldiers Medal; 3 Battle Stars; Pres Unit Cit; Num Commends; pa/Life Mem NEA; AAUP; NASA; Phi Delta Kappa; Past Pres Sigma Tau Delta; Advr Delta Sigma; IPA; Past Advr TEPS Ed Com; Assn Higher Ed; NSSE; Others; cp/Bd Mem Num Groups incl'g: YMCA; Scouts; Camp Fire Orgs, Brownies, Bluebirds, Civic Improvemt Groups; Commun Little Theatre; Authors Soc; Past Pres Kiwanis Clb; Lions Clb; Others; r/Prot: Lay Min, SS Sch & Bible Sch Instr, Ch Bd; hon/Most Popular Tchr; Most Popular & Respected Prof; Outstg Sch Supt Awd, Neb; Commun Awds for Yth Efforts; Neb W/W Bicent; Nat Am Legion Aux Awd for Popular Yth Radio-TV Progs; PTA Awds; Civic-Commun Ldrship Awds; Biogl Listings; Others.

WEI, DIANA YUN-DEE oc/Professor; b/Jun 8, 1930; h/1152 Janaf Pl, Norfolk, VA 23502; ba/Norfolk; m/Benjamin Min; c/Victor Mark; p/Fan Sou-Kang and Tong Chi-Ying, Taipei, Taiwan; ed/BS Taiwan Normal Univ; MS Univ Neb; PhD McGill Univ; pa/Prof Math Norfolk St Col; Am Math Soc; Canadian Math Cong; r/Prot; hon/Nat Res Coun Canada F'ship; Grantee; Profl Pubs; Num Biogl Listings.

WEIDEMANN, ANTON FREDRICK oc/Farm Manager; Poet; b/Mar 26, 1917; h/Star Rt, Box 407, Pala, CA 92059; ba/Same; m/Thelma Louise; c/Jeanne Rollins, Ronald Edward; p/Jacob and Harriett Byng Weidemann (dec); pa/Pub'd 4 Books Poetry: *Roses And Thorns* 1976, *Seasons And Seasoning* 1974, *Through A Poet's Window* 1974, *Golden Years of Youth* 1973; Nat Poetry Soc; cp/Past Mem Panma Val Commun Assn; C of C; IPA; IBA; U Amateur Press; r/Luth; hon/Walter Perkins, Bicent Trophy; 2 Awds, Clover Intl Poetry Competition; Apprec Awd, Quid Nunc; Masters of Mod Poetry Awd; Centro Studi E Scambi Internazionali (Rome, Italy); Others.

WELCH, JOHN WILEY oc/Businessman; Building Executive; b/Jun 29, 1928; h/713 Welshire Dr, La Crescent, MN 55947; ba/La Crescent; m/Jann Deen; c/Kendra Deen, Brent John, James Allen; p/Ralph O Welch (dec); Dorothy Abbott, La Crescent; ed/BS Univ Wis 1955; Arch Drafting: WWTI 1965, Weaver Sch Realty 1966; pa/Pres: CBS Homes Inc (La Crescent), Crescent Bldg Prods (La Crescent), J F Enterprises; Owner: Brookhill Apts, Brookhill Homes, NRG Homes; Nat Assn Home Bldrs; Nat Assn Home Mfrs; NW Lumberman's Assn; Wood Structural & Component Assn; Houston Co Home Bldrs: Former Mem, Secy, Bd Dirs, Jt Com Mem; La Crosse Area Home Bldrs Assn: Mem, Co-Drafted By-laws & Constitution 1972, Publicity Chm 1972, Entertainmt Chm 1973-74, Auction & Rummage Com 1976, Leg Chm 1976, Assoc of Yr 1976, Spike Mem 1977; cp/La Crescent Am Legion Post 595; Former Mem La Crescent City Rec Bd Dirs; Current Mem La Crescent Apple Fest Bd; La Crescent C of C: Past Pres, Past Mem Bd Dirs; Var Mason Activs; Del Repub St, Dist & Co Convs; Former Chm La Crosse Bus & Profl Couples Clb; Others; r/Bethany Evang Ch: Chm Planning & Expansion Com, Chapel Com Conslt for Evang Camp Grounds, Adult SS Substitute; Former Mem U Meth Ch La

Crescent; hon/Hon Skipper Awd, Minneapolis Aquatennial; Dir's Awd, Mpls Aquatennial (as Pres of La Crescent Apple Fest); Recipient & Finalist Minn Small Bus of Yr Awd, Small Bus Assn; Biogl Listings.

WELCH, RONALD MAURICE oc/- Atmospheric Researcher; b/Dec 30, 1943; h/-77 Am Sonnigen Hang, 65 Mainz, Marien-born 32, West Germany; ba/W Germany; m/Tatyana E Dmitrieva; p/Graydon Lawrence and Margaret Ann Welch, Los Lunas, NM; ed/MA 1967; PhD (Physics) 1971; PhD (Meteorol) 1976; pa/Atmospheric Res Institut fur Meteorologie, Univ Manz; Atmospheric Res Colo St Univ (Currently on leave of absence), Ft Collins, Colo; AAAS; Sigma Xi; NY Acad Sci; Am Phy Soc; Am Meteorol Soc; Am Geophys Soc; Coun of Envir Resources Ctr; hon/Notable Ams Bicent Era; W/W in W; Am Men & Wom Sci; DIB; Commun Ldrs & Noteworthy Ams; Men Achmt; Phi Beta Kappa.

WELLS, HAROLD W oc/Farmer; Fuel Distributor; b/Dec 12, 1937; h/Box 705, McGehee, AR 71654; ba/Same; m/Mary Chatham; c/Timothy F, Terry W, Tony F; p/Otho F Wells (dec); Elsie Wells, Dumas, AR; pa/Secy-Treas Desha Co Farm Bur; Pres Ark Agri Movemt Assn; cp/Var Activs St & Nat Elections; r/Bapt.

WELLS, JERRY LEE oc/Horse Rancher; b/Nov 9, 1940; h/Rt 2, Box 43, Purcell, OK 73080; ba/Same; m/Betty; c/Marty, Nancy; p/L V Wells, Oklahoma City, OK; Leona Wells, Sulphur, OK; pa/Profl Horse Trainer; r/Bapt; hon/Made 1st Supreme Champ of AQHA; Won 7 World Champ Awds.

WELLS, ROSEMARY S oc/Assistant Professor; b/Dec 12, 1930; h/1219 Scott, Winnetka, IL 60093; ba/Chicago, IL; m/Warren Wells; c/Wendy Rose, Jeffrey Joe, Jerrold Patrick; p/Joe Siplon (dec); Emma Wogsland Siplon, Libertyville, IL; ed/BA

1951; MA 1953; PhD 1973; pa/Author: 2 Eng Work Texts, 2 Prog'g Hlth Ed Books, Articles to Profl Jours; cp/Gilbert & Sullivan Operetta Group: Asst Music Dir, Past Pres; Sect Ldr of 2nd Violins, Evanston Symph Orch; r/Meth; hon/World W/W Wom; DIB; W/W Am Wom; 2000 Wom Achmt; Other Listings.

WENDELBURG, NORMA RUTH oc/Musician; b/Mar 26, 1918; h/Rt No 2, Stafford, KS 67578; ba/Haviland, KS; p/Henry and Anna Moeckel Wendelburg (dec); ed/BMus Bethany Col; MMus Univ Mich; MMus, PhD Eastman Sch Music; pa/Composer Num Works (Perf'd & Pub'd)

Piano Recitals; Col & Univ Tchr Var Sts: Ks, Tex, Ia, Neb; Fdr & Orgr Annual Music Fest (Abilene, Tex); Promoter & Performer New Music; r/Prot: Ch Sch Tchr; hon/F'ship, Composers' Conf (Middlebury, Vt); Composition S'ship, Berkshire Ctr (Lenox, Mass); Fulbright Awd; Other F'ships; "Meet the Composer" Awd; Biogl Listings.

WENDT, L BIRDELL ELIASON oc/Art-ist; Designer; b/Mar 17; h/12 N Owen St, Mt Prospect, IL 60056; ba/Mt Prospect; m/Howard A; c/Nancy W Berry, Mary W Tagge, Charmaine (dec); p/Herman and Stella Berenice Fenney Eliason (dec); ed/Budget Beauty Sch; Advt'g Art Sch; Pvt Studies; mil/Oreg Wom's Ambulance Corps; pa/Art Dir Americana Hlth Care Ctr 1973-76; Seascape Mural 1976; Indian Mural 1976; Ill Chd's Book; Art Conslt Photog Studio, Portland, Oreg; Art Tchr Zion Luth Sch; Art Dir Yrbook; Designed & Constructed 4-ft Scale Model Luth HS; cp/Res for Hist of Mtly Ill 1971; Portrait for Mt Prospect Hist Soc 1976; Channel 11 Auction (Public TV) 7 Yrs; r/Luth; Designed Banners, Bultns, Plaques, Booklets for Var Luth Chs; hon/Commun Ser Awds; $100 Bicent Awd for Garage Door; Bicent Awd for Gay '90's Bathing Suit; Gold Medal Rel Painting, Pencil Sketch; 2nd Pl St Oreg; Grand Prize Portland; Var Awds for Painting & Piano.

WENDTLAND, WILLIAM W oc/Band Director, Educator; b/May 18, 1918; h/1816 Frost, Rosenberg, TX 77471; ba/Sealy, TX; m/Polly Ann; c/Walt, Lisa, Steve; p/William W and Polly Ann Wendtland, Rosenberg; ed/BA; BME; MA; MusD; mil/USAF WWII, Inf; pa/Sealy HS: Dir Bands, Supt Music; TBA; TMEA; TSTA; NEA; CBDNA; NJE; ASBDA; NBA; Phi Beta Mu; cp/Tex St Guard; Shrine Clb; Repub Party; r/Meth; hon/Outstg US Edr; Bandmaster of Yr 1975; W/W: Music, S&SW; Notable Ams; Commun Ldrs; Personalities of S; Book of Honor; Men Achmt; Intl W/W Intells.

WERLIN, ROSELLA HARWOOD oc/- Writer; Teacher; Lecturer; Travel Counselor; b/Sept 23, 1912; h/2340 Underwood Blvd, Houston, TX 77025; m/Joseph Sidney; c/2 Sons, 1 Daugh; ed/BS Univ Houston; MS; pa/Journalist: San Antonio, Galvaston News, Chgo Sun Times; Feature Articles Houston Post 1971-72; Author Brochure on Hist of Univ Tex Med Sch; Contbr: *Ency Britannica, Christian Sci Monitor, NY Times, Dallas News, Life, Time, Am Mag, Milwaukee Jour,*

Houston Chronicle, Houston Post; Theta Sigma Phi; Tex Wom's Press; Houston Press Assn Tchrs; Houston Fashion Group; cp/Brandeis Univ Hadassah; Galveston Hist Soc; Houston Hist Soc; Eng Spkg Union; Friends Rice Univ; Alumni Univ Houston; hon/US Treasury Dept Awd, War Savings Comm; Kappa Alpha Mu, Houston Photog Soc Awd; Tchg Awd Excell, Tex Press Assn; Houston Grit Iron Awd, IPA; W/W in Am.

WERNER, VICTOR EMILE oc/Manage-ment Consultant; Memory Expert; Author; Lecturer; b/Sept 22, 1894; h/7418 Holly Ave, Takoma Park, MD 20012; ba/Same; m/Geraldine Thompson; p/Charles A and Cathrine Marie Frisk Werner (dec); ed/Mil Dipls; AA 1958, BBA 1963 Geo Wash Univ;

mil/AUS Ordnance, w Am Exped Forces & Army of Occup 1917-19; pa/Lectr & Instr Sci of Mnemonics 1956-; Army Ofc Chief of Staff, Pentagon; Army Fin Ofc; Picatinny Arsenal; Noval Dental Ofc Sch; Internal Revenue Ser; Cath Univ; Am Univ; Geo Wash Univ; Gallaudet Col for Deaf; Col Univ Coll; Adult Ed Prog, Arlington, Va; TV & Radio; Num Former Positions; Profl Assns; cp/VFW; Life Mem US, Cmdr Quentin Roosevelt Post 10, Assoc Ed Kings Co Bltn, Aide-de-Camp to Sev Cmdrs-in-Chief; Mason; Cand Coun-man, Takoma Park; r/Prot; hon/Army Awds: Patriotic Civilian Ser, Cert of Achmt, Occup Medal, Silver Medal, Order of Leopold II of Belgium, Victory Medal; Others.

WEST, ANN oc/Physician; b/Nov 7, 1901; h/6620 Yosemite Ln, Dallas, TX 75214; ba/Dallas; p/William Jackson and Iona Carter West (dec); ed/MD Baylor Med Col 1930; Intern Baylor Hosp, Dallas 1930-31; pa/Gen Pract: Lynn Co (Tex) 1932-36, Dallas 1936-;

Mem Staff Baylor, Parkland Hosps; Clin Asst, Prof Internal Med SWn Med Sch Univ Tex-Dallas; cp/Red Cross; Repub; Others; r/Bapt; hon/Fellow IBA; Intl W/W Commun Ser; 2000 Wom Achmt; DIB; World W/W Wom; W/W Tex; Notable Ams Bicent Era; Commun Ldrs & Noteworthy Ams; Others.

WEST, DANIEL JONES JR oc/Medical Administrator; b/Sep 19, 1949; h/Elmer Ave, Rt 4, Box 4425, Pottsville, PA 17901; ba/P'ville; m/Linda Jean Werdt; c/Jeffrey Bryan, Christopher Jones; p/Daniel J West Sr, Frackville, PA; Mildred Wilkinson, Frackville; ed/BS cum laude 1971, MEd cum laude, Penn St Univ 1972; Currently Pursuing PhD; pa/Instr Cont'g Ed, Penn St Univ (Schuylkill Campus) 1973-; Pt-time Pvt Pract Behavioral Therapist 1975-; Pvt Conslt on Drug & Alcohol Abuse 1974-; Dir of Ambulatory & Outreach Sers, Good Samaritan Hosp 1979-; Cert'd Rehab Cnslr; Am Psychol Assn; Pa Psychol Assn; Assn Advmt of Behavioral Therapy; APGA; Coun of Rehab Cnslr Edrs; Alcohol & Drug Probs Assn of N Am; Am Ednl Res Assn; Assn Mtl Hlth Admrs; Am Mgmt Assn; Am Public Hlth Assn; Other Profl Assns; Participant in Profl Confs; cp/Penn St Alumni Assn; En Pa Inst of Alcohol Studies Alumni Assn; Alumni Assn, Summer Schs of Rutgers Univ; Schuylkill Co Alumni Assn of Penn St Univ; r/Prot; hon/Elks Hon Student; Art Awd; Iota Alpha Delta; Dedication & Ldrship Awd, Gov's Coun on Drug & Alcohol Abuse; Keystone Hon Soc, Penn St Univ; W/W: Fin & Indust, E; Others.

WEST, IVA JEAN oc/Pharmacist; b/Nov 20, 1934; h/2815 W 19th, Plainview, TX 79072; ba/Plainview; m/Jess Wayne; c/Marc Hunter, Mason Drew; p/Thomas John and Hester Belle Hobbs Shrum (dec); ed/Att'd: Tex Tech, McNeese St Col; pa/West Pharm; Served on Tex Wom's Aus to Tex Pharm Assn 4 Yrs; cp/Hale Co Hist Comm 9 Yrs; Wom's Div C of C; Llano Estacado Mus Assn; Plainview Jr Ser Leag 10 Yrs; r/Bapt; hon/Plainview's Wom of Yr 1974.

WEST, JULIAN RALPH oc/Consultant; Teacher; b/Dec 12, 1915; h/1955 N Tamarind Ave, Los Angeles, CA 90068; m/Marvel E Knorr; c/Stuart J, R Bruce, Judy E Hagedorn

(Mrs Jerome H); p/Joseph C and Helen E Nason West (dec); ed/BLiberal Studies Univ Okla; CPA (Cal); Cert'd Profl Contracts/Mgr; Cert'd Internal Auditor; pa/Public Acct'g 1946-49; w Ofc Auditor Gen USAF 1949-62; Ofc Secy of Def, Arlington, Va: Audit Policy Div 1962-67, Chief Procuremt Review Div 1967-73; Conslt 1973-; Tchr UCLA Ext Univ 1977-; Am Inst CPAs; Nat Contract Mgmt Assn, Former Nat Dir; IPA; cp/UN Assn of USA; LA Co Mus Art; Smithsonian Assocs; Olmsted Cir, Hollywood Presb Med Ctr; Oceanic Soc; Wilderness Soc; Earthwatch; LA Ath Clb; Var Travel Clbs; r/Hollywood 1st Presb Ch: Mem, Deacon; hon/Fellow, ABI; Mem IBA; Commun Ldrs & Noteworthy Ams; Personalities W&MW; Book of Honor; Notable Ams; Others.

WESTBROOK, SCOTT CHARLES III oc/School Administrator; b/Feb 27, 1939; h/5096 Buckingham Pl, Troy, MI 48098; ba/Pontiac, MI; m/Ruth Devereaux; c/Scott Charles IV, Reseda Kathryn; p/Scott C Jr and Kathryn E Westbrook (dec); ed/BA Prairie View A&M; MEd Tex So Univ; EdD Wayne St Univ; pa/Sch Admr Pontiac Sch Dist; Mich Occupl Ed Assn; Com Mem Am Voc Assn; Pres Mich Occupl Spec Needs Assn; Nat Assn Voc Ed Spec Needs Pers; Nat Assn for Advmt of Black Ams in Voc Ed; Mich Assn St & Fed Prog Specialists; Pontiac Assn Sch Admrs; Ed Com Oakland Livingston Human Ser Agy; Others; cp/Bd Mem Pontiac Area Urban Leag; Life Mem Kappa Alpha Psi; Advr Detroit Kappa Leag; Chm Oakland Co Yth Assistance Coun, Employmt Com; Growth Chm Pontiac Dist BSA; Others; r/F'ship U Meth Ch, Troy, Mich: Mem; hon/Ser Awd, Detroit Area Clb, Prairie View A&M Alumni Assn; Ser Awd, Houston Alumni Chapt Kappa Alpha Psi; Acad Awds HS & Col; Biogl Listings.

WESTERBERG, RUSSELL A oc/Executive Accountant; b/Feb 28, 1943; h/5910 Twin Springs, Boise, ID 032705; ba/Boise; m/Lucille; c/Kimberly, Selina; p/Elaine Wallentine, Preston, ID; mil/AUS; cp/Mem St Leg 2 Terms.

WESTERHAUS, CATHERINE K oc/Social Worker; b/Oct 13, 1910; h/613 N Plum, Newton, KS 67114; m/George H; p/Anthony J and Permelia A Mathes Kannapel (dec); ed/BMus Ed; MSW; mil/USNR WWII; pa/Nat Assn Social Wkrs; Ks Soc for Clin Social Work; cp/LWV; r/Cath; hon/Ks Social Wkr of Yr 1975; Am Legion Chd & Yth Awd, 5th Dist; W/W Am Wom.

WESTHAUSEN, GARY H oc/Educator; b/Mar 14, 1932; h/4633 Blackberry Lane, Batavia, OH 45103; ba/Batavia; m/Kathleen R; c/David, Debi, Denis; p/Gustav H Westhausen (dec); Florence M Westhausen, Northridge, CA; ed/BA Univ Minn 1956; MA Univ Notre Dame 1971; MEd Univ Cinc 1975; mil/USAF, Ret'd Lt/Col; pa/Asst Prof of Hist, Clermont Gen & Tech Col; Soc Hist Ed; AAUP; hon/USAF Merit Ser Medal; USAF Commend Medal w OLC.

WHARTON, JAMES R oc/Strategy Simulator; b/Jul 26, 1951; h/5465 Atlantic Ave, Long Beach, CA 90805; ed/Student Long Bch City Col 1978-; Att'd: Univ Md 1974-76, Univ Cal-B 1973, San Francisco St Univ 1973, De Anza Jr Col (San Jose, Cal) 1969-70; mil/S/Sgt Adjutant Gen Corps 1970-78; S/Sgt Intell Corps, USAR 1978-; pa/Currently w Intl

Gamers Assn Long Bch; Chm Exec Com Intl Gamers Assn; Intl Soc Polit Psychol; cp/Col Confed AF; 3/VCmdr AMVETS Post 48; US Nav Inst; The Psywar Soc; So Cal Motorcycle Roadriders Assn; Tex Motorcycle Roadriders Assn; hon/Strategy Simulations Hall of Fame, 100th Bronze Game 1978, 200th Silver Game 1979; Dist'd Grad, 61TAAS IPW Course 1979; W/W Am HS Grads.

WHEADON, ROSETTA FAY oc/College President; b/Dec 27, 1934; h/2600 St Louis Ave, East St Louis, IL 62205; ba/E St Louis; m/A Wendell; c/Michael Wendell; p/Roosevelt Dawkins Sr (dec); Wilma Dawkins Agnew (dec); ed/BS; MS; PhD; pa/Pres St Commun Col of E St Louis; AACJC; AAUA; CBAA; cp/Alpha Kappa Alpha; E St Louis Wom's Clb; Friends of Artist Guild; r/Wesley-Bethel U Meth Ch; hon/W/W: Black Am, Am Wom.

WHEELER, ARLINE ZILPHA oc/Educator; Businesswoman; b/Jul 16, 1908; h/RR 2, Rogers, AR 72756; ba/Same; m/Dock; p/Wiley Claud and Rosa E Fuqua Frank (dec); ed/BS; MS; Dipl Adv'd Study in Cnslr Ed; pa/Ret'd Edr & Bus-wom; Ret'd Tchrs Assns: St & NW Ark; Treas Rogers Br AAUW; cp/Benton Co Anti-Cruelty Soc; r/1st Christian Ch; hon/Hon Awd for Superior, Fed Bur Indian Affairs; Other Indian Ser Hons; Biogl Listings.

WHEELER, JANICE A oc/Assistant Comptroller; b/Jan 9, 1956; h/1310 Capri St, Coral Gables, FL 33134; ba/Miami, FL; p/Robert H Wheeler, Miami; Jean S Wheeler, Coral Gables; ed/AA; pa/Omni Intl; cp/DAR; En Star; Repub; r/Bapt; hon/Morris Goldstein Awd; Am Legion Awd; L'Allegro Pres, FSU Secy 1974.

WHELAN, PAUL A oc/University President; b/Jul 26, 1929; h/908 Buell, Joliet, IL 60435; ba/Romeoville, IL; m/Patricia; c/Steven, Timothy, Michael, Monica, Kevin, Thomas, Patrick, Gregory, Martin, Matthew, Daniel, Moira; p/Augustine and Margaret Whelan; ed/BS; MA; PhD; mil/USAF Ret'd Col, Command Pilot; pa/Pres Lewis Univ; Chair Coun Liberal Arts Dean; Ala Coun of Ed; Chair Mobile U Ed Comm; Ala 1202 Task Force Comm; Am Assn Col & Univ Adm; Am Hist Assn; cp/Lions Intl; Dir Joliet YMCA; Joliet Rotary Clb; Exec Bd Boy Scouts Explorer Unit; r/Rom Cath; hon/Dist'd Flying Cross; Bronze Star; AF Meritorious Ser Medal; AF Commend Medals; USAF Acad & AF Inst of Technol Outstg Tchr Awds; Outstg Civic Ldr Awd.

WHETTEN, JOHN DILWORTH oc/Consumer Products Company Executive; b/Jun 8, 1940; h/2250 Loch Ln, Walnut Creek, CA 94598; ba/Oakland, CA; m/Carma Rebecca Pearse; c/Carma Rebecca, Rebecca Kate, Mary Coza; p/Lester B and Kate Allred Whetten; ed/BS Brigham Yg Univ 1965; MBA Univ Cal-B 1967; mil/USAR 1958-67; pa/Clorox Co, Oakland, Cal 1967-: Mgr New Prods & Acquisitions 1971-73, Mgr Advt'g & Mktg 1973-77, Mgr Acquisitions & Bus Devel 1977-; Lectr Princeton Res Inst on Corp & Acquisition Strategies; cp/Bd Trustees E Bay Botanical & Zool Soc; Commonwealth Clb San Francisco; Oakland Ath Clb; Chm Brigham Yg Univ Exec Tng Conf for No Cal; r/Ch Jesus Christ LDS: Mem; hon/Author "The Intro of a New Product; A Case Hist of Clorox 2", Univ Cal Grad Sch Bus.

WHIPPLE, CHARLES M JR oc/Professor; Author; b/Jul 11, 1938; h/327 Sundance, Edmond, OK 73034; ba/Edmond; c/Christian Von, Michelle Dyanne; p/Charles and Julia Whipple, Oklahoma City, OK; ed/BA; MA; PhD; EdD; LittD; pa/Prof Psychol Ctl St Univ; Author 7 Books; Dir Pubs Okla Psychol Assn; r/Congreg.

WHITE, CHARLES DENNY oc/Minister; b/Mar 3, 1914; h/6800 Abbotswood Dr, Charlotte, NC 28211; ba/Charlotte; m/Lucille Everhart (dec); 2nd Cornelia Thompson;

c/Charles D Jr, Delbert Leon, Judith Ramsey, LaDean Giles, Zenda R, David Lee; p/John Charles and Mayme York White (dec); ed/AB High Point Col; BD Duke Div; DD High Point; pa/Min Local Chs 1940-67; Dist Supt; Adm Asst to Bishop; Secy of Dist, Annual, Jurisdiction & Gen Confs; Col Chd's Home, Home for Aging Trustee; cp/Lion; Rotarian; Mason; r/U Meth.

WHITE, HARRY CLIFFORD oc/Minister; b/Jul 21, 1930; h/271 Winfield Dr, Hillbrook Forest, Spartanburg, SC 29302; ba/S'burg; m/Addie Jane Douglas; c/Martha Miller, Harry C Jr; p/James Dale White (dec); Mary Jo Allison White, Hickory Grove, SC; ed/AB Erskine Col 1951; JDiv Erskine Theol Sem 1959; Postgrad Work Luth Theol So Sem; mil/USN 1951-55, USNR 1955-59; Chaplain Asst to Base Chaplain, Prot, Moffett Field (Cal) 1953-55; Called to Active Duty w 1st Battalion, 131st Medium Tank Battalion (Camp Irwin, Cal) 1961; Grad Command & Gen Staff Col Course 1976; Group Chaplain 228th Signal Group, SC Army NG (Current); pa/Pastorates: Spartanburg ARP Ch 1968-, Rogers Meml ARP Ch, Rock Hill (SC) 1964-68, 1st ARP Ch, Charlotte (NC) 1960-64, 1st Pastorate Garrison Meml ARP Ch, Bessemer City (NC) 1959, 60; Ordained by Catawba Presby, Hickory Grove (NC) 1959; Lic'd by Catawba Presby 1959; 2nd Presby: Com on Christian Ed 1974-78, Chm Com on Stewardship 1974-77, Com on Stewardship 1974-75, Moderator 1970; Catawba Presby: Com on Christian Ed 1964-68, Moderator 1966; Mem Bd Stewardship 1969-73; Com on Investmts of Stewardship Bd & Mem ARP Foun Inc 1975-76; Com on Worship 1978-; Sr High Yth Dir 1974-; Moderator 1st Presby 1960-61; Other Profl Activs; Contbr Articles to Denom & Secular Pubs; cp/BSA: Dir Coun Camporee (Former), Chm Coun Activs Com (Former), S'burg, Currently Mem-at-Large Palmetto Coun & Advr to Pres or Chm of Coun; Mem Palmetto Lodge A&FM, Lodge #289, Sharon (SC); Resv Ofcr's Assn US; SC & Nat NG Assns; Mil Chaplains Assn US; Mem People & Assocs Inc, Drug & Alcohol Coun, S'burg; Dem; Mem Citizens for Decency; r/Assoc Reformed Presb Ch; hon/Guardsman Medal, SC; Meritorious Ser Awd, Army (SC); Resv Component Medal, Army; Navy: Good Conduct Medal, Nat Def Medal; Biogl Listings.

WHITE, JAMES oc/Purchasing Agent; b/Jul 7, 1942; h/5 Marianna Pl, Morristown, NJ 07960; ba/M'town; m/Carolyn H; p/Erma White, Frierson, LA; ed/BS Grambling Col 1965; mil/AUS 1966-69; pa/Purchasing Agt Allied Chem Corp, M'town 1975-; Pricing Analyst Fiat-Allis Constrn Machinery Inc (Formerly Allis Chalmers Corp) 1970-75; Tchr: Caddo Parish Sch Sys, Shreveport, La

1969-70, LaSalle Parish Sch Sys, Jena, La 1965-66; r/Presb.

WHITE, NORMA RUTH S oc/Curriculum Coordinator; b/Nov 17; h/6042 Ribault Rd, Jacksonville, FL 32209; ba/J'ville; c/Marcel Kevin; p/Ruth Cummings Solomon, J'ville; ed/BS; MA; pa/Curric Coor Ribault Sr HS; Jr HS Band Dir (1st Female Band Dir in Sch Dist); Curric Writer Duval Co Sch Dist; Tchr Instrumental Music Resource; Dir Public Relats Sum Musical Prodns; Coor Instrumental Music Duval Co Sch Dist; Tchr Adult Ed Prog Fla Jr Col, J'ville; Charter Mem Nat Bandmasters Assn; Secy: Fla Assn Band Dirs, Fla Band Dirs; Dist Chm Dist IV Fla Jr High Band Dirs; Co Chm Jr High Band Dirs; Fla Orch Assn; Fla Bandmasters Assn; ASCD; Duval Co Assn Sec'dy Sch Admrs; Fla Music Supvrs Assn; Fla Music Edrs Assn; Bd Dirs J'ville Univ MAT Prog; Curric Review Com; Arts Assembly; Bd Dirs Music Interaction; Wkshop Conslt; Alpha Kappa Alpha: S Atl Reg Dir 1974-78, Nat Prog Com 1970-74, Visitation Team 1972-74, Others; cp/NAACP; YWCA; Charter Mem J'ville Sect Nat Coun Negro Wom; Bd Dirs: Girl's Clb, Day Nursery Assn, NE Fla Area Adv Coun of Fla Soc for Preven of Blindness; Fla A&M Univ Alumni Assn Century Clb; Bus Mgr Kevinette Clb; J'ville Coun on Citizen Involvemt; Phi Delta Kappa; r/St Philips Epis Ch: Mem; hon/Secy Kappa Delta Pi; Profl Pubs; 1978 Reg Conf: Undergrad Awd, Hall of Fame Awd; Bethune Elem Sch PTA for Meritorious Ser; Cert of Apprec for Meritorious & Dedicated Ser, W Union Bapt Ch; Outstg Achmt & Dedicated Ser, Darnell Cookman Band Parents; Hons from Var Band Dirs Assns; Others.

WHITE, SALLY FOX oc/Public Relations Manager; h/6410 Colewood Ct NW, Atlanta, GA 30328; ba/Atlanta; m/Joseph A; c/Clair Fox; p/J Gilbert Fox (dec); Nelia Alma Carter Fox Atkins (dec); ed/BJ cum laude Univ Tex; pa/Current Public Relats Mgr Neiman-Marcus; Retail Promotion Account Mgr The Merchandising Group Inc, New York, NY; Free-lance Fashion Commentator/Publicist: Chgo, Dallas, New Orleans; Asst to Merchandising Editor *Ladies' Home Jour*; Other Profl Positions; Charter Mem Atl Press Clb; Wom in Communs: Chapt Pres, Chm Var Projs); The Fashion Group Inc: Reg Dir, Treas; AAUW; BPW Assn; cp/Atlanta Wom's C of C: Dogwood Fest & Intl City Com Chm; Atlanta Hist Soc, Tullie Smith House Restoration Com; Rabun Gap-Nacoochee Clb; High Mus Art, Hospitality Com; Atlanta C of C, Bus Mbrship; LWV; North Sprgs PTA; Atlanta Metro U Way Solicitation Com; Atlanta Meml Art Assn; r/Presb; hon/Ga C of C Awds: Hist Soc Proj, Advt'g Awd for Bus; Ldg Ladies of Atlanta 1975; Ser Awd, The Fashion Group; Dogwood Fest Awd, Wom's C of C; Parade Honor, WSB-TV 1976; Ser Awd, Atlanta Med Aux; W/W Am Wom.

WHITE, STANLEY ARCHIBALD oc/-Engineering Management; b/Sept 25, 1931; h/1541 Amberwood Dr, Santa Ana, CA 92705; ba/Anaheim, CA; m/Edda Maria Castano-Benitez; c/Dianne Louella, Stanley Archibald Jr, Paul Joseph, John Clarence; p/Clarence Archibald White (dec); Lou Ella Arford, Fullerton, CA; ed/BSEE 1957; MSEE 1959; PhD Purdue Univ 1965; mil/Inf 1949-51; USAF 1951-55; pa/Lectr: USC, UCLA, UCI, UCD; Sr Mem IEEE; Author 50 Pubs; cp/Chm Adv Bd for Master Plan for Spec Ed (Orange Co); Chm Fair Housing Coun; Chm Commun Assistance Fund; r/Rom Cath: Lay Minister, Liturgist, Musician; hon/Eta Kappa Nu; Tau Beta Pi; Sigma Xi; NAm Aviation Sci-Engrg Fellow.

WHITE, WILLIAM LOUIS oc/University Professor; b/Aug 24, 1941; h/3175 Robinson Rd, Apt D-20, Jackson, MS 39209; ba/Jackson; m/Dessie B; c/Patrise A, William J; p/Bruce V White (dec); Earlease White, Holly Springs, MS; ed/BS; MA; PhD; pa/Prof Jackson St Univ; VChm Math Div Miss Acad Sci; Advr Pre-Engrg Clb; Advr Freshman Class; Served on Panel of Evaluators: MISIP, SSTP; r/Epis; hon/Nat F'ship Fund F'ship; Jackson St Fac Res Grant.

WHITEHURST, LOWELL E oc/Engineer; b/Jun 20, 1948; h/3702 The Alameda, Baltimore, MD 21218; ba/Balto; m/Sandra Eiken; c/Landis Eirin, Sherrod Elliott; p/Booker T Whitehurst, Balto, MD; Eulah B Jacobs, Balto, MD; ed/Grad Balto Polytechnic Inst 1966; Cert of Completion, Balto City Plumbing Code 1968; Cert of Completion, Elects thru Microwaves, Chanute AFB 1969; Att'd Johns Hopkins Univ & Morgan St Univ; mil/USAF 1968-72, Missile Sys Analyst Specialist; pa/VP, Egli & Gompf Inc 1979-; Ofc Engr, Nash/Bridges 1978-79; Mech Designer, Henry Adams Inc 1976-78; Designer, Harold A Schlenger 1976; Other Former Positions; Provides Bldg Types for Residential & Commercial Structures; Am Soc Heating, Refrigeration & Air Conditioning Engrs; Am Soc Plumbing Engrs; Nat Tech Assn; hon/Cert of Professionalism, USAF; Cert of Apprec, Pres Richard M Nixon.

WHITESIDES, GLENN E oc/College President; b/Dec 23, 1935; h/2104 Luther St, Newberry, SC 29108; ba/Newberry; m/Jerri Anne Hoke; c/Jane, Anna, John; p/Wright M and Emma Whitesides, Chester, SC; ed/BA Erskine Col; MA; PhD Fla St Univ; Postdoct Work Harvard Univ; pa/Pres Newberry Col; Pres's Adv Bd Nat Assn Intercollegiate Ath; Nat Exec Comm Consortium of Small Pvt Cols; St Exec Com SC Coun Cols & Univs; cp/Bd Dirs SC Nat Bk; Kiwanis Clb; Exec Com SC U Way; r/Redeemer Luth Ch; hon/Biogl Listings.

WHITE-WARE, GRACE ELIZABETH oc/Educator; b/Oct 5, 1921; h/14701 Milverton Rd, Cleveland, OH 44120; ba/Cleve; c/Oloye Kunle Adeyemon; p/James Eathel and Madree Penn White (dec); ed/BA Stowe Tchr's Col; pa/Adult Ed Tchr Cleve Bd Ed 1965-; Hd Tchr Hd Start Prog 1965; Tchr: Quincy Elem Sch (Cleve) 1961-, Gladstone Elem Sch (Cleve) 1954-61, Dunbar Sch (Kinlock, Mo) 1952, Lincoln Sch (Richmond, Mo) 1951, Ross Elem Sch (Chgo) 1951, Others; Tchr TV Tonight Sch, Lessons for Adults, Cleve 1972; Tri-Owner, VP, Social Editor *Style* Mag, St Louis 1947-49; Owner/Mgr Wentworth Record Distributors, Chgo 1947-51; Supr Accts Receivable Div Spiegel Inc, Chgo 1947-52; Other Profl Positions; Ohio & Cleve Ed Assns; Nat Assn Public Sch Adult Ed; IPA; Eta Phi Beta; Phi Delta Kappa, 1/VP Cleve 1971-73; Delta Sigma Theta, Pres Cleve 1969-73; cp/NAACP; Phillis Wheatley Assn; Moreland Commun Assn; Nat Coun

Negro Wom; Dem; Novelette Bridge Clb; Treas Jr Wom's Civic Leag; Cleve Bd Afro-Am Cult & Hist Soc; Wom's Aux Bd Talbert Clin & Day Care Ctr, Cleve; Adv Bd Langston Hughes Lib; Mem Forest City Hosp Aux Bd; Tots & Teens Inc: Charter Mem, Fin Secy; Mem Cleve Chapt Cong Racial Equality; Mem Cleve Coun Human Relats; VChm Cleve Com Yth for Understanding Teenage Union; Mem Child Devel Parent Bd Gtr Cleve Neighborhood Ctrs Assn; Others; r/Prot; hon/Most Outstg Vol of Yr, NY Fdn Settlemts 1944; Ldg Tchr Commun, Cleve *Call & Post*; Martha Holden Jennings Scholar Awd; Martha Holden Jennings Foun, Cleve; Spec Outstg Tchrs Awd; Outstg Ser Awd, Black Ec Union; Cert Apprec, City Cleve; Charter Mem & 1/VP Top Ladies of Distn; Num Biogl Listings.

WHITFIELD, VALLIE JO oc/Aide &

Broker; b/Mar 18, 1922; h/1841 Pleasant Hill Rd, Pleasant Hill, CA 94523; ba/Pleasant Hill; m/Robert Edward; c/Christa, Robert (dec), James David, Joanne Vallie; p/Joseph Edward Fox (dec); Valley Schiefer Fox-Westkamper; ed/AA; BA Cand; pa/Real Est Broker; Realtor Whitfield Realty; Writer; Pubr Whitfield Books; cp/Commun Ser Aide; r/Cath; hon/Life Mem PTA; Nom Citizen of Yr, Pleasant Hill; Sev Hons & Awds.

WHITING, BRUCE RANDOLPH oc/-Psychologist; b/Jun 7, 1946; h/6 Mt Vernon St, Somerville, MA 02145; m/Patricia; c/Orange Blossom; p/Cuthbert R and Virginia T Whiting, Saddle River, NJ; ed/AB Rutgers Univ; MA, PhD Boston Univ; cp/Intl Soc for Philosophical Enquiry; hon/Nat Merit Finalist; Capt US Physical Fitness Team.

WHITING, CUTHBERT RANDOLPH oc/Business Executive; Scientific Consultant; b/May 29, 1909; h/12 N Church Rd, Saddle River, NJ 07458; ba/Same; m/Virginia Turpin; c/Bruce Randolph; p/William A Whiting (dec); Anne Williams Whiting, Prescott, AZ; ed/BS NYU 1937; Grad Schs Rutgers & Columbia Univs; Adv'd Ofcr's Grad, USAR; Var Engrg & Bus Schs; Other Studies; mil/USAR Ret'd, Lt Col; 1941-45, 2/Lt to Maj; Silver Star Medal for Gallantry in Action; Bronze Arrowhead for Assault Troops; Philippine Liberation Medal w 2 Bronze Stars; 10 Campaign or Battle Stars for Combat in Pacific Theater; pa/Chm Bd Dirs PROBE Inc, NJ 1975-; Engrg VP Med Electronics & Elect Vehicle Firms (NY) 1971-75; Asst to Dean of Engrg Grad Sch West

Point (NY) 1960-70; Chief Engr Distant Early Warning (DEW) Radar Experimental Line on Alaskan Arctic Shore 1953-54; Engr to Sr Staff Engr & Intermed Mgmt Bell Sys (15 Yrs); Former Mem Soc Nav Engrs; Intl Pres Intl Soc for Phil Enquiry 1975-; Life Mem Telephone Pioneers Am; Mem Elect Vehicle Coun 1972-; IEEE; cp/Trustee & Life Mem Vets of Seventh Regiment; Past Pres Vet's Crusaders; Ret'd Ofcrs Assn; SAR; Other Orgs; r/Prot; hon/NY St Conspicuous Ser Awd & Cit; Lttr of Commend for Indust Invention, AT&T; Cert of Commend in Recog of DEW Line Ser in Arctic; Lttr of Commend for Saving Life of Seriously Injured Boy, NY Telephone Co; Lttr of Commend, US Cong-man for Invention Given to NASA; Sr Fellow, Intl Soc for Phil Enquiry; Coauthor *Early Warnings* 1962; Pub'd Papers; Patents on Inventions.

WHITNEY, JOHN FREEMAN JR oc/Professor; Mayor; b/Feb 14, 1944; h/18 Pheasant Run Dr, Chatham, IL 62629;

ba/Springfield, IL; m/Carolyn Nordyke; c/Cristina Elizabeth, John Freeman III, William David; p/John Freeman and Agnese Taliaferro Whitney, Lutherville, MD; ed/BA Baylor Univ; MS Tex A&I Univ; Postgrad Fla St Univ; pa/Prof Polit Sci Lincoln Land Col; Pi Sigma Alpha; cp/Mayor, Chatham; Conslt NBC Election Ctl; Leg Staff Intern St of Fla; Adm Asst Ill St Fair Campaign Mgr; Former Mem Gov's Transition Task Force; r/So Bapt; hon/VFW Awd; Ford Foun Fellow.

WHITNEY, VIRGINIA KOOGLER oc/Librarian; b/Feb 6, 1927; h/502 Orchard St, Aztec, NM 87410; ba/Aztec; c/Barbara Jo Petersen, James Thomas; p/C V and Josephine Clements Koogler, Aztec; ed/BA; MEd;

pa/Aztec Ed Assn; Pres NM Sch Libns; NM A-V Assn: Pres, Secy 3 Yrs; St Pres KKI; cp/Repub Ctl Com, NM; Trustee Aztec Public Lib; r/Meth: Ch Bd; hon/Author: *Koogler Fam of Va & Tennille Fam*; Coauthor: *Aztec, Anasazi to Statehood* & *Wom in Ed in NM*.

WHITTED, MILDRED M oc/Professor; b/Sept 11, 1929; h/8140 Tulane, University City, MO 63130; ba/St Louis, MO; m/Jack J; p/Willie Mason (dec); Lillie M Mason, E St Louis, IL; ed/BS; MS; Doct Mktg & DE; pa/Presently Full Prof Bus Forest Park Commun Col; Former Dir "Operation Consumer Insight" (Consumer Ed Prog for Disadvantaged); Former Tchg Assoc Ind Univ 2 Yrs; Former Bus Instr E St Louis Sr HS 6 Yrs; Other Former Positions; AAUP; Nat Bus Tchrs Assn; Kappa Delta Pi; Delta Pi Epsilon; Pi Lambda Theta; Am Voc Assn; NEA; Am Mktg Assn; Mo Assn Jr Cols, Chm Bus & Ecs Div 1971-72; Area Bus Tchrs Assn; Coun for Distributive Tchr Ed; Other Profl Activs; cp/Univ City LWV, Voter Registration Com; U-City Commun Adv Coun; 1/VP Creve-Coeur Dem Clb; Chm Bus Adv Com St Louis Cath Archdiocese; Iota Phi Lambda; Mem Consumer Adv Coun Better Bus Bur; Columnist Var Pubs; r/Third Bapt Ch; hon/Cited for Unique Contbn to Bus Ed, Mildred Louise Bus Col; Wom in the New Awd, Alpha Kappa Alpha; IPA; 1972 Outstg Wom of Yr, Iota Phi Lambda; Nom'd as Outstg HS Tchr, Jack & Jill Clb Am Inc 1964; Served as Queen of Love & Beauty for Nat Coun for·Negro Wom 1960; Pubs; Biogl Listings.

WHITTEN, JAMES ROBERT oc/Pharmacist; Investments; b/Aug 11, 1926; h/5505 N Walnut Rd, N Little Rock, AR 72116; ba/Little Rock; m/Marguerite; c/James R II, Carol Christine W Hobbs; p/Samuel Orrin and Elsa Ann Ohls Whitten (dec); ed/BS; mil/USAAF WWII; pa/Am Soc Hosp Pharmacists, Pres Ark Chapt 1970-71; cp/Past Mem Rotary; Sertoma; Toastmasters; Bd Mem Am Cancer Soc; Cand St Rep & St Senate; Others; r/Presb: Ordained 1959; hon/Pres's Awd; Squibb Ldrship Awd.

WHITTENBURG, GRACE EVELYN McKEE oc/Homemaker; b/Aug 19, 1919; h/3214 Ong St, Amarillo, TX 79109; m/Roy R; c/Grace Evelyn Coltrin (Mrs Don), Jewel Anne Johnston (Mrs Murray Jr), George Allen II, Louis Palma McKee, John Burkhart, Mary Lois Lockhart (Mrs Jerry), Roy Robert Jr; p/Louis Palma McKee (dec); Jewel Porter McKee, Amarillo; ed/AA En NM Jr Col (now ENMU); Addit Study W Tex Univ; cp/Bd Dirs: Girlstown USA, Mtl Hlth Assn Tex, Mtl

Hlth Assn Tex Panhandle; Jr Leag Amarillo; Amarillo: Symph Guild, Art Ctr Assn, Art Alliance, Coun of Garden Clbs, Christian Wom's Clb, Fed'd Wom's Clb, Bkr's Wives Clb; Jr Leag Garden Clb; Tex Cowbelles; Repub Wom's Clb; Assn of the W's; Discovery Ctr; Panhandle-Plains Hist Soc; W Tex Ex-Student Assn; Phoenix Clb; ENMU Alumni; Life Mem YWCA; The Wom's Forum; Tex Fdn Wom's Clbs; Acad Amarillo Foun for Hlth & Sci Ed (Charter Mem); Others; r/Paramount Terrace Christian Ch: Ladies' Assn, Bible Study; hon/Book of Honor; DIB; Personalities of S; Intl W/W Commun Ser.

WICKERSHAM, LAMONT TITUS III oc/Attorney; b/Feb 14, 1933; ba/110 Montgomery Ave, Bala, PA 19004; m/Davis P W; c/Lamont Titus IV, Claudia Davis, Cadwalader T; p/Lamont Titus Jr and Claudia Pepper Wickersham; ed/BA Harvard 1954; DEcon Princeton 1957; LLB Yale 1960; JD Vienna Inst Intl & Comparative Law 1962; mil/AUS 1963-64, Adjutant to Lt Col Peat M Mitchell; pa/Asst Gen Counsel IBM World Trade Corp 1960-63; STaff Counsel US Embassy, Rangoon, Burma 1964-68; Partner Dewey, Cheatham & Howe 1968-; cp/Intl Chds Wel Fund; r/Epis; hon/AUS: Silver Star, Malta Cross, Croix de Guerre.

WIDNER, ROSE oc/Teacher; Homemaker; b/Nov 29, 1921; h/709 Broadmoor, Blytheville, AR 72315; m/J D; c/Mike, Patricia; ed/BSE, MSE Ark St Univ; pa/Tchr Gosnell Elem Sch 13 Yrs; AFMC: Ext Chm, Pres NE Dist; Pres Orpheus Clb; Writer for Chd (Inst of Chd's Lit); r/1st Bapt Ch: Mem, Ch Choir, Pres Choir, Class Tchr, Other Activs; hon/Awd of Merit for Outstg Participation in Nat Music Week 1978, NFMC; Nat Kanzanian Awd (in tchg Ec Ed); Delta Kappa Gamma; Life Mem Orpheus Clb.

WIEDEBUSCH, LARRY oc/State Delegate; Businessman; ba/403 Fern Dr, Glen Dale, WV 26038; m/Married; c/3 Chd; pa/-Self-employed Bus-man; cp/Elected to WVa Ho of Dels 1974, 76, 78: Chm Com on Indust & Labor 4 Yrs, Mem Leg Rule-Making Com, Others; Loyal Order of Moose; Lions Clb; Am Legion; BPO Elks Lodge 282; Garibaldi Lodge; Gov's Manpower Prog; Glen Dale PTA; Exec Bd U Way; Ohio Val Labor Adv Coun, Marshall Co; Dem Men's Clb; Mech Maintenance Assn; Bd Dirs Marshall Co Sr Citizens; Bd Dirs Marshall Co Cancer Soc; Com-man BSA; Past Pres Utility Wkrs Am; Former Chaplain Civitans; Hon Mem Marshall Co Sch Aux Pers; Del to Dem St Conv; hon/W/W Am Polits.

WIERNIK, PETER H oc/Physician; b/Jun 16, 1939; h/5026 Round Tower Pl, Columbia, MD 21044; ba/Baltimore, MD; m/Roberta Fuller; c/Julie Anne, Lisa Britt, Peter Harrison; p/Harris and Molly Emmerman Wiernik, Waco, TX; ed/BA 1961, MD Univ Va 1965; mil/Comm'd Ofcr, US Public Hlth Ser; pa/Dir, Balto Cancer Res Prog; Chief Clin Oncology Br & Prof of Med, Univ of Md Sch of MEd; Prog Com, Am Soc Clin Oncology 1970; Am Assn Cancer Res; Fellow, Intl Soc Hematology; r/Jewish; hon/Phi Beta Kappa; Phi Sigma; Alpha Omega Alpha.

WILBER, CLARE MARIE oc/Musician; Educator; Orchestra Manager; b/Mar 21, 1928; h/900 Edwards St, Ft Collins, CO 80524;

ba/Ft Collins; m/Charles G; c/Maureen, Charles, Michael, Thomas (dec), Kathleen, Aileen, John Joseph; p/Thomas A and Kathleen M Brennan O'Keefe; ed/AB cum laude Loretto Hgts Col; MS Fordham Univ; MMus Colo St Univ; pa/Edr Dept Music Colo St Univ; Orch Mgr Ft Collins Symph Orch; Ft Collins Music Tchrs Assn: Mem, Treas 1976-; Delta Omicron; Certn Bd, Colo St Music Tchrs 1977-; Am Symph Orch Leag; MTNA; Colo Music Tchrs Assn; Elite Music Co: Dir 1975-, VP 1975-; Composer; Secy Assn Colo Orchs; cp/Wom's Guild Ft Collins Symph; Colo St Univ Wom's Adv Bd; Lincoln Commun Ctr; r/Rom Cath; hon/Spec Ser Awd, Delta Omicron.

WILBUN, RUBYE KNOWLES oc/Teacher; b/Feb 3, 1922; h/1548 Gold Ave, Memphis, TN 38106; ba/Memphis; m/S A; c/Shepperson Jr, Gary R; p/Isaiah and Jessie K Knowles (dec); ed/BS; MA; pa/5th Grade Tchr; NEA; MEA; WTA; Cooperating Tchr for Student Tchrs; cp/Ward 47 Civic Clb; Chm Keep Am Beautiful; Mem; Chm Art for Primary Dept SS; hon/Newspaper in the Classroom S'ship; AM Newspaper Pubrs Awd; Key to City of Memphis; Author "Tchr's Notebook" 1973-75.

WILDE, JAMES A oc/Assistant Professor; b/May 1, 1939; h/3095 Norwood Ave, Decatur, IL 62526; ba/Decatur; m/Monique; c/Adam; p/W W and Marguerite A Wilde, Royalton, MN; ed/BA; MDiv; MA; PhD w distn; pa/Asst Prof Rel Millikin Univ; Soc Biblical Lit; Cath Biblical Assn; Chgo Soc Biblical Res; r/Rom Cath; hon/Cit, Drew Univ.

WILDER, DEAN oc/Professional Tenor; College Professor; b/Nov 10, 1938; h/Betsy Ross Cir, Liberty, MO 64068; ba/Liberty; m/Kay Wordsworth; c/Anne Elizabeth; p/Lester and Ethel Boring, Milwaukie, OR; ed/BA Cascade Col 1963; MMus New England Conservatory of Music 1970; pa/Dir Vocal Studies William Jewell Col; Nat Assn Tchrs Singing; Am Guild Musical Artists; So Bapt Ch Music Conf; Over 100 Concerts & Recitals Yrly; Master Classes & Wkshops throughout US; r/Second Bapt Ch, Liberty: Mem; hon/Outstg Yg Men Am; Outstg Edrs Am; World W/W Musicians; Cult Exc Cit, Republic of Korea; Outstg Grad, Cascade Col; Men of Achmt; Personalities W&MW.

WILES, MARILYN McCALL oc/Assistant Professor; Consultant; b/Aug 21, 1944; h/1337 Dana Dr, Oxford, OH 45056; ba/Oxford; m/David Kimball; c/Corey

Kimball, Matthew Alexander; p/Dorothy Peoples McCall, Miami, FL; ed/BS; MEd; EdD; pa/Conslt Ednl Adaptations Inc; AERA; ASCD; r/Prot; hon/Phi Delta Kappa; Pi Kappa Phi; Personalities W&MW.

WILKES, HELEN T oc/Artist; h/1831 Crestmont Ct, Glendale, CA 91208; ba/Same; m/Peter F; c/Patricia W, Peter T (dec); c/Wilber and La Belle Townsend (dec); ed/BA Univ Cal-B; pa/Juror; Lectr; Gallery Dir; Tchr; Bd Mem Art Org; Juror City Shows; Dir All-City Exhibit; Coor Vincent Price Shows; CoFdr Glendale Fine Arts Gallery; Docent for Art Ctr; cp/Citizen's Adv Bd, Glendale; r/Epis; hon/Juried Awds; Los Angeles Mayor's Cert of Apprec; Order of Shield; Zeta

Tau Alpha.

WILKINSON, HAZEL WILEY oc/Microbiologist; b/Aug 4, 1941; h/400 Sassafras Rd, Roswell, GA 30076; ba/Atlanta, GA; m/James Nathaniel Parkman; p/Joseph Edgar Wilkinson Jr (dec); Alida Livingston Wilkinson, Selma, AR; ed/BS; MS; PhD;

pa/Res Microbiologist Ctr for Disease Control; Chief Spec Immunol Lab; Edit Bd Mem *Jour of Clin Microbiol*; Am Soc for Microbiol; Specialist Microbiologist; Sigma Xi; AAAS; Lancefield Soc; r/Epis; hon/Pres' Awd, Am Soc for Microbiol SE Br; Wom in Hlth, Dept HEW.

WILKS, THOMAS MILTON oc/Metro Campus Minister; b/Feb 14, 1945; h/347 Parma Dr, Manchester, MO 63011; ba/St Louis, MO; m/Jacquelin Holsomback; c/Thomas David, Bryan Emerson; p/Milton Emerson and Bernice Thompson Wilks, Bastrop, LA; ed/BA La Col; ThM New Orleans Bapt Theol Sem; DMin So Bapt Theol Sem; pa/Metro Campus Min St Louis Metro Area; Pres Charleston Min Assn; Chm & Mem Num Denom Coms; Spkr & Tchr St Assemblies; cp/Commun Better Com; City Park Bd; Chm Child Wel Adv Com; C of C Rec Com; r/So Bapt; hon/W/W: Am Cols & Univs, Rel, W&MW; Men of Achmt; Pres' Cup for Excell in Debate, La Col; Outstg Yg Men Am.

WILL, CHARLES A oc/Life Insurance Underwriter; b/Apr 10, 1917; h/81 River Rd, Grand View, NY 10960; ba/Stamford, CT; m/Kathleen Joan O'Donnell; c/John Barry, Mary Kathleen, Peter Joseph; p/Charles A Will (dec); Gertrude Zauner Will, New York, NY; ed/BS NYU; mil/USNR 1944-46; pa/Authority on Life Ins Underwriting; Pubr of Newsletter in US, Canada & 15 Other Countries; Inst Home Ofc Underwriters (Pres 1958); Home Ofc Life Underwriters Assn; Jt Ad Hoc Coms of IHOU & HOLUA; COINTRA; Canadian HOLUA; Canadian Reinsurance Conf; Hon Mem, S African Assn of Med Dirs & Assurance Med Soc of Gt Britain; r/1st Park Commr, Village of S Nyack (NY); r/Cath.

WILLARD, CAROL J PETZOLD oc/Teacher; b/Dec 26, 1915; h/301 Dick Ave, Hamilton, OH 45013; ba/H'ton; m/Jack A; c/John T, Patricia R; p/H O and Florence Jeffries Petzold (dec); ed/BS & Postgrad Work Miami Univ (Ohio); MEd Xavier Univ; pa/Tchr Devel Disabilities Pierce Elem Sch; CEC; AAUW; BPW; Life Mem NEA; OEA; cp/Musical Arts Clb; Commun Sers; Past

Mem Butler Co Mtl Hlth Adv Bd; Cath Charities; Play for Style Shows for S'ship Funds; Nat 2/VP Intl Fdn Cath Alumnae; r/Cath; hon/Awd Statues for Excell in Bach, Beethoven, Mozart, Brahms, Chopin, Cinc Conservatory of Music; World W/W Wom; Personalities of W&MW; W/W Am Child Devel.

WILLIAMS, ANNIE JOHN oc/Teacher; Researcher; b/Aug 26, 1913; h/2021 Sprunt Ave, Durham, NC 27705; p/John Wesley and Martha Anne Walker Williams; ed/AB Greensboro Col 1933; MA Univ NC-CH 1939; Grad Studies; pa/Tchr Num Schs in NC; Tchr Blackstone Col (Va) 1934-35; Adj Asst Prof Math & Sci Ed NC St Univ, Raleigh, NC 1966-73; Tchr Durham HS, Durham (Prior to Retiremt); NEA; Life Mem: NC Assn Edrs, NCTM, Math Assn Am; Nat Ret'd Tchrs Assn; NC Ret'd Govtl Employees' Assn; Durham City-Co Ret'd Sch Pers; NC Coun Tchrs Math; Sch Sci & Math Assn; Eta Chapt Delta Kappa Gamma; cp/Pierian Lit Clb; Assn for Preserv of Eno River Val; Durham-Chapel Hill Chapt Greensboro Col Alumni Assn; Coor'g Coun for Sr Citizens, Durham; r/Duke Meml U Meth Ch, Durham: UMW; hon/Contbr to Num Profl Jours; Coauthor *Algebra, First Course* & *Algebra, Second Course*; Hon Mem, Mu Alpha Theta; Shell Merit F'ship for Study at Cornell Univ; W W Rankin Meml Awd for Excell in Math Ed, NC Coun Tchrs Math; Book of Honor; Intl Reg Profiles.

WILLIAMS, BEVERLY JEAN oc/Physician; b/Aug 16, 1943; h/5590 Clarke Address, Memphis, TN 38118; ba/Memphis; p/John Ed and Odessa Williams, Memphis; ed/BS; MD; pa/Pres M-S Hlth Profls; Bluff City Med Soc;

Am Col Physicians; cp/NAACP; Am Heart Assn; Bd Dirs Am Diabetes Assn; r/Friendship Bapt Ch: Mem; hon/HS Class Valedictorian; Grad w Hons: Howard Univ, Univ Tenn Med Sch; Recipient 3 Yr Tchg & Res Awd, Am Col Physicians.

WILLIAMS, C E oc/Pastor; b/Dec 22, 1917; h/14134-130 NE, Kirkland, WA 98033; ba/Seattle, WA; m/Gwen; c/Keith, Mona Lisa, Lillie Mae Wade, John Lee Jr, Leon, Rhonda Hall; p/Charlie and Ellen Williams (dec); ed/Doct; cp/Chaplain Grand Lodge Masons 14 Yrs; Accounts & Claim Nat Bapt Conv Am; Cherry Hill Coalition Commun Work; r/Bapt; hon/Biogl Listings.

WILLIAMS, DAVID ROGERSON JR oc/Engineering Executive; b/Oct 20, 1921; h/Oak Bar Ranch, Nogales, AZ 85621; ba/Tulsa, OK; m/Pauline Bolton; c/Pauline W d'Aguin, David R III, Rachel K; p/David R and Martha Hill Williams (dec); ed/BS Yale Univ; mil/USAF Capt; pa/Chm: The Resource Scis Corp (Tulsa), Williams Brothers Engrg Co (Tulsa), Williams Brothers Canada Limited (Calgary, Ontario, Canada); Dir: Alaskan Resource Scis Corp (Anchorage), Filtrol Corp (Los Angeles, Cal), Gt Wn Bk & Trust (Phoenix, Ariz), Holmes & Narver Inc (Orange, Cal), Koehring Co (Milwaukee, Wis), Patagonia Corp (Tucson, Ariz), No Resources Inc (Billings, Mont), Williams Brothers Engrg Limited (London, England), Others; Trustee: Desert Res Inst (Reno, Nev), Hudson Inst (Croton-on-Hudson, NY); Mem Royal Soc Arts (London).

WILLIAMS, DAVID RUSSELL oc/Associate Professor; b/Oct 21, 1932; h/520 East Ave, Rochester, NY 14607; ba/Rochester; m/Elsa; p/H Russell and Mary Dean Williams, Indianapolis, IN; ed/AB Columbia Col; MA Columbia Univ; PhD Univ Rochester; mil/AUS 1957-59; pa/Assoc Prof Music Theory Eastman Sch Music; Secy Col Music Soc 1973-; Secy, Bd Dirs Rochester Philharm Orch 1976-; VP, Bd Dirs Rochester Chamber Orch; Bd Dirs Opera Theatre of Rochester; r/Epis; hon/Pub Awd, Eastman Sch of Music; W/W in E; Intl W/W in Music; DIB.

WILLIAMS, DONALD J oc/Electrical Engineer; b/Dec 28, 1925; h/1818 W State Ave, Phoenix, AZ 85021; ba/Litchfield Park, AZ; m/Nancy Ruth Thompson; c/Jeffrey Robert, Lynn Ruth, Jennifer Louise; p/William John Williams, Iron Mtn, MI; Jessie Coad Williams (dec); ed/BSEE Mich Tech; MSE Ariz

St Univ; mil/AUS Pacific Theater; pa/Elect Engr (Specialist in Elec Systems) Goodyear Aerospace; Sr Mem IEEE; Past Tech Conslt USAF; Former Lectr Glendale (Ariz) Col; cp/Soloist on Highland Bagpipe; London Soc; Mason; Shriner; r/Meth; hon/Instr's Cert on Highland Bagpipe, Col of Piping (Glasgow, Scotland); Men of Achmt; W/W in W.

WILLIAMS, EDWARD DONALD oc/Airline Public Relations; b/Feb 5, 1925; h/713 Eastman Dr, Mt Prospect, IL 60056; m/Dorothy Elizabeth Schroepel; c/Lee, Marc, Gregg, Faith Munger (Mrs Gary H), Joy Siehr (Mrs Patrick J); p/Edward J Williams; Ann P Williams, Chicago, IL; mil/USMC 1942-46; Air Medal; pa/Public Relats Rep United Airlines. Chgo 1974-; Reporter-Aviation Writer Milwaukee Jour 1961-74; Reporter: Chgo's Am 1958-61, Chgo Daily News

1952-58; Reporter-Photog Sheboygan (Wis) Press 1951-52; Mem Headline Clb, Chgo; Press Vets; Exptl Aircraft Assn; Aviation/Space Writers Assn; Aircraft Owners & Pilots Assn; Pt-time Assoc Editor Vintage Airplane Mag; r/Rom Cath; hon/Recipient Awds: AF Assn, Wis Wing CAP, Resv Ofcrs Assn, AFR, Wis Aviation Trades Assn, Wis Coun on Aeros; Contbr Articles to Aviation Jours & Popular Mags; Awd of Merit, United Airlines; Biogl Listings.

WILLIAMS, ELSIE M oc/Social Worker; b/Apr 6, 1931; h/Rt 8, Box 116, Leon Dr, Anderson, SC 29621; ba/Anderson; m/Broy Jr; c/Lee Andrews, Jerome B, Jimmy L, Randy C, Annie F, Lillian M; p/James and Lillian M Brown (dec); ed/AA; BA; pa/Vol Dept Social Sers; r/Prot; hon/2 Yr S'ship; Personalities of S.

WILLIAMS, HARLAN BRYAN oc/Minister; b/Jun 27, 1946; h/PO Box 1126, Apison, TN 37302; ba/Apison; m/Brenda Jeane Denton; c/Matthew Harlan; p/James H and Amy Jewell Isom Williams, Chattanooga, TN; ed/BA Belmont Col 1968; MDiv New Orleans Bapt Theol Sem 1978; pa/Ordained Min So Bapt Conv 1966; Pastor 1st Bapt Ch, Apison 1978-; Interim Pastor Pilgrim Rest Bapt Ch, Covington, La 1978; Pastor: Jerusalem Bapt Ch (Bush, La) 1976-77, Allons Bapt Ch (Allons, Tenn) 1974-75, Wolf Creek Bapt Ch (Spring City, Tenn) 1970-74, Rucker Bapt Ch (Murfreesboro, Tenn) 1967-68; Big Spring Bapt Ch (Cleveland, Tenn) 1968-70: Assoc Pastor, Mission Pastor, Yth Dir; Other Former

Pastorates; Mem Credentials Com Hamilton Co Assn Bapt 1978-; Mem Yth Com St Tammany Parish Assn Bapt (Covington, La) 1976-77; Riverside Assn Bapts (Livingston, Tenn): SS Dir 1974-75, Hospitality Chm World Mission Conf 1975, Chm Adm Com 1974-75; Tenn Val Assn Bapt (Dayton, Tenn): Ch Tng Dir 1970-72, VModerator 1971-72, Annual Message Preacher 1971, Chm Constitutional Com 1971, Chm Promotional Com 1971-72, Moderator 1972-74; cp/NAm Assn Ventriloquists; Lingberg Hist Soc; Collectors Guild; Belmont Alumni Assn; Nat Locksmith Assn; r/So Bapt; hon/DIB; Commun Ldrs & Noteworthy Ams; Men Achmt; Personalities of S; Notable Ams; W/W Rel.

WILLIAMS, HARRISON ARLINGTON JR oc/United States Senator; b/Dec 10, 1919; h/Bedminster, NJ; ba/352 Russell Senate Ofc Bldg, Washington, DC 20510; m/Jeanette Smith; c/Peter, Nina, Jonathan, Wendy; p/Harrison Arlington Williams Sr (dec); Isabel Lamson; ed/AB Oberlin Col 1941; LLB Columbia Law Sch 1948; 10 Hon Degs; mil/USN Pilot, USNR; pa/Elected to 83rd Cong (Mem Ho of Reps) 1953, Re-elected 1954; Elected US Senate 1958, 64, 70, 76: Chm Human Resources Com, Chm Subcom on Labor, Mem Bkg, Housing & Urban Affairs Com, Other Com Mbrships; Author Var Key Leg; NJ & Am Bar Assns; Nat Trans Policy Study Comm; Nat Ocean Policy Study Group; Adv Coun Woodrow Wilson Sch of Public & Intl Affairs at Princeton Univ; cp/Dem, Var Nat Coms & Couns; r/U Presb Ch: Mem; hon/Author; Trumpeter Awd, Nat Consumers Leag; Awds incl: Nat Cong Hispanic-Am Citizens, Intl Fund for Animal Wel, Am Civil Liberties Union of NJ; Person of Yr, Nat Coun on Commun Sers for Commun & Jr Cols 1978; Commun Ser Awd, AFL-CIO & Ctr of Alcohol Studies (Rutgers Univ); "Knight of the Yr," Bayley Seton Leag, Seton Hall Univ; Awd of Merit, Fed Adm Law Judges Conf; Hope Chest Awd, Nat MS Soc; Gertrude F Zimand Meml Awd, Nat Child Labor Coun; Others.

WILLIAMS, HARVEY oc/Psychologist; b/Oct 4, 1928; h/3900 Parkview Ln No 21B, Irvine, CA 92715; c/3 Daughs; ed/BA; MS; PhD; DDiv; pa/Current Psychologist Univ Cal-Irvine, Asst Dir Career Planning & Placemt Ctr; Present VChm Statutory Com of Extended Opportunity, Progs & Sers for Cal Commun Cols; Guest Lectr Dept Psychi & Human Behavior Univ Cal-I Col of Med; Lectr; Advr; Orange Co Hlth Planning Coun, US Dept HEW, Ctr for Wn Hemispheric Studies Inc, Assn Am Med Cols, Govt of India (on Hlth), 4 US Presidents (on Nat Hlth); Former Dir HEW Funded Grant for City of

Long Bch (Involving Crisis Ctr, Hdstart Prog & Ednl Opports Prog); St Ed Com; Am Soc Tng & Devel; Am Mgmt Assn; IPA; cp/BSA; Co Hlth Coun; NAACP; Am Civil Liberties Union; hon/Hon ThD Deg; Man of Yr, City of Long Bch 1968, 69; Annual Awd, Am Civil Liberties Union; Student Awd, Univ Cal-I; Biogl Listings.

WILLIAMS, HERMETTA ELAINE oc/-Administrative Assistant; b/May 28, 1943; h/423 W Wisconsin, Chicago, IL 60614; ba/Chgo; p/Herman Williams (dec); Fannye W Whitfield, Midway, AL; ed/ABA Ctl YMCA Commun Col; BA DePaul Univ 1978; MS 1979; pa/Adm Asst Clin Lab; Am Public Hlth Assn; Am Soc Med Technol; Nat Assn Hosp Purchasing Mgmt; Hosp Mgmt Systems Soc; Am Registry Med Asst: Past Pres, Mem

Bd Dirs; Nat Secys Assn, Intl; Commun Resource Advr Depaul Univ; Chm Hlth Careers Am Assn Med Assts; Clin Lab Mgmt Assn; Coor Am Cancer Soc Sum S'ship Prog, Roosevelt Meml Hosp; cp/Notary Public; r/1st Ch of Deliverance Spiritual Ch: Yth Wkr; hon/Fellow, Intl Col Med Technol; Merit Awd for Ldrship, Am Assn Med Pers; Dist'd Cit Awd for Exceptl Profl Ser, Am Assn Med Pers; Ser Awd, Roosevelt Meml Hosp; Chgo Public Schs Cooperative Ed Awd for Participation in Coop Hlth Occups Prog.

WILLIAMS, IRA JOSEPH oc/Minister; Ambassador of Goodwill; b/Aug 5, 1926; h/3763 Brennan Ave, Norfolk, VA 23502; m/Elsie Moore; c/3 Chd; p/Moses and Alethia Williams; ed/BTh Store Col 1952; BD Kingsley Sch Rel 1954; DD Am Bible Col 1961; AB Union Christian Bible Inst 1972; MA Pacific Col 1974; Certs; Addit Studies; pa/Former Pastorates: NY, Va, NC; Former Rec Dir Wash; Former Moderator Wash Area Mins Alliance; Orgr & Past Pres Qtrly Meeting Union (Wash); Former Exec Secy NC Bapt Dist Conv; Former Exec Secy U Christian Front for Brotherhood; Former Exec Secy Tidewater Metro Bapt Mins Conf; Past Chancellor Union Christian Bible Inst, Norfolk Ext; Pastor Antioch Bapt Ch, Norfolk; Nat Pres U Christian Front for Brotherhood; Moderator Old Dominion Missionary Bapt Assn; Exec Bd Mem Old En Bapt Assn NC; Exec Bd Mem Va Bapt St Conv; Mem Fgn Mission Bd; cp/Orgr & 1/Pres Wash Br NAACP; Tidewater Coun BSA; Tidewater Ctr for Sickle Cell Anemia; 32° Deg Mason; Former Bd Mem Alpha Phi Alpha; Life Mem NAACP; hon/Author; Cert of Recog, Gov Commonwealth of Va (John N Dalton); "Dr I Joseph Williams Day" (Aug 5, 1974), City of Norfolk; Intl Reg Profiles.

WILLIAMS, JEAN TAYLOR oc/Artist; h/2801 Mountain Brook Pkwy, Birmingham, AL 35223; ba/B'ham; m/James Hayes (dec); c/James Richard, Hayes Taylor, Mary Jean; p/Woodie Richard and Ella Harrison Taylor (dec); ed/BS Univ Montevallo; Spec Study; pa/Instr Sec'dy Sch 1933-35; Art Chm Mtn Brook Jr HS 1966; Juror St of Ala HSs Art S'ship Awd Competition 1971, 72; Portrait & Figure Painter; Am Artists Profl Leag (NY); Nat Leag Am Pen Wom; Nat Soc Arts & Lttrs; B'ham Art Assn; Ala Art Leag; Fac Woms Clb Univ Ala; Beta Beta Beta; Delta Phi Alpha; cp/B'ham Symph Assn; Vestavia CC; Turtlepoint Yacht & CC; The Clb; B'ham Symph Assn Fund-raising Proj; Vol Activs; r/Indep Presb Ch, B'ham; hon/Exhibited &

Won Awds Num Shows incl'g: Tenn Val Reg, Nat Leag Am Pen Wom (St), Ala St Exhbn, Grand Awd in Oil Painting, B'ham Mus Art & St's Traveling Exhibit, Others; One-Wom Exhbns incl: Samford Univ, Buchanan Gallery, Nat Soc Arts & Lttrs, The Clb, B'ham, AAUW; Presented Gold Key to City of Bessemer (Ala); Work Rep's in Num Pvt Collections incl'g: Univ Ala Med Ctr, Okolona Bapt Ch; Biogl Listings.

WILLIAMS, JOHNNY oc/Law Enforcement Agent; b/Aug 1, 1948; h/305 Brook-Green Dr, Columbia, SC 29210; ba/Columbia; m/Janet G; c/Johnte G; p/Ashpy Williams (dec); Eliza Williams, Sumter, SC;

ed/Assoc Degs: Crim Justice, Correctl Adm; Cert in Study of Human Relats Ocean Co Col (NJ); mil/AUS 6 Yrs; pa/Agt SC St Law Enforcemt Div 1972-; cp/Boys Clb; St Govt; r/Bapt; hon/AUS: Sharp Shooting Awd, Soldier of the Month Awd, Safe Driving Awd.

WILLIAMS, LARRY ALBERT oc/Dentist; h/Rt 1, Benson, NC 27504; ba/Benson, NC; m/Dorothy Lou Warren; c/Warren Albert, Larry Gregory; p/Wilton Albert and Edith Belk Williams, Tabor City, NC; ed/BS; DDS; FAGD; FACD; pa/Johnston Co Dental Soc: Pres, VP; 4th Dist Dental Soc: VP, Pres; Pres, Holland Dental Study Clb; Pres, NC Dental Soc Anesthesiology; NC Med Peer Review; Prog Chm, NC Dental Soc Conv 1980; Pres, NC Acad Gen Dentistry; Acad Gen Dentistry Long Range Planning; cp/Dir, Benson C of C; Pres, Lions Clb; Mason Lodge; Ancient & Accepted Scottish Rite; Shrine Clb; Mule Days Com; Former BSA Vol; r/Benson Bapt Ch: Deacon, Chm Bd Deacons (2 yrs), Asst SS Tchr, Past Dir SS Yth Dept, Choir Mem; hon/F'ships: Acad of Gen Dentistry, Am Col Dentists.

WILLIAMS, MARTHA OLIVER oc/Poet; Writer; Office Manager & Accountant; b/May 15, 1925; h/1015 Harrison St, El Dorado, AR 71730; ba/El Dorado; m/Carl S; c/Larry Carl, Mark Oliver; ed/Ofc Mgr & Acct Ark Chems Inc (Chem Mfg Plant); Self-employed 1948-70; TV Broadcaster 1954-57; Radio Broadcaster 1959-62; Instr Fundamentals of Poetry So Ark Univ, El Dorado Br Commun Ser; Poets Roundtable Ark; Nat Leag Am Pen Wom: N La Br, Mbrship Chm Local Br 1976-78, Secy La 1976-78; Books Pub'd: *Lines From Living* 1973 (2nd Printing 1974), *Windows* 1976, *Why the Snow* 1978; Contbr to Mags & Other Pubs; cp/PTA: Past Local Pres, Former St VP & St Mag Chm; Past VP & Mbrship Chm El Dorado Commun Concert Assn; r/Bible Class Tchr; hon/Poets Roundtable Monthly Contest (Oct 1975, Mar 1977); Maj Poets Sevenelle;

Maj Poets Grand Prize; Biogl Listings.

WILLIAMS, MELVIN oc/Social Services Administrator; b/Mar 1, 1946; h/708 Marquette Dr, Louisville, KY 40222; ba/L'ville; m/Brenda Harvey; c/Guy Bivins; p/John Melvin Williams, Memphis, TN; Rosie Lee Williams (dec); ed/BS Fisk Univ; MEd Univ L'ville; pa/Assoc Exec Dir Progs, Plans & Operations, L'ville Urban Leag; Former Dept Mgr & Asst Div Mgr F W Woolworth Inc; Golden Circle, Memphis (Life Ins Co): Former Debit Mgr, Former Bldr, Former Staff Tnr/Supvr; Other Former Positions; VP Assn Asst Chief Execs; Alpha Phi Alpha; cp/ARC, VChm Supplemental Income Security Prog; Adv Com: Neighborhood Awds Prog, Dept Hlth-Swine Flue Immunization Prog (L'ville); Bd Mem Emer Med Ser; Frat Order of Masonry So Cross Lodge; Human Needs & Budget Priorities Coalition's Task Force; NAACP; Vol U Ser Org; U Negro Col Fund; YMCA; r/U Ch of Christ; hon/Apprec Awd, Supplemental Income Security Prog; Apprec Awd & Cit for Meritorious Ser, MUW; Field Instr Cert of Apprec, Univ L'ville, Kent Sch of Social Work; High Achiever Perf Awd, L'ville Public Schs Campaign Chm, MUW.

WILLIAMS, MELVIN EMANUEL oc/Technical/Administrative Advisor to Local Governments; b/Dec 8, 1940; h/PO Box 1515, Tallahassee, FL 32302; m/Helen Deloris; c/Melvin Pierre, Manuel Delano; p/Thomas Samuel and Amelia David Williams (dec); ed/BA Wilberforce Univ 1963; MPA Univ RI 1968; mil/USN 1963-67; pa/Instr Mgmt & Ecs Ky Bus Col, Danville, Ky 1978-; Public Mgmt & Tng Conslt Blue Grass Area Devel Dist Inc, Lexington, Ky 1977-; Tech & Tng Resources Specialist-Conslt Garrard Co, Lincoln Co, City of Lancaster & City of Stanford (Ky) 1977-; Opers & Planning Advr Country Rds Hlth Plan Inc, Beckley, WVa 1976-77; Tng Sers Advr for Consumer Hlth Protection Ky Bur for Hlth Sers 1975-76; Prog Devel Conslt for Drug Abuse Rehab Sers Ctl Commun Hlth Bd of Hamilton Co Inc, Cincinnati, Ohio 1973-74; Other Former Positions; Am Soc for Public Adm; Am Soc for Tng & Devel; cp/Garrard & Lincoln Counties (Ky): Advr Bi-co Mgmt Assistance Prog, Secy Bi-co Ec Adjustmt Com; r/Ch of God of Am Inc: Ordained Elder 1974; Sponsor & Host Friendly Gospel Gathering, WIXI Radio (Lancaster, Ky).

WILLIAMS, NORMA PAINTER oc/-Educational Diagnostician; b/Sept 18, 1934; h/114 Bailey, Dumas, TX 79029; ba/Dumas; m/Bill H; c/Gregory Kirk, Bradford Dirk; p/Frank and Cora Painter, Sunray, TX; ed/BS; MEd; pa/N Plains Assn for Chd w LD, Leg Chm; Tex Assn for Chd w LD; Secy Ednl

Diagnosticians of the Golden Spread; Secy Tex Profl Edrs Moore Co; Coun of Ednl Diagnosticians; Tex Assn Ednl Diagn; CEC; Classroom Tchrs Assn; cp/Moore Co Mus Fdr; Charter Mem Moore Co Hist Soc Former Bd Mem & Ofcr: U Way, YMCA, Moore Co Dem Wom, Dilletant Study Clb; r/Presb: Ruling Elder, Past Deacon.

WILLIAMS, PARKER oc/Dean of Library Sciences; b/Jul 26, 1929; h/10404 Belfast Rd, LaPorte, TX 77571; ba/Pasadena, TX; p/James Cill and Bonnie Pearl Williams (dec); ed/BA; MEd; PhD; pa/San Jacinto Col, Pasadena: Dean Lib Sers 1974-. Hd Libn Lee

Davis Lib 1961-74; Hd Libn Pasadena Public Lib 1955-61; Sys-wide Libn Grand Saline Public Schs, Grand Saline, TX 1949-55; Tex Jr Col Assn: Chm Nom'g Com 1975-76, Chm Lng Resource Div 1974-75, VChm Lib Div 1973-74, Profl Devel Com 1971-75, Social Chm 1971-72; Tex Lib Assn: VChm & Chm Elected Adm Round Table 1975-76, Local Arrangemts Com (in Houston), Chm Col Univ Div 1971-72, Others; Zeta Omega Chapt Delta Kappa Gamma; Bd Mem Pasadena Public Lib 1967-74; SWn Lib Assn; Adv Dir 1st Nat Bk, Deer Park (Tex) 1974-; cp/Adv Bd Mem Marquis Biogl Soc; San Jacinto Wom's Clb; Kappa Delta Phi; Beta Sigma Phi; Rho Sigma Chapt Epsilon Sigma Alpha; Former Mem Pasadena Fine Arts Coun; Others; r/Bapt; hon/Contbr to Tex Lib Jours; Num Biogl Listings.

WILLIAMS, ROGER JOHN oc/Biochemist; b/Aug 14, 1893; h/1604 Gaston Ave, Austin, TX 78703; ba/Austin; m/M Phyllis; c/Roger John Jr, Janet, Arnold, John Hobson; p/Robert Runnels and Alice Evelyn Mills Williams (dec); ed/BS; MS; PhD; DSc; pa/Univ Tex: Prof Chem, Dir Clayton Foun Biochem Inst 1939-63; r/Prot; hon/Hon DSc: Redlands, Columbia Univ, Oreg St; Mead Johnson Awd, Am Inst Nutrition; Chandler Medal, Columbia Univ.

WILLIAMS, VERNON ALBRIGHT oc/Industrial Engineer; b/Jan 31, 1955; h/7300 Cedar Post Rd, Liverpool, NY 13088; ba/Syracuse, NY; p/Raymond P and Willie Mae Williams, High Point, NC; ed/BS NC A&T SU; pa/Am Soc for Metals; Soc Mfg Engrs; hon/W/W Among Students in Am Univs & Cols.

WILLIAMSON, PETER ARTHUR oc/-Assistant Professor; b/Apr 22, 1944; h/1118 Bond Ave, Auburn, AL 36830; ba/Auburn; m/Susan Ford; c/Traci; p/Arthur J and Mary H Williamson; ed/BA Williams Col 1966; MS Bank St Col of Ed 1975; EdD Univ Ga 1978; pa/Asst Prof Early Childhood Ed Auburn Univ; Am Ednl Res Assn; Assn for Childhood Ed Intl; Nat Assn for Ed of Yg Chd; Phi Delta Kappa; Treas Lee Co Assn of Yg Chd; r/Congreg; hon/Judd Awd for Excell in Res, Phi Delta Kappa; Outstg Yg Men Am.

WILLIAMSON, WILLIAM HARVEY oc/Artist; Muralist; h/Granada Inn, 2375 W Lincoln, Anaheim, CA 92801; m/Elizabeth Carter; p/William W and Erma Mural Williamson; pa/Nat Soc of Mural Painters; Intl Assn of Plastic Arts; IPA; Life Fellow Intl

Inst of Arts & Lttrs; hon/Num Biogl Listings; Num Exhbns in Am & Europe incl'g: Tower Observation Gallery (the Mall, Albany, NY) 1977-78, Galerie du Chardon (Left Bank Paris, France), Galerie Vallombreuse (Biarritz, France) 1978, I C A Inst Contemp Arts Lib (London, England), Carmel Art Assn Galleries (Carmel, Cal), Pebble Bch Art Gallery (Cal), Num Others; Num Biogl Listings.

WILLINGHAM, ELIZABETH MOORE oc/Sales Promotion Director; Public Relations; Educator; Editor; b/Oct 14, 1948; h/3600 Fort Ave, Waco, TX 76710; ba/Waco; m/John; c/Emily Jane, Thomas Carl; p/Elmo Moore, Lake Striker, TX; Sue Whitaker Nichols, Lake Mexia, TX; ed/BA magna cum laude 1973, MA 1979 Baylor Univ; pa/Mod

Lang Assn; Conf on Christianity & Lit; Am Studies Assn, Tex Chapt; AAUP; Intl Browning Soc; NEA; Sev Papers; cp/St & Local Dem Party; hon/Tchg Asst'ship, Baylor Univ; Browning F'ship; Danforth Foun Finalist.

WILLIS, W MARTY JR oc/Regional Manager; b/Feb 27, 1938; h/3814 Treadway Dr, Valrico, FL 33594; ba/Tampa, FL; c/W Marty III, W Melody; p/W M Sr and Cora Lee Willis, Memphis, TN; pa/Reg Mgr Quality Inns Intl Inc 1975-; Asst VP Opers Consolidated Inns (Holiday Inns) 1974-75; Gen Mgr & Fla Supvr Quality Inns Inc 1971-74; ITT Sheraton Properties 1967-71; Mgr Pvt Clbs 1964-67; Profl Show & Recording Musician 1957-64; cp/Kiwanis Clb; Chm Tourist Com Daytona Bch C of C; Mem Egypt Temple Shrine; 32°, Scottish Rite; hon/Quality Inns Inc: Top Prodr, Advt'g/Promotion Awd; Appt'd a "Friendly Floridian", Fla Dept of Commerce 1974; Bd Dirs Daytona Bch Motel/Hotel Assn 1971; Gold Record for White Silver Sands; Biogl Listings.

WILLS, EDWINA FLORENCE WHEELER oc/Professional Musician; Professional Artist, Poet; h/8270 SE Poppy Ln, Portland, OR 97222; ba/Same; m/L Max; c/Victoria Brown (Mrs R M), Byron S, David M, Mary Beth W Conyac (dec); p/Edwina Morris and Jessie Goble Wheeler (dec); ed/BA Grinnell Col 1937; Masters Equiv Wash St 1939; Addit Studies; pa/Profl Musician: Perf'g Cellist & Contralto, Tchr Piano; Prin Cellist, Portland Chamber Orch 1973-; Vol Music Therapy Oreg St Hosp 1960-67; Sch Music Tchr: Elem, Jr High, HSs 1958-69; Tchr Cols: Wash St, Lewis & Clark Col 1962-67; Pvt Tchr of Cello & Piano 1935-; cp/F'ship of Reconciliation; Wom's Clb; r/Prot: Comm Evang; hon/1st Nat MOE Music Comp Awd (Perf), 26th Am Music Fest (NYC) 1965; Wash Fdn Music Clbs 1st Music Comkp Awd (Perf), Commun Concerts Assn 1973; Featured Spkr; Var Art Awds; Exhibited at Inst of Chgo; Biogl Listings; Others.

WILLS, ELIZABETH WOOD oc/Director of Christian Education, Administrative Assistant; b/Dec 4, 1908; h/1815 Potomac Cir, Lansing, MI 48910; ba/Lansing; m/Theodore O M (dec); c/Theodore O M II, David Wood; p/David Edwards and Jessie Lochore Aird Wood (dec); ed/BA Univ Del 1935; BMus Westminster Choir Col 1938; pa/Min of Music: 1st Presb Ch, Portland, Ind 1939-45, S Shore Presb Ch, Chgo, Ill 1945-50; Dir of Christian Ed & Min of Music: Laurel Hgts Meth Ch, San Antonio, Tex 1951-52, 1st U Meth Ch, Monrovia, Cal 1942-63; Dir Christian Ed 1st U Presb Ch, Lansdowne, Pa 1963-64; Dir Christian Ed & Adm Asst 1st U Presb Ch, Lansing 1965-; Charter Mem Assn Mins of Music of U Meth Ch; Mem, Num Ofcs: Assn Dirs of Christian Ed of Meth Ch in So Cal, Interdenom Assn Dirs Christian Ed of Cal; Nat Assn Dirs Christian Ed in U Presb Ch USA; Reg Assn Dirs Christian Ed in MW of U Presb Ch; Local Chapts of Presb & Interdenom Dirs Christian Ed; Nat Childhood Ed Assn; Christian Ed Com Phila Presby & Grand River Presby; Pers Com Lake Mich Presby of U Presb Ch; Nat Coun Chs, Del Nat Assembly 1964; AAUW; Nat Curric Plan'g Com for U Presb Ch 1964; Interdenom Nat Curric Plan'g Com 1962-63; cp/Past Mem Bd Dirs S Shore YMCA, Chgo; Mem, Ofcr Music Clbs: Portland, Ind, Chgo; Lit Socs: Portland, Springfield, Ill, Chgo, San Antonio; Symph Orch, Concert, Drama Bds & Orgs; Nat Woms Clb; Past Mem Commun Integration & Clearing Bd, Monrovia, Cal; Nat Coun Chs Ednl Com, Lansing; U Ch Wom; Rel Advrs Assn, Mich St Univ; Public Spkr & Singer; Fdr & Dir Mary Poppins Nursery Sch, Lansing; Caledonia Clb, Detroit; Assoc Mem Iona Commun, Isle of Iona, Scotland; Intl Ecumenical F'ship, London; r/Presby Soc, Woms Assn of Lake Mich Presby; Ordained Min of Music & Min of Christian Ed, U Meth Ch USA; Comm'd Ch Wkr in U Presb Ch USA; hon/Phi Kappa Phi; Campfire Girl Wom of Yr 1959 Monrovia; Nat Hon Mbrships: Woms Assn U Meth Ch in USA, Woms Assn U Presb Ch in USA; Prayer

Chapel Opened & Named in Her Hon, 1st Meth Ch, Monrovia 1960; Biogl Listings.

WILSON, BENJAMIN CALVIN oc/-Assistant Professor; b/Mar 30, 1947; ba/814 Sprau Tower, Wn Mich Univ, Kalamazoo, MI 49008; m/Patricia Ann; c/Nikki Kai, Ayanna Tene; p/Benjamin C Wilson (dec); Winifred J Wilson; ed/BA; MA; PhD; pa/Asst Prof Black Am Studies Wn Mich Univ; Black Edrs Kalamazoo Co; cp/Human Relats Instr Reg Police Acad; r/Bapt; hon/Outstg Yg Man Am.

WILSON, CHARLES WILLIAM oc/-Physician, Surgeon; b/Aug 12, 1916; h/4655 Basque Dr, Santa Maria, CA 93454; ba/Santa Maria; m/Frances Presha Stephenson; c/Charles William II, Walter Stephen, Cherrie, James Robin; p/Jacob Resor Wilson (dec); Estella Cherrie Wilson (dec); ed/BA Wichita Univ; MD Univ Ks; mil/USN 1943-46, Lt (sg) MC; pa/Phys & Surg

Specializing in Psychi & Med Hypnosis; Staff Psychiatrist, Atascadero, Cal 1975-; Pvt Pract Psychi & Med Hypnosis 1971-; Reschr & Developer Four Rapid Psychotherapies; So Cal Psychi Soc; Am Psychi Assn; Am Soc Clin Hypnosis; Soc Clin & Experimtl Hypnosis; Acad Parapsychol & Med; AAAS; cp/BSA 23 Yrs: Scout, Scoutmaster, Explorer Ldr, Asst Dist & Neighbor Commr, Tchr of Tnrs; Rotary Intl; Am Legion; Elem Sch Bd, St Francis (Ks); Mason; Phi Beta Pi; Men of Webster; Delta Upsilon; Lions Clb 2 Yrs; r/Meth Ch: Lay Ldr; hon/BSA: Eagle Scout, Explorer Silver Awd, Scoutmaster's Key, Wood Badge; Biogl Listings.

WILSON, DONALD M oc/Composer; Associate Professor; b/Jun 30, 1937; h/550 W Wooster, Bowling Green, OH 43402; ba/Bowling Green; m/Claire P; c/Sheilah C, Susannah B; p/William George and Dora L Wilson, Plainfield, IL; ed/BA Univ Chgo 1959; MA 1962, DMA 1965 Cornell Univ; pa/BGSU: Coor Modular Curric & Aural Skills 1977-, Chm Composition/Hist Dept 1973-77, Dir Bd Tutors 1969-, Assoc Prof Music Theory & Composition 1972-, Asst Prof 1969-72, Instr 1967-69; WUHY-FM, Philadelphia (Pa): Prog Dir 1966-67, Music Dir 1965-66; Other Former Positions; Am Music Ctr; Phila Composers Forum; Am Composers Alliance; Music Tchrs' Nat Assn; Ohio Music Tchrs' Assn; Ohio Theory-Composition Tchrs Assn; Other Profl Activs; r/Epis; hon/Pub'd Compositions; Num Public Perfs; 4 Am Music Awds for Promotion & Perf of Am Music (on behalf of BGSU), Nat Fdn Music Clbs; Delius Fest's Instrumental Best-in-Category Awd for SETT 1974; Hon Mention, Oreg Col of Ed's 1970 Sum Arts Fest; Other Awds; Biogl Listings; Pub'd Articles.

WILSON, GEORGE WILTON oc/-Professor; b/Feb 15, 1928; h/2325 Woodstock Pl, Bloomington, IN 47401; ba/B'ton; m/Marie; c/Ronald, Douglas, Suzanne; p/-Walter and Ida Wilson (dec); ed/BComm Carleton Univ 1950; MA Univ Ky 1951; PhD Cornell Univ 1955; pa/Prof Ecs & Bus Ind Univ; Chm Dept Ec 1966-70; Dean Col of Arts & Scis 1970-73; Pres Trans Res Forum 1969; Pres Task Force on Trans; Conslt to World Bk, Var Govts & Businesses; Author Num Books & Articles on Ec, Trans; hon/Dist'd Prof, Ind Univ; Alumni Awd, Carleton Univ; Vis Dist'd Scholar, Univ Tenn.

WILSON, HUGH EDWARD oc/Engineer; b/Oct 13, 1919; h/19122 Challe Cir W, Spring, TX; m/Betty Jean; c/Marsha Ruth, Stephen Emil, Hugh Edward Jr; p/Hugh Emil and Maude Wilson (dec); ed/AS (EE) N Tex Agri Col; BS (EE) So Meth Univ; mil/AUS 1940-45, Chief Warrant Ofcr; Bronze Star Medal; Am Def Ser Medal; European Theater of Opers Campaign Medal w 4 Battle Stars; Victory Medal; pa/Sr Staff Mgr Elec Engrg Forest Prods Dept, Brown & Root Inc, Houston, TX; IEEE: Sr Mem, (Houston Sect:) Treas 1968-69, Secy 1969-70, VChm 1970-71, Chm 1971-72; Power Engrg Soc; Indust Applications Soc; Am Inst Elec Engrs: Mem, Dir Houston Sect 1962-63; Tech Assn of Pulp & Paper Indust; Houston Engrg & Sci Soc; r/Ch of Christ; hon/Author Sev Profl Articles; Chm or CoChm Var Tech Confs; W/W Tex; Notable Ams; Personalities of S; Men of Achmt; Intl W/W: Intells, Commun Ser; Others.

WILSON, NEVADA PEARL BROWN oc/Secretary; Manufacturing Company Employee; b/Jan 19, 1930; h/1841 Kit Carson Dr, Dyersburg, TN 38024; ba/Ethridge, TN; m/Charles A; c/D E Brown, Barbara Sue Brown, Beverly Hope Brown Bailey; p/Jady Clay Beatty (dec); Esther Lee Nutt (dec); ed/Cert Gen Ofc Pract; BS Cand; pa/Presently Assoc'd w Murray Ohio Mfg Co, Lawrenceburg, Tenn; Farm Mgr; Pvt Secy; cp/Commun Civic Clb, Ethridge; Vol; Hist Soc Lawrence Co; Ornithological Soc; r/Hillcrest Bapt Ch, D'burg: Mem; Meth Lay Spkr; Vaughn Meml Ch of Nazarene: Choir Mem; Others.

WILSON, ROSE CONFEF oc/Educator; Counselor; Resource Specialist; b/Jun 14, 1924; h/1529 Tennessee St, Lake Charles, LA 70605; ba/Lake Charles; m/Clarence Jr (dec); chd/Michael C T, C Patrick, James R, Marguerite R, S Timothy; p/Irven J Confer, Pittsburgh, PA; Marguerite Rose Kelley Confer (dec); ed/BA; MEd; EdS; EdD; pa/Parish Sch Bd 1963-; Resource Spec for Spec Sers 1978 & 1979-, Coor Title IV Occupl Readiness Prog 1978-79, Tchr LaGrange Mid Sch (Lake Charles) 1977-78, Coor Commun Ed Sch (Evenings) 1978, Others; Cnslr: SW La Hlth Cnslg Ser (Summer 1978 & Vol Cnslr 1971-78), The Guid Clin (Lake Charles) 1977-, Others; Speaker on Var Topics for Civic Orgs & Profl Groups; Vis Lectr on Mtl Hygiene, McNeese St Univ (Lake Charles) 1977; Adv

Com on Autism for St of La Dept of Ed 1979; Phi Delta Kappa; Alpha Delta Kappa; APGA; LPGA; La Ed Res Assn; Assn for Cnslr Ed & Supvn; La Assn for Cnslr Ed & Supvn; Am Sch Cnslr Assn; LSCA; Am Voc Assn; NEA; Profl Adv Bd, SW La Hlth Cnslg Ser; Others; cp/Profl Adv Bd, La Epilepsy Assn; Past Chm, SW La Mayors' Com on Employmt of Handicapped; Lake Charles Civic Symph Aux 1969-; Past Mem Telephone Com; Nat Soc for Autistic Chd; United Cerebral Palsy of SW La; W Calcasieu Assn for Retarded Citizens; Others; r/St Margaret Cath Ch: Catechism Tchr 3 Yrs, Secy 1978-80, Liturgy Planner 1974-79, Lay Min for Eucharist 1977-, Others; hon/Alpha Phi of Delta Kappa Gamma S'ship; Tchrs Medal, Freedoms Foun at Val Forge; Keys to City of Lake Charles, presented by Mayor James Sudduth; Cert of Awd, Lake Charles Assn for Retarded Citizens; Wom of Yr, QUOTA Clb of Lake Charles 1975; Others.

WILSON, SADIE LUCILLE oc/Resource Teacher; b/May 29, 1934; h/949 E 84th St, 1st Floor, Chicago, IL 60619; ba/Chgo; c/Daniel Rutherford; p/Smith Daniel Wilson (dec); Rachel I WIlson, Chgo; ed/BE; MA; Masters Guid & Cnslg; pa/Resource Tchr Grades 5-8 (Rdg Improvemt); Orgr Field Trips for Students & Adults; Org'd Winter & Sum Social Ctr Prog; Sponsor: Sch Newspaper, Yrbook, Book Fair, Drama Group, Cheerleaders, Student Coun; Coor Tutorial Prog; Mem Planning Com for Career Conf (Sch); Chperson Publicity Com Provident Hosp; Resource Person to Aid Students to Win S'ships; Corr Secy Profl Wom's Aux Provident Hosp; Sch Store Mgr; Camp Advr to Students, Elem & HS; APGA; ANWC; cp/PWA; Les Amies Charitable Clb; r/Presb.

WILSON, SHIRLEY SCHAUB oc/Athletic Director; b/Sept 26, 1926; h/430 Devonshire Ln, Burlington, NC 27215; ba/Durham, NC; m/Katie; c/John, Cathy, Steve; p/John L and Georgia K Wilson (dec); ed/BS Davidson Col; MEd UNC; mil/USN WWII; pa/Asst Dir Aths Duke Univ; Nat Ftball Coaches Assn; Nat Assn Ath Dirs; cp/Rotary Clb; Exec Bd Boy Scouts; Trustee Pop Warner Ftball; r/Presb: Deacon, Elder, SS Tchr; hon/Runner-Up Nat Ftball Coach of Yr, NAIA; Num Conf & Dist Hons for Ftball Coach of Yr.

WILTSE, DORR NORMAN oc/Casualty Insurance Executive; City Assessor; b/Sept 20, 1911; h/708 W Sherman, Caro, MI 48723; ba/Caro; m/Gladys May Garner; c/Dorr Norman Jr, Saire Christina; p/Norman Anson Wiltse (dec); Evie Markham McCartney (dec); ed/Att'd En Mich Univ & Ctl Mich Univ; pa/Mich Assessor's Assn; ICA Planning Comm; VP Caro Devel Corp; Pres Caro Hist Comm; cp/Pres Caro Masonic Bldg Assn; Caro Area Bicent Comm Chm; Dem; Mem Com to Elect Pres Ford; Nat Trust for Hist Preserv; Hist Soc Mich; r/Presb: Ordained Elder; hon/Hon 33° Mason; Citizen of Yr Awd, Caro C of C 1975; Royal Order of Scotland; Grand High Priest, Grand Chapt Royal Arch Masons Mich 1966-67; Mich Bicent Awd of Merit; Nat De Molay Legion of Merit Awd.

WIMMER, GLEN ELBERT oc/Professional Engineer; b/Feb 16, 1903; h/3839-48 Vista Campana S, Oceanside, CA 92054; ba/Same; m/Mildred G McCullough; c/Frank Thomas; ed/BSME 1925, MSME 1933 Ia St Univ; MBA NWn Univ 1935; mil/USAR Ofcr Activs 1925-28; Inactive to 1938; pa/Draftsman GE Co Ft Wayne, Ind 1925-29; Asst Engr Wn Elect Co, Chgo, Ill 1929-32; Mech Engr Instr, Mich Col Mining & Technol 1936-37; Machine Designer Firestone Tire & Rubber Co, Akron, Ohio 1937-38; Engr in Charge of Design for Ditto Inc, Chgo 1938-39; Asst to Chief Engr of Victorgraph Corp Chgo 1939-40; Detroit, Mich: Designer of Tools & Machinery for Pioneer Engrg & Mfg Co 1940-41, Designer & Checker Assoc Designers 1941-42, Designer & Checker Engrg Ser Corp 1942, Checker & Asst Supt Design for Norman E Miller & Assocs 1942, Engrg Checker Lee Engrg Co 1942-45; Chgo: Hd Design & Devel Dept Cummins Perforator Co 1943-45, Staff Engr Charge of Design & Devel Tammen & Denison Inc 1945-58, Instr of Cost Analysis Evening Course, Ill Inst Technol 1946-47, Engr w Barnes & Reineck Inc 1958-60, 61-68, Devel Engr B H Bunn Co 1960-61; Pvt Pract 1968-; Dir Ill Engrg Coun 1958-66; Mem Ill Soc Profl Engrs; Nat Soc Profl Engrs; IPA; r/Meth; hon/Delta Chi; Cert by Nat Bur Engrg Bds; W/W: Engrg, W; Ldrs Am Sci; Intl Blue Book World Notables; Nat Social Dir; Soc Dirs of US & Cal; The Blue Book; Ill Lives; 2000 Men Achmt; DIB; Intercont Biog Assn; Men Achmt; Personalities of W&MW; Cal Register; Intl Reg Profiles; Intl W/W: Intells, Commun Ser; Commun Ldrs Am; Notable Ams Bicent Era; Book of Honor.

WINCHESTER, CLARENCE FLOYD oc/Consultant; b/Oct 14, 1901; h/2124 Sudbury Pl NW, Washington, DC 20012;

ba/Same; m/Alma Tatsch; c/Maxine Claire W Cloon (Mrs Robert); p/Leon Alpheus and Nina Pearl T Winchester (dec); ed/BS 1924, MS 1935 Univ Cal-B; PhD Univ Mo-C 1939; mil/USAAF 1942-47, 1/Lt to Capt; pa/Instr Cal Schs 1924-31; Res Scist: Univ New Hampshire 1931-32, Univ Cal-Davis 1932-37, Univ Mo-C 1937-47; Res Scist USDA, Beltsville, Md 1949-61; Lectr in Nutrition Howard Univ 1966-75; Conslt in Animal & Human Nutrition 1975-; hon/Sigma Xi; Gamma Sigma Delta.

WING, MARY CAROL oc/Staff Physician; Laboratory Director; b/Dec 15, 1946; h/PO Box 513, Niwor, CO 80544; ba/Boulder, CO; m/Gary Stephen; p/Chas E and Geraldine M Soulliard, Tucson, AZ; ed/BS magna cum laude 1968, MD 1973 Univ Ariz; pa/Wardenburg SHS, Univ Colo: Staff Phys, Dir Clin Lab; Nat Assn Residents & Interns; Am Med Wom's Assn; cp/Lectr Local Groups; r/Rom Cath; hon/Alpha Lambda Delta; Beta Beta Beta; Phi Beta Kappa; Phi Kappa Phi.

WINKELMANN, JOHN PAUL oc/Pharmacist; h/1012 Surrey Hills Dr, St Louis, MO 63117; ba/Same; m/Margaret Ann; chd/John Damian & James Paul, Joseph Peter, Christopher Louis; p/Clarence Henry Winkelmann (dec); Alyce Marie Winkelmann, St Louis; mil/USAFR: Capt, Armed Forces Courier Ofcr 1956-57; pa/Nat Cath Pharms Guild of US: Pres 1968-70 & 1979-, Exec Dir 1970-, Fdg Mem 1962, Fdg Editor Cath Pharm 1967-; St Louis Col of Pharm: Histn 1960-, Bd Trustees 1961-, Chm Audit Com 1968-; r/Cath; hon/Knight of Malta, Pope Paul VI; Cath Pharm of Yr 1970; Knight of the Holy Sepulchre, Pope John Paul II.

WINKLEMAN, JACK DUANE oc/Farmer; b/Oct 17, 1943; h/Rt 5, Kirksville, MO 63501; ba/K'ville; m/Rosemary Clinkenbeard; c/Patrick Lee, Lisa Jo, Barry Jay; p/Gene and Margaret Reynolds Winkleman, Greentop, MO; mil/AUS (Europe) 1961-64; pa/Owner & Operator of Commercial Livestock & Grain Farm; Fdr & Pres, Wintock Inc (Land Holding Co) 1974-; Fdr & Pres, KRC Inc (Rec Ctr) 1979-; Asst Dir Grain Dept, NFO (Corning, Iowa) 1969; Bd Dirs, Mo Corn Growers Assn 1978-; Bd Dirs, Nat Corn Growers Assn 1978-; cp/Past Com-man, Clay Twp (Mo); Del to Var Co, Dist & St Polit Convs; r/Sperry Bapt Ch (Sperry, Mo); hon/W/W: MW, Am; Men of Achmt.

WINTERS, GEORGE ARCHER oc/- Professional Musician; b/Dec 3, 1950; h/6515 Spring Well, San Antonio, TX 78249; p/-

Russell R and Doris A Winters, Hills, CA; ed/BMus Univ Colo; Masters Eastmann Sch; pa/Composer; Bassist San Antonio Symph Conductor Winters Chamber Orch; cp/Tex Arts Alliance; r/Epis; hon/S'ship, Aspen Music Fest 1976; Brockport Conductors Fest 1978; Grad Cum Laude.

WINTHROP, AMORY oc/Horse Trainer; Horse Show Rider & Judge; b/Dec 14, 1931; h/"Winley", Millbrook, NY 12545; p/Robert Winthrop; Theodora A Randolph; ed/Grad Bradford Jr Col; pa/Reg'd Am Horse Show, Judge of Jumpers, Hunters, Hunt Seat Equitation; cp/Bd Dirs Fund for Animals Inc; Assistance Dogs Intl; NY Animal Adoption Soc; Pres Taconic Animal Protectors; Bd Dirs Coun New England Inst of Comparative Med; NY St Humane Assn; Pres Winley Foun; r/Epis.

WISEMAN, BERNARD oc/Author, Illustrator; b/Aug 26, 1922; h/868 Lake Hill Rd, W Eau Gallie, Mel, FL 32935; ba/Same; m/Susan Nadine; c/Michael Avram, (Stepson) Peter F Cranis; p/Abraham Zalman and Yetta Leah Wiseman (dec); mil/USCG WWII, 4½ Yrs; pa/Author & Illustrator Chd's Books; Cartoonist; r/Hebrew.

WISER, SARA POPPLETON oc/Realtor; b/Dec 23, 1909; h/435 E 3rd W, Logan, UT 84321; m/LaMoin H (dec); c/Gerald L, Dean C (dec), Marie W Daines, Judy W Brooks, Joyce W Watterson, John Steve; p/John Mitton and Mary Owen Gunnell Poppleton; pa/Real Est Saleslady Weber Real Est, Logan 1962-63; Real Est Broker; Propr Wiser Real Est 1963-; Nat Assn Realtors; Logan Real Est Bd; cp/C of C, Logan; Soroptimist Clb, Logan; r/LDS Ch: Mem.

WITHAM, WILLIAM TASKER oc/- University Professor; b/May 20, 1914; h/2323 Washington Ave, Terre Haute, IN 47803; ba/- Terre Haute; m/Drusilla Goodwin; c/- Raymond, Suzanne (dec), Kathleen (dec), Lawrence; p/Raymond Lee and Marion Tasker Witham (dec); ed/BA Drew 1936; MA Columbia 1940; PhD Ill 1961; pa/Ind St Univ:

Prof Eng 1967-80, Assoc Prof 1963-67, Asst Prof 1959-63; Hartwick Col: Assoc Prof 1949-59, Asst Prof 1943-49; AAUP; Col Eng Assn; Conf on Col Compos & Commun; Mod Lang Assn; Mod Humanities Res Assn; NCTE; cp/Actor, Dir & Bd Mem Commun Theatres in Terre Haute & Oneonta (NY); Pres Peace Couns Terre Haute & Oneonta; Former Cubmaster BSA; r/U Presb: Deacon, Elder, Mem Synod Coms; hon/Phi Kappa Phi; Sigma Tau Delta; Mark Twain Soc; Eugene Field Soc; Danforth Foun Awd; Pub'd Author.

WITHERSPOON, INA LORRENE McAULEY oc/Hairdresser; Free-lance

Writer; b/Dec 22, 1920; h/1011 Pittman Rd, Hot Springs, AR 71901; ba/Same; m/Clayton H; c/Charles R, Sherri Kay Meredith (Mrs J D); p/Howard R and Rilla J Alexander McAuley, Hobbs, NM; ed/Grad Ark Beauty Col; pa/Beauty Salon (Witherspoon's Beauty Salon) Owner & Operator 1962-; Mem Nat Writer's Clb; Poets Roundtable; cp/Past Pres PTA; Beta Sigma Phi; Smithsonian Nat Assn; Nat Archives; r/So Bapt; hon/Intl W/W Poets; Ark Gazette Foun Awd; 1st Hon Mention; Num Pub'd Poems & Var Books of Poetry.

WITTEN, LAURENCE CLAIBORNE II oc/Antiquarian Book Seller; b/Apr 3, 1926; ba/PO Box 490, Southport, CT 06490; m/Cora Nell Williams; c/Julia, Patricia, Cecile; p/Laurence Claiborne and Julia Eleanora M Witten; ed/BA Williams Col 1948; MusB Yale 1951; mil/AUS 1944-46; pa/Owner & Mgr Laurence Witten Rare Books: Bethany, Conn 1951-53, New Haven 1953-66, Monroe, Conn 1966-76, Southport 1976-; Lectr on Early Musical Instruments; Advr & CoFdr Yale Univ Collection for Hist Sound Recs; Mem Nat Adv Bd Ctr for the Book, Lib of Cong 1978-; Antiquarian Booksellers Assn Am: Secy 1975-78, Pres 1978-; Intl Leag Antiquarian Booksellers; Medieval Soc Am; Renaissance Soc Am; Manuscript Soc Am; Music Instruments Soc, Dir 1975-77; Grolier Clb; Pres Old Book Table 1973-75; cp/Former Mem Budget Com UF; Former Mem Bd Dirs: New Haven Symph, Neighborhood Music Sch (New Haven); Former Mem Easton (Conn) Planning & Zoning Comm; Repub; hon/Contbr Articles to Var Pubs; Biogl Listings.

WITTMAN, NORA EDNA oc/Educator; Retired University Professor; b/Feb 13, 1897; h/307 Locust Ln, State College, PA 16801; p/John M and Margaret M Dill Wittman (dec); ed/BA Pa St Univ 1926; MA Cornell Univ 1932; Grad Study; pa/Tchr: Grade Schs 1915-22, HS 1926-30; Instr & Asst Prof German PSU 1932-60; Prof: Kent St Univ

1960, Lehigh Univ 1962, 64, Cedar Crest Col 1965; Lectr Bucknell Univ 1966-67; Chm Nat AATG-FLES Com; Fdr & Secy-Treas Ctl Pa AATG; Secy-Treas Pa St MLA; AAUP; MLA; PS Ret'd Staff Clb; Fac Wom's Clb; r/Cath; hon/Treas Pi Lambda Theta; Delta Gamma Soc, Treas Beta Xi Chapt; World W/W Wom; Dir Am Scholars; World W/W Wom; W/W Color Photo; Pub'd Author.

WOEPPEL, LOUISE BELLE WILHELMINA oc/Independent Consultant; h/831 S 30 St, Omaha, NE 68105; ba/Same; p/Frederick Wilhelm and Hanna W Woeppel (dec); ed/BA

Univ Neb-O 1938; MA Creighton Univ 1941; MM Eastman Sch Music 1949; Addit Wkshops & Sems; pa/Indep Conslt in Fine Arts; Fine Arts Specialist: Ralston (Neb) to 1946, Dana Col 1946-48, Drake Univ Col Fine Arts 1949-51, Millard Sch 1951-53, TV & Elects Inst 1953-55; Creighton Univ 1954-76: Eng Ed, Fine Arts; AAUP; MENC; Intl Soc for Music Ed; cp/Mem Landmarks Wn Heritage Mus; Nat Hist Trust; Past Del Douglas Co & Neb St Convs (Repub); Joslyn Mus; Joslyn Wom's Org; Joslyn Chamber Music Com; Tuesday Musical Concert Series; Neb Sinfonia Concert Series; Others; r/Kountze Meml Luth Ch, LCA: Lib Chm 1969-; hon/Grad S'ship; Eastman; Delta Kappa Gamma; Sigma Alpha Iota; Profl Pubs.

WOERNER, EARL LaVERN oc/Dentist; b/Apr 30, 1934; h/1313 S Weatherfield, St Louis, MO 63141; ba/St Louis; m/Marilyn Jean; c/Barclay Lane; p/Earl A Woerner (dec); Ruby O Woerner, Vandalia, IL; ed/DDS; pa/Conslt: Amber Ridge Sch for Handicapped, Jewish Hosp Home Care Dept;

Dental Staff the Jewish Staff, Secy; Asst Prof SIU Sch Dental Med; Former Chief U Cerebral Palsy Dental Clin; Am Dental Assn; Am Soc Dentistry for Chd; Am Assn Hosp Dentists; cp/Mem Conservation Fdn Mo; r/Meth; hon/Gratitude Awd, U Cerebral Palsy Assn St Louis; Elizabeth Wright Steidley Prize in Chem, Blackburn Col.

WOLANIN, SOPHIE MAE oc/Educator; Scholar; Tutor; Secretary; b/Jun 11, 1915; h/232 Meyran Ave, Pittsburgh, PA 15213; ba/Pgh; p/Stephen and Mary F Wolanin (dec); ed/BS cum laude Univ SC 1948; PhD honoris causa Colo St Christian Col 1972; pa/Westinghouse Credit Corp, Pgh: Charter Employee 1954-, Exec Secy 1954-72, Sr Secy 1972-, Reporter WCC News 1967-68, Asst Editor WCC News 1968-71, Assoc Editor 1971-76; Confidential Secy Westinghouse Elect Corp, Pgh 1949-54; Instr Math, Bus Adm & Secretarial Sci Univ SC, Columbia (SC) 1946-48; Other Former Positions; Life Mem: Allegheny Co S'ship Assn (Pgh), AAUW, Am Cnslrs Soc; BPW Clb Pgh; Intl Fdn Univ Wom; IPA; Nat Assn Exec Secys; Nat Fdn BPW Clbs Inc; Nat Soc Lit & Arts; Pa Fdn BPW Clbs Inc; Westinghouse Vet Employees' Assn, E Pgh; Assoc Mem Am Mus Natural Hist; Fdg Mem Nat Hist Soc; The Early Am Soc; Fdg Charter Mem Anglo-Am Hist Soc; Life Mem Mercer Co (Pa) Hist Soc; Nat Trust for Hist Preserv; Polish Am Ednl & Cult Soc; Nat Charter Mem Smithsonian Instn Assocs; UN Assn USA; Var Alumni Assns; Hostess Spec Events & Progs Allegheny Soc for Crippled Chd & Adults; Repub Party; Nat Adv Bd Am Security Coun; Fdr Ctr for Intl Security Studies of Am Security Coun Ed

Foun; Allegheny Co LWV; Am Acad Polit & Social Sci; Life Mem Acad Polit Sci; Num Other Mbrships & Activs, Past & Present; r/Rom Cath; Am Bible Soc; Life Mem Liturgical Conf NAm; St Paul's Cathedral Altar Soc (Pgh); hon/Fellow: ABI, Univ SC Ednl Foun; Life Fellow, Intl Inst Commun Ser; Charter Mem The Pres's Coun, Univ SC Ednl Foun; Wom of Yr, BPW Clb Pgh 1972; "Summo Cum Honore" Hons Shield, Honors Reg (E Berlin, Pa); Cited in US Congl Record for Hist Portrayal of Betsy Ross; Girl Friday Cit, Trans World Airlines; Num Biogl Listings; Num Others.

WOLCOTT, ROGER LODGE oc/Retired; Association Executive; Inventor; b/May 19, 1912; h/4796 Waterloo Rd, Atwater, OH 44201; m/Dorothy Kenty; c/Vange Elene Firestone (Mrs Charles L), Kent Edward, Janet Louise; p/Duncan Brewster and Daisy Lodge Wolcott (dec); ed/BS Kent St Univ 1935; pa/Tchr Public Schs: Garrettsville (Ohio), Cleve, Alliance (Ohio), Rootstown (Ohio), N Jackson (Ohio), Ravenna (Ohio), Mantua (Ohio), Edinburg (Ohio); Taylorcraft Aviation Corp, Alliance: 1936-46, Chief Insp 1943-46; Specialist Aeromech Res & Devel Engrg Dept Goodyear Aerospace Corp, Akron 1946-71; Balloon Pilot for TV & Movies; Zoning Inspector 1971-; Balloon Flyers Akron: Charter Mem, Treas 1956-59, VP 1960, Pres 1961-62; Lighter Than Air Soc, Akron: Charter Mem, Pres 1952-54, 55-57, VP 1959-61; Balloon Fdn Am: Fdg Mem, VP 1961, Charter; OX5 Aviation Pioneers; Soc Exptl Stress Analysis; Smithsonian Instn; Akron Area Pilots Assn; Assn Balloon & Airship Constructors; Wn Res Engrg Assn; Goodyear Foremen's Clb; Am Balloon Corps Vets; cp/Former Com-man BSA; USCG Aux; JCs, Kent; Airplane Model Leag Am; hon/Ldrship Awds, Kent St Univ; Richard Pollard Trophy Awd, Wingfoot Sect, Ward T Van Orman Thermal Balloon Trophy; Pilot of Yr, Balloon Flyers Akron 1961; Patentee in Field; W/W in MW.

WOLFE, ESTEMORE ALVIS oc/Educator; Executive; b/Dec 29, 1919; h/10 W Adams Ave, Detroit, MI 48226; ba/Detroit; p/Henry Sr and Vinia Crump Wolfe (dec); ed/BS; MA; MEd; EdD; DLitt; DFA; DHL; mil/AUS Med Station Hosp 4 Yrs; pa/VP & Secy, Wright Mutual Ins Co Inc; cp/Pres Nat Alumni Assn, Jackson St Univ; Bd Dirs, Friends of AMISTAD Inc; Bd Dirs, Boston Nat Alumni Assn; Perf'g Arts Dir, Detroit Bd Ed; Dem Clb; Politic Action Com; Others; r/Ctl United Meth Ch (Detroit); hon/Alumnus of Yr (2); Hon Degs; Rec'd Medallions (3); Rec'd Plaques & Cits; Keys to Sev Cities; Scrolls Apprec; Num Others.

WOLFERT, EILEEN PATRICIA oc/Homemaker; b/Nov 7, 1917; m/Edward C; c/Helen Patricia W Kozero; p/James Henry Sterling (dec) Elizabeth Adeline Grace, El Paso, TX; mil/AUS Auditor, Fiscal Sect (Tokyo, Japan); Clerk Ordnance Office, 2nd Army (Ft Meade, Md); cp/Wom's C of C; Woms Aux, Univ Tex-EP; Univ Tex Civic Opera Guild; Sante Fe (NM) Opera Guild; Life Mem & Past Publicity Chm, Christ Child Soc; El Paso Rehab Soc; Treas, Our Lady of Assumption Altar Soc; Arthritis Foun; Goodwill Foun; El Paso Mus of Art; VP, Rel Commun; Past Pres & Life Mem, Hotel Dieu Hosp & Med Ctr Aux; Smithsonian Inst; Pres, Kappa Delta Mothers Clb; r/Cath; hon/Plaque Apprec, Hotel Dieu Aux.

WOLVERTON, TERRY LYNN oc/Writer; Theater Director; b/Aug 23, 1954; h/1020½ Laguna Ave, Los Angeles, CA 90026; ba/LA; p/Donald E Wolverton; Ruth Lenore McCarthy, Southfield, MI; ed/BPh; pa/Co-dir, Lesbian Art Proj; Pub'd *Blue Moon;* cp/Speaker, Feminist Conf on Pornography; r/Wiccan; hon/Wom of Yr, Fam of Wom.

WONG, BENJAMIN YAU-CHEUNG oc/Assistant Director; b/Jul 15, 1943; h/2231 English Ct, Walnut Creek, CA 94598;

m/Beatrice Bei-Chu Wong; c/2; p/Hung Wong and Ku Yip; ed/BS; MS; PhD; pa/Asst Dir, Dept Operational Res & Evaluation; Var Positions Fields Med Care Delivery Sys, Bldg Sys, Earthquake Engrg, Disaster Planning, Technol Transfer & Computer Progs; hon/Scholastic & Achmt Awds; Notable Ams.

WONG, CHING oc/Artist; b/Oct 24, 1932; h/3669 Hilo Pl, Hon, HI 96816; m/Carrick Git Yee; c/Rena Ying, Carla Mun; ed/Pratt Inst Graphics Ctr (NY); Arts Students Leag (NY); pa/Art Exhbns; hon/Rec'd Art Awd, Honolulu Acad Arts; Acquisition Awds, St Foun on Cult.

WOOD, EARL RAY oc/Minister; b/Aug 17, 1941; h/307 S Waverly, Holland, MI 49423; ba/Holland; m/Ruth Eleanor; c/Suzanne Marie, Rebecca Rae; p/Lyman Clyde and Mildred Berniece Wood, Fulton, MO; ed/BD, MDiv, DMin Luther Rice Theol

Sem; mil/AUS; pa/Mich St Bapt Exec Bd; Chm Fin Com, Assn Bible Tchg Dir; cp/Crisis Intervention Staff, Ottawa Co; r/Holland So Bapt Ch: Pastor; hon/Rec'd Plaques & Certs for Work in Mtl Hlth (Franklin, Ill); W/W Rel; DIB; Men Achmt; Personalities of W&MW.

WOOD, KATHLEEN WILKINSON W oc/Retired; b/Jan 27, 1890; h/PO Box 325, Sea Island, GA 31561; ba/Same; m/James Augustus II (dec); p/Asbury Taylor Wilkinson (dec); Elizabeth Catherine Gaston (dec); ed/BA Randolph Macon, Sullins Col; MA Columbia Univ; Spec Work Under Med Specs in Hosps & Med Cols; pa/Chatauqua & Lyceum Lectr; Appt'd Head Hlth Dept Ga Col 1917, Emeritus Prof Hlth 1954; Author 6 Col Textbooks, Col Bulletins, Mag Articles; Fellow, Life Mem Am Public Hlth Assn; Confs Intl TB Assn (Wash, DC) 1926; Participating Mem, Am Child Hlth Assn Confs; Confs on Col Hygiene 1931, 36, 47; 1st White House Conf on Child Hlth; Columbia Univ Conf on Hlth of Fam 1929; AMA Confs on Phys' Part in Hlth Ed 1947, 49, 51; Royal Soc Hlth; Fellow: AAAS, AHPER (Nat Hon Awd 1944, Hon Fellow 1960); Visiting Prof Hlth, Wash St Univ; Lectr Other Wash St Cols; Visiting Prof Hlth, Berea Col 1958-59; cp/Past Regent, DAR; Nat Soc Colonial Dames of Am; Past Town Com Chm & St Bd Mem; Nat Soc Magna Charta Dames; Descs of Lords of Md Manors; Huguenot Soc SC; Conservative Repub; Ala, Ga & Coastal Ga Hist Socs; Nat Trust for Hist Preserv; So Cal Camellia Soc; Mozart Soc; Sea Island Bch Clb; Golf Clb; Cottage Owners Clb; r/Meth; hon/Honorarium Am Child Hlth Assn; W/W: Am Ed, Am Wom, Am Col Profs, S&SW; Intl W/W Intellectuals.

WOOD, LARRY (MARYLAIRD) oc/Journalist; Educator; h/6161 Castle Dr, Oakland, CA 94611; c/Mary, Marcia, Barry; p/Edward Hayes and Alice McNeel Small; ed/BA magna cum laude, 1939, MA w Highest Hons 1940 Univ Wash; Addit Studies; pa/Byline Columnist: *Oakland Cal Tribune, San Francisco Chronicle* 1946-; Feature Writer Wn Region *Christian Sci Monitor, Tribune Register* (Des Moines, Iowa) & Worldwide CSM Syndicate 1973-; Feature Writer, *Travelday;* Cal Correspondent, *Seattle Times Sunday Mag;* Free-lance Writer Var Nat Mags incl'g *Parents', Am Home, Sports Illustrated, Sea Frontiers* 1946-; Author & Contbg Editor, *Eng for Social Living* (McGraw-Hill); Author, *Journalism Qtrly* 1978; Regional

Correspondent, *Spokane Mag;* CSM Radio Syndicate; San Diego St Univ: Asst Prof Journalism 1974-, Tenure Track Asst Prof 1976-, Visiting Prof Journalism 1974-; Ext Prof, Cal St Univ-H & Ext Div Univ Cal-B; Others; Speaker: 1969 Cal Writers Conf, Oakland C of C, Cal Writers Clb, Sci Writing Conv (Nat Assn Ed in Journalism 1978), Others; Am Assn Ed in Journalism; Soc Am Travel Writers; Nat Press Photogs Assn; Eastbay Wom's Press Clb; Charter Mem, Investigative Reporters & Editors Inc; Cal Assn Envir Profls & Cal Acad Envir News Writers; SF Press Clb; Others; cp/Public Relats Work for: Chd's Med Ctr Nn Cal, GSA, YMCA, Am Cancer Soc, Oakland & Mills Col, ARC, Num Others; Envir Conslt N Am; Conslt US Forest Ser; Author Awd Winning Series on Bay Area Hlth Care, *Oakland Tribune;* Public Relats Soc Am; Nat Soc Public Relats Assn; Intl Oceanographic Soc; Univ Wash Ocean Scis Alumni Assn; Sierra Clb; Nat Wildlife Fdn; Audubon Soc; Others; hon/Public Relats Dir & Alumna, Phi Beta Kappa; Chi Omega; Pi Lambda Theta; Sigma Delta Chi; Rec'd Cit, US Forest Ser for Feature Article on Pacific Crest Trail; Rec'd Accolade for Feature on Yellowstone Grizzlies, Nat Park Ser; Elected Nat Assn Sci Writers; Bd Mem, Cal St Parks Foun; Rec'd Cits from: Wildlife Refugees of World, 15 Endangered Animals & Birds, Railroads of W, Others; Biogl Listings.

WOOD, ROBERT W JR oc/Plastic Surgeon; b/Jan 10, 1931; h/#15 Pine Hill, Houston, TX 77019; ba/Houston; m/Sarah Lee Norman; c/Robert William III, John Willard Guy, James Norman; p/Robert William Wood (dec); Mary J Peters, Escondide, CA; ed/BS 1951, MD 1955 Univ Ill; Internship, Baylor Univ Hosp (Dallas, Tex) 1955-56; Gen Surg Residency, Dallas Vets Hosp 1960-63; Plastic & Reconstructive Surg Progs, Christ Hosp (Cinc, Ohio) 1963-65; Addit Studies; mil/USAF: Chief Dept Ob-gyn, Bergstrom AFB; pa/Clinical Asst Prof Dept Plastic Surg, Baylor Col Med 1970-; Clinical Assoc, Univ Tex Col Med (Houston) 1973-; Other Positions; VP Houston Soc Plastic Surgs 1977-78; Pres, Intl Soc Clinical Plastic Surgs 1977-79; Pres, Tex Soc Plastic Surg 1978-79; Intl Soc Aesthetic Plastic Surg; Intl Confederation Plastic & Reconstructive Surgs; Tex Med Assn; Am Soc Plastic & Reconstructive Surgs; Houston Surgical Soc; Harris Co Med Soc; Diplomate, Am Bd Plastic Surg; Am Cleft Palate Assn; Am Burn Assn; Others; Contbr Num Articles Profl Jours; Speaker Profl Meetings; IPA; r/Meth; hon/Pi Kappa Epsilon; Phi Beta Pi; W/W Tex; Nat Register Prominent Ams & Intl Notables; Outstg Am in S; W/W S&SW.

WOOD, SAMELLYN JONES oc/Educator; Consultant; b/Jun 13, 1945; h/4313 SW Admiral Ct, Portland, OR 97221; m/Harold Wayne; c/Tamara Leigh, Benjamin Allen, Joel Hinckley; p/Ivan Charles and Helen Hinckley Jones, Altadena, CA; ed/BA; MA; pa/Tchr; Conf Presenter; Writer; Curric Developer; r/Ch of Jesus Christ LDS; hon/Outstg Yg Wom Am; DIB; Personalities of W.

WOOD, SUMNER SR oc/Lawyer; Author; b/Mar 2, 1902; h/19430 Beallsville Rd, Beallsville, MD 20704; m/Peggy Angel; c/Sumner Jr, David E, Judson R, Wriley C A, Brooks C B, Octavia W Cooper; p/Isaac Sumner and Octavia Byrne Wood (dec); ed/SB Harvard; JD w Hons Geo Washington Law Sch; pa/Trust, Wills & Real Estate Lwyr; Montgomery Co (Md) Bar Assn; cp/Harvard Clb of Wash (DC); Soc of Mayflower Descendents; Hist Soc of Montgomery Co; r/Epis; hon/Author: *The Virginia Bishop* (1961), *Cupid's Path in Ancient Plymouth* (1957), *Laws Everyone Should Know: An Am Citizens Handbook* (1941, 51, 60, 68), Others.

WOOD, WAYNE BARRY oc/Photographer; Travel Writer; b/Jun 23, 1958; h/6161 Castle Dr, Oakland, CA; p/W B and Larry Wood; ed/Cal St Univ-Hayward; pa/Syndicated Photographer for CSM New Ser; Freelancer for Oceanographic Mags, *Sea Frontiers* and *Oceans,* Others; Sigma Delta

Chi; Nat Press Photogs Assn; PR Assns; r/Prot; hon/Var Col Awds for Student Ser; Cal PR Press Awds.

WOODALL, STELLA oc/Poet; b/Jan 15, 1899; h/3915 SW Military Dr, San Antonio, TX 78211; ba/Same; m/(dec); c/Ruth W James, Anna W Frost, Clara Elizabeth W Urban; p/(dec); ed/DLit; DHL; mil/20 Yrs Civil Ser; Ret'd Air Force Histn-Writer; pa/Author: *Twelve Air Force Histories* (& Num Other Books for Air Force), *Wom of the Bible, Lectures on the Book of Ruth, Lectures on St John, Inspirational Poems, Adventures in Friendship, Golden Treasures, Anthol of Tex Poems* (Winner Gold Awd), *Dr Stella Woodall's Collected Poems* (Winner Gold Awd), Num Others; Editor & Pubr: *Adventures in Poetry Mag, Am Poetry Leag Mag;* Editor & Advr Bd, *Intl W/W Poetry;* Conducts Monthly Poetry-writing Contests for Stella Woodall Poetry Soc, Annual Nat Contests for Am Poetry Leag, Continual Contests for *Adventures in Poetry Mag* & Intl Contests for Patriotic Poetry Seminar; Pres, Stella Woodall Poetry Soc Intl; Nat Pres, Am Poetry Leag; Pres-Dir, Patriotic Poetry Seminar; Nat Leag Am Pen Wom: Orgr & Charter Pres (San Antonio Branch), St Music Chm, Nat Lttrs Bd; Fdr-Fellow & VChancellor, Intl Acad Poets; Nat Public Relats Dir, United Poets Laureate Intl; Nat

Liaison Ofcr, World Poetry Soc; Nat CoChm, Promote Poetry Am; Judge, Regional Rep, Speaker & Symposium Chm, World Cong of Poets; Centro Studi E Scambi Internazionali; Tex Comm on Arts & Humanities; Others; cp/Tex Senate Adv Coun on Leg Affairs; Dir, Beautify San Antonio Assn; Nat Assn Ret'd Fed Employees; Past Pres, Armed Forces Writers' Leag; Past Pres, Senior Citizens Clb; Past Chm Stategy Bd Round Table & Publicity Chm Round Tabel Lttrs, San Antonio Wom's Clb; Past Treas, Civilian Wel Assn USAF; Others; r/Meth; hon/Intl Wom 1975 & 1976 w Lareate Hons; Poet Laureate Intl & Poet Laureate Tex; Intl Hall of Fame Wom of Distinction; Rec'd 2 Gold Laurel Leaf Crowns, United Poets Laureate Intl; Churchmanship Awd; Presented Silver Bowl, Strategy Bd Round Table; Gold Plaque, Stella Woodall Poetry Soc; Dist'd Ser Cit, World Poetry Soc; KBAT-Tex Star Awd; Coun of Pres' Awd; Rec'd Gold Plaque for Sers During Bicent; *Stella Woodall's Collected Poems* Nom'd for Pulitzer Prize; Hon Awd, Freedoms Foun Val Forge; Poet Laureate, Intl Poets' Shrine; Num Others; Biogl Listings.

WOODEN, JOSEPHINE ANN oc/Professor; b/Jan 9, 1939; h/Box 447, Cleveland, GA 30528; ba/Cleveland; c/Jeffrey Alvin; p/Ira and Leomia Cook Wooden,

Chattanooga, TN; ed/BS Univ Tenn-C 1961; MACT UNC-CH 1968; pa/Prof Eng, Truett-McConnell Col; Prof Eng, DeKalb Commun Col 1968-76; Editor, Economy Ednl Pubrs 1965-67; Master Tchr, Dalewood Jr HS 1963-65; Eng & Social Studies Tchr, Brainerd HS (Chattanooga) 1961-63; NEA; AAUP; CCCC; SCETC; cp/Yg Dems; PTA; r/Cleveland Meth Ch; hon/Rec'd 4-H Clb Nat Foods & Nutrition S'ship; R J Reynolds Ecs F'ship; DeKalb Fac F'ship; Nat Master Tchrs Seminar (Portland, Maine); Personalities of S; Intl W/W Wom Ed; World W/W Wom.

WOODLIN, ALMA THOMPSON oc/-Nurse's Aid; b/Feb 4, 1912; h/80 Riverdale Ave, Yonkers, NY 10701; ba/Yonkers; m/-Arthur (dec); p/Robert and Sarah Thompson (dec); pa/Ret'd, Jewish Guild for Blind; Yonkers Child Care Bd; NCNW; cp/Voter Registration; Life Mem & Past Pres, BPW; Bd Mem, YWCA; r/Messiah Bapt Ch: Past SS Tchr; Yonkers Coun of Chs; hon/"This is Your Life."

WOODS, LARRY DAVID oc/Lawyer; Teacher; b/Sept 10, 1944; h/1530 Graybar Ln, Nashville, TN 37215; ba/Nashville; m/Nancy; c/Rachel, Allen, Sarah; p/Allen Noel and Loyce L Woods; ed/BA Emory Univ; JD NWn Univ; pa/Tenn Bar Assn; AAUP; cp/Chm, Tenn Adv Com on Legal Sers; Bd Trustees, Ctl St Psychi Hosp; Chm, Tenn St Univ Grievance Com; Tenn St Univ Fac Rank & Tenure Com; hon/Pres, Delta Sigma Rho; Tau Kappa Alpha.

WOODS, MARGARET STAEGER oc/-Educator; b/Aug 21, 1911; h/40 W Cremona, Seattle, WA 98119; ba/Seattle; c/Pamela Fay W Reiman, Frederick Waring; p/Carl P Staeger (dec); Olivia Waring Staeger, Centralia, WA; ed/BA Wash St Univ; MEd Univ Wash; pa/Active Prof Emeritus, Seattle Pacific Univ; Ednl Conslt; Ednl Ldrship Am Inc; Devel'd 1st Master's Deg Prog in Elem Ed w Emphasis on Creative Ed; Fdr, Commun-sponsored Prog in Creative Dramatics in Public Libs for Yg Chd, "Let's Pretend w Fours & Fives" 1953-76; Author, *Wonderwork*; Contbr Articles Profl Jours; Author Self-Instrnl Guides for Parents & Tchrs in Creative Ed; Lectr & Dir Workshops US, Jamaica, Australia, Newfoundland & Puerto Rico; cp/Arts for Yth; r/Congreg; hon/Rec'd Dist'd Ser Awd, Zeta Phi Eta; Nat Delta Zeta Wom of Yr; Personality of Day, NY Worlds Fair.

WOODSON, MARY F oc/Teacher; b/Jul 15, 1932; h/831 Easterling St, Prichard, AL 36610; ba/Mobile, AL; m/Cecil Lee Sr (dec); c/Cecilia Beatrice; p/James Cleon Fairley Sr (dec); Mary Ella Slaughter Fairley Jones (dec); ed/BS w Hons ASU; Attended Dillard Univ; pa/Elem Tchr, Woodcock Sch; MCEA; AEA; NEA; AFT; cp/Vol Worker: NAACP, YWCA, Mayor, Commun Theatre, Drug Addiction; Commun Choir; r/Mt Olive AME Zion Ch (Prichard): Pianist & Organist 25 Yrs, Choir, SS Tchr; hon/Zeta Phi Beta; Rec'd Plaques, Trophies, Others.

WOOLF, VICTOR VERNON oc/Thera-pist; b/Dec 17, 1937; h/1234 Aspen Ave, Provo, UT 84601; ba/Orem, UT; m/Marlene; c/Kim, Trevor, Vickie, Kent, Derick, Kendra, Chad, Mindi, Nicole, Brandon Todd; p/Victor Amos Woolf; Lena Ross, Alberta, Canada; ed/BSEd, MREd, PhD Brigham Yg Univ; pa/Exec Dir, Marriage & Fam Therapy Ctr; Instr LDS Sem Inst & BYU; Exec Dir, Tri-Co Drug Rehab Prog; Pres, Utah Co Mtl Hlth Bd; Crim Adjudication & Adult Parole Com, Nat Inst Drug Abuse; cp/Mountainland Assn Govs; r/LDS: High Coun-man, High Priest; hon/Rec'd Awd for Outstg Contbn Mtl Hlth Utah Co.

WOON, PAUL SAM oc/Research Scientist; b/Jul 1, 1942; h/1009 E Florida Ave, Appleton, WI 54911; ba/Neenah, WI; m/Lin-Sun; c/Audrey Hui; p/Ramon Woon (dec); Rita Woon; ed/BS 1965, MS 1968 Univ Iowa; PhD Univ Akron 1974; pa/Kimberly-Clark Corp: Sr Res Scist 1978-, Res Scist 1976-77; Staff Res Assoc, Appleton Papers (Div of NCR) 1974-76; Instr Chem, Cuyahoga Col 1972-73; Res Chem, PPG Industs 1968-71; Res

Chem, Clinical Res Ctr, Univ Iowa 1965-68; Author Var Profl Pubs; hon/Patentee in Field.

WOOTTON, LUTIAN ROBERT oc/Professor; b/Jun 2, 1916; h/794 Rockinwood Dr, Athens, GA 30606; ba/Athens; m/Margaret Joy Parrish; c/Robert Frank; p/Samuel Francis and Permelia Russel Pattillo Wootton (dec); ed/BS Austin Peay St Univ; MA Peabody Univ; EdD Univ Va; pa/Prof Curric & Supv, Univ Ga; Reschr; Lectr; Pubr; So Assn Conslt, Evaluator & Dir; r/Presb: Elder, Choir Mem, Campus Christ Life Ldr; hon/W/W: Am Ed, S&SE; Men Achmt; Ldrs Ed; Notable Ams; Personalities of S.

WORKER, GEORGE F JR oc/Agrono-mist; b/Jun 1, 1923; h/1004 E Holton Rd, El Centro, CA 92243; ba/El Centro; m/Donna R; c/Kent, Stephanie, Cathy, Mindy; p/George R Sr and Eleanor Worker, Homelake, CO; ed/BS Colo St Univ; MS Univ Neb; mil/USAAC 1943-46; pa/Agronomist & Supt

Imperial Val Field Station, Univ Cal; Grain Release Conslt: Kufra Agri Proj (Libya) 1969-70, Hawaiian Agronomics Co (Iran) 1973; Agronomy Soc Am; Wn Section Crop Sci, Cal Chapter Agronomy (Sacramento); cp/Rotary Clb; Former Sch Bd Mem, Meadows Union & Holtville Unified Sch Dists; r/Cath; hon:/Gamma Sigma Delta.

WORRALL, WILLIAM CHARLES oc/Publisher; b/Mar 23, 1936; h/8525 S Passons Blvd, Pico Rivera, CA 90660; ba/Downey, CA; ed/Long Beach City Col; MA Atlanta So Univ; NY Ext Univ; Univ Cal-I; San Luis Obispo; Notre Dame Col; pa/Pubr: *Organist Mag*, *Keyboard World Mag* (Australia), *Tasten-Welt Mag* (Switzerland), *Keyboard World Mag* (Am); Intl Fdr, Yg Organists Assn Intl; Dir, Home Organist Adventures; Organist, Pianist, Comedian, Entertainer, Record'g Artist; Concerts Am, Canada, Mexico & Australia; Bd Mem, Electronic Arts Foun; Intl Assn Organ Tchrs; Keyboard World Hall of Fame; Chm Bd, Keyboard World Inc; Past Pres, Long Beach Profl Organists Clb; VP LA Profl Organists Clb 1977; Hollywood Comedy Clb; Orange Co Profl Organists Clb; Wn Pubrs Conf; Am Theatre Organ Soc; cp/Vol Sers, Exceptional Chd's Foun; LA World Affairs Coun; Downey C of C; Toastmasters; hon/Finalist Judge, Yamaha Electone Fest (Canada).

WRIGHT, ELDON MILLARD oc/Attor-ney; Counselor; b/Jun 14, 1912; h/405 W Sixth St, N Manchester, IN 46962; ba/Manchester; m/Frances Ada Gibble; c/Renee Carmen, Glen Eldon; p/Glen Ellis Wright, Manchester; Grace Ellen Wright (dec); ed/BA Manchester Col; LLB, JD Valparaiso Univ; HHD Kingston Univ; mil/AUS WWII; pa/Judge, N Manchester Mun Ct 5 Yrs; Real Estate Broker; Wabash Co & Ind St Bar Assns; cp/Former Trustee, Town of N Manchester; Bd Trustees, Bethel Home for Boys (Gaston, Ind); Mason; r/Christian F'ship Prot Ch; hon/Ky Col.

WRIGHT, EUGENE BOX oc/Lawyer; Executive; b/Feb 21, 1943; h/3607 Highgreen Dr, Kingwood, TX 77339; ba/Cleveland, TX; m/Linda Gatlin; c/Laura, Alan, Julia; p/Hugh F and Madeline B Wright, Cleveland; ed/BBA

SMU 1965; JD Univ Houston 1968; pa/Admit'd Tex Bar 1968, US Supr Ct Bar 1976; Individual Law Pract 1968-; City Atty (Cleveland) 1969-72; Pres, Wright Energy Corp 1978; Dir, Splendora Lumber Co 1974-76; Secy & Dir Cleveland Pub'g Co Inc, Triangle Press Inc, Gtr Beaumont Pub'g Co Inc & Olympic Inc; Am, Tex, Liberty-Chambers, Cos Bar Assns; cp/Chm Bicent Com; UN Day Chm; r/Meth; hon/Phi Mu Alpha Sinfonia; Delta Sigma Pi; Beta Gamma Sigma; Phi Delta Phi; Ky Col; W/W: Tex, Am Law; Outstg Yg Men Am; DIB.

WRIGHT, FLOYD VERNON oc/Execu-tive; b/Dec 26, 1916; h/5028 Purdue Dr, Metairie, LA 70003; ba/New Orleans, LA; m/Kate Elizabeth Harry; c/Lisa W Kitchens, Richard Vernon; p/Floyd E and Pearl Elvira Thompson Wright (dec); ed/Grad: NE Mo St Tchr Col 1937, Wash & Jefferson Col 1943, Biarritz (France) Am Univ 1946, Am Mgmt Assn 1962, Brookings Instn 1965; mil/USAAF 1943-46; pa/Pres, Fed Intermediate Credit Bank New Orleans 1970-; Deputy Gov & Dir, Farm Credit Adm 1961-70; Asst VP, Fed Intermediate Credit Bank (St Louis, Mo) 1960-61; Mgr, Illini Prodn Credit Assn 1958-60; Other Positions; Secy, Assn Mo Prodn Credit Assns; Am Mgmt Assn & Pres' Assn AMA; IPA; So Farm Forum; Dir-at-Lrg, La Commercial Agri Assn; cp/Past Secy, Farmington Citizens Commun Better Schs; Past Bd Mem, Farmington Commun Expan-sion Corp; Agri-bus Com, New Orleans C of C; Former VP, Farmington C of C; Rotary Clb; IOOF; Mo Soc Wash; r/Bapt; hon/Past Pres, Pi Omega Pi.

WRIGHT, HAROLD HANNON oc/-Minister; b/Oct 8, 1895; h/1201 W Main, Du-rant, OK 74701; m/Mary Elizabeth Ritchey; c/Harold Hannon Jr; p/Ernest Gilbert and Eva Fances Hannon Wright (dec); ed/BA Yale Col 1916; Chgo Theol Sem 1931-33; mil/Field Artillery; pa/Ret'd Min Emeritus, Congreg-

Unit Ch (Ft Collins, Colo); Pres, Coun Chs (Ft Collins) & Min Alliance; Editor, *Thoughts of Mary Ritchey Wright in Poetry & Prose*; cp/Chm, Colo Congl Conf Social Action; hon/Phi Beta Kappa.

WRIGHT, JOAN DUNBAR oc/Principal; b/Oct 3, 1934; h/5602 S Blackstone Ave, Chicago, IL 60637; ba/Chgo; c/Wendi Waldeen; p/Harry Sr and Waldeen Ramsey Dunbar, Chgo; ed/BS Univ Ill 1955; MA Univ Chgo 1959; EdD Nova Univ 1976; Addit Studies; pa/Prin, O Westcott Elem Sch 1971-; Prin, Howland Elem Sch 1969-71; Chgo Public Schs: Adjustmt Tchr, Guid Cnslr, ESEA Read'g Conslt, Curric Conslt, Asst Prin 1966-69; Conslt, NEn Ill St Univ Ctr Urban Ed 1978-; Chrperson, Dist 20 New Progs Com 1977-; Coor Title VI Summer Progs, Chgo Bd Ed Dept Spec Ed 1977-78; Chrperson, Chgo Prin Assn & Chgo Bd Ed Annual Conf 1977-79; Instr Kennedy-King Col & NEn Ill St Univ 1975; Other Positions; Chgo Area Read'g Assn; Assn for Supvn & Curric Devel; Am Assn Sch Admrs; Adm Wom Ed; Chgo Prins Assn; cp/Coun Exceptional Chd; Former Mem Bd Dirs, SW Mtl Hlth Ctr; Former Conslt, Accounters Commun Ctr; r/Meth; hon/Delta Kappa Gamma; Phi Delta Kappa; Delta Sigma Theta.

WRIGHT, LOU oc/Psychic; Instructor;

b/Oct 17, 1936; h/6650 Quitman Ct, Arvada, CO 80003; ba/Westminster, CO; m/Donald Burnworth; c/Teresa Kay W Gibbs, Jack Bryant; p/Verner E and Olive Kay Ellis Conner, Boonville, IN; ed/NY Sch Interior Design; pa/Instr, Univ Colo; Radio Show, KIMN & TV Show Channel 2 KWGN; cp/DAR; r/Meth Ch (Wheat Ridge, Colo); Mem; hon/Featured in: *Denver Mag, Country Style, Midnight Globe, Photoplay, Nat Enquirer,* Others; Key to City New Orleans; Hon Mem: Kiwanis, Rotary Clb, Others.

WRIGHT, WILLIAM E oc/Professor; b/Nov 5, 1926; h/18200 Honeysuckle Ln, Deephaven, MN 55391; ba/Minneapolis, MN; m/Norma Louise Lacy; c/Mariellen Lacy; p/Cecil Augustus Wright (dec); Leila Myrtle Wright, Long Beach, CA; ed/BS 1951, MA 1953, PhD 1957 Univ Colo; mil/AUS 1945-47; pa/Univ Minn: Dir Grad Studies (Dept Hist) 1968-69, Assoc Dean Intl Progs 1969, Assoc VP Intl Progs 1969-76, Dir Austrian Studies Ctr 1977-, Prof Hist; cp/Past Cand Minn St Senate; Former Chm Leg Task Force; Past Mgr, Congl Campaign D Fraser; Citizens Leag Mpls; r/Prot; hon/McKnight Awd Humanities; Phi Alpha Theta Best Work in Hist; Fulbright F'ships.

WU, SHI TSAN oc/Professor; b/Jul 31, 1933; h/2602 Fanelle Cir, Huntsville, AL 35801; ba/Huntsville; m/Mai K; c/Cheyenne Y T, Rosalind Y M, Patricia Y B; p/Shu-Zee and Dawn Min Bau Wu, Taipei, Taiwan; ed/BSME Nat Taiwan Univ 1955; MSME Ill Inst Technol 1959; PhD Univ Colo 1967; Addit Studies; pa/Univ Ala-H: Act'g Chm Dept Mech Engrg 1976-77, Prof Engr 1972-, Adj Prof Physics 1976-, Others; Australian-Am Ed Foun Prof Physics, La Trobe Univ (Melbourne, Australia) 1975-76; Res Asst, High Altitude Observatory, Nat Ctr Atmospheric Res 1964-67; Conslt Space Envir Lab, ERL, Nat Oceanic & Atmospheric Adm, Dept Commerce 1974-; Conslt, Wyle Labs

(H'ville) 1970-; Conslt, Northrop Corp (H'ville) 1969-; AIAA: Assoc Dir Ed (Ala Sect), Nat Com on Space & Atmospheric Physics 1972-, Others; Mem Div III, Magnetospheric Phenomena, IAGA; Coor Solar Physics, Study of Interplanetary Phenomena & Inter-Union Comm on Solar-Terrestrial Physics (Nat Acad Sci); Team Ldr to Visit Taipei to Devel Coop Sci Prog; Guest Investigator OSO-VII, Goddard Space Flight Ctr (NASA) 1973-; Prin Investigator NASA & DOE Contracts; Reviewer for Papers & Proposals: *Applied Mechs Review, Jour of Mech ASCE, Jour Geophysical Res, Solar Physics Jour,* AIAA, NOAA, Dept Commerce, Others; Editor: *Physics of Space Envir* (w R E Smith 1972), *Application of Solar Energy* (w D Christensen, R Head & W Whitacre 1975), Others; Vol Editor, *Study of Traveling Interplanetary Phenomena* (1977); Lectr; Other Positions & Activs; hon/Outstg Ser Awd, Sigma Xi; Sr Fulbright-Hays Scholar; NSF Summer Fellow, Univ Colo; NSF Pre-doct Fellow, Univ Colo & Princeton Univ; W/W: Am, Am Ed, S&SW; Intl Scholars Directory; Am Men Sci.

WU, WILLIAM L S oc/Physician; b/Sept 1, 1921; h/2030 Menalto Ave, Menlo Park, CA 94025; ba/Same; ed/BA Stanford Univ 1943; MD 1946; MS Tulane Univ 1955; Dipls, US Naval Sch Aviation Med 1956 & USAF Sch Aviation Med 1961; Cert Tng Aviation Med

(FAA), Univ Cal 1962, 64; mil/USNR 1954-57, Cmdr Med Corp; pa/Asst Visiting & Visiting Physician, Charity Hosp & Hutchinson Meml Tchg & Diagnostic Clinics 1948-54; Staff Physician Aviation, Space & Radiation Med Group, Gen Dynamics/Convair 1958-61; Aerospace Med Spec & Med Monitor All Manned Tests Perf'd by Life Scist Sect, Dynamics/Astronautics 1961-65; Aerospace Med & Bioastronautical Space, Lovelace Foun for Med Ed & Res (Albuquerque, NM) 1965; Staff Phys, Laguna Honda Hosp (San Francisco) 1968-74; Fellow, San Diego Biomed Res Inst; NY Acad Scis; Am Inst Aeronauts & Astronauts; IEEE; Inst Envir Scis; IPA; Author Sci Profl Papers; cp/Bd Dirs, Little House (Menlo Park); hon/Rec'd 3 Gold Medals, 4 Silver Medals & 2 Bronze Medals; DIB; Commun Ldrs & Noteworthy Ams; 2000 Men Achmt; Intl W/W Commun Ser; W/W; Nat Social Directory; Others.

WURSTER, MARGUERITE RAY SMITH oc/Librarian; b/Sept 7, 1916; h/6514 27th Ave N, St Petersburg, FL 33710; ba/St Petersburg; m/Robert Frederick; c/Hal S Batey, Marilyn B Holeman, Diana B Pettengill; p/William Edward and Alma Inez Ray Smith (dec); ed/BA Univ Fla 1963; MA Univ So Fla 1973; pa/Spec Libs Assn: Exec Bd & Pres Fla Chapt 1970-71, Chm Bylaws Com; Fla Lib Assn: Former Chm Col & Spec Libs Div, Currently Ser'g Cits & Awds Com; cp/Dem Party; r/St Luke's Meth Ch (St Petersburg); Mem; hon/Kappa Delta Pi; Chapt Correspond'g Secy, Delta Kappa Gamma.

WYAND, MARTIN JUDD oc/Professor; b/May 28, 1931; h/15740 E Greenwood Dr, Aurora, CO 80013; ba/Denver, CO; m/Margaret Allison Knox; c/Charles S and Marian A Wyand, State College, PA; ed/BA 1953, MA 1954 Penn St Univ; JD Univ Denver 1969; PhD Univ Ill 1964; mil/USAF 1954-56; USAFR 1956-; pa/Prof Ecs, Univ Denver;

Author Num Articles Profl Jours; Rocky Mountain Social Sci Assn; Am Ec Assn; Am Col Schs Bus; N Ctl Assn Cols & Univs; Air Force Assn; Reserve Ofcrs Assn; Others; cp/Bd Dirs, Colo Right-to-Work Org; r/Washington Park Meth Ch (Denver): Adm Bd Dirs; hon/Rec'd Shell Oil Res Grant; Appointed Acad Instr, Air Intell Tng Ctr; Rec'd Univ Denver Fac Res Grant Awd Ecs; Others; Biogl Listings.

WYATT, ANGELA JANE oc/Student; b/Sept 29, 1959, h/Rt 1, Salem, IL 62881, p/John Lowell and Darlene Fry Wyatt, Salem; ed/Theatre & Dance Major, So Ill Univ; pa/Centralia Little Theatre Players; Centralia Cult Soc Prodns: *Blithe's Spirit, Oliver, Godspell, Bye Bye Birdie;* Salem Little Theatre, *The Gong Show;* SIUE Prodns: *The Miser, Cabaret;* Others; Charter Mem, Little Egypt Regional Theatre; Choreographer, Salem Little Theatre; cp/Pres, Gen Marion Soc, Chd Am Revolution; Isach Hull Chapt, DAR; Marion Co Teen Chm, March of Dimes; 4-H Ldr; Co & St Winner, Am Legion Jr Aux; Intl Order Rainbow for Girls, Co-Editor *Ill Rainbow News,* Co-Capt Rainbow Pom-Pom Team; Others; hon/Grand Cross of Color; Gov Ogilvie Hostess; Outstg Dramatist of Yr 1977; Wom's Clb Mus S'ship, Ill Weslyan Univ; Outstg Ser, Mus, Speech, Radio, Journalism & Speech Regional Awds; Var Dance & Vocal Awds; Dean's List; Others; W/W Among Am HS Students; Notable Ams; DIB; World W/W Commun Ser; Intl Yth Achmt.

WYATT, DARLA JEAN oc/Student; b/Jun 29, 1963; h/Rt 1, Salem, IL 62881; p/John L and Darlene Fry Wyatt, Salem; ed/Salem Commun HS; pa/Speech Team; Readers Theatre; French Clb; Marching Band; FHA; Concert Choir; Girls Glee Clb; Madrigal Singers; Voice & Theatre Student; Tap, Jazz & Ballet at Lalla Bauman Sch of Dance (St Louis); Jan Pegg Sch of Dance (Centralia, Ill); One-Way Singers; Centralia Cult Soc & Little Theatre; Salem Little Theatre; Others; cp/Intl Order Rainbow Girls; GSA; Am Legion Jr Aux; Marion Co Chapt, March of Dimes;

Salem-Centralia Shriners Football Game Chm (Shriners Burn Ctr Benefit Game); r/Grace United Meth Ch: Mem; hon/Top Teen & Entertainer Awd, Ill St Fair; Num 1st Pl Awds, Ill St Solo & Ensemble Contests; Winner, Modern Woodmen Oration Contest; Intl Order Rainbow for Girls: Girl of Month, Ill Grand Assembly, Go-Getter Awd, Grand Choir, Grand Cross of Colors, Others; 4-H Awds; IPA.

WYATT, DARLENE FRY oc/Teacher's Aide; b/Nov 14, 1938; h/Rt 1, Salem, IL

62881; m/John Lowell; c/Darla Jean, Angela Jane; p/Zekel E and Pansy O Fry, Salem; ed/Lindenwood Col for Wom.

WYATT, HAZEL FRANCES oc/Service Worker; b/Jan 28, 1919; h/Box 141, Rt 2, Huntington, TN 38344; ba/Huntington; p/Ed

Wyatt (dec); Tara Wyatt, Huntington; ed/BS Bether Col; Grad Univ Tenn-M; cp/Heart Assn; Home Demo Clb; r/Primitive Bapt; hon/Wom of Yr, Home Demo Clb.

WYATT, JOHN LOWELL oc/Cattle Rancher; b/Sept 4, 1932; h/Rt 1, Salem, IL 62881; ba/Same; m/Darlene Fry; c/Angela Jane, Darla Jane; p/Russell Lowell and Florence Finn Wyatt, Salem; ed/So Ill Univ; mil/Korean War; pa/NFOASC; cp/Repub Nat Com Fund; r/Grace United Meth Ch.

WYLER, PAUL oc/Lawyer; Administrative Law Judge; h/1311 Talmadge St, Los Angeles, CA 90027; ba/Los Angeles, CA; m/Lorraine; c/Jill, David; p/Jacob and Dura Wilensky (dec); ed/BSS; LLB; LLM; Addit Studies; pa/Employed by Var Law Firms in NYC 1953-58; Employed in LA & Beverly Hills (Cal) w Pvt Law Firm 1959-67; Referee & Adm Law Judge, Cal Unemployment Ins Appeals Bd 1967-; Lectr in Cal Unemployment Ins Law, UCLA Ext 1972, 74, 75; Admitted to NY Bar 1953, Bar of US Supreme Ct 1958, Cal Bar 1959; ABA: Conf of Adm Law Judges 1972-, Com on Mbrship 1973-75, Com on Labor 1974-, Pvt Bar in Legal Sers to Poor 1974-, Com on Benefits to Unemployed Persons 1976-, Chm Subcom on Adm Due Process Thereof 1975-, Others; Com on Adm Agys & Tribunals, Cal St Bar 1970-74; LA Co Bar Assn: Bar Bulletin Com 1961-63, Com on Adm Agys 1960-73, Alt Del to Cal State Conf of Dels 1973-77; Cal Adm Referees Assn (State Assn): Chm Com on Profl Advmt 1970-73, Mem & Contbr to Edit Bd of ARA Review 1971-, VP 1973-74, Pres 1974-75, Others, (So Cal Chapt): VP 1969-73, Pres 1973-74, Panelist, Others; hon/1 of 4 Finalists in 1974 Competition for Arthur Altmeyer F'ship, US Dept of Labor.

WYLIE, WOODROE WILSON oc/Cattle Rancher; b/Jun 19, 1918; h/Rt 1, Carthage, TX 75633; ba/Same; p/James Euin and Florence Hennigan Wylie, Carthage; cp/Active Repub Politics; Poetry Cirs; Rusk Co Poetry Soc; Known for Political Writings; r/Meth; hon/Author, "The Imprint of Judy Garland"; Others.

WYNDEWICKE, KIONNE ANNETTE oc/Teacher; h/533 E 33rd Pl, Apt 1100, Chicago, IL 60616; ba/Chgo; p/Charles Thomas Johnson (dec); Missouria Jackson Johnson; ed/BS Ill St Normal Univ 1960; pa/IPA; CARA; IRA; cp/Profl Wom's Aux, Provident Hosp; YWCA; PUSH; r/Christ the Mediator Luth Ch: Mem; hon/1 of 25 Black Wom Selected in Chgo for Kizzy Image Awd; Commun Ser Awd, Beatrice Caffrey Yth Ser

Inc S Ctl Com; Wom of Day, WAIT Radio Station; Selected to Attend Innovative Tchr Tng Seminar, Williams Col.

WYNNE, EASTELLA JANE oc/Teacher; b/May 10, 1908; h/114 Marcy E, #13, Montesano, WA 98563; ed/BA 1936; MA 1948; BMus 1949; DMus 1950; Perm Certs Lib Sci; pa/Sister Rel Order; Tchr Mus, Piano, Rel 1927-74; St Joseph Parish 1974-: Rel Ed Coor, Liturgy Coor, Eucharistic Min, Organist 2 Parishes; Rel Ed Bd, Archdiocesan Rel Ed Assn; Sacred Mus & Lit Comm; Parish Coun; Nat Guild Piano Tchrs; Am Col Musicians; Wash St Mus Tchrs Assn; Eligible for Emeritus Cert for Piano Tchrs, Nat Assn Mus Tchrs; Nationally Accredited Piano Tchr; Cert'd Rel Ed Tchr; cp/Working w Sr Citizens; r/Dominican Sisters of Edmonds, Wash; hon/Nat Guild Piano Tchrs Hall of Fame; Biogl Listings.

WYSONG, EARL M JR oc/Educator; Consultant; b/Jun 3, 1925; h/213 Farmgate Lane, Silver Spring, MD 20904; m/Lois A; c/Joyce W Gordy, Cheryl W Dankulich; p/Mary E Wysong, Silver Spring, MD; ed/BA En Washington Univ 1961; MBA 1964, DBA Geo Washington Univ 1972; mil/US Army 1943-46; USAF 1949-62 (Rank of Major); pa/Acct, En Air Lines 1946-49; EDP Auditor & Sys Acct, US Gen Acct'g Ofc 1962-80; Prof of Acct'g Loyola Col 1980-; Intl Dir, Assn for Sys Mgmt; Chm ADP Com, Assn Govt Accts; Am Inst CPAs; Acad Mgmt; cp/Calverton Citizens Assn; Treas 1966, Bd Dirs 1967-70; r/Prot; hon/Cert'd Public Acct; Cert'd Data Processing Auditor; Cert'd Mgr; Dist'd Ser Awd, Assn for Sys Mgmt; Achmt of Yr Awd, Assn Govt Accts.

WYSS, NORMA TOPPING oc/Supervisor; b/Jan 7, 1919; h/Rt 2, Box 196, Perdido Terrace, Pensacola, FL 32506; ba/Pensacola; m/Werner Oscar; p/Eugene L Topping (dec); Sylvia Schubert, Warrington, FL; ed/BA 1949, MS 1960 Fla St Univ; pa/Area I Cnslg Supvr, Fla St Dept Commerce; APGA; NECA; FPGA; ACES; cp/Pensacola C of C; r/Luth;

hon/Alpha Delta Kappa (Fla's 1st Pres); W/W Am Wom; 2000 Wom Achmt; World W/W Wom.

WYSZYNSKI, RICHARD CHESTER oc/Musician; Writer; Teacher; b/Feb 15, 1933; h/851 N Leavitt St, Chicago, IL 60622; p/Ignatius John Wyszynski, Chgo; Victoria Wyszynski (dec); ed/BM, BME NWn Univ 1955; Pvt Study w Marcel Moyse 1961-65; Grad Studies, Univ So Cal 1965; pa/Instr Mus: MONACEP Adult Ed (Chgo) 1977-, Ctl Commun Col 1975, USC-LA 1973, Others; Editor & Pubr, *Interplay Mag*; Mus Critic & Columnist, *Old Town Voice*; Writer Editor Sers, Columbia Records (NY); Prodr-Broadcaster, WHPK-FM (Chgo); Free-lance Articles; Author Film Script Sev 16mm

Documentaries & First Prize Winners NY Film Fest, Venice, Edinburgh, Brussels, Others; Maj Roles Commun Theatre; Minor Role in Ross Hunter Film, *The Pad & How to Use It*; Conductor, Lincolnwood (Ill) Commun Theatre 1976; Free-lance Profl Flutist & Conductor; Fdr & Dir, Interguild Chamber Mus Workshop 1951-54; Solo Flute: NC Symph Orch 1960, Shreveport (La) Symph Orch 1960-61, Others; Mus Coor & Conductor Films by Harry Atwood, Charles Dee Sharp, Others; Mus Dir, Cardinal Chamber Orch 1968-; Others; cp/Exec Dir, Consolidated Ath Comm (Chgo); r/Rom Cath; hon/Dedications of Mus Compositions; Biog Pub'd Anthol by Bob Brier; Others.

Y

YADAO, ALEX PERALTA oc/Physician; Surgeon; b/Jan 20, 1938; h/9323 Old Mt Vernon Rd, Alexandria, VA 22309; ba/A'ria; m/Nilda Zorrilla Alcasabas; c/Albert, Glynn, Melissa, Cherie; p/Leo and Felisa Peralta Yadao, Cubao, Quezon City, Philippines; ed/AA 1958, MD 1963 Univ Santo Tomas Col Med & Surg; Internships: Vets Meml Hosp 1963, Sinai Hosp Baltimore; Residency Wash Hosp Ctr 1965-69; mil/Philippine Army Lt 1960; pa/Currently Vascular & Gen Surg No Va; Surg House Ofcr Fairfax Hosp 1969-73; AMA; Am Trauma Soc; So & Bd Councilors Philippine Med Assns; Fairfax, Prince William Co, A'ria & Va St Med Socs; Orgr & Pres Va Assn Philippine Phys; Pres Barangay Intl; Va & Dir Nat Hypoglycemia Soc; Phy Advr Am Assn Med Asst; Assn Philippine Practicing Phys Am; Soc Philippine Surgs Am; Am Soc Abdominal Surgs; Intl Col Surgs; Am Col Intl Phys; Va Med Arbitration Bd; Am Soc Bariatric Phys; cp/Com Programming & Planning Potomac Hosp; Com Emer & Programming Commonwlth Hosp; No Va Foun Med Care Profl Standard Review Org; Va Med Polit Soc; Am Assn Fgn Med Grads; Pres: UST Med Alumni, Potomac Triangle Med Assocs Ltd; Va Cult Laureatte; Dir Philippine Heritage Fdn; Optimist Clb; Del 8th World Jamboree Canada 1955; Del 10th World Scout Jamboree Philippines 1959; r/Rom Cath; hon/Phys Recog Awd: 3 AMA, Va St; BSA: Eagle Scout w Silver Palms, Woodbager; Mil Marksmanship Awd; Num Biogl Listings.

YAMANE, STANLEY JOEL oc/Physician; b/Mar 13, 1943; h/98-336 Kaonohi St, Aiea, HI 96701; ba/Waipahu, HI; m/Joyce; c/Stanley, Karen; p/Tooru and Yukiko Yamane, Kapaa, HI; ed/BS 1966, OD 1966 Pacific Univ; pa/Dr Optometry Pvt Pract 1967-; Added Partner Kuwabara 1973 & Assoc Nishizawa 1978; Conslt Chds House Inc; Lectr: Am Cancer Soc, Ctl Mich Univ, Hi Pharm Assn, Bausch & Lomb, Others; Am Acad Optometry; Am Optometric Assn: Com Optometric Paraoptmetric Pers, Del Annual Nat Conv, Lectr Post-Nat Cong Cont'g Ed Prog; Hi Optometric Assn: Pres, 2nd VP, Div Dir, Leg Lobbyist, Chm Num Coms; Am Optometric Foun; APHA; Better Vision Inst; Col Optometrists Vision Devel; cp/Hi Optometric Polit Action Com; Hi Vision Sers; BSA; Friends Waipahu Cult Garden Park; Hi Assn Chd Lng Disabilities; Hi Assn Intellectually Gifted Chd; Leeward Mtl Hlth Adv Coun; Oahu JCs; Leilani Estates Commun Assn; Pearl Ridge Elem Sch Parent-Tchr Group; Village W Commun Assn; Waipahu: Bus Assn, HS Adv Coun, Bus Adv Coun; r/Conserv Bapt; Yg Mens Christian Assn; hon/Leeward Oahu JCs: Dist'd Ser Awd, Top Outstg Yg Man Awd; Nat Eye Res Foun: Merit Awd, Dist'd Ser Awd; Bus-man of Mo Awd, Waipahu Bus Assn; Man of Yr Awd, Hi Optometric Assn; Num Biogl Listings.

YANISH, ELIZABETH oc/Sculptor; h/131 Fairfax, Denver, CO 80220; m/Nathan; c/Ronald, Mindy, Marilyn Ginsburg; p/Sam and Fannie May Yaffe, Denver; pa/Num Sculpture Exhbns US & Europe; VPres Nat & Pres Colo Artists Equity Assns; cp/Pres: Gtr Denver Coun Arts & Humanities, Disabled Am Vets Aux; Chm Visual Arts Fest Com; Bd Trustees Denver Ctr Performing Arts; Mayors Cont'g Com Child Abuse; Bd Ed Com Arts Elem Ed; Resource Artist Denver Public Schs; hon/W/W: World Wom, Am Art, Am Wom, W; Notable Ams.

YANOSKO, ELIZABETH JUANITA oc/-Homemaker; b/Feb 26, 1924; h/Box 101 Bartholow St, St John, WA 99171; ba/Same; m/-Michael; c/Barbara Cheney, Michael; p/-John Imbler (dec); Jessie Howry Imbler, Toledo, OR; pa/St John Sch 1978-79; Am Shopper Panel Whitman Co 1978; Record Rater EARS 1978; Foster Home Chd 1963-64 & 1975-79; Motel Mgr Oreg 1969-72; Other Past

Positions; cp/Early Am Soc; Nat Audubon Soc; Intl Assn Turtles; US Olympic Soc; Couture Soc; Intl Platform Assn; Secy Am Legion; Altar Soc; Brownie Ldr; Chm Girl Scout Troop Com; Den Mother; Chm Legion Aux Hosp Holidays; Chm PTA Hospitality Com; Vol Helper Cand St Gov; Red Cross; Band Booster; r/Cath; Tchr Catechizem Class; hon/Cert Merit: Potpourri Cookery, KWSU Radio Sta; PHT En Wash St Col; 2nd Prize, Idaho St Fair; Cand Mother of Yr.

YARBOROUGH, BARBARA LOUISE oc/Educator; b/Jun 29, 1940; h/PO Box 173, Elon Col, NC 27244; ba/EC; p/Olin and Louise Yarborough, Fort Mill, SC; ed/BS Winthrop Col; MAT UNC-CH; pa/Elon Col: Asst Prof PE, Volleyball & Cheerldr Coach; Instr UNC-CH 6 Yrs; Rec Dir Florence Crittenton Home 1 Yr; Tchr: Indep HS 2 Yrs, Coulwood Jr HS 4 Yrs; Rep Assembly Del Nat Conv AAHPER; NCAHPER: Pres, VPres PE Div, Nom'g Com Chm, Rep Assembly Del So Dist; SDAAHPER: Pres & VPres PE Div, Nom'g Com, Future Directions Com; SAPECW; NAPECW; NCDGWS: Golf, Gymnastics & Cheerldr Chm; US Gymnastics Fdn; World Futurist Org; US Assn Indep Gymnastics Clb; cp/NCS Public Affairs Team; r/Mem Front St U Meth Ch, Burlington; hon/Outstg Yg Wom Am 1971; W/W NC; Intl W/W Intells; Personalities Am.

YARBROUGH, KAREN MARGUERITE oc/Geneticist; b/Mar 4, 1938; h/Rt 9 Box 795, Hattiesburg, MS 39401; ba/H'burg; p/David Yarbrough (dec); Marguerite Hartsfield Yarbrough, Biloxi, MS; ed/BS 1961, MS 1963 Miss St Univ; PhD NCSU 1967; pa/Univ So Miss: Asst Dean & Res Coor Col Sci & Technol 1976-, Dir Inst Genetics 1976-, Prof Microbiol 1976-, Assoc Prof 1970-72, Asst

Prof 1967-70, Col Sci & Technol Rep Num Univ Couns, Univ Com on Coms, Chm Instnl Self Study Com Fac, Col Sci & Technol Curric Com, Acad Coun; Res Asst: NCSU 1963-67, MSU 1961-63; Genetics Soc Am; Miss & NY Acads Scis; Am Soc Human Genetics; Am Genetics Assn; hon/Sigma Xi; Phi Sigma; Phi Theta Kappa; Delta Kappa Gamma; USM Excell Tchg Awd; Cardinal Key; Zeta Tau Alpha Foun Scholar; John Rust Trust Fund Scholar; Personalities S; Outstg Edrs Am; DIB; W/W: Am Wom, S&SW, World Wom Edrs; Commun Ldrs & Noteworthy Ams.

YARSHATER, EHSAN oc/Professor; b/Apr 3, 1921; h/450 Riverside Dr, New York, NY 10027; ba/New York, NY; m/Latifeh Alvieh; p/Hashem and Rouhaniyeh Yarshater (dec); ed/BA; DLit; PhD; pa/Prof of Iranian Studies & Dir Iranian Studies, Columbia Univ; Editor: Ency Iranica, Persian Heritage Series, Modern Persian Literature Series; hon/Unesco Awd for Best Book for Yg People.

YASKULSKI, SHARON GAY oc/Veterinary Dermatologist; b/Nov 17, 1948; h/2837 Bonifacio St, Concord, CA 04519; ba/Walnut Creek, CA; p/Stephen and Dorothy Lee Yaskulski, Whiting, IN; ed/DVM; pa/AAHA; Am, Cal, So Cal & Peninsula VMA; AALAS; hon/NIH Res Ser Awd 1977-78.

YATES, HATTYE SCOTT oc/Nurse; b/Dec 16, 1924; h/537 Montgomery Rd, Tuskegee Inst, AL 36088; ba/Tuskegee;

m/Clayton Sr; c/Deidre Y Duncan, Clayton III; p/Gilbert and Naomi Scott (dec); ed/BS; pa/Nurse VA Hosp; Am, Ala & Macon Co Nurses Assns; Nat Assn Col Wom; Chi Eta Phi; cp/T'gee Inst Grad Nurses Clb; T'gee Alumni Clb; NAACP; Nat Coun Negro Wom; Delta Sigma Theta; OES; Daughs Isis; Order Golden Cir; Jack & Jill Am; r/Cath; St Josephs Solidarity BVM; hon/Superior Perf, W/W Am Wom; Spec Achmt Awd.

YATSEVITCH, MICHAEL M oc/Conservationist; Forester; Farmer; Administrator; b/May 25, 1913; h/Fernald Hill Farm, Cornish, NH 03746; ba/Same; m/Claudia E; c/Mary M, Margaret M, Michael M, Stephanie, McGregor J; p/Michael G and Margaret Thomas Yatsevitch (dec); pa/Independent Land Owner, Forester, Farmer; Dir, NH Timberland Owners Assn; Tree Farmer, Am Tree Farm Sys; Soc Protection of NH Forests; Sullivan Co Stabilization & Conservation Ser; Soc of NJ Conserv Comms; Am Farm Bur Fdn; Nat Grange; Assn NH Assessors; cp/NH Sch Bds Assn; NH Mun Assn; Dir, Windsor Vis'g Nurse Assn; Cornish Selectman 19 Yrs (Chm); Trustee, Town of Cornish Trust Funds 15 Yrs; Cornish Sch Bd 21 Yrs (Chm); Cornish Planning Bd; Cornish Conserv Comm; Dir, Cornish Fair Assn; Chm, Cornish Woodsmen's Field Day 16 Yrs; Others; r/Russian Orthodox.

YEAGER, FREDA KNOBLETT oc/-Professor; b/Feb 23, 1928; h/2720 C Parkwood Pl #102, Huntsville, TX 77340; ba/-H'ville; c/Debra Y Manning; p/Fred and Julia Knoblett (dec); ed/BA magna cum laude Franklin Col 1965; MA Sam Houston St Univ 1970; PhD Tex A&M Univ 1977; pa/SHSU: Currently Asst Prof Eng, Instr 1971, Fellow 1968-70; Pt-time Instr Tex A&M Univ 1970-71; Tchr Columbus Sr HS 1965-68; r/Mem St Thomas Epis Ch, H'ville; hon/Kappa Delta Pi; Phi Alpha Theta; Alpha; Knobe Prize Awds 1964 & 65.

YEAGLEY, JOAN oc/Poet; b/Jan 25, 1930; h/Rt 1, Stella, MO 64867; m/H A; c/Jan, Donn, Jeff, Jeanne; p/H E Howerton (dec); Jeannette Howerton; pa/Author: 4 Bookmark Poets, KC Out Loud, Mo Poets; Poems Num Mags & Jours incl'g: Saturday Review, Poetry Bag, Review La Booche, Fine Arts Discovery, KC Star; r/Epis; hon/1st Prize, Ks City Star Contest.

YEP, WALLEN L B oc/Administrator; b/Jul 23, 1943; h/601 Montclair Ave, Oakland, CA 94610; ba/Berkeley, CA; m/Yong Sun; c/Suk; p/Hong Wey and Chin Gee Yep, San Carlos, CA; ed/AA Col San Mateo 1972; BA Cal St Univ-SF 1975; MBA Golden Gate Univ 1977; Cert Contract Adm Univ Cal 1976; mil/AUS 1967-69; pa/MTC Hotel Claremont; Asst Prof Intl Bus Mgmt & Asian Mktg Lincoln Univ 1978-; Free Lance Advr Firms/Individuals Domestic & Intl Bus; Author Ref Book Occupl Cert & Lic'g-Main Requirements; Monographs: Hidden Fallacies Fgn Mkt Data-Main Elements & Formats Used, Fin Status Peoples Republic China; Nat Assn Purchasing Mgmt; Purchasing Mgmt Assn No Cal; Oakland World Trade Assn; Assn MBA Execs; Cert'd Profl Contracts Mgr NCMA; Cert'd Purchasing Mgr NAPM; cp/Oakland Unified Sch Dist Affirmative Action Purchasing Adv Coun; CoChm N Bch Chinatown Yth Sers Ctr; Chinese Affirmative Action; Cal & Golden Gate Alumni; Repub; Num Commun Agys Bay Area; hon/KABL Radio Sta Citizen of Day Awd; Nom Duncan S Gregg Awd; W/W: Fin & Indust, W; Personalities W&MW; Men Achmt; DIB; Notable Ams.

YIP, JETHRO SUTHERLAND oc/Entomologist; Agricultural Chemist; b/Jul 28, 1895; h/3901 E Dakota Ave, Fresno, CA 93726; ba/Same; ed/BS 1921, MS 1923 Univ Cal-B; pa/Chem Coast Lab 1966-67; Chem & Entomologist Twining Lab 1941-65; Res Assoc Div Plant Nutrition Univ Cal-B 1936-41; Entomol Bur Plant Indust US Dept Agri 1934-36; Other Past Positions; Contbr:

Pyrethrum Cult, Pa Farmer, Jour Ec Entomol; hon/Cal Recog Awd, Chinese Consolidated Benevolent Assn; Dist'd Ser Entomologist Awd, DIB; 2000 Men Achmt Awds; Intl W/W Commun Ser; Commun Ldrs & Noteworthy Ams Annual Awds; W/W Inc; Book Hon; Notable Ams Bicent Era Awd; Ldrs Am Sci; Intl Register Profiles Awd; People Who Matter.

YODER, LUELLA MAY NAFZINGER oc/Educator; b/May 17, 1913; h/Star Rt, Box 3, Belleville, PA 17004; m/Urie Phillip; p/John Nafzinger, McVeytown, PA; Ida Belle Zook, B'ville; ed/BS Shippensburg St Tchrs Col; MEd Pa St Univ; Addit Studies; mil/AUS Spec Tng Unit Instr 3rd Ser Command, Indiantown Gap Mil Reservation; Army Libn Aberdeen

Proving Grounds; pa/Chm Eng Dept Kishacoquillas Jr-Sr HS; Eng Tchr: Menno-Union Joint HS, Bratton-McVeytown-Oliver Joint HS, Derry Township HS; r/Luth; hon/Delta Kappa Gamma; W/W: Am Ed, World Wom; Creative & Successful Personalities Intl Pers Res; DIB.

YOGIJI, HARBHAJAN SINGH KHALSA oc/Minister; Administrator; b/Aug 26, 1929; h/1905 Preuss Rd, Los Angeles, CA 90035; ba/LA; m/Inderjit Kaur Puri; c/Ranbir Singh, Kulbir Singh, Kamaljit Kaur Puri; p/Kartar Singh and Harkrishan Kaur Puri, New Delhi, India; ed/BA Punjab Univ; mil/Indian Army; pa/Min & Rel Adm Head Sikh Dharma W Hemisphere; Dir Spir Ed 3HO Foun; Tchr Kundalini Yoga: UCLA, USC; Interrel Coun So Cal; CoPres World Parliament Rels; Am Coun Execs Rel; cp/LA World Affairs Coun; LA Bombay Sisters; Rotary Intl; r/Sikh Dharma; hon/Friendship Scrool & Key Miami; Hon Titles: Bhai Sahib 1974, The Siri Singh Sahib 1971; Debate Awds, Punjab Univ.

YOKEN, MELVIN BARTON oc/Professor; b/Jun 25, 1939; h/97 Delcar St, Fall River, MA 02720; ba/N Dartmouth, MA; c/Cynthia Stein; c/Andrew; p/Albert Yoken (dec); Sylvia Yoken, FR; ed/BA Univ Mass; MAT Brown Univ; PhD 1972; pa/Prof Mod Langs &

Lit SMU; MLA; AATF; ACTFL; Platform Assn Am; P L Courier Assn; Paul Claudel Assn; New Eng Mod Lang Assn; cp/Franco-phone Clb; Pres & Bd Dirs Friends of FR Public Lib; Pubs Dir FR C of C; hon/Dist'd Ser Awd, City FR.

YOST, CHARLES EDWARD oc/Priest; Professor; Librarian; b/May 4, 1932; h/7335 S Lovers Ln Rd, Hales Corners, WI 53130; ba/Same; p/Edward Yost (dec); Mary Becker

Yost, Pittsburgh, PA; ed/STL 1960, MSLS 1961 Cath Univ Am; pa/Libn & Prof Hist Theol Sacred Heart Sch Theol; Am & Cath Lib Assns; Cath Hist Soc; Am Philatelic Assn; r/Mem Cong Priests Sacred Heart; Ordained Rom Cath Priest 1958; Rel Superior Sacred Heart Monastery 1977-.

YOU, RICHARD W oc/Physician; Surgeon; b/Dec 23, 1916; h/1104 Alewa Dr, Honolulu, HI 96817; ba/H'lulu; m/Eleanor; c/Pamela, Aleta; p/Dong Men and Mary Choy You (dec); ed/BS Univ Hi 1939; MD Creighton Med Sch 1943; Addit Studies; mil/Hi NG Sgt 1932-39; US Med Corps: 1st Lt to Capt 1944-46, Post & Compound Surg Prisoner of War Camp 1945-46, Capt 117th Sta Hosp 1946, Capt Hi NG 1947-50; pa/Chm Hawaiian AAU Tae Kwon Do Com; US Olympic Com; Pres Hi Chapt US Olympians 1958-77; AAU: US Olympic Com 1956-77, Nat Conv 1953-77, Wn Assn of US 1959-77, Nat Karate Med Com 1973-77, Nat Tau Kwon Do Com 1976-77, Nat Sports Med Com 1965-77, Other Coms; Judge: US Sullivan Awd Panel 1954-77, US Olympic & Nat Weightlifting Championships 1956; Cert'd Nat AAU Weightlifting Referee 1963-77; Weightlifting as an Ofcl Var Capacities and as an Ath 1932-; Judge Mr Am, Miss Hi-Universe, Miss Hi-Intl & Other Beauty, Hlth & Physique Contests 1944-77; Diplomat Nat Bd Med Examrs 1952-77; US Olympic Soc; Mgr, Coach & Tnr: Hi Weightlifting Team, Hi Woms & Girls Track & Field Team; Coach,

Tnr & Developer Num Nat & World Champions in Weightlifting, Boxing, Long Distance Running, Baseball, Swimming, Track & Field; Num Other Orgs, Ofcs, Coms; cp/Bd Mgrs Hawaiian AAU; Chm Nat AAU Hospitality Com; Phys: Hi Sr Leag Football, St Louis HS Football Team, Hula Bowl Football Games; Pres: Olympic Boxing Clb, Korean Univ Clb, Boxing Mgrs Guild, Hi Assn AAU, Korean C of C, Korean Commun Coun, York Ath Clb, Kamaaina Magic Cir; VP: Korean Vil, H'lulu Stadium Ltd, York Intl Traders, H'lulu Qtrback Clb; VChm: Action Com Govs Yth Fitness Com, Univ Hi Bd Regents; Dir & Advr Num XDR Clbs; Trustee: Univ Hi Foun, Univ Hi Ath Foun; Secy & Treas Creighton Univ Alumni Assn; Capt Nuuanu YMCA Fund Dr; Num Other Civic Activs; hon/Invited to Moscow to check Olympic Facilities for 1980 Moscow Olympic Games 1977; Invited to Intl Biog Centre Royal Jubilee Conf on Arts & Communs 1977; Intl Helms Hall of Fame Weightlifting 1968; US Olympian Awd of Merit for Contbns in Olympic Sports 1976-77; US Wisdom Hall of Fame & Wisdom Awd of Hon 1970; World Brotherhood: Outstg Indiv Awd Winner, Man of Yr Awd; Hi Sportman of Yr; Father of Yr Sports Awd, H'lulu C of C; Dist'd Achmt Awd, Field Humanities; Asiatic-Pacific Ser Medal; WW-II Victory Medal; Pub'd Author; Num Biogl Listings.

YOUMANS, ELSIE oc/Educator; b/Jul 25, 1912; h/11562 Monette Rd, Riverview, FL 33569; ba/R'view; m/Travis; p/H D and Alice Williams, Tampa, FL; ed/AB; MA; pa/Sch Tchr Orange Grove; cp/Pres Civic Clb; Pres Garden Clb; r/Mem 1st Bapt Ch, R'view; hon/Delta Kappa Gamma.

YOUNG, CARLENE oc/Professor; ba/301 S 5th St, San Jose, CA 95192; c/Howard, Loren; p/James Herb (dec); Florence Herb, Detroit, MI; ed/BA 1955; MA

1960; EdD 1967; PhD 1976; pa/Prof & Chair Afro-Am Studies Dept San Jose St Univ 1969-; Am Sociol Assn; Am Acad Polit & Social Scis; AAUP: Treas 1975-76, VP 1976-77, Exec Com; U Profs Cal; Cal Wom Higher Ed; Cal Col & Univ Fac Assn; Alpha Kappa Alpha; cp/Soc Psychol Study Social Issues; Bd Dirs Cath Social Sers; Chair & Adv Com Oral Hist Black Ams; Bd Dirs Afro-Am Commun Ctr; Secy & Steering Com Nat Coun Black Studies; Chair & Bd Dir No Reg Cal Black Fac & Staff Assn; hon/Phi Kappa Phi; Alpha Phi Alpha Awd; Assn 3rd World Wom Ldrship Awd; Outstg Work Pan-African Cult Heritage, Min Commun Hotline; Phi Delta Kappa Nat Register Ednl Reschrs; W/W: Intl Commun, Intl Intells, World Wom Ed, Am Wom, Am Higher Ed; Commun Ldrs & Noteworthy Ams; Personalities W&MW; Notable Ams; Outstg Edrs Am

YOUNG, DENNIS HUGH oc/Southern Baptist Minister; b/Mar 31, 1954; h/Rt 1 Box 618, Carrollton, GA 30117; ba/Same; p/Hugh and Mertha McLendon Young, Carrollton; pa/Min Music Roopville, Ga 1971-75; Assoc Pastor Temple 1st Bapt Ch 1975-78; r/Bapt; hon/W/W Rel; Commun Ldrs & Noteworthy Ams; Intl Dic Biog Records.

YOUNG, EDNA LESTINA oc/Educator; b/Oct 11, 1924; h/1722 Oak St, Columbia, SC 29204; ba/C'bia; p/Charles Young, Teaneck, NJ; Mary Young (dec); ed/BS Hampton Inst; MA NYU; pa/Unit Ldr 4th & 5th Grades Open Space Sch; Nat, SC & Richland Co Ed Assns; Nat Coun Tchrs Math; NAUW; cp/NAACP; YWCA; Alpha Kappa Alpha; Vol Muscular Dystrophy; r/Mem Bethel AME Ch; hon/Ser Awd, Alpha Kappa Alpha; Nat Sci Grant Elem Tchrs & Pers Math.

YOUNG, ELEANOR ANNE oc/Professor; b/Oct 8, 1925; h/1701 Alametos, San Antonio, TX 78201; ba/SA; p/Carl and Eleanor Hamilton Young (dec); ed/BA Incarnate Word Col 1947; MEd St Louis Univ 1955; PhD Univ Wisc 1968; RD; pa/Assoc Prof & CoDir Div Human Nutrition, Dept Med Univ Tex Hlth Sci Ctr 1977-; Former Assoc Prof & Chm Dept Home Ec Incarnate Word Col; Conslt: Surg Gen AUS 1976-, Audie L Murphy Vets Adm Hosp 1973-, Luth Gen Hosp N 1977, Med Staff Bexar Co Hosp Dist 1971-; Assn Wom Sci; Am Inst Nutrition; Am Soc Clin Nutrition; Am Fdn Clin Res; Am, Tex & San Antonio Dietetic Assns; Am & Tex Public Hlth Assns; AHEA; ASAS; Am Soc Parenteral & Enteral Nutrition; NY Acad Sci; Soc Nutrition Ed; Tex Home Ec Assn; Tex St Nutrition Coun; Tex Assoc'd Nutrition Advr; cp/Tex Affil Nutrition Subcom AHA; S Tex Kidney Foun; S Tex Hlth Ed Ctr; Tex St Dept Hlth; Coun & Chm Res Sect Tex St Nutrition Coun; Chm Nutrition Task Force Camino Real Hlth Sys Agy; r/Mem Sister Charity of Incarnate Word; hon/Sigma Xi; Grants: US Dept Agri Univ Wisc, Chds Bur Univ Ia; Gen Food F'ship, Univ Wisc; Pub'd Author; W/W: Wom, Am Wom, World Wom, S&SW; Am Men & Wom Sci; Outstg Edr Am.

YOUNG, ELIZABETH BELL oc/Professor; b/Jul 2, 1929; h/8104 W Bch Dr NW, Washington, DC 20012; ba/Wash, DC; m/Charles Alexander Jr; p/Joseph and Eulalia Miller Bell (dec); ed/BA, MA NC Ctl Univ; PhD Ohio St Univ; pa/Cath Univ Am: Prof Grad & Undergrad Sch 1966-, Supvr Spch & Hearing Clin 1966-; Bd Am Spch & Hearing

Assn; cp/Adv Bd U Negro Col Fund; r/Bapt; hon/Outstg Alumni Awd, Ohio St Univ; Certs Apprec: DC Dental Soc, DC Comm Status Wom; Evalutor Outstg Ed Texts, Pi Lambda Theta; Num Biogl Listings.

YOUNG, JAMES N oc/Firefighter; b/Nov 1, 1924; h/1406 Wenasoga Rd, Corinth, MS 38834; m/Elva Marie Dobbins; c/2 Daughs; ed/Att'd NE Miss Jr Col; mil/USMC 3rd Marine Div WW-II 3 Yrs; pa/Constrn TVA 1946-61; Policeman City of Corinth 1961-64; Corinth Fire Dept: Fireman 1964-, Dept Chief 1978-; Est'g Fire Protection Prog 3 Co Area NE Miss & Devel'g Tng Acad for Corinth & NE Miss Fire Depts; Intl Soc Fire Ser Instrs; Miss Fire Chiefs Assn; Miss Fire Fighters Assn; cp/Com Yellow Creek Watershed Emer Planning Group; VFW; Am Legion; hon/Fireman of Yr, VFW; Book Hon.

YOUNG, LLOYD EMORY oc/Administrator; Counselor; b/Nov 15, 1936; h/603 Elizabeth Ave, Newark, NJ 07112; ba/Newark; m/Juanita; c/Donald; p/George C L and Lelia M Young (dec); ed/BS Morgan St Univ; MA Kean Col; mil/AUS 1960-62; pa/Recorder & Quality Control Ofcr, Tri-State Transportation Com (E Orange, NJ) 1962-63; Mgr, Men's Dept, Ohrbach's Deptartment Store (Newark) 1963-65; Guided Group Interaction Spec, Sr Group Ldr, Sect Supvr & Cnslr, Kilmer Job Corps Ctr (Edison, NJ) 1965-68; Essex County Col: Coor of Student Activs, Dir Student Activs, Asst Dean Student Affairs 1968-74, Assoc Dean for Admissions, Assessment & Records 1974-79; Dir Student Support Sers for ECC Extension Ctrs 1979-; Cnslr & Lectr in Field; Century Assn for Excell in Ed; APGA; AAHE; EACDAS; ACPA; NJCCDA; CBAA (NE Region); cp/Mary McLeod Bethune Foun Inc; Mayor's Com on Fire Preven 1971-73; Bethany Lodge #31, PHA Worshipful Master; Worthy Patron OES; Excell High Priest, HRAM; Others; r/Meth; hon/Cert of Merit, Bethany Chapt OES; Most Worshipful Prince Hall Grand Lodge of NJ; Cert of Proficiency, Essex Co Col; Cert of Ser Awd; W/W E; Phi Delta Kappa; Others.

YOUNG, PATRICK H oc/Architect; b/Mar 17, 1930; h/PO Box 2396, Jackson, MS 39205; m/Hildegard Luise Vassmer; ed/Dipl-Ingenieur, Architekt 1962; pa/Arch Designer Hong Kong 1949-54; Arch Bremen, Germany 1962-67; Acoustical Conslt NYC 1967-68; Arch: NYC 1968-72, Cocoa Bch 1972-74, Jackson, Miss 1974-; Am Inst Archs; Am Inst Phys; Acoustical Soc Am; Intl Platform Assn; hon/Recipient Archtl Design Competition, Cong/Concert Hall Germany 1963-64.

YOUNG, ROBERT MICHAEL oc/Systems Analyst; b/Nov 5, 1947; h/18520 Eagles Roost Dr, Germantown, MD 20767; ba/Rockville, MD; m/Elaine Catherine; c/Dawn Yateem, Louis Yateem; p/Philip Clark and Mary Helen Young, Ocala, FL; ed/BS 1969; MS 1973; MS 1978; pa/Sr Sys Analyst, Info Planning Assocs; Tech Conslt to Var Agys (DOT, NOAA, DOI, EPA, FAA); CoAuthor, *A Primer for MLAB*; cp/Germantown Alliance; Fredericktown Players; r/Prot; hon/NSF Summer Res Fellow; IAESTE-UN Summer Exchange Student; W/W E.

YOUNG, ROSALIE oc/Psychologist; b/Nov 30, 1936; ba/Harlen Valley Psychiatric

Ctr, Wingdale, NY 12594; m/Bernard; c/Sue, Maura, Sandy, Joe, Barry; ed/MS; MSW; PhD; pa/Pvt Pract Psychotherapist; Cert'd Sex Therapist; AASECT; Nat Assn Social Workers; APGA; Nat Rehab Assn; NY St Mtl Hlth Adm; Nat Coun on Aging; Pub'd Author; cp/Common Cause; Others; hon/W/W E.

YOUNG, SARAH HAMILTON oc/-Nurse; b/Jan 5, 1930; h/17820 Buehler Rd, Olney, MD 20832; ba/Bethesda, MD; p/William and Marian Kerr Young, Pittsburg, PA; ed/RN; Addit Studies; pa/Clin Nurse Expert Neurology Nsg Ser, NIH Clin Ctr; Am & Md Nurses Assns; cp/Metro Assn Parkinsons Disease; CoFdr Wash Chapt Alzheimers Soc; r/Rom Cath; hon/Indiv & Group Merit Awds, NIH.

YOURITZIN, GLENDA GREEN oc/Artist; Lecturer; Educator; b/Feb 4, 1945; h/1721 Oakwood Dr, Norman, OK 73069; ba/Same; m/Victor Koshkin; p/Allen and Alma Green, Weatherford, TX; ed/BA magna cum laude Tex Christian Univ 1967; MA Kress F'ship Tulane Univ 1970; pa/Univ Okla: Vis Instr Art 1975-76, Guest Artist Fac 1972-75, Spec Instr 1973-75; Tulane Univ: Pt-time Instr Art Hist 1969-72, Curator Collections Newcomb Art Sch 1968-72; Res Asst Kimbell Art Mus Summers 1968 & 69; 1 Wom Exhbns Num Mus & Gallerys incl'g: Philbrook Art Ctr, Okla Mus Art, Artsplace II, Mus SW; Num Other Juried & Selected Exhbns; Paintings Public Collections: Smithsonian Instn, Mus of City NY, Williams Col Mus Art, St Okla Art Collection, Univ Okla; hon/Featured Var Mags.

YOUSE, GLAD ROBINSON oc/Composer; Author; b/Oct 22, 1898; h/532 E 12th St, Baxter Springs, KS 66713; m/C E (dec); c/Madolyn Y Babcock; p/James and Catherine Robinson (dec); pa/ASCAP; SAI; Nat Leag Am Pen Wom; Nat Fdn Music Clbs; r/Presb; hon/AFD Baker Univ; Achmt Awd, Stephens Col; Matrix Table Awd, Theta Sigma Phi; Ring Excell, Sigma Alpha Iota; Beta Sigma Phi.

YOUTCHEFF, JOHN SHELDON oc/-Program Manager; b/Apr 16, 1925; h/543 Midland Ave, Berwyn, PA 19312; ba/Wash, DC; m/Elsie Marianne Koerner; c/Karen, John Jr, Mark, Heidi, Lisa; p/Slav and

Florence Davidson Youtcheff, Cincinnati, OH; ed/BA; MA; PhD; mil/USNR Cmdr; pa/Prog Mgr US Postal Ser Hdqtrs; NSPE; Fellow AAAS; cp/Past Pres Optimist Clb; r/Rom Cath.

YOVICICH-JONES, GEORGE STEVEN

oc/Civil Engineer; b/Jun 2, 1927; h/PO Box 712, Skokie, IL 60076; m/Sofia; c/1 Son; ed/BSCE 1951; MSCE 1956; PhD NWn Univ 1958; mil/AUS 1954-56; pa/Overseas & Domestic Projs US Corps Engrs 1951-54; Civil Engr Hollabird & Root 1956-57; Arcadia Engrg Intl Inc: Prof Engr & Gen Mgr 1956-70, Bd Chm 1970-; Prof Structural Engrg NWn Univ; Chm Ec Univ Ill; Author: *The Pneumatic Tube Goes Mod, Opports in Constrn, Mgmt & Labor; Contbr Engrg News Record; ASCE; Prof Engrs Soc USA; cp/Leg Asst Ill Gen Assembly; Bd Chm Oakton Col; Pres: Hamilton St Univ, Tetrakear & Assoc Inc; Dir & Bd 1st Nat Bank Chicago & Skokie Commun Hosp; hon/Doct Ec Univ Fla; PhD Hamilton St Univ.

YUEH, NORMA N oc/Director Library Services; b/Jan 21, 1928; h/15 Timothy Rd, Wayne, NJ 07470; ba/Mahwah, NJ; c/Brenda, Dara; ed/BS; MLS; DLS; pa/Pres Coun NJ St Col & Univ Libs 1978-79; NJ Lib Assn: Insts Com 1978-79, Adm Sect Prog Com 1977-78, Pers Adm Com 1974-77; Planning Com Reg Conf Prelude Govs Conf Lib & Info Sers 1978-79; Doct Com Sch Lib Ser Columbia Univ 1977-79; Discussion Ldr Assn Col & Res Libs Am Lib Assn 1978; Standing Com on Interlib Coop Coun St Cols 1976-; Steering Com Coor'g Coun Ridgewood Area Libs 1974-; Accreditation Vistor Middle Sts Assn Col & Sec'dy Sch 1974-; hon/Grant Columbia Univ Sch Lib Ser; William Paterson Col: Fac Devel Fund, Incentive Bonus Awd.

YUTHAS, LADESSA JOHNSON oc/-Educator; b/Oct 9, 1928; h/495 W 4 Ave Dr, Broomfield, CO 80020; ba/Denver, CO; m/-John Yuthas (dec); ba/2nd Wayne Winters; c/-Lynn, John, Kristi, Susan; p/James and Mary Johnson, Ft Collins, CO; ed/BS Colo St Univ 1949; MS Purdue Univ 1954; PhD Univ Colo-B 1969; Addit Studies; pa/Metro St Col: Prof Rdg, Dept Chm 1965-; Dir EPDA Inst Univ Colo Summers 1970 & 71; Rdg Supvr W Lafayette Public Schs 1952-55; Vis Prof:

Purdue Univ, Univ Colo, Colo St Univ, Ft Lewis Col; Conslt: Adams Co SJ/29 J Bennett 1975-76, Div Yth Sers St Colo 1969-71, Colo Dept Ed 1973-76, Bur Indian Affairs St New Mexico 1969-70, ESEA Migrant Ed Colo St Dept Ed 1968-71; Num Spchs & Wkshops; Wn Col Rdg Assn; IRA: Nom'g Com, Chm Trans Com, Chm Friday Prog; Colo Coun IRA: Bd Dirs, Pres, Chm Num Coms; cp/Pres & Bd Dirs Rocky Mtn Rdg Specs; Adv Bd Annual Forum Vision & Lng; Adv Bd Chds Hosp; Colo Lang Arts Soc; r/Meth; hon/Outstg Scholar, Pi Gamma Mu; Outstg Dissertation Rdg, CCIRA; Pub'd Author; Outstg Edrs Am; W/W: Colo, Child Devel Profls, World Wom Ed, World Wom, Intl Intells, Intl Commun Ser; Personalities W&MW; Commun Ldrs & Noteworthy Ams; DIB.

Z

ZABOROWSKI, ROBERT RONALD oc/Provincial Archbishop; b/Mar 14, 1946; h/2803 Tenth St, Wyandotte, MI 48192; ba/Wyandotte; ed/Attended Holy Cross Old Cath Sem; DD 1971, JCD 1974, STD & PhD 1976 St Ignatius Bishop & Martyr Old Cath Sem; pa/Former Organist & Choirmaster: St Elizabeth's Rom Cath Ch (Wyandotte), St Henry's Rom Cath Ch (Lincoln Park, Mich), St John Cantius Polish Rom Cath Ch (Detroit, Mich), Others; Converted from Rom Catholicism to Old Catholicism; Ordained: Sacred Order Subdiaconate 1966, Sacred Order Diaconate 1967, Sacred Priesthood Old Cath Ch (Non-Rom) by Most Rev Joseph Anthony Mazur 1968; Parochial Asst, Holy Cross Polish Old Cath Ch (Chgo) 1968; Established Parochial Mission of Old Cath Ch for Dissident & Ostracized Rom Caths, Epis & Others (Wyandotte) 1969; Consecrated to Sacred Episcopate by Archbishops Joseph Maurice Francois Giraud, Joseph Matthew Nevilloy & Others 1972; Archbishop 1976; Re-established & Re-organized Former Province of N Am Mariavite Old Cath Ch of Poland 1974; Currently Sers as Prime Bishop, Mariavite Old Cath Ch, Province of N Am; Author: "The Work of Great Mercy", What is Mariavitism?", "Missa Solemnis", Num Others Pub'd Rel Jours; 2nd Pres, The Vilatte Guild; Hon Mem, St Irenaeus Inst (France); Knight of Grand Cross, Sovereign Order of St John of Jerusalem Knights of Malta (Rome); Knight of Justice, Sovereign Order of St John of Jerusalem Knights Hospitaller (Malta); St Stephen Albert I Policastro, Prince of Manche-Normandia, Titular Prime Sovereign of Crete-Conte della Civitas (Count of City Sovereign); Hon Mem, Cong of Lit & Arts (France); Others; r/Mariavite Old Cath; hon/Rec'd Hon Doct Moral & Dogmatic Theol & Hon Doct Divine Scis, Inst Sainte Pierre (France).

ZABSKY, JOHN MITCHELL oc/-Mechanical Engineer; b/Apr 18, 1933; h/3640C S Main St, Santa Ana, CA 92707; ba/-Irvine, CA; p/Joseph A Zabsky (dec); Joan Lucas, Joplin, MO; ed/AS; BSME, MSME; pa/AIAA; ASME; Nat Soc Profl Engrs; hon/Patentee; Rec'd Synergism Awds.

ZACHARIAH, MATHEW oc/Sociologist; Educator; b/Feb 17, 1930; h/Rt 4, Box 217, Whitewater, WI 53190; ba/Whitewater; m/Kunjamma M; c/Elizabeth, George; p/George and Elizabeth Zachariah (dec); ed/BA Univ Madras (India) 1952; MA Univ Kerala (India) 1965; MA 1966, PhD 1968 Univ Minn; pa/Assoc Prof Dept Sociol, Univ Wis 1970-; Asst Prof Sociol, Marquette Univ (Milwaukee, Wis) 1968-70; Univ Minn: Tchg Asst 1967-68, Res Asst 1965-67; Lectr Sociol, Univ Kerala 1965; Others; Assoc Editor, Intl

Jour of Comparative & Applied Criminal Justice 1976-; Life Mem, Sociol Soc India; Am Sociol Assn; MW Sociol Soc; Wis Sociol Assn; cp/Former Secy to the Syrian Christian Assn (Madras, India); Former Secy to Madras Christian Col Malayalee Assn; Former Gen Secy, Loyola Col Assn (Trivandrum, India); r/En Orthodox Ch; hon/Alpha Kappa Delta; Rec'd Padmanabha Menon Meml Prize, Madras; First Rank for MA, Univ Kerala; Am Men Sci; Nat Directory Sociol of Ed & Ednl Sociol; Outstg Edrs Am; W/W: Am, MW; DIB; Men Achmt; Others.

ZAFFIRINI, JUDITH oc/Director Communications; b/Feb 13, 1946; h/1505 O'Kane, Apt 5, Laredo, TX 78040; ba/Laredo; m/Carlos M; p/George and Nieves M Pappas, Laredo; ed/BS; MA; PhD; pa/Am Assn Wom in Commun & Jr Cols; Assn Borderland Scholars; Commun Col Journalism Assn; Wom's Inst for Freedom of Press; Tex Assn for Commun Sers & Cont'g Ed; Assn for Ed in Journalism; Tex Jr Col Tchrs Assn; So Speech Communication Assn; Speech Communication Assn; Coun for Advmt & Support Ed; Intl Communication Assn; Tex Journalism Tchrs Assn; Tex Press Wom & Nat Fdn Press Wom; Tex Public Relats Assn; Blue Ribbon Com on Ed, Appointed by Gen John Hill; cp/Nat Coun for Commun Relats; Chrperson Campaign Fund; Am Heart Assn; Soc Martha Washington; Attractions Com & Commun Activs Com, Laredo C of C; Laredo Art Assn; Laredo Little Theatre; Former Mem Bd Dirs, Laredo High Hope Vols; Former Mem: Tex Assn for Emotionally Disturbed Chd, Tex Assn for Mentally Retarded Chd & Tex Mtl Hlth Assn (Bd Dirs); Steer'g Com, Amigas de John Hill Gubernatorial Election; St Dem Exec Com-wom; Webb Co Wom's Polit Caucus; Nat, Mexican & Am Wom's Polit Caucuses; Del Tex Dem Party St Convs; 1 of 3 Webb Co Coors for Jimmy Carter, Organized Ralley for Chip Carter; Others; r/Cath; hon/Rec'd Awds for Entries, Sch & Col Pubs (Sponsored by *Nation's Sch Report*); Rec'd Editing & Writing Awds, Tex Press Wom Communs Contest; Top 10 Tex Press Wom; 1 of 10 Best Dressed Wom, *The Laredo Times*; W/W: Tex, Am Wom; World W/W Wom Ed; Outstg Yg Wom Am; Wom Achmt, Dist IV Tex Press Wom.

ZAGUSTIN, ELENA oc/Professor; h/16862 Morse Circle, Huntington Beach, CA 92649; ba/Long Beach, CA; p/Anatol Zagustin, Huntington Beach; Taisa Zagustin (dec); ed/MS, PhD Stanford Univ; pa/Prof Civil Engrg, Cal St Univ-LB; Am Math Soc; Am Geophysical Soc; EERI; Others; r/Orthodox; hon/Rec'd Creole S'ship & Univ S'ship, Stanford Univ; Sigma Xi.

ZAJICEK, CHARLES JOSEPH oc/-Professor; b/Jan 26, 1917; h/937 Sutton Dr, San Antonio, TX 78228; ba/San Antonio; m/-Sarita Soto; c/Charles Joseph II, Linda Louise; p/Joseph J and Louise Elizabeth Josten Zajicek (dec); ed/BA; BS; MFA; MEd; mil/AUS;

pa/Prof & Ednl Cnslr, San Antonio Col; cp/Local Political Campaigns; Others; r/La Trinidad United Meth Ch; hon/Rec'd F'ships, Tex Christian Univ; Kellogg Foun F'ship; NDEA, Univ Tex-A.

ZAJICEK, SARITA HERRERA SOTO

oc/Educator; b/Oct 12, 1916; h/937 Sutton Dr, San Antonio, TX 78228; ba/San Antonio; m/Charles Joseph; c/Charles Joseph II, Linda Louise Z Beal; p/Benjamin Enriques and Herlinda Herrera Soto, San Antonio; ed/BA, MA, PhD Univ Tex-A; mil/USN Dept Censorship; pa/Prof & Supvr Spec Read'g Tchrs, San Antonio Col; cp/Local Political Campaigns; r/La Trinidad United Meth Ch: Mem; hon/Rec'd Carnegie Res Awd; IPA; Adelante, An Emerging Design for Mexican Am Ed; Commun Ldrs & Noteworthy Ams; Ldrs in Ed; W/W: Am Ed, Mexican Am Affairs, Meth Ch, Am Wom, US, S&SW, Others; Intl Scholar's Directory; World W/W Wom Ed; Others.

ZAMORA, MARIO D oc/Professor; b/Jul 27, 1935; h/1442-B N Mt Vernon St, Williamsburg, VA 23185; ba/Williamsburg; m/Ducella N; c/Gregory Ronald, Nerissa Caridad, Morris Edward, Lili, Sarah Elizabeth; p/Leon B Zamora, Tarlac, Philippines; Caridad Zamora (dec); ed/BA cum laude, MA Univ Philippines; PhD Cornell Univ; pa/Prof Anthropol, Col of William & Mary; Former Dean, Prof & Chm Dept Anthropol, Univ Philippines; Visiting Prof Sociol & Anthropol, En Montana Col & Col William & Mary; Exchange Scholar to Delhi Univ (New Delhi, India); Former Dir-Gen,

Tribal Res Ctr, Comm on Integration, Govt of Philippines; Former Dir, Museum & Inst Ethnology & Archaeol, Univ Philippines; Co-fdr & Editor, *Studies in Third World Societies*; Assoc Editor, *Jour of Asian & African Studies*; Fellow, Am Anthropol Assn; Royal Anthropol Inst Gt Brit & Ireland; Life Mem, Indian Anthropol Assn; Indian Sociol Soc; Ethnographic & Folk Culture Soc (India); Indian Inst Public Adm; Indian Political Sci Assn; Others; r/Cath; hon/Fulbright/Smith-Mundt Fellow, Cornell Univ; Adlai Stevenson Fellow to United Nations Inst for Tng & Res; Class Valedictorian; Cornell Grad Fellow; Fellow, Coun on Ec & Cult Affairs (NY); Phi Kappa Phi; Pi Gamma Mu; 1 of 10 Outstg Yg Men Philippine Republic; Num Others; Biogl Listings.

ZAMPELLA, EDWARD FRANCIS oc/Chief Judge; b/Jun 3, 1915; h/53 Magnolia Ave, Jersey City, NJ 07306; ba/Jersey City; m/Maria Lee; c/Edward Ronald, Arthur Francis; p/Erminio and Filomena Lettieri Zampella (dec); ed/LLB John Marshall Law Sch 1936; mil/1942-45; pa/Admit'd Pract 1938; Admit'd Supr Ct USA 1956, US Ct Appeals 1962; Judge Mun Ct Jersey City 1949-52; Secy to Cong-man T James Tumulty 1954-56; Secy to Dir Public Safety, Revenue & Fin 1957; Asst Prosecutor Hudson Co 1958-62; Chief Judge, Mun Ct NJ 1976-; Coms: Chm Unauthorized Pract of Law Com, Crim Law Com & Future Lwyrs Com (Hudson Co Bar Assn), Video Tape Com (NJ Bar Assn), Supr Ct Com on Mun Cts; Hudson Co, NJ & Fed Bar Assns; cp/Former Bd Dirs, Paul Revere Boys Clb; Helped Raise Funds to Buy Snow Plow for Citizens of Capracotta (Italy); Former Jersey City Chm, Muscular Dystrophy Drive; Master Ceremonies 8 Consecutive Yrs, Annual Flag Day Parade (Sponsored by Veterans Alliance Hudson Co); Helped Erect Christopher Columbus Monument at Journal Square; Chm Vets' Group Which Erected Vets' Meml Flagpole Journal Square; Chm, Drive to Help People of Po Val (Italy); Helped Establish Med Sch Jersey City; Co-fdr & 1st Pres, Italian Advmt Assn; Fund Raiser for St Anthony of Padua Soc (Now Hon Pres); Toastmaster.

Dinner-Dance to Raise Funds for Pack Foun for Cancer Res; Others; r/Rom Cath; hon/Cit'd by Father Cassidy for Work Done for Father Cassidy Home on the Range for Homeless Boys; Man of Yr, Unico National 1972; Cit'd by Christopher Columbus Com for 25 Yrs Ser; Others.

ZANI, FREDERICK CAESAR oc/Guidance Counselor; b/Jun 9, 1929; h/709 Holmes Rd, N Attleboro, MA 02760; ba/Attleboro; m/Dorothy Ann Menezes; c/Gregory Robert, Elizabeth Ann; p/John and Catherine Voluletti Zani (dec); ed/BSEd cum laude, Salem St Col 1954; MEd Boston Univ 1959; Addit Studies; pa/Guid Cnslr, Attleboro HS; NEA; MTA; ATA; Nat Edrs F'ship Inc; cp/Lions Clb; Parent Org of Exceptional Chd; Boston Chd's Hosp Ctr; r/Assembly of God; hon/Pres Student Body, Salem St Col.

ZAYAC, IVAN BOHDAN SEMEN oc/Architect; b/Oct 6, 1910; h/68-49 Exeter St, Forest Hills, NY 11375; ba/New York, NY; c/Maria Falina; p/Juljan Zajac and Falina Knight Radwan von Pawencki (dec); ed/ML Univ Jan Kasimierz (Poland) 1932; M Diplomatic Scis 1934; Dipl Mus, Lviv Conservatory Mus 1933; Postgrad in Law Sorbonne, Univ Paris 1946-48; Postgrad in Arch, Ecole Superieure Nationale des Beaux Arts (Paris) 1947-48; Cooper Union 1953; pa/Judge, Pres of Ct, Asst Prof Law (Poland) 1935-44; Law Cnslr Allgemeine Electrizitat Gesellschaft (Bratislava, Czechoslovakia) 1944-45; Var Arch Firms NYC 1950-53; w Eggers & Higgins Co (NYC) 1953-57; Philip C Johnson & Assocs (NYC) 1957-60; Edward Durell Stone & Assocs (NYC) 1963-70; I M Pei & Partners (NYC) 1971-74; Prin Ivan Zayac, Architect (Forest Hills) 1974-; Shevchenko Sci Soc; Ukrainian Acad Art & Scis; Ukrainian Engrs Soc Am (Past Pres NY Chapt); Ukrainian Artists Assn; Designer: Ukrainian Cult Ctr & Mus Ukrainian Art (Hunter, NY); cp/World Cong Free Ukrainians (Div Chm); Ukrainian Nat Assn; Selfreliance Assn Am Ukrainians (Past Dir); r/Ukrainian Orthodox; hon/Spec Hon Mention, Sch Design Competition; First Prize, Esquisse Art Show; Others.

ZEIMET, EDWARD JOSEPH oc/Professor; b/Jan 16, 1925; h/445 S 19th St, La Crosse, WI 54601; ba/La Crosse; m/Frances Ann Ward; c/Edward Evan, Stephanie Lynn, Anna Marie, Thomas Anthony, Samantha Frances; p/Anthony J and Stella M Orlowicz Zeimet; ed/BS 1948, MS 1950, PhD 1970 Univ Wis; mil/AUS 1943-46; pa/Prof, Univ Wis; SALT; AECT; IVLA; Asst Editor, *WAVA Dispatch*; Coor, Ednl Media Prog; cp/Commun Care Org Conslt; Dem Party; Campus Coor, Cong-man Alvin Baldus; Others; hon/Cert of Apprec, WAVA.

ZEITLIN, JOSEPH oc/Rabbi; Professor; Author; b/May 18; h/25 E 86 St, New York, NY 10028; ba/NYC; m/Married; c/3 Chd; p/Issac and Mathilde Zeitlin (dec); ed/BA CCNY 1926; MHL Jewish Theological Sem of Am 1930; MA Columbia Univ 1941; PhD 1945; Dipl, Phila Sch of Expression; mil/Religious Trio, WWII; pa/Rabbi: Temple Bnai Jeshurun (Phila) 1930-32, Temple Ansche Chesed (NYC) 1932-50, Riverside Temple (NYC) 1950-, Now Emeritus; Preacher-Chaplain, Mt Sinai Hosp 1973-; Rabbinical Assembly Am: Exec Com, Chm Social Justice Com; Chm Ch & St Exec Co, NY Bd of Rabbis; Exec Com, Syn Coun of Am; Exec Com, UJA Fdn of NY; cp/Town Clb Foun Exec Com; Sr Chaplain, Hon Legion NY Police Dept; Author: *Disciples of the Wise* (Religious Book of the Month Selection), *Hebrew Made Easy, Speech Power (How to Convince People), Speech Power (Through Listening)*; r/Hebrew; hon/Medal of Hon, La Fundacion Internacional Eloy Alfaro; Hon Legion Medal of Hon; Plaques, Cits & Testimonials, UJA Fdn of NY.

ZELNER, ESTELLE M oc/Secretary; b/Aug 7, 1934; h/3950 N Lake Shore Dr, Chicago, IL 60613; p/Sam and Irene Mogill

(dec); pa/Writer; Regular Contbr: *Lake View News* (1976-77), *A Different Drummer* (1977-78), *Paranassus Mag, CSP World News*, Others; Author: "Jennie" (Short Story), *The Reincarnation of Elizabeth Barrett Browning* (Narrative) 1977, *Courage Without Cause* (Play) 1978, Others; Composer 5 Musical Pieces; Poetry incl'd: *Intl Clover Poetry Socs Anthols, New Voices of Am Poetry Anthols, Winds of the World, From Sea to Sea in Song, A Search of the Soul*, Others; hon/Winner 2nd Prize, *Lake View News* & Chgo Press Wom's Clb; Rec'd Awd for Poetry & Recog of Achmt, Intl Clover Poetry Soc; Commun Ldrs & Noteworthy Ams; Intl Authors & Writers W/W; DIB; CSP World Yrbook; World W/W Wom; Others.

ZEPEDA, DAVID GEORGE oc/Assistant Professor; b/Sep 27, 1946; h/209 S 29th Ave #109, Hattiesburg, MS 39401; ba/H'burg; p/J P Zepeda, Ft Worth, TX; Juanita Zepeda (dec); ed/BA Tex Wesleyan Col 1970; MM Tex Tech Univ; pa/Asst Prof of Voice, Univ So Miss 1977-; Musical & Opera Roles (Tex Tech Univ Perfs) incl: "Goro" in *Madame Butterfly*, "Dancairo" in *Carmen*, "Senex" in *A Funny Thing Happened on the Way to the Forum*, Others; Vocal Perfs at: Tex Tech Univ, Wn Tex Col, Tarrant Co Jr Col, Lubbock Christian Col, Univ So Miss; Other Appearances: PBS-TV (Lubbock), ABC-TV (Local Programming), VI Intl Tchaikovsky Competition (Moscow, USSR), Birmingham Symph, Others; Pi Kappa Lambda; Phi Mu Alpha Sinfonia; Sigma Phi Epsilon; r/Presb; hon/Amon G Carter Music S'ship; Pressor Music S'ship; TTU Music S'ship; Tex St S'ship; 3rd Place & 2nd Place Tie, Shreveport Symph Auditions.

ZERWAS, MARY ALEXANDER oc/Environmental Health Scientist; b/Nov 16, 1947; h/14 Moonbeam Dr, Mountain View, CA 94043; ba/Menlo Park, CA; m/George William; c/Michelle Ann; p/Theron and Marie Alexander, Jenkintown, PA; ed/BA 1969; MPh 1975; pa/Mgr Res Support Group, Ctr for Occupational & Envir Safety & Hlth (Stanford Res Inst); Reschr: Envir Hlth Dept

(Sch of Public Hlth, Univ Cal-B) 1975, Univ Cinc 1969-74; Pediatric Res Lab (Univ Iowa) 1967-69, Clinical Res Lab (Univ Iowa) 1966-67, Infectious Disease Lab (Univ Iowa) 1964-65; Former Conf Rep & Treas, Am Indust Hygiene Assn; Publicity Chrperson, Wn Occupational Hlth Conf 1977; Pub'd Res Articles; r/Presb.

ZIEBARTH, PHYLLIS ANN oc/Graphic Designer; b/Jan 23, 1926; h/3782½ Curtis St,

San Diego, CA 92106; ba/San Diego; c/Charles Michael, John C, Patricia Z Boukeroui; p/George B and Elda Wade Tjaden, Colton, SD; ed/Dipls: NY Sch Interior Design, Nat Photo Color'g Sch Chgo, SDAV Advance Cake Decorat'g, SFAE Creat Advtg, Floral Design Sch (San Diego); pa/Nat Leag Am Pen Wom (Pres, Pt Loma-Ocean Beach Branch); San Diego Communicating Arts Group; Histn, Cal Press Wom; cp/Life Mem, San Diego Maritime Mus; Save Our Heritage Org; San Diego Hist Soc; La Jolla Toastmistress (Former Editor); r/Prot; hon/Book Accepted for Consideration for US Awd in Poetry (Univ Pittsburgh Press); World W/W Wom; Intl W/W Intells; DIB; W/W Commun Ser.

ZIMMERMAN, ELEANOR HOWITT oc/Civic Worker; b/1904; h/4700 Townsend Ave, Los Angeles, CA 90041; m/John Russell; c/John Irvine, Lois Z Wheeler (Mrs John C); p/Richard Irvine and Lois Hall Howitt (dec); ed/Univ Cal-B; cp/Fdr Eagle Rock Val Hist Soc; Eagle Rock Repub Wom; Parliamentn; Genealogist; r/Epis; hon/Histn's Awd, Verdugo Dist Fdn Wom's Clbs; 7th Cent Awd, Wom's 20th Cent Clb; Epsilon Sigma Epsilon.

ZIMMERMAN, NAOMA oc/Counselor; b/Aug 2, 1914; h/456 Drexel Ave, Glencoe, IL 60022; ba/Highland Park, IL; ed/MA Univ Chgo 1940; pa/Caseworker Therapist IV & Staff Conslt, Fam Ser of S Lake Co 1958-; Therapist, Jewish Chd's Bur Chgo 1937-41; Summer Fac Mem, Univ Chgo 1967-70; Conslt, Guid Depts 6 Schs; Other Positions; Lectr; Workshop Ldr; Author: *Sleepy Forest* (1943), *The Party Dress* (1943), *Baby Animals* 1955, *Corky Meets a Spaceman* (1960), Others; Nat Assn Social Work; Am Orthopsychiatric Assn; Cert'd Social Worker, St of Ill & Nat Assn Social Workers; hon/Foremost Wom Communication; Outstg Profls Human Sers; DIB; Writer's Directory; Contemp Authors; World W/W Wom; Others.

ZINK, JOHN S oc/Executive; b/Oct 17, 1928; ba/Tulsa, OK; m/Bette Lee; c/Darton, Whitney, Colin, Neel; p/John Steele and Swannie Smith Zink (dec); ed/BSME; pa/Pres, John Zink Co; Bd Dirs, Sunbeam Corp & Exec Com (Chgo); Dir, Utica Nat Bank & Trust Co (Tulsa); Dir US Auto Clb, Speedway (Indiaba); cp/Trustee, Hillcrest Med Ctr (Tulsa); Trustee, John Zink Foun (Skiatook, Okla); Active, BSA; Repub Party; r/Prot; hon/Pi Tau Sigma; Okla St Univ Engrg Hall of Fame.

ZINKE, ERNEST EDWARD oc/Minister; b/Mar 16, 1945; h/1909 Armond Ln, Silver Spring, MD 20904; ba/Washington, DC; m/Lenora Ann Christensen; c/David Dwayne, Douglas Edward; p/David and Maxine Anderson Zinke, Exeter, CA; ed/BA; MDiv; MA; pa/Res Asst, Biblical Res Inst, Gen Conf SDA; Author: *God is Like This* (1975), *God is Not Silent* (1976), "The Nature of Scripture," *The Advent Review & Sabbath Herald* (Jan 15, 1976), "Freedom in the New Testament," *Liberty* (May-Jun 1976), "Approaches to Theol," *The Ministry* (Oct 1977), Others; r/SDA; hon/MDiv summa cum laude, Andrews Univ.

ZINN, GLADYS AVERY oc/Retired Teacher; b/Jan 21, 1899; h/W Friendship Haven, Fort Dodge, IA 50501; m/Ferdinand R (dec); p/Milo and Jennie Dudley Avery (dec); ed/BA St Univ Iowa; pa/Pub'd 3 Vols Poetry; Author Short Stories; Iowa Poetry Assn; Nat Leag Am Pen Wom; r/Meth; hon/Hon Life Mem; Mark Twain Soc, Eugene Field Soc, Others; World W/W Wom; DIB; 2000 Wom Achmt; World W/W Poetry; Personalities of W&MW; Notable Ams.

ZIOMEK, HENRYK oc/Professor; b/Jan 8, 1922; h/370 Rivermont Rd, Athens, GA 30606; ba/Athens; m/Patricia Ann De Moor; c/Stanley, John Josef, Paul; p/Walenty Ziomek (dec); Jozefs Ziomek, Poland; ed/BA Ind St Univ; MA Ind Univ; PhD Univ Minn; mil/Polish Underground 1941-45; pa/Prof Romance Langs, Univ Ga; Author 9 Books on

Spanish Golden Age Drama; Pub'd Num Articles Profl Jours; Modern Lang Assn; S Atl Modern Lang Assn; Am Assn Tchrs Spanish & Portuguese; Assn Internacional de Hispanistas; Comediantes; cp/Polish Inst Arts & Sci Am; r/Epis; hon/Sigma Delta Pi.

ZIRKLE, VIRGINIA IRENE oc/Extension Home Economist; b/Sept 18, 1923; h/1165 E Third St, Ottawa, OH 45875; ba/Ottawa; p/Paul and Gladys Fern Calvert Zirkle (dec); ed/BS; MA; pa/Participated Regular TV Prog on Consumer Topics Over 18 Yrs (Toledo); Participated ½hr Radio Prog, WOWO 10 Yrs (Ft Wayne, Ind); Currently Working on Weekly Radio Broadcast (Ottawa); Prepares Newslttrs & Sends to Homemakers; Contributed to Independent Study Course for Yg Homemakers; Compiled 1st Hlth Handbook for Putnam Co 1974; Conducts Demos & Surveys: Fam Eating (USDA), Farm Accidents, Money Mgmt, Others; Ohio Coop Extension Agents Assn: 1st Wom Pres 1973-74, Bd Dirs 1951-53 & 1973-75, Others; Nat Assn Extension Home Economists: Pres 1976-77, Var Coms; Ohio Home Economics Assn; Am Home Economics Assn; Allen Co Home Economics Assn; BPW 1951-75; Adv Com, Sch of Home Ec (Ohio St Univ) 1974-78; Affirmative Action & Equal Opportunity Com, Ohio Coop Ext Ser 1974-78; Ser'd St Com on Ext Tng & Res; Others; cp/Past Pres, Ohio St Univ Alumni Assn; Ser'd All Chairs, OES; Bd Mem & Secy, Putnam Co Unit Am Cancer Soc; Ednl Com Chm, TB & Respiratory Disease Com; Friends of Lib; Team for Assess'g Head Start Prog Putnam Co; Putnam Co Soc for Crippled Chd; Civic Mus Assn; Others; r/St Marks Luth Ch: Choir Mem; hon/Nu Alpha Theta; Omicron Nu; Epsilon Sigma Phi; Ohio's Nom for Dist'd Ser Ruby Awd, Epsilon Sigma Phi; Rec'd Moses S'ship; Pfeizer F'ship; Dist'd Ser Awd, Nat Assn Ext Home Ecs & Sch of Home Ec (Ohio St Univ); USDA Superior Recog Awd; W/W; Am Wom, Hon Soc Am, MW, Am, Ohio; DIB; Intl W/W Commun Ser; World W/W Wom; Others.

ZISHKA, RONALD LOUIS oc/Sociologist; b/Mar 27, 1935; h/1080 Beechwood Dr, Lancaster, OH 43130; ba/Columbus, OH; c/Mary L, John L, Cathy A; p/Louie F and Wilma M Zishka, Montebello, CA; ed/AA;

BA Capital Univ; MDiv Luth Theol Sem; MA Case Wn Reserv Univ; PhD Ohio St Univ; pa/Prof Social Psychol, Ohio Univ; Dir, Eastland Psychol Ctr; Fam Cnslr; r/Am Luth Ch: Clergyman; hon/W/W MW; Outstg Profls Human Sers.

ZITKO, HOWARD JOHN oc/Director;

Author; b/Oct 26, 1911; h/711 E Blacklidge Dr, Tucson, AZ 85719; c/3; ed/Univ Wis 1929-31; Univ Cal-LA 1946-48; DD Golden St Univ 1949; Co-fdr & Author Basic Phil, Lemurian F'ship 1936-46; Min, Temple of Jewelled Cross (Los Angeles, Cal) 1942-46; Fdr & Chief Exec, World Univ Roundtable 1946-; Min, Ch of Abundant Life (Huntington Park, Cal) 1955-59; Fdr & Pres Bd Trustees, World Univ 1967-; Author: *The Lemurian Theo-Christian Conception* (1936), *Be It Resolved* (1940), Others; Contbr Articles Profl Jours; Editor & Pubr, "Intl Newslttr to World Univ" Over 25 Yrs; Lectr; Hon Mem: L'Assn Francaise pour l'Avancement de Sciences de l'Homme (Paris, France), Intl Inst Cult Asst (Columbus Assn), Universala Ordeno de Antares (Trieste, Italy), Sancta Maria Gloriosa Serenissimus Militaris Ordo (Rome, Italy), Gran Fraternidad Universal (Caracas, Venezuela), Arbeitsgemeinschaft Der Esoteriker (Oberhausen, Germany), Others; Ordained Min, Am Min Assn; cp/Am Civil Liberties Union; Am Assn Ret'd Persons; r/Unitarian-Universalist Ch (Tucson); hon/Rec'd Malayan Kris, Homeopaths of Malaya; Bronze Medal, St Olaf's Acad (London, England); Silver Chalice, World Univ Roundtable; Hon Degs: DHL Am World Patriarchates (NY), DMH L'Universite Libre Asie (Karachi, Pakistan), Doct Am Ethnical Heritage (Universidad De Los Pueblos De Las Americas, NY), Doct Indian Phil (Indian Assn Am), DLit Min Tng Col (Sheffield, England); Hon Pres: Solomon Gbadebo Col (Nigeria), Gt China Arts Col (Hong Kong), Institut Nord-Africain D'Etudes Metapsychiques (Algeria); Ky Col; Biogl Listings.

ZODHIATES, SPIROS G oc/Executive; b/Mar 13, 1922; ba/Chattanooga, TN; m/Joan; c/Lois Z Jenks (Mrs Paul), Priscilla, Philip, Mary; p/George Zodhiates, Cyprus; Mary Zodhiates (dec); ed/ThB Nat Bible Inst; MA NYU; ThD Luther Rice Sem 1978; mil/British Army; pa/Pres, AMG Intl; Pres, CLW Communs Group; Pres, Inspirational Tours; Author; Lectr; Ordained Bapt Min; r/Prot; hon/Gold Medal, Greek Red Cross; Cits, Var Greek Orgs & Philanthropic Insts.

ZOLOTOW, CHARLOTTE oc/Author; Editor; b/Jun 26, 1915; h/29 Elm Place, Hastings-on-Hudson, NY 10706; ba/New York, NY; c/Stephen, Ellen; p/Louis J and Ella Bernstein Shapiro (dec); pa/VP & Assoc Pubr, Harper Jr Books (Harper & Row); Author Over 50 Chd's Books incl'g, *The Park Book* (1944), *Over & Over* 1957), *My Grandson Lew* (1974), *Janey* (1973), *The Sky Was Blue* (1963), *An Overpraised Season: 10 Stories of Yth* (Anthol for Teenagers); PEN; Authors Leag; r/Jewish; hon/Rec'd Harper Gold Medal Awd for Editor Excell.

ZOOK, MARY ANN oc/Pianist; Teacher; b/Aug 10, 1939; h/4 E St, Oneonta, NY 13820; ba/Oneonta; p/J Harold Zook (dec); Anne Moore Zook, Mifflintown, PA; ed/BME Penn St Univ; MM Ind Univ; pa/Mus Tchr,

Hartwick Col; Advr Col Chapt, MENC; MTNA; NY St MTA; ISME; AAUP; r/Meth; hon/Mu Phi Epsilon; Iota Kappa Lambda; Pi Lambda Theta; Rec'd Hons as Piano Soloist & Accompanist.

ZOTTER, THOMAS FRANK oc/Student; b/Oct 22, 1958; h/224 Chestnut Hill Rd, Torrington, CT 06790; ba/Washington, DC;

p/Frank John and Elvira E Zotter, Torrington; ed/Student, Univ Mass; pa/Dir, Mt Vernon Assocs; cp/Chm & Dir, Col Repubs Univ Mass; Regional Dir, Col Repubs Nat Com; Staff Mem: Ford for Pres, Upson for Cong, Chase for Cong, Garwyach for St Senator, Rome for St Senator; hon/Dean's List.

ZSIGMOND, ELEMER K oc/Physician; Anesthesiologist; b/May 16, 1930; h/2265 Delaware, Ann Arbor, MI 48103; ba/Ann Arbor; m/Kathryn Fogarasi; c/William Zoltan; p/Zsigmond Elemer and Kartori Terez (dec); ed/MD Univ Budapest Med Sch (Hungary); Anesthesiol Residency, Allegheny Gen Hosp; pa/Dir, Anesthesiol Res Lab, Mercy Hosp (Pittsburgh, Pa); Anesthesiol & Dir Anesthesiol Res Lab, Allegheny Gen Hosp (Pgh); Prof Anesthesiol, Univ Mich Med Sch.

ZSUFFA, MARY MARGARET oc/Administrative Manager; b/May 25, 1943; h/6307 Lake Sunrise Dr, Apollo Beach, FL 33570; p/Eugene and Mary Zsuffa, Apollo Bch; ed/BS; MS; MBA; pa/Nat Assn Female Execs; AAUP; Am Soc Tng & Devel; cp/Vol Tng Spec, United Way; r/Cath; hon/Kappa Delta Pi.

ZUCCO, KAREN KAY oc/Teacher; b/Apr 19, 1944; h/1201 Knoll Crest Dr, Washington, IL 61571; ba/E Peoria, IL; m/Richard Leon; c/Ronda Kay; p/Claude D and Mildred Mishler, Eureka, IL; ed/BS Ill St Univ 1965; Cert Grades 7-12; Addit Studies; pa/Prof Social Sci, Ill Ctl Col 1968-; Tchr, Metamora Jr HS (Ill) 1967-68; Tchr, Oakland Park Jr HS (Streator, Ill) 1965-67; Fam Cnslr; Pvt Security (Completed Ill Ctl Col Police Sci Prog); Yth Activs Reporter (Radio); Speaker; Contbr Articles Profl Jours; AAUW; MW & Ill Sociol Assns; Nat Coun of Crime & Delinquency; Acad Crim Justice Scis; Multi-

Co Juv Ofcrs Leag; Ill Assn Crim Justice Edrs; Commun Col Social Sci Assn; Ill Commun Col Fac Assn (Exec Com 8 Yrs); Pres-Elect, Ill Ctrl Col Fac Forum; Ill Commun Col Bd Self-Study & Evaluation Com; Editor Bd, *Commun Col Frontiers*; Others; cp/Pres, Italian-Am Concordia Soc Ladies Aux; Eureka Hosp Aux; Wom's Repub Clb (Wash); r/Calvary Mennonite Ch (Wash): Mem, Choir; hon/World W/W: Wom, Wom Ed; Personalities of W&MW; Commun Ldrs & Noteworthy Ams; Intl W/W Commun Ser.

ZUFELT, DAVID L oc/Professor; b/Apr 28, 1933; h/Station #1, PO Box 2323, Kingsville, TX 78363; ba/Kingsville; p/LeRoy M Zufelt, Liverpool, NY; Mary H Zufelt (dec); ed/BS 1954, MS 1957 St Univ NY; EdD Univ Neb 1967; Addit Studies; pa/Prof Ed & Chm Supvr Com Bilingual Ed Ctr, Tex A&I Univ

1970-; Prof Elem Ed, Univ Neb 1971-74 & 1976-78; Col of St Scholastica (Duluth, Minn): Assoc Prof & Coor Elem Ed 1968-70, Chm Div Ed 1969-70; Assoc Prof & Curric Spec (K-12), Coteau Hills Resource Ctr & Univ ND 1967-68; Other Positions; Co-author: *Envir Ed for Classroom Tchrs* (w S Audean Allman & O W Kopp 1976), *Cognates: Vocabulary Enrichment for Bilinguals - Spanish/Eng* (w Joe R Gonzales 1973), *Individualized Tchr Renewal: A Profl Model for Tchr Ed* (w Noel R Jackson 1975), Others; Contbr Articles Profl Jours; Intl Presentations; r/Prot; hon/Kappa Delta Pi; Phi Delta Kappa; Grad F'ship, Univ Pgh; Grad Asst'ship, Univ Pgh & Univ Neb; Outstg Edr Am; Rec'd Res Grants.

ZUNDELL-WEINER, CLAIRE oc/Director; b/Jun 19, 1933; h/4438 Carfax Ave, Lakewood, CA 90713; m/Michael H; c/Aaryn Anne, Elliot Michael; p/Edward Shapiro (dec); Mary Shapiro, Worcester, MA; pa/Resident Dir: Gold Crown Dinner Theatre (Cal), Coffee Ground Players (NY), NY Chd's Mime Theatre, The Unit (Exptl Workshop), Suitcase Theatre Co (Jr Theatre); Instr & Dir: Theatre Games & Nonverbals Workshop (City Cult Activs, NY), Theatre in the Park (NY St Coun on Arts), Theatre Games (Title I Govt Prog), Norwich Sr HS Theatre Ensemble (Bd Ed), Founs in Theatre (Roberson Ctr for Arts, NY), Theatre for Yth (Dade Co Comm Schs, Fla); Others; Free-lance Writer; cp/Coor & Advr, NY St Coun on Arts "10 Towns" Proj; Dir Summer Cult Activs, Norwich Yth Comm; hon/W/W Am Wom; World W/W Wom; Notable Ams.

ZURCHER, LOUIS ANTHONY JR oc/College Administrator; b/May 13, 1936; h/Room 334, Donaldson Brown Cont'g Ed Ctr, Blacksburg, VA 24060; ba/Blacksburg; m/Susan Lee; c/Anthony Walsh, Nora Breen; p/Louis Anthony Sr and Kathleen Ursula Zurcher (dec); ed/BA Univ SF (Cal) 1961; MA 1963, PhD 1965 Univ Ariz; Cert'd Social Psychologist, Am Sociol Assn 1968; mil/USNR Lt/Cmdr; pa/VPI & St Univ: Prof Sociol, Assoc Provost & Dean Grad Sch 1978-, Num Coms & Positions; Univ Tex-A: Prof 1973-78, Assoc Prof 1969-73, Asst Prof 1968-69, Act'g Chrperson Dept Sociol 1974-75, Assoc Dean Grad Sch 1975-78, Coms; Adj Prof: Antioch Union Grad Sch 1969-, Ctr for Innovative Ed (Pepperdine Univ) 1974-; Chrperson Poverty & Human Resources Div, Soc for Study of Social Probs 1968-71; Adv Editor, *Social Sci Qtrly* (1968-75) & *Sociological Symposium* (1972-); Conslt'g Editor, *Jour Applied Behavioral Scis* (1968-71); Editor Bd, *Jour Voluntary Action Res* (1976-); Assoc Editor, *Deviant Behavior: An Interdisciplinary Jour* (1978-); Bd Dirs, Assn Vol Scholars 1976-; Exec Coun, Inter-Univ Seminar on Armed Forces & Society 1978-; Speaker Spec TV Progs; Conslt: Office Smoking & Hlth (Dept HEW) 1978-, Disaster Res Ctr (Nat Sci Foun) 1977, Smoking & Hlth Branch (Nat Cancer Inst 1975-), Ed & Public Affairs Inc (Wash, DC) 1971-73, Num Others; Author: *Poverty Warriors: The Human Experience of Planned Social Intervention* (1970), *The Mutable Self: A Self-Concept for Social Change* (1977); Co-author Sev Books; Contbr Articles Profl Jours; Presentations Profl Meetings; Fellow: Am Sociol Assn, Am Psychol Assn, Others; hon/BA cum laude; Acad S'ship, Univ SF; Hon Mention, Woodrow Wilson Fellow; Nat Sci Foun Grad F'ship; Abraham Maslow Visiting Fellow, Wn Behavioral Scis Inst; Alpha Kappa Delta; Psi Chi; Sigma Xi; Phi Beta Kappa; Rec'd Num Res Grants; Am Men & Wom Sci; W/W: Am Cols & Univs, S&SW; DIB; World W/W Authors; Intl Authors & Writers W/W; Contemp Authors; Others.

ZYTKOSKEE, TATE VAN EMAN oc/Clergyman; b/Sept 15, 1912; h/11 Tree Line Dr, Liverpool, NY 13088; ba/Syracuse, NY; m/Mary Alice Fernald; c/Jacquie Marie Z Hall, Taryl Beth Z Cordone; p/A E and Laura Brown Tate Zytkoskee (dec); ed/BA Union Col 1949; MA Md Univ 1959; mil/Med Dept Army 4½ Yrs; pa/Ordained 1952; Prin & Tchr, Edgecombe Acad (Baltimore, Md) 1949-50; Supt Ed & Yth Dir, Chesapeake Conf (Baltimore) 1950-55; Supt Ed & Yth Dir, Temperance of NJ Conf 1955-57; Yth Dir & Temp Dir, Potomac Conf (Stautnon, Va)

1957-59; Ed Dir & Yth Dir, Indonesia Union 1959-60; Pres, Korean Union Col (Seoul) 1960-65; Ed Secy, Far En Div (Singapore) 1965-68; Civilian Chaplain, Korean Union Servicemen's Ctr (Seoul) 1968-70; Ed Supt NY Conf 1970-, Communs Dir 1976; Others; r/SDA; hon/Rec'd Hon Awd, Korean Union Col; Army Awds: Bronze Star Medal w 2 Oak Leaf Clusters, Asiatic-Pacific Campaign Medal w 1 Bronze Arrowhead & 2 Bronze Ser Stars, Meritorious Unit Emblem, Philippine Liberation Ribbon, Philippine Pres Unit Cit, Philippine Independence Ribbon, Am Defense Medal, Am Campaign Medal, WWII Victory Medal, Good Conduct Medal; Biogl Listings.

ADDENDUM

AAGAARD, GEORGE NELSON oc/-Professor; b/Aug 16, 1913; h/3810 49th Ave NE, Seattle, WA 98105; ba/Seattle; m/Lorna D; c/Diane Louise, George Nelson, Richard Nelson, David Nelson, Stephen Nelson; p/(dec); ed/BS 1934, MB 1936, MD 1937 Univ Minn; pa/Univ Wash Sch Med: Dist'd Prof 1978, Prof of Med & Hd Div Clin Pharmacol 1964-, Dean & Prof of Internal Med 1954-64; Dean & Prof of Internal Med, SWn Med Sch, Univ Tex 1952-54; Univ Minn: Assoc Prof of Med & Dir of Continuation Med Ed 1948-51, F'ship in Internal Med w Promotions to Instr & Asst Prof 1941-47; Gen Med Pract, Mpls, Minn 1937-41; Diplomate, Am Bd Internal Med; Fellow, Am Col Physicians; AMA; Am Med Writer's Assn; Am Public Hlth Assn; Am Rehab Found; Am Therapeutic Soc; Assn Am Med Cols; King Co Med Soc; Dallas Co Med Soc; Nat Insts Hlth; Tex Acad Internal Med; Wash St Soc Internal Med; Wn Pharmacology Soc; Edit Bd, Wn Jour Med 1977-; cp/Am Heart Assn; Wash Chapt, Am Heart Assn; Ariz Med Sch Study Adv Com; r/Univ Congreg Ch: Active Mem; hon/Profl Pubs.

ABBOTT, DEAN FREDERICK oc/Landscape Architect; Urban Designer; b/Feb 18, 1939; h/1899 Marshall, St Paul, MN 55104; c/Lange, Marisa; p/Fred Abbott; Marion Folhemus Abbott (dec); ed/BS Mich St Univ 1961; MLA Harvard Univ 1963; pa/Positions w: Zion & Breen, NYC, M Paul Friedburg, NYC, Sasaki, Walker & Assoc, San Fran 2 Yrs, Lawrence Halprin Assocs, NYC (Co-Dir NYC Ofc 1974) 7 Yrs; Teaching Positions: Univ Ga Sch Envirl Design 1964-67, Vis Univ Va, Rutgers Univ, City Univ NY, Univ Minn, Mpls; Reg'd Landscape Arch, Ga; ARTEKA; hon/Harvard S'ship; W/W Midwest; Design & Envir's Awd for Design Excell (Battery Park City Urban Open Spaces, NYC) 1975; CUE (Com for Urban Envir) Awd 1975; 2nd Pl, Rainbow Ctr Plaza Intl Design Competition, Niagra, NY 1973.

BOSS, JUDY oc/Author; Lecturer; Songwriter; b/Nov 26, 1935; h/1855 Summit Ave, St Paul, MN 55105; m/W Andrew; c/Kevin, Kathleen, Michael, Mary, James; (Stepchd:) Cathleen, Christine, David, Wallace; p/David Alford (dec); Florence Weisner (dec); ed/BS; pa/Author: In Silence They Return, A Garden of Joy, Dying to Live, Somewhere Alive & Then, Now and Forever; cp/Intl Platform Spkrs; r/Christian; hon/F'ship Spiritual Frontiers; Intl Authors & Writers; W/W Comtemp Authors; Worlds W/W Authors.

HANNUM, ALBERTA PIERSON oc/Writer; b/Aug 3, 1906; h/52 Arlington Dr, Howard Place, Wheeling, WV; m/Robert Fulton (dec); c/Kay Bartlett (Mrs Lawrence R), Sara Lee Chase (Mrs John T); p/James Ellsworth and Carolina Adelle Evans Pierson; ed/BA Ohio St Univ 1927; Grad Work Columbia Univ 1928; pa/Writer & Lectr W Coltston Leigh Inc, New York 1939-40; Author: Thursday April 1931, The Hills Step Lightly 1934, The Gods and One 1941, The Mountain People 1943, Roseanna McCoy, Spin A Silver Dollar 1946 (title changed to Blue Horse), Paint the Wind 1958, Look Back With Love 1969; hon/Annual Book Awd, AAUW 1971; Daugh of Yr, WWVa Soc of Washington, DC; AAUP Awd for Commun Ser; Contemp Authors Awd, Gale Res Co; Awds for Roseanna McCoy: Made into Motion Picture 1949, Included in Reader's Digest Condensation 1946; 2 Books Made into Lib of Cong Talking Books for Blind & Handicapped; World W/W Wom; Others.

HANRAHAN, JOYCE YANCEY oc/Elementary School Principal; b/Sept 29, 1933; h/62 Marcy St, Portsmouth, NH 03801; ba/York, ME; m/Edward John; p/Odell and Nellie Yancey, Langdale, AL; ed/BA Univ Ala; MEd 1964, MEd 1968 Univ NH; pa/Prin Village Elem Sch; Spkr: Elem Prins' Conv (Miami) 1972, Num New Eng & St Meetings on Open Ed & Chd's Thinking; Appeared on Ednl TV (Issues concerning young chd); Pres

NH Assn Non-Profit Day Care Dirs; cp/City Coun-person, P'mouth (2 terms); Pres P'mouth Altrusa Clb; r/Prot; hon/Outstg Yg Edr.

HANRAHAN, ROBERT J oc/Professor; b/Jan 7, 1932; h/3730 NW 16th Pl, Gainesville, FL 32605; ba/G'ville; m/Mary Ellen Hogan; c/Ann Marie, Sheila Frances, Robert Joseph Jr, Margaret Evyleen; p/James R Hanrahan (dec); Lucille Florence Granger Hanrahan, Woodstock, IL; ed/BS Loyola Univ; PhD Univ Wis-Madison; pa/Prof Chem Univ Fla-G; Am Chem Soc; Am Phy Soc; Radiation Res Soc; Am Soc for Mass Spectrometry; Inter-Am Photochem Soc; r/Rom Cath; hon/US Nat Sci Fellow (Leeds, England); Vis Scist, Hahn-Meitner Inst (Berlin, Germany); Author Profl Papers; W/W S&SE.

HANNAH, FRANKLIN (JESSE) oc/Administrator; b/Apr 30, 1945; h/303 E Whiteside, Springfield, MO 65807; ba/S'field; m/Gloria Kay; c/Kenneth Edward, Kevin Dewayne, Kimberly Michelle; p/Charley Edward Hannah (dec); Rosia Z Hannah, Searcy, AR; ed/BS Ark St Univ; pa/Fin Secy Gen Coun of Assemblies of God, Div Fgn Missions; Pres Adm Mgmt Soc, S'field Chapt 1978-79; cp/Kiwanis Clb, Wynne, Ark; Chm Mbrship Com U Way S'field; Exec Loan Ofcr; r/Gen Coun Assemblies of God: Ordained Min; Outpost #6 Royal Ranger Cmdr, Assemblies of God, S'field; hon/Dean's List, Ark St Univ: Former Mem Pres' Cabinet, Union Life Ins Co.

HANNON, MARIAN EDWARDS oc/Apartment Owner; b/Dec 16, 1912; h/1930 Mt Vernon Ct #7, Mt View, CA 94040; c/Brian, Denis, Neill, Maureen; p/LeRoy M and Cornelia E Edwards (dec); ed/MA; MS; pa/Owner 7 Apts; AAUW; cp/PWP; r/Prot; hon/W/W Am Wom.

HANNS, CHRISTIAN ALEXANDER oc/Community Educator; Consultant; b/Sept 12, 1948; h/312 Jefferson Ave, Linden, NJ 07036; p/Christian J and Elizabeth Branch Hanns; ed/Dipl & FCC 3rd Class Radio Lic, Career Acad Broadcasting 1966; Dipl Jour & Public Relats Def Info Sch 1967; BA 1972, MA 1973 Kean Col NJ; Doct Tng Rutgers Univ Grad Sch Ed 1973-; Currently Working on Adm & Supvn Credentials; mil/AUS 1966-69, Specialist 5th Class; pa/Union Col, Plainfield, NJ 1972-76: Col & Voc Cnslg & Placemt, Dir Cnslg & Testing; Ednl Resource Inst, Elizabeth, NJ 1974-76: Career & Voc Cnslg, Dir Cnslg & Curric & Devel; Watchung Hills Adult Sch, Warren, NJ 1975-: Coor Adult Ed Progs, Cnslr & Instr; Proj Coor Union Co Coalition for Human Sers, Linden 1976-77; Conslt, Test Admr, Interviewer, APL Proj, Rutgers Univ 1977; Voc Cnslr Integrity House Inc, Berkeley Heights, NJ 1978; Cnslr & Instr Adult Ed Progs Franklin Twp Adult Sch, Somerset, NJ 1978-; Employmt Specialist NJ Dept Hlth, Div Narcotic & Drug Abuse Control, E Orange, NJ 1978-; Conslt CLEP & Broker Ed/Curric Devel, E Orange Bd Ed 1978-; Coor Life Skills Ed E Orange Bd Ed 1979-; Adult Commun Ed Assn; Substance Abuse Cnslr Assn; Nat Rehab Assn; APGA; AVA; cp/Exec Bd Dirs ARC, En Union Co; Adv Coun Jt Planning Com on Vietnam Era Vets, VA Reg Ofc, Newark; hon/2 Awds for Sers Rendered, ARC En Union Co; Golden Quill in Jour, Ft Banjamin Harrison, Ind; Profl Pubs; Biogl Listings.

HAYES, ALVIN JR oc/Lawyer; b/Apr 11, 1932; h/5662 S 83rd E Ave, Tulsa, OK 74145; ba/Tulsa; m/Julia Mae; c/Alvin III, Robert; p/Alvin B and Josephine Hayes, S Sioux City, NE; ed/BA Morningside Col; LLB Univ SD; mil/Hon Disch; pa/Okla Bar; la Bar; Fed Ct Bar; Bd Dirs Bus & Intl Devel Corp; r/Bapt; hon/Urban Leag; Boy Scouts; Local Human Rts Coun.

JONES, ANDREW MELVIN oc/Teacher; b/Mar 10, 1932; h/809 Pecan St, Cleveland, MS 38732; ba/Cleveland; m/Elizabeth Reid; c/Amy Elizabeth, John R; p/Clint Jones, Clinton, MS; Opal Irene Peeler Jones (dec); ed/BA; MA; EdD; mil/AUS; pa/Instr Delta St Univ; Exec Secy Miss Speech Assn; Dir Miss

Yth Cong; Miss Assn Sch Admrs; cp/Crosstie Art Fest; Lion's Clb; Dem Party; r/Bapt; hon/Phi Delta Kappa; Kappa Delta Pi; Pi Kappa Delta; Ser Awd Phi Delta Kappa.

JONES, BILLY L oc/Patrolman; b/May 18, 1933; h/2706 Morgan Rd, Murfreesboro, TN 37130; ba/Nashville, TN; m/Betty; c/Edward, Patricia; p/Hassell and Mildred Jones, Goodlettsville, TN; ed/Grad FBI Acad; mil/USN 1952-56; pa/Col Tenn Hwy Patrol; FOP; Tenn Law Enforcemt Ofcrs Assn; r/Bapt.

LAMBERT, MARY ANDERSEN oc/Learning Disabilities Therapist; b/Nov 15, 1930; h/15 Fenway Ct, Walnut Creek, CA 94598; ba/Orinda, CA; m/Walker W (dec); c/Stephen Winston; p/Theodore Neils; p/Theodore N and Mary F Andersen, Brooklyn, NY; ed/BS Univ Conn 1951; MS Cal St Univ-H 1974; mil/USN Lt; cp/Ret'd Ofcrs Assn; Delta Zeta Alumni; r/Prot; hon/Outstg Ldrs Sec'dy Ed; Phi Upsilon Omicron; W/W Am Cols.

MARCHIONE, MARGHERITA FRANCES oc/Professor; b/Feb 19, 1922; h/Villa Walsh, Morristown, NJ 07960; ba/Madison, NJ; p/(dec); ed/BA Georgian Ct Col; MA, PhD Columbia Univ; pa/Sister of Rel Order; Prof Italian, Col of Arts & Scis, Farleigh Dickinson Univ; Dir NDEA & FDU Italian Insts; Former Pres Walsh Col; Pres AAIS; Exec Coun AIHA; Lectr US & Abroad; Author: L'imagine Tesa (1960), 20th Cent Italian Poetry (1974), Clemente Rebora, Others; Contbr Articles Profl Jours; Am Italian Assn; Modern Lang Assn; AAUP; Others; cp/Grad Fac Alumni, Columbia Univ; Ital Hist Records Comm; United Nations Assn; r/Rom Cath: Rel Tchrs of St Lucy Filippini; hon/Giuseppe Garibaldi Scholar, Columbia Univ; Rec'd NDEA Grant, Univ Ky; Fulbright Scholar, Univ Rome; Rec'd Cert of Merit, FDU Evening Coun; Rec'd AMITA Achmt Awd Ed; Recipient FDU Res Grants; Wom of Yr; W/W: Am Wom, Authors & Journalists, Am Col & Univ Adm, Am, E; DIB; Intl W/W Commun Ser; Others.

MEREDITH, FANNIE MAE oc/Executive Secretary; b/Sept 29, 1917; ba/Phoenix, AZ 85061; m/Daniel Thomas; c/Gloria M Walton, James Harris, Daniel Robert; p/R J Howell, Waco, TX; ed/BA Grand Canyon Col; pa/Exec Secy Alumni Assn, Grand Canyon Col; CASE; cp/Repub Party; Former Mem Region Bd of Am Bapt Chs; r/1st Bapt Ch (Phoenix): Mem; hon/Rec'd Ser Awd, Alumni Assn Grand Canyon Col; Alumnus of Yr Awd, Alumni Assn GCC 1972.

MILLER, DONALD GEORGE oc/Retired Clergyman; Educator; b/Oct 30, 1909; h/2219 Line Bridge Rd, Whiteford, MD 21160; m/Eleanor C; c/Lynne, Douglas, Richard; p/C Herbert and Alma L Miller (dec); ed/BA Greenville Col 1930; STB 1933, STM 1934 Biblical Sem NY; MA 1934, PhD 1935 NYU; pa/Pastor, Presb Ch (Laurinburg, NC) 1970-74; Pres, Pittsburgh Theol Sem (Penn) 1962-70; Prof New Testament, Union Theol Sem 1943-62; Other Former Positions; Writer; Speaker; r/Presb; hon/Rockefeller Brothers Fac F'ship; Dist'd Alumnus Awd, Greenville Col.

MOMIYAMA, NANAE oc/Artist; h/Woodland Dr, Rye Town, NY 10573; ba/Greenwich, CT; p/Tokutaro and Kimie Momiyama, Tokyo, Japan; ed/BA Bunka Gakuin Col (Japan); MA Tokyo Wom's Col; Art Students Leag (Sponsored, Japanese Govt); Pvt Res, France & Italy; pa/Art Instr, St Univ NY (Col at Purchase) 1973-; Westchester Co Art Workshop (White Plains, NY); Rippowam HS, Cont'g Ed (Stanford, Conn) 1971-76; Other Positions; Exhbns: Grand Prix Humanitaire de France 1975, 23e Grand Prix Intl de Peinture de Deauville (France) 1972, Nat Acad Annual Exhbn (NY) 1968-78, Nat Mus Modern Arts (Tokyo) 1953, Metro Mus Tokyo, Nat Assn Wom Artists Annual (NY) 1968-75, Galeries Raymond Duncan (Paris) 1975, Num Others; Lectr; Art Moden Arts Assn (NY Chapt); Assn Internationale des Artists Plastiques, l'UNESCO (Paris); Japanese Artist Assn; Nat

Assn Wom Artists; Japanese Artists Assn NY; Author, *Sumi-e, An Intro to Ink Painting;* Illustrator; r/Buddhist; hon/Charles Woodbury Meml Prize, NAWA Annual (Nat Acad NY); Madaille d'Argent, Grand Prix Humanitaire de France; Jury Awd, 23e Grand Prix International de Peinture de Deauville; Mbrship Awds: Modern Arts Assn Tokyo, France & Jiyu Bijitsuka Kyokai; One-man Shows: Ligoa Duncan Gallery (NY), Seibu Gallery (Tokyo), Bruce Mus (G'wich), Gima's Gallery (Honolulu), Forum Gallery (Tokyo), Others; Perm Jury Mem, Modern Arts Assn.

MONDY, NELL IRENE oc/Professor; b/Oct 27, 1921; h/130 College, Ithaca, NY 14850; ba/Ithaca; p/D D and E C Mondy (dec); ed/BS, BA (Both suma cum laude) Ouachita Univ 1943; MS Tex Univ 1945; PhD Cornell Univ 1953; pa/Asst & Assoc Prof Food & Nutrition, Cornell Univ 1953-; Supvr Food Spec, US Dept Agri (Wash, DC) 1960; Food Conslt, R T French Co (Rochester, NY) 1966; Prof Food & Nutrition, Fla St Univ 1969-71; Food Conslt, Holmen Brenderi (Gjovik, Norway) 1972-73; Other Positions: AAAS; Am Chem Soc; Inst Food Technologists; NY Acad Scis; Fellow, Am Inst Chemists; European Assn Potato Res; Potato Assn Am; Soc Cryobiology; Am Home Ec Assn; AAUP; Grad Wom Sci; Others; Contbr Num Articles Profl Jours; cp/Cornell United Rel Work; Cornell Campus Clb (Intl Hospitality Com); NY Coun Churches; Historic Ithaca; r/First Bapt Ch (Ithaca): Trustee; hon/Rec'd Sigma Xi F'ship, Cornell Univ; Danforth Awd, Penn St Univ & Univ Cal-B; Res Featured in *Res at Cornell* (1959); Nat Sci Foun Awd, Col & Univ Tchrs Chem; Dist'd Alumni Awd, Ouachita Univ; NATO Awd (to Participate in Seminar, Royal Col Food Sci Technol), Glasgow, Scotland; Higher Ed Act Awd, Cornell Univ; Nat F'ship Bd & Gen Coor Nat Awds, Grad Wom Sci; Iota Sigma Pi; Sigma Delta Epsilon; Phi Kappa Phi; Omicron Nu; Pi Lambda Theta; Phi Tau Sigma; Sigma Xi; Biogl Listings.

MONTES, LEOPOLDO F oc/Physician; Researcher; Educator; b/Nov 22, 1929; h/4319 Kennesaw Dr, Birmingham, AL 35213; ba/B'ham; m/Maria Mercedes Pfeiffer; c/Carolina, Mercedes, Ana, Leopoldo, Teresa, William; p/Leopoldo A Montes (dec); Celia G Montes, Buenos Aires, Argentina; ed/MS; DMSc; MD; pa/Univ Ala Med Ctr & Med Col 1966-: Prof Dermatology 1969-, Assoc Prof Microbiol 1968-; Pract Med (Spec Dermatol): Buenos Aires 1960-63, Houston 1963-66, B'ham 1966-; Adj Prof Large Animal Surg & Med, Auburn Univ Sch Veterinary Med 1977-; Editor, *Cutaneous Pathology* (Jour) 1974-; Other Positions: Reschr; Fellow, Am Acad Dermatology; Am Acad Microbiol; Royal Col Phys & Surgs Canada; Am Soc Microbiol; Soc Investigative Dermatol; Histochem Soc; Am Soc Cell Biol; AAAS; Am Fdn Clinical Res; Electron Microscope Soc Am; Intl Soc Tropical Dermatol (Asst Secy-Gen 1969-74); Am Dermatol Assn; r/Cath; hon/Rec'd Res Career Devel Awd, USPHS; Rec'd Grants: USPHS, NSF, Kresge Foun; Sigma Xi; Others.

RUSSELL, DIANA E H oc/Professor; b/Nov 6, 1938; h/2432 Grant St, Berkeley, CA 94703; ba/Oakland, CA; p/James and Kathleen Russell, Cape Town, S Africa; ed/BA Univ CT 1959; MA 1967, PhD 1970 Harvard Univ; Dipl w distns London Sch Ec 1961; pa/Prin Investigator Rape & Sexual Assault Nat Inst Mtl Hlth 1977-79; Div Social Sci Mills Col: Assoc Prof Sociol 1975, Asst Prof Sociol 1969-75; Res Assoc Ctr Intl Studies Princeton Univ 1967-68; Res Asst: Dept Psychi Groote Schuur Hosp & Univ CT 1963, Dept Social Anthropology London Sch Ec & Polit Sci 1961-62; Lectr Profl Confs & Orgs; Secy-Treas Sect Sex Roles Am Sociol Assn; Assoc Woms Inst Freedom of Press; Res Assoc Inst Sci Analysis; Coor Com Intl Tribunal Crimes Against Wom; AAUW; cp/US Del World Cong IWY; Feminist Activist Against Sexual Assault & Other Violence; Intl Solidarity Wom; hon/Mostyn Lloyd Meml Prize, London Sch Ec; Harvard F'ships 1963-64 & 1965-66; Pub'd Author; Num Biogl Listings.

SCHNEIDER, ROBERT NOEL oc/Clinical Psychologist; b/Feb 16, 1933; h/11670 Chieftain Dr, St Louis, MO 63141; ba/St Louis; m/Kathryn Lednick; c/Jeff, Eric; p/Daniel F and Adele C Schneider, High Ridge. MO; ed/BA 1957, MA 1960, PhD 1962 Univ Mo-Columbia; pa/Staff Psychologist VA Med Ctr; Pt-time Pvt Pract; hon/Phi Beta Kappa; Sigma Xi.

SCOTT, VIRGINIA BRYAN oc/Teacher; Administrator; b/Oct 9, 1929; h/Box 197, William Carey Col, Hattiesburg, MS 39401; c/Randall, Kathryn, Sid; p/George N Bryan (dec); Theta Bryan, H'burg; ed/BS; ME; pa/Cnslr, Adm Wm Carey Col; r/Bapt; hon/DIB; Notable Ams Bicent Era; W/W Am Wom; Ldrs in Ed; World W/W Wom.

SOMERVILLE, EARNESTINE oc/Student; b/Oct 18, 1955; h/3929 E 120th, Cleveland, OH 44105; p/Earnest Lee and Ella Ruth Somerville, Cleve; ed/BA; BS; pa/Active Mem Alpha Psi Chapt Phi Gamma Nu; cp/Epsilon Iota Chapt Delta Sigma Theta: Past Treas, Pres; Ohio Univ Nat Pan-Hellenic Coun: Past Treas, VP; Asst Treas Black Student Cult Prog'g Bd; Student Senate Rep; Col Rep Caucus; VP & Dean Student Adv Com; Univ Prof Selection Com; Others; r/Bapt; hon/Freshman S'ship, Ohio Univ; Seelbach Ednl Foun S'ship; Cleve S'ship Prog; World W/W Wom; W/W Among Students in Am Univs & Cols; Outstg Greek Ldr Awd; Sr Ldr Awd; Intl W/W Commun Ser; Commun Ldrs & Noteworthy Ams.

VAUGHN, CLARENCE BENJAMIN oc/Physician; b/Dec 14, 1928; h/19410 Canterbury Rd, Detroit, MI 48221; ba/Southfield, MI; m/Sarah Campbell; c/Steven, Annette, Carl, Ronald; p/Albert and Aretha Johnson Vaughn; ed/BS Benedict Col; MS; MD Howard Univ; PhD Wayne St Univ; mil/USAFR Col, Flight Surg; pa/Phys Oncology & Clinical Res, Providence Hosp; Wayne St Univ: Asst Prof Oncology & Assoc Dept Biochem; cp/Former Pres Wayne Co Unit, Am Cancer Soc; hon/Rec'd Outstg AFRES Flight Surg Awd.

WILLIAMS, DUANE EDWARD oc/US Army Officer; b/Feb 6, 1944; h/23 Hunt St, Ft Bragg, NC 28307; ba/Ft Bragg; m/Donna; c/Nicole; ed/BS Va Mil Inst; mil/AUS Ofcr, Major Field Arty; pa/IEEE; cp/Shrine; r/Epis Ch: Lay Rdr; hon/Bronze Star; Air Medal; Meritorious Ser; Army Commend Medal.

Appendix I

State-Locator Index

ALABAMA

Abbott, Jr., Benjamin Edward
Appleton, Bobby J.
Askew, Edward L.
Averhart, Lula
Ayers, James Wilbur
Baggett, Agnes
Baker, Mary Jane
Banks, Rosa Maria Taylor
Barnett, Ed Willis
Barrett, Len Gary
Barton, Larry H.
Beacham, Louise H.
Beazley, Curtis Edward
Bethea, Barron
Bettis, Dorothy D.
Bevill, Tom
Bilbo, Thomas E.
Blackston, Joe Ronald
Blake, Jean Alestine Lloyd
Bridges, Jr., James Edward
Brooks, Betty Jean
Browder, Johnie Mae Gomillion
Bruce, Jerry Wayne
Bryant, Elizabeth Ann
Butterfield, Huber Edward
Campbell, III, Robert Craig
Cannon, Lena F.
Cantrell, Clyde Hull
Carter, Frances Tunnell
Cason, Cleo Stargel
Cates, Annette Bingham
Cates, Curtis Anthony
Cavanaugh, Caroline Seale
Christopher, Thomas Weldon
Church, Avery Grenfell
Cobb, Bernice Coar
Coleman, Claudette T.
Colle, Barbara W.
Connell, James F. L.
Dansby, Huddie
Dewberry, Inez Stephens
Diener, Urban Lowell
Dorough, Virginia Ann
Duffey, Paul A.
Dunn, Ross
Eich, III, Wilbur Foster
Ejimofor, Cornelius Ogu
Emerson, Geraldine Mariellen
Essenwanger, Oskar M.
Estis, Willis Cleve
Eyster, Henry Clyde
Fletcher, Dixie Chafin
Floyd, John Alex
Foster, Caroline Robinson
Franklin, Harold Alonza
Frey, Edith Turner
Fudge, Edward William
Gann, Louise Weeks
Garside, Jo-Ann Doreen
Gay, William Teague
Gibbons, Jean Dickinson
Gibson, John Thomas
Gilmore, Laurene S.
Gravlee, Jr., Leland Clark
Greenberg, Stan Shimen
Gutierrez-Mazorra, Juan Francisco
Hadley, Rosa Louise
Hall, III, Samuel Jonathan
Hamilton, Eugene Leverett
Hankins, Anna Lou
Harris, Thomas Lee
Harrison, George Brooks
Henderson, Carol Morner
Hester, Ruby
Higgins, Earl Bernard

Hodgens, Sr., Paul Morton
Huff, Ozzie
Ingram, Betty E.
Johnson, David Pittman
Johnson, Herman Bluitt
Johnson, Sallie Kathryn
Jones, Mildred Josephine
Julich, Dorothy Louise
Kinney, Marguerite Rodgers
Kirby, Mayme Clark
Koch, Christine Hodges
Kuby, Jr., Carl Joseph
Labram, Cale Deane
Lambright, Carolina Gale
Logel, Annie Wheeler
Lucas, William R.
Lumpkin, Thomas Riley
Lyman, Ruth Ann
McAuley, Van Alfon
McCord, Charles Edward
McDonald, William Lindsey
McKemie, Isabelle McKenzie
Maness, Doris Kay
Marks, Henry S.
Marks, Marsha Kass
Marston, Jr., Joseph G. Lanaux
Martin, Cola Allen
Martin, Dale Alison
Mason, Clifford Gene
Maynor, Jr., Hal W.
Merritt, George William
Montes, Leopoldo
Morgado, Sadie Dawn
Moss, Frances P.
Musgrove, Zula Hyche
Navia, Juan
Neighbors, Joyce LaRue
Nesbit, Phyllis Schneider
Nixon, John William
Noel, Mark Gerard
O'Gwynn, Olive Lillian
Oldham, Henry Nevel
Orr, Paul G.
Osborn, III, Prime F.
Patterson, Edwin
Phelps, Wayne Arnita
Pickett, Joseph C.
Plyler, Bonnie D.
Primm, Bob Bruner
Ringsdorf, Jr., Warren Marshall
Rodenburg, Carl E.
Rosen, Dorah Sterne
Rushton, William James
Schaffner, Winnie Mae
Seibel, Jr., George Henry
Sessions, Anne Claire
Smith, Nelson Henry
Smith, Troy Alvin
Stallworth, Charles D.
Stone, Lettie Irene
Stover, Iva Clemmons
Tanner, Billy Charles
Taylor, Jr., Ernest Austin
Thompson, Jr., Andrew Boyd
Torbert, Jr., C. C.
Traylor, Josephine Z.
Traylor, Orba F.
Turner, Jr., Rex Allwin
Tyson, III, John Caius
Uhlig, George Ernest
Vann, David Johnson
Vickrey, Jr., James F.
Walden, Kathryn C.
Walker, William Hood
Williams, Jean Taylor
Williamson, Peter Arthur
Woodson, Mary F.
Wu, Shi Tsan
Yates, Hattye Scott

ALASKA

Banks, Iola K.
Berrie, Peter Michael
Buswell, Arthur Wilcox
Faust, Nina Hope
Godbey, William Givens
Hammond, Jay S.
Hemenway, Robert B.
Hickel, Walter Joseph
Knaebel, Jeff
Kolber, James S.
Mathews, James R.
Sanders, Frances Beyer
Stewart, Oro Rozella

ARIZONA

Backus, Charles Edward
Bahill, S. Larry
Ballantyne, III, Reginald Malcolm
Barr, Elsie S.
Baumbach, Donald Otto
Bell, Leslie
Bredlow, Thomas Gayle
Brown, Edith Petrie
Bullock, Dorothy Dodson
Burge, Ethel
Bushman, Clarence Earl
Cahill, Mary Paula
Clark, LaVerne Harrell
Coombes, Mariel
Cree, Allan
Darby, Wesley Andrew
De Concini, Dennis
Diethrich, Edward Bronson
Elliott, Shirley Ann White
Fairbanks, Justin Fox
Ferguson, Evelyn Cook
Fisher, Mary Hannah
Foyle, Dolores Hartley
Francis, Marilyn A.
Fredericks, Donald Grey
Golder, Esther Barnes
Gordon, Guanetta Stewart
Gore, Louise Cantrell
Griffen, Joyce Jones
Hansen, Jo Ann Brown
Hanson, Freddie Phelps
Harte, Joseph Meakin
Herron, Bettie Jane
Hines, Dorothy Lynn
Houghton, Neal Doyle
Hudson, John W.
Jamison, Sara Moyne
John, Elizabeth Beaman
Johnson, John M.
Johnston, Lillian Beatrice
Jordan, Barbara Leslie
King, Carl Stanely
Kissinger, Dorothy Vale
Liggett, Frances J.
Lincoln-Smith, Dorothy
McCaleb, Ann Child
Merchant, Vasant V.
Millard, Vivian Turner
Mitchell, Wayne Lee
Nagy, Bartholomew Stephen
Onufrock, Richard Shade
Osler, Edith Petrie
Peterson, David Lawrence
Philpott, Emalee Isola
Price, Robert W.
Ranahan, Sandi Manning

Kessner, Daniel Aaron
Kho, James Wang
Kim, Keith
Kimbell, Marion Joel
King, Helen Blanche
Kintner, Janet Ide
Klein, Kenneth Robert
Kleinberg, Philip Reuben
Klopsteg, Paul Ernest
Knight, Granville F.
Kockinos, Constantin Neophytos
Kolawole, Lawrence Compton
Kolosvary, Eva J.
Kordus, Henry
Kraus, Pansy Daegling
Kucingis, John Anthony
Kuhner, Susan Mary
Kutger, Joseph Peter
Lacey, Walter H.
LaCour, Vivienne
Cambro, Phillip
Lampp, Barrett Maurice
Landers, Newlin J.
Landers, Vernette Trosper
Landgarten, Helen
Lang, Jr., James DeVore
Langer, Eliezer
Lanouette, Etta May
Larson, Larry Gale
Lashley, Virginia Stephenson
La Sor, William Sanford
Latts, Leatrice Lynne
Lauer, Frances Louise
Lawrence, Gladys Wilkinson
Lawrence, Jaye A.
Leask, Barbara Glenn
Lehrhoff, Irwin
Lennox, William R.
Lesko, Leonard Henry
Levin, Lawrence Lee
Levin, Sheila E.
Lindholm, Helge Waldemar
Lippitt, Elizabeth Charlotte
Lipton, Lenny
Livesay, Jr., George Benton
Livesay, Richard Wyman
Lloyd-Wayne, Letha Memorie
Lobb, Margaret E.
Loeb, Barbara Snyder
Loeffler, Dan Theodore
Loiseaux, Pierre Roland
London, Kurt L.
Lowe, Warren
Lowery, John Stewart
Lundstrom, Jean Louise
Lyons, George W. C.
Maas, Thelma Maxine
McAllister, Bernice Jacklyn
McCarroll, Stephen James
McCaslin, Leon H.
McCullogh, Constance Mary
McDonald, John William
McDonald, Marianne
McDonnell, M. Geraldine
McKee, Timothy Gene
McKig, Eloise
McKnight, Lenore Ravin
McKuen, Rod
McLaughlin, Glen
McLevie, Elaine Marianne
McLevie, John Gilwell
McReavy, John Morgan
McWilliams, Margaret Edgar
McEwen, Colin Ellis
McGlynn, Betty Lochrie
McGowan-Sass, Brenda Kathleen
Machorro, Margaret Ozuna
Mack, Brenda Lee
Mahan, Jr., Jack Lee
Manahan, Manny Celectino
Manske, Charles Louis
Maron, Milford Alvin
Marshall, Helen E.
Marshall, Ira Bruce
Martin, Margaret Allison

Martin, Patricia Miles
Mason, Dean Towle
Mathisen, Helen Alice
Maughan, Meredith Gail
Maupin, Benita M.
Maust, Ezma M. Cobb
Meeks, Elsie M.
Merrill, Girldine Fallon
Miethe, Terry Lee
Mollenhauer, Bernhard
Moore, Jr., Charles August
Moore, Phyllis Jeanette
Morgenstern, Donald Earl
Morgenthaler, Helen Marie
Morrisey, Robert Brewster
Moses, Jr., James Anthony
Moungovan, Julia Longfellow
Murphy, Winifred Lee
Myers, Hector Franklin
Myers, Rochelle Gruskin
Nadon, John Douglas
Nagy, Gabor
Neil, Jessie M.
Nolan, David Brian
Nolen, Milton Wayne
Nong
Nowels-Lloyd, Diana Marie
Nyun-Han, Norman
O'Donnel, Patrick Albert
Orr, John Berk
Ostrkamp, Dalene M.
Overholser, J. Homer
Pallasch, Thomas John
Panajotovic, Elena Maria
Parker, Robert Miles
Parlee, Norman Allen
Petersen, Gary Michael
Pethel, Dorothy Lorene
Pfiester, Ralph Gerald
Philips-Silvernail, Leslie J.
Pittman, Floyd E.
Pittman, Jim Paul
Platt, W. Gerald
Pollard, Joseph Kieran
Polley, Elizabeth Marie
Potthoff, Jerome J.
Powell, Russell Francis
Power, Paul Wayne
Prendergast, Gwen Diana
Ragle, Karen Louise
Rashmir, Rose Lillian
Ratliff, Frances Anne
Reeva, Mona R.
Reidenbach, Albert James
Rende, Giandomenico
Resch, Gerald William
Richardson, Delroy McCoy
Richmond, John
Rigney, Robert Buford
Riley, Miles O'Brien
Ringrose, Josph Stephen
Robbins, Arthur Freeman
Roberts, Mary Annette
Robeson, Lillyan Rose
Robinson, Clayton David
Robinson, Gary Garth
Robinson, Gay Elizabeth
Robinson, Richard Harden
Rodenrys, John J.
Roettger, Dorye
Rogers, Gayle
Rohrer, William Glen
Romine, Joanne Barbara
Roney, Alice Mann
Ross, Charlotte Pack
Rothman, Barry Kenneth
Rummerfield, Walter Glen
Russell, Christopher Thomas
Rye, Sven
Sachs, William
Sarafian, Armen
Sarafian, Sylvia Annette
Sartor, Carolyn Denise
Savitsky, Helen
Schultz, Clara Peck

Schwartz, Jerome L.
Schwarzott, Wilhelm
Scollay, Patricia Ann
Seddon, Lisa Ruth
Seegall, Manfred Ismar
Semones, Jo Ann
Seto, Edward Leung
Shaddeau, Donna May
Shannon, K. Ann
Shawstad, Raymond Vernon
Sheley, Vernita Loree
Shelton, Joel Edward
Shephard, Lenese Ivory
Sherman, Edna Schultz
Shilds, Ruby
Shiffman, Max
Shipley, L. Earle
Shirley, Fehl Lorayne
Shumway, James McBride
Simpson, Gwen-Holly
Simonini, David Michael
Singletary, Lillian Darlington
Sison, Ramon Canlas
Skaalegaard, Hans Martin
Skoll, Sergius
Sliwinski, Mitchell Stanley
Smith, Bernard J.
Smith, David E.
Smith, Merrett T.
Smith, Robert J.
Snell, Patricia Poldervaart
Snyder, Myra C.
Sperry, Sally Baxter
Spillane, John H.
Stamendovic, Hrista
Stern, Doris L.
Stone, Idella Purnell
Stott, Jr., Kenhelm Welburn
Sturiale, Glory
Summer, Carol Rochelle
Summers, Kathryn J.
Sun, Teresa Chi-Ching
Sviland, Mary Ann
Swannack, Cheryl
Swartout, Bruce Edwin
Swarthout, Walter Emmet
Sykes, Ruby Lee
Taggart, Marion Ewing
Tanaka, Hisako
Tarson, Herbert Harvey
Tautenhahn, Gunther
Thomas, Jess
Thomas, William Victor
Thompson, Jesse Jackson
Thomson, John Ansel
Thornton, Joy Leah
Tillman, Donald C.
Todd, Vivian Edmiston
Toliver, Raymond Frederick
Tracy, Louise
Tucker, Wanda Hall
Turner, Clayton Duane
Uhland, Ruth Ellen
Van Hagan, Charles Edward
Vaughn, Mary
Vega, Benjamin Urbizo
Vlachos, Estella Maria
Wade, Dorothy R.
Wadia, Maneck S.
Wald, Edwin Prescott
Waters, Raymond Woolsey
Waters, Rowena Joyce
Watson, Jerry D.
Webb, Rozana
Weber, Irwin Jack
Weber, Sheila K.
Weidemann, Anton Frederick
West, Julian Ralph
Wharton, James R.
Whetten, John Dilworth
White, Stanley Archibald
Whitfield, Vallie Jo
Wilkes, Helen T.
Williams, Harvey
Williamson, William Harvey

Wilson, Charles William
Wimmer, Glen Elbert
Wolverton, Terry Lynn
Wong, Benjamin Yau-Cheung
Wood, Larry (Marylaird)
Wood, Wayne Barry
Worker, Jr., George F.
Worrall, William Charles
Wu, William L. S.
Wyler, Paul
Yaskulski, Sharon Gay
Yep, Wallen L. B.
Yip, Jethro Sutherland
Yogji, Harbhajan Singh
Young, Carlene
Zabsky, John Mitchell
Zagustin, Elena
Zerwas, Mary Alexander
Ziebarth, Phyllis Ann
Zimmerman, Eleanor Howitt
Zundell-Weiner, Claire

COLORADO

Anderson, Herbert Frederick
Andrews, James Warren
Atkins, Jr., Walter J.
Axton, Florence Gotthelf
Bansemer, Richard Frederick
Barnewall, Gordon Gouverneur
Benson, Mavis
Betts, Clifford Allen
Blackhurst, James Herbert
Bortz, Libby Joffe
Bowling, Franklin Lee
Buxton, Charles Roberts
Callaway, Howard Hollis
Carver, Jr., Ralph Daniel
Cicchinelli, Louis Frank
Cobb, Annetta P.
Colburn, Gary Lee
Conley, George Emery
Counter, Benjamin Frink
Cowperthwaite, Blanche Hallack
Creer, Thomas Laselle
Demarest, Bruce Alvin
Derr, Mary Louise
Douglass, Katherine Mooney
Evans, Joseph Robert
Evridge, Carolyn Haldane
Fiore, Genevieve Natalina
Fishman, Susan
Flanders, Eleanor Carlson
Fly, Claude Lee
Franklin, Cecil Loyd
Furness, Edna Lue
Futrell, John Carroll
Gaumer, Veronica G.
Genova, David Joseph
Gibson, Verda Kay
Girard, Judith
Grant-Easter, Evonne Ella
Gregory, Dennis A.
Griffith, Mary C.
Grkovic, George M.
Hoffman, Ruth Irene
Huth, Allen J.
Johnson, June Beverly
Johnson, Robert Leland
Joslen, Robert A.
Joy, Carol Marie
Kaslow, David Martin
Kellner, Theda Aileen
Kutchinsky, Leigh Elena
Lane, Irene Elisabeth
Langlois, Aimee
Lantz, Alma E.
Leininger, Hazel Lucille
Lockwood, Barbara J.
Lord, Gayle Kay
Lord, Ruth S.
Lyons, Sarah Pearl

Miller, Margaret Faye
Mishra, Bipin Bihari
Murphy, Frederick A.
Norman, John Edward
Norwood, III, James Madison
Olson, Donald George
Pennington, Lillian Boyer
Rankin, Kathleen Elizabeth
Rhiger, Sula Marie
Sadeh, Willy Zeev
Schuetzenduebel, Wolfram Gerhard
Shannon, Dale E.
Shaw, Mildred Hart
Shepperd, Walter Robert
Siegenthaler, Kenneth Eugene
Srivastava, Jaya Nidhi
Steiner, Nancy Miller
Sullivant, Bryan Sterling
Thompson, Dorothy McElrath
Track, Gerhard
Truesdell, Jerry Lynn
Wachernagel, Hans Beat
Waite, Sarah Frances
Wilber, Clare Marie
Wilder, Dean
Wing, Mary Carol
Wright, Lou
Wyand, Martin Judd
Yanish, Elizabeth
Yuthas, Ladessa Johnson

CONNECTICUT

Allen, George Howard
Anderson, Douglas Scranton Hesley
Bertone, C. M.
Blumberg, Phillip Irvin
Boyea, Ruthe Wright
Brown, Otha N.
Burke, Thomas J. M.
Byron, Leonard J.
Bysiewicz, Shirley Raissi
Chappell, Bette Tyson
Collier, Charlene Mitchell
Danko, Bohdan
Dent, V. Edward
Diamant, Herbert Arthur
Di Corleto, Helen Theresa
Drenosky, Lillian F.
Duleep, Kodendera Subbiah
Ellig, Bruce Robert
Eurich, Alvin Christian
Farkas, Jack John S.
Fawcett, Mrs. Roscoe Kent
Fitzgerald, Terence Sean
Flaker, James Henry
Forman, Joseph Charles
Fox, Lucille Montrose
Freedman, Gerald Stanley
Frink, Charles Richard
Fry, Johan Trilby
Fuller, Brent Davis
Gansberg, Judith M.
Giaimo, Robert Nicholas
Goetcheus, John Stewart
Gomes, Albert
Hall, Ann Louise
Hazlitt, Henry
Herren, Peter Hans
Jay, Hilda Lease
Koskoff, Theodore I.
Koussa, Harold Alan
Kratz, Elizabeth Ellen
Kurau, Warren Peter
Lack, Sylvia Anne
Liebson, Alice Ruth
Lo, Hang Hsin
McDannald, Clyde Elliott
Macnair, Sandra
Marrett, Michael McFarlene
Migrdichan, Vartkes
Miller, Carol Miller
Momiyama, Nanae

Muller, Janet Sloane
Olson, Harold Roy
Park, Cynthia
Pastor, Lucille E.
Pellerin, Mary Ann
Radler, Louis
Randall, Gerald Robert
Sanford, G. Marshall
Sasso, Ruth Maryann
Satchidananda, Sri Swami
Selby, Jr., Hubert
Small, Rosemary
Snow, Helen Foster
Stave, Bruce Martin
Taylor, Russel Reid
Will, Charles A.
Witten, II, Laurence Claiborne
Zotter, Thomas Frank

DELAWARE

Allen, Alma Coppedge
Balick, Bernard
Beamish, Patricia Mary
Becker, Jr., Paul Erdman
Biden, Joseph R.
Davis, Lenwood G.
King, Jr., Edward Beverly
MacKenzie, Malcolm Lewis
Organist, Donna Marie

DISTRICT OF COLUMBIA

Baer, Max Frank
Bayh, Marvella Hern
Booker, Janice A.
Booker, Merrel Daniel
Brosnan, Carol Raphael
Bryant, Claudine Moss Gay
Capone, Helen Diana
Carter, William Beverly
Chennault, Anna Chan
Clipper, Joseph Daniel
Cohen, David
Coleman, Sarah Williamson
Conyers, Jr., John
Dennis, Francis Alfonso
Dixon, Paul Rand
Dunlap, Estelle Cecilia Diggs
Edwards, Cecile Hoover
Edwards, Jack
Edwards, Virginia Lee
Elson, Edward Lee Roy
Epremian, Edward
Erlenborn, John N.
Farrar, Margaret Marian
Frauens, Marie
Gale, James Elwin
Garthoff, Raymond Leonard
Gibbs, Carroll Robert
Glickman, Dan
Goldwin, Robert A.
Griffin, Kathleen Mary
Griffin, Robert P.
Griffith, Ernest S.
Groseclose, Elgin
Gustason, Gerilee
Hammerschmidt, John Paul
Hance, Kent R.
Hartke, Vance
Hay, George Austin
Henschel, Beverly Jean Smith
Herndon, Terry Eugene
Hill, Sandra Vernice
Hill, Wilhelmina
Hinson, Jon
Holland, Ken
Holt, Marhorie Seawell
Holtzman, Elizabeth
Hope, Walter Barrington

Hosmer, Craig
Howe, William E.
Huckenpahler, Victoria
Huggins, James Bernard
Hunter, Robert E.
Jamme, Albert Joseph
Jessner, Lucie Ney
Jones, Kelsey A.
Jones, Lillian Hogan
Jones, Walter Alfred
Jones, Walter Beamon
Kloze, Ida Iris
Kraus, Mozelle Bigelow
Lacy, Barbara
Leahy, Miriam Kramer
Levin, A. Leo
Lord, Margaret Plunkett
McGee, Gale W.
Madigan, Edward R.
Magnuson, Warren G.
Manor, Filomena Roberta
Martin, James Grubbs
Martin, Ruth M.
Mikus, Joseph A.
Miller, Mary Jeannette
Montie, Irene C.
Morgan, Roy L.
Moss, Robert Sheriffs
Newman, Linda Elaine
Neimeyer, Grover Charles
Ortiz de la Renta
Palmatier, Anna Curran
Parham, Gladys Bolt
Phillips, Marjorie
Pulvari, Charles F.
Robbins, Dorothy Bradshaw
Russell, Phebe Gale
Scally, Mary Anthony
Simko, Jan
Sloan, Edith Barksdale
Stockton, Barbara Marshall
Sutherland, William Anderson
Tate, Merze
Timbrell, Charles
Toutorsky, Basil P.
Tower, John Goodwin
Wallace, Joan S.
Winchester, Clarence Floyd
Young, Elizabeth Bell

FLORIDA

Abdullah, Tariq Husam
Abrhamson, Bergljot
Adams, Harland Morrison
Allen, Don L.
Allen, E. Ross
Allen, John Eldridge
Alvarez, Thelma Lucia
Ammarell, John Samuel
Anderson, Ira Dennis
Anderson, James William
Arboleya, Carlos Jose
Arora, Chandra K.
Asam, Julia McCain Lampkin
Atchley, Edward Noah
Averbach, Philip Fred
Babette, Anita
Bafalis, Louis Arthur
Bailey, III, Charles Williams
Baker, Carleton Harold
Baker, Jr., James L.
Balistrieri, Thomas Joseph
Barnard, Clare A.
Barnhill, Laura Ruth
Baron, Howard N.
Barrowman, Kino Mary
Barry, Jr, Thomas Martin
Bauer, Charles Ronald
Baxter, Gene Kenneth
Bay, Magdalena Charlotte
Bayless, Dan J.

Beach, Dorothy R.
Bell, Jerry Sheridan
Benedict, John L.
Benham, Jack Edward
Bennett, Charles Edward
Bhatkar, Awinash P.
Blank, Ralph John
Blankenbaker, Ronald Gail
Book, Ronald Lee
Borkan, William Noah
Boyette, Robert E.
Brandsness, Margaret Carson
Brevetti, Anne Anna
Brock, Vandall Kline
Bromby, Carol Hogan
Bronson, Oswald Perry
Buckalew, Louis Walter
Buford, Olivette H.
Burkman, Jr., Ernest
Caccamise, Genevra Louise
Campbell, Marie Mallory
Canova, Sayer Joseph
Capps, Robert VanBuren
Cardoso, Anthony A.
Carey, Eileen Frances
Carner, Rebecca L.
Carnevale, Dario
Carr, Elizabeth Stephens
Carroll, Lillian Rebecca
Carson, William Edwards
Carswell, David Clements
Cheary, Brian Sidney
Cherry, Gwendolyn Sawyer
Chow, Chen-Ying Leung
Clark, John Richard
Clark, Julie Ann
Clark, Jr., Robert Julian
Clemons, Mae O.
Coke, C. Eugene
Coleman, Georgia Forbes
Colsky, Jacob
Conibear, Jo W.
Constable, Loraine Loder
Costello, Evelyn M.
Covell, Cranston Edwards
Crenshaw, Tena Lula
Crews, Essie J.
Critchlow, Susan Melissa
Crump, Richard Loy
Cummings, Patricia C.
Curtiss, George C.
Davidson, Mabel Elizabeth
Davisson, Mona June Garner
Deutsch, Paul Michael
DeYoung, Muriel Herrick-Maurer
Dillin, Jr, Jake Thomas
Dixon, Eva Crawford Johnson
Dockery, Christine
Dopico, Elvira Marta
Douglas, Barton Thrasher
Dragstedt, Jr., Carl Albert
Draper, Line Bloom
Dubsky, Vaclav Paul
Dugan, Charles C.
Eadie, Donald
Ehrenkranz, Elaine
Eisenstein, Alfred
Elkins, Larry Owen
Elliot, Larion J.
Elliott, Emanuel John
Ellis, Aileen Virginia
Ellis, Michael
Evans, Marilyn Bailey
Everidge, Mary Jim
Fascell, Dante B.
Feinstein, Edward
Field, Elizabeth Ashlock
Fishman, Joseph
Fitzgerald, Jr., Joseph Michael
Fleming, Lois DeLavan
Fordyce, Phillip Randall
Forkner, Claude Ellis
Forman, Max L.
Fowles, Beth H.
Fox, Lauretha Ewing

Frederick, Margie Garrett
French, Jeana Turner
Friedman, Richard Nathan
Fuller, Jams Howe
Funke, Francis Joseph
Gainer, Ruby Jackson
Gale, Steven H.
Geltz, Charles Gottlieb
Gentry, Doris Garner
Gibson, James Eugene
Gibson, Robert
Gil, Emigdio Antonio
Gildred, Victoria
Glenn, Carolyn Love
Gold, Kenneth R.
Goldberg, Lillian
Goodwin, Dave
Gray, Nolan Kenneth
Greaves, Richard Lee
Greenan, Gary Collins
Gregorio, Peter Anthony
Guglielmino, Paul Joseph
Gunter, Jr., William Dawson
Haight, Hildred Dray
Halfon, Ann H.
Hamrick, Joyce McCleskey
Hanrahan, Robert J.
Harrell, Hardy Matthew
Harris, Martin Harvey
Hart, Valerie O.
Hasty, Beatrice Giroux Jones
Helganz, Beverly Buzhardt
Hendley, Graham Fisher
Hendrix, Daniel W.
Hermelee, Laurence Stephan
Hershey, Philip
Hiaasen, Carl Andreas
Hirt, Fred Denis
Hoade, Jane Richter
Holland, Earl Stafford
Hornsby, J. Russell
Horwitz, Thomas Arthur
Hunt, Mary Alice
Hutchinson, Richard Charles
Hyatt, Guy William
Jackson, B. Gordon
Jackson, Norman Allen
Jackson, Vonicle Barnes
Jacobson, Alan Frank
James, Shaylor Lorenza
Jenkins, Edwin Garth
Jennings, John J.
Jernigan, Rawlin Cleveland
Jett, Claribel B.
Johnson, Franklyn Arthur
Jones, Avalene Chumbley
Jones, Kenneth Maxwell
Jones, Marcus Earl
Joyce, Edwin Anthony
Juergensen, Hans
Kahler, Woodland
Kapp, John Paul
Katz, Annette Sara
Keith, Gladys Pauline
Kelley, Ronald D.
Kennedy, D. James
Keys, Raymond R.
Kirby, II, Charles D.
Kirk, Barbara Ellen
Kirk, Colleen Jean
Knoebel, Daniel McClellan
Kolin, Irving Seymour
Kosmach, Frank P.
Kucsera, Abbie Kent
Kurzweg, Ulrich Hermann
Kushner, David Zakeri
Lakela, Olga
Lang, Franz
Lasbury, Leah B.
Last, Sondra Carole
Leaver, Vincent Wayne
Lee, Anna Marie
Leeds, Sylvia C.
Lightfoot, Harriett Anna
Litkenhaus, Raymond Arthur

McCord, III, James Richard
McCurdy, Martha Elizabeth
McGinty, Helen
Maish, James Ivan
Maloof, Joyce Morgan
Manka, III, Walter Ralph
Marbury, III, Ritchey McGuire
Martin, David Edward
Masterson, Thomas Robert
Matthews, Evan Jan
Mauldin, Jean
Maurer, Michele Lynne
May, John C.
Maynard, Kenneth Delano
Melton, Sr., Ira B.
Mercer, James Lee
Mills, William A.
Mitchell, Marion Faulkner
Mohanty, Santosh Kumar
Moring, Felix Cleveland
Morse, Jean Alston
Moseley, Mary Mac
Murray, Vincent D.
Myrick, Jr., Fred Lee
Nimmons, Billy Truett
O'Leary, Jr., William Colden
Olkowski, Zbigniew L.
Palms, John M.
Parkman, James N.
Payne, Emily Clement
Pollack, Robert Harvey
Porter, Garland Burns
Pou, Emily Quinn
Powell, Ruth Hill
Pryor, Jr., George Walter
Pryor, III, Shepherd Green
Raines, Lawrence Wesley
Ramsey, Ira Clayton
Ransom, Raymond Lincoln
Redmond, John Durham
Reed, Dale Charles
Riggsby, Dutchie Sellers
Riggsby, Ernest Duward
Robbins, Linda S.
Robinson, Charlynn Chamberlin
Roesel, Catherine Elizabeth
Rogers, Herbert Francis
Romo, Oscar I.
Roper, John Warren
Roper, Roberta Johnson
Rose, Jr., Aubert V.
Sanders, III, Walter MacDonald
Scott, Sherry Jones
Scott, Wilton C.
Shaffer, Frances Annette
Smith, Dorothy Lasseter
Smith, Warren Thomas
Snipes, Lawrence Paul
Spikes, Jesse James
Steine, Lyon
Stern, Ellen
Thompson, Roscoe Mullins
Tippett, John Thomas
Warren, Marie Haley
Waters, John W.
White, Sally Fox
Wilkinson, Hazel Wiley
Wood, Kathleen Wilkinson
Wootton, Lutian Robert
Young, Dennis Hugh
Ziomek, Henryk

GUAM

Bordallo, Ricardo Jerome
Cristobal, Adrian Loreto
Eliason, Phyllis Marie

HAWAII

Adams, William Mansfield
Ariyoshi, George Ryoichi
Ball, Robert Jerome
Bourke, Gerard Joseph
Bunson, Margaret R.
Campbell, Charles M.
Cattell, Raymond Bernard
Ching, Ernest K. S.
Chong, Anson
Christian, James Howard
Chun, Dai Ho
Chung, May Evelyn Kirkpatrick
Crispin, Charles Honnold
Doi, Nelson Kiyoshi
Duley, Alvin J.
Freeman, Jr., Ralph Carter
Hammer, Norman Lyle
Hazzard, Don Philip
Hirayama, Tetsu
Jasper, Ruth Mowbray
Kaulili, Alvina Nye
Kelley, Beverly Gwyn
Knowlton, Jr., Edgar Colby
Krause, Lloyd Thomas
Loui, Beatrice Lan Que
Lum, Jean L. J.
Makk, Americo Imre
Makk, Eva Holusa
Min, Frank K.
Moir, Gertrude M.
Moir, Jr., John Troup
Nakama, Christian S.
Niedzielski, Henryk Zygmunt
Numano, Allen Stanislaus
Peterson, Barbara Ann
Roberts, Gertrud
Salzman, Barnett Seymour
Straub, Nellie Cora
Thompson, Donnis Hazel
Trumbull, Robert Oliver
Wong, Ching
Yamane, Stanley Joel
You, Richard W.

IDAHO

Anderjack, George Michael
Anderson, Moselle Wilcox
Bolton, Thomas Porteous
Chapman, John Sherwood
Cox, Marygrace
Crane, Charles Arthur
Garrison-McDowell, Margaret Frances
Grayson, Edwin M.
Hafen, Bruce Clark
Harding, Ralph
Heath, Mildred
Hendren, Merlyn Churchill
Jarboe, Robert Nolen
Jensen, Mary Donna
Johnston, William James
Lilly, James Alexander
Lyons, James Felton
Smitherman, Charleton K.
Tartoue, Cassie Eugenia
Westerberg, Russell A.

ILLINOIS

Abbasy, Iftikharul Haque
Abdallah, Salam Mohamed
Abrahamson, Diane M.
Adams, Herbert Richards
Albin, Richard Joel
Alesia, James J.
Alexander, Wilma Jean
Ames, John Dawes
Anderson, John Bayard
Apea, Joseph B. K.
Ashland, Emelyn Ida Andrea

Aston, Katharine Oline
Aubin, Barbara
Ayachi, Helen
Baertschi, Walter
Baerwald, John E.
Bagby, Marvin Orville
Baker, Betty Louise
Baladad, Juanito T.
Barnard, George Hugh
Barnard, Janet Kay
Barnes, Frances Ramona
Barr, Charlotte Anne
Barrett, John Frances
Barter, Alice Knar
Beem, Jack D.
Below, Jr., Fred
Benckendorff, Nancy L.
Benstock, Bernard
Berland, Theodore
Berryman, Esther B.
Bingham, Johnella Woods
Black, Donald Raymond
Blanchard, B. Everard
Bousley, Gloria Diana Parrish
Boyle, Paul Michael
Brewster, Ethel H.
Brezinski, Paul Frank
Brock, William Allen
Brown, Harold Ogden Jospeh
Brutus, Dennis V.
Burg, Lawrence Edward
Burnett, Donald Ewing
Burtschi, Mary Pauline
Balcagni, Frank J.
Campbell, Jr., Calvin Arthur
Campbell, Charles George
Campbell, Mary Lou
Caroline, J. C.
Carpenter, Allan
Carter, Warrick L.
Chapman, Carolyn
Chapman, Douglas K.
Childs, John Lawrence
Chipain, George Chris
Chrisman, James Edward
Christensen, Jerry Melvin
Christman, Luther
Chung, Frank Huan-Chen
Cissik, John Henry
Clark, Jr., Warren Seeley
Clarke, William R.
Clausen, Robert Howard
Clay, Sr. Willie B.
Clayton, Sheryl Anne
Coleman, Linda E.
Colemon, Johnnie M.
Collins, David Raymond
Compton, Roger E.
Cook, Kenneth John
Cooley, Adelaide Nation
Cordero, Roque
Cormier, Romae Joseph
Cothran, Gladys Williams
Coutts, Francis Isabel
Cromeenes, James Richard
Curatolo, Alphonse Frank
Daily, James Lee
Dale, Richard
Dallianis, Jean Demas
Davis, Willie L.
Dayringer, Richard Lee
Dedowicz, Christine Dorothy
de la Huerga, Jesus
Del Valle, Helen C.
Desmond, Terrence T.
Devera, Adele King
Donegan, Charles Edward
Donovan, Margaret Henderlite
Dres, Demetrios William
Driskell, Claude Evans
Dunn, Dorothy Fay
Dykstra, Gail Lynn
Edelson, David
Edmunds, Palmer Daniel
Ehrhard, Hugh-Bert

Ekren, Marguerite Martha
Emrick, Raymond Terry
Erickson, J. Irving
Erlenbach, Johanna Maria
Faber, Jr., John
Fako, Nancy Jordan
Faulkner, Bernice Taylor
Fawell, Michael K.
Feldman, Leon
Fenn, Carl E.
Field, Mary
Finch, Donald George
Fitzgerald, Gerald Joseph
Flaherty, Susanne Alice
Flynn, Michael Francis
Ford, Judith Anne
Ford, Ruth Van Sickle
Formeller, Shirley Anne
Fox, Samuel
Fox, Theodore A.
Franks, Dorothy Seybold
Freeman, Harold F.
Frey, Thomas L.
Fromberg, LaVerne Charlotte Ray
Fulton, Alvenia Moody
Fults, Anna Carol
Fuqua, Hugh G.
Frantz, Olive S.
Gallagher, Blanche Marie
Gallup, Grant Morris
Genskow, Jack D.
Gillespie, Kathryn A.
Gillet, Pamela Alice
Gilpin, Dorothea Hayman
Gordon, Robert Thomas
Gospodaric, Mimi
Grady, John Donovan
Gray, Milton H.
Green, Chester R.
Green, Roland James
Greenwald, Barry S.
Gregor, Harold Laurence
Grillot, Jr., Francis A.
Gross, James Dehnert
Gullan, Ann Mary
Gunderson, Gerladine Maxine
Gustafson, Anita Virginia
Gustafson, Marjorie Lillian
Guyton, Geneva
Guyton, Ricky Tyrone
Habig, Marion Alphonse
Hackamack, Beatrice Irene
Hackamack, David Lee
Hahn, Ralph Crane
Halbe, Donald James
Hanson, Robert Leonard
Harris, Petra J.
Hasbargen, Arthur
Hayman, Marlene Rhodes
Hefner, Christine Ann
Heller, Melvin Paul
Henrikson, Arthur Allen
Hensler, Mary Elsie
Higgins, F. Edward
Hill, Michael Emmanuel
Hindsley, Mark Hubert
Hoffmann, Wilma M.
Horan, Catherine Anne
Howe, Jonathan Thomas
Howser, John William
Huebner, Donald Frank
Huebner, Nancy Minor
Hughes, Irene F.
Hughes, Margaret Cyrena
Huyck, Margaret Hellie
Hyde, Hazel Marguerite

Israel, Jeannette Nemecek
Issel, Richard Phillip
Jackson, Ruth Frances
Jacobson, Michael H.
Jacobson, Selma Maria
Jani, Subhash Natwerlal
Jasper, A. William
Jautokas, Victor

Jenkins, Dorothy
Jilani, Atiq A.
Joffe, Eunice Claire
Johnson, Elsie
Johnson, Francis Willard
Johnson, Frederic Henry
Johnson, Josephine L.
Jones, Nelson
Jupin, Laura Rose
Kahn, Julian
Kaiser, Jr., Walter Christian
Kaistha, Krishan Kuman
Kamii, Constance Kazuko
Kantzer, Kenneth Sealer
Kapacinskas, Joseph
Kaufman, Gary Edward
Kaufmann, Marion Kenneth
Kearin, Anita M.
Keen, Maria Elizabeth
Kelly, Michael John
Kent, Mary Lou
Kessman, Alan S.
Kilbert, Florence Jane
Kirk, Sara
Klimley, Nancy E.
Kona, Martha M.
Konkel, Wilbur Stanton
Korshak, Margie
Koulogeorge, Patricia Andrea
Kozelka, Tressie Masocco
Krasic, Ljubo
Kurz, Albert Leslie
Kuzniar, Zofina
Lad, Prakash Shripad
La Harry, Norman
Lancaster, F. Wilfred
Landwehr, Arthur J.
Lane, Stanley Gwin
Langston, Judy Ann
LaVelle, Faith Wilson
Leavitt, Gladys G.
LaCompte, Peggy Lewis
Leiferman, Silvia Weiner
Lemke, Arthur Athniel
Levy, Batia Goodman
Little, James Earl
Loftus, Darlene Joyce
Lohrer, Alice
Lumicao, Benjamin Guiab
McCombs, Sherwin
McCormack, Frank A.
McDonald, Theresa Beatrice
MacLin, Melvin Marlo
McElwain, John Allen
McGeever, Margaret E.
McGuire, Jennie Rae
McGuire, Mary Lynn
McKee, John Walter
Maile, Carlton Arthur
Makkai, Adam
Malik, Raymond Howard
Mardell-Czudnowski, Carol
Martinek, Robert George
Mathews, Henry James
Matson, Virginia F.
May, Marion Louise
Mehlinger, Kermit Thorpe
Melancon, Donald
Miller, Ida Mae
Miller, Laverne G.
Mills, Frederick Van Fleet
Mitchell, Barbara Jean
Mosak, Harold H.
Murdock, Percy
Neff, Clarence E.
Newman, Barbara Mae
Nguyen, Vietson Van
Northup, Wiliam Carlton

O'Brien, Charles Richard
O'Brien, Pamela Renee
Oryshkevich, Roman Sviatoslav
Ottaway, Lois Marie
Palmer, Robert Gerald
Parke, Scott James

Parks, James Hays
Parsons, Donald James
Pastine, Maureen Diane
Pavelka, Elaine Blanche
Pawlikowski, John Thaddeus
Peckwas, Edward Alan
Peckwas, Jane Ann
Pollitt, Gertrude
Pomerantz, Louis
Pont, John
Popovic, Deyan
Porter, Leonard
Prentice, Stewart Webster
Ramsey, Victor Eugene
Regensteiner, Else
Reich, Minna Lerich
Robinson, Edward Arlen
Robinson, Renault A.
Ropp, Ronald David
Ruskamp, Jr., John Arthur
Rzeminski, Peter Joseph
Salter, Marilyn Burke
Scharlemann, Herbert Karl
Scheer, Wilbert E.
Schmidt, Wayne William
Schneider, Marjorie Louise
Schroeder, Leonard W.
Schusky, Ernest L.
Schwan, LeRoy Bernard
Shapey, Ralph
Silber, Mark B.
Simpson, Marshall Wayne
Sing, Eric John
Solovy, Ellen Bransky
Springer, William Lee
Stanley, Frances Kniftun
Stauder, Paul Wenzel
Steinburg, Charles Louise
Stillman, Alexander
Streff, John D.
Swartz, Janet A. Maule
Till, Sandra L.
Tingley, Donald Fred
Tinsley-Brown, Betty Ann
Tulis, Allen Joseph
Turner, Lynn Warren
Turner, Vera Arbogast
Tuteur, Muriel Friedman
Underwood, Robert Charles
Unfer, Beulah M.
Velardo, Jospeh Thomas
Vogele, Dorothy Dixon
Voobus, Arthur
Wager, Scott Thomas
Wagner, Joseph Crider
Washburn, Paul Arthur
Washington, William Elbert
Weathers, Lena Jane
Webb, Michael Richard
Wells, Rosemary S.
Wendt, L. Birdell Eliason
Wheadon, Rosetta Fay
Whelan, Paul. A.
Whitney, Jr., John Freeman
Wilde, James A.
Williams, Edward Donald
Williams, Hermetta Elaine
Wilson, Sadie Lucille
Wright, Joan Dunbar
Wyatt, Angela Jane
Wyatt, Darlene Fay
Wyatt, John Lowell
Wyndewicke, Kionne Annette
Wyszynski, Richard Chester
Yovicich-Jones, George Steven
Zelner, Estelle M.
Zimmerman, Naoma
Zucco, Karen Kay

INDIANA

Abbott, John David

Adair, Edwin Ross
Ade, Walter Frank Charles
Andrews, Theodora Anne
Archibald, Patricia Ann
Avery, David Roger
Axeen, Marina Esther
Barber, Sandra Powell
Baringer, Clara Ellen
Barrick, Louise Grider
Benjamin, Jr., Adam
Bennett, Ivan Frank
Betts, Jo Ann
Bex, Brian William Louis
Birchfield, Robert Boyd
Bookwalter, Karl Webber
Bowen, Otis Ray
Bridgewater, Walter Cleveland
Bundrent, Durwood Creed
Caldwell, Robert Graham
Claybaugh, Glenn A.
Clise, Dorothea V.
Clouse, John D.
Coatie, Charles E.
Cole, Eugene Roger
Conrad, Larry Allen
Doornbos, Jr., Roy
Dudley, Glenna Tolbert
Duncan, Bert Logan
Durnil, Gordon K.
Erickson, Fred Harvey
Erwin, William Walter
Fisher, Marjorie Helen
Fisher, Thomas G.
Ford, Lee Ellen
Free, Helen M.
Freeland, Jr., Robert Lenward
Freeman, Donald McKinley
Fuller, Ray W.
Garmel, Marion Bess Simon
Garner, La Forrest Dean
Geddes, LaNelle Evelyn
Gibson, Milton Eugene
Gilman, David Alan
Gowings, Dan Douglas
Greenwood, Charles Huddie
Greer, Martin Luther
Griffin, George Ann
Grunkemeyer, Florence Bernadette
Hall, Inez Jean
Hall, Robert Malcolm
Hamilton, Christina Dee
Hamrick, Chalres Robert
Hansen, William Freeman
Harper, Mitch Van
Harshbarger, J. Arlene
Hart, Sr., Ronald Cary
Hayashi, Tetsumaro
Hayes, Arthur C.
Hayes, John Marion
Headlee, William Hugh
Henzlik, Raymond Eugene
Herd, Richard Murlen
Hignite, Robert E.
Hudnut, III, William H.
Hummer, Glen Sharp
Ipes, Thomas Peter
Jackson, Linda Duff
Jimerson, Sr., James Compere
Jocelyn, Wayne Lewis
Johnson, Charles Bruce
Jones, Ruby Aileen
Kaiser, Beverly A.
Kempf, Jane E.
King, Jr., Leroy H.
King, Mae Elizabeth
Kline, Tex Ray
Lair, Helen M.
Lang, Maud Ora
Leiman, Robert W.
Leskow, Olive
Liggett, Delmore
Lippert, Catherine Beth
Livingston, Von E.
Lucas, Georgetta Marie
Maass, Vera Sonja

McLaughlin, Jerry Loren
Maddigan, Ruth Jean
McKaig, Patricia Lyn
Malola, Mary E.
Manders, Karl Lee
Markley, Roger Bruce
Masterson, Mary Eileen
Matusik, Walter Michael
Meeker, Duane
Miller, Frances Fox
Munger, Elizabeth Mack
Nash, Edward Merl
Parker, E. Camille
Pendergrass, Presley Wade
Pettit, Anne
Phillips, Michael Joseph
Platt, David D.
Riggs, Donald Eugene
Scherle, Phyllis Joyce
Schulz, Victor Arthur
Scott, Glen D.
Shafer, Wilma Clare
Shoemaker, Fern Catherine
Smith, Mary Demetria
Strickler, Paul Edwin
Taylor, Joseph Thomas
Weaver, Elvin Paul
Weaver, Richard Donald
Weber, Frank E.
Wilson, George Wilton
Witham, William Tasker
Wright, Eldon Millard

IOWA

Arnold, Jr., Duane
Asadzadehfrad, Murlene Wallace
Barta, Marie Laura
Bartachek, Judith Diane
Bigley, Christine Ruth
Buswell, Henrietta Arlene
Bygness, Hazel Isabella
Cathcart, Mildred Dooley
Cooper, Reginald R.
Cox, Dean Freeman
Crahan, Jack B.
Degener, Veneta M.
Draper, Marian E.
Fathie, Kazem
Foley, Gerald Kevin
Fox, Margaret Gertrude
Frank, Sam Hager
Gould, James John
Harrison, Leanne Kay
Howlett, Phyllis L.
Huffman, James Hudson
Hunt, John DuBois
Husseiny, Abdo Ahmed
Huston, Jeffrey Charles
Hynes, George P.
Johnson, Curtis William
Johnson, David Bascomb
Kirchner, John Howard
Kelley, Beverly Gwyn
Knowlton, Jr., Edgar Colby
Krause, Lloyd Franklin
Laposky, Ben Francis
Laughlin, Mildred Knight
Lehman, Hyla Beroen
Lounsberry, Robert Horace
McLure, Gail Thomas
Marquis, Gerladine M.
Mather, Roger Frederick
Morris, Eugene
Murray, Rochelle Ann
Noble, Weston Henry
Riemer, Leroy Erwin
Seger, Robert Morse
Sheils, George Arthur
Silliman, Benjamin DeWayne
Solbrig, Ingeborg Hildegard
Stauffacher, Dean Worthing

Tolle, Eugenia M. Venner
Zinn, Gladys Avery

KANSAS

Ammar, Raymond G.
Barnes, Rachel Carter
Beacham, Woodard Davis
Beahon, Mary Ann Eggers
Beck, Michael Warren
Bennett, Robert F.
Birch, Lonah Kay
Bishop, Bessie Emily
Boyd, Rodney Carney
Budge, Melba Cornwell
Burger, Henry G
Burnett, Barbara Ann
Bush, Marcia Kay
Cheng, Chia-Chung
Christoph, Mildred
Christopherson, Marie Lucille
Cook, Charles Eberle
Coombs, Thelma H
Coons, Jr., Eldo J.
Cray, Jr., Cloud Lanor
Crowther, Robert Hamblett
Darby, Harry
Driever, Steven Leiby
Ediger, Michael Lee
Feagles, Gerald Franklin
Flora, Jan Leighton
Fung, Adrian K.
Guthrie, Richard A.
Haralick, Robert M.
Hawk, Gary Dean
Hay, Frances T.
Hensley, Betty Austin
Hershman, Joann Oppenheimer
Hiebert, Elizabeth Blake
Hines, Donald Diebert
Holmes, Betty Jean
Homburger, Richard H.
Hughes, Margaret Cline
Kaufman, Donald David
Kennedy, M. Patrice
Lingenfelser, Angelus Joseph
Lown, Wilford Franklin
McLean, Ruth Ann
McIlvain, Terry Mack
Mathewson, Hugh Spalding
Miller, Albert Raymond
Miller, Dorothea Welsh
Moscript, Dorotha Marguertie
Neuenschwander, Joyce Evonne
O'Hare, John Michael
Page-Stocks, Barbara Ann
Parks, Sherman A.
Pendley, Patricia Ellis
Peters, Elmer Sylvester
Priestley, Violet Arta
Ritter, Olive Mai
Robinett, Patricia Mildred
Sanford, Paul Everett
Scarlett, Dorothy Gladys
Smith, Norvel E.
Snyder, Merle L.
Speir, Kenneth G.
Thomen, Phyllis, Ann
Varner, Charleen LaVern
Wendelburg, Norma Ruth
Westerhaus, Catherine K.
Youse, Glad Robinson

KENTUCKY

Ahmed, Alice Pearce
Amyx, Katherine McClure
Anderson, Thomas Harold
Applegate, Walter Thomas
Bailey, Harry Hudson

Baldinger, Charlene Lois
Baldwin, Charlotte Eads
Bandy, Bette Linde
Barton, Nelda Ann Lambert
Bastawi, Aly Eloui
Begley, Robert Jennings
Bennett, Ivan Stanley
Bentley, Ruth Shearer
Bertram, Randall Byron
Blaylock, Donald Lynn
Bowden, Elizabeth Chandler
Boyer, Theodore Stanley
Bradbury, Lynn Allen
Brown, Maggie Cole
Brown, Robert Paul
Burchard, Forrest J.
Campbell, Carey Walton
Cangemi, Joseph P.
Carr, James Rogers
Carter, Lizzie E. Hill
Cawood, Billie Jean
Clark, Odis Morrison
Clark, Ruth Wallace
Clarkson, Hazel Lillian Sanders
Cleveland, Gene Rickey
Cole, Margaret Evelyn
Coleman, Jr., J. Winston
Collins, Courtney W.
Collins, Martha Layne
Cornett, Frances Bernice
Cosper, Barry Floyd
Crockett, Anne Allen
Crockett, H. Dale
Culpepper, Jetta C.
Culpepper, Richard Alan
Davis, Phillip Reuben
Dean, Lloyd
Debusman, Paul Marshall
Dorsey, Harold Winston
Earles, Pat S.
Elam, J. Phillip
Embry, Jr., Carlos Brogdon
Evans, Martha Alice
Fawbush, John Ray
Ford, Jr., Gordon Buell
Freeman, Jerome Warren
Freibert, Lucy M.
Funk, James E.
Fuson, Benjamin Willis
Galloway, Rex Farmer
Gleitz, George Phillip
Gobar, Ash
Golstein, Jane
Graham, Jr., Bruce M.
Graham, Nancy Guilfoil
Griffin, Lucille Slaughter
Gunn, Mary Laura
Gwaltney, Mildred
Harper, Paul Gordon
Hatcher, Joseph Carroll
Heflin, Harold
Hehl, Lambert Lawrence
Hentschel, Alza J. Stratton
Hixson, Allie Corbin
Holt, Carol E.
Howard, James Tommy
Howell, Henry Garland
Hurt, Billy Grey
Jackson, Earl J.
Jent, Sue Allen
Johnson, Harvey Marshall
Johnson, Robert Eugene
Jones, Calvin Paul
Kadaba, Pankaja Kooveli
Kinzer, Dennis Ray
Knudson, Martha Ailene
Komosa, Adam Anthony
Lamar, Carl Fletcher
Larimore, Leon
Lay, Frances Ballard
Lay, Mary Alice
Linville, Nannie Lou
Livingston, George Herbert
McAninch, Robert D.
McClure, Michael Wayne

McCubbin, Nicholas David
McMillon, Jr., Raymond Cecil
Machen, Roy Walter
Malloy, Martha Reuss
Martin, Melvin D.
Mason, Jr., Ernest
Melton, C. Alan
Milburn, Theresa Holtzclaw
Milburn, William Isaac
Morgan, Barbara Ann
Morris, Roger Dale
Morris, Vista Lorene
Mundy, Ella Mae
Music, Edward C.
Osborne, John Randolph
Palmer, Stephen Donald
Parks, Agatha E.
Peckham, III, William Henry
Perkins, David William
Phillips, William Henry
Piersol, Edna Wagner
Powers, Georgia M.
Pratt, Willia Devaughn
Priest, Helen Rubyor
Rangel, Carlos Enrique
Rich, Isadore Alexander
Richardson, Mildred Copelin
Roberts, Heyward Delain
Roberts Jeanette L.
Robinson, Ralph Rollin
Rodgers, Sr., William Harry
Roemer, William Nicholas
Ross, Sue G.
Roszell, Jr., Calvert Theodore
Schwendeman, Joseph Raymond
Seeger, Charles Ronald
Shah, Swarupchand M.
Shah, Vinod M.
Simeck, Clyde Frederick
Sinders, Mary Galley
Sledd, Gertrude Lee
Snider, Ruth A.
Spencer, Aida Besancon
Spencer, William David
Stapleton, Kathy J.
Stewart, Arthur Van
Stilwell, III, William Earle
Summers, Sally W.
Teegarden, Maude Boggs
Thom, Robert T. Anderson
Thomas, Patrick Aloysius
Thompson, Brent Druien
Traina, Robert Angelo
Tuck, William Powell
Wan, Richard T. C.
Williams, Melvin

LOUISIANA

Adams, Cecile Neomia
Adams, John Quincy
Aguilar, Rodolto Jesus
Allen, Karen Sue
Allen, Jr., L. Calhoun
Arndt, Hilda C. M.
Attales, Gerald Bruce
Barr, Nona Lee
Beason, Donald Ray
Berard, Dailey J.
Billingsley, David Lewis
Biundo, Jr., Joseph James
Bogan, Carmen Page
Boutte, Margaret Ann
Bracewell, Mervill Winzer
Braden, IV, Henry English
Bradford, Louise Mathilde
Brian, Jr., Alexis Morgan
Calub, Alfonso de Guzman
Carter, Maxine, Goodman
Carter, Jr., Prentiss Henson
Cazalas, Mary Williams
Claudel, Calvin Andre

Collier, Louis M.
Comeaux, Allen Joseph
Connelly, Michael Robert
Crump, Kenny Sherman
Davidge, Billy Lloyd
Davis, Donald Fred
DeFelice, Jr., Davd John
Deinhardt, Carol Lucy
Dessauer, Herbert C.
Driskell, Hermione Marie
Dupree, Leonard Larkin
Edwards, Edwin W.
Emerson, Robert Biscal
Emmer, John Wiltz
Epley, William Arnold
Epps, Anna Cherrie
Evans, Patricia Terrell
Fontenot, Jr., Martin Mayance
Ford, Elmer Lee
Forester, Jean Martha
Foret, George Joseph
Foster, Julia F.
Fourcard, Inez Garey
Foxworth, Charles Leonard
Galliano, Vernon Frederick
Galloway, III, Louie Altheimer
Gautreaux, Marcelian Francis
Gay, Clara Flournoy
Giammerse, Jr., Jack
Good, Mary Lowe
Gorman, Joyce Marie
Graser, Earl John
Graves, Mary Jo
Grodman, Pyrrha Gladys
Grue, Lee Meitzen
Guillaume, Jr., Alfred Joseph
Hardesty, Patricia E.
Harris, Arthur Lee
Harrison, Shirley M.
Henderson, James H.
Hines, Dorothy Anne
Horton, Janet E.
Huckaby, Thomas Gerald
Jackson, Morris K.
Johnson, Johnny Ray
Jordan, Eddie Jack
Judson, Lorraine Anderson
Karkalits, Olin Carroll
Kelly, Cecilia Mary
Kerans, Lawrence Clinton
Kerr, III, Charles MacDonald
Kleiner, Janellyn Pickering
Lewis, Winderlean Smith
Lippman, Alfred
Lipstate, Eugene J.
Little, Anne Sharpe
Little, Florence Herbert
Lovelady, Joe Render
McBroom, Ruby Careington
McCallion, William J.
Magee, Jr., Thomas Eston
Malone, June C.
Matson, Larry James
Morial, Ernest Nathan
Nugent, Donald York
Odom, Roy Harris
Owen, Dolores Bullock
Pearce, Charles Wellington
Pearce, Dorothy DeLorenzo
Prejean, L. Wayne
Qadir, Syed M. A.
Rault, Jr., Joseph Matthew
Reeder, James Arthur
Rees, Paul Klein
Regan, Carroll Robert
Rivard, Robert Cooper
Robinson, James William
Ryder, William Henderson
Seale, Margaret R.
Segel, Kenneth Ian
Sensat, Lloyd Lester
Smith, Jane Lynette
Smith, Pauline Giles
Snyder, Marjorie Sims
Sumner, William Edward

Sumrell, Gene
Tahir, Ash H.
Tan, Owen T.
Vaughn, Pearl Henderson
Venditto, James Joseph
Washington, Charles Lloyd
Wilson, Rose Confer
Wright, Floyd Vernon

MAINE

Davy, Gloria-Jeanne
Freilinger, James Edward
Hankins, John Erskine
Hathaway, William Dodd
Heald, Bruce Day
Hichens, Walter W.
Randall, Eudora Patricia
Taylor, Alan J.
Tracy, Marilyn Louise

MARYLAND

Adams, Henry Hitch
Allen, Aris T.
Anderson, Kenneth Allen
App, Austin J.
Arbuckle, Wendell Sherwood
Asbury, Claud Logan
Auerbach, Barry B.
Bailey, Elizabeth Ellery
Baily, Nathan A.
Bainum, Peter M.
Banik, Promila
Barbeito, Manuel Serafino
Bata, Evelyn Joan
Bawden, Monte Paul
Beckles, Frances N.
Benzinger, Maria
Benzinger, Theodor Hannes
Boehm, Jr., Edward Gordon
Borra, Ranjan
Bosworth, Margaret Wamsley
Boykin, Lorraine Stith
Braddox, Miamah Mietta
Braude, Herman M.
Brown, Robert Joseph
Burke, Gerard Patrick
Buskell, Zelma Jean
Buxbaum, Martin
Calhoun, William Carl
Capozzi, Marian R.
Chakrabarty, Rameswar
Church, Lloyd E.
Clark, Bill P.
Clark, William James
Cox, Jack C.
Dannenberg, Jr., Arthur M.
Davis, Curtis Carroll
De Michele, Margaret M.
Derucher, Kenneth Noel
de Vries, Margaret Garritsen
Docter, Charles Alfred
Dogger, Ada Ruth Carolyn
Domenici, Pete Vichi
Dubey, Satya Deva
Dunham, Daniel Bentley
Dyer, George Carroll
Edinger, Stanley Evan
Ellis, Mary L.
Eskut, Billie Lee
Esposito, Luigi
Fisher, Carl A.
Foresti, Jr., Roy
Fox, Roxanne Elaine
Frimer, Norman E.
Funn, Courtney H.
Furr, Quint E.
Gamson, Leland Pablo

Gattone, Vincent H.
Gay, Anna Belle Graham
Gazin, Charles Lewis
Gee, Zilphia Toni
Genoa, Jr., John
Gerhardt, Louise Burger
Gershowitz, Sonya
Gilbert, Robert Lee
Giolito, Carolyn Hughes
Gormley, Michael Brodt
Goslee, Reba Elena
Gragg, Henry Williford
Hamberger, Loren Dahlhamer
Hanford, William Edwrd
Hawkins, Sarah Margarett
Hayes, Margaret Smithey
Hegstad, Roland Rex
Hill, Ethel Brown
Hoenack, Peg Course
Hoffman, Mary Ann
Holcomb, Gerard Frank
Houck, Jr., Lewis Daniel
Hume, John Chandler
Hummel, Frances Cope
Huntley, William Robert
Inyart, Gene
Irving, Jr., George W..
Jascourt, Hugh Donald
Jeng, Helene Wu
Jordan-Cox, Carmen
Kafka, Marian Stern
Karna, Maya Tolani
Kemp, Lamar Elliott
Klebanoff, Philip Samuel
Klisch, Karen
Lehman, Leonard
Lewis, Jr., William Chesley
Little, Dainty Margo
Long, Lewis M. K.
Luzarraga, Marlene Kathryn
MacLennan, Beryce W.
Maxson, Harmon David
Melvin, Mary Lee
Merrick, Robert Graff
Morahan, Daniel Michael
Morgan, James Emerous
Myers, Sr., Samuel Lloyd
Nichols, Thomas S.
O'Connor, John Joseph
Orem, Reginald Calvert
O'Toole, Edward Thomas
Paffenbarger, George Corbly
Passwater, Richard Albert
Pearman, Reginald A.
Pemberton, Janette E.
Pemberton, S. MacPherson
Polis, Harry John
Polydoroff, Susan Wills
Prewitt, Judith Martha
Rice, Frederick Anders
Sanger, Isaac Jacob
Schaller, Jerome D.
Schoettler, Ellouise
Shalowtiz, Erwin Emmanuel
Shapere, Dudley
Sonnemann, Nell Battle
Spruce, Frances Blythe
Stehling, Kurt Richard
Stroube, Jr., William Bryan
Subasic, Frank J.
Swanson, Roger Fulton
Tarpley, Jr., Thomas Marvin
Thomas, Walter Scott
Werner, Victor Emile
Whitehurst, Lowell E.
Wiernik, Peter J.
Wood, Sr., Sumner
Wysong, Jr., Earl M.
Young, Robert Michael
Young, Sarah Hamilton
Zinke, Ernest Edward

MASSACHUSETTS

Abramovitz, Morton I.
Aitken, Molly Bennett-Marks
Allison, Jr., Graham Tillett
Allukian, Myron
Ambrose, Joseph Mark
Austen, William Gerald
Barbour, Walworth
Barstow, Paul Rogers
Beale, Everett M.
Bliss, Jr., Edward L.
Breslin, Donald Joseph
Buczko, Thaddeus
Burke, Daniel Anthony
Butler, Yvonne Janet
Chase, Joseph Russell
Christian, Walter P.
Colny, Jean Poindexter
Coulter, William Goddard
Darity, Evangeline Royall
Dauber, Jonathan M.
Davis, Robert James
Deanin, Rudolph Dreskin
de Mesne, Eugene
Diamant, Marilyn Charlotte
Edwards, Mattie S.
Eldridge, Jessie Cannon
Epstein, David Mayer
Fioravanti, Nancy Eleanor
Gallagher, Helen Kizik
Garabedian, Martha Ann
Gawienowski, Anthony Michael
Gil, David Georg
Giunier, Ewart
Glynn, Neil Held
Granahan, John Joseph
Greenberg, Frank Joseph
Gregory, Lydia May Jencks
Grodberg, Marcus Gordon
Grout, Geraldine Isabel
Hall, Robert Arthur
Hall, Wilfred McGregor
Harutunian, John Martin
Harvey, Eleanor Thornton Moss
Haugh, Richard Stanley
Hillery, Mary Jane
Hollomon, J. Herbert
Horovitz, Samuel Bertram
Ide, Judith H.
Janosik, Steven M.
Jean, Gabrielle Lucille
Johnson, Joyce
Johnson, Roger Alan
Jones, Ralph E.
Jones, Vernon
Kaliski, Judith Putnam
Keefe, Mildred Jones
Kenney, Alan
Kessler, Minuetta Shumiatcher
Knox, William Franklin
Koehler, Isabel Winifred
Lamkin, Selma H.
Lichtenstadter, Ilse
McCarthy, Mary Frances
McLendon, Dorothy
Maginnis, Iva-Anne
Maginnis, John Joseph
Manazir, Flora Mary
Marelli, John Vincent
Marsh, Milton Rutolph
Martin, Anna Miriam
Massod, Mary Fatette
Maxwell, Stanley Fielding
Mhlaba, Sondlo L.
Mickel, Hubert Sheldon
Miller, Ruth M. H.
Munroe, Barbara
Pfeiffer, David Graham
Rambauske, Werner Robert
Rathbone, Perry Townsen
Ross, Mary Jane
Rosselli, Charles Anthony
Seifert, Ralph Hammond
Serenyi, Peter
Shapiro, Lynn Irene
Stamm, Ann Waidelich

Starbard, Barbara Earl
Strang, Peter MacDonald
Toman, Kurt
Turner, Naomi Cocke
Vallely, Anne Elizabeth
Ward, Thomas Vincent
Whiting, Bruce Randolph
Yoken, Melvin Barton
Zani, Frederick Caesar

MICHIGAN

Adams, Betsy
Adrounie, V. Harry
Agrawal, Chandra P.
Akmakjian, Alan Paul
Arnett, Harold Edward
Bachman, Jerald Graybill
Bale, James F.
Ballentine, Krim Menelik
Bank, II, Theodore Paul
Barkley, Owen Herbert
Bellville, Miriam Priscilla
Bond, Floyd Alden
Bonner, Ophelia Calloway
Bowles, Hazel Elizabeth
Bragg, Dennis W.
Branch, Hira E.
Briede, Robert Paul
Brown, Garry E.
Buhl, Lloyd F.
Cederberg, Elford A.
Chandan, Ramesh C.
Chuang, Marisa Yuen
Cisaruk, Andrew A.
Collier, Betty F.
Connellan, Jr., Thomas Kennedy
Covert, Richard Lee
Crain, Ada Elizabeth
Crawford, Jr., Clan
Crippen, Edward Filmore
Daldin, Herman J.
Dean, Wanda Elizabeth
De Gaetano, Carolyn Hall
Dias, Donaldo De Souza
Dohring, Grace Helen
Dukes, Dorothy
Dukes, Lauretta
Dulisch, Mary L.
Edwards, E. Dean
Eisenmann, Lois Eleanor
Elder, Jean Katherine
Elliott, George Algimon
Everett, Warren S.
Farmakis, George Leonard
Feindt, Mary Clarissa
Fitzgerald, Harold Alvin
Frank, Ruth Marie Finley
Freedman, David Noel
Frumkin, Robert Martin
Gage, Lois Waite
Giles, William Mitchell
Grant, Lowell Dean
Greig, Walter
Grody, William Charles
Gunn, Willie Cosdena Thomas
Gunnings, Thomas Sylvester
Hall, Mildred Verzola
Hamachek, Alice Lavonne
Hamachek, Don E.
Hamilton, Theophilus Elliott
Hamlar, Portia Y. T.
Hatfield, Cordella M.
Hawkins, Leonard J.
Hedrick, Banius C.
Hildebrand, Verna L.
Hill, May Davis
Hoffer, Janice Ann
Hudson, Roy D.
Humphrey, Lawrence Ceaphus

Issari, M. Ali
Jackson, Jr., Harvey L.
Jackson, Herbert Cross
Jackson, Wilma
Jacobs, Herb Fred
Jenkins, Alma Rice
Jenks, Halsey Denton
Johnson, Terence Elwyn
Jones, Frank Warren
Jones, Lethonee Angela
Jones, Suzanne Taffy
Kales, Robert G.
Karampelas, Napoleom Dimetrius
Karunakaran, Kizhakepat Pisharath
Katz, Irving I.
Kilsdonk, Ann Gabriel
Kochen, Manfred
Krupp, Guinevere Ann
Land, Robert Donald
Leinonen, Ellen A.
Leipprandt, Mary Mitin
Liebrenz, Marilyn Louise
Likins, William Henry
Long, Mattie Lee
Lougheed, Jacqueline Isobel
Luahiwa, Judith Bagwell
MacMahan, Jr., Horace Arthur
McGehee, Jr., H. Coleman
McGowan, Marjorie Frances
Martin, Charles Allen
Mason, Dorothy Allison
Mioduszewski, Thomas Phillip
Neville, Laurine
Nobes, Leon D.
Ongwela, Gado Appollo
Parker, Phyllis Hepburn
Peske, Patric O.
Plumb, Forrest Leo
Porter, Milton Clyde
Powell, Richard Keith
Price, Ruth Puph
Raniville, Francis Oliver
Rao, Desiraju B.
Reynolds, Judy LaCoe
Roberts, Annye Pearl-Hardy
Roeper, George A.
Rutherford, James William
Sachtleben, Carl Henry
Seiler, Charlotte Woody
Sharland, Teresa C.
Sheppard, Ronald John
Stickney, Kenneth Arthur
Strome, Cloyce P. A.
Strong, Blondell M.
Tooke, Florence L.
Turner, Arthur Edward
Van Plew, Wright Henry
Varner, Nellie M.
Vickers, Robert Clemons
Volz, Paul Albert
Walkinshaw, Lawrence Harvey
Wallace, George John
Ward, Donald Maxwell
Wedding, Erling Solheim
Westbrok, III, Scott Charles
Wills, Elizabeth Wood
Wilson, Benjamin Calvin
Wiltse, Dorr Norman
Wolfe, Estemore Alvis
Wood, Earl Ray
Zaborowski, Robert Ronald
Zsigmond, Elemer K.

MINNESOTA

Baker, John Stevenson
Baker, Lurline Juanita
Benn, Bradley W. M.
Berg, Julia Irene
Berggren, Paul Walter

Brekke, Arnold
Brown, David Millard
Bryant, Antusa Santos
Carlson, Helen Hedman
Carlson, Mary Jean Callery
Carrington, Laura Ann
Clague, Thomas Eugene
Clauson, Alberta Ayer
Comty, Christina Mary
Cottone, Ronald Anthony
Decker, Sr., Robert D.
Dorweiler, Paul Lawrence
Eckert, Ernst R. G.
Epstein, Alvin
Ericksen, Sylvia M.
Erickson, Ellsworth Burch
Ernest, David John
Farah, Caesar Elie
Fergus, Patricia Marguerita
Firl, Donald Harold
Flick, Paul John
Follingstad, Henry George
Foreman, Gertrude Evelyn
Formanek, Elizabeth Mary
Formanek, Luella Helen
Foster, Lowell Walter
Friddle, Dale J.
Gandrud, Ebenhard Stewart
Gish, Sandra Louise
Glaus, Marlene Anne
Graubard, Mark Aaron
Gregerson, Doris Elaine
Hansen, Edward A.
Hansen, Susan Marie
Hanson, Norma Lee
Harrison, George Louis
Herman, John Allen
Higgins, Barbara
Hoistad, Louise Marie
Hooten, Ann Bratrud
Hopkins, Jr., William Barton
Hsi, Eugene Yu-Tseng
Jenks, Mary Ellen
Jodock, Darrell Harland
Johnson, Gordon Gilbert
Johnson, Ray Arvin
Kieselhorst, Lois Genevieve
Kugler, Ida Carolyn
Latz, Robert
Liggett, Delmas E.
Lindahl, Lorraine Elsie
Lundquist, Carl Henry
McCarthy, Eleanor Edith
Massman, Virgil Frank
Micke, Marilyn
Miller, Elizabeth Louise
Mundahl, Frances Mae
Orlich, Margaret Roberta
Pantell, Phyllis Ross
Posz, Albert Conrad
Puh, Chiung
Richardson, Joseph L.
Ryan, Nancy Wilhelmson
Ryan, Robert Dale
Sykora, Sylvia Esther
Taylor, Curtis L.
Thierer, Judith Ann
Tschirki, Robert Dean
van Appledorn, E. Ruth
Weaton, George Frederic
Welch, John Wiley
Wright, William E.

MISSISSIPPI

Ables, James Whit
Adams, Jr., John Melvin
Ahern, Hugh Stephen
Ammerman, Gale Richard
Anthony, Sandra Harris

Ard, Harold J.
Austin, Barbara Elizabeth
Backstrom, Martha Carolyn Murphree
Bahr, George Richard
Balam, Baxish Singh
Bangham, P. Jerald
Barksdale, Lucy Ann
Bates, Lura Wheeler
Beam, Bittena Carter
Bell, Jr., George Guice
Bell, Robbie Lloyd
Blackburn, Bertha Maiden
Blue, David Robert
Boatright, Barbara Reba-Hall
Bonner, Lilly Annelle
Breland, James Andrew
Brewer, Wilmon
Browne, Walter Broach
Bullock, William Joseph
Busby, Flornece Robinson
Byrd, Joseph Keys
Chain, Bobby Lee
Cleveland, Gaines Hightower
Cleveland, Jr., Ollie Ancil
Coker, Daisy Linnie
Corlew, John G.
Crowe, Hilda Faye
Cunningham, Beatrice
Dabbs, Miriam Adair
Davis, Carole Elizabeth
Dillon, Rae Evelyn
Dollar, Dennis Earl
Donaldson, Mary Howe
Dorsey, Michael A.
Douglas, Denna Mae
Eaton, Blaine Haskin
Edwards, Brian Alfred
Evans, Bruce A.
Fant, Sadie Patton
Ford, Clara Agnes
Fordham, Willmon Albert
Freundt, Jr., Albert Henry
Gandy, Edythe Evelyn
Geer, Patricia Boyle
Glenn, Judy N.
Green, Lacy August
Grissett, J. Ray
Hamilton, Charles Granville
Hamilton, Mary Elizabeth Casey
Hankinson, Mel Darwin
Harkins, Bobbye Roberts
Harper, Ed
Headrick, Flora Runnels
Henderson, Robbye Robinson
Hickok, Leslie George
Hicks, William Trotter
Holcombe, Troy Leon
Holliday, Josephine Crain
Holmes, Clifton
Hood, III, Burrel Samuel
Hooper, Virginia Fite
Hornsby, J. Marie
Izlar, Robert Lee
Jackson, Charlie Wilton
Jamieson, Addie Mae
Jasper, Martin Theophilus
Jones, Letha Parker
Kay, Kasmir Stanley
Kelly, Robert Emmett
Khatena, Joe
Lewis, Charles Bady
Lewis, Di Ann Bartee
Lindsey, O. Russell
Lopez, Ana Maria
Lowry, Bernice Gertrude
Lunardini, Robert Christopher
Lyells, Ruby E.
McDowall, Mary Ruth
McKay, George William
Macon, Myra Faye
Malbon, Janice Crotts
Marshall, O. B.
Mitchell, Roy DeVoy
Montgomery, Gillespie V.
Morrison, Francis Secrest

Musgrave, Ray Sigler
Nelson, Charles Lamar
Noone, John Thomas
Papasan, Mavour Ruth
Paul, Bani
Paul, Madhabendra Prasad
Peterson, Eulah Leana
Powell, Anice Carpenter
Purvis, III, Robert Craig
Riggs, Jr., Karl A.
Roberts, Charles Truitt
Rose, Allen
Shirley, Ollye Brown
Simmons, Jewell Phillips
Sisk, Kathern Ivous
Smith, Stanley G.
Stennis, John Cornelius
Swearingen, John Neafus
Thomas, Garnett Jett
Thomas, Jonathan Griffen
Trotter, Sr., Jesse L.
Van Groningen, Gerard
Ward, Rosie Graham
White, William Louis
Yarbrough, Karen Marguerite
Young, James N.
Young, Patrick H.
Zepeda, David George

MISSOURI

Abramovitz, Joseph Henry
Ahl, Sally W.
Alger, Don McKay
Ashcraft, Jesse Morris
Baebler, Arthur George
Bailey, Robert Edson
Baker, Raymond E.
Ballew, Susie Lee
Barnes, Jim Weaver
Bennett, Bobby
Bolte, Jr., Carl Eugene
Briscoe, Frank Earl
Bujac, Jr., James Norman
Bull, Stanley Raymond
Capps, Norman E.
Carter, Joan Haselman
Christ-Janer, Arland F.
Claar, Richard Lee
Clare, Stewart
Clark, William Merle
Clevenger, Horace Marshall
Clinton, William Christopher
Coles, Richard W.
Collins, Janet Reed
Copper, James Vernon
Cowen, Gerald Preston
Cox, Hardin Charles
Crouch, Philip Andrew
Crowley, Frances Felicia
Dalton, Glenn Laque
Dannov, Fred
Darnell, Edna Erle
David, Keith Raymond
Davis, Evelyn Marguerite
Day, Delbert Edwin
DeLange, Kenneth Allen
Dorff, Marcella Adabelle
Durbney, Clydrow John
East, Anna Mary
Engle, Patricia A.
Farrell, Odessa Wright
Flower, Joseph R.
Gentry, Alwyn Howard
Getman, Clyde J.
Glaser, Kurt
Gravens, Daniel Lee
Gray, Richard Alan
Green, Rice Andrew
Guenther, Charles John
Haley, Johnetta Randolph
Haley, Karen Louise

Hall, Judy A.
Hamra, Jr., Sam F.
Hannah, Franklin Jesse
Happ, Lawrence Raymond
Hardin Clifford Morris
Harris, Beverly Howard
Harshaw, Jack Raymond
Hayes, Paul Wesley
Hazel, Erik Richard
Heaton, Jane
Hedley, Katherine Henby
Hedrick, Harold Burdette
Hellmuth, George Francis
Henderson, Morris
Herbertt, Stanley
Heyward, Jr., John Wesley
Hitchcock, Carl D.
Hoard, Yvonne Walker
Hoelscher, Harold E.
Hollander, Doris A.
Holzum, Helen Marie
Howard, Jim M.
Huser, Carl Frank
Ichord, Richard H.
James, William J.
Johnson, Grace Manchester
Jones, Alice Hanston
June, Willa Dee
Klobe, Martha Patricia
Koch, Mary Therese
Korte, Adele D. J.
Lampo, Stephen Frederick
Larson, Eva Hilborg
Leitner, Stanley Allen
Liu, Henry
Lloyd, Corrine Avis
Lovinger, Warren Conrad
Lucido, Joseph L.
Lyman, Janice Kay
Lyons, Jerry L.
McClain, Chalres J.
McClure, Enos Swain
McClure, Ruby-Ellen
Maples, Evelyn Lucille
Marsh, Gwendolyn
Meyer, Walter
Miller, Carrie Eulah
Miner, Lorine Verna
Moore, Charles Lee
Moore, Elizabeth T.
Moore, Hershell Edward
Morgan, J. Derald
Moseley, Robert Carter
Mosley, Maxine V.
Murdock, Daryl Lynn
Murphy, Jerry John
Newton, Patricia A.
Norfolk, Glenn Dale
Orland, Henry
Owen, Jeannine Dolores
Penn, Winona Elizabeth
Pepper, Henry Cornelius
Pilson, Susan C. M.
Reddin, Opal Laurene
Reinhardt, Siegried Gerhard
Replogle, Eleanor
Rodriguez, John Albert
Rolston, Margaret Elizabeth
Sauer, Mary Louise
Scarborough, Curtiss Clinton
Scharlemann, Martin Henry
Smith, Wayne Delarmie
Staton, Knofel L.
Steinberg, Dora, Ellen
Stock, Mary-Jule Schrautnagel
Suelflow, August R.
Sullivan, Jessie Pauline
Thurman, Arthur Odell
Thurman, Leona Pouncey
Turner, Herman Nathaniel
Twaddle, Melvin Lawrence
Unger, William Ernst
VanGilder, Marvin Lee
Wagner, Jimmy Wayne
Ware, Larry Gordon

Warmsley, Ernestine Laura
Whitted, Mildred
Wilks, Thomas Milton
Winkelmann, John Paul
Winkleman, Jack Duane
Woerner, Earl LaVern
Yeagley, Joan

MONTANA

Brault, Raymond Wilfred
Cuelho, Antie Joseph
Donovan, Roberta Marie
Hartmann, M. Clare
Keil, Norma Fern
Rosell, Antoinette Fraser
Roset, Wilfred Laurier
Sicotte, Grace Darling

NEBRASKA

Alexis, Mildred Elizabeth
Andre, Paul Revere
Badeer, Henry Sarkis
Chesser, Barbara Jo
Clatanoff, Doris Ann
Crain, Hazel Mae
D'Agnese, Helen Jean
Deupree, Jean Durley
Edmunds, Niel Arthur
Fox, H. Ronald
Gingery, Burneil E.
Harpster, V. Aileen
Laughlin, Joan Marie
Lennox, Marjorie Elizabeth
Lynch, Benjamin Leo
Maier, Charles Robert
Meier, William Henry
Oldham, Howell G.
Roads, Jr., Leo Franklin
Rogers, Gifford E.
Sallquist, Gary A.
Spelts, Jr., Richard E.
Swoboda, Joseph Stephen
Wehrer, Charles S.
Woeppel, Louise Belle

NEVADA

Alderman, Minnis Amelia
Altvater, Helen M.
Babero, Bert Bell
Badik, Eleanor Rose
Byerly, Joan B.
Davis, William Claude
Dill, David Bruce
Gowdy, Anni C.
Hernandez, Alfredo
Jones, Clarence Klotz
Neidert, Kalo Edward
Noble, George Washington
Rhodig, Russel Delmer
Storz, Lester Gilbert
Trimmer, Jr., Harvey W.

NEW HAMPSHIRE

Alosa, Janet Allard
Cumming, Roger A.
Desai, Veena Balvantrai
Graf, Leonard Grant
Hanrahan, Joyce Yancey
Hodgdon, Shirley Lamson

Kelly, Doris Lillian
Laffin, Shirley Eleanor
Larson, Walter Ramey
Leedy, Dwight Adrian
Masters, Roger D.
Selle, Elaine Louise
Taffe, Betty Jo
Yatsevitch, Michael M.

NEW JERSEY

Allen, Edgard Yan
Amorelli, Anna Marie
Anzalone, Alfred Mark
Aronowitz, Alfred G.
Austin, Stanley Stuart
Baatz, Charles Albert
Bais, Daljit S.
Baker, Elsworth Fredrick
Baker, William Oliver
Baretski, Charles Allan
Barrett, Claire Rondeau
Bauer, Raymond G.
Beck, Gasper Paul
Bishop, Robert Milton
Bontempo, Paul N.
Borman, Iris
Brady, Winifred B.
Brannan, Ethel Ford
Brody, Stuart Martin
Brothers, Joyce Diane
Buckley, Harold Donald
Buttinger, Joseph
Chong, Luis A.
Chryssatopoulos, Hanka Wanda
Chu, Florence Chien Hwa
Claytor, Anne Marie
Clemens, David Allen
Cole, John Dean
Coon, Thomas Francis
Costa, Sylvia Allen
Cox, Elizabeth L.
Crozier, Vivian
Daniels, Rose Lynn
Davis, Nathaniel
Delgado, Ramon Louis
Dennis, Dorothy
de Planque, E. Gail
DeSalvo, Louise A.
Deutsch, Stuart Thomas
Dickerson, Loren Lester
Drake, Josephine Eleanor
Drinkwater, Robert Edwrd
Dugan, Constance Marie
Edwards, Ray Conway
Estill, Ann
Eves, Jr., James H.
Eyramya, Carmen Stanley
Farley, Dorothy A.
Fatemi, Nasrollah S.
Fink, Aaron
Fitchue, Leah Gaskin
Fitts, Leonard Donald
Fleischman, Alan Isadore
Flicker, Paul Leo
Flynn, Martha Connelly
Foster, Florence Perey
Fox, Danielle Daley
Friedlieb, Leslie Aaron
Friedman, Jacob Sander
Friis, Erik J.
Fuchs, Helmuth Hans
Gaul, Thomas Joseph
Gips, Walter F.
Golan, Lawrence Peter
Gold, Milton
Goldberg, Arthur Abba
Goldblatt, Barry Lance
Greco, Albert Nicholas
Greenaway, Millicent Dickenson
Griffing, William E.
Gruber, Jerome Martin

Grundy, John Owen
Hadley, Wayne Nelson
Halpern, Teodoro
Hanns, Christian Alexander
Harris, Yvonne J.
Hawley, Elizabeth Hoover
Hawley, Willard Hayden
Hayes, Edward James
Hayes, Mary Margaret
Hayes, Paul James
Heier, Dorothy Ruth
Hellman, Hal
Hinnant, Ollen B.
Hirshberg, Ruth
Howarth, Patricia Harriet
Ibok, Effiong Etukudo
Jacbsen, Albert
Janowsky, Oscar I.
Jecko, Perry Timothy
Job, Kenneth A.
Johnson, Fielding Holmes
Johnson, Selina Tetzlaff
Jones, James Robert
Kandravy, John
Keller, Suzanne
Killeen, Catherine D.
King, Lis
Kingery, Bernard Troy
Kmetz, Donald William
Knauf, Janine Bernice
Korn, Elizabeth P.
Kuzmak, Lubomyr I.
Lange, Adeline Rose
Lekus, Diana Rose
LoBoves, Janet Margaret
Lukas, Richard Anthony
McCarthy, Mary Theresa
McCreath, William Callan
McNabb, Talmadge Ford
Machione, Margherita Frances
MacKay, John Alexander
Makar, Nadia Eissa
Manogue, Helen Smith
March, Katherine B.
Mason, Lucile Gertrude
May, Judy Gail
Nicol, Marjorie Carmichael
Ohl, Ronald Edward
Perlberg, William
Petillo, John Joseph
Pigman, Gladys Hargreaves
Ratliff, Gerald Lee
Robinette, Joseph Allen
Rutherford, Jr., John Elmer
Ruzicka, Mary Frances
Salimi, Mostafa
Schlert, Mary Esther
Scialabba, Elmerinda Caccavo
Shay, Joseph Leo
Skidmore, Jr., James Albert
Smoler, Eleanor C.
Starnes, William Herbert
Stein, Hilton Larry
Szemborski, Eleanor
Szilassy, Sandor
Tanner, Jack Gene
Thorman, Lillian Joan
Tonnesen, Stanley T.
Treirat, Eduard
Trigg, Christine Elizabeth
Turton, III, Robert Straker
Turton, Sandra H. Bross
Vozza, Evelyn Markert
Walko, Mary Ann
White, James
Whiting, Cuthbert Randolph
Williams, Jr., Harrison Arlington
Young, Lloyd Emory
Yueh, Norma N.
Zampella, Edward Francis

NEW YORK

Abzug, Bella Savitzky
Accurso, Anthony Salvatore
Ackerman, Carolyn S.
Adams, Carolyn E.
Adams, Marianne Kathryn
Agli, Roemary
Ailey, Alvin
Alboum, Lawrence
Algard, Ole
Alger, Philip Langdon
Allen, Gary Irving
Allers, Franz
Amara, Lucine
Amerasinghe, Hamilton Shirley
Anbinder, Paul
Andrews, Benny
Antony, Yancey Lamar
Archibald, Reginald MacGregor
Archimovich, Alexaner Sinovious
Arnold, Jr., Lester E.
Arrington, Abner Atman
Ashe, Arthur Robert
Assatourian, Alice Husisian
Assatourian, Haig Gourji Khan
Atkins, Charles Agee
Aversa, Alarico
Aynes, Edith Annette
Badalamente, Marie Ann
Baer, Norbert Sebastian
Bagchi, Prenab
Bahr, Lauren S.
Baker, Barton
Baker, Bernice Maude
Baker, Dorothy Gillam
Bakhru, Hassa
Balderston, Jean Merrill
Barba, Harry
Barnes, Bruce Ernest
Barone, Stephen
Barron, David Milton
Barry, B. Austin
Bartalos, Mihaly
Bartova, Florence
Baryshnikov, Mikhail
Bass, Hyman
Basu, Samarendra
Battersby, Harold Ronald
Beck, Robert Alfred
Beeton, Diana Lafay
Bell, James Milton
Bell, Maud Melinda
Bender, Beverly Sterl
Benner, Lora Merle
Benskina, Margarita Orelia
Berg, Louis Leslie
Berger, Miriam E.
Bergleitner, Jr., George C.
Berkowitz, David
Berman, Herbert Lawrence
Bernardo, Jose Raul
Berns, Harmon Gordon
Bernstein, Leonard
Bertoni, Dante H.
Bertoni, Mae Henriksen
Beverly, Laura Elizabeth
Biddle, Jane Lammert
Bloom, Melvyn Harold
Blum, June
Boal, Sara Metzner
Bobrow, Edwin E.
Boley, Bolaffio Rita
Bonney, Arthur Peres
Bowers, Faubion
Bowman, Jr., Joseph E.
Brady, Emily F.
Bramwell, Henry
Breckel, Susanne
Brook, David
Brook, Nathan Harry
Brothers, Jack Anthony
Brown, Bruce Robert
Bryant, John William
Buckel, Ronald Paul
Byam, Milton S.
Callner, Richard

Cameron, Nina Rao
Cammarata, Joan Frances
Canterino, Serafina
Caruso, Paul John
Carvalho, Alan Dean
Cathcart, Alan
Cawein, Kathrin
Cecconi-Bates, Augusta
Chertow, Doris S.
Ciancone, Lucy
Ciuca, Eugen
Cleveland, Hattye Mae
Cohen, Aaron E.
Cohen, Gail Debbie
Cohen, Irwin
Comstock, Ruth B.
Connell, Louise Fox
Cook, Blanche Wiesen
Cook, Jeannine Salvo
Cooke, Robert Wayne
Cornell, II, George Washington
Cortlandt, Lynn
Cosnotti, Richard Louis
Coval, Naomi Miller
Cowen, Emory L.
Cox, Joseph Mason
Cranny, Titus Francis
Crawford, Shirley Eagley
Crihan, Joan G.
Crooke, Stanley Thomas
Crowley, Ralph Manning
Crumb, Anne Marie Theresa
Cuervo, Robert Felix
Daniel, Samuel M.
D'Anjou, Henry Genet
Davis, Jr., Ernest
Davis, Francis Raymond
Day, Beth F.
Day, John H.
DeGregorio, Robert Eugene
Delli, Helga Bertrun
De Long, Harold William
Del Percio, Gloria M.
Demetrius, James Kleon
DeVito, Albert Kenneth
Deyrup, Astrith Johnson
Dickinson, June McWade
Diedolf, John T.
Dillard, Emil Lee
Dizer, Jr., John Thomas
Donahue, Grace Helen Serverino
Douglas, William Richard
Dragonette, Jessica
Draper, Thomas John
Drummond, Malcom McAllister
Du Broff, Diana D.
Dudley, Willie Margurie
Duroska, Emilia O.
Dykshoorn, Marinus Bernardus
Eaves, Elsie
Edson, Carroll Andrew
Edwards, Cynthia Adele
Ehrlich, Helene Hedy
Einach, Charles Donald
Eisenhart, Charles Donald
El Ghamry, Mohamed T.
Elkins, Dov Peretz
Elliott, Marjorie Reeve
Engel, Eliot L.
Erlich, Elizabeth Ann
Eschner, Edward G.
Espina, Angel Beaunoni
Esposito, Kathy Ann
Exton, Jr., William
Facci, Domenico A.
Falk, Carolyn Rosenstein
Farian, Babette Sommerich
Fay, Thomas J.
Feldsher, Howard M.
Ferguson, Karen Anne
Ferris, Charles Birdsall
Fields, Joan Ross
Finn, William F.
Fiser, James Ronald
Flatt, Jane Dee

Fleming, Ronald Howard
Fleysher, Ellen
Flickinger, Bonnie Gordon
Foss, Lukas
Foster, Carno Augustus
Foster, Holland
Foxe, Arthur Norman
Francis, Neville Andrew
Francoeur, Romaine D.
Frankel, George Joseph
Frederick, Jonathan Elbert
Freeman, Leonard Murray
Frey, Barbara R.
Fu, Lorraine S.
Fudin, Carole Ellen
Gadol-Kelly, Joan
Garner, Gerald J.
Garnett, Adrienne Wilma
Garretto, Jr., Leonard A.
Gartner, Lawrence Mitchel
Gary, Gayle H. M.
Gatti, Corinne
Gazzola, Richard Peter
Geiger, Loren Dennis
Gershoy, Eugenia
Gersoni, Diane Claire
Gerstman, Judith R.
Gewald, Robert M.
Gilman, Benjamin Arthur
Giraudier, Antonio
Gittler, Joseph Bertram
Glasberg, H. Mark
Gocek, Matilda Arkenbout
Godfrey, John Carl
Goldin, Augusta
Goldman, Martin Jerome
Goldman, Simon
Gollub, Monica
Gordon, Harry William
Gorin, Jr., Robert Murray
Gouldthrope, Kennet Alfred
Goulian, Dicran
Graber, Harris David
Grafton, Connie Ernestine
Green, Ernestine R.
Green, S. William
Greene, Robert Ford
Greenspan, Adam
Greenstein, Michael
Greenstein, Teddy
Greenwald, Douglas
Gunter, Lester William
Habberton, John
Hammer, Lillian
Hancock, Gerre Edward
Hanson, John Robert
Hardon, John Anthony
Harkness, Rebekah West
Harris, Elisabeth Tamlyn
Harris, Ernest E.
Harriss, Clement Lowell
Hart, Agnes
Hastings, Baird
Hauge, Gabriel
Helpern, Joan M. G.
Henkin, Louis
Herscher, Irenaeus Joseph
Hill, Carol
Hirschberg, Besse Bryna
Holley, Edgar Merritt
Holling-Kaemmerer, Janice A.
Holman, Ottilie Ann
Horan, Linda
Hornblass, Albert
Horwich, Diana M.
Houston, Carol S.
Hsu, Joseph Jen-Yuan
Hughes, Stacy E.
Hundredmark, III, Bert A.
Hunter, Jacqueline
Inez, Colette
Ingalls, George Lewis
Irvine, Jr., Raymond Gerald
Jackson, Barbara Williams
Jakeway, Kevin W.

Cunningham, William
Daniel, Edith Short
Davis, III, Egbert Lawrence
Davis, Mollie Camp
Daye, Charles Edward
Dedmon, Richard Kendrick
Diamond, Harvey J.
D'Ignazio, III, Silvio Frederick
Dodson, Don C.
Dore, Mary D.
Doster, Harold Charles
Dougherty, Jr., William Howard
Draper, Sr., Howard Dennis
Dupin, Clyde C.
Dyar, William Heller
Edwards, Mary Janice
Elebash, Hunley Agee
Evans, H. C.
Evans, Raymond
Farwell, Jr., Harold Frederick
Fawcett, George D.
Ferrell, III, Excell Osborne
Fitzgerald, Ernest A.
Flack, Jr., Charles Zorah
Freeman, Doris Blanton
Freese, Howard Lee
Freeze, Elizabeth Bouldin
Freeze, Mattie Elizabeth
Fuller, Albert Clinton
Funderburk, David B.
Gaddis, Roger Gary
Galloway, Ray Maynes
Galvin, Hoyt R.
Gardner, Barry Lynn
Garner, Mildred Maxine
Gibson, Jr., John Albert
Giddens, Beulah M.
Giduz, Roland
Gilbert, Judy Mavin
Giles, Barbara Ann
Giles, Carl Howard
Gilliatt, Cecil Lee
Goldman, Bert A.
Gordley, Marilyn Classe
Gordley, Metz Tranbarger
Graham, Virginia Bryant
Grant, Ann Baum Dudley
Grossnickle, William Foster
Gulati, Jagjit
Guyer, II, Charles Grayson
Hackney, III, James Acra
Haggard, William Henry
Hairston, Peter Wilson
Hales, Celia Elaine
Hampton, Carol Dean
Hampton, Carolyn Hutchins
Haritun, Rosalie Ann
Harper, James Cunningham
Harrell, Charles H.
Harris, Betsey Matthis
Harris, Jean W.
Harris, Jr., Jordan Clifton
Hathorn, Suzette Flowers
Hay, Jr., Russell Earl
Hayes, Kyle
Heath, Charles Chastain
Heffernan, Thomas Patrick
Hefner, W. G.
Hemby, Jr., James Benjamin
Henderson, John Baxter
Henson, A. Miriam Morgan
Henson, Jr., O'Dell Williams
Hershey, H. Garland
Hicks, Eva Pauline
Hiers, Gerald Lamar
Hodges, Luther Hartwell
Hodgin, Sidney LaRue
Hogan, Judy
Holsti, Ole Rudolf
Holtzman, Eva Seaman
Hope, Kate Jeffreys
Horne, Annie Pearl
Hubbard, Hampton
Humenik, Frank James
Hunter, Lena Virginia

Hurr, Doris Smith
Husketh, Alma Ormond
Jackson, Marion Thomas
Jackson, Jr., Maynard Holbrook
Jackson, Zane Gray
Jessup, Belvin J.
Johnson, George
Johnston, Billy Gray
Johnston, Jr., Wilbur Lee
Jones, Hattie Elizabeth
Jones, James Grady
Jordan, Jr., John Richard
Kell, Jean Marie
Kendrick, Diane Priscilla
Kiser, Elizabeth Quinter
Kistler, Jr., Donald D.
Knight, James Wesley
Lathrop, Gertrude Adams
Laws, Milas Timothy
Ledford, Horace B.
Ledford, Kenneth Avery
Lee, Felicia S. W.
Lind, Viiu Saral
Long, Shirley Dobbins
Love, Dorothy Bryan
Lutz, Paul Eugene
McClelland, Golda Page
McCotter, Jr., Charles Kennedy
McCoy, Almo N.
McCoy, Narviar Walker
McKeel, Marion Elizabeth
McLauchlin, Beatrice Hall
McLean, Stephen Alderman
Maddox, Irene Newcomb
Mahler, Mary Lee
Mallard, Elizabeth Keith
Merritt, Doreatha Frost
Merritt, Peggy F.
Miller, J. D.
Montgomery, Royce Lee
Moore, Ruby Johnson
Mumford, Patrick Wayne
Neller, Jr., Arthur Agustus
Newman, James Samuel
O'Neal, Robert P.
Parker, Jr., Walter Raleigh
Patterson, Esther Fleming
Pegram, Jr., Elias H.
Perkins, Kenneth Warren
Pittman, Benny Ray
Powell, Charles Edwin
Price, Jr., Earnest
Puckett, Dorothy Williford
Quinn, Joseph Earl
Raiford, Ernest Lee
Raney, Richard Beverly
Rauch, Marshall Arthur
Reed, Dennis Lee
Rivenbark, Rembert Reginald
Royce, Rosemary T.
Salt, Albert Alexander
Satterfield, G. Howard
Selkinghaus, Walter Eugene
Shelton, Raymond Fryar
Smith, Jr., Dock G.
Smith, Doretta Frenna
Smith, Janet Fay
Smitherman, Guy Vernon
Spaeth, Shirley Turner
Sparks, Charles E.
Speer, Allen Paul
Spurlock, Lassena Clark
Stimson, Richard Alden
Stoessel, Carole Jean
Van Landingham, Eugenia P.
Walston, George Stancill
White, Charles Denny
Williams, Annie John
Williams, Larry Albert
Wilson, Shirley Schaub
Yarborough, Barbara Louise

NORTH DAKOTA

Clark, Alice T.
Dorgan, Byron Leslie
Hagen, Orville West
Hektner, Vernon E.
Herslip, Larry
Jukkala, Peggy J.
Klingensmith, Don Joseph
Mack, Arlene
Merrick, Mary James
Schmidt, Cletus J.
Scriba, Joelyn A.

OHIO

Abrahamson, Jr., Ira A.
Adams, Leroy
Allen, Alice Shoecraft
Ammer, William
Arnett, James Edward
Austin, Michael Herschel
Ballard, Irma L. Parrett
Balthorpe, Jacqueline Morehead
Bardis, Panos D.
Bernard, Lowell Francis
Bidart, Mary Florecita
Blazer, Sondra Kay Gordon
Boecklin, Peg Pitman
Bondurant, Byron Lee
Bower, True Gehman
Bowman, Georgiana Hood
Brandel, Mary Hermengild
Brasey, Henry L.
Brophy, Jr., Charles A.
Bryan, Janet Major
Carnahan, Jean Ann
Carraher, Jr., Charles E.
Cessna, John Curtis
Chen, Wai-Kai
Childs, Francine C.
Clema, Joe Kotouc
Cleveland, Jr., Cromwell-Cook
Clinger, Grace June
Clouden, LaVerne Carole
Cohen, Armond E.
Coleman, Nancy Jean
Collins, Edward Milton
Colombi, Viloa Marie
Cook, Lee William
Copeland, Carolyn Davis
Copeland, William Mack
Coran, Aubert Y.
Corcoran, M. Jerome
Cousins, Albert Newton
Couts, Woody Charles
Cox, Catherine Neff
Craig, Vernon Eugene
Critelli, Ida Joann
Crosby, Fred McClellan
Cummins, Kenneth Burdette
Daarud, Bertha Mae
D'Amato, Al
Dargusch, Carlton Spencer
Davis, Ronald Byron
Davis, Sara Jacqueline
DeForest, Julie Morrow
Dewire, Norman Edward
Doermann, Ralph Walter
Dornette, Ralph Meredith
Dunlap, Jane B.
Dunn, Robert Garvin
Eakin, Thomas Capper
Edse, Ilsedore Maria
Eglistis, Irma
Ezzo, Carolyn
Favret, J. Raymond
Fawcett, Novice G.
Ferguson, Harry
Fincher, Glen Eugene
Finney, Clara
Florence, Franklin Delano
Floto, William Mathew
Foley, Kevin Michael

Forbes, Fred William
Francis, Marion David
Frohnapfel, Wilhelmina
Frost, William P.
Gartland, Beverly Patterson
Gehres, Helen Roop
Geisinger, William Robert
Gerla, Morton
Ghering, Mary Virgil
Gibson, Curtis A.
Gilfillen, Jr., George C.
Gilliom, Bonnie Lee Cherp
Gleser, Goldine
Glover, Betty S.
Gobetz, Giles Edward
Gordon, Gilbert
Green, Galen Lee
Greenwald, Herbert A.
Greive, William Henry
Grinstead Leonard S.
Hackney, Howard Smith
Hambourger, Linda S. Mintz
Haque, Azeez C.
Haque, Malika Hakim
Hawes, Miriam Lucille
Heimlich, Henry Jay
Henry, Edwin Roscoe
Heurich, Betty Eleanor
Holtkamp, Dorsey Emil
Hostetler, David Lee
Houchins, June Farley
Howard, John Malone
Hoyt, Claremont Earl
Hrinko, Jean Ayr
Hulley, Clair Montrose
Innis, Robert William
Jan, George P.
Jensen, Fred Charles
Jestice, Lois Burnez
Johnson, Lewis Neil
Johnson, Mary Elizabeth
Johnson, Roman E.
Jones, Worth Roosevelt
Juvancic, Richard William
Kardos, James Wesley
Kawahara, Fred Katsumi
Kelley, Elbert Hollis
Kemp, Dorothy Elizabeth
Kerestan, Richard Michael
King, Laura Jane
Kiriazis, James William
Kline, Lenore Marie
Koesters, Mary Justina
Kohn, Mary Louise
Kovach, Kenneth Julius
Kovalchuk, Feodor Sawa
Kropf, Joan R.
Krysiak, Joseph Edward
Kuriger, Jr., Frank Joseph
Kurtz, Freda W.
Kyriazis, Andreas P.
Laabs, Ernst A.
Leidig, Melvin Dwight
Line, James V.
Lockhart, III, George
Lowry, Mary Ann
McCormick, William Edward
Mackey, R. Elizabeth
McMahan, Rebecca Sue
Macebuh, Sandy
Maciuszko, Jerzy J.
Markley, Blanch Luciel
Markworth, Alan John
Metz, M. Jean
Mitchell, Melvin James
Moore, Dan Tyler
Moore, Thadelua
Newbern, Captola D.
Niffenegger, James Albert
Norman, Patricia J.
Nye, Bernard Carl
Oh, Kong Tatt
Orze, Wladzia Helene
Ostlund, Leonard Alexander
Overholser, Ronald Lee

Parch, Joseph Raymond
Parmer, Opal E.
Phillips, Chandler Allen
Phillips, Marell Knott
Pikaart, Len
Poole, Marjorie Hartman
Pope, Myra Joe
Raftopoulos, Demetrios Dionysios
Rancour, Joann Sue
Redman, J. James
Renick, Patricia Ann
Richmond, Quinton B.
Rieg, Daniel Joseph
Rivkin, Ellis
Rogers, A. Robert
Roth, Frederic Hull
Salisbury, Jane Jefford
Schirripa, Dennis James
Schmucker, Ruby Elvy
Seitzinger, Mary Lou
Shaffer, Dale Eugene
Shapton, William Robert
Shaw, Elizabeth Christine
Sheard, Kevin
Shonkwiler, John A.
Smith, Robert Lee
Stahl, Daniel L.
Stone, Ivy Goldhamer
Thrall, Jr., Richard Cameron
Tiemeyer, Hope Johnson
Turner, Gladys T.
Vlahos, George Efthymios
Walker, Jr., C. R.
Westhausen, Gary H.
White-Ware, Grace Elizabeth
Wiles, Marilyn McCall
Willard, Carol J. Petzold
Wilson, Donald M.
Wolcott, Roger Lodge
Zirkle, Virginia Irene
Zishka, Ronald Louis

OKLAHOMA

Abercrombie, Betty Webber
Alexander, Ashley Harry
Allen, Annie Bell
Allen, Loretta Belle
Atkins, Hannah Diggs
Auten, Melvin R.
Badger, Daniel Delano
Banks, Glenna Mae
Barkley, Fred Alexander
Barnett, Franklin Dewees
Baumann, Daniel Bruce
Bayazeed, Abdo Fares
Beach, Paul Thomas
Bendure, Leona Jensen
Berry, Jr., Lemuel
Bigda, Richard James
Biolchini, Robert F.
Blackburn, Ella Mae
Blair, F. Joe
Blair, Marie Lenore
Bonham, Tal D.
Boulton, Grace W.
Bridgman, Joyce Marie
Brooks, June Brooks
Bruner, Inez W.
Burch, Loren William
Buse, Sylvia Tweedt
Byrum, James Knox
Cargill, Jr., O. A.
Champlin, H. H.
Chavers, Pasqual Dean
Cleaver, Edgar M.
Clifton, Rose Mary
Cochran, Walter Martin
Coleman, Harold John
Collins, Corliss Jean
Cooper, Arthur Earnest
Crumbo, Minisa

Dannelley, Jr., Paul Edward
Deadmon, Gertrude Valivia
Dennis, Cherry Nixon
Dombrowski, Madge Cohea
Domstead, Mary M.
Donahue, Hayden H.
Douglass, Richard Bary
Duerksen, Mable Vogt
Eisel, Joyce Mary
Elder, Mark Lee
Evans, Rodney Earl
Fisher, Ada Sipuel
Fite, Boneta Lebeau
Fite, Elwin
Ford, Clyde Gilpin
Ford, William Gerald Francis
Francke, Harry Carl
Freeland, Phillip Loy
Fuller, Gerald Ralph
Garrard, Thomas Edward
Gaunt, Dona Ophelia Jennings
George, Preston W.
Gilbreath, Alice Marie
Gooden, William J.
Hada, Jerrianne
Harris, Loyd Ervin
Harrison, William Earl
Hayes, Deanne
Herring, Michael Morris
Hickman, Kathryn Theresa
Higgins, Lester Edward
Hoke, Sheila Wilder
Hudlin, Grace Elizabeth
Hudson, Leonard Lester
Hunter, Cameron Kreg
Hunter, Ramona E.
Ingram, Charles Dean
Javellas, Ina J.
Jones, Dale Paschal
Jones, Linda Lee
Kahle, Naomi Ruth
Keefer, Evelyn Mae
Kelleher, Pamela Ruth
Kerr, Mildred Hoover
Kirkham, M. B.
Lackey, Guy Annadale
Landman, Georgina B.
Lewis, Gladys Sherman
London, Janice B.
Long, Mona Pybas
Ludwig, Ruby Ballard
Lyons, Dan
McCombs, Solomon
Martin, Philip Joe
Martin, Robert Leo
Matthews, Elsie C. Spears
Meinders, Hildred McCants
Mohd, Maqsood Ahmed
Mowdy, Al
Murphy, Polly Lewis
Norfleet, Almeta Faye
Northcross-Walker, David
Oberle, George Hurley
O'Dell, William George
O'Donoghue, Don H.
Parham, Ruby Inez
Parr, Frank Robert
Peer, Gary G.
Phelps, Edna Mae
Prichard, Thora Inez
Privett, A. Rex
Read, Nelda Joyce
Reed, Kathlyn Louise
Reed, Robert De Hart
Rex, Lonnie Royce
Ricker, Norman Hurd
Schoolcraft, Victoria Lynn
Shipp, Victor Ray
Smith, Valentine Joy
Southerland, Randy
Sparks, Marie Catherine
Stevens, Myrtle Chandler
Surber, Joe Robert
Trombley, Charles Cyprian

Turpen, Michael Craig
Wade, Geraldine Elizabeth
Wells, Jerry Lee
Whipple, Jr., Charles M.
Wright, Harold Hannon
Youritzin, Glenda Green
Zink, John S.

OREGON

Alexander, Ann M.
Bailey, Exine Margaret Anderson
Bailey, III, Henry John
Baker, James Hallead
Baldwin, Stanley C.
Bancroft, Barbara Ayleen
Bennett, Beverley Loree
Benson, Lester R.
Bliesner, Gustav Henry
Brazauskas, Pius
Browne, Joseph Peter
Cargo, David Francis
Clark, Donald Edward
Cleland, John George P.
Coe, Wendell Lynn
Duff, W. Jack
Ebinger, John B.
Edwards, Roberta Elaine
Eliander, Kevin Spurlin
Erickson, Patricia Loeberl
Flowers, Donna Lee
Fortt, Inez Julia Long
Foster, Atwood
Gray, Lawrence Alston
Green, Edith
Hackett, William David
Hales, Loyde Wesley
Hall, Frederick Columbus
Hamilton, Ethel Macy
Hilton, Harvey Lee
Hunt, Howard Lee
Isham, Jr., Quentin Delbert
Lehl, Mabel Bowman
Lum, Paul P.
McCawley, Elton Leeman
Munter, Pamela Osborne
Murray, Juls Maree
Oakland, Sam-Adolf
O'Connor, Helene Allen
Pamplin, Jr., Robert Boisseau
Propst, E. Allen
Rahimtoola, Shahbudin H.
Rand, Nancy Geraldine
Ransom, Jay Ellis
Rollins, David T.
Row, Edna Berniece
Scott, Kathryn Louise
Smith, Gloria Felecia
Soderstrom, Dorothy Marie
Staffanson, Ruth C.
Taylor, Wesley Daniel
Wills, Edwina Florence
Wood, Samellyn Jones

PENNSYLVANIA

Ahlgren, Roy B.
Alger, Ferris Eugene
Allshouse, Gary Wayne
Alvarez, Marcelo A.
Anderson, Sarah Anderson
Andrews, Charles Lawrence
Arabia, Anthony John
Ashbaugh, Laura Frances
Axam, John Arthur
Bachman, Leonard
Baker, Justine Clara
Balada, Leonardo
Balas, Egon
Barrett, Robert Owen

Bendik, John Joseph
Benovitz, Madge Klein
Beretsky, Metodij
Berg, Jean Horton
Bishop, Bernice Angeline
Brafford, William C.
Britt, Jr., George G.
Byington, Frederick D.
Cale, David Lee
Carpenter, II, Charles Whitney
Carr, Owen C.
Cascario, Elizabeth Frinzi
Cassidy, Michael Edward
Charlton, Jr., George N.
Charyna, Myroslav
Clark, Jr., Fred
Coates, Charles R.
Cohn, Priscilla N.
Coppersmith, Mimi Ungar
Coppes, Leonard John
Cox, Elinor Driver
Crabtree, Arthur Bamford
Cresson, Ruth Elizabeth Haynes
Curtis, Dorothy Stevenson
Daggett, Bradford I.
de Marzia, Violette
Detzel, Wilma Marie
DeVane, Evelyn Gaynelle
Dickie, Lois Galbraith
Dickstein, Jack
Diefenderfer, Omie Tilton
Di Luzio, Jean Baptiste
Donahey, Jean Elizabeth
Dorian, Harry A.
Dorsey, Lois Lee
Eckman, Bertha Elizabeth
Eckman, Carol Ann
Egan, Mary Joan
Engel, Randy V.
Evans, Theda
Federico, Peter George
Fischer, Roger Raymond
Fontain, Gregory
Forehan, L. Marie Farrow
Friedman, Philip Harvey
Galbraith, Lilyan King
Garner, Marie Grillo
Garszcznski, Suzanne M.
Geigle, Ralph C.
Gessner-Asten, Erika V.
Golany, Gideon S.
Goodwin, Carlton Byron
Gordon, George N.
Gorman, M. Adele Francis
Gradisar, Helen Margaret
Greenfeld, Yeshayahu
Gregorian, Vartan
Greulich, Kathryn Sullivan
Griglak, Martin Samuel
Gross, John Hammes
Guhl, Dale Thane
Gulnac, Jon Crawford
Gupta, Venu Gopal
Guthrie, Marion B.
Habboushe, Christa Parhad
Hahn, Ruth Freeman
Hall, Jr., Edwin Arthur
Halstead-McFarland, Diane Claire
Hart, Eleanore Hays
Hasley, Robert Nathan
Hauptfuhrer, Barbara Barnes
Hawley, Robert Patrick
Heard, Rowita Charlene
Henisch, Heinz Kurt
Kenney, Robert Lee
Henry, Aaron E.
Hepburn, Eileen Harkins
Herder, Thomas G.
Hineman, Anna L.
Hingson, Robert Andrew
Hitchens, Charles Norwood
Hostetler, Shirley Ann
Houseal, Reuben Arthur
Houseal, Ruth Arnold
Houts, Earl

Huffman, Virginia M.
Hughes, Philip Edgcumbe
Hurd, Priscilla Alden
Jacobs, Allan Duane
Jacobs, Augusta Adele
Jacobsen, William Dutton
Johnson, William H. E.
Jones, Sondra Michelle
Joyner, Christopher Clayton
Joyner, Nancy Douglas
Karn, Gloria Stoll
Kaye, William Mark
Kellinger, Josef Michael
Kellner, Davena Mae
Kerr, Gretchen H.
Klein, Martin John
Knight, Kathleen
Kostem, Celal Nizamettin
Krantz, Marilyn
Krasner, William
Kratz, Mildred Sands
Ksiazek, Marilynn C.
Kurjakovic-Bogunovich, Mira
Kwik, Christine
La Costa Gonzales, Carlos
Lent, John Anthony
Levi, Henry Thomas
Lindsay, Henry E. H.
Logan, Sr., Thomas Wilson
McDonnell, Lois Eddy
Mangargal, Larry E.
Manka, Dan Paul
Marino, Vincent Joseph
Marsh, Kenneth Stanley
Mazelauskas, M. Gabrielle
Megill, Jr., Virgil Glen
Metcalf, Gertrude Rothenberger
Mitra, Gopal C.
Mobley, Herbert Brooks
Nelson, Jean Ann
Oliver, Judith A.
Paladino, Madaline
Palmer, Arnold Daniel
Park, Virginia R.
Pedrone, Dino J.
Pellow, Rita Boll
Philipps, Winfred Marshall
Popescu-Judetz, Eugenia
Posy, Carl Jeffrey
Prescott, Patsy
Prevoznik, Stephen J.
Ramov, Edward Samuel
Rangos, Joh G.
Raphael, Carl S.
Reeder, Clarence Charles
Reichle, Frederick A.
Reisdorf, Shirley Carman
Ridgely, Josephine Jones
Riedlinger, Marilyn Wood
Roberts, Thelma Aneinetta
Rochowicz, Jr., John Anthony
Romain, Margaret A.
Ross, Becky Anne
RuDusky, Basil Michael
Schmidt, Mark Otto
Sebastianelli, Mario Joseph
Shallcross, Virginia Carter
Solczanyk, Andrij Darian
Strayer, Vernon John
Stueber, Gustav
Swiecicka-Ziemianek, Maria
Szegho, Emeric
Tarnawsky, Ostap E. M.
Taylor, Horace Melvin
Taylor, John Calvin
Thoma, Shirley Christoff
Tily, III, Stephen Bromley
Tucker, C. DeLores
Turnbach, Marie
Vazquez-Santander, Jose
Ward, Victoria Francine
West, Jr., Daniel Jones
Wickersham, III, Lamont Titus
Wittman, Nora Edna
Wolanin, Sophie Mae

Yoder, Luella May
Youtcheff, John Sheldon

PUERTO RICO

Altieri, Pablo I.
Alvarado-Torres, Thilda I.
Batista De Rodriguez, Adelaida
Bhajan, William Rudolph
Calderon-Serrano, Alfredo
Contreras-Bordallo, Fermin
Cruz, Carlos
de la Sierra, Angell O.
Delgado de Torres, Alma
de Maldonado, Quinones Aida
Deynes, Wanda N.
Gimenez, Miguel Angel
Girod, Alberic O.
Gomez, Berrios Nelida
Gonzalez, Charles John
Gonzalez, Rafael A.
Gonzalez-Alcover, Jose Carmelo
Guzman, Alberto Porrata
Landron Villamil, Jose
Larde, Enrique Roberto
Masso, Gonzalez Gildo
Mayol, Pedro Magdiel
Mendez, Felix G.
Menendez-Monroig, Jose
Nogueras, Rivera Nocolas
Ramirez-Rivera, Jose
Rivera, Nicolas Nogueras
Robinson, Nancy Margaret
Roman de Jesus, Jose C.
Romero-Barcelo, Carlos A.
Ruiz, Aldelmo
Schmidt, Sandra Estrella
Sierra, Angell O. de la
Soto-Munoz, Manuel
Torres-Aybar, Francisco G.
Torres-Delgado, R.
Ulmos, Guillermo Enrique
Villalon, Manuel Felipe
Vizcarra, Ginoris

RHODE ISLAND

Batastini, Jr., Armando Emilio
Fairleigh, James Parkinson
Galamaga, Donald Peter
Halo, Hugo H.
Harris, Louise
Ibranyi, Francis Joseph
Kelly, Helen S.
Neusner, Jacob
Palumbo, Louis Alexander
Shaw, Anne P.
Straton, Andrew Charles
Tordoff, Harry Slocum

SOUTH CAROLINA

Adams, L. Wayne
Amos, Marjorie R.
Arthur, Gladys Bean
Bakanic, Eunice Yvonne
Baldwin, Esther Lillian
Bates, Jamie Louise
Baum, Charles J.
Bell, Louise Matheson
Berger, Leonard
Black, Margaret C.
Blasius, Jack Michael
Boatman, Becky L.
Bowen, III, Ernest Thomas Harrison
Boykin, John Wyant
Brannock, Jr., Durant York

Brannon, Thomas J.
Brisbon, Bobby Leroy
Brister, Dougals Woodrow
Burrell, Ronald Eugene
Burton, William Joseph
Busha, Charles Henry
Byrd, Alma C. Weaver
Cain, Elise Gasque
Carpenter, William Levy
Carroll, Charles Edward
Cauthen, Deloris Helen
Chapman, Jr., James Alfred
Chavis, Earl B.
Cooper, Herbert Press
Cooper, Luther Grady
Cooper, Robert Perry
Covington, Rick
Crumbly, John Quantock
Curry, Mary Earle Lowry
Curry, Peden Gene
Davis, Mattie
Demetrious, Mary
Du Bose, Jerry Davis
Duncan, Inez Boyd
Erb, Richard L.
Evans, Beatrice Singleton
Ezell, Earl Geer
Figg, Jr., Robert McCormick
Flood, Dorothea Rehfuss
Floyd, Jr., Eldra Moore
Franklin, III, William H.
Frederick, Carolyn Essig
Friedman, Julian Richard
Fudenberg, H. Hugh
Fullwood, Joseph Michael
Gaillard, William Lucas
Gibbes, William Holman
Gill, Mrs. Elijah
Glassman, Armand B.
Goggins, Horace
Gordon, Ethel M.
Hardin, James Neal
Harrell, Flynn Thomas
Harrison, Anne Thelma
Harrison, Winnie M.
Hart, Elizabeth Johnson
Harvey, Harold Michael
Headstrom, Birger Richard
Heiser, Jr., Joseph Miller
Heyward, Joseph Edwsard
Hickson, Charlestine Dawson
Holland, Gene Grigsby
Howe, Evelyn Freeman
Hudson, Maxine Taylor
Hudson, Sallie Margaret
Huffman, John William
Hunter, Elizabeth Shealy
Hyder, Nancy Elizabeth
Jenkins, Mary Elizabeth
Katona, Anna Barbara
Keepler, Manuel
Kelley, Callie Imojean
Kelly, Margaret McLaurin
Kinney, Jr., William Light
Lang, Mary P.
Langer, Sandra Lois
Larisey, Marian Laura
Left, Joseph Daniel
McAbee, Alvin Aiken
McLafferty, Dee Hartmann
McMillian, Fredrina Tolbert
McMullen, Linda Addilene
Mann, James Robert
Means, Willerma Frazier
Mesic, Harry Randolph
Mims, Thomas Jerome
Mlott, Sylvester Roman
Morgan, Harold Clifford
Morris, R. Edwin
Mozingo, Margaret Johnson
Mullins, Jr., Edward Wade
Oliver, DeLoris Ham
Owens, Andrea Shirley
Owens, Hilda Faye

Parker, Jack DuPree
Parson, Hazel Snipes
Pate, William Wilson
Pratt, Samuel B.
Rakestraw, Gary Ray
Ravoira, James
Sandrapaty, Ramachandra Rao
Shah, Dinesh Ochhavlal
Shah, Nandkumar S.
Smelkinson, Marsha Ellen
Smiley, Gertrude C.
Smith, Charles Foster
Smith, John Gettys
Smith, Paul Abraham
Spence, Floyd Davidson
Stallings, R. W.
Stroman, Samuel David
Tangeman, Delbert Ray
Twiggs, Doris Davis
Tyler, Carolyn Smith
White, Harry Clifford
Whitesides, Glenn E.
Williams, Elsie M.
Williams, Johnny
Young, Edna Lestina

SOUTH DAKOTA

Ager, Alma Clyde
Briggs, Hilton, Marshall
Edelen, Mary Beaty
Finch, Bernie O.
Hayes, Harrold Henry
Helgeland, Les L.
Huls, James Joseph
Lamont, Frances Stiles
Lein, Charles D.
Mitten, Louis Otto
Pyles, Loran Ray
Shelver, Janet
Stofferahn, Kenneth Darrell

TENNESSEE

Allen, Donald Harold
Allen, Lullavee Rogers
Allison, William Landon
Anderson, Evelyn Rocella
Anderson, Jack Roy
Anderson, Thomas J.
Anderson, Vivian M.
Austin, Ella Frances Neal
Axton, Mae Boren
Baer, Charles Gordon
Baird, Jr., James Catchings
Baker, Kathryn Taylor
Baker, Norman Ottis
Balentine, III, John Leroy
Balnicky, Robert G.
Beets, Sara Sullenberger
Bell, Charmie Poore
Bell, Lorraine Petties
Bird, Agnes Thornton
Bisson, Wheelock Alexander
Blue, Edna Gossage
Bogdanowicz, Walter Andrew
Borthick, Mavis Ary
Bowers, Sharon Faye
Boyd, Sallie McFerren
Brady, Dale E.
Bridges, Dorothy Louise
Brooks, Virginia Walton
Bunten, Carolyn Melba
Bush, Wendall
Campbell, Agnes Knight
Carney, Frank Nelson
Cates, Paul William
Chapman, Michael Ray
Childress, Denver Ray

Chisolm, Charles Smith
Chu, Tien-Yung Julian
Clarke, Ann Neistadt
Clements, Louie O.
Clevenger, Ernest Allen
Cobb, James Petersen
Cockrell, Jr., Claude O'Flynn
Cockrell, Pearl Hand
Cooper, Robrt Elbert
Cotton, Cynthia Lee
Cougill, Mary Ann
Cox, Nancy Ingle
Craven, Douglas Charles
Crim, Claire Gamble
Crosser, Carolyn Hays
Crum, Patsy Young
Crum, Paul Edward
Cummings, Donald Eugene
Davis, Jr., John Clarence
Day, Randall L.
Dean, Jr., Robert Gayle
DeLay, Wayne Tilden
Deweese, Charles William
Donaldson, Fletcher William
East, Daniel Sidney
Elg, Robert George
Erwin, Jean Hocking
Fair, Vivian Rose
Feinstein, Abraham J.
Fisher, Howard L.
Floyd, Winford Ray
Ford, Harold Eugene
Foster, Edwin Powell
Fowler, Watson Rodney
Fox, Portland Porter
Freas, Annie Belle Hamilton
Freed, Curtis B.
Fry, Sr., Malcolm Craig
Gardner, E. Claude
Gilmore, James W.
Godwin, Paul Milton
Goethert, Bernhard Herman
Griggs, Patsy Ann
Gunter, Evelyn Coleman
Hampton, Ophina L.
Haslam, III, James A.
Hatmaker, Carolyn L.
Haun, Frances Conway
Heath, Barbara J.
Heilman, Marilyn Patton
Hibbett, Eugene P.
Hickman, Hoyt Leon
Hiles, Jr., William Gayle
Hill, James Mark
Hill, Malcolm Lansden
Hobbs, Sonia A. B.
Holcombe, Jr., Cressie Earl
Holloway, Evelyn Ann
Holloway, James Franklin
Howard, Noah Eugene
Howe, III, Lyman H.
Hunt, Lula Mai
Hurst, George Samuel
Inman, Jr., Franklin P.
Jenkins, Dorothy Davis
Joe, Young-Choon Charles
Johnson, Charlie James
Johnson, Jack R.
Jones, Brian Keith
Jones, Donald Collins
Jones, Elise J.
Jones, Kathleen Roberts
Jones, Lois Monahon
Jones, Jr., W. Allan
Katzman, Louise Brooks
Keever, Rosalie Ausmus
King, Alma Gean
King, Dennis R.
Klein, George
LaFon, John Walter
Lane, L. Quentin
La Prad, Quentin
Lawrence, Reggie Ray
Lawson, Verna Rebecca
Leete-Spaulding, Helen

Little, Mary E.
Long, Beatrice Powell
Love, Russell Jacques
Lyle, Mary Emma
Lynn, Sara Gaw
McCray, Robert Dewey
McInteer, Jim Bill
Makansi, Munzer
Mardis, Elma Hubbard
Marshall, John David
Meagher, Charles Franklin
Moran, Ann Elizabeth
Myhre, Trygve Chatham
Nakarai, Toyozo W.
Navratil, Robert Norman
Neff, Sr., Robert Lee
Norton, Dorothea Oliver
Ogilvie, Margaret Pruett
Olsen, Martha Brown
Overman, Frances Henson
Parham, Dorothy I.
Parker, Clyde J.
Partridge, Lloyd D.
Patterson, Virginia G.
Pierson, J. O.
Piper, Henry Burton
Prince, Arthur Hessel
Purkey, Roger Franklin
Purvis, Mary Belle
Ring, Larry Richard
Rives, James Henry
Roaden, Arliss Lloyd
Robbins, James Tate
Rogers, Mary Virginia
Ruane, Richard James
St. Charles, Paul W.
Scott, Charlotte Lawana
Seets, Ethel B.
Shackelford, Jr., Robert Paisley
Smith, Allie Maitland
Smith, Mary Isabelle
Snodderly, Louise Davis
Sordinas, Augustus
Sorrells, Frank Douglas
Soyars, Crystine Yates
Spear, Ruby Louise
Steele, Robert Miller
Stewart, Mary Estella
Suarez, Manuel L.
Swain, James O.
Swink, Esther Elaine

Tarwater, Ella Floyd
Thomas, Andrew Christie
Thomas, Wade Hamilton
Thorp, Dorothy F.
Tolleson, Sherwell Klawyn
Ulmer, William Douglas
Vaden, Norma Jean
Vaughan, John Nolen
Wade, Eugene Howard
Wanderman, Richad Gordon
Webster, Burnice Hoyle
Wilbun, Rubye Knowles
Williams, Beverly Jean
Williams, Harlan Bryan
Wilson, Nevada Pearl
Wooden, Josephine Ann
Wyatt, Hazel Frances
Zodhiates, Spiros G.

TEXAS

Abels, Mac Jon
Abraham, John P.
Adams, Ernestine
Adams, J. T.
Addison, Harold V.
Afuvai, Dianna Sue
Akin, Jr., Ralph Hardie
Albright, Cooper Eugene
Alexopoulos, Constantine John
Alford, Betty Bohon

Allen, Fred Edwin
Allred, William David
Almendarez, Yolanda Carbajal
Amir-Moez, Ali Reza
Anderson, Harriet Idell
Anderson, Owanah Pickens
Anderson, W. E.
Arnold, Marietta R.
Ashby, Jr., John Edmund
Asher, Fred M.
Asher, Vernon
Atkinson, D. Franklin
Atwater, Jr., Milton
Aue, Julia Newton
Ayers, III, Curtis Proper
Baggett, Jimmy D.
Bailey, Sr., Leo Lynn
Bain, Emily Johnston
Baker, Betty Ruth
Baker, Tommye Pitts
Baker, William Duncan
Balzer, Larry Dale
Barfield, Marguerite Irl
Barkley, G. Richard
Barlow, Jr., Herman Zulch
Barnes, Maggie Lue Shifflett
Barnhart, Joe Edward
Barrera, Eustolia R.
Barrientes, Guadalupe
Bartsch, Richard Allen
Bass, Charles Daniel
Bassett, Henrietta Elizabeth
Bateman, John Roger
Bates, Enid May
Battista, Orlando Aloysius
Bean, Alan L.
Beauchamp, Jeffery Oliver
Beck, Jr., Arthello
Beck, Hubert Frederick
Becker, Robert Dean
Beckstrom, Harriett Mae
Bell, Bilie Joe
Bentley, Kenton Earl
Bentley, Virgil Temple
Berg, Jerald Allan
Bergeron, Jimmie Leon
Berry, Charles Alden
Bettencourt, Margaret Rowan
Bieser, Albert Howard
Birkelbach, Mary Ruth
Birnell, Dorisa Leon
Bishop, Eliza H.
Bisquerra, Jose
Black, Shirley Jean
Black, Wendell Ray
Blackburn, William Kenton
Blair, Jr., John Doherty
Blakeney, Roger Neal
Blankinship, Ann Roberta
Blend, Henrietta Boronstein
Blessing, Vinnie Maleta
Blythe, Jr., William Jackson
Bodey, Gerald Paul
Bogle, Ennis Odelle
Bohmfalk, Johnita Schuessler
Boren, Edward Daniel
Bott, Harvey John
Bott, Margaret Deats
Bowen, Mildred Hazel
Boynton, Irene Ruth
Branham, Henry Hamilton
Braunagel, Helen May
Brelsford, Jeanne Kaye
Brennan, Richard Oliver
Brereton, Thomas F.
Brieger, Alton
Brightman, Tom C.
Britt, Chester Olen
Broeker, Annie Barr
Brown, Gwendolyn Ruth
Brown, Robert Wade
Bruff, Beverly Olive
Bruhn, John Glyndon
Bryan, Edward Raymond
Bryan, Jane Campbell

Hernandez, Cruz G.
Hill, Connie Virginia
Hill, Don Robert
Hill, Earline Sankey
Hill, Gerald Wayne
Hlavinka, Anthony Charles
Hoag, Charles Richard
Hobby, William Pettus
Hoffman, Elise
Hoffman, Garlyn Odell
Hohf, Jerome Chalmers
Holland, John Gordon
Hollin, Shelby W.
Hood, Ann Wallace
Houston, Lillian Pearl
Hoyt, Stephen Lee
Hubbard, Jere
Hubenak, Joe A.
Hudson, Gladys W.
Huey, Mary Evelyn
Huff, Cherry Lee
Huff, Ima Kelling
Hughes, Anne F.
Huibregtse, Doris Marie
Huibregtse, Harlan Howard
Hunter, Cannie Mae
Igbokwe, Emmanuel Chukwuemeka
Iverson, John W.
Jackson, Colon Ray
Jackson, Larry Dean
Jackson, Narah Thellis
Jahn, Sr., Edward Louis
James, Jr., Advergus Dell
Jasek, Diane Martha
Jenkins, Jr., Hays
Jenkins, Roy L.
Jennings, Robert Wendell
Jernigan, Nancy Franklin
Jobe, Jr., Madison Alphonso
Johnson, Eddie Bernice
Johnson, Elliott A.
Johnson, Frederick Dean
Johnson, Gary Reid
Johnson, Gordon, Gustav
Johnson, II, Jerry Kenneth
Johnson, Joe David
Johnson, Johnny Albert
Johnson, Mary Lynn
Johnson, Rita B.
Johnson, Thomas
Jones, Beulah Agnes
Jones, Kenneth W.
Jones, Viola
Jordan, W. A.
Jordan, William Thomas
Jorgensen, Charles Conrad
Kanda, Janice Humphrey
Kavanaugh, Robert Lee
Keele, Marjorie Sue
Keller, Ernestine Christy
Kennedy, Martin Travis
Kimbrough, Alynda Kay
King, Charles Willis
King, John Quill
Kistler, Ernest Losson
Klein, Mildred Lucille
Knowles, Thomas George
Kouw, Willy Alexander
Kreager, David J.
Kueker, John David
Kunitz, Sharon Lee
Kuntz, Rosalie Lois
Kurk, Anna Jean
Kwie, William Wie Liam
LaBelle, Donald Joseph
Lagow, Richard J.
Laing, Betty Jean
Lamb, Jr., Charles William
Lary, Eugene
Latham, William Peters
Latimer, Fred Hollis
Law, Ralph Aregood
Lawson, Theodore Earl
Leatherbury, Jr., John Raymond
LeBlanc, Vera Adore

Leiske, Robert Warren
Le Tourneau, Richard
Levine, Hernand Eugene
Lindner, Gayle Lee
Lindsay, Jon Stephen
Lipscomb, Peggy Elaine
Liu, David Ta-Ching
Lockett, Allan Neil
Lodhi, M. A. K.
Logan, Jr., Ralph Howard
Logan, Robert Allen
Longoria, Earlene Moorman
Lopez, Miguel
Lovvorn, Martin Craft
Lowry, K. Patricia
Luna, David G.
Luttrull, Ronald Ray
Lutz, Raymond Price
Lyda, Hap
Lyons, Sharon Lynn
Ma, Chen-Luan
Maa, Peter Sheng-Shyong
McCarley, Carolyn Josephine
McConn, James J.
McConnell, Dorothy F.
McCraney, Willard Kary
McCraw, Ronald Kent
McDaniel, Elizabeth L.
McDaniel, Jan L.
McDowell, Joslin David
McKinley, Jimmie Joe
McKnight, Harry F.
McMillan, Mae Frances
McMillian, Marie Y.
McMurry, Claudia Pauline
McNelly, Juanita R.
McPhaul, Lonnie Richard
McGill, Dennie W.
McIlveene, Charles Steele
McKay, Gwendolyn Sickles
McKay, Lawrence Brian
Mahood, Violeta Tanner
Manning, Walter Scott
Marcom, Orval Weldon
Martin, Everett S.
Martin, Lois E.
Martin, Richard Fred
Massengill, Ellen Webb
Matthews, Myreta Julia
Mattox, James Albon
Mays, Larry Wesley
Meador, Lenora Melissa
Mefferd, Jr., Roy B.
Melgar, Julio
Mergele, Harriette Gant
Merrill, Janet Louise
Milford, Murray Hudson
Miller, Jr., L. T.
Mitchell, Jerry Don
Mitchell, Lawrence Du-Wayne
Moberley, Connie M.
Moon, Willie Margaret
Moore, Colleen N.
Moore, Jr., Dalton
Moore, Doyle H.
Morgan, James Leland
Morris, Ida Toth
Morrison, Francine Reese
Morse, Samuel Alton
Moss, Tommye Atkinson
Mountain, Clifton Fletcher
Muller, Gene Alan
Murphy, John B.
Murphy, Natalie Owen
Naylor, Pleas Coleman
Neal, Timmie Ann
Newby, Charles David
Nicholas, Rose Catherine
Northrop, Monroe
Nowotny, Erhard Peter
Oakes, Herbert C.
Oberhauser, Joseph Francis
O'Neal, Mary Lois
O'Neill, Jr., Joseph Ignatius
Osterhaus, Leo B.

Palmer, Jeannette Ursula
Palmer, John David
Palmer, Ralph Thomas
Palmer, Raynor W.
Pamoja, Imani
Parker, Jacquelyn Susan
Parker, Thomas Lyles
Parks, Jackelee A.
Parrott, Barbara Marie
Patterson, Noble Festus
Patton, Celestel Hightower
Paul, Grace
Pearson, Jim Berry
Peel, Valerie Stovall
Pender, Pollard Eugene
Perram, Steven William
Perritt, Henry Hardy
Persch, 'Ruth Lucille
Pettit, Katherine Denshaw
Porter, Para Wright
Porter, Jr., William Howard
Potts, Donald Ralph
Potts, Nancy D.
Prather, Melvin
Price, Beth D.
Progar, Dorothy Ruth
Ptaszkowski, Jr., Stanley Edward
Pugh, Jessie Truman
Pugh, Julian Franklin
Qualls, Marshall David
Quisenberry, John Henry
Ragan, Bryant Timmons
Ragan, Seaborn Bryant
Ramsey, Elliott
Rasbury, Avery Guinn
Rentfro, Ethel Chilton
Reul, Jr., George John
Richardson, James Milton
Ries, Edward Richard
Robinett, Leslie White
Rodriguez, Johnny Gomez
Roetschke, Ronald Clay
Rogers, Lorene Lane
Roppolo, John Wayne
Rowe, Iris Guider
Rudenberg, Frank Hermann
Russell, Janalynn
Russell, Vicki Roseann
Saari, Dorothy Reynolds
Sanchez, Maria N.
Sanderlin, Eva May
Sassin, Carol Ann
Schaff, Robert Adair
Schwartz, Joseph
Sears, William John
Seelers, Fred Court
Settles, Carl E.
Shaffer, Ma Luisa
Shelton, June Pollet
Shoebothem, Ann White
Shorter, Louise R.
Shoulders, Harlan Robert
Sidwell, Derek
Silva, Jose Angel
Silva, Valeriano
Simpson, Wade Bland
Skinner, Walter Nathaniel
Skipworth, Eldon Robert
Smith, Johnny Eugene
Smith, Sr., Travis I.
Snipes, Felix Earl
Sol, Carlos David
Solberg, Jr., Ruell Floyd
Somerville, Hazel Doris
Spiller, Ellen Brubaker
Spinks, William Herschel
Stanley, Garland Maurice
Starnes, Paul M.
Statman, Jan B.
Steward, George Edmond
Stewart, Louis Alvin
Stodghill, Patsy Ann
Stokes, Vernon L.
Strothoff, Carl Frederick
Sweeten, Jr., John Marbrooks

Swiggett, Hal
Tadlock, Lila Clementa
Tevis, Betty W.
Thompson, Esther Lee
Tobias, Donna R.
Towles, Betty Lorraine
Towles, Charles Clifford
Trabulsi, Jr., Richard Joseph
Treadwell, III, Hubert Thomas
Trevino, Estella L.
Trevino, Lee Buck
Tschatschula, Marvin Edward
Tufts, Mary Ann
Tuma, June M.
Updegrove, Pat Ford
Vanzant, Jimmie Lou
Vickers, Mozelle Carver
Walker, Lucile Hill
Walker, Margaret Phillips
Wallace, J. B.
Wallace, III, John Francis
Ware, Eunice Letiria
Watkins, Jr., Albert Burrow
Wendtland, William W.
Werlin, Rosella Harwood
West, Ann
West, Iva Jean
Whittenburg, Grace Evelyn
Williams, Norma Painter
Williams, Parker
Williams, Roger
Willingham, Elizabeth Moore
Wilson, Hugh Edward
Winters, George Archer
Wolfert, Eileen Patricia
Wood, Jr., Robert W.
Woodall, Stella
Wright, Eugene Box
Wylie, Woodrow Wilson
Yeager, Freda Knoblett
Young, Eleanor Anne
Zaffirini, Judith
Zajicek, Charles Joseph
Zajicek, Sarita Herrera
Zufelt, David L.

UTAH

Adams, Beverly Decker
Aland, Kent Merrel
Ashworth, Brent Ferrin
Ashworth, Dell Shepherd
Belliston, Angus Henry
Berrett, Lamar Cecil
Birrell, Verla Leone
Bowles, David Stanley
Cheesman, Paul R.
Clark, Carol Lois
Clark, Dorothy Corbin
Clark, Ruth Millburn
Copeland, Drusilla Gail
Cowley, Au-Deane Shepherd
Crandall, Vern J.
Davis, France A.
de la Torre de San Braulio, IV,
    Enrique Carlos
de la Torre de San Braulio,
    Maria-Luisa
Dilley, Groegory D.
Dilley, William G.
Eyring, Henry
Fabian, Josephine Cunningham
Gregerson, Edna J.
Grenney, William James
Haddock, Jay Lamar
Hill, George B.
Johnson, Annette R. M.
Johnson, Ralph M.
Kovalenko, Virgil Nicholas
Kulkarni, Hemant
Kunz, McKay Heber
Loveridge, Della L.

McCloud, Susan Evans
Marsh, Bettie Jean
Oaks, Dallin Harris
Pollei, Paul Cannon
Robinson, Patricia Isabell
Robinson, Christine Hinckley
Salisbury, Frank B.
Saxena, Vinod Kumar
Simpkins, Mark Adelbert
Snyder, Gladys Reid
Stewart, Ora Pate
Stout, Mary Kathryn
Sweitzer, Harry Phillips
Turner, Ruth Elaine
Wallace, Glenn Walker
Wiser, Sara Poppleton
Woolf, Victor Vernon

VERMONT

Barret, Richard Carter
Francois, Ewart Ian
French, Ruth Evelyn
Garellick, Arwin F. B.
Hunter, William A.
Jackson, Edgar Newman
Johnson, Philip M.
Neiburg, Gladys Eudas
Nesti, Richard Pierre
Sexauer, Arwin, F. B.
Svetlova, Marina

VIRGIN ISLANDS

Burgess, Frances Marian
Cancryn, Addelita
Hatchette, Edwin Ersdale
Moorehead, George A.

VIRGINIA

Adams, Andrew Stanford
Adams, Jean
Aiken, Thomas Worthen
Al-Abdulla, Hamid M.
Anderson, Glroia B.
Anderson, Howard Palmer
Applegate, Harry Alvin
Armstrong, Jr., William Harrison
Baker, Daniel R.
Ball, Catherine Brodie
Ball, Harold G.
Bartlett, Joe
Baucom, James E.
Baxter, Robert Francis
Baxter, Ruth Howell
Beach, Sr., Paul Cole
Bennett, Bonnie C.
Bergsten, Fred G.
Bernhardt, John Peter Ashley
Binford, Linwood Thomas
Birch, Robert Louis
Biship, Sid G.
Blunt, Jane Antoinette Lomas
Boiter, Kenneth Alan
Booker, Henry Marshall
Books, Earl James Eugene
Borsi, Peter N.
Brand, Frances Christian
Breaux, John B.
Broderick, Grace Margaret
Brown, Jr., James Thomas
Bryant, Sylvia Leigh
Bulcao, Douglas William
Burmahln, Elmer Fred
Burnette, Jerry Edward

Busbee, Elizabeth Divers
Byler, Gary C.
Cannon, Howard W.
Cantrell, Robert Wendell
Carlton, Ruby Stewart
Carr, Jess
Carter, Jr., Leonard Clyde
Carvalho, Julie Ann
Cayce, Hugh Lynn
Chadhuri, Tapan Kuman
Chopra, Kuldip Prakash
Christiansen, Marjorie Miner
Clark, James Arthur
Clark, Wayne Douglas
Cline, Ray Steiner
Cochran, Samuel Lynn
Cooper, Lee P.
Cordaro, John Benedict
Cornett, Leota Rae
Couch, James Vance
Cox, III, Edwin
Coxe, Nelson Y.
Creekmore, Frederick Hillary
Cregger, Mildred Rodgers
Crotts, Stephen Michael
Crowder, Camellia Huffman
Culberson, Randall Edward
Currey, Virginia May
Cuthrell, Carl Edward
Damon, Carolyn Eleanore
Daniel, Jr., Robert Williams
Darracott, Halvor Thomas
Dash, James Ellis
Davis, Agnes Marion
Davis, Robert Pickens
Dean, Halsey Albert
Dean, Lydia Margaret Carter
Deaton, Fae Adams
De Genaro, Guy Joseph
De Genaro, Jennie Jennings
Dent, Myra Lena
Dewton, Johannes Leopold
Dillon, Viloa May
Downing, Thomas Nelms
Doyle, Brian Bowles
Draper, Cecil Norman
Draper, Marjorie F.
Dudley, William M.
Durrett, Madison Winfrey
Earman, John Gary
Eggleston, Louise Mavis Way
Ernouf, Anita B.
Ethell, Jeffrey Lance
Evans, John Derby
Filicky, Joseph George
Fishburn, Charles George
Fisher, Charles Harold
Fitton, Jr., H. Nelson
Fleming, Deryl Ray
Francis, Elizabeth Lincoln
Freeman, Hugh Ward
Freeman, James Goodrich
Friedman, Lora R.
Friend, Edith Overton
Funk, Lisa Ann
Gandy, Gerald Larmon
Gangstad, Edward Otis
Gardner, William Leonard
Gibson, Charles Walter
Gill, Robert Monroe
Goff, Lousella Holland
Gonano, John Roland
Griffith, Margaret Arnold
Grinstead, Audrey Hudson
Guerrant, Doris Jeanne
Gurnsey, Ronald Allen
Hackenberg, Larry Michael
Hadgopoulos, Saralyn Poole
Hagood, Lacy Edmunds
Hammett, Eugene Kirby
Hamner, Sharon Boone
Hancock, Sr., George H.
Hankla, Velma Cash
Harbour, Patricia Moore

Hardley, Gary Kaye
Harllee, John
Harris, Nancy Edwards
Hauxwell, Gerald Dean
Havelos, Sam George
Hilldrup, Lucille Penney
Hobbs, Cecil
Hoekstra, Harold Derk
Holcomb, Dorothy Turner
Hopewell, Harry Lynn
Hopkins, Margaret Lail
Houtmann, Jacques Georges
Hudson, Elizabeth Desmond
Hudson, Worth McLane
Huebner, Richard Allen
Huffman, Phyllis
Hugin, Adolph Charles
I'Anson, Lawrence Warren
James, Allix Bledsoe
Jenkins, Clara Barnes
Jenkins, Jr., Robert Warls
Johnson, Jean Ationell
Johnson, Larry W.
Jones, Patricia
Judy, William Lee
Karafyllakis, Antonios A.
Kaufman, Irene Mathias
Keder, Virko
Keesling, Karen R.
Keith, Virgie Irene
Kellam, Jeffrey Stanton
Kiko, Philip George
Kimmitt, Joseph Stanley
King, Algin Braddy
King, Joyce Pauline
Kittrell, Flemmie P.
Kurtz, S. James
Lacey, V. Duane
Lanciano, Jr., Claude Olwen
Layman, John Whitney
Lazarow, Arthur
Leitch, Alma
Lewis, Charlton Scott
Link, Amelia Gwin
Lipovich, II, George Jay
Long, Eula Kennedy

Mabe, David Linwood
McAlister, James Douglas
McCormick, Michael Patrick
McCoul, Vicky Jean
Maddox, Jr., Robert Lee
McGavock, Polly P.
McInturff, Ernest Robert
Madeira, Dashiell Livingston
Madry-Taylor, Jacquelyn
Martin, Henry Lawrence
Marx, Gary D.
Massey, Donald Wayne
Meiselman, E. Anne
Merricks, David Lee
Miller, Fannie Roll
Miller, Michael Douglass
Mitchell, Gregory Jerome
Moomaw, G. Dunbar
Moore, Doris Elizabeth
Moore, Sr., James Kenneth
Moore, Lorena Lauterbach
Morlang, Barbara Blauvelt
Morris, Harriet Jones
Motter, Roberta Lee
Mueller, William Fegley
Murray, Philip Allen
Neeper, Ralph Arnold
Nickols, John
Norris, Ruby Lee
Nuckels, Robert Lee
O'Dell, V. Edwin
Palmer, Forrest Charles
Parker, Dorothy
Parker, James Lee
Paterson, Lois Stone
Payne, Sandra Glenda
Pendell, Elmer
Pendleton, Roger Lee

Perlik, Jr., Charles Andrew
Peterson, James Neal
Petry, James Wesley
Pinion, Richard Lewis
Pollard, III, William Francis
Price, David Lee
Quigg, Dorothy Quay
Redd, Vivian Cortezza
Reinl, Harry Charles
Rice, Ronald Lee
Roberts, Louise Venable
Roberts, Phyllis Vreeland
Robertson, Ralph Byron
Ryder, Georgia Atkins
Sakhadeo, Shrihari S.
Saliba, Selma G.
Sansaver, James Leroy
Sehgal, Robert
Seward, Estelle Beale
Shirk, Frank Charles
Singh, Tara
Sneade, Daniel Carson
Spencer, Chauncey Edward
Spradlin-Hanson, Frances
Steele, James E.
Stevens, Genevieve Johnson
Stevens, Mary Coggin
Swartz, Christian LeFevre
Telleen, Judy Gertrude
Tillinghast, Meta Ione
Trudinger, L. Paul
Vache, Claude Charles
Vance, Hubert R.
Vass, Larry Ivan
Venable, Josephine Dott
Walker, Eunice Arnaud
Walsh, Nancy Lee
Weedon, William Stone
Wei, Diana Yun-Dee
Williams, Ira Joseph
Yadao, Alex Peralta
Zamora, Mario D.
Zurcher, Jr., Louis Anthony

WASHINGTON

Anderson, Gordon Lee
Barrows, Margaret Bentley Hamilton
Bechtel, Jean Robinson
Beck, Clifford Wallace
Bethel, James Samuel
Blahovich, Joseph Sameul
Brown, Barbara June
Buchanan, Jerry Major
Burnett, Alta Hazel
Christian, Gary Dale
Cook, Blanche Helen McLane
Coole, Walter Alton
Coombs, C'Ceal P.
Corr, Michael William
Cremora, Gouda
Crisman, Mary Frances B.
Davis, Charles Ronald
Davis, Julia Elizabeth
Fenske, Virginia E.
Fowler, Betty Janmae
Fudala, Janet Barker
Gallagher, Patrick J.
Garrison, Etta Josephine
Garrison, William Dougals
Gessel, Stanley P.
Gies, Frederick John
Godfrey, Dorothy Doud
Gridley, Beryl Smith
Griffith, Charles Allen
Hansen, June Allshouse
Holmes, Thomas Hall
Houston, Harry Rollins
Jackson, W. A. Douglas
Jensen, Harry Robert
Kathren, Ronald L.
Kenny, Bettie Ilene

King, Joseph Jerone
Klein, James Albert
Knapp, Mary Elizabeth
Lauglin, Joy Judge
Lewis, Loraine Ruth
Liebe, Ruth Dorothy
Lonneker, ArLeen Patterson
McLeron, Lee Marie
McReynolds, Neil Lawrence
McFarlin, Barbara Ann
Michaelsen, Shirley Ann
Milander, Henry Martin
Miller, Earl Beauford
Mscichowski, Lois I.
Murillo-Rohde, Ildaura
Murphy, Herta Albrecht
Nicholls, James Harold
Olson, Robert William
Ostrom, Cyrus Warren
Parlotz, Robert David
Peterson, William David
Phibbs, Philip Monford
Powell, Donnie Melvin
Powell, Willa Dene
Reel, Rita M.
Reifler, Henrietta
Schauss, Alexander George
Schiller, John A.
Schuetz, Gordon William
Selby, John Marshall
Sletager, Janice Rae
Smedvig, Egil
Smith, Helen Brekke
Smith, Samuel J.
Velamoor, Sashadri Rajagopal
Waddell, Robert Malcolm
Williams, C. E.
Woods, Margaret Staeger
Wynne, Eastella Jane
Yanosko, Elizabeth Juanita

WEST VIRGINIA

Ayers, Anne Louise
Babb, Thomas Jackson
Bailes, Tressie Nona
Balanis, Constantine A.
Baylor, Richard P.
Briggs, Everett Francis
Burdette, Patricia Ann
Corpuz-Ambrosio, Erlinda Balancio
De La Pena, Cordell Amado
Derrington, Kenneth Edward
Devereaux, Elizabeth Baker
Dodds, Edna Corder
Dulaney, Allena Faye
Dulaney, Annie Harvey
Eddington, Alan Michael
Fairbanks, Harold Vincent
Foose, Don Holt
Fowler, Sandra
Frantz, Ann Browning
Glazer, Frederic Jay
Hannum, Alberta Pierson
Herndon, Judith A.
Hinkle, Blanche Elizabeth
Howard, Martha Cummins
Lackey, Marilyn Louise
Leasure, Betty Jean
Lockhart, James Lemuel
Lovejoy, Dallas Landon
Ludwig, Ray Woodrow
McClanahan, Louise Ann
McCullough, John Phillip
Martin, III, Clarence E.
Maxwell, Robert E.
Molina, Maria Teresa
Myers, Mary Pell
Neville, Genevieve Jewel
Noble, Alma Nease
Peterson, Frederick Alvin
Scott, John Edward

Shrivastava, Krishna Kumar
Simpson, Ervin Peter
Snyder, Robert Martin
Stanley, Charles Richard
Van Puffelen, John Herman
Wiedbusch, Larry

WISCONSIN

Bakken, Henry H.
Barsi, Louis Michael
Bartel, Bruce Allan
Biever, Bruce Francis
Buchanan-Davidson, Dorothy Jean
Freiman, Marshall
Gade, Clifford W.
Gruberg, Martin
Harrold, William Eugene

Heinzen, Raymond Frank
Heybl, Laurice
Kendro, Richard Joseph
Kitchen, Dennis Lee
Matty, Richard P.
Nikolai, Lorraine C.
O'Brien, Elizabeth Jones
O'Brien, Francis Tucker
O'Brien, Warren Sylvester
O'Donnell, David Richardson
Refior, Everett Lee
Strandell, Marjatta
Swanson, David H.
van der Poel, Cornelius
Woon, Paul Sam
Yost, Charles Edward
Zachariah, Mathew
Zeimet, Edward Joseph

WYOMING

Eskens, Esther Pauline
Fox, Abraham H.
Francis, Shirley A.
Glatz, Myron Lee
Goddard, Dean Allen
Hahon, Nicholas
Hammond, Russell Irving
Haygood, Carolyn Marie
Hess, Irene Rose
Higginbotham, Doris Ross
Homer, Frederick D.
Hord, Violet Catherine
Hursh, John Ray
Kamback, Marvin Carl
Kinney, James W.
Lantz, Everett D.
Lynde, Joseph Ernest
Movsky, Myron B.
Perryman, Bruce Clark
Smetak, Larry Anthony
Sowerwine, Jr., Elbert Orla

During editorial scheduling, the following listees have recently relocated outside the geographical scope of this publication. All have contributed more than a majority of dedicated efforts to the nation, either through professional or personal involvements.

AUSTRIA

Gill, Trudi H.

CANADA

Colby, Robert Lester
Dow, Marguerite Ruth
Drapeau, Jean
Firestone, O. John
Franklyn, Gaston Joseph

Hartling, Marjorie-Anne
Holland, Ray G. L.
Jeremiah, Lester Earl
King, Ethel Marguerite
Kirkland-Casgrain, Claire
O'Connor, Mary Catherine
Olah, Susan Rose
Pasternak, Eugenia
Pearson, Norman
Rodkiewicz, Czeslae Mateusz
Sablatash, Mike
Salvary, Stanley C. W.
Schreyer, Edward Richard
Swamy, Mayasandra N. S.
Tremblay, Jean-Louis
Vachon, Louis-Albert
Veale, Warren Lorne

KENYA

Cole, William Joseph

NICARAGUA

Eudaly, Jr., Nate

SWITZERLAND

Baker, Carl Gwin

The **State-Locator Index** is one of the Institute's newest and most functional publication innovations. This **Index** guarantees easy accessibility of all individuals listed in this publication, presented according to alphabetical positions by separate states.

Appendix II

Charlotte Mae Brett, F.A.B.I., L.F.A.B.I.
218 East 4th Street, Apartment 4A, Spencer, Iowa 51301
Family Genealogist; Retired Educator

Juanita Sumner Brightwell, F.A.B.I.
1037 Hancock Drive, Americus, Georgia 31709
Retired Director of Library Services, Lake Blackshear Regional Library,
Americus; Former President, Georgia Library Association
Researcher, Administrator, Librarian

Sylvia Leigh Bryant, F.I.B.A., L.A.A.B.I.
Route 5, Box 498A, Madison Heights, Virginia 24572
Editor-Publisher, *The Anthology Society*
Poet, Free-Lance Writer, Editor

Frederick D. Byington, Ed.D., F.A.B.I.
1500 Locust Street, No. P305, Philadelphia, Pennsylvania 19102
Director, Byton Private School, Philadelphia
Administrator, Educator, Consultant

Juan B. Calatayud, M.D., F.A.C.A.
1712 Eye Street, NW, Suite 1004, Washington, D.C. 20006
Professor, George Washington University School of Medicine;
Private Physician

Joseph Peter Cangemi, M.D., F.A.C.A.
Psychology Department, Western Kentucky University, Bowling Green,
Kentucky 42101
Professor of Psychology, Western Kentucky University
Management Consultant, Researcher, Educator

Avery G. Church, F.A.A.A., F.A.B.I., F.I.A.P.
351 Azalea Road, Apartment B-28, Mobile, Alabama 36609
Research Staff and Board of Directors, The Sociological and Anthropological
Services Institute, Inc.; Lecturer in Anthropology, University of Southern
Alabama
Educator, Scientist, Poet

C. Eugene Coke, Ph.D.
F.R.S.C., F.A.B.I., F.S.D.C., F.T.I., F.C.I.C.
26 Aqua Vista Drive, Ormond Beach, Florida 32074
President, Coke and Associate Consultants
Researcher, Author, Scientist, International Authority on Man-Made Fibers

Vera Estelle Sellars Colyer
Post Office Box 70, Grandfield, Oklahoma 73546
President-Agent, Colyer Insurance Agency, Inc.

James F. L. Connell, Ph.D., C.P.G.
Box 144, Montevallo, Alabama 35115
Professor of Geology and Geography; Independent Consulting Geologist

Grover F. Daussman, Ph.D.
1910 Colice Road, SE, Huntsville, Alabama 35801
Engineering Consultant; Former United States Government Engineer

Elias D. Dekazos, Ph.D.
408 Sandstone Drive, Athens, Georgia 30605
Plant Physiologist, R. Russell Agriculture Research Center

Veena B. Desai, M.D.
M.R.C.O.G., F.A.C.O.G., F.A.C.S., F.I.C.S.
110 Court Street, Portsmouth, New Hampshire 03801
Private Practice of Obstetrics and Gynecology

The Prince Vladimir E. Doggett-Eletsky
The Chalet of Runsulpag, 799 Mountain Circle, Tahoe Vista, California 95732
President, Doggett and Doggett Enterprises
Business Executive

Mildred C. Dugan, M.D.
7158 Tamarack Road, Fort Worth, Texas 76116
Physician

Gertrude Ballou Dunbar
2413 Brook Road, Charlottesville, Virginia 22901
Historian, Genealogist

James Don Edwards, Ph.D.
School of Accounting, College of Business Administration, University of
Georgia, Athens, Georgia 30602
J. M. Tull Professor of Accounting, University of Georgia
Researcher, Educator

Henri C. Flesher, D.D. (Ret.), B.L.D., Ph.D., F.I.B.C., F.A.B.I.
Route 1, Box 218-11 West Scorpio, Silverbell Estates, Eloy, Arizona 85231
Retired Publisher and Journalist

Sandra Fowler, F.A.B.I., L.A.A.B.I.
West Columbia, West Virginia 25287
Associate Editor, *Ocarina* and *The Album*
Editor, Publisher

Lorraine S. Gall, Ph.D., F.A.B.I.
6812 Academy, Apartment 605, Houston, Texas 77025
President, Bacti-Consult Associates; Senior Microbiological Consultant, Private Business
Researcher, Space Scientist, Educator

Carrie Leigh George, Ph.D., M.Div., Ed.S., D.Rel.
1652 Detroit Avenue, NW, Atlanta, Georgia 30314
Senior Counselor and Assistant Professor of Curriculum and Instruction, Georgia State University; Ordained Clergywoman
Researcher, Consultant, Educator

Vivian W. Giles
Post Office Box 31, Danville, Virginia 24541
Owner-Manager, Vivian Giles Business Services

Antonio Giraudier, F.A.B.I., L.P.A.B.I.
215 East 68th Street, New York City, New York 10021
Writer, Author, Poet, Artist

Admiral A. B. Hammett
2500 East Las Olas Boulevard, Apt. 705, Fort Lauderdale, Florida 33302
Retired United States Naval Reserve Commander

Marjorie S. Hooper, L.H.D., L.F.A.B.I.
101 Skye Loch Drive, West, Dunedin, Florida 33528
Retired Research Associate for Visual Disabilities Track of the College of Education, Florida State University; Editor-Emeritus, American Printing House for the Blind
Researcher, Editor1Publisher Management and Production

Lewis Daniel Houck, Jr., Ph.D., L.F.I.B.A., F.A.B.I.
11111 Woodson Avenue, Kensington, Maryland 20795
Project Leader for Economic Research Service, United States Department of Agriculture
Management Consultant, Author, Educator, Businessman

Geraldine Grosvenor Hunnewell, D.L.
F.I.B.A., F.A.B.I., A.F.S., F.T.L.A., F.I.P.A.
10799 Sherman Grove Avenue, No. 39, Sunland, California 91040
Researcher, Naturalist, Author, Scholar

Anna M. Jackson, Ph.D., A.B.P.P., F.A.B.I.
4200 East Ninth Avenue, Box C258, Denver, Colorado 80262
Director of Medical Student Advisory Office and Associate Professor of Psychiatry, University of Colorado; Clinical Psychologist
Researcher, Educator

Greta Kempton, F.A.B.I.
14 East 75 Street, New York City, New York 10021
National Portrait Artist

Catherine Earl Bailey Kerr, L.P.A.B.I.
14-12 West Hendricks, Roswell, New Mexico 88201
Owner-Manager, Kerr International School of Art
International Artist

Mozelle Bigelow Kraus, Ed.D., L.A.A.B.I.
1660 L Street, NW, Suite 212, Washington, D.C. 20036
Private Psychology Practice

Enrique Roberto Larde, M.G.A., F.A.B.I.
PO Box 2992, Old San Juan, Puerto Rico 00903
Director and Treasurer, South Continental Insurance Agency, Inc.; Director
and Executive Vice President, Corporacion Insular de Seguros; Director and
First Vice President, Asociacion de Companias de Seguros Incorporadas en
Puerto Rico, Inc.
Researcher, Business Executive

Shu-Tien Li, Ph.D., P.E., Eng.D.
F.A.S.C.E., F.A.A.A.S., F.A.C.I.
Post Office Drawer 5505, Orange, California 92667
Founder and President, Li Institution of Science and Technology; President,
World Open University
Researcher, Educator, Administrator, Consultant

Florence E. H. Little, F.I.B.A, F.A.B.I., L.F.A.B.I.
1093A Belle Terre Drive, La Place, Louisiana 70068
Genealogist, Educator, Musician

Ruby E. Stutts Lyells, L.H.D.
1116 Isiah Montgomery Street, Jackson, Mississippi 39203
Federal Jury Commissioner, United States District Court, Southern District of
Mississippi; Trustee, Prentiss Institute
Researcher, Writer, Librarian

Krishna Shankar Manudhane, Ph.D., F.A.B.I.
7839 Stonehill Drive, Cincinnati, Ohio 45230
Vice President, Research and Development, ICN Pharmaceuticals, Inc.
Researcher

Robert C. McGee, Jr., F.A.B.I.
Route 2, Box 396, River Road, Richmond, Virginia 23233
President, Swan, Inc.
Business Executive, Aeronautical Engineer, Consultant, Administrator

Rod McKuen
Post Office Box G, Beverly Hills, California 90213

Poet, Composer-Lyricist, Author, Performer
President: Stanyan Records, Discus New Gramophone Society, Mr. Kelly
Productions, Montcalm Productions, Stanyan Books, Cheval Books, Biplane
Books, Rod McKuen Enterprises

Herbert B. Mobley, D.D., L.P.A.B.I.
Post Office Box 165, Summit Station, Pennsylvania 17979

President and Editor-in-Chief, Jan-Bert Press, Inc.; Emeritus Pastor, St.
Mark's (Brown's) United Church of Christ, Summit Station

Irving Morris, M.L.S., F.A.B.I.
21-15 34th Avenue, Apt. 2D, Long Island City, New York 11106

Educator and Library Media Specialist, L. D. Brandeis High School Annex,
New York City

Makio Murayama, Ph.D.
5010 Benton Avenue, Bethesda, Maryland 20814

Research Biochemist, National Institute of Health

Virginia Simmons Nyabongo, Ph.D.
936 34th Avenue North, Nashville, Tennessee 37209

Professor Emeritus of French, Research, Tennessee State University
Researcher, Author, Educator

George Robert Overby, Ph.D., F.A.B.I., L.P.A.B.I.
5927 Windhover Drive, Orlando, Florida 32805

Chancellor, Freedom University; Founder, President, The International
Association of Christian Education
Author, Lecturer, Consultant, Educator

Loislee M. Parker, Ed.D.
1601 South Shade Avenue, Sarasota, Florida 33579

Educator

D. C. Parks, F.A.B.I.
2639 Belle Terrace, Bakersfield, California 93304

Founder, President, Addictive Drugs Educational Foundation
Consultant, Counselor, Analyst

Sartell Prentice, Jr.
1404 Chamberlain Road, Pasadena, California 91103

Independent Lecturer and Consultant on Incentive Employee Profit Sharing
Plans

Jarnagin Bernard Ricks, F.A.B.I.
Post Office Box 3336, Main Office, Shreveport, Louisiana 71103
Writer, Composer, Professional Astrologer, International Clairvoyant

Roland B. Scott, M.D.
1723 Shepherd Street, NW, Washington, D.C. 20011
Professor of Pediatrics and Child Health and Director Sickle Cell Center, Howard University
Educator, Administrator

Delphia Frazier Smith, F.I.P.S.
20229th Street, Mammoth Spring, Arkansas 72554
Writer, Poet, Artist, Musician

Herbert H. Tarson, Ph.D., F.A.B.I.
4611 Denwood Road, La Mesa, California 92041
Vice President for Academic Affairs, National University, San Diego
Researcher, Educator

Andrew B. Thompson, Jr., F.I.B.A., L.A.A.B.I.
Post Office Box 3008, Montgomery, Alabama 36109
Vice President, General Manager, Editor, National Photo Pricing Service, Inc.

Basil P. Toutorsky, D.Mus., L.P.A.B.I., F.A.B.I., L.F.I.B.A.
1720 16th Street, NW, Washington, D.C. 20009
Director, Toutorsky Academy of Music
Professor, Composer, Pianist

Aliyah W. M. von Nussbaumer, Ph.D., D.Th.
11110 Hazen Road, Houston, Texas 77072
Research Librarian, Published Author, Educator

Marian Williams, L.F.A.B.I.
1289 Mathews Avenue, Lakewood, Ohio 44107
Free-Lance Writer and Poet, Researcher

Roger Lodge Wolcott
4796 Waterloo Road, Atwater, Ohio 44201
Former Specialist in Aeromechanical Research and Development, Engineering Department, Goodyear Aerospace Corporation, Akron; Secretary, The Lighter Than Air Society
Aviation Pioneer, Inventor, Association Executive

Stella Woodall, D.Lit., F.A.B.I.
206 Patricia Drive, Junction, Texas 76849

President-Director, Stella Woodall Poetry Society International; Editor-Publisher, *Adventures in Poetry Magazine*
Author, Editor, Publisher, Poet

Howard John Zitko, D.D., D.L.
711 East Blacklidge Drive, Tucson, Arizona 85719

President and Chairman of the Board, World University

Appendix III

Roster of Fellow Members
American Biographical Institute

Christian Campbell Abrahamsen
Bergljot Abrahamson
Diane M. Abrahamson
Anthony (Tony) Salvatore Accurso
Louise Ida Acker
Cecile Neomi Walker Adams
Rev. Leroy Adams
Harold V. Addison
Steven V. Agid
Hugh Stephen Ahern
John Madison Airy
Ralph Hardie Akin, Jr.
Esther Ann Teel Albright
Signe Henreitte Johnson Aldeboigh
Larry J. Alexander, Ed.D.
Byron Paul Allen
Edgard Yan Allen
John Eldridge Allen
Rev. Thomas G. Allen
Frank E. Allison, Sr.
Mujahid Al-Sawwaf, Ph.D.
Peter C. Altner, M.D.
Thelma L. Alvarez
Ali Reza Amir-Moez, Ph.D.
Doris Ehlinger Anderson, J.D.
Gloria Long Anderson, Ph.D.
Harriet Idell Anderson
Herbert Frederick Anderson, M.D.
Rozena Hammond Anderson
Ursula M. Anderson, M.D., D.P.H., M.R.C.S.,
    L.R.C.P., D.C.H., F.A.A.P.
George Fredrick Andreasen, D.D.S.
Hyrum Leslie Andrus, Ph.D.
Walter Thomas Applegate, Ph.D., D.D.
Mahmoud Zaky Arafat, Ph.D.
Pedro Alfonzo Araya
Wendell Sherwood Arbuckle, Ph.D.
Violet Balestreri Archer, D.Mus.
Sylvia Argow
Floro Fernando Arive, M.D.
Edward James Arlinghaus
Claris Marie Armstrong
Naomi Young Armstrong, D.H.L.
William Harrison Armstrong, Jr.
Kenneth D. Arn, M.D.
James Edward Arnett, Ph.D.
Dwight Lester Arnold, Ph.D.
Florence M. Arnold
Edward Lee Arrington, Jr.
Albert J. Arsenault, Jr.
Franzi Ascher-Nash
Dell Shepherd Ashworth
Chuck Aston
Katharine Oline Aston
Grace Marie Smith Auer
Aurelia Marie Richard Augustus
Beryl David Averbook, M.D.
William Marvin Avery, Jr.
Florence M. Gotthelf Axton, Ph.D.
Roderick Honeyman Aya
Anne Louise Ayers
James Wilbur Ayers
Catherine Beatrice Aymar
Edith Annette Aynes

Peter J. Babris, Ph.D.
Rosalie Wride Bacher
Manson Harvey Bailey, Jr.
Daljit S. Bais
Judge Anna Dorthea Baker

Elsworth Fredrick Baker
John A. Baker
Justine Clara Baker
Roberta Rymer Balfe
Howard Balin, M.D.
Iris Georgia Ball
Louis Alvin Ball
Joseph G. Ballard, Sr.
Susan Lee Ballew
Betsy Ross Anne Ballinger
Lloyd Kenneth Balthrop, Th.D.
Barbara A. Bancroft
Helen Virginia Bangs
Candace Dean Bankhead
Jean Bare
Vivian Miller Barfield
Alexander John Barket
Herman Zulch Barlow, Jr., Ed.D.
George Hugh Barnard, J.D.
Frances Ramona Barnes
Marylou Riddleberger Barnes, Ed.D.
Melver Raymond Barnes
Charlotte A. Barr
Nona Lee Barr
Kathleen Corlelia Parker Barriss
Margaret Bentley Hamilton Barrows
Mihaly Bartalos, M.D.
Arline Ruth Barthlein
Larry H. Barton
Florence S. Bartova
G. Robert Bartron, M.D.
Nina M. Barwick
Henrietta Elizabeth (Beth) Bassett
Harold Ronald Eric Battersby
R. Ray Battin, Ph.D.
Ethel Hines Battle
Carl Edward Baum, Ph.D.
Donald Otto Baumbach, Ph.D.
Magdalena Charlotte Bay ('Magdalena')
Everett Minot Beale
Gary Floyd Beard
Donald Ray Beason
Roberta Ann Beaton
Mary Dawn Thomas Beavers
Adeline C. Becht
Harriet Perry Beckstrom, D.O.
Rexine Ellen Beecher
Phyllis Tenney Belcher
Lenore Breetwor Belisle, Ed.D.
George Wilbur Bell
James Milton Bell, M.D., F.A.P.A., F.A.C.P.
Harold James Bender
John A. Benedict
Christopher Aaron Bennett
Margarita Orelia Benskina
Betty Jones Benson
Dailey J. Berard
Julia Irene Berg
Muriel Mallin Berman
Harmon Gordon Berns
Leonard Bernstein
Frank Weldon Berry, Sr.
Irving Aaron Berstein
Norman M. Better, Ed.D.
Clifford Allen Betts
Laura Elizabeth Beverly
Brian William Louis Bex
Awinash P. Bhatkar, Ph.D.
Henrietta DeWitte Bigelow
Annette C. Billie

Novella Stafford Billions
Carol H. Bird
Donald Raymond Black
Harold Stephen Black
Willa Brown Black
Joe Ronald Blackston
Frank Blair
Ilene Mills Blake
Terri Blake (AKA-Theresa Blalack)
William H. Blakely, Jr.
Roger Neal Blakeney, Ph.D.
B. Everard Blanchard, D.Div.
Ronald Gail Blankenbaker, M.D.
Maija Sibilla Blaubergs
Gustav Henry Bliesner
Edna J. Gossage Blue
Wendell Norman Bodden
Carmen Page Bogan
Johnita Schuessler Bohmfalk
Gerald L. Boland
Oran Edward Bollinger, Ph.D.
Robert Howard Boltz
Suzanne Poljacik Bolwell
Loraine Mary Bomkamp
Dr. Floyd A. Bond
Drew Adrian Bondy
Tal D. Bonham, Th.D.
Ophelia Calloway Bonner
Earl James Eugene Books
Emily Clark Kidwell Linder Boone
Myron Vernon Boor
Mary Elizabeth Borst
Metodij Boretsky, Ph.D.
Raymond Paul Botch
Shirley Marie Oakes Bothwell
Harvey John Bott
Wilhelmina Wotkyns Botticher
Badi Mansour Boulous, M.D., Ph.D.
Mary Bancroft Boulton
Jean A. H. Bourget
Geoffrey Howard Bourne, D.Sc., D.Phil.
Gloria Diane Parrish Bousley, Ph.D.
Mildred Hazel Bowen
Theodore Stanley Boyer
Frances L. Boykin
Mervell Winzer Bracewell, R.N., DR.P.H.
Margaret Anowell Brame, Jr. II
Sister M. Teresa Bramsiepe
Wayne Keith Brattain
Helen Raymond Braunschweiger
Pius Brazauskas
Ruby Blanche Franklin Breads
Virginia Huffman Break
Arnold Brekke, Ph.D.
George Matthew Brembos
Lynn D. Brenneman
Charlotte Mae Brett
Anne A. Brevetti
Virginia Rose Alexander Brewer
Ethel Craig Brewster
A. Morgan Brian, Jr.
Joan Briggs
Juanita Sumner Brightwell
Angie R. Brinkley
Willis R. Brinkmeyer
Bobby Leroy Brisbon, Ed.D.
Jan Leeman Brooks
June Brooks Brooks
Margaret Alyce Page Brooks
Edith Petrie Brown, M.D.
Edward Kinard Brown, Ed.D.
Gwendolyn Ruth Brown
Hazel Claire MacCalla Brown
Jerry Joseph Brown
Joseph Leandrew Brown
Louis Daniel Brown, J.D.
Luther Daniel Brown, Ph.D.
Thomas Cartwright Brown
Thomas Lewis Brown
May L. Brumfield
Nancy Louise Bruner
Lillian Sholtis Brunner
Jacob Franklin Bryan, III

Elizabeth Ann Bryant
Kathryn Henriette Bryant
Richard John Brzustowicz
Wesley F. Buchele
Henry L. Buckardt
Bronius Budriunas
Richard S. Budzik
Vera Mildred Buening
Elizabeth Whitney Buffim
Ethel Munday Bullard
Claire R. Cohen Burch
Jewel Calvin Burchfield
Patricia Ann Burdette
Suanna Jeanette Burnau
Alta Hazel Burnett
William Earl Burney, D.R.E.
Grover Preston Burns, D.Sc.
Billie Burrow
Barbara J. Burton
Elizabeth Allene Burtt
Anna Gardner Butler
Broadus Nathaniel Butler, Ph.D.
Elaine Ruth Marjorie Mallory Butler, Ph.D.
Joseph Buttinger
Mercy Lynne Buttorff
Frederick D. Byington
Joseph Keys Byrd

Mary Catherine Coleman
Zelia S. Coleman
Dr. Johnnie Colemon
Barbara W. Colle
Louis Malcolm Collier
Evelyn Padgett Collins
Zelma Mitchell Collins
Bundy Colwell, J.D.
Allen J. Comeaux
Archimedes Abad Concon, M.D.
Jo W. Conibear
James Frederick Louis Connell, Ph.D.
James H. Conrod, D.Min.
Patricia Cochran Cook
J. F. Cooley, D.C.L., D.D.
Robert Tytus Coolidge
Mariel Coombes
George Augustin Cooney, J.D.
Eldo J. Coons, Jr., Ph.D.
Herbert Press Cooper, Ph.D.
Jimmy Lee Cooper
Patricia Evelyn Pennington Cooper
Gretchen J. Corbitt
George Bronnie Corder
Erlinda Balancio Corpuz-Ambrosio
Leota Rae Cornett
Ernest S. Corso
Lyn Cortlandt
Evelyn M. Costello
Robert W. Costley, Sr.
Constantinos Haralampos Coulianos
Naomi Miller Coval, D.D.S.
Mary E. Cox
Yvonne Peery Cox
Ella Hobbs Craig
Vernon Eugene Craig
Marlene Rae Cram
Ira Carlton Crandall, Ph.D., D.S.Sc., D.Litt., Ed.D.
Josephine Lackey Crawford
Ioan Crihan
Adrian Loreto Cristobal
Charles Harrison Criswell
Tillie Victoria Swanson Croft
Charles Marion Cromer
Rev. Irvie Keil Cross
Joe George Crowell, D.D.S.
Carolyn Ann Crutchfield, Ed.D.
Randall Edward Culberson
Alfred Samuel Cummin, Ph.D.
Sylvia E. Cummin
Anne Bernice Smith Cunningham
David S. Cunningham, Jr.
Frank Earl Curran

Alton Kenneth Curtis, Ph.D.
Dorothy Massie Custer
Patsy Smith Czvik

Rev. Lawrence C. Dade
Bradford Ivan Daggett
Leola Lenora Dahlberg
Abdulhusein S. Dalal, Ph.D.
Charlotte Owens Dalo
Ruth C. Dameron
Frances Mueller Danforth
Huddie Dansby
Wayne Martel Daubenspeck
Ethel Hinton Daughtridge
Mabel Elizabeth Davidson
Alexander Schenck Davis
Beatrice Grace Davis, J.D.
Chaplain Rev. Dr. Clarence Davis, Jr.
Claudine Davis
Ernest Davis, Jr.
Evelyn Marguerite Bailey Davis
Father Francis R. Davis
Col. Gordon William Davis
Irma Blanche Davis
Lowell Livingston Davis
Mable Wilson Davis
Robert Wilson Davis
William Ackelson Davis
William Claude Davis
Kenneth Arthur Davison
Mary McCoy Deal
Michael Thomas Dealy
Robert Gayle Dean, Jr.
Walter John Deane
Patricia Ann de Champlain
David Michael DeDonato
Thelma B. DeGraff, Ph.D.
Dolores Tejeda de Hamilton
Michael Dei-Anang, Litt.D.
Jose C. Roman de Jesus
Elias Demetrios Dekazos, Ph.D.
Curtis Martin Delahoussaye
Violette de Mazia
Aryola Marieanne Demos
Judianne Densen-Gerber
Sarah Lee Creech Denton
Mary Jane Denton-Learn, Ed.D.
Adelaida Batista De Rodriquez
Lawrence Aloysius DeRosa
Veena Balvantrai DeSai
Kenneth Noel Derucher
Ruth S. de Treville
Robert Marshall DeuPree
Adele K. Devera
Julia Anne Bonjour DeVere
Albert Kenneth De Vito, Ph.D., Mus.D.
Inez Stephens Dewberry
Franklin Roosevelt DeWitt, J.D.
Muriel Herrick DeYoung
Tejpal Singh Dhillon, M.D.
G. Di Antonio
Darrell Thomas Dibona
June M. Dickinson
Joan T. Diedolf
Russell E. Diethrick, Jr.
H. Brent Dietsche, Ph.D.
Rudolph Gerard Di Girolamo
Anne Holden Dill
William G. Dilley
Otis B. Dillon
Priya Chitta Dimantha
Evelyn Lois Dittmann
Loy Henderson Dobbins, Ph.D.
Sofia Hilario Doctor
Jeannette Betts Dodd
Elizabeth C. Doherty, Ph.D.
Henry Dolezal
Sylvia Maida Dominiguez, Ph.D.
Norbert Frank Dompke
Richard Francis Domurat
Mary H. O'Neill Dooley
Susan Sherley Dorsey

Robert F. Doster
Richard Bary Douglass
Helen Jeannette Dow, Ph.D.
Marguerite Ruth Dow
Charyl Wayne Kennedy Dragoo
Josephine Eleanor Drake
Zelphia Pollard Drake
Claude Evans Driskell, D.D.S.
Eugene Ardent Drown
Satya Deva Dubey, Ph.D.
Diana D. DuBroff
George William Dudley
Anne Marie Marcelle Dumouchel
Deidra Renee Duncan
Dyna Duncan
William Archibald Duncan
Helen Faye Kindle Dungee
Lawrence Dunkel, Ph.D.
Estelle Cecilia Diggs Dunlap
Elsie Hyder Dunn
Mildred Elaine Dunn
Clydrow John Durbney
Lewis M. Durden, D.D., Ph.D.
Nancy E. Dworkin, Ph.D.
Robert Francis Dyer, Jr., M.D.
Edith Wuergler Dylan

Thomas Capper Eakin
John Benjamin Ebinger (d. 1979)
Bertha Elizabeth Eckman
Elly Helen Economou, Ph.D.
Alan Michael Eddington
Harold W. Edmonson
Adrian Rose Edwards
Louis Mavis Way Eggleston, D.Litt. (d. 1979)
Gordon Frederick Ehret, P.E.
Lois Eleanor Eisenmann
Alfred Eisenstein
Monday U. Ekpo
Oscar Reed Elam, Jr.
Norman Orville Eldred
Mohamed Tawfik El Ghamry, Ph.D.
Sami El Hage, Ph.D.
Johnnie Carl Eli, Jr., D.D.S.
Rosemary Taylor Elias
Afton Yeates Eliason
Donald J. Ely
Bessie Miriam Embree
Raymond Terry Emrick, Ph.D.
Elizabeth Lois English, Ph.D.
Charles Thomas Epps, Ph.D., Ped.D.
Rev. William Saxe Epps
Eugenia Eres
Ellsworth Burch Erickson
Anita Bonilla Ernouf, Ph.D.
Dorothy W. Erskine
Jean Hocking Erwin, Ph.D.
Billie Lee Eskut
Oskar M. Essenwanger, Ph.D.
Gene Gordon Essert, M.D.
Ann H. M. Estill
Eddie Estrada
L. Ken Evans, D.D.S.
Louise Evans, Ph.D

Tuula Jokinen Fabrizio, D.M.S.
Mary Waring Falconer
Sally Basiga Famarin
Sadie Patton Fant
Francisco Cabreros Farinas
Dr. Dorothy Anne Farley
George Leonard Farmakis, Ph.D.
Helen Horne Farr, Ed.D.
Margaret Marion Farrar, Ph.D.
George E. Farrell, M.D.
Darlene Faucher
George D. Fawcett
Marie Ann Formanek Fawcett
Blair Fearon, M.D.
Eugene W. Fedorenko, Ph.D.
Shirley Feinstein

Gary Spencer Felton, Ph.D.
Tse-Yun Feng, Ph.D.
Nicholas Vasilievich Feodoroff
Patricia Marguerita Fergus
Anthony Ralph Fernicola, M.D.
Elizabeth Ashlock Field
Donald George Finch
Donnie Wayne Finch
Alice Elizabeth Fine
Richard I. Fine, Ph.D.
Aaron Fink, Ph.D.
Joan Lockwood Finn
William Francis Finn, M.D.
Carmine Fiorentino
O. Y. Firestone, J.D.
Charles Frederick Fisher, D.Ed.
Mary Hannah Fisher
H. William Fister, M.D.
Leonard Donald Fitts, Ph.D.
Stanton T. Fitts
Admiral Gerald Joseph FitzGerald
Harold Alvin Fitzgerald
Paul Leo Flicker, M.D.
Edward Francis Flint, Jr.
William Mathew Floto
Donald Ray Flowers, Sr.
Henry Bascom Floyd, III
Lyman John Floyd
Luella Lancaster Floyd, D.Min.
Claude Lee Fly, Ph.D.
Frank Foglio
Elinor R. Ford, L.H.D., LL.D.
Prof. Dr. Gordon Buell Ford, Jr.
Judith Anne Ford
Lee Ellen Ford, J.D.
Ruth VanSickle Ford
Gary Walton Fordham
Willmon Albert Fordham
Luella Helen Formanek
Virginia Ransom Forrest
Jane L. Forsyth, Ph.D.
Caroline Robinson Foster,
Marietta Allen Foster
Inez Garey Fourcard
Clara M. Fouse
Abraham Harvey Fox
Lauretta Ewing Fox, Ph.D.
Arthur Norman Foxe, M.D.
Charles Leonard Foxworth, Ph.D.
Florence Gerald Foxworth
Dr. Irving A. Fradkin
Dorothy Killian Franchino
Donald Ely Frank
Elaine Koenigsdorf Frank
Richard Symons Frazer, Ph.D.
Danny Lee Fread, Ph.D.
Annie Belle Hamilton Freas
Eldine A. Frederick
Leonard Harland Frederick
Elizabeth Hicks Freeman
Elizabeth Bouldin Freeze
Ruth Evelyn French
Joyce Chlarson Frisby
Mary Elizabeth Louise Froustet
Louise Scott Fry
Wilhelmine E. Fuhrer
Fred Franklin Fulton
Gary Sudberry Funderburk
Mrs. Courtney H. Funn
Quint E. Furr

Diana Ruth Gabhart
Ruby Jackson Gainer, Ph.D.
Dorothy L. W. Gaither
John J. Gajec
Lilyan King Galbraith, Ed.D.
Lorraine S. Gall, Ph.D.
Joan Mildred Gallipeau
Mario R. Garcia-Palmieri, M.D.
Arwin F. B. Garellick
Lawrence Garrison
Ricardo F. Garzia

Sharon Lee Gates
Alexander V. J. Gaudieri
Charles Gottliev Geltz
Meta Wade George
Sonya Ziporkin Gershowitz
Mary Frances Gibson
Milton Eugene Gibson, M.D.
Weldon B. Gibson, Ph.D.
Katherine Jefferson Strait Giffin
Margaret Gill
Edna Avery Gillette
Rev. Perry Eugene Gillum
Antonio Giraudier
Perry Aaron Glick
Alberic O. Girod
Emilio R. Giuliani, M.D.
Arthur G. Glass
Joseph William Givens Godbey, Ph.D.
Joseph Gold
Patricia Anne Goler, Ph.D.
Nelida Gomez
William Raymond Gommel
E. Larry Gomoll
Carlos La Costa Gonzalez
Rafael A. Gonzalez-Torres, Ph.D.
Pamela J. Gonzlik
Hope K. Goodale, Ph.D.
Robert Thomas Gordon, M.D.
Mimi Gospodaric
Edna Jenkins Gossage
William B. Graham
Queenette Faye Grandison
Peter Hendricks Grant, Ph.D.
Edwin Milton Grayson
Frank Joseph Greenberg, Ed.D., Ph.D., L.F.I.B.A.
Janelle Garlow Greene
Edna Jensen Gregerson
Walter Greig, Sci.D., D.C.S.
Charles Allen Griffith, M.D.
Ione Quinby Griggs
Wilbur Wallace Griggs, Jr.
James Dehnert Gross, M.D.
Clarence Edward Grothaus, Ph.D.
Ivan H. Grove
Raymond Louis Guarnieri
Halldor Viktor Gudnason, M.D., Ph.D.
Laura Guggenbuhl, Ph.D.
Sr. St. Michael Guinan, Ph.D.
Rev. Jon Crawford Gulnac
Howard L. Gunn
Evelyn Coleman Gunter
Nina Nadine Gutierrez
Mildred Dorothy Guy

Merrill W. Haas
Maj. William David Hackett
Howard Smith Hackney
Lorena Grace Hahn
Major Arnold Wayne Hale
Dr. Tenny Hale
Gladys Murphy Haley
Karen Louise Haley
David Gunther Hall
Mildred Verzola Hall
Wilbur A. Hall
Jean-Pierre Hallet
Gerald Halpin, Ed.D.
Glennelle Halpin, Ph.D.
Earle Hartwell Hamilton
Madrid Turner Hamilton
Lillian Hammer
Eugene Kirby Hammett, Jr.
Frances LaCoste Hampson
Charles Robert Hamrick
Dr. Joyce McCleskey Hamrick
Laura Alice Green Hamrick
Franklin Jesse Hannah
Alberta Pierson Hannum
Kathryn G. Hansen
Freddie Phelps Hanson, Ph.D.
Vera Doris Hanson
Maria Harasevych

Jakob Harich, Ph.D.
Bobbye Roberts Harkins
Ethel Harper
V. Aileene Harpster, D.D., Th.D.
Hardy Matthew Harrell
Florence H. Harrill
Paul R. Harrington, M.D.
Louise Harris
Mary Imogene Harris, Ed.D.
Thomas Lee Harris
Virgil William Harris, III, Ph.D.
Daniel D. Harrison, Ph.D.
Shirley M. Harrison
Winnie M. Harrison
Newman Wendell Harter, D.D.S.
William O. Hartsaw, Ph.D.
Eleanor T. M. Harvey
Frances Marie Kirkland Harz
Nora Mae Rucker Hashbarger
James S. Haskins
Beatrice Giroux Jones Hasty
Col. Benjamin Frank Hatfield
Robert S. Hatrak
Jacob Hauser
Orressa Harris Hauser
Joseph Key Hawkins
Robert A. Hawkins, Ed.D.
Willard Hayden Hawley
Mildred Fleming Haworth
George Austin Hay
Arthur C. Hayes
Charles Patrick Hayes
D. Virginia Pate Hayes
Mary Katherine Jackson Hays
Mattie Sue Martin Hays
H. Lynn Hazlett, D.B.A.
William Hugh Headlee, Ph.D.
Gladys Levonia Moyers Heath
Robert Hezron Heckart, D.D.
Henrietta Irene Henderson
Morris Henderson
Graham Fisher Hendley
Donald Wayne Hendon, Ph.D.
Phyllis Jean Hendrickson
Robert Lee Henney, Ph.D.
Martha Alice Grebe Henning
Beverly Jean Smith Henschel, Ed.D.
Kirby James Hensley
Peter Hans Herren
Howard Duane Herrick, M.D.
Lettie Marie Herrman
Irene Rose Hess
Ah Kewn Hew
Carl Andreas Hiaasen, J.D.
Elizabeth Blake Hiebert
Doris Ross Higginbotham
Claudette D. Hill
George B. Hill
William Harwood Hinton, Ph.D.
Aurora Tagala Hipolito, M.D.
Charles Norwood Hitchens
Lore Hirsch, M.D.
Jane Richter Hoade, J.D.
Sidney LaRue Hodgin
Loren H. Hoeltke
Elise Hoffman, Ph.D.
Judy Hogan
Edward Lionel Holbrook
Dorothy Turner Holcomb
Gene 'Scotty' Grigsby Holland
Ray G. L. Holland, M.D.
Ruby Love Holland
Shelby W. Hollin, J.D.
Lawrence Milton Holloway, M.D.
Helen Marie Holzum
Daisy Bishop Honor
Burrell S. Hood, III, Ed.D.
Thomas Richard Hood
Marjorie Seaton Hooper
Alice Elizabeth Hoopes
Albert Bartow Hope
Annie Pearl Cooke Horne
J. Marie Hornsby

J. Russell Hornsby
Louis A. Horwitz
Franziska Porges Hosken
Lewis Daniel Houck, Jr., Ph.D.
Reuben Arthur Houseal, Th.D., Ph.D., LL.D.
Ruth Arnold Houseal, D.R.E., L.H.D.
Edmund L. Housel, M.D.
Edna Gertrude Houser
Thelma L. Howard, M.D.
Lyman H. Howe, III, Ph.D.
John S. Hoyt, Jr., Ph.D.
Jean Ayr Wallace Hrinko
Joseph Jen-Yuan Hsu, Ph.D.
Wen-ying Hsu
Yao Tsai Huang
Elizabeth Desmond Hudson
Norman Nelson Huff
Phyllis Huffman
Edwin McCulloc Hughes, Ed.D.
Janice Baxter Hull
S. Loraine Boos Hull, Ph.D.
Hazel Lucia Humphrey
Lugene G. Hungerford
Geraldine Grosvenor Hunnewell
John DuBois Hunt, J.D.
Lula Mai Hunt
Cannie Mae Hunter
Miriam Eileen Hunter
Priscilla Payne Hurd, D.D.
Abdo Ahmed Husseiny, Ph.D.
Edward Lee Husting, Ph.D.
Janet Lois Hutchinson
Colonel John K. Hyun, J.D.

Francis Joseph Ibranyi, Ph.D., D.S.T.
Celina Sua Lin Ing
Thomas Peter Ipes, D.Min.
Linda Jean Garver Iungerich

Anna Mitchell Jackson, Ph.D.
Carolyn Jane Jackson
Harvey L. Jackson, Jr.
Ruby L. Jackson
Thomas William Jackson
Gordon Waldemar Jacobs, M.D.
Benjamin William Henry Jacobs
Michael Harold Jacobson
Edward Louis John, Sr.
Paula Hermine Sophie Jahn
Advergus Dell James, Jr.
Robert Bleakley James, Jr.
Isabel Jansen
Nana Belle Clay Jarrell
Diane M. Jasek
Ina J. Javellas
Maria Bustos Jefferson
Woodie Rauschers Jenkins, Jr.
Ronald Paul Jensh, Ph.D.
Sue Allen Jent
Lester Earl Jeremiah, Ph.D.
Ann Elizabeth Jewett, Ed.D.
Hugh Judge Jewett, M.D.
Mary Alice Jezyk
Herta Helena Jogland, Ph.D.
Rev. Charlie James Johnson
Dorothy P. Johnson
Esta D. Johnson
James Andrew Johnson, Sr.
Patricia Lee Johnson
Colonel Rufus Winfield Johnson
Scott Edwin Johnson
Rev. William R. Johnson, Sr.
Agueda Iglesias Johnston, D.H.L.
Lillian B. Spinner Johnston
George Jones
Faye C. Jones
Mallory Millett Jones
Myrtis Idelle Jones
Patricia Jones, Ed.D.
Professor Vernon A. Jones
Gary Blake Jordan, Ph.D.

Lan Jordan, Ph.D.
Carmen A. Jordan-Cox
Kathleen Doris Jorgenson
Leslie James Judd
John Louis Juliano
Felix Joseph Jumonville, Jr., Ed.D.
Willa Dee June
Msgr. Francis M. Juras
Ioliene Justus

Woodland Kahler
Faith Hope Kahn, R.N., O.R.N., R.M.S.
Julian Kahn
Krishan K. Kaistha, Ph.D.
Nora Evelyn Kalbhin
Robert Gray Kales
Shirley M. Kales
Ted Reimann Kalua
Robert Kiyoshi Kanagawa
Joseph Kapacinskas
Anne Kaplan
Dorothy Theresa Karl
Marian Joan Karpen
Nikolai Kasak
Michael Kasberg
Nicolai Nicolaevich Kashin
Robert Stephen Kaszynski
Hilda Katz
Alvina Nye Kaulili
Rita Davidson Kaunitz
Lawrence Kayton, M.D.
Anita M. Kearin
Helen Revenda Kearney, Ph.D.
Jean Clarke Keating
Rosalie Ausmus Keever
Shirley Yvonne Kellam, M.D.
Paul Dudley Keller, M.D., F.A.C.S.
Louise Salter Kelley
Doris Lillian Kelly
Margaret McLaurin Ricaud Kelly
Greta Kempton
Charles William Kenn
D. James Kennedy, D.D., Ph.D.
Bettie Ilene Cruts 'Bik' Kenny
Donald Keith Kenny
Ethel Marie Kerchner
Minuetta Shumiatcher Kessler
Maj. Frank Howard Kiesewetter
Joseph Eungchan Kim
Keith Kim
Mary Lee Evans Kimball
Dr. Clifton W. King
Ethel Marguerite King, Ph.D.
Helen Blanche King
J. B. King, Jr.
Joseph Jerone King
Louise Willis King
Sarah Nell King
Mattie Armstrong Kinsey
Ellen Irene Groves Kirby
Henry Vance Kirby, M.D.
Mayme Clark Kirby
Nellie Woll Kirkpatrick
Sister Joan Kister, F.M.M.
Dorothea M. Klajbor
Dr. Edgar Albert Klein
I. Maxine Klein
Martin John Herman Klein
Jean Ross Kline
Tex R. Kline
Kurt L. Klippstatter
Paul E. Klopsteg, Ph.D., Sc.D.
Arthur Alexander Knapp, D.Opth.
Gloria Ann Mackey Knight
William Albert Koch
Dr. Boris Kochanowsky
Dr. Constantin Neophytos Kockinos
Dorothy June Koelbl
Lawrence Compton Kolawole
Adam Anthony Komosa, Ph.D.
Jin Au Kong, Ph.D.
Elaine Ferris Decker ('Sunny') Korn

D. G. Kousoulas
Father William Armstrong Kraft
Father Ljubo Krasic
Mozelle De Witte Bigelow Kraus
Pansy Daegling Kraus
Dr. Rev. Violet Joan Krech-Cisowski
Adrian Henry Kreig
James Morrison Kress
Adrian Henry Krieg
Albertine Krohn, Ph.D.
Yu Hsiu Ku, Sc.D., LL.D.
Ruth Peyton Kube
Isaac Newton Kugelmass, M.D.
Ida Carolyn Kugler, Ph.D.
William John Kugler
Stanley A. Kulpinski, Th.D.
Ina West Kurzhals
Leigh Elena Kutchinsky, Ph.D., M.D.
Lubomyr Ihor Kuzmak, M.D., D.Sc.
Christine Irene Kwik-Kostek, M.D.

V. Duane Lacey
Lloyd Hamilton Lacy
Shue-Lock Lam, Ph.D.
Lawrence Webster Lamb
Eleanor Lambert
E. Henry Lamkin, Jr., M.D.
Selma H. Lamkin
Labelle David Lance
Edward Clark Lander
Newlin J. Landers
Vernette Trosper Landers, Ed.D.
Georgina Barbara Landman
Mary Frances Kernell Lane
Audrey Pearl Knight Laney
Enrique Roberto Larde
Lena Schultz Larsen
Agnes D. Lattimer, M.D.
Elaine Marie Laucks
Frances Louise Peacock Lauer
Ralph Aregood Law, Jr.
Betty N. Lawson
Verna Rebecca Lawson
Obert M. Lay, M.D.
Harry Christopher Layton, D.D., Ph.D.,
    D.F.A., H.H.D.
Lillian Frances Warren Lazanberry
Albert Lazarus Leaf, Ph.D.
Miriam Leahy
Walden Albert Leecing
Sylvia Leeds
Dwight Adrian Leedy
Helen Ames Leete-Spaulding
Frank Edward LeGrand, Ph.D.
Silvia Weiner Leiferman
Ellen A. Leinonen, Ph.D.
Yoko Ono Lennon
Professor William Robert Lennox
John Anthony Lent, Ph.D.
Màe Grace Leone, Ph.D.
Barbara C. LeRoy
William M. Lester
Lois May Letch
Elmer A. Letchworth, Ed.D.
Harold A. Levenson
Philip Levine, M.D.
Keith Kerton Lewin
Eldwyn Ernest Lewis, Ph.D.
Leon Starks Lewis
Loraine Ruth Lewis
Shirley Jeane Lewis
William Howard Lewis, D.D.
Carol Ann Liaros
Eugene Aaron Lichtman
Ruth Dorothy Liebe
Morris B. Lieberman, Ph.D.
Luan Eng Lie-Injo, M.D.
Janis Lielmezs
Carol Asnin Liff
Rosalind Caribelle Lifquist
David Arthur Liggett
Dr. Delmore Liggett

Harriett Anna Grimm Lightfoot
Ping-Wha Lin, Ph.D., P.E.
Dorothy Insley Linker
Ivan L. Lindahl
Helge W. Lindholm
Mary Frances Lindsley, D.H.L., D.L.A.
Timothy Young Ling, Ph.D.
Elizabeth Charlotte Lippitt
Peggy Elaine Lipscomb
Darin V. Liska, P.E.
Robert Barry Litman, M.D.
Bertha Felder Littell
Florence Elizabeth Herbert Little
Terril D. Littrell, Ph.D., D.D.
Si-kwang Liu, Ph.D.
Richard W. Livesay, M.D.
Von Edward Livingston, J.D.
Addie Mae Curbo Lloyd
Dame Jean Loach, D.C.M.S.A., D.C.T., C.C.A.,
    F.M.L., F.I.B.A.
Floyd Otto Lochner, Ed.D.
L. W. Locke
David M. Lockwood, Ph.D.
Louisa Loeb
Sarah Elizabeth Larkin Loening
Hazel Anderson Loewenstein
Leslie Celeste Logan
Dr. Jennifer Mary Hildreth Loggie
Pauline Teresa Di Bitose Longo
ArLeen Patterson Lonneker
Rita A. Lopes
Anna M. Gonzalez Lopez
Maria Trinidad Lopez
Evelyn June Lorenzen, Ph.D., M.D.
Ann Louise Lotko
Joann Love
Dallas Landon Lovejoy, L.L.S.
Thelma Spessard Loyd
Judith Bagwell Luahiwa
Lilibel Pazoureck Lucy
Ruby Ballard Ludwig
Archie William Luper
Edythe Lutzker
Adelheid Wilhelmine Luhr
Ruby Elizabeth Stutts Lyells
Angela Yaw-Guo Lyie
Jerry Lee Lyons, P.E.

Vera Sonja Maass, Ph.D.
Roy Walter Machen, Th.D., D.D., D.R.E., D.Min.
Ruth Jean Maddigan
Eugenie Cassatt Madeina
Visweswara Laxminarayana Madhyastha, Ph.D.
William August Maesen, D.S.W.
Larry Elliot Magargal, M.D.
Albert A. Magee, Jr.
Thomas Harold Mahan
Francis Elizabeth Dougherty Maierhauser
James I. Maish, Ph.D.
Americo Bartholomew Makk
Raymond Howard Malik, Ph.D.
Wilfred Michael Mallon, S.J.
Mary E. Tranbarger Malola
June Culler Malone
Dr. Lucinda Johnson Malone
Joyce Morgan Maloof
Rt. Rev. Lucien Malouf, B.S.O.
James Darwin Mann
Santa Singh Mann
Colonel Filomena Roberta Manor
Krishna Shankar Manudhane, Ph.D.
Mamie Jane Jimerson Marbley
Paula Dee Thompson Markham
John D. Marks
V. Steven Markstrom
Don Welch Marsh
Milton Marsh
Otis 'Dock' Marston
James Larence Martin, D.D.S.
Melvin D. Martin
Paul J. Martin, Ph.D.
Peggy Smith Martin

Ernesto Pedregon Martinez
John S. Martinez, Ph.D.
Ellen Marxer
Aretha H. Mason
Dean T. Mason
Frank Henry Mason
Madeline Mason
Joseph F. Masopust
Elinor Tripato Massoglia, Ed.D.
John Ross Matheson, C.D., U.E.
Helen K. Mathews
Hugh Spalding Mathewson, M.D.
Bill G. Matson
Jean Foster Matthew, Ph.D.
Alvin Leon Matthews
Elsie Catherine Spears Matthews
Norma Jean Humphries Mauldin
Rev. Charles Alexander Maxell
Katherine Gant Maxwell, Ph.D.
Wythel Louween Killen Mayborn
Cynthia Francis May-Cole
Frederick J. Mayer
Edythe Beam Mayes
James Thomas Mayne
Lawrence Clayton McAlister
Bernice Jacklyn Lyons McAllister
Van A. McAuley
Honorable Rita Cloutier McAvoy
William V. McBride
Judge Daniel Thompson McCall, Jr.
Robert John McCandliss, M.D.
William Harroll McCarroll, M.D.
Mildred M. McCleave
Dr Sherwin D. C. McCombs
Grace McCormack
Irene McCrystal, Ph.D.
Constance M. McCullough, Ph.D.
John Phillip McCullough, Ph.D.
(Betty) Martha Elizabeth McCurdy, Ph.D.
Henry Arwood McDaniel, Jr.
Khlar Elwood McDonald, M.D.
Theresa Beatrice Pierce McDonald
Barbara Ann McFarlin
Ambassador Gale W. McGee
Robert C. McGee, Jr.
William A. McGee, III
Helen McGinty
Marjorie Frances McGowan
Sterling Fisher McIlhany
Donald D. McKee
Marion Elizabeth McKell
Malcolm F. McKesson
Harry J. McKinnon, Jr., M.D.
Mary Cannon McLean, Ed.D.
Robert George McLendon
Gwen Edith McMillan
Ambrose M. McNamara
Thomas Parnell McNamara, Sr.
Esther M. Mealing
Dr. M. S. Megahed
Ira B. Melton, Sr.
Sol Mendelson, Ph.D.
Carlos Mendez-Santos
Samuel D. Menin
Vasant V. Merchant, Ph.D.
Addie Hylton Merrimee
Ruth Evelyn Parks Mertz
Juozas Meskauskas, Ph.D., M.D.
Dorothy Taylor Mesney
Maqbul A. Mian, M.D.
Cyril Michael
Barbara Falgout Michaelis
Hubert Sheldon Mickel, M.D.
Capt. Alfred Alexander Mickalow, Jr.
Mildred M. Milazzo
Charles E. Miles
Robert Wiliam Miles
Vivian Turner Millard
C. Edward Miller
Carol Miller Miller
Dolphus O. Miller
Dorothea Welsh Miller
Earl Beauford Miller

Maj. Gen. Frank Dickson Miller
J. Malcolm Miller
Jeanne-Marie A. Miller, Ph.D.
L. T. Miller, Jr., Ph.D.
Mary Frances Miller
Robert J. Miller
William A. Mills
Jewel Brooks Milner
John Herbert Milnes
Frank Kuipong Min
Giulio Romano Antonio Minchella, M.D., D.S.
Horst Minkofski-Garrigues
Barry Leonard Steffan Mirenburg
George Miskovsky, J.D.
Kegham Aram Mississyan, Ph.D.
Barbara Jean Mitchell
George E. Mixon, M.D.
Marjorie Frances Griner Mixon
Dr. Herbert Brooks Mobley
Edward Francis Mohler, Jr.
Gertrude M. F. Moir
John Troup Moir, Jr.
Eleanor Moore Montgomery
Lt. Gen. Richard M. Montgomery
Dan Tyler Moore
Frank E. Moore
Hershell Edward Moore
Paul Richard Moore
Phyllis Clark Moore, Ph.D.
Dr. George Alexander Moorehead
Daniel M. Morahan
Kenneth Carol Morgan
Felix Cleveland Moring
Alvin E. Morris, Ed.D.
Eugene Morris
Florence Eden Morris
Irving Morris
Ruth Morris
Sue Hannah Morris
Francine Reese Morrison, D.S.M., D.D.
Leger R. Morrison, Ed.D.
Samuel Alton Morse, D.B.A.
Hans Birger Mortensen
Helen Luella Morton, M.D.
Walter Graydon Morton
Wilbur Young Morton
Dr. Herbert Frederick Moseley
Dr. James Anthony Moses, Jr.
James P. Mosley
Tommye Atkinson Moss
Beatrice Carroll Mullen
J. B. Mumford
Walter John Mumm, Ph.D.
Makio Murayama, Ph.D.
Walter John Mumm, Ph.D.
Wanda M. Penrod Munson, M.A.
Noveree Murdaugh
Percy Murdock
Mary Kathleen Connors Murphy, Ph.D.
William Joseph Murphy, Jr.
Joan Murray
Edward Cecil Music
Tofigh Varcaneh Mussivand, Ph.D.
Fred L. Myrick, Jr., Ph.D.

Toyozo W. Nakarai, Ph.D.
Hiromu Nakamura, Ph.D.
John B. Nanny
Sunil Baran Nath, Ph.D.
Pleas C. Naylor, Jr.
William Arthur Nebel, M.D.
Lucien Needham
Clarence E. Neff
America Elizabeth Nelson, M.D.
Lorraine Lavington Nelson
Robert Lee Nelson, Ph.D., D.D.
Thomas Harry Nelson
Elsie Paschal Nespor
Lois H. Neuman
Sister Laurine Neville, O.P.
Joyce Nevitt
Capitola Dent Newbern, Ed.D.

Martha R. Newby, Ed.D.
Virginia Shaw Newell
Emma Read Newton
Annette Evelyn Nezelek
Rev. James Harold Nicholls
Thomas S. Nichols
William Roger Niehaus
Mary Martin Niepold
Masami 'Sparky' Niimi
Lorraine C. Nikolai
George Washington Noble
Mark Gerard Noel
Patricia Joyce Brownson Norman
William Carlton Northup
Joachim Robert Nortmann
Marie A. Norton
Allen Stanislaus Motoyuki Numano
Walenty Nowacki
Crosby Llewelle Grant Nurse

Gene S. Obert
Paul M. Obert, M.D.
Robert Paul O'Block
D. Susan J. O'Brien
James P. O'Flarity
Wilson Reid Ogg
Clifton Oliver, Jr.
Hester Grey Ollis
Jaime Alberto Olmo, M.D.
Carl Edwin Olsen
M. Eugene Olsen
Benedict Bernard O'Malley, Ph.D.
William Joseph O'Malley
Col. Robert Palmer O'Neal
Paul de Verez Onffroy, Ph.D.
Helen Marie Opsahl
William Dabney O'Riordan, M.D.
Henry Orland, Ph.D.
Margaret Roberta Carlson Orlich
Robert Louis Ory, Ph.D.
Roman Sviatoslav Oryshkevich, D.D.S., M.D.
Prime F. Osborn, III
Cyrus Warren Ostrom
Marshall Voigt Otis
Edward Thomas O'Toole, Ph.D.
Marie Louise Molera O'Toole
George Robert Overby, Ph.D.
J. Homer Harold Overholser
Ronald Overholser
Edwin Dean Overton
Esen Sever Ozgener, Ed.D.

Margaret Ann Pace
Edward Thurston Pagat, M.D.
Marcelo Pagat, Jr.
Matthew John Page, M.D.
Thomas J. Pallasch, D.D.S.
Kayton R. Palmer
Rt. Rev. Dr. Louis Alexander Palumbo, Jr.
Robert Boisseau Pamplin, Jr.
Marciano Vega Pangilinan
John Pao
Spyros Demitrios Papalexiou
Leah Ann Pape
Margaret Pardee
Ruby Inex Myers McCollum Parham
Margaret Bittner Parke, Ed.D.
Boots Farthing Parker
Charles W. Parker, Jr.
Earl Melvin Parker, Sr.
Jacquelyn Susan Parker
Loislee M. Parker
Marilyn Morris Parker
William Dale Parker, Ph.D., Sc.D.
Belvidera Ashleigh Dry Parkinson, Ph.D.
D. C. Parks
Olivia Maxine Parks
Sandra Lou Parks
George N. Parris, J.D.
Andrew Mentlow Parsley, Ph.D.
Eugenia Pasternak

E. 'Steve' M. Sadang, M.D.V., Ph.D.
Stanley Cecil Winston Salvary, Ph.D.
Dorothy Vermelle Sampson, J.D.
Archbishop Mar Athanasius Yeshue Samuel
Carol Lee Sanchez
James Julian Sanchez, M.D.
Betty M. Sandella
Sylvia Ann Santos
Mary Louise Steinhilber Sauer
Robert Leonard Sawyer, Sr., Th.D.
Frank John Scallon
Helen Carol Schabbel
Lucrezia C. Schiavone
William Michael Schimmel, D.M.A.
Dolores F. Schjaastad
Minnie Anne Schmidt
Carl E. Schmollinger
George Ferdinand Schnack, M.D.
Mary E. Schwappach, M.D.
Wilhlem Schwarzotto
James L. Scott
Marie M. Scott
Col. Wilton C. Scott
Clara Kalhoefer Searles
Lorraine E. King Seay
Margielea Stonestreet See
JoAnn Semones
Doris Shay Serstock
John George Sevcik, J.D.
Dr. John Charles Sevier
Flossie Tate Sewell
George Miller Shadle, M.D.
Lucille M. Hogue Shealy
Ernest Shell
Vincent George Sheridan
Roy Allen Shive, Ph.D.
Mary F. Barnie Shuhi
Carrie Spivey Shumate
James McBride Shumway
C. Leroy Shuping, Jr., J.D.
Myrtis Irene Siddon
Howard M. Siegler, M.D.
Jan Simko, Ph.D.
Alyne Johnson Simpkins
Marion Carlyn Simpson
Eric John Sing, Ph.D.
Bhagwant Singh, Ph.D.
Kathern Ivous Sisk
James Dudley Sistrunk
Lydia Arlene Sitler, Ed.D.
Florence K. Slack
James Merritt Small, D.D.
Mary Ann U. Small
Ada Mae Blanton Smith, Ph.D.
Bettye L. Sebree Smith
Dock G. Smith, Jr.
Jessie Addie Smith
Norvel Emory Smith
Robert J. Smith
Wayne Delarmie Smith, D.V.M.
John Joseph Snyder, O.D.
Birger Kristoffer Soby
Walter W. Sohl
Ruell Floyd Solberg, Jr.
Donald Wayne Solomon, M.D., Ph.D.
Donald Henry Soucek, D.D.S.
Hattie T. Spain
Ellen Wilkerson Spears
James Parker Spillers
William Herschel Spinks
Ruth Evans Stadel
Edwin Henry Stamberger
Jacqueline J. Stanley
Linnie Marie Stearman
Lt. David Eric Stein
Andre Louis Steiner, D.Sc.
William Mark Stenzler
Dorothy Elizabeth Shay Stickman
Barbara Marshall Stockton
Willard Stone, D.H.A.
Jeremy Averill Stowell, M.D.
Dr. John George Strachan
Peter MacDonald Strang

Nellie Cora Straub
C. Clarke Straughan
Gustav Stueber
Glory Sturiale
Lakshminarayana Subramaniam
Eugene Y. C. Sung
M. N. Srikanta Swamy, Ph.D.
Arleen Wiley Swanson
Bonnie Ethel Wolfe Swickard
Maria Swiecicka-Ziemianek, Ph.D.
Ruby B. Sykes, D.D.S.
Emeric Szegho, J.D.

Neva Bennett Talley-Morris, M.Ed.
Peter J. Talso, M.D.
Noboru Tashiro, L.L.B.
Gunther Tautenhahn
Bertrand Leroy Taylor III
Grier Corbin Taylor
Rev. Horace Melvin Taylor, Th.M.
Lisa Taylor
Wesley Daniel Taylor, M.D.
Neal Gary Tepper
Esther Irene Test
Harry Pemberton Thatcher
Joseph Theodore, Jr.
Kadakampallil G. Thimotheose, Ph.D.
Alan Thomas, Ph.D.
J. C. Thomas, Jr.
Lowell Thomas
Minna Lee Thomas
Mary Diel Thomason
Henry George Thompson
William LaMont Thompson
Jean Kaye Tinsley
Betty Ann Tinsley-Brown
George John Tiss, M.D.
Vivian Edmiston Todd, Ph.D.
Hugh Pat Tomlinson
Francisco G. Torres-Aybar, M.D.
Basil P. Toutorsky, L.L.M.
Dennis Takeshi Toyomura
June Traska
Evelyn Ladene Trennt
Harvey W. Trimmer, Jr.
Laura McCleese G. Trusedell
Wanda Hall Tucker
Dr. Arthur E. Turner
Herman Nathaniel Turner, Jr.
Helen Flynn Tyson

Robert Takeo Uda
Friedrich Karl Urschler, M.D.

M. Lois Valakis
Henry Valent
Verne Leroy van Breemen, M.D., Ph.D.
Barbara Jane Dixon VanGilder
Richard C. Van Vrooman
Henry Varner, Jr.
Larry Ivan Vass, D.D.S.
Mary Vaughn
Prudence Melvina Veatch
June J. Veckerelli
Marion G. Vedder
James Joseph Venditto
Josefina Vera
Sister Mary Vernice (Makovic), S.N.D.
Santos Luis Villar, Ph.D.
Anthony Joseph Viscido, D.D.S.
Estella Maria Vlachos
John J. Vollmann, Ph.D.
Robert Volpe, M.D., F.R.C.P.
Arthur Voobus, Th.D.
Greta Evona Wade
Gerald Richard Wagner, Ph.D.
Betty Joanne Wahl
Mary Lee Sellers Wainwright
Edwin Prescott Wald

Kathryn Law Carroll Walden
Roy Willard Walholm, Jr.
Claudius R. Walker, Jr.
Iris Walker
Westbrook Arthur Walker, Ph.D.
William David Waller
James Arthur Waln
Doris E. Walsh
Bert Mathew Walter
Robert Ancil Walters
Rosie Reella Graham Ward
Marie Haley Warren
Lillian Frances Warren-Lazenberry
John Edward Warthen
Sharon Margaret Washburn
Lidia Cherie Wasowicz
Sydney Earle Watt
George Frederic Weaton, Jr.
Henry Weaver
Dr. Bernice Larson Webb
Ernest Packard Webb
Rozana Webb
Earl C. Weber
Gertrude Christian Weber
Sheila K. Weber, Ph.D.
Burnice Hoyle Webster, S.T.D., D.Sc., D.D., Ph.D.
Ernest Wesley Webster
Ruth S. Wedgworth
George C. Wee, M.D.
Milo Pershing Weeren
Diana Yun-Dee Wei, Ph.D.
Charles Kenneth Weidner
Norman Sidney Weiser
James Athanasius Weisheipl, Ph.D., D.Phil.
John W. Welch
Fay Gillis Wells
Josephine Mildred Wenck
L. Birdell Eliason Wendt
William W. Wendtland, Mus.D.
Wasyl Weresh, Ph.D.
Julian Ralph West
Lee Roy West, L.L.M.
Robert Warren Whalin, Ph.D.
William Polk Wharton, Jr., Ph.D.
Arline Z. Wheeler
James Edwin Wheeler
Charles Safford White
Ethyle Herman White
Frances R. Marjorie White
John Dudley White, Jr.
Mary Geraldine White
Saundra Sue White
Thurman James White, Ph.D.
Anna Whitefield
Alice McLemore Jones Whitehead
Edward Augustus Whitescarver
Vallie Jo Fox Whitfield
Cuthbert Randolph Whiting
Edward G. Whittaker
Grace Evelyn McKee Whittenburg
Carol Ann Wick
Jetie Boston Wilds, Jr.
William Garfield Wilkerson, M.D.
Harold Lloyd Wilkes, D.D.
Anne Oldham Willard
Carol Jane Petzold Willard, M.Ed.
Jack A. Willard
Albert J. Williams, Jr.
Anita T. J. L. Williams
Annie John Williams
Ather Williams, Jr.
Charlotte Evelyn Forrester Williams

Clarence Leon Williams, Ph.D.
Donald Jacob Williams
Dorothy Parmley Williams
Harvey Williams, Ph.D., D.Div.
Jean Taylor Williams
Leola K. Williams
William Harvey Williamson, Ph.D.
Francena Willingham
Mary Jane Willingham
James H. Willis
William Clarence Willmot
David Roger Willour, N.G.T.S.
Parker O. Willson
Charles William Wilson, M.D.
Cora Morgan Wilson
E. C. Wilson, Jr.
Hugh Edward Wilson
James Walter Wilson, Ph.D.
Leigh R. Wilson
Nevada Pearl Brown Wilson
Dorr Norman Wiltse, Sr.
Glen Elbert Wimmer
Lt. Gregory Lynn Winters
Nora Edna Wittman
Sophie Mae Wolanin, Ph.D.
Seymour "Sy" Wolf
Bradley Allen Wolfe
Deborah Cannon Partridge Wolfe, Ed.D.
Rev. Francis Wolle
Muriel Sibell Wolle
Colin Chockson Wong, D.D.S., F.R.S.H.
    F.A.G.D., F.A.D.I., F.I.C.D., F.A.C.D.
Marylaird (Larry) Wood
Stella Woodall, D.Lit., D.H.L.
Geraldine Pittman Woods, Ph.D., D.Sc.
Margaret Herbert Ratrie Woods
Margaret S. Woods
Clifton Ward Woolley, M.D., F.A.A.P.
Darrell Wayne Woolwine
Bertrand Ray Worsham, M.D.
Elizabeth Wrancher
John Lawrence Wray
Eugene Box Wright, J.D.
Inez Meta Maria Wright
Kenneth Kun-Yu Wu, M.D.
William Lung-Shen Wu, M.D.
Doris Stork Wukasch
Angela Jane Wyatt
Rev. Claude S. Wyatt, Jr.
Kionne Annette Wyndewicke
Darlene Fry Wyatt

Alex Peralta Yadao, M.D.
Elizabeth Juanita Yanosko
Claude Lee Yarbro, Jr., Ph.D.
James Edgar Yarbrough
Fowler Redford Yett, Ph.D.
Jethro Sutherland Yip
Luella May Nafzinger Yoder
Ronald Eugene Yokely
James N. Young
Patrick J. H. Young
Adele Linda Younis, Ph.D.
Lawrence Thomas Zagar, Ph.D.
Edward Francis Zampella
Estelle M. Zelner
Dr. Melvin Eddie Zichek
Gladys Avery Zinn
Howard John Zitko, D.D.
Herman David Zweiban

Appendix IV

Roster of Life and Annual Members American Biographical Institute Research Association

The *AMERICAN BIOGRAPHICAL INSTITUTE RESEARCH ASSOCIATION (ABIRA)* was established in 1979 to further extend the biographical research started by the American Biographical Institute in 1967 when it published its first reference volume on prominent Americans. All members of the *ABIRA* are chosen by an Executive Council based on professional, academic and community achievement(s). At present, over 500 individuals belong to the *ABIRA*. All are like-minded in their search for cultural and social enrichment and their desire for sharing important knowledge and discoveries. There are three different levels of membership, all of which have certain benefits.

The *ABIRA* publishes an annual *MEMBERSHIP ROSTER* which contains a concise and up-to-date biography on each member, including addresses, family, education, career history, community work, religion, published works and honors received. The *ABIRA* also publishes, periodically, a magazine entitled *ABIRA DIGEST*. This magazine keeps members in touch with one another in addition to announcing current projects of the Institute.

It is expected that during 1982 the *ABIRA* will grow by at least 20-25%.

PROFESSIONAL/ADMINISTRATIVE STAFF

Chairman..Janet Mills Evans
Vice Chairman...J. S. Thomson
Registrar...Andrew R. Holland
Communications Assistant...Sandra J. Brown

Reference: *Gale Encyclopedia of Associations*
Send all communications or membership inquiries to:
    205 West Martin Street, P.O. Box 226
    Raleigh, North Carolina 27602 U.S.A.

Abrams, Rosalie
Abrell, Ronald L.
Acker, Louise
Allen, Arcola
Allen, Loretta
Allison, Frank E.
Allison, William L.
Ames, John D.
Anderson, Thelma Bills
Anderson, Ursula
Anderson, Vivian M.
Arrington, Abner Atman
Ashbaugh, Laura
Ashiofu, Anthony I.
Aston, Katherine O.
Aust, Ruth Ann
Averell, Lois H.
Averhart, Lula
Ayers, Anne L.

Babb, Mattie A.

Bacher, Rosalie Wride
Bair, Mary Helen
Baker, Elsworth L.
Balogh, Endre
Barbour, Judy
Barcynski, Leon
Bardis, Panos D.
Bare, Jean
Barnes, Melver Raymond
Barr, Nona Lee
Barthlein, Arline R.
Baum, Carl E.
Baxter, Ruth H.
Bay, Magdalena
Beardmore, Glenn E.
Belisle, Lenore
Bell, Deanne
Bell, Leslie
Bell, Marilyn Ann
Bemley, Jesse L.
Benskina, Margarita Orelia
Benton, Suzanne

Berg, Julia I.
Berkey, Maurice E.
Binford, Linwood Thomas
Birdine, John C.
Black, Harold S.
Black, Larry K.
Blakeney, Roger N.
Bohmfalk, Johnita
Bomkamp, Loraine Mary
Bothwell, Shirley M.
Botticher, Wilhelmina W.
Bourne, Geoffrey
Bouvier, Alexandria
Boyer, Theodore S.
Boykin, Frances Lewis
Bradley, Ramona K.
Brame, Arden H.
Brandel, Hermengild
Break, Virginia Huffman
Breazeale, Morris H.
Brett, Charlotte Mae
Briggs, Nancy E.

Brody, Stuart M.
Brost, Eileen Marie
Brownell, Daphne
Bruce, John I.
Brumagim, Duane T.
Brunson, Marion Bailey
Bryan, Jacob F.
Bryant, Sylvia L.
Buhisan, Angelito T.
Bullard, Ethel M.
Burke, Thomas J. M.
Burley-Allen, Madelyn F.
Butts, Ruby
Bye, Raymond S.

Callahan, Wilma Jean
Campbell, Caroline K.
Cardinale, Kathleen
Carnevale, Dario
Carpenter, Charles W.
Carroll, Beatrice J.
Carson, William E.
Carter, Lillie Mae Bland
Carter, Marion Elizabeth
Carver, J. A.
Case, Paul C.
Cates, Paul W.
Cauthen, Deloris Vaughan
Cecconi-Bates, Augusta
Cellini, William Q.
Chaudhuri, Tapan K.
Chilton, Howard Goodner
Chin, Sue S.
Christensen, Don E.
Christensen, R. M.
Ciancone, Lucy
Clark, Ellery H.
Clark, Mary Otis
Cleveland, Hattye M.
Cohen, Irwin
Cole, Eddie-Lou
Connell, Louise Fox
Conner, William T.
Cook, David H.
Corsello, Lily Joann
Couch, M. Douglass
Cox, Donald J.
Craig, Robert John
Crawford, Josephine L.
Crihan, Ioan G.
Croxton, Thomas C.
Cucin, Robert L.

Daniel, Eunice B.
Dansby, Huddie
Davidson, Mabel E.
Davis, Alexander S.
Davis, Evelyn M.
Davis, Gordon W.
Davis, Rosie L.
de Czege, Albert W.
de Shaffer, Maria Luisa
Dennison, Jerry L.
Denton, Thomas S.
DeRosa, Lawrence A.
Di Ponio, Concetta Celia
DiSimone, Marion Elizabeth
Doherty, Elizabeth C.
Dolezal, Henry
Domec, Ethel M.
Dosick, Wayne D.
Dow, Marguerite R.
Drake, Josephine E.
Drummond, Malcolm
Dubard, Walter Highgate
DuBroff, Diana D.
Dumouchel, Anne Marcelle
Dunbar, Gertrude
Duncan, Becky
Duncan, Gertrude
Duncan, Dyna
Dunlap, Estelle Cecilia

Dunn, Helen Elizabeth
Durbney, Clydrow J.

Edmunds, E. Wayne
Edwards, Ray C.
El Ghamry, Mohamed T.
Emrick, Raymond T.
Eng, Joe Y.
Engle, Patricia A.
Erwin, Jean
Essenwanger, Oskar M.
Ester, Mary Ellen
Evans, Raymond

Farley, Dorothy A.
Farmakis, George Leonard
Farrar, Margaret M.
Fawcett, James D.
Fay, Thomas J.
Fenske, Virginia
Fergus, Patricia M.
Ferguson, Harry
Field, Elizabeth A.
Finch, Thomas Wesley
Fink, Aaron
Fisher, Mary
Foley, Kevin M.
Forbes, Fred W.
Ford, Gordon B.
Forman, Ruth Love
Fowler, Sandra
Fox, Portland P.
Franchino, Dorothy K.
Franks, Dorothy S.
Freeze, Elizabeth
French, Ruth E.
Freund, E. Frances
Fuchs, Helmuth Hans

Gaither, Dorothy L. W.
Galamaga, Donald Peter
Gale, James E.
Galvan, Sabino
Garciagodoy, M.
Gardine, Juanita F.
Garrett, Samuel J.
Garrison, Patricia M.
Gary, Gayle Harriet
Gauthier, Thomas R.
Gebo, Robert D.
German, Fin L.
Gerrard-Maisson, Emile A.
Gershowitz, Sonya
Gerstman, Judith R.
Ghattas, Sonia R.
Gibson, Curtis A.
Gibson, Weldon B.
Giraudier, Antonio
Glaze, Diana L.
Goff, Louella H.
Gomez, Nelida
Gospodaric, Mimi
Gray, Dora E. C.
Green, Ruth G.
Greenaway, Millicent D.
Greenlee, Betty
Gregory, Sheila E. H.
Grigory, Mildred A.
Grove, Jeffrey L.

Hackett, William D.
Hackney, Howard S.
Hale, Arnold W.
Hall, Wilfred McGregor
Hamilton, Madrid
Hamilton, Ethel M.
Hanf, James A.
Hankla, Velma Cash
Hanns, Christian A.
Hansen, Kathryn G.

Hanson, Freddie P.
Harding, Jeanne C.
Haritun, Rosalie Ann
Harpster, V. Aileen
Harrell, Hardy M.
Harris, Jane Maddox
Harris, Louise
Harris, Thomas Lee
Harris, Vander E.
Harrison, Winnie M.
Harz, Frances M.
Hasty, Beatrice G. J.
Havelos, Sam George
Havilland, Ben
Hays, Tina Athena
Hearn, Charles V.
Henderson, William D.
Henney, R. Lee
Herren, Peter H.
Hobdy, Frances L.
Holland, Ray G. L.
Holland, Ruby Love
Holloway, Lawrence M.
Hooper, Marjorie S.
Horan, Linda M.
Horn, Marion
Hornsby, J. Russell
Houseal, Reuben Arthur
Houseal, Ruth Arnold
Hsu, Wen-ying
Hunnewell, Geraldine G.
Hunter, Cannie Mae
Huraj, Helen Icea
Husseiny, A. A.

Ibok, Effiong E.
Ibranyi, Francis
Irvine, R. Gerald

Jackson, Linda D.
Jacobsen, William D.
James, Shaylor L.
Johnson, Iris M.
Johnson, Peggy McKinney
Johnson, Rufus W.
Jones, Myrtle J.
Jordan, Lan
Jordan, W. A.

Kales, Robert G.
Kalvinskas, John J.
Kanagawa, Robert K.
Kar, Anil Krishna
Karl, Dorothy T.
Karr, Don John
Kasparian, Alice E.
Kaufman, Irene Mathias
Keroher, Grace Cable
Kerr, Catherine E. B.
Kiehm, Tae Gee
King, Helen B.
King, Joseph Jerone
Kline, Tex R.
Knaebel, Jeff
Knauf, Janine B.
Koch, Frances T.
Koehlr, Isabel W.
Kokenzie, Henry
Kraus, Mozelle B.
Kraus, Pansy D.
Ksiazek, Marilyn C.
Kurjakovic, Mira B.

Lair, Helen
Landers, Newlin J.
Landers, Vernette
Lane, Mary Frances
Larde, Enrique Robert
Laudenslager, Wanda Lee
Lauer, Frances L. P.

Lawson, Verna
Leahy, Miriam K.
Leavitt, Charles L.
Leba, Samuel
Lee, Gerald F.
Leeds, Sylvia
Lennox, William R.
Lester, William M.
Lewis, Loraine R.
Lindberg, Elayne V.
Little, Florence
Loening, Sarah
Long, Shirley D.
Lonneker, ArLeen P.
Loper, Marilyn S.
Lovelace, Dennis J.
Lowry, Dolores E.
Luahiwa, Judith Bagwell

Maass, Vera S.
Mabe, Ruth A.
MacLellan, Helen M.
MacLennan, Beryce W.
Magargal, Larry E.
Malone, June C.
Manahan, Manny C.
Manogura, Ben J.
Marchetti, Jean W.
Martin, Deborah Louise
Mason, Aretha H.
Mason, Madeline
Mathewson, Hugh S.
Matthews, Elsie S.
Mauldin, Jean
McAnally-Miller, Virginia
McCoin, John M.
McCoy, Patricia Alice
McCullough, Constance M.
McCune, Weston E.
McDowell, Margaret F. G.
McKee, John W.
McMillian, Marie Y.
McNabb, Martha Sue
Meeks, Elsie M.
Mendelson, Sol
Merchant, Vasant V.
Mestnik, Irmtraut M.
Michna, Marienka
Migrdichian, Vartkes
Miles, Donald M.
Miller, C. Edward
Miller, Laverne G.
Miller, Robert J.
Mills, William A.
Min, Frank K.
Mitra, Gopal C.
Mitten, Robert L.
Mobley, Herbert B.
Mollenhauer, Bernhard
Moore, Dalton
Moore, Elizabeth T.
Morahan, Daniel M.
Morgan, Branch
Mori, Marianne M.
Morler, Edward E.
Morris, Richard
Morrison, Francine R.
Mott, Bob
Motter, Roberta T.
Mowrey, Shirley D.
Mozingo, Margaret J.
Mscichowski, Lois I.
Murray, Avery
Music, Edward C.

Naylor, Pleas C.
Nelson, Lorraine L.
Nelson, Robert L.
Nelson, Thomas H.
Nevel, Eva Mary
Newbern, Captola D.
Newell, Virginia S.